Baseball america®
2015 ALMANAC

D1516112

BASEBALL AMERICA INC. · DURHAM, N.C.

BaseBall america
2015 ALMANAC

Editor
Josh Leventhal

Assistant Editors
Ben Badler, J.J. Cooper, Matt Eddy, Aaron Fitt,
Vincent Lara-Cinisomo, Will Lingo, Clint Longenecker,
John Manuel, Josh Norris, Jim Shonerd

Database and Application Development
Brent Lewis

Contributing Writer
John Perrotto

Photo Editor
Jim Shonerd

Editorial Assistants
Jacob Emert, Bill Woodward

Design & Production
Sara Hiatt McDaniel,
Linwood Webb

Programming & Technical Development
Brent Lewis

Cover Photo
Clayton Kershaw by Bill Nichols

©2014 Baseball America Inc. No portion of this book may be reprinted or reproduced without the written consent of the publisher. For additional copies, visit our Website at BaseballAmerica.com or call 1-800-845-2726 to order. US $23.95-$26.95, plus shipping and handling per order. Expedited shipping available.

Distributed by Simon & Schuster ISBN-13: 978-1-932391-54-1

Statistics provided by Major League Baseball Advanced Media and compiled by Baseball America

BaseBall america
THE TEAM

GENERAL MANAGER Will Lingo @willingo

EDITORIAL
EDITOR IN CHIEF John Manuel @johnmanuelba
MANAGING EDITOR J.J. Cooper @jjcoop36
NEWS EDITOR Josh Leventhal @joshlev44
ASSOCIATE EDITOR Matt Eddy @matteddyba
WEB EDITOR Vincent Lara-Cinisomo @vincelara
NATIONAL WRITERS Ben Badler @benbadler
Aaron Fitt @aaronfitt
ASSISTANT EDITORS Clint Longenecker @clint_ba
Josh Norris @jnorris427
Jim Shonerd @jimshonerdba

PRODUCTION
DESIGN &
PRODUCTION DIRECTOR Sara Hiatt McDaniel
MULTIMEDIA MANAGER Linwood Webb

ADVERTISING
ADVERTISING
DIRECTOR George Shelton
DIRECT MARKETING
MANAGER Ximena Caceres
MARKETPLACE
MANAGER Kristopher M. Lull
ADVERTISING ACCOUNT
EXECUTIVE Abbey Langdon

BUSINESS
CUSTOMER SERVICE Ronnie McCabe, C.J. McPhatter
ACCOUNTING/
OFFICE MANAGER Hailey Carpenter
TECHNOLOGY MANAGER Brent Lewis

STATISTICAL SERVICE
MAJOR LEAGUE BASEBALL ADVANCED MEDIA

ACTION/
OUTDOOR GROUP

MANAGEMENT
PRODUCTION
DIRECTOR Kasey Kelley
EDITORIAL DIRECTOR,
DIGITAL Chris Mauro
FINANCE DIRECTOR Adam Miner
DIRECTOR OF SALES/
OUTDOOR Chris Engelsman
DIRECTOR OF SALES/
ACTION Adam Cozens

DIGITAL GROUP
DIGITAL DIRECTOR,
ENGINEERING Jeff Kimmel
SENIOR PRODUCT
MANAGER Rishi Kumar
SENIOR PRODUCT
MANAGER Marc Bartell
CREATIVE DIRECTOR Peter Tracy

MANUFACTURING & PRODUCTION
OPERATIONS
VP, MANUFACTURING &
AD OPERATIONS Greg Parnell
SENIOR DIRECTOR,
Ad OPERATIONS Pauline Atwood
PRODUCTION
MANAGER Jason Jopling
ARCHIVIST Thomas Voehringer

SOURCE INTERLINK
MEDIA, LLC

CHAIRMAN Peter Englehart
CHIEF EXECUTIVE
OFFICER Scott P. Dickey
EVP, CHIEF FINANCIAL
OFFICER Bill Sutman
EVP, CHIEF CREATIVE
OFFICER Alan Alpanian
EVP, SPORTS &
ENTERTAINMENT Norb Garrett
EVP, CHIEF CONTENT
OFFICER Angus MacKenzie
EVP, OPERATIONS Kevin Mullan
SVP, ENTERPRISES Tyler Schulze
EVP, SALES &
MARKETING Eric Schwab
SVP, DIGITAL
OPERATIONS Dan Bednar
VP, SALES
OPERATIONS Matt Boice
SVP, FINANCIAL
PLANNING Mike Cummings
SVP, AUTOMOTIVE
DIGITAL Geoff DeFrance
VP, EDITORIAL
OPERATIONS Amy Diamond
EVP, AFTERMARKET
AUTOMOTIVE Doug Evans
SVP, CONTENT
STRATEGY,AUTOMOTIVE David Freiburger
SVP, DIGITAL, SPORTS
& ENTERTAINMENT Greg Morrow
VP, DIGITAL
MONETIZATION Elisabeth Murray
SVP, MARKETING Ryan Payne
EVP, MIND OVER EYE Bill Wadsworth

CONSUMER MARKETING,
ENTHUSIAST MEDIA SUBSCRIPTION
COMPANY, INC.
SVP, CIRCULATION Tom Slater
VP, RETENTION &
OPERATIONS
FULFILLMENT Donald T. Robinson III

TABLE OF CONTENTS

BILL NICHOLS

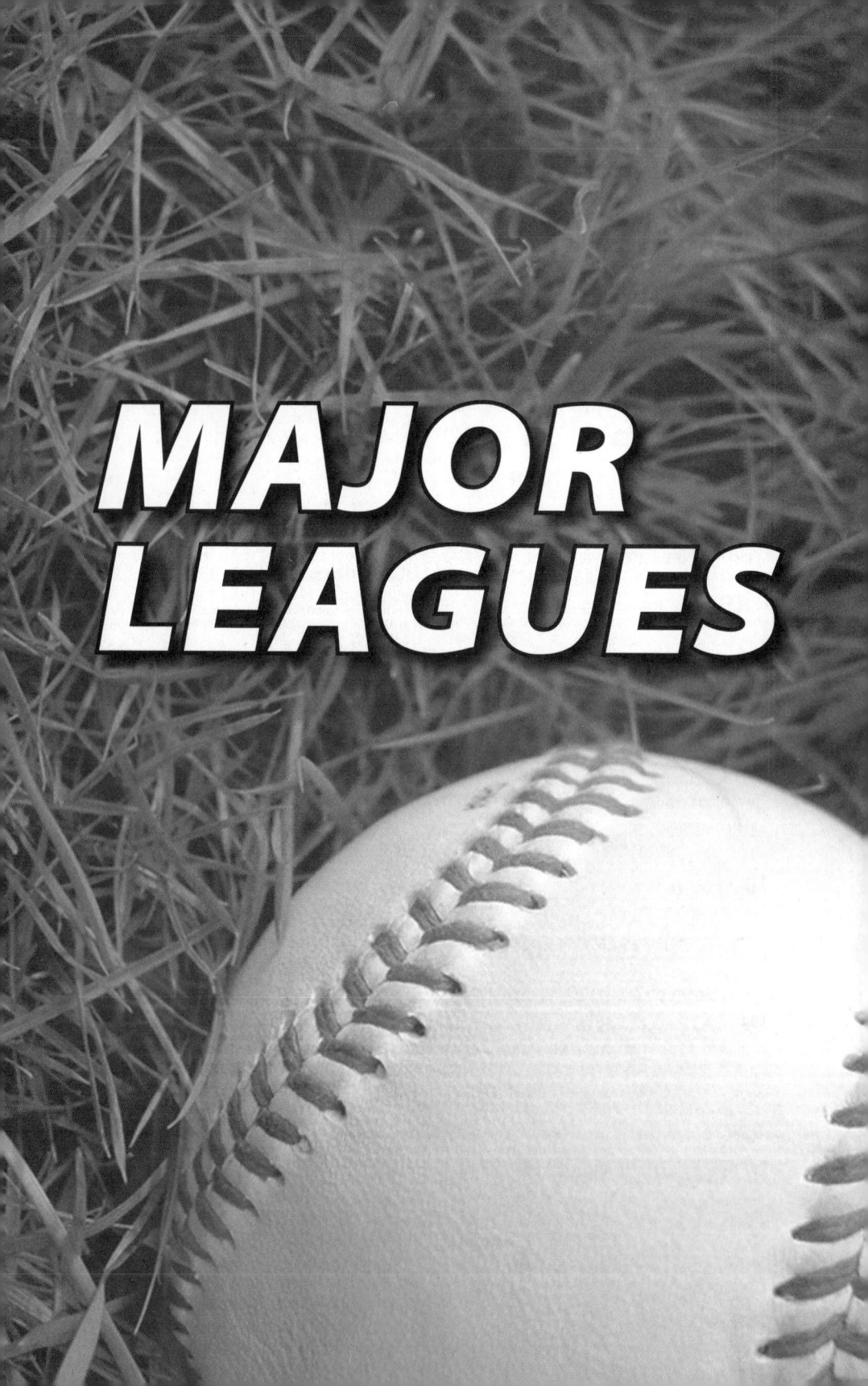

MAJOR LEAGUES

Prominent departures, and a dominant Dodger

BY JOHN PERROTTO

The 2014 season will be remembered more for who said goodbye than who said hello.

Yankees shortstop Derek Jeter retired after 20 seasons and after cementing himself as one of the legends of the game for its most-storied franchise.

Bud Selig announced he would be stepping down in January after 22 years as commissioner, a time in which the game saw a number of significant changes.

Without the fanfare of Jeter, White Sox first baseman Paul Konerko also retired following an 18-year career and was honored by the unveiling of a statue outside U.S. Cellular Field on the next-to-last day of his career.

Jeter's final game came on the last day of the regular season at Fenway Park in Boston but was actually anticlimactic after his dramatic Yankee Stadium finale three days earlier.

Jeter started as the designated hitter against the Red Sox in his final game and had an RBI infield single off Clay Buchholz in his second at-bat in the third inning for his 3,465th career hit. He then exited for pinch-runner Brian McCann as the sold-out crowd of 36,879 gave him a long standing ovation.

"I felt like the time was right," said Jeter, who finished his career with a .310 batting average. "My emotions were so all over the place on Thursday in New York, and when I got here I was ready. I was ready for my career to be over with. I'm happy I had an opportunity to come up and play here a couple of games. I'm ready for this to be the end."

The emotion was nowhere what it was in New York when Jeter hit a game-winning, opposite-field single to right field in the bottom of the ninth inning off Even Meek to give the Yankees a 6-5 victory over the Orioles.

It appeared Jeter would have no chance to be the hero as the Yankees took a 5-2 lead into the ninth. However, the Orioles rallied to tie the game against closer David Robertson as Adam Jones hit a two-run home run and Steve Pearce added a solo shot.

That gave the Yankees one last at-bat and Jose Pirela led off with a single. Brett Gardner then bunted pinch-runner Antoan Richardson to second base, setting the stage for Jeter's dramatic

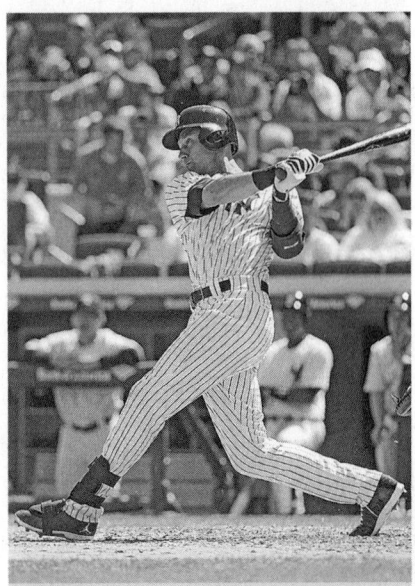

Yankees captain Derek Jeter was cheered at each stop of his retirement tour

TOMASSO DeROSA

moment.

"Sort of an out-of-body experience," Jeter said.

"You can't even dream this stuff up," Yankees manager Joe Girardi added.

After Jeter did the obligatory postgame television and radio interviews in front of the Yankees' dugout, he was joined by former teammates Andy Pettitte, Mariano Rivera, Jorge Posada, Tino Martinez and Bernie Williams along with Hall of Fame manager Joe Torre. Jeter's family, at the urging of Girardi, also came onto the field.

The 40-year-old Jeter had one final act. He walked to shortstop, a towel covering his face so the always-stoic team captain could hide his emotions from the fans and TV cameras, and took one last look around before acknowledging the crowd.

"I want to take something special from Yankee Stadium and the view from shortstop here tonight is what I want to take home from it," Jeter said.

Jeter helped the Yankees win 13 American League titles, seven pennants and five World Series. He also appeared in the 14 All-Star Games.

"It's been a blessing," Girardi said. "To play

along with such a great player, to manage a guy that is what you want in every player, what you want every player to care about, what you want every player to fight for, what you want every player to do. It's been a real blessing."

Selig has not been nearly as universally loved and respected as Jeter. In fact, he has been a polarizing figure with some of the changes he has brought to the game—interleague play and the wild card, to name a couple that upset traditionalists—and the long labor battles he was part of until relations between the owners and union improved in recent years.

Selig took over as the game's head in September, 1992, following the forced resignation of Fay Vincent. Selig became the chairman of baseball's executive council until being elected commissioner in 1998. Though he had talked about retiring many times in the past, the 80-year-old Selig finally followed through with the promise as Major League Baseball chief operating officer Rob Manfred was elected in August to succeed him in January 2015.

While Selig's strength has been to consistently build a consensus among the sport's 30 owners, Manfred defeated Red Sox chairman Tom Werner in the first contested vote for a commissioner in 46 years. Tim Brosnan was a third candidate but the MLB executive vice president of business withdrew just before the start of balloting.

While the results of the voting were not revealed, it reportedly took six votes before Manfred received the necessary 75 percent—23 votes—to be elected. The remaining seven dissenters then changed their votes to make it a unanimous vote in a show of solidarity.

"What I said to the owners after the vote is that I didn't really want to even think about who was on what side of what issue at points in the process and that my commitment to the owners was that I would work extremely hard day in and day out to convince all 30 of them that they had made a great decision," said Manfred, who will become the sport's 10th commissioner.

Selig had backed Manfred's candidacy since announcing his retirement.

"There is no doubt in my mind he has the training, the temperament, the experience to be a very successful commissioner, and I have justifiably very high expectations," Selig said.

Konerko bowed out in his typical low-key fashion on the season's final day. He played five innings at first base in the White Sox's 6-4 loss to the Royals, going 0-for-3. He took his position at first base in the sixth inning then was replaced

by rookie Andy Wilkins as the crowd of 32,266 chanted "Paulie, Paulie."

Konerko spent his final 16 seasons with the White Sox, helping them to a World Series title in 2005, after beginning his career with brief stints with the Dodgers and Reds. He finished with 439 home runs and 1,412 RBIs.

"This whole thing blew me away," Konerko said. "I know I've been here a while and I knew there'd be something at the end that would be commemorating me being here for a while. But this whole thing, the fans and all that last night, I never thought that I was one of those guys that gets that."

After the game, Konerko took an impromptu lap around the field, waving to the fans.

"I saw people crying," Konerko said. "That's crazy, just because I play a game. But I get it. It's something you do for closure for them as well."

The 38-year-old shed no tears, though, because his .207 batting average in 81 games told him it was time to move on.

"It was my time," he said. "I walk away with no what-ifs."

Dominant Dodger

Dodgers lefthander Clayton Kershaw started and won the season-opener March 22 against the Diamondbacks at the Sydney Cricket Grounds in Australia, then developed a sore muscle in his upper back on the long flight home.

The injury landed Kershaw on the disabled list for 41 days but didn't stop him from having one of the top seasons by a pitcher in recent history, going 21-3, 1.77 in 27 starts. Kershaw became the first pitcher to lead the major leagues in ERA for four straight seasons and the first to lead the NL in that category four years in a row since the Dodgers' Sandy Koufax did so five seasons in a row from 1962-66.

Kershaw's ERA was the lowest by an NL pitcher since Greg Maddux posted a 1.63 mark for the 1995 Braves.

The performance came following an offseason in which Kershaw signed a seven-year, $210-million extension, the largest contract given to a pitcher in major league history. However, the windfall did not make Kershaw complacent and he led the majors in wins.

"I don't ever want to fail, that's a big part of why I keep doing what I do every day," Kershaw said. "There's a responsibility to your teammates and to your organization. The Dodgers have invested a lot of money in all of us—a lot in me, especially—and there's a responsibility there to work as hard as you

BILL NICHOLS

Mariners ace Felix Hernandez turned in another dominant season on the mound but required a little help from an official scoring change to earn his second American League ERA title

can and earn that money. You should never lose sight of that."

While duly impressed by the work of his batterymate, Dodgers catcher A.J. Ellis doesn't believe 2014 will go down as Kershaw's best season.

"It's hard to say someone as decorated as Clayton is still evolving into a pitcher but I think he's becoming more a power pitcher, as opposed to that overpowering thrower," Ellis said. "He's attacking the strike zone. You get a lot of weaker swings when you are ahead in the count. You have a tendency to get more defensive-type swings and you see that when he pitches."

Mariners righthander Felix Hernandez won his second AL ERA title, though there was some controversy. He pitched 5 ⅓ scoreless innings against the Angels on the final day of the season then was removed not long after the Mariners were eliminated from playoff contention when the Athletics qualified by beating the Rangers.

The day before the start, Hernandez's ERA dipped from 2.34 to 2.18 when Major League Baseball executive vice president of baseball operations Joe Torre, upon appeal by the pitcher's agent, changed a hit to an error in his previous start against the Blue Jays, causing four runs allowed to become unearned.

Hernandez was removed from the game by Mariners manager Lloyd McClendon when his ERA dropped to 2.14, putting him ahead of White Sox lefthander Chris Sale and his 2.17 mark.

"Felix gutted it out all year and he deserved it," McClendon said of helping put Hernandez in position to win his second ERA title.

There was also a bit of controversy surrounding Astros second baseman Jose Altuve winning his first AL batting title, also the first in franchise history.

Interim manager Tom Lawless' original lineup for the season finale against the Mets did not include Altuve because the Astros wanted to protect his three-point lead over Tigers designated hitter Victor Martinez. However, Altuve insisted he wanted to play.

The Astros relented and Altuve went 2-for-4 to finish with a .341 average. Martinez went 0-for-3 in his game against the Twins to finish at .335.

"I think this is way better than just sitting on the bench and waiting for something," Altuve said. "If you want to win something, you've got to win it on the field."

Altuve also struck a blow for the little guy. The Astros list him at 5-foot-5, though he insists he is an inch taller.

CONTINUED ON PAGE 11

PLAYER OF THE YEAR

Kershaw looks ahead

BILL SHAIKIN

On the morning that would deliver to the Dodgers their greatest pitcher in two generations, Clayton Kershaw awoke with a thought.

The draft was not televised in 2006. If you wanted to know which team had drafted you, you had to wait for a phone call or follow along on the Internet

"I thought I was going to the Tigers," Kershaw said.

Luckily for the Dodgers, he fell to them with the seventh pick in the 2006 draft and ended up in L.A.

"We were hoping and praying Clayton would get to us," scouting director Logan White said.

Kershaw led the majors in ERA for an unprecedented fourth straight season, this time at 1.77. He topped the majors with 21 wins, despite spotting the league five weeks because of injury. The Dodgers went 23-4 in his starts.

In June, he threw a no-hitter with 15 strikeouts. In September, he startled Nationals center fielder Bryce Harper by running from first base to third on a softly-hit single. In the NL West division clincher, he fielded a ground ball between his legs—with his back turned to home plate—and tripled home the tying run.

What is so stunning about Kershaw's success is that he has gotten so much better after winning two Cy Young Awards in three years.

"You don't want to just shut it down in the offseason and say, 'Try again next year and do the same stuff,'" Kershaw said.

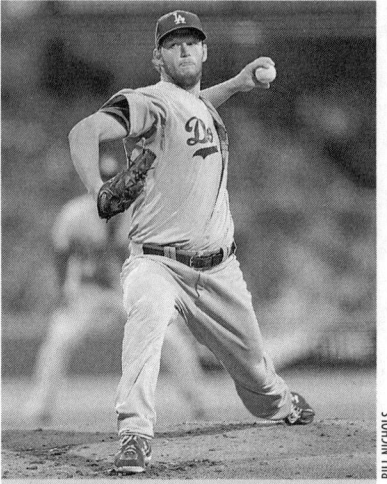

BILL NICHOLS

Clayton Kershaw is making a run at Sandy Koufax as best pitcher in Dodgers history

For example, he became more groundball-oriented this season, with nearly 52 percent of balls hit in play against him staying out of the air. He also threw fewer fastballs and more sliders, and he threw his curve for strikes early in the count as well as for strike three.

"It's ironic to me that the big knock on him when he came up was, this guy couldn't command the ball, couldn't throw strikes," Ellis said. "He was almost sent back to the minor leagues due to his inability to go deep into games because his pitch count was so high.

"And now it's almost to the point where you're saying, 'Hey, Clayton, maybe you're throwing too many strikes?'"

Kershaw has positioned himself to do long considered the unthinkable: surpass Sandy Koufax as greatest pitcher in Dodgers history.

Koufax was 26 when he embarked on five magnificent seasons. He led the NL in ERA each season from 1962-66, winning three Cy Young trophies and one MVP award. He retired at age 30, because of an arthritic elbow.

Kershaw, 26, and just won his third Cy Young Award.

PREVIOUS POY WINNERS

2004: Barry Bonds, of, Giants
2005: Albert Pujols, 1b, Cardinals
2006: Johan Santana, lhp, Twins
2007: Alex Rodriguez, ss, Yankees
2008: C.C. Sabathia, lhp, Indians/Brewers
2009: Joe Mauer, c, Twins
2010: Roy Halladay, rhp, Phillies
2011: Matt Kemp, of, Dodgers
2012: Mike Trout, Angels
2013: Mike Trout, Angels

Full list: BaseballAmerica.com/awards

CONTINUED FROM PAGE 9

Rockies first baseman Justin Morneau took advantage of playing his home games in the thin air of Denver by winning the NL batting title with a .319 mark in his first season with Colorado after signing as a free agent in the offseason. He became the seventh Rockies player to win the crown in the franchise's 22-year history, joining Andres Galarraga (1994), Larry Walker (1998, 1999, 2001), Todd Helton (2000), Matt Holliday (2007), Carlos Gonzalez (2010) and another former Twin, Michael Cuddyer (2013).

Morneau had the lowest average for a batting champ in either league since Tony Gwynn hit .313 for the 1988 Padres. Morneau won by four points over Pirates third baseman Josh Harrison, who finished with a .315 average.

"I'm most proud that I was consistent all season," Morneau said. "Sometimes you get hot for a while and hit .450, but I think I was consistent all season and I focused and concentrated on that."

Orioles designated hitter/outfielder Nelson Cruz found little interest on the free agent market after serving a 50-game suspension late in the 2013 season for violating Major League Baseball's drug program. However, he led the major leagues with 40 home runs and proved to be a bargain on a one-year, $8-million contract that he signed after spring training had already started. It was the first AL homer title for Cruz.

"We just felt like it was a good fit with his

mindset going into the season," Orioles manager Buck Showalter said. "It was not a vindictiveness, Nelson knows things were self-inflicted. He really wanted to reestablish himself and we thought we could provide a real good opportunity for him and the sky might be the limit."

Marlins right fielder Giancarlo Stanton topped the NL with 37 homers despite missing the final 17 games of the season after being hit in the face by a pitch from Brewers righthander Mike Fiers. Stanton had surgery to repair facial fractures.

Dodgers first baseman Adrian Gonzalez drove in 116 runs to lead the majors. Angels center fielder Mike Trout led the AL with 111, the fewest for an RBI champ in that league in a non-shortened season since Lee May had 109 for the 1976 Orioles.

The Brewers' Jonathan Lucroy set the major league single-season record for doubles by a catcher with 46, one more than Ivan Rodriguez had with the 1996 Rangers. Lucroy hit 53 doubles overall to lead the NL and become the first player who was primarily a catcher to top his league in that category.

Tigers lefthander David Price paced the majors with 271 strikeouts, including eight on the final day of regular season when he beat the Twins to clinch Detroit's fourth consecutive AL Central title. Price had 189 of those strikeouts with the Rays before being traded July 31 and finished with two more whiffs than Indians righthander Corey

CONTINUED ON PAGE 13

AMERICAN LEAGUE STANDINGS

EAST	W	L	PCT	GB	Manager	General Manager	Attendance	Average	Last Penn.
Baltimore	96	66	.593	-	Buck Showalter	Dan Duquette	2,464,473	30,805	1983
NY Yankees	84	78	.519	12	Joe Girardi	Brian Cashman	3,401,624	42,520	2009
Toronto	83	79	.512	13	John Gibbons	Alex Anthopoulos	2,375,525	29,327	1993
Tampa Bay	77	85	.475	19	Joe Maddon	Andrew Friedman	1,446,464	17,857	2008
Boston	71	91	.438	25	John Farrell	Ben Cherington	2,956,089	36,494	2013
CENTRAL	W	L	PCT	GB	Manager	GM	Attendance	Average	Last Penn.
Detroit	90	72	.556	-	Brad Ausmus	Dave Dombrowski	2,917,209	36,014	2012
*Kansas City	89	73	.549	1	Ned Yost	Dayton Moore	1,956,482	24,154	1985
Cleveland	85	77	.525	5	Terry Francona	Chris Antonetti	1,437,393	18,428	1997
Chicago Sox	73	89	.451	17	Robin Ventura	Rick Hahn	1,650,821	20,896	2005
Minnesota	70	92	.432	20	Ron Gardenhire	Terry Ryan	2,250,606	27,785	1991
WEST	W	L	PCT	GB	Manager	GM	Attendance	Average	Last Penn.
LA Angels	98	64	.605	-	Mike Scioscia	Jerry Dipoto	3,095,935	38,221	2002
*Oakland	88	74	.543	10	Bob Melvin	Billy Beane	2,003,628	25,045	2011
Seattle	87	75	.537	11	Lloyd McClendon	Jack Zduriencik	2,064,334	25,485	None
Houston	70	92	.432	28	Bo Porter/Tom Lawless	Jeff Luhnow	1,751,829	21,627	2005
Texas	67	95	.414	31	Ron Washington/Tim Bogar	Jon Daniels	2,718,733	33,564	2011

*Wild card

PLAYOFFS—Wild Card: Royals defeated A's 9-8. **Division Series:** Orioles defeated Tigers 3-0 and Royals defeated Angels 3-0 in best-of-five series. **Championship Series:** Royals defeated Orioles 4-0 in best-of-seven series.

ROOKIE OF THE YEAR

Abreu quiets critics

BEN BADLER

When Jose Abreu came out of Cuba—and even before then—one highly respected scout after another came back with the same report on the slugger who had decimated Serie Nacional pitching.

His bat is too slow. He's a restricted athlete with a bad body. He can't lay off hard sliders away. Sure, he has huge raw power, but there are too many holes in his swing. He'd make a great softball player.

"He's turning 27 years old and has a career full of 85 to 87 mile an hour fastballs," one international scout said. "He's not an athlete and he doesn't have bat speed. You're asking a 27-year-old non-athlete to go to the big leagues and make an adjustment. Against 97 (mph), this guy has no chance. All of us who know him are all saying the same thing."

All this for one of the greatest hitters Cuba has ever produced, who regularly posted an on-base percentage north of .500 and slugged over .800 in Serie Nacional, including a ridiculous .453/.597/.986 MVP campaign with 33 homers in 293 plate appearances in the 2010-11 season. Abreu had scouts who believed in him, but despite a record contract for a first-year Cuban player of six years, $68 million, plenty more were skeptical.

One year later, Abreu has silenced his critics on his way to winning Baseball America's Rookie of the Year Award. Abreu, 27, hit .317/.383/.581 with 36 home runs, leading the majors in slugging with a 5.5 Wins Above Replacement (WAR), per Baseball-Reference.com.

So, how did the White Sox get it right while so many other talented scouts whiffed so badly on Abreu?

The majority of their scouting on Abreu came from Marco Paddy, the team's special assistant to the general manager in charge of international operations. The White Sox didn't have anyone at the 2013 World Baseball Classic, but Paddy had scouted Abreu at four or five international tournaments, including while he ran Toronto's international scouting

CLIFF WELCH

Jose Abreu slugged 36 home runs in his first season to win Rookie of the Year

until the White Sox hired him after the 2011 season.

The White Sox didn't see any issues with Abreu's bat speed. At Abreu's showcase, they saw him face pitchers throwing in the low-90s, and watched the first fastball he saw land over the right-center field fence. That showcase just helped solidify their enthusiasm. As Abreu's bidding shows, if hitting a baseball is one of the hardest things to do in sports, determining who can hit major league pitching is still one of the hardest things to do in scouting.

PREVIOUS ROY WINNERS

2004: Khalil Greene, ss, Padres
2005: Huston Street, rhp, Athletics
2006: Justin Verlander, rhp, Tigers
2007: Ryan Braun, 3b, Brewers
2008: Geovany Soto, c, Cubs
2009: Andrew McCutchen, of, Pirates
2010: Jason Heyward, of, Braves
2011: Jeremy Hellickson, rhp, Rays
2012: Mike Trout, Angels
2013: Jose Fernandez, Marlins
Full list: BaseballAmerica.com/awards

Kluber, who had 269. Kluber's 18 wins tied Angels righthander Jered Weaver for the AL lead.

Reds righthander Johnny Cueto wound up tied with Nationals righthander Jordan Zimmermann for the NL strikeouts lead with 242 after whiffing seven Pirates on the season's last day.

Altuve also led the AL in stolen bases with 56 while Dodgers second baseman Dee Gordon's 64 paced the NL.

Mariners righthander Fernando Rodney led the majors in 48 saves. Braves closer Craig Kimbrel was first in the NL with 47, the fourth year in a row he either led or tied for the league lead.

Twins righthander Phil Hughes set a major league single-season record with an 11.63 strikeout/walk ratio as he struck out 186 and walked just 16 in 209 ⅔ innings. He broke the record of 11.00 set by Bret Saberhagen during the strike-shortened 1994 season with the Mets. Hughes' record came just a year after he had a pedestrian 2.88 ratio with the Yankees.

Angels In The Clouds

The Angels came into the season having not qualified for the postseason for four straight years, leading to speculation that the jobs of longtime manager Mike Scioscia and general manager Jerry Dipoto were on the line.

However, the Angels responded with the best record in the regular season at 98-64 while storming past the Athletics to win the AL West. Down six games to Oakland on June 21, the Angels wound up winning the division by 10 games in a season that included Albert Pujols' 500th home run.

"I couldn't be prouder of these guys," Scioscia said after the Angels' 5-0 victory over the Mariners on Sept. 17 wrapped up the division title. "These guys are awesome. They worked so hard throughout the summer. You just don't pick up that much ground in such a short amount of time without playing at an incredible level and we did."

The Orioles won their first AL East title since 1996 with a 96-66 record, 12 games better than the second-place Yankees. A 90-72 record was enough to give the Tigers their fourth AL Central championship in a row after edging the Royals by one game.

However, the Royals won the first AL wild card, enabling them to make their first postseason appearance since 1985 when they won their lone World Series title. The 29-year drought was the longest active one in major North American professional team sports.

"It feels better than expected," designated hitter Billy Butler, the Royals' first-round draft pick in 2004, said after his team clinched a playoff berth Sept. 26 with a 3-1 victory over the White Sox at Chicago. "It's a great thing. I'm proud to bring this organization something they envisioned when they drafted me."

The Athletics hung on for the second wild card.

The pressure was on the Dodgers to win the

NATIONAL LEAGUE STANDINGS

EAST	W	L	PCT	GB	Manager	General Manager	Attendance	Average	Last Penn.
*-Washington	96	66	.593	-	Matt Williams	Mike Rizzo	2,579,389	31,844	None
NY Mets	79	83	.488	17	Terry Collins	Sandy Alderson	2,148,808	26,860	2000
Atlanta	79	83	.488	17	Fredi Gonzalez	Frank Wren	2,354,305	29,065	1999
Miami	77	85	.475	19	Mike Redmond	Dan Jennings	1,732,283	21,386	2003
Philadelphia	73	89	.451	23	Ryne Sandberg	Ruben Amaro Jr.	2,423,852	29,924	2009
CENTRAL	W	L	PCT	GB	Manager	GM	Attendance	Average	Last Penn.
x-St. Louis	90	72	.556	-	Mike Matheny	John Mozeliak	3,540,649	43,711	2013
y-Pittsburgh	88	74	.543	2	Clint Hurdle	Neal Huntington	2,442,564	30,155	1979
Milwaukee	82	80	.506	8	Ron Roenicke	Doug Melvin	2,797,384	34,535	1982
Cincinnati	76	86	.469	14	Bryan Price	Walt Jocketty	2,476,664	30,576	1990
Chicago Cubs	73	89	.451	17	Rick Renteria	Jed Hoyer	2,652,113	32,742	1945
WEST	W	L	PCT	GB	Manager	GM	Attendance	Average	Last Penn.
x-LA Dodgers	94	68	.580	-	Don Mattingly	Ned Colletti	3,782,337	46,695	1988
y-San Francisco	88	74	.543	6	Bruce Bochy	Brian Sabean	3,368,697	41,588	2012
San Diego	77	85	.475	17	Bud Black	Josh Byrnes/AJ Preller	2,195,373	27,103	1998
Colorado	66	96	.407	28	Walt Weiss	Dan O'Dowd	2,680,329	33,090	2007
Arizona	64	98	.395	30	Kirk Gibson/Alan Trammell	Kevin Towers/Dave Stewart	2,073,730	25,601	2001

*Wild card

PLAYOFFS—Wild Card: Giants defeated Pirates 8-0 in one-game playoff. Division Series: Giants defeated Nationals 3-1 and Cardinals defeated Dodgers 3-1 in best-of-five series. Championship Series: Giants defeated Cardinals 4-1 in best-of-seven series.

NL West after beginning the season with a payroll of $234 million, the largest in baseball history, according to calculations by The Associated Press. While they did finish first, it was not without a struggle.

The Dodgers fell 10 games behind the Giants in the division standings on June 8 and had a 33-31 record. They then went 51-37 the rest of the season to finish 94-68 and six games ahead of San Francisco.

The Nationals finished with the best record in the NL at 96-66 while rolling to the East title by 17 games over the Braves and Marlins.

The Cardinals won their second straight NL Central crown with a 90-72 record, holding off the Pirates by two games. The Brewers, who held a 6 ½-game at the beginning of July, collapsed as they went 31-47 over the final three months to finish eight games behind.

"It's been a hard year," Brewers manager Ron Roenicke said on the last day of the season.

Hall Of Braves

Cooperstown resembled the South on Hall of Fame induction weekend.

Seemingly every other person walking the tree-lined streets of the quaint village in central New York was wearing Braves' caps, jerseys and T-shirts. Buses from Georgia, South Carolina and North Carolina were everywhere.

Six players and managers were inducted and all but one had at least some sort of tie to the Braves. The one who didn't was born and raised in Georgia and was a big Atlanta fan while growing up.

Manager Bobby Cox led the Braves to an unprecedented run of success with 14 consecutive division titles from 1991-2005 (the 1994 post-season was canceled because of a players' strike). Lefthander Tom Glavine and righthander Greg Maddux played a major part in the Braves' success in that period.

Furthermore, Joe Torre was a star player then later managed the Braves, Tony La Russa spent one season as a utility infielder in Atlanta before becoming one of the game's greatest skippers. Slugging designated hitter/first baseman Frank Thomas spent his entire career in the AL but was born and raised in Columbus, Ga.

Cox managed in the major leagues for 29 seasons with the Braves and Blue Jays and his 2,504 victories are the fourth-highest total in major league history. He led Atlanta to five NL pennants and the city's only major professional sports championship when the Braves won the 1995 World Series.

Bobby Cox entered the Hall of Fame with pitchers Tom Glavine and Greg Maddux

"To go into the Hall of Fame and have two of your big three pitchers join you, with a third likely to go in next year, is unbelievable," Cox said, referring to John Smoltz being eligible for election for the first time in 2015. "You've got a better chance of hitting the lottery than something like this happen. There's no more magical place than Cooperstown and this proves it."

Glavine won 305 games over 22 seasons with the Braves and Mets, the fourth-highest total ever by a lefty. He won the NL Cy Young Award in 1991 and 1998 and called being inducted "the ultimate honor of a career in baseball."

"My career saw a lot of ups and downs, a lot of sacrifices on and off the field and more than a few times when I questioned what I was doing," Glavine said. "There are no more questions now, only gratitude toward those who were so helpful along the way."

Maddux finished with 355 wins in 23 seasons with the Cubs, Braves, Padres and Dodgers and won four consecutive NL Cy Youngs from 2002-05. He has the eighth-most wins in major league history.

Always cool, calm and collected on the mound, Maddux admitted he was extremely nervous while giving the first public speech of his life. However, he mixed in humor with thank yous and explained while there is no logo on the cap on his plaque.

"I played in Chicago for 11 years and I played

ALL-ROOKIE TEAM 2014

Pos	PLAYER, TEAM	AGE	AB	AVG	OBP	SLG	2B	HR	RBI	SB	RUNDOWN
C	Travis d'Arnaud, Mets	25	385	.242	.302	.416	22	13	41	1	Lived up to offensive projections after return to Triple-A
1B	Jose Abreu, White Sox	27	556	.317	.383	.581	35	36	107	3	Cuban led majors in slugging and second in OPS
2B	Mookie Betts, Red Sox	22	189	.291	.368	.444	12	5	18	7	All the ingredients to be a hitting star
3B	Nick Castellanos, Tigers	22	533	.259	.306	.394	31	11	66	2	Solid gap power and high line-drive rate
SS	Danny Santana, Twins	24	405	.319	.353	.472	27	7	40	20	Top five for rookies in extra-base hits (41) and SBs
CF	Billy Hamilton, Reds	23	563	.250	.292	.355	25	6	48	56	Second in NL in SBs and third in putouts
OF	Kevin Kiermaier, Rays	24	331	.263	.315	.450	16	10	35	5	Led team in slugging and OPS
OF	George Springer, Astros	24	295	.231	.336	.468	8	20	51	5	Power balanced 33-percent strikeout rate
DH	Kennys Vargas, Twins	23	215	.274	.316	.456	10	9	38	0	One of highest contact rates for rookies in strike zone

Pos	PITCHER, TEAM	AGE	W	L	SV	ERA	IP	SO	BB	RUNDOWN
SP	Jacob deGrom, Mets	26	9	6	0	2.69	140	144	43	Former college shortstop led rookies in ERA
SP	Collin McHugh, Astros	27	11	9	0	2.73	155	157	41	Logged lowest WHIP (1.02) of any rookie with at least 100 IP
SP	Marcus Stroman, Blue Jays	23	11	6	0	3.65	131	111	28	Led Toronto's primary five in WHIP, SO/BB ratio, home run rate
SP	Masahiro Tanaka, Yankees	25	13	5	0	2.77	136	141	21	Elbow injury dampened first-half dominance
SP	Yordano Ventura, Royals	23	14	10	0	3.20	183	159	69	Only Garrett Richards threw faster fastball among starters
RP	Dellin Betances, Yankees	26	5	0	1	1.40	90	135	24	5.6 SO/BB ratio and unhittable two-pitch mix (.149 average)

in Atlanta for 12 years," Maddux said. "I learned how to pitch in Chicago and I learned how to win and raise my family in Atlanta. I love both cities and fans equally, and I'd never be able to choose one over the other."

Thomas made a lot of memories by hitting 521 home runs in 19 seasons with the White Sox, Athletics and Blue Jays and won back-to-back AL Most Valuable Player awards in 1993-94. He became the first player to play more than half his games at DH and make the Hall of Fame.

While his boyhood dream of playing for the Braves was never fulfilled, being elected to the Hall of Fame was a nice consolation prize.

"When you're a kid, you dream about playing in the big leagues, playing in All-Star Games, playing in World Series," Thomas said. "I don't think any kid dreams about going into the Hall of Fame. It just seems so out of reach, so impossible."

Frank Thomas will be remembered as the greatest hitter in the history of the White Sox, the team that gave La Russa his first major league manager's job. La Russa also managed the Athletics and Cardinals and won 2,728 games in 33 seasons to rank third on the all-time list while winning six pennants and three World Series.

The White Sox hired La Russa when he was 34 years old and managing their Triple-A Iowa farm club. La Russa thought general manager Roland Hemond was calling to tell him catcher Mike Colbern was being called up to the major leagues. Instead, it was La Russa who got the call after Chicago manager Don Kessinger had resigned.

"I got a call at 1 p.m. and was told they were announcing a new manager at 4 p.m.," La Russa said. "I never dreamed it would end up here in Cooperstown all these years later."

While Torre is remembered by younger fans for managing the Yankees, he was an outstanding player as a catcher and third baseman. He played for 18 seasons, participated in nine All-Star Games and was the NL MVP in 1971 while with the Cardinals.

Torre also won six pennants and four World Series during 12 years as the Yankees' manager. He managed 29 seasons, in all, as he also had stints with New York Mets, Braves and Dodgers, finishing with 2,326 wins—fifth on the all-time list.

"Baseball is a game of life," Torre said. "It's not perfect, but it feels like it is. That's the magic of it. We are responsible for giving it the respect it deserves. Our sport is part of the American soul, and it's ours to borrow—just for a while.

"If all of us who love baseball and are doing our jobs, then those who get the game from us will be as proud to be a part of it as we were. And we are. This game is a gift, and I am humbled, very humbled, to accept its greatest honor."

Roger Angell, who has authored seven best-selling books on baseball, received the J.G. Taylor Spink Award for meritorious service to baseball writing and Rangers radio play-by-play announcer Eric Nadel received the Ford C. Frick Award for excellence in broadcasting.

Elbow Epidemic

Elbow injuries have become more common in the game as pitchers throw harder and put more torque on their arms with their breaking pitches. However, it seemed that elbow injuries became an epidemic in 2014. A week rarely went by without another pitcher going under the knife.

A 2013 survey showed 25 percent of big league pitchers and 15 percent of minor league pitchers

had undergone the procedure. Though MLB did not release updated numbers during the 2014 season, it seemed certain that the percentages rose. A total of 84 pitchers had the surgery between the majors and minors, including five former all-stars: the Diamondbacks' Bronson Arroyo and Patrick Corbin, the Marlins' Jose Fernandez, the Padres' Josh Johnson and the Rays' Matt Moore.

"It's a problem. There's no question about it," commissioner Bud Selig said. "I'm almost afraid to pick up the paper every day because there's some bad news. We've got to find ways to prevent these injuries from happening. I don't know how we're going to do it but we need to find a way to keep pitchers healthy."

MLB held a summit meeting at its headquarters in May that included Dr. James Andrews, one of the nation's foremost orthopedic surgeons. Andrews admitted, though, that he and some of the other top elbow experts had yet to put their finger on why so many ligaments were being torn.

"We don't know quite what to say at this point," Andrews said.

Ulnar collateral reconstruction surgery had

UNDER THE KNIFE

Eighty-seven players had Tommy John surgery in 2014, according to the accounting of Hardball Times writer Jon Roegele.

Player	Surgery	Team	Pos	Throws	Age
Anthony Prieto	1/1/14	CHC	P	L	20
Jose Lopez	1/1/14	CIN	P	R	20
Tyler Stirewalt	1/1/14	MIN	P	R	23
Javier Herrera	1/1/14	SF	OF	R	29
Jacob Bray	3/1/14	BAL	P	R	21
Barret Loux	3/1/14	CHC	P	R	25
Miguel Sano	3/12/14	MIN	3B	R	21
Clay Holmes	3/19/14	PIT	P	R	21
Jace Chancellor	3/19/14	SD	P	R	23
Connor Sadzeck	3/26/14	TEX	P	R	22
Corey Williams	4/1/14	MIN	P	L	23
Nick McBride	4/1/14	TEX	P	R	23
Ross Stripling	4/2/14	LAD	P	R	24
Jameson Taillon	4/9/14	PIT	P	R	22
Wes Benjamin	4/10/14	TEX	P	L	20
Brian Moran	4/15/14	LAA	P	L	25
Junior Morillo	4/22/14	CIN	P	L	22
Ben Smith	4/24/14	HOU	P	L	21
Jose Campos	4/25/14	NYY	P	R	21
Johnny Hellweg	4/29/14	MIL	P	R	25
Mac Williamson	4/29/14	SF	OF	R	23
Matt Reistetter	5/7/14	WAS	C	R	22
Danny Rosenbaum	5/8/14	WAS	P	L	26
Tyler Bashlor	5/13/14	NYM	P	R	21
Raul Alcantara	5/14/14	OAK	P	R	21
Jeff Hoffman	5/14/14	TOR	P	R	21
Chad Jones	5/20/14	CIN	P	L	25
Anthony Fernandez	5/22/14	SEA	P	L	24
Scott McGough	5/27/14	MIA	P	R	24
Clinton Hollon	5/27/14	TOR	P	R	19
Brad Renner	5/28/14	CHC	P	R	23
Randy Rosario	5/28/14	MIN	P	L	20
Keith Butler	5/28/14	STL	P	R	25
Matt Purke	5/29/14	WAS	P	L	23
Caleb Ferguson	5/30/14	LAD	P	L	17
Erick Fedde	6/3/14	WAS	P	R	21
Duke Welker	6/5/14	PIT	P	R	28
Daniel Moskos	6/17/14	LAD	P	L	28
Jeff Walters	6/17/14	NYM	P	R	26
Josh Pennington	6/24/14	BOS	P	R	18
Derek Law	6/24/14	SF	P	R	23
Daniel Winkler	7/1/14	COL	P	R	24
Endrys Briceno	7/1/14	DET	P	R	22
Fernando Romero	7/1/14	MIN	P	R	19
Chris Flexen	7/1/14	NYM	P	R	19
Marvin Gorgas	7/1/14	SEA	P	R	18
Tom Robson	7/15/14	TOR	P	R	21
Dylan Cease	7/22/14	CHC	P	R	18
Dustin Houle	7/22/14	MIL	C	R	20
Hector Hernandez	7/25/14	ARI	P	L	23
Stephen Fife	7/30/14	LAD	P	R	27
Dillon Peters	7/31/14	MIA	P	L	21
Ramon Morla	8/1/14	SEA	3B	R	24
Tyler Saladino	8/14/14	CHW	SS	R	24
Neil Wagner	8/19/14	TOR	P	R	30
Max Fried	8/20/14	SD	P	L	20
Jeff Ibarra	9/24/14	SD	P	L	26
Mark Clark	9/24/14	TB	C	R	18
Cory Luebke	2/18/14	SD	P	L	29
Kris Medlen	3/18/14	ATL	P	R	28
Luke Hochevar	3/18/14	KC	P	R	30
Brandon Beachy	3/21/14	ATL	P	R	27
Jarrod Parker	3/24/14	OAK	P	R	25
Patrick Corbin	3/25/14	ARI	P	L	24
Bruce Rondon	3/29/14	DET	P	R	23
David Hernandez	4/1/14	ARI	P	R	29
Peter Moylan	4/1/14	LAD	P	R	35
Erik Davis	4/2/14	WAS	P	R	27
Bobby Parnell	4/8/14	NYM	P	R	29
Cory Gearrin	4/16/14	ATL	P	R	28
Matt Moore	4/22/14	TB	P	L	25
Josh Johnson	4/24/14	SD	P	R	30
Ivan Nova	4/29/14	NYY	P	R	27
A.J. Griffin	4/30/14	OAK	P	R	26
Pedro Figueroa	4/30/14	TEX	P	L	28
Jose Fernandez	5/16/14	MIA	P	R	21
Martin Perez	5/19/14	TEX	P	L	23
Jose Cisnero	5/28/14	HOU	P	R	25
Chris Withrow	6/3/14	LAD	P	R	25
Sean Burnett	6/5/14	LAA	P	L	31
Matt Wieters	6/17/14	BAL	C	R	28
Bronson Arroyo	7/15/14	ARI	P	R	37
Tyler Chatwood	7/23/14	COL	P	R	24
Nate Jones	7/29/14	CHW	P	R	28
Tyler Skaggs	8/13/14	LAA	P	L	22
Jonny Venters	9/17/14	ATL	P	L	29
Jeremy Hefner	10/9/14	NYM	P	R	28

increased tenfold in the first decade of the 21st century, Andrews and Dr. Jeremy Bruce wrote in the May issue of the Journal of the American Academy of Orthopaedic Surgeons, citing a paper by J.R. Dugas. Experts think young pitchers throw far more often now than they did a decade or two ago.

"Baseball, once considered a seasonal sport, has become a year-round event in some regions of the United States, with increased team travel play and sponsored tournaments," Andrews and Bruce wrote.

Dr. Bert Mandelbaum, Major League Baseball's director of medical research, began collecting data on injuries and lengths of layoffs in both the major leagues and minor leagues going back to 2010.

"We're looking at it in terms of the demographics: Can we predict who is going to get this injury? Is there something in their training? Is there something in their biomechanics?" said Dr. Gary Green, MLB's medical director.

Dr. Frank Jobe pioneered the operation in 1974 when he operated on John. There were no more than four similar surgeries performed on a major league pitcher until a spike to 12 in 1996, according to research by Jon Roegele, a writer for the Hardball Times. The figure rose to 43 by 2003 and 69 in 2012 before dropping to 49 last year then jumped to 84 in 2014.

John told The Associated Press that he believes too much weight training has led to weakened ligaments and more operations bearing his name.

"These guys today, they spend more time in the weight room than they do on the mound. Strengths and weights are fine, but if that was everything, then Arnold Schwarzenegger would be a 20-game winner," he said. "They just get so big and strong that there's very little elasticity in their arms."

Can't Manage It

Two managers were fired during the season and the ax fell on a third the day after the season ended.

However, the biggest surprise managerial change came when the Rangers' Ron Washington resigned Sept. 5, saying he needed to devote his full attention to an "off-the-field personal matter." A few weeks later, Washington held a brief news conference saying he had been unfaithful to his wife.

Washington's resignation came a day after his team lost its sixth straight game to fall to 53-87 and become the first team in the major leagues mathematically eliminated from playoff contention. It was a steep drop from 2010-11, when the Rangers made the first two World Series appear-

AMERICAN LEAGUE BEST TOOLS

A Baseball America survey of American League managers, conducted at midseason 2014, ranked players with the best tools.

BEST HITTER
1. Miguel Cabrera, Tigers
2. Mike Trout, Angels
3. Robinson Cano, Mariners

BEST POWER
1. Jose Abreu, White Sox
2. Miguel Cabrera, Tigers
3. Edwin Encarnacion, Blue Jays

BEST BUNTER
1. Erick Aybar, Angels
2. Brett Gardner, Yankees
3. Alcides Escobar, Royals

BEST STRIKE-ZONE JUDGMENT
1. Victor Martinez, Tigers
2. Miguel Cabrera, Tigers
3. Carlos Santana, Indians

BEST HIT-AND-RUN ARTIST
1. Erick Aybar, Angels
2 (tie). Jose Altuve, Astros
2 (tie). Michael Brantley, Indians

BEST BASERUNNER
1. Jose Altuve, Astros
2. Jacoby Ellsbury, Yankees
3. Coco Crisp, Athletics

FASTEST BASERUNNER
1. Jarrod Dyson, Royals
2. Rajai Davis, Tigers
3. Mike Trout, Angels

MOST EXCITING PLAYER
1. Mike Trout, Angels
2. Miguel Cabrera, Tigers
3. Jose Altuve, Astros

BEST PITCHER
1. Felix Hernandez, Mariners
2. Masahiro Tanaka, Yankees
3. Jon Lester, Red Sox/Athletics

BEST FASTBALL
1. Garrett Richards, Angels
2. Jake McGee, Rays
3. Yordano Ventura, Royals

BEST CURVEBALL
1. Dellin Betances, Yankees
2. Corey Kluber, Indians
3. Justin Verlander, Tigers

BEST SLIDER
1. Yu Darvish, Rangers
2 (tie). Chris Sale, White Sox
2 (tie). Max Scherzer, Tigers

BEST CHANGEUP
1. Felix Hernandez, Mariners
2 (tie). Max Scherzer, Tigers
2 (tie). James Shields, Royals

BEST CONTROL
1. David Price, Rays/Tigers
2. Hisashi Iwakuma, Mariners
3. Phil Hughes, Twins

BEST PICKOFF MOVE
1. Mark Buehrle, Blue Jays
2. James Shields, Royals
3. Ryan Feierabend, Rangers

BEST RELIEVER
1. Greg Holland, Royals
2. Dellin Betances, Yankees
3. Koji Uehara, Red Sox

BEST DEFENSIVE CATCHER
1. Salvador Perez, Royals
2. Alex Avila, Tigers
3. Yan Gomes, Indians

BEST DEFENSIVE 1B
1. Eric Hosmer, Royals
2. James Loney, Rays
3. Mark Teixeira, Yankees

BEST DEFENSIVE 2B
1. Dustin Pedroia, Red Sox
2. Robinson Cano, Mariners
3. Ian Kinsler, Tigers

BEST DEFENSIVE 3B
1. Adrian Beltre, Rangers
2. Evan Longoria, Rays
3. Josh Donaldson, Athletics

BEST DEFENSIVE SS
1. Alcides Escobar, Royals
2. Erick Aybar, Angels
3. J.J. Hardy, Orioles

BEST INFIELD ARM
1. Adrian Beltre, Rangers
2. Manny Machado, Orioles
3. Yunel Escobar, Rays

BEST DEFENSIVE OF
1. Alex Gordon, Royals
2. Adam Jones, Orioles
3. Mike Trout, Angels

BEST OUTFIELD ARM
1. Yoenis Cespedes, Athletics/Red Sox
2. Leonys Martin, Rangers
3. Jose Bautista, Blue Jays

BEST MANAGER
1. Bob Melvin, Athletics
2. Mike Scioscia, Angels
3. Joe Maddon, Rays

ances in franchise history under Washington.

"It's like losing your dad," Rangers lefthander Derek Holland said. "I was extremely close with

CONTINUED ON PAGE 19

ORGANIZATION OF THE YEAR

Worth wait for Royals

J.J. COOPER

When Dayton Moore was hired as the Royals' general manager in 2006, he said that this front office would bring the Royals back to prominence through an emphasis on player development via the draft and international signings.

Eight years later, he's been a man of his word. The Royals have not won a title, but they came as close as you could in 2014. In Game Seven of the World Series, the Royals' left the tying run at third base in the bottom of the ninth inning.

But even in falling short, the Royals revitalized what once was a baseball hotbed but had fallen into disrepair.

As a small-market team, the only way the Royals can sustain success is through stellar scouting and player development. Eight of the nine regulars, four of the five starting pitchers and the two setup men and closer were homegrown or acquired when the Royals traded homegrown talent. It took longer than most expected–a lot longer.

But Baseball America ranked the Royals farm system 28th in the game in 2005 and 23rd heading into 2006. The farm system Moore's staff took over in 2006 featured Alex Gordon, Billy Butler and Mike Aviles. That was it. Not one pitching prospect in the organization at the time of Moore's hiring went on to have a significant big league career. Of the Royals' five Class A and rookie-level clubs at the time, just three position players (Ed Lucas, Irving Falu and Jeff Bianchi) made the majors.

When Moore agreed to take the job, he

Catcher Salvador Perez emerged as a team leader and defensive stalwart

BILL NICHOLS

PREVIOUS WINNERS

2003: Florida Marlins
2004: Minnesota Twins
2005: Atlanta Braves
2006: Los Angeles Dodgers
2007: Colorado Rockies
2008: Tampa Bay Rays
2009: Philadelphia Phillies
2010: San Francisco Giants
2011: St. Louis Cardinals
2012: Cincinnati Reds
2013: St. Louis Cardinals

Full list: BaseballAmerica.com/awards

got a commitment from the Glass family that they would spend significant money on player development. The Royals spent at least $6.6 million on every draft class from 2007-2014 and have averaged nearly $9 million a year in draft spending. The Royals hired Rene Francisco and revitalized an international scouting program.

Mike Moustakas, Danny Duffy and Greg Holland were part of Moore's 2007 draft class. Salvador Perez and Kelvin Herrera were signed on the new front office's first significant Latin American scouting trip in 2006.

Eric Hosmer, Yordano Ventura and other contributors arrived at the tail end of a new wave of prospects. Wil Myers was shipped off to bring back James Shields and Wade Davis.

After putting together a run to the World Series, the Royals now need to prove that they have a second act. When they were finishing assembling their first wave of prospects, they talked of the need for a second and third wave.

Moore lived up to his promise to build a winner. Now he gets a chance to try to make it last.

CONTINUED FROM PAGE 17

him. He's taught me a lot both on and off the field and I didn't see any of this coming at all. I'm lost for words."

Washington had received a one-year contract extension in spring training that covered the 2015 season and general manager Jon Daniels said the team had not considered changing managers during an injury-ravaged year.

Washington joined the Rangers in 2007 and had a 664-611 record.

Bench coach Tim Bogar replaced Washington on an interim basis but Pirates bench coach Jeff Banister was hired after the season as the permanent replacement.

Astros manager Bo Porter, in just his second season, was fired Sept. 1. Houston was 59-79 at the time, a marked improvement over his first year when they had the worst record in the major leagues for a third consecutive season at 51-111.

"I hope he realizes that he was doing as well as he could, given the circumstances," Astros right-hander Scott Feldman said. "It's tough to see, but Bo's a strong guy and I'm sure he'll be back on his feet and back in the game whenever he wants to be."

Former Diamondbacks manager A.J. Hinch, who had been serving as a special assistant to the general manager with the Padres, was hired to replace Porter after Astros minor league infield coordinator Tom Lawless finished out the last month of the season on an interim basis.

Diamondbacks manager Kirk Gibson was let go with three games left, not a surprise as the organization figured to undergo sweeping changes after Hall of Fame manager Tony La Russa was hired to the newly created position of chief baseball officer in May.

The Diamondbacks finished the season with a 64-98 record, the worst in the major leagues. They won the NL West under Gibson in 2011 but he finished with a 353-375 record in his five-year stint. Athletics bench coach Chip Hale, once a coach and minor league manager for Arizona, was hired as Gibson's replacement.

Kevin Towers was also fired as GM and La Russa tabbed Dave Stewart, his former ace pitcher when he managed the Athletics, as the replacement. Stewart had most recently worked as a player agent.

Ron Gardenhire's 13-year run as the Twins' manager ended when he was canned the day after the season ended. The affable skipper led Minnesota to the postseason six times in his first

MAJOR LEAGUES

NATIONAL LEAGUE BEST TOOLS

A Baseball America survey of National League managers, conducted at midseason 2014, ranked players with the best tools.

BEST HITTER
1. Troy Tulowitzki, Rockies
2. Andrew McCutchen, Pirates
3. Paul Goldschmidt, D-backs

BEST POWER
1. Giancarlo Stanton, Marlins
2. Paul Goldschmidt, D-backs
3. Yasiel Puig, Dodgers

BEST BUNTER
1. Dee Gordon, Dodgers
2. Billy Hamilton, Reds
3. Everth Cabrera, Padres

BEST STRIKE-ZONE JUDGMENT
1. Andrew McCutchen, Pirates
2. Joey Votto, Reds
3. Matt Carpenter, Cardinals

BEST HIT AND RUN ARTIST
1. Yadier Molina, Cardinals
2 (tie). Martin Prado, D-backs/Yankees
2 (tie). Jonathan Lucroy, Brewers

BEST BASERUNNER
1. Billy Hamilton, Reds
2. Dee Gordon, Dodgers
3. Andrew McCutchen, Pirates

FASTEST BASERUNNER
1. Billy Hamilton, Reds
2. Dee Gordon, Dodgers
3. Ben Revere, Phillies

MOST EXCITING PLAYER
1. Andrew McCutchen, Pirates
2. Yasiel Puig, Dodgers
3. Carlos Gomez, Brewers

BEST PITCHER
1. Clayton Kershaw, Dodgers
2. Adam Wainwright, Cardinals
3. Johnny Cueto, Reds

BEST FASTBALL
1. Aroldis Chapman, Reds
2. Craig Kimbrel, Braves
3. Edinson Volquez, Pirates

BEST CURVEBALL
1. Adam Wainwright, Cardinals
2. Clayton Kershaw, Dodgers
3. Julio Teheran, Braves

BEST SLIDER
1. Craig Kimbrel, Braves
2. Clayton Kershaw, Dodgers
3. Jose Fernandez, Marlins

BEST CHANGEUP
1. Cole Hamels, Phillies
2. Johnny Cueto, Reds

3. Stephen Strasburg, Nationals

BEST CONTROL
1. Adam Wainwright, Cardinals
2. Clayton Kershaw, Dodgers
3. Zack Greinke, Dodgers

BEST PICKOFF MOVE
1. Madison Bumgarner, Giants
2. Julio Teheran, Braves
3. Johnny Cueto, Reds

BEST RELIEVER
1. Craig Kimbrel, Braves
2. Aroldis Chapman, Reds
3. Kenley Jansen, Dodgers

BEST DEFENSIVE CATCHER
1. Yadier Molina, Cardinals
2. Jonathan Lucroy, Brewers
3. Russell Martin, Pirates

BEST DEFENSIVE 1B
1. Adam LaRoche, Nationals
2. Paul Goldschmidt, D-backs
3. Freddie Freeman, Braves

BEST DEFENSIVE 2B
1. Brandon Phillips, Reds
2. D.J. LeMahieu, Rockies
3. Chase Utley, Phillies

BEST DEFENSIVE 3B
1. Nolan Arenado, Rockies
2. David Wright, Mets
3. Todd Frazier, Reds

BEST DEFENSIVE SS
1. Andrelton Simmons, Braves
2. Troy Tulowitzki, Rockies
3. Ian Desmond, Nationals

BEST INFIELD ARM
1. Andrelton Simmons, Braves
2. Troy Tulowitzki, Rockies
3. Ian Desmond, Nationals

BEST DEFENSIVE OF
1. Andrew McCutchen, Pirates
2. Carlos Gomez, Brewers
3. Gerardo Parra, D-backs

BEST OUTFIELD ARM
1. Yasiel Puig, Dodgers
2. Gerardo Parra, D-backs
3. Carlos Gonzalez, Rockies

BEST MANAGER
1. Bruce Bochy, Giants
2. Mike Matheny, Cardinals
3. Fredi Gonzalez, Braves

nine years from 2002-10—though they went just 6-21 in the playoffs—but the Twins lost at least 92 games in each of his final four seasons.

CONTINUED ON PAGE 21

MAJOR LEAGUE *ALL-STARS*

BILL NICHOLS

Mike Trout topped the American League in runs, total bases, RBIs and strikeouts

BILL NICHOLS

Buster Posey helped the Giants to a World Series title while batting a team-best .311

FIRST TEAM

Pos.	Player, Team	AVG	OBP	SLG	AB	R	H	2B	3B	HR	RBI	BB	SO	SB	CS
C	Jonathan Lucroy	.301	.373	.465	585	73	176	53	2	13	69	66	71	4	4
1B	Jose Abreu	.317	.383	.581	556	80	176	35	2	36	107	51	131	3	1
2B	Jose Altuve	.341	.377	.453	660	85	225	47	3	7	59	36	53	56	9
3B	Adrian Beltre	.324	.388	.492	549	79	178	33	1	19	77	57	74	1	1
SS	Hanley Ramirez	.283	.369	.448	449	64	127	35	0	13	71	56	84	14	5
CF	Andrew McCutchen	.314	.410	.542	548	89	172	38	6	25	83	84	115	18	3
OF	Mike Trout	.287	.377	.561	602	115	173	39	9	36	111	83	184	16	2
OF	Giancarlo Stanton	.288	.395	.555	539	89	155	31	1	37	105	94	170	13	1
DH	Victor Martinez	.335	.409	.565	561	87	188	33	0	32	103	70	42	3	2

Pos.	Pitcher, Team	W	L	ERA	G	GS	SV	IP	H	R	ER	HR	BB	SO	WHIP
SP	* Clayton Kershaw, LAD	21	3	1.77	27	27	0	198	139	42	39	9	31	239	0.86
SP	Corey Kluber, CLE	18	9	2.44	34	34	0	236	207	72	64	14	51	269	1.09
SP	Felix Hernandez, SEA	15	6	2.14	34	34	0	236	170	68	56	16	46	248	0.92
SP	Johnny Cueto, CIN	20	9	2.25	34	34	0	245	169	69	61	22	65	242	0.96
SP	Adam Wainwright, STL	20	9	2.38	32	32	0	227	184	64	60	10	50	179	1.03
RP	Dellin Betances, NYY	5	0	1.40	70	0	1	90	46	15	14	4	24	135	0.78

SECOND TEAM

Pos.	Player, Team	AVG	OBP	SLG	AB	R	H	2B	3B	HR	RBI	BB	SO	SB	CS
C	Buster Posey	.311	.364	.490	547	72	170	28	2	22	89	47	69	0	1
1B	Miguel Cabrera	.313	.371	.524	611	101	191	52	1	25	109	60	117	1	1
2B	* Robinson Cano	.314	.382	.454	595	77	187	37	2	14	82	61	68	10	3
3B	Anthony Rendon	.287	.351	.473	613	111	176	39	6	21	83	58	104	17	3
SS	Jhonny Peralta	.263	.336	.443	560	61	147	38	0	21	75	58	112	3	2
CF	* Michael Brantley	.327	.385	.506	611	94	200	45	2	20	97	52	56	23	1
OF	Jose Bautista	.286	.403	.524	553	101	158	27	0	35	103	104	96	6	2
OF	Yasiel Puig	.296	.382	.480	558	92	165	37	9	16	69	67	124	11	7
DH	Paul Goldschmidt	.300	.396	.542	406	75	122	39	1	19	69	64	110	9	3
DH	Nelson Cruz	.271	.333	.525	613	87	166	32	2	40	108	55	140	4	5

Pos.	Pitcher, Team	W	L	ERA	G	GS	SV	IP	H	R	ER	HR	BB	SO	WHIP
SP	Chris Sale, CHW	12	4	2.17	26	26	0	174	129	48	42	13	39	208	0.97
SP	Cole Hamels, PHI	9	9	2.46	30	30	0	205	176	60	56	14	59	198	1.15
SP	Jon Lester, BOS/OAK	16	11	2.46	32	32	0	220	194	76	60	16	48	220	1.10
SP	Garrett Richards, LAA	13	4	2.61	26	26	0	169	124	51	49	5	51	164	1.04
SP	Jordan Zimmermann WAS	14	5	2.66	32	32	0	200	185	67	59	13	29	182	1.07
RP	Wade Davis, KC	9	2	1.00	71	0	0	72	38	8	8	0	23	109	0.85

EXECUTIVE OF THE YEAR

Dan Duquette spent 10 years in baseball's wilderness after being cast out in March 2002 by the new Red Sox ownership group of John Henry, Tom Werner and Larry Lucchino. He was criticized as aloof and arrogant and came to rue his comments about Roger Clemens being in the twilight of his career when he left Boston in 1996. A return to baseball seemed less and less likely as the years passed—although Duquette said he turned down other offers—until the Orioles came calling in November 2011, a hiring that stunned observers and fans. But Duquette, as he's done in previous stints with the Expos and Red Sox, worked the roster margins well, adding useful, inexpensive pieces that led to great depth for an Orioles team that in 2014 ran away with a weakened AL East.

Dan Duquette

PREVIOUS WINNERS

2002: Billy Beane, Athletics **2008:** Theo Epstein, Red Sox
2003: Brian Sabean, Giants **2009:** Dan O'Dowd, Rockies
2004: Terry Ryan, Twins **2010:** Jon Daniels, Rangers
2005: Mark Shapiro, Indians **2011:** Doug Melvin, Brewers
2006: Dave Dombrowski, Tigers **2012:** Billy Beane, Athletics
2007: Jack Zduriencik, Brewers **2013:** Dan Duquette, Orioles

Full list: BaseballAmerica.com/awards

MANAGER OF THE YEAR

Inflexible. Intractable. Wears out his welcome— quick. Those were the criticisms lobbed at Buck Showalter, who was not a part of a Major League organization from 2007-09 after he was fired by the Rangers following the 2006 season. But he was hired to turn around the listing Orioles for the final third of the 2010 season and after a 93-loss 2011 season, got them pointed in the right direction, culminating in a 96-win season and their first AL East title since 1997. Showalter's strength is in utilizing his roster depth to great results, getting useful at-bats from players such as Steve Pearce, Jimmy Paredes and Caleb Joseph and allowing rookies such as Jonathan Schoop to play through struggles. At 58 and in his fourth managerial job, Showalter, appears to have taken lessons from previous stops.

DIAMOND IMAGES

Buck Showalter

PREVIOUS WINNERS

2002: Mike Scioscia, Angels **2008:** Ron Gardenhire, Twins
2003: Jack McKeon, Marlins **2009:** Mike Scioscia, Angels
2004: Bobby Cox, Braves **2010:** Bobby Cox, Braves
2005: Ozzie Guillen, White Sox **2011:** Joe Maddon, Rays
2006: Jim Leyland, Tigers **2012:** Buck Showalter, Orioles
2007: Terry Francona, Red Sox **2013:** Clint Hurdles, Pirates

Full list: BaseballAmerica.com/awards

CONTINUED FROM PAGE 19

"I'm gone, I'm outta here because we didn't win," Gardenhire said. "That's what it gets down to in baseball. That's what it should get down to. You have to win on the field and these last four years have been tough for all of us."

Towers was one of six GMs who were either fired, resigned, switched jobs or were reassigned. The Braves' Frank Wren and Padres' Josh Byrnes were also jettisoned.

The Braves decided to make a move with Wren with one week left in just the sixth of the last 23 completed seasons in which they failed to make the playoffs. Citing problems with the organization's scouting and player development, club president John Schuerholz said it was time to get back to "The Braves Way."

Byrnes was dismissed June 22, in the middle of

his third year on the job, with the Padres on their way to their fourth straight losing season. Under Byrnes, the Padres payroll increased nearly $40 million to $89 million but the franchise made little progress.

"This ownership group is committed to fielding a team that consistently competes for postseason play," Padres CEO Mike Dee said. "After a lengthy evaluation of every facet of our baseball operations, we have decided to make this change today."

The Padres hired Rangers assistant GM A.J. Preller as their new GM on Aug. 5.

Dan O'Dowd, who had been stripped of much of his power with the Rockies in recent years, turned down a two-year contract extension at the end of the season and decided to resign. While on the job for 15 seasons—a virtual eternity in today's game—O'Dowd produced just four teams

with winning records and two postseason berths, including 2007, when the Rockies were swept by the Red Sox in the franchise's lone World Series appearance.

Senior vice president of baseball operations Bill Geivett, who had been making most of the baseball decisions in recent years, was fired. The Rockies stayed inside the organization for their new GM, promoting senior director of player development Jeff Bridich.

After leading the small-market Rays to four postseason appearances in the span of six years from 2008-13, vice president of baseball operation Andrew Friedman decided to move on to one of the biggest markets as he was hired by the Dodgers to be their president of baseball operations.

Dodgers GM Ned Colletti was reassigned to the job of special adviser to club president and CEO Stan Kasten. Team president Matt Silverman was put in charge of the Rays' baseball operations.

Shortly thereafter, manager Joe Maddon exercised an opt-out clause in his contract and eventually took over the helm of the Cubs.

Handful Of No-Nos

The season was highlighted by five no-hitters, the first thrown by a pitcher in his final season when Dodgers righthander Josh Beckett pitched his gem at Philadelphia on May 25. The 34-year-old would win just three more games before going on the disabled list Aug. 4 with a hip injury then deciding to retire at the end of the season.

It was the first no-hitter of Beckett's 14-year career and came after he was limited to eight starts in 2013—going 0-5, 5.19—before undergoing surgery to repair a nerve condition.

"You don't think at this point of your career that you're going to do that," Beckett said after the no-hitter.

The Phillies were also on the positive side of a no-hitter Sept. 1 when four pitchers combined to shut down the Braves in Atlanta. Lefthander Cole Hamels pitched the first six innings but was removed from the game with his pitch count at 108. Set-up reliever Jake Diekman, rookie Ken Giles and closer Jonathan Papelbon finished with one scoreless inning each.

"I think having a combined no-hitter is very difficult because guys have to come right in and get the guys out, no matter what the situation is," Hamels said. "It's a little more dramatic to be able to see that you're trying to play the cards as best you can against the lineup."

Giants righthander Tim Lincecum made history when he became the first pitcher to throw two no-

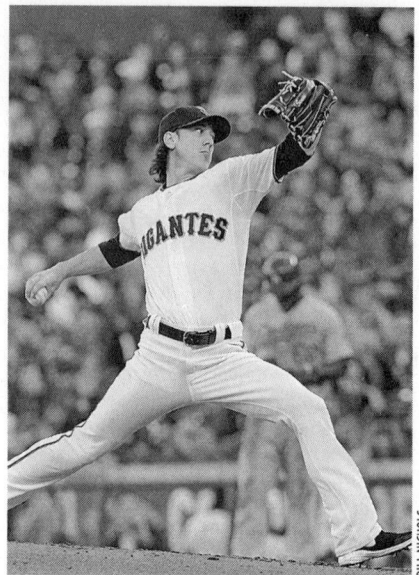

BILL NICHOLS

Tim Lincecum pitched a no-hitter against the Padres for the second year in a row

hitters against the same team, pulling off the feat at home against the Padres on June 25 for the second straight season.

"It's hard enough to do one," Giants manager Bruce Bochy said. "To do two, that puts you in a little different class."

Dodgers lefthander Clayton Kershaw had the season's most dominant no-hitter June 18 versus the Rockies. Kershaw struck out 15 and did not walk a batter as the only runner he allowed reached on a two-base error by shortstop Hanley Ramirez on a ball hit by Corey Dickerson to lead off the seventh inning.

Even the opposition was awestruck by Kershaw's performance.

"When there's a special moment for someone, you want to watch how a guy responds," Rockies shortstop Troy Tulowitzki said. "It was nice for me to see how much it means for him. If something can bring tears to someone's eyes, it means you really care—and he cares a lot about this game."

For the second year in a row, there was a no-hitter on the last day of the season as Nationals righthander Jordan Zimmermann tossed a no-no against the visiting Marlins. Rookie left fielder Steven Souza, inserted into the game for defensive purposes at the start of the ninth inning by manager Matt Williams, preserved the gem by making

CONTINUED ON PAGE 24

Fitting finale for Jeter

ALL-STAR GAME

Derek Jeter's final season included a storybook All-Star Game send off

BILL NICHOLS

JOHN PERROTTO

The All-Star Game, for the second year in a row, turned out to be more about honoring a retiring New York Yankees legend than the game itself.

Derek Jeter made his 14th and final All-Star Game a memorable one, going 2-for-2 and helping the American League earn a 5-3 victory over the National League at Target Field in Minneapolis.

The shortstop started a three-run run first inning with a double. He also singled in the third, then took his position in the field to start the fourth inning. AL manager John Farrell of the Boston Red Sox sent out the White Sox's Alexei Ramirez to replace Jeter, who received a long ovation.

"I really appreciated the response, from the crowd and from the players on both teams," Jeter said. "It was very humbling."

Farrell had Jeter's exit planned in advance.

"We tried to get him two at-bats and then having him come out," Farrell said. "You know what, he has a flair for the dramatic. Two base hits and scored the first run. It worked out pretty well."

It was reminiscent of the 2013 All-Star Game at Citi Field in New York when Yankees closer Mariano Rivera was the focus of the festivities. Rivera was named the game's Most Valuable Player after pitching the ninth for the save.

Jeter wasn't the MVP in 2014, though.

Fittingly, Los Angeles Angels center fielder Mike Trout, who seems poised to replace Jeter as the face of Major League Baseball, won the honor. He went 2-for-3 with two extra-base hits and two RBIs.

"Derek Jeter was my role model growing up," Trout said. "To be the MVP in his last All-Star Game is really special to me."

Trout's double in a two-run fifth inning off St. Louis Cardinals reliever Pat Neshek broke a 3-3 tie and proved to be the game-winning hit.

Oakland Athletics left fielder Yoenis Cespedes won the All-Star Home Run Derby for the second straight season, then was traded to the Red Sox later in the month.

JULY 15, 2014

American League 5, National League 3

National	AB	R	H	BI	American	AB	R	H	BI
McCutchen, CF	3	0	1	0	Jeter, SS	2	1	2	0
Blackmon, CF	2	0	0	0	Al.Ramirez, SS	2	1	1	0
Puig, RF	3	0	0	0	Aybar, SS	0	0	0	0
Pence, RF	1	0	0	0	Trout, LF	3	1	2	2
Tulowitzki, SS	3	0	1	0	Moss, RF	1	0	0	0
Castro, S, SS	1	0	0	0	Cano, 2B	2	0	0	0
Goldschmidt, 1B	3	0	0	0	Altuve, 2B	0	0	0	1
Freeman, F, 1B	1	0	1	0	d-Kinsler, PH-2B	1	0	0	0
Stanton, DH	3	0	0	0	M.Cabrera, 1B	3	1	1	2
a-Rizzo, PH-DH	1	0	0	0	Abreu, 1B	1	0	0	0
Ramirez, Ar, 3B	3	1	2	0	Bautista, RF	2	0	0	0
Frazier, 3B	0	0	0	0	Cespedes, LF	2	0	0	0
Utley, 2B	1	1	1	1	N.Cruz, DH	2	0	0	0
b-Gordon, D, PR-2B	1	0	0	0	c-Seager, PH-DH	2	0	0	0
Murphy, Dn, 2B	1	0	0	0	Ad.Jones, CF	2	0	0	0
Lucroy, C	2	0	2	2	A.Beltre, 3B	0	0	0	0
Mesoraco, C	1	0	0	0	Donaldson, 3B	2	0	0	0
M.Montero, C	1	0	0	0	Brantley, CF	1	0	0	0
C.Gomez, LF	2	0	0	0	S.Perez, C	1	0	0	0
J.Harrison, LF	2	0	0	0	D.Norris, C	2	1	1	0
					K.Suzuki, C	0	0	0	0
Totals	**35**	**3**	**8**	**3**	**Totals**	**31**	**5**	**7**	**5**

National	0	2	0	1	0 0 0 0 0	—	3
American	3	0	0	0	2 0 0 0 x	—	5

a-Struck out for Stanton in the 8th; b-Ran for Utley in the 4th; c-Grounded out for Cruz, N in the 6th; d-Struck out for Altuve in the 7th.

LOB—American 4, National 7. E: Freeman. 2B: Utley, Lucroy 2, Tulowitzki, Ar.Ramirez, Jeter, Trout. 3B: Trout. HR: M.Cabrera. SB: McCutchen, Al.Ramirez.

National	IP	H	ER	BB	SO	American	IP	H	ER	BB	SO
Wainwright	1	3	3	0	2	Hernandez	1	1	0	0	2
Kershaw	1	0	0	0	1	Lester	1	3	2	0	0
Simon	1	1	0	0	1	Darvish	1	0	0	0	1
Greinke	1	0	0	0	2	Sale	1	1	1	0	1
Neshek (L)	1/3	3	2	0	0	Scherzer (W)	1	1	0	0	0
Clippard	2/3	0	0	0	0	Kazmir	2/3	1	0	0	0
Rodriguez	1	0	0	1	0	Uehara	1/3	0	0	0	0
Kimbrel	1	0	0	0	3	Holland	1	0	0	0	1
Watson	1/3	0	0	0	0	Doolittle	2/3	1	0	0	2
Chapman	2/3	0	0	0	0	Rodney	1/3	0	0	0	1
						Perkins (S)	1	0	0	0	1

T—3:13. **A**—41,048.

a spectacular diving catch of a drive by Christian Yelich for the final out.

The losing pitcher was Henderson Alvarez, who just happened to throw a no-hitter against the Tigers on the final day of the 2013 season.

"I thought there was no way this would ever happen," Zimmermann said. "My career numbers are something like one hit per inning, so I figure if I can make it out of the first, the hit's coming in the second. But today was one of those special days."

Truly Offensive

It shouldn't have been surprising that so many no-hitters were thrown in a season in which scoring and power were again on the wane.

Research by Baseball America's Matt Eddy noted that 2014 was the first year in which power-on-contact was demonstrably lower than before—the lowest since 1993, in fact. In past seasons, all the extra strikeouts were reducing the number of balls in play, thus the number of opportunities for raw homers and other extra-base hits.

But in 2014, the MLB-wide rate for isolated slugging-on-contact dipped to .173. It had hovered between .180 and .190 since 1994.

Home runs-on-contact dipped to 3.2 percent of all plate appearances this season, the lowest rate since 1993, when it was 3.1 percent. So, yes, batters were now making much less contact, and in 2014 at least, they were not hitting the ball as hard when they did connect.

Major league hitters batted .251, down two

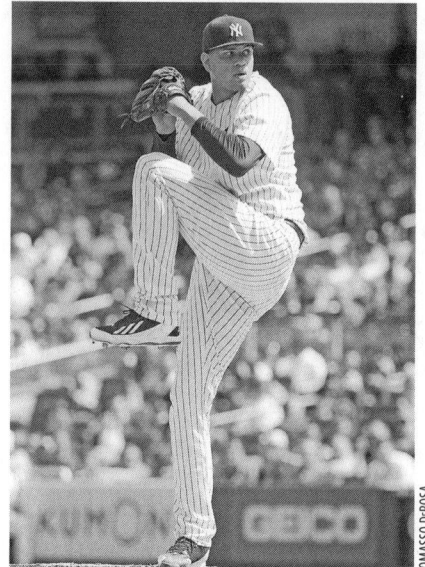

TOMASSO DeROSA

Yankees reliever Dellin Betances typified the dominance pitchers had in 2014

points from last season and 20 points from 1999, the height of the steroids era. The last time the average was when it dipped to .244 in 1972, prompting the AL to put the designated hitter rule into effect the following season.

Teams averaged 4.07 runs per game, the lowest since 1981 and down from 5.14 in 2000. Teams also averaged 0.87 homers a game, the lowest figure since 1992.

The Royals hit just 95 homers but became the first AL team to reach the postseason despite being last in the majors in homers since the 1959 White Sox hit 97.

"The sport is changing. Pitching has been dominant," commissioner Bud Selig said. "There are a lot of theories about it. But everything does go in cycles. There are a lot of good, young hitters coming in, so I'm not concerned about it."

Let's Make A Deal

July featured a number of blockbuster deals in advance of the July 31 non-waiver trading deadline.

The Athletics were involved in two of them and got the action start early when they dealt top shortstop prospect Addison Russell and two other minor leaguers to the Cubs on July 4 for right-handers Jeff Samardzija and Jason Hammel. Then on July 31, Oakland acquired ace lefthander Jon Lester and outfielder Jonny Gomes from the Red

ACTIVE LEADERS

Career leaders among players who played in a game in 2014. Batters require 3,000 plate appearances and pitchers 1,000 innings to qualify for percentage titles.

BATTERS			PITCHERS		
AVG	Miguel Cabrera	.320	ERA	Clayton Kershaw	2.48
OBP	Joey Votto	.417	SO/9	Max Scherzer	9.59
SLG	Albert Pujols	.588	BB/9	Dan Haren	1.86
OPS	Albert Pujols	.991	HR/9	Clayton Kershaw	0.54
R	Alex Rodriguez	1,919	W	Tim Hudson	214
H	Alex Rodriguez	2,939	L	Mark Buehrle	152
2B	Albert Pujols	561	SV	Joe Nathan	376
3B	Carl Crawford	120	IP	Mark Buehrle	3,084
HR	Alex Rodriguez	654	SO	CC Sabathia	2,437
RBI	Alex Rodriguez	1,969	BB	AJ Burnett	1,051
BB	Jason Giambi	1,366	AVG	Clayton Kershaw	.209
SO	Adam Dunn	2,379	G	LaTroy Hawkins	1,000
XBH	Alex Rodriguez	1,203	GS	Mark Buehrle	461
SB	Ichiro Suzuki	487	HR	Mark Buehrle	339

Sox for left fielder Yoenis Cespedes and a competitive balance pick in the 2015 amateur draft.

The Athletics led the AL West by 2 ½ games when they acquired Lester and expected that the addition of three veteran pitchers would lead to their third consecutive division title. Instead, Oakland finished 10 games behind the Angels and didn't clinch the second wild card until the last day of the season.

The Red Sox, on their way to a last-place finish in the AL East a year after winning the World Series, also continued their retooling by trading righthander John Lackey to the Cardinals for righthander Joe Kelly and right fielder Allen Craig.

"It speaks to where we are as a team," Red Sox general manager Ben Cherington said. "There's nothing sort of celebratory about this. These moves are made because, collectively as an organization, we haven't performed well enough, in this year anyway."

The Tigers added a third Cy Young winner to their starting rotation when they acquired lefthander David Price from the Rays in a three-way trade that also involved the Mariners as he joined Max Scherzer and Justin Verlander. The trade paid off when Price beat the Twins on the last day of the regular season to clinch the Tigers' fourth AL Central title in a row.

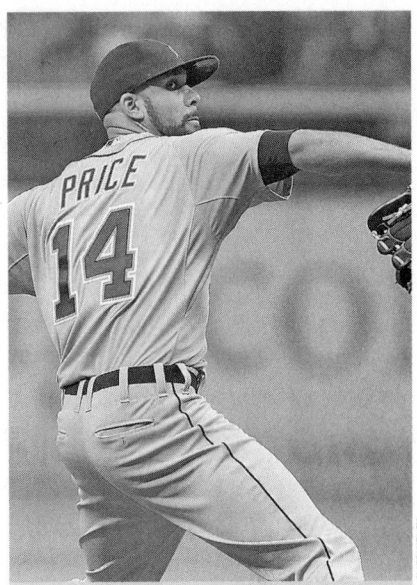

The Tigers landed David Price from the Rays but fell short of the World Series

CLIFF WELCH

International Flavor

The influx of international professional players into the major leagues continued with White Sox first baseman Jose Abreu and Yankees rigthhander Masahiro Tanaka making the biggest impacts of the newcomers.

Abreu, a Cuban defector, was signed to a six-year, $68 million contract and yielded a large return on the White Sox's investment. The 27-year-old led the AL with a .581 slugging percentage while hitting .317 with 36 home runs and 107 RBIs in 145 games. Many scouts were skeptical about Abreu's ability to make the transition from Cuba to the major leagues, believing pitchers would find his weaknesses and exploit them. The

White Sox, though, were convinced he was a star in the making after his performance at the 2013 World Baseball Classic.

"The plus-plus power was what got him the most notoriety, but we viewed him as a more complete hitter than that." general manager Rick Hahn said. "It wasn't just an all-or-nothing, big swing home run guy, it was someone who had the ability to adjust and be a professional hitter."

Tanaka arrived from Japan with great fanfare after he was signed for seven years and $155 million. He was everything the Yankees hoped for, going 13-5 with a 2.77 ERA in 20 starts. However, he was on the disabled list from July 9-Sept. 20 with a sprained elbow ligament, though the good news was that he was able to rehab the injury rather than undergoing Tommy John surgery, for now.

"I will come back stronger next season," Tanaka vowed after his final start.

IMPORTED GOODS

Masahiro Tanaka's debut was cut short by injury but still compares favorably to other Japanese pitchers' first seasons in the U.S.

Year	Player, Team	W	L	ERA	IP	H	R	ER	BB	SO
1995	Hideo Nomo, LAD	13	6	2.54	191	124	63	54	78	236
1997	Hideki Irabu, NYY	5	4	7.09	53	69	47	42	20	56
2007	Daisuke Matsuzaka, Bos	15	12	4.40	205	191	100	100	80	201
2008	Hiroki Kuroda, LAD	9	10	3.73	183	181	85	76	42	116
2012	Yu Darvish, TEX	16	9	3.90	191	156	89	83	89	221
2014	Masahiro Tanaka, NYY	13	5	2.77	136	123	47	42	21	141

MAJOR LEAGUE *DEBUTS*

ARIZONA DIAMONDBACKS

Nick Ahmed	June 29
Chase Anderson	May 11
Mike Bolsinger	April 14
Andrew Chafin	Aug. 13
Bradin Hagens	Aug. 14
Ender Inciarte	May 2
Jake Lamb	Aug. 7
Evan Marshall	May 6
David Peralta	June 1
Bo Schultz	March 23
Matt Stites	June 19
Ryan Buchter	June 20

ATLANTA BRAVES

Juan Jaime	June 20
Tommy La Stella	May 28
Gus Schlosser	March 31
Chasen Shreve	July 19
Shae Simmons	May 31
Ian Thomas	March 31

BALTIMORE ORIOLES

Caleb Joseph	May 7
Christian Walker	Sept. 17

BOSTON RED SOX

Matt Barnes	Sept. 9
Mookie Betts	June 29
Bryce Brentz	Sept. 17
Dan Butler	Aug. 10
Rusney Castillo	Sept. 17
Garin Cecchini	June 1
Edwin Escobar	Aug. 27
Alex Hassan	June 1
Anthony Ranaudo	Aug. 1
Carlos Rivero	Aug. 29
Christian Vazquez	July 9

CHICAGO CUBS

Arismendy Alcantara	July 9
Javier Baez	Aug. 5
Dallas Beeler	June 28
Kyle Hendricks	July 10
Eric Jokisch	Sept. 7
Rafael Lopez	Sept. 2
Neil Ramirez	April 25
Jorge Soler	Aug. 27
Matt Szczur	Aug. 17
Tsuyoshi Wada	July 8

CHICAGO WHITE SOX

Jose Abreu	March 31
Chris Bassitt	Aug. 30
Scott Carroll	April 27
Adrian Nieto	April 2
Carlos Sanchez	July 13
Scott Snodgress	Sept. 3
Taylor Thompson	July 20
Andy Wilkins	Aug. 31

CINCINNATI REDS

Tucker Barnhart	April 3
Carlos Contreras	June 21
Daniel Corcino	Aug. 26
Ryan Dennick	Sept. 2
Jumbo Diaz	June 20
Yorman Rodriguez	Sept. 4

CLEVELAND INDIANS

Austin Adams	July 12
Jesus Aguilar	May 15
Kyle Crockett	May 16
Tyler Holt	July 6
T.J. House	May 17
Roberto Perez	July 10
Bryan Price	Sept. 1

COLORADO ROCKIES

Cristhian Adames	July 29
Christian Bergman	June 9
Brooks Brown	May 22

DETROIT TIGERS (cont.)

Eddie Butler	June 6
Yohan Flande	June 25
Tommy Kahnle	April 3
Chris Martin	April 26
Tyler Matzek	June 11
Kyle Parker	June 16
Ben Paulsen	May 22
Jackson Williams	Aug. 27
Rafael Ynoa	Sept. 1

DETROIT TIGERS

Tyler Collins	March 31
Buck Farmer	Aug. 13
Blaine Hardy	June 16
Corey Knebel	May 24
Kyle Lobstein	Aug. 23
James McCann	Sept. 1
Pat McCoy	June 22
Melvin Mercedes	Aug. 15
Justin Miller	April 18
Steven Moya	Sept. 1
Robbie Ray	May 6
Kyle Ryan	Aug. 30
Chad Smith	June 22
Eugenio Suarez	June 4
Drew VerHagen	July 19

HOUSTON ASTROS

Jake Buchanan	June 21
Michael Foltynewicz	Aug. 2
Enrique Hernandez	July 1
Rudy Owens	May 23
Domingo Santana	July 1
Jon Singleton	June 3
George Springer	April 16
Nick Tropeano	Sept. 10

KANSAS CITY ROYALS

Lane Adams	Sept. 1
Aaron Brooks	May 3
Christian Colon	July 1
Brandon Finnegan	Sept. 6
Terrance Gore	Aug. 31
Michael Mariot	April 11
Justin Marks	April 20
Francisco Pena	May 20
Wilking Rodriguez	June 3

LOS ANGELES ANGELS

Cam Bedrosian	June 3
C.J. Cron	May 3
Jairo Diaz	Sept. 8
Jarrett Grube	May 31
Mike Morin	April 30
Shawn O'Malley	Sept. 7
Drew Rucinski	July 10

LOS ANGELES DODGERS

Erisbel Arruebarrena	May 23
Pedro Baez	May 5
Daniel Coulombe	Sept. 16
Carlos Frias	Aug. 4
Yimi Garcia	Sept. 1
Alex Guerrero	March 22
Red Patterson	May 1
Joc Pederson	Sept. 1
Miguel Rojas	June 6
Jamie Romak	May 28

MIAMI MARLINS

Justin Bour	June 5
Anthony DeSclafani	May 14
Andrew Heaney	June 19
J.T. Realmuto	June 5

MILWAUKEE BREWERS

Matt Clark	Sept. 2
Jason Rogers	Sept. 2
Wei-Chung Wang	April 14

MINNESOTA TWINS

A.J. Achter	Sept. 3

Gregory Polanco

GEORGE GOJKOVICH

Logan Darnell	May 6
Trevor May	Aug. 9
Yohan Pino	June 19
Jorge Polanco	June 26
Danny Santana	May 5
Kennys Vargas	Aug. 1

NEW YORK METS

Dario Alvarez	Sept. 3
Eric Campbell	May 10
Jacob deGrom	May 15
Erik Goeddel	Sept. 1
Dilson Herrera	Aug. 29
Rafael Montero	May 14

NEW YORK YANKEES

Dean Anna	April 4
Shane Greene	April 24
Bryan Mitchell	Aug. 10
Jose Pirela	Sept. 22
Jose Ramirez	June 4
Yangervis Solarte	April 2
Masahiro Tanaka	April 4
Zelous Wheeler	July 3
Chase Whitley	May 15

OAKLAND ATHLETICS

Billy Burns	July 28

PHILADELPHIA PHILLIES

Aaron Altherr	June 16
David Buchanan	May 24
Maikel Franco	Sept. 2
Ken Giles	June 12
Miguel Alfredo Gonzalez	Sept. 3
Mario Hollands	April 1
Hector Neris	Aug. 5

PITTSBURGH PIRATES

John Holdzkom	Sept. 2
Gregory Polanco	June 10
Casey Sadler	May 2

ST. LOUIS CARDINALS

Eric Fornataro	April 21
Greg Garcia	April 28
Marco Gonzales	June 25
Nick Greenwood	June 16
Randal Grichuk	April 28
Tommy Pham	Sept. 9
Jorge Rondon	June 29
Xavier Scruggs	Sept. 4
Oscar Taveras	May 31
Sam Tuivailala	Sept. 9

SAN DIEGO PADRES

R.J. Alvarez	Sept. 3
Leonel Campos	Sept. 3
Odrisamer Despaigne	June 23
Frank Garces	Aug. 19
Jake Goebbert	June 20
Jesse Hahn	June 3
Rymer Liriano	Aug. 11
Jace Peterson	April 25
Kevin Quackenbush	April 25

Donn Roach	April 2
Cory Spangenberg	Sept. 1

SAN FRANCISCO GIANTS

Brett Bochy	Sept. 13
Gary Brown	Sept. 3
Erik Cordier	Sept. 3
Chris Dominguez	Sept. 3
Matt Duffy	May 22
Adam Duvall	June 26
Chris Heston	Sept. 13
Joe Panik	May 22
Hunter Strickland	Sept. 1
Andrew Susac	May 22

SEATTLE MARINERS

Roenis Elias	April 3
James Jones	April 18
Dominic Leone	April 6
Stefen Romero	April 1
Carson Smith	Sept. 1
Chris Taylor	July 24

TAMPA BAY RAYS

Vince Belnome	July 3
Curt Casali	July 18
Cole Figueroa	May 16
C.J. Riefenhauser	April 19
Kirby Yates	June 7

TEXAS RANGERS

Lisalverto Bonilla	Sept. 4
Alex Claudio	Aug. 13
Jon Edwards	Aug. 15
Phil Klein	Aug. 1
Nick Martinez	April 5
Roman Mendez	July 8
Rougned Odor	May 8
Spencer Patton	Sept. 4
Daniel Robertson	April 29
Guilder Rodriguez	Sept. 9
Seth Rosin	March 31
Ben Rowen	June 15
Ryan Rua	Aug. 29
Luis Sardinas	April 20
Jake Smolinski	July 7
Tomas Telis	Aug. 25
Matt West	July 10

TORONTO BLUE JAYS

Brad Glenn	June 27
Kendall Graveman	Sept. 5
Daniel Norris	Sept. 5
Dalton Pompey	Sept. 2
Rob Rasmussen	May 20
Aaron Sanchez	July 23
Marcus Stroman	May 4

WASHINGTON NATIONALS

Aaron Barrett	March 31
Taylor Hill	June 25
Steven Souza	April 13
Michael Taylor	Aug. 12
Blake Treinen	April 12

CLUB BATTING

	AVG	G	AB	R	H	2B	3B	HR	RBI	BB	SO	SB	OBP	SLG
Detroit	.277	162	5630	757	1557	325	26	155	731	443	1144	106	.331	.426
Kansas City	.263	162	5545	651	1456	286	29	95	604	380	985	153	.314	.376
Los Angeles	.259	162	5652	773	1464	304	31	155	729	492	1266	81	.322	.406
Toronto	.259	162	5549	723	1435	282	24	177	690	502	1151	78	.323	.414
Baltimore	.256	162	5596	705	1434	264	16	211	681	401	1285	44	.311	.422
Texas	.256	162	5460	637	1400	260	28	111	597	417	1162	105	.314	.375
Minnesota	.254	162	5567	715	1412	316	27	128	675	544	1329	99	.324	.389
Chicago	.253	162	5543	660	1400	279	32	155	625	417	1362	85	.310	.398
Cleveland	.253	162	5575	669	1411	284	23	142	644	504	1189	104	.317	.389
Tampa Bay	.247	162	5516	612	1361	263	24	117	586	527	1124	63	.317	.367
New York	.245	162	5497	633	1349	247	26	147	591	452	1133	112	.307	.380
Boston	.244	162	5551	634	1355	282	20	123	601	535	1337	63	.316	.369
Oakland	.244	162	5545	729	1354	253	33	146	686	586	1104	83	.320	.381
Seattle	.244	162	5450	634	1328	247	32	136	600	396	1232	96	.300	.376
Houston	.242	162	5447	629	1317	240	19	163	596	495	1442	122	.309	.383

CLUB PITCHING

	ERA	G	CG	SHO	SV	IP	H	R	ER	HR	BB	SO	AVG
Seattle	3.17	162	2	9	51	1452	1240	554	512	137	463	1317	.230
Oakland	3.22	162	7	13	31	1463	1269	572	524	147	406	1244	.233
Baltimore	3.43	162	3	13	53	1461	1342	593	557	151	472	1174	.244
Kansas City	3.51	162	3	14	53	1450	1386	624	565	128	440	1168	.250
Cleveland	3.56	162	6	15	40	1468	1398	653	581	135	464	1450	.250
Tampa Bay	3.56	162	3	22	37	1463	1292	625	579	145	482	1437	.234
Los Angeles	3.58	162	3	13	46	1482	1307	630	590	126	504	1342	.236
New York	3.75	162	5	10	48	1453	1392	664	605	164	398	1370	.250
Toronto	4.00	162	3	16	45	1443	1400	686	642	151	490	1199	.253
Boston	4.01	162	3	7	36	1465	1458	715	653	154	482	1213	.260
Detroit	4.01	162	5	8	41	1454	1475	705	648	127	462	1244	.263
Houston	4.11	162	7	3	31	1438	1437	723	657	139	484	1137	.260
Chicago	4.29	162	3	6	36	1441	1468	758	687	140	557	1152	.265
Texas	4.49	162	6	17	33	1426	1510	773	711	160	505	1110	.272
Minnesota	4.57	162	2	7	38	1435	1588	777	728	147	408	1031	.280

CLUB FIELDING

TEAM	FPCT	PO	A	E	DP	TEAM	FPCT	PO	A	E	DP
Baltimore	.986	4384	1604	87	156	Detroit	.983	4362	1538	101	153
Los Angeles	.986	4448	1482	83	127	Houston	.983	4316	1704	106	151
Seattle	.986	4356	1608	82	139	Kansas City	.983	4352	1512	104	122
Boston	.985	4397	1610	92	155	Chicago	.982	4323	1682	107	170
Tampa	.985	4391	1309	88	96	Oakland	.982	4390	1634	111	150
Toronto	.985	4329	1528	87	130	Texas	.982	4279	1413	106	155
Minnesota	.984	4305	1579	97	136	Cleveland	.981	4405	1599	116	139
New York	.984	4359	1474	92	107						

INDIVIDUAL BATTING LEADERS

	AVG	G	AB	R	H	2B	3B	HR	RBI	BB	SO	SB
Altuve, Jose, Houston	.341	158	660	85	225	47	3	7	59	36	53	56
Martinez, Victor, Detroit	.335	151	561	87	188	33	0	32	103	70	42	3
Brantley, Michael, Cleveland	.327	156	611	94	200	45	2	20	97	52	56	23
Beltre, Adrian, Texas	.324	148	549	79	178	33	1	19	77	57	74	1
Abreu, Jose, Chicago	.317	145	556	80	176	35	2	36	107	51	131	3
Cano, Robinson, Seattle	.314	157	595	77	187	37	2	14	82	61	68	10
Cabrera, Miguel, Detroit	.313	159	611	101	191	52	1	25	109	60	117	1
Cain, Lorenzo, Kansas City	.301	133	471	55	142	29	4	5	53	24	108	28
Cabrera, Melky, Toronto	.301	139	568	81	171	35	3	16	73	43	67	6
Eaton, Adam, Chi White Sox	.300	123	486	76	146	26	10	1	35	43	83	15

INDIVIDUAL PITCHING LEADERS

	W	L	ERA	G	GS	CG	SV	IP	H	R	ER	BB	SO
Hernandez, Felix, Seattle	15	6	2.14	34	34	0	0	236	170	68	56	46	248
Sale, Chris, Chicago	12	4	2.17	26	26	2	0	174	129	48	42	39	208
Kluber, Corey, Cleveland	18	9	2.44	34	34	3	0	235	207	72	64	51	269
Lester, Jon, Boston, Oakland	16	11	2.46	32	32	1	0	219	194	76	60	48	220
Richards, Garrett, Los Angeles	13	4	2.61	26	26	1	0	168	124	51	49	51	164
Cobb, Alex, Tampa Bay	10	9	2.87	27	27	0	0	166	142	56	53	47	149
Keuchel, Dallas, Houston	12	9	2.93	29	29	5	0	200	187	71	65	48	146
Gray, Sonny, Oakland	14	10	3.08	33	33	2	0	219	187	84	75	74	183
Scherzer, Max, Detroit	18	5	3.15	33	33	1	0	220	196	80	77	63	252
Ventura, Yordano, Kansas City	14	10	3.20	31	30	0	0	183	168	70	65	69	159

AWARD WINNERS

Selected by Baseball Writers Association of America

MOST VALUABLE PLAYER

Player	1st	2nd	3rd	Total
Mike Trout, Angels	30			420
Victor Martinez, Tigers		16	4	229
Michael Brantley, Indians		8	6	185
Jose Abreu, White Sox		1	6	145
Robinson Cano, Mariners		1	1	124
Jose Bautista, Blue Jays		1	1	122
Nelson Cruz, Orioles			6	102
Josh Donaldson, Athletics		1	2	96
Miguel Cabrera, Tigers		1	2	82
Felix Hernandez, Mariners		2	1	48
Corey Kluber, Indians			1	45
Alex Gordon, Royals				44
Jose Altuve, Astros				41
Adam Jones, Orioles				34
Adrian Beltre, Rangers				22
Greg Holland, Royals				13
Albert Pujols, Angels				5
Howie Kendrick, Angels				3
James Shields, Royals				3
Kyle Seager, Mariners				1

CY YOUNG AWARD

Pitcher	1st	2nd	3rd	Total
Corey Kluber, Indians	17	11	2	169
Felix Hernandez, Mariners	13	17		159
Chris Sale, White Sox		2	19	78
Jon Lester, Red Sox/Athletics			3	46
Max Scherzer, Tigers			4	32
David Price, Rays/Tigers			2	16
Phil Hughes, Twins				6
Wade Davis, Royals				3
Greg Holland, Royals				1

ROOKIE OF THE YEAR

Player	1st	2nd	3rd	Total
Jose Abreu, White Sox	30			150
Matt Shoemaker, Angels		12	4	40
Dellin Betances, Yankees		7	6	27
Collin McHugh, Astros		6	3	21
Masahiro Tanaka, Yankees		3	7	16
Yordano Ventura, Royals		1	6	9
Danny Santana, Twins		1		3
Nick Castellanos, Tigers			1	1
Brock Holt, Red Sox			1	1
Jake Odorizzi, Rays			1	1
George Springer, Astros			1	1

MANAGER OF THE YEAR

Manager	1st	2nd	3rd	Total
Buck Showalter, Orioles	25	3	1	132
Mike Scioscia, Angels	4	11	8	61
Ned Yost, Royals		11	8	41
Lloyd McClendon, Mariners	1	5	9	29
Terry Francona, Indians			2	2
Joe Girardi, Yankees			1	1
Bob Melvin, Athletics			1	1

GOLD GLOVE WINNERS

Selected by AL managers

C—Salvador Perez, Kansas City. 1B—Eric Hosmer, Kansas City. 2B—Dustin Pedroia, Boston. SS—J.J. Hardy, Baltimore. 3B—Kyle Seager, Seattle. LF—Alex Gordon, Kansas City. CF—Adam Jones, Baltimore. RF—Nick Markakis, Baltimore. P—Dallas Keuchel, Houston.

DEPARTMENT LEADERS

BATTING

GAMES
Alcides Escobar, Kansas City	162
Evan Longoria, Tampa Bay	162
Ian Kinsler, Detroit	161
5 players	159

AT-BATS
Ian Kinsler, Detroit	684
Jose Altuve, Houston	660
Adam Jones, Baltimore	644
Nick Markakis, Baltimore	642
Albert Pujols, Los Angeles	633

PLATE APPEARANCES
Ian Kinsler, Detroit	726
Nick Markakis, Baltimore	710
Jose Altuve, Houston	707
Brian Dozier, Minnesota	707
Mike Trout, Los Angeles	705

RUNS
Mike Trout, Los Angeles	115
Brian Dozier, Minnesota	112
Jose Bautista, Toronto	101
Miguel Cabrera, Detroit	101
Ian Kinsler, Detroit	100

HITS
Jose Altuve, Houston	225
Michael Brantley, Cleveland	200
Miguel Cabrera, Detroit	191
Ian Kinsler, Detroit	188
Victor Martinez, Detroit	188

TOTAL BASES
Mike Trout, Los Angeles	338
Jose Abreu, Chicago	323
Nelson Cruz, Baltimore	322
Miguel Cabrera, Detroit	320
Victor Martinez, Detroit	317

DOUBLES
Miguel Cabrera, Detroit	52
Jose Altuve, Houston	47
Michael Brantley, Cleveland	45
Ian Kinsler, Detroit	40
Trevor Plouffe, Minnesota	40

TRIPLES
Michael Bourn, Cleveland	10
Adam Eaton, Chicago	10
Mike Trout, Los Angeles	9
4 players	8

EXTRA-BASE HITS
Mike Trout, Los Angeles	84
Miguel Cabrera, Detroit	78
Nelson Cruz, Baltimore	74
Jose Abreu, Chicago	73
Michael Brantley, Cleveland	67

HOME RUNS
Nelson Cruz, Baltimore	40
Chris Carter, Houston	37
Jose Abreu, Chicago	36
Mike Trout, Los Angeles	36
2 players	35

RUNS BATTED IN
Mike Trout, Los Angeles	111
Miguel Cabrera, Detroit	109
Nelson Cruz, Baltimore	108
Jose Abreu, Chicago	107
Albert Pujols, Los Angeles	105

SACRIFICES
Brett Gardner, New York	13
Jose Ramirez, Cleveland	13
Mike Aviles, Cleveland	11
3 players	9

SACRIFICE FLIES
Miguel Cabrera, Detroit	11
Mike Trout, Los Angeles	10
4 players	9

HIT BY PITCH
Mike Zunino, Seattle	17
Shin-Soo Choo, Texas	12
Adam Jones, Baltimore	12
3 players	11

WALKS
Carlos Santana, Cleveland	113
Jose Bautista, Toronto	104
Brian Dozier, Minnesota	89

Mike Trout, Los Angeles	83
Mike Napoli, Boston	78

STOLEN BASES
Jose Altuve, Houston	56
Jacoby Ellsbury, New York	39
Rajai Davis, Detroit	36
Jarrod Dyson, Kansas City	36
2 players	31

CAUGHT STEALING
Elvis Andrus, Texas	15
Leonys Martin, Texas	12
Rajai Davis, Detroit	11
Alejandro De Aza, Chi/Bal,	10
4 players	9

Jose Altuve

STOLEN-BASE PERCENTAGE
James Jones, Seattle	0.96
Michael Brantley, Cleveland	0.96
Jose Reyes, Toronto	0.94
Craig Gentry, Oakland	0.91
Jacoby Ellsbury, New York	0.89

STRIKEOUTS
Mike Trout, Los Angeles	184
Chris Carter, Houston	182
Chris Davis, Baltimore	173
Adam Dunn, Chi/Oak	159
Tyler Flowers, Chicago	159

TOUGHEST TO STRIKE OUT (AT-BATS PER STRIKEOUT)
Victor Martinez, Detroit	13.36
Jose Altuve, Houston	12.45
Michael Brantley, Cleveland	10.91
Nori Aoki, Kansas City	10.02
Kurt Suzuki, Minnesota	9.83

GROUNDED INTO DOUBLE PLAYS
Albert Pujols, Los Angeles	28
Matt Dominguez, Houston	23
Salvador Perez, Kansas City	22
5 players	21

MULTI-HIT GAMES
Jose Altuve, Hou	69
Michael Brantley, Cle	59
Victor Martinez, Det	57
Robinson Cano, Sea	56
Miguel Cabrera, Det	55
Adam Jones, Bal	55
Ian Kinsler, Det	55

ON-BASE PERCENTAGE
Victor Martinez, Detroit	.409
Jose Bautista, Toronto	.403
Adrian Beltre, Texas	.388
Michael Brantley, Cleveland	.385
Jose Abreu, Chicago	.384

SLUGGING PERCENTAGE
Jose Abreu, Chicago	.581
Victor Martinez, Detroit	.565
Mike Trout, Los Angeles	.561
Edwin Encarnacion, Toronto	.547
Nelson Cruz, Baltimore	.525

ON-BASE-PLUS SLUGGING
Victor Martinez, Detroit	.974
Jose Abreu, Chicago	.964
Mike Trout, Los Angeles	.939
Jose Bautista, Toronto	.928
Edwin Encarnacion, Toronto	.901

LOWEST AVERAGE
Jason Castro, Houston	.222
Adam Dunn Chi/Oak	.219
Mark Teixeira, New York	.216
Matt Dominguez, Houston	.215
Chris Davis, Baltimore	.196

PITCHING

WINS
Corey Kluber, Cleveland	18
Jered Weaver, Los Angeles	18
Max Scherzer, Detroit	18
4 players	16

LOSSES
Colby Lewis, Texas	14
6 players	13

GAMES
Bryan Shaw, Cleveland	80
Joe Smith, Los Angeles	76

Victor Martinez

BILL NICHOLS

CLIFF WELCH

Cody Allen, Cleveland 76
Kevin Jepsen, Los Angeles 74
5 players 735

GAMES STARTED
7 players 34

GAMES FINISHED
Fernando Rodney, Seattle 64
Greg Holland, Kansas City 60
Glen Perkins, Minnesota 56
David Robertson, New York 55
Joe Nathan, Detroit 54

COMPLETE GAMES
Dallas Keuchel, Houston 5
Corey Kluber, Cleveland 3
David Price, TB/Det 3
Rick Porcello, Detroit 3
Masahiro Tanaka, New York 3

SHUTOUTS
Rick Porcello, Detroit 3
Clay Buchholz, Boston 2
Martin Perez, Texas 2
Sonny Gray, Oakland 2
22 players 1

SAVES
Fernando Rodney, Seattle 48
Greg Holland, Kansas City 46
David Robertson, New York 39
Zach Britton, Baltimore 37
Joe Nathan, Detroit 35

INNINGS PITCHED
David Price, TB/Det 248.1
Felix Hernandez, Seattle 236
Corey Kluber, Cleveland 235.2
James Shields, Kansas City 227
Max Scherzer, Detroit 220.1

HITS ALLOWED
David Price, TB/Det 230
Mark Buehrle, Toronto 228
James Shields, Kansas City 224
Justin Verlander, Detroit 223
Phil Hughes, Minnesota 221

RUNS ALLOWED
Justin Verlander, Detroit 114
Clay Buchholz, Boston 108
Colby Lewis, Texas 107

Dallas Keuchel

CLIFF WELCH

John Danks, Chicago 106
R.A. Dickey, Toronto 101

HOME RUNS ALLOWED
Hector Noesi, Sea/Chi/Tex, 28
Jered Weaver, Los Angeles 27
R.A. Dickey, Toronto 26
Chris Young, Seattle 26
4 players 25

WALKS
C.J. Wilson, Los Angeles 85
Ubaldo Jimenez, Baltimore 77
R.A. Dickey, Toronto 74
John Danks, Chicago 74
Sonny Gray, Oakland 74

WALKS PER NINE INNINGS
Phil Hughes, Minnesota 0.69
Hisashi Iwakuma, Seattle 1.06

David Price, TB/Det 1.38
Hiroki Kuroda, New York 1.58
Wei-Yin Chen, Baltimore 1.79

HIT BATTERS
R.A. Dickey, Toronto 14
Jeremy Guthrie, Kansas City 14
Bud Norris, Baltimore 14
Scott Carroll, Chicago 12
7 players 11

STRIKEOUTS
David Price, TB/Det 271
Corey Kluber, Cleveland 269
Max Scherzer, Detroit 252
Felix Hernandez, Seattle 248
Jon Lester, Bos/Oak 220

STRIKEOUTS PER NINE INNINGS
Chris Sale, Chicago 10.76

Max Scherzer, Detroit 10.29
Corey Kluber, Cleveland 10.27
David Price, TB/Det 9.82
Felix Hernandez, Seattle 9.46

**STRIKEOUTS PER NINE INNINGS
(RELIEVERS)**
Andrew Miller, Bos/Bal 14.87
Brad Boxberger, Tampa Bay 14.47
Wade Davis, Kansas City 13.63
Dellin Betances, New York 13.5
David Robertson, New York 13.43

DOUBLE PLAYS
Dallas Keuchel, Houston 36
Rick Porcello, Detroit 30
Mark Buehrle, Toronto 24
C.J. Wilson, Los Angeles 23
Roenis Elias, Seattle 23

PICKOFFS
Drew Smyly, Det/TB, 7
Hector Santiago, Los Angeles 6
Danny Duffy, Kansas City 6
4 players 4

WILD PITCHES
Garrett Richards, Los Angeles 22
Felix Hernandez, Seattle 18
Sonny Gray, Oakland 15
Yu Darvish, Texas 14
2 players 13

WALKS-PLUS-HITS PER INNING
Felix Hernandez, Seattle 0.92
Chris Sale, Chicago 0.97
Garrett Richards, Los Angeles 1.04
Hisashi Iwakuma, Seattle 1.05
David Price, TB/Det 1.08

OPPONENT AVERAGE
Felix Hernandez, Seattle .200
Garrett Richards, Los Angeles .201
Chris Sale, Chicago .205
Alex Cobb, Tampa Bay .231
Sonny Gray, Oakland .232

WORST ERA
Clay Buchholz, Boston 5.34
Colby Lewis, Texas 5.18
Hector Noesi, Sea/Chi/Tex 4.75
John Danks, Chicago 4.74
Justin Verlander, Detroit 4.54

FIELDING

PITCHER
PCT.	Wei-Yin Chen, Baltimore	1.000
	Roenis Elias, Seattle	1.000
	Scott Feldman, Houston	1.000
	Kyle Gibson, Minnesota	1.000
	Corey Kluber, Cleveland	1.000
	Jake Odorizzi, Tampa Bay	1.000
	Jose Quintana, Chicago	1.000
	Chris Sale, Chicago	1.000
PO	Kyle Gibson, Minnesota	30
A	Dallas Keuchel, Houston	47
DP	Burke Badenhop, Boston	6
	Jose Quintana, Chi White Sox	6
E	Jeremy Guthrie, Kansas City	6
	Justin, Verlander, Detroit	6

CATCHER
PCT	Brian McCann, New York	.998
A	Mike Zunino, Seattle	84
DP	Alex Avila, Detroit	9
DP	Yan Gomes, Cleveland	9
E	Yan Gomes, Cleveland	14

PB	Yan Gomes, Cleveland	6
PO	Yan Gomes, Cleveland	1052
TC	Yan Gomes, Cleveland	11390

FIRST BASE
A	Miguel Cabrera, Detroit	98
DP	Jose Abreu, Chicago	105
E	Jon Singleton, Houston	11
PCT	Albert Pujols, Los Angeles	.997
PO	James Loney, Tampa Bay	1111
TC	James Loney, Tampa Bay	11782

SECOND BASE
A	Brian Dozier, Minnesota	475
DP	Jose Altuve, Houston	105
E	Brian Dozier, Minnesota	15
PCT	Dustin Pedroia, Boston	.997
PO	Ian Kinsler, Detroit	290
TC	Ian Kinsler, Detroit	766

THIRD BASE
A	Josh Donaldson, Oakland	328
DP	Josh Donaldson, Oakland	43
E	Josh Donaldson, Oakland	23

PCT	Kyle Seager, Seattle	.981
PO	Adrian Beltre. Texas	144
TC	Josh Donaldson, Oakland	482

SHORTSTOP
A	Alexei Ramirez, Chicago	486
DP	Alexei Ramirez, Chicago	119
E	Jose Reyes, Toronto	19
PCT	Erick Aybar, LA Angels	.982
PO	Elvis Andrus, Texas	237
TC	Alexei Ramirez, Chicago	696

OUTFIELD
A	Yoenis Cespedes, Oak/Bos	16
DP	Jackie Bradley Jr., Boston	8
E	Leonys Martin, Texas	8
E	Dayan Viciedo, Chi ago	8
G	Alex Gordon, Kansas City	156
PCT	Desmond Jennings, Tampa Bay	1
PCT	Nick Markakis, Baltimore	1
PO	Leonys Martin, Texas	415
TC	Leonys Martin, Texas	434

MAJOR LEAGUES

CLUB BATTING

	AVG	G	AB	R	H	2B	3B	HR	RBI	BB	SO	SB	OBP	SLG
Colorado	.276	162	5612	755	1551	307	41	186	721	397	1281	85	.327	.445
Los Angeles	.265	162	5560	718	1476	302	38	134	686	519	1246	138	.333	.406
Pittsburgh	.259	162	5536	682	1436	275	30	156	659	520	1244	104	.330	.404
San Francisco	.255	162	5523	665	1407	257	42	132	636	427	1245	56	.311	.388
Miami	.253	162	5538	645	1399	254	36	122	614	501	1419	58	.317	.378
St. Louis	.253	162	5426	619	1371	275	21	105	585	471	1133	57	.320	.369
Washington	.253	162	5542	686	1403	265	27	152	635	517	1304	101	.321	.393
Milwaukee	.250	162	5462	650	1366	297	28	150	617	423	1197	102	.311	.397
Arizona	.248	162	5552	615	1379	259	47	118	573	398	1165	86	.302	.376
Philadelphia	.242	162	5603	619	1356	251	27	125	584	443	1306	109	.302	.363
Atlanta	.241	162	5468	573	1316	240	22	123	545	472	1369	95	.305	.360
Chicago	.239	162	5508	614	1315	270	31	157	590	442	1477	65	.300	.385
New York	.239	162	5472	629	1306	275	19	125	602	516	1264	101	.308	.364
Cincinnati	.238	162	5395	595	1282	254	20	131	562	415	1252	122	.296	.365
San Diego	.226	162	5294	535	1199	224	30	109	500	468	1294	91	.292	.342

CLUB PITCHING

	ERA	G	CG	SHO	SV	IP	H	R	ER	HR	BB	SO	AVG
Washington	3.03	162	5	19	45	1470	1351	555	495	110	352	1288	.244
San Diego	3.27	162	4	10	41	1438	1300	577	523	117	462	1284	.241
Atlanta	3.38	162	5	13	54	1455	1369	597	547	121	472	1301	.251
Los Angeles	3.40	162	7	16	47	1464	1338	617	554	142	429	1373	.242
Pittsburgh	3.47	162	2	7	48	1456	1341	631	562	128	499	1228	.247
New York	3.49	162	1	11	42	1463	1370	618	568	141	509	1303	.248
San Francisco	3.50	162	8	12	46	1449	1305	614	564	133	389	1211	.241
St. Louis	3.50	162	8	23	55	1448	1321	603	564	123	470	1221	.242
Cincinnati	3.59	162	5	13	44	1446	1282	612	576	163	507	1290	.237
Milwaukee	3.67	162	3	9	45	1457	1386	657	594	167	431	1246	.250
Miami	3.78	162	3	16	42	1457	1481	674	613	114	458	1190	.264
Philadelphia	3.79	162	2	12	40	1468	1396	687	619	134	521	1255	.252
Chicago	3.91	162	1	11	37	1463	1398	707	636	115	504	1311	.252
Arizona	4.26	162	2	4	35	1444	1467	742	683	154	469	1278	.265
Colorado	4.84	162	1	4	24	1431	1528	818	770	173	531	1074	.276

CLUB FIELDING

TEAM	FPCT	PO	A	E	DP	TEAM	FPCT	PO	A	E	DP
Cincinnati	.988	4338	1588	72	120	Washington	.984	4412	1625	100	139
Philadelphia	.987	4405	1673	83	133	Arizona	.983	4333	1645	101	147
Atlanta	.986	4365	1527	85	143	Chicago	.983	4390	1668	103	137
St. Louis	.985	4346	1617	88	145	Colorado	.983	4293	1808	106	146
Miami	.984	4373	1700	97	154	Los Angeles	.983	4394	1707	107	145
Milwaukee	.984	4373	1602	99	130	New York	.983	4391	1617	104	158
San Francisco	.984	4347	1699	100	155	Pittsburgh	.983	4369	1838	109	148
						San Diego	.983	4316	1560	101	124

INDIVIDUAL BATTING LEADERS

	AVG	G	AB	R	H	2B	3B	HR	RBI	BB	SO	SB
Morneau, Justin, Colorado	.319	135	502	62	160	32	3	17	82	34	60	0
Harrison, Josh, Pittsburgh	.315	143	520	77	164	38	7	13	52	22	81	18
McCutchen, Andrew, Pittsburgh	.314	146	548	89	172	38	6	25	83	84	115	18
Posey, Buster, San Francisco	.311	147	547	72	170	28	2	22	89	47	69	0
Revere, Ben, Philadelphia	.306	151	601	71	184	13	7	2	28	13	49	49
Span, Denard, Washington	.302	147	610	94	184	39	8	5	37	50	65	31
Lucroy, Jonathan, Milwaukee	.301	153	585	73	176	53	2	13	69	66	71	4
Puig, Yasiel, LA Dodgers	.296	148	558	92	165	37	9	16	69	67	124	11
Werth, Jayson, Washington	.292	147	534	85	156	37	1	16	82	83	113	9
Castro, Starlin, Chicago	.292	134	528	58	154	33	1	14	65	35	100	4

INDIVIDUAL PITCHING LEADERS

	W	L	ERA	G	GS	CG	SV	IP	H	R	ER	BB	SO
Kershaw, Clayton, Los Angeles	21	3	1.77	27	27	6	0	198	139	42	39	31	239
Cueto, Johnny, Cincinnati	20	9	2.25	34	34	4	0	243	169	69	61	65	242
Wainwright, Adam, St. Louis	20	9	2.38	32	32	5	0	227	184	64	60	50	179
Fister, Doug, Washington	16	6	2.41	25	25	1	0	164	153	52	44	24	98
Hamels, Cole, Philadelphia	9	9	2.46	30	30	0	0	204	176	60	56	59	198
Alvarez, Henderson, Miami	12	7	2.65	30	30	3	0	187	198	65	55	33	111
Zimmermann, Jordan, Wash.	14	5	2.66	32	32	3	0	199	185	67	59	29	182
Greinke, Zack, LA Dodgers	17	8	2.71	32	32	0	0	202	190	69	61	43	207
Lynn, Lance, St. Louis	15	10	2.74	33	33	2	0	203	185	72	62	72	181
Wood, Alex, Atlanta	11	11	2.78	35	24	1	0	171	151	58	53	45	170

AWARD WINNERS

Selected by Baseball Writers Association of America

MOST VALUABLE PLAYER

Player	1st	2nd	3rd	Total
Clayton Kershaw, Dodgers	18	9	1	355
Giancarlo Stanton, Marlins	8	10	12	298
Andrew McCutchen, Pirates	4	10	15	271
Jonathan Lucroy, Brewers			1	167
Anthony Rendon, Nationals			1	155
Buster Posey, Giants			1	152
Adrian Gonzalez, Dodgers				57
Adam Wainwright, Cardinals				53
Josh Harrison, Pirates				52
Anthony Rizzo, Cubs				37
Hunter Pence, Giants				34
Johnny Cueto, Reds				22
Russell Martin, Pirates				21
Matt Holliday, Cardinals				17
Jhonny Peralta, Cardinals				17
Carlos Gomez, Brewers				13
Justin Upton, Braves				10
Jayson Werth, Nationals				9
Denard Span, Nationals				8
Yasiel Puig, Dodgers				8
Devin Mesoraco, Reds				5
Lucas Duda, Mets				3
Freddie Freeman, Braves				2
Justin Morneau, Rockies				2
Dee Gordon, Dodgers				1
Troy Tulowitzki, Rockies				1

CY YOUNG AWARD

Pitcher	1st	2nd	3rd	Total
Clayton Kershaw, Dodgers	30			210
Johnny Cueto, Reds		23	6	112
Adam Wainwright, Cardinals		7	23	97
Madison Bumgarner, Giants				28
Jordan Zimmermann, Nationals			1	25
Cole Hamels, Phillies				17
Zack Greinke, Dodgers				6
Doug Fister, Nationals				5
Jake Arrieta, Cubs				3
Craig Kimbrel, Braves				3
Stephen Strasburg, Nationals				3
Henderson Alvarez, Marlins				1

ROOKIE OF THE YEAR

Player	1st	2nd	3rd	Total
Jacob deGrom, Mets	26	4		142
Billy Hamilton, Reds	4	23	3	92
Kolten Wong, Cardinals		1	11	14
Ken Giles, Phillies		2	2	8
Ender Inciarte, Diamondbacks			4	4
Joe Panik, Giants			3	3
Travis d'Arnaud, Mets			2	2
Jeurys Familia, Mets			2	2
Kyle Hendricks, Cubs			2	2
Chase Anderson, Diamondbacks			1	1

MANAGER OF THE YEAR

Manager	1st	2nd	3rd	Total
Matt Williams, Nationals	18	6	1	109
Clint Hurdle, Pirates	8	12	4	80
Bruce Bochy, Giants	3	3	6	30
Mike Matheny, Cardinals		5	3	18
Mike Redmond, Marlins	1	2	5	16
Don Mattingly, Dodgers		1	9	12
Ron Roenicke, Brewers		1		3
Bud Black, Padres		1		1
Terry Collins, Mets		1		1

GOLD GLOVE WINNERS

Selected by NL managers

C—Yadier Molina, St.Louis. 1B—Adrian Gonzalez, Los Angeles. 2B—DJ LeMahieu, Colorado. SS—Andrelton Simmons, Atlanta. 3B— Nolan Arenado, Colorado. LF— Christian Yelich, Miami. CF—Juan Lagares, New York. RF—Jason Heyward, Atlanta. P—Zack Greinke, Los Angeles.

GAMES
Freddie Freeman, Atlanta	162
Hunter Pence, San Francisco	162
Casey McGehee, Miami	160
Adrian Gonzalez, Los Angeles	159
Matt Carpenter, St. Louis	158

AT-BATS
Hunter Pence, San Francisco	650
Casey McGehee, Miami	616
Anthony Rendon, Washington	613
Denard Span, Washington	610
Dee Gordon, Los Angeles	609

PLATE APPEARANCES
Matt Carpenter, St. Louis	709
Freddie Freeman, Atlanta	708
Hunter Pence, San Francisco	708
Casey McGehee, Miami	691
Anthony Rendon, Wash	683

RUNS
Anthony Rendon, Washington	111
Hunter Pence, San Francisco	106
Matt Carpenter, St. Louis	99
Carlos Gomez, Milwaukee	95
2 players	94

HITS
Ben Revere, Philadelphia	184
Denard Span, Washington	184
Hunter Pence, San Francisco	180
Casey McGehee, Miami	177
3 players	176

TOTAL BASES
Giancarlo Stanton, Miami	299
Andrew McCutchen, Pittsburgh	297
Anthony Rendon, Wash	290
Hunter Pence, San Francisco	289
Adrian Gonzalez, Los Angeles	285

DOUBLES
Jonathan Lucroy, Milwaukee	53
Freddie Freeman, Atlanta	43
Adrian Gonzalez, Los Angeles	41
3 players	39

TRIPLES
Dee Gordon, Los Angeles	12
Brandon Crawford, S.F.	10
Adeiny Hechavarria, Miami	10
Hunter Pence, San Francisco	10
2 players	9

EXTRA-BASE HITS
Andrew McCutchen, Pittsburgh	69
Giancarlo Stanton, Miami	69
Adrian Gonzalez, Los Angeles	68
Jonathan Lucroy, Milwaukee	68
2 players	66

HOME RUNS
Giancarlo Stanton, Miami	37
Anthony Rizzo, Chicago	32
Lucas Duda, New York	30
Todd Frazier, Cincinnati	29
Justin Upton, Atlanta	29

RUNS BATTED IN
Adrian Gonzalez, Los Angeles	116
Giancarlo Stanton, Miami	105
Justin Upton, Atlanta	102
Ryan Howard, Philadelphia	95
2 players	92

SACRIFICES
Shelby Miller, St. Louis	13

Dee Gordon

DAVID SEELIG

Johnny Cueto, Cincinnati	12
Zack Wheeler, New York	12
Tanner Roark, Washington	11
Jean Segura, Milwaukee	10

SACRIFICE FLIES
Adrian Gonzalez, Los Angeles	11
Brandon Crawford, S.F.	10
Matt Carpenter, St. Louis	9
Chase Utley, Philadelphia	9
4 players	8

HIT BY PITCH
Jon Jay, St. Louis	20
Carlos Gomez, Milwaukee	19
Matt Holliday, St. Louis	17
Starling Marte, Pittsburgh	17
2 players	15

WALKS
Matt Carpenter, St. Louis	95
Giancarlo Stanton, Miami	94
Freddie Freeman, Atlanta	90
Andrew McCutchen, Pittsburgh	84
Jayson Werth, Washington	83

STOLEN BASES
Dee Gordon, Los Angeles	64
Billy Hamilton, Cincinnati	56
Ben Revere, Philadelphia	49
Carlos Gomez, Milwaukee	34
Denard Span, Washington	31

CAUGHT STEALING
Billy Hamilton, Cincinnati	23
Dee Gordon, Los Angeles	19
Carlos Gomez, Milwaukee	12
Starling Marte, Pittsburgh	11

Andrew McCutchen

BILL NICHOLS

2 players	10

STOLEN-BASE PERCENTAGE
Drew Stubbs, Colorado	87
Ender Inciarte, Arizona	86
Ben Revere, Philadelphia	86
Andrew McCutchen, Pittsburgh	86
Anthony Rendon, Wash.	85

STRIKEOUTS
Ryan Howard, Philadelphia	190
Marlon Byrd, Philadelphia	185
Ian Desmond, Washington	183
B.J. Upton, Atlanta	173
Justin Upton, Atlanta	171

TOUGHEST TO STRIKE OUT
(AT-BATS PER STRIKEOUT)
Ben Revere, Philadelphia	12.27
Denard Span, Washington	9.38
Andrelton Simmons, Atlanta	9
Justin Morneau, Colorado	8.37
Jonathan Lucroy, Milwaukee	8.24

GROUNDED INTO DOUBLE PLAYS
Casey McGehee, Miami	31
Andrelton Simmons, Atlanta	25
Chris Johnson, Atlanta	23
David Wright, New York	22
2 players	21

MULTI-HIT GAMES
Denard Span, Washington	58
Ben Revere, Philadelphia	56
Jonathan Lucroy, Milwaukee	53
Hunter Pence, San Francisco	50
Christian Yelich, Miami	50

ON-BASE PERCENTAGE
Andrew McCutchen, Pittsburgh	.410
Giancarlo Stanton, Miami	.395
Jayson Werth, Washington	.394
Anthony Rizzo, Chicago	.386
Freddie Freeman, Atlanta	.386

SLUGGING PERCENTAGE
Giancarlo Stanton, Miami	.555
Andrew McCutchen, Pitt.	.542
Anthony Rizzo, Chicago	.527
Matt Kemp, Los Angeles	.506
Justin Morneau, Colorado	.496

ON-BASE-PLUS SLUGGING
Andrew McCutchen, Pitt	.952
Giancarlo Stanton, Miami	.950
Anthony Rizzo, Chicago	.913
Yasiel Puig, Los Angeles	.863
Justin Morneau, Colorado	.860

LOWEST AVERAGE

PITCHING

WINS
Clayton Kershaw, Los Angeles	21
Adam Wainwright, St. Louis	20
Johnny Cueto, Cincinnati	20
Madison Bumgarner, S.F.	18
2 players	17

LOSSES
A.J. Burnett, Philadelphia	18
Eric Stults, San Diego	17
Edwin Jackson, Chicago	15
Tyson Ross, San Diego	14
Nathan Eovaldi, Miami	14

GAMES
Tony Watson, Pittsburgh	78
Will Smith, Milwaukee	78

Jeurys Familia, New York	76
3 players	75

GAMES STARTED

A.J. Burnett, Philadelphia	34
Johnny Cueto, Cincinnati	34
Stephen Strasburg, Wash.	34
8 players	33

GAMES FINISHED

Francisco Rodriguez, Mil.	66
Trevor Rosenthal, St. Louis	59
Kenley Jansen, Los Angeles	57
Steve Cishek, Miami	55
Addison Reed, Arizona	55

COMPLETE GAMES

Clayton Kershaw, Los Angeles	6
Adam Wainwright, St. Louis	5
Johnny Cueto, Cincinnati	4
Madison Bumgarner, S.F. 4	
Julio Teheran, Atlanta	42

SHUTOUTS

Adam Wainwright, St. Louis	3
Henderson Alvarez, Miami	3
7 players	21

SAVES

Craig Kimbrel, Atlanta	47
Trevor Rosenthal, St. Louis	45
Francisco Rodriguez, Mil.	44
Kenley Jansen, Los Angeles	44
2 player	39

INNINGS PITCHED

Johnny Cueto, Cincinnati	243.2
Adam Wainwright, St. Louis	227
Julio Teheran, Atlanta	221
Madison Bumgarner, S.F.	217.1
Stephen Strasburg, Wash.	215.2

HITS ALLOWED

Nathan Eovaldi, Miami	223
Bartolo Colon, New York	218
Mike Leake, Cincinnati	217
Aaron Harang, Atlanta	215
Kyle Kendrick, Philadelphia	21407

RUNS ALLOWED

A.J. Burnett, Philadelphia	122
Travis Wood, Chicago	110
Kyle Kendrick, Philadelphia	108
Nathan Eovaldi, Miami	107
Edwin Jackson, Chicago	105

Craig Kimbrel

ED WOLFSTEIN

HOME RUNS ALLOWED

Marco Estrada, Milwaukee	29
Dan Haren, Los Angeles	27
Eric Stults, San Diego	26
Kyle Kendrick, Philadelphia	25
Franklin Morales, Colorado	24

WALKS

A.J. Burnett, Philadelphia	96
Francisco Liriano, Pittsburgh	81
Zack Wheeler, New York	79
Travis Wood, Chicago	76
Wade Miley, Arizona	75

WALKS PER NINE INNINGS

Jordan Zimmermann, Wash	.1.31
Doug Fister, Washington	1.32

Bartolo Colon, New York	1.33
Clayton Kershaw, Los Angeles	1.41
Henderson Alvarez, Miami	1.59

HIT BATTERS

Charlie Morton, Pittsburgh	19
A.J. Burnett, Philadelphia	16
Johnny Cueto, Cincinnati	15
Edinson Volquez, Pittsburgh	14
Mike Leake, Cincinnati	13

STRIKEOUTS

Johnny Cueto, Cincinnati	242
Stephen Strasburg, Was	242
Clayton Kershaw, L.A.	239
Madison Bumgarner, S.F	.219
2 players	204

STRIKEOUTS PER NINE INNINGS

Clayton Kershaw, LA	10.85
Stephen Strasburg, Was	10.13
Francisco Liriano, Pittsburgh	9.7
Ian Kennedy, San Diego	9.27
Zack Greinke, Los Angeles	9.21

STRIKEOUTS PER NINE INNINGS (RELIEVERS)

Aroldis Chapman, Cin.	17.67
Kenley Jansen, Los Angeles	13.91
Craig Kimbrel, Atlanta	13.86
Jake Diekman, Philadelphia	12.68
Will Smith, Milwaukee	11.79

DOUBLE PLAYS

Adam Wainwright, St. Louis	24
Wily Peralta, Milwaukee	24
Henderson Alvarez, Miami	24
Charlie Morton, Pittsburgh	22
3 players	21

PICKOFFS

Madison Bumgarner, S.F.	6
Julio Teheran, Atlanta	6
4 players	5

WILD PITCHES

Edinson Volquez, Pittsburgh	15
Tim Lincecum, San Francisco	15
Zack Greinke, Los Angeles	12
Francisco Liriano, Pittsburgh	12
Tyson Ross, San Diego	12

WALKS-PLUS-HITS PER INNING

Clayton Kershaw, L.A.	0.86
Johnny Cueto, Cincinnati	0.96
Adam Wainwright, St. Louis	1.03
Jordan Zimmermann, Was	1.07
Doug Fister, Washington	1.08

OPPONENT AVERAGE

Johnny Cueto, Cincinnati	.194
Clayton Kershaw, Los Angeles	.196
Francisco Liriano, Pittsburgh	.218
Adam Wainwright, St. Louis	.222
Tyson Ross, San Diego	.230

WORST ERA

Travis Wood, Chicago	5.03
Kyle Kendrick, Philadelphia	4.61
A.J. Burnett, Philadelphia	4.59
Nathan Eovaldi, Miami	4.37
Wade Miley, Arizona	4.34

FIELDING

PITCHER

A	Johnny Cueto, Cincinnati	39
DP	Zack Greinke, LA Dodgers	8
E	Bartolo Colon, NY Mets	5
E	Franklin Morales, Colorado	5
G	Will Smith, Milwaukee	78
G	Tony Watson, Pittsburgh	78
PCT	10 players	1.000
PO	Zack Greinke, LA Dodgers	28
TC	Johnny Cueto, Cincinnati	63

CATCHER

A	Welington Castillo, Chi Cubs	93
DP	Miguel Montero, Arizona	12
E	Jarrod Saltalamacchia, Miami	15
PB	Jarrod Saltalamacchia, Miami	6
PCT	Yadier Molina, St. Louis	.998
PO	Miguel Montero, Arizona	1037
TC	Miguel Montero, Arizona	1115

FIRST BASE

A	Adrian Gonzalez, LA Dodgers	118
A	Anthony Rizzo, Chi Cubs	118
DP	Freddie Freeman, Atlanta	130
E	Garrett Jones, Miami	13
PCT	Justin Morneau, Colorado	.997
PO	Adrian Gonzalez, LA Dodgers	1318
TC	Adrian Gonzalez, LA Dodgers	1442

SECOND BASE

A	Chase Utley, Philadelphia	423
DP	DJ LeMahieu, Colorado	99
E	Daniel Murphy, NY Mets	15
PCT	Brandon Phillips, Cincinnati	.996
PO	Chase Utley, Philadelphia	292
TC	Chase Utley, Philadelphia	726

THIRD BASE

A	Matt Carpenter, St. Louis	288
DP	Casey McGehee, Miami	34
E	Pedro Alvarez, Pittsburgh	25
PCT	Casey McGehee, Miami	.979

PO	Anthony Rendon, Washington	106
TC	Matt Carpenter, St. Louis	394

SHORTSTOP

A	Segura, Jean, Milwaukee	447
DP	Simmons, Andrelton, Atlanta	99
E	Desmond, Ian, Washington	24
G	Desmond, Ian, Washington	154
PCT	Rollins, Jimmy, Philadelphia	.988
PO	Simmons, Andrelton, Atlanta	217
TC	Hechavarria, Adeiny, Miami	652

OUTFIELD

A	Yasiel Puig, LA Dodgers	15
DP	7 players	3
E	Justin Upton, Atlanta	8
G	Hunter Pence, San Francisco	161
PCT	Will Venable, San Diego	1
PO	Denard Span, Washington	377
TC	Denard Span, Washington	388

BILL NICHOLS

Madison Bumgarner's dominant postseason run earned him MVP honors in the National League Championship Series and World Series, and helped the Giants to a third title in five years

Dynasty? Champ Giants loathe to call it that

JOHN PERROTTO

There were two questions left hanging after the Giants became the second franchise in this century to win three World Series.

One, does three titles in five years enable the Giants to be considered a dynasty after they did not make the playoffs in the other two seasons and averaged just more than 87 wins a season in that span?

Two, is Madison Bumgarner human?

The Giants said they would let history decide if they have put together a dynasty, a word manager Bruce Bochy flinched at after his team downed the Pittsburgh Pirates in the National League wild card game, the Nationals in four games in the NL Division Series, the Cardinals in five games in the NL Championship Series and finally the Royals in

seven games in the World Series.

"A lot has to go right," Bochy said. "First off, it starts with the talent. I mean, you need that, which we have. Then you have to deal with a lot of things maybe during the season. Every manager says, 'Hey, we're fine, we have a good chance to get there if we stay healthy.' But that doesn't always happen."

What Bumgarner, the lanky 25-year-old lefthander, did in the postseason almost never happens.

Bumgarner pitched 52 ⅔ innings, more than any pitcher ever has in a single postseason, and posted an outstanding 1.03 ERA as the Giants won the World Series for the third straight World Series in an even-numbered year after also doing so in 2010 and 2012. The Red Sox are the only other team to win three World Series since 2000.

Bumgarner also threw a pair of shutouts, both four-hitters, with the first coming at Pittsburgh against the Pirates and the other in Game Five of the World Series at San Francisco that gave the Giants a 3-2 lead in the best-of-seven series.

However, Bumgarner's greatest moment occurred in the final game of the season when he came on in relief and closed out a 3-2 victory with five scoreless innings for the save in Game Seven. It was his first relief appearance since 2010 and he threw 68 pitches just three days after a 117-pitch effort in his shutout.

"It's like the guy isn't human," Giants outfielder/first baseman Michael Morse said. "What can you say? He did everything."

Not surprisingly, Bumgarner was named MVP of the series after allowing just one run in 21 innings while going 2-0 with the save and dashing the Royals' hopes of winning it all in their first postseason trip since 1985, when they won the franchise's lone World Series title.

"We had opportunities but not many and you've got to give him a lot of credit for that," Royals first baseman Eric Hosmer said. "He pitched great the entire series. He was the difference in the series, pretty obviously."

The Giants became the first road team to win a Game Seven since the 1979 Pirates beat the Orioles, and Bumgarner became just the third pitcher to work in relief after throwing a shutout earlier in the World Series. The last man to do so was Randy Johnson for the 2001 Diamondbacks.

Yet Bumgarner did not seem all that impressed, speaking in his usual monotone in a postgame press conference.

"I was just thinking of making outs," he said. "I thank the team for leaving me in there and trusting me to go out there."

Bochy said he would have had a hard time taking Bumgarner out, regardless of the pitch count, because he was pitching so well.

"In fact, I was staying away from him every inning," Bochy said, "because I was hoping he wouldn't go, 'I'm starting to get a little tired.' "

The teams split the opening two games of the series in Kansas City. The Giants took Game One by a score of 7-1 behind Bumgarner then the Royals won 7-2 in Game Two as they broke a 2-2 tie with a five-run sixth inning that included a two-run double by catcher Salvador Perez and a two-run home run by second baseman Omar Infante.

The Giants then took two of three when the series shifted to San Francisco, though the Royals eked out a 3-2 victory in Game Three as relievers

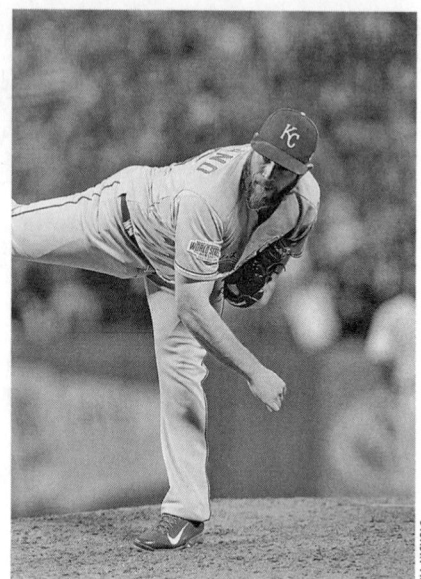

Greg Holland is the final piece of a rock-solid Royals bullpen

BILL NICHOLS

Brandon Finnegan, Kelvin Herrera, Wade Davis and Greg Holland combined for four hitless innings to preserve the one-run lead.

In Game Four, the Giants evened the series at 2-2 as right fielder Hunter Pence keyed an 11-4 victory with three hits and three RBIs. Bumgarner then threw his second shutout of the postseason in Game Five to put San Francisco back in the lead with the series returning to Kansas City.

The Royals turned Game Six game into a rout early, scoring seven runs in the second inning on the way to a 10-0 victory. Center fielder Lorenzo Cain had two hits and three RBIs while 23-year-old righthander Yordano Ventura pitched seven innings and combined with Jason Frasor and Tim Collins on a six-hit shutout to force a winner-take-all Game Seven where Bumgarner worked his magic one last time.

Quick Work In LCS

Both pennant winners made short work of their opponents in the League Championship Series with the Giants beating the Cardinals in five games and the Royals sweeping the Orioles.

The NLCS ended in dramatic fashion when journeyman first baseman Travis Ishikawa, playing left field because of an injury to Morse, hit a three-run home run in the bottom of the ninth inning off Michael Wacha to give the Giants a 6-3 victory in Game Five.

Ishikawa began the season as the Pirates' starting first baseman but was released three weeks later. He then spent three months with the Giants' Triple-A Fresno farm club before being called up to the majors July 29.

Yet he wound up hitting the first series-ending home run for the Giants since Bobby Thomson's "Shot Heard 'Round The World' beat the Brooklyn Dodgers for the 1951 NL pennant, seven seasons before the franchise moved from New York to the Bay Area.

Ishikawa was originally drafted by the Giants in the 21st round in 2002 out of high school in Federal Way, Wash.

"It's gratifying," Ishikawa said. "If there's an organization I'd want to do it for, it would be this one."

Bumgarner was the MVP of the NLCS after pitching 7 ⅔ scoreless innings in winning Game One and allowing three runs in eight innings in Game Five, though he did not factor in the decision.

"He's just so consistent, he really is," catcher Buster Posey said of Bumgarner. "It doesn't matter the situation, that's what makes him so good."

All of the Royals' wins were by two runs or fewer as their pitching staff shut down the Orioles, including holding them to two runs in the final two games of the series.

"That's what you dream of as a kid," said Holland, who had a save in all four games. "Punch your ticket to the World Series, especially before your home crowd. These fans have been waiting a long time. They deserve it."

Cain was named the ALCS MVP to end quite

a week. He went home to Oklahoma between the end of the Royals' sweep of the Angels in the American League Division Series and the start of ALCS when his wife Jenny gave birth to the couple's first child, a boy named Cameron Loe.

Fatherhood seemed to agree with Cain as he went 8-for-15 (.533) against the Orioles while scoring five runs. He also made a number of outstanding catches, ranging far into both gaps to steal hits.

"Unbelievable feeling," Cain said. "I've enjoyed every moment of it."

Short Division

None on the four Division Series went the distance.

Both NL series lasted four games with the Giants knocking off the Nationals, and the Cardinals downing the Dodgers. There were a pair of sweeps in the AL with the Royals upsetting the Angels, whose 98-64 regular season record was the best in the major leagues, and the Orioles taking out the Tigers.

The Royals stunned the Angels by winning the first two games at Anaheim on 11th-inning home runs. Third baseman Mike Moustakas' solo shot gave Kansas City a 3-2 victory in Game One and Hosmer's three-run blast in Game Two catapulted the Royals to a 4-1 win.

The Royals then rolled to an 8-3 home victory in Game Three, knocking out Angels lefthander C.J. Wilson during a four-run first inning that included a three-run double by Alex Gordon.

"I've never seen this group of kids so confident on a big stage," Royals manager Ned Yost said.

AMERICAN LEAGUE CHAMPIONS, 1995–2014

American League postseason results in Wild Card Era, 1995-present, where (*) denotes wild card playoff entrant.

YEAR	CHAMPIONSHIP SERIES	ALCS MVP	DIVISION SERIES 1	DIVISION SERIES 2
2014	Kansas City* 4, Baltimore 0	Lorenzo Cain, of, Kansas City	Kansas City 3, Los Angeles 0	Baltimore 3, Detroit 0
2013	Boston 4, Detroit 2	Koji Uehara, rhp, Boston	Boston 3, Tampa Bay* 1	Detroit, 3, Oakland 2
2012	Detroit 4, New York 0	Delmon Young, of, Detroit	New York 3, Baltimore* 2	Detroit 3, Oakland 2
2011	Texas 4, Detroit 2	Nelson Cruz, of, Texas	Detroit 3, New York 2	Texas 3, Tampa Bay* 1
2010	Texas 4, New York 2	Josh Hamilton, of, Texas	Texas 3, Tampa Bay 2	New York* 3, Minnesota 0
2009	New York 4, Los Angeles 2	C.C. Sabathia, lhp, New York	New York 3, Minnesota 0	Los Angeles 3, Boston* 0
2008	Tampa Bay 4, Boston 3	Matt Garza, rhp, Tampa Bay	Boston* 3, Los Angeles 1	Tampa Bay 3, Chicago 1
2007	Boston 4, Cleveland 3	Josh Beckett, rhp, Boston	Boston 3, Los Angeles 0	Cleveland 3, New York* 1
2006	Detroit 4, Oakland 0	Placido Polanco, 2b, Detroit	Detroit* 3, New York 1	Oakland 3, Minnesota 0
2005	Chicago 4, Los Angeles 1	Paul Konerko, 1b, Chicago	Chicago 3, Boston* 0	Los Angeles 3, New York 2
2004	Boston 4, New York 3	David Ortiz, dh, Boston	Boston* 3, Anaheim 0	New York 3, Minnesota 1
2003	New York 4, Boston 3	Mariano Rivera, rhp, New York	New York 3, Minnesota 1	Boston* 3, Oakland 2
2002	Anaheim 4, Minnesota 1	Adam Kennedy, 2b, Anaheim	Anaheim* 3, New York 1	Minnesota 3, Oakland 2
2001	New York 4, Seattle 1	Andy Pettitte, lhp, New York	Seattle 3, Cleveland 2	New York 3, Oakland* 2
2000	New York 4, Seattle 2	David Justice, of, New York	New York 3, Oakland 2	Seattle* 3, Chicago 0
1999	New York 4, Boston 1	Orlando Hernandez, rhp, New York	Boston* 3, Cleveland 2	New York 3, Texas 0
1998	New York 4, Cleveland 2	David Wells, lhp, New York	Cleveland 3, Boston* 1	New York 3, Texas 0
1997	Cleveland 4, Baltimore 2	Marquis Grissom, of, Cleveland	Cleveland 3, New York* 2	Baltimore 3, Seattle 1
1996	New York 4, Baltimore 1	Bernie Williams, of, New York	Baltimore* 3, Cleveland 1	New York 3, Texas 1
1995	Cleveland 4, Seattle 2	Orel Hershiser, rhp, Cleveland	Cleveland 3, Boston 0	Seattle 3, New York* 2

It was an unexpectedly quick ending for the Angels.

"Anything happens in the playoffs," Los Angeles manager Mike Scioscia said. "You don't go in with any badge saying you won the most games, and you're certainly not going to get any points for that going into the playoffs."

After winning the AL East by 12 games, the Orioles carried that momentum into the post-season by making quick work of the Tigers for their first postseason series victory since 1997. Designated hitter Nelson Cruz—who led the majors in homers with 40—put the finishing touch on the series with a two-run home run in the Orioles' 2-1 victory in Game Three at Detroit, his eighth career postseason homer against the Tigers.

"If you tell me before the series we were going to sweep, I don't believe it," Cruz said.

It would have been hard to believe that Dodgers ace lefthander Clayton Kershaw would lose twice in the same series after going 21-3 in the regular season, but the Cardinals beat him twice.

Kershaw couldn't hold a 6-2 lead in the Game One at Los Angeles as Matt Carpenter's three-run double keyed an eight-run seventh as the Cardinals rallied for a 10-9 win. Matt Adams' three-run homer in the seventh inning powered the Cardinals to a 3-2 victory in the decisive Game Four at St. Louis.

"I don't think I touched the ground the whole way around the bases," Adams said. "Definitely the highlight of my career."

The Nationals had the NL's best regular season record at 96-66 but managed just nine runs in four games against the Giants.

The turning point came in Game Two, an 18-inning marathon that lasted six hours and 23 minutes, which the Giants won 2-1 on first base-man Brandon Belt's solo home run off Tanner Roark that put San Francisco ahead 2-0 in the series. It was the longest game, time-wise, in post-season history and tied for the longest by innings.

"These guys, they're relentless," Bochy said. "They're warriors on the road."

Mild And Wild

The Giants and Royals took their first steps toward the World Series by surviving the winner-take-all wild-card games to start their postseason runs.

The Giants won the NL game easily, routing the Pirates 8-0 as Bumgarner began his postseason for the ages by pitching a four-hit shutout. Brandon Crawford broke a scoreless tie in the fourth inning by becoming the first shortstop in postseason history to hit a grand slam, connecting off Edinson Volquez.

"We thrive in these pressure situations," Crawford said. "I don't what it is. We just keep fighting no what the circumstance is."

Conversely, the Royals rallied for a 9-8 victory in 12 innings over the visiting Athletics.

Down 7-3 going into the bottom of the eighth inning against ace Jon Lester, the Royals scored three runs before adding another in the ninth to force extra innings. The Athletics pulled ahead 8-7 in the top of the 12th but the Royals scored twice in the bottom of the inning with Perez singling in the winning run with two outs on a night Kansas City tied a postseason record by stealing seven bases.

NATIONAL LEAGUE CHAMPIONS, 1995–2014

National League postseason results in Wild Card Era, 1995-present, where (*) denotes wild card playoff entrant.

YEAR	CHAMPIONSHIP SERIES	NLCS MVP	DIVISION SERIES	DIVISION SERIES
2014	San Francisco* 4, St. Louis 1	Madison Bumgarner, lhp, San Francisco	San Francisco 3, Washington 1	St. Louis 3, Los Angeles 1
2013	St. Louis 4, Los Angeles 2	Michael Wacha, rhp, St. Louis	St. Louis 3, Pittsburgh* 2	Los Angeles 3, Atlanta 1
2012	San Francisco 4, St. Louis 3	Marco Scutaro, 2b, San Francisco	St. Louis* 3, Washington 2	San Francisco 3, Cincinnati 2
2011	St. Louis 4, Milwaukee 2	David Freese, 3b, St. Louis	St. Louis 3, Philadelphia 2	Milwaukee 3, Arizona 2
2010	San Francisco 4, Philadelphia 2	Cody Ross, of, San Francisco	Philadelphia 3, Cincinnati 0	San Francisco 3, Atlanta* 1
2009	Philadelphia 4, Los Angeles 1	Ryan Howard, 1b, Philadelphia	Los Angeles 3, St. Louis 0	Philadelphia 3, Colorado* 1
2008	Philadelphia 4, Los Angeles 1	Cole Hamels, lhp, Philadelphia	Los Angeles 3, Chicago 0	Philadelphia 3, Milwaukee* 1
2007	Colorado 4, Arizona 0	Matt Holliday, of, Colorado	Arizona 3, Chicago 0	Colorado* 3, Philadelphia 0
2006	St. Louis 4, New York 3	Jeff Suppan, rhp, St. Louis	New York 3, Los Angeles* 0	St. Louis 3, San Diego 1
2005	Houston 4, St. Louis 2	Roy Oswalt, rhp, Houston	St. Louis 3, San Diego 0	Houston* 3, Atlanta 1
2004	St. Louis 4, Houston 3	Albert Pujols, 1b, St. Louis	St. Louis 3, Los Angeles 1	Houston* 3, Atlanta 2
2003	Florida 4, Chicago 3	Ivan Rodriguez, c, Florida	Florida* 3, San Francisco 1	Chicago 3, Atlanta 2
2002	San Francisco 4, St. Louis 1	Benito Santiago, c, San Francisco	San Francisco* 3, Atlanta 2	St. Louis 3, Arizona 0
2001	Arizona 4, Atlanta 1	Craig Counsell, ss, Arizona	Atlanta 3, Houston 0	Arizona 3, St. Louis* 2
2000	New York 4, St. Louis 1	Mike Hampton, lhp, New York	St. Louis 3, Atlanta 0	New York* 3, San Francisco 1
1999	Atlanta 4, New York 2	Eddie Perez, c, Atlanta	Atlanta 3, Houston 1	New York* 3, Arizona 1
1998	San Diego 4, Atlanta 2	Sterling Hitchcock, lhp, San Diego	Atlanta 3, Chicago* 0	San Diego 3, Houston 1
1997	Florida 4, Atlanta 2	Livan Hernandez, rhp, Florida	Florida* 3, San Francisco 0	Atlanta 3, Houston 0
1996	Atlanta 4, St. Louis 3	Javy Lopez, c, Atlanta	Atlanta 3, Los Angeles* 0	St. Louis 3, San Diego 0
1995	Atlanta 4, Cincinnati 0	Mike Devereaux, of, Atlanta	Atlanta 3, Colorado* 1	Cincinnati 3, Los Angeles 0

The Giants won their third title in five years

Year	Winner	Loser	Result
1903	Boston (AL)	Pittsburgh (NL)	5-3
1904	NO SERIES		
1905	New York (NL)	Philadelphia (AL)	4-1
1906	Chicago (AL)	Chicago (NL)	4-2
1907	Chicago (NL)	Detroit (AL)	4-0
1908	Chicago (NL)	Detroit (AL)	4-1
1909	Pittsburgh (NL)	Detroit (AL)	4-3
1910	Philadelphia (AL)	Chicago (NL)	4-1
1911	Philadelphia (AL)	New York (NL)	4-2
1912	Boston (AL)	New York (NL)	4-3-1
1913	Philadelphia (AL)	New York (NL)	4-1
1914	Boston (NL)	Philadelphia (AL)	4-0
1915	Boston (AL)	Philadelphia (NL)	4-1
1916	Boston (AL)	Brooklyn (NL)	4-1
1917	Chicago (AL)	New York (NL)	4-2
1918	Boston (AL)	Chicago (NL)	4-2
1919	Cincinnati (NL)	Chicago (AL)	5-3
1920	Cleveland (AL)	Brooklyn (NL)	5-2
1921	New York (NL)	New York (AL)	5-3
1922	New York (NL)	New York (AL)	4-0
1923	New York (AL)	New York (NL)	4-2
1924	Washington (AL)	New York (NL)	4-3
1925	Pittsburgh (NL)	Washington (AL)	4-3
1926	St. Louis (NL)	New York (AL)	4-3
1927	New York (AL)	Pittsburgh (NL)	4-0
1928	New York (AL)	St. Louis (NL)	4-0
1929	Philadelphia (AL)	Chicago (NL)	4-1
1930	Philadelphia (AL)	St. Louis (NL)	4-2
1931	St. Louis (NL)	Philadelphia (AL)	4-3
1932	New York (AL)	Chicago (NL)	4-0
1933	New York (NL)	Washington (AL)	4-1
1934	St. Louis (NL)	Detroit (AL)	4-3
1935	Detroit (AL)	Chicago (NL)	4-2
1936	New York (AL)	New York (NL)	4-2
1937	New York (AL)	New York (NL)	4-1
1938	New York (AL)	Chicago (NL)	4-0
1939	New York (AL)	Cincinnati (NL)	4-0
1940	Cincinnati (NL)	Detroit (AL)	4-3
1941	New York (AL)	Brooklyn (NL)	4-1
1942	St. Louis (NL)	New York (AL)	4-1
1943	New York (AL)	St. Louis (NL)	4-1
1944	St. Louis (NL)	St. Louis (AL)	4-2
1945	Detroit (AL)	Chicago (NL)	4-3
1946	St. Louis (NL)	Boston (AL)	4-3
1947	New York (AL)	Brooklyn (NL)	4-3
1948	Cleveland (AL)	Boston (NL)	4-2
1949	New York (AL)	Brooklyn (NL)	4-1
1950	New York (AL)	Philadelphia (NL)	4-0
1951	New York (AL)	New York (NL)	4-2
1952	New York (AL)	Brooklyn (NL)	4-3
1953	New York (AL)	Brooklyn (NL)	4-2
1954	New York (NL)	Cleveland (AL)	4-0
1955	Brooklyn (NL)	New York (AL)	4-3
1956	New York (AL)	Brooklyn (NL)	4-3
1957	Milwaukee (NL)	New York (AL)	4-3
1958	New York (AL)	Milwaukee (NL)	4-3
1959	Los Angeles (NL)	Chicago (AL)	4-2
1960	Pittsburgh (NL)	New York (AL)	4-3
1961	New York (AL)	Cincinnati (NL)	4-1
1962	New York (AL)	San Francisco (NL)	4-3
1963	Los Angeles (NL)	New York (AL)	4-0
1964	St. Louis (NL)	New York (AL)	4-3
1965	Los Angeles (NL)	Minnesota (AL)	4-3
1966	Baltimore (AL)	Los Angeles (NL)	4-0
1967	St. Louis (NL)	Boston (AL)	4-3
1968	Detroit (AL)	St. Louis (NL)	4-3
1969	New York (NL)	Baltimore (AL)	4-1
1970	Baltimore (AL)	Cincinnati (NL)	4-1
1971	Pittsburgh (NL)	Baltimore (AL)	4-3
1972	Oakland (AL)	Cincinnati (NL)	4-3
1973	Oakland (AL)	New York (NL)	4-3
1974	Oakland (AL)	Los Angeles (NL)	4-1
1975	Cincinnati (NL)	Boston (AL)	4-3
1976	Cincinnati (NL)	New York (AL)	4-0
1977	New York (AL)	Los Angeles (NL)	4-2
1978	New York (AL)	Los Angeles (NL)	4-2
1979	Pittsburgh (NL)	Baltimore (AL)	4-3
1980	Philadelphia (NL)	Kansas City (AL)	4-2
1981	Los Angeles (NL)	New York (AL)	4-2
1982	St. Louis (NL)	Milwaukee (AL)	4-3
1983	Baltimore (AL)	Philadelphia (NL)	4-1
1984	Detroit (AL)	San Diego (NL)	4-1
1985	Kansas City (AL)	St. Louis (NL)	4-3
1986	New York (NL)	Boston (AL)	4-3
1987	Minnesota (AL)	St. Louis (NL)	4-3
1988	Los Angeles (NL)	Oakland (AL)	4-1
1989	Oakland (AL)	San Francisco (NL)	4-0
1990	Cincinnati (NL)	Oakland (AL)	4-0
1991	Minnesota (AL)	Atlanta (NL)	4-3
1992	Toronto (AL)	Atlanta (NL)	4-2
1993	Toronto (AL)	Philadelphia (NL)	4-2
1994	NO SERIES		
1995	Atlanta (NL)	Cleveland (AL)	4-2
1996	New York (AL)	Atlanta (NL)	4-2
1997	Florida (NL)	Cleveland (AL)	4-3
1998	New York (AL)	San Diego (NL)	4-0
1999	New York (AL)	Atlanta (NL)	4-0
2000	New York (AL)	New York (NL)	4-1
2001	Arizona (NL)	New York (AL)	4-3
2002	Anaheim (AL)	San Francisco (NL)	4-3
2003	Florida (NL)	New York (AL)	4-2
2004	Boston (AL)	St. Louis (NL)	4-0
2005	Chicago (AL)	Houston (NL)	4-0
2006	St. Louis (NL)	Detroit (AL)	4-1
2007	Boston (AL)	Colorado (NL)	4-0
2008	Philadelphia (NL)	Tampa Bay (AL)	4-1
2009	New York (AL)	Philadelphia (NL)	4-2
2010	San Francisco (NL)	Texas (AL)	4-1
2011	St. Louis (NL)	Texas (AL)	4-3
2012	San Francisco (NL)	Detroit (AL)	4-0
2013	Boston (AL)	St. Louis (NL)	4-2
2014	San Francisco (NL)	Kansas City (AL)	4-3

WORLD SERIES BOX SCORES

GAME 1 October 21, 2014

SAN FRANCISCO 7, KANSAS CITY 1

SAN FRANCISCO	AB	R	H	RBI	BB	SO	LOB	AVG
Blanco, G, CF	3	2	1	1	2	0	1	.333
Panik, 2B	5	1	1	1	0	1	5	.200
Posey, C	5	0	1	0	0	0	4	.200
Sandoval, 3B	5	1	2	2	0	0	0	.400
Pence, RF	3	2	2	2	2	0	0	.667
Belt, 1B	4	1	1	0	1	2	4	.250
Morse, DH	5	0	1	1	0	3	5	.200
Ishikawa, LF	1	0	0	0	0	0	0	.000
a-Perez, J, PH-LF	2	0	0	0	0	1	0	.000
Crawford, B, SS	3	0	1	0	1	0	0	.333
TOTALS	36	7	10	7	6	7	19	

a-Hit a sacrifice bunt for Ishikawa in the 4th.

KANSAS CITY	AB	R	H	RBI	BB	SO	LOB	AVG
Escobar, A, SS	4	0	1	0	0	1	2	.250
Aoki, RF	4	0	0	0	0	1	3	.000
Cain, L, CF	2	0	0	0	1	1	0	.000
Hosmer, 1B	4	0	0	0	0	0	4	.000
Butler, B, DH	3	0	1	0	0	0	0	.333
a-Willingham, PH-DH	1	0	0	0	0	1	0	.000
Gordon, A, LF	3	0	0	0	0	1	1	.000
Perez, S, C	3	1	1	1	0	1	1	.333
Infante, 2B	3	0	0	0	0	0	0	.000
Moustakas, 3B	3	0	1	0	0	1	0	.333
TOTALS	30	1	4	1	1	7	11	

a-Struck out for Butler, B in the 9th. 2B: Sandoval, Pence, Moustakas. 3B: Panik. HR: Pence, Perez, S. GIDP: Perez, S, Aoki. SF LOB: 9; KC LOB: 4.

SAN FRANCISCO	IP	H	R	ER	BB	SO	HR	ERA
Bumgarner (W, 1-0)	7	3	1	1	1	5	1	1.29
Lopez, Jav	1	1	0	0	0	0	0	0.00
Strickland	1	0	0	0	0	2	0	0.00

KANSAS CITY	IP	H	R	ER	BB	SO	HR	ERA
Shields (L, 0-1)	3	7	5	5	1	1	1	15.00
Duffy	3	1	2	2	3	3	0	6.00
Collins	2	2	0	0	1	2	0	0.00
Frasor	1	0	0	0	1	1	0	0.00

Shields pitched to 3 batters in the 4th. Duffy pitched to 2 batters in the 7th. WP: Shields, Collins. HBP: Cain, L.

GAME 2 October 22, 2014

KANSAS CITY 7, SAN FRANCISCO 2

SAN FRANCISCO	AB	R	H	RBI	BB	SO	LOB	AVG
Blanco, G, CF	4	1	1	1	1	1	2	.286
Panik, 2B	4	0	1	0	0	0	3	.222
Posey, C	4	0	1	0	0	1	3	.222
Sandoval, 3B	4	1	1	0	0	1	1	.444
Pence, RF	4	0	1	0	0	1	1	.429
Belt, 1B	4	0	1	1	0	1	2	.250
Morse, DH	3	0	1	0	0	0	3	.250
a-Susac, PH-DH	1	0	0	0	0	1	0	.000
Ishikawa, LF	4	0	1	0	0	2	1	.200
Crawford, B, SS	3	0	1	0	1	0	1	.333
TOTALS	35	2	9	2	2	8	17	

a-Struck out for Morse in the 9th.

KANSAS CITY	AB	R	H	RBI	BB	SO	LOB	AVG
Escobar, A, SS	4	0	2	1	0	1	1	.375
Aoki, RF	3	0	0	0	0	0	2	.000
Dyson, J, CF	1	0	0	0	0	0	0	.000
Cain, L, CF-RF	4	2	2	0	0	0	0	.333
Hosmer, 1B	2	1	0	0	2	1	0	.000
Butler, B, DH	3	0	2	2	0	0	0	.500
1-Gore, PR-DH	0	1	0	0	0	0	0	.000
a-Willingham, PH-DH	1	0	0	0	0	1	0	.000
Gordon, A, LF	4	0	0	0	0	0	4	.000
Perez, S, C	4	1	1	2	0	1	0	.286
Infante, 2B	3	2	2	2	0	0	0	.333
Moustakas, 3B	3	0	1	0	0	0	1	.333

TOTALS (continued, top of right column)

TOTALS	32	7	10	7	2	4	8

a-Struck out for Gore in the 8th. 1-Ran for Butler, B in the 6th. 2B: Sandoval, Belt; Cain, L, Infante, Escobar, A, Perez, S. HR: Blanco, G; Infante. CS: Escobar, A.

SAN FRANCISCO	IP	H	R	ER	BB	SO	HR	ERA
Peavy (L, 0-1)	5	6	4	4	2	1	0	7.20
Machi	0	1	1	1	0	0	0	-.--
Lopez, Jav	1/3	0	0	0	0	0	0	0.00
Strickland	0	2	2	2	0	0	1	18.00
Affeldt	2/3	1	0	0	0	0	0	0.00
Lincecum	1 2/3	0	0	0	0	2	0	0.00
Casilla, S	1/3	0	0	0	0	1	0	0.00

KANSAS CITY	IP	H	R	ER	BB	SO	HR	ERA
Ventura	5 1/3	8	2	2	0	2	1	3.38
Herrera, K (W, 1-0)	1 2/3	0	0	0	2	1	0	0.00
Davis, W	1	0	0	0	0	2	0	0.00
Holland, G	1	1	0	0	0	3	0	0.00

Peavy pitched to 2 batters in the 6th. Machi pitched to 1 batter in the 6th. Strickland pitched to 2 batters in the 6th. WP: Strickland.

GAME 3 October 24, 2014

KANSAS CITY 3, SAN FRANCISCO 2

KANSAS CITY	AB	R	H	RBI	BB	SO	LOB	AVG
Escobar, A, SS	4	2	2	0	0	1	0	.417
Gordon, A, LF	4	1	1	1	0	1	1	.091
Cain, L, RF	4	0	0	1	0	1	1	.300
Hosmer, 1B	4	0	1	0	0	1	0	.100
Moustakas, 3B	4	0	1	0	0	1	1	.300
Infante, 2B	3	0	0	0	1	2	0	.222
Perez, S, C	3	0	0	0	0	0	2	.200
Dyson, J, CF	3	0	1	0	0	0	2	.250
Guthrie, P	2	0	0	0	0	0	0	.000
Herrera, K, P	1	0	0	0	0	0	1	.000
Finnegan, P	0	0	0	0	0	0	0	.000
Davis, W, P	0	0	0	0	0	0	0	.000
Holland, G, P	0	0	0	0	0	0	0	.000
TOTALS	32	3	6	3	1	7	8	

SAN FRANCISCO	AB	R	H	RBI	BB	SO	LOB	AVG
Blanco, G, CF	3	0	0	0	1	0	0	.200
Panik, 2B	4	0	0	0	0	1	2	.154
Posey, C	4	0	0	1	0	1	0	.154
Sandoval, 3B	4	0	0	0	0	1	1	.308
Pence, RF	3	0	1	0	1	0	0	.400
Belt, 1B	3	0	1	0	0	1	1	.273
Ishikawa, LF	2	0	0	0	0	0	1	.143
b-Perez, J, PH-LF	1	0	0	0	0	0	1	.000
Crawford, B, SS	3	1	1	0	0	1	1	.333
Affeldt, P	0	0	0	0	0	0	0	.000
Casilla, S, P	0	0	0	0	0	0	0	.000
Hudson, T, P	1	0	0	0	0	0	0	.000
Lopez, Jav, P	0	0	0	0	0	0	0	.000
a-Morse, PH	1	1	1	1	0	0	0	.333
Romo, P	0	0	0	0	0	0	0	.000
Arias, SS	1	0	0	0	0	1	0	.000
TOTALS	30	2	4	2	2	4	8	

a-Doubled for Lopez, Jav in the 6th. b-Flied out for Ishikawa in the 7th. 2B: Escobar, A, Gordon, A; Morse. KC LOB: 3. SF LOB: 3.

KANSAS CITY	IP	H	R	ER	BB	SO	HR	ERA
Guthrie (W, 1-0)	5	4	2	2	0	0	0	3.60
Herrera, K (H, 1)	1 1/3	0	0	0	2	1	0	0.00
Finnegan (H, 1)	2/3	0	0	0	0	1	0	0.00
Davis, W (H, 1)	1	0	0	0	0	2	0	0.00
Holland, G (S, 1)	1	0	0	0	0	0	0	0.00

SAN FRANCISCO	IP	H	R	ER	BB	SO	HR	ERA
Hudson, T (L, 0-1)	5 2/3	4	3	3	1	2	0	4.76
Lopez, Jav	1/3	1	0	0	0	1	0	0.00
Romo	1 1/3	1	0	0	0	3	0	0.00
Affeldt	1 1/3	0	0	0	0	0	0	0.00
Casilla, S	1/3	0	0	0	0	1	0	0.00

GAME 4 October 25, 2014

SAN FRANCISCO 11, KANSAS CITY 4

KANSAS CITY	AB	R	H	RBI	BB	SO	LOB	AVG
Escobar, A, SS	5	0	1	0	0	1	0	.353
Gordon, A, LF	5	1	1	0	0	1	1	.125
Cain, L, RF	5	1	2	0	0	1	1	.267
Hosmer, 1B	5	1	3	1	0	1	2	.267
Moustakas, 3B	3	1	0	0	1	0	2	.231
Collins, P	0	0	0	0	0	0	0	.000
Infante, 2B	4	0	1	2	0	1	1	.231
Perez, S, C	4	0	3	1	0	0	1	.357
Dyson, J, CF	3	0	1	0	1	0	2	.286
Vargas, P	2	0	0	0	0	1	3	.000
Frasor, P	0	0	0	0	0	0	0	.000
Duffy, P	0	0	0	0	0	0	0	.000
a-Aoki, PH	1	0	0	0	0	0	1	.000
Finnegan, P	0	0	0	0	0	0	0	.000
Nix, J, 3B	1	0	0	0	0	0	1	.000
TOTALS	38	4	12	4	2	7	15	

a-Grounded into a double play for Duffy in the 6th.

SAN FRANCISCO	AB	R	H	RBI	BB	SO	LOB	AVG
Blanco, G, CF	5	3	2	0	1	0	3	.267
Panik, 2B	4	2	2	2	0	0	2	.235
Posey, C	3	1	1	1	2	0	2	.188
Pence, RF	5	2	3	3	0	0	4	.467
Sandoval, 3B	5	0	2	2	0	2	4	.333
Belt, 1B	3	0	1	1	2	1	0	.286
Perez, J, LF	4	0	1	1	0	1	4	.143
Crawford, B, SS	5	1	1	0	0	2	3	.286
Vogelsong, P	0	0	0	0	0	0	0	.000
Machi, P	0	0	0	0	0	0	0	.000
a-Duffy, PH	1	1	1	0	0	0	0	1.000
Petit, Y, P	1	0	1	0	0	0	0	1.000
b-Arias, PH	1	0	1	0	0	0	0	.500
Affeldt, P	0	0	0	0	0	0	0	.000
c-Morse, PH	0	1	0	0	1	0	0	.333
Romo, P	0	0	0	0	0	0	0	.000
d-Ishikawa, PH	1	0	0	0	0	0	0	.125
Strickland, P	0	0	0	0	0	0	0	.000
TOTALS	38	11	16	10	6	6	22	

a-Singled for Machi in the 3rd. b-Singled for Petit, Y in the 6th. c-Walked for Affeldt in the 7th. d-Lined out for Romo in the 8th. 2B: Hosmer, Gordon, A; Panik 2, Pence.

KANSAS CITY	IP	H	R	ER	BB	SO	HR	ERA
Vargas	4	6	3	3	2	3	0	6.75
Frasor	1/3	1	1	1	0	0	0	6.75
Duffy	2/3	1	0	0	1	1	0	4.91
Finnegan (L, 0-1)	1	5	5	5	2	0	0	27.00
Collins	2	3	2	2	1	2	0	4.50

SAN FRANCISCO	IP	H	R	ER	BB	SO	HR	ERA
Vogelsong	2 2/3	7	4	4	1	2	0	13.50
Machi	1/3	0	0	0	1	1	0	27.00
Petit, Y (W, 1-0)	3	2	0	0	0	2	0	0.00
Affeldt (H, 1)	1	1	0	0	0	0	0	0.00
Romo	1	1	0	0	0	1	0	0.00
Strickland	1	1	0	0	0	1	0	9.00

Vargas pitched to 1 batter in the 5th. Finnegan pitched to 2 batters in the 7th.

GAME 5 *October 26, 2014*

SAN FRANCISCO 5, KANSAS CITY 0

KANSAS CITY	AB	R	H	RBI	BB	SO	LOB	AVG
Escobar, A, SS	4	0	0	0	0	0	0	.286
Gordon, A, LF	4	0	0	0	0	1	0	.100
Cain, L, RF-CF	4	0	1	0	0	0	0	.263
Hosmer, 1B	4	0	1	0	0	1	1	.263
Perez, S, C	3	0	1	0	0	0	1	.353
Moustakas, 3B	3	0	0	0	0	1	2	.188
Infante, 2B	3	0	1	0	0	1	2	.250
Herrera, K, P	0	0	0	0	0	0	0	.000
Davis, W, P	0	0	0	0	0	0	0	.000
Dyson, J, CF	2	0	0	0	0	2	2	.222
a-Butler, B, PH	1	0	0	0	0	1	0	.429
Aoki, RF	0	0	0	0	0	0	0	.000
Shields, P	2	0	0	0	0	1	1	.000

Nix, J, 2B	1	0	0	0	0	0	0	.000
TOTALS	31	0	4	0	0	8	9	

a-Struck out for Dyson, J in the 8th.

SAN FRANCISCO	AB	R	H	RBI	BB	SO	LOB	AVG
Blanco, G, CF	5	0	0	0	0	1	1	.200
Panik, 2B	3	0	1	0	1	0	0	.250
Posey, C	3	0	1	0	0	0	1	.211
Sandoval, 3B	4	2	2	0	0	1	3	.364
Pence, RF	4	2	2	0	0	1	3	.474
Belt, 1B	4	0	1	0	0	2	3	.278
Ishikawa, LF	3	0	2	0	0	0	2	.273
1-Perez, J, PR-LF	1	1	1	2	0	0	0	.250
Crawford, B, SS	4	0	2	3	0	0	2	.333
Bumgarner, P	4	0	0	0	0	2	5	.000
TOTALS	35	5	12	5	2	7	20	

1-Ran for Ishikawa in the 6th. 2B: Perez, J; Infante. KC LOB: 4. SF LOB: 8. E: Escobar, A (1, throw). DP: (Nix, J-Escobar, A-Hosmer).

KANSAS CITY	IP	H	R	ER	BB	SO	HR	ERA
Shields (L, 0-2)	6	8	2	2	1	4	0	7.00
Herrera, K	1	2	2	2	1	0	0	4.50
Davis, W	1	2	1	0	0	3	0	0.00

SAN FRANCISCO	IP	H	R	ER	BB	SO	HR	ERA
Bumgarner (W, 2-0)	9	4	0	0	0	8	0	0.56

Herrera, K pitched to 2 batters in the 8th.

GAME 6 *October 28, 2014*

KANSAS CITY 10, SAN FRANCISCO 0

SAN FRANCISCO	AB	R	H	RBI	BB	SO	LOB	AVG
Blanco, G, CF	4	0	0	0	1	2	3	.167
Panik, 2B	3	0	1	0	1	0	0	.261
Posey, C	3	0	0	0	0	0	3	.182
Susac, C	1	0	0	0	0	0	1	.000
Sandoval, 3B	3	0	1	0	1	0	0	.360
Arias, 3B	0	0	0	0	0	0	0	.500
Pence, RF	4	0	1	0	0	0	3	.435
Belt, 1B	4	0	1	0	0	2	3	.273
Morse, DH	4	0	0	0	0	2	2	.231
Ishikawa, LF	2	0	0	0	1	2	0	.231
Perez, J, LF	1	0	1	0	0	0	0	.333
Crawford, B, SS	2	0	1	0	1	0	0	.350
Duffy, SS	1	0	0	0	0	1	1	.500
TOTALS	32	0	6	0	5	7	16	

KANSAS CITY	AB	R	H	RBI	BB	SO	LOB	AVG
Escobar, A, SS	5	1	2	1	0	0	1	.308
Aoki, RF	3	1	1	1	1	1	1	.091
Dyson, J, CF	1	0	0	0	0	0	0	.200
Cain, L, CF-RF	3	1	2	3	2	0	1	.318
Hosmer, 1B	5	1	2	2	0	2	4	.292
Butler, B, DH	4	0	1	1	1	0	3	.364
Gordon, A, LF	4	1	1	0	0	1	2	.125
Perez, S, C	4	1	2	0	0	0	1	.381
Moustakas, 3B	4	2	2	2	0	0	1	.250
Infante, 2B	4	2	2	0	0	1	2	.300
TOTALS	37	10	15	10	4	5	16	

2B: Moustakas, Hosmer, Butler, B, Infante, Cain, L., Escobar, A; Pence. HR: Moustakas. SF LOB: 10. KC LOB: 7.

SAN FRANCISCO	IP	H	R	ER	BB	SO	HR	ERA
Peavy (L, 0-2)	1 1/3	6	5	5	1	2	0	12.79
Petit, Y	2/3	3	2	2	0	0	0	4.91
Machi	3	5	2	2	1	2	0	8.10
Strickland	2	1	1	1	1	0	1	6.75
Vogelsong	1	0	0	0	1	1	0	9.82

KANSAS CITY	IP	H	R	ER	BB	SO	HR	ERA
Ventura (W, 1-0)	7	3	0	0	5	4	0	1.46
Frasor	1	2	0	0	0	1	0	3.86
Collins	1	1	0	0	0	2	0	3.60

WP: Petit, Y.Umpires: HP: Jeff Kellogg. 1B: Jeff Nelson. 2B: Eric Cooper. 3B: Jim Reynolds. LF: Ted Barrett. RF: Hunter Wendelstedt. Weather: 58 degrees, clear.

GAME 7 October 29, 2014
SAN FRANCISCO 3, KANSAS CITY 2

SAN FRANCISCO	AB	R	H	RBI	BB	SO	LOB	AVG
Blanco, G, CF	4	0	0	0	0	0	0	.143
Panik, 2B	4	0	0	0	0	3	0	.222
Posey, C	4	0	0	0	0	2	0	.154
Sandoval, 3B	3	2	3	0	0	0	0	.429
Pence, RF	4	1	2	0	0	0	2	.444
Belt, 1B	4	0	2	0	0	0	2	.308
Morse, DH	3	0	1	2	0	2	1	.250
Crawford, B, SS	3	0	0	1	0	3	2	.304
Perez, J, LF	3	0	0	0	0	2	3	.250
TOTALS	32	3	8	3	0	12	10	

KANSAS CITY	AB	R	H	RBI	BB	SO	LOB	AVG
Escobar, A, SS	3	0	1	0	0	1	0	.310
Aoki, RF	3	0	0	0	1	0	3	.071
Cain, L, CF	4	0	1	0	0	1	2	.308
Hosmer, 1B	4	0	0	0	0	2	2	.250
Butler, B, DH	4	1	1	0	0	0	0	.333
Gordon, A, LF	3	1	2	1	0	0	0	.185
Perez, S, C	3	0	0	0	0	2	0	.333
Moustakas, 3B	3	0	0	0	0	2	0	.217
Infante, 2B	2	0	1	1	0	1	0	.318
TOTALS	29	2	6	2	1	5	11	

2B: Gordon, A; Sandoval. SF LOB: 5. KC LOB: 5.

SAN FRANCISCO	IP	H	R	ER	BB	SO	HR	ERA
Hudson, T	1²/₃	3	2	2	1	1	0	6.14
Affeldt (W, 1-0)	2¹/₃	1	0	0	0	0	0	0.00
Bumgarner (S, 1)	5	2	0	0	0	4	0	0.43

KANSAS CITY	IP	H	R	ER	BB	SO	HR	ERA
Guthrie (L, 1-1)	3¹/₃	4	3	3	0	3	0	5.40
Herrera, K	2²/₃	3	0	0	0	4	0	2.70
Davis, W	2	1	0	0	0	3	0	0.00
Holland, G	1	0	0	0	0	2	0	0.00

HBP: Sandoval (by Guthrie), Perez, S (by Hudson, T), Gordon, A (by Affeldt). Umpires: HP: Jeff Nelson. 1B: Eric Cooper. 2B: Jim Reynolds. 3B: Ted Barrett. LF: Hunter Wendelstedt. RF: Jeff Kellogg.

AMERICAN LEAGUE WILD CARD GAME
KANSAS CITY ROYALS VS OAKLAND ATHLETICS

PLAYER, POS	AVG	G	AB	R	H	2B	3B	HR	RBI	BB	SO	SB
Alberto Callaspo, 1B	1.000	1	1	0	1	0	0	0	1	0	0	0
Coco Crisp, CF	.333	1	6	1	2	0	0	0	1	0	3	0
Josh Donaldson, 3B	.400	1	5	1	2	0	0	0	0	1	2	0
Nate Freiman, 1B	.000	1	1	0	0	0	0	0	0	0	0	0
Sam Fuld, LF	.400	1	5	1	2	0	0	0	0	1	1	0
Jed Lowrie, SS	.000	1	5	0	0	0	0	0	0	0	0	0
Brandon Moss, DH	.400	1	5	2	2	0	0	2	5	1	2	0
Derek Norris, C	.200	1	5	1	1	0	0	0	1	0	2	0
Nick Punto, 2B	.000	1	2	0	0	0	0	0	0	0	1	0
Josh Reddick, RF	.500	1	4	2	2	0	0	0	0	2	0	0
Eric Sogard, 2B	.250	1	4	0	1	0	0	0	0	0	2	0
Geovany Soto, C	.000	1	1	0	0	0	0	0	0	0	1	0
Stephen Vogt, 1B	.000	1	3	0	0	0	0	0	0	0	1	0
Totals	.277	1	47	8	13	0	0	2	8	6	15	0

PITCHER	W	L	ERA	G	GS	SV	IP	H	R	ER	BB	SO
Fernando Abad	0	0	0.00	1	0	0	0.1	0	0	0	0	0
Sean Doolittle	0	0	4.50	1	0	0	2.0	2	1	1	0	0
Luke Gregerson	0	0	0.00	1	0	0	0.2	1	0	0	1	2
Jason Hammel	0	0	-	1	0	0	0.0	1	0	0	0	0
Jon Lester	0	0	7.36	1	1	0	7.1	8	6	6	2	5
Dan Otero	0	1	13.50	1	0	0	1.1	3	2	2	0	1
Totals	0	1	6.94	1	1	0	11.2	15	9	9	3	8

PLAYER, POS	AVG	G	AB	R	H	2B	3B	HR	RBI	BB	SO	SB
Nori Aoki, RF	.000	1	4	1	0	0	0	0	1	0	0	1
Billy Butler, DH	.500	1	4	0	2	0	0	0	0	2	0	1
Lorenzo Cain, CF	.333	1	6	2	2	1	0	0	2	0	0	1
Christian Colon, PH	1.000	1	1	1	1	0	0	0	1	0	0	1
Jarrod Dyson, CF	-	1	0	1	0	0	0	0	0	0	0	1
Alcides Escobar, SS	.500	1	4	1	2	0	0	0	0	0	0	1
Alex Gordon, LF	.000	1	5	0	0	0	0	0	0	1	2	1
Eric Hosmer, 1B	.750	1	4	2	3	0	1	0	1	2	0	0
Omar Infante, 2B	.400	1	5	0	2	0	0	0	0	0	2	0
Mike Moustakas, 3B	.333	1	3	1	1	0	0	0	0	0	0	0
Jayson Nix, 3B	.000	1	1	0	0	0	0	0	0	0	1	0
Salvador Perez, C	.167	1	6	0	1	0	0	0	1	0	2	0
Josh Willingham, PH	1.000	1	1	0	1	0	0	0	0	0	0	0
Totals	.341	1	44	9	15	1	1	0	8	3	8	6

PITCHER	W	L	ERA	G	GS	SV	IP	H	R	ER	BB	SO
Wade Davis	0	0	0.00	1	0	0	1.0	0	0	0	0	1
Brandon Finnegan	0	0	3.86	1	0	0	2.1	1	1	1	1	3
Jason Frasor	1	0	0.00	1	0	0	0.2	1	0	0	0	1
Kelvin Herrera	0	0	5.40	1	0	0	1.2	4	1	1	0	3
Greg Holland	0	0	0.00	1	0	0	1.0	0	0	0	3	1
James Shields	0	0	7.20	1	1	0	5.0	5	4	4	2	6
Yordano Ventura	0	0	54.00	1	0	0	0.1	2	2	2	0	0
Totals	1	0	6.00	1	1	0	12.0	13	8	8	6	15

LOB—Oakland 10, Kansas City 8. DP—Kansas City. SAC—Lowrie, Colon, Dyson, Escobar 2. SF—Aoki. IBB—Moss (by Holland). SB—Aoki, Cain, Colon, Dyson, Escobar, Gordon, Gore. CS—Hosmer. WP—Gregerson, Frasor, Ventura. PB—Perez.

SCORE BY INNINGS

Oakland	200 005 000 001—8
Kansas City	102 000 031 002—9

AMERICAN LEAGUE DIVISION SERIES
LOS ANGELES ANGELS VS KANSAS CITY ROYALS

PLAYER, POS	AVG	G	AB	R	H	2B	3B	HR	RBI	BB	SO	SB
Nori Aoki, RF	.333	3	12	2	4	0	0	0	1	1	1	0
Billy Butler, DH	.000	3	9	1	0	0	0	0	0	3	1	1
Lorenzo Cain, CF	.154	3	13	2	2	0	0	0	1	0	3	0
Jarrod Dyson, CF	.000	3	2	0	0	0	0	0	0	0	0	0
Alcides Escobar, SS	.214	3	14	1	3	1	0	0	1	0	5	0
Alex Gordon, LF	.300	3	10	2	3	2	0	0	4	3	2	2
Eric Hosmer, 1B	.400	3	10	3	4	1	0	2	4	3	4	0
Omar Infante, 2B	.000	3	11	0	0	0	0	0	1	1	4	0
Mike Moustakas, 3B	.273	3	11	3	3	0	0	2	2	1	2	0
Salvador Perez, C	.154	3	13	0	2	0	0	0	1	0	4	0
Josh Willingham, PH	.000	1	1	0	0	0	0	0	0	0	0	0
Totals	.198	3	106	15	21	4	0	4	15	12	26	3

PITCHER	W	L	ERA	G	GS	SV	IP	H	R	ER	BB	SO
Tim Collins	0	0	0.00	1	0	0	0.2	0	0	0	0	1
Wade Davis	0	0	2.70	3	0	0	3.1	3	1	1	2	3
Danny Duffy	1	0	0.00	1	0	0	1.0	1	0	0	0	1
Brandon Finnegan	1	0	0.00	2	0	0	1.2	0	0	0	1	0
Jason Frasor	0	0	0.00	2	0	0	1.1	0	0	0	1	0
Kelvin Herrera	0	0	0.00	3	0	0	1.0	0	0	0	1	1
Greg Holland	0	0	0.00	3	0	2	3.0	0	0	0	0	6
James Shields	1	0	3.00	1	1	0	6.0	6	2	2	2	6
Jason Vargas	0	0	3.00	1	1	0	6.0	3	2	2	1	2
Yordano Ventura	0	0	1.29	1	1	0	7.0	5	1	1	5	5
Totals	3	0	1.74	3	3	2	31.0	18	6	6	9	25

PLAYER, POS	AVG	G	AB	R	H	2B	3B	HR	RBI	BB	SO	SB
Erick Aybar, SS	.455	3	11	0	5	1	0	0	0	0	1	1
Gordon Beckham, 3B	.000	2	1	0	0	0	0	0	0	0	1	0
Kole Calhoun, RF	.333	3	15	1	5	0	0	0	0	1	1	0
Hank Conger, PH	.000	1	1	0	0	0	0	0	0	0	1	0
C.J. Cron, PH	.111	3	9	0	1	0	0	0	2	4	0	
David Freese, 3B	.125	3	8	1	1	0	0	1	2	4	0	
Josh Hamilton, LF	.000	3	13	0	0	0	0	0	1	0	2	0
Chris Iannetta, C	.100	3	10	1	1	0	0	1	1	2	0	
Howie Kendrick, 2B	.154	3	13	1	2	1	0	0	0	0	5	0
Efren Navarro, PH	.000	1	1	0	0	0	0	0	0	0	1	0
Albert Pujols, 1B	.167	3	12	1	2	0	0	0	2	1	1	0
Mike Trout, CF	.083	3	12	1	1	0	0	1	3	2	0	
Totals	.170	3	106	6	18	3	0	4	6	9	25	1

PITCHER	W	L	ERA	G	GS	SV	IP	H	R	ER	BB	SO
Jason Grilli	0	0	0.00	2	0	0	2.0	0	0	0	0	2
Kevin Jepsen	0	1	13.50	3	0	0	2.0	4	4	3	4	1
Mike Morin	0	0	18.00	1	0	0	1.0	3	2	2	0	1
Vinnie Pestano	0	0	0.00	2	0	0	1.0	1	0	0	0	1
Cory Rasmus	0	0	0.00	1	0	0	2.2	0	0	0	1	2
Fernando Salas	0	1	6.75	2	0	0	1.1	1	1	1	0	1
Hector Santiago	0	0	13.50	1	0	0	1.1	1	2	2	2	0
Matt Shoemaker	0	0	1.50	1	1	0	6.0	5	1	1	0	6
Joe Smith	0	0	0.00	2	0	0	2.0	0	0	0	0	2
Huston Street	0	0	0.00	2	0	0	3.0	0	0	0	2	3
Jered Weaver	0	0	2.57	1	1	0	7.0	3	2	2	2	6
C.J. Wilson	0	1	40.50	1	1	0	0.2	3	3	3	1	1
Totals	**0**	**4**	**3.20**	**3**	**3**	**0**	**30.0**	**21**	**15**	**14**	**12**	**26**

E—Infante, Iannetta. LOB—Kansas City 16, Los Angeles 20. DP—Kansas City 3, Los Angeles 1. GIDP—Butler, Freese, Hamilton. SAC—Escobar, Aybar 2. SF—Cain, Infante. HBP—Beckham (by Collins), Freese (by Shields). IBB—Gordon 2 (by Jepsen, by Street). SB—Butler, Gordon 2, Gore 2, Aybar. CS—Trout. WP—Davis, Shields, Morin.

SCORE BY INNINGS

Kansas City	313 211 000 004—15
LA Angels	101 111 010 000—6

BALTIMORE ORIOLES VS· DETROIT TIGERS

PLAYER, POS	AVG	G	AB	R	H	2B	3B	HR	RBI	BB	SO	SB
Alex Avila, C	.222	3	9	0	2	1	0	0	0	0	4	0
Miguel Cabrera, 1B	.364	3	11	2	4	1	0	1	1	1	2	0
Ezequiel Carrera, CF	.000	3	1	0	0	0	0	0	0	1	0	1
Nick Castellanos, 3B	.100	3	10	1	1	0	0	1	1	2	1	0
Rajai Davis, CF	.333	3	6	0	2	0	0	0	0	0	0	0
Bryan Holaday, C	.000	1	2	0	0	0	0	0	0	0	1	0
Torii Hunter, RF	.200	3	10	2	2	0	0	0	0	2	2	0
Don Kelly, CF	.500	2	2	0	1	0	0	0	0	0	1	1
Ian Kinsler, 2B	.083	3	12	0	1	0	0	0	0	1	3	0
J.D. Martinez, LF	.250	3	12	2	3	1	0	2	5	0	4	0
Victor Martinez, DH	.333	3	12	3	4	2	0	1	3	0	4	0
Hernan Perez, PH	.000	2	2	0	0	0	0	0	0	0	0	0
Andrew Romine, SS	.182	3	11	0	2	0	0	0	0	0	4	0
Eugenio Suarez, PH	.000	1	1	0	0	0	0	0	0	0	0	0
Totals	**.218**	**3**	**101**	**10**	**22**	**5**	**0**	**5**	**10**	**7**	**26**	**2**

PITCHER	W	L	ERA	G	GS	SV	IP	H	R	ER	BB	SO
Joba Chamberlain	0	0	108.00	2	0	0	0.1	3	5	4	0	0
Phil Coke	0	0	27.00	1	0	0	0.1	1	1	1	1	0
Joe Nathan	0	0	0.00	1	0	0	1.0	0	0	0	0	1
David Price	0	1	2.25	1	1	0	8.0	5	2	2	2	6
Anibal Sanchez	0	0	0.00	1	0	0	2.0	0	0	0	0	2
Max Scherzer	0	1	6.14	1	1	0	7.1	7	5	5	1	6
Joakim Soria	0	1	45.00	2	0	0	1.0	4	5	5	2	0
Justin Verlander	0	0	5.40	1	1	0	5.0	6	3	3	1	4
Totals	**0**	**3**	**7.20**	**3**	**3**	**0**	**25.0**	**26**	**21**	**20**	**7**	**19**

PLAYER, POS	AVG	G	AB	R	H	2B	3B	HR	RBI	BB	SO	SB
Nelson Cruz, DH	.500	3	12	4	6	0	0	2	5	0	3	0
Alejandro De Aza, LF	.375	2	8	1	3	2	0	0	2	0	0	0
Ryan Flaherty, 3B	.222	3	9	2	2	0	0	0	1	1	2	0
J.J. Hardy, SS	.300	3	10	3	3	0	0	1	2	2	1	0
Nick Hundley, C	.000	3	8	0	0	0	0	0	0	1	2	0
Kelly Johnson, 3B	.000	1	1	0	0	0	0	0	0	0	0	0
Adam Jones, CF	.182	3	11	4	2	0	0	0	0	1	3	1
Caleb Joseph, C	.000	1	3	0	0	0	0	0	0	0	2	0
David Lough, LF	.000	1	1	0	0	0	0	0	0	0	0	0
Nick Markakis, RF	.250	3	12	3	3	0	0	1	3	1	2	0
Steve Pearce, 1B	.300	3	10	2	3	0	0	0	1	1	1	0
Jonathan Schoop, 2B	.300	3	10	2	3	1	0	0	2	1	1	1
Delmon Young, LF	.250	2	4	0	1	0	0	0	3	0	2	0
Totals	**.263**	**3**	**99**	**21**	**26**	**4**	**0**	**4**	**20**	**7**	**19**	**2**

PITCHER	W	L	ERA	G	GS	SV	IP	H	R	ER	BB	SO
Brad Brach	1	0	0.00	1	0	0	0.2	0	0	0	0	0
Zach Britton	0	0	3.86	3	0	2	2.1	2	1	1	1	2
Wei-Yin Chen	0	0	12.27	1	1	0	3.2	7	5	5	0	3
Kevin Gausman	0	0	2.45	1	0	0	3.2	3	1	1	1	5
Tommy Hunter	0	0	0.00	1	0	0	1.0	2	0	0	1	1
Andrew Miller	0	0	0.00	2	0	0	3.1	0	0	0	1	3

Bud Norris	1	0	0.00	1	1	0	6.1	2	0	0	2	6
Darren O'Day	0	0	9.00	1	0	0	1.0	2	1	1	0	0
Chris Tillman	1	0	3.60	1	1	0	5.0	4	2	2	1	6
Totals	**3**	**0**	**3.33**	**3**	**3**	**2**	**27.0**	**22**	**10**	**10**	**7**	**26**

E—Davis, Romine, Hardy. LOB—Detroit 17, Baltimore 13. DP—Detroit 1, Baltimore 3. GIDP—Cabrera, Perez, Jones. HBP—De Aza (by Scherzer), Jones (by Chamberlin), Pearce (by Price). IBB—Castellanos (by Britton), Hardy (by Soria). SB—Carrera, Kelly, Jones, Schoop. WP—Coke, Norris.

SCORE BY INNINGS

Detroit	020 500 021—10
Baltimore	212 102 1(12)0—21

AMERICAN LEAGUE CHAMPIONSHIP SERIES

BALTIMORE ORIOLES VS· KANSAS CITY ROYALS

PLAYER, POS	AVG	G	AB	R	H	2B	3B	HR	RBI	BB	SO	SB
Nori Aoki, RF	.273	4	11	3	3	0	0	0	0	2	0	0
Billy Butler, DH	.286	4	14	1	4	2	0	0	3	1	2	0
Lorenzo Cain, CF	.533	4	15	5	8	2	0	0	1	2	3	1
Jarrod Dyson, CF	.000	4	1	0	0	0	0	0	0	1	2	0
Alcides Escobar, SS	.278	4	18	3	5	1	0	1	2	1	1	0
Alex Gordon, LF	.250	4	12	1	3	1	0	1	5	2	7	0
Terrance Gore, DH	-	2	0	1	0	0	0	0	0	0	0	0
Eric Hosmer, 1B	.400	4	15	0	6	0	0	0	3	2	4	0
Omar Infante, 2B	.308	4	13	0	4	0	0	0	3	0	3	0
Mike Moustakas, 3B	.200	4	15	2	3	0	0	2	3	0	4	0
Salvador Perez, C	.067	4	15	1	1	0	0	0	0	1	2	0
Totals	**.280**	**4**	**132**	**18**	**37**	**6**	**0**	**4**	**17**	**15**	**28**	**1**

PITCHER	W	L	ERA	G	GS	SV	IP	H	R	ER	BB	SO
Wade Davis	2	0	0.00	4	0	0	5.0	2	0	0	0	6
Brandon Finnegan	0	0	27.00	2	0	0	0.1	3	1	1	1	0
Jason Frasor	1	0	0.00	1	0	0	1.0	0	0	0	0	0
Jeremy Guthrie	0	0	1.80	1	1	0	5.0	3	1	1	2	2
Kelvin Herrera	0	0	0.00	4	0	0	5.2	2	0	0	1	6
Greg Holland	0	0	2.25	4	0	4	4.0	3	1	1	2	3
James Shields	0	0	7.20	1	1	0	5.0	10	4	4	1	3
Jason Vargas	1	0	1.69	1	1	0	5.1	2	1	1	3	6
Yordano Ventura	0	0	6.35	1	1	0	5.2	5	4	4	3	3
Totals	**4**	**0**	**2.92**	**4**	**4**	**4**	**37.0**	**30**	**12**	**12**	**13**	**29**

PLAYER, POS	AVG	G	AB	R	H	2B	3B	HR	RBI	BB	SO	SB
Nelson Cruz, DH	.250	4	16	1	4	1	0	0	2	2	2	0
Alejandro De Aza, LF	.308	4	13	3	4	1	0	0	1	1	1	0
Ryan Flaherty, 3B	.333	4	12	2	4	0	0	1	3	3	5	0
J.J. Hardy, SS	.200	4	15	0	3	1	0	0	1	1	4	0
Nick Hundley, C	.143	2	7	0	1	0	0	0	0	0	3	0
Kelly Johnson, 3B	.000	1	1	0	0	0	0	0	0	0	0	0
Adam Jones, CF	.250	4	16	2	4	0	0	0	3	2	5	0
Caleb Joseph, C	.333	2	6	0	2	0	0	0	1	0	2	0
Nick Markakis, RF	.263	4	19	1	5	1	0	0	0	1	1	0
Jimmy Paredes, PH	-	1	0	0	0	0	0	0	0	0	1	0
Steve Pearce, 1B	.059	4	17	2	1	1	0	0	0	1	2	0
Jonathan Schoop, 2B	.091	4	11	1	1	0	0	0	0	0	2	3
Delmon Young, DH	.200	2	5	0	1	0	0	0	1	0	1	0
Totals	**.217**	**4**	**138**	**12**	**30**	**5**	**0**	**2**	**12**	**13**	**29**	**2**

PITCHER	W	L	ERA	G	GS	SV	IP	H	R	ER	BB	SO
Brad Brach	0	0	0.00	1	0	0	1.2	1	0	0	2	1
Zach Britton	0	0	3.86	3	0	0	2.1	3	1	1	4	3
Wei-Yin Chen	0	1	3.38	1	1	0	5.1	7	2	2	1	4
Kevin Gausman	0	0	0.00	2	0	0	4.1	1	0	0	1	2
Miguel Gonzalez	0	1	1.59	1	1	0	5.2	4	2	1	4	4
Tommy Hunter	0	0	0.00	1	0	0	0.2	1	0	0	0	0
Brian Matusz	0	0	13.50	1	0	0	0.2	1	1	1	0	1
Andrew Miller	0	0	0.00	3	0	0	4.0	1	0	0	0	5
Bud Norris	0	0	8.31	1	1	0	4.1	9	4	4	0	3
Darren O'Day	0	2	16.20	3	0	0	1.2	2	3	3	1	2
Chris Tillman	0	0	10.38	1	1	0	4.1	7	5	5	2	3
Totals	**0**	**4**	**4.37**	**4**	**4**	**0**	**35.0**	**37**	**18**	**17**	**15**	**28**

E—Herrera, Moustakas, Flaherty, Joseph, Schoop. LOB—Kansas City 31, Baltimore 29. DP—Kansas City 3, Baltimore 4. GIDP—Butler, Infante, Moustakas, Cruz, Young 2. SAC—Cain, Moustakas. SF—Butler

2, Joseph. HBP—Aoki (by Gonzalez), Gordon 2 (by Miller, by Gonzalez). IBB—Hosmer (by Gonzalez), Infante (by Britton). SB—Cain, Markakis, Schoop. CS—Dyson 2. WP—Gonzalez.

SCORE BY INNINGS

Kansas City	405 211 002 003—18	
Baltimore	024 041 000 001—12	

NATIONAL LEAGUE WILD CARD GAME
PITTSBURGH PIRATES VS· SAN FRANCISCO GIANTS

PLAYER, POS	AVG	G	AB	R	H	2B	3B	HR	RBI	BB	SO	SB
Brandon Belt, 1B	.667	1	3	1	2	0	0	0	3	2	0	0
Gregor Blanco, CF	.000	1	4	1	0	0	0	0	0	0	1	0
Madison Bumgarner, P	.000	1	4	0	0	0	0	0	0	0	3	0
Brandon Crawford, SS	.200	1	5	1	1	0	0	1	4	0	2	0
Travis Ishikawa, LF	.000	1	2	0	0	0	0	0	0	1	1	0
Joe Panik, 2B	.600	1	5	0	3	0	0	0	0	0	0	0
Hunter Pence, RF	.250	1	4	2	1	0	0	0	0	1	0	0
Juan Perez, LF	.000	1	1	0	0	0	0	0	0	0	0	0
Buster Posey, C	.400	1	5	1	2	0	0	0	1	0	0	0
Pablo Sandoval, 3B	.500	1	4	2	2	0	0	0	0	1	1	0
Totals	.297	1	37	8	11	0	0	1	8	6	7	0

PITCHER	W	L	ERA	G	GS	SV	IP	H	R	ER	BB	SO
Madison Bumgarner	1	0	0.00	1	1	0	9.0	4	0	0	1	10
Totals	1	0	0.00	1	1	0	9.0	4	0	0	1	10

PLAYER, POS	AVG	G	AB	R	H	2B	3B	HR	RBI	BB	SO	SB
Josh Harrison, 3B	.500	1	4	0	2	0	0	0	0	0	1	0
Starling Marte, LF	.250	1	4	0	1	0	0	0	0	0	1	0
Russell Martin, C	.250	1	4	0	1	0	0	0	0	0	0	0
Andrew McCutchen, CF	.000	1	3	0	0	0	0	0	0	1	1	0
Jordy Mercer, SS	.000	1	4	0	0	0	0	0	0	0	2	0
Brent Morel, PH	.000	1	1	0	0	0	0	0	0	0	0	0
Gaby Sanchez, 1B	.000	1	3	0	0	0	0	0	0	0	0	0
Travis Snider, RF	.000	1	2	0	0	0	0	0	0	0	2	0
Jose Tabata, RF	.000	1	2	0	0	0	0	0	0	0	1	0
Edinson Volquez, P	.000	1	1	0	0	0	0	0	0	0	0	0
Neil Walker, 2B	.000	1	4	0	0	0	0	0	0	0	2	0
Totals	.125	1	32	0	4	0	0	0	0	1	10	0

PITCHER	W	L	ERA	G	GS	SV	IP	H	R	ER	BB	SO
John Holdzkom	0	0	9.00	1	0	0	1.0	2	1	1	1	1
Jared Hughes	0	0	18.00	1	0	0	1.0	3	2	2	1	1
Bobby LaFromboise	0	0	0.00	1	0	0	0.2	0	0	0	0	0
Mark Melancon	0	0	0.00	1	0	0	1.0	0	0	0	0	1
Edinson Volquez	0	1	9.00	1	1	0	5.0	5	5	5	3	3
Justin Wilson	0	0	0.00	1	0	0	0.1	1	0	0	1	1
Totals	0	1	8.00	1	1	0	9.0	11	8	8	6	7

E—Arias, Crawford. LOB—San Francisco 8, Pittsburgh 6. DP—Pittsburgh. GIDP—Crawford. WP—Wilson.

SCORE BY INNINGS

San Francisco	000 401 210—8	
Pittsburgh	000 000 000—0	

NATIONAL LEAGUE DIVISION SERIES
WASHINGTON NATIONALS VS· SAN FRANCISCO GIANTS

PLAYER, POS	AVG	G	AB	R	H	2B	3B	HR	RBI	BB	SO	SB
Brandon Belt, 1B	.278	4	18	1	5	0	0	1	2	1	4	0
Gregor Blanco, CF	.111	4	18	0	2	0	0	0	1	2	1	1
Gary Brown, PH	.000	1	1	0	0	0	0	0	0	0	1	0
Madison Bumgarner, P	.000	1	1	0	0	0	0	0	0	1	1	0
Brandon Crawford, SS	.294	4	17	1	5	1	0	0	1	4	0	0
Matt Duffy, PH	.000	4	4	0	0	0	0	0	0	0	1	0
Tim Hudson, P	.000	1	1	0	0	0	0	0	0	0	1	0
Travis Ishikawa, LF	.182	4	11	1	2	0	0	0	1	1	1	0
Joe Panik, 2B	.211	4	19	3	4	0	1	0	2	1	0	0
Jake Peavy, P	.000	1	2	0	0	0	0	0	0	0	0	0
Hunter Pence, RF	.278	4	18	1	5	2	0	0	1	3	3	1
Juan Perez, LF	.000	3	7	1	0	0	0	0	0	1	1	0
Yusmeiro Petit, P	.000	1	1	0	0	0	0	0	0	0	0	0
Buster Posey, C	.389	4	18	0	7	0	0	0	1	1	1	0

PLAYER, POS	AVG	G	AB	R	H	2B	3B	HR	RBI	BB	SO	SB
Pablo Sandoval, 3B	.211	4	19	1	4	1	0	0	1	1	4	0
Andrew Susac, PH	.000	1	1	0	0	0	0	0	0	0	0	0
Ryan Vogelsong, P	.500	1	2	0	1	0	0	0	0	0	1	0
Totals	.222	4	158	9	35	4	1	1	8	11	24	2

PITCHER	W	L	ERA	G	GS	SV	IP	H	R	ER	BB	SO
Jeremy Affeldt	0	0	0.00	3	0	0	1.2	1	0	0	0	1
Madison Bumgarner	0	1	2.57	1	1	0	7.0	6	3	2	1	6
Santiago Casilla	0	0	0.00	3	0	2	3.0	0	0	0	1	2
Tim Hudson	0	0	1.23	1	1	0	7.1	7	1	1	0	8
Javier Lopez	0	0	0.00	3	0	0	0.2	0	0	0	1	1
Jean Machi	0	0	4.50	2	0	0	2.0	1	1	1	0	1
Jake Peavy	1	0	0.00	1	1	0	5.2	2	0	0	3	3
Yusmeiro Petit	1	0	0.00	1	0	0	6.0	1	0	0	3	7
Sergio Romo	0	0	0.00	3	0	0	3.0	2	0	0	0	2
Hunter Strickland	1	0	9.00	3	0	1	3.0	4	3	3	1	4
Ryan Vogelsong	0	0	1.59	1	1	0	5.2	2	1	1	2	4
Totals	3	1	1.60	4	4	3	45.0	26	9	8	12	39

PLAYER, POS	AVG	G	AB	R	H	2B	3B	HR	RBI	BB	SO	SB
Asdrubal Cabrera, 2B	.200	4	15	2	3	1	0	1	2	0	5	0
Ian Desmond, SS	.167	4	18	2	3	0	0	0	0	1	6	1
Danny Espinosa, 2B	.000	2	4	0	0	0	0	0	0	0	1	0
Doug Fister, P	.000	1	3	0	0	0	0	0	0	0	1	0
Kevin Frandsen, PH	.000	1	1	0	0	0	0	0	0	0	0	0
Gio Gonzalez, P	.000	1	1	0	0	0	0	0	0	0	1	0
Bryce Harper, LF	.294	4	17	4	5	1	0	3	4	2	3	0
Adam LaRoche, 1B	.056	4	18	0	1	0	0	0	0	1	4	0
Wilson Ramos, C	.118	4	17	1	2	0	0	0	1	0	6	0
Anthony Rendon, 3B	.368	4	19	0	7	0	0	0	1	1	2	1
Tanner Roark, P	.000	2	1	0	0	0	0	0	0	0	0	0
Nate Schierholtz, PH	1.000	4	1	0	1	0	0	0	2	0	0	0
Denard Span, CF	.105	4	19	0	2	0	0	0	0	1	3	0
Stephen Strasburg, P	.000	1	0	0	0	0	0	0	0	0	0	0
Jayson Werth, RF	.059	4	17	0	1	0	0	0	0	3	5	0
Ryan Zimmerman, PH	.250	4	4	0	1	0	0	0	0	0	1	0
Jordan Zimmermann, P	.000	1	3	0	0	0	0	0	0	0	2	0
Totals	.164	4	159	9	26	3	0	4	7	12	39	2

PITCHER	W	L	ERA	G	GS	SV	IP	H	R	ER	BB	SO
Aaron Barrett	0	0	0.00	2	0	0	0.1	1	0	0	2	0
Jerry Blevins	0	0	0.00	3	0	0	3.1	0	0	0	0	2
Tyler Clippard	0	0	0.00	3	0	0	3.0	1	0	0	1	2
Doug Fister	1	0	0.00	1	1	0	7.0	4	0	0	3	3
Gio Gonzalez	0	0	0.00	1	1	0	4.0	4	2	0	1	1
Tanner Roark	0	1	3.38	2	0	0	2.2	3	1	1	0	3
Rafael Soriano	0	0	0.00	2	0	0	2.1	1	0	0	0	1
Craig Stammen	0	0	2.25	2	0	0	4.0	3	1	1	0	2
Drew Storen	0	0	6.75	2	0	0	1.1	4	1	1	0	1
Stephen Strasburg	0	1	1.80	1	1	0	5.0	8	2	1	1	2
Matt Thornton	0	1	3.86	3	0	0	2.1	3	1	1	2	1
Jordan Zimmermann	0	0	1.04	1	1	0	8.2	3	1	1	1	6
Totals	1	3	1.23	4	4	0	44.0	35	9	6	11	24

E—Bumgarner, Gonzalez. LOB—San Francisco 34, Washington 28. DP—San Francisco 2, Washington 3. GIDP—Posey, Ramos, Span. SAC—Blanco, Hudson, Peavy, Perez, Ramos. SF—Crawford. HBP—Posey (by Strasburg). IBB—Posey (by Thornton), Sandoval (by Barrett), Schierholtz (by Petit). SB—Blanco, Pence, Desmond, Rendon. CS—Belt, Pence, Posey. WP—Barrett. PB—Ramos.

SCORE BY INNINGS

San Francisco	021 100 202 000 000 001—9	
Washington	001 010 601 000 000 000—9	

LOS ANGELES DODGERS VS· ST· LOUIS CARDINALS

PLAYER, POS	AVG	G	AB	R	H	2B	3B	HR	RBI	BB	SO	SB
Matt Adams, 1B	.250	4	12	2	3	0	0	1	4	3	2	0

PLAYER, POS	AVG	G	AB	R	H	2B	3B	HR	RBI	BB	SO	SB
Peter Bourjos, CF	.000	3	1	0	0	0	0	0	0	0	1	0
Matt Carpenter, 3B	.375	4	16	4	6	3	0	3	7	1	4	0
Daniel Descalso, 2B	-	1	0	0	0	0	0	0	0	0	0	0
Randal Grichuk, RF	.188	4	16	2	3	0	0	1	1	1	7	0
Matt Holliday, LF	.267	4	15	3	4	0	0	1	3	1	5	0
Jon Jay, CF	.455	4	11	1	5	0	0	0	1	1	2	0
Pete Kozma, 2B	.000	2	5	0	0	0	0	0	0	0	3	0
John Lackey, P	.000	1	2	0	0	0	0	0	0	0	0	0
Lance Lynn, P	.000	1	2	0	0	0	0	0	0	0	2	0
Shelby Miller, P	.000	1	1	0	0	0	0	0	0	0	1	0
Yadier Molina, C	.200	4	15	2	3	1	0	0	0	0	3	0
Jhonny Peralta, SS	.214	4	14	2	3	1	0	0	0	1	4	0
Oscar Taveras, PH	.250	4	4	1	1	0	0	0	0	0	1	0
Adam Wainwright, P	.000	1	1	0	0	0	0	0	0	0	0	0
Kolten Wong, 2B	.182	3	11	1	2	1	0	1	2	0	2	0
Totals	**.238**	**4**	**126**	**18**	**30**	**6**	**0**	**7**	**18**	**8**	**37**	**0**

PITCHER	W	L	ERA	G	GS	SV	IP	H	R	ER	BB	SO
Randy Choate	0	0	*.**	1	0	0	0.0	1	1	1	0	0
Sam Freeman	0	0	-	1	0	0	0.0	1	0	0	0	2
Marco Gonzales	2	0	0.00	3	0	0	3.0	2	0	0	1	2
John Lackey	1	0	1.29	1	1	0	7.0	5	1	1	1	8
Lance Lynn	0	0	3.00	1	1	0	6.0	7	2	2	2	8
Seth Maness	0	0	0.00	2	0	0	1.0	1	0	0	0	1
Carlos Martinez	0	0	6.75	1	0	0	1.1	0	1	1	1	1
Shelby Miller	0	0	3.18	1	1	0	5.2	5	2	2	3	4
Pat Neshek	0	1	2.45	4	0	0	3.2	2	1	1	0	3
Trevor Rosenthal	0	0	3.00	3	0	3	3.0	5	1	1	1	4
Adam Wainwright	0	0	12.46	1	1	0	4.1	11	6	6	1	5
Totals	**3**	**1**	**3.86**	**4**	**4**	**3**	**35.0**	**39**	**15**	**15**	**12**	**36**

PLAYER, POS	AVG	G	AB	R	H	2B	3B	HR	RBI	BB	SO	SB
Carl Crawford, LF	.294	4	17	2	5	1	0	0	1	0	7	0
A.J. Ellis, C	.538	4	13	4	7	1	0	1	2	4	1	0
Andre Ethier, CF	.250	2	4	0	1	0	0	0	0	2	1	0
Adrian Gonzalez, 1B	.188	4	16	1	3	0	0	1	3	1	2	0
Dee Gordon, 2B	.176	4	17	0	3	0	0	0	2	2	6	1
Zack Greinke, P	.667	1	3	1	2	0	0	0	0	0	0	0
Matt Kemp, RF	.353	4	17	1	6	0	0	1	2	0	3	0
Clayton Kershaw, P	.500	2	2	0	1	0	0	0	0	0	1	0
Yasiel Puig, CF	.250	4	12	4	3	0	1	0	1	1	8	0
Hanley Ramirez, SS	.429	4	14	2	6	1	0	0	2	1	0	1
Miguel Rojas, SS	.000	1	1	0	0	0	0	0	0	0	0	0
Hyun-Jin Ryu, P	.000	1	1	0	0	0	0	0	0	0	1	0
Justin Turner, PH	.000	2	2	0	0	0	0	0	0	0	1	0
Juan Uribe, 3B	.118	4	17	0	2	0	0	0	1	0	6	0
Scott Van Slyke, PH	.000	1	1	0	0	0	0	0	0	0	0	0
Totals	**.285**	**4**	**137**	**15**	**39**	**4**	**1**	**3**	**14**	**12**	**36**	**2**

PITCHER	W	L	ERA	G	GS	SV	IP	H	R	ER	BB	SO
Pedro Baez	0	0	7.71	2	0	0	2.1	1	2	2	1	2
Scott Elbert	0	1	13.50	2	0	0	1.1	3	2	2	0	2
Zack Greinke	0	0	0.00	1	1	0	7.0	2	0	0	2	7
J.P. Howell	0	0	13.50	3	0	0	1.1	5	2	2	0	0
Kenley Jansen	0	0	0.00	1	0	1	1.0	0	0	0	0	2
Clayton Kershaw	0	2	7.82	2	2	0	12.2	12	11	11	2	19
Brandon League	1	0	0.00	4	0	0	2.0	1	0	0	1	0
Hyun-Jin Ryu	0	0	1.50	1	1	0	6.0	5	1	1	1	4
Brian Wilson	0	0	0.00	1	0	0	0.1	1	0	0	1	1
Totals	**1**	**3**	**4.76**	**4**	**4**	**1**	**34.0**	**30**	**18**	**18**	**8**	**37**

E—Neshek. LOB—St. Louis 18, Los Angeles 35. DP—St. Louis 3, Los Angeles 4. GIDP—Adams, Peralta, Wong 2, Crawford, Kemp, Ramirez. SAC—Descalso, Jay, Kershaw 3, Ryu. HBP—Jay 2 (by Greinke, by Baez), Puig (by Wainwright), Ramirez (by Miller). IBB—Adams 2 (by League, by Wilson), Ellis (by Lynn). SB—Gordon, Ramirez. WP—Wainwright, Greinke, Kershaw. PB—Molina.

SCORE BY INNINGS

St. Louis	101 001 (13)20—18
LA Dodgers	004 223 031—15

NATIONAL LEAGUE CHAMPIONSHIP SERIES

ST-LOUIS CARDINALS VS-SAN FRANCISCO GIANTS

PLAYER, POS	AVG	G	AB	R	H	2B	3B	HR	RBI	BB	SO	SB
Joaquin Arias, PH	.500	3	2	2	1	0	0	0	1	0	0	0

PLAYER, POS	AVG	G	AB	R	H	2B	3B	HR	RBI	BB	SO	SB
Brandon Belt, 1B	.214	5	14	3	3	0	0	0	1	5	4	0
Gregor Blanco, CF	.227	5	22	3	5	1	0	0	2	1	3	0
Madison Bumgarner, P	.000	2	6	0	0	0	0	0	0	0	2	0
Brandon Crawford, SS	.125	5	16	3	2	1	0	0	0	3	3	0
Matt Duffy, PH	-	2	0	1	0	0	0	0	0	0	0	0
Tim Hudson, P	.500	1	2	0	1	0	0	0	0	0	0	0
Travis Ishikawa, LF	.385	5	13	1	5	2	0	1	7	1	3	0
Michael Morse, PH	.500	4	4	1	2	0	0	1	1	0	0	0
Joe Panik, 2B	.182	5	22	1	4	0	0	1	3	1	1	0
Jake Peavy, P	.000	1	1	0	0	0	0	0	0	0	1	0
Hunter Pence, RF	.235	5	17	2	4	1	0	0	3	3	4	1
Juan Perez, LF	.400	4	5	1	2	0	0	0	0	1	1	0
Yusmeiro Petit, P	.000	1	1	0	0	0	0	0	0	0	0	0
Buster Posey, C	.200	5	20	3	4	0	0	0	3	2	3	0
Pablo Sandoval, 3B	.400	5	20	3	8	3	0	0	2	2	2	0
Andrew Susac, PH	1.000	1	1	0	1	0	0	0	0	0	0	0
Totals	**.253**	**5**	**166**	**24**	**42**	**8**	**0**	**3**	**21**	**19**	**27**	**1**

PITCHER	W	L	ERA	G	GS	SV	IP	H	R	ER	BB	SO
Jeremy Affeldt	1	0	0.00	4	0	0	4.2	1	0	0	2	1
Madison Bumgarner	1	0	1.72	2	2	0	15.2	9	3	3	3	12
Santiago Casilla	0	0	0.00	4	0	2	3.2	2	0	0	2	3
Tim Hudson	0	0	5.68	1	1	0	6.1	7	4	4	0	5
Javier Lopez	0	0	0.00	3	0	0	1.1	2	0	0	0	2
Jean Machi	0	0	27.00	2	0	0	0.1	2	1	1	0	0
Jake Peavy	0	0	4.50	1	1	0	4.0	4	2	2	3	2
Yusmeiro Petit	1	0	0.00	1	0	0	3.0	1	0	0	1	4
Sergio Romo	1	1	5.40	4	0	0	1.2	2	1	1	0	1
Hunter Strickland	0	0	6.75	1	0	0	1.1	1	1	1	0	1
Ryan Vogelsong	0	0	12.00	1	1	0	3.0	7	4	4	2	1
Totals	**4**	**1**	**3.20**	**5**	**5**	**2**	**45.0**	**38**	**16**	**16**	**13**	**32**

PLAYER, POS	AVG	G	AB	R	H	2B	3B	HR	RBI	BB	SO	SB
Matt Adams, 1B	.222	5	18	3	4	0	0	2	3	2	3	0
Peter Bourjos, CF	.000	2	1	0	0	0	0	0	0	0	0	0
Matt Carpenter, 3B	.200	5	20	2	4	1	0	1	1	2	8	0
Tony Cruz, C	.200	4	5	2	1	0	0	1	1	2	2	0
Daniel Descalso, 1B	.000	3	2	0	0	0	0	0	0	0	0	0
Marco Gonzales, P	-	3	0	0	0	0	0	0	0	0	0	0
Randal Grichuk, RF	.158	5	19	1	3	0	0	1	2	0	6	0
Matt Holliday, LF	.227	5	22	2	5	1	0	0	0	0	1	0
Jon Jay, CF	.500	5	18	2	9	1	0	0	1	2	1	0
John Lackey, P	.000	1	1	0	0	0	0	0	0	0	1	0
Lance Lynn, P	.000	1	2	0	0	0	0	0	0	0	1	0
Shelby Miller, P	.000	1	1	0	0	0	0	0	0	0	0	0
Yadier Molina, C	.333	2	6	0	2	0	0	0	0	0	0	0
Jhonny Peralta, SS	.118	5	17	0	2	0	0	0	1	3	2	0
A.J. Pierzynski, C	.167	2	6	0	1	0	0	0	1	1	1	0
Oscar Taveras, RF	.667	3	3	1	2	0	0	1	1	0	0	0
Adam Wainwright, P	.000	2	3	0	0	0	0	0	0	0	2	0
Kolten Wong, 2B	.278	5	18	3	5	2	1	2	4	1	3	1
Totals	**.233**	**5**	**163**	**16**	**38**	**5**	**1**	**8**	**15**	**13**	**32**	**1**

PITCHER	W	L	ERA	G	GS	SV	IP	H	R	ER	BB	SO
Randy Choate	0	1	9.00	4	0	0	1.0	1	2	1	3	1
Marco Gonzales	0	1	9.00	3	0	0	3.0	2	3	3	1	2
John Lackey	0	0	6.00	1	1	0	6.0	5	4	4	1	3
Lance Lynn	0	0	3.18	1	1	0	5.2	6	2	2	1	3
Seth Maness	1	0	0.00	4	0	0	4.2	4	0	0	0	1
Carlos Martinez	0	0	0.00	3	0	0	2.2	3	0	0	3	1
Shelby Miller	0	0	7.36	1	1	0	3.2	6	3	3	2	3
Pat Neshek	0	0	2.25	4	0	0	4.0	1	1	1	0	3
Trevor Rosenthal	0	0	13.50	1	0	0	0.2	2	1	1	2	1
Michael Wacha	0	1	81.00	1	0	0	0.1	2	3	3	1	0
Adam Wainwright	0	1	3.09	2	2	0	11.2	10	5	4	5	9
Totals	**1**	**4**	**4.57**	**5**	**5**	**0**	**43.1**	**42**	**24**	**22**	**19**	**27**

E—Carpenter, Choate. LOB—San Francisco 37, St. Louis 30. DP—San Francisco 6, St. Louis 4. GIDP—Panik, Sandoval 2, Adams, Carpenter, Molina, Peralta 2. SAC—Blanco, Duffy, Perez, Gonzales, Molina, Wainwright. SF—Belt, Posey. HBP—Sandoval (by Lackey), Jay (by Bumgarner), Lackey (by Hudson). IBB—Belt (by Lackey), Wong (by Peavy). SB—Pence, Wong. CS—Jay. WP—Rosenthal. PB—Cruz.

SCORE BY INNINGS

San Francisco	525 014 114 001—24
St. Louis	114 501 211 000—16

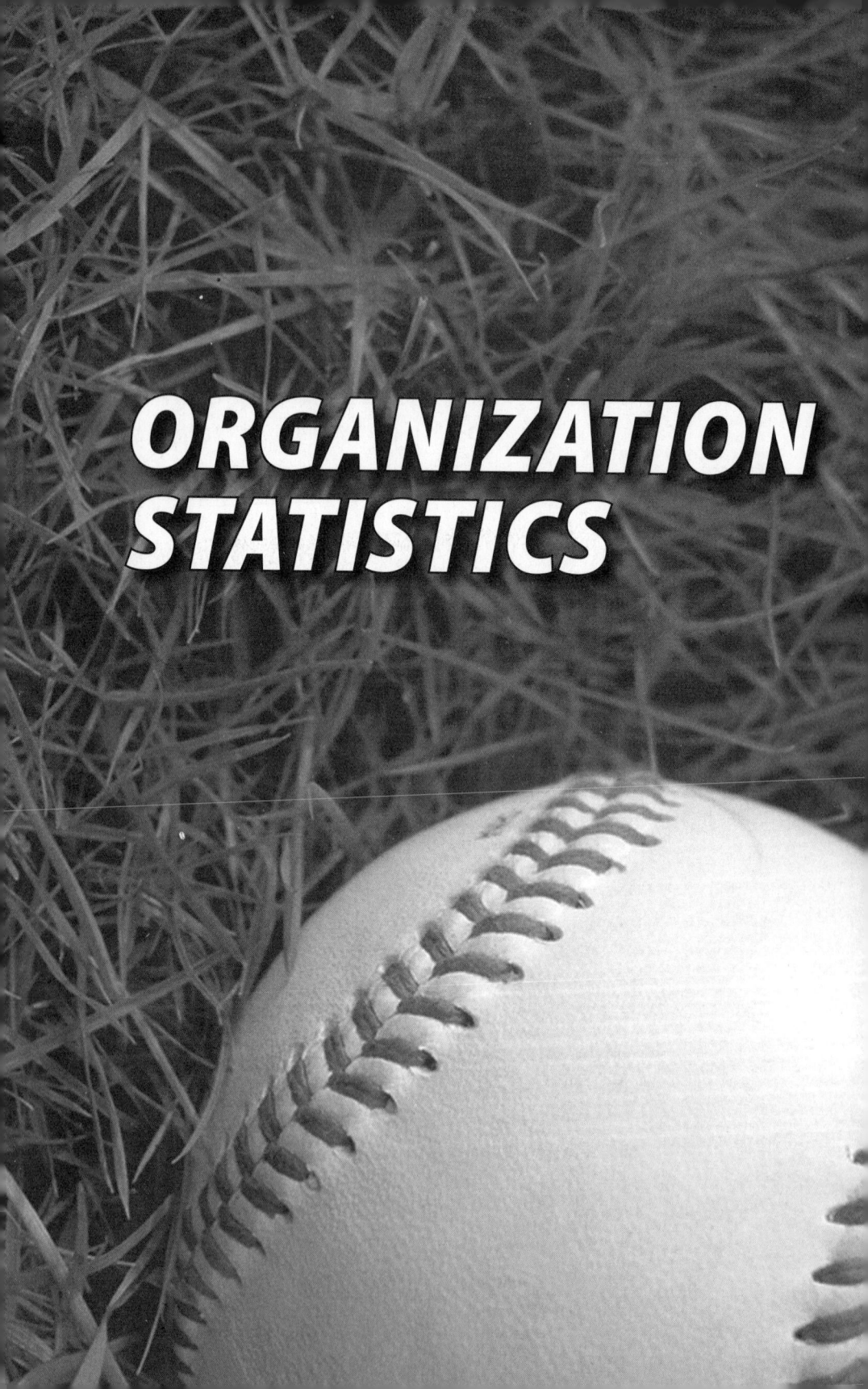

ORGANIZATION STATISTICS

Arizona Diamondbacks

SEASON IN A SENTENCE: The losses of starter Patrick Corbin and reliever David Hernandez to UCL tears as well as a 9-22 start portended an awful season for Arizona, which culminated in a 64-98 record.

HIGH POINT: A 14-13 record in July moved the Diamondbacks to their literal high point—third place as of July 22—when they defeated the Tigers. That good feeling wouldn't last.

LOW POINT: Having dropped 8 of 9 to fall to 63-96, the Diamondbacks fired manager Kirk Gibson, the Manager of the Year in 2011, as bench coach Alan Trammell took over for the final three games. General manager Kevin Towers had been dismissed in early September.

NOTABLE ROOKIES: After spending three seasons in the independent leagues, David Peralta, who signed with the Cardinals as a pitcher out of Venezuela in 2004, signed with the Diamondbacks in July 2014. By 2015, the 26-year-old now-outfielder was one of the league's most surprising and successful rookies, ending up at .286/.320/.450 with 29 extra-base hits. Shortstop Chris Owings played in just 91 games because of a left shoulder strain and other injuries, but still hit .261/.300/.406. Chase Anderson was called up from Double-A Mobile in early May and went 9-7, 4.01 in 21 starts. Third baseman Jake Lamb climbed from Double-A after tearing up Triple-A in a brief stint and posted a .636 OPS in the majors.

KEY TRANSACTIONS: Arizona shed the remaining $25 million of Martin Prado's contract—including $22 million for 2015-16—when they traded the versatile righthanded hitter to the Yankees for slugging prospect Peter O'Brien. O'Brien hit 34 homers for the Yankees and Diamondbacks organizations, but lacks a position although the Diamondbacks believe he can catch given more reps.

DOWN ON THE FARM: Shortstop Nick Ahmed is touted by scouts and PCL managers as a Gold Glove player to be, with slick actions and an above-average arm. He might force the team to trade from its shortstop surplus sooner than later. Righthanders Archie Bradley, Braden Shipley and Aaron Blair are racing to see who reaches the majors first. Third baseman Brandon Drury would be the organization's top hitting prospect if not for Lamb. He should play next season at Triple-A.

OPENING DAY PAYROLL: $111,798,833 (12th)

PLAYERS OF THE YEAR

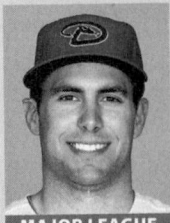

MAJOR LEAGUE	MINOR LEAGUE
Paul Goldschmidt	**Jake Lamb**
1b	**3b**
.300/.396/.542	.327/.407/.566
19 HR in 109 games	(Double-A/Triple-A)
Led team in HR, AVG	39 2Bs, 15 homers.

ORGANIZATION LEADERS

BATTING   *Minimum 250 AB

MAJORS

* AVG	Pollock, A.J.	.302
* OPS	Goldschmidt, Paul	.938
HR	Goldschmidt, Paul	19
RBI	Montero, Miguel	72

MINORS

* AVG	Marte, Andy, Reno	.329
8 OBP	Lamb, Jake, Mobile, Reno	.407
* SLG	Lamb, Jake, Mobile, Reno	.566
R	Almadova, Breland, South Bend, Visalia	95
H	Drury, Brandon, Visalia, Mobile	160
TB	Flores, Rudy, Visalia	277
2B	Drury, Brandon, Visalia, Mobile	42
3B	Velazquez, Andrew, South Bend	15
HR	Flores, Rudy, Visalia	28
RBI	Flores, Rudy, Visalia	100
BB	Harrell, Lucas, Reno	77
SO	Blair, Aaron, South Bend, Visalia, Mobile	171
SB	Velazquez, Andrew, South Bend	50

PITCHING   #Minimum 75 IP

MAJORS

W	Collmenter, Josh	11
# ERA	Collmenter, Josh	3.46
SO	Miley, Wade	183
SV	Reed, Addison	32

MINORS

W	Sinnery, Brandon, Visalia	14
L	Brewer, Charles, Mobile, Reno	12
# ERA	Schugel, A.J., Mobile	3.47
G	Gibson, Daniel, South Bend, Visalia	58
GS	Brewer, Charles, Mobile, Reno	29
SV	Burgos, Enrique, Visalia	29
IP	Sinnery, Brandon, Visalia	170
BB	Harrell, Lucas, Reno	77
SO	Blair, Aaron, South Bend, Visalia, Mobile	171
AVG	Blair, Aaron, South Bend, Visalia, Mobile	.218

General Manager: Kevin Towers. **Farm Director:** Mike Bell. **Scouting Director:** Ray Montgomery

Class	Team	League	W	L	PCT	Finish	Manager
Majors	Arizona Diamondbacks	National	64	98	.395	30th (30)	Kirk Gibson
Triple-A	Reno Aces	Pacific Coast	81	63	.563	t-1st (16)	Phil Nevin
Double-A	Mobile Bay Bears	Southern	79	58	.577	3rd (10)	Andy Green
High A	Visalia Rawhide	California	75	65	.536	4th (10)	Robby Hammock
Low A	South Bend Silver Hawks	Midwest	83	56	.597	2nd (16)	Mark Haley
Short season	Hillsboro Hops	Northwest	48	28	.632	1st (8)	J.R. House
Rookie	Missoula Osprey	Pioneer	36	40	.474	7th (8)	Audo Vicente
Rookie	Diamondbacks	Arizona	29	27	.518	5th (8)	Luis Urueta
Overall 2015 Minor League Record			431	337	.561	2nd (30)	

ORGANIZATION STATISTICS

ARIZONA DIAMONDBACKS

NATIONAL LEAGUE

Batting	B-T	HT	WT	DOB	AVG	vLH	vRH	G	AB	R	H	2B	3B	HR	RBI	BB	HBP	SH	SF	SO	SB	CS	SLG	OBP
Ahmed, Nick	R-R	6-3	205	3-15-90	.200	.176	—	25	70	9	14	2	0	1	4	3	0	2	0	10	0	1	.271	.233
Campana, Tony	L-L	5-8	165	5-30-86	.150	.000	—	26	60	4	9	1	1	0	3	0	1	0	0	10	4	1	.200	.164
Chavez, Eric	L-R	6-1	215	12-7-77	.246	.167	—	44	69	6	17	3	1	3	8	11	0	0	1	19	2	0	.449	.346
Evans, Nick	R-R	6-2	220	1-30-86	.273	.294	—	18	22	2	6	2	0	2	7	1	0	0	0	10	0	0	.636	.304
Goldschmidt, Paul	R-R	6-3	245	9-10-87	.300	—	—	109	406	75	122	39	1	19	69	64	2	0	3	110	9	3	.542	.396
Gosewisch, Tuffy	R-R	5-11	200	8-17-83	.225	.222	—	41	129	6	29	8	0	1	7	3	0	0	0	24	0	0	.310	.242
Gregorius, Didi	L-R	6-2	205	2-18-90	.226	.137	—	80	270	35	61	9	5	6	27	22	3	2	2	52	3	0	.363	.290
Hill, Aaron	R-R	5-11	205	3-21-82	.244	.242	—	133	501	52	122	26	3	10	60	28	5	0	7	92	4	3	.367	.287
Inciarte, Ender	L-L	5-10	165	10-29-90	.278	.273	—	118	418	54	116	18	2	4	27	25	4	0	5	33	19	3	.359	.318
Jackson, Brett	L-R	6-2	220	8-2-88	.000	—	—	7	4	0	0	0	0	0	0	1	0	0	0	1	0	0	.000	.200
Kieschnick, Roger	L-R	6-3	220	1-21-87	.195	.000	—	25	41	2	8	1	0	1	2	0	0	0	0	16	0	0	.293	.195
Lamb, Jake	L-R	6-3	220	10-9-90	.230	.136	—	37	126	15	29	4	1	4	11	6	0	0	1	37	1	1	.373	.263
Marte, Alfredo	R-R	5-11	195	3-31-89	.170	.242	—	44	106	8	18	5	1	2	9	6	1	1	0	34	1	0	.292	.221
Marte, Andy	R-R	6-1	205	10-21-83	.188	.167	—	6	16	1	3	0	0	1	3	0	0	0	0	3	0	0	.375	.188
Montero, Miguel	L-R	5-11	210	7-9-83	.243	.198	—	136	489	40	119	23	0	13	72	56	9	0	6	97	0	4	.370	.329
Owings, Chris	R-R	5-10	190	8-12-91	.261	.309	—	91	310	34	81	15	6	6	26	16	2	2	2	67	8	1	.406	.300
Pacheco, Jordan	R-R	6-1	205	1-30-86	.272	.324	—	47	81	6	22	4	0	0	8	3	0	1	0	12	0	0	.321	.298
2-team total (22 Colorado)					.255	—	—	69	153	10	39	10	1	0	16	9	1	1	1	27	0	0	.333	.299
Parra, Gerardo	L-L	5-11	200	5-6-87	.259	.212	—	104	406	51	105	18	3	6	30	24	4	4	2	72	5	5	.362	.305
2-team total (46 Milwaukee)					.261	—	—	150	529	64	138	22	4	9	40	32	5	6	2	100	9	7	.369	.308
Paul, Xavier	L-R	5-9	205	2-25-85	.100	.000	—	14	20	2	2	0	0	0	0	1	0	0	0	8	0	0	.100	.143
Pennington, Cliff	B-R	5-10	195	6-15-84	.254	.265	—	68	177	21	45	5	3	2	10	20	3	1	0	36	6	1	.350	.340
Peralta, David	L-L	6-2	215	8-14-87	.286	.197	—	88	329	40	94	12	9	8	36	16	1	1	1	60	6	3	.450	.320
Pollock, A.J.	R-R	6-1	195	12-5-87	.302	.280	—	75	265	41	80	19	6	7	24	19	2	1	0	46	14	3	.498	.353
Prado, Martin	R-R	6-1	190	10-27-83	.270	—	—	106	403	44	109	17	4	5	42	23	6	0	4	57	2	1	.370	.317
Reimold, Nolan	R-R	6-4	205	10-12-83	.294	—	—	7	17	2	5	1	0	1	4	0	0	0	1	10	0	0	.529	.278
Ross, Cody	R-L	5-10	195	12-23-80	.252	.254	—	83	202	15	51	8	0	2	15	15	1	0	1	44	0	0	.322	.306
Trumbo, Mark	R-R	6-4	235	1-16-86	.235	.250	—	88	328	37	77	15	1	14	61	28	1	0	5	89	2	3	.415	.293
Wilson, Bobby	R-R	6-0	220	4-8-83	.250	.000	—	2	4	0	1	0	0	0	0	0	0	0	0	0	0	0	.250	.250

Pitching	B-T	HT	WT	DOB	W	L	ERA	G	GS	CG	SV	IP	H	R	ER	HR	BB	SO	AVG	vLH	vRH	K/9	BB/9
Anderson, Chase	R-R	6-0	190	11-30-87	9	7	4.01	21	21	0	0	114	117	56	51	16	40	105	.268	.225	.302	8.27	3.15
Arroyo, Bronson	R-R	6-3	195	2-24-77	7	4	4.08	14	14	1	0	86	92	40	39	10	19	47	.279	.233	.331	4.92	1.99
Bolsinger, Mike	R-R	6-2	210	1-29-88	1	6	5.50	10	9	0	0	52	66	36	32	7	17	48	.308	.337	.284	8.25	2.92
Cahill, Trevor	R-R	6-4	220	3-1-88	3	12	5.61	32	17	0	1	111	123	76	69	9	55	105	.285	.346	.226	8.54	4.47
Chafin, Andrew	R-L	6-2	220	6-17-90	0	1	3.86	3	3	0	0	14	13	6	6	0	8	10	.265	.231	.278	6.43	5.14
Collmenter, Josh	R-R	6-4	235	2-7-86	11	9	3.46	33	28	1	1	179	163	75	69	18	39	115	.246	.282	.207	5.77	1.96
De La Rosa, Eury	L-L	5-9	165	2-24-90	2	0	2.95	25	0	0	0	37	37	12	12	2	14	32	.262	.309	.233	7.85	3.44
Delgado, Randall	R-R	6-3	200	2-9-90	4	4	4.87	47	4	0	0	78	71	44	42	6	35	86	.239	.234	.244	9.97	4.06
Hagens, Bradin	R-R	6-3	210	5-12-89	0	1	3.38	2	0	0	0	3	4	1	1	0	3	2	.400	.667	.286	6.75	10.13
Harris, Will	R-R	6-4	225	8-28-84	0	3	4.34	29	0	0	0	29	27	14	14	3	9	35	.252	.255	.250	10.86	2.79
Hudson, Daniel	R-R	6-3	225	3-9-87	0	1	13.50	3	0	0	0	3	4	4	4	0	0	2	.308	.250	.400	6.75	0.00
Marshall, Evan	R-R	6-2	220	4-18-90	4	4	2.74	57	0	0	0	49	50	17	15	3	17	54	.266	.300	.246	9.85	3.10
McCarthy, Brandon	R-R	6-7	200	7-7-83	3	10	5.01	18	18	0	0	110	131	65	61	15	20	93	.298	.323	.273	7.63	1.64
Miley, Wade	L-L	6-0	220	11-13-86	8	12	4.34	33	33	0	0	201	207	103	97	23	75	183	.269	.265	.270	8.19	3.35
Nuno, Vidal	L-L	5-11	195	7-26-87	0	7	3.76	14	14	0	0	84	71	37	35	10	20	69	.228	.155	.249	7.42	2.15
Paterson, Joe	R-L	6-0	190	5-19-86	0	0	33.75	3	0	0	0	1	4	5	5	0	1	0	.571	.333	.750	0.00	6.75
Perez, Oliver	L-L	6-3	220	8-15-81	3	4	2.91	68	0	0	7	59	50	25	19	5	24	76	.226	.281	.184	11.66	3.68
Putz, J.J.	R-R	6-5	250	2-22-77	1	1	6.59	18	0	0	0	14	17	10	10	1	6	14	.315	.600	.147	9.22	3.95
Reed, Addison	L-R	6-4	220	12-27-88	1	7	4.25	62	0	0	32	59	57	31	28	11	15	69	.244	.219	.267	10.47	2.28
Rowland-Smith, Ryan	L-L	6-3	220	1-26-83	0	0	4.91	6	0	0	0	7	7	5	4	0	4	9	.269	.273	.267	11.05	4.91
Schultz, Bo	R-R	6-3	220	9-25-85	0	1	7.88	4	0	0	0	8	13	7	7	1	1	5	.382	.353	.412	5.63	1.13
Spruill, Zeke	B-R	6-5	190	9-11-89	1	1	3.57	6	1	0	0	23	27	11	9	0	4	14	.300	.289	.311	5.56	1.59

Stites, Matt	R-R	5-11	195	5-28-90	0	0	5.73	37	0	0	0	33	33	23	21	6	16	26	.260	.192	.307	7.09	4.36
Thatcher, Joe	L-L	6-2	230	10-4-81	1	0	2.63	37	0	0	0	24	23	10	7	3	3	25	.247	.241	.256	9.38	1.13
Ziegler, Brad	R-R	6-4	210	10-10-79	5	3	3.49	68	0	0	1	67	60	29	26	5	24	54	.243	.183	.279	7.25	3.22

Fielding

Catcher	PCT	G	PO	A	E	DP	PB
Gosewisch	.996	35	241	18	1	1	1
Montero	.988	131	1037	65	13	12	5
Wilson	1.000	2	10	1	0	0	0

First Base	PCT	G	PO	A	E	DP
Evans	1.000	3	9	2	0	1
Goldschmidt	.993	109	934	80	7	83
Pacheco	1.000	11	71	4	0	5
Trumbo	.992	43	363	18	3	42

Second Base	PCT	G	PO	A	E	DP
Ahmed	1.000	2	2	5	0	2
Gregorius	.975	11	13	26	1	3
Hill	.988	116	215	347	7	69
Owings	1.000	18	32	48	0	11
Pacheco	1.000	1	1	0	0	0

	PCT	G	PO	A	E	DP
Pennington	1.000	18	34	48	0	12
Prado	.909	4	8	12	2	4

Third Base	PCT	G	PO	A	E	DP
Chavez	1.000	11	5	10	0	2
Evans	1.000	1	1	2	0	1
Gregorius	1.000	2	2	1	0	0
Hill	1.000	7	2	13	0	1
Lamb	.987	34	14	61	1	5
Marte	1.000	4	1	7	0	1
Pacheco	.500	3	0	1	1	0
Pennington	1.000	8	5	19	0	2
Prado	.954	99	67	181	12	19

Shortstop	PCT	G	PO	A	E	DP
Ahmed	.970	18	25	40	2	11
Gregorius	.983	67	98	189	5	39

	PCT	G	PO	A	E	DP
Owings	.957	61	77	165	11	36
Pennington	.975	23	24	54	2	13

Outfield	PCT	G	PO	A	E	DP
Campana	1.000	16	34	0	0	0
Evans	—	1	0	0	0	0
Inciarte	.982	114	266	10	5	0
Jackson	1.000	5	7	0	0	0
Kieschnick	.917	8	11	0	1	0
Marte	.953	27	40	1	2	1
Parra	.980	103	186	8	4	2
Paul	1.000	5	3	0	0	0
Peralta	.972	84	132	6	4	2
Pollock	.994	70	151	8	1	2
Reimold	1.000	4	7	0	0	0
Ross	.971	56	61	5	2	1
Trumbo	1.000	41	65	5	0	0

RENO ACES   TRIPLE-A

PACIFIC COAST LEAGUE

Batting	B-T	HT	WT	DOB	AVG	vLH	vRH	G	AB	R	H	2B	3B	HR	RBI	BB	HBP	SH	SF	SO	SB	CS	SLG	OBP
Ahmed, Nick	R-R	6-3	205	3-15-90	.312	.315	—	104	407	57	127	26	4	4	47	37	3	4	1	55	14	6	.425	.373
Borenstein, Zach	L-R	6-0	225	7-23-90	.260	.136	—	20	73	12	19	4	1	5	15	7	0	0	1	22	0	1	.548	.321
2-team total (30 Salt Lake)					.258	—	—	50	190	23	49	8	1	7	37	10	1	1	2	55	0	3	.421	.296
Bortnick, Tyler	R-R	5-11	185	7-3-87	.224	.240	—	41	85	13	19	2	1	0	5	10	1	2	0	21	3	0	.273	.313
Campana, Tony	L-L	5-8	165	5-30-86	.288	—	—	47	163	31	47	5	4	0	17	12	2	3	1	28	8	2	.368	.343
2-team total (53 Salt Lake)					.277	—	—	100	365	62	101	11	6	0	34	30	3	9	1	67	17	11	.340	.336
Cedeno, Ronny	R-R	6-0	195	2-2-83	.343	—	—	41	134	29	46	8	2	3	23	14	2	1	1	25	6	0	.500	.411
Clark, Tyler	B-R	6-5	210	3-30-92	—	—	—	1	0	0	0	0	0	0	0	0	0	0	0	0	0	0	.000	—
Cunningham, Aaron	R-R	5-11	215	4-24-86	.255	.330	—	92	243	33	62	16	3	0	31	29	5	0	4	46	2	1	.346	.342
Diaz, Argenis	R-R	6-0	190	2-12-87	.281	.227	—	39	135	11	38	9	1	0	12	11	1	3	0	28	0	1	.363	.340
Dorn, Danny	L-L	6-2	205	7-20-84	.304	.195	—	73	247	42	75	13	6	12	47	32	2	1	6	57	1	1	.551	.380
Evans, Nick	R-R	6-2	220	1-30-86	.354	.328	—	51	198	42	70	18	2	11	47	23	3	0	3	28	0	0	.631	.423
Freeman, Mike	L-R	6-0	190	8-4-87	.307	.200	—	71	218	37	67	11	7	1	25	21	0	0	2	25	6	0	.436	.365
Gregorius, Didi	L-R	6-2	205	2-18-90	.310	.304	—	57	226	42	70	14	4	3	25	24	6	3	1	26	3	0	.447	.389
Inciarte, Ender	L-L	5-10	165	10-29-90	.312	—	—	26	109	22	34	4	2	2	12	10	0	0	1	21	7	2	.440	.367
Jackson, Brett	L-R	6-2	220	8-2-88	.188	.111	—	11	16	2	3	0	0	1	3	3	0	0	0	9	1	0	.375	.316
2-team total (81 Iowa)					.208	—	—	92	240	25	50	8	4	6	23	27	4	0	0	103	5	6	.350	.299
Jacobs, Mike	L-R	6-3	210	10-30-80	.299	.324	—	135	501	79	150	37	0	19	97	60	3	0	11	120	0	0	.487	.370
Kieschnick, Roger	L-R	6-2	220	1-21-87	.260	.222	—	95	369	57	96	25	1	14	49	28	3	0	1	88	5	1	.461	.317
Lalli, Blake	L-R	6-1	210	5-12-83	.275	.069	—	93	284	31	78	17	1	3	29	27	1	0	0	57	0	2	.373	.340
Lamb, Jake	L-R	6-3	220	10-9-90	.500	—	—	5	18	3	9	4	0	1	5	3	0	0	0	4	2	0	.889	.571
Marte, Alfredo	R-R	5-11	195	3-31-89	.319	—	—	78	270	46	86	15	3	11	45	39	4	0	4	60	6	0	.519	.407
Marte, Andy	R-R	6-1	205	10-21-83	.329	—	—	126	471	81	155	32	3	19	80	48	1	0	6	62	1	0	.531	.388
Martin, Dustin	L-L	6-2	215	4-4-84	.209	—	—	18	43	6	9	2	0	2	7	4	0	0	0	8	1	0	.395	.277
McQuail, Steve	R-R	6-2	225	6-10-89	.200	—	—	2	5	1	1	0	0	1	1	0	0	0	0	2	0	0	.800	.200
Oeltjen, Trent	L-L	6-1	205	2-28-83	.219	.111	—	13	32	5	7	0	0	1	3	0	0	0	0	12	1	1	.313	.286
Owings, Chris	R-R	5-10	190	8-12-91	.250	—	—	10	40	6	10	1	0	0	1	0	0	0	0	9	3	0	.275	.250
Pacheco, Jordan	R-R	6-1	205	1-30-86	.286	.250	—	4	14	3	4	1	0	0	3	1	0	0	0	1	0	0	.357	.333
Paul, Xavier	L-R	5-9	205	2-25-85	.000	—	—	1	4	0	0	0	0	0	1	0	0	1	0	0	0	0	.000	.000
Pennington, Cliff	B-R	5-10	175	6-15-84	.385	—	—	4	13	3	5	0	0	0	3	1	0	0	0	1	1	0	.385	.529
Pollock, A.J.	R-R	6-1	195	12-5-87	.163	.077	—	13	49	4	8	1	1	0	9	2	0	0	1	4	0	0	.224	.192
Ross, Cody	R-L	5-10	195	12-23-80	.290	—	—	9	31	2	9	1	0	0	7	1	0	0	0	5	0	0	.323	.313
Tarleton, Dallas	L-R	5-11	200	8-5-87	.000	—	—	3	2	0	0	0	0	0	0	1	0	0	0	2	0	0	.000	.333
Tekotte, Blake	L-R	5-11	180	5-24-87	.222	.000	—	7	18	2	4	2	1	0	6	1	1	0	2	8	0	0	.444	.273
Trumbo, Mark	R-R	6-4	235	1-16-86	.455	—	—	3	11	6	5	0	0	3	6	1	0	0	0	2	0	0	1.273	.500
Weber, Garrett	R-R	5-10	165	3-29-89	.353	.327	—	54	201	38	71	13	3	7	30	15	4	0	2	43	0	1	.552	.405
Wilson, Bobby	R-R	6-0	220	4-8-83	.267	.288	—	76	270	29	72	11	0	3	38	23	1	3	2	45	0	2	.341	.324

Pitching	B-T	HT	WT	DOB	W	L	ERA	G	GS	CG	SV	IP	H	R	ER	HR	BB	SO	AVG	vLH	vRH	K/9	BB/9
Barrett, Jake	R-R	6-3	230	7-22-91	1	0	3.72	30	0	0	16	29	22	13	12	3	15	23	.220	.250	.192	7.14	4.66
Bolsinger, Mike	R-R	6-2	210	1-29-88	8	3	3.93	17	16	0	0	92	92	40	40	6	32	88	.261	.263	.260	8.64	3.14
Bradley, Archie	R-R	6-4	235	8-10-92	1	4	5.18	5	5	0	0	24	26	14	14	0	12	23	.277	.303	.262	8.51	4.44
Brewer, Charles	R-R	6-3	205	4-7-88	8	10	4.99	22	22	0	0	126	146	74	70	10	34	96	.293	.311	.277	6.84	2.42
Brooks, Eric	R-R	6-2	200	8-29-90	0	0	0.00	3	1	0	0	7	2	0	0	0	3	0	.095	.000	.133	0.00	3.86
Cahill, Trevor	R-R	6-4	220	3-1-88	2	2	3.49	6	6	0	0	28	21	12	11	4	20	27	.214	.279	.164	8.58	6.35
Chafin, Andrew	R-L	6-2	220	6-17-90	5	5	5.34	17	16	0	0	93	111	62	55	11	39	73	.298	.267	.307	7.09	3.79
Cooper, Blake	R-R	5-11	190	3-30-88	1	0	6.00	17	0	0	0	24	25	16	16	1	17	20	.281	.242	.304	7.50	6.38
De La Rosa, Eury	L-L	5-9	165	2-24-90	2	4	2.52	36	0	0	2	39	33	18	11	3	20	36	.224	.150	.276	8.24	4.58
Eitel, Derek	R-R	6-4	200	11-21-87	5	1	2.70	30	0	0	0	47	44	15	14	5	23	60	.254	.238	.264	11.57	4.44

Pitching	B-T	HT	WT	DOB	W	L	ERA	G	GS	CG	SV	IP	H	R	ER	HR	BB	SO	AVG	vLH	vRH	K/9	BB/9
Hagens, Bradin	R-R	6-3	210	5-12-89	1	1	2.55	4	4	1	0	25	21	11	7	1	9	9	.226	.302	.160	3.28	3.28
Harrell, Lucas	B-R	6-2	205	6-3-85	6	4	5.15	22	20	0	0	107	115	64	61	12	77	67	.285	.294	.275	5.65	6.50
Harris, Will	R-R	6-4	225	8-28-84	3	2	0.99	43	0	0	1	46	34	10	5	3	20	44	.207	.194	.216	8.67	3.94
Hessler, Keith	L-L	6-4	215	3-15-89	0	0	3.00	1	1	0	0	3	4	1	1	1	2	4	.333	.000	.500	12.00	6.00
Hudson, Daniel	R-R	6-3	225	3-9-87	0	0	0.00	2	2	0	0	2	1	0	0	0	1	2	.167	.500	.000	9.00	4.50
Lee, Mike	R-R	6-7	235	11-18-86	1	1	3.48	2	2	0	0	10	9	4	4	1	2	4	.237	.182	.259	3.48	1.74
Loe, Kameron	R-R	6-8	245	9-10-81	0	0	9.00	6	0	0	0	10	15	10	10	1	3	8	.349	.350	.348	7.20	2.70
2-team total (7 Omaha)					0	0	6.43	13	0	0	1	21	22	15	15	2	10	12	—	—	—	5.14	4.29
Marshall, Evan	R-R	6-2	220	4-18-90	0	1	0.54	14	0	0	1	17	10	1	1	0	5	19	.175	.250	.135	10.26	2.70
Munson, Kevin	R-R	6-1	215	1-3-89	4	3	2.60	56	0	0	2	62	49	19	18	5	22	82	.215	.338	.149	11.84	3.18
Paredes, Willy	R-R	6-3	180	2-2-89	0	0	27.00	1	0	0	0	1	5	3	3	1	0	0	.625	.667	.600	0.00	0.00
Paterson, Joe	R-L	6-0	190	5-19-86	0	2	2.95	56	0	0	0	43	45	16	14	1	19	33	.274	.198	.359	6.96	4.01
Putz, J.J.	R-R	6-5	250	2-22-77	0	0	0.00	2	0	0	0	2	1	0	0	0	2	2	.167	.000	.250	10.80	10.80
Richard, Clayton	L-L	6-5	245	9-12-83	1	0	4.26	1	1	0	0	6	5	3	3	1	1	6	.407	.308	.500	1.42	1.42
Sanabia, Alex	R-R	6-2	210	9-8-88	0	1	8.10	8	4	0	0	23	41	23	21	8	8	11	.394	.391	.397	4.24	3.09
2-team total (20 New Orleans)					7	5	4.70	28	23	0	0	134	159	77	70	18	40	104	—	—	—	6.99	2.69
Schultz, Bo	R-R	6-3	220	9-25-85	10	8	6.18	28	23	1	0	135	174	109	93	17	46	82	.311	.343	.281	5.45	3.06
Schuster, Patrick	R-L	6-2	185	10-30-90	0	0	4.50	21	0	0	0	18	21	10	9	2	10	20	.300	.194	.385	10.00	5.00
Serrano, Mark	L-R	6-1	185	9-14-85	6	0	3.78	22	4	0	0	50	49	24	21	7	20	46	.250	.288	.228	8.28	3.60
Spruill, Zeke	B-R	6-5	190	9-11-89	3	7	6.04	28	11	0	1	79	89	58	53	10	21	71	.280	.259	.300	8.09	2.39
Stites, Matt	R-R	5-11	195	5-20-90	0	0	2.25	17	0	0	12	16	13	6	4	1	6	15	.228	.240	.219	8.44	3.38
Todd, Jess	R-R	5-11	210	4-20-86	8	2	3.61	53	0	0	5	72	68	32	29	5	27	66	.253	.252	.253	8.21	3.36
Van Grouw, Justin	R-R	6-7	225	9-7-90	0	0	0.00	3	0	0	0	6	4	0	0	0	2	4	.190	.300	.091	6.00	3.00
Wolf, Randy	L-L	6-0	205	8-22-76	5	1	4.50	6	6	0	0	34	40	18	17	1	18	35	.299	.310	.295	9.26	4.76
2-team total (7 Salt Lake)					6	2	4.65	13	13	0	0	72	85	38	37	6	30	66	—	—	—	8.29	3.77

Fielding

Catcher	PCT	G	PO	A	E	DP	PB
Clark	1.000	1	2	0	0	0	1
Lalli	.992	79	541	52	5	6	4
Pacheco	1.000	1	3	0	0	0	
Wilson	.997	74	548	58	2	9	4

First Base	PCT	G	PO	A	E	DP
Dorn	1.000	26	212	21	0	23
Evans	.986	15	132	13	2	13
Freeman	1.000	1	5	1	0	0
Jacobs	.995	102	940	69	5	92
Lamb	1.000	1	6	0	0	1
Marte	1.000	2	10	0	0	1
McQuail	1.000	1	9	0	0	0
Weber	1.000	6	36	2	0	5

Second Base	PCT	G	PO	A	E	DP
Ahmed	.955	14	19	45	3	9
Bortnick	.973	22	24	49	2	6
Cedeno	.992	31	45	81	1	19
Diaz	.976	7	13	28	1	8

	PCT	G	PO	A	E	DP
Freeman	.972	22	48	56	3	15
Gregorius	.977	38	66	104	4	32
Owings	.947	8	8	28	2	3
Pacheco	1.000	2	2	5	0	1
Pennington	1.000	2	0	4	0	0
Weber	.990	22	37	60	1	17

Third Base	PCT	G	PO	A	E	DP
Bortnick	.833	6	2	3	1	0
Diaz	.867	4	7	6	2	2
Evans	.905	15	7	31	4	4
Lamb	1.000	5	5	5	0	0
Marte	.956	121	67	236	14	19
Pennington	.667	1	0	2	1	0
Weber	.667	6	1	7	4	0

Shortstop	PCT	G	PO	A	E	DP
Ahmed	.979	91	123	307	9	65
Cedeno	1.000	10	22	24	0	8
Diaz	.976	28	37	85	3	22
Gregorius	.945	19	35	68	6	15

	PCT	G	PO	A	E	DP
Owings	1.000	1	1	1	0	0
Pennington	1.000	1	2	3	0	0

Outfield	PCT	G	PO	A	E	DP
Borenstein	.969	20	29	2	1	0
Campana	.971	38	65	3	2	0
Cunningham	.979	67	91	4	2	0
Dorn	.980	41	44	4	1	2
Evans	1.000	12	18	1	0	0
Freeman	.983	44	55	2	1	1
Inciarte	.979	26	42	5	1	0
Jackson	.800	11	4	0	1	0
Kieschnick	.978	89	172	3	4	0
Marte	.942	71	95	3	6	0
Martin	1.000	14	17	1	0	0
Oeltjen	1.000	11	13	0	0	0
Pollock	.903	13	26	2	3	0
Ross	1.000	9	9	2	0	0
Tekotte	.846	6	11	0	2	0
Trumbo	1.000	3	3	0	0	0
Weber	1.000	16	23	1	0	0

MOBILE BAYBEARS
SOUTHERN LEAGUE
DOUBLE-A

Batting	B-T	HT	WT	DOB	AVG	vLH	vRH	G	AB	R	H	2B	3B	HR	RBI	BB	HBP	SH	SF	SO	SB	CS	SLG	OBP
Belza, Tom	L-R	6-0	190	7-31-89	.305	—	—	123	413	56	126	21	5	1	31	50	7	5	3	89	9	3	.387	.387
Borenstein, Zach	L-R	6-0	225	7-23-90	.241	.158	—	23	87	13	21	4	2	3	14	12	1	0	2	17	3	0	.437	.333
Bowman, Dan	R-L	6-0	210	9-2-89	.160	.000	—	13	25	2	4	0	0	0	1	2	0	0	0	9	0	0	.160	.222
Clark, Tyler	B-R	6-5	210	3-30-92	.000	.000	—	3	6	0	0	0	0	0	0	0	1	0	0	3	0	0	.000	.143
Court, Ryan	R-R	6-2	210	5-28-88	.243	.208	—	61	136	18	33	12	1	2	16	18	3	1	2	40	4	1	.390	.340
Davis, Lars	L-R	6-3	205	11-7-85	.182	.250	—	8	22	2	4	3	0	0	2	4	1	0	0	4	0	0	.318	.333
Diaz, Argenis	R-R	6-0	190	2-12-87	.292	—	—	19	65	11	19	3	0	0	2	5	0	0	0	13	1	0	.338	.343
Drury, Brandon	R-R	6-2	190	8-21-92	.295	—	—	29	105	12	31	7	0	4	14	7	2	0	2	19	0	0	.476	.345
Freeman, Mike	L-R	6-0	190	8-4-87	.214	.167	—	52	196	27	42	7	3	5	16	20	2	2	1	41	7	1	.357	.292
Glaesmann, Todd	R-R	6-4	220	10-24-90	.211	.214	—	49	166	17	35	9	0	1	14	8	2	0	1	51	5	0	.283	.254
Gomez, Raywilly	B-R	5-11	195	1-25-90	.273	.324	—	55	150	16	41	4	0	3	22	19	1	1	2	20	0	0	.360	.355
Greene, Justin	R-R	6-0	185	10-10-85	.174	.185	—	30	92	10	16	4	1	0	7	5	9	0	0	1	28	0	4	.239	.245
Griffin, Jon	R-R	6-6	230	4-29-89	.218	.238	—	109	353	43	77	14	0	15	53	31	8	0	4	111	0	0	.385	.293
Haniger, Mitch	R-R	6-2	215	12-23-90	.333	—	—	8	24	5	8	3	0	0	5	3	2	0	1	4	0	0	.458	.433
2-team total (67 Huntsville)					.262	—	—	75	267	46	70	10	1	10	39	22	6	2	4	45	4	0	.419	.328
Harbin, Taylor	R-R	5-9	171	2-13-86	.125	—	—	10	32	4	4	0	0	1	3	0	2	0	1	7	0	1	.219	.171
Jamieson, Sean	R-R	6-0	195	3-2-89	.298	.235	—	91	329	56	98	18	5	5	33	31	4	7	3	61	6	7	.429	.362
Lamb, Jake	R-L	6-3	220	10-9-90	.318	—	—	103	374	60	119	35	5	14	79	50	6	0	9	99	0	0	.551	.399
Martin, Dustin	L-L	6-2	215	4-4-84	.291	.327	—	67	230	43	67	15	0	8	38	36	1	0	1	52	5	3	.461	.388
Marzilli, Evan	L-L	6-0	185	3-13-91	.246	.260	—	81	285	33	70	12	6	3	35	30	6	2	2	67	8	5	.361	.328
Montilla, Gerson	R-R	5-10	168	11-13-89	.271	.329	—	107	336	40	91	12	3	6	40	28	3	2	7	65	1	6	.378	.326
O'Brien, Pete	R-R	6-3	215	7-15-90	.385	—	—	4	13	1	5	0	0	1	4	1	0	0	0	5	0	0	.615	.429
Parraz, Jordan	R-R	6-3	215	10-8-84	.190	.238	—	26	84	10	16	4	1	2	7	10	2	0	0	20	0	2	.333	.292

Batting	B-T	HT	WT	DOB	AVG	vLH	vRH	G	AB	R	H	2B	3B	HR	RBI	BB	HBP	SH	SF	SO	SB	CS	SLG	OBP
Peralta, David	L-L	6-2	215	8-14-87	.297	.231	—	53	202	33	60	17	1	6	46	18	2	0	1	21	2	0	.480	.359
Rodriguez, Steven	L-R	6-1	200	1-8-90	.267	.261	—	39	105	17	28	9	0	0	11	15	1	4	2	26	0	1	.352	.358
Samson, Nate	R-R	6-1	190	8-19-87	.274	.182	—	46	117	20	32	6	1	4	9	15	2	2	1	25	5	2	.444	.363
Tarleton, Dallas	L-R	5-11	200	8-5-87	.367	—	—	10	30	2	11	3	0	0	6	0	0	0	0	7	0	0	.467	.367
Thomas, Mark	R-R	6-1	225	5-5-88	.191	—	—	61	204	22	39	8	2	9	33	15	2	0	2	65	0	1	.382	.251
Weber, Garrett	R-R	5-10	165	3-29-89	.282	.276	—	57	195	23	55	9	1	2	18	8	5	0	0	37	0	0	.369	.327

Pitching	B-T	HT	WT	DOB	W	L	ERA	G	GS	CG	SV	IP	H	R	ER	HR	BB	SO	AVG	vLH	vRH	K/9	BB/9
Anderson, Kyle	R-L	6-2	205	5-24-90	0	0	0.00	1	0	0	1	1	1	0	0	0	0	0	.333	—	.333	0.00	0.00
Anderson, Chase	R-R	6-0	190	11-30-87	4	2	0.69	6	6	0	0	39	22	4	3	1	6	38	.159	.150	.163	8.77	1.38
Barrett, Jake	R-R	6-3	230	7-22-91	1	2	2.39	25	0	0	12	26	25	7	7	0	12	24	.260	.278	.250	8.20	4.10
Blair, Aaron	R-R	6-5	230	5-26-92	4	1	1.94	8	8	0	0	46	30	11	10	4	16	46	.185	.220	.165	8.94	3.11
Bradley, Archie	R-R	6-4	235	8-10-92	2	3	4.12	12	12	1	0	55	45	27	25	2	36	46	.231	.268	.210	7.57	5.93
Brewer, Charles	R-R	6-3	205	4-7-88	3	2	2.91	7	7	0	0	43	36	14	14	3	14	42	.231	.091	.286	8.72	2.91
Brooks, Eric	R-R	6-2	200	8-29-90	1	0	0.00	1	1	0	0	5	2	0	0	0	0	5	.125	.167	.100	9.00	0.00
Chafin, Andrew	R-L	6-2	220	6-17-90	4	1	1.96	9	9	0	0	55	49	14	12	4	19	41	.243	.278	.235	6.71	3.11
Cooper, Blake	R-R	5-11	190	3-30-88	3	2	1.85	24	0	0	0	34	26	11	7	2	10	31	.213	.158	.238	8.21	2.65
2-team total (8 Tennessee)					3	3	1.62	32	0	0	1	44	31	12	8	2	13	48	—	—	—	9.74	2.64
Fitzgerald, Justin	R-R	6-5	230	3-3-86	7	2	4.02	15	11	0	1	65	68	34	29	5	32	51	.272	.313	.251	7.06	4.43
Fleck, Kaleb	R-R	6-2	190	1-24-89	7	3	2.56	56	0	0	17	63	55	18	18	4	28	79	.237	.203	.253	11.23	3.98
Furney, Sean	R-R	6-5	220	6-2-91	0	1	4.50	1	1	0	0	4	7	2	2	0	2	3	.467	.600	.400	6.75	4.50
Godfrey, Graham	R-R	6-3	215	8-9-84	0	1	6.48	2	2	0	0	8	12	6	6	1	3	9	.333	.214	.409	9.72	3.24
Hagens, Bradin	R-R	6-3	210	5-12-89	8	6	4.15	24	18	0	0	111	108	65	51	7	50	60	.259	.261	.258	4.88	4.07
Hively, R.J.	R-R	6-2	225	11-27-88	3	5	2.76	55	0	0	3	62	56	26	19	1	29	54	.245	.342	.196	7.84	4.21
Lee, Mike	R-R	6-7	235	11-18-86	7	5	4.49	19	19	1	0	104	110	58	52	6	29	61	.273	.348	.235	5.26	2.50
Paredes, Willy	R-R	6-3	180	2-2-89	5	2	2.33	43	3	0	0	66	60	19	17	2	31	45	.252	.250	.253	6.17	4.25
Richard, Clayton	L-L	6-5	245	9-12-83	0	2	6.60	3	3	0	0	15	23	13	11	2	4	7	.359	.429	.340	4.20	2.40
Schugel, A.J.	R-R	5-11	210	6-27-89	6	4	3.47	26	26	0	0	148	142	60	57	3	50	117	.260	.238	.271	7.13	3.05
Schuster, Patrick	R-L	6-2	185	10-30-90	3	2	2.03	36	0	0	0	27	12	7	6	2	15	19	.141	.125	.156	6.41	5.06
Serrano, Mark	L-R	6-1	185	9-14-85	0	0	1.80	1	0	0	0	5	5	1	1	0	1	5	.263	.429	.167	9.00	1.80
Sherfy, Jimmie	R-R	6-0	175	12-27-91	3	1	4.97	37	0	0	1	38	34	21	21	4	18	45	.241	.306	.219	10.66	4.26
Shipley, Braden	R-R	6-3	190	2-22-92	1	2	3.60	4	4	0	0	20	14	8	8	3	10	18	.203	.227	.191	8.10	4.50
Simmons, Seth	R-R	5-9	170	6-14-88	1	1	1.51	35	0	0	2	48	28	10	8	1	18	60	.168	.258	.147	11.33	3.40
Sogard, Alex	L-L	6-3	215	7-25-87	0	1	9.64	15	0	0	0	19	30	20	20	6	10	16	.370	.375	.368	7.71	4.82
Stites, Matt	R-R	5-11	195	5-28-90	0	1	3.75	12	0	0	3	12	10	5	5	0	3	8	.244	.400	.194	6.00	2.25
Wheeler, Cody	L-L	5-11	160	8-19-89	2	0	0.40	20	0	0	0	22	6	2	1	0	20	27	.087	.074	.095	10.88	8.06
Winkler, Kyle	R-R	5-11	195	6-18-90	3	1	4.34	20	0	0	0	29	30	19	14	4	20	35	.254	.243	.259	10.86	6.21
Woodall, Bryan	R-R	6-1	200	10-24-86	1	4	3.76	10	7	0	0	38	35	17	16	4	11	28	.240	.186	.276	6.57	2.58

Fielding

Catcher	PCT	G	PO	A	E	DP	PB
Clark	1.000	2	12	0	0	0	1
Davis	.987	8	69	5	1	0	2
Gomez	.982	31	200	19	4	1	0
O'Brien	1.000	3	12	0	0	0	1
Rodriguez	1.000	38	229	28	0	4	4
Tarleton	.986	9	65	6	1	0	2
Thomas	.992	59	429	50	4	11	6

First Base	PCT	G	PO	A	E	DP
Belza	.990	40	276	17	3	30
Court	.994	28	160	15	1	16
Freeman	—	1	0	0	0	0
Gomez	1.000	1	3	0	0	0
Griffin	.991	90	747	27	7	74
Peralta	.909	1	10	0	1	0

Second Base	PCT	G	PO	A	E	DP
Belza	1.000	5	7	14	0	7
Drury	1.000	2	3	4	0	1

	PCT	G	PO	A	E	DP
Freeman	.989	24	34	59	1	11
Harbin	1.000	5	5	14	0	1
Jamieson	.929	3	6	7	1	4
Montilla	.972	80	135	217	10	45
Samson	.967	9	8	21	1	8
Weber	1.000	39	84	102	0	30

Third Base	PCT	G	PO	A	E	DP
Belza	—	1	0	0	0	0
Court	.927	11	9	29	3	3
Drury	.982	28	15	39	1	4
Lamb	.959	97	50	207	11	20
Montilla	—	2	0	0	0	0
Samson	1.000	1	1	0	0	0
Weber	1.000	5	3	10	0	0

Shortstop	PCT	G	PO	A	E	DP
Diaz	.949	19	29	46	4	22
Freeman	.968	15	19	41	2	7
Harbin	1.000	3	4	4	0	1

	PCT	G	PO	A	E	DP
Jamieson	.971	86	116	258	11	54
Samson	.982	25	31	77	2	13

Outfield	PCT	G	PO	A	E	DP
Belza	.992	79	119	4	1	1
Borenstein	1.000	21	34	2	0	1
Bowman	.947	10	18	0	1	0
Court	1.000	1	3	0	0	0
Freeman	1.000	25	50	1	0	0
Glaesmann	1.000	46	68	4	0	0
Greene	1.000	30	51	1	0	0
Haniger	1.000	7	7	1	0	0
Harbin	1.000	1	2	0	0	0
Martin	.984	63	115	5	2	1
Marzilli	.990	81	188	3	2	1
Montilla	.941	15	16	0	1	0
O'Brien	1.000	1	1	0	0	0
Parraz	1.000	24	59	4	0	0
Peralta	.976	46	78	2	2	0
Samson	—	1	0	0	0	0

VISALIA RAWHIDE

HIGH CLASS A

CALIFORNIA LEAGUE

Batting	B-T	HT	WT	DOB	AVG	vLH	vRH	G	AB	R	H	2B	3B	HR	RBI	BB	HBP	SH	SF	SO	SB	CS	SLG	OBP
Almadova, Breland	R-R	6-1	195	10-18-90	.295	—	—	42	173	36	51	8	2	1	18	12	2	6	2	36	9	4	.382	.344
Bowman, Dan	R-L	6-0	210	9-2-89	.237	.214	—	25	93	13	22	5	0	2	7	8	2	0	0	31	3	1	.355	.311
Brito, Socrates	L-L	6-2	200	9-6-92	.293	.269	—	128	518	82	152	30	5	10	62	36	2	0	5	109	38	10	.429	.339
Court, Ryan	R-R	6-2	210	5-28-88	.272	.209	—	46	173	23	47	13	2	4	21	20	1	0	1	58	4	3	.439	.349
Drury, Brandon	R-R	6-2	210	8-21-92	.300	.275	—	107	430	73	129	35	1	19	81	41	5	0	2	76	4	3	.519	.366
Flores, Rudy	L-R	6-3	205	12-12-90	.301	.217	—	132	525	76	158	35	0	28	100	33	13	0	6	189	3	2	.528	.354
Freeman, Ronnie	R-R	6-1	190	1-8-91	.278	.284	—	91	306	43	85	24	1	3	41	30	2	1	6	55	1	1	.392	.340
Gebhardt, Ryan	R-R	5-10	185	10-5-91	.356	—	—	43	160	27	57	6	1	0	18	10	3	0	1	19	2	3	.406	.402
Glenn, Alex	L-L	5-11	180	6-18-91	.285	.288	—	124	488	85	139	30	8	24	89	44	3	0	3	116	22	3	.527	.346
Jacobs, Brandon	R-R	6-1	225	12-8-90	.210	.182	—	89	310	42	65	10	2	16	36	30	6	0	1	111	3	3	.410	.291
Marzilli, Evan	L-L	6-0	185	3-13-91	.244	.257	—	52	176	30	43	8	3	5	18	31	2	1	2	54	7	4	.409	.360

	B-T	HT	WT	DOB	AVG	vLH	vRH	G	AB	R	H	2B	3B	HR	RBI	BB	HBP	SH	SF	SO	SB	CS	SLG	OBP
McQuail, Steve	R-R	6-2	225	6-10-89	.225	.276	—	49	187	22	42	8	1	10	35	10	3	0	1	61	1	0	.439	.274
Medrano, Kevin	L-R	6-1	155	5-21-90	.284	.261	—	114	422	50	120	19	4	4	45	28	4	6	6	62	19	9	.377	.330
Navarro, Raul	R-R	5-10	170	2-5-92	.304	.316	—	114	437	72	133	20	6	7	53	37	6	8	4	78	18	9	.426	.364
Pena, Fidel	R-R	5-11	165	7-19-91	.236	.269	—	64	233	36	55	5	1	7	27	10	2	3	2	39	10	2	.356	.271
Queliz, Jose	R-R	6-3	200	8-7-92	.195	.207	—	42	133	12	26	2	0	2	9	3	2	0	0	34	0	1	.256	.225
Roberts, George	R-R	6-0	206	4-17-90	.295	—	—	25	88	7	26	7	0	0	7	7	2	0	1	19	2	0	.375	.357
Rodriguez, Steven	L-R	6-1	200	1-8-90	.250	—	—	9	28	4	7	3	2	0	4	7	0	0	1	7	0	0	.500	.389
Tarleton, Dallas	L-R	5-11	200	8-5-87	.278	—	—	10	36	3	10	1	0	0	5	5	1	0	0	11	0	0	.306	.381

Pitching	B-T	HT	WT	DOB	W	L	ERA	G	GS	CG	SV	IP	H	R	ER	HR	BB	SO	AVG	vLH	vRH	K/9	BB/9
Arroyo, Spencer	L-L	6-2	166	8-9-88	6	7	4.62	28	27	0	0	166	185	98	85	17	49	124	.282	.292	.278	6.74	2.66
Barbosa, Andrew	R-L	6-8	205	11-18-87	7	2	3.71	19	19	0	0	87	84	45	36	12	39	117	.249	.265	.243	12.06	4.02
Blair, Aaron	R-R	6-5	230	5-26-92	4	2	4.35	13	13	0	0	72	70	37	35	6	21	81	.251	.209	.280	10.08	2.61
Bradley, J.R.	R-R	6-3	185	6-9-92	2	1	2.41	18	0	0	2	19	14	5	5	2	9	25	.200	.214	.190	12.05	4.34
Brooks, Eric	R-R	6-2	200	8-29-90	0	2	16.20	2	2	0	0	7	14	13	12	4	4	4	.400	.364	.417	5.40	5.40
Burgos, Enrique	R-R	6-4	200	11-23-90	3	3	2.47	55	0	0	29	55	37	17	15	5	26	83	.188	.127	.222	13.66	4.28
Cahill, Trevor	R-R	6-4	220	3-1-88	0	1	18.00	1	1	0	0	2	2	4	4	1	0	4	.250	.500	.000	18.00	0.00
Darrah, Jesse	L-R	6-2	190	3-28-90	3	5	6.08	16	16	0	0	84	114	63	57	16	35	68	.317	.299	.327	7.26	3.74
Garcia, Henry	L-L	6-1	170	6-15-90	5	3	5.23	40	0	0	0	72	82	42	42	9	23	46	.286	.287	.285	5.72	2.86
Gibson, Daniel	R-L	6-2	221	10-16-91	4	3	9.13	21	0	0	0	23	31	28	23	3	12	22	.316	.333	.305	8.74	4.76
Hernandez, Hector	B-L	6-1	190	2-20-91	2	4	5.79	6	6	0	0	37	51	27	24	6	7	21	.325	.200	.368	5.06	1.69
Hessler, Keith	L-L	6-4	215	3-15-89	4	2	4.40	44	0	0	1	59	79	31	29	3	18	78	.319	.344	.303	11.83	2.73
Krehbiel, Joe	R-R	6-2	185	12-20-92	1	0	1.42	22	0	0	3	25	13	5	4	1	9	28	.149	.129	.161	9.95	3.20
2-team total (4 Inland Empire)					1	0	1.53	26	0	0	3	29	15	7	5	2	10	34	—	—	—	10.43	3.07
Omahen, Johnny	R-R	6-0	190	3-15-89	3	3	5.03	18	8	0	0	59	80	39	33	5	15	45	.324	.348	.310	6.86	2.29
Schepel, Kyle	L-R	6-1	230	8-7-90	3	3	4.87	39	0	0	1	41	36	26	22	1	28	33	.240	.296	.208	7.30	6.20
Sherfy, Jimmie	R-R	6-0	175	12-27-91	2	0	3.27	11	0	0	6	11	6	5	4	2	5	23	.158	.182	.148	18.82	4.09
Shipley, Braden	R-R	6-3	190	2-22-92	2	4	4.03	10	10	0	0	60	57	32	27	7	21	68	.258	.219	.277	10.14	3.13
Shuttlesworth, Johnny	R-R	6-1	220	9-30-89	0	1	2.08	14	0	0	2	17	13	4	4	3	6	13	.200	.136	.233	6.75	3.12
Simmons, Seth	R-R	5-9	170	6-14-88	2	2	6.08	13	0	0	1	13	16	10	9	3	9	18	.302	.500	.231	12.15	6.08
Sinnery, Brandon	R-R	6-4	170	1-26-90	14	7	4.02	28	28	3	0	170	175	92	76	19	44	109	.266	.317	.240	5.76	2.32
Slaats, Josh	R-R	6-5	225	12-22-88	0	0	7.36	3	0	0	0	4	5	3	3	1	4	2	.357	.500	.250	4.91	9.82
Van Grouw, Justin	R-R	6-7	225	9-7-90	0	1	6.00	19	0	0	0	30	43	20	20	3	10	23	.331	.362	.313	6.90	3.00
Watts, Daniel	L-L	6-3	190	10-26-89	0	0	6.19	7	1	0	0	16	22	12	11	4	7	14	.333	.385	.321	7.88	3.94
Weller, Blayne	R-R	6-5	220	1-30-90	4	2	4.73	9	9	0	0	46	40	27	24	5	21	70	.230	.250	.218	13.80	4.14
Wheeler, Cody	L-L	5-11	160	8-19-89	3	4	2.35	25	0	0	0	38	25	11	10	1	18	53	.181	.150	.194	12.44	4.23
Winkler, Kyle	R-R	5-11	195	6-18-90	1	3	3.53	23	0	0	0	36	31	19	14	3	17	37	.237	.244	.233	9.34	4.29

Fielding

Catcher	PCT	G	PO	A	E	DP	PB
Freeman	.992	90	693	70	6	4	8
Pena	1.000	6	5	1	0	1	1
Queliz	.995	42	355	25	2	5	6
Rodriguez	.979	9	85	10	2	1	0
Tarleton	.985	8	62	5	1	1	2

First Base	PCT	G	PO	A	E	DP
Court	1.000	13	105	9	0	14
Flores	.985	111	864	40	14	63
McQuail	.993	16	121	15	1	6
Roberts	1.000	2	7	0	0	0

Second Base	PCT	G	PO	A	E	DP
Gebhardt	.958	16	29	40	3	9
Medrano	.980	74	123	166	6	28
Pena	.965	58	102	144	9	34

Third Base	PCT	G	PO	A	E	DP
Court	.722	7	4	9	5	0
Drury	.947	94	45	188	13	13
Gebhardt	1.000	1	2	1	0	0
Navarro	1.000	28	10	44	0	1
Roberts	.909	16	10	30	4	2

Shortstop	PCT	G	PO	A	E	DP
Gebhardt	.962	28	25	75	4	6
Medrano	.966	34	41	72	4	11
Navarro	.950	82	98	208	16	43

Outfield	PCT	G	PO	A	E	DP
Almadova	.992	42	111	6	1	0
Bowman	.934	25	54	3	4	2
Brito	.960	119	282	3	12	0
Court	.833	5	5	0	1	0
Gebhardt	—	1	0	0	0	0
Glenn	.945	121	214	9	13	1
Jacobs	.990	60	93	4	1	0
Marzilli	.981	52	149	2	3	1

SOUTH BEND SILVER HAWKS   LOW CLASS A

MIDWEST LEAGUE

Batting	B-T	HT	WT	DOB	AVG	vLH	vRH	G	AB	R	H	2B	3B	HR	RBI	BB	HBP	SH	SF	SO	SB	CS	SLG	OBP
Almadova, Breland	R-R	6-1	195	10-18-90	.269	.324	—	90	312	59	84	16	2	6	39	42	6	4	0	79	26	10	.391	.367
Ard, Taylor	R-R	6-2	230	1-31-90	.000	—	—	2	4	0	0	0	0	0	0	1	1	0	0	1	0	0	.000	.333
Bell, Carter	R-R	6-1	195	6-12-90	.250	—	—	1	4	0	1	0	0	0	0	0	0	0	0	1	0	0	.250	.250
Bowman, Dan	R-L	6-0	210	9-2-89	.265	.296	—	30	102	19	27	5	2	4	19	3	3	0	1	29	1	0	.471	.303
Bray, Colin	B-L	6-4	205	6-18-93	.267	—	—	9	30	3	8	1	1	1	5	1	1	0	0	12	2	1	.467	.313
Esquerra, Zach	R-R	6-4	215	12-3-90	.204	.173	—	59	201	32	41	12	0	4	25	22	5	0	0	74	5	1	.323	.298
Gebhardt, Ryan	R-R	5-10	185	10-5-91	.266	.222	—	25	79	12	21	6	1	0	11	7	1	0	3	13	1	0	.367	.322
Herum, Marty	R-R	6-3	215	12-16-91	.273	.293	—	83	319	41	87	12	5	4	38	10	1	2	4	53	2	4	.379	.293
Lopez, B.J.	R-R	5-9	185	9-29-94	.202	.258	—	27	89	6	18	0	0	0	12	8	1	3	2	24	1	0	.202	.270
McQuail, Steve	R-R	6-2	225	6-10-89	.304	.250	—	29	112	21	34	6	2	6	20	9	3	0	1	30	0	1	.554	.368
Mitsui, Trevor	R-R	6-5	225	10-1-92	.400	—	—	2	5	1	2	1	0	0	1	0	0	0	0	1	0	0	.600	.400
Munoz, Joe	R-R	6-3	195	12-28-93	.246	.221	—	80	297	48	73	18	1	9	44	31	4	0	5	88	1	1	.404	.320
Nelson, Grant	R-R	6-1	215	9-8-91	.175	.308	—	20	57	5	10	1	1	0	3	8	0	1	0	24	0	0	.228	.277
Palka, Daniel	L-L	6-2	220	10-8-91	.250	.233	—	117	452	62	113	23	5	22	82	55	4	0	6	127	9	3	.469	.333
Parr, Josh	R-R	5-11	170	9-11-89	.077	.000	—	11	39	2	3	0	0	0	2	3	0	1	0	7	1	0	.077	.143
Pena, Fidel	R-R	5-11	165	7-19-91	.267	.250	—	42	150	19	40	5	5	2	20	7	0	1	1	22	2	5	.407	.297
Perez, Michael	L-R	6-0	180	8-7-92	.238	.225	—	98	319	53	76	21	4	9	35	62	2	1	4	92	1	3	.414	.362
Queliz, Jose	R-R	6-3	200	8-7-92	.391	.000	—	6	23	3	9	4	0	0	3	1	0	0	0	8	0	0	.565	.417
Roberts, George	R-R	6-0	206	4-17-90	.235	.295	—	44	166	21	39	6	2	2	11	12	4	0	2	42	8	1	.331	.299

Batting	B-T	HT	WT	DOB	AVG	vLH	vRH	G	AB	R	H	2B	3B	HR	RBI	BB	HBP	SH	SF	SO	SB	CS	SLG	OBP
Taylor, Chuck	B-L	5-9	185	9-21-93	.288	.313	—	108	396	60	114	17	4	3	50	60	5	1	6	74	11	6	.374	.383
Trahan, Stryker	L-R	5-11	215	4-25-94	.198	.116	—	95	368	47	73	21	1	13	52	30	4	1	4	146	3	0	.367	.264
Velazquez, Andrew	B-R	5-8	175	7-14-94	.291	.317	—	133	540	94	157	18	15	9	56	62	7	4	5	135	50	15	.430	.368
Westbrook, Jamie	R-R	5-9	170	6-18-95	.259	.231	—	130	505	69	131	27	4	8	49	38	5	3	6	98	6	3	.376	.314
Williams, Justin	L-R	6-2	215	8-20-95	.286	.308	—	27	98	16	28	6	3	2	22	7	3	0	0	22	0	1	.469	.352

Pitching	B-T	HT	WT	DOB	W	L	ERA	G	GS	CG	SV	IP	H	R	ER	HR	BB	SO	AVG	vLH	vRH	K/9	BB/9
Allen, Brad	L-R	6-4	220	3-26-89	3	0	4.64	4	4	0	0	21	18	11	11	3	10	25	.222	.259	.204	10.55	4.22
2-team total (15 Lansing)					7	5	3.44	19	19	0	0	97	89	41	37	10	33	107	—	—	—	9.96	3.07
Banda, Anthony	L-L	6-2	190	8-10-93	3	0	1.54	6	6	0	0	35	32	7	6	2	7	34	.237	.400	.200	8.74	1.80
2-team total (20 Wisconsin)					9	6	3.03	26	20	0	2	119	116	47	40	6	45	117	—	—	—	8.87	3.41
Blair, Aaron	R-R	6-5	230	5-26-92	1	2	4.04	6	6	1	0	36	25	19	16	2	14	44	.188	.244	.159	11.10	3.53
Bracho, Silvino	R-R	5-11	179	7-14-92	3	2	2.08	45	0	0	26	43	25	10	10	3	8	70	.167	.196	.149	14.54	1.66
Bradley, J.R.	R-R	6-3	185	6-9-92	1	1	0.00	13	0	0	5	12	9	5	0	0	4	21	.205	.167	.231	16.20	3.09
Byo, Alex	R-R	6-2	218	9-2-90	0	0	3.00	10	0	0	0	21	11	8	7	1	7	17	.157	.107	.190	7.29	3.00
Doran, Ryan	R-R	6-1	185	8-5-90	4	0	3.00	6	5	1	0	33	27	12	11	1	4	27	.223	.190	.241	7.36	1.09
Eckels, Ben	R-R	5-11	193	1-27-94	1	2	6.16	5	3	0	0	19	24	13	13	2	15	13	.312	.300	.324	6.16	7.11
Furney, Sean	R-R	6-5	220	6-2-91	9	8	4.22	22	22	1	0	124	144	66	58	11	25	80	.290	.313	.275	5.82	1.82
Gibson, Daniel	R-L	6-2	221	10-16-91	3	2	1.98	37	0	0	3	36	27	8	8	1	14	45	.203	.097	.235	11.15	3.47
Hathaway, Steve	L-L	6-1	185	9-13-90	0	0	3.68	8	0	0	1	15	12	9	6	0	6	18	.207	.188	.214	11.05	3.68
Hernandez, Hector	B-L	6-1	190	2-20-91	5	4	3.45	11	11	0	0	63	68	42	24	4	15	51	.272	.314	.265	7.32	2.15
Jameson, Tom	R-R	6-7	245	8-4-91	1	0	4.05	27	0	0	0	47	50	22	21	3	5	37	.276	.286	.271	7.14	0.96
Jeter, Bud	R-R	6-3	205	10-27-91	4	2	2.43	31	0	0	0	41	46	17	11	0	9	34	.289	.286	.291	7.52	1.99
Jones, Brent	R-R	6-3	215	1-10-93	5	2	2.80	8	8	1	0	35	41	18	11	1	12	27	.285	.353	.224	6.88	3.06
Jose, Jose	L-L	6-2	175	7-21-90	1	1	2.58	38	0	0	0	45	28	16	13	2	17	51	.176	.162	.180	10.13	3.38
Locante, Will	L-L	6-1	190	2-2-90	3	0	1.53	43	0	0	4	53	31	14	9	1	23	57	.168	.064	.204	9.68	3.91
Martinez, Jose	R-R	6-1	160	4-14-94	1	1	6.00	2	2	0	0	6	8	5	4	1	4	3	.348	.385	.300	4.50	6.00
Miller, Adam	R-R	6-0	185	12-28-89	5	1	3.40	24	8	0	0	53	54	23	20	3	19	40	.261	.278	.250	6.79	3.23
Omahen, Johnny	R-R	6-0	190	3-15-89	4	6	3.72	14	10	0	1	65	65	33	27	4	10	46	.257	.256	.258	6.34	1.38
Perry, Blake	R-R	6-5	190	2-3-92	9	6	4.21	25	25	0	0	135	115	68	63	11	66	126	.233	.265	.215	8.42	4.41
Platt, Austin	R-R	6-3	203	3-5-92	1	1	6.67	10	3	0	0	30	36	25	22	5	17	22	.303	.244	.338	6.67	5.16
Roberts, Jake	R-R	6-0	215	1-25-91	1	1	2.84	12	0	0	1	13	7	7	4	1	9	11	.163	.167	.160	7.82	6.39
Sarianides, Nick	R-R	6-1	200	8-29-89	1	1	2.33	20	0	0	1	27	22	9	7	3	9	31	.210	.216	.206	10.33	3.00
Schepel, Kyle	L-R	6-1	230	8-7-90	1	1	1.50	13	0	0	1	18	13	4	3	1	10	16	.197	.167	.208	8.00	5.00
Shipley, Braden	R-R	6-3	190	2-22-92	4	2	3.74	8	8	0	0	46	46	22	19	1	11	41	.263	.291	.240	8.08	2.17
Shuttlesworth, Johnny	R-R	6-1	220	9-30-89	2	2	3.98	21	0	0	0	32	37	14	14	3	10	28	.301	.300	.301	7.96	2.84
Slaats, Josh	R-R	6-5	225	12-22-88	0	1	4.15	1	1	0	0	4	3	3	2	0	3	2	.167	.143	.182	4.15	6.23
Solbach, Markus	R-R	6-5	205	8-26-91	2	2	4.45	5	5	1	0	28	34	15	14	2	4	17	.271	.242	.297	5.40	1.27
Weller, Blayne	R-R	6-5	220	1-30-90	5	4	4.03	21	11	1	0	83	82	41	37	7	29	91	.259	.278	.249	9.91	3.16

Fielding

Catcher	PCT	G	PO	A	E	DP	PB
Lopez	.996	27	201	24	1	0	3
Nelson	1.000	20	115	20	0	0	1
Perez	.993	89	756	73	6	6	10
Queliz	.977	4	36	7	1	0	0
Trahan	.920	4	20	3	2	0	0

First Base	PCT	G	PO	A	E	DP
Herum	.997	35	288	16	1	26
McQuail	.970	5	30	2	1	4
Palka	.988	93	831	67	11	57
Roberts	1.000	8	63	1	0	3
Westbrook	1.000	1	5	0	0	1

Second Base	PCT	G	PO	A	E	DP
Gebhardt	1.000	9	12	30	0	8
Palka	.833	1	1	4	1	1

	PCT	G	PO	A	E	DP
Parr	.933	4	1	13	1	2
Pena	1.000	8	13	30	0	5
Westbrook	.956	119	194	308	23	59

Third Base	PCT	G	PO	A	E	DP
Ard	1.000	1	1	0	0	0
Bell	1.000	1	2	3	0	0
Gebhardt	1.000	11	9	17	0	1
Herum	.921	30	17	53	6	4
McQuail	1.000	2	2	1	0	1
Munoz	.878	63	29	122	21	6
Parr	1.000	4	5	5	0	0
Pena	1.000	7	5	21	0	0
Roberts	.982	22	7	47	1	5

Shortstop	PCT	G	PO	A	E	DP
Gebhardt	1.000	4	11	8	0	4

	PCT	G	PO	A	E	DP
Munoz	.893	7	11	14	3	3
Parr	.667	2	1	1	1	0
Velazquez	.941	129	188	372	35	65

Outfield	PCT	G	PO	A	E	DP
Almadova	.996	89	234	12	1	3
Bowman	1.000	25	59	0	0	0
Bray	1.000	9	12	1	0	0
Esquerra	.950	49	70	6	4	1
Palka	1.000	12	26	5	0	0
Parr	1.000	1	1	0	0	0
Pena	.951	21	36	3	2	1
Taylor	.981	103	148	5	3	0
Trahan	.951	84	124	13	7	2
Williams	1.000	27	44	3	0	0

HILLSBORO HOPS

NORTHWEST LEAGUE

Batting	B-T	HT	WT	DOB	AVG	vLH	vRH	G	AB	R	H	2B	3B	HR	RBI	BB	HBP	SH	SF	SO	SB	CS	SLG	OBP
Ard, Taylor	R-R	6-2	230	1-31-90	.267	—	—	10	30	7	8	1	0	1	3	9	1	0	0	5	0	0	.400	.450
Baker, Tyler	L-R	5-9	179	3-8-93	.250	.321	—	23	84	10	21	3	1	1	10	10	1	0	0	15	1	2	.345	.337
Carrasco, Cesar	R-R	6-2	185	10-3-93	.192	.250	—	7	26	2	5	3	0	0	4	1	0	0	1	8	0	0	.308	.214
Cribbs, Galli	L-R	6-0	170	10-8-92	.191	.226	—	40	110	15	21	2	0	0	14	12	3	1	2	37	7	4	.209	.283
Cron, Kevin	R-R	6-5	245	2-17-93	.287	.324	—	31	129	23	37	8	0	6	17	10	1	0	2	29	0	0	.488	.338
Esquerra, Zach	R-R	6-4	215	12-3-90	.167	.185	—	26	96	9	16	4	1	2	15	8	2	0	0	39	3	0	.292	.245
Garcia, Yorman	R-R	6-1	197	3-17-94	.229	.304	—	20	70	9	16	2	0	1	8	5	1	1	0	15	5	1	.300	.289
Glaesmann, Todd	R-R	6-4	220	10-24-90	.404	—	—	14	57	12	23	8	0	2	9	4	0	0	0	18	0	0	.649	.443
Gonzalez, Justin	R-R	6-2	191	6-24-91	.198	.262	—	40	131	21	26	4	1	6	19	20	2	2	0	49	1	3	.382	.314
Heyman, Grant	L-R	6-4	209	11-7-93	.315	—	—	57	222	31	70	10	0	5	37	7	8	0	2	58	8	1	.428	.356
Ijames, Stewart	L-R	6-0	220	8-21-88	.143	.250	—	2	7	3	1	0	0	0	0	1	0	0	0	3	0	0	.143	.250
Irving, Nate	R-R	6-0	235	10-17-92	.190	.250	—	8	21	5	4	1	0	0	1	4	2	1	1	8	1	0	.238	.357
Mayers, Jacob	R-R	6-1	215	8-8-90	.296	.231	—	32	125	14	37	6	2	0	10	11	2	0	0	31	1	3	.376	.362
Nyisztor, Steve	R-R	6-1	200	5-2-91	.309	.314	—	44	178	32	55	12	4	3	23	14	4	2	2	28	10	3	.472	.369

	B-T	HT	WT	DOB	AVG	vLH	vRH	G	AB	R	H	2B	3B	HR	RBI	BB	HBP	SH	SF	SO	SB	CS	SLG	OBP
Parr, Jordan	R-R	6-2	195	11-29-90	.265	.308	—	62	226	35	60	16	0	6	26	23	4	2	2	53	17	5	.416	.341
Ratliff, Taylor	L-R	6-2	161	6-25-92	.191	.113	—	57	188	33	36	2	1	1	17	31	3	4	5	52	19	7	.229	.308
Roberts, George	R-R	6-0	206	4-17-90	.276	.318	—	21	76	6	21	6	0	0	19	7	0	0	3	14	4	1	.355	.326
Robertson, Nate	R-R	6-2	200	11-16-92	.235	.254	—	57	200	27	47	5	0	0	14	12	1	3	0	55	15	3	.260	.282
Robinson, Bennie	L-R	6-3	219	10-1-90	.235	.182	—	23	81	11	19	1	0	0	9	11	1	0	0	8	2	1	.247	.333
Ruiz, Pedro	B-R	5-9	186	8-30-91	.244	.224	—	62	234	30	57	11	1	4	28	32	4	7	2	48	7	2	.350	.342
Soto, Elvin	B-R	5-10	210	2-12-92	.256	.167	—	51	180	26	46	10	5	3	23	20	1	2	1	43	2	4	.417	.332
Trahan, Stryker	L-R	5-11	215	4-25-94	.257	.242	—	30	113	15	29	7	1	6	22	15	1	0	2	23	2	2	.496	.344

Pitching	B-T	HT	WT	DOB	W	L	ERA	G	GS	CG	SV	IP	H	R	ER	HR	BB	SO	AVG	vLH	vRH	K/9	BB/9
Anderson, Kyle	R-L	6-2	205	5-24-90	2	3	3.99	12	4	0	0	29	32	15	13	1	9	22	.286	.194	.329	6.75	2.76
Baker, Nick	R-R	6-1	190	8-2-92	3	1	3.20	16	5	0	1	56	64	22	20	5	2	38	.282	.253	.300	6.07	0.32
Byo, Alex	R-R	6-2	218	9-2-90	2	0	2.33	10	0	0	0	19	19	7	5	0	7	13	.264	.250	.271	6.05	3.26
Cetta, Mike	R-R	5-11	198	12-30-92	2	3	6.51	19	1	0	0	28	45	31	20	3	17	22	.360	.458	.299	7.16	5.53
Curtis, Zac	L-L	5-9	179	7-4-92	2	1	1.00	24	0	0	14	27	18	5	3	0	12	42	.188	.222	.174	14.00	4.00
Doran, Ryan	R-R	6-1	185	8-5-90	4	3	2.56	10	10	0	0	63	69	24	18	3	10	48	.278	.250	.290	6.82	1.42
Eckels, Ben	R-R	5-11	193	1-27-94	3	1	2.66	10	10	0	0	47	38	14	14	0	14	57	.222	.187	.250	10.84	2.66
Geyer, Cody	R-R	5-10	224	5-4-92	3	1	3.77	26	0	0	3	31	24	17	13	0	19	23	.211	.139	.244	6.68	5.52
Jones, Brent	R-R	6-3	215	1-10-93	2	1	3.90	6	6	0	0	28	22	12	12	2	10	18	.218	.313	.174	5.86	3.25
Keller, Brad	R-R	6-5	230	7-27-95	1	0	0.00	1	1	0	0	6	1	0	0	0	1	8	.053	.000	.125	12.00	1.50
Loggins, Dustin	R-R	6-4	223	8-1-90	1	1	1.18	27	0	0	4	38	21	5	5	1	18	47	.164	.196	.143	11.13	4.26
McCullough, Mason	R-R	6-4	245	1-7-93	1	0	3.55	13	0	0	1	13	6	5	5	0	12	16	.146	.154	.143	11.37	8.53
Miller, Jared	L-L	6-7	240	8-21-93	1	1	3.58	8	5	0	0	28	21	11	11	3	9	21	.204	.229	.191	6.83	2.93
Pedrotty, John	L-L	6-4	219	11-28-89	0	2	16.20	7	0	0	0	8	12	15	15	0	15	5	.333	.400	.323	5.40	16.20
Perez, Felipe	R-R	6-3	200	1-22-94	3	0	2.14	4	4	0	0	21	20	7	5	0	5	12	.256	.182	.286	5.14	2.14
Placido, Anderson	L-L	6-0	190	9-24-93	2	0	2.35	3	3	0	0	15	11	4	4	1	8	18	.212	—	.212	10.57	4.70
Platt, Austin	R-R	6-3	203	3-5-92	3	3	6.49	13	11	0	0	53	59	48	38	5	27	41	.268	.284	.258	7.01	4.61
Ramirez, Luis	R-R	6-3	240	7-12-92	0	0	2.08	13	0	0	1	13	9	3	3	0	4	17	.191	.059	.267	11.77	2.77
Roberts, Jake	R-R	6-0	215	1-25-91	0	0	5.40	4	0	0	1	3	6	3	2	0	4	2	.375	.000	.462	5.40	10.80
Savas, Dan	R-R	6-5	241	7-11-92	3	0	3.98	21	1	0	0	43	38	21	19	2	18	37	.236	.193	.260	7.74	3.77
Schultz, Scott	R-R	6-2	212	12-15-91	5	5	4.57	14	12	0	0	69	81	41	35	3	20	37	.297	.292	.300	4.83	2.61
Solbach, Markus	R-R	6-5	205	8-26-91	2	1	2.57	4	3	0	0	21	16	8	6	2	1	16	.203	.212	.196	6.86	0.43
Toyfair, Tyler	R-R	6-5	230	4-12-90	0	1	5.50	10	0	0	0	18	17	11	11	0	6	18	.274	.381	.220	9.00	3.00
Wort, Rob	R-R	6-1	155	2-7-89	3	0	1.04	7	0	0	0	9	6	1	1	1	2	13	.194	.308	.111	13.50	2.08

Fielding

Catcher	PCT	G	PO	A	E	DP	PB
Baker	.986	19	115	29	2	1	0
Irving	.986	8	62	6	1	0	1
Soto	.985	39	297	25	5	2	6
Trahan	.977	15	111	16	3	2	3

First Base	PCT	G	PO	A	E	DP
Ard	.917	2	10	1	1	0
Carrasco	1.000	1	4	1	0	1
Cron	.990	27	268	23	3	22
Mayers	.987	16	137	15	2	12
Parr	1.000	5	43	2	0	5
Roberts	.988	8	81	2	1	7
Robinson	1.000	20	166	6	0	12

Second Base	PCT	G	PO	A	E	DP
Cribbs	1.000	24	39	73	0	15

	PCT	G	PO	A	E	DP
Nyisztor	.976	21	26	57	2	10
Ruiz	.948	33	69	94	9	20

Third Base	PCT	G	PO	A	E	DP
Ard	1.000	5	2	7	0	1
Carrasco	1.000	1	0	1	0	0
Cron	.667	1	0	2	1	0
Gonzalez	.833	4	1	9	2	2
Mayers	.750	5	3	15	6	1
Roberts	1.000	11	6	20	0	2
Robertson	.913	38	15	58	7	2
Ruiz	.974	15	10	28	1	3

Shortstop	PCT	G	PO	A	E	DP
Cribbs	.947	14	16	38	3	7
Gonzalez	.914	36	53	118	16	17
Nyisztor	.875	1	4	3	1	1

	PCT	G	PO	A	E	DP
Robertson	.942	15	15	34	3	7
Ruiz	1.000	16	25	56	0	6

Outfield	PCT	G	PO	A	E	DP
Esquerra	.902	23	35	2	4	0
Garcia	.925	18	34	3	3	0
Glaesmann	1.000	11	20	1	0	1
Heyman	.966	48	84	0	3	0
Ijames	1.000	2	6	0	0	0
Nyisztor	.920	19	22	1	2	0
Parr	.974	50	107	5	3	2
Ratliff	.976	55	118	5	3	1
Robertson	1.000	1	2	0	0	0
Trahan	1.000	6	7	1	0	1

AZL DIAMONDBACKS   ROOKIE

ARIZONA LEAGUE

Batting	B-T	HT	WT	DOB	AVG	vLH	vRH	G	AB	R	H	2B	3B	HR	RBI	BB	HBP	SH	SF	SO	SB	CS	SLG	OBP
Abreu, Mike	R-R	5-11	185	9-29-93	.130	.000	—	10	23	0	3	0	0	0	2	3	1	0	0	10	1	1	.130	.259
Branigan, Michael	R-R	5-10	175	1-9-96	.136	.000	—	10	22	1	3	0	0	0	3	2	1	0	0	2	0	0	.136	.240
Castillo, Henry	B-R	6-0	180	12-8-94	.331	—	—	28	124	22	41	6	9	1	22	1	3	1	0	29	1	2	.548	.352
Clark, Tyler	B-R	6-5	210	3-30-92	.333	—	—	7	24	5	8	1	1	0	2	3	0	0	1	5	2	0	.458	.393
Cordero, Jacob	R-R	5-10	174	11-14-94	.263	—	—	38	114	15	30	4	1	0	15	22	3	2	1	29	6	4	.316	.393
Diaz, Isan	L-R	5-10	185	5-27-96	.187	.156	—	49	182	22	34	7	5	3	21	25	2	1	2	56	6	5	.330	.289
Dorn, Danny	L-L	6-2	205	7-20-84	.500	—	—	2	8	3	4	2	0	0	3	0	0	0	1	1	0	0	.750	.444
Garcia, Yorman	R-R	6-1	197	3-17-94	.284	—	—	19	67	11	19	5	1	0	9	6	2	0	1	13	1	1	.388	.355
Graciano, Vicson	R-R	6-1	155	11-23-95	.194	.083	—	32	93	8	18	2	0	0	10	14	0	0	2	27	0	1	.215	.294
Haniger, Mitch	R-R	6-2	215	12-23-90	.200	.250	—	4	15	4	3	1	0	1	4	1	0	0	0	6	0	0	.467	.250
Hernandez, Gerard	L-L	5-10	195	10-16-94	.293	.132	—	47	184	29	54	4	6	1	24	8	2	1	1	48	4	2	.397	.328
Herrera, Jose	B-R	5-10	185	2-24-97	.227	.273	—	43	154	24	35	4	1	0	14	23	4	0	3	37	1	0	.266	.337
Ijames, Stewart	L-R	6-0	220	8-21-88	.267	—	—	5	15	4	4	2	0	0	3	3	0	0	0	4	0	0	.400	.389
McPhearson, Matt	L-L	5-8	164	5-12-96	.281	.265	—	43	160	32	45	2	0	0	16	23	4	2	2	43	23	3	.294	.381
Munoz, Joe	R-R	6-3	195	12-28-93	.294	—	—	4	17	1	5	0	0	0	2	3	0	0	0	3	0	0	.294	.368
Owings, Chris	R-R	5-10	190	8-12-91	.571	—	—	3	7	1	4	0	0	0	2	3	0	0	0	5	0	0	.571	.700
Pacheco, Jordan	R-R	6-1	205	1-30-86	.250	—	—	4	12	1	3	0	0	0	3	2	0	0	1	2	0	0	.250	.333
Pena, Ismael	L-L	6-3	175	12-15-95	.193	.132	—	46	166	24	32	2	4	2	18	25	2	0	3	40	0	1	.289	.301
Pennington, Cliff	B-R	5-10	195	6-15-84	.421	—	—	5	19	2	8	1	0	0	5	3	0	0	0	4	0	0	.474	.500

Name	B-T	HT	WT	DOB	AVG	vLH	vRH	G	AB	R	H	2B	3B	HR	RBI	BB	HBP	SH	SF	SO	SB	CS	SLG	OBP
Pollock, A.J.	R-R	6-1	195	12-5-87	.333	—	—	2	3	0	1	1	0	0	0	0	1	0	0	1	0	0	.667	.500
Rondon, Alvaro	B-R	5-10	160	9-6-90	.286	—	—	19	77	16	22	4	1	0	2	4	0	0	0	13	4	0	.364	.321
Samboy, Raul	R-R	5-11	155	9-25-93	.240	.282	—	42	154	24	37	10	6	1	18	15	1	0	4	56	2	0	.403	.305
Sanchez, Richi	L-R	5-10	185	5-6-94	.233	.167	—	24	60	6	14	1	0	0	3	10	0	1	0	14	0	0	.250	.343
Trumbo, Mark	R-R	6-4	235	1-16-86	.462	—	—	4	13	5	6	1	0	2	6	1	0	0	0	3	0	0	1.000	.500
Veras, Luis	R-R	6-1	180	11-4-93	.385	—	—	17	65	8	25	5	0	1	14	3	0	0	1	21	0	1	.508	.406
Wilson, Marcus	R-R	6-3	175	8-15-96	.206	.219	—	39	131	15	27	2	2	1	22	16	1	0	0	40	4	2	.275	.297

Pitching	B-T	HT	WT	DOB	W	L	ERA	G	GS	CG	SV	IP	H	R	ER	HR	BB	SO	AVG	vLH	vRH	K/9	BB/9
Anderson, Kyle	R-L	6-2	205	5-24-90	0	0	0.00	1	0	0	0	2	1	0	0	0	0	2	.143	.000	.167	9.00	0.00
Barbosa, Andrew	R-L	6-8	205	11-18-87	0	0	0.00	1	0	0	0	2	2	0	0	0	1	2	.222	.500	.143	9.00	4.50
Basora, Anthony	L-L	6-4	205	2-17-95	1	2	6.75	12	0	0	0	15	25	19	11	3	4	11	.373	.375	.373	6.75	2.45
Bazzani, Anthony	R-R	6-5	215	10-7-90	0	1	2.35	8	0	0	3	8	5	4	2	0	2	6	.185	.250	.133	7.04	2.35
Benitez, Anfernee	L-L	6-1	176	7-24-95	2	5	3.38	15	6	0	0	56	47	31	21	3	16	50	.229	.182	.247	8.04	2.57
Bradley, Archie	R-R	6-4	235	8-10-92	0	0	4.50	1	1	0	0	4	5	2	2	0	1	6	.278	.286	.273	13.50	2.25
Cancio, Roberto	L-L	6-1	160	8-8-95	0	0	4.00	9	0	0	0	9	7	4	4	0	12	9	.219	.429	.160	9.00	12.00
Castillo, Luis	R-R	6-2	180	3-10-95	3	3	4.40	15	1	0	2	43	57	25	21	2	7	30	.322	.323	.322	6.28	1.47
Clark, Cody	R-R	6-2	215	7-22-93	1	0	2.00	9	0	0	4	9	7	2	2	0	2	8	.212	.286	.158	8.00	2.00
Godfrey, Graham	R-R	6-3	215	8-9-84	1	0	1.13	4	0	0	0	8	8	3	1	0	4	5	.276	.429	.227	5.63	4.50
Helmink, Holden	R-R	6-4	180	11-10-93	0	0	4.50	2	0	0	0	2	2	1	1	0	2	3	.333	1.000	.200	13.50	9.00
Hudson, Daniel	R-R	6-3	225	3-9-87	0	0	2.25	4	4	0	0	4	4	1	1	0	0	5	.250	.000	.308	11.25	0.00
Keller, Brad	R-R	6-5	230	7-27-95	4	0	2.30	6	3	0	0	31	30	8	8	2	9	20	.265	.179	.294	5.74	2.59
Kostuk, Kurtis	L-R	6-2	200	9-8-95	0	1	22.24	6	0	0	0	6	13	15	14	0	8	3	.448	.364	.500	4.76	12.71
Medick, Spencer	L-L	6-3	220	5-23-91	3	0	1.17	15	0	0	2	31	29	6	4	1	5	32	.250	.261	.247	9.39	1.47
Miller, Adam	R-R	6-0	185	12-28-89	0	0	0.00	3	0	0	0	3	1	0	0	0	0	6	.111	.000	.143	18.00	0.00
Montero, Merkis	R-R	6-2	155	12-1-95	2	2	5.03	4	0	0	0	20	23	14	11	1	6	17	.295	.258	.319	7.78	2.75
Newton, Dallas	L-R	6-5	215	9-3-94	1	1	3.78	3	2	0	0	17	9	9	7	1	5	13	.148	.053	.190	7.02	2.50
Perez, Felipe	R-R	6-3	200	1-22-94	0	1	5.23	6	0	0	0	21	30	12	12	0	5	14	.361	.286	.417	6.10	2.18
Perez, Gabriel	R-R	6-0	185	6-3-91	2	1	1.89	4	2	0	0	19	12	6	4	0	5	28	.171	.316	.118	13.26	2.37
Potter, Andrew	R-R	6-0	208	2-9-94	0	0	9.00	10	0	0	0	15	22	16	15	1	8	14	.344	.292	.375	8.59	4.91
Ramirez, Luis	R-R	6-3	240	7-12-92	0	0	0.00	3	0	0	0	3	2	3	0	0	3	4	.200	.000	.222	13.50	10.13
Ramirez, Yefrey	R-R	6-2	165	11-28-93	4	2	1.93	7	4	0	0	37	26	9	8	0	4	48	.186	.260	.144	11.57	0.96
Reed, Cody	L-L	6-3	245	6-7-96	0	1	2.18	10	7	0	0	21	17	7	5	0	5	26	.218	.182	.232	11.32	2.18
Roberts, Jake	R-R	6-0	215	1-25-91	0	0	2.00	7	0	0	0	9	8	2	2	0	1	1	.242	.333	.208	1.00	1.00
Rodriguez, Santos	L-L	6-6	190	1-2-88	0	0	0.00	2	2	0	0	2	3	0	0	0	0	2	.375	1.000	.286	9.00	0.00
Smith, Josh	R-R	6-3	181	7-8-96	1	0	10.80	5	0	0	0	3	5	4	4	0	3	3	.313	.800	.091	8.10	8.10
Spruill, Zeke	R-R	6-5	190	9-11-89	0	2	7.50	3	2	0	0	6	8	5	5	0	1	6	.320	.300	.333	9.00	1.50
Takahashi, Rodrigo	R-R	5-11	180	1-23-97	3	4	4.39	10	4	0	0	41	34	22	20	1	12	34	.224	.211	.235	7.46	2.63
Toussaint, Touki	R-R	6-3	185	6-20-96	1	1	4.80	7	5	0	0	15	14	12	8	0	12	17	.237	.130	.306	10.20	7.20
Wasserman, Zak	L-L	6-6	225	8-30-90	0	0	3.60	16	0	0	2	25	25	14	10	2	2	20	.243	.250	.241	7.20	0.72
Woodall, Bryan	R-R	6-1	200	10-24-86	0	0	0.00	3	3	0	0	3	2	0	0	0	0	6	.167	.250	.125	18.00	0.00

Fielding

Catcher	PCT	G	PO	A	E	DP	PB
Branigan	1.000	5	38	9	0	0	5
Clark	.967	4	27	2	1	0	0
Herrera	.982	41	331	42	7	3	7
Sanchez	.984	12	52	11	1	0	4

First Base	PCT	G	PO	A	E	DP
Clark	1.000	1	8	1	0	2
Cordero	1.000	1	3	0	0	1
Dorn	1.000	1	10	3	0	3
Graciano	1.000	1	7	1	0	0
Pena	.984	29	226	17	4	22
Samboy	.978	25	209	12	5	19

Second Base	PCT	G	PO	A	E	DP
Abreu	1.000	6	10	10	0	2
Castillo	.948	23	45	64	6	9

	PCT	G	PO	A	E	DP
Cordero	1.000	6	9	7	0	3
Diaz	.920	11	18	28	4	6
Owings	1.000	1	0	4	0	4
Pacheco	1.000	2	1	2	0	0
Rondon	.978	9	24	21	1	6
Sanchez	1.000	6	12	12	0	4

Third Base	PCT	G	PO	A	E	DP
Abreu	1.000	1	0	2	0	0
Castillo	1.000	2	0	2	0	1
Cordero	.899	26	21	50	8	5
Graciano	.889	28	11	37	6	3
Samboy	.846	4	2	9	2	0

Shortstop	PCT	G	PO	A	E	DP
Cordero	.884	8	13	25	5	6
Diaz	.925	39	54	93	12	23

	PCT	G	PO	A	E	DP
Owings	1.000	2	2	2	0	0
Pennington	.917	3	3	8	1	2
Rondon	.913	10	12	30	4	8

Outfield	PCT	G	PO	A	E	DP
Garcia	1.000	17	29	3	0	1
Haniger	1.000	2	6	0	0	0
Hernandez	.912	44	77	6	8	0
Ijames	1.000	4	7	1	0	0
McPhearson	.965	42	78	4	3	0
Pena	.955	11	20	1	1	0
Pollock	1.000	2	1	0	0	0
Samboy	.944	13	17	0	1	0
Trumbo	1.000	2	1	0	0	0
Veras	.933	6	12	2	1	1
Wilson	1.000	37	76	3	0	2

MISSOULA OSPREY   ROOKIE

PIONEER LEAGUE

Batting	B-T	HT	WT	DOB	AVG	vLH	vRH	G	AB	R	H	2B	3B	HR	RBI	BB	HBP	SH	SF	SO	SB	CS	SLG	OBP
Abreu, Mike	R-R	5-11	185	9-29-93	.171	.222	—	13	41	4	7	1	0	0	2	2	2	1	0	7	3	0	.195	.244
Alcantara, Sergio	B-R	5-10	150	7-10-96	.244	.200	—	70	266	48	65	11	0	1	18	48	1	4	1	62	8	4	.297	.361
Ard, Taylor	R-R	6-2	230	1-31-90	.342	—	—	22	76	8	26	7	1	3	16	6	5	0	1	16	0	0	.579	.420
Baker, Tyler	L-R	5-9	179	3-8-93	.291	.158	—	23	86	8	25	6	0	3	14	5	1	0	0	25	0	1	.465	.337
Castillo, Henry	B-R	6-0	180	12-8-94	.271	.318	—	24	85	7	23	3	0	1	4	5	0	0	0	16	1	1	.341	.311
Clark, Tyler	B-R	6-5	210	3-30-92	.263	.167	—	10	38	5	10	2	1	1	6	2	0	0	0	8	1	0	.447	.300
Cron, Kevin	R-R	6-5	245	2-17-93	.295	.300	—	33	132	31	39	10	0	6	28	10	7	0	1	16	0	0	.508	.373
Ehmcke, Maik	L-L	6-2	200	7-14-94	.221	.156	—	47	136	20	30	5	1	0	3	14	2	1	0	34	4	2	.272	.303
Gutierrez, Yosbel	R-R	5-10	170	1-20-93	.250	.250	—	18	56	6	14	1	1	2	14	7	3	0	1	17	0	0	.411	.358
Hernandez, Gerard	L-L	5-10	195	10-16-95	.405	.222	—	10	37	6	15	3	1	1	9	2	0	1	1	5	1	1	.622	.444
Herrera, Jose	B-R	5-10	185	2-24-97	.286	—	—	2	7	2	2	1	0	0	2	1	2	0	0	0	2	0	.429	.444
Humphreys, Tyler	R-R	6-2	212	9-23-93	.233	.250	—	51	180	11	42	9	1	0	20	13	1	1	1	52	2	1	.294	.287

Name	B-T	HT	WT	DOB	AVG	vLH	vRH	G	AB	R	H	2B	3B	HR	RBI	BB	HBP	SH	SF	SO	SB	CS	SLG	OBP
Ijames, Stewart	L-R	6-0	220	8-21-88	.327	—	—	30	101	26	33	3	0	12	36	22	1	0	1	26	0	0	.713	.448
Lopez, B.J.	R-R	5-9	185	9-29-94	.252	.160	—	33	119	7	30	2	0	1	11	7	2	2	0	24	0	1	.294	.305
Mayers, Jacob	R-R	6-1	215	8-8-90	.385	—	—	11	39	5	15	1	1	0	2	5	1	0	1	8	1	1	.462	.457
McFarland, Dane	R-R	6-4	210	10-24-94	.253	.269	—	66	241	38	61	8	3	7	29	14	3	0	3	79	15	4	.398	.299
Mitsui, Trevor	R-R	6-5	225	10-1-92	.330	.308	—	68	264	46	87	17	2	12	52	16	9	0	1	60	1	3	.545	.386
Nelson, Grant	R-R	6-1	215	9-8-91	.500	—	—	1	2	0	1	0	0	0	1	2	0	0	0	1	0	0	.500	.750
Ozuna, Fernery	B-R	5-8	165	11-9-95	.264	.237	—	73	303	54	80	14	2	7	28	19	1	2	4	55	4	3	.393	.306
Railey, Matt	L-L	5-11	190	3-16-95	.267	—	—	13	45	7	12	5	1	2	7	4	0	0	0	7	1	1	.556	.327
Robinson, Bennie	L-R	6-3	219	10-1-90	.222	.111	—	15	45	5	10	1	0	1	3	3	0	0	0	8	1	0	.311	.271
Smith, Damion	L-R	6-3	170	2-14-94	.235	.267	—	30	85	9	20	4	0	0	12	11	1	1	0	29	1	1	.282	.330
Williams, Justin	L-R	6-2	215	8-20-95	.386	—	—	46	189	31	73	6	2	2	23	17	0	0	2	44	1	1	.471	.433

Pitching	B-T	HT	WT	DOB	W	L	ERA	G	GS	CG	SV	IP	H	R	ER	HR	BB	SO	AVG	vLH	vRH	K/9	BB/9
Bazzani, Anthony	R-R	6-5	215	10-7-90	1	1	3.09	11	0	0	4	12	7	4	4	1	4	14	.171	.091	.263	10.80	3.09
Bolton, Tyler	R-R	6-4	205	1-27-93	5	4	6.00	15	12	0	0	72	101	56	48	10	19	54	.334	.356	.317	6.75	2.38
Brooks, Eric	R-R	6-2	200	8-29-90	0	0	1.42	3	0	0	0	6	4	1	1	0	1	6	.190	.167	.200	8.53	1.42
Cape, Derek	R-R	6-3	190	5-22-90	0	3	5.67	22	0	0	0	33	43	25	21	3	10	36	.319	.295	.338	9.72	2.70
Clark, Cody	R-R	6-2	215	7-22-93	0	0	1.80	10	0	0	0	10	5	4	2	0	6	15	.152	.167	.133	13.50	5.40
Greer, Brody	R-R	6-1	190	5-15-91	1	2	4.94	25	0	0	10	27	30	18	15	4	15	37	.278	.235	.316	12.18	4.94
Helmink, Holden	R-R	6-4	180	11-10-93	0	1	4.50	12	0	0	0	14	12	8	7	2	10	11	.222	.286	.182	7.07	6.43
Hernandez, Carlos	R-R	5-11	170	4-26-94	5	4	4.22	14	14	0	0	70	76	42	33	4	36	61	.288	.262	.310	7.81	4.61
Keller, Brad	R-R	6-5	230	7-27-95	1	4	6.95	8	8	0	0	34	50	31	26	6	18	30	.347	.254	.429	8.02	4.81
Landsheft, Will	R-R	6-1	205	7-27-92	1	0	4.41	22	0	0	1	33	32	18	16	1	15	34	.256	.241	.268	9.37	4.13
Mateo, Wagner	L-L	6-2	190	3-30-93	1	0	8.16	12	0	0	0	14	8	13	13	0	19	17	.170	.227	.120	10.67	11.93
Moya, Gabriel	L-L	6-0	175	1-9-95	5	4	6.00	15	12	0	0	63	82	47	42	8	19	67	.318	.295	.329	9.71	2.71
Newton, Dallas	L-R	6-5	215	9-3-94	4	5	5.13	11	11	0	0	53	58	42	30	7	18	40	.274	.321	.242	6.84	3.08
Pardo, Lawrence	L-L	6-0	180	10-22-91	1	1	4.79	18	0	0	0	21	14	11	11	3	12	23	.187	.091	.226	10.02	5.23
Ramirez, Yefrey	R-R	6-2	165	11-28-93	2	1	4.45	6	6	0	0	30	32	16	15	8	7	17	.271	.298	.246	5.04	2.08
Reed, Cody	L-L	6-3	245	6-7-96	0	1	2.25	4	4	0	0	12	3	3	3	1	7	14	.081	.091	.077	10.50	5.25
Simmons, Kevin	R-R	6-1	185	9-1-93	2	3	3.61	18	0	0	2	47	39	23	19	9	11	43	.222	.254	.202	8.18	2.09
Solbach, Markus	R-R	6-5	205	8-26-91	2	2	5.33	6	4	0	0	25	30	16	15	2	5	22	.300	.250	.339	7.82	1.78
Solis, Jency	R-R	6-1	180	2-22-93	3	1	4.95	27	0	0	2	40	36	25	22	3	10	34	.247	.302	.205	7.65	2.25
Toussaint, Touki	R-R	6-3	185	6-20-96	1	3	12.51	5	5	0	0	14	24	22	19	5	6	15	.381	.217	.475	9.88	3.95
Toyfair, Tyler	R-R	6-5	230	4-12-90	1	0	4.50	14	0	0	1	18	24	16	9	2	6	21	.308	.300	.313	10.50	3.00

Fielding

Catcher	PCT	G	PO	A	E	DP	PB
Baker	.994	20	148	23	1	1	2
Clark	1.000	6	48	4	0	0	1
Gutierrez	.978	15	108	26	3	3	2
Herrera	1.000	2	21	2	0	0	0
Lopez	.990	33	266	42	3	2	10
Nelson	1.000	1	9	0	0	0	0

First Base	PCT	G	PO	A	E	DP
Ard	1.000	8	62	5	0	7
Cron	.985	22	185	11	3	18
Mayers	1.000	4	28	7	0	2
Mitsui	.987	42	368	20	5	34

Robinson	—	1	0	0	0	0

Second Base	PCT	G	PO	A	E	DP
Abreu	.944	9	22	12	2	2
Castillo	.870	11	16	24	6	5
Ozuna	.962	57	96	158	10	35

Third Base	PCT	G	PO	A	E	DP
Ard	.893	13	8	17	3	1
Humphreys	.935	50	35	95	9	7
Mayers	.778	4	4	3	2	1
Ozuna	.913	10	6	15	2	1

Shortstop	PCT	G	PO	A	E	DP
Alcantara	.950	70	114	225	18	42

	PCT	G	PO	A	E	DP
Ozuna	.971	7	17	16	1	5

Outfield	PCT	G	PO	A	E	DP
Clark	—	3	0	0	0	0
Ehmcke	.985	44	62	2	1	0
Hernandez	.875	10	11	3	2	0
Ijames	.932	30	39	2	3	0
McFarland	.945	66	108	13	7	2
Railey	1.000	13	11	0	0	0
Smith	.979	27	44	2	1	0
Williams	.986	45	68	5	1	0

DSL DIAMONDBACKS   ROOKIE

DOMINICAN SUMMER LEAGUE

Batting	B-T	HT	WT	DOB	AVG	vLH	vRH	G	AB	R	H	2B	3B	HR	RBI	BB	HBP	SH	SF	SO	SB	CS	SLG	OBP
Alcantara, Frankies	R-R	6-1	190	8-23-95	.203	.261	—	35	118	17	24	9	1	1	15	14	8	0	1	46	3	3	.322	.326
Bracho, Didimo	R-R	5-11	170	9-2-96	.272	.238	—	61	217	44	59	10	0	2	30	31	10	0	3	45	37	14	.346	.383
De Leon, Jose	R-R	6-2	160	8-9-95	.222	.176	—	18	54	7	12	2	0	0	7	4	1	0	0	13	3	1	.259	.288
Feliciano, Frangel	B-R	6-2	190	4-8-96	.151	.125	—	15	53	4	8	1	1	0	3	7	1	0	0	21	0	1	.208	.262
Garcia, Oswaldo	R-R	6-3	210	11-28-95	.232	.225	—	53	198	21	46	10	3	0	29	21	5	0	5	33	4	2	.313	.314
Hernandez, Ramon	R-R	6-4	195	3-2-96	.230	.196	—	63	239	30	55	12	2	3	35	28	8	0	2	47	0	3	.335	.329
Herrera, Josue	R-R	6-0	165	2-3-97	.178	.231	—	17	45	4	8	2	0	0	3	11	2	0	0	7	0	0	.222	.362
Jimenez, Gerson	R-R	6-1	200	12-2-94	.251	.154	—	63	227	33	57	11	2	0	31	38	8	0	2	43	8	3	.317	.375
Lopez, Jose	R-R	6-0	181	12-15-96	.160	.200	—	31	81	16	13	1	1	0	8	19	5	2	2	28	3	0	.198	.346
Martinez, Francis	B-R	6-4	187	6-28-97	.230	.260	—	64	230	45	53	12	1	9	32	34	13	0	0	71	0	2	.409	.361
Mendez, Jacser	R-R	5-11	180	3-2-95	.148	.105	—	18	61	6	9	1	0	0	4	5	1	1	1	9	0	0	.164	.221
Mezquita, Melvin	B-R	6-3	175	6-2-95	.234	.273	—	55	205	30	48	2	7	0	16	29	5	1	1	36	13	5	.312	.342
Ordaz, Jose	L-L	6-1	170	8-11-96	.307	.304	—	47	179	29	55	5	3	0	13	14	4	1	1	28	16	5	.369	.369
Ovalles, Adony	R-R	6-2	185	5-10-94	.154	.000	—	25	78	7	12	4	0	1	11	13	0	0	1	29	2	1	.244	.272
Sanchez, Yan	R-R	6-2	170	8-31-96	.218	.175	—	55	193	23	42	7	2	0	10	19	6	1	0	43	8	2	.275	.307
Santana, Rafael	R-R	6-2	185	10-24-95	.276	—	—	45	134	22	37	6	1	0	22	29	8	3	1	30	9	5	.336	.430

Pitching	B-T	HT	WT	DOB	W	L	ERA	G	GS	CG	SV	IP	H	R	ER	HR	BB	SO	AVG	vLH	vRH	K/9	BB/9
Acosta, Geovanny	R-R	6-2	165	8-15-93	3	0	2.53	18	0	0	6	32	17	9	9	0	17	38	.152	.139	.158	10.69	4.78
Colon, Frangy	R-R	6-2	170	1-18-93	0	0	3.18	12	0	0	5	17	13	12	6	0	16	15	.200	.214	.196	7.94	8.47
Cordoba, Enorbe	R-R	6-1	190	1-2-95	0	2	3.95	9	0	0	0	14	15	16	6	1	14	7	.288	.208	.357	4.61	9.22
Duval, Starling	R-R	6-6	200	11-28-94	0	1	6.75	17	0	0	0	20	20	22	15	1	15	9	.260	.238	.268	4.05	6.75

		Ht	Wt	DOB	W	L	ERA	G	GS	CG	SV		IP	H	R	ER		BB	SO	AVG	vLH	vRH		
Espinosa, Geremia	R-R	6-4	180	6-11-96	0	0	9.00	2	0	0	0	2	3	2	2	0	0	0	.333	.000	.375	0.00	0.00
Felix, Wellinton	R-R	6-1	185	11-25-94	4	1	2.70	16	2	0	0	40	35	13	12	0	12	25	.238	.265	.230	5.63	2.70
Ferrand, Javier	L-L	6-0	185	4-26-96	1	1	4.00	9	6	0	0	27	28	15	12	0	13	26	.259	.333	.244	8.67	4.33
Garcia, Willi	R-R	5-11	180	3-14-95	0	1	4.71	16	0	0	4	21	25	17	11	0	6	16	.291	.387	.236	6.86	2.57
Gonzalez, Erbert	R-R	5-10	170	10-21-95	6	1	1.42	14	0	0	2	32	25	6	5	0	11	32	.214	.273	.190	9.09	3.13
Guzman, Carlos	R-R	6-3	180	3-22-97	2	1	5.26	14	0	0	0	26	29	16	15	0	12	20	.305	.237	.351	7.01	4.21
Hiciano, Argeny	R-R	6-3	160	10-19-96	1	1	5.84	4	2	0	0	12	11	8	8	1	5	15	.229	.333	.205	10.95	3.65
Madero, Luis	R-R	6-3	175	4-15-97	6	4	2.70	13	13	0	0	67	46	21	20	0	22	76	.192	.167	.202	10.26	2.97
Montero, Merkis	R-R	6-2	155	12-1-95	4	3	1.66	12	12	0	0	70	56	18	13	1	10	69	.216	.258	.202	8.83	1.28
Nunez, Anthony	R-R	6-2	180	4-30-95	2	2	4.07	17	3	0	2	42	51	27	19	0	12	31	.295	.304	.291	6.64	2.57
Ovalles, Melvin	R-R	6-2	180	11-21-96	1	3	3.15	10	8	0	0	34	35	19	12	0	13	29	.261	.313	.233	7.60	3.41
Pujols, Rafael	R-R	6-6	175	8-21-95	5	0	3.02	16	0	0	3	42	36	16	14	0	8	38	.228	.211	.233	8.21	1.73
Santana, Yeison	R-R	6-0	160	10-25-96	3	3	3.03	13	13	0	0	65	60	25	22	0	20	68	.247	.203	.264	9.37	2.76
Soto, Alvaro	R-R	6-0	165	7-16-94	0	0	9.00	5	0	0	0	6	8	7	6	0	8	8	.308	.167	.350	12.00	12.00
Vargas, Emilio	R-R	6-3	200	8-12-96	4	4	2.21	11	11	0	0	61	52	23	15	0	17	46	.224	.227	.222	6.79	2.51

Fielding

Catcher	PCT	G	PO	A	E	DP	PB
Garcia	.961	30	226	18	10	0	6
Mendez	.993	18	134	10	1	1	5
Ovalles	.966	25	207	23	8	1	6

First Base	PCT	G	PO	A	E	DP
Garcia	.982	12	106	4	2	14
Hernandez	.983	32	268	20	5	21
Jimenez	.986	29	265	14	4	27

Second Base	PCT	G	PO	A	E	DP
Bracho	.949	55	93	132	12	27
De Leon	.944	7	4	13	1	2
Herrera	.919	8	18	16	3	5

	PCT	G	PO	A	E	DP
Mezquita	.900	2	5	4	1	1
Sanchez	1.000	9	15	21	0	5

Third Base	PCT	G	PO	A	E	DP
Bracho	1.000	1	0	4	0	0
De Leon	.813	10	7	19	6	3
Hernandez	.930	33	30	103	10	12
Herrera	.571	2	2	2	3	0
Mezquita	.867	4	5	8	2	1
Sanchez	.908	24	15	54	7	3

Shortstop	PCT	G	PO	A	E	DP
Bracho	.889	2	3	5	1	2
De Leon	1.000	1	1	2	0	0

	PCT	G	PO	A	E	DP
Mezquita	.947	48	71	144	12	25
Sanchez	.882	25	34	78	15	11

Outfield	PCT	G	PO	A	E	DP
Alcantara	.964	17	26	1	1	0
Feliciano	1.000	3	3	0	0	0
Jimenez	1.000	19	30	0	0	0
Lopez	.953	29	58	3	3	1
Martinez	.944	58	79	5	5	0
Ordaz	.966	46	81	3	3	1
Santana	.974	44	71	4	2	2

Atlanta Braves

SEASON IN A SENTENCE: Seventy-four days in first place collapsed into a below .500 record, and a 7-18 September cost general manager Frank Wren his job and caused an overhaul of the team's front office.

HIGH POINT: The Braves won nine in a row from June 27 to July 5, which left them at their high-water mark of 11 games over .500. They had a 1 1/2-game lead in the NL East and seemed destined for a playoff spot.

LOW POINT: Let us present a few: There was a 5-0 loss to the Mets that dropped the Braves below .500 and came in the midst of a 1-10 stretch that doomed the team to a losing record. There was the three-game sweep to the lowly—at least in 2015—Texas Rangers in mid-September that was part of a five-game losing streak. And then, near the end of the season, Atlanta fired general manager Frank Wren in what turned out to be a front-office shakeup.

NOTABLE ROOKIES: Righthanded reliever Shae Simmons came up from Double-A Mississippi to strike out more than a batter per inning. Tommy La Stella stepped in when Dan Uggla was released and hit .251/.328/.317. Phil Gosselin, 25, who hit .344 at Triple-A Gwinnett, provided decent production when he arrived in July. Catcher Christian Bethancourt showed in flashes that he could be ready to assume the full-time catching duties and had 26 extra-base hits at Gwinnett.

KEY TRANSACTIONS: Within about a week in March, the Braves lost Kris Medlen and Brandon Beachy to Tommy John surgery, weakening their rotation depth and forcing them to sign 36-year-old Aaron Harang, who surpassed expectations with a 12-12, 3.57 season. At the trade deadline looking for a boost, the Braves sent away catching prospect Victor Caratini, the 65th overall pick in 2014, to the Cubs for versatile Emilio Bonifacio and lefty reliever James Russell, but that move could not stem the foundering club.

DOWN ON THE FARM: Righthander Lucas Sims was not as dominant as he was in 2014, but finished on a strong note. Jose Peraza might be ready to solve the Braves' second base issues as soon as 2016. Jason Hursh, the 2014 first-rounder, reached Double-A and won 11 games. 2011 third-round pick Kyle Kubitza led the organization's minor leaguers in total bases, on-base percentage and triples.

OPENING DAY PAYROLL: $97,855,673 (17th)

PLAYERS OF THE YEAR

MAJOR LEAGUE	MINOR LEAGUE
Justin Upton of	**Kyle Kubitza** 3b
.270/.342/.491	(Double-A)
3rd in NL in RBI (102)	.295/.405/.470
T-4th in NL in HR (29)	50 extra-base hits

ORGANIZATION LEADERS

BATTING   *Minimum 250 AB

MAJORS

* AVG	Hill, Aaron	.244
* OPS	Montero, Miguel	.699
HR	Goldschmidt, Paul	19
RBI	Montero, Miguel	72

MINORS

* AVG	Gosselin, Phil, Gwinnett	.344
* OBP	Kubitza, Kyle, Mississippi	.405
* SLG	Hunter, Cedric, Mississippi	.495
R	Peraza, Jose, Lynchburg, Mississippi	79
H	Peraza, Jose, Lynchburg, Mississippi	159
TB	Kubitza, Kyle, Mississippi	207
	Peraza, Jose, Lynchburg, Mississippi	207
2B	Ahrens, Kevin, Lynchburg	41
3B	Kubitza, Kyle, Mississippi	11
	Peraza, Jose, Lynchburg, Mississippi	11
HR	Terdoslavich, Joey, Gwinnett	15
RBI	Hunter, Cedric, Mississippi	72
BB	Brosius, Tyler, Rome	59
SO	Kubitza, Kyle, Mississippi	133
SB	Peraza, Jose, Lynchburg, Mississippi	60

PITCHING   #Minimum 75 IP

MAJORS

W	Collmenter, Josh	11
# ERA	Collmenter, Josh	3.46
SO	Miley, Wade	183
SV	Reed, Addison	32

MINORS

W	Ross, Greg, Lynchburg, Mississippi	12
L	Rodriguez, Hector Daniel, Gwinnett	13
ERA	Ross, Greg, Lynchburg, Mississippi	2.80
G	Hoyt, James, Gwinnett, Mississippi	52
GS	Miller, Jarrett, Lynchburg	28
GS	Sims, Lucas, Lynchburg	28
SV	Jaime, Juan, Gwinnett	18
IP	Ross, Greg, Lynchburg, Mississippi	158
BB	Brosius, Tyler, Rome	59
SO	Martin, Cody, Gwinnett	142
AVG	Ross, Greg, Lynchburg, Mississippi	.236

General Manager: Frank Wren. **Farm Director:** Ronnie Richardson. **Scouting Director:** Tony DeMacio.

Class	Team	League	W	L	PCT	Finish	Manager
Majors	Atlanta Braves	National	79	83	.488	t-16th (30)	Fredi Gonzalez
Triple-A	Gwinnett Braves	International	65	77	.458	11th (14)	Brian Snitker
Double-A	Mississippi Braves	Southern	83	56	.597	1st (10)	Aaron Holbert
High A	Lynchburg Hillcats	Carolina	68	71	.489	4th (8)	Luis Salazar
Low A	Rome Braves	South Atlantic	56	84	.400	t-12th (14)	Jonathan Schuerholz
Rookie	Danville Braves	Appalachian	38	30	.559	2nd (10)	Randy Ingle
Rookie	Braves	Gulf Coast	29	30	.492	9th (16)	Rocket Wheeler
Overall 2015 Minor League Record			339	348	.493	19th (30)	

ORGANIZATION STATISTICS

ATLANTA BRAVES

NATIONAL LEAGUE

Batting	B-T	HT	WT	DOB	AVG	vLH	vRH	G	AB	R	H	2B	3B	HR	RBI	BB	HBP	SH	SF	SO	SB	CS	SLG	OBP
Bethancourt, Christian	R-R	6-2	205	9-2-91	.248	.409	.209	31	113	7	28	3	0	0	9	3	1	0	0	26	1	1	.274	.274
Bonifacio, Emilio	B-R	5-11	205	4-23-85	.212	.273	.188	41	118	12	25	3	1	1	6	10	0	0	0	36	12	2	.280	.273
2-team total (69 Chicago)					.259	—		110	394	47	102	17	4	3	24	26	0	6	0	85	26	8	.345	.305
Constanza, Jose	L-L	5-9	185	9-1-83	.000	.000	.000	12	4	1	0	0	0	0	0	0	0	0	0	1	0	0	.000	.000
Doumit, Ryan	B-R	6-1	220	4-3-81	.197	.167	.205	100	157	11	31	4	0	5	17	7	1	0	1	49	1	0	.318	.235
Freeman, Freddie	L-R	6-5	225	9-12-89	.288	.260	.300	162	607	93	175	43	4	18	78	90	8	0	3	145	3	4	.461	.386
Gattis, Evan	R-R	6-4	260	8-18-86	.263	.343	.244	108	369	41	97	17	1	22	52	22	8	0	2	97	0	0	.493	.317
Gosselin, Phil	R-R	6-1	200	10-3-88	.266	.275	.260	46	128	17	34	4	0	1	3	5	2	1	0	27	2	2	.320	.304
Heyward, Jason	L-L	6-5	245	8-9-89	.271	.169	.304	149	573	74	155	26	3	11	58	67	6	0	3	98	20	4	.384	.351
Johnson, Chris	R-R	6-3	225	10-1-84	.263	.395	.231	153	582	43	153	27	0	10	58	23	2	2	2	159	6	0	.361	.292
La Stella, Tommy	L-R	5-11	185	1-31-89	.251	.311	.236	93	319	22	80	16	1	1	31	36	1	3	1	40	2	1	.317	.328
Laird, Gerald	R-R	6-1	230	11-13-79	.204	.186	.211	53	152	12	31	8	0	0	10	14	1	0	0	33	0	0	.257	.275
Pastornicky, Tyler	R-R	5-11	180	12-13-89	.200	.350	.050	28	40	4	8	0	1	0	2	6	0	1	0	11	0	1	.250	.304
Pena, Ramiro	B-R	5-11	200	7-18-85	.245	.286	.235	81	147	9	36	6	0	3	9	13	0	4	1	38	1	0	.347	.304
Schafer, Jordan	L-L	6-1	205	9-4-86	.163	.071	.182	63	80	9	13	4	0	0	2	10	0	3	0	20	15	2	.213	.256
Simmons, Andrelton	R-R	6-2	195	9-4-89	.244	.250	.243	146	540	44	132	18	4	7	46	32	0	2	2	60	4	5	.331	.286
Terdoslavich, Joey	B-R	6-2	200	9-9-88	.300	.429	.000	9	10	1	3	2	0	0	2	0	0	1	0	3	0	0	.500	.364
Uggla, Dan	R-R	5-11	210	3-11-80	.162	.138	.168	48	130	13	21	3	0	2	10	10	4	0	1	40	0	0	.231	.241
2-team total (4 San Francisco)					.149	—		52	141	14	21	3	0	2	10	11	4	0	1	46	0	0	.213	.229
Upton, Justin	R-R	6-2	205	8-25-87	.270	.286	.266	154	566	77	153	34	2	29	102	60	6	0	8	171	8	4	.491	.342
Upton, B.J.	R-R	6-3	185	8-21-84	.208	.200	.210	141	519	67	108	19	5	12	35	57	1	3	2	173	20	7	.333	.287

Pitching	B-T	HT	WT	DOB	W	L	ERA	G	GS	CG	SV	IP	H	R	ER	HR	BB	SO	AVG	vLH	vRH	K/9	BB/9
Avilan, Luis	L-L	6-2	220	7-19-89	4	1	4.57	62	0	0	0	43	47	22	22	2	21	25	.287	.264	.312	5.19	4.36
Beato, Pedro	R-R	6-6	230	10-27-86	0	0	0.00	3	0	0	0	4	3	0	0	0	3	3	.188	.111	.286	6.23	6.23
Buchter, Ryan	L-L	6-3	240	2-13-87	1	0	0.00	1	0	0	0	1	0	0	0	0	1	1	.000	—	.000	9.00	9.00
Carpenter, David	R-R	6-2	230	7-15-85	6	4	3.54	65	0	0	3	61	61	27	24	5	16	67	.256	.220	.287	9.89	2.36
Floyd, Gavin	R-R	6-4	235	1-27-83	2	2	2.65	9	9	0	0	54	55	23	16	6	13	45	.266	.301	.231	7.45	2.15
Hale, David	R-R	6-2	210	9-27-87	4	5	3.30	45	6	0	0	87	89	38	32	5	39	44	.264	.289	.243	4.53	4.02
Harang, Aaron	R-R	6-7	260	5-9-78	12	12	3.57	33	33	0	0	204	215	88	81	15	71	161	.273	.289	.259	7.09	3.13
Jaime, Juan	R-R	6-2	250	8-2-87	0	0	5.84	16	0	0	0	12	14	8	8	1	9	18	.280	.333	.241	13.14	6.57
Kimbrel, Craig	R-R	5-11	220	5-28-88	0	3	1.61	63	0	0	47	62	30	13	11	2	26	95	.142	.147	.135	13.86	3.79
Minor, Mike	L-L	6-4	220	12-26-87	6	12	4.77	25	25	0	0	145	165	77	77	21	44	120	.285	.357	.265	7.43	2.72
Russell, James	L-L	6-4	200	1-8-86	0	0	2.22	22	1	0	0	24	21	6	6	0	4	16	.233	.259	.222	5.92	1.48
2-team total (44 Chicago)					0	2	2.97	66	1	0	1	58	45	20	19	3	20	42	—	—	—	6.55	3.12
Santana, Ervin	R-R	6-2	185	12-12-82	14	10	3.95	31	31	0	0	196	193	90	86	16	63	179	.266	.291	.235	8.22	2.89
Schlosser, Gus	R-R	6-4	225	10-20-88	0	1	7.64	15	0	0	0	18	23	16	15	2	6	8	.329	.333	.326	4.08	3.06
Shreve, Chasen	L-L	6-3	190	7-12-90	0	0	0.73	15	0	0	0	12	10	1	1	0	3	15	.217	.273	.167	10.95	2.19
Simmons, Shae	R-R	5-11	175	9-3-90	1	2	2.91	26	0	0	1	22	15	8	7	1	11	23	.197	.122	.286	9.55	4.57
Teheran, Julio	R-R	6-2	200	1-27-91	14	13	2.89	33	33	4	0	221	188	82	71	22	51	186	.232	.239	.223	7.57	2.08
Thomas, Ian	L-L	6-4	215	4-20-87	1	2	4.22	16	0	0	0	11	10	5	5	6	13	.250	.318	.110	10.97	5.06
Varvaro, Anthony	R-R	6-0	190	10-31-84	3	3	2.63	61	0	0	0	55	46	18	16	5	13	50	.228	.149	.273	8.23	2.14
Walden, Jordan	R-R	6-5	250	11-16-87	0	2	2.88	58	0	0	3	50	33	17	16	2	27	62	.186	.188	.185	11.16	4.86
Wood, Alex	L-L	6-4	215	1-12-91	11	11	2.78	35	24	1	0	172	151	58	53	16	45	170	.239	.247	.236	8.91	2.36

Fielding

Catcher	PCT	G	PO	A	E	DP	PB
Bethancourt	.987	31	216	15	3	1	6
Doumit	.952	2	19	1	1	1	0
Gattis	.994	93	723	49	5	2	5
Laird	.995	48	339	28	2	4	7

First Base	PCT	G	PO	A	E	DP
Freeman	.996	162	1271	116	5	130
Johnson	1.000	1	1	0	0	0

Terdoslavich	1.000	2	2	0	0	0

Second Base	PCT	G	PO	A	E	DP
Bonifacio	1.000	5	11	8	0	2
Gosselin	.973	26	32	40	2	10
La Stella	.984	88	146	216	6	54
Pastornicky	.967	10	11	18	1	5
Pena	.976	38	36	46	2	11
Uggla	.944	35	58	95	9	19

Third Base	PCT	G	PO	A	E	DP
Gosselin	.950	9	4	15	1	3
Johnson	.978	150	56	209	6	18
Pena	1.000	17	4	9	0	1

Shortstop	PCT	G	PO	A	E	DP
Bonifacio	.900	3	4	5	1	2
Gosselin	1.000	8	8	13	0	4
Pena	.917	15	25	30	5	10

Simmons	.978	146	217	411	14	99

Outfield	PCT	G	PO	A	E	DP
Bonifacio	1.000	25	54	1	0	0

Constanza	1.000	3	2	0	0	0
Doumit	1.000	18	35	0	0	0
Gosselin	—	1	0	0	0	0
Heyward	.997	149	365	9	1	2

Schafer	1.000	30	42	0	0	0
Terdoslavich	1.000	2	3	0	0	0
Upton	.972	150	271	5	8	0
Upton	.980	139	329	9	7	3

GWINNETT BRAVES   TRIPLE-A
INTERNATIONAL LEAGUE

Batting	B-T	HT	WT	DOB	AVG	vLH	vRH	G	AB	R	H	2B	3B	HR	RBI	BB	HBP	SH	SF	SO	SB	CS	SLG	OBP
Bethancourt, Christian	R-R	6-2	205	9-2-91	.283	.280	.284	91	343	33	97	17	1	8	48	13	2	1	6	61	7	1	.408	.308
Boggs, Brandon	B-R	6-0	210	1-9-83	.256	.273	.249	92	297	36	76	17	3	7	33	25	5	2	2	67	5	1	.404	.322
Constanza, Jose	L-L	5-9	185	9-1-83	.293	.275	.300	111	447	65	131	10	2	0	36	37	0	9	4	49	30	10	.324	.344
Cunningham, Todd	B-R	6-0	205	3-20-89	.287	.282	.290	120	470	59	135	28	2	8	58	35	10	13	3	79	19	8	.406	.347
Gattis, Evan	R-R	6-4	260	8-18-86	.188	.400	.091	4	16	2	3	0	0	0	2	0	0	0	0	7	0	0	.188	.188
Gosselin, Phil	R-R	6-1	200	10-3-88	.344	.398	.321	96	378	58	130	29	5	5	31	19	3	6	1	62	6	1	.487	.379
Greene, Tyler	R-R	6-2	200	8-17-83	.200	.000	.276	12	40	5	8	2	1	1	4	0	0	1	1	17	1	1	.375	.195
Hamilton, Mark	L-L	6-4	215	7-29-84	.233	.043	.276	81	257	41	60	13	1	7	35	41	2	0	2	78	0	1	.374	.341
Jones, Mycal	R-R	5-10	190	5-30-87	.000	—	.000	1	1	0	0	0	0	0	0	0	0	0	0	1	0	0	.000	.000
Kazmar, Sean	R-R	5-9	180	8-5-84	.297	.371	.265	67	232	34	69	18	1	4	34	19	1	3	4	28	2	2	.435	.348
La Stella, Tommy	L-R	5-11	185	1-31-89	.293	.236	.321	47	167	18	49	6	1	1	23	25	2	0	4	14	1	1	.359	.384
Leonard, Joe	R-R	6-5	220	8-26-88	.278	.262	.286	41	133	13	37	8	1	2	17	11	0	2	1	29	0	0	.398	.331
Lerud, Steve	L-R	6-1	220	10-13-84	.250	.128	.288	60	164	23	41	9	1	4	19	28	5	3	0	43	1	0	.390	.376
Martinez, Ozzie	R-R	5-10	200	5-7-88	.288	.302	.284	78	243	26	70	11	2	0	22	20	0	4	2	29	4	0	.350	.340
Mejia, Ernesto	R-R	6-5	260	12-2-85	.354	.308	.377	20	79	12	28	5	0	7	24	7	2	0	0	22	0	0	.684	.420
Mitchell, Derrick	R-R	6-3	210	1-5-87	.217	.219	.217	42	92	14	20	5	0	3	9	19	1	0	0	21	3	3	.370	.357
Murphy, Donnie	R-R	5-10	190	3-10-83	.167	.182	.161	10	42	6	7	2	0	2	10	0	1	0	1	12	0	0	.357	.182
2-team total (10 Louisville)					.160	—	—	20	75	7	12	3	0	3	13	2	2	0	1	17	0	0	.320	.200
Pastornicky, Tyler	R-R	5-11	180	12-13-89	.290	.276	.297	47	176	13	51	5	1	1	17	11	0	1	1	23	7	2	.347	.330
Reyes, Elmer	R-R	5-11	175	11-26-90	.286	.320	.276	55	206	27	59	16	2	3	24	5	6	1	3	45	2	0	.427	.318
Salcedo, Edward	R-R	6-3	210	7-30-91	.212	.245	.200	110	364	50	77	21	1	10	44	40	4	1	4	97	13	5	.357	.294
Simunic, Andy	R-R	6-0	170	8-7-85	.250	.286	.200	8	12	1	3	0	0	0	0	0	0	0	0	4	0	0	.250	.250
Terdoslavich, Joey	B-R	6-2	200	9-9-88	.256	.271	.249	136	507	62	130	18	1	15	61	61	1	0	0	106	1	3	.385	.337
Yepez, Jose	R-R	6-0	210	6-19-81	.222	.258	.188	28	63	9	14	3	0	0	7	9	1	0	0	20	0	0	.270	.329

Pitching	B-T	HT	WT	DOB	W	L	ERA	G	GS	CG	SV	IP	H	R	ER	HR	BB	SO	AVG	vLH	vRH	K/9	BB/9
Atkins, Mitch	R-R	6-4	225	10-1-85	1	3	4.72	11	5	0	0	34	33	18	18	1	17	20	.260	.319	.182	5.24	4.46
Avilan, Luis	L-L	6-2	220	7-19-89	0	1	5.40	9	0	0	0	12	13	8	7	0	11	6	.310	.308	.310	4.63	8.49
Beato, Pedro	R-R	6-6	230	10-27-86	2	0	4.10	42	2	0	6	48	43	23	22	7	17	45	.240	.276	.214	8.38	3.17
Buchter, Ryan	L-L	6-3	240	2-13-87	3	3	3.29	49	0	0	1	63	51	23	23	5	40	63	.229	.200	.248	9.00	5.71
Carpenter, David	R-R	6-2	230	7-15-85	0	0	0.00	2	2	0	0	2	0	0	0	0	0	4	.000	.000	.000	18.00	0.00
Doyle, Terry	R-R	6-4	250	11-2-85	4	4	2.93	23	7	0	1	58	52	22	19	3	20	44	.240	.233	.246	6.79	3.09
Fisher, Carlos	R-R	6-4	220	2-22-83	3	1	3.00	23	0	0	2	33	26	13	11	1	14	41	.217	.250	.194	11.18	3.82
Floyd, Gavin	R-R	6-4	235	1-27-83	1	1	3.26	5	5	0	0	19	17	8	7	3	9	11	.239	.205	.281	5.12	4.19
Hoyt, James	R-R	6-5	220	9-30-86	1	1	5.46	24	0	0	1	28	38	18	17	4	14	34	.314	.339	.290	10.93	4.50
Jaime, Juan	R-R	6-2	250	8-2-87	1	0	3.51	43	0	0	18	41	27	18	16	1	36	63	.181	.243	.120	13.83	7.90
Lamm, Mark	R-R	6-4	215	3-8-88	1	3	5.93	16	0	0	0	27	35	23	18	2	18	24	.321	.396	.250	7.90	5.93
Loe, Kameron	R-R	6-8	245	9-10-81	1	2	8.83	12	0	0	0	17	30	18	17	4	3	16	.380	.458	.345	8.31	1.56
Martin, Cody	R-R	6-3	230	9-4-89	7	8	3.52	27	26	1	1	156	151	66	61	17	56	142	.254	.265	.240	8.19	3.23
Maya, Yunesky	R-R	6-0	210	8-28-81	3	3	2.63	17	14	0	0	86	96	33	25	6	20	64	.280	.308	.253	6.72	2.10
Minor, Mike	R-L	6-4	220	12-26-87	2	0	3.24	2	1	0	0	8	5	3	3	1	3	8	.172	.000	.227	8.64	3.24
Northcraft, Aaron	R-R	6-4	230	5-28-90	0	7	6.54	13	12	0	0	65	86	50	47	6	31	51	.317	.372	.273	7.10	4.31
Obispo, Wirfin	R-R	6-2	215	9-26-84	2	1	4.66	19	0	0	0	19	17	11	10	0	12	21	.233	.171	.289	9.78	5.59
2-team total (26 Indianapolis)					2	3	4.13	45	0	0	0	48	42	24	22	2	27	50	—	—	—	9.38	5.06
Reyes, Jorge	R-R	6-3	195	12-7-87	1	3	4.61	8	0	0	0	14	10	10	7	0	9	15	.213	.200	.222	9.88	5.93
Rodriguez, Daniel	L-L	5-11	195	12-11-84	6	13	5.04	29	21	0	0	125	134	76	70	16	49	111	.276	.241	.287	7.99	3.53
Russell, Andy	R-R	6-0	200	4-27-84	0	1	10.38	4	0	0	0	4	8	5	5	0	2	5	.364	.333	.385	10.38	4.15
Santana, Ervin	R-R	6-2	185	12-12-82	1	0	8.44	1	1	0	0	5	8	6	5	1	4	3	.333	.333	.333	5.06	6.75
Schlosser, Gus	R-R	6-4	225	10-20-88	7	6	4.17	25	15	0	0	99	93	49	46	7	48	70	.249	.247	.251	6.34	4.35
Severino, Atahualpa	L-L	5-11	220	11-6-84	5	3	3.22	40	0	0	2	45	33	16	16	2	20	54	.205	.203	.207	10.88	4.03
Shreve, Chasen	L-L	6-3	190	7-12-90	2	1	3.72	10	0	0	2	10	9	4	4	2	3	11	.273	.214	.316	10.24	2.79
Simmons, Shae	R-R	5-11	175	9-3-90	0	1	36.00	2	2	0	0	1	3	4	4	0	2	1	.600	.667	.500	9.00	18.00
Stewart, Zach	R-R	6-2	205	9-28-86	7	4	4.58	20	14	0	0	106	134	61	54	6	34	59	.311	.307	.315	5.01	2.89
Texeira, Kanekoa	R-R	6-2	190	2-6-86	3	5	4.86	13	10	0	0	70	77	39	38	7	36	33	.288	.272	.303	4.22	4.61
Thomas, Ian	L-L	6-4	215	4-20-87	0	1	3.95	6	1	0	1	14	12	6	6	1	5	16	.245	.083	.297	10.54	3.29
Vasquez, Luis	R-R	6-4	200	4-3-86	1	0	11.91	11	0	0	0	11	15	16	15	3	11	15	.333	.348	.318	11.91	8.74
Walden, Jordan	R-R	6-5	250	11-16-87	0	1	10.80	2	2	0	0	2	1	2	2	1	1	5	.143	.250	.000	27.00	5.40
Wood, Alex	L-L	6-4	215	1-12-91	0	0	1.04	2	2	0	0	9	7	1	1	0	4	8	.233	.333	.222	8.31	4.15

Fielding

Catcher	PCT	G	PO	A	E	DP	PB
Bethancourt	.986	80	608	42	9	5	10
Gattis	1.000	2	10	0	0	0	0
Lerud	.987	54	354	32	5	2	6
Yepez	.990	14	88	10	1	1	3

First Base	PCT	G	PO	A	E	DP
Gosselin	—	1	0	0	0	0
Hamilton	.996	59	443	22	2	56
Leonard	1.000	16	123	7	0	15
Mejia	.992	13	107	11	1	9
Terdoslavich	.984	65	452	36	8	57

Second Base	PCT	G	PO	A	E	DP
Gosselin	.970	25	35	61	3	16
Kazmar	.956	13	17	26	2	6
La Stella	.990	40	79	113	2	27
Martinez	.972	31	50	90	4	24
Pastornicky	.981	41	56	97	3	31

Third Base	PCT	G	PO	A	E	DP
Gosselin	.929	41	30	61	7	10
Greene	—	1	0	0	0	0
Kazmar	1.000	29	11	52	0	9
Leonard	.980	22	16	33	1	3
Martinez	1.000	4	2	2	0	1
Murphy	1.000	8	6	13	0	2
Salcedo	.868	47	31	74	16	10

Shortstop	PCT	G	PO	A	E	DP
Gosselin	.943	20	33	49	5	17
Greene	.976	10	13	28	1	7
Kazmar	.989	24	38	50	1	9
Martinez	.978	42	59	115	4	34
Reyes	.987	54	94	134	3	33
Outfield	**PCT**	**G**	**PO**	**A**	**E**	**DP**
Boggs	1.000	72	148	2	0	2

Constanza	.974	107	181	4	5	0
Cunningham	.991	119	319	11	3	4
Gosselin	1.000	8	13	0	0	0
Mitchell	.985	40	63	1	1	0
Pastornicky	.750	1	3	0	1	0
Salcedo	.906	48	72	5	8	1
Simunic	1.000	6	7	0	0	0
Terdoslavich	.974	49	76	0	2	0

MISSISSIPPI BRAVES   DOUBLE-A

SOUTHERN LEAGUE

Batting	B-T	HT	WT	DOB	AVG	vLH	vRH	G	AB	R	H	2B	3B	HR	RBI	BB	HBP	SH	SF	SO	SB	CS	SLG	OBP
Carroll, Dan	R-R	6-1	180	1-6-89	.149	.222	.132	19	47	5	7	0	0	0	3	3	9	3	1	10	3	1	.149	.317
Castro, Daniel	R-R	5-11	170	11-14-92	.277	.389	.248	51	173	23	48	9	1	4	20	5	1	0	1	18	2	1	.410	.300
Castro, Erik	L-R	6-4	200	11-13-87	.229	.143	.250	12	35	3	8	0	0	1	6	7	0	0	0	7	0	0	.314	.357
Hefflinger, Robby	R-R	6-5	235	1-3-90	.119	.100	.122	18	59	4	7	3	1	0	3	9	0	0	0	25	0	0	.203	.235
Hunter, Cedric	L-L	6-0	195	3-10-88	.295	.395	.272	120	400	60	118	30	4	14	72	56	7	1	6	52	12	5	.495	.386
Jones, Mycal	R-R	5-10	190	5-30-87	.255	.262	.254	108	380	52	97	22	2	3	41	42	8	7	6	72	21	7	.347	.337
Kennelly, Matt	R-R	6-1	200	3-21-89	.266	.340	.249	68	252	29	67	10	1	0	21	22	2	0	1	39	1	1	.313	.329
Kleinknecht, Barrett	R-R	6-0	200	7-30-88	.280	.349	.261	100	293	43	82	19	3	9	38	15	3	3	5	51	2	3	.457	.316
Kubitza, Kyle	L-R	6-3	215	7-15-90	.295	.326	.288	132	440	76	130	31	11	8	55	77	7	0	5	133	21	6	.470	.405
Landoni, Emerson	B-R	5-11	180	2-19-89	.271	.321	.261	59	181	24	49	6	0	1	12	20	8	4	0	29	5	3	.320	.368
Leonard, Joe	R-R	6-5	220	8-26-88	.246	.308	.238	36	114	11	28	3	0	0	7	10	0	0	1	25	2	1	.272	.304
Lipka, Matt	R-R	6-1	200	4-15-92	.189	.000	.230	28	106	12	20	6	0	0	6	9	1	0	0	15	10	2	.245	.259
Loman, Seth	L-R	6-4	235	12-16-85	.261	.241	.265	90	318	47	83	20	0	12	59	25	12	0	4	77	4	0	.437	.334
Mitchell, Derrick	R-R	6-3	210	1-5-87	.214	.125	.235	17	42	10	9	1	0	1	7	8	0	1	3	7	1	0	.310	.321
Nunez, Gustavo	B-R	5-10	170	2-8-88	.301	.235	.314	97	306	46	92	10	3	2	31	24	1	7	0	57	10	6	.373	.353
Peraza, Jose	R-R	6-0	165	4-30-94	.335	.282	.349	44	185	35	62	7	3	1	17	7	1	2	0	15	25	8	.422	.363
Poythress, Rich	R-R	6-4	235	8-11-87	.289	.391	.254	30	90	12	26	3	0	2	14	9	0	0	0	15	1	0	.389	.354
2-team total (46 Jacksonville)					.260	—	—	76	250	31	65	9	0	6	31	24	2	0	1	36	2	1	.368	.329
Reyes, Elmer	R-R	5-11	175	11-26-90	.303	.188	.324	58	211	25	64	16	1	2	28	7	6	1	3	48	3	2	.417	.339
Rohm, David	R-R	6-4	225	1-22-90	.255	.250	.257	114	364	33	93	19	5	0	46	20	5	1	2	93	3	4	.335	.302
Schlehuber, Braeden	R-R	6-2	210	1-7-88	.230	.244	.227	77	239	20	55	10	1	3	41	24	5	7	5	30	2	0	.318	.308
Wren, Kyle	L-L	5-10	175	4-23-91	.283	.295	.280	56	205	28	58	11	4	0	16	16	1	5	0	40	13	5	.376	.338

Pitching	B-T	HT	WT	DOB	W	L	ERA	G	GS	CG	SV	IP	H	R	ER	HR	BB	SO	AVG	vLH	vRH	K/9	BB/9
Atkins, Mitch	R-R	6-4	225	10-1-85	6	1	3.45	17	17	1	0	107	100	43	41	13	19	90	.248	.283	.226	7.57	1.60
Batista, Lay	R-R	6-2	200	8-4-89	0	1	8.22	3	1	0	0	8	8	7	7	0	7	2	.296	.250	.333	2.35	8.22
Berger, Eric	L-L	6-2	205	4-22-86	1	1	8.22	11	0	0	0	15	21	16	14	0	6	15	.323	.238	.364	8.80	3.52
Bromberg, David	L-R	6-6	245	9-14-87	2	3	4.14	8	8	0	0	37	35	23	17	3	15	37	.246	.222	.258	9.00	3.65
Cornely, John	R-R	6-1	205	5-17-89	7	3	2.49	46	0	0	7	69	45	19	19	2	34	71	.186	.164	.195	9.31	4.46
Cunniff, Brandon	R-R	6-0	185	10-7-88	3	0	2.05	33	0	0	0	53	39	14	12	2	20	50	.210	.218	.206	8.54	3.42
Doyle, Terry	R-R	6-4	250	11-2-85	1	0	2.79	5	0	0	0	10	9	3	3	1	0	8	.243	.091	.308	7.45	0.00
2-team total (8 Birmingham)					5	4	5.33	8	1	0	0	51	59	32	30	5	16	35	—	—	—	6.22	2.84
Fassold, Cody	R-R	6-2	230	10-2-88	0	0	6.00	6	0	0	0	9	9	6	6	1	4	10	.250	.250	.250	10.00	4.00
Floyd, Gavin	R-R	6-4	235	1-27-83	0	1	7.71	1	1	0	0	5	4	5	4	0	1	6	.222	.200	.231	11.57	1.93
Gardner, Joe	R-R	6-4	220	3-18-88	2	1	2.81	3	3	0	0	16	13	5	5	1	3	7	.228	.292	.182	3.94	1.69
2-team total (7 Tennessee)					3	3	3.40	10	10	0	0	53	45	20	20	4	13	24	—	—	—	4.08	2.21
Graham, J.R.	R-R	6-0	195	1-14-90	1	5	5.55	27	19	0	0	71	79	47	44	2	26	50	.289	.250	.311	6.31	3.28
Harper, Ryne	R-R	6-3	215	3-27-89	9	5	2.58	48	0	0	1	77	69	24	22	5	24	93	.242	.294	.220	10.92	2.82
Hoyt, James	R-R	6-5	220	9-30-86	2	2	1.14	28	0	0	6	32	19	5	4	1	10	43	.170	.214	.143	12.22	2.84
Hursh, Jason	R-R	6-3	200	10-2-91	11	7	3.58	27	26	1	0	148	151	70	59	5	43	83	.272	.253	.282	5.04	2.61
Kelly, Ryan	R-R	6-2	180	10-30-87	2	2	3.21	22	0	0	5	28	18	10	10	3	10	35	.176	.086	.224	11.25	3.21
Minor, Mike	R-L	6-4	220	12-26-87	0	2	8.00	2	2	0	0	9	14	8	8	5	0	7	.359	.500	.323	7.00	0.00
Northcraft, Aaron	R-R	6-4	230	5-28-90	7	3	3.68	13	12	0	0	66	57	21	21	2	24	62	.228	.278	.208	8.50	3.29
Pacheco, Ronan	L-L	6-6	195	7-29-88	2	1	10.80	9	0	0	0	8	7	10	10	0	14	3	.241	.000	.318	3.24	15.12
Perez, Carlos	L-L	6-3	220	11-20-91	0	0	19.29	4	0	0	0	2	2	6	5	0	11	2	.200	.167	.250	7.71	42.43
Perez, Williams	R-R	6-1	230	5-21-91	7	6	2.91	26	25	0	0	133	119	49	43	4	39	94	.241	.278	.223	6.36	2.64
Reyes, Jorge	B-R	6-3	195	12-7-87	0	1	2.25	19	0	0	1	32	19	12	8	4	12	30	.168	.188	.160	8.44	3.38
Robinson, Andrew	R-R	6-1	185	2-13-88	5	0	2.54	17	0	0	1	28	27	8	8	2	3	29	.243	.286	.217	9.21	0.95
Ross, Greg	R-R	6-3	200	9-6-89	7	3	2.08	13	12	1	0	78	63	22	18	4	20	44	.216	.172	.240	5.08	2.31
Shreve, Chasen	L-L	6-3	190	7-12-90	3	2	2.48	36	0	0	7	54	42	16	15	2	9	76	.213	.259	.196	12.59	1.49
Simmons, Shae	R-R	5-11	175	9-3-90	0	0	0.78	20	0	0	14	23	15	2	2	0	6	30	.183	.212	.163	11.74	2.35
Thomas, Ian	L-L	6-4	215	4-20-87	0	0	5.40	4	0	0	0	3	4	2	2	1	2	4	.308	.500	.273	10.80	5.40
Weber, Ryan	R-R	6-0	180	8-12-90	5	6	4.53	32	13	0	0	101	129	59	51	7	16	62	.317	.353	.299	5.51	1.42

Fielding

Catcher	PCT	G	PO	A	E	DP	PB
Kennelly	.997	68	547	28	2	3	1
Kleinknecht	1.000	1	2	0	0	0	0
Schlehuber	.993	76	505	54	4	4	1
Leonard	1.000	15	105	5	0	8	
Loman	.993	73	652	51	5	56	
Poythress	.988	22	158	13	2	13	
Rohm	1.000	3	6	0	0	0	

	PCT	G	PO	A	E	DP
Kleinknecht	.983	29	43	71	2	14
Landoni	.985	45	70	123	3	21
Nunez	.970	26	39	59	3	18
Peraza	.988	41	76	93	2	18
Reyes	.944	9	11	23	2	5

First Base	PCT	G	PO	A	E	DP
Castro	1.000	10	68	8	0	10
Kleinknecht	1.000	34	209	13	0	20

Second Base	PCT	G	PO	A	E	DP
Castro	1.000	3	7	8	0	2
Jones	—	1	0	0	0	0

Third Base	PCT	G	PO	A	E	DP
Kleinknecht	.818	8	3	15	4	0

	PCT	G	PO	A	E	DP
Kubitza	.924	120	80	225	25	15
Landoni	—	1	0	0	0	0
Leonard	.958	15	4	19	1	2
Nunez	.750	2	1	2	1	0
Poythress	—	1	0	0	0	0
Shortstop	**PCT**	**G**	**PO**	**A**	**E**	**DP**
Castro	.974	44	56	134	5	24
Kleinknecht	1.000	6	5	13	0	2
Landoni	1.000	3	7	6	0	3
Nunez	.969	50	58	130	6	28
Reyes	.957	44	55	125	8	21
Outfield	**PCT**	**G**	**PO**	**A**	**E**	**DP**
Carroll	1.000	16	22	0	0	0
Hefflinger	1.000	16	19	1	0	0
Hunter	.989	101	176	3	2	0
Jones	.991	102	221	7	2	1
Kleinknecht	1.000	15	17	1	0	0
Kubitza	—	1	0	0	0	0
Lipka	.981	28	49	4	1	1
Loman	—	1	0	0	0	0
Mitchell	.971	12	33	1	1	0
Nunez	1.000	12	10	0	0	0
Robinson	—	1	0	0	0	0
Rohm	.989	102	170	8	2	2
Wren	.991	50	114	1	1	0

LYNCHBURG HILLCATS   HIGH CLASS A
CAROLINA LEAGUE

Batting	B-T	HT	WT	DOB	AVG	vLH	vRH	G	AB	R	H	2B	3B	HR	RBI	BB	HBP	SH	SF	SO	SB	CS	SLG	OBP
Ahrens, Kevin	B-R	6-1	195	4-26-89	.266	.259	.268	129	478	68	127	41	1	7	65	48	5	—	5	82	1	1	.400	.336
Bello, Yenier	R-R	5-11	225	2-12-85	.333	.375	.313	7	24	2	8	1	0	1	0	0	1	0	2	0	0	.375	.333
Bloxom, Justin	R-B	6-1	205	4-29-88	.244	.222	.250	44	160	14	39	13	2	2	20	22	0	—	3	28	3	0	.388	.330
Brown, Blake	R-R	6-0	185	6-30-91	.261	.326	.235	50	161	20	42	9	1	1	17	24	0	—	1	50	9	4	.348	.355
Camargo, Johan	B-R	6-0	160	12-13-93	.259	.476	.135	17	58	7	15	2	0	1	6	1	0	1	2	13	0	0	.345	.262
Carroll, Dan	R-R	6-1	180	1-6-89	.201	.115	.234	63	189	28	38	11	0	3	18	22	12	5	3	62	18	4	.307	.319
Castro, Daniel	R-R	5-11	170	11-14-92	.292	.288	.293	70	257	33	75	16	3	1	34	10	1	10	1	20	7	4	.389	.320
Elander, Josh	R-R	6-1	220	3-19-91	.219	.318	.200	37	137	19	30	9	0	2	21	20	2	0	4	32	6	0	.328	.319
Garcia, Eric	L-R	5-11	175	2-18-91	.238	.212	.246	82	277	39	66	14	1	0	23	34	0	3	0	50	9	6	.296	.322
Godfrey, Sean	R-R	6-2	180	1-2-92	.333	.250	.385	11	42	3	14	4	1	0	6	1	3	1	0	9	4	2	.476	.391
Hyams, Levi	L-R	6-2	205	10-6-89	.238	.205	.247	108	370	50	88	21	6	2	41	48	3	—	6	82	2	2	.343	.326
Kleinknecht, Barrett	R-R	6-0	200	7-30-88	.000	.000	.000	5	11	0	0	0	0	0	0	3	1	0	0	4	0	0	.000	.267
Landoni, Emerson	B-R	5-11	180	2-19-89	.270	.241	.282	52	185	23	50	6	0	1	21	21	1	—	2	36	1	2	.319	.344
Martinez, Jose	R-R	6-7	210	7-25-88	.319	.277	.333	66	257	32	82	14	3	4	34	26	0	—	5	37	5	1	.444	.375
Nick, David	R-R	6-2	180	2-3-90	.294	.321	.284	73	282	41	83	13	4	6	35	19	1	—	1	58	5	4	.433	.340
Nunez, Anthony	R-R	6-3	215	2-4-90	.175	.167	.179	15	40	7	7	1	0	0	2	5	2	1	1	10	0	0	.200	.292
Odom, Joseph	R-R	6-2	205	1-9-92	.205	.115	.241	61	185	18	38	7	0	6	20	29	1	—	2	48	1	3	.341	.313
Peraza, Jose	R-R	6-0	165	4-30-94	.342	.435	.312	66	284	44	97	13	8	1	27	10	3	3	4	32	35	7	.454	.365
Piloto, Alejandro	R-R	6-0	185	4-8-92	.133	.118	.143	15	45	2	6	1	0	7	6	0	1	2	15	1	1	.178	.226
Sanchez, Edison	R-R	6-4	195	11-1-90	.218	.204	.222	60	211	17	46	13	0	1	19	13	9	1	1	68	1	2	.294	.291
Skinner, Will	R-R	6-0	210	6-9-89	.253	.245	.255	109	392	60	99	31	1	11	52	27	13	—	5	122	5	3	.421	.318
Tewell, Tyler	L-R	5-11	185	7-17-91	.251	.286	.241	80	283	40	71	12	3	8	45	12	6	—	6	44	0	3	.399	.290
Wren, Kyle	L-L	5-10	175	4-23-91	.296	.305	.292	76	291	46	86	10	4	0	27	30	2	7	6	39	33	9	.357	.359

Pitching	B-T	HT	WT	DOB	W	L	ERA	G	GS	CG	SV	IP	H	R	ER	HR	BB	SO	AVG	vLH	vRH	K/9	BB/9
Batista, Lay	R-R	6-2	200	8-4-89	2	2	6.61	8	8	0	0	31	38	24	23	3	11	25	.292	.306	.284	7.18	3.16
Bierman, Sean	L-L	6-0	195	10-20-88	0	0	0.00	1	0	0	0	1	0	0	0	0	0	1	.000	.000	.000	9.00	0.00
2-team total (5 Winston-Salem)					0	0	2.84	6	0	0	0	6	5	3	2	1	4	7	—	—	—	9.95	5.68
Cabrera, Mauricio	R-R	6-2	180	9-22-93	1	1	5.59	19	3	0	0	29	24	22	18	1	19	28	.226	.170	.271	8.69	5.90
Carela, Danny	R-R	6-3	230	9-18-87	0	0	0.00	2	0	0	0	2	1	0	0	0	2	2	.167	.000	.250	9.00	9.00
Chaffee, Matt	L-L	6-0	185	12-19-88	1	2	8.63	20	0	0	0	24	30	26	23	2	22	32	.306	.263	.316	12.00	8.25
Cunniff, Brandon	R-R	6-0	185	10-7-88	1	0	0.00	9	0	0	3	16	5	1	0	0	7	21	.102	.091	.105	12.06	4.02
Fassold, Cody	R-R	6-2	230	10-2-88	3	0	1.46	12	0	0	1	12	10	2	2	1	10	15	.217	.200	.250	10.95	7.30
Feigl, Brady	R-L	6-3	175	12-27-90	3	2	2.05	13	0	0	1	22	11	5	5	0	4	23	.155	.080	.196	9.41	1.64
Holmes, Colby	R-R	5-11	190	10-24-90	1	1	4.91	4	0	0	0	7	10	4	4	0	1	7	.345	.800	.250	8.59	1.23
Hyatt, Nathan	R-R	6-0	185	9-26-90	5	3	2.71	37	0	0	3	63	60	26	19	3	27	73	.246	.253	.242	10.43	3.86
Jadofsky, Zach	R-R	6-3	210	6-17-90	3	4	5.51	27	2	0	1	51	51	32	31	7	21	43	.258	.296	.231	7.64	3.73
Kelly, Ryan	R-R	6-2	180	10-30-87	1	1	2.25	8	0	0	5	12	4	3	3	1	2	14	.098	.118	.083	10.50	1.50
Marksberry, Matt	L-L	6-1	200	8-25-90	1	0	10.80	2	0	0	0	3	4	4	4	0	2	2	.286	.333	.273	5.40	5.40
Miller, Jarrett	R-R	6-1	195	9-28-89	8	9	4.04	29	28	0	0	151	164	76	68	13	50	127	.271	.288	.257	7.55	2.97
Moore, Navery	R-R	6-2	212	8-10-90	1	2	5.20	25	0	0	0	45	57	33	26	5	19	42	.310	.366	.274	8.40	3.80
Pacheco, Ronan	L-L	6-6	195	7-29-87	2	1	4.59	20	0	0	0	33	31	18	17	2	20	18	.254	.233	.261	4.86	5.40
Parsons, Wes	R-R	6-5	190	9-6-92	4	7	5.00	23	23	0	0	113	119	73	63	10	34	96	.271	.277	.267	7.62	2.70
Peterson, Dave	R-R	6-5	205	1-4-90	1	1	4.50	19	0	0	2	30	39	15	15	2	7	29	.317	.305	.328	8.70	2.10
Pfisterer, Eric	L-L	6-2	225	5-18-90	0	2	6.87	9	0	0	0	18	22	19	14	2	7	21	.297	.263	.309	10.31	3.44
Pruneda, Benino	R-R	5-9	170	8-8-88	2	2	5.82	31	0	0	2	43	48	29	28	1	22	50	.279	.310	.257	10.38	4.57
Ross, Greg	R-R	6-3	200	9-6-89	5	3	3.50	15	11	0	0	80	78	34	31	6	18	66	.255	.305	.229	7.46	2.03
Scarpetta, Cody	R-R	6-3	250	8-25-88	3	6	4.50	12	11	0	0	58	53	36	29	4	29	52	.244	.280	.214	8.07	4.50
Schrader, Clay	L-R	5-11	200	4-28-90	0	1	9.00	3	0	0	0	4	5	5	4	0	7	2	.333	.571	.125	4.50	15.75
Scoggin, Patrick	R-R	6-4	230	2-21-91	0	2	8.74	7	1	0	0	11	16	16	11	2	11	8	.348	.533	.258	6.35	8.74
Sims, Lucas	R-R	6-2	195	5-10-94	8	11	4.19	28	28	0	0	157	146	81	73	12	57	107	.247	.256	.242	6.15	3.27
Walters, Blair	L-L	6-0	200	11-8-89	6	1	2.33	8	7	0	0	46	41	12	12	3	11	33	.241	.125	.287	6.41	2.14
Waszak, Andrew	R-R	6-1	205	10-8-90	0	0	9.20	5	4	0	0	15	22	18	15	2	8	9	.333	.300	.348	5.52	4.91
Watts, Daniel	L-L	6-3	190	10-26-89	2	4	4.59	14	13	0	0	67	74	41	34	7	22	60	.278	.250	.286	8.10	2.97
Wilson, Alex	R-R	6-5	225	4-3-91	4	3	2.02	42	0	0	16	62	49	14	14	3	18	57	.216	.193	.229	8.23	2.60

Fielding

Catcher	PCT	G	PO	A	E	DP	PB
Bello	1.000	7	51	14	0	0	0
Nunez	.950	14	84	11	5	0	3
Odom	.990	59	445	42	5	3	5
Tewell	.989	63	480	41	6	2	10

First Base	PCT	G	PO	A	E	DP
Ahrens	1.000	5	38	2	0	5
Bloxom	.982	36	306	17	6	23
Hyams	.997	42	329	18	1	16
Kleinknecht	1.000	3	22	3	0	1
Martinez	.947	2	13	5	1	2
Nunez	1.000	1	10	0	0	1

Sanchez	.988	57	491	15	6 36

Second Base	PCT	G	PO	A	E	DP
Garcia	.985	27	49	85	2	11
Hyams	.969	31	46	78	4	18
Landoni	.958	16	21	48	3	9
Nick	1.000	10	13	9	0	2
Peraza	.965	58	87	134	8	25

Third Base	PCT	G	PO	A	E	DP
Ahrens	.958	108	62	187	11	19
Garcia	.931	13	4	23	2	2
Hyams	.952	16	11	29	2	0

	PCT	G	PO	A	E	DP
Kleinknecht	1.000	2	1	5	0	0
Landoni	.917	6	2	9	1	1
Shortstop	PCT	G	PO	A	E	DP
Camargo	.956	17	25	40	3	10
Castro	.978	70	97	219	7	30
Garcia	.927	23	35	66	8	13
Landoni	.956	25	24	63	4	5
Peraza	1.000	7	7	21	0	5
Outfield	PCT	G	PO	A	E	DP
Brown	.989	46	82	4	1	0
Carroll	1.000	54	108	3	0	0

Elander	.982	32	51	3	1	0
Garcia	—	1	0	0	0	0
Godfrey	1.000	11	22	0	0	0
Martinez	.973	42	67	4	2	0
Nick	.989	53	89	2	1	0
Piloto	1.000	12	20	0	0	0
Sanchez	1.000	3	3	1	0	0
Skinner	.975	99	190	9	5	2
Wren	.974	76	181	3	5	3

ROME BRAVES — LOW CLASS A

SOUTH ATLANTIC LEAGUE

Batting	B-T	HT	WT	DOB	AVG	vLH	vRH	G	AB	R	H	2B	3B	HR	RBI	BB	HBP	SH	SF	SO	SB	CS	SLG	OBP
Brown, Blake	R-R	6-0	185	6-30-91	.239	.208	.247	66	218	29	52	14	3	4	25	36	2	0	0	70	10	2	.385	.352
Camargo, Johan	B-R	6-0	160	12-13-93	.267	.339	.241	115	420	53	112	16	4	0	40	34	2	15	7	50	7	6	.324	.320
Caratini, Victor	B-R	6-0	195	8-17-93	.279	.297	.273	87	323	42	90	18	4	5	42	34	4	1	3	59	1	1	.406	.352
Carroll, Dan	R-R	6-1	180	1-6-89	.342	.308	.360	10	38	7	13	2	1	0	6	4	1	0	1	10	5	1	.447	.409
Chin, Gerald	L-R	5-10	160	5-9-93	.211	.214	.211	21	71	4	15	5	0	0	6	6	1	0	1	14	1	0	.282	.278
Curcio, Keith	L-R	5-10	170	12-28-92	.316	.154	.667	8	19	4	6	2	0	1	5	0	3	2	0	2	0	1	.579	.409
De La Rosa, Bryan	R-R	5-8	193	3-26-94	.092	.100	.091	22	65	3	6	1	0	0	4	6	1	0	0	30	0	1	.108	.181
Franco, Carlos	R-R	6-2	170	12-20-91	.255	.204	.272	123	443	54	113	20	4	9	49	45	1	1	1	84	7	2	.379	.324
Garcia, Eric	L-R	5-11	175	2-18-91	.226	.083	.260	15	62	9	14	1	2	1	5	6	0	0	1	10	0	2	.355	.290
Giardina, Sal	B-R	6-4	215	4-30-92	.266	.214	.291	37	128	12	34	3	0	2	16	10	4	0	0	30	0	2	.336	.338
Godfrey, Sean	R-R	6-2	180	1-2-92	.275	.290	.270	35	142	23	39	4	3	3	24	7	1	3	0	27	11	0	.408	.313
Harper, Reed	R-R	6-2	200	12-21-90	.193	.229	.183	48	166	18	32	5	0	0	7	17	1	2	1	19	2	0	.223	.270
Kirby-Jones, A.J.	R-R	5-10	215	10-2-88	.156	.125	.162	13	45	5	7	1	0	3	7	8	0	0	1	14	0	0	.378	.278
Krietemeier, Tanner	B-R	6-2	210	5-11-92	.254	.400	.226	19	63	5	16	1	1	0	13	12	1	0	1	12	1	1	.302	.377
Lien, Connor	R-R	6-3	205	3-15-94	.275	.288	.271	85	309	41	85	17	3	5	36	21	9	4	2	84	16	4	.398	.337
Livesay, Cody	L-L	6-0	160	7-6-93	.286	.474	.216	22	70	7	20	0	0	1	5	0	2	1	2	5	3	.286	.329
Luna, Ronald	R-R	6-0	145	8-18-92	.191	.056	.225	24	89	7	17	3	0	0	8	6	0	1	0	12	0	1	.225	.242
McElroy, Codey	R-R	6-5	195	12-13-92	.217	.176	.241	13	46	7	10	1	0	2	5	5	3	0	0	16	2	0	.370	.333
Meneses, Joey	R-R	6-3	190	5-6-92	.283	.180	.315	58	212	30	60	15	3	8	29	22	2	1	1	48	2	1	.495	.354
Moranda, Seth	R-R	6-2	180	9-26-92	.197	.273	.180	15	61	7	12	2	0	0	7	4	0	0	0	14	1	0	.230	.246
Morel, Jose	B-R	6-1	195	8-2-93	.174	.000	.200	8	23	2	4	2	1	0	1	1	0	0	0	7	0	0	.348	.208
Nunez, Anthony	R-R	6-3	215	2-4-90	.138	.000	.148	9	29	2	4	1	0	0	2	4	1	0	0	6	0	1	.172	.265
Oliver, Connor	R-R	6-0	180	10-13-93	.252	.247	.253	101	405	64	102	19	6	3	26	38	8	2	2	95	13	8	.351	.327
Piloto, Alejandro	R-R	6-0	185	4-8-92	.208	.353	.164	21	72	7	15	1	0	1	7	2	1	1	2	17	1	1	.264	.234
Reyes, Victor	L-R	6-3	170	10-5-94	.259	.149	.291	89	332	32	86	13	0	0	34	24	1	2	2	58	12	7	.298	.309
Reynolds, Mikey	B-R	5-9	170	8-19-90	.188	.231	.176	18	64	9	12	2	1	0	3	7	0	0	0	13	4	2	.250	.268
Sanchez, Carlos	R-R	6-0	178	11-5-93	.173	.208	.158	25	81	11	14	4	0	0	12	3	2	1	0	19	0	0	.222	.221
Sanchez, Edison	R-R	6-4	195	11-1-90	.176	.100	.286	5	17	1	3	1	0	0	1	2	0	0	0	11	0	0	.235	.263
Schrader, Jake	R-R	6-2	215	3-1-91	.290	.200	.319	88	328	51	95	17	5	11	55	24	6	0	2	82	2	3	.473	.347
Sears, Orrin	R-R	6-3	225	3-20-91	.188	.231	.158	9	32	5	6	2	0	0	1	2	2	0	0	7	0	1	.250	.278
Sprowl, Trevor	L-R	6-0	185	2-2-93	.189	.333	.091	12	37	2	7	1	0	0	1	9	0	1	0	7	0	2	.216	.348
Wilson, Ross	R-R	5-11	185	11-9-88	.244	.225	.250	74	275	33	67	15	3	7	40	29	9	2	8	57	3	2	.396	.327

Pitching	B-T	HT	WT	DOB	W	L	ERA	G	GS	CG	SV	IP	H	R	ER	HR	BB	SO	AVG	vLH	vRH	K/9	BB/9
Barker, Brandon	R-R	6-3	200	8-20-92	5	2	3.93	12	5	0	0	34	39	16	15	1	12	32	.289	.310	.273	8.39	3.15
Bierman, Sean	L-L	6-0	195	10-20-88	2	0	0.00	2	0	0	0	10	7	2	0	0	4	11	.175	.133	.200	9.58	3.48
2-team total (2 Kannapolis)					2	1	3.26	4	2	0	0	19	20	9	7	2	8	16	—	—	—	7.45	3.72
Briceno, Rafael	R-R	6-2	175	10-29-90	0	0	12.71	6	0	0	0	11	23	18	16	1	2	11	.390	.476	.342	8.74	1.59
Brosius, Tyler	R-R	6-4	230	1-7-92	5	7	4.51	28	15	0	1	108	106	74	54	5	59	65	.257	.281	.238	5.43	4.93
Buchanan, Chuck	L-L	6-5	220	7-14-90	1	3	3.23	7	7	0	0	31	31	17	11	0	16	28	.261	.393	.220	8.22	4.70
Cordero, Daniel	R-R	6-0	180	6-7-93	1	1	6.67	6	6	0	0	27	39	24	20	1	15	15	.348	.356	.340	5.00	5.00
Dettmann, Jared	L-L	6-3	180	5-18-92	0	3	6.95	5	5	0	0	22	31	20	17	1	11	15	.330	.400	.288	6.14	4.50
Diaz, Chris	L-L	6-0	195	5-24-93	0	0	2.97	10	9	0	0	33	21	12	11	1	21	36	.178	.227	.149	9.72	5.67
Dirks, Caleb	R-R	6-3	225	6-9-93	1	0	2.74	14	0	0	3	23	25	8	7	2	10	21	.281	.313	.263	8.22	3.91
Feigl, Brady	R-L	6-3	175	12-27-90	2	3	3.50	25	0	0	0	44	49	21	17	2	9	37	.275	.258	.284	7.63	1.85
Flores, Michael	L-L	6-0	180	4-26-93	1	1	6.87	7	1	0	0	18	22	16	14	1	10	13	.289	.188	.328	6.38	4.91
Gil, Yean Carlos	R-R	6-2	195	12-10-90	7	6	3.35	27	22	1	0	126	117	54	47	3	26	93	.248	.220	.264	6.63	1.85
Holland, Adam	R-R	6-5	225	12-15-89	2	3	7.96	12	4	0	0	32	45	33	28	1	19	19	.333	.328	.338	5.40	5.40
Holmes, Colby	R-R	5-11	190	10-24-90	2	1	5.29	13	2	0	0	32	48	27	19	1	11	21	.336	.352	.319	5.85	3.06
Jadofsky, Zach	R-R	6-3	210	6-17-90	0	0	2.70	9	0	0	1	10	10	3	3	1	5	10	.263	.471	.095	9.00	4.50
Janas, Stephen	R-R	6-6	198	4-21-92	2	6	4.52	18	17	0	0	98	108	61	49	8	29	61	.283	.284	.283	5.62	2.67
Kimbrel, Matt	R-R	6-0	190	3-13-90	2	3	7.40	13	0	0	1	21	34	18	17	3	16	14	.382	.432	.333	6.10	6.97
LaFreniere, Frank	R-R	6-5	185	6-2-90	1	3	8.83	4	4	0	0	17	20	19	17	2	5	13	.282	.292	.277	6.75	2.60
Lopez, Cesar	R-R	6-3	210	12-3-90	1	0	3.86	4	0	0	0	7	8	3	3	1	3	4	.276	.357	.200	5.14	3.86
Marksberry, Matt	L-L	6-1	200	8-25-90	5	10	3.55	22	22	0	0	112	100	54	44	10	51	98	.240	.257	.230	7.90	4.11
Minor, Ryan	R-L	6-4	200	12-26-87	0	0	0.00	1	1	0	0	5	1	0	0	0	1	4	.063	.000	.000	7.20	1.80
Moore, Navery	R-R	6-2	212	8-10-90	0	0	4.50	4	0	0	0	6	7	3	3	2	0	8	.304	.214	.444	12.00	0.00
Otero, Andy	L-L	5-9	165	6-3-92	4	4	3.60	30	0	0	3	55	55	26	22	4	22	60	.262	.288	.246	9.82	3.60

Name	B-T	HT	WT	DOB	W	L	ERA	G	GS	CG	SV	IP	H	R	ER	HR	BB	SO	vLH	vRH	SLG	K/9	BB/9
Parmenter, Race	R-R	6-0	180	5-24-91	0	1	8.10	5	0	0	0	7	12	7	6	2	2	5	.375	.294	.467	6.75	2.70
Perez, Carlos	L-L	6-3	220	11-20-91	0	0	0.00	4	0	0	0	4	2	3	0	0	3	6	.125	.286	.000	12.46	6.23
Perez, Pete	R-R	5-10	200	12-8-90	0	4	3.28	44	0	0	7	58	63	30	21	3	15	59	.273	.262	.282	9.21	2.34
Salazar, Carlos	R-R	6-0	200	11-23-94	1	6	10.60	10	10	0	0	36	47	45	42	2	38	27	.320	.368	.268	6.81	9.59
Sims, Matt	R-R	6-3	190	2-13-92	0	2	4.67	10	0	0	0	17	20	9	9	2	6	9	.299	.310	.289	4.67	3.12
Swanner, Michael	R-R	6-4	190	9-23-92	4	2	4.32	36	0	0	0	58	62	33	28	5	31	47	.266	.286	.250	7.25	4.78
Tate, Richie	R-R	6-6	225	4-11-92	5	5	3.68	45	0	0	5	66	64	33	27	5	36	52	.251	.221	.278	7.09	4.91
Ubiera, Andry	R-R	6-0	170	5-22-93	0	4	9.95	5	4	0	0	19	21	21	21	3	15	16	.288	.200	.368	7.58	7.11
Vail, Tyler	R-R	6-0	220	3-3-93	0	3	5.86	18	1	0	0	35	49	25	23	4	17	32	.327	.408	.243	8.15	4.33
Waszak, Andrew	R-R	6-1	205	10-8-90	0	0	11.25	2	0	0	0	4	8	5	5	0	2	5	.400	.545	.222	11.25	4.50
Watts, Daniel	L-L	6-3	190	10-26-89	2	1	3.16	5	5	0	0	26	23	9	9	3	6	22	.237	.226	.242	7.71	2.10
Weaver, Matt	R-R	6-0	175	1-27-90	0	0	12.15	7	0	0	0	7	16	11	9	2	7	5	.432	.438	.429	6.75	9.45

Fielding

Catcher	PCT	G	PO	A	E	DP	PB
Caratini	.991	70	494	51	5	2	6
De La Rosa	.979	22	118	20	3	1	4
Giardina	.994	21	135	19	1	1	2
Nunez	.987	9	61	14	1	1	0
Sanchez	.994	22	139	21	1	1	6
Sears	1.000	2	6	1	0	0	0

First Base	PCT	G	PO	A	E	DP
Costantino	1.000	2	14	3	0	2
Giardina	.966	11	102	11	4	4
Harper	1.000	1	8	1	0	1
Kirby-Jones	1.000	4	30	1	0	2
Krietemeier	.983	12	108	9	2	8
Luna	1.000	4	42	1	0	1
Meneses	.981	29	246	14	5	10
Sanchez	1.000	5	38	4	0	2
Schrader	.991	61	524	34	5	53
Wilson	1.000	17	134	9	0	11

Second Base	PCT	G	PO	A	E	DP
Chin	.931	14	18	36	4	9
Garcia	.956	10	21	22	2	6
Harper	.965	28	50	89	5	14
Luna	.933	13	21	21	3	5
Moranda	.839	14	19	33	10	8
Reynolds	.985	16	24	41	1	4
Sprowl	.967	8	11	18	1	2
Wilson	.967	38	55	119	6	19

Third Base	PCT	G	PO	A	E	DP
Caratini	.917	10	6	16	2	1
Franco	.909	110	76	204	28	21
Garcia	.571	3	0	4	3	0
Harper	.875	5	2	5	1	0
Luna	.882	6	7	8	2	0
Sprowl	1.000	1	1	0	0	0
Wilson	.968	9	7	23	1	1

Shortstop	PCT	G	PO	A	E	DP
Camargo	.938	114	165	330	33	57

	PCT	G	PO	A	E	DP
Garcia	.909	2	6	4	1	2
Harper	.974	9	14	23	1	4
Luna	.857	1	2	4	1	1
McElroy	.926	13	34	29	5	7
Reynolds	.500	1	0	1	1	0
Wilson	1.000	3	3	7	0	2

Outfield	PCT	G	PO	A	E	DP
Brown	.974	57	109	5	3	0
Carroll	1.000	8	15	1	0	0
Curcio	1.000	5	19	2	0	0
Godfrey	1.000	35	61	3	0	1
Krietemeier	1.000	1	1	0	0	0
Lien	.963	82	147	7	6	0
Livesay	.982	21	52	2	1	1
Meneses	.957	12	21	1	1	0
Morel	1.000	7	13	0	0	0
Oliver	.975	97	229	6	6	3
Piloto	1.000	17	25	1	0	0
Reyes	.976	79	159	7	4	2
Sears	1.000	2	4	0	0	0

DANVILLE BRAVES

ROOKIE

APPALACHIAN LEAGUE

Batting	B-T	HT	WT	DOB	AVG	vLH	vRH	G	AB	R	H	2B	3B	HR	RBI	BB	HBP	SH	SF	SO	SB	CS	SLG	OBP
Albies, Ozhaino	B-R	5-9	150	1-7-97	.356	.390	.340	38	135	25	48	4	3	1	14	17	2	5	2	17	15	3	.452	.429
Austin, Blake	R-R	6-1	220	7-1-92	.000	.000	.000	3	4	0	0	0	0	0	1	0	0	0	2	0	0	.000	.200
Black, Justin	R-R	6-0	195	5-20-93	.262	.255	.267	52	145	29	38	9	1	2	16	17	3	2	1	61	9	5	.379	.349
Chin, Gerald	L-R	5-10	160	5-29-93	.429	.667	.400	9	28	7	12	4	0	1	11	0	1	0	0	5	1	0	.679	.448
Curcio, Keith	L-R	5-10	170	12-28-92	.259	.500	.240	8	27	6	7	2	0	0	4	3	0	0	1	5	1	0	.333	.323
Daris, Joseph	L-R	5-10	170	11-22-91	.264	.333	.248	37	125	20	33	1	0	1	9	10	4	2	0	31	7	4	.296	.338
Davidson, Braxton	L-L	6-2	210	6-18-96	.167	.083	.208	13	36	1	6	2	0	0	3	9	1	0	0	10	0	0	.222	.348
De La Rosa, Bryan	R-R	5-8	193	3-26-94	.176	.278	.140	23	68	8	12	3	0	0	2	9	1	0	0	24	0	0	.221	.282
Dodig, Mike	L-R	6-4	210	7-8-93	.250	.188	.269	47	140	13	35	8	1	1	15	18	0	0	1	51	2	3	.343	.333
Edgerton, Jordan	R-R	6-1	190	8-30-93	.275	.296	.265	59	218	31	60	13	1	3	43	29	1	1	11	34	3	2	.385	.347
Godfrey, Sean	R-R	6-2	180	1-2-92	.412	.333	.440	16	68	17	28	9	1	0	9	2	1	0	1	9	3	0	.574	.431
Grullon, Yeudi	B-R	6-1	170	7-18-94	.241	.242	.240	30	83	8	20	0	0	3	11	0	2	0	19	1	2	.241	.330
Krietemeier, Tanner	B-R	6-2	210	5-11-92	.280	.429	.222	8	25	1	7	3	0	0	6	6	2	0	0	6	0	0	.400	.455
Livesay, Cody	L-L	6-0	160	7-6-93	.500	.000	.538	5	14	7	7	1	0	0	1	3	0	0	0	2	2	1	.571	.588
McElroy, Codey	R-R	6-5	195	12-13-92	.242	.225	.250	35	120	19	29	8	2	0	15	11	5	1	3	30	3	0	.342	.324
Monasterio, Luis	R-R	6-0	170	11-11-94	.213	.105	.286	18	47	5	10	0	0	0	6	8	0	1	1	9	0	0	.213	.321
Morel, Jose	B-R	6-1	195	8-2-93	.208	.205	.211	35	120	17	25	1	1	1	6	6	1	1	2	30	5	2	.258	.248
Murphy, Tanner	R-R	6-1	215	2-27-95	.242	.205	.257	50	157	21	38	8	0	5	19	30	1	0	3	38	2	1	.389	.361
Nevarez, Wigberto	R-R	6-3	230	7-17-91	.224	.212	.235	23	67	6	15	2	0	2	9	6	2	1	0	14	1	0	.343	.307
Obregon, Omar	B-R	5-10	150	4-18-94	.297	.404	.248	58	182	29	54	5	2	0	20	24	3	6	2	25	5	5	.346	.384
Piloto, Alejandro	R-R	6-0	185	4-8-92	.273	.317	.250	34	121	13	33	5	1	3	20	5	0	0	1	25	2	2	.405	.299
Sanchez, Carlos	R-R	6-0	178	11-5-93	.300	.333	.286	7	20	2	6	4	0	0	3	3	1	0	0	6	0	0	.500	.417
Sanchez, Fernelys	R-R	6-3	210	3-1-94	.262	.286	.255	54	141	19	37	10	1	2	18	17	1	0	2	57	8	2	.390	.342
Sprowl, Trevor	L-R	6-0	185	2-2-93	.278	.222	.296	15	36	4	10	0	0	0	4	1	1	2	0	8	0	1	.278	.316
Tellor, Matt	B-R	6-5	210	9-24-91	.228	.229	.227	37	123	12	28	6	0	4	25	13	1	0	4	40	2	1	.374	.298

Pitching	B-T	HT	WT	DOB	W	L	ERA	G	GS	CG	SV	IP	H	R	ER	HR	BB	SO	AVG	vLH	vRH	K/9	BB/9
Barker, Brandon	R-R	6-3	200	8-20-92	0	0	0.00	2	0	0	0	2	2	0	0	0	0	2	.250	.000	.286	9.00	0.00
Caicedo, Oriel	L-L	5-11	190	1-14-94	1	0	0.95	3	3	0	0	19	12	6	2	1	8	9	.176	.091	.217	4.26	3.79
Cordero, Daniel	R-R	6-0	180	6-7-93	4	3	3.81	12	12	0	0	59	58	27	25	4	17	50	.260	.257	.262	7.63	2.59
Dirks, Caleb	R-R	6-3	225	6-9-93	0	0	0.96	7	0	0	2	9	8	2	1	0	3	16	.222	.286	.182	15.43	2.89
Emmons, Dustin	R-R	6-2	175	10-29-91	1	0	1.86	8	0	0	0	10	9	6	2	0	0	9	.243	.231	.250	8.38	0.00
Flores, Michael	L-L	6-0	180	8-8-92	2	1	2.83	16	1	0	0	29	18	9	9	2	9	36	.178	.143	.188	11.30	2.83
Grosser, Alec	R-R	6-2	190	1-12-95	4	3	3.68	13	12	0	0	64	60	29	26	0	22	63	.244	.264	.229	8.91	3.11
Gunther, Ryan	R-R	6-2	190	11-17-90	0	0	8.31	9	0	0	0	13	17	13	12	0	7	13	.321	.333	.314	9.00	4.85
Holmes, Colby	R-R	5-11	190	10-24-90	1	2	4.05	13	0	0	0	20	29	12	9	1	2	17	.326	.314	.333	7.65	0.90

	B-T	HT	WT	DOB	W	L	ERA	G	GS	CG	SV	IP	H	R	ER	HR	BB	SO	AVG	vLH	vRH	K/9	BB/9
Kimbrel, Matt	R-R	6-0	190	3-13-90	2	0	1.69	6	0	0	1	11	9	2	2	1	2	12	.214	.263	.174	10.13	1.69
Kinman, Kyle	L-L	5-11	185	9-25-90	3	0	2.43	19	0	0	4	30	24	10	8	1	6	43	.222	.148	.247	13.04	1.82
Marte, Felix	R-R	6-1	180	11-14-90	0	0	2.19	10	0	0	0	12	9	3	3	1	4	9	.209	.143	.241	6.57	2.92
Miranda, Fernando	R-R	5-11	180	9-5-94	3	2	2.33	18	0	0	4	27	21	8	7	2	7	31	.208	.139	.246	10.33	2.33
Povse, Max	R-R	6-8	185	8-23-93	4	2	3.42	12	11	0	0	47	42	19	18	1	11	37	.235	.226	.239	7.04	2.09
Roney, Bradley	R-R	6-2	180	9-1-92	2	3	4.03	18	0	0	1	22	14	13	10	1	20	34	.184	.167	.196	13.70	8.06
Salazar, Carlos	R-R	6-0	200	11-23-94	2	1	2.51	17	0	0	0	29	15	14	8	0	18	34	.147	.189	.123	10.67	5.65
Sims, Matt	R-R	6-3	190	2-13-92	1	1	3.18	7	0	0	0	11	5	4	4	0	4	10	.147	.200	.125	7.94	3.18
Stiffler, Ian	L-R	6-1	175	2-12-95	0	1	8.71	4	2	0	0	10	11	10	10	1	11	5	.282	.400	.208	4.35	9.58
Ubiera, Andry	R-R	6-0	170	5-22-93	4	3	3.68	14	13	0	0	64	57	30	26	4	26	56	.239	.258	.228	7.92	3.68
Vail, Tyler	R-R	6-0	220	3-3-93	0	1	1.42	12	0	0	0	19	14	4	3	1	4	23	.194	.217	.184	10.89	1.89
Waszak, Andrew	R-R	6-1	205	10-8-90	4	7	4.44	14	14	0	0	73	73	37	36	2	18	51	.264	.261	.267	6.29	2.22
Weaver, Matt	R-R	6-0	175	1-27-90	0	0	1.29	4	0	0	1	7	2	1	1	0	1	11	.087	.182	.000	14.14	1.29
Zavala, Jorge	R-R	6-4	200	6-10-94	0	0	3.86	2	0	0	0	2	4	1	1	1	1	4	.364	.000	.571	15.43	3.86

Fielding

Catcher	PCT	G	PO	A	E	DP	PB
Austin	1.000	3	4	0	0	0	0
De La Rosa	.984	17	105	20	2	0	2
Murphy	.989	42	328	26	4	2	7
Nevarez	.983	17	103	11	2	1	2
Sanchez	1.000	4	22	2	0	0	3

First Base	PCT	G	PO	A	E	DP
Daris	1.000	1	8	1	0	0
Dodig	.981	32	235	17	5	20
Grullon	1.000	3	6	1	0	2
Krietemeier	1.000	5	38	3	0	3
Monasterio	.976	7	39	1	1	3
Nevarez	1.000	5	37	4	0	5
Tellor	.990	28	198	10	2	22

Second Base	PCT	G	PO	A	E	DP
Chin	.917	9	14	19	3	4
Grullon	.964	12	18	35	2	8
Monasterio	1.000	6	5	11	0	3
Obregon	.992	47	102	136	2	26
Sprowl	.900	5	4	5	1	1

Third Base	PCT	G	PO	A	E	DP
Edgerton	.926	55	28	110	11	10
Grullon	1.000	3	0	2	0	0
McElroy	1.000	8	7	9	0	1
Monasterio	1.000	7	3	8	0	3
Sprowl	.000	1	0	0	1	0

Shortstop	PCT	G	PO	A	E	DP
Albies	.950	37	39	95	7	24
Grullon	.862	10	5	20	4	1

	PCT	G	PO	A	E	DP
McElroy	.890	19	25	40	8	6
Obregon	.958	6	7	16	1	1
Sanchez	1.000	1	1	2	0	1

Outfield	PCT	G	PO	A	E	DP
Black	.987	47	73	3	1	0
Curcio	1.000	7	18	1	0	0
Daris	.987	33	74	1	1	0
Davidson	.889	10	15	1	2	0
Dodig	1.000	1	1	0	0	0
Godfrey	1.000	16	35	0	0	0
Livesay	1.000	5	5	0	0	0
Morel	.957	30	41	3	2	0
Obregon	—	1	0	0	0	0
Piloto	.939	29	30	1	2	0
Sanchez	.982	45	53	1	1	0

GCL BRAVES   ROOKIE
GULF COAST LEAGUE

Batting	B-T	HT	WT	DOB	AVG	vLH	vRH	G	AB	R	H	2B	3B	HR	RBI	BB	HBP	SH	SF	SO	SB	CS	SLG	OBP
Albies, Ozhaino	B-R	5-9	150	1-7-97	.381	.438	.362	19	63	16	24	3	0	0	5	11	2	1	1	6	7	2	.429	.481
Austin, Blake	R-R	6-1	220	7-1-92	.176	.111	.200	18	34	4	6	1	0	1	6	4	2	0	0	13	0	1	.294	.300
Azuaje, Franklin	R-R	6-1	170	3-31-95	.289	.250	.303	13	45	11	13	4	0	0	6	4	4	0	0	7	2	0	.378	.396
Bello, Yenier	R-R	5-11	225	2-12-85	.286	.167	.375	8	28	3	8	1	0	1	3	1	0	0	1	0	0	0	.429	.300
Cruz, Jared	R-R	6-1	175	3-29-95	.182	.333	.148	24	66	4	12	2	0	0	4	7	1	0	1	14	1	0	.212	.267
Daris, Joseph	L-R	5-10	170	11-22-91	.349	.400	.333	14	43	8	15	2	0	0	4	3	1	1	0	8	4	0	.395	.404
Davidson, Braxton	L-L	6-2	210	6-18-96	.243	.194	.263	37	111	23	27	7	1	0	8	22	7	0	0	32	0	0	.324	.400
Didder, Ray-Patrick	R-R	6-0	170	10-1-94	.274	.368	.244	45	157	22	43	6	5	0	16	15	5	6	1	33	4	4	.376	.354
Dykstra, Luke	R-R	6-1	195	11-7-95	.262	.279	.255	44	149	16	39	11	0	2	28	9	4	1	3	12	7	2	.376	.315
Estevez, Kelvin	R-R	6-1	190	11-17-95	.200	.206	.198	47	145	16	29	7	1	1	22	10	2	2	1	35	3	0	.283	.259
Flores, Alejandro	B-R	6-1	180	12-27-95	.250	.222	.257	38	92	17	23	4	1	4	15	12	2	0	0	20	0	0	.446	.349
Franco, J.J.	R-R	5-9	180	2-1-95	.347	.406	.319	31	101	17	35	2	0	1	14	10	3	1	0	16	1	4	.396	.421
Gaylor, Stephen	L-R	6-1	180	10-4-91	.325	.250	.357	9	40	7	13	1	0	2		1	1	1	0	8	2	0	.400	.357
Grullon, Yeudi	B-R	6-1	170	7-18-94	.250	.250	.250	5	8	1	2	0	0	0	2	2	0	1	0	0	0	0	.250	.400
Hagenmiller, Ian	R-R	6-1	215	9-9-94	.168	.161	.170	41	125	6	21	4	1	1	7	10	4	1	1	40	2	0	.240	.250
Harper, Reed	R-R	6-2	200	12-21-90	.333	.000	.429	3	9	3	3	0	0	0	0	1	1	0	0	1	0	1	.333	.455
Hass, Nathan	R-R	6-0	195	3-7-94	.154	.200	.125	12	13	1	2	0	0	0	1	4	0	0	0	2	0	0	.154	.353
Hoschke, Karl	R-R	6-3	185	7-1-95	.120	.125	.118	10	25	5	3	0	1	0	4	1	0	1	0	14	0	0	.200	.258
Lipka, Matt	R-R	6-1	200	4-15-92	.267	.400	.200	4	15	3	4	2	0	0	1	0	0	0	0	6	0	0	.400	.313
Livesay, Cody	L-L	6-0	160	7-6-93	.231	.250	.226	14	39	12	9	2	0	0		13	0	0	0	6	4	2	.282	.423
Manwaring, Dylan	R-R	6-3	210	9-27-94	.200	.107	.230	39	115	15	23	7	0	0	16	18	4	3	2	43	0	2	.261	.324
Martinez, Carlos	R-R	5-11	200	5-4-95	.243	.294	.228	32	74	9	18	4	0	0	2	4	2	3	0	7	1	0	.297	.300
Mendez, Erison	R-R	5-11	170	5-4-92	.277	.386	.226	45	137	23	38	7	0	0	29	6	3	0	1	17	9	4	.328	.349
Meneses, Joey	R-R	6-3	190	5-6-92	.357	.000	.385	4	14	3	5	2	0	0	4	0	0	0	0	0	0	0	.500	.357
Monasterio, Luis	R-R	6-0	170	11-11-94	.283	.313	.270	16	53	10	15	3	0	0	5	11	0	0	1	10	1	1	.340	.400
Morel, Jose	B-R	6-1	195	8-2-93	.279	.278	.279	19	61	13	17	5	1	0	8	7	1	0	0	8	5	0	.393	.362
Nevarez, Wigberto	R-R	6-3	230	7-17-91	.308	.000	.444	10	26	3	8	2	0	0	3	1	1	0	0	5	0	0	.385	.357
Obrochta, Connor	R-R	6-0	195	8-7-92	.219	.222	.217	19	64	6	14	2	2	0	10	7	1	0	2	16	2	0	.313	.297
Pina, Jose	R-R	6-2	180	9-23-94	.273	.167	.313	15	44	7	12	3	1	1	6	7	0	0	1	17	2	2	.455	.365
Puello, Juan	R-R	6-2	214	4-20-92	.118	.200	.083	11	17	1	2	0	0	0	4	0	0	0	0	8	0	0	.118	.286
Reiher, Kevin	R-R	5-10	190	5-24-94	.000	.000	.000	5	7	0	0	0	0	0	0	0	1	0	0	5	0	0	.000	.125
Salcedo, Edward	R-R	6-3	210	7-30-91	.211	.571	.000	5	19	2	4	1	0	2	7	1	0	0	0	2	1	0	.579	.250

Pitching	B-T	HT	WT	DOB	W	L	ERA	G	GS	CG	SV	IP	H	R	ER	HR	BB	SO	AVG	vLH	vRH	K/9	BB/9
Beech, Caleb	R-R	6-4	215	4-18-93	0	0	14.40	4	0	0	0	5	11	9	8	0	3	1	.423	.455	.400	1.80	5.40
Brocker, Cole	R-R	6-2	220	4-17-90	2	0	3.26	13	0	0	0	19	13	9	7	0	7	21	.186	.259	.140	9.78	3.26
Cabrera, Mauricio	R-R	6-2	180	9-22-93	0	0	6.75	3	2	0	0	4	3	3	3	0	2	3	.214	.200	.222	6.75	4.50
Caicedo, Oriel	L-L	5-11	190	1-14-94	4	2	2.81	10	7	0	0	48	46	17	15	0	3	32	.250	.179	.263	6.00	0.56
Cundari, Rocco	R-R	6-1	200	10-20-90	0	0	13.50	2	0	0	0	3	6	5	5	1	2	1	.500	1.000	.400	2.70	5.40

Name	B-T	HT	WT	DOB	W	L	ERA	G	GS	CG	SV	IP	H	R	ER	HR	BB	SO	AVG	vLH	vRH	K/9	BB/9
Dettmann, Jared	L-L	6-3	180	5-18-92	2	3	4.10	17	0	0	1	26	23	13	12	0	18	17	.240	.200	.247	5.81	6.15
Espinosa, Abraham	R-R	6-1	175	6-3-93	2	1	4.50	14	0	0	0	26	29	16	13	0	9	21	.274	.154	.313	7.27	3.12
Falcon, Felix	L-L	6-2	190	8-7-95	0	1	13.50	1	1	0	0	3	3	4	4	1	3	3	.250	.000	.273	10.13	10.13
Fulenchek, Garrett	R-R	6-4	205	6-7-96	0	7	4.78	12	10	0	0	38	34	21	20	2	22	29	.238	.265	.223	6.93	5.26
Gamez, Luis	R-R	6-2	175	6-25-96	2	0	4.74	17	0	0	0	19	20	12	10	0	17	11	.274	.143	.356	5.21	8.05
Gonzalez, Francisco	R-R	6-0	170	9-21-94	3	3	4.06	12	7	0	0	58	64	31	26	2	17	41	.283	.359	.253	6.40	2.65
Gunther, Ryan	R-R	6-2	190	11-17-90	0	0	5.06	4	0	0	0	5	6	4	3	2	0	4	.261	.500	.133	6.75	0.00
Lamm, Mark	R-R	6-4	215	3-8-88	0	1	8.44	4	1	0	0	5	8	5	5	1	4	7	.381	.333	.400	11.81	6.75
Martinez, Jhon	L-L	6-0	165	2-9-95	1	1	6.14	5	3	0	1	15	14	12	10	1	8	15	.255	.154	.286	9.20	4.91
Mejia, Dilmer	L-L	5-11	160	7-9-97	1	0	3.60	3	3	0	0	15	15	6	6	2	4	8	.273	.000	.306	4.80	2.40
Osnowitz, Mitchell	R-R	6-5	245	7-2-91	1	0	5.74	13	0	0	2	16	12	10	10	1	8	18	.218	.200	.225	10.34	4.60
Perez, Carlos	L-L	6-3	220	11-20-91	0	0	10.38	6	4	0	0	4	1	6	5	0	12	6	.067	.000	.083	12.46	24.92
Peterson, Dave	R-R	6-5	205	1-4-90	0	0	4.50	1	0	0	0	2	2	1	1	0	0	3	.250	.000	.286	13.50	0.00
Rodriguez, Rafael	R-R	6-1	180	9-22-92	0	3	2.29	13	0	0	0	20	14	5	5	1	8	16	.200	.160	.222	7.32	3.66
Sambola, Clayvon	R-R	6-2	180	11-19-92	0	1	5.06	4	0	0	0	5	7	9	3	1	7	7	.318	.286	.333	11.81	11.81
Santana, Jordany	R-R	6-0	190	7-17-95	3	2	4.45	12	9	0	0	57	61	31	28	1	18	30	.277	.354	.245	4.76	2.86
Sechler, Jordan	R-L	6-2	215	11-8-91	1	2	3.26	15	0	0	4	19	20	9	7	0	6	18	.267	.353	.241	8.38	2.79
Silva, Aldo	R-R	6-1	240	10-19-95	1	1	1.71	14	0	0	0	21	16	8	4	0	10	10	.219	.208	.224	4.29	4.29
Stewart, Zach	R-R	6-2	205	9-28-86	0	1	4.50	2	2	0	0	4	5	3	2	1	2	2	.313	.200	.364	4.50	4.50
Stuart, Dylan	L-L	5-10	175	9-1-92	1	0	3.24	5	0	0	0	8	10	4	3	3	1	9	.294	.250	.300	9.72	1.08
Thomas, Ian	L-L	6-4	215	4-20-87	0	0	4.50	3	3	0	0	6	7	3	3	1	0	7	.304	.400	.278	10.50	0.00
Torres, Yeralf	R-R	6-1	175	9-21-95	0	0	40.50	1	1	0	0	1	3	3	3	0	2	0	.600	1.000	.500	0.00	27.00
Webb, Jacob	R-R	6-1	200	8-15-93	2	1	2.14	11	6	0	0	34	30	9	8	2	8	31	.231	.225	.233	8.29	2.14
Zavala, Jorge	R-R	6-4	200	6-10-94	3	0	0.38	18	0	0	7	24	9	1	1	0	7	27	.115	.120	.113	10.13	2.63

Fielding

Catcher	PCT	G	PO	A	E	DP	PB
Austin	1.000	13	49	7	0	0	2
Bello	1.000	6	23	4	0	0	0
Flores	.993	31	135	6	1	1	1
Hass	.943	12	29	4	2	0	1
Martinez	.994	32	135	19	1	2	3
Nevarez	1.000	4	19	1	0	0	0
Reiher	1.000	5	11	2	0	1	0

First Base	PCT	G	PO	A	E	DP
Austin	1.000	2	6	0	0	1
Azuaje	.875	2	12	2	2	2
Cruz	.992	17	118	3	1	10
Hagenmiller	.977	39	287	12	7	21
Meneses	1.000	3	27	0	0	4
Monasterio	.981	7	47	4	1	4
Nevarez	.963	4	26	0	1	1

Second Base	PCT	G	PO	A	E	DP
Cruz	1.000	7	10	13	0	4
Didder	.952	6	7	13	1	2
Dykstra	.958	23	40	52	4	10
Franco	1.000	30	53	73	0	15
Grullon	1.000	4	5	5	0	2
Harper	1.000	1	3	1	0	0

Third Base	PCT	G	PO	A	E	DP
Azuaje	.935	9	8	21	2	4
Harper	.800	1	0	4	1	0
Manwaring	.920	39	20	95	10	9
Mendez	1.000	5	3	12	0	1
Monasterio	.880	9	6	16	3	2

Shortstop	PCT	G	PO	A	E	DP
Albies	.923	16	23	49	6	9
Cruz	1.000	1	3	0	0	0
Didder	.931	34	51	112	12	19

	PCT	G	PO	A	E	DP
Dykstra	.944	10	15	19	2	4
Grullon	1.000	1	2	1	0	0
Mendez	.833	2	3	2	1	2

Outfield	PCT	G	PO	A	E	DP
Daris	.935	14	29	0	2	0
Davidson	.925	28	35	2	3	0
Estevez	.943	43	62	4	4	1
Gaylor	1.000	9	26	0	0	0
Hoschke	1.000	5	8	0	0	0
Lipka	1.000	4	6	0	0	0
Livesay	1.000	14	22	0	0	0
Mendez	1.000	34	57	2	0	1
Morel	.958	15	21	2	1	1
Obrochta	1.000	19	38	1	0	1
Pina	.952	12	18	2	1	0
Puello	1.000	8	2	0	0	0
Salcedo	1.000	3	5	1	0	1

DSL BRAVES

ROOKIE

DOMINICAN SUMMER LEAGUE

Batting	B-T	HT	WT	DOB	AVG	vLH	vRH	G	AB	R	H	2B	3B	HR	RBI	BB	HBP	SH	SF	SO	SB	CS	SLG	OBP
Arias, Elias	L-L	6-1	180	6-30-94	.297	.278	.303	62	232	35	69	8	1	2	33	38	5	3	1	39	21	12	.366	.406
Barrios, Rafael	R-R	6-0	165	3-4-97	.091	—	.091	5	11	1	1	1	0	0	1	0	0	1	0	2	0	0	.182	.091
Cabrera, Jeyson	R-R	6-0	185	11-21-95	.231	.182	.246	50	182	22	42	9	2	1	15	12	7	0	2	37	2	2	.319	.300
Castro, Carlos	R-R	6-1	195	5-24-94	.308	.406	.285	49	169	26	52	12	3	2	28	9	10	0	0	22	2	2	.450	.378
Cleofa, Nisandro	R-R	5-11	180	10-25-93	.091	.000	.125	11	11	5	1	0	0	0	0	1	0	1	0	4	1	0	.091	.167
Cortes, Jorge	R-R	6-2	175	11-15-95	.210	.270	.194	55	181	22	38	13	2	0	19	13	16	1	1	40	2	3	.304	.318
George, Jose	B-R	6-2	200	6-14-94	.213	.208	.214	44	136	14	29	5	0	0	11	7	3	1	0	43	1	1	.250	.314
Guerrero, Jan	L-R	6-3	195	7-18-96	.206	.136	.224	27	107	11	22	4	1	1	16	7	1	0	1	26	1	1	.290	.259
Guillermo, Ronny	R-R	6-1	170	8-2-96	.186	.226	.171	43	113	18	21	4	0	0	9	17	1	1	1	32	7	3	.221	.295
Josephina, Kevin	B-R	6-0	170	12-6-96	.171	.375	.111	9	35	5	6	1	0	0	5	4	2	0	1	10	1	0	.200	.286
Josephina, Terrence	R-R	6-2	185	12-5-94	.243	.407	.204	43	140	15	34	3	2	1	13	16	3	0	0	17	3	2	.314	.333
Lar, Yunior	R-R	6-1	190	1-23-96	.036	.250	.000	16	28	2	1	1	0	0	0	1	0	0	0	10	0	1	.071	.069
Mercuri, Mattia	R-R	6-0	190	8-20-94	.213	.222	.211	43	94	10	20	4	2	0	6	11	6	2	1	23	0	4	.298	.330
Perez, Ruben	R-R	6-0	180	9-21-95	.329	.417	.313	44	155	28	51	7	4	1	18	6	8	1	0	37	7	7	.445	.385
Philips, Bryan	B-R	5-11	150	8-12-95	.190	.192	.190	50	147	18	28	3	0	0	7	13	4	5	0	34	5	5	.211	.274
Salazar, Alejandro	R-R	6-0	170	10-5-96	.303	.269	.312	66	241	35	73	3	4	1	28	19	2	3	3	41	6	3	.361	.355
Tejada, Ledernin	R-R	6-3	168	3-20-96	.234	.324	.208	57	167	25	39	9	0	0	13	21	5	8	0	40	4	5	.287	.337
Todd, Ruddy	R-R	6-3	200	4-3-94	.205	.167	.218	33	73	13	15	2	0	0	4	16	1	2	0	11	2	1	.233	.356
Vasquez, Carlos	B-R	6-2	160	2-25-95	.100	.000	.125	9	20	2	2	1	0	0	1	3	0	0	1	3	1	0	.150	.208
Willems, Reangelo	B-R	6-2	165	9-21-94	.229	.192	.236	46	153	18	35	7	2	0	19	10	4	0	1	38	0	3	.301	.292

Pitching	B-T	HT	WT	DOB	W	L	ERA	G	GS	CG	SV	IP	H	R	ER	HR	BB	SO	AVG	vLH	vRH	K/9	BB/9
Barrios, Luis	L-L	6-4	210	3-4-97	2	6	6.53	18	8	0	0	41	35	36	30	0	33	52	.227	.238	.226	11.32	7.19
Gavidia, Angel	R-R	6-2	180	5-16-95	0	5	4.62	17	10	0	0	51	59	30	26	2	16	46	.294	.219	.336	8.17	2.84
Gil, Frank	R-R	6-2	165	9-24-96	1	1	7.97	17	1	0	1	20	25	19	18	0	14	13	.305	.304	.305	5.75	6.20
Henry, Gabriel	R-R	6-3	180	11-16-95	2	0	2.38	20	0	0	1	34	23	11	9	1	21	23	.187	.241	.170	6.09	5.56
Joaquin, Victor	R-R	6-5	220	12-29-93	3	4	3.89	9	6	0	0	35	27	28	15	0	15	47	.206	.222	.200	12.20	3.89

Jones, Jesus	R-R	6-2	165	5-31-95	0	1	3.00	18	0	0	0	24	21	14	8	0	21	23	.239	.263	.232	8.63	7.88
Laguna, Jason	R-R	5-11	170	1-8-96	3	3	6.03	19	0	0	0	34	39	27	23	0	23	27	.300	.318	.291	7.08	6.03
Ledezma, Carlos	R-R	6-1	175	8-31-95	1	0	0.84	6	1	0	0	11	7	2	1	0	6	14	.179	.143	.188	11.81	5.06
Leiva, Darrel	R-R	6-1	185	7-31-94	1	1	4.50	2	0	0	0	2	3	1	1	0	1	1	.375	.000	.600	4.50	4.50
Manzanares, Osman	R-R	6-2	192	3-6-95	1	0	4.02	7	0	0	1	16	14	8	7	1	10	7	.246	.273	.239	4.02	5.74
Mejia, Dilmer	L-L	5-11	160	7-9-97	4	1	1.68	11	11	0	0	59	40	18	11	0	11	52	.190	.206	.186	7.93	1.68
Mora, Luis	R-R	6-4	160	6-17-95	0	5	10.18	19	9	0	0	38	41	49	43	2	42	34	.291	.326	.274	8.05	9.95
Moreno, Ramon	R-R	6-0	190	10-25-89	4	3	2.50	29	0	0	13	40	34	14	11	1	2	32	.236	.186	.257	7.26	0.45
Orozco, Evertz	R-R	6-5	192	9-16-94	0	3	2.93	11	5	0	0	28	26	16	9	0	12	21	.245	.364	.192	6.83	3.90
Perez, Luis	R-R	6-1	180	4-7-97	1	0	4.91	11	7	0	0	29	27	27	16	0	29	12	.257	.355	.216	3.68	8.90
Sanchez, Javier	L-R	6-4	210	10-3-96	1	2	6.35	15	9	0	0	51	63	38	36	1	13	30	.310	.383	.280	5.29	2.29
Silvestre, Alvaro	R-R	6-3	165	1-23-94	3	0	7.65	12	0	0	0	20	18	17	17	0	12	19	.247	.188	.263	8.55	5.40
Tavers, Ramon	R-R	6-1	200	8-31-95	0	0	3.86	11	0	0	0	14	11	9	6	0	11	8	.216	.286	.189	5.14	7.07
Torres, Yeralf	R-R	6-1	175	9-21-95	0	3	4.41	14	3	0	0	35	29	27	17	0	24	47	.230	.256	.217	12.20	6.23

Fielding

Catcher	PCT	G	PO	A	E	DP	PB
Castro	.970	40	242	54	9	2	6
Perez	.958	18	120	16	6	2	9
Todd	.979	29	169	21	4	0	11

First Base	PCT	G	PO	A	E	DP
Castro	.957	4	20	2	1	3
Cortes	.992	31	223	15	2	21
Guerrero	.985	25	187	11	3	14
Lar	.986	14	69	2	1	6
Mercuri	.931	7	63	4	5	7
Perez	1.000	1	1	0	0	0
Philips	1.000	1	1	0	0	0
Willems	—	1	0	0	0	0

Second Base	PCT	G	PO	A	E	DP
Barrios	.800	5	4	4	2	1
Cabrera	.963	28	64	66	5	15
Josephina	1.000	7	14	11	0	5
Josephina	1.000	1	2	1	0	0
Mercuri	.971	30	47	52	3	12
Philips	.959	20	39	32	3	9

Third Base	PCT	G	PO	A	E	DP
Cabrera	1.000	1	0	1	0	0
Guillermo	.885	28	32	45	10	6
Josephina	.891	36	31	59	11	5
Mercuri	—	3	0	0	0	0
Salazar	.923	12	3	21	2	3
Vasquez	1.000	4	2	1	0	1

Shortstop	PCT	G	PO	A	E	DP
Guillermo	1.000	1	2	0	0	0
Josephina	1.000	2	3	5	0	1
Philips	.960	27	35	62	4	11
Salazar	.923	51	69	135	17	24

Outfield	PCT	G	PO	A	E	DP
Arias	.927	62	134	5	11	1
Cabrera	.882	5	14	1	2	0
Cleofa	1.000	7	7	1	0	1
Cortes	.935	25	26	3	2	0
George	.897	44	68	2	8	2
Tejada	.933	56	75	8	6	2
Willems	.957	42	60	7	3	2

Baltimore Orioles

SEASON IN A SENTENCE: Dan Duquette and Buck Showalter pieced together their third straight playoff team, this one reaching the American League Championship Series despite a rotation short on aces and a lineup weakened by injuries to Matt Wieters and Manny Machado.

HIGH POINT: The O's rolled to the AL East title by 12 games, rallied from a three-run deficit in Game Two of the AL Division Series before sweeping the Tigers and reached the ALCS for the first time since 1997. Baltimore boasted a home run champ for the second straight year in Nelson Cruz.

LOW POINT: The O's managed just 10 runs during a four-game sweep by the Royals in the ALCS. After a breakout 2013 campaign, Machado had a forgettable 2014. He slumped after missing most of April while recovering from surgery on his left knee, instigated a benches-clearing fight against the Athletics in May, then suffered a season-ending injury to his right knee in August. Meanwhile, Chris Davis hit just .196 and was suspended 25 games in August for amphetamine use.

NOTABLE ROOKIES: Righthander Kevin Gausman bounced between Triple-A Norfolk and Baltimore during the first half before becoming one of Baltimore's most reliable starters over the final two months. He worked out of the bullpen in the postseason and halted a Tigers rally in Game Two of the ALDS by striking out five of the first eight batters he faced. Jonathan Schoop filled in admirably for Machado at third in April before becoming the regular second baseman.

KEY TRANSACTIONS: Duquette's one-year, $8 million gamble on Cruz paid off. The same could not be said of the four-year, $50 million deal given to Ubaldo Jimenez, the presumptive ace who was pulled from the rotation in August. Baltimore released then re-signed Steve Pearce in April, and he responded by hitting 21 homers. Journeyman malcontent Delmon Young provided the critical blow in the Game Two rally against the Tigers.

DOWN ON THE FARM: Baltimore returned one pitching prospect to the mound in June, when Dylan Bundy made his first apperance since missing all of 2013 while recovering from Tommy John surgery, and lost another one month later when 2013 first-rounder Hunter Harvey was shut down with elbow inflamation. Christian Walker belted 26 home runs between Double-A and Triple-A, and Cuban outfielder Dariel Alvarez slugged .472 while rising to Triple-A in his second full season.

OPENING DAY PAYROLL: $105,084,121 (14th).

PLAYERS OF THE YEAR

MAJOR LEAGUE	MINOR LEAGUE
Nelson Cruz	**Christian Walker**
of/dh	1b
.271/.333/.525	(AA/AAA)
40 HR, .858 OPS	.288/.357/.459
Led majors in HR	26 HR, 96 RBI

ORGANIZATION LEADERS

BATTING		*Minimum 250 AB
MAJORS		
* AVG	Pearce, Steve	.293
* OPS	Pearce, Steve	.930
HR	Cruz, Nelson	40
RBI	Cruz, Nelson	108
MINORS		
* AVG	Sisco, Chance, Delmarva	.340
* OBP	Romero, Niuman, Bowie	.417
* SLG	Burgess, Michael, Frederick, Bowie	.552
R	Yastrzemski, Mike, Delmarva, Frederick, Bowie	96
H	Alvarez, Dariel, Bowie, Norfolk	163
TB	Yastrzemski, Mike, Delmarva, Frederick, Bowie	262
2B	Alvarez, Dariel, Bowie, Norfolk	37
3B	Yastrzemski, Mike, Delmarva, Frederick, Bowie	16
HR	Walker, Christian, Bowie, Norfolk	26
RBI	Walker, Christian, Bowie, Norfolk	96
BB	Romero, Niuman, Bowie	84
SO	Walker, Christian, Bowie, Norfolk	132
SB	Lorenzo, Gregory, Delmarva, Frederick	42

PITCHING		#Minimum 75 IP
MAJORS		
W	Chen, Wei-Yin	16
# ERA	Britton, Zach	1.65
SO	Tillman, Chris	150
SV	Britton, Zach	37
MINORS		
W	Wilson, Tyler, Bowie, Norfolk	14
L	Horacek, Mitch, Delmarva, Frederick	11
	Wright, Mike, Norfolk	11
# ERA	Brault, Steven, Delmarva, Frederick	2.77
G	Drake, Oliver, Bowie	50
GS	Wilson, Tyler, Bowie, Norfolk	28
SV	Drake, Oliver, Bowie	31
IP	Wilson, Tyler, Bowie, Norfolk	167
BB	Bridwell, Parker, Frederick	70
SO	Wilson, Tyler, Bowie, Norfolk	157
AVG	Brault, Steven, Delmarva, Frederick	.216

2014 PERFORMANCE

General Manager: Dan Duquette. **Farm Director:** Kent Qualls. **Scouting Director:** Gary Rajsich.

Class	Team	League	W	L	PCT	Finish	Manager
Majors	Baltimore Orioles	American	96	66	.593	t-2nd (30)	Buck Schowalter
Triple-A	Norfolk Tides	International	65	79	.451	13th (14)	Ron Johnson
Double-A	Bowie Baysox	Eastern	72	70	.507	6th (12)	Gary Kendall
High A	Frederick Keys	Carolina	65	72	.474	t-7th (10)	Luis Pujols
Low A	Delmarva Shorebirds	South Atlantic	66	73	.475	7th (14)	Ryan Minor
Short season	Aberdeen IronBirds	New York-Penn	27	48	.360	14th (14)	Matt Murrullo
Rookie	Orioles	Gulf Coast	29	31	.483	10th (16)	Orlando Gomez
Overall 2015 Minor League Record			324	373	.465	25th (30)	

ORGANIZATION STATISTICS

BALTIMORE ORIOLES

AMERICAN LEAGUE

Batting	B-T	HT	WT	DOB	AVG	vLH	vRH	G	AB	R	H	2B	3B	HR	RBI	BB	HBP	SH	SF	SO	SB	CS	SLG	OBP
Berry, Quintin	L-L	6-0	175	11-21-84	.000	.000	.000	10	2	3	0	0	0	0	0	0	0	0	0	1	1	0	.000	.000
Casilla, Alexi	B-R	5-9	170	7-20-84	.000	.000	.000	1	4	0	0	0	0	0	0	0	0	0	0	1	0	0	.000	.000
Clevenger, Steve	L-R	6-0	195	4-5-86	.225	.143	.232	35	89	8	20	8	1	0	8	8	0	0	0	19	0	0	.337	.289
Cruz, Nelson	R-R	6-2	230	7-1-80	.271	.314	.258	159	613	87	166	32	2	40	108	55	5	0	5	140	4	5	.525	.333
Davis, Chris	L-R	6-3	230	3-17-86	.196	.188	.199	127	450	65	88	16	0	26	72	60	9	1	5	173	2	1	.404	.300
De Aza, Alejandro	L-L	6-0	195	4-11-84	.293	.364	.282	20	82	11	24	5	3	3	10	6	0	1	0	19	2	3	.537	.341
2-team total (122 Chicago)					.252	—	—	142	477	56	120	24	8	8	41	39	6	3	3	119	17	10	.386	.314
Flaherty, Ryan	L-R	6-3	210	7-27-86	.221	.174	.230	102	281	33	62	15	1	7	32	22	5	3	1	68	1	0	.356	.288
Hardy, J.J.	R-R	6-1	190	8-19-82	.268	.226	.283	141	529	56	142	28	0	9	52	29	4	3	4	104	0	0	.372	.309
Hundley, Nick	R-R	6-1	200	9-8-83	.233	.227	.234	50	159	17	37	4	0	5	19	10	0	2	3	50	1	0	.352	.273
Johnson, Kelly	L-R	6-1	200	2-22-82	.231	.000	.243	19	39	7	9	4	0	1	4	6	0	0	0	11	0	1	.410	.333
3-team total (10 Boston, 77 New York)					.215	—	—	106	265	29	57	14	2	7	27	29	2	0	1	71	2	2	.362	.296
Jones, Adam	R-R	6-3	225	8-1-85	.281	.344	.261	159	644	88	181	30	2	29	96	19	12	0	7	133	7	1	.469	.311
Joseph, Caleb	R-R	6-3	180	6-18-86	.207	.202	.210	82	246	22	51	9	0	9	28	17	3	6	3	69	0	1	.354	.264
Lombardozzi Jr., Steve	B-R	6-0	200	9-20-88	.288	.071	.339	20	73	6	21	1	1	0	2	0	1	0	0	14	1	0	.329	.297
Lough, David	L-L	5-11	180	1-20-86	.247	.100	.266	112	174	31	43	6	3	4	16	15	1	6	1	33	8	5	.385	.309
Machado, Manny	R-R	6-2	180	7-6-92	.278	.240	.294	82	327	38	91	14	0	12	32	20	3	2	2	68	2	0	.431	.324
Markakis, Nick	L-L	6-1	190	11-17-83	.276	.280	.274	155	642	81	177	27	1	14	50	62	4	0	2	84	4	2	.386	.342
Paredes, Jimmy	B-R	6-3	200	11-25-88	.302	.444	.273	18	53	9	16	4	0	2	8	2	0	0	0	13	2	0	.491	.327
2-team total (9 Kansas City)					.286	—	—	27	63	12	18	4	0	2	8	2	0	0	0	16	4	0	.444	.308
Pearce, Steve	R-R	5-11	210	4-13-83	.293	.327	.279	102	338	51	99	26	0	21	49	40	4	0	1	76	5	0	.556	.373
Phelps, Cord	B-R	6-1	210	1-23-87	.000	.000	.000	3	3	0	0	0	0	0	0	0	0	0	0	0	0	0	.000	.000
Schoop, Jonathan	R-R	6-2	210	10-16-91	.209	.200	.212	137	455	48	95	18	0	16	45	13	8	5	0	122	2	0	.354	.244
Walker, Christian	R-R	6-0	220	3-28-91	.167	.200	.154	6	18	1	3	1	0	1	1	1	0	0	0	9	0	0	.389	.211
Weeks, Jemile	B-R	5-9	165	1-26-87	.273	—	.273	3	11	2	3	0	1	0	0	0	0	2	0	0	0	0	.455	.273
2-team total (14 Boston)					.297	—	—	17	37	8	11	3	1	0	3	4	1	2	1	2	2	0	.432	.372
Wieters, Matt	B-R	6-5	240	5-21-86	.308	.238	.325	26	104	13	32	5	0	5	18	6	0	2	0	19	0	1	.500	.339
Young, Delmon	R-R	6-3	240	9-14-85	.302	.282	.312	83	242	27	73	11	1	7	30	10	3	0	0	51	2	0	.442	.337

Pitching	B-T	HT	WT	DOB	W	L	ERA	G	GS	CG	SV	IP	H	R	ER	HR	BB	SO	AVG	vLH	vRH	K/9	BB/9
Brach, Brad	R-R	6-6	215	4-12-86	7	1	3.18	46	0	0	0	62	48	24	22	6	25	54	.216	.250	.192	7.80	3.61
Britton, Zach	L-L	6-3	195	12-22-87	3	2	1.65	71	0	0	37	76	46	17	14	4	23	62	.178	.170	.182	7.31	2.71
Chen, Wei-Yin	L-L	6-0	195	7-21-85	16	6	3.54	31	31	0	0	186	193	77	73	23	35	136	.266	.268	.266	6.59	1.70
Gausman, Kevin	R-R	6-3	190	1-6-91	7	7	3.57	20	20	1	0	113	111	48	45	7	38	88	.260	.254	.269	6.99	3.02
Gonzalez, Miguel	R-R	6-1	170	5-27-84	10	9	3.23	27	26	1	0	159	155	61	57	25	51	111	.255	.259	.249	6.28	2.89
Guilmet, Preston	R-R	6-2	200	7-27-87	0	1	5.23	10	0	0	0	10	8	6	6	2	1	12	.200	.111	.273	10.45	1.74
Hunter, Tommy	R-R	6-3	260	7-3-86	3	2	2.97	60	0	0	11	61	55	22	20	4	12	45	.244	.245	.243	6.68	1.78
Jimenez, Ubaldo	R-R	6-5	210	1-22-84	6	9	4.81	25	22	0	0	125	113	68	67	14	77	116	.241	.244	.238	8.33	5.53
Matusz, Brian	L-L	6-4	200	2-11-87	2	3	3.48	63	0	0	0	52	51	23	20	7	17	53	.250	.223	.277	9.23	2.96
McFarland, T.J.	L-L	6-3	220	6-8-89	4	2	2.76	37	1	0	0	59	70	22	18	2	13	34	.300	.266	.324	5.22	1.99
Meek, Evan	R-R	6-0	225	5-12-83	0	4	5.79	23	0	0	0	23	26	16	15	3	11	16	.289	.318	.261	6.17	4.24
Miller, Andrew	L-L	6-7	210	5-21-85	2	0	1.35	23	0	0	1	20	8	3	3	1	4	34	.119	.188	.057	15.30	1.80
2-team total (50 Boston)					5	5	2.02	73	0	0	1	62	33	16	14	3	17	103	—	—	—	14.87	2.45
Norris, Bud	R-R	6-0	220	3-2-85	15	8	3.65	28	28	0	0	165	149	68	67	20	52	139	.242	.255	.226	7.57	2.83
O'Day, Darren	R-R	6-4	220	10-22-82	5	2	1.70	68	0	0	4	69	42	14	13	6	19	73	.174	.189	.164	9.57	2.49
Patton, Troy	B-L	6-1	180	9-3-85	0	1	8.10	9	0	0	0	7	9	6	6	1	4	5	.333	.308	.357	6.75	5.40
Ramirez, Ramon	R-R	5-11	200	8-31-81	0	0	0.00	1	0	0	0	1	0	0	0	0	1	2	.000	.000	.000	18.00	9.00
Saunders, Joe	L-L	6-3	215	6-16-81	0	0	13.50	6	0	0	0	3	3	5	5	1	4	1	.250	.000	.500	2.70	10.80
2-team total (8 Texas)					0	5	6.70	14	8	0	0	43	65	37	32	9	24	23	—	—	—	4.81	5.02
Stinson, Josh	R-R	6-4	210	3-14-88	0	0	6.23	8	0	0	0	13	16	9	9	2	6	6	.302	.259	.346	4.15	4.15
Tillman, Chris	R-R	6-5	210	4-15-88	13	6	3.34	34	34	1	0	207	189	83	77	21	66	150	.238	.249	.225	6.51	2.86
Webb, Ryan	R-R	6-6	245	2-5-86	3	3	3.83	51	0	0	0	49	50	21	21	2	12	37	.259	.212	.283	6.75	2.19

BALTIMORE ORIOLES

Fielding

Catcher	PCT	G	PO	A	E	DP	PB
Clevenger	1.000	25	130	10	0	2	0
Hundley	.995	49	362	25	2	4	2
Joseph	.993	78	539	42	4	4	7
Wieters	.994	22	169	5	1	0	0

First Base	PCT	G	PO	A	E	DP
Clevenger	.929	3	13	0	1	1
Davis	.996	115	909	52	4	97
Flaherty	1.000	3	12	0	0	1
Joseph	1.000	4	10	0	0	0
Markakis	1.000	2	23	1	0	1
Pearce	.998	51	399	37	1	34
Walker	.979	6	45	2	1	5

Second Base	PCT	G	PO	A	E	DP
Casilla	—	1	0	0	0	0
Flaherty	.986	30	47	91	2	17
Johnson	.857	3	3	3	1	1
Lombardozzi Jr.	.988	20	29	52	1	14
Paredes	—	1	0	0	0	0
Schoop	.987	123	206	338	7	89
Weeks	1.000	1	0	1	0	0

Third Base	PCT	G	PO	A	E	DP
Casilla	.500	1	0	1	1	0
Davis	.886	21	9	22	4	3
Flaherty	.936	43	13	60	5	7
Johnson	.938	17	4	11	1	0
Machado	.962	82	61	168	9	17
Paredes	.900	13	7	20	3	2

	PCT	G	PO	A	E	DP
Schoop	.902	17	13	24	4	0

Shortstop	PCT	G	PO	A	E	DP
Flaherty	.965	29	32	51	3	10
Hardy	.978	141	187	394	13	99

Outfield	PCT	G	PO	A	E	DP
Berry	1.000	5	2	0	0	1
Cruz	1.000	70	132	2	0	0
De Aza	.977	20	41	1	1	0
Flaherty	—	2	0	0	0	0
Jones	.984	155	374	7	6	3
Lough	.993	103	135	4	1	0
Markakis	1.000	147	295	11	0	1
Pearce	1.000	40	75	5	0	1
Young	1.000	28	32	4	0	1

NORFOLK TIDES   TRIPLE-A
INTERNATIONAL LEAGUE

Batting	B-T	HT	WT	DOB	AVG	vLH	vRH	G	AB	R	H	2B	3B	HR	RBI	BB	HBP	SH	SF	SO	SB	CS	SLG	OBP
Adams, David	R-R	6-1	205	5-15-87	.214	.273	.188	21	70	7	15	3	1	2	8	6	2	0	0	22	0	0	.371	.295
Almanzar, Michael	R-R	6-3	190	12-2-90	.118	.200	.083	5	17	1	2	0	0	1	2	1	0	0	0	5	0	0	.294	.167
Alvarez, Dariel	R-R	6-2	180	11-7-88	.301	.333	.287	44	173	23	52	17	2	1	19	8	0	0	2	27	1	1	.439	.328
Berry, Quintin	L-L	6-0	175	11-21-84	.285	.195	.309	112	365	53	104	19	1	3	35	57	2	5	3	84	25	6	.367	.382
Borbon, Julio	L-L	6-0	195	2-20-86	.288	.288	.287	124	466	68	134	9	4	5	44	38	1	6	1	73	34	10	.356	.342
Britton, Buck	L-R	5-11	160	5-16-86	.254	.167	.280	59	205	24	52	12	1	8	35	15	2	0	4	33	0	0	.439	.305
Casilla, Alexi	B-R	5-9	170	7-20-84	.264	.286	.255	56	197	25	52	8	0	1	19	14	1	0	1	28	9	2	.320	.315
Clevenger, Steve	L-R	6-0	195	4-5-86	.305	.333	.294	64	226	28	69	13	0	2	30	23	1	0	4	30	1	0	.389	.366
De Jesus Jr., Ivan	R-R	5-11	200	5-1-87	.282	.298	.276	113	411	54	116	19	5	5	56	50	1	3	4	84	2	1	.389	.358
2-team total (2 Pawtucket)					.281	—	—	115	417	54	117	19	5	5	57	52	1	4	4	85	2	1	.386	.359
Freitas, David	R-R	6-3	225	3-18-89	.364	1.000	.333	8	22	2	8	1	0	1	4	6	0	0	0	3	0	0	.545	.500
Joseph, Caleb	R-R	6-3	180	6-18-86	.261	.467	.161	22	92	8	24	7	0	2	11	3	0	0	0	22	0	0	.402	.284
Lombardozzi Jr., Steve	B-R	6-0	200	9-20-88	.270	.259	.276	78	270	26	73	9	1	0	30	17	0	2	6	32	6	4	.311	.307
Marrero, Chris	R-R	6-3	229	7-2-88	.239	.122	.289	37	138	17	33	7	1	3	14	10	1	0	2	35	0	0	.370	.291
Monell, Johnny	L-R	6-0	210	3-27-86	.209	.167	.215	30	91	10	19	4	0	1	7	8	1	0	0	16	1	0	.286	.280
Paredes, Jimmy	B-R	6-3	200	11-25-88	.258	.222	.276	32	132	11	34	7	1	3	23	6	0	0	2	31	4	0	.394	.286
Paul, Xavier	L-R	5-9	205	2-25-85	.254	.288	.246	81	295	45	75	12	2	12	56	27	2	0	5	83	1	1	.431	.316
Peguero, Francisco	R-R	6-0	190	6-1-88	.273	.299	.261	78	304	41	83	16	1	3	33	11	4	0	1	69	4	2	.362	.306
Phelps, Cord	B-R	6-1	210	1-23-87	.259	.248	.265	99	343	61	89	13	5	7	51	52	4	1	3	60	2	5	.388	.361
Urrutia, Henry	L-R	6-3	180	2-13-87	.270	.276	.267	51	204	14	55	12	1	0	17	5	0	0	2	50	2	1	.338	.284
Walker, Christian	R-R	6-0	220	3-28-91	.259	.212	.281	44	166	15	43	10	0	6	19	18	2	0	2	49	0	0	.428	.335
Wallace, Brett	L-R	6-2	235	8-26-86	.265	.194	.285	90	339	50	90	12	0	10	35	29	4	0	2	98	0	1	.389	.329
2-team total (38 Buffalo)					.282	—	—	128	472	62	133	17	0	17	58	44	7	0	2	131	0	1	.426	.350
Ward, Brian	R-R	5-11	210	10-17-85	.227	.241	.220	64	185	24	42	5	0	2	20	28	2	4	3	44	2	0	.286	.330
Weeks, Jemile	B-R	5-9	165	1-26-87	.280	.271	.285	63	207	29	58	12	4	1	19	37	3	7	3	30	8	4	.391	.392

Pitching	B-T	HT	WT	DOB	W	L	ERA	G	GS	CG	SV	IP	H	R	ER	HR	BB	SO	AVG	vLH	vRH	K/9	BB/9
Additon, Nick	L-L	6-5	215	12-16-87	6	5	4.32	27	9	0	0	90	94	48	43	5	39	67	.274	.265	.278	6.72	3.91
Alderson, Tim	R-R	6-6	220	11-3-88	2	4	6.12	28	0	0	0	50	59	35	34	6	19	37	.292	.215	.341	6.66	3.42
Bell, Heath	R-R	6-3	250	9-29-77	2	0	4.22	10	0	0	1	11	15	6	5	0	6	11	.341	.250	.450	9.28	5.06
2-team total (5 Scranton/W-B)					2	1	5.40	15	0	0	2	17	22	11	10	1	12	19	—	—	—	10.26	6.48
Bischoff, Matt	R-R	6-0	190	5-21-87	0	0	0.00	1	0	0	0	3	4	0	0	0	2	1	.308	.250	.400	3.00	6.00
Brach, Brad	R-R	6-6	215	4-12-86	3	1	3.47	17	0	0	1	23	26	10	9	1	6	43	.286	.275	.294	16.59	2.31
Chalas, Miguel	R-R	5-11	155	6-27-92	1	1	1.29	2	0	0	0	7	2	1	1	0	6	5	.091	.083	.100	6.43	7.71
Coello, Robert	R-R	6-5	250	11-23-84	4	1	1.90	20	0	0	2	24	13	10	5	2	15	25	.167	.156	.174	9.51	5.70
2-team total (26 Scranton/W-B)					6	2	1.78	46	0	0	6	56	34	17	11	3	36	69	—	—	—	11.16	5.82
De La Cruz, Kelvin	L-L	6-5	190	8-1-88	1	4	5.98	37	0	0	1	50	61	40	33	8	31	49	.305	.209	.353	8.88	5.62
Escalona, Edgmer	R-R	6-4	235	10-6-86	1	2	6.10	6	3	0	0	21	27	14	14	4	5	14	.310	.364	.256	6.10	2.18
2-team total (19 Scranton/W-B)					2	4	3.71	25	4	0	4	51	53	23	21	5	10	37	—	—	—	6.53	1.76
Gamboa, Eddie	R-R	6-1	200	12-21-84	4	5	4.06	14	12	0	0	78	70	41	35	7	28	74	.241	.216	.270	8.58	3.24
Gausman, Kevin	R-R	6-3	190	1-6-91	1	3	3.32	11	11	0	0	43	41	18	16	5	18	44	.246	.261	.227	9.14	3.74
Gonzalez, Miguel	R-R	6-1	170	5-27-84	1	0	3.00	2	2	0	0	9	6	3	3	1	2	1	.182	.400	.087	1.00	2.00
Guilmet, Preston	R-R	6-2	200	7-27-87	4	2	3.91	40	0	0	10	48	42	25	21	6	10	54	.227	.211	.244	10.06	1.86
Gurka, Jason	L-L	6-0	170	1-10-88	0	2	9.45	2	2	0	0	7	8	8	7	1	1	6	.286	.333	.273	8.10	1.35
Huntzinger, Brock	R-R	6-3	200	7-2-88	4	3	3.00	47	0	0	1	81	70	29	27	8	25	76	.232	.202	.261	8.44	2.78
Jimenez, Ubaldo	R-R	6-5	210	1-22-84	0	0	1.50	1	1	0	0	6	5	1	1	0	2	3	.208	.250	.188	4.50	3.00
Johnson, Steve	R-R	6-1	220	8-31-87	0	2	7.11	13	13	0	0	38	47	31	30	9	30	32	.297	.289	.305	7.58	7.11
Jones, Chris	L-L	6-2	205		8	8	3.61	35	14	0	0	120	124	62	48	4	36	85	.266	.200	.289	6.39	2.71
McFarland, T.J.	L-L	6-3	220	6-8-89	0	1	3.75	5	1	0	0	24	21	11	10	0	8	25	.226	.185	.242	9.38	3.00
Meek, Evan	R-R	6-0	225	5-12-83	2	0	1.94	39	0	0	16	42	33	13	9	2	4	37	.214	.206	.220	7.99	0.86
Patton, Troy	B-L	6-1	180	9-3-85	0	0	3.86	4	0	0	0	5	4	2	2	1	3	2	.222	.000	.400	3.86	5.79
Pettit, Jake	L-L	6-1	185	10-28-86	0	1	8.53	1	1	0	0	6	7	6	6	1	2	2	.269	.500	.167	2.84	2.84
Ramirez, Ramon	R-R	5-11	200	8-31-81	1	1	2.28	18	0	0	0	24	22	10	6	0	8	30	.247	.171	.296	11.41	3.04

	B-T	HT	WT	DOB	W	L	ERA	G	GS	CG	SV	IP	H	R	ER	HR	BB	SO	AVG	vLH	vRH	K/9	BB/9
Rapada, Clay	R-L	6-5	195	3-9-81	2	0	7.23	18	0	0	1	19	28	17	15	2	7	12	.359	.344	.370	5.79	3.38
Saunders, Joe	L-L	6-3	215	6-16-81	0	1	1.50	10	0	0	0	12	11	2	2	0	6	8	.250	.211	.280	6.00	4.50
Stinson, Josh	R-R	6-4	210	3-14-88	5	5	5.48	22	13	1	1	85	78	54	52	14	38	80	.242	.221	.257	8.44	4.01
Vasquez, Anthony	L-L	6-0	190	9-19-86	0	1	8.22	3	1	0	0	8	11	7	7	2	3	5	.344	.250	.400	5.87	3.52
Webb, Ryan	R-R	6-6	245	2-5-86	0	2	4.76	11	0	0	0	11	13	8	6	1	2	10	.277	.267	.281	7.94	1.59
Wilson, Tyler	R-R	6-2	185	9-25-89	4	3	3.60	12	12	0	0	70	61	30	28	8	21	66	.239	.246	.234	8.49	2.70
Wolf, Randy	L-L	6-0	205	8-22-76	0	0	4.20	6	1	0	0	15	18	9	7	1	5	12	.305	.333	.293	7.20	3.00
Wright, Mike	R-R	6-6	215	1-3-90	5	11	4.61	26	26	0	0	143	159	87	73	10	41	103	.281	.247	.318	6.50	2.59
Yoon, Suk-Min	R-R	6-0	190	7-24-86	4	8	5.74	23	18	0	0	96	125	69	61	15	26	67	.317	.325	.310	6.30	2.45

Fielding

Catcher	PCT	G	PO	A	E	DP	PB
Clevenger	.991	48	321	23	3	5	5
Freitas	1.000	8	49	5	0	0	0
Joseph	.994	21	166	13	1	0	2
Monell	1.000	18	103	11	0	2	3
Ward	.977	60	433	40	11	4	4

First Base	PCT	G	PO	A	E	DP
Britton	.950	2	17	2	1	1
Clevenger	.957	3	21	1	1	1
Freitas	—	0	0	0	0	0
Marrero	.965	18	131	8	5	10
Monell	.984	6	53	7	1	12
Phelps	1.000	5	20	1	0	1
Walker	.989	44	359	15	4	27
Wallace	.992	72	545	49	5	48

Second Base	PCT	G	PO	A	E	DP
Adams	1.000	3	2	10	0	1

		1.000	1	3	4	0	1
Britton	1.000	1	3	4	0	1
Casilla	1.000	34	33	89	0	15
De Jesus Jr.	1.000	8	14	16	0	5
Lombardozzi Jr.	.969	38	62	96	5	19
Paredes	.952	5	9	11	1	1
Phelps	1.000	31	47	76	0	17
Weeks	.958	30	53	83	6	20

Third Base	PCT	G	PO	A	E	DP
Adams	.886	15	13	18	4	1
Almanzar	1.000	5	4	11	0	2
Britton	.932	54	30	94	9	10
De Jesus Jr.	1.000	1	0	1	0	0
Lombardozzi Jr.	.939	16	13	18	2	2
Paredes	.933	27	17	39	4	2
Phelps	.970	28	24	41	2	4
Walker	—	1	0	0	0	0
Wallace	.938	7	6	9	1	1

Shortstop	PCT	G	PO	A	E	DP
Casilla	.949	21	41	53	5	13
De Jesus Jr.	.966	98	160	243	14	57
Lombardozzi Jr.	.933	5	4	10	1	1
Phelps	.950	6	5	14	1	1
Weeks	.932	17	20	35	4	7

Outfield	PCT	G	PO	A	E	DP
Alvarez	.968	43	87	4	3	1
Berry	.989	107	255	11	3	3
Borbon	.994	122	318	4	2	3
Britton	1.000	2	2	0	0	0
Lombardozzi Jr.	.972	22	35	0	1	0
Marrero	1.000	3	5	0	0	0
Paul	.960	20	23	1	1	0
Peguero	.985	65	124	4	2	2
Phelps	1.000	31	44	4	0	0
Urrutia	.962	34	73	2	3	0
Weeks	.917	7	11	0	1	0

BOWIE BAYSOX   DOUBLE-A

EASTERN LEAGUE

Batting	B-T	HT	WT	DOB	AVG	vLH	vRH	G	AB	R	H	2B	3B	HR	RBI	BB	HBP	SH	SF	SO	SB	CS	SLG	OBP
Adams, David	R-R	6-1	205	5-15-87	.265	.282	.255	84	306	39	81	16	3	7	40	26	7	1	3	47	3	1	.405	.333
Alvarez, Dariel	R-R	6-2	180	11-7-88	.309	.360	.286	91	359	52	111	20	1	14	68	13	2	1	6	35	7	4	.487	.332
Bermudez, Ronald	R-R	6-0	195	8-25-86	.291	.331	.262	94	357	42	104	22	0	3	32	17	2	3	6	61	2	2	.378	.322
Britton, Buck	L-R	5-11	160	5-16-86	.317	.290	.333	61	252	46	80	14	1	7	32	22	3	1	1	23	3	1	.464	.378
Burgess, Michael	L-L	5-11	195	10-20-88	.148	.286	.100	7	27	1	4	2	0	0	2	1	0	0	0	5	0	1	.222	.179
Chavez, Zane	L-R	5-10	200	12-30-86	.167	.286	.118	14	48	4	8	0	1	0	5	0	0	0		11	0	0	.208	.245
Chiang, Chih-Hsien	L-R	6-2	195	2-21-88	.219	.140	.245	56	201	20	44	12	1	3	20	12	1	1	2	28	0	1	.333	.264
Davis, Chris	L-R	6-3	230	3-17-86	.250	1.000	.000	1	4	1	1	0	0	0	0	0	0	0	0	2	0	0	.250	.250
Davis, Glynn	R-R	6-3	170	12-7-91	.313	.357	.294	26	96	9	30	6	0	1	12	2	1	1	3	20	3	1	.406	.330
Freitas, David	R-R	6-3	225	3-18-89	.250	.268	.241	53	168	22	42	11	0	5	25	19	1	1	1	24	0	0	.405	.328
Kang, K.D.	L-L	6-2	200	2-6-88	.282	.311	.270	100	376	50	106	22	3	12	37	32	1	1	2	86	2	2	.452	.338
Marrero, Chris	R-R	6-3	229	7-2-88	.235	.259	.220	61	217	30	51	10	1	10	42	20	2	0	2	40	0	0	.429	.303
Ohlman, Mike	R-R	6-5	215	12-14-90	.236	.217	.246	113	403	40	95	25	1	2	33	43	2	2	4	86	0	0	.318	.310
Reimold, Nolan	R-R	6-4	205	10-12-83	.315	.450	.235	17	54	10	17	3	0	2	9	12	0	0	3	13	1	1	.481	.420
Romero, Niuman	B-R	6-1	190	1-24-85	.320	.286	.336	130	482	86	154	30	1	5	48	84	2	5	8	63	7	2	.417	.417
Rosa, Garabez	R-R	6-2	166	10-12-89	.282	.296	.274	124	465	59	131	27	1	11	69	12	1	3	4	95	7	2	.415	.299
Ruettiger, John	L-L	6-1	193	9-21-89	.282	.204	.320	61	149	24	42	6	1	0	10	11	1	3	0	22	8	4	.336	.335
Schoop, Sharlon	R-R	6-2	190	4-15-87	.217	.214	.219	77	267	29	58	13	0	3	25	24	3	3	1	56	0	3	.300	.288
Starr, Sammie	R-R	5-8	165	5-31-88	.176	.200	.158	15	34	3	6	0	0	1	4	0	0	0	0	2	0	0	.265	.176
Walker, Christian	R-R	6-0	220	3-28-91	.301	.283	.309	95	366	58	110	15	2	20	77	38	3	0	4	83	2	1	.516	.367
Ward, Brian	R-R	5-11	210	10-17-85	.346	.429	.250	7	26	4	9	1	0	0	2	4	0	0	0	3	0	1	.385	.433
Yastrzemski, Mike	L-L	5-11	180	8-23-90	.250	.211	.278	43	184	23	46	13	4	3	12	14	2	1	0	34	1	2	.413	.310

Pitching	B-T	HT	WT	DOB	W	L	ERA	G	GS	CG	SV	IP	H	R	ER	HR	BB	SO	AVG	vLH	vRH	K/9	BB/9
Additon, Nick	L-L	6-5	215	12-16-87	1	1	2.45	5	5	0	0	29	27	9	8	1	9	25	.245	.250	.244	7.67	2.76
Ayala, Luis	R-R	6-2	205	1-12-78	1	0	5.06	5	0	0	0	5	11	3	3	0	2	5	.423	.438	.400	8.44	3.38
Berry, Tim	L-L	6-3	180	3-18-91	6	7	3.51	23	23	0	0	133	122	57	52	12	45	108	.249	.212	.263	7.29	3.04
Bischoff, Matt	R-R	6-0	190	5-21-87	3	5	5.21	23	10	0	0	67	81	41	39	11	26	57	.305	.270	.333	7.62	3.48
Castillo, Fabio	R-R	6-1	235	2-19-89	0	1	5.14	18	0	0	0	28	30	22	16	3	20	22	.273	.310	.231	7.07	6.43
Davies, Zach	R-R	6-0	150	2-7-93	10	7	3.35	21	20	0	0	110	106	50	41	8	32	109	.249	.230	.267	8.92	2.62
DePaula, Julio	R-R	6-0	180	12-31-82	1	5	4.97	21	1	0	3	38	44	22	21	2	13	43	.282	.296	.271	10.18	3.08
Drake, Oliver	R-R	6-4	215	1-13-87	2	4	3.08	50	0	0	31	53	41	19	18	2	17	71	.214	.208	.219	12.13	2.91
Escat, Gene	R-R	6-2	195	9-3-89	1	0	0.00	4	0	0	0	8	6	0	0	0	2	6	.231	.250	.214	6.48	2.16
Gamboa, Eddie	R-R	6-1	200	12-21-84	1	2	3.19	5	5	0	0	31	19	14	11	1	18	30	.171	.143	.188	8.71	5.23
Givens, Mychal	R-R	6-0	207	5-13-90	0	0	3.91	18	0	0	0	25	19	12	11	0	23	28	.209	.262	.163	9.95	8.17
Gonzalez, Miguel	R-R	6-1	170	5-29-84	0	0	0.00	1	1	0	0	4	0	0	0	0	1	5	.000	.143	.333	10.38	2.08
Gurka, Jason	L-L	6-0	170	1-10-88	3	1	2.38	30	3	0	0	64	50	21	17	4	18	60	.212	.160	.236	8.39	2.52
Hensley, Steven	R-R	6-3	190	12-27-86	3	1	2.09	37	0	0	5	60	46	17	14	4	27	57	.213	.220	.209	8.50	4.03
Kline, Branden	R-R	6-3	210	9-29-91	0	2	5.94	3	3	0	0	17	18	11	11	1	9		.290	.378	.160	4.86	5.94
Morillo, Juan	R-R	6-3	190	11-5-83	2	0	4.67	22	0	0	0	35	35	19	18	1	28	41	.267	.328	.214	10.64	7.27
Norris, Bud	R-R	6-0	220	3-2-85	0	1	6.23	1	1	0	0	4	4	3	3	0	5	7	.250	.222	.286	14.54	10.38

BALTIMORE ORIOLES

	B-T	HT	WT	DOB	W	L	ERA	G	GS	CG	SV	IP	H	R	ER	HR	BB	SO	AVG	vLH	vRH	K/9	BB/9
Petrini, Chris	R-L	6-0	205	2-11-87	2	2	6.35	15	0	0	0	23	26	16	16	5	6	14	.306	.286	.316	5.56	2.38
Pettit, Jake	L-L	6-1	185	10-28-86	4	8	6.14	25	19	0	0	110	134	81	75	16	37	62	.304	.263	.321	5.07	3.03
Prado, Marcel	R-R	6-4	230	11-22-87	7	3	4.54	41	0	0	4	75	66	45	38	4	33	59	.235	.246	.226	7.05	3.94
Rodriguez, Eduardo	L-L	6-2	200	4-7-93	3	7	4.79	16	16	1	0	83	90	50	44	5	29	69	.274	.186	.310	7.51	3.16
2-team total (6 Portland)					6	8	3.60	22	22	1	0	120	120	54	48	6	37	108	—	—	—	8.10	2.78
Santana, Alexander	B-R	5-11	170	8-26-91	1	0	0.00	2	0	0	0	2	0	0	0	0	0	2	.000	.000	.000	9.00	9.00
Tolliver, Ashur	L-L	6-0	170	1-24-88	3	1	3.18	18	1	0	0	23	27	9	8	1	5	25	.293	.241	.317	9.93	1.99
Vasquez, Anthony	L-L	6-0	190	9-19-86	8	7	4.73	24	18	0	0	116	137	70	61	16	37	87	.295	.277	.304	6.75	2.87
Wilson, Tyler	R-R	6-2	185	9-25-89	10	5	3.72	16	16	0	0	97	101	47	40	10	22	91	.266	.264	.269	8.47	2.05

Fielding

Catcher	PCT	G	PO	A	E	DP	PB
Chavez	1.000	8	57	13	0	0	1
Freitas	.993	40	284	18	2	0	4
Ohlman	.987	91	695	63	10	6	10
Ward	1.000	5	44	2	0	0	1

First Base	PCT	G	PO	A	E	DP
Britton	.982	6	52	3	1	4
Davis	1.000	1	10	0	0	0
Freitas	1.000	1	11	0	0	2
Marrero	.998	44	378	27	1	29
Walker	.989	91	771	67	9	79

Second Base	PCT	G	PO	A	E	DP
Adams	.981	69	119	195	6	38
Britton	.979	22	32	60	2	10

	PCT	G	PO	A	E	DP
Romero	1.000	3	7	10	0	4
Rosa	.988	36	58	102	2	20
Schoop	1.000	11	13	37	0	3
Starr	1.000	6	5	12	0	2

Third Base	PCT	G	PO	A	E	DP
Adams	1.000	2	1	2	0	0
Britton	.905	30	15	42	6	1
Romero	.960	94	52	165	9	22
Rosa	.500	1	1	0	1	0
Schoop	.953	18	8	33	2	4
Starr	—	1	0	0	0	0

Shortstop	PCT	G	PO	A	E	DP
Romero	.957	29	44	68	5	18
Rosa	.932	63	101	172	20	29

	PCT	G	PO	A	E	DP
Schoop	.966	47	66	131	7	26
Starr	1.000	5	10	13	0	4

Outfield	PCT	G	PO	A	E	DP
Alvarez	.987	90	213	10	3	4
Bermudez	.988	93	152	7	2	1
Burgess	1.000	7	13	2	0	0
Chiang	1.000	52	77	3	0	0
Davis	.979	26	44	2	1	0
Kang	.912	46	58	4	6	0
Marrero	1.000	6	7	0	0	0
Reimold	1.000	8	10	2	0	1
Rosa	1.000	24	57	3	0	1
Ruettiger	.986	51	67	4	1	1
Yastrzemski	.974	42	113	1	3	1

FREDERICK KEYS   HIGH CLASS A
CAROLINA LEAGUE

Batting	B-T	HT	WT	DOB	AVG	vLH	vRH	G	AB	R	H	2B	3B	HR	RBI	BB	HBP	SH	SF	SO	SB	CS	SLG	OBP
Almanzar, Michael	R-R	6-3	190	12-2-90	.118	.000	.154	5	17	1	2	2	0	0	2	1	1	0	0	4	0	0	.235	.211
Boss, Torsten	L-R	6-0	190	12-27-90	.333	.000	.500	1	3	1	1	1	0	0	0	1	0	0	0	1	0	0	.667	.500
2-team total (42 Carolina)					.218	—	—	43	147	16	32	7	1	5	17	20	2	0	1	46	1	2	.381	.318
Burgess, Michael	L-L	5-11	195	10-20-88	.315	.315	.314	83	321	51	101	32	4	15	68	26	3	0	5	61	6	2	.579	.366
Chavez, Zane	R-R	5-10	200	12-30-86	.302	.204	.356	37	139	18	42	5	0	6	17	9	1	1	2	23	0	0	.468	.344
Chiang, Chih-Hsien	L-R	6-2	195	2-21-88	.221	.222	.221	34	122	13	27	4	0	4	12	14	0	0	0	21	0	3	.352	.301
Davis, Glynn	R-R	6-3	170	12-7-91	.295	.326	.284	89	352	65	104	21	4	1	31	36	2	4	1	69	20	8	.386	.363
Esposito, Jason	R-R	6-2	200	7-19-90	.272	.356	.240	127	470	50	128	31	5	9	50	17	5	0	6	103	5	4	.417	.301
Herbst, Lucas	L-L	6-0	185	9-9-90	.237	.212	.250	54	194	21	46	9	2	1	22	9	4	1	2	46	7	0	.320	.282
Hutter, Joel	R-R	6-1	210	2-28-90	.226	.212	.233	61	186	24	42	7	1	2	25	27	5	1	1	39	2	0	.306	.338
Kimmel, Sam	L-R	6-0	185	11-3-89	.200	.500	.154	4	15	2	3	0	0	0	2	0	0	0	1	0	1	0	.200	.188
Lorenzo, Gregory	R-R	6-0	160	5-31-91	.000	—	.000	1	3	0	0	0	0	0	0	0	0	0	0	2	0	0	.000	.000
Machado, Manny	R-R	6-2	180	7-6-92	.667	.571	.800	3	12	5	8	4	1	0	2	1	0	0	0	1	1	0	1.167	.692
Mancini, Trey	R-R	6-4	215	3-18-92	.251	.219	.262	69	275	37	69	19	0	7	41	14	4	0	2	43	0	1	.396	.295
Marin, Adrian	R-R	6-0	180	3-8-94	.232	.230	.233	115	431	40	100	30	1	5	42	21	3	3	2	103	12	4	.341	.271
Mosby, Michael	R-R	6-0	195	10-30-89	.000	.000	.000	3	12	0	0	0	0	0	0	0	0	0	0	4	0	0	.000	.000
Mummey, Trent	L-L	5-9	170	1-5-89	.182	.000	.235	7	22	1	4	0	0	0	4	0	0	0	0	8	0	2	.182	.308
Nathans, Tucker	L-R	6-0	200	11-6-88	.271	.253	.277	90	329	39	89	17	0	3	26	22	1	1	1	75	4	0	.350	.317
Pena, Jerome	B-R	5-11	185	11-6-88	.269	.276	.266	93	309	47	83	19	4	5	39	31	2	4	5	103	4	2	.405	.334
Perez, Pedro	R-R	5-11	170	5-8-91	.229	.500	.148	11	35	3	8	0	0	0	3	1	0	0	1	6	0	0	.229	.243
Ruettiger, John	L-L	6-1	193	9-21-89	.231	.159	.262	38	147	16	34	3	1	1	14	17	0	0	1	20	15	5	.286	.309
Russell, Steel	L-R	6-0	195	9-5-90	.181	.150	.192	25	72	10	13	2	0	1	3	5	1	1	0	19	0	0	.250	.244
Sawyer, Wynston	R-R	6-3	205	11-14-91	.250	.210	.262	81	272	29	68	14	0	4	33	33	2	1	8	40	0	0	.346	.327
Simpson, Creede	R-R	6-2	185	9-8-89	.214	.338	.160	58	215	30	46	18	0	7	22	24	2	1	1	52	2	1	.395	.298
Starr, Sammie	R-R	5-8	165	5-31-88	.257	.200	.302	33	113	16	29	10	1	4	19	9	2	1	0	13	3	2	.469	.323
Webb, Brenden	L-L	6-1	185	2-24-90	.230	.165	.251	105	374	48	86	21	3	11	49	39	1	0	6	122	8	5	.390	.300
Wynns, Austin	R-R	6-2	205	12-10-90	.214	.250	.200	5	14	3	3	1	0	0	4	3	0	1	1	0	0	0	.286	.333
Yastrzemski, Mike	L-L	5-11	180	8-23-90	.312	.450	.274	23	93	21	29	7	2	1	19	8	2	0	4	16	5	0	.462	.364

Pitching	B-T	HT	WT	DOB	W	L	ERA	G	GS	CG	SV	IP	H	R	ER	HR	BB	SO	AVG	vLH	vRH	K/9	BB/9
Beal, Jesse	B-R	6-6	210	7-12-90	2	1	3.48	23	5	0	4	41	46	17	16	2	13	36	.275	.284	.270	7.84	2.83
Blackmar, Mark	R-R	6-3	215	4-28-92	10	1	3.18	26	18	1	1	130	109	54	46	5	32	83	.229	.245	.216	5.73	2.21
Brault, Steven	L-L	6-1	175	4-29-92	2	0	0.55	3	3	1	0	16	7	1	1	0	2	9	.127	.083	.140	4.96	1.10
Bridwell, Parker	R-R	6-4	190	2-2-91	7	10	4.45	26	26	1	0	142	123	75	70	11	70	142	.234	.223	.242	9.02	4.45
Bundy, Dylan	R-R	6-1	195	11-15-92	1	2	4.78	6	6	0	0	26	28	14	14	0	13	15	.283	.273	.291	5.13	4.44
Chalas, Miguel	R-R	5-11	155	6-27-92	2	3	4.80	28	0	0	0	69	76	41	37	7	20	49	.276	.215	.315	6.36	2.60
Escat, Gene	R-R	6-2	195	9-3-89	2	5	3.49	31	1	0	1	57	50	26	22	4	26	58	.239	.179	.275	9.21	4.13
Givens, Mychal	R-R	6-0	207	5-13-90	1	2	3.24	18	0	0	0	33	21	20	12	2	16	27	.174	.159	.182	7.29	4.32
Hauser, Matt	R-R	6-2	195	3-30-88	0	4	7.04	11	0	0	2	15	22	15	12	2	9	16	.349	.321	.371	9.39	5.28
Hernandez, Ivan	R-R	6-2	249	7-28-91	0	0	5.40	2	0	0	0	5	7	4	3	0	2	2	.333	.545	.100	3.60	3.60
Hobgood, Matt	R-R	6-4	245	8-1-90	3	4	4.48	29	0	0	4	64	64	46	32	3	30	48	.254	.245	.260	6.72	4.20
Horacek, Mitch	L-L	6-5	185	12-3-91	0	1	7.50	1	1	0	0	6	7	5	5	0	3	3	.333	.125	.462	4.50	4.50
Keller, Jon	R-R	6-5	210	8-8-92	0	0	8.31	2	0	0	0	4	8	5	4	0	7	5	.400	.400	.400	10.38	14.54
Kline, Branden	R-R	6-3	210	9-29-91	8	6	3.84	23	23	0	0	127	143	60	54	9	32	95	.288	.325	.269	6.75	2.27
Price, Matt	R-R	6-2	215	9-8-89	3	4	6.43	21	0	0	3	28	39	22	20	6	16	35	.317	.333	.307	11.25	5.14

BALTIMORE ORIOLES

Rheault, Dylan	R-R	6-9	245	3-21-92	0	3	3.38	4	0	0	0	5	5	3	2	0	5	2	.263	.444	.100	3.38	8.44
Rutledge, Lex	L-L	6-1	195	6-28-91	4	3	2.97	35	0	0	8	58	43	21	19	2	37	46	.205	.164	.219	7.18	5.77
Taylor, Matt	R-L	6-1	185	4-1-91	6	2	3.69	13	13	0	0	63	72	30	26	2	33	22	.294	.254	.308	3.13	4.69
Tolliver, Ashur	L-L	6-0	170	1-24-88	0	1	2.45	9	0	0	2	15	14	4	4	1	2	15	.241	.273	.234	9.20	1.23
Torres, Dennis	R-R	6-3	200	5-17-90	2	2	3.66	19	2	0	6	39	39	17	16	1	12	21	.267	.343	.203	4.81	2.75
Vader, Sebastian	R-R	6-4	175	6-3-92	3	4	4.60	9	9	0	0	47	47	24	24	7	26	34	.263	.214	.294	6.51	4.98
Van Meter, Joe	R-R	6-2	195	10-18-88	3	2	4.91	9	9	0	0	48	46	27	26	9	19	30	.247	.309	.221	5.66	3.59
Wager, Brady	R-R	6-3	190	11-17-90	6	8	5.32	26	21	1	0	115	137	77	68	11	50	71	.295	.340	.263	5.56	3.91
Yacabonis, Jimmy	R-R	6-3	205	3-21-92	0	4	8.58	17	0	0	0	28	34	27	27	2	28	23	.301	.256	.329	7.31	8.89

Fielding

Catcher	PCT	G	PO	A	E	DP	PB
Chavez	.994	22	159	14	1	0	5
Perez	.977	11	70	14	2	2	1
Russell	.993	25	127	11	1	1	7
Sawyer	.991	79	501	43	5	5	2
Wynns	1.000	5	35	4	0	0	1

First Base	PCT	G	PO	A	E	DP
Hutter	.994	17	156	5	1	12
Mancini	.993	69	671	35	5	62
Mosby	1.000	2	12	1	0	1
Simpson	.992	51	450	30	4	28

Second Base	PCT	G	PO	A	E	DP
Hutter	.953	16	34	48	4	9
Nathans	1.000	22	35	68	0	10

Pena	.970	82	131	263	12	57
Starr	.975	19	23	54	2	5

Third Base	PCT	G	PO	A	E	DP
Almanzar	1.000	3	1	4	0	0
Esposito	.960	118	83	257	14	19
Hutter	.976	14	10	31	1	6
Machado	.875	2	2	5	1	0
Mosby	.889	1	1	7	1	1
Starr	.750	1	1	2	1	0

Shortstop	PCT	G	PO	A	E	DP
Hutter	1.000	2	2	5	0	1
Marin	.972	115	179	334	15	67
Pena	1.000	10	14	36	0	8
Starr	1.000	12	21	27	0	2

Outfield	PCT	G	PO	A	E	DP
Boss	1.000	1	3	0	0	0
Burgess	.961	62	117	7	5	1
Chiang	.980	29	43	5	1	1
Davis	.984	88	176	4	3	2
Herbst	.937	49	71	3	5	1
Kimmel	1.000	4	4	0	0	0
Lorenzo	1.000	1	4	0	0	0
Mummey	.952	6	19	1	1	0
Nathans	1.000	12	16	2	0	0
Ruettiger	1.000	38	78	1	0	1
Simpson	1.000	3	5	0	0	0
Webb	.976	101	195	6	5	1
Yastrzemski	1.000	23	41	1	0	0

DELMARVA SHOREBIRDS

LOW CLASS A

SOUTH ATLANTIC LEAGUE

Batting	B-T	HT	WT	DOB	AVG	vLH	vRH	G	AB	R	H	2B	3B	HR	RBI	BB	HBP	SH	SF	SO	SB	CS	SLG	OBP
Bierfeldt, Conor	R-R	6-2	220	4-2-91	.196	.093	.235	111	397	44	78	27	1	12	67	38	5	1	1	107	3	0	.360	.274
Breen, Jared	R-R	5-11	185	5-11-91	.217	.226	.215	70	244	27	53	13	0	0	29	23	6	3	2	65	1	2	.270	.298
Caronia, Anthony	L-R	6-0	170	5-22-91	.364	.367	.363	53	176	25	64	8	1	1	18	13	1	3	0	41	12	6	.438	.411
Castagnini, Federico	R-R	6-0	165	3-15-91	.234	.273	.224	33	107	17	25	1	0	0	5	16	1	4	2	18	0	2	.243	.333
Dosch, Drew	L-R	6-2	200	6-24-92	.314	.333	.308	128	500	76	157	22	4	5	50	47	6	2	1	97	5	3	.404	.379
Hart, Josh	L-L	6-1	180	10-2-94	.255	.274	.250	85	326	22	83	5	1	1	28	21	2	0	3	86	11	5	.285	.301
Herbst, Lucas	L-L	6-0	185	9-9-90	.198	.182	.203	24	96	10	19	2	0	1	8	4	3	2	1	18	5	0	.250	.250
Kemp, Jeff	R-R	6-0	190	3-23-90	.254	.233	.260	108	437	52	111	28	3	4	42	17	10	3	6	98	4	3	.359	.294
Kimmel, Sam	L-R	6-0	185	11-3-89	.158	.000	.231	8	19	2	3	0	0	0	0	1	0	0	0	6	1	0	.158	.200
Lartiguez, Oswill	R-R	6-1	179	8-11-92	.200	.333	.143	4	10	1	2	1	0	0	1	0	0	0	0	3	1	0	.300	.200
Ledesma, Ronarsy	R-R	5-11	170	4-19-93	.308	.125	.600	3	13	1	4	0	1	1	4	0	0	0	0	3	0	0	.692	.308
Lorenzo, Gregory	R-R	6-0	160	5-31-91	.263	.272	.260	125	472	64	124	14	8	1	34	30	7	6	0	127	42	11	.333	.316
Mancini, Trey	R-R	6-4	215	3-18-92	.317	.375	.305	68	268	30	85	13	3	8	42	14	5	0	4	52	1	1	.422	.357
Murphy, Alex	R-R	5-11	210	10-5-94	.200	.250	.182	4	15	0	3	1	0	0	1	0	0	0	0	6	0	0	.267	.200
Murphy, Tanner	L-R	6-1	190	7-4-92	.333	.400	.286	3	12	2	4	1	0	1	1	0	0	0	0	4	0	0	.667	.333
Rust, Tanner	B-R	6-2	200	8-3-90	.188	.208	.178	23	69	7	13	2	0	1	6	7	2	0	0	18	0	1	.261	.282
Simpson, Creede	R-R	6-2	185	9-8-89	.302	.333	.291	64	245	46	74	16	0	4	29	23	2	1	3	61	2	2	.416	.363
Sisco, Chance	L-R	6-2	193	2-24-95	.340	.267	.360	114	426	56	145	27	2	5	63	42	7	0	3	79	1	2	.448	.406
Vega, Anthony	L-R	6-0	190	12-6-90	.208	.217	.206	59	178	21	37	11	5	1	18	22	0	0	1	63	7	5	.343	.294
Veloz, Hector	R-R	6-2	192	2-1-94	.160	.091	.189	25	75	3	12	5	0	1	6	3	0	0	0	31	0	0	.267	.192
Viele, Justin	R-R	5-11	185	11-13-94	.134	.120	.139	29	97	10	13	3	0	0	9	7	4	1	0	30	2	2	.165	.222
Wynns, Austin	R-R	6-2	205	12-10-90	.252	.270	.246	85	313	24	79	16	0	1	33	22	3	1	2	52	0	2	.313	.306
Yastrzemski, Mike	L-L	5-11	180	8-23-90	.306	.283	.311	63	258	52	79	14	10	10	44	19	6	1	2	64	12	4	.554	.365

Pitching	B-T	HT	WT	DOB	W	L	ERA	G	GS	CG	SV	IP	H	R	ER	HR	BB	SO	AVG	vLH	vRH	K/9	BB/9
Bleeker, Derrick	R-R	6-5	220	3-11-91	0	0	2.19	6	0	0	1	12	8	4	3	1	0	14	.170	.000	.258	10.22	0.00
Brault, Steven	L-L	6-1	175	4-29-92	9	8	3.05	22	21	1	0	130	107	47	44	4	28	115	.227	.224	.228	7.96	1.94
Cortright, Garrett	R-R	6-5	208	10-2-91	1	3	3.94	19	0	0	1	32	35	14	14	3	11	22	.282	.268	.294	6.19	3.09
Cunningham, Nick	R-R	6-2	205	5-21-91	2	5	10.09	11	5	0	0	36	59	45	40	6	15	15	.369	.354	.383	3.79	3.79
Delgado, Dariel	R-R	5-11	185	8-24-93	0	3	4.09	9	5	0	0	33	33	23	15	7	10	25	.248	.281	.217	6.82	2.73
Gonzalez, Luis	L-L	6-2	170	1-17-92	6	4	4.83	17	16	0	0	76	73	45	41	3	29	72	.249	.202	.271	8.49	3.42
Hart, Donnie	L-L	5-11	180	9-6-90	1	3	3.68	24	0	0	4	29	25	13	12	2	11	31	.227	.200	.246	9.51	3.38
Harvey, Hunter	R-R	6-3	175	12-9-94	7	5	3.18	17	17	0	0	88	66	39	31	5	33	106	.209	.209	.208	10.88	3.39
Hess, David	R-R	6-2	180	7-10-93	0	0	3.38	2	2	0	0	8	7	3	3	0	0	12	.333	.333	.083	13.50	0.00
Horacek, Mitch	L-L	6-5	185	12-3-91	6	10	3.80	24	24	0	0	137	139	73	58	8	35	151	.262	.192	.291	9.90	2.29
Hunter, Tommy	R-R	6-3	260	7-3-86	0	0	0.00	1	0	0	0	1	0	0	0	0	0	2	.000	.000	—	18.00	0.00
Keller, Jon	R-R	6-5	210	8-8-92	3	0	1.59	24	0	0	5	57	39	11	10	1	14	66	.192	.198	.188	10.48	2.22
Louico, Williams	R-R	6-0	200	4-10-90	1	1	3.94	32	1	0	0	62	64	38	27	3	30	48	.262	.255	.267	7.01	4.38
Nowottnick, Nik	R-R	6-4	195	12-5-91	1	0	3.38	7	0	0	0	8	7	5	3	0	4	6	.219	.267	.176	6.75	4.50
Parry, Bennett	L-L	6-6	225	8-7-91	1	3	2.63	16	5	0	0	38	32	18	11	1	17	45	.222	.137	.269	10.55	4.06
Rennie, Luc	R-R	6-2	200	4-26-94	3	7	6.21	17	15	0	0	87	131	71	60	8	21	72	.348	.369	.332	7.45	2.17
Rheault, Dylan	R-R	6-9	245	3-21-92	8	4	2.82	34	0	0	3	67	60	24	21	2	25	50	.248	.243	.252	6.72	3.36
Richardson, David	R-R	5-11	170	1-31-91	0	0	1.95	18	0	0	1	32	24	8	7	2	11	24	.209	.229	.194	6.68	3.06
Santana, Alexander	B-R	5-11	170	8-26-91	1	1	4.55	15	0	0	0	28	23	14	14	3	8	35	.219	.196	.245	11.39	2.60
Severino, Janser	R-R	6-2	140	9-16-91	3	4	5.16	9	9	0	0	45	57	31	26	3	13	42	.310	.319	.301	8.34	2.58

	B-T	HT	WT	DOB	W	L	ERA	G	GS	CG	SV	IP	H	R	ER	HR	BB	SO	AVG	vLH	vRH	K/9	BB/9
Torres, Dennis	R-R	6-3	200	5-17-90	1	3	3.31	17	0	0	3	35	31	13	13	0	17	28	.240	.273	.216	7.13	4.33
Urban, Austin	L-R	6-1	185	7-8-92	3	4	4.01	27	6	0	5	61	65	32	27	4	32	38	.278	.317	.248	5.64	4.75
Vader, Sebastian	R-R	6-4	175	6-3-92	8	4	3.04	13	13	1	0	83	79	32	28	4	15	55	.245	.226	.261	5.96	1.63
Yacabonis, Jimmy	R-R	6-3	205	3-21-92	1	1	1.07	21	0	0	14	25	9	3	3	0	15	31	.113	.133	.100	11.01	5.33

Fielding

Catcher	PCT	G	PO	A	E	DP	PB
Murphy	1.000	2	22	1	0	0	0
Murphy	.968	3	29	1	1	0	0
Sisco	.990	74	558	61	6	3	16
Wynns	.995	62	473	72	3	0	8

First Base	PCT	G	PO	A	E	DP
Kemp	1.000	1	13	0	0	0
Mancini	.994	66	573	54	4	45
Rust	.958	9	64	4	3	4
Simpson	.990	61	544	33	6	42
Veloz	.966	5	26	2	1	2

Second Base	PCT	G	PO	A	E	DP
Caronia	.963	49	73	137	8	25

	PCT	G	PO	A	E	DP
Castagnini	.992	31	50	69	1	18
Kemp	.950	40	69	121	10	25
Viele	.966	21	29	57	3	10

Third Base	PCT	G	PO	A	E	DP
Dosch	.931	120	62	222	21	10
Kemp	.867	6	3	10	2	0
Ledesma	.917	3	4	7	1	0
Rust	.800	2	0	4	1	0
Veloz	.773	10	4	13	5	2

Shortstop	PCT	G	PO	A	E	DP
Breen	.951	70	93	197	15	37
Castagnini	1.000	1	0	3	0	0
Kemp	.947	61	93	191	16	38

Viele	.800	7	10	18	7	4

Outfield	PCT	G	PO	A	E	DP
Bierfeldt	.980	59	91	9	2	2
Castagnini	1.000	1	2	0	0	0
Hart	.982	85	160	4	3	0
Herbst	.978	24	39	6	1	2
Kimmel	.833	5	5	0	1	0
Lartiguez	1.000	3	6	0	0	0
Lorenzo	.979	125	218	16	5	3
Rust	1.000	8	9	1	0	0
Vega	.991	59	113	3	1	1
Veloz	1.000	3	3	0	0	0
Yastrzemski	.975	60	104	13	3	2

ABERDEEN IRONBIRDS   SHORT-SEASON
NEW YORK-PENN LEAGUE

Batting	B-T	HT	WT	DOB	AVG	vLH	vRH	G	AB	R	H	2B	3B	HR	RBI	BB	HBP	SH	SF	SO	SB	CS	SLG	OBP
Anderson, Austin	L-R	5-11	190	6-18-92	.307	.344	.299	49	176	16	54	12	1	1	19	12	1	1	0	21	2	1	.403	.354
Capellan, Byron	R-R	5-11	150	8-9-93	.273	.500	.222	4	11	1	3	1	0	0	0	0	0	0	0	4	0	0	.364	.273
Casilla, Alexi	B-R	5-9	170	7-20-84	.467	—	.467	4	15	4	7	2	0	0	1	1	0	0	0	2	0	1	.600	.500
Castagnini, Federico	R-R	6-0	165	3-15-91	.200	.297	.171	51	160	16	32	7	0	0	7	11	3	1	1	35	1	2	.244	.263
Clevenger, Steve	L-R	6-0	195	4-5-86	.667	1.000	.500	2	6	2	4	2	0	1	5	1	0	0	0	0	0	0	1.500	.714
Coluccio, Brandon	R-R	6-0	200	8-15-92	.048	.000	.063	15	21	0	1	1	0	0	2	0	0	0	0	7	0	0	.095	.048
Gassaway, Randolph	R-R	6-4	210	5-23-95	.204	.091	.233	17	54	4	11	1	1	1	9	2	0	0	2	18	1	0	.315	.224
Gold, Tad	L-L	6-1	195	3-1-91	.109	.000	.128	21	55	5	6	1	1	0	1	10	0	2	0	14	1	1	.164	.246
Gonzalez, Jay	L-L	5-9	170	12-11-91	.259	.194	.270	59	216	28	56	7	1	0	10	26	0	1	0	68	14	9	.301	.339
Heim, Jonah	B-R	6-3	190	6-27-95	.143	.143	.143	20	70	2	10	2	0	1	2	2	0	0	1	15	0	0	.214	.164
Hernandez, Manuel	R-R	6-1	190	8-19-92	.231	.500	.111	8	13	2	3	0	0	0	1	7	0	0	0	3	0	1	.231	.500
Kimmel, Sam	L-R	6-0	185	11-3-89	.318	.000	.350	6	22	2	7	1	0	0	0	5	0	0	0	2	0	3	.500	.444
Kneeland, Cameron	R-R	6-1	195	6-23-90	.000	—	.000	2	6	0	0	0	0	0	0	0	0	0	0	1	0	0	.000	.000
Lartiguez, Oswill	R-R	6-1	179	8-11-92	.254	.265	.252	53	177	12	45	6	3	0	10	13	0	2	2	53	5	8	.322	.302
Ledesma, Ronarsy	R-R	5-11	170	4-19-93	.267	.333	.250	3	15	2	4	0	0	1	3	1	0	0	0	3	0	0	.467	.313
Mercedes, Alexander	R-R	6-0	160	3-20-92	.500	—	.500	4	4	0	2	1	0	0	0	1	0	0	0	1	0	1	.750	.500
Merullo, Nick	B-R	5-11	211	3-8-92	.000	—	.000	2	2	0	0	0	0	0	0	0	0	0	0	0	0	0	.000	.000
Moquete, Jamill	R-R	6-3	215	2-13-92	.208	.237	.201	60	192	26	40	11	2	8	25	19	8	0	3	58	5	4	.411	.302
Murphy, Alex	R-R	5-11	210	10-5-94	.277	.273	.278	54	195	21	54	12	0	3	25	15	2	0	3	42	2	1	.385	.330
Murphy, Tanner	L-R	6-1	190	7-4-92	.284	.111	.284	31	90	7	24	4	0	0	10	2	0	1	1	19	1	1	.311	.280
Palmer, Riley	L-R	6-4	215	11-15-91	.273	.267	.274	59	194	27	53	11	2	5	21	8	7	0	1	61	2	1	.428	.324
Peterson, Derek	R-R	6-3	195	3-6-91	.000	—	.000	2	2	0	0	0	0	0	0	0	0	0	0	0	0	0	.000	.000
Pfeiffer, Austin	R-R	6-4	225	5-25-91	.167	.200	.162	13	42	5	7	1	0	0	3	1	1	0	0	16	2	0	.190	.205
Segui, Cory	R-R	6-1	200	12-20-91	.133	.138	.132	38	105	6	14	2	0	0	3	5	1	0	1	50	0	0	.152	.179
Veloz, Hector	R-R	6-2	192	2-1-94	.236	.244	.233	68	225	24	53	6	3	7	26	28	3	1	1	78	6	5	.382	.327
Viele, Justin	R-R	5-11	185	11-13-90	.185	.280	.164	45	135	14	25	5	0	0	14	22	3	6	1	32	9	3	.222	.311
Weeks, Jemile	R-R	5-9	165	1-26-87	.364	—	.364	3	11	1	4	1	0	0	2	0	0	0	0	1	1	0	.455	.462
Wilkerson, Steve	B-R	6-1	169	1-11-92	.190	.114	.206	60	210	19	40	9	1	2	15	14	3	0	3	42	3	6	.271	.248
Zorrilla, Andrickson	B-L	6-2	195	3-15-91	.222	.000	.286	3	9	1	2	0	0	0	0	0	0	0	0	6	0	0	.222	.222

Pitching	B-T	HT	WT	DOB	W	L	ERA	G	GS	CG	SV	IP	H	R	ER	HR	BB	SO	AVG	vLH	vRH	K/9	BB/9
Adamek, Brady	R-R	6-5	230	4-13-90	0	1	3.60	4	0	0	0	5	7	3	2	0	1	4	.368	.222	.500	7.20	1.80
Albin, Zach	R-R	6-2	195	6-30-93	0	0	12.46	2	0	0	0	4	7	6	6	0	1	3	.350	.375	.333	6.23	2.08
Bill, Augey	L-L	6-9	225	3-22-91	0	2	4.09	13	0	0	0	33	37	15	15	2	6	27	.285	.220	.315	7.36	1.64
Bleeker, Derrick	R-R	6-5	220	3-11-91	1	2	3.09	13	0	0	2	23	24	9	8	0	4	23	.261	.250	.268	8.87	1.54
Bundy, Dylan	B-R	6-1	195	11-15-92	0	1	0.60	3	3	0	0	15	10	1	1	0	3	22	.189	.200	.182	13.20	1.80
Bundy, Bobby	R-R	6-2	215	1-13-90	0	0	5.40	3	0	0	0	5	3	3	3	0	2	5	.167	.250	.100	9.00	3.60
Burke, Mike	R-R	6-2	200	8-27-92	1	0	0.00	3	0	0	1	5	2	0	0	0	1	9	.118	.000	.200	16.20	1.80
Chleborad, Tanner	R-R	6-6	185	11-4-92	0	3	2.78	10	8	0	0	32	38	13	10	0	11	15	.295	.220	.357	4.18	3.06
Connaughton, Pat	R-R	6-5	215	1-6-93	0	1	2.45	6	4	0	0	15	13	9	4	0	3	10	.228	.222	.233	6.14	1.84
Cortright, Garrett	R-R	6-5	208	10-2-91	0	1	0.93	4	0	0	1	10	5	2	1	0	5	5	.143	.100	.160	4.66	4.66
Crichton, Stefan	R-R	6-3	200	2-29-92	2	5	4.47	20	1	0	1	44	56	26	22	2	7	40	.311	.372	.244	8.12	1.42
Cunningham, Nick	R-R	6-2	205	5-21-91	0	1	3.00	3	3	0	0	15	13	7	5	1	4	5	.228	.152	.333	3.00	2.40
Delgado, Dariel	R-R	5-11	185	8-24-93	1	2	3.10	9	0	0	2	20	22	7	7	1	4	21	.286	.385	.235	9.30	1.77
Dominguez, Dioni	B-R	6-1	175	10-20-90	0	1	0.00	2	0	0	0	3	4	2	0	0	1	2	.333	.000	.500	6.75	3.38
Gausman, Kevin	R-R	6-3	190	1-6-91	0	0	0.00	1	1	0	0	2	1	1	0	0	1	1	.143	.000	.250	4.50	4.50
Gonzalez, Brian	R-L	6-3	190	5-10-95	0	1	5.00	2	2	0	0	9	11	5	5	0	2	11	.286	.583	.130	11.00	2.00
Green, Eric	L-L	6-1	200	4-18-90	0	0	1.08	3	0	0	0	8	5	1	1	0	6	14	.185	.133	.250	15.12	6.48
Grimes, Matt	R-R	6-5	185	9-4-91	1	3	5.32	10	5	0	0	22	23	17	13	2	8	14	.274	.250	.300	5.73	3.27
Hernandez, Ivan	R-R	6-2	249	7-28-91	1	2	3.47	18	0	0	4	23	11	9	1	6	24		.261	.333	.218	9.26	2.31
Hess, David	R-R	6-2	180	7-10-93	2	1	3.20	8	5	0	0	25	22	9	9	1	8	24	.242	.293	.200	8.53	2.84

Jimenez, Ubaldo	R-R	6-5	210	1-22-84	0	0	0.00	1	1	0	0	5	5	1	0	0	3	3	.294	.286	.300	5.79	5.79
Johnson, Steve	R-R	6-1	220	8-31-87	0	1	3.38	3	3	0	0	8	3	3	3	1	6	5	.115	.067	.182	5.63	6.75
Long, Lucas	R-R	6-0	195	10-7-92	0	4	9.00	5	5	0	0	17	28	18	17	0	5	16	.378	.355	.395	8.47	2.65
McFarland, T.J.	L-L	6-3	220	6-8-89	1	0	0.00	1	0	0	0	1	0	0	0	0	1	2	.000	.000	.000	18.00	9.00
McGranahan, Zeke	R-R	6-4	215	1-3-91	0	0	5.06	4	0	0	0	5	7	5	3	1	4	4	.292	.167	.333	6.75	6.75
Means, John	L-L	6-3	195	4-24-93	1	3	3.41	10	9	0	0	37	42	15	14	1	2	33	.282	.206	.304	8.03	0.49
Nootbaar, Nigel	R-R	6-0	180	3-24-93	2	1	7.43	14	0	0	0	23	25	19	19	2	13	19	.287	.303	.278	7.43	5.09
Nowottnick, Nik	R-R	6-4	195	12-5-91	2	2	3.30	14	0	0	0	30	28	13	11	1	14	18	.246	.152	.309	5.40	4.20
Parry, Bennett	L-L	6-6	225	8-7-91	2	0	1.09	6	5	0	0	25	16	4	3	1	14	24	.186	.158	.194	8.76	5.11
Pinales, Elias	L-L	6-4	155	11-7-92	0	0	3.38	1	0	0	0	3	2	1	1	0	0	1	.200	.143	.333	3.38	0.00
Rennie, Luc	R-R	6-2	200	4-26-94	2	2	8.10	7	1	0	1	27	29	25	24	3	10	24	.274	.276	.271	8.10	3.38
Santana, Alexander	B-R	5-11	170	8-26-91	0	0	0.00	3	0	0	0	10	2	0	0	0	11	.067	.125	.045	10.24	0.00
Schuh, Max	L-L	6-4	210	3-13-92	2	0	5.25	9	0	0	0	12	15	7	7	0	4	12	.319	.400	.281	9.00	3.00
Severino, Janser	R-R	6-2	140	9-16-91	0	1	2.31	5	4	0	0	23	24	9	6	1	7	24	.267	.310	.229	9.26	2.70
Tarpley, Stephen	R-L	6-1	180	2-17-93	3	5	3.66	13	12	0	0	66	69	32	27	4	24	60	.279	.317	.266	8.14	3.26
Trowbridge, Matt	L-L	5-10	175	3-24-93	0	1	5.14	10	0	0	0	14	18	12	8	0	10	20	.310	.318	.306	12.86	6.43
Walker, Josh	R-R	6-2	175	12-18-91	1	1	3.80	13	0	0	1	24	22	11	10	1	8	17	.250	.290	.228	6.46	3.04

Fielding

Catcher	PCT	G	PO	A	E	DP	PB
Clevenger	1.000	1	8	1	0	0	0
Coluccio	1.000	9	20	2	0	0	1
Heim	.980	18	171	30	4	1	6
Merullo	1.000	1	3	0	0	0	0
Murphy	.982	35	237	35	5	3	4
Murphy	.964	20	123	12	5	1	3

First Base	PCT	G	PO	A	E	DP
Palmer	.982	25	255	13	5	23
Segui	.988	19	151	8	2	10
Veloz	.984	34	335	26	6	27

Second Base	PCT	G	PO	A	E	DP
Casilla	.944	2	8	9	1	3
Castagnini	.981	29	26	75	2	14
Ledesma	1.000	2	6	3	0	1
Pfeiffer	1.000	1	0	1	0	1

	PCT	G	PO	A	E	DP	PB
Veloz	.667	1	1	1	1	0	
Viele	1.000	4	2	9	0	2	
Weeks	1.000	1	4	4	0	0	
Wilkerson	.963	45	57	153	8	33	

Third Base	PCT	G	PO	A	E	DP
Anderson	.932	26	18	51	5	5
Castagnini	.974	20	11	26	1	4
Kneeland	1.000	2	0	3	0	0
Palmer	.917	4	4	7	1	0
Pfeiffer	.778	2	2	5	2	1
Segui	.800	3	1	3	1	0
Veloz	.868	30	14	52	10	2

Shortstop	PCT	G	PO	A	E	DP
Anderson	.949	10	12	25	2	4
Capellan	.941	4	8	8	1	1
Casilla	1.000	1	2	3	0	1

	PCT	G	PO	A	E	DP
Castagnini	.960	6	10	14	1	2
Peterson	1.000	1	1	0	0	0
Pfeiffer	.962	7	13	12	1	4
Viele	.960	41	56	135	8	30
Wilkerson	.914	15	17	36	5	5

Outfield	PCT	G	PO	A	E	DP
Castagnini	1.000	4	3	0	0	0
Gassaway	.944	14	17	0	1	0
Gold	.949	18	37	0	2	0
Gonzalez	1.000	55	101	7	0	0
Hernandez	1.000	6	2	0	0	0
Kimmel	1.000	6	6	0	0	0
Lartiguez	.988	52	73	6	1	1
Mercedes	1.000	2	1	0	0	0
Moquete	.961	57	71	2	3	0
Palmer	.964	21	24	3	1	2
Zorrilla	1.000	2	3	0	0	0

GCL ORIOLES   ROOKIE

GULF COAST LEAGUE

Batting	B-T	HT	WT	DOB	AVG	vLH	vRH	G	AB	R	H	2B	3B	HR	RBI	BB	HBP	SH	SF	SO	SB	CS	SLG	OBP
Aguilar, Andres	R-R	5-11	175	1-12-94	.267	.167	.333	5	15	0	4	1	1	0	2	0	0	0		1	0	0	.467	.353
Almanzar, Michael	R-R	6-3	190	12-2-90	.125	.000	.250	2	8	0	1	1	0	0	0	0	0	0	0	3	0	0	.250	.125
De La Cruz, Alexander	R-R	6-1	185	8-22-91	.316	.000	.429	11	19	2	6	1	0	0	4	3	0	1	1	4	0	0	.368	.391
Fajardo, Daniel	R-R	6-1	170	11-19-94	.132	.000	.172	15	38	1	5	0	0	0	5	2	0	0	0	7	0	0	.132	.175
Franco, Daniel	R-R	6-0	165	10-31-94	.208	.140	.245	44	144	22	30	2	1	0	5	10	1	3	0	44	15	4	.236	.265
Gassaway, Randolph	R-R	6-4	210	5-23-95	.167	.158	.172	13	48	5	8	2	0	1	3	1	0	0	0	13	3	0	.271	.184
Grim, Gerrion	R-R	6-2	190	9-17-93	.197	.048	.255	26	76	4	15	3	1	0	6	11	1	0	1	27	2	5	.263	.303
Hart, Josh	L-L	6-1	180	10-2-94	.167	.286	.118	6	24	2	4	0	1	0	0	1	0	0	0	2	2	0	.250	.200
Harwick, Clinton	R-R	6-2	190	8-10-91	.194	.174	.204	26	72	6	14	2	0	0	7	8	5	3	0	13	2	0	.222	.318
Heim, Jonah	B-R	6-3	190	6-27-95	.244	.273	.222	26	78	8	19	9	0	0	5	6	1	1	0	9	3	0	.359	.306
Juvier, Alejandro	L-R	6-1	180	1-20-96	.178	.233	.159	40	118	16	21	4	1	0	9	8	2	0	0	32	5	0	.229	.242
Labrador, Alexander	R-R	6-2	190	10-27-94	.500	1.000	.000	2	2	0	1	0	0	0	0	0	0	0	0	1	0	0	.500	.500
Ledesma, Ronarsy	R-R	5-11	170	4-19-93	.289	.344	.257	50	166	21	48	10	2	5	21	14	2	1	1	32	3	3	.464	.350
Lee, Alexander	R-R	6-3	205	1-14-91	.214	.160	.231	36	103	11	22	3	0	0	7	20	2	1	0	29	1	0	.243	.352
Mercedes, Alexander	R-R	6-0	160	3-20-92	.203	.184	.210	45	138	22	28	8	3	0	11	13	3	2	0	21	8	2	.304	.286
Merullo, Nick	B-R	5-11	211	3-8-92	.045	.000	.063	10	22	1	1	0	0	0	2	3	1	1	0	6	0	0	.045	.192
Olesczuk, T.J.	R-R	6-1	205	2-5-92	.265	.172	.301	34	102	8	27	8	1	0	12	2	3	0	1	26	3	2	.363	.296
Peterson, Derek	R-R	6-3	195	3-6-91	.289	.270	.305	31	97	7	28	8	3	0	18	7	1	0	1	23	1	2	.433	.340
Pfeiffer, Austin	R-R	6-4	225	5-25-91	.313	.000	.417	4	16	3	5	0	1	1	2	1	0	0	0	3	0	0	.625	.353
Reyes, Jomar	R-R	6-3	220	2-20-97	.285	.367	.248	53	186	23	53	10	2	4	29	15	1	0	5	38	1	0	.425	.333
Rifaela, Ademar	L-L	5-10	180	11-20-94	.242	.364	.208	34	99	17	24	3	0	4	11	14	0	3	0	17	0	0	.394	.336
Rona, Pita	R-R	6-7	205	7-25-94	.205	.400	.138	16	39	5	8	1	0	0	1	2	3	0	0	17	0	0	.231	.295
Salas, Guillermo	B-R	6-0	175	4-21-94	.200	.333	.143	24	60	9	12	1	0	0	0	1	0	0	0	8	1	4	.217	.213
Soto, Ronald	R-R	6-4	220	10-5-94	.205	.091	.250	37	88	9	18	2	1	0	2	3	0	0	0	12	0	1	.308	.262
Urrutia, Henry	L-R	6-3	180	2-13-87	.184	.214	.176	14	49	4	9	1	0	0	2	3	0	0	0	11	0	0	.204	.231
Vargas, Yariel	R-R	6-0	180	9-25-94	.282	.417	.208	29	78	5	22	5	1	0	8	10	2	1	1	15	1	0	.372	.374
Vasquez, Oscar	B-R	5-11	150	11-22-93	.200	.300	.104	16	35	2	7	0	1	1	7	2	0	1	3	0	0	6	0	.408	.345
Weeks, Jemile	B-R	5-9	165	1-26-87	.563	.571	.556	5	16	5	9	3	1	0	3	3	0	0	0	3	1	0	.875	.632

Pitching	B-T	HT	WT	DOB	W	L	ERA	G	GS	CG	SV	IP	H	R	ER	HR	BB	SO	AVG	vLH	vRH	K/9	BB/9
Albin, Zach	R-R	6-2	195	6-14-93	3	0	1.77	11	0	0	0	20	16	4	4	0	6	17	.225	.154	.267	7.52	2.66
Almonte, Jefferies	R-R	6-2	190	5-29-92	2	3	6.23	16	0	0	3	22	25	18	15	2	14	25	.275	.200	.321	10.38	5.82
Alvarado, Cristian	R-R	6-3	175	9-20-94	1	2	5.40	11	4	0	1	23	24	16	14	1	9	26	.258	.222	.281	10.03	3.47
Aquino, Wilmer	L-L	5-9	170	12-5-91	0	0	3.86	2	0	0	0	5	2	4	2	0	4	3	.125	.000	.222	5.79	7.71

Ayers, Danny	L-L	6-3	210	3-24-95	0	4	5.53	12	9	0	0	28	30	25	17	1	22	15	.270	.310	.256	4.88	7.16
Baker, Patrick	R-R	6-3	215	8-15-93	0	0	0.56	9	0	0	1	16	9	2	1	0	7	20	.167	.217	.129	11.25	3.94
Bundy, Bobby	R-R	6-2	215	1-13-90	0	0	10.13	3	3	0	0	3	4	4	3	0	2	4	.364	.250	.429	13.50	6.75
Burke, Mike	R-R	6-2	200	8-27-92	1	0	2.45	11	0	0	1	18	11	5	5	1	1	20	.175	.214	.143	9.82	0.49
Cosme, Jean	R-R	6-2	155	5-24-96	2	0	4.70	9	1	0	0	15	13	8	8	1	8	17	.228	.217	.235	9.98	4.70
Fermin, Yeraldo	R-R	5-11	140	10-2-91	0	0	7.71	2	1	0	0	5	3	4	4	0	4	6	.167	.286	.091	11.57	7.71
Floranus, Wendell	R-R	6-0	158	4-16-95	2	0	3.45	12	0	0	0	29	28	18	11	0	8	17	.243	.216	.266	5.34	2.51
Ghidotti, Keegan	R-R	6-4	210	4-4-92	3	1	1.37	16	0	0	5	20	9	4	3	0	8	10	.143	.222	.083	4.58	3.66
Gonzalez, Brian	R-L	6-3	230	10-25-95	0	0	0.00	8	8	0	0	25	11	1	0	0	8	25	.134	.160	.123	9.12	2.92
Grendell, Kevin	L-L	6-2	210	8-22-93	2	3	3.79	10	5	0	0	36	30	17	15	2	18	39	.229	.250	.224	9.84	4.54
Isenia, Jonatan	R-R	6-2	180	3-31-93	2	3	2.30	10	8	0	1	43	27	18	11	1	15	46	.178	.175	.179	9.63	3.14
Jimenez, Francisco	R-R	6-1	160	10-4-94	0	3	3.98	11	6	0	0	43	43	23	19	0	13	32	.261	.257	.263	6.70	2.72
Johnson, Steve	R-R	6-1	220	8-31-87	0	0	0.00	1	1	0	0	2	0	0	0	0	2	3	.000	—	.000	16.20	10.80
Joseph, Michael	R-R	6-7	215	9-12-90	0	0	0.00	2	0	0	1	2	1	1	0	0	2	1	.167	.250	.000	0.00	9.00
Koch, Brandon	R-R	6-4	210	12-7-95	1	1	1.93	4	0	0	0	5	1	3	1	0	8	3	.071	.000	.167	5.79	15.43
Lin, Yi-Hsiang	L-L	6-0	175	12-16-92	1	0	2.91	12	0	0	0	22	13	10	7	1	11	21	.171	.190	.164	8.72	4.57
Long, Lucas	R-R	6-0	195	10-7-92	1	1	2.25	6	2	0	0	16	15	5	4	0	1	13	.250	.231	.265	7.31	0.56
McAdams, Sean	R-R	6-6	210	11-17-93	0	0	9.00	2	0	0	0	2	0	2	2	0	2	2	.000	.000	.000	9.00	9.00
McCracken, Jason	R-R	6-4	225	9-4-91	0	0	14.73	3	0	0	0	4	7	6	6	0	3	3	.389	.375	.400	7.36	7.36
McGranahan, Zeke	R-R	6-4	215	1-3-91	2	1	1.50	15	0	0	4	18	9	5	3	0	9	13	.150	.222	.119	6.50	4.50
McLeod, John	L-L	6-4	220	6-3-92	1	1	3.00	5	2	0	0	12	12	7	4	0	6	7	.261	.308	.242	5.25	4.50
Means, John	L-L	6-3	195	4-24-93	0	1	4.50	1	1	0	0	2	3	1	1	0	0	3	.333	1.000	.250	13.50	0.00
Novak, Jan	R-L	6-3	190	1-19-94	1	0	0.00	3	0	0	0	3	1	0	0	0	2	2	.100	.000	.167	6.00	6.00
Pinales, Elias	L-L	6-4	155	11-7-92	1	1	2.00	12	0	0	0	27	19	7	6	0	14	20	.194	.083	.230	6.67	4.67
Pintar, Jake	L-R	6-7	200	2-13-94	0	0	2.25	3	0	0	0	4	3	2	1	0	2	3	.231	.000	.333	6.75	4.50
Scott, Tanner	R-L	6-2	220	7-22-94	1	5	6.26	10	8	0	0	23	21	22	16	0	20	23	.236	.259	.226	9.00	7.83
Taylor, Matt	R-L	6-1	185	4-1-91	1	1	6.14	2	1	0	0	7	8	5	5	0	2	8	.276	.333	.261	9.82	2.45
Trowbridge, Matt	L-L	5-10	175	3-24-93	1	0	0.00	1	0	0	0	1	0	0	0	0	0	2	.000	.000	.000	18.00	0.00
Yoon, Jeong-Hyeon	L-L	6-2	220	5-17-93	0	0	1.93	2	0	0	0	5	5	1	1	0	1	4	.294	.333	.273	7.71	1.93

Fielding

Catcher	PCT	G	PO	A	E	DP	PB
De La Cruz	.983	11	44	14	1	0	1
Fajardo	1.000	15	80	10	0	0	2
Heim	1.000	25	182	34	0	5	10
Labrador	1.000	2	2	0	0	0	0
Merullo	.983	9	50	9	1	0	4
Soto	.979	13	85	10	2	0	5

First Base	PCT	G	PO	A	E	DP
Lee	.971	33	250	18	8	17
Peterson	1.000	20	142	10	0	8
Reyes	1.000	1	5	1	0	2
Rona	.949	16	105	7	6	10

Second Base	PCT	G	PO	A	E	DP
Juvier	.922	36	50	68	10	10

	PCT	G	PO	A	E	DP
Ledesma	.990	24	41	55	1	12
Vargas	—	1	0	0	0	0
Vasquez	1.000	3	3	5	0	2
Weeks	.923	5	3	9	1	0

Third Base	PCT	G	PO	A	E	DP
Almanzar	.000	1	0	0	2	0
Ledesma	.946	18	7	28	2	0
Peterson	1.000	3	0	2	0	0
Reyes	.897	45	35	78	13	4
Vargas	1.000	1	0	1	0	0

Shortstop	PCT	G	PO	A	E	DP
Harwick	.902	26	35	57	10	11
Ledesma	.667	1	1	3	2	2
Peterson	.968	7	13	17	1	4

	PCT	G	PO	A	E	DP
Pfeiffer	.778	3	2	5	2	1
Salas	.953	22	25	56	4	9
Vargas	—	1	0	0	0	0
Vasquez	.933	7	10	18	2	4

Outfield	PCT	G	PO	A	E	DP
Aguilar	1.000	5	4	0	0	0
Franco	.986	39	69	3	1	1
Gassaway	1.000	10	13	0	0	0
Grim	.974	25	36	2	1	0
Hart	1.000	4	7	0	0	0
Mercedes	.978	43	81	6	2	6
Olesczuk	.951	31	35	4	2	1
Rifaela	.979	30	46	0	1	0
Urrutia	1.000	10	9	0	0	0
Vargas	1.000	7	5	0	0	0

DSL ORIOLES1   ROOKIE
DOMINICAN SUMMER LEAGUE

Batting	B-T	HT	WT	DOB	AVG	vLH	vRH	G	AB	R	H	2B	3B	HR	RBI	BB	HBP	SH	SF	SO	SB	CS	SLG	OBP
Acosta, Rauel	R-R	6-4	210	12-23-95	244	327	223	67	242	24	59	8	2	1	25	37	5	0	1	47	0	4	306	354
Adames, Angel	R-R	6-00	179	05-22-96	248	152	286	34	117	11	29	6	0	2	15	13	1	1	1	35	3	2	350	326
Alexander, Rochendrick	R-R	6-3	189	11-10-94	176	222	164	67	216	21	38	5	1	0	18	15	5	5	3	61	7	2	208	243
Alvarado, Nicanor	R-R	6-3	205	06-22-94	180	190	177	32	100	10	18	6	1	1	8	5	3	0	1	39	0	0	290	239
Andujar, Ricardo	B-R	6-00	160	08-06-92	318	298	323	63	239	34	76	12	3	0	18	32	2	0	2	35	15	12	393	400
Betemit, Felipe		5-11	182	07-06-91	105	—	—	7	19	1	2	0	0	0	1	0	2	0	0	7	1	0	105	190
Carrillo, Jean	R-R	6-00	200	06-16-97	202	194	205	36	104	9	21	4	0	0	10	16	8	4	0	20	0	1	240	352
Chaves, Luis	R-R	6-2	190	11-26-94	227	204	235	60	220	28	50	6	13	3	23	15	4	2	3	62	5	3	414	285
Colla, Richard	R-R	5-9	180	10-27-93	164	000	189	20	61	6	10	3	0	0	3	12	0	0	0	25	1	0	213	301
De Freitas, Nelio	R-R	6-00	210	02-22-93	150	143	152	13	40	4	6	0	0	0	4	2	3	1	2	6	1	0	150	234
De Los Santos, Manuel	R-R	6-00	180	01-15-96	148	—	—	28	88	6	13	0	0	0	5	5	5	0	1	33	2	2	148	232
De Oleo, Jesus	R-R	6-00	180	03-27-95	222	240	217	31	117	9	26	5	1	0	7	6	1	1	2	29	4	0	282	262
Diaz, Carlos	L-L	6-2	220	12-16-96	241	237	243	50	174	12	42	8	0	1	16	32	3	2	0	49	1	1	305	365
Engelhardt, Rachid	R-R	5-11	190	11-09-95	233	—	—	43	133	16	31	5	4	1	21	7	6	2	1	21	5	3	353	299
Flores, Pedro	B-R	5-10	141	04-18-96	224	219	226	36	116	18	26	2	1	0	10	17	2	1	1	20	6	1	259	331
Galastica, Gonzalo	B-R	5-11	190	08-14-96	208	286	190	33	72	14	15	1	0	0	5	5	0	3	1	19	4	1	222	256
Gil, Geremias	R-R	6-2	190	01-22-96	165	077	181	27	85	5	14	4	0	0	8	7	2	0	3	23	1	0	212	237
Gil, Jorge	R-R	6-4	200	04-13-94	269	277	267	65	223	23	60	5	1	0	21	39	1	1	0	40	9	1	300	380
Gonzalez, Alfredo	R-R	6-00	165	12-14-95	219	136	241	32	105	7	23	2	0	0	4	9	1	2	1	12	4	1	238	284
Grasso, Carlos	R-R	6-2	245	08-28-96	180	—	—	24	61	4	11	2	0	0	4	9	1	1	1	26	0	1	213	292
Guerra, Byron	R-R	5-10	180	10-27-93	179	150	187	49	95	10	17	0	1	0	7	8	3	0	1	23	2	0	200	262
Lamas, Sergio	B-R	6-00	176	11-26-93	192	167	198	42	99	14	19	4	3	0	13	15	5	3	1	34	2	2	293	325
Laureano, Carlos	R-R	6-3	175	06-27-94	230	273	220	64	226	33	52	6	5	1	12	39	4	4	1	69	14	8	314	352

Player	B-T	HT	WT	DOB	AVG	vLH	vRH	G	AB	R	H	2B	3B	HR	RBI	BB	HBP	SH	SF	SO	SB	CS	OBP	SLG
Lizardo, Yeridolfo	R-R	6-3	195	06-29-93	222	314	201	57	194	20	43	16	1	0	21	23	8	1	1	55	2	4	314	327
Llewellyn, Phildrick	B-R	6-1	205	09-25-93	283	250	289	30	92	13	26	5	1	2	14	14	1	4	0	14	6	3	424	383
Martinez, Gregory	R-R	6-1	190	12-05-95	115	000	130	8	26	1	3	0	1	0	2	4	0	0	0	12	0	0	192	233
Medina, Robertico	R-R	6-00	170	01-12-94	200	289	170	57	180	32	36	7	1	3	20	42	8	1	1	71	7	2	300	372
Medina, Victor	R-R	6-00	180	11-20-94	201	267	185	45	154	15	31	5	1	0	11	4	0	1	2	51	1	0	247	219
Montes, Juan	B-R	6-2	185	05-15-95	216	130	232	44	148	21	32	5	1	1	19	22	6	1	1	35	1	5	284	339
Mora, Ivan	R-R	6-1	171	07-22-94	263	—	—	40	114	19	30	2	4	0	15	9	1	4	2	30	8	2	351	317
Pichardo, Miguel	L-L	6-1	160	10-21-94	137	091	154	44	124	15	17	1	2	1	9	22	2	3	1	49	8	1	202	275
Ramirez, Ramon	R-R	5-10	175	02-27-92	286	250	298	32	126	28	36	5	2	0	14	15	3	0	0	20	8	4	357	375
Rodriguez, Carlos	R-R	6-1	160	03-22-95	191	125	213	51	162	20	31	4	1	0	8	11	11	1	1	37	12	5	228	286
Salas, Guillermo	B-R	6-00	175	04-21-94	340	250	387	12	47	9	16	2	1	0	2	3	2	2	0	4	4	1	426	404
Santana, Brandon	R-R	6-2	180	10-13-95	173	273	146	15	52	3	9	2	0	0	0	3	3	0	0	24	0	0	212	259
Soto, Ronald	R-R	6-4	220	10-05-94	286	417	239	29	91	15	26	6	1	3	14	16	3	0	1	19	2	3	473	405
Tucen, Adony	R-R	6-00	175	05-10-95	103	—	—	33	87	9	9	1	0	0	2	12	9	3	1	36	6	2	115	275
Vizcaino, Fabian	R-R	5-11	178	05-27-95	229	167	250	20	48	9	11	1	0	0	6	8	0	1	0	10	1	2	250	339

Pitching	B-T	HT	WT	DOB	W	L	ERA	G	GS	CG	SV	IP	H	R	ER	HR	BB	SO	AVG	vLH	vRH	K/9	BB/9
Bautista, Miguel	R-R	5-11	158	12-11-92	9	1	1.61	15	5	0	1	61	42	15	11	0	16	63	192	270	160	9.24	2.35
Cuevas, Yanuel	R-R	5-11	180	10-25-93	2	1	96	25	0	0	15	38	23	6	4	0	10	36	169	217	144	8.60	2.39
Diaz, Elvis	R-R	6-3	185	02-06-93	2	1	4.40	5	4	0	0	14	17	7	7	0	3	10	293	500	250	6.28	1.88
Encarnacion, Erick	L-L	6-1	180	04-04-96	0	0	12.21	15	0	0	0	14	17	21	19	0	20	21	304	250	313	13.50	12.86
Encarnacion, Virgilio	R-R	6-2	190	02-08-92	1	1	1.91	13	0	0	3	33	31	9	7	0	9	23	254	400	169	6.27	2.45
Floranus, Wendell	R-R	6-00	158	04-16-95	1	1	1.69	4	4	0	0	21	23	6	4	0	2	10	284	345	250	4.22	84
Florian, Wildyn	R-R	6-1	185	10-29-92	0	0	3.38	3	0	0	0	3	2	1	1	0	6	3	250	000	286	113	225
Jhonson, Barry	R-R	6-2	190	12-20-92	3	0	2.08	10	4	0	1	30	16	10	7	1	19	35	155	250	127	138	5.64
Jimenez, Francisco	R-R	6-1	160	10-04-94	3	0	00	4	4	0	0	25	13	1	0	0	5	26	155	143	161	9.49	1.82
Jimenez, Julin	R-R	6-1	200	01-29-93	1	1	5.31	13	0	0	2	20	20	14	12	0	11	15	253	176	274	6.64	4.87
Leoncio, Tomas	R-R	6-2	180	03-03-95	5	1	2.10	14	14	0	0	73	66	21	17	0	32	51	247	266	239	6.29	3.95
Marrugo, Yeizer	R-R	6-00	170	10-01-94	6	2	2.20	9	9	0	0	45	48	15	11	0	9	42	271	275	270	8.40	1.80
Martinez, Leybi	R-R	6-4	180	01-20-95	1	2	4.05	15	8	0	0	53	50	30	24	0	34	44	253	250	254	7.43	5.74
Medina, Cesar	R-R	6-3	180	06-16-94	1	1	2.13	18	0	0	2	38	18	9	9	2	18	25	145	184	128	5.92	4.26
Mesa, Victor	R-R	6-2	170	11-26-93	5	2	1.64	14	5	0	0	44	27	13	8	0	14	37	178	171	180	7.57	2.86
Palumbo, Angelo	R-R	6-3	180	11-10-95	2	5	1.95	15	9	0	1	55	42	20	12	0	23	36	213	259	194	5.86	3.74
Ramirez, Victor	R-R	6-1	190	05-12-95	3	1	64	19	0	0	6	28	15	4	2	0	4	28	143	121	153	8.89	1.27
Alvarado, Cristian	R-R	6-3	175	09-20-94	3	0	36	4	3	0	0	25	15	1	1	0	3	12	181	143	208	4.32	1.08
Bonilla, Miguel Angel	R-R	6-3	180	09-29-94	0	0	2.13	6	0	0	0	13	7	3	3	0	4	14	149	053	214	9.95	2.84
Fabian, Edward	R-R	6-3	170	08-23-95	2	2	95	8	0	0	0	19	18	8	2	0	11	19	254	240	261	9.00	5.21
Feliz, Henry	R-R	6-00	185	05-23-92	0	0	00	3	0	0	0	3	1	1	0	0	3	3	111	500	000	9.00	9.00
Ferrer, Gerald	R-R	6-2	160	04-20-92	0	1	4.20	11	0	0	0	15	19	10	7	2	13	15		—	—	9.00	7.80
Herrera, Alvin	R-R	6-1	165	03-15-93	5	3	3.51	22	0	0	8	41	32	16	16	1	9	36	222	208	231	7.90	1.98
LeFranc, Lu Franc-Cito	R-R	6-4	220	03-03-93	0	2	113	10	1	0	0	13	12	15	15	1	15	10	240	071	306	6.75	113
Morel, Luis	R-R	6-2	188	09-14-93	1	2	4.44	10	0	0	0	24	25	18	12	0	12	12	260	281	250	4.44	4.44
Pacheco, Johalis	L-L	6-00	170	03-29-94	5	5	2.22	14	14	0	0	73	55	31	18	3	30	54	208	178	214	6.66	3.70
Peluffo, Jhon	R-R	6-2	160	06-16-97	3	4	4.35	14	4	0	0	39	44	21	19	4	22	30	289	311	275	6.86	5.03
Peralta, Ofelky	R-R	6-5	195	04-20-97	0	0	3.12	11	11	0	0	43	28	20	15	0	37	33	187	158	204	6.85	7.68
Polanco, Miguel	L-L	6-4	200	01-28-94	0	2	8.28	14	1	0	0	25	38	28	23	1	16	11	365	133	404	3.96	5.76
Rojas, Edwin	R-R	6-6	200	09-26-95	0	0	19.13	9	0	0	0	8	17	19	17	3	10	3	425	500	393	3.38	11.25
Romero, Victor	R-R	6-3	170	02-17-95	1	6	1.75	14	14	0	0	72	58	24	14	4	12	67	217	216	218	8.38	1.50
Rosario, Jose	R-R	6-1	160	02-22-94	4	4	2.95	13	11	0	0	76	75	40	25	3	12	65	246	290	224	7.66	1.41
Valdez, Juan	R-R	6-2	160	02-06-91	6	5	1.77	14	14	1	0	87	68	21	17	2	14	65	—	—	—	6.75	1.45

Fielding

Catcher	PCT	G	PO	A	E	DP	PB
Carrillo	983	34	241	45	5	3	4
De Freitas	974	13	99	13	3	1	3
Gonzalez	988	32	212	34	3	0	3
Grasso	988	24	139	25	2	0	6
Llewellyn	989	13	74	17	1	0	1
Martinez	984	8	53	9	1	0	2
Soto	990	12	93	11	1	1	3
Vizcaino	960	18	97	23	5	2	6

First Base	PCT	G	PO	A	E	DP
Acosta	987	49	425	23	6	37
Alvarado	987	9	76	1	1	5
Andujar	1.000	1	1	0	0	1
Diaz	965	42	363	23	14	23
Gil	983	7	57	2	1	2
Guerra	993	36	128	10	1	17
Lizardo	1.000	1	7	0	0	1
Llewellyn	1.000	11	87	6	0	9
Medina	906	4	27	2	3	2
Soto	991	12	107	2	1	11

Second Base	PCT	G	PO	A	E	DP
Adames	948	17	31	42	4	7
Andujar	967	16	33	56	3	16
Betemit	867	3	8	5	2	2
Colla	911	13	17	34	5	3
Engelhardt	1.000	2	1	3	0	0
Flores	963	35	70	85	6	15
Galastica	956	18	32	33	3	10
Guerra	1.000	6	13	20	0	3
Lamas	992	34	55	72	1	10
Ramirez	986	13	29	41	1	13
Santana	1.000	2	3	5	0	1

Third Base	PCT	G	PO	A	E	DP
Adames	1.000	1	1	1	0	0
Andujar	920	8	5	18	2	2
Betemit	—	1	0	0	0	0
Guerra	895	10	5	12	2	0
Lizardo	894	55	35	108	17	7
Medina	908	54	35	104	14	5
Pichardo	800	1	1	3	1	1
Ramirez	1.000	4	7	11	0	2
Santana	806	11	7	22	7	5

Shortstop	PCT	G	PO	A	E	DP
Adames	867	7	6	20	4	0
Andujar	949	32	51	97	8	20
De Oleo	932	31	82	82	12	17
Galastica	917	4	5	6	1	1
Lamas	824	5	9	19	6	3
Pichardo	932	40	62	103	12	22
Ramirez	950	16	33	43	4	8
Salas	925	12	22	27	4	5

Outfield	PCT	G	PO	A	E	DP
Alexander	960	66	133	11	6	4
Chaves	989	56	88	6	1	2
De Los Santos	927	27	36	2	3	0
Engelhardt	983	35	55	4	1	1
Gil	946	57	85	3	5	1
Laureano	966	64	136	7	5	1
Llewellyn	1.000	3	4	0	0	0
Medina	1.000	10	17	1	0	0
Montes	968	38	57	4	2	0
Mora	1.000	35	47	1	0	0
Rodriguez	986	46	66	6	1	0
Tucen	971	28	31	3	1	0

DOMINICAN SUMMER LEAGUE

Batting	B-T	HT	WT	DOB	AVG	vLH	vRH	G	AB	R	H	2B	3B	HR	RBI	BB	HBP	SH	SF	SO	SB	CS	SLG	OBP
Adames, Angel	R-R	6-0	179	5-22-96	.248	.152	.286	34	117	11	29	6	0	2	15	13	1	1	1	35	3	2	.350	.326
Betemit, Felipe	B-R	5-11	182	7-6-91	.000	.000	.000	2	7	0	0	0	0	0	0	0	0	0	0	3	0	0	.000	.000
2-team total (5 Orioles1)					.105	—	—	7	19	1	2	0	0	0	1	0	2	0	0	7	1	0	.105	.190
Colla, Richard	R-R	5-9	180	10-27-93	.164	.000	.189	20	61	6	10	3	0	0	3	12	0	0	0	25	1	0	.213	.301
De Los Santos, Manuel	R-R	6-0	180	1-15-96	.071	.000	.100	9	28	0	2	0	0	0	0	2	1	0	0	16	1	0	.071	.161
2-team total (19 Orioles1)					.148	—	—	28	88	6	13	0	0	0	5	5	5	0	1	33	2	2	.148	.232
De Oleo, Jesus	R-R	6-0	180	3-27-95	.222	.240	.217	31	117	9	26	5	1	0	7	6	1	1	2	29	4	0	.282	.262
Diaz, Carlos	L-L	6-2	220	12-16-96	.241	.237	.243	50	174	12	42	8	0	1	16	32	3	0	2	49	1	1	.305	.365
Engelhardt, Rachid	R-R	5-11	190	11-9-95	.206	.400	.125	9	34	2	7	0	2	0	7	3	1	0	1	6	0	1	.324	.282
2-team total (34 Orioles1)					.233	—	—	43	133	16	31	5	4	1	21	7	6	2	1	21	5	3	.353	.299
Gil, Geremias	R-R	6-2	190	1-22-96	.165	.077	.181	27	85	5	14	4	0	0	8	7	2	0	3	23	1	0	.212	.237
Gonzalez, Alfredo	R-R	6-0	165	12-14-95	.219	.136	.241	32	105	7	23	2	0	0	4	9	1	2	1	12	4	1	.238	.284
Grasso, Victor	R-R	6-2	245	8-28-96	.188	.300	.136	13	32	4	6	1	0	0	2	5	0	0	1	13	0	1	.219	.289
2-team total (11 Orioles1)					.180	—	—	24	61	4	11	2	0	0	4	9	1	1	1	26	0	1	.213	.292
Lamas, Sergio	R-R	6-0	176	11-26-93	.192	.167	.198	42	99	14	19	4	3	0	13	15	5	3	1	34	2	2	.293	.325
Laureano, Carlos	R-R	6-3	175	6-27-94	.230	.273	.220	64	226	33	52	6	5	1	12	39	4	4	1	69	14	8	.314	.352
Lizardo, Yeridolfo	R-R	6-3	195	6-29-93	.222	.314	.201	57	194	20	43	16	1	0	21	23	8	1	1	55	2	4	.314	.327
Llewellyn, Phildrick	B-R	6-1	205	9-25-93	.283	.250	.289	30	92	13	26	5	1	2	14	14	1	4	0	14	6	3	.424	.383
Martinez, Gregory	R-R	6-1	190	12-5-95	.115	.000	.130	8	26	1	3	0	1	0	2	4	0	0	0	12	0	0	.192	.233
Medina, Victor	R-R	6-0	180	11-20-94	.201	.267	.185	45	154	15	31	5	1	0	11	4	0	1	2	51	1	0	.247	.219
Montes, Juan	B-R	6-2	185	5-15-95	.216	.130	.232	44	148	21	32	5	1	1	19	22	6	1	1	35	1	5	.284	.339
Mora, Ivan	R-R	6-1	171	7-22-94	.225	.267	.214	22	71	11	16	2	2	0	11	6	1	4	1	17	4	1	.310	.291
2-team total (18 Orioles1)					.263	—	—	40	114	19	30	2	4	0	15	9	1	4	2	30	8	2	.351	.317
Ramirez, Ramon	R-R	5-10	175	2-27-92	.286	.250	.298	32	126	28	36	5	2	0	14	15	3	0	0	20	8	4	.357	.375
Rodriguez, Carlos	R-R	6-1	160	3-22-95	.191	.125	.213	51	162	20	31	4	1	0	8	11	1	1	1	37	12	5	.228	.286
Salas, Guillermo	R-R	6-0	175	4-21-94	.340	.250	.387	12	47	9	16	2	1	0	2	3	2	2	0	4	4	1	.426	.404
Santana, Brandon	R-R	6-2	180	10-13-95	.173	.273	.146	15	52	3	9	2	0	0	0	3	3	0	0	24	0	0	.212	.259
Soto, Ronald	R-R	6-4	220	10-5-94	.286	.417	.239	29	91	15	26	6	1	3	14	16	3	0	1	19	2	3	.473	.405
Tucen, Adony	R-R	6-0	175	5-10-95	.103	.091	.106	21	58	5	6	1	0	0	2	9	4	3	1	25	5	2	.121	.264
2-team total (12 Orioles1)					.103	—	—	33	87	9	9	1	0	0	2	12	9	3	1	36	6	2	.115	.275

Pitching	B-T	HT	WT	DOB	W	L	ERA	G	GS	CG	SV	IP	H	R	ER	HR	BB	SO	AVG	vLH	vRH	K/9	BB/9
Alvarado, Cristian	R-R	6-3	175	9-20-94	3	0	0.36	4	3	0	0	25	15	1	1	0	3	12	.181	.143	.208	4.32	1.08
Bonilla, Miguel Angel	R-R	6-3	185	9-29-94	0	0	2.13	6	0	0	0	13	7	3	3	0	4	14	.149	.053	.214	9.95	2.84
Fabian, Edward	R-R	6-3	170	8-23-95	2	2	0.95	8	0	0	0	19	18	8	2	0	11	19	.254	.240	.261	9.00	5.21
Feliz, Henry	R-R	6-0	185	5-23-92	0	0	0.00	3	0	0	0	3	1	1	0	0	3	3	.111	.500	.000	9.00	9.00
Ferrer, Gerald	R-R	6-2	160	4-20-92	0	0	3.18	8	0	0	0	11	14	7	4	2	7	10	.311	.250	.324	7.94	5.56
2-team total (3 Orioles1)					0	1	4.20	11	0	0	0	15	19	10	7	2	13	15	—	—	—	9.00	7.80
Herrera, Alvin	R-R	6-1	165	3-15-93	5	3	3.51	22	0	0	8	41	32	16	16	1	9	36	.222	.208	.231	7.90	1.98
LeFranc, Lu Franc-Cito	R-R	6-4	220	3-3-93	0	2	10.13	10	1	0	0	13	12	15	15	1	15	10	.240	.071	.306	6.75	10.13
Morel, Luis	R-R	6-2	188	9-14-93	1	2	4.44	10	0	0	0	24	25	18	12	0	12	12	.260	.281	.250	4.44	4.44
Pacheco, Johalis	L-L	6-0	170	3-29-94	5	5	2.22	14	14	0	0	73	55	31	18	3	30	54	.208	.178	.214	6.66	3.70
Peluffo, Jhon	R-R	6-2	160	6-16-97	3	4	4.35	14	4	0	0	39	44	21	19	4	22	30	.289	.311	.275	6.86	5.03
Peralta, Ofelky	R-R	6-5	195	4-20-97	0	4	3.12	11	11	0	0	43	28	20	15	0	37	33	.187	.158	.204	6.85	7.68
Polanco, Miguel	L-L	6-4	200	8-28-95	0	2	8.28	14	1	0	0	25	38	28	23	1	16	11	.365	.133	.404	3.96	5.76
Rojas, Edwin	R-R	6-0	200	9-26-95	0	0	19.13	9	0	0	0	8	17	19	17	3	10	3	.425	.500	.393	3.38	11.25
Romero, Victor	R-R	6-3	170	2-17-95	1	6	1.75	14	14	0	0	72	58	24	14	4	12	67	.217	.216	.218	8.38	1.50
Rosario, Jose	R-R	6-1	160	2-22-94	4	4	2.95	13	11	0	0	76	75	40	25	3	12	65	.246	.290	.224	7.66	1.41
Valdez, Juan	R-R	6-2	160	2-6-91	4	3	2.07	10	10	1	0	61	49	16	14	2	9	46	.217	.205	.224	6.79	1.33
2-team total (4 Orioles1)					6	5	1.77	14	14	1	0	87	68	21	17	2	14	65	—	—	—	6.75	1.45

Fielding

Catcher	PCT	G	PO	A	E	DP	PB
Gonzalez	.988	32	212	34	3	0	3
Grasso	.973	13	62	10	2	0	1
Llewellyn	.989	13	74	17	1	0	1
Martinez	.984	8	53	9	1	0	2
Soto	.990	12	93	11	1	1	3

First Base	PCT	G	PO	A	E	DP
Diaz	.965	42	363	23	14	23
Gil	.983	7	57	2	1	2
Lizardo	1.000	1	7	0	0	1
Llewellyn	1.000	11	87	6	0	9
Medina	.906	4	27	2	3	2
Soto	.991	12	107	2	1	11

Second Base	PCT	G	PO	A	E	DP
Adames	.948	17	31	42	4	7

	PCT	G	PO	A	E	DP
Betemit	.667	1	2	0	1	0
Colla	.911	13	17	34	5	3
Engelhardt	1.000	3	1	3	0	0
Lamas	.992	34	55	72	1	10
Ramirez	.986	13	29	41	1	13
Santana	1.000	2	3	5	0	1

Third Base	PCT	G	PO	A	E	DP
Adames	1.000	1	1	1	0	0
Lizardo	.894	55	35	108	17	7
Ramirez	1.000	4	7	11	0	2
Santana	.806	11	7	22	7	5

Shortstop	PCT	G	PO	A	E	DP
Adames	.867	7	6	20	4	0
De Oleo	.932	31	82	82	12	17
Lamas	.824	5	9	19	6	3

	PCT	G	PO	A	E	DP
Ramirez	.950	16	33	43	4	8
Salas	.925	12	22	27	4	5

Outfield	PCT	G	PO	A	E	DP
De Los Santos	1.000	9	14	0	0	0
Engelhardt	1.000	5	8	2	0	1
Gil	.889	14	22	2	3	0
Laureano	.966	64	136	7	5	1
Llewellyn	1.000	3	4	0	0	0
Medina	1.000	10	17	1	0	0
Montes	.968	38	57	4	2	0
Mora	1.000	18	31	0	0	0
Rodriguez	.986	46	66	6	1	0
Tucen	.958	17	20	3	1	0

Boston Red Sox

SEASON IN A SENTENCE: Use any cliché you'd like—first to worst will do—but Boston went from winning the World Series in 2014 to trading its best pitcher and finishing dead last in the AL East.

HIGH POINT: The Red Sox spent one day in first place—April 3—and then lost three in a row on the way to a 13-13 April.

LOW POINT: After winning eight of nine following a rout of the Blue Jays on July 21, the Red Sox lost eight of nine, prompting the deadline selloff of Jon Lester, John Lackey, Andrew Miller and Stephen Drew.

NOTABLE ROOKIES: Mookie Betts jumped from Double-A to Triple-A to center field and then second base in Fenway Park, hitting .291/.368/.444 in 189 at-bats. Rusney Castillo made an even bigger jump, crossing from Cuba and then inactivity for 18 months to make an impact in minor league playoff games and going 12-for-36 in a brief audition for Boston at the end of the season. Pitchers Allen Webster, Anthony Ranaudo, Matt Barnes, Heath Hembree and Edwin Escobar all made appearances to varying degrees of success as the Red Sox auditioned for a mostly redone pitching staff in 2015.

KEY TRANSACTIONS: With 2015 down the drain, Boston traded Lester to Oakland on July 31 for righthanded slugger Yoenis Cespedes, then swapped Lackey to St. Louis for righthanded starter Joe Kelly and first baseman Allen Craig, and finally sent Miller to Baltimore for the Orioles' No. 2 prospect Eduardo Rodriguez, a lefthanded starter. In smaller deals, Boston sent away Drew to the Yankees for IF/OF Kelly Johnson. In an earlier deal, Boston traded righthanded starter Jake Peavy to the Giants for Hembree and Escobar.

DOWN ON THE FARM: With Betts and catcher Christian Vazquez graduating, Boston still has a farm system worthy of envy. Lefthanders Henry Owens and Brian Johnson reached Triple-A Pawtucket and could make bids for the 2015 major league rotation. Catcher Blake Swihart has louder tools than Vazquez and could push him for the job by 2016. Sean Coyle is the latest diminutive Red Sox second baseman pushing for playing time. First baseman Sam Travis, drafted out of Indiana in 2015, is an advanced college bat. Deven Marrero is a wizard at short, and center fielder Manuel Margot had a breakout season.

OPENING DAY PAYROLL: $154,380,395 (5th)

PLAYERS OF THE YEAR

MAJOR LEAGUE	MINOR LEAGUE
David Ortiz dh	**Mookie Betts,** **2b/of**
.263/.355/.517	(Double-A/Triple-A)
35 HR, 104 RBI	.346/.431/.529
6th in AL in HR, RBI	65 RBI, 33 SB

ORGANIZATION LEADERS

BATTING		*Minimum 250 AB
MAJORS		
* AVG	Holt, Brock	.281
* OPS	Ortiz, David	.872
HR	Ortiz, David	35
RBI	Ortiz, David	104
MINORS		
* AVG	Betts, Mookie, Portland, Pawtucket	.346
* OBP	Betts, Mookie, Portland, Pawtucket	.431
* SLG	Asuaje, Carlos, Greenville, Salem	.533
R	Johnson, Matty, Salem	104
H	Witte, Jantzen, Greenville, Salem	153
TB	Asuaje, Carlos, Greenville, Salem	256
2B	Witte, Jantzen, Greenville, Salem	44
3B	Asuaje, Carlos, Greenville, Salem	12
HR	Shaw, Travis, Portland, Pawtucket	21
RBI	Asuaje, Carlos, Greenville, Salem	101
BB	Kukuk, Cody, Greenville, Salem	83
SO	Hassan, Alex, Pawtucket	109
SB	Margot, Manuel, Greenville, Salem	42

PITCHING		#Minimum 75 IP
MAJORS		
W	Lackey, John	11
# ERA	Lester, Jon	2.52
SO	Lester, Jon	149
SV	Uehara, Koji	26
MINORS		
W	Owens, Henry, Portland, Pawtucket	17
L	Callahan, Jamie, Greenville	13
# ERA	Johnson, Brian, Salem, Portland	2.13
G	Britton, Drake, Pawtucket	45
GS	Owens, Henry, Portland, Pawtucket	26
SV	Ramirez, Noe, Portland	18
IP	Owens, Henry, Portland, Pawtucket	159
BB	Kukuk, Cody, Greenville, Salem	83
SO	Owens, Henry, Portland, Pawtucket	170
AVG	Johnson, Brian, Salem, Portland	.197

General Manager: Ben Cherington. **Farm Director:** Ben Crockett. **Scouting Director:** Amiel Sawdaye.

Class	Team	League	W	L	PCT	Finish	Manager
Majors	Boston Red Sox	American	71	91	.438	25th (30)	John Farrell
Triple-A	Pawtucket Red Sox	International	79	65	.549	t-2nd (14	Kevin Boles
Double-A	Portland Sea Dogs	Eastern	88	54	.620	1st (12)	Billy McMillon
High A	Salem Red Sox	Carolina	68	68	.500	3rd (8)	Carlos Febles
Low A	Greenville Drive	South Atlantic	60	79	.432	10th (14)	Darren Fenster
Short season	Lowell Spinners	New York-Penn	37	38	.493	t-6th (14)	Joe Oliver
Rookie	Red Sox	Gulf Coast	36	24	.600	4th (16)	Tom Kotchman
Overall 2015 Minor League Record			368	328	.529	5th (30)	

ORGANIZATION STATISTICS

BOSTON RED SOX

AMERICAN LEAGUE

Batting	B-T	HT	WT	DOB	AVG	vLH	vRH	G	AB	R	H	2B	3B	HR	RBI	BB	HBP	SH	SF	SO	SB	CS	SLG	OBP
Betts, Mookie	R-R	5-9	155	10-7-92	.291	.328	.275	52	189	34	55	12	1	5	18	21	2	1	0	31	7	3	.444	.368
Bogaerts, Xander	R-R	6-1	210	10-1-92	.240	.263	.230	144	538	60	129	28	1	12	46	39	8	2	7	138	2	3	.362	.297
Bradley, Jackie	L-R	5-10	195	4-19-90	.198	.231	.180	127	384	45	76	19	2	1	30	31	5	1	2	121	8	0	.266	.265
Brentz, Bryce	R-R	6-0	210	12-30-88	.308	.571	.211	9	26	5	8	2	0	0	2	0	0	0	0	9	0	0	.385	.308
Brown, Corey	L-L	6-1	210	11-26-85	.000	.000	—	3	1	0	0	0	0	0	0	0	0	0	0	1	0	0	.000	.000
Butler, Dan	R-R	5-10	210	10-17-86	.211	.167	.231	7	19	1	4	3	0	0	2	1	0	0	0	5	0	0	.368	.250
Carp, Mike	L-R	6-2	210	6-30-86	.198	.143	.215	42	86	9	17	5	1	0	9	11	5	0	1	17	0	1	.279	.320
2-team total (17 Texas)					.175	—	—	59	126	11	22	5	1	0	13	16	5	0	2	31	0	1	.230	.289
Castillo, Rusney	R-R	5-8	186	9-7-87	.333	.250	.357	10	36	6	12	1	0	2	6	3	1	0	0	6	3	0	.528	.400
Cecchini, Garin	L-R	6-3	220	4-20-91	.258	.000	.320	11	31	6	8	3	0	1	4	3	2	0	0	11	0	0	.452	.361
Cespedes, Yoenis	R-R	5-10	210	10-18-85	.269	.119	.308	51	201	27	54	10	3	5	33	7	2	0	3	48	4	0	.423	.296
2-team total (101 Oakland)					.260	—	—	152	600	89	156	36	6	22	100	35	3	0	7	128	7	2	.450	.301
Craig, Allen	R-R	6-2	215	7-18-84	.128	.167	.109	29	94	7	12	3	0	1	2	9	4	0	0	36	1	0	.191	.234
Drew, Stephen	L-R	6-0	190	3-16-83	.176	.097	.200	39	131	11	23	6	1	4	11	14	0	0	0	39	1	1	.328	.255
2-team total (46 New York)					.162	—	—	85	271	18	44	14	1	7	26	27	0	0	2	75	1	1	.299	.237
Gomes, Jonny	R-R	6-1	230	11-22-80	.234	.302	.151	78	209	22	49	7	0	6	32	26	6	0	5	70	0	0	.354	.329
2-team total (34 Oakland)					.234	—	—	112	273	28	64	8	0	6	37	35	6	0	7	88	0	0	.330	.327
Hassan, Alex	R-R	6-3	220	4-1-88	.125	.167	.000	3	8	1	1	0	0	0	0	1	0	0	0	5	0	0	.125	.222
Herrera, Jonathan	B-R	5-9	180	11-3-84	.233	.250	.222	42	90	10	21	1	2	0	9	7	3	3	1	24	1	3	.289	.307
Holt, Brock	L-R	5-10	185	6-11-88	.281	.293	.274	106	449	68	126	23	5	4	29	33	2	5	3	98	12	2	.381	.331
Johnson, Kelly	L-R	6-1	200	2-22-82	.160	.200	.150	10	25	1	4	1	0	0	1	0	0	0	0	10	0	0	.200	.160
3-team total (19 Baltimore, 77 New York)					.215	—	—	106	265	29	57	14	2	7	27	29	2	0	1	71	2	2	.362	.296
Lavarnway, Ryan	R-R	6-4	240	8-7-87	.000	.000	.000	9	10	0	0	0	0	0	0	0	0	0	0	3	0	0	.000	.000
Middlebrooks, Will	R-R	6-3	220	9-9-88	.191	.170	.198	63	215	14	41	10	0	2	19	15	4	0	0	70	1	1	.265	.256
Napoli, Mike	R-R	6-0	220	10-31-81	.248	.300	.230	119	415	49	103	20	0	17	55	78	4	0	3	133	3	2	.419	.370
Nava, Daniel	B-L	5-11	200	2-22-83	.270	.159	.293	113	363	41	98	21	0	4	37	33	10	0	2	81	4	2	.361	.361
Ortiz, David	L-L	6-4	230	11-18-75	.263	.275	.256	142	518	59	136	27	0	35	104	75	3	0	6	95	0	0	.517	.355
Pedroia, Dustin	R-R	5-8	165	8-17-83	.278	.250	.288	135	551	72	153	33	0	7	53	51	1	0	6	75	6	6	.376	.337
Pierzynski, A.J.	L-R	6-3	235	12-30-76	.254	.198	.282	72	256	19	65	10	1	4	31	9	4	1	4	40	0	0	.348	.286
Rivero, Carlos	R-R	6-3	200	5-20-88	.571	.500	.667	4	7	1	4	2	0	1	3	1	0	0	0	0	0	0	1.286	.625
Roberts, Ryan	R-R	5-11	185	9-19-80	.105	.000	.250	8	19	1	2	0	0	0	3	0	0	0	0	7	0	0	.105	.227
Ross, David	R-R	6-2	230	3-19-77	.184	.228	.158	50	152	16	28	7	0	7	15	16	0	2	1	58	0	1	.368	.260
Sizemore, Grady	L-L	6-2	200	8-2-82	.216	.154	.241	52	185	14	40	10	2	2	15	19	0	0	1	41	5	0	.324	.288
Vazquez, Christian	R-R	5-9	195	8-21-90	.240	.189	.254	55	175	15	42	9	0	1	20	19	0	3	4	33	0	0	.309	.308
Victorino, Shane	B-R	5-9	190	11-30-80	.268	.325	.241	30	123	14	33	6	1	2	12	6	1	1	2	21	2	0	.382	.303
Weeks, Jemile	B-R	5-9	165	1-26-87	.308	.000	.381	14	26	6	8	3	0	0	3	4	1	0	1	2	2	0	.423	.406
2-team total (3 Baltimore)					.297	—	—	17	37	8	11	3	1	0	3	4	1	2	1	2	2	0	.432	.372

Pitching	B-T	HT	WT	DOB	W	L	ERA	G	GS	CG	SV	IP	H	R	ER	HR	BB	SO	AVG	vLH	vRH	K/9	BB/9
Badenhop, Burke	R-R	6-5	220	2-8-83	0	3	2.29	70	0	0	1	71	70	20	18	1	19	40	.268	.255	.276	5.09	2.42
Barnes, Matt	R-R	6-4	205	6-17-90	0	0	4.00	5	0	0	0	9	11	4	4	1	2	8	.306	.333	.286	8.00	2.00
Breslow, Craig	L-L	6-1	190	8-8-80	2	4	5.96	60	0	0	1	54	73	40	36	8	28	37	.319	.291	.341	6.13	4.64
Britton, Drake	L-L	6-2	215	5-22-89	0	0	0.00	7	0	0	0	7	5	0	0	2	4	0	.000	.263	5.40	2.70	
Buchholz, Clay	L-R	6-3	190	8-14-84	8	11	5.34	28	28	2	0	170	182	108	101	17	54	132	.273	.284	.259	6.97	2.85
Capuano, Chris	L-L	6-3	215	8-19-78	1	1	4.55	28	0	0	0	32	34	17	16	3	15	29	.270	.333	.217	8.24	4.26
2-team total (12 New York)					3	4	4.35	40	12	0	0	97	101	51	47	10	34	84	—	—	—	7.77	3.14
De La Rosa, Rubby	R-R	6-1	205	3-4-89	4	8	4.43	19	18	0	0	102	116	51	50	12	35	74	.293	.305	.279	6.55	3.10
Doubront, Felix	L-L	6-2	225	10-23-87	2	4	6.07	17	10	0	0	59	69	45	40	10	26	43	.282	.329	.260	6.52	3.94
Escobar, Edwin	L-L	6-1	185	4-22-92	0	0	4.50	2	0	0	0	2	1	1	1	0	0	2	.143	.000	.167	9.00	0.00
Hembree, Heath	R-R	6-4	210	1-13-89	0	0	4.50	6	0	0	0	10	11	5	5	1	5	6	.289	.364	.259	5.40	4.50
Kelly, Joe	R-R	6-1	175	6-9-88	4	2	4.11	10	10	0	0	61	47	29	28	5	32	41	.215	.183	.250	6.02	4.70
Lackey, John	R-R	6-6	235	10-23-78	11	7	3.60	21	21	1	0	137	137	60	55	15	32	116	.256	.244	.273	7.60	2.10
Layne, Tommy	L-L	6-2	190	11-2-84	2	1	0.95	30	0	0	0	19	14	4	2	0	8	14	.212	.159	.318	6.63	3.79
Lester, Jon	L-L	6-4	240	1-7-84	10	7	2.52	21	21	0	0	143	128	52	40	9	32	149	.238	.254	.234	9.38	2.01

Pitcher	B-T	HT	WT	DOB	W	L	ERA	G	GS	CG	SHO	SV	IP	H	R	ER	HR	BB	SO	AVG	vLH	vRH	K/9	BB/9
2-team total (11 Oakland)					16	11	2.46	32	32	1	0	0	220	194	76	60	16	48	220	—	—	—	9.01	1.97
Miller, Andrew	L-L	6-7	210	5-21-85	3	5	2.34	50	0	0	0	0	42	25	13	11	2	13	69	.168	.150	.180	14.67	2.76
2-team total (23 Baltimore)					5	5	2.02	73	0	0	0	1	62	33	16	14	3	17	103	—	—	—	14.87	2.45
Mujica, Edward	R-R	6-3	225	5-10-84	2	4	3.90	64	0	0	0	8	60	69	28	26	6	14	43	.294	.315	.276	6.45	2.10
Peavy, Jake	R-R	6-1	195	5-31-81	1	9	4.72	20	20	0	0	0	124	131	67	65	20	46	100	.273	.268	.279	7.26	3.34
Ranaudo, Anthony	R-R	6-7	230	9-9-89	4	3	4.81	7	7	0	0	0	39	39	21	21	10	16	15	.260	.280	.240	3.43	3.66
Tazawa, Junichi	R-R	5-11	200	6-6-86	4	3	2.86	71	0	0	0	0	63	58	23	20	5	17	64	.240	.241	.238	9.14	2.43
Uehara, Koji	R-R	6-2	195	4-3-75	6	5	2.52	64	0	0	0	26	64	51	18	18	10	8	80	.216	.197	.240	11.19	1.12
Webster, Allen	R-R	6-2	190	2-10-90	5	3	5.03	11	11	0	0	0	59	58	35	33	3	28	36	.264	.250	.279	5.49	4.27
Wilson, Alex	R-R	6-0	215	11-3-86	1	0	1.91	18	0	0	0	0	28	20	8	6	3	5	19	.198	.250	.151	6.04	1.59
Workman, Brandon	R-R	6-5	225	8-13-88	1	10	5.17	19	15	0	0	0	87	88	57	50	11	36	70	.263	.262	.264	7.24	3.72
Wright, Steven	R-R	6-1	220	8-30-84	0	1	2.57	6	1	0	0	0	21	21	8	6	2	4	22	.256	.250	.261	9.43	1.71

Fielding

Catcher	PCT	G	PO	A	E	DP	PB
Butler	.977	7	41	2	1	0	2
Pierzynski	.994	64	464	28	3	2	5
Ross	.983	50	381	27	7	3	3
Vazquez	.987	54	338	32	5	4	8

First Base	PCT	G	PO	A	E	DP
Carp	1.000	20	115	11	0	10
Craig	1.000	17	131	14	0	12
Herrera	1.000	1	1	0	0	0
Holt	.986	8	62	9	1	15
Johnson	1.000	5	32	4	0	3
Lavarnway	1.000	6	23	3	0	0
Middlebrooks	1.000	1	2	0	0	1
Napoli	.992	110	904	71	8	92
Nava	.983	11	51	6	1	5
Ortiz	1.000	5	37	2	0	9

Second Base	PCT	G	PO	A	E	DP
Betts	.955	14	25	38	3	7
Herrera	1.000	9	3	13	0	1
Holt	1.000	11	12	23	0	4
Johnson	—	1	0	0	0	0
Pedroia	.997	135	247	405	2	96
Weeks	1.000	6	7	14	0	1

Third Base	PCT	G	PO	A	E	DP
Bogaerts	.910	44	37	64	10	2
Carp	—	1	0	0	0	0
Cecchini	.952	9	7	13	1	2
Herrera	.947	14	4	14	1	0
Holt	.945	39	30	73	6	5
Johnson	1.000	2	1	3	0	0
Middlebrooks	.972	62	38	99	4	9
Rivero	.833	3	1	4	1	0
Roberts	.929	8	3	10	1	1

Shortstop	PCT	G	PO	A	E	DP
Bogaerts	.975	99	138	256	10	54
Drew	.989	39	66	107	2	34
Herrera	1.000	16	14	38	0	13
Holt	1.000	12	14	41	0	6
Weeks	1.000	3	3	8	0	2

Outfield	PCT	G	PO	A	E	DP
Betts	.989	37	84	3	1	2
Bradley	.997	125	304	13	1	8
Brentz	1.000	8	14	0	0	0
Brown	1.000	1	1	0	0	0
Carp	1.000	12	8	0	0	0
Castillo	1.000	10	31	1	0	0
Cespedes	.977	43	81	4	2	0
Craig	1.000	13	20	0	0	0
Gomes	.971	75	97	2	3	0
Hassan	1.000	2	1	0	0	0
Holt	1.000	44	80	1	0	0
Johnson	—	1	0	0	0	0
Nava	.984	100	178	9	3	1
Sizemore	.990	51	100	3	1	1
Victorino	1.000	30	56	1	0	0

PAWTUCKET RED SOX   TRIPLE-A

INTERNATIONAL LEAGUE

Batting	B-T	HT	WT	DOB	AVG	vLH	vRH	G	AB	R	H	2B	3B	HR	RBI	BB	HBP	SH	SF	SO	SB	CS	SLG	OBP
Betts, Mookie	R-R	5-9	155	10-7-92	.335	.426	.304	45	185	31	62	12	2	5	31	26	0	0	0	30	11	4	.503	.417
Bradley, Jackie	L-R	5-10	195	4-19-90	.212	.087	.279	14	66	6	14	1	0	1	5	3	0	0	0	18	0	1	.273	.246
Brentz, Bryce	R-R	6-0	210	12-30-88	.243	.288	.223	63	230	42	56	11	2	12	53	32	3	0	2	58	0	1	.465	.341
Brown, Corey	L-L	6-1	210	11-26-85	.231	.220	.236	91	325	35	75	15	2	17	42	28	2	0	2	106	6	2	.446	.294
Butler, Dan	R-R	5-10	210	10-17-86	.241	.247	.238	83	286	35	69	19	0	4	30	29	5	0	5	71	0	0	.350	.317
Carp, Mike	L-R	6-2	210	6-30-86	.238	.000	.278	7	21	2	5	1	0	1	3	1	0	0	0	7	0	0	.429	.273
Cecchini, Garin	L-R	6-3	220	4-20-91	.263	.242	.272	114	407	52	107	21	1	7	57	44	5	1	1	99	11	1	.371	.341
Craig, Allen	R-R	6-2	215	7-18-84	.200	.000	.250	2	5	1	1	0	0	0	2	1	0	0	0	1	0	0	.200	.333
De Jesus Jr., Ivan	R-R	5-11	200	5-1-87	.167	.000	.250	2	6	0	1	0	0	0	1	2	0	1	0	1	0	0	.167	.375
2-team total (113 Norfolk)					.281	—	—	115	417	54	117	19	5	5	57	52	1	4	4	85	2	1	.386	.359
Drew, Stephen	L-R	6-0	190	3-16-83	.154	.250	.111	4	13	0	2	1	0	0	0	1	0	0	0	5	0	0	.231	.214
Gibson, Derrik	R-R	6-1	170	12-5-89	.244	.200	.259	21	78	9	19	2	2	2	9	4	1	0	2	15	2	0	.397	.282
Hassan, Alex	R-R	6-3	220	4-1-88	.287	.333	.267	114	408	66	117	31	1	8	55	60	2	0	4	109	2	2	.426	.378
Henry, Justin	L-R	6-2	190	4-30-85	.251	.164	.281	73	215	29	54	9	3	1	22	31	0	3	1	39	5	1	.335	.344
Hernandez, Jayson	R-R	5-10	200	9-2-88	.000	.000	.000	1	4	0	0	0	0	0	0	0	0	0	0	2	0	0	.000	.000
Herrera, Jonathan	B-R	5-9	180	11-3-84	.309	.211	.361	13	55	11	17	2	1	0	4	4	0	1	1	11	1	1	.382	.350
Hissey, Pete	L-L	6-1	180	1-17-90	.000	—	.000	2	2	0	0	0	0	0	1	0	0	0	1	0	0	0	.000	.000
Holt, Brock	L-R	5-10	185	6-11-88	.315	.300	.324	27	108	19	34	8	2	1	7	8	4	0	1	12	7	1	.454	.380
Lavarnway, Ryan	R-R	6-4	240	8-7-87	.283	.297	.277	62	219	22	62	10	0	3	20	33	5	0	0	45	0	0	.370	.389
Marrero, Deven	R-R	6-1	195	8-25-90	.210	.244	.200	50	186	23	39	11	0	1	20	12	1	2	1	37	4	1	.285	.260
Martinez, Mario	R-R	6-3	220	11-13-89	.000	—	.000	1	1	0	0	0	0	0	0	0	0	0	0	1	0	0	.000	.000
McCoy, Mike	R-R	5-9	180	4-2-81	.181	.198	.172	88	259	31	47	14	0	1	25	41	2	7	3	55	7	2	.247	.295
Meneses, Heiker	R-R	5-9	200	7-1-91	.241	.417	.118	16	58	3	14	2	1	0	3	3	0	2	0	10	0	1	.310	.279
Middlebrooks, Will	R-R	6-3	220	9-9-88	.231	.217	.235	29	104	13	24	1	1	4	8	6	1	0	1	30	0	0	.375	.277
Nava, Daniel	B-L	5-11	200	2-22-83	.253	.231	.263	24	83	12	21	3	0	3	14	12	1	0	2	21	2	1	.398	.347
Rivero, Carlos	R-R	6-3	200	5-20-88	.286	.329	.271	74	273	32	78	14	2	5	36	23	2	0	4	66	0	2	.407	.341
Roberts, Ryan	R-R	5-11	185	9-19-80	.277	.307	.263	72	274	40	76	22	1	7	32	23	2	1	1	53	2	3	.442	.337
Shaw, Travis	L-R	6-4	225	4-16-90	.262	.189	.291	81	313	43	82	21	1	10	41	28	1	0	4	76	2	0	.431	.321
Snyder, Brandon	R-R	6-2	225	11-23-86	.216	.247	.200	35	126	13	26	6	0	8	19	11	3	0	1	50	1	0	.444	.284
Spring, Matt	R-R	6-2	215	11-7-84	.265	.750	.200	12	34	7	9	5	0	2	7	3	1	0	1	15	0	0	.588	.333
Swihart, Blake	B-R	6-1	175	4-3-92	.261	.375	.200	18	69	6	18	3	1	1	9	2	0	0	0	15	1	0	.377	.282
Torres, Andres	B-R	5-10	195	1-26-78	.292	.450	.231	18	72	8	21	4	0	3	8	1	1	1	0	17	1	2	.472	.311
Vazquez, Christian	R-R	5-9	195	8-21-90	.279	.267	.284	66	244	35	68	17	0	3	20	21	1	2	2	52	0	1	.385	.336
Victorino, Shane	B-R	5-9	190	11-30-80	.138	.000	.200	9	29	3	4	1	0	0	0	0	0	0	0	6	0	0	.172	.138
Wilkerson, Shannon	R-R	6-0	200	7-20-88	.234	.100	.281	25	77	8	18	2	1	0	6	3	0	3	0	21	1	0	.286	.263

Pitching	B-T	HT	WT	DOB	W	L	ERA	G	GS	CG	SV	IP	H	R	ER	HR	BB	SO	AVG	vLH	vRH	K/9	BB/9
Barnes, Matt	R-R	6-4	205	6-17-90	8	9	3.95	23	22	0	0	128	119	60	56	8	46	103	.247	.217	.277	7.26	3.24
Boscan, Wilfredo	R-R	6-2	160	10-26-89	2	0	0.00	2	0	0	0	4	0	0	0	0	2	4	.000	.000	.000	9.82	4.91
Breslow, Craig	L-L	6-1	190	8-8-80	1	0	0.00	3	1	0	0	3	1	0	0	0	2	1	.111	.000	.125	3.38	6.75
Britton, Drake	L-L	6-2	215	5-22-89	2	3	5.86	45	0	0	5	58	77	41	38	8	38	37	.326	.276	.350	5.71	5.86
Buchholz, Clay	L-R	6-3	190	8-14-84	0	1	2.53	2	2	0	0	11	6	3	3	2	2	10	.167	.211	.118	8.44	1.69
Celestino, Miguel	R-R	6-6	205	10-10-89	1	3	5.16	16	0	0	3	23	19	13	13	6	12	26	.226	.316	.152	10.32	4.76
De La Rosa, Rubby	R-R	6-1	205	3-4-89	2	4	3.45	12	12	0	0	60	50	27	23	1	25	57	.229	.273	.185	8.55	3.75
Doubront, Felix	L-L	6-2	225	10-23-87	0	0	1.86	2	2	0	0	10	6	2	2	0	5	13	.182	.000	.214	12.10	4.66
Ely, John	R-R	6-2	210	5-13-86	1	1	2.52	25	1	0	1	39	40	15	11	3	14	35	.261	.270	.253	8.01	3.20
Escobar, Edwin	L-L	6-1	185	4-22-92	0	2	4.28	5	5	0	0	27	33	15	13	3	8	20	.297	.300	.297	6.59	2.63
Hembree, Heath	R-R	6-4	210	1-13-89	0	1	2.70	7	0	0	2	7	5	2	2	0	5	9	.192	.000	.278	12.15	6.75
Hernandez, Chris	L-L	6-2	195	12-14-88	5	9	4.08	33	16	1	1	117	117	60	53	5	60	75	.267	.216	.285	5.77	4.62
Hill, Rich	L-L	6-5	220	3-11-80	3	3	3.23	25	0	0	2	39	29	15	14	0	17	45	.206	.196	.211	10.38	3.92
2-team total (4 Scranton/W-B)					3	3	2.93	29	0	0	2	43	31	15	14	0	18	55	—	—	—	11.51	3.77
Hinojosa, Dalier	R-R	6-1	195	2-10-86	3	5	3.79	41	0	0	3	62	39	27	26	5	33	65	.183	.179	.186	9.49	4.82
Kehrt, Jeremy	R-R	6-2	190	12-21-85	0	4	5.45	13	4	0	0	33	43	23	20	1	12	20	.312	.359	.270	5.45	3.27
Layne, Tommy	L-L	6-2	190	11-2-84	5	1	1.50	37	0	0	11	48	29	8	8	1	20	53	.173	.136	.193	9.94	3.75
McCarthy, Mike	R-R	6-3	185	11-18-87	0	0	2.45	1	0	0	0	4	2	1	1	0	1	3	.154	.286	.000	7.36	2.45
Owens, Henry	L-L	6-6	205	7-21-92	3	1	4.03	6	6	0	0	38	32	17	17	4	12	44	.230	.172	.245	10.42	2.84
Ranaudo, Anthony	R-R	6-7	230	9-9-89	14	4	2.61	24	24	1	0	138	112	45	40	9	54	111	.223	.213	.232	7.24	3.52
Resop, Chris	R-R	6-3	225	11-4-82	4	1	4.42	25	0	0	2	39	34	19	19	3	14	36	.236	.237	.235	8.38	3.26
Valdez, Jose	R-R	6-4	200	1-22-83	0	1	2.41	11	0	0	0	19	20	9	5	1	7	15	.267	.294	.244	7.23	3.38
Verdugo, Ryan	L-L	6-0	205	4-10-87	2	1	3.45	10	3	0	2	29	26	11	11	2	11	38	.241	.185	.259	11.93	3.45
Villareal, Brayan	R-R	6-0	170	5-10-87	1	0	5.40	9	0	0	1	10	4	7	6	0	12	12	.118	.154	.095	10.80	10.80
Webster, Allen	R-R	6-2	190	2-10-90	4	4	3.10	21	20	1	1	122	107	45	42	9	44	100	.234	.223	.247	7.38	3.25
Wilson, Alex	R-R	6-0	215	11-3-86	6	1	4.35	35	0	0	5	41	38	21	20	2	23	40	.248	.271	.234	8.71	5.01
Workman, Brandon	R-R	6-5	225	8-13-88	7	1	4.11	11	11	0	0	61	61	28	28	10	17	55	.263	.248	.276	8.07	2.49
Wright, Steven	R-R	6-1	220	8-30-84	5	5	3.41	15	15	1	0	95	86	43	36	9	22	68	.240	.182	.279	6.44	2.08

Fielding

Catcher	PCT	G	PO	A	E	DP	PB
Butler	.995	54	384	41	2	4	7
Lavarnway	1.000	15	109	4	0	0	1
Spring	1.000	11	70	5	0	0	0
Swihart	1.000	16	131	8	0	1	0
Vazquez	.996	52	413	39	2	4	5

First Base	PCT	G	PO	A	E	DP
Carp	1.000	3	12	0	0	2
Hassan	1.000	17	143	17	0	9
Henry	1.000	4	17	1	0	2
Lavarnway	.985	31	242	18	4	28
Martinez	1.000	1	1	0	0	0
Nava	1.000	3	21	0	0	1
Shaw	.998	75	568	51	1	59
Snyder	.992	16	118	10	1	13
Spring	1.000	1	1	0	0	0

Second Base	PCT	G	PO	A	E	DP
Betts	.964	6	10	17	1	5
De Jesus Jr.	.857	1	3	3	1	3
Gibson	1.000	10	16	21	0	4
Henry	.973	35	56	88	4	21
Herrera	.944	11	16	35	3	8

Holt	1.000	4	11	22	0	2
McCoy	.978	23	40	50	2	12
Meneses	.962	6	10	15	1	1
Roberts	.983	55	97	133	4	31

Third Base	PCT	G	PO	A	E	DP
Cecchini	.923	84	61	130	16	10
Holt	1.000	4	4	6	0	1
McCoy	.857	6	1	5	1	1
Middlebrooks	1.000	17	8	27	0	4
Rivero	.938	37	24	66	6	2
Roberts	1.000	3	1	2	0	0
Shaw	1.000	6	6	7	0	1
Snyder	.750	1	0	3	1	0

Shortstop	PCT	G	PO	A	E	DP
De Jesus Jr.	1.000	1	0	4	0	0
Drew	1.000	4	4	10	0	5
Gibson	1.000	2	4	4	0	0
Herrera	1.000	2	5	3	0	1
Holt	.961	19	30	44	3	8
Marrero	.973	50	76	137	6	34
McCoy	.994	45	61	107	1	26
Meneses	.940	10	19	28	3	10

	Rivero	.969	17	21	42	2	14

Outfield	PCT	G	PO	A	E	DP
Betts	1.000	37	83	3	0	1
Bradley	1.000	14	40	1	0	0
Brentz	.990	51	91	6	1	1
Brown	.990	87	199	1	2	0
Carp	—	2	0	0	0	0
Cecchini	1.000	26	46	1	0	0
Craig	—	1	0	0	0	0
Gibson	1.000	8	17	0	0	0
Hassan	.989	90	177	6	2	1
Henry	.983	33	57	2	1	0
Hissey	1.000	2	1	0	0	0
McCoy	1.000	13	28	2	0	1
Nava	1.000	18	36	1	0	0
Rivero	1.000	12	21	2	0	1
Roberts	1.000	5	6	0	0	0
Snyder	1.000	7	9	0	0	0
Torres	1.000	15	26	0	0	0
Victorino	.667	9	4	0	2	0
Wilkerson	1.000	24	57	0	0	0

PORTLAND SEA DOGS   DOUBLE-A

EASTERN LEAGUE

Batting	B-T	HT	WT	DOB	AVG	vLH	vRH	G	AB	R	H	2B	3B	HR	RBI	BB	HBP	SH	SF	SO	SB	CS	SLG	OBP
Almanzar, Michael	R-R	6-3	190	12-2-90	.277	.273	.279	49	166	18	46	9	0	5	25	12	9	0	1	39	2	0	.422	.356
Bethea, Danny	R-R	6-1	210	1-31-90	.250	1.000	.143	2	8	0	2	1	0	0	3	1	0	0	0	1	0	0	.375	.333
Betts, Mookie	R-R	5-9	155	10-7-92	.355	.442	.307	54	214	56	76	18	3	6	34	35	1	0	3	20	22	3	.551	.443
Blair, Carson	R-R	6-1	190	10-18-89	.288	.200	.306	17	59	11	17	6	1	2	8	10	1	0	1	19	0	0	.525	.394
Brenly, Mike	R-R	6-3	220	10-14-86	.168	.158	.171	46	143	10	24	7	1	2	18	13	2	1	1	37	1	0	.273	.245
Chester, David	R-R	6-5	270	3-31-89	.231	.264	.214	61	212	21	49	9	0	7	31	18	3	0	2	68	0	2	.373	.298
Coyle, Sean	R-R	5-8	175	1-17-92	.295	.328	.277	96	336	60	99	23	1	16	61	38	5	1	4	95	13	1	.512	.371
De La Cruz, Keury	L-L	5-11	170	11-28-91	.295	.209	.341	70	258	30	76	15	0	7	30	14	0	0	3	55	3	2	.434	.327
Dent, Ryan	R-R	6-0	190	3-15-89	.238	.125	.278	37	122	12	29	8	1	1	6	6	5	2	0	33	0	6	.344	.301
Gibson, Derrik	R-R	6-1	170	12-5-89	.302	.358	.269	85	291	49	88	15	3	2	26	38	5	4	2	54	8	7	.395	.390
Greenwell, Bo	L-L	6-0	185	10-15-88	.182	.105	.207	25	77	9	14	2	0	1	7	9	2	2	0	13	3	1	.247	.284
Heller, Kevin	R-R	5-10	195	9-12-89	.167	.143	.174	10	30	2	5	1	0	0	3	6	0	0	0	8	0	0	.200	.306
Hissey, Pete	L-L	6-1	180	1-17-90	.287	.296	.282	51	181	22	52	7	3	0	18	14	3	2	0	45	5	5	.359	.348
Johnson, Kelly	L-R	6-1	200	2-22-82	.000	.000	.000	2	6	1	0	0	0	0	0	2	0	0	0	3	0	0	.000	.250
Lavarnway, Ryan	R-R	6-4	240	8-7-87	.273	.333	.250	3	11	2	3	0	0	1	2	1	0	0	0	1	0	0	.545	.333
Marrero, Deven	R-R	6-1	195	8-25-90	.291	.312	.280	68	268	42	78	19	2	5	39	34	2	0	3	57	12	7	.433	.371

	B-T	HT	WT	DOB	AVG	vLH	vRH	G	AB	R	H	2B	3B	HR	RBI	BB	HBP	SH	SF	SO	SB	CS	SLG	OBP
Meneses, Heiker	R-R	5-9	200	7-1-91	.190	.202	.182	95	306	36	58	9	1	1	23	20	6	7	3	52	9	6	.235	.251
Miller, Mike	R-R	5-9	170	9-27-89	.301	.261	.314	23	93	15	28	4	0	3	12	6	2	0	0	14	3	1	.441	.356
Ramos, Henry	B-R	6-2	190	4-15-92	.326	.356	.306	48	181	26	59	9	2	2	23	11	1	1	0	38	2	4	.431	.368
Rivero, Carlos	R-R	6-3	200	5-20-88	.214	.200	.221	31	117	14	25	6	0	2	17	8	4	0	1	24	0	0	.316	.285
Roof, Jonathan	R-R	6-1	175	1-23-89	.255	.246	.260	59	188	24	48	11	2	3	20	19	5	2	0	46	1	3	.383	.340
Shaw, Travis	L-R	6-4	225	4-16-90	.305	.272	.333	47	177	35	54	8	1	11	37	29	1	1	0	23	5	3	.548	.406
Spring, Matt	R-R	6-2	215	11-7-84	.233	.234	.232	31	103	17	24	7	0	6	23	10	3	0	4	32	0	0	.476	.308
Swihart, Blake	R-R	6-1	175	4-3-92	.300	.275	.315	92	347	47	104	23	3	12	55	29	1	0	3	65	7	1	.487	.353
Welch, Stefan	L-R	6-3	190	8-12-88	.222	.200	.235	105	333	48	74	16	3	8	49	48	12	1	6	99	1	1	.360	.336
Wilkerson, Shannon	R-R	6-0	200	7-20-88	.266	.298	.250	105	384	51	102	23	3	2	43	30	1	8	4	69	11	4	.357	.317

Pitching	B-T	HT	WT	DOB	W	L	ERA	G	GS	CG	SV	IP	H	R	ER	HR	BB	SO	AVG	vLH	vRH	K/9	BB/9
Augliera, Mike	R-R	6-0	200	6-8-90	8	10	4.56	25	24	1	0	148	171	82	75	12	20	76	.292	.290	.294	4.62	1.22
Boscan, Wilfredo	R-R	6-2	160	10-26-89	1	7	3.88	20	5	0	1	63	75	38	27	6	15	44	.299	.321	.281	6.32	2.15
Celestino, Miguel	R-R	6-6	205	10-10-89	1	2	3.07	23	0	0	6	29	25	10	10	2	8	34	.229	.182	.262	10.43	2.45
Couch, Keith	L-R	6-2	210	11-5-89	8	2	2.96	18	17	2	1	100	105	41	33	3	22	72	.266	.299	.243	6.46	1.97
Diaz, Dayan	R-R	5-10	190	2-10-89	2	1	2.76	11	0	0	1	16	16	5	5	0	7	16	.236	.229	.229	8.82	3.86
Diaz, Luis	R-R	6-3	210	4-9-92	3	4	3.72	13	13	1	0	77	71	34	32	7	26	63	.247	.221	.268	7.33	3.03
Doubront, Felix	L-L	6-2	225	10-23-87	0	0	4.50	1	1	0	0	4	4	2	2	0	0	2	.267	.125	.429	4.50	0.00
Haley, Justin	R-R	6-5	230	6-16-91	3	2	1.19	6	6	0	0	38	30	5	5	2	16	33	.222	.222	.222	7.88	3.82
Johnson, Brian	L-L	6-3	225	12-7-90	10	2	1.75	20	20	2	0	118	78	29	23	6	32	99	.189	.169	.195	7.55	2.44
Kehrt, Jeremy	R-R	6-2	190	12-21-85	1	2	6.00	7	3	0	0	24	33	16	16	4	8	15	.324	.310	.333	5.63	3.00
Kraus, Kyle	R-R	5-11	185	1-19-90	0	0	21.60	1	0	0	0	2	7	4	4	1	2	0	.700	.667	.750	0.00	10.80
Kurcz, Aaron	R-R	6-0	175	8-8-90	3	2	2.14	34	0	0	3	42	32	11	10	0	22	54	.204	.283	.155	11.57	4.71
McCarthy, Mike	R-R	6-3	185	11-18-87	10	4	4.82	27	12	0	0	97	100	54	52	13	21	68	.267	.235	.289	6.31	1.95
Olmsted, Michael	R-R	6-6	280	5-2-87	3	0	4.45	12	0	0	1	32	29	21	16	4	24	37	.230	.191	.253	10.30	6.68
Ott, Matty	R-R	6-1	190	4-20-90	1	2	6.11	12	0	0	0	18	23	12	12	0	7	11	.315	.276	.341	5.60	3.57
Owens, Henry	L-L	6-6	205	7-21-92	14	4	2.60	20	20	3	0	121	89	36	35	6	47	126	.201	.216	.196	9.37	3.50
Pena, Miguel	L-L	6-2	175	10-24-90	2	2	6.41	13	13	0	0	60	75	44	43	6	25	47	.306	.417	.279	7.01	3.73
Ramirez, Noe	R-R	6-3	180	12-22-89	2	1	2.14	42	0	0	18	67	56	17	16	0	16	56	.230	.233	.227	7.49	2.14
Reed, Nate	R-R	6-3	180	12-1-87	0	1	6.75	6	0	0	0	13	23	10	10	1	6	11	.383	.529	.326	7.43	4.05
Rodriguez, Eduardo	L-L	6-2	200	4-7-93	3	1	0.96	6	6	0	0	37	30	4	4	1	8	39	.222	.297	.194	9.40	1.93
2-team total (16 Bowie)					6	8	3.60	22	22	1	0	120	120	54	48	6	37	108	—	—		8.10	2.78
Ruiz, Pete	R-R	6-2	205	8-21-87	3	2	4.15	12	0	0	0	26	24	12	12	1	10	21	.250	.237	.259	7.27	3.46
Scott, Robby	B-L	6-3	190		8	2	1.96	35	1	0	3	60	55	17	13	3	15	51	.249	.417	.186	7.69	2.26
Valdez, Jose	R-R	6-4	200	1-22-83	0	1	1.59	13	0	0	4	17	18	4	3	1	4	13	.269	.250	.277	6.88	2.12
Wright, Steven	R-R	6-1	220	8-30-84	1	0	3.60	1	1	0	0	5	5	3	2	1	1	4	.278	.200	.375	7.20	1.80

Fielding

Catcher	PCT	G	PO	A	E	DP	PB
Blair	1.000	15	114	5	0	0	2
Brenly	.996	32	230	29	1	0	0
Spring	1.000	14	78	4	0	1	2
Swihart	.987	81	578	46	8	2	0

First Base	PCT	G	PO	A	E	DP
Almanzar	1.000	8	62	2	0	7
Brenly	1.000	6	54	6	0	2
Chester	.992	16	118	7	1	8
Johnson	1.000	1	8	1	0	1
Lavarnway	1.000	2	14	2	0	1
Shaw	.993	35	280	15	2	25
Spring	1.000	2	6	0	0	0
Welch	.997	79	628	46	2	60

Second Base	PCT	G	PO	A	E	DP
Betts	.980	40	80	121	4	23
Coyle	.982	61	107	166	5	35
Dent	.966	7	14	14	1	5
Gibson	.875	5	8	13	3	1
Meneses	1.000	17	36	44	0	9
Miller	1.000	11	20	36	0	7
Roof	.938	4	6	9	1	3

Third Base	PCT	G	PO	A	E	DP
Almanzar	.928	39	24	79	8	5
Brenly	1.000	2	0	2	0	0
Coyle	.842	18	14	18	6	1
Dent	.947	7	6	12	1	2
Gibson	.909	3	2	8	1	1
Johnson	1.000	1	0	2	0	0
Meneses	.963	31	18	61	3	5
Miller	.952	8	2	18	1	2
Rivero	.878	13	9	27	5	2
Roof	.932	14	14	27	3	2
Shaw	.875	6	2	12	2	1
Welch	.957	10	9	13	1	2

Shortstop	PCT	G	PO	A	E	DP
Dent	.983	13	21	38	1	8
Gibson	.983	16	15	43	1	8
Marrero	.978	66	87	178	6	36
Meneses	.985	46	60	140	3	31
Miller	1.000	4	5	12	0	2

Outfield	PCT	G	PO	A	E	DP
Betts	1.000	12	30	0	0	0
Brenly	—	3	0	0	0	0
De La Cruz	.983	62	113	3	2	0
Dent	.952	13	20	0	1	0
Gibson	.973	59	106	3	3	2
Greenwell	.957	24	42	2	2	0
Heller	.950	10	19	0	1	0
Hissey	.989	51	92	1	1	1
Ramos	.958	47	88	3	4	0
Rivero	1.000	11	21	0	0	0
Roof	1.000	41	65	3	0	1
Wilkerson	.996	105	249	6	1	2

SALEM RED SOX   HIGH CLASS A

CAROLINA LEAGUE

Batting	B-T	HT	WT	DOB	AVG	vLH	vRH	G	AB	R	H	2B	3B	HR	RBI	BB	HBP	SH	SF	SO	SB	CS	SLG	OBP
Asuaje, Carlos	R-R	5-9	160	11-2-91	.323	.205	.362	39	155	27	50	14	2	4	28	18	2	0	1	34	1	3	.516	.398
Blair, Carson	R-R	6-1	190	10-18-89	.261	.261	.260	67	238	40	62	19	2	9	41	48	2	0	3	88	0	0	.471	.385
Chester, David	R-R	6-5	270	3-31-89	.220	.136	.250	22	82	11	18	3	2	3	15	13	1	0	3	18	0	0	.415	.323
Dent, Ryan	R-R	6-0	190	3-15-89	.248	.266	.242	72	254	32	63	20	3	3	31	37	4	2	2	56	15	2	.386	.350
Escobar, Leonel	R-R	5-10	175	9-4-90	.148	.048	.183	28	81	10	12	3	0	0	7	10	0	2	0	17	0	0	.185	.242
Gedman, Matt	L-R	6-2	205	9-26-88	.201	.186	.206	49	184	15	37	8	0	0	18	9	1	0	1	28	2	0	.245	.241
Gragnani, Reed	B-R	5-11	180	9-5-90	.300	.282	.305	99	360	64	108	19	8	1	53	64	3	5	1	51	8	4	.406	.409
Greenwell, Bo	L-L	6-0	185	10-15-88	.200	.167	.214	6	20	5	4	2	0	0	1	4	2	0	0	1	0	1	.300	.385
Guerrero, Dreily	B-R	5-11	165	12-10-90	.224	.212	.228	59	156	24	35	6	3	3	16	10	0	2	1	59	7	3	.359	.269
Heller, Kevin	R-R	5-10	195	9-12-89	.253	.324	.231	94	316	41	80	21	2	7	48	45	17	1	2	90	12	5	.399	.374
Hernandez, Jayson	R-R	5-10	200	9-2-88	.234	.350	.193	23	77	7	18	8	0	1	6	5	1	0	1	18	0	0	.377	.286
Johnson, Matty	B-R	5-8	165	4-10-88	.276	.182	.310	132	510	104	141	18	10	4	55	74	10	6	3	85	40	17	.375	.377

Name	B-T	HT	WT	DOB	AVG	vLH	vRH	G	AB	R	H	2B	3B	HR	RBI	BB	HBP	SH	SF	SO	SB	CS	SLG	OBP
King, Aaron	L-L	6-5	230	4-27-89	.167	.250	.083	7	24	3	4	0	0	0	1	1	0	0	0	10	0	0	.167	.200
Mager, Kevin	R-R	6-2	185	5-16-89	.111	.048	.133	25	81	8	9	2	0	0	6	11	2	0	1	22	0	0	.136	.232
Margot, Manuel	R-R	5-11	170	9-28-94	.340	.308	.351	16	50	4	17	5	0	2	14	2	1	1	2	5	3	2	.560	.364
Martinez, Mario	R-R	6-3	220	11-13-89	.268	.263	.270	118	463	50	124	28	2	9	62	13	2	0	4	96	1	1	.395	.288
Miller, Mike	R-R	5-9	170	9-27-89	.307	.333	.301	49	192	24	59	8	0	0	18	15	3	6	0	25	7	4	.349	.367
Moore, Nick	B-R	6-2	200	12-9-92	.167	.000	.200	5	12	1	2	0	0	0	0	2	0	0	0	5	1	0	.167	.286
Perkins, Kendrick	L-R	6-2	225	9-12-91	.181	.000	.250	23	72	12	13	4	0	2	5	9	1	0	0	35	0	0	.319	.280
Roberson, Tim	R-R	5-10	190	7-19-89	.219	.167	.235	40	151	17	33	10	1	2	20	12	0	0	0	41	0	0	.338	.276
Romanski, Jake	R-R	5-11	185	12-22-90	.291	.350	.257	17	55	8	16	7	0	2	9	1	0	0	0	5	1	1	.527	.304
Roof, Jonathan	R-R	6-1	175	1-23-89	.301	.382	.268	50	193	39	58	15	2	4	23	27	1	0	3	32	2	1	.461	.384
Tavarez, Aneury	L-R	5-9	175	4-14-92	.250	.219	.257	93	344	52	86	16	5	11	50	17	8	4	3	97	18	5	.422	.298
Vinicio, Jose	B-R	5-11	150	7-10-93	.264	.243	.272	39	129	16	34	5	1	0	10	4	2	1	2	29	0	6	.318	.292
Weems, Jordan	L-R	6-3	175	11-7-92	.329	.353	.323	24	82	13	27	4	0	1	6	9	2	1	0	24	2	0	.415	.409
Witte, Jantzen	R-R	6-2	195	1-4-90	.296	.355	.277	65	257	21	76	20	4	4	39	18	2	0	5	41	2	1	.451	.340

Pitching	B-T	HT	WT	DOB	W	L	ERA	G	GS	CG	SV	IP	H	R	ER	HR	BB	SO	AVG	vLH	vRH	K/9	BB/9
Aro, Jonathan	R-R	6-0	172	10-10-90	2	0	1.80	7	1	0	1	20	12	6	4	1	7	24	.176	.231	.143	10.80	3.15
Cuevas, William	R-R	6-0	160	10-14-90	2	6	4.70	24	10	0	1	96	92	57	50	7	32	80	.253	.252	.253	7.53	3.01
Dahlstrand, Jacob	R-R	6-5	205	3-26-92	3	0	2.81	6	5	0	0	32	31	16	10	3	8	21	.252	.240	.260	5.91	2.25
Diaz, Dayan	R-R	5-10	190	2-10-89	0	1	1.34	24	0	0	6	34	21	8	5	1	14	40	.179	.146	.197	10.69	3.74
Diaz, Luis	R-R	6-3	210	4-9-92	6	3	3.33	13	13	0	0	68	71	31	25	3	18	48	.268	.284	.260	6.38	2.39
Grover, Taylor	R-R	6-3	195	4-22-91	0	1	1.46	5	0	0	1	12	7	2	2	0	6	19	.167	.125	.192	13.86	4.38
Gunkel, Joe	R-R	6-5	225	12-30-91	3	5	4.64	10	10	1	0	52	62	32	27	3	13	39	.294	.213	.344	6.71	2.24
Haley, Justin	R-R	6-5	230	6-16-91	7	4	2.82	19	11	1	1	93	77	34	29	4	23	74	.229	.232	.227	7.19	2.23
Jimenez, Ellis	R-R	6-2	175	6-26-92	0	0	3.38	2	0	0	0	3	2	1	1	1	0	0	.200	.000	.286	0.00	0.00
Johnson, Brian	L-L	6-3	225	12-7-90	3	1	3.86	5	5	0	0	26	23	13	11	0	7	33	.230	.214	.236	11.57	2.45
Kraus, Kyle	R-R	5-11	185	1-19-90	7	4	4.43	27	3	0	3	83	100	49	41	9	16	59	.300	.308	.295	6.37	1.73
Kukuk, Cody	L-L	6-4	200	4-10-93	4	7	5.26	20	20	0	0	79	71	53	46	2	71	87	.248	.244	.249	9.95	8.12
Light, Pat	R-R	6-5	195	3-29-91	6	6	4.93	22	22	1	0	115	135	67	63	10	33	57	.295	.283	.303	4.46	2.58
Littrell, Corey	L-L	6-3	185	3-21-92	5	5	3.60	19	18	0	0	100	101	43	40	8	38	91	.266	.280	.261	8.19	3.42
Maddox, Austin	R-R	6-2	220	5-13-91	1	1	5.82	10	0	0	1	22	20	14	14	5	3	22	.244	.219	.260	9.14	1.25
Martin, Kyle	R-R	6-7	220	1-18-91	4	5	4.02	35	0	0	10	81	84	41	36	11	16	82	.268	.265	.269	9.15	1.79
Mercedes, Simon	R-R	6-4	200	2-17-92	5	10	4.76	19	14	0	1	85	85	50	45	6	38	74	.261	.184	.308	7.84	4.02
Ott, Matty	R-R	6-1	190	4-20-90	2	1	2.36	17	0	0	4	27	20	10	7	0	6	25	.204	.194	.210	8.44	2.03
Quevedo, Heri	R-R	6-2	211	6-7-90	1	1	4.29	4	4	0	0	21	22	11	10	0	6	25	.250	.265	.250	10.71	2.57
Reed, Nate	R-R	6-3	180	12-1-87	3	1	3.83	20	0	0	0	47	39	20	20	3	33	36	.238	.190	.254	6.89	6.32
Stroup, Kyle	R-R	6-6	235	3-13-90	1	2	8.25	18	0	0	1	24	39	28	22	1	21	20	.368	.300	.409	7.50	7.88
Younginer, Madison	R-R	6-4	195	11-3-90	3	3	4.08	35	0	0	2	57	61	31	26	0	25	55	.275	.329	.245	8.63	3.92

Fielding

Catcher	PCT	G	PO	A	E	DP	PB
Blair	.980	51	399	32	9	3	5
Escobar	.986	27	182	23	3	4	1
Hernandez	.966	22	151	21	6	2	3
Roberson	1.000	2	12	1	0	0	0
Romanski	1.000	16	111	24	0	1	0
Weems	.982	22	152	13	3	1	2

First Base	PCT	G	PO	A	E	DP
Chester	.993	15	140	7	1	11
Gedman	.993	20	134	7	1	13
Guerrero	1.000	1	3	0	0	0
Martinez	1.000	34	272	22	0	27
Roberson	.984	30	226	14	4	23
Witte	.995	42	351	25	2	32

Second Base	PCT	G	PO	A	E	DP
Asuaje	.974	16	26	48	2	9
Dent	.977	17	37	48	2	13

Third Base	PCT	G	PO	A	E	DP
Gragnani	.961	65	133	166	12	35
Guerrero	1.000	22	34	50	0	12
Miller	1.000	14	32	41	0	11
Roof	.917	3	6	5	1	1
Witte	1.000	1	2	2	0	0

Third Base	PCT	G	PO	A	E	DP
Asuaje	1.000	1	0	4	0	0
Dent	.818	3	2	7	2	2
Gragnani	1.000	6	6	11	0	1
Guerrero	.950	10	8	11	1	1
Mager	.833	5	3	12	3	2
Martinez	.960	69	45	146	8	14
Miller	1.000	3	0	4	0	0
Roof	.940	27	25	54	5	7
Witte	.951	16	12	27	2	2

Shortstop	PCT	G	PO	A	E	DP
Dent	.966	45	74	122	7	32

	PCT	G	PO	A	E	DP
Guerrero	.913	21	28	45	7	7
Miller	.961	31	43	79	5	15
Roof	.905	8	10	28	4	4
Vinicio	.948	37	54	93	8	16

Outfield	PCT	G	PO	A	E	DP
Asuaje	1.000	19	28	2	0	1
Dent	.900	7	8	1	1	0
Gragnani	1.000	7	9	0	0	0
Greenwell	1.000	4	3	0	0	0
Heller	.988	85	155	6	2	1
Johnson	.986	132	275	10	4	4
King	1.000	6	12	3	0	0
Mager	1.000	14	27	3	0	1
Margot	1.000	16	29	0	0	0
Moore	1.000	3	1	1	0	0
Perkins	.926	21	25	0	2	0
Roof	.895	10	17	0	2	0
Tavarez	.932	90	168	9	13	0

GREENVILLE DRIVE

LOW CLASS A

SOUTH ATLANTIC LEAGUE

Batting	B-T	HT	WT	DOB	AVG	vLH	vRH	G	AB	R	H	2B	3B	HR	RBI	BB	HBP	SH	SF	SO	SB	CS	SLG	OBP
Allday, Forrestt	R-R	5-11	190	4-24-91	.274	.340	.250	52	186	29	51	12	2	0	18	25	8	9	2	42	5	6	.360	.380
Asuaje, Carlos	R-R	5-9	160	11-2-91	.305	.304	.305	90	325	59	99	24	10	11	73	41	9	2	6	56	7	4	.542	.391
Bethea, Danny	R-R	6-1	210	1-31-90	.290	.214	.313	17	62	9	18	0	0	2	7	4	0	0	0	9	0	1	.387	.333
Coste, Carlos	R-R	6-2	186	5-11-93	.259	.263	.258	27	81	5	21	0	0	1	6	4	3	1	0	31	0	0	.296	.318
Drew, Stephen	L-R	6-0	190	3-16-83	.375	.333	.400	3	8	1	3	2	0	0	2	1	0	0	0	4	0	0	.625	.444
Greenwell, Bo	L-L	6-0	185	10-15-88	.275	.281	.273	29	120	24	33	6	1	3	14	11	1	0	3	21	5	1	.417	.333
Guzman, Franklin	R-R	5-11	185	2-4-94	.241	.160	.259	39	141	23	34	11	0	3	11	10	0	4	1	40	6	0	.383	.289
Kapstein, Zach	R-R	6-2	195	5-28-92	.280	.184	.302	66	200	26	56	8	1	1	26	24	3	2	2	76	2	1	.345	.362
King, Aaron	L-L	6-5	230	4-27-89	.091	.000	.125	3	11	1	1	1	0	0	1	0	0	0	0	3	0	0	.182	.091
Lin, Tzu-Wei	L-R	5-9	155	2-15-94	.229	.282	.209	102	402	55	92	22	1	1	42	54	0	4	7	74	10	7	.296	.315
Lorenzana, Hector	R-R	5-11	190	9-29-91	.193	.235	.183	28	88	5	17	3	0	0	7	12	0	0	0	18	2	0	.227	.290
Loya, Jesus	L-R	5-11	175	6-15-92	.170	.200	.156	15	47	8	8	0	0	0	6	0	1	0	8	2	0	.170	.264

Batting	B-T	HT	WT	DOB	AVG	vLH	vRH	G	AB	R	H	2B	3B	HR	RBI	BB	HBP	SH	SF	SO	SB	CS	SLG	OBP
Mager, Kevin	R-R	6-2	185	5-16-89	.230	.286	.211	73	257	36	59	15	1	7	33	34	1	3	0	61	0	0	.377	.322
Margot, Manuel	R-R	5-11	170	9-28-94	.286	.360	.259	99	370	61	106	20	5	10	45	37	2	4	0	49	39	13	.449	.355
Mars, Danny	B-R	6-0	195	1-22-94	.167	.000	.286	10	36	4	6	0	0	0	0	3	0	1	0	6	4	0	.167	.231
Peralta, Aneudis	R-R	5-11	195	8-21-93	.269	.368	.243	30	93	11	25	5	0	0	7	6	0	0	0	24	2	1	.323	.313
Perkins, Kendrick	L-R	6-2	225	9-12-91	.296	.347	.275	51	169	23	50	10	1	6	26	10	6	1	2	71	2	2	.473	.353
Procyshen, Jordan	L-R	5-10	185	3-11-93	.300	.300	.300	9	30	2	9	1	0	1	3	3	0	0	0	8	0	0	.433	.364
Rider, Jimmy	R-R	5-8	175	5-9-90	.256	.269	.251	105	348	57	89	20	2	3	37	58	6	0	4	71	6	2	.351	.368
Rijo, Wendell	R-R	5-11	170	9-4-95	.254	.269	.249	111	409	56	104	27	6	9	46	56	4	2	2	103	16	6	.416	.348
Roberson, Tim	R-R	5-10	190	7-19-89	.238	.315	.209	71	269	29	64	16	0	8	32	24	2	0	1	64	0	0	.387	.304
Romanski, Jake	R-R	5-11	185	12-22-90	.270	.197	.293	78	300	30	81	16	2	1	44	24	1	3	3	39	10	5	.347	.323
Sturgeon, Cole	L-L	6-0	180	9-17-91	.284	.314	.273	48	183	28	52	10	0	2	25	16	3	2	2	31	4	1	.372	.348
Travis, Sam	L-R	6-0	195	8-27-93	.290	.406	.240	27	107	12	31	11	1	3	14	7	0	0	1	14	0	1	.495	.330
Weems, Jordan	L-R	6-3	175	11-7-92	.166	.143	.178	50	163	16	27	4	2	0	9	25	2	2	1	68	6	0	.215	.283
Witte, Jantzen	R-R	6-2	195	1-4-90	.330	.391	.308	65	233	50	77	24	2	8	54	36	5	0	8	56	4	3	.554	.418

Pitching

Pitching	B-T	HT	WT	DOB	W	L	ERA	G	GS	CG	SV	IP	H	R	ER	HR	BB	SO	AVG	vLH	vRH	K/9	BB/9
Adams, Mike	L-L	6-3	215	10-4-90	2	3	2.82	30	0	0	4	51	43	19	16	4	9	49	.213	.238	.201	8.65	1.59
Alcantara, Mario	R-R	6-2	170	12-27-92	1	2	8.31	16	7	0	0	43	60	46	40	5	34	24	.326	.383	.282	4.98	7.06
Aro, Jonathan	R-R	6-0	172	10-10-90	1	3	2.27	25	0	0	7	67	52	27	17	3	22	74	.211	.170	.241	9.89	2.94
Ball, Trey	L-L	6-6	185	6-27-94	5	10	4.68	22	22	0	0	100	111	69	52	9	39	68	.280	.299	.273	6.12	3.51
Buttrey, Ty	L-R	6-6	230	3-31-93	0	5	6.85	11	11	0	0	46	59	41	35	5	24	40	.306	.264	.331	7.83	4.70
Callahan, Jamie	R-R	6-2	205	8-24-94	3	13	6.96	25	25	0	0	109	137	95	84	12	66	89	.309	.291	.324	7.37	5.47
Dahlstrand, Jacob	R-R	6-5	205	3-26-92	5	5	2.93	22	1	0	3	74	75	29	24	2	20	54	.266	.214	.311	6.60	2.44
Ely, John	R-R	6-2	210	5-13-86	1	0	5.63	6	0	0	0	8	11	5	5	0	5	7	.314	.500	.217	7.88	5.63
Garcia, Jason	R-R	6-0	185	11-21-92	2	1	3.79	9	3	0	3	36	31	16	15	0	17	37	.242	.281	.211	9.34	4.29
Gomez, Sergio	R-R	6-3	155	8-24-93	1	2	6.75	20	1	0	2	77	88	62	58	8	49	57	.291	.211	.355	6.63	5.70
Grover, Taylor	R-R	6-3	195	4-22-91	1	5	4.73	20	0	1	6	46	39	26	24	7	13	43	.222	.226	.217	8.47	2.56
Gunkel, Joe	R-R	6-5	225	12-30-91	3	0	2.28	17	5	0	2	51	26	15	13	3	11	62	.149	.133	.163	10.87	1.93
Jimenez, Ellis	R-R	6-2	175	6-26-92	0	1	12.79	3	0	0	1	6	10	9	9	1	5	5	.400	.385	.417	7.11	7.11
Kukuk, Cody	L-L	6-4	200	4-10-93	3	0	1.88	5	5	0	0	24	18	6	5	1	12	29	.217	.258	.192	10.88	4.50
Light, Pat	R-R	6-5	195	3-29-91	2	0	4.15	3	3	0	0	17	16	9	8	1	4	19	.231	.167	.310	9.87	2.08
McGrath, Daniel	R-L	6-3	205	7-7-94	6	6	4.07	19	19	1	0	97	80	51	44	9	52	81	.223	.200	.232	7.49	4.81
Perez, Oscar	R-R	6-1	185	11-9-91	0	1	7.24	5	0	0	0	14	23	12	11	0	3	4	.397	.483	.310	2.63	1.98
Ruiz, Pete	R-R	6-2	205	8-21-87	0	0	3.26	11	0	0	2	19	13	7	7	0	10	27	.194	.219	.171	12.57	4.66
Smith, Myles	R-R	6-1	175	3-23-92	5	10	5.82	26	12	0	1	104	121	75	67	9	62	73	.298	.277	.319	6.34	5.38
Stankiewicz, Teddy	R-R	6-4	200	11-25-93	11	8	3.72	25	25	0	0	140	141	64	58	9	29	102	.260	.288	.238	6.54	1.86
Taveras, German	R-R	6-2	180	2-15-93	0	1	4.13	11	0	0	5	28	28	15	13	4	13	19	.259	.250	.265	6.04	4.13
Vellette, Raynel	R-R	6-2	165	6-10-91	7	3	3.04	23	0	0	0	47	45	21	16	1	28	36	.254	.260	.250	6.85	5.32

Fielding

Catcher	PCT	G	PO	A	E	DP	PB
Bethea	.989	12	81	8	1	2	1
Coste	.979	22	130	9	3	0	3
Procyshen	.970	8	61	3	2	1	1
Roberson	.958	7	38	8	2	1	0
Romanski	.986	61	445	52	7	5	5
Weems	.981	35	236	20	5	1	1

First Base	PCT	G	PO	A	E	DP
Mager	.983	7	57	2	1	5
Peralta	.971	9	65	3	2	3
Rider	1.000	3	12	1	0	1
Roberson	.992	48	360	24	3	27
Travis	.989	23	166	20	2	18
Witte	.996	57	441	35	2	50

Second Base	PCT	G	PO	A	E	DP
Asuaje	.982	24	45	63	2	13

	PCT	G	PO	A	E	DP
Lorenzana	.941	9	13	19	2	4
Rider	1.000	2	0	6	0	0
Rijo	.959	106	205	284	21	60

Third Base	PCT	G	PO	A	E	DP
Asuaje	.976	38	20	62	2	3
Lorenzana	.872	14	8	26	5	1
Mager	1.000	1	0	1	0	0
Peralta	.833	15	12	13	5	1
Rider	.898	68	48	101	17	11
Witte	.920	10	5	18	2	0

Shortstop	PCT	G	PO	A	E	DP
Asuaje	1.000	6	7	17	0	1
Drew	.875	2	3	4	1	0
Lin	.947	101	148	279	24	64
Lorenzana	1.000	3	6	6	0	1
Rider	.955	31	51	76	6	14

Outfield	PCT	G	PO	A	E	DP
Allday	.957	50	89	1	4	1
Asuaje	.962	17	25	0	1	0
Greenwell	.984	29	62	1	1	0
Guzman	.921	38	66	4	6	0
Kapstein	.978	52	85	2	2	0
King	1.000	3	2	0	0	0
Loya	.935	15	29	0	2	0
Mager	.984	39	57	5	1	1
Margot	.992	96	253	5	2	0
Mars	1.000	10	25	0	0	0
Perkins	.959	39	67	3	3	0
Sturgeon	.984	48	112	8	2	2

LOWELL SPINNERS   SHORT-SEASON

NEW YORK-PENN LEAGUE

Batting	B-T	HT	WT	DOB	AVG	vLH	vRH	G	AB	R	H	2B	3B	HR	RBI	BB	HBP	SH	SF	SO	SB	CS	SLG	OBP
Bethea, Danny	R-R	6-1	210	1-31-90	.067	.000	.100	8	15	1	1	0	0	0	1	3	0	0	1	4	0	0	.067	.211
Betts, Jordan	R-R	6-3	220	10-6-91	.269	.333	.247	64	242	32	65	17	2	10	40	25	0	0	3	76	1	2	.479	.333
Brentz, Bryce	R-R	6-0	210	12-30-88	.125	.000	.143	2	8	2	1	0	0	0	1	1	0	0	1	2	0	0	.125	.200
Dubon, Mauricio	R-R	6-0	160	7-19-94	.320	.344	.313	66	256	40	82	8	1	3	34	9	0	4	5	26	7	8	.395	.337
Flores, Raymel	B-R	5-9	155	9-22-94	.282	.333	.263	61	206	31	58	6	3	1	12	16	4	6	1	67	14	4	.354	.344
Guzman, Franklin	R-R	5-11	185	2-4-92	.241	.278	.222	15	54	7	13	3	0	2	6	2	1	0	1	15	3	2	.407	.276
Hudson, Bryan	L-R	6-1	185	2-10-95	.237	.178	.255	52	194	27	46	5	3	0	11	25	1	1	0	43	8	5	.294	.327
Longhi, Nick	R-L	6-2	205	8-16-95	.330	.310	.338	30	109	19	36	10	1	0	10	11	0	0	1	22	0	3	.440	.388
Lopez, Deiner	B-R	6-0	165	5-30-94	.277	.235	.296	48	159	24	44	6	1	2	16	10	5	4	1	33	15	4	.365	.337
Mars, Danny	B-R	6-0	195	1-22-94	.311	.220	.346	44	177	28	55	9	3	2	17	14	2	2	0	37	12	6	.429	.368
McKeon, Alex	R-R	6-2	215	5-20-93	.000	.000	.000	2	5	0	0	0	0	0	0	0	2	0	0	1	0	0	.000	.286
Meyers, Mike	R-R	6-1	175	12-28-93	.215	.193	.224	56	209	25	45	6	9	0	27	9	1	0	3	52	5	3	.330	.248
Monge, Joseph	R-R	6-0	170	5-18-95	.288	.400	.247	31	111	17	32	9	1	0	10	3	4	3	3	31	4	2	.387	.322
Moore, Nick	B-R	6-2	200	12-9-92	.264	.200	.283	37	129	13	34	10	0	4	21	7	1	2	4	45	10	1	.434	.298

	B-T	HT	WT	DOB	AVG	vLH	vRH	G	AB	R	H	2B	3B	HR	RBI	BB	HBP	SH	SF	SO	SB	CS	SLG	OBP
Peralta, Aneudis	R-R	5-11	195	8-21-93	.269	.241	.289	19	67	6	18	3	1	0	6	4	2	0	0	12	0	0	.343	.329
Procyshen, Jordan	L-R	5-10	185	3-11-93	.259	.231	.268	19	54	3	14	3	0	0	6	7	0	0	1	6	0	1	.315	.339
Sopilka, David	R-R	6-0	170	8-30-93	.153	.185	.138	27	85	3	13	1	0	1	10	2	2	2	0	25	2	0	.200	.191
Sturgeon, Cole	L-L	6-0	180	9-17-91	.276	.250	.280	7	29	3	8	0	2	0	5	0	1	0	0	5	2	0	.414	.300
Suarez, Alixon	R-R	6-1	180	7-25-94	.209	.182	.214	40	134	14	28	8	4	2	13	9	2	2	1	50	0	1	.373	.267
Tellez, Cisco	L-L	5-11	217	6-5-92	.250	.077	.298	37	120	13	30	4	0	0	11	13	1	2	2	27	0	1	.283	.324
Torres, Andres	B-R	5-10	195	1-26-78	.211	.000	.222	5	19	1	4	2	0	1	3	1	0	0	0	4	0	0	.474	.250
Travis, Sam	R-R	6-0	195	8-27-93	.333	.422	.300	40	165	28	55	5	1	4	30	4	4	1	0	18	5	1	.448	.364
Victorino, Shane	B-R	5-9	190	11-30-80	.000	—	.000	4	9	0	0	0	0	0	0	2	0	0	2	0	0	0	.000	.182

Pitching

	B-T	HT	WT	DOB	W	L	ERA	G	GS	CG	SV	IP	H	R	ER	HR	BB	SO	AVG	vLH	vRH	K/9	BB/9
Alcantara, Mario	R-R	6-2	170	12-27-92	2	3	8.00	11	0	0	0	18	20	17	16	2	14	20	.282	.219	.333	10.00	7.00
Buttrey, Ty	L-R	6-6	230	3-31-93	0	0	3.09	3	2	0	0	12	11	6	4	0	7	12	.244	.238	.250	9.26	5.40
Drehoff, Jake	L-L	6-4	195	6-5-92	3	4	3.54	14	14	0	0	69	75	30	27	4	23	48	.281	.294	.276	6.29	3.01
Ethington, Willie	R-R	6-3	190	12-8-93	2	1	4.66	6	2	0	0	19	22	11	10	1	8	12	.293	.240	.320	5.59	3.72
Fernandez, Jeffry	R-R	6-3	180	3-25-93	0	3	5.30	4	4	0	0	19	22	14	11	2	6	4	.293	.320	.240	1.93	2.89
Garcia, Edwar	R-R	6-4	175	11-19-93	0	0	7.67	16	0	0	1	27	31	26	23	1	18	26	.272	.296	.250	8.67	6.00
Garcia, Jason	R-R	6-0	185	11-21-92	1	1	3.48	5	4	0	0	21	19	10	8	0	7	22	.238	.311	.143	9.58	3.05
Harris, Ryan	R-R	6-2	195	1-25-93	0	0	7.71	4	0	0	0	5	4	4	4	0	3	3	.211	.125	.273	5.79	5.79
Jimenez, Ellis	R-R	6-2	175	6-26-92	4	2	3.90	17	0	0	1	32	30	18	14	0	14	22	.244	.290	.197	6.12	3.90
Martinez, Enfember	R-R	5-11	140	8-9-94	1	0	3.28	16	0	0	0	25	23	9	9	1	15	15	.247	.214	.275	5.47	5.47
McAvoy, Kevin	R-R	6-4	210	7-21-93	0	2	1.91	11	11	0	0	28	23	7	6	0	3	23	.221	.250	.182	7.31	0.95
McEachern, Kuehl	R-R	6-4	195	5-7-93	1	1	2.93	13	0	0	2	28	28	12	9	0	4	22	.262	.241	.286	7.16	1.30
Mercedes, Simon	R-R	6-4	200	2-17-92	0	0	1.64	3	1	0	0	11	13	2	2	0	3	5	.317	.259	.429	4.09	2.45
Perez, Oscar	R-R	6-1	185	11-9-91	1	0	3.30	12	0	0	0	30	30	15	11	3	6	19	.254	.250	.258	5.70	1.80
Perez, Randy	L-L	5-10	165	4-1-94	2	2	2.78	5	5	0	0	23	24	8	7	0	8	16	.273	.273	.273	6.35	3.18
Pinales, Carlos	R-R	6-1	180	4-5-92	1	3	5.58	25	0	0	15	31	37	20	19	3	9	24	.303	.327	.286	7.04	2.64
Quevedo, Heri	R-R	6-2	211	6-7-90	5	3	7.17	11	9	0	0	54	65	45	43	8	20	40	.295	.300	.292	6.67	3.33
Reilly, Reed	R-R	6-4	220	1-5-92	0	1	3.89	10	10	0	0	39	43	18	17	2	6	30	.274	.280	.267	6.86	1.37
Romero, Dioscar	R-R	6-3	230	4-17-95	0	0	0.00	1	1	0	0	4	1	0	0	0	4	3	.091	.000	.143	7.36	9.82
Shepherd, Chandler	R-R	6-3	185	8-25-92	4	3	4.05	16	1	0	0	33	33	18	15	3	8	35	.254	.254	.254	9.45	2.16
Show, Brandon	R-R	6-2	180	10-31-92	1	1	7.13	12	0	0	0	18	18	14	14	0	12	11	.269	.314	.219	5.60	6.11
Smorol, Rob	L-L	6-1	185	2-22-91	0	4	4.18	17	1	0	0	32	27	18	15	2	18	22	.227	.154	.263	6.12	5.01
Taveras, German	R-R	6-2	180	2-15-93	3	1	2.76	7	0	0	0	16	9	5	5	0	5	17	.161	.208	.125	9.37	2.76
Whitson, Karsten	R-R	6-3	195	8-25-91	0	1	7.71	4	2	0	0	7	8	6	6	1	5	5	.296	.286	.308	6.43	6.43
Wilkerson, Aaron	R-R	6-3	190	5-24-89	5	1	1.62	8	8	0	0	50	32	11	9	3	11	54	.183	.238	.132	9.72	1.98

Fielding

Catcher	PCT	G	PO	A	E	DP	PB
Bethea	1.000	7	25	1	0	0	0
McKeon	1.000	2	18	6	0	1	0
Procyshen	.989	12	76	13	1	1	0
Sopilka	.983	25	159	16	3	2	2
Suarez	.982	38	238	31	5	4	6

First Base	PCT	G	PO	A	E	DP
Longhi	1.000	2	7	1	0	0
Moore	.971	14	117	15	4	10
Peralta	.989	11	85	4	1	9
Tellez	.989	22	167	9	2	14
Travis	.980	33	263	26	6	21

Second Base	PCT	G	PO	A	E	DP
Flores	.987	47	91	135	3	31
Lopez	.943	30	52	80	8	14

Third Base	PCT	G	PO	A	E	DP
Betts	.944	60	34	101	8	8
Lopez	.935	12	11	32	3	3
Peralta	.900	3	1	8	1	0

Shortstop	PCT	G	PO	A	E	DP
Dubon	.947	64	130	189	18	38
Flores	.904	11	22	25	5	8

Outfield	PCT	G	PO	A	E	DP
Brentz	1.000	1	2	0	0	0
Guzman	.974	14	35	3	1	1
Hudson	.990	52	97	4	1	2
Longhi	.919	23	34	0	3	0
Mars	1.000	44	95	2	0	1
Meyers	.976	48	75	7	2	4
Monge	1.000	31	75	1	0	0
Moore	.857	6	6	0	1	0
Sturgeon	.929	7	13	0	1	0
Torres	1.000	4	5	1	0	0
Victorino	.800	4	3	1	1	0

GCL RED SOX

ROOKIE

GULF COAST LEAGUE

Batting	B-T	HT	WT	DOB	AVG	vLH	vRH	G	AB	R	H	2B	3B	HR	RBI	BB	HBP	SH	SF	SO	SB	CS	SLG	OBP
Acosta, Victor	R-R	5-11	160	6-2-96	.268	.295	.260	42	149	31	40	11	0	2	21	14	4	2	1	30	13	1	.383	.345
Austin, Jordon	R-R	5-11	195	3-14-95	.163	.069	.214	31	86	14	14	4	1	0	7	11	3	1	0	43	5	0	.233	.280
Basabe, Luis Alexander	B-R	6-0	160	8-26-96	.248	.290	.230	32	105	15	26	5	0	1	13	13	1	1	3	23	2	4	.324	.328
Brentz, Bryce	R-R	6-0	210	12-30-88	.056	.143	.000	7	18	1	1	1	0	0	3	0	0	0	0	5	0	0	.111	.190
Chavis, Michael	R-R	5-10	190	8-11-95	.269	.333	.247	39	134	21	36	12	3	1	16	15	1	0	0	38	5	3	.425	.347
Devers, Rafael	L-R	6-0	195	10-24-96	.312	.214	.351	42	157	21	49	11	2	4	36	14	2	0	1	30	1	0	.484	.374
Fisher, Devon	R-R	6-0	215	5-1-96	.210	.105	.256	22	62	8	13	1	0	0	6	15	0	0	1	13	0	0	.226	.364
Gravel, Simon	R-R	6-2	190	5-19-94	.267	.375	.143	6	15	2	4	0	0	0	3	3	0	0	0	1	0	0	.267	.389
Guerra, Javier	L-R	5-11	155	9-25-95	.269	.306	.254	51	201	21	54	14	4	2	26	5	0	1	0	42	1	5	.408	.286
Hill, Tyler	R-R	6-0	195	3-4-96	.000	.000	.000	4	7	1	0	0	0	0	0	1	1	0	0	2	0	1	.000	.222
Kemp, Trenton	R-R	6-2	195	9-30-95	.225	.209	.234	38	120	21	27	8	0	3	20	12	3	0	0	36	3	2	.367	.311
Lavarnway, Ryan	R-R	6-4	240	8-7-87	.400	—	.400	2	5	1	2	1	0	0	2	1	0	0	0	1	0	0	.600	.500
Lorenzana, Hector	R-R	5-11	190	9-29-91	.167	.000	.235	8	24	5	4	0	0	0	1	4	1	0	0	6	0	1	.167	.310
McKeon, Alex	R-R	6-2	215	5-20-93	.250	.250	.250	26	56	6	14	5	0	0	6	3	2	0	0	9	0	0	.339	.311
Miller, Derek	R-R	6-2	180	7-18-92	.281	.259	.293	54	192	31	54	12	0	1	24	27	6	0	0	34	15	5	.359	.387
Monge, Joseph	R-R	6-0	170	5-18-95	.266	.222	.289	19	64	19	17	4	1	2	17	9	4	0	0	14	5	1	.453	.390
Moore, Ben	R-R	6-1	195	9-22-92	.288	.292	.291	28	80	20	23	4	1	0	16	12	5	0	1	12	0	0	.363	.408
Nunez, Jhon	B-R	5-9	165	12-5-94	.293	.286	.296	16	41	6	12	4	0	0	4	6	0	0	1	8	0	1	.390	.375
Ockimey, Josh	L-R	6-1	215	10-18-95	.188	.176	.195	36	112	17	21	3	1	0	14	14	3	0	1	37	1	0	.232	.292
Oliveras, Rafael	R-R	5-10	180	1-4-95	.260	.316	.236	39	127	23	33	4	0	0	14	17	4	4	1	18	3	1	.291	.362

	B-T	HT	WT	DOB	AVG	vLH	vRH	G	AB	R	H	2B	3B	HR	RBI	BB	HBP	SH	SF	SO	SB	CS	SLG	OBP
Pena, Darwin	L-L	6-0	180	3-5-93	.200	.250	.174	39	105	10	21	2	0	0	13	12	1	0	5	24	0	1	.219	.276
Rivera, Jeremy	B-R	5-9	150	1-30-95	.178	.250	.120	14	45	9	8	2	0	0	6	5	1	0	0	9	2	0	.222	.275
Vinicio, Jose	B-R	5-11	150	7-10-93	.429	.750	.300	5	14	3	6	1	1	0	2	7	0	1	1	2	4	3	.643	.591

Pitching	B-T	HT	WT	DOB	W	L	ERA	G	GS	CG	SV	IP	H	R	ER	HR	BB	SO	AVG	vLH	vRH	K/9	BB/9
Almonte, Jose	R-R	6-2	185	9-8-95	2	3	3.02	11	8	0	0	48	46	20	16	3	17	33	.254	.217	.286	6.23	3.21
Beeks, Jalen	L-L	5-11	180	7-10-93	0	0	0.00	2	0	0	0	5	3	0	0	0	0	8	.167	.000	.188	14.40	0.00
Buttrey, Ty	L-R	6-6	230	3-31-93	0	0	1.80	2	2	0	0	5	2	1	1	0	1	4	.118	.200	.083	7.20	1.80
Cosart, Jake	R-R	6-2	175	2-11-94	0	1	2.25	7	7	0	0	16	7	7	4	0	11	16	.132	.091	.161	9.00	6.19
Couch, Keith	L-R	6-2	210	11-5-89	0	0	2.00	6	3	0	0	6	2	0	0	0	0	6	.150	.000	.188	8.53	0.00
Fernandez, Jeffry	R-R	6-3	180	3-25-93	1	1	4.71	9	8	0	0	36	31	21	19	1	6	22	.231	.245	.224	5.45	1.49
Garcia, Carlos	L-L	6-0	170	12-15-94	1	1	3.32	14	0	0	2	22	22	8	8	0	12	13	.272	.333	.261	5.40	4.98
Goetze, Pat	R-R	6-6	200	3-3-94	1	3	3.72	13	0	0	3	29	33	16	12	0	3	20	.282	.304	.268	6.21	0.93
Gomez, Sergio	R-R	6-3	155	8-24-93	0	1	6.00	3	2	0	0	6	7	4	4	0	2	9	.280	.000	.583	13.50	3.00
Gunn, Michael	L-L	6-0	205	1-25-93	0	0	3.60	3	0	0	0	5	4	2	2	0	3	4	.250	.333	.231	7.20	5.40
Heras, Keivin	R-R	6-1	160	9-21-94	3	0	0.00	14	0	0	2	27	21	6	0	0	4	16	.202	.176	.214	5.27	1.32
Jimenez, Dedgar	L-L	6-3	240	3-6-96	3	3	3.28	11	10	0	0	49	54	26	18	3	8	37	.273	.135	.304	6.75	1.46
Kopech, Michael	R-R	6-3	195	4-30-96	0	1	4.61	8	8	0	0	14	11	7	7	0	9	16	.216	.118	.265	10.54	5.93
McEachern, Kuehl	R-R	6-4	195	5-7-93	1	0	0.00	4	0	0	2	6	3	0	0	0	0	3	.167	.182	.143	4.76	0.00
Nunez, Taylor	R-R	6-4	185	7-28-92	0	2	2.30	11	0	0	2	16	9	4	4	0	9	13	.176	.200	.161	7.47	5.17
Pimentel, Yankory	R-R	6-2	210	9-29-93	3	0	2.93	13	0	0	1	31	27	13	10	0	7	25	.225	.205	.235	7.34	2.05
Ramos, Luis	L-L	6-1	180	6-5-95	4	3	2.93	12	1	0	0	43	40	15	14	0	7	29	.242	.185	.254	6.07	1.47
Rodriguez, Javier	L-L	6-2	165	5-1-95	8	0	1.44	10	3	0	0	44	32	10	7	0	21	34	.205	.174	.211	7.01	4.33
Speier, Gabe	R-R	6-0	175	4-12-95	3	0	1.55	9	6	0	0	29	22	6	5	0	1	26	.210	.257	.186	8.07	0.31
Steen, Kevin	R-R	6-1	170	7-24-96	0	1	4.50	3	2	0	0	6	8	4	3	0	2	5	.348	.200	.462	7.50	3.00
Trader, K.J.	R-R	5-10	160	6-17-94	0	3	5.65	12	0	0	3	14	13	9	9	1	15	10	.250	.211	.273	6.28	9.42
Villareal, Brayan	R-R	6-0	170	5-10-87	0	0	0.00	3	1	0	0	4	3	0	0	0	1	6	.214	1.000	.154	13.50	2.25
Williams, Jalen	R-R	6-4	210	4-21-95	1	1	4.35	10	0	0	1	21	23	13	10	0	6	12	.288	.258	.306	5.23	2.61

Fielding

Catcher	PCT	G	PO	A	E	DP	PB
Fisher	.964	18	93	13	4	1	8
Gravel	1.000	4	14	0	0	0	1
McKeon	.991	25	106	9	1	1	1
Moore	.964	19	116	18	5	0	6
Nunez	1.000	14	60	11	0	1	3

First Base	PCT	G	PO	A	E	DP
Lavarnway	1.000	1	6	1	0	0
Ockimey	.976	31	240	8	6	18
Pena	.990	39	278	24	3	28

Second Base	PCT	G	PO	A	E	DP
Acosta	.979	21	32	60	2	11

	PCT	G	PO	A	E	DP
Lorenzana	1.000	7	7	19	0	2
Oliveras	.974	25	47	64	3	12
Rivera	.980	11	21	28	1	5

Third Base	PCT	G	PO	A	E	DP
Acosta	.903	21	20	45	7	2
Chavis	.917	10	3	19	2	1
Devers	.905	29	25	70	10	6
Lorenzana	1.000	1	0	2	0	1

Shortstop	PCT	G	PO	A	E	DP
Chavis	.915	13	15	39	5	4
Guerra	.944	43	70	117	11	27
Rivera	1.000	1	2	2	0	0

	PCT	G	PO	A	E	DP
Vinicio	1.000	3	7	12	0	4

Outfield	PCT	G	PO	A	E	DP
Austin	.982	29	52	3	1	0
Basabe	1.000	32	67	5	0	2
Brentz	1.000	3	1	2	0	0
Hill	1.000	4	4	0	0	0
Kemp	.986	37	68	2	1	1
Miller	.977	53	82	3	2	1
Monge	.973	19	34	2	1	0
Oliveras	1.000	14	10	1	0	0

DSL RED SOX   ROOKIE

DOMINICAN SUMMER LEAGUE

Batting	B-T	HT	WT	DOB	AVG	vLH	vRH	G	AB	R	H	2B	3B	HR	RBI	BB	HBP	SH	SF	SO	SB	CS	SLG	OBP
Aybar, Yoan	L-L	6-2	165	7-3-97	.271	.195	.289	56	214	33	58	12	9	0	26	11	4	1	1	54	7	6	.411	.317
Baldwin, Roldani	R-R	5-11	180	3-16-96	.269	.160	.297	65	242	36	65	10	3	4	42	27	7	0	1	41	3	1	.384	.357
Barriento, Juan	R-R	6-2	201	4-28-96	.255	.154	.289	26	102	14	26	0	1	1	11	6	1	0	0	16	2	1	.304	.303
Basabe, Luis Alexander	B-R	6-0	160	8-26-96	.284	.161	.316	40	148	38	42	7	11	0	26	30	3	0	3	36	13	2	.480	.408
Basabe, Luis Alejandro	B-R	5-9	160	8-26-96	.222	.227	.221	30	99	19	22	3	1	0	6	28	2	3	0	25	9	1	.273	.403
Benoit, Luis	L-R	5-10	165	11-29-94	.188	.238	.172	34	85	20	16	2	1	2	12	15	7	1	0	26	3	5	.294	.355
Carrizalez, Gerardo	R-R	6-1	175	7-28-95	.231	.214	.235	46	147	25	34	10	1	1	23	17	4	3	3	37	3	1	.333	.322
Devers, Rafael	L-R	6-0	195	10-24-96	.337	.167	.372	28	104	26	35	6	3	3	21	21	1	0	2	20	4	1	.538	.445
Hernandez, Juan	L-R	5-10	155	4-9-96	.300	.333	.293	42	140	23	42	2	1	0	15	20	2	3	1	19	10	5	.329	.393
Lameda, Raiwinson	L-R	5-11	175	10-7-95	.307	.500	.269	51	199	39	61	7	4	2	32	14	5	2	4	27	13	6	.412	.360
Lozada, Jose	R-R	5-11	165	2-4-97	.242	.357	.212	28	66	18	16	1	1	0	7	15	0	0	1	19	4	0	.288	.378
Lucena, Isaias	B-R	5-11	180	11-15-94	.272	.241	.280	41	147	17	40	13	1	0	22	28	1	0	1	31	3	0	.374	.390
Miranda, Samuel	L-R	6-1	175	8-21-97	.241	.429	.205	26	87	11	21	5	0	0	12	7	4	1	2	11	3	1	.299	.320
Nieva, Fabian	B-R	6-0	175	8-18-95	.000	.000	.000	9	15	1	0	0	0	0	0	1	0	0	0	14	0	0	.000	.063
Perez, Jesus	L-L	6-3	184	10-23-95	.233	.273	.219	37	129	24	30	9	2	1	20	13	7	0	2	61	3	3	.357	.331
Toribio, Rafael	R-R	5-8	160	1-26-96	.149	.192	.132	31	94	10	14	2	1	0	12	8	2	2	2	25	3	3	.191	.226
Tovar, Carlos	R-R	5-11	170	8-20-95	.241	.222	.245	65	245	46	59	10	3	2	22	36	7	6	2	44	11	4	.331	.352
Urena, Pablo	R-R	6-0	175	10-17-94	.207	.250	.197	30	87	13	18	3	1	1	10	4	1	0	2	23	3	2	.299	.245
Yovera, Luis	R-R	6-2	170	10-15-95	.268	.353	.231	23	56	7	15	1	0	2	7	7	2	1	0	14	0	0	.393	.369

Pitching	B-T	HT	WT	DOB	W	L	ERA	G	GS	CG	SV	IP	H	R	ER	HR	BB	SO	AVG	vLH	vRH	K/9	BB/9
Ardiles, Yeferson	R-R	6-0	175	5-31-97	3	1	4.74	12	1	0	1	25	26	14	13	2	11	19	.260	.260	.260	6.93	4.01
Bautista, Gerson	R-R	6-2	168	5-31-95	2	1	1.03	13	12	0	0	61	37	15	7	1	21	32	.174	.214	.154	4.72	3.10
Caceres, Carlos	R-R	6-3	200	9-30-94	4	0	1.57	17	0	0	6	29	22	10	5	1	17	25	.212	.275	.172	7.85	5.34
De Jesus, Enmanuel	L-L	6-0	190	12-10-96	5	5	3.15	14	14	0	0	60	55	28	21	2	18	55	.239	.200	.245	8.25	2.70
Diaz, Jhonathan	L-L	6-0	170	9-13-96	6	2	1.63	14	14	0	0	66	46	15	12	1	16	54	.197	.229	.191	7.33	2.17
El Halaby, Samir	R-R	6-3	175	7-5-95	2	1	4.28	17	0	0	2	34	48	28	16	2	7	20	.338	.209	.394	5.35	1.87
Gonzalez, Daniel	R-R	6-5	180	2-9-96	9	0	2.25	15	15	0	0	72	61	20	18	2	14	56	.235	.211	.247	7.00	1.75

BOSTON RED SOX

Name	B-T	Ht	Wt	DOB	W	L	ERA	G											AVG	vLH	vRH		
Hernandez, Darwinzon	L-L	6-2	180	12-17-96	1	1	2.89	14	1	0	0	28	24	12	9	0	19	15	.231	.000	.255	4.82	6.11
Lacrus, Shair	R-R	6-1	170	12-22-96	3	1	3.72	13	4	0	0	36	31	17	15	1	12	23	.230	.292	.195	5.70	2.97
Lantigua, Marcos	R-R	6-3	200	12-14-95	0	0	7.50	8	0	0	1	12	13	16	10	0	13	10	.250	.182	.268	7.50	9.75
Martinez, Algenis	R-R	6-1	185	9-12-93	6	2	1.85	20	0	0	6	58	39	13	12	2	15	49	.195	.254	.170	7.56	2.31
Mendoza, Ritzi	R-R	6-2	175	1-10-96	4	1	3.40	12	9	0	1	45	46	21	17	1	16	23	.254	.277	.241	4.60	3.20
Perez, Juan	L-L	5-11	180	9-9-96	0	1	7.46	12	0	0	0	25	29	23	21	3	17	13	.293	.300	.292	4.62	6.04
Requena, Hildemaro	R-R	6-2	170	7-20-97	1	0	1.17	5	0	0	0	8	8	5	1	0	7	6	.267	.500	.182	7.04	8.22
Rodriguez, Alejandro	L-L	6-1	160	10-30-96	2	1	4.50	10	0	0	1	20	18	11	10	2	7	16	.243	.273	.238	7.20	3.15
Tena, Francisco	L-L	6-3	160	3-4-95	0	0	0.00	5	0	0	1	7	2	0	0	0	5	5	.083	.200	.053	6.14	6.14
Torrealba, Jervis	L-L	6-0	165	6-9-95	2	2	1.80	18	0	0	4	50	28	11	10	1	18	44	.163	.086	.182	7.92	3.24

Fielding

Catcher	PCT	G	PO	A	E	DP	PB
Baldwin	.968	17	114	8	4	1	4
Lucena	.990	31	178	23	2	0	5
Miranda	.988	22	135	23	2	3	4
Urena	1.000	5	33	3	0	0	1

First Base	PCT	G	PO	A	E	DP
Barriento	1.000	14	139	4	0	13
Carrizalez	.983	37	332	23	6	36
Nieva	1.000	5	24	2	0	1
Perez	.941	4	30	2	2	3
Urena	.986	20	132	10	2	8
Yovera	1.000	1	7	0	0	0

Second Base	PCT	G	PO	A	E	DP
Basabe	.966	30	59	85	5	23
Benoit	.970	15	23	41	2	5
Lozada	.922	16	28	43	6	11
Toribio	.944	14	20	31	3	9
Tovar	1.000	4	8	12	0	3

Third Base	PCT	G	PO	A	E	DP
Baldwin	.921	29	17	65	7	6
Benoit	.931	11	7	20	2	3
Carrizalez	.926	9	9	16	2	1
Devers	.905	22	23	53	8	3
Lozada	.667	4	0	2	1	0
Toribio	1.000	2	2	5	0	0
Tovar	1.000	1	2	3	0	0

Shortstop	PCT	G	PO	A	E	DP
Benoit	.810	8	8	9	4	1
Lozada	1.000	1	0	2	0	1
Toribio	.842	6	5	11	3	2
Tovar	.954	60	101	187	14	37

Outfield	PCT	G	PO	A	E	DP
Aybar	.992	55	115	4	1	0
Barriento	.913	10	20	1	2	0
Basabe	.976	36	72	9	2	5
Hernandez	.963	41	74	5	3	2
Lameda	.981	46	98	3	2	2
Perez	.959	25	44	3	2	0
Yovera	.895	17	16	1	2	0

Chicago Cubs

SEASON IN A SENTENCE: The Cubs didn't come close to contending under first-year manager Rick Renteria, with their fifth straight fifth-place finish, but they did engender hopes of a turnaround with an infusion of prospects to the major leagues, such as Arismendy Alcantara, Javier Baez and Jorge Soler, as well as bounce-back seasons from Starlin Castro and Anthony Rizzo.

HIGH POINT: Jake Arrieta began emerging as a needed frontline starter, narrowly missing two no-hitters. He left after 7²/₃ innings and one hit in a June 30 win at Boston, then threw a 13-strikeout one-hitter in his penultimate home start, a 7-0 complete game win against the Reds.

LOW POINT: Any Edwin Jackson start could suffice here. The less-than-mighty Padres hung eight runs on him in May, and he's 14-33 in two seasons with the Cubs. He's under contract through 2016 for $22 million more.

NOTABLE ROOKIES: Alcantara got the longest look, while Baez also exceeded his rookie eligibility. Both struggled with strikeouts, as did Mike Olt, who nonetheless ranked among rookie leaders in home runs. The top rookie performer was pitchability righty Kyle Hendricks, who allowed just four homers in 80 innings and had the rotation's best ERA.

KEY TRANSACTIONS: The Cubs were already in last place when they traded Jeff Samardzija and Jason Hammel to Oakland, receiving the Athletics' last two first-round picks—shortstop Addison Russell and outfielder Billy McKinney—in return. They made several minor moves as well, buying low on potential starters such as Felix Doubront and Jacob Turner.

DOWN ON THE FARM: Kris Bryant, the No. 2 pick in the 2013 draft, won the Minor League Player of the Year award after leading the minors in homers and batting .325/.438/.661 between Double-A Tennessee and Triple-A Iowa. Manny Ramirez joined Iowa as a player/coach and earned plaudits for his work with hitters such as Baez and Soler. C.J. Edwards made just 10 appearances, but was pitching in the Arizona Fall League and remains perhaps the Cubs' top arm. Kyle Schwarber, the team's top pick in 2014, blazed through three levels and posted a 1.063 OPS with 18 homers. Low Class A Kane County, led by Minor League Manager of the Year Mark Johnson, won 91 games and the Midwest League playoffs as well.

OPENING DAY PAYROLL: $74,546,356 (28th)

PLAYERS OF THE YEAR

MAJOR LEAGUE	MINOR LEAGUE
Anthony Rizzo	**Kris Bryant**
1b	3b
.286/.386/.527	.325/.438/.661
32 HR, 78 RBI	(Double-A, Triple-A)
Led team in HR	43 HR, 110 RBI

ORGANIZATION LEADERS

BATTING		*Minimum 250 AB
MAJORS		
* AVG	Castro, Starlin	.292
* OPS	Rizzo, Anthony	.913
HR	Rizzo, Anthony	32
RBI	Rizzo, Anthony	78
MINORS		
* AVG	Bryant, Kris, Tennessee, Iowa	.325
* OBP	Bryant, Kris, Tennessee, Iowa	.438
* SLG	Bryant, Kris, Tennessee, Iowa	.661
R	Bryant, Kris, Tennessee, Iowa	118
H	Bryant, Kris, Tennessee, Iowa	160
TB	Bryant, Kris, Tennessee, Iowa	325
2B	Villanueva, Christian, Iowa, Tennessee	38
3B	Caro, Roberto, DSL Cubs	15
HR	Bryant, Kris, Tennessee, Iowa	43
RBI	Bryant, Kris, Tennessee, Iowa	110
BB	Bryant, Kris, Tennessee, Iowa	86
SO	Bryant, Kris, Tennessee, Iowa	162
SB	Hannemann, Jacob, Kane County, Daytona	37

PITCHING		#Minimum 75 IP
MAJORS		
W	Arrieta, Jake	10
# ERA	Hendricks, Kyle	2.46
SO	Arrieta, Jake	167
SV	Rondon, Hector	29
MINORS		
W	Francescon, P.J., Tennessee	11
	Torrez, Daury, Kane County	11
L	Rusin, Chris, Iowa	13
# ERA	Torrez, Daury, Kane County	2.74
G	Rivero, Armando, Tennessee, Iowa	49
GS	Jokisch, Eric, Iowa	26
	Scott, Tayler, Daytona	26
SV	Parker, Blake, Iowa	25
IP	Jokisch, Eric, Iowa	158
BB	Black, Corey, Tennessee	71
SO	Jokisch, Eric, Iowa	143
AVG	Black, Corey, Tennessee	.224

2014 PERFORMANCE

General Manager: Jed Hoyer. **Farm Director:** Jaron Madison. **Scouting Director:** Matt Dorey.

Class	Team	League	W	L	PCT	Finish	Manager:
Majors	Chicago Cubs	National	73	89	.451	t-22nd (30)	Rick Renteria
Triple-A	Iowa Cubs	Pacific Coast	74	70	.514	t-7th (16)	Marty Pevey
Double-A	Tennessee Smokies	Southern	66	73	.475	5th (10)	Buddy Bailey
High A	Daytona Cubs	Florida State	67	69	.493	8th (12)	Dave Keller
Low A	Kane County Cougars	Midwest	91	49	.650	1st (18)	Mark Johnson
Short season	Boise Hawks	Northwest	41	35	.539	3rd (8)	Gary Van Tol
Rookie	Cubs	Arizona	22	34	.393	12th (13)	Jimmy Gonzalez
Overall Minor League Record			361	330	.522	7th (30)	

ORGANIZATION STATISTICS

CHICAGO CUBS

NATIONAL LEAGUE

Batting	B-T	HT	WT	DOB	AVG	vLH	vRH	G	AB	R	H	2B	3B	HR	RBI	BB	HBP	SH	SF	SO	SB	CS	SLG	OBP
Alcantara, Arismendy	B-R	5-10	170	10-29-91	.205	.244	.190	70	278	31	57	11	2	10	29	17	2	1	2	93	8	5	.367	.254
Baez, Javier	R-R	6-0	190	12-1-92	.169	.143	.177	52	213	25	36	6	0	9	20	15	1	0	0	95	5	1	.324	.227
Baker, John	L-R	6-1	215	1-20-81	.192	.161	.199	68	182	9	35	7	0	0	15	19	2	3	2	58	0	0	.231	.273
Barney, Darwin	R-R	5-10	185	11-8-85	.230	.293	.205	72	204	18	47	10	2	2	16	9	1	2	1	31	1	0	.328	.265
2-team total (22 Los Angeles)					.241	—	—	94	237	24	57	11	2	3	23	17	4	2	2	34	1	0	.342	.300
Bonifacio, Emilio	B-R	5-11	205	4-23-85	.279	.408	.234	69	276	35	77	14	3	2	18	16	0	6	0	49	14	6	.373	.318
2-team total (41 Atlanta)					.259	—	—	110	394	47	102	17	4	3	24	26	0	6	0	85	26	8	.345	.305
Castillo, Welington	R-R	5-10	210	4-24-87	.237	.301	.216	110	380	28	90	19	0	13	46	26	7	2	2	102	0	0	.389	.296
Castro, Starlin	R-R	6-0	190	3-24-90	.292	.304	.288	134	528	58	154	33	1	14	65	35	4	0	2	100	4	4	.438	.339
Coghlan, Chris	L-R	6-0	195	6-18-85	.283	.247	.294	125	385	50	109	28	5	9	41	39	3	3	2	81	7	4	.452	.352
Kalish, Ryan	L-L	6-0	215	3-28-88	.248	.333	.241	57	121	13	30	4	4	0	5	8	0	1	0	28	3	2	.347	.295
Lake, Junior	R-R	6-3	215	3-27-90	.211	.213	.210	108	308	30	65	10	3	9	25	14	1	1	2	110	7	3	.351	.246
Lopez, Rafael	L-R	5-9	190	10-2-87	.182	.333	.125	7	11	0	2	0	0	0	1	2	0	0	1	4	0	0	.182	.286
Olt, Mike	R-R	6-2	210	8-27-88	.160	.165	.158	89	225	23	36	8	0	12	33	25	3	0	5	100	0	1	.356	.248
Rizzo, Anthony	L-L	6-3	240	8-8-89	.286	.300	.281	140	524	89	150	28	1	32	78	73	15	0	4	116	5	4	.527	.386
Ruggiano, Justin	R-R	6-1	210	4-12-82	.281	.305	.268	81	224	29	63	13	1	6	28	18	3	1	4	70	2	4	.429	.337
Schierholtz, Nate	L-R	6-2	215	2-15-84	.192	.197	.190	99	313	29	60	10	3	6	33	18	4	0	6	76	4	3	.300	.240
2-team total (23 Washington)					.195	—	—	122	353	32	69	11	4	7	37	20	4	0	6	84	4	5	.309	.243
Soler, Jorge	R-R	6-4	215	2-25-92	.292	.286	.294	24	89	11	26	8	1	5	20	6	0	0	2	24	1	0	.573	.330
Sweeney, Ryan	L-L	6-4	225	2-20-85	.251	.292	.246	77	207	22	52	9	0	3	20	15	1	2	1	33	0	0	.338	.304
Szczur, Matt	R-R	6-1	195	7-20-89	.226	.346	.139	33	62	6	14	2	0	2	5	4	0	0	0	11	0	0	.355	.273
Valaika, Chris	R-R	5-11	205	3-14-85	.231	.263	.217	44	121	10	28	4	0	3	13	7	2	0	1	35	1	0	.339	.282
Valbuena, Luis	L-R	5-10	200	11-30-85	.249	.217	.256	149	478	68	119	33	4	16	51	65	2	1	1	113	1	2	.435	.341
Watkins, Logan	L-R	5-11	195	8-29-89	.246	.143	.259	31	65	10	16	3	0	1	6	1	1	1	0	16	1	0	.338	.269
Whiteside, Eli	R-R	6-2	220	10-22-79	.120	.000	.136	8	25	0	3	1	0	0	2	0	0	0	1	6	0	0	.160	.115

Pitching	B-T	HT	WT	DOB	W	L	ERA	G	GS	CG	SV	IP	H	R	ER	HR	BB	SO	AVG	vLH	vRH	K/9	BB/9
Arrieta, Jake	R-R	6-4	225	3-6-86	10	5	2.53	25	25	1	0	157	114	46	44	5	41	167	.203	.198	.207	9.59	2.36
Beeler, Dallas	R-R	6-5	210	6-12-89	0	2	3.27	2	2	0	0	11	10	5	4	0	7	6	.263	.294	.238	4.91	5.73
Doubront, Felix	L-L	6-2	225	10-23-87	2	1	3.98	4	4	0	0	20	22	9	9	2	7	8	.278	.360	.241	3.54	3.10
Fujikawa, Kyuji	L-R	6-0	190	7-21-80	0	0	4.85	15	0	0	0	13	18	8	7	2	6	17	.327	.385	.276	11.77	4.15
Grimm, Justin	R-R	6-3	210	8-16-88	5	2	3.78	73	0	0	0	69	59	32	29	4	27	70	.230	.188	.250	9.13	3.52
Hammel, Jason	R-R	6-6	225	9-2-82	8	5	2.98	17	17	0	0	109	88	36	36	10	23	104	.222	.231	.217	8.61	1.90
Hendricks, Kyle	R-R	6-3	190	12-7-89	7	2	2.46	13	13	0	0	80	72	24	22	4	15	47	.242	.237	.247	5.27	1.68
Jackson, Edwin	R-R	6-3	210	9-9-83	6	15	6.33	28	27	0	0	141	168	105	99	18	63	123	.302	.341	.268	7.87	4.03
Jokisch, Eric	R-L	6-2	185	7-29-89	0	0	1.88	4	1	0	0	14	18	6	3	3	4	10	.290	.300	.288	6.28	2.51
Parker, Blake	R-R	6-3	225	6-19-85	1	1	5.14	18	0	0	0	21	24	13	12	3	4	24	.279	.171	.353	10.29	1.71
Ramirez, Neil	R-R	6-4	190	5-25-89	3	3	1.44	50	0	0	3	44	29	11	7	2	17	53	.184	.200	.173	10.92	3.50
Rondon, Hector	R-R	6-3	180	2-26-88	4	4	2.42	64	0	0	29	63	52	21	17	2	15	63	.218	.255	.188	8.95	2.13
Rosscup, Zac	R-L	6-2	205	6-9-88	1	0	9.45	18	0	0	0	13	14	14	14	2	12	21	.259	.200	.310	14.18	8.10
Rusin, Chris	L-L	6-2	195	10-22-86	0	0	7.11	4	0	0	0	13	16	10	10	1	5	8	.308	.208	.393	5.68	3.55
Russell, James	L-L	6-4	200	1-8-86	0	2	3.51	44	0	0	1	33	24	14	13	3	16	26	.202	.295	.103	7.02	4.32
2-team total (22 Atlanta)					0	2	2.97	66	0	1	1	58	45	20	19	3	20	42	—	—	—	6.55	3.12
Samardzija, Jeff	R-R	6-5	225	1-23-85	2	7	2.83	17	17	0	0	108	99	44	34	7	31	103	.245	.257	.236	8.58	2.58
Schlitter, Brian	R-R	6-5	235	12-21-85	2	3	4.15	61	0	0	0	56	58	29	26	2	19	31	.270	.288	.261	4.95	3.04
Straily, Dan	R-R	6-2	215	12-1-88	0	1	11.85	7	1	0	0	14	20	20	18	1	9	13	.323	.214	.412	8.56	5.93
Strop, Pedro	R-R	6-1	220	6-13-85	2	4	2.21	65	0	0	2	61	40	19	15	2	25	71	.187	.214	.169	10.48	3.69
Turner, Jacob	R-R	6-5	215	5-21-91	2	4	6.49	8	6	0	0	35	42	27	25	4	10	17	.313	.352	.288	4.41	2.60
2-team total (20 Miami)					6	11	6.13	28	18	0	0	113	148	81	77	12	33	71	—	—	—	5.65	2.63
Veras, Jose	R-R	6-6	240	10-20-80	0	1	8.10	12	0	0	0	13	12	12	12	2	11	13	.255	.222	.276	8.78	7.43
Villanueva, Carlos	R-R	6-2	215	11-28-83	5	7	4.64	42	5	0	2	78	89	42	40	6	19	72	.282	.268	.290	8.34	2.20
Vizcaino, Arodys	R-R	6-0	190	11-13-90	0	0	5.40	5	0	0	0	5	5	3	3	1	3	4	.263	.000	.455	7.20	5.40
Wada, Tsuyoshi	L-L	5-11	180	2-21-81	4	4	3.25	13	13	0	0	69	67	28	25	7	19	57	.254	.184	.270	7.40	2.47
Wood, Travis	R-L	5-11	175	2-6-87	8	13	5.03	31	31	0	0	174	190	110	97	20	76	146	.277	.220	.297	7.57	3.94
Wright, Wesley	R-L	5-11	185	1-28-85	0	3	3.17	58	0	0	0	48	48	19	17	2	19	37	.262	.273	.255	6.89	3.54

Fielding

Catcher	PCT	G	PO	A	E	DP	PB
Baker	.996	55	437	30	2	2	5
Castillo	.993	106	784	93	6	6	7
Lopez	1.000	4	23	1	0	0	0
Whiteside	1.000	8	49	3	0	1	1

First Base	PCT	G	PO	A	E	DP
Olt	1.000	12	93	4	0	10
Rizzo	.993	140	1184	118	9	104
Valaika	.982	15	99	12	2	13

Second Base	PCT	G	PO	A	E	DP
Alcantara	.989	25	31	63	1	9
Baez	.957	25	60	51	5	18
Barney	.987	67	83	140	3	27

	PCT	G	PO	A	E	DP	PB
Bonifacio	.968	26	38	52	3	17	
Valaika	1.000	12	17	27	0	4	
Valbuena	1.000	21	24	41	0	4	
Watkins	.908	16	30	29	6	9	

Third Base	PCT	G	PO	A	E	DP
Bonifacio	1.000	7	1	9	0	1
Olt	.929	52	20	72	7	4
Valaika	1.000	8	8	16	0	2
Valbuena	.969	124	78	202	9	17

Shortstop	PCT	G	PO	A	E	DP
Baez	.964	30	45	89	5	22
Bonifacio	1.000	1	1	3	0	0
Castro	.973	133	148	386	15	74

	PCT	G	PO	A	E	DP
Valaika	1.000	2	5	5	0	3

Outfield	PCT	G	PO	A	E	DP
Alcantara	.958	48	111	3	5	0
Bonifacio	.977	48	83	1	2	1
Coghlan	.978	103	171	5	4	2
Kalish	.982	38	55	0	1	0
Lake	.955	85	145	3	7	1
Ruggiano	.991	57	115	1	1	0
Schierholtz	1.000	81	152	9	0	3
Soler	.958	24	44	2	2	1
Sweeney	.990	56	94	7	1	1
Szczur	1.000	26	48	1	0	1
Watkins	1.000	2	4	0	0	0

IOWA CUBS

TRIPLE-A

PACIFIC COAST LEAGUE

Batting	B-T	HT	WT	DOB	AVG	vLH	vRH	G	AB	R	H	2B	3B	HR	RBI	BB	HBP	SH	SF	SO	SB	CS	SLG	OBP
Alcantara, Arismendy	B-R	5-10	170	10-29-91	.307	.374	.280	89	335	62	103	25	11	10	41	25	0	3	3	83	21	3	.537	.353
Anderson, Lars	L-L	6-4	215	9-25-87	.287	.278	.290	34	87	12	25	5	0	4	19	11	1	1	1	18	0	0	.483	.370
Baez, Javier	R-R	6-0	190	12-1-92	.260	.241	.268	104	388	64	101	24	2	23	80	34	5	0	7	130	16	8	.510	.323
Bote, David	R-R	5-11	185	4-7-93	.400	.667	.286	4	10	3	4	0	0	1	3	2	0	0	0	1	1	0	.700	.500
Bryant, Kris	R-R	6-5	215	1-4-92	.295	.313	.289	70	244	57	72	14	1	21	52	43	9	0	1	85	7	2	.619	.418
Castillo, Welington	R-R	5-10	210	4-24-87	.375	—	.375	2	8	0	3	0	0	0	1	2	0	0	0	1	0	0	.375	.500
Coghlan, Chris	L-R	6-0	195	6-18-85	.243	.192	.273	24	70	9	17	5	0	0	6	13	3	1	1	18	6	1	.314	.379
Ely, Andrew	L-R	5-10	180	1-23-93	.229	.000	.242	9	35	4	8	1	0	1	9	5	0	0	1	7	0	0	.343	.317
Flores, Luis	R-R	5-10	195	11-2-86	.253	.258	.250	31	87	16	22	3	0	2	8	27	2	2	0	13	0	0	.356	.440
Gonzalez, Edgar	R-R	6-0	182	6-14-78	.500	.333	.600	5	8	2	4	0	0	1	0	0	0	0	0	2	0	0	.500	.500
Ha, Jae-Hoon	R-R	6-1	185	10-29-90	.286	.500	.227	8	28	6	8	1	0	1	2	0	0	1	0	4	0	0	.429	.286
Jackson, Brett	L-R	6-2	220	8-2-88	.210	.153	.230	81	224	23	47	8	4	5	20	24	4	0	0	94	4	6	.348	.298
2-team total (11 Reno)					.208	—		92	240	25	50	8	4	6	23	27	4	0	0	103	5	6	.350	.299
Kalish, Ryan	L-L	6-0	215	3-28-88	.251	.256	.249	87	287	34	72	14	3	8	37	28	2	2	0	74	12	4	.404	.322
Lake, Junior	R-R	6-3	215	3-27-90	.262	.308	.250	14	65	11	17	3	0	2	7	6	0	0	0	15	2	1	.400	.324
Lopez, Rafael	L-R	5-9	190	10-2-87	.285	.242	.303	61	207	17	59	4	1	1	27	28	3	1	0	52	0	0	.329	.378
Mota, Jonathan	R-R	6-0	200	6-1-87	.261	.341	.228	47	142	18	37	5	1	3	18	5	0	1	4	36	1	0	.373	.278
Olt, Mike	R-R	6-2	210	8-27-88	.302	.341	.277	28	106	16	32	9	0	7	24	8	0	1	1	33	1	0	.585	.348
Ramirez, Manny	R-R	6-0	225	5-30-72	.222	.269	.196	24	72	6	16	2	0	3	10	5	0	0	0	27	0	0	.375	.273
Ruggiano, Justin	R-R	6-1	210	4-12-82	.143	.000	.250	6	21	3	3	1	0	0	3	1	0	0	0	6	0	0	.190	.280
Rymel, Lance	R-R	6-0	195	5-2-90	.000	—	.000	2	2	0	0	0	0	0	0	0	0	0	0	0	0	0	.000	.000
Soler, Jorge	R-R	6-4	215	2-25-92	.282	.263	.292	32	110	22	31	11	1	8	29	17	0	0	0	26	0	1	.618	.378
Soto, Elliot	R-R	5-9	160	8-21-89	.241	.250	.237	29	108	13	26	4	0	1	11	8	0	0	3	21	1	0	.306	.286
Szczur, Matt	R-R	6-1	195	7-20-89	.261	.223	.282	116	414	52	108	16	1	1	24	30	3	9	1	78	30	7	.312	.315
Valaika, Chris	R-R	5-11	205	8-14-85	.278	.254	.292	102	352	43	98	21	0	10	50	31	7	2	5	76	2	1	.423	.344
Villanueva, Christian	R-R	5-11	210	6-19-91	.211	.212	.210	64	223	22	47	18	0	6	26	21	2	1	1	64	2	1	.372	.283
Vitters, Josh	R-R	6-2	200	8-27-89	.213	.187	.228	112	375	33	80	14	0	11	38	23	5	1	0	107	4	1	.339	.268
Watkins, Logan	L-R	5-11	195	8-29-89	.256	.226	.267	103	324	59	83	21	1	4	38	33	2	7	2	77	23	4	.364	.327
Wells, Casper	R-R	6-2	220	11-23-84	.197	.241	.156	26	61	6	12	2	0	0	8	0	0	0	0	20	0	0	.230	.290
Whiteside, Eli	R-R	6-2	220	10-22-79	.214	.200	.220	63	206	14	44	13	0	6	21	18	5	0	1	50	0	0	.364	.291

Pitching	B-T	HT	WT	DOB	W	L	ERA	G	GS	CG	SV	IP	H	R	ER	HR	BB	SO	AVG	vLH	vRH	K/9	BB/9
Antigua, Jeffry	R-L	6-1	205	6-23-90	1	0	4.37	13	0	0	0	23	26	11	11	2	7	15	.289	.231	.333	5.96	2.78
Batista, Frank	R-R	5-10	170	4-26-89	0	0	3.86	8	0	0	1	7	5	3	3	1	4	2	.200	.231	.167	2.57	5.14
Beeler, Dallas	R-R	6-5	210	6-12-89	9	6	3.40	20	20	1	0	124	112	48	47	8	32	83	.245	.283	.209	6.01	2.32
Cabrera, Alberto	R-R	6-4	210	10-25-88	4	2	3.29	40	0	0	2	66	46	26	24	9	30	61	.197	.158	.227	8.36	4.11
Coleman, Casey	L-R	6-0	185	7-3-87	0	0	36.00	1	0	0	0	1	4	5	4	0	2	1	.571	1.000	.500	9.00	18.00
2-team total (34 Omaha)					5	1	2.65	35	0	0	3	68	55	24	20	4	28	54	—	—	—	7.15	3.71
Doubront, Felix	L-L	6-2	225	10-23-87	0	1	5.40	2	2	0	0	10	12	6	6	0	3	11	.300	.333	.286	9.90	2.70
Figueroa, Eduardo	R-R	6-1	185	11-30-88	1	1	3.46	8	1	0	0	13	15	9	5	0	5	9	.278	.308	.250	6.23	3.46
Fujikawa, Kyuji	L-R	6-0	190	7-21-80	0	0	1.50	6	0	0	0	6	5	1	1	0	1	4	.250	.125	.333	6.00	1.50
Hatley, Marcus	R-R	6-5	220	3-26-88	2	6	4.60	45	0	0	1	47	52	27	24	6	13	58	.283	.284	.282	11.11	2.49
Heesch, Michael	R-L	6-5	245	5-15-90	1	0	0.00	1	0	0	0	3	1	0	0	0	2	4	.091	.000	.111	10.80	5.40
Hendricks, Kyle	R-R	6-3	190	12-7-89	10	5	3.59	17	17	0	0	103	98	46	41	5	23	97	.256	.274	.239	8.50	2.02
Hermans, Zak	R-R	6-2	190	6-21-91	0	0	5.40	1	1	0	0	3	4	2	2	0	2	2	.286	.250	.300	5.40	5.40
Jokisch, Eric	R-L	6-2	185	7-29-89	9	10	3.58	26	26	1	0	158	155	76	63	12	31	143	.255	.236	.263	8.13	1.76
Mateo, Marcos	R-R	6-1	220	4-18-84	3	0	3.86	33	0	0	2	37	34	18	16	3	17	43	.248	.274	.227	10.37	4.10
Negrin, Yoanner	R-R	5-11	190	4-29-84	1	3	5.34	25	3	0	1	59	66	39	35	5	35	47	.289	.284	.293	7.17	5.34
Parker, Blake	R-R	6-3	225	6-19-85	0	1	1.77	35	0	0	25	36	28	8	7	3	12	52	.214	.159	.274	13.12	3.28
Pimentel, Carlos	R-R	6-3	180	12-1-89	4	9	5.35	29	15	0	0	101	109	66	60	17	52	95	.281	.284	.278	8.47	4.63
Rakkar, Jasvir	R-R	6-2	200	4-27-91	0	0	0.00	1	0	0	0	1	0	0	0	0	0	1	.000	—	.000	9.00	0.00
Ramirez, Neil	R-R	6-4	190	5-25-89	0	0	7.71	6	0	0	0	7	7	6	6	2	5	11	.250	.231	.267	14.14	6.43
Rhee, Dae-Eun	L-R	6-2	190	3-23-89	3	2	3.75	9	8	0	0	48	53	23	20	4	16	36	.293	.284	.300	6.75	3.00
Rivero, Armando	R-R	6-4	190	2-1-88	3	0	2.97	23	0	0	1	30	25	10	10	4	12	46	.227	.200	.246	13.65	3.56
Rosscup, Zac	R-L	6-2	205	6-9-88	2	0	2.10	29	0	0	4	30	18	7	7	0	15	38	.173	.231	.138	11.40	4.50

CHICAGO CUBS

Rusin, Chris	L-L	6-2	195	10-22-86	8	13	4.31	23	23	1	0	146	163	75	70	15	38	97	.293	.280	.298	5.97	2.34
Sanchez, Jonathan	L-L	6-0	200	11-19-82	0	0	67.50	1	0	0	0	1	1	5	5	1	3	1	.333	.500	.000	13.50	40.50
Schlitter, Brian	R-R	6-5	235	12-21-85	0	0	3.38	7	0	0	3	8	10	4	3	0	3	4	.294	.235	.353	4.50	3.38
Straily, Dan	R-R	6-2	215	12-1-88	3	5	4.09	10	10	0	0	55	59	34	25	7	20	56	.273	.284	.264	9.16	3.27
2-team total (10 Sacramento)					7	8	4.42	20	20	0	0	118	113	67	58	16	46	123	—	—	—	9.38	3.51
Vizcaino, Arodys	R-R	6-0	190	11-13-90	0	0	5.40	17	0	0	0	18	25	11	11	1	11	16	.325	.346	.314	7.85	5.40
Wada, Tsuyoshi	L-L	5-11	180	2-21-81	10	6	2.77	19	18	0	0	114	104	36	35	13	28	120	.241	.250	.238	9.50	2.22

Fielding

Catcher	PCT	G	PO	A	E	DP	PB
Castillo	1.000	2	14	2	0	0	0
Flores	.993	31	241	31	2	3	1
Lopez	.991	56	429	33	4	4	6
Rymel	1.000	1	2	0	0	0	0
Whiteside	.990	57	452	33	5	2	4
Valaika	.911	15	15	26	4	7	
Watkins	.920	16	15	31	4	9	

First Base	PCT	G	PO	A	E	DP
Anderson	1.000	28	198	21	0	20
Coghlan	1.000	5	31	1	0	2
Mota	.994	21	157	18	1	17
Olt	.990	26	182	19	2	29
Valaika	.998	52	415	41	1	45
Vitters	.960	16	92	5	4	12
Watkins	1.000	10	64	7	0	4
Whiteside	.974	4	27	10	1	1

Second Base	PCT	G	PO	A	E	DP
Alcantara	.964	70	103	168	10	33
Baez	.976	16	37	46	2	11

Bote	1.000	2	3	4	0	1
Ely	1.000	7	15	26	0	5
Mota	1.000	3	5	11	0	3
Valaika	1.000	12	14	27	0	7
Watkins	.982	44	73	91	3	32

Third Base	PCT	G	PO	A	E	DP
Bote	1.000	1	0	2	0	0
Bryant	.963	67	50	133	7	17
Mota	1.000	5	1	10	0	1
Olt	1.000	2	0	3	0	1
Valaika	.900	12	8	10	2	0
Villanueva	.966	63	41	128	6	11
Watkins	1.000	3	0	1	0	0

Shortstop	PCT	G	PO	A	E	DP
Alcantara	.941	6	4	12	1	0
Baez	.965	85	146	212	13	53
Mota	—	2	0	0	0	0
Soto	.992	29	45	79	1	30

Outfield	PCT	G	PO	A	E	DP
Alcantara	.955	11	21	0	1	0
Anderson	—	1	0	0	0	0
Coghlan	.962	18	25	0	1	0
Ha	1.000	8	21	1	0	0
Jackson	.964	68	105	1	4	1
Kalish	.965	75	108	2	4	0
Lake	.960	13	24	0	1	0
Mota	1.000	13	20	0	0	0
Ramirez	1.000	4	5	0	0	0
Ruggiano	1.000	5	8	0	0	0
Soler	1.000	27	52	0	0	0
Szczur	.996	111	225	12	1	2
Valaika	1.000	2	4	0	0	0
Vitters	.956	73	84	3	4	0
Watkins	.980	32	48	0	1	0
Wells	.968	18	28	2	1	1

TENNESSEE SMOKIES

DOUBLE-A

SOUTHERN LEAGUE

Batting	B-T	HT	WT	DOB	AVG	vLH	vRH	G	AB	R	H	2B	3B	HR	RBI	BB	HBP	SH	SF	SO	SB	CS	SLG	OBP
Almora, Albert	R-R	6-2	180	4-16-94	.234	.217	.237	36	141	20	33	7	2	2	10	2	1	0	0	23	0	1	.355	.250
Anderson, Lars	L-L	6-4	215	9-25-87	.315	.071	.345	37	124	14	39	11	1	2	12	16	0	0	1	20	0	0	.468	.390
Andreoli, John	R-R	6-1	215	6-9-90	.211	.229	.205	61	209	37	44	4	2	0	8	34	4	3	2	49	28	2	.249	.329
Bonifacio, Emilio	B-R	5-11	205	4-23-85	.250	.600	.091	4	16	1	4	0	0	0	0	0	0	0	0	2	0	1	.250	.250
Brown, Kevin	L-R	6-0	195	10-30-90	.333	.400	.316	6	24	4	8	1	1	0	4	3	0	0	0	8	0	0	.458	.407
Bruno, Stephen	R-R	5-9	165	11-17-90	.276	.313	.268	105	384	54	106	26	5	3	42	27	16	1	4	77	6	2	.393	.346
Bryant, Kris	R-R	6-5	215	1-4-92	.355	.442	.337	68	248	61	88	20	0	22	58	43	5	0	1	77	8	2	.702	.458
Chen, Pin-Chieh	L-R	6-1	170	7-23-91	.232	.250	.231	48	155	20	36	8	1	0	10	24	2	1	0	16	5	1	.297	.343
Cutler, Charlie	L-R	6-0	200	7-29-86	.310	.286	.312	102	284	48	88	14	0	5	42	44	9	2	3	34	1	0	.412	.415
Darvill, Wes	R-R	6-2	175	9-10-91	.231	.231	.231	39	121	13	28	4	1	1	13	9	1	2	1	23	2	2	.306	.288
Davis, Taylor	R-R	5-11	185	11-28-89	.319	.333	.311	53	138	19	44	11	1	4	29	12	1	0	1	14	0	0	.500	.375
DeVoss, Zeke	B-R	5-10	175	7-17-90	.120	.182	.109	23	75	7	9	1	2	1	6	10	2	1	0	19	5	2	.227	.241
Flores, Luis	R-R	5-10	195	11-2-86	.252	.150	.276	36	107	19	27	5	0	3	13	14	1	1	2	24	0	0	.383	.339
Geiger, Dustin	R-R	6-2	180	12-2-91	.223	.198	.230	124	399	48	89	25	0	12	47	44	3	2	0	106	2	1	.376	.305
Giansanti, Anthony	R-R	5-10	195	9-28-88	.239	.212	.250	90	222	24	53	6	1	3	19	15	1	4	1	36	3	1	.315	.289
Ha, Jae-Hoon	R-R	6-1	185	10-29-90	.226	.202	.232	117	434	40	98	18	0	5	49	26	4	4	5	73	5	5	.302	.273
Lopez, Rafael	L-R	5-9	190	10-12-87	.297	.111	.323	45	148	21	44	13	0	4	24	29	0	0	0	26	1	1	.466	.412
Mota, Jonathan	R-R	6-0	200	6-1-87	.246	.300	.234	52	175	12	43	8	1	1	10	9	0	2	1	34	2	1	.320	.281
Papaccio, Giuseppe	R-R	6-1	185	6-8-91	.000	.000	.000	2	2	0	0	0	0	0	0	0	0	0	0	1	0	0	.000	.000
Russell, Addison	R-R	6-0	195	1-23-94	.294	.370	.281	50	194	32	57	11	0	12	36	9	2	0	0	35	2	2	.536	.332
Rymel, Lance	R-R	6-0	195	5-2-90	.125	.250	.000	5	8	1	1	0	0	0	1	0	0	0	1	0	0	0	.125	.300
Silva, Rubi	L-R	5-11	180	6-25-89	.246	.269	.241	81	301	27	74	13	4	6	38	16	2	1	3	73	7	7	.375	.286
Soler, Jorge	R-R	6-4	215	2-25-92	.415	.389	.426	22	65	13	27	9	1	6	22	12	0	0	2	15	0	0	.862	.494
Soto, Elliot	R-R	5-9	160	8-21-89	.246	.290	.233	40	134	14	33	8	0	0	12	21	0	2	0	21	3	0	.306	.348
Valdez, Jeudy	R-R	5-10	190	5-5-89	.225	.156	.248	58	182	17	41	5	2	3	20	15	1	2	1	38	3	2	.324	.286
Villanueva, Christian	R-R	5-11	210	6-19-91	.248	.289	.238	62	234	31	58	20	0	4	32	19	3	1	2	42	0	1	.385	.310

Pitching	B-T	HT	WT	DOB	W	L	ERA	G	GS	CG	SV	IP	H	R	ER	HR	BB	SO	AVG	vLH	vRH	K/9	BB/9
Antigua, Jeffry	R-L	6-1	205	6-23-90	0	2	3.58	9	4	0	0	33	31	15	13	2	13	19	.265	.346	.242	5.23	3.58
Arrieta, Jake	R-R	6-4	225	3-6-86	1	1	1.26	4	4	0	0	14	8	4	2	0	5	11	.157	.071	.189	6.91	3.14
Batista, Frank	R-R	5-10	170	4-26-89	4	2	1.63	32	0	0	10	39	33	12	7	4	9	32	.234	.300	.208	7.45	2.09
Black, Corey	R-R	5-11	175	8-4-91	6	7	3.47	26	25	0	0	124	100	55	48	13	71	119	.224	.161	.258	8.61	5.14
Castillo, Lendy	R-R	6-1	170	4-8-89	1	1	3.95	36	0	0	1	41	32	22	18	4	39	41	.212	.261	.190	9.00	8.56
Cates, Zach	R-R	6-3	200	12-17-89	2	1	6.00	23	0	0	1	27	21	22	18	0	22	22	.242	.217		7.33	7.33
Cervenka, Hunter	L-L	6-1	215	1-3-90	4	4	3.79	48	0	0	1	62	44	28	26	1	31	65	.202	.151	.228	9.49	4.52
Cooper, Blake	R-R	5-11	190	3-30-88	0	1	0.87	8	0	0	1	10	5	1	1	0	3	17	.139	.231	.087	14.81	2.61
2-team total (24 Mobile)					3	3	1.62	32	0	0	1	44	31	12	8	2	13	48	—	—		9.74	2.64
Doubront, Felix	L-L	6-2	225	10-23-87	0	1	6.23	1	1	0	0	4	5	4	3	0	5	3	.294	.500	.231	10.38	6.23
Edwards, C.J.	R-R	6-2	155	9-3-91	1	2	2.44	10	10	0	0	48	30	14	13	1	21	46	.180	.197	.168	8.63	3.94
Figueroa, Eduardo	R-R	6-1	185	11-30-88	2	1	4.44	12	11	0	0	49	50	28	24	3	21	27	.270	.323	.244	4.99	3.88
Francescon, Patrick	R-R	5-11	185	1-4-89	11	6	3.52	43	0	0	1	69	64	30	27	4	31	48	.252	.254	.251	6.26	4.04
Gardner, Joe	R-R	6-4	220	3-18-88	1	2	3.65	7	7	0	0	37	32	15	15	3	10	17	.241	.250	.233	4.14	2.43

	B-T	HT	WT	DOB	W	L	ERA	G	GS	CG	SV	IP	H	R	ER	HR	BB	SO	AVG	vLH	vRH	K/9	BB/9
2-team total (3 Mississippi)					3	3	3.40	10	10	0	0	53	45	20	20	4	13	24	—	—	—	4.08	2.21
Johnson, Pierce	R-R	6-3	170	5-10-91	5	4	2.55	18	17	0	0	92	60	27	26	8	54	91	.194	.194	.194	8.93	5.30
Kirk, Austin	L-L	6-1	200	5-22-90	1	4	4.84	13	0	0	0	22	22	16	12	5	10	12	.265	.276	.259	4.84	4.03
Loosen, Matt	R-R	6-2	205	4-10-89	5	5	5.77	26	19	0	0	106	93	72	68	10	69	96	.238	.297	.206	8.15	5.86
Lorick, Jeff	L-L	6-0	205	12-18-87	2	3	4.52	46	0	0	1	64	59	40	32	5	29	58	.241	.264	.227	8.20	4.10
McKirahan, Andrew	R-L	6-2	195	2-8-90	0	3	3.45	21	0	0	2	29	28	13	11	3	6	24	.257	.343	.216	7.53	1.88
Pena, Felix	R-R	6-2	190	2-25-90	2	4	7.48	6	6	0	0	28	30	23	23	5	17	26	.294	.308	.286	8.46	5.53
Pineiro, Joel	R-R	6-0	200	9-25-78	0	1	4.43	4	4	0	0	22	29	15	11	5	4	10	.309	.357	.269	4.03	1.61
Pineyro, Ivan	R-R	6-1	200	9-29-91	0	4	5.55	11	11	0	0	49	58	35	30	7	23	41	.293	.235	.323	7.58	4.25
Rhee, Dae-Eun	L-R	6-2	190	3-23-89	5	4	3.27	18	16	0	0	105	89	42	38	5	40	61	.238	.252	.231	5.25	3.44
Rivero, Armando	R-R	6-4	190	2-1-88	2	1	1.56	26	0	0	10	35	18	7	6	2	16	54	.153	.200	.128	14.02	4.15
Rodriguez, Julio	R-R	6-4	195	8-29-90	1	2	5.52	3	3	0	0	15	9	10	9	1	13	10	.176	.300	.097	6.14	7.98
Searle, Ryan	R-R	6-0	190	6-22-89	3	1	6.63	9	0	0	0	19	22	14	14	2	9	17	.289	.409	.241	8.05	4.26
Veras, Jose	R-R	6-6	240	10-20-80	2	0	0.00	4	1	0	0	5	1	0	0	2	3	.067	.250	.000	5.79	3.86	
Vizcaino, Arodys	R-R	6-0	190	11-13-90	1	1	2.63	14	0	0	1	14	7	4	4	1	3	16	.149	.171	.172	10.54	1.98
Zych, Tony	R-R	6-3	190	8-7-90	4	5	5.09	45	0	0	2	58	75	36	33	3	18	35	.329	.344	.323	5.40	2.78

Fielding

Catcher

Catcher	PCT	G	PO	A	E	DP	PB
Cutler	.997	41	282	27	1	0	5
Davis	.993	35	260	19	2	0	3
Flores	.991	30	195	25	2	1	2
Lopez	.987	39	267	41	4	1	3
Rymel	.947	3	17	1	1	0	0

First Base

First Base	PCT	G	PO	A	E	DP
Anderson	.981	23	151	7	3	14
Cutler	1.000	19	123	8	0	16
Darvill	1.000	1	1	0	0	0
Davis	1.000	1	1	0	0	0
Geiger	.996	111	876	54	4	82
Giansanti	1.000	4	6	0	0	0
Mota	1.000	6	42	1	0	6
Valdez	1.000	1	4	0	0	0

Second Base

Second Base	PCT	G	PO	A	E	DP
Bonifacio	1.000	2	5	7	0	3
Bruno	.973	93	159	243	11	59
Darvill	.963	16	27	52	3	10
Giansanti	1.000	13	20	17	0	6
Mota	.978	12	18	27	1	9
Soto	.950	4	9	10	1	2
Valdez	.976	10	16	25	1	6
Villanueva	1.000	3	1	4	0	1

Third Base

Third Base	PCT	G	PO	A	E	DP
Bryant	.923	62	46	122	14	12
Darvill	.800	2	1	3	1	0
Geiger	1.000	4	1	3	0	0
Giansanti	.846	6	2	9	2	1
Mota	.943	11	10	23	2	2
Villanueva	.923	61	31	125	13	13

Shortstop

Shortstop	PCT	G	PO	A	E	DP
Darvill	.906	19	14	44	6	7
Giansanti	1.000	3	3	3	0	0
Mota	1.000	3	7	11	0	0
Russell	.990	47	61	147	2	36
Soto	.982	36	56	111	3	21
Valdez	.915	43	55	96	14	21

Outfield

Outfield	PCT	G	PO	A	E	DP
Almora	.985	32	62	2	1	0
Anderson	1.000	17	20	0	0	0
Andreoli	.991	57	112	2	1	0
Bonifacio	.667	2	2	1	0	0
Brown	1.000	6	12	0	0	0
Chen	1.000	45	87	3	0	1
Cutler	.800	4	4	0	1	0
Darvill	1.000	1	5	0	0	0
DeVoss	1.000	22	34	1	0	1
Geiger	1.000	2	1	0	0	0
Giansanti	.983	45	50	7	1	1
Ha	.980	112	233	9	5	1
Mota	.971	23	32	1	1	0
Silva	.988	79	155	9	2	2
Soler	.955	16	21	0	1	0

DAYTONA CUBS   HIGH CLASS A

FLORIDA STATE LEAGUE

Batting	B-T	HT	WT	DOB	AVG	vLH	vRH	G	AB	R	H	2B	3B	HR	RBI	BB	HBP	SH	SF	SO	SB	CS	SLG	OBP
Almora, Albert	R-R	6-2	180	4-16-94	.283	.301	.276	89	367	55	104	20	2	7	50	12	2	0	4	46	6	3	.406	.306
Amaya, Gioskar	R-R	5-11	175	12-13-92	.276	.296	.268	112	369	56	102	16	3	4	35	53	9	—	2	90	14	7	.369	.379
Candelario, Jeimer	B-R	6-1	180	11-24-93	.193	.203	.188	62	218	24	42	10	2	5	26	23	2	0	1	44	0	3	.326	.275
Carhart, Ben	R-R	5-10	200	1-21-90	.340	.500	.200	13	47	6	16	5	0	0	7	4	0	0	0	9	1	0	.447	.392
Chen, Pin-Chieh	L-R	6-1	170	7-23-91	.275	.219	.297	65	229	36	63	14	6	0	18	28	2	4	0	38	8	8	.389	.359
Contreras, Willson	R-R	6-1	175	5-13-92	.242	.179	.266	80	281	40	68	14	2	5	37	28	5	—	2	66	5	5	.359	.320
Darvill, Wes	L-R	6-2	175	9-10-91	.257	.259	.257	60	206	26	53	13	1	1	24	17	0	1	4	42	6	0	.345	.308
DeVoss, Zeke	B-R	5-10	175	7-17-90	.174	.152	.186	43	132	14	23	5	0	1	13	24	6	—	1	42	7	4	.235	.325
Hankins, Jordan	L-R	5-10	191	2-18-92	.218	.179	.232	33	110	12	24	5	0	2	17	13	4	—	0	25	2	0	.318	.323
Hannemann, Jacob	L-L	6-1	195	4-29-91	.241	.238	.243	36	145	17	35	9	0	2	12	11	1	2	0	34	5	3	.345	.299
Hernandez, Marco	L-R	6-0	170	9-6-92	.270	.227	.288	122	441	61	119	13	7	3	55	30	2	—	6	90	22	8	.351	.315
Krist, Chadd	R-R	5-11	190	1-28-90	.220	.228	.217	52	186	20	41	9	0	4	18	17	2	0	1	42	3	1	.333	.291
2-team total (8 Jupiter)					.218	—		60	216	21	47	11	0	4	19	17	2	0	1	54	3	1	.324	.280
McKinney, Billy	L-L	6-1	195	8-23-94	.301	.375	.267	51	176	30	53	12	4	1	36	25	4	—	5	42	1	0	.432	.390
Papaccio, Giuseppe	R-R	6-1	185	6-8-91	.080	.083	.077	8	25	1	2	1	0	0	0	0	0	0	0	6	0	0	.120	.080
Rademacher, Bijan	L-L	6-0	200	6-15-91	.281	.308	.269	111	384	58	108	22	6	10	56	42	9	—	3	87	4	8	.448	.363
Rymel, Lance	R-R	6-0	195	5-2-90	.182	.000	.250	3	11	0	2	1	0	0	0	1	0	1	0	3	0	0	.273	.182
Saunders, Tim	R-R	6-0	180	5-17-90	.210	.265	.173	36	124	10	26	9	1	2	15	7	2	3	1	40	10	2	.347	.261
Schwarber, Kyle	L-R	6-0	235	3-5-93	.302	.265	.318	44	159	31	48	9	1	6	28	36	1	0	5	38	4	6	.560	.393
Shoulders, Rock	L-R	6-2	225	9-26-91	.223	.253	.211	91	310	46	69	16	1	12	42	55	1	—	1	112	1	2	.397	.341
Vogelbach, Dan	L-L	6-0	250	12-17-92	.268	.212	.294	132	482	71	129	28	1	16	76	66	5	—	7	91	4	4	.429	.357
Zapata, Oliver	B-R	5-9	180	9-13-92	.129	.167	.105	11	31	4	4	0	0	0	4	2	0	0	1	12	0	0	.129	.176

Pitching	B-T	HT	WT	DOB	W	L	ERA	G	GS	CG	SV	IP	H	R	ER	HR	BB	SO	AVG	vLH	vRH	K/9	BB/9
Amlung, Justin	R-R	6-1	185	5-21-90	4	4	4.37	15	9	0	1	60	72	32	29	3	19	45	.300	.340	.269	6.79	2.87
Arrieta, Jake	R-R	6-4	225	3-6-86	0	0	4.76	1	1	0	0	6	5	5	3	3	2	7	.227	.250	.167	11.12	3.18
Bremer, Tyler	R-R	6-2	210	12-7-89	0	1	4.70	8	0	0	0	15	14	8	8	2	7	12	.241	.185	.290	7.04	4.11
Cates, Zach	R-R	6-3	200	12-17-89	1	1	2.08	13	0	0	1	26	22	7	6	0	3	18	.247	.300	.232	6.23	1.04
Concepcion, Gerardo	L-L	6-2	180	2-29-92	0	1	1.17	8	0	0	1	15	8	2	2	0	6	14	.157	.158	.156	8.22	3.52
Davis, Josh	R-R	6-3	210	11-3-90	0	0	6.75	1	0	0	0	3	6	2	2	0	1	2	.462	.125	1.000	6.75	3.38
Dorris, Nathan	L-L	6-3	185	12-9-90	5	6	5.91	19	11	0	0	75	90	51	49	6	32	53	.305	.250	.327	6.39	3.86
Figueroa, Eduardo	R-R	6-1	185	11-30-88	0	1	11.25	1	1	0	0	4	2	5	5	2	3	2	.143	.200	.000	4.50	6.75
Godley, Zack	R-R	6-3	235	4-21-90	3	2	3.57	29	0	0	8	40	40	21	16	3	17	52	.253	.268	.241	11.60	3.79
Graham, Trevor	R-R	6-3	220	11-21-91	2	0	0.00	3	0	0	3	9	5	0	0	0	4	8	.185	.182	.188	8.31	4.15

Name	B-T	HT	WT	DOB	W	L	ERA	G	GS	CG	SV	IP	H	R	ER	HR	BB	SO	AVG	vLH	vRH	K/9	BB/9
Ihrig, Tyler	L-L	6-0	190	9-17-91	0	0	7.00	3	1	0	0	9	10	7	7	1	3	8	.303	.353	.250	8.00	3.00
Jensen, Michael	R-R	6-1	185	12-10-90	7	4	2.85	36	0	0	1	60	59	26	19	2	30	62	.252	.207	.279	9.30	4.50
Kirk, Austin	L-L	6-1	200	5-22-90	1	0	3.23	26	1	0	2	47	36	20	17	3	27	34	.208	.188	.220	6.46	5.13
McKirahan, Andrew	R-L	6-2	195	2-8-90	2	1	0.99	23	0	0	8	36	29	6	4	1	8	33	.213	.263	.194	8.17	1.98
Paniagua, Juan Carlos	R-R	6-1	175	4-4-90	2	4	6.14	8	7	0	0	29	36	25	20	4	21	23	.305	.280	.324	7.06	6.44
Pena, Felix	R-R	6-2	190	2-25-90	4	6	3.19	19	19	1	0	96	88	43	34	6	34	76	.240	.275	.216	7.13	3.19
Perakslis, Steve	R-R	6-1	185	1-15-91	5	0	3.93	35	0	0	3	69	62	32	30	4	28	55	.244	.183	.299	7.21	3.67
Peralta, Starling	R-R	6-4	180	11-11-90	6	3	3.43	33	2	0	2	81	64	41	31	7	25	86	.213	.256	.183	9.52	2.77
Rakkar, Jasvir	R-R	6-2	200	4-27-91	0	0	4.50	5	0	0	0	6	8	3	3	0	0	1	.320	.313	.333	1.50	0.00
Reed, Austin	R-R	6-3	200	10-31-91	0	1	4.62	17	0	0	2	25	28	14	13	1	12	18	.280	.282	.279	6.39	4.26
Rosario, Jose	R-R	6-1	170	8-29-90	5	8	5.44	26	16	0	0	101	127	70	61	12	50	92	.305	.331	.286	8.20	4.46
Scott, Tayler	R-R	6-3	165	6-1-92	8	8	4.34	26	26	0	0	135	142	79	65	14	52	79	.268	.262	.274	5.28	3.48
Skulina, Tyler	R-R	6-5	255	9-18-91	0	2	7.27	3	3	0	0	9	11	9	7	0	9	7	.367	.455	.316	7.27	9.35
Vizcaino, Arodys	R-R	6-0	190	11-13-90	0	0	1.00	9	0	0	1	9	6	1	1	0	4	10	.194	.000	.286	10.00	4.00
Wang, Yao-Lin	R-R	6-0	180	2-5-91	4	7	5.57	24	11	0	0	65	69	47	40	5	24	48	.271	.260	.278	6.68	3.34
Wells, Ben	R-R	6-3	220	9-10-92	2	4	6.55	8	5	0	0	22	27	17	16	1	23	18	.303	.321	.295	7.36	9.41
Zastryzny, Rob	R-L	6-3	205	3-26-92	4	6	4.66	23	23	0	0	110	121	58	57	10	33	110	.279	.288	.275	9.00	2.70

Fielding

Catcher	PCT	G	PO	A	E	DP	PB
Carhart	1.000	2	16	2	0	0	1
Contreras	.998	73	495	72	1	1	11
Krist	.988	50	313	30	4	2	7
Rymel	1.000	3	20	1	0	0	0
Schwarber	.981	9	93	12	2	0	3

First Base	PCT	G	PO	A	E	DP
Contreras	1.000	2	2	0	0	0
Shoulders	.988	33	290	39	4	28
Vogelbach	.995	103	908	44	5	80

Second Base	PCT	G	PO	A	E	DP
Amaya	.972	107	167	278	13	54
Chen	1.000	1	2	1	0	0

	PCT	G	PO	A	E	DP
Darvill	.972	15	23	47	2	11
Papaccio	1.000	1	1	1	0	1
Saunders	.988	15	34	50	1	12

Third Base	PCT	G	PO	A	E	DP
Candelario	.950	57	40	131	9	10
Carhart	.955	11	6	15	1	2
Darvill	.980	32	25	71	2	6
Hankins	.937	31	17	72	6	3
Papaccio	1.000	3	1	4	0	1
Saunders	.933	5	3	11	1	1

Shortstop	PCT	G	PO	A	E	DP
Darvill	.944	6	3	14	1	2
Hernandez	.949	122	174	370	29	69

	PCT	G	PO	A	E	DP
Papaccio	1.000	2	0	7	0	2
Saunders	.921	8	9	26	3	6

Outfield	PCT	G	PO	A	E	DP
Almora	.995	87	211	8	1	0
Chen	.979	64	93	2	2	0
DeVoss	.968	40	58	2	2	0
Hannemann	1.000	36	83	6	0	0
McKinney	.958	32	69	0	3	0
Rademacher	.934	100	151	5	11	0
Schwarber	.980	26	47	3	1	0
Shoulders	1.000	28	38	2	0	0
Zapata	1.000	10	14	1	0	0

KANE COUNTY COUGARS   LOW CLASS A

MIDWEST LEAGUE

Batting	B-T	HT	WT	DOB	AVG	vLH	vRH	G	AB	R	H	2B	3B	HR	RBI	BB	HBP	SH	SF	SO	SB	CS	SLG	OBP
Baez, Jeffrey	R-R	6-0	180	10-30-93	.236	.257	.225	31	106	14	25	7	1	6	15	10	0	1	1	38	2	2	.491	.299
Balaguert, Yasiel	R-R	6-2	215	1-9-93	.252	.250	.253	93	369	45	93	17	2	7	53	20	1	0	2	86	0	2	.366	.291
Bote, David	R-R	5-11	185	4-7-93	.210	.283	.186	58	186	19	39	12	0	1	21	20	1	1	—	49	3	4	.290	.323
Brockmeyer, Cael	R-R	6-5	235	10-8-91	.297	.286	.302	77	256	31	76	14	2	8	43	18	13	—	5	48	0	0	.461	.366
Brown, Kevin	L-R	6-0	195	10-30-90	.221	.105	.259	22	77	6	17	2	0	2	10	7	0	1	2	15	1	2	.325	.279
Candelario, Jeimer	B-R	6-1	180	11-24-93	.250	.169	.279	63	244	32	61	19	3	6	37	18	0	—	1	45	0	1	.426	.300
Canela, Danny	L-R	5-11	200	12-24-90	.278	.364	.256	14	54	7	15	1	0	1	6	2	0	0	0	12	0	0	.352	.304
Caratini, Victor	B-R	6-0	195	8-17-93	.264	.313	.243	14	53	7	14	4	1	0	13	4	0	0	1	10	0	0	.377	.310
Carhart, Ben	R-R	6-0	200	1-21-90	.262	.292	.262	102	386	56	104	18	1	5	43	37	6	—	5	40	1	0	.360	.339
Dunston Jr., Shawon	L-R	6-2	170	2-5-93	.268	.282	.265	96	328	53	88	17	2	3	37	18	2	4	7	59	27	6	.381	.304
Hankins, Jordan	L-R	5-10	191	2-18-92	.322	.278	.333	50	180	22	58	16	0	3	34	11	1	0	2	24	1	1	.461	.361
Hannemann, Jacob	L-L	6-1	195	4-29-91	.254	.316	.236	88	342	57	87	14	5	6	39	31	4	—	3	77	32	4	.377	.321
Lockhart, Danny	L-R	5-11	165	11-4-92	.284	.297	.281	89	327	55	93	18	4	0	28	33	1	3	4	47	12	5	.364	.348
Martin, Trey	R-R	6-2	188	12-11-92	.247	.264	.242	112	368	50	91	16	1	5	37	27	0	—	2	100	29	7	.337	.297
Papaccio, Giuseppe	R-R	6-1	185	6-8-91	.056	.000	.071	6	18	0	1	0	0	0	0	1	0	0	0	9	0	0	.056	.105
Penalver, Carlos	R-R	6-0	170	5-17-94	.211	.187	.218	128	478	55	101	17	4	1	40	33	2	—	4	100	21	10	.270	.263
Remillard, Will	R-R	6-1	195	9-18-92	.286	.333	.271	49	168	19	48	13	0	1	26	21	2	2	0	31	0	0	.381	.372
Rogers, Jacob	L-R	6-5	195	8-23-89	.268	.255	.273	129	447	76	120	27	2	16	67	64	3	—	4	116	2	1	.445	.361
Saunders, Tim	R-R	6-0	180	5-17-90	.333	.000	1.000	1	3	0	1	1	0	0	1	0	0	0	0	1	0	0	.667	.333
Schwarber, Kyle	L-R	6-0	235	3-5-93	.361	.400	.345	23	83	17	30	8	0	4	15	11	2	—	0	17	1	1	.602	.448
Sweeney, Ryan	L-L	6-4	225	2-20-85	.000	—	.000	2	5	0	0	0	0	0	0	1	0	0	0	1	0	0	.000	.167
Valerio, Antonio	R-R	6-0	190	3-21-91	.143	.000	.333	2	7	1	1	0	0	0	0	1	0	0	0	2	0	0	.286	.250
Young, Chesny	R-R	6-1	180	10-6-92	.324	.414	.289	27	105	14	34	6	2	0	9	5	0	2	2	22	2	1	.419	.348
Zagunis, Mark	R-R	6-0	205	2-5-93	.280	.133	.343	14	50	11	14	6	1	0	4	10	2	0	0	9	5	0	.440	.419

Pitching	B-T	HT	WT	DOB	W	L	ERA	G	GS	CG	SV	IP	H	R	ER	HR	BB	SO	AVG	vLH	vRH	K/9	BB/9
Amlung, Justin	R-R	6-1	185	5-21-90	4	0	1.54	12	4	0	0	47	34	8	8	4	7	40	.204	.206	.202	7.71	1.35
Arias, Jose	R-R	6-6	235	1-17-91	1	1	1.77	25	0	0	3	41	24	13	8	1	17	51	.168	.190	.150	11.29	3.76
Blackburn, Paul	R-R	6-2	185	12-4-93	9	4	3.23	24	24	0	0	117	108	48	42	6	31	75	.247	.249	.244	5.77	2.38
Bremer, Tyler	R-R	6-2	210	12-7-89	5	1	2.43	28	0	0	12	37	28	11	10	2	15	51	.201	.250	.172	12.41	3.65
Carrillo, Francisco	R-R	6-0	190	3-15-90	0	1	1.35	12	0	0	6	13	9	2	2	0	7	16	.196	.174	.217	10.80	4.73
Concepcion, Gerardo	L-L	6-2	180	2-29-92	2	2	3.89	19	0	0	0	42	38	19	18	1	15	38	.248	.146	.295	8.21	3.24
Davis, Josh	R-R	6-3	210	11-3-90	1	2	4.11	7	1	0	0	15	22	13	7	0	2	11	.344	.333	.350	6.46	1.17
Diaz, Alberto	L-L	5-9	157	6-12-91	0	0	23.63	2	0	0	0	3	5	7	7	1	4	1	.417	.000	.500	3.38	13.50
Dorris, Nathan	L-L	6-3	185	12-9-90	4	2	2.49	13	0	0	2	22	14	7	6	0	14	21	.184	.143	.200	8.72	5.82
Frazier, Scott	R-R	6-7	215	12-3-91	0	1	162.00	2	0	0	0	2	8	6	6	0	5	0	.667	.667	—	0.00	135.00
Fujikawa, Kyuji	L-R	6-0	190	7-21-80	0	0	0.00	2	0	0	1	4					1	4	.143	.000	.167	21.60	5.40
Garner, David	R-R	6-1	180	9-21-92	1	0	4.02	10	0	0	1	16	16	7	7	1	10	13	.262	.333	.194	7.47	5.74

	B-T	HT	WT	DOB	W	L	ERA	G	GS	CG	SV	IP	H	R	ER	HR	BB	SO	AVG	vLH	vRH	K/9	BB/9
Godley, Zack	R-R	6-3	235	4-21-90	1	1	1.80	11	0	0	7	15	9	3	3	0	7	25	.170	.133	.184	15.00	4.20
Heesch, Michael	R-L	6-5	245	5-15-90	3	1	2.18	24	0	0	0	45	32	12	11	1	20	59	.198	.273	.169	11.71	3.97
Hermans, Zak	R-R	6-2	190	6-21-91	3	3	3.92	20	0	0	0	39	35	21	17	4	19	36	.240	.255	.231	8.31	4.38
Hoffner, Corbin	R-R	6-5	235	7-30-93	2	1	5.64	16	0	0	0	30	33	19	19	0	16	26	.289	.294	.286	7.71	4.75
Ihrig, Tyler	L-L	6-0	190	9-17-91	3	1	2.30	5	4	0	1	27	24	7	7	2	5	20	.238	.370	.189	6.59	1.65
Johnson, Pierce	R-R	6-3	170	5-10-91	0	1	2.45	2	2	0	0	11	4	3	3	1	3	8	.118	.231	.048	6.55	2.45
Martinez, Jonathan	R-R	6-1	203	6-27-94	4	0	2.31	5	5	1	0	23	22	6	6	2	2	15	.244	.271	.214	5.79	0.77
2-team total (19 Great Lakes)					11	5	3.26	24	24	1	0	130	132	49	47	10	21	106	—	—	—	7.36	1.46
Paniagua, Juan Carlos	R-R	6-1	175	4-4-90	6	4	3.36	17	14	0	1	80	71	32	30	7	36	75	.242	.215	.262	8.40	4.03
Pugliese, James	R-R	6-3	195	8-12-92	4	0	1.66	31	0	0	3	54	39	14	10	1	15	56	.198	.208	.188	9.28	2.48
Rakkar, Jasvir	R-R	6-2	200	4-27-91	3	1	0.87	12	0	0	1	21	10	2	2	0	6	21	.143	.158	.125	9.15	2.61
Skulina, Tyler	R-R	6-5	255	9-18-91	4	7	3.21	18	18	0	0	90	71	36	32	3	35	68	.218	.244	.201	6.83	3.51
Torrez, Daury	R-R	6-3	170	6-11-93	11	7	2.74	23	23	1	0	131	110	50	40	8	21	81	.226	.210	.235	5.55	1.44
Tseng, Jen-Ho	L-R	6-1	210	10-3-94	6	1	2.40	19	17	1	0	105	76	29	28	7	15	85	.204	.194	.212	7.29	1.29
Underwood, Duane	R-R	6-2	205	7-20-94	6	4	2.50	22	21	0	0	101	85	37	28	10	36	84	.231	.219	.239	7.51	3.22
Wagner, Michael	R-R	6-3	175	10-3-91	3	3	3.23	28	0	0	2	61	70	23	22	8	26	60	.293	.313	.274	8.80	3.82
Wells, Ben	R-R	6-3	220	9-10-92	4	0	2.23	7	7	0	0	36	25	11	9	1	25	20	.208	.246	.175	4.95	6.19

Fielding

Catcher	PCT	G	PO	A	E	DP	PB
Brockmeyer	.982	48	347	31	7	0	3
Caratini	1.000	9	58	10	0	2	2
Carhart	.996	31	216	39	1	1	4
Remillard	.997	44	335	42	1	2	7
Schwarber	1.000	9	65	11	0	0	1
Valerio	1.000	1	6	0	0	0	0
Zagunis	.960	3	21	3	1	0	0

First Base	PCT	G	PO	A	E	DP
Brockmeyer	1.000	6	55	2	0	3
Carhart	.987	9	66	10	1	7
Rogers	.993	127	991	121	8	78

Second Base	PCT	G	PO	A	E	DP
Bote	.990	28	37	65	1	11
Carhart	.891	13	14	27	5	4
Lockhart	.983	78	135	207	6	38
Papaccio	1.000	4	4	6	0	1
Saunders	1.000	1	2	1	0	0
Young	.987	17	32	46	1	15

Third Base	PCT	G	PO	A	E	DP
Bote	.859	24	14	41	9	3
Candelario	.965	62	45	120	6	11
Carhart	.800	6	1	7	2	0
Hankins	.926	43	16	84	8	9
Young	.917	6	4	7	1	1

Shortstop	PCT	G	PO	A	E	DP
Bote	1.000	2	6	7	0	0
Lockhart	.925	11	17	20	3	5

	PCT	G	PO	A	E	DP
Papaccio	1.000	1	3	1	0	0
Penalver	.964	127	208	376	22	65

Outfield	PCT	G	PO	A	E	DP
Baez	.985	31	60	4	1	1
Balaguert	.976	79	160	5	4	1
Bote	1.000	5	7	0	0	0
Brown	.968	18	29	1	1	0
Dunston Jr.	.988	82	164	4	2	2
Hannemann	.969	87	182	8	6	2
Martin	.996	110	229	5	1	1
Schwarber	1.000	8	11	0	0	0
Sweeney	—	2	0	0	0	0
Zagunis	1.000	7	16	0	0	0

BOISE HAWKS — SHORT-SEASON

NORTHWEST LEAGUE

Batting	B-T	HT	WT	DOB	AVG	vLH	vRH	G	AB	R	H	2B	3B	HR	RBI	BB	HBP	SH	SF	SO	SB	CS	SLG	OBP
Baez, Jeffrey	R-R	6-0	180	10-30-93	.267	.150	.306	38	161	31	43	6	2	7	30	14	4	—	0	40	15	6	.460	.341
Blair, Zak	L-R	5-10	190	12-19-89	.250	.250	.250	10	32	7	8	0	0	0	1	5	0	0	6	0	0	.250	.351	
Bote, David	R-R	5-11	185	4-7-93	.260	.367	.195	37	131	22	34	11	0	2	16	18	4	1	0	24	9	3	.389	.366
Brown, Kevin	L-R	6-0	195	10-30-90	.270	.306	.257	34	137	24	37	11	3	3	23	13	0	0	1	26	2	2	.460	.331
Burks, Charcer	R-R	6-0	170		.313	.292	.325	37	128	25	40	6	2	0	20	21	3	2	2	31	4	3	.391	.416
Canela, Danny	L-R	5-11	200	12-24-90	.295	.164	.342	66	254	34	75	16	0	6	48	23	0	—	3	55	2	1	.429	.350
Castillo, Erick	B-R	5-11	180	2-25-93	.200	.000	.250	3	10	1	2	0	0	0	0	1	0	0	0	1	0	0	.200	.273
Crawford, Rashad	B-R	6-3	185	10-15-93	.259	.213	.279	71	297	45	77	13	7	1	34	16	1	—	3	83	14	5	.360	.297
Cuevas, Varonex	B-R	6-0	165	7-24-92	.118	.000	.154	12	34	4	4	1	0	1	3	4	0	0	0	10	0	0	.235	.211
Flete, Bryant	B-R	5-10	146	1-31-93	.256	.300	.236	36	129	19	33	6	0	0	12	18	2	1	2	27	2	5	.302	.351
Graves, Calvin	R-R	5-9	170	3-18-91	.222	.182	.240	15	36	6	8	0	1	0	4	1	0	0	7	2	0	.278	.317	
Hodges, Jesse	R-R	6-1	212	3-29-94	.265	.246	.271	73	272	39	72	14	1	7	44	25	4	—	6	84	1	1	.401	.329
Lockhart, Danny	L-R	5-11	165	11-4-92	.421	.091	.875	4	19	6	8	2	0	0	3	0	0	0	0	6	1	0	.526	.421
Malave, Mark	B-R	6-3	185	1-5-95	.263	.347	.216	41	137	18	36	8	0	0	15	18	1	0	2	42	0	0	.321	.348
Marra, Justin	L-R	5-10	190	1-18-93	.279	.171	.305	58	208	39	58	17	0	9	38	25	1	—	2	68	0	1	.490	.356
Papaccio, Giuseppe	R-R	6-1	185	6-8-91	.222	.250	.217	23	72	14	16	2	0	0	8	11	2	1	3	13	0	0	.250	.330
Schwarber, Kyle	L-R	6-0	235	3-5-93	.600	.400	.667	5	20	7	12	1	1	4	10	2	1	0	1	2	0	1.350	.625	
Tomasovich, Alex	R-R	6-3	185	11-6-91	.311	.250	.345	37	132	18	41	6	1	0	18	9	4	0	0	26	1	0	.371	.372
Torres, Gleyber	R-R	6-1	175	12-13-96	.393	.250	.450	7	28	4	11	2	3	1	4	4	0	0	0	7	2	0	.786	.469
Vosler, Jason	L-R	6-1	190	9-6-93	.266	.227	.278	30	94	13	25	1	3	1	11	12	2	—	0	16	0	2	.372	.361
White, Charlie	L-L	5-9	180	11-13-91	.200	.176	.206	36	85	14	17	3	1	0	8	11	2	—	0	19	2	0	.259	.306
Young, Chesny	R-R	6-0	180	10-6-92	.354	.368	.368	15	48	13	17	3	0	0	9	8	2	—	0	8	1	0	.417	.466
Zagunis, Mark	R-R	6-0	205	2-5-93	.299	.317	.292	41	154	32	46	9	2	2	27	31	5	—	1	31	11	2	.422	.429
Zapata, Oliver	B-R	5-9	180	9-13-92	.200	.000	.227	7	25	3	5	3	0	0	4	6	0	0	1	9	0	1	.320	.344

Pitching	B-T	HT	WT	DOB	W	L	ERA	G	GS	CG	SV	IP	H	R	ER	HR	BB	SO	AVG	vLH	vRH	K/9	BB/9
Alzolay, Adbert	R-R	6-0	179	3-1-95	0	0	3.00	1	0	0	0	3	2	1	1	0	1	2	.182	.000	.222	6.00	3.00
Carrillo, Francisco	R-R	6-0	190	3-15-90	1	2	2.42	14	0	0	1	26	22	8	7	1	5	33	.233	.211	11.42	1.73
Clifton, Trevor	R-R	6-4	170	5-11-95	4	2	3.69	13	13	0	0	61	59	30	25	3	30	54	.257	.329	.219	7.97	4.43
Conway, Josh	R-R	6-1	175	4-12-91	0	1	1.96	13	13	0	0	37	25	11	8	1	9	24	.187	.111	.225	5.89	2.21
Davis, Josh	R-R	6-3	210	11-3-90	1	1	6.62	12	0	0	0	18	28	17	13	3	4	18	.354	.269	.396	9.17	2.04
Diaz, Alberto	L-L	5-9	157	6-21-91	0	2	6.85	14	0	0	0	24	33	19	18	5	12	18	.327	.304	.333	6.85	4.56
Eregua, Greyfer	R-R	5-11	160	10-15-93	1	0	6.23	7	0	0	0	13	11	9	9	4	5	13	.224	.333	.161	9.00	3.46
Farris, James	R-R	6-2	210	4-4-92	0	0	2.57	7	0	0	0	14	12	4	4	0	3	21	.240	.313	.206	13.50	1.93
Frazier, Scott	R-R	6-7	215	12-3-91	0	0	—	1	0	0	0	1	0	0	0	1	4	4	0	1.000	—1.000	—	
Garner, David	R-R	6-1	180	9-21-92	1	1	3.60	12	0	0	2	15	15	7	6	1	6	23	.259	.174	.314	13.80	3.60
Graham, Trevor	R-R	6-3	220	11-21-91	4	4	5.58	11	10	1	0	50	65	38	31	4	19	49	.316	.282	.333	8.82	3.42

Name	B-T	HT	WT	DOB	W	L	ERA	G	GS	CG	SV	IP	H	R	ER	HR	BB	SO	AVG	vLH	vRH	K/9	BB/9
Hoffner, Corbin	R-R	6-5	235	7-30-93	1	2	3.12	6	0	0	2	9	10	6	3	0	6	9	.294	.364	.261	9.35	6.23
Ihrig, Tyler	L-L	6-0	190	9-17-91	4	2	4.44	8	8	0	0	47	50	25	23	4	6	36	.276	.387	.253	6.94	1.16
Lang, Trey	R-R	6-3	225	5-18-92	2	1	4.89	20	0	0	0	35	27	23	19	0	21	28	.220	.118	.258	7.20	5.40
Leal, Erick	R-R	6-3	180	3-17-95	6	2	3.73	13	13	0	0	63	68	34	26	7	18	31	.272	.311	.250	4.45	2.59
Lewis, Daniel	R-R	6-0	200	3-26-91	1	0	0.87	8	0	0	0	10	6	1	1	0	6	13	.171	.154	.182	11.32	5.23
Llano, Carlos	R-R	6-0	185	2-28-92	0	0	3.00	2	0	0	0	3	1	1	1	0	2	3	.100	.000	.143	9.00	6.00
Maples, Dillon	R-R	6-2	195	5-9-92	0	2	12.23	6	6	0	0	18	29	30	24	0	20	13	.358	.321	.377	6.62	10.19
Markey, Brad	R-R	5-11	185	3-3-92	1	1	3.00	13	0	0	2	27	26	9	9	3	5	27	.250	.278	.235	9.00	1.67
Masek, Trey	R-R	6-0	175	1-9-92	0	0	9.82	2	0	0	0	4	6	4	4	0	4	5	.353	.200	.417	12.27	9.82
McNeil, Ryan	R-R	6-3	210	2-1-94	0	5	8.44	8	0	0	0	16	20	16	15	6	10	12	.308	.333	.298	6.75	5.63
Morel, Yomar	R-R	6-1	180	11-18-93	1	0	6.10	11	0	0	0	21	32	15	14	5	2	12	.356	.355	.356	5.23	0.87
Norwood, James	R-R	6-2	205	12-24-93	0	2	7.00	8	4	0	0	18	16	14	14	3	7	18	.239	.261	.227	9.00	3.50
Null, Jeremy	R-R	6-7	200	9-27-93	2	0	1.29	5	1	0	0	14	12	2	2	0	2	11	.231	.294	.200	7.07	1.29
Rakkar, Jasvir	R-R	6-2	200	4-27-91	0	1	7.98	7	0	0	0	15	21	14	13	2	5	17	.328	.353	.319	10.43	3.07
Stinnett, Jake	R-R	6-4	202	4-25-92	0	0	2.84	2	2	0	0	6	3	2	2	1	2	7	.130	.200	.111	9.95	2.84
Thorpe, Tommy	L-L	6-0	185	9-20-92	1	0	3.38	8	0	0	0	19	12	7	7	0	7	21	.185	.136	.209	10.13	3.38
Wang, Yao-Lin	R-R	6-0	180	2-5-91	0	0	0.00	2	0	0	0	3	2	0	0	0	0	5	.182	.000	.333	15.00	0.00
Wells, Ben	R-R	6-3	220	9-10-92	2	2	3.86	6	6	0	0	28	27	15	12	1	15	22	.248	.361	.192	7.07	4.82
Williams, Ryan	R-R	6-4	220	11-1-91	1	1	1.46	9	0	0	1	25	20	7	4	2	3	26	.227	.192	.242	9.49	1.09
Wilson, Sam	L-L	6-2	200	7-30-91	5	1	3.62	16	0	0	3	32	25	14	13	1	12	40	.216	.103	.253	11.13	3.34

Fielding

Catcher	PCT	G	PO	A	E	DP	PB
Canela	1.000	5	31	4	0	0	1
Castillo	1.000	3	30	2	0	0	0
Malave	.976	25	186	16	5	2	3
Marra	.986	30	250	26	4	3	5
Schwarber	.926	2	23	2	2	0	0
Zagunis	.972	15	93	11	3	0	3

First Base	PCT	G	PO	A	E	DP
Bote	1.000	3	3	1	0	1
Canela	.984	56	471	31	8	46
Malave	.982	6	53	2	1	4
Tomasovich	1.000	18	151	12	0	15

Second Base	PCT	G	PO	A	E	DP
Blair	.917	10	22	22	4	6
Bote	.962	23	42	60	4	19
Cuevas	1.000	4	4	10	0	3

	PCT	G	PO	A	E	DP
Flete	.976	6	16	24	1	5
Lockhart	1.000	3	3	4	0	2
Papaccio	1.000	1	2	2	0	1
Tomasovich	.891	10	16	25	5	6
Vosler	.976	12	12	29	1	5
Young	.985	13	25	42	1	7

Third Base	PCT	G	PO	A	E	DP
Bote	1.000	2	0	4	0	0
Brown	1.000	1	0	1	0	0
Cuevas	—	1	0	0	0	0
Hodges	.930	72	46	141	14	13
Tomasovich	.667	3	1	5	3	1
Vosler	1.000	2	2	3	0	1

Shortstop	PCT	G	PO	A	E	DP
Bote	1.000	1	2	2	0	1
Cuevas	.857	6	7	11	3	2

	PCT	G	PO	A	E	DP
Flete	.927	30	43	123	13	21
Papaccio	.952	22	18	61	4	13
Tomasovich	1.000	1	2	2	0	0
Torres	.881	7	10	27	5	6
Vosler	.903	12	17	39	6	6
Young	.857	2	0	6	1	0

Outfield	PCT	G	PO	A	E	DP
Baez	.971	37	61	6	2	2
Bote	.909	8	10	0	1	0
Brown	.949	28	35	2	2	0
Burks	1.000	36	58	2	0	1
Crawford	.988	70	162	3	2	1
Graves	1.000	11	19	0	0	0
Schwarber	1.000	2	3	0	0	0
White	1.000	30	29	2	0	1
Zagunis	.909	14	20	0	2	0
Zapata	.900	7	9	0	1	0

AZL CUBS   ROOKIE

ARIZONA LEAGUE

Batting	B-T	HT	WT	DOB	AVG	vLH	vRH	G	AB	R	H	2B	3B	HR	RBI	BB	HBP	SH	SF	SO	SB	CS	SLG	OBP
Alamo, Tyler	R-R	6-4	200	5-2-95	.215	.313	.195	31	93	12	20	2	0	0	10	4	3	1	1	18	0	0	.237	.267
Alcala, Roney	R-R	6-1	223	2-15-94	.242	.300	.223	38	124	19	30	6	1	2	10	7	3	0	2	29	2	0	.355	.294
Balaguert, Yasiel	R-R	6-2	215	1-9-93	.250	.333	.222	3	12	1	3	0	2	0	0	1	0	0	0	1	0	0	.583	.308
Bonifacio, Emilio	B-R	5-11	205	4-23-85	.300	—	.300	3	10	1	3	0	0	0	0	1	0	0	0	2	1	0	.300	.364
Burks, Charcer	R-R	6-0	170	3-9-95	.308	.375	.298	20	65	14	20	4	1	1	10	3	1	0	1	20	9	1	.446	.343
Calero, Arnaldo	R-R	6-1	185	11-16-93	.182	.000	.286	5	11	1	2	0	0	0	2	1	0	0	0	7	0	0	.182	.250
Castillo, Erick	B-R	5-11	180	2-25-93	.264	.385	.225	17	53	3	14	4	0	0	2	3	1	0	0	5	0	0	.340	.316
Cuevas, Varonex	B-R	6-0	165	7-24-92	.318	.318	.318	26	88	12	28	4	3	1	6	7	0	0	0	16	3	2	.466	.368
Ely, Andrew	L-R	5-10	180	1-23-93	.326	.250	.343	25	86	11	28	4	1	4	7	3	2	0	0	16	1	2	.535	.363
Flete, Bryant	B-R	5-10	146	1-31-93	.315	.400	.295	19	54	10	17	2	0	0	7	6	1	1	0	9	3	0	.352	.393
Graves, Calvin	R-R	5-9	170	3-18-91	.313	.250	.333	15	32	4	10	2	0	0	3	2	1	0	1	3	4	1	.375	.361
Jimenez, Eloy	R-R	6-4	205	11-27-96	.227	.167	.242	42	150	13	34	8	2	3	27	10	0	0	4	32	3	1	.367	.268
Marcano, Ricardo	L-R	6-2	190	10-18-94	.265	.212	.279	43	155	23	41	10	0	2	14	7	2	2	2	37	5	1	.368	.301
Martarano, Joe	R-R	6-4	235	7-28-94	.154	.000	.167	4	13	2	2	0	0	0	1	0	0	0	0	6	0	0	.154	.214
Mineo, Alberto	L-R	5-10	170	7-23-94	.241	.192	.252	43	137	12	33	8	1	1	24	27	2	0	3	36	0	2	.336	.367
Mitchell, Kevonte	R-R	6-4	185	8-12-95	.294	.310	.289	39	143	30	42	3	4	0	12	14	5	0	1	32	19	1	.371	.374
Ortiz, Dalfis	B-R	5-10	160	2-10-92	.111	.000	.167	5	9	1	1	0	0	0	3	0	0	0	4	2	0	0	.111	.333
Paula, Adonis	R-R	6-1	185	6-21-94	.228	.172	.242	47	149	14	34	7	1	1	15	10	2	1	1	47	1	1	.309	.284
Pearson, Tyler	R-R	6-0	185	4-15-92	.235	.417	.179	21	51	9	12	2	1	2	6	2	5	0	1	16	1	2	.431	.322
Silva, Rubi	L-R	5-11	180	6-25-89	.385	.500	.455	3	13	2	5	1	0	0	2	1	0	0	0	4	1	0	.462	.429
Soler, Jorge	R-R	6-4	215	2-25-92	.400	1.000	.348	8	25	7	10	3	0	1	6	4	1	0	0	7	0	0	.640	.500
Son, Ho-young	R-R	5-11	170	8-23-94	.254	.091	.283	25	71	12	18	2	1	0	9	7	0	0	0	11	12	3	.310	.321
Torrealba, Yorvit	R-R	5-11	200	7-19-78	.385	.500	.273	4	13	3	4	3	0	0	0	0	0	0	0	2	0	0	.538	.308
Torres, Gleyber	R-R	6-1	175	12-13-96	.279	.391	.260	43	154	33	43	6	3	1	29	25	0	0	4	33	8	7	.377	.372
Ubiera, Shamil	R-R	6-0	190	9-28-92	.206	.280	.183	34	107	9	22	7	0	1	14	5	3	0	1	14	7	3	.299	.259
Vargas, Eufran	R-R	5-11	178	7-14-94	.200	.333	.143	3	10	2	2	1	0	0	3	0	0	0	0	4	0	0	.300	.200
Young, Chesny	R-R	6-1	180	10-16-92	.167	—	.167	2	6	0	1	0	0	0	1	1	0	0	0	2	0	0	.167	.286
Zagunis, Mark	R-R	6-0	205	2-5-93	.125	.000	.143	8	8	1	1	1	0	0	1	1	0	0	0	2	0	0	.250	.222

Pitching	B-T	HT	WT	DOB	W	L	ERA	G	GS	CG	SV	IP	H	R	ER	HR	BB	SO	AVG	vLH	vRH	K/9	BB/9
Alzolay, Adbert	R-R	6-0	179	3-1-95	2	5	8.51	9	3	0	0	24	31	28	23	3	11	26	.298	.300	.297	9.62	4.07

Name	B-T	HT	WT	DOB	W	L	ERA	G	GS	CG	SV	IP	H	R	ER	HR	BB	SO	AVG	vLH	vRH	K/9	BB/9
Araujo, Pedro	R-R	6-3	214	7-2-93	0	0	2.76	10	0	0	1	16	12	6	5	1	8	27	.197	.095	.250	14.88	4.41
Arias, Jose	R-R	6-6	235	1-17-91	0	0	6.75	2	0	0	0	3	4	2	2	0	0	3	.308	.333	.300	10.13	0.00
Brink, Jordan	L-R	6-0	200	3-18-93	0	1	13.50	2	0	0	0	3	5	4	4	1	2	3	.385	.250	.444	10.13	6.75
Carreno, Marcelo	R-R	6-1	170	6-26-91	0	1	4.76	3	3	0	0	6	6	3	3	1	4	4	.261	.333	.214	6.35	6.35
Castillo, Jesus	R-R	6-2	165	8-27-95	1	0	2.67	11	4	0	0	30	28	12	9	0	16	23	.252	.320	.197	6.82	4.75
Concepcion, Gerardo	L-L	6-2	180	2-29-92	0	0	6.75	2	0	0	0	3	1	2	2	0	2	3	.100	—	.100	10.13	6.75
Diaz, Alberto	L-L	5-9	157	6-12-91	0	0	3.00	3	0	0	0	6	2	5	2	0	7	2	.105	.000	.143	3.00	10.50
Diaz, Andin	L-L	6-0	182	9-2-92	2	2	3.60	15	0	0	0	25	25	14	10	0	10	25	.263	.185	.294	9.00	3.60
Edwards, C.J.	R-R	6-2	155	9-3-91	0	0	1.59	2	2	0	0	6	2	1	1	0	4	8	.111	.083	.167	12.71	6.35
Frazier, Scott	R-R	6-7	215	12-3-91	0	1	36.00	2	1	0	0	1	0	8	4	0	8	2	.000	—	.000	18.00	72.00
Fujikawa, Kyuji	L-R	6-0	190	7-21-80	0	0	0.00	4	2	0	0	4	1	0	0	0	1	5	.071	.000	.125	11.25	2.25
Griggs, Tanner	R-R	6-2	165	6-14-94	1	1	3.45	9	0	0	0	16	17	7	6	0	4	11	.274	.321	.235	6.32	2.30
Hedges, Zach	R-R	6-4	195	10-21-92	2	1	1.37	12	0	0	0	20	18	6	3	0	2	23	.237	.231	.240	10.53	0.92
Hernandez, Luis	R-R	6-5	210	3-13-95	1	1	5.11	8	3	0	0	25	27	18	14	4	8	24	.276	.235	.297	8.76	2.92
Knighton, John Michael	R-R	6-2	190	4-30-94	0	1	3.38	5	1	0	0	8	10	5	3	2	1	5	.313	.222	.348	5.63	1.13
Llano, Carlos	R-R	6-0	185	2-28-92	0	2	5.79	4	0	0	1	5	8	4	3	0	3	5	.381	.429	.357	9.64	5.79
Maples, Dillon	R-R	6-2	195	5-9-92	0	2	3.48	4	4	0	0	10	6	4	4	0	6	10	.167	.091	.200	8.71	5.23
Markey, Brad	R-R	5-11	185	3-3-92	0	0	4.50	2	0	0	0	2	2	1	1	0	0	2	.286	.667	.000	9.00	0.00
Mejia, Jefferson	R-R	6-7	195	8-2-94	2	4	2.48	12	2	0	0	40	30	25	11	1	17	45	.204	.233	.192	10.13	3.83
Minch, Jordan	L-L	6-3	180	7-16-93	0	0	3.38	7	0	0	2	11	11	6	4	2	1	14	.250	.250	.250	11.81	0.84
Morel, Yomar	R-R	6-1	180	11-18-93	1	0	0.00	7	0	0	3	11	5	2	0	0	1	10	.128	.167	.095	8.44	0.84
Norwood, James	R-R	6-2	205	12-24-93	0	0	13.50	2	0	0	0	2	4	3	3	0	1	2	.500	.333	.600	9.00	4.50
Null, Jeremy	R-R	6-7	200	9-27-93	0	0	9.00	2	0	0	0	2	3	2	2	0	0	2	.375	.333	.400	9.00	0.00
Paulino, Jose	L-L	6-2	165	4-9-95	3	4	5.98	12	7	0	0	47	55	41	31	3	20	42	.294	.298	.293	8.10	3.86
Perez, Hector	R-R	6-1	157	6-25-93	0	1	4.41	11	0	0	1	16	14	15	8	0	11	24	.215	.250	.189	13.22	6.06
Pineyro, Ivan	R-R	6-1	200	9-29-91	0	2	5.56	4	4	0	0	11	15	9	7	1	2	9	.319	.231	.353	7.15	1.59
Pugliese, James	R-R	6-3	195	8-12-92	0	0	0.00	2	0	0	1	3	0	0	0	0	0	5	.000	.000	.000	15.00	0.00
Ramirez, Neil	R-R	6-4	190	5-25-89	0	0	6.75	2	0	0	0	1	2	2	1	0	2	2	.286	.333	.250	13.50	13.50
Salazar, Victor	R-R	6-3	178	1-21-93	0	0	0.00	4	0	0	0	3	0	1	0	0	0	3	.000	.000	.000	9.00	0.00
Sands, Carson	L-L	6-3	195	3-28-95	3	1	1.89	9	4	0	0	19	15	7	4	0	7	20	.221	.133	.245	9.47	3.32
Santana, Alex	R-R	6-1	150	10-23-93	3	2	2.55	11	5	0	0	42	36	15	12	1	14	36	.231	.237	.227	7.65	2.98
Schlitter, Brian	R-R	6-5	235	12-21-85	0	0	0.00	1	0	0	0	1	0	0	0	0	0	0	.000	—	.000	0.00	0.00
Steele, Justin	L-L	6-1	180	7-11-95	0	0	2.89	9	4	0	0	19	15	6	6	0	8	25	.217	.176	.231	12.05	3.86
Stinnett, Jake	R-R	6-4	202	4-25-92	0	1	7.71	3	2	0	0	5	9	4	4	0	3	3	.409	.455	.364	5.79	0.00
Thorpe, Tommy	L-L	6-0	185	9-20-92	0	0	0.00	2	0	0	0	2	1	0	0	0	2	1	.125	.000	.143	9.00	0.00
Williams, Ryan	R-R	6-4	220	11-1-91	1	0	0.00	2	0	0	0	2	1	0	0	0	0	3	.143	.333	.000	13.50	0.00
Willis, Austyn	R-R	6-6	205	6-13-96	0	1	4.20	10	2	0	0	15	13	11	7	0	7	9	.228	.105	.289	5.40	4.20
Wilson, Sam	L-L	6-2	200	7-30-91	0	0	6.00	2	0	0	0	3	3	3	2	0	1	0	.300	.250	.333	0.00	3.00

Fielding

Catcher	PCT	G	PO	A	E	DP	PB
Alamo	.991	14	102	14	1	0	6
Castillo	.986	17	124	22	2	4	2
Graves	1.000	1	1	0	0	0	0
Mineo	.986	9	56	14	1	0	4
Pearson	.970	19	111	20	4	1	3
Torrealba	1.000	4	24	1	0	0	0
Vargas	1.000	3	15	2	0	0	1
Zagunis	.875	1	7	0	1	0	0

First Base	PCT	G	PO	A	E	DP
Alamo	.952	10	68	11	4	8
Alcala	.982	32	259	15	5	26
Marcano	1.000	2	23	0	0	0
Martarano	.905	2	18	1	2	3
Mineo	.977	15	119	11	3	9

Second Base	PCT	G	PO	A	E	DP
Alcala	1.000	4	3	16	0	4

	PCT	G	PO	A	E	DP
Bonifacio	1.000	1	0	2	0	0
Cuevas	.941	6	4	12	1	2
Ely	.974	24	48	63	3	13
Flete	.917	11	15	29	4	9
Ortiz	.833	2	4	6	2	3
Son	.900	14	24	30	6	7
Young	1.000	2	6	3	0	1

Third Base	PCT	G	PO	A	E	DP
Alcala	.800	1	0	4	1	0
Cuevas	.875	10	3	18	3	2
Flete	1.000	1	1	1	0	0
Martarano	.800	2	3	5	2	0
Ortiz	1.000	2	0	3	0	1
Paula	.883	47	20	86	14	8
Pearson	.500	1	0	1	1	0

Shortstop	PCT	G	PO	A	E	DP
Cuevas	.952	6	6	14	1	6

	PCT	G	PO	A	E	DP
Flete	.929	3	6	7	1	2
Son	.828	7	9	15	5	4
Torres	.931	43	64	125	14	25

Outfield	PCT	G	PO	A	E	DP
Alcala	1.000	1	1	0	0	0
Balaguert	1.000	2	1	1	0	0
Bonifacio	1.000	1	1	0	0	0
Burks	.969	20	31	0	1	0
Calero	.667	4	2	0	1	0
Cuevas	1.000	6	6	0	0	0
Flete	—	1	0	0	0	0
Graves	1.000	11	15	0	0	0
Jimenez	.974	24	36	1	1	0
Marcano	.909	41	34	6	4	1
Mitchell	.965	34	54	1	2	1
Silva	1.000	2	3	0	0	0
Soler	.833	6	4	1	1	0
Ubiera	.870	29	38	2	6	0

DSL CUBS1   ROOKIE

DOMINICAN SUMMER LEAGUE

Batting	B-T	HT	WT	DOB	AVG	vLH	vRH	G	AB	R	H	2B	3B	HR	RBI	BB	HBP	SH	SF	SO	SB	CS	SLG	OBP
Acosta, Luis	R-R	6-2	195	11-28-94	.186	.000	.242	13	43	10	8	2	0	1	8	9	0	0	1	12	3	2	.302	.321
Caro, Roberto	B-R	6-0	185	9-25-93	.289	.225	.301	66	246	66	71	6	15	3	37	48	8	5	3	47	35	7	.472	.416
Delarosa, Frandy	B-R	6-1	180	1-24-96	.281	.195	.298	61	249	38	70	19	4	1	50	19	4	1	5	39	12	5	.402	.336
Emeterio, Jenner	R-R	6-1	170	3-19-93	.309	.133	.345	56	178	38	55	11	3	0	32	44	5	3	3	31	24	10	.404	.452
Garcia, Robert	B-R	5-10	170	12-6-93	.316	.333	.312	52	171	37	54	5	3	1	25	12	12	5	1	32	24	5	.398	.398
Gonzalez, Antonio	B-R	5-10	170	1-27-94	.250	.133	.310	18	44	12	11	4	1	0	6	10	0	2	1	16	5	2	.386	.382
Gonzalez, Erick	R-R	5-10	175	9-2-96	.254	.167	.277	19	59	3	15	2	0	1	11	3	1	2	1	14	2	0	.322	.297
Hodwalker, Martin	B-R	5-11	180	4-1-95	.094	.167	.077	17	32	4	3	0	0	0	2	0	1	0	10	2	1	.094	.147
Jimenez, Carlos	R-R	5-10	175	7-3-93	.301	.394	.284	57	216	41	65	14	3	3	33	19	8	2	2	13	21	6	.435	.376
Matos, Manuel	R-R	6-0	175	10-6-96	.289	.318	.285	53	194	36	56	9	4	6	39	26	3	0	2	47	7	2	.469	.378
Nunez, Richard	R-R	5-10	170	3-14-95	.175	.083	.200	21	57	5	10	4	0	0	4	6	0	0	0	23	0	0	.246	.288
Paniagua, Jose	R-R	6-2	180	6-7-94	.305	.265	.312	67	233	44	71	22	4	6	40	35	2	2	3	56	20	4	.511	.396

Name	B-T	HT	WT	DOB	AVG	vLH	vRH	G	AB	R	H	2B	3B	HR	RBI	BB	HBP	SH	SF	SO	SB	CS	SLG	OBP
Pena, Jhonny	R-R	6-0	190	5-24-92	.220	.250	.217	22	50	1	11	2	0	0	8	10	2	0	0	12	0	0	.260	.371
Ramirez, Carlos	R-L	5-9	185	5-27-92	.273	.286	.267	10	22	3	6	0	0	2	5	5	0	0	0	1	1	0	.545	.407
Ruiz, Miguel	B-R	6-1	170	11-5-96	.237	.059	.276	57	186	33	44	3	6	0	28	34	4	1	1	47	7	8	.317	.364
Tineo, Franklin	R-R	6-1	176	12-30-94	.213	.182	.220	56	160	28	34	9	1	0	15	23	2	1	1	45	6	7	.281	.317
Ubiera, Luis	R-R	6-2	170	9-17-96	.207	.273	.197	30	82	18	17	3	0	0	7	18	3	1	0	26	3	4	.244	.369
Valerio, Antonio	R-R	6-0	190	3-21-91	.256	.250	.258	38	117	15	30	4	0	1	13	12	3	0	2	12	3	0	.316	.336

Pitching

Name	B-T	HT	WT	DOB	W	L	ERA	G	GS	CG	SV	IP	H	R	ER	HR	BB	SO	AVG	vLH	vRH	K/9	BB/9
Aquino, Assael	R-R	6-3	180	7-16-92	1	1	2.11	18	0	0	3	43	31	19	10	1	30	39	.208	.136	.238	8.23	6.33
Araujo, Pedro	R-R	6-3	214	7-2-93	2	1	1.35	4	3	0	0	20	17	3	3	0	6	14	.230	.194	.256	6.30	2.70
De La Cruz, Oscar	R-R	6-4	200	3-4-95	8	1	1.80	14	14	0	0	75	56	24	15	2	19	64	.199	.165	.219	7.68	2.28
Diaz, Andin	L-L	6-0	182	9-2-92	3	1	1.21	4	3	0	0	22	14	5	3	0	9	18	.179	.063	.210	7.25	3.63
Escanio, Luiz	R-R	6-5	190	7-31-92	0	2	5.47	15	0	0	7	25	26	20	15	0	13	31	.271	.244	.291	11.31	4.74
Hernandez, Jeffry	R-R	6-5	215	1-19-95	2	2	7.77	16	0	0	1	22	26	21	19	0	11	15	.302	.351	.265	6.14	4.50
Marte, Junior	R-R	6-0	170	6-6-95	2	2	3.52	14	6	0	0	31	24	19	12	0	25	27	.220	.341	.138	7.92	7.34
Morel, Jose	L-R	6-6	204	11-13-94	5	1	3.16	14	13	0	0	63	55	31	22	0	21	57	.233	.243	.229	8.19	3.02
Moreno, Erling	R-R	6-3	200	1-13-97	0	1	1.08	4	4	0	0	8	6	2	1	0	3	6	.194	.286	.118	6.48	3.24
Perez, Jesus	L-L	6-1	160	10-20-95	0	0	216.00	1	0	0	0	0	5	8	8	0	3	0	.833	—	.833	0.00	81.00
Pieters, Chris	L-L	6-3	185	9-21-94	1	0	9.56	15	1	0	0	16	22	21	17	1	25	15	.328	.267	.346	8.44	14.06
Ramirez, Moises	R-R	6-0	160	12-11-95	0	1	13.50	1	0	0	0	2	6	4	3	0	1	2	.500	.750	.375	9.00	4.50
Rodriguez, Santiago	R-R	6-0	185	6-14-94	8	1	1.67	17	11	0	1	81	68	20	15	2	13	71	.225	.223	.227	7.89	1.44
Rondon, Andri	R-R	6-2	190	9-16-95	3	3	4.33	12	6	0	0	44	44	29	21	1	22	30	.270	.154	.306	6.18	4.53
Rosario, Aneuris	R-R	6-0	165	3-4-95	1	5	3.79	24	0	0	4	40	49	25	17	2	19	34	.308	.222	.352	7.59	4.24
Silverio, Pedro	R-R	6-2	210	6-29-94	4	2	2.61	16	8	0	1	69	53	25	20	0	20	50	.212	.255	.182	6.52	2.61
Torres, Deibi	R-R	6-3	190	12-8-94	1	3	4.83	13	1	0	3	32	39	23	17	1	15	23	.300	.340	.277	6.54	4.26
Vasquez, Dilson	R-R	6-3	200	2-7-92	1	1	9.70	16	0	0	1	21	24	28	23	1	31	24	.276	.429	.203	10.13	13.08

Fielding

Catcher	PCT	G	PO	A	E	DP	PB
Gonzalez	.993	19	131	20	1	1	4
Hodwalker	1.000	12	53	3	0	1	1
Matos	.966	36	220	39	9	0	12
Nunez	1.000	6	23	2	0	0	2
Pena	1.000	1	10	1	0	0	0
Ramirez	.970	5	28	4	1	0	1
Valerio	.981	12	43	10	1	2	0

First Base	PCT	G	PO	A	E	DP
Acosta	.778	1	7	0	2	1
Garcia	1.000	1	1	1	0	0
Matos	.981	10	49	3	1	5
Nunez	1.000	5	19	1	0	1
Paniagua	.986	47	337	18	5	24
Pena	1.000	10	66	2	0	8
Ramirez	1.000	4	24	1	0	2
Tineo	1.000	3	11	1	0	1

	PCT	G	PO	A	E	DP
Valerio	.975	10	73	6	2	2

Second Base	PCT	G	PO	A	E	DP
Delarosa	.958	16	39	30	3	6
Emeterio	.889	3	5	3	1	1
Gonzalez	.963	5	10	16	1	3
Jimenez	1.000	6	6	11	0	2
Matos	—	1	0	0	0	0
Ruiz	.980	15	24	26	1	5
Tineo	.962	32	57	70	5	17

Third Base	PCT	G	PO	A	E	DP
Emeterio	.889	7	1	7	1	1
Gonzalez	.833	5	4	6	2	0
Jimenez	.963	9	6	20	1	4
Matos	1.000	2	2	4	0	1
Nunez	.857	2	0	6	1	0
Paniagua	.714	3	3	2	2	0
Ruiz	.935	34	27	60	6	3

	PCT	G	PO	A	E	DP
Tineo	.769	6	0	10	3	1
Valerio	.943	17	19	31	3	3

Shortstop	PCT	G	PO	A	E	DP
Delarosa	.892	15	22	36	7	6
Gonzalez	.909	6	4	16	2	2
Jimenez	.922	44	58	120	15	14
Ruiz	.912	12	11	20	3	5
Tineo	.750	5	4	5	3	2

Outfield	PCT	G	PO	A	E	DP
Acosta	1.000	10	14	1	0	0
Caro	.983	65	166	4	3	0
Emeterio	.990	51	90	7	1	2
Garcia	.934	49	92	7	7	1
Matos	1.000	1	1	0	0	0
Paniagua	.963	27	24	2	1	1
Ubiera	.897	27	26	0	3	0

VSL CUBS   ROOKIE

VENEZUELAN SUMMER LEAGUE

Batting	B-T	HT	WT	DOB	AVG	vLH	vRH	G	AB	R	H	2B	3B	HR	RBI	BB	HBP	SH	SF	SO	SB	CS	SLG	OBP
Ayala, Luis	R-L	6-0	176	12-21-95	.209	.152	.223	53	163	23	34	0	2	0	14	21	4	0	5	55	14	8	.233	.306
Colasante, Moises	R-R	5-9	176	9-19-94	.205	.455	.121	17	44	4	9	2	0	0	2	4	0	0	0	16	2	0	.250	.271
Galindo, Wladimir	R-R	6-3	210	11-6-96	.278	.366	.250	62	223	29	62	18	1	7	30	20	7	0	0	55	3	2	.462	.356
Garcia, Humberto	B-R	5-10	165	5-20-94	.275	.273	.276	56	160	22	44	8	5	0	18	17	2	3	1	31	20	9	.388	.350
Gomez, Victor	R-R	6-2	180	5-25-95	.182	.000	.216	27	88	11	16	1	2	0	2	6	3	1	0	21	2	3	.239	.258
Gonzalez, Jesus	R-R	5-10	145	12-10-95	.224	.154	.236	39	85	13	19	3	0	0	4	5	1	2	0	26	2	3	.259	.275
Gonzalez, Jose	R-R	6-1	160	1-12-96	.232	.231	.232	64	259	31	60	4	2	0	24	19	4	1	1	34	12	6	.263	.293
Gonzalez, Leonardo	R-R	6-1	178	2-17-95	.152	.125	.155	31	79	10	12	2	0	0	6	4	2	2	1	19	3	1	.177	.209
Gutierrez, Danny	R-R	5-7	152	3-1-91	.285	.241	.298	36	123	12	35	8	0	0	12	8	6	0	1	20	7	7	.350	.355
Hidalgo, Luis	R-R	6-1	160		.318	.320	.317	46	151	22	48	8	0	3	19	9	4	0	1	13	9	5	.430	.370
Matos, Fidel	R-R	6-0	200	2-6-95	.250	.167	.269	34	96	8	24	4	0	1	9	8	1	0	0	27	4	2	.323	.314
Monasterio, Andrews	B-R	6-0	175	5-30-97	.292	.269	.297	36	137	28	40	5	1	0	9	15	2	1	1	19	14	1	.343	.368
Pedra, Henrry	R-R	5-11	175	4-26-94	.254	.222	.260	46	118	20	30	3	1	0	10	9	2	4	0	29	9	3	.297	.318
Pereda, Jhonny	R-R	6-1	170	4-18-96	.228	.250	.223	63	215	24	49	6	1	1	14	23	4	1	0	16	1	4	.279	.314
Rico, Miguel	R-R	6-2	204	9-15-93	.252	.175	.269	64	222	29	56	12	0	5	33	28	12	0	3	24	1	2	.374	.362
Vahlis, Roberto	R-R	5-10	190	11-19-93	.216	.143	.236	53	134	13	29	5	0	2	14	24	4	3	2	19	2	3	.299	.348

Pitching	B-T	HT	WT	DOB	W	L	ERA	G	GS	CG	SV	IP	H	R	ER	HR	BB	SO	AVG	vLH	vRH	K/9	BB/9
Arias, Jesus	R-R	6-1	185	9-29-93	2	1	4.02	22	1	0	5	40	40	26	18	1	27	39	.261	.275	8.70	6.02	
Bermudez, Harrinson	R-R	6-4	190	3-6-95	1	5	5.47	13	12	0	0	51	57	41	31	1	20	24	.279	.217	.311	4.24	3.53
Colorado, Alejandro	R-R	6-1	170	6-22-96	0	0	1.80	2	0	0	0	5	5	1	1	0	2	2	.294	.500	.182	3.60	3.60
De Los Rios, Enrique	R-R	6-1	175	5-2-95	2	5	3.76	14	14	0	0	67	74	33	28	4	9	42	.278	.280	.277	5.64	1.21
Gomez, Yapson	L-L	5-10	160	10-2-93	6	2	1.51	13	12	1	0	71	50	19	12	0	8	37	.193	.114	.209	4.67	1.01
Jerez, Salvador	R-R	6-4	205	3-28-93	2	2	4.63	13	0	0	0	23	19	19	12	2	15	12	.216	.200	.224	4.63	5.79
Leidenz, Jose	R-R	6-1	171	10-16-94	3	3	3.28	20	0	0	2	36	24	18	13	1	15	22	.183	.128	.207	5.55	3.79

Lima, Gabriel	R-R	6-2	180	5-2-96	0	2	4.03	9	7	0	0	29	24	16	13	0	11	24	.218	.231	.211	7.45	3.41
Lovera, Yeiker	R-R	6-0	175	1-23-93	0	1	2.92	6	0	0	1	12	19	7	4	0	2	11	.358	.294	.389	8.03	1.46
Medina, Ivan	R-R	6-3	162	2-26-96	0	1	9.75	9	0	0	0	12	25	19	13	1	5	7	.424	.412	.429	5.25	3.75
Mejias, Angel	L-L	6-3	180	10-30-93	1	2	3.28	16	1	0	0	36	51	18	13	0	13	28	.331	.286	.341	7.07	3.28
Moreno, Erling	R-R	6-3	200	1-13-97	0	0	0.00	1	0	0	0	3	4	0	0	0	0	3	.400	.250	.500	9.00	0.00
Pacheco, Alex	L-L	6-3	184	9-20-94	1	1	3.38	16	0	0	0	19	17	10	7	0	16	11	.254	.308	.241	5.30	7.71
Palma, Eugenio	L-L	5-11	170	11-26-96	1	1	1.69	12	0	0	0	21	14	4	4	0	3	18	.175	.235	.159	7.59	1.27
Pieters, Chris	L-L	6-3	185	9-21-94	0	1	18.00	3	0	0	0	4	9	8	8	0	5	3	.450	.667	.357	6.75	11.25
Ramirez, Moises	R-R	6-0	160	12-11-95	2	2	5.06	6	5	0	0	21	26	13	12	2	4	11	.310	.261	.328	4.64	1.69
Rengifo, Juan	R-R	6-3	206	6-12-94	1	1	3.38	9	0	0	1	13	13	5	5	0	3	14	.271	.375	.219	9.45	2.03
Rodriguez, Carlos A.	L-L	5-11	178	7-18-95	0	3	1.23	12	10	0	0	58	53	19	8	1	5	56	.236	.216	.241	8.64	0.77
Sanchez, Julio	R-R	5-11	165	9-28-91	5	2	3.53	20	0	0	1	36	31	24	14	3	24	25	.240	.167	.276	6.31	6.06
Valera, Ramon	R-R	6-2	180	9-27-94	0	1	16.50	6	0	0	1	6	9	18	11	0	13	3	.281	.357	.222	4.50	19.50
Vides, Mauro	R-R	6-2	207	10-19-95	1	3	2.73	13	6	0	0	33	34	19	10	0	12	16	.258	.173	.313	4.36	3.27

Fielding

Catcher	PCT	G	PO	A	E	DP	PB
Gonzalez	.951	11	33	6	2	0	3
Hidalgo	1.000	1	5	0	0	0	0
Pereda	.982	53	267	59	6	2	8
Vahlis	.982	18	91	19	2	0	4

First Base	PCT	G	PO	A	E	DP
Galindo	.980	11	91	8	2	7
Gonzalez	.991	13	108	0	1	6
Hidalgo	1.000	1	5	2	0	0
Matos	1.000	9	57	3	0	5
Pedra	1.000	1	1	0	0	0
Pereda	1.000	7	54	3	0	4
Rico	.983	35	278	10	5	19
Vahlis	.971	5	31	2	1	1

Second Base	PCT	G	PO	A	E	DP
Garcia	.882	4	5	10	2	2
Gonzalez	.892	32	42	57	12	6
Gutierrez	.923	21	37	47	7	9
Pedra	.948	29	44	65	6	7

Third Base	PCT	G	PO	A	E	DP
Galindo	.857	46	45	93	23	7
Garcia	1.000	1	0	2	0	0
Gutierrez	1.000	1	0	2	0	0
Matos	.750	2	1	2	1	0
Pedra	1.000	1	1	1	0	0
Rico	.838	23	17	45	12	0

Shortstop	PCT	G	PO	A	E	DP
Garcia	.839	22	47	52	19	17
Gonzalez	.800	1	2	2	1	0
Gutierrez	.903	7	9	19	3	4
Monasterio	.935	35	49	108	11	13
Pedra	.854	8	18	17	6	4

Outfield	PCT	G	PO	A	E	DP
Ayala	.936	50	93	10	7	2
Colasante	1.000	16	29	4	0	0
Galindo	—	1	0	0	0	0
Garcia	.971	29	63	4	2	1
Gomez	.900	27	61	2	7	0
Gonzalez	.966	51	131	10	5	0
Gonzalez	1.000	2	1	0	0	0
Gutierrez	.800	10	11	1	3	0
Hidalgo	.976	31	37	3	1	0
Jerez	1.000	1	1	0	0	0
Matos	1.000	14	21	1	0	0
Pedra	—	1	0	0	0	0
Rico	1.000	1	1	0	0	0

CHICAGO CUBS

Chicago White Sox

SEASON IN A SENTENCE: In Paul Konerko's farewell season, Cuban rookie Jose Abreu proved a worthy replacement, while ace Chris Sale continued to do his thing, helping the White Sox improve by 10 games over their 2014 results. But poor pitching, both in the rotation and in the bullpen, doomed the White Sox to another losing season.

HIGH POINT: As late as June 11, the White Sox were realistically in the race. They reached the .500 mark by throttling the Tigers 8-2 at home, chasing Justin Verlander in the sixth and getting seven strong innings from John Danks while Abreu homered and drove in his 50th run. But the South Siders lost 11 of their next 14 games, and a July rally couldn't keep the Sox from falling out of the race.

LOW POINT: August was a 9-19 slog that saw the White Sox trade regulars such as Gordon Beckham, Alejandro de Aza and Adam Dunn to contenders. A 16–0 loss to the Rangers on Aug. 5 presaged the drudgery of August, as Colby Lewis shut out the White Sox while Dunn mopped up by pitching the bottom of the eighth.

NOTABLE ROOKIES: Abreu was BA's Rookie of the Year, but most other rookies faltered for the Sox. Marcus Semien had his moments, hitting .234/.300/.372, and Rule 5 pick Adrian Nieto proved a capable reserve catcher. But righty Erik Johnson, expected to be a key rotation piece, had an awful season, and righthanders Jake Petricka and Daniel Webb were good but not great at the back of the bullpen.

KEY TRANSACTIONS: Signing Abreu for six years and $68 million proved shrewd, and an offseason deal for outfielder Adam Eaton provided a spark, though Addison Reed's absence was felt in the bullpen. Dealing Beckham, De Aza and Dunn brought only one potential prospect, hard-throwing righty Nolan Sanburn.

DOWN ON THE FARM: Picking third overall—their highest pick since taking Harold Baines No. 1 overall in 1977—the White Sox drafted N.C. State lefthander Carlos Rodon, who entered the year as the draft's top prospect. They signed him for a club-record $6,582,000, the largest bonus of any 2015 draftee. He finished the year in Triple-A Charlotte, which led the minors in attendance in its first year in a new, downtown ballpark. No full-season Sox team posted a winning record, and only the Phillies had a worse record for domestic farm clubs.

OPENING DAY PAYROLL: $89,551,982 (20th)

PLAYERS OF THE YEAR

MAJOR LEAGUE

Jose Abreu
1b
.317/.383/.581
36 HR, 107 RBI
Led rookies in HR, RBI

MINOR LEAGUE

Andy Wilkins
1b
(Triple-A)
.293/.338/.558
Led org with 30 HR

ORGANIZATION LEADERS

BATTING *Minimum 250 AB

MAJORS

* AVG	Abreu, Jose	.317
* OPS	Abreu, Jose	.964
HR	Abreu, Jose	36
RBI	Abreu, Jose	107

MINORS

* AVG	Recchia, Mike, Winston-Salem, Birmingham	.223
* OBP	Ravelo, Rangel, Birmingham	.386
* SLG	Wilkins, Andy, Charlotte	.558
R	Thompson, Trayce, Birmingham	86
H	Ravelo, Rangel, Birmingham	147
TB	Wilkins, Andy, Charlotte	274
2B	Coats, Jason, Winston-Salem, Birmingham	38
	Wilkins, Andy, Charlotte	38
3B	Engel, Adam, AZL White Sox, Kannapolis, W-Salem	10
	May, Jacob, Winston-Salem	10
HR	Wilkins, Andy, Charlotte	30
RBI	Wilkins, Andy, Charlotte	85
BB	Mitchell, Andrew, Kannapolis	67
SO	Morris, Jacob, Kannapolis	179
SB	Engel, Adam, AZL White Sox, Kannapolis, W-Salem	39

PITCHING #Minimum 75 IP

MAJORS

W	Sale, Chris	12
# ERA	Sale, Chris	2.17
SO	Sale, Chris	208
SV	Petricka, Jake	14

MINORS

W	Recchia, Mike, Winston-Salem, Birmingham	10
L	Bucciferro, Tony, Winston-Salem, Birmingham	12
L	Jaye, Myles, Winston-Salem, Birmingham	12
ERA	Danish, Tyler, Kannapolis, Winston-Salem	2.08
G	Fuentes, Nelvin, Charlotte, Birmingham	44
	Kussmaul, Ryan, Birmingham, Charlotte	44
	Molina, Nestor, Birmingham	44
GS	Jaye, Myles, Winston-Salem, Birmingham	28
SV	Bengard, Jon, Great Falls	8
	Hardin, Brandon, Birmingham, Winston-Salem	8
IP	Bucciferro, Tony, Winston-Salem, Birmingham	165
BB	Mitchell, Andrew, Kannapolis	67
SO	Recchia, Mike, Winston-Salem, Birmingham	134
AVG	Recchia, Mike, Winston-Salem, Birmingham	.223

CHICAGO WHITE SOX

General Manager: Rick Hahn. **Farm Director:** Nick Capra. **Scouting Director:** Doug Laumann.

Class	Team	League	W	L	PCT	Finish	Manager
Majors	Chicago White Sox	American	73	89	.451	t-22nd (30)	Robin Ventura
Triple-A	Charlotte Knights	International	63	81	.438	14th (14)	Joel Skinner
Double-A	Birmingham Barons	Southern	60	80	.429	t-9th (10)	Julio Vinas
High A	Winston-Salem Dash	Carolina	61	78	.439	8th (8)	Tommy Thompson
Low A	Kannapolis Intimidators	South Atlantic	62	75	.453	8th (14)	Pete Rose Jr.
Rookie	Great Falls Voyagers	Pioneer	39	37	.513	4th (8)	Charles Poe
Rookie	White Sox	Arizona	30	25	.545	t-4th (13)	Mike Gellinger
Overall Minor League Record			315	376	.456	27th (30)	

ORGANIZATION STATISTICS

CHICAGO WHITE SOX
AMERICAN LEAGUE

Batting	B-T	HT	WT	DOB	AVG	vLH	vRH	G	AB	R	H	2B	3B	HR	RBI	BB	HBP	SH	SF	SO	SB	CS	SLG	OBP
Abreu, Jose	R-R	6-3	255	1-29-87	.317	.353	.305	145	556	80	176	35	2	36	107	51	11	0	4	131	3	1	.581	.383
Beckham, Gordon	R-R	6-0	185	9-16-86	.221	.309	.191	101	390	43	86	24	0	7	36	19	5	3	5	70	3	0	.336	.263
2-team total (26 Los Angeles)					.226	—	—	127	446	53	101	27	0	9	44	22	7	3	5	81	3	0	.348	.271
Danks, Jordan	L-R	6-4	215	8-7-86	.222	.150	.237	51	117	14	26	2	0	2	10	14	0	0	1	46	5	3	.291	.303
De Aza, Alejandro	L-L	6-0	195	4-11-84	.243	.105	.276	122	395	45	96	19	5	5	31	33	6	2	3	100	15	7	.354	.309
2-team total (20 Baltimore)					.252	—	—	142	477	56	120	24	8	8	41	39	6	3	3	119	17	10	.386	.314
Dunn, Adam	L-R	6-6	285	11-9-79	.220	.154	.232	106	363	43	80	17	0	20	54	65	3	0	4	132	1	1	.433	.340
2-team total (25 Oakland)					.219	—	—	131	429	49	94	18	0	22	64	71	7	0	4	159	1	1	.415	.337
Eaton, Adam	L-L	5-8	185	12-6-88	.300	.299	.301	123	486	76	146	26	10	1	35	43	5	2	2	83	15	9	.401	.362
Flowers, Tyler	R-R	6-4	245	1-24-86	.241	.255	.236	127	407	42	98	16	1	15	50	25	8	1	1	159	0	1	.396	.297
Garcia, Avisail	R-R	6-4	240	6-12-91	.244	.333	.213	46	172	19	42	8	0	7	29	14	2	0	2	44	4	1	.413	.305
Garcia, Leury	B-R	5-8	170	3-18-91	.166	.161	.169	73	145	13	24	3	0	1	6	5	0	4	1	48	11	1	.207	.192
Gillaspie, Conor	L-R	6-1	195	7-18-87	.282	.221	.300	130	464	50	131	31	5	7	57	36	3	0	3	78	0	4	.416	.336
Konerko, Paul	R-R	6-2	220	3-5-76	.207	.252	.146	81	208	15	43	8	0	5	22	10	4	0	2	51	0	0	.317	.254
Nieto, Adrian	B-R	6-0	200	11-12-89	.236	.273	.226	48	106	8	25	5	0	2	7	8	1	3	0	38	0	1	.340	.296
Phegley, Josh	R-R	5-10	225	2-12-88	.216	.200	.222	11	37	4	8	2	0	3	7	0	0	0	1	11	0	0	.514	.211
Ramirez, Alexei	R-R	6-2	180	9-22-81	.273	.273	.274	158	622	82	170	35	2	15	74	24	6	1	4	81	21	4	.408	.305
Sanchez, Carlos	B-R	5-11	195	6-29-92	.250	.364	.194	28	100	6	25	5	0	0	5	3	0	0	1	25	1	1	.300	.269
Semien, Marcus	R-R	6-1	195	9-17-90	.234	.271	.212	64	231	30	54	10	2	6	28	21	1	2	0	70	3	0	.372	.300
Sierra, Moises	R-R	6-1	220	9-24-88	.276	.276	.275	83	127	20	35	8	2	2	7	7	0	0	1	34	3	1	.417	.311
2-team total (13 Toronto)					.230	—	—	96	161	22	37	8	2	2	9	8	0	0	1	43	3	1	.342	.265
Taylor, Michael	R-R	6-5	255	12-19-85	.250	.231	.267	11	28	3	7	1	0	0	5	0	0	0	0	9	0	0	.286	.364
Viciedo, Dayan	R-R	5-11	240	3-10-89	.231	.221	.235	145	523	65	121	22	3	21	58	32	5	0	3	122	0	1	.405	.281
Wilkins, Andy	L-R	6-1	220	9-13-88	.140	.333	.125	17	43	2	6	2	0	0	2	2	0	0	0	22	0	0	.186	.178

Pitching	B-T	HT	WT	DOB	W	L	ERA	G	GS	CG	SV	IP	H	R	ER	HR	BB	SO	AVG	vLH	vRH	K/9	BB/9
Bassitt, Chris	R-R	6-5	210	2-22-89	1	1	3.94	6	5	0	0	30	34	13	13	0	13	21	.286	.317	.250	6.37	3.94
Belisario, Ronald	R-R	6-3	240	12-31-82	4	8	5.56	62	0	0	8	66	78	46	41	4	18	47	.295	.315	.281	6.38	2.44
Carroll, Scott	R-R	6-4	215	9-24-84	5	10	4.80	26	19	0	0	129	147	81	69	13	45	64	.289	.292	.284	4.45	3.13
Cleto, Maikel	R-R	6-3	250	5-1-89	0	1	4.60	28	0	0	0	29	24	18	15	3	23	32	.214	.170	.254	9.82	7.06
Danks, John	L-L	6-1	210	4-15-85	11	11	4.74	32	32	0	0	194	205	106	102	25	74	129	.269	.275	.275	5.99	3.44
Downs, Scott	L-L	6-2	220	3-17-76	0	2	6.08	38	0	0	1	24	24	17	16	1	15	22	.258	.224	.295	8.37	5.70
2-team total (17 Kansas City)					0	4	4.97	55	0	0	1	38	36	24	21	2	20	25	—	—	—	5.92	4.74
Francisco, Frank	R-R	6-2	250	9-11-79	0	0	12.27	4	0	0	0	4	7	6	5	2	3	5	.368	.400	.333	12.27	7.36
Guerra, Javy	R-R	6-1	190	10-31-85	2	4	2.91	42	0	0	1	46	41	15	15	3	20	38	.246	.217	.280	7.38	3.88
Johnson, Erik	R-R	6-3	230	12-30-89	1	1	6.46	5	5	0	0	24	27	18	17	1	15	18	.297	.342	.264	6.85	5.70
Jones, Nate	R-R	6-5	220	1-28-86	0	0	—	2	0	0	0	0	2	4	4	0	3	0	1.000	1.000	1.000	—	—
Leesman, Charlie	L-L	6-4	215	3-10-87	0	1	20.25	1	1	0	0	3	9	6	6	1	1	0	.600	1.000	.538	0.00	3.38
Lindstrom, Matt	R-R	6-2	215	2-11-80	2	2	5.03	35	0	0	6	34	47	23	19	3	12	18	.338	.303	.381	4.76	3.18
Noesi, Hector	R-R	6-3	205	1-26-87	8	11	4.39	28	27	1	0	166	167	88	81	27	54	117	.264	.241	.293	6.34	2.93
3-team total (2 Seattle, 3 Texas)					8	12	4.75	33	27	1	0	172	180	98	91	28	56	123	—	—	—	6.42	2.92
Paulino, Felipe	R-R	6-3	270	10-5-83	0	2	11.29	4	4	0	0	18	35	24	23	6	12	14	.389	.333	.452	6.87	5.89
Petricka, Jake	R-R	6-5	205	6-5-88	1	6	2.96	67	0	0	14	73	67	24	24	3	33	55	.253	.310	.208	6.78	4.07
Putnam, Zach	R-R	6-2	225	7-3-87	5	3	1.98	49	0	0	6	55	39	14	12	2	20	46	.205	.235	.170	7.57	3.29
Quintana, Jose	L-L	6-1	220	1-24-89	9	11	3.32	32	32	0	0	200	197	87	74	10	52	178	.257	.268	.253	8.00	2.34
Rienzo, Andre	R-R	6-3	190	7-5-88	4	5	6.82	18	11	0	0	65	82	54	49	12	33	51	.304	.299	.309	7.10	4.59
Sale, Chris	L-L	6-6	180	3-30-89	12	4	2.17	26	26	2	0	174	129	48	42	13	39	208	.205	.165	.214	10.76	2.02
Snodgress, Scott	L-L	6-6	225	9-20-89	0	0	15.43	4	0	0	0	2	8	7	4	1	3	1	.500	.429	.556	3.86	11.57
Surkamp, Eric	L-L	6-5	220	7-16-87	2	0	4.81	35	0	0	0	24	22	14	13	3	13	20	.244	.174	.318	7.40	4.81
Thompson, Taylor	R-R	6-5	225	6-18-87	0	0	10.13	5	0	0	0	5	9	6	6	1	4	4	.391	.455	.333	6.75	6.75
Veal, Donnie	L-L	6-4	235	9-18-84	0	0	7.50	7	0	0	0	6	6	5	5	0	7	6	.261	.200	.308	9.00	10.50
Webb, Daniel	R-R	6-3	215	8-18-89	6	5	3.99	57	0	0	0	68	59	31	30	6	42	58	.238	.217	.256	7.71	5.59

CHICAGO WHITE SOX

Fielding

Catcher	PCT	G	PO	A	E	DP	PB
Flowers	.991	124	863	70	8	6	9
Nieto	.995	46	201	14	1	0	6
Phegley	.989	11	75	13	1	1	2

First Base	PCT	G	PO	A	E	DP
Abreu	.994	109	970	69	6	105
Dunn	.995	23	207	7	1	24
Konerko	1.000	23	168	9	0	25
Viciedo	1.000	4	25	0	0	1
Wilkins	1.000	13	75	4	0	7

Second Base	PCT	G	PO	A	E	DP
Beckham	.981	100	202	312	10	74

Garcia	.943	14	18	32	3	14
Sanchez	.992	27	49	72	1	18
Semien	.970	26	51	78	4	23

Third Base	PCT	G	PO	A	E	DP
Garcia	.972	15	10	25	1	1
Gillaspie	.961	127	79	216	12	26
Semien	.896	33	14	72	10	9

Shortstop	PCT	G	PO	A	E	DP
Garcia	.917	9	2	9	1	2
Ramirez	.978	158	195	486	15	119
Sanchez	1.000	1	1	5	0	0
Semien	1.000	3	0	3	0	1

Outfield	PCT	G	PO	A	E	DP
Danks	.989	47	93	1	1	0
De Aza	.992	120	231	5	2	1
Dunn	.923	6	12	0	1	0
Eaton	.988	121	312	9	4	1
Garcia	.978	46	84	4	2	0
Garcia	.950	19	18	1	1	0
Sierra	.965	73	79	4	3	1
Taylor	1.000	8	13	2	0	0
Viciedo	.965	128	215	5	8	0

CHARLOTTE KNIGHTS   TRIPLE-A
INTERNATIONAL LEAGUE

Batting	B-T	HT	WT	DOB	AVG	vLH	vRH	G	AB	R	H	2B	3B	HR	RBI	BB	HBP	SH	SF	SO	SB	CS	SLG	OBP
Black, Dan	L-R	6-5	240	7-2-87	.267	.293	.252	48	165	22	44	8	0	6	21	21	0	0	3	42	0	0	.424	.344
Danks, Jordan	L-R	6-4	215	8-7-86	.270	.240	.283	93	348	51	94	18	0	16	57	47	3	0	8	103	2	0	.460	.355
Davidson, Matt	R-R	6-2	225	3-26-91	.199	.176	.208	130	478	59	95	18	0	20	55	49	8	1	3	164	0	0	.362	.283
Eaton, Adam	L-L	5-8	185	12-6-88	.313	.333	.308	4	16	2	5	1	0	0	2	0	0	0	0	4	2	0	.375	.313
Garcia, Avisail	R-R	6-4	240	6-12-91	.340	.333	.343	13	50	9	17	3	0	1	3	1	2	0	0	16	0	0	.460	.377
Gillaspie, Conor	L-R	6-1	195	7-18-87	.167	.000	.200	3	12	1	2	0	0	1	1	0	0	0	0	2	0	0	.417	.167
Gimenez, Hector	B-R	5-10	230	9-28-82	.109	.143	.098	16	55	5	6	1	0	1	4	9	0	0	0	14	0	0	.182	.234
2-team total (3 Buffalo)					.129	—	—	19	62	6	8	1	0	1	5	11	0	0	1	14	0	0	.194	.257
Gonzalez, Miguel	R-R	5-11	220	12-3-90	.245	.217	.254	27	94	11	23	6	0	2	7	5	0	0	0	13	0	0	.372	.283
Hernandez, Gorkys	R-R	6-1	190	9-7-87	.233	.210	.246	47	176	19	41	10	0	0	8	13	2	1	1	44	6	0	.290	.292
Jirschele, Justin	L-R	5-11	195	4-15-90	.250	.286	.243	14	44	3	11	1	0	0	6	2	0	1	1	4	0	0	.273	.277
Johnson, Micah	L-R	6-0	190	12-18-90	.275	.301	.263	65	273	30	75	10	5	2	28	16	1	9	3	42	12	6	.370	.314
Johnson, Michael	L-R	5-9	170	10-28-88	.000	.000	.000	4	6	0	0	0	0	0	0	0	0	0	0	3	0	0	.000	.000
Liddi, Alex	R-R	6-4	225	8-14-88	.171	.179	.167	22	76	6	13	1	0	3	7	3	0	2	0	27	1	1	.303	.203
Mitchell, Jared	L-L	6-0	205	10-13-88	.230	.143	.261	81	269	41	62	8	2	9	30	49	8	5	5	111	11	7	.375	.360
Phegley, Josh	R-R	5-10	225	2-12-88	.274	.271	.276	107	419	69	115	30	4	23	75	31	8	2	7	72	0	1	.530	.331
Phipps, Denis	R-R	6-2	220	7-22-85	.159	.250	.086	19	63	6	10	4	0	1	3	6	2	0	1	17	2	0	.270	.250
Richmond, Josh	R-R	6-3	205	6-14-89	.212	.000	.250	11	33	6	7	1	1	2	8	4	1	0	0	10	0	0	.485	.316
Saladino, Tyler	R-R	6-0	200	7-20-89	.310	.330	.300	82	294	41	91	16	4	9	43	27	1	1	2	50	7	1	.483	.367
Sanchez, Carlos	B-R	5-11	195	6-29-92	.293	.222	.325	110	437	60	128	19	6	7	57	36	5	10	6	84	16	4	.412	.349
Semien, Marcus	R-R	6-1	195	9-17-90	.267	.321	.249	83	303	57	81	20	3	15	52	53	5	0	5	59	7	2	.502	.380
Sierra, Luis	L-R	5-11	150	7-23-87	.000	.000	.000	1	3	0	0	0	0	0	0	0	0	0	0	0	0	0	.000	.000
Sierra, Moises	R-R	6-1	220	9-24-88	.250	.500	.167	4	16	2	4	0	0	0	2	0	0	0	0	3	2	0	.250	.333
Taylor, Michael	R-R	6-5	255	12-19-85	.306	.306	.306	64	219	41	67	8	2	6	38	29	2	0	4	50	1	0	.489	.386
Tekotte, Blake	L-R	5-11	180	5-24-87	.251	.176	.278	81	283	37	71	18	1	11	35	28	3	3	1	81	1	4	.438	.324
Tuiasosopo, Matt	R-R	6-2	225	5-10-86	.277	.291	.271	63	195	42	54	10	0	11	32	46	4	0	0	56	0	0	.497	.424
2-team total (59 Buffalo)					.240	—	—	122	409	59	98	18	0	13	50	71	5	0	2	120	1	1	.379	.357
Wagner, Daniel	L-R	6-0	185	7-12-88	.100	.200	.000	3	10	0	1	0	0	0	0	0	0	0	0	1	0	0	.100	.100
Wilkins, Andy	L-R	6-1	220	9-13-88	.293	.285	.297	127	491	79	144	38	1	30	85	34	1	0	3	91	0	1	.558	.338

Pitching	B-T	HT	WT	DOB	W	L	ERA	G	GS	CG	SV	IP	H	R	ER	HR	BB	SO	AVG	vLH	vRH	K/9	BB/9
Axelrod, Dylan	R-R	6-0	195	7-30-85	6	7	4.50	18	16	0	0	88	96	47	44	9	36	76	.287	.322	.243	7.77	3.68
2-team total (6 Louisville)					8	9	4.01	24	22	1	0	130	127	61	58	12	43	108	—	—	—	7.46	2.97
Barnette, Tyler	R-R	6-3	190	5-28-92	0	0	9.53	3	0	0	0	6	10	11	6	0	3	6	.357	.375	.333	9.53	4.76
Beck, Chris	R-R	6-3	225	9-4-90	1	3	4.05	7	7	0	0	33	36	16	15	1	13	28	.265	.283	.250	7.56	3.51
Boggs, Mitchell	R-R	6-4	235	2-15-84	2	3	9.50	25	0	0	1	36	64	41	38	3	17	18	.400	.429	.373	4.50	4.25
Cales, David	R-R	5-11	205	7-27-87	0	1	9.00	1	1	0	0	4	7	4	4	0	1	1	.389	.400	.375	2.25	2.25
Carroll, Scott	R-R	6-4	215	9-24-84	1	1	1.57	4	4	0	0	23	18	8	4	0	9	13	.228	.250	.185	5.09	3.52
Casey, Jarrett	R-L	6-0	185	10-27-87	1	3	3.44	12	0	0	1	18	21	14	7	2	10	6	.292	.286	.294	2.95	4.91
Cleto, Maikel	R-R	6-3	250	5-31-89	0	3	5.91	22	0	0	3	35	37	23	23	7	15	50	.272	.317	.233	12.86	3.86
De Los Santos, Frank	L-L	6-0	165	11-17-87	1	1	5.75	24	0	0	0	36	46	23	23	3	17	17	.322	.289	.337	4.25	4.25
Doran, Bobby	R-R	6-6	235	3-21-89	5	2	5.56	9	9	0	0	45	47	28	28	5	23	35	.267	.242	.296	6.95	4.57
Francisco, Frank	R-R	6-2	250	9-11-79	0	0	0.00	6	0	0	1	8	4	1	0	0	1	12	.154	.154	.154	13.50	1.13
Frazier, Parker	R-R	6-5	175	11-11-88	0	1	5.08	15	0	0	0	28	33	17	16	3	13	19	.295	.353	.246	6.04	4.13
Fuentes, Nelvin	L-L	6-0	206	4-7-89	1	2	5.61	22	0	0	0	34	31	22	21	5	15	23	.248	.286	.229	6.15	4.01
Guerra, Javy	R-R	6-1	190	10-31-85	1	1	2.33	14	0	0	3	19	19	8	5	1	8	11	.271	.314	.229	5.12	3.72
Hanson, Tommy	R-R	6-6	220	8-28-86	3	5	6.16	10	10	0	0	50	49	36	34	9	28	32	.254	.211	.296	5.80	5.07
Heath, Deunte	R-R	6-4	240	8-8-85	5	1	3.22	22	8	0	0	64	54	27	23	7	32	73	.231	.327	.140	10.21	4.48
Hill, Shawn	R-R	6-2	225	4-28-81	2	4	4.81	10	9	0	0	58	74	35	31	8	9	27	.307	.322	.294	4.19	1.40
3-team total (6 Buffalo, 4 Toledo)					7	6	4.49	20	17	0	0	112	133	61	56	13	27	56	—	—	—	4.49	2.16
Johnson, Erik	R-R	6-3	230	12-30-89	5	7	6.73	20	20	1	0	106	136	82	79	11	54	63	.319	.346	.293	5.37	4.60
Kussmaul, Ryan	R-R	6-4	190	9-19-86	2	5	3.81	33	1	0	5	52	41	24	22	7	26	57	.216	.241	.194	9.87	4.50
Leesman, Charlie	L-L	6-4	215	3-10-87	2	6	4.10	14	12	0	0	68	69	36	31	7	32	66	.270	.319	.251	8.74	4.24
Lindstrom, Matt	R-R	6-3	215	2-11-80	0	1	13.50	5	0	0	0	5	9	7	7	0	3	3	.474	.400	.500	5.79	5.79
McCutchen, Daniel	R-R	6-2	215	9-26-82	0	2	10.59	7	5	0	0	26	41	31	31	7	10	16	.366	.293	.444	6.15	3.42
Paulino, Felipe	R-R	6-3	270	10-5-83	5	5	0	0	3	9.61	5	0	0	20	29	24	21	5	16	16	.349	.333	.379	7.32	7.32

	B-T	HT	WT	DOB	W	L	ERA	G	GS	CG	SV	IP	H	R	ER	HR	BB	SO	AVG	vLH	vRH	K/9	BB/9
Purcey, David	L-L	6-5	245	4-22-82	0	2	4.58	12	0	0	2	20	19	10	10	3	14	15	.268	.222	.295	6.86	6.41
Putnam, Zach	R-R	6-2	225	7-3-87	1	0	0.00	5	0	0	0	7	4	0	0	0	1	12	.160	.188	.111	15.43	1.29
Rienzo, Andre	R-R	6-3	190	7-5-88	1	4	4.05	10	9	0	0	47	44	23	21	4	24	43	.242	.209	.271	8.29	4.63
Rodon, Carlos	L-L	6-3	234	12-10-92	0	0	3.00	3	3	0	0	12	9	4	4	0	8	18	.209	.000	.243	13.50	6.00
Rodriguez, Henry	R-R	6-1	225	2-25-87	0	1	21.60	3	0	0	0	2	5	4	4	0	8	3	.556	.667	.333	16.20	43.20
Sale, Chris	L-L	6-6	180	3-30-89	0	0	0.00	1	1	0	0	4	1	0	0	0	2	11	.077	.250	.000	24.75	4.50
Snodgress, Scott	L-L	6-6	225	9-20-89	0	1	4.96	8	0	0	0	16	17	9	9	4	4	16	.266	.000	.370	8.82	2.20
Surkamp, Eric	L-L	6-5	220	7-16-87	4	5	4.69	18	11	0	0	79	95	46	41	8	20	86	.304	.314	.301	9.84	2.29
Thompson, Taylor	R-R	6-5	225	6-18-87	3	0	2.14	39	0	0	7	59	48	15	14	3	29	68	.215	.259	.171	10.37	4.42
Veal, Donnie	L-L	6-4	235	9-18-84	4	5	5.94	37	0	0	4	50	57	36	33	4	27	49	.289	.250	.305	8.82	4.86
Wang, Chien-Ming	R-R	6-4	225	3-31-80	5	3	5.06	9	9	0	0	53	71	36	30	2	12	23	.326	.350	.304	3.88	2.03
2-team total (19 Louisville)					13	8	4.12	28	28	0	0	173	200	94	79	6	57	73	—	—	—	3.81	2.97
Zaleski, Matt	R-R	6-1	205	12-2-81	2	1	4.17	14	4	0	0	37	35	19	17	2	11	20	.254	.301	.200	4.91	2.70

Fielding

Catcher	PCT	G	PO	A	E	DP	PB
Gimenez	.965	13	76	7	3	1	0
Gonzalez	.988	27	149	18	2	2	2
Phegley	.991	105	799	86	8	7	14
Sierra	1.000	1	5	2	0	0	0

First Base	PCT	G	PO	A	E	DP
Black	.995	22	189	11	1	19
Gimenez	1.000	3	28	0	0	2
Johnson	1.000	1	3	0	0	1
Liddi	1.000	5	29	3	0	4
Saladino	.990	10	100	4	1	13
Tuiasosopo	.986	8	67	4	1	5
Wilkins	.994	99	846	57	5	93

Second Base	PCT	G	PO	A	E	DP
Jirschele	1.000	10	10	23	0	3
Johnson	.967	58	108	159	9	39
Johnson	1.000	2	1	0	1	0
Saladino	1.000	4	9	9	0	1

	PCT	G	PO	A	E	DP PB
Sanchez	.988	64	119	206	4	64
Semien	1.000	8	14	15	0	4
Tuiasosopo	1.000	1	2	4	0	0
Wagner	.950	3	7	12	1	3

Third Base	PCT	G	PO	A	E	DP
Davidson	.943	111	64	185	15	16
Gillaspie	1.000	3	0	12	0	2
Liddi	.944	8	5	12	1	1
Saladino	1.000	3	3	6	0	0
Sanchez	1.000	2	4	1	0	0
Semien	.981	17	14	38	1	5
Tuiasosopo	1.000	2	1	6	0	0

Shortstop	PCT	G	PO	A	E	DP
Davidson	1.000	2	3	5	0	1
Jirschele	1.000	4	7	9	0	3
Liddi	.950	4	6	13	1	2
Saladino	.973	50	66	152	6	44
Sanchez	.970	44	63	131	6	28

	PCT	G	PO	A	E	DP
Semien	.973	42	68	114	5	24

Outfield	PCT	G	PO	A	E	DP
Danks	.991	91	227	3	2	0
Eaton	1.000	3	4	0	0	0
Garcia	1.000	7	13	0	0	0
Hernandez	.990	44	89	9	1	2
Johnson	.500	1	1	0	1	0
Liddi	1.000	6	10	2	0	0
Mitchell	.956	76	124	7	6	1
Phipps	1.000	16	17	1	0	0
Richmond	1.000	10	15	0	0	0
Saladino	.842	8	15	1	3	0
Semien	1.000	11	27	1	0	0
Sierra	.800	3	4	0	1	0
Taylor	.973	56	102	6	3	2
Tekotte	.940	72	121	4	8	2
Tuiasosopo	.982	37	53	3	1	0

BIRMINGHAM BARONS   DOUBLE-A

SOUTHERN LEAGUE

Batting	B-T	HT	WT	DOB	AVG	vLH	vRH	G	AB	R	H	2B	3B	HR	RBI	BB	HBP	SH	SF	SO	SB	CS	SLG	OBP
Anderson, Tim	R-R	6-1	180	6-23-93	.364	.500	.357	10	44	7	16	3	0	1	7	0	0	1	0	9	0	1	.500	.364
Beckham, Gordon	R-R	6-0	185	9-16-86	.163	.500	.108	12	43	5	7	2	0	1	6	4	0	0	0	6	1	0	.279	.234
Black, Dan	L-R	6-5	240	7-2-87	.260	.243	.265	44	169	17	44	11	0	5	22	22	1	1	3	34	3	1	.414	.344
Buckner, Grant	R-R	6-2	225	3-21-88	.189	.200	.185	12	37	6	7	3	0	2	5	3	1	0	0	8	1	0	.432	.268
Coats, Jason	R-R	6-2	200	2-24-90	.265	.154	.291	19	68	5	18	3	1	0	9	3	1	2	3	9	1	1	.338	.293
Curley, Chris	R-R	6-0	185	8-25-87	.286	.351	.270	131	504	64	144	31	4	5	53	28	6	4	4	73	8	3	.393	.328
De Pinto, Joe	R-R	6-1	190	4-3-89	.160	.154	.162	15	50	4	8	2	0	1	4	2	0	0	0	6	4	0	.260	.250
DeMichele, Joey	L-R	5-11	190	2-5-91	.154	.063	.173	24	91	9	14	3	2	0	9	6	1	1	0	22	1	0	.231	.214
Dowdy, Jeremy	R-R	6-2	215	7-13-90	.250	.333	.200	3	8	1	2	0	0	0	1	1	0	0	0	2	0	0	.250	.333
Earley, Michael	R-R	6-0	200	3-15-88	.251	.206	.262	94	354	28	89	16	2	3	39	17	1	1	1	62	4	1	.333	.287
Farrell, Jeremy	R-R	6-3	200	11-11-86	.247	.194	.267	80	243	31	60	15	2	2	29	23	4	2	3	68	2	2	.350	.319
Gonzalez, Miguel	R-R	5-11	220	12-3-90	.269	.286	.267	16	52	6	14	5	1	0	4	4	2	1	0	7	0	0	.404	.345
Heisler, Adam	L-R	5-10	165	6-7-88	.240	1.000	.208	9	25	5	6	1	2	0	2	1	3	0	7	0	1	.440	.321
Johnson, Micah	L-R	6-0	190	12-18-90	.329	.229	.360	37	146	18	48	9	1	3	16	21	1	1	1	27	10	7	.466	.414
Johnson, Michael	L-R	5-9	170	10-28-88	.250	—	.250	2	4	0	1	0	0	0	1	0	0	0	0	0	1	0	.250	.250
Keppinger, Jeff	R-R	6-0	185	4-21-80	.256	.400	.235	11	39	3	10	1	0	1	4	6	0	1	1	2	0	0	.359	.348
Marrero, Christian	L-L	6-1	185	7-30-86	.298	.250	.305	50	161	27	48	11	0	7	36	30	0	2	4	34	4	1	.497	.400
Medina, Martin	R-R	6-0	200	3-4-88	.333	.286	.343	17	42	9	14	4	0	0	6	7	1	0	0	9	1	0	.429	.440
Mitchell, Jared	L-L	6-0	205	10-13-88	.299	.324	.293	39	157	32	47	5	3	10	26	16	2	2	2	40	4	5	.561	.367
Pedroza, Jaime	B-R	5-8	180	9-12-86	.225	.121	.251	78	289	34	65	12	3	5	35	21	2	3	1	55	3	4	.339	.281
Ravelo, Rangel	R-R	6-2	210	4-24-92	.309	.379	.293	133	476	72	147	37	4	11	66	56	9	2	8	77	10	6	.473	.386
Richmond, Josh	R-R	6-3	205	6-14-89	.247	.231	.252	100	356	47	88	17	5	9	51	32	11	1	4	85	9	2	.399	.325
Sierra, Luis	L-R	5-11	150	7-23-87	.197	.000	.227	25	76	4	15	3	0	0	8	1	1	3	1	13	1	0	.237	.215
Smith, Kevan	R-R	6-4	230	6-28-88	.290	.342	.278	106	389	45	113	21	3	10	48	46	9	2	3	68	1	1	.437	.376
Thompson, Trayce	R-R	6-3	210	3-15-91	.237	.253	.234	133	518	86	123	34	6	16	59	65	4	3	5	151	20	5	.419	.324
Wagner, Daniel	L-R	6-0	185	7-12-88	.203	.107	.231	80	251	24	51	10	2	2	21	12	1	6	1	37	6	4	.283	.242
Walker, Keenyn	B-R	6-3	190	8-12-90	.155	.130	.161	32	110	15	17	1	1	2	4	11	0	1	0	55	11	2	.236	.231

Pitching	B-T	HT	WT	DOB	W	L	ERA	G	GS	CG	SV	IP	H	R	ER	HR	BB	SO	AVG	vLH	vRH	K/9	BB/9
Bassitt, Chris	R-R	6-5	210	2-22-89	3	1	1.56	6	6	0	0	35	26	10	6	2	14	36	.206	.281	.145	9.35	3.63
Beck, Chris	R-R	6-3	225	9-4-90	5	8	3.39	20	20	1	0	117	116	50	44	7	31	57	.258	.250	.263	4.40	2.39
Blough, Bryan	R-R	6-1	190	8-29-89	2	4	4.21	18	7	0	0	62	62	31	29	4	23	35	.266	.292	.248	5.08	3.34
Bucciferro, Tony	R-R	6-3	205	12-27-89	2	2	5.00	6	6	0	0	36	45	20	20	3	6	21	.300	.360	.240	5.25	1.50
Cales, David	R-R	5-11	205	7-27-87	2	1	4.61	28	4	0	1	55	59	29	28	6	24	53	.277	.324	.254	8.73	3.95
Casey, Jarrett	R-L	6-0	185	10-27-87	1	0	1.98	20	0	0	1	41	26	9	9	2	17	26	.184	.095	.222	5.71	3.73
Crawford, Evan	R-L	6-2	190	9-2-86	0	1	5.40	15	0	0	0	18	20	15	11	1	20	16	.299	.304	.295	6.87	9.82
De Los Santos, Frank	L-L	6-0	165	11-17-87	0	0	1.04	5	0	0	0	9	7	1	1	0	2	4	.226	.222	.227	4.15	2.08

Pitching	B-T	HT	WT	DOB	W	L	ERA	G	GS	CG	SV	IP	H	R	ER	HR	BB	SO	AVG	vLH	vRH	K/9	BB/9
Doyle, Terry	R-R	6-4	250	11-2-85	4	4	5.93	8	8	1	0	41	50	29	27	4	16	27	.303	.246	.340	5.93	3.51
2-team total (5 Mississippi)					5	4	5.33	13	8	1	0	51	59	32	30	5	16	35	—	—		6.22	2.84
Frazier, Parker	R-R	6-5	175	11-11-88	2	4	3.70	27	0	0	1	41	47	24	17	4	10	25	.276	.291	.270	5.44	2.18
Fuentes, Nelvin	L-L	6-0	206	4-7-89	0	3	3.23	22	0	0	1	31	25	11	11	0	19	43	.223	.205	.235	12.62	5.58
Hansen, Kyle	R-R	6-8	200	4-20-91	0	0	4.70	4	0	0	0	8	6	4	4	1	6	6	.240	.125	.444	7.04	7.04
Hardin, Brandon	R-R	6-0	200	2-17-90	0	2	6.91	21	0	0	3	27	40	21	21	1	16	15	.339	.350	.333	4.94	5.27
Jaye, Myles	B-R	6-3	170	12-28-91	4	12	5.32	24	24	1	0	132	146	87	78	10	53	73	.287	.283	.290	4.98	3.61
Kussmaul, Ryan	R-R	6-4	190	9-19-86	3	0	4.96	11	0	0	0	16	18	10	9	1	5	17	.281	.200	.318	9.37	2.76
Marin, Terance	R-R	6-1	170	8-21-89	0	2	4.97	2	2	0	0	13	18	7	7	1	2	12	.346	.350	.344	8.53	1.42
McCully, Nick	R-R	5-11	195	9-5-88	4	9	5.79	22	19	0	0	96	113	66	62	12	44	35	.297	.373	.259	3.27	4.11
Molina, Nestor	R-R	6-1	220	1-9-89	7	4	4.55	44	0	0	7	61	58	40	31	7	22	46	.249	.247	.250	6.75	3.23
Montas, Francellis	R-R	6-2	185	3-21-93	0	0	0.00	1	1	0	0	5	1	1	0	0	1	1	.063	.000	.071	1.80	1.80
Olacio, Jefferson	L-L	6-7	270	1-16-94	0	0	6.14	9	0	0	0	15	19	11	10	0	8	13	.311	.360	.278	7.98	4.91
Ortiz, Braulio	R-R	6-5	205	12-20-91	0	2	9.00	15	0	0	1	18	16	19	18	0	30	25	.235	.154	.286	12.50	15.00
Recchia, Mike	R-R	6-1	210	4-2-89	6	4	3.10	19	19	1	0	107	96	43	37	10	35	87	.236	.286	.203	7.30	2.93
Sanchez, Angel	R-R	6-1	190	11-28-89	1	2	6.60	3	3	0	0	15	22	14	11	2	5	9	.349	.267	.375	5.40	3.00
3-team total (12 Jacksonville, 2 Montgomery)					1	11	6.96	17	17	0	0	76	102	66	59	6	25	45	—	—		5.31	2.95
Snodgress, Scott	L-L	6-6	225	9-20-89	6	7	3.89	21	21	0	0	123	119	60	53	9	52	79	.256	.221	.263	5.80	3.82
Vance, Kevin	R-R	6-0	208	7-8-90	7	4	4.48	43	0	0	6	62	58	32	31	3	30	61	.250	.236	.259	8.81	4.33
Winiarski, Cody	R-R	6-3	205	8-27-89	1	4	8.34	34	0	0	5	45	62	44	42	3	20	54	.321	.422	.271	10.72	3.97

Fielding

Catcher	PCT	G	PO	A	E	DP	PB
Dowdy	1.000	2	13	1	0	0	0
Gonzalez	1.000	16	89	10	0	0	2
Medina	1.000	16	102	11	0	1	1
Sierra	1.000	8	64	5	0	0	0
Smith	.985	103	596	73	10	7	10

First Base	PCT	G	PO	A	E	DP
Black	.993	17	134	9	1	16
Buckner	1.000	1	5	1	0	0
Farrell	1.000	7	41	1	0	5
Marrero	.991	13	103	8	1	11
Ravelo	.996	108	943	51	4	87

Second Base	PCT	G	PO	A	E	DP
Beckham	.917	6	13	20	3	8
Curley	.977	31	53	75	3	27
DeMichele	1.000	24	42	62	0	11
Farrell	1.000	1	3	2	0	1

	PCT	G	PO	A	E	DP
Johnson	.969	30	53	73	4	17
Johnson	1.000	1	4	5	0	1
Keppinger	.800	1	2	2	1	0
Pedroza	—	1	0	0	0	0
Sierra	1.000	5	8	14	0	5
Wagner	.985	48	76	116	3	26

Third Base	PCT	G	PO	A	E	DP
Buckner	.842	7	8	8	3	2
Curley	.953	57	48	133	9	15
Farrell	.964	60	52	110	6	15
Keppinger	.857	7	2	10	2	0
Ravelo	.800	2	1	3	1	1
Sierra	1.000	12	4	20	0	4
Wagner	1.000	4	2	5	0	0

Shortstop	PCT	G	PO	A	E	DP
Anderson	.942	10	17	32	3	5
Curley	.968	35	42	107	5	18

	PCT	G	PO	A	E	DP
Pedroza	.944	76	112	208	19	46
Wagner	.892	23	28	46	9	9

Outfield	PCT	G	PO	A	E	DP
Buckner	1.000	5	8	0	0	0
Coats	.980	19	49	0	1	0
De Pinto	.929	9	13	0	1	0
Earley	.978	75	129	5	3	1
Farrell	1.000	2	2	0	0	0
Heisler	.944	8	17	0	1	0
Marrero	1.000	13	21	2	0	1
Mitchell	1.000	39	88	2	0	0
Richmond	.983	96	229	9	4	0
Thompson	.985	131	329	7	5	1
Walker	.967	32	86	1	3	1

WINSTON-SALEM DASH HIGH CLASS A

CAROLINA LEAGUE

Batting	B-T	HT	WT	DOB	AVG	vLH	vRH	G	AB	R	H	2B	3B	HR	RBI	BB	HBP	SH	SF	SO	SB	CS	SLG	OBP
Anderson, Tim	R-R	6-1	180	6-23-93	.297	.329	.286	68	286	48	85	18	7	6	31	7	5	0	2	68	10	3	.472	.323
Barnum, Keon	L-L	6-5	225	1-16-93	.253	.199	.273	132	491	49	124	29	1	8	60	37	2	1	2	163	3	0	.365	.306
Basto, Nick	R-R	6-2	210	4-1-94	.263	.248	.271	87	315	39	83	14	2	7	35	19	5	0	3	66	1	4	.387	.313
Beatty, C.J.	B-R	5-10	190	9-28-88	.222	.083	.273	13	45	7	10	1	0	1	6	4	0	1	1	8	2	1	.311	.280
Buckner, Grant	R-R	6-2	225	3-21-88	.276	.267	.281	61	203	23	56	14	1	4	26	9	4	0	1	24	2	2	.414	.318
Coats, Jason	R-R	6-2	200	2-24-90	.291	.304	.286	115	429	64	125	35	2	15	72	35	6	2	4	65	5	2	.487	.350
DeMichele, Joey	L-R	5-11	190	2-5-91	.264	.203	.291	105	386	50	102	25	4	4	42	34	2	4	4	65	6	3	.381	.324
Engel, Adam	R-R	6-1	215	12-9-91	.239	.280	.222	21	88	11	21	0	0	0	5	6	2	2	2	21	9	1	.239	.296
Hawkins, Courtney	R-R	6-3	220	11-12-93	.249	.190	.272	122	449	65	112	25	4	19	84	53	5	1	7	143	11	3	.450	.331
Heisler, Adam	L-R	5-10	165	6-7-88	.283	.261	.289	33	113	15	32	5	3	2	9	11	0	2	0	15	7	3	.434	.347
Jirschele, Justin	L-R	5-11	195	4-15-90	.315	.167	.340	40	124	14	39	6	0	0	4	9	0	3	0	7	4	0	.363	.361
Johnson, Michael	L-R	5-9	170	10-28-88	.156	.050	.205	22	64	6	10	2	0	0	6	9	0	1	3	13	0	2	.188	.250
Marjama, Mike	R-R	6-2	205	7-20-89	.266	.300	.247	70	248	26	66	16	2	3	17	8	2	2	3	33	2	3	.383	.292
May, Jacob	B-R	5-10	180	1-23-92	.258	.266	.254	109	415	66	107	31	10	2	27	42	1	12	2	71	37	8	.395	.326
Medina, Martin	R-R	6-0	200	3-24-90	.270	.222	.289	37	126	12	34	6	1	0	16	10	1	0	2	35	3	0	.333	.324
Michalczewski, Trey	B-R	6-3	210	2-27-95	.194	.190	.196	19	72	5	14	2	0	0	5	9	1	2	0	21	1	0	.222	.293
Narvaez, Omar	B-R	5-10	175	2-10-92	.279	.111	.319	47	140	18	39	8	0	2	16	27	2	1	4	21	1	2	.379	.393
Peter, Jake	L-R	6-1	185	4-5-93	.236	.167	.254	23	89	8	21	4	1	0	5	4	1	0	0	13	1	0	.303	.277
Rondon, Cleuluis	R-R	6-0	155	4-13-94	.247	.303	.220	53	198	24	49	10	4	1	24	19	1	3	1	33	3	4	.354	.315
Voight, Zach	R-R	6-0	185	8-26-90	.222	.135	.268	35	108	11	24	8	1	2	14	14	1	4	0	25	0	2	.370	.317
Walker, Keenyn	B-R	6-3	190	8-12-90	.217	.145	.245	70	230	27	50	8	3	0	21	25	2	3	1	85	20	3	.278	.298

Pitching	B-T	HT	WT	DOB	W	L	ERA	G	GS	CG	SV	IP	H	R	ER	HR	BB	SO	AVG	vLH	vRH	K/9	BB/9
Barnette, Tyler	R-R	6-3	190	5-28-92	0	0	15.00	2	0	0	0	3	7	7	5	0	2	3	.438	.455	.400	9.00	6.00
Bautista, Jose	L-L	6-1	175	3-31-92	1	1	5.46	24	0	0	0	31	31	22	19	4	24	37	.244	.182	.266	10.63	6.89
Bierman, Sean	L-L	6-0	195	10-20-88	0	0	3.38	5	0	0	0	5	5	3	2	1	4	6	.227	.167	.250	10.13	6.75
2-team total (1 Lynchburg)					0	0	2.84	6	0	0	0	6	5	3	2	1	4	7	—	—		9.95	5.68
Blough, Bryan	R-R	6-1	190	8-29-89	1	2	1.93	13	1	0	4	19	17	7	4	1	5	20	.230	.179	.261	9.64	2.41
Blount, Nick	R-R	6-6	225	9-1-90	0	1	7.00	4	2	0	0	9	11	7	7	2	9	9	.314	.357	.286	9.00	2.00
Brennan, Brandon	R-R	6-4	220	7-26-91	2	0	2.93	6	6	0	0	31	32	11	10	1	12	20	.286	.333	.246	6.46	3.52
Brewster, Ben	L-R	6-3	215	11-14-91	0	1	1.80	4	0	0	0	5	5	2	1	0	5	5	.238	.286	.214	9.00	9.00

					W	L	ERA	G	GS	CG	SV	IP	H	R	ER	HR	BB	SO	AVG	vLH	vRH	K/9	BB/9
Bucciferro, Tony	R-R	6-3	205	12-27-89	7	10	3.90	21	21	2	0	129	139	68	56	8	16	94	.270	.260	.275	6.54	1.11
Casey, Jarrett	R-L	6-0	185	10-27-87	1	0	0.00	6	0	0	2	8	5	0	0	0	2	11	.179	.333	.136	12.38	2.25
Crawford, Evan	R-L	6-2	190	9-2-86	0	1	3.38	2	0	0	0	3	1	2	1	0	2	6	.100	.000	.111	20.25	6.75
Danish, Tyler	R-R	6-0	205	9-12-94	5	3	2.65	18	18	0	0	92	87	35	27	7	23	78	.249	.283	.227	7.66	2.26
Dykstra, James	R-R	6-4	195	11-22-90	3	3	4.89	9	9	0	0	53	73	33	29	3	6	46	.322	.322	.321	7.76	1.01
Fernandez, Raul	R-R	6-2	180	6-22-90	2	3	2.49	14	0	0	0	22	14	7	6	1	17	20	.192	.200	.186	8.31	7.06
Goldberg, Brad	R-R	6-4	228	2-21-90	4	4	5.23	35	7	0	2	76	90	59	44	2	46	62	.300	.279	.312	7.37	5.47
Hagan, Sean	L-L	6-6	215	3-5-91	2	1	3.70	36	0	0	1	56	53	29	23	3	21	35	.242	.221	.252	5.63	3.38
Hansen, Kyle	R-R	6-8	200	4-20-91	8	4	3.33	31	0	0	2	51	48	22	19	1	20	52	.245	.224	.256	9.12	3.51
Hardin, Brandon	R-R	6-0	200	2-17-90	0	2	1.86	19	0	0	5	19	16	7	4	2	8	19	.225	.333	.159	8.84	3.72
Isler, Zach	R-R	6-5	230	10-31-90	1	8	5.18	37	0	0	4	42	59	33	24	2	25	44	.326	.354	.310	9.50	5.40
Jaye, Myles	B-R	6-3	170	12-28-91	3	0	1.55	4	4	1	0	29	22	8	5	2	5	15	.200	.406	.115	4.66	1.55
Leyer, Euclides	R-R	6-2	175	12-28-90	1	3	4.53	34	0	0	3	56	55	32	28	3	29	50	.261	.209	.285	8.08	4.69
Lopez, Adam	R-R	6-5	195	2-21-90	0	1	5.14	4	0	0	0	7	4	4	4	0	5	9	.174	.222	.143	11.57	6.43
Marin, Terance	R-R	6-1	170	8-21-89	4	3	4.22	14	10	0	0	70	77	44	33	5	16	60	.274	.265	.279	7.68	2.05
Montas, Francellis	R-R	6-2	185	3-21-93	4	0	1.60	10	10	1	0	62	45	16	11	2	14	56	.202	.273	.164	8.13	2.03
Olacio, Jefferson	L-L	6-7	270	1-16-94	0	5	4.69	29	4	0	0	56	65	43	29	2	31	58	.288	.237	.305	9.38	5.01
Ortiz, Braulio	R-R	6-5	205	12-20-91	0	8	5.05	20	9	0	3	52	64	34	29	3	33	51	.309	.283	.320	8.88	5.75
Putman, David	R-R	6-1	205	2-28-90	0	0	3.18	10	0	0	2	11	10	6	4	0	9	19	.233	.176	.269	15.09	7.15
Recchia, Mike	R-R	6-1	210	4-2-89	4	3	2.90	7	7	0	0	40	27	15	13	3	10	47	.188	.228	.161	10.49	2.23
Rodon, Carlos	L-L	6-3	234	12-10-92	0	0	1.86	4	2	0	0	10	7	3	2	0	5	15	.189	.143	.200	13.97	4.66
Sanchez, Angel	R-R	6-1	190	11-28-89	1	1	4.26	2	2	0	0	13	13	7	6	1	3	9	.271	.333	.256	6.39	2.13
Wendelken, J.B.	R-R	6-0	190	3-24-93	7	10	5.25	27	27	1	0	146	181	105	85	15	33	129	.304	.349	.275	7.97	2.04

Fielding

Catcher	PCT	G	PO	A	E	DP	PB
Marjama	.994	63	473	52	3	6	2
Medina	.996	34	267	17	1	2	3
Narvaez	.992	46	339	45	3	2	6

First Base	PCT	G	PO	A	E	DP
Barnum	.985	130	1146	67	19	99
Buckner	.987	10	72	2	1	1
Marjama	1.000	3	26	0	0	2

Second Base	PCT	G	PO	A	E	DP
DeMichele	.972	103	194	293	14	58
Jirschele	1.000	1	1	4	0	0
Johnson	.926	6	10	15	2	2
Peter	.991	23	25	89	1	15

Voight	1.000	6	7	15	0	3

Third Base	PCT	G	PO	A	E	DP
Basto	.788	58	26	89	31	1
Buckner	.900	25	14	49	7	6
Jirschele	.917	24	8	47	5	5
Johnson	1.000	2	0	2	0	0
Michalczewski	.909	17	9	31	4	3
Voight	.938	16	9	36	3	4

Shortstop	PCT	G	PO	A	E	DP
Anderson	.897	66	71	200	31	35
Johnson	.953	11	15	26	2	5
Rondon	.955	53	73	158	11	38
Voight	.911	10	14	27	4	5

Outfield	PCT	G	PO	A	E	DP
Basto	1.000	7	7	1	0	0
Beatty	.960	11	21	3	1	0
Buckner	1.000	11	10	0	0	0
Coats	.952	99	189	10	10	1
Engel	.979	18	44	3	1	1
Hawkins	.928	113	170	11	14	0
Heisler	1.000	15	24	0	0	0
Jirschele	1.000	6	6	0	0	0
Johnson	1.000	1	1	0	0	0
May	.979	94	181	4	4	1
Walker	.958	52	88	3	4	0

KANNAPOLIS INTIMIDATORS   LOW CLASS A

SOUTH ATLANTIC LEAGUE

Batting	B-T	HT	WT	DOB	AVG	vLH	vRH	G	AB	R	H	2B	3B	HR	RBI	BB	HBP	SH	SF	SO	SB	CS	SLG	OBP
Alvarez, Eddy	B-R	5-9	175	1-30-90	.431	.385	.441	18	72	12	31	6	0	3	14	7	1	0	0	10	4	4	.639	.488
Austin, Brett	B-R	6-1	190	11-24-92	.235	.310	.207	42	153	16	36	12	0	0	15	18	1	3	3	47	1	1	.314	.314
Clarke, Chevy	B-R	6-0	200	1-9-92	.176	.067	.208	20	68	12	12	3	1	1	3	9	1	1	1	26	0	1	.294	.278
Danner, Michael	L-R	5-10	186	9-18-91	.229	.429	.195	14	48	8	11	1	1	0	4	4	0	0	0	13	0	0	.292	.288
Dowdy, Jeremy	R-R	6-2	215	7-13-90	.302	.352	.283	53	199	19	60	10	2	1	22	16	2	1	0	35	2	0	.387	.359
Earley, Nolan	L-L	6-0	205	3-27-91	.306	.222	.333	19	72	8	22	4	2	1	8	5	2	1	0	13	1	1	.458	.367
Engel, Adam	R-R	6-1	215	12-9-91	.261	.205	.279	74	307	54	80	14	7	6	30	29	5	0	0	86	28	11	.410	.334
Fisher, Zac	L-R	6-2	195	12-13-91	.158	.200	.143	5	19	1	3	1	0	0	2	2	0	0	0	3	0	0	.211	.238
Hayes, Danny	L-R	6-4	210	9-21-90	.283	.268	.288	130	473	65	134	33	4	11	75	73	4	5	4	119	1	1	.440	.381
Jones, Hunter	R-R	6-2	185	8-17-91	.205	.241	.197	41	156	27	32	5	1	5	15	16	7	0	1	45	11	2	.346	.306
Kiser, Kale	B-R	5-10	180	3-31-90	.239	.176	.254	27	88	7	21	6	4	1	5	9	3	2	0	21	1	0	.432	.330
Leonards, Ryan	R-R	5-11	195	7-22-91	.239	.279	.225	48	163	21	39	6	1	2	16	16	6	0	5	34	9	0	.325	.321
Michalczewski, Trey	B-R	6-3	210	2-27-95	.273	.302	.264	116	432	57	118	25	7	10	70	45	8	4	6	140	6	3	.433	.348
Morris, Jacob	R-R	6-3	195	12-19-90	.220	.202	.225	132	495	69	109	36	2	8	44	57	6	1	2	179	12	6	.349	.307
Narvaez, Omar	R-R	5-10	175	2-10-92	.291	.077	.316	38	127	7	37	3	0	0	20	9	1	0	5	11	0	0	.315	.331
Rondon, Cleuluis	R-R	6-0	155	4-13-94	.233	.242	.230	77	301	35	70	9	0	0	16	26	2	4	3	65	13	8	.262	.295
Shryock, Tyler	L-R	6-0	170	3-28-91	.166	.150	.168	48	151	13	25	2	0	0	8	16	2	0	0	28	4	4	.179	.254
Stringer, Christian	L-R	5-11	185	6-25-90	.259	.263	.258	76	293	41	76	14	2	9	39	23	2	1	3	51	7	1	.413	.315
Thomas, Toby	R-R	5-11	190	12-9-93	.215	.286	.194	25	93	11	20	7	1	2	12	7	1	1	1	20	0	2	.376	.275
Thomore, Carl	R-R	6-2	212	1-13-93	.225	.238	.221	113	374	42	84	17	0	4	46	43	9	4	7	124	12	3	.302	.314
Voight, Zach	R-R	6-0	185	8-26-90	.240	.200	.256	34	125	9	30	7	0	1	12	6	0	0	0	34	1	1	.320	.275
Williams, Tyler	R-R	6-2	205	1-5-91	.202	.121	.223	92	317	34	64	13	2	7	39	30	5	2	1	114	5	2	.322	.280

Pitching	B-T	HT	WT	DOB	W	L	ERA	G	GS	CG	SV	IP	H	R	ER	HR	BB	SO	AVG	vLH	vRH	K/9	BB/9
Abramson, Matt	R-R	6-2	185	3-22-90	3	8	5.40	30	0	0	6	58	62	39	35	4	33	43	.276	.386	.185	6.63	5.09
Banks, Tanner	L-L	6-1	205	10-24-91	0	0	0.00	1	0	0	0	2	2	0	0	0	0	2	.222	.500	.000	7.71	0.00
Barnette, Tyler	R-R	6-3	190	5-29-92	2	8	5.08	25	11	0	1	85	100	58	48	4	21	52	.302	.296	.308	5.51	2.22
Bautista, Jose	L-L	6-1	175	3-31-92	1	1	0.92	10	0	1	0	20	14	5	2	0	6	26	.192	.138	.227	11.90	2.75
Bierman, Sean	L-L	6-0	195	10-20-88	0	1	7.00	2	2	0	0	9	13	7	7	2	4	5	.333	.273	.357	5.00	4.00
2-team total (2 Rome)					2	1	3.26	4	2	0	0	19	20	9	7	2	8	16	—	—	—	7.45	3.72
Brennan, Brandon	R-R	6-4	220	7-26-91	2	0	2.55	3	3	0	0	18	11	5	5	0	6	15	.172	.235	.100	7.64	3.06
Brewster, Ben	L-L	6-3	215	11-14-91	2	0	1.72	8	0	0	1	16	9	4	3	0	5	17	.164	.158	.167	9.77	2.87

Name	B-T	HT	WT	DOB	W	L	ERA	G	GS	CG	SV	IP	H	R	ER	HR	BB	SO	AVG	vLH	vRH	K/9	BB/9
Brito, Jose	R-R	6-0	175	10-10-90	3	2	5.40	33	1	0	2	70	73	50	42	8	38	34	.269	.301	.237	4.37	4.89
Bruening, Brett	R-R	6-6	210	12-30-88	0	0	3.00	3	0	0	0	3	3	3	1	0	1	1	.231	.167	.286	3.00	3.00
Chavez, Dylan	L-L	6-3	190	4-16-91	4	5	2.93	31	0	0	3	58	47	27	19	4	27	42	.214	.214	.213	6.48	4.17
Danish, Tyler	R-R	6-0	205	9-12-94	3	0	0.71	7	7	0	0	38	28	8	3	0	10	25	.206	.143	.250	5.92	2.37
Dykstra, James	R-R	6-4	195	11-22-90	6	8	2.64	16	16	1	0	99	101	33	29	3	10	82	.262	.227	.297	7.45	0.91
Freudenberg, Chris	L-L	6-3	195	6-19-93	3	1	4.34	6	6	0	0	29	28	14	14	2	13	30	.257	.433	.190	9.31	4.03
Guerrero, Jordan	L-L	6-3	190	5-31-94	6	2	3.46	27	9	0	0	78	81	33	30	5	27	80	.266	.269	.265	9.23	3.12
Hagan, Sean	L-L	6-6	215	3-5-91	0	1	2.35	4	0	0	0	8	6	2	2	1	1	5	.240	.250	.235	5.87	1.17
Leyer, Robin	R-R	6-2	175	3-13-93	5	9	3.81	25	25	1	0	135	144	73	57	9	43	86	.282	.241	.319	5.75	2.87
Lowry, Thaddius	R-R	6-4	215	10-4-94	4	6	4.76	17	17	1	0	87	103	52	46	5	29	43	.308	.273	.346	4.45	3.00
McKenzie, Jeff	L-L	6-0	170	5-15-91	3	5	5.60	13	10	1	0	63	79	41	39	8	15	36	.313	.385	.282	5.17	2.15
Mendonca, Tanner	R-R	6-4	215	6-18-92	0	0	4.50	3	0	0	1	4	2	2	2	0	7	6	.154	.167	.143	13.50	15.75
Mitchell, Andrew	R-R	6-3	205	11-9-91	4	3	5.37	31	5	0	0	65	51	42	39	3	67	83	.222	.216	.229	11.43	9.23
Powers, Alex	R-R	6-4	180	2-26-92	0	2	4.84	13	0	0	1	22	25	12	12	2	8	16	.275	.220	.341	6.45	3.22
Putman, David	R-R	6-1	205	2-28-90	0	3	3.13	19	0	0	5	23	29	10	8	0	15	32	.299	.267	.327	12.52	5.87
Salgado, Brad	R-R	6-1	185	7-15-91	2	2	3.38	13	0	0	3	32	33	15	12	3	4	27	.258	.293	.229	7.59	1.13
Sanchez, Jake	R-R	6-1	205	8-19-89	5	4	2.80	15	9	1	3	61	56	26	19	6	14	66	.232	.224	.241	9.74	2.07
Throne, Storm	R-R	6-7	215	9-3-90	0	1	11.57	4	0	0	1	7	9	9	9	1	4	4	.300	.182	.368	5.14	5.14
Walsh, Connor	L-R	6-2	176	10-18-92	1	0	9.45	4	0	0	0	7	10	7	7	0	2	6	.357	.286	.381	8.10	2.70
Wheeler, Andre	L-L	6-1	170	9-27-91	3	3	2.84	28	16	0	0	98	85	38	31	5	32	111	.233	.195	.253	10.16	2.93

Fielding

Catcher	PCT	G	PO	A	E	DP	PB
Austin	.985	42	281	40	5	3	5
Dowdy	.993	53	373	41	3	4	4
Fisher	1.000	5	36	3	0	0	1
Narvaez	.980	38	266	33	6	4	5

First Base	PCT	G	PO	A	E	DP
Hayes	.991	111	1004	71	10	87
Williams	.972	27	236	11	7	30

Second Base	PCT	G	PO	A	E	DP
Alvarez	.933	9	22	20	3	7
Shryock	.943	41	74	126	12	30
Stringer	.974	68	118	220	9	48

	PCT	G	PO	A	E	DP
Thomas	1.000	1	3	4	0	1
Voight	.979	20	31	64	2	13

Third Base	PCT	G	PO	A	E	DP
Leonards	1.000	2	0	2	0	0
Michalczewski	.918	114	73	183	23	16
Shryock	1.000	1	0	5	0	0
Thomas	.923	19	11	49	5	6
Voight	1.000	2	0	4	0	0

Shortstop	PCT	G	PO	A	E	DP
Alvarez	.941	6	9	23	2	4
Leonards	.947	46	58	137	11	26
Rondon	.956	77	142	246	18	65

	PCT	G	PO	A	E	DP
Shryock	.778	5	1	6	2	0
Thomas	1.000	2	3	3	0	1
Voight	.750	2	1	2	1	0

Outfield	PCT	G	PO	A	E	DP
Clarke	.970	20	30	2	1	0
Danner	1.000	13	23	1	0	0
Earley	1.000	10	18	0	0	0
Engel	.983	74	166	7	3	1
Jones	.987	40	76	2	1	1
Kiser	.952	24	38	2	2	0
Morris	.974	132	249	14	7	3
Thomore	.979	100	179	10	4	1
Williams	1.000	1	1	0	0	0

AZL WHITE SOX · ROOKIE

ARIZONA LEAGUE

Batting	B-T	HT	WT	DOB	AVG	vLH	vRH	G	AB	R	H	2B	3B	HR	RBI	BB	HBP	SH	SF	SO	SB	CS	SLG	OBP
Adolfo, Micker	R-R	6-3	200	9-11-96	.218	.167	.231	46	179	27	39	10	2	5	21	14	2	1	2	85	0	0	.380	.279
Alvarez, Eddy	B-R	5-9	175	1-30-90	.291	.154	.333	27	110	20	32	5	1	2	12	20	0	0	0	24	5	6	.409	.400
Anderson, Tim	R-R	6-1	180	6-23-93	.200	.000	.333	5	15	2	3	0	0	2	2	2	0	0	0	5	0	1	.600	.294
Ayala, Sammy	L-R	6-2	195	7-12-94	.000	—	.000	1	3	0	0	0	0	0	0	0	0	0	0	2	0	0	.000	.000
Barraza, Jose	L-R	6-1	220	7-28-94	.287	.310	.280	37	136	28	39	5	2	5	19	13	2	0	1	62	1	0	.463	.355
Basto, Nick	R-R	6-2	210	4-3-94	.282	.273	.286	9	39	7	11	3	2	1	10	1	1	0	0	7	0	0	.538	.317
Cruz, Johan	R-R	6-2	170	10-8-95	.179	.000	.194	22	78	12	14	3	0	1	7	9	1	1	0	18	0	1	.256	.273
Danner, Michael	L-R	5-10	186	9-18-91	.229	.286	.220	13	48	6	11	1	2	0	7	5	1	0	1	5	0	1	.333	.309
Engel, Adam	R-R	6-1	215	12-9-91	.364	.125	.440	8	33	6	12	3	3	1	3	3	2	0	0	6	2	0	.727	.447
Flores, Marc	L-R	6-5	225	6-11-92	.222	.269	.209	32	117	19	26	5	3	1	9	16	1	0	1	24	1	0	.342	.319
Garcia, Joxelier	R-R	5-10	185	4-30-94	.000	.000	.000	6	8	0	0	0	0	0	0	0	0	0	0	3	0	0	.000	.000
Hollenbeck, Michael	L-R	6-2	205	6-4-92	.227	.263	.213	24	66	7	15	2	1	0	7	14	0	1	0	20	0	1	.288	.363
Jarvis, Jake	R-R	5-10	175	2-23-95	.221	.250	.213	29	95	11	21	4	0	0	11	10	6	1	0	30	1	0	.263	.333
Macias, Sam	R-R	6-0	195	12-9-91	.149	.250	.114	21	47	9	7	0	0	0	3	6	0	1	0	20	3	1	.149	.245
Moore, Blair	L-R	6-2	200	2-25-91	.260	.125	.300	29	104	17	27	3	3	0	15	11	2	2	1	28	0	0	.346	.339
Plourde, Ryan	R-R	6-0	210	2-26-92	.290	.167	.320	14	31	6	9	1	2	1	8	8	0	0	0	8	1	0	.548	.436
Rodriguez, Antonio	R-R	6-0	180	5-16-95	.257	.289	.248	43	167	20	43	9	1	4	20	9	0	0	3	47	4	1	.395	.291
Santana, Audry	R-R	5-11	170	2-22-92	.120	.111	.125	7	25	0	3	0	0	0	1	0	0	0	0	12	0	0	.120	.120
Santos, Jeffy	B-R	6-2	150	1-4-93	.295	.231	.323	13	44	11	13	4	0	0	6	15	1	0	0	12	3	2	.386	.483
Silverio, Louis	R-R	6-2	195	12-15-93	.301	.238	.323	25	83	9	25	5	2	2	18	8	1	0	0	20	2	0	.482	.370
Suiter, Michael	R-R	6-1	193	4-9-92	.263	.114	.306	42	156	29	41	7	1	4	31	15	10	0	1	28	14	3	.397	.363
Swick, Kevin	R-R	6-0	195	7-27-91	.184	.267	.167	26	87	10	16	2	0	0	7	9	1	2	2	20	1	1	.207	.263
Velasquez, Victor	B-R	5-11	195	2-5-95	.151	.071	.179	16	53	6	8	0	0	0	4	3	2	3	0	14	1	0	.151	.224
Yount, Cody	L-R	6-1	200	8-19-88	.250	.281	.239	34	124	16	31	5	0	0	11	28	1	0	1	23	0	0	.290	.390

Pitching	B-T	HT	WT	DOB	W	L	ERA	G	GS	CG	SV	IP	H	R	ER	HR	BB	SO	AVG	vLH	vRH	K/9	BB/9
Adams, Spencer	R-R	6-3	171	4-13-96	3	3	3.67	10	9	0	0	42	49	22	17	4	4	59	.282	.225	.330	12.74	0.86
Banks, Tanner	L-L	6-1	205	10-24-91	1	1	1.64	14	0	0	3	22	14	4	4	0	6	31	.184	.043	.245	12.68	2.45
Bassitt, Chris	R-R	6-5	210	2-22-89	0	0	4.15	3	2	0	0	9	9	4	4	0	3	13	.257	.278	.235	13.50	3.12
Blount, Nick	R-R	6-6	225	9-1-90	0	0	0.00	2	1	0	0	4	2	0	0	0	3	3	.167	.167	.167	6.75	6.75
Brewster, Ben	L-L	6-3	215	11-14-91	0	0	0.00	2	0	0	0	4	1	0	0	0	2	6	.083	.000	.100	13.50	4.50
Bruening, Brett	R-R	6-6	210	12-30-88	0	0	6.00	3	0	0	0	3	2	2	2	0	3	5	.200	.000	.333	15.00	9.00
Davis, Devon	L-L	6-4	215	8-20-91	0	0	0.00	2	0	0	0	2	3	0	0	0	0	8	.154	.333	.100	19.64	0.00
Done, Victor	R-R	6-3	195	9-3-95	2	3	4.18	11	10	0	0	47	47	29	22	2	32	52	.257	.260	.255	9.89	6.08
Easterling, Brannon	R-R	6-4	230	8-1-90	2	3	2.70	14	0	0	1	33	34	14	10	2	4	34	.264	.273	.257	9.18	1.08

	B-T	HT	WT	DOB	W	L	ERA	G	GS	CG	SV	IP	H	R	ER	HR	BB	SO	AVG	vLH	vRH	K/9	BB/9
Einhardt, Evin	R-R	6-3	191	7-2-91	2	1	7.33	14	1	0	0	23	29	23	19	1	15	19	.305	.212	.355	7.33	5.79
Gomez, Mike	L-L	6-1	195	10-17-91	2	0	1.27	13	0	0	1	21	8	6	3	0	16	33	.113	.105	.115	13.92	6.75
Goossen-Brown, Josh	R-R	6-2	210	2-21-91	1	2	3.80	15	0	0	3	21	18	10	9	2	5	27	.228	.185	.250	11.39	2.11
Leesman, Charlie	L-L	6-4	215	3-10-87	0	0	4.91	2	2	0	0	4	5	2	2	0	2	4	.385	.667	.300	9.82	4.91
Lopez, Adam	R-R	6-5	195	2-21-90	0	0	0.00	3	0	0	0	5	3	0	0	0	4	8	.176	.000	.250	15.43	7.71
Martinez, Andre	L-L	6-0	185	6-22-93	0	0	13.50	1	0	0	0	2	3	3	3	1	1	1	.333	.500	.286	4.50	4.50
Martinez, Luis	R-R	6-4	190	1-29-95	3	2	4.09	7	6	0	0	33	31	20	15	3	16	40	.244	.273	.222	10.91	4.36
Mendonca, Tanner	R-R	6-4	215	6-18-92	1	2	3.80	15	0	0	2	21	16	9	9	0	6	41	.208	.233	.191	17.30	2.53
Montas, Francellis	R-R	6-2	185	3-21-93	1	0	1.29	4	4	0	0	14	6	3	2	1	7	23	.128	.188	.097	14.79	4.50
Patterson, Jamie	R-R	6-4	165	12-7-93	2	1	3.65	14	0	0	1	25	22	18	10	2	8	15	.224	.333	.169	5.47	2.92
Peralta, Yelmison	R-R	6-0	190	3-3-95	4	2	3.55	13	1	0	1	38	35	21	15	1	9	29	.254	.188	.289	6.87	2.13
Rodon, Carlos	L-L	6-3	234	12-10-92	0	0	6.00	2	1	0	0	3	4	2	2	0	0	5	.308	.333	.300	15.00	0.00
Rodriguez, Henry	R-R	6-1	225	2-25-87	0	0	6.75	5	0	0	0	5	3	4	4	0	5	14	.143	.250	.077	23.63	8.44
Shearrow, Luke	R-R	6-4	225	2-10-91	2	2	4.06	12	9	0	0	44	38	23	20	2	27	42	.242	.293	.212	8.53	5.48
Trexler, David	R-R	6-3	185	9-4-90	0	0	0.00	4	0	0	0	7	5	2	0	0	0	6	.179	.273	.118	7.71	0.00
Valerio, Kelvis	R-R	6-1	160	9-26-91	4	2	3.07	9	6	0	0	44	42	20	15	0	7	39	.244	.293	.219	7.98	1.43

Fielding

Catcher	PCT	G	PO	A	E	DP	PB
Ayala	1.000	1	9	0	0	0	1
Barraza	.981	31	280	31	6	2	24
Garcia	1.000	5	22	5	0	0	0
Hollenbeck	.985	23	183	16	3	1	9
Plourde	1.000	7	48	5	0	0	3

First Base	PCT	G	PO	A	E	DP
Flores	.987	26	213	10	3	15
Yount	.975	30	257	17	7	22

Second Base	PCT	G	PO	A	E	DP
Alvarez	.951	16	26	52	4	9

Jarvis	.963	25	39	65	4	14
Santana	.844	7	11	16	5	3
Santos	1.000	1	3	4	0	2
Velasquez	.943	8	11	22	2	4

Third Base	PCT	G	PO	A	E	DP
Basto	.913	9	6	15	2	2
Macias	—	1	0	0	0	0
Moore	.864	24	9	29	6	1
Swick	.980	24	11	39	1	2

Shortstop	PCT	G	PO	A	E	DP
Alvarez	.900	10	11	34	5	6

Anderson	1.000	5	7	18	0	3
Cruz	.925	22	30	68	8	11
Santos	.879	12	15	36	7	9
Velasquez	.953	8	13	28	2	4

Outfield	PCT	G	PO	A	E	DP
Adolfo	.937	43	58	1	4	0
Danner	1.000	12	16	1	0	0
Engel	1.000	8	15	1	0	0
Macias	1.000	18	18	0	0	0
Rodriguez	.985	37	57	7	1	1
Silverio	1.000	23	21	3	0	0
Suiter	.981	34	50	3	1	1

GREAT FALLS VOYAGERS   ROOKIE

PIONEER LEAGUE

Batting	B-T	HT	WT	DOB	AVG	vLH	vRH	G	AB	R	H	2B	3B	HR	RBI	BB	HBP	SH	SF	SO	SB	CS	SLG	OBP
Clarke, Chevy	B-R	6-0	200	1-9-92	.215	.414	.178	47	181	37	39	9	0	10	31	40	1	5	0	67	10	5	.431	.360
Fish, Zach	R-R	6-1	200	11-5-92	.250	.366	.221	56	204	34	51	11	0	5	22	24	3	1	2	62	0	0	.377	.335
Fisher, Zac	L-R	6-2	195	12-13-91	.348	.400	.336	45	178	28	62	11	3	8	46	19	1	0	2	35	0	0	.579	.410
Gross, Ethan	R-R	6-0	193	9-4-92	.230	.061	.270	48	174	18	40	6	1	0	22	19	3	0	2	31	0	0	.276	.313
Haupt, Dillon	R-R	6-5	225	10-8-91	.290	.209	.319	43	162	27	47	9	2	9	28	13	6	0	0	53	0	0	.537	.365
Jones, Hunter	R-R	6-2	185	8-17-91	.351	.250	.386	28	111	28	39	7	3	4	15	12	0	0	1	24	9	1	.577	.411
Jones, Ryan	L-L	6-4	215	6-27-91	.244	.286	.235	46	160	25	39	10	1	3	16	14	6	0	2	30	0	0	.375	.324
Laumann, Jackson	R-R	6-3	220	5-21-93	.193	.237	.179	43	150	12	29	5	1	4	19	9	2	0	2	44	0	0	.320	.245
Lechich, Louie	L-L	6-4	200	11-19-91	.254	.174	.275	61	228	32	58	13	2	5	22	10	2	0	1	56	4	1	.395	.290
Leonards, Ryan	R-R	5-11	195	7-22-91	.333	.333	.333	9	36	6	12	1	2	0	2	2	0	0	0	3	0	0	.472	.368
Palmeiro, Patrick	R-R	6-3	210	3-6-90	.260	.357	.235	54	208	34	54	9	1	10	30	15	0	0	1	62	0	1	.457	.308
Peter, Jake	L-R	6-1	185	4-5-93	.388	.375	.392	37	152	26	59	11	6	2	21	13	4	0	2	13	1	1	.579	.444
Robbins, Mason	L-L	6-0	200	2-1-93	.304	.304	.304	54	230	28	70	11	3	7	32	11	0	0	1	43	1	3	.470	.335
Shryock, Tyler	L-R	6-0	170	3-28-91	.301	.160	.337	32	123	11	37	2	0	0	8	9	0	2	0	15	9	1	.317	.348
Stoner, Zach	L-R	6-3	200	12-16-93	.245	.118	.272	29	98	12	24	4	1	1	7	14	2	0	0	30	0	0	.337	.351
Thomas, Toby	R-R	5-11	190	12-9-93	.274	.188	.291	24	95	11	26	8	2	2	13	8	1	3	0	21	1	2	.463	.337
Ziznewski, John	R-R	6-2	190	4-28-91	.243	.290	.231	43	152	23	37	7	0	0	13	23	0	3	1	39	4	1	.289	.341

Pitching	B-T	HT	WT	DOB	W	L	ERA	G	GS	CG	SV	IP	H	R	ER	HR	BB	SO	AVG	vLH	vRH	K/9	BB/9
Ball, Matt	R-R	6-5	200	1-23-95	3	6	7.26	14	13	0	0	57	81	60	46	6	21	42	.319	.331	.308	6.63	3.32
Bengard, Jon	R-R	6-4	185	1-7-91	2	0	2.76	22	0	0	8	33	37	12	10	3	6	42	.274	.266	.282	11.57	1.65
Brennan, Brandon	R-R	6-4	220	7-26-91	1	1	3.20	5	5	0	0	20	17	8	7	2	7	12	.243	.256	.226	5.49	3.20
Bummer, Aaron	L-L	6-3	200	9-21-93	0	0	2.45	16	0	0	1	22	18	7	6	1	6	28	.222	.214	.226	11.45	2.45
Clark, Brian	R-L	6-3	225	4-27-93	3	4	3.35	15	9	0	0	48	47	27	18	1	14	52	.251	.208	.266	9.68	2.61
Cooper, Matt	R-R	6-0	190	9-30-91	4	2	3.18	21	0	0	1	34	32	12	12	3	10	47	.246	.250	.242	12.44	2.65
Davis, Devon	L-L	6-4	215	8-20-91	0	1	2.77	15	0	0	2	26	17	9	8	0	11	31	.183	.172	.188	10.73	3.81
Freudenberg, Chris	L-L	6-3	195	6-19-93	3	3	3.17	9	9	0	0	48	54	21	17	3	15	38	.280	.245	.293	7.08	2.79
Fry, Jace	L-L	6-1	190	7-9-93	1	0	2.79	7	0	0	0	10	7	3	3	0	3	10	.206	.200	.208	9.31	2.79
Martinez, Luis	R-R	6-4	190	1-29-95	2	1	1.42	5	5	0	0	25	24	4	4	2	10	22	.261	.422	.106	7.82	3.55
McKenzie, Jeff	L-L	6-0	170	5-15-91	1	0	1.54	2	2	0	0	12	7	4	2	1	0	4	.167	.200	.162	3.09	0.00
Monroe, Grant	R-R	6-4	220	9-29-91	1	3	4.50	18	1	0	0	32	36	20	16	3	7	27	.295	.386	.244	7.59	1.97
Peralta, Yelmison	R-R	6-0	190	3-3-95	0	1	3.68	2	2	0	0	7	8	3	3	0	9	4	.308	.250	.400	4.91	11.05
Powers, Alex	R-R	6-0	180	2-26-92	3	1	1.54	11	0	0	2	23	15	5	4	0	3	29	.185	.147	.213	11.19	1.16
Salgado, Brad	R-R	6-1	185	7-15-91	1	0	2.57	3	0	0	1	7	6	2	2	0	2	12	.231	.200	.250	15.43	2.57
Santiago, Anthony	R-R	5-11	200	9-22-89	3	3	6.13	17	2	0	0	40	44	33	27	4	20	27	.291	.355	.247	4.54	4.54
Sharrer, Charlie	R-R	6-1	205	6-27-91	1	1	5.65	18	0	0	1	29	33	20	18	3	11	19	.289	.241	.333	5.97	3.45
Stone, Dane	R-R	6-7	225	6-14-91	6	3	3.99	15	15	0	0	79	95	41	35	4	20	76	.291	.272	.312	8.66	2.28
Thompson, Zach	R-R	6-6	185	10-23-93	2	3	3.27	11	11	0	0	44	43	21	16	2	16	22	.262	.238	.286	5.32	2.86
Trexler, David	R-R	6-3	185	9-4-90	1	2	3.42	14	0	0	0	24	24	11	9	5	9	27	.258	.279	.240	10.27	3.42
Valerio, Kelvis	R-R	6-1	160	9-26-91	0	1	1.64	2	2	0	0	11	9	2	2	1	1	5	.237	.353	.143	4.09	0.82
Walsh, Connor	L-R	6-2	176	10-18-92	1	1	2.66	15	0	0	2	20	15	8	6	0	14	23	.200	.276	.152	10.18	6.20

Fielding

Catcher	PCT	G	PO	A	E	DP	PB
Fisher	.988	30	214	28	3	0	3
Haupt	.995	26	194	12	1	1	4
Stoner	.986	22	185	26	3	0	4

First Base	PCT	G	PO	A	E	DP
Jones	.977	37	323	23	8	31
Laumann	.981	38	340	26	7	26
Palmeiro	1.000	4	41	3	0	2

Second Base	PCT	G	PO	A	E	DP
Gross	.976	21	26	55	2	7

	PCT	G	PO	A	E	DP
Peter	.944	23	35	67	6	19
Thomas	.953	23	38	83	6	19
Ziznewski	.957	10	12	33	2	5

Third Base	PCT	G	PO	A	E	DP
Gross	1.000	2	1	3	0	0
Palmeiro	.926	47	30	82	9	10
Ziznewski	.972	28	17	52	2	4

Shortstop	PCT	G	PO	A	E	DP
Gross	.953	25	35	67	5	18
Leonards	.939	8	9	22	2	5

	PCT	G	PO	A	E	DP
Peter	.984	11	16	47	1	7
Shryock	.919	31	30	84	10	11
Ziznewski	1.000	2	4	6	0	1

Outfield	PCT	G	PO	A	E	DP
Clarke	.954	46	96	8	5	1
Fish	1.000	50	81	4	0	1
Jones	1.000	27	49	3	0	1
Lechich	.969	56	88	6	3	2
Robbins	.978	52	80	7	2	2

DSL WHITE SOX · ROOKIE

DOMINICAN SUMMER LEAGUE

CHICAGO WHITE SOX

Batting	B-T	HT	WT	DOB	AVG	vLH	vRH	G	AB	R	H	2B	3B	HR	RBI	BB	HBP	SH	SF	SO	SB	CS	SLG	OBP
Ariza, Jose	R-R	6-2	183	12-23-93	.200	—	.200	3	5	2	1	0	0	0	0	4	0	1	0	2	0	0	.200	.556
Beltre, Ramon	R-R	5-11	160	10-18-96	.259	.250	.260	60	239	47	62	3	5	0	31	37	3	4	4	33	22	8	.314	.360
Cruz, Johan	R-R	6-2	170	10-8-95	.329	.429	.321	22	85	10	28	7	1	1	7	12	2	4	0	18	5	4	.471	.424
Dalmasi, Gesel	R-R	6-2	236	3-10-93	.250	.333	.241	18	64	9	16	2	1	0	10	8	5	0	0	19	0	1	.313	.377
De Jesus, Jhan	R-R	6-2	165	1-30-92	.189	.000	.200	16	53	5	10	6	0	0	9	5	0	1	1	9	1	0	.302	.254
Feliz, Maiker	R-R	6-0	195	8-17-97	.198	.214	.197	59	212	24	42	5	1	0	27	32	4	3	0	53	4	5	.231	.315
Gideon, Yolberth	R-R	5-11	155	2-6-96	.185	.667	.164	45	146	25	27	0	0	0	8	38	5	1	0	24	1	5	.185	.370
Gonzalez, Carlos	R-R	6-1	175	8-30-93	.268	.350	.259	57	205	26	55	11	1	1	18	19	4	2	3	39	2	4	.346	.338
Gonzalez, Daniel	R-R	6-1	190	12-6-95	.288	.450	.268	47	177	22	51	6	0	0	19	15	5	1	1	12	1	1	.322	.359
Hernandez, Nelson	L-R	6-0	180	2-29-96	.131	.200	.125	25	61	5	8	0	2	0	2	6	2	1	1	19	2	1	.197	.229
Mejia, Carlos	R-R	6-3	190	9-27-95	.210	.000	.221	30	100	11	21	2	2	0	4	9	0	0	1	34	0	0	.270	.273
Mejia, Droherlin	R-R	6-1	180	8-20-94	.287	.500	.271	37	115	19	33	6	1	0	13	13	6	1	2	27	9	4	.357	.382
Otano, Hanleth	R-R	6-3	195	7-16-96	.220	.250	.216	62	214	23	47	14	3	2	27	12	6	0	1	77	0	1	.341	.279
Perez, Carlos	R-R	5-10	160	9-10-96	.305	.200	.311	31	95	10	29	2	0	0	9	7	1	0	1	7	2	0	.326	.356
Ramos, Roger	R-R	6-2	174	10-9-94	.256	.800	.234	44	133	22	34	10	3	1	16	19	5	1	1	46	10	4	.398	.367
Reyes, Victor	R-R	6-0	155	9-24-96	.257	.143	.270	26	70	9	18	3	0	0	5	4	0	3	0	17	3	4	.300	.297
Tejeda, Anderson	L-R	6-0	165	8-1-96	.295	.600	.274	33	78	16	23	2	0	0	9	12	0	1	2	25	8	0	.321	.380
Valdez, Bradley	L-R	6-0	195	12-11-94	.259	.385	.248	44	170	16	44	9	0	0	16	15	4	0	0	25	1	1	.312	.333
Villarroel, Ylexander	B-R	6-2	190	6-4-97	.268	.143	.275	37	138	7	37	4	1	0	7	5	3	0	0	28	1	3	.312	.308

Pitching	B-T	HT	WT	DOB	W	L	ERA	G	GS	CG	SV	IP	H	R	ER	HR	BB	SO	AVG	vLH	vRH	K/9	BB/9
Acosta, Nelson	R-R	6-3	195	8-22-97	0	4	2.35	14	12	0	1	46	25	18	12	0	28	36	.163	.162	.165	7.04	5.48
Aponte, Luis	R-R	6-2	180	8-27-97	0	5	8.87	10	9	0	0	23	31	25	23	0	24	13	.348	.316	.373	5.01	9.26
Arias, Feny	L-L	6-0	175	5-6-91	0	1	1.29	4	0	0	0	7	6	2	1	0	0	9	.222	.250	.217	11.57	0.00
Arteaga, Luis	R-R	6-1	185	10-19-94	3	3	1.75	14	2	0	0	51	38	16	10	1	16	40	.208	.270	.165	7.01	2.81
Coroba, Josbel	L-L	6-0	180	5-18-97	2	1	2.95	19	2	0	1	37	23	15	12	0	23	42	.176	.083	.185	10.31	5.65
De La Cruz, Leonardo	L-L	6-4	180	4-29-94	1	3	2.82	13	0	0	0	22	21	12	7	0	16	27	.239	.100	.256	10.88	6.45
Diaz, Carlos	L-L	6-0	186	1-1-94	5	1	1.29	20	0	0	1	49	32	14	7	0	16	54	.181	.182	.181	9.99	2.96
Escorcia, Kevin	L-L	6-1	170	1-5-95	4	2	1.92	13	12	0	0	56	44	18	12	0	12	73	.215	.192	.218	11.66	1.92
Espinosa, Ramon	R-R	6-2	185	11-30-93	1	5	5.94	18	0	0	2	33	23	25	22	0	23	25	.190	.185	.191	6.75	6.21
Guerrero, Yeuris	R-R	6-3	180	9-20-95	0	2	1.88	15	1	0	3	24	21	10	5	0	8	33	.223	.290	.190	12.38	3.00
Herrera, Antonio	R-R	6-4	195	9-26-94	1	0	2.41	12	3	0	0	34	29	15	9	0	14	15	.232	.226	.234	4.01	3.74
Ledo, Luis	R-R	6-4	208	5-28-95	3	2	5.64	14	3	0	0	22	29	16	14	0	16	24	.319	.304	.324	9.67	6.45
Mora, Hansel	R-R	6-4	185	8-10-94	1	4	6.40	12	10	0	0	32	39	31	23	2	19	26	.302	.353	.284	7.24	5.29
Percel, Eriberto	R-R	6-5	200	8-2-92	3	1	1.86	19	0	0	2	39	24	11	8	0	17	35	.183	.237	.161	8.15	3.96
Perez, Victor	L-R	6-3	195	8-11-95	1	0	3.75	9	1	0	0	12	9	5	5	0	6		.231	.500	.200	4.50	14.25
Quijada, Jhoan	L-L	6-3	210	12-27-94	1	3	3.63	14	3	0	0	52	65	34	21	1	15	38	.302	.375	.286	6.58	2.60
Rocha, Jaider	R-R	6-1	185	5-23-93	2	1	2.05	13	12	0	0	53	41	18	12	0	21	58	.217	.246	.205	9.91	3.59
Rodriguez, Juan	L-R	6-0	185	8-2-92	2	1	1.09	20	0	0	5	33	22	10	4	0	23	29	.186	.313	.167	7.91	6.27
Rodriguez, Wilmy	R-R	6-4	225	11-8-90	0	1	13.50	1	0	0	0	1	1	1	1	0	2	0	.333	.000	.500	0.00	27.00

Fielding

Catcher	PCT	G	PO	A	E	DP	PB
Gonzalez	.988	45	360	42	5	3	16
Perez	.975	25	178	18	5	1	3
Villarroel	.925	7	47	2	4	0	1

First Base	PCT	G	PO	A	E	DP
Ariza	1.000	2	18	0	0	0
Gonzalez	.980	38	327	22	7	28
Reyes	1.000	1	3	0	0	0
Valdez	.993	31	256	10	2	30
Villarroel	.750	1	4	2	2	0

Second Base	PCT	G	PO	A	E	DP
Beltre	.927	20	47	55	8	9

	PCT	G	PO	A	E	DP
Gideon	.971	31	53	81	4	24
Gonzalez	1.000	7	15	17	0	6
Reyes	.935	14	32	26	4	7

Third Base	PCT	G	PO	A	E	DP
Beltre	1.000	2	2	1	0	0
Feliz	.923	59	44	137	15	20
Gideon	.778	3	3	4	2	0
Gonzalez	.912	13	7	24	3	2

Shortstop	PCT	G	PO	A	E	DP
Beltre	.943	37	70	128	12	23
Cruz	.927	21	38	63	8	10
Gideon	.923	9	19	17	3	3

	PCT	G	PO	A	E	DP
Reyes	.889	4	4	12	2	2

Outfield	PCT	G	PO	A	E	DP
Dalmasi	.889	4	8	0	1	0
De Jesus	1.000	15	19	1	0	1
Hernandez	.946	23	35	0	2	0
Mejia	.919	25	30	4	3	1
Mejia	.968	36	55	5	2	1
Otano	.965	58	83	0	3	0
Ramos	.946	44	63	7	4	1
Reyes	—	2	0	0	0	0
Tejeda	.892	29	29	4	4	1

Cincinnati Reds

SEASON IN A SENTENCE: New manager Bryan Price's first year can only be termed a disaster as the Reds fell apart in the second half, failing to live up to the playoff hopes predicted for them before the season.

HIGH POINT: On July 13, Johnny Cueto picked up his 10th win of the season when the Reds beat the Pirates 6-3 on the day before the all-star break to improve to 51-44, 1.5 games out of first place in the NL Central.

LOW POINT: Cincinnati's bullpen fell apart in a 14-5 loss to the Mets on Sept. 5. The loss was Cincinnati's fourth straight and its 17th in 23 games. It dropped the Reds to 66-75 overall. That was one of many low points over the final two months of the season. The Reds had two six-game losing streaks over the final two months and a third stretch where they lost six of seven.

NOTABLE ROOKIES: Center fielder Billy Hamilton had a very streaky season at the plate. He started very slowly, but warmed up to hit 10 doubles and three home runs in an extremely productive June. He then tailed off again in the second half of the season. Defensively, he was excellent in center field. Righthanded reliever Jumbo Diaz made his big league debut as a 30-year-old to provide surprisingly effective relief work as a setup man.

KEY TRANSACTIONS: First baseman Joey Votto was placed on the disabled list on May 21 with a quad injury. He came off the disabled list, then reaggravated the injury and went back on the disabled list in early July. He never returned to action. His lost season was crushing for the Reds as Cincinnati had no one ready to adequately replace him. Votto's replacements at first base hit .257/.312/.382.

DOWN ON THE FARM: Righthander Ben Lively, a 2014 fourth-round pick, was a surprise standout. Lively was dominant (10-1, 2.28) in the first half of the season in high Class A Bakersfield, and pitched well for Double-A Pensacola (3-6, 3.88). Reds 2014 supplemental first-rounder Michael Lorenzen showed good control at Pensacola. Jesse Winker posted a .917 OPS through two levels before an injury ended his season. The news wasn't as good for 2013 first-rounder Phillip Ervin. Ervin hit just .237/.305/.376 at low Class A Dayton. No. 1 prospect Robert Stephenson struggled with his control, going 7-10, 4.74.

OPENING DAY PAYROLL: $112.4 million (11th).

PLAYERS OF THE YEAR

MAJOR LEAGUE	MINOR LEAGUE
Johnny Cueto	**Jesse Winker**
rhp	of
20-9, 2.25, 0.96 WHIP	.287/.399/.518
244 IP, 169 H, 242 SO	(High-A, Double-A)
Tied for NL lead in SO	15 HR, 57 RBI

ORGANIZATION LEADERS

BATTING *Minimum 250 AB

MAJORS

* AVG	Mesoraco, Devin	.273
* OPS	Mesoraco, Devin	.893
HR	Frazier, Todd	29
RBI	Frazier, Todd	80
	Mesoraco, Devin	80

MINORS

* AVG	Waldrop, Kyle, Bakersfield, Pensacola	.338
* OBP	Smith, Marquez, Pensacola, Bakersfield	.424
* SLG	Smith, Marquez, Pensacola, Bakersfield	.601
R	Smith, Marquez, Pensacola, Bakersfield	93
H	Waldrop, Kyle, Bakersfield, Pensacola	165
TB	Smith, Marquez, Pensacola, Bakersfield	274
2B	Waldrop, Kyle, Bakersfield, Pensacola	37
3B	Ovalle, Gabriel, DSL Reds	8
HR	Smith, Marquez, Pensacola, Bakersfield	30
RBI	Smith, Marquez, Pensacola, Bakersfield	131
BB	Smith, Marquez, Pensacola, Bakersfield	85
SO	Mattair, Travis, Pensacola	133
SB	Silva, Juan, Bakersfield	34

PITCHING #Minimum 75 IP

MAJORS

W	Cueto, Johnny	20
# ERA	Cueto, Johnny	2.25
SO	Cueto, Johnny	242
SV	Chapman, Aroldis	36

MINORS

W	Travieso, Nick, Dayton	14
	Wright, Daniel, Dayton, Bakersfield	14
L	Corcino, Daniel, Pensacola, Louisville	12
	Peralta, Wandy, Bakersfield	12
# ERA	Travieso, Nick, Dayton	3.03
G	Dennick, Ryan, Pensacola, Louisville	58
GS	Moscot, Jon, Pensacola, Louisville	28
	Peralta, Wandy, Bakersfield	28
	Romano, Sal, Dayton	28
SV	Dyer, Shane, Pensacola	22
IP	Moscot, Jon, Pensacola, Louisville	167
BB	Corcino, Daniel, Pensacola, Louisville	74
	Stephenson, Robert, Pensacola	74
SO	Lively, Ben, Bakersfield, Pensacola	171
AVG	Lively, Ben, Bakersfield, Pensacola	.215

General Manager: Walt Jocketty. **Farm Director:** Jeff Graupe. **Scouting Director:** Chris Buckley.

Class	Team	League	W	L	PCT	Finish	Manager
Majors	Cincinnati Reds	National	76	86	.469	21st (30)	Bryan Price
Triple-A	Louisville Bats	International	68	75	.476	9th (14)	Jim Riggleman
Double-A	Pensacola Blue Wahoos	Southern	60	80	.429	t-9th (10	Delino DeShields
High A	Bakersfield Blaze	California	78	62	.557	t-2nd (10)	Pat Kelly
Low A	Dayton Dragons	Midwest	68	70	.493	8th (16)	Jose Nieves
Rookie	Billings Mustangs	Pioneer	41	35	.539	3rd (8)	Dick Schofield
Rookie	Reds	Arizona	24	32	.429	11th (13)	Eli Marrero
Overall Minor League Record			339	354	.489	20th (30)	

ORGANIZATION STATISTICS

CINCINNATI REDS

NATIONAL LEAGUE

Batting	B-T	HT	WT	DOB	AVG	vLH	vRH	G	AB	R	H	2B	3B	HR	RBI	BB	HBP	SH	SF	SO	SB	CS	SLG	OBP
Barnhart, Tucker	B-R	5-11	195	1-7-91	.185	.083	.214	21	54	3	10	0	0	1	1	4	0	2	0	10	0	0	.241	.241
Bernadina, Roger	L-L	6-2	200	6-12-84	.153	.182	.146	44	59	3	9	3	0	0	5	10	1	1	0	16	2	1	.203	.286
2-team total (9 Los Angeles)					.167	—	—	53	66	5	11	3	0	1	9	10	3	1	0	19	2	1	.258	.304
Bourgeois, Jason	R-R	5-9	190	1-4-82	.242	.400	.214	18	33	5	8	0	1	0	1	1	0	0	0	6	0	0	.303	.265
Bruce, Jay	L-L	6-3	215	4-3-87	.217	.161	.235	137	493	71	107	21	1	18	66	44	2	1	5	149	12	3	.373	.281
Cozart, Zack	R-R	6-0	195	8-12-85	.221	.262	.211	147	506	48	112	18	5	4	38	25	7	5	0	79	7	0	.300	.268
Elmore, Jake	R-R	5-9	185	6-15-87	.182	.000	.200	5	11	0	2	0	0	0	0	1	0	0	0	4	0	0	.182	.250
Frazier, Todd	R-R	6-3	220	2-12-86	.273	.254	.278	157	597	88	163	22	1	29	80	52	7	0	4	139	20	8	.459	.336
Hamilton, Billy	B-R	6-0	160	9-9-90	.250	.264	.246	152	563	72	141	25	8	6	48	34	1	9	4	117	56	23	.355	.292
Hannahan, Jack	L-R	6-2	210	3-4-80	.188	.000	.191	26	48	3	9	3	0	0	2	2	0	0	0	17	0	0	.250	.220
Heisey, Chris	R-R	6-1	210	12-14-84	.222	.205	.229	119	275	34	61	15	2	8	22	15	2	5	2	64	9	2	.378	.265
Ludwick, Ryan	R-L	6-2	215	7-13-78	.244	.253	.241	112	357	28	87	20	0	9	45	31	4	1	4	94	0	2	.375	.308
Lutz, Donald	L-R	6-3	250	2-6-89	.176	.333	.167	28	51	2	9	4	0	0	1	3	0	0	0	16	0	0	.255	.222
Mesoraco, Devin	R-R	6-1	220	6-19-88	.273	.291	.269	114	384	54	105	25	0	25	80	41	12	0	3	103	1	3	.534	.359
Negron, Kris	R-R	6-0	195	2-1-86	.271	.318	.250	49	144	19	39	10	1	6	17	12	1	1	0	40	5	0	.479	.331
Pena, Brayan	R-B	5-9	230	1-7-82	.253	.184	.272	115	348	23	88	18	1	5	26	20	1	0	3	42	2	3	.353	.291
Phillips, Brandon	R-R	6-0	200	6-28-81	.266	.229	.278	121	462	44	123	25	0	8	51	23	6	2	6	74	2	3	.372	.306
Rodriguez, Yorman	R-R	6-3	195	8-15-92	.222	.167	.238	11	27	3	6	0	0	0	2	1	1	0	0	12	0	1	.222	.276
Santiago, Ramon	B-R	5-11	175	8-31-79	.246	.362	.205	75	179	20	44	8	0	2	17	24	3	7	1	38	2	1	.324	.343
Schumaker, Skip	L-L	5-10	195	2-3-80	.235	.222	.238	83	247	22	58	12	0	2	22	18	1	3	2	50	2	1	.308	.287
Soto, Neftali	R-R	6-1	215	2-28-89	.100	.200	.000	21	30	1	3	1	0	0	1	0	0	0	1	8	1	0	.133	.097
Votto, Joey	L-R	6-2	220	9-10-83	.255	.293	.241	62	220	32	56	16	0	6	23	47	3	0	2	49	1	1	.409	.390

Pitching	B-T	HT	WT	DOB	W	L	ERA	G	GS	CG	SV	IP	H	R	ER	HR	BB	SO	AVG	vLH	vRH	K/9	BB/9
Axelrod, Dylan	R-R	6-0	195	7-30-85	2	1	2.95	5	4	0	0	18	14	6	6	5	4	20	.206	.111	.268	9.82	1.96
Bailey, Homer	R-R	6-4	230	5-3-86	9	5	3.71	23	23	1	0	146	134	60	60	16	45	124	.247	.270	.230	7.66	2.78
Bell, Trevor	L-R	6-2	205	10-12-86	0	0	67.50	2	0	0	0	1	5	5	5	0	2	0	.714	.500	.800	0.00	27.00
Broxton, Jonathan	R-R	6-4	295	6-16-84	4	2	1.86	51	0	0	7	48	32	10	10	3	17	37	.190	.219	.173	6.89	3.17
2-team total (11 Milwaukee)					4	3	2.30	62	0	0	7	59	41	15	15	4	19	49	—	—	—	7.52	2.91
Chapman, Aroldis	L-L	6-4	205	2-28-88	0	3	2.00	54	0	0	36	54	21	12	12	1	24	106	.121	.132	.118	17.67	4.00
Christiani, Nick	R-R	6-0	190	7-17-87	0	1	5.54	10	0	0	0	13	12	8	8	2	6	8	.240	.429	.167	5.54	4.15
Cingrani, Tony	L-L	6-4	215	7-5-89	2	8	4.55	13	11	0	0	63	63	33	32	12	35	61	.258	.204	.272	8.67	4.97
Contreras, Carlos	R-R	5-11	205	1-8-91	0	1	6.52	17	0	0	0	19	19	16	14	2	17	19	.250	.216	.282	8.84	7.91
Corcino, Daniel	R-R	5-11	210	8-26-90	0	2	4.34	5	3	0	0	19	13	9	9	2	10	15	.188	.167	.200	7.23	4.82
Cueto, Johnny	R-R	5-11	215	2-15-86	20	9	2.25	34	34	4	0	244	169	69	61	22	65	242	.194	.194	.194	8.94	2.40
Dennick, Ryan	L-L	6-0	185	1-10-87	0	0	11.57	8	0	0	0	5	7	7	6	2	4	3	.350	.143	.462	5.79	7.71
Diaz, Jumbo	R-R	6-4	315	2-27-84	0	1	3.38	36	0	0	0	35	29	13	13	3	14	37	.230	.275	.209	9.61	3.63
Francis, Jeff	L-L	6-5	220	1-8-81	0	1	5.40	1	1	0	0	5	5	3	3	1	0	4	.250	.000	.278	7.20	0.00
Holmberg, David	R-L	6-3	225	7-19-91	2	2	4.80	7	5	0	0	30	27	16	16	8	16	18	.243	.280	.233	5.40	4.80
Hoover, J.J.	R-R	6-3	230	8-13-87	1	10	4.88	54	0	0	0	63	56	36	34	13	31	75	.236	.333	.159	10.77	4.45
Latos, Mat	R-R	6-6	245	12-9-87	5	5	3.25	16	16	0	0	102	92	42	37	9	26	74	.240	.237	.244	6.51	2.29
Leake, Mike	R-R	5-10	190	11-12-87	11	13	3.70	33	33	0	0	214	217	93	88	23	50	164	.263	.290	.242	6.89	2.10
LeCure, Sam	R-R	6-0	205	5-4-84	1	4	3.81	62	0	0	0	57	62	27	24	6	24	48	.283	.215	.333	7.62	3.81
Marshall, Sean	L-L	6-7	225	8-30-82	0	0	7.71	15	0	0	0	14	23	14	12	1	12	14	.354	.458	.293	9.00	7.71
Ondrusek, Logan	R-R	6-8	230	2-13-85	3	3	5.49	40	0	0	0	41	50	26	25	5	16	42	.296	.306	.290	9.22	3.51
Parra, Manny	L-L	6-3	215	10-30-82	0	3	4.66	53	0	0	1	37	39	20	19	4	18	34	.272	.256	.305	8.35	4.42
Partch, Curtis	R-R	6-5	240	2-13-87	1	0	0.00	6	0	0	0	7	2	0	0	0	7	6	.087	.200	.000	7.71	9.00
Simon, Alfredo	R-R	6-6	265	5-8-81	15	10	3.44	32	32	0	0	196	181	80	75	22	56	127	.245	.251	.238	5.82	2.57
Villarreal, Pedro	R-R	6-1	230	12-9-87	0	2	4.30	12	0	0	0	15	11	7	7	1	7	12	.208	.176	.222	7.36	4.30

Fielding

Catcher	PCT	G	PO	A	E	DP	PB
Barnhart	1.000	20	110	14	0	2	3
Mesoraco	.997	109	832	55	3	5	9
Pena	.995	46	361	20	2	3	1

First Base	PCT	G	PO	A	E	DP
Bernadina	1.000	1	10	0	0	0

	PCT	G	PO	A	E	DP
Bruce	.875	3	14	0	2	0
Frazier	.985	43	297	27	5	21
Hannahan	.985	13	58	6	1	7

Lutz	.975	6	36	3	1	3
Pena	.997	53	365	23	1	35
Soto	1.000	7	20	1	0	0
Votto	.988	61	499	63	7	39

Second Base	PCT	G	PO	A	E	DP
Elmore	1.000	2	5	2	0	0
Negron	1.000	17	22	46	0	8
Phillips	.996	121	216	307	2	68
Santiago	.986	20	25	47	1	8
Schumaker	.957	19	28	39	3	7

Third Base	PCT	G	PO	A	E	DP
Frazier	.970	124	85	204	9	16

Negron	.983	25	18	41	1	4
Santiago	.932	28	22	33	4	2
Soto	1.000	2	1	1	0	0

Shortstop	PCT	G	PO	A	E	DP
Cozart	.984	147	204	400	10	73
Elmore	1.000	3	2	5	0	1
Negron	1.000	2	5	6	0	1
Santiago	1.000	20	17	50	0	8

Outfield	PCT	G	PO	A	E	DP
Bernadina	1.000	26	23	0	0	0
Bourgeois	.929	10	12	1	1	0
Bruce	.980	131	231	8	5	2

Hamilton	.994	144	342	10	2	3
Heisey	1.000	77	131	0	0	0
Ludwick	1.000	92	135	1	0	0
Lutz	1.000	6	11	1	0	1
Negron	—	1	0	0	0	0
Rodriguez	1.000	8	12	0	0	0
Santiago	—	1	0	0	0	0
Schumaker	.987	52	71	3	1	1

LOUISVILLE BATS

TRIPLE-A

INTERNATIONAL LEAGUE

Batting	B-T	HT	WT	DOB	AVG	vLH	vRH	G	AB	R	H	2B	3B	HR	RBI	BB	HBP	SH	SF	SO	SB	CS	SLG	OBP
Anderson, Bryan	L-R	6-1	200	12-16-86	.302	.185	.326	52	162	20	49	12	1	5	24	19	2	3	1	29	0	1	.481	.380
Barnhart, Tucker	B-R	5-11	195	1-7-91	.246	.138	.278	78	256	18	63	9	3	1	29	28	1	4	3	34	0	1	.316	.319
Berset, Chris	B-R	6-0	195	1-27-88	.000	—	.000	1	3	0	0	0	0	0	0	0	0	0	0	1	0	0	.000	.000
Bourgeois, Jason	R-R	5-9	190	1-4-82	.278	.194	.307	136	551	76	153	29	3	4	43	40	3	3	3	51	24	9	.363	.328
Chang, Ray	R-R	6-1	195	8-24-83	.250	.000	.500	1	4	0	1	0	0	0	0	0	0	0	0	0	0	0	.500	.250
Costanzo, Mike	L-R	6-2	205	9-9-83	.194	.059	.214	43	129	9	25	4	0	4	15	16	0	0	2	47	0	1	.318	.279
Diaz, Argenis	R-R	6-0	190	2-12-87	.245	.250	.243	53	163	21	40	8	0	1	18	10	1	7	1	30	2	2	.313	.291
Duncan, Shelley	R-R	6-5	215	9-29-79	.200	.222	.192	14	35	4	7	1	0	1	4	6	1	1	0	7	0	0	.314	.333
Elmore, Jake	R-R	5-9	185	6-15-87	.279	.250	.288	25	86	14	24	2	0	0	6	15	0	1	2	15	3	0	.302	.379
Fellhauer, Josh	L-L	5-11	175	3-24-88	.222	.667	.167	9	27	4	6	3	0	0	4	2	0	0	0	7	0	0	.333	.276
Gotay, Ruben	B-R	5-11	175	12-25-82	.255	.231	.263	136	518	86	132	22	1	17	59	61	1	0	4	127	3	3	.400	.332
Hannahan, Jack	L-R	6-2	210	3-4-80	.286	.167	.318	8	28	1	8	2	0	0	5	2	0	0	1	4	0	0	.357	.323
Iribarren, Hernan	L-R	6-1	195	6-29-84	.233	.240	.231	99	249	29	58	9	2	1	20	27	0	4	4	45	1	1	.297	.304
LaMarre, Ryan	R-L	6-1	205	11-21-88	.200	.143	.241	17	50	6	10	2	0	1	6	8	0	1	0	17	1	1	.300	.310
Lutz, Donald	L-R	6-3	250	2-6-89	.236	.259	.227	52	195	26	46	9	2	6	33	17	4	0	2	68	4	0	.395	.307
Mesoraco, Devin	R-R	6-1	220	6-19-88	.300	.250	.333	3	10	2	3	0	0	1	2	0	0	0	0	1	0	0	.600	.300
Miller, Corky	R-R	6-1	250	3-18-76	.190	.200	.184	23	63	4	12	3	0	0	5	1	0	0	0	14	0	0	.238	.203
Murphy, Donnie	R-R	5-10	190	3-10-83	.152	.200	.143	10	33	1	5	1	0	1	3	2	1	0	0	5	0	0	.273	.222
2-team total (10 Gwinnett)					.160	—	—	20	75	7	12	3	0	1	3	13	2	2	0	1	17	0	0	.320	.200
Navarro, Rey	B-R	5-10	185	12-22-89	.296	.237	.316	65	230	24	68	17	0	3	24	19	1	0	1	26	1	1	.409	.351
Neal, Thomas	R-R	6-2	220	8-17-87	.255	.260	.254	106	364	44	93	18	1	4	38	36	5	2	2	70	2	2	.343	.329
Negron, Kris	R-R	6-0	195	2-1-86	.269	.234	.284	75	219	33	59	15	3	3	25	14	5	2	0	54	9	2	.406	.328
Nelson, Chris	R-R	5-11	205	9-3-85	.274	.382	.231	63	237	26	65	9	0	4	38	18	3	0	3	52	0	2	.363	.330
Perez, Felix	L-L	6-2	190	11-14-84	.280	.235	.296	122	460	62	129	36	3	12	74	29	4	1	5	85	0	2	.450	.325
Perez, Rossmel	R-R	5-9	200	8-26-89	.214	.143	.238	9	28	1	6	1	0	0	3	2	0	0	0	3	0	0	.250	.267
Phillips, Brandon	R-R	6-0	200	6-28-81	.000	.000	.000	2	5	0	0	0	0	0	0	1	0	0	0	0	0	0	.000	.167
Ramirez, Max	R-R	5-11	220	10-11-84	.192	.208	.179	20	52	5	10	0	0	0	2	16	0	0	0	11	0	0	.192	.382
Schumaker, Skip	L-R	5-10	195	2-3-80	.417	.500	.375	4	12	1	5	4	0	0	3	1	0	0	0	3	0	0	.750	.462
Selsky, Steve	R-R	6-0	203	7-20-89	.240	.244	.238	55	121	15	29	7	1	1	11	21	2	0	1	47	0	0	.339	.359
Silverio, Juan	R-R	6-1	175	4-18-91	.247	.130	.290	31	85	10	21	6	0	1	5	2	0	0	0	22	0	0	.353	.264
Soto, Neftali	R-R	6-1	215	2-28-89	.302	.321	.297	75	278	27	84	23	0	2	34	21	1	0	3	41	0	0	.406	.350
Votto, Joey	L-R	6-2	220	9-10-83	.333	.333	.333	2	6	1	2	0	0	0	0	0	0	0	0	2	0	0	.333	.333
Wilson, Mike	R-R	6-2	245	6-29-83	.205	.263	.160	29	88	9	18	5	0	3	7	11	0	0	0	26	0	0	.364	.293

Pitching	B-T	HT	WT	DOB	W	L	ERA	G	GS	CG	SV	IP	H	R	ER	HR	BB	SO	AVG	vLH	vRH	K/9	BB/9
Axelrod, Dylan	R-R	6-0	195	7-30-85	2	2	2.98	6	6	1	0	42	31	14	14	3	7	32	.203	.279	.141	6.80	1.49
2-team total (18 Charlotte)					8	9	4.01	24	22	1	0	130	127	61	58	12	43	108	—	—	—	7.46	2.97
Bell, Trevor	L-R	6-2	205	10-12-86	0	0	0.00	1	0	0	0	1	0	0	0	0	1	1	.000	—	.000	9.00	9.00
Castillo, Fabio	R-R	6-1	235	2-19-89	2	1	2.74	15	0	0	1	23	17	8	7	0	12	15	.205	.222	.196	5.87	4.70
Chapman, Aroldis	L-L	6-4	205	2-28-88	0	1	72.00	2	1	0	0	1	7	8	8	0	2	2	.700	.500	.833	18.00	18.00
Christiani, Nick	R-R	6-0	190	7-17-87	3	0	6.75	24	0	0	0	28	45	23	21	2	18	14	.372	.444	.329	4.50	5.79
Corcino, Daniel	R-R	5-11	210	8-26-90	0	1	7.20	1	1	0	0	5	3	4	4	3	6	4	.176	.000	.429	10.80	7.20
Crabbe, Tim	R-R	6-4	195	2-20-88	5	7	4.13	30	12	0	2	94	104	50	43	8	37	60	.281	.260	.299	5.73	3.56
Dennick, Ryan	L-L	6-0	185	1-10-87	4	0	2.36	57	0	0	3	50	42	15	13	0	18	39	.231	.209	.253	7.07	3.26
Diamond, Scott	L-L	6-3	220	7-30-86	1	5	6.65	9	7	0	0	43	65	34	32	5	10	19	.346	.367	.338	3.95	2.08
2-team total (17 Rochester)					5	12	6.57	26	22	1	0	123	174	96	90	15	32	66	—	—	—	4.82	2.34
Diaz, Jumbo	R-R	6-4	315	2-27-84	2	2	1.35	30	0	0	18	33	25	6	5	1	10	31	.208	.268	.156	8.37	2.70
Francis, Jeff	L-L	6-5	220	1-8-81	4	3	3.33	8	8	0	0	49	52	25	18	3	12	45	.272	.238	.289	8.32	2.22
Freeman, Justin	R-R	5-11	175	10-22-86	3	1	4.25	29	0	0	6	30	34	16	14	1	8	23	.293	.302	.288	6.98	2.43
Gonzalez, Edgar	R-R	6-2	210	2-23-83	0	0	4.50	2	0	0	0	2	2	1	1	0	2	5	.250	.000	.333	22.50	9.00
Holmberg, David	R-L	6-3	225	7-19-91	2	6	4.66	18	18	0	0	93	119	53	48	4	33	56	.316	.407	.287	5.44	3.21
Hoover, J.J.	R-R	6-3	230	8-13-87	0	0	0.00	4	0	0	0	5	3	1	0	0	2	7	.150	.143	.167	12.60	3.60
Hyde, Lee	R-L	6-2	210	2-14-85	0	1	5.68	25	0	0	0	25	24	18	16	1	13	27	.258	.257	.259	9.59	4.62
Jurrjens, Jair	R-R	6-1	200	1-29-86	2	3	4.46	6	6	0	0	34	42	19	17	1	13	27	.311	.393	.243	7.08	3.41
Latos, Mat	R-R	6-6	245	12-9-87	2	0	2.33	4	4	1	0	19	17	5	5	1	7	13	.243	.346	.182	6.05	3.26
Maloney, Matt	L-L	6-4	210	1-16-84	0	2	16.20	2	2	0	0	7	25	16	12	2	0	3	.595	.750	.579	4.05	0.00
Marmol, Carlos	R-R	6-1	235	10-14-82	0	1	7.36	3	0	0	0	4	2	3	3	1	6	6	.167	.500	.000	14.73	14.73

Marshall, Brett	R-R	6-1	195	3-22-90	1	10	6.53	16	15	0	0	70	77	62	51	9	51	59	.279	.324	.248	7.55	6.53
Marshall, Sean	L-L	6-7	225	8-30-82	0	0	4.50	2	2	0	0	2	2	1	1	1	1	2	.250	.333	.200	9.00	4.50
Moscot, Jon	R-R	6-4	205	8-15-91	1	1	5.71	3	3	0	0	17	15	11	11	5	7	9	.224	.231	.220	4.67	3.63
O'Brien, Mikey	R-R	5-11	190	3-3-90	0	2	4.65	7	5	0	0	31	28	19	16	5	11	22	.248	.280	.222	6.39	3.19
Ondrusek, Logan	R-R	6-8	230	2-13-85	0	0	0.00	1	1	0	0	1	2	0	0	0	0	0	.500	.000	.667	0.00	0.00
Partch, Curtis	R-R	6-5	240	2-13-87	4	1	4.75	41	0	0	6	47	46	28	25	3	25	54	.258	.246	.266	10.27	4.75
Ramirez, Elvin	R-R	6-3	210	10-10-87	2	4	6.05	16	0	0	1	19	21	14	13	2	10	16	.276	.276	.277	7.45	4.66
Reineke, Chad	R-R	6-6	230	4-9-82	0	4	9.20	11	4	0	0	30	46	32	31	4	14	19	.343	.375	.326	5.64	4.15
Rogers, Chad	R-R	5-11	205	8-3-89	2	0	4.08	35	0	0	1	53	58	30	24	7	37	34	.276	.318	.248	5.77	6.28
Rowland-Smith, Ryan	L-L	6-3	250	1-26-83	0	0	4.20	12	1	0	0	15	19	9	7	0	4	9	.317	.409	.263	5.40	2.40
2-team total (12 Buffalo)					1	0	4.66	24	1	0	0	29	29	17	15	4	7	20	—	—	—	6.21	2.17
Russell, Adam	R-R	6-8	280	4-14-83	2	2	4.33	27	0	0	2	35	39	18	17	2	19	34	.289	.352	.247	8.66	4.84
Schmidt, Nick	L-L	6-5	245	10-10-85	0	1	7.53	10	0	0	0	14	20	12	12	1	10	11	.339	.240	.412	6.91	6.28
Smith, Josh	R-R	6-2	220	8-7-87	10	7	4.70	28	24	1	0	159	174	90	83	8	66	123	.275	.271	.278	6.96	3.74
Villarreal, Pedro	R-R	6-1	230	12-9-87	6	2	3.20	42	2	0	2	56	57	20	20	5	13	50	.261	.173	.333	7.99	2.08
Wang, Chien-Ming	R-R	6-4	225	3-31-80	8	5	3.70	19	19	0	0	119	129	58	49	4	45	50	.282	.248	.310	3.77	3.39
2-team total (9 Charlotte)					13	8	4.12	28	28	0	0	173	200	94	79	6	57	73	—	—	—	3.81	2.97
Williamson, Fabian	R-L	6-2	175	10-20-88	0	0	4.50	1	0	0	0	2	1	1	1	0	2	2	.143	.000	.167	9.00	9.00

Fielding

Catcher	PCT	G	PO	A	E	DP	PB
Anderson	.996	40	264	11	1	2	1
Barnhart	.992	75	450	54	4	5	1
Berset	1.000	1	7	1	0	0	0
Mesoraco	1.000	3	11	0	0	0	0
Miller	.993	21	133	6	1	2	2
Perez	.960	8	47	1	2	0	1
Ramirez	1.000	6	43	0	0	1	0

First Base	PCT	G	PO	A	E	DP
Anderson	.972	7	31	4	1	5
Chang	1.000	1	6	1	0	1
Costanzo	.967	29	191	12	7	27
Duncan	1.000	4	24	1	0	3
Gotay	.982	8	51	4	1	6
Hannahan	1.000	3	23	1	0	2
Lutz	.990	15	92	5	1	9
Miller	1.000	1	8	1	0	0
Neal	.994	53	443	17	3	51
Nelson	1.000	2	6	0	0	1
Ramirez	.986	10	65	3	1	5
Silverio	1.000	1	2	0	0	0
Soto	.993	35	252	17	2	28
Votto	1.000	2	12	2	0	3

Second Base	PCT	G	PO	A	E	DP
Bourgeois	1.000	1	0	1	0	0
Diaz	.913	3	9	12	2	3
Elmore	1.000	14	28	40	0	9
Gotay	.981	80	161	204	7	64
Iribarren	.978	29	52	80	3	20
Murphy	1.000	6	16	18	0	7
Navarro	.952	16	19	40	3	10
Negron	1.000	5	3	13	0	1
Nelson	.917	2	3	8	1	4
Phillips	.923	2	7	5	1	3
Schumaker	—	1	0	0	0	0

Third Base	PCT	G	PO	A	E	DP
Costanzo	.818	5	3	6	2	0
Diaz	1.000	2	2	4	0	1
Elmore	1.000	2	1	1	0	0
Gotay	.906	23	12	46	6	1
Iribarren	.922	29	9	38	4	5
Negron	.857	3	2	4	1	0
Nelson	.957	51	25	86	5	9
Silverio	.920	24	15	31	4	4
Soto	.934	37	22	63	6	7

Shortstop	PCT	G	PO	A	E	DP
Diaz	.955	48	63	128	9	26
Elmore	1.000	8	10	20	0	5
Iribarren	.889	7	2	14	2	1
Murphy	1.000	2	4	2	0	1
Navarro	.979	51	61	130	4	23
Negron	.981	47	69	140	4	40

Outfield	PCT	G	PO	A	E	DP
Bourgeois	.991	130	315	9	3	4
Costanzo	1.000	5	4	2	0	0
Elmore	1.000	2	3	0	0	0
Fellhauer	.867	8	13	0	2	0
Gotay	.967	14	28	1	1	0
Iribarren	1.000	35	37	2	0	1
LaMarre	.980	17	46	2	1	1
Lutz	1.000	39	67	7	0	1
Murphy	1.000	1	3	0	0	0
Neal	1.000	17	38	1	0	0
Negron	.975	26	39	0	1	0
Nelson	.905	10	18	1	2	0
Perez	.989	116	258	14	3	3
Schumaker	1.000	4	10	0	0	0
Selsky	.977	49	83	1	2	0
Wilson	.963	18	26	0	1	0

PENSACOLA BLUE WAHOOS

SOUTHERN LEAGUE

DOUBLE-A

Batting	B-T	HT	WT	DOB	AVG	vLH	vRH	G	AB	R	H	2B	3B	HR	RBI	BB	HBP	SH	SF	SO	SB	CS	SLG	OBP
Amaral, Beau	L-L	5-10	177	2-11-91	.167	.143	.174	10	30	7	5	2	0	0	2	5	0	0	0	5	1	0	.233	.286
Anderson, Bryan	L-R	6-1	200	12-16-86	.343	.375	.326	21	70	11	24	2	2	5	19	11	0	0	1	14	0	1	.643	.427
Berset, Chris	B-R	6-0	195	1-27-88	.187	.161	.194	42	139	12	26	2	0	0	9	18	1	1	2	28	0	1	.201	.281
Chang, Ray	R-R	6-1	195	8-24-83	.234	.219	.239	53	145	17	34	9	0	0	14	12	2	3	1	23	0	1	.297	.300
Duran, Juan	R-R	6-7	230	9-2-91	.243	.197	.256	100	338	40	82	18	3	17	51	23	3	0	0	130	1	1	.464	.297
Fellhauer, Josh	L-L	5-11	175	3-24-88	.243	.143	.250	34	107	12	26	3	2	0	10	18	0	1	0	28	1	1	.308	.352
2-team total (39 Huntsville)					.268	—	—	73	235	24	63	12	4	0	19	34	0	3	1	60	2	2	.353	.359
Gonzalez, Yovan	R-R	5-10	190	11-11-89	.143	.222	.105	8	28	3	4	1	0	0	0	0	1	0	0	4	0	0	.179	.143
Greene, Brodie	R-R	6-1	195	9-25-87	.227	.244	.221	113	362	41	82	15	1	3	29	37	1	6	5	51	10	4	.298	.296
Lohman, Devin	R-R	6-1	185	4-14-89	.245	.278	.235	108	330	37	81	16	2	5	29	27	7	4	7	74	8	6	.352	.310
Lutz, Donald	L-R	6-3	250	2-6-89	.360	.294	.375	23	89	16	32	7	2	6	16	7	1	0	0	17	1	0	.685	.412
Marson, Lou	R-R	6-1	205	6-26-86	.217	.400	.167	7	23	2	5	0	0	2	5	0	0	0	0	3	1	0	.217	.379
Mattair, Travis	R-R	6-5	210	12-21-88	.238	.274	.228	131	474	56	113	27	2	13	69	39	5	1	1	133	3	1	.386	.303
Mejias-Brean, Seth	R-R	6-2	216	4-5-91	.235	.313	.213	65	226	23	53	7	2	3	22	32	2	3	1	50	1	4	.323	.333
Mesoraco, Devin	R-R	6-1	220	6-19-88	.000	—	.000	3	5	0	0	0	0	0	0	2	0	0	1	1	0	0	.000	.250
Navarro, Rey	B-R	5-10	185	12-22-89	.271	.259	.274	67	255	40	69	17	2	9	33	27	0	5	4	32	4	7	.459	.336
Perez, Rossmel	B-R	5-9	200	8-26-89	.333	.205	.357	72	252	34	84	16	2	4	48	23	2	1	2	21	2	4	.460	.391
Rodriguez, Yorman	R-R	6-3	195	8-15-92	.262	.294	.255	119	450	69	118	20	5	9	40	47	1	1	3	117	12	5	.389	.331
Selsky, Steve	R-R	6-0	203	7-20-89	.301	.293	.304	64	166	23	50	8	0	1	21	29	5	0	5	42	2	4	.367	.410
Silverio, Juan	R-R	6-1	175	4-18-91	.270	.214	.286	79	259	34	70	12	2	10	31	12	3	2	3	51	2	0	.448	.307
Smith, Bryson	R-R	6-1	195	12-17-88	.227	.108	.274	46	132	6	30	3	0	1	12	8	4	2	1	18	1	2	.273	.290
Smith, Marquez	R-R	5-10	185	3-20-85	.156	.429	.080	14	32	4	5	2	0	1	5	2	0	0	0	12	0	0	.313	.206
Waldrop, Kyle	L-L	6-2	216	11-26-91	.315	.300	.318	66	232	27	73	17	3	8	35	17	0	1	2	44	3	4	.517	.359
Winker, Jesse	L-L	6-3	210	8-17-93	.208	.250	.193	21	77	15	16	5	0	2	8	14	0	0	1	22	0	0	.351	.326
Wright, Ryan	R-R	6-1	200	12-3-89	.205	.300	.184	62	219	23	45	12	0	2	17	10	3	3	2	51	2	1	.288	.248

Pitching

Pitching	B-T	HT	WT	DOB	W	L	ERA	G	GS	CG	SV	IP	H	R	ER	HR	BB	SO	AVG	vLH	vRH	K/9	BB/9
Adleman, Tim	R-R	6-5	200	11-13-87	3	8	2.85	30	6	0	0	79	70	28	25	7	20	69	.242	.174	.271	7.86	2.28
Bender, Joel	L-L	6-4	210	8-3-91	0	0	4.50	1	1	0	0	4	3	2	2	0	1	3	.214	.333	.182	6.75	2.25
Black, Sean	R-R	6-3	185	4-23-88	1	1	10.57	5	0	0	0	8	10	9	9	1	5	9	.313	.111	.391	10.57	5.87
Broxton, Jonathan	R-R	6-4	295	6-16-84	0	0	0.00	2	2	0	0	2	1	0	0	0	0	2	.143	.250	.000	9.00	0.00
Castillo, Fabio	R-R	6-1	235	2-19-89	0	0	2.35	7	0	0	0	8	10	5	2	2	3	5	.323	.273	.350	5.87	3.52
Contreras, Carlos	R-R	5-11	205	1-8-91	2	1	2.70	9	3	0	0	20	15	7	6	0	11	27	.195	.231	.176	12.15	4.95
Corcino, Daniel	R-R	5-11	210	8-26-90	10	11	4.13	26	25	0	0	144	123	73	66	16	70	113	.230	.227	.232	7.08	4.39
Dennick, Ryan	L-L	6-0	185	1-10-87	0	0	0.00	1	0	0	0	2	0	0	0	0	0	1	.667	.000	1.000	27.00	0.00
Dyer, Shane	R-R	6-3	185	3-9-88	0	3	3.26	43	0	0	22	50	50	21	18	3	19	35	.263	.207	.288	6.34	3.44
Freeman, Justin	R-R	5-11	175	10-22-86	1	0	4.24	15	0	0	2	17	17	10	8	2	4	16	.254	.286	.239	8.47	2.12
Gonzalez, Carlos	R-R	6-1	195	6-12-90	3	0	3.63	21	0	0	0	22	28	9	9	2	14	19	.315	.407	.274	7.66	5.64
Hayes, Drew	R-R	6-1	205	9-3-87	5	3	4.04	52	1	0	4	71	63	33	32	4	39	76	.241	.275	.229	9.59	4.92
Hyde, Lee	R-L	6-2	210	2-14-85	0	0	6.75	4	0	0	0	4	3	3	3	1	3	3	.214	.143	.286	6.75	6.75
Klimesh, Ben	R-R	6-4	220	5-14-90	1	1	6.19	15	0	0	1	16	17	11	11	1	7	24	.270	.263	.273	13.50	3.94
Latos, Mat	R-R	6-6	245	12-9-87	0	0	6.75	1	1	0	0	4	7	5	3	1	2	3	.350	.400	.300	6.75	4.50
Lively, Ben	R-R	6-4	190	3-5-92	3	6	3.88	13	13	0	0	72	60	32	31	7	36	76	.232	.247	.226	9.50	4.50
Lorenzen, Michael	R-R	6-3	195	1-4-92	4	6	3.13	24	24	0	0	121	112	50	42	9	44	84	.253	.222	.266	6.27	3.28
Maine, Scott	L-L	6-3	225	2-2-85	1	0	6.10	13	0	0	0	10	12	10	7	1	6	8	.300	.333	.263	7.84	6.97
McMyne, Kyle	R-R	5-11	220	10-18-89	0	1	5.91	7	0	0	0	11	15	7	7	1	6	8	.357	.375	.346	6.75	5.06
Moscot, Jon	R-R	6-4	205	8-15-91	7	10	3.13	25	25	2	0	149	145	60	52	11	43	111	.255	.268	.249	6.69	2.59
Nelo, Hector	R-R	6-1	205	11-5-86	0	0	7.04	5	0	0	0	8	9	8	4	1	4	9	.300	.600	.240	10.57	4.70
2-team total (21 Chattanooga)					1	0	6.98	26	0	0	0	39	50	36	30	5	23	41	—	—	—	9.54	5.35
O'Brien, Mikey	R-R	5-11	190	3-3-90	3	3	3.80	19	11	1	0	66	63	38	28	4	28	54	.250	.267	.243	7.33	3.80
Pinckard, Brooks	L-R	6-1	190	8-15-88	1	1	6.21	22	0	0	0	29	32	21	20	2	19	11	.291	.296	.289	3.41	5.90
Quezada, Radhames	R-R	6-2	175	7-6-90	0	0	0.00	1	0	0	0	1	0	0	0	0	0	1	.000	—	.000	9.00	0.00
Ramirez, Elvin	R-R	6-3	210	10-10-87	0	2	5.06	16	0	0	0	21	21	12	12	0	10	10	.253	.280	.241	4.22	4.22
Renken, Daniel	R-R	6-3	190	7-5-89	0	0	4.61	8	1	0	0	14	15	11	7	1	10	18	.278	.250	.286	11.85	6.59
Stephenson, Robert	R-R	6-3	195	2-24-93	7	10	4.74	27	26	0	0	137	114	81	72	18	74	140	.240	.186	.246	9.22	4.87
Walczak, Jamie	R-R	6-2	195	5-4-87	6	7	4.52	51	1	0	4	74	67	41	37	6	40	85	.254	.232	.262	10.38	4.89
Williamson, Fabian	R-L	6-2	175	10-20-88	2	6	4.03	50	0	0	1	58	55	32	26	5	28	66	.249	.306	.221	10.24	4.34

Fielding

Catcher	PCT	G	PO	A	E	DP	PB
Anderson	.987	20	144	8	2	1	3
Berset	.983	40	312	25	6	5	1
Gonzalez	.986	7	59	10	1	2	0
Marson	.980	7	49	1	1	0	0
Mesoraco	1.000	3	25	1	0	0	0
Perez	.996	68	492	49	2	4	7

First Base	PCT	G	PO	A	E	DP
Chang	1.000	8	40	1	0	7
Mattair	.996	118	927	66	4	89
Perez	1.000	1	6	0	0	0
Selsky	.987	14	68	9	1	5
Silverio	1.000	1	3	0	0	0
Smith	.979	7	45	2	1	2
Waldrop	1.000	2	12	1	0	1

Second Base	PCT	G	PO	A	E	DP
Chang	.984	21	25	36	1	8
Greene	.970	28	38	60	3	17
Lohman	.963	16	26	26	2	12
Navarro	.967	39	65	82	5	21
Wright	.987	56	92	134	3	39

Third Base	PCT	G	PO	A	E	DP
Chang	.960	13	8	16	1	0
Lohman	1.000	1	0	1	0	0
Mattair	.938	10	7	8	1	0
Mejias-Brean	.956	63	56	119	8	15
Silverio	.938	62	46	119	11	13

Shortstop	PCT	G	PO	A	E	DP
Greene	.975	47	54	103	4	26

	PCT	G	PO	A	E	DP
Lohman	.927	82	97	181	22	43
Navarro	.942	30	27	71	6	15

Outfield	PCT	G	PO	A	E	DP
Amaral	1.000	8	21	1	0	0
Chang	1.000	1	1	0	0	0
Duran	.929	88	175	8	14	3
Fellhauer	1.000	27	63	1	0	0
Greene	.984	35	56	5	1	0
Lutz	.977	22	41	2	1	0
Rodriguez	.973	114	238	13	7	0
Selsky	1.000	37	53	4	0	2
Silverio	1.000	7	12	0	0	0
Smith	.987	41	73	3	1	0
Waldrop	.980	57	95	3	2	1
Winker	1.000	20	38	2	0	0

BAKERSFIELD BLAZE

HIGH CLASS A

CALIFORNIA LEAGUE

Batting	B-T	HT	WT	DOB	AVG	vLH	vRH	G	AB	R	H	2B	3B	HR	RBI	BB	HBP	SH	SF	SO	SB	CS	SLG	OBP
Amaral, Beau	L-L	5-10	177	2-11-91	.295	.298	.294	85	339	55	100	23	4	6	33	26	5	3	1	56	13	10	.440	.353
Arias, Junior	R-R	6-1	200	1-9-92	.271	.154	.298	17	70	15	19	2	0	3	10	5	2	0	0	18	9	3	.429	.338
Benedetto, Nick	R-R	6-0	150	2-27-93	.136	.111	.143	13	44	3	6	4	0	0	2	1	0	—	0	15	0	0	.227	.156
Berset, Chris	B-R	6-0	195	1-27-88	.310	.667	.291	16	58	7	18	5	0	2	9	7	2	0	0	8	0	0	.500	.403
Buckley, Sean	R-R	6-3	224	9-3-89	.312	.400	.284	61	231	40	72	13	0	11	43	13	7 —	3	55	3	4	.511	.362
Diaz, Sammy	B-R	5-10	192	2-28-91	.327	.432	.254	34	107	16	35	10	0	1	16	5	0	1	2	13	1	1	.449	.351
Elizalde, Sebastian	L-R	6-0	175	11-20-91	.272	.250	.279	66	243	35	66	17	1	9	37	19	3 —	2	44	10	7	.461	.330
Gelalich, Jeff	L-R	6-0	210	3-16-91	.252	.277	.243	61	234	42	59	11	0	9	28	25	3	1	1	72	9	1	.415	.331
Gonzalez, Yovan	R-R	5-10	190	11-11-89	.242	.220	.247	72	244	27	59	8	0	1	22	24	3 —	3	34	0	0	.287	.314
Hudson, Joe	R-R	6-0	205	5-21-91	.289	.438	.207	14	45	9	13	3	0	5	9	2	0	0	0	9	0	1	.689	.319
Matthews, Jon	R-R	6-0	175	4-5-91	.333	.000	.359	13	42	9	14	3	0	0	4	4	0	0	1	11	7	1	.405	.383
Mejias-Brean, Seth	R-R	6-2	216	4-5-91	.300	.386	.276	69	267	56	80	8	3	11	45	44	0	0	2	49	7	1	.476	.396
Morillo, Julio	R-R	5-10	175	12-27-92	.282	.250	.286	14	39	4	11	1	0	0	2	2	0	3	1	6	0	0	.308	.310
Perez, Juan	L-R	5-11	185	11-11-91	.267	.346	.243	120	445	60	119	28	2	13	70	28	1 —	8	83	15	7	.427	.307
Peterson, Brent	R-R	5-10	175	10-20-92	.281	.150	.304	39	135	14	38	5	0	0	9	9	3	0	1	31	1	0	.319	.338
Riggins, Harold	R-R	6-2	240	3-6-90	.232	.233	.232	35	125	12	29	10	0	3	12	15	0 —	0	58	2	0	.384	.314
Silva, Juan	L-L	5-11	204	1-8-91	.310	.443	.267	67	252	51	78	14	3	4	42	48	2	3	2	49	34	9	.437	.421
Smith, Bryson	R-R	6-1	195	12-17-88	.238	.000	.294	7	21	4	5	2	0	0	6	1	1 —	0	1	0	0	.333	.429
Smith, Marquez	R-R	5-10	205	3-20-85	.323	.404	.301	120	424	89	137	32	4	29	126	83	8 —	5	93	1	0	.623	.438
Tolisano, John	B-R	5-11	190	10-7-88	.204	.244	.191	56	186	29	38	10	0	7	33	29	0	1	7	48	1	2	.371	.302
Vidal, David	R-R	5-11	185	10-23-89	.260	.295	.241	50	177	25	46	14	0	4	34	20	0	0	4	41	0	0	.407	.335
Vincej, Zach	R-R	5-11	177	5-1-91	.271	.267	.272	115	428	72	116	23	1	1	40	44	3 —	2	73	11	8	.336	.342

	B-T	HT	WT	DOB	AVG	vLH	vRH	G	AB	R	H	2B	3B	HR	RBI	BB	HBP	SH	SF	SO	SB	CS	SLG	OBP
Waldrop, Kyle	L-L	6-2	216	11-26-91	.359	.224	.391	65	256	54	92	20	1	6	32	22	3	2	5	56	11	2	.516	.409
Winker, Jesse	L-L	6-3	210	8-17-93	.317	.327	.314	53	205	42	65	15	0	13	49	40	1	0	3	46	5	1	.580	.426
Wright, Ryan	R-R	6-1	200	12-3-89	.311	.271	.324	55	241	46	75	17	2	8	41	10	3	0	1	32	7	1	.498	.345

Pitching	B-T	HT	WT	DOB	W	L	ERA	G	GS	CG	SV	IP	H	R	ER	HR	BB	SO	AVG	vLH	vRH	K/9	BB/9
Adleman, Tim	R-R	6-5	200	11-13-87	0	1	12.38	8	0	0	0	8	18	13	11	3	7	8	.439	.333	.522	9.00	7.88
Allen, James	R-R	6-1	197	11-20-89	4	7	6.23	36	10	0	0	87	121	64	60	16	22	64	.340	.381	.315	6.65	2.28
Amezcua, Tony	R-R	5-11	184	5-27-91	0	0	0.00	2	0	0	0	2	3	0	0	0	3	1	.333	.667	.167	3.86	11.57
Black, Sean	R-R	6-3	185	4-23-88	1	0	5.94	8	1	0	0	17	14	13	11	0	11	15	.215	.192	.231	8.10	5.94
Cisco, Drew	L-R	5-11	201	7-29-91	5	6	6.78	27	27	0	0	143	210	119	108	24	24	78	.341	.310	.363	4.90	1.51
Dennhardt, Mike	R-R	6-1	205	6-1-90	7	8	4.52	29	24	0	0	139	145	81	70	14	61	117	.271	.310	.237	7.56	3.94
Gonzalez, Carlos	R-R	6-1	195	6-12-90	2	0	0.57	26	0	0	15	31	17	2	2	1	7	34	.156	.158	.155	9.77	2.01
Guillon, Ismael	L-L	6-2	210	2-13-92	1	6	6.79	12	11	0	0	58	68	52	44	13	28	45	.291	.377	.248	6.94	4.32
Johnson, Jacob	R-R	6-4	215	9-12-90	5	1	2.75	43	0	0	8	72	76	28	22	7	16	52	.274	.307	.252	6.50	2.00
Kemp, Ryan	R-R	6-4	210	9-26-90	1	0	4.50	17	0	0	0	28	28	17	14	4	8	25	.248	.229	.262	8.04	2.57
Klimesh, Ben	R-R	6-4	220	5-14-90	4	1	4.34	35	0	0	6	46	40	27	22	5	14	53	.227	.205	.243	10.45	2.76
Lively, Ben	R-R	6-4	190	3-5-92	10	1	2.28	13	13	0	0	79	57	20	20	6	16	95	.201	.250	.167	10.82	1.82
Lucas, Sean	R-L	6-1	200	4-6-89	3	2	4.96	33	1	0	1	53	57	31	29	5	18	54	.279	.227	.310	9.23	3.08
McMyne, Kyle	R-R	5-11	220	10-18-89	4	1	4.76	38	0	0	4	45	51	26	24	6	21	35	.291	.226	.327	6.95	4.17
Moran, Jimmy	R-R	6-1	180	6-7-90	7	5	4.54	45	1	0	1	69	79	43	35	9	18	65	.290	.329	.274	8.44	2.34
Muhammad, El'Hajj	R-R	6-2	200	7-7-91	0	2	3.68	17	1	0	0	22	22	11	9	1	18	20	.275	.240	.291	8.18	7.36
O'Brien, Mikey	R-R	5-11	190	3-3-90	1	0	6.23	3	3	0	0	17	23	15	12	4	4	13	.319	.400	.262	6.75	2.08
Pearl, Brian	L-R	6-1	190	5-17-88	0	2	8.74	11	0	0	0	11	17	12	11	1	5	5	.378	.250	.448	3.97	3.97
Peralta, Wandy	L-L	6-0	210	7-27-91	7	12	4.82	28	28	0	0	142	164	92	76	19	55	93	.290	.245	.308	5.89	3.49
Pinckard, Brooks	L-R	6-1	190	8-15-88	3	0	0.66	7	0	0	0	14	8	2	1	0	3	8	.167	.235	.129	5.27	1.98
Renken, Daniel	R-R	6-3	190	7-5-89	0	0	0.00	1	0	0	0	1	1	0	0	0	1	3	.333	.500	.000	13.50	0.00
Somsen, Layne	R-R	6-0	190	6-5-89	2	2	3.86	21	2	0	1	40	32	21	17	4	16	38	.224	.190	.250	8.62	3.63
Wright, Daniel	R-R	6-2	205	4-3-91	11	5	4.14	18	18	0	0	109	105	56	50	15	15	99	.251	.263	.243	8.20	1.24

Fielding

Catcher	PCT	G	PO	A	E	DP	PB
Berset	.984	16	109	14	2	0	2
Gonzalez	.991	72	505	47	5	3	5
Hudson	.983	14	104	10	2	1	4
Morillo	.990	13	82	13	1	2	0
Vidal	.996	32	228	27	1	4	13

First Base	PCT	G	PO	A	E	DP
Elizalde	1.000	4	32	1	0	2
Morillo	1.000	1	2	1	0	1
Perez	1.000	2	13	0	0	0
Riggins	.973	30	258	29	8	29
Smith	.995	83	710	52	4	59
Tolisano	1.000	7	54	5	0	8
Vidal	.993	16	130	10	1	11
Waldrop	.923	4	22	2	2	2

Second Base	PCT	G	PO	A	E	DP
Diaz	1.000	2	3	6	0	1

Perez	.982	88	175	258	8	57
Peterson	.938	4	8	7	1	0
Tolisano	.930	15	30	36	5	8
Wright	.982	34	66	94	3	25

Third Base	PCT	G	PO	A	E	DP
Diaz	.879	14	9	20	4	2
Mejias-Brean	.959	68	63	145	9	6
Perez	.923	4	4	8	1	0
Peterson	.910	22	11	50	6	6
Riggins	1.000	1	1	2	0	0
Smith	.944	29	21	63	5	6
Tolisano	.778	4	3	4	2	0
Vidal	.750	3	1	2	1	0

Shortstop	PCT	G	PO	A	E	DP
Diaz	1.000	3	2	6	0	1
Perez	.974	26	34	78	3	15
Peterson	1.000	4	7	15	0	3

Vincej	.956	114	150	325	22	76

Outfield	PCT	G	PO	A	E	DP
Amaral	.984	85	176	10	3	1
Arias	.920	17	22	1	2	0
Benedetto	1.000	13	32	3	0	0
Diaz	1.000	10	13	1	0	0
Elizalde	.972	59	102	3	3	1
Gelalich	.956	60	106	2	5	1
Matthews	.957	12	22	0	1	0
Perez	—	1	0	0	0	0
Peterson	1.000	11	15	0	0	0
Riggins	—	2	0	0	0	0
Silva	.975	55	115	1	3	0
Smith	1.000	7	11	0	0	0
Tolisano	1.000	3	1	0	0	0
Waldrop	.968	56	87	5	3	1
Winker	.972	48	66	4	2	0

DAYTON DRAGONS   LOW CLASS A

MIDWEST LEAGUE

Batting	B-T	HT	WT	DOB	AVG	vLH	vRH	G	AB	R	H	2B	3B	HR	RBI	BB	HBP	SH	SF	SO	SB	CS	SLG	OBP
Amaral, Beau	L-L	5-10	177	2-11-91	.329	.250	.339	17	70	13	23	5	3	1	11	5	1	2	1	15	9	2	.529	.377
Benedetto, Nick	R-R	6-0	150	2-27-93	.221	.242	.214	40	131	14	29	8	0	2	17	2	1	0	1	58	1	1	.328	.233
Blandino, Alex	R-R	6-0	190	11-6-92	.261	.278	.255	34	134	20	35	10	1	4	16	13	2	0	3	42	1	2	.440	.329
Buckley, Sean	R-R	6-3	224	9-3-89	.185	.231	.177	24	92	11	17	5	0	2	16	5	2	0	1	29	5	1	.304	.240
Bueno, Ronald	B-R	5-10	154	10-4-92	.253	.250	.254	54	182	19	46	7	3	0	13	13	2	7	0	39	4	5	.324	.310
Daal, Carlton	R-R	6-2	160	8-1-93	.296	.329	.287	95	345	46	102	10	3	1	29	19	1	5	0	60	13	3	.351	.334
Dailey, Brandon	R-R	5-10	170	2-10-92	.216	.273	.200	17	51	10	11	1	0	3	6	5	2	1	0	20	0	0	.412	.310
Diaz, Sammy	B-R	5-10	192	2-28-91	.259	.225	.268	51	189	23	49	11	3	1	21	17	0	1	2	18	4	0	.365	.317
Elizalde, Sebastian	L-R	6-0	175	11-20-91	.311	.216	.336	55	183	29	57	12	1	7	34	41	2	1	2	48	9	10	.503	.439
Ervin, Phil	R-R	5-10	205	7-15-92	.237	.240	.236	132	498	68	118	34	7	7	68	46	7	0	10	110	30	5	.376	.305
Gelalich, Jeff	L-R	6-0	210	3-16-91	.222	.257	.215	55	212	30	47	7	3	2	21	24	3	3	1	59	12	4	.311	.308
Hannahan, Jack	L-R	6-2	210	3-4-80	.333	.333	.333	4	12	0	4	1	0	0	1	1	0	0	0	5	0	0	.417	.385
Hudson, Joe	R-R	6-0	205	5-21-91	.216	.250	.208	80	269	34	58	14	2	3	30	33	6	2	1	54	2	1	.316	.314
Mateo, Danny	B-R	6-1	178	8-10-91	.229	.222	.231	24	83	13	19	7	0	1	7	10	0	1	1	14	0	0	.349	.309
Matthews, Jon	R-R	6-1	195	4-6-91	.314	.429	.278	67	236	34	74	7	3	2	21	28	5	1	0	48	13	9	.394	.398
McGruder, Jamodrick	L-R	5-8	155	8-4-91	.235	.154	.254	97	349	51	82	11	7	5	30	58	3	4	2	74	12	8	.350	.347
Morillo, Julio	R-R	5-10	175	12-27-92	.250	.000	.286	5	16	2	4	0	0	0	3	1	0	0	0	4	0	0	.250	.294
Ortiz, Jose	R-R	5-11	205	6-11-94	.198	.147	.216	39	131	12	26	7	1	3	14	8	1	1	0	39	0	0	.336	.250
Phillips, Brandon	R-R	6-0	200	6-28-81	.667	1.000	.600	1	3	0	2	1	0	0	0	0	1	0	0	1	0	0	1.000	.750
Pigott, Daniel	R-R	6-2	205	10-4-89	.257	.290	.248	38	140	18	36	5	1	0	16	11	4	2	1	26	2	5	.307	.327
Rachal, Avain	R-R	6-0	195	2-11-94	.193	.245	.179	74	244	23	47	8	2	2	24	21	5	3	3	78	13	2	.266	.267
Rahier, Tanner	R-R	5-11	198	10-12-93	.238	.284	.224	117	421	51	100	19	2	9	54	33	6	2	6	98	2	2	.356	.298
Ramirez, Robert	L-R	6-0	190	7-18-92	.288	.271	.295	45	177	26	51	12	4	6	25	9	4	1	1	58	0	3	.503	.335

	B-T	HT	WT	DOB	AVG	vLH	vRH	G	AB	R	H	2B	3B	HR	RBI	BB	HBP	SH	SF	SO	SB	CS	SLG	OBP
Reynoso, Jonathan	R-R	6-3	177	1-7-93	.229	.256	.221	52	175	20	40	4	1	0	13	14	4	4	2	41	8	1	.263	.297
Rosa, Gabriel	R-R	6-4	185	7-2-93	.170	.122	.189	45	147	13	25	5	1	3	12	14	4	1	2	46	9	2	.279	.257
Tromp, Chadwick	R-R	5-9	180	3-21-95	.231	.250	.222	5	13	1	3	0	0	0	0	1	0	1	0	3	0	0	.231	.286
Valor, Humberto	R-R	6-0	208	9-9-92	.036	.000	.040	9	28	1	1	0	0	0	1	2	0	0	0	8	0	0	.036	.100

Pitching	B-T	HT	WT	DOB	W	L	ERA	G	GS	CG	SV	IP	H	R	ER	HR	BB	SO	AVG	vLH	vRH	K/9	BB/9
Amezcua, Tony	R-R	5-11	184	5-27-91	2	2	5.09	26	0	0	0	46	47	29	26	1	21	45	.267	.316	.244	8.80	4.11
Becker, Nolan	R-L	6-6	225	6-13-91	1	2	2.17	26	0	0	1	37	28	16	9	5	9	44	.203	.152	.219	10.61	2.17
Bender, Joel	L-L	6-4	210	8-3-91	6	3	4.66	45	1	0	2	64	69	33	33	1	20	70	.290	.269	.300	9.90	2.83
Brattvet, Scott	R-R	6-1	195	7-21-91	3	6	4.08	36	0	0	10	46	48	23	21	2	18	36	.281	.203	.321	6.99	3.50
Chacin, Alejandro	R-R	5-11	202	6-24-93	4	4	2.34	48	0	0	20	65	52	23	17	2	28	84	.216	.233	.206	11.57	3.86
Chapman, Aroldis	L-L	6-4	205	2-28-88	0	0	0.00	2	2	0	0	2	0	0	0	0	1	3	.000	.000	.000	13.50	4.50
Diaz, Pedro	R-R	6-0	234	4-29-93	2	2	5.34	39	0	0	2	56	67	45	33	5	20	50	.290	.247	.315	8.08	3.23
Garrett, Amir	L-L	6-5	210	5-3-92	7	8	3.65	27	27	2	0	133	115	65	54	11	51	127	.231	.248	.226	8.57	3.44
Guillon, Ismael	L-L	6-2	210	2-13-92	4	1	3.17	13	12	0	0	63	41	27	23	3	27	69	.186	.196	.183	9.51	3.72
Howard, Nick	R-R	6-3	215	4-6-93	2	1	3.74	11	5	0	0	34	28	15	14	4	11	23	.233	.333	.173	6.15	2.94
Kemp, Ryan	R-R	6-4	210	9-26-90	1	3	5.35	20	0	0	0	34	41	26	20	3	13	29	.304	.347	.279	7.75	3.48
Langfield, Dan	R-R	6-2	196	1-21-91	3	2	4.62	21	9	0	0	60	45	33	31	7	43	81	.205	.179	.218	12.08	6.41
Mitchell, Evan	R-R	6-2	175	3-18-92	2	3	4.22	26	0	0	0	32	30	18	15	1	13	29	.252	.156	.311	8.16	3.66
Moran, Luke	R-R	6-2	200	3-6-92	0	0	0.00	1	1	0	0	4	3	0	0	0	3	3	.200	.167	.222	6.75	6.75
Morillo, Junior	L-L	6-0	175	10-30-91	0	1	1.69	1	1	0	0	5	4	1	1	0	2	2	.222	.000	.286	3.38	3.38
Muehring, Austin	R-R	6-3	185	5-18-91	0	0	0.00	2	0	0	0	3	3	0	0	0	0	3	.250	.250	.250	8.10	0.00
Quezada, Radhames	R-R	6-2	175	7-6-90	1	2	2.75	15	0	0	0	20	16	10	6	0	18	18	.235	.250	.227	8.24	8.24
Romano, Sal	R-R	6-4	250	10-12-93	8	11	4.12	28	28	0	0	149	169	87	68	9	42	128	.288	.303	.279	7.75	2.54
Romero, Franderlyn	R-R	6-1	190	2-21-93	0	0	3.60	1	1	0	0	5	5	3	2	1	0	3	.263	.250	.273	5.40	0.00
Routt, Nick	L-L	6-4	215	8-28-90	0	0	3.12	3	3	0	0	17	14	7	6	1	4	14	.219	.304	.171	7.27	2.08
Somsen, Layne	R-R	6-0	190	6-5-89	1	1	1.40	11	1	0	2	19	12	3	3	1	4	26	.174	.107	.220	12.10	1.86
Stephens, Jackson	R-R	6-3	205	5-11-94	2	7	4.81	14	14	0	0	67	70	40	36	8	22	54	.271	.222	.294	7.22	2.94
Travieso, Nick	R-R	6-2	215	1-31-94	14	5	3.03	26	26	1	0	143	123	62	48	10	44	114	.229	.191	.256	7.19	2.78
Weiss, Zack	R-R	6-1	200	6-16-92	2	4	2.42	34	0	0	3	63	50	18	17	4	21	80	.217	.233	.208	11.37	2.98
Wright, Daniel	R-R	6-2	205	4-3-91	3	2	2.06	10	7	0	0	44	36	11	10	5	7	42	.225	.194	.247	8.66	1.44

Fielding

Catcher	PCT	G	PO	A	E	DP	PB
Dailey	.986	16	131	12	2	1	6
Hudson	.988	80	650	84	9	8	10
Morillo	1.000	3	31	5	0	0	6
Ortiz	.991	38	306	29	3	3	3
Tromp	1.000	5	40	6	0	0	0

First Base	PCT	G	PO	A	E	DP
Diaz	.988	10	74	8	1	5
Elizalde	.988	18	152	12	2	14
Mateo	.995	23	177	27	1	26
Pigott	.978	31	252	16	6	27
Rachal	.993	19	138	9	1	22
Ramirez	.976	41	342	25	9	30

Second Base	PCT	G	PO	A	E	DP
Bueno	.964	36	67	94	6	26

	PCT	G	PO	A	E	DP
Diaz	.970	21	37	60	3	21
McGruder	.954	71	154	180	16	44
Phillips	1.000	1	1	3	0	2
Rachal	.963	12	25	27	2	6
Valor	1.000	3	3	9	0	1

Third Base	PCT	G	PO	A	E	DP
Bueno	.960	8	7	17	1	2
Diaz	1.000	10	4	24	0	4
Rachal	.857	9	2	16	3	0
Rahier	.948	113	57	234	16	31
Valor	1.000	3	3	7	0	1

Shortstop	PCT	G	PO	A	E	DP
Blandino	.947	34	34	108	8	20
Bueno	.963	8	10	16	1	5
Daal	.911	93	147	253	39	54

	PCT	G	PO	A	E	DP
Diaz	1.000	2	3	5	0	0
Valor	.889	2	5	3	1	1

Outfield	PCT	G	PO	A	E	DP
Amaral	1.000	16	32	3	0	2
Benedetto	.977	37	82	3	2	2
Diaz	1.000	8	13	0	0	0
Elizalde	.958	32	44	2	2	1
Ervin	.995	123	212	9	1	1
Gelalich	.990	53	93	3	1	1
Matthews	.974	56	68	6	2	0
McGruder	1.000	2	2	0	0	0
Pigott	1.000	7	16	0	0	0
Rachal	—	1	0	0	0	0
Reynoso	.921	49	68	2	6	0
Rosa	.988	42	77	5	1	0

AZL REDS   ROOKIE

ARIZONA LEAGUE

Batting	B-T	HT	WT	DOB	AVG	vLH	vRH	G	AB	R	H	2B	3B	HR	RBI	BB	HBP	SH	SF	SO	SB	CS	SLG	OBP
Arias, Junior	R-R	6-1	200	1-9-92	.167	.333	.133	12	36	4	6	1	0	0	9	0	1	0	14	0	0	.194	.333	
Carter, Dalton	L-L	6-2	200	4-3-95	.230	.143	.253	30	100	17	23	6	0	0	10	8	2	0	2	32	0	0	.290	.295
Crook, Narciso	R-R	6-3	205	7-12-95	.255	.167	.283	42	149	27	38	9	2	4	20	13	1	0	3	45	12	1	.423	.313
Duarte, Jose	R-R	6-2	190	4-23-93	.200	.000	.222	4	10	1	2	0	0	1	2	0	0	0	1	0	0	.500	.273	
Florentino, Olivel	B-R	6-1	160	2-3-94	.160	.105	.177	26	81	8	13	3	0	0	10	4	0	1	0	27	2	2	.198	.200
Freeland, Jarrett	L-R	6-7	210	6-24-94	.190	.214	.186	29	84	6	16	1	0	0	4	14	0	0	0	22	1	1	.202	.306
Gonzalez, Luis	R-R	6-0	175	7-28-94	.277	.348	.256	32	94	7	26	6	1	0	11	2	0	3	0	22	5	3	.362	.292
Guerrero, Francis	R-R	6-3	185	11-16-94	.111	.000	.125	4	9	1	1	0	0	0	0	0	0	0	0	4	0	0	.111	.111
Hargreaves, Elliott	L-L	5-10	175	1-4-94	.000	.000	.000	2	7	1	0	0	0	0	0	2	0	0	0	2	0	0	.000	.222
Kronenfeld, Paul	L-R	6-3	225	9-27-91	.234	.205	.247	44	128	16	30	6	2	2	21	20	2	0	1	35	2	1	.359	.344
LaValley, Gavin	R-R	6-3	235	12-28-94	.286	.333	.267	59	219	29	54	10	2	5	30	26	2	0	2	44	3	0	.439	.374
Lofstrom, Morgan	L-R	6-1	185	8-17-95	.215	.133	.234	24	79	4	17	4	0	0	5	1	2	0	0	21	0	0	.266	.244
Mardirosian, Shane	L-R	5-10	175	10-13-95	.164	.214	.149	35	122	11	20	2	3	0	10	12	4	0	0	25	5	4	.230	.261
Martijn, Jonathan	R-R	6-2	200	2-23-94	.230	.152	.278	32	87	5	20	5	1	0	10	5	2	0	0	27	0	0	.310	.287
Medina, Reydel	L-L	6-0	195	2-14-93	.244	.256	.241	46	176	26	43	10	4	6	31	4	2	3	3	61	3	5	.449	.265
Mendez, Miguel	L-R	5-10	160	4-16-93	.250	.000	.286	7	16	1	4	0	0	0	2	1	0	0	1	3	0	0	.250	.278
Ramirez, Robert	L-R	6-0	190	7-18-92	.238	.200	.273	6	21	4	5	1	2	0	6	2	2	0	1	3	0	0	.476	.346
Siri, Jose	R-R	6-2	175	7-22-95	.248	.256	.246	46	157	31	39	6	4	2	11	12	2	1	0	35	12	2	.376	.310
Smith, Bryson	R-R	6-1	195	12-17-88	.176	.000	.200	5	17	2	3	0	0	0	2	1	1	0	1	7	0	0	.176	.250
Trees, Mitch	R-R	6-0	200	7-18-95	.057	.000	.071	14	35	2	2	0	0	0	4	1	0	2	0	21	0	0	.057	.167
Tromp, Chadwick	R-R	5-9	180	3-21-95	.323	.222	.364	25	93	14	30	8	0	3	13	3	2	0	1	16	0	1	.505	.354
Valor, Geraldo	R-R	5-10	155	5-2-94	.167	—	.167	5	6	1	1	0	0	0	0	0	0	0	0	2	0	0	.167	.167

CINCINNATI REDS

Batting	B-T	HT	WT	DOB	AVG	vLH	vRH	G	AB	R	H	2B	3B	HR	RBI	BB	HBP	SH	SF	SO	SB	CS	SLG	OBP
Vargas, Hector	R-R	6-2	170	1-27-95	.297	.359	.276	41	155	28	46	8	4	1	9	5	0	3	0	18	3	2	.419	.319
Veras, Josciel	R-R	5-8	175	12-7-92	.242	.200	.261	10	33	5	8	0	1	0	4	5	2	0	0	11	1	0	.303	.375

Pitching	B-T	HT	WT	DOB	W	L	ERA	G	GS	CG	SV	IP	H	R	ER	HR	BB	SO	AVG	vLH	vRH	K/9	BB/9
Anselmi, Davide	R-R	6-2	210	1-11-95	0	0	3.78	12	0	0	0	17	21	10	7	1	6	18	.313	.333	.302	9.72	3.24
Antone, Tejay	R-R	6-4	205	12-5-93	0	0	4.70	3	2	0	0	8	12	5	4	1	2	6	.343	.556	.269	7.04	2.35
Arias, Junior Joselin	R-R	3	170	11-10-93	1	6	6.05	13	7	0	0	39	59	37	26	3	12	39	.351	.444	.295	9.08	2.79
Armstrong, Mark	R-R	6-2	210	11-26-94	4	3	4.23	14	13	0	0	62	62	37	29	4	14	56	.250	.307	.219	8.17	2.04
Boyles, Ty	R-L	6-3	270	9-30-95	4	2	3.35	13	5	0	0	46	30	22	17	3	16	52	.175	.094	.212	10.25	3.15
Cerreto, P.J.	R-R	6-3	225	3-18-91	0	0	0.00	2	0	0	0	2	2	0	0	0	0	2	.286	.000	.333	10.80	0.00
Constante, Jacob	L-L	6-4	215	3-22-94	0	5	4.09	11	9	0	0	33	42	27	15	2	11	31	.307	.318	.301	8.45	3.00
Correll, Zac	R-R	6-6	230	1-28-96	0	0	0.00	4	4	0	0	10	7	0	0	0	3	11	.179	.059	.273	9.58	2.61
Crouse, Shane	R-R	6-3	195	7-17-93	3	1	5.30	13	0	0	1	19	19	12	11	1	7	20	.268	.143	.320	9.64	3.38
Cuevas, Israel	R-R	6-1	178	9-19-95	1	1	4.54	13	1	0	0	34	30	18	17	2	18	29	.244	.291	.206	7.75	4.81
Damian, Pedro	R-R	6-1	170	11-29-92	1	1	4.15	3	0	0	0	4	0	2	2	0	3	5	.000	.000	.000	10.38	6.23
De Sousa, Jose	L-L	6-0	180	5-15-92	1	0	3.72	8	0	0	1	10	10	5	4	0	9	12	.286	.250	.316	11.17	8.38
Ehret, Jake	R-R	6-3	190	3-18-93	1	1	3.78	13	0	0	0	17	17	10	7	1	13	10	.274	.250	.289	5.40	7.02
Gomez, Wagner	B-R	5-11	205	12-2-91	0	1	3.18	8	0	0	0	11	9	7	4	0	3	16	.214	.154	.241	12.71	2.38
Ismail, Ross	R-R	6-0	195	2-19-97	0	1	12.00	4	0	0	0	3	6	4	4	1	3	3	.400	.500	.333	9.00	9.00
Izold, Jakub	R-L	6-4	205	7-16-93	0	0	6.65	15	0	0	0	22	28	22	16	1	8	12	.304	.277		4.98	3.32
Krauss, Conor	R-R	6-5	205	6-14-91	1	1	1.42	9	0	0	2	13	13	5	2	0	6	17	.260	.261	.259	12.08	4.26
Martinez, Juan	L-L	6-2	175	7-15-92	0	2	4.10	14	5	0	0	48	46	27	22	1	14	51	.250	.264	.244	9.50	2.61
Muehring, Austin	R-R	6-3	185	5-18-91	0	0	2.70	3	0	0	0	3	2	1	1	0	3	3	.167	.000	.286	8.10	8.10
Muhammad, El'Hajj	R-R	6-2	200	7-7-91	0	1	3.38	3	1	0	0	3	2	1	1	0	1	3	.250	.200	.133	10.13	3.38
Parmenter, Tyler	R-R	6-2	185	5-4-93	0	1	1.69	13	0	0	0	16	11	3	3	2	4	22	.183	.235	.163	12.38	2.25
Paulson, Jake	R-R	6-6	210	2-17-92	4	1	3.72	18	0	0	4	19	21	15	8	0	9	27	.273	.375	.226	12.57	4.19
Pearl, Brian	L-R	6-1	190	5-17-88	0	1	1.80	8	5	0	0	10	10	3	2	0	2	8	.263	.385	.200	7.20	1.80
Ramirez, Bernardo	R-R	6-2	180	2-2-93	2	2	3.00	11	4	0	0	27	26	13	9	2	13	30	.255	.294	.216	10.00	4.33
Sullivan, Michael	L-L	6-0	210	1-14-94	1	2	1.93	17	0	0	2	19	12	9	4	0	5	27	.176	.185	.171	13.02	2.41

Fielding

Catcher	PCT	G	PO	A	E	DP	PB
Duarte	.960	3	21	3	1	0	2
Guerrero	1.000	4	24	1	0	0	1
Lofstrom	.984	21	163	18	3	1	13
Trees	.982	14	94	14	2	0	14
Tromp	.987	21	198	22	3	1	5

First Base	PCT	G	PO	A	E	DP
Freeland	.974	28	210	17	6	15
Kronenfeld	.968	33	255	13	9	17

Second Base	PCT	G	PO	A	E	DP
Florentino	1.000	1	0	2	0	0
Mardirosian	.922	34	54	88	12	16

	PCT	G	PO	A	E	DP
Mendez	.913	5	10	11	2	3
Valor	1.000	1	1	0	0	0
Vargas	.949	18	30	45	4	5
Veras	.889	4	3	13	2	0

Third Base	PCT	G	PO	A	E	DP
Florentino	.850	9	7	10	3	0
Gonzalez	1.000	12	4	18	0	4
LaValley	.854	39	25	57	14	4
Ramirez	.867	4	3	10	2	1

Shortstop	PCT	G	PO	A	E	DP
Florentino	.837	12	7	34	8	4
Gonzalez	.935	21	36	65	7	10

	PCT	G	PO	A	E	DP
Mendez	—	1	0	0	0	
Valor	.750	2	1	2	1	0
Vargas	.910	22	26	55	8	11
Veras	1.000	5	10	13	0	3

Outfield	PCT	G	PO	A	E	DP
Arias	.857	9	6	0	1	0
Carter	.818	25	26	1	6	0
Crook	.955	36	55	8	3	2
Hargreaves	1.000	2	1	0	0	0
Martijn	.857	22	18	0	3	0
Medina	.923	41	69	3	6	1
Siri	.990	43	90	6	1	2
Smith	—	2	0	0	0	0

BILLINGS MUSTANGS

ROOKIE

PIONEER LEAGUE

Batting	B-T	HT	WT	DOB	AVG	vLH	vRH	G	AB	R	H	2B	3B	HR	RBI	BB	HBP	SH	SF	SO	SB	CS	SLG	OBP
Aldazoro, Argenis	L-L	6-2	160	9-17-92	.325	.238	.347	57	212	44	69	10	5	11	39	11	0	3	2	39	9	1	.575	.356
Aquino, Aristides	R-R	6-4	190	4-22-94	.292	.275	.298	71	284	48	83	23	5	16	64	15	7	0	1	66	21	5	.577	.342
Benedetto, Nick	R-R	6-0	150	2-27-93	.269	.294	.260	22	67	13	18	1	0	1	5	11	2	0	0	21	4	1	.328	.388
Blandino, Alex	R-R	6-0	190	11-6-92	.309	.294	.312	29	110	20	34	10	1	4	16	16	4	0	1	36	6	3	.527	.412
Boulware, Garrett	R-R	6-2	200	9-9-92	.266	.486	.203	44	158	20	42	11	1	2	22	17	7	0	1	33	0	0	.386	.361
Chavez, Alberti	R-R	5-10	170	7-21-95	.206	.103	.244	31	107	13	22	4	0	0	6	5	1	3	0	18	1	2	.243	.248
Duarte, Jose	R-R	6-2	190	4-23-93	.236	.167	.270	18	55	4	13	2	0	1	8	2	1	0	0	13	0	0	.327	.276
Franklin, K.J.	R-R	6-1	220	11-24-94	.211	.232	.204	61	237	28	50	11	2	4	30	7	3	0	2	65	4	1	.325	.241
Greer, Alex	R-R	6-0	185	10-18-92	.256	.214	.276	41	129	18	33	7	4	4	23	8	3	0	2	45	7	1	.465	.310
LaValley, Gavin	R-R	6-3	235	12-28-94	.190	.500	.158	5	21	2	4	0	0	1	2	0	1	0	0	10	0	0	.333	.227
Long, Shedric	L-R	5-10	175	8-22-95	.172	.100	.194	29	87	6	15	3	0	0	6	5	0	1	0	18	2	1	.207	.217
O'Grady, Brian	L-R	6-2	215	5-17-92	.257	.211	.267	62	214	44	55	17	3	6	42	35	4	0	5	45	7	0	.449	.354
Paula, Daniel	R-R	5-11	220	11-21-92	.200	.091	.263	8	30	4	6	0	0	2	5	0	0	0	0	6	1	0	.400	.200
Pickens, Jimmy	L-R	6-0	220	3-08-91	.281		.191	51	173	24	36	9	2	3	19	18	3	2	3	50	4	2	.335	.268
Sparks, Taylor	R-R	6-4	200	4-3-93	.232	.227	.234	55	198	41	46	7	7	10	30	31	7	3	0	84	14	1	.490	.350
Thompson, Cory	R-R	5-11	180	9-23-94	.245	.262	.240	66	253	45	62	13	1	6	28	13	7	2	3	47	13	0	.375	.297
Veras, Josciel	R-R	5-8	175	12-7-92	.292	.313	.281	18	48	7	14	2	0	3	8	7	0	0	0	11	4	1	.521	.336
Washington, Ty	R-R	6-0	160	9-1-93	.288	.167	.333	50	198	40	57	15	0	4	22	16	0	1	3	28	20	3	.424	.336

Pitching	B-T	HT	WT	DOB	W	L	ERA	G	GS	CG	SV	IP	H	R	ER	HR	BB	SO	AVG	vLH	vRH	K/9	BB/9
Antone, Tejay	R-R	6-4	205	12-5-93	2	3	5.94	12	12	0	0	47	72	37	31	3	16	28	.358	.376	.340	5.36	3.06
Bernardino, Brennan	L-L	6-4	180	1-15-92	1	1	1.01	22	0	0	9	27	17	4	3	0	9	31	.177	.122	.218	10.46	3.04
Brattvet, Scott	R-R	6-1	195	7-21-91	0	1	5.11	10	0	0	0	12	16	8	7	2	4	15	.320	.409	.250	10.95	2.92
Gomez, Wagner	B-R	5-11	205	12-2-91	1	1	5.93	11	0	0	0	14	17	12	9	1	11	14	.288	.243	.364	9.22	7.24
Guzman, Jose	R-R	6-3	178	9-8-91	0	0	9.00	9	1	0	0	16	21	17	16	3	13	15	.328	.361	.286	8.44	7.31
Hunter, Brian	R-R	6-3	215	11-22-92	2	0	1.95	21	0	0	9	28	20	6	6	2	9	31	.208	.260	.152	10.08	2.93
Kivel, Jeremy	R-R	6-1	200	10-16-93	1	4	5.31	13	9	0	0	41	54	28	24	4	21	44	.312	.380	.235	9.74	4.65

Name	B-T	HT	WT	DOB	W	L	ERA	G	GS	CG	SV	IP	H	R	ER	HR	BB	SO	AVG	vLH	vRH	K/9	BB/9
Krauss, Conor	R-R	6-5	205	6-14-93	1	2	6.89	8	2	0	0	16	15	16	12	1	5	12	.242	.267	.219	6.89	2.87
Mahle, Tyler	R-R	6-2	175	9-29-94	5	4	3.87	15	15	2	0	77	80	43	33	5	15	71	.263	.284	.244	8.33	1.76
Marquez, Soid	R-R	6-3	165	1-3-95	6	2	4.03	18	4	0	1	45	45	24	20	3	16	32	.262	.256	.268	6.45	3.22
Moody, Jacob	R-L	5-9	185	10-29-92	2	0	4.56	21	0	0	0	24	24	13	12	0	19	31	.250	.300	.214	11.79	7.23
Moran, Luke	R-R	6-2	200	3-6-92	5	5	4.60	15	15	0	0	74	77	43	38	13	12	60	.262	.287	.241	7.26	1.45
Remer, Jordan	L-L	6-2	210	3-19-90	0	1	2.37	18	0	0	0	19	20	13	5	0	10	25	.250	.097	.347	11.84	4.74
Roman, Fabian	R-R	6-0	200	11-22-91	3	2	4.41	19	0	0	1	33	43	23	16	1	7	17	.312	.258	.361	4.68	1.93
Romero, Franderlyn	R-R	6-1	190	2-21-93	0	0	7.71	1	1	0	0	5	6	5	4	0	3	4	.333	.200	.500	7.71	5.79
Saunders, Mike	R-R	6-2	210	3-7-91	1	1	8.51	18	2	0	0	24	42	29	23	2	11	21	.375	.418	.333	7.77	4.07
Sterner, Ty	L-L	6-1	208	12-9-92	3	1	2.83	21	0	0	0	29	30	13	9	0	21	31	.265	.209	.300	9.73	6.59
Strahan, Wyatt	R-R	6-3	190	4-18-93	0	3	2.76	14	14	0	0	42	48	23	13	0	12	40	.277	.213	.354	8.50	2.55
Varner, Seth	L-L	6-3	225	1-27-92	4	3	4.91	13	1	0	0	37	49	24	20	2	8	33	.320	.305	.330	8.10	1.96
Williams, Jose	R-R	6-5	200	2-17-91	3	1	3.21	18	0	0	0	34	31	13	12	1	7	19	.238	.271	.211	5.08	1.87

Fielding

Catcher	PCT	G	PO	A	E	DP	PB
Boulware	.984	42	325	33	6	1	7
Duarte	.972	10	64	6	2	0	0
Long	.978	24	158	19	4	3	17
Paula	.978	5	39	6	1	0	2

First Base	PCT	G	PO	A	E	DP
Aldazoro	.967	27	220	16	8	15
Duarte	1.000	1	8	0	0	0
Franklin	.978	44	360	33	9	32
O'Grady	.984	8	56	6	1	7

Second Base	PCT	G	PO	A	E	DP
Chavez	.970	20	40	56	3	9

	PCT	G	PO	A	E	DP
Thompson	.919	13	28	51	7	9
Veras	.927	7	17	21	3	6
Washington	.944	36	57	112	10	13

Third Base	PCT	G	PO	A	E	DP
Chavez	.889	6	2	6	1	0
Franklin	.814	14	5	30	8	2
LaValley	1.000	2	0	1	0	0
O'Grady	.833	3	2	3	1	1
Sparks	.913	52	35	91	12	5
Veras	.600	1	0	3	2	0

Shortstop	PCT	G	PO	A	E	DP
Blandino	.941	25	40	71	7	16

	PCT	G	PO	A	E	DP
Chavez	.810	4	6	11	4	2
Thompson	.932	47	79	140	16	26
Veras	1.000	1	0	3	0	0

Outfield	PCT	G	PO	A	E	DP
Aldazoro	.939	20	28	3	2	1
Aquino	.963	65	118	13	5	1
Benedetto	1.000	22	57	1	0	0
Chavez	—	1	0	0	0	0
Greer	.965	37	53	2	2	1
O'Grady	.938	45	85	6	6	1
Pickens	.941	44	62	2	4	0
Veras	1.000	8	14	1	0	1

DSL REDS
ROOKIE

DOMINICAN SUMMER LEAGUE

Batting	B-T	HT	WT	DOB	AVG	vLH	vRH	G	AB	R	H	2B	3B	HR	RBI	BB	HBP	SH	SF	SO	SB	CS	SLG	OBP
Bernabel, Ery	R-R	6-1	175	7-2-94	198	179	201	51	167	16	33	4	1	0	21	18	5	1	2	42	9	4	234	292
Capitillo, Derik	R-R	5-11	205	4-11-95	240	180	257	64	225	30	54	8	3	1	29	29	9	1	1	40	12	3	316	348
De Los Santos, Tomas	L-R	6-3	180	4-16-95	267	214	278	22	86	14	23	4	1	0	4	8	2	0	0	21	6	5	337	344
De Luna, Jose	R-R	6-3	194	3-11-94	250	200	259	49	172	19	43	7	2	0	18	6	3	2	2	34	3	3	314	284
Doval, Sucre	R-R	6-3	175	9-6-96	164	233	140	41	116	14	19	3	3	0	2	10	0	2	0	47	1	3	241	230
Gabo, Erick	R-R	6-2	195	2-22-95	255	273	252	38	141	14	36	9	2	0	17	9	1	0	0	30	3	3	348	305
Guerrero, Raynay	R-R	6-4	190	2-24-93	234	211	239	38	128	15	30	7	0	0	11	12	4	1	3	29	2	1	289	313
Manzanero, Pabel	R-R	6-3	170	1-30-96	165	143	170	36	109	6	18	3	0	0	8	9	2	0	0	29	1	2	193	242
Martinez, Valentin	R-R	6-0	175	9-19-94	250	364	226	24	64	8	16	3	1	0	3	13	4	1	0	18	8	0	328	407
Mejia, Cesar	L-R	6-1	165	12-8-94	200	111	224	25	85	6	17	3	1	0	7	10	0	1	0	21	1	1	259	284
Mejia, Diohanky	R-R	6-3	190	9-29-95	188	200	184	16	48	3	9	0	0	0	4	8	0	0	0	12	1	0	188	304
Ovalle, Gabriel	B-R	6-2	170	12-10-94	210	220	208	69	257	36	54	10	8	0	11	24	4	6	0	54	21	4	311	288
Rivero, Carlos	L-R	6-0	175	4-30-97	197	093	224	57	208	28	41	1	4	0	11	19	2	10	1	46	15	4	240	270
Santana, Leandro	R-R	6-2	175	2-19-97	303	368	291	40	122	21	37	6	4	0	14	28	1	0	1	38	6	3	418	434
Saunders, Dario	R-R	5-9	165	3-8-93	200	—	—	44	125	22	25	1	2	0	6	24	6	0	0	31	26	7	240	355
Vargas, Franklin	R-R	5-11	170	11-8-96	147	136	150	36	102	9	15	0	0	1	7	11	0	2	0	31	3	2	176	230
Wallace, Raul	R-R	6-2	180	8-19-95	217	195	222	60	212	28	46	5	4	1	19	18	7	0	2	49	4	2	292	297
Azcona, Francis	B-R	5-10	155	11-20-95	243	351	223	62	230	31	56	8	3	0	21	35	2	4	1	49	18	5	304	347
Beltre, Michael	R-R	6-3	180	7-3-95	278	194	302	49	162	25	45	7	1	1	9	26	8	1	1	44	12	4	352	401
Guerrero, Francis	R-R	6-3	185	11-16-94	215	182	224	56	209	18	45	6	1	3	22	19	2	0	1	62	0	0	297	286
Hernandez, Luis	R-R	6-2	180	7-21-94	194	231	188	51	175	19	34	4	4	1	14	14	6	1	0	57	2	3	280	277
Jimenez, Daniel	R-R	5-11	175	4-23-96	222	156	236	63	248	26	55	8	4	1	22	9	8	4	3	35	10	6	298	269
Jimenez, Olvis	L-L	6-4	175	11-8-96	253	333	244	30	95	11	24	3	0	1	5	15	0	2	0	18	4	1	316	355
Liberatore, Ernesto	R-R	6-0	180	3-26-96	225	077	247	38	102	11	23	6	0	1	13	8	7	4	1	34	1	3	314	322
Lopez, Maikel	B-R	6-2	185	10-31-93	250	320	232	39	120	6	30	7	1	0	22	10	3	0	1	18	0	0	325	321
Martinez, Victor	R-R	6-1	170	1-29-97	152	114	162	57	198	16	30	1	0	1	7	10	4	2	1	50	6	2	172	207
Mateo, Carlos	R-R	6-3	175	5-17-95	215	206	218	48	158	17	34	2	0	0	10	5	7	4	0	37	3	3	228	271
Monegro, Jose	R-R	6-2	165	10-20-95	194	320	163	38	129	8	25	11	0	1	14	18	2	2	0	37	1	0	302	302
Noel, Yoel	R-R	6-2	180	2-24-95	119	143	115	19	59	2	7	0	0	0	5	2	2	2	2	23	2	0	119	169
Rubicondo, Anthony	R-R	6-1	175	4-14-96	206	162	215	56	209	25	43	6	2	3	11	10	6	3	0	46	2	4	297	262
Saba, Vidauri	R-R	6-2	170	9-17-95	148	167	143	18	27	4	4	0	0	0	3	9	0	1	0	9	2	0	148	361
Sugilio, Andy	B-R	6-2	170	10-26-96	259	400	239	55	158	12	41	2	2	0	16	12	1	2	1	32	4	5	297	314

Pitching	B-T	HT	WT	DOB	W	L	ERA	G	GS	CG	SV	IP	H	R	ER	HR	BB	SO	AVG	vLH	vRH	K/9	BB/9
Acevedo, Pedro	L-L	6-5	178	1-16-95	0	1	13.03	12	3	0	0	19	31	32	28	0	28	21	—	—	—	9.78	13.03
Bautista, Wendolyn	R-R	6-0	185	3-27-93	4	4	3.22	14	14	1	0	73	74	39	26	1	16	53	265	250	270	6.56	1.98
Damian, Pedro	R-R	6-1	170	11-29-92	2	4	1.90	10	10	0	0	47	32	13	10	1	17	72	186	255	160	13.69	3.23
Encarnacion, Marcos	R-R	6-2	180	11-28-95	3	3	2.44	14	12	0	0	55	51	24	15	1	28	57	238	314	201	9.27	4.55
Garcia, Eriberto	R-R	5-11	180	11-7-95	0	3	6.53	18	0	0	9	21	28	18	15	1	7	13	329	313	340	5.66	3.05
Jimenez, Hector	L-L	6-0	160	4-3-95	0	0	6.12	15	0	0	1	25	27	24	17	1	16	22	267	250	270	7.92	5.76
Laguna, Jose	R-R	6-2	180	2-16-96	2	0	1.29	6	2	0	0	14	11	5	2	0	6	8	239	471	103	5.14	3.86
Martinez, Jairo	L-L	6-1	175	3-21-93	4	3	3.67	17	0	0	3	34	28	19	14	3	15	38	222	125	236	9.96	3.93
Mateo, Alfredo	R-R	6-1	185	10-24-93	1	1	2.78	18	0	0	4	32	26	14	10	0	15	35	—	—	—	9.74	4.18

Mena, Alfredo	R-R	6-3	205	12-6-93	2	3	1.93	15	3	0	1	47	43	18	10	1	18	33	243	333	203	6.36	3.47
Moncion, Isaac	R-R	6-5	210	8-11-95	0	1	12.00	3	0	0	1	3	5	4	4	0	4	4	385	000	500	12.00	12.00
Montilla, Franklin	R-R	6-4	203	6-28-94	0	4	2.79	15	15	0	0	71	58	30	22	1	27	54	230	200	244	6.85	3.42
Nayib, David	R-R	6-5	180	8-31-94	0	0	5.12	12	0	0	0	19	26	18	11	2	10	8	—	—	—	3.72	4.66
Paredes, Yean	R-R	6-3	185	8-17-95	3	1	6.20	16	0	0	0	20	25	17	14	0	21	18	313	286	318	7.97	9.30
Reinoso, Gregory	L-L	6-1	170	11-17-95	1	2	2.25	14	9	0	0	48	30	22	12	1	42	40	—	—	—	7.50	7.88
Roman, Jesus	R-R	6-2	195	2-2-97	5	2	3.99	19	0	0	2	38	37	20	17	1	24	36	252	325	224	8.45	5.63
Santos, Yerry	R-R	6-4	180	11-30-94	0	2	3.05	17	0	0	1	38	27	18	13	0	27	38	200	143	220	8.92	6.34
Telleria, Adolfi	R-R	6-1	170	4-12-94	5	6	3.68	14	14	0	0	71	77	35	29	2	15	73	268	250	275	9.25	1.90
Veras, Jose	R-R	6-4	180	2-10-94	2	0	4.50	17	0	0	1	42	46	27	21	2	13	26	—	—	—	5.57	2.79
Corcino, Jairon	R-R	5-11	185	7-27-94	0	0	3.47	14	0	0	0	23	17	9	9	0	12	16	205	056	246	6.17	4.63
De Jesus, Yoel	R-R	6-2	180	10-8-94	1	8	2.93	14	14	0	0	68	69	42	22	2	31	59	256	176	292	7.85	4.12
De Leon, John	R-R	6-4	205	10-13-93	0	5	9.54	20	0	0	0	39	55	44	41	2	32	21	344	326	350	4.89	7.45
Encarnacion, Carlos	R-R	6-3	180	11-15-93	0	0	5.06	4	0	0	0	5	7	3	3	0	1	5	350	333	357	8.44	1.69
Estevez, Miguel	R-R	6-3	160	10-31-93	0	6	4.20	14	13	0	0	64	73	40	30	1	23	52	290	256	306	7.27	3.22
Guzman, Hernando	R-R	6-2	170	3-12-96	4	4	3.58	21	0	0	0	33	34	16	13	0	17	20	266	263	267	5.51	4.68
Jimenez, Felix	R-R	6-3	170	9-29-95	1	1	6.75	14	0	0	0	27	26	30	20	0	26	21	252	323	222	7.09	8.78
Jones, David	R-R	6-4	200	4-26-94	0	8	5.60	10	10	0	0	35	48	39	22	1	14	25	298	259	320	6.37	3.57
Lara, Jean	R-R	6-3	200	4-15-93	4	1	2.23	20	0	0	6	40	37	15	10	0	10	28	245	152	286	6.25	2.23
Lugo, Sandy	R-R	6-0	170	3-26-94	3	3	2.90	19	2	0	2	50	43	24	16	0	16	61	229	288	206	11.05	2.90
Pena, Warlin	L-L	6-2	170	7-17-95	1	2	5.56	10	1	0	0	23	23	18	14	1	17	24	258	188	274	9.53	6.75
Perez, Alexander	R-R	6-3	195	4-23-95	2	2	4.33	12	7	0	0	44	56	30	21	1	8	40	289	296	285	8.24	1.65
Salas, Jose	R-R	6-3	190	2-7-95	2	7	4.90	12	12	0	0	61	66	42	33	2	10	42	273	327	236	6.23	1.48

Fielding

Catcher	PCT	G	PO	A	E	DP	PB
Guerrero	980	13	89	11	2	0	5
Liberatore	967	29	208	23	8	2	5
Lopez	962	37	212	41	10	2	10
Capitillo	980	30	208	31	5	2	8
Manzanero	980	32	249	39	6	1	4
Martinez	983	15	102	12	2	1	5

First Base	PCT	G	PO	A	E	DP
Capitillo	984	31	241	12	4	24
De Luna	979	7	44	2	1	4
Guerrero	969	64	478	24	16	36
Jimenez	941	4	30	2	2	1
Liberatore	968	9	60	1	2	5
Lopez	857	2	6	0	1	1
Manzanero	1.000	3	23	6	0	3
Martinez	1.000	1	4	0	0	0
Mejia	867	3	11	2	2	1
Monegro	970	28	220	10	7	10
Rubicondo	1.000	7	30	3	0	1

Second Base	PCT	G	PO	A	E	DP
Azcona	938	61	96	174	18	23
Bernabel	895	5	6	11	2	2
Mateo	—	1	0	0	0	
Mejia	1.000	3	1	1	0	0
Ovalle	1.000	8	18	20	0	2
Rivero	975	34	79	78	4	20
Rubicondo	974	12	17	21	1	0
Saba	864	7	11	8	3	2
Vargas	894	26	47	46	11	17

Third Base	PCT	G	PO	A	E	DP
Bernabel	844	16	18	36	10	7
Manzanero	1.000	1	1	0	0	0
Monegro	667	1	1	3	2	0
Ovalle	1.000	1	1	2	0	0
Rivero	906	9	10	19	3	2
Rubicondo	876	45	32	67	14	6
Saba	857	3	2	4	1	0
Santana	842	38	37	59	18	5
Sugilio	797	35	22	33	14	1
Vargas	840	8	4	17	4	0
Wallace	400	1	0	2	3	0

Shortstop	PCT	G	PO	A	E	DP
Martinez	896	57	102	140	28	18
Ovalle	929	58	95	166	20	28
Rivero	908	14	22	37	6	5
Sugilio	842	21	18	46	12	4

Outfield	PCT	G	PO	A	E	DP
Beltre	930	40	78	2	6	0
Bernabel	1.000	24	50	7	0	0
De Los Santos	1.000	21	33	3	0	0
De Luna	973	28	31	5	1	0
Doval	941	35	47	1	3	0
Gabo	1.000	16	30	1	0	1
Hernandez	916	44	104	5	10	2
Jimenez	978	68	127	9	3	1
Mateo	913	42	67	6	7	2
Mejia	906	20	24	5	3	1
Noel	944	10	17	0	1	0
Ovalle	1.000	1	2	0	0	0
Rubicondo	—	1	0	0	0	0
Saunders	965	40	76	6	3	2
Wallace	978	58	126	5	3	2

Cleveland Indians

SEASON IN A SENTENCE: The Indians overcame a slow start to post a second straight winning season, but their push for a return to the playoffs petered out in September.

HIGH POINT: Corey Kluber's Cy Young-caliber season was the biggest revelation for the Tribe in 2015. The righty put together a spectacular 1.73 ERA after the all-star break, and for a time it looked like the Indians might repeat 2014's late-season charge to the playoffs. The Indians went 18-9 in August and finished the month by sweeping a three-game series in Kansas City to pull within 2 ½ games of first place, but that was as close as they would get.

LOW POINT: The Indians sputtered out of the gate to the tune of an 11-17 record through the end of April. Disappointing seasons from expected stalwarts Jason Kipnis and Nick Swisher, among others, held the offense back, and the Indians were also a porous defensive team.

NOTABLE ROOKIES: Several first-timers made an impact on Cleveland's pitching staff. Lefty Kyle Crockett became the first 2013 draftee to reach the majors and became a key cog out of the bullpen in the second half, holding lefthanded hitters to a .206 average. Trevor Bauer, the third overall pick in 2011, stuck in Cleveland's rotation after an up-and-down minor-league career, while lefty T.J. House, a high-dollar signing out of the 2008 draft, finally broke through to the majors.

KEY TRANSACTIONS: Other than losing Ubaldo Jimenez and Scott Kazmir in free agency— losses which were offset by Kluber's emergence— the Indians brought back the core of their 2013 playoff team. They did sell off a couple of soon-to-be free-agent veterans at the trade deadline, sending Asdrubal Cabrera to the Nationals and the struggling Justin Masterson to the Cardinals.

DOWN ON THE FARM: Shortstop Francisco Lindor, Cleveland's 2011 first-round pick, was the youngest player to play in the International League in 2014 at age 20, while outfielder Tyler Naquin, its 2012 first-rounder, was having a strong season in Double-A before it was cut short by a broken hand. Triple-A Columbus won a division title, and three of the Indians' four full-season affiliates reached postseason play. The Rookie-level Arizona League team took home a championship behind the heroics of 2014 third-round pick Bobby Bradley, who won the AZL triple crown.

OPENING DAY PAYROLL: $82,500,800 (24th).

General Manager: Chris Antonetti. **Farm Director:** Ross Atkins. **Scouting Director:** John Mirabelli

Class	Team	League	W	L	PCT	Finish	Manager
Majors	Cleveland Indians	American	85	77	.525	12th (30)	Terry Francona
Triple-A	Columbus Clippers	International	79	65	.549	t-2nd (14)	Chris Tremie
Double-A	Akron RubberDucks	Eastern	73	69	.514	t-3rd (12)	Dave Wallace
High A	Carolina Mudcats	Carolina	62	74	.456	7th (8)	Scooter Tucker
Low A	Lake County Captains	Midwest	65	74	.468	11th (16)	Mark Budzinski
Short season	Mahoning Valley Scrappers	New York-Penn	33	42	.440	11th (14)	Ted Kubiak
Rookie	Indians	Arizona	37	16	.698	1st (13)	Anthony Medrano
Overall Minor League Record			349	340	.507	15th (30)	

ORGANIZATION STATISTICS

CLEVELAND INDIANS

AMERICAN LEAGUE

Batting	B-T	HT	WT	DOB	AVG	vLH	vRH	G	AB	R	H	2B	3B	HR	RBI	BB	HBP	SH	SF	SO	SB	CS	SLG	OBP
Aguilar, Jesus	R-R	6-3	250	6-30-90	.121	.167	.067	19	33	2	4	0	0	0	3	4	0	0	1	13	0	0	.121	.211
Aviles, Mike	R-R	5-10	205	3-13-81	.247	.259	.239	113	344	38	85	16	1	5	39	13	1	11	5	49	14	5	.343	.273
Bourn, Michael	L-R	5-10	180	12-27-82	.257	.224	.272	106	444	57	114	17	10	3	28	35	3	3	2	114	10	6	.360	.314
Brantley, Michael	L-L	6-2	200	5-15-87	.327	.307	.337	156	611	94	200	45	2	20	97	52	8	0	5	56	23	1	.506	.385
Cabrera, Asdrubal	R-R	6-0	205	11-13-85	.246	.248	.245	97	378	54	93	22	2	9	40	27	7	0	4	79	7	2	.386	.305
Chisenhall, Lonnie	L-R	6-2	190	10-4-88	.280	.294	.276	142	478	62	134	29	1	13	59	39	8	4	3	99	3	1	.427	.343
Dickerson, Chris	L-L	6-4	230	4-10-82	.224	.250	.221	41	98	12	22	4	0	2	6	12	0	2	0	38	3	0	.327	.309
Giambi, Jason	L-R	6-3	240	1-8-71	.133	—	.133	26	60	3	8	2	0	2	5	9	1	0	0	12	0	0	.267	.257
Gimenez, Chris	R-R	6-2	220	12-27-82	.000	.000	.000	8	9	0	0	0	0	0	0	1	0	0	0	3	0	0	.000	.100
2-team total (33 Texas)					.241	—	—	41	116	13	28	10	0	0	11	12	0	0	0	29	0	1	.328	.313
Gomes, Yan	R-R	6-2	215	7-19-87	.278	.331	.256	135	485	61	135	25	3	21	74	24	3	0	6	120	0	4	.472	.313
Holt, Tyler	R-R	5-10	190	3-10-89	.268	.311	.192	36	71	4	19	2	0	0	2	3	1	1	0	25	2	2	.296	.307
Johnson, Elliot	B-R	6-1	190	3-9-84	.105	.133	.000	7	19	1	2	2	0	0	0	0	0	1	0	7	0	0	.211	.105
Kipnis, Jason	L-R	5-11	190	4-3-87	.240	.208	.256	129	500	61	120	25	1	6	41	50	2	1	2	100	22	3	.330	.310
Kottaras, George	L-R	6-0	200	5-10-83	.286	.000	.333	10	21	4	6	0	0	3	4	4	0	1	1	10	0	0	.714	.385
2-team total (4 Toronto)					.240	—	—	14	25	4	6	0	0	3	4	5	0	1	1	14	0	0	.600	.355
Morgan, Nyjer	L-L	5-10	180	7-2-80	.341	.000	.350	15	41	8	14	1	0	1	6	7	0	3	1	6	3	0	.439	.429
Murphy, David	L-L	6-3	210	10-18-81	.262	.238	.268	129	416	40	109	25	1	8	58	36	2	1	7	61	2	3	.385	.319
Perez, Roberto	R-R	5-11	225	12-23-88	.271	.167	.311	29	85	10	23	5	0	1	4	5	0	5	0	26	0	0	.365	.311
Raburn, Ryan	R-R	6-0	185	4-17-81	.200	.195	.208	74	195	18	39	7	0	4	22	13	1	0	3	51	0	0	.297	.250
Ramirez, Jose	B-R	5-9	165	9-17-92	.262	.291	.247	68	237	27	62	10	2	2	17	13	1	13	2	35	10	1	.346	.300
Santana, Carlos	B-R	5-11	210	4-8-86	.231	.271	.212	152	541	68	125	25	0	27	85	113	3	0	3	124	5	2	.427	.365
Sellers, Justin	R-R	5-10	160	2-1-86	.188	.200	.182	17	16	1	3	0	0	0	3	0	2	0	4	0	1	.188	.316
Shuck, J.B.	L-L	5-11	195	6-18-87	.077	.333	.043	16	26	2	2	0	0	0	0	0	0	0	0	1	0	0	.077	.077
2-team total (22 Los Angeles)					.145	—	—	38	110	12	16	1	0	2	9	3	0	1	0	12	2	0	.209	.168
Swisher, Nick	B-L	6-0	200	11-25-80	.208	.168	.224	97	360	33	75	20	0	8	42	36	0	1	4	111	0	0	.331	.278
Walters, Zach	B-R	6-2	210	9-5-89	.170	.241	.136	30	88	9	15	2	0	7	12	5	1	0	0	32	0	0	.432	.223

Pitching	B-T	HT	WT	DOB	W	L	ERA	G	GS	CG	SV	IP	H	R	ER	HR	BB	SO	AVG	vLH	vRH	K/9	BB/9
Adams, Austin	R-R	5-11	190	8-19-86	0	0	9.00	6	0	0	0	7	9	7	7	1	1	4	.310	.273	.333	5.14	1.29
Allen, Cody	R-R	6-1	210	11-20-88	6	4	2.07	76	0	0	24	70	48	21	16	7	26	91	.194	.141	.250	11.76	3.36
Atchison, Scott	R-R	6-2	200	3-29-76	6	0	2.75	70	0	0	2	72	60	24	22	4	14	49	.227	.267	.207	6.13	1.75
Axford, John	R-R	6-5	220	4-1-83	2	3	3.92	49	0	0	10	44	34	21	19	6	30	51	.214	.207	.221	10.51	6.18
Bauer, Trevor	R-R	6-1	190	1-17-91	5	8	4.18	26	26	0	0	153	151	76	71	16	60	143	.259	.249	.268	8.41	3.53
Carrasco, Carlos	R-R	6-3	210	3-21-87	8	7	2.55	40	14	1	1	134	103	40	38	7	29	140	.209	.196	.221	9.40	1.95
Crockett, Kyle	L-L	6-2	170	12-15-91	4	1	1.80	43	0	0	0	30	26	6	6	2	8	28	.239	.206	.283	8.40	2.40
Hagadone, Nick	L-L	6-5	230	1-1-86	1	0	2.70	35	0	0	0	23	18	7	7	3	6	27	.214	.217	.211	10.41	2.31
House, T.J.	R-L	6-1	205	9-29-89	5	3	3.35	19	18	0	0	102	113	41	38	10	22	80	.284	.252	.297	7.06	1.94
Kluber, Corey	R-R	6-4	215	4-10-86	18	9	2.44	34	34	3	0	236	207	72	64	14	51	269	.233	.244	.220	10.27	1.95
Lee, C.C.	R-R	5-11	190	10-21-86	1	1	4.50	37	0	0	0	28	30	15	14	3	12	26	.275	.250	.284	8.36	3.86
Lowe, Mark	L-R	6-3	210	6-7-83	0	1	3.86	7	0	0	0	7	10	7	3	2	6	6	.313	.300	.318	7.71	7.71
Masterson, Justin	R-R	6-6	250	3-22-85	4	6	5.51	19	19	0	0	98	106	66	60	6	56	93	.279	.330	.214	8.54	5.14
McAllister, Zach	R-R	6-6	240	12-8-87	4	7	5.23	22	15	0	0	86	96	54	50	7	28	74	.280	.286	.275	7.74	2.93
Outman, Josh	L-L	6-1	205	9-14-84	4	0	3.28	31	0	0	0	25	22	10	9	4	16	24	.234	.180	.295	8.76	5.84
2-team total (9 New York)					4	0	2.86	40	0	0	0	28	24	10	9	4	16	26	—	—	—	8.26	5.08
Pestano, Vinnie	R-R	6-0	200	2-20-85	0	1	5.00	13	0	0	0	9	13	7	5	2	1	13	.333	.538	.231	13.00	1.00
2-team total (12 Los Angeles)					0	1	2.89	25	0	0	0	19	18	8	6	3	5	26	—	—	—	12.54	2.41
Price, Bryan	R-R	6-4	215	11-13-86	0	0	20.25	3	0	0	0	3	8	6	6	3	1	1	.500	.500	.500	3.38	3.38
Rzepczynski, Marc	L-L	6-2	220	8-29-85	0	3	2.74	73	0	0	1	46	42	19	14	1	19	46	.246	.180	.338	9.00	3.72
Salazar, Danny	R-R	6-0	190	1-11-90	6	8	4.25	20	20	1	0	110	117	57	52	13	35	120	.272	.246	.289	9.82	2.86
Shaw, Bryan	B-R	6-1	210	11-8-87	5	5	2.59	80	0	0	2	76	61	26	22	6	22	64	.216	.294	.168	7.55	2.59
Tomlin, Josh	R-R	6-1	190	10-19-84	6	9	4.76	25	16	1	0	104	120	66	55	18	14	94	.281	.250	.314	8.13	1.21
Wood, Blake	R-R	6-5	240	8-8-85	0	1	7.11	7	0	0	0	6	4	5	5	0	7	7	.182	.167	.200	9.95	9.95

Fielding

Catcher	PCT	G	PO	A	E	DP	PB
Gimenez	1.000	2	1	1	0	0	0
Gomes	.988	126	1052	73	14	9	6
Kottaras	1.000	9	61	3	0	1	0
Perez	.988	29	217	24	3	2	1
Santana	1.000	11	94	10	0	1	2

First Base	PCT	G	PO	A	E	DP
Aguilar	.974	12	71	4	2	4
Chisenhall	1.000	11	52	1	0	5
Gimenez	1.000	5	17	1	0	4
Raburn	1.000	1	0	2	0	0
Santana	.995	94	842	64	5	71
Swisher	.980	52	400	39	9	42

Second Base	PCT	G	PO	A	E	DP
Aviles	.993	33	52	86	1	19

	PCT	G	PO	A	E	DP
Johnson	.833	2	3	7	2	2
Kipnis	.989	123	181	347	6	63
Ramirez	1.000	11	14	24	0	6
Sellers	1.000	7	0	2	0	0
Walters	1.000	4	5	9	0	3

Third Base	PCT	G	PO	A	E	DP
Aguilar	—	1	0	0	0	0
Aviles	.909	36	21	49	7	1
Chisenhall	.931	114	60	182	18	9
Gimenez	—	1	0	0	0	0
Johnson	—	1	0	0	0	0
Santana	.909	26	25	35	6	3
Sellers	—	4	0	0	0	0

Shortstop	PCT	G	PO	A	E	DP
Aviles	1.000	15	21	37	0	7

	PCT	G	PO	A	E	DP
Cabrera	.963	92	115	254	14	57
Ramirez	.983	56	76	155	4	34
Sellers	1.000	6	9	14	0	4

Outfield	PCT	G	PO	A	E	DP
Aviles	1.000	33	28	1	0	1
Bourn	.992	105	235	5	2	1
Brantley	.996	147	271	12	1	2
Dickerson	.964	34	50	3	2	0
Holt	1.000	35	43	0	0	0
Johnson	1.000	3	6	0	0	0
Morgan	1.000	14	23	0	0	0
Murphy	.986	122	205	6	3	1
Raburn	.960	44	45	3	2	1
Shuck	1.000	9	12	0	0	0
Swisher	1.000	6	7	0	0	0
Walters	.917	6	11	0	1	0

COLUMBUS CLIPPERS

TRIPLE-A

INTERNATIONAL LEAGUE

Batting	B-T	HT	WT	DOB	AVG	vLH	vRH	G	AB	R	H	2B	3B	HR	RBI	BB	HBP	SH	SF	SO	SB	CS	SLG	OBP
Abraham, Adam	R-R	6-0	228	3-27-87	.273	.267	.275	18	55	10	15	1	0	2	9	8	0	1	3	10	0	0	.400	.348
Aguilar, Jesus	R-R	6-3	250	6-30-90	.304	.295	.309	118	427	69	130	31	0	19	77	64	3	0	5	96	0	0	.511	.395
Bourn, Michael	L-R	5-10	180	12-27-82	.150	.143	.154	5	20	1	3	1	0	0	2	0	0	0	0	3	0	0	.200	.150
Branyan, Russell	L-R	6-4	235	12-19-75	.333	.333	.333	4	12	1	4	1	0	0	3	3	0	0	0	3	0	0	.417	.467
Brown, Dusty	R-R	6-0	195	6-19-82	.185	.125	.211	17	54	7	10	3	0	3	4	11	0	0	0	18	0	0	.407	.323
Carlin, Luke	B-R	5-10	195	12-20-80	.217	.186	.232	61	184	22	40	6	1	3	23	29	2	3	0	39	0	0	.370	.330
Carson, Matt	R-R	6-2	200	7-1-81	.259	.239	.269	82	274	47	71	13	1	10	32	27	6	1	3	85	11	1	.423	.335
Ciriaco, Audy	R-R	6-3	195	6-16-87	.255	.239	.262	112	373	41	95	25	3	15	70	30	3	3	4	83	1	1	.458	.312
Cooper, David	L-L	6-0	200	2-12-87	.224	.167	.258	40	143	13	32	7	0	0	14	20	0	0	0	14	0	0	.273	.319
Fedroff, Tim	L-R	5-10	200	2-4-87	.247	.250	.245	70	231	37	57	14	0	0	18	52	0	1	0	64	4	5	.307	.385
Hankins, Todd	R-R	5-9	175	11-18-90	.286	.000	1.000	2	7	0	2	1	0	0	1	0	0	1	0	2	0	0	.429	.286
Holt, Tyler	R-R	5-10	190	3-10-89	.308	.384	.273	59	227	61	70	15	0	2	16	39	3	3	0	45	20	4	.401	.416
Johnson, Elliot	B-R	6-1	190	3-9-84	.236	.252	.227	87	314	43	74	14	6	5	37	43	1	3	4	82	10	1	.366	.326
Kipnis, Jason	L-R	5-11	190	4-3-87	.111	.000	.167	3	9	1	1	0	0	1	3	0	0	0	0	2	0	0	.444	.111
Kottaras, George	L-R	6-0	200	5-10-83	.119	.071	.143	14	42	4	5	0	0	1	5	4	0	1	0	10	0	0	.190	.196
2-team total (13 Buffalo)					.190			27	84	10	16	1	0	4	13	11	0	1	0	32	0	0	.345	.284
LaHair, Bryan	L-R	6-5	240	11-5-82	.114	.100	.133	10	35	2	4	2	0	0	4	1	0	0	0	10	0	0	.171	.139
Lindor, Francisco	B-R	5-11	175	11-14-93	.273	.320	.252	38	165	24	45	4	0	5	14	9	0	4	2	36	3	7	.388	.307
Moncrief, Carlos	L-R	6-0	220	11-3-88	.271	.281	.265	132	480	64	130	33	4	12	63	38	4	6	2	130	8	3	.431	.328
Morgan, Nyjer	L-L	5-10	180	7-2-80	.200	.233	.167	15	60	4	12	4	0	1	7	3	0	0	1	16	1	0	.317	.234
Perez, Roberto	R-R	5-11	225	12-23-88	.305	.296	.308	53	174	29	53	11	1	8	43	29	1	4	1	51	1	0	.517	.405
Raburn, Ryan	R-R	6-0	185	4-17-81	.059	.000	.067	4	17	2	1	0	0	0	0	1	0	0	0	2	0	0	.059	.111
Ramirez, Jose	B-R	5-9	165	9-17-92	.302	.309	.298	60	245	37	74	15	2	5	29	25	0	2	5	30	19	11	.441	.360
Ramsey, James	L-R	6-0	190	12-19-89	.284	.194	.329	28	109	17	31	9	1	3	16	13	2	1	2	34	1	0	.468	.365
Rohlinger, Ryan	R-R	6-0	195	10-7-83	.233	.330	.187	85	292	31	68	16	0	5	27	24	5	5	2	48	0	0	.339	.300
Sellers, Justin	R-R	5-10	160	2-1-86	.254	.254	.253	102	355	31	90	18	1	3	40	25	5	4	6	48	3	1	.335	.307
Toole, Justin	R-R	6-0	180	9-10-86	—			1	0	0	0	0	0	0	0	0	0	0	0	0	0	0	—	—
Urshela, Giovanny	R-R	6-0	197	10-11-91	.276	.254	.285	104	395	63	109	27	6	13	65	30	3	1	1	51	0	2	.473	.331
Wallace, Chris	R-R	6-0	220	4-27-88	.170	.333	.034	18	53	7	9	2	0	1	5	5	0	0	0	16	0	0	.264	.241
Walters, Zach	R-B	6-2	210	9-5-89	.387	.538	.278	7	31	4	12	4	0	2	8	0	0	0	0	5	0	0	.710	.387
2-team total (60 Syracuse)					.310			67	268	42	83	22	5	17	56	20	2	1	1	67	0	2	.619	.367

Pitching	B-T	HT	WT	DOB	W	L	ERA	G	GS	CG	SV	IP	H	R	ER	HR	BB	SO	AVG	vLH	vRH	K/9	BB/9
Adams, Austin	R-R	5-11	190	8-19-86	3	2	2.50	42	0	0	5	54	44	16	15	4	16	52	.224	.241	.211	8.67	2.67
Arias, Gabriel	R-R	6-2	185	12-6-89	7	4	4.15	15	13	0	0	80	83	48	37	9	21	49	.264	.273	.254	5.49	2.35
Armstrong, Shawn	R-R	6-2	210	9-11-90	0	0	5.40	5	0	0	0	5	4	3	3	1	3	4	.235	.429	.100	7.20	5.40
Banwart, Travis	R-R	6-3	220	2-14-86	5	2	3.12	16	16	0	0	89	73	32	31	8	33	78	.224	.244	.204	7.86	3.32
Barnes, Scott	L-L	6-4	200	9-5-87	3	2	3.69	25	1	0	0	32	22	14	13	3	16	35	.193	.191	.194	9.95	4.55
Bauer, Trevor	R-R	6-1	190	1-17-91	4	1	2.15	7	7	1	0	46	36	11	11	5	14	44	.216	.195	.238	8.61	2.74
Brach, Brett	R-R	6-2	190	3-28-90	0	2	8.10	3	2	0	0	7	12	8	6	0	2	7	.387	.467	.313	9.45	2.70
Cloyd, Tyler	R-R	6-3	210	5-16-87	10	8	3.89	27	26	3	0	167	181	78	72	26	31	118	.277	.280	.275	6.37	1.67
Cooper, Jordan	R-R	6-2	190	5-10-89	0	1	4.91	2	1	0	0	7	6	4	4	0	5	3	.222	.200	.250	3.68	6.14
Crockett, Kyle	L-L	6-2	170	12-15-91	0	0	1.04	6	0	0	0	9	7	4	1	0	0	6	.219	.071	.333	6.23	0.00
Davies, Kyle	R-R	6-1	210	9-9-83	9	8	4.11	21	21	0	0	125	130	65	57	10	33	80	.273	.277	.269	5.78	2.38
Hagadone, Nick	L-L	6-5	230	1-1-86	3	4	3.77	23	0	0	1	29	26	16	12	5	12	41	.250	.205	.283	12.87	3.77
Herrmann, Frank	L-R	6-4	220	5-30-84	1	1	6.37	28	0	0	0	30	32	21	21	6	19	30	.274	.263	.283	9.10	5.76
House, T.J.	L-R	6-1	205	9-18-89	1	4	3.79	10	10	0	0	57	56	25	24	3	16	42	.264	.179	.303	6.63	2.53
Lee, C.C.	R-R	5-11	190	10-21-86	0	1	3.30	25	0	0	3	30	29	12	11	1	9	42	.250	.292	.221	11.10	2.70
Lowe, Mark	L-R	6-3	210	6-7-83	4	3	5.62	41	0	0	17	42	46	28	26	4	17	47	.280	.278	.282	10.15	3.67
Marcum, Shaun	R-R	6-0	195	12-14-81	1	0	2.35	8	1	0	0	15	10	5	4	1	6	10	.192	.200	.182	5.87	3.52
Maronde, Nick	B-L	6-2	205	9-5-89	0	0	0.00	1	1	0	0	6	2	0	0	0	1	8	.100	.100	.100	12.00	1.50
Masterson, Justin	R-R	6-6	250	3-22-85	0	1	5.40	2	2	0	0	12	9	7	7	0	8	10	.220	.087	.389	7.71	6.17

CLEVELAND INDIANS

	B-T	HT	WT	DOB	W	L	ERA	G	GS	CG	SV	IP	H	R	ER	HR	BB	SO	AVG	vLH	vRH	K/9	BB/9
McAllister, Zach	R-R	6-6	240	12-8-87	7	1	2.09	11	11	0	0	69	57	19	16	3	14	59	.224	.256	.196	7.70	1.83
Miller, Adam	R-R	6-4	215	11-26-84	0	0	0.00	1	0	0	0	1	0	0	0	0	0	2	.000	.000	.000	18.00	0.00
Murata, Toru	L-R	6-0	175	5-20-85	5	3	5.38	14	12	0	0	72	79	44	43	14	20	44	.283	.346	.230	5.50	2.50
Outman, Josh	L-L	6-1	205	9-14-84	3	1	4.43	23	1	0	0	22	21	12	11	2	8	20	.266	.189	.333	8.06	3.22
Pestano, Vinnie	R-R	6-0	200	2-20-85	2	4	1.78	32	0	0	6	30	23	8	6	0	12	37	.209	.302	.149	10.98	3.56
Price, Bryan	R-R	6-4	215	11-13-86	0	1	2.73	20	0	0	4	26	19	8	8	3	10	28	.200	.220	.185	9.57	3.42
Ramirez, J.C.	R-R	6-4	250	8-16-88	1	3	3.45	25	0	0	2	31	33	16	12	5	11	15	.280	.339	.226	4.31	3.16
Salazar, Danny	R-R	6-0	190	1-11-90	4	6	3.71	11	11	2	0	61	58	28	25	7	28	76	.243	.250	.237	11.27	4.15
Sturdevant, Tyler	R-R	6-0	185	12-20-85	1	1	4.05	22	0	0	1	27	26	13	12	3	8	24	.257	.316	.222	8.10	2.70
Suarez, Benny	R-R	6-1	190	9-28-91	0	0	30.86	2	0	0	0	2	6	8	8	4	3	1	.500	.500	.500	3.86	11.57
Tejeda, Enosil	R-R	6-0	175	6-21-89	0	0	0.00	1	0	0	0	1	0	0	0	0	1	1	.000	.000	.000	9.00	9.00
Tomlin, Josh	R-R	6-1	190	10-19-84	2	1	2.25	6	6	1	0	40	26	10	10	5	10	33	.191	.178	.206	7.43	2.25
von Schamann, Duke	R-R	6-5	220	6-3-91	1	0	6.52	2	2	0	0	10	12	7	7	2	2	2	.293	.353	.250	1.86	1.86
Wood, Blake	R-R	6-5	240	8-8-85	0	0	1.13	9	0	0	0	8	7	3	1	0	11	7	.226	.273	.200	7.88	12.38
Zagurski, Mike	L-L	6-0	240	1-27-83	2	0	2.76	16	0	0	0	16	11	5	5	1	10	22	.183	.280	.114	12.12	5.51
2-team total (30 Buffalo)					4	1	2.08	46	0	0	0	61	42	16	14	1	29	83	—	—	—	12.31	4.30

Fielding

Catcher	PCT	G	PO	A	E	DP	PB
Brown	.981	14	92	9	2	0	3
Carlin	.989	58	409	27	5	1	5
Kottaras	1.000	14	109	4	0	2	1
Perez	.993	53	423	31	3	4	2
Wallace	1.000	10	56	3	0	1	4

First Base	PCT	G	PO	A	E	DP
Abraham	1.000	9	68	6	0	9
Aguilar	.994	82	605	60	4	70
Branyan	1.000	2	8	0	0	1
Brown	1.000	1	4	0	0	0
Ciriaco	.989	35	252	20	3	27
Cooper	.983	16	106	9	2	8
Johnson	.857	2	6	0	1	1
LaHair	.958	3	21	2	1	4
Rohlinger	1.000	2	9	1	0	2
Wallace	.970	5	29	3	1	5

Second Base	PCT	G	PO	A	E	DP
Ciriaco	.985	30	53	76	2	18
Hankins	1.000	2	1	4	0	0

	PCT	G	PO	A	E	DP
Johnson	1.000	13	18	30	0	7
Kipnis	.889	3	4	4	1	2
Ramirez	.993	35	46	105	1	24
Rohlinger	.996	51	92	133	1	38
Sellers	.978	18	35	52	2	12
Toole	—	1	0	0	0	0
Walters	.944	3	5	12	1	2

Third Base	PCT	G	PO	A	E	DP
Abraham	1.000	2	2	0	0	0
Aguilar	—	1	0	0	0	0
Ciriaco	.917	14	9	13	2	1
Johnson	1.000	1	0	1	0	0
Ramirez	1.000	1	0	1	0	0
Rohlinger	.921	31	17	41	5	1
Sellers	.667	2	0	1	2	0
Urshela	.977	98	59	156	5	17
Walters	1.000	1	1	3	0	0

Shortstop	PCT	G	PO	A	E	DP
Ciriaco	.945	17	16	53	4	14
Johnson	.909	3	2	8	1	2

	PCT	G	PO	A	E	DP
Lindor	.981	38	54	104	3	25
Ramirez	.967	21	32	55	3	15
Rohlinger	.857	2	6	6	2	3
Sellers	.939	67	89	142	15	39
Urshela	1.000	1	3	0	0	0

Outfield	PCT	G	PO	A	E	DP
Bourn	1.000	3	10	0	0	0
Carson	.993	71	135	7	1	2
Ciriaco	—	1	0	0	0	0
Fedroff	.990	62	98	0	1	0
Holt	.987	58	144	3	2	1
Johnson	.969	55	125	2	4	0
LaHair	1.000	3	5	0	0	0
Moncrief	.972	129	256	22	8	6
Morgan	1.000	13	24	2	0	1
Ramirez	1.000	4	11	0	0	0
Ramsey	1.000	28	81	2	0	2
Sellers	.973	17	36	0	1	0
Walters	1.000	2	5	0	0	0

AKRON RUBBERDUCKS

DOUBLE-A

EASTERN LEAGUE

Batting	B-T	HT	WT	DOB	AVG	vLH	vRH	G	AB	R	H	2B	3B	HR	RBI	BB	HBP	SH	SF	SO	SB	CS	SLG	OBP
Abraham, Adam	R-R	6-0	228	3-27-87	.231	.182	.266	29	108	11	25	8	0	1	9	12	1	0	1	15	1	1	.333	.311
Bourn, Michael	L-R	5-10	180	12-27-82	.000	.200	.000	6	23	0	2	0	0	0	2	0	0	0	0	2	0	0	.087	.160
Fedroff, Tim	L-R	5-10	200	2-4-87	.216	.220	.214	29	111	12	24	5	0	2	14	8	2	0	2	29	1	0	.315	.276
Ferrell, Cody	R-R	5-10	195	4-29-90	.308	.000	.400	5	13	1	4	0	0	0	2	0	1	0	2	3	2	0	.308	.400
Gallas, Anthony	R-R	6-2	210	12-14-87	.293	.344	.266	73	280	35	82	16	2	16	49	21	1	0	7	71	0	1	.536	.337
Giambi, Jason	L-R	6-3	240	1-8-71	.118	.000	.200	6	17	1	2	2	0	0	1	2	0	0	0	9	0	0	.235	.211
Gonzalez, Erik	R-R	6-0	175	8-31-91	.357	.257	.394	31	129	21	46	6	3	1	16	7	0	0	0	23	6	1	.473	.390
Holt, Tyler	R-R	5-10	190	3-10-89	.298	.306	.295	39	124	13	37	4	1	0	14	27	0	2	3	26	11	2	.347	.416
LaHair, Bryan	L-R	6-5	240	11-5-82	.234	.195	.251	101	364	38	85	17	2	5	60	50	0	0	3	91	1	1	.332	.324
Lavisky, Alex	R-R	6-1	209	1-13-91	.278	.232	.310	67	241	26	67	10	0	4	25	12	1	1	1	44	1	1	.369	.314
Lindor, Francisco	B-R	5-11	175	11-14-93	.278	.313	.255	88	342	51	95	12	4	6	48	40	1	1	3	61	25	9	.389	.352
Linton, Ollie	L-L	5-8	160	4-7-86	.253	.255	.253	49	150	22	38	7	2	1	13	17	3	3	0	34	12	3	.347	.341
Lowery, Jake	L-R	6-0	200	7-21-90	.201	.156	.219	66	219	27	44	7	3	5	19	33	2	0	4	71	1	0	.329	.306
Myles, Bryson	R-R	5-11	230	9-18-89	.263	.304	.245	84	300	39	79	15	3	6	30	26	6	4	1	87	12	5	.393	.333
Naquin, Tyler	L-R	6-3	190	4-24-91	.313	.260	.335	76	304	54	95	12	5	4	30	29	2	1	5	71	14	3	.424	.371
Pedroza, Jaime	R-R	5-8	180	9-12-86	.358	.200	.426	21	67	17	24	4	2	2	7	3	2	2	0	8	1	0	.567	.403
Raburn, Ryan	R-R	6-0	185	4-17-81	.455	.333	.500	3	11	2	5	0	0	0	4	1	0	0	0	3	0	0	.455	.500
Rodriguez, Ronny	R-R	6-0	170	4-17-92	.228	.211	.236	118	413	52	94	25	0	5	34	25	1	2	6	92	4	5	.324	.270
Sabourin, Jerrud	L-L	6-2	210	11-4-89	.152	.143	.154	12	33	2	5	1	0	0	2	3	0	1	2	4	0	0	.182	.189
Smith, Jordan	L-R	6-4	205	7-5-90	.248	.236	.255	126	459	52	114	24	4	2	50	33	2	0	3	82	9	8	.331	.300
Swisher, Nick	B-L	6-0	200	11-25-80	.500	.000	.750	2	6	0	3	2	0	0	2	0	0	0	0	1	0	0	.833	.500
Toole, Justin	R-R	6-0	180	9-10-86	.275	.280	.273	77	236	25	65	13	1	0	25	14	5	1	1	32	3	3	.339	.328
Urshela, Giovanny	R-R	6-0	197	10-11-91	.300	.314	.291	24	90	15	27	9	0	1	16	1	1	0	1	16	1	1	.567	.347
Valerio, Charlie	B-R	6-0	204	11-7-90	.259	.091	.375	9	27	6	7	0	0	0	1	3	0	0	0	7	1	0	.259	.333
Wendle, Joe	L-R	5-11	190	4-26-90	.253	.265	.247	87	336	46	85	20	5	8	50	26	4	0	4	55	3	2	.414	.311
Wolters, Tony	L-R	5-10	180	6-9-92	.249	.222	.265	94	341	36	85	15	1	4	36	43	3	2	6	74	3	2	.314	.319

Pitching	B-T	HT	WT	DOB	W	L	ERA	G	GS	CG	SV	IP	H	R	ER	HR	BB	SO	AVG	vLH	vRH	K/9	BB/9
Anderson, Cody	R-R	6-4	220	9-14-90	4	11	5.44	25	25	0	0	126	141	78	76	17	45	81	.285	.345	.233	5.80	3.22
Araujo, Elvis	L-L	6-6	215	7-15-91	1	0	2.57	18	0	0	3	21	20	7	6	2	15	21	.270	.242	.293	9.00	6.43
Arias, Gabirel	R-R	6-2	185	12-6-89	7	2	3.13	12	12	0	0	69	66	27	24	4	21	42	.257	.336	.185	5.48	2.74
Armstrong, Shawn	R-R	6-2	210	9-11-90	6	2	2.12	44	0	0	15	51	39	12	12	3	19	68	.211	.244	.187	12.00	3.35

	B-T	HT	WT	DOB	W	L	ERA	G	GS	CG	SV	IP	H	R	ER	HR	BB	SO	AVG	vLH	vRH	K/9	BB/9
Colon, Joseph	R-R	6-0	167	2-18-90	8	7	3.39	25	25	1	0	138	132	56	52	8	55	96	.256	.245	.266	6.26	3.59
Cooper, Jordan	R-R	6-2	190	5-10-89	7	3	4.96	35	4	0	0	78	72	44	43	12	31	61	.244	.260	.233	7.04	3.58
Crockett, Kyle	L-L	6-2	170	12-15-91	0	0	0.57	15	0	0	6	16	8	1	1	0	3	17	.145	.118	.158	9.77	1.72
Davies, Kyle	R-R	6-1	210	9-9-83	2	1	3.03	5	5	0	0	30	28	18	10	7	7	18	.252	.289	.227	5.46	2.12
Haley, Trey	R-R	6-4	205	6-21-90	0	0	7.02	15	0	0	0	17	19	13	13	4	13	15	.292	.257	.333	8.10	7.02
Head, Louis	R-R	6-1	180	4-23-90	1	1	2.97	29	0	0	3	36	35	14	12	3	16	39	.255	.295	.224	9.66	3.96
Maronde, Nick	B-L	6-3	205	9-5-89	0	2	12.38	2	2	0	0	8	19	12	11	2	2	9	.487	.444	.524	10.13	2.25
Martin, Josh	R-R	6-5	230	12-30-89	0	0	0.00	1	0	0	0	2	0	0	0	0	0	4	.000	.000	.000	18.00	0.00
Miller, Adam	R-R	6-4	215	11-26-84	1	2	5.44	28	0	0	0	41	39	28	25	6	14	43	.239	.194	.271	9.36	3.05
Morimando, Shawn	L-L	5-11	195	11-20-92	2	6	3.83	10	10	0	0	56	63	31	24	2	17	38	.281	.292	.277	6.07	2.72
Murata, Toru	L-R	6-0	175	5-20-85	5	4	4.61	13	8	0	0	55	60	31	28	6	18	35	.284	.327	.238	5.76	2.96
Nixon, Robert	R-R	6-1	225	11-1-88	0	0	13.50	1	0	0	0	1	1	2	2	1	1	2	.200	.333	.000	0.00	6.75
Packer, Matt	L-L	6-0	200	8-28-87	1	1	8.68	2	2	0	0	9	12	9	9	1	4	7	.324	.500	.303	6.75	3.86
Price, Bryan	R-R	6-4	215	11-13-86	1	0	1.80	8	0	0	1	10	7	3	2	2	2	16	.189	.200	.182	14.40	1.80
Ramirez, J.C.	R-R	6-4	250	8-16-88	1	0	2.08	10	0	0	1	13	5	3	3	1	8	14	.111	.125	.095	9.69	5.54
Roberts, Will	L-R	6-5	195	8-17-90	12	12	4.08	27	27	0	0	161	170	81	73	13	36	98	.276	.268	.283	5.48	2.01
Sides, Grant	R-R	6-4	215	6-22-89	0	0	0.00	1	0	0	0	1	0	0	0	0	2	0	.000	.000	.000	0.00	18.00
Soto, Giovanni	L-L	6-2	190	5-18-91	0	2	3.23	37	0	0	1	53	45	24	19	2	12	49	.230	.141	.280	8.32	2.04
Sturdevant, Tyler	R-R	6-0	185	12-20-85	1	1	1.45	24	0	0	7	31	19	5	5	1	9	30	.179	.234	.136	8.71	2.61
Sulser, Cole	R-R	6-0	190	3-12-90	0	1	3.27	2	2	0	0	11	9	6	4	2	2	9	.225	.238	.211	7.36	1.64
Tejeda, Enosil	R-R	6-0	175	6-21-89	4	2	3.23	44	0	0	6	56	49	22	20	5	13	60	.238	.242	.235	9.70	2.10
Valera, Francisco	R-R	6-1	170	10-19-89	1	1	7.11	8	0	0	0	13	19	10	10	3	6	7	.352	.333	.367	4.97	4.26
von Schamann, Duke	R-R	6-5	220	6-3-91	8	8	4.20	24	20	0	1	135	140	68	63	15	34	68	.271	.248	.291	4.53	2.27

Fielding

Catcher	PCT	G	PO	A	E	DP	PB
Lavisky	.995	51	376	35	2	6	5
Lowery	.974	25	131	20	4	1	1
Wolters	1.000	66	439	52	0	4	4

First Base	PCT	G	PO	A	E	DP
Abraham	1.000	7	52	6	0	4
Gallas	—	1	0	0	0	0
LaHair	.995	80	681	44	4	68
Lowery	.985	23	194	4	3	21
Rodriguez	.988	23	151	10	2	15
Sabourin	.990	11	94	6	1	7
Swisher	1.000	2	8	0	0	1
Valerio	.966	7	51	5	2	7

Second Base	PCT	G	PO	A	E	DP
Pedroza	.857	3	2	4	1	0

	PCT	G	PO	A	E	DP
Rodriguez	.977	45	77	133	5	25
Toole	1.000	8	11	25	0	8
Wendle	.984	80	160	280	7	73
Wolters	.978	10	16	28	1	5

Third Base	PCT	G	PO	A	E	DP
Abraham	.977	15	16	26	1	3
Pedroza	.900	6	3	6	1	0
Rodriguez	.948	40	32	60	5	8
Toole	.993	66	44	93	1	6
Urshela	.938	23	12	48	4	5

Shortstop	PCT	G	PO	A	E	DP
Gonzalez	.959	30	35	82	5	26
Lindor	.967	88	133	251	13	62
Pedroza	.946	12	9	26	2	4
Rodriguez	.914	8	10	22	3	8

	PCT	G	PO	A	E	DP
Wolters	.969	8	7	24	1	0

Outfield	PCT	G	PO	A	E	DP
Abraham	1.000	5	9	2	0	0
Bourn	1.000	6	16	0	0	0
Fedroff	.982	27	52	2	1	0
Ferrell	.889	5	7	1	1	0
Gallas	.990	50	99	0	1	0
Holt	.981	31	47	5	1	0
Linton	.990	47	101	2	1	0
Myles	1.000	69	111	5	0	1
Naquin	.995	74	179	9	1	1
Raburn	1.000	2	2	0	0	0
Smith	.986	121	279	10	4	0
Toole	—	2	0	0	0	0

CAROLINA MUDCATS   HIGH CLASS A
CAROLINA LEAGUE

Batting	B-T	HT	WT	DOB	AVG	vLH	vRH	G	AB	R	H	2B	3B	HR	RBI	BB	HBP	SH	SF	SB	CS	SLG	OBP
Battaglia, Ryan	R-R	6-1	202	6-29-92	.112	.167	.092	31	89	5	10	5	0	1	8	12	2	1	1			.202	.231
Boss, Torsten	L-R	6-0	190	12-27-90	.215	.200	.218	42	144	15	31	6	1	5	17	19	2	0	1	45	1	2	.375	.313
2-team total (1 Frederick)					.218	—	—	43	147	16	32	7	1	5	17	20	2	0	1	46	1	2	.381	.318
Diaz, Yandy	R-R	6-2	185	8-8-91	.286	.267	.293	76	283	42	81	7	2	2	37	49	3	—	1	35	3	3	.367	.396
Ferrell, Cody	R-R	5-10	195	4-29-90	.125	.000	.143	6	8	1	1	0	0	0	0	2	0	0	0	2	0	1	.125	.300
Gallas, Anthony	R-R	6-2	210	12-14-87	.276	.228	.293	58	221	29	61	21	0	8	31	17	1	0	0	52	4	1	.480	.331
Gonzalez, Erik	R-R	6-0	175	8-31-91	.289	.228	.310	74	308	44	89	14	7	3	46	23	0	—	2	65	15	6	.409	.336
Haase, Eric	R-R	5-10	180	12-18-92	.185	.238	.159	16	65	4	12	4	0	1	6	5	0	0	0	19	0	1	.292	.243
Hankins, Todd	R-R	5-9	175	11-18-90	.258	.235	.267	88	349	50	90	21	5	5	42	31	6	—	2	96	25	5	.390	.327
Linton, Ollie	L-L	5-8	160	4-7-86	.320	.364	.313	23	75	9	24	7	0	0	9	12	2	1	2	17	4	4	.413	.418
Lucas, Jeremy	R-L	6-1	205	1-10-91	.267	.255	.272	101	378	62	101	24	3	12	58	52	6	—	2	69	1	1	.442	.363
Medina, Yhoxian	R-R	5-10	165	5-11-90	.288	.277	.293	99	385	60	111	19	2	1	36	39	3	—	2	61	12	5	.356	.357
Monsalve, Alex	R-R	6-2	225	4-22-92	.265	.183	.303	93	359	37	95	20	4	5	51	25	6	—	2	67	2	1	.384	.321
Roberts, James	R-R	6-2	180	12-11-91	.268	.226	.284	117	407	44	109	9	0	4	57	34	12	6	4	75	0	3	.319	.339
Rodriguez, Luigi	B-R	5-11	160	11-13-92	.250	.245	.252	99	336	50	84	13	4	6	30	50	1	—	2	88	15	8	.366	.347
Sabourin, Jerrud	L-L	6-2	210	11-2-89	.295	.244	.314	89	322	37	95	19	1	5	45	39	1	—	2	61	2	1	.407	.371
Sever, Joe	R-R	6-0	205	8-12-90	.263	.239	.271	72	270	34	71	10	0	3	36	30	9	2	5	47	2	0	.333	.350
Valerio, Charlie	B-R	6-0	204	11-7-90	.245	.286	.231	17	53	6	13	4	1	0	4	10	0	0	0	10	0	0	.358	.365
Vick, Logan	L-R	5-11	185	10-22-90	.183	.237	.167	82	263	44	48	16	1	3	21	58	3	3	3	81	13	6	.285	.333
Washington, LeVon	L-R	5-11	170	7-26-91	.294	.295	.293	70	252	39	74	11	1	4	28	45	2	—	2	73	3	3	.393	.402

Pitching	B-T	HT	WT	DOB	W	L	ERA	G	GS	CG	SV	IP	H	R	ER	HR	BB	SO	AVG	vLH	vRH	K/9	BB/9
Araujo, Elvis	L-L	6-6	215	7-15-91	1	1	4.03	25	0	0	8	29	23	16	13	1	13	29	.217	.133	.231	9.00	4.03
Baker, Dylan	R-R	6-2	215	4-6-92	3	3	4.05	9	9	0	0	47	45	25	21	3	18	28	.250	.268	.229	5.40	3.47
Brown, D.J.	R-R	6-6	205	11-28-90	3	8	4.51	26	20	0	0	124	144	74	62	8	33	83	.287	.294	.283	6.04	2.40
Clevinger, Mike	R-R	6-4	220	12-21-90	0	1	4.79	5	4	0	0	21	20	12	11	1	11	15	.270	.282	.257	6.53	4.79
Cook, Clayton	R-R	6-3	175	7-23-90	2	4	6.02	20	1	0	1	40	47	29	27	4	15	31	.288	.173	.386	6.92	3.35
DeJesus, Luis	R-R	6-3	175	12-16-91	0	0	5.40	2	0	0	0	2	3	1	1	1	2	1	.375	.400	.333	5.40	10.80
Head, Louis	R-R	6-1	180	4-23-90	0	3	2.21	17	0	0	9	20	10	5	5	0	7	34	.141	.182	.122	15.05	3.10
Heller, Ben	R-R	6-3	205	8-5-91	1	0	2.25	17	0	0	1	16	8	6	4	1	13	17	.148	.172	.120	9.56	7.31

CLEVELAND INDIANS

Name	B-T	HT	WT	DOB	W	L	ERA	G	GS	CG	SV	IP	H	R	ER	HR	BB	SO	AVG	vLH	vRH	K/9	BB/9
Lee, Jacob	R-R	6-1	190	10-25-89	4	0	2.99	41	1	0	2	72	67	28	24	5	18	53	.241	.235	.244	6.59	2.24
Martin, Josh	R-R	6-5	230	12-30-89	5	6	2.92	38	0	0	3	65	47	23	21	4	21	65	.199	.163	.222	9.05	2.92
Melo, Carlos	R-R	6-3	180	2-27-91	0	1	10.13	12	0	0	0	11	14	16	12	0	15	7	.326	.357	.310	5.91	12.66
Merritt, Ryan	L-L	6-0	165	2-21-92	13	3	2.58	25	25	2	0	160	128	56	46	12	25	127	.216	.197	.221	7.13	1.40
Morimando, Shawn	L-L	5-11	195	11-20-92	8	3	2.99	18	18	0	0	96	72	42	32	7	35	70	.203	.212	.201	6.54	3.27
Nixon, Robert	R-R	6-1	225	11-1-88	1	6	4.62	31	0	0	1	49	50	33	25	3	19	32	.263	.269	.259	5.92	3.51
Peoples, Scott	R-R	6-5	190	9-5-91	7	8	4.34	26	17	0	0	102	106	58	49	7	42	101	.271	.268	.274	8.94	3.72
Plutko, Adam	R-R	6-3	195	10-3-91	4	9	4.08	18	18	0	0	97	99	47	44	11	18	76	.265	.262	.268	7.24	1.67
Sides, Grant	R-R	6-4	215	6-22-89	4	2	2.67	43	0	0	6	54	43	17	16	1	27	50	.221	.260	.195	8.33	4.50
Suarez, Benny	R-R	6-1	190	9-28-91	2	3	3.81	37	0	0	2	57	57	26	24	1	23	37	.266	.293	.246	5.88	3.65
Sulser, Cole	R-R	6-0	190	3-12-90	4	13	5.62	25	23	0	0	125	135	92	78	9	35	120	.274	.254	.289	8.64	2.52

Fielding

Catcher	PCT	G	PO	A	E	DP	PB
Battaglia	.987	20	145	10	2	0	2
Haase	.981	8	47	6	1	1	1
Lucas	.994	63	449	47	3	2	5
Monsalve	.992	45	327	29	3	4	10
Valerio	1.000	2	6	3	0	0	0

First Base	PCT	G	PO	A	E	DP
Battaglia	1.000	2	8	1	0	1
Lucas	.989	10	85	2	1	5
Sabourin	.994	54	460	38	3	33
Sever	.989	59	476	47	6	45
Valerio	1.000	14	103	11	0	8

Second Base	PCT	G	PO	A	E	DP
Boss	.950	16	34	42	4	8
Hankins	.950	34	53	80	7	19
Medina	.991	26	41	68	1	8
Roberts	.957	58	114	153	12	31
Sever	1.000	2	3	5	0	2

Third Base	PCT	G	PO	A	E	DP
Diaz	.944	74	59	126	11	7
Medina	.931	7	6	21	2	2
Roberts	.869	53	26	100	19	11
Sever	.889	4	1	7	1	0

Shortstop	PCT	G	PO	A	E	DP
Gonzalez	.954	74	91	200	14	32

	PCT	G	PO	A	E	DP
Medina	.958	63	104	167	12	38

Outfield	PCT	G	PO	A	E	DP
Boss	1.000	22	42	2	0	1
Ferrell	1.000	4	6	0	0	0
Gallas	1.000	50	79	2	0	0
Hankins	.993	54	141	0	1	0
Linton	.981	23	50	1	1	1
Medina	1.000	3	3	0	0	0
Rodriguez	.947	93	194	4	11	0
Sabourin	1.000	29	48	1	0	0
Sever	1.000	3	1	0	0	0
Vick	.966	80	162	7	6	1
Washington	.970	60	97	1	3	0

LAKE COUNTY CAPTAINS   LOW CLASS A
MIDWEST LEAGUE

Batting	B-T	HT	WT	DOB	AVG	vLH	vRH	G	AB	R	H	2B	3B	HR	RBI	BB	HBP	SH	SF	SO	SB	CS	SLG	OBP
Battaglia, Ryan	R-R	6-1	202	6-29-92	.000	.000	.000	1	3	0	0	0	0	0	0	0	0	0	0	1	0	0	.000	.000
Bautista, Claudio	R-R	5-11	170	11-29-93	.249	.176	.266	119	461	65	115	21	7	13	54	12	5	3	2	103	11	3	.410	.275
Boss, Torsten	L-R	6-0	190	12-27-90	.198	.000	.225	37	126	15	25	6	1	4	16	22	2	0	0	44	0	2	.357	.327
Castillo, Ivan	B-R	5-11	150	5-30-95	.260	.292	.252	84	315	37	82	12	3	5	26	11	5	10	3	61	11	6	.365	.293
Ferrell, Cody	R-R	5-10	195	4-29-90	.199	.156	.210	48	151	21	30	6	0	3	11	20	2	0	0	40	6	3	.298	.301
Fink, Grant	R-R	6-3	215	12-14-90	.225	.164	.237	118	409	59	92	20	1	13	60	61	1	1	2	174	0	1	.374	.326
Frazier, Clint	R-R	6-1	190	9-6-94	.266	.301	.257	120	474	70	126	18	6	13	50	56	7	1	4	161	12	6	.411	.349
Haase, Eric	R-R	5-10	180	12-18-92	.270	.275	.269	77	296	48	80	16	4	16	42	28	3	0	1	84	1	2	.514	.338
Hamilton, Nick	B-R	6-1	200	11-19-89	.000	—	.000	1	1	0	0	0	0	0	0	0	0	0	0	0	0	0	.000	.000
Hendrix, Paul	R-R	6-2	187	11-18-91	.287	.259	.294	115	415	63	119	21	5	12	46	49	4	0	4	138	2	2	.448	.364
Loopstok, Sicnarf	R-R	5-11	195	4-26-93	.278	.714	.172	10	36	7	10	2	1	1	2	3	2	0	0	7	2	0	.472	.366
Martinez, Jorge	B-R	6-1	183	3-29-93	.128	.211	.104	26	86	4	11	2	0	0	9	9	0	0	2	31	0	1	.151	.206
Papi, Mike	L-R	6-2	190	9-19-92	.178	.147	.188	39	135	21	24	4	0	3	15	26	0	1	3	32	2	0	.274	.305
Paulino, Dorssys	R-R	6-0	175	11-21-94	.251	.291	.240	113	427	51	107	25	5	3	35	33	6	3	3	101	5	6	.354	.311
Rodriguez, Nellie	R-R	6-2	225	6-12-94	.268	.200	.285	130	485	67	130	32	3	22	88	60	2	0	3	142	0	0	.482	.349
Rowland, Shane	L-R	6-0	200	11-22-91	.111	.250	.071	5	18	0	2	0	0	0	2	1	0	0	0	8	0	0	.111	.158
Ruiz, Brian	R-R	6-3	180	9-11-92	.260	.308	.247	85	292	29	76	18	1	3	28	14	6	1	0	93	0	4	.360	.308
Santander, Anthony	B-R	6-2	190	10-19-94	.184	.083	.201	43	163	16	30	9	1	1	10	17	0	0	1	49	2	0	.270	.260
Schubert, Josh	R-R	6-4	210	1-25-94	.198	.263	.183	28	101	5	20	1	1	0	6	6	1	0	1	43	2	1	.228	.248
Stock, Richard	R-R	6-2	190	9-2-89	.261	.241	.265	52	184	15	48	12	2	4	26	6	4	1	2	40	1	1	.413	.296
Vick, Logan	L-R	5-11	185	10-22-90	.237	.235	.238	16	59	7	14	2	1	1	13	11	0	0	0	3	0	0	.356	.357
Zimmer, Bradley	L-R	6-4	185	11-27-92	.273	1.000	.200	3	11	4	3	1	0	2	2	2	0	0	0	3	1	0	.909	.385

Pitching	B-T	HT	WT	DOB	W	L	ERA	G	GS	CG	SV	IP	H	R	ER	HR	BB	SO	AVG	vLH	vRH	K/9	BB/9
Aviles, Robbie	L-R	6-4	200	12-17-91	2	1	2.55	25	9	0	1	85	73	33	24	2	11	49	.233	.211	.246	5.21	1.17
Beras, Wander	L-R	6-0	160	7-18-88	3	2	5.21	40	0	0	2	67	57	50	39	6	36	63	.225	.190	.237	8.42	4.81
Brady, Sean	L-L	6-0	175	6-9-94	0	1	13.50	1	1	0	0	3	6	6	4	2	2	2	.429	.500	.400	6.75	6.75
Brantley, Justin	R-R	5-11	167	3-5-91	4	1	1.31	25	0	0	2	41	31	7	6	3	15	47	.204	.170	.222	10.23	3.27
Brown, Mitch	R-R	6-1	195	4-13-94	8	8	3.31	27	27	0	0	139	113	60	51	6	55	127	.226	.227	.226	8.24	3.57
DeJesus, Luis	R-R	6-3	175	12-16-91	0	0	8.10	8	0	0	0	13	22	12	12	3	2	14	.367	.333	.385	9.45	1.35
Doane, Kerry	R-R	5-11	175	9-3-90	0	1	6.06	7	0	0	0	16	16	13	11	2	7	10	.262	.296	.235	5.51	3.86
Frank, Trevor	R-R	6-0	195	6-23-91	5	4	2.63	50	0	0	18	55	40	20	16	3	9	62	.205	.294	.157	10.21	1.48
Garcia, Justin	R-R	6-1	180	9-16-92	0	0	4.15	4	0	0	0	9	9	5	4	0	3	10	.265	.455	.174	10.38	3.12
Hamrick, Caleb	R-R	6-2	210	9-25-93	3	9	6.64	30	12	0	1	99	126	81	73	7	51	63	.313	.317	.311	5.73	4.64
Heller, Ben	R-R	6-3	205	8-5-91	4	1	2.43	28	0	0	4	37	19	10	10	3	16	64	.147	.093	.174	15.57	3.89
Kime, Dace	R-R	6-3	200	3-6-92	7	14	5.22	28	28	0	0	136	148	90	79	12	56	108	.276	.258	.286	7.13	3.70
Lugo, Luis	L-L	6-5	200	3-5-94	10	9	4.92	27	22	0	0	126	124	79	69	16	40	146	.255	.315	.237	10.40	2.85
Mathews, Kenny	L-L	6-3	205	8-6-93	2	2	2.04	8	0	0	0	18	12	6	4	0	6	14	.200	.286	.174	7.13	3.06
McAllister, Zach	R-R	6-6	240	12-8-87	0	0	6.23	1	1	0	0	4	9	3	3	0	1	4	.429	.455	.400	8.31	2.08
Melo, Carlos	R-R	6-3	180	2-27-91	3	1	4.94	25	0	0	4	27	24	19	15	2	23	39	.229	.231	.227	12.84	7.57
Milbrath, Jordan	R-R	6-6	215	8-1-91	3	12	3.95	26	23	1	0	125	127	65	55	8	49	77	.271	.257	.281	5.53	3.52
Paredes, Alexis	R-R	6-3	175	1-24-92	3	5	6.19	38	0	0	0	68	87	52	47	10	32	49	.310	.278	.325	6.45	4.21
Plutko, Adam	R-R	6-3	195	10-3-91	3	1	3.93	10	10	0	0	53	49	26	23	1	12	66	.241	.263	.228	11.28	2.05
Polanco, Anderson	L-L	6-3	190	9-6-92	3	0	1.95	19	6	0	0	51	32	16	11	1	17	62	.178	.278	.153	11.01	3.02

Stokes, Jim	R-R	6-6	225	10-9-90	0	0	2.45	11	0 0 1	15	8	4	4	0	12	19	.160	.111	.188	11.66	7.36
Whitehouse, Matt	L-L	6-1	175	4-13-91	2	1	5.51	11	0 0 0	33	39	28	20	3	11	33	.289	.244	.311	9.09	3.03

Fielding

Catcher	PCT	G	PO	A	E	DP	PB
Haase	.977	77	606	79	16	8	19
Loopstok	.990	10	94	8	1	1	4
Rowland	1.000	3	28	1	0	0	2
Stock	.977	51	384	42	10	4	11

First Base	PCT	G	PO	A	E	DP
Fink	.973	21	169	13	5	17
Papi	1.000	2	14	2	0	0
Rodriguez	.990	118	1047	54	11	82

Second Base	PCT	G	PO	A	E	DP
Bautista	.970	116	233	314	17	62

Boss	1.000	1	2	3	0	1
Castillo	1.000	1	2	3	0	1
Hendrix	.981	23	48	55	2	12

Third Base	PCT	G	PO	A	E	DP
Fink	.939	93	81	179	17	18
Hendrix	.978	50	29	107	3	7

Shortstop	PCT	G	PO	A	E	DP
Castillo	.950	80	101	219	17	44
Hendrix	.956	37	36	95	6	18
Paulino	.849	24	29	44	13	8

Outfield	PCT	G	PO	A	E	DP
Boss	.956	26	43	0	2	0
Castillo	—	1	0	0	0	0
Ferrell	.962	46	100	2	4	2
Frazier	.962	112	193	8	8	0
Martinez	.980	24	44	4	1	1
Papi	.982	35	54	2	1	1
Paulino	.935	82	124	6	9	1
Ruiz	.966	52	83	3	3	1
Schubert	.982	28	47	7	1	3
Vick	1.000	15	27	6	0	1
Zimmer	1.000	2	4	0	0	0

MAHONING VALLEY SCRAPPERS   SHORT-SEASON

NEW YORK-PENN LEAGUE

Batting	B-T	HT	WT	DOB	AVG	vLH	vRH	G	AB	R	H	2B	3B	HR	RBI	BB	HBP	SH	SF	SO	SB	CS	SLG	OBP
Allen, Greg	B-R	6-0	175	3-15-93	.244	.340	.219	57	225	46	55	8	2	0	19	27	15	1	2	26	30	5	.298	.361
Castillo, Leonardo	R-R	6-2	190	7-9-93	.260	.209	.271	64	231	20	60	11	3	6	49	26	2	2	3	44	0	0	.411	.336
Cervenka, Martin	R-R	6-1	175	8-3-92	.181	.235	.167	25	83	7	15	3	0	0	8	8	0	1	1	15	1	0	.217	.250
De La Cruz, Juan	B-R	6-1	195	8-5-93	.192	.167	.203	28	99	11	19	7	1	2	6	4	1	2	0	18	0	0	.343	.231
Fisher, Austin	L-R	6-1	195	1-8-92	.196	.152	.208	46	158	13	31	1	0	1	10	13	2	3	0	35	2	0	.222	.266
Hamilton, Nick	B-R	6-1	200	11-19-89	.000	—	.000	3	7	1	0	0	0	0	0	0	0	0	0	1	0	0	.000	.000
Martinez, Jorge	B-R	6-1	183	3-29-93	.283	.100	.333	12	46	6	13	3	1	2	13	3	0	0	0	14	1	0	.522	.327
2-team total (4 Tri-City)					.245	—		16	53	6	13	3	1	2	13	3	0	0	0	16	1	0	.453	.286
McClure, D'vone	B-R	6-3	190	1-22-94	.225	.162	.242	49	169	15	38	9	1	1	9	15	2	1	1	38	2	5	.308	.294
Mejia, Francisco	B-B	5-10	175	10-27-95	.282	.236	.295	66	248	32	70	17	4	2	36	18	5	0	3	47	2	4	.407	.339
Mejia, Joel	R-R	5-11	160	4-7-93	.138	.167	.130	7	29	2	4	0	0	1	1	1	0	0	7	1	0	.138	.194
Mendoza, Yonathan	B-R	5-11	167	2-10-94	.239	.222	.244	63	213	30	51	7	0	1	19	26	0	2	0	26	4	1	.286	.322
Murphy, Taylor	L-R	6-2	200	11-3-92	.262	.325	.245	53	187	23	49	9	1	3	23	26	4	0	2	37	1	1	.369	.361
Papi, Mike	L-R	6-2	190	9-19-92	.222	.000	.250	2	9	2	2	0	0	0	3	0	0	0	0	0	0	0	.222	.222
Patterson, Steven	L-R	5-9	205	8-3-92	.269	.229	.280	54	216	38	58	20	1	4	26	25	2	1	3	43	1	1	.426	.346
Roberts, Drake	B-S	5-8	155	1-6-92	.175	.174	.175	34	120	9	21	7	1	0	13	7	3	0	0	39	2	1	.250	.238
Rowland, Shane	L-R	6-0	200	11-22-91	.250	.500	.167	9	32	2	8	2	0	0	3	3	0	0	0	7	0	0	.313	.314
Schubert, Josh	B-R	6-4	210	1-25-94	.194	.278	.173	26	93	10	18	3	1	0	5	6	2	0	0	38	0	0	.247	.257
Smith, Garrett	B-R	6-3	180	2-7-90	.000	—	.000	2	5	0	0	0	0	0	0	0	0	0	0	1	0	0	.000	.000
Valdez, Ordomar	B-R	5-9	150	4-27-94	.274	.333	.253	38	124	16	34	4	1	0	4	14	0	1	0	17	9	7	.323	.348
Zimmer, Bradley	L-R	6-4	185	11-27-92	.304	.372	.280	45	168	32	51	11	2	4	30	19	9	0	1	30	11	4	.464	.401

Pitching	B-T	HT	WT	DOB	W	L	ERA	G	GS	CG	SV	IP	H	R	ER	HR	BB	SO	AVG	vLH	vRH	K/9	BB/9
Brady, Sean	L-L	6-0	175	6-9-94	2	4	2.79	14	14	0	0	71	68	28	22	2	27	44	.250	.191	.270	5.58	3.42
Carter, Jordan	R-R	6-4	195	9-29-9i	1	2	2.60	12	2	0	1	35	33	13	10	0	4	24	.246	.309	.203	6.23	1.04
Cox, Cortland	R-R	6-1	185	11-3-94	0	2	3.24	6	0	0	0	8	8	3	3	1	1	7	.258	.214	.294	7.56	1.08
DeJesus, Luis	R-R	6-3	175	12-16-91	3	3	4.44	10	3	0	0	26	24	13	13	0	9	21	.247	.280	.213	7.18	3.08
DeMasi, Dominic	R-R	6-3	190	5-18-93	0	2	4.91	15	0	0	0	18	22	10	10	1	10	13	.301	.239	.407	6.38	4.91
Estrella, Edward	R-R	6-1	170	1-28-94	3	0	4.21	10	0	0	0	36	33	17	17	5	15	24	.234	.194	.270	5.94	3.72
Eubank, Luke	R-R	6-0	180	2-24-94	0	1	2.25	17	0	0	3	20	21	6	5	0	5	16	.276	.286	.271	7.20	2.25
Feyereisen, J.P.	R-R	6-2	215	2-7-93	3	0	1.00	15	0	0	4	18	9	2	2	0	2	26	.150	.231	.088	12.71	0.53
Garcia, Justin	R-R	6-1	180	9-16-92	3	2	3.62	14	0	0	0	32	32	15	13	3	11	23	.262	.242	.283	6.40	3.06
Gomez, Luis	L-L	6-0	195	9-15-92	4	0	6.67	15	0	0	1	28	25	21	21	6	18	41	.234	.205	.250	13.02	5.72
Hill, Cameron	R-R	6-1	185	5-24-94	1	2	1.76	14	12	0	0	56	39	11	11	1	20	33	.202	.204	.200	5.27	3.20
House, T.J.	R-L	6-1	185	9-29-89	0	0	0.00	1	1	0	0	5	2	0	0	0	4	1	.133	.000	.154	7.20	0.00
Lovegrove, Kieran	R-R	6-4	185	7-28-94	2	2	3.90	8	0	0	0	30	28	14	13	0	23	14	.255	.222	.277	4.20	6.90
Maronde, Nick	B-L	6-3	205	9-5-89	0	0	1.00	3	3	0	0	9	4	1	1	0	1	8	.133	.167	.111	8.00	1.00
Melo, Carlos	R-R	6-3	180	2-27-91	0	0	0.00	1	0	0	0	2	1	0	0	0	2	1	.455	.500	.400	4.50	9.00
Merryweather, Julian	R-R	6-4	200	10-14-91	7	3	3.66	13	12	0	0	47	47	22	19	2	13	35	.260	.326	.191	6.75	2.51
Rodriguez, Ramon	R-R	5-11	176	3-1-94	3	0	3.80	13	1	0	0	24	22	11	10	2	7	15	.253	.268	.239	5.70	2.66
Santana, Juan	R-R	6-2	170	7-2-93	1	9	5.09	14	14	0	0	64	80	48	36	6	22	37	.308	.295	.321	5.23	3.11
Shane, Casey	R-R	6-4	190	8-23-95	1	0	0.82	2	2	0	0	11	8	1	1	0	1	5	.205	.235	.182	4.09	0.82
Speer, David	L-L	6-1	185	8-14-92	3	1	2.74	14	1	0	0	43	42	13	13	2	8	47	.261	.179	.305	9.91	1.69
Stokes, Jim	R-R	6-6	225	10-9-90	0	2	5.68	5	0	0	2	6	5	5	4	0	2	8	.200	.286	.091	11.37	2.84
Vizcaya, Anthony	R-R	6-0	180	10-24-93	1	6	10.64	15	1	0	0	33	54	42	39	3	20	27	.380	.387	.373	7.36	5.45
Zapata, Jose	R-R	6-4	200	5-21-93	1	2	2.97	20	1	0	1	36	34	16	12	0	20	26	.248	.180	.287	6.44	4.95

Fielding

Catcher	PCT	G	PO	A	E	DP	PB
Cervenka	.969	25	143	15	5	0	8
De La Cruz	1.000	1	1	0	0	0	0
Mejia	.972	52	335	53	11	2	9
Rowland	1.000	2	9	3	0	0	1

First Base	PCT	G	PO	A	E	DP
Castillo	.995	59	526	36	3	38

De La Cruz	.993	16	132	14	1	12
Hamilton	1.000	1	7	2	0	0
Rowland	.917	2	10	1	1	2

Second Base	PCT	G	PO	A	E	DP
Mendoza	.933	3	7	7	1	1
Patterson	.962	50	98	152	10	26
Roberts	.952	5	10	10	1	2

Smith	1.000	1	1	2	0	1
Valdez	.960	16	29	43	3	9

Third Base	PCT	G	PO	A	E	DP
Castillo	1.000	1	2	0	0	0
De La Cruz	1.000	1	1	0	0	0
Fisher	1.000	2	0	4	0	1
Mendoza	.976	32	14	69	2	5

CLEVELAND INDIANS

Patterson	.750	3	4	8	4	2
Roberts	.931	20	18	36	4	4
Valdez	1.000	18	14	37	0	3
Shortstop	**PCT**	**G**	**PO**	**A**	**E**	**DP**
Fisher	.963	44	70	112	7	15
Mendoza	.973	27	46	61	3	13

Roberts	.950	6	7	12	1	1
Outfield	**PCT**	**G**	**PO**	**A**	**E**	**DP**
Allen	.991	54	108	7	1	3
Armendariz	1.000	10	19	1	0	0
De La Cruz	.875	3	7	0	1	0
Hamilton	1.000	1	2	0	0	0

Martinez	1.000	12	15	1	0	1
McClure	.957	35	66	0	3	0
Mejia	.909	6	9	1	1	1
Murphy	.964	46	74	6	3	3
Papi	.750	1	2	1	1	0
Schubert	.961	22	49	0	2	0
Zimmer	.971	42	49	3	3	1

AZL INDIANS ROOKIE

ARIZONA LEAGUE

Batting	B-T	HT	WT	DOB	AVG	vLH	vRH	G	AB	R	H	2B	3B	HR	RBI	BB	HBP	SH	SF	SO	SB	CS	SLG	OBP
Bautista, Gerald	R-R	6-0	190	7-20-94	.132	.300	.093	16	53	3	7	1	0	0	2	3	0	0	0	18	1	0	.151	.179
Bradley, Bobby	L-R	6-1	225	5-29-96	.361	.238	.407	39	155	39	56	13	4	8	50	16	3	0	2	36	3	0	.652	.426
Cabral, Victor	R-R	6-2	180	11-5-93	.167	.125	.182	8	30	4	5	1	1	0	5	2	1	0	0	8	0	0	.267	.242
Calderon, Kevin	R-R	5-11	180	4-4-94	.286	.375	.265	16	42	5	12	2	0	0	7	1	0	0	1	5	0	0	.333	.295
Caro, Hector	R-R	6-3	195	10-3-95	.167	.250	.136	9	30	3	5	1	0	0	4	4	0	1	0	8	0	0	.200	.265
Carter, Jodd	R-R	5-10	170	7-20-96	.291	.343	.272	37	127	25	37	5	0	1	17	15	1	1	3	28	7	2	.354	.363
Castro, Willi	B-R	6-1	165	4-24-97	.239	.250	.234	43	155	31	37	5	3	2	11	6	4	5	0	33	9	4	.348	.285
Chang, Yu-Cheng	R-R	6-1	175	8-18-95	.346	.385	.333	42	159	39	55	9	4	6	25	18	3	0	1	28	6	1	.566	.420
Chu, Li-Jen	R-R	5-11	200	3-13-94	.348	.222	.403	29	89	22	31	13	0	3	19	11	2	1	0	18	0	0	.596	.431
Cruz, Grofi	R-R	6-2	175	4-3-96	.156	.125	.167	19	64	4	10	0	0	5	4	0	0	0	13	1	0	.156	.206
Gonzalez, Gianpaul	R-R	6-0	185	1-11-96	.176	.077	.238	11	34	4	6	0	0	0	5	6	0	0	0	9	0	0	.176	.300
Ison, Bobby	L-L	5-8	170	7-5-93	.240	.250	.236	32	121	21	29	2	0	0	9	15	3	1	0	11	7	5	.256	.338
Loopstok, Sicnarf	R-R	5-11	195	4-26-93	.467	.000	.500	5	15	6	7	0	1	4	6	3	0	0	0	4	0	0	1.400	.556
Lucas, Simeon	L-R	6-2	195	2-7-96	.217	.111	.243	16	46	7	10	3	0	0	5	8	0	0	0	25	1	1	.326	.345
Miguel, Francisco	R-R	6-3	206	3-24-95	.190	.100	.220	33	121	8	23	5	0	2	19	6	2	2	0	52	2	0	.281	.228
Myles, Bryson	R-R	5-11	230	9-18-89	.500	.500	.500	5	20	5	10	5	0	2	9	0	0	0	0	2	3	1	1.050	.500
Pantoja, Alexis	B-R	5-11	150	1-18-96	.250	.282	.238	40	144	24	36	5	0	0	11	12	1	1	1	17	13	0	.285	.310
Sayles, Silento	R-R	5-9	185	3-28-95	.262	.258	.263	35	130	25	34	1	3	0	10	17	1	2	2	35	16	5	.315	.347
Shorto, Ben	R-R	6-1	170	3-23-95	.000	.000	—	1	1	0	0	0	0	0	0	0	0	0	0	0	0	0	.000	.000
Tapia, Emmanuel	L-L	6-3	215	2-26-96	.315	.286	.329	39	127	23	40	8	1	4	27	17	3	0	1	35	2	2	.488	.405
Wendle, Joe	L-R	5-11	190	4-26-90	.455	.750	.389	6	22	8	10	1	1	0	4	4	0	0	0	4	1	1	.591	.538
Winfrey, Nate	R-R	6-2	195	9-29-94	.211	.176	.218	28	95	18	20	3	3	1	20	20	5	1	2	32	1	0	.337	.369

Pitching	B-T	HT	WT	DOB	W	L	ERA	G	GS	CG	SV	IP	H	R	ER	HR	BB	SO	AVG	vLH	vRH	K/9	BB/9
Algarin, Erick	R-R	6-1	195	3-31-95	2	1	2.32	11	0	0	1	31	25	8	8	1	8	33	.219	.306	.179	9.58	2.32
Angulo, Argenis	R-R	6-3	220	2-26-94	2	0	7.80	13	0	0	1	15	20	13	13	1	6	27	.313	.250	.350	16.20	3.60
Baker, Dylan	R-R	6-2	215	4-6-92	0	0	1.59	3	3	0	0	6	2	1	1	1	1	13	.105	.400	.000	20.65	1.59
Capps, Matt	R-R	6-2	250	9-3-83	0	0	7.20	4	2	0	0	5	6	5	4	1	2	4	.300	.333	.273	7.20	3.60
Chen, Ping-Hsueh	R-R	6-2	195	7-8-94	0	0	2.70	15	0	0	4	17	8	6	5	0	9	23	.138	.148	.129	12.42	4.86
Chiang, Shao-Ching	R-R	6-0	175	11-10-93	4	2	4.53	10	8	0	0	46	45	26	23	1	3	34	.260	.275	.250	6.70	0.59
Cox, Cortland	R-R	6-1	185	11-3-94	3	1	2.40	13	0	0	1	15	12	4	4	0	3	17	.222	.211	.229	10.20	1.80
Dunatov, Jordan	R-R	6-5	190	10-20-92	0	0	0.00	10	0	0	0	9	6	5	0	0	10	7	.200	.250	.182	7.00	10.00
Haley, Trey	R-R	6-4	205	6-21-90	1	0	1.93	5	2	0	0	5	3	1	1	0	1	6	.176	.200	.167	11.57	1.93
Hashimoto, Naoki	R-R	5-11	180	6-7-90	0	0	0.00	1	0	0	0	1	0	0	0	0	0	2	.000	.000	.000	18.00	0.00
Hentges, Sam	L-L	6-6	245	7-18-96	1	0	0.69	8	0	0	0	13	4	3	1	0	5	10	.095	.154	.069	6.92	3.46
Hockin, Grant	R-R	6-4	200	3-5-96	0	0	3.86	9	7	0	0	21	21	9	9	1	4	19	.266	.269	.264	8.14	1.71
Linares, Leandro	R-R	6-3	205	1-27-94	2	3	7.62	11	3	0	0	39	39	38	33	4	29	38	.262	.304	.243	8.77	6.69
Lopez, Francisco	R-R	6-0	195	2-13-94	1	0	1.46	4	1	0	0	12	10	5	2	0	5	17	.213	.267	.188	12.41	3.65
Marcum, Shaun	R-R	6-0	195	12-14-81	0	0	0.00	1	1	0	0	2	1	0	0	1	3	.167	.000	.200	13.50	4.50
Marquina, Yoiber	R-R	5-10	190	2-3-96	3	1	2.57	18	0	0	7	21	19	13	6	0	12	29	.235	.263	.209	12.43	5.14
Mathews, Kenny	L-L	6-3	205	8-6-93	0	1	27.00	2	1	0	0	2	6	5	5	1	0	2	.600	.500	.625	10.80	0.00
Miniard, Micah	R-R	6-7	195	4-12-96	0	0	5.25	6	0	0	1	12	9	10	7	2	5	8	.196	.167	.206	6.00	3.75
Pannone, Thomas	L-L	6-0	180	4-28-94	5	0	3.20	11	7	0	0	45	32	24	16	1	24	62	.194	.200	.192	12.40	4.80
Puello, Johan	R-R	5-11	165	1-5-94	2	1	1.69	14	0	0	0	27	17	16	5	0	16	28	.177	.263	.121	9.45	5.40
Radeke, Mason	R-R	6-1	175	6-13-90	0	0	0.00	2	2	0	0	2	1	0	0	0	3	3	.250	.200	.333	13.50	10.00
Rayl, Mike	L-L	6-5	180	11-1-88	0	1	5.40	3	3	0	0	5	5	3	3	1	3	6	.263	.333	.231	10.80	5.40
Robinson, Jared	R-R	6-0	190	11-20-94	0	2	1.23	9	0	0	0	22	14	7	3	2	7	19	.177	.136	.193	7.77	2.86
Rodriguez, Ramon	R-R	5-11	176	3-1-94	0	0	5.40	5	0	0	0	2	3	3	1	3	11	.111	.200	.077	19.80	5.40
Romero, Jean	R-R	6-1	175	6-6-96	0	0	0.00	1	0	0	0	1	0	0	0	0	1	0	.000	.000	.000	0.00	9.00
Shane, Casey	R-R	6-4	200	8-23-95	5	0	2.72	10	9	0	0	46	38	22	14	1	15	40	.226	.304	.172	7.77	2.91
Sheffield, Justus	L-L	5-10	196	5-13-96	3	1	4.79	8	4	0	0	21	24	16	11	0	9	29	.286	.200	.322	12.63	3.92
Valladares, Randy	L-L	5-11	155	7-6-94	1	2	3.70	14	0	0	3	24	16	14	10	0	14	19	.188	.240	.167	7.03	5.18

Fielding

Catcher	PCT	G	PO	A	E	DP	PB
Calderon	.973	15	96	12	3	1	4
Chu	.975	25	174	20	5	0	7
Gonzalez	.982	11	98	12	2	0	4
Loopstok	1.000	2	6	1	0	0	1
Lucas	.962	15	117	9	5	0	11

First Base	PCT	G	PO	A	E	DP
Bautista	.933	4	25	3	2	5
Bradley	.980	33	274	21	6	23

Tapia	.950	19	141	12	8	13
Second Base	**PCT**	**G**	**PO**	**A**	**E**	**DP**
Bautista	1.000	2	3	4	0	0
Castro	.971	29	57	76	4	15
Pantoja	.958	20	46	69	5	17
Shorto	—	1	0	0	0	0
Wendle	.947	5	11	7	1	1

Third Base	PCT	G	PO	A	E	DP
Bautista	1.000	1	0	3	0	0

Chang	.894	16	9	33	5	1
Cruz	.806	18	7	18	6	1
Winfrey	.891	21	11	30	5	2
Shortstop	**PCT**	**G**	**PO**	**A**	**E**	**DP**
Castro	.904	15	10	37	5	6
Chang	.945	22	24	45	4	15
Pantoja	.933	21	22	48	5	9
Outfield	**PCT**	**G**	**PO**	**A**	**E**	**DP**
Armendariz	.875	15	14	0	2	0

Bautista	—	2	0	0	0	0	Carter	.951	35	37	2	2	0	Myles	.875	4	7	0	1	0
Cabral	1.000	7	12	0	0	0	Ison	.982	31	55	0	1	0	Sayles	.964	34	51	2	2	0
Caro	.900	9	17	1	2	0	Miguel	.904	33	45	2	5	0							

DSL INDIANS   ROOKIE

DOMINICAN SUMMER LEAGUE

Batting	B-T	HT	WT	DOB	AVG	vLH	vRH	G	AB	R	H	2B	3B	HR	RBI	BB	HBP	SH	SF	SO	SB	CS	SLG	OBP
Almonte, Elvio	R-R	6-4	195	11-24-93	.279	.241	.288	45	140	19	39	11	0	2	24	10	3	1	1	33	1	3	.400	.338
Andujar, Yoan	R-R	6-2	180	5-26-96	.200	.000	.222	3	10	1	2	1	0	0	2	1	0	0	1	6	0	0	.300	.250
Beltre, Enmanuel	R-R	6-3	215	4-27-95	.198	.208	.195	34	101	7	20	2	1	2	19	9	1	0	1	25	0	2	.297	.268
Caro, Hector	R-R	6-3	195	10-3-95	.209	.185	.219	23	91	4	19	9	0	0	7	4	0	0	1	21	1	1	.308	.240
Cerda, Erlin	R-R	5-9	170	5-5-94	.313	.382	.289	65	214	48	67	14	6	0	33	35	6	3	4	36	23	2	.435	.417
De Los Santos, Alexis	R-R	6-3	0	8-22-94	.190	.167	.196	18	58	7	11	4	1	0	5	7	1	2	0	12	0	0	.293	.288
Eladio, Miguel	R-R	6-1	160	5-10-96	.226	.180	.241	61	195	30	44	3	4	0	9	12	3	1	0	43	16	6	.282	.281
Garcia, Juan	R-R	6-3	195	8-17-97	.218	.176	.231	43	142	10	31	6	0	3	19	9	2	0	1	39	1	2	.324	.273
Marte, Francisco	R-R	6-2	180	4-16-97	.182	.200	.176	6	22	2	4	0	1	0	3	1	0	0	0	8	1	0	.273	.217
Medina, Jose	L-L	6-1	185	2-14-95	.320	.357	.306	67	250	41	80	21	5	2	55	26	7	2	3	35	12	6	.468	.395
Mejia, Gabriel	B-R	5-11	160	7-30-95	.335	.309	.344	70	263	67	88	6	5	0	20	51	1	1	1	50	72	20	.395	.443
Moncion, Juan Carlos	L-L	6-2	210	10-24-93	.280	.143	.333	7	25	6	7	0	0	0	3	7	0	0	0	2	2	1	.280	.438
Mora, Ronnys	R-R	6-1	195	10-2-96	.189	.167	.200	25	37	5	7	3	0	0	10	16	1	0	0	11	0	0	.270	.444
Mujica, Yosmar	R-R	6-2	170	12-25-96	.136	.111	.154	18	22	9	3	0	0	0	2	1	0	0	1	11	5	0	.136	.240
Ortega, Efrin	R-R	6-0	165	7-20-97	.197	.200	.196	33	71	7	14	0	0	0	4	4	1	1	0	18	10	9	.197	.250
Ramirez, Wagner	R-R	5-11	170	12-11-94	.152	.214	.125	22	46	6	7	1	0	0	0	3	1	1	0	13	1	1	.174	.220
Rodriguez, Jason	R-R	5-11	180	1-11-95	.200	.233	.186	49	140	13	28	4	0	1	18	9	4	1	4	16	1	0	.250	.261
Rodriguez, Jorma	R-R	5-10	150	3-25-96	.330	.298	.343	61	197	45	65	9	3	1	33	46	3	9	3	30	13	11	.421	.458
Soto, Junior	R-R	3	175	1-21-97	.221	.228	.219	58	208	32	46	5	3	1	21	31	2	0	2	41	11	8	.288	.325
Torrealba, Hazzent	R-R	6-0	170	10-21-96	.158	.000	.231	12	19	3	3	1	0	0	0	3	1	0	0	6	0	1	.211	.304
Vicente, Jose	R-R	5-11	175	11-13-95	.216	.211	.218	34	97	11	21	6	0	0	15	6	1	0	1	14	1	1	.278	.267

Pitching	B-T	HT	WT	DOB	W	L	ERA	G	GS	CG	SV	IP	H	R	ER	HR	BB	SO	AVG	vLH	vRH	K/9	BB/9
Arosemena, Julio	R-R	6-1	190	7-20-95	5	4	3.18	22	0	0	4	40	31	19	14	2	26	33	.228	.209	.237	7.49	5.90
Diaz, Darlin	R-R	6-8	220	12-1-95	0	0	8.64	6	0	0	0	8	6	9	8	1	21	12	.222	.444	.111	12.96	22.68
Florez, Rainer	R-R	6-1	160	9-13-96	0	0	1.00	7	0	0	0	9	2	1	1	0	6	7	.077	.125	.056	7.00	6.00
Gomez, Daniel	R-R	6-1	185	6-2-94	7	3	1.39	14	10	0	0	65	45	16	10	0	10	55	.196	.190	.199	7.65	1.39
Izaguirre, Alejandro	R-R	6-0	175	3-5-97	1	2	5.09	15	0	0	2	23	27	19	13	4	19	22	.290	.333	.273	8.61	7.43
Jimenez, Domingo	R-R	6-3	175	8-29-93	2	3	2.34	13	11	0	0	50	30	22	13	0	45	50	.176	.217	.161	9.00	8.10
Jimenez, Luis	R-R	6-4	170	1-2-95	4	3	1.67	13	10	0	0	54	39	17	10	0	20	39	.206	.155	.237	6.50	3.33
Martinez, Henry	R-R	6-1	175	4-27-94	2	1	2.70	20	0	0	7	37	33	15	11	3	12	28	.252	.308	.228	6.87	2.95
Mejia, Jean Carlos	R-R	6-4	205	8-26-96	3	0	2.70	16	0	0	1	33	22	14	10	0	15	29	.182	.211	.169	7.83	4.05
Mena, Bijelic	R-R	6-1	180	9-28-95	0	1	7.20	5	3	0	0	10	15	12	8	1	5	5	.357	.286	.393	4.50	4.50
Nina, Jose	R-R	6-0	175	7-10-94	1	1	3.47	17	0	0	6	23	25	14	9	0	11	15	.272	.357	.234	5.79	4.24
Ramirez, Jesus	R-R	6-4	190	3-14-95	1	1	9.39	4	0	0	0	8	12	10	8	0	5	5	.375	.308	.421	5.87	5.87
Rodriguez, Jose	R-R	6-0	185	3-18-95	2	2	3.00	14	14	0	0	66	60	25	22	3	23	60	.245	.238	.250	8.18	3.14
Tati, Felix	R-R	6-2	190	4-1-97	1	1	3.54	8	3	0	1	20	19	11	8	2	6	16	.257	.278	.250	7.08	2.66
Tineo, Ramon	R-L	6-0	170	1-31-96	3	2	3.94	19	0	0	2	30	27	15	13	1	17	32	.235	.273	.226	9.71	5.16
Ventura, Cesar	R-R	6-0	195	3-14-95	7	2	2.56	14	7	0	0	63	62	18	18	1	19	40	.261	.237	.272	5.68	2.70
Ventura, Jhon	R-R	6-5	200	3-12-95	1	2	2.02	11	8	0	1	36	27	13	8	0	30	26	.211	.276	.192	6.56	7.57
Villasmil, Rodolfo	R-R	6-0	160	1-20-95	1	0	7.71	16	0	0	0	19	17	21	16	2	19	12	.227	.182	.245	5.79	9.16
Vizcaino, Gabriel	R-R	6-2	190	3-26-94	0	0	1.91	7	4	0	0	28	20	11	6	0	19	17	.196	.189	.200	5.40	6.04

Fielding

Catcher	PCT	G	PO	A	E	DP	PB
Ramirez	.991	22	95	10	1	1	7
Rodriguez	.975	48	314	43	9	3	9
Vicente	.966	22	99	14	4	1	7

First Base	PCT	G	PO	A	E	DP
Beltre	.962	27	194	8	8	12
De Los Santos	.917	4	22	0	2	2
Medina	.990	31	269	16	3	20
Mejia	1.000	1	4	0	0	0
Moncion	1.000	7	70	3	0	8
Mora	.976	20	77	4	2	6

Second Base	PCT	G	PO	A	E	DP
Cerda	.940	17	35	44	5	9
Mejia	1.000	2	5	1	0	0

	PCT	G	PO	A	E	DP	
Ortega	.955	20	38	46	4	6	
Rodriguez	.964	34	52	83	5	17	
Torrealba	1.000	12	9	14	0	3	

Third Base	PCT	G	PO	A	E	DP
Cerda	.891	42	43	80	15	4
De Los Santos	.923	16	12	36	4	3
Eladio	1.000	1	1	1	0	0
Mora	1.000	2	2	5	0	0
Ortega	1.000	1	1	0	0	0
Rodriguez	.882	14	8	22	4	1

Shortstop	PCT	G	PO	A	E	DP
Eladio	.912	58	85	165	24	26
Medina	1.000	1	1	2	0	0

	PCT	G	PO	A	E	DP
Rodriguez	.964	18	36	44	3	10

Outfield	PCT	G	PO	A	E	DP
Almonte	.867	12	13	0	2	0
Andujar	1.000	2	1	1	0	0
Caro	.923	22	45	3	4	2
Garcia	.955	12	19	2	1	0
Marte	1.000	5	7	0	0	0
Medina	.951	42	52	6	3	0
Mejia	.977	68	118	9	3	3
Mujica	1.000	11	8	0	0	0
Rodriguez	1.000	1	2	0	0	0
Soto	.971	58	98	3	3	0

Colorado Rockies

SEASON IN A SENTENCE: A promising start to the season ended with a thud for a team that was tied for first in the American League West as late as May 7 before tallying a 16-37 mark across June and July, all but ending any hopes of contending.

HIGH POINT: After beating the Rangers for the third game in a row on May 7, the Rockies were tied for first. Jorge De La Rosa got his fourth win, Carlos Gonzalez slammed his seventh homer and things were looking up. Gonzalez hit just four homers the rest of the season and played in just 70 games before being shut down to have knee surgery.

LOW POINT: The Rocks hit rock bottom—32 games below .500—on Sept. 15 before a six-game winning streak prettied things up for the final ledger. Gonzalez missed more than half the season, Troy Tulowitzki played in just 91 games and rookie Eddie Butler didn't resemble the rising star of last season while missing time with a sore shoulder.

NOTABLE ROOKIES: Butler made three starts and if healthy could be a part of the 2015 rotation. Tyler Matzek, a 2009 first-round pick impressed at times (6-11, 4.05) and showed promising command. Rule 5 pickup Tommy Kahnle has a big fastball, but needs to work on control to be a key part of the bullpen in 2015.

KEY TRANSACTIONS: Kahnle was fairly effective after being picked up from the Yankees in the Rule 5 draft; 23-year-old righthander Jordan Lyles, the key figure in the deal that sent Dexter Fowler to the Astros, was 7-4, 4.33 in 127 big league innings. Lefthander Franklin Morales, the Rockies top prospect in 2007, was reacquired from the Red Sox in December for Jonathan Herrera and posted a 6-9, 5.37 record in 142 innings with Colorado.

DOWN ON THE FARM: The Rockies have intriguing prospects at all levels, including a couple who could help as soon as next season. Righthanders Butler and 2014 No. 3 overall pick Jon Gray were effective in spots in 2015, although both were slowed by injuries. Bats such as Raimel Tapia, David Dahl, Ryan McMahon, Forrest Wall, Max George and Kevin Padlo all had outstanding offensive seasons. But none are particularly close to helping the major league team, although some, such as McMahon, could be prime trade bait, depending on what the team signs Nolan Arenado long term, for example, or if they attempt to cash in Corey Dickerson.

OPENING DAY PAYROLL: 99,579,071 (16th).

PLAYERS OF THE YEAR

TONY FARLOW

MAJOR LEAGUE	MINOR LEAGUE
Corey Dickerson of	**Ryan McMahon** 3b/1b
.312/.364/.567	(Low-A)
24 HR, 76 RBI	.282/.358/.502
Led team in homers	46 2B, 102 RBI

ORGANIZATION LEADERS

BATTING *Minimum 250 AB

MAJORS

* AVG	Tulowitzki, Troy	.340
* OPS	Tulowitzki, Troy	1.035
HR	Dickerson, Corey	24
RBI	Morneau, Justin	82

MINORS

* AVG	Tapia, Raimel, Asheville	.326
* OBP	Tapia, Raimel, Asheville	.382
* OPS	Paulsen, Ben, Colorado Springs	.533
R	McMahon, Ryan, Asheville	93
R	Tapia, Raimel, Asheville	93
H	Tapia, Raimel, Asheville	157
TB	Prime, Correlle, Asheville	264
2B	Prime, Correlle, Asheville	47
3B	Piron, Jonathan, DSL Rockies	9
HR	Prime, Correlle, Asheville	21
RBI	Prime, Correlle, Asheville	102
BB	Dwyer, Sean, Modesto, Tri-City	61
SO	White, Max, Asheville	153
SB	Tapia, Raimel, Asheville	33

PITCHING #Minimum 75 IP

MAJORS

W	De La Rosa, Jorge	14
ERA	Matzek, Tyler	4.05
SO	De La Rosa, Jorge	139
SV	Hawkins, LaTroy	23

MINORS

W	Senzatela, Antonio, Asheville	15
L	Alsup, Ben, Modesto	14
ERA	Anderson, Tyler, Tulsa	1.98
G	Daniel, Trent, Asheville	53
GS	Alsup, Ben, Modesto	28
SV	White, Cole, Col. Springs, Tulsa	16
IP	Flemer, Matt, Modesto	165
BB	Alsup, Ben, Modesto	72
SO	Flemer, Matt, Modesto	130
AVG	Anderson, Tyler, Tulsa	.216

COLORADO ROCKIES

2014 PERFORMANCE

General Manager: Dan O'Dowd. **Farm Director:** Jeff Bridich. **Scouting Director:** Bill Schmidt.

Class	Team	League	W	L	PCT	Finish	Manager
Majors	Colorado Rockies	National	66	96	.407	29th (30)	Walt Weiss
Triple-A	Colorado Springs Sky Sox	Pacific Coast	53	91	.368	16th (16)	Glenallen Hill
Double-A	Tulsa Drillers	Texas	71	68	.511	4th (8)	Kevin Riggs
High A	Modesto Nuts	California	43	97	.307	10th (10)	Don Sneddon
Low A	Asheville Tourists	South Atlantic	89	49	.645	1st (14)	Fred Ocasio
Short season	Tri-City Dust Devils	Northwest	33	43	.434	6th (8)	Drew Saylor
Rookie	Grand Junction Rockies	Pioneer	43	33	.566	1st (8)	Anthony Sanders
Overall Minor League Record			332	381	.466	24th (30)	

ORGANIZATION STATISTICS

COLORADO ROCKIES
NATIONAL LEAGUE

Batting	B-T	HT	WT	DOB	AVG	vLH	vRH	G	AB	R	H	2B	3B	HR	RBI	BB	HBP	SH	SF	SO	SB	CS	SLG	OBP
Adames, Cristhian	B-R	6-0	180	7-26-91	.067	.500	.000	7	15	1	1	0	0	0	0	0	0	0	0	5	0	0	.067	.067
Arenado, Nolan	R-R	6-2	205	4-16-91	.287	.313	.278	111	432	58	124	34	2	18	61	25	4	1	5	58	2	1	.500	.328
Barnes, Brandon	R-R	6-2	210	5-15-86	.257	.259	.256	132	292	37	75	17	4	8	27	15	0	6	0	100	5	4	.425	.293
Blackmon, Charlie	L-L	6-3	210	7-1-86	.288	.267	.296	154	593	82	171	27	3	19	72	31	13	6	5	96	28	10	.440	.335
Cuddyer, Michael	R-R	6-2	220	3-27-79	.332	.412	.302	49	190	32	63	15	1	10	31	14	0	0	1	30	3	0	.579	.376
Culberson, Charlie	R-R	6-0	200	4-10-89	.195	.172	.204	95	210	17	41	7	2	3	24	12	5	4	2	62	2	2	.290	.253
Dickerson, Corey	L-R	6-1	205	5-22-89	.312	.253	.328	131	436	74	136	27	6	24	76	37	1	0	4	101	8	7	.567	.364
Gonzalez, Carlos	L-L	6-1	220	10-17-85	.238	.241	.237	70	260	35	62	15	1	11	38	19	1	0	1	70	3	0	.431	.292
LeMahieu, D.J.	R-R	6-4	205	7-13-88	.267	.286	.261	149	494	59	132	15	5	5	42	33	2	7	2	97	10	10	.348	.315
McBride, Matt	R-R	6-2	215	5-23-85	.226	.313	.133	21	31	6	7	2	0	2	6	2	1	0	0	12	0	0	.484	.294
McKenry, Michael	R-R	5-10	205	3-4-85	.315	.279	.328	57	168	23	53	9	0	8	22	22	1	1	0	42	0	3	.512	.398
Morneau, Justin	L-R	6-4	220	5-15-81	.319	.254	.341	135	502	62	160	32	3	17	82	34	6	0	8	60	0	3	.496	.364
Pacheco, Jordan	R-R	6-1	205	1-30-86	.236	.217	.245	22	72	4	17	6	1	0	8	6	1	0	1	15	0	0	.347	.300
2-team total (47 Arizona)					.255	—	—	69	153	10	39	10	1	0	16	9	1	1	1	27	0	0	.333	.299
Parker, Kyle	R-R	6-0	205	9-30-89	.192	.125	.222	18	26	1	5	1	0	0	1	0	0	0	0	14	0	0	.231	.192
Paulsen, Ben	L-R	6-4	205	10-27-87	.317	.333	.314	31	63	8	20	4	0	4	10	2	1	0	0	19	0	0	.571	.348
Pridie, Jason	L-R	6-1	205	10-9-83	.000	—	.000	2	4	1	0	0	0	0	0	0	0	0	0	2	0	0	.000	.000
Rosario, Wilin	R-R	5-11	220	2-23-89	.267	.317	.249	106	382	46	102	25	0	13	54	23	0	0	5	70	1	0	.435	.305
Rutledge, Josh	R-R	6-1	190	4-21-89	.269	.309	.254	105	309	44	83	16	7	4	33	20	6	5	2	83	2	3	.405	.323
Stubbs, Drew	R-R	6-4	205	10-4-84	.289	.328	.268	132	388	67	112	22	4	15	43	30	1	2	3	136	20	3	.482	.339
Tulowitzki, Troy	R-R	6-3	215	10-10-84	.340	.397	.321	91	315	71	107	18	1	21	52	50	5	0	5	57	1	1	.603	.432
Wheeler, Ryan	L-R	6-3	235	7-10-88	.232	.167	.240	31	56	6	13	2	0	2	13	5	0	0	3	12	0	0	.375	.281
Williams, Jackson	R-R	5-11	200	5-14-86	.214	.000	.231	7	14	1	3	0	0	1	3	2	0	0	0	4	0	0	.429	.313
Ynoa, Rafael	R-R	6-0	185	8-7-87	.343	.318	.356	19	67	5	23	6	1	0	13	4	0	0	0	9	0	0	.463	.380

Pitching	B-T	HT	WT	DOB	W	L	ERA	G	GS	CG	SV	IP	H	R	ER	HR	BB	SO	AVG	vLH	vRH	K/9	BB/9
Anderson, Brett	L-L	6-4	225	2-1-88	1	3	2.91	8	8	0	0	43	44	18	14	1	13	29	.267	.326	.244	6.02	2.70
Belisle, Matt	R-R	6-4	225	6-6-80	4	7	4.87	66	1	0	0	65	74	35	35	5	19	43	.292	.289	.295	5.98	2.64
Bergman, Christian	R-R	6-1	180	5-4-88	3	5	5.93	10	10	0	0	55	75	37	36	9	10	31	.318	.280	.346	5.10	1.65
Bettis, Chad	R-R	6-1	200	4-26-89	0	2	9.12	21	0	0	0	25	42	26	25	4	10	13	.378	.345	.411	4.74	3.65
Brothers, Rex	L-L	6-0	210	12-18-87	4	6	5.59	74	0	0	0	56	65	38	35	7	39	55	.288	.309	.271	8.79	6.23
Brown, Brooks	L-R	6-3	205	6-20-85	0	1	2.77	28	0	0	0	26	20	9	8	3	5	21	.208	.209	.208	7.27	1.73
Butler, Eddie	B-R	6-2	180	3-13-91	1	1	6.75	3	3	0	0	16	23	12	12	2	7	3	.343	.423	.293	1.69	3.94
Chacin, Jhoulys	R-R	6-3	215	1-7-88	1	7	5.40	11	11	0	0	63	63	38	38	8	28	42	.265	.245	.280	5.97	3.98
Chatwood, Tyler	R-R	6-0	185	12-16-89	1	0	4.50	4	4	0	0	24	21	13	12	4	8	20	.226	.160	.333	7.50	3.00
De La Rosa, Jorge	L-L	6-1	215	4-5-81	14	11	4.10	32	32	0	0	184	161	90	84	21	67	139	.238	.196	.250	6.79	3.27
Flande, Yohan	L-L	6-2	180	1-27-86	0	6	5.19	16	10	0	0	59	55	34	34	5	16	34	.257	.164	.294	5.19	2.44
Friedrich, Christian	R-L	6-4	215	7-8-87	0	4	5.92	16	3	0	0	24	25	21	16	3	10	27	.263	.138	.318	9.99	3.70
Hawkins, LaTroy	R-R	6-5	220	12-21-72	4	3	3.31	57	0	0	23	54	52	23	20	3	13	32	.246	.238	.255	5.30	2.15
Hernandez, Pedro	L-L	5-10	210	4-12-89	0	1	4.76	1	1	0	0	6	6	3	3	0	2	2	.316	.429	.250	3.18	3.18
Jurrjens, Jair	R-R	6-1	200	1-29-86	0	1	10.61	2	2	0	0	9	20	11	11	4	3	9	.435	.448	.412	8.68	2.89
Kahnle, Tommy	R-R	6-1	230	8-7-89	2	1	4.19	54	0	0	0	69	51	39	32	7	31	63	.206	.184	.228	8.26	4.06
Logan, Boone	R-L	6-5	215	8-13-84	2	3	6.84	35	0	0	0	25	31	20	19	6	11	32	.310	.318	.304	11.52	3.96
Lopez, Wilton	R-R	6-0	200	7-19-83	0	0	11.37	4	0	0	0	6	18	8	8	3	0	4	.514	.385	.591	5.68	0.00
Lyles, Jordan	R-R	6-4	215	10-19-90	7	4	4.33	22	22	0	0	127	127	64	61	12	46	90	.262	.289	.235	6.39	3.27
Martin, Chris	R-R	6-8	215	6-2-86	0	0	6.89	16	0	0	0	16	22	12	12	2	4	14	.338	.333	.341	8.04	2.30
Masset, Nick	R-R	6-5	235	5-17-82	2	0	5.80	51	0	0	0	45	56	31	29	3	24	36	.316	.368	.284	7.20	4.80
Matzek, Tyler	L-L	6-3	210	10-19-90	6	11	4.05	20	19	1	0	118	120	53	53	9	44	91	.267	.147	.306	6.96	3.37
Morales, Franklin	L-L	6-1	210	1-24-86	6	9	5.37	38	22	0	0	142	166	90	85	24	65	100	.296	.253	.313	6.32	4.11
Nicasio, Juan	R-R	6-3	210	8-31-86	6	6	5.38	33	14	0	0	94	107	59	56	19	31	63	.289	.309	.273	6.05	2.98
Ottavino, Adam	L-R	6-5	230	11-22-85	1	4	3.60	75	0	0	1	65	67	26	26	6	16	70	.271	.347	.238	9.69	2.22
Scahill, Rob	R-R	6-2	220	2-15-87	1	0	4.80	12	0	0	0	15	17	8	8	3	9	11	.283	.391	.216	6.60	5.40

Fielding

Catcher	PCT	G	PO	A	E	DP	PB
McKenry	.982	50	312	24	6	1	5
Pacheco	.993	19	132	7	1	0	3
Rosario	.989	96	585	54	7	5	12
Williams	1.000	7	37	2	0	0	0

First Base	PCT	G	PO	A	E	DP
Cuddyer	.990	14	92	7	1	6
Culberson	1.000	4	31	3	0	0
LeMahieu	—	1	0	0	0	0
McBride	1.000	5	28	1	0	6
Morneau	.997	131	1170	86	4	122
Pacheco	1.000	4	13	3	0	0
Parker	1.000	2	15	1	0	2
Paulsen	1.000	15	110	8	0	7
Rosario	1.000	4	25	0	0	7
Wheeler	1.000	5	21	2	0	3

Second Base	PCT	G	PO	A	E	DP
Adames	1.000	2	2	6	0	2
Culberson	.988	20	35	44	1	13
LeMahieu	.991	144	257	413	6	99
Pacheco	—	1	0	0	0	0
Rutledge	.963	17	25	27	2	6
Ynoa	1.000	1	1	3	0	0

Third Base	PCT	G	PO	A	E	DP
Arenado	.959	111	69	280	15	31
Cuddyer	1.000	3	1	4	0	0
Culberson	.971	32	11	56	2	5
LeMahieu	1.000	7	2	5	0	0
Rutledge	.818	5	1	8	2	1
Wheeler	1.000	12	7	18	0	1
Ynoa	1.000	13	15	34	0	3

Shortstop	PCT	G	PO	A	E	DP
Adames	1.000	5	6	10	0	2

Culberson	.987	23	28	47	1	14	
LeMahieu	—	1	0	0	0	0	
Rutledge	.961	69	64	159	9	34	
Tulowitzki	.990	89	119	269	4	59	
Ynoa	1.000	2	2	11	0	3	

Outfield	PCT	G	PO	A	E	DP
Barnes	.983	74	114	3	2	1
Blackmon	.979	142	317	6	7	2
Cuddyer	1.000	35	56	5	0	1
Dickerson	.977	105	171	2	4	0
Gonzalez	.990	65	97	3	1	1
McBride	1.000	4	3	1	0	1
Parker	1.000	4	4	1	0	0
Paulsen	1.000	3	5	0	0	0
Pridie	1.000	2	3	0	0	0
Stubbs	.969	113	215	7	7	1

COLORADO SPRINGS SKY SOX   TRIPLE-A
PACIFIC COAST LEAGUE

Batting	B-T	HT	WT	DOB	AVG	vLH	vRH	G	AB	R	H	2B	3B	HR	RBI	BB	HBP	SH	SF	SO	SB	CS	SLG	OBP
Adames, Cristhian	B-R	6-0	180	7-26-91	.338	.333	.339	38	145	19	49	12	0	1	14	13	0	5	0	25	5	1	.441	.392
Arenado, Nolan	R-R	6-2	205	4-16-91	.350	.300	.400	5	20	2	7	2	0	0	3	0	0	0	0	3	0	0	.450	.350
Cleary, Delta	B-R	6-2	220	8-14-89	.250	.211	.273	16	52	5	13	3	0	0	7	6	0	0	0	14	2	2	.308	.328
Cuddyer, Michael	R-R	6-2	220	3-27-79	.000	—	.000	1	1	0	0	0	0	0	0	1	0	0	0	0	0	0	.000	.500
Culberson, Charlie	R-R	6-0	200	4-10-89	.429	.333	.500	2	7	1	3	2	0	0	1	0	0	0	0	2	0	0	.714	.500
Dickerson, Corey	L-R	6-1	205	5-22-89	.385	.250	.444	3	13	2	5	1	1	0	1	1	0	0	0	4	0	0	.615	.429
Frey, Evan	L-L	6-0	170	6-7-86	.211	.244	.198	63	161	21	34	8	1	1	15	21	0	1	1	30	2	3	.292	.301
Garcia, Drew	B-R	6-1	175	4-24-85	.237	.240	.235	96	304	31	72	19	1	4	36	20	4	6	0	100	6	2	.345	.293
Garneau, Dustin	R-R	6-0	200	8-13-87	.216	.159	.240	44	148	17	32	9	2	5	22	14	3	1	0	21	1	1	.405	.297
Gonzalez, Carlos	L-L	6-1	220	10-17-85	.385	.400	.375	4	13	4	5	1	1	2	6	1	1	0	0	3	0	0	1.077	.467
Gonzalez, Jose	R-R	6-1	165	6-23-87	.500	.667	.000	2	4	2	2	0	0	1	3	1	0	0	0	1	0	0	1.250	.600
Janish, Paul	R-R	6-2	200	10-12-82	.234	.246	.230	67	209	18	49	9	1	1	19	13	2	1	1	35	1	2	.301	.284
2-team total (46 Omaha)					.268	—	—	113	362	35	97	20	2	3	36	28	2	5	1	53	1	5	.359	.323
Kandilas, David	R-R	6-2	195	9-14-90	.111	.167	.000	2	9	0	1	0	0	0	0	0	0	0	0	2	0	0	.111	.111
McBride, Matt	R-R	6-2	215	5-24-85	.305	.313	.302	51	187	27	57	11	1	7	35	12	2	0	5	19	0	1	.487	.345
McKenry, Michael	R-R	5-10	205	3-4-85	.313	.385	.281	23	83	15	26	6	0	3	12	7	1	1	1	13	3	0	.494	.370
Morneau, Justin	L-R	6-4	220	5-15-81	.500	1.000	.333	1	4	0	2	0	0	0	0	0	0	0	0	0	0	0	.500	.500
Nina, Angelys	R-R	5-11	165	11-16-88	.279	.280	.279	107	390	51	109	18	3	7	53	23	2	4	3	64	6	7	.395	.321
Parker, Kyle	R-R	6-0	205	9-30-89	.289	.266	.298	128	502	73	145	30	3	15	72	33	4	0	3	102	4	3	.450	.336
Paulsen, Ben	L-R	6-4	205	10-27-87	.294	.262	.308	117	435	76	128	32	6	20	76	58	2	0	2	119	4	5	.533	.378
Pridie, Jason	L-R	6-1	205	10-9-83	.278	.246	.291	108	418	61	116	17	6	12	51	40	1	2	2	74	28	6	.433	.341
Ramirez, Michael	R-R	5-10	165	4-27-90	.208	.000	.238	7	24	1	5	0	0	1	4	0	0	2	1	8	0	0	.333	.200
Rosario, Wilin	R-R	5-11	220	2-23-89	.333	—	.333	2	6	0	2	1	0	0	0	0	0	0	0	1	0	0	.500	.333
Rutledge, Josh	R-R	6-1	190	4-21-89	.333	.500	.250	15	54	7	18	3	0	1	5	7	1	1	1	12	3	3	.444	.413
Smalling, Tim	R-R	6-3	207	10-14-87	.265	.257	.269	61	215	33	57	15	3	4	22	20	2	0	2	46	4	4	.419	.331
Wheeler, Ryan	L-R	6-3	235	7-10-88	.243	.246	.241	59	210	18	51	9	0	4	20	15	1	1	3	43	0	2	.343	.293
2-team total (25 Salt Lake)					.268	—	—	84	302	31	81	10	0	6	35	23	1	1	5	62	0	2	.361	.317
Wheeler, Tim	L-R	6-4	205	1-21-88	.233	.252	.226	119	416	51	97	25	3	11	45	36	13	5	2	109	9	10	.387	.313
Williams, Jackson	R-R	5-11	200	5-5-86	.256	.383	.214	72	242	26	62	15	0	4	34	37	1	3	3	57	3	3	.368	.353
Ynoa, Rafael	R-R	6-0	185	8-7-87	.297	.287	.302	115	427	66	127	31	3	5	32	38	2	4	2	78	7	7	.419	.356

Pitching	B-T	HT	WT	DOB	W	L	ERA	G	GS	CG	SV	IP	H	R	ER	HR	BB	SO	AVG	vLH	vRH	K/9	BB/9
Anderson, Brett	L-L	6-4	225	2-1-88	1	0	0.96	2	2	0	0	9	8	1	1	0	2	8	.229	.250	.217	7.71	1.93
Bergman, Christian	R-R	6-1	180	5-4-88	5	5	4.19	15	15	0	0	92	96	48	43	11	18	60	.269	.253	.283	5.85	1.75
Betancourt, Rafael	R-R	6-2	220	4-29-75	1	0	10.50	7	0	0	6	6	10	7	7	2	3	4	.370	.375	.368	6.00	4.50
Bettis, Chad	R-R	6-1	200	4-26-89	3	4	3.09	20	5	0	3	55	45	22	19	1	21	55	.225	.235	.218	8.95	3.42
Brown, Brooks	L-R	6-3	205	6-20-85	1	1	4.18	37	0	0	7	47	50	29	22	4	17	46	.275	.325	.235	8.75	3.23
Burke, Greg	R-R	6-4	215	9-21-82	3	3	7.59	36	0	0	1	53	67	45	45	10	26	64	.303	.317	.292	10.80	4.39
Burres, Brian	L-L	6-1	175	4-8-81	1	6	5.75	15	13	0	0	67	87	54	43	8	38	57	.330	.291	.340	7.70	5.13
Butler, Eddie	B-R	6-2	180	3-13-91	0	1	10.13	1	1	0	0	5	8	7	6	0	3	4	.348	.429	.313	6.75	5.06
Capuano, Chris	L-L	6-3	215	8-19-78	1	0	3.07	3	3	0	0	15	12	5	5	2	3	14	.226	.133	.263	8.59	1.84
Chacin, Jhoulys	R-R	6-3	215	1-7-88	1	1	2.53	2	2	0	0	11	9	5	3	0	5	8	.220	.357	.148	6.75	4.22
Chatwood, Tyler	R-R	6-0	185	12-16-89	1	0	1.42	1	1	0	0	6	5	1	1	1	0	8	.217	.250	.143	11.37	0.00
Corpas, Manny	R-R	6-3	210	12-3-82	1	2	5.29	28	1	0	0	48	63	29	28	6	10	42	.315	.352	.284	7.93	1.89
Flande, Yohan	L-L	6-2	190	1-27-86	3	11	5.60	18	16	0	0	88	112	58	55	9	33	67	.315	.339	.303	6.83	3.36
Friedrich, Christian	R-L	6-4	215	7-8-87	2	9	5.02	17	13	0	1	91	114	76	71	16	39	83	.306	.274	.320	8.18	3.84
Gomez, Leuris	R-R	6-0	170	10-20-86	2	2	4.47	33	3	0	0	54	56	31	27	2	33	66	.267	.222	.300	10.93	5.47
Hernandez, Pedro	L-L	5-10	210	4-12-89	6	7	6.42	19	17	1	0	88	125	66	63	10	30	53	.336	.364	.324	5.40	3.06
Houser, James	L-L	6-4	205	3-19-84	1	1	6.94	5	2	0	0	12	.11	9	9	2	7	8	.244	.500	.233	6.17	5.40
Houston, Dan	R-R	6-3	205	10-24-86	2	6	6.12	31	7	0	1	65	76	48	44	7	29	46	.298	.289	.303	6.40	4.04
Jurrjens, Jair	R-R	6-1	200	1-29-86	0	5	4.60	8	8	2	0	47	52	29	24	6	16	24	.280	.263	.292	4.60	3.06

Name	B-T	HT	WT	DOB	W	L	ERA	G	GS	CG	SV	IP	H	R	ER	HR	BB	SO	AVG	vLH	vRH	K/9	BB/9
Kulik, Ryan	L-L	5-11	205	12-3-85	0	1	21.60	1	0	0	0	3	10	8	8	1	2	2	.556	.364	.857	5.40	5.40
Logan, Boone	R-L	6-5	215	8-13-84	0	0	1.50	7	0	0	1	6	3	1	1	1	3	6	.150	.000	.273	9.00	4.50
Lopez, Wilton	R-R	6-0	200	7-19-83	1	2	4.57	23	1	0	0	43	58	24	22	4	6	35	.320	.307	.330	7.27	1.25
Lyles, Jordan	R-R	6-4	215	10-19-90	1	0	0.00	1	0	0	0	5	3	0	0	0	2	4	.200	.143	.250	7.71	3.86
Martin, Chris	R-R	6-8	215	6-2-86	1	3	4.39	25	0	0	5	27	33	15	13	2	9	36	.308	.311	.306	12.15	3.04
Masset, Nick	R-R	6-5	235	5-17-82	1	0	0.00	9	0	0	1	9	2	0	0	0	1	9	.069	.091	.056	9.35	1.04
Matzek, Tyler	L-L	6-3	210	10-19-90	5	4	4.05	12	12	0	0	67	70	40	30	8	31	61	.265	.256	.270	8.24	4.19
McClendon, Mike	R-R	6-5	225	4-3-85	2	6	7.04	17	8	0	1	63	101	57	49	14	18	37	.366	.370	.362	5.31	2.59
Nicasio, Juan	R-R	6-3	210	8-31-86	3	2	4.54	10	4	0	1	36	41	21	18	4	15	36	.304	.294	.310	9.08	3.79
Roenicke, Josh	R-R	6-3	205	8-4-82	0	1	10.45	6	0	0	0	10	22	14	12	3	4	8	.440	.417	.447	6.97	3.48
Scahill, Rob	R-R	6-2	220	2-15-87	2	3	4.32	41	0	0	2	58	59	32	28	6	18	53	.261	.255	.266	8.18	2.78
Seidel, R.J.	R-R	6-5	225	9-3-87	0	2	10.02	9	0	0	0	21	31	26	23	4	11	20	.373	.333	.387	8.71	4.79
Tomko, Brett	R-R	6-4	220	4-7-73	2	3	5.85	10	10	0	0	40	58	28	26	5	9	28	.339	.266	.402	6.30	2.03
2-team total (9 Omaha)					6	6	4.74	19	18	0	0	87	104	49	46	11	28	60	—	—	—	6.18	2.89
White, Cole	R-R	6-2	195	1-22-88	0	0	6.00	3	0	0	0	3	2	2	2	1	4	1	.200	.286	.000	3.00	12.00

Fielding

Catcher	PCT	G	PO	A	E	DP	PB
Garneau	.986	42	308	38	5	4	1
Gonzalez	.833	1	5	0	1	0	0
McKenry	.990	22	186	11	2	1	2
Ramirez	.981	6	49	4	1	1	1
Rosario	1.000	2	11	1	0	0	0
Williams	.994	72	508	33	3	1	5

First Base	PCT	G	PO	A	E	DP
Cuddyer	1.000	1	5	0	0	0
McBride	1.000	7	51	4	0	3
Morneau	1.000	1	6	2	0	1
Parker	.987	40	347	26	5	44
Paulsen	.992	93	780	69	7	90
Smalling	.923	1	10	2	1	0
Wheeler	1.000	4	30	1	0	6

Second Base	PCT	G	PO	A	E	DP
Adames	1.000	3	5	3	0	1
Garcia	.984	28	56	64	2	17

	PCT	G	PO	A	E	DP
Janish	.976	15	28	52	2	14
Nina	.971	87	200	261	14	71
Rutledge	1.000	2	2	3	0	1
Smalling	1.000	1	1	4	0	0
Ynoa	.986	18	30	41	1	8

Third Base	PCT	G	PO	A	E	DP
Adames	.960	16	8	40	2	1
Arenado	1.000	4	2	8	0	1
Garcia	.944	11	9	25	2	3
Janish	.881	11	9	28	5	1
Nina	.789	7	5	10	4	1
Smalling	.923	11	7	17	2	1
Wheeler	.912	46	23	81	10	7
Ynoa	.964	44	19	89	4	7

Shortstop	PCT	G	PO	A	E	DP
Adames	.977	18	32	53	2	16
Culberson	1.000	2	4	8	0	2
Garcia	.953	37	42	122	8	32

	PCT	G	PO	A	E	DP
Janish	.991	28	32	74	1	22
Nina	1.000	4	5	10	0	1
Rutledge	.979	13	13	34	1	7
Ynoa	.991	46	72	148	2	35

Outfield	PCT	G	PO	A	E	DP
Cleary	.958	14	21	2	1	0
Dickerson	1.000	3	10	0	0	0
Frey	.985	44	64	3	1	0
Garcia	1.000	6	8	1	0	0
Gonzalez	1.000	3	2	0	0	0
Kandilas	.833	2	5	0	1	0
McBride	.962	30	51	0	2	0
Parker	.952	83	115	4	6	0
Paulsen	1.000	6	9	0	0	0
Pridie	.983	100	224	6	4	2
Smalling	1.000	44	57	3	0	1
Wheeler	1.000	5	5	0	0	0
Wheeler	.972	108	195	10	6	3

TULSA DRILLERS
TEXAS LEAGUE

DOUBLE-A

Batting	B-T	HT	WT	DOB	AVG	vLH	vRH	G	AB	R	H	2B	3B	HR	RBI	BB	HBP	SH	SF	SO	SB	CS	SLG	OBP
Adames, Cristhian	B-R	6-0	180	7-26-91	.267	.247	.274	88	330	42	88	9	4	2	38	29	2	13	6	58	7	9	.336	.324
Bergin, David	R-R	6-2	235	8-25-89	.241	.167	.294	12	29	4	7	1	0	1	2	7	1	0	0	7	0	0	.379	.405
Casteel, Ryan	R-R	5-11	205	6-6-91	.280	.261	.289	113	436	63	122	22	1	16	56	39	3	0	3	94	3	3	.445	.341
Cleary, Delta	R-R	6-2	220	8-14-89	.251	.250	.252	102	354	49	89	9	4	3	25	37	3	12	3	83	23	7	.325	.325
Cuddyer, Michael	R-R	6-2	220	3-27-79	.182	—	.182	3	11	2	2	0	0	0	0	2	0	0	0	0	0	0	.182	.308
Featherston, Taylor	R-R	6-1	185	10-8-89	.260	.297	.244	127	497	69	129	33	4	16	57	38	9	3	3	114	14	6	.439	.322
Garneau, Dustin	R-R	6-0	200	8-13-87	.270	.242	.280	34	115	14	31	7	0	2	20	14	4	0	2	19	2	3	.383	.363
Gonzalez, Jose	R-R	6-1	165	6-23-87	.238	.240	.236	25	80	6	19	2	2	0	9	11	0	1	1	24	1	0	.313	.326
Humphries, Brian	L-R	6-3	205	3-20-90	.276	.255	.283	112	402	35	111	17	6	4	45	11	4	7	5	74	9	6	.378	.299
Kandilas, Ryan	R-R	6-2	195	9-14-90	.194	.167	.208	21	72	10	14	2	1	4	13	3	1	1	0	16	1	1	.417	.237
Langfels, Jayson	R-R	6-2	205	8-17-88	.277	.220	.304	98	307	46	85	8	3	4	35	42	9	0	3	102	14	8	.362	.377
Massey, Tyler	L-L	6-1	205	7-21-89	.260	.259	.261	125	469	61	122	19	5	8	47	33	1	4	2	91	28	3	.373	.309
Murphy, Tom	R-R	6-1	220	4-3-91	.213	.171	.237	27	94	16	20	4	0	5	15	14	1	0	0	27	0	0	.415	.321
O'Dowd, Chris	B-R	5-11	190	10-14-90	.269	.226	.282	39	134	12	36	7	0	0	16	15	3	3	0	30	7	1	.321	.355
Ramirez, Michael	R-R	5-10	165	4-27-90	.250	.500	.000	2	4	1	1	0	0	0	0	0	0	0	0	2	0	0	.250	.250
Riggins, Harold	R-R	6-2	240	3-6-90	.263	.319	.227	58	179	20	47	8	2	7	25	21	4	0	1	79	2	3	.447	.351
Rivera, Jose	R-R	5-10	170	4-8-90	.250	.290	.231	37	96	11	24	7	2	0	15	5	3	0	1	21	0	1	.365	.305
Simon, Jared	R-R	6-0	230	3-9-89	.222	.271	.198	91	293	28	65	14	0	11	43	29	4	0	2	88	6	1	.382	.299
Smalling, Tim	R-R	6-3	207	10-14-87	.260	.267	.257	16	50	7	13	5	0	0	6	6	1	1	1	7	4	1	.360	.345
Story, Trevor	R-R	6-1	175	11-15-92	.200	.179	.208	56	205	29	41	8	1	9	20	28	2	2	0	82	3	1	.380	.302
Swanner, Will	R-R	6-1	195	9-10-91	.279	.379	.240	32	104	12	29	5	0	4	14	4	0	0	0	35	1	4	.442	.306
Wong, Joey	L-R	5-10	185	12-12-88	.221	.185	.230	83	258	30	57	13	2	1	17	24	0	3	2	54	5	1	.298	.285

Pitching	B-T	HT	WT	DOB	W	L	ERA	G	GS	CG	SV	IP	H	R	ER	HR	BB	SO	AVG	vLH	vRH	K/9	BB/9
Anderson, Tyler	L-L	6-4	215	12-30-89	7	4	1.98	23	23	0	0	118	91	37	26	3	40	106	.216	.257	.203	8.06	3.04
Aquino, Jayson	L-L	6-1	180	11-22-92	0	0	3.00	2	2	0	0	12	9	4	4	0	8	9	.205	.000	.237	6.75	6.00
Arrowood, Ryan	R-R	6-3	190	8-24-90	7	0	3.80	40	2	0	1	88	83	41	37	6	34	46	.250	.218	.274	4.72	3.49
Bergman, Christian	R-R	6-1	180	5-4-88	0	1	3.00	2	2	0	0	9	8	3	3	1	5	5	.258	.188	.333	5.00	5.00
Broyles, Shane	R-R	6-1	180	8-19-91	0	1	1.17	3	1	0	0	8	5	1	1	0	1	5	.185	.077	.286	5.87	1.17
Butler, Eddie	R-R	6-2	180	3-13-91	6	9	3.58	18	18	0	0	108	104	46	43	10	32	63	.256	.246		5.25	2.67
Capuano, Chris	L-L	6-3	215	8-19-78	0	0	1.93	1	1	0	0	5	4	1	1	0	2	7	.235	.667	.143	13.50	3.86
Castillo, Richard	R-R	5-11	165	10-11-89	3	12	5.41	25	25	0	0	136	153	97	82	17	46	69	.284	.292	.279	4.56	3.04
Erbe, Brandon	R-R	6-4	190	12-25-87	0	0	16.62	5	0	0	0	4	6	8	8	1	8	6	.333	.222	.444	12.46	16.62
Gomez, Leuris	R-R	6-0	170	10-20-86	0	0	4.50	3	0	0	0	4	1	2	2	0	3	6	.083	.000	.091	13.50	6.75
Gonzalez, Nelson	R-R	6-1	168	2-15-90	6	3	4.14	47	0	0	0	67	63	39	31	3	26	54	.247	.275	.229	7.22	3.48

Name	B-T	HT	WT	DOB	W	L	ERA	G	GS	CG	SV	IP	H	R	ER	HR	BB	SO	AVG	vLH	vRH	K/9	BB/9
Gray, Jon	R-R	6-4	235	11-5-91	10	5	3.91	24	24	0	0	124	107	58	54	10	41	113	.237	.241	.233	8.18	2.97
Hernandez, Carlos	L-L	5-11	155	3-4-87	5	7	2.68	28	20	0	0	124	130	49	37	6	21	94	.267	.227	.279	6.80	1.52
Houston, Dan	R-R	6-3	205	10-24-86	0	1	7.11	3	0	0	0	6	7	6	5	0	7	6	.280	.100	.400	8.53	9.95
Kern, Bruce	R-R	6-1	175	4-24-88	0	1	0.00	1	0	0	0	1	1	2	0	0	1	0	.333	.000	1.000	0.00	13.50
Kulik, Ryan	L-L	5-11	205	12-3-85	1	3	7.92	6	5	0	0	25	39	23	22	3	13	17	.361	.318	.372	6.12	4.68
McClendon, Mike	R-R	6-5	225	4-3-85	1	0	5.14	1	1	0	0	7	8	5	4	1	0	4	.296	.200	.318	5.14	0.00
Mueller, Josh	R-R	6-4	215	1-18-89	2	0	2.89	16	0	0	0	19	17	6	6	0	18	14	.246	.143	.317	6.75	8.68
Oberg, Scott	R-R	6-2	205	3-13-90	0	1	2.63	27	0	0	15	27	22	8	8	1	6	21	.218	.163	.259	6.91	1.98
Piazza, Mike	R-R	6-4	220	11-24-86	0	2	3.94	4	2	0	0	16	18	7	7	1	10	7	.290	.212	.379	3.94	5.63
Roberts, Kenny	L-L	6-1	200	3-9-88	9	2	2.30	47	0	0	2	78	52	22	20	3	20	54	.193	.192	.194	6.20	2.30
Seidel, R.J.	R-R	6-5	225	9-3-87	0	1	6.57	5	1	0	0	12	16	14	9	3	6	9	.308	.227	.367	6.57	4.38
Sitton, Kraig	L-L	6-5	190	7-13-88	4	8	3.68	48	0	0	4	66	63	35	27	8	24	43	.254	.167	.294	5.86	3.27
Striz, Nate	R-R	6-2	220	10-15-88	2	2	6.34	29	0	0	0	38	49	30	27	4	19	31	.310	.322	.303	7.28	4.46
White, Cole	R-R	6-2	195	1-22-88	3	3	2.96	44	0	0	16	49	36	21	16	3	33	42	.211	.293	.168	7.77	6.10
Winkler, Dan	R-R	6-1	200	2-2-90	5	2	1.41	12	12	1	0	70	33	11	11	5	17	71	.139	.179	.103	9.13	2.19

Fielding

Catcher	PCT	G	PO	A	E	DP	PB
Casteel	.985	39	244	20	4	2	5
Garneau	.974	24	167	19	5	0	0
Gonzalez	.989	23	161	17	2	8	2
Murphy	.988	23	148	11	2	2	1
O'Dowd	.975	25	146	9	4	0	1
Ramirez	1.000	1	7	0	0	0	0
Swanner	1.000	8	47	3	0	0	0

First Base	PCT	G	PO	A	E	DP
Bergin	.949	6	54	2	3	9
Casteel	.985	59	478	39	8	37
Cuddyer	1.000	1	10	0	0	2
Garneau	1.000	3	30	2	0	2
Gonzalez	1.000	2	10	2	0	2
Langfels	.992	14	113	9	1	14

	PCT	G	PO	A	E	DP
Massey	.923	1	11	1	1	2
Riggins	.989	46	401	43	5	35
Swanner	.971	11	95	4	3	10

Second Base	PCT	G	PO	A	E	DP
Adames	.984	14	30	31	1	9
Featherston	.980	72	169	225	8	52
Rivera	.985	26	51	79	2	20
Smalling	.933	3	4	10	1	1
Story	.957	5	9	13	1	4
Wong	.947	24	41	49	5	10

Third Base	PCT	G	PO	A	E	DP
Adames	.884	13	5	33	5	3
Langfels	.943	82	45	185	14	15
Smalling	1.000	4	3	6	0	0
Story	.913	6	3	18	2	1

	PCT	G	PO	A	E	DP
Wong	.963	44	19	86	4	9

Shortstop	PCT	G	PO	A	E	DP
Adames	.955	50	64	147	10	26
Featherston	.959	39	68	118	8	22
Story	.954	43	75	113	9	31
Wong	.929	7	8	18	2	1

Outfield	PCT	G	PO	A	E	DP
Cleary	.984	100	234	7	4	1
Cuddyer	—	2	0	0	0	0
Humphries	.995	104	182	7	1	2
Kandilas	1.000	20	35	3	0	1
Massey	.957	119	252	17	12	5
Simon	.988	81	161	7	2	3
Smalling	.714	5	4	1	2	1

MODESTO NUTS   HIGH CLASS A

CALIFORNIA LEAGUE

Batting	B-T	HT	WT	DOB	AVG	vLH	vRH	G	AB	R	H	2B	3B	HR	RBI	BB	HBP	SH	SF	SO	SB	CS	SLG	OBP
Bergin, David	R-R	6-2	235	8-25-89	.202	.140	.235	34	124	16	25	6	1	9	25	9	2	0	2	47	0	0	.484	.263
Ciriaco, Juan	R-R	5-9	165	7-6-90	.283	.343	.264	81	283	35	80	8	6	1	33	8	3	5	3	55	24	9	.364	.306
Dahl, David	L-R	6-2	195	4-1-94	.267	.375	.227	29	120	14	32	8	2	4	14	5	0	0	0	27	3	0	.467	.296
Dwyer, Sean	L-L	6-0	200	12-5-91	.204	.111	.238	76	274	23	56	11	2	3	30	36	0	0	4	67	2	3	.292	.293
Espy, Dean	R-R	6-1	210	10-30-89	.213	.179	.226	69	268	37	57	14	1	9	28	7	2	2	0	61	2	1	.373	.238
Herrera, Rosell	R-R	6-3	190	10-16-92	.244	.138	.287	72	275	31	67	11	1	4	23	24	0	1	2	52	9	7	.335	.302
Jones, Derek	L-L	6-0	210	6-3-90	.227	.108	.261	113	366	43	83	14	6	9	34	34	8	5	1	134	9	3	.372	.306
Kandilas, David	R-R	6-3	195	9-14-90	.272	.250	.279	68	254	42	69	17	6	1	21	30	6	2	2	51	15	6	.398	.360
Mehrten, Alec	R-R	6-3	190	7-24-90	.188	.167	.200	7	16	2	3	1	0	0	2	2	0	0	0	3	0	0	.250	.278
Mende, Sam	R-R	6-3	195	1-9-90	.155	.077	.178	17	58	6	9	3	1	0	0	4	5	1	0	12	2	1	.241	.269
2-team total (18 San Jose)					.175	—	—	35	126	11	22	5	2	0	1	8	5	1	0	38	2	2	.246	.252
O'Dowd, Chris	B-R	5-11	190	10-4-90	.272	.239	.282	74	287	40	78	20	3	5	32	22	2	2	3	67	16	4	.415	.325
Ramirez, Michael	R-R	5-10	165	4-27-90	.200	.190	.203	27	85	9	17	3	0	1	11	1	3	3	0	17	0	1	.271	.236
Ribera, Jordan	L-R	6-0	225	12-22-88	.257	.232	.265	117	408	45	105	22	1	9	64	40	2	0	4	88	3	1	.382	.324
Rivera, Jose	R-R	5-10	170	4-18-90	.150	.286	.077	7	20	2	3	1	0	1	6	1	0	0	1	4	1	0	.350	.182
San Juan, Alex	R-R	5-11	210	4-30-91	.189	.107	.226	27	90	8	17	4	0	1	9	4	0	0	0	32	1	0	.267	.223
Soriano, Wilson	R-R	5-9	140	12-31-91	.174	.250	.091	9	23	3	4	0	0	0	0	1	0	1	0	3	3	0	.174	.208
Sosa, Francisco	R-R	6-4	210	2-27-90	.223	.234	.219	65	224	27	50	12	3	6	27	22	4	4	2	70	5	7	.384	.302
Story, Trevor	R-R	6-1	175	11-15-92	.332	.500	.265	50	184	38	61	17	7	5	28	31	3	0	0	59	20	4	.582	.436
Swanner, Will	R-R	6-1	210	9-10-91	.261	.267	.259	82	310	36	81	16	3	9	41	32	2	1	3	106	7	5	.419	.331
Tauchman, Mike	L-L	6-2	200	12-3-90	.294	.246	.318	53	197	33	58	11	4	4	18	29	1	0	1	41	9	3	.452	.386
Valaika, Pat	R-R	5-11	200	9-9-92	.272	.242	.284	86	331	46	90	14	5	8	47	24	1	4	2	101	7	6	.417	.321
Von Tungeln, Kyle	L-L	5-9	175	9-18-90	.245	.341	.206	45	143	17	35	7	1	0	14	17	1	2	0	44	4	5	.308	.329
Wessinger, Matt	R-R	6-0	180	9-20-90	.214	.190	.226	110	359	35	77	13	2	4	40	26	7	4	3	46	7	4	.295	.278

Pitching	B-T	HT	WT	DOB	W	L	ERA	G	GS	CG	SV	IP	H	R	ER	HR	BB	SO	AVG	vLH	vRH	K/9	BB/9
Alsup, Ben	R-R	6-3	180	9-9-88	3	14	5.40	28	28	0	0	155	181	112	93	21	72	107	.294	.270	.309	6.21	4.18
Aquino, Jayson	L-L	6-1	180	11-22-92	5	10	5.40	16	16	1	0	95	113	66	57	7	30	74	.305	.314	.301	7.01	2.84
Brazoban, Huascar	R-R	6-3	155	10-15-89	0	0	4.50	3	0	0	0	4	4	2	2	0	3	5	.267	.400	.200	11.25	6.75
Brown, Andrew	R-R	6-2	195	11-11-89	1	5	7.80	9	8	0	0	43	59	39	37	6	18	20	.333	.363	.309	4.22	3.80
Broyles, Shane	R-R	6-1	180	8-19-91	2	2	3.43	41	0	0	1	63	55	29	24	7	21	68	.234	.297	.194	9.71	3.00
Burke, Devin	R-R	6-1	205	2-20-91	6	12	5.94	23	23	0	0	120	143	91	79	21	43	103	.288	.319	.270	7.75	3.23
Butler, Eddie	R-R	6-2	180	3-13-91	0	0	6.75	1	1	0	0	4	2	3	3	2	0	2	.125	.250	.083	4.50	4.50
Carpenter, Ryan	L-L	6-5	210	8-22-90	2	6	3.94	13	13	0	0	78	74	43	34	3	29	54	.245	.230	.251	6.26	3.36
Chacin, Jhoulys	R-R	6-3	215	1-7-88	0	2	8.59	2	2	0	0	7	8	7	7	1	3	4	.276	.118	.500	4.91	3.68
Erbe, Brandon	R-R	6-4	190	12-25-87	0	0	0.60	12	0	0	0	15	13	3	1	0	9	19	.236	.261	.219	11.40	5.40
Fernandez, Raul	R-R	6-2	180	6-22-90	0	1	7.00	29	0	0	7	27	37	28	21	2	15	20	.322	.278	.342	6.67	5.00
Flemer, Matt	R-R	6-2	210	11-22-90	13	10	4.53	28	27	1	0	165	178	93	83	18	36	130	.272	.270	.273	7.09	1.96

Name	B-T	HT	WT	DOB	W	L	ERA	G	GS	CG	SV	IP	H	R	ER	HR	BB	SO	AVG	vLH	vRH	K/9	BB/9
Gagnon, Tyler	R-R	6-2	175	3-22-89	0	2	3.32	18	3	0	0	43	44	18	16	3	12	23	.270	.292	.253	4.78	2.49
Gibbard, Ryan	R-R	6-3	220	11-28-89	0	5	6.44	9	9	0	0	36	47	28	26	1	26	20	.324	.350	.306	4.95	6.44
Gonzalez, Rayan	R-R	6-3	175	10-18-90	4	5	3.99	50	0	0	11	56	65	28	25	0	22	64	.290	.194	.359	10.22	3.51
Keck, Jon	L-L	6-6	215	6-18-88	2	4	4.72	34	0	0	1	34	35	20	18	4	15	35	.265	.250	.274	9.17	3.93
Kern, Bruce	R-R	6-1	175	4-24-88	0	4	5.60	29	0	0	0	27	33	17	17	0	16	23	.308	.429	.250	7.57	5.27
Kulik, Ryan	L-L	5-11	205	12-3-85	2	2	4.44	4	4	0	0	24	30	12	12	2	7	21	.297	.194	.343	7.77	2.59
Lyles, Jordan	R-R	6-4	215	10-19-90	0	0	0.00	1	1	0	0	4	3	0	0	0	2	4	.214	.300	.000	9.82	4.91
Mejias, Alving	R-R	6-0	200	12-26-91	1	1	4.48	45	0	0	0	78	85	44	39	8	30	85	.277	.286	.271	9.77	3.45
Newberry, Jacob	R-R	6-2	210	10-10-90	1	0	4.00	23	0	0	0	36	41	19	16	1	13	42	.277	.276	.278	10.50	3.25
Piazza, Mike	R-R	6-4	220	11-24-86	0	5	7.91	5	5	0	0	19	35	18	17	7	7	9	.398	.421	.380	4.19	3.26
Striz, Nate	R-R	6-2	220	10-15-88	1	0	3.91	16	0	0	0	23	24	13	10	2	10	25	.273	.222	.308	9.78	3.91
Tago, Peter	R-R	6-3	190	7-5-92	0	6	6.00	43	0	0	0	60	64	51	40	4	47	48	.281	.260	.291	7.20	7.05

Fielding

Catcher	PCT	G	PO	A	E	DP	PB
O'Dowd	.978	54	362	36	9	3	12
Ramirez	.985	27	178	22	3	5	7
San Juan	.979	26	173	17	4	1	6
Swanner	.988	40	287	34	4	2	3
Rivera	.955	7	9	12	1		5
Valaika	.962	27	51	76	5		21
Wessinger	.949	38	71	79	8		23
Story	.951	39	56	117	9		28
Valaika	.973	54	74	117	7		38
Wessinger	1.000	2	2	3	0		1

First Base	PCT	G	PO	A	E	DP
Bergin	.970	15	118	11	4	10
Dwyer	.984	13	114	11	2	10
Espy	.982	8	47	9	1	6
Jones	1.000		3	2	0	1
Ribera	.990	85	637	41	7	67
Swanner	.996	28	216	7	1	32

Second Base	PCT	G	PO	A	E	DP
Ciriaco	.961	72	138	210	14	55
Mehrten	.909	2	4	6	1	3

Third Base	PCT	G	PO	A	E	DP
Espy	.929	41	26	66	7	5
Herrera	.905	30	8	49	6	9
Mehrten	1.000	1	0	2	0	0
Mende	.947	14	13	23	2	5
Story	.885	8	8	15	3	1
Wessinger	.928	50	30	86	9	13

Shortstop	PCT	G	PO	A	E	DP
Ciriaco	.944	3	5	12	1	1
Herrera	.911	40	54	119	17	23
Mehrten	.889	2	2	6	1	0
Mende	.800	1	3	1	1	1

Outfield	PCT	G	PO	A	E	DP
Ciriaco	—	1	0	0	0	0
Dahl	.955	29	82	3	4	1
Dwyer	.942	49	94	3	6	0
Espy	1.000	2	1	0	0	0
Jones	.987	109	222	7	3	4
Kandilas	.981	68	140	12	3	5
Soriano	.889	8	14	2	2	0
Sosa	.945	60	116	5	7	2
Tauchman	.983	53	111	2	2	1
Von Tungeln	.980	44	95	1	2	0
Wessinger	.917	15	19	3	2	2

ASHEVILLE TOURISTS
LOW CLASS A
SOUTH ATLANTIC LEAGUE

Batting	B-T	HT	WT	DOB	AVG	vLH	vRH	G	AB	R	H	2B	3B	HR	RBI	BB	HBP	SH	SF	SO	SB	CS	SLG	OBP
Benjamin Jr., Mike	R-R	6-0	190	3-18-92	.341	.336	.343	78	311	70	106	22	6	12	47	18	6	5	3	70	25	8	.566	.385
Briceno, Jose	R-R	6-1	210	9-19-92	.283	.264	.293	84	315	38	89	23	1	12	50	16	10	8	1	57	8	4	.476	.336
Dahl, David	L-R	6-2	195	4-1-94	.309	.326	.300	90	392	69	121	33	6	10	41	23	1	4	2	65	18	5	.500	.347
Galvez, Cesar	B-R	5-9	145	7-24-91	.230	.143	.271	23	87	14	20	1	0	0	7	10	0	2	1	8	9	6	.241	.306
Graeter, Ashley	R-R	6-1	190	10-3-89	.309	.369	.273	60	223	36	69	19	1	9	40	15	6	1	4	49	8	3	.525	.363
Jimenez, Emerson	L-R	6-1	160	12-16-94	.259	.236	.268	73	266	36	69	11	4	1	28	5	2	8	2	58	16	7	.342	.276
McMahon, Ryan	L-R	6-2	185	12-14-94	.282	.220	.310	126	482	93	136	46	3	18	102	54	7	2	7	143	8	5	.502	.358
Mehrten, Alec	R-R	6-3	190	7-24-90	.246	.182	.293	42	130	10	32	5	0	0	16	4	8	1		26	1	3	.285	.317
Osborne, Zach	R-R	5-8	155	4-2-90	.268	.263	.272	68	231	28	62	11	1	2	24	21	4	1		22	6	6	.351	.339
Patterson, Jordan	L-L	6-4	215	2-12-92	.278	.245	.295	125	453	69	126	27	0	14	66	46	17	6	10	118	25	8	.430	.359
Prime, Correlle	R-R	6-5	222	2-18-94	.291	.273	.302	127	508	84	148	47	3	21	102	36	1	2	5	131	8	2	.520	.336
Rodriguez, Wilfredo	R-R	5-10	200	1-25-94	.310	.347	.290	75	281	36	87	16	0	3	37	21	4	3	6	33	2	3	.399	.359
Tapia, Raimel	L-L	6-2	160	2-4-94	.326	.313	.333	122	481	93	157	32	1	9	72	35	11	8	4	90	33	16	.453	.382
Thomas, Dillon	L-L	6-1	195	12-10-92	.317	.278	.333	32	126	15	40	10	1	1	10	5	3	0	0	38	8	3	.437	.358
Valaika, Pat	R-R	5-11	200	9-9-92	.370	.488	.310	34	127	25	47	12	1	4	23	9	1	4	3	26	12	2	.575	.407
White, Max	L-L	6-2	175	10-10-93	.229	.238	.225	103	350	56	80	15	6	6	39	37	6	5	2	132	22	2	.363	.311

Pitching	B-T	HT	WT	DOB	W	L	ERA	G	GS	CG	SV	IP	H	R	ER	HR	BB	SO	AVG	vLH	vRH	K/9	BB/9
Balog, Alex	R-R	6-5	210	7-16-92	8	5	3.95	27	24	0	1	150	158	81	66	12	41	114	.273	.252	.289	6.82	2.45
Blank, Trent	R-R	6-2	190	8-31-89	5	0	2.48	40	0	0	4	62	44	19	17	4	10	49	.203	.261	.160	7.15	1.46
Brown, Andrew	R-R	6-2	195	11-11-89	4	2	6.91	14	2	0	3	27	41	29	21	1	12	14	.353	.217	.443	4.61	3.95
Burke, Devin	R-R	6-1	205	2-20-91	0	1	3.09	3	2	0	0	12	9	6	4	2	1	8	.220	.286	.185	6.17	0.77
Carasiti, Matt	R-R	6-3	205	7-23-91	6	2	3.08	46	0	0	2	76	71	31	26	6	28	76	.247	.248	.247	9.00	3.32
Daniel, Trent	L-L	6-2	190	7-1-90	5	2	3.12	53	0	0	15	61	47	25	21	2	26	54	.214	.132	.271	8.01	3.86
Estevez, Carlos	R-R	6-4	210	12-28-92	1	3	4.73	33	0	0	0	53	62	34	28	4	11	50	.294	.348	.252	8.44	1.86
Firth, Scott	R-R	6-0	170	1-2-91	0	1	13.50	3	0	0	0	3	4	6	5	1	5	0	.286	.400	.222	0.00	13.50
Freeland, Kyle	L-L	6-3	170	5-14-93	2	0	0.83	5	5	0	0	22	14	4	2	1	4	18	.179	.059	.213	7.48	1.66
Hernandez, Jefri	R-R	6-1	170	4-27-91	0	2	6.30	23	0	0	1	20	25	20	14	1	13	25	.305	.342	.273	11.25	5.85
Jemiola, Zach	R-R	6-3	200	4-6-94	9	10	5.06	27	27	0	0	142	165	96	80	18	46	92	.297	.300	.295	5.82	2.91
Jiminian, Johendi	R-R	6-3	170	10-14-92	14	6	3.99	28	27	0	0	151	158	79	67	7	45	120	.269	.269	.270	7.15	2.68
Magliaro, Marc	R-R	5-11	175	2-17-90	0	0	6.00	3	0	0	0	3	3	2	2	0	1	1	.273	.200	.333	3.00	3.00
Neiman, Troy	R-R	6-1	195	11-13-90	7	1	1.59	47	0	0	6	79	52	16	14	2	21	89	.183	.153	.210	10.14	2.38
Norris, Logan	R-R	5-10	175	8-27-90	1	1	3.79	16	0	0	1	19	23	9	8	1	9	15	.295	.313	.283	7.11	4.26
Palo, Daniel	R-R	6-4	215	11-30-90	0	0	10.80	6	0	0	0	7	7	8	8	1	7	5	.269	.444	.176	6.75	9.45
Pierpont, Matt	R-R	6-2	215	1-25-91	3	0	2.96	17	0	0	1	27	24	9	9	5	7	27	.220	.234	.189	9.00	2.30
Senzatela, Antonio	R-R	6-1	180	1-21-95	15	2	3.11	26	26	0	0	145	134	61	50	11	36	89	.243	.201	.282	5.54	2.24
Stamey, Dylan	R-R	6-2	185	1-7-92	1	3	4.54	36	0	0	11	36	41	22	18	2	11	33	.291	.343	.243	8.33	5.30
Wade, Konner	L-R	6-3	190	12-3-91	8	8	3.61	27	25	0	1	142	154	79	57	16	35	94	.278	.263	.293	5.96	2.22

Fielding

Catcher	PCT	G	PO	A	E	DP	PB
Briceno	.977	75	492	99	14	7	11
Graeter	.963	21	146	12	6	1	8
Rodriguez	.994	44	310	22	2	2	6

First Base	PCT	G	PO	A	E	DP
Graeter	.966	5	47	10	2	2

Patterson	1.000	11	92	13 0 11	
Prime	.986	122	1185	65 18 107	

Second Base	PCT	G	PO	A	E	DP
Benjamin Jr.	.972	61	128	180	9	52
Galvez	.972	22	32	71	3	10
Mehrten	.963	30	35	96	5	19
Osborne	.973	31	60	85	4	16

Third Base	PCT	G	PO	A	E	DP
Benjamin Jr.	.951	10	9	30	2	3
Galvez	.833	1	0	5	1	1
Graeter	.667	2	1	3	2	0
McMahon	.916	118	99	248	32	28
Mehrten	1.000	9	11	17	0	2

Shortstop	PCT	G	PO	A	E	DP
Benjamin Jr.	.750	3	1	2	1	0
Jimenez	.926	73	101	211	25	40

Osborne	.971	35	39	94	4	18
Valaika	.953	31	52	89	7	24

Outfield	PCT	G	PO	A	E	DP
Dahl	.982	83	203	11	4	2
Patterson	.954	103	171	14	9	2
Tapia	.934	112	209	2	15	0
Thomas	1.000	28	62	2	0	0
White	.964	91	156	6	6	1

TRI-CITY DUST DEVILS   SHORT-SEASON

NORTHWEST LEAGUE

COLORADO ROCKIES

Batting	B-T	HT	WT	DOB	AVG	vLH	vRH	G	AB	R	H	2B	3B	HR	RBI	BB	HBP	SH	SF	SO	SB	CS	SLG	OBP
Bergin, David	R-R	6-2	235	8-25-89	.371	.333	.379	10	35	5	13	4	1	2	12	2	1	0	1	9	1	0	.714	.410
Bumpers, Sam	R-R	6-0	180	11-24-92	.258	.239	.265	46	178	20	46	9	3	0	23	15	3	0	1	41	8	3	.343	.325
Derkes, Marcos	R-R	6-0	155	9-12-91	.249	.218	.261	54	193	41	48	10	3	2	9	28	6	3	1	58	22	2	.363	.360
Dilone, Miguel	L-R	6-2	175	7-8-93	.225	.172	.242	36	120	14	27	3	1	3	23	18	0	2	3	36	5	5	.342	.319
Dwyer, Sean	L-L	6-0	200	12-5-91	.295	.340	.278	46	176	28	52	16	1	5	28	25	3	0	1	43	7	3	.483	.390
Fuentes, Josh	R-R	6-2	215	2-19-93	.260	.314	.243	41	150	20	39	7	0	1	16	13	5	2	2	39	6	2	.327	.335
Galvez, Cesar	B-R	5-9	145	7-24-91	.276	.308	.269	35	134	13	37	4	0	0	15	9	0	3	0	14	13	9	.306	.322
Garvey, Ryan	R-R	6-1	190	3-30-93	.233	.250	.226	41	150	17	35	8	3	3	15	12	5	0	2	42	6	2	.387	.308
Hoelscher, Shane	R-R	6-0	195	9-21-91	.332	.379	.311	53	193	31	64	16	2	2	27	29	3	1	0	39	11	6	.466	.427
Jenkins, Renaldo	R-R	6-0	190	3-1-93	.162	.038	.229	25	74	7	12	3	0	0	6	5	0	2	1	27	5	0	.203	.213
Parris, Jordan	R-R	6-3	205	7-2-92	.105	.214	.070	21	57	6	6	0	0	0	3	8	2	1	0	23	0	0	.105	.239
Perkins, Robbie	R-R	6-0	175	5-29-94	.202	.162	.217	38	129	17	26	7	1	1	7	14	0	0	0	42	3	0	.295	.280
Polonia, Rodney	L-R	5-10	160	9-9-93	.286	.250	.294	7	21	5	6	2	0	1	2	1	0	1	0	3	2	1	.524	.318
Prigatano, Richard	R-R	6-3	195	9-24-92	.172	.184	.168	47	157	11	27	7	1	0	9	17	2	1	1	54	9	2	.229	.260
Rabago, Chris	R-R	5-11	185	4-22-93	.225	.239	.220	47	169	13	38	6	0	0	12	14	6	2	4	42	6	6	.260	.301
Ramos, Roberto	L-R	6-5	220	12-28-94	.220	.111	.244	15	50	5	11	2	0	2	7	4	0	0	0	16	0	0	.380	.278
Richardson, Denzel	R-R	6-2	174	1-7-94	.200	.231	.191	18	60	7	12	4	0	1	6	6	0	0	0	14	5	2	.317	.273
Rosario, Jairo	R-R	5-10	175	1-21-93	.213	.318	.172	24	80	7	17	2	2	1	5	5	0	0	0	25	1	1	.325	.259
Soriano, Wilson	R-R	5-9	140	12-31-91	.385	.294	.429	14	52	6	20	4	2	0	5	1	1	0	0	3	6	4	.538	.407
Sosa, Francisco	R-R	6-4	210	2-3-93	.324	.333	.322	20	74	7	24	3	0	1	10	7	1	0	1	12	7	2	.405	.386
Story, Trevor	R-R	6-1	175	11-15-92	.286	.000	.400	2	7	2	2	1	0	0	1	0	0	0	0	3	0	0	.429	.375
Tauchman, Mike	L-L	6-2	200	12-3-90	.280	.500	.238	7	25	5	7	1	0	0	4	4	0	0	1	2	6	0	.320	.367
Thomas, Dillon	L-L	6-1	195	12-10-92	.209	.071	.245	18	67	8	14	4	2	0	9	3	0	0	2	22	2	2	.358	.243
Weeks, Drew	R-R	6-1	180	6-9-93	.281	.345	.258	56	217	33	61	15	4	2	26	19	2	2	1	47	9	6	.415	.343

Pitching	B-T	HT	WT	DOB	W	L	ERA	G	GS	CG	SV	IP	H	R	ER	HR	BB	SO	AVG	vLH	vRH	K/9	BB/9
Brazoban, Huascar	R-R	6-3	155	10-15-89	1	0	3.23	20	0	0	0	31	24	13	11	3	8	23	.203	.271	.157	6.75	2.35
Bryant, Tony	R-R	6-7	220	4-18-91	0	1	13.50	1	1	0	0	4	8	6	6	0	1	2	.444	.545	.286	4.50	2.25
Castellani, Ryan	R-R	6-3	193	4-1-96	1	2	3.65	10	10	0	0	37	35	20	15	2	9	25	.248	.269	.236	6.08	2.19
DeLuca, Evan	L-L	6-1	195	3-9-91	0	0	7.43	13	0	0	0	13	11	12	11	3	20	13	.216	.353	.147	8.78	13.50
Firth, Scott	R-R	6-0	170	1-2-91	0	2	3.47	24	0	0	10	23	21	14	9	3	10	19	.236	.258	.224	7.33	3.86
Gagnon, Tyler	R-R	6-2	175	3-22-89	0	3	6.11	4	4	0	0	18	24	15	12	1	6	6	.348	.333	.359	3.06	3.06
Magliaro, Marc	R-R	5-11	175	2-17-90	1	0	16.20	1	0	0	0	2	3	3	3	1	1	2	.375	.250	.500	10.80	5.40
McCrummen, Jerad	R-R	6-1	190	9-11-90	4	2	3.15	23	0	0	2	40	41	18	14	1	10	37	.263	.222	.284	8.33	2.25
Michalec, Josh	R-R	6-2	185	6-20-92	1	3	5.40	27	0	0	8	27	27	17	16	1	11	28	.262	.270	.258	9.45	3.71
Moll, Sam	L-L	5-10	185	1-18-92	0	1	4.15	9	0	0	0	13	17	6	6	1	4	7	.327	.462	.282	4.85	2.77
Mueller, Josh	R-R	6-4	215	1-18-89	0	0	1.93	5	0	0	0	5	3	1	1	0	2	10	.176	.200	.143	19.29	3.86
Newberry, Jacob	R-R	6-2	210	10-10-90	0	0	18.00	3	0	0	0	3	8	6	6	2	1	1	.471	.500	.467	3.00	3.00
Norris, Logan	R-R	5-10	175	8-27-90	0	0	9.95	3	1	0	0	6	10	8	7	0	4	5	.345	.500	.235	7.11	5.68
Payamps, Joel	R-R	6-2	170	4-7-94	0	2	6.10	7	6	0	0	21	20	15	14	1	22	22	.278	.259	.289	9.58	9.58
Rodriguez, Helmis	L-L	5-11	155	6-10-94	4	7	1.97	15	15	0	0	91	82	30	20	2	18	41	.236	.232	.238	4.04	1.77
Rohrbach, Andrew	R-R	6-3	195	4-10-92	0	0	4.50	2	2	0	0	4	5	2	2	0	0	2	.313	.167	.400	4.50	0.00
Sawyer, Logan	R-R	6-5	215	1-18-92	3	2	3.43	15	6	0	0	58	62	23	22	2	11	35	.267	.301	.248	5.46	1.72
Sheehan, John	R-R	5-11	190	8-16-90	4	0	3.70	15	0	0	0	24	22	13	10	2	6	21	.239	.212	.254	7.77	2.22
Shouse, Blake	R-R	6-2	185	3-9-93	3	6	4.68	14	14	0	0	67	68	42	35	5	31	35	.272	.247	.288	4.68	4.14
Stamey, Dylan	R-R	6-2	185	1-7-92	2	0	4.61	11	0	0	0	14	12	7	7	0	5	17	.235	.333	.182	11.20	3.29
Thompson, Dylan	L-R	6-3	195	9-4-92	3	2	8.89	18	0	0	0	26	41	30	26	1	14	18	.357	.370	.348	6.15	4.78
Vasto, Jerry	L-L	6-2	195	2-12-92	0	0	0.00	1	0	0	0	1	0	0	0	0	1	0	.000	—	.000	9.00	0.00
Waltrip, Billy	L-L	6-2	215	7-1-92	2	1	5.58	25	0	0	0	31	36	21	19	1	19	31	.283	.333	.259	9.10	5.58
Warner, Ryan	L-R	6-7	195	1-21-94	1	4	6.20	11	11	0	0	41	39	34	28	3	38	24	.262	.279	.250	5.31	8.41
Wiest, Grahamm	R-R	6-3	195	8-9-91	1	3	3.90	8	6	0	0	30	39	16	13	3	8	23	.315	.308	.319	6.90	2.40
Yan, Carlos	R-R	6-5	192	1-28-91	2	1	6.59	26	0	0	0	29	38	22	21	4	16	26	.319	.354	.296	8.16	5.02
Zurat, Chad	R-R	6-2	215	11-22-91	1	0	8.14	10	0	0	0	21	36	23	19	0	5	19	.367	.444	.323	8.14	2.14

Fielding

Catcher	PCT	G	PO	A	E	DP	PB
Parris	.986	21	128	13	2	1	4
Perkins	.977	38	223	29	6	3	8
Rosario	.970	24	140	19	5	2	11

First Base	PCT	G	PO	A	E	DP
Bergin	.988	9	73	10	1	6

Dilone	.979	16	136	6	3	15
Dwyer	.985	41	380	24	6	40
Fuentes	.975	8	68	11	2	10
Ramos	1.000	5	38	2	0	5

Second Base	PCT	G	PO	A	E	DP
Bumpers	.974	45	91	137	6	29

Dilone	.944	7	11	23	2	2
Galvez	.980	7	20	28	1	9
Hoelscher	1.000	1	2	3	0	1
Jenkins	.987	18	37	41	1	9
Rabago	1.000	1	2	5	0	2

Third Base	PCT	G	PO	A	E	DP
Fuentes	.905	26	22	54	8	6
Galvez	.955	5	7	14	1	0
Hoelscher	.931	44	39	83	9	8
Jenkins	.889	3	1	7	1	1

Shortstop	PCT	G	PO	A	E	DP
Bumpers	.833	1	2	3	1	2
Fuentes	.941	3	6	10	1	4

Galvez	.929	18	22	56	6	9
Polonia	.906	6	13	16	3	3
Rabago	.928	46	81	178	20	38
Story	1.000	2	1	3	0	1

Outfield	PCT	G	PO	A	E	DP
Derkes	.974	50	112	2	3	0
Garvey	.936	36	68	5	5	1
Jenkins	1.000	1	1	0	0	0

Prigatano	.951	39	56	2	3	1
Richardson	1.000	13	25	0	0	0
Soriano	1.000	12	32	1	0	1
Sosa	.969	15	31	0	1	0
Tauchman	1.000	6	6	2	0	1
Thomas	.963	13	25	1	1	1
Weeks	.989	48	88	4	1	1

GRAND JUNCTION ROCKIES   ROOKIE

PIONEER LEAGUE

Batting	B-T	HT	WT	DOB	AVG	vLH	vRH	G	AB	R	H	2B	3B	HR	RBI	BB	HBP	SH	SF	SO	SB	CS	SLG	OBP
Carrizales, Omar	L-L	6-0	175	1-30-95	.307	.115	.346	45	153	28	47	5	3	0	13	18	0	2	2	33	14	10	.379	.376
Castro, Luis	R-R	6-1	187	9-19-95	.301	.280	.306	34	123	28	37	3	0	2	16	15	2	1	2	25	6	3	.374	.380
Causey, Nate	L-R	6-2	205	3-6-93	.221	.273	.209	39	113	27	25	10	0	4	19	27	4	0	1	39	2	1	.416	.386
Cuddyer, Michael	R-R	6-2	220	3-27-79	.579	1.000	.500	5	19	5	11	6	0	0	9	1	1	0	1	0	0	0	.895	.591
Daza, Yonathan	R-R	6-2	190	2-28-94	.370	.405	.361	47	192	38	71	11	0	4	35	11	4	1	0	25	19	7	.490	.415
Garcia, Henry	R-R	6-2	195	9-21-93	.327	.316	.329	27	104	20	34	2	0	3	20	4	3	0	2	27	2	1	.433	.363
George, Max	S-9	180	4-7-96	.301	.435	.274	46	136	30	41	8	1	4	19	25	8	5	2	44	10	3	.463	.433
Jean, Luis	R-R	6-1	150	8-17-94	.285	.357	.269	44	158	22	45	5	4	1	25	10	2	3	3	19	13	8	.386	.329
Jenkins, Renaldo	R-R	6-0	190	3-1-93	.444	.583	.375	9	36	9	16	4	1	1	3	0	1	0	5	3	2	.694	.487
Jones, Wesley	R-R	6-2	180	8-12-95	.263	.121	.301	42	156	15	41	5	0	0	16	5	3	1	1	24	2	2	.295	.297
Marte, Hamlet	R-R	5-10	180	2-3-94	.329	.409	.301	44	167	34	55	14	2	4	33	17	4	0	0	37	6	5	.509	.404
McBride, Matt	R-R	6-2	215	5-23-85	.615	—	.615	4	13	6	8	3	0	0	5	3	0	0	0	1	1	0	.846	.688
McClure, Terry	R-R	6-2	190	9-29-95	.254	.179	.273	41	138	23	35	7	0	2	21	24	2	4	1	50	7	3	.348	.370
Nunez, Dom	L-R	6-0	175	1-17-95	.313	.294	.317	46	176	30	55	12	0	8	40	21	0	0	1	28	5	7	.517	.384
Padlo, Kevin	R-R	6-2	200	7-15-96	.300	.346	.291	48	160	32	48	15	4	8	44	31	4	1	2	38	6	1	.594	.421
Ramos, Roberto	L-R	6-5	220	12-28-94	.208	.188	.214	24	72	6	15	3	0	1	10	6	3	0	1	23	1	1	.292	.293
Reyes, Randy	R-R	6-0	175	9-4-92	.321	.351	.314	50	193	40	62	11	6	8	40	8	3	0	4	47	12	4	.565	.351
Richardson, Denzel	R-R	6-2	174	1-7-94	.213	.063	.250	22	80	12	17	6	2	0	7	7	0	0	1	18	7	3	.338	.273
Rogers, Wes	R-R	6-3	180	3-7-94	.283	.400	.265	30	113	25	32	3	2	3	16	13	1	4	0	25	15	1	.425	.362
Soriano, Wilson	S-9	140	12-31-91	.295	.381	.270	28	95	14	28	1	0	1	11	5	3	1	1	7	15	4	.337	.346
Stein, Troy	R-R	6-1	210	4-17-92	.350	.222	.455	5	20	7	7	2	0	1	3	2	0	0	0	4	3	0	.600	.409
Wall, Forrest	L-R	6-0	176	11-20-95	.318	.478	.291	41	157	48	50	6	6	3	24	27	0	3	1	32	18	5	.490	.416

Pitching	B-T	HT	WT	DOB	W	L	ERA	G	GS	CG	SV	IP	H	R	ER	HR	BB	SO	AVG	vLH	vRH	K/9	BB/9
Bello, Yoely	L-L	6-2	150	12-16-90	4	1	1.17	26	0	0	0	31	19	12	4	2	12	44	.170	.083	.234	12.91	3.52
Betancourt, Rafael	R-R	6-2	220	4-29-75	1	0	2.03	14	0	0	0	13	18	7	3	0	5	11	.310	.310	.310	7.43	3.38
Black, Taylor	R-R	6-2	190	12-16-91	3	1	2.65	20	1	0	3	34	39	13	10	0	8	22	.293	.323	.268	5.82	2.12
Brothers, Hunter	L-R	6-1	210	12-20-91	1	0	5.59	17	0	0	0	19	21	16	12	0	10	16	.284	.368	.194	7.45	4.66
Bryant, Tony	R-R	6-7	220	4-18-91	3	0	4.50	9	2	0	0	22	23	12	11	2	7	22	.274	.171	.372	9.00	2.86
Crawford, Alec	R-R	6-2	205	1-10-92	0	5	5.18	24	0	0	9	24	32	19	14	3	3	22	.302	.348	.267	8.14	1.11
Freeland, Kyle	L-L	6-3	170	5-14-93	1	0	1.56	5	5	0	0	17	16	4	3	0	2	15	.254	.167	.289	7.79	1.04
Glanz, Gavin	R-R	6-2	205	12-13-91	1	4	4.34	23	0	0	4	29	30	18	14	1	11	26	.265	.288	.246	8.07	3.41
Howard, Sam	R-L	6-3	170	3-5-93	1	3	5.40	14	13	0	0	53	73	34	32	6	10	42	.333	.327	.335	7.09	1.69
Kenilvort, Alec	R-R	6-6	230	1-7-93	0	1	6.53	19	0	0	0	21	27	17	15	2	11	20	.307	.333	.283	8.71	4.79
Lomangino, James	R-R	6-0	205	10-5-91	3	1	3.18	15	8	0	0	45	44	23	16	7	8	34	.251	.182	.322	6.75	1.59
Magliaro, Marc	R-R	5-11	175	2-17-90	1	1	5.72	19	0	0	1	28	39	26	18	4	16	22	.331	.379	.283	6.99	5.08
Musgrave, Harrison	L-L	6-1	205	3-3-92	2	4	5.44	13	11	0	0	48	60	40	29	10	14	50	.303	.317	.296	9.38	2.63
Norris, Logan	R-R	5-10	175	8-27-90	5	0	2.88	16	1	0	0	25	29	8	8	1	5	20	.293	.304	.283	7.20	1.80
Palacios, Javier	R-R	6-1	165	9-29-93	6	5	6.21	16	15	0	0	83	103	69	57	15	19	61	.301	.348	.248	6.64	2.07
Pierpont, Matt	R-R	6-2	215	1-25-91	1	0	2.79	8	0	0	3	10	8	5	3	1	1	9	.216	.095	.375	8.38	0.93
Polanco, Carlos	R-R	6-2	175	2-18-94	6	5	5.62	15	15	0	0	75	99	58	47	11	27	66	.321	.325	.317	7.88	3.23
Quintin, Cristian	R-R	6-3	165	12-27-93	0	0	10.13	16	0	0	0	19	35	25	21	6	6	14	.389	.354	.429	6.75	2.89
Rodriguez, Alex	L-L	6-4	206	9-14-93	0	1	7.20	10	1	0	0	10	17	17	8	1	3	10	.347	.211	.433	9.00	2.70
Schlitter, Craig	R-R	6-0	195	5-16-92	3	1	2.41	20	4	0	1	41	38	18	11	5	11	41	.244	.243	.244	9.00	2.41

Fielding

Catcher	PCT	G	PO	A	E	DP	PB
Causey	.875	5	26	2	4	0	0
Marte	.982	34	233	34	5	0	12
Nunez	.987	37	263	41	4	1	13
Stein	1.000	3	25	8	0	1	1

First Base	PCT	G	PO	A	E	DP
Castro	1.000	5	48	7	0	7
Causey	.988	28	238	15	3	27
Cuddyer	1.000	2	14	0	0	1
Garcia	.976	26	217	25	6	21
McBride	1.000	2	14	4	0	0
Ramos	.971	22	166	3	5	15

Second Base	PCT	G	PO	A	E	DP
George	.800	1	2	2	1	0

Jean	.951	6	11	28	2	5
Jenkins	.946	9	14	21	2	5
Jones	.940	31	45	95	9	17
Soriano	.667	1	1	3	2	0
Wall	.962	30	46	79	5	20

Third Base	PCT	G	PO	A	E	DP
Castro	.921	22	13	45	5	3
Jean	.857	6	5	7	2	2
Jenkins	.500	1	0	1	1	0
Jones	.850	6	5	12	3	1
Padlo	.917	45	27	72	9	8
Soriano	1.000	2	0	1	0	0

Shortstop	PCT	G	PO	A	E	DP
George	.906	45	70	133	21	31

Jean	.917	32	60	95	14	18
Soriano	1.000	1	1	2	0	1

Outfield	PCT	G	PO	A	E	DP
Carrizales	.989	45	86	4	1	1
Cuddyer	1.000	1	1	0	0	0
Daza	.950	45	70	6	4	1
Jean	1.000	1	3	0	0	0
McBride	1.000	2	2	0	0	0
McClure	.944	38	65	2	4	1
Reyes	.921	40	54	4	5	0
Richardson	.939	18	26	5	2	1
Rogers	1.000	30	35	0	0	0
Soriano	1.000	24	44	5	0	2

DOMINICAN SUMMER LEAGUE

Batting	B-T	HT	WT	DOB	AVG	vLH	vRH	G	AB	R	H	2B	3B	HR	RBI	BB	HBP	SH	SF	SO	SB	CS	SLG	OBP
Brito, Antony	R-R	5-11	180	2-15-95	.254	.206	.267	51	169	19	43	8	0	0	15	14	1	5	0	30	5	3	.302	.315
Brito Jr., Luis	L-L	6-0	165	1-28-96	.275	.207	.290	52	160	17	44	8	2	0	13	20	0	2	2	39	13	7	.350	.352
Diaz, Joel	R-R	6-1	175	9-18-95	.224	.281	.210	45	170	15	38	5	0	0	16	7	4	2	1	22	2	2	.253	.269
Gomez, Jose	R-R	6-0	170	12-10-96	.263	.269	.262	67	243	36	64	13	1	0	18	17	6	7	0	33	20	12	.325	.327
Gonzalez, Hidekel	R-R	5-11	175	10-7-96	.250	.200	.262	17	52	3	13	6	0	0	7	3	2	0	1	14	1	1	.365	.310
Herrera, Carlos	L-R	6-0	145	9-23-96	.230	.100	.266	36	139	18	32	7	0	0	11	11	1	8	1	25	6	4	.281	.289
Jimenez, Anderson	R-R	6-1	180	7-31-97	.217	.206	.221	41	138	15	30	4	0	2	19	12	3	0	2	37	3	2	.290	.290
Jimenez, Wilkyns	R-R	6-2	180	7-18-95	.214	.367	.174	44	145	8	31	4	0	0	12	9	1	4	0	33	0	2	.241	.265
Marcelino, Ramon	L-R	6-1	175	12-23-96	.235	.234	.235	59	226	23	53	13	3	1	24	14	9	0	4	46	8	8	.332	.300
Melendez, Manuel	L-L	5-11	165	1-10-97	.227	.271	.216	64	233	25	53	9	2	1	16	18	5	5	2	33	11	7	.296	.295
Paulino, Elvin	R-R	6-1	195	12-3-94	.163	.118	.177	42	147	15	24	6	1	2	11	7	4	0	2	42	3	1	.259	.219
Piron, Jonathan	L-R	6-0	175	11-14-94	.267	.260	.269	63	247	29	66	14	9	2	17	14	0	5	1	50	20	7	.421	.305
Rodriguez, Jose	L-R	5-10	135	2-23-96	.209	.240	.200	40	115	13	24	6	0	0	5	5	2	3	0	24	3	7	.261	.254

Pitching	B-T	HT	WT	DOB	W	L	ERA	G	GS	CG	SV	IP	H	R	ER	HR	BB	SO	AVG	vLH	vRH	K/9	BB/9
Brazoban, Gustavo	R-R	6-3	159	8-13-91	0	0	0.00	2	0	0	0	1	0	0	0	0	2	0	.000	.000	.000	0.00	13.50
Eusebio, Breiling	L-L	6-1	175	10-21-96	1	2	3.72	11	5	0	0	29	29	16	12	2	11	33	.261	.133	.281	10.24	3.41
Fernandez, Julian	R-R	6-2	160	12-5-95	1	0	5.60	18	0	0	0	18	13	12	11	1	17	15	.206	.174	.225	7.64	8.66
Franco, Kelvin	R-R	6-1	165	10-29-94	3	1	2.17	21	0	0	3	29	20	12	7	1	13	32	.200	.162	.222	9.93	4.03
Garcia, Henry	R-R	6-5	195	3-29-97	2	2	2.11	13	0	0	0	21	17	8	5	0	10	8	.236	.214	.241	3.38	4.22
Guillen, Adonis	R-R	6-2	175	11-23-95	5	6	2.72	27	2	0	8	36	33	24	11	2	16	34	.231	.257	.222	8.42	3.96
Guzman, Luis	L-L	6-1	165	2-27-96	3	1	1.54	13	3	0	0	41	20	7	7	0	10	21	.156	.111	.164	4.61	2.20
Harvey, Ronald	R-R	6-0	165	3-15-95	0	0	3.86	2	0	0	0	2	4	1	1	0	1	0	.444	.500	.429	0.00	3.86
Julio, Erick	R-R	6-1	175	9-22-96	2	5	2.45	13	13	0	0	66	51	26	18	2	11	45	.211	.192	.219	6.14	1.50
Justo, Salvador	R-R	6-5	210	10-14-94	1	3	7.50	16	0	0	4	12	13	11	10	1	9	13	.295	.313	.286	9.75	6.75
Lopez, Carlos	R-R	6-2	175	4-24-96	0	0	7.04	9	0	0	1	8	9	7	6	0	6	9	.290	.417	.211	10.57	7.04
Matos, Andres	R-R	6-2	165	3-13-96	2	1	3.80	13	0	0	0	24	23	12	10	1	14	25	.256	.103	.328	9.51	5.32
Oviedo, Jorge	L-L	6-2	180	10-6-96	4	3	2.49	13	13	1	0	69	54	24	19	2	8	61	.212	.333	.190	8.00	1.05
Ozuna, Lorenz	R-R	6-0	175	9-22-94	4	1	1.93	12	6	0	0	47	36	14	10	2	15	37	.222	.275	.205	7.14	2.89
Pena, Juan	R-R	6-2	175	8-25-95	4	2	1.16	13	10	0	0	70	50	18	9	2	10	54	.202	.194	.205	6.94	1.29
Perez, Esmerlin	R-R	6-0	165	1-8-96	0	0	1.35	4	0	0	0	7	2	1	1	0	5	4	.095	.000	.154	5.40	6.75
Quintana, Yohander	R-R	6-3	175	4-9-97	1	1	2.28	14	0	0	1	28	18	10	7	1	7	11	.188	.300	.136	3.58	2.28
Requena, Alejandro	R-R	6-0	185	11-29-96	1	2	3.96	13	5	0	0	39	37	22	17	0	9	28	.247	.196	.269	6.52	2.09
Villarroel, Cesar	R-R	6-3	188	7-27-94	0	0	0.00	4	0	0	0	6	2	0	0	0	1	6	.086	.083	.000	9.00	1.50
Villarroel, Hector	L-L	6-3	150	8-12-95	1	2	2.22	13	11	0	0	49	28	18	12	2	31	44	.167	.200	.161	8.14	5.73
Viloria, Ismael	R-R	6-1	165	3-31-95	0	2	3.13	11	2	0	0	23	24	11	8	1	10	13	.267	.375	.227	5.09	3.91

Fielding

Catcher	PCT	G	PO	A	E	DP	PB
Diaz	1.000	1	7	1	0	0	1
Gonzalez	.990	13	80	15	1	0	3
Jimenez	.982	41	270	57	6	1	11
Paulino	.939	23	136	17	10	0	3

First Base	PCT	G	PO	A	E	DP
Brito	1.000	2	14	0	0	0
Diaz	.995	40	402	23	2	24
Gomez	1.000	2	6	0	0	0
Jimenez	.963	3	26	0	1	0
Paulino	.977	18	158	9	4	9
Suero	.964	14	100	6	4	8

Second Base	PCT	G	PO	A	E	DP
Brito	1.000	6	8	7	0	0
Gomez	1.000	19	37	53	0	7
Herrera	1.000	4	8	13	0	1
Piron	.964	41	84	106	7	23
Rodriguez	1.000	6	5	10	0	1

Third Base	PCT	G	PO	A	E	DP
Brito	.874	25	22	61	12	3
Diaz	1.000	1	3	2	0	1
Gomez	.946	25	25	81	6	7
Jimenez	.855	21	22	49	12	2
Piron	—	1	0	0	0	0

Shortstop	PCT	G	PO	A	E	DP
Gomez	.933	21	38	74	8	8
Herrera	.929	32	65	91	12	14
Piron	.899	22	32	66	11	3

Outfield	PCT	G	PO	A	E	DP
Brito	1.000	1	1	0	0	0
Brito Jr.	.930	46	60	6	5	0
Gomez	1.000	1	1	0	0	0
Marcelino	.933	59	75	9	6	0
Melendez	.984	63	122	4	2	0
Rodriguez	1.000	5	7	0	0	0
Suero	.961	45	70	3	3	0

Detroit Tigers

SEASON IN A SENTENCE: Another strong season, but another year without an elusive World Series ring for the Tigers, who won their fourth consecutive American League Central title but lost to the Orioles in a Division Series sweep, marking the team's earliest exit during that stretch.

HIGH POINT: After a July 24 victory over the Angels' best starter, Garrett Richards, the Tigers held a seven-game lead in the AL Central with two months left in the season, and looked like a surefire bet to march into the postseason. Miguel Cabrera, Victor Martinez, and breakout sensation J.D. Martinez led an offense that ranked second in the majors in runs scored. They did end up winning the division, but ...

LOW POINT: ... the Tigers went just 33-30 the rest of the season, narrowly edged the Royals by a game for the AL Central crown, then saw their season quickly disappear with 12-3, 7-6 and 2-1 losses to the Orioles in the ALDS. Bullpen issues yet again plagued the Tigers, who couldn't count on Joe Nathan or Joba Chamberlain in high-leverage situations.

NOTABLE ROOKIES: Third baseman Nick Castellanos showed flashes of his offensive potential, but he struggled moving back to the hot corner from the outfield and generally underwhelmed with his .259/.306/.394 performance. When Jose Iglesias got injured, shortstop Eugenio Suarez got fast-tracked to Detroit and provided steady insurance, hitting .242/.316/.336 in 85 games.

KEY TRANSACTIONS: With Max Scherzer's pending free agency, Justin Verlander scuffling and Anibal Sanchez hurting, the Tigers acquired David Price in a three-way trade at the deadline, sending center fielder Austin Jackson to Seattle, with lefthander Drew Smyly and rising young shortstop prospect Willy Adames to the Rays. They also tried to fix their bullpen problems by giving righthanders Jake Thompson and Corey Knebel to the Rangers for Joakim Soria, but that did little to help, as Soria didn't pitch well for the Tigers and manager Brad Ausmus was reluctant to use him in critical situations.

DOWN ON THE FARM: Most of the Tigers' top players aren't homegrown talent, a trend that will likely have to continue with a relatively thin farm system. Second baseman Devon Travis is a polished hitter with nowhere to play, while outfielder Steven Moya has a high ceiling but remains raw despite a strong year in Double-A.

OPENING DAY PAYROLL: $163,078,526 (4th)

PLAYERS OF THE YEAR

MAJOR LEAGUE	MINOR LEAGUE
Max Scherzer **rhp**	**Steven Moya** **of**
18-5, 3.15	(Double-A)
Led AL in wins	.276/.306/.555
3rd in AL with 252 SO	35 HR, 105 RBI

ORGANIZATION LEADERS

BATTING · *Minimum 250 AB

MAJORS

* AVG	Martinez, Victor	.335
* OPS	Martinez, Victor	.974
HR	Martinez, Victor	32
RBI	Cabrera, Miguel	109

MINORS

* AVG	Bernard, Wynton, West Michigan	.323
* OBP	Bernard, Wynton, West Michigan	.394
* SLG	Moya, Steven, Erie	.555
R	Bernard, Wynton, West Michigan	91
H	Bernard, Wynton, West Michigan	164
TB	Moya, Steven, Erie	286
2B	Rhymes, Raph, West Michigan	35
3B	Adames, Willy, West Michigan	12
HR	Moya, Steven, Erie	35
RBI	Moya, Steven, Erie	105
BB	Lennerton, Jordan, Toledo	73
SO	Moya, Steven, Erie	161
SB	Bernard, Wynton, West Michigan	45

PITCHING · #Minimum 75 IP

MAJORS

W	Scherzer, Max	18
# ERA	Scherzer, Max	3.15
SO	Scherzer, Max	252
SV	Nathan, Joe	35

MINORS

W	Farmer, Buck, West Michigan, Erie, Toledo	12
L	Hankins, Derek, Toledo	14
# ERA	Ziomek, Kevin, West Michigan	2.27
G	Nesbitt, Angel, Lakeland, Erie	48
GS	Hankins, Derek, Toledo	27
	Saupold, Warwick, Erie	27
SV	Nesbitt, Angel, Lakeland, Erie	20
	Whelan, Kevin, Toledo	20
IP	Ryan, Kyle, Erie, Toledo	160
BB	Saupold, Warwick, Erie	65
SO	Ziomek, Kevin, West Michigan	152
AVG	Ziomek, Kevin, West Michigan	.201

General Manager: Dave Dombrowski. **Farm Director:** Dan Lunetta. **Scouting Director:** Scott Pleis.

Class	Team	League	W	L		Finish	Manager
Majors	Detroit Tigers	American	90	72	.556	t-5th (30)	Brad Ausmus
Triple-A	Toledo Mud Hens	International	69	74	.483	8th (14)	Larry Parrish
Double-A	Erie SeaWolves	Eastern	71	71	.500	7th (12)	Lance Parrish
High A	Lakeland Flying Tigers	Florida State	62	75	.453	10th (12)	Dave Huppert/Bill Dancy
Low A	West Michigan Whitecaps	Midwest	82	58	.586	3rd (16)	Andrew Graham
Short season	Connecticut Tigers	New York-Penn	42	34	.553	t-4th (14)	Mike Rabelo
Rookie	Tigers	Gulf Coast	34	25	.576	6th (16)	Basilio Cabrera
Overall Minor League Record			360	337	.516	9th (30)	

ORGANIZATION STATISTICS

DETROIT TIGERS
AMERICAN LEAGUE

Batting	B-T	HT	WT	DOB	AVG	vLH	vRH	G	AB	R	H	2B	3B	HR	RBI	BB	HBP	SH	SF	SO	SB	CS	SLG	OBP
Avila, Alex	L-R	5-11	210	1-29-87	.218	.226	.215	124	390	44	85	22	0	11	47	61	3	1	2	151	0	3	.359	.327
Cabrera, Miguel	R-R	6-4	240	4-18-83	.313	.301	.317	159	611	101	191	52	1	25	109	60	3	0	11	117	1	1	.524	.371
Carrera, Ezequiel	L-L	5-10	185	6-11-87	.261	.357	.236	45	69	12	18	4	1	0	2	3	1	0	0	14	7	1	.348	.301
Castellanos, Nick	R-R	6-4	210	3-4-92	.259	.237	.266	148	533	50	138	31	4	11	66	36	3	0	7	140	2	2	.394	.306
Collins, Tyler	L-L	5-11	215	6-6-90	.250	.200	.263	18	24	3	6	0	0	1	4	1	0	0	0	4	0	0	.375	.280
Davis, Rajai	R-R	5-9	195	10-19-80	.282	.356	.247	134	461	64	130	27	2	8	51	22	5	3	3	75	36	11	.401	.320
Gonzalez, Alex	R-R	6-1	210	2-15-77	.167	.200	.160	9	30	4	5	0	1	0	2	2	0	0	0	4	0	0	.233	.219
Holaday, Bryan	R-R	6-0	205	11-19-87	.231	.151	.301	62	156	14	36	5	1	0	15	8	1	2	4	37	1	1	.276	.266
Hunter, Torii	R-R	6-2	225	7-18-75	.286	.308	.278	142	549	71	157	33	2	17	83	23	7	0	7	89	4	3	.446	.319
Jackson, Austin	R-R	6-1	185	2-1-87	.273	.330	.252	100	374	52	102	25	5	4	33	35	2	1	8	85	9	4	.398	.332
2-team total (54 Seattle)					.256	—	154	597	71	153	30	6	4	47	47	2	1	9	144	20	6	.347	.308
Kelly, Don	L-R	6-4	190	2-15-80	.245	.120	.268	95	163	24	40	5	1	0	7	20	1	1	0	29	6	1	.288	.332
Kinsler, Ian	R-R	6-0	200	6-22-82	.275	.281	.273	161	684	100	188	40	4	17	92	29	5	3	5	79	15	4	.420	.307
Martinez, J.D.	R-R	6-3	220	8-21-87	.315	.307	.318	123	441	57	139	30	3	23	76	30	3	0	6	126	6	3	.553	.358
Martinez, Victor	B-R	6-2	210	12-23-78	.335	.371	.323	151	561	87	188	33	0	32	103	70	4	0	6	42	3	2	.565	.409
McCann, James	R-R	6-2	210	6-13-90	.250	.167	.333	9	12	2	3	1	0	0	0	0	0	0	0	2	1	0	.333	.250
Moya, Steven	L-R	6-6	230	8-9-91	.375	.000	.429	11	8	2	3	0	0	0	0	0	0	0	0	2	0	0	.375	.375
Perez, Hernan	R-R	6-1	185	3-26-91	.200	.000	.333	8	5	1	1	0	0	0	0	1	0	0	0	1	0	0	.200	.333
Romine, Andrew	L-R	6-1	200	12-24-85	.227	.333	.198	94	251	30	57	6	0	2	12	18	0	4	0	60	12	2	.275	.279
Suarez, Eugenio	B-R	5-11	180	7-18-91	.242	.238	.244	85	244	33	59	9	1	4	23	22	5	5	1	67	3	2	.336	.316
Worth, Danny	R-R	6-1	185	9-30-85	.167	.087	.263	18	42	5	7	1	0	0	5	2	1	0	1	12	0	1	.190	.217

Pitching	B-T	HT	WT	DOB	W	L	ERA	G	GS	CG	SV	IP	H	R	ER	HR	BB	SO	AVG	vLH	vRH	K/9	BB/9
Alburquerque, Al	R-R	6-0	195	6-10-86	3	1	2.51	72	0	0	1	57	46	16	16	7	21	63	.219	.245	.190	9.89	3.30
Chamberlain, Joba	R-R	6-2	250	9-23-85	2	5	3.57	69	0	0	2	63	57	26	25	3	24	59	.245	.252	.237	8.43	3.43
Coke, Phil	L-L	6-1	210	7-19-82	5	2	3.88	62	0	0	1	58	69	28	25	5	20	41	.299	.257	.333	6.36	3.10
Farmer, Buck	L-R	6-4	225	2-20-91	0	1	11.57	4	2	0	0	9	12	12	12	2	5	11	.308	.364	.235	10.61	4.82
Hardy, Blaine	L-L	6-2	230	3-14-87	2	1	2.54	38	0	0	0	39	34	12	11	1	20	31	.238	.203	.266	7.15	4.62
Johnson, Jim	R-R	6-6	240	6-27-83	1	0	6.92	16	0	0	0	13	9	13	10	0	12	14	.191	.182	.200	9.69	8.31
2-team total (38 Oakland)					5	2	7.09	54	0	0	2	53	69	46	42	5	35	42	—	—	—	7.09	5.91
Knebel, Corey	R-R	6-3	195	11-26-91	0	0	6.23	8	0	0	0	9	11	7	6	0	3	11	.306	.300	.313	11.42	3.12
Krol, Ian	L-L	6-1	210	5-9-91	0	0	4.96	45	0	0	1	33	42	23	18	6	13	28	.304	.261	.348	7.71	3.58
Lobstein, Kyle	L-L	6-3	200	8-12-89	1	2	4.35	7	6	0	0	39	35	20	19	3	14	27	.236	.217	.245	6.18	3.20
McCoy, Pat	L-L	6-3	200	8-3-88	0	0	3.86	14	0	0	0	14	21	6	6	0	13	11	.344	.208	.432	7.07	8.36
Mercedes, Melvin	R-R	6-3	250	11-2-90	0	0	0.00	1	0	0	0	2	0	0	0	0	2	0	.000	.000	.000	9.00	9.00
Miller, Justin	R-R	6-3	215	6-13-87	1	0	5.11	8	0	0	0	12	14	9	7	2	2	5	.292	.222	.333	3.65	1.46
Nathan, Joe	R-R	6-4	230	11-22-74	5	4	4.81	62	0	0	35	58	60	32	31	5	29	54	.265	.280	.245	8.38	4.50
Ortega, Jose	R-R	5-11	185	10-12-88	0	1	27.00	1	0	0	0	1	4	3	3	0	3	1	1.000	.000	.000	6.75	27.00
Porcello, Rick	R-R	6-5	200	12-27-88	15	13	3.43	32	31	3	0	205	211	89	78	18	41	129	.268	.268	.268	5.67	1.80
Price, David	L-L	6-6	210	8-26-85	4	4	3.59	11	11	1	0	78	74	32	31	5	15	82	.243	.264	.235	9.50	1.74
2-team total (23 Tampa Bay)					15	12	3.26	34	34	3	0	248	230	100	90	25	38	271	—	—	—	9.82	1.38
Putkonen, Luke	R-R	6-6	215	5-10-86	0	0	27.00	2	0	0	0	3	6	8	8	2	2	1	.400	.333	.444	3.38	6.75
Ray, Robbie	L-L	6-2	195	10-1-91	1	4	8.16	9	6	0	0	29	43	26	26	5	11	19	.350	.351	.349	5.97	3.45
Reed, Evan	R-R	6-4	255	12-31-85	0	1	4.18	32	0	0	0	32	39	19	15	2	12	26	.302	.305	.300	7.24	3.34
Ryan, Kyle	L-L	6-5	180	9-25-91	2	0	2.61	6	1	0	0	10	10	3	3	0	2	4	.256	.300	.241	3.48	1.74
Sanchez, Anibal	R-R	6-0	205	2-27-84	8	5	3.43	22	21	0	0	126	108	55	48	4	30	102	.228	.219	.241	7.29	2.14
Scherzer, Max	R-R	6-3	220	7-27-84	18	5	3.15	33	33	1	0	220	196	80	77	18	63	252	.238	.242	.232	10.29	2.57
Smith, Chad	R-R	6-3	215	10-2-89	0	0	5.40	10	0	0	0	12	15	7	7	1	3	9	.319	.417	.217	6.94	2.31
Smyly, Drew	L-L	6-3	190	6-13-89	6	9	3.93	21	18	0	0	105	111	48	46	14	31	89	.271	.176	.309	7.60	2.65
2-team total (7 Tampa Bay)					9	10	3.24	28	25	1	0	153	136	57	55	18	42	133	—	—	—	7.82	2.47
Soria, Joakim	R-R	6-3	200	5-18-84	1	1	4.91	13	0	0	1	11	13	7	6	2	2	6	.289	.238	.333	4.91	1.64
2-team total (35 Texas)					2	4	3.25	48	0	0	18	44	38	19	16	2	6	48	—	—	—	9.74	1.22
VerHagen, Drew	R-R	6-6	230	10-22-90	0	1	5.40	1	1	0	0	5	5	3	3	0	3	4	.294	.308	.250	7.20	5.40
Verlander, Justin	R-R	6-5	225	2-20-83	15	12	4.54	32	32	0	0	206	223	114	104	18	65	159	.275	.239	.321	6.95	2.84
Whelan, Kevin	R-R	5-11	205	1-8-84	0	0	13.50	1	0	0	0	1	3	2	2	2	2	1	.429	.250	.667	6.75	13.50

Fielding

Catcher	PCT	G	PO	A	E	DP	PB
Avila	.995	122	883	52	5	9	3
Holaday	.981	58	333	23	7	2	4
Martinez	.926	2	23	2	2	0	1
McCann	1.000	6	22	1	0	0	0

First Base	PCT	G	PO	A	E	DP
Avila	—	1	0	0	0	0
Cabrera	.995	126	978	98	5	100
Kelly	.988	30	72	7	1	10
Martinez	.989	35	251	16	3	24
Worth	.000	1	0	0	1	0

Second Base	PCT	G	PO	A	E	DP
Kelly	—	1	0	0	0	0

	PCT	G	PO	A	E	DP
Kinsler	.988	160	290	467	9	101
Perez	1.000	5	1	2	0	1
Romine	1.000	12	7	5	0	2
Worth	1.000	3	2	0	0	0

Third Base	PCT	G	PO	A	E	DP
Cabrera	.950	10	6	13	1	2
Castellanos	.950	145	75	212	15	22
Gonzalez	—	1	0	0	0	0
Kelly	.975	41	8	31	1	3
Perez	—	2	0	0	0	0
Suarez	1.000	2	1	1	0	0

Shortstop	PCT	G	PO	A	E	DP
Gonzalez	.903	9	7	21	3	5

	PCT	G	PO	A	E	DP
Perez	1.000	1	2	0	0	0
Romine	.975	83	111	206	8	46
Suarez	.968	81	113	189	10	49
Worth	1.000	13	27	31	0	14

Outfield	PCT	G	PO	A	E	DP
Carrera	1.000	39	51	1	0	0
Collins	1.000	11	14	0	0	0
Davis	.983	125	277	6	5	1
Hunter	.978	128	218	5	5	1
Jackson	.984	100	247	2	4	1
Kelly	1.000	25	50	0	0	0
Martinez	.980	111	198	1	4	0
Moya	—	5	0	0	0	0

TOLEDO MUD HENS

TRIPLE-A

INTERNATIONAL LEAGUE

Batting	B-T	HT	WT	DOB	AVG	vLH	vRH	G	AB	R	H	2B	3B	HR	RBI	BB	HBP	SH	SF	SO	SB	CS	SLG	OBP
Carrera, Ezequiel	L-L	5-10	185	6-11-87	.307	.290	.315	97	374	68	115	15	5	6	41	48	3	5	4	65	43	13	.422	.387
Collins, Tyler	L-L	5-11	215	6-6-90	.263	.233	.275	121	468	63	123	17	2	18	62	49	4	0	5	116	12	4	.423	.335
Crowe, Trevor	B-R	5-10	190	11-17-83	.240	.217	.247	66	258	27	62	16	0	4	26	19	0	0	1	40	8	7	.349	.291
Dirks, Andy	L-L	6-0	195	1-24-86	.400	—	.400	2	5	1	2	1	0	0	1	0	0	0	0	0	2	0	0	.600	.400
Douglas, Brandon	R-R	6-0	200	8-27-85	.228	.234	.225	82	263	32	60	14	1	4	28	24	2	6	4	43	5	2	.335	.294
Exposito, Luis	R-R	6-3	210	12-20-87	.177	.152	.190	29	96	9	17	4	0	3	10	9	1	0	1	29	0	0	.313	.252
Fields, Daniel	L-R	6-2	215	1-23-91	.219	.259	.202	75	274	29	60	10	3	6	26	15	6	2	2	76	8	2	.343	.273
Gaynor, Wade	R-R	6-3	225	4-19-88	.221	.308	.190	84	299	37	66	21	2	7	34	23	2	3	3	100	12	1	.375	.278
Guez, Ben	R-R	5-11	180	1-24-87	.230	.296	.204	119	404	55	93	24	3	16	50	37	17	2	2	129	7	6	.423	.320
Hanzawa, Troy	R-R	5-9	155	9-12-85	.103	.214	.000	10	29	1	3	0	0	0	1	0	0	1	0	8	0	0	.103	.103
2-team total (14 Lehigh Valley)					.119			24	67	3	8	1	0	0	4	2	2	1	16	0	1	.134	.167
Hessman, Mike	R-R	6-5	215	3-5-78	.248	.222	.256	116	420	62	104	18	2	28	64	53	3	0	9	116	5	2	.500	.330
Kengor, Will	L-R	6-3	180	7-24-92	.000	.000	.000	1	3	0	0	0	0	0	0	0	0	0	0	0	0	0	.000	.000
Lemon, Marcus	L-R	5-11	173	6-3-88	.132	.111	.136	21	53	3	7	1	0	0	1	6	0	0	0	13	0	1	.151	.220
Lennerton, Jordan	L-L	6-2	230	2-16-86	.249	.211	.262	121	410	54	102	26	2	10	53	73	1	2	2	114	0	1	.395	.362
Martinez, J.D.	R-R	6-3	220	8-21-87	.308	.125	.367	17	65	16	20	3	1	10	22	3	0	0	0	17	2	0	.846	.366
McCann, James	B-R	6-2	210	6-13-90	.295	.342	.276	109	417	49	123	34	0	7	54	25	9	2	7	90	9	2	.427	.343
Perez, Hernan	R-R	6-1	185	3-26-91	.287	.280	.290	133	547	69	157	32	7	6	53	36	2	7	4	65	21	6	.404	.331
Pina, Manny	R-R	6-0	215	6-5-87	.268	.138	.303	38	138	18	37	4	0	3	16	11	1	1	3	19	2	0	.362	.320
Suarez, Eugenio	B-R	5-11	180	7-18-91	.302	.429	.241	12	43	6	13	4	0	2	7	6	2	0	1	9	2	0	.535	.404
Worth, Danny	R-R	6-1	185	9-30-85	.211	.273	.196	66	223	19	47	15	1	1	18	27	0	1	0	87	9	0	.300	.296

Pitching	B-T	HT	WT	DOB	W	L	ERA	G	GS	CG	SV	IP	H	R	ER	HR	BB	SO	AVG	vLH	vRH	K/9	BB/9
Augenstein, Bryan	R-R	6-6	230	7-11-86	0	0	0.00	2	0	0	0	2	1	0	0	0	0	2	.143	.333	.000	7.71	7.71
Belfiore, Mike	R-L	6-3	220	10-3-88	5	7	3.25	35	13	0	0	91	92	38	33	10	36	60	.262	.262	.262	5.91	3.55
Below, Duane	L-L	6-3	220	11-15-85	8	5	3.70	22	21	0	0	117	124	51	48	11	41	62	.283	.219	.306	4.78	3.16
Burgos, Alex	L-L	5-11	195	12-1-90	0	0	—	1	0	0	0	0	0	0	0	0	1	0	—	—	—	—	—
Crosby, Casey	R-L	6-5	225	9-17-88	0	0	5.71	11	0	0	0	17	15	15	11	2	13	12	.227	.304	.186	6.23	6.75
Farmer, Buck	L-R	6-4	225	2-20-91	1	1	9.82	2	2	0	0	7	11	9	8	1	4	2	.355	.368	.333	2.45	4.91
Faulk, Kenny	L-L	6-0	235	5-27-87	1	0	1.62	11	0	0	0	17	5	3	3	0	11	20	.093	.000	.125	10.80	5.94
Hankins, Derek	R-R	6-4	195	7-1-83	7	14	5.15	28	27	1	0	152	189	94	87	16	38	71	.306	.284	.332	4.20	2.25
Hardy, Blaine	L-L	6-2	230	3-14-87	3	2	2.68	20	6	0	0	47	35	14	14	2	13	53	.208	.214	.205	10.15	2.49
Hill, Shawn	R-R	6-2	225	4-28-81	3	1	3.28	4	4	0	0	25	28	9	9	0	4	8	.295	.280	.311	2.92	1.46
3-team total (6 Buffalo, 10 Charlotte)					7	6	4.49	20	17	0	0	112	133	61	56	13	27	56	—	—	—	4.49	2.16
Johnson, Jim	R-R	6-6	240	6-27-83	0	1	3.86	4	0	0	0	5	4	3	2	1	2	2	.211	.222	.200	3.86	1.93
Knebel, Corey	R-R	6-3	195	11-26-91	1	1	1.96	14	0	0	2	18	6	4	4	0	9	20	.109	.115	.103	9.82	4.42
Krol, Ian	L-L	6-1	210	5-9-91	0	0	3.86	8	0	0	0	7	11	3	3	1	1	12	.344	.375	.333	15.43	1.29
Lobstein, Kyle	L-L	6-3	200	8-12-89	9	11	4.07	26	25	1	0	146	174	71	66	10	42	127	.293	.302	.283	7.83	2.59
Marinez, Jhan	R-R	6-1	200	8-12-88	1	2	8.84	12	0	0	0	18	23	20	18	4	21	21	.315	.500	.154	10.31	10.31
McCoy, Pat	L-L	6-3	220	8-3-88	2	0	2.59	21	0	0	0	31	25	10	9	3	6	25	.225	.194	.240	7.18	1.72
Mercedes, Melvin	R-R	6-3	250	11-2-90	0	3	4.92	46	0	0	3	60	69	35	33	8	16	31	.284	.309	.267	4.62	2.39
Miller, Justin	R-R	6-3	215	6-13-87	2	1	1.81	38	0	0	5	45	30	9	9	2	12	39	.194	.205	.183	7.86	2.42
Ortega, Jose	R-R	5-11	185	10-12-88	2	3	3.57	43	1	0	1	58	50	25	23	4	36	48	.228	.248	.212	7.45	5.59
Putkonen, Luke	R-R	6-6	215	5-10-86	0	0	11.25	2	0	0	0	4	7	5	5	1	1	0	.389	.500	.300	0.00	2.25
Ray, Robbie	L-L	6-2	195	10-1-91	7	6	4.22	20	19	0	0	100	106	51	47	6	44	75	.277	.273	.279	6.73	3.95
Reed, Evan	R-R	6-4	255	12-31-85	0	1	4.24	17	1	0	0	23	26	11	11	0	5	26	.289	.275	.300	10.03	1.93
Robertson, Nate	R-L	6-2	225	9-3-77	0	2	3.43	14	0	0	0	21	20	13	8	0	13	12	.250	.290	.224	5.14	5.57
Ryan, Kyle	L-L	6-5	180	9-25-91	3	0	1.64	5	5	0	0	33	21	8	6	0	5	20	.184	.091	.207	5.45	1.36
Schlereth, Daniel	L-L	6-0	210	5-9-86	1	1	4.50	17	0	0	0	18	19	13	9	1	11	16	.264	.400	.212	8.00	5.50
2-team total (21 Indianapolis)					2	3	5.89	38	0	0	0	37	37	32	24	3	29	34	—	—	—	8.35	7.12
Sitz, Scott	R-R	5-10	210	9-10-90	1	0	0.00	1	0	0	0	1	1	0	0	0	2	2	.250	.000	.333	18.00	0.00
Smith, Chad	R-R	6-3	215	10-2-89	4	3	5.00	22	0	0	0	27	38	15	15	2	5	22	.345	.316	.361	7.33	1.67
Startup, Will	L-L	6-0	195	8-4-84	0	0	0.00	1	0	0	0	3	2	0	0	0	1	2	.182	.000	.250	5.40	2.70
VerHagen, Drew	R-R	6-6	230	10-22-90	6	7	3.67	19	19	0	0	110	117	47	45	5	25	63	.275	.298	.251	5.14	2.04
Whelan, Kevin	R-R	5-11	205	1-8-84	2	3	2.70	41	0	0	20	43	30	13	13	0	21	54	.190	.167	.209	11.22	4.36

DETROIT TIGERS

DETROIT TIGERS

Fielding

Catcher	PCT	G	PO	A	E	DP	PB
Exposito	.965	19	129	8	5	1	3
McCann	.993	98	630	44	5	7	5
Pina	1.000	26	162	22	0	2	3

First Base	PCT	G	PO	A	E	DP
Douglas	1.000	1	2	0	0	0
Gaynor	.994	24	170	7	1	18
Hessman	1.000	2	8	2	0	1
Lennerton	1.000	121	1058	69	0	107
Worth	1.000	2	10	1	0	1

Second Base	PCT	G	PO	A	E	DP
Douglas	.985	69	151	184	5	42
Hanzawa	.973	9	15	21	1	4

Kengor	1.000	1	1	3	0	0
Lemon	.983	13	19	38	1	5
Perez	1.000	14	20	38	0	12
Worth	.977	43	90	127	5	43

Third Base	PCT	G	PO	A	E	DP
Douglas	.895	12	10	24	4	2
Gaynor	.931	40	28	66	7	3
Hessman	.960	86	58	179	10	25
McCann	.500	1	0	1	1	0
Worth	.938	10	1	14	1	0

Shortstop	PCT	G	PO	A	E	DP
Lemon	1.000	2	4	7	0	2
Perez	.970	118	175	334	16	71

Suarez	.960	12	21	27	2	8
Worth	.985	12	22	43	1	9

Outfield	PCT	G	PO	A	E	DP
Carrera	.992	94	231	4	2	0
Collins	.962	118	217	13	9	1
Crowe	1.000	14	24	0	0	0
Dirks	—	1	0	0	0	0
Douglas	—	1	0	0	0	0
Exposito	1.000	1	1	0	0	0
Fields	1.000	72	175	2	0	0
Gaynor	.964	18	27	0	1	0
Guez	.992	105	242	7	2	3
Lemon	1.000	4	1	0	0	0
Martinez	1.000	12	19	0	0	0

ERIE SEAWOLVES — DOUBLE-A

EASTERN LEAGUE

Batting	B-T	HT	WT	DOB	AVG	vLH	vRH	G	AB	R	H	2B	3B	HR	RBI	BB	HBP	SH	SF	SO	SB	CS	SLG	OBP
Albernaz, Craig	R-R	5-8	185	10-30-82	.181	.208	.165	66	204	19	37	6	0	0	17	10	4	13	1	43	7	2	.211	.233
Cabrera, Ramon	B-R	5-8	195	11-5-89	.277	.305	.259	107	394	42	109	17	0	5	47	33	0	0	4	37	1	0	.358	.329
2-team total (12 Altoona)					.273	—	—	119	440	47	120	22	0	6	52	36	0	0	4	43	1	1	.364	.325
Fields, Daniel	L-R	6-2	215	1-23-91	.286	.556	.158	8	28	4	8	3	1	0	9	6	1	0	0	7	2	0	.464	.429
Gaynor, Wade	R-R	6-3	225	4-19-88	.293	.405	.175	27	82	17	24	10	1	6	16	9	0	0	0	30	0	0	.659	.363
Green, Dean	L-R	6-4	255	6-30-89	.311	.349	.293	113	409	51	127	26	1	10	65	28	8	0	2	80	0	1	.452	.365
Hanover, Tyler	R-R	5-7	170	8-25-89	.125	.000	.250	2	8	0	1	1	0	0	0	0	0	0	0	2	0	0	.250	.125
Johnson, Jamie	L-R	5-9	180	4-26-87	.258	.233	.272	118	446	71	115	20	5	5	37	63	1	7	5	52	11	5	.359	.348
Jones, Corey	L-R	6-0	205	9-14-87	.304	.231	.333	113	415	42	126	31	2	5	42	24	6	4	4	73	5	7	.424	.347
Krizan, Jason	L-R	6-0	185	6-28-89	.293	.217	.327	124	464	68	136	31	2	7	56	53	1	3	4	47	14	7	.414	.364
Lemon, Marcus	L-R	5-11	173	6-3-88	.252	.368	.215	50	159	24	40	9	1	3	14	12	1	3	1	31	1	3	.377	.306
Longley, Andrew	R-R	6-3	215	10-5-88	.240	.429	.167	8	25	4	6	0	1	0	3	1	0	0	0	12	0	0	.320	.269
Loy, Brandon	R-R	6-0	190	5-3-90	.209	.160	.278	14	43	7	9	2	0	0	2	4	0	2	0	6	0	0	.256	.277
Machado, Dixon	R-R	6-1	170	2-22-92	.305	.295	.310	90	292	45	89	23	1	5	32	40	3	4	3	36	8	7	.442	.391
Martinez, Francisco	R-R	6-2	210	9-1-90	.224	.295	.169	93	317	33	71	12	0	1	29	18	1	1	3	72	21	3	.271	.265
Moya, Steven	L-R	6-6	230	8-9-91	.276	.262	.284	133	515	81	142	33	3	35	105	23	3	0	8	161	16	4	.555	.306
Suarez, Eugenio	B-R	5-11	180	7-18-91	.284	.393	.213	42	155	26	44	14	1	6	29	15	0	0	0	38	7	2	.503	.347
Travis, Devon	R-R	5-9	195	2-21-91	.298	.254	.320	100	396	68	118	20	7	10	52	37	2	2	4	60	16	5	.460	.358
Westlake, Aaron	L-R	6-4	235	12-27-88	.236	.211	.251	116	419	53	99	20	1	15	49	32	3	0	4	120	8	5	.396	.293

Pitching	B-T	HT	WT	DOB	W	L	ERA	G	GS	CG	SV	IP	H	R	ER	HR	BB	SO	AVG	vLH	vRH	K/9	BB/9
Augenstein, Bryan	R-R	6-6	230	7-11-86	4	1	5.44	28	0	0	1	45	47	28	27	4	12	41	.266	.292	.250	8.26	2.42
Avila, Nick	R-R	6-2	220	8-29-88	0	4	6.15	16	4	0	0	34	47	32	23	10	14	20	.324	.370	.278	5.35	3.74
Burgos, Alex	L-L	5-11	195	12-1-90	0	0	0.00	1	0	0	0	1	0	0	0	0	1	2	.000	.000	.000	18.00	9.00
Collier, Tommy	R-R	6-2	205	12-3-89	4	7	5.88	17	17	1	0	86	86	61	56	14	39	48	.263	.267	.260	5.04	4.10
Crouse, Matt	L-L	6-4	185	7-1-90	0	0	2.08	2	1	0	0	4	4	2	1	0	3	4	.235	.500	.200	8.31	6.23
Farmer, Buck	R-R	6-4	225	2-20-91	1	0	3.00	2	2	0	0	12	10	4	4	1	4	11	.222	.136	.304	8.25	3.00
Faulk, Kenny	L-L	6-0	235	5-27-87	2	3	5.24	31	1	0	1	45	37	29	26	4	30	57	.231	.278	.208	11.49	6.04
Ferrell, Jeff	R-R	6-3	185	11-23-90	10	9	5.54	25	25	0	0	138	174	85	85	17	38	92	.309	.304	.313	6.00	2.48
Knebel, Corey	R-R	6-3	195	11-26-91	3	0	1.20	11	0	0	1	15	8	4	2	1	8	23	.154	.158	.152	13.80	4.80
Knudson, Guido	R-R	6-1	185	8-5-89	1	6	4.26	28	2	0	2	61	64	31	29	4	26	66	.274	.306	.250	9.68	3.82
Mantiply, Joe	R-L	6-4	215	3-1-91	0	0	3.38	8	0	0	1	11	12	5	4	1	3	10	.293	.333	.269	8.44	2.53
McCoy, Pat	L-L	6-3	220	8-3-88	1	0	3.95	9	0	0	1	14	16	8	6	0	3	9	.286	.235	.308	5.93	1.98
Nesbitt, Angel	R-R	6-1	237	12-4-90	1	0	2.23	24	0	0	6	32	20	8	8	3	15	36	.177	.125	.228	10.02	4.18
Palacios, Wilsen	R-R	6-3	180	12-15-89	10	4	4.58	26	25	0	0	134	158	75	68	15	55	90	.292	.314	.270	6.06	3.70
Robowski, Ryan	L-L	6-0	185	2-3-88	4	1	4.06	39	5	0	4	78	71	37	35	9	34	77	.241	.219	.253	8.92	3.94
Ryan, Kyle	L-L	6-5	180	9-25-91	7	10	4.55	21	21	1	0	127	140	67	64	15	32	78	.285	.224	.306	5.54	2.27
Saupold, Warwick	R-R	6-1	195	1-16-90	8	11	5.01	27	27	2	0	140	141	92	78	16	65	125	.266	.285	.247	8.04	4.18
Smith, Brennan	R-R	6-3	200	8-4-89	0	1	6.75	8	0	0	0	11	12	8	8	2	1	11	.279	.176	.346	9.28	1.69
Smith, Chad	R-R	6-3	215	10-2-89	1	0	1.35	12	0	0	1	20	15	3	3	0	6	18	.208	.188	.225	8.10	2.70
Smith, Slade	R-R	6-2	190	9-26-90	3	6	5.92	33	1	0	0	52	78	38	34	4	11	25	.350	.354	.346	4.35	1.92
Startup, Will	L-L	6-0	195	8-4-84	5	1	5.47	36	0	0	0	49	59	32	30	7	21	31	.295	.322	.284	5.66	3.83
Thompson, Jake	R-R	6-4	235	1-31-94	1	0	2.45	2	2	0	0	11	10	3	3	0	4	7	.238	.233	.250	5.73	3.27
Turley, Josh	L-L	6-0	185	8-26-90	3	4	3.78	9	9	0	0	50	53	22	21	8	16	28	.273	.250	.281	5.04	2.88
Valdez, Jose	R-R	6-1	200	3-1-90	2	3	4.11	47	0	0	18	57	56	27	26	6	26	66	.257	.269	.248	10.42	4.11

Fielding

Catcher	PCT	G	PO	A	E	DP	PB
Albernaz	.986	66	430	63	7	6	3
Cabrera	.994	73	480	29	3	1	4
Longley	.985	8	60	6	1	0	2

First Base	PCT	G	PO	A	E	DP
Gaynor	1.000	2	10	0	0	2
Green	.979	22	173	12	4	18
Jones	.977	10	79	5	2	5

Westlake	.990	113	840	76	9	74

Second Base	PCT	G	PO	A	E	DP
Jones	.990	26	42	62	1	14
Lemon	.900	10	12	24	4	7
Loy	.981	13	22	31	1	7
Travis	.974	95	183	235	11	42

Third Base	PCT	G	PO	A	E	DP
Gaynor	.800	4	2	6	2	0
Jones	.932	60	31	92	9	7
Martinez	.927	85	53	151	16	15

Shortstop	PCT	G	PO	A	E	DP
Lemon	.974	13	15	23	1	3
Loy	.500	1	0	1	1	0
Machado	.965	90	164	222	14	42

	PCT	G	PO	A	E	DP			PCT	G	PO	A	E	DP			PCT	G	PO	A	E	DP
Martinez	.700	3	2	5	3	1		Gaynor	1.000	11	23	1	0	0		Krizan	.993	120	261	6	2	0
Suarez	.962	42	71	106	7	31		Hanover	1.000	2	6	0	0	0		Lemon	1.000	23	46	2	0	2
Outfield	PCT	G	PO	A	E	DP		Johnson	.979	115	270	9	6	1		Moya	.989	131	271	8	3	3
Fields	1.000	8	13	0	0	0		Jones	1.000	18	32	0	0	0		Travis	1.000	3	7	0	0	0

LAKELAND FLYING TIGERS

HIGH CLASS A

FLORIDA STATE LEAGUE

Batting	B-T	HT	WT	DOB	AVG	vLH	vRH	G	AB	R	H	2B	3B	HR	RBI	BB	HBP	SH	SF	SO	SB	CS	SLG	OBP
Castro, Harold	L-R	6-0	165	11-30-93	.299	.222	.319	57	211	17	63	5	0	0	10	9	3	8	1	40	8	8	.322	.335
Dirks, Andy	L-L	6-0	195	1-24-86	.313	—	.313	7	16	4	5	1	0	0	1	2	0	0	0	4	0	2	.375	.389
Durham, Lance	L-R	5-11	210	2-20-88	.221	.119	.251	106	375	37	83	17	3	4	47	44	2	0	3	126	1	1	.315	.304
Gibson, Tyler	L-R	6-2	210	6-17-93	.107	.000	.136	19	56	7	6	0	1	1	2	9	0	1	0	28	0	0	.196	.231
Gonzalez, David	R-R	5-9	140	12-1-93	.125	.000	.143	5	8	3	1	0	0	0	0	1	0	0	0	1	0	0	.125	.222
Green, Austin	R-R	6-1	200	2-22-90	.263	.252	.267	107	403	47	106	17	3	15	53	20	6	1	3	73	2	2	.432	.306
Hanover, Tyler	R-R	5-7	170	8-25-89	.242	.223	.250	116	376	44	91	21	7	2	28	25	5	10	3	50	6	5	.351	.296
Harrell, Connor	R-R	6-3	215	3-24-91	.270	.242	.280	131	485	66	131	26	3	14	66	37	19	0	3	135	15	3	.423	.344
Holm, Jeff	L-L	6-3	220	10-17-88	.215	.051	.286	34	130	14	28	6	1	4	18	17	1	0	3	26	1	2	.369	.305
Longley, Andrew	R-R	6-3	215	10-5-88	.203	.146	.232	37	123	6	25	3	0	0	8	6	0	1	1	38	0	1	.228	.238
Loy, Brandon	R-R	6-0	190	5-3-90	.182	.182	.182	7	22	1	4	0	0	0	1	2	0	1	0	4	3	0	.182	.250
Machado, Dixon	R-R	6-1	170	2-22-92	.252	.254	.250	41	159	30	40	8	1	1	8	23	1	3	1	34	2	1	.333	.348
McVaney, Jeff	R-R	6-2	210	1-16-90	.273	.218	.292	132	494	61	135	29	6	11	74	45	12	0	5	87	17	7	.423	.345
Negron, Steven	B-R	5-8	175	5-13-93	.000	—	.000	1	2	0	0	0	0	0	0	0	0	0	0	1	0	0	.000	.000
Powell, Curt	R-R	6-0	180	4-30-91	.266	.216	.284	117	443	49	118	19	6	2	44	27	3	7	1	113	9	2	.350	.312
Reaves, Jared	R-R	5-10	185	7-20-90	.236	.202	.247	94	335	31	79	12	1	3	21	21	4	4	1	69	4	3	.304	.288
Robbins, James	L-L	6-0	225	9-26-90	.231	.182	.247	124	458	47	106	27	0	17	55	18	6	3	5	154	0	2	.402	.267
Thomas, Michael	R-R	5-11	210	1-27-91	.118	.000	.200	6	17	0	2	0	0	0	1	0	0	0	0	9	0	0	.118	.118
Wright, Chad	L-R	5-10	198	7-27-89	.249	.197	.272	121	457	62	114	19	1	3	35	52	2	4	2	88	9	3	.315	.327

Pitching	B-T	HT	WT	DOB	W	L	ERA	G	GS	CG	SV	IP	H	R	ER	HR	BB	SO	AVG	vLH	vRH	K/9	BB/9
Bailey, Tanner	R-R	6-6	240	7-6-90	2	4	3.75	8	6	2	0	36	32	18	15	4	12	14	.242	.262	.224	3.50	3.00
Briceno, Endrys	R-R	6-5	171	2-7-92	0	0	3.38	3	3	0	0	16	16	6	6	1	3	7	.262	.297	.208	3.94	1.69
Burgos, Alex	L-L	5-11	195	12-1-90	2	4	4.26	25	2	0	2	61	58	33	29	4	34	58	.257	.264	.252	8.51	4.99
Clark, Tyler	B-R	6-2	185	1-4-89	3	3	6.15	25	0	0	0	34	37	26	23	4	26	35	.264	.263	.265	9.36	6.95
Collier, Tommy	R-R	6-2	205	12-3-89	3	3	3.80	9	9	0	0	47	49	24	20	5	16	40	.271	.239	.301	7.61	3.04
De La Rosa, Edgar	R-R	6-8	235	11-12-90	7	9	3.30	26	26	1	0	139	116	64	51	13	53	91	.230	.211	.246	5.89	3.43
Drummond, Calvin	R-R	6-3	200	9-22-89	3	3	3.97	35	0	0	1	45	44	31	20	4	33	65	.242	.247	.237	12.90	6.55
Edwards, Chase	R-R	6-1	180	2-4-94	0	0	3.00	1	0	0	0	3	4	1	1	1	0	3	.364	.250	.429	0.00	0.00
Ehlers, Logan	L-L	6-1	190	10-30-91	4	4	4.97	26	5	0	0	71	89	43	39	6	23	46	.312	.314	.311	5.86	2.93
Eichhorn, Kevin	R-R	6-0	175	2-6-90	5	2	2.40	17	14	0	0	94	83	26	25	4	26	63	.243	.241	.244	6.05	2.50
Ford, Tyler	L-L	5-8	175	9-11-91	1	1	2.89	4	0	0	0	9	8	3	3	2	2	7	.222	.154	.261	6.75	1.93
Fury, Nate	R-R	5-11	200	2-6-91	0	3	3.65	9	0	0	0	12	14	7	5	0	8	16	.280	.278	.281	11.68	5.84
Gillies, Charlie	R-R	6-2	200	8-30-90	0	0	9.00	1	1	0	0	2	2	2	2	1	0	1	.222	.250	.000	4.50	0.00
Huber, Brett	R-R	6-3	190	3-23-90	0	0	4.50	1	0	0	0	2	3	1	1	0	3	4	.333	.250	.400	18.00	13.50
John, Jordan	R-L	6-3	200	7-5-90	1	1	7.82	3	3	0	0	13	12	11	11	0	7	8	.255	.000	.279	5.68	4.97
Kellogg, Micah	R-R	6-4	195	11-29-89	0	1	2.70	3	2	0	0	10	9	3	3	1	7	4	.243	.118	.350	3.60	6.30
Knudson, Guido	R-R	6-1	185	8-5-89	2	1	3.06	12	0	0	5	18	13	6	6	1	6	23	.203	.308	.132	11.72	3.06
Longstreth, Ryan	L-L	6-1	205	4-16-90	0	2	2.27	16	1	0	0	32	28	10	8	0	7	15	.241	.250	.237	4.26	1.99
Lopez, Yorfrank	R-R	6-2	232	12-1-90	5	12	5.04	26	26	1	0	134	153	90	75	12	52	86	.291	.295	.278	5.78	3.49
Mayberry, Whit	R-R	6-0	190	5-29-90	1	0	1.69	10	0	0	0	21	14	4	4	0	3	21	.182	.162	.200	8.86	1.27
Nesbitt, Angel	R-R	6-1	237	12-4-90	2	0	0.79	24	0	0	14	34	23	3	3	0	8	36	.189	.172	.203	9.44	2.10
Norris, Daryl	R-R	6-1	220	6-12-91	0	2	9.98	6	1	0	0	15	25	17	17	2	10	8	.373	.444	.290	4.70	5.87
Sanchez, Eduardo	R-R	5-11	180	2-16-89	0	2	18.00	3	0	0	0	2	6	4	4	0	2	6	.600	.667	.500	9.00	9.00
Sitz, Scott	R-R	5-10	210	9-10-90	0	1	2.20	13	0	0	8	16	11	5	4	1	7	9	.200	.231	.172	4.96	3.86
Smith, Brennan	R-R	6-3	200	8-4-89	2	7	3.12	32	0	0	7	52	40	22	18	0	28	51	.221	.256	.194	8.83	4.85
Smith, Slade	R-R	6-2	200	9-26-90	0	1	4.66	6	0	0	0	10	9	8	5	0	7	2	.243	.571	.167	1.86	6.52
St. John, Locke	L-L	6-3	180	1-31-93	2	4	5.67	8	8	0	0	40	54	27	25	3	15	18	.342	.321	.353	4.08	3.40
Startup, Will	L-L	6-0	195	8-4-84	2	0	2.57	4	0	0	0	7	7	2	2	1	2	7	.269	.071	.500	9.00	2.57
Szkutnik, Trent	R-L	6-0	195	8-21-93	0	0	1.00	4	0	0	0	9	4	1	1	1	5	8	.133	.000	.222	8.00	5.00
Thompson, Jake	R-R	6-4	235	1-31-94	6	4	3.14	16	16	0	0	83	75	31	29	3	25	79	.244	.291	.207	8.57	2.71
Todd, Jade	R-L	6-2	190	3-22-90	2	0	5.40	24	1	0	0	33	37	20	20	3	19	34	.291	.263	.314	9.18	5.13
Turley, Josh	L-L	6-0	185	8-26-90	7	1	1.85	18	13	0	0	97	70	21	20	2	23	81	.205	.146	.224	7.49	2.13

Fielding

Catcher	PCT	G	PO	A	E	DP	PB
Green	.990	95	638	65	7	4	14
Longley	.993	37	257	23	2	2	3
Thomas	.952	6	38	2	2	0	2

First Base	PCT	G	PO	A	E	DP
Durham	1.000	3	13	4	0	2
Holm	.988	7	80	3	1	5
Powell	1.000	9	49	6	0	5
Robbins	.994	121	1077	70	7	99

Second Base	PCT	G	PO	A	E	DP
Castro	.991	48	82	131	2	27

	PCT	G	PO	A	E	DP
Hanover	1.000	14	23	56	0	12
Loy	1.000	7	15	12	0	3
Powell	.964	69	114	183	11	40

Third Base	PCT	G	PO	A	E	DP
Castro	.938	7	4	11	1	7
Hanover	.954	96	65	207	13	18
Powell	.929	24	11	41	4	5
Reaves	1.000	13	6	25	0	1

Shortstop	PCT	G	PO	A	E	DP
Gonzalez	.786	3	4	7	3	2
Machado	.972	41	63	112	5	23

	PCT	G	PO	A	E	DP
Powell	.964	15	22	31	2	11
Reaves	.961	81	117	204	13	47

Outfield	PCT	G	PO	A	E	DP
Dirks	1.000	6	4	0	0	0
Gibson	.978	19	44	1	1	0
Hanover	1.000	5	9	0	0	0
Harrell	.997	126	296	9	1	1
Holm	1.000	14	25	1	0	0
McVaney	.974	129	254	4	7	1
Wright	.991	118	223	9	2	3

DETROIT TIGERS

WEST MICHIGAN WHITECAPS

LOW CLASS A

MIDWEST LEAGUE

Batting	B-T	HT	WT	DOB	AVG	vLH	vRH	G	AB	R	H	2B	3B	HR	RBI	BB	HBP	SH	SF	SO	SB	CS	SLG	OBP
Adames, Willy	R-R	6-1	180	9-2-95	.269	.271	.268	98	353	40	95	14	12	6	50	39	3	4	1	96	3	6	.428	.346
2-team total (27 Bowling Green)					.271	—	—	125	450	55	122	19	14	8	61	54	4	4	2	126	6	6	.429	.353
Bernard, Wynton	R-R	6-2	200	9-24-90	.323	.302	.331	131	507	91	164	30	6	6	47	56	5	12	3	86	45	19	.442	.394
Betancourt, Javier	R-R	6-0	180	5-8-95	.269	.252	.275	134	558	67	150	18	3	6	54	26	7	15	6	81	9	6	.344	.307
Castro, Harold	L-R	6-0	165	11-30-93	.250	.318	.220	20	72	8	18	5	0	0	3	5	1	4	1	7	3	2	.319	.304
Contreras, Francisco	R-R	6-1	180	12-3-91	.222	.227	.220	79	275	30	61	9	1	3	28	23	3	6	6	78	6	0	.295	.283
Dirks, Andy	L-L	6-0	195	1-24-86	.214	.000	.250	5	14	2	3	1	0	0	3	0	0	0	0	1	1	0	.286	.353
Ficociello, Dominic	R-R	6-4	205	4-10-92	.275	.299	.267	134	530	66	146	25	6	6	53	40	8	0	2	116	11	8	.379	.334
Gerber, Mike	L-R	6-2	175	7-8-92	.387	.000	.400	8	31	4	12	3	0	0	5	4	0	0	0	3	1	0	.484	.457
Gibson, Tyler	L-R	6-2	210	6-17-93	.272	.067	.312	28	92	14	25	6	0	0	9	16	1	0	0	33	4	4	.337	.385
Greiner, Grayson	R-R	6-6	215	10-11-92	.322	.407	.286	26	90	11	29	5	0	2	16	11	1	0	2	18	0	0	.444	.394
Harrison, Brett	R-R	6-0	205	6-9-92	.191	.238	.170	19	68	6	13	4	0	0	3	3	1	0	1	21	0	1	.250	.233
Holm, Jeff	L-L	6-3	220	10-17-88	.258	.315	.239	80	299	50	77	12	1	11	48	39	5	1	1	64	7	3	.415	.352
Kivett, Ross	R-R	6-0	195	10-19-91	.215	.222	.214	19	65	3	14	2	0	0	7	6	2	2	1	8	3	0	.246	.297
Leyba, Domingo	B-R	5-11	160	9-11-95	.397	.292	.424	30	116	20	46	7	0	1	7	6	1	1	0	13	1	2	.483	.431
Leyland, Patrick	R-R	6-2	210	10-11-91	.140	.159	.130	36	121	3	17	2	0	1	9	2	0	1	0	16	0	0	.182	.154
Perez, Arvicent	R-R	5-10	178	1-14-94	.348	.600	.317	14	46	7	16	2	0	0	6	1	1	2	0	5	1	1	.391	.375
Pickar, Bennett	R-R	6-2	210	9-14-90	.184	.135	.202	80	272	15	50	9	0	0	22	22	3	1	0	81	2	0	.217	.253
Powell, Curt	R-R	6-0	180	4-30-91	.265	.167	.318	8	34	1	9	1	1	0	2	0	0	0	0	4	0	0	.353	.265
Remes, Tim	R-R	6-0	205	6-17-92	.159	.150	.162	27	88	9	14	1	0	2	9	13	1	4	1	32	1	0	.239	.272
Rhymes, Raph	R-R	6-0	190	10-22-89	.256	.234	.263	134	527	72	135	35	2	9	71	52	8	0	6	74	4	6	.381	.329
Schotts, Austin	R-R	5-11	180	9-16-93	.211	.167	.228	62	228	23	48	10	3	2	14	16	2	4	1	63	7	6	.307	.267
Verlander, Ben	R-R	6-4	200	1-31-92	.208	.279	.181	56	216	16	45	7	1	1	23	9	0	0	4	45	3	3	.264	.236
Zambrano, Jose	B-R	5-7	155	11-4-93	.233	.208	.241	58	215	16	50	2	0	1	14	11	0	4	0	25	4	0	.256	.270

Pitching	B-T	HT	WT	DOB	W	L	ERA	G	GS	CG	SV	IP	H	R	ER	HR	BB	SO	AVG	vLH	vRH	K/9	BB/9
Crawford, Jonathon	R-R	6-2	205	11-1-91	8	3	2.85	23	23	0	0	123	93	41	39	3	50	85	.220	.235	.212	6.22	3.66
Davenport, Matt	R-R	6-8	200	10-11-89	5	6	2.92	32	6	0	3	89	98	35	29	0	22	74	.278	.287	.273	7.46	2.22
Farmer, Buck	L-R	6-4	225	2-20-91	10	5	2.60	18	18	0	0	104	91	37	30	6	24	116	.233	.254	.223	10.07	2.08
Felix, Julio	R-R	6-1	210	2-23-92	3	2	3.38	44	0	0	13	77	70	31	29	2	15	71	.244	.217	.260	8.26	1.75
Fury, Nate	R-R	5-11	200	2-6-91	2	0	0.59	10	0	0	0	15	13	2	1	0	5	18	.224	.227	.222	10.57	2.93
Green, Chad	L-R	6-3	210	5-24-91	6	4	3.11	23	23	0	0	130	121	51	45	8	28	125	.251	.290	.223	8.63	1.93
Krol, Ian	L-L	6-1	210	5-9-91	0	0	0.00	1	0	0	0	1	0	0	0	0	1	.000	—	.000	9.00	0.00
Kubitza, Austin	R-R	6-5	225	11-16-91	10	2	2.34	23	23	0	0	131	98	46	34	5	43	140	.202	.215	.192	9.62	2.95
LaMarche, Will	R-R	6-3	220	8-7-91	2	0	4.99	26	0	0	1	40	30	23	22	1	24	40	.211	.212	.211	9.08	5.45
Lewicki, Artie	R-R	6-3	195	4-8-92	2	2	2.45	10	1	0	2	26	19	8	7	2	9	22	.213	.333	.143	7.71	3.16
Longstreth, Ryan	L-L	6-1	205	4-16-90	0	1	2.08	7	0	0	0	13	16	3	3	0	1	10	.308	.333	.297	6.92	0.69
Maciel, Jon	R-R	6-2	225	11-17-92	6	8	4.07	27	20	0	0	128	138	66	58	10	26	91	.277	.285	.271	6.38	1.82
Mantiply, Joe	R-L	6-4	215	3-1-91	6	3	2.40	38	0	0	8	71	57	19	19	2	19	76	.221	.215	.223	9.59	2.40
Putkonen, Luke	R-R	6-6	215	5-10-86	0	1	13.50	3	0	0	0	3	4	4	4	1	2	0	.333	.667	.222	0.00	6.75
Ravenelle, Adam	R-R	6-3	185	10-5-92	0	0	0.00	2	0	0	1	3	0	0	0	0	0	5	.000	.000	.000	15.00	0.00
Reininger, Zac	B-R	6-3	170	1-28-93	4	4	2.54	33	0	0	11	57	42	18	16	3	17	58	.203	.260	.172	9.21	2.70
Robertson, Montreal	R-R	6-4	205	6-19-90	6	5	3.23	43	0	0	8	75	84	34	27	3	28	59	.285	.345	.247	7.05	3.35
Sitz, Scott	R-R	5-10	210	9-10-90	2	5	5.31	29	0	0	2	42	49	31	25	6	10	40	.295	.397	.233	8.50	2.13
Szkutnik, Trent	L-L	6-0	195	8-21-93	0	1	4.42	9	0	0	0	18	20	11	9	0	4	14	.294	.182	.348	6.87	1.96
Thompson, Jeff	R-R	6-6	245	9-23-91	0	0	6.75	3	3	0	0	8	10	7	6	1	9	10	.323	.400	.250	11.25	10.13
Ziomek, Kevin	R-L	6-3	200	3-21-92	10	6	2.27	23	23	0	0	123	89	45	31	5	53	152	.201	.194	.204	11.12	3.88

Fielding

Catcher	PCT	G	PO	A	E	DP	PB
Greiner	.991	26	211	14	2	0	1
Perez	.967	14	105	12	4	0	1
Pickar	.991	80	620	73	6	2	16
Remes	.978	27	246	22	6	1	4

First Base	PCT	G	PO	A	E	DP
Contreras	1.000	3	22	1	0	2
Ficociello	.993	109	998	67	8	94
Holm	.995	22	197	12	1	21
Leyland	.958	10	60	8	3	7

Second Base	PCT	G	PO	A	E	DP
Betancourt	.973	104	201	312	14	75
Castro	1.000	11	23	29	0	7

Contreras	1.000	1	2	1	0	1
Leyba	.973	13	28	45	2	14
Zambrano	.956	13	21	44	3	8

Third Base	PCT	G	PO	A	E	DP
Betancourt	.929	4	2	11	1	0
Contreras	.925	75	40	145	15	17
Ficociello	.971	11	10	23	1	5
Harrison	.919	18	9	48	5	2
Zambrano	.942	37	16	65	5	2

Shortstop	PCT	G	PO	A	E	DP
Adames	.952	97	132	289	21	63
Betancourt	.940	18	26	53	5	9
Leyba	.961	17	24	50	3	11

Powell	.905	7	5	14	2	2
Zambrano	.833	2	1	4	1	3

Outfield	PCT	G	PO	A	E	DP
Bernard	.984	129	246	7	4	0
Contreras	1.000	3	4	0	0	0
Dirks	1.000	3	1	0	0	0
Gerber	1.000	8	21	0	0	0
Gibson	1.000	28	50	3	0	0
Holm	1.000	19	27	1	0	1
Kivett	1.000	18	49	2	0	0
Rhymes	.987	111	153	4	2	0
Schotts	1.000	62	153	4	0	2
Verlander	1.000	48	63	1	0	0

CONNECTICUT TIGERS

SHORT-SEASON

NEW YORK-PENN LEAGUE

Batting	B-T	HT	WT	DOB	AVG	vLH	vRH	G	AB	R	H	2B	3B	HR	RBI	BB	HBP	SH	SF	SO	SB	CS	SLG	OBP
Brown, Rashad	L-L	5-11	180	12-17-93	.236	.139	.256	55	208	27	49	5	1	0	18	26	1	1	2	36	9	5	.269	.321
Coffman, Kasey	L-R	6-3	201	9-8-91	.268	.269	.268	44	153	19	41	10	2	1	16	12	4	0	3	35	6	0	.379	.331
Crafort, Samuel	B-R	6-0	147	7-31-93	.143	.000	.200	2	7	0	1	0	0	0	0	0	0	0	0	3	0	0	.143	.143
Fuentes, Steven	B-R	5-11	180	10-21-94	.295	.100	.344	55	200	30	59	13	7	3	19	16	3	3	0	51	6	2	.475	.356

	B-T	HT	WT	DOB	AVG	vLH	vRH	G	AB	R	H	2B	3B	HR	RBI	BB	HBP	SH	SF	SO	SB	CS	SLG	OBP
Gerber, Mike	L-R	6-2	175	7-8-92	.286	.275	.289	57	217	40	62	16	4	7	37	17	7	0	2	48	8	4	.493	.354
Gonzalez, David	R-R	5-9	140	12-1-93	.115	.100	.125	6	26	0	3	0	0	0	0	1	0	0	0	2	0	0	.115	.148
Hill, Derek	R-R	6-2	195	12-30-95	.203	.286	.183	19	74	8	15	1	1	0	3	2	2	0	0	26	2	1	.243	.244
Kapstein, Jacob	B-R	6-2	215	2-24-94	.248	.290	.236	44	141	18	35	9	0	1	19	15	0	2	2	36	0	0	.333	.316
Kivett, Ross	R-R	6-1	195	10-19-91	.289	.250	.300	47	190	26	55	10	2	1	26	14	2	2	1	24	1	3	.379	.343
Leyba, Domingo	B-R	5-11	160	9-11-95	.264	.194	.287	37	144	20	38	11	1	1	17	8	0	2	0	17	1	2	.375	.303
Maddox, Will	L-R	5-10	180	6-11-92	.270	.371	.245	48	178	28	48	7	1	0	12	15	3	7	1	23	13	1	.320	.335
Mattlage, Garrett	B-R	5-10	175	2-25-93	.230	.238	.228	45	165	28	38	8	1	0	8	28	3	1	0	47	4	1	.291	.352
Navarro, Franklin	B-R	5-10	181	10-17-94	.250	.195	.267	45	172	14	43	10	1	3	23	5	0	4	0	25	0	0	.372	.271
Negron, Steven	B-R	5-8	175	5-13-93	.143	.500	.000	4	7	1	1	0	0	0	2	2	0	0	1	2	0	0	.143	.300
Pankake, Joey	R-R	6-2	185	11-23-92	.292	.404	.261	64	240	37	70	16	2	2	36	22	0	0	5	44	2	0	.400	.345
Pirtle, Brett	B-R	5-9	175	3-23-91	.294	.083	.336	40	143	15	42	11	1	1	26	7	3	2	2	15	1	2	.406	.335
Remes, Tim	R-R	6-0	205	6-17-92	.243	.273	.237	24	70	7	17	3	0	2	8	11	0	0	1	24	0	0	.371	.341
Salgado, Ismael	R-R	6-1	165	1-11-93	.263	.333	.231	5	19	0	5	1	0	0	3	1	0	0	0	2	0	1	.316	.300
Taladay, Chris	L-R	6-1	220	5-22-91	.250	.200	.273	4	16	3	4	0	0	0	1	2	0	0	0	4	0	0	.250	.333
Thomas, Michael	R-R	5-11	210	1-27-91	.136	.143	.133	7	22	0	3	0	0	0	1	0	0	0	0	6	0	0	.136	.136
Tovar, Orvin	R-R	5-11	180	8-6-93	.179	.250	.130	10	39	2	7	1	0	0	3	3	0	0	0	10	0	0	.205	.238
Verlander, Ben	R-R	6-4	200	1-31-92	.240	.275	.226	43	146	22	35	6	0	2	19	15	1	1	1	25	1	0	.322	.313

Pitching

	B-T	HT	WT	DOB	W	L	ERA	G	GS	CG	SV	IP	H	R	ER	HR	BB	SO	AVG	vLH	vRH	K/9	BB/9
Bailey, Tanner	R-R	6-6	240	7-6-90	1	2	1.88	7	7	0	0	38	35	9	8	1	4	32	.252	.239	.264	7.51	0.94
Belisario, Johan	R-R	5-11	165	8-13-93	5	0	0.79	19	0	0	3	34	21	4	3	0	8	34	.172	.196	.155	9.00	2.12
Burgos, Cesar	R-R	6-2	185	3-1-93	1	0	3.38	4	0	0	1	5	9	2	2	1	0	5	.360	.286	.389	8.44	0.00
Chavez, Emanuel	R-R	6-3	175	1-19-95	0	1	1.93	4	0	0	0	9	10	4	2	0	3	11	.263	.154	.320	10.61	2.89
Edwards, Chase	R-R	6-1	180	2-4-94	6	3	2.99	15	15	0	0	87	99	41	29	5	13	52	.280	.335	.235	5.36	1.34
Elam, Cale	R-R	6-2	210	9-22-90	0	0	108.00	1	0	0	0	0	3	4	4	0	1	0	.750	1.000	.500	0.00	27.00
Fischer, Jack	R-R	6-1	175	8-28-91	0	1	4.88	17	0	0	1	28	34	20	15	0	11	22	.301	.275	.323	7.16	3.58
Ford, Tyler	L-L	5-8	175	9-11-91	0	1	20.25	2	0	0	0	1	3	3	3	0	3	0	.000	.000	.000	0.00	20.25
Heddinger, Josh	R-R	6-4	220	1-16-93	1	2	3.20	10	8	0	0	20	17	8	7	0	4	12	.239	.281	.205	5.49	1.83
Hemmer, Gabe	R-R	6-3	220	6-22-90	2	1	2.13	20	0	0	4	25	19	8	6	0	6	41	.204	.229	.190	14.57	2.13
Jimenez, Joe	R-R	6-3	220	1-17-95	3	2	2.70	23	0	0	4	27	22	10	8	1	6	41	.218	.291	.130	13.84	2.03
Kellogg, Micah	R-R	6-4	195	11-29-89	0	2	1.93	5	0	0	1	9	7	5	2	1	4	6	.206	.188	.222	5.79	3.86
Kirkland, Johnnie	R-R	6-1	200	8-25-89	1	1	2.97	13	1	0	0	33	26	13	11	0	9	31	.210	.250	.176	8.37	2.43
Ladwig, A.J.	R-R	6-5	180	12-24-92	0	5	5.73	10	10	0	0	22	27	16	14	2	2	12	.293	.250	.341	4.91	0.82
LaMarche, Will	R-R	6-3	220	8-7-91	1	0	2.38	4	0	0	0	11	4	3	3	1	3	17	.105	.125	.091	13.50	2.38
Lara, Confesor	R-R	6-2	170	8-7-90	2	2	2.70	13	3	0	0	57	44	26	17	3	21	43	.203	.225	.183	6.83	3.34
Laxer, Josh	R-R	6-0	195	6-7-93	3	0	3.00	14	0	0	1	30	26	13	10	1	5	27	.236	.218	.255	8.10	1.50
Norris, Daryl	R-R	6-1	220	6-12-91	0	0	4.05	4	0	0	0	7	4	5	3	0	5	6	.182	.429	.067	8.10	6.75
Perez, Fernando	R-R	6-3	181	12-17-93	6	4	3.63	14	14	0	0	69	71	35	28	2	24	58	.267	.360	.200	7.53	3.12
Pritcher, Austin	R-R	6-1	190	2-13-91	7	3	3.97	14	7	0	0	68	68	35	30	4	19	45	.265	.294	.245	5.96	2.51
Smith, Gage	R-R	6-2	185	2-13-91	3	1	1.53	15	0	0	2	29	29	5	5	0	7	20	.248	.246	.250	6.14	2.15
Turnbull, Spencer	R-R	6-3	215	9-18-92	0	2	4.45	11	11	0	0	28	31	16	14	1	14	19	.270	.306	.242	6.04	4.45
Voelker, Paul	R-R	5-10	185	8-19-92	0	1	2.52	16	0	0	1	25	18	8	7	1	9	31	.209	.200	.217	11.16	3.24

Fielding

Catcher	PCT	G	PO	A	E	DP	PB
Navarro	.989	44	339	34	4	0	5
Remes	.989	24	154	20	2	1	2
Taladay	1.000	4	33	6	0		2
Thomas	.944	6	33	1	2	0	1

First Base	PCT	G	PO	A	E	DP
Fuentes	1.000	4	19	2	0	1
Kapstein	.976	37	295	37	8	21
Maddox	.992	38	362	23	3	29

Second Base	PCT	G	PO	A	E	DP
Leyba	.993	35	59	88	1	16

	PCT	G	PO	A	E	DP
Maddox	.904	9	21	26	5	4
Pirtle	.960	33	50	95	6	13

Third Base	PCT	G	PO	A	E	DP
Fuentes	.897	41	25	80	12	7
Negron	.600	4	1	2	2	0
Pankake	.893	34	28	47	9	1

Shortstop	PCT	G	PO	A	E	DP
Fuentes	.938	7	7	23	2	4
Gonzalez	.865	6	12	20	5	4
Leyba	1.000	3	1	6	0	0
Mattlage	.879	42	60	114	24	19

	PCT	G	PO	A	E	DP
Pankake	.893	16	24	43	8	11
Pirtle	.875	3	2	5	1	0

Outfield	PCT	G	PO	A	E	DP
Brown	.957	46	66	1	3	0
Coffman	1.000	28	58	3	0	0
Crafort	1.000	1	1	0	0	0
Gerber	.990	53	92	3	1	0
Hill	.964	19	27	0	1	0
Kivett	1.000	45	84	6	0	2
Salgado	1.000	5	9	1	0	0
Tovar	1.000	3	2	0	0	0
Verlander	.973	32	69	2	2	0

GCL TIGERS   ROOKIE

GULF COAST LEAGUE

Batting	B-T	HT	WT	DOB	AVG	vLH	vRH	G	AB	R	H	2B	3B	HR	RBI	BB	HBP	SH	SF	SO	SB	CS	SLG	OBP
Baptist, Corey	R-R	6-4	215	4-19-95	.268	.306	.250	42	153	20	41	14	0	1	23	9	1	0	1	19	4	2	.379	.311
Brugnoni, Giancarlo	R-R	6-3	225	2-25-91	.277	.263	.284	37	112	22	31	7	0	7	16	21	2	0	0	33	5	0	.527	.400
Castano, Adrian	L-L	6-3	180	8-20-95	.283	.480	.143	19	60	7	17	3	0	0	7	6	0	1	0	11	1	0	.333	.348
Crafort, Samuel	R-R	6-0	147	7-31-93	.183	.148	.200	34	82	11	15	4	0	1	8	21	1	1	3	28	4	0	.268	.352
Fields, Daniel	L-R	6-2	215	1-23-91	.167	.000	.200	2	6	2	1	1	0	0	0	0	1	0	0	2	0	0	.333	.286
Gibson, Tyler	L-R	6-2	210	6-17-93	.333	—	.333	4	9	0	3	0	0	0	1	0	0	1	0	0	2	0	0	.333	.455
Gonzalez, David	R-R	5-9	140	12-1-93	.326	.431	.267	49	181	26	59	12	1	2	23	22	1	3	2	19	6	5	.436	.398
Hill, Derek	R-R	6-2	195	12-30-95	.212	.300	.174	28	99	12	21	2	2	2	11	16	2	1	1	19	9	1	.333	.331
Kengor, Will	L-R	6-3	180	7-24-92	.278	.259	.287	48	162	30	45	9	2	0	21	21	1	3	4	31	6	3	.358	.356
McAlpine, Duncan	L-R	5-10	215	4-10-91	.259	.167	.286	10	27	5	7	2	0	1	2	8	3	0	0	7	1	0	.444	.474
Negron, Steven	R-R	5-8	175	5-13-93	.128	.143	.121	31	86	8	11	1	1	0	8	13	2	1	4	25	4	3	.163	.248
Ordonez Jr., Magglio	R-R	6-1	200	10-14-95	.118	.333	.040	15	34	2	4	0	0	0	3	5	0	2	0	14	0	0	.118	.231
Padron, Victor	L-R	5-8	160	7-5-94	.226	.194	.243	38	106	21	24	3	0	0	13	28	0	4	1	19	5	3	.255	.385

Name	B-T	HT	WT	DOB	AVG	vLH	vRH	G	AB	R	H	2B	3B	HR	RBI	BB	HBP	SH	SF	SO	SB	CS	SLG	OBP
Perez, Arvicent	R-R	5-10	178	1-14-94	.309	.231	.345	27	81	14	25	6	1	3	20	1	1	1	4	7	3	0	.519	.310
Philibossian, James	R-R	5-10	180	2-6-96	.120	.250	.059	15	25	5	3	1	0	0	2	3	1	0	0	8	0	0	.160	.241
Salgado, Ismael	R-R	6-1	165	1-11-93	.300	.268	.317	46	160	26	48	6	3	0	17	12	1	1	3	26	6	3	.375	.347
Sayers, Aaron	L-R	6-1	175	5-25-94	.259	.311	.224	32	112	10	29	1	1	1	16	10	2	2	1	21	2	4	.313	.328
Shepherd, Zach	R-R	6-3	185	9-14-95	.301	.298	.302	51	173	34	52	12	5	4	29	21	2	0	5	44	5	1	.497	.373
Taladay, Chris	L-R	6-1	220	5-22-91	.289	.200	.314	16	45	8	13	1	2	1	11	5	1	1	0	8	1	0	.467	.373
Thomas, Michael	R-R	5-11	210	1-27-91	.333	.500	.200	2	9	3	3	0	0	0	1	0	0	0	0	2	1	0	.333	.333
Tovar, Orvin	R-R	5-11	180	8-6-93	.289	.276	.294	32	97	16	28	6	0	0	14	8	1	0	1	13	2	2	.351	.346
Zeile, Shane	R-R	6-1	195	6-14-93	.222	.320	.158	21	63	10	14	1	1	2	6	4	1	1	1	14	0	1	.365	.275

Pitching

Name	B-T	HT	WT	DOB	W	L	ERA	G	GS	CG	SV	IP	H	R	ER	HR	BB	SO	AVG	vLH	vRH	K/9	BB/9
Baez, Sandy	R-R	6-2	180	11-25-93	1	2	3.06	12	12	0	0	62	62	27	21	3	16	48	.258	.278	.250	7.01	2.34
Burgos, Cesar	R-R	6-2	185	3-1-93	2	2	2.78	11	0	0	0	32	37	16	10	2	7	23	.276	.343	.253	6.40	1.95
Carter, Nate	R-R	6-2	180	8-13-91	1	0	2.25	4	0	0	1	8	7	3	2	1	1	8	.107	.167	.063	9.00	1.13
Castillo, Oswaldo	R-R	6-0	193	8-18-96	1	3	3.20	9	9	1	0	45	37	17	16	3	14	32	.236	.196	.255	6.40	2.80
Castro, Anthony	R-R	6-0	174	4-13-95	6	3	4.10	13	12	0	0	59	53	32	27	1	30	50	.241	.186	.276	7.58	4.55
Chavez, Emanuel	R-R	6-3	175	1-19-95	2	0	3.86	8	0	0	1	12	11	6	5	0	5	16	.239	.154	.273	12.34	3.86
Elam, Cale	R-R	6-2	210	9-22-90	1	0	0.00	1	0	0	0	3	0	0	0	0	0	1	.000	.000	.000	3.00	0.00
Ford, Tyler	L-L	5-8	175	9-11-91	4	1	1.69	10	0	0	3	21	10	5	4	0	7	25	.145	.188	.132	10.55	2.95
Fury, Nate	R-R	5-11	200	2-6-91	0	0	0.00	1	0	0	0	3	2	0	0	0	0	5	.154	.000	.167	15.00	0.00
Gillies, Charlie	R-R	6-2	200	8-30-90	0	1	1.13	2	2	0	0	8	7	2	1	0	1	10	.233	.571	.130	12.38	1.13
Gutierrez, Alfred	R-R	6-0	143	6-12-95	0	1	7.04	3	2	0	0	8	11	7	6	0	3	9	.355	.500	.304	10.57	3.52
Heddinger, Josh	R-R	6-4	220	1-16-93	0	0	3.00	2	0	0	0	3	4	1	1	0	1	2	.364	.000	.400	6.00	3.00
Kellogg, Micah	R-R	6-4	195	11-29-89	3	1	2.25	9	0	0	0	20	13	6	5	2	3	15	.188	.174	.196	6.75	1.35
Ladwig, A.J.	R-R	6-5	180	12-24-92	0	2	3.00	3	0	0	0	6	6	2	2	0	2	4	.300	.000	.375	6.00	3.00
Lakatos, Alex	R-R	6-2	210	11-24-91	0	0	6.75	3	0	0	0	7	11	6	5	0	1	3	.393	.556	.316	4.05	1.35
Lara, Carlos	R-R	6-2	170	3-2-94	6	1	3.48	13	5	0	0	44	34	24	17	2	27	46	.206	.158	.220	9.41	5.52
Lara, Confesor	R-R	6-2	170	8-7-90	1	0	0.00	1	1	0	0	6	5	1	0	0	1	4	.250	.333	.235	6.00	1.50
Laxer, Josh	R-R	6-0	195	6-7-93	0	0	0.00	2	0	0	0	3	0	0	0	0	2	2	.000	.000	.000	6.00	6.00
Lewicki, Artie	R-R	6-3	195	4-8-92	0	0	0.00	2	2	0	0	2	2	0	0	0	1	4	.222	.000	.286	18.00	4.50
Mayberry, Whit	R-R	6-0	190	5-29-90	0	0	0.00	2	0	0	0	4	2	0	0	0	2	5	.167	.333	.111	12.27	4.91
Moreno, Gerson	R-R	6-0	175	9-10-95	1	1	4.40	14	1	0	0	29	32	19	14	0	17	22	.283	.345	.262	6.91	5.34
Norris, Daryl	R-R	6-1	220	6-12-91	1	5	7.43	7	3	0	1	23	27	20	19	1	12	10	.297	.242	.328	3.91	4.70
Paulino, Brenny	R-R	6-4	170	2-21-93	0	0	7.04	14	1	0	0	15	19	20	12	0	21	11	.297	.267	.306	6.46	12.33
Ravenelle, Adam	R-R	6-3	185	10-5-92	0	0	0.00	1	0	0	0	0	0	0	0	0	0	0	.000	—	.000	0.00	0.00
Smith, Jordan	R-R	6-1	210	4-23-92	0	0	0.00	4	0	0	2	8	3	0	0	0	3	6	.115	.182	.067	6.48	3.24
Smith, Gage	R-R	6-2	185	2-13-91	1	0	0.00	3	0	0	0	3	0	0	0	0	1	6	.136	.400	.059	8.53	1.42
St. John, Locke	L-L	6-3	180	1-31-93	0	0	1.50	2	2	0	0	6	4	1	1	0	3	7	.200	.143	.231	10.50	4.50
Szkutnik, Trent	R-L	6-0	195	8-21-93	0	0	3.48	4	0	0	0	10	13	4	4	1	3	7	.333	.000	.382	6.10	2.61
Turnbull, Spencer	R-R	6-3	215	9-18-92	0	1	3.00	1	1	0	0	3	2	1	1	1	1	4	.200	—	.200	12.00	3.00
Voelker, Paul	R-R	5-10	185	8-19-92	0	0	0.00	2	0	0	1	2	0	0	0	0	0	4	.000	.000	.000	18.00	0.00
Watkins, Spenser	R-R	6-1	190	8-27-92	3	2	3.83	10	8	0	0	42	38	20	18	4	20	43	.244	.319	.211	9.14	4.25

Fielding

Catcher	PCT	G	PO	A	E	DP	PB
Perez	.990	25	161	32	2	1	2
Philibossian	1.000	12	23	2	0	0	0
Taladay	.982	15	103	4	2	1	4
Thomas	1.000	2	14	6	0	0	1
Zeile	.971	21	111	21	4	0	6

First Base	PCT	G	PO	A	E	DP
Baptist	.987	34	291	3	4	27
Brugnoni	.987	28	217	10	3	22
Ordonez Jr.	1.000	3	12	1	0	3

Second Base	PCT	G	PO	A	E	DP
Gonzalez	.986	27	69	67	2	18
Negron	.972	28	51	54	3	18
Sayers	.952	8	20	20	2	4

Third Base	PCT	G	PO	A	E	DP
McAlpine	1.000	4	1	7	0	1
Sayers	.800	1	2	6	2	0
Shepherd	.922	51	32	109	12	12

Shortstop	PCT	G	PO	A	E	DP
Gonzalez	.965	22	33	78	4	15
Kengor	.966	26	27	86	4	8
Sayers	.922	11	12	35	4	9

Outfield	PCT	G	PO	A	E	DP
Castano	.964	17	26	1	1	0
Crafort	.941	31	46	2	3	0
Fields	1.000	2	4	0	0	0
Gibson	1.000	3	4	0	0	0
Hill	.963	28	50	2	2	1
Ordonez Jr.	.857	7	6	0	1	0
Padron	.939	37	44	2	3	0
Salgado	.989	44	86	1	1	0
Tovar	.958	29	41	5	2	2

DSL TIGERS
ROOKIE

DOMINICAN SUMMER LEAGUE

Batting	B-T	HT	WT	DOB	AVG	vLH	vRH	G	AB	R	H	2B	3B	HR	RBI	BB	HBP	SH	SF	SO	SB	CS	SLG	OBP
Alcantara, Randel	L-R	6-1	180	5-13-97	.255	.361	.232	55	200	37	51	8	1	7	31	24	8	0	1	48	1	3	.410	.356
Beltre, Moises	R-R	5-11	190	11-15-90	.357	.500	.300	14	14	3	5	1	0	0	2	1	1	0	0	2	0	0	.429	.438
2-team total (1 Padres)					.353	—	—	15	17	3	6	2	0	0	2	1	1	0	0	3	0	0	.471	.421
De La Cruz, Israel	R-R	6-0	150	6-15-97	.252	.200	.262	47	151	33	38	5	7	0	15	15	3	3	0	53	4	4	.377	.331
Delgado, Alwin	R-R	6-3	175	11-3-92	.239	.304	.227	51	155	34	37	7	0	3	19	28	2	4	2	44	5	2	.342	.358
Gonzalez, Cesar	R-R	6-2	175	5-31-95	.342	.432	.324	59	225	57	77	15	6	1	29	29	7	0	2	52	31	9	.476	.430
Hidalgo, Gregoris	R-R	5-10	160	12-18-93	.238	.208	.244	41	143	28	34	5	2	2	24	17	7	1	2	27	9	4	.343	.343
Joseph, Manuel	R-R	5-11	160	6-16-94	.379	.472	.360	60	211	55	80	10	7	7	45	27	8	0	6	23	16	9	.592	.456
Martinez, Hector	R-R	5-11	175	11-1-96	.271	.222	.279	42	181	33	49	15	1	2	19	7	5	2	0	47	4	6	.398	.316
Mejia, Sauris	L-L	5-9	150	11-8-96	.207	.190	.211	46	116	23	24	3	1	0	8	20	5	0	2	29	10	5	.250	.343
Pena, Yerison	B-R	6-1	180	7-18-91	.313	.317	.312	65	230	60	72	19	5	2	53	46	2	0	1	44	22	7	.465	.430
Rodriguez, Sandy	R-R	6-1	180	10-19-94	.158	.000	.176	10	19	5	3	1	0	0	6	7	3	0	0	5	3	0	.211	.448
Sanjur, Mario	R-R	5-7	174	12-23-95	.230	.286	.219	49	135	19	31	7	1	1	26	19	1	3	3	12	6	2	.319	.323
Santana, Felix	R-R	5-10	180	8-14-94	.358	.310	.366	53	193	40	69	14	2	2	29	21	13	0	1	36	14	5	.482	.452
Serrano, Ariel	R-R	5-10	174	6-23-96	.248	.212	.258	47	161	24	40	10	1	0	22	15	2	2	1	30	10	3	.323	.318

	B-T	HT	WT	DOB	AVG	vLH	vRH	G	AB	R	H	2B	3B	HR	RBI	BB	HBP	SH	SF	SO	SB	CS	SLG	OBP
Tejeda, Bryan	R-R	6-0	190	1-17-96	.211	.136	.230	34	109	15	23	4	0	0	10	7	2	2	0	21	4	0	.248	.271
Valdez, Ignacio	R-R	6-3	195	7-16-95	.263	.222	.271	62	224	47	59	20	6	4	43	28	7	0	4	58	9	6	.460	.357

Pitching	B-T	HT	WT	DOB	W	L	ERA	G	GS	CG	SV	IP	H	R	ER	HR	BB	SO	AVG	vLH	vRH	K/9	BB/9
Alcantara, Juan	R-R	6-4	195	7-30-94	2	0	2.45	10	4	0	2	29	27	15	8	0	8	27	.241	.176	.269	8.28	2.45
Almonte, Yei	R-R	6-2	210	10-8-95	7	1	2.47	14	8	0	0	51	51	21	14	0	17	30	.258	.190	.286	5.29	3.00
Baez, Jorge	R-R	6-2	185	5-9-95	3	1	3.53	15	4	0	1	43	40	27	17	1	26	29	.245	.238	.250	6.02	5.40
Batista, Franchi	R-R	6-0	170	5-26-96	0	0	2.25	3	0	0	1	4	5	2	1	0	1	4	.313	.250	.333	9.00	2.25
Cabrera, Rusbell	R-R	6-3	170	9-29-95	2	3	4.20	14	8	0	3	45	36	24	21	1	27	28	.217	.230	.210	5.60	5.40
De Pena, Enrique	R-R	6-2	175	2-19-96	0	0	3.86	4	0	0	0	5	7	4	2	0	7	3	.333	.200	.375	5.79	13.50
Espinal, Derlin	L-L	6-0	160	10-3-94	2	0	2.00	12	0	0	0	18	13	5	4	0	7	9	.220	.286	.200	4.50	3.50
German, Francisco	R-R	6-2	160	12-26-96	2	1	2.66	16	6	0	1	44	30	13	13	0	16	37	.192	.268	.150	7.57	3.27
Jacobs, Vijandrick	L-L	5-10	185	2-20-94	5	2	4.31	19	0	0	0	40	45	34	19	1	25	38	.268	.111	.298	8.62	5.67
Manzanillo, Rafael	R-R	6-6	190	10-24-91	2	0	3.21	3	3	0	0	14	11	9	5	0	8	12	.204	.185	.222	7.71	5.14
Martinez, Malvin	R-R	6-0	170	4-19-95	3	0	5.87	17	0	0	3	23	26	15	15	2	9	24	.283	.433	.210	9.39	3.52
Martinez, Stanley	R-R	6-3	185	11-29-94	2	1	5.23	15	6	0	1	52	61	35	30	1	21	33	.293	.225	.328	5.75	3.63
Mateo, Jhonny	R-R	6-3	170	8-19-94	3	1	2.59	15	11	0	1	59	47	28	17	0	23	42	.213	.241	.197	6.41	3.51
Mueses, Victor	R-R	6-1	175	10-13-95	2	2	2.41	16	4	0	3	41	33	22	11	1	21	31	.219	.273	.188	6.80	4.61
Obispo, Janry	R-R	6-3	205	10-10-93	1	2	3.28	22	0	0	11	25	19	10	9	0	6	15	.213	.156	.246	5.47	2.19
Rosario, Harold	R-R	5-11	198	10-23-92	4	1	2.45	14	0	0	0	18	18	7	5	0	10	22	.269	.333	.239	10.80	4.91
Soto, Gregory	L-L	6-1	180	2-11-95	5	3	3.20	16	10	0	0	51	41	24	18	0	25	57	.224	.000	.250	10.13	4.44
Tejada, Andres	R-R	6-5	190	2-2-95	5	2	3.15	19	1	0	3	34	27	17	12	0	19	30	.208	.250	.191	7.86	4.98
Viloria, Felix	L-L	6-1	165	12-2-96	1	0	2.28	14	6	0	1	47	33	16	12	2	17	50	.194	.087	.211	9.51	3.23

Fielding

Catcher	PCT	G	PO	A	E	DP	PB
Beltre	.975	14	37	2	1	0	1
Rodriguez	.984	10	50	12	1	1	1
Sanjur	.994	49	314	44	2	2	12
Tejeda	.988	27	144	22	2	1	6

First Base	PCT	G	PO	A	E	DP
Delgado	.984	22	175	14	3	15
Pena	.992	52	461	33	4	37
Sanjur	1.000	1	2	0	0	0
Tejeda	1.000	6	24	3	0	2
Valdez	.800	1	4	0	1	0

Second Base	PCT	G	PO	A	E	DP
Alcantara	1.000	1	1	1	0	0

	PCT	G	PO	A	E	DP
De La Cruz	.864	5	7	12	3	1
Hidalgo	.960	39	79	87	7	21
Joseph	.980	9	19	30	1	3
Martinez	.906	21	37	50	9	11
Pena	.962	7	10	15	1	2

Third Base	PCT	G	PO	A	E	DP
Alcantara	.817	48	37	97	30	8
Delgado	.894	27	25	51	9	1
Hidalgo	—	1	0	0	0	0
Joseph	.967	10	7	22	1	0
Pena	—	2	0	0	0	0
Sanjur	1.000	1	1	0	0	0

Shortstop	PCT	G	PO	A	E	DP
De La Cruz	.894	39	71	107	21	26
Delgado	1.000	5	6	12	0	1
Hidalgo	—	1	0	0	0	0
Joseph	.923	24	36	60	8	11
Martinez	.878	12	12	24	5	3
Pena	1.000	1	1	0	0	0

Outfield	PCT	G	PO	A	E	DP
Gonzalez	.989	45	82	5	1	2
Joseph	1.000	2	2	1	0	0
Mejia	.887	36	44	3	6	1
Santana	.940	47	60	3	4	0
Serrano	.973	46	66	7	2	2
Valdez	.966	60	75	9	3	4

VSL TIGERS

ROOKIE

VENEZUELAN SUMMER LEAGUE

Batting	B-T	HT	WT	DOB	AVG	vLH	vRH	G	AB	R	H	2B	3B	HR	RBI	BB	HBP	SH	SF	SO	SB	CS	SLG	OBP
Alfaro, Adrian	L-R	5-9	176	9-19-95	.256	.190	.279	65	242	43	62	10	5	0	16	37	2	3	3	26	17	7	.339	.356
Arias, Franklin	R-R	6-0	165	1-9-97	.269	.158	.305	50	156	19	42	5	1	0	23	21	6	1	0	32	4	5	.314	.377
Aristigueta, Keyder	R-R	5-11	165	2-2-96	.168	.250	.143	42	119	19	20	3	1	0	5	13	2	1	1	22	1	3	.210	.259
Azocar, Jose	R-R	5-11	165	5-11-96	.340	.297	.355	65	250	39	85	7	6	1	36	11	4	1	3	48	13	5	.428	.373
Azuaje, Jheyser	R-R	5-9	165	2-12-97	.239	.226	.244	34	113	10	27	7	0	0	14	5	2	1	2	15	4	1	.301	.279
Bello, Moises	R-R	5-10	160	6-13-97	.216	.375	.143	15	51	9	11	2	1	0	1	3	2	2	0	8	2	1	.294	.286
Castillo, Eliezer	R-R	6-1	169	1-10-95	.313	.405	.278	37	134	21	42	7	1	1	15	7	6	3	3	30	7	2	.403	.367
Cortez, Victor	L-L	6-1	176	2-14-96	.229	.300	.205	39	118	16	27	1	2	0	6	14	1	0	1	19	0	2	.271	.313
Escobar, Elys	R-R	6-0	190	9-21-96	.297	.424	.247	38	118	12	35	10	1	0	13	10	2	0	0	22	2	0	.398	.362
Flores, Dilinyer	R-R	5-9	187	5-1-96	.095	.143	.071	10	21	0	2	0	0	0	0	1	0	2	0	12	0	1	.095	.136
Hernandez, Hector	L-R	6-0	175	2-23-96	.194	.204	.190	56	170	23	33	8	1	0	11	18	4	2	0	44	6	1	.253	.286
Ledezma, Junnell	R-R	5-9	165	11-9-95	.326	.382	.299	46	172	31	56	5	8	1	29	14	5	0	4	20	11	1	.465	.385
Pereira, Anthony	R-R	6-0	170	11-28-96	.250	.234	.256	65	228	48	57	15	4	4	30	29	5	3	3	39	19	5	.404	.343
Sthormes, Andres	R-R	5-10	171	8-7-96	.284	.323	.274	49	155	22	44	7	2	0	21	6	2	0	1	12	7	3	.355	.317
Torrealba, Luis	R-R	5-11	175	9-23-96	.261	.271	.257	60	226	30	59	12	3	0	30	25	9	0	1	63	4	6	.341	.356

Pitching	B-T	HT	WT	DOB	W	L	ERA	G	GS	CG	SV	IP	H	R	ER	HR	BB	SO	AVG	vLH	vRH	K/9	BB/9
Cabrera, Ray	R-R	6-1	170	10-18-94	3	0	3.43	20	0	0	0	21	21	8	8	1	5	10	.276	.316	.263	4.29	2.14
Cedeno, Luis	R-R	6-1	185	10-2-93	1	3	3.75	13	2	0	2	36	37	22	15	0	9	29	.255	.256	.255	7.25	2.25
Del Valle, Esmeiro	R-R	6-6	193	10-9-93	0	1	1.71	10	2	0	0	21	16	6	4	0	8	11	.219	.227	.216	4.71	3.43
Figueroa, Ken	R-R	6-0	165	5-30-96	3	2	2.89	13	11	0	0	53	48	25	17	1	17	48	.239	.150	.297	8.15	2.89
Fuentes, Jose	R-R	6-1	165	10-6-94	3	1	1.80	13	8	0	0	50	49	23	10	0	11	22	.254	.259	.252	3.96	1.98
Guillen, Victor	R-R	5-11	180	12-22-94	0	0	6.30	10	0	0	0	10	8	7	7	1	9	5	.229	.400	.160	4.50	8.10
Gutierrez, Alfred	R-R	6-0	143	6-12-95	5	3	2.68	14	10	0	0	54	53	21	16	4	8	50	.255	.245	.258	8.39	1.34
Hidrogo, Eudis	L-L	6-1	198	6-6-95	4	1	0.91	13	12	1	0	59	44	15	6	0	12	42	.203	.179	.208	6.37	1.82
Ledezma, Luis	R-R	6-0	150	1-27-97	0	0	1.13	6	0	0	0	8	5	1	1	0	3	6	.192	.000	.250	6.75	3.38
Lopez, Jose	R-R	5-9	164	5-25-95	1	0	3.22	15	1	0	2	36	36	18	13	0	15	25	.257	.286	.219	6.19	3.72
Moreno, Willians	R-R	6-0	182	3-30-96	2	1	4.01	16	0	0	0	25	13	11	11	0	18	18	.155	.143	.159	6.57	4.01
Paricaguan, Jesus	R-R	6-0	165	12-3-95	5	2	2.28	13	6	0	1	43	40	14	11	1	6	26	.250	.286	.237	5.40	1.25
Perez, Gerbinson	L-R	5-8	178	5-24-95	5	2	2.32	19	0	0	0	31	27	9	8	0	4	39	.237	.167	.250	11.32	1.16
Rodriguez, Hector	R-R	6-4	210	12-4-96	1	1	2.35	5	0	0	0	8	5	3	2	0	3	5	.263	.158		5.87	3.52
Vasquez, Angel	R-R	6-5	190	10-8-93	8	2	1.71	13	13	1	0	68	48	17	13	3	10	32	.198	.173	.210	4.21	1.32

Verastegui, Adenson	R-R	5-11	205	2-19-93	3	3	1.53	28	0	0	18	29	18	7	5	1	9	23	.173	.152	.183	7.06	2.76
Yanez, Wildenson	R-R	6-1	165	11-23-96	1	1	2.84	13	3	0	1	38	33	15	12	0	9	21	.224	.125	.262	4.97	2.13

Fielding

Catcher	PCT	G	PO	A	E	DP	PB
Azuaje	.987	24	134	22	2	1	0
Escobar	.981	22	143	15	3	3	7
Sthormes	.972	30	151	24	5	1	8
Aristigueta	.920	33	53	51	9	15	
Bello	.917	2	7	4	1	0	
Castillo	1.000	6	3	13	0	2	
Ledezma	1.000	4	10	17	0	4	
Pereira	.942	10	20	29	3	8	

First Base	PCT	G	PO	A	E	DP
Castillo	1.000	7	35	2	0	1
Cortez	.984	28	239	13	4	20
Ledezma	.996	29	226	10	1	15
Torrealba	.992	13	128	3	1	14

Second Base	PCT	G	PO	A	E	DP
Alfaro	.969	25	53	71	4	20

Third Base	PCT	G	PO	A	E	DP
Bello	1.000	10	6	30	0	2
Castillo	.959	24	16	54	3	3
Ledezma	.952	13	15	25	2	3
Pereira	.883	26	22	46	9	1
Torrealba	.700	6	3	4	3	0

Shortstop	PCT	G	PO	A	E	DP
Alfaro	.894	41	54	115	20	18
Bello	.938	4	6	9	1	1
Pereira	.914	30	49	111	15	22

Outfield	PCT	G	PO	A	E	DP
Arias	.968	49	88	4	3	1
Azocar	.958	64	145	13	7	1
Cortez	1.000	13	15	0	0	0
Flores	.800	8	4	0	1	0
Hernandez	.943	52	74	8	5	3
Torrealba	.970	40	61	4	2	2

Houston Astros

SEASON IN A SENTENCE: The Astros improved by 19 wins over 2014, but the season but the season was hardly a success with manager Bo Porter fired at the start of September, No. 1 overall pick Brady Aiken not signing and No. 1 prospect Carlos Correa missing half the season with a fractured right fibula.

HIGH POINT: Houston was a much stronger club after the all-star break, playing 30-36 ball and winning six of seven in late August into September, including series wins over the Angels, A's and Mariners—playoff contenders all. The Astros were 15-14 in August, one of two winning months in the season.

LOW POINT: Not signing the No. 1 overall pick—just the third time that's happened since the draft was instituted in 1965—was bad enough, but the ensuing bad press over alleged leaks of Aiken's medical history led to unflattering comments from Aiken's agent, the respected Casey Close. Jacob Nix, the team's fifth-round choice, filed a grievance after the club allegedly pulled its agreement with him after the deal with Aiken wasn't completed.

NOTABLE ROOKIES: The Astros began promoting their top prospects in 2015 and George Springer (20 HR, .804 OPS) and Jon Singleton (13 HR) made quick impacts. Righthander Nick Tropeano made four representative starts down the stretch and could be a part of the rotation next season. Right fielder Domingo Santana, acquired in the Hunter Pence deal, looked overmatched in the majors, striking out 14 of the 18 times he came to the plate.

KEY TRANSACTIONS: The Astros have long been fans of Colin Moran—they nearly drafted him No. 1 in 2013—and they acquired him in a six-player deal that netted them outfielder Jake Marisnick and sleeper prospect Frances Martes. The club believes Moran will hit for power eventually and be an average defender at third, so they parted with righthander Jarred Cosart to get him.

DOWN ON THE FARM: High Class A Lancaster won the California League title behind the hitting exploits of Brett Phillips, who went 3-for-4 in the deciding victory over Visalia. Third baseman Rio Ruiz had three hits as well. Carlos Correa was having a wonderful season until the injury in June, but still ended up leading the organization with a .325 average (.926 OPS). Several pitchers had 10 wins, including impressive lefthander Josh Hader and righthander Tropeano, who reached the majors.

OPENING DAY PAYROLL: $ 44,985,800 (29th).

PLAYERS OF THE YEAR

MAJOR LEAGUE	MINOR LEAGUE
Jose Altuve	**Carlos Correa**
2b	**ss**
.341/.377/.453	(High A)
59 RBI, 56 SB	.325/.416/.510
Led AL in batting	6 HR, 57 RBI, 20 SB

ORGANIZATION LEADERS

BATTING		*Minimum 250 AB
MAJORS		
* AVG	Altuve, Jose	.341
* OPS	Altuve, Jose	.83
HR	Carter, Chris	37
RBI	Carter, Chris	88
MINORS		
* AVG	Kemp, Tony, Lancaster, Corpus Christi	.316
* OBP	Kemp, Tony, Lancaster, Corpus Christi	.411
* SLG	Hernandez, Teoscar, Lancaster, Corpus Christi	.535
R	Kemp, Tony, Lancaster, Corpus Christi	121
H	Kemp, Tony, Lancaster, Corpus Christi	167
TB	Phillips, Brett, Quad Cities, Lancaster	261
2B	Ruiz, Rio, Lancaster	37
3B	Phillips, Brett, Quad Cities, Lancaster	14
HR	Tucker, Preston, Corpus Christi, Oklahoma City	24
BB	McCullers, Lance, Lancaster	56
SO	Hernandez, Teoscar, Lancaster, Corpus Christi	153
SB	DeShields, Delino, Corpus Christi	54

PITCHING		#Minimum 75 IP
MAJORS		
W	Keuchel, Dallas	12
# ERA	McHugh, Colin	2.73
SO	McHugh, Collin	157
SV	Qualls, Chad	19
MINORS		
W	Devenski, Chris, Lancaster, Corpus Christi	10
	Hader, Josh, Lancaster, Corpus Christi	10
	Scribner, Troy, Corpus Christi, Tri-City, Quad Cities	10
L	Rodgers, Brady, Oklahoma City, Corpus Christi	12
# ERA	Shirley, Tommy, Corpus Christi, Oklahoma City	2.53
G	Stoffel, Jason, Oklahoma City	54
GS	Cruz, Luis, Corpus Christi, Oklahoma City	22
SV	Cotton, Jamaine, Lancaster	12
	Perez, Tyson, Lancaster, Corpus Christi	12
	Thompson, Ryan, Tri-City	12
	Walter, Andrew, Quad Cities, Lancaster	12
IP	Owens, Rudy, Oklahoma City	135
BB	McCullers, Lance, Lancaster	56
SO	Hernandez, Teoscar, Lancaster, Corpus Christi	153
AVG	Tropeano, Nick, Oklahoma City	.202

2014 PERFORMANCE

General Manager: Jeff Luhnow. **Farm Director:** Quinton McCracken. **Scouting Director:** Mike Elias.

Class	Team	League	W	L	PCT	Finish	Manager
Majors	Houston Astros	American	70	92	.432	t-26th (30)	Bo Porter/Tom Lawless
Triple-A	Oklahoma City RedHawks	Pacific Coast	74	70	.514	t-7th (16)	Tom Lawless/ Tony DeFrancesco
Double-A	Corpus Christi Hooks	Texas	33	37	.471	t-5th (8)	Keith Bodie
High A	Lancaster JetHawks	California	78	62	.557	t-2nd (10)	Rodney Linares
Low A	Quad Cities River Bandits	Midwest	70	69	.504	7th (16)	Omar Lopez
Short season	Tri-City ValleyCats	New York-Penn	48	28	.632	t-1st (14)	Ed Romero
Rookie	Greeneville Astros	Appalachian	32	34	.485	8th (10)	Josh Bonifay
Rookie	Astros	Gulf Coast	28	32	.467	11th (16)	Marty Malloy
Overall Minor League Record			363	332	.522	8th (30)	

ORGANIZATION STATISTICS

HOUSTON ASTROS

AMERICAN LEAGUE

Batting	B-T	HT	WT	DOB	AVG	vLH	vRH	G	AB	R	H	2B	3B	HR	RBI	BB	HBP	SH	SF	SO	SB	CS	SLG	OBP
Altuve, Jose	R-R	5-6	175	5-6-90	.341	.414	.319	158	660	85	225	47	3	7	59	36	5	1	5	53	56	9	.453	.377
Carter, Chris	R-R	6-4	250	12-18-86	.227	.244	.220	145	507	68	115	21	1	37	88	56	5	0	4	182	5	2	.491	.308
Castro, Jason	L-R	6-3	215	6-18-87	.222	.237	.216	126	465	43	103	21	2	14	56	34	9	1	3	151	1	0	.366	.286
Corporan, Carlos	B-R	6-2	245	1-7-84	.235	.222	.245	55	170	22	40	6	0	6	19	14	3	1	2	37	0	0	.376	.302
Dominguez, Matt	R-R	6-1	215	8-28-89	.215	.242	.204	157	564	51	121	17	0	16	57	29	5	2	7	125	0	1	.330	.256
Fowler, Dexter	B-R	6-4	190	3-22-86	.276	.327	.260	116	434	61	120	21	4	8	35	66	3	1	1	108	11	4	.399	.375
Gonzalez, Marwin	B-R	6-1	205	3-14-89	.277	.333	.268	103	285	33	79	15	1	6	23	17	4	4	0	58	2	4	.400	.327
Grossman, Robbie	B-L	6-0	195	9-16-89	.233	.216	.239	103	360	42	84	14	2	6	37	55	2	3	2	105	9	3	.333	.337
Guzman, Jesus	R-R	6-1	200	6-14-84	.188	.183	.197	69	165	10	31	4	0	2	9	19	0	0	0	52	3	0	.248	.272
Hernandez, Enrique	R-R	5-11	170	8-24-91	.284	.263	.290	24	81	10	23	4	2	1	8	8	0	0	0	11	0	0	.420	.348
Hoes, L.J.	R-R	6-0	200	3-5-90	.172	.227	.107	55	122	12	21	5	0	3	11	10	0	1	3	31	0	0	.287	.230
Krauss, Marc	L-R	6-2	245	10-5-87	.194	.400	.182	67	186	16	36	6	0	6	21	21	1	0	0	54	0	0	.323	.279
Marisnick, Jake	R-R	6-4	225	3-30-91	.272	.375	.241	51	173	18	47	8	0	3	19	5	3	2	3	48	6	3	.370	.299
Petit, Gregorio	R-R	5-10	195	12-10-84	.278	.379	.235	37	97	14	27	8	0	2	9	1	2	0	0	25	0	1	.423	.300
Presley, Alex	L-L	5-10	190	7-25-85	.244	.375	.230	89	254	22	62	6	1	6	19	13	1	1	2	44	5	1	.346	.281
Santana, Domingo	R-R	6-5	225	8-5-92	.000	.000	.000	6	17	1	0	0	0	0	0	1	0	0	0	14	0	0	.000	.056
Singleton, Jon	L-L	6-2	255	9-18-91	.168	.247	.142	95	310	42	52	13	0	13	44	50	1	0	1	134	2	3	.335	.285
Springer, George	R-R	6-3	205	9-19-89	.231	.194	.242	78	295	45	68	8	1	20	51	39	9	0	2	114	5	2	.468	.336
Stassi, Max	R-R	5-10	200	3-15-91	.350	.333	.353	7	20	2	7	2	0	0	4	0	0	0	0	6	0	0	.450	.350
Villar, Jonathan	B-R	6-1	205	5-2-91	.209	.230	.199	87	263	31	55	13	2	7	27	19	2	4	1	80	17	4	.354	.267

Pitching	B-T	HT	WT	DOB	W	L	ERA	G	GS	CG	SV	IP	H	R	ER	HR	BB	SO	AVG	vLH	vRH	K/9	BB/9
Albers, Matt	L-R	6-1	225	1-20-83	0	0	0.90	8	0	0	0	10	10	1	1	0	3	8	.263	.261	.267	7.20	2.70
Bass, Anthony	R-R	6-2	200	11-1-87	1	1	6.33	21	0	0	2	27	32	20	19	6	7	7	.294	.259	.333	2.33	2.33
Buchanan, Jake	R-R	6-0	235	9-24-89	1	3	4.58	17	2	0	0	35	41	19	18	4	12	20	.297	.307	.286	5.09	3.06
Chapman, Kevin	L-L	6-3	225	2-19-88	2	0	4.64	21	0	0	0	21	22	11	11	3	11	19	.268	.261	.278	8.02	4.64
Cisnero, Jose	R-R	6-3	245	4-11-89	0	0	9.64	5	0	0	0	5	8	5	5	0	4	5	.400	.400	.400	9.64	7.71
Clemens, Paul	R-R	6-4	200	2-14-88	0	1	5.84	13	0	0	0	25	28	20	16	5	13	16	.275	.236	.319	5.84	4.74
Cosart, Jarred	R-R	6-3	195	5-25-90	9	7	4.41	20	20	0	0	116	119	61	57	7	51	75	.267	.262	.274	5.80	3.95
De Leon, Jorge	R-R	6-0	185	8-15-87	0	0	4.91	8	0	0	0	7	9	4	4	2	3	4	.310	.308	.313	4.91	3.68
Deduno, Sam	R-R	6-3	190	7-2-83	0	1	3.12	5	1	0	0	9	5	4	3	0	5	9	.172	.105	.300	9.35	5.19
2-team total (30 Minnesota)					2	6	4.47	35	9	0	0	101	97	53	50	9	46	83	—	—	—	7.42	4.11
Downs, Darin	R-L	6-3	210	12-26-84	2	1	5.45	45	0	0	0	35	28	22	21	2	19	27	.226	.203	.255	7.01	4.93
Farnsworth, Kyle	R-R	6-4	230	4-14-76	0	0	6.17	16	0	0	0	12	14	8	8	3	8	.311	.083	.394	6.17	6.94
Feldman, Scott	L-R	6-7	230	2-7-83	8	12	3.74	29	29	2	0	180	185	86	75	16	50	107	.266	.270	.261	5.34	2.50
Fields, Josh	R-R	6-0	190	8-19-85	4	6	4.45	54	0	0	4	55	50	29	27	2	17	70	.242	.268	.218	11.52	2.80
Foltynewicz, Mike	R-R	6-4	220	10-7-91	0	1	5.30	16	0	0	0	19	23	11	11	3	7	14	.299	.333	.263	6.75	3.38
Harrell, Lucas	R-R	6-2	205	6-3-85	0	3	9.49	3	3	0	0	12	19	14	13	2	9	9	.345	.333	.360	6.57	6.57
Keuchel, Dallas	L-L	6-3	210	1-1-88	12	9	2.93	29	29	5	0	200	187	71	65	11	48	146	.252	.243	.255	6.57	2.16
Martinez, David	R-R	6-2	220	8-4-87	0	0	5.14	3	0	0	0	7	5	4	4	1	2	6	.192	.200	.182	7.71	2.57
McHugh, Collin	R-R	6-2	195	6-19-87	11	9	2.73	25	25	0	0	155	117	53	47	13	41	157	.208	.220	.190	9.14	2.39
Oberholtzer, Brett	L-L	6-1	225	7-1-89	5	13	4.39	24	24	0	0	144	170	73	70	12	28	94	.295	.292	.295	5.89	1.75
Owens, Rudy	L-L	6-3	240	12-18-87	0	1	7.94	1	1	0	0	6	9	5	5	1	2	1	.360	.417	.308	1.59	3.18
Peacock, Brad	R-R	6-1	210	2-2-88	4	9	4.72	28	24	0	0	132	136	80	69	20	70	119	.267	.273	.259	8.13	4.78
Qualls, Chad	R-R	6-4	240	8-17-78	1	5	3.33	58	0	0	19	51	54	22	19	5	5	43	.265	.303	.229	7.54	0.88
Sipp, Tony	L-L	6-0	190	7-12-83	4	3	3.38	56	0	0	4	51	28	19	19	5	17	63	.157	.138	.176	11.19	3.02
Tropeano, Nick	R-R	6-4	200	8-27-90	1	3	4.57	4	4	0	0	22	19	12	11	0	9	13	.241	.241	.246	5.40	3.74
Valdes, Raul	L-L	5-11	190	11-27-77	0	0	12.27	8	0	0	1	4	5	5	5	2	3	4	.313	.429	.222	9.82	7.36
Veras, Jose	R-R	6-6	240	10-20-80	4	0	3.03	34	0	0	1	33	25	13	11	4	16	37	.203	.190	.210	10.19	4.41
Williams, Jerome	R-R	6-3	240	12-4-81	1	4	6.04	26	0	0	0	48	59	33	32	7	16	38	.301	.283	.320	7.17	3.02
2-team total (2 Texas)					2	5	6.71	28	2	0	0	58	77	44	43	7	19	44	—	—	—	6.87	2.97
Zeid, Josh	R-R	6-4	235	3-24-87	0	0	6.97	23	0	0	0	21	30	18	16	6	7	18	.345	.455	.278	7.84	3.05

Fielding

Catcher	PCT	G	PO	A	E	DP	PB
Castro	.995	114	767	55	4	4	11
Corporan	.992	54	359	25	3	4	1
Stassi	.964	6	22	5	1	0	2

First Base	PCT	G	PO	A	E	DP
Carter	.978	14	123	12	3	13
Gonzalez	1.000	1	2	0	0	0
Guzman	.994	52	300	24	2	29
Krauss	.986	33	257	30	4	24
Singleton	.987	91	776	53	11	75

Second Base	PCT	G	PO	A	E	DP
Altuve	.986	156	268	459	10	105
Gonzalez	1.000	11	12	21	0	4
Hernandez	—	1	0	0	0	0

Third Base	PCT	G	PO	A	E	DP
Petit	1.000	4	2	4	0	1
Dominguez	.972	153	109	278	11	22
Gonzalez	.875	10	2	12	2	1
Guzman	—	1	0	0	0	0
Petit	1.000	12	9	16	0	2

Shortstop	PCT	G	PO	A	E	DP
Gonzalez	.979	71	76	200	6	36
Hernandez	1.000	5	3	10	0	3
Petit	.973	19	22	50	2	14
Villar	.949	82	104	229	18	45

Outfield	PCT	G	PO	A	E	DP
Carter	1.000	6	12	0	0	0
Fowler	.980	111	238	4	5	1
Gonzalez	1.000	4	3	0	0	0
Grossman	.984	102	177	6	3	1
Guzman	1.000	8	5	0	0	0
Hernandez	.959	19	45	2	2	1
Hoes	.974	48	70	4	2	0
Krauss	1.000	23	37	1	0	1
Marisnick	.984	49	122	4	2	1
Presley	1.000	80	115	3	0	0
Santana	1.000	5	6	1	0	0
Sipp	—	2	0	0	0	0
Springer	.960	77	163	6	7	2

OKLAHOMA CITY REDHAWKS   TRIPLE-A
PACIFIC COAST LEAGUE

Batting	B-T	HT	WT	DOB	AVG	vLH	vRH	G	AB	R	H	2B	3B	HR	RBI	BB	HBP	SH	SF	SO	SB	CS	SLG	OBP
Amador, Japhet	R-R	6-4	310	1-19-87	.214	.333	.158	7	28	0	6	2	0	0	8	2	0	0	1	7	0	0	.286	.258
Aplin, Andrew	L-L	6-0	205	3-21-91	.260	.286	.256	28	96	14	25	3	1	0	15	15	0	1	4	15	5	3	.313	.348
Castro, Erik	L-R	6-4	200	11-13-87	.175	.048	.207	35	103	9	18	4	1	2	6	13	1	1	0	34	0	0	.291	.274
Chambers, Adron	L-L	5-10	200	10-8-86	.281	.229	.315	25	89	14	25	6	0	2	15	10	1	1	1	14	1	3	.416	.356
Duffy, Matt	R-R	6-3	227	2-6-89	.285	.316	.267	85	309	46	88	11	3	12	49	21	6	4	5	68	0	3	.456	.337
Fowler, Dexter	B-R	6-4	190	3-22-86	.300	.000	.429	4	10	1	3	0	0	0	1	2	0	0	0	0	0	0	.300	.417
Grossman, Robbie	B-L	6-0	195	9-16-89	.337	.433	.287	44	175	30	59	16	0	4	15	22	2	0	0	38	10	8	.497	.417
Guzman, Jesus	R-R	6-1	200	6-14-84	.615	.000	.727	4	13	3	8	3	0	0	5	3	0	0	1	2	0	0	.846	.647
Hernandez, Enrique	R-R	5-11	170	8-24-91	.337	.325	.342	67	264	41	89	17	2	8	31	18	2	2	3	25	6	5	.508	.380
2-team total (21 New Orleans)					.318	—	—	88	336	49	107	22	2	10	37	28	3	2	4	38	6	6	.485	.372
Hoes, L.J.	R-R	6-0	200	3-5-90	.297	.278	.304	35	128	21	38	6	0	2	15	16	2	1	1	30	5	4	.391	.381
Krauss, Marc	L-R	6-2	245	10-5-87	.283	.283	.292	40	152	22	43	11	0	5	37	21	1	0	2	41	1	0	.454	.369
McCurdy, Ryan	R-R	5-10	175	12-28-87	.000	.000	.000	10	17	1	0	0	0	0	0	0	0	0	0	4	0	0	.000	.000
Meyer, Jonathan	R-R	6-1	230	11-1-90	.221	.195	.230	43	154	19	34	4	0	2	10	12	2	0	2	30	0	0	.286	.282
Mier, Jio	R-R	6-2	180	8-26-90	.242	.125	.289	39	99	14	24	3	0	1	8	12	1	3	0	30	1	3	.303	.330
Perez, Carlos	R-R	6-0	210	10-27-90	.258	.279	.251	87	299	33	77	16	2	6	34	28	1	6	3	53	3	0	.385	.320
Petit, Gregorio	R-R	5-10	195	12-10-84	.296	.290	.300	84	314	45	93	19	1	10	42	20	3	3	3	51	1	3	.459	.341
Santana, Domingo	R-R	6-5	225	8-5-92	.296	.353	.271	124	443	63	131	27	2	16	81	64	2	0	4	149	6	4	.474	.384
Sclafani, Joe	B-R	5-11	190	4-22-90	.339	.340	.338	60	186	36	63	7	3	2	25	26	1	7	0	26	7	2	.441	.423
Simunic, Andy	R-R	6-0	170	8-7-85	.263	.290	.250	30	95	11	25	5	0	1	10	10	0	1	0	22	1	2	.347	.333
Singleton, Jon	L-L	6-2	255	9-18-91	.267	.309	.244	54	195	37	52	10	1	14	43	42	0	1	1	52	1	1	.544	.397
Sosa, Ruben	B-R	5-7	170	9-23-90	.268	.286	.265	26	56	11	15	4	1	1	9	5	0	3	1	14	5	3	.429	.323
Springer, George	R-R	6-3	205	9-19-89	.353	.333	.361	13	51	17	18	4	1	3	9	9	1	0	0	15	4	0	.647	.459
Stassi, Max	R-R	5-10	200	3-15-91	.247	.272	.237	100	389	48	96	20	2	9	45	22	6	3	2	101	1	0	.378	.296
Torreyes, Ronald	R-R	5-10	150	9-2-92	.300	.284	.302	124	454	64	136	20	5	2	45	24	10	21	2	26	11	9	.379	.347
Tucker, Preston	L-L	6-0	215	7-6-90	.286	.319	.277	71	269	38	77	18	0	7	50	30	0	3	2	74	2	0	.431	.354
Villar, Jonathan	B-R	6-1	205	5-2-91	.262	.222	.269	50	187	34	49	2	3	3	27	30	1	2	1	58	24	6	.353	.365
Wates, Austin	R-R	6-1	180	9-2-88	.303	.293	.302	72	277	43	84	11	3	2	29	41	1	4	0	43	30	4	.386	.395
2-team total (27 New Orleans)					.289	—	—	99	388	61	112	18	4	2	29	50	2	4	0	65	36	6	.371	.373

Pitching	B-T	HT	WT	DOB	W	L	ERA	G	GS	CG	SV	IP	H	R	ER	HR	BB	SO	AVG	vLH	vRH	K/9	BB/9
Bass, Anthony	R-R	6-2	200	11-1-87	0	2	3.31	14	0	0	0	16	15	9	6	4	6	14	.246	.100	.317	7.71	3.31
Buchanan, Jake	R-R	6-0	235	9-24-89	7	5	3.87	16	15	1	0	88	95	44	38	7	16	46	.275	.253	.297	4.69	1.63
Chapman, Kevin	L-L	6-3	225	2-19-88	2	1	1.23	42	0	0	9	44	37	11	6	0	24	64	.230	.133	.311	13.09	4.91
Cisnero, Jose	R-R	6-3	245	4-11-89	0	0	2.45	6	0	0	0	11	5	3	3	1	4	18	.105	.143	.105	14.73	3.27
Clemens, Paul	R-R	6-4	200	2-14-88	6	3	4.08	19	5	0	1	46	37	21	21	4	23	41	.216	.233	.204	7.96	4.47
Cruz, Luis	L-L	5-9	200	9-10-90	1	2	5.92	5	5	0	0	24	31	16	16	4	13	26	.323	.240	.352	9.62	4.81
Cruz, Rhiner	R-R	6-2	210	11-1-86	1	1	2.25	14	0	0	0	20	19	8	5	0	7	19	.247	.265	.233	8.55	3.15
De Leon, Jorge	R-R	6-0	185	8-15-87	3	3	2.66	30	0	0	2	47	45	16	14	0	16	43	.258	.232	.281	8.18	3.04
Doran, Bobby	R-R	6-6	235	3-21-89	2	4	5.36	21	9	0	0	81	94	52	48	7	29	41	.298	.305	.293	4.57	3.24
Downs, Darin	R-L	6-3	210	12-26-84	1	0	5.54	9	0	0	0	13	17	8	8	0	4	15	.327	.364	.300	10.38	2.77
Fields, Josh	R-R	6-0	190	8-19-85	0	0	0.00	3	0	0	1	3	0	0	0	0	1	4	.000	.000	.000	12.00	3.00
Foltynewicz, Mike	R-R	6-4	220	10-7-91	7	7	5.08	21	18	0	0	103	98	63	58	10	52	102	.260	.279	.244	8.94	4.56
Lo, Chia-Jen	R-R	5-11	205	4-7-86	1	0	4.74	16	0	0	0	19	27	10	10	2	12	17	.346	.343	.349	8.05	5.68
Martinez, David	R-R	6-2	200	8-4-87	5	6	5.64	22	13	0	0	83	94	54	52	5	30	62	.289	.372	.222	6.72	3.25
McHugh, Collin	R-R	6-2	195	6-19-87	0	0	3.79	5	3	0	0	19	13	9	8	6	13	.217	.214	.222	6.16	2.84
Oberholtzer, Brett	L-L	6-1	225	7-1-89	1	2	4.65	5	5	0	0	31	35	17	16	9	3	31	.282	.333	.261	9.00	0.87
Owens, Rudy	L-L	6-3	240	12-18-87	7	5	4.48	24	20	0	1	129	130	68	64	10	30	97	.263	.299	.244	6.78	2.10
Peacock, Brad	R-R	6-1	210	2-2-88	1	0	4.76	1	1	0	0	6	7	3	3	1	1	5	.292	.214	.400	7.94	1.59
Robinson, Andrew	R-R	6-1	185	2-13-88	0	2	4.50	6	0	0	1	8	9	5	4	0	0	7	.273	.250	.294	7.88	0.00
Rodgers, Brady	R-R	6-2	187	9-17-90	1	0	0.00	1	1	0	0	6	2	0	0	0	1	4	.111	.167	.000	6.00	1.50
Rodriguez, Richard	R-R	6-4	205	3-4-90	2	0	3.49	16	0	0	0	28	19	11	11	3	6	23	.196	.200	.193	7.31	1.91
Seaton, Ross	L-R	6-4	200	9-18-89	1	1	6.87	8	1	0	0	18	24	18	14	3	10	9	.316	.300	.326	4.42	4.91
Shirley, Tommy	R-L	6-5	200	11-11-88	0	2	3.96	12	2	0	0	25	30	12	11	0	13	20	.293	.282	.299	7.20	4.68

HOUSTON ASTROS

	B-T	HT	WT	DOB	W	L	ERA	G	GS	CG	SV	IP	H	R	ER	HR	BB	SO	AVG	vLH	vRH	K/9	BB/9
Stoffel, Jason	R-R	6-1	235	9-15-88	5	3	2.94	53	0	0	11	64	65	27	21	3	28	68	.270	.262	.275	9.51	3.92
Tiburcio, Frederick	R-R	6-3	192	11-1-90	0	0	0.00	1	0	0	0	2	2	0	0	0	3	1	.333	.333	.333	4.50	13.50
Tropeano, Nick	R-R	6-4	200	8-27-90	9	5	3.03	23	20	0	0	125	90	44	42	11	33	120	.202	.156	.241	8.66	2.38
Urckfitz, Pat	L-L	6-4	200	7-21-88	0	1	4.10	25	0	0	0	26	27	14	12	2	15	20	.273	.256	.286	6.84	5.13
Valdes, Raul	L-L	5-11	190	11-27-77	1	0	3.48	8	0	0	0	10	9	4	4	1	0	13	.220	.150	.286	11.32	0.00
Veras, Jose	R-R	6-6	240	10-20-80	0	0	0.00	2	0	0	0	2	1	0	0	0	1	4	.143	.250	.000	18.00	4.50
White, Alex	R-R	6-3	220	8-29-88	3	6	6.50	25	10	0	0	64	78	51	46	7	31	53	.301	.314	.293	7.49	4.38
Wojciechowski, Asher	R-R	6-4	240	12-21-88	4	4	4.74	15	14	0	0	76	89	46	40	10	21	59	.293	.338	.253	6.99	2.49
Zeid, Josh	R-R	6-4	235	3-24-87	2	2	2.41	17	0	0	7	19	14	8	5	2	9	21	.212	.250	.190	10.13	4.34

Fielding

Catcher	PCT	G	PO	A	E	DP	PB
McCurdy	1.000	5	16	0	0	0	0
Perez	.981	74	579	41	12	4	8
Stassi	.994	72	500	41	3	4	3

First Base	PCT	G	PO	A	E	DP
Amador	1.000	1	10	0	0	1
Castro	.990	13	91	7	1	11
Duffy	.995	55	407	30	2	53
Guzman	1.000	1	9	0	0	0
Hernandez	1.000	1	2	0	0	0
Krauss	.996	25	222	17	1	23
Perez	1.000	5	23	0	0	3
Singleton	.987	51	433	28	6	49
Tucker	.917	3	28	5	3	2

Second Base	PCT	G	PO	A	E	DP
Hernandez	.991	26	44	68	1	24
Mier	.979	12	18	29	1	9
Sclafani	.978	42	67	113	4	30
Simunic	1.000	4	3	6	0	1

	PCT	G	PO	A	E	DP
Sosa	1.000	2	2	5	0	1
Torreyes	.979	73	123	203	7	53

Third Base	PCT	G	PO	A	E	DP
Duffy	1.000	35	16	59	0	7
Hernandez	.894	14	7	35	5	3
Meyer	.936	42	34	69	7	10
Mier	1.000	15	13	17	0	3
Petit	.967	12	8	21	1	3
Sclafani	.893	14	3	22	3	1
Simunic	—	1	0	0	0	0
Sosa	1.000	1	0	0	0	0
Torreyes	.964	24	13	40	2	5

Shortstop	PCT	G	PO	A	E	DP
Hernandez	.971	13	20	47	2	10
Mier	.896	12	16	27	5	8
Petit	.967	65	95	200	10	41
Sclafani	—	1	0	0	0	0
Torreyes	.952	14	16	43	3	8
Villar	.965	48	66	125	7	39

Outfield	PCT	G	PO	A	E	DP
Aplin	.986	27	71	2	1	2
Castro	—	1	0	0	0	0
Chambers	1.000	22	46	1	0	0
Duffy	—	1	0	0	0	0
Fowler	1.000	2	2	0	0	0
Grossman	1.000	42	90	0	0	0
Hernandez	1.000	13	22	3	0	0
Hoes	.962	34	76	0	3	0
Krauss	1.000	6	10	0	0	0
Santana	.981	110	202	6	4	2
Simunic	1.000	24	45	2	0	1
Sosa	1.000	19	31	3	0	0
Springer	1.000	13	21	1	0	0
Torreyes	.976	16	38	2	1	0
Tucker	.979	55	90	4	2	0
Wates	.991	63	106	5	1	0

CORPUS CHRISTI HOOKS

DOUBLE-A

TEXAS LEAGUE

Batting	B-T	HT	WT	DOB	AVG	vLH	vRH	G	AB	R	H	2B	3B	HR	RBI	BB	HBP	SH	SF	SO	SB	CS	SLG	OBP
Aplin, Andrew	L-L	6-0	205	3-21-91	.267	.216	.286	98	356	49	95	11	1	6	50	65	2	6	5	56	21	8	.354	.379
Cokinos, M.P.	R-R	6-2	215	6-18-90	.271	.205	.289	60	203	17	55	7	0	1	22	9	1	4	0	23	2	3	.320	.305
DeShields, Delino	R-R	5-9	210	8-16-92	.236	.269	.226	114	411	75	97	14	2	11	57	61	11	18	6	112	54	14	.360	.346
Duffy, Matt	R-R	6-3	227	2-6-89	.302	.481	.240	49	202	23	61	11	1	6	35	7	5	1	1	36	2	1	.455	.340
Epps, Chris	L-R	6-2	172	12-10-88	.156	.250	.145	23	77	10	12	1	1	3	11	16	0	0	1	27	4	2	.312	.298
Fontana, Nolan	L-R	5-11	190	6-6-91	.262	.167	.287	66	229	33	60	21	1	1	26	61	2	11	2	76	5	8	.376	.418
Garcia, Rene	R-R	6-0	205	3-21-90	.244	.284	.232	75	270	34	66	14	0	5	23	9	4	5	0	32	5	3	.352	.279
Gregor, Conrad	L-L	6-3	225	2-27-92	.239	.105	.267	33	109	14	26	4	1	3	13	13	1	0	1	21	0	1	.376	.323
Heineman, Tyler	B-R	5-11	195	6-19-91	.242	.226	.246	78	265	34	64	15	3	1	26	24	13	2	2	37	3	3	.332	.332
Heras, Leonardo	L-R	5-9	190	5-29-90	.236	.254	.232	96	313	39	74	13	6	5	36	52	5	5	0	58	19	4	.364	.354
Hernandez, Enrique	R-R	5-11	170	8-24-91	.325	.438	.250	10	40	9	13	3	0	1	5	3	0	0	0	3	0	0	.475	.372
Hernandez, Teoscar	R-R	6-2	180	10-15-92	.284	.300	.280	23	95	12	27	4	1	4	10	2	0	1	0	36	2	3	.474	.299
Kemp, Tony	L-R	5-6	165	10-31-91	.292	.218	.315	59	233	42	68	11	4	4	21	28	7	5	2	32	13	6	.425	.381
Meredith, Brandon	R-R	6-2	225	12-19-89	.236	.233	.237	41	127	22	30	7	0	8	22	24	2	3	1	35	4	3	.480	.364
Meyer, Jonathan	R-R	6-1	230	11-1-90	.212	.318	.181	77	293	26	62	9	2	2	41	19	5	3	2	63	2	1	.276	.270
Mier, Jio	R-R	6-2	180	8-26-90	.216	.273	.196	79	255	33	55	10	3	0	27	23	2	8	5	59	5	1	.302	.281
Moran, Colin	L-R	6-4	215	10-1-92	.304	.385	.279	28	112	12	34	6	0	2	22	9	0	0	2	23	0	1	.411	.350
Nash, Telvin	R-R	6-1	248	2-20-91	.227	.215	.231	84	273	46	62	4	0	22	49	34	9	3	2	112	1	1	.484	.330
Perdomo, Carlos	R-R	5-10	160	4-25-90	.246	.366	.214	60	195	26	48	4	0	2	17	22	2	5	0	29	3	3	.297	.329
Sclafani, Joe	B-R	5-11	190	4-22-90	.285	.115	.322	36	144	14	41	4	2	1	15	10	1	1	1	13	2	2	.361	.333
Scott, Jordan	L-R	6-2	180	9-22-91	.167	.000	.333	4	6	0	1	0	0	0	0	0	0	2	0	1	0	0	.167	.167
Sosa, Ruben	B-R	5-7	170	9-23-90	.267	.367	.229	50	180	31	48	8	5	3	26	22	1	12	1	53	20	4	.417	.348
Tucker, Preston	L-L	6-0	215	7-6-90	.276	.339	.260	65	261	41	72	17	0	17	43	26	3	0	0	46	3	3	.536	.348
Wik, Marc	L-R	5-11	220	7-18-92	.429	.000	.500	2	7	3	3	1	0	1	3	0	1	0	0	1	0	1	1.000	.500

Pitching	B-T	HT	WT	DOB	W	L	ERA	G	GS	CG	SV	IP	H	R	ER	HR	BB	SO	AVG	vLH	vRH	K/9	BB/9
Alaniz, R.J.	R-R	6-4	175	6-14-91	0	0	6.44	14	1	0	0	29	27	22	21	2	26	15	.255	.214	.281	4.60	7.98
Appel, Mark	R-R	6-5	225	7-15-91	1	2	3.69	7	6	1	0	39	35	17	16	2	13	38	.236	.164	.287	8.77	3.00
Ballew, Travis	R-R	6-0	160	5-1-91	6	3	6.14	37	0	0	4	51	60	37	35	5	33	41	.299	.353	.259	7.19	5.79
Cain, Colton	L-L	6-3	256	2-5-91	0	3	6.28	14	7	0	0	39	51	30	27	6	26	33	.327	.321	.330	7.68	6.05
Cruz, Luis	L-L	5-9	200	9-10-90	7	6	3.14	21	17	0	1	100	86	39	35	12	25	92	.231	.258	.221	8.25	2.24
De Leon, Jorge	R-R	6-0	185	8-15-87	1	2	3.92	15	0	0	2	21	18	10	9	5	7	18	.231	.200	.245	7.83	3.05
Devenski, Chris	R-R	6-3	195	11-13-90	5	3	3.92	10	5	0	0	41	33	21	18	7	18	37	.213	.143	.261	8.06	3.92
Dimock, Michael	R-R	6-2	194	10-26-89	1	4	3.29	16	0	0	1	27	26	12	10	1	7	21	.252	.294	.232	6.91	2.30
2-team total (23 San Antonio)					2	7	3.47	39	0	0	1	57	55	32	22	6	17	61	—	—	—	9.63	2.68
Downs, Darin	R-L	6-3	210	12-26-84	0	1	5.40	2	2	0	0	2	3	1	1	0	2	3	.429	.500	.400	16.20	10.80
Geith, T.J.	L-L	6-5	175	6-27-89	0	0	0.00	1	0	0	0	0	0	0	0	0	0	0	.000	.000	—	0.00	0.00
Hader, Josh	L-L	6-3	160	4-7-94	1	1	6.30	5	4	0	0	20	16	14	14	2	16	24	.216	.067	.254	10.80	7.20
Hauschild, Mike	R-R	6-3	210	1-22-90	2	9	4.29	20	16	0	1	99	95	53	47	5	25	87	.258	.307	.225	7.94	2.28
Heidenreich, Matt	L-R	6-5	185	1-17-91	1	0	8.02	12	5	0	1	34	51	34	30	4	21	30	.347	.352	.342	8.02	5.61

	B-T	HT	WT	DOB	W	L	ERA	G	GS	CG	SV	IP	H	R	ER	HR	BB	SO	AVG	vLH	vRH	K/9	BB/9
Jankowski, Jordan	R-R	6-2	200	5-17-89	5	6	3.58	30	14	0	3	108	90	44	43	12	26	120	.227	.293	.180	10.00	2.17
Lambson, Mitchell	L-L	6-1	205	7-20-90	3	1	1.36	23	0	0	1	33	25	8	5	4	5	35	.207	.213	.203	9.55	1.36
Minaya, Juan	R-R	6-4	195	9-18-90	0	0	3.12	6	0	0	0	9	9	3	3	1	4	11	.265	.125	.308	11.42	4.15
Perez, Tyson	R-R	6-3	215	12-27-89	4	0	2.09	30	0	0	11	39	25	11	9	3	14	29	.187	.163	.198	6.75	3.26
Robinson, Andrew	R-R	6-1	185	2-13-88	4	2	1.89	20	0	0	2	33	31	7	7	0	11	32	.240	.224	.250	8.64	2.97
Rodgers, Brady	R-R	6-2	187	9-17-90	5	12	4.77	26	17	0	2	121	135	73	64	15	19	87	.287	.292	.282	6.49	1.42
Rodriguez, Richard	R-R	6-4	205	3-4-90	0	2	3.05	11	0	0	0	21	21	7	7	1	2	28	.256	.343	.191	12.19	0.87
Rollins, David	L-L	6-1	195	12-4-89	3	4	3.81	27	12	0	1	78	74	38	33	7	22	77	.243	.256	.239	8.88	2.54
Scribner, Troy	R-R	6-3	190	7-2-91	2	0	2.70	3	1	0	0	7	5	2	2	1	3	7	.208	.200	.214	9.45	4.05
Seaton, Ross	L-R	6-4	200	9-18-89	0	1	2.65	4	2	0	0	17	16	7	5	1	6	16	.250	.200	.310	8.47	3.18
Shirley, Tommy	R-L	6-5	220	11-11-88	7	3	1.88	17	13	0	1	86	63	24	18	7	17	78	.201	.186	.206	8.13	1.77
Smith, Kyle	R-R	6-0	170	9-10-92	5	5	4.34	21	13	0	0	95	92	47	46	14	25	96	.251	.234	.261	9.06	2.36
Sogard, Alex	L-L	6-3	215	7-25-87	1	1	2.91	25	0	0	2	43	33	22	14	7	20	25	.210	.171	.224	5.19	4.15
Urckfitz, Pat	L-L	6-4	200	7-21-88	1	1	1.32	22	0	0	3	27	24	8	4	0	5	22	.238	.200	.254	7.24	1.65
Weiland, Kyle	L-R	6-4	195	9-12-86	0	0	14.40	5	0	0	0	5	12	8	8	4	4	3	.462	.300	.563	5.40	7.20
West, Aaron	R-R	6-1	195	6-1-90	2	1	5.55	7	5	0	0	24	22	15	15	4	10	13	.242	.277	.205	4.81	3.70

Fielding

Catcher	PCT	G	PO	A	E	DP	PB
Cokinos	1.000	2	7	0	0	0	0
Garcia	.992	71	542	55	5	4	6
Heineman	.994	70	566	72	4	3	2

First Base	PCT	G	PO	A	E	DP
Cokinos	.982	20	160	5	3	13
Duffy	1.000	16	116	9	0	9
Gregor	.995	24	182	11	1	11
Meredith	1.000	5	44	0	0	1
Nash	.990	68	546	31	6	46
Perdomo	.989	10	88	4	1	10
Tucker	1.000	8	42	5	0	6

Second Base	PCT	G	PO	A	E	DP
Fontana	.968	41	75	104	6	24
Hernandez	1.000	10	15	31	0	9
Kemp	.996	56	101	128	1	25

	PCT	G	PO	A	E	DP
Meyer	1.000	7	10	14	0	5
Mier	.966	9	13	15	1	6
Perdomo	1.000	6	7	6	0	1
Sclafani	.967	12	28	31	2	11
Sosa	1.000	3	9	5	0	2

Third Base	PCT	G	PO	A	E	DP
Duffy	.934	35	22	77	7	4
Meyer	.904	60	45	125	18	8
Mier	.938	7	4	11	1	1
Moran	1.000	28	11	51	0	4
Perdomo	1.000	1	0	1	0	0
Sclafani	.868	17	5	28	5	0

Shortstop	PCT	G	PO	A	E	DP
Fontana	.992	25	37	82	1	19
Meyer	.853	10	5	24	5	4
Mier	.955	63	95	182	13	34

	PCT	G	PO	A	E	DP
Perdomo	.960	39	53	91	6	15
Sosa	.895	6	6	11	2	2

Outfield	PCT	G	PO	A	E	DP
Aplin	.982	95	207	13	4	3
Cokinos	1.000	1	1	0	0	0
DeShields	.970	108	222	3	7	0
Epps	.947	14	18	0	1	0
Heras	.993	85	146	4	1	0
Hernandez	1.000	23	50	1	0	1
Kemp	1.000	3	6	0	0	0
Meredith	1.000	17	36	1	0	0
Perdomo	1.000	1	1	1	0	0
Sclafani	1.000	3	2	0	0	0
Scott	1.000	3	2	0	0	0
Sosa	1.000	32	57	3	0	0
Tucker	.990	48	99	3	1	0
Wik	1.000	2	4	0	0	0

LANCASTER JETHAWKS

HIGH CLASS A

CALIFORNIA LEAGUE

Batting	B-T	HT	WT	DOB	AVG	vLH	vRH	G	AB	R	H	2B	3B	HR	RBI	BB	HBP	SH	SF	SO	SB	CS	SLG	OBP
Borchering, Bobby	B-R	6-2	205	10-25-90	.238	.200	.250	16	63	3	15	4	1	0	7	8	0	0	0	24	0	0	.333	.324
Correa, Carlos	R-R	6-4	205	9-22-94	.325	.172	.378	62	249	50	81	16	6	6	57	36	5	0	3	45	20	4	.510	.416
Elkins, Austin	B-R	5-11	195	12-21-90	.252	.333	.234	36	115	20	29	4	0	2	9	23	6	1	0	25	0	0	.339	.403
Gominsky, Justin	R-R	6-4	185	8-26-89	.333	.500	.300	5	12	2	4	0	0	0	1	1	0	1	0	2	0	0	.333	.385
Gregor, Conrad	L-R	6-3	225	1-29-92	.367	.286	.397	47	180	43	66	14	3	12	45	27	3	0	4	25	1	1	.678	.449
Gulbransen, Dan	L-R	5-11	205	1-5-91	.261	.250	.265	72	253	41	66	15	4	6	46	38	2	2	4	68	2	1	.423	.357
Hernandez, Teoscar	R-R	6-2	180	10-15-92	.294	.217	.323	96	391	72	115	33	8	17	75	49	5	5	5	117	31	6	.550	.376
Kemmer, Jon	L-L	6-2	220	11-17-90	.294	.250	.308	39	153	32	45	10	1	12	33	4	1	0	1	33	0	1	.608	.314
Kemp, Tony	L-L	5-6	165	10-31-91	.336	.250	.363	72	295	79	99	19	4	4	37	45	8	5	3	35	28	7	.468	.433
Mathis, Tanner	L-L	5-11	195	6-27-91	.258	.314	.237	40	132	24	34	7	2	2	19	18	2	2	1	39	3	6	.386	.353
Mayfield, Jack	R-R	5-11	190	9-30-90	.293	.351	.267	66	246	39	72	22	2	7	39	20	4	3	4	50	1	6	.484	.350
McDonald, Chase	R-R	6-4	265	6-2-92	.000	—	.000	1	1	0	0	0	0	0	0	0	0	0	0	0	0	0	.000	.000
Meredith, Brandon	R-R	6-2	225	12-19-89	.242	.233	.245	39	153	27	37	3	2	7	22	17	3	0	0	35	0	1	.425	.329
Mitchell, Ronnie	L-L	5-11	200	6-21-91	.248	.273	.241	27	101	12	25	5	0	3	11	12	1	1	0	21	0	1	.386	.333
Moon, Chan	L-R	6-0	185	3-23-91	.286	.393	.254	59	241	36	69	9	3	4	36	21	1	2	4	59	10	7	.398	.341
Morales, Jobduan	B-R	5-10	211	6-7-91	.216	.231	.212	45	171	26	37	8	1	4	28	19	0	0	5	50	1	2	.345	.287
Pena, Roberto	B-R	6-0	217	6-8-92	.249	.265	.242	93	350	48	87	19	0	13	54	25	1	5	5	63	1	2	.414	.306
Perdomo, Carlos	R-R	5-10	160	4-25-90	.328	.400	.309	36	119	26	39	3	3	1	17	15	2	2	3	14	8	2	.429	.403
Phillips, Brett	R-R	6-0	175	6-2-94	.339	.321	.346	27	109	19	37	8	2	4	10	14	2	2	1	20	5	4	.560	.421
Ramsay, James	L-L	5-11	200	3-2-92	.222	.400	.154	5	18	3	4	1	0	0	3	1	1	0		6	1	1	.389	.364
Rodriguez, Jake	R-R	5-9	175	1-24-92	.116	.231	.067	15	43	3	5	0	0	0	5	5	1	0	0	8	1	0	.116	.224
Ruiz, Rio	L-R	6-2	215	5-22-94	.293	.312	.286	131	516	76	151	37	2	11	77	82	0		4	91	4	4	.436	.387
Scott, Jordan	L-R	6-2	180	5-22-94	.297	.212	.325	58	212	35	63	13	7	1	31	19	1	7	2	34	9	4	.439	.355
Sosa, Ruben	B-R	5-7	170	9-23-90	.238	.167	.273	40	130	24	31	6	4	1	12	19	1	7	2	36	14	3	.369	.336
Vasquez, Danry	L-R	6-3	177	1-8-94	.291	.160	.334	114	423	67	123	30	2	5	47	40	2	8	2	68	1	2	.407	.353
White, Tyler	R-R	5-11	225	10-19-90	.267	.250	.272	43	150	28	40	13	1	8	23	28	7	0	1	27	0	0	.527	.403
Wik, Marc	L-R	5-11	220	7-18-92	.143	—	.143	2	7	2	1	1	0	0	0	2	0	0	0	1	0	0	.286	.333

Pitching	B-T	HT	WT	DOB	W	L	ERA	G	GS	CG	SV	IP	H	R	ER	HR	BB	SO	AVG	vLH	vRH	K/9	BB/9
Appel, Mark	R-R	6-5	225	7-15-91	2	5	9.74	12	12	0	0	44	74	51	48	9	11	40	.372	.347	.394	8.12	2.23
Brunnemann, Tyler	R-R	6-2	200	8-9-91	0	0	2.03	8	0	0	1	13	7	3	3	1	5	18	.152	.143	.156	12.15	3.38
Christensen, Pat	R-R	6-3	195	9-22-91	1	0	5.60	13	0	0	0	27	44	23	17	2	9	23	.367	.333	.385	7.57	2.96
Cotton, Chris	R-L	5-10	166	11-21-90	1	0	16.88	3	0	0	0	3	6	5	5	3	0	1	.462	.500	.429	3.38	0.00
Cotton, Jamaine	R-R	6-1	205	9-27-90	2	4	4.60	37	0	0	12	45	53	24	23	8	15	29	.305	.305	.304	5.80	3.00
Devenski, Chris	R-R	6-3	195	11-13-90	5	5	4.11	17	11	0	2	77	70	42	35	8	12	77	.233	.212	.243	9.04	1.41

	B-T	HT	WT	DOB	W	L	ERA	G	GS	CG	SV	IP	H	R	ER	HR	BB	SO	AVG	vLH	vRH	K/9	BB/9
Emanuel, Kent	L-L	6-3	225	6-4-92	9	5	4.59	21	14	0	2	102	111	55	52	12	19	76	.278	.243	.297	6.71	1.68
Grills, Evan	L-L	6-4	205	6-13-92	2	3	4.70	10	6	0	2	44	58	33	23	6	4	26	.319	.346	.308	5.32	0.82
Hader, Josh	L-L	6-3	160	4-7-94	9	2	2.70	22	15	0	2	103	76	41	31	9	38	112	.206	.227	.199	9.75	3.31
Hauschild, Mike	R-R	6-3	210	1-22-90	2	1	4.41	8	4	0	0	35	40	17	17	3	9	31	.310	.333	.299	8.05	2.34
Heidenreich, Matt	L-R	6-5	185	1-17-91	3	4	5.40	16	6	0	2	53	74	38	32	6	14	54	.323	.312	.331	9.11	2.36
Holmes, Brian	L-L	6-4	210	1-30-91	5	2	4.53	20	10	0	2	87	86	50	44	13	23	82	.259	.265	.256	8.45	2.37
Lambson, Mitchell	L-L	6-1	205	7-20-90	1	1	3.32	17	0	0	2	22	21	8	8	3	4	28	.263	.318	.241	11.63	1.66
McCullers Jr., Lance	L-R	6-2	205	10-2-93	3	6	5.47	25	18	0	4	97	95	63	59	18	56	115	.255	.230	.274	10.67	5.20
Minaya, Juan	R-R	6-4	195	9-18-90	2	3	4.40	29	1	0	1	45	43	25	22	6	22	53	.247	.300	.219	10.60	4.40
Minor, Daniel	R-R	5-11	195	2-9-91	9	3	4.25	36	0	0	3	53	52	26	25	6	17	51	.254	.286	.228	8.66	2.89
Morton, Zach	R-R	6-1	180	7-12-90	1	1	4.94	22	7	0	2	71	80	42	39	6	22	30	.289	.272	.303	3.80	2.79
Osborne, J.D.	R-L	6-5	205	11-13-90	2	1	8.28	17	0	0	0	25	21	26	23	2	25	19	.221	.192	.232	6.84	9.00
Perez, Tyson	R-R	6-3	215	12-27-89	0	3	5.87	9	0	0	1	15	22	12	10	0	9	15	.349	.391	.325	8.80	5.28
Rodriguez, Richard	R-R	6-4	205	3-4-90	0	0	5.06	7	0	0	0	11	10	6	6	2	2	16	.250	.389	.136	13.50	1.69
Sanudo, Gonzalo	L-R	6-3	235	1-10-92	0	0	6.02	19	6	0	0	52	65	35	35	7	9	39	.308	.266	.333	6.71	1.55
Smith, Kyle	R-R	6-0	170	9-10-92	4	0	2.60	7	3	0	0	28	18	10	8	3	12	31	.178	.143	.197	10.08	3.90
Velasquez, Vince	B-R	6-3	203	6-7-92	7	4	3.74	15	10	0	0	55	45	24	23	6	23	72	.223	.264	.208	11.71	3.74
Walter, Andrew	R-R	6-4	200	10-18-90	0	2	5.14	7	0	0	3	7	13	6	4	2	1	8	.382	.429	.350	10.29	1.29
Westwood, Kyle	R-R	6-3	190	4-13-91	8	7	4.23	27	17	0	2	132	146	70	62	8	26	88	.283	.287	.281	6.00	1.77

Fielding

Catcher	PCT	G	PO	A	E	DP	PB
Morales	.987	38	275	22	4	2	1
Pena	.996	93	755	84	3	9	7
Rodriguez	.977	14	120	9	3	0	0

First Base	PCT	G	PO	A	E	DP
Borchering	.991	14	105	7	1	10
Gregor	.993	44	371	33	3	36
Gulbransen	1.000	8	71	2	0	5
Kemmer	.964	2	27	0	1	0
Meredith	.989	30	248	17	3	25
Perdomo	1.000	4	40	4	0	3
White	.991	38	304	25	3	25

Second Base	PCT	G	PO	A	E	DP
Elkins	.947	23	54	54	6	8
Kemp	.980	64	124	164	6	42

	PCT	G	PO	A	E	DP
Mayfield	.969	44	87	131	7	29
Morales	.500	1	0	2	2	2
Perdomo	.921	8	14	21	3	4
Sosa	.500	2	1	0	1	0

Third Base	PCT	G	PO	A	E	DP
Mayfield	1.000	8	5	12	0	0
Morales	—	1	0	0	0	0
Perdomo	.889	10	3	21	3	2
Ruiz	.948	122	72	218	16	16
White	1.000	1	0	1	0	0

Shortstop	PCT	G	PO	A	E	DP
Correa	.969	59	110	204	10	35
Elkins	1.000	1	0	1	0	0
Mayfield	.932	11	11	30	3	8
Moon	.934	57	85	170	18	27

	PCT	G	PO	A	E	DP
Perdomo	.955	13	9	33	2	3

Outfield	PCT	G	PO	A	E	DP
Gominsky	1.000	4	7	1	0	0
Gulbransen	1.000	23	31	0	0	0
Hernandez	.963	96	224	10	9	4
Kemmer	.974	19	35	2	1	0
Mathis	.984	39	59	3	1	0
Meredith	1.000	9	16	2	0	0
Mitchell	.983	25	57	1	1	0
Phillips	.966	27	54	3	2	1
Ramsay	1.000	5	6	0	0	0
Scott	.978	49	85	3	2	0
Sosa	.973	38	67	6	2	1
Vasquez	.980	93	139	9	3	0
Wik	1.000	2	2	0	0	0

QUAD CITIES RIVER BANDITS

LOW CLASS A

MIDWEST LEAGUE

Batting	B-T	HT	WT	DOB	AVG	vLH	vRH	G	AB	R	H	2B	3B	HR	RBI	BB	HBP	SH	SF	SO	SB	CS	SLG	OBP
Booth, Brett	R-R	5-11	215	10-12-90	.242	.167	.269	56	182	20	44	10	1	5	24	18	4	0	1	52	2	0	.390	.322
Bottger, Ryan	B-R	6-0	210	4-14-93	.227	.258	.216	34	119	13	27	2	0	1	8	8	2	0	3	22	6	2	.269	.280
Boyd, Bobby	L-R	5-9	180	1-4-93	.219	.350	.170	20	73	9	16	0	1	0	6	7	0	2	0	15	6	1	.247	.288
Davis, J.D.	R-R	6-3	215	4-27-93	.303	.297	.305	43	155	20	47	9	0	8	32	13	2	0	1	41	4	0	.516	.363
Elkins, Austin	B-R	5-11	195	12-21-90	.256	.125	.310	26	82	8	21	5	1	0	9	6	1	4	0	14	4	1	.341	.315
Fernandez, Leon	R-R	6-1	170	5-20-93	.279	.192	.301	40	129	21	36	7	2	3	21	17	0	0	0	41	9	4	.434	.363
Gonzalez, Alex	R-R	5-11	165	7-7-91	.250	.167	.286	6	20	4	5	2	0	0	5	2	0	0	0	4	0	0	.350	.318
Gregor, Conrad	L-R	6-3	225	2-27-92	.298	.360	.287	44	161	26	48	13	1	1	28	28	3	0	2	34	0	0	.410	.407
Holberton, Brian	L-R	5-10	200	6-10-92	.253	.206	.265	85	297	34	75	18	1	6	34	33	2	1	1	42	0	1	.380	.330
Kemmer, Jon	L-L	6-2	220	11-17-90	.289	.324	.280	52	199	29	52	15	1	4	17	20	3	1	0	39	3	1	.450	.369
Lindauer, Thomas	R-R	6-2	175	12-2-91	.183	.250	.162	92	301	30	55	14	0	5	31	25	0	4	0	78	4	2	.279	.245
Mathis, Tanner	L-L	5-11	195	6-27-91	.261	.250	.264	36	119	16	31	7	2	0	7	20	1	1	0	23	7	2	.353	.371
Mayfield, Jack	R-R	5-11	190	6-30-90	.265	.375	.244	39	147	24	39	9	0	2	16	13	1	0	2	26	2	1	.367	.325
McDonald, Chase	R-R	6-4	265	6-2-92	.279	.348	.256	102	362	57	101	25	0	16	67	44	5	0	2	116	0	0	.481	.363
Mejia, Brauly	R-R	6-0	185	10-28-94	.143	.200	.111	5	14	0	2	0	0	0	1	0	0	0	0	8	0	0	.143	.143
Melendez, Alexander	R-R	6-1	185	4-21-95	.167	.000	.250	6	12	1	2	0	0	0	2	0	1	0	0	5	0	0	.167	.286
Mitchell, Ronnie	L-L	5-11	200	6-21-91	.285	.204	.308	72	249	39	71	12	1	13	46	29	2	1	3	64	5	6	.498	.360
Moon, Chan	L-R	6-0	185	3-23-91	.279	.269	.282	68	233	40	65	9	7	2	24	31	0	10	1	41	25	6	.403	.362
Morales, Jobduan	B-R	5-10	211	6-7-91	.310	.250	.333	20	71	11	22	7	0	1	11	10	0	0	1	20	1	0	.451	.390
Parker, Rene	R-R	5-10	190	6-22-91	.164	.045	.190	37	122	9	20	4	0	2	11	8	1	1	2	28	0	1	.246	.218
Phillips, Brett	L-R	6-0	175	5-30-94	.302	.266	.311	103	384	68	116	21	12	13	58	36	4	12	7	76	18	10	.521	.362
Ramsay, James	L-L	5-11	200	3-2-92	.247	.271	.240	118	434	70	107	26	10	3	35	59	5	5	6	101	33	7	.373	.339
Reed, A.J.	L-R	6-4	240	5-10-93	.272	.167	.305	34	125	21	34	9	1	7	24	8	2	0	0	32	0	0	.528	.326
Rodriguez, Jake	R-R	5-9	175	1-24-92	.160	.067	.182	25	81	6	13	2	0	1	8	6	1	1	0	28	0	0	.222	.227
Springer, George	R-R	6-3	205	9-19-89	.250	—	.250	3	4	1	1	0	0	0	0	3	0	0	0	1	2	0	.500	.571
White, Tyler	R-R	5-11	225	10-29-90	.305	.231	.326	71	239	41	73	20	1	7	41	35	12	0	4	40	0	1	.485	.414
Wik, Marc	L-R	5-11	220	7-18-92	.252	.209	.264	59	206	38	52	14	3	4	33	3	1	3	3	55	11	7	.408	.343

Pitching	B-T	HT	WT	DOB	W	L	ERA	G	GS	CG	SV	IP	H	R	ER	HR	BB	SO	AVG	vLH	vRH	K/9	BB/9
Bass, Anthony	R-R	6-2	200	11-1-87	0	0	0.00	3	1	0	0	6	2	0	0	0	0	6	.125	.000	.250	13.50	0.00
Brunnemann, Tyler	R-R	6-2	200	8-9-91	0	2	1.86	25	0	0	3	48	33	12	10	3	10	51	.192	.180	.198	9.50	1.86
Christensen, Pat	R-R	6-3	205	12-27-90	3	1	2.39	17	0	0	0	26	24	8	7	0	9	23	.242	.308	.219	7.86	3.08
Comer, Kevin	R-R	6-3	205	8-1-92	2	5	4.24	21	11	0	3	76	80	41	36	4	26	64	.269	.308	.234	7.55	3.07
Cotton, Chris	R-L	5-10	166	11-21-90	1	3	3.40	32	1	0	3	56	55	26	21	2	11	49	.255	.254	.255	7.92	1.78

	B-T	HT	WT	DOB	W	L	ERA	G	GS	CG	SV	IP	H	R	ER	HR	BB	SO	AVG	vLH	vRH	K/9	BB/9
Emanuel, Kent	L-L	6-3	225	6-4-92	0	2	2.45	6	4	0	0	22	20	12	6	3	4	17	.241	.333	.221	6.95	1.64
Feliz, Michael	R-R	6-4	210	6-28-93	8	6	4.03	25	19	0	0	103	104	53	46	6	37	111	.263	.323	.225	9.73	3.24
Frias, Edison	R-R	6-1	180	12-18-90	8	5	4.82	17	12	0	0	75	84	49	40	7	15	60	.282	.346	.230	7.23	1.81
Grills, Evan	L-L	6-4	205	6-13-92	3	3	2.70	16	10	2	1	77	84	28	23	4	11	47	.287	.267	.292	5.52	1.29
Gustave, Jandel	R-R	6-2	160	10-12-92	5	5	5.01	23	14	0	2	79	94	57	44	3	29	82	.289	.271	.297	9.34	3.30
Houser, Adrian	R-R	6-4	228	2-2-93	5	6	4.14	25	17	0	0	109	99	55	50	5	37	93	.242	.231	.251	7.70	3.06
Lee, Chris	L-L	6-4	175	8-17-92	8	6	3.66	28	16	0	0	113	120	56	46	7	51	75	.275	.236	.284	5.97	4.06
Mills, Jordan	L-L	6-5	200	5-11-92	0	0	5.87	7	0	0	0	8	6	5	5	2	9	5	.214	.083	.313	10.57	5.87
Minnis, Albert	R-L	6-0	190	11-5-91	2	2	3.76	24	0	0	0	41	49	21	17	1	11	35	.293	.270	.300	7.75	2.43
Morton, Zach	R-R	6-1	180	7-12-90	2	1	2.86	12	0	0	0	22	19	7	7	1	7	17	.241	.217	.250	6.95	2.86
Rivera, Raul	R-R	6-3	185	2-5-91	0	0	2.08	3	0	0	0	4	8	1	1	0	1	6	.381	.250	.556	12.46	2.08
Sanudo, Gonzalo	L-R	6-3	235	1-10-92	0	3	1.14	7	2	0	0	24	15	3	3	0	6	16	.181	.118	.224	6.08	2.28
Scribner, Troy	R-R	6-3	190	7-2-91	1	2	3.52	5	3	0	1	23	22	12	9	4	10	35	.250	.220	.277	13.70	3.91
Sims, Blaine	L-L	6-0	185	3-10-89	4	4	3.40	12	9	0	1	56	61	31	21	2	37	47	.281	.245	.293	7.60	5.98
Thurman, Andrew	R-R	6-3	225	12-10-91	7	9	5.38	26	20	0	1	115	122	75	69	9	40	107	.275	.287	.267	8.35	3.12
Tiburcio, Frederick	R-R	6-3	192	11-1-90	4	3	3.05	27	0	0	7	41	31	19	14	3	14	47	.205	.291	.156	10.23	3.05
Vaughn, Aaron	R-R	5-11	195	12-16-91	0	0	0.00	1	0	0	0	2	0	0	0	0	0	2	.000	.000	.000	10.80	0.00
Walter, Andrew	R-R	6-4	200	10-18-90	4	3	3.21	33	0	0	9	48	41	20	17	3	19	48	.238	.190	.263	9.06	3.59
Yuhl, Keegan	R-R	6-0	220	1-23-92	0	0	3.07	9	0	0	2	15	10	5	5	1	4	16	.192	.087	.276	9.82	2.45

Fielding

Catcher	PCT	G	PO	A	E	DP	PB
Booth	.991	38	316	28	3	3	10
Holberton	.981	66	488	40	10	4	12
Morales	.980	18	133	15	3	0	3
Rodriguez	.981	19	142	13	3	2	7

First Base	PCT	G	PO	A	E	DP
Gregor	.997	35	302	36	1	31
Kemmer	.995	22	183	11	1	21
McDonald	.995	65	537	37	3	46
Reed	1.000	18	132	12	0	12
White	1.000	2	15	3	0	2

Second Base	PCT	G	PO	A	E	DP
Elkins	.977	18	37	49	2	14
Fernandez	.917	24	50	60	10	8
Mayfield	1.000	6	11	19	0	4
Moon	.974	52	104	158	7	37

	PCT	G	PO	A	E	DP
Morales	1.000	1	2	1	0	0
Parker	.985	23	19	47	1	13
Wik	.980	25	34	63	2	13

Third Base	PCT	G	PO	A	E	DP
Davis	.950	41	27	69	5	3
Elkins	.889	8	2	14	2	0
Gonzalez	.929	6	1	12	1	1
Mayfield	.950	10	6	13	1	0
Moon	.857	6	1	5	1	0
White	.916	62	25	117	13	13
Wik	.929	9	7	24	0	3

Shortstop	PCT	G	PO	A	E	DP
Elkins	1.000	1	1	2	0	1
Lindauer	.946	92	131	237	21	42
Mayfield	.929	22	22	57	6	11
Moon	.918	11	18	27	4	11

	PCT	G	PO	A	E	DP
Parker	.931	17	16	51	5	7
Wik	1.000	1	1	3	0	0

Outfield	PCT	G	PO	A	E	DP
Bottger	.977	31	42	1	1	0
Boyd	1.000	20	40	1	0	0
Fernandez	.625	12	5	0	3	0
Kemmer	.975	24	38	1	1	0
Mathis	.959	32	45	2	2	0
McDonald	1.000	2	8	0	0	0
Mejia	.600	5	2	1	2	0
Melendez	1.000	5	4	0	0	0
Mitchell	.981	62	103	3	2	1
Phillips	.981	102	195	14	4	2
Ramsay	.995	116	209	5	1	3
Springer	1.000	1	1	0	0	0
Wik	1.000	19	24	5	0	0

TRI-CITY VALLEYCATS

SHORT-SEASON

NEW YORK-PENN LEAGUE

Batting	B-T	HT	WT	DOB	AVG	vLH	vRH	G	AB	R	H	2B	3B	HR	RBI	BB	HBP	SH	SF	SO	SB	CS	SLG	OBP
Bottger, Ryan	B-R	6-0	210	4-14-93	.313	.476	.269	27	99	22	31	6	0	4	17	10	4	0	1	16	2	3	.495	.395
Boyd, Bobby	L-R	5-9	180	1-4-93	.333	.273	.349	42	159	30	53	6	0	0	9	17	2	6	0	18	13	5	.371	.404
Davis, J.D.	R-R	6-3	215	4-27-93	.279	.240	.291	30	111	18	31	7	1	5	20	15	4	0	1	25	1	0	.495	.382
Fisher, Derek	L-R	6-1	207	8-21-93	.303	.355	.289	41	152	31	46	4	3	2	18	16	3	0	1	35	17	4	.408	.378
Gingras, Ricky	L-R	6-2	205	10-18-90	.252	.125	.276	46	147	11	37	7	0	3	15	8	5	1	2	26	0	0	.361	.309
Gonzalez, Alfredo	R-R	6-1	190	7-13-92	.246	.222	.253	46	122	19	30	4	1	3	9	15	4	0	0	24	5	5	.369	.348
Hernandez, Alex	R-R	5-8	190	2-4-92	.210	.154	.228	56	162	22	34	5	0	2	14	27	4	3	0	33	0	2	.278	.337
Hyde, Mott	R-R	5-10	190	3-10-92	.254	.236	.259	70	244	35	62	18	3	3	31	23	6	15	2	51	3	1	.389	.331
Joyce, Terrell	R-R	6-3	235	5-29-92	.231	.250	.225	53	182	24	42	13	1	11	32	20	1	2	1	67	1	1	.495	.309
Martin, Jason	L-R	5-10	175	9-5-95	.222	.071	.254	21	81	7	18	3	1	1	2	7	0	2	0	13	5	3	.321	.284
Martinez, Jorge	B-R	6-1	183	3-29-93	.000	—	.000	4	7	0	0	0	0	0	0	0	0	0	0	2	0	0	.000	.000
2-team total (12 Mahoning Valley)					.245	—		16	53	6	13	3	1	2	13	3	0	0	0	16	1	0	.453	.286
Nelubowich, Adam	L-R	6-2	195	4-28-91	.176	—	.176	5	17	3	3	2	0	0	2	0	0	0	0	4	0	0	.294	.176
Ovando, Ariel	L-L	6-4	226	9-15-93	.237	.295	.220	58	194	17	46	7	0	1	14	14	0	1	1	45	0	0	.289	.287
Parker, Dayne	R-R	5-10	190	6-22-91	.333	—	.333	1	3	0	1	0	0	0	0	0	0	0	0	1	0	0	.333	.333
Presley, Alex	L-L	5-10	190	7-25-85	.200	1.000	.000	2	5	1	1	0	1	0	0	1	0	0	0	1	0	0	.600	.333
Reed, A.J.	L-R	6-4	240	5-10-93	.306	.167	.351	34	124	22	38	11	0	5	30	22	3	0	1	22	2	0	.516	.420
Ritchie, Jamie	R-R	6-2	190	4-9-93	.331	.219	.364	47	142	19	47	12	2	1	24	29	5	1	2	26	5	1	.465	.455
Rodriguez, Jake	R-R	5-9	175	1-24-92	.063	.000	.071	11	32	1	2	0	0	1	2	0	0	0	0	15	0	0	.156	.063
Santana, Juan	R-R	6-1	176	8-16-94	.239	.154	.253	26	92	8	22	4	0	0	10	6	0	2	1	16	0	1	.304	.283
Santana, Ravel	R-R	6-2	160	5-1-92	.125	.333	.065	13	40	7	5	1	1	1	8	9	1	0	1	8	0	0	.275	.294
Solano, Jose	R-R	6-2	175	3-15-92	.241	.324	.213	56	145	19	35	9	2	1	15	4	1	2	0	36	6	4	.352	.267
Tanielu, Nick	R-R	5-11	205	9-4-92	.300	.250	.314	62	233	29	70	16	2	3	40	16	4	1	2	48	2	1	.425	.353
Trompiz, Kristian	R-R	6-1	170	12-2-95	.500	.667	.400	3	8	2	4	3	0	0	1	0	0	1	0	2	0	0	.875	.500
Wik, Marc	L-R	5-11	220	7-18-92	.220	.214	.222	12	50	8	11	1	0	1	5	6	0	2	0	9	4	3	.300	.304

Pitching	B-T	HT	WT	DOB	W	L	ERA	G	GS	CG	SV	IP	H	R	ER	HR	BB	SO	AVG	vLH	vRH	K/9	BB/9
Chrismon, Austin	R-R	6-2	230	9-16-92	6	3	3.69	16	13	0	0	68	65	32	28	2	15	49	.250	.255	.245	6.45	1.98
Davis, Zach	L-L	6-3	220	12-16-91	1	0	16.88	2	0	0	0	3	6	5	5	0	2	2	.462	.500	.444	6.75	6.75
Fant, Randall	L-L	6-4	180	1-28-91	2	3	4.62	12	5	0	0	37	48	22	19	1	6	39	.310	.389	.286	9.49	1.46
Ferguson, Kevin	L-L	6-0	180	7-4-91	0	0	5.23	11	0	0	0	10	9	6	6	3	9	10	.214	.188	.231	8.71	7.84
Garcia, Junior	L-L	6-1	180	10-1-95	0	0	0.00	1	0	0	0	2	1	0	0	0	1	0	.143	.000	.200	4.50	0.00
Gause, Jay	R-R	6-2	225	4-24-92	0	1	9.45	9	3	0	0	13	15	15	14	2	9	13	.273	.323	.208	8.78	6.08

Name	B-T	HT	WT	DOB	W	L	ERA	G	GS	CG	SV	IP	H	R	ER	HR	BB	SO	AVG	vLH	vRH	K/9	BB/9
Holley, Krishawn	R-R	6-0	195	2-8-92	0	0	0.00	3	0	0	0	3	6	5	0	0	2	1	.353	.444	.250	2.70	5.40
Kahana, Robert	R-R	6-1	180	5-16-93	1	3	3.48	5	5	0	0	21	27	13	8	0	3	15	.290	.212	.333	6.53	1.31
Kessay, Sebastian	L-L	6-2	215	6-19-93	1	0	8.03	5	2	0	0	12	13	11	11	2	5	20	.271	.333	.256	14.59	3.65
McNitt, Brandon	R-R	5-11	175	1-9-92	2	1	2.78	12	3	0	0	32	22	10	10	2	11	30	.188	.200	.181	8.35	3.06
Mengden, Daniel	R-R	6-2	190	2-19-93	0	0	1.93	2	1	0	0	5	5	1	1	0	1	6	.278	.400	.231	11.57	1.93
Mills, Jordan	L-L	6-5	200	5-11-92	1	2	1.88	21	0	0	2	24	21	7	5	0	9	30	.233	.308	.203	11.25	3.38
Munnelly, Chris	R-R	6-2	200	2-16-91	2	0	3.38	15	0	0	4	27	24	11	10	2	8	31	.231	.255	.211	10.46	2.70
Musgrove, Joe	R-R	6-5	230	12-4-92	7	1	2.81	15	13	0	0	77	64	25	24	4	10	67	.224	.203	.248	7.83	1.17
Ordosgoitti, Luis	R-R	6-4	180	9-22-92	2	5	4.53	14	9	0	0	60	60	37	30	3	19	53	.259	.248	.268	7.99	2.87
Radziewski, Bryan	L-L	6-0	180	2-21-92	2	0	3.04	15	1	0	1	27	18	9	9	0	13	29	.194	.156	.213	9.79	4.39
Ramirez, Francis	R-R	6-5	205	1-12-92	2	5	3.62	15	8	1	0	50	45	24	20	3	21	45	.242	.269	.222	8.15	3.81
Rivera, Raul	R-R	6-3	185	2-5-91	3	0	3.09	19	0	0	0	32	26	15	11	3	11	32	.217	.194	.241	9.00	3.09
Scribner, Troy	R-R	6-3	190	7-2-91	7	1	1.38	10	10	1	0	52	36	11	8	1	14	60	.190	.207	.175	10.38	2.42
Sims, Blaine	L-L	6-0	185	3-10-89	1	0	3.06	5	3	0	0	18	15	6	6	1	10	13	.242	.250	.240	6.62	5.09
Thompson, Ryan	R-R	6-5	215	6-26-92	2	1	2.96	23	0	0	12	24	22	9	8	2	9	19	.244	.143	.309	7.03	3.33
Vaughn, Aaron	R-R	5-11	195	12-16-91	2	0	1.15	14	0	0	0	16	12	2	2	1	4	15	.214	.194	.240	8.62	2.30
Velazquez, Derick	R-R	6-4	200	11-28-93	2	1	1.57	18	0	0	4	23	18	4	4	1	2	24	.217	.226	.212	9.39	0.78
Weiland, Kyle	L-R	6-4	195	9-12-86	1	0	0.00	5	0	0	0	6	4	0	0	0	1	6	.190	.100	.273	9.00	1.50
Wheeland, Vince	R-R	5-11	190	1-10-92	1	1	5.89	15	0	0	0	18	26	12	12	0	6	10	.329	.257	.386	4.91	2.95

Fielding

Catcher	PCT	G	PO	A	E	DP	PB
Gingras	.962	9	42	8	2	2	1
Gonzalez	.976	44	324	38	9	4	6
Ritchie	.991	27	201	18	2	0	2
Rodriguez	.957	9	63	4	3	0	3

First Base	PCT	G	PO	A	E	DP
Gingras	.982	18	163	4	3	11
Joyce	1.000	5	26	3	0	2
Ovando	.987	32	223	11	3	18
Reed	.988	31	306	16	4	21
Ritchie	1.000	2	1	0	0	0

Second Base	PCT	G	PO	A	E	DP
Hernandez	.991	49	81	140	2	27
Hyde	1.000	1	2	2	0	0
Parker	1.000	1	0	5	0	0

Shortstop (cont.)	PCT	G	PO	A	E	DP
Santana	.938	17	20	55	5	7
Tanielu	.976	16	30	50	2	7
Trompiz	1.000	1	2	1	0	0
Wik	1.000	1	1	2	0	1

Third Base	PCT	G	PO	A	E	DP
Davis	.871	27	13	61	11	3
Nelubowich	.667	3	2	0	1	0
Santana	.947	6	6	12	1	2
Tanielu	.933	44	25	87	8	6
Trompiz	1.000	1	0	1	0	0

Shortstop	PCT	G	PO	A	E	DP
Hernandez	.962	6	6	19	1	6
Hyde	.958	69	90	204	13	36
Santana	.875	4	5	2	1	1
Trompiz	.667	1	1	1	1	0

	PCT	G	PO	A	E	DP
Wik	1.000	1	0	2	0	0

Outfield	PCT	G	PO	A	E	DP
Bottger	.973	24	32	4	1	0
Boyd	.976	42	79	3	2	1
Davis	1.000	1	2	0	0	0
Fisher	.964	39	52	2	2	0
Joyce	.963	25	26	0	1	0
Martin	1.000	21	42	0	0	0
Martinez	—	4	0	0	0	0
Nelubowich	1.000	2	4	1	0	0
Ovando	.943	31	30	3	2	1
Presley	1.000	1	2	0	0	0
Santana	1.000	12	11	3	0	0
Solano	1.000	46	46	4	0	0
Wik	.923	10	12	0	1	0

GREENEVILLE ASTROS   ROOKIE

APPALACHIAN LEAGUE

Batting	B-T	HT	WT	DOB	AVG	vLH	vRH	G	AB	R	H	2B	3B	HR	RBI	BB	HBP	SH	SF	SO	SB	CS	SLG	OBP
Carrasco, Cesar	R-R	6-2	185	10-3-93	.228	.212	.233	35	123	18	28	9	0	1	9	18	0	1	0	39	1	0	.325	.326
Cesar, Randy	R-R	6-1	180	1-11-95	.300	.100	.333	1	10	4	3	1	0	1	3	1	0	0	0	1	0	0	.700	.364
Clements, Brett	B-R	5-9	185	9-23-90	.116	.100	.121	15	43	4	5	1	0	0	2	5	1	0	1	12	0	1	.140	.220
Goedert, Connor	R-R	6-2	190	12-14-93	.125	.059	.154	17	56	5	7	3	0	0	4	8	1	1	1	19	0	1	.179	.242
Gonzalez, Richard	R-R	5-9	180	11-18-93	.125	.000	.167	4	8	1	1	0	0	0	0	3	0	0	0	1	1	0	.125	.364
Laureano, Ramon	R-R	5-11	175	7-15-94	.189	.364	.143	16	53	8	10	0	0	1	2	7	0	1	0	16	4	0	.245	.283
Marte, Ydarqui	R-R	6-1	188	10-10-92	.269	.279	.265	51	175	27	47	8	0	1	18	11	1	0	1	29	2	1	.383	.338
Martin, Jason	L-R	5-10	175	9-5-95	.274	.233	.289	42	164	32	45	11	6	0	21	24	0	2	2	30	8	6	.415	.363
McMullen, Sean	L-L	5-9	190	6-4-92	.256	.281	.250	42	156	22	40	9	1	2	25	11	1	1	4	35	3	2	.365	.302
Medina, Edwin	R-R	5-8	170	2-11-93	.246	.308	.231	23	65	11	16	3	0	0	3	17	1	3	0	20	10	4	.292	.410
Mejia, Yonathan	B-R	6-2	175	9-19-92	.235	.241	.233	50	183	17	43	8	2	3	18	16	1	0	2	41	3	2	.350	.297
Melendez, Alexander	R-R	6-1	185	4-21-95	.393	.286	.429	12	28	3	11	2	0	0	5	3	2	0	1	11	3	2	.464	.500
Muniz, Bryan	R-R	6-2	200	6-5-93	.220	.192	.228	36	127	11	28	4	1	2	12	16	2	0	1	21	1	1	.315	.315
Nottingham, Jacob	R-R	6-3	200	4-3-95	.230	.245	.224	48	174	25	40	10	1	5	28	18	3	1	4	54	3	2	.385	.307
Nunez, Antonio	R-R	5-9	165	1-10-93	.190	.154	.202	52	158	25	30	6	1	0	10	36	1	7	1	26	2	3	.241	.342
Parker, Dayne	R-R	5-10	190	6-22-91	.500	1.000	.400	3	12	2	6	0	0	0	2	0	0	0	0	4	0	0	.500	.571
Reynoso, Luis	R-R	6-1	170	9-2-94	.233	.162	.261	36	129	16	30	4	0	2	13	11	1	0	0	42	2	3	.310	.298
Roa, Hector	R-R	6-0	195	3-1-95	.236	.226	.240	29	106	15	25	4	1	4	13	6	1	0	1	44	1	0	.406	.281
Santana, Juan	R-R	6-1	176	8-16-94	.368	.381	.364	21	87	20	32	6	0	2	16	3	0	3	2	9	3	1	.506	.380
Santos, Jeffy	B-R	6-2	180	1-4-93	.218	.241	.210	34	110	12	24	4	1	0	15	10	1	1	2	31	1	1	.273	.285
Trompiz, Kristian	R-R	6-1	170	12-2-95	.245	.222	.254	30	94	6	23	6	0	0	13	10	0	3	0	16	2	1	.309	.317
Woodward, Trent	R-R	6-2	200	2-4-92	.234	.200	.246	27	94	19	22	7	1	2	14	17	4	0	3	21	1	1	.394	.364

Pitching	B-T	HT	WT	DOB	W	L	ERA	G	GS	CG	SV	IP	H	R	ER	HR	BB	SO	AVG	vLH	vRH	K/9	BB/9
Arauz, Harold	R-R	6-2	185	5-29-95	1	0	1.46	3	1	0	0	12	7	4	2	1	2	15	.152	.176	.138	10.95	1.46
Barrios, Agapito	R-R	6-2	167	11-30-93	5	0	2.09	13	6	0	0	56	39	15	13	0	11	46	.193	.141	.226	7.39	1.77
Davis, Zach	L-L	6-3	220	12-16-91	2	0	2.04	13	0	0	4	18	16	4	4	0	4	24	.232	.118	.269	12.23	2.04
De Leon, Ambiorix	L-L	6-3	235	7-8-91	0	0	0.00	3	0	0	0	4	1	0	0	0	0	5	.077	.000	.091	12.27	0.00
De Los Santos, Samil	R-R	6-4	175	1-8-94	0	1	7.11	4	0	0	0	6	5	5	5	0	4	13	.240	.000	.286	18.47	5.68
Deetz, Dean	R-R	6-1	190	11-29-93	2	4	8.88	13	4	0	0	25	30	29	25	1	19	24	.297	.270	.313	8.53	6.75
Delis, Juan	R-R	6-1	195	5-29-94	0	0	6.48	7	0	0	0	8	8	7	6	1	6	8	.258	.600	.192	8.64	6.48
Dykxhoorn, Brock	R-R	6-8	225	7-2-94	3	3	4.31	13	5	0	0	31	30	17	15	2	8	36	.254	.293	.234	10.34	2.30
German, Devonte	R-R	6-5	240	10-14-94	1	2	3.94	13	9	0	0	48	51	23	21	2	28	33	.277	.358	.231	6.19	5.25
Greenwood, Aaron	R-R	6-3	215	8-19-91	3	1	4.66	17	0	0	0	29	33	16	15	4	3	35	.275	.216	.301	10.86	0.93

Name	B-T	HT	WT	DOB	W	L	ERA	G	GS	CG	SV	IP	H	R	ER	HR	BB	SO	AVG	vLH	vRH	K/9	BB/9
Guduan, Reymin	L-L	6-4	185	3-16-92	2	5	4.47	13	9	0	0	44	53	32	22	2	27	58	.286	.211	.306	11.77	5.48
Hernandez, Elieser	R-R	6-1	170	5-3-95	1	0	0.00	4	1	0	0	10	6	0	0	0	5	8	.167	.000	.214	7.20	4.50
Holley, Krishawn	R-R	6-0	195	2-8-92	0	0	7.59	10	0	0	0	11	17	12	9	1	5	7	.340	.500	.250	5.91	4.22
James, Josh	R-R	6-3	200	3-8-93	1	3	2.72	13	6	0	0	40	35	13	12	0	15	45	.245	.259	.235	10.21	3.40
Juarez, Gerardo	R-R	6-2	175	9-10-92	0	0	6.35	2	1	0	0	6	7	4	4	0	1	5	.333	.400	.313	7.94	1.59
Kahana, Robert	R-R	6-1	180	5-16-93	1	1	3.64	9	3	0	0	30	22	16	12	1	9	22	.195	.196	.194	6.67	2.73
Montero, Jose	R-R	6-4	190	1-22-93	1	2	3.38	8	5	0	0	32	26	13	12	2	14	36	.222	.250	.203	10.13	3.94
Nicely, Austin	B-L	6-1	170	12-13-94	2	6	3.88	12	10	0	0	49	56	31	21	1	25	28	.292	.342	.279	5.18	4.62
Perez, Jorge	R-R	6-0	175	7-30-93	2	3	2.97	18	0	0	0	30	32	18	10	0	17	39	.264	.310	.241	11.57	5.04
Peterson, Eric	R-R	6-4	195	3-8-93	1	0	2.35	19	0	0	7	23	18	9	6	0	7	32	.209	.182	.226	12.52	2.74
Santos, Juan	R-R	6-4	240	8-30-95	0	2	6.30	9	4	0	0	20	15	17	14	0	19	31	.205	.182	.216	13.95	8.55
Yuhl, Keegan	R-R	6-0	220	1-23-92	0	0	1.25	9	2	0	0	22	21	3	3	0	4	17	.244	.195	.289	7.06	1.66

Fielding

Catcher	PCT	G	PO	A	E	DP	PB
Clements	1.000	15	117	12	0	0	1
Gonzalez	.977	4	39	4	1	0	0
Nottingham	.988	45	371	54	5	3	7
Woodward	1.000	5	43	4	0	0	2

First Base	PCT	G	PO	A	E	DP
Mejia	.988	38	300	17	4	24
Muniz	.975	18	147	12	4	14
Roa	.962	7	49	1	2	4
Woodward	1.000	7	53	5	0	8

Second Base	PCT	G	PO	A	E	DP
Nunez	.963	41	64	90	6	19
Parker	1.000	2	4	5	0	1

	PCT	G	PO	A	E	DP
Reynoso	.943	7	12	21	2	6
Santana	1.000	11	26	38	0	9
Trompiz	.939	8	14	17	2	7

Third Base	PCT	G	PO	A	E	DP
Carrasco	.789	19	1	29	8	3
Cesar	.875	3	2	5	1	0
Goedert	.710	16	6	16	9	0
Reynoso	.942	19	13	36	3	2
Santana	—	1	0	0	0	0
Trompiz	.944	15	7	27	2	1

Shortstop	PCT	G	PO	A	E	DP
Nunez	.944	9	13	21	2	7
Parker	.333	1	0	1	2	1

	PCT	G	PO	A	E	DP
Reynoso	.938	4	6	9	1	2
Santana	.857	9	15	33	8	9
Santos	.930	34	37	82	9	17
Trompiz	.976	11	12	28	1	6

Outfield	PCT	G	PO	A	E	DP
Laureano	1.000	16	26	0	0	0
Marte	.937	49	85	4	6	0
Martin	.990	42	99	4	1	2
McMullen	.955	41	62	2	3	0
Medina	1.000	21	37	0	0	0
Melendez	1.000	12	18	0	0	0
Reynoso	1.000	8	7	0	0	0
Roa	.875	16	20	1	3	0
Woodward	1.000	6	8	0	0	0

GCL ASTROS   ROOKIE

GULF COAST LEAGUE

Batting	B-T	HT	WT	DOB	AVG	vLH	vRH	G	AB	R	H	2B	3B	HR	RBI	BB	HBP	SH	SF	SO	SB	CS	SLG	OBP
Avea, Marlon	R-R	6-1	195	8-31-93	.279	.375	.250	21	68	11	19	5	0	0	12	8	4	1	1	9	1	1	.353	.383
Bowey, Jake	L-R	6-0	205	7-16-96	.222	.250	.214	6	18	3	4	2	1	0	4	2	0	0	1	5	0	0	.444	.286
Castro, Ruben	L-R	5-10	182	7-10-96	.241	.077	.293	20	54	4	13	1	0	0	5	7	2	1	0	10	0	1	.259	.349
Cesar, Randy	R-R	6-1	180	1-11-95	.272	.263	.274	49	184	19	50	11	0	2	12	9	1	1	2	42	0	2	.364	.306
Coa, Pedro	R-R	6-2	190	12-21-92	.286	—	.286	3	7	2	2	0	0	0	3	0	1	0	2	1	0	0	.286	.300
Duarte, Osvaldo	R-R	5-9	160	1-18-96	.280	.280	.280	20	75	13	21	3	1	0	6	8	0	3	2	16	9	4	.347	.341
Dupont, Will	L-R	6-0	170	12-1-93	.235	.333	.214	6	17	4	4	0	1	0	3	3	1	0	0	7	0	0	.353	.381
Estrella, Jean	L-R	5-11	170	4-16-96	.218	.294	.197	24	78	9	17	2	0	0	4	12	0	3	0	18	4	5	.244	.322
Fernandez, Frankeny	R-R	6-1	170	12-7-96	.250	.077	.291	19	68	9	17	1	1	0	5	9	0	2	2	23	5	4	.294	.329
Fisher, Derek	R-R	6-1	207	8-21-93	.667	—	.667	1	3	0	2	1	0	0	0	1	0	0	0	0	0	0	1.000	.750
Goedert, Connor	R-R	6-2	190	12-14-93	.179	.200	.175	21	78	7	14	3	0	0	4	6	1	2	0	22	0	1	.218	.247
Gonzalez, Richard	R-R	5-9	180	11-18-93	.214	.235	.209	29	84	8	18	5	0	1	8	10	6	3	1	26	0	0	.310	.337
Martinez, Jorge	R-R	6-1	183	3-29-93	.275	.182	.300	15	51	8	14	5	0	3	10	3	0	0	2	16	4	1	.549	.304
Mauricio, Joan	L-R	5-11	160	10-22-96	.127	.083	.136	22	71	11	9	4	1	0	4	14	0	0	0	25	4	1	.211	.271
McCall, Dex	R-R	6-1	220	1-29-94	.258	.250	.260	50	178	17	46	8	2	1	29	21	1	0	1	40	1	0	.343	.338
Medina, Edwin	R-R	5-8	170	2-11-93	.265	.444	.215	27	83	20	22	3	1	0	6	16	1	5	1	15	18	2	.325	.386
Mejia, Brauly	R-R	6-0	185	10-28-94	.273	.172	.295	49	161	29	44	7	6	2	25	26	8	1	3	35	9	10	.429	.394
Melendez, Alexander	R-R	6-1	185	4-21-95	.351	.269	.380	30	97	17	34	3	1	0	11	8	5	6	0	22	17	3	.402	.427
Michelena, Arturo	R-R	5-11	160	10-15-94	.235	.088	.277	45	153	11	36	5	1	1	20	20	0	5	2	31	5	1	.301	.320
Payano, Luis	R-R	6-1	175	5-12-96	.257	.281	.250	42	140	18	36	6	2	5	18	12	0	6	1	47	4	9	.436	.314
Pena, Brian	R-R	6-1	185	6-14-94	.260	.357	.222	17	50	4	13	2	0	0	4	3	1	1	0	17	0	0	.300	.315
Roa, Hector	R-R	6-0	195	3-1-95	.280	.160	.320	26	100	16	28	11	1	3	14	7	0	0	1	31	2	1	.500	.324
Tejada, Nestor	L-L	5-11	170	4-17-97	.169	.000	.196	19	59	3	10	2	0	0	4	4	3	2	0	11	3	1	.203	.258
Trompiz, Kristian	R-R	6-1	170	12-2-95	.317	.429	.286	19	63	14	20	7	0	1	8	8	2	2	1	11	5	1	.476	.405

Pitching	B-T	HT	WT	DOB	W	L	ERA	G	GS	CG	SV	IP	H	R	ER	HR	BB	SO	AVG	vLH	vRH	K/9	BB/9
Acosta, Yhoan	L-L	6-1	175	6-17-95	1	3	3.00	8	3	0	1	33	35	15	11	0	9	33	.278	.160	.307	9.00	2.45
Alaniz, R.J.	R-R	6-4	175	6-14-91	1	1	6.94	3	3	0	0	12	23	15	9	0	2	7	.411	.286	.452	5.40	1.54
Arauz, Harold	R-R	6-2	185	5-29-95	4	2	3.76	11	6	0	2	41	30	18	17	3	17	53	.200	.300	.175	11.73	3.76
Ballew, Travis	R-R	6-0	160	5-11-91	0	0	0.84	7	0	0	1	11	11	4	1	0	3	13	.250	.214	.267	10.97	2.53
Cain, Colton	L-L	6-3	256	2-5-91	0	0	1.00	3	2	0	0	9	7	1	1	0	3	8	.233	.667	.185	8.00	3.00
De Leon, Ambiorix	L-L	6-3	235	7-8-91	0	0	0.00	3	2	0	0	4	2	0	0	0	1	5	.133	.000	.182	11.25	2.25
De Los Santos, Samil	R-R	6-4	175	1-9-94	1	1	3.38	11	1	0	0	13	13	6	5	0	8	15	.255	.278	.242	10.13	5.40
Delis, Juan	R-R	6-1	195	5-29-94	2	0	3.09	10	0	0	4	12	8	4	4	0	5	9	.205	.300	.172	6.94	3.86
Fant, Randall	L-L	6-4	180	1-28-91	1	0	0.71	4	1	0	0	13	9	3	1	0	3	18	.205	.400	.179	12.79	2.13
Ferrell, Justin	R-R	6-7	190	4-21-94	1	3	3.67	12	5	0	1	34	33	15	14	3	12	39	.246	.347	.188	10.22	3.15
Garcia, Junior	L-L	6-1	180	10-15-95	0	1	3.02	12	8	0	0	42	47	18	14	1	19	27	.283	.167	.315	5.83	4.10
Gatlin, John	R-R	6-4	220	12-14-90	1	3	1.29	13	0	0	2	14	12	4	2	0	11	15	.240	.158	.290	9.64	7.07
Gehrs, Kyle	L-L	5-9	175	6-10-91	1	0	4.95	16	0	0	0	20	23	18	11	0	11	16	.288	.313	.281	7.20	4.95
Hernandez, Elieser	R-R	6-1	170	5-3-95	4	1	2.78	8	3	1	0	36	26	12	11	2	8	34	.206	.190	.214	8.58	2.02
Hernandez, Juan	R-R	6-3	170	1-24-93	0	1	13.50	3	0	0	0	4	7	6	6	0	6	5	.368	.333	.385	11.25	13.50
Holley, Krishawn	R-R	6-0	195	2-8-92	0	0	9.00	2	0	0	0	2	3	2	2	0	2	2	.333	.500	.200	9.00	9.00

					W	L	ERA	G	GS	CG	SV	IP	H	R	ER	HR	BB	SO	AVG	vLH	vRH	K/9	BB/9
Juarez, Gerardo	R-R	6-2	175	9-10-92	0	0	0.00	3	0	0	1	2	2	0	0	0	0	3	.222	.000	.333	11.57	0.00
Martes, Francis	R-R	6-0	170	11-24-95	1	1	0.82	4	3	0	0	11	5	3	1	0	3	12	.132	.214	.083	9.82	2.45
2-team total (8 Marlins)					3	3	4.09	12	9	0	0	44	34	24	20	0	23	45	—	—	—	9.20	4.70
Mengden, Daniel	R-R	6-2	190	2-19-93	0	0	4.26	4	0	0	0	6	4	3	3	0	0	11	.167	.250	.125	15.63	0.00
Minnis, Albert	R-L	6-0	190	11-5-91	0	1	6.75	3	0	0	0	7	11	6	5	0	4	7	.355	.111	.455	9.45	5.40
Montero, Jose	R-R	6-4	190	1-22-93	0	0	0.00	1	1	0	0	1	0	0	0	0	0	1	.000	.000	.000	9.00	0.00
Osborne, J.D.	R-L	6-5	205	11-13-90	1	1	7.17	19	0	0	0	21	19	21	17	0	27	14	.250	.444	.224	5.91	11.39
Perdomo, Christian	L-L	6-6	180	11-9-93	2	2	6.75	17	0	0	0	19	17	18	14	2	19	20	.236	.267	.228	9.64	9.16
Pinales, Joselo	R-R	6-1	180	11-16-94	0	3	4.66	13	4	0	1	39	37	22	20	2	18	24	.262	.254	.270	5.59	4.19
Sanchez, Starlyng	L-L	5-11	170	8-6-94	1	2	9.00	7	1	0	0	19	28	20	19	2	10	10	.337	.375	.328	4.74	4.74
Santamaria, Cristhopher	L-L	5-11	175	6-19-96	2	2	4.91	10	5	0	0	33	43	27	18	5	6	30	.303	.345	.292	8.18	1.64
Seaton, Ross	L-R	6-4	200	9-18-89	1	0	2.57	4	4	0	0	14	17	5	4	0	1	11	.304	.321	.286	7.07	0.64
Solarte, Alejandro	L-L	6-4	180	9-22-94	2	1	4.88	17	0	0	1	24	30	17	13	3	13	19	.316	.450	.280	7.13	4.88
Vaughn, Aaron	R-R	5-11	195	12-16-91	0	1	2.89	7	0	0	3	9	7	3	3	0	2	6	.206	.273	.174	5.79	1.93
Velasquez, Vince	B-R	6-3	203	6-7-92	0	1	2.08	3	3	0	0	9	5	2	2	0	2	19	.167	.000	.250	19.73	2.08
Weiland, Kyle	R-R	6-4	195	9-12-86	1	1	1.50	4	2	0	0	6	2	1	1	0	1	5	.105	.000	.143	7.50	1.50
West, Aaron	R-R	6-1	195	6-1-90	0	0	2.70	3	3	0	0	10	10	3	3	0	1	6	.270	.250	.280	5.40	0.90

Fielding

Catcher	PCT	G	PO	A	E	DP	PB
Avea	.963	15	90	15	4	0	7
Castro	.980	7	43	7	1	0	2
Coa	1.000	3	11	2	0	1	0
Gonzalez	.985	29	237	28	4	1	10
Pena	.976	17	113	10	3	1	5

First Base	PCT	G	PO	A	E	DP
Avea	1.000	3	25	0	0	2
Bowey	1.000	6	44	4	0	4
Cesar	1.000	5	38	1	0	2
Goedert	1.000	2	6	2	0	2
McCall	.981	36	287	16	6	30
Roa	1.000	13	116	9	0	6

Second Base	PCT	G	PO	A	E	DP
Dupont	1.000	4	6	7	0	1

	PCT	G	PO	A	E	DP
Estrella	.971	9	17	16	1	5
Fernandez	.907	17	50	38	9	11
Hernandez	1.000	1	0	1	0	1
Michelena	.983	24	55	62	2	15
Trompiz	1.000	10	19	28	0	4

Third Base	PCT	G	PO	A	E	DP
Cesar	.880	34	24	71	13	6
Estrella	.929	12	3	23	2	2
Goedert	.886	10	13	18	4	1
Michelena	.943	11	6	27	2	2

Shortstop	PCT	G	PO	A	E	DP
Cesar	1.000	1	0	2	0	0
Duarte	.912	17	29	33	6	6
Estrella	1.000	2	0	3	0	0
Mauricio	.899	22	32	57	10	9

	PCT	G	PO	A	E	DP
Michelena	.956	11	23	42	3	11
Trompiz	.911	9	9	32	4	3

Outfield	PCT	G	PO	A	E	DP
Duarte	1.000	3	5	1	0	0
Estrella	1.000	4	5	1	0	0
Fisher	1.000	1	2	0	0	0
Martinez	.950	13	15	4	1	0
Medina	1.000	26	54	4	0	1
Mejia	.950	47	53	4	3	0
Melendez	.955	30	41	1	2	0
Payano	.970	41	60	5	2	1
Roa	1.000	7	8	1	0	0
Tejada	.967	19	28	1	1	0

DSL ASTROS   ROOKIE

DOMINICAN SUMMER LEAGUE

Batting	B-T	HT	WT	DOB	AVG	vLH	vRH	G	AB	R	H	2B	3B	HR	RBI	BB	HBP	SH	SF	SO	SB	CS	SLG	OBP
Almonte, Marcos	R-R	5-10	163	3-28-96	233	—	—	67	258	44	60	17	4	2	27	42	9	4	0	44	20	9	353	359
Amador, Wilson	R-R	6-1	160	12-14-96	245	264	240	64	245	49	60	7	2	1	30	24	17	4	3	67	29	13	302	349
Ayarza, Rodrigo	B-R8-May	145	2-20-95	274	—	—	61	223	35	61	12	2	1	42	40	5	8	6	30	13	5	359	387	
Beltre, Reiny	R-R	6-0	180	7-16-96	231	—	—	34	121	17	28	6	0	0	15	20	9	1	0	21	4	3	281	380
Benjamin, Jose	R-R	6-2	170	12-16-95	235	—	—	42	136	28	32	6	2	0	13	20	6	2	4	24	4	2	309	349
Bermejo, Jesus	R-R	6-1	180	4-8-94	148	053	169	34	108	14	16	5	0	0	7	15	3	3	1	39	4	0	194	268
Bernal, Ihan	R-R	6-1	195	10-20-96	200	242	189	52	155	26	31	7	0	2	19	51	6	2	2	47	4	2	284	411
Bowey, Jake	L-R	6-0	205	7-16-96	212	267	182	27	85	12	18	6	0	2	13	22	0	1	1	26	3	2	353	370
Bracamonte, Gabriel	R-R	5-9	165	5-15-95	378	375	378	15	45	10	17	2	2	0	4	6	3	2	0	9	1	1	511	481
Campos, Oscar	R-R	5-10	170	12-8-96	200	294	152	14	50	7	10	1	1	0	7	4	1	3	0	5	0	0	260	273
Canelon, Carlos	R-R	5-11	170	12-14-94	181	143	197	32	94	14	17	2	0	0	6	10	6	6	0	29	0	0	202	300
De La Cruz, Bryan	R-R	6-2	175	12-16-96	262	—	—	59	183	33	48	5	1	1	24	34	5	2	3	51	6	3	317	387
De Leon, Angel	R-R	6-1	170	5-26-96	162	—	—	30	105	15	17	5	1	1	10	12	2	0	0	46	0	5	257	261
Duarte, Osvaldo	R-R	5-9	160	1-18-96	270	200	306	15	74	12	20	4	2	0	13	4	2	4	0	15	7	3	378	325
Fernandez, Frankeny	R-R	6-1	170	12-7-96	320	444	297	50	175	45	56	12	3	1	32	34	7	0	7	48	30	2	440	435
Franco, Wander	B-R	6-1	189	10-11-96	244	348	203	68	246	41	60	15	0	4	35	48	1	0	4	37	0	0	354	365
Fuente, Juan	R-R	6-0	155	11-8-93	300	—	—	58	180	33	54	7	1	1	23	27	12	5	1	41	11	10	367	423
Lorenzo, Edgar	R-R	5-11	160	1-15-97	236	—	—	56	182	34	43	15	1	2	21	30	6	2	1	50	15	3	363	361
Lucas, Felix	R-R	6-3	195	3-27-97	144	—	—	39	132	10	19	4	0	3	15	19	7	0	0	64	1	0	242	285
Luciano, Christopher	R-R	6-0	180	5-31-96	251	—	—	62	215	30	54	11	1	3	39	50	5	3	3	68	2	2	353	399
MacDonald, Connor	R-R	6-5	200	2-27-96	328	378	308	35	128	26	42	9	1	2	24	19	8	0	1	31	1	2	461	442
Marquez, Orlando	R-R	5-10	180	3-12-96	296	455	250	28	98	15	29	8	1	1	20	10	4	0	1	25	6	1	429	381
Matute, Jonathan	R-R	6-0	170	4-28-97	246	229	253	69	256	37	63	12	0	3	25	43	9	9	3	53	12	5	328	370
Mauricio, Joan	L-R	5-11	160	10-22-96	275	195	304	43	153	22	42	5	9	1	29	26	0	4	2	39	3	1	444	376
Peralta, Anardo	B-R	5-11	170	5-11-96	165	—	—	41	121	20	20	2	1	1	13	31	5	0	0	39	1	3	223	357
Pineda, Andy	L-R	6-1	165	11-11-96	279	—	—	65	215	37	60	1	3	0	16	30	8	8	2	54	23	12	312	384
Sanchez, Vicente	L-R	5-11	170	10-4-96	281	304	276	32	121	30	34	3	3	5	30	22	1	5	2	23	7	7	479	390
Tejada, Nestor	L-L	5-11	175	4-17-97	186	220	173	46	145	24	27	1	6	0	15	28	6	4	0	32	2	2	276	341
Timberlake, Hayden	R-R	6-0	185	3-5-96	188	—	—	22	64	8	12	2	1	0	5	10	1	0	1	20	0	0	250	303
Toribio, Oliver	R-R	5-10	180	7-16-96	222	333	179	42	117	17	26	4	1	1	18	35	8	3	1	35	2	3	299	429

Pitching	B-T	HT	WT	DOB	W	L	ERA	G	GS	CG	SV	IP	H	R	ER	HR	BB	SO	AVG	vLH	vRH	K/9	BB/9
Abreu, Albert	R-R	6-2	175	9-26-95	3	2	2.78	14	14	0	0	68	48	25	21	1	29	54	197	167	208	7.15	3.84
Abreu, Bryan	R-R	6-1	175	4-22-97	0	2	6.55	16	0	0	2	22	19	20	16	0	20	23	238	300	200	9.41	8.18
Acosta, Yhoan	L-L	6-1	175	6-17-95	2	3	5.29	8	7	0	0	34	43	22	20	1	13	34	309	238	322	9.00	3.44
Almengo, Diogenes	R-R	6-2	190	6-2-95	1	0	3.50	6	0	0	1	18	19	7	7	0	6	13	271	310	244	6.50	3.00

Player	B-T	HT	WT	DOB	W	L	ERA	G	GS	CG	SV	IP	H	R	ER	HR	BB	SO	AVG	vLH	vRH	SO/9	BB/9
Almonte, Antonio	R-R	6-2	170	8-20-95	3	1	5.06	10	2	0	0	32	35	26	18	1	11	24	265	241	284	6.75	3.09
Arias, Luis	L-L	5-11	170	1-3-94	0	1	2.25	7	0	0	0	8	8	5	2	1	3	9	258	000	286	113	3.38
Belboder, Joel	R-R	6-0	185	10-5-95	4	2	3.38	20	1	0	2	40	38	19	15	2	15	25	—	—	—	5.63	3.38
Benzant, Gerald	R-R	6-2	185	12-21-94	1	3	7.17	14	7	0	0	38	49	41	30	1	23	39	—	—	—	9.32	5.50
Chavez, Enrique	R-R	5-11	194	4-13-96	2	2	5.56	5	0	0	0	11	17	11	7	0	4	6	362	462	324	4.76	3.18
Cuevas, Juan	R-R	6-0	195	5-4-94	1	5	5.44	19	0	0	3	45	60	36	27	2	14	36	—	—	—	7.25	2.82
De La Cruz, Yan	R-R	5-11	165	8-5-93	0	0	4.82	9	0	0	0	9	13	8	5	0	4	7	310	231	345	6.75	3.86
Hernandez, Juan	R-R	6-3	170	1-24-93	2	3	5.90	10	2	0	0	29	33	28	19	0	15	22	284	222	324	6.83	4.66
Hiraldo, Carlos	L-L	5-10	175	7-15-96	0	0	3.81	15	10	0	0	52	48	29	22	2	27	39	244	300	234	6.75	4.67
Lopez, Tomas	R-R	6-2	175	5-6-94	1	1	13.69	13	0	0	0	24	24	39	36	0	27	7	273	273	273	2.66	127
Madden, Lachlan	R-R	5-11	170	6-3-96	2	1	3.27	15	0	0	5	22	21	8	8	0	7	16	266	250	275	6.55	2.86
Madera, Ezequiel	R-R	6-2	180	3-22-96	0	0	7.36	9	0	0	0	11	8	11	9	1	8	13	195	154	214	164	6.55
Martinez, Saul	R-R	6-2	185	6-21-95	0	0	00	1	0	0	0	2	1	0	0	0	1	0	167	333	000	00	4.50
Montano, Salvador	L-L	6-3	150	7-14-94	7	3	2.24	15	11	0	0	64	55	21	16	1	23	87	236	194	243	12.17	3.22
Paulino, Hansel	R-R	6-2	170	1-3-96	0	1	12.71	6	0	0	0	6	13	13	8	0	15	5	—	—	—	7.94	23.82
Pena, Adonis	R-R	6-4	195	10-29-93	2	4	5.92	15	10	0	1	49	62	60	32	0	31	44	286	284	287	8.14	5.73
Pinales, Erasmo	R-R	5-11	180	11-25-94	3	1	2.13	15	14	0	0	72	50	23	17	2	18	63	—	—	—	7.91	2.26
Pinales, Joselo	R-R	6-1	180	11-16-94	1	2	4.43	4	4	0	0	20	15	11	10	1	4	14	197	143	218	6.20	1.77
Pirela, Gabriel	R-R	6-1	165	5-1-94	0	1	5.54	7	0	0	0	13	17	10	8	0	6	10	321	200	394	6.92	4.15
Pizzolato, Carlos	R-R	6-2	170	3-6-96	2	3	2.59	13	6	0	1	42	36	24	12	2	16	29	228	151	267	6.26	3.46
Polanco, Moreno	R-R	6-3	180	7-29-94	2	3	2.27	13	12	0	0	48	38	21	12	1	29	32	221	317	165	6.04	5.48
Ramirez, Luis	L-L	5-10	160	11-27-95	1	2	2.55	7	0	0	2	18	12	7	5	0	6	15	203	333	189	7.64	3.06
Ramos, Jose	R-R	6-1	160	8-4-96	0	1	6.57	19	0	0	5	25	33	18	18	1	17	28	320	242	357	122	6.20
Richez, Michael	R-R	6-1	173	5-15-97	0	0	16.88	3	0	0	0	3	5	10	5	1	7	4	385	500	286	13.50	23.63
Rodriguez, Ramon	R-R	6-4	196	3-23-93	2	1	3.98	12	0	0	0	20	19	12	9	0	7	11	—	—	—	4.87	3.10
Rosario, Jose	R-R	6-6	180	2-15-95	2	4	3.80	16	3	0	1	47	44	23	20	0	11	35	240	222	250	6.65	2.09
Saldana, Abdiel	R-R	5-11	195	3-13-96	4	1	3.44	15	4	0	1	50	46	25	19	3	15	44	—	—	—	7.97	2.72
Sanabria, Carlos	R-R	6-0	165	1-24-97	2	2	2.82	15	3	0	0	38	44	23	12	0	18	25	—	—	—	5.87	4.23
Sanchez, Starlyng	L-L	5-11	170	8-6-94	1	3	5.40	8	7	0	0	32	42	27	19	1	9	30	—	—	—	8.53	2.56
Sandoval, Edgardo	R-R	6-0	170	7-9-96	3	0	2.84	12	7	0	1	51	47	24	16	1	11	46	237	222	248	8.17	1.95
Santamaria, Cristhopher	L-L	5-11	175	6-19-96	1	1	2.20	6	5	0	0	29	22	12	7	1	5	25	208	167	216	7.85	1.57
Severino, Miguel	R-R	6-3	180	5-30-93	0	0	15.19	5	2	0	0	5	2	9	9	0	11	4	125	000	167	6.75	18.56
2-team total (4 Padres)					0	0	257	9	2	0	0	7	5	17	16	0	20	8	—	—	—	129	25.71
Taveras, Starlyn	R-R	6-3	205	4-21-94	0	1	14.34	10	0	0	0	11	12	17	17	0	18	11	273	400	207	9.28	15.19
Uribe, Josue	R-R	6-0	180	2-6-95	2	2	1.08	16	0	0	4	25	11	6	3	0	14	16	129	231	085	5.76	5.04
Valdez, Gabriel	R-R	6-2	185	10-25-95	4	4	3.47	18	0	0	0	47	49	21	18	2	10	34	—	—	—	6.56	1.93
Villarroel, Edwin	L-L	6-3	165	5-18-95	3	4	4.10	14	9	0	1	59	64	42	27	4	13	41	—	—	—	6.22	1.97

HOUSTON ASTROS

Fielding

Catcher	PCT	G	PO	A	E	DP	PB
Bermejo	1.000	3	3	1	0	0	0
Bernal	980	40	259	34	6	1	12
Bowey	1.000	1	7	0	0	0	0
Bracamonte	955	10	68	16	4	0	3
Campos	912	11	66	17	8	0	2
Canelon	992	29	209	35	2	0	7
Marquez	962	15	104	21	5	0	5
Timberlake	961	16	91	31	5	0	9
Toribio	990	30	176	32	2	0	11

First Base	PCT	G	PO	A	E	DP
Beltre	958	3	23	0	1	2
Bermejo	978	28	245	23	6	11
Bernal	927	3	38	0	3	2
Bowey	993	15	130	13	1	7
Franco	1.000	6	29	1	0	1
Lucas	983	18	157	12	3	9
Luciano	978	37	338	13	8	29
MacDonald	979	34	297	23	7	22
Marquez	—	1	0	0	0	0
Toribio	1.000	4	26	1	0	1

Second Base	PCT	G	PO	A	E	DP
Almonte	1.000	3	8	11	0	2
Ayarza	938	12	32	28	4	6
Beltre	1.000	1	1	1	0	0
Fernandez	925	45	106	115	18	14
Fuente	1.000	3	5	9	0	0
Matute	972	64	132	175	9	28
Peralta	951	20	45	53	5	9

Third Base	PCT	G	PO	A	E	DP
Almonte	875	12	7	21	4	1
Amador	833	10	11	24	7	1
Ayarza	828	6	6	13	5	2
Beltre	907	30	30	77	11	7
Franco	927	59	57	133	15	18
Fuente	—	1	0	0	0	0
Luciano	923	10	9	15	2	2
MacDonald	1.000	1	1	0	0	0
Matute	950	6	7	12	1	2
Peralta	923	13	10	26	3	3

Shortstop	PCT	G	PO	A	E	DP
Almonte	937	35	52	97	10	17
Amador	855	47	69	119	32	13
Ayarza	794	8	5	22	7	2
Duarte	880	11	13	31	6	5
Fuente	500	1	0	1	1	0
Mauricio	922	41	56	109	14	12
Peralta	833	6	6	9	3	0

Outfield	PCT	G	PO	A	E	DP
Almonte	1.000	17	20	1	0	0
Ayarza	1.000	29	47	3	0	0
Benjamin	948	40	69	4	4	0
Bermejo	1.000	1	1	0	0	0
De La Cruz	941	53	75	5	5	0
De Leon	853	17	29	0	5	0
Duarte	857	3	6	0	1	0
Fuente	947	47	87	2	5	1
Lorenzo	954	53	81	2	4	0
Lucas	1.000	3	3	0	0	0
MacDonald	—	1	0	0	0	0
Peralta	—	1	0	0	0	0
Pineda	976	61	118	3	3	1
Sanchez	930	29	62	4	5	0
Tejada	974	44	72	2	2	1
Vasquez	922	44	69	2	6	1

Kansas City Royals

SEASON IN A SENTENCE: The best season in nearly three decades for Kansas City ended up one win short of the promised land, but it was a fun ride along the way.

HIGH POINT: Trailing by four in the eighth inning of the wild card game, facing Jon Lester, the Royals improbably managed to tie the game. After falling behind again in the 12th inning, the Royals rallied with two runs of their own in the bottom of the inning. Three weeks later, Kansas City was playing in the World Series.

LOW POINT: Salvador Perez's pop fly to end Game 7 of the World Series with the tying run at third base will be the moment Royals' fans replay over and over in the aftermath of their playoff run. But the situation was much tougher in early July. Just after the all-star break, Lester shut out the Royals 6-0 to finish off the Boston's three-game sweep, dropping Kansas City seven games behind the Tigers in the AL Central.

NOTABLE ROOKIES: Righthander Yordano Ventura immediately became the club's No. 2 starter as a rookie. The hardest-throwing starter in baseball, Ventura maintained his stuff throughout the season, finishing off with seven shutout innings in a Game 6 win in the World Series. Lefthander Brandon Finnegan became the first player ever to pitch in the College World Series and the World Series in the same season.

KEY TRANSACTIONS: The Royals signed lefthander Jason Vargas to a four-year, $32 million free agent deal before the season. Vargas responded by going 11-10, 3.71 in 30 starts. Right fielder Nori Aoki was acquired in an offseason trade that sent lefthander Will Smith to Milwaukee. After a slow start, he was a vital part of the club's postseason run. But probably the most notable move was the team's decision to be a buyer at the trade deadline instead of a seller even though the club was 11 games back in the Central at the time. Less than a month later, the Royals were in first place.

DOWN ON THE FARM: Righthander Kyle Zimmer, the club's 2012 first-round pick, was expected to help the big league club at some point. Instead he missed almost the entire season with a variety of injuries. Shortstop Raul Mondesi struggled at high Class A Wilmington and 2013 first-round pick Hunter Dozier was excellent in Wilmington but not nearly as good after a promotion to Double-A. Triple-A Omaha won its third Pacific Coast League title in four years.

OPENING DAY PAYROLL: $90.5 million (18th).

PLAYERS OF THE YEAR

BRAD GLAZIER

MAJOR LEAGUE	MINOR LEAGUE
Alex Gordon	**Glenn Sparkman**
lf	**rhp**
.261/.351/.432	(high Class A)
34 2B, 19 HR,	8-3, 1.56
Led team in OPS, HR	117 SO in 121 IP

ORGANIZATION LEADERS

BATTING		*Minimum 250 AB
MAJORS		
* AVG	Cain, Lorenzo	0.301
* OPS	Gordon, Alex	0.783
HR	Gordon, Alex	19
RBI	Gordon, Alex	74
MINORS		
AVG	Merrifield, Whit, NW Arkansas, Omaha	0.319
OBP	Giavotella, Johnny, Omaha	0.373
SLG	Peguero, Carlos, Omaha	0.563
R	Merrifield, Whit, NW Arkansas, Omaha	79
H	Merrifield, Whit, NW Arkansas, Omaha	154
TB	Fields, Matt, Omaha	239
2B	Merrifield, Whit, NW Arkansas, Omaha	41
3B	Mondesi, Raul, Wilmington	12
HR	Peguero, Carlos, Omaha	30
RBI	Fields, Matt, Omaha	81
BB	Dozier, Hunter, Wilmington, NW Arkansas	66
SO	Fields, Matt, Omaha	156
SB	Gore, Terrance, Wilmington, Omaha	47

PITCHING		#Minimum 75 IP
MAJORS		
W	Shields, James	14
	Ventura, Yordano	14
# ERA	Duffy, Danny	2.53
SO	Shields, James	180
SV	Holland, Greg	46
MINORS		
W	Brooks, Aaron, Omaha	12
W	Ferguson, Andy, NW Arkansas, Omaha	12
L	Farrell, Luke, Lexington, NW Arkansas	13
# ERA	Sparkman, Glenn, Wilmington	1.56
G	Alexander, Scott, NW Arkansas, Omaha	46
GS	Lamb, John, Omaha	26
	Melville, Tim, NW Arkansas	26
SV	Peterson, Mark, Wilmington, NW Arkansas	25
IP	Ferguson, Andy, NW Arkansas, Omaha	159.2
BB	Lamb, John, Omaha	68
	Melville, Tim, NW Arkansas	68
SO	Manaea, Sean, Wilmington	146
AVG	Sparkman, Glenn, Wilmington	0.213

2014 PERFORMANCE

General Manager: Dayton Moore. **Farm Director:** Scott Sharp. **Scouting Director:** Lonnie Goldberg

Class	Team	League	W	L	PCT	Finish	Manager
Majors	Kansas City Royals	American	89	73	.549	7th (30)	Ned Yost
Triple-A	Omaha Storm Chasers	Pacific Coast	76	67	.531	6th (16)	Brian Poldberg
Double-A	Northwest Arkansas Naturals	Texas	53	87	.379	8th (8)	Vance Wilson
High A	Wilmington Blue Rocks	Carolina	65	72	.474	t-5th (8)	Darryl Kennedy
Low A	Lexington Legends	South Atlantic	57	83	.407	11th (14)	Brian Buchanan
Rookie	Burlington Royals	Appalachian	28	40	.412	9th (10	Tommy Shields
Rookie	Idaho Falls Chukars	Pioneer	38	38	.500	5th (8)	Omar Ramirez
Overall Minor League Record			317	387	.450	28th (30)	

ORGANIZATION STATISTICS

KANSAS CITY ROYALS

AMERICAN LEAGUE

Batting	B-T	HT	WT	DOB	AVG	vLH	vRH	G	AB	R	H	2B	3B	HR	RBI	BB	HBP	SH	SF	SO	SB	CS	SLG	OBP
Adams, Lane	R-R	6-4	190	11-13-89	.000	—	.000	6	3	1	0	0	0	0	0	0	0	0	0	2	0	0	.000	.000
Aoki, Norichika	L-R	5-9	180	1-5-82	.285	.363	.259	132	491	63	140	22	6	1	43	43	6	8	1	49	17	8	.360	.349
Butler, Billy	R-R	6-1	240	4-18-86	.271	.321	.255	151	549	57	149	32	0	9	66	41	5	0	8	96	0	0	.379	.323
Cain, Lorenzo	R-R	6-2	205	4-13-86	.301	.313	.297	133	471	55	142	29	4	5	53	24	4	0	3	108	28	5	.412	.339
Ciriaco, Pedro	R-R	6-0	180	9-27-85	.213	.100	.243	25	47	7	10	2	0	0	2	0	1	1	0	9	4	0	.255	.229
Colon, Christian	R-R	5-10	190	5-14-89	.333	.375	.310	21	45	8	15	5	1	0	6	3	0	1	0	4	2	0	.489	.375
Dyson, Jarrod	L-R	5-10	160	8-15-84	.269	.250	.274	120	260	33	70	4	4	1	24	22	0	6	2	52	36	7	.327	.324
Escobar, Alcides	R-R	6-1	185	12-16-86	.285	.313	.275	162	579	74	165	34	5	3	50	23	6	8	4	83	31	6	.377	.317
Giavotella, Johnny	R-R	5-8	185	7-10-87	.216	.125	.241	12	37	8	8	1	0	1	5	1	2	0	1	5	0	1	.324	.268
Gordon, Alex	L-R	6-1	220	2-10-84	.266	.256	.271	156	563	87	150	34	1	19	74	65	11	0	4	126	12	3	.432	.351
Gore, Terrance	R-R	5-7	165	6-8-91	.000	.000	—	11	1	5	0	0	0	0	0	0	1	0	0	0	5	0	.000	.500
Hayes, Brett	R-R	6-0	215	2-13-84	.135	.053	.182	27	52	3	7	1	0	1	2	1	0	0	0	12	0	0	.212	.151
Hosmer, Eric	L-L	6-4	225	10-24-89	.270	.264	.273	131	503	54	136	35	1	9	58	35	3	0	6	93	4	2	.398	.318
Ibanez, Raul	L-R	6-2	225	6-2-72	.188	.000	.221	33	80	7	15	3	1	2	5	10	0	0	0	16	0	0	.325	.278
2-team total (57 Los Angeles)					.167	—		90	246	23	41	8	3	5	26	33	0	0	1	59	3	2	.285	.264
Infante, Omar	R-R	5-11	195	12-26-81	.252	.217	.264	135	528	50	133	21	3	6	66	33	2	5	7	68	9	3	.337	.295
Kratz, Erik	R-R	6-4	240	6-15-80	.276	.250	.294	13	29	4	8	1	0	2	3	1	0	0	1	10	0	0	.517	.290
2-team total (34 Toronto)					.218	—	—	47	110	12	24	4	0	5	13	4	0	0	1	22	0	0	.391	.243
Maxwell, Justin	R-R	6-5	225	11-6-83	.150	.087	.235	20	40	4	6	1	0	0	3	2	2	0	1	20	0	1	.175	.222
Moustakas, Mike	L-R	6-0	195	9-11-88	.212	.172	.223	140	457	45	97	21	1	15	54	35	3	1	4	74	1	0	.361	.271
Nix, Jayson	R-R	5-11	195	8-26-82	.000	.000	.000	7	8	0	0	0	0	0	1	0	0	0	1	6	0	0	.000	.000
Paredes, Jimmy	B-R	6-3	200	11-25-88	.200	.000	.222	9	10	3	2	0	0	0	0	0	0	0	0	3	2	0	.200	.200
2-team total (18 Baltimore)					.286	—		27	63	12	18	4	0	2	8	2	0	0	0	16	4	0	.444	.308
Peguero, Carlos	L-L	6-5	250	2-22-87	.222	.000	.250	4	9	1	2	1	0	0	1	1	0	0	0	5	0	0	.333	.300
Pena, Francisco	R-R	6-2	230	10-12-89	—	—	—	1	0	0	0	0	0	0	0	0	0	0	0	0	0	0	—	—
Perez, Salvador	R-R	6-3	240	5-10-90	.260	.226	.270	150	578	57	150	28	2	17	70	22	3	0	3	85	1	0	.403	.289
Valencia, Danny	R-R	6-2	220	9-19-84	.282	.354	.178	36	110	8	31	5	0	2	11	7	1	0	1	27	0	0	.382	.328
2-team total (50 Toronto)					.258	—	—	86	264	20	68	16	1	4	30	14	2	0	4	62	1	1	.371	.296
Willingham, Josh	R-R	6-2	220	2-17-79	.233	.316	.204	24	73	14	17	5	0	2	6	11	2	0	0	24	1	0	.384	.349
2-team total (68 Minnesota)					.215	—		92	297	48	64	10	1	14	40	53	9	0	5	102	2	0	.397	.346

Pitching	B-T	HT	WT	DOB	W	L	ERA	G	GS	CG	SV	IP	H	R	ER	HR	BB	SO	AVG	vLH	vRH	K/9	BB/9
Brooks, Aaron	R-R	6-4	220	4-27-90	0	1	43.88	2	1	0	0	3	12	13	13	1	3	2	.667	.714	.636	6.75	10.13
Bueno, Francisley	L-L	5-11	205	3-5-81	0	0	4.18	30	0	0	0	32	36	16	15	3	7	20	.277	.206	.343	5.57	1.95
Chen, Bruce	L-L	6-2	215	6-19-77	2	4	7.45	13	7	0	0	48	69	40	40	7	16	36	.343	.310	.357	6.70	2.98
Coleman, Louis	R-R	6-4	205	4-4-86	1	0	5.56	31	0	0	1	34	39	21	21	6	18	24	.291	.233	.319	6.35	4.76
Coleman, Casey	L-R	6-0	185	7-3-87	1	0	5.25	10	0	0	0	12	16	8	7	0	6	5	.327	.333	.321	3.75	4.50
Collins, Tim	L-L	5-7	170	8-21-89	0	3	3.86	22	0	0	0	21	18	9	9	2	11	15	.247	.273	.235	6.43	4.71
Crow, Aaron	R-R	6-3	195	11-10-86	6	1	4.12	67	0	3	59	52	32	27	10	24	34		.240	.271	.215	5.19	3.66
Davis, Wade	R-R	6-5	220	9-7-85	9	2	1.00	71	0	0	3	72	38	8	8	0	23	109	.151	.189	.112	13.63	2.88
Downs, Scott	L-L	6-2	220	3-17-76	0	2	3.14	17	0	0	0	14	12	7	5	1	5	3	.231	.226	.238	1.88	3.14
2-team total (38 Chicago)					0	4	4.97	55	0	0	1	38	36	24	21	2	20	25	—	—	—	5.92	4.74
Duffy, Danny	L-L	6-3	205	12-21-88	9	12	2.53	31	25	0	0	149	113	52	42	12	53	113	.209	.137	.230	6.81	3.19
Finnegan, Brandon	L-L	5-11	185	4-14-93	0	1	1.29	7	0	0	0	7	6	1	1	0	1	10	.222	.333	.167	12.86	1.29
Frasor, Jason	R-R	5-9	180	8-9-77	3	0	1.53	23	0	0	0	18	13	3	3	1	4	16	.217	.286	.179	8.15	2.04
2-team total (38 Texas)					4	1	2.66	61	0	0	0	47	40	17	14	3	18	46	—	—	—	8.75	3.42
Guthrie, Jeremy	R-R	6-1	205	4-8-79	13	11	4.13	32	32	1	0	203	215	100	93	23	49	124	.272	.297	.241	5.51	2.18
Hendriks, Liam	R-R	6-1	205	2-10-89	0	2	4.66	6	3	0	0	19	26	12	10	0	3	15	.325	.297	.349	6.98	1.40
2-team total (3 Toronto)					1	2	5.23	9	6	0	0	33	38	21	19	3	7	23	—	—	—	6.34	1.93
Herrera, Kelvin	R-R	5-10	200	12-31-89	4	3	1.41	70	0	0	0	70	54	12	11	0	26	59	.214	.244	.186	7.59	3.34
Holland, Greg	R-R	5-10	205	11-20-85	1	3	1.44	65	0	0	46	62	37	13	10	3	20	90	.170	.177	.160	12.99	2.89
Joseph, Donnie	L-L	6-3	190	11-1-87	0	0	81.00	1	0	0	0	1	5	6	6	1	1	2	.714	.000	.833	27.00	13.50
Mariot, Michael	R-R	6-0	190	10-20-88	1	0	6.48	17	0	0	0	25	31	21	18	2	12	21	.298	.321	.271	7.56	4.32

	B-T	HT	WT	DOB	W	L	ERA	G	GS	CG	SV	IP	H	R	ER	HR	BB	SO	AVG	vLH	vRH	K/9	BB/9
Marks, Justin	L-L	6-3	205	1-12-88	0	0	13.50	1	0	0	0	2	4	3	3	0	3	2	.400	.333	.429	9.00	13.50
Rodriguez, Wilking	R-R	6-1	180	3-2-90	0	0	0.00	2	0	0	0	2	1	0	0	0	1	1	.167	.333	.000	4.50	4.50
Shields, James	R-R	6-3	215	12-20-81	14	8	3.21	34	34	1	0	227	224	95	81	23	44	180	.256	.261	.251	7.14	1.74
Vargas, Jason	L-L	6-0	215	2-2-83	11	10	3.71	30	30	1	0	187	197	82	77	19	41	128	.267	.268	.266	6.16	1.97
Ventura, Yordano	R-R	6-0	180	6-3-91	14	10	3.20	31	30	0	0	183	168	70	65	14	69	159	.240	.232	.250	7.82	3.39

Fielding

Catcher	PCT	G	PO	A	E	DP	PB
Hayes	1.000	27	94	5	0	2	1
Kratz	1.000	11	47	1	0	1	0
Pena	1.000	1	0	1	0	0	0
Perez	.992	146	1037	72	9	5	5

First Base	PCT	G	PO	A	E	DP
Butler	.993	37	272	24	2	26
Hosmer	.991	130	1043	88	10	85
Ibanez	1.000	3	14	3	0	2
Nix	1.000	1	3	0	0	0

Second Base	PCT	G	PO	A	E	DP
Ciriaco	1.000	13	17	27	0	7
Colon	1.000	11	15	26	0	4

	PCT	G	PO	A	E	DP
Giavotella	.979	12	15	31	1	5
Infante	.978	134	187	304	11	67
Paredes	1.000	2	0	1	0	0
Valencia	1.000	6	5	6	0	0

Third Base	PCT	G	PO	A	E	DP
Ciriaco	1.000	3	4	1	0	0
Colon	.800	5	2	6	2	1
Moustakas	.947	138	97	241	19	14
Nix	1.000	4	1	2	0	0
Paredes	1.000	3	1	2	0	1
Valencia	.966	26	11	46	2	5

Shortstop	PCT	G	PO	A	E	DP
Ciriaco	—	2	0	0	0	0

	PCT	G	PO	A	E	DP
Colon	1.000	2	0	2	0	0
Escobar	.976	162	213	440	16	91
Nix	1.000	2	2	1	0	0

Outfield	PCT	G	PO	A	E	DP
Adams	1.000	2	3	0	0	0
Aoki	.991	120	212	5	2	1
Cain	.994	133	338	8	2	0
Dyson	.983	108	228	4	4	0
Gordon	.994	156	341	8	2	0
Gore	1.000	2	1	0	0	0
Ibanez	.957	10	22	0	1	0
Maxwell	1.000	14	16	1	0	0
Peguero	1.000	4	3	0	0	0
Willingham	1.000	1	3	0	0	0

OMAHA STORM CHASERS   TRIPLE-A

PACIFIC COAST LEAGUE

Batting	B-T	HT	WT	DOB	AVG	vLH	vRH	G	AB	R	H	2B	3B	HR	RBI	BB	HBP	SH	SF	SO	SB	CS	SLG	OBP
Bocock, Brian	R-R	5-11	185	3-9-85	.279	.296	.273	97	340	44	95	18	2	2	20	26	1	7	3	71	3	5	.362	.330
Cain, Lorenzo	R-R	6-2	205	4-13-86	.000	—	.000	2	7	0	0	0	0	0	0	0	0	0	0	0	0	0	.000	.000
Ciriaco, Pedro	R-R	6-0	180	9-27-85	.302	.313	.298	62	205	27	62	17	3	2	24	6	1	1	2	35	6	0	.444	.322
Colon, Christian	R-R	5-10	190	5-14-89	.311	.350	.295	86	344	55	107	18	0	8	47	30	3	6	5	29	15	4	.433	.366
Cuthbert, Cheslor	R-R	6-1	190	11-16-92	.264	.115	.323	25	91	12	24	5	0	2	16	9	0	0	0	12	1	1	.385	.330
Davis, Logan	L-R	6-2	175	8-23-91	.294	.000	.333	5	17	2	5	0	0	0	1	1	0	0	0	5	0	0	.294	.368
Donald, Jason	R-R	6-1	195	9-4-84	.231	.118	.262	25	78	7	18	3	0	1	5	3	2	0	2	21	1	1	.308	.271
2-team total (44 Round Rock)					.234			69	222	29	52	9	2	4	13	18	2	3	3	65	4	2	.347	.294
Eibner, Brett	R-R	6-3	195	12-2-88	.241	.197	.255	74	274	42	66	13	2	7	27	30	2	2	3	78	5	2	.380	.317
Fields, Matt	R-R	6-5	235	7-8-85	.262	.333	.233	125	465	67	122	29	2	28	81	36	9	0	2	156	1	1	.514	.326
Fletcher, Brian	R-R	6-0	190	10-26-88	.298	.214	.323	35	124	14	37	4	1	2	15	10	1	0	1	40	3	3	.395	.353
Flores, Jesus	R-R	6-1	210	10-26-84	.248	.206	.262	40	137	18	34	5	0	5	21	11	0	2	0	32	0	0	.394	.304
Giavotella, Johnny	R-R	5-8	185	7-10-87	.308	.280	.320	114	441	66	136	33	2	7	61	47	1	0	4	36	20	4	.440	.373
Gore, Terrance	R-R	5-7	165	6-8-91	.250	.500	.222	17	20	8	5	0	0	0	2	1	3	0		4	11	3	.250	.348
Graterol, Juan	R-R	6-1	205	2-14-89	.250	.273	.222	7	20	0	5	0	0	0	2	0	0	0	1	4	0	0	.250	.238
Hayes, Brett	R-R	6-0	215	2-13-84	.310	.333	.296	10	42	8	13	3	0	3	8	2	0	0	0	14	1	0	.595	.341
Hernandez, Gorkys	R-R	6-1	190	9-7-87	.231	.500	.182	4	13	3	3	0	0	0	1	1	0	0	0	2	2	1	.231	.286
Hosmer, Eric	L-L	6-4	225	10-24-89	.300	.500	.250	2	10	2	3	0	0	1	3	1	0	0	0	3	0	0	.600	.364
Infante, Omar	R-R	5-11	195	12-26-81	.364	1.000	.300	3	11	1	4	1	0	0	1	0	0	0	0	4	0	0	.455	.364
Janish, Paul	R-R	6-2	200	10-12-82	.314	.245	.350	46	153	17	48	11	1	2	17	15	0	4	0	18	0	3	.438	.375
2-team total (67 Colorado Springs)					.268			113	362	35	97	20	2	3	36	28	2	5	1	53	1	5	.359	.323
Maggi, Beau	R-R	6-1	208	11-11-90	.125	1.000	.000	4	8	1	1	0	0	0	0	2	0	0	0	5	0	0	.125	.300
Maxwell, Justin	R-R	6-5	225	11-6-83	.285	.353	.252	56	207	32	59	11	1	8	29	20	3	0	3	75	3	2	.464	.352
Merrifield, Whit	R-R	6-1	175	1-24-89	.340	.349	.335	76	321	57	109	28	3	3	29	17	2	2	3	52	11	7	.474	.373
Mesa, Melky	R-R	6-1	190	1-31-87	.284	.316	.273	23	74	11	21	3	0	5	10	4	3	0	0	26	1	0	.527	.346
Morin, Parker	L-R	5-11	195	7-2-91	.000	—	.000	1	3	0	0	0	0	0	0	1	0	0	0	1	0	0	.000	.250
Moustakas, Mike	L-R	6-0	195	9-11-88	.355	.250	.391	8	31	3	11	3	0	1	5	3	0	0	0	6	0	0	.548	.412
Orlando, Paulo	R-R	6-2	210	11-1-85	.301	.250	.322	136	501	61	151	21	9	6	63	39	5	5	4	86	34	9	.415	.355
Paredes, Jimmy	B-R	6-3	200	11-25-88	.305	.299	.307	65	269	37	82	18	4	5	36	11	0	0	0	78	17	1	.457	.332
Peguero, Carlos	L-L	6-5	250	2-22-87	.266	.198	.290	104	368	64	98	17	1	30	76	45	3	0	2	138	11	4	.563	.349
Pena, Francisco	R-R	6-2	230	10-12-89	.240	.268	.229	96	342	53	82	13	0	27	61	16	5	2	5	65	0	3	.515	.280
Valencia, Danny	R-R	6-2	220	9-19-84	.273	—	.273	3	11	2	3	0	0	1	3	0	0	0	1	0			.545	.429

Pitching	B-T	HT	WT	DOB	W	L	ERA	G	GS	CG	SV	IP	H	R	ER	HR	BB	SO	AVG	vLH	vRH	K/9	BB/9
Adam, Jason	R-R	6-4	225	8-4-91	1	1	2.35	8	0	0	0	15	17	4	4	0	4	11	.288	.167	.341	6.46	2.35
Alexander, Scott	L-L	6-2	190	7-10-89	1	2	6.16	11	0	0	0	19	23	16	13	4	10	13	.311	.321	.304	6.16	4.74
Baumann, Buddy	L-L	5-10	175	12-9-87	2	4	3.19	40	11	0	2	90	85	35	32	6	31	68	.252	.226	.264	6.77	3.09
Binford, Christian	R-R	6-6	217	12-20-92	0	1	5.40	4	0	0	0	10	16	7	6	1	5	9	.348	.375	.318	8.10	4.50
Brooks, Aaron	R-R	6-4	220	4-27-90	12	3	3.88	25	23	1	1	139	151	67	60	14	25	97	.278	.273	.282	6.28	1.62
Bueno, Francisley	L-L	5-11	205	3-5-81	0	2	5.52	9	3	0	0	15	14	10	9	1	4	17	.250	.000	.412	10.43	2.45
Chen, Bruce	L-L	6-2	215	6-19-77	0	1	8.76	3	3	0	0	12	21	12	12	1	3	13	.396	.294	.444	9.49	2.19
Coleman, Louis	R-R	6-4	205	4-4-86	2	1	3.86	28	1	0	7	40	32	20	17	6	15	53	.215	.180	.232	12.03	3.40
Coleman, Casey	L-R	6-0	185	7-3-87	5	1	2.15	34	0	0	3	67	51	19	16	4	26	53	.213	.176	.235	7.12	3.49
2-team total (1 Iowa)					5	1	2.65	35	0	0	3	68	55	24	20	4	28	54	—	—	—	7.15	3.71
Collins, Tim	L-L	5-7	170	8-21-89	2	1	2.76	23	1	0	3	42	26	13	13	6	16	56	.177	.204	.161	11.91	3.40
Culver, Malcom	R-R	6-1	205	2-9-90	0	1	7.36	3	0	0	1	4	6	3	3	1	1	3	.375	.300	.500	7.36	2.45
Duffy, Danny	L-L	6-3	205	12-21-88	1	0	3.00	1	1	0	0	6	5	2	2	1	1	4	.238	.143	.286	6.00	1.50
Dwyer, Chris	R-L	6-3	210	4-10-88	4	4	5.59	28	5	0	2	66	64	44	41	8	39	65	.253	.235	.262	8.86	5.32
Ferguson, Andy	R-R	6-1	195	9-2-88	1	1	6.00	2	2	0	0	12	12	8	8	5	3	6	.255	.292	.217	4.50	2.25

Name	B-T	HT	WT	DOB	W	L	ERA	G	GS	CG	SV	IP	H	R	ER	HR	BB	SO	AVG	vLH	vRH	K/9	BB/9
Hendriks, Liam	R-R	6-1	205	2-10-89	4	1	2.83	5	5	0	0	35	33	13	11	1	6	35	.254	.284	.222	9.00	1.54
Joseph, Donnie	L-L	6-3	190	11-1-87	1	1	3.86	19	0	0	1	26	26	15	11	3	20	30	.255	.319	.200	10.52	7.01
2-team total (9 New Orleans)					2	1	5.50	28	0	0	1	36	44	29	22	7	32	35	—	—		8.75	8.00
Lamb, John	L-L	6-4	205	7-10-90	8	10	3.97	27	26	0	0	138	137	78	61	19	68	131	.258	.269	.254	8.52	4.42
Loe, Kameron	R-R	6-8	245	9-10-81	0	0	4.09	7	0	0	1	11	7	5	5	1	7	4	.184	.158	.211	3.27	5.73
2-team total (6 Reno)					0	0	6.43	13	0	0	1	21	22	15	15	2	10	12	—	—		5.14	4.29
Marimon, Sugar Ray	R-R	6-1	194	9-30-88	5	4	3.56	15	15	0	0	83	88	36	33	10	26	67	.276	.306	.247	7.24	2.81
Mariot, Michael	R-R	6-0	190	10-20-88	2	1	4.95	14	0	0	2	20	19	11	11	2	7	25	.238	.313	.188	11.25	3.15
Marks, Justin	L-L	6-3	205	1-12-88	3	2	5.64	13	2	0	0	30	38	25	19	4	11	27	.292	.246	.333	8.01	3.26
3-team total (5 Round Rock, 4 Sacramento)					3	3	5.03	22	2	0	0	39	44	28	22	4	16	37	—	—		8.47	3.66
Mortensen, Clayton	R-R	6-4	185	4-10-85	5	4	4.74	16	15	0	0	76	86	43	40	11	22	62	.281	.230	.322	7.34	2.61
Patton, Spencer	R-R	6-1	185	2-20-88	4	3	4.08	34	0	0	14	46	26	21	21	9	22	60	.161	.162	.161	11.65	4.27
2-team total (15 Round Rock)					5	4	3.90	49	0	0	18	62	42	27	27	10	25	85	—	—		12.27	3.61
Rodriguez, Wilking	R-R	6-1	180	3-2-90	1	1	2.87	13	0	0	0	16	13	5	5	0	8	15	.224	.118	.268	8.62	4.60
Saunders, Joe	L-L	6-3	215	6-16-81	1	2	6.75	4	4	0	0	19	27	17	14	4	5	6	.355	.320	.373	2.89	2.41
2-team total (2 Round Rock)					1	3	4.99	6	6	0	0	31	42	20	17	5	10	14	—	—		4.11	2.93
Selman, Sam	R-L	6-3	195	11-14-90	0	0	13.50	5	0	0	0	4	7	6	6	0	7	7	.368	.286	.417	15.75	15.75
Tomko, Brett	R-R	6-4	220	4-7-73	4	3	3.80	9	8	0	0	47	46	21	20	6	19	32	.256	.239	.273	6.08	3.61
2-team total (10 Colorado Springs)					6	6	4.74	19	18	0	0	87	104	49	46	11	28	60	—	—		6.18	2.89
Triggs, Andrew	R-R	6-4	210	3-16-89	0	0	0.00	1	0	0	1	1	0	0	0	0	0	0	.000	.000	—	0.00	0.00
Troncoso, Ramon	R-R	6-2	215	2-16-83	1	6	4.30	24	1	0	0	44	46	22	21	3	11	33	.267	.273	.263	6.75	2.25
Verdugo, Ryan	L-L	6-0	205	4-10-87	5	2	4.24	9	9	0	0	47	38	23	22	6	14	44	.228	.216	.231	8.49	2.70
Wade, Cory	R-R	6-2	185	5-28-83	0	0	6.57	7	0	0	0	12	17	10	9	2	4	4	.333	.333	.333	2.92	2.92
Walters, P.J.	R-R	6-4	215	3-12-85	1	4	7.97	10	8	0	0	41	52	40	36	8	19	34	.301	.294	.310	7.52	4.20
Wood, Blake	R-R	6-5	240	8-8-85	0	0	6.38	14	0	0	0	18	18	14	13	2	16	21	.265	.261	.267	10.31	7.85

Fielding

Catcher	PCT	G	PO	A	E	DP	PB
Flores	.992	40	338	23	3	1	6
Graterol	1.000	6	41	5	0	1	0
Hayes	1.000	10	64	3	0	1	0
Maggi	1.000	3	15	1	0	0	0
Pena	.992	90	667	60	6	8	8

First Base	PCT	G	PO	A	E	DP
Bocock	.991	32	213	19	2	24
Cuthbert	1.000	9	81	4	0	11
Donald	1.000	2	16	1	0	1
Fields	.985	101	751	53	12	80
Hosmer	1.000	2	19	4	0	2

Second Base	PCT	G	PO	A	E	DP
Bocock	1.000	7	9	18	0	5
Ciriaco	.963	21	28	49	3	8
Colon	.976	35	66	94	4	20
Donald	.905	8	7	12	2	2
Giavotella	.976	65	128	154	7	45

Infante	1.000	2	2	2	0	0
Janish	1.000	3	11	6	0	3
Merrifield	.857	2	3	3	1	2
Paredes	.975	10	15	24	1	4

Third Base	PCT	G	PO	A	E	DP
Bocock	.920	43	30	73	9	10
Ciriaco	.944	11	7	27	2	4
Colon	.967	13	9	20	1	2
Cuthbert	.923	15	5	19	2	0
Davis	1.000	1	0	2	0	0
Donald	.875	3	2	5	1	0
Giavotella	.901	29	23	41	7	4
Moustakas	1.000	2	1	16	0	1
Paredes	1.000	28	17	51	0	4
Valencia	1.000	2	3	0	0	0

Shortstop	PCT	G	PO	A	E	DP
Bocock	.962	15	17	33	2	11
Ciriaco	.932	28	32	64	7	13

	PCT	G	PO	A	E	DP
Colon	.988	35	69	102	2	25
Donald	.977	12	18	25	1	7
Janish	.975	43	44	110	4	21
Paredes	.925	14	17	32	4	7

Outfield	PCT	G	PO	A	E	DP
Cain	1.000	1	2	0	0	0
Davis	.875	3	7	0	1	0
Eibner	.987	71	145	4	2	1
Fletcher	1.000	8	9	0	0	0
Gore	.909	7	10	0	1	0
Hernandez	1.000	4	9	0	0	0
Maxwell	.977	54	126	2	3	1
Merrifield	.993	72	127	7	1	0
Mesa	1.000	23	41	1	0	0
Orlando	.994	131	329	7	2	4
Paredes	.933	10	13	1	1	0
Peguero	.932	63	104	5	8	1

NORTHWEST ARKANSAS NATURALS

DOUBLE-A

TEXAS LEAGUE

Batting	B-T	HT	WT	DOB	AVG	vLH	vRH	G	AB	R	H	2B	3B	HR	RBI	BB	HBP	SH	SF	SO	SB	CS	SLG	OBP
Adams, Lane	R-R	6-4	190	11-13-89	.269	.185	.304	105	405	65	109	25	3	11	36	45	9	2	4	86	38	9	.427	.352
Aoki, Norichika	L-R	5-9	180	1-5-82	.100	.000	.143	3	10	1	1	0	0	0	0	0	0	0	0	1	0	0	.100	.182
Bocock, Brian	R-R	5-11	185	3-9-85	.160	.100	.200	7	25	5	4	2	0	0	2	5	1	2	0	4	1	0	.240	.323
Bonifacio, Jorge	R-R	6-1	195	6-4-93	.230	.199	.242	132	505	49	116	20	4	4	51	50	5	0	6	127	8	3	.309	.302
Calixte, Orlando	R-R	5-11	160	2-3-92	.241	.246	.238	96	374	43	90	15	1	11	37	27	0	6	5	92	9	5	.374	.288
Chapman, Ethan	L-R	6-0	180	1-5-90	.235	.242	.232	106	298	31	70	7	2	1	28	32	1	14	2	74	11	9	.282	.309
Colon, Christian	R-R	5-10	190	5-14-89	.250	.500	.000	2	8	1	2	1	0	0	0	1	0	0	0	2	1	0	.375	.333
Cuthbert, Cheslor	R-R	6-1	190	11-16-92	.276	.274	.277	96	355	35	98	19	1	10	48	36	1	0	3	67	9	3	.420	.342
Davis, Logan	L-R	6-2	175	8-23-91	.091	.000	.125	6	11	0	1	0	0	0	1	0	0	1	0	2	0	0	.091	.091
Dozier, Hunter	R-R	6-4	220	8-22-91	.209	.197	.215	64	234	33	49	12	0	4	21	31	1	0	1	70	3	2	.312	.303
Fletcher, Brian	R-R	6-0	190	10-26-88	.254	.143	.316	17	59	9	15	1	0	5	14	5	1	0	5	17	1	0	.525	.300
Franco, Angel	B-R	5-10	155	5-23-90	.234	.260	.219	94	338	36	79	9	2	2	26	27	1	14	3	50	8	5	.290	.290
Gibbs, Micah	B-R	5-11	205	7-27-88	.217	.186	.235	52	161	8	35	10	0	2	17	18	0	2	2	35	3	1	.317	.293
Graterol, Juan	R-R	6-1	205	2-14-89	.280	.232	.299	70	246	17	69	17	0	4	28	9	3	5	1	29	0	0	.398	.313
Maier, Mitch	L-R	6-3	210	6-30-82	.233	.212	.246	25	90	14	21	5	0	3	8	9	0	0	0	30	0	0	.389	.303
Merrifield, Whit	R-R	6-1	175	1-24-89	.278	.356	.248	44	162	22	45	13	1	5	20	22	1	4	1	27	5	4	.463	.366
Morin, Parker	L-R	5-11	195	7-2-91	.206	.190	.214	55	189	13	39	7	0	3	16	12	2	4	0	59	0	1	.291	.261
Ramirez, Max	R-R	5-11	220	10-11-84	.260	.346	.200	36	127	14	33	5	1	3	16	15	0	0	0	37	0	0	.386	.338
Rincon, Edinson	R-R	6-1	215	8-11-90	.237	.287	.204	69	224	16	53	11	0	1	15	21	3	4	1	51	0	7	.299	.309
Schlehuber, Jared	R-R	6-3	220	12-24-88	.177	.085	.216	45	158	9	28	5	0	2	12	16	3	2	1	47	0	0	.247	.264
Threlkeld, Mark	R-R	6-1	201	5-2-90	.246	.260	.239	85	301	37	74	13	1	9	40	23	2	3	1	79	1	3	.385	.303
Trapp, Justin	R-R	5-10	165	10-7-90	.239	.217	.251	113	364	47	87	9	1	4	26	32	3	7	1	81	12	6	.302	.305

Pitching	B-T	HT	WT	DOB	W	L	ERA	G	GS	CG	SV	IP	H	R	ER	HR	BB	SO	AVG	vLH	vRH	K/9	BB/9
Adam, Jason	R-R	6-4	225	8-4-91	4	8	5.03	19	18	0	0	98	107	62	55	9	30	89	.279	.259	.297	8.15	2.75

KANSAS CITY ROYALS

	B-T	HT	WT	DOB	W	L	ERA	G	GS	CG	SV	IP	H	R	ER	HR	BB	SO	AVG	vLH	vRH	K/9	BB/9
Alexander, Scott	L-L	6-2	190	7-10-89	1	2	3.88	35	0	0	3	49	42	26	21	3	16	36	.235	.220	.242	6.66	2.96
Arguelles, Noel	L-L	6-4	220	1-12-90	1	2	7.15	42	0	0	1	62	70	61	49	9	44	44	.287	.295	.283	6.42	6.42
Baez, Angel	R-R	6-3	226	2-14-91	1	5	4.65	35	0	0	0	62	58	33	32	9	29	71	.251	.207	.300	10.31	4.21
Billo, Greg	R-R	6-4	220	7-15-90	0	2	7.41	6	3	0	0	17	25	18	14	2	13	17	.347	.350	.344	9.00	6.88
Binford, Christian	R-R	6-6	217	12-20-92	3	2	3.19	8	8	0	0	48	45	19	17	7	6	38	.247	.181	.318	7.13	1.13
Chen, Bruce	L-L	6-2	215	6-19-77	0	0	6.00	1	1	0	0	3	3	2	2	2	0	3	.533	.250	.636	9.00	0.00
Crow, Aaron	R-R	6-3	195	11-10-86	1	0	3.00	2	0	0	0	3	3	1	1	1	1	1	.300	.400	.200	3.00	3.00
Culver, Malcom	R-R	6-1	205	2-9-90	4	4	4.40	41	0	0	7	61	67	35	30	3	28	57	.283	.313	.254	8.36	4.11
Davis, Tripp	L-L	6-1	200	2-12-91	0	3	8.74	3	2	0	0	11	18	11	11	1	5	4	.400	.500	.371	3.18	3.97
Farrell, Luke	R-R	6-6	210	6-7-91	0	1	6.17	2	2	0	0	12	11	8	8	2	2	11	.250	.304	.190	8.49	1.54
Fassold, Cody	R-R	6-2	230	10-2-88	1	2	3.57	23	2	0	0	40	45	20	16	1	11	43	.281	.259	.304	9.60	2.45
Ferguson, Andy	R-R	6-1	195	9-2-88	11	10	2.93	25	23	2	0	148	130	51	48	13	41	118	.237	.229	.245	7.19	2.50
Finnegan, Brandon	L-L	5-11	185	4-14-93	0	3	2.25	8	0	0	0	12	15	9	3	2	2	13	.283	.111	.371	9.75	1.50
Marimon, Sugar Ray	R-R	6-1	194	9-30-88	0	1	2.14	4	4	0	0	21	18	5	5	0	7	9	.243	.211	.278	3.86	3.00
Melville, Tim	R-R	6-5	210	10-9-89	2	11	5.50	26	26	0	0	129	144	92	79	14	68	105	.282	.325	.242	7.31	4.73
Murray, Matt	R-R	6-4	225	12-28-89	1	6	4.28	28	10	0	0	76	78	42	36	4	23	61	.263	.288	.238	7.26	2.74
Nina, Aroni	R-R	6-4	178	4-9-90	0	1	4.76	6	1	0	0	11	7	6	6	0	6	7	.179	.200	.158	5.56	4.76
Pena, Hassan	R-R	6-2	210	3-25-85	1	0	4.50	5	0	0	1	10	9	5	5	1	8	9	.243	.261	.214	8.10	7.20
Perez, Kevin	R-R	6-0	205	8-1-93	0	0	4.15	2	0	0	0	4	6	2	2	1	3	2	.375	.286	.444	4.15	6.23
Peterson, Mark	R-R	6-0	190	9-7-90	0	1	1.72	12	0	0	3	16	16	3	3	1	6	14	.271	.360	.206	8.04	3.45
Rodriguez, Wilking	R-R	6-1	180	3-2-90	1	0	1.64	11	0	0	0	11	11	3	2	2	4	12	.256	.263	.250	9.82	3.27
Selman, Sam	R-L	6-3	195	11-14-90	4	6	3.87	28	16	0	0	93	81	42	40	7	49	87	.233	.234	.232	8.42	4.74
Sulbaran, J.C.	R-R	6-2	220	11-9-89	8	10	3.25	25	23	0	0	127	128	58	46	11	54	116	.264	.257	.272	8.20	3.82
Triggs, Andrew	R-R	6-4	210	3-16-89	4	3	2.93	43	1	0	19	61	55	28	20	4	16	38	.235	.264	.210	5.58	2.35
Williams, Ali	R-R	6-2	185	7-8-89	5	3	5.18	25	0	0	0	40	34	25	23	8	21	46	.227	.209	.241	10.35	4.73
Wood, Blake	R-R	6-5	240	8-8-85	0	1	8.10	6	0	0	0	7	11	6	6	1	2	13	.393	.571	.214	17.55	2.70

Fielding

Catcher	PCT	G	PO	A	E	DP	PB
Gibbs	.990	49	368	30	4	1	0
Graterol	.987	42	327	63	5	10	3
Morin	.988	54	375	49	5	5	8

First Base	PCT	G	PO	A	E	DP
Cuthbert	.988	28	225	15	3	16
Franco	1.000	1	2	0	0	0
Graterol	1.000	25	203	11	0	18
Ramirez	.985	17	127	6	2	12
Rincon	1.000	2	8	0	0	1
Schlehuber	.981	23	195	9	4	15
Threlkeld	.981	52	391	29	8	31

Second Base	PCT	G	PO	A	E	DP
Cuthbert	.833	3	4	6	2	1
Davis	.900	3	6	3	1	0

Franco	.992	57	84	172	2	36
Merrifield	.925	14	23	26	4	8
Trapp	.949	71	108	173	15	32

Third Base	PCT	G	PO	A	E	DP
Calixte	.667	1	0	2	1	0
Cuthbert	.891	60	48	107	19	6
Dozier	.911	61	31	92	12	3
Franco	1.000	5	1	10	0	2
Rincon	1.000	1	1	1	0	0
Schlehuber	.857	16	8	22	5	1

Shortstop	PCT	G	PO	A	E	DP
Bocock	.964	7	9	18	1	5
Calixte	.940	92	166	227	25	52
Colon	1.000	2	6	6	0	3
Davis	1.000	1	0	2	0	0

Franco	.948	33	41	86	7	10
Merrifield	.978	9	21	23	1	6

Outfield	PCT	G	PO	A	E	DP
Adams	.985	104	262	3	4	1
Aoki	1.000	2	1	0	0	0
Bonifacio	.960	125	212	6	9	3
Chapman	1.000	98	209	13	0	4
Davis	—	1	0	0	0	0
Fletcher	1.000	2	6	0	0	0
Maier	.977	21	39	3	1	0
Merrifield	1.000	21	39	4	0	0
Rincon	1.000	30	42	2	0	0
Schlehuber	1.000	1	3	0	0	0
Trapp	.971	35	65	3	2	1

WILMINGTON BLUE ROCKS
CAROLINA LEAGUE

HIGH CLASS A

Batting	B-T	HT	WT	DOB	AVG	vLH	vRH	G	AB	R	H	2B	3B	HR	RBI	BB	HBP	SH	SF	SO	SB	CS	SLG	OBP
Antonio, Mike	R-R	6-2	190	10-26-91	.242	.220	.249	68	227	30	55	18	2	5	32	12	1	3	5	40	0	1	.405	.278
Chavez, Johermyn	R-R	6-3	220	1-26-89	.224	.091	.272	36	125	13	28	3	0	3	17	12	5	0	3	34	0	0	.320	.310
Chism, Tyler	R-R	6-0	205	10-6-88	.227	.400	.176	8	22	1	5	2	0	0	0	2	1	0	0	6	1	1	.318	.320
Davis, Logan	L-R	6-2	175	8-23-91	.220	.000	.225	13	41	2	9	0	2	0	3	1	0	2	0	9	1	0	.317	.238
Diekroeger, Kenny	R-R	6-2	190	11-5-90	.212	.265	.197	47	151	17	32	2	1	1	8	18	0	2	0	37	6	1	.258	.296
Donato, Mark	L-L	6-2	225	11-18-91	.185	.188	.184	44	135	7	25	6	2	1	14	12	3	0	2	32	0	0	.281	.263
Dozier, Hunter	R-R	6-4	220	8-22-91	.295	.288	.297	66	224	36	66	18	0	4	39	35	5	0	3	56	7	3	.429	.397
Eibner, Brett	R-R	6-3	195	12-2-88	.220	.100	.258	13	41	5	9	3	0	1	3	10	0	0	0	16	3	2	.366	.373
Evans, Zane	R-R	6-2	209	11-29-91	.226	.198	.238	101	371	34	84	24	0	5	36	27	3	2	0	92	2	1	.332	.284
Ford, Fred	R-R	6-5	200	4-10-92	.152	.100	.167	17	46	5	7	1	0	2	6	4	0	0	0	18	0	0	.304	.220
Gallagher, Cam	R-R	6-3	210	12-6-92	.228	.200	.236	96	312	24	71	18	0	5	34	37	1	5	6	38	1	0	.333	.306
Gore, Terrance	R-R	5-7	165	6-8-91	.218	.204	.222	89	252	34	55	8	1	0	15	20	4	9	2	66	36	4	.258	.284
Lopez, Jack	R-R	5-9	165	12-16-92	.215	.245	.205	108	405	34	87	19	2	1	29	27	6	5	0	66	23	9	.279	.274
Maggi, Beau	L-R	6-1	208	11-11-90	.000	—	.000	2	4	0	0	0	0	0	1	1	0	0	0	1	0	0	.000	.333
Mondesi, Raul A.	B-R	6-1	165	7-27-95	.211	.219	.209	110	435	54	92	14	12	8	33	24	3	8	2	122	17	4	.354	.256
Rockett, Daniel	R-R	6-2	200	11-9-90	.205	.263	.189	116	351	38	72	14	5	3	28	21	5	5	2	87	7	1	.299	.259
Schlehuber, Jared	R-R	6-3	220	12-24-88	.252	.219	.260	48	155	20	39	9	0	6	20	19	2	0	1	31	2	0	.426	.339
Schwindel, Frank	R-R	6-1	205	6-29-92	.241	.313	.214	16	58	6	14	3	0	2	5	2	1	0	0	12	0	0	.397	.279
Starling, Bubba	R-R	6-4	180	8-3-92	.218	.310	.189	132	482	67	105	23	4	9	54	49	13	0	5	150	17	2	.338	.304
Stubbs, Cody	L-L	6-4	215	1-14-91	.223	.119	.247	92	314	27	70	11	4	10	39	23	6	1	2	92	2	1	.379	.287
Threlkeld, Mark	R-R	6-1	201	5-2-90	.242	.091	.275	17	62	7	15	1	0	2	4	3	1	0	0	20	1	0	.355	.288
Torres, Ramon	B-R	5-10	155	1-22-93	.248	.323	.229	44	149	14	37	5	3	0	8	10	1	6	1	16	5	2	.322	.298

Pitching	B-T	HT	WT	DOB	W	L	ERA	G	GS	CG	SV	IP	H	R	ER	HR	BB	SO	AVG	vLH	vRH	K/9	BB/9
Almonte, Miguel	R-R	6-2	180	4-4-93	6	8	4.49	23	22	0	0	110	107	60	55	9	32	101	.259	.290	.236	8.24	2.61
Bartsch, Kyle	L-L	5-10	210	3-10-91	5	5	2.29	41	0	0	7	55	45	16	14	3	12	52	.227	.213	.234	8.51	1.96
Binford, Christian	R-R	6-6	217	12-20-92	5	4	2.40	14	14	0	0	83	72	28	22	2	11	92	.231	.217	.240	10.02	1.20

Name	B-T	HT	WT	DOB	W	L	ERA	G	GS	CG	SV	IP	H	R	ER	HR	BB	SO	AVG	vLH	vRH	K/9	BB/9
Caramo, Yender	R-R	6-0	175	8-25-91	4	8	3.59	35	4	0	3	83	94	42	33	1	12	42	.285	.231	.321	4.57	1.31
Davis, Tripp	L-L	6-1	200	2-12-91	0	0	2.70	2	0	0	0	7	8	2	2	0	1	8	.286	.333	.263	10.80	1.35
Dziedzic, Jonathan	R-L	6-0	165	2-4-91	6	7	2.52	24	24	0	0	125	122	40	35	5	37	113	.263	.284	.257	8.14	2.66
Edwards, Andrew	R-R	6-6	265	10-7-91	0	4	5.79	11	0	0	1	19	22	12	12	1	7	15	.297	.333	.257	7.23	3.38
Finnegan, Brandon	L-L	5-11	185	4-14-93	0	1	0.60	5	5	0	0	15	5	1	1	1	2	13	.106	.000	.147	7.80	1.20
Manaea, Sean	R-L	6-5	235	2-1-92	7	8	3.11	25	25	1	0	122	102	54	42	5	54	146	.228	.211	.234	10.80	3.99
Murray, Matt	R-R	6-4	225	12-28-89	0	1	2.50	8	0	0	0	18	9	5	5	1	7	19	.148	.091	.179	9.50	3.50
Nina, Aroni	R-R	6-4	178	4-9-90	3	1	4.53	23	0	0	0	44	37	27	22	2	25	45	.231	.203	.250	9.27	5.15
Peterson, Mark	R-R	6-0	190	9-7-90	1	2	1.31	33	0	0	22	41	31	8	6	1	12	32	.211	.255	.185	6.97	2.61
Pounders, Brooks	R-R	6-4	270	9-26-90	0	1	4.02	3	3	0	0	16	16	9	7	0	7	18	.262	.323	.200	10.34	4.02
Santos, Luis	R-R	6-0	185	2-11-91	4	4	5.00	16	11	0	0	72	68	42	40	6	18	52	.250	.281	.222	6.50	2.25
Sneed, Zeb	R-R	6-4	195	3-19-91	5	3	2.71	38	0	0	1	63	56	28	19	2	14	48	.238	.167	.288	6.86	2.00
Sparkman, Glenn	B-R	6-2	210	5-11-92	8	3	1.56	29	18	0	1	121	94	28	21	2	25	117	.213	.198	.225	8.70	1.86
Stumpf, Daniel	L-L	6-2	200	1-4-91	3	8	3.77	32	8	0	2	74	82	34	31	1	19	79	.281	.247	.293	9.61	2.31
Walter, John	R-R	6-5	225	5-20-91	6	3	3.80	30	3	0	0	64	66	27	27	3	22	44	.270	.242	.290	6.19	3.09
Williams, Ali	R-R	6-2	185	7-8-89	0	0	1.88	12	0	0	0	24	16	5	5	2	11	37	.200	.238	.186	13.88	4.13
Wood, Blake	R-R	6-5	240	8-8-85	2	1	0.93	5	0	0	0	10	4	1	1	1	2	10	.125	.000	.160	9.31	1.86

Fielding

Catcher	PCT	G	PO	A	E	DP	PB
Evans	.987	50	363	25	5	4	7
Gallagher	.991	89	691	101	7	4	7
Maggi	1.000	2	14	2	0	0	1

First Base	PCT	G	PO	A	E	DP
Antonio	.986	9	65	4	1	5
Donato	.996	41	267	17	1	16
Schlehuber	.972	13	101	2	3	10
Schwindel	.985	15	122	8	2	9
Stubbs	.992	49	365	20	3	28
Threlkeld	.994	16	146	11	1	14

Second Base	PCT	G	PO	A	E	DP
Davis	.933	4	4	10	1	2

	PCT	G	PO	A	E	DP
Diekroeger	.965	37	55	82	5	17
Lopez	.983	76	171	184	6	41
Torres	.970	22	32	65	3	13

Third Base	PCT	G	PO	A	E	DP
Antonio	.952	11	4	16	1	1
Davis	1.000	6	2	7	0	0
Diekroeger	.960	9	4	20	1	1
Dozier	.948	62	36	91	7	7
Lopez	1.000	2	2	4	0	2
Schlehuber	.938	33	20	56	5	4
Torres	.857	21	5	25	5	2

Shortstop	PCT	G	PO	A	E	DP
Davis	1.000	3	5	4	0	1

	PCT	G	PO	A	E	DP
Lopez	.940	29	40	69	7	13
Mondesi	.963	106	129	282	16	48
Torres	1.000	1	0	2	0	0

Outfield	PCT	G	PO	A	E	DP
Chavez	.984	34	60	1	1	0
Chism	.909	7	10	0	1	0
Diekroeger	—	1	0	0	0	0
Eibner	.917	10	11	0	1	0
Ford	.939	16	29	2	2	0
Gore	.989	86	179	6	2	0
Rockett	.967	111	197	11	7	1
Schlehuber	1.000	1	2	0	0	0
Starling	.993	130	265	14	2	5
Stubbs	.980	35	47	2	1	0

LEXINGTON LEGENDS

LOW CLASS A

SOUTH ATLANTIC LEAGUE

Batting	B-T	HT	WT	DOB	AVG	vLH	vRH	G	AB	R	H	2B	3B	HR	RBI	BB	HBP	SH	SF	SO	SB	CS	SLG	OBP
Antonio, Mike	R-R	6-2	190	10-26-91	.313	.212	.354	32	112	21	35	6	0	4	23	13	2	0	1	16	0	0	.473	.391
Arteaga, Humberto	R-R	6-1	160	1-23-94	.198	.194	.199	122	450	33	89	13	2	2	31	17	3	12	1	111	7	6	.249	.231
Chism, Tyler	R-R	6-0	205	10-6-88	.267	.250	.273	9	30	7	8	2	0	2	4	0	1	0	0	7	3	0	.533	.290
Diekroeger, Kenny	R-R	6-2	190	11-5-90	.265	.189	.294	51	189	24	50	9	1	5	21	11	3	2	4	34	6	3	.402	.309
Duenez, Samir	L-R	6-1	195	6-11-96	.232	.150	.246	41	142	12	33	9	2	0	9	7	0	0	0	19	2	1	.324	.268
Escalera, Alfredo	R-R	6-1	180	2-17-95	.221	.265	.202	104	438	62	97	17	4	9	38	18	10	7	2	111	11	3	.340	.267
Ford, Fred	R-R	6-5	200	4-10-92	.206	.200	.208	101	335	44	69	21	1	10	46	39	6	0	5	128	8	3	.364	.296
Garcia, Carlos	R-R	5-10	175	3-18-92	.272	.227	.289	80	276	38	75	11	3	2	36	24	5	5	1	49	31	5	.355	.340
Hernandez, Elier	R-R	6-3	200	11-21-94	.264	.295	.252	111	420	54	111	19	4	9	34	16	4	3	3	99	5	5	.393	.296
Johnson, Chad	R-R	6-0	190	5-31-94	.233	.179	.252	105	365	47	85	16	1	4	39	46	7	1	7	137	2	3	.315	.325
Kjerstad, Dex	R-R	6-1	210	1-19-92	.275	.236	.294	80	276	33	76	14	5	6	33	18	7	1	0	59	9	6	.428	.336
Kuntz, Kevin	B-R	6-1	185	5-29-90	.300	.308	.296	16	40	6	12	2	0	0	2	6	0	2	0	8	3	0	.350	.391
Ramos, Mauricio	R-R	6-1	160	2-2-92	.279	.258	.289	109	419	47	117	27	3	9	54	22	14	1	2	75	0	3	.422	.335
Rivera, Alexis	L-L	6-2	225	6-17-94	.191	.146	.207	50	162	14	31	8	1	0	17	18	2	1	0	60	9	2	.253	.280
Schwindel, Frank	R-R	6-1	205	6-29-92	.286	.312	.274	102	406	48	116	29	2	20	70	17	1	0	4	68	0	1	.515	.313
Shin, Jin-Ho	R-R	6-2	200	10-20-91	.333	—	.333	1	3	0	1	0	0	0	0	0	0	0	0	0	0	0	.333	.333
Taylor, Dominique	R-R	6-1	190	8-11-92	.300	.296	.302	89	333	51	100	16	5	7	40	18	8	5	3	49	18	4	.441	.348
Torres, Ramon	B-R	5-10	155	1-22-93	.304	.292	.310	73	276	46	84	15	2	5	26	16	2	15	1	40	15	5	.428	.346
Villegas, Luis	R-R	5-10	170	12-2-92	.276	.300	.263	8	29	4	8	2	0	0	1	2	1	1	0	6	0	0	.345	.344

Pitching	B-T	HT	WT	DOB	W	L	ERA	G	GS	CG	SV	IP	H	R	ER	HR	BB	SO	AVG	vLH	vRH	K/9	BB/9
Alvarez, Matt	R-R	6-2	190	1-11-91	5	7	5.15	30	7	0	3	73	63	45	42	3	52	72	.230	.230	.230	8.84	6.38
Black, Alex	R-R	6-3	210	2-27-91	3	1	5.59	19	0	0	1	37	49	29	23	4	20	33	.322	.360	.286	8.03	4.86
Brockett, Andrew	R-R	5-11	185	7-5-92	0	0	1.45	10	0	0	1	19	14	5	3	0	8	14	.203	.125	.270	6.75	3.86
Davis, Tripp	L-L	6-1	200	2-12-91	2	2	4.95	16	2	0	0	44	57	25	24	5	13	40	.315	.194	.386	8.24	2.68
Eaton, Todd	R-R	6-1	190	5-9-92	0	0	16.20	1	0	0	0	2	3	4	3	1	2	1	.375	.400	.333	5.40	10.80
Edwards, Andrew	R-R	6-6	265	10-7-91	3	5	4.76	22	6	0	1	68	87	44	36	2	29	48	.311	.336	.288	6.35	3.84
Fairchild, Austin	R-L	6-1	195	3-25-94	0	2	11.05	2	2	0	0	7	2	10	9	0	9	7	.080	.000	.100	8.59	11.05
Farrell, Luke	R-R	6-6	210	6-7-91	2	12	5.25	23	19	0	1	108	117	76	63	13	47	102	.273	.262	.284	8.50	3.92
Fernandez, Pedro	R-R	6-0	175	5-25-94	1	8	4.99	16	8	0	3	61	50	36	34	6	33	60	.225	.234	.217	8.80	4.84
Goudeau, Ashton	R-R	6-5	205	7-23-92	0	0	6.62	7	0	0	0	18	23	16	13	2	6	18	.324	.406	.256	9.17	3.06
Hill, Tim	L-L	6-2	200	2-10-90	2	0	1.26	15	0	0	8	14	4	2	2	1	7	18	.087	.000	.143	11.30	4.40
Junis, Jake	R-R	6-2	225	9-16-92	9	8	4.30	26	22	0	0	136	136	74	65	16	38	109	.262	.270	.254	7.21	2.51
McCarthy, Kevin	R-R	6-3	200	2-22-92	1	0	0.00	2	0	0	0	4	2	0	0	0	2	1	.182	.000	.333	2.25	4.50
Mills, Chad	R-R	6-4	185	11-30-91	2	1	1.18	7	7	0	0	38	25	6	5	0	10	33	.198	.214	.186	7.82	2.37
Ogando, Cesar	R-L	6-3	210	6-6-92	1	1	7.50	6	0	0	0	12	16	13	10	0	5	8	.314	.286	.324	6.00	3.75
Perez, Kevin	R-R	6-0	205	8-1-93	2	3	4.60	29	0	0	3	59	54	36	30	3	30	62	.247	.265	.231	9.51	4.60

KANSAS CITY ROYALS

Name	B-T	HT	WT	DOB	W	L	ERA	G	GS	CG	SV	IP	H	R	ER	HR	BB	SO	AVG	vLH	vRH	K/9	BB/9
Reed, Cody	L-L	6-5	220	4-15-93	3	9	5.46	19	19	0	0	84	105	66	51	5	36	58	.312	.263	.338	6.21	3.86
Rico, Luis	L-L	6-1	175	11-29-93	3	8	4.38	25	16	0	1	109	121	65	53	9	44	88	.281	.307	.267	7.27	3.63
Rodriguez, Jose	R-R	6-2	192	9-18-92	5	1	4.84	30	1	0	5	67	68	40	36	5	28	54	.268	.333	.217	7.25	3.76
Santos, Luis	R-R	6-0	185	2-11-91	4	1	1.76	9	6	1	2	46	33	11	9	3	5	34	.198	.220	.176	6.65	0.98
Simmons, Crawford	R-L	6-2	185	6-10-91	1	3	6.75	16	3	0	0	43	47	33	32	7	21	35	.283	.254	.303	7.38	4.43
Stephenson, Niklas	R-R	6-2	195	11-16-93	1	0	4.00	2	2	0	0	9	11	5	4	0	3	4	.306	.286	.318	4.00	3.00
Swab, Kenny	R-R	6-2	215	8-20-88	0	0	5.40	4	0	0	1	8	8	5	5	0	5	2	.286	.333	.250	2.16	5.40
Tenuta, Matt	L-L	6-4	208	12-16-93	6	10	5.43	26	20	0	1	126	147	82	76	9	33	84	.297	.258	.319	6.00	2.36
Yambati, Robinson	R-R	6-3	185	1-15-91	1	1	2.84	9	0	0	0	13	14	9	4	1	4	14	.275	.400	.222	9.95	2.84

Fielding

Catcher	PCT	G	PO	A	E	DP	PB
Johnson	.988	94	678	76	9	4	15
Schwindel	.993	38	256	42	2	4	13
Shin	1.000	1	9	1	0	1	0
Villegas	.982	8	50	4	1	0	3

First Base	PCT	G	PO	A	E	DP
Duenez	.984	33	281	20	5	29
Ford	.985	31	249	14	4	21
Rivera	.963	18	175	6	7	13
Schwindel	.993	63	530	26	4	60

Second Base	PCT	G	PO	A	E	DP
Arteaga	.978	9	18	26	1	6

	PCT	G	PO	A	E	DP
Diekroeger	1.000	27	56	95	0	21
Garcia	.951	44	78	116	10	26
Kuntz	.964	16	19	35	2	5
Torres	.969	48	85	162	8	43

Third Base	PCT	G	PO	A	E	DP
Antonio	.806	16	6	23	7	1
Diekroeger	1.000	7	2	14	0	0
Garcia	.863	22	13	31	7	3
Ramos	.928	99	52	204	20	15
Torres	.500	2	0	1	1	0

Shortstop	PCT	G	PO	A	E	DP
Arteaga	.970	108	191	321	16	76

	PCT	G	PO	A	E	DP
Diekroeger	.983	13	19	39	1	6
Torres	.940	20	34	60	6	19

Outfield	PCT	G	PO	A	E	DP
Chism	1.000	8	15	0	0	0
Duenez	—	1	0	0	0	0
Escalera	.967	98	206	1	7	0
Ford	.951	43	72	6	4	0
Hernandez	.978	99	176	4	4	0
Kjerstad	.938	74	120	2	8	0
Rivera	1.000	20	25	2	0	0
Taylor	.969	83	153	4	5	3

BURLINGTON ROYALS   ROOKIE

APPALACHIAN LEAGUE

Batting	B-T	HT	WT	DOB	AVG	vLH	vRH	G	AB	R	H	2B	3B	HR	RBI	BB	HBP	SH	SF	SO	SB	CS	SLG	OBP
Adams, Lane	R-R	6-4	190	11-13-89	.500	.500	.500	3	10	3	5	2	2	0	4	4	0	0	0	1	0	0	1.100	.643
Banuelos, Josh	R-R	6-2	215	9-3-91	.302	.333	.291	56	199	28	60	13	1	3	26	17	10	0	0	21	7	2	.422	.385
Burt, D.J.	R-R	5-9	160	10-13-95	.215	.140	.248	49	144	17	31	1	0	2	9	15	3	0	1	25	7	3	.264	.301
Cano, Cristian	R-R	6-2	170	2-9-94	.207	.185	.214	38	111	16	23	4	3	1	11	9	2	1	2	30	1	1	.324	.274
Castellano, Angelo	R-R	6-0	170	1-13-95	.183	.208	.176	42	115	11	21	6	0	0	8	6	2	3	2	15	4	0	.235	.232
Clemmons, Leland	R-R	5-9	170	6-17-93	.224	.105	.258	26	85	19	19	3	1	5	18	11	5	0	1	29	13	1	.459	.343
Dale, Ryan	R-R	6-3	180	3-16-96	.171	.250	.143	34	105	6	18	1	0	0	10	6	3	1	1	36	0	3	.181	.235
Dulin, Brandon	L-R	6-3	225	12-29-92	.201	.065	.231	50	174	21	35	5	1	7	25	11	7	0	2	50	4	1	.362	.273
Estades, Ariel	L-R	5-11		4-27-94	.111	.000	.125	4	9	1	1	0	0	0	2	0	0	0	0	0	0	0	.111	.111
Fernandez, Xavier	R-R	5-11	197	7-15-95	.152	.214	.138	26	79	5	12	5	0	0	2	8	1	1	0	12	0	0	.215	.239
Fletcher, Brian	R-R	6-0	190	10-26-88	.167	.000	.188	7	18	2	3	0	0	0	1	4	0	0	0	9	0	0	.167	.318
Fukofuka, Amalani	R-R	6-1	180	9-25-95	.183	.109	.209	51	180	19	33	2	7	1	12	19	2	1	2	66	7	7	.289	.266
Gasparini, Marten	R-B	6-0	165	5-24-97	.191	.120	.233	19	68	11	13	2	1	0	1	3	0	1	0	32	4	1	.250	.225
King, Riley	R-L	6-4	210	4-23-94	.238	.273	.222	37	105	9	25	2	0	1	13	8	4	0	1	35	4	3	.286	.314
Lara, Luis	R-R	5-11	170	3-2-95	.258	.333	.227	13	31	2	8	1	0	0	1	5	0	0	0	5	1	0	.290	.361
Martinez, Jose	B-R	5-10	150	8-15-96	.229	.163	.247	56	201	18	46	8	1	1	23	12	0	3	2	26	9	3	.294	.270
Moon, Logan	R-R	6-2	195	2-15-92	.332	.339	.329	59	226	23	75	10	5	2	24	10	0	0	2	40	16	2	.447	.357
Newman, Alex	R-R	6-1	200	12-7-92	.273	.200	.333	8	22	1	6	2	0	0	3	0	0	0	1	8	2	1	.364	.261
Olloque, Manny	R-R	6-2	165	5-11-96	.333	.400	.317	25	75	17	25	5	1	0	7	2	2	0	2	6	6	0	.427	.358
Taylor, Dominique	R-R	6-1	190	8-11-92	.231	.167	.286	4	13	2	3	0	0	0	0	1	0	0	0	1	3	0	.231	.286
Vallot, Chase	R-R	6-0	215	8-21-96	.215	.159	.232	53	186	29	40	14	0	7	27	26	7	0	3	81	0	1	.403	.329
Viloria, Meibrys	L-R	5-11	175	2-15-97	.200	.077	.259	13	40	4	8	2	0	1	5	10	1	0	0	10	0	0	.325	.373

Pitching	B-T	HT	WT	DOB	W	L	ERA	G	GS	CG	SV	IP	H	R	ER	HR	BB	SO	AVG	vLH	vRH	K/9	BB/9
Beal, Evan	R-R	6-5	195	8-2-93	0	0	6.23	9	0	0	4	9	13	7	6	0	3	5	.361	.375	.350	5.19	3.12
Blewett, Scott	R-R	6-6	210	4-10-96	1	2	4.82	8	7	0	0	28	27	16	15	3	15	29	.262	.261	.263	9.32	4.82
Brockett, Andrew	R-R	5-11	185	7-5-92	3	1	2.16	5	0	0	1	8	7	2	2	1	2	11	.226	.333	.158	11.88	2.16
Camacho, Enmanuel	L-L	6-0	160	1-9-95	0	1	6.98	11	0	0	1	19	28	16	15	3	5	16	.333	.200	.351	7.45	2.33
Cordero, Estarlin	L-L	6-0	145	3-3-93	2	2	7.20	15	0	0	5	27	22	10	8	1	7	30	.224	.333	.195	10.13	2.36
Cruz, Antonio	L-L	5-11	200	10-7-91	0	0	0.00	4	0	0	1	6	0	0	0	4	10	.000	.000	.000	15.00	6.00
Darhower, Chase	R-R	6-4	215	1-12-93	3	2	3.03	11	4	0	1	36	34	17	12	4	12	27	.258	.320	.220	6.81	3.03
Eaton, Todd	R-R	6-1	190	5-9-92	1	0	4.15	10	0	0	0	13	17	6	6	1	7	14	.340	.400	.300	9.69	4.85
Flecha, Christian	L-L	6-2	150	5-9-95	2	3	6.00	11	2	0	0	30	28	24	20	5	21	34	.241	.316	.227	10.20	6.30
Griffin, Foster	L-L	6-3	200	7-27-95	0	2	3.21	11	11	0	0	28	19	10	10	2	12	19	.186	.200	.184	6.11	3.86
Henry, Brennan	L-L	6-4	200	10-23-91	0	0	3.65	10	0	0	0	12	10	9	5	0	10	11	.217	.222	.216	8.03	7.30
Herrera, Carlos	L-L	6-3	180	7-4-93	0	2	6.04	10	3	0	0	28	37	29	19	5	15	26	.308	.258	.326	8.26	4.76
Hope, Carter	L-R	6-3	195	2-5-95	1	3	3.71	10	8	0	0	53	54	26	22	2	19	41	.256	.316	.207	6.92	3.21
Machado, Andres	R-R	6-0	175	4-22-93	1	2	3.63	7	0	0	0	17	12	9	7	2	11	15	.182	.143	.200	7.79	5.71
Marte, Yunior	R-R	6-2	195	2-2-95	4	3	3.44	11	9	0	1	52	45	23	20	3	19	40	.233	.213	.250	6.88	3.27
Munoz, Jairo	R-R	6-0	180	8-12-91	0	0	6.75	1	0	0	0	1	5	2	1	0	0	1	.556	.400	.750	6.75	0.00
Pinto, Julio	R-R	6-3	185	11-18-95	4	3	4.83	11	2	0	0	41	41	25	22	2	24	28	.268	.200	.312	6.15	5.27
Ray, Corey	R-R	6-4	175	12-15-92	1	2	3.05	11	9	0	0	38	48	15	15	1	10	36	.282	.333	.252	7.31	2.03
Rodgers, Colin	L-L	5-10	180	12-2-93	0	4	7.36	6	6	0	0	17	17	10	9	0	6	19	.340	.200	.375	9.82	2.45
Sandness, Eric	R-R	6-6	210	10-14-94	0	0	4.40	11	0	0	0	14	12	8	7	1	9	10	.222	.333	.167	6.28	5.65
Sons, Dylan	L-L	6-3	176	7-15-93	1	2	3.78	10	1	0	0	17	16	8	7	0	15	14	.258	.182	.275	7.56	8.10
Stephenson, Niklas	R-R	6-2	195	11-16-93	3	3	2.14	11	6	0	0	59	45	25	14	2	9	47	.205	.224	.193	7.17	1.37
Tompkins, Ian	L-L	6-0	195	3-23-93	1	0	2.13	10	0	0	0	13	9	7	3	0	16	16	.205	.111	.229	11.37	11.37

	B-T	HT	WT	DOB	W	L	ERA	G	GS	CG	SV	IP	H	R	ER	HR	BB	SO	AVG	vLH	vRH	K/9	BB/9
Way, Cole	L-L	6-11	235	10-23-91	0	1	5.40	7	0	0	1	10	12	6	6	1	4	8	.300	.111	.355	7.20	3.60
Yambati, Robinson	R-R	6-3	185	1-15-91	0	2	8.64	7	0	0	0	8	11	9	8	1	6	10	.314	.471	.167	10.80	6.48

Fielding

Catcher	PCT	G	PO	A	E	DP	PB
Fernandez	.967	26	170	32	7	2	5
Lara	.971	12	55	12	2	1	5
Vallot	.988	32	227	28	3	2	12
Viloria	1.000	5	31	7	0	0	0

First Base	PCT	G	PO	A	E	DP
Banuelos	.996	53	419	39	2	33
Castellano	—	1	0	0	0	0
Dulin	.972	16	161	10	5	13

Second Base	PCT	G	PO	A	E	DP
Burt	.981	44	88	115	4	27
Castellano	1.000	17	23	42	0	5

Martinez	.976	9	15	26	1	6

Third Base	PCT	G	PO	A	E	DP
Burt	1.000	1	0	1	0	0
Castellano	.976	18	9	31	1	3
Dale	.846	34	19	58	14	8
Olloque	.843	23	10	33	8	2

Shortstop	PCT	G	PO	A	E	DP
Burt	.750	2	5	4	3	2
Castellano	1.000	4	4	9	0	2
Gasparini	.866	18	24	47	11	7
Martinez	.930	47	55	117	13	19

Outfield	PCT	G	PO	A	E	DP
Adams	1.000	3	3	0	0	0
Cano	.964	30	47	6	2	1
Clemmons	1.000	25	50	3	0	0
Dulin	.962	14	24	1	1	0
Estades	1.000	3	5	0	0	0
Fletcher	1.000	6	9	0	0	0
Fukofuka	.974	44	107	4	3	0
King	.952	33	37	3	2	0
Moon	.991	55	98	10	1	0
Newman	.882	8	15	0	2	0
Taylor	1.000	4	5	0	0	0

IDAHO FALLS CHUKARS   ROOKIE
PIONEER LEAGUE

Batting	B-T	HT	WT	DOB	AVG	vLH	vRH	G	AB	R	H	2B	3B	HR	RBI	BB	HBP	SH	SF	SO	SB	CS	SLG	OBP
Allen, Jerrell	R-R	6-2	180	9-6-92	.211	.167	.231	6	19	3	4	1	0	0	3	0	0	0	0	3	1	1	.263	.318
Clark, DonAndre	B-R	5-10	180	7-31-92	.248	.389	.226	37	133	23	33	3	2	0	10	11	2	1	0	35	14	5	.301	.315
Davis, Logan	L-R	6-2	175	8-23-91	.214	.000	.250	5	14	1	3	1	0	0	1	6	0	0	1	0	0	0	.286	.450
Downes, Brandon	R-R	6-2	175	9-29-92	.308	.303	.309	41	169	31	52	13	4	3	23	10	5	1	3	41	6	4	.485	.358
Duenez, Samir	L-R	6-1	195	6-11-96	.304	.450	.278	39	135	16	41	7	1	1	27	10	0	2	2	20	4	2	.393	.347
Flores, Jecksson	R-R	5-11	145	10-28-92	.244	.241	.244	49	160	20	39	7	3	0	16	10	1	2	2	18	6	4	.325	.289
Franco, Wander	R-R	6-2	170	12-13-94	.323	.394	.304	42	158	19	51	13	3	3	19	8	5	0	0	36	3	1	.500	.374
Gasparini, Marten	B-R	6-0	165	5-24-97	.455	1.000	.333	4	11	4	5	0	0	1	3	1	0	0	0	2	2	0	.727	.500
Gomez, Brawlun	R-R	6-2	185	8-5-92	.290	.321	.282	39	145	35	42	8	5	4	22	13	3	0	1	38	8	2	.497	.358
Gonzalez, Cesar	R-R	6-3	185	11-20-93	.204	.286	.191	20	54	8	11	1	0	0	6	2	3	2	0	12	0	1	.222	.271
Gonzalez, Pedro	R-R	6-2	162	1-28-92	.279	.333	.268	22	68	9	19	4	0	2	10	1	2	0	1	13	0	1	.426	.306
Henry, Desmond	R-R	6-1	175	7-7-93	.173	.167	.175	32	75	16	13	1	0	0	5	16	0	3	0	28	13	2	.187	.319
Hill, Mike	L-R	6-2	195	1-29-92	.288	.205	.305	63	229	30	66	11	8	3	32	20	1	0	2	47	3	1	.445	.345
Morin, Parker	L-R	5-11	195	7-2-91	.200	.000	.231	7	30	3	6	1	0	1	4	0	0	0	0	7	0	0	.333	.200
O'Hearn, Ryan	L-L	6-3	200	7-26-93	.361	.286	.377	64	249	61	90	16	1	13	54	39	1	0	4	59	3	2	.590	.444
Pehl, Robert	R-R	6-1	205	9-23-92	.332	.244	.350	63	241	38	80	16	1	3	41	23	5	0	1	37	4	2	.444	.400
Pollock, Kyle	R-R	6-0	200	8-16-92	.299	.406	.268	42	144	18	43	11	0	2	26	14	1	1	3	16	1	0	.417	.358
Rivera, Alexis	L-L	6-2	225	6-17-94	.222	.125	.243	11	45	7	10	2	0	1	5	1	1	0	0	10	1	0	.333	.255
Thomasson, Brandon	R-R	6-4	220	3-15-92	.239	.278	.233	40	138	16	33	11	1	2	27	7	0	0	3	38	1	4	.377	.270
Torrence, Devon	R-R	6-0	190	5-8-89	.250	1.000	.000	1	4	0	1	0	0	0	0	0	1	0	0	2	0	0	.250	.250
Toups, Corey	R-R	5-10	170	2-12-93	.335	.419	.313	57	203	49	68	20	3	3	32	43	4	2	4	38	7	0	.507	.453
Valenzuela, Luis	L-R	5-10	150	8-25-93	.259	.036	.293	57	216	39	56	8	5	2	29	14	1	2	1	45	5	0	.370	.306

Pitching	B-T	HT	WT	DOB	W	L	ERA	G	GS	CG	SV	IP	H	R	ER	HR	BB	SO	AVG	vLH	vRH	K/9	BB/9
Brickhouse, Bryan	R-R	6-0	195	6-6-92	1	2	4.88	9	8	0	0	28	30	18	15	3	10	22	.275	.280	.271	7.16	3.25
Checo, Mariel	R-R	6-3	190	10-16-89	0	0	8.18	8	0	0	0	11	12	14	10	3	5	14	.250	.250	11.45	4.09
Deshazier, Torey	R-R	6-0	160	9-16-93	5	3	3.17	13	6	0	0	65	59	30	23	7	22	66	.243	.190	.280	9.09	3.03
Fairchild, Austin	R-L	6-0	195	3-25-94	1	1	13.20	12	2	0	0	15	16	22	22	1	28	18	.276	.267	.279	10.80	16.80
Fitzsimmons, Jon	R-R	6-2	205	11-29-91	0	1	5.40	13	0	0	3	18	13	12	11	0	16	19	.197	.192	.200	9.33	7.85
Goudeau, Ashton	R-R	6-6	205	7-23-92	1	0	1.69	8	0	0	0	16	12	3	3	1	4	15	.203	.259	.156	8.44	2.25
Green, Nick	R-L	6-2	190	9-21-90	0	1	3.52	14	0	0	4	15	18	8	6	0	1	13	.310	.250	.353	7.63	0.59
Guevara, Cruz	L-L	6-0	155	5-29-94	0	0	5.47	15	0	0	2	25	25	15	15	2	11	23	.278	.310	.262	8.39	4.01
Halley, Shane	B-R	6-1	200	9-8-89	2	1	6.87	16	0	0	0	18	29	16	14	3	8	13	.358	.250	.463	6.38	3.93
Hill, Tim	L-L	6-2	200	2-10-90	1	1	2.35	5	0	0	0	8	3	2	2	1	2	12	.115	.000	.167	14.09	2.35
Jeffreys, Mike	R-R	6-4	190	10-29-91	2	3	6.13	12	7	0	0	47	59	36	32	6	13	37	.306	.291	.316	7.09	2.49
Lewis, Sam	R-R	6-2	195	10-9-91	3	1	3.63	14	0	0	3	35	28	15	14	4	13	44	.226	.310	.183	11.42	3.38
Lovvorn, Zach	R-R	6-0	185	5-26-94	3	6	5.00	14	5	0	1	67	83	44	37	3	15	56	.303	.267	.329	7.56	2.03
Marimon, Sugar Ray	R-R	6-1	194	9-30-88	0	1	2.38	3	2	0	0	11	12	3	3	2	2	8	.293	.316	.273	6.35	1.59
Mills, Alec	R-R	6-4	185	11-30-91	2	2	4.66	7	6	0	0	19	20	12	10	0	4	14	.278	.462	.174	6.52	1.86
Newberry, Jake	R-R	6-2	195	11-20-94	6	4	4.50	13	10	1	0	68	74	37	34	3	22	65	.286	.317	.256	8.60	2.91
Ogando, Emilio	L-L	6-2	180	8-13-93	2	2	2.97	13	5	0	0	30	25	14	10	2	17	27	.229	.214	.235	8.01	5.04
Pounders, Brooks	R-R	6-4	270	9-26-90	0	1	4.80	6	5	0	0	15	13	9	8	0	5	19	.241	.250	.231	11.40	3.00
Reynoso, Javier	B-L	5-11	185	10-31-92	1	4	7.56	8	3	0	1	25	25	23	21	0	20	27	.266	.077	.338	9.72	7.20
Rodgers, Colin	L-L	5-10	180	12-2-93	0	0	3.00	1	1	0	0	3	1	2	1	0	3	1	.100	.143	.000	3.00	9.00
Rodriguez, Alberto	R-R	6-1	225	12-24-91	0	0	7.16	13	0	0	0	16	23	19	13	2	16	10	.319	.296	.333	5.51	8.82
Skoglund, Eric	L-L	6-7	200	10-26-92	0	2	5.09	9	8	0	0	23	30	17	13	2	9	25	.316	.407	.279	9.78	3.52
Stout, Eric	L-L	6-3	185	3-17-93	5	2	3.58	13	1	0	1	33	31	15	13	2	10	27	.254	.226	.264	7.44	2.76
Strahm, Matt	R-L	6-4	180	11-12-91	1	0	2.29	10	1	0	1	20	10	6	5	1	10	27	.149	.227	.111	12.36	4.58
Thomas, Brandon	L-L	5-11	200	9-16-93	2	0	7.24	11	0	0	0	14	14	11	11	5	10	14	.275	.353	.235	9.22	6.59
Zimmer, Kyle	R-R	6-3	215	9-13-91	0	0	1.93	6	5	0	0	5	5	1	1	0	4	5	.263	.091	.500	9.64	7.71

Fielding

Catcher	PCT	G	PO	A	E	DP	PB
Gonzalez	.969	19	113	13	4	0	4

Gonzalez	.989	21	156	22	2	2	1
Morin	1.000	4	27	7	0	1	0

Pollock	.980	42	297	49	7	2	8

First Base	PCT	G	PO	A	E	DP
Duenez	.978	27	204	17	5	22
Gonzalez	1.000	1	8	0	0	1
O'Hearn	.998	40	383	22	1	29
Rivera	1.000	3	30	5	0	2
Thomasson	.985	10	59	7	1	6

Second Base	PCT	G	PO	A	E	DP
Davis	1.000	1	0	2	0	0
Flores	.992	25	47	83	1	15
Valenzuela	.958	54	85	141	10	35

Third Base	PCT	G	PO	A	E	DP
Davis	.923	4	0	12	1	1
Flores	.941	5	4	12	1	1
Franco	.914	10	13	19	3	2
Hill	.914	60	33	115	14	7

Shortstop	PCT	G	PO	A	E	DP
Flores	.977	19	29	55	2	16
Gasparini	.789	4	3	12	4	4
Toups	.933	57	69	154	16	28
Valenzuela	.750	1	1	2	1	0

Outfield	PCT	G	PO	A	E	DP
Allen	1.000	6	7	0	0	0
Clark	.984	34	60	2	1	0
Downes	.987	40	69	8	1	1
Gomez	.897	34	61	0	7	0
Henry	1.000	29	28	1	0	0
O'Hearn	.950	15	19	0	1	0
Pehl	.968	51	59	1	2	0
Rivera	.900	6	9	0	1	0
Thomasson	.941	24	32	0	2	0
Torrence	1.000	1	1	1	0	0

DSL ROYALS

ROOKIE

DOMINICAN SUMMER LEAGUE

Batting	B-T	HT	WT	DOB	AVG	vLH	vRH	G	AB	R	H	2B	3B	HR	RBI	BB	HBP	SH	SF	SO	SB	CS	SLG	OBP
Arias, Joel	R-R	6-0	160	4-6-97	.250	.125	.277	55	180	28	45	12	1	0	21	18	0	2	2	61	8	2	.328	.315
Atencio, Jesus	R-R	5-10	165	8-22-96	.211	.227	.206	33	90	9	19	2	0	0	7	14	1	2	2	16	0	0	.233	.318
Caraballo, Jose	R-R	6-1	180	1-7-97	.245	.233	.248	55	192	27	47	8	4	2	30	12	5	2	1	42	5	3	.359	.305
Collado, Offerman	R-L	5-10	140	6-10-96	.287	.200	.304	53	178	27	51	2	3	1	21	33	2	1	2	28	8	9	.348	.400
Diaz, Carlos	B-R	5-8	145	11-15-92	.279	.432	.245	68	240	32	67	9	4	0	23	13	4	4	1	19	21	10	.350	.326
Martinez, Yorly	R-R	6-0	190	8-23-94	.232	.318	.208	63	203	31	47	10	2	1	27	23	9	2	7	30	4	0	.315	.326
Melo, Yeison	R-R	6-1	180	7-30-95	.298	.405	.273	63	225	30	67	8	6	2	29	24	0	0	5	39	4	2	.413	.358
Mogollon, Jose	R-R	6-1	170	5-17-96	.182	.500	.150	40	44	6	8	1	0	0	5	5	0	0	2	13	3	1	.205	.255
Nunez, Oliver	B-R	5-10	170	2-21-95	.234	.188	.250	46	128	24	30	5	2	0	11	38	1	3	2	26	12	6	.305	.408
Ortiz, Dalfis	B-R	5-10	160	2-10-92	.210	.222	.208	22	62	9	13	4	1	0	7	8	0	3	1	3	6	3	.306	.296
Saez, Alberto	R-R	6-1	155	7-11-96	.119	.143	.115	20	59	4	7	4	0	0	3	5	2	0	0	19	1	1	.186	.212
Sanchez, Jose	L-L	5-10	155	7-21-94	.260	.367	.233	55	150	27	39	5	4	0	14	29	2	8	4	34	7	3	.347	.378
Tejeda, Gustavo	R-R	6-0	185	8-2-95	.231	.000	.333	10	26	2	6	2	0	0	1	5	0	0	0	10	0	0	.308	.355
Torres, Jose	R-R	6-0	175	9-30-95	.149	.125	.155	37	87	12	13	3	0	0	7	12	6	2	0	22	2	5	.184	.295
Tovar, Roberto	B-R	6-1	180	11-16-94	.219	.158	.232	45	114	7	25	5	0	0	15	15	0	2	2	12	1	2	.263	.305
Valerio, Cornelio	L-L	5-10	175	3-7-94	.220	.167	.229	14	41	0	9	1	1	0	3	1	0	1	0	5	0	1	.293	.238
Vasquez, Cristhian	L-L	6-0	175	9-11-96	.155	.000	.191	18	58	6	9	1	1	1	7	13	1	0	0	18	2	3	.259	.319
Venegas, Ariel	R-R	5-11	155	5-5-95	.273	.316	.255	36	66	16	18	2	1	0	4	10	3	3	0	8	4	1	.333	.392
Viloria, Meibrys	L-R	5-11	175	2-15-97	.306	.150	.341	33	111	16	34	8	1	2	20	14	1	1	2	18	1	1	.450	.383
Vital, Jose	R-R	6-2	180	3-25-96	.122	.083	.138	24	41	6	5	1	0	0	3	4	2	0	1	21	4	0	.146	.229

Pitching	B-T	HT	WT	DOB	W	L	ERA	G	GS	CG	SV	IP	H	R	ER	HR	BB	SO	AVG	vLH	vRH	K/9	BB/9
Acevedo, Wilson	R-R	6-4	175	2-15-93	2	1	6.94	9	0	0	1	12	13	13	9	1	5	7	.271	.500	.133	5.40	3.86
Adames, Samuel	R-R	6-4	190	9-27-94	2	0	2.36	14	1	0	0	34	25	10	9	0	9	24	.203	.125	.241	6.29	2.36
Cepin, Reinaldo	L-L	6-1	160	1-10-94	6	1	3.38	15	1	0	0	48	39	23	18	1	20	46	.218	.111	.237	8.63	3.75
Cruz, Aronny	L-L	6-2	175	7-23-95	1	0	1.77	13	4	0	2	36	26	9	7	0	16	27	.218	.217	.219	6.81	4.04
Diaz, Frandy	L-L	5-10	155	3-25-95	0	1	4.50	11	0	0	1	16	9	9	8	1	9	18	.164	.000	.209	10.13	5.06
Garabito, Gerson	R-R	6-0	160	8-19-95	2	1	1.28	13	13	0	0	49	24	12	7	1	27	61	.143	.135	.147	11.13	4.93
Gomez, Ofreidy	R-R	6-3	190	7-6-95	0	4	6.17	12	4	0	1	35	35	33	24	1	20	35	.246	.245	.247	9.00	5.14
Hernandez, Arnaldo	R-R	6-0	175	2-9-96	1	1	2.55	7	3	0	1	18	13	8	5	1	7	19	.213	.200	.220	9.68	3.57
Maldonado, Ismael	R-R	6-4	170	9-28-95	0	0	13.50	7	0	0	0	12	18	15	0	13	7	.293	.071	.407	6.30	11.70
Mateo, Yeison	R-R	6-2	185	4-17-93	6	1	1.65	15	0	0	1	27	22	8	5	1	14	12	.232	.222	.235	3.95	4.61
Medrano, Miguel	R-R	6-2	175	6-19-95	3	5	3.96	14	6	0	2	36	29	19	16	2	10	20	.213	.167	.234	4.95	2.48
Melendez, Cesar	R-R	6-1	162	3-20-95	4	1	4.07	15	0	0	3	24	23	13	11	0	9	19	.261	.333	.218	7.03	3.33
Pena, Yimauri	R-R	6-2	160	10-15-93	2	1	2.67	14	12	0	0	67	65	25	20	4	10	55	.251	.247	.253	7.35	1.34
Quinonez, Starling	R-R	6-5	170	7-2-95	0	0	9.64	2	0	0	0	5	6	5	5	0	3	2	.333	.429	.273	3.86	5.79
Reyes, Junior	L-L	6-0	165	3-29-96	3	2	3.36	14	13	0	0	64	55	35	24	2	24	49	.230	.173	.246	6.85	3.36
Rodriguez, Jorge	L-L	6-0	160	6-30-96	2	1	1.80	13	8	0	1	40	18	14	8	0	25	49	.137	.045	.156	11.03	5.63
Terrero, Franco	R-R	6-0	180	5-20-95	7	5	4.01	16	4	0	1	52	53	29	23	1	9	36	.266	.339	.236	6.27	1.57
Veras, Jose	R-R	6-1	170	7-15-94	1	3	2.15	18	1	0	7	46	34	16	11	1	8	36	.202	.236	.186	7.04	1.57

Fielding

Catcher	PCT	G	PO	A	E	DP	PB
Arias	1.000	1	7	1	0	0	1
Atencio	.984	23	98	22	2	1	2
Tejeda	.981	7	48	5	1	0	0
Torres	.992	21	100	17	1	0	5
Tovar	.978	16	79	9	2	1	2
Viloria	.980	25	167	26	4	1	2

First Base	PCT	G	PO	A	E	DP
Atencio	.963	10	71	6	3	7
Martinez	.966	30	251	6	9	10
Mogollon	1.000	3	16	0	0	0
Torres	.991	14	103	3	1	8
Tovar	.995	26	197	14	1	15

Second Base	PCT	G	PO	A	E	DP
Collado	.959	49	85	127	9	20

Diaz	1.000	8	11	19	0	1
Martinez	—	1	0	0	0	0
Nunez	.870	4	10	10	3	1
Ortiz	.981	14	26	25	1	5
Torres	—	1	0	0	0	0
Venegas	1.000	3	4	7	0	4

Third Base	PCT	G	PO	A	E	DP
Diaz	.918	17	14	31	4	0
Martinez	.952	32	17	63	4	2
Nunez	.500	2	0	2	2	0
Ortiz	1.000	6	5	5	0	2
Torres	.667	2	1	3	2	0
Venegas	.864	24	17	34	8	5

Shortstop	PCT	G	PO	A	E	DP
Diaz	.929	43	54	103	12	14

Nunez	.950	36	44	88	7	13

Outfield	PCT	G	PO	A	E	DP
Arias	.964	53	103	4	4	1
Atencio	1.000	1	2	0	0	0
Caraballo	.952	45	76	4	4	0
Melo	.959	37	65	6	3	4
Mogollon	1.000	36	31	1	0	1
Saez	.813	16	10	3	3	0
Sanchez	.979	54	90	4	2	2
Valerio	1.000	7	10	0	0	0
Vital	1.000	12	20	3	0	0

Los Angeles Angels

SEASON IN A SENTENCE: The Angels, picked by most observers to finish fourth in a loaded AL West, had their bullpen rebuilt on the fly by general manager Jerry Dipoto, moved into first place in August and ran away with the division.

HIGH POINT: The Angels won eight of nine from Aug. 12-21 to surge into first place ahead of Oakland and never let go, finishing 10 games ahead in the division. Mike Trout's usual excellence, Albert Pujols' 100-RBI season and Kole Calhoun's breakout season gave Los Angeles a boost.

LOW POINT: After the stirring finish to the season, Los Angeles was steamrolled by the surprising Royals in the AL Division Series, getting swept 3-0 and losing two of the games in the 11th inning on homers by Mike Moustakas and Eric Hosmer.

NOTABLE ROOKIES: Nondrafted free agent Matt Shoemaker, at 27, surprised the Angels by winning 16 games after the team lost ace Garrett Richards and lefthander Tyler Skaggs to injuries. C.J. Cron, the 2011 first-rounder from Utah, contributed 24 extra-base hits in 242 at-bats. Efren Navarro, the 28-year-old first baseman, had 10 doubles in limited playing time. North Carolina alum Mike Morin made 60 appearances out of the bullpen and struck out 8.24 per nine with a 2.90 ERA. Righthanded reliever Cam Bedrosian made 17 appearances and struck out more than a batter per inning.

KEY TRANSACTIONS: Rebuilding the bullpen was the key and it came via several moves. The first deal came on June 27, when the Pirates and Angels swapped underperforming righthanders with Jason Grilli headed west and Ernesto Frieri headed to the Pirates. Grilli struck out more than a batter per inning in 40 appearances with a 3.48 ERA, while Frieri was designated for assignment later in the season. About a week later, the Angels acquired lefthander Joe Thatcher from Arizona, and then on July 19, sent four of their top 10 prospects to San Diego for closer Huston Street, who posted a 1.71 ERA and had 17 saves.

DOWN ON THE FARM: The trades of Taylor Lindsey, Jose Rondon, Zach Borenstein and R.J. Alvarez took a chunk of the Angels farm system, but lefthander Ricardo Sanchez, just 17, struck out 10.01 per nine. Second baseman Alex Yarbrough is a below-average defender, but has shown an innate ability to hit.

OPENING DAY PAYROLL: $128,046,500 (10th)

PLAYERS OF THE YEAR

MAJOR LEAGUE	MINOR LEAGUE
Mike Trout of	**Cam Bedrosian** rhp
.287/.377/.561	(High A/Double-A/
36 HR, 111 RBI	Triple-A)
Led team in HR, RBI	2-1, 2.00, 21 SV

ORGANIZATION LEADERS

BATTING		*Minimum 250 AB
MAJORS		
* AVG	Kendrick, Howie	.293
* OPS	Trout, Mike	.938
HR	Trout, Mike	36
RBI	Trout, Mike	111
MINORS		
* AVG	Boesch, Brennan, Salt Lake	.332
* OPS	Boesch, Brennan, Salt Lake	1.017
* SLG	Boesch, Brennan, Salt Lake	.636
R	Johnson, Sherman, Inland Empire	107
H	Hernandez, Brian, Inland Empire, Arkansas	156
TB	Johnson, Sherman, Inland Empire	246
2B	Yarbrough, Alex, Arkansas	38
3B	Johnson, Sherman, Inland Empire	13
HR	Raben, Dennis, Inland Empire	31
RBI	Raben, Dennis, Inland Empire	94
BB	Johnson, Sherman, Inland Empire	88
SO	Eaves, Kody, Burlington	142
SB	Hinshaw, Chad, Burlington, Inland Empire	41

PITCHING		#Minimum 75 IP
MAJORS		
W	Weaver, Jered	18
# ERA	Smith, Joe	1.81
SO	Weaver, Jered	169
SV	Street, Huston	17
MINORS		
W	DeLoach, Tyler, Inland Empire, Arkansas	14
L	Sappington, Mark, Arkansas, Inland Empire	11
	Sneed, Kramer, Arkansas	11
# ERA	Roth, Michael, Arkansas	2.62
G	Diaz, Jairo, Inland Empire, Arkansas	56
GS	Grube, Jarrett, Salt Lake	27
SV	Bedrosian, Cam, Inland Empire, Arkansas, Salt Lake	18
IP	Rucinski, Drew, Arkansas	149
BB	Sappington, Mark, Arkansas, Inland Empire	79
SO	DeLoach, Tyler, Inland Empire, Arkansas	161
AVG	DeLoach, Tyler, Inland Empire, Arkansas	.198

General Manager: Jerry Dipoto. **Farm Director:** Bobby Scales. **Scouting Director:** Ric Wilson.

Class	Team	League	W	L	PCT	Finish	Manager
Majors	Los Angeles Angels	American	98	64	.605	1st (30)	Mike Scioscia
Triple-A	Salt Lake Bees	Pacific Coast	60	84	.417	15th (16)	Keith Johnson
Double-A	Arkansas Travelers	Texas	75	65	.536	3rd (8)	Phillip Wellman
High A	Inland Empire 66ers	California	62	78	.443	9th (10)	Denny Hocking
Low A	Burlington Bees	Midwest	68	71	.489	9th (16)	Bill Richardson
Rookie	Orem Owlz	Pioneer	42	33	.560	2nd (8)	Dave Stapleton
Rookie	Angels	Arizona	30	25	.545	t-4th (13)	Elio Sarmiento
Overall Minor League Record			337	356	.486	21st (30)	

ORGANIZATION STATISTICS

LOS ANGELES ANGELS

AMERICAN LEAGUE

Batting	B-T	HT	WT	DOB	AVG	vLH	vRH	G	AB	R	H	2B	3B	HR	RBI	BB	HBP	SH	SF	SO	SB	CS	SLG	OBP
Aybar, Erick	B-R	5-10	180	1-14-84	.278	.248	.290	156	589	77	164	30	4	7	68	36	5	3	8	62	16	9	.379	.321
Beckham, Gordon	R-R	6-0	185	9-16-86	.268	.211	.297	26	56	10	15	3	0	2	8	3	2	0	0	11	0	0	.429	.328
2-team total (101 Chicago)					.226	—	—	127	446	53	101	27	0	9	44	22	7	3	5	81	3	0	.348	.271
Boesch, Brennan	L-L	6-4	235	4-12-85	.187	.333	.181	27	75	6	14	2	0	2	7	2	0	0	2	19	3	0	.293	.203
Buck, John	R-R	6-3	245	7-7-80	.200	.250	.000	5	5	0	1	0	0	0	0	0	0	0	0	2	0	0	.200	.200
2-team total (27 Seattle)					.225	—	—	32	89	9	20	2	0	1	6	8	0	0	0	26	0	0	.281	.289
Calhoun, Kole	L-L	5-10	200	10-14-87	.272	.252	.277	127	493	90	134	31	3	17	58	38	2	2	2	104	5	3	.450	.325
Campana, Tony	L-L	5-8	165	5-30-86	.333	.500	.273	18	15	6	5	0	0	0	2	0	0	0	0	6	0	1	.333	.333
Conger, Hank	B-R	6-2	220	1-29-88	.221	.188	.223	80	231	24	51	12	0	4	25	22	2	4	1	57	0	2	.325	.293
Cowgill, Collin	R-L	5-9	185	5-22-86	.250	.288	.215	106	260	37	65	10	1	5	21	26	5	2	0	74	4	0	.354	.330
Cron Jr., C.J.	R-R	6-4	235	1-5-90	.256	.258	.255	79	242	28	62	12	1	11	37	10	1	0	6	61	0	0	.450	.289
Freese, David	R-R	6-2	225	4-28-83	.260	.320	.243	134	462	53	120	25	1	10	55	38	6	0	5	124	1	3	.383	.321
Green, Grant	R-R	6-3	180	9-27-87	.273	.356	.204	43	99	7	27	5	0	1	11	2	0	0	2	20	1	4	.354	.282
Hamilton, Josh	L-L	6-4	240	5-21-81	.263	.330	.239	89	338	43	89	21	0	10	44	32	5	0	6	108	3	3	.414	.331
Iannetta, Chris	R-R	6-0	230	4-8-83	.252	.272	.240	108	306	41	77	22	0	7	43	54	8	0	5	91	3	0	.392	.373
Ibanez, Raul	L-R	6-2	225	6-2-72	.157	.034	.182	57	166	16	26	5	2	3	21	23	0	0	1	43	3	2	.265	.258
2-team total (33 Kansas City)					.167	—	—	90	246	23	41	8	3	5	26	33	0	0	1	59	3	2	.285	.264
Jimenez, Luis	R-R	6-1	205	1-18-88	.162	.174	.143	18	37	3	6	2	0	0	2	0	2	2	0	13	0	0	.216	.205
Kendrick, Howie	R-R	5-10	210	7-12-83	.293	.327	.282	157	617	85	181	33	5	7	75	48	4	3	2	110	14	5	.397	.347
McDonald, John	R-R	5-9	185	9-24-74	.171	.192	.160	95	76	4	13	2	0	0	5	7	2	5	1	18	1	1	.197	.256
Navarro, Efren	L-L	6-0	210	5-14-86	.245	.321	.229	64	159	17	39	10	1	1	14	13	0	2	0	27	1	3	.340	.302
O'Malley, Shawn	R-R	5-11	165	12-28-87	.188	.400	.091	14	16	3	3	0	0	0	1	0	0	0	0	8	2	0	.188	.188
Pujols, Albert	R-R	6-3	230	1-16-80	.272	.263	.275	159	633	89	172	37	1	28	105	48	5	0	9	71	5	1	.466	.324
Shuck, J.B.	L-L	5-11	195	6-18-87	.167	.105	.185	22	84	10	14	1	0	2	9	3	0	1	0	11	2	0	.250	.195
2-team total (16 Cleveland)					.145	—	—	38	110	12	16	1	0	2	9	3	0	1	0	12	2	0	.209	.168
Stewart, Ian	R-R	6-3	215	4-5-85	.176	.300	.155	24	68	8	12	2	3	2	7	3	1	0	0	31	1	0	.382	.222
Trout, Mike	R-R	6-2	230	8-7-91	.287	.275	.291	157	602	115	173	39	9	36	111	83	10	0	10	184	16	2	.561	.377

Pitching	B-T	HT	WT	DOB	W	L	ERA	G	GS	CG	SV	IP	H	R	ER	HR	BB	SO	AVG	vLH	vRH	K/9	BB/9
Alvarez, Jose	L-L	5-11	180	5-6-89	0	0	0.00	2	0	0	0	1	1	0	0	0	0	1	.333	.000	1.000	13.50	0.00
Bedrosian, Cam	R-R	6-0	205	10-2-91	0	1	6.52	17	0	0	0	19	23	17	14	2	12	20	.288	.350	.225	9.31	5.59
Burnett, Sean	L-L	6-1	180	9-17-82	0	0	13.50	3	0	0	0	1	1	1	1	0	0	0	.333	.333	—	0.00	0.00
Carpenter, David	R-R	6-3	180	9-1-87	0	0	0.00	1	0	0	0	3	1	0	0	0	0	0	.100	.000	.200	0.00	0.00
De La Rosa, Dane	R-R	6-7	245	2-1-83	0	0	11.57	3	0	0	0	2	3	3	3	0	3	0	.375	.250	.500	0.00	11.57
Diaz, Jairo	R-R	6-0	195	5-27-91	0	0	3.18	5	0	0	0	6	4	2	2	0	3	8	.200	.143	.333	12.71	4.76
Frieri, Ernesto	R-R	6-2	205	7-19-85	0	3	6.39	34	0	0	11	31	33	22	22	8	9	38	.268	.238	.326	11.03	2.61
Grilli, Jason	R-R	6-4	235	11-11-76	1	3	3.48	40	0	0	1	34	29	15	13	0	10	36	.238	.288	.200	9.62	2.67
Grube, Jarrett	R-R	6-4	220	11-5-81	0	0	13.50	1	0	0	0	1	1	1	1	0	0	0	.333	—	.333	0.00	0.00
Herrera, Yoslan	R-R	6-2	200	4-28-81	1	1	2.70	20	0	0	0	17	22	5	5	0	9	13	.324	.406	.250	7.02	4.86
Hill, Rich	L-L	6-5	220	3-11-80	0	0	—	2	0	0	0	0	1	1	0	3	0	1.000	—	1.000	—	—
2-team total (14 New York)					0	0	3.38	16	0	0	0	5	7	2	2	0	6	9	—	—	—	15.19	10.13
Jepsen, Kevin	R-R	6-3	235	7-26-84	0	2	2.63	74	0	0	2	65	45	19	19	4	23	75	.192	.219	.167	10.38	3.18
Kohn, Michael	R-R	6-2	200	6-26-86	2	1	3.04	25	0	0	0	24	11	9	8	1	20	26	.141	.108	.171	9.89	7.61
LeBlanc, Wade	L-L	6-3	215	8-7-84	1	1	3.45	10	3	0	0	29	25	11	11	2	6	21	.236	.242	.233	6.59	1.88
2-team total (1 New York)					1	1	3.94	11	3	0	0	30	27	13	13	2	7	21	—	—	—	6.37	2.12
Maronde, Nick	B-L	6-3	205	9-5-89	0	0	12.79	11	0	0	0	6	12	9	9	0	7	7	.429	.385	.467	9.95	9.95
Morin, Mike	R-R	6-4	220	5-3-91	4	4	2.90	60	0	0	0	59	51	22	19	3	19	54	.234	.283	.181	8.24	2.90
Pestano, Vinnie	R-R	6-0	200	2-20-85	0	0	0.93	12	0	0	0	10	5	1	1	1	4	13	.152	.333	.048	12.10	3.72
2-team total (13 Cleveland)					0	1	2.89	25	0	0	0	19	18	8	6	3	5	26	—	—	—	12.54	2.41
Rasmus, Cory	R-R	6-0	200	11-6-87	3	2	2.57	30	6	0	0	56	42	17	16	5	17	57	.204	.234	.179	9.16	2.73
Richards, Garrett	R-R	6-3	210	5-27-88	13	4	2.61	26	26	1	0	169	124	51	49	5	51	164	.201	.194	.209	8.75	2.72
Roth, Michael	L-L	6-1	210	2-15-90	1	0	8.76	7	0	0	0	12	16	12	12	2	9	9	.340	.286	.364	6.57	6.57
Rucinski, Drew	R-R	6-2	190	12-30-88	0	0	4.91	3	0	0	0	7	9	4	4	0	2	8	.290	.154	.389	9.82	2.45

	B-T	HT	WT	DOB	W	L	ERA	G	GS	CG	SV	IP	H	R	ER	HR	BB	SO	AVG	vLH	vRH	K/9	BB/9
Salas, Fernando	R-R	6-2	210	5-30-85	5	0	3.38	57	0	0	0	59	50	22	22	5	14	61	.228	.188	.271	9.36	2.15
Santiago, Hector	R-L	6-0	210	12-16-87	6	9	3.75	30	24	0	0	127	120	63	53	15	53	108	.248	.244	.249	7.63	3.75
Shoemaker, Matt	R-R	6-2	225	9-27-86	16	4	3.04	27	20	0	0	136	122	49	46	14	24	124	.241	.257	.222	8.21	1.59
Skaggs, Tyler	L-L	6-4	215	7-13-91	5	5	4.30	18	18	0	0	113	107	59	54	9	30	86	.253	.290	.242	6.85	2.39
Smith, Joe	R-R	6-2	205	3-22-84	7	2	1.81	76	0	0	15	75	45	16	15	4	15	68	.172	.206	.136	8.20	1.81
Street, Huston	R-R	6-0	195	8-2-83	1	2	1.71	28	0	0	17	26	24	5	5	1	7	23	.240	.182	.311	7.86	2.39
Thatcher, Joe	L-L	6-2	230	10-4-81	1	1	8.53	16	0	0	0	6	13	6	6	0	1	2	.433	.409	.500	2.84	1.42
Wall, Josh	R-R	6-6	215	1-21-87	0	0	54.00	2	0	0	0	1	5	6	6	0	3	0	.714	1.000	.667	0.00	27.00
Weaver, Jered	R-R	6-7	210	10-4-82	18	9	3.59	34	34	1	0	213	193	87	85	27	65	169	.239	.255	.212	7.13	2.74
Wilson, C.J.	L-L	6-1	210	11-18-80	13	10	4.51	31	31	1	0	176	169	95	88	17	85	151	.258	.201	.277	7.74	4.35

Fielding

Catcher	PCT	G	PO	A	E	DP	PB
Buck	1.000	5	11	0	0	0	
Conger	.989	79	599	37	7	1	1
Iannetta	.997	104	744	36	2	5	4
Green	1.000	10	7	23	0	6	
Kendrick	.984	154	267	406	11	83	
McDonald	1.000	2	4	3	0	1	
O'Malley	1.000	1	0	1	0	0	
Beckham	.938	6	4	11	1	4	
Green	1.000	1	0	5	0	0	
McDonald	.950	16	19	19	2	4	

First Base	PCT	G	PO	A	E	DP
Calhoun	1.000	2	4	0	0	0
Cron Jr.	.996	36	221	12	1	23
Green	1.000	1	4	0	0	1
Ibanez	1.000	5	21	2	0	2
Navarro	.992	28	124	8	1	10
Pujols	.997	116	879	80	3	78
Stewart	1.000	6	24	1	0	1

Second Base	PCT	G	PO	A	E	DP
Beckham	1.000	5	3	7	0	1

Third Base	PCT	G	PO	A	E	DP
Beckham	.933	13	10	18	2	3
Freese	.966	122	67	162	8	18
Green	1.000	5	2	3	0	0
Jimenez	1.000	16	9	18	0	5
McDonald	.970	73	16	48	2	5
Pujols	1.000	1	0	1	0	0
Stewart	.962	16	10	15	1	0

Shortstop	PCT	G	PO	A	E	DP
Aybar	.982	155	194	359	10	75

Outfield	PCT	G	PO	A	E	DP
Boesch	.933	12	14	0	1	0
Calhoun	.996	123	230	9	1	1
Campana	1.000	13	15	0	0	0
Cowgill	.984	97	175	4	3	2
Green	1.000	17	18	0	0	0
Hamilton	.972	74	169	3	5	1
Ibanez	1.000	16	26	0	0	0
Navarro	.982	27	52	2	1	0
O'Malley	1.000	6	5	0	0	0
Shuck	1.000	21	43	2	0	0
Trout	.992	149	383	4	3	1

SALT LAKE BEES

TRIPLE-A

PACIFIC COAST LEAGUE

Batting	B-T	HT	WT	DOB	AVG	vLH	vRH	G	AB	R	H	2B	3B	HR	RBI	BB	HBP	SH	SF	SO	SB	CS	SLG	OBP
Albitz, Vance	R-R	5-7	170	1-31-88	.325	.368	.309	60	206	27	67	17	5	2	25	7	1	3	1	19	2	3	.485	.349
Boesch, Brennan	L-L	6-4	235	4-12-85	.332	.283	.348	95	374	68	124	25	7	25	85	29	2	1	6	86	10	4	.636	.381
Borenstein, Zach	L-R	6-0	225	7-23-90	.256	.176	.270	30	117	11	30	4	0	2	22	3	1	1	1	33	0	2	.342	.279
2-team total (20 Reno)					.258	—	—	50	190	23	49	8	1	7	37	10	1	1	2	55	0	3	.421	.296
Buck, John	R-R	6-3	245	7-7-80	.294	.258	.307	33	119	13	35	8	0	2	15	13	2	0	1	22	0	0	.412	.370
Calhoun, Kole	L-L	5-10	200	10-14-87	.500	.000	.550	5	22	7	11	2	1	1	5	0	0	0	0	3	0	1	.818	.500
Campana, Tony	L-L	5-8	165	5-30-86	.267	.304	.253	53	202	31	54	6	2	0	17	18	1	6	0	39	9	9	.317	.330
2-team total (47 Reno)					.277	—	—	100	365	62	101	11	6	0	34	30	3	9	1	67	17	11	.340	.352
Cowgill, Collin	R-L	5-9	185	5-22-86	.333	.333	.333	3	12	4	4	2	0	0	2	0	0	0	0	2	0	0	.500	.429
Cron Jr., C.J.	R-R	6-4	235	1-5-90	.316	.275	.331	49	190	30	60	14	1	7	33	18	4	0	1	40	2	1	.511	.385
De La Rosa, Anderson	R-R	5-11	190	8-1-84	.256	.000	.294	10	39	3	10	3	0	0	6	0	0	0	0	9	0	0	.333	.256
Field, Tommy	R-R	5-10	185	2-22-87	.285	.352	.264	80	302	55	86	18	4	7	33	28	5	3	4	63	5	1	.440	.351
Freese, David	R-R	6-2	225	4-28-83	.200	—	.200	3	10	4	2	0	0	2	4	4	0	0	0	1	0	0	.800	.429
Good, Riley	L-R	6-0	185	3-7-92	.500	—	.500	1	2	0	1	0	0	0	0	0	0	0	0	0	0	0	.500	.500
Green, Grant	R-R	6-3	180	9-27-87	.333	.352	.326	48	198	36	66	17	3	5	42	13	2	0	1	31	4	2	.525	.379
Hamilton, Josh	L-L	6-4	240	5-21-81	.462	.000	.500	3	13	2	6	2	0	0	0	0	0	0	0	2	0	0	.615	.462
Heid, Drew	L-R	5-10	175	12-14-87	.250	.231	.254	24	80	9	20	1	2	0	10	5	0	2	2	18	1	0	.313	.287
Hester, John	R-R	6-2	210	9-14-83	.261	.214	.276	71	241	31	63	16	1	6	29	26	3	1	2	70	3	0	.411	.338
Jimenez, Luis	R-R	6-1	205	1-18-88	.286	.306	.280	117	469	67	134	34	3	21	76	24	2	2	4	75	12	4	.505	.321
Komatsu, Erik	L-L	5-10	175	10-1-87	.067	.000	.091	7	15	1	1	1	0	0	1	2	0	1	0	3	0	0	.133	.176
Lindsey, Taylor	L-L	6-0	195	12-2-91	.247	.231	.251	75	295	50	73	13	4	8	30	31	2	5	0	44	7	2	.400	.323
2-team total (41 El Paso)					.238	—	—	116	468		105	19	5	10	40		4	5	2	59	7	4	.372	.306
Long, Matt	L-R	5-11	190	4-30-87	.261	.200	.272	64	241	48	63	11	1	5	29	37	0	3	0	65	18	1	.378	.360
Lopez, Roberto	R-R	6-0	195	10-1-85	.293	.345	.278	115	400	51	117	21	2	11	56	25	7	2	6	70	4	5	.438	.340
Martinez, Luis	R-R	6-0	210	4-3-85	.262	.333	.254	53	191	25	50	15	0	4	22	15	4	2	0	33	0	0	.403	.329
2-team total (14 Sacramento)					.242	—	—	67	231	26	56	16	0	4	25	20	6	2	0	43	0	0	.364	.319
Navarro, Efren	L-L	6-0	210	5-14-86	.326	.233	.360	72	273	45	89	19	3	4	50	43	1	0	1	47	2	1	.462	.418
O'Malley, Shawn	R-R	5-11	165	12-28-87	.330	.360	.321	89	318	60	105	19	9	3	38	39	7	9	3	44	13	4	.475	.411
Shuck, J.B.	L-L	5-11	195	6-30-87	.320	.355	.307	102	406	64	130	18	9	5	57	43	3	4	9	30	9	6	.446	.382
Stewart, Ian	L-R	6-3	215	4-5-85	.198	.042	.237	36	121	21	24	3	0	5	13	18	2	0	1	42	1	0	.347	.310
Swift, Jimmy	R-R	6-2	190	12-21-87	.247	.500	.225	21	77	10	19	4	0	1	12	2	1	2	2	17	0	0	.338	.268
Wheeler, Ryan	L-R	6-3	215	7-10-88	.326	.371	.298	25	92	13	30	1	0	2	15	8	0	0	2	19	0	0	.402	.373
2-team total (59 Colorado Springs)					.268	—	—	84	302	31	81	10	6	0	35	23	1	1	5	62	0	2	.361	.317
Zaneski, Zach	R-R	6-2	215	6-27-86	.250	—	.250	5	12	0	3	1	0	0	0	0	0	1	0	6	0	0	.333	.250

Pitching	B-T	HT	WT	DOB	W	L	ERA	G	GS	CG	SV	IP	H	R	ER	HR	BB	SO	AVG	vLH	vRH	K/9	BB/9
Alvarez, Jose	L-L	5-11	180	5-6-89	0	2	6.75	6	6	0	0	31	35	25	23	8	15	17	.285	.196	.338	4.99	4.40
Bedrosian, Cam	R-R	6-0	205	10-2-91	1	1	7.71	8	0	0	2	7	5	6	6	0	10	12	.192	.125	.222	12.86	7.71
Berg, Jeremy	R-R	6-0	180	7-17-86	3	2	7.50	38	0	0	0	48	68	47	40	4	14	46	.332	.397	.291	8.63	2.63
Boshers, Buddy	L-L	6-3	205	5-9-88	1	0	6.23	11	0	0	0	13	10	9	9	1	13	12	.227	.250	.214	8.31	9.00
Boyd, Jake	R-R	6-3	200	1-6-90	0	0	0.00	2	0	0	0	3	0	0	0	0	1	1	.273	.000	.333	2.70	2.70
Brady, Mike	R-R	6-0	210	3-21-87	0	2	7.01	17	1	0	2	26	30	21	20	1	13	21	.294	.265	.321	7.36	4.56
Carpenter, David	R-R	6-3	180	9-1-87	2	1	3.34	21	1	0	3	30	30	11	11	0	12	22	.263	.317	.233	6.67	3.64

Name	B-T	HT	WT	DOB	W	L	ERA	G	GS	CG	SV	IP	H	R	ER	HR	BB	SO	AVG	vLH	vRH	G/9	BB/9
Carson, Robert	L-L	6-4	240	1-23-89	0	1	10.34	14	0	0	0	16	23	18	18	2	13	9	.343	.345	.342	5.17	7.47
2-team total (18 Albuquerque)					2	6	7.30	32	0	0	0	41	58	36	33	5	25	39	—	—	—	8.63	5.53
Castillo, Yeiper	R-R	6-3	185	9-6-88	1	0	0.00	1	0	0	0	3	0	0	0	0	0	2	.000	.000	.000	5.40	0.00
Chaffee, Ryan	R-R	6-2	195	5-18-88	1	2	6.08	31	0	0	2	37	42	25	25	2	28	45	.290	.436	.200	10.95	6.81
Clay, Caleb	R-R	6-2	180	2-15-88	3	7	5.09	12	12	1	0	76	87	44	43	14	17	45	.288	.273	.299	5.33	2.01
De La Rosa, Dane	R-R	6-7	245	2-1-83	3	2	5.33	27	0	0	3	25	21	16	15	2	18	21	.226	.244	.208	7.46	6.39
Grube, Jarrett	R-R	6-4	220	11-5-81	8	9	5.56	27	27	1	0	147	164	99	91	26	41	121	.279	.307	.255	7.39	2.50
Herrera, Yoslan	R-R	6-2	200	4-28-81	4	4	2.52	41	0	0	5	50	51	16	14	3	16	47	.266	.267	.265	8.46	2.88
Johnson, Kevin	L-R	6-4	240	8-19-88	0	0	40.50	1	0	0	0	1	4	3	3	1	1	0	.667	.667	.667	9.00	13.50
Kohn, Michael	R-R	6-2	200	6-26-86	1	1	4.76	33	0	0	8	34	28	24	18	6	27	33	.228	.227	.228	8.74	7.15
LeBlanc, Wade	L-L	6-3	215	8-7-84	10	4	4.43	22	22	1	0	128	143	68	63	11	42	119	.288	.259	.300	8.37	2.95
Lerew, Anthony	L-R	6-4	225	10-28-82	4	6	6.75	22	14	0	0	83	116	67	62	12	34	56	.336	.311	.352	6.10	3.70
Lyon, Brandon	R-R	6-1	200	8-10-79	0	6	4.08	20	0	0	0	18	33	11	8	0	8	9	.398	.447	.356	4.58	4.08
Maronde, Nick	B-L	6-3	205	9-5-89	0	0	9.35	9	0	0	0	9	11	9	9	0	15	12	.314	.400	.250	12.46	15.58
Martinez, Joe	L-R	6-2	190	2-26-83	0	3	16.36	3	3	0	0	11	25	23	20	4	9	14	.424	.250	.581	11.45	7.36
Morin, Mike	R-R	6-4	220	5-3-91	0	1	12.00	4	0	0	2	3	7	5	4	1	0	5	.438	.444	.429	15.00	0.00
Newby, Kyler	R-R	6-4	225	2-22-85	0	4	3.98	30	2	0	0	41	50	21	18	3	11	32	.313	.299	.323	7.08	2.43
Nieve, Fernando	R-R	6-0	220	7-15-82	0	2	5.29	15	1	0	0	17	21	10	10	0	12	12	.323	.375	.293	11.65	6.35
2-team total (18 Sacramento)					2	3	6.33	33	1	0	3	43	59	32	30	4	26	46	—	—	—	9.70	5.48
Pestano, Vinnie	R-R	6-0	200	2-20-85	1	1	2.25	6	0	0	0	8	7	3	2	1	4	12	.219	.308	.158	13.50	4.50
Pineiro, Joel	R-R	6-0	200	9-25-78	1	2	7.48	4	4	0	0	22	36	20	18	3	7	11	.375	.400	.357	4.57	2.91
Raley, Brooks	L-L	6-3	200	6-29-88	0	3	10.57	6	5	0	0	23	39	27	27	1	12	15	.379	.447	.338	5.87	4.70
Rasmus, Cory	R-R	6-0	200	11-6-87	2	1	4.18	22	0	0	2	28	23	14	13	2	16	24	.223	.191	.250	7.71	5.14
Reynolds, Danny	R-R	6-0	170	5-2-91	0	0	0.00	1	0	0	0	2	1	0	0	0	1	3	.143	.200	.000	13.50	4.50
Richardson, Dustin	L-L	6-6	220	1-9-84	3	3	7.69	36	3	0	2	53	64	49	45	7	26	56	.302	.279	.317	9.57	4.44
Salas, Fernando	R-R	6-2	210	5-30-85	0	0	0.00	3	0	0	1	3	2	0	0	0	0	6	.200	.250	.000	0.00	0.00
Santiago, Hector	R-L	6-0	210	12-16-87	1	1	6.43	3	3	0	0	14	23	12	10	0	7	9	.371	.400	.357	5.79	4.50
Shoemaker, Matt	R-R	6-2	225	9-27-86	1	0	6.31	5	5	0	0	26	34	18	18	2	9	26	.327	.371	.262	9.12	3.16
Sisk, Brandon	L-L	6-2	220	7-13-85	0	1	13.09	17	0	0	0	11	15	16	16	2	5	11	.313	.208	.417	9.00	4.09
Skaggs, Tyler	L-L	6-4	215	7-13-91	0	1	6.00	1	1	0	0	3	5	7	2	0	5	6	.357	.250	.400	6.00	15.00
Spomer, Kurt	B-R	6-2	215	7-10-89	1	1	0.00	9	0	0	0	10	9	2	0	0	5	4	.250	.222	.278	3.60	4.50
Thomas, Justin	L-L	6-3	220	1-18-84	4	8	5.99	20	20	0	0	113	148	80	75	21	41	95	.329	.338	.324	7.59	3.28
Volstad, Chris	R-R	6-8	230	9-23-86	2	1	6.18	7	7	0	0	39	48	28	27	7	12	24	.298	.267	.326	5.49	2.75
Wall, Josh	R-R	6-6	215	1-21-87	0	0	4.22	8	0	0	0	11	11	7	5	0	5	11	.262	.313	.231	9.28	4.22
Wolf, Randy	L-L	6-0	205	8-22-76	1	1	4.78	7	7	0	0	38	45	20	20	5	12	31	.306	.348	.298	7.41	2.87
2-team total (6 Reno)					6	2	4.65	13	13	0	0	72	85	38	37	6	30	66	—	—	—	8.29	3.77

Fielding

Catcher	PCT	G	PO	A	E	DP	PB
Buck	1.000	22	161	11	0	2	2
De La Rosa	.979	9	84	9	2	3	1
Hester	.996	66	450	30	2	6	3
Martinez	.992	48	370	25	3	1	6
Zaneski	1.000	2	13	1	0	0	0

First Base	PCT	G	PO	A	E	DP
Buck	1.000	2	12	3	0	3
Cron Jr.	.986	42	322	24	5	36
Green	.975	5	37	2	1	6
Jimenez	.972	11	65	5	2	5
Lopez	.994	38	287	30	2	40
Navarro	.997	31	285	22	1	31
Stewart	.990	14	90	14	1	11
Wheeler	.984	8	58	5	1	7
Zaneski	.833	1	4	1	1	2

Second Base	PCT	G	PO	A	E	DP
Albitz	.990	43	87	109	2	30
Field	1.000	15	23	48	0	12
Green	1.000	4	11	11	0	4
Lindsey	.977	71	127	171	7	47
Long	1.000	1	1	4	0	0
O'Malley	1.000	13	26	49	0	16
Stewart	1.000	2	3	10	0	2

Third Base	PCT	G	PO	A	E	DP
Field	.846	16	14	30	8	4
Freese	1.000	2	0	3	0	0
Green	.944	15	9	25	2	5
Jimenez	.942	81	48	148	12	25
Long	.909	6	3	7	1	1
Lopez	1.000	5	0	7	0	1
O'Malley	1.000	5	5	8	0	2
Stewart	1.000	9	5	12	0	2
Swift	.909	6	2	8	1	0
Wheeler	.966	10	7	21	1	1

Shortstop	PCT	G	PO	A	E	DP
Albitz	.985	14	26	38	1	9
Field	.946	48	61	115	10	37
Green	.944	18	18	33	3	6
O'Malley	.967	56	93	139	8	29
Swift	.986	15	28	44	1	7

Outfield	PCT	G	PO	A	E	DP
Boesch	.977	81	124	4	3	0
Borenstein	.980	30	45	5	1	1
Calhoun	1.000	4	6	0	0	0
Campana	1.000	52	129	1	0	0
Cowgill	1.000	2	1	1	0	0
Good	—	1	0	0	0	0
Green	1.000	7	22	0	0	0
Hamilton	1.000	2	1	0	0	0
Heid	.958	20	44	2	2	0
Komatsu	1.000	7	11	0	0	0
Long	.976	52	123	0	3	0
Lopez	.979	60	91	1	2	0
Navarro	.980	27	50	0	1	0
O'Malley	.955	12	19	2	1	1
Shuck	.985	89	187	5	3	2
Wheeler	1.000	1	3	0	0	0

ARKANSAS TRAVELERS

DOUBLE-A

TEXAS LEAGUE

Batting	B-T	HT	WT	DOB	AVG	vLH	vRH	G	AB	R	H	2B	3B	HR	RBI	BB	HBP	SH	SF	SO	SB	CS	SLG	OBP
Albitz, Vance	R-R	5-7	170	1-31-88	.230	.242	.222	25	87	10	20	8	0	1	6	9	1	0	0	13	3	0	.356	.309
Allbritton, Alex	R-R	6-2	185	12-9-90	.235	.200	.250	5	17	2	4	2	0	0	1	0	0	0	0	5	0	0	.353	.278
Bandy, Jett	R-R	6-4	235	3-26-90	.250	.247	.251	93	312	38	78	12	0	13	40	33	15	1	2	63	2	4	.413	.348
Bianucci, Mike	R-R	6-1	215	6-26-86	.274	.273	.274	62	241	36	66	17	1	12	49	11	2	0	4	55	1	0	.502	.306
Borenstein, Zach	L-R	6-0	225	7-23-90	.266	.304	.243	48	184	23	49	13	2	5	28	21	0	0	2	53	6	4	.440	.338
Cowart, Kaleb	B-R	6-3	225	6-2-92	.223	.202	.232	126	435	48	97	18	4	6	54	43	3	2	4	99	26	7	.324	.295
De La Rosa, Anderson	R-R	5-11	190	8-1-84	.200	.216	.191	41	145	12	29	11	0	2	18	7	1	0	2	38	0	1	.317	.239
Gonzalez, Maikol	R-R	5-10	175	3-25-86	.270	.265	.272	89	319	57	86	10	3	1	21	52	1	7	2	52	30	7	.329	.372
Gowens, Brennan	L-R	6-0	195	3-14-90	.208	.000	.250	9	24	3	5	1	0	0	3	5	0	0	0	10	0	0	.250	.296
Heid, Drew	L-R	5-10	175	12-14-87	.250	.214	.259	82	272	35	68	7	5	2	22	29	2	2	1	47	7	4	.335	.326
Hernandez, Brian	R-R	6-1	195	11-25-88	.308	.314	.305	119	458	53	141	25	0	7	60	39	6	0	5	85	5	5	.408	.366
Hudson, Kyle	L-L	5-11	175	1-7-87	.244	.184	.281	55	197	29	48	4	1	0	15	28	0	5	0	39	11	5	.274	.338

Batting	B-T	HT	WT	DOB	AVG	vLH	vRH	G	AB	R	H	2B	3B	HR	RBI	BB	HBP	SH	SF	SO	SB	CS	SLG	OBP
Komatsu, Erik	L-L	5-10	175	10-1-87	.179	.111	.211	20	56	2	10	1	1	2	5	7	0	0	1	19	2	1	.339	.266
Long, Matt	L-R	5-11	190	4-30-87	.223	.250	.213	50	175	32	39	8	2	4	15	20	0	1	4	52	6	2	.360	.296
Melker, Adam	L-L	5-11	180	1-31-88	.258	.181	.286	83	275	29	71	6	1	5	32	19	5	3	0	51	12	4	.342	.318
O'Malley, Shawn	R-R	5-11	165	12-28-87	.188	.200	.182	11	32	3	6	0	1	0	5	6	0	1	1	8	1	0	.250	.308
Ross, Chance	R-R	6-0	180	2-28-90	.333	.500	.000	1	3	2	1	0	0	0	0	1	0	0	0	1	1	0	.333	.500
Snyder, Mike	R-R	6-4	230	6-17-90	.211	.185	.223	47	166	15	35	9	0	3	17	12	1	0	2	54	1	0	.319	.265
Stamets, Eric	R-R	6-0	190	9-25-91	.235	.287	.212	106	344	46	81	13	1	4	23	24	5	7	2	62	11	1	.314	.293
Swift, Jimmy	R-R	6-2	190	12-21-87	.179	.167	.191	29	95	6	17	2	0	2	7	4	0	1	0	24	0	2	.263	.212
Workman, Andy	R-R	6-1	200	11-16-88	.188	.118	.242	39	117	13	22	4	0	2	17	14	4	3	0	30	2	4	.274	.296
Yarbrough, Alex	B-R	6-0	195	8-3-91	.285	.244	.305	136	544	66	155	38	4	5	77	33	1	3	11	124	6	6	.397	.321
Zaneski, Zach	R-R	6-2	215	6-27-86	.279	.353	.250	19	61	9	17	3	0	3	7	5	0	0	0	12	0	0	.475	.333
2-team total (3 Frisco)					.239	—	—	22	71	9	17	3	0	3	7	6	0	0	0	14	0	0	.408	.308

Pitching

Pitching	B-T	HT	WT	DOB	W	L	ERA	G	GS	CG	SV	IP	H	R	ER	HR	BB	SO	AVG	vLH	vRH	K/9	BB/9
Alvarez, R.J.	R-R	6-1	200	6-8-91	0	0	0.33	21	0	0	1	27	13	2	1	0	10	38	.149	.231	.083	12.67	3.33
2-team total (17 San Antonio)					0	1	1.25	38	0	0	7	43	29	7	6	0	13	61	—	—	—	12.67	2.70
Arenas, Orangel	R-R	6-0	200	3-31-89	6	8	3.86	26	20	0	0	114	113	58	49	7	44	51	.266	.232	.291	4.01	3.46
Bedrosian, Cam	R-R	6-0	205	10-2-91	1	0	1.11	30	0	0	15	32	10	5	4	1	10	57	.097	.125	.079	15.87	2.78
Boshers, Buddy	L-L	6-3	205	5-9-88	2	3	2.66	29	8	0	0	61	47	21	18	1	27	70	.211	.221	.206	10.33	3.98
Brady, Mike	R-R	6-0	210	3-21-87	1	4	2.98	28	2	0	2	42	41	16	14	3	10	42	.256	.242	.265	8.93	2.13
Burnett, Sean	L-L	6-1	180	9-17-82	0	0	5.06	6	0	0	0	5	6	3	3	0	3	7	.286	.333	.267	11.81	5.06
Carpenter, David	R-R	6-3	180	9-1-87	2	1	1.10	24	0	0	6	33	24	4	4	1	13	36	.209	.341	.135	9.92	3.58
Castillo, Yeiper	R-R	6-3	185	9-6-88	3	3	5.36	8	0	0	0	42	39	25	25	2	26	33	.248	.278	.224	7.07	5.57
Chaffee, Ryan	R-R	6-2	195	5-18-88	3	0	2.31	13	0	0	0	23	22	7	6	0	9	30	.242	.194	.267	11.57	3.47
De La Rosa, Dane	R-R	6-7	245	2-1-83	0	0	0.00	2	0	0	0	2	1	0	0	0	0	2	.167	.000	.250	9.00	0.00
DeLoach, Tyler	R-L	6-6	240	4-12-91	4	0	2.29	6	0	0	0	35	17	9	9	3	17	39	.144	.152	.141	9.93	4.33
Diaz, Jairo	R-R	6-0	195	5-27-91	2	1	2.20	27	0	0	11	33	30	8	8	2	10	48	.252	.306	.214	13.22	2.76
Giardina, Carmine	L-L	6-3	225	2-20-88	2	1	4.45	49	0	0	0	57	53	33	28	6	30	45	.251	.188	.282	7.15	4.76
Gott, Trevor	R-R	6-0	190	8-26-92	2	1	1.53	13	0	0	2	18	11	3	3	0	7	18	.186	.167	.195	9.17	3.57
2-team total (10 San Antonio)					2	1	2.76	23	0	0	2	29	22	11	9	0	16	29	—	—	—	8.90	4.91
Johnson, Kevin	L-R	6-4	240	8-19-88	4	4	2.98	41	0	0	0	60	73	24	20	2	29	35	.312	.317	.309	5.22	4.33
Maronde, Nick	B-L	6-3	205	9-5-89	0	0	13.50	7	0	0	1	7	6	11	11	4	15	10	.222	.000	.286	12.27	18.41
McGowin, Kyle	R-R	6-3	180	11-27-91	0	1	5.40	1	1	0	0	5	6	3	3	1	0	3	.286	.000	.364	5.40	0.00
Morin, Mike	R-R	6-4	220	5-3-91	1	0	0.00	5	0	0	3	5	3	0	0	0	0	6	.176	.286	.100	10.80	0.00
Reynolds, Danny	R-R	6-0	170	5-2-91	3	2	3.60	30	0	0	2	40	42	16	16	1	15	41	.273	.226	.297	9.23	3.38
Roth, Michael	L-L	6-1	210	2-15-90	11	7	2.62	22	22	0	0	141	121	48	41	9	53	79	.238	.200	.248	5.05	3.39
Rucinski, Drew	R-R	6-2	190	12-30-88	10	6	3.15	26	26	2	0	149	142	61	52	7	41	140	.257	.238	.272	8.48	2.48
Sappington, Mark	R-R	6-5	210	11-17-90	1	4	6.44	9	0	0	0	43	44	31	31	2	36	34	.255	.254	.290	7.06	7.48
Sisk, Brandon	L-L	6-2	220	7-13-85	0	2	3.95	13	0	0	1	14	11	6	6	0	5	16	.220	.308	.189	10.54	3.29
Smith, Nate	L-L	6-3	200	8-28-91	5	3	2.89	11	11	0	0	62	48	21	20	3	30	67	.218	.217	.218	9.67	4.33
Sneed, Kramer	L-L	6-3	185	10-7-88	8	11	4.68	28	26	0	0	138	136	80	72	18	66	109	.255	.269	.250	7.09	4.29
Spomer, Kurt	B-R	6-2	215	7-10-89	3	3	3.70	16	0	0	0	24	21	11	10	1	12	10	.244	.240	.246	3.70	4.44
Wilson, C.J.	L-L	6-1	210	11-18-80	1	0	3.38	1	1	0	0	5	4	2	2	1	2	7	.211	.000	.267	11.81	3.38

Fielding

Catcher	PCT	G	PO	A	E	DP	PB
Bandy	.996	91	703	84	3	4	7
De La Rosa	.994	39	293	46	2	5	6
Zaneski	.966	15	80	6	3	0	1

First Base	PCT	G	PO	A	E	DP
Bianucci	.882	2	13	2	2	0
De La Rosa	1.000	1	5	0	0	1
Hernandez	.991	98	803	46	8	74
Snyder	.997	36	278	17	1	17
Swift	1.000	7	53	5	0	5

Second Base	PCT	G	PO	A	E	DP
Albitz	1.000	2	1	4	0	2
Gonzalez	.895	4	8	9	2	4
O'Malley	.800	1	1	3	1	0
Ross	1.000	1	2	0	0	0
Yarbrough	.982	132	250	297	10	76

Third Base	PCT	G	PO	A	E	DP
Cowart	.929	120	81	219	23	20
Hernandez	.975	17	12	27	1	3
Swift	.950	6	5	14	1	0

Shortstop	PCT	G	PO	A	E	DP
Albitz	.962	23	40	61	4	11
Allbritton	.909	2	2	8	1	2
Gonzalez	.939	7	10	21	2	3
Hernandez	1.000	1	3	2	0	1
O'Malley	1.000	1	2	3	0	0
Stamets	.976	106	153	333	12	63
Swift	1.000	2	3	3	0	1

Outfield	PCT	G	PO	A	E	DP
Bianucci	.944	11	16	1	1	0
Borenstein	.984	42	57	5	1	1
Gonzalez	.972	66	101	3	3	1
Gowens	1.000	4	8	0	0	0
Heid	.987	78	147	9	2	1
Hudson	1.000	49	108	0	0	0
Komatsu	1.000	15	21	0	0	0
Long	1.000	50	100	4	0	1
Melker	.976	75	156	5	4	2
O'Malley	1.000	3	2	1	0	0
Swift	1.000	9	17	2	0	0
Workman	.972	31	67	2	2	0

INLAND EMPIRE 66ERS   HIGH CLASS A

CALIFORNIA LEAGUE

Batting	B-T	HT	WT	DOB	AVG	vLH	vRH	G	AB	R	H	2B	3B	HR	RBI	BB	HBP	SH	SF	SO	SB	CS	SLG	OBP
Aguilera, Eric	L-L	6-2	218	7-3-90	.279	.167	.297	11	43	3	12	3	0	0	2	2	0	1	0	10	0	0	.349	.311
Allbritton, Alex	R-R	6-2	185	12-9-90	.241	.186	.262	110	369	43	89	26	1	2	37	34	2	8	3	112	7	5	.333	.306
Baker, Abel	L-R	6-1	200	10-26-90	.143	.050	.175	25	77	3	11	3	0	0	3	4	0	0	0	31	0	0	.182	.185
Bayardi, Brandon	R-R	6-2	235	11-27-90	.321	.200	.348	7	28	9	9	0	0	1	5	0	1	0	0	4	2	0	.429	.345
Bemboom, Anthony	L-R	6-2	190	1-18-90	.244	.125	.280	46	172	21	42	6	2	3	30	8	1	0	1	27	2	2	.355	.280
Cayones, Exicardo	L-L	6-0	185	10-9-91	.284	.234	.307	44	148	30	42	10	1	0	14	17	1	1	0	39	6	2	.365	.361
Clarke, Chevy	B-R	6-0	190	7-13-91	.173	.250	.151	36	110	4	19	1	0	1	5	13	1	4	0	35	3	2	.209	.266
Davis, Quinten	R-R	6-1	185	8-1-92	.200	.500	.000	7	5	1	1	0	0	0	1	0	0	0	0	2	0	0	.200	.200
Gomez, Rolando	L-R	5-7	145	6-18-89	.210	.200	.212	23	81	9	17	3	1	0	7	10	0	1	0	24	3	1	.272	.297
Good, Riley	L-R	6-0	185	3-7-92	.246	.225	.252	49	167	15	41	9	1	0	12	4	0	1	0	39	11	3	.311	.263
Gowens, Brennan	L-R	6-0	195	3-14-90	.205	.182	.208	25	83	9	17	4	2	0	6	9	1	1	0	16	5	3	.301	.290

Name	B-T	HT	WT	DOB	AVG	vLH	vRH	G	AB	R	H	2B	3B	HR	RBI	BB	HBP	SH	SF	SO	SB	CS	SLG	OBP
Hernandez, Brian	R-R	6-1	195	11-25-88	.190	.067	.219	19	79	5	15	4	0	2	10	3	1	0	1	17	2	1	.316	.226
Hinkle, Wade	L-L	6-0	225	9-5-89	.295	.214	.327	82	292	48	86	25	3	9	46	40	15	0	1	69	2	0	.493	.405
Hinshaw, Chad	R-R	6-1	205	9-10-90	.261	.259	.262	65	264	49	69	14	8	10	46	15	15	1	3	65	16	7	.489	.333
Johnson, Sherman	L-R	5-10	180	7-15-90	.276	.318	.262	136	529	107	146	23	13	17	78	88	5	4	3	104	26	12	.465	.382
O'Loughlin, Nick	R-R	6-0	200	4-2-90	.107	.000	.125	10	28	3	3	1	0	0	1	3	0	0	0	9	0	0	.143	.194
Raben, Dennis	L-L	6-3	220	7-31-87	.292	.257	.306	105	397	63	116	15	3	31	94	38	8	0	5	96	4	3	.579	.362
Ray, Andrew	R-R	6-1	195	5-1-91	.110	.190	.091	35	109	9	12	3	0	2	8	14	0	1	0	52	3	2	.193	.211
Rondon, Jose	R-R	6-1	160	3-3-94	.327	.357	.317	72	297	40	97	17	5	0	24	17	0	9	1	50	8	6	.418	.362
2-team total (37 Lake Elsinore)					.319	—	—	109	433	58	138	26	5	1	36	30	2	12	1	73	11	7	.409	.365
Rosa, Angel	R-R	6-2	185	9-19-92	.348	.355	.346	28	112	14	39	7	3	0	18	6	3	1	2	21	4	3	.464	.390
Ross, Chance	R-R	6-0	180	2-28-90	.245	.214	.256	29	106	10	26	3	1	1	9	2	1	1	1	30	2	2	.321	.264
Shannon, Mark	L-L	6-0	185	4-12-91	.288	.299	.283	107	420	58	121	23	1	10	53	19	7	5	4	86	17	6	.419	.327
Towey, Cal	L-R	6-1	215	2-6-90	.279	.321	.262	128	477	72	133	24	6	10	63	51	15	1	3	137	21	15	.417	.364
Weik, Joe	R-R	6-2	215	4-21-88	.179	.174	.182	21	67	8	12	2	0	1	5	10	0	1	1	8	0	0	.254	.282
Wright, Zach	R-R	6-1	205	1-10-90	.243	.227	.250	89	309	49	75	11	2	9	43	36	6	3	3	95	3	1	.379	.331

Pitching

Name	B-T	HT	WT	DOB	W	L	ERA	G	GS	CG	SV	IP	H	R	ER	HR	BB	SO	AVG	vLH	vRH	K/9	BB/9
Adams, Austin	R-R	6-2	180	5-5-91	3	2	3.79	42	0	0	1	59	27	28	25	3	53	80	.141	.102	.159	12.13	8.04
Bedrosian, Cam	R-R	6-0	205	10-2-91	0	0	0.00	5	0	0	1	6	1	0	0	0	2	15	.056	.143	.000	23.82	3.18
Billo, Greg	R-R	6-4	220	7-15-90	0	2	14.40	2	2	0	0	5	11	8	8	1	6	4	.478	.600	.385	7.20	10.80
Blackford, Alex	R-R	5-11	200	11-16-90	0	0	7.36	5	0	0	0	11	10	10	9	1	5	10	.250	.188	.292	8.18	4.09
Boyd, Jake	R-R	6-3	200	1-6-90	1	2	5.10	27	0	0	0	48	56	29	27	4	17	36	.298	.253	.327	6.80	3.21
Castillo, Yeiper	R-R	6-3	185	9-6-88	0	1	9.82	2	1	0	0	4	6	5	4	0	4	1	.375	.375	.375	2.45	9.82
2-team total (6 Stockton)					1	2	9.11	8	6	0	0	27	42	30	27	4	22	9	—	—	—	3.04	7.43
Clevinger, Mike	R-R	6-4	220	12-21-90	1	3	5.37	13	13	0	0	55	58	41	33	8	27	58	.272	.303	.246	9.43	4.39
Crowley, Ryan	L-L	6-3	190	11-15-90	0	6	6.07	9	7	0	0	43	63	33	29	7	6	23	.356	.276	.372	4.81	1.26
De La Rosa, Dane	R-R	6-7	245	2-1-83	0	0	0.00	1	0	0	0	1	0	0	0	0	0	1	.000	.000	.000	9.00	0.00
DeLoach, Tyler	R-L	6-6	240	4-12-91	10	4	3.21	21	19	0	0	112	87	46	40	6	49	122	.213	.222	.210	9.80	3.94
Diaz, Jairo	R-R	6-0	195	5-27-91	2	3	4.78	29	0	0	4	32	31	18	17	2	10	37	.244	.163	.286	10.41	2.81
Foss, Trevor	R-R	6-3	175	11-15-89	3	0	4.54	11	7	0	0	42	48	26	21	6	11	25	.300	.349	.295	5.40	2.38
Gordon, Grant	R-R	6-3	175	9-10-90	0	1	8.71	11	0	0	0	10	18	11	10	3	6	6	.375	.368	.379	5.23	5.23
Hanson, Ray	R-R	6-7	235	2-27-90	4	5	5.00	12	12	1	0	72	67	37	32	6	31	55	.245	.235	.251	6.88	3.88
Hernandez, Matt	L-L	6-2	190	6-14-91	0	0	7.56	5	0	0	0	8	9	8	7	1	4	5	.290	.400	.238	5.40	4.32
Hurtado, Daniel	R-R	6-3	180	7-25-92	0	1	2.45	2	0	0	0	4	2	1	1	1	0	8	.154	1.000	.083	19.64	0.00
Keudell, Alex	R-R	6-2	205	2-25-90	1	5	10.08	7	7	0	0	28	48	34	31	3	14	22	.375	.457	.344	7.16	4.55
Krehbiel, Joe	R-R	6-2	185	12-20-92	0	0	2.25	4	0	0	0	4	2	2	1	1	1	6	.133	.000	.200	13.50	2.25
2-team total (22 Visalia)					1	0	1.53	26	0	0	3	29	15	7	5	2	10	34	—	—	—	10.43	3.07
McGowin, Kyle	R-R	6-2	180		1	5	2.93	10	10	0	0	58	51	24	19	4	16	48	.236	.304	.204	7.41	2.47
Miranda, Danny	L-L	6-0	225	8-25-90	3	1	4.80	8	0	0	1	15	17	9	8	2	6	10	.309	.211	.361	6.00	3.60
Morin, Mike	R-R	6-4	220	5-3-91	0	0	0.00	1	0	0	1	1	1	0	0	0	0	2	.250	.500	.000	18.00	0.00
Morris, Elliot	R-R	6-4	210	4-26-92	3	3	4.17	9	9	0	0	45	37	23	21	5	28	40	.220	.244	.198	7.94	5.56
2-team total (8 Lake Elsinore)					6	6	3.86	17	17	0	0	93	77	42	40	12	39	73	—	—	—	7.04	3.76
Murillo, David	R-R	5-11	190	1-3-92	0	0	0.00	1	0	0	0	3	1	0	0	0	1	3	.100	.000	.250	9.00	3.00
O'Grady, Chris	L-L	6-4	220	4-17-90	4	4	3.33	45	2	0	5	84	84	40	31	5	17	81	.263	.239	.275	8.71	1.83
Ortman, Dillon	R-R	6-2	198	6-13-92	1	0	5.87	4	2	0	0	15	17	10	10	4	5	5	.279	.160	.361	2.93	2.93
Reynolds, Danny	R-R	6-0	170	5-2-91	0	0	1.80	11	0	0	0	20	11	6	4	0	7	19	.159	.143	.167	8.55	3.15
Salas, Fernando	R-R	6-2	210	5-30-85	0	0	0.00	1	0	0	0	1	0	0	0	0	0	1	.000	.000	.000	9.00	0.00
Santos, Eduard	R-R	6-2	220	10-22-89	4	4	5.36	42	0	0	1	49	56	33	29	5	16	72	.283	.305	.267	13.32	2.96
Sappington, Mark	R-R	6-5	210	11-17-90	3	7	5.76	33	8	0	5	70	80	50	45	11	43	80	.288	.325	.261	10.24	5.50
Sharp, Clint	R-R	6-2	215	3-20-91	3	3	6.87	8	8	0	0	37	43	28	28	5	18	23	.295	.286	.301	5.65	4.42
Smith, Michael	R-R	6-0	195	1-31-90	1	1	3.99	29	1	0	2	47	45	21	21	7	14	39	.257	.260	.255	7.42	2.66
Smith, Nate	L-L	6-3	200	8-28-91	6	3	3.07	10	10	0	0	56	41	22	19	3	14	51	.201	.295	.175	8.25	2.26
Spomer, Kurt	B-R	6-2	215	7-10-89	3	2	1.79	32	0	0	8	40	28	8	8	2	13	28	.197	.302	.135	6.25	2.90
Tobik, Dan	R-R	6-4	195	1-8-91	4	8	4.69	21	18	0	1	117	131	74	61	10	44	79	.287	.290	.285	6.08	3.38
Trygg, Spencer	R-R	6-2	210	6-2-90	0	1	5.92	17	0	0	0	24	43	19	16	2	9	11	.398	.472	.327	4.07	3.33
Wood, Austin	R-R	6-4	225	7-11-90	0	0	1.74	4	4	0	0	10	6	3	2	0	3	9	.158	.167	.150	7.84	2.61

Fielding

Catcher	PCT	G	PO	A	E	DP	PB
Baker	1.000	24	150	26	0	0	2
Bemboom	.988	23	144	24	2	0	4
O'Loughlin	.981	9	47	6	1	0	2
Towey	.974	8	33	5	1	0	9
Wright	.987	84	689	97	10	2	13

First Base	PCT	G	PO	A	E	DP
Aguilera	1.000	8	72	5	0	8
Allbritton	1.000	13	111	11	0	11
Bayardi	1.000	1	7	0	0	1
Hernandez	1.000	9	75	3	0	6
Hinkle	.984	61	507	35	9	55
Raben	.987	51	440	33	6	40
Ross	1.000	1	13	0	0	0
Towey	1.000	1	13	0	0	0

Second Base	PCT	G	PO	A	E	DP
Allbritton	.983	39	71	107	3	24

Gomez	—	1	0	0	0	0
Johnson	.991	97	205	247	4	72
Ross	.963	8	6	20	1	5

Third Base	PCT	G	PO	A	E	DP
Allbritton	.959	37	27	67	4	10
Bemboom	.857	4	0	6	1	0
Hernandez	.966	9	6	22	1	3
Johnson	.976	15	11	30	1	4
Rosa	.500	1	1	0	1	0
Ross	.911	16	12	29	4	2
Towey	.923	67	44	123	14	14

Shortstop	PCT	G	PO	A	E	DP
Allbritton	.978	25	46	44	2	9
Gomez	.846	3	4	7	2	4
Johnson	.974	22	31	44	2	11
Rondon	.963	71	95	221	12	45
Rosa	.943	27	29	70	6	18

Outfield	PCT	G	PO	A	E	DP
Aguilera	1.000	2	5	0	0	0
Bayardi	1.000	2	3	0	0	0
Cayones	1.000	38	70	1	0	0
Clarke	.929	32	39	0	3	0
Davis	1.000	1	2	0	0	0
Gomez	.972	20	35	0	1	0
Good	.947	47	70	2	4	0
Gowens	.957	25	44	1	2	0
Hinkle	—	1	0	0	0	0
Hinshaw	.994	64	149	7	1	2
Johnson	1.000	2	2	0	0	0
Raben	.974	17	36	1	1	0
Ray	.939	30	30	1	2	0
Ross	.800	4	4	0	1	0
Shannon	.991	106	208	7	2	3
Towey	.948	38	52	3	3	0
Weik	1.000	14	23	0	0	0

BURLINGTON BEES

LOW CLASS A

MIDWEST LEAGUE

Batting	B-T	HT	WT	DOB	AVG	vLH	vRH	G	AB	R	H	2B	3B	HR	RBI	BB	HBP	SH	SF	SO	SB	CS	SLG	OBP
Aguilera, Eric	L-L	6-2	218	7-3-90	.292	.265	.301	124	469	59	137	22	4	14	71	35	7	1	12	101	17	3	.446	.342
Alberto, Ranyelmy	R-R	6-2	175	5-27-94	.169	.154	.175	96	343	29	58	11	2	8	35	29	0	2	3	121	5	6	.283	.232
Bayardi, Brandon	R-R	6-2	235	11-27-90	.272	.343	.254	48	173	15	47	9	1	5	20	13	4	1	1	40	5	1	.422	.335
Bemboom, Anthony	L-R	6-2	190	1-18-90	.217	.294	.186	19	60	8	13	3	2	2	13	4	1	0	0	7	1	0	.433	.277
Cayones, Exicardo	L-L	6-0	185	10-9-91	.256	.143	.297	51	160	20	41	11	1	2	21	34	1	3	2	42	1	2	.375	.386
Dalton, Ryan	R-R	6-1	200	7-24-91	.207	.243	.194	79	266	28	55	8	0	5	24	31	4	2	4	68	1	0	.293	.295
Dionicio, Ismael	B-R	5-10	165	7-19-91	.245	.235	.248	53	159	12	39	3	0	0	13	12	1	2	3	39	0	3	.264	.297
Eaves, Kody	L-R	6-0	175	7-8-93	.268	.225	.282	130	549	74	147	37	7	10	45	29	5	0	4	142	25	10	.415	.308
Fish, Mike	R-R	6-1	190	1-3-91	.252	.228	.260	110	428	51	108	25	6	9	57	30	5	2	4	78	8	3	.402	.306
Gretzky, Trevor	L-L	6-4	190	9-14-92	.201	.200	.201	50	179	14	36	7	1	3	12	4	0	3	0	47	5	0	.302	.219
Hinshaw, Chad	R-R	6-1	205	9-10-90	.282	.296	.276	59	206	51	58	13	3	6	24	28	14	0	0	63	25	8	.461	.403
Houchins, Zach	R-R	6-3	185	9-16-92	.200	.250	.176	28	110	8	22	6	0	0	10	7	2	0	1	26	3	0	.255	.258
McGee, Stephen	R-R	6-3	230	2-7-91	.217	.079	.252	99	313	30	68	12	1	2	29	50	9	2	5	80	1	1	.281	.337
Moye, Cambric	R-R	6-1	185	4-21-92	.148	.163	.137	40	122	11	18	6	0	2	12	15	2	0	0	45	0	0	.246	.252
Palmer, Tyler	R-R	5-11	189	9-20-91	.160	.320	.101	27	94	6	15	2	1	0	7	2	1	2	2	24	2	2	.202	.229
Pellant, Kirby	L-R	5-10	175	7-13-90	.095	.000	.118	8	21	1	2	1	0	0	1	2	0	0	1	7	3	0	.143	.167
Rosa, Angel	R-R	6-2	185	9-19-92	.246	.242	.247	99	395	43	97	23	3	7	46	25	6	2	1	103	15	5	.372	.300
Salcedo, Erick	B-R	5-10	155	6-28-93	.239	.233	.242	128	422	48	101	5	3	0	24	32	2	10	2	57	21	10	.265	.295
Shannon, Mark	L-L	6-0	185	4-28-91	.284	.179	.328	26	95	12	27	9	0	3	16	7	0	0	2	12	3	1	.474	.327
Way, Bo	L-L	6-0	180	11-17-91	.339	.344	.337	29	115	21	39	4	2	1	10	13	4	1	0	16	6	4	.461	.424

Pitching	B-T	HT	WT	DOB	W	L	ERA	G	GS	CG	SV	IP	H	R	ER	HR	BB	SO	AVG	vLH	vRH	K/9	BB/9
Alcantara, Alfonso	R-R	6-2	190	4-3-93	7	6	3.81	27	20	0	1	125	98	57	53	6	60	117	.219	.254	.194	8.40	4.31
Almonte, Yency	B-R	6-3	185	6-4-94	2	5	4.93	9	9	0	0	42	40	23	23	5	14	32	.252	.241	.263	6.86	3.00
Blackford, Alex	R-R	5-11	200	11-16-90	2	4	2.89	20	6	0	0	53	41	22	17	2	16	67	.207	.250	.167	11.38	2.72
Busenitz, Alan	R-R	6-1	180	8-22-90	4	5	1.94	49	0	0	17	70	55	18	15	2	21	62	.217	.243	.200	8.01	2.71
Carlson, Ben	R-R	6-3	215	11-30-90	3	2	2.60	52	0	0	14	66	69	27	19	2	17	62	.266	.234	.289	8.50	2.33
Clevinger, Mike	R-R	6-4	220	12-21-90	3	0	1.88	5	5	0	0	24	16	5	5	2	5	27	.186	.259	.153	10.13	1.88
Cooney, Harrison	R-R	6-2	175	3-23-92	9	8	2.65	25	22	1	1	129	108	50	38	5	51	91	.227	.253	.205	6.35	3.56
Etsell, Ryan	R-R	6-4	180	12-18-91	5	4	4.11	18	15	0	0	81	89	44	37	10	24	70	.281	.341	.235	7.78	2.67
Foss, Trevor	R-R	6-3	175	11-15-89	3	6	2.77	24	1	0	0	49	37	18	15	2	20	46	.219	.239	.206	8.51	3.70
Gordon, Grant	R-R	6-0	175	9-10-90	2	3	4.37	30	0	0	1	56	51	36	27	3	36	45	.245	.237	.252	7.28	5.82
Hurtado, Daniel	R-R	6-3	180	7-25-92	2	4	2.95	16	12	0	0	64	63	27	21	7	20	64	.267	.221	.293	9.00	2.81
Jimenez, Eswarlin	L-L	6-1	187	11-27-91	1	2	9.87	12	0	0	0	17	34	23	19	3	8	18	.415	.318	.450	9.35	4.15
Krehbiel, Joe	R-R	6-2	185	12-20-92	0	0	1.93	13	0	0	5	14	8	4	3	0	6	17	.163	.200	.125	10.93	3.86
Loconsole, Brian	R-R	6-2	215	8-10-90	5	4	1.68	34	0	0	3	70	53	20	13	1	16	51	.208	.167	.235	6.59	2.07
Mahle, Greg	L-L	6-2	230	4-17-93	0	1	3.38	18	0	0	1	29	20	12	11	1	12	38	.190	.237	.164	11.66	3.68
Morris, Elliot	R-R	6-4	210	4-26-92	2	1	2.25	8	7	0	0	40	29	14	10	2	13	44	.200	.213	.190	9.90	2.93
Muck, Ronnie	R-R	6-0	195	7-20-91	2	3	4.64	11	0	0	0	21	26	18	11	1	8	25	.286	.317	.260	10.55	3.38
Newcomb, Sean	L-L	6-5	240	6-12-93	0	1	6.94	4	4	0	0	12	13	9	9	1	5	15	.289	.250	.297	11.57	3.86
Nuss, Garrett	R-R	6-1	180	4-15-93	5	1	3.76	20	20	0	0	105	105	51	44	4	39	85	.265	.258	.269	7.26	3.33
Sharp, Clint	R-R	6-2	215	3-20-91	6	5	5.03	18	18	0	0	91	98	61	51	13	32	54	.275	.313	.252	5.32	3.15
Smith, Michael	R-R	6-0	195	1-31-90	3	2	4.05	15	0	0	0	27	25	13	12	4	7	25	.250	.294	.227	8.44	2.36
Swanson, Cole	L-L	6-5	200	4-5-92	1	3	4.35	37	0	0	0	50	35	24	24	4	23	69	.196	.176	.203	12.50	4.17
Trygg, Spencer	R-R	6-2	210	6-2-90	0	1	4.50	3	0	0	0	4	3	2	2	1	3	4	.200	.300	.000	9.00	6.75

Fielding

Catcher	PCT	G	PO	A	E	DP	PB
Bemboom	.993	18	117	22	1	2	1
Dalton	.857	2	5	1	1	0	0
McGee	.989	93	742	77	9	10	10
Moye	.983	36	272	18	5	2	6

First Base	PCT	G	PO	A	E	DP
Aguilera	.990	88	766	53	8	71
Bayardi	1.000	6	43	2	0	4
Dalton	.995	44	416	25	2	34
Gretzky	1.000	4	40	4	0	2
Shannon	1.000	1	1	0	0	0

Second Base	PCT	G	PO	A	E	DP
Dionicio	1.000	3	2	8	0	1

	PCT	G	PO	A	E	DP
Eaves	.949	126	196	359	30	72
Pellant	1.000	1	2	1	0	1
Salcedo	.978	12	17	28	1	9

Third Base	PCT	G	PO	A	E	DP
Dalton	.907	19	17	22	4	2
Dionicio	.926	29	21	54	6	3
Houchins	.944	21	21	30	3	4
Pellant	.667	4	0	6	3	1
Rosa	.907	73	61	144	21	17

Shortstop	PCT	G	PO	A	E	DP
Houchins	.941	5	6	10	1	3
Rosa	.953	22	32	70	5	19
Salcedo	.971	114	167	330	15	59

Outfield	PCT	G	PO	A	E	DP
Alberto	.968	93	173	11	6	3
Bayardi	.986	36	63	6	1	0
Cayones	.967	38	58	1	2	1
Dalton	1.000	5	9	1	0	0
Dionicio	1.000	3	4	1	0	0
Fish	.959	82	133	6	6	3
Gretzky	.982	41	53	1	1	0
Hinshaw	.991	57	108	3	1	1
Palmer	.981	27	51	0	1	0
Shannon	1.000	23	36	0	0	0
Way	1.000	27	57	3	0	1

AZL ANGELS

ROOKIE

ARIZONA LEAGUE

Batting	B-T	HT	WT	DOB	AVG	vLH	vRH	G	AB	R	H	2B	3B	HR	RBI	BB	HBP	SH	SF	SO	SB	CS	SLG	OBP
Abbott, Alex	L-R	5-11	187	11-2-94	.202	.138	.225	31	109	21	22	6	1	0	8	13	7	1	0	30	3	7	.275	.326
Armstrong, Patrick	R-R	6-1	210	7-16-91	.210	.226	.204	35	124	21	26	5	2	2	12	18	11	1	1	40	2	2	.331	.357
Bayardi, Brandon	R-R	6-2	235	11-27-90	.400	.500	.364	4	15	3	6	4	0	0	2	3	0	0	0	1	1	0	.667	.500
Bemboom, Anthony	R-R	6-2	190	1-18-90	.167	.000	.200	2	6	3	1	0	1	0	0	3	0	0	0	2	0	0	.500	.444
Everett, Dillon	R-R	6-0	190	1-27-92	.271	.353	.250	26	85	15	23	3	1	1	9	8	3	2	1	12	5	2	.365	.351
Gildea, Brandon	R-R	6-0	205	8-7-92	.321	.407	.281	25	84	12	27	4	3	0	12	5	2	0	0	18	6	2	.440	.374

LOS ANGELES ANGELS

Batting	B-T	HT	WT	DOB	AVG	vLH	vRH	G	AB	R	H	2B	3B	HR	RBI	BB	HBP	SH	SF	SO	SB	CS	SLG	OBP
Herrera, Jose	B-R	6-0	155	1-14-93	.269	.231	.283	41	145	20	39	9	1	1	23	11	1	1	1	28	1	5	.366	.323
Lavalli, Cody	R-R	6-4	190	1-22-92	.239	.167	.259	31	109	18	26	8	0	1	8	9	2	0	1	49	6	4	.339	.306
Lindsey, Taylor	L-R	6-0	195	12-2-91	.333	—	.333	1	3	1	1	0	0	0	0	1	0	0	0	0	0	0	.333	.500
Long, Matt	L-R	5-11	190	4-30-87	.333	.000	.500	1	3	0	1	0	0	0	0	1	1	0	0	0	0	0	.333	.500
Martinez, Mario	R-R	5-10	185	7-31-96	.186	.067	.218	23	70	7	13	2	0	0	7	6	2	—	1	24	0	0	.214	.266
Martinez, Ricky	R-R	6-2	180	11-30-95	.257	.289	.246	43	152	28	39	8	1	1	22	20	1	0	0	43	2	4	.342	.347
Mateo, Steven	R-R	6-2	188	8-19-92	.306	.303	.306	45	157	20	48	9	3	1	26	21	2	1	0	31	2	2	.420	.394
Moreno, Juan	R-R	6-1	160	11-17-94	.245	.353	.216	44	159	28	39	10	0	0	23	22	0	1	3	26	10	6	.308	.332
O'Malley, Shawn	R-R	5-11	165	12-28-87	.300	.250	.333	3	10	3	3	0	1	1	4	1	0	1	0	4	1	0	.800	.364
Perez, Ayendy	L-R	5-9	160	9-10-93	.279	.350	.259	48	183	35	51	7	4	0	14	14	0	6	2	31	16	3	.361	.327
Rodriguez, Jose	R-R	5-11	163	11-3-95	.209	.192	.213	35	115	10	24	4	1	0	15	10	1	1	2	36	1	2	.261	.273
Rondon, Jose	R-R	6-1	160	3-3-94	.125	—	.125	2	8	3	1	0	0	0	0	1	1	0	0	0	2	1	.125	.300
Seiz, Ryan	B-R	6-1	227	12-8-91	.000	.000	.000	3	9	0	0	0	0	0	1	1	0	0	1	6	0	0	.000	.091
Snyder, Mike	R-R	6-4	230	6-17-90	.353	.000	.462	5	17	2	6	1	0	2	2	2	0	0	0	7	1	0	.529	.421
Spivey, Eason	R-R	6-1	205	5-16-92	.125	.222	.097	12	40	1	5	1	0	0	4	2	0	1	0	14	0	0	.150	.167
Torres, Franklin	R-R	6-1	170	10-27-96	.254	.321	.233	32	114	12	29	1	2	0	11	17	0	0	1	27	3	3	.298	.348
Whitten, Fran	L-R	6-4	230	12-1-90	.343	.346	.341	28	108	27	37	7	3	2	19	14	3	0	2	30	5	1	.519	.425
Wiggins, Ryan	R-R	6-1	200	4-6-92	.282	.273	.286	15	39	5	11	2	1	0	8	7	1	0	1	16	0	1	.385	.396

Pitching	B-T	HT	WT	DOB	W	L	ERA	G	GS	CG	SV	IP	H	R	ER	HR	BB	SO	AVG	vLH	vRH	K/9	BB/9
Almonte, Yency	B-R	6-3	185	6-4-94	0	1	17.18	2	2	0	0	4	7	7	7	0	1	5	.467	.714	.250	12.27	2.45
Alonzo, Eric	B-R	6-2	210	8-28-91	2	1	2.01	16	0	0	1	31	31	12	7	1	9	27	.252	.241	.262	7.76	2.59
Alvarez, Jose	L-L	5-11	180	5-6-89	0	0	0.00	1	1	0	0	1	0	0	0	0	1	0	.000	—	.000	0.00	9.00
Anderson, Justin	L-R	6-3	190	9-28-92	0	0	5.14	2	2	0	0	7	9	4	4	0	3	6	.310	.313	.308	7.71	3.86
Boyd, Jake	R-R	6-5	200	1-6-90	0	0	0.00	3	0	0	0	4	4	0	0	0	0	2	.286	.000	.364	4.50	0.00
Carpenter, Tyler	R-R	6-5	225	2-25-92	1	0	0.00	2	0	0	0	3	1	0	0	0	0	3	.100	.200	.000	9.00	0.00
De La Rosa, Dane	R-R	6-7	245	2-1-83	0	0	13.50	2	1	0	0	2	2	3	3	1	0	2	.250	.500	.167	9.00	0.00
Etsell, Ryan	R-R	6-4	180	12-18-91	0	0	6.75	2	1	0	0	4	4	3	3	1	1	1	.286	.571	.000	2.25	2.25
Fitzgerald, Sean	R-R	6-2	178	12-24-91	0	0	27.00	1	0	0	0	2	1	1	0	0	1	0	1.000	1.000	1.000	0.00	0.00
Frye, Josh	R-R	6-7	215	10-23-91	1	1	8.04	17	0	0	0	28	32	26	25	0	18	27	.286	.295	.279	8.68	5.79
Gatto, Joe	R-R	6-3	204	6-14-95	2	1	5.40	10	6	0	0	25	33	17	15	1	9	15	.320	.378	.288	5.40	3.24
Jewell, Jake	R-R	6-3	200	5-16-93	1	0	1.48	9	6	0	0	30	23	6	5	0	12	26	.213	.220	.207	7.71	3.56
Kopra, Jacob	R-R	6-4	205	10-25-90	1	0	0.00	1	0	0	0	2	1	0	0	0	0	3	.143	.000	.167	13.50	0.00
Lopez, Eduar	R-R	6-0	180	2-21-95	0	3	4.68	11	8	0	0	42	41	27	22	1	25	53	.258	.338	.198	11.27	5.31
Maronde, Nick	B-L	6-3	205	9-5-89	0	0	4.50	2	0	0	0	2	1	0	2	1	0	4	.000	.000	.000	9.00	18.00
McCreery, Adam	L-L	6-8	195	12-31-92	1	1	4.58	15	0	0	0	20	12	11	10	0	19	21	.179	.125	.209	9.61	8.69
McGowin, Kyle	R-R	6-3	180	11-27-91	0	0	0.00	1	1	0	0	2	2	0	0	0	1	2	.250	.250	.250	9.00	4.50
Mendoza, Jose	R-R	6-2	165	7-29-94	3	6	5.89	12	10	0	0	55	81	48	36	6	11	28	.340	.367	.324	4.58	1.80
Miller, Zak	R-R	6-3	205	9-28-91	3	0	2.20	12	0	0	1	16	13	5	4	0	11	14	.220	.166	.275	7.71	6.06
Murillo, David	R-R	5-11	190	1-3-92	3	3	2.38	16	0	0	1	34	23	13	9	1	3	33	.178	.206	.168	8.74	0.79
Newby, Kyler	R-R	6-4	225	2-22-85	0	0	0.00	2	0	0	0	3	0	0	0	0	0	6	.000	.000	.000	18.00	0.00
Newcomb, Sean	L-L	6-5	240	6-12-93	0	0	3.00	2	2	0	0	3	3	1	1	1	1	3	.273	—	.273	9.00	3.00
Ortman, Dillon	R-R	6-2	198	6-13-92	3	0	0.93	10	0	0	1	19	18	8	2	0	3	15	.247	.214	.267	6.98	1.40
Petersen, Jake	L-L	6-4	205	4-12-91	0	0	0.00	2	0	0	1	2	1	0	0	0	0	2	.167	.500	.000	9.00	0.00
Piche, Jordan	R-R	6-1	180	9-3-91	1	0	0.79	8	0	0	0	11	11	4	1	0	2	11	.244	.300	.200	8.74	1.59
Rodriguez, Jose	R-R	6-2	155	8-29-91	2	1	4.85	9	4	0	1	26	34	15	14	1	5	29	.312	.270	.333	10.04	1.73
Sanchez, Ricardo	L-L	5-11	170	4-11-97	2	2	3.49	12	9	0	0	39	40	22	15	0	22	43	.258	.242	.262	10.01	5.12
Talley, Ryan	R-R	6-2	200	6-11-91	1	1	7.56	9	0	0	0	8	3	8	7	0	12	11	.111	.000	.158	11.88	12.96
Tromblee, Stephen	L-L	5-11	205	4-3-89	0	0	0.00	1	0	0	0	1	0	0	0	0	0	0	.000	.000	—	0.00	0.00
Wagner, Nick	R-R	6-3	210	10-26-90	2	0	2.75	16	0	0	2	20	14	7	6	0	4	32	.194	.161	.220	14.64	1.83
Watson, Tyler	L-L	5-11	160	6-9-93	1	1	3.97	15	0	0	0	23	20	13	10	1	8	32	.227	.120	.270	12.71	3.18
Wood, Austin	R-R	6-4	225	7-11-90	0	1	0.69	5	3	0	0	13	7	2	1	0	4	11	.149	.118	.167	7.62	2.77
Young, Austin	R-R	6-4	220	4-20-92	0	2	2.14	12	0	0	4	21	14	5	5	1	1	17	.179	.225	.132	7.29	0.43

Fielding

Catcher	PCT	G	PO	A	E	DP	PB
Bemboom	1.000	2	12	0	0	0	1
Gildea	.988	20	144	24	2	1	3
Martinez	.974	19	126	24	4	0	2
Spivey	.991	12	98	10	1	1	2
Wiggins	.976	10	71	10	2	0	2

First Base	PCT	G	PO	A	E	DP
Armstrong	1.000	11	96	6	0	9
Herrera	1.000	3	14	2	0	2
Mateo	.983	29	261	21	5	23
Seiz	.913	2	21	0	2	2
Snyder	1.000	4	37	3	0	2
Whitten	.986	12	128	8	2	10
Wiggins	1.000	1	1	0	0	0

Second Base	PCT	G	PO	A	E	DP
Everett	.980	21	35	65	2	13
Lindsey	1.000	1	1	0	0	1
Moreno	.956	24	48	83	6	14
Rodriguez	1.000	3	3	7	0	2
Torres	.917	9	11	22	3	7

Third Base	PCT	G	PO	A	E	DP
Everett	1.000	3	2	3	0	0
Herrera	.936	38	21	96	8	7
Moreno	.857	9	3	15	3	1
Rodriguez	.850	8	3	14	3	0

Shortstop	PCT	G	PO	A	E	DP
Moreno	.895	11	16	35	6	8
O'Malley	1.000	2	2	2	0	1
Rodriguez	.857	1	2	4	1	0
Rodriguez	.931	24	29	66	7	10
Rondon	1.000	2	4	9	0	2
Torres	.860	21	27	53	13	16

Outfield	PCT	G	PO	A	E	DP
Abbott	.979	31	44	3	1	0
Armstrong	.920	22	22	1	2	0
Bayardi	1.000	3	11	0	0	0
Lavalli	.938	30	28	2	2	0
Long	1.000	1	3	0	0	0
Martinez	.985	41	61	5	1	2
O'Malley	1.000	2	3	1	0	0
Perez	.947	48	85	4	5	1

OREM OWLZ   ROOKIE

PIONEER LEAGUE

Batting	B-T	HT	WT	DOB	AVG	vLH	vRH	G	AB	R	H	2B	3B	HR	RBI	BB	HBP	SH	SF	SO	SB	CS	SLG	OBP
Adams, Caleb	R-R	6-0	185	1-26-93	.252	.302	.236	61	210	37	53	9	2	7	28	21	2	1	1	70	7	1	.414	.325

	B-T	HT	WT	DOB	AVG	vLH	vRH	G	AB	R	H	2B	3B	HR	RBI	BB	HBP	SH	SF	SO	SB	CS	SLG	OBP
Daniel, Andrew	R-R	6-1	190	1-27-93	.340	.360	.335	63	259	49	88	20	3	6	39	23	8	1	2	42	13	3	.510	.408
Davis, Quinten	R-R	6-1	185	8-1-92	.274	.304	.267	36	124	20	34	7	2	5	18	6	1	2	0	24	2	3	.484	.313
Delgado, Natanael	L-L	6-1	170	10-23-95	.301	.250	.307	38	153	23	46	8	4	3	21	5	3	0	1	34	4	0	.464	.333
Everett, Dillon	R-R	6-0	190	1-27-92	.143	.286	.071	6	21	3	3	0	0	0	0	1	2	0	0	3	2	0	.143	.250
Gretzky, Trevor	L-L	6-4	190	9-14-92	.429	.000	.439	11	42	9	18	3	1	0	7	2	0	0	0	6	2	1	.548	.455
Hermosillo, Michael	R-R	5-9	190	1-17-95	.244	.351	.217	54	180	36	44	10	4	3	23	29	4	1	2	48	10	4	.394	.358
Houchins, Zach	R-R	6-3	185	9-16-92	.388	.455	.376	36	139	39	54	13	1	6	39	13	2	0	2	15	1	0	.626	.442
Linares, Raul	B-R	5-11	160	10-4-90	.270	.265	.272	50	196	35	53	12	5	3	33	22	0	1	2	33	7	3	.429	.341
Lindsey, Taylor	L-R	6-0	195	12-2-91	.200	—	.200	1	5	0	1	1	0	0	1	0	0	0	0	0	0	0	.400	.200
Long, Matt	L-R	5-11	190	4-30-87	.667	—	.667	1	3	2	2	0	1	1	1	2	0	0	0	1	1	0	2.333	.800
Moreno, Juan	R-R	6-1	160	11-17-94	.200	.286	.154	5	20	4	4	1	0	0	3	0	0	0	0	4	0	0	.250	.200
Palmer, Tyler	R-R	5-11	189	9-20-91	.300	.276	.308	34	120	27	36	8	2	2	17	11	3	1	2	16	10	1	.450	.368
Pizarro, Pedro	R-R	5-10	205	12-19-93	.193	.188	.195	16	57	7	11	0	0	2	9	1	1	0	0	14	0	0	.298	.220
Santigate, R.J.	L-R	6-3	195	5-25-91	.230	.188	.250	31	100	15	23	1	0	0	11	9	0	0	0	27	4	0	.240	.294
Seiz, Ryan	B-R	6-1	227	12-8-91	.261	.300	.248	39	165	35	43	8	2	8	31	12	0	1	3	51	0	2	.479	.306
Soto, Wendell	R-R	5-9	170	5-11-92	.259	.188	.277	50	162	30	42	6	1	6	27	26	1	7	4	37	2	1	.420	.358
Spivey, Eason	R-R	6-1	205	5-16-92	.208	.214	.206	15	48	10	10	2	0	0	8	14	0	0	0	7	0	0	.250	.387
Strentz, Michael	R-R	6-1	215	11-10-91	.330	.325	.331	43	176	29	58	15	2	4	29	6	3	0	1	41	6	1	.506	.360
Toribio, Pedro	R-R	5-10	158	7-21-90	.455	—	.455	3	11	4	5	0	0	0	1	1	0	0	0	3	4	1	.455	.500
Wass, Wade	R-R	6-0	210	9-23-91	.341	.423	.321	39	132	21	45	14	0	7	20	21	10	0	2	42	0	0	.606	.461
Way, Bo	L-L	6-0	180	11-17-91	.354	.400	.345	32	130	29	46	12	4	2	27	8	2	6	1	13	7	5	.554	.397
Whitten, Fran	L-R	6-4	230	12-1-92	.261	.171	.291	33	138	20	36	7	1	9	33	5	1	0	1	40	3	0	.522	.290
Yacinich, Jake	R-R	6-1	180	3-2-93	.176	.000	.188	6	17	5	3	1	0	0	2	4	1	0	0	6	1	0	.235	.364

Pitching	B-T	HT	WT	DOB	W	L	ERA	G	GS	CG	SV	IP	H	R	ER	HR	BB	SO	AVG	vLH	vRH	K/9	BB/9
Anderson, Justin	L-R	6-3	190	9-28-92	1	4	9.00	11	5	0	0	22	31	29	22	1	12	13	.316	.244	.377	5.32	4.91
Bolaski, Michael	R-R	6-3	185	2-5-92	5	3	4.52	13	12	0	0	68	62	40	34	4	32	51	.244	.308	.197	6.78	4.26
Carpenter, Tyler	R-R	6-5	225	2-25-92	0	0	3.74	10	0	0	1	22	26	11	9	2	2	15	.289	.366	.224	6.23	0.83
Ellis, Chris	R-R	6-4	190	9-22-92	0	1	6.89	9	2	0	0	16	17	12	12	2	8	16	.309	.280	.333	9.19	4.60
Fernandez, Arjenis	R-R	6-4	195	7-29-93	9	5	4.23	15	14	0	0	79	103	51	37	6	19	46	.316	.394	.263	5.26	2.17
Gatto, Joe	R-R	6-3	204	6-14-95	0	0	4.50	1	1	0	0	2	3	1	1	0	1	1	.375	.333	.400	4.50	0.00
Guerra, Angel	R-R	6-1	180	2-2-93	4	1	5.79	14	5	0	0	42	55	31	27	4	21	13	.313	.268	.351	2.79	4.50
Jewell, Jake	R-R	6-3	200	5-16-93	0	2	8.76	3	3	0	0	12	22	12	12	1	4	9	.386	.444	.333	6.57	2.92
Kipper, Jordan	R-R	6-4	185	10-6-92	3	2	2.73	14	0	0	0	26	26	10	8	1	8	21	.257	.341	.200	7.18	2.73
Klonowski, Alex	R-R	6-4	195	4-1-92	1	2	6.00	14	2	0	1	27	31	19	18	0	11	26	.290	.278	.296	8.67	3.67
Kopra, Jacob	R-R	6-4	205	10-25-90	0	0	3.60	14	0	0	4	15	16	6	6	2	5	15	.258	.261	.256	9.00	3.00
Mahle, Greg	L-L	6-2	230	4-17-93	1	1	0.00	5	0	0	1	8	5	5	0	0	3	11	.172	.125	.190	12.38	3.38
Middleton, Keynan	R-R	6-2	185	9-12-93	5	4	6.45	14	14	0	0	67	69	58	48	9	30	53	.260	.211	.298	7.12	4.03
Muck, Ronnie	R-R	6-0	195	8-23-91	1	0	1.84	8	0	0	0	15	10	4	3	2	0	23	.192	.316	.121	14.11	0.00
Ortman, Dillon	R-R	6-2	198	6-13-92	0	0	27.00	2	0	0	0	1	5	4	4	1	2	2	.625	.667	.600	13.50	13.50
Paredes, Eduardo	R-R	6-1	170	3-6-95	2	1	1.33	19	0	0	7	20	8	4	3	0	8	31	.114	.172	.073	13.72	3.54
Petersen, Jake	L-L	6-4	205	4-12-91	2	1	5.96	14	0	0	1	23	31	18	15	4	8	15	.326	.250	.373	5.96	3.18
Rhoades, Jeremy	R-R	6-4	225	2-12-93	2	1	4.42	14	7	0	0	39	43	25	19	3	15	40	.279	.267	.287	9.31	3.49
Robichaux, Austin	R-R	6-5	170	11-23-92	2	3	4.91	15	8	0	0	40	44	25	22	5	8	27	.286	.224	.333	6.02	1.79
Rodriguez, Nataniel	L-L	5-10	185	8-27-90	0	0	12.00	2	0	0	0	3	6	6	4	1	2	0	.400	.500	.364	0.00	6.00
Rodriguez, Ramon	R-R	6-0	180	9-20-93	2	1	2.80	19	0	0	0	35	32	16	11	2	17	39	.252	.169	.324	9.93	4.33
Varela, Zach	R-R	6-2	220	8-19-92	2	1	3.29	14	0	0	0	27	27	14	10	0	1	19	.250	.300	.221	6.26	0.33
Watson, Tyler	L-L	5-11	160	6-9-93	0	0	4.50	2	0	0	0	2	4	2	1	0	1	1	.444	.500	.429	4.50	4.50
Wesely, Jonah	L-L	6-2	205	12-8-94	0	0	4.08	16	2	0	2	35	29	19	16	3	18	38	.218	.149	.256	9.68	4.58

Fielding

Catcher	PCT	G	PO	A	E	DP	PB
Pizarro	.939	16	75	17	6	2	2
Spivey	.991	13	89	16	1	1	2
Strentz	.972	28	212	35	7	0	7
Wass	.973	20	126	18	4	0	6

First Base	PCT	G	PO	A	E	DP
Gretzky	.979	8	88	5	2	4
Santigate	1.000	1	3	0	0	0
Seiz	.979	35	351	19	8	31
Wass	.964	5	52	2	2	6
Whitten	.974	27	252	13	7	20

Second Base	PCT	G	PO	A	E	DP
Daniel	.976	57	103	178	7	43

	PCT	G	PO	A	E	DP
Everett	1.000	6	13	12	0	2
Linares	.948	12	22	33	3	7
Lindsey	1.000	1	3	2	0	0
Soto	—	1	0	0	0	0
Toribio	1.000	1	3	3	0	2

Third Base	PCT	G	PO	A	E	DP
Houchins	.923	25	25	71	8	10
Linares	.914	28	20	54	7	3
Santigate	.922	30	19	52	6	4

Shortstop	PCT	G	PO	A	E	DP
Daniel	.923	4	4	8	1	1
Houchins	.940	13	22	41	4	8
Moreno	.952	5	8	12	1	2

	PCT	G	PO	A	E	DP
Soto	.934	50	75	150	16	36
Toribio	.750	2	3	9	4	0
Yacinich	.774	6	5	19	7	1

Outfield	PCT	G	PO	A	E	DP
Adams	.950	61	88	8	5	0
Davis	.940	30	45	2	3	0
Delgado	.958	20	18	5	1	0
Hermosillo	.989	49	81	5	1	1
Linares	1.000	10	8	2	0	0
Long	1.000	1	2	0	0	0
Palmer	.981	32	52	1	1	0
Way	.909	31	37	3	4	0
Whitten	1.000	3	2	1	0	0

DSL ANGELS
ROOKIE

DOMINICAN SUMMER LEAGUE

Batting	B-T	HT	WT	DOB	AVG	vLH	vRH	G	AB	R	H	2B	3B	HR	RBI	BB	HBP	SH	SF	SO	SB	CS	SLG	OBP
Almao, Angel	R-R	5-10	145	11-5-94	.254	.231	.261	63	213	32	54	8	1	0	12	33	11	3	0	23	20	8	.300	.381
Arias, Jonathan	R-R	6-2	150	1-31-96	.308	.200	.330	32	117	13	36	4	2	0	8	2	3	1	0	17	4	6	.376	.336
Castillo, Deyvi	R-R	6-1	175	8-13-97	.238	.255	.232	52	202	20	48	9	1	0	21	13	2	1	1	41	13	5	.292	.289
Diaz, Argenis	R-R	6-2	160	9-17-96	.158	.143	.163	57	183	25	29	4	1	0	13	18	5	3	3	59	14	6	.191	.249
Garcia, Julio	R-R	6-0	175	7-31-97	.162	.083	.179	18	68	6	11	1	0	0	5	7	0	2	2	19	2	2	.176	.234
Garcia, Stevens	R-R	6-2	170	7-30-97	.181	.182	.180	35	83	8	15	1	0	0	6	8	0	—	1	44	1	0	.193	.250

Genao, Angel R-R 6-2 175 3-22-93 .296 .192 .319 45 142 18 42 7 1 1 16 14 2 0 1 26 7 2 .380 .365
Mills, Goldny B-R 5-11 170 12-11-95 .192 .216 .185 55 172 20 33 3 2 0 13 28 3 3 1 45 6 7 .233 .314
Molina, Angel R-R 6-0 175 8-20-97 .241 .200 .250 18 54 6 13 2 0 0 8 3 0 0 0 8 5 0 .278 .281
Mota, Darlyn B-R 6-1 165 8-2-96 .218 .214 .219 42 124 19 27 7 1 0 9 21 4 2 1 33 7 4 .290 .347
Pedie, Junior R-R 6-3 185 6-17-97 .193 .179 .196 58 192 25 37 10 1 0 21 24 2 2 5 71 6 5 .255 .283
Pina, Keinner R-R 5-10 165 2-12-97 .214 .243 .205 47 154 19 33 1 0 0 14 31 7 1 1 34 8 9 .221 .368
Richiez, Danny R-R 6-2 175 8-13-96 .208 .214 .207 29 96 14 20 6 1 0 7 16 2 2 0 41 9 3 .292 .333
Sanchez, Jeyson R-R 5-10 174 7-4-94 .219 .163 .232 66 224 32 49 12 1 1 23 32 13 0 4 26 12 2 .295 .344
Santana, Gabriel R-R 6-2 180 8-18-95 .248 .213 .257 64 234 32 58 6 1 6 30 21 6 1 2 28 11 6 .359 .323
Tejada, Miguel L-L 6-3 165 9-13-95 .095 .167 .067 11 21 2 2 1 0 0 1 7 0 0 0 8 1 0 .143 .321

Pitching	B-T	HT	WT	DOB	W	L	ERA	G	GS	CG	SV	IP	H	R	ER	HR	BB	SO	AVG	vLH	vRH	K/9	BB/9
Araujo, Cesar	R-R	6-2	160	6-17-97	1	0	7.58	14	0	0	0	19	24	18	16	2	18	16	.300	.192	.352	7.58	8.53
Barria, Jaime	R-R	6-1	180	7-18-96	4	4	3.03	16	8	0	1	59	57	27	20	1	11	55	.252	.372	.189	8.34	1.67
Galan, Lianmy	R-R	6-3	165	8-23-96	1	0	1.50	9	3	0	1	24	13	4	4	0	6	13	.157	.053	.244	4.88	2.25
Gonzalez, Raymundo	R-R	6-3	190	9-8-95	3	3	3.95	16	0	0	0	41	41	21	18	2	6	30	.263	.167	.298	6.59	1.32
Heredia, Andres	R-R	6-3	175	8-15-96	3	3	4.25	12	8	0	1	42	33	22	20	0	18	36	.216	.204	.222	7.65	3.83
Mieses, Crusito	R-R	6-5	190	4-18-96	3	6	1.83	13	12	0	0	64	46	21	13	0	24	56	.207	.172	.222	7.88	3.38
Molina, Cristopher	R-R	6-3	170	6-10-97	1	3	3.49	13	11	0	0	49	42	29	19	2	22	43	.228	.282	.195	7.90	4.04
Montilla, Anderson	R-R	6-4	180	10-23-95	0	1	33.75	2	0	0	0	1	3	5	5	0	3	2	.429	.000	.500	13.50	20.25
Pena, Luis	R-R	5-11	170	8-24-95	1	0	0.55	10	0	0	2	16	7	1	1	0	3	12	.130	.105	.143	6.61	1.65
Peralta, Alexis	R-R	6-3	170	11-3-96	1	2	4.84	15	0	0	1	22	22	13	12	0	20	27	.259	.265	.255	10.88	8.06
Pimentel, Yunior	L-L	6-4	180	9-9-94	4	5	4.24	15	13	0	1	70	64	35	33	2	34	57	.245	.210	.256	7.33	4.37
Pina, Shakiro	L-L	5-11	170	3-4-97	0	0	13.50	17	0	0	0	15	17	31	22	1	21	19	.274	.125	.326	11.66	12.89
Rondon, Manuel	L-L	6-1	165	3-7-95	0	5	2.30	14	14	0	0	67	59	30	17	3	25	66	.237	.244	.236	8.91	3.38
Rosales, Engerberg	L-L	6-1	160	4-16-96	0	0	6.91	11	0	0	0	14	10	11	11	1	20	16	.204	.182	.211	10.05	12.56
Rosario, Edisson	L-L	6-0	180	8-13-94	0	0	6.17	7	1	0	0	12	17	15	8	0	12	9	.333	.300	.341	6.94	9.26
Salomon, Franklin	L-L	5-11	160	3-17-95	0	2	3.48	6	0	0	0	10	10	5	4	0	5	13	.256	.167	.273	11.32	4.35
Terrero, Delfo	L-L	6-4	200	12-17-96	0	2	2.57	12	0	0	0	21	19	11	6	1	14	13	.241	.286	.231	5.57	6.00
Valdez, Alexander	R-R	6-0	175	1-28-94	7	2	2.38	24	0	0	5	42	37	15	11	0	10	41	.240	.276	.219	8.86	2.16
Yan, Jefry	L-L	6-3	170	8-17-96	2	1	7.92	17	0	0	3	25	34	27	22	3	13	17	.306	.238	.322	6.12	4.68

Fielding

Catcher	PCT	G	PO	A	E	DP	PB
Genao	.993	23	117	31	1	0	2
Molina	.988	10	74	11	1	2	2
Pina	.993	31	219	48	2	4	9
Sanchez	.993	15	120	18	1	2	3

First Base	PCT	G	PO	A	E	DP
Almao	1.000	1	13	1	0	1
Arias	.917	3	11	0	1	1
Castillo	—	1	0	0	0	0
Genao	—	1	0	0	0	0
Pina	1.000	4	24	1	0	2
Richiez	.929	1	12	1	1	0
Sanchez	.950	8	55	2	3	5
Santana	.989	57	490	32	6	40

Second Base	PCT	G	PO	A	E	DP
Almao	1.000	3	6	5	0	1
Arias	.951	10	19	20	2	1
Mills	.931	53	100	116	16	26
Mota	.949	14	27	29	3	6
Sanchez	.800	2	3	1	1	0

Third Base	PCT	G	PO	A	E	DP
Almao	.930	33	27	66	7	6
Arias	.861	9	11	20	5	1
Mota	1.000	2	1	0	0	0
Richiez	.887	23	21	34	7	7
Sanchez	.926	11	11	14	2	2

Shortstop	PCT	G	PO	A	E	DP
Almao	.944	17	23	45	4	5
Arias	.837	12	10	31	8	8
Garcia	.917	18	26	29	5	4
Mota	.891	30	50	65	14	13
Richiez	—	1	0	0	0	0

Outfield	PCT	G	PO	A	E	DP
Almao	.938	7	14	1	1	0
Arias	1.000	2	1	0	0	0
Castillo	.965	50	81	2	3	0
Diaz	.957	56	104	7	5	2
Garcia	.870	31	38	2	6	1
Genao	.957	10	21	1	1	1
Pedie	.908	58	80	9	9	4
Sanchez	.923	8	12	0	1	0
Tejada	1.000	9	8	2	0	1

Los Angeles Dodgers

SEASON IN A SENTENCE: A 94-win year wasn't good enough for the Dodgers, whose season ended in the playoffs against the Cardinals for the second straight season, this time in the National League Division Series thanks in part to a shaky bullpen.

HIGH POINT: After the all-star break, the Dodgers went 40-25, including a 17-8 mark in September to run away with their second straight National League West crown. Matt Kemp's second-half resurgence was critical to the Dodgers' success, as the outfielder hit .309/.365/.606 after the all-star break, with 17 of his 25 home runs in 64 games in the second half. The lineup had few holes when everyone was healthy, with Kemp, Yasiel Puig, Adrian Gonzalez and Hanley Ramirez each posting an OPS over .800. Zack Greinke and Clayton Kershaw anchored the pitching staff, while Josh Beckett threw a no-hitter on May 25.

LOW POINT: After Puig struggled in the first three games of the NLDS, manager Don Mattingly benched arguably the team's best hitter in Game 4, then used him as a pinch-runner instead of a pinch-hitter down 3-2 in the ninth inning as the Cardinals held on for the victory to eliminate the Dodgers from the postseason.

NOTABLE ROOKIES: Very few rookies played much for the Dodgers, who relied more on high-priced veterans than cost-controlled young talent. Miguel Rojas filled in at shortstop and provided stellar defense but had one of the lightest bats in the big leagues.

KEY TRANSACTIONS: Instead of dealing away their top prospects, the Dodgers held on to their blue-chip talent at the trade deadline. They did acquire righthander Roberto Hernandez from the Phillies in August in exchange for a pair of prospects at low Class A Great Lakes, second baseman Jesmuel Valentin and righthander Victor Arano.

DOWN ON THE FARM: The Dodgers have three of the best prospects in baseball, though the depth in the system thins out quickly after them.

Blocked by a crowded outfield in Los Angeles, Joc Pederson was left to rake in Triple-A Albuquerque, where he had a 30-30 season with 33 home runs, 30 stolen bases and a .305/.437/.586 slash line. Shortstop Corey Seager showed why he's one of the best hitters in the minors as he reached Double-A. Lefthander Julio Urias had little difficulty handling the high Class A California League, where he had a 2.36 ERA and 109 strikeouts in 88 innings despite not turning 18 until August.

OPENING DAY PAYROLL: $241,128,402 (1st)

PLAYERS OF THE YEAR

MAJOR LEAGUE	MINOR LEAGUE
Clayton Kershaw	**Corey Seager,**
lhp	**ss**
21-3, 1.77	(High Class A/
Led majors in ERA for	Double-A)
fourth year in a row	.349/.402/.602

).

ORGANIZATION LEADERS

BATTING		*Minimum 250 AB
MAJORS		
* AVG	Turner, Justin	.340
* OPS	Turner, Justin	.897
HR	Gonzalez, Adrian	27
RBI	Gonzalez, Adrian	116
MINORS		
* AVG	Seager, Corey, R. Cucamonga, Chattanooga	.349
* OBP	Pederson, Joc, Albuquerque	.435
* SLG	Seager, Corey, R. Cucamonga, Chattanooga	.602
R	Pederson, Joc, Albuquerque	106
H	Seager, Corey, R. Cucamonga, Chattanooga	166
TB	Seager, Corey, R. Cucamonga, Chattanooga	286
2B	Seager, Corey, R. Cucamonga, Chattanooga	50
3B	Schebler, Scott,Chattanooga	14
HR	Pederson, Joc,Albuquerque	33
RBI	Seager, Corey, R. Cucamonga, Chattanooga	97
BB	Pederson, Joc, Albuquerque	100
SO	Baldwin, James, Rancho Cucamonga	169
SB	Holland, Malcolm, Great Lakes	42

PITCHING		#Minimum 75 IP
MAJORS		
W	Kershaw, Clayton	21
# ERA	Kershaw, Clayton	1.77
SO	Kershaw, Clayton	239
SV	Jansen, Kenley	44
MINORS		
W	Windle, Tom, Rancho Cucamonga	12
L	Bird, Zachary, Great Lakes	17
# ERA	Bennett, Jeff, Albuquerque	3.83
G	Gonzalez, Juan, Chattanooga	54
GS	Reed, Chris, Chattanooga, Albuquerque	28
SV	Baez, Pedro, Chattanooga, Albuquerque	12
IP	Reed, Chris, Chattanooga, Albuquerque	158
BB	Martinez, Fabio, R. Cucamonga, Albuquerque	93
SO	Anderson, Chris, Rancho Cucamonga	146
AVG	Cotton, Jharel ,Rancho Cucamonga	.239

General Manager: Ned Coletti. **Farm Director:** De Jon Watson. **Scouting Director:** Logan White.

Class	Team	League	W	L	PCT	Finish	Manager
Majors	Los Angeles Dodgers	National	94	68	.580	4th (30)	Don Mattingly
Triple-A	Albuquerque Isotopes	Pacific Coast	62	80	.437	14th (16)	Damon Berryhill
Double-A	Chattanooga Lookouts	Southern	61	77	.442	8th (10)	Razor Shines
High A	Rancho Cucamonga Quakes	California	65	75	.464	8th (10)	P.J. Forbes
Low A	Great Lakes Loons	Midwest	66	73	.475	10th (16)	Bill Haselman
Rookie	Ogden Raptors	Pioneer	37	38	.493	6th (8)	Jack McDowell
Rookie	Dodgers	Arizona	25	31	.446	9th (13)	John Shoemaker
Overall Minor League Record			316	374	.458	26th (30)	

ORGANIZATION STATISTICS

LOS ANGELES DODGERS

NATIONAL LEAGUE

Batting	B-T	HT	WT	DOB	AVG	vLH	vRH	G	AB	R	H	2B	3B	HR	RBI	BB	HBP	SH	SF	SO	SB	CS	SLG	OBP
Arruebarrena, Erisbel	R-R	6-0	200	3-25-90	.195	.222	.188	22	41	4	8	1	0	0	4	3	0	0	1	17	0	0	.220	.244
Barney, Darwin	R-R	5-10	185	11-8-85	.303	.182	.364	22	33	6	10	1	0	1	7	8	3	0	1	3	0	0	.424	.467
2-team total (72 Chicago)					.241	—	—	94	237	24	57	11	2	3	23	17	4	2	2	34	1	0	.342	.300
Baxter, Mike	L-R	6-0	205	12-7-84	.000	.000	.000	4	7	0	0	0	0	0	0	1	0	0	0	2	0	0	.000	.125
Bernadina, Roger	L-L	6-2	200	6-12-84	.286	.000	.400	9	7	2	2	0	0	1	4	0	2	0	0	3	0	0	.714	.444
2-team total (44 Cincinnati)					.167	—	—	53	66	5	11	3	0	1	9	10	3	1	0	19	2	1	.258	.304
Butera, Drew	R-R	6-1	200	8-9-83	.188	.216	.180	61	170	16	32	6	1	3	14	17	2	1	2	41	0	0	.288	.267
Crawford, Carl	L-L	6-2	225	8-5-81	.300	.321	.296	105	343	56	103	14	3	8	46	16	6	0	4	55	23	6	.429	.339
Ellis, A.J.	R-R	6-3	220	4-9-81	.191	.215	.183	93	283	21	54	9	0	3	25	53	4	3	4	57	0	0	.254	.323
Ethier, Andre	L-L	6-2	225	4-10-82	.249	.222	.253	130	341	29	85	17	6	4	42	31	6	1	1	74	2	2	.370	.322
Federowicz, Tim	R-R	5-10	215	8-5-87	.113	.190	.080	23	71	2	8	3	0	1	5	3	1	2	1	18	0	0	.197	.158
Figgins, Chone	B-R	5-8	180	1-22-78	.217	.174	.243	38	60	8	13	3	0	0	1	14	1	1	0	15	4	1	.267	.373
Gonzalez, Adrian	L-L	6-2	225	5-8-82	.276	.201	.303	159	591	83	163	41	0	27	116	56	2	0	11	112	1	1	.482	.335
Gordon, Dee	L-R	5-11	170	4-22-88	.289	.295	.287	148	609	92	176	24	12	2	34	31	4	3	3	107	64	19	.378	.326
Guerrero, Alex	R-R	5-10	205	11-20-86	.077	.000	.143	11	13	0	1	0	0	0	0	0	0	0	0	6	0	0	.077	.077
Kemp, Matt	R-R	6-4	215	9-23-84	.287	.264	.295	150	541	77	155	38	3	25	89	52	0	0	6	145	8	5	.506	.346
Olivo, Miguel	R-R	6-0	230	7-15-78	.217	.000	.250	8	23	4	5	0	1	0	2	1	0	0	1	12	0	0	.304	.240
Pederson, Joc	L-L	6-1	185	4-21-92	.143	.000	.174	18	28	1	4	0	0	0	0	9	0	1	0	10	0	0	.143	.351
Puig, Yasiel	R-R	6-3	235	12-7-90	.296	.258	.307	148	558	92	165	37	9	16	69	67	12	2	1	124	11	7	.480	.382
Ramirez, Hanley	R-R	6-2	225	12-23-83	.283	.282	.283	128	449	64	127	35	0	13	71	56	6	0	1	84	14	5	.448	.369
Robinson, Clint	L-L	6-5	225	2-16-85	.333	.000	.429	9	9	3	3	0	0	0	2	1	0	0	0	1	0	0	.333	.400
Rojas, Miguel	R-R	6-0	150	2-24-89	.181	.061	.216	85	149	16	27	3	0	1	9	10	2	1	0	28	0	0	.221	.242
Romak, Jamie	R-R	6-2	220	9-30-85	.048	.000	.100	15	21	2	1	1	0	0	3	2	0	0	0	8	0	0	.095	.130
Triunfel, Carlos	R-R	5-11	195	2-27-90	.133	.000	.167	12	15	3	2	0	0	1	1	1	0	0	0	5	0	0	.333	.188
Turner, Justin	R-R	6-0	210	11-23-84	.340	.323	.349	109	288	46	98	21	1	7	43	28	4	0	2	58	6	1	.493	.404
Uribe, Juan	R-R	6-0	235	3-22-79	.311	.291	.317	103	386	36	120	23	0	9	54	15	1	0	2	77	0	1	.440	.337
Van Slyke, Scott	R-R	6-5	220	7-24-86	.297	.315	.279	98	212	32	63	13	1	11	29	28	4	0	2	71	4	2	.524	.386

Pitching	B-T	HT	WT	DOB	W	L	ERA	G	GS	CG	SV	IP	H	R	ER	HR	BB	SO	AVG	vLH	vRH	K/9	BB/9
Baez, Pedro	R-R	6-2	230	3-11-88	0	0	2.63	20	0	0	0	24	16	7	7	3	5	18	.188	.179	.196	6.75	1.88
Beckett, Josh	R-R	6-5	230	5-15-80	6	6	2.88	20	20	1	0	116	96	41	37	17	39	107	.226	.252	.198	8.33	3.03
Correia, Kevin	R-R	6-3	200	8-24-80	2	4	8.03	9	4	0	0	25	34	28	22	7	8	18	.324	.379	.255	6.57	2.92
Coulombe, Danny	L-L	5-10	185	10-26-89	0	0	4.15	5	0	0	0	4	5	3	2	1	2	4	.250	.375	.167	8.31	4.15
Dominguez, Jose	R-R	6-0	200	8-7-90	0	0	11.37	5	0	0	0	6	7	8	8	2	3	8	.269	.167	.357	11.37	4.26
Elbert, Scott	L-L	6-2	225	8-13-85	1	0	2.08	7	0	0	0	4	4	1	1	0	1	2	.235	.364	.000	4.15	2.08
Fife, Stephen	R-R	6-3	220	10-4-86	0	0	6.00	1	1	0	0	6	7	4	4	3	1	5	.280	.333	.231	7.50	1.50
Frias, Carlos	R-R	6-4	170	11-13-89	1	1	6.12	15	2	0	0	32	33	22	22	4	7	29	.254	.317	.200	8.07	1.95
Garcia, Yimi	R-R	6-1	175	8-18-90	0	0	1.80	8	0	0	0	10	6	2	2	2	1	9	.171	.077	.227	8.10	0.90
Greinke, Zack	R-R	6-2	195	10-21-83	17	8	2.71	32	32	0	0	202	190	69	61	19	43	207	.247	.246	.248	9.21	1.91
Haren, Dan	R-R	6-5	215	9-17-80	13	11	4.02	32	32	0	0	186	183	101	83	27	36	145	.252	.227	.277	7.02	1.74
Hernandez, Roberto	R-R	6-4	230	8-30-80	2	3	4.74	9	9	0	0	44	48	27	23	6	18	30	.282	.333	.225	6.18	3.71
2-team total (23 Philadelphia)					8	11	4.10	32	29	0	0	165	156	84	75	19	73	105	—	—	—	5.74	3.99
Howell, J.P.	L-L	6-0	185	4-25-83	3	3	2.39	68	0	0	0	49	31	14	13	2	25	48	.183	.170	.198	8.82	4.59
Jansen, Kenley	B-R	6-5	265	9-30-87	2	3	2.76	68	0	0	44	65	55	20	20	5	19	101	.224	.284	.169	13.91	2.62
Kershaw, Clayton	L-L	6-3	225	3-19-88	21	3	1.77	27	27	6	0	198	139	42	39	9	31	239	.196	.193	.197	10.85	1.41
League, Brandon	R-R	6-2	215	3-16-83	2	3	2.57	63	0	0	0	63	65	23	18	0	27	38	.278	.313	.260	5.43	3.86
Maholm, Paul	L-L	6-2	245	6-25-82	1	5	4.84	30	8	0	0	71	82	44	38	8	28	34	.297	.289	.301	4.33	3.57
Patterson, Red	R-R	6-3	220	11-5-87	0	0	1.93	1	1	0	0	5	2	1	1	0	3	1	.133	.125	.143	1.93	5.79
Perez, Chris	R-R	6-4	230	7-1-85	1	3	4.27	49	0	0	1	46	38	23	22	6	25	39	.228	.200	.247	7.58	4.86
Rodriguez, Paco	L-L	6-3	220	4-16-91	1	0	3.86	19	0	0	0	14	12	6	6	1	4	14	.250	.241	.263	9.00	2.57
Ryu, Hyun-Jin	L-L	6-2	255	3-25-87	14	7	3.38	26	26	0	0	152	152	60	57	8	29	139	.257	.283	.249	8.23	1.72
Wilson, Brian	R-R	6-1	205	3-16-82	2	4	4.66	61	0	0	1	48	49	26	25	5	29	54	.259	.297	.235	10.06	5.40
Withrow, Chris	R-R	6-4	215	4-1-89	0	0	2.95	20	0	0	0	21	10	8	7	1	18	28	.143	.000	.233	11.81	7.59
Wright, Jamey	R-R	6-6	240	12-24-74	5	4	4.35	61	1	0	1	70	72	35	34	3	27	54	.271	.238	.299	6.91	3.45

Fielding

Catcher	PCT	G	PO	A	E	DP	PB
Butera	1.000	57	434	30	0	2	9
Ellis	.995	92	737	68	4	4	2
Federowicz	.983	22	150	19	3	1	1
Olivo	.981	8	47	4	1	1	0

First Base	PCT	G	PO	A	E	DP
Butera	.800	1	4	0	1	0
Ethier	1.000	1	5	0	0	0
Gonzalez	.996	157	1318	118	6	118
Robinson	1.000	3	7	0	0	1
Romak	1.000	1	14	1	0	3
Turner	1.000	2	13	2	0	2
Van Slyke	.975	21	70	7	2	8

Second Base	PCT	G	PO	A	E	DP
Barney	.966	12	13	15	1	2

	PCT	G	PO	A	E	DP	PB
Figgins	1.000	5	3	13	0	3	
Gordon	.981	144	256	375	12	84	
Rojas	1.000	3	2	11	0	2	
Turner	.954	14	23	39	3	8	

Third Base	PCT	G	PO	A	E	DP
Figgins	.958	10	4	19	1	0
Rojas	.923	19	8	28	3	2
Romak	—	1	0	0	0	0
Turner	.961	59	23	99	5	10
Uribe	.979	102	60	215	6	25

Shortstop	PCT	G	PO	A	E	DP
Arruebarrena	.930	21	14	26	3	6
Barney	1.000	2	0	5	0	0
Figgins	1.000	2	1	0	0	0
Ramirez	.961	115	148	246	16	53

	PCT	G	PO	A	E	DP
Rojas	.973	66	41	101	4	25
Triunfel	.889	10	7	9	2	2
Turner	.922	15	11	36	4	4

Outfield	PCT	G	PO	A	E	DP
Baxter	1.000	1	3	0	0	0
Bernadina	—	4	0	0	0	0
Crawford	.978	94	132	1	3	0
Ethier	.994	92	153	1	1	0
Figgins	1.000	1	1	0	0	0
Guerrero	1.000	3	2	0	0	0
Kemp	.971	143	227	7	7	2
Pederson	1.000	12	16	0	0	0
Puig	.989	144	254	15	3	3
Rojas	—	1	0	0	0	0
Romak	1.000	3	3	0	0	0
Van Slyke	.977	60	83	1	2	0

ALBUQUERQUE ISOTOPES
TRIPLE-A
PACIFIC COAST LEAGUE

Batting	B-T	HT	WT	DOB	AVG	vLH	vRH	G	AB	R	H	2B	3B	HR	RBI	BB	HBP	SH	SF	SO	SB	CS	SLG	OBP
Arruebarrena, Erisbel	R-R	6-0	200	3-25-90	.333	.467	.259	26	84	7	28	3	2	1	11	10	0	0	1	26	1	1	.452	.400
Barney, Darwin	R-R	5-10	185	11-8-85	.257	.667	.219	9	35	5	9	1	0	0	1	3	0	0	0	5	0	0	.286	.316
Baxter, Mike	L-R	6-0	205	12-7-84	.289	.276	.295	119	412	72	119	25	8	7	36	45	0	—	3	87	12	5	.439	.365
Bernadina, Roger	L-L	6-2	200	6-12-84	.246	.273	.229	23	57	8	14	2	2	0	2	12	1	—	1	23	2	0	.351	.380
Buss, Nick	L-R	6-2	190	12-15-86	.261	.258	.262	26	92	12	24	3	3	1	16	8	2	1	1	22	2	3	.391	.330
2-team total (110 Sacramento)					.299	—	—	136	542	91	162	20	5	5	68	53	6	1	6	87	14	6	.382	.364
Cannon, John	R-R	6-0	180	5-11-90	.571	.000	.667	6	7	1	4	0	0	0	0	0	0	0	0	1	0	0	.571	.571
Cavazos-Galvez, Brian	R-R	6-0	215	5-17-87	.313	.200	.342	23	48	8	15	2	0	2	11	2	0	—	1	10	0	0	.479	.333
Crawford, Carl	L-L	6-2	225	8-5-81	.455	—	.455	4	11	4	5	0	2	0	1	0	0	0	0	2	1	1	.818	.455
Ellis, A.J.	R-R	6-3	220	4-9-81	.400	1.000	.250	2	5	1	2	0	0	1	2	1	0	0	0	1	0	0	1.000	.500
Erickson, Gorman	B-R	6-4	220	3-11-88	.297	.288	.301	60	155	19	46	10	1	7	29	21	1	1	0	31	1	1	.510	.384
Federowicz, Tim	R-R	5-10	215	8-5-87	.328	.418	.288	78	299	51	98	26	0	14	48	26	2	—	2	66	1	0	.555	.383
Figgins, Chone	B-R	5-8	180	1-22-78	.286	.321	.257	19	63	12	18	3	0	0	3	11	0	0	0	14	2	1	.333	.392
Grider, Casio	R-R	6-1	165	5-19-87	.286	.000	.364	5	14	3	4	2	1	0	3	2	0	—	0	7	0	0	.786	.375
Guerrero, Alex	R-R	5-10	205	11-20-86	.329	.397	.300	65	243	38	80	14	5	15	49	10	4	0	1	44	4	0	.613	.364
Harris, Brendan	R-R	6-1	200	8-26-80	.333	.667	.250	6	15	1	5	1	0	0	1	4	0	0	0	2	0	0	.400	.474
Hazelbaker, Jeremy	L-R	6-3	200	8-14-87	.222	.267	.200	22	90	12	20	3	2	4	11	2	0	0	0	27	6	2	.433	.239
Ibarra, Walter	B-R	5-11	180	11-1-87	.269	.207	.293	97	338	32	91	11	0	5	32	14	2	—	1	68	6	4	.346	.301
Liddi, Alex	R-R	6-4	225	8-14-88	.219	.188	.235	44	146	22	32	8	0	6	16	19	1	0	0	53	0	2	.397	.313
Meggs, Joe	R-R	6-0	195	4-30-90	.000	—	.000	1	1	0	0	0	0	0	0	0	0	0	0	0	0	0	.000	.000
Monell, Johnny	L-R	6-0	210	3-27-86	.261	.192	.281	38	115	11	30	8	1	3	17	10	0	0	1	24	3	0	.426	.317
Morales, Delvis	B-R	6-2	175	8-29-90	.269	.238	.283	29	67	7	18	3	0	0	7	10	2	—	0	14	1	1	.313	.380
Olivo, Miguel	R-R	6-0	210	7-15-78	.368	.360	.373	20	76	10	28	6	0	4	20	3	2	0	0	25	0	0	.605	.407
Pederson, Joc	L-L	6-1	185	4-21-92	.303	.299	.306	121	445	106	135	17	4	33	78	100	5	—	2	149	30	13	.582	.435
Peterson, Brock	R-R	6-3	230	11-20-83	.387	.476	.354	45	155	32	60	15	1	9	36	18	2	—	0	30	1	0	.671	.457
Robinson, Clint	L-L	6-5	225	2-16-85	.312	.261	.341	119	429	77	134	31	5	18	80	64	2	0	4	84	0	0	.534	.401
Robinson, Trayvon	B-R	5-10	200	9-1-87	.235	.276	.218	117	400	51	94	23	2	6	30	35	2	4	2	112	11	7	.348	.298
Rojas, Miguel	R-R	6-0	150	2-24-89	.302	.326	.292	51	159	27	48	9	0	4	13	10	3	0	1	21	7	3	.434	.353
Romak, Jamie	R-R	6-2	220	9-30-85	.280	.292	.276	108	418	65	117	30	3	24	85	34	4	—	6	107	4	1	.538	.335
Triunfel, Carlos	R-R	5-11	195	2-27-90	.223	.235	.219	89	300	28	67	12	4	4	40	12	2	4	3	55	2	1	.330	.256

Pitching	B-T	HT	WT	DOB	W	L	ERA	G	GS	CG	SV	IP	H	R	ER	HR	BB	SO	AVG	vLH	vRH	K/9	BB/9
Abreu, Juan	R-R	6-0	185	4-8-85	0	0	7.11	8	0	0	0	6	9	5	5	0	7	4	.346	.300	.375	5.68	9.95
Baez, Pedro	R-R	6-0	230	3-11-88	0	0	4.76	23	0	0	6	23	27	12	12	4	4	20	.303	.448	.233	7.94	1.59
Bennett, Jeff	R-R	6-3	200	6-10-80	8	6	3.83	21	21	1	0	120	137	63	51	11	44	82	.287	.332	.245	6.15	3.30
Billings, Bruce	R-R	6-0	210	11-18-85	1	1	6.75	5	0	0	0	15	26	13	11	2	8	16	.394	.406	.382	9.82	4.91
Carpenter, Drew	R-R	6-3	240	5-18-85	3	1	7.74	16	6	0	1	48	67	49	41	3	20	40	.332	.338	.328	7.55	3.78
Carson, Robert	L-L	6-4	240	1-23-89	2	5	5.40	18	0	0	0	25	35	18	15	3	12	30	.315	.256	.353	10.80	4.32
2-team total (14 Salt Lake)					2	6	7.30	32	0	0	0	41	58	36	33	5	25	39	—	—	—	8.63	5.39
Demel, Sam	R-R	6-0	210	10-23-85	1	2	6.41	21	0	0	5	46	55	33	33	9	18	43	.294	.309	.278	8.35	3.50
Dominguez, Jose	R-R	6-0	200	8-7-90	1	2	3.24	31	0	0	10	33	31	15	12	1	18	39	.244	.228	.257	10.53	4.86
Edlefsen, Steve	B-R	6-2	195	6-27-85	0	1	11.88	6	0	0	0	8	15	11	11	0	10	2	.417	.563	.300	2.16	10.80
Elbert, Scott	L-L	6-2	195	8-13-85	0	2	4.91	18	0	0	0	15	17	10	8	2	7	15	.304	.421	.243	9.20	4.30
Enright, Barry	R-R	6-3	220	3-30-86	0	4	8.10	8	5	0	0	33	53	31	30	8	8	16	.366	.318	.405	4.32	2.16
Fife, Stephen	R-R	6-3	220	10-4-86	2	2	7.01	11	9	0	0	44	65	35	34	2	15	27	.351	.310	.377	5.56	3.09
Frias, Carlos	R-R	6-4	210	11-13-89	8	4	5.01	16	15	2	0	92	114	57	51	4	21	65	.307	.314	.301	6.38	2.06
Garcia, Yimi	R-R	6-1	175	8-18-90	4	2	3.10	47	0	0	5	61	58	23	21	5	18	69	.249	.323	.200	10.18	2.66
Germano, Justin	R-R	6-2	210	8-6-82	1	1	9.88	3	2	0	0	14	20	15	15	4	2	14	.339	.424	.231	9.22	1.32
2-team total (21 Round Rock)					5	14	5.02	24	23	3	0	145	165	87	81	26	24	96	—	—	—	5.94	1.49
Hynes, Colt	L-L	5-11	200	6-28-85	1	3	4.08	42	0	0	2	53	56	25	24	6	10	46	.271	.261	.277	7.81	1.70
Judy, Josh	R-R	6-4	210	2-9-86	2	2	5.79	23	0	0	2	28	35	20	18	1	8	24	.315	.396	.241	7.71	2.57
Lee, Zach	R-R	6-3	195	9-13-91	7	13	5.38	28	27	0	0	151	177	105	90	18	54	97	.297	.273	.317	5.79	3.23

Player	B-T	HT	WT	DOB	W	L	ERA	G	GS	CG	SV	IP	H	R	ER	HR	BB	SO	AVG	vLH	vRH	K/9	BB/9
Magill, Matt	R-R	6-3	210	11-10-89	7	6	5.21	36	12	0	0	85	80	53	49	8	59	70	.254	.283	.229	7.44	6.27
Martinez, Fabio	R-R	6-3	190	10-29-89	1	0	3.18	5	0	0	0	6	6	4	2	0	2	3	.300	.182	.444	4.76	3.18
Moskos, Daniel	R-L	6-1	200	4-28-86	1	0	6.52	9	0	0	0	10	10	7	7	0	5	8	.270	.353	.200	7.45	4.66
Patterson, Red	R-R	6-3	220	5-11-87	5	8	5.79	29	20	0	1	121	140	79	78	21	43	104	.293	.291	.294	7.71	3.19
Ravin, Josh	R-R	6-5	225	1-21-88	1	0	4.22	11	0	0	2	11	12	6	5	1	7	8	.286	.368	.217	6.75	5.91
Reed, Chris	L-L	6-4	195	5-20-90	0	3	10.97	5	5	0	0	21	37	28	26	5	11	18	.378	.350	.385	7.59	4.64
Rodriguez, Paco	L-L	6-3	220	4-16-91	2	3	4.40	32	0	0	1	29	25	16	14	4	17	35	.231	.224	.240	10.99	5.34
Smith, Steve	R-R	6-2	215	5-15-86	2	4	7.32	21	6	0	0	63	81	52	51	16	23	37	.312	.325	.301	5.31	3.30
Sosa, Henry	R-R	6-1	210	7-28-85	1	2	3.72	7	7	0	0	36	39	21	15	1	12	27	.273	.296	.258	6.69	2.97
Souza, Justin	R-R	6-1	185	10-22-85	1	1	7.13	12	0	0	0	18	24	14	14	3	4	12	.333	.424	.256	6.11	2.04
Struck, Nick	R-R	6-0	205	10-7-89	0	1	5.63	2	1	0	0	8	13	6	5	2	0	2	.394	.333	.467	2.25	0.00

Fielding

Catcher	PCT	G	PO	A	E	DP	PB
Cannon	1.000	1	6	1	0	0	0
Ellis	1.000	2	21	2	0	0	0
Erickson	.982	39	253	14	5	0	2
Federowicz	.987	69	476	56	7	6	5
Monell	.991	16	106	10	1	0	4
Olivo	.971	18	118	16	4	1	4

First Base	PCT	G	PO	A	E	DP
Erickson	1.000	1	2	0	0	0
Liddi	1.000	2	20	0	0	1
Monell	.975	6	33	6	1	8
Peterson	.992	29	231	15	2	29
Robinson	.994	99	874	65	6	92
Romak	1.000	11	96	6	0	11

Second Base	PCT	G	PO	A	E	DP
Arruebarrena	1.000	3	8	10	0	3
Figgins	1.000	8	13	0	1	
Grider	.944	5	6	11	1	2
Guerrero	.973	51	81	138	6	37
Harris	1.000	1	4	1	0	0

Ibarra	.994	42	67	108	1	25
Morales	.976	24	29	54	2	15
Rojas	.978	8	14	30	1	5
Triunfel	.954	24	29	74	5	20

Third Base	PCT	G	PO	A	E	DP
Arruebarrena	1.000	4	2	11	0	2
Barney	.600	3	1	2	2	2
Figgins	1.000	5	2	10	0	0
Guerrero	—	1	0	0	0	0
Harris	1.000	2	0	3	0	0
Ibarra	.933	5	3	11	1	0
Liddi	.943	34	18	65	5	10
Rojas	1.000	16	12	29	0	4
Romak	.921	77	33	118	13	9
Triunfel	1.000	7	2	10	0	1

Shortstop	PCT	G	PO	A	E	DP
Arruebarrena	.965	18	27	55	3	12
Barney	.906	6	10	19	3	6
Figgins	1.000	4	9	16	0	7
Guerrero	1.000	4	2	8	0	1

Ibarra	.969	42	68	122	6	27
Morales	1.000	2	4	2	0	1
Rojas	1.000	23	30	57	0	12
Triunfel	.965	59	86	159	9	40

Outfield	PCT	G	PO	A	E	DP
Baxter	.978	109	171	11	4	0
Bernadina	.958	17	22	1	1	0
Buss	.974	23	36	2	1	0
Cavazos-Galvez	.813	13	11	2	3	0
Crawford	1.000	4	4	0	0	0
Figgins	.857	4	5	1	1	0
Guerrero	1.000	9	11	1	0	0
Hazelbaker	1.000	20	35	1	0	1
Liddi	1.000	2	2	1	0	0
Pederson	.974	117	257	7	7	3
Peterson	1.000	11	15	0	0	0
Robinson	1.000	2	5	0	0	0
Robinson	.986	103	206	1	3	0
Romak	.970	20	30	2	1	0

CHATTANOOGA LOOKOUTS

DOUBLE-A

SOUTHERN LEAGUE

Batting	B-T	HT	WT	DOB	AVG	vLH	vRH	G	AB	R	H	2B	3B	HR	RBI	BB	HBP	SH	SF	SO	SB	CS	SLG	OBP
Adams, Ryan	R-R	5-11	185	4-21-87	.312	.278	.318	44	125	21	39	12	0	1	10	9	3	0	0	26	0	1	.432	.372
Arruebarrena, Erisbel	R-R	6-0	200	3-25-90	.208	.143	.220	25	96	10	20	4	1	1	6	4	2	2	1	31	0	0	.302	.252
Bates, Aaron	R-R	6-4	230	3-10-84	.176	.333	.091	11	17	1	3	2	0	0	4	0	0	0	4	0	0	.294	.333
Boscan, J.C.	R-R	6-2	215	12-26-79	.168	.190	.164	52	131	11	22	6	0	1	7	15	1	0	0	32	1	0	.237	.259
Cavazos-Galvez, Brian	R-R	5-11	215	5-17-87	.227	.345	.206	64	194	16	44	12	1	2	20	8	1	0	0	32	4	2	.330	.261
Coyle, Bobby	L-L	6-1	215	3-6-89	.289	.292	.288	47	142	17	41	9	1	5	20	6	0—	3	23	0	0	.472	.311
Cuevas, Noel	R-R	6-2	187	10-2-91	.231	.231	.231	131	425	50	98	12	9	7	44	31	—	1	92	6	3	.351	.285
Dickson, O'Koyea	R-R	5-11	215	2-9-90	.269	.177	.288	126	461	71	124	36	3	17	73	38	14—	5	67	5	6	.471	.340
Garcia, Jon	R-R	5-11	175	11-11-91	.071	.000	.111	9	28	3	2	1	0	0	5	0	0	6	0	0	.143	.212
Grider, Casio	R-R	6-1	165	8-17-87	.195	.200	.195	51	128	17	25	1	1	3	10	12	3	1	0	49	9	3	.289	.280
Hazelbaker, Jeremy	L-R	6-3	200	8-14-87	.251	.275	.247	87	271	31	68	9	8	4	33	30	0—	0	70	15	7	.387	.326
Ibarra, Walter	B-R	5-11	180	11-1-87	.222	.000	.240	7	27	3	6	2	0	0	5	2	0	0	7	0	1	.296	.276
Liddi, Alex	R-R	6-4	225	8-14-88	.216	.161	.235	36	116	16	25	4	2	2	12	13	2—	1	47	2	2	.336	.303
Martinez, Ozzie	R-R	5-10	200	5-7-88	.176	.091	.198	33	108	10	19	2	1	2	11	9	1	2	2	20	1	0	.269	.242
Mayora, Daniel	R-R	5-11	175	7-27-85	.302	.325	.298	131	493	69	149	27	4	9	75	43	4—	10	63	6	4	.428	.356
O'Brien, Chris	B-R	6-0	219	7-24-89	.266	.246	.270	116	354	33	94	32	4	7	53	41	3—	7	66	3	0	.438	.341
Oguisten, Faustino	R-R	6-2	165	1-17-91	.000	.000	.000	1	2	0	0	0	0	0	0	0	0	1	0	0	.000	.000
Rosario, Alberto	R-R	5-10	190	1-10-87	.277	.231	.294	25	47	3	13	1	0	1	7	3	0	0	15	0	0	.362	.320
Sanchez, Angel	R-R	6-1	205	9-20-83	.251	.182	.273	54	183	19	46	6	2	2	16	12	1	2	3	27	0	0	.339	.296
Schebler, Scott	L-R	6-1	208	10-6-90	.280	.282	.280	135	489	82	137	23	14	28	73	45	22—	3	110	10	4	.556	.365
Seager, Corey	L-R	6-4	215	4-27-94	.345	.244	.383	38	148	28	51	16	3	2	27	10	0	1	2	39	1	1	.534	.381
Songco, Angelo	L-R	6-0	190	9-9-88	.000	.—	.000	3	12	0	0	0	0	0	0	1	0	0	6	0	0	.000	.077
Sweeney, Darnell	B-R	6-1	180	2-1-91	.288	.279	.290	132	490	88	141	34	5	14	57	77	5—	4	117	15	16	.463	.387

Pitching	B-T	HT	WT	DOB	W	L	ERA	G	GS	CG	SV	IP	H	R	ER	HR	BB	SO	AVG	vLH	vRH	K/9	BB/9
Baez, Pedro	R-R	6-2	230	3-11-88	2	1	2.79	17	0	0	6	19	15	7	6	0	9	18	.208	.143	.235	8.38	4.19
Brummett, Tyson	R-R	6-0	185	8-15-84	4	5	2.79	14	13	0	0	71	69	29	22	2	21	57	.246	.300	.206	7.23	2.66
Cabrera, Freddie	R-R	6-5	210	1-25-90	0	1	2.70	12	1	0	0	23	23	9	7	0	6	9	.261	.241	.271	3.47	2.31
Carson, Robert	L-L	6-4	240	1-23-89	1	1	2.12	11	0	0	2	17	15	7	4	3	7	14	.242	.250	.239	7.41	3.71
Cash, Ralston	R-R	6-3	215	8-20-91	0	0	3.24	6	0	0	0	8	5	3	3	0	6	10	.179	.222	.158	10.80	6.48
Coulombe, Danny	L-L	5-10	185	10-26-89	0	0	2.57	18	0	0	1	21	18	9	6	1	10	31	.231	.250	.217	13.29	4.29
Eadington, Eric	R-L	6-2	220	2-9-88	0	0	3.38	5	0	0	0	8	6	3	3	1	7	8	.214	.333	.182	9.00	7.88
Frias, Carlos	R-R	6-4	170	11-13-89	2	1	3.38	5	5	0	0	32	34	16	12	2	9	14	.274	.262	.280	3.94	2.53
Gonzalez, Juan	R-R	6-2	200	4-5-90	4	8	3.34	54	0	0	0	70	65	34	26	2	47	48	.245	.225	.256	6.17	6.04
Gould, Garrett	R-R	6-2	190	7-19-91	1	6	7.34	16	11	0	0	61	81	54	50	12	28	41	.308	.263	.335	6.02	4.11
Kehrt, Jeremy	R-R	6-2	190	12-21-85	2	0	1.69	5	4	0	0	21	18	5	4	0	7	8	.231	.227	.232	3.38	2.95
Kershaw, Clayton	L-L	6-3	225	3-19-88	0	0	1.80	1	1	0	0	5	6	2	1	0	2	9	.286	.167	.333	16.20	3.60

LOS ANGELES DODGERS

	B-T	HT	WT	DOB	W	L	ERA	G	GS	CG	SV	IP	H	R	ER	HR	BB	SO	AVG	vLH	vRH	K/9	BB/9
Marinez, Jhan	R-R	6-1	200	8-12-88	7	1	4.91	21	0	0	0	22	19	15	12	1	11	25	.232	.407	.145	10.23	4.50
Martin, Jarret	L-L	6-3	230	8-14-89	1	1	3.29	46	0	0	7	55	34	22	20	1	48	64	.182	.194	.176	10.54	7.90
Nelo, Hector	R-R	6-1	205	11-5-86	1	0	6.97	21	0	0	0	31	41	28	24	4	19	32	.306	.302	.309	9.29	5.52
2-team total (5 Pensacola)					1	0	6.98	26	0	0	0	39	50	36	30	5	23	41	—	—	—	9.54	5.35
Noriega, Juan	R-R	5-7	145	9-3-90	5	5	3.58	39	0	1	50	49	25	20	1	17	46	.257	.274	.248	8.23	3.04
Ravin, Josh	R-R	6-5	225	1-21-88	1	1	3.07	12	0	0	4	15	12	7	5	1	7	17	.218	.238	.206	10.43	4.30
Reed, Chris	L-L	6-4	195	5-20-90	4	8	3.22	23	23	0	0	137	114	70	49	10	55	116	.226	.260	.217	7.62	3.61
Sanchez, Raydel	R-R	6-3	180	3-11-90	2	6	5.79	16	13	0	0	65	70	43	42	11	25	26	.278	.347	.236	3.58	3.44
Santiago, Andres	R-R	6-1	218	10-26-89	6	8	4.47	26	24	1	0	129	131	77	64	16	53	98	.263	.256	.267	6.84	3.70
Shelton, Matt	R-R	6-4	205	11-30-88	4	4	4.15	27	16	0	1	87	83	50	40	7	47	74	.253	.263	.248	7.68	4.88
Slama, Anthony	R-R	6-3	195	1-6-84	0	2	6.00	5	0	0	0	6	13	6	4	0	3	6	.419	.250	.478	9.00	4.50
Smith, Blake	L-R	6-2	225	12-9-87	1	4	4.05	26	0	0	2	33	35	19	15	2	16	33	.263	.300	.247	8.91	4.32
Smith, Steve	R-R	6-2	215	5-15-86	3	2	2.76	8	7	2	0	46	36	16	14	1	15	28	.208	.262	.179	5.52	2.96
Stem, Craig	R-R	6-5	215	1-5-90	0	3	8.06	19	0	0	0	26	36	24	23	0	19	19	.360	.389	.344	6.66	6.66
Struck, Nick	R-R	6-0	205	10-7-89	5	6	5.47	21	19	0	0	100	119	65	61	7	45	58	.299	.331	.278	5.20	4.03
Thomas, Mike	L-L	6-2	185	1-6-89	4	3	2.73	48	0	0	3	59	51	22	18	3	41	76	.239	.307	.203	11.53	6.22
von Schamann, Duke	R-R	6-5	220	6-3-91	1	0	0.00	1	1	0	0	7	2	0	0	0	0	2	.083	.000	.133	2.57	0.00

Fielding

Catcher	PCT	G	PO	A	E	DP	PB
Boscan	.982	42	293	36	6	0	4
O'Brien	.990	102	652	74	7	8	11
Rosario	.981	11	41	10	1	0	0

First Base	PCT	G	PO	A	E	DP
Bates	.909	1	10	0	1	2
Cavazos-Galvez	1.000	6	48	1	0	5
Coyle	1.000	1	9	0	0	1
Dickson	.983	116	978	76	18	72
Liddi	.984	14	118	8	2	17
Mayora	.952	3	19	1	1	2
Songco	1.000	1	6	1	0	1

Second Base	PCT	G	PO	A	E	DP
Adams	.939	25	45	47	6	4
Grider	.979	15	18	28	1	7
Ibarra	.960	5	10	14	1	3

Martinez	1.000	2	5	2	0	0
Mayora	.978	8	17	28	1	9
Oguisten	.667	1	2	0	1	0
Sanchez	.986	21	26	46	1	8
Sweeney	.958	81	164	197	16	48

Third Base	PCT	G	PO	A	E	DP
Adams	.333	5	0	1	2	0
Grider	1.000	2	0	1	0	0
Liddi	.880	11	11	11	3	1
Martinez	.912	11	10	21	3	2
Mayora	.935	119	76	256	23	26

Shortstop	PCT	G	PO	A	E	DP
Arruebarrena	.962	25	31	71	4	14
Grider	.875	5	4	3	1	2
Ibarra	.917	2	2	9	1	2
Martinez	.934	23	28	57	6	9

Sanchez	.959	32	32	85	5	12
Seager	.938	35	54	96	10	26
Sweeney	.897	28	44	61	12	11

Outfield	PCT	G	PO	A	E	DP
Bates	.857	5	5	1	1	0
Cavazos-Galvez	.944	39	64	3	4	0
Coyle	1.000	28	44	3	0	1
Cuevas	.978	125	262	10	6	1
Dickson	1.000	2	3	0	0	0
Garcia	1.000	8	10	1	0	0
Grider	.964	24	26	1	1	0
Hazelbaker	.974	75	146	4	4	1
O'Brien	—	2	0	0	0	0
Schebler	.972	132	233	8	7	2
Sweeney	.922	23	46	1	4	0

RANCHO CUCAMONGA QUAKES   HIGH CLASS A

CALIFORNIA LEAGUE

Batting	B-T	HT	WT	DOB	AVG	vLH	vRH	G	AB	R	H	2B	3B	HR	RBI	BB	HBP	SH	SF	SO	SB	CS	SLG	OBP
Arruebarrena, Erisbel	R-R	6-0	200	3-25-90	.245	.400	.227	12	49	8	12	4	1	2	11	2	0	0	3	24	1	0	.490	.259
Baldwin III, James	L-R	6-3	205	10-10-91	.217	.207	.220	112	374	62	81	20	6	14	43	36	4	4	1	169	28	4	.414	.292
Capellan, Jose	R-R	6-0	210	10-10-90	.210	.167	.228	25	81	7	17	3	0	0	4	7	0	1	1	20	1	0	.247	.270
Dixon, Brandon	R-R	6-2	215	1-29-92	.262	.221	.272	94	390	59	102	23	4	9	46	12	2	8	4	103	8	7	.410	.284
Farmer, Kyle	R-R	6-0	200	8-17-90	.238	.162	.269	36	130	8	31	5	1	0	15	10	3	2	1	28	2	0	.292	.306
Garcia, Jon	R-R	5-11	175	11-11-91	.214	.064	.262	46	192	27	41	9	0	11	29	7	0	0	2	56	0	0	.432	.239
Garvey, Robbie	L-L	5-8	165	4-26-89	.229	.187	.240	114	424	69	97	15	10	7	45	32	6	13	3	105	22	5	.361	.290
Grider, Casio	R-R	6-1	165	8-17-87	.217	.243	.205	29	115	16	25	5	1	2	8	7	1	1	0	32	10	1	.330	.268
Guerrero, Alex	R-R	5-10	205	11-20-86	.368	.400	.357	5	19	3	7	4	1	0	2	2	0	0	0	2	0	0	.684	.429
Jacobs, Chris	R-R	6-5	257	11-25-88	.266	.276	.263	126	451	68	120	28	1	25	94	75	17	0	5	117	1	2	.499	.387
Law, Adam	R-R	6-0	193	2-5-90	.273	.221	.289	106	403	65	110	20	2	0	37	41	9	10	5	69	19	10	.333	.349
Maynard, Pratt	L-R	6-0	215	11-19-89	.282	.303	.277	49	174	15	49	19	1	2	27	19	0	1	3	38	0	0	.437	.347
McDonald, James	B-R	5-10	170	12-16-91	.211	.125	.273	6	19	3	4	2	0	0	2	0	0	0	0	5	0	0	.316	.211
Miller, Aaron	L-L	6-3	200	9-18-87	.257	.175	.279	102	374	53	96	28	6	14	60	51	5	0	4	123	2	0	.476	.350
Morales, Delvis	B-R	6-2	175	8-29-90	.333	.333	—	1	3	0	1	0	0	0	0	1	0	0	0	1	0	0	.333	.500
Moyer, Dillon	R-R	6-0	200	7-18-91	.205	.179	.213	37	117	9	24	6	0	1	7	9	4	3	0	38	0	1	.282	.285
Ogle, Tyler	R-R	5-10	210	8-9-90	.273	.208	.297	81	267	40	73	15	2	7	54	44	4	1	1	59	0	1	.423	.383
Proscia, Steve	R-R	6-2	210	6-26-90	.233	.214	.238	115	430	50	100	19	2	14	60	30	8	3	6	104	9	3	.384	.291
Rathjen, Jeremy	R-R	6-5	195	1-28-90	.269	.250	.276	92	342	54	92	20	2	16	44	39	5	9	3	93	9	2	.480	.350
Rodriguez, Leo	R-R	5-11	160	12-11-91	.313	.211	.356	35	128	16	40	2	1	0	6	5	0	1	1	13	1	1	.344	.336
Seager, Corey	L-R	6-4	215	4-27-94	.352	.400	.337	80	327	61	115	34	2	18	70	30	5	0	3	76	5	1	.633	.411
Turner, Justin	R-R	6-0	210	11-23-84	.200	.000	1.000	5	1	1	0	0	0	0	0	2	0	0	0	0	0	0	.200	.429
Uribe, Juan	R-R	6-0	235	3-22-79	.316	.111	.500	5	19	4	6	2	0	0	3	0	0	0	0	2	0	0	.421	.316
Wingo, Scott	L-R	5-11	175	3-25-89	.091	.000	.100	5	11	1	1	0	0	0	0	0	0	0	0	3	0	0	.091	.286

Pitching	B-T	HT	WT	DOB	W	L	ERA	G	GS	CG	SV	IP	H	R	ER	HR	BB	SO	AVG	vLH	vRH	K/9	BB/9
Anderson, Chris	R-R	6-4	215	7-29-92	7	7	4.62	27	25	0	0	134	147	77	69	11	63	146	.282	.303	.265	9.78	4.22
Araujo, Victor	R-R	5-11	171	11-9-92	0	1	7.20	5	0	0	0	5	5	4	4	1	2	4	.250	.222	.273	7.20	3.60
Beckett, Josh	R-R	6-5	230	5-15-80	0	1	6.75	1	1	0	0	4	5	3	3	2	3	5	.313	.500	.286	11.25	6.75
Billingsley, Chad	R-R	6-1	240	7-29-84	0	1	6.00	2	2	0	0	3	3	3	2	0	3	3	.250	.143	.400	9.00	9.00
Brown, Geoff	L-L	5-11	188	1-20-89	4	6	4.50	41	4	0	1	88	93	55	44	10	34	78	.274	.231	.297	7.98	3.48
Cabrera, Freddie	R-R	6-5	210	1-25-90	3	1	4.68	23	0	0	0	42	41	26	22	5	18	18	.258	.289	.229	3.83	3.83
Carson, Robert	L-L	6-4	240	1-23-89	0	1	5.40	4	0	0	0	5	6	3	3	1	3	3	.316	.300	.333	1.80	5.40
Caughel, Lindsey	R-R	6-3	205	8-13-90	8	5	3.53	15	12	0	0	87	94	39	34	7	20	81	.270	.281	.260	8.41	2.08
Chirinos, Luis	R-R	6-2	205	4-22-90	0	2	6.04	7	5	0	0	28	25	19	19	2	9	27	.236	.196	.273	8.58	2.86

Cotton, Jharel	R-R	5-11	195	1-19-92	6	10	4.05	25	20	1	0	127	113	70	57	18	34	138	.239	.230	.245	9.81	2.42
Coulombe, Danny	L-L	5-10	185	10-26-89	3	0	3.05	31	0	0	5	44	33	16	15	3	17	61	.206	.182	.223	12.38	3.45
Elbert, Scott	L-L	6-2	225	8-13-85	0	0	3.86	5	1	0	0	5	4	2	2	1	2	3	.222	.250	.200	5.79	3.86
Fernandez, Yasmanys	L-L	6-1	214	5-10-87	1	0	3.38	22	0	0	0	21	21	10	8	1	16	22	.259	.219	.286	9.28	6.75
Garcia, Onelki	L-L	6-3	225	8-2-89	0	1	27.00	1	1	0	0	1	2	2	2	0	1	0	.500	.000	.667	0.00	13.50
Gomez, Gustavo	R-R	6-1	150	5-24-91	2	2	6.66	26	1	0	0	49	61	39	36	9	30	38	.313	.302	.318	7.03	5.55
Jones, Owen	R-R	6-1	190	6-12-89	2	1	6.28	21	0	0	3	29	43	23	20	6	6	16	.339	.418	.278	5.02	1.88
Kershaw, Clayton	L-L	6-3	225	3-19-88	0	0	1.80	1	1	0	0	5	2	1	1	1	1	6	.118	.000	.200	10.80	1.80
Martinez, Brandon	R-R	6-4	162	11-25-90	0	1	7.20	1	1	0	0	5	8	4	4	1	0	1	.400	.143	.538	1.80	0.00
Martinez, Fabio	R-R	6-3	190	10-29-89	5	6	4.97	23	17	0	0	100	82	71	55	9	91	86	.223	.244	.207	7.77	8.22
McGeary, Jack	L-L	6-3	195	3-19-89	1	0	7.20	7	0	0	0	10	11	9	8	0	20	9	.297	.333	.273	8.10	18.00
Mesa, Luis	R-R	6-4	200	7-13-90	3	2	6.05	24	0	0	0	39	45	28	26	4	13	24	.296	.370	.255	5.59	3.03
Ozoria, Arismendy	R-R	6-1	195	8-7-90	0	0	0.00	2	0	0	0	3	3	0	0	0	0	4	.273	.200	.333	13.50	0.00
Perez, Chris	R-R	6-4	230	7-1-85	0	1	9.00	4	2	0	0	5	6	5	5	0	1	2	.316	.111	.500	3.60	1.80
Rogers, Rob	R-R	5-11	205	10-25-90	2	9	4.59	49	0	0	8	65	69	44	33	6	20	66	.268	.276	.264	9.19	2.78
Shelton, Matt	R-R	6-4	205	11-30-88	1	1	1.76	8	0	0	0	15	13	3	3	0	1	16	.228	.304	.176	8.22	0.59
Smith, Blake	L-R	6-2	225	12-9-87	1	3	3.54	22	0	0	9	28	23	13	11	2	13	28	.221	.255	.193	9.00	4.18
Stem, Craig	R-R	6-5	215	1-5-90	0	2	3.82	26	0	0	2	35	41	22	15	3	12	30	.283	.367	.224	7.64	3.06
Tillman, Daniel	R-R	6-1	185	3-14-89	2	1	5.92	36	0	0	2	49	55	41	32	4	23	38	.275	.306	.258	7.03	4.25
Urias, Julio	L-L	5-11	160	8-12-96	2	2	2.36	25	20	0	0	88	60	25	23	4	37	109	.194	.175	.202	11.19	3.80
Wilson, Brian	R-R	6-1	205	3-16-82	0	0	0.00	2	2	0	0	2	1	0	0	0	0	2	.143	.000	.333	9.00	0.00
Windle, Tom	L-L	6-4	215	3-10-92	12	8	4.26	26	25	0	0	139	147	82	66	14	44	111	.271	.257	.276	7.17	2.84

Fielding

Catcher	PCT	G	PO	A	E	DP	PB
Capellan	.984	25	161	24	3	4	3
Farmer	.988	30	221	31	3	2	4
Maynard	.985	30	236	33	4	1	5
Ogle	.993	61	523	42	4	3	22

First Base	PCT	G	PO	A	E	DP
Jacobs	.993	114	995	84	8	95
Miller	1.000	11	76	10	0	9
Ogle	.986	7	67	4	1	2
Proscia	1.000	11	87	8	0	9

Second Base	PCT	G	PO	A	E	DP
Dixon	.956	94	172	258	20	49
Grider	.958	8	10	13	1	3
Guerrero	1.000	2	5	3	0	2
Law	.992	29	50	76	1	19

	PCT	G	PO	A	E	DP
McDonald	1.000	1	3	5	0	3
Morales	.833	1	2	3	1	2
Rodriguez	.951	9	16	23	2	9

Third Base	PCT	G	PO	A	E	DP
Arruebarrena	1.000	8	3	14	0	3
Guerrero	1.000	2	1	3	0	1
Law	.912	19	7	24	3	1
McDonald	.571	3	0	4	3	0
Proscia	.907	101	76	188	27	16
Rodriguez	.793	10	7	16	6	3
Turner	—	1	0	0	0	0
Uribe	1.000	3	0	7	0	0
Wingo	1.000	1	1	0	0	0

Shortstop	PCT	G	PO	A	E	DP
Arruebarrena	.947	4	9	9	1	2

	PCT	G	PO	A	E	DP
Grider	.952	10	9	31	2	6
Guerrero	1.000	1	0	4	0	1
Moyer	.978	37	51	125	4	23
Rodriguez	.934	16	17	40	4	9
Seager	.966	77	103	238	12	40

Outfield	PCT	G	PO	A	E	DP
Baldwin III	.969	110	247	7	8	2
Garcia	.989	44	85	6	1	1
Garvey	.959	111	200	9	9	4
Grider	1.000	12	13	0	0	0
Law	.975	56	73	6	2	1
McDonald	—	1	0	0	0	0
Miller	.909	11	18	2	2	1
Proscia	1.000	1	2	1	0	1
Rathjen	.966	84	133	11	5	2
Wingo	1.000	2	4	0	0	0

GREAT LAKES LOONS   LOW CLASS A
MIDWEST LEAGUE

Batting	B-T	HT	WT	DOB	AVG	vLH	vRH	G	AB	R	H	2B	3B	HR	RBI	BB	HBP	SH	SF	SO	SB	CS	SLG	OBP
Ahart, Devan	L-R	6-1	175	10-21-92	.304	.385	.286	16	69	5	21	6	0	0	4	1	0	1	1	8	3	0	.391	.310
Capellan, Jose	R-R	6-0	210	10-19-89	.221	.217	.222	26	86	4	19	1	0	0	4	0	0	2	1	15	1	3	.233	.218
Chigbogu, Justin	L-L	6-1	240	7-8-94	.156	.000	.169	24	90	13	14	4	1	3	12	5	0	1	0	39	1	0	.322	.200
Cordero, Josmar	R-R	5-10	175	9-10-91	.244	.267	.236	103	389	41	95	18	1	11	41	20	10	1	1	86	10	5	.380	.298
Curletta, Joey	R-R	6-4	245	3-8-94	.277	.250	.285	133	516	60	143	30	1	7	68	41	4	3	4	111	15	9	.380	.333
Farmer, Kyle	R-R	6-0	200	8-17-90	.310	.314	.309	57	229	25	71	16	4	2	35	15	3	0	2	24	9	3	.441	.357
Hoenecke, Paul	L-R	6-2	205	7-8-90	.247	.136	.277	128	482	59	119	37	2	15	61	47	4	0	6	99	8	4	.425	.315
Holland, Malcolm	R-R	5-11	165	6-18-92	.206	.244	.194	112	374	47	77	7	5	0	21	62	2	10	2	103	42	11	.251	.320
Morales, Delvis	B-R	6-2	175	8-29-90	.149	.217	.114	23	67	5	10	0	0	3	11	0	3	0	21	1	2	.149	.269
Moyer, Dillon	R-R	6-0	200	7-18-91	.228	.185	.243	78	254	35	58	13	3	0	25	28	3	8	0	60	16	6	.303	.312
Navin, Spencer	R-R	6-1	185	8-11-92	.234	.267	.223	53	175	25	41	6	1	1	13	10	15	5	1	67	5	2	.297	.328
Oguisten, Faustino	R-R	6-1	165	1-17-91	.121	.154	.100	13	33	2	4	0	0	0	3	0	3	0	16	2	0	.121	.194
Rivas, Webster	R-R	6-2	218	8-8-90	.254	.189	.273	91	319	25	81	18	2	5	32	23	0	3	1	56	2	1	.370	.303
Rodriguez, Leo	R-R	5-11	160	12-11-91	.224	.083	.270	13	49	1	11	1	0	0	3	3	1	0	0	8	2	0	.245	.283
Santana, Alex	R-R	6-4	200	8-21-93	.241	.318	.220	111	390	43	94	20	0	3	33	36	4	7	6	140	13	5	.315	.307
Scavuzzo, Jacob	R-R	6-4	200	1-15-94	.209	.125	.232	108	402	46	84	18	4	5	35	32	6	3	1	126	17	4	.311	.227
Trinkwon, Brandon	L-R	6-1	170	3-30-92	.247	.268	.242	94	308	40	76	15	2	3	29	54	1	8	2	39	11	4	.338	.359
Valentin, Jesmuel	B-R	5-9	180	5-12-94	.280	.250	.292	108	407	73	114	22	9	7	47	38	7	7	3	72	24	7	.430	.349
Wampler, Tyler	R-R	6-0	175	9-11-91	.071	.000	.088	14	42	2	3	1	0	0	3	4	1	2	1	10	1	0	.095	.167

Pitching	B-T	HT	WT	DOB	W	L	ERA	G	GS	CG	SV	IP	H	R	ER	HR	BB	SO	AVG	vLH	vRH	K/9	BB/9
Arano, Victor	R-R	6-2	200	2-7-95	4	7	4.08	22	15	0	3	86	88	42	39	11	20	83	.260	.294	.235	8.69	2.09
Araujo, Victor	R-R	5-11	171	11-9-92	5	2	1.32	42	0	0	6	68	39	13	10	2	15	74	.167	.222	.132	9.79	1.99
Barlow, Scott	R-R	6-3	170	12-18-92	6	7	4.50	23	21	0	1	106	113	64	53	11	35	104	.269	.283	.261	8.83	2.97
Baune, Jamie	R-R	6-3	190	9-27-91	1	0	5.30	6	0	0	1	19	27	11	11	4	3	14	.365	.409	.300	6.75	1.45
Bird, Zach	R-R	6-4	205	7-14-94	6	17	4.25	26	24	1	0	119	118	65	56	9	55	110	.259	.289	.239	8.34	4.17
Campbell, James	R-R	6-1	195	9-20-91	1	1	4.91	4	4	0	0	18	24	12	10	1	13	4	.324	.238	.438	1.96	6.38
Campbell, Matt	R-R	5-10	195	9-28-91	0	1	2.00	26	0	0	4	36	28	8	8	2	10	45	.220	.255	.194	11.25	2.50
Cash, Ralston	R-R	6-3	215	8-20-91	3	1	2.84	29	0	0	1	51	33	16	16	1	22	62	.188	.183	.190	11.01	3.91
Chirinos, Luis	R-R	6-2	205	4-22-90	5	4	4.48	21	8	0	0	60	73	38	30	6	25	46	.300	.330	.282	6.86	3.73

	B-T	HT	WT	DOB	W	L	ERA	G	GS	CG	SV	IP	H	R	ER	HR	BB	SO	AVG	vLH	vRH	K/9	BB/9
De Leon, Jose	R-R	6-2	185	8-7-92	2	0	1.19	4	4	0	0	23	14	4	3	1	2	42	.171	.121	.204	16.68	0.79
De Paula, Luis	L-L	6-1	170	4-23-92	1	2	5.74	9	5	0	1	31	39	22	20	2	14	24	.305	.303	.305	6.89	4.02
Harris, Greg	R-R	6-2	170	8-17-94	7	6	4.45	22	16	0	0	87	88	50	43	7	28	92	.258	.250	.263	9.52	2.90
Hershiser, Jordan	R-R	6-8	245	9-15-88	2	2	2.28	30	4	0	0	59	43	19	15	6	23	62	.211	.250	.189	9.40	3.49
Hooper, Kyle	R-R	6-4	195	5-28-91	1	0	3.07	27	0	0	1	41	32	14	14	3	18	54	.213	.196	.222	11.85	3.95
Johnson, Michael	L-L	6-1	185	1-3-91	4	3	1.83	50	0	0	1	64	46	17	13	2	25	91	.198	.214	.191	12.80	3.52
Martinez, Brandon	R-R	6-4	162	11-25-90	1	8	4.91	28	15	0	0	103	127	60	56	13	33	78	.309	.326	.300	6.84	2.89
Martinez, Jonathan	R-R	6-1	203	6-27-94	7	5	3.47	19	19	0	0	106	110	43	41	8	19	91	.271	.293	.257	7.70	1.61
2-team total (5 Kane County)					11	5	3.26	24	24	1	0	130	132	49	47	10	21	106	—	—	—	7.36	1.46
McGeary, Jack	L-L	6-3	195	3-19-89	0	0	7.20	3	0	0	0	5	7	4	4	0	2	9	.333	.333	.333	16.20	3.60
Pope, Mark	R-R	6-2	203	8-29-89	4	3	2.26	49	0	0	9	64	51	22	16	2	15	52	.221	.207	.228	7.35	2.12
Rhame, Jacob	R-R	6-1	190	3-16-93	5	4	2.00	51	0	0	9	67	48	16	15	3	14	90	.198	.163	.215	12.03	1.87
Richy, John	R-R	6-4	215	7-28-92	0	0	1.65	4	4	0	0	16	14	4	3	0	7	14	.230	.273	.205	7.71	3.86
Vanegas, A.J.	R-R	6-3	205	8-16-92	1	0	0.00	5	0	0	1	8	3	0	0	0	7		.111	.000	.176	7.56	0.00
Villa, Francisco	R-R	6-1	175	1-24-92	0	0	6.97	7	0	0	0	10	18	11	8	2	3	8	.367	.391	.346	6.97	2.61

Fielding

Catcher

	PCT	G	PO	A	E	DP	PB
Capellan	.992	24	227	26	2	3	1
Farmer	.997	44	359	34	1	3	8
Navin	.986	46	380	54	6	0	8
Rivas	.993	29	261	29	2	0	6

First Base

	PCT	G	PO	A	E	DP
Chigbogu	.984	22	168	13	3	17
Cordero	.994	90	727	41	5	49
Hoenecke	1.000	11	66	4	0	8
Rivas	.989	23	168	10	2	21

Second Base

	PCT	G	PO	A	E	DP
Holland	.963	10	12	14	1	5
Morales	1.000	1	3	1	0	2
Oguisten	.955	6	8	13	1	3
Rodriguez	.980	13	17	33	1	3
Trinkwon	.962	15	21	30	2	3
Valentin	.976	105	218	271	12	56

Third Base

	PCT	G	PO	A	E	DP
Cordero	1.000	1	1	0	0	0
Hoenecke	.930	111	51	202	19	16
Morales	.944	8	5	12	1	2
Oguisten	1.000	1	0	1	0	0
Rodriguez	—	1	0	0	0	0
Trinkwon	.932	29	17	52	5	6
Valentin	—	1	0	0	0	0

Shortstop

	PCT	G	PO	A	E	DP
Morales	.920	12	21	25	4	5
Moyer	.976	78	128	203	8	49
Oguisten	1.000	3	6	8	0	1
Trinkwon	.956	38	41	88	6	13
Wampler	.967	14	21	37	2	8

Outfield

	PCT	G	PO	A	E	DP
Ahart	1.000	16	28	0	0	0
Curletta	.979	126	215	13	5	4
Holland	.987	75	152	2	2	0
Morales	—	1	0	0	0	0
Oguisten	1.000	3	13	0	0	0
Santana	.978	104	170	5	4	1
Scavuzzo	.964	99	184	2	7	0

AZL DODGERS   ROOKIE

ARIZONA LEAGUE

Batting	B-T	HT	WT	DOB	AVG	vLH	vRH	G	AB	R	H	2B	3B	HR	RBI	BB	HBP	SH	SF	SO	SB	CS	SLG	OBP
Adams, Ryan	R-R	5-11	185	4-21-87	.250	1.000	.000	1	4	1	1	0	0	0	0	0	0	0	0	3	0	0	.250	.250
Arruebarrena, Erisbel	R-R	6-0	200	3-25-90	.222	.000	.267	5	18	3	4	2	0	2	4	0	0	0	0	10	0	0	.667	.222
Bellinger, Cody	L-L	6-4	180	7-13-95	.150	.000	.200	5	20	2	3	1	0	0	1	0	0	0	0	5	0	0	.200	.190
Bereszniewicz, Billy	L-L	5-10	170	9-11-91	.308	.000	.400	11	26	3	8	1	0	0	2	1	2	0	2	3	3	2	.346	.419
Canellas, Daniel	R-R	6-0	185	2-23-95	.224	.154	.244	18	58	5	13	6	0	0	4	2	1	0	0	16	0	0	.328	.262
Castillo, Deivy	L-L	6-3	170	7-21-95	.248	.194	.267	42	141	23	35	3	1	1	18	4	3	0	0	38	10	4	.305	.350
Celli, Federico	R-R	6-3	215	2-15-95	.343	.714	.250	17	35	5	12	2	0	0	4	5	1	0	0	8	3	1	.400	.439
De Jong, Scott	R-R	6-4	235	4-26-93	.220	.226	.218	35	109	19	24	2	0	6	20	15	4	0	2	47	4	1	.404	.331
Dixon, Brandon	R-R	6-2	215	1-29-92	.000	.000	.000	1	3	0	0	0	0	0	0	0	0	0	0	0	0	0	.000	.000
Estrella, Alberto	R-R	6-3	190	5-22-97	.172	.154	.179	31	93	11	16	2	1	3	9	10	3	0	0	57	0	2	.312	.274
Freeman, Clint	L-R	6-1	195	5-25-91	.305	.353	.295	32	95	16	29	5	3	2	20	7	0	0	2	26	1	1	.484	.346
Gomez, Cristian	R-R	5-11	185	1-11-96	.286	.353	.256	19	56	9	16	4	0	1	12	5	2	5	0	16	0	0	.411	.365
Guerrero, Alex	R-R	5-10	205	11-20-86	.348	.200	.389	7	23	6	8	1	0	2	6	3	1	0	2	5	0	0	.652	.414
Hennessey, Blake	R-R	6-0	172	9-28-94	.273	.182	.295	23	55	5	15	6	0	0	8	7	2	1	0	14	1	1	.382	.375
Isabel, Ibandel	R-R	6-4	185	6-20-95	.238	.132	.283	38	130	16	31	7	1	3	20	10	2	0	0	48	1	0	.377	.303
Jones, Matt	L-R	6-7	250	3-9-94	.182	.125	.200	23	66	4	12	2	0	0	4	7	0	0	0	33	3	0	.212	.260
Maynard, Pratt	L-R	6-0	215	11-19-89	.100	.000	.143	4	10	2	1	1	0	0	2	0	0	0	0	2	0	0	.200	.250
Medina, Michael	R-R	6-2	190	8-24-96	.274	.333	.258	36	117	17	32	9	1	5	16	18	3	1	0	52	5	0	.496	.384
Rodriguez, Luis	R-R	5-11	180	2-12-95	.125	.000	.200	2	8	1	1	0	0	0	0	0	0	0	0	5	0	0	.125	.125
Sandoval, Ariel	R-R	6-2	180	11-6-95	.221	.302	.186	46	140	18	31	7	1	2	16	7	0	3	0	29	6	0	.329	.259
Scott, Ryan	R-R	6-1	180	2-7-95	.170	.067	.211	22	53	8	9	1	0	1	5	12	3	0	0	22	0	0	.245	.353
Tirado, Lucas	L-R	6-2	180	11-13-96	.177	.107	.200	39	113	15	20	6	0	0	12	11	3	3	1	50	3	0	.230	.266
Ulmer, Deion	R-R	5-9	170	7-18-94	.237	.320	.215	37	118	19	28	6	0	0	4	7	1	3	0	29	5	2	.288	.286
Verdugo, Alex	L-L	6-0	200	5-15-96	.347	.325	.354	49	170	29	59	14	3	3	33	20	4	0	2	14	8	0	.518	.423
Walker, Jared	L-R	6-2	195	2-4-96	.231	.267	.216	38	104	18	24	5	1	1	13	20	3	1	0	34	6	4	.327	.367
Wampler, Tyler	R-R	6-0	175	9-11-91	.210	.357	.167	19	62	14	13	1	0	0	4	8	3	0	0	7	3	0	.226	.329
Whiting, Brant	L-R	5-9	190	2-6-92	.393	.385	.396	25	61	14	24	1	1	0	6	13	6	0	0	9	0	0	.443	.538

Pitching	B-T	HT	WT	DOB	W	L	ERA	G	GS	CG	SV	IP	H	R	ER	HR	BB	SO	AVG	vLH	vRH	K/9	BB/9
Baranik, Carson	R-R	6-3	205	11-6-92	3	2	2.86	15	1	0	0	28	25	11	9	3	11	29	.231	.205	.246	9.21	3.49
Carpenter, Drew	R-R	6-3	240	5-18-85	0	1	6.75	3	1	0	0	4	7	3	3	0	1	2	.389	.500	.357	4.50	2.25
Cruz, Oscar	R-R	6-1	170	8-25-94	1	0	5.52	11	0	0	0	15	17	13	9	0	11	8	.283	.211	.317	4.91	6.75
De Paula, Luis	L-L	6-1	170	4-23-92	0	0	0.00	2	0	0	0	3	0	0	0	0	0	6	.000	.000	.000	18.00	3.00
Felix, Carlos	R-R	6-2	240	11-6-95	3	1	2.93	12	5	0	0	43	37	19	14	0	11	37	.232	.252		7.74	2.30
Fife, Stephen	R-R	6-2	220	10-4-86	0	0	1.50	1	1	0	0	6	3	1	1	1	0	5	.136	.100	.167	7.50	0.00
Gonzalez, Yeuri	R-R	6-2	170	12-22-92	1	3	3.73	10	6	0	0	41	41	20	17	4	6	36	.248	.293	.211	7.90	1.32
Guzman, Kevin	R-R	6-3	165	11-6-94	3	4	3.33	12	12	1	0	54	50	31	20	4	12	48	.239	.244	.236	8.00	2.00
Harcksen, Misja	R-R	6-2	165	4-19-95	0	0	4.91	7	2	0	0	11	14	9	6	0	4	5	.292	.286	.294	4.09	3.27
Holmes, Grant	L-R	6-1	215	3-22-96	1	2	3.00	7	6	0	0	30	20	11	10	2	7	33	.187	.250	.149	9.90	2.10

LOS ANGELES DODGERS

Player	B-T	HT	WT	DOB	W	L	ERA	G	GS	CG	SV	IP	H	R	ER	HR	BB	SO	AVG	vLH	vRH	K/9	BB/9
Kowalczyk, Karch	R-R	6-1	216	3-31-91	0	1	1.69	5	0	0	3	5	2	1	1	1	2	6	.111	.200	.077	10.13	3.38
Martinez, Francisco	R-R	6-0	190	12-3-91	3	1	1.94	9	9	0	0	42	31	15	9	1	9	36	.197	.197	.198	7.78	1.94
Numata, Takumi	R-R	6-1	190	3-4-94	1	2	5.46	10	7	0	1	28	31	25	17	1	13	29	.274	.250	.288	9.32	4.18
Osuna, Lenix	R-R	6-1	220	11-11-95	0	1	13.50	2	0	0	0	1	4	2	2	0	0	1	.571	.500	.600	6.75	0.00
Pacheco, Jairo	L-L	6-0	165	7-6-96	4	3	2.27	12	6	0	0	48	39	20	12	1	16	54	.228	.298	.202	10.20	3.02
Richter, Harlan	R-R	6-6	225	9-24-92	0	2	2.25	11	0	0	1	12	8	6	3	1	8	11	.186	.176	.192	8.25	6.00
Rivero, Adrian	L-L	6-3	185	5-30-91	1	1	4.60	13	0	0	0	16	16	12	8	0	9	14	.250	.320	.205	8.04	5.17
Rossman, Bubby	B-R	6-5	220	6-29-92	0	2	4.74	13	0	0	1	19	19	11	10	1	8	23	.257	.231	.271	10.89	3.79
Schuller, Sven	R-R	6-3	205	1-17-96	0	0	3.38	6	0	0	0	5	4	5	2	0	3	5	.200	.000	.286	8.44	5.06
Serrano, Wellington	L-L	6-0	170	9-5-94	1	0	1.62	15	0	0	0	17	9	5	3	0	9	17	.155	.167	.152	9.18	4.86
Soto, William	R-R	6-4	185	2-13-96	0	0	0.00	2	0	0	0	2	0	0	0	0	0	3	.000	.000	.000	13.50	0.00
Sylvester, Derrick	R-R	6-6	200	4-19-91	2	2	1.16	15	0	0	3	23	15	4	3	0	3	26	.172	.133	.193	10.03	1.16
Uter, Kam	R-R	6-3	200	1-26-96	0	1	3.38	5	0	0	0	5	7	4	2	0	3	8	.318	.300	.333	13.50	5.06
Villegas, M.J.	R-R	6-2	190	9-6-94	1	2	4.18	12	0	0	1	24	22	14	11	0	9	29	.227	.176	.254	11.03	3.42

Fielding

Catcher	PCT	G	PO	A	E	DP	PB
Canellas	.973	18	131	12	4	1	6
Maynard	1.000	3	8	1	0	0	0
Rodriguez	.957	2	18	4	1	0	2
Scott	.989	22	161	20	2	4	0
Whiting	.988	23	153	17	2	2	4

First Base	PCT	G	PO	A	E	DP
Bellinger	1.000	5	35	4	0	3
De Jong	.981	19	146	6	3	9
Freeman	.990	15	92	6	1	9
Hennessey	1.000	1	1	0	0	0
Isabel	.987	26	205	16	3	12

Second Base	PCT	G	PO	A	E	DP
Dixon	1.000	1	0	1	0	0
Gomez	.964	8	7	20	1	3
Guerrero	1.000	1	0	4	0	0
Hennessey	.975	14	12	27	1	4
Ulmer	.979	34	48	91	3	17
Wampler	.938	10	9	21	2	2

Third Base	PCT	G	PO	A	E	DP
Estrella	.719	24	9	37	18	3
Guerrero	1.000	1	1	1	0	1
Hennessey	.909	8	4	6	1	0
Walker	.832	34	19	75	19	5

Shortstop	PCT	G	PO	A	E	DP
Arruebarrena	.900	3	1	8	1	0
Gomez	.941	13	15	33	3	6
Guerrero	1.000	2	3	2	0	1
Tirado	.842	38	41	82	23	14
Wampler	1.000	9	11	23	0	6

Outfield	PCT	G	PO	A	E	DP
Bereszniewicz	1.000	10	6	0	0	0
Castillo	.962	36	74	1	3	0
Celli	1.000	11	17	0	0	0
Freeman	.667	2	2	0	1	0
Isabel	—	1	0	0	0	0
Jones	.957	15	21	1	1	0
Medina	1.000	33	44	7	0	4
Sandoval	.929	42	50	2	4	0
Verdugo	.977	45	80	4	2	0
Wampler	—	1	0	0	0	0

OGDEN RAPTORS — ROOKIE

PIONEER LEAGUE

Batting	B-T	HT	WT	DOB	AVG	vLH	vRH	G	AB	R	H	2B	3B	HR	RBI	BB	HBP	SH	SF	SO	SB	CS	SLG	OBP
Ahart, Devan	L-R	6-1	175	10-21-92	.358	.278	.377	48	190	40	68	11	4	2	20	15	0	0	3	18	16	10	.489	.399
Ahmed, Mike	R-R	6-2	195	1-20-92	.285	.378	.254	53	179	32	51	8	4	0	18	29	3	0	0	37	7	1	.374	.393
Alexander, Theo	L-R	6-1	195	8-25-94	.217	.043	.255	43	129	16	28	6	0	3	15	12	0	0	1	41	0	4	.333	.282
Allen, Jimmy	R-R	5-10	170	1-4-92	.271	.174	.301	53	192	28	52	14	4	0	20	6	5	3	1	35	2	3	.385	
.309 Bellinger, Cody	L-L	6-4	180	7-13-95	.328	.375	.316	46	195	49	64	13	6	3	34	14	0	0	3	38	5	8	.503	.368
Bereszniewicz, Billy	L-L	5-10	170	9-11-91	.286	.091	.337	35	105	16	30	2	4	0	7	5	2	5	1	13	4	3	.381	.327
Cannon, John	R-R	6-0	180	5-11-90	.278	.375	.250	11	36	7	10	1	0	2	7	2	0	1	0	4	2	0	.472	.316
Capellan, Yensys	R-R	6-2	190	10-4-93	.227	.259	.213	31	88	16	20	6	0	3	13	15	0	1	2	19	6	0	.398	.333
Chigbogu, Justin	L-L	6-1	240	7-8-94	.248	.109	.286	67	254	65	63	7	1	20	56	26	3	0	4	101	3	2	.520	.321
Cowen, Austin	R-R	5-11	195	9-15-89	.286	.364	.258	15	42	5	12	4	1	1	7	4	0	0	0	5	0	1	.500	.348
Godbold, Andrew	R-R	6-3	230	3-18-92	.268	.348	.212	21	56	7	15	2	1	3	14	7	2	0	0	12	4	2	.500	.369
Gomez, Cristian	R-R	5-11	185	1-11-96	.108	.167	.080	19	37	0	4	0	0	0	1	2	1	0	0	8	0	1	.108	.175
Harris, Jaylen	B-R	5-9	175	9-25-93	.250	.000	.381	13	32	7	8	1	0	0	4	6	0	1	0	7	7	2	.281	.368
Henderson, Stefen	R-R	6-1	200	1-11-92	.190	.182	.200	13	21	2	4	0	0	0	1	2	0	0	1	12	1	0	.190	.292
Hering, Colin	L-L	6-3	215	2-14-91	.293	.200	.311	47	147	33	43	10	2	3	20	14	5	1	2	24	6	1	.449	.369
Leon, Julian	R-R	5-11	215	1-24-96	.332	.328	.333	63	223	39	74	14	1	12	57	31	6	0	4	53	1	1	.565	.420
McDonald, James	B-R	5-10	170	12-16-91	.200	—	.200	2	5	0	1	0	0	0	0	0	0	0	0	3	0	0	.200	.200
Meggs, Joe	R-R	6-0	195	4-30-90	.238	.229	.245	33	84	23	20	3	0	0	7	11	8	1	0	13	7	1	.274	.379
Ramos, Kelvin	R-R	5-10	170	12-21-93	.225	.280	.203	33	89	11	20	3	1	0	10	9	0	1	1	16	3	3	.281	.293
Redman, Hunter	R-R	5-10	180	8-25-92	.239	.167	.265	18	46	7	11	1	0	2	5	3	1	0	0	13	1	0	.391	.300
Santana, Melvin	R-R	5-10	160	10-4-91	.257	.417	.208	32	101	10	26	6	2	0	17	7	1	1	2	19	8	4	.356	.306
Scavuzzo, Jacob	R-R	6-4	200	1-15-94	.289	.333	.267	14	45	6	13	6	0	1	5	3	0	0	0	10	2	0	.489	.333
Scott, Ryan	R-R	6-1	180	2-7-95	.143	—	.143	4	7	1	1	0	0	0	0	1	0	0	0	3	0	0	.286	.250
Vela, Osvaldo	L-R	6-3	205	9-15-92	.307	.333	.303	48	137	14	42	10	0	3	22	15	1	1	3	32	3	3	.445	.377
Verdugo, Alex	L-L	6-0	200	5-15-96	.400	.400	.400	5	20	3	8	1	0	0	8	0	0	0	0	4	3	0	.450	.400
Wampler, Tyler	R-R	6-0	175	9-11-91	.286	.333	.250	11	21	1	6	0	0	0	2	2	0	0	0	5	1	0	.286	.348
Wolfe, Brian	L-L	6-4	210	10-16-90	.230	.200	.233	40	113	10	26	6	0	3	8	6	3	0	0	13	0	1	.363	.287

Pitching	B-T	HT	WT	DOB	W	L	ERA	G	GS	CG	SV	IP	H	R	ER	HR	BB	SO	AVG	vLH	vRH	K/9	BB/9
Baune, Jamie	R-R	6-3	190	9-27-91	0	0	9.20	5	1	0	0	15	23	20	15	3	7	6	.359	.417	.325	3.68	4.30
Bock, Edinson	R-R	6-2	190	4-15-94	1	0	8.36	10	0	0	0	14	14	13	13	3	11	14	.259	.360	.172	9.00	7.07
Bolt, Garrett	R-R	6-4	215	9-23-89	0	0	54.00	1	0	0	0	1	6	6	6	1	3	1	.857	1.000	.833	9.00	27.00
Brigham, Jeff	R-R	6-0	200	2-16-92	0	3	3.58	11	10	0	0	33	32	14	13	2	16	33	.267	.290	.241	9.09	4.41
Broussard, Joe	R-R	6-1	220	1-28-91	2	2	3.35	18	0	0	4	46	43	21	17	2	13	56	.246	.241	.250	11.04	2.56
De Leon, Jose	R-R	6-2	185	8-7-92	5	0	2.65	10	8	0	0	54	44	25	16	2	19	77	.217	.259	.189	12.75	3.15
Dominguez, Jose	R-R	6-0	200	8-7-90	0	0	13.50	2	0	0	0	1	1	2	2	0	1	2	.200	.333	.000	13.50	6.75
Elbert, Scott	L-L	6-2	225	8-13-85	0	1	40.50	1	1	0	0	1	2	3	3	1	1	1	.500	1.000	.333	13.50	13.50
Flamion, Billy	L-L	6-1	190	1-19-93	1	2	3.33	22	0	0	3	27	21	13	10	0	24	34	.216	.184	.237	11.33	8.00
Gonzalez, Victor	L-L	6-0	200	11-16-95	4	5	6.09	12	12	0	0	55	79	45	37	7	22	41	.343	.220	.386	6.75	3.62
Hayward, Vaughn	R-R	6-2	210	4-7-91	0	1	5.52	17	1	0	0	31	37	27	19	0	15	35	.308	.333	.286	10.16	4.35

Name	B-T	HT	WT	DOB	W	L	ERA	G	GS	CG	SV	IP	H	R	ER	HR	BB	SO	AVG	vLH	vRH	K/9	BB/9
Holmes, Grant	L-R	6-1	215	3-22-96	1	1	4.91	4	4	0	0	18	19	10	10	1	6	25	.271	.355	.205	12.27	2.95
Keller, Danny	R-R	6-5	190	6-30-92	0	0	6.75	3	0	0	0	4	3	5	3	0	3	1	.214	.500	.167	2.25	6.75
Kowalczyk, Karch	R-R	6-1	216	3-31-91	1	0	4.71	14	0	0	1	21	29	17	11	4	12	19	.326	.390	.271	8.14	5.14
Martinez, Francisco	R-R	6-0	190	12-3-91	1	0	0.00	2	0	0	0	4	5	5	0	0	2	3	.263	.333	.200	6.75	4.50
Oaks, Trevor	R-R	6-3	220	3-26-93	5	2	6.31	14	3	0	0	36	41	27	25	2	13	29	.283	.243	.324	7.32	3.28
Osuna, Lenix	R-R	6-1	220	11-11-95	0	2	4.02	16	0	0	3	16	20	8	7	2	5	18	.313	.393	.250	10.34	2.87
Pacheco, Jairo	L-L	6-0	165	7-6-96	0	0	0.00	2	0	0	0	0	1	1	0	0	2	0	.333	.500	.000	0.00	54.00
Reyes, Bernardo	R-R	6-0	175	7-22-95	3	5	5.28	17	6	0	1	58	71	45	34	8	19	52	.298	.305	.292	8.07	2.95
Richy, John	R-R	6-4	215	7-28-92	0	0	5.71	8	5	0	0	17	20	15	11	1	4	17	.278	.344	.225	8.83	2.08
Rivero, Adrian	L-L	6-3	185	5-30-91	1	0	5.40	4	0	0	0	5	5	3	3	0	5	3	.294	.250	.308	5.40	9.00
Stewart, Brock	L-R	6-3	170	10-9-91	3	2	3.41	17	1	0	3	34	36	20	13	1	17	45	.259	.269	.250	11.80	4.46
Sylvester, Derrick	R-R	6-6	200	4-19-91	0	0	0.00	2	0	0	0	3	2	0	0	1	0	.250	.500	.167	0.00	3.38
Taylor, Ryan	R-R	6-0	195	7-2-92	2	0	6.05	12	0	0	0	19	18	16	13	2	15	15	.254	.200	.306	6.98	6.98
Teodo, Wascar	R-R	6-4	185	6-25-94	0	2	17.36	3	0	0	0	5	12	10	9	0	4	5	.545	.714	.467	9.64	7.71
Underwood, J.D.	L-R	6-2	215	9-2-92	4	5	6.75	14	13	0	0	56	68	50	42	7	29	49	.292	.340	.254	7.88	4.66
Vanegas, A.J.	R-R	6-3	205	8-16-92	1	0	1.89	16	0	0	4	19	14	4	4	0	14	26	.203	.286	.146	12.32	6.63
Velasquez, Abdiel	R-R	6-3	184	3-4-93	2	5	5.35	15	10	0	0	66	77	52	39	11	29	41	.281	.284	.279	5.62	3.97

Fielding

Catcher	PCT	G	PO	A	E	DP	PB
Cannon	.941	11	86	9	6	0	0
Cowen	1.000	6	27	5	0	0	0
Leon	.991	50	404	53	4	3	8
Redman	.973	15	102	6	3	0	0
Scott	1.000	4	19	3	0	1	0

First Base	PCT	G	PO	A	E	DP
Bellinger	.983	43	387	24	7	19
Chigbogu	.975	28	221	16	6	17
Wolfe	.982	8	56	7	0	11

Second Base	PCT	G	PO	A	E	DP
Allen	.954	49	68	119	9	17
McDonald	1.000	1	3	2	0	0

	PCT	G	PO	A	E	DP
Santana	.951	27	39	77	6	14
Wampler	.714	2	1	4	2	0

Third Base	PCT	G	PO	A	E	DP
Ahmed	.921	51	32	96	11	7
Allen	.667	2	0	2	1	0
Capellan	.882	27	12	55	9	3
Vela	1.000	5	3	5	0	1

Shortstop	PCT	G	PO	A	E	DP
Ahmed	.909	2	4	6	1	1
Gomez	.912	19	22	40	6	9
McDonald	1.000	1	1	0	0	0
Ramos	.936	33	49	68	8	20
Vela	.845	35	35	74	20	10

	PCT	G	PO	A	E	DP
Wampler	.960	9	7	17	1	3

Outfield	PCT	G	PO	A	E	DP
Ahart	.960	46	91	6	4	2
Alexander	.946	36	47	6	3	1
Bereszniewicz	1.000	31	59	4	0	1
Godbold	.867	17	13	0	2	0
Harris	.944	16	16	1	1	0
Henderson	.938	9	13	2	1	0
Hering	.917	43	51	4	5	0
Meggs	.963	29	25	1	1	0
Scavuzzo	.941	14	14	2	1	1
Verdugo	.667	3	2	0	1	0
Wolfe	.912	23	29	2	3	1

DSL DODGERS   ROOKIE

DOMINICAN SUMMER LEAGUE

Batting	B-T	HT	WT	DOB	AVG	vLH	vRH	G	AB	R	H	2B	3B	HR	RBI	BB	HBP	SH	SF	SO	SB	CS	SLG	OBP
Albert, Shakir	R-R	6-0	185	12-24-96	.275	.265	.278	61	218	34	60	11	3	3	20	18	8	4	2	64	12	7	.394	.350
Aquino, Carlos	B-R	6-0	165	10-20-95	.281	.324	.268	48	146	27	41	7	5	0	10	20	1	2	1	29	11	6	.397	.369
Clementina, Hendrik	R-R	6-0	165	6-17-95	.275	.348	.250	49	182	22	50	11	1	2	18	6	5	0	1	32	3	3	.379	.314
Gomez, Rafael	B-R	6-0	170	1-5-95	.208	.125	.250	15	24	6	5	0	1	0	1	4	1	2	0	10	3	4	.292	.345
Lugo, Julio	R-R	6-4	180	7-7-97	.120	.167	.114	23	50	3	6	2	0	0	2	3	1	3	0	15	0	0	.160	.185
Mosquera, Carlos	B-L	5-9	150	1-9-96	.181	.321	.136	50	116	19	21	1	4	0	10	17	1	6	2	25	8	4	.259	.287
Nunez, Felix	R-R	5-11	170	3-21-97	.200	.053	.255	26	70	8	14	2	0	1	9	4	2	3	0	18	0	1	.271	.263
Ortiz, Samuel	B-R	5-11	170	8-4-96	.230	.240	.229	53	165	23	38	3	1	0	12	35	3	3	3	25	10	3	.261	.366
Padilla, Daniel	R-R	6-2	175	2-16-97	.252	.344	.226	42	147	22	37	1	4	0	11	14	3	4	1	27	10	6	.313	.327
Paz, Luis	L-R	6-1	190	5-7-96	.193	.086	.219	59	181	16	35	5	1	1	24	21	3	2	1	41	3	5	.249	.286
Peguero, Alex	L-L	6-7	190	12-23-95	.147	.182	.138	33	102	4	15	3	0	0	7	2	0	0	0	41	1	1	.176	.163
Perez, Jimy	R-R	6-2	185	2-12-94	.200	.400	.133	6	20	4	4	0	0	1	3	4	0	0	0	4	2	1	.350	.333
Perez, Moises	R-R	5-10	150	7-18-97	.222	.184	.230	55	203	20	45	13	1	0	16	13	1	4	1	52	11	8	.296	.271
Pitre, Gersel	R-R	6-0	180	7-19-96	.236	.214	.246	36	89	11	21	3	0	0	9	10	2	0	1	8	3	1	.270	.324
Santana, Cristian	R-R	6-2	175	2-24-97	.203	.211	.202	38	118	7	24	7	1	0	11	6	0	1	1	29	2	2	.280	.240
Subero, Luis	R-R	5-11	185	3-21-95	.182	.333	.169	31	77	3	14	3	0	0	5	5	2	0	1	9	0	0	.221	.247
Valera, Joel	B-R	6-0	185	2-23-96	.145	.125	.153	30	83	6	12	1	1	0	5	10	1	0	2	40	2	1	.181	.240

Pitching	B-T	HT	WT	DOB	W	L	ERA	G	GS	CG	SV	IP	H	R	ER	HR	BB	SO	AVG	vLH	vRH	K/9	BB/9
Almonte, Adriel	L-L	6-0	160	10-11-94	2	1	3.97	19	0	0	0	23	26	14	10	0	16	16	.306	.438	.275	6.35	6.35
Bautista, Angel	R-R	6-3	190	4-25-95	1	3	2.53	19	0	0	2	32	31	11	9	0	11	27	.263	.286	.250	7.59	3.09
Canizales, Jesus	R-R	6-4	190	5-25-96	1	0	7.53	10	1	0	0	14	13	14	12	1	16	7	.245	.313	.216	4.40	10.05
Chica, Dennys	L-L	6-3	175	8-31-95	0	3	2.60	15	12	0	1	52	49	26	15	2	10	50	.239	.302	.222	8.65	1.73
Diaz, Johan	R-R	6-2	195	11-1-92	4	1	2.61	19	0	0	3	31	20	16	9	1	16	29	.180	.270	.135	8.42	4.65
Escudero, Jose	R-R	5-11	170	5-24-95	0	0	0.00	2	0	0	0	2	1	1	0	0	0	2	.167	.500	.000	10.80	0.00
Fernandez, Roberth	L-L	6-1	165	3-21-95	3	2	2.14	14	13	0	0	67	50	19	16	2	20	49	.213	.200	.215	6.55	2.67
Forbes, Melvyn	R-R	6-3	185	12-2-93	1	0	4.60	13	0	0	0	16	9	9	8	0	17	6	.173	.118	.200	3.45	9.77
German, Angel	R-R	6-4	185	5-25-96	1	5	8.63	13	1	0	0	24	31	29	23	1	18	23	.320	.371	.290	8.63	6.75
Gooding, Max	L-L	5-11	165	3-7-96	1	1	3.00	18	0	0	0	24	19	11	8	0	10	16	.221	.333	.191	6.00	3.75
Londono, Miguel	L-L	6-1	160	4-30-96	0	0	4.05	15	0	0	0	20	23	16	9	1	15	11	.295	.364	.284	4.95	6.75
Longa, Roniel	R-R	6-2	180	7-12-94	1	0	5.06	16	0	0	2	21	24	18	12	0	14	16	.279	.313	.259	6.75	5.91
Mora, Gregor	R-R	6-1	185	8-28-95	2	1	2.25	18	4	0	2	44	36	14	11	1	17	35	.224	.281	.192	7.16	3.48
Perez, Edward	R-R	6-2	174	11-25-95	3	0	1.78	14	0	0	5	39	17	7	5	1	11	10	.195	.219	.182	3.55	3.91
Ramirez, Osiris	R-R	6-3	185	9-14-95	4	2	2.59	14	13	0	0	59	57	25	17	3	18	42	.246	.237	.250	6.41	2.75
Rodriguez, Hector	R-R	6-3	190	10-17-94	4	4	1.98	14	11	0	0	64	43	15	14	0	12	42	.185	.238	.155	5.94	1.70
Soto, Algenis	R-R	6-4	185	5-24-96	1	3	12.00	11	1	0	0	9	9	14	12	1	15	6	.257	.364	.208	6.00	15.00
Suero, Angel	R-R	6-7	220	10-8-96	0	0	4.15	3	0	0	0	4	3	2	2	0	2	3	.188	.286	.111	6.23	4.15
Urena, Miguel	R-R	6-8	210	2-27-95	5	5	1.60	13	13	0	0	62	50	18	11	0	18	36	.223	.213	.228	5.23	2.61

Fielding

Catcher	PCT	G	PO	A	E	DP	PB
Clementina	.964	26	164	21	7	0	7
Nunez	1.000	2	2	1	0	0	0
Paz	1.000	1	4	0	0	0	0
Pitre	.981	33	168	36	4	4	5
Subero	.974	28	124	28	4	1	6

First Base	PCT	G	PO	A	E	DP
Nunez	1.000	1	1	0	0	0
Paz	.990	55	469	23	5	24
Peguero	.963	26	176	8	7	19
Perez	1.000	1	7	2	0	0
Subero	1.000	2	4	1	0	0

Second Base	PCT	G	PO	A	E	DP
Aquino	.960	27	64	57	5	7

	PCT	G	PO	A	E	DP
Gomez	.923	7	6	6	1	0
Nunez	1.000	2	1	7	0	2
Ortiz	.949	46	69	119	10	22
Perez	1.000	2	3	1	0	0

Third Base	PCT	G	PO	A	E	DP
Aquino	.933	15	6	8	1	0
Gomez	—	1	0	0	0	0
Nunez	.905	20	12	45	6	4
Perez	.783	5	3	15	5	1
Santana	.800	17	14	30	11	3
Valera	.800	28	17	39	14	4

Shortstop	PCT	G	PO	A	E	DP
Aquino	.875	3	3	4	1	1
Nunez	—	1	0	0	0	0

	PCT	G	PO	A	E	DP
Ortiz	.920	5	12	11	2	1
Perez	.931	51	84	174	19	25
Santana	.879	17	16	35	7	4

Outfield	PCT	G	PO	A	E	DP
Albert	.967	53	81	6	3	1
Gomez	1.000	4	5	2	0	0
Lugo	.957	17	21	1	1	1
Mieses	.979	53	130	11	3	4
Mosquera	.974	41	69	5	2	2
Osorio	1.000	21	41	3	0	0
Padilla	.989	39	83	5	1	1

Miami Marlins

SEASON IN A SENTENCE: A year after losing 100 games, the Marlins made a 17-game improvement and finished with 77 victories, underscored by an MVP-type season from Giancarlo Stanton, breakout seasons from Marcell Ozuna and Henderson Alvarez and an emergent season from Christian Yelich.

HIGH POINT: On July 29, the Marlins won their sixth in a row as Alvarez shut out the Nationals and Stephen Strasburg, 3-0. The win left Miami at 53-53 and just five games out of first place. Although the Marlins would get back over .500 in August, the magnitude of the victory makes this their shining moment.

LOW POINT: They had two. No. 1 was the loss of ace righthander Jose Fernandez to Tommy John surgery, a blow so severe all of major league baseball mourned on social media. No. 2 was much uglier as Stanton, who was on his way to a 40-homer season, was hit in the face with a pitch from Milwaukee's Mike Fiers. Stanton sustained facial fractures and tooth damage and did not play again, but still led the NL with 37 homers.

NOTABLE ROOKIES: Never shy about assertively promoting, the Marlins in 2015 employed top 10 prospects such as catcher J.T. Realmuto, righthander Anthony DeSclafani and No. 1 prospect Andrew Heaney, the lefthander from Oklahoma State. None stayed around long or had great success, but the Marlins are especially hopeful that Heaney will command a spot in the 2015 rotation. Outfielder Jake Marisnick was around briefly before being swapped to Houston, and 26-year-old Justin Bour is a favorite of Triple-A manager Andy Haines.

KEY TRANSACTIONS: The Marlins, sensing a shot at a wild card and down a pitcher with the loss of Fernandez, swapped Marisnick, 2014 first-rounder Colin Moran and potential sleeper Frances Martes, a righthanded pitcher, to Houston for righthanded starter Jarred Cosart. Cosart, just 24, pitched very well (4-4, 2.39) and will pair with Fernandez at the top of the Marlins' rotation next season.

DOWN ON THE FARM: Even with the promotions, the Marlins have a solid minor league system, including pitchability lefthander Justin Nicolino, another part of the impressive haul from Toronto in the Jose Reyes deal. Further away, Dominican righthander Domingo German excelled at low Class A.

OPENING DAY PAYROLL: $41,836,900 (30th)

PLAYERS OF THE YEAR

MAJOR LEAGUE	MINOR LEAGUE
Giancarlo Stanton rf	**Domingo German** rhp
.288/.395/.555	(Low Class A)
Led NL with 37 HR	9-3, 2.48
2nd in NL in OPS, RBI	113 SO in 123 IP

ORGANIZATION LEADERS

BATTING		*Minimum 250 AB
MAJORS		
* AVG	Stanton, Giancarlo	.288
* OPS	Stanton, Giancarlo	.950
HR	Stanton, Giancarlo	37
RBI	Stanton, Giancarlo	105
MINORS		
* AVG	Lopez, Carlos, Greensboro	.323
* OBP	Wallach, Chad, Jupiter, Greensboro	.431
* SLG	Bour, Justin, New Orleans	.517
R	Lopez, Carlos, Greensboro	85
H	Lopez, Carlos, Greensboro	164
TB	Jensen, Kyle, New Orleans	239
2B	Juengel, Matt, New Orleans, Jupiter	32
3B	six tied at	6
HR	Jensen, Kyle, New Orleans	27
RBI	Rosa, Viosergy, Jupiter, Jacksonville	95
BB	Nola, Austin, Jacksonville	77
SO	Jensen, Kyle, New Orleans	147
SB	Perez, Yefri, Greensboro	30

PITCHING		#Minimum 75 IP
MAJORS		
W	Alvarez, Henderson	12
# ERA	Alvarez, Henderson	2.65
SO	Koehler, Tom	153
SV	Cishek, Steve	39
MINORS		
W	Nicolino, Justin, Jacksonville	14
L	Lyman, Scott, Jacksonville, Jupiter	12
L	Milroy, Matt, Greensboro, Jupiter	12
# ERA	German, Domingo, Greensboro	2.48
G	Wittgren, Nick, Jacksonville	52
GS	Nicolino, Justin, Jacksonville	28
SV	Wittgren, Nick, Jacksonville	20
IP	Nicolino, Justin, Jacksonville	170
BB	Milroy, Matt, Greensboro, Jupiter	61
SO	Heaney, Andrew, Jacksonville, New Orleans	143
AVG	Milroy, Matt, Greensboro, Jupiter	.220

General Manager: Dan Jennings. **Farm Director:** Brian Chattin. **Scouting Director:** Stan Meek

Class	Team	League	W	L	PCT	Finish	Manager
Majors	Miami Marlins	National	77	85	.475	t-18th (30)	Mike Redmond
Triple-A	New Orleans Zephyrs	Pacific Coast	70	74	.486	t-11th (16)	Andy Haines
Double-A	Jacksonville Suns	Southern	81	59	.579	2nd (10)	Andy Barkett
High A	Jupiter Hammerheads	Florida State	50	87	.365	11th (12)	Brian Schneider
Low A	Greensboro Grasshoppers	South Atlantic	87	53	.621	t-3rd (14)	Dave Berg
Short season	Batavia Muckdogs	New York-Penn	34	42	.447	10th (14)	Angel Espada
Rookie	Marlins	Gulf Coast	25	35	.417	t-12th (16)	Julio Garcia
Overall Minor League Record			347	350	.498	17th (30)	

ORGANIZATION STATISTICS

MIAMI MARLINS

NATIONAL LEAGUE

Batting	B-T	HT	WT	DOB	AVG	vLH	vRH	G	AB	R	H	2B	3B	HR	RBI	BB	HBP	SH	SF	SO	SB	CS	SLG	OBP
Baker, Jeff	R-R	6-2	220	6-21-81	.264	.319	.191	90	208	27	55	10	4	3	28	13	1	0	3	51	1	0	.394	.307
Bour, Justin	L-R	6-4	250	5-28-88	.284	.200	.290	39	74	10	21	3	0	1	11	9	0	0	0	19	0	0	.365	.361
Dietrich, Derek	L-R	6-0	205	7-18-89	.228	.143	.241	49	158	31	36	6	2	5	17	13	10	2	0	38	1	0	.386	.326
Dobbs, Greg	L-R	6-1	205	7-2-78	.077	—	.077	15	13	0	1	0	0	0	0	0	0	0	0	4	0	0	.077	.077
2-team total (21 Washington)					.171	—	—	36	41	0	7	1	0	0	2	1	0	0	1	8	0	0	.195	.186
Furcal, Rafael	B-R	5-8	195	10-24-77	.171	.200	.167	9	35	4	6	0	1	0	2	2	0	0	0	7	0	0	.229	.216
Hechavarria, Adeiny	R-R	5-11	185	4-15-89	.276	.321	.265	146	536	53	148	20	10	1	34	26	1	4	6	86	7	5	.356	.308
Hernandez, Enrique	R-R	5-11	170	8-24-91	.175	.091	.207	18	40	3	7	2	1	2	6	4	1	0	0	10	0	1	.425	.267
Johnson, Reed	R-R	5-10	190	12-8-76	.235	.303	.198	113	187	24	44	15	0	2	25	1	8	2	3	37	0	1	.348	.266
Jones, Garrett	L-L	6-5	235	6-21-81	.246	.221	.250	146	496	59	122	33	2	15	53	46	1	0	4	116	0	1	.411	.309
Lucas, Ed	R-R	6-3	215	5-21-82	.251	.329	.198	69	179	19	45	5	0	1	9	8	0	2	0	48	1	0	.296	.283
Marisnick, Jake	R-R	6-4	225	3-30-91	.167	.111	.179	14	48	3	8	0	0	0	3	0	0	0	0	19	5	0	.167	.216
Mathis, Jeff	R-R	6-0	205	3-31-83	.200	.273	.176	64	175	12	35	7	0	2	12	15	0	5	0	64	0	0	.274	.263
McGehee, Casey	R-R	6-1	220	10-12-82	.287	.219	.303	160	616	56	177	29	1	4	76	67	1	0	7	102	4	2	.357	.355
Ozuna, Marcell	R-R	6-1	230	11-12-90	.269	.245	.275	153	565	72	152	26	5	23	85	41	1	0	5	164	3	1	.455	.317
Realmuto, J.T.	R-R	6-1	215	3-18-91	.241	1.000	.214	11	29	4	7	1	1	0	9	1	0	0	0	8	0	0	.345	.267
Saltalamacchia, Jarrod	B-R	6-3	235	5-2-85	.220	.216	.221	114	373	43	82	20	0	11	44	55	2	0	5	143	0	1	.362	.320
Solano, Donovan	R-R	5-9	205	12-17-87	.252	.243	.254	111	310	26	78	11	1	3	28	19	3	7	1	61	1	2	.323	.300
Stanton, Giancarlo	R-R	6-6	240	11-8-89	.288	.343	.274	145	539	89	155	31	1	37	105	94	3	0	2	170	13	1	.555	.395
Valdespin, Jordany	L-R	6-0	190	12-23-87	.214	.429	.198	52	98	8	21	2	1	3	10	9	0	6	0	16	1	0	.347	.280
Yelich, Christian	L-R	6-3	200	12-5-91	.284	.317	.273	144	582	94	165	30	6	9	54	70	3	3	2	137	21	7	.402	.362

Pitching	B-T	HT	WT	DOB	W	L	ERA	G	GS	CG	SV	IP	H	R	ER	HR	BB	SO	AVG	vLH	vRH	K/9	BB/9
Alvarez, Henderson	R-R	6-0	205	4-18-90	12	7	2.65	30	30	3	0	187	198	65	55	14	33	111	.275	.274	.276	5.34	1.59
Caminero, Arquimedes	R-R	6-4	250	6-16-87	0	1	10.80	6	0	0	0	7	8	8	8	2	4	8	.296	.250	.316	10.80	5.40
Capps, Carter	R-R	6-4	230	8-7-90	0	0	3.98	17	0	0	0	20	19	9	9	1	5	25	.244	.324	.182	11.07	2.21
Cishek, Steve	R-R	6-6	215	6-18-86	4	5	3.17	67	0	0	39	65	58	26	23	3	21	84	.237	.213	.266	11.57	2.89
Cosart, Jarred	R-R	6-3	195	5-25-90	4	4	2.39	10	10	0	0	64	54	19	17	2	22	40	.231	.228	.233	5.63	3.09
DeSclafani, Anthony	R-R	6-1	190	4-18-90	2	2	6.27	13	5	0	0	33	40	23	23	4	5	26	.303	.333	.273	7.09	1.36
Dunn, Mike	L-L	6-0	210	5-23-85	10	6	3.16	75	0	0	1	57	47	25	20	4	22	67	.220	.220	.219	10.58	3.47
Dyson, Sam	R-R	6-1	205	5-7-88	3	1	2.14	31	0	0	0	42	41	14	10	1	15	33	.255	.284	.234	7.07	3.21
Eovaldi, Nate	R-R	6-2	215	2-13-90	6	14	4.37	33	33	0	0	200	223	107	97	14	43	142	.282	.296	.266	6.40	1.94
Fernandez, Jose	R-R	6-2	225	7-31-92	4	2	2.44	8	8	0	0	52	36	19	14	4	13	70	.188	.247	.126	12.19	2.26
Flynn, Brian	L-L	6-7	250	4-19-90	0	1	9.00	2	1	0	0	7	12	7	7	0	3	6	.375	.333	.385	7.71	3.86
Gregg, Kevin	R-R	6-6	245	6-20-78	0	0	10.00	12	0	0	0	9	11	10	10	2	5	6	.306	.304	.308	6.00	5.00
Hand, Brad	L-L	6-3	220	3-20-90	3	8	4.38	32	16	0	1	111	112	56	54	10	39	67	.264	.224	.280	5.43	3.16
Hatcher, Chris	R-R	6-1	205	1-12-85	0	3	3.38	52	0	0	0	56	55	22	21	4	12	60	.252	.222	.277	9.64	1.93
Heaney, Andrew	L-L	6-2	185	6-5-91	0	3	5.83	7	5	0	0	29	32	19	19	6	7	20	.281	.212	.309	6.14	2.15
Jennings, Dan	L-L	6-3	210	4-17-87	0	2	1.34	47	0	0	0	40	45	11	6	3	17	38	.281	.299	.265	8.48	3.79
Koehler, Tom	R-R	6-2	235	6-29-86	10	10	3.81	32	32	0	0	191	177	84	81	16	71	153	.248	.241	.256	7.20	3.34
Marmol, Carlos	R-R	6-1	235	10-14-82	0	3	8.10	15	0	0	0	13	16	12	12	3	10	14	.291	.414	.154	9.45	6.75
Morris, Bryan	L-R	6-3	225	3-28-87	4	1	0.66	39	0	0	0	41	33	6	3	2	12	36	.221	.242	.205	7.97	2.66
2-team total (21 Pittsburgh)					8	1	1.82	60	0	0	0	64	58	17	13	6	24	50	—	—	—	6.99	3.36
Penny, Brad	R-R	6-4	230	5-24-78	2	1	6.58	8	4	0	0	26	34	20	19	3	13	13	.327	.279	.361	4.50	4.50
Ramos, A.J.	R-R	5-10	205	9-20-86	7	0	2.11	68	0	0	0	64	36	16	15	1	43	73	.164	.151	.172	10.27	6.05
Rodriguez, Henry	R-R	6-1	225	2-25-87	0	0	10.80	2	0	0	0	2	2	2	2	0	5	1	.333	.250	.500	5.40	27.00
Slowey, Kevin	R-R	6-3	205	5-4-84	1	1	5.30	17	2	0	0	37	53	23	22	3	9	24	.353	.338	.366	5.79	2.17
Turner, Jacob	R-R	6-5	215	5-21-91	4	7	5.97	20	12	0	0	78	106	54	52	8	23	54	.328	.290	.354	6.20	2.64
2-team total (8 Chicago)					6	11	6.13	28	18	0	0	113	148	81	77	12	33	71	—	—	—	5.65	2.63
Wolf, Randy	L-L	6-0	205	8-22-76	1	3	5.26	6	4	0	1	26	33	17	15	4	6	19	.311	.235	.326	6.66	2.10

Fielding

Catcher	PCT	G	PO	A	E	DP	PB								First Base	PCT	G	PO	A	E	DP
Mathis	.998	62	389	39	1	4	3	Realmuto	.982	9	51	3	1	1	0	First Base					
								Saltalamacchia	.981	107	741	45	15	6	6	Baker	.993	43	263	15	2	23

	PCT	G	PO	A	E	DP
Bour	1.000	15	116	10	0	13
Jones	.988	129	990	107	13	103
Lucas	1.000	6	8	0	0	0

Second Base	PCT	G	PO	A	E	DP
Baker	.985	21	21	45	1	9
Dietrich	.950	44	58	134	10	24
Furcal	1.000	8	13	19	0	8
Hernandez	1.000	3	4	8	0	2
Lucas	.988	20	29	56	1	10
Solano	.997	73	139	212	1	47
Valdespin	.961	17	28	45	3	8

Third Base	PCT	G	PO	A	E	DP
Baker	—	2	0	0	0	0
Dietrich	.000	1	0	0	1	0
Hernandez	1.000	3	0	5	0	0
Lucas	.857	4	0	6	1	0
McGehee	.979	158	78	241	7	34
Solano	1.000	2	2	2	0	1

Shortstop	PCT	G	PO	A	E	DP
Hechavarria	.979	146	200	438	14	87
Lucas	.985	19	19	45	1	11
Solano	1.000	4	7	14	0	4

Outfield	PCT	G	PO	A	E	DP
Hernandez	1.000	9	16	1	0	1
Johnson	.979	34	42	4	1	1
Jones	1.000	9	8	0	0	0
Lucas	.875	7	7	0	1	0
Marisnick	1.000	13	47	2	0	1
Ozuna	.987	151	356	10	5	1
Stanton	.982	143	319	7	6	1
Valdespin	1.000	11	15	0	0	0
Yelich	.993	144	271	6	2	1

NEW ORLEANS ZEPHYRS   TRIPLE-A

PACIFIC COAST LEAGUE

Batting	B-T	HT	WT	DOB	AVG	vLH	vRH	G	AB	R	H	2B	3B	HR	RBI	BB	HBP	SH	SF	SO	SB	CS	SLG	OBP
Angle, Matt	L-R	5-9	185	9-10-85	.213	.153	.233	88	239	22	51	9	0	1	16	20	3	3	2	62	4	1	.264	.280
Benson, Joe	R-R	6-1	215	3-5-88	.000	.000	.000	5	7	0	0	0	0	0	0	2	0	0	0	3	0	1	.000	.222
Black, Danny	L-R	6-3	185	8-19-88	.198	.280	.141	47	121	15	24	3	1	2	11	11	0	0	0	26	5	0	.289	.265
Bogusevic, Brian	L-L	6-3	215	2-18-84	.260	.243	.267	79	265	43	69	14	4	6	33	32	6	4	4	56	5	7	.411	.349
Bour, Justin	L-R	6-4	250	5-28-88	.306	.252	.330	103	385	59	118	27	0	18	72	39	3	0	3	57	3	1	.517	.372
Brantly, Rob	L-R	6-1	195	7-14-89	.255	.243	.261	101	364	38	93	15	2	4	37	20	1	0	7	61	0	0	.341	.291
Canha, Mark	R-R	6-1	200	2-15-89	.303	.284	.311	127	465	83	141	28	3	20	82	57	8	0	7	112	3	1	.505	.384
Cox, Zack	L-R	5-11	225	5-9-89	.282	.219	.301	104	312	40	88	18	3	8	35	29	1	1	1	65	2	0	.436	.344
Diaz, Juan	B-R	6-4	220	12-12-88	.278	.164	.316	131	464	54	129	27	1	12	63	22	3	2	7	117	5	3	.418	.310
Dietrich, Derek	L-R	6-0	205	7-18-89	.317	.176	.354	21	82	15	26	3	0	7	16	4	6	0	0	18	1	0	.610	.391
Harbin, Taylor	R-R	5-9	171	2-13-86	.133	.048	.208	14	45	3	6	1	0	1	4	2	0	1	0	19	0	0	.222	.170
Hernandez, Enrique	R-R	5-11	170	8-24-91	.250	.438	.196	21	72	8	18	5	0	2	6	10	1	0	1	13	0	1	.403	.345
2-team total (67 Oklahoma City)					.318	—	—	88	336	49	107	22	2	10	37	28	3	2	4	38	6	6	.485	.372
Jensen, Kyle	R-L	6-3	250	5-20-88	.260	.280	.251	133	497	70	129	29	0	27	92	48	7	0	4	147	1	0	.481	.331
Juengel, Matt	R-R	6-2	185	1-13-90	.231	.333	.143	3	13	1	3	0	0	1	3	0	0	0	0	2	0	0	.462	.231
Krick, Taylor	R-R	6-1	215	3-31-88	.182	.333	.000	6	11	0	2	0	0	0	0	1	0	0	0	3	0	0	.182	.250
Lucas, Ed	R-R	6-3	215	5-21-82	.261	.400	.194	14	46	5	12	1	0	0	3	7	1	0	3	10	0	0	.283	.351
Marisnick, Jake	R-R	6-4	225	3-30-91	.277	.239	.295	89	343	50	95	16	4	10	40	17	9	6	2	64	24	6	.434	.326
Rodriguez, Josh	R-R	6-0	185	12-18-84	.259	.236	.272	122	424	60	110	21	2	11	44	46	6	1	5	112	7	4	.396	.337
Silverio, Alfredo	R-R	6-1	215	5-6-87	.156	.077	.188	13	45	5	7	2	0	1	2	1	0	0	0	9	0	0	.267	.174
Skipworth, Kyle	L-R	6-4	230	3-1-90	.216	.191	.228	70	204	24	44	7	1	10	30	16	6	0	0	75	1	2	.407	.292
Solano, Donovan	R-R	5-9	205	12-17-87	.095	.000	.125	6	21	2	2	1	0	0	3	0	0	0	1	5	0	0	.143	.091
Valdespin, Jordany	L-R	6-0	190	12-23-87	.270	.274	.269	61	222	39	60	9	2	8	29	36	2	3	2	29	15	10	.437	.374
Wates, Austin	R-R	6-1	180	9-2-88	.252	.265	.247	27	111	18	28	7	1	0	0	9	1	0	0	2	6	2	.333	.314
2-team total (74 Oklahoma City)					.286	—	—	101	392	62	112	18	4	2	30	52	3	0	0	67	37	6	.367	.374
Yelich, Christian	L-R	6-3	200	12-5-91	.111	—	.111	2	9	1	1	0	0	1	0	4	0	0	0	5	0	0	.444	.111

Pitching	B-T	HT	WT	DOB	W	L	ERA	G	GS	CG	SV	IP	H	R	ER	HR	BB	SO	AVG	vLH	vRH	K/9	BB/9
Ames, Steve	R-R	6-1	205	3-15-88	1	1	5.93	9	0	0	0	14	16	9	9	2	7	4	.314	.333	.300	2.63	4.61
Caminero, Arquimedes	R-R	6-4	250	6-16-87	4	1	4.86	42	0	0	10	63	70	36	34	7	30	79	.276	.273	.278	11.29	4.29
Capps, Carter	R-R	6-4	230	8-7-90	0	1	1.64	7	0	0	0	11	8	3	2	0	6	17	.211	.182	.222	13.91	4.91
Cargill, Collin	R-R	6-2	190	10-6-87	0	1	6.92	11	0	0	0	13	16	12	10	2	11	8	.296	.316	.286	5.54	7.62
Conley, Adam	L-L	6-3	215	5-24-90	3	5	6.00	12	11	0	0	60	65	41	40	3	26	48	.279	.242	.292	7.20	3.90
Dayton, Grant	L-L	6-1	205	11-25-87	2	2	3.72	39	0	0	1	56	53	24	23	10	22	61	.249	.236	.255	9.86	3.56
DeSclafani, Anthony	R-R	6-1	190	4-18-90	3	3	3.49	12	11	0	0	59	48	23	23	2	21	59	.218	.268	.179	8.95	3.19
Dyson, Sam	R-R	6-1	205	5-7-88	2	1	2.49	13	0	0	1	25	21	8	7	0	10	20	.231	.200	.246	7.11	3.55
Evans, Bryan	R-R	6-2	200	2-25-87	5	8	4.42	36	14	0	2	112	101	63	55	15	45	105	.239	.243	.237	8.44	3.62
Flynn, Brian	L-L	6-7	250	4-19-90	8	10	4.06	25	25	1	0	140	169	83	63	13	50	104	.302	.261	.316	6.70	3.22
Gregg, Kevin	R-R	6-6	245	6-20-78	1	0	3.00	5	0	0	0	6	2	2	0	0	2	3	.250	.250	.250	4.50	3.00
Hand, Brad	L-L	6-3	220	3-20-90	2	0	3.27	4	4	0	0	22	18	8	8	3	9	22	.234	.241	.229	9.00	3.68
Hatcher, Chris	R-R	6-1	205	1-12-85	1	2	2.01	15	0	0	5	22	16	5	5	2	6	25	.200	.133	.240	10.07	2.42
Heaney, Andrew	L-L	6-2	185	6-5-91	5	4	3.87	15	15	1	0	84	75	45	36	9	23	91	.234	.205	.245	9.79	2.47
Jennings, Dan	L-L	6-3	210	4-17-87	0	0	3.38	6	0	0	0	8	6	4	3	0	7	6	.207	.100	.263	10.13	7.88
Joseph, Donnie	L-L	6-3	190	11-1-87	1	0	9.58	9	0	0	0	10	18	14	11	4	12	5	.367	.308	.389	4.35	10.45
2-team total (19 Omaha)					2	1	5.50	28	0	0	1	36	44	29	22	7	32	35	—	—	—	8.75	8.00
McCarthy, Casey	R-R	6-4	215	4-13-90	0	0	29.45	3	0	0	0	4	12	12	12	2	7	1	.632	.143	.917	2.45	17.18
Montgomery, Matt	R-R	6-4	210	7-21-87	0	4	9.82	4	3	0	0	11	18	13	12	1	8	6	.391	.375	.400	4.91	6.55
Morey, Robert	R-R	6-1	185	11-27-88	1	1	4.96	4	3	0	0	16	23	10	9	1	7	16	.329	.344	.316	8.82	3.86
Nappo, Greg	L-L	5-10	195	8-25-88	1	0	8.44	5	0	0	0	5	9	5	5	1	4	4	.375	.500	.333	6.75	6.75
Nygren, James	R-R	6-0	195	3-8-89	0	0	5.40	2	0	0	0	5	5	3	3	0	3	5	.263	.250	.286	9.00	5.40
O'Gara, Joey	R-R	6-7	205	4-20-88	0	0	13.50	3	0	0	0	3	5	4	4	2	1	4	.417	.500	.333	3.38	6.75
Olmos, Edgar	L-L	6-4	220	4-12-90	2	3	3.86	33	0	0	1	51	49	24	22	4	17	44	.257	.263	.254	7.71	2.98
Penny, Brad	R-R	6-4	230	5-24-78	2	2	2.28	5	5	0	0	28	26	12	7	0	7	26	.252	.231	.266	8.46	2.93
Rodriguez, Henry	R-R	6-1	225	2-25-87	0	1	4.26	17	0	0	1	25	10	12	12	1	38	41	.122	.167	.089	14.57	13.50
Roe, Chaz	R-R	6-5	190	10-9-86	3	3	3.66	47	0	0	14	64	53	30	26	5	21	72	.229	.276	.195	10.13	2.95
Rogers, Jared	R-R	6-7	205	5-9-88	1	1	6.98	8	6	0	0	30	42	24	23	1	14	13	.333	.407	.269	3.94	4.25
Sanabia, Alex	R-R	6-2	210	9-8-88	7	4	3.98	20	19	0	0	111	118	54	49	10	32	93	.271	.253	.285	7.56	2.60
2-team total (8 Reno)					7	5	4.70	28	23	0	0	134	159	77	70	18	40	104	—	—	—	6.99	2.69
Sanchez, Jesus	R-R	5-11	200	9-24-87	0	5	7.47	23	1	0	1	31	45	30	26	3	13	26	.331	.305	.351	7.47	3.73

MIAMI MARLINS

	B-T	HT	WT	DOB	W	L	ERA	G	GS	CG	SV	IP	H	R	ER	HR	BB	SO	AVG	vLH	vRH	K/9	BB/9
Spence, Josh	L-L	6-2	195	1-22-88	0	0	3.97	11	0	0	0	11	13	5	5	2	7	12	.302	.059	.462	9.53	5.56
Varner, Rett	R-R	6-3	210	2-3-88	5	1	7.16	27	0	0	0	33	42	28	26	4	25	26	.309	.263	.327	7.16	6.89
Villanueva, Elih	R-R	6-2	230	7-27-86	10	10	4.47	27	27	0	0	137	148	77	68	18	47	104	.274	.260	.284	6.83	3.09

Fielding

Catcher	PCT	G	PO	A	E	DP	PB
Brantly	.992	92	706	51	6	2	9
Skipworth	.988	60	472	32	6	3	13

First Base	PCT	G	PO	A	E	DP
Bour	.997	91	705	53	2	59
Canha	.994	40	332	17	2	39
Jensen	.983	16	115	4	2	12

Second Base	PCT	G	PO	A	E	DP
Black	1.000	20	30	41	0	8
Dietrich	.978	21	36	55	2	16
Harbin	.957	13	19	26	2	4
Hernandez	1.000	11	28	29	0	9
Lucas	1.000	8	13	19	0	4
Rodriguez	.985	47	80	112	3	30
Solano	.800	1	2	2	1	1
Valdespin	.965	35	56	80	5	18

Third Base	PCT	G	PO	A	E	DP
Canha	.909	18	10	20	3	1
Cox	.937	73	30	118	10	11
Diaz	.909	4	3	7	1	3
Hernandez	1.000	2	0	7	0	0
Krick	1.000	2	0	4	0	0
Lucas	.714	4	0	5	2	0
Rodriguez	.935	48	20	95	8	8
Solano	1.000	3	3	8	0	0
Valdespin	.875	3	2	5	1	0

Shortstop	PCT	G	PO	A	E	DP
Black	.962	9	8	17	1	6
Diaz	.960	122	156	325	20	70
Hernandez	1.000	8	17	14	0	6
Lucas	.750	2	0	3	1	0
Rodriguez	.942	15	17	32	3	4

	PCT	G	PO	A	E	DP
Solano	1.000	1	1	2	0	0

Outfield	PCT	G	PO	A	E	DP
Angle	1.000	69	124	5	0	2
Benson	1.000	2	1	0	0	0
Black	.909	9	9	1	1	0
Bogusevic	.985	69	124	5	2	0
Canha	.983	61	110	5	2	1
Jensen	.990	101	185	8	2	1
Juengel	1.000	3	4	1	0	0
Lucas	1.000	1	3	0	0	0
Marisnick	.986	85	205	4	3	1
Silverio	1.000	11	28	1	0	0
Valdespin	.946	21	34	1	2	0
Wates	.963	26	52	0	2	0
Yelich	1.000	2	7	0	0	0

JACKSONVILLE SUNS   DOUBLE-A

SOUTHERN LEAGUE

Batting	B-T	HT	WT	DOB	AVG	vLH	vRH	G	AB	R	H	2B	3B	HR	RBI	BB	HBP	SH	SF	SO	SB	CS	SLG	OBP
Barnes, Austin	R-R	5-9	185	12-28-89	.296	.167	.315	78	284	56	84	20	2	12	43	50	6	3	5	36	8	0	.507	.406
Benson, Joe	R-R	6-1	215	3-5-88	.264	.237	.268	124	417	71	110	23	4	10	62	57	13	3	8	96	15	4	.410	.364
Black, Danny	L-R	6-3	185	8-19-88	.224	.300	.211	69	210	25	47	7	4	2	32	36	1	4	1	57	4	1	.324	.339
Burg, Alex	R-R	6-0	190	8-9-87	.264	.238	.270	76	227	34	60	9	1	7	29	33	3	1	1	66	2	2	.405	.364
Dayleg, Terrence	R-R	6-0	170	9-19-87	.241	.040	.270	59	199	25	48	15	0	2	33	9	5	2	1	48	1	1	.347	.290
Fisher, Ryan	L-R	6-3	195	4-24-88	.207	.231	.204	36	111	13	23	2	0	5	15	10	6	0	1	33	0	1	.360	.305
Furcal, Rafael	B-R	5-8	195	10-24-77	.297	.400	.281	10	37	5	11	2	0	0	3	0	0	0	0	2	4	0	.351	.350
Galloway, Isaac	R-R	6-2	190	10-10-89	.217	.241	.212	110	314	38	68	11	6	4	39	15	2	3	4	109	8	2	.328	.254
Gimenez, Wilfredo	R-R	5-11	235	12-18-90	.243	.280	.236	44	148	9	36	8	0	1	21	3	0	0	1	18	2	0	.318	.257
Guerra, Yosmany	B-R	5-10	10	4-27-83	.143	.000	.147	12	35	1	5	1	0	1	1	5	0	1	0	9	0	1	.257	.250
Keys, Brent	L-R	6-0	185	7-14-90	.242	.167	.257	89	293	45	71	9	1	0	18	54	3	7	4	34	7	4	.280	.362
Lopez, Alfredo	R-R	5-10	160	10-7-89	.216	.273	.201	84	213	20	46	10	0	0	14	22	3	3	0	41	11	4	.263	.298
Morales, Angel	R-R	6-1	180	11-24-89	.125	.000	.167	13	32	3	4	2	0	0	0	0	0	0	0	10	4	0	.188	.125
Nola, Austin	R-R	6-0	190	12-28-89	.259	.250	.260	134	499	68	129	21	5	1	53	77	12	2	5	94	8	5	.327	.368
Poythress, Rich	R-R	6-4	235	8-11-87	.244	.238	.245	46	160	19	39	6	0	4	17	15	2	0	1	21	1	1	.356	.315
2-team total (30 Mississippi)					.260	—	—	76	250	31	65	9	0	6	31	24	2	0	1	36	2	1	.368	.329
Realmuto, J.T.	R-R	6-1	215	3-18-91	.299	.305	.297	97	375	66	112	25	6	8	62	41	3	0	4	59	18	5	.461	.369
Rieger, Ryan	L-L	6-2	205	8-10-90	.250	.200	.256	43	100	8	25	9	1	1	9	6	0	0	1	21	0	0	.390	.290
Rosa, Viosergy	L-L	6-3	185	6-16-90	.292	.273	.295	20	72	15	21	4	1	2	17	14	2	0	1	13	0	0	.458	.416
Shoemaker, Brady	R-R	6-0	200	5-10-87	.274	.115	.296	123	413	65	113	26	2	12	71	67	3	1	6	90	2	1	.433	.374
Silverio, Alfredo	R-R	6-1	215	5-6-87	.212	.154	.221	74	274	17	58	7	1	3	36	9	3	0	5	69	2	3	.277	.241
Tejada, Miguel	R-R	5-9	220	5-25-74	.357	—	.357	4	14	2	5	1	0	0	0	0	0	0	0	0	0	0	.429	.357
Wilson, Ross	R-R	5-11	185	11-9-88	.000	—	.000	3	5	0	0	0	0	0	0	0	0	0	0	2	0	0	.000	.000

Pitching	B-T	HT	WT	DOB	W	L	ERA	G	GS	CG	SV	IP	H	R	ER	HR	BB	SO	AVG	vLH	vRH	K/9	BB/9
Ames, Steve	R-R	6-1	205	3-15-88	2	2	1.64	9	0	0	0	11	8	3	2	0	4	9	.195	.250	.172	7.36	3.27
Cargill, Collin	R-R	6-2	190	10-6-87	5	1	3.22	32	0	0	0	36	34	21	13	1	10	19	.243	.381	.184	4.71	2.48
Dayton, Grant	L-L	6-1	205	11-25-87	0	1	1.10	11	0	0	3	16	17	2	2	0	4	18	.262	.278	.255	9.92	2.20
DeSclafani, Anthony	R-R	6-1	190	4-18-90	3	4	4.19	8	8	0	0	43	45	20	20	4	10	38	.278	.216	.306	7.95	2.09
Effertz, Joel	R-R	6-3	235	9-27-90	0	0	0.00	1	0	0	0	2	1	0	0	0	4	1	.167	—	.167	4.50	18.00
Heaney, Andrew	L-L	6-2	185	6-5-91	4	2	2.35	9	8	0	0	54	45	16	14	2	13	52	.223	.154	.239	8.72	2.18
Higgins, Tyler	R-R	6-1	215	4-22-91	2	0	4.97	15	0	0	0	29	40	18	16	4	8	17	.336	.375	.322	5.28	2.48
Leverton, James	R-L	6-1	215	5-13-86	0	1	4.15	7	0	0	0	9	8	5	4	1	3	7	.250	.500	.100	7.27	3.12
Link, Jon	R-R	6-0	205	3-23-84	1	0	2.25	2	2	0	0	12	10	3	3	0	1	16	.217	.357	.156	12.00	0.75
Logan, Blake	R-R	6-1	245	1-12-92	0	0	0.00	5	0	0	0	11	6	0	0	0	1	11	.158	.077	.200	9.00	0.82
Lyman, Scott	R-R	6-4	215	3-21-90	0	1	10.80	1	1	0	0	5	8	7	6	0	2	3	.471	.250	.538	5.40	3.60
Manzueta, Jheyson	R-R	6-2	180	12-5-89	4	2	4.44	29	0	0	2	47	48	24	23	2	22	28	.271	.317	.246	5.40	4.24
McCarthy, Casey	R-R	6-4	215	4-13-90	1	1	1.93	5	0	0	0	9	8	2	2	2	2	6	.229	.400	.100	5.79	1.93
Montgomery, Matt	R-R	6-4	210	7-21-87	1	1	4.45	11	3	0	0	28	37	17	14	2	7	17	.311	.364	.280	5.40	2.22
Morey, Robert	R-R	6-1	185	11-27-88	3	2	5.09	11	6	0	0	41	50	25	23	3	20	19	.329	.355	.313	4.20	4.43
Moseley, Dustin	R-R	6-4	215	12-26-81	1	1	2.89	5	5	0	0	28	20	12	9	1	4	14	.194	.200	.190	4.50	1.29
Nappo, Greg	L-L	5-10	195	8-25-88	2	0	1.74	34	0	0	1	47	28	9	9	4	7	40	.170	.119	.187	7.71	1.35
Nicolino, Justin	L-L	6-3	190	11-22-91	14	4	2.85	28	28	2	0	170	162	68	54	10	20	81	.249	.211	.259	4.28	1.06
Nygren, James	R-R	6-0	195	3-8-89	4	2	3.46	34	5	0	2	65	70	30	25	8	10	37	.270	.270	.271	5.12	1.38
O'Gara, Joey	R-R	6-7	205	4-20-88	1	0	3.12	8	0	0	1	9	9	3	3	0	2	6	.265	.143	.296	8.31	2.08
Olmos, Edgar	L-L	6-4	220	4-12-90	1	0	4.44	18	0	0	2	26	22	16	13	5	13	16	.232	.242	.226	5.47	4.44
Owings, Micah	R-R	6-5	220	9-28-82	1	1	5.40	2	2	0	0	8	12	5	5	2	3	10	.353	.333	.360	10.80	3.24
Ramos, A.J.	R-R	5-10	205	9-20-86	0	0	9.00	1	0	0	0	1	1	1	1	0	1	1	.400	.500	.333	9.00	9.00
Ramsey, Matt	R-R	5-11	205	9-24-89	0	2	1.95	20	0	0	8	28	19	12	6	2	7	34	.190	.220	.169	11.06	2.28

Player	B-T	HT	WT	DOB	W	L	ERA	G	GS	CG	SV	IP	H	R	ER	HR	BB	SO	AVG	vLH	vRH	K/9	BB/9
2-team total (24 Montgomery)					3	2	1.47	44	0	0	14	61	35	16	10	2	30	80	—	—	—	11.74	4.40
Redman, Reid	R-R	6-0	180	11-22-88	1	0	1.38	9	0	0	1	13	8	3	2	0	3	10	.174	.000	.250	6.92	2.08
Reed, Frankie	L-L	6-1	185	2-12-88	2	0	3.86	20	0	0	0	30	29	14	13	3	10	29	.261	.194	.293	8.60	2.97
Rogers, Jared	R-R	6-7	205	5-9-88	7	5	4.40	19	17	1	0	94	108	52	46	8	19	53	.294	.300	.291	5.07	1.82
Sanchez, Angel	R-R	6-1	190	11-28-89	0	8	6.88	12	12	0	0	52	69	44	40	2	18	30	.314	.259	.348	5.16	3.10
3-team total (3 Birmingham, 2 Montgomery)					1	11	6.96	17	17	0	0	76	102	66	59	6	25	45	—	—	—	5.31	2.95
Smith, Chipper	L-L	6-2	195	1-22-90	3	4	4.27	14	14	0	0	65	52	36	31	11	31	57	.217	.179	.224	7.85	4.27
Urena, Jose	R-R	6-2	195	9-12-91	13	8	3.33	26	25	0	0	162	155	65	60	14	29	121	.255	.279	.240	6.72	1.61
Williams, Trevor	R-R	6-3	228	4-25-92	0	1	6.00	3	3	0	0	15	22	12	10	0	6	14	.344	.308	.368	8.40	3.60
Wittgren, Nick	R-R	6-2	215	5-29-91	5	5	3.55	52	0	0	20	66	73	31	26	6	14	56	.281	.284	.279	7.64	1.91

Fielding

Catcher	PCT	G	PO	A	E	DP	PB
Barnes	.990	29	186	7	2	2	1
Gimenez	.985	26	124	9	2	1	4
Realmuto	.989	88	595	41	7	6	9

First Base	PCT	G	PO	A	E	DP
Burg	1.000	15	102	7	0	5
Fisher	1.000	9	60	1	0	7
Gimenez	.991	12	108	5	1	13
Poythress	.987	42	357	26	5	35
Rieger	1.000	21	160	9	0	20
Rosa	.995	20	173	10	1	15
Shoemaker	.987	35	300	11	4	22

Second Base	PCT	G	PO	A	E	DP
Barnes	.962	30	66	87	6	22
Black	.989	45	73	111	2	26
Dayleg	1.000	8	17	23	0	5
Furcal	.976	10	17	23	1	4
Guerra	.955	8	12	30	2	3
Lopez	.975	40	62	97	4	23
Nola	1.000	7	10	18	0	4
Wilson	1.000	1	1	2	0	1

Third Base	PCT	G	PO	A	E	DP
Barnes	.886	15	6	33	5	2
Burg	.915	36	20	66	8	5
Dayleg	.957	45	19	93	5	13
Fisher	.885	24	13	56	9	4
Lopez	.938	26	13	47	4	2
Nola	1.000	4	4	9	0	2
Tejada	.778	4	0	7	2	1
Wilson	—	1	0	0	0	0

Shortstop	PCT	G	PO	A	E	DP
Black	.942	16	22	43	4	10
Dayleg	.923	2	4	8	1	2
Guerra	.800	1	2	2	1	0
Nola	.962	125	180	381	22	73

Outfield	PCT	G	PO	A	E	DP
Benson	.986	119	274	11	4	5
Black	1.000	6	8	0	0	0
Burg	.971	19	32	1	1	0
Galloway	.991	101	228	5	2	0
Keys	.961	85	163	9	7	0
Morales	1.000	9	21	0	0	0
Rieger	.900	8	9	0	1	0
Shoemaker	1.000	49	72	2	0	0
Silverio	.972	67	131	6	4	2

JUPITER HAMMERHEADS   HIGH CLASS A
FLORIDA STATE LEAGUE

Batting	B-T	HT	WT	DOB	AVG	vLH	vRH	G	AB	R	H	2B	3B	HR	RBI	BB	HBP	SH	SF	SO	SB	CS	SLG	OBP
Adams, Josh	R-R	5-11	185	3-7-89	.148	.133	.154	30	108	5	16	2	2	1	10	8	0	1	0	24	0	0	.231	.207
Avila, Juan	R-R	6-1	180	10-18-91	.208	.286	.195	14	48	2	10	4	0	0	4	2	0	1	0	9	1	0	.292	.240
Barber, Blake	R-R	5-10	180	4-4-90	.252	.246	.255	106	357	48	90	18	3	9	42	28	2	3	1	77	8	6	.395	.309
Barnes, Austin	R-R	5-9	185	12-28-89	.317	.286	.331	44	180	24	57	11	2	1	14	19	1	0	0	35	3	3	.417	.385
Bohn, Justin	R-R	6-0	180	11-2-92	.296	.271	.307	48	199	29	59	9	3	0	12	16	0	1	1	45	7	3	.372	.347
Dayleg, Terrence	R-R	6-0	170	9-19-87	.278	.258	.288	55	212	25	59	8	0	1	15	14	6	2	0	38	1	2	.330	.341
Dietrich, Derek	L-R	6-0	205	7-18-89	.313	.000	.385	5	16	4	5	1	1	1	2	2	1	0	0	5	0	0	.688	.421
Flynn, Cameron	L-L	6-0	195	2-24-90	.247	.244	.248	39	158	17	39	5	2	1	15	4	1	3	3	23	2	0	.323	.265
Furcal, Rafael	B-R	5-8	195	10-24-77	.316	.375	.300	11	38	6	12	0	0	1	5	1	0	0	5	1	0	.316	.409
Goetz, Ryan	L-R	5-10	185	5-16-88	.242	.276	.229	109	385	28	93	11	2	0	39	40	1	8	4	83	24	4	.281	.312
Gomez, Anthony	R-R	6-0	190	11-26-90	.218	.225	.214	65	216	17	47	5	0	0	12	7	0	3	1	22	3	2	.241	.241
Guerra, Yosmany	R-R	6-0	10	4-27-83	.414	.500	.400	9	29	5	12	3	0	0	3	5	0	0	2	0	0	.517	.500
Harris, Alonzo	R-R	5-11	165	1-16-89	.094	.182	.048	11	32	3	3	1	1	0	4	5	0	1	0	6	2	0	.188	.216
Hechavarria, Adeiny	R-R	5-11	185	4-15-89	.125		.167	2	8	0	1	1	0	0	0	0	0	0	8	0	0	.250	.125
Johnson, Coco	R-R	5-11	205	5-3-91	.067	.000	.071	5	15	0	1	0	0	0	0	1	0	0	0	8	0	0	.067	.125
Juengel, Matt	R-R	6-2	185	1-13-90	.272	.315	.255	132	511	80	139	32	6	6	65	36	10	2	3	75	23	2	.393	.330
Keefer, Cody	L-R	6-1	185	11-6-90	.232	.216	.236	57	198	22	46	7	4	2	19	14	1	2	2	26	1	3	.338	.284
Krist, Chadd	R-R	5-11	190	1-28-90	.200	.000	.214	8	30	1	6	2	0	0	1	0	0	0	0	12	0	0	.267	.200
2-team total (52 Daytona)					.218	—	—	60	216	21	47	11	0	4	19	17	2	0	1	54	3	1	.324	.280
Lucas, Ed	R-R	6-3	215	5-21-82	.429	.667	.364	3	14	3	6	0	0	0	2	2	0	0	0	2	0	0	.429	.500
Morales, Angel	R-R	6-1	180	11-24-89	.306	.400	.269	10	36	6	11	3	0	1	6	2	0	1	0	12	0	1	.472	.342
Moran, Colin	L-R	6-4	215	10-1-92	.294	.264	.310	89	361	34	106	21	0	5	33	28	0	0	3	53	1	2	.393	.342
Othman, Sharif	B-R	6-0	195	3-23-89	.133	.214	.097	29	90	9	12	2	0	3	8	14	0	7	1	26	0	0	.256	.248
Perio, Noah	L-R	6-0	170	11-14-91	.241	.147	.270	96	294	35	71	11	1	1	29	20	0	5	1	38	6	1	.296	.289
Rieger, Ryan	L-L	6-2	205	8-10-90	.220	.200	.224	18	59	4	13	2	0	0	3	10	2	0	0	10	0	0	.254	.352
Romero, Avery	R-R	5-8	190	5-11-93	.320	.269	.338	26	100	12	32	8	0	0	10	7	1	0	0	13	4	1	.400	.370
Rosa, Viosergy	L-L	6-3	185	6-16-90	.291	.271	.301	116	446	52	130	25	1	13	78	42	5	0	5	98	0	0	.439	.355
Saltalamacchia, Jarrod	B-R	6-3	235	5-2-85	.286	—	.286	2	7	0	2	0	0	0	0	1	0	0	0	1	0	0	.286	.375
Sanz, Luis	R-R	5-10	165	2-23-91	.154	.000	.200	7	13	2	2	0	0	1	2	1	3	1	1	0	0	.154	.294
Solorzano, Jesus	R-R	6-0	190	8-8-90	.233	.167	.256	85	301	27	70	8	4	3	19	9	1	6	3	78	18	7	.316	.255
Wallach, Chad	R-R	6-3	210	11-4-91	.328	.389	.304	19	64	4	21	3	0	0	8	12	1	0	1	7	0	0	.375	.436
Wilson, Ross	R-R	5-11	185	11-9-88	.239	.278	.226	20	71	5	17	2	0	1	9	4	2	1	1	19	0	2	.310	.295
Yelich, Christian	L-R	6-3	200	12-5-91	.333	—	.333	2	6	2	2	0	0	0	1	1	0	0	0	1	0	0	.333	.429

Pitching	B-T	HT	WT	DOB	W	L	ERA	G	GS	CG	SV	IP	H	R	ER	HR	BB	SO	AVG	vLH	vRH	K/9	BB/9
Alvis, Sam	R-L	6-0	195	6-11-92	0	0	3.06	11	0	0	0	18	21	9	6	2	5	13	.292	.263	.324	6.62	2.55
Bautista, Nestor	L-L	6-3	200	5-13-92	0	0	0.00	1	0	0	0	1	0	0	0	0	1	2	.000	.000	.000	18.00	9.00
Brice, Austin	R-R	6-4	205	6-19-92	8	9	3.60	25	24	0	0	127	114	66	51	5	55	109	.241	.268	.218	7.70	3.89
Buckelew, James	L-L	6-2	155	8-4-91	0	0	15.00	2	0	0	0	3	5	5	5	1	1	2	.357	.375	.333	6.00	3.00
Capps, Carter	R-R	6-4	230	8-7-90	0	0	0.00	1	1	0	0	2	0	0	0	0	0	2	.000	.000	.000	9.00	0.00
Conley, Adam	L-L	6-3	215	5-24-90	0	1	5.06	1	1	0	0	5	9	6	3	0	2	2	.346	.333	.353	3.38	3.38
Crabaugh, Cody	L-R	6-6	210	12-25-90	1	2	8.44	5	3	0	0	16	22	17	15	1	5	7	.310	.343	.278	3.94	2.81
Donatello, Sean	R-R	6-2	205	8-24-90	1	2	4.02	15	0	0	6	16	19	7	7	1	4	13	.317	.348	.297	7.47	2.30

MIAMI MARLINS

	B-T	HT	WT	DOB	W	L	ERA	G	GS	CG	SV	IP	H	R	ER	HR	BB	SO	AVG	vLH	vRH	K/9	BB/9
Ellington, Brian	R-R	6-4	200	8-4-90	2	2	4.75	35	0	0	0	47	51	28	25	2	24	56	.271	.243	.289	10.65	4.56
Esch, Jacob	R-R	6-4	190	3-27-90	6	6	4.05	25	24	1	0	136	147	73	61	7	34	105	.276	.301	.254	6.97	2.26
Fermin, Miguel	R-R	5-11	175	2-11-85	0	2	5.59	7	0	0	0	10	14	7	6	1	3	6	.341	.333	.348	5.59	2.79
Fischer, Kyle	R-R	6-3	205	2-11-91	0	0	4.50	1	0	0	0	2	4	1	1	0	0	2	.400	.286	.667	9.00	0.00
Gregg, Kevin	R-R	6-6	245	6-20-78	0	0	9.00	2	0	0	0	1	3	4	1	1	0	2	.429	.500	.000	18.00	0.00
Greve, Greg	R-R	6-3	200	1-5-92	0	0	0.00	2	0	0	0	3	1	0	0	0	1	4	.091	.167	.000	10.80	2.70
Hand, Brad	L-L	6-3	220	3-20-90	0	0	0.75	2	2	0	0	12	4	1	1	0	2	14	.103	.200	.069	10.50	1.50
Hodges, Josh	R-R	6-7	235	6-21-91	0	6	7.34	13	13	0	0	65	90	59	53	6	22	34	.327	.267	.386	4.71	3.05
Jennings, Dan	L-L	6-3	210	4-17-87	0	0	0.00	3	3	0	0	6	3	0	0	0	0	8	.136	.286	.067	12.00	0.00
Kane, Tyler	R-R	6-1	190	8-23-92	0	0	11.57	2	0	0	0	2	5	3	3	0	4	1	.455	.500	.444	3.86	15.43
Lazo, Raudel	L-L	5-9	165	4-12-89	0	0	9.00	3	0	0	0	3	3	3	3	0	2	1	.273	.500	.222	3.00	6.00
Logan, Blake	R-R	6-1	245	1-12-92	1	3	3.45	22	2	0	2	44	38	18	17	1	9	41	.230	.279	.196	8.32	1.83
Lowell, Charlie	L-L	6-4	235	10-25-90	0	3	30.68	10	1	0	0	7	23	27	25	0	14	8	.511	.471	.536	9.82	17.18
Lyman, Scott	R-R	6-4	215	3-21-90	5	11	3.53	24	24	1	0	135	137	62	53	7	49	95	.265	.243	.287	6.33	3.27
Manzueta, Jheyson	R-R	6-2	180	12-5-89	1	0	4.15	8	0	0	0	13	13	7	6	0	3	9	.265	.100	.379	6.23	2.08
McCarthy, Casey	R-R	6-4	215	4-13-90	3	4	3.32	23	0	0	2	41	36	16	15	1	14	30	.245	.197	.284	6.64	3.10
Milroy, Matt	L-R	6-2	185	10-5-90	2	9	7.20	12	11	0	0	50	49	43	40	4	38	37	.257	.244	.265	6.66	6.84
Mincey, Brad	R-R	6-0	190	12-9-88	0	4	6.87	23	0	0	0	38	63	34	29	2	5	26	.375	.444	.323	6.16	1.18
Montgomery, Matt	R-R	6-4	210	7-21-87	1	0	3.00	1	0	0	0	3	2	1	1	0	0	2	.222	.200	.250	6.00	0.00
Nygren, James	R-R	6-0	195	3-8-89	0	0	0.00	2	0	0	0	4	0	0	0	0	1	2	.000	.000	.000	4.50	2.25
O'Gara, Joey	R-R	6-7	205	4-20-88	1	0	0.54	15	0	0	0	8	17	10	2	1	0	12	.164	.128	.227	6.48	0.54
Penny, Brad	R-R	6-4	230	5-24-78	0	2	5.06	2	2	0	0	11	10	6	6	0	0	4	.250	.250	.250	3.38	0.00
Porter, Kyle	L-L	6-2	200	6-1-92	0	0	10.80	1	0	0	0	2	2	2	2	0	3	3	.286	1.000	.167	16.20	16.20
Redman, Reid	R-R	6-0	180	11-22-88	4	1	2.22	35	0	0	6	49	42	12	12	1	9	58	.231	.325	.157	10.73	1.66
Reed, Frankie	L-L	6-1	185	2-12-88	2	2	3.22	20	0	0	1	36	38	17	13	5	10	21	.264	.191	.299	5.20	2.48
Robinson, C.J.	R-R	6-0	215	5-11-93	0	1	7.36	5	0	0	0	7	11	6	6	1	2	4	.393	.250	.450	4.91	2.45
Scott, Alan	L-L	6-5	230	10-29-90	1	0	0.00	2	0	0	0	5	2	0	0	0	2	4	.125	.200	.091	7.20	3.60
Smith, Chipper	L-L	6-2	195	1-22-90	1	3	1.65	12	1	0	0	27	21	7	5	0	7	30	.212	.219	.209	9.88	2.30
Sosa, Juan	R-R	6-2	165	10-11-89	0	1	3.60	4	0	0	0	5	8	3	2	0	2	1	.381	.417	.333	1.80	3.60
Suggs, Colby	R-R	5-11	235	10-25-91	1	6	5.09	46	0	0	3	58	59	36	33	3	25	47	.266	.234	.297	7.25	3.86
Turner, Jacob	R-R	6-5	215	5-21-91	1	1	2.45	2	2	0	0	11	7	3	3	1	1	10	.179	.240	.071	8.18	0.82
Wertenberger, Ryan	R-R	6-2	215	1-22-90	0	0	8.10	4	0	0	0	7	9	6	6	0	2	4	.360	.615	.083	5.40	2.70
Williams, Trevor	R-R	6-3	228	4-25-92	8	6	2.79	23	23	0	0	129	138	49	40	5	29	90	.277	.278	.275	6.28	2.02

Fielding

Catcher	PCT	G	PO	A	E	DP	PB
Adams	.991	30	199	29	2	2	5
Barnes	.988	44	294	36	4	2	0
Krist	1.000	8	48	7	0	1	0
Othman	.991	29	207	21	2	3	0
Saltalamacchia	1.000	1	11	2	0	0	0
Sanz	.956	7	40	3	2	0	0
Wallach	.993	18	138	10	1	1	2

First Base	PCT	G	PO	A	E	DP
Barber	1.000	4	19	1	0	2
Goetz	1.000	1	2	0	0	0
Gomez	1.000	7	42	2	0	8
Juengel	.988	9	80	3	1	8
Lucas	1.000	1	6	0	0	0
Perio	.985	14	120	11	2	8
Rieger	1.000	6	57	3	0	5
Rosa	.988	102	955	49	12	84

Second Base	PCT	G	PO	A	E	DP
Barber	.973	16	21	50	2	9
Bohn	.900	5	12	6	2	4

	PCT	G	PO	A	E	DP
Dayleg	1.000	2	4	9	0	1
Dietrich	1.000	5	12	17	0	3
Furcal	.977	11	18	25	1	6
Gomez	.977	28	36	94	3	19
Lucas	.875	2	3	4	1	2
Perio	.966	68	101	214	11	30
Romero	.988	16	23	56	1	13

Third Base	PCT	G	PO	A	E	DP
Avila	.857	14	8	22	5	1
Barber	.947	15	11	25	2	0
Bohn	1.000	2	0	3	0	0
Goetz	1.000	1	0	3	0	1
Gomez	1.000	2	1	3	0	0
Lucas	.000	1	0	0	1	0
Moran	.975	86	42	150	5	18
Romero	.833	6	3	7	2	1
Wilson	.936	13	11	33	3	1

Shortstop	PCT	G	PO	A	E	DP
Bohn	.947	40	51	110	9	20
Dayleg	.932	51	71	135	15	30

	PCT	G	PO	A	E	DP
Goetz	.927	11	12	26	3	5
Gomez	.922	26	40	66	9	16
Guerra	.977	9	12	30	1	5
Hechavarria	1.000	2	4	4	0	2
Lucas	.857	1	2	4	1	1

Outfield	PCT	G	PO	A	E	DP
Barber	.963	32	50	2	2	0
Flynn	.989	38	88	2	1	0
Goetz	.984	94	178	10	3	2
Harris	.947	9	18	0	1	0
Johnson	1.000	4	6	0	0	0
Juengel	.951	86	111	6	6	1
Keefer	.978	50	86	2	2	0
Morales	1.000	10	25	0	0	0
Perio	1.000	5	8	0	0	0
Solorzano	.973	85	169	8	5	1
Wilson	.867	8	12	1	2	1
Yelich	1.000	2	3	0	0	0

GREENSBORO GRASSHOPPERS   LOW CLASS A

SOUTH ATLANTIC LEAGUE

Batting	B-T	HT	WT	DOB	AVG	vLH	vRH	G	AB	R	H	2B	3B	HR	RBI	BB	HBP	SH	SF	SO	SB	CS	SLG	OBP
Anderson, Brian	R-R	6-3	175	5-19-93	.314	.313	.314	39	153	27	48	7	0	8	37	13	4	0	2	28	0	0	.516	.378
Avila, Juan	R-R	6-1	180	10-18-91	.248	.233	.254	77	286	37	71	18	2	6	30	25	10	6	1	58	1	0	.388	.329
Bohn, Justin	R-R	6-0	180	11-2-92	.293	.294	.293	63	239	39	70	16	2	6	47	39	3	3	1	49	4	2	.452	.397
Castro, Victor	R-R	6-1	198	1-10-92	.143	.167	.136	15	56	4	8	4	0	1	4	2	3	0	0	15	0	0	.268	.213
Cordova, Rehiner	R-R	6-0	150	1-11-94	.248	.257	.245	76	266	38	66	4	1	1	27	24	4	8	1	51	3	0	.282	.319
Davis, Mason	B-R	5-9	175	1-11-93	.259	.308	.214	7	27	3	7	2	0	0	3	4	0	0	0	6	0	1	.333	.355
Dean, Austin	R-R	6-1	190	10-14-93	.308	.325	.301	99	403	67	124	20	4	9	58	38	4	1	3	72	4	4	.444	.371
Dewitt, Kentrell	L-R	5-11	180	3-20-91	.266	.274	.264	84	308	57	82	14	6	8	44	33	3	3	1	80	9	4	.429	.342
Duran, Carlos	L-R	6-1	195	5-24-92	.077	.000	.083	4	13	1	1	0	0	0	2	1	0	0	1	2	0	0	.077	.133
Haynal, Brad	R-R	6-3	215	8-21-91	.226	.333	.195	13	53	5	12	2	0	1	6	3	1	0	0	12	0	0	.321	.281
Hoo, Chris	R-R	5-9	190	2-19-92	.382	.364	.391	13	34	5	13	2	0	0	3	9	3	2	0	8	0	0	.441	.543
Jimenez, Joel	R-R	5-11	170	4-30-92	.191	.200	.188	27	94	2	18	0	0	0	9	0	1	1	0	25	0	0	.191	.200
Johnson, Coco	R-R	5-11	205	5-3-91	.220	.091	.261	26	91	12	20	2	1	3	17	5	3	0	1	14	3	0	.363	.280
Keefer, Cody	L-R	6-1	185	11-6-90	.319	.267	.339	43	166	33	53	6	2	4	23	11	1	1	2	24	0	0	.452	.361
Lopez, Carlos	L-R	6-2	210	7-16-89	.323	.301	.331	130	507	85	164	27	5	7	74	59	1	5	4	64	5	2	.438	.392

	B-T	HT	WT	DOB	AVG	vLH	vRH	G	AB	R	H	2B	3B	HR	RBI	BB	HBP	SH	SF	SO	SB	CS	SLG	OBP
Lopez, Javier	R-R	6-3	180	9-13-94	.205	.200	.207	26	117	11	24	11	0	0	9	4	1	2	0	20	0	0	.299	.238
Martinez, Hiram	B-R	5-11	155	9-30-92	.182	.000	.200	3	11	1	2	0	0	0	0	1	0	0	0	1	0	0	.182	.250
Munoz, Felix	L-L	6-2	170	4-27-92	.300	.319	.293	126	494	81	148	31	4	16	91	57	1	0	8	74	1	2	.476	.368
Othman, Sharif	B-R	6-0	195	3-23-89	.219	.125	.246	20	73	7	16	3	0	2	9	4	0	2	0	19	0	0	.342	.260
Perez, Yefri	R-R	5-11	165	2-24-91	.287	.267	.294	118	421	65	121	17	0	1	29	26	5	8	2	54	30	9	.335	.335
Riddle, J.T.	L-R	6-3	175	10-12-91	.280	.252	.290	103	435	65	122	17	4	9	60	26	4	6	6	55	5	1	.400	.323
Romero, Avery	R-R	5-8	190	5-11-93	.320	.253	.345	92	366	51	117	23	1	5	46	25	3	3	2	47	6	4	.429	.366
Wallach, Chad	R-R	6-3	210	11-4-91	.321	.243	.350	78	271	50	87	19	1	7	49	50	4	2	3	39	3	0	.476	.430

Pitching	B-T	HT	WT	DOB	W	L	ERA	G	GS	CG	SV	IP	H	R	ER	HR	BB	SO	AVG	vLH	vRH	K/9	BB/9
Adames, Jose	R-R	6-2	165	1-17-93	2	2	3.07	10	8	0	0	44	46	23	15	4	18	38	.261	.276	.247	7.77	3.68
Alvis, Sam	R-L	6-0	195	6-11-92	1	0	3.00	9	0	0	0	18	17	11	6	0	8	16	.258	.333	.182	8.00	4.00
Arias, Jose	R-R	6-6	235	1-17-91	0	1	2.70	7	0	0	1	13	13	4	4	0	1	20	.245	.259	.231	13.50	0.68
Bremer, Tyler	R-R	6-2	210	12-7-89	1	0	1.13	7	0	0	2	8	5	1	1	0	2	12	.179	.222	.100	13.50	2.25
Carreras, Alexander	L-L	6-1	200	1-9-90	0	0	9.00	1	0	0	0	1	1	1	1	0	2	0	.333	.000	.500	0.00	18.00
Crabaugh, Cody	L-R	6-6	210	12-25-90	4	3	4.48	18	9	0	1	66	77	38	33	5	16	41	.294	.317	.267	5.56	2.17
De La Rosa, Esmerling	R-R	6-2	199	5-15-91	5	2	2.28	32	0	0	3	51	49	14	13	6	18	55	.266	.253	.281	9.64	3.16
Del Orbe, Ramon	R-R	5-11	190	2-17-92	3	2	5.09	16	0	0	1	41	49	24	23	4	21	32	.318	.343	.299	7.08	4.65
Del Pozo, Miguel	L-L	6-1	180	10-14-92	2	6	4.91	41	0	0	4	66	59	37	36	5	19	85	.243	.186	.284	11.59	2.59
Donatello, Sean	R-R	6-2	205	8-24-90	3	0	3.79	30	0	0	11	38	43	18	16	4	6	51	.279	.260	.296	12.08	1.42
Easley, Josh	R-R	6-3	190	12-9-90	3	2	3.63	14	0	0	1	17	18	10	7	2	4	13	.254	.250	.256	6.75	2.08
Effertz, Joel	R-R	6-2	235	9-27-90	0	0	2.38	7	0	0	0	11	8	4	3	2	3	10	.195	.053	.318	7.94	2.38
Fischer, Kyle	R-R	6-5	205	2-11-91	1	1	3.38	8	2	0	0	21	21	10	8	1	9	20	.259	.214	.308	8.86	3.80
Garcia, Jarlin	L-L	6-2	170	1-18-93	10	5	4.38	25	25	0	0	134	152	78	65	13	21	111	.286	.273	.290	7.47	1.41
Garner, Max	R-R	6-3	200	6-11-90	3	4	3.91	13	13	0	0	71	76	39	31	5	20	59	.269	.302	.240	7.44	2.52
German, Domingo	R-R	6-2	175	8-4-92	9	3	2.48	25	25	0	0	123	116	43	34	6	25	113	.249	.269	.228	8.25	1.82
Kane, Tyler	R-R	6-1	190	8-23-92	2	0	4.18	18	0	0	2	32	36	16	15	2	10	20	.295	.338	.246	5.57	2.78
Kinley, Tyler	R-R	6-4	205	1-31-91	3	1	2.70	28	0	0	10	30	20	12	9	3	10	30	.183	.160	.203	9.00	3.00
Logan, Blake	R-R	6-1	245	1-12-92	1	1	5.93	10	0	0	1	14	12	14	9	1	8	9	.240	.182	.286	5.93	5.27
McCarthy, Casey	R-R	6-4	215	1-30-90	2	0	3.27	7	0	0	0	11	10	4	4	1	5	12	.250	.158	.333	9.82	4.09
Milroy, Matt	L-R	6-2	185	10-5-90	6	3	2.56	14	9	0	0	63	44	25	18	1	23	87	.190	.168	.208	12.36	3.27
Moseley, Dustin	R-R	6-4	215	12-26-81	0	0	3.60	1	1	0	0	5	5	4	2	0	0	4	.238	.250	.222	7.20	0.00
Newell, Ryan	R-R	6-2	215	6-18-91	8	7	3.36	19	19	1	0	110	110	48	41	8	21	94	.263	.313	.211	7.71	1.72
Robinson, C.J.	R-R	6-5	215	5-11-93	6	4	4.10	32	0	0	1	48	48	22	22	1	26	38	.261	.303	.221	7.08	4.84
Sadberry, Chris	L-L	6-0	195	11-8-91	4	1	2.65	7	6	0	0	34	22	10	10	3	7	29	.179	.083	.240	7.68	1.85
Townsley, Sean	L-L	6-7	240	9-19-90	6	3	2.25	20	14	1	3	96	88	29	24	2	18	87	.242	.256	.236	8.16	1.69
Wertenberger, Ryan	R-R	6-2	215	1-22-90	2	1	4.42	16	9	0	0	53	60	35	26	8	19	42	.287	.293	.282	7.13	3.23
Wooster, James	L-L	6-1	200	6-19-89	0	1	2.16	13	0	0	2	17	6	4	4	0	11	17	.109	.100	.114	9.18	5.94

Fielding

Catcher	PCT	G	PO	A	E	DP	PB
Haynal	.973	13	100	10	3	0	2
Hoo	.991	12	91	16	1	3	2
Jimenez	1.000	26	171	18	0	1	8
Othman	.989	19	156	18	2	1	2
Wallach	.994	73	597	69	4	2	8

First Base	PCT	G	PO	A	E	DP
Avila	.979	5	46	0	1	3
Cordova	1.000	1	10	0	0	0
Duran	1.000	1	1	0	0	1
Lopez	.994	17	159	11	1	15
Munoz	.994	118	1093	67	7	85

Second Base	PCT	G	PO	A	E	DP
Anderson	.964	9	23	30	2	9
Bohn	.979	23	34	58	2	13

	PCT	G	PO	A	E	DP
Cordova	.984	13	27	33	1	10
Davis	1.000	2	0	3	0	0
Martinez	1.000	1	0	6	0	0
Perez	.920	12	16	30	4	2
Riddle	.947	6	7	11	1	1
Romero	.969	77	113	226	11	44

Third Base	PCT	G	PO	A	E	DP
Anderson	.933	26	22	48	5	7
Avila	.947	47	31	112	8	6
Cordova	.939	32	24	53	5	6
Martinez	1.000	2	1	1	0	0
Riddle	.907	35	27	61	9	6

Shortstop	PCT	G	PO	A	E	DP
Bohn	.957	34	38	95	6	13
Cordova	.966	27	40	75	4	16

	PCT	G	PO	A	E	DP
Lopez	.898	22	32	74	12	10
Perez	1.000	1	1	3	0	0
Riddle	.958	58	90	185	12	38

Outfield	PCT	G	PO	A	E	DP
Avila	.964	21	24	3	1	1
Castro	.929	9	13	0	1	0
Cordova	1.000	4	9	0	0	0
Davis	1.000	4	6	0	0	0
Dean	.974	82	107	7	3	0
Dewitt	.984	60	117	4	2	1
Johnson	.933	15	27	1	2	0
Keefer	.986	39	72	1	1	0
Lopez	.969	93	138	16	5	1
Perez	.995	103	192	7	1	1

BATAVIA MUCKDOGS   SHORT-SEASON

NEW YORK-PENN LEAGUE

Batting	B-T	HT	WT	DOB	AVG	vLH	vRH	G	AB	R	H	2B	3B	HR	RBI	BB	HBP	SH	SF	SO	SB	CS	SLG	OBP
Anderson, Brian	R-R	6-3	175	5-19-93	.273	.316	.259	20	77	11	21	3	1	3	12	6	1	1	0	11	1	1	.455	.333
Aper, Ryan	R-R	6-3	175	6-6-93	.218	.133	.234	58	188	25	41	9	1	1	21	10	3	8	1	62	4	3	.293	.267
Blanton, Aaron	R-R	6-2	175	9-1-93	.264	.348	.247	70	261	41	69	6	5	0	28	18	5	2	3	48	10	10	.326	.321
Cabrera, Rony	R-R	5-11	175	1-29-96	.303	.286	.308	7	33	4	10	2	0	0	1	0	0	0	0	7	1	0	.364	.303
Carcaise, Scott	L-L	6-5	230	5-13-92	.122	.000	.161	12	41	3	5	1	0	0	0	8	0	0	0	15	0	0	.146	.265
Castillo, Felix	R-R	5-11	170	6-20-91	.250	.000	.286	5	16	2	4	0	0	0	2	0	1	0	0	5	0	0	.250	.294
Castro, Victor	R-R	6-1	198	1-10-92	.225	.167	.235	34	120	8	27	7	1	1	14	7	3	0	1	26	2	1	.325	.282
Cranmer, Ryan	R-R	6-2	195	6-23-92	.346	.000	.375	9	26	6	9	1	0	2	4	5	0	0	1	5	0	0	.615	.438
Davis, Mason	B-R	5-9	175	1-11-93	.319	.331	.320	56	216	39	69	13	5	3	29	24	3	4	1	35	9	7	.468	.393
Duran, Carlos	L-R	6-1	195	5-24-92	.278	.083	.308	46	180	20	50	10	0	0	18	11	1	0	1	20	0	0	.333	.321
Fisher, Eric	L-L	6-3	205	3-10-92	.248	.188	.265	38	149	12	37	5	0	3	17	4	1	1	2	21	1	0	.342	.269
Grove, Kevin	R-R	6-4	225	12-28-90	.241	.400	.205	42	162	22	39	9	1	2	17	9	2	0	0	51	1	1	.346	.289
Haynal, Brad	R-R	6-3	215	8-21-91	.271	.375	.255	30	118	13	32	6	0	2	21	7	2	0	2	39	0	1	.373	.318
Hoo, Chris	R-R	5-9	190	2-19-92	.321	.667	.227	10	28	1	9	4	0	0	1	1	4	1	0	3	0	0	.464	.424
Jimenez, Joel	R-R	5-11	170	4-30-92	.125	.000	.143	2	8	1	1	0	0	0	1	0	0	0	0	3	0	0	.250	.125

Name	B-T	HT	WT	DOB	AVG	vLH	vRH	G	AB	R	H	2B	3B	HR	RBI	BB	HBP	SH	SF	SO	SB	CS	SLG	OBP
Johnson, Coco	R-R	5-11	205	5-3-91	.000	—	.000	1	4	0	0	0	0	0	0	0	0	0	0	0	0	0	.000	.000
Lopez, Javier	R-R	6-3	180	9-13-94	.234	.233	.234	45	175	22	41	7	3	0	8	8	4	5	3	38	3	1	.309	.279
Martinez, Hiram	B-R	5-11	155	9-30-92	.235	.176	.250	28	85	9	20	2	0	0	9	4	3	0	1	9	0	0	.259	.290
Norwood, John	R-R	6-1	185	9-24-92	.256	.500	.212	20	78	4	20	1	1	0	6	3	0	0	0	25	0	0	.295	.284
Olivencia, Iramis	R-R	5-9	175	11-6-94	.219	.364	.189	21	64	5	14	5	0	0	1	1	2	0	18	2	0	.297	.242	
Pujols, Wildert	L-L	6-1	175	6-7-94	.264	.238	.269	47	140	13	37	8	1	0	14	10	1	5	1	27	4	1	.336	.316
Rivera, Christian	R-R	5-10	165	2-10-94	.176	.333	.143	7	17	3	3	0	0	0	0	6	1	0	0	4	0	1	.176	.417
Sanz, Luis	R-R	5-10	165	2-23-91	.212	.235	.204	21	66	4	14	1	0	0	4	8	2	1	0	2	0	0	.227	.316
Vigil, Rodrigo	R-R	6-0	164	1-3-93	.280	.235	.289	32	107	9	30	5	1	1	10	6	2	2	0	9	1	0	.374	.330
Williams, Miles	R-R	5-10	185	7-18-92	.150	.071	.174	21	60	9	9	2	0	1	6	6	4	0	0	32	0	0	.233	.271
Woods, K.J.	L-R	6-3	230	7-9-95	.219	.118	.239	29	105	8	23	6	1	1	10	8	2	0	2	33	2	1	.324	.282

Pitching	B-T	HT	WT	DOB	W	L	ERA	G	GS	CG	SV	IP	H	R	ER	HR	BB	SO	AVG	vLH	vRH	K/9	BB/9
Adames, Ayron	B-R	6-0	190	3-1-94	0	0	20.25	1	0	0	0	1	4	3	3	1	0	1	.500	1.000	.333	6.75	0.00
Adames, Jose	R-R	6-2	165	1-17-93	4	0	1.32	7	2	0	0	27	26	6	4	0	11	28	.263	.283	.245	9.22	3.62
Alvis, Sam	R-L	6-0	195	6-11-92	0	0	2.25	2	0	0	0	4	5	1	1	0	4	4	.294	.250	.333	9.00	9.00
Beltre, Andy	R-R	6-4	195	7-6-93	1	1	6.00	3	3	0	0	12	14	9	8	2	4	15	.286	.400	.105	11.25	3.00
Buckelew, James	L-L	6-2	155	8-4-91	0	3	4.43	11	0	0	0	20	26	11	10	0	6	21	.325	.208	.375	9.30	2.66
Carreras, Alexander	L-L	6-1	200	1-9-90	5	3	2.28	21	0	0	2	43	39	12	11	0	14	38	.242	.191	.263	7.89	2.91
Castellanos, Gabriel	L-L	6-1	165	12-28-93	2	6	4.65	13	13	0	0	62	52	45	32	1	41	54	.224	.222	.225	7.84	5.95
Cavanerio, Jorgan	R-R	6-1	155	8-18-94	4	6	4.56	14	14	0	0	79	98	47	40	9	14	55	.314	.309	.321	6.27	1.59
Del Orbe, Ramon	R-R	5-11	190	2-17-92	0	0	0.00	6	0	0	2	15	4	0	0	0	4	12	.082	.125	.000	7.04	2.35
Farnworth, Steven	R-R	6-2	175	9-6-93	1	1	4.86	18	4	0	1	37	39	26	20	4	11	28	.269	.281	.259	6.81	2.68
Fermin, Miguel	R-R	6-1	175	2-11-85	1	0	0.00	2	0	0	0	3	0	0	0	0	1	3	.000	.000	.000	9.00	3.00
Fox, Hayden	R-L	6-4	200	3-1-91	2	0	6.56	16	0	0	0	23	35	22	17	1	9	23	.337	.400	.316	8.87	3.47
Hodges, Josh	R-R	6-7	235	6-21-91	3	5	2.63	22	0	0	7	38	34	12	11	3	9	42	.238	.217	.257	10.04	2.15
Holmes, Ben	L-L	6-1	195	9-12-91	0	2	2.95	11	11	0	0	40	47	17	13	5	12	31	.320	.275	.336	7.03	2.72
Kane, Tyler	R-R	6-1	190	8-23-92	0	1	4.50	6	0	0	2	10	9	8	5	0	1	6	.220	.200	.238	5.40	0.90
MacDonald, Christian	L-L	6-4	210	2-26-92	0	2	6.23	15	0	0	0	22	29	16	15	0	9	18	.330	.182	.379	7.48	3.74
Mader, Michael	L-L	6-2	195	2-18-94	1	0	2.00	12	12	0	0	45	31	11	10	3	16	28	.199	.250	.176	5.60	3.20
Martinez, Juancito	R-R	6-1	170	6-10-89	2	1	2.51	21	0	0	6	29	23	11	8	0	11	33	.215	.250	.176	10.36	3.45
Mendoza, Yeims	R-R	6-2	155	2-27-93	0	4	6.75	7	2	0	0	13	12	12	10	5	8	10	.240	.261	.222	6.75	5.40
Overton, Connor	R-R	6-0	190	7-24-93	1	2	4.71	17	0	0	1	21	24	15	11	2	14	20	.289	.238	.341	8.57	6.00
Oviedo, Ramon	R-R	6-4	175	7-24-90	0	0	5.63	5	0	0	0	8	8	5	5	0	5	7	.267	.250	.278	7.88	5.63
Ramos, Felix	B-L	6-0	175	12-2-93	0	0	20.25	1	0	0	0	1	3	3	3	0	3	1	.429	.500	.400	6.75	20.25
Sadberry, Chris	L-L	6-0	195	11-8-91	0	1	4.09	4	0	0	0	11	13	5	5	0	2	11	.302	.250	.323	9.00	1.64
Smigelski, Jacob	R-R	6-3	200	6-20-92	2	2	4.95	13	5	0	0	44	46	28	24	3	16	24	.266	.293	.245	4.95	3.30
Squier, Scott	R-L	6-5	185	9-17-92	4	2	3.17	13	6	0	0	48	43	20	17	1	18	40	.239	.125	.280	7.45	3.35
Wertenberger, Ryan	R-R	6-2	215	1-22-90	1	0	3.00	2	0	0	0	3	5	2	1	0	0	3	.333	.333	.333	9.00	0.00

Fielding

Catcher	PCT	G	PO	A	E	DP	PB
Castillo	1.000	5	24	4	0	0	0
Haynal	1.000	11	78	12	0	1	4
Hoo	1.000	10	65	11	0	2	0
Jimenez	1.000	2	8	2	0	0	0
Sanz	.994	21	139	22	1	2	2
Vigil	.985	32	226	38	4	3	11

First Base	PCT	G	PO	A	E	DP
Carcaise	1.000	8	54	11	0	4
Duran	.982	34	300	20	6	22
Fisher	.973	35	293	37	9	35

Second Base	PCT	G	PO	A	E	DP
Anderson	.987	17	31	45	1	10

	PCT	G	PO	A	E	DP
Cabrera	.975	7	14	25	1	3
Davis	.972	39	89	123	6	26
Martinez	1.000	4	8	17	0	3
Olivencia	.981	9	28	25	1	8
Rivera	1.000	1	1	0	0	0

Third Base	PCT	G	PO	A	E	DP
Blanton	.932	42	21	75	7	7
Cranmer	.818	5	2	7	2	1
Davis	1.000	9	3	16	0	2
Martinez	.868	18	12	21	5	2
Rivera	.889	6	7	9	2	2

Shortstop	PCT	G	PO	A	E	DP
Blanton	.924	29	39	82	10	17

	PCT	G	PO	A	E	DP
Lopez	.928	43	84	134	17	30
Martinez	.926	6	7	18	2	1

Outfield	PCT	G	PO	A	E	DP
Aper	.960	56	117	2	5	0
Castro	.911	31	47	4	5	2
Davis	1.000	6	13	1	0	2
Grove	1.000	38	62	0	0	0
Johnson	1.000	1	3	1	0	1
Norwood	.977	18	42	1	1	0
Olivencia	1.000	9	16	1	0	1
Pujols	.938	36	56	4	4	0
Williams	.960	20	23	1	1	0
Woods	.955	19	21	0	1	0

GCL MARLINS   ROOKIE
GULF COAST LEAGUE

Batting	B-T	HT	WT	DOB	AVG	vLH	vRH	G	AB	R	H	2B	3B	HR	RBI	BB	HBP	SH	SF	SO	SB	CS	SLG	OBP
Anderson, Blake	R-R	6-3	180	1-5-96	.108	.000	.125	26	74	6	8	2	0	0	5	12	7	0	1	33	0	1	.135	.287
Bogusevic, Brian	L-L	6-3	215	2-18-84	.333	.500	.286	3	9	2	3	0	0	1	3	2	0	0	0	2	1	1	.667	.455
Brewster, Travis	L-L	5-9	210	1-21-92	.217	.000	.238	9	23	2	5	0	0	0	1	2	0	0	0	8	4	0	.217	.280
Cabrera, Rony	R-R	5-11	175	1-29-96	.265	.381	.246	47	155	10	41	9	0	0	14	2	0	0	3	26	4	1	.323	.269
Castillo, Felix	R-R	5-1	170	6-20-91	.333	.500	.273	5	15	1	5	1	0	0	1	0	0	0	0	1	0	0	.400	.375
Cranmer, Ryan	R-R	6-2	195	6-23-92	.143	.000	.182	3	14	0	2	0	0	0	0	0	0	0	0	7	0	0	.143	.143
Fisher, Ryan	L-R	6-3	195	4-24-88	.333	—	.333	3	6	2	2	0	0	1	2	2	0	0	0	2	0	0	.833	.500
Garrett, Stone	R-R	6-2	195	11-22-95	.236	.333	.212	40	148	17	35	3	1	0	11	7	0	0	1	31	4	1	.270	.269
Guerra, Yosmany	B-R	5-10	10	4-27-83	.353	.429	.300	5	17	5	6	0	1	1	4	5	0	0	0	2	0	0	.647	.500
Hoo, Chris	R-R	5-9	190	2-19-92	.188	.250	.167	7	16	1	3	0	0	0	1	2	0	0	0	0	0	0	.188	.316
Lopez, Javier	R-R	6-3	180	9-13-94	.231	.000	.250	4	13	0	3	0	0	0	1	1	0	0	0	1	0	0	.231	.286
Moscat, Galvi	R-R	6-0	180	6-29-94	.209	.250	.203	27	86	7	18	1	0	1	7	6	1	0	1	7	0	0	.256	.266
Olivencia, Iramis	R-R	5-9	175	11-6-94	.156	.200	.148	14	32	2	5	1	1	0	4	8	0	0	0	9	1	0	.250	.325
Reyes, Angel	R-R	6-0	175	5-6-95	.203	.214	.200	26	79	13	16	6	1	1	9	10	1	0	0	24	1	0	.342	.300
Richards, Jonathan	B-R	6-0	180	6-16-95	.247	.333	.233	26	85	7	21	2	0	0	2	1	0	0	0	15	1	0	.271	.256
Schales, Brian	R-R	6-1	170	2-13-96	.243	.152	.264	49	173	24	42	8	0	1	23	16	5	2	4	28	2	5	.306	.318

	B-T	HT	WT	DOB	AVG	vLH	vRH	G	AB	R	H	2B	3B	HR	RBI	BB	HBP	SH	SF	SO	SB	CS	SLG	OBP
Seymour, Anfernee	R-R	5-11	165	6-24-95	.245	.222	.250	26	98	24	24	0	1	0	3	12	1	1	0	27	11	2	.265	.333
Smith, Austen	R-R	6-4	240	1-2-92	.288	.261	.292	47	153	25	44	5	1	7	34	20	12	0	2	41	0	0	.471	.406
Soltis, Casey	L-L	6-1	185	6-8-95	.264	.182	.283	33	121	13	32	3	0	0	8	14	3	0	0	33	2	1	.289	.355
Soto, Isael	L-L	6-0	190	11-2-96	.251	.240	.253	50	183	26	46	9	1	7	23	10	4	0	2	47	1	2	.426	.302
Sullivan, Zach	R-R	6-3	180	11-26-95	.280	.214	.291	30	93	12	26	3	1	2	11	16	2	0	2	19	9	1	.398	.389
Twine, Justin	R-R	5-11	205	10-7-95	.229	.273	.218	44	166	19	38	8	5	1	16	6	7	0	0	52	5	1	.355	.285
Woods, K.J.	L-R	6-3	230	7-9-95	.240	.273	.231	15	50	5	12	1	0	1	9	4	0	0	0	20	0	1	.320	.296

Pitching	B-T	HT	WT	DOB	W	L	ERA	G	GS	CG	SV	IP	H	R	ER	HR	BB	SO	AVG	vLH	vRH	K/9	BB/9
Adames, Ayron	B-R	6-0	190	3-1-94	3	2	4.07	14	4	0	0	42	33	23	19	0	25	40	.224	.291	.185	8.57	5.36
Ames, Steve	R-R	6-1	205	3-15-88	0	0	1.50	5	0	0	0	6	3	1	1	0	1	4	.150	.111	.182	6.00	1.50
Aquino, Francisco	L-L	6-3	185	9-15-92	2	3	4.32	15	3	1	1	33	25	21	16	1	21	26	.207	.244	.188	7.02	5.67
Bautista, Nestor	L-L	6-3	200	5-13-92	2	1	2.48	13	3	0	0	36	30	12	10	0	10	30	.229	.216	.234	7.43	2.48
Buckelew, James	L-L	6-2	155	8-4-91	1	0	1.13	4	0	0	0	8	6	3	1	0	3	8	.214	.250	.200	9.00	3.38
Capps, Carter	R-R	6-4	230	8-7-90	0	0	0.00	2	2	0	0	1	0	1	0	0	2	2	.000	.000	.000	13.50	13.50
De La Rosa, Leurys	R-R	6-2	160	11-5-94	1	2	4.15	18	0	0	2	30	41	19	14	1	9	21	.325	.292	.346	6.23	2.67
Fischer, Kyle	R-R	6-3	205	2-11-91	0	0	11.12	9	0	0	0	11	22	16	14	1	5	14	.386	.450	.351	11.12	3.97
Greve, Greg	R-R	6-3	200	1-5-92	1	2	3.62	20	0	0	1	32	32	16	13	0	8	19	.258	.333	.205	5.29	2.23
Grim, Nick	R-R	6-3	200	1-16-91	0	0	0.00	2	0	0	0	1	0	0	0	0	0	3	.000	.000	.000	9.00	20.25
Hepner, Justin	R-R	6-3	200	2-4-92	0	0	12.27	3	0	0	0	4	8	6	5	0	2	2	.400	.333	.429	4.91	4.91
Holloway, Jordan	R-R	6-4	190	6-13-96	1	3	6.41	10	6	0	0	27	38	24	19	0	8		.352	.412	.324	2.70	2.70
Jennings, Dan	L-L	6-3	210	4-17-87	0	0	0.00	1	0	0	0	1	0	0	0	0	0	1	.000	.000	.000	9.00	0.00
Kolek, Tyler	R-R	6-5	260	12-15-95	0	3	4.50	9	8	0	0	22	22	17	11	0	13	18	.275	.314	.244	7.36	5.32
Lazo, Raudel	L-L	5-9	165	4-12-89	0	0	3.60	5	3	0	0	5	2	2	2	0	2	5	.118	.000	.154	9.00	0.00
Martes, Francis	R-R	6-0	170	11-24-95	2	2	5.18	8	6	0	0	33	29	21	19	0	20	33	.232	.244	.225	9.00	5.45
2-team total (4 Astros)					3	3	4.09	12	9	0	0	44	34	24	20	0	23	45	—	—	—	9.20	4.70
Mendoza, Yeims	R-R	6-2	155	2-27-93	1	0	5.79	5	0	0	0	9	8	6	6	0	10	8	.235	.364	.174	7.71	9.64
Morey, Robert	R-R	6-1	185	11-27-88	0	1	0.93	3	3	1	0	10	8	3	1	0	1	11	.216	.250	.176	10.24	0.93
O'Gara, Joey	R-R	6-7	205	4-20-88	0	2	5.06	5	1	0	0	5	4	3	3	0	4	6	.200	.111	.273	6.75	0.00
Porter, Kyle	L-L	6-2	200	6-1-92	3	2	5.18	17	0	0	0	24	23	16	14	0	9	29	.242	.281	.222	10.73	3.33
Ramos, Felix	B-L	6-0	175	12-2-93	0	4	7.63	14	4	0	3	31	48	28	26	2	11	19	.358	.405	.340	5.58	3.23
Rojas, Keivi	R-R	6-0	170	2-26-93	0	0	5.63	6	0	0	1	8	9	6	5	0	6	3	.290	.385	.222	3.38	6.75
Scott, Alan	L-L	6-5	230	10-29-90	1	0	2.08	15	0	0	2	22	24	6	5	0	9	15	.300	.429	.254	6.23	3.74
Smith, Chipper	L-L	6-2	195	1-22-90	1	0	0.00	2	2	0	0	8	4	2	0	0	0	4	.143	.000	.190	4.50	0.00
Sosa, Juan	R-R	6-2	165	10-11-89	0	0	0.00	3	0	0	0	3	1	0	0	0	0	3	.100	.000		9.00	0.00
Steckenrider, Drew	R-R	6-5	215	1-10-91	0	0	0.00	1	0	0	1	1	0	0	0	0	0	1	.000	—	.000	9.00	0.00
Varner, Rett	R-R	6-3	210	2-3-88	1	2	11.25	4	2	0	0	4	5	5	5	0	3	2	.313	.400	.273	4.50	6.75
White, Nick	R-R	6-3	205	10-15-95	1	1	2.61	9	2	0	0	21	16	10	6	0	15	14	.211	.167	.239	6.10	6.53
Williams, Nick	R-R	6-2	225	11-15-91	4	5	3.92	12	4	0	0	44	41	22	19	1	16	27	.256	.333	.210	5.56	3.30
Zulueta, Nelson	R-R	6-3	175	8-10-94	0	0	9.00	5	1	0	0	5	5	5	5	0	2	2	.263	.400	.111	3.60	3.60

Fielding

Catcher	PCT	G	PO	A	E	DP	PB
Anderson	.983	26	156	21	3	0	13
Castillo	1.000	3	12	1	0	0	0
Hoo	1.000	7	34	9	0	0	0
Morales	.988	25	146	20	2	3	10
Reyes	1.000	3	22	4	0	0	2

First Base	PCT	G	PO	A	E	DP
Cabrera	1.000	9	57	7	0	5
Fisher	1.000	1	10	0	0	0
Reyes	.949	7	51	5	3	5
Smith	.985	45	428	18	7	37

Second Base	PCT	G	PO	A	E	DP
Cabrera	.962	24	29	73	4	14
Guerra	.923	2	4	8	1	3

	PCT	G	PO	A	E	DP
Olivencia	.960	14	11	37	2	0
Richards	.980	22	34	62	2	13
Schales	1.000	3	12	1	2	0

Third Base	PCT	G	PO	A	E	DP
Cabrera	.955	14	14	28	2	3
Cranmer	.667	2	1	3	2	0
Fisher	1.000	2	0	3	0	0
Richards	.818	3	3	6	2	1
Schales	.911	40	28	85	11	3

Shortstop	PCT	G	PO	A	E	DP
Cabrera	1.000	1	3	4	0	3
Guerra	.923	3	5	7	1	2
Lopez	1.000	3	5	13	0	0
Reyes	1.000	1	1	2	0	1

	PCT	G	PO	A	E	DP
Richards	1.000	1	2	3	0	0
Schales	.938	4	6	9	1	2
Seymour	.840	7	9	12	4	4
Twine	.946	43	66	126	11	25

Outfield	PCT	G	PO	A	E	DP
Bogusevic	1.000	3	4	0	0	0
Brewster	1.000	5	7	0	0	0
Cabrera	—	1	0	0	0	0
Garrett	.898	31	42	2	5	0
Moscat	.961	26	45	4	2	2
Seymour	.944	19	34	0	2	0
Soltis	.939	27	42	4	3	0
Soto	.973	40	71	0	2	0
Sullivan	.980	25	47	2	1	1
Woods	1.000	11	18	0	0	0

DSL MARLINS

ROOKIE

DOMINICAN SUMMER LEAGUE

Batting	B-T	HT	WT	DOB	AVG	vLH	vRH	G	AB	R	H	2B	3B	HR	RBI	BB	HBP	SH	SF	SO	SB	CS	SLG	OBP
Acosta, Leisman	L-R	5-9	150	1-12-97	.311	.360	.297	58	235	30	73	12	1	0	26	18	1	0	0	30	13	6	.370	.362
Alcala, Luis	L-R	6-2	180	9-21-96	.169	.167	.170	40	124	16	21	2	1	0	9	26	2	0	1	39	1	2	.202	.320
Almonte, Erwin	L-L	6-0	170	2-22-95	.304	.213	.329	70	289	39	88	15	6	2	37	14	2	1	2	21	2	2	.419	.339
Avello, Roger	B-R	6-2	189	12-5-94	.282	.311	.274	54	202	35	57	12	2	0	22	9	8	1	1	38	10	6	.361	.336
Garcia, Pablo	B-R	5-10	170	9-26-96	.287	.413	.252	53	209	35	60	10	3	1	31	18	2	3	5	38	2	3	.378	.342
Guaba, Endy	R-R	6-2	195	3-31-95	.100	—		5	10	2	1	0	0	0	0	3	0	0	0	5	0	1	.100	.308
Guerrero, Jesus	R-R	6-0	180	8-30-96	.170	.174	.169	28	88	11	15	3	1	1	10	5	5	1	0	26	2	0	.261	.255
Guzman, Josue	L-L	6-3	175	5-30-96	.203	.107	.221	61	177	19	36	8	1	0	15	30	6	2	1	43	2	5	.260	.336
Lara, Garvis	L-R	6-2	170	5-19-96	.237	.340	.209	54	219	34	52	6	5	0	17	14	4	1	2	54	8	8	.311	.293
Olivo, Benito	R-R	6-0	185	7-11-94	.326	.333	.324	14	46	9	15	3	2	1	6	6	1	0	0	12	1	1	.543	.415
Pena, Ermel	R-R	6-1	170	8-26-96	.240	.179	.254	52	150	21	36	4	2	1	14	13	4	1	1	36	11	5	.313	.315
Pinto, Yobanis	R-R	5-11	190	2-15-96	.234	.212	.242	36	124	15	29	4	0	0	15	15	8	0	3	12	0	0	.266	.347
Reyes, Yefry	L-R	5-10	170	12-18-96	.242	.265	.236	45	178	17	43	8	0	1	25	8	4	0	1	30	4	2	.303	.288
Santos, Jhonny	R-R	6-0	160	10-2-96	.223	.322	.195	65	264	36	59	9	4	0	19	21	5	1	7	35	10	5	.288	.286

Pitching	B-T	HT	WT	DOB	W	L	ERA	G	GS	CG	SV	IP	H	R	ER	HR	BB	SO	AVG	vLH	vRH	K/9	BB/9
Arias, Jesus	L-L	5-9	150	4-16-93	0	3	2.25	10	7	0	1	24	23	11	6	0	4	24	.247	.412	.211	9.00	1.50
Artiles, Carlos	R-R	6-4	210	8-20-91	0	3	6.29	12	7	0	0	24	20	20	17	0	27	19	.263	.421	.211	7.03	9.99
Atizol, Mauricio	L-L	6-3	180	9-2-96	0	0	3.92	9	4	0	0	21	13	11	9	1	12	17	.178	.176	.179	7.40	5.23
Bautista, Felix	R-R	6-5	190	6-20-95	0	1	12.41	8	1	0	0	12	11	17	17	0	20	7	.250	.462	.161	5.11	14.59
Cuello, Eliezer	R-R	6-2	195	11-18-96	2	3	2.76	15	9	0	1	65	54	31	20	0	29	51	.228	.243	.222	7.03	3.99
Diaz, Jose	R-R	6-2	180	5-7-93	1	5	4.48	15	5	0	0	72	85	53	36	2	23	53	.294	.245	.318	6.59	2.86
Gonzalez, Eddy	R-R	6-6	175	9-28-94	0	3	9.98	8	3	0	0	15	13	22	17	0	23	8	.228	.222	.231	4.70	13.50
Hernandez, Elias	R-R	6-3	185	5-14-96	0	1	18.90	4	0	0	0	7	20	16	14	1	4	6	.513	.643	.440	8.10	5.40
Jaramillo, Jose	R-R	6-1	180	12-2-95	5	2	1.89	19	1	0	3	48	39	16	10	1	19	28	.228	.196	.240	5.29	3.59
Lara, Erick	R-R	6-2	150	3-24-94	3	4	4.38	11	6	0	0	49	40	37	24	0	25	35	.209	.222	.204	6.39	4.56
Olmos, Cristian	R-R	6-2	180	6-2-94	0	2	4.91	15	0	0	4	33	35	23	18	1	17	29	.271	.333	.255	7.91	4.64
Osoria, Aneury	R-R	6-7	170	11-15-93	1	2	8.68	8	3	0	0	19	28	19	18	1	11	19	.341	.313	.348	9.16	5.30
Ovalle, Jeremy	R-R	6-3	185	1-17-97	6	2	3.04	16	9	0	0	77	80	38	26	1	24	52	.270	.277	.268	6.08	2.81
Perez, Yonqueli	R-R	6-4	175	6-6-93	0	1	3.68	9	6	0	0	22	17	12	9	0	20	22	.224	.360	.157	9.00	8.18
Quijada, Jose	L-L	6-0	175	11-9-95	5	5	2.91	16	8	0	1	74	69	30	24	2	23	66	.245	.355	.231	7.99	2.78
Rodriguez, Jonathan	R-R	6-0	160	9-22-95	0	2	6.06	11	0	0	0	16	10	13	11	0	26	11	.200	.000	.244	6.06	14.33
Rodriguez, Manuel	L-L	6-2	160	12-23-96	1	2	5.23	11	1	0	0	21	28	18	12	1	11	14	.318	.100	.346	6.10	4.79
Ulloa, Brayan	L-L	6-1	180	2-25-95	2	2	5.91	6	0	0	1	11	10	8	7	0	8	11	.227	.250	.225	9.28	6.75
Vergara, Jefferson	R-R	5-11	165	5-8-97	1	0	4.30	10	0	0	1	15	15	11	7	0	14	11	.268	.333	.244	6.75	8.59

Fielding

Catcher	PCT	G	PO	A	E	DP	PB
Garcia	.973	49	332	72	11	2	21
Guaba	1.000	1	3	0	0	0	0
Guerrero	.960	18	100	21	5	0	2
Olivo	1.000	2	8	3	0	0	6
Pinto	1.000	5	38	5	0	0	1

First Base	PCT	G	PO	A	E	DP
Almonte	.987	49	410	29	6	28
Guaba	1.000	2	12	1	0	0
Guerrero	1.000	1	7	0	0	0
Pena	.952	3	20	0	1	0
Pinto	.981	21	144	9	3	12

Second Base	PCT	G	PO	A	E	DP
Acosta	.925	44	101	83	15	16
Pena	.917	9	18	15	3	1
Reyes	.954	23	43	40	4	12
Solano	1.000	1	4	3	0	2

Third Base	PCT	G	PO	A	E	DP
Alcala	.817	26	17	59	17	6
Pena	.925	15	19	30	4	4
Reyes	.847	21	14	36	9	3
Solano	.949	15	18	38	3	4

Shortstop	PCT	G	PO	A	E	DP
Acosta	.714	1	2	3	2	2
Alcala	.891	12	22	27	6	5

	PCT	G	PO	A	E	DP
Lara	.915	43	68	136	19	19
Pena	.985	18	31	36	1	5
Reyes	.909	3	5	5	1	1
Solano	—	1	0	0	0	0

Outfield	PCT	G	PO	A	E	DP
Acosta	1.000	5	2	2	0	0
Almonte	1.000	2	1	0	0	0
Avello	.927	54	98	3	8	1
Guzman	.955	59	102	5	5	3
Olivo	.929	8	10	3	1	0
Pena	.917	10	8	3	1	0
Reyes	—	1	0	0	0	0
Santos	.987	65	136	13	2	3
Solano	.938	27	44	1	3	0

Milwaukee Brewers

SEASON IN A SENTENCE: The Brewers spent more than four months in first place, but a disastrous second half took Milwaukee out of the playoff race entirely, to the point that they barely finished over .500.

HIGH POINT: The Brewers' exhilarating first half reached its apex on June 28, a day they beat the Rockies 7-4 behind Matt Garza. At that moment, the Brewers' owned the National League's best record at 51-32 and a 6 1/2-game lead on the Cardinals in the NL Central. Catcher Jonathan Lucroy earned his first all-star nod, hitting .301 and leading the NL in doubles (53), and the Brewers sent four players to the mid-summer classic—Lucroy, Carlos Gomez, Aramis Ramirez and Francisco Rodriguez.

LOW POINT: Milwaukee's true biggest loss was scouting director Bruce Seid's unexpected passing in early September. On the field, the Brewers went into a tailspin in the second half as their offense dried up—Milwaukee scored just 3.4 runs per game after the all-star break, compared to 4.4 before it. After they peaked at 19 games over .500 on June 28, they went just 31-48 the rest of the way, the third-worst record in the NL.

NOTABLE ROOKIES: Top prospect Jimmy Nelson joined the rotation full-time after a dominant stint in Triple-A, though he went just 2-9, 4.93 in the majors. Righthanders Rob Wooten and Jeremy Jeffress pitched regularly out of the bullpen, the latter posting a 1.88 ERA in 29 appearances after joining the team in late July.

KEY TRANSACTIONS: The Brewers made a splash in free agency, signing Garza to a four-year, $50 million deal. He delivered a good but not great first season in Milwaukee, going 8-8, 3.64. Trying to upgrade their lineup, Milwaukee parted with one of its better prospects, outfielder Mitch Haniger, to get Gerardo Parra from Arizona at the trade deadline, but Parra would hit just .268 with three homers in 46 games with the Brewers.

DOWN ON THE FARM: Nelson won the minor league ERA title and Pacific Coast League pitcher of the year honors, going 10-2, 1.46 in 111 innings for Triple-A Nashville before being called up for good in July. Catcher Clint Coulter, a 2012 first-round pick, tied for the Midwest League home run lead (22) and had the league's top on-base percentage (.410). Shortstop Orlando Arcia, just 20, hit .289/.346/.392 with 29 doubles, 50 RBIs and 31 stolen bases.

OPENING DAY PAYROLL: $102,724,338 (15th)

PLAYERS OF THE YEAR

MAJOR LEAGUE

Jonathan Lucroy
c
.301/.373/.465
13 HR, 53 2B, 69 RBI
Led NL hitters in WAR

MINOR LEAGUE

Jimmy Nelson
rhp
(Triple-A)
10-2, 1.46 in 111 IP
Led minors in ERA

ORGANIZATION LEADERS

BATTING   *Minimum 250 AB

MAJORS

* AVG	Lucroy, Jonathan	.301
* OPS	Lucroy, Jonathan	.838
HR	Gomez, Carlos	23
RBI	Braun, Ryan	81

MINORS

* AVG	Velez, Eugenio, Nashville	.309
* OBP	Coulter, Clint, Wisconsin	.410
* SLG	Coulter, Clint, Wisconsin	.520
R	Ratterree, Michael, Huntsville, Wisconsin	93
H	Rogers, Jason, Huntsville, Nashville	146
TB	Rogers, Jason, Huntsville, Nashville	241
2B	Taylor, Tyrone, Brevard County, Huntsville	36
3B	Rivera, Yadiel, Brevard County, Huntsville	8
HR	Coulter, Clint, Wisconsin	22
RBI	Coulter, Clint, Wisconsin	89
BB	Brennan, Taylor, Wisconsin	87
SO	Ratterree, Michael, Huntsville, Wisconsin	166
SB	Garcia, Omar, Wisconsin	44

PITCHING   #Minimum 75 IP

MAJORS

W	Peralta, Wily	17
# ERA	Gallardo, Yovani	3.51
SO	Peralta, Wily	154
SV	Rodriguez, Francisco	44

MINORS

W	Wagner, Tyler, Brevard County	13
L	Bradley, Jed, Brevard County, Huntsville	10
	Jungmann, Taylor, Huntsville, Nashville	10
	Lopez, Jorge, Brevard County	10
	Suter, Brent, Huntsville	10
# ERA	Wagner, Tyler, Brevard County	1.86
G	Leach, Brent, Huntsville, Nashville	63
GS	Gagnon, Drew, Huntsville	28
SV	Goforth, David, Huntsville	27
IP	Gagnon, Drew, Huntsville	155
BB	Pena, Ariel, Nashville	75
SO	Jungmann, Taylor, Huntsville, Nashville	147
AVG	Pena, Ariel, Nashville	.208

2014 PERFORMANCE

General Manager: Doug Melvin. **Farm Director:** Reid Nichols. **Scouting Director:** Bruce Seid.

Class	Team	League	W	L	PCT	Finish	Manager
Majors	Milwaukee Brewers	National	82	80	.506	15th (30)	Ron Roenicke
Triple-A	Nashville Sounds	Pacific Coast	77	67	.535	5th (16)	Rick Sweet
Double-A	Huntsville Stars	Southern	77	63	.550	4th (10)	Carlos Subero
High A	Brevard County Manatees	Florida State	73	62	.541	6th (12)	Joe Ayrault
Low A	Wisconsin Timber Rattlers	Midwest	72	67	.518	t-5th (16)	Matt Erickson
Rookie	Helena Brewers	Pioneer	27	49	.355	8th (8)	Tony Diggs
Rookie	Brewers	Arizona	24	31	.436	10th (13)	Nestor Corredor
Overall Minor League Record			350	339	.508	14th (30)	

ORGANIZATION STATISTICS

MILWAUKEE BREWERS

NATIONAL LEAGUE

Batting	B-T	HT	WT	DOB	AVG	vLH	vRH	G	AB	R	H	2B	3B	HR	RBI	BB	HBP	SH	SF	SO	SB	CS	SLG	OBP
Bianchi, Jeff	R-R	5-11	185	10-5-86	.171	.240	.133	29	70	4	12	1	0	0	6	3	0	0	1	17	0	0	.186	.203
Braun, Ryan	R-R	6-2	200	11-17-83	.266	.279	.262	135	530	68	141	30	6	19	81	41	6	0	3	113	11	5	.453	.324
Clark, Matt	L-R	6-5	230	12-10-86	.185	—	.185	16	27	4	5	0	0	3	7	2	0	0	2	8	0	0	.519	.226
Davis, Khris	R-R	5-11	190	12-21-87	.244	.258	.239	144	501	70	122	37	2	22	69	32	10	0	6	122	4	1	.457	.299
Falu, Irving	B-R	5-10	180	6-6-83	.000	.000	.000	11	10	0	0	0	0	0	1	1	0	0	1	1	0	0	.000	.083
2-team total (11 San Diego)					.100	—	—	22	30	0	3	0	0	0	1	4	0	0	1	5	1	0	.100	.200
Gennett, Scooter	L-R	5-10	170	5-1-90	.289	.103	.307	137	440	55	127	31	3	9	54	22	0	8	4	67	6	3	.434	.320
Gindl, Caleb	L-L	5-9	210	8-31-88	.158	.333	.125	8	19	0	3	0	0	0	0	4	0	0	0	5	0	0	.158	.304
Gomez, Carlos	R-R	6-3	220	12-4-85	.284	.258	.291	148	574	95	163	34	4	23	73	47	19	1	3	141	34	12	.477	.356
Gomez, Hector	R-R	6-0	200	3-5-88	.150	.333	.071	15	20	2	3	1	0	0	1	1	0	0	0	9	0	0	.200	.190
Herrera, Elian	B-R	5-10	195	2-1-85	.274	.226	.288	69	135	14	37	7	1	0	5	3	0	1	1	36	4	1	.341	.288
Lucroy, Jonathan	R-R	6-0	195	6-13-86	.301	.304	.300	153	585	73	176	53	2	13	69	66	2	0	2	71	4	4	.465	.373
Maldonado, Martin	R-R	6-0	230	8-16-86	.234	.250	.224	52	111	14	26	5	0	4	16	11	3	1	0	32	0	0	.387	.320
Overbay, Lyle	L-L	6-2	235	1-28-77	.233	.185	.238	121	258	24	60	14	0	4	35	36	1	0	1	60	2	0	.333	.328
Pagnozzi, Matt	R-R	6-2	215	11-10-82	—	—	—	1	0	0	0	0	0	0	0	0	0	0	0	0	0	—	—
Parra, Gerardo	L-L	5-11	200	5-6-87	.268	.167	.279	46	123	13	33	4	1	3	10	8	1	2	0	28	4	2	.390	.318
2-team total (104 Arizona)					.261	—	—	150	529	64	138	22	4	9	40	32	5	6	2	100	9	7	.369	.308
Ramirez, Aramis	R-R	6-1	205	6-25-78	.285	.327	.275	133	494	47	141	23	1	15	66	21	13	0	3	75	3	0	.427	.330
Reynolds, Mark	R-R	6-2	220	8-3-83	.196	.173	.204	130	378	47	74	9	0	22	45	47	3	1	4	122	5	1	.394	.287
Rogers, Jason	R-R	6-2	245	3-13-88	.111	.167	.000	8	9	1	1	0	0	0	1	0	0	0	1	0	0	0	.222	.200
Schafer, Logan	L-L	6-1	195	9-8-86	.181	.214	.176	65	116	13	21	9	1	0	8	15	1	3	1	27	2	1	.276	.278
Segura, Jean	R-R	5-10	205	3-17-90	.246	.182	.263	146	513	61	126	14	6	5	31	28	4	10	2	70	20	9	.326	.289
Weeks, Rickie	R-R	5-10	220	9-13-82	.274	.256	.294	121	252	36	69	19	1	8	29	25	8	0	1	73	3	4	.452	.357

Pitching	B-T	HT	WT	DOB	W	L	ERA	G	GS	CG	SV	IP	H	R	ER	HR	BB	SO	AVG	vLH	vRH	K/9	BB/9
Broxton, Jonathan	R-R	6-4	295	6-16-84	0	1	4.35	11	0	0	0	10	9	5	5	1	2	12	.225	.235	.217	10.45	1.74
2-team total (51 Cincinnati)					4	3	2.30	62	0	0	7	59	41	15	15	4	19	49	—	—	—	7.52	2.91
Duke, Zach	L-L	6-2	210	4-19-83	5	1	2.45	74	0	0	0	59	49	19	16	3	17	74	.223	.198	.242	11.35	2.61
Estrada, Marco	R-R	6-0	200	7-5-83	7	6	4.36	39	18	0	0	151	137	77	73	29	44	127	.241	.226	.254	7.59	2.63
Fiers, Mike	R-R	6-2	190	6-15-85	6	5	2.13	14	10	0	0	72	46	19	17	7	17	76	.181	.188	.175	9.54	2.13
Figaro, Alfredo	R-R	6-0	190	7-7-84	0	1	7.27	6	0	0	0	9	11	7	7	2	1	8	.297	.238	.375	8.31	1.04
Gallardo, Yovani	R-R	6-2	210	2-27-86	8	11	3.51	32	32	0	0	192	195	86	75	21	54	146	.261	.235	.279	6.83	2.53
Garza, Matt	R-R	6-4	215	11-26-83	8	8	3.64	27	27	1	0	163	143	77	66	12	50	126	.223	.241	.241	6.94	2.76
Gorzelanny, Tom	L-L	6-3	210	7-12-82	0	0	0.86	23	0	0	0	21	22	3	2	1	8	23	.259	.324	.216	9.86	3.43
Henderson, Jim	L-R	6-5	220	10-21-82	2	1	7.15	14	0	0	0	11	14	10	9	3	4	17	.311	.429	.258	13.50	3.18
Jeffress, Jeremy	R-R	6-1	205	9-21-87	1	1	1.88	29	0	0	0	29	27	6	6	1	7	25	.260	.372	.180	7.85	2.20
Kintzler, Brandon	R-R	5-10	190	8-1-84	3	3	3.24	64	0	0	0	58	62	22	21	8	16	31	.284	.250	.304	4.78	2.47
Lohse, Kyle	R-R	6-2	210	10-4-78	13	9	3.54	31	31	2	0	198	183	87	78	22	45	141	.246	.254	.239	6.40	2.04
Nelson, Jimmy	R-R	6-6	245	6-5-89	2	9	4.93	14	12	0	0	69	62	42	38	6	19	57	.292	.275	.309	7.40	2.47
Peralta, Wily	R-R	6-1	245	5-8-89	17	11	3.53	32	32	0	0	199	198	88	78	23	61	154	.261	.305	.217	6.98	2.76
Rodriguez, Francisco	R-R	6-0	195	1-7-82	5	5	3.04	69	0	0	44	68	49	23	23	14	18	73	.198	.176	.221	9.66	2.38
Smith, Will	R-L	6-5	250	7-10-89	1	3	3.70	78	0	0	1	66	62	31	27	6	31	86	.248	.167	.299	11.79	4.25
Thornburg, Tyler	R-R	5-11	190	9-29-88	3	1	4.25	27	0	0	0	30	24	14	14	1	21	28	.222	.119	.288	8.49	6.37
Wang, Wei-Chung	L-L	6-1	180	4-25-92	0	0	10.90	14	0	0	0	17	25	22	21	3	8	13	.361	.333	.375	6.75	4.15
Wooten, Rob	R-R	6-1	195	7-21-85	1	4	4.72	40	0	0	0	34	42	18	18	1	8	29	.307	.306	.307	7.60	2.10

Fielding

Catcher	PCT	G	PO	A	E	DP	PB
Lucroy	.996	136	1013	65	4	5	5
Maldonado	.978	42	250	22	6	2	2
Pagnozzi	1.000	1	2	0	0	0	0

First Base	PCT	G	PO	A	E	DP
Clark	.982	9	51	3	1	5
Lucroy	.992	19	113	9	1	9
Maldonado	.889	2	6	2	1	0

Second Base	PCT	G	PO	A	E	DP
Bianchi	1.000	4	2	6	0	1
Gennett	.981	119	201	268	9	61
Gomez	1.000	1	0	1	0	0
Herrera	1.000	7	4	6	0	1

	PCT	G	PO	A	E	DP
Overbay	.992	83	553	34	5	41
Reynolds	.996	91	627	60	3	58
Rogers	.923	4	12	0	1	1

	PCT	G	PO	A	E	DP
Weeks	.969	62	92	126	7	31

Third Base	PCT	G	PO	A	E	DP
Bianchi	.923	9	11	13	2	3
Falu	1.000	3	0	1	0	1
Gomez	1.000	6	1	3	0	0
Herrera	1.000	1	1	8	0	0
Ramirez	.963	126	74	184	10	12
Reynolds	.964	42	13	67	3	6

Shortstop	PCT	G	PO	A	E	DP
Bianchi	.975	10	10	29	1	3
Falu	.800	2	1	3	1	0
Gomez	.944	7	3	14	1	3
Herrera	.927	14	17	34	4	7
Segura	.975	144	180	447	16	83

Outfield	PCT	G	PO	A	E	DP
Braun	.993	134	263	5	2	2
Davis	.988	134	252	2	3	2
Gennett	—	1	0	0	0	0
Gindl	1.000	6	11	0	0	0
Gomez	.986	145	355	7	5	2

Herrera	1.000	26	38	0	0	0
Parra	.957	39	66	1	3	1
Reynolds	1.000	3	1	0	0	0
Schafer	.983	47	54	4	1	2

NASHVILLE SOUNDS
TRIPLE-A

PACIFIC COAST LEAGUE

Batting	B-T	HT	WT	DOB	AVG	vLH	vRH	G	AB	R	H	2B	3B	HR	RBI	BB	HBP	SH	SF	SO	SB	CS	SLG	OBP
Bianchi, Jeff	R-R	5-11	185	10-5-86	.276	.269	.278	24	98	11	27	5	0	3	12	6	0	0	1	19	2	0	.418	.314
Clark, Matt	L-R	6-5	230	12-10-86	.313	.348	.295	53	195	35	61	9	0	16	37	15	3	—	0	52	0	0	.605	.371
Diaz, Robinzon	R-R	5-11	220	9-19-83	.232	.300	.206	38	142	14	33	6	0	3	13	4	0	2	0	15	0	0	.338	.253
Falu, Irving	B-R	5-10	180	6-6-83	.291	.360	.245	76	247	28	72	8	1	2	18	21	0	1	3	22	9	9	.356	.343
Gindl, Caleb	L-L	5-9	210	8-31-88	.227	.152	.257	110	362	40	82	20	1	8	32	42	2	—	1	88	2	2	.354	.310
Gomez, Hector	R-R	6-3	200	3-5-88	.282	.283	.281	121	408	59	115	25	6	15	49	21	7	—	4	80	5	3	.483	.325
Green, Taylor	L-R	6-0	195	11-2-86	.245	.208	.262	53	155	15	38	9	0	3	18	8	4	2	1	24	0	0	.361	.298
Halton, Sean	R-R	6-4	260	6-7-87	.293	.342	.263	122	416	63	122	29	3	8	63	30	3	—	4	90	0	1	.435	.342
Hermida, Jeremy	L-R	6-3	220	1-30-84	.256	.283	.244	108	340	52	87	20	0	16	67	62	2	—	4	90	0	2	.456	.370
Herrera, Elian	R-R	5-10	195	2-1-85	.304	.319	.294	33	115	21	35	9	2	0	9	8	0	1	0	19	5	1	.417	.350
Mattison, Kevin	L-L	6-1	195	9-20-85	.212	.197	.219	91	217	30	46	11	3	7	29	22	4	—	2	80	13	4	.387	.294
May, Lucas	R-R	6-0	200	10-24-84	.200	.278	.118	15	35	1	7	3	0	0	4	3	0	0	2	10	1	0	.286	.250
Morris, Hunter	L-R	6-2	225	10-7-88	.279	.283	.277	91	330	46	92	21	1	11	42	20	3	0	3	74	0	0	.448	.323
Orr, Pete	L-R	6-1	195	6-8-79	.301	.244	.320	113	359	55	108	20	6	4	41	12	3	3	0	76	7	4	.423	.329
Pagnozzi, Matt	R-R	6-2	215	11-10-82	.215	.291	.169	71	228	29	49	5	0	11	29	20	7	4	0	63	1	0	.382	.298
Rogers, Jason	R-R	6-2	245	3-13-88	.316	.290	.328	57	206	36	65	11	4	11	39	22	1	—	3	38	0	0	.568	.379
Schafer, Logan	L-L	6-1	195	9-8-86	.273	.318	.256	41	161	27	44	13	4	3	18	21	0	2	1	33	4	1	.460	.355
Statia, Hainley	B-R	5-10	178	1-19-86	.262	.217	.316	23	42	3	11	3	0	0	3	3	0	0	0	10	1	0	.333	.311
Velez, Eugenio	B-R	6-1	170	5-16-82	.309	.252	.341	116	404	57	125	24	4	7	51	31	4	—	2	68	27	15	.441	.363
Weisenburger, Adam	R-R	5-10	185	12-13-88	.237	.429	.194	13	38	5	9	2	0	1	4	4	1	1	0	10	0	0	.368	.326
Zarraga, Shawn	R-R	6-0	248	1-21-89	.213	.235	.200	17	47	1	10	2	0	0	7	5	2	—	2	7	0	0	.255	.304

Pitching	B-T	HT	WT	DOB	W	L	ERA	G	GS	CG	SV	IP	H	R	ER	HR	BB	SO	AVG	vLH	vRH	K/9	BB/9
Blazek, Michael	R-R	6-0	200	3-16-89	4	4	4.13	37	17	0	1	102	106	51	47	9	40	87	.256	.278		7.65	3.52
Buckner, Billy	R-R	6-2	205	8-27-83	1	1	6.00	4	2	0	0	12	9	8	8	1	3	15	.205	.241	.133	11.25	2.25
2-team total (15 El Paso)					5	6	5.83	19	16	0	0	76	94	60	49	11	36	59	—	—		7.02	4.28
Burgos, Hiram	R-R	5-11	210	8-4-87	1	3	6.50	4	4	0	0	18	22	16	13	2	10	20	.297	.353	.281	10.00	5.00
Cravy, Tyler	R-R	6-3	195	7-13-89	0	0	2.70	1	1	0	0	3	3	1	1	0	3	4	.250	.167	.333	10.80	8.10
De La Torre, Jose	R-R	5-10	195	10-17-85	4	3	5.97	21	0	0	0	29	36	21	19	2	16	36	.316	.346	.290	11.30	5.02
Dillard, Tim	R-R	6-4	220	7-19-83	0	0	14.54	4	0	0	0	4	11	8	7	2	1	3	.478	.636	.333	6.23	2.08
Fiers, Mike	R-R	6-2	190	6-15-85	8	5	2.55	17	17	1	0	102	80	34	29	8	17	129	.212	.158	.243	11.35	1.50
Figaro, Alfredo	R-R	6-0	190	7-7-84	5	2	3.71	42	2	0	2	70	80	31	29	5	22	55	.288	.268	.301	7.04	2.82
Gorzelanny, Tom	L-L	6-3	210	7-12-82	0	0	0.93	7	2	0	0	10	8	1	1	0	1	7	.222	.308	.174	6.52	0.93
Hand, Donovan	R-R	6-3	235	4-20-86	4	8	5.20	47	8	0	13	80	100	51	46	9	22	71	.304	.299	.307	8.02	2.49
Heckathorn, Kyle	R-R	6-6	225	6-17-88	3	2	5.70	28	4	0	0	47	51	31	30	7	21	30	.273	.280	.267	5.70	3.99
Hellweg, Johnny	R-R	6-9	210	10-29-88	1	2	4.95	4	4	0	0	20	21	11	11	1	15	12	.288	.400	.245	5.40	6.75
Henderson, Jim	L-R	6-5	220	10-21-82	0	1	6.75	3	0	0	0	3	2	2	2	1	2	2	.222	.400	.000	5.50	6.75
Jackson, Jay	R-R	6-1	195	10-27-87	0	3	5.06	6	6	0	0	27	29	15	15	4	16	28	.282	.340	.220	9.45	5.40
Jeffress, Jeremy	R-R	6-1	205	9-21-87	4	1	1.51	30	0	0	5	42	38	8	7	0	18	45	.224	.242	.210	9.72	3.89
Jungmann, Taylor	R-R	6-6	210	12-18-89	8	6	3.98	19	18	0	0	102	88	48	45	7	46	101	.235	.179	.284	8.94	4.07
Leach, Brent	L-L	6-5	215	11-18-82	4	3	3.28	59	1	0	0	60	51	25	22	6	28	69	.243	.237	.248	10.29	4.18
Leon, Arcenio	R-R	6-1	220	9-22-86	1	3	5.26	28	0	0	0	39	44	27	23	3	19	32	.278	.292	.267	7.32	4.35
Lowe, Johnnie	R-R	6-5	215	3-21-85	1	4	5.55	18	5	0	0	36	40	24	22	6	15	35	.280	.185	.337	8.83	3.79
Marzec, Eric	R-R	5-11	210	1-13-88	0	0	1.32	6	1	0	0	14	10	4	2	0	4	12	.192	.231	.154	7.90	2.63
Mills, Brad	L-L	6-0	185	3-5-85	4	2	1.56	14	12	0	0	75	51	18	13	5	18	77	.190	.193	.190	9.24	2.16
Molleken, Dustin	L-R	6-4	230	8-21-84	5	2	4.84	54	0	0	4	74	71	44	40	7	35	89	.252	.280	.234	10.78	4.24
Nelson, Jimmy	R-R	6-6	245	6-5-89	10	2	1.46	17	16	0	0	111	70	23	18	3	32	114	.179	.192	.170	9.24	2.59
Pena, Ariel	R-R	6-3	240	5-20-89	9	8	4.56	25	24	0	0	128	96	69	65	12	75	140	.208	.201	.212	9.82	5.26
Wooten, Rob	R-R	6-1	195	7-21-85	0	2	5.82	21	0	0	14	22	24	16	14	1	5	21	.267	.308	.235	8.72	2.08

Fielding

Catcher	PCT	G	PO	A	E	DP	PB
Diaz	1.000	38	353	29	0	1	3
May	1.000	12	96	7	0	1	0
Pagnozzi	.995	68	540	52	3	5	9
Weisenburger	.984	13	113	8	2	1	1
Zarraga	1.000	16	128	10	0	1	1

First Base	PCT	G	PO	A	E	DP
Clark	.995	50	383	22	2	26
Halton	.995	25	163	24	1	14
Morris	.978	68	608	42	6	48
Orr	1.000	1	1	0	0	0

Second Base	PCT	G	PO	A	E	DP
Bianchi	1.000	8	12	23	0	3
Falu	.991	29	47	59	1	12
Gomez	.857	2	1	5	1	0

	PCT	G	PO	A	E	DP
Herrera	.958	12	19	27	2	10
Orr	.977	74	109	186	7	32
Statia	.964	10	14	13	1	3
Velez	.973	33	39	69	3	10

Third Base	PCT	G	PO	A	E	DP
Bianchi	.750	7	3	3	2	1
Falu	.961	23	15	34	2	0
Gomez	1.000	3	1	7	0	2
Green	.976	44	19	62	2	3
Herrera	1.000	6	3	9	0	0
Orr	.935	21	15	28	3	2
Rogers	.951	56	35	101	7	5
Statia	1.000	1	0	2	0	0

Shortstop	PCT	G	PO	A	E	DP
Bianchi	.974	9	18	20	1	2

	PCT	G	PO	A	E	DP
Falu	.981	28	35	71	2	9
Gomez	.969	111	146	290	14	61
Orr	1.000	6	15	11	0	2
Statia	1.000	1	1	1	0	1

Outfield	PCT	G	PO	A	E	DP
Clark	1.000	3	3	0	0	0
Gindl	.994	104	160	6	1	1
Halton	.990	80	97	3	1	0
Hermida	.967	87	115	2	4	0
Herrera	1.000	17	21	1	0	0
Mattison	.965	83	132	4	5	1
Orr	1.000	5	5	0	0	0
Schafer	.969	41	90	5	3	1
Velez	.971	64	64	4	2	0

MILWAUKEE BREWERS

HUNTSVILLE STARS

DOUBLE-A

SOUTHERN LEAGUE

MILWAUKEE BREWERS

Batting	B-T	HT	WT	DOB	AVG	vLH	vRH	G	AB	R	H	2B	3B	HR	RBI	BB	HBP	SH	SF	SO	SB	CS	SLG	OBP
Davis, Kentrail	L-R	5-9	200	6-29-88	.245	.244	.245	108	359	53	88	23	2	2	37	59	4	6	5	75	14	7	.337	.354
Diaz, Robinzon	R-R	5-11	220	9-19-83	.293	.395	.252	45	150	12	44	7	0	0	10	7	0	0	3	15	1	0	.340	.319
Fellhauer, Josh	L-L	5-11	175	3-24-88	.289	.258	.299	39	128	12	37	9	2	0	9	16	0	2	1	32	1	1	.391	.366
2-team total (34 Pensacola)					.268	—	—	73	235	24	63	12	4	0	19	34	0	3	1	60	2	2	.353	.359
Gimenez, Hector	B-R	5-10	230	9-28-82	.250	.300	.231	40	148	16	37	11	0	8	29	8	1	0	2	34	0	0	.486	.289
Green, Taylor	L-R	6-0	195	11-2-86	.167	.500	.136	6	24	1	4	0	0	0	1	2	0	0	0	3	0	0	.167	.231
Haniger, Mitch	R-R	6-2	215	12-23-90	.255	.333	.231	67	243	41	62	7	1	10	34	19	4	2	3	41	4	0	.416	.316
2-team total (8 Mobile)					.262	—	—	75	267	46	70	10	1	10	39	22	6	2	4	45	4	0	.419	.328
Hopkins, Greg	R-R	6-1	200	11-22-88	.206	.159	.218	72	209	24	43	6	2	6	24	26	4	2	2	41	5	4	.340	.303
Kjeldgaard, Brock	R-R	6-5	235	1-22-86	.176	.286	.148	20	34	4	6	0	1	1	8	8	0	0	0	13	1	1	.324	.333
Komatsu, Erik	L-L	5-10	175	10-1-87	.214	.182	.220	54	140	14	30	6	0	3	15	14	0	2	0	33	4	2	.321	.286
Macias, Brandon	R-R	5-10	185	10-10-88	.250	.500	.000	1	4	0	1	0	0	0	1	0	0	0	0	1	0	0	.250	.250
May, Lucas	R-R	6-0	200	10-24-84	.214	.333	.200	9	28	4	6	1	0	1	4	1	0	1	0	2	0	0	.357	.241
Morris, Hunter	L-R	6-2	225	10-7-88	.269	.182	.333	7	26	3	7	0	0	0	2	1	0	0	0	4	0	0	.269	.296
Paciorek, Joey	R-R	6-2	225	9-20-88	.235	.154	.271	44	85	11	20	3	0	2	10	12	2	0	0	22	0	0	.341	.343
Prince, Josh	R-R	6-0	180	1-26-88	.246	.189	.262	111	345	55	85	15	0	5	35	56	4	9	2	73	37	10	.333	.356
Ramirez, Nick	L-L	6-3	225	8-1-89	.231	.244	.226	133	490	71	113	21	5	19	82	55	4	0	3	152	1	4	.410	.312
Ratterree, Michael	R-R	6-1	190	2-9-91	.115	.250	.091	7	26	2	3	1	0	1	5	4	0	0	0	12	1	0	.269	.233
Richardson, D'Vontrey	R-R	6-1	200	7-30-88	.239	.308	.224	77	289	44	69	12	3	5	36	21	3	3	2	49	15	2	.353	.295
Rivera, Yadiel	R-R	6-2	175	5-2-92	.262	.268	.261	58	183	31	48	9	6	2	13	10	1	2	0	36	5	2	.410	.304
Rogers, Jason	R-R	6-2	245	3-13-88	.282	.316	.274	77	287	42	81	18	2	7	43	31	3	0	3	56	5	1	.432	.355
Sermo, Jose	B-R	6-0	190	3-22-91	.000	.000	.000	2	2	0	0	0	0	0	0	0	0	0	0	1	0	0	.000	.000
Shaw, Nick	R-R	5-11	160	8-25-88	.270	.297	.264	113	356	47	96	14	3	0	40	64	5	11	5	71	6	9	.326	.384
Stang, Chad	R-R	6-2	190	3-26-89	.083	.250	.000	9	12	0	1	0	0	0	2	0	0	1	0	6	1	0	.083	.083
Statia, Hainley	B-R	5-10	178	1-19-86	.278	.317	.266	60	180	29	50	8	1	5	26	39	2	2	1	21	5	5	.417	.410
Taylor, Tyrone	R-R	6-0	185	1-22-94	.077	—	.077	5	13	0	1	0	0	0	0	1	0	0	0	5	1	0	.077	.143
Vucinich, Shea	R-R	6-1	185	12-1-88	.191	.140	.207	79	183	24	35	9	2	2	22	27	3	5	0	52	7	1	.295	.305
Weisenburger, Adam	R-R	5-10	185	12-13-88	.259	.314	.240	68	201	24	52	10	1	2	23	32	5	9	2	34	1	1	.348	.371
Zarraga, Shawn	R-R	6-0	248	1-21-89	.303	.368	.322	75	215	34	71	16	0	1	30	42	4	1	5	24	1	1	.419	.440

Pitching	B-T	HT	WT	DOB	W	L	ERA	G	GS	CG	SV	IP	H	R	ER	HR	BB	SO	AVG	vLH	vRH	K/9	BB/9
Barnes, Jacob	R-R	6-2	230	4-14-90	2	6	4.26	23	21	0	0	106	94	57	50	9	38	75	.244	.350	.182	6.39	3.24
Barreda, Manuel	R-R	5-11	195	10-8-88	0	1	1.99	17	0	0	0	23	17	7	5	3	14	20	.207	.182	.217	7.94	5.56
Bradley, Jed	L-L	6-4	225	6-12-90	5	8	4.55	17	17	0	0	87	106	52	44	8	36	71	.307	.231	.330	7.34	3.72
Cravy, Tyler	R-R	6-3	195	7-13-89	8	1	1.72	14	12	0	0	73	47	17	14	7	15	64	.184	.217	.166	7.85	1.84
De La Torre, Jose	R-R	5-10	195	10-17-85	1	0	1.93	9	0	0	2	14	8	3	3	2	6	16	.163	.294	.094	10.29	3.86
Dillard, Tim	R-R	6-4	220	7-19-83	5	3	3.13	43	0	0	1	60	44	25	21	3	16	53	.200	.180	.208	7.91	2.39
Gagnon, Drew	R-R	6-4	195	6-26-90	11	6	3.96	28	28	0	0	155	135	77	68	18	62	118	.239	.235	.242	6.87	3.61
Goforth, David	R-R	5-10	205	10-11-88	5	4	3.76	54	0	0	27	65	60	28	27	2	29	46	.242	.268	.229	6.40	4.04
Hall, Brooks	R-R	6-5	230	6-26-90	2	1	2.77	5	5	0	0	26	24	9	8	1	7	16	.264	.344	.220	5.54	2.42
Henderson, Jim	L-R	6-5	220	10-21-82	0	0	0.00	3	0	0	0	4	1	1	0	0	1	4	.077	.000	.100	9.00	2.25
Holle, Greg	R-R	6-8	240	11-16-88	3	2	2.31	23	0	0	0	35	27	9	9	2	6	22	.218	.200	.228	5.66	1.54
Jungmann, Taylor	R-R	6-6	210	12-18-89	4	4	2.77	9	9	0	0	52	52	21	16	4	15	46	.264	.247	.274	7.96	2.60
Leach, Brent	L-L	6-5	215	11-18-82	0	0	2.25	4	0	0	0	4	1	1	1	1	4	.077	.000	.111	9.00	2.25
Leon, Arcenio	R-R	6-1	220	9-22-86	2	0	2.18	24	0	0	3	33	23	9	8	0	8	29	.193	.243	.171	7.91	2.18
Lowe, Johnnie	R-R	6-5	215	3-21-85	1	0	4.22	5	0	0	0	11	12	5	5	3	2	8	.286	.286	.286	6.75	1.69
Marzec, Eric	R-R	5-11	210	1-13-88	1	4	3.34	32	6	0	1	73	78	34	27	6	27	50	.269	.321	.239	6.19	3.34
Medlen, Casey	R-R	6-0	155	8-4-89	4	0	2.82	29	0	0	1	38	31	13	12	4	21	38	.223	.269	.195	8.92	4.93
Moye, Andy	R-R	6-5	180	9-11-87	4	2	4.50	11	10	0	0	48	54	25	24	6	14	30	.284	.246	.304	5.63	2.63
Poppe, Tanner	R-R	6-6	225	7-19-90	1	1	3.21	23	0	0	0	28	28	15	10	4	11	25	.264	.286	.254	8.04	3.54
Ross, Austin	R-R	6-2	200	8-12-88	2	3	3.12	5	5	0	0	26	31	12	9	2	8	28	.290	.286	.292	9.69	2.77
Shackelford, Kevin	R-R	6-5	210	4-8-89	2	4	4.86	40	0	0	1	50	60	33	27	3	17	25	.297	.333	.277	4.50	3.06
Strong, Mike	L-L	6-0	195	11-17-88	0	0	0.00	1	0	0	0	4	0	0	0	0	1	6	.000	.000	.000	13.50	2.25
Suter, Brent	R-L	6-5	195	8-29-89	10	10	3.96	28	27	1	0	152	144	72	67	14	53	118	.255	.294	.246	6.97	3.13
Toledo, Tommy	R-R	6-3	198	12-13-88	4	3	4.68	38	0	0	0	58	61	31	30	8	19	57	.271	.239	.286	8.90	2.97

Fielding

Catcher	PCT	G	PO	A	E	DP	PB
Diaz	.985	24	122	11	2	1	0
May	.959	7	44	3	2	0	1
Paciorek	1.000	12	53	8	0	1	3
Weisenburger	.984	63	445	35	8	5	7
Zarraga	.991	51	305	38	3	4	1

First Base	PCT	G	PO	A	E	DP
Gimenez	.982	8	53	1	1	7
Hopkins	1.000	5	30	2	0	3
Morris	1.000	4	44	2	0	4
Paciorek	1.000	5	29	0	0	3
Ramirez	.995	125	1084	63	6	114
Statia	1.000	2	9	0	0	1
Vucinich	1.000	1	3	0	0	0
Zarraga	1.000	3	11	0	0	0

Second Base	PCT	G	PO	A	E	DP
Hopkins	.988	39	71	97	2	27
Prince	.984	41	89	99	3	25
Shaw	.972	42	67	104	5	30
Statia	.973	17	25	47	2	7
Vucinich	.978	22	36	53	2	8

Third Base	PCT	G	PO	A	E	DP
Diaz	.889	14	5	27	4	1
Green	1.000	5	2	8	0	0
Hopkins	.983	24	10	47	1	1
Macias	1.000	1	1	2	0	0
Paciorek	.500	1	0	1	1	0
Prince	1.000	5	1	8	0	1
Rogers	.928	66	45	136	14	16
Statia	1.000	30	16	62	0	7

Vucinich	.957	19	5	17	1	0

Shortstop	PCT	G	PO	A	E	DP
Rivera	.940	57	97	168	17	47
Shaw	.965	71	72	174	9	32
Statia	1.000	6	8	11	0	4
Vucinich	.927	26	27	75	8	15

Outfield	PCT	G	PO	A	E	DP
Davis	.964	105	176	10	7	2
Diaz	.000	2	0	0	0	0
Fellhauer	.989	37	81	9	1	1
Gimenez	.957	28	21	1	1	1
Haniger	.964	67	123	9	5	3
Kjeldgaard	1.000	16	19	0	0	0
Komatsu	1.000	49	82	1	0	0
Paciorek	1.000	11	8	1	0	0

Prince	.989	55	86	3	1	0	Shaw	1.000	1	2	0	0	0	Taylor	1.000	5	12	1	0	1
Ratterree	1.000	7	12	0	0	0	Stang	1.000	6	6	0	0	0	Vucinich	1.000	9	6	1	0	0
Richardson	.974	75	176	8	5	2	Statia	1.000	4	1	0	0	0							

BREVARD COUNTY MANATEES · HIGH CLASS A
FLORIDA STATE LEAGUE

Batting	B-T	HT	WT	DOB	AVG	vLH	vRH	G	AB	R	H	2B	3B	HR	RBI	BB	HBP	SH	SF	SO	SB	CS	SLG	OBP
Arcia, Orlando	R-R	6-0	165	8-4-94	.289	.281	.292	127	498	65	144	29	5	4	50	42	2	3	1	65	31	11	.392	.346
Berberet, Parker	R-R	6-3	205	10-20-89	.277	.364	.243	51	159	15	44	12	0	2	17	15	2	2	2	28	2	0	.390	.343
Cooper, Garrett	R-R	6-6	230	12-25-90	.238	.229	.241	53	164	23	39	11	0	2	16	18	5	0	1	51	1	0	.341	.330
Delmonico, Nick	L-R	6-2	200	7-12-92	.262	.156	.294	37	141	11	37	8	0	4	15	7	1	0	1	34	2	2	.404	.300
Garfield, Cameron	R-R	6-0	190	5-23-91	.229	.238	.226	95	362	31	83	19	1	2	41	17	4	0	5	64	9	3	.304	.268
Garza, Mike	R-R	6-1	195	3-11-90	.286	.260	.293	97	339	29	97	17	4	1	25	19	2	3	0	58	8	3	.369	.328
Hopkins, Greg	R-R	6-1	200	11-22-88	.167	.245	.23	67	9	15	3	0	0	3	10	0	2	0	10	2	0	.269	.325
Macias, Brandon	R-R	5-10	185	10-10-88	.254	.283	.245	81	264	30	67	12	0	2	28	20	4	3	4	41	3	3	.322	.312
Orf, Nathan	R-R	5-9	180	2-1-90	.288	.369	.262	123	451	66	130	30	4	2	43	55	22	4	6	74	7	6	.386	.388
Reed, Michael	R-R	6-0	190	11-18-92	.255	.253	.256	110	365	50	93	20	5	5	47	78	9	2	3	79	33	13	.378	.396
Rivera, Yadiel	R-R	6-2	175	5-2-92	.255	.323	.231	66	231	35	59	8	2	3	17	16	4	1	2	50	5	3	.346	.312
Roache, Victor	R-R	6-1	225	9-17-91	.226	.220	.228	122	433	46	98	17	2	18	54	37	8	1	2	138	11	4	.400	.298
Rodriguez, Alfredo	R-R	6-0	175	5-26-90	.255	.286	.246	82	263	30	67	9	1	2	27	31	4	1	1	33	16	6	.319	.341
Schafer, Logan	L-L	6-1	195	9-8-86	.250	.000	.500	2	4	1	1	1	0	0	1	1	0	0	0	0	0	0	.500	.400
Sermo, Jose	B-R	6-0	190	3-22-91	.221	.182	.233	37	95	12	21	2	0	2	10	9	0	5	1	31	1	1	.305	.286
Taylor, Tyrone	R-R	6-0	185	1-22-94	.278	.323	.263	130	507	69	141	36	3	6	68	39	4	3	6	58	22	6	.396	.331

Pitching	B-T	HT	WT	DOB	W	L	ERA	G	GS	CG	SV	IP	H	R	ER	HR	BB	SO	AVG	vLH	vRH	K/9	BB/9
Barnes, Jacob	R-R	6-2	230	4-14-90	0	0	1.23	3	0	0	0	7	3	1	1	1	0	8	.125	.167	.083	9.82	0.00
Bradley, Jed	L-L	6-4	225	6-12-90	5	2	2.98	10	10	0	0	60	54	21	20	4	10	53	.240	.154	.275	7.91	1.49
De La Torre, Jose	R-R	5-10	195	10-17-85	0	0	2.25	3	0	0	0	4	3	1	1	1	0	6	.188	.000	.273	13.50	0.00
Gorzelanny, Tom	L-L	6-3	210	7-12-82	0	1	1.50	3	0	0	0	3	1	1	1	1	1	5	.158	.000	.250	7.50	1.50
Holle, Greg	R-R	6-8	240	11-16-88	0	0	1.50	8	0	0	0	12	9	2	2	1	1	13	.200	.278	.148	9.75	0.75
Huizinga, Jon	R-R	6-4	200	10-16-79	0	0	1.35	5	0	0	2	7	7	1	1	0	3	8	.280	.333	.231	10.80	4.05
Johnson, Hobbs	R-L	5-11	205	4-29-91	12	8	2.93	25	24	1	0	148	118	59	48	10	43	105	.221	.238	.212	6.40	2.62
Lieser, Scott	R-R	6-3	195	4-23-90	1	1	4.61	17	0	0	2	27	25	17	14	5	5	20	.245	.232	.261	6.59	1.65
Lopez, Jorge	R-R	6-4	165	2-10-93	10	10	4.58	25	25	1	0	138	144	80	70	12	46	119	.273	.251	.294	7.78	3.01
Magnifico, Damien	R-R	6-1	185	5-24-91	8	6	3.74	22	22	2	0	120	110	61	50	11	43	76	.244	.276	.212	5.68	3.22
Peterson, Stephen	L-L	6-3	210	11-6-87	5	4	2.98	34	0	0	4	60	53	22	20	3	20	45	.235	.189	.265	6.71	2.98
Pierce, Chad	R-R	6-1	215	11-20-87	3	8	4.60	27	6	0	1	61	68	37	31	7	28	55	.291	.317	.261	8.16	4.15
Poppe, Tanner	R-R	6-6	225	7-19-90	0	1	2.25	12	0	0	9	16	15	4	4	1	3	16	.250	.290	.207	9.00	1.69
Ross, Austin	R-R	6-2	200	8-12-88	7	5	3.76	21	11	0	0	91	84	40	38	7	24	82	.250	.267	.232	8.11	2.37
Seidenberger, Trevor	L-L	6-2	200	6-9-92	0	1	8.59	11	0	0	0	15	21	14	14	3	8	18	.339	.417	.289	11.05	4.91
Shackelford, Kevin	R-R	6-5	210	4-7-89	0	0	0.87	12	0	0	5	21	19	2	2	0	4	16	.260	.353	.179	6.97	1.74
Spurlin, Tyler	R-R	6-3	195	6-17-91	1	0	5.87	8	0	0	1	8	10	7	5	3	4	6	.313	.313	.313	7.04	4.70
Strong, Mike	L-L	6-0	195	11-17-88	2	2	2.50	30	6	1	4	76	56	22	21	6	23	78	.207	.241	.184	9.28	2.74
Toledo, Tommy	R-R	6-3	198	12-13-88	0	2	1.00	7	0	0	4	9	9	2	1	0	4	9	.257	.200	.300	9.00	4.00
Viramontes, Martin	R-R	6-5	225	7-12-89	3	3	3.70	31	0	0	2	58	45	26	24	8	29	66	.210	.205	.216	10.18	4.47
Wagner, Tyler	R-R	6-3	195	1-24-91	13	6	1.86	25	25	1	0	150	118	41	31	10	48	118	.221	.229	.212	7.08	2.88
Wang, Wei-Chung	L-L	6-1	180	4-25-92	1	0	1.86	2	1	0	0	10	7	2	2	0	0	9	.219	.167	.250	8.38	0.00
Williams, Mark	R-R	6-3	240	8-12-89	1	0	1.61	19	0	0	10	22	9	5	4	0	9	21	.127	.143	.116	8.46	3.63
Williams, Taylor	B-R	5-11	165	7-21-91	1	2	4.26	5	5	1	0	25	29	14	12	4	5	25	.290	.302	.270	8.88	1.78

Fielding

Catcher	PCT	G	PO	A	E	DP	PB						
Berberet	.994	47	304	37	2	1	4	Hopkins	1.000	3	1	3	0	2	Macias	.920	8	10	13	2	2
Garfield	.987	90	684	57	10	5	3	Orf	.978	55	87	132	5	32	Orf	—	1	0	0	0	0
Orf	—	1	0	0	0	0	0	Rivera	.968	28	40	80	4	16	Rivera	.979	38	58	128	4	27
								Rodriguez	.986	17	32	41	1	9	Rodriguez	—	1	0	0	0	0

First Base	PCT	G	PO	A	E	DP
Berberet	1.000	3	0	0	0
Cooper	.990	52	441	31	5	39
Garza	.988	64	552	37	7	55
Hopkins	1.000	1	3	0	0	1
Orf	—	1	0	0	0	0
Rodriguez	.995	24	165	17	1	21

Third Base	PCT	G	PO	A	E	DP
Delmonico	.948	34	14	78	5	6
Garza	.969	14	8	23	1	2
Hopkins	1.000	18	9	33	0	6
Macias	.953	68	41	100	7	10
Orf	1.000	4	4	6	0	1
Sermo	1.000	1	0	1	0	0

Outfield	PCT	G	PO	A	E	DP
Macias	1.000	6	11	1	0	0
Orf	1.000	41	68	3	0	1
Reed	.987	101	140	10	2	3
Roache	.969	106	149	8	5	3
Schafer	1.000	2	2	0	0	0
Sermo	.947	26	35	1	2	0
Taylor	.993	129	290	7	2	1

Second Base	PCT	G	PO	A	E	DP
Arcia	.988	36	53	114	2	24

Shortstop	PCT	G	PO	A	E	DP
Arcia	.961	90	174	273	18	65

WISCONSIN TIMBER RATTLERS · LOW CLASS A
MIDWEST LEAGUE

Batting	B-T	HT	WT	DOB	AVG	vLH	vRH	G	AB	R	H	2B	3B	HR	RBI	BB	HBP	SH	SF	SO	SB	CS	SLG	OBP
Castillo, Francisco	B-R	5-10	166	6-4-93	.221	.059	.241	45	154	21	34	5	1	0	17	8	1	2	1	26	2	4	.266	.262
Cooper, Garrett	R-R	6-6	230	12-25-90	.333	.000	.370	9	30	2	10	3	0	1	8	0	2	0	0	4	0	0	.533	.375
Coulter, Clint	R-R	6-3	222	7-30-93	.287	.347	.268	126	429	84	123	28	3	22	89	73	21	0	6	103	6	6	.520	.410
Davis, Johnny	B-R	5-10	177	4-26-90	.258	.297	.250	110	430	57	111	3	4	0	16	35	3	13	2	116	32	21	.284	.317
DeMuth, Dustin	L-R	6-3	200	7-30-91	.193	.048	.242	23	83	11	16	3	2	1	12	6	4	3	0	29	1	1	.313	.280
Denson, David	L-R	6-3	254	1-17-95	.243	.146	.265	68	226	37	55	10	1	4	29	43	0	0	0	80	3	3	.350	.364

MILWAUKEE BREWERS

	B-T	HT	WT	DOB	AVG	vLH	vRH	G	AB	R	H	2B	3B	HR	RBI	BB	HBP	SH	SF	SO	SB	CS	SLG	OBP
Eshleman, Paul	R-R	6-3	220	9-3-90	.237	.275	.220	39	131	13	31	5	1	2	11	9	4	4	0	29	0	0	.336	.306
Garcia, Omar	R-R	5-11	170	8-1-93	.263	.308	.250	113	391	57	103	17	3	0	23	35	13	14	3	77	44	21	.322	.342
Halcomb, Steven	R-R	5-10	180	8-27-90	.222	.167	.234	78	243	19	54	6	0	1	25	24	2	3	4	42	3	4	.259	.293
Matos, Sthervin	R-R	6-1	185	2-13-94	.103	.154	.077	11	39	2	4	0	0	1	7	1	0	2	1	12	1	0	.179	.122
McFarland, Chris	R-R	6-0	190	11-24-92	.284	.337	.268	100	394	55	112	17	3	6	39	24	6	9	5	88	30	9	.388	.331
Neda, Rafael	R-R	6-1	215	10-12-88	.254	.262	.252	85	287	42	73	16	0	3	30	34	11	0	3	30	3	3	.341	.352
Ortega, Angel	R-R	6-2	170	9-11-93	.231	.250	.227	110	389	36	90	18	4	4	54	13	3	10	6	88	11	4	.329	.258
Pena, Jose	R-R	6-2	192	3-3-91	.234	.267	.224	112	398	49	93	18	2	9	63	24	5	1	4	93	2	4	.357	.283
Ramirez, Aramis	R-R	6-1	205	6-25-78	.333	.500	.250	2	6	0	2	0	0	0	0	0	0	0	0	0	1	0	0	.333	.333
Ratterree, Michael	R-R	6-1	190	2-9-91	.235	.248	.231	125	447	91	105	33	5	18	71	75	8	0	7	154	4	6	.452	.350
Smith-Brennan, Taylor	R-R	6-0	210	1-31-92	.241	.237	.243	129	435	68	105	18	4	16	76	87	1	1	4	131	8	5	.411	.366

Pitching	B-T	HT	WT	DOB	W	L	ERA	G	GS	CG	SV	IP	H	R	ER	HR	BB	SO	AVG	vLH	vRH	K/9	BB/9
Alexander, Tyler	L-L	6-1	180	9-22-91	5	4	4.68	20	9	0	2	65	72	43	34	3	32	73	.273	.309	.257	10.06	4.41
Archer, Tristan	R-R	6-2	200	10-18-90	7	6	3.42	26	13	0	5	113	109	51	43	6	43	88	.256	.261	.252	7.01	3.42
Astin, Barrett	R-R	6-1	210	10-22-91	8	7	4.96	27	18	0	4	122	132	76	67	12	36	81	.277	.307	.253	5.99	2.66
Banda, Anthony	L-L	6-2	190	8-10-93	6	6	3.66	20	14	0	2	84	84	40	34	4	38	83	.263	.267	.261	8.93	4.09
2-team total (6 South Bend)					9	6	3.03	26	20	0	2	119	116	47	40	6	45	117	—	—	—	8.87	3.41
Curtis, Luke	R-R	6-1	195	12-31-91	1	0	3.70	12	0	0	1	24	17	14	10	3	7	23	.200	.222	.184	8.51	2.59
Diaz, Victor	R-R	6-1	170	10-6-93	3	5	4.86	23	10	0	1	87	73	51	47	10	41	66	.226	.248	.206	6.83	4.24
Fernandez, Rodolfo	R-R	6-2	220	3-21-90	1	0	2.87	14	0	0	2	31	26	11	10	1	14	24	.222	.229	.217	6.89	4.02
Gainey, Preston	R-R	6-3	205	2-13-91	5	9	4.18	24	24	0	0	125	127	74	58	13	49	113	.261	.278	.245	8.14	3.53
Harvey, Seth	L-R	6-2	205	1-20-88	0	1	3.21	8	0	0	0	14	8	6	5	0	6	19	.170	.083	.261	12.21	3.86
Linehan, Tyler	L-L	6-0	240	8-30-91	1	1	10.03	5	0	0	0	12	18	16	13	0	9	8	.353	.429	.324	6.17	6.94
Martin, Harvey	L-L	6-1	200	7-12-89	5	6	5.96	28	0	0	1	54	80	39	36	5	15	54	.333	.330	.336	8.94	2.48
Moore, Brandon	R-R	6-3	230	2-27-92	0	0	7.45	5	0	0	0	10	11	9	8	1	3	11	.282	.300	.263	10.24	2.79
Moye, Andy	R-R	6-5	180	9-11-87	1	0	1.69	1	1	0	0	5	7	1	1	0	0	4	.350	.364	.333	6.75	0.00
Quintana, Zach	R-R	5-11	180	4-15-94	4	5	5.70	25	16	0	2	85	100	60	54	4	49	58	.296	.307	.286	6.12	5.17
Razo, Chris	R-R	5-11	210	6-22-90	2	1	4.70	28	0	0	3	46	56	30	24	0	18	52	.293	.282	.301	10.17	3.52
Salas, Javi	R-R	6-4	210	3-20-92	1	2	3.82	6	6	0	0	33	34	14	14	4	5	23	.301	.243	.365	6.27	1.36
Seidenberger, Trevor	L-L	6-2	200	6-9-92	6	1	1.59	20	0	0	1	40	26	9	7	3	11	37	.193	.205	.187	8.39	2.50
Spurlin, Tyler	R-R	6-3	195	6-17-91	3	1	2.96	16	0	0	0	27	21	11	9	2	13	16	.223	.239	.208	5.27	4.28
Terry, Clint	L-L	6-2	195	6-9-92	3	5	2.49	17	9	0	0	76	66	23	21	3	26	70	.233	.233	.233	8.29	3.08
Thompson, Chad	R-R	6-7	207	2-6-91	2	2	5.04	7	4	0	0	25	35	16	14	0	12	22	.324	.296	.352	7.92	4.32
Wang, Wei-Chung	L-L	6-1	180	4-25-92	0	2	3.29	3	3	0	0	14	13	6	5	0	4	10	.250	.188	.278	6.59	2.63
Williams, Mark	R-R	6-3	240	8-12-89	0	2	2.70	5	0	0	0	7	5	2	2	0	4	4	.227	.091	.364	5.40	5.40
Williams, Taylor	B-R	5-11	165	7-21-91	8	1	2.36	22	12	1	4	107	78	34	28	4	23	112	.201	.215	.190	9.42	1.93

Fielding

Catcher	PCT	G	PO	A	E	DP	PB
Coulter	.978	61	402	46	10	4	17
Eshleman	.980	28	203	38	5	2	8
Neda	.992	51	449	38	4	4	6
Smith-Brennan	.989	21	163	10	2		12

First Base	PCT	G	PO	A	E	DP
Cooper	.974	9	69	7	2	6
Denson	.982	66	514	44	10	41
Eshleman	.965	9	75	8	3	3
Halcomb	1.000	11	67	3	0	3
Neda	.996	30	211	23	1	19

Second Base	PCT	G	PO	A	E	DP
Castillo	.946	31	58	65	7	10
Halcomb	.991	24	38	70	1	13
McFarland	.954	88	135	219	17	47

Third Base	PCT	G	PO	A	E	DP
DeMuth	.857	19	20	28	8	2
Halcomb	1.000	14	4	22	0	2
Matos	.813	7	2	11	3	1
Ramirez	1.000	1	0	1	0	0

Shortstop	PCT	G	PO	A	E	DP
Halcomb	.967	30	45	71	4	15
Ortega	.932	110	200	295	36	55

Outfield	PCT	G	PO	A	E	DP
Smith-Brennan	.922	101	64	173	20	14
Castillo	.923	11	12	0	1	0
Davis	.961	107	267	6	11	3
Garcia	.976	113	196	11	5	3
Pena	.957	78	108	4	5	0
Ratterree	.992	119	240	10	2	2

AZL BREWERS

ROOKIE

ARIZONA LEAGUE

Batting	B-T	HT	WT	DOB	AVG	vLH	vRH	G	AB	R	H	2B	3B	HR	RBI	BB	HBP	SH	SF	SO	SB	CS	SLG	OBP
Belonis, Carlos	R-R	6-3	175	8-19-94	.271	.317	.257	45	177	27	48	8	1	1	15	10	1	3	0	61	17	8	.345	.314
Cooper, Garrett	R-R	6-6	230	12-25-90	.375	.500	.333	5	16	3	6	1	0	1	3	3	0	0	0	3	0	0	.625	.474
Denson, David	L-R	6-3	254	1-17-95	.250	.000	.333	5	16	2	4	2	0	0	3	6	0	0	0	8	0	0	.375	.455
Gatewood, Jacob	R-R	6-5	190	9-25-95	.206	.238	.198	50	204	19	42	6	0	3	32	13	0	1	4	71	7	8	.279	.249
Harrison, Monte	R-R	6-3	200	8-10-95	.261	.205	.277	50	180	37	47	7	2	1	20	31	12	0	1	48	32	2	.339	.402
Leonardo, Daniel	B-R	5-9	160	8-28-95	.256	.160	.280	38	125	23	32	3	1	0	11	14	3	4	1	32	3	2	.296	.343
Martin, Matt	R-R	6-0	187	10-14-92	.311	.176	.351	28	74	17	23	5	1	1	11	5	10	0	0	19	0	1	.446	.427
Matos, Sthervin	R-R	6-1	185	2-13-94	.196	.250	.184	11	46	7	9	5	0	2	7	4	0	1	0	10	4	1	.435	.260
Morris, Hunter	L-R	6-2	225	10-7-88	.200	.333	.167	5	15	2	3	1	1	0	3	0	0	0	0	3	0	0	.400	.333
Narron, Connor	B-R	6-3	215	11-12-91	.139	.250	.125	11	36	4	5	1	0	0	5	6	1	0	0	10	0	1	.222	.279
Norton, Tanner	L-R	6-0	190	7-9-95	.250	.179	.269	40	132	14	33	3	0	0	15	16	4	1	0	28	0	0	.273	.349
Oquendo, Jonathan	B-R	6-3	170	3-21-96	.204	.222	.200	30	98	7	20	0	0	0	8	9	0	1	1	21	1	2	.204	.269
Ortiz, Juan	L-R	6-1	175	9-20-94	.263	.323	.245	36	133	19	35	5	2	3	21	13	0	0	2	37	1	7	.398	.324
Otano, Leudi	R-R	5-11	180	2-21-91	.189	.238	.176	28	95	10	18	3	1	0	11	16	0	1	1	31	1	1	.242	.304
Post, Milan	R-R	6-1	185	3-22-94	.106	.000	.127	23	66	7	7	3	0	0	1	10	3	1	0	23	0	2	.152	.253
Quiterio, Jorge	R-R	6-0	171	12-10-94	.151	.208	.137	38	119	14	18	4	0	2	14	7	0	2	1	38	4	2	.235	.197
Rubio, Elvis	R-R	6-3	215	7-2-94	.147	.250	.091	11	34	7	5	0	0	1	4	1	1	0	1	7	1	0	.235	.189
Santana, Yunior	R-R	6-3	210	9-10-93	.177	.267	.160	30	96	11	17	2	0	1	6	12	0	0	1	40	16	3	.229	.266
Stokes, Troy	R-R	5-8	182	2-2-96	.262	.225	.273	47	172	29	45	10	1	0	18	24	5	3	3	47	19	3	.331	.363

Pitching	B-T	HT	WT	DOB	W	L	ERA	G	GS	CG	SV	IP	H	R	ER	HR	BB	SO	AVG	vLH	vRH	K/9	BB/9
Alexander, Tyler	L-L	6-1	180	9-22-91	0	2	5.17	6	2	0	1	16	22	17	9	1	9	21	.328	.333	.326	12.06	5.17
Blau, Bubba	R-R	6-2	190	8-3-92	1	4	4.05	11	6	0	1	27	25	20	12	5	9	21	.231	.220	.241	7.09	3.04

Name	B-T	HT	WT	DOB	W	L	ERA	G	GS	CG	SV	IP	H	R	ER	HR	BB	SO	AVG	vLH	vRH	K/9	BB/9
Burkhalter, David	R-R	6-3	190	7-25-95	0	5	7.15	10	4	0	0	23	34	21	18	1	7	19	.327	.318	.333	7.54	2.78
Carver, David	L-L	6-3	180	10-25-91	1	1	5.68	8	1	0	0	19	25	14	12	2	3	20	.309	.276	.327	9.47	1.42
Cravy, Tyler	R-R	6-3	195	7-13-89	0	1	0.00	2	2	0	0	6	2	1	0	0	2	8	.100	.000	.133	12.00	3.00
Diaz, Miguel	R-R	6-1	175	11-28-94	4	2	4.21	13	5	0	0	47	42	24	22	3	20	53	.232	.173	.280	10.15	3.83
Earls, Kaleb	R-R	6-5	185	3-17-93	0	2	2.08	9	0	0	3	17	11	5	4	0	4	24	.175	.160	.184	12.46	2.08
Gomez, Milton	R-R	6-1	172	4-22-94	3	3	3.81	14	8	0	0	57	64	39	24	4	23	49	.271	.243	.295	7.78	3.65
Harvey, Seth	L-R	6-2	205	1-20-88	0	0	7.84	8	1	0	0	10	17	9	9	0	1	11	.362	.444	.310	9.58	0.87
Henderson, Jim	R-R	6-5	220	10-21-82	0	0	0.00	3	2	0	0	4	3	0	0	0	0	5	.214	.286	.143	12.27	0.00
Hillis, Andy	R-R	6-6	218	11-6-90	0	0	24.30	9	0	0	0	7	8	20	18	2	15	11	.276	.200	.316	14.85	20.25
Hudgens, Brock	R-R	6-0	190	10-16-91	3	1	1.17	11	0	0	1	15	10	7	2	0	7	18	.185	.179	.192	10.57	4.11
Lavandero, Alex	L-R	6-3	180	11-21-93	0	1	14.54	5	0	0	0	4	6	7	7	1	5	5	.375	.400	.364	10.38	10.38
Leal, Carlos	L-R	5-11	180	7-13-91	0	0	8.53	6	0	0	0	6	6	6	6	1	4	9	.261	.154	.400	12.79	5.68
Medeiros, Kodi	L-L	6-2	180	5-25-96	0	2	7.13	9	4	0	1	18	24	21	14	2	13	26	.308	.105	.373	13.25	6.62
Reeves, Chad	L-L	6-2	190	2-4-91	0	1	5.93	10	0	0	1	14	17	9	9	0	10	11	.333	.154	.395	7.24	6.59
Rizzo, Gian	R-R	6-1	160	9-5-93	1	0	2.22	10	0	0	4	28	19	8	7	4	3	32	.184	.195	.177	10.16	0.95
Smith, Caleb	R-R	6-4	215	4-22-93	1	2	4.68	14	2	0	2	25	16	15	13	2	26	17	.184	.200	.175	6.12	9.36
Stark, Taylor	R-R	5-11	165	10-7-91	0	0	9.72	8	0	0	0	8	14	11	9	0	8	5	.368	.500	.308	5.40	8.64
Torres, Joshua	R-R	6-0	160	4-26-94	4	0	1.92	14	7	0	0	52	47	15	11	1	10	37	.239	.212	.259	6.45	1.74
Ventura, Angel	R-R	6-2	185	4-7-93	6	3	5.19	14	6	0	0	50	56	33	29	2	9	46	.283	.316	.262	8.23	1.61
Walla, Max	L-L	5-11	205	4-12-91	0	0	9.28	9	0	0	0	11	15	14	11	0	10	8	.326	.231	.364	6.75	8.44
Wang, Wei-Chung	L-L	6-1	180	4-25-92	0	0	0.00	2	2	0	0	4	1	0	0	0	0	3	.077	.000	.100	7.36	0.00
Yamamoto, Jordan	R-R	6-0	185	5-11-96	0	1	4.57	10	3	0	0	22	22	12	11	3	13	22	.262	.300	.241	9.14	5.40

Fielding

Catcher	PCT	G	PO	A	E	DP	PB
Martin	.991	13	100	10	1	0	6
Narron	.979	8	43	13	1	0	4
Norton	.967	4	27	2	1	0	3
Otano	.974	17	135	13	4	1	5
Post	.974	22	168	20	5	2	8

First Base	PCT	G	PO	A	E	DP
Denson	1.000	5	32	1	0	6
Matos	1.000	2	14	1	0	3
Morris	.969	4	29	2	1	2
Norton	.986	35	261	17	4	21
Ortiz	1.000	14	100	7	0	9

	PCT	G	PO	A	E	DP
Otano	1.000	2	11	4	0	1

Second Base	PCT	G	PO	A	E	DP
Leonardo	.959	35	76	112	8	19
Oquendo	.984	14	29	33	1	7
Quiterio	.969	9	14	17	1	3

Third Base	PCT	G	PO	A	E	DP
Cooper	.824	5	4	10	3	2
Matos	.786	10	6	16	6	2
Narron	—	1	0	0	0	0
Oquendo	.737	8	4	10	5	0
Otano	.880	9	7	15	3	1
Quiterio	.781	29	5	52	16	6

Shortstop	PCT	G	PO	A	E	DP
Gatewood	.955	44	74	117	9	19
Leonardo	.824	4	4	10	3	2
Oquendo	.868	9	11	35	7	5

Outfield	PCT	G	PO	A	E	DP
Belonis	.959	42	93	1	4	2
Harrison	.914	46	71	3	7	0
Ortiz	.875	11	14	0	2	0
Quiterio	—	1	0	0	0	0
Rubio	1.000	7	3	0	0	0
Santana	.921	20	33	2	3	0
Stokes	1.000	46	65	2	0	0

HELENA BREWERS

ROOKIE

PIONEER LEAGUE

Batting	B-T	HT	WT	DOB	AVG	vLH	vRH	G	AB	R	H	2B	3B	HR	RBI	BB	HBP	SH	SF	SO	SB	CS	SLG	OBP
Aviles, Luis	R-R	6-1	170	3-16-95	.251	.300	.238	53	187	24	47	8	4	2	19	14	0	4	0	57	11	4	.369	.303
Castillo, Francisco	B-R	5-10	166	6-4-93	.273	.267	.275	41	161	20	44	9	1	1	16	13	0	0	0	28	9	5	.360	.328
Cleary, Jack	R-R	6-2	212	6-20-90	.282	.400	.267	24	85	9	24	4	0	1	11	8	2	1	0	18	3	1	.365	.358
DeMuth, Dustin	L-R	6-3	200	7-30-91	.333	.364	.327	31	120	16	40	7	1	2	12	9	4	0	1	18	2	2	.458	.396
Diaz, Brandon	R-R	5-11	175	4-14-95	.261	.217	.271	67	253	46	66	9	3	4	26	33	6	4	3	65	22	9	.368	.356
Hinojosa, Dionis	R-R	6-0	192	8-14-90	.256	.533	.200	29	90	15	23	5	0	1	18	7	3	1	2	15	5	3	.344	.324
Matos, Sthervin	R-R	6-1	185	2-13-94	.317	.241	.336	34	142	20	45	9	1	6	31	3	2	0	1	28	4	0	.521	.338
McCall, Greg	R-R	6-1	195	12-25-91	.326	.370	.305	23	86	15	28	6	0	2	15	6	2	0	2	28	0	0	.465	.375
Mejia, Natanael	R-R	6-0	175	7-10-92	.215	.071	.241	25	93	6	20	2	0	1	11	4	2	1	1	23	0	0	.269	.260
Meyer, Mitch	L-R	6-2	190	2-18-92	.252	.130	.287	55	210	28	53	11	3	7	26	19	3	3	0	71	8	4	.433	.323
Munoz, Gregory	L-R	5-9	160	2-6-94	.295	.303	.294	58	220	40	65	12	1	0	15	17	1	5	0	42	21	6	.359	.349
Narron, Connor	B-R	6-3	215	11-12-91	.258	.313	.239	17	62	8	16	3	0	1	2	11	1	0	0	11	1	3	.355	.378
Neuhaus, Tucker	L-R	6-3	190	6-18-95	.233	.294	.215	61	232	31	54	13	0	3	21	20	1	4	0	76	9	2	.328	.296
Rivera, Edgardo	L-R	6-0	155	4-12-94	.245	.070	.297	57	188	28	46	6	0	0	11	22	1	2	0	52	14	6	.277	.327
Rubio, Elvis	R-R	6-3	215	7-2-94	.270	.308	.258	29	115	16	31	5	0	1	15	9	4	0	0	28	1	1	.339	.344
Sharkey, Alan	L-L	6-1	185	11-8-93	.254	.167	.272	53	177	19	45	13	2	3	24	29	3	3	1	42	6	4	.401	.367
Williams, Eric	R-R	5-10	190	4-25-95	.230	.250	.224	42	135	17	31	3	1	1	9	21	1	1	0	27	8	7	.289	.338

Pitching	B-T	HT	WT	DOB	W	L	ERA	G	GS	CG	SV	IP	H	R	ER	HR	BB	SO	AVG	vLH	vRH	K/9	BB/9
Carver, David	L-L	6-3	180	10-25-91	1	1	5.24	6	2	0	0	22	24	18	13	3	8	7	.267	.346	.234	2.82	3.22
Cox, Wesley	R-R	6-3	200	5-2-92	1	0	7.45	15	0	0	4	19	26	16	16	2	5	13	.321	.273	.354	6.05	2.33
Curtis, Luke	R-R	6-1	195	12-31-91	0	2	4.15	5	0	0	2	4	4	2	2	0	1	5	.250	.200	.273	10.38	2.08
Deeter, Ryan	R-R	6-0	180	7-27-91	0	3	3.68	17	0	0	0	22	18	13	9	3	16	21	.222	.294	.170	8.59	6.55
Earls, Kaleb	R-R	6-5	185	3-17-93	1	0	3.60	2	0	0	0	5	4	3	2	0	4	2	.222	.000	.333	3.60	7.20
Ghelfi, Drew	R-R	6-3	190	9-10-90	0	1	9.00	9	0	0	0	11	14	11	11	2	4	8	.318	.267	.345	6.55	3.27
Hirsch, Zach	L-L	6-4	220	7-6-90	2	2	3.73	15	5	0	1	41	43	20	17	5	5	40	.267	.276	.262	8.78	1.10
Hissa, Donnie	R-R	6-2	240	1-9-92	0	2	6.52	15	0	0	1	19	26	16	14	2	5	11	.325	.262	.395	5.12	2.33
Kole, J.B.	R-R	6-4	200	1-26-93	2	3	7.64	13	0	0	1	35	48	34	30	7	14	23	.320	.299	.342	5.86	3.57
Linehan, Tyler	L-L	6-0	240	8-30-91	2	0	4.64	16	1	0	2	33	31	21	17	0	19	44	.246	.211	.261	12.00	5.18
Moore, Brandon	R-R	6-3	230	2-27-92	1	0	3.86	12	0	0	2	30	36	15	13	0	6	25	.283	.293	.279	7.42	1.78
Ortega, Jorge	R-R	6-1	165	6-20-93	4	5	4.23	15	15	0	0	83	90	45	39	13	8	46	.274	.286	.265	4.99	0.87
Ortega, Luis	L-L	5-10	155	4-20-93	3	9	9.44	14	9	0	0	48	81	62	50	5	24	40	.382	.347	.393	7.55	4.53
Rincon, Junior	R-R	6-2	185	12-7-91	0	1	10.31	16	0	0	0	18	29	21	21	3	20	17	.358	.353	.362	8.35	9.82
Salas, Javi	R-R	6-4	210	3-20-92	0	3	6.92	8	4	0	1	26	33	23	20	1	9	16	.308	.350	.284	5.54	3.12
Sneed, Cy	R-R	6-4	185	10-1-92	0	2	5.92	11	6	0	1	38	50	31	25	4	14	31	.311	.310	.311	7.34	3.32

Name	B-T	HT	WT	DOB	W	L	ERA	G	GS	CG	SV	IP	H	R	ER	HR	BB	SO	AVG	vLH	vRH	K/9	BB/9
Thompson, Chad	R-R	6-7	207	2-6-91	3	2	3.41	7	4	0	0	29	24	15	11	4	10	28	.226	.178	.262	8.69	3.10
Uhen, Josh	R-R	6-4	185	4-7-92	2	4	4.28	15	8	0	0	55	53	30	26	7	14	37	.251	.238	.264	6.09	2.30
Williams, Devin	R-R	6-3	165	9-21-94	4	7	4.48	15	8	0	0	66	74	39	33	5	20	66	.282	.299	.269	8.95	2.71
Woodruff, Brandon	R-R	6-4	215	2-10-93	1	2	3.28	14	8	0	0	47	48	35	17	2	16	37	.262	.254	.268	7.14	3.09

Fielding

Catcher	PCT	G	PO	A	E	DP	PB
Cleary	1.000	24	147	18	0	2	6
McCall	.972	18	124	15	4	2	3
Mejia	.957	23	157	21	8	2	4
Narron	.990	13	92	8	1	1	3

First Base	PCT	G	PO	A	E	DP
DeMuth	.979	14	126	12	3	11
Matos	1.000	13	112	10	0	9
Sharkey	.983	50	411	44	8	34

Second Base	PCT	G	PO	A	E	DP
Castillo	.941	29	43	84	8	12
Munoz	.979	49	82	155	5	26

Third Base	PCT	G	PO	A	E	DP
DeMuth	.826	11	8	11	4	1
Matos	.839	16	15	32	9	6
Mejia	.667	1	1	1	1	0
Neuhaus	.891	50	36	95	16	4

Shortstop	PCT	G	PO	A	E	DP
Aviles	.924	53	99	158	21	32

	PCT	G	PO	A	E	DP
Castillo	.942	12	23	26	3	6
Munoz	.918	10	17	28	4	3
Neuhaus	1.000	2	2	7	0	2

Outfield	PCT	G	PO	A	E	DP
Diaz	.994	62	153	6	1	4
Hinojosa	.974	23	35	2	1	0
Meyer	.961	44	69	4	3	0
Rivera	.964	48	79	2	3	0
Rubio	1.000	21	35	1	0	1
Williams	.982	32	47	7	1	1

DSL BREWERS

ROOKIE

DOMINICAN SUMMER LEAGUE

Batting	B-T	HT	WT	DOB	AVG	vLH	vRH	G	AB	R	H	2B	3B	HR	RBI	BB	HBP	SH	SF	SO	SB	CS	SLG	OBP
Atencio, Johel	R-R	5-10	180	9-17-96	.290	.326	.280	55	214	32	62	11	0	1	25	10	5	0	3	19	1	0	.355	.332
Chal, Roosevert	L-R	5-9	155	4-9-94	.254	.280	.239	25	71	7	18	2	0	0	11	3	1	1	0	10	0	2	.282	.293
Colatosti, Raphachel	R-R	6-1	173	7-3-93	.256	.216	.266	54	176	23	45	4	0	0	24	24	3	1	2	28	3	4	.278	.351
Correa, Henry	L-R	6-0	160	1-29-97	.161	.059	.186	34	87	11	14	3	0	0	7	12	3	2	0	30	2	5	.195	.284
De Los Santos, Juan	R-R	5-11	170	1-11-94	.236	.143	.261	61	199	25	47	10	0	2	28	32	7	0	2	44	4	3	.317	.358
Fernandez, Dilson	R-R	5-11	185	5-9-94	.250	.333	.227	21	56	5	14	3	2	0	4	4	0	0	0	11	1	0	.375	.300
Mallen, Franly	R-R	6-1	160	5-27-97	.235	.220	.238	63	243	38	57	11	0	1	23	26	9	1	4	69	4	5	.292	.326
Martinez, Kevin	B-R	5-10	180	1-11-95	.254	.244	.257	59	189	25	48	9	3	0	24	21	2	2	1	33	4	0	.333	.333
Martinez, Yerald	R-R	6-2	180	12-3-95	.256	.286	.248	68	262	48	67	14	6	5	46	28	8	0	2	72	10	8	.412	.343
Mendez, Julio	R-R	5-10	140	10-24-96	.234	.184	.248	58	171	25	40	8	2	0	14	22	7	2	1	21	7	4	.304	.343
Pena, Franmy	B-R	5-10	175	6-8-92	.167	.333	.111	19	36	8	6	0	2	0	4	8	1	0	0	11	1	0	.278	.333
Pierre, Nicolas	R-R	6-3	170	11-13-96	.258	.237	.264	60	252	36	65	14	2	6	27	13	8	1	1	58	9	5	.401	.314
Santana, Geuris	L-R	6-3	195	6-30-95	.222	.000	.235	8	18	1	4	0	0	0	1	2	1	0	0	3	0	0	.222	.333
Segovia, Joantgel	R-R	6-1	175	11-8-96	.384	.500	.354	58	224	40	86	6	4	0	21	24	7	3	1	19	6	8	.446	.457
Valderrey, Nicol	R-R	6-2	180	1-20-97	.223	.057	.262	53	184	19	41	7	0	5	24	20	5	0	1	56	0	0	.342	.314
Vasquez, Yoel	R-R	6-1	180	8-20-96	.286	.200	.333	8	14	1	4	0	1	0	1	3	3	1	0	5	0	0	.429	.500

Pitching	B-T	HT	WT	DOB	W	L	ERA	G	GS	CG	SV	IP	H	R	ER	HR	BB	SO	AVG	vLH	vRH	K/9	BB/9
Arias, Doni	R-R	6-3	187	7-26-92	3	1	1.42	10	0	0	5	13	9	3	2	0	6	8	.191	.071	.242	5.68	4.26
Benoit, Rodrigo	R-R	6-2	170	2-23-94	1	3	4.73	8	7	0	0	27	36	25	14	3	4	16	.313	.316	.312	5.40	1.35
Brea, Jesus	R-R	6-3	194	12-25-95	1	0	6.55	15	0	0	1	22	29	23	16	0	12	15	.309	.375	.259	6.14	4.91
Cordero, Axel	R-R	6-4	175	7-13-91	0	1	8.25	19	0	0	2	24	34	29	22	2	12	12	.343	.366	.328	4.50	4.50
De La Cruz, Joan	L-L	6-3	175	9-30-94	4	2	3.86	12	12	0	0	61	62	29	26	3	26	70	.261	.311	.249	10.38	3.86
Diaz, Juan	R-R	6-0	185	9-24-92	1	2	4.81	21	0	0	1	39	39	30	21	1	26	45	.247	.216	.262	10.30	5.95
Diplan, Nattino	R-R	6-3	180	12-30-93	0	5	6.80	11	9	0	0	45	59	46	34	2	23	28	.322	.358	.308	5.60	4.60
Flores, Junior	R-R	6-1	175	10-13-94	2	3	4.81	13	11	0	0	58	48	35	31	0	35	50	.230	.203	.240	7.76	5.43
Hernandez, Nelson	R-R	6-2	170	3-13-97	1	6	7.81	11	11	0	0	55	83	51	48	4	33	44	.352	.333	.360	5.37	1.30
Leal, Yosmer	R-R	6-4	170	2-26-96	1	6	4.45	12	12	0	0	57	60	39	28	2	31	45	.267	.198	.318	7.15	4.92
Luna, Carlos	R-R	6-1	175	9-25-96	1	2	3.51	12	0	0	3	33	39	16	13	0	10	16	.302	.196	.372	4.32	2.70
Nova, Boanerges	L-L	6-2	170	2-6-93	0	0	3.94	18	0	0	0	32	30	18	14	2	13	28	.240	.353	.222	7.88	3.66
Padilla, Marcos	L-L	6-2	175	1-1-94	1	2	9.68	16	0	0	0	18	25	24	19	3	22	19	.321	.308	.323	9.68	11.21
Peguero, Pedro	R-R	6-6	215	8-10-93	2	3	6.23	11	3	0	0	26	19	20	18	0	36	31	.198	.103	.239	10.73	12.46
Tejada, Melvin	R-R	6-3	175	1-24-95	3	4	2.98	21	1	0	3	51	53	37	17	1	25	35	.257	.125	.317	6.14	4.38
Torrez, Orlando	R-R	6-3	195	4-14-92	6	3	4.69	19	4	0	1	56	47	31	29	1	21	41	.228	.212	.234	6.63	3.40

Fielding

Catcher	PCT	G	PO	A	E	DP	PB
Atencio	.990	24	180	11	2	0	11
Fernandez	.955	11	35	7	2	0	5
Martinez	.956	36	184	34	10	2	6
Pena	.935	12	62	10	5	2	3
Vasquez	.942	8	44	5	3	0	6

First Base	PCT	G	PO	A	E	DP
Colatosti	1.000	16	127	5	0	11
De Los Santos	.975	6	37	2	1	2
Fernandez	1.000	2	11	0	0	2
Martinez	1.000	4	24	1	0	4
Pena	—	1	0	0	0	0
Santana	.857	3	5	1	1	1
Valderrey	.974	49	429	24	12	23

Second Base	PCT	G	PO	A	E	DP
Chal	.968	17	23	37	2	9
Colatosti	1.000	7	13	16	0	5
Correa	.963	17	32	46	3	9
De Los Santos	1.000	2	4	3	0	0
Mallen	.846	3	3	8	2	1
Mendez	.946	34	59	82	8	13

Third Base	PCT	G	PO	A	E	DP
Chal	.750	5	4	5	3	1
Colatosti	.913	23	21	63	8	4
Correa	.875	4	5	9	2	3
De Los Santos	.876	34	27	72	14	7
Mendez	.875	12	8	20	4	4
Santana	.778	4	0	7	2	1

Shortstop	PCT	G	PO	A	E	DP
Correa	1.000	1	2	1	0	1
Mallen	.904	60	103	160	28	19
Mendez	.891	14	10	31	5	6

Outfield	PCT	G	PO	A	E	DP
Colatosti	1.000	11	11	2	0	0
De Los Santos	.909	21	18	2	2	0
Martinez	.946	68	111	11	7	3
Mendez	—	1	0	0	0	0
Pena	1.000	2	0	1	0	0
Pierre	.947	60	138	6	8	2
Santana	.000	1	0	0	1	0
Segovia	.951	56	90	7	5	0

Minnesota Twins

SEASON IN A SENTENCE: Twins fans had few expectations for the 2015 season when it began, and those low expectations were right in line with what happened–last place in the AL Central for the third time in the past four seasons.

HIGH POINT: Minneapolis-St. Paul was an excellent host for the All-Star Game as the eyes of the baseball world turned to Target Field for the mid-summer classic. In the regular season, Minnesota posted a winning record in April, their first winning record in a month since June 2012.

LOW POINT: The all-star weekend was also supposed to be a chance for Twins fans to see the club's top two prospects, Miguel Sano and Byron Buxton, in person at the Futures Game, but both were unable to attend because of long-term injuries.

NOTABLE ROOKIES: Versatile center fielder/shortstop Danny Santana finished second on the club in runs scored (70) and stolen bases (20). He hit an impressive .319/.353/.472 in extensive action. First baseman Kennys Vargas had a loud big league debut, hitting .274/.316/.456 after a midseason callup. Lefty Yohan Pino surprisingly found himself in the big league rotation as a 30-year-old rookie. He struggled after a strong start, finishing 2-5, 5.07 in 11 starts. Trevor May (3-6, 7.88) got an even ruder introduction to the big leagues.

KEY TRANSACTIONS: Catcher Kurt Suzuki (.288/.345/.383) and righthander Phil Hughes (16-10, 3.52) proved to be a pair of valuable, reasonably inexpensive free agent acquisitions. The Twins were impressed enough by Suzuki that they added a multi-year extension to his one-year deal during the season. Another free agent signing, righthander Ricky Nolasco (6-12, 5.38), didn't work out nearly as well. A fourth straight season of more than 90 losses cost manager Ron Gardenhire his job.

DOWN ON THE FARM: Before the season began, the Twins announced that Sano would miss the entire season because of Tommy John surgery on his throwing arm. The news got worse when Buxton missed most of the first half of the season with a wrist injury, then missed most of the second half of the season after suffering a concussion in a frightening outfield collision. Even with the injuries, the Twins' system finished with the sixth-best overall record in 2015, and every Twins minor league club with the exception of the GCL Twins finished above .500. The Fort Myers Twins won the Florida State League title.

OPENING DAY PAYROLL: $84.9 million (22nd).

PLAYERS OF THE YEAR

MAJOR LEAGUE	MINOR LEAGUE
Brian Dozier 2b	**Jose Berrios** rhp
.242/.345/.416	(High A, Double-A,
23 HR, 21 SB	Triple-A)
Led Twins in HR, SB	12-8, 2.70

ORGANIZATION LEADERS

BATTING   *Minimum 250 AB

MAJORS

* AVG	Santana, Danny	.319
* OPS	Santana, Danny	.824
HR	Dozier, Brian	23
RBI	Plouffe, Trevor	80

MINORS

AVG	Garver, Mitch, Cedar Rapids	.298
OBP	Garver, Mitch, Cedar Rapids	.399
SLG	Rodriguez, Reynaldo, Rochester, New Britain	.495
R	Christensen, Chad, Cedar Rapids	84
H	Polanco, Jorge, Fort Myers, New Britain	151
TB	Rodriguez, Reynaldo, Rochester, New Britain	244
2B	Rodriguez, Reynaldo, Rochester, New Britain	37
3B	Kanzler, Jason, Cedar Rapids, Fort Myers	9
HR	Walker II, Adam Brett, Fort Myers	25
RBI	Walker II, Adam Brett, Fort Myers	94
BB	Harrison, Travis, Fort Myers	64
SO	Walker II, Adam Brett, Fort Myers	156
SB	Goodrum, Niko, Fort Myers	35

PITCHING   #Minimum 75 IP

MAJORS

W	Hughes, Phil	16
# ERA	Hughes, Phil	3.52
SO	Hughes, Phil	186
SV	Perkins, Glen	34

MINORS

W	Duffey, Tyler, Ft. Myers, N. Britain, Rochester	13
L	Eades, Ryan, Cedar Rapids	11
# ERA	Wheeler, Jason, Ft. Myers, Roch., N. Britain	2.67
G	O'Rourke, Ryan, New Britain, Rochester	51
GS	Meyer, Alex, Rochester	27
SV	Oliveros, Lester, New Britain, Rochester	18
IP	Wheeler, Jason, Ft. Myers, Roch., N. Britain	158
BB	Meyer, Alex, Rochester	64
SO	Meyer, Alex, Rochester	153
AVG	Berrios, Jose, Ft. Myers, N. Britain, Roch.	.227

General Manager: Terry Ryan. **Farm Director:** Brad Steil. **Scouting Director:** Deron Johnson.

Class	Team	League	W	L	PCT	Finish	Manager
Majors	Minnesota Twins	American	70	92	.432	t-25th (30)	Ron Gardenhire
Triple-A	Rochester Red Wings	International	77	67	.535	5th (14)	Gene Glynn
Double-A	New Britain Rock Cats	Eastern	73	69	.514	t-4th (12)	Jeff Smith
High A	Fort Myers Miracle	Florida State	82	57	.590	1st (12)	Doug Mientkiewicz
Low A	Cedar Rapids Kernels	Midwest	73	67	.521	4th (16)	Jake Mauer
Rookie	Elizabethton Twins	Appalachian	38	30	.559	t-2nd (10)	Ray Smith
Rookie	Twins	Gulf Coast	23	37	.383	t-14th (16)	Ramon Borrego
Overall Minor League Record			366	327	.528	6th (30)	

ORGANIZATION STATISTICS

MINNESOTA TWINS

AMERICAN LEAGUE

Batting	B-T	HT	WT	DOB	AVG	vLH	vRH	G	AB	R	H	2B	3B	HR	RBI	BB	HBP	SH	SF	SO	SB	CS	SLG	OBP
Arcia, Oswaldo	L-R	6-0	220	5-9-91	.231	.198	.249	103	372	46	86	16	3	20	57	31	6	0	1	127	1	2	.452	.300
Bartlett, Jason	R-R	6-0	190	10-30-79	.000	—	.000	3	3	3	0	0	0	0	0	0	1	0	0	3	0	0	.000	.250
Bernier, Doug	R-R	6-1	185	6-24-80	.286	.333	.250	7	7	2	2	0	0	0	1	1	0	0	0	2	0	0	.286	.444
Colabello, Chris	R-R	6-4	220	10-24-83	.229	.211	.239	59	205	17	47	13	0	6	39	14	1	0	0	66	0	2	.380	.282
Dozier, Brian	R-R	5-11	190	5-15-87	.242	.264	.233	156	598	112	145	33	1	23	71	89	9	3	8	129	21	7	.416	.345
Escobar, Eduardo	B-R	5-10	175	1-5-89	.275	.328	.252	133	433	52	119	35	2	6	37	24	2	4	2	93	1	1	.406	.315
Florimon, Pedro	B-R	6-2	180	12-10-86	.092	.111	.082	33	76	7	7	1	1	0	1	8	0	2	0	22	6	0	.132	.179
Fryer, Eric	R-R	6-2	215	8-26-85	.213	.206	.220	28	75	11	16	4	0	1	5	5	1	0	0	15	1	0	.307	.272
Fuld, Sam	L-L	5-10	175	11-20-81	.274	.326	.256	53	164	15	45	10	0	1	17	26	0	3	2	29	12	3	.354	.370
2-team total (60 Oakland)					.239	—	—	113	351	40	84	16	4	4	36	43	0	6	2	63	21	4	.342	.321
Herrmann, Chris	L-R	6-0	200	11-24-87	.213	.250	.203	33	75	8	16	3	0	0	4	4	0	0	0	17	1	0	.253	.253
Hicks, Aaron	B-R	6-2	190	10-2-89	.215	.279	.178	69	186	22	40	8	0	1	18	36	0	2	1	56	4	3	.274	.341
Kubel, Jason	L-R	6-0	220	5-25-82	.224	.194	.233	45	156	12	35	6	1	1	13	19	1	0	0	59	1	0	.295	.313
Mastroianni, Darin	R-R	5-11	190	8-26-85	.000	.000	.000	7	11	3	0	0	0	0	1	0	0	0	0	5	1	0	.000	.083
2-team total (14 Toronto)					.116	—	—	21	43	7	5	0	0	1	2	1	0	0	0	10	1	0	.186	.136
Mauer, Joe	L-R	6-5	230	4-19-83	.277	.268	.282	120	455	60	126	27	2	4	55	60	1	0	2	96	3	0	.371	.361
Morales, Kendrys	B-R	6-1	225	6-20-83	.234	.250	.225	39	154	12	36	11	0	1	18	6	0	0	2	27	0	0	.325	.259
2-team total (59 Seattle)					.218	—	—	98	367	28	80	20	0	8	42	27	3	0	4	68	0	0	.338	.274
Nunez, Eduardo	R-R	6-0	185	6-15-87	.250	.232	.267	72	204	26	51	7	4	4	24	5	1	3	0	31	9	3	.382	.271
Parmelee, Chris	L-L	6-1	220	2-24-88	.256	.325	.225	87	250	27	64	11	0	7	28	17	2	0	1	64	0	3	.384	.307
Pinto, Josmil	R-R	5-11	210	3-31-89	.219	.186	.236	57	169	25	37	8	0	7	18	24	1	0	3	50	0	1	.391	.315
Plouffe, Trevor	R-R	6-2	205	6-15-86	.258	.278	.249	136	520	69	134	40	2	14	80	53	4	0	5	109	2	1	.423	.328
Polanco, Jorge	B-R	5-11	165	7-5-93	.333	—	.333	5	6	2	2	1	1	0	2	3	0	0	2	0	0	.833	.500
Santana, Danny	B-R	5-11	175	11-7-90	.319	.301	.326	101	405	70	129	27	7	7	40	19	3	2	1	98	20	4	.472	.353
Schafer, Jordan	L-L	6-1	205	9-4-86	.285	.171	.326	41	130	17	37	5	1	1	13	12	0	5	0	28	15	5	.362	.345
Suzuki, Kurt	R-R	5-11	230	10-4-83	.288	.331	.270	131	452	37	130	34	0	3	61	34	9	1	7	46	0	1	.383	.345
Vargas, Kennys	B-R	6-5	275	8-1-90	.274	.228	.309	53	215	26	59	10	1	9	38	12	3	0	4	63	0	0	.456	.316
Willingham, Josh	R-R	6-2	230	2-17-79	.210	.243	.195	68	224	34	47	5	1	12	34	42	7	0	5	78	1	0	.402	.345
2-team total (24 Kansas City)					.215	—	—	92	297	48	64	10	1	14	40	53	9	0	5	102	2	0	.397	.346

Pitching	B-T	HT	WT	DOB	W	L	ERA	G	GS	CG	SV	IP	H	R	ER	HR	BB	SO	AVG	vLH	vRH	K/9	BB/9
Achter, A.J.	R-R	6-5	205	8-27-88	1	0	3.27	7	0	0	0	11	14	7	4	2	3	5	.304	.389	.250	4.09	2.45
Burton, Jared	R-R	6-5	225	6-2-81	3	5	4.36	68	0	0	3	64	58	34	31	6	25	46	.241	.227	.250	6.47	3.52
Correia, Kevin	R-R	6-3	200	8-24-80	5	13	4.94	23	23	0	0	129	157	76	71	13	32	61	.297	.296	.298	4.24	2.23
Darnell, Logan	L-L	6-2	210	2-2-89	0	2	7.13	7	4	0	0	24	31	20	19	5	8	22	.307	.348	.295	8.25	3.00
Deduno, Sam	R-R	6-3	190	7-2-83	2	5	4.60	30	8	0	0	92	92	49	47	9	41	74	.261	.271	.251	7.24	4.01
2-team total (5 Houston)					2	6	4.47	35	9	0	0	101	97	53	50	9	46	83	—	—	—	7.42	4.11
Duensing, Brian	L-L	6-0	205	2-22-83	3	3	3.31	62	0	0	0	54	52	20	20	6	20	33	.254	.242	.264	5.47	3.31
Fien, Casey	R-R	6-2	205	10-21-83	6	6	3.98	73	0	0	1	63	64	29	28	7	10	51	.262	.255	.269	7.25	1.42
Gibson, Kyle	R-R	6-6	220	10-23-87	13	12	4.47	31	31	0	0	179	178	91	89	12	57	107	.258	.268	.245	5.37	2.86
Guerrier, Matt	R-R	6-3	195	8-2-78	0	1	3.86	27	0	0	0	28	30	12	12	1	10	12	.273	.288	.259	3.86	3.21
Hughes, Phil	R-R	6-5	240	6-24-86	16	10	3.52	32	32	1	0	210	221	88	82	16	16	186	.268	.249	.289	7.98	0.69
Johnson, Kris	L-L	6-4	205	10-14-84	0	1	4.73	3	3	0	0	13	17	7	7	2	9	12	.315	.250	.353	8.10	6.08
May, Trevor	R-R	6-5	215	9-23-89	3	6	7.88	10	9	0	0	46	59	41	40	7	22	44	.314	.298	.327	8.67	4.34
Milone, Tommy	L-L	6-0	205	2-16-87	0	1	7.06	6	5	0	0	22	37	21	17	4	11	14	.363	.238	.395	5.82	4.57
2-team total (16 Oakland)					6	4	4.19	22	21	0	0	118	128	63	55	16	37	75	—	—	—	5.72	2.82
Nolasco, Ricky	R-R	6-2	225	12-13-82	6	12	5.38	27	27	1	0	159	203	96	95	22	38	115	.316	.334	.297	6.51	2.15
Oliveros, Lester	R-R	6-0	235	5-28-88	0	1	7.11	7	0	0	0	6	6	5	5	2	3	5	.261	.000	.375	7.11	4.26
Pelfrey, Mike	R-R	6-7	250	1-14-84	0	3	7.99	5	5	0	0	24	29	23	21	5	18	10	.305	.196	.462	3.80	6.85
Perkins, Glen	L-L	6-0	205	3-2-83	4	3	3.65	63	0	0	34	62	62	29	25	7	11	66	.258	.284	.249	9.63	1.61
Pino, Yohan	R-R	6-2*	190	12-26-83	2	5	5.07	11	11	0	0	60	66	37	34	8	14	50	.278	.284	.272	7.46	2.09
Pressly, Ryan	R-R	6-3	205	12-15-88	2	0	2.86	21	0	0	0	28	30	10	9	3	8	14	.278	.308	.261	4.45	2.54
Swarzak, Anthony	R-R	6-4	210	9-10-85	3	2	4.60	50	4	0	0	86	100	48	44	5	28	47	.288	.282	.293	4.92	2.93
Thielbar, Caleb	L-L	6-0	195	1-31-87	2	1	3.40	54	0	0	0	48	51	19	18	3	16	35	.280	.289	.271	6.61	3.02

	B-T	HT	WT	DOB	W	L	ERA	G	GS	CG	SV	IP	H	R	ER	HR	BB	SO	AVG	vLH	vRH	K/9	BB/9
Thompson, Aaron	L-L	6-3	195	2-28-87	0	0	2.45	7	0	0	0	7	8	2	2	0	2	6	.286	.294	.273	7.36	2.45
Tonkin, Mike	R-R	6-7	220	11-19-89	0	0	4.74	25	0	0	0	19	23	13	10	2	6	16	.307	.333	.292	7.58	2.84

Fielding

Catcher	PCT	G	PO	A	E	DP	PB
Fryer	.994	24	152	6	1	1	1
Herrmann	1.000	1	1	0	0	0	0
Pinto	.973	25	173	8	5	0	4
Suzuki	.995	119	737	39	4	1	3

First Base	PCT	G	PO	A	E	DP
Colabello	.989	23	162	18	2	18
Mauer	.997	100	830	82	3	85
Morales	1.000	13	102	5	0	8
Parmelee	.995	33	167	18	1	15
Vargas	.970	13	88	9	3	3

Second Base	PCT	G	PO	A	E	DP
Bernier	1.000	2	2	3	0	1
Dozier	.980	156	261	475	15	98

	PCT	G	PO	A	E	DP
Escobar	.966	9	12	16	1	5
Nunez	1.000	2	1	0	0	0

Third Base	PCT	G	PO	A	E	DP
Escobar	.944	25	12	39	3	7
Nunez	.909	20	15	15	3	0
Plouffe	.960	127	109	226	14	25

Shortstop	PCT	G	PO	A	E	DP
Bernier	1.000	3	1	4	0	0
Escobar	.986	98	130	224	5	49
Florimon	.982	31	28	84	2	18
Nunez	.970	20	19	46	2	7
Polanco	1.000	4	3	6	0	3
Santana	.983	34	53	65	2	15

Outfield	PCT	G	PO	A	E	DP
Arcia	.975	100	191	8	5	0
Bartlett	—	2	0	0	0	0
Colabello	.960	19	22	2	1	1
Escobar	1.000	3	5	2	0	0
Fuld	.987	53	153	3	2	1
Herrmann	.970	24	32	0	1	0
Hicks	.989	65	173	4	2	2
Kubel	1.000	40	76	0	0	0
Mastroianni	1.000	7	5	1	0	0
Nunez	.938	18	28	2	2	1
Parmelee	.991	54	102	4	1	3
Santana	.977	69	167	5	4	0
Schafer	.977	41	83	2	2	0
Willingham	1.000	53	103	3	0	2

ROCHESTER RED WINGS
INTERNATIONAL LEAGUE

TRIPLE-A

Batting	B-T	HT	WT	DOB	AVG	vLH	vRH	G	AB	R	H	2B	3B	HR	RBI	BB	HBP	SH	SF	SO	SB	CS	SLG	OBP
Arcia, Oswaldo	L-R	6-0	220	5-9-91	.312	.313	.311	22	77	16	24	7	0	5	18	5	2	0	1	17	1	0	.597	.365
Beresford, James	L-R	6-1	170	1-19-89	.276	.237	.293	131	507	65	140	28	2	2	47	36	1	8	4	75	7	4	.351	.323
Bernier, Doug	R-R	6-1	185	6-24-80	.280	.265	.286	124	404	53	113	25	2	6	54	40	5	12	5	78	5	4	.396	.348
Colabello, Chris	R-R	6-4	220	10-24-83	.268	.293	.254	61	213	28	57	13	0	10	38	21	2	0	2	55	0	0	.469	.336
Farris, Eric	R-R	5-9	180	3-3-86	.280	.315	.264	133	483	59	135	23	1	4	44	26	3	4	7	57	16	8	.356	.316
Florimon, Pedro	B-R	6-2	180	12-10-86	.257	.250	.261	85	280	38	72	17	4	4	29	30	1	0	3	82	12	2	.389	.328
Fryer, Eric	R-R	6-2	215	8-26-85	.252	.355	.213	36	111	12	28	7	1	0	11	12	0	1	1	29	5	0	.333	.323
Hanson, Nate	R-R	6-0	195	2-8-87	.241	.241	.241	23	83	12	20	7	0	2	11	4	2	0	1	15	0	0	.398	.289
Herrmann, Chris	L-R	6-0	200	11-24-87	.304	.284	.319	60	204	31	62	18	4	5	26	21	2	0	1	45	4	1	.505	.373
Hicks, Aaron	B-R	6-2	190	10-2-89	.278	.258	.293	24	72	9	20	5	0	1	8	9	0	1	2	13	1	1	.389	.349
Mastroianni, Darin	R-R	5-11	190	8-26-85	.450	—	.450	4	20	4	9	2	0	0	2	0	0	0	0	4	0	1	.550	.450
2-team total (88 Buffalo)					.277	—	—	92	364	56	101	20	1	5	23	40	4	3	2	71	20	6	.379	.354
Nelson, Brad	L-R	6-2	255	12-23-82	.229	.268	.216	71	227	27	52	11	0	5	30	28	1	0	4	43	0	1	.344	.312
Nunez, Eduardo	R-R	6-0	185	6-15-87	.282	.200	.294	11	39	7	11	1	0	1	6	1	0	0	1	8	1	0	.385	.293
Ortiz, Danny	L-L	5-11	175	1-5-90	.256	.231	.266	73	242	36	62	13	3	8	33	9	1	0	2	51	0	0	.434	.283
Parmelee, Chris	L-L	6-1	220	2-24-88	.305	.385	.283	32	118	13	36	7	0	7	23	14	1	0	2	24	0	0	.542	.378
Pinto, Josmil	R-R	5-11	210	3-31-89	.279	.317	.264	60	208	24	58	17	1	6	35	31	2	0	1	37	0	1	.457	.376
Rahl, Chris	R-R	5-10	185	12-5-83	.259	.280	.251	104	332	41	86	17	1	7	43	7	1	1	5	82	9	6	.380	.272
Ramirez, Wilkin	R-R	6-2	230	10-25-85	.262	.333	.230	107	386	44	101	23	3	4	41	22	4	0	5	104	8	2	.368	.305
Rodriguez, Reynaldo	R-R	6-0	200	7-2-86	.156	.000	.185	10	32	2	5	1	0	1	4	3	0	0	0	8	0	0	.281	.229
Rohlfing, Dan	R-R	6-0	200	2-12-89	.205	.200	.208	75	219	29	45	17	0	2	23	28	5	0	2	56	0	1	.311	.307
Romero, Deibinson	R-R	6-1	215	9-24-86	.265	.269	.263	123	419	50	111	31	2	8	45	60	8	0	5	88	0	1	.406	.364
Santana, Danny	B-R	5-11	175	11-7-90	.268	.273	.267	24	97	15	26	7	2	0	7	6	0	2	0	28	4	1	.381	.311
Willingham, Josh	R-R	6-2	230	2-17-79	.185	.182	.188	8	27	3	5	2	0	1	3	1	1	0	0	8	0	0	.370	.241

Pitching	B-T	HT	WT	DOB	W	L	ERA	G	GS	CG	SV	IP	H	R	ER	HR	BB	SO	AVG	vLH	vRH	K/9	BB/9
Achter, A.J.	R-R	6-5	205	8-27-88	4	4	2.38	40	0	0	6	72	44	20	19	4	24	69	.176	.144	.201	8.63	3.00
Berrios, Jose	R-R	6-0	187	5-27-94	0	1	18.00	1	1	0	0	3	7	6	6	0	3	3	.438	.444	.429	9.00	9.00
Darnell, Logan	L-L	6-2	210	2-2-89	7	6	3.60	23	19	1	0	115	108	63	46	16	49	90	.246	.218	.256	7.04	3.83
Diamond, Scott	L-L	6-3	220	7-30-86	4	7	6.53	17	15	1	0	80	109	62	58	10	22	47	.328	.231	.358	5.29	2.48
2-team total (9 Louisville)					5	12	6.57	26	22	1	0	123	174	96	90	15	32	66	—	—	—	4.82	2.34
Duffey, Tyler	R-R	6-3	230	12-27-90	2	0	3.94	3	3	0	0	16	16	7	7	3	6	16	.258	.278	.231	9.00	3.38
Gilmartin, Sean	L-L	6-2	190	5-8-90	2	4	4.28	14	14	0	0	74	69	39	35	7	28	59	.250	.190	.276	7.21	3.42
Guerra, Deolis	R-R	6-5	245	4-17-89	2	2	4.33	36	1	0	0	52	51	28	25	5	18	54	.250	.261	.241	9.35	3.12
Guerrier, Matt	R-R	6-3	195	8-2-78	0	1	7.20	4	0	0	1	5	7	4	4	2	2	3	.318	.500	.214	5.40	3.60
Hamburger, Mark	R-R	6-4	195	2-5-87	4	4	3.79	14	6	0	1	55	51	27	23	1	22	37	.249	.257	.240	6.09	3.62
Hoffman, Matt	L-L	6-2	224	11-8-88	1	0	3.80	14	0	0	2	21	24	10	9	4	9	19	.293	.267	.308	8.02	3.80
2-team total (3 Lehigh Valley)					1	0	3.91	17	0	0	2	25	29	12	11	4	11	20	—	—	—	7.11	3.91
Ibarra, Edgar	L-L	6-0	190	5-31-89	5	0	3.44	31	0	0	0	50	50	19	19	1	23	42	.259	.267	.256	7.61	4.17
Johnson, Kris	L-L	6-4	205	10-14-84	10	7	3.48	23	23	2	0	132	115	58	51	8	55	102	.232	.165	.256	6.95	3.75
May, Trevor	R-R	6-5	215	9-23-89	8	6	2.84	18	18	1	0	98	75	33	31	4	39	94	.209	.179	.235	8.60	3.57
Meyer, Alex	R-R	6-9	220	1-3-90	7	7	3.52	27	27	0	0	130	116	58	51	10	64	153	.241	.269	.214	10.57	4.42
Milone, Tommy	L-L	6-0	205	2-16-87	0	1	1.29	1	1	0	0	7	6	1	1	0	2	3	.240	.333	.227	3.86	2.57
O'Rourke, Ryan	R-L	6-3	220	4-30-88	0	0	0.00	1	0	0	0	1	1	0	0	0	0	1	.250	.500	.000	9.00	0.00
Oliveros, Lester	R-R	6-0	235	5-28-88	1	2	2.29	24	0	0	6	35	27	10	9	0	13	52	.208	.159	.254	13.25	3.31
Pelfrey, Mike	R-R	6-7	250	1-14-84	1	0	0.90	2	2	0	0	10	9	1	1	0	3	3	.250	.294	.211	2.70	2.70
Pino, Yohan	R-R	6-2	190	12-26-83	10	2	2.47	16	9	2	0	73	47	21	20	9	24	72	.180	.231	.139	8.88	2.96
Pressly, Ryan	R-R	6-3	205	12-15-88	1	4	2.98	35	0	0	6	60	55	25	20	1	21	63	.238	.247	.232	9.40	3.13
Pryor, Stephen	R-R	6-4	245	7-23-89	1	0	0.89	14	0	0	2	20	6	2	2	2	16	22	.094	.080	.103	9.74	7.08
Raley, Brooks	L-L	6-3	200	6-29-88	0	1	3.68	8	1	0	1	15	17	7	6	1	11	19	.283	.200	.325	11.66	6.75
Thompson, Aaron	L-L	6-3	195	2-28-87	3	3	3.98	46	0	0	3	52	49	27	23	5	26	51	.250	.200	.272	8.83	4.50

				W	L	ERA	G	GS	CG	SV	IP	H	R	ER	HR	BB	SO	AVG	vLH	vRH	K/9	BB/9
Tonkin, Mike	R-R	6-7	220	11-19-89	3	4	2.80	39	0	0	10	45	41	18	14	2	12	46	.246	.274	.223	9.20	2.40
Vasquez, Virgil	R-R	6-3	205	6-7-82	1	1	4.50	3	3	1	0	16	16	8	8	2	6	17	.262	.333	.206	9.56	3.38
Wheeler, Jason	L-L	6-6	251	10-27-90	0	0	3.60	1	1	0	0	5	5	2	2	0	2	3	.263	.143	.333	5.40	3.60

Fielding

Catcher	PCT	G	PO	A	E	DP	PB
Fryer	.996	32	262	17	1	2	2
Herrmann	.985	26	182	12	3	3	1
Pinto	.993	34	285	8	2	2	3
Rohlfing	.996	58	430	22	2	3	3

First Base	PCT	G	PO	A	E	DP
Bernier	1.000	1	6	2	0	0
Colabello	.991	54	393	33	4	40
Hanson	.986	17	128	16	2	12
Herrmann	—	1	0	0	0	0
Nelson	.994	45	308	22	2	37
Parmelee	.993	22	135	15	1	10
Rodriguez	1.000	3	31	1	0	2
Rohlfing	1.000	6	30	1	0	4
Romero	1.000	4	40	0	0	5

Second Base	PCT	G	PO	A	E	DP
Beresford	.982	128	272	325	11	85
Bernier	.978	12	16	28	1	4
Farris	1.000	3	3	2	0	0
Florimon	1.000	7	9	15	0	6

Third Base	PCT	G	PO	A	E	DP
Beresford	1.000	3	3	1	0	0
Bernier	.952	44	17	63	4	6
Florimon	.846	11	6	16	4	1
Hanson	1.000	2	2	3	0	0
Nunez	.500	4	0	2	2	1
Romero	.907	98	61	145	21	14

Shortstop	PCT	G	PO	A	E	DP
Bernier	.974	53	84	174	7	33
Florimon	.942	65	70	156	14	33
Nunez	1.000	4	5	8	0	3

	PCT	G	PO	A	E	DP
Santana	.918	20	20	36	5	10
Outfield	**PCT**	**G**	**PO**	**A**	**E**	**DP**
Arcia	1.000	16	26	1	0	0
Bernier	1.000	8	10	0	0	0
Colabello	1.000	2	1	0	0	0
Farris	1.000	127	281	8	0	3
Herrmann	1.000	30	51	1	0	0
Hicks	1.000	23	36	0	0	0
Mastroianni	1.000	3	7	0	0	0
Nunez	1.000	1	3	0	0	0
Ortiz	.973	65	106	3	3	1
Parmelee	1.000	9	21	1	0	1
Rahl	.986	102	211	4	3	3
Ramirez	.990	71	95	3	1	1
Rodriguez	1.000	7	12	0	0	0
Rohlfing	1.000	4	7	0	0	0
Willingham	1.000	4	5	0	0	0

NEW BRITAIN ROCK CATS   DOUBLE-A

EASTERN LEAGUE

Batting	B-T	HT	WT	DOB	AVG	vLH	vRH	G	AB	R	H	2B	3B	HR	RBI	BB	HBP	SH	SF	SO	SB	CS	SLG	OBP
Boyer, Brad	L-R	6-0	185	10-4-83	.246	.231	.251	79	256	19	63	7	3	0	26	13	1	4	5	33	14	3	.297	.280
Buxton, Byron	R-R	6-2	190	12-18-93	.000	.000	—	1	3	0	0	0	0	0	0	0	0	0	0	3	0	0	.000	.000
Fuld, Sam	L-L	5-10	175	11-20-81	.429	.500	.375	4	14	4	6	2	0	1	2	2	0	0	1	0	0	0	.786	.500
Gonzales, Mike	L-R	6-6	264	6-16-88	.264	.281	.257	31	106	14	28	7	0	3	18	9	3	0	0	26	0	0	.415	.339
Hanson, Nate	R-R	6-0	195	2-8-87	.259	.241	.266	96	367	53	95	26	0	4	46	34	10	0	4	54	1	0	.362	.335
Hicks, Aaron	B-R	6-2	190	10-2-89	.297	.304	.294	43	148	30	44	11	1	4	21	28	0	—	2	27	2	3	.466	.404
Knudson, Kyle	R-R	6-3	210	9-12-87	.215	.236	.203	83	247	15	53	16	0	0	33	13	5	—	3	57	0	0	.279	.265
Koch, Matt	R-R	6-0	220	11-21-88	.212	.176	.228	73	217	23	46	9	0	2	19	27	2	3	1	58	2	1	.281	.304
Kvasnicka, Mike	R-R	6-2	200	12-7-88	.257	.263	.254	112	370	35	95	23	0	10	55	26	0	—	3	80	5	3	.400	.303
Mejia, Aderlin	B-R	5-11	170	5-12-92	.275	.222	.303	15	51	6	14	1	0	0	4	6	0	2	0	9	2	1	.294	.351
Michael, Levi	B-R	5-10	180	2-9-91	.340	.409	.290	15	53	13	18	1	0	1	7	3	0	0	1	11	4	1	.358	.444
Nunez, Eduardo	R-R	6-0	185	6-15-87	.400	.750	.167	4	10	1	4	0	1	0	3	0	0	0	0	2	1	0	.600	.538
Ortiz, Danny	L-L	5-11	175	1-5-90	.324	.382	.290	49	182	22	59	16	2	4	31	4	1	1	1	34	3	1	.500	.340
Pettersen, Adam	R-R	5-9	162	11-19-88	.203	.320	.118	27	59	5	12	4	0	0	2	10	1	3	0	17	1	1	.271	.329
Polanco, Jorge	B-R	5-11	165	7-5-93	.281	.333	.257	37	146	13	41	6	0	1	16	9	0	2	0	28	7	3	.342	.323
Ray, Lance	L-R	6-1	195	9-2-89	.208	.333	.167	8	24	4	5	2	1	0	4	2	2	—	1	10	0	0	.375	.310
Rodriguez, Jairo	R-R	5-11	180	8-24-88	.192	.429	.105	9	26	2	5	0	0	0	1	2	0	0	0	2	1	0	.192	.250
Rodriguez, Reynaldo	R-R	6-0	200	7-2-86	.286	.313	.274	126	461	81	132	36	2	21	66	39	7	—	10	77	6	4	.510	.344
Rosario, Eddie	L-R	6-1	180	9-28-91	.237	.252	.230	79	316	40	75	20	3	8	36	17	1	—	2	68	8	4	.396	.277
Thomas, Tony	R-R	5-10	180	7-10-86	.241	.287	.216	129	453	71	109	29	6	12	45	37	4	—	3	141	14	4	.411	.302
Vargas, Kennys	B-R	6-5	275	8-1-90	.281	.294	.274	97	356	50	100	17	0	17	63	43	3	0	3	68	0	2	.472	.360
Waring, Brandon	R-R	6-3	215	1-2-86	.212	.220	.207	106	345	40	73	28	0	13	43	40	10	—	1	150	2	0	.406	.311
Wickens, Stephen	R-R	5-10	170	3-5-89	.217	.240	.207	57	161	20	35	6	0	0	12	10	3	—	1	29	5	3	.255	.271
Wilson, Kenny	B-R	5-11	195	1-30-90	.195	.200	.192	11	41	6	8	3	0	0	1	6	2	1	0	3	1	0	.268	.327
2-team total (44 New Hampshire)					.232	—	—	55	211	30	49	7	4	2	16	17	6	6	2	58	17	6	.332	.305
Wimberly, Corey	B-R	5-8	170	10-26-83	.252	.256	.250	72	246	32	62	13	5	0	19	15	5	7	1	37	17	4	.346	.307

Pitching	B-T	HT	WT	DOB	W	L	ERA	G	GS	CG	SV	IP	H	R	ER	HR	BB	SO	AVG	vLH	vRH	K/9	BB/9
Achter, A.J.	R-R	6-5	205	8-27-88	0	0	0.00	3	0	0	1	7	3	0	0	0	1	11	.136	.143	.133	14.85	1.35
Adam, Jason	R-R	6-4	225	8-4-91	0	0	5.14	2	1	0	0	7	10	4	4	0	2	3	.333	.333	.333	3.86	2.57
Baxendale, D.J.	R-R	6-2	190	12-8-90	0	3	5.76	7	4	0	0	25	32	20	16	2	5	14	.311	.205	.375	5.04	1.80
Berrios, Jose	R-R	6-0	187	5-27-94	3	4	3.54	8	8	1	0	41	33	17	16	2	12	28	.226	.238	.217	6.20	2.66
Boer, Madison	R-R	6-4	215	11-9-89	0	0	2.70	2	0	0	0	3	4	1	1	0	2	2	.286	.667	.182	5.40	5.40
Dean, Pat	L-L	6-1	180	5-25-89	8	9	4.81	26	26	1	0	144	192	91	77	20	31	83	.320	.307	.324	5.19	1.94
Duffey, Tyler	R-R	6-3	230	12-27-90	8	3	3.80	18	18	0	0	111	104	52	47	14	19	84	.248	.271	.229	6.79	1.54
Fuller, Jim	L-L	5-10	180	6-1-87	3	1	2.41	38	0	0	1	56	48	16	15	2	30	68	.227	.214	.232	10.93	4.82
Gilmartin, Sean	L-L	6-2	190	5-8-90	3	3	3.13	12	12	0	0	72	76	30	25	2	16	74	.275	.215	.294	9.25	2.00
Guerrier, Matt	R-R	6-3	195	8-2-78	0	0	0.00	3	0	0	0	4	4	1	0	0	2	5	.286	.600	.111	11.25	4.50
Hamburger, Mark	R-R	6-4	195	2-5-87	0	1	3.38	8	1	0	1	16	16	9	6	2	5	17	.258	.391	.179	9.56	2.81
Hermsen, B.J.	R-R	6-5	240	12-1-89	0	0	13.50	3	0	0	0	4	9	8	6	0	2	2	.429	.500	.333	4.50	4.50
Ibarra, Edgar	L-L	6-0	190	5-31-89	2	1	6.91	9	0	0	1	14	17	12	11	1	5	16	.309	.067	.400	10.05	3.14
Johnson, Cole	R-R	6-3	200	10-6-88	3	8	3.84	49	2	0	9	73	71	36	31	6	21	82	.251	.216	.271	10.16	2.60
Melotakis, Mason	R-L	6-2	206	6-28-91	1	0	2.25	13	0	0	2	16	17	5	4	0	3	17	.274	.250	.283	9.56	1.69
O'Rourke, Ryan	R-L	6-2	220	4-30-88	2	4	3.98	50	0	0	4	41	36	24	18	5	16	52	.232	.103	.333	11.51	3.54
Oliveros, Lester	R-R	6-0	235	5-28-88	3	1	0.89	26	0	0	12	30	17	6	3	0	14	36	.162	.216	.132	10.68	4.15
Rogers, Taylor	L-L	6-3	175	12-17-90	11	6	3.29	24	24	1	0	145	150	63	53	4	37	113	.268	.217	.285	7.01	2.30
Salcedo, Adrian	R-R	6-4	175	2-5-91	3	9	4.19	39	6	0	2	73	78	39	34	2	24	76	.272	.265	.275	9.37	2.96
Summers, Matt	R-R	6-1	205	8-17-89	2	4	6.79	28	6	0	1	53	64	46	40	5	21	54	.300	.337	.276	9.17	3.57

	B-T	HT	WT	DOB	G	GS	CG	SV	IP	ERA...																	

Name	B-T	HT	WT	DOB				IP	H	R	ER	HR	BB	SO	AVG	vLH	vRH	K/9	BB/9
Turpen, Dan	R-R	6-4	245	8-17-86	5	2	4.48	40	1	0	3	62	53	33	31	5	30	62	.226	.276	.203	8.95	4.33
Vasquez, Virgil	R-R	6-3	205	6-7-82	6	6	4.09	22	20	3	0	123	118	58	56	12	31	92	.252	.254	.250	6.71	2.26
Wheeler, Jason	L-L	6-6	251	10-27-90	5	4	2.78	12	12	1	0	74	69	23	23	9	16	55	.242	.214	.251	6.66	1.94
Wimmers, Alex	L-R	6-2	212	11-1-88	1	0	3.74	13	1	0	1	22	19	9	9	3	6	27	.229	.250	.213	11.22	2.49

Fielding

Catcher	PCT	G	PO	A	E	DP	PB
Knudson	.995	82	586	41	3	1	8
Koch	.992	64	445	32	4	5	6
Rodriguez	1.000	7	48	3	0	1	0

First Base	PCT	G	PO	A	E	DP
Gonzales	.989	23	165	7	2	16
Hanson	1.000	21	115	13	0	10
Koch	1.000	4	12	0	0	0
Rodriguez	1.000	23	164	13	0	13
Vargas	.994	81	621	33	4	62
Waring	.933	3	12	2	1	1

Second Base	PCT	G	PO	A	E	DP
Boyer	1.000	30	47	50	0	14
Hanson	.980	13	19	29	1	9
Michael	.983	14	30	27	1	11
Polanco	.882	4	8	7	2	1
Rosario	.975	16	37	41	2	12

	PCT	G	PO	A	E	DP	PB
Thomas	.969	53	97	92	6	25
Wickens	.986	22	28	45	1	10
Wimberly	1.000	5	10	9	0	1

Third Base	PCT	G	PO	A	E	DP
Hanson	.950	31	13	44	3	4
Kvasnicka	1.000	1	0	2	0	0
Nunez	.800	1	2	2	1	0
Thomas	1.000	3	3	3	0	1
Waring	.961	91	56	163	9	13
Wickens	.970	28	14	50	2	6

Shortstop	PCT	G	PO	A	E	DP
Boyer	.907	39	32	66	10	13
Mejia	.917	15	24	53	7	8
Nunez	1.000	1	1	1	0	0
Pettersen	.928	25	27	50	6	11
Polanco	.922	33	29	90	10	18
Thomas	.955	33	39	87	6	18

	PCT	G	PO	A	E	DP
Wickens	1.000	3	2	13	0	4
Wimberly	.769	4	4	6	3	2

Outfield	PCT	G	PO	A	E	DP
Buxton	1.000	1	2	1	0	0
Fuld	.917	4	10	1	1	0
Hanson	1.000	6	7	0	0	0
Hicks	.980	38	97	2	2	1
Kvasnicka	.977	106	200	8	5	2
Nunez	—	1	0	0	0	0
Ortiz	.953	46	74	8	4	0
Pettersen	—	1	0	0	0	0
Ray	1.000	6	15	0	0	0
Rodriguez	.992	61	120	5	1	3
Rosario	1.000	65	155	6	0	1
Thomas	.989	39	82	5	1	2
Wickens	1.000	4	5	0	0	0
Wilson	.913	11	19	2	2	0
Wimberly	1.000	62	118	4	0	0

FORT MYERS MIRACLE

FLORIDA STATE LEAGUE

HIGH CLASS A

Batting	B-T	HT	WT	DOB	AVG	vLH	vRH	G	AB	R	H	2B	3B	HR	RBI	BB	HBP	SH	SF	SO	SB	CS	SLG	OBP
Buxton, Byron	R-R	6-2	190	12-18-93	.240	.324	.207	30	121	19	29	4	2	4	16	10	3	0	0	33	6	2	.405	.313
Gonzales, Mike	L-R	6-6	264	6-16-88	.274	.196	.291	78	281	44	77	22	0	9	53	30	5	0	3	62	0	0	.448	.351
Goodrum, Niko	B-R	6-3	198	2-28-92	.249	.283	.236	122	438	63	109	19	5	3	49	58	2	2	4	99	35	4	.336	.337
Grimes, Tyler	R-R	5-10	187	7-3-90	.232	.238	.230	79	263	34	61	14	2	3	38	25	8	7	4	69	1	2	.335	.313
Haar, Bryan	R-R	6-3	215	12-9-89	.226	.000	.259	10	31	3	7	3	0	0	5	4	0	0	1	12	0	0	.323	.306
Harrison, Travis	R-R	6-1	215	10-17-92	.269	.255	.273	129	458	80	123	33	1	3	59	64	7	0	8	86	7	5	.365	.361
Hicks, D.J.	L-R	6-5	247	4-2-90	.262	.243	.269	118	423	69	111	24	2	11	76	57	1	0	10	94	1	1	.407	.344
Kanzler, Jason	R-R	6-0	190	8-20-90	.267	.368	.239	27	86	23	23	3	1	3	11	12	3	0	0	33	12	0	.430	.376
Kepler, Max	L-L	6-4	205	2-10-93	.264	.273	.261	102	364	53	96	20	6	5	59	34	5	2	2	62	6	2	.393	.333
Mejia, Aderlin	B-R	5-11	170	5-12-92	.273	.326	.254	95	348	48	95	14	0	1	40	48	3	5	5	43	23	6	.322	.361
Michael, Levi	R-R	5-10	180	2-9-91	.305	.366	.287	45	177	28	54	9	2	1	21	19	2	1	2	25	4	3	.395	.375
Murphy, Jonathan	R-R	6-1	189	6-23-90	.197	.214	.192	21	66	9	13	3	0	0	8	9	0	0	0	24	2	2	.242	.293
Pettersen, Adam	R-R	5-9	162	11-19-88	.263	.333	.250	7	19	3	5	1	0	0	2	1	1	1	1	4	0	0	.316	.318
Polanco, Jorge	B-R	5-11	165	7-5-93	.291	.242	.307	94	378	61	110	17	6	6	45	46	1	1	6	60	10	8	.415	.364
Ray, Lance	L-R	6-1	195	9-2-89	.286	.300	.283	18	63	9	18	8	0	2	9	4	2	7	4	12	0	0	.508	.333
Roberts, Nate	L-L	6-1	200	2-25-89	.276	.300	.263	19	58	12	16	9	1	0	8	10	1	0	0	11	0	0	.466	.391
Rodriguez, Jairo	R-R	5-11	180	8-24-88	.227	.200	.232	29	97	10	22	7	0	0	14	5	3	1	3	16	0	0	.299	.278
Rosario, Eddie	L-R	6-1	180	9-28-91	.300	.385	.235	8	30	5	9	0	0	4	4	0	0	0	5	1	1	.300	.382
Santana, Danny	B-R	5-11	175	11-7-90	.000	.000	.000	3	11	0	0	0	0	0	0	1	0	0	0	3	1	0	.000	.083
Swim, Alex	B-R	5-11	180	3-26-91	.333	—	.333	1	3	0	1	0	0	0	0	0	0	0	0	0	0	0	.333	.333
Turner, Stuart	R-R	6-2	230	12-27-91	.249	.232	.255	93	325	49	81	16	2	7	40	31	5	1	2	61	7	0	.375	.322
Valera, Rafael P	R-R	5-11	180	8-15-94	.111	.250	.000	3	9	0	1	0	0	0	1	0	0	0	0	3	0	0	.222	.200
Walker, Adam Brett	R-R	6-4	225	10-18-91	.246	.225	.252	132	505	78	124	19	1	25	94	44	2	0	3	156	9	5	.436	.307
Wickens, Stephen	R-R	5-10	170	3-5-89	.310	.294	.317	15	58	11	18	2	1	1	12	6	0	0	2	12	4	1	.431	.364

Pitching	B-T	HT	WT	DOB	W	L	ERA	G	GS	CG	SV	IP	H	R	ER	HR	BB	SO	AVG	vLH	vRH	K/9	BB/9
Baxendale, D.J.	R-R	6-2	190	12-8-90	4	4	6.02	11	11	1	0	58	70	39	39	7	12	41	.297	.294	.299	6.33	1.85
Berrios, Jose	R-R	6-0	187	5-27-94	9	3	1.96	16	16	1	0	96	78	29	21	4	23	109	.218	.243	.193	10.18	2.15
Boer, Madison	R-R	6-4	215	11-9-89	1	2	4.08	40	1	0	6	53	43	26	24	4	22	37	.222	.163	.269	6.28	3.74
Burdi, Nick	R-R	6-5	215	1-19-93	2	0	0.00	7	0	0	1	7	5	0	0	0	2	12	.208	.300	.143	14.73	2.45
Duffey, Tyler	R-R	6-3	230	12-27-90	3	0	2.82	4	4	0	0	22	22	8	7	0	5	13	.244	.341	.152	5.24	2.01
Gilbert, Brian	R-R	6-1	215	8-9-92	2	4	4.93	32	0	0	5	46	53	28	25	4	24	38	.291	.372	.231	7.49	4.73
Gruver, Steven	L-L	6-2	209	6-30-89	4	6	2.79	42	10	0	2	87	82	32	27	1	35	58	.253	.230	.267	6.00	3.62
Hermsen, B.J.	R-R	6-5	240	12-1-89	1	2	6.62	20	3	0	0	34	49	26	25	5	16	17	.340	.300	.362	4.50	4.24
Hurlbut, David	L-L	6-3	221	11-24-89	3	3	2.05	11	8	1	0	57	53	19	13	2	11	31	.249	.200	.268	4.89	1.74
Johnson, D.J.	L-R	6-4	235	8-30-89	2	0	2.84	12	0	0	0	13	14	6	4	0	4	12	.269	.211	.303	8.53	2.84
Jones, Rafael	R-R	6-4	247	3-1-91	3	3	3.73	40	0	0	13	51	49	27	21	2	23	53	.255	.301	.220	9.41	4.09
Jones, Zack	R-R	6-1	185	12-4-90	0	0	0.00	5	0	0	3	5	3	0	0	0	2	5	.167	.111	.222	9.00	3.60
Lee, Brett	L-L	6-4	206	9-20-90	10	5	2.45	21	19	2	0	106	111	42	29	0	33	54	.272	.213	.301	4.57	2.79
Melotakis, Mason	R-L	6-2	206	6-28-91	3	1	3.45	25	2	0	1	47	50	20	18	3	24	45	.269	.186	.307	8.62	4.60
Mildren, Ethan	R-R	6-4	215	6-4-91	3	3	5.47	10	10	1	0	53	62	34	32	6	18	29	.292	.327	.263	4.96	3.08
Muren, Alex	R-R	6-3	200	11-6-91	1	1	2.41	13	0	0	0	19	18	6	5	1	4	11	.250	.250	.250	5.30	1.93
Peterson, Brandon	R-R	6-1	190	9-23-91	1	1	1.80	31	1	0	1	45	28	10	9	0	17	65	.177	.197	.163	13.00	3.40
Shibuya, Tim	R-R	6-1	190	9-14-89	7	4	3.64	28	10	2	2	89	95	39	36	5	11	59	.269	.297	.249	5.97	1.11
Slegers, Aaron	R-R	6-10	245	9-4-92	2	1	3.32	3	3	0	0	19	14	7	7	2	4	12	.209	.222	.194	5.68	1.89
Tomshaw, Matt	L-L	6-2	200	12-17-88	11	6	3.50	25	21	1	2	136	152	67	53	10	28	82	.285	.287	.284	5.41	1.85

Van Steensel, Todd	R-R	6-1	190	1-14-91	1	0	1.52	16	0	0	1	24	15	4	4	0	15	26	.181	.226	.154	9.89	5.70
Wheeler, Jason	L-L	6-6	251	10-27-90	6	5	2.51	13	13	1	0	79	77	31	22	2	19	57	.253	.206	.279	6.49	2.16
Wimmers, Alex	L-R	6-2	212	11-1-88	3	3	4.04	18	7	0	0	62	71	44	28	2	25	70	.284	.267	.299	10.11	3.61

Fielding

Catcher	PCT	G	PO	A	E	DP	PB
Grimes	.992	19	112	12	1	0	3
Rodriguez	.981	29	192	10	4	0	5
Swim	1.000	1	9	1	0	0	0
Turner	.996	92	612	57	3	7	8

First Base	PCT	G	PO	A	E	DP
Gonzales	.990	13	95	9	1	12
Haar	1.000	3	19	0	0	1
Hicks	.992	109	989	61	8	112
Kepler	.978	12	121	10	3	10
Mejia	1.000	6	39	4	0	3

Second Base	PCT	G	PO	A	E	DP
Goodrum	.913	4	7	14	2	3
Grimes	.974	34	48	101	4	23
Mejia	.983	45	94	137	4	44
Michael	.977	43	78	138	5	24

	PCT	G	PO	A	E	DP
Pettersen	1.000	1	1	0	0	0
Polanco	.955	6	9	12	1	5
Rosario	1.000	2	0	5	0	1
Valera	1.000	2	3	5	0	1
Wickens	.957	8	6	16	1	2

Third Base	PCT	G	PO	A	E	DP
Goodrum	.942	92	63	179	15	12
Grimes	.900	5	3	6	1	2
Haar	.750	4	2	4	2	0
Harrison	.781	15	10	15	7	1
Mejia	.931	19	6	48	4	4
Wickens	1.000	7	3	12	0	2

Shortstop	PCT	G	PO	A	E	DP
Goodrum	.948	26	36	92	7	27
Mejia	.981	24	34	70	2	17
Pettersen	.933	3	3	11	1	2

	PCT	G	PO	A	E	DP
Polanco	.939	86	120	266	25	63
Santana	1.000	1	2	0	0	0
Outfield	PCT	G	PO	A	E	DP
Buxton	1.000	29	81	3	0	0
Grimes	.981	21	49	4	1	0
Harrison	.988	98	163	3	2	0
Kanzler	1.000	25	59	4	0	2
Kepler	.988	87	161	6	2	1
Murphy	1.000	19	44	2	0	0
Pettersen	1.000	3	11	1	0	0
Ray	1.000	15	18	2	0	1
Roberts	1.000	5	7	0	0	0
Rosario	1.000	7	11	0	0	0
Santana	1.000	2	6	1	0	1
Valera	1.000	1	5	0	0	0
Walker	.975	110	223	7	6	2

CEDAR RAPIDS KERNELS

LOW CLASS A

MIDWEST LEAGUE

Batting	B-T	HT	WT	DOB	AVG	vLH	vRH	G	AB	R	H	2B	3B	HR	RBI	BB	HBP	SH	SF	SO	SB	CS	SLG	OBP
Altobelli, Bo	R-R	6-1	200	2-6-91	.224	.250	.216	44	143	22	32	8	0	1	5	13	7	2	0	22	0	0	.301	.319
Avila, Carlos	R-R	5-10	180	3-28-90	.333	.500	.286	3	9	0	3	1	0	0	2	2	0	0	0	2	0	0	.444	.455
Christensen, Chad	R-R	6-3	210	10-6-90	.272	.289	.267	127	492	84	134	24	7	9	73	42	11	2	6	133	30	5	.404	.339
Garver, Mitch	R-R	6-1	220	1-15-91	.298	.323	.290	120	430	65	128	29	1	16	79	61	12	0	1	65	7	5	.481	.399
Granite, Zach	L-L	6-1	175	9-17-92	.291	.450	.237	21	79	9	23	2	2	0	2	4	0	1	1	8	1	4	.367	.321
Haar, Bryan	R-R	6-3	215	12-9-89	.267	.221	.279	108	401	46	107	20	5	14	63	30	3	0	5	127	1	2	.446	.319
Hinojoso, Jonatan	B-R	5-11	150	10-23-92	.341	.259	.379	20	85	16	29	2	4	1	15	5	0	2	0	20	2	2	.494	.378
Kanzler, Jason	R-R	6-0	190	8-20-90	.286	.299	.282	84	315	48	90	8	8	9	48	16	8	1	2	105	15	7	.448	.334
Larson, Zach	R-R	6-2	185	10-8-93	.265	.231	.277	41	151	19	40	11	0	1	20	10	4	2	1	35	4	0	.358	.325
Licon, Joel	R-R	5-10	180	12-21-90	.201	.310	.171	43	134	10	27	4	0	0	8	17	2	2	1	39	3	1	.231	.299
Mauer, Joe	L-R	6-5	230	4-19-83	.400	.500	.364	4	15	2	6	0	0	0	1	0	0	0	0	1	0	0	.400	.400
Murphy, Jonathan	R-R	6-1	189	6-23-90	.207	.243	.194	47	145	12	30	5	0	1	9	20	0	—	1	49	4	3	.262	.301
Murphy, Max	R-R	5-11	195	11-17-92	.242	.139	.284	32	124	15	30	7	0	4	15	8	5	—	0	40	1	1	.395	.314
Pineda, Jeremias	B-R	5-11	187	11-16-90	.163	.100	.179	15	49	7	8	0	1	1	6	6	1	0	0	18	4	1	.265	.268
Quesada, Michael	R-R	6-1	205	2-1-90	.205	.255	.190	60	200	22	41	13	0	4	26	22	2	2	2	47	1	1	.330	.288
Santy, Bryan	R-R	6-1	201	6-28-90	.204	.400	.159	15	54	5	11	3	0	2	9	3	1	1	0	9	0	0	.370	.259
Swim, Alex	B-R	5-11	180	3-26-91	.311	.241	.332	63	238	27	74	9	0	0	31	15	1	1	2	26	0	2	.349	.352
Thomas, Ivory	R-R	5-9	193	8-24-91	.163	.077	.179	36	80	14	13	1	0	2	8	37	2	1	1	39	3	1	.250	.433
Vavra, Tanner	R-R	5-11	180	7-6-89	.258	.242	.256	81	279	39	72	14	1	1	22	26	11	11	0	69	7	3	.326	.345
Vielma, Engelb	B-R	5-11	157	6-22-94	.266	.225	.277	112	418	63	111	13	4	1	33	28	3	5	5	71	10	6	.323	.313
Wade, Logan	B-R	6-1	190	11-13-91	.233	.286	.213	75	279	36	65	12	4	7	38	16	0	3	3	64	4	7	.380	.272
Walker, Ryan	L-R	6-1	170	3-26-92	.239	.149	.258	76	268	38	64	8	4	0	24	23	1	1	5	60	9	3	.299	.296
Williams, J.D.	B-R	5-11	183	11-20-90	.245	.292	.230	75	261	34	64	19	4	3	30	29	5	1	2	71	7	2	.383	.330

Pitching	B-T	HT	WT	DOB	W	L	ERA	G	GS	CG	SV	IP	H	R	ER	HR	BB	SO	AVG	vLH	vRH	K/9	BB/9
Batts, Mat	R-L	5-11	190	7-6-91	2	0	2.20	6	5	0	0	29	21	8	7	1	3	34	.208	.185	.216	10.67	0.94
Bixler, Brandon	R-L	5-11	180	12-31-91	7	4	2.68	41	0	0	0	74	49	25	22	2	37	77	.191	.175	.198	9.36	4.50
Boyd, Hudson	R-R	6-3	235	10-18-92	4	4	4.34	44	0	0	7	58	52	32	28	5	31	45	.240	.244	.237	6.98	4.81
Burdi, Nick	R-R	6-5	215	1-19-93	0	0	4.15	13	0	0	4	13	8	6	6	0	8	26	.174	.333	.071	18.00	5.54
Eades, Ryan	R-R	6-2	200	12-15-91	10	11	5.14	26	25	1	0	133	147	85	76	11	50	98	.285	.287	.283	6.63	3.38
Gallant, Dallas	R-R	6-1	195	1-25-89	2	1	0.64	21	0	0	5	28	12	3	2	0	9	46	.125	.171	.108	14.79	2.89
Gilbert, Brian	R-R	6-1	215	8-9-92	1	0	0.90	6	0	0	0	10	5	1	1	0	2	12	.135	.188	.095	10.80	1.80
Gonsalves, Stephen	L-L	6-5	190	7-8-94	2	3	3.19	8	8	0	0	37	31	17	13	1	11	44	.228	.256	.215	10.80	2.70
Hu, Chih-Wei	R-R	6-1	209	11-4-93	7	2	2.29	10	9	0	0	55	40	20	14	0	13	48	.201	.164	.222	7.85	2.13
Jorge, Felix	R-R	6-2	170	1-2-94	2	5	9.00	12	8	0	0	39	57	40	39	9	20	23	.354	.304	.374	5.31	4.62
Landa, Yorman	R-R	6-0	175	6-11-94	3	1	2.88	13	0	0	0	25	18	9	8	1	13	30	.200	.152	.228	10.80	4.68
Mazza, Chris	R-R	6-4	180	10-17-89	4	4	2.79	25	0	0	0	48	47	16	15	1	11	62	.254	.284	.234	11.54	2.05
Mildren, Ethan	R-R	6-4	215	6-4-91	3	5	4.03	14	13	0	0	74	78	35	33	6	16	54	.277	.246	.299	6.60	1.95
Montanez, Josue	L-L	6-1	217	1-15-92	2	4	6.67	24	6	0	0	57	63	50	42	2	27	58	.275	.250	.285	9.21	4.29
Muren, Alex	R-R	6-3	200	11-16-91	3	1	2.89	29	0	0	1	56	47	19	18	2	8	44	.232	.256	.215	7.07	1.29
Nolasco, Ricky	R-R	6-2	225	12-13-82	0	0	2.89	2	2	0	0	9	10	3	3	1	1	8	.278	.429	.182	7.71	0.96
Penilla, Derrick	L-L	6-2	180	12-31-91	1	2	5.64	7	3	0	0	22	25	16	14	4	10	22	.287	.385	.270	8.87	4.03
Peterson, Brandon	R-R	6-1	190	9-23-91	1	0	0.71	9	0	0	0	13	9	1	1	0	2	19	.196	.357	.125	13.50	1.42
Powell, Christian	L-R	6-4	230	7-3-91	0	1	7.56	10	0	0	0	17	20	15	14	0	16	17	.294	.286	.300	9.18	8.64
Reed, Jake	R-R	6-2	190	9-29-92	3	0	0.36	16	0	0	5	25	10	2	1	0	3	31	.116	.139	.100	11.16	1.08
Romero, Fernando	R-R	6-0	215	12-24-94	0	0	3.00	3	3	0	0	12	15	9	7	2	8	4	.289	.353	.250	6.75	3.75
Rosario, Randy	L-L	6-1	160	5-18-94	0	1	5.40	3	3	0	0	12	15	9	7	2	8	4	.333	.375	.324	3.09	6.17
Slegers, Aaron	R-R	6-10	245	9-4-92	7	7	4.53	20	20	1	0	113	118	66	57	7	20	90	.268	.292	.251	7.15	1.59
Stewart, Kohl	R-R	6-3	195	10-7-94	3	5	2.59	19	19	0	0	87	75	36	25	4	24	62	.233	.266	.207	6.41	2.48
Sulbaran, Miguel	L-L	5-10	209	3-19-94	0	0	0.00	1	0	0	0	1	1	1	0	0	1		.200	.000	.250	9.00	0.00

	B-T	HT	WT	DOB	W	L	ERA	G	GS	CG	SV	IP	H	R	ER	HR	BB	SO	AVG	vLH	vRH	K/9	BB/9
Thorpe, Lewis	R-L	6-1	160	11-23-95	3	2	3.52	16	16	0	0	72	62	37	28	7	36	80	.232	.247	.226	10.05	4.52
Van Steensel, Todd	R-R	6-1	190	1-14-91	0	0	1.30	23	0	0	8	35	23	5	5	4	9	45	.189	.240	.153	11.68	2.34
Wilson, Jared	R-R	6-4	210	4-26-90	3	4	2.95	32	0	0	0	58	46	26	19	6	25	56	.219	.257	.199	8.69	3.88

Fielding

Catcher	PCT	G	PO	A	E	DP	PB
Altobelli	1.000	13	105	10	0	0	0
Garver	.986	63	516	58	8	4	8
Quesada	.991	53	418	38	4	3	4
Santy	.960	4	22	2	1	0	1
Swim	1.000	12	84	3	0	0	3

First Base	PCT	G	PO	A	E	DP
Altobelli	.981	30	240	19	5	21
Christensen	.992	90	719	40	6	68
Garver	.944	4	31	3	2	5
Haar	1.000	16	136	7	0	13
Mauer	1.000	3	23	2	0	2
Quesada	1.000	2	12	1	0	1

Second Base	PCT	G	PO	A	E	DP
Avila	.500	1	1	0	1	0

	PCT	G	PO	A	E	DP
Licon	.917	5	11	11	2	5
Vavra	.963	63	101	135	9	34
Vielma	.963	7	13	13	1	1
Wade	.968	31	40	80	4	21
Walker	.983	39	73	99	3	23

Third Base	PCT	G	PO	A	E	DP
Haar	.923	88	48	157	17	21
Hinojoso	.800	17	12	16	7	3
Licon	.936	19	8	36	3	1
Wade	.846	18	14	30	8	4

Shortstop	PCT	G	PO	A	E	DP
Hinojoso	.750	1	1	2	1	0
Licon	.938	5	6	9	1	3
Vielma	.964	105	164	294	17	65
Wade	1.000	2	2	6	0	0

	PCT	G	PO	A	E	DP
Walker	.946	31	39	84	7	8

Outfield	PCT	G	PO	A	E	DP
Avila	1.000	2	1	0	0	0
Christensen	.984	36	56	4	1	1
Granite	1.000	21	30	1	0	0
Kanzler	.986	83	198	12	3	4
Larson	.966	39	52	5	2	2
Licon	.933	11	12	2	1	1
Murphy	.987	44	72	3	1	0
Murphy	.987	32	73	5	1	1
Pineda	1.000	14	15	1	0	1
Swim	.948	46	64	9	4	1
Thomas	.952	36	56	3	3	1
Wade	.952	12	18	2	1	0
Williams	.961	55	71	2	3	0

ELIZABETHTON TWINS   ROOKIE

APPALACHIAN LEAGUE

Batting	B-T	HT	WT	DOB	AVG	vLH	vRH	G	AB	R	H	2B	3B	HR	RBI	BB	HBP	SH	SF	SO	SB	CS	SLG	OBP
Deol, Dutch	R-R	6-3	200	10-20-92	.181	.125	.198	32	105	7	19	3	0	0	8	11	1	0	4	29	0	0	.210	.263
Diemer, Austin	R-R	6-1	180	4-28-93	.227	.221	.230	55	203	26	46	6	0	2	12	11	12	1	0	53	10	2	.286	.305
Doe, Brett	R-R	5-10	170	6-12-90	.207	.188	.214	23	58	7	12	3	1	1	5	4	5	0	0	13	0	0	.345	.313
English, Tanner	R-R	5-10	160	3-11-93	.316	.485	.247	32	114	20	36	5	2	3	16	8	7	2	0	27	5	1	.474	.439
Fernandez, Jorge	B-R	6-3	188	3-30-94	.321	.222	.341	33	109	13	35	6	2	1	25	8	0	0	2	23	1	1	.440	.361
Gordon, Nick	L-R	6-0	160	10-24-95	.294	.338	.275	57	235	46	69	6	4	1	28	11	5	0	4	45	11	7	.366	.333
Hinojoso, Jonatan	B-R	5-11	150	10-23-92	.247	.143	.276	32	97	15	24	1	2	0	8	7	0	0	2	22	2	0	.299	.292
Hurt, Will	R-R	5-11	175	12-22-93	.235	.056	.300	25	68	7	16	0	0	0	5	7	0	0	1	26	0	1	.235	.303
Kelly, Pat	R-R	5-10	165	11-19-92	.242	.243	.242	39	128	16	31	7	1	0	7	8	1	0	1	36	4	0	.313	.290
Kuresa, Tyler	L-L	6-3	190	11-17-92	.298	.265	.313	46	161	28	48	14	0	5	44	21	3	0	4	28	1	1	.478	.381
Mautner, Tyler	R-R	6-2	220	4-8-93	.210	.263	.181	45	162	19	34	13	0	5	25	14	9	0	1	41	0	1	.383	.306
Murphy, Max	R-R	5-11	195	11-17-92	.378	.381	.377	35	119	34	45	7	2	10	26	22	6	0	4	34	4	0	.723	.483
Navarreto, Brian	R-R	6-4	220	12-29-94	.194	.250	.167	31	108	16	21	8	1	3	15	7	0	0	1	33	0	0	.370	.241
Pineda, Jeremias	B-R	5-11	187	11-16-90	.237	.333	.194	58	232	39	55	6	3	1	15	21	3	2	0	64	23	6	.302	.309
Real, Alex	R-R	6-0	210	1-19-93	.284	.281	.286	28	88	9	25	5	0	1	11	4	2	0	2	23	1	1	.375	.323
Schmit, Blake	R-R	6-1	185	2-27-92	.162	.053	.200	22	74	9	12	1	0	0	4	7	2	1	1	12	1	2	.176	.250
Vavra, Trey	R-R	6-2	185	9-11-91	.319	.393	.287	50	185	32	59	20	1	1	34	18	5	0	1	37	1	2	.454	.392
White, T.J.	R-R	5-10	200	1-24-92	.294	.200	.333	5	17	2	5	1	0	0	1	4	0	0	0	2	0	0	.353	.429

Pitching	B-T	HT	WT	DOB	W	L	ERA	G	GS	CG	SV	IP	H	R	ER	HR	BB	SO	AVG	vLH	vRH	K/9	BB/9
Batts, Mat	R-L	5-11	190	7-6-91	2	0	2.05	4	4	0	0	22	15	5	5	2	3	24	.203	.143	.209	9.82	1.23
Booser, Cameron	L-L	6-3	225	5-4-92	1	5	2.01	19	0	0	2	31	28	22	7	0	14	42	.231	.258	.222	12.06	4.02
Burris, Josh	R-R	5-10	183	11-28-91	0	0	1.29	4	0	0	0	7	5	1	1	0	1	9	.192	.273	.133	11.57	1.29
Cederoth, Michael	R-R	6-6	195	11-25-92	4	2	3.55	11	10	0	0	46	41	26	18	1	18	42	.227	.237	.219	8.28	3.55
Clay, Sam	L-L	6-2	190	6-21-93	2	1	5.59	19	0	0	0	29	35	20	18	0	17	44	.285	.257	.295	13.66	5.28
Curtiss, John	R-R	6-4	200	4-5-93	2	1	2.30	9	6	0	0	31	33	8	8	1	7	41	.273	.226	.309	11.78	2.01
Gibbons, Sam	L-R	6-4	190	12-12-93	4	5	3.88	12	12	0	0	65	63	29	28	3	18	63	.259	.241	.275	8.72	2.49
Gonsalves, Stephen	L-L	6-5	190	7-8-94	2	0	2.79	6	6	0	0	29	23	12	9	1	10	26	.225	.222	.227	8.07	3.10
Hildenberger, Trevor	R-R	6-2	200	12-15-90	0	0	0.00	1	0	0	0	1	0	0	0	0	0	2	.000	—	.000	18.00	0.00
Hu, Chih-Wei	R-R	6-1	209	11-4-93	1	0	1.69	3	3	0	0	16	7	3	3	0	2	16	.127	.174	.094	9.00	1.13
Irby, C.K.	R-R	6-1	200	5-6-92	1	1	1.35	19	0	0	2	33	26	8	5	0	13	51	.206	.245	.178	13.77	3.51
Jorge, Felix	R-R	6-2	170	1-2-94	4	2	2.59	12	12	0	0	66	58	20	19	2	14	61	.237	.318	.174	8.32	1.91
LeBlanc, Randy	R-R	6-4	185	3-7-92	1	3	2.70	17	2	0	1	37	40	20	11	1	4	34	.278	.358	.231	8.35	0.98
Lo, Kuo Hua	R-R	5-10	195	10-28-92	3	0	3.69	19	1	0	0	32	27	14	13	1	10	37	.229	.321	.154	10.52	2.84
Montanez, Josue	L-L	6-1	217	1-15-92	2	2	3.60	10	0	0	0	15	17	8	6	0	4	21	.266	.167	.304	12.60	2.40
Penilla, Derrick	L-L	6-2	180	12-31-91	5	4	4.53	13	11	0	0	52	59	30	26	2	10	50	.288	.457	.239	8.71	1.74
Poulson, Brandon	R-R	6-6	240	12-16-90	0	1	8.59	6	1	0	0	7	7	7	7	1	13	9	.250	.571	.143	11.05	15.95
Reed, Jake	R-R	6-2	190	9-29-92	0	0	0.00	4	0	0	3	6	1	0	0	0	0	8	.053	.100	.000	12.00	0.00
Steele, Keaton	R-R	6-3	225	10-30-91	2	1	2.93	19	0	0	0	31	30	12	10	1	9	33	.254	.200	.288	9.68	2.64
Tillery, Zach	R-R	6-3	210	1-12-93	0	0	3.00	1	0	0	0	3	2	1	1	0	0	2	.182	.333	.125	6.00	0.00

Fielding

Catcher	PCT	G	PO	A	E	DP	PB
Doe	.966	21	128	14	5	0	12
Fernandez	.990	22	175	17	2	2	5
Navarreto	1.000	27	236	25	0	5	4
Real	.977	12	75	9	2	0	2

First Base	PCT	G	PO	A	E	DP
Kuresa	.991	39	305	22	3	33
Mautner	.941	2	16	0	1	0
Vavra	.980	27	235	14	5	16

Second Base	PCT	G	PO	A	E	DP
Hinojoso	.964	10	22	31	2	6
Hurt	.986	20	23	50	1	8
Kelly	.977	39	67	101	4	25

Third Base	PCT	G	PO	A	E	DP
Hinojoso	.818	19	8	28	8	3
Mautner	.895	43	16	61	9	3
Schmit	.778	3	2	5	2	1
White	.800	5	3	9	3	3

Shortstop	PCT	G	PO	A	E	DP
Gordon	.964	49	67	145	8	27
Schmit	.910	19	23	48	7	4

Outfield	PCT	G	PO	A	E	DP
Deol	.952	30	37	3	2	0
Diemer	.958	55	89	2	4	0
English	.983	26	59	0	1	0
Murphy	.974	29	37	0	1	0
Pineda	.977	55	80	6	2	2
Vavra	1.000	13	15	2	0	0

GCL TWINS

ROOKIE

GULF COAST LEAGUE

Batting	B-T	HT	WT	DOB	AVG	vLH	vRH	G	AB	R	H	2B	3B	HR	RBI	BB	HBP	SH	SF	SO	SB	CS	SLG	OBP
Baez, Dubal	R-R	6-0	175	6-14-93	.281	.171	.326	40	121	21	34	6	0	0	9	10	3	4	0	20	12	5	.331	.351
Barrie, Jack	R-R	6-4	250	2-23-96	.205	.192	.213	25	73	1	15	2	0	0	4	7	1	0	0	26	2	1	.233	.284
Davis, Tyree	B-R	6-3	175	9-4-95	.087	.075	.095	38	103	11	9	2	2	0	3	14	2	0	0	43	7	1	.146	.210
Encarnacion, Frank	R-L	6-1	195	11-1-95	.198	.300	.137	26	81	3	16	3	0	0	3	4	1	2	0	26	6	2	.235	.244
Gonzalez, Roberto	L-L	6-0	195	3-14-95	.233	.083	.290	13	43	3	10	3	0	0	6	5	0	0	0	19	4	1	.302	.313
Granite, Zach	L-L	6-1	175	9-17-92	.214	.222	.200	4	14	4	3	0	0	0	0	2	0	0	0	4	3	0	.214	.313
Guzman, Manuel	B-R	5-9	160	2-10-95	.283	.302	.272	47	145	26	41	5	2	0	13	22	2	4	0	19	18	8	.345	.385
Larson, Zach	R-R	6-2	185	10-8-93	.320	.286	.333	9	25	2	8	1	0	0	3	5	0	0	1	3	1	0	.360	.419
Michael, Levi	B-R	5-10	180	2-9-91	.308	.400	.250	5	13	1	4	1	0	0	2	2	0	0	2	0	0	1	.385	.353
Minier, Amaurys	B-R	6-2	190	1-30-96	.292	.278	.299	53	171	25	50	11	2	8	33	29	4	0	1	52	2	2	.520	.405
Molina, Nelson	L-R	6-3	175	4-30-95	.243	.146	.284	45	136	15	33	0	3	0	12	13	0	4	2	19	12	2	.287	.305
Montesino, Ariel	B-R	5-10	170	9-21-95	.165	.147	.173	43	109	15	18	4	1	0	10	10	0	1	1	24	10	3	.220	.233
Ojeda, Gabriel	R-R	6-0	195	8-1-95	.169	.190	.160	25	71	4	12	2	0	0	8	8	1	0	0	18	2	1	.197	.263
Polanco, Joel	R-R	5-11	175	8-15-92	.248	.268	.237	32	117	16	29	6	0	2	14	5	2	0	0	30	4	0	.350	.296
Poteete, Jarrard	L-R	6-1	200	11-12-93	.220	.265	.200	34	109	6	24	6	0	1	17	9	2	1	0	25	0	0	.303	.292
Ramirez, Joel	R-R	6-0	170	9-4-93	.176	.194	.167	43	108	16	19	2	0	0	5	12	2	2	1	32	10	2	.194	.268
Silva, Rainis	R-R	6-1	183	3-20-96	.270	.224	.298	41	152	11	41	9	1	0	20	6	0	0	2	25	0	0	.342	.294
Valera, Rafael P	R-R	5-11	180	8-15-94	.254	.175	.286	47	138	23	35	8	2	0	14	21	5	1	1	17	13	2	.341	.370
Verkerk, Lucas	L-R	6-3	185		.147	.200	.125	25	68	7	10	0	0	0	3	5	1	2	0	20	0	2	.147	.216
Wade, Logan	B-R	6-1	190	11-13-91	.132	.083	.154	10	38	3	5	2	0	0	1	3	0	0	0	8	2	0	.184	.195
White, T.J.	R-R	5-10	200	1-24-92	.148	.000	.200	8	27	2	4	0	0	1	4	1	0	1	4	0	0	.148	.273
Wimberly, Corey	B-R	5-8	170	10-26-83	.222	.286	.182	6	18	3	4	1	0	0	2	1	0	1	0	3	0	0	.278	.318

Pitching	B-T	HT	WT	DOB	W	L	ERA	G	GS	CG	SV	IP	H	R	ER	HR	BB	SO	AVG	vLH	vRH	K/9	BB/9
Batts, Mat	R-L	5-11	190	7-6-91	0	1	0.00	3	1	0	0	10	4	1	0	0	1	9	.118	.000	.143	8.10	0.90
Baxendale, D.J.	R-R	6-2	190	12-8-90	0	0	0.00	7	1		0	7	1	1	0	0	2	8	.045	.111	.000	10.29	2.57
Burris, Josh	B-R	5-10	183	11-28-91	0	2	4.91	4	2	0	0	7	7	9	4	0	6		.250	.211		9.82	7.36
Del Rosario, Eduardo	R-R	6-0	145	5-19-95	4	1	3.49	11	0	0	1	28	27	17	11	1	9	25	.237	.129	.277	7.94	2.86
Easton, Brandon	L-L	6-5	190	9-21-92	2	2	2.70	12	10	0	0	50	48	22	15	2	20	46	.253	.297	.242	8.28	3.60
Farfan, Onas	L-L	5-11	185	6-23-93	0	1	4.80	6	3	0	0	15	14	8	8	0	11	15	.241	.267	.233	9.00	6.60
Gonzalez, Miguel	R-R	6-1	180	10-12-94	1	2	8.78	5	3	0	0	13	23	15	13	0	2	12	.371	.471	.333	8.10	1.35
Guyer, Josh	R-R	6-2	185	5-27-94	1	1	5.01	12	8	0	0	47	51	31	26	2	17	26	.283	.267	.292	5.01	
3.28 Hayden, Zach	R-R	6-2	215	10-29-91	0	0	3.38	8	0	0	0	5	2	6	2	0	11	7	.111	.000	.167	11.81	18.56
Hernandez, Onesimo	R-R	5-11	200	2-16-92	1	3	3.73	8	7	0	0	31	29	18	13	1	16	35	.243	.273	.217	10.05	4.60
Hildenberger, Trevor	R-R	6-2	200	12-15-90	1	4	2.57	23	0	0	10	28	27	12	8	1	5	30	.243	.273	.231	9.64	1.61
Hurlbut, David	L-L	6-3	221	11-24-89	0	1	3.24	3	3	0	0	8	9	4	3	0	2	4	.265	.143	.296	4.32	2.16
Jones, Zack	R-R	6-1	185	12-4-90	0	0	3.38	6	1	0	0	5	3	2	2	0	4	9	.158	.143	.167	15.19	6.75
Liranzo, Wilfredy	R-R	5-11	185	10-26-94	0	0	1.04	3	2	0	0	9	5	1	1	0	5	13	.167	.200	.150	13.50	5.19
Nordgren, Miles	R-R	6-2	190	6-12-92	1	3	2.23	16	1	0	3	44	48	17	11	0	8	20	.277	.333	.245	4.06	1.62
Pearce, Callan	R-R	6-3	190	8-1-95	1	2	6.04	18	0	0	0	25	26	17	17	2	13	23	.268	.200	.292	8.17	4.62
Silva, Jhon	B-R	5-11	160	6-5-93	0	0	2.45	12	0	0	0	18	17	9	5	2	7	19	.254	.261	.250	9.33	3.44
Tapia, Alexis	R-R	6-2	195	8-10-95	5	2	3.20	12	8	0	0	45	41	18	16	2	6	36	.236	.204	.250	7.20	1.20
Theofanopoulos, Michael	L-L	6-1	185	8-5-92	2	3	4.23	11	5	0	0	28	35	27	13	2	10	30	.292	.333	.281	9.76	3.25
Tillery, Zach	R-R	6-3	210	1-12-93	2	3	2.31	11	5	0	0	35	27	11	9	0	9	25	.214	.250	.198	6.43	2.31
Wagner, Seth	L-L	6-7	220	12-27-94	0	1	5.67	18	0	0	2	27	21	18	17	2	16	19	.223	.346	.176	6.33	5.33
Zazueta, Leonel	R-R	6-0	170	9-27-94	2	2	3.60	8	0	0	1	10	11	6	4	1	7	9	.262	.267	.259	8.10	6.30
Zoquiel, Reyson	L-L	5-11	175	11-5-93	0	3	10.97	10	0	0	0	11	16	13	0		18	5	.262	.250	.267	4.22	15.19

BaseballAmerica.com

Fielding

Catcher	PCT	G	PO	A	E	DP	PB
Ojeda	.967	7	27	2	1	0	2
Polanco	1.000	13	81	16	0	0	5
Poteete	.994	24	147	21	1	2	5
Silva	.984	24	157	29	3	1	5

First Base	PCT	G	PO	A	E	DP
Barrie	.984	18	123	4	2	11
Minier	.990	15	92	10	1	8
Molina	.980	7	45	5	1	2
Montesino	1.000	2	9	0	0	1
Polanco	.994	16	156	7	1	15
Poteete	1.000	1	10	0	0	0
Ramirez	1.000	3	13	1	0	2
Silva	.987	10	72	6	1	7
Valera	1.000	1	1	1	0	0

Second Base	PCT	G	PO	A	E	DP
Guzman	.963	21	29	48	3	10
Michael	1.000	1	1	7	0	1

	PCT	G	PO	A	E	DP
Molina	.800	2	3	1	1	0
Montesino	.946	8	17	18	2	6
Ramirez	.920	8	12	11	2	1
Valera	.959	20	35	59	4	12
Wade	1.000	5	8	12	0	3
Wimberly	1.000	3	7	3	0	2

Third Base	PCT	G	PO	A	E	DP
Baez	.714	2	3	2	2	1
Molina	.929	18	8	31	3	3
Montesino	.929	7	3	10	1	0
Ramirez	1.000	4	2	3	0	0
Valera	.857	16	7	29	6	1
Verkerk	.891	21	12	29	5	1
Wade	.857	2	2	4	1	1
White	.786	8	4	18	6	2

Shortstop	PCT	G	PO	A	E	DP
Guzman	.965	23	37	73	4	17
Michael	.714	3	1	4	2	2

	PCT	G	PO	A	E	DP
Molina	.931	14	21	33	4	10
Montesino	.900	1	5	4	1	3
Ramirez	.913	25	28	56	8	6
Valera	1.000	2	2	2	0	0

Outfield	PCT	G	PO	A	E	DP
Baez	1.000	36	54	1	0	1
Davis	.955	37	62	1	3	1
Encarnacion	.925	24	35	2	3	0
Gonzalez	.867	12	12	1	2	0
Granite	1.000	3	5	0	0	0
Guzman	1.000	3	1	0	0	0
Larson	1.000	8	8	0	0	0
Minier	.962	34	48	3	2	0
Molina	1.000	8	9	1	0	0
Montesino	.979	26	45	1	1	0
Ramirez	1.000	3	4	1	0	1
Valera	.955	13	21	0	1	0
Wimberly	1.000	3	5	1	0	0

DSL TWINS   ROOKIE
DOMINICAN SUMMER LEAGUE

Batting	B-T	HT	WT	DOB	AVG	vLH	vRH	G	AB	R	H	2B	3B	HR	RBI	BB	HBP	SH	SF	SO	SB	CS	SLG	OBP
Alvarez, Jhonathan	R-R	6-0	190	2-18-96	.211	.182	.218	34	109	14	23	1	1	0	9	20	2	1	0	27	0	2	.239	.344
Amarante, Junior	L-L	5-11	185	3-21-95	.287	.379	.270	53	181	34	52	5	2	0	17	24	4	6	0	42	22	2	.337	.383
Andrade, Jorge	B-R	5-10	170	12-7-94	.287	.333	.274	51	174	38	50	5	8	0	18	26	4	3	2	53	22	6	.408	.388
Arraez, Luis	L-R	5-10	155	4-9-97	.348	.316	.354	31	115	23	40	6	0	0	15	16	2	1	1	9	10	5	.400	.433
Diaz, Eugenio	R-R	6-2	200	11-7-94	.167	.200	.158	14	48	11	8	0	0	0	6	8	4	0	2	11	0	0	.167	.323
Diaz, Lewin	L-L	6-3	180	11-19-96	.257	.333	.242	43	144	17	37	13	0	5	27	26	4	0	0	24	0	0	.451	.385
Franco, Edwin	B-R	5-11	160	10-7-94	.093	.000	.100	19	43	8	4	0	0	0	5	9	0	0	0	16	7	3	.093	.250
Hernandez, Francisco	B-R	5-10	165	9-20-95	.210	.156	.230	42	119	20	25	0	0	0	13	27	3	2	0	36	7	6	.210	.369
Herrera, Edgar	L-L	6-0	180		.259	.313	.243	43	139	17	36	2	2	0	15	23	1	1	3	23	5	5	.302	.361
Martinez, Carlos	R-R	5-11	170	4-6-94	.182	.000	.207	10	33	5	6	1	0	1	3	8	1	0	1	5	3	1	.303	.349
Martinez, Luis	B-R	5-11	170	10-25-95	.328	.333	.327	23	58	12	19	3	1	0	9	11	1	0	0	11	14	4	.414	.443
Molina, Robert	B-R	5-11	170	9-16-96	.206	.160	.216	43	141	14	29	7	2	0	11	20	2	0	0	25	3	2	.284	.313
Morel, Emmanuel	R-R	5-10	150	5-4-97	.240	.190	.256	55	171	34	41	2	3	1	29	19	6	6	3	39	7	2	.304	.332
Palacios, Jermaine	R-R	6-0	145	7-19-96	.270	.313	.260	49	178	40	48	11	6	0	29	35	7	2	3	37	14	3	.399	.404
Parra, Jorge	R-R	6-0	176	6-14-95	.260	.389	.227	52	177	31	46	9	3	0	19	23	5	4	3	41	2	1	.345	.356
Tapia, Roni	R-R	6-3	175	4-3-97	.269	.243	.275	50	197	19	53	15	4	0	26	10	1	0	1	56	0	1	.386	.306
Tovar, Antonio	R-R	6-0	196	6-1-96	.253	.222	.259	61	194	23	49	6	5	0	32	41	3	1	6	35	9	11	.335	.381
Ynfante, Gabriel A.	B-R	5-11	158	11-15-94	.226	.333	.198	39	115	19	26	7	1	0	13	28	11	1	1	25	6	4	.304	.419

Pitching	B-T	HT	WT	DOB	W	L	ERA	G	GS	CG	SV	IP	H	R	ER	HR	BB	SO	AVG	vLH	vRH	K/9	BB/9
Aponte, Carlos	R-R	5-11	185	9-13-95	3	4	2.89	23	0	0	2	44	37	18	14	2	24	26	.237	.212	.244	5.36	4.95
Balbuena, Erick	R-R	6-2	175	6-4-96	1	2	7.17	17	0	0	1	21	15	25	17	0	23	22	.183	.222	.172	9.28	9.70
Cabrera, Robener	R-R	6-3	205	1-25-94	3	3	4.03	15	5	0	0	45	36	23	20	0	17	42	.228	.161	.244	8.46	3.43
Gomez, Moises	R-R	6-1	192	2-8-97	1	2	2.03	9	5	0	0	27	26	11	6	1	10	30	.252	.267	.247	10.13	3.38
Hernandez, Luis	R-R	6-2	185	1-28-96	2	4	3.04	17	7	0	1	47	43	25	16	0	27	38	.238	.304	.215	7.23	5.13
Herrera, Juan	R-R	6-3	170	1-28-96	2	2	3.31	12	1	0	3	16	14	11	6	2	7	8	.233	.182	.441		3.86
Jimenez, Jadison	L-L	6-0	180	3-19-94	6	3	2.19	13	13	0	0	74	51	23	18	0	16	56	.191	.100	.203	6.81	1.95
Martinez, Jose	R-R	6-2	175	10-29-96	2	2	1.91	16	7	0	0	57	46	22	12	1	11	33	.221	.074	.273	5.24	1.75
Perez, Randolph	R-R	6-0	170	4-23-94	3	0	1.32	16	3	0	2	48	26	12	7	0	19	37	.163	.175	.158	6.99	3.59
Quezada, Johan	R-R	6-6	200	8-25-94	1	0	3.99	18	0	0	0	29	13	17	13	0	46	38	.135	.111	.141	11.66	14.11
Ramirez, Jose	R-R	6-0	170	8-19-92	4	0	2.25	14	14	0	0	64	45	23	16	0	33	55	.204	.231	.195	7.73	4.64
Ramirez, Williams	R-R	6-1	200	8-8-92	4	1	1.81	16	15	0	0	75	46	31	15	1	33	81	.176	.179	.176	9.76	3.98
Rosario, Gabriel	R-R	6-1	185	9-8-94	1	0	9.82	4	0	0	0	7	8	9	8	2	7	6	.296	.250	.304	7.36	8.59
Silva, Argenis	R-R	6-0	190	7-24-95	6	1	4.33	22	0	0	1	35	39	20	17	2	16	27	.285	.286	.284	6.88	4.08

Fielding

Catcher	PCT	G	PO	A	E	DP	PB
Alvarez	.970	31	224	32	8	0	10
Martinez	.939	7	42	4	3	0	2
Molina	.980	41	266	32	6	3	10

First Base	PCT	G	PO	A	E	DP
Arraez	1.000	1	11	0	0	1
Diaz	.990	12	88	11	1	4
Diaz	.983	40	391	17	7	35
Molina	1.000	1	10	0	0	1
Parra	.986	22	137	8	2	13
Tapia	.931	4	23	4	2	3
Ynfante	1.000	2	12	1	0	0

Second Base	PCT	G	PO	A	E	DP
Andrade	.975	33	79	76	4	21
Arraez	.971	25	54	82	4	19
Franco	1.000	1	2	0	0	1
Palacios	1.000	3	3	3	0	1
Ynfante	.984	15	32	28	1	3

Third Base	PCT	G	PO	A	E	DP
Martinez	1.000	1	0	1	0	0
Palacios	.925	40	22	102	10	12
Tapia	.800	25	21	59	20	8
Ynfante	.708	10	5	12	7	2

Shortstop	PCT	G	PO	A	E	DP
Arraez	1.000	3	6	9	0	1

	PCT	G	PO	A	E	DP
Franco	.861	10	9	22	5	3
Morel	.908	52	59	148	21	19
Palacios	.975	8	17	22	1	4
Ynfante	.857	5	10	14	4	3

Outfield	PCT	G	PO	A	E	DP
Amarante	.882	40	42	3	6	0
Andrade	.000	3	0	0	1	0
Hernandez	.984	40	61	2	1	1
Herrera	.975	40	76	3	2	1
Martinez	.950	16	19	0	1	0
Parra	.939	34	28	3	2	0
Tovar	.980	59	91	5	2	1

New York Mets

LEAD IN: A promising March and April (15-11) devolved into a debilitating May and June (22-35), dooming the Mets to a sixth consecutive losing season.

HIGH POINT: After the May and June swoon, the Mets went 15-10 in July, twice winning four in a row in the month. After beating the Padres on July 18, the Mets were 46-50. Four games below .500 was the closest New York got to break even the remainder of the season, finishing at 79-83, although they did go 15-10 in September to close on a strong note.

LOW POINT: The Fifth of July was no picnic for the Mets, who lost to Texas to fall to a season-worst 11 games below .500. They won eight of nine following that game to reach their high point.

NOTABLE ROOKIES: Jacob deGrom, overlooked in a Las Vegas rotation that included Noah Syndergaard and Rafael Montero, posted a 9-6, 2.69 mark with 144 strikeouts in 140 innings, remarkable for the former lanky college shortstop, who used a strong three-pitch mix to lead all rookie starters in ERA. Catcher Travis d'Arnaud lived up to offensive projections—although it took a return to Triple-A Las Vegas—hitting .272/.319/.486 with 10 home runs in 69 games after returning from the minors on June 24. Wilmer Flores did enough (.664 OPS) to warrant consideration as the starting shortstop in 2015.

KEY TRANSACTIONS: The Mets finally settled their first base conundrum by trading Ike Davis to Pittsburgh for righthander Zach Thornton and lefty Blake Taylor. That move allowed Lucas Duda to take over first, and the lefthanded hitter led the team with 30 homers and an .830 OPS. The signing of outfielder Chris Young to a one-year, $7.25 million deal did not work out as well, as Young hit just .205/.283/.346 before he was released and became a hero across town for the Yankees in September.

DOWN ON THE FARM: Syndergaard did not have a strong statistical season, but evaluators remain bullish about his talent and temperament. He could make his debut in 2015. Montero showed flashes, and evaluators see a No. 4-5 starter with solid command. Catcher Kevin Plawecki continued to be a contact-making machine, striking out just 48 times in 419 at-bats. Shortstop Matt Reynolds raised his profile on the Mets' radar with an .859 OPS, although scouts expressed skepticism about his shortstop ability.

OPENING DAY PAYROLL: $84,281,011 (23rd)

PLAYERS OF THE YEAR

MAJOR LEAGUE	MINOR LEAGUE
Lucas Duda	**Matt Reynolds**
1b	**ss**
.253/.349/.481	(Double-A/Triple-A)
30 HR, 92 RBI	.343/.405/.454
Led Mets in HR, OPS	21 2Bs, 6 HR, 20 SB

ORGANIZATION LEADERS

BATTING		*Minimum 250 AB
MAJORS		
* AVG	Murphy, Daniel	.289
* OPS	Duda, Lucas	.830
HR	Duda, Lucas	30
RBI	Duda, Lucas	92
MINORS		
* AVG	Rivera, T.J., St. Lucie, Binghamton	.349
* OBP	Dykstra, Allan, Las Vegas	.426
* SLG	den Dekker, Matt, Las Vegas	.540
R	Herrera, Dilson, St. Lucie, Binghamton	98
H	Herrera, Dilson, St. Lucie, Binghamton	169
TB	Herrera, Dilson, St. Lucie, Binghamton	251
2B	Herrera, Dilson, St. Lucie, Binghamton	33
3B	Nimmo, Brandon, St. Lucie, Binghamton	9
HR	Burgamy, Brian, Binghamton	23
RBI	Mazzilli, L.J., Savannah, St. Lucie, Las Vegas	79
BB	Nimmo, Brandon, St. Lucie, Binghamton	86
SO	Lawley, Dustin, Binghamton	134
SB	Pierre, Ysidro, DSL Mets2, DSL Mets1	33

PITCHING		#Minimum 75 IP
MAJORS		
W	Colon, Bartolo	15
# ERA	Familia, Jeurys	2.21
SO	Wheeler, Zack	187
SV	Mejia, Jenrry	28
MINORS		
W	Peavey, Greg, Las Vegas, Binghamton	12
L	Fulmer, Michael, St. Lucie, Binghamton	11
# ERA	Matz, Steven, St. Lucie, Binghamton	2.24
G	Bradford, Chase, Binghamton, Las Vegas	57
GS	Verrett, Logan, Las Vegas	28
SV	Bradford, Chase, Binghamton, Las Vegas	16
	Morris, Akeel, Savannah	16
IP	Verrett, Logan, Las Vegas	162
BB	Alvarado, Giancarlo, Las Vegas	51
	Tapia, Domingo, St. Lucie	51
SO	Syndergaard, Noah, Las Vegas	145
AVG	McGowan, Kevin, Savannah, St. Lucie	.226

2014 PERFORMANCE

General Manager: Sandy Alderson. **Farm Director:** Paul DePodesta. **Scouting Director:** Tommy Tanous.

Class	Team	League	W	L	PCT	Finish	Manager
Majors	New York Mets	National	79	83	.488	t-16th (30)	Terry Collins
Triple-A	Las Vegas 51s	Pacific Coast	81	63	.563	t-1st (16)	Wally Backman
Double-A	Binghamton Mets	Eastern	83	59	.585	2nd (12)	Pedro Lopez
High A	St. Lucie Mets	Florida State	76	62	.551	4th (12)	Ryan Ellis
Low A	Savannah Sand Gnats	South Atlantic	85	51	.625	2nd (14)	Luis Rojas
Short season	Brooklyn Cyclones	New York-Penn	42	34	.553	t-4th (14)	Tom Gamboa
Rookie	Kingsport Mets	Appalachian	34	34	.500	6th (10)	Jose Leger
Rookie	Mets	Gulf Coast	33	27	.550	7th (16)	Jose Carreno
Overall Minor League Record			434	330	.568	1st (30)	

ORGANIZATION STATISTICS

NEW YORK METS

NATIONAL LEAGUE

Batting	B-T	HT	WT	DOB	AVG	vLH	vRH	G	AB	R	H	2B	3B	HR	RBI	BB	HBP	SH	SF	SO	SB	CS	SLG	OBP
Abreu, Bobby	L-R	6-0	220	3-11-74	.248	.200	.254	78	133	12	33	9	0	1	14	20	0	0	2	21	1	0	.338	.342
Brown, Andrew	R-R	6-0	200	9-10-84	.182	.133	.207	19	44	6	8	1	0	2	7	3	1	0	1	15	0	0	.341	.245
Campbell, Eric	R-R	6-3	205	4-9-87	.263	.250	.276	85	190	16	50	9	0	3	16	17	1	0	3	55	3	0	.358	.322
Centeno, Juan	L-R	5-9	195	11-16-89	.200	.000	.222	10	30	1	6	0	0	0	2	3	0	0	0	5	0	0	.200	.273
d'Arnaud, Travis	R-R	6-2	210	2-10-89	.242	.242	.241	108	385	48	93	22	3	13	41	32	2	1	1	64	1	0	.416	.302
Davis, Ike	L-L	6-4	220	3-22-87	.208	.000	.250	12	24	4	5	1	0	1	5	6	0	0	0	4	0	0	.375	.367
2-team total (131 Pittsburgh)					.233	—	—	143	360	43	84	19	0	11	51	63	0	0	4	78	0	4	.378	.344
den Dekker, Matt	L-L	6-1	210	8-10-87	.250	.200	.255	53	152	23	38	11	0	0	7	21	1	0	0	34	7	4	.322	.345
Duda, Lucas	L-R	6-4	255	2-3-86	.253	.180	.273	153	514	74	130	27	0	30	92	69	9	0	4	135	3	2	.481	.349
Flores, Wilmer	R-R	6-3	205	8-6-91	.251	.119	.290	78	259	28	65	13	1	6	29	12	1	1	1	31	1	0	.378	.286
Granderson, Curtis	L-R	6-1	200	3-16-81	.227	.245	.220	155	564	73	128	27	2	20	66	79	6	0	5	141	8	2	.388	.326
Herrera, Dilson	R-R	5-10	150	3-3-94	.220	.182	.229	18	59	6	13	0	1	3	11	7	0	0	0	17	0	0	.407	.303
Lagares, Juan	R-R	6-1	215	3-17-89	.281	.349	.264	116	416	46	117	24	3	4	47	20	7	3	6	87	13	4	.382	.321
Murphy, Daniel	L-R	6-1	215	4-1-85	.289	.274	.293	143	596	79	172	37	2	9	57	39	2	0	5	86	13	5	.403	.332
Nieuwenhuis, Kirk	L-R	6-3	225	8-7-87	.259	.222	.262	61	112	16	29	14	1	3	16	16	0	0	2	39	4	0	.482	.346
Quintanilla, Omar	L-R	5-9	185	10-24-81	.207	.333	.192	15	29	2	6	1	0	0	3	2	0	0	0	5	0	0	.241	.258
Recker, Anthony	R-R	6-2	240	8-29-83	.201	.114	.223	58	174	18	35	9	0	7	27	10	1	2	2	64	1	1	.374	.246
Satin, Josh	R-R	6-2	215	12-23-84	.086	.130	.000	25	35	2	3	2	0	0	3	6	2	0	0	14	0	0	.143	.256
Teagarden, Taylor	R-R	6-0	210	12-21-83	.143	.000	.167	9	28	1	4	0	0	1	2	5	2	0	0	7	0	0	.250	.200
Tejada, Ruben	R-R	5-11	200	10-27-89	.237	.238	.236	119	355	30	84	11	0	5	34	50	8	4	2	73	1	2	.310	.342
Tovar, Wilfredo	R-R	5-10	180	8-11-91	.000	—	.000	2	3	0	0	0	0	0	0	0	0	0	0	0	0	0	.000	.000
Wright, David	R-R	6-0	205	12-20-82	.269	.342	.241	134	535	54	144	30	1	8	63	42	4	0	5	113	8	5	.374	.324
Young, Chris	R-R	6-2	200	9-5-83	.205	.136	.229	88	254	31	52	12	0	8	35	25	4	1	3	54	7	3	.346	.283
Young Jr., Eric	B-R	5-10	195	5-25-85	.229	.225	.230	100	280	48	64	10	5	1	17	24	5	5	2	60	30	6	.311	.299

Pitching	B-T	HT	WT	DOB	W	L	ERA	G	GS	CG	SV	IP	H	R	ER	HR	BB	SO	AVG	vLH	vRH	K/9	BB/9
Alvarez, Dario	L-L	6-1	170	1-17-89	0	0	13.50	4	0	0	0	1	4	2	2	1	0	1	.500	.500	.500	6.75	0.00
Black, Vic	R-R	6-4	210	5-23-88	2	3	2.60	41	0	0	0	35	26	12	10	2	19	32	.206	.208	.205	8.31	4.93
Carlyle, Buddy	L-R	6-3	210	12-21-77	1	1	1.45	27	0	0	0	31	23	6	5	2	5	28	.204	.250	.158	8.13	1.45
Colon, Bartolo	R-R	5-11	285	5-24-73	15	13	4.09	31	31	0	0	202	218	97	92	22	30	151	.273	.260	.287	6.72	1.33
deGrom, Jake	L-R	6-4	180	6-19-88	9	6	2.69	22	22	0	0	140	117	44	42	7	43	144	.228	.224	.231	9.24	2.76
Edgin, Josh	L-L	6-1	245	12-17-86	1	1	1.32	47	0	0	0	27	19	6	4	2	6	28	.196	.185	.219	9.22	1.98
Eveland, Dana	L-L	6-1	235	10-29-83	1	1	2.63	30	0	0	1	27	24	8	8	2	6	27	.229	.241	.216	8.89	1.98
Familia, Jeurys	R-R	6-3	240	10-10-89	2	5	2.21	76	0	0	5	77	59	26	19	3	32	73	.209	.293	.134	8.50	3.72
Farnsworth, Kyle	R-R	6-4	230	4-14-76	0	3	3.18	19	0	0	3	17	18	6	6	2	6	10	.281	.367	.206	5.29	3.18
Gee, Dillon	R-R	6-1	205	4-28-86	7	8	4.00	22	22	0	0	137	128	61	61	18	43	94	.250	.254	.246	6.16	2.82
Germen, Gonzalez	R-R	6-1	200	9-23-87	0	0	4.75	25	0	0	0	30	30	16	16	7	14	31	.256	.321	.203	9.20	4.15
Goeddel, Erik	R-R	6-3	190	12-20-88	0	0	2.70	6	0	0	0	7	3	2	2	0	4	6	.136	.250	.071	8.10	5.40
Lannan, John	L-L	6-4	235	9-27-84	1	0	15.75	5	0	0	0	4	7	7	7	3	2	2	.368	.364	.375	4.50	4.50
Matsuzaka, Daisuke	R-R	6-0	205	9-13-80	3	3	3.89	34	9	0	1	83	62	38	36	6	50	78	.209	.209	.209	8.42	5.40
Mejia, Jenrry	R-R	6-0	205	10-11-89	6	6	3.65	63	7	0	28	94	98	41	38	9	41	98	.265	.239	.289	9.42	3.94
Montero, Rafael	R-R	6-0	185	10-17-90	1	3	4.06	10	8	0	0	44	44	21	20	8	23	42	.257	.293	.215	8.53	4.67
Niese, Jon	L-L	6-3	220	10-27-86	9	11	3.40	30	30	0	0	188	193	80	71	17	45	138	.268	.254	.273	6.62	2.16
Parnell, Bobby	R-R	6-3	205	9-8-84	0	0	9.00	1	0	0	0	1	2	1	1	0	1	1	.400	.500	.333	9.00	9.00
Rice, Scott	L-L	6-6	225	9-21-81	1	2	5.93	32	0	0	0	14	15	9	9	1	12	13	.288	.262	.400	8.56	7.90
Torres, Carlos	R-R	6-1	180	10-22-82	8	6	3.06	73	1	0	2	97	89	35	33	11	38	96	.246	.218	.262	8.91	3.53
Valverde, Jose	R-R	6-4	265	3-24-78	0	1	5.66	21	0	0	2	21	24	16	13	4	10	23	.282	.200	.340	10.02	4.35
Wheeler, Zack	R-R	6-4	195	5-30-90	11	11	3.54	32	32	1	0	185	167	84	73	14	79	187	.240	.259	.223	9.08	3.84

Fielding

Catcher	PCT	G	PO	A	E	DP	PB
Centeno	.971	9	63	4	2	0	1
d'Arnaud	.990	105	829	38	9	2	12

Recker	.988	52	378	28	5	2	3
Teagarden	1.000	9	54	6	0	0	

First Base	PCT	G	PO	A	E	DP
Campbell	.992	18	125	5	1	15
Davis	1.000	7	67	3	0	4

Duda	.994	146	1108	82	7	125			
Murphy	—	1	0	0	0	0			
Satin	1.000	8	50	3	0	4			

Second Base	PCT	G	PO	A	E	DP
Campbell	1.000	1	3	3	0	2
Flores	.989	19	40	46	1	13
Herrera	.963	17	29	49	3	16
Murphy	.974	126	209	347	15	88
Quintanilla	—	2	0	0	0	0
Young Jr.	1.000	2	3	2	0	0

Third Base	PCT	G	PO	A	E	DP
Campbell	.971	19	5	28	1	3
Flores	—	1	0	0	0	0
Murphy	1.000	16	6	26	0	4
Satin	1.000	1	0	1	0	0
Wright	.954	133	83	231	15	21

Shortstop	PCT	G	PO	A	E	DP
Campbell	1.000	2	1	1	0	0
Flores	.979	51	54	135	4	33
Quintanilla	.973	11	16	20	1	7
Tejada	.984	114	147	339	8	79
Tovar	1.000	1	0	1	0	0

Outfield	PCT	G	PO	A	E	DP
Abreu	.949	31	37	0	2	0
Brown	1.000	12	14	0	0	0
Campbell	1.000	23	24	2	0	1
den Dekker	.986	45	69	4	1	0
Duda	1.000	1	1	0	0	0
Granderson	.994	151	305	8	2	1
Lagares	.984	112	293	6	5	0
Nieuwenhuis	.981	35	47	5	1	0
Young	.993	78	133	5	1	3
Young Jr.	.993	73	128	6	1	1

LAS VEGAS 51S   TRIPLE-A
PACIFIC COAST LEAGUE

Batting	B-T	HT	WT	DOB	AVG	vLH	vRH	G	AB	R	H	2B	3B	HR	RBI	BB	HBP	SH	SF	SO	SB	CS	SLG	OBP
Abreu, Bobby	L-R	6-0	220	3-11-74	.360	.364	.359	26	75	11	27	8	0	1	18	16	0	0	0	14	0	0	.507	.473
Allen, Brandon	L-R	6-2	235	2-12-86	.266	.361	.238	98	320	64	85	11	2	13	52	51	2	0	2	67	2	1	.434	.368
Brown, Andrew	R-R	6-0	200	9-10-84	.283	.323	.270	103	385	65	109	26	1	21	69	52	5	0	4	87	2	0	.519	.372
Campbell, Eric	R-R	6-3	205	4-9-87	.355	.469	.321	33	141	39	50	15	0	3	24	20	2	0	0	20	3	1	.525	.442
Carrillo, Xorge	R-R	6-1	220	4-12-89	.313	1.000	.154	8	16	3	5	2	0	0	3	1	2	0	1	1	0	0	.438	.400
Centeno, Juan	L-R	5-9	195	11-16-89	.291	.318	.287	53	179	19	52	5	0	1	17	15	1	4	3	26	2	0	.335	.343
d'Arnaud, Travis	R-R	6-2	210	2-10-89	.436	.389	.459	15	55	13	24	8	0	6	16	3	1	0	0	5	0	0	.909	.475
den Dekker, Matt	L-L	6-1	210	8-10-87	.334	.272	.354	93	335	70	112	31	7	8	46	40	3	3	3	65	9	5	.540	.407
Dykstra, Allan	L-R	6-5	215	5-21-87	.280	.239	.290	117	343	62	96	23	3	16	74	84	7	0	5	97	0	0	.504	.426
Flores, Wilmer	R-R	6-3	205	8-6-91	.323	.333	.320	55	220	43	71	11	2	13	57	16	1	1	3	39	0	2	.568	.367
Gronauer, Kai	R-R	6-1	215	11-28-86	.167	.250	.125	19	24	3	4	3	0	1	7	4	1	3	1	9	0	1	.417	.300
Lagares, Juan	R-R	6-1	215	3-17-89	.444	1.000	.375	3	9	2	4	1	0	0	0	0	1	0	0	1	0	0	.556	.500
Lutz, Zach	R-R	6-1	220	6-3-86	.291	.294	.290	59	227	39	66	11	2	7	37	29	7	0	1	50	1	1	.449	.386
Mazzilli, L.J.	R-R	6-1	190	9-6-90	.200	—	.200	1	5	0	1	0	0	0	0	0	0	0	0	1	0	0	.200	.200
Muno, Danny	B-R	5-11	190	2-9-89	.259	.270	.254	117	359	74	93	13	1	14	62	60	7	5	4	82	9	5	.418	.372
Nieuwenhuis, Kirk	L-R	6-3	225	8-7-87	.265	.234	.274	57	211	34	56	13	3	11	32	15	2	0	1	56	3	3	.512	.319
Plawecki, Kevin	R-R	6-2	225	2-26-91	.283	.372	.248	43	152	25	43	6	0	5	21	14	1	2	1	21	0	0	.421	.345
Puello, Cesar	R-R	6-2	220	4-1-91	.252	.312	.220	105	318	59	80	20	2	7	37	30	21	2	0	72	13	1	.393	.355
Quintanilla, Omar	L-R	5-9	185	10-24-81	.232	.207	.238	46	155	19	36	10	2	3	27	7	2	4	2	21	1	1	.381	.271
Reynolds, Matt	R-R	6-1	198	12-3-90	.333	.393	.306	68	267	54	89	16	4	5	40	21	5	2	6	60	14	4	.479	.385
Sandoval, Rylan	R-R	5-10	185	8-10-87	.167	—	.167	2	6	1	1	1	0	0	3	2	0	0	1	0	0	0	.333	.333
Satin, Josh	R-R	6-2	215	12-23-84	.289	.300	.285	100	374	50	108	27	1	9	49	61	1	0	4	79	1	3	.439	.386
Seratelli, Anthony	B-R	5-10	190	2-27-83	.279	.271	.282	93	244	45	68	10	4	5	40	41	3	3	3	64	8	7	.414	.385
Teagarden, Taylor	R-R	6-0	210	12-21-83	.303	.405	.231	55	178	32	54	7	0	14	39	30	1	0	2	59	0	0	.579	.403
Vaughn, Cory	R-R	6-3	225	5-1-89	.228	.316	.174	65	197	31	45	8	1	7	30	26	3	1	1	59	7	0	.386	.326
Young, Chris	R-R	6-2	200	9-5-83	.667	.600	.714	3	12	7	8	2	0	2	5	2	0	0	0	2	1	0	1.333	.714

Pitching	B-T	HT	WT	DOB	W	L	ERA	G	GS	CG	SV	IP	H	R	ER	HR	BB	SO	AVG	vLH	vRH	K/9	BB/9
Alvarado, Giancarlo	R-R	6-4	210	1-24-78	3	6	7.29	24	13	0	0	84	103	72	68	10	51	58	.293	.290	.297	6.21	5.46
Black, Vic	R-R	6-4	210	5-23-88	0	1	1.45	17	0	0	7	19	12	5	3	0	17	18	.194	.241	.152	8.68	8.20
Bowman, Matt	R-R	6-0	165	5-31-91	3	2	3.47	7	6	0	0	36	38	15	14	1	9	32	.268	.279	.257	7.93	2.23
Bradford, Chase	R-R	6-1	230	8-5-89	3	2	3.52	34	0	0	5	46	54	21	18	6	4	41	.290	.341	.248	8.02	0.78
Carlyle, Buddy	L-R	6-3	210	12-21-77	4	2	2.16	30	0	0	3	33	27	11	8	6	12	36	.223	.368	.094	9.72	3.24
Carreno, Joel	R-R	6-2	255	3-7-87	2	4	4.76	20	7	0	0	59	66	33	31	7	23	49	.300	.275	.322	7.52	3.53
Church, John	R-R	6-2	250	11-4-86	1	3	4.50	26	0	0	1	34	41	20	17	4	11	28	.304	.259	.338	7.41	2.91
deGrom, Jake	L-R	6-4	180	6-19-88	4	0	2.58	7	7	0	0	38	39	13	11	2	10	29	.267	.266	.268	6.81	2.35
Edgin, Josh	L-L	6-1	245	12-17-86	3	0	4.97	17	0	0	2	13	16	7	7	1	11	12	.327	.250	.400	8.53	7.82
Eveland, Dana	L-L	6-1	235	10-29-83	4	1	3.91	12	8	0	0	46	55	22	20	5	12	58	.291	.235	.312	11.35	2.35
Germen, Gonzalez	R-R	6-1	200	9-23-87	3	1	2.38	18	0	0	6	23	20	6	6	2	10	21	.233	.135	.306	8.34	3.97
Goeddel, Erik	R-R	6-3	190	12-20-88	3	2	5.37	49	0	0	0	64	77	41	38	6	30	64	.296	.261	.322	9.05	4.24
Gorski, Darin	L-L	6-4	210	10-6-87	2	3	4.56	10	9	0	0	47	57	33	24	8	19	51	.303	.244	.322	9.70	3.61
Lannan, John	L-L	6-4	235	9-27-84	3	2	6.75	8	6	0	0	35	51	30	26	6	14	19	.340	.348	.337	4.93	3.63
Leathersich, Jack	R-L	5-11	200	7-14-90	0	0	5.40	11	0	0	0	8	8	6	5	2	7	14	.242	.167	.333	15.12	7.56
Matsuzaka, Daisuke	R-R	6-0	205	9-13-80	0	0	2.25	2	2	0	0	12	7	3	3	0	6	12	.171	.063	.240	9.00	4.50
Mazzoni, Cory	R-R	6-1	200	12-19-89	5	1	4.67	9	9	0	0	52	54	29	27	6	12	49	.284	.257	.248	8.48	2.08
Montero, Rafael	R-R	6-0	185	10-17-90	6	4	3.60	16	16	0	0	80	69	43	32	4	34	80	.231	.236	.225	9.00	3.83
Peavey, Greg	R-R	6-2	185	7-11-88	1	5	11.62	6	6	0	0	29	49	37	37	7	17	24	.377	.338	.419	7.53	5.34
Pill, Tyler	R-R	6-1	185	5-29-90	0	0	7.71	1	1	0	0	5	6	4	4	0	3	4	.300	.273	.333	7.71	5.79
Reid, Ryan	L-R	5-11	210	4-24-85	5	2	4.91	48	0	0	4	70	88	41	38	3	30	56	.310	.354	.273	7.23	4.26
Rice, Scott	L-L	6-6	225	9-21-81	0	0	3.38	6	0	0	0	5	4	2	2	1	4	6	.222	.308	.000	10.13	6.75
Socolovich, Miguel	R-R	6-1	195	7-24-86	2	2	3.64	51	0	0	3	59	68	26	24	5	19	68	.286	.302	.276	10.31	2.88
Syndergaard, Noah	L-R	6-6	240	8-29-92	9	7	4.60	26	26	0	0	133	154	77	68	11	43	145	.293	.284	.300	9.81	2.91
Thornton, Zach	R-R	6-3	220	5-19-88	1	5	4.22	50	0	0	1	60	61	36	28	5	21	66	.257	.289	.236	9.80	3.17
Verrett, Logan	R-R	6-2	190	6-19-90	11	5	4.33	28	28	1	0	162	188	94	78	17	34	119	.291	.311	.274	6.61	1.89
Walters, Jeff	R-R	6-3	210	11-6-87	3	3	8.86	23	0	0	6	21	38	21	21	3	8	14	.409	.359	.444	5.91	3.38

Fielding														
Catcher	PCT	G	PO	A	E	DP	PB							
Carrillo	1.000	7	42	2	0	0	1	Centeno	.990	52	361	28	4	3	10	Gronauer	1.000	5	35	1	0	0	0
								d'Arnaud	.975	10	75	2	2	0	2	Plawecki	.992	40	339	14	3	0	1

	PCT	G	PO	A	E	DP
Teagarden	.992	44	342	23	3	2 5
First Base	**PCT**	**G**	**PO**	**A**	**E**	**DP**
Allen	.991	59	397	32	4	46
Brown	1.000	4	39	4	0	3
Campbell	1.000	17	85	16	0	12
Dykstra	.981	61	434	39	9	56
Flores	1.000	2	12	0	0	0
Plawecki	1.000	1	7	0	0	1
Satin	.988	25	152	14	2	15
Teagarden	.964	7	51	3	2	8
Second Base	**PCT**	**G**	**PO**	**A**	**E**	**DP**
Campbell	.971	13	28	40	2	11
Flores	.930	12	20	33	4	10
Mazzilli	1.000	1	2	4	0	1
Muno	.967	69	107	153	9	41

	PCT	G	PO	A	E	DP
Quintanilla	1.000	5	3	11	0	2
Reynolds	.975	8	9	30	1	7
Satin	.986	17	24	46	1	11
Seratelli	.959	43	75	112	8	36
Third Base	**PCT**	**G**	**PO**	**A**	**E**	**DP**
Brown	.500	1	0	1	1	0
Campbell	1.000	6	8	11	0	1
Flores	1.000	7	6	11	0	1
Lutz	.931	58	27	81	8	9
Muno	.905	24	11	27	4	2
Satin	.954	59	27	118	7	9
Shortstop	**PCT**	**G**	**PO**	**A**	**E**	**DP**
Campbell	.833	2	6	4	2	2
Flores	.948	32	47	99	8	27
Muno	.955	21	28	35	3	7

	PCT	G	PO	A	E	DP
Quintanilla	.983	40	60	110	3	34
Reynolds	.967	58	73	161	8	39
Sandoval	.889	2	3	5	1	3
Seratelli	1.000	1	0	1	0	0
Outfield	**PCT**	**G**	**PO**	**A**	**E**	**DP**
Abreu	1.000	9	16	2	0	0
Allen	1.000	44	67	2	0	0
Brown	.974	89	140	7	4	0
Campbell	1.000	6	11	0	0	0
den Dekker	.989	89	168	4	2	1
Lagares	1.000	2	4	1	0	1
Nieuwenhuis	.991	56	109	6	1	3
Puello	.942	91	121	9	8	1
Seratelli	.982	43	54	0	1	0
Vaughn	.990	57	94	2	1	0
Young	1.000	3	8	0	0	0

BINGHAMTON METS

DOUBLE-A

EASTERN LEAGUE

Batting	B-T	HT	WT	DOB	AVG	vLH	vRH	G	AB	R	H	2B	3B	HR	RBI	BB	HBP	SH	SF	SO	SB	CS	SLG	OBP
Boyd, Jayce	R-R	6-3	185	12-30-90	.293	.297	.291	119	413	60	121	22	2	8	59	52	9	0	3	67	2	1	.414	.382
Burgamy, Brian	B-R	5-10	190	6-27-81	.276	.244	.293	121	450	80	124	32	1	23	76	71	3	0	3	101	6	2	.504	.376
Carrillo, Xorge	R-R	6-1	220	4-12-89	.283	.262	.292	58	191	28	54	7	0	2	19	11	10	1	2	32	0	0	.351	.350
Cecchini, Gavin	R-R	6-1	180	12-22-93	.250	.000	.333	1	4	1	1	0	0	0	0	0	0	0	0	1	0	0	.250	.250
Ceciliani, Darrell	L-L	6-1	220	6-22-90	.289	.339	.266	106	395	59	114	17	4	7	54	22	6	1	6	89	16	7	.405	.331
Centeno, Juan	L-R	5-9	195	11-16-89	.286	.206	.349	21	77	8	22	5	0	8	6	0	0	0	11	0	1	.351	.337
Clark, Matt	L-R	6-5	230	12-10-86	.297	.247	.322	67	219	32	65	14	0	10	46	25	7	0	4	45	0	0	.498	.380
d'Arnaud, Travis	R-R	6-2	210	2-10-89	.125	.250	.000	3	8	2	1	0	0	1	2	1	0	0	0	0	0	.500	.222
Gronauer, Kai	R-R	6-1	215	11-28-86	.176	.444	.080	11	34	3	6	1	0	1	4	4	1	0	0	7	0	0	.294	.282
Herrera, Dilson	R-R	5-10	150	3-3-94	.340	.368	.325	61	241	50	82	17	3	10	48	29	2	0	6	52	9	4	.560	.406
Johnson, Kyle	R-R	6-0	180	11-9-89	.259	.277	.250	103	359	61	93	25	4	4	39	42	7	1	5	80	12	9	.384	.344
Lagares, Juan	R-R	6-1	215	3-17-89	.250	1.000	.000	2	8	2	2	0	0	0	1	1	0	0	0	0	0	.250	.333
Lawley, Dustin	R-R	6-1	205	4-11-89	.235	.245	.229	120	447	61	105	29	1	20	69	35	2	0	3	134	4	3	.438	.292
Maron, Cam	R-R	6-1	175	1-20-91	.500	1.000	.000	1	2	0	1	0	0	0	0	0	0	0	0	1	0	0	.500	.500
Nimmo, Brandon	L-R	6-3	205	3-27-93	.238	.152	.291	65	240	38	57	12	4	6	26	36	1	2	0	54	5	1	.396	.339
Plawecki, Kevin	R-R	6-2	225	2-26-91	.326	.297	.340	58	224	33	73	18	0	6	43	16	5	0	4	27	0	0	.487	.378
Reynolds, Matt	R-R	6-1	198	12-3-90	.355	.319	.374	58	211	33	75	5	3	1	21	29	0	0	2	41	6	3	.422	.430
Rivera, T.J.	R-R	6-1	190	10-27-88	.358	.367	.352	54	201	28	72	13	0	1	28	11	4	0	5	27	1	0	.438	.394
Sandoval, Rylan	R-R	5-10	185	8-10-87	.262	.357	.228	38	107	14	28	4	0	1	9	4	0	0	0	33	1	1	.327	.319
Taijeron, Travis	R-R	6-2	200	1-20-89	.248	.271	.234	101	330	57	82	30	0	15	64	48	8	0	1	107	1	3	.476	.357
Tovar, Wilfredo	R-R	5-10	180	8-11-91	.282	.292	.277	78	255	31	72	8	1	2	29	21	5	1	3	22	8	6	.345	.345
Vaughn, Cory	R-R	6-2	235	5-1-89	.190	.200	.185	50	174	19	33	9	0	3	10	15	8	0	2	47	5	1	.293	.281
Young Jr., Eric	B-R	5-10	195	5-25-85	.000	.000	.000	3	9	2	0	0	0	0	0	2	0	0	3	1	0	.000	.182
Zapata, Nelfi	R-R	6-0	203	12-13-90	.185	.222	.167	14	27	5	5	2	0	1	3	1	0	0	4	0	0	.259	.290

Pitching	B-T	HT	WT	DOB	W	L	ERA	G	GS	CG	SV	IP	H	R	ER	HR	BB	SO	AVG	vLH	vRH	K/9	BB/9
Alvarez, Dario	L-L	6-1	170	1-17-89	1	0	0.00	5	0	0	1	6	4	0	0	0	9	.200	.182	.222	14.29	0.00
Bennett, Hamilton	R-L	6-1	180	6-26-88	0	0	3.38	10	1	0	0	16	23	9	6	2	3	12	.329	.259	.372	6.75	1.69
Bowman, Matt	R-R	6-0	165	5-31-91	7	6	3.11	17	17	0	0	98	102	45	34	7	27	92	.266	.278	.256	8.42	2.47
Bradford, Chase	R-R	6-1	230	8-9-89	1	2	2.03	23	0	0	11	27	26	8	6	0	6	25	.245	.289	.213	8.44	2.03
Cessa, Luis	R-R	6-3	190	4-25-92	0	1	12.27	1	1	0	0	4	7	5	5	2	2	3	.412	.444	.375	7.36	4.91
Chism, T.J.	L-L	5-10	190	8-9-88	1	0	7.65	16	0	0	0	20	27	17	17	1	12	16	.338	.200	.420	7.20	5.40
Church, John	R-R	6-2	250	11-4-86	2	0	3.13	18	0	0	1	23	21	8	8	1	5	28	.241	.323	.196	10.96	1.96
Cuan, Angel	L-L	5-11	150	5-29-89	3	5	6.23	8	8	1	0	39	50	31	27	5	11	29	.309	.327	.306	6.69	2.54
Fontanez, Randy	R-R	6-1	205	5-18-89	0	1	4.86	22	0	0	2	33	37	21	18	3	14	33	.268	.236	.289	8.91	3.78
Fraser, Ryan	R-R	6-3	190	8-27-88	3	2	6.39	19	0	0	0	25	30	20	18	3	11	15	.294	.150	.387	5.33	3.91
Fulmer, Michael	R-R	6-3	200	3-15-93	0	1	16.20	1	1	0	0	3	6	6	6	1	1	3	.375	.500	.000	2.70	8.10
Gorski, Darin	L-L	6-4	210	10-6-87	4	2	2.22	9	9	1	0	53	41	16	13	8	12	54	.212	.250	.203	9.23	2.05
Huchingson, Chase	L-L	6-5	200	4-14-89	4	1	3.10	25	0	0	0	29	21	12	10	2	16	26	.200	.250	.151	8.07	4.97
Kolarek, Adam	L-L	6-2	205	1-14-89	1	0	6.07	48	0	0	2	56	77	45	38	2	21	43	.314	.352	.285	6.87	3.36
Lara, Rainy	R-R	6-4	180	3-14-91	6	4	4.31	20	20	0	0	109	123	60	52	12	26	71	.283	.326	.241	5.88	2.15
Leathersich, Jack	R-L	5-11	200	7-14-90	3	3	2.93	37	0	0	1	46	38	17	15	1	21	79	.221	.254	.200	15.46	4.11
Matsuzaka, Daisuke	R-R	6-0	205	9-13-80	1	0	1.50	1	1	0	0	6	3	1	1	0	0	3	.143	.250	.000	4.50	0.00
Matz, Steve	R-L	6-2	200	5-29-91	6	5	2.27	12	12	1	0	71	66	23	18	3	14	69	.248	.211	.258	8.71	1.77
Mazzoni, Cory	R-R	6-1	200	10-19-89	2	0	4.50	2	2	0	0	12	10	6	6	0	4	10	.217	.136	.292	7.50	3.00
Pantelidis, Alex	L-L	6-2	235	7-7-90	0	1	12.27	1	1	0	0	4	7	5	5	0	2	2	.412	.400	.417	4.91	4.91
Peavey, Greg	R-R	6-2	185	7-11-88	11	3	2.90	18	18	1	0	115	93	39	37	7	26	99	.221	.219	.223	7.75	2.03
Peterson, Tim	R-R	6-1	190	2-22-91	0	1	108.00	1	0	0	0	4	5	4	4	1	0	1	.667	.500	1.000	0.00	27.00
Pill, Tyler	R-R	6-1	185	5-29-90	9	5	3.83	22	21	0	0	125	115	55	53	11	29	120	.246	.235	.256	8.66	2.09
Robles, Hansel	R-R	5-11	185	8-13-90	7	6	4.31	30	18	1	0	111	107	57	53	10	43	106	.255	.254	.257	8.62	3.50
Satterwhite, Cody	R-R	6-4	205	1-27-87	3	2	2.33	48	0	0	15	58	42	17	15	3	22	63	.204	.191	.214	9.77	3.41
Sewald, Paul	R-R	6-2	190	5-26-90	1	0	4.15	3	0	0	0	4	3	2	2	0	3	7	.188	.000	.333	14.54	6.23
Velasquez, Jon	R-R	6-0	170	10-15-85	4	4	3.62	44	0	0	1	55	45	23	22	2	13	49	.223	.244	.210	8.07	2.14
Ynoa, Gabriel	R-R	6-2	158	5-26-93	3	2	4.21	11	11	2	0	66	74	32	31	9	12	42	.281	.355	.216	5.70	1.63

NEW YORK METS

Fielding

Catcher	PCT	G	PO	A	E	DP	PB
Carrillo	.991	55	399	32	4	0	4
Centeno	1.000	21	140	12	0	0	0
d'Arnaud	1.000	2	4	0	0	0	0
Gronauer	.989	11	84	6	1	0	1
Maron	1.000	1	1	0	0	0	0
Plawecki	.994	54	452	31	3	4	4
Zapata	.957	4	22	0	1	0	0

First Base	PCT	G	PO	A	E	DP
Boyd	.994	73	576	49	4	50
Burgamy	.987	32	221	11	3	17
Clark	.986	40	253	23	4	22
Lawley	1.000	1	3	0	0	0

Second Base	PCT	G	PO	A	E	DP
Burgamy	.964	31	54	54	4	12

Herrera	.975	55	90	146	6	34
Lawley	1.000	1	0	3	0	1
Reynolds	1.000	13	22	30	0	6
Rivera	.960	8	8	16	1	2
Sandoval	.955	13	19	23	2	3
Tovar	.984	30	41	85	2	17

Third Base	PCT	G	PO	A	E	DP
Burgamy	.921	52	19	63	7	3
Carrillo	1.000	1	0	2	0	0
Lawley	.892	71	38	102	17	5
Rivera	.963	15	6	20	1	4
Sandoval	.929	6	2	11	1	2
Zapata	.857	4	1	5	1	0

Shortstop	PCT	G	PO	A	E	DP
Cecchini	1.000	1	2	4	0	0

Herrera	.962	8	7	18	1	1
Reynolds	.958	46	64	117	8	21
Rivera	.956	29	50	79	6	18
Sandoval	.962	16	22	28	2	8
Tovar	.983	47	56	113	3	20

Outfield	PCT	G	PO	A	E	DP
Ceciliani	.996	98	244	7	1	2
Clark	1.000	2	6	0	0	0
Johnson	.986	94	203	14	3	2
Lagares	1.000	2	5	0	0	0
Lawley	.985	44	59	7	1	0
Nimmo	.993	62	143	3	1	1
Taijeron	.982	85	156	5	3	0
Vaughn	.990	47	88	7	1	2
Young Jr.	1.000	2	5	0	0	0

ST. LUCIE METS
FLORIDA STATE LEAGUE

HIGH CLASS A

Batting	B-T	HT	WT	DOB	AVG	vLH	vRH	G	AB	R	H	2B	3B	HR	RBI	BB	HBP	SH	SF	SO	SB	CS	SLG	OBP
Allen, Brandon	L-R	6-2	235	2-12-86	.471	.143	.700	5	17	3	8	3	0	0	5	7	1	0	0	2	0	0	.647	.640
Cecchini, Gavin	R-R	6-1	180	12-22-93	.236	.286	.220	68	233	36	55	10	1	5	31	32	1	0	5	40	3	3	.352	.325
Cordero, Albert	R-R	5-11	175	1-14-90	.196	.218	.186	51	168	17	33	5	0	4	17	11	2	1	2	34	1	1	.298	.251
de la Cruz, Maikis	R-R	5-11	174	9-6-90	.267	.261	.268	125	450	70	120	24	0	5	47	25	1	4	3	82	12	3	.353	.305
Evans, Phillip	R-R	5-10	185	9-10-92	.247	.273	.237	111	389	34	96	16	0	4	39	39	2	1	6	59	0	1	.319	.314
Frenzel, Cole	L-R	6-2	208	3-13-90	.197	.111	.216	49	152	8	30	9	0	2	17	11	2	0	1	37	1	1	.296	.259
Gomez, Gilbert	R-R	6-3	190	3-8-92	.217	.228	.214	99	313	51	68	19	4	4	27	65	2	2	2	89	10	6	.342	.353
Herrera, Dilson	R-R	5-10	150	3-3-94	.307	.310	.307	67	283	48	87	16	2	3	28	18	4	2	2	44	14	3	.410	.355
King, Jared	B-L	5-11	200	10-12-91	.287	.327	.271	49	181	11	52	11	1	2	28	15	1	0	1	36	0	1	.392	.343
Lagares, Juan	R-R	6-1	215	3-17-89	.250	—	.250	1	4	0	1	0	0	0	0	0	0	0	0	1	0	0	.250	.250
Maron, Cam	L-R	6-1	175	1-20-91	.282	.253	.292	98	348	50	98	15	2	3	50	61	2	0	5	68	1	1	.362	.387
Mazzilli, L.J.	R-R	6-1	190	9-6-90	.312	.237	.335	64	250	40	78	20	2	4	34	16	5	1	2	33	3	3	.456	.363
McNeil, Jeff	L-R	6-1	165	4-8-92	.246	.208	.258	58	207	31	51	8	2	1	13	22	4	7	1	25	2	2	.319	.329
Nimmo, Brandon	L-R	6-3	205	3-27-93	.322	.333	.316	62	227	59	73	9	5	4	25	50	2	0	0	51	9	3	.458	.448
Perez, Jairo	R-R	5-10	160	6-10-88	.353	.365	.349	65	249	39	88	13	3	10	50	8	7	0	5	33	4	2	.550	.383
Pina, Eudy	R-R	6-3	188	4-12-91	.263	.289	.253	126	430	62	113	21	6	9	59	37	7	2	4	98	5	6	.402	.328
Rivera, T.J.	R-R	6-1	190	10-27-88	.341	.342	.341	61	252	42	86	16	0	4	47	14	5	0	3	37	2	1	.452	.383
Rodriguez, Aderlin	R-R	6-3	210	11-18-91	.242	.287	.224	89	339	32	82	20	2	6	54	16	4	1	0	73	0	0	.366	.284
Ruiz, Yeixon	R-R	6-0	155	3-19-91	.333	.571	.261	7	30	2	10	1	0	0	5	0	1	1	0	3	1	1	.367	.355
Shields, Robbie	R-R	6-1	195	12-7-87	.242	.000	.400	10	33	3	8	2	0	0	4	0	0	0	0	8	0	1	.303	.324
Teagarden, Taylor	R-R	6-0	210	12-21-83	.333	.333	.333	2	6	1	2	0	0	0	0	0	0	0	0	2	0	0	.333	.333
Tovar, Wilfredo	R-R	5-10	180	8-11-91	.353	.222	.500	5	17	2	6	1	0	0	3	0	0	0	0	1	2	0	.588	.522
Young Jr., Eric	R-R	5-10	195	5-25-85	.250	—	.250	1	4	2	1	0	0	0	0	1	0	0	0	0	0	0	.250	.400

Pitching	B-T	HT	WT	DOB	W	L	ERA	G	GS	CG	SV	IP	H	R	ER	HR	BB	SO	AVG	vLH	vRH	K/9	BB/9
Alvarez, Dario	L-L	6-1	170	1-17-89	2	0	0.00	4	0	0	0	6	1	0	0	0	3	10	.059	.167	.000	14.21	4.26
Carnevale, Hunter	R-R	5-11	200	8-27-88	1	0	4.35	7	0	0	0	10	5	5	5	1	6	8	.143	.263	.000	6.97	5.23
2-team total (5 Dunedin)					1	0	4.30	12	0	0	0	15	10	7	7	1	10	10	—	—	—	6.14	6.14
Cessa, Luis	R-R	6-3	190	4-25-92	7	8	4.00	20	20	1	0	115	110	54	51	7	27	83	.253	.276	.230	6.51	2.12
Chism, T.J.	L-L	5-10	190	8-9-88	0	4	4.07	24	0	0	4	24	20	12	11	4	7	27	.227	.146	.325	9.99	2.59
Coles, Robby	R-R	6-0	180	8-20-91	0	0	4.62	19	0	0	2	25	28	18	13	1	19	22	.280	.306	.255	7.82	6.75
Cuan, Angel	L-L	5-11	150	5-29-89	0	0	6.00	2	2	0	0	9	10	7	6	0	1	4	.278	.125	.321	4.00	1.00
Fontanez, Randy	R-R	6-1	205	5-18-89	2	1	2.56	24	0	0	10	32	26	11	9	2	7	33	.220	.246	.189	9.38	1.99
Fraser, Ryan	R-R	6-3	190	8-27-88	1	1	3.43	14	0	0	2	21	23	9	8	0	9	12	.267	.357	.182	5.14	3.86
Fulmer, Michael	R-R	6-3	190	3-15-93	6	10	3.97	19	19	0	0	95	112	52	42	7	31	86	.286	.299	.273	8.15	2.93
Germen, Gonzalez	R-R	6-1	200	9-23-87	0	0	0.00	6	0	0	5	5	0	0	0	0	3	8	.227	.250	.200	13.50	5.06
Hefner, Jeremy	R-R	6-4	205	3-11-86	0	0	9.00	3	3	0	0	8	8	8	8	1	9	9	.267	.333	.167	10.13	10.13
Hilario, Julian	R-R	6-1	180	8-17-90	1	1	5.79	33	0	0	0	51	56	36	33	4	39	41	.273	.224	.318	7.19	6.84
Huchingson, Chase	L-L	6-5	200	4-14-89	0	0	7.11	6	0	0	0	6	5	5	5	1	5	5	.217	.273	.167	9.95	7.11
Koch, Matt	L-R	6-3	185	11-2-90	10	4	4.64	22	22	0	0	120	141	67	62	7	32	63	.294	.294	.294	4.71	2.39
Kuebler, Jake	R-R	6-5	200	9-3-89	3	2	3.86	33	0	0	3	58	66	34	25	3	25	56	.283	.298	.271	8.64	3.86
Lannan, John	L-L	6-4	235	9-27-84	0	3	6.75	6	6	0	0	21	30	16	16	2	7	7	.326	.320	.328	4.64	2.95
Lugo, Seth	R-R	6-4	185	11-17-89	8	3	4.11	27	4	0	3	105	100	55	48	12	38	114	.244	.188	.294	9.77	3.26
Matsuzaka, Daisuke	R-R	6-0	205	9-13-80	0	0	0.00	1	1	0	0	3	1	0	0	0	0	3	.091	.000	.167	9.00	0.00
Matz, Steve	R-L	6-2	200	5-29-91	3	3	2.21	12	12	0	0	69	66	21	17	0	21	62	.255	.301	.233	8.05	2.73
Mazzoni, Cory	R-R	6-1	200	10-19-89	0	0	5.02	2	0	0	0	9	11	5	5	0	3	9	.297	.333	.263	9.00	3.00
McGowan, Kevin	R-R	6-6	215	10-18-91	3	5	5.06	11	10	0	0	59	57	37	33	3	24	30	.251	.336	.171	4.60	3.68
Mitchell, Bret	R-R	6-2	190	12-10-88	1	0	4.91	7	0	0	0	11	7	6	6	0	9	10	.189	.190	.188	8.18	7.36
Montero, Rafael	R-R	6-0	185	10-17-90	0	0	0.00	1	1	0	0	4	2	0	0	0	1	4	.154	.333	.100	9.00	2.25
Panteliodis, Alex	L-L	6-2	235	7-7-90	1	0	3.38	2	1	0	0	8	10	3	3	0	0	6	.303	.333	.278	6.75	0.00
Peterson, Tim	R-R	6-1	190	2-22-91	2	1	5.70	13	0	0	0	24	29	18	15	0	12	26	.299	.304	.294	9.89	4.56
Sewald, Paul	R-R	6-2	190	5-26-90	4	1	1.73	40	0	0	11	52	38	11	10	1	16	62	.201	.247	.163	10.73	2.77
Tapia, Domingo	R-R	6-4	185	12-16-91	6	8	3.96	21	21	0	0	109	104	53	48	5	51	56	.255	.256	.254	4.62	4.21

	B-T	HT	WT	DOB	W	L	ERA	G	GS	CG	SV	IP	H	R	ER	HR	BB	SO	AVG	vLH	vRH	K/9	BB/9
Wheeler, Beck	R-R	6-3	215	12-13-88	4	4	5.88	33	0	0	9	41	35	27	27	3	24	63	.226	.157	.282	13.72	5.23
Ynoa, Gabriel	R-R	6-2	158	5-26-93	8	2	3.95	14	14	0	0	82	95	40	36	7	13	64	.288	.256	.325	7.02	1.43

Fielding

Catcher	PCT	G	PO	A	E	DP	PB
Cordero	.985	45	284	38	5	2	1
Maron	.988	96	713	53	9	6	5
Teagarden	1.000	1	4	0	0	0	

First Base	PCT	G	PO	A	E	DP
Allen	1.000	3	30	1	0	0
Cordero	1.000	6	40	6	0	7
Frenzel	.994	46	317	28	2	26
Perez	.991	23	194	18	2	25
Rivera	.995	25	201	18	1	13
Rodriguez	.977	42	328	15	8	29
Shields	1.000	3	17	1	0	0

Second Base	PCT	G	PO	A	E	DP
Evans	.943	24	38	62	6	13
Herrera	.959	43	82	126	9	23

	PCT	G	PO	A	E	DP
Mazzilli	.954	53	89	138	11	32
McNeil	1.000	1	1	6	0	1
Rivera	.943	18	36	46	5	14
Ruiz	1.000	1	2	1	0	1
Shields	1.000	1	1	2	0	0

Third Base	PCT	G	PO	A	E	DP
Evans	.977	20	11	32	1	4
McNeil	.946	48	29	76	6	3
Perez	.905	19	10	28	4	3
Rivera	.963	11	10	16	1	1
Rodriguez	.880	39	24	64	12	5
Shields	.917	5	5	6	1	0

Shortstop	PCT	G	PO	A	E	DP
Cecchini	.935	59	67	149	15	28
Evans	.954	53	76	152	11	32

	PCT	G	PO	A	E	DP
Herrera	.976	19	21	59	2	11
Ruiz	.952	6	7	13	1	2
Tovar	1.000	3	8	11	0	3

Outfield	PCT	G	PO	A	E	DP
Allen	1.000	1	1	0	0	0
de la Cruz	.973	113	214	6	6	0
Gomez	.963	91	202	7	8	1
King	.985	38	66	1	1	0
Lagares	1.000	1	2	0	0	0
McNeil	1.000	1	1	1	0	1
Nimmo	.992	56	128	1	1	0
Perez	—	2	0	0	0	0
Pina	.952	116	208	10	11	2
Young Jr.	1.000	1	2	0	0	0

SAVANNAH SAND GNATS

LOW CLASS A

SOUTH ATLANTIC LEAGUE

Batting	B-T	HT	WT	DOB	AVG	vLH	vRH	G	AB	R	H	2B	3B	HR	RBI	BB	HBP	SH	SF	SO	SB	CS	SLG	OBP
Biondi, Patrick	L-R	5-9	165	1-9-91	.233	.214	.239	115	404	58	94	12	4	2	18	54	3	12	1	88	24	12	.297	.327
Cecchini, Gavin	R-R	6-1	180	12-22-93	.259	.214	.273	57	228	42	59	17	4	3	25	25	2	1	3	41	7	1	.408	.333
Cruzado, Victor	B-R	5-11	180	6-3-92	.273	.214	.295	107	359	64	98	14	6	7	50	58	0	0	4	78	10	7	.404	.371
Frenzel, Cole	L-R	6-2	208	3-13-90	.304	.222	.333	22	69	7	21	4	0	2	10	11	2	0	1	13	1	0	.449	.410
Glenn, Jeff	R-R	6-3	185	9-22-91	.208	.149	.228	59	183	19	38	10	2	0	20	20	0	1	2	58	0	1	.284	.283
Guillorme, Luis	L-R	5-10	170	9-27-94	.333	.333	.333	3	9	2	3	0	0	0	0	1	0	1	0	0	0	0	.333	.400
Johnson, Jonathan	L-R	5-9	170	10-27-88	.238	.333	.203	39	101	10	24	5	1	0	10	23	3	0	0	17	8	0	.307	.394
King, Jared	B-L	5-11	200	10-12-91	.231	.280	.215	31	104	14	24	4	4	1	21	23	2	0	3	14	4	2	.375	.371
Leroux, Jon	R-R	6-1	205	9-19-90	.227	.250	.211	28	97	13	22	5	2	4	10	9	1	0	0	30	0	0	.443	.299
Mazzilli, L.J.	R-R	6-1	190	9-6-90	.292	.365	.261	66	250	39	73	9	2	7	45	29	1	0	4	48	11	1	.428	.363
McNeil, Jeff	L-R	6-1	165	4-8-92	.332	.387	.312	59	232	38	77	20	2	2	38	20	8	3	2	34	15	3	.461	.401
Oberste, Matt	R-R	6-2	220	8-9-91	.274	.245	.285	91	336	48	92	22	4	8	47	19	5	1	3	68	1	1	.435	.320
Plaia, Colton	R-R	6-2	205	9-25-90	.261	.213	.279	84	272	34	71	13	1	4	30	28	3	1	4	68	1	0	.360	.332
Rivero, Jorge	B-R	6-0	185	1-6-89	.235	.253	.227	81	268	27	63	9	1	5	31	33	0	2	1	60	6	3	.332	.318
Rosario, Amed	R-R	6-2	170	11-20-95	.133	.091	.158	7	30	2	4	0	1	1	4	1	0	0	0	11	0	0	.300	.161
Ruiz, Yeixon	B-R	6-0	155	3-19-91	.255	.241	.261	67	263	36	67	5	6	5	36	19	1	0	5	4	52	15	3	.376	.301
Sabol, Stefan	R-R	6-0	200	2-2-92	.199	.214	.192	101	327	46	65	13	5	8	54	56	1	1	3	105	16	5	.339	.315
Smith, Dominic	L-L	6-0	185	6-15-95	.271	.311	.255	126	461	52	125	26	1	1	44	51	2	1	3	77	5	4	.338	.344
Stuart, Champ	R-R	6-0	175	10-11-92	.256	.218	.273	81	285	50	73	5	5	3	28	36	3	2	4	97	29	4	.340	.341
Zapata, Nelfi	R-R	6-0	203	12-13-90	.236	.360	.167	42	140	18	33	10	1	0	12	12	4	0	0	34	1	0	.321	.314

Pitching	B-T	HT	WT	DOB	W	L	ERA	G	GS	CG	SV	IP	H	R	ER	HR	BB	SO	AVG	vLH	vRH	K/9	BB/9
Acosta, Octavio	R-R	6-0	165	8-3-90	1	2	3.14	5	4	0	1	29	25	13	10	1	14	18	.238	.349	.161	5.65	4.40
Alvarez, Dario	L-L	6-1	170	1-17-89	7	1	1.32	20	6	0	1	61	43	12	9	2	14	95	.192	.182	.197	13.94	2.05
Carnevale, Hunter	R-R	5-11	200	8-27-88	3	1	6.27	16	0	0	0	19	22	15	13	3	10	15	.282	.233	.343	7.23	4.82
Coles, Robby	R-R	6-0	180	8-20-91	0	2	1.95	21	0	0	11	28	27	6	6	0	5	32	.255	.354	.172	10.41	1.63
Diaz, Miller	R-R	6-1	210	6-22-92	6	1	2.25	13	11	1	2	68	44	19	17	3	27	79	.183	.186	.180	10.46	3.57
Flexen, Chris	R-R	6-3	215	7-1-94	3	5	4.83	13	13	0	0	69	75	41	37	5	37	46	.276	.299	.255	6.00	4.83
Frias, Darwin	R-R	6-0	192	2-18-92	5	2	2.98	43	0	0	4	57	44	23	19	4	27	76	.212	.232	.198	11.93	4.24
Gant, John	R-R	6-3	175	8-6-92	11	5	2.56	21	21	2	0	123	107	47	35	5	40	114	.231	.217	.241	8.34	2.93
Gsellman, Robert	R-R	6-4	200	7-18-93	10	6	2.55	20	20	4	0	116	122	42	33	2	34	92	.275	.271	.278	7.12	2.63
Knapp, Ricky	R-R	6-1	195	5-20-92	7	7	4.34	22	20	2	0	120	140	72	58	8	39	92	.283	.256	.302	6.88	2.92
McGowan, Kevin	R-R	6-6	215	10-18-91	4	2	2.14	10	10	1	0	59	42	17	14	2	22	44	.198	.208	.189	6.71	3.36
Mincone, John	L-L	6-1	215	7-23-89	2	3	4.61	34	0	0	1	55	72	33	28	1	17	46	.314	.311	.316	7.57	2.80
Mitchell, Bret	R-R	6-2	190	12-10-88	2	1	2.57	19	0	0	1	28	32	11	8	0	8	34	.288	.279	.294	10.93	2.57
Morris, Akeel	R-R	6-1	170	11-14-92	4	1	0.63	41	0	0	16	57	19	5	4	1	22	89	.103	.141	.075	14.05	3.47
Paez, Paul	L-L	5-9	185	4-29-92	1	2	4.08	21	0	0	1	29	32	19	16	2	11	29	.237	.350	.147	7.39	2.80
Panteliodis, Alex	L-L	6-2	235	7-7-90	5	5	4.52	13	13	1	0	78	104	50	39	5	16	39	.323	.326	.322	4.52	1.85
Peterson, Tim	R-R	6-1	190	2-22-91	3	0	2.05	19	0	0	1	31	16	8	7	2	4	44	.151	.196	.109	12.91	1.17
Taylor, Logan	R-R	6-5	205	12-13-91	1	3	2.77	8	8	0	0	49	41	19	15	7	14	39	.227	.246	.217	7.21	2.59
Vanderheiden, Tyler	R-R	6-2	175	6-27-90	1	1	6.43	13	0	0	1	21	25	16	15	0	12	13	.309	.282	.333	5.57	5.14
Whalen, Rob	R-R	6-2	200	1-31-94	9	1	2.01	11	10	0	0	63	44	18	14	2	19	53	.192	.247	.154	7.61	2.73

Fielding

Catcher	PCT	G	PO	A	E	DP	PB
Glenn	.994	59	405	54	3	4	11
Plaia	.985	84	637	100	11	4	11

First Base	PCT	G	PO	A	E	DP
Oberste	1.000	28	220	14	0	14
Smith	.993	110	953	53	7	76

Second Base	PCT	G	PO	A	E	DP
Johnson	.979	37	56	81	3	10
Mazzilli	.971	49	90	146	7	31
Rivero	.964	55	76	141	8	20
Ruiz	1.000	1	2	6	0	0

Third Base	PCT	G	PO	A	E	DP
Frenzel	.930	21	11	29	3	1

	PCT	G	PO	A	E	DP
Leroux	.500	2	0	4	4	0
McNeil	.955	57	33	117	7	9
Oberste	.750	2	2	1	1	0
Rivero	.894	20	12	30	5	1
Rosario	1.000	1	0	1	0	0
Ruiz	1.000	1	1	1	0	0
Zapata	.918	38	18	60	7	5

Shortstop	PCT	G	PO	A	E	DP
Cecchini	.947	53	80	134	12	22
Guillorme	.933	3	3	11	1	1
Mazzilli	.897	14	15	20	4	7
Rivero	1.000	4	3	6	0	3

	PCT	G	PO	A	E	DP
Rosario	.833	2	0	5	1	0
Ruiz	.899	65	98	161	29	29
Outfield	PCT	G	PO	A	E	DP
Biondi	.981	115	199	6	4	2

	PCT	G	PO	A	E	DP
Cruzado	.977	99	203	5	5	1
King	1.000	23	26	3	0	0
Rivero	1.000	5	9	0	0	0
Sabol	.985	91	131	3	2	1
Stuart	.983	79	165	4	3	2

BROOKLYN CYCLONES
SHORT-SEASON
NEW YORK-PENN LEAGUE

Batting	B-T	HT	WT	DOB	AVG	vLH	vRH	G	AB	R	H	2B	3B	HR	RBI	BB	HBP	SH	SF	SO	SB	CS	SLG	OBP
Abreu, Adrian	R-R	6-0	185	6-14-91	.236	.250	.232	53	174	25	41	8	0	2	17	24	0	0	2	35	5	2	.316	.325
Arrizurieta, Luis	R-R	5-10	160	8-10-91	.200	.250	.182	10	15	3	3	0	1	0	2	5	0	0	0	3	0	0	.333	.400
Bernal, Michael	R-R	6-1	195	12-27-91	.240	.286	.230	71	233	29	56	8	4	5	36	17	6	0	1	95	12	6	.373	.307
Chavez, Anthony	R-R	6-2	185	11-8-92	.170	.316	.133	52	94	10	16	6	0	0	6	11	4	2	0	44	3	1	.234	.284
Conforto, Michael	L-R	6-1	211	3-1-93	.331	.324	.333	42	163	30	54	10	0	3	19	16	5	0	2	29	3	0	.448	.403
Diehl, Jeff	R-R	6-4	195	9-30-93	.263	.250	.266	36	118	8	31	7	0	1	13	4	0	1	0	38	1	1	.347	.287
Fulmer, William	R-R	5-10	185	1-8-92	.197	.333	.169	24	71	9	14	2	0	1	8	6	2	0	1	16	0	1	.268	.275
Katz, Michael	R-R	6-3	235	8-6-92	.275	.333	.265	42	153	17	42	9	1	0	18	12	0	0	2	45	5	1	.346	.323
Moore, Tyler	L-R	6-2	213	8-8-93	.240	.286	.236	63	192	17	46	11	2	1	18	24	1	1	4	49	1	0	.333	.321
Mora, John	L-L	5-10	165	5-31-93	.292	.208	.323	24	89	15	26	3	1	0	5	5	1	1	3	20	3	2	.348	.321
Nido, Tomas	R-R	6-0	190	4-12-94	.277	.317	.265	58	188	20	52	6	1	1	21	14	0	0	1	41	2	2	.335	.325
Perez, Pedro	R-B	6-1	190	8-31-94	.193	.167	.200	22	83	9	16	2	0	0	4	5	0	0	1	18	3	1	.217	.236
Ponce, Dimas	R-R	5-11	140	1-22-91	.109	.000	.128	32	55	4	6	2	1	0	2	4	1	3	0	12	0	0	.182	.183
Reyes, Alfredo	R-R	6-2	170	10-4-93	.258	.167	.280	10	31	3	8	0	0	0	1	0	0	2	0	13	1	0	.258	.258
Rodriguez, Jean	B-R	6-0	160	9-3-92	.286	.500	.200	3	7	1	2	0	1	0	3	1	0	0	0	0	0	0	.571	.375
Rosario, Amed	R-R	6-2	170	11-20-95	.289	.322	.280	68	266	39	77	11	5	1	23	17	3	2	2	47	7	3	.380	.337
Tharp, Tucker	R-R	5-10	195	11-26-91	.213	.300	.191	66	202	23	43	5	1	0	6	12	2	5	1	52	9	5	.248	.263
Tuschak, Joe	L-R	6-0	185	10-17-92	.211	.250	.208	36	114	15	24	4	0	2	11	10	5	1	1	38	0	2	.298	.300
Urena, Jhoan	B-R	6-1	200	9-1-94	.300	.300	.300	75	283	30	85	20	1	5	47	27	0	0	5	58	7	9	.431	.356

Pitching	B-T	HT	WT	DOB	W	L	ERA	G	GS	CG	SV	IP	H	R	ER	HR	BB	SO	AVG	vLH	vRH	K/9	BB/9
Acosta, Octavio	R-R	6-0	165	8-3-90	3	3	2.80	8	8	0	0	45	33	19	14	2	11	36	.208	.130	.267	7.20	2.20
Arias, Martires	R-R	6-7	210	11-10-90	2	0	2.11	4	4	0	0	21	19	5	5	0	10	26	.238	.222	.250	10.97	4.22
Baldonado, Alberto	L-L	6-2	160	2-1-93	3	4	4.34	12	9	0	0	48	55	28	23	1	20	43	.288	.288	.288	8.12	3.78
Bay, Shane	L-L	6-2	225	2-29-92	0	1	1.59	20	0	0	15	23	19	4	4	0	3	22	.232	.120	.281	8.74	1.19
Bumgardner, Gaither	R-R	6-6	210	1-29-91	0	2	2.30	12	0	0	2	31	20	14	8	1	15	27	.180	.261	.123	7.76	4.31
Gee, Dillon	R-R	6-1	205	4-28-86	0	1	2.08	2	2	0	0	9	7	2	2	0	2	16	.212	.167	.238	16.62	2.08
Griffin, Cameron	R-R	6-3	200	6-25-91	0	0	1.08	12	0	0	0	17	12	3	2	0	5	15	.190	.208	.179	8.10	2.70
Hepple, Mike	R-R	6-6	210	6-5-90	2	0	1.93	13	0	0	0	23	22	10	5	0	11	18	.234	.222	.245	6.94	4.24
Mateo, Luis	R-R	6-3	185	3-22-90	0	0	7.20	4	0	0	0	5	7	4	4	1	4		.333	.222	.417	7.20	1.80
Matsuzaka, Daisuke	R-R	6-0	205	9-13-80	1	0	0.00	1	1	0	0	5	2	0	0	0	2	7	.118	.100	.143	12.60	3.60
Meisner, Casey	R-R	6-7	190	5-22-95	5	3	3.75	13	13	0	0	62	67	35	26	4	18	67	.271	.260	.280	9.67	2.60
Molina, Marcos	R-R	6-3	188	3-9-95	7	3	1.77	12	12	0	0	76	46	18	15	2	18	91	.170	.202	.142	10.73	2.12
Oswalt, Corey	R-R	6-4	200	9-3-93	6	2	2.26	12	11	0	0	68	55	20	17	1	15	59	.218	.242	.197	7.85	2.00
Paez, Paul	L-L	5-9	185	4-29-92	1	0	0.00	6	0	0	0	9	5	0	0	0	2	7	.111	.125	.100	11.81	3.38
Prevost, Josh	R-R	6-8	225	1-15-92	1	2	1.83	11	0	0	1	20	17	6	4	0	4	14	.233	.235	.231	6.41	2.75
Rengel, Luis	R-R	6-2	165	3-19-90	0	1	5.00	9	0	0	0	9	9	10	5	1	5	11	.257	.353	.167	11.00	5.00
Reyes, Scarlyn	R-R	6-3	190	12-10-89	2	3	2.39	12	7	0	1	49	39	19	13	1	17	47	.219	.228	.209	8.63	3.12
Secrest, Kelly	L-L	6-0	215	9-13-91	3	1	1.82	20	0	0	0	25	20	6	5	0	12	30	.222	.235	.214	10.95	4.38
Urbina, Juan	L-L	6-2	170	3-15-93	1	0	3.75	11	0	0	1	12	14	8	5	1	11	14	.286	.250	.310	10.50	8.25
Valdez, Carlos	L-L	6-2	170	9-30-90	2	2	3.99	12	6	0	0	38	32	22	17	2	22	30	.225	.205	.233	7.04	5.17
Villasmil, Edioglis	R-R	6-2	164	4-10-92	0	3	2.95	21	0	0	0	21	18	9	7	0	10	22	.222	.241	.212	9.28	4.22
Welch, Brandon	R-R	6-1	185	8-24-91	2	2	5.18	14	3	0	0	33	34	21	19	4	12	21	.276	.320	.247	5.73	3.27
Wieck, Brad	L-L	6-9	255	10-14-91	1	1	1.40	16	0	0	0	26	17	6	4	1	6	39	.181	.114	.220	13.68	2.10

Fielding

Catcher	PCT	G	PO	A	E	DP	PB
Abreu	.974	36	295	36	9	2	9
Arrizurieta	1.000	8	57	5	0	1	1
Moore	.957	14	64	3	3	1	2
Nido	.974	31	240	24	7	0	4

First Base	PCT	G	PO	A	E	DP
Abreu	1.000	2	14	0	0	2
Chavez	—	1	0	0	0	0
Diehl	.985	14	121	7	2	8
Fulmer	.925	7	60	2	5	4
Katz	.990	30	276	13	3	14
Moore	.963	3	26	0	1	1
Nido	1.000	2	11	0	0	0

	PCT	G	PO	A	E	DP
Perez	1.000	22	175	12	0	19
Second Base	PCT	G	PO	A	E	DP
Chavez	.954	47	51	94	7	21
Fulmer	.904	16	17	30	5	5
Moore	.956	25	32	55	4	9
Ponce	.982	21	22	34	1	4
Rodriguez	1.000	3	3	7	0	1
Third Base	PCT	G	PO	A	E	DP
Chavez	1.000	2	1	2	0	1
Perez	—	1	0	0	0	0
Urena	.909	75	45	125	17	10
Shortstop	PCT	G	PO	A	E	DP
Ponce	.967	10	10	19	1	5

	PCT	G	PO	A	E	DP
Reyes	.941	10	9	23	2	8
Rosario	.926	64	73	178	20	27
Outfield	PCT	G	PO	A	E	DP
Bernal	.943	69	106	9	7	2
Conforto	.905	41	52	5	6	0
Diehl	.800	5	4	0	1	0
Fulmer	.750	3	3	0	1	0
Katz	1.000	13	12	0	0	0
Moore	1.000	1	1	0	0	0
Mora	.892	21	32	1	4	0
Tharp	1.000	65	116	0	0	0
Tuschak	.981	32	51	1	1	0

KINGSPORT METS
ROOKIE
APPALACHIAN LEAGUE

Batting	B-T	HT	WT	DOB	AVG	vLH	vRH	G	AB	R	H	2B	3B	HR	RBI	BB	HBP	SH	SF	SO	SB	CS	SLG	OBP
Arrizurieta, Luis	R-R	5-10	160	8-10-91	.095	.000	.111	10	21	0	2	0	0	0	1	4	1	0	1	7	0	0	.095	.259

Batting	B-T	HT	WT	DOB	AVG	vLH	vRH	G	AB	R	H	2B	3B	HR	RBI	BB	HBP	SH	SF	SO	SB	CS	SLG	OBP
Becerra, Wuilmer	R-R	6-4	190	10-1-94	.300	.348	.286	58	207	37	62	10	2	7	29	14	4	0	3	55	7	3	.469	.351
Brosher, Brandon	R-R	6-3	225	2-17-95	.387	.500	.360	7	31	6	12	0	0	4	8	2	0	0	0	11	1	0	.774	.424
Canelon, Leon	R-R	5-11	150	9-10-91	.178	.167	.182	42	101	10	18	2	0	0	6	11	0	0	0	26	3	1	.198	.259
Caraballo, Oswald	R-R	6-2	180	1-5-93	.289	.279	.293	62	249	36	72	18	0	4	38	12	0	0	4	26	5	1	.410	.317
Figuera, Jose	R-R	6-2	180	6-10-93	.104	.053	.125	27	67	5	7	1	0	0	2	8	0	1	0	23	0	0	.119	.200
Garcia, Eudor	R-R	6-1	215	1-19-94	.262	.189	.279	55	202	22	53	9	1	2	28	16	5	0	3	32	0	0	.347	.327
Garcia, Jose	B-R	6-0	200	11-3-94	.215	.154	.223	30	107	7	23	3	0	0	13	5	0	0	2	30	0	2	.243	.246
Guillorme, Luis	L-R	5-10	170	9-27-94	.282	.310	.276	57	238	38	67	10	0	0	17	17	3	6	0	28	6	4	.324	.337
Kaupe, Branden	B-R	5-7	175	4-10-94	.260	.296	.250	41	123	26	32	3	3	0	9	16	2	0	1	31	4	1	.333	.352
Leal, Miguel	R-R	6-0	184	7-4-91	.273	.500	.206	13	44	7	12	2	0	1	7	2	1	0	1	6	0	0	.386	.313
Lupo, Vicente	R-R	6-0	180	11-26-93	.278	.387	.245	44	133	28	37	9	0	7	24	29	2	1	0	52	7	0	.504	.415
Mathieu, Zach	R-R	6-7	265	11-25-91	.270	.211	.289	47	152	13	41	17	0	3	29	19	4	0	4	53	1	1	.441	.358
Ortega, Luis	R-R	5-10	187	4-5-93	.282	.270	.287	46	131	22	37	10	0	2	16	10	4	0	2	19	5	1	.405	.347
Perez, Pedro	B-R	6-1	190	8-31-94	.242	.281	.231	43	149	22	36	10	0	3	19	19	5	0	2	38	3	1	.369	.343
Rodriguez, Jean	B-R	6-0	160	9-3-92	.312	.214	.331	49	173	30	54	4	3	3	17	17	4	3	0	35	4	2	.422	.387
Wilson, Ivan	R-R	6-3	220	5-26-95	.176	.125	.186	58	188	26	33	5	1	1	17	27	3	2	1	99	4	0	.388	.254

Pitching	B-T	HT	WT	DOB	W	L	ERA	G	GS	CG	SV	IP	H	R	ER	HR	BB	SO	AVG	vLH	vRH	K/9	BB/9
Almonte, Gaby	R-R	6-0	185	8-15-92	0	7	5.00	11	11	0	0	54	56	37	30	4	16	29	.276	.250	.293	4.83	2.67
Arias, Martires	R-R	6-7	210	11-10-90	4	0	0.50	8	3	0	2	36	18	4	2	0	12	34	.154	.083	.203	8.58	3.03
Beeler, Bryce	L-R	6-2	180	3-9-93	4	2	3.13	14	0	0	0	23	16	12	8	0	7	18	.198	.208	.193	7.04	2.74
Blackham, Matt	R-R	5-11	150	1-7-93	2	0	1.42	11	0	0	0	19	10	6	3	2	9	25	.149	.143	.152	11.84	4.26
Blank, Nicco	R-R	5-9	165	10-29-92	0	0	11.57	10	0	0	0	9	11	13	12	0	13	10	.314	.417	.261	9.64	12.54
Buchmann, Connor	R-R	6-1	190	7-11-93	0	0	32.40	3	0	0	0	2	6	6	6	0	7	0	.545	.500	.556	0.00	37.80
Church, Andrew	R-R	6-2	190	10-7-94	3	5	4.61	11	11	1	0	53	73	39	27	1	14	31	.326	.366	.303	5.30	2.39
Duff, Jimmy	R-R	6-6	200	11-15-93	3	1	1.83	13	1	0	0	34	27	9	7	1	7	24	.211	.218	.205	6.29	1.83
Estevez, Ramon	R-R	6-0	165	10-27-90	1	1	3.86	15	0	0	3	23	22	14	10	1	6	22	.237	.257	.224	8.49	2.31
German, Audry	R-R	5-11	163	8-16-92	0	1	15.68	5	1	0	0	10	21	18	18	0	10	8	.429	.294	.500	6.97	8.71
Gonzalez, Yoan	L-L	6-0	178	1-29-91	1	4	5.53	8	5	0	0	28	33	18	17	1	11	19	.289	.240	.303	6.18	3.58
Massie, Andrew	R-R	6-1	170	1-27-94	1	5	4.91	10	10	0	0	44	48	35	24	2	20	22	.282	.281	.283	4.50	4.09
Missigman, Craig	R-R	6-4	175	8-5-93	1	0	7.43	9	0	0	0	13	17	12	11	0	10	16	.304	.250	.344	10.80	6.75
Montgomery, Christian	R-R	6-1	230	11-20-92	0	2	6.48	12	4	0	0	33	32	29	24	3	32	43	.250	.240	.256	11.61	8.64
Nuez, Yoryi	R-R	6-1	153	2-13-93	5	4	3.66	11	11	0	0	47	31	33	19	4	38	41	.183	.212	.165	7.91	7.33
Palsha, Alex	R-R	6-1	195	5-10-92	0	0	2.08	3	0	0	1	4	2	2	1	0	2	2	.143	.500	.083	4.15	4.15
Rengel, Luis	R-R	6-2	165	3-19-90	0	0	0.00	4	0	0	0	6	3	2	0	0	2	8	.261	.125	.333	12.00	3.00
Reyes, Persio	R-R	6-2	151	3-19-93	2	0	1.34	8	4	0	1	34	19	5	5	0	11	31	.173	.175	.171	8.29	2.94
Reyes, Ruben	R-R	6-4	178	9-22-90	2	0	3.09	13	0	0	1	23	18	13	8	1	13	25	.212	.313	.151	9.64	5.01
Roseboom, David	L-L	6-3	215	5-17-92	1	0	1.59	16	0	0	4	23	18	5	4	0	8	30	.202	.091	.239	11.91	3.18
Taylor, Blake	L-L	6-3	220	8-17-95	2	1	5.34	8	7	0	0	30	41	21	18	1	23	20	.342	.300	.350	5.93	6.82
Williams, Ty	R-R	6-2	195	2-21-94	1	1	3.27	14	0	0	1	22	17	9	8	0	13	20	.224	.286	.188	8.18	5.32

Fielding

Catcher	PCT	G	PO	A	E	DP	PB
Arrizurieta	.944	8	47	4	3	0	4
Brosher	1.000	2	17	2	0	0	2
Garcia	.967	30	206	32	8	5	13
Leal	.991	13	94	11	1	0	1
Ortega	.980	22	121	25	3	2	8

First Base	PCT	G	PO	A	E	DP
Arrizurieta	1.000	1	2	0	0	0
Mathieu	.990	44	372	26	4	27
Ortega	.975	15	73	5	2	9
Perez	.979	16	133	4	3	12

Second Base	PCT	G	PO	A	E	DP
Canelon	.986	18	25	44	1	12
Kaupe	.923	32	50	81	11	18
Perez	1.000	1	2	3	0	1
Rodriguez	.946	24	49	57	6	11

Third Base	PCT	G	PO	A	E	DP
Canelon	1.000	7	3	4	0	0
Garcia	.889	42	36	60	12	7
Kaupe	1.000	1	1	3	0	1
Perez	.933	16	12	30	3	1
Rodriguez	.850	16	14	20	6	4

Shortstop	PCT	G	PO	A	E	DP
Canelon	.917	14	15	40	5	6
Guillorme	.947	57	79	187	15	33
Rodriguez	.941	2	6	10	1	1

Outfield	PCT	G	PO	A	E	DP
Becerra	.990	56	96	7	1	0
Caraballo	.940	52	74	4	5	1
Figuera	.935	26	28	1	2	0
Lupo	.854	27	40	1	7	0
Ortega	—	1	0	0	0	0
Rodriguez	1.000	4	1	0	0	0
Wilson	.973	57	139	5	4	4

GCL METS   ROOKIE
GULF COAST LEAGUE

Batting	B-T	HT	WT	DOB	AVG	vLH	vRH	G	AB	R	H	2B	3B	HR	RBI	BB	HBP	SH	SF	SO	SB	CS	SLG	OBP
Berrios, Arnaldo	B-R	5-9	175	1-15-96	.272	.227	.284	31	103	13	28	7	0	0	12	8	0	1	0	26	5	2	.340	.324
Burdick, Dale	R-R	6-0	175	10-12-95	.170	.130	.183	40	94	19	16	2	0	1	8	19	5	3	1	23	3	4	.223	.336
Correa, Franklin	R-R	5-9	176	1-1-96	.000	.000	.000	5	16	1	0	0	0	0	1	1	0	0	0	6	0	0	.000	.059
Evans, Phillip	R-R	5-10	185	9-10-92	.667	1.000	.000	1	3	0	2	0	0	0	0	0	0	0	0	1	0	0	.667	.667
Figuera, Jose	R-R	6-2	180	6-10-93	.333	.500	.300	4	12	2	4	0	1	0	2	3	0	0	1	6	2	0	.500	.438
Fulmer, William	R-R	5-10	185	1-8-92	.333	.750	.182	4	15	1	5	1	0	0	4	1	0	0	0	2	0	1	.400	.375
Hilario, Manuel	R-R	5-10	172	2-10-92	.232	.217	.237	33	99	14	23	3	0	1	12	7	3	0	1	20	4	2	.293	.300
King, Jared	B-L	5-11	190	1-21-92	.364	.000	.444	3	11	4	4	0	1	1	2	1	0	0	0	0	1	0	.818	.417
Knight, Darryl	R-R	6-2	220	2-26-93	.273	.667	.171	14	44	4	12	3	2	0	5	3	2	0	1	14	2	1	.432	.340
Lagares, Juan	R-R	6-1	215	3-17-89	.000	.000	.000	2	8	0	0	0	0	0	0	0	0	0	0	0	0	0	.000	.000
Leal, Miguel	R-R	6-0	184	7-4-91	.273	.250	.280	12	33	4	9	2	0	0	6	3	1	0		4	0	0	.333	.429
Maracaro, Alvin	R-R	5-9	178	2-10-93	.210	.211	.209	37	105	16	22	3	0	1	12	13	3	1	2	19	4	1	.267	.309
Marte, Santo	R-R	5-9	170	9-30-93	.167	.167	.167	4	12	0	2	1	0	0	1	0	0	0	0	2	0	0	.250	.231
Mora, John	L-L	5-10	165	5-31-93	.318	.222	.337	32	110	29	35	6	3	0	12	20	3	1	1	13	14	4	.427	.433
Perez, Jairo	R-R	5-10	160	6-10-88	.583	.500	.600	4	12	1	7	2	0	0	3	2	0	0	0	1	0	1	.750	.643
Ramirez, Raphael	L-L	5-11	175	12-15-95	.256	.161	.287	41	125	24	32	4	4	0	16	10	1	1	3	43	18	3	.352	.309

Name	B-T	HT	WT	DOB	AVG	vLH	vRH	G	AB	R	H	2B	3B	HR	RBI	BB	HBP	SH	SF	SO	SB	CS	SLG	OBP
Ramos, Milton	R-R	5-11	158	10-26-95	.241	.139	.269	51	166	20	40	9	5	0	29	14	1	1	3	34	6	6	.355	.299
Ramos, Natanael	R-R	5-10	170	6-19-93	.217	.233	.211	33	106	8	23	4	0	0	8	8	2	1	1	14	2	2	.255	.282
Reyes, Alfredo	R-R	6-2	160	10-4-93	.236	.297	.217	46	157	22	37	7	0	0	18	8	0	4	1	38	9	2	.280	.271
Rodriguez, Dionis	R-R	6-0	183	2-15-95	.205	.316	.169	25	78	14	16	4	0	1	9	7	2	2	2	26	2	0	.295	.281
Rojas, Hengelbert	R-R	6-1	188	10-27-93	.224	.167	.239	36	116	12	26	7	0	1	14	17	7	0	0	29	0	1	.310	.357
Sanchez, Elvis	R-R	6-2	190	2-8-94	.111	.000	.125	3	9	0	1	0	0	0	1	0	0	0	0	3	0	0	.111	.111
Teagarden, Taylor	R-R	6-0	210	12-21-83	.200	.500	.125	4	10	0	2	2	0	0	0	1	1	0	0	6	0	0	.400	.333
Tovar, Wilfredo	R-R	5-10	180	8-11-91	.333	—	.333	2	6	0	2	1	0	0	2	1	0	0	0	1	0	1	.500	.429
Valencia, Gregory	R-R	6-3	185	3-19-93	.308	.333	.300	8	26	6	8	3	0	0	4	3	0	0	0	9	2	1	.423	.379
Winningham, Dash	L-L	6-2	230	10-11-95	.231	.273	.221	52	169	23	39	10	1	5	36	17	8	0	5	39	2	1	.391	.322
Zabala, Emmanuel	R-R	6-0	185	9-29-94	.301	.311	.298	55	196	33	59	7	3	0	20	13	6	4	4	23	13	12	.367	.356

Pitching	B-T	HT	WT	DOB	W	L	ERA	G	GS	CG	SV	IP	H	R	ER	HR	BB	SO	AVG	vLH	vRH	K/9	BB/9
Almeida, Adrian	L-L	6-0	150	5-2-92	3	2	2.13	10	7	0	0	38	26	14	9	0	23	40	.198	.136	.230	9.47	5.45
Arias, Eucebio	R-R	6-1	173	9-20-94	2	2	3.86	6	6	0	0	19	16	15	8	0	10	8	.229	.357	.143	3.86	4.82
Badamo, Tyler	R-R	6-2	190	8-8-92	1	0	1.74	10	4	0	0	31	25	9	6	2	6	26	.216	.191	.232	7.55	1.74
Bernard, Derrick	R-R	6-2	190	4-8-92	0	0	3.86	6	0	0	0	7	6	6	3	0	9	8	.231	.077	.385	10.29	11.57
Buchanan, Connor	R-R	6-1	190	7-11-93	0	0	3.38	6	0	0	0	5	5	3	2	0	6	4	.217	.000	.333	6.75	10.13
Canelon, Kevin	L-L	6-1	175	1-16-94	1	2	1.45	12	5	0	1	37	26	9	6	1	1	30	.200	.213	.193	7.23	0.24
Celas, Jose	R-R	6-1	180	1-12-91	1	2	3.28	11	7	0	0	36	38	17	13	0	22	37	.264	.226	.274	9.34	5.55
Crismatt, Nabil	R-R	6-1	197	12-25-94	1	1	2.25	19	0	0	2	28	15	8	7	1	10	33	.161	.143	.172	10.61	3.21
Durham, Alex	R-R	6-4	185	9-16-96	1	0	6.00	7	0	0	0	6	2	4	4	0	7	6	.100	.000	.143	9.00	10.50
Feliz, Gabriel	L-L	5-11	160	11-12-92	2	0	2.55	21	0	0	1	18	17	8	5	1	15	18	.262	.333	.227	9.17	7.64
Gee, Dillon	R-R	6-1	205	4-28-86	0	0	0.00	1	1	0	0	2	1	0	0	0	0	2	.125	.000	.167	9.00	0.00
German, Audry	R-R	5-11	163	8-25-94	3	2	3.94	6	5	1	0	30	37	14	13	1	3	16	.316	.302	.324	4.85	0.91
Griffin, Cameron	R-R	6-3	200	6-25-91	0	0	0.00	2	0	0	0	2	0	0	0	0	0	2	.000	.000	.000	9.00	0.00
Hefner, Jeremy	R-R	6-4	205	3-11-86	0	0	3.00	3	3	0	0	6	4	2	2	0	0	2	.200	.400	.133	3.00	0.00
Herrmann, Dan	R-R	6-5	205	9-2-94	0	1	18.47	11	0	0	0	6	5	13	13	1	19	0	.200	.250	.176	0.00	27.00
Horne, Kurtis	L-L	6-5	190	8-5-96	1	0	1.08	7	0	0	0	8	7	2	1	1	4	3	.226	.429	.059	3.24	4.32
Huertas, Joel	B-L	6-3	210	2-14-96	1	0	6.35	8	0	0	0	11	8	9	8	0	12	14	.200	.250	.179	11.12	9.53
Llanes, Gabe	R-R	6-3	185	1-15-96	2	0	4.85	8	0	0	0	13	15	8	7	1	6	8	.288	.353	.257	5.54	4.15
Manoah, Erik	R-R	6-2	215	12-22-95	3	0	2.63	8	3	0	0	24	20	8	7	0	10	18	.238	.286	.214	6.75	3.75
Marte, Juan	R-R	6-3	208	8-29-90	0	1	9.00	2	0	0	0	2	3	2	2	0	1	1	.375	.400	.333	4.50	4.50
Mateo, Luis	R-R	6-3	185	3-22-90	0	0	1.69	4	0	0	1	5	4	1	1	1	6	.182	.143	.200	10.13	1.69
Mazzoni, Cory	R-R	6-1	200	10-19-89	0	1	4.50	1	1	0	0	4	5	2	2	0	1	7	.294	.125	.444	15.75	2.25
McMinn, Brent	R-R	6-2	195	12-2-90	0	2	2.31	11	1	0	2	12	8	8	3	0	8	10	.205	.154	.231	7.71	6.17
Medina, Jose	L-L	6-2	180	8-25-96	0	2	9.12	11	3	0	0	25	39	29	25	3	7	22	.368	.343	.380	8.03	2.55
Mitchell, Bret	R-R	6-2	190	12-10-88	0	0	0.00	1	0	0	0	2	0	0	0	0	3	.000	.000	.000	13.50	0.00
Montero, Rafael	R-R	6-0	185	10-17-90	0	0	4.50	1	1	0	0	2	3	1	1	0	3	.333	.250	.400	13.50	0.00
Ortega, Flabio	R-R	6-0	180	8-19-90	2	0	2.19	10	0	0	1	12	10	4	3	1	5	5	.238	.250	.231	3.65	3.65
Palsha, Alex	R-R	6-1	195	5-10-92	0	1	0.69	14	0	0	10	13	11	2	1	0	3	17	.239	.059	.345	11.77	2.08
Ramos, Darwin	R-R	6-1	195	11-23-95	2	4	3.96	10	7	0	0	39	39	26	17	0	12	30	.262	.250	.270	6.98	2.79
Rodriguez, Waldo	L-L	5-11	176	10-20-90	2	3	5.14	16	0	0	1	14	23	9	8	0	11	10	.390	.400	.386	6.43	7.07
Taylor, Blake	L-L	6-3	220	8-17-95	2	0	0.00	3	1	0	0	11	1	2	0	0	7	10	.029	.000	.045	8.44	5.91
Taylor, Logan	R-R	6-5	205	12-13-91	2	0	1.13	3	3	0	0	16	14	2	2	0	2	16	.237	.174	.278	9.00	1.13
Uceta, Adonis	R-R	6-1	195	5-10-94	1	0	5.11	4	0	0	1	12	12	7	7	4	2	9	.255	.235	.267	6.57	1.46
Whalen, Rob	R-R	6-2	200	1-31-94	0	1	1.29	3	2	0	0	7	4	1	1	0	2	10	.160	.222	.125	12.86	2.57

Fielding

Catcher	PCT	G	PO	A	E	DP	PB
Hilario	1.000	2	4	1	0	0	1
Knight	.954	10	76	7	4	1	3
Leal	.971	6	32	2	1	0	1
Ramos	.991	28	191	27	2	2	4
Rodriguez	.981	18	135	22	3	3	6
Teagarden	2	3	0	0	0	0

First Base	PCT	G	PO	A	E	DP
Burdick	1.000	2	4	0	0	0
Hilario	.995	22	190	12	1	15
Leal	.938	5	25	5	2	2
Sanchez	1.000	3	21	4	0	3
Winningham	.980	35	284	11	6	26

Second Base	PCT	G	PO	A	E	DP
Burdick	1.000	14	21	32	0	9

	PCT	G	PO	A	E	DP
Correa	.900	2	7	2	1	1
Fulmer	.909	4	4	6	1	1
Maracaro	1.000	6	1	10	0	1
Marte	.933	3	7	7	1	1
Ramos	.976	20	27	56	2	13
Reyes	.888	16	23	48	9	11

Third Base	PCT	G	PO	A	E	DP
Burdick	.889	20	6	26	4	3
Correa	1.000	1	1	0	0	0
Hilario	.917	4	3	8	1	1
Maracaro	.915	31	18	68	8	7
Perez	1.000	3	1	7	0	0
Valencia	.840	8	6	15	4	1

Shortstop	PCT	G	PO	A	E	DP
Burdick	1.000	2	4	7	0	0

	PCT	G	PO	A	E	DP
Correa	.800	1	2	2	1	0
Evans	.667	1	1	1	1	0
Ramos	.940	29	50	75	8	13
Reyes	.966	29	41	99	5	23
Tovar	1.000	2	0	3	0	0

Outfield	PCT	G	PO	A	E	DP
Berrios	.906	28	27	2	3	0
Burdick	—	1	0	0	0	0
Figuera	1.000	4	7	2	0	0
Hilario	1.000	4	5	0	0	0
King	—	1	0	0	0	0
Lagares	1.000	2	1	0	0	0
Mora	.980	29	45	3	1	2
Ramirez	.978	38	85	3	2	0
Rojas	.973	30	33	3	1	0
Zabala	.989	52	81	7	1	1

DSL METS   ROOKIE

DOMINICAN SUMMER LEAGUE

Batting	B-T	HT	WT	DOB	AVG	vLH	vRH	G	AB	R	H	2B	3B	HR	RBI	BB	HBP	SH	SF	SO	SB	CS	SLG	OBP
Aybar, Cecilio	R-R	6-0	165	11-23-93	.286	.429	.257	11	42	13	12	2	2	1	8	2	4	0	0	12	4	1	.500	.375
Carpio, Luis	R-R	6-0	165	7-11-97	.234	.182	.248	60	209	35	49	9	1	1	20	33	4	2	2	33	12	4	.301	.347
Carrion, Junior	R-R	6-0	198	12-16-93	.208	—	—	33	106	15	22	3	0	4	15	5	10	1	1	32	2	1	.349	.303
Cespedes, Ricardo	L-L	6-1	160	8-24-97	.266	—	—	54	218	29	58	9	3	0	17	14	1	0	2	36	7	5	.335	.311
Correa, Franklin	R-R	5-9	176	1-1-96	.260	.171	.282	53	177	28	46	12	1	4	20	34	3	4	2	41	11	3	.407	.384

Player	B-T	HT	WT	DOB	AVG	vLH	vRH	G	AB	R	H	2B	3B	HR	RBI	BB	HBP	SH	SF	SO	SB	CS	OBP	SLG
Crisostomo, Luis	L-R	6-1	180	12-9-93	.270	.278	.268	67	237	40	64	14	2	2	31	23	4	7	3	31	5	3	.371	.341
De Aza, Yeffry	R-R	6-0	170	1-14-97	.300	—	—	52	203	25	61	12	1	1	22	10	1	0	1	36	4	1	.384	.335
Diaz, Alejandro	B-R	6-0	150	3-2-96	.244	.185	.274	32	100	17	25	1	1	0	10	13	1	4	0	13	2	4	.280	.342
Diaz, Edwin	L-R	6-2	180	11-30-95	.228	—	—	46	136	18	31	4	4	1	26	16	0	0	2	41	2	2	.338	.305
Dirocie, Anthony	R-R	6-0	160	4-24-97	.221	.267	.213	33	95	16	21	6	0	0	14	15	1	0	3	22	3	1	.284	.325
Geraldo, Claudio	L-L	6-1	185	4-28-97	.240	.263	.235	29	100	11	24	6	3	0	13	12	2	1	1	31	1	3	.360	.330
Guzman, Rafael	R-R	6-1	175	10-5-95	.226	—	—	51	155	15	35	6	2	2	19	13	5	4	0	48	6	10	.329	.306
Infante, Santos	R-R	6-3	195	4-15-95	.126	.095	.136	32	87	7	11	3	0	1	10	3	0	2	2	45	0	2	.195	.152
Jimenez, Grabiel	L-L	6-2	180	1-16-95	.220	.167	.234	60	209	23	46	5	1	0	20	22	4	1	1	39	12	11	.254	.305
Lebron, Luis	R-R	6-0	170	1-6-97	.231	.250	.227	21	52	5	12	2	0	0	1	5	0	1	0	18	1	1	.269	.298
Maria, Jose	R-R	5-9	194	11-30-94	.257	—	—	53	187	34	48	10	2	5	26	14	8	0	0	40	9	3	.412	.335
Martinez, Jose	R-R	6-1	159	1-18-94	.250	—	—	2	4	0	1	0	0	0	1	0	0	0	1	0	1	0	1	.250	.400
Medina, Jose	R-R	6-3	170	10-21-96	.286	—	—	55	210	34	60	9	4	2	33	22	4	0	2	25	7	4	.395	.361
Montero, Luis	R-R	6-2	190	1-16-96	.302	.229	.328	49	182	26	55	9	0	1	20	16	4	1	3	19	4	5	.368	.366
Moreno, Hansel	B-R	6-3	157	11-3-96	.204	.250	.195	29	103	14	21	1	1	0	7	17	0	3	1	34	3	1	.233	.314
Moscote, Victor	R-R	6-1	155	5-10-96	.308	—	—	63	227	31	70	8	1	1	30	21	1	1	3	52	5	2	.366	.365
Ortiz, Hanser	L-R	6-0	195	6-2-94	.224	—	—	56	201	16	45	5	1	0	21	16	0	0	1	33	5	2	.259	.280
Pascual, Oliver	B-R	5-10	155	11-16-96	.229	.224	.231	62	227	28	52	8	0	0	27	36	3	8	4	40	12	8	.264	.337
Patino, Miguel	R-R	5-11	155	12-17-95	.263	—	—	52	175	28	46	10	1	0	15	10	4	5	2	24	7	8	.331	.314
Paulino, Dionis	L-L	6-3	190	6-20-94	.250	.273	.244	49	160	33	40	3	4	1	16	27	3	0	2	39	15	7	.338	.365
Pierre, Ysidro	B-R	6-1	171	11-30-93	.241	—	—	60	212	41	51	7	2	0	16	24	7	3	1	53	33	13	.292	.336
Rasquin, Walter	R-R	5-9	160	3-21-96	.321	.303	.326	58	165	33	53	11	2	1	23	25	7	1	1	22	12	4	.430	.429
Sanchez, Ali	R-R	6-0	175	1-20-97	.303	.341	.291	50	175	21	53	7	0	3	24	27	4	2	1	31	6	6	.394	.406
Sanchez, Carlos	R-R	5-11	170	6-6-96	.245	.318	.224	27	98	14	24	6	0	0	11	11	3	0	2	18	1	2	.306	.333
Terrazas, Rigoberto	B-R	6-0	160	4-11-96	.239	—	—	59	201	19	48	5	1	0	25	18	2	4	3	46	3	3	.274	.304

Pitching	B-T	HT	WT	DOB	W	L	ERA	G	GS	CG	SV	IP	H	R	ER	HR	BB	SO	AVG	vLH	vRH	K/9	BB/9
Alvarez, Jean	R-R	6-1	160	5-1-95	0	0	2.25	5	0	0	0	3	0	6	0		9	0	.000	.000	.000		3.38
Batista, Brian	L-L	6-0	175	8-27-95	1	0	18.00	13	0	0	0	13	17	28	26	1	21	10	.304	.154	.349	6.92	14.54
Berihuete, Enmanuel	R-R	6-0	174	11-5-93	6	6	4.66	25	0	0	2	68	71	44	35	3	15	57	.268	.222	.285	7.58	2.00
Blanco, Rolgenis	R-R	6-0	160	2-7-93	0	0	11.66	9	0	0	0	15	29	22	19	0	9	10	.420	.423	.419	6.14	5.52
Carreno, Luis	R-R	6-0	169	8-12-95	2	5	1.60	14	14	0	0	56	40	22	10	2	24	48	.203	.240	.180	8.63	4.31
Castillo, Yrelvis	R-R	6-4	197	7-13-91	3	2	6.54	25	0	0	3	43	43	37	31	1	33	38	.270	.268	.272	8.02	6.96
Celis, Jorge	L-L	5-10	160	9-11-94	2	1	3.17	25	0	0	0	48	38	20	17	2	31	46	—	—	—	8.57	5.77
Cespedes, Jorge	R-R	6-5	174	12-4-94	1	0	6.75	4	0	0	0	7	9	5	5	0	1	5	.310	.250	.320	6.75	1.35
Cuello, Ederi	L-L	6-0	170	10-10-96	0	0	8.10	4	0	0	0	7	8	8	6	1	4	6	.276	.400	.250	8.10	5.40
Debora, Nicolas	R-R	6-5	170	12-6-93	0	0	3.69	11	8	0	0	46	46	21	19	1	14	41	—	—	—	7.96	2.72
Encarnacion, Rafael	L-L	6-2	178	9-2-94	3	2	4.61	19	0	0	2	41	45	25	21	1	14	38	.288	.280	.290	8.34	3.07
Estevez, Gregorix	R-R	6-5	200	4-12-94	2	2	3.09	13	3	0	2	35	22	15	12	0	16	40	.179	.140	.200	1.29	4.11
Familia, Misael	R-R	6-2	190	1-27-95	1	2	3.47	12	0	0	3	23	23	12	9	0	6	17	—	—	—	6.56	2.31
Fernandez, Wuender	R-R	6-2	185	1-15-97	0	0	19.13	9	0	0	0	8	19	18	17	0	12	9	.422	.529	.357	1.13	13.50
Geraldo, Jose	R-R	6-0	185	7-14-95	1	0	3.68	6	1	0	1	15	17	6	6	0	3	13	.274	.286	.268	7.98	1.84
Gonzalez, Harol	R-R	6-0	160	3-2-95	1	0	3.24	15	7	0	2	50	51	26	18	1	11	53	—	—	—	9.54	1.98
Gonzalez, Merandy	R-R	6-1	175	10-9-95	3	1	3.54	13	12	0	0	56	50	28	22	2	15	47	—	—	—	7.55	2.41
Guedez, Ronald	R-R	6-1	160	1-26-96	2	0	3.04	14	13	0	0	68	62	26	23	2	16	49	—	—	—	6.49	2.12
Gutierrez, Miguel	L-L	6-0	180	12-3-94	1	4	2.77	14	1	0	1	26	24	14	8	1	17	26	.247	.125	.288	9.00	5.88
Hernandez, Carlos	R-R	6-0	165	11-3-94	3	5	5.61	17	9	0	1	59	61	44	37	2	33	37	.271	.284	.264	5.61	5.01
Laguerre, Ramon	R-R	6-4	170	4-28-96	0	1	1.38	4	4	0	0	13	11	8	2	0	1	11	.220	.211	.226	7.62	.69
Leon, Nelson	R-R	6-1	175	3-1-95	0	0	3.52	6	0	0	0	8	7	3	3	1	2	6	.259	.250	.263	7.04	2.35
Marte, Juan	R-R	6-3	208	8-24-94	4	2	4.28	14	6	0	0	48	59	31	23	6	16	32	.294	.364	.267	5.96	2.98
Mateo, Luis	R-R	6-6	180	4-7-93	0	0	9.92	13	0	0	0	16	22	20	18	0	23	13	—	—	—	7.16	12.67
Mendez, Jose	R-R	6-7	230	12-29-94	0	0	16.88	8	4	0	0	11	14	21	20	2	25	9	—	—	—	7.59	21.09
Merilan, Claudio	R-R	6-1	184	5-3-94	1	3	4.22	15	10	0	0	60	54	34	28	2	25	40	.239	.242	.237	6.03	3.77
Montijo, Marbin	R-R	6-0	160	7-4-96	2	3	2.82	13	12	0	0	54	53	22	17	2	15	37	.268	.231	.292	6.13	2.48
Moreno, Jose	R-R	6-4	168	7-31-96	0	0	6.43	5	0	0	0	7	9	5	5	1	6	5	.360	.200	.400	6.43	7.71
Olivo, Aneury	L-L	6-2	159	10-24-94	1	2	4.84	21	2	0	6	45	40	28	24	2	21	49	—	—	—	9.87	4.23
Reina, Richard	R-R	6-2	183	2-7-95	1	2	4.03	21	3	0	2	45	47	22	20	1	26	51	—	—	—	1.28	5.24
Rodriguez, Alban	R-R	6-0	150	3-15-96	2	1	1.56	7	1	0	1	17	14	6	3	1	8	20	.226	.143	.250	1.38	4.15
Rodriguez, Edgar	R-R	6-2	155	8-31-94	1	4	7.62	19	7	0	0	39	44	36	33	0	30	31	.286	.250	.297	7.15	6.92
Rodriguez, Jhonaiker	R-R	6-0	160	4-8-96	0	1	4.82	7	0	0	2	9	7	6	5	0	6	10	.212	.000	.250	9.64	5.79
Rodriguez, Ramon	R-R	5-11	169	12-27-91	0	1	4.41	12	8	0	1	49	45	30	24	1	13	40	—	—	—	7.35	2.39
Rondon, Ygnacio	R-R	6-3	174	5-16-95	0	1	3.27	4	0	0	0	11	13	7	4	0	4	13	.289	.278	.296	3.27	3.27
Silva, Luis	R-R	6-0	170	11-17-96	0	0	1.80	3	1	0	0	5	2	1	1	0	1	8	.111	.111	.111	14.40	1.80
Suazo, Randinson	R-R	6-0	190	4-19-95	1	0	4.86	20	0	0	0	33	40	29	18	1	17	20	—	—	—	5.40	4.59
Uceta, Adonis	R-R	6-1	195	5-10-94	3	2	2.33	10	10	0	0	54	50	25	14	2	9	36	.240	.317	.207	6.00	1.50
Vallejo, Bladimil	R-R	6-1	180	10-10-91	0	0	1.69	4	0	0	2	5	5	1	1	0	0	2	.278	.000	.313	3.38	.00

Fielding

Catcher	PCT	G	PO	A	E	DP	PB
Guzman	.976	31	213	27	6	0	9
Lebron	.967	18	106	10	4	0	5
Maria	.979	13	82	13	2	0	2
Martinez	1.000	2	0	0	0	0	0
Moscote	.979	9	37	10	1	0	1
Ortiz	.969	24	161	26	6	0	11
Rasquin	1.000	5	24	3	0	0	1
Sanchez	.986	64	421	77	7	0	16

First Base	PCT	G	PO	A	E	DP
Castillo	1.000	1	2	0	0	1
Crisostomo	1.000	3	11	0	0	1
Diaz	1.000	1	1	0	0	0
Guzman	.977	18	125	5	3	12
Maria	.952	17	117	3	6	9
Martinez	1.000	2	14	0	0	0

	PCT	G	PO	A	E	DP
Montero	.989	19	167	6	2	14
Moscote	.990	47	371	16	4	28
Ortiz	.986	20	130	14	2	20
Patino	.982	18	105	4	2	9
Paulino	.986	12	66	2	1	5
Rasquin	.943	15	95	5	6	9
Sanchez	1.000	1	7	0	0	1
Terrazas	1.000	3	11	1	0	2

Second Base	PCT	G	PO	A	E	DP
Aybar	1.000	2	5	5	0	3
Carpio	.973	33	65	80	4	14
Correa	.969	50	120	133	8	32
Crisostomo	1.000	6	13	10	0	4
De Aza	.973	17	29	42	2	5
Diaz	1.000	5	4	5	0	0
Guzman	1.000	1	1	3	0	0
Moreno	1.000	3	6	5	0	3
Pascual	.957	6	7	15	1	3
Patino	.974	19	37	39	2	11
Paulino	—	1	0	0	0	0
Rasquin	—	1	0	0	0	0
Terrazas	.900	12	15	30	5	4

Third Base	PCT	G	PO	A	E	DP
Carpio	1.000	1	0	3	0	0
Cespedes	—	1	0	0	0	0
Correa	.600	3	2	1	2	0

	PCT	G	PO	A	E	DP
Crisostomo	.895	6	6	11	2	1
De Aza	.854	17	9	26	6	4
Diaz	.913	52	41	95	13	9
Montero	.769	7	5	5	3	1
Moscote	.826	9	7	12	4	1
Patino	.868	16	15	31	7	4
Rasquin	.920	23	15	31	4	4
Sanchez	—	1	0	0	0	0
Terrazas	.946	28	20	50	4	2

Shortstop	PCT	G	PO	A	E	DP
Aybar	.840	5	9	12	4	5
Carpio	.927	26	44	70	9	16
De Aza	.892	15	20	54	9	6
Diaz	.947	9	11	25	2	2
Moreno	.909	21	38	52	9	9
Pascual	.934	56	91	162	18	31
Patino	.800	4	4	4	2	1
Terrazas	.892	16	19	39	7	7

Outfield	PCT	G	PO	A	E	DP
Carrion	.939	23	29	2	2	1
Cespedes	.992	50	115	12	1	1
Crisostomo	.961	56	93	6	4	5
Diaz	.938	30	30	0	2	0
Dirocie	.964	27	51	3	2	2
Geraldo	1.000	26	54	3	0	1
Guzman	1.000	3	1	0	0	0
Infante	.933	22	25	3	2	0
Jimenez	.957	54	86	2	4	0
Lebron	.000	1	0	0	2	0
Maria	.800	3	4	0	1	0
Medina	.908	51	90	9	10	1
Montero	1.000	20	18	2	0	0
Patino	—	1	0	0	0	0
Paulino	.970	36	58	6	2	0
Pierre	.985	58	122	8	2	2
Rasquin	1.000	7	6	0	0	0
Terrazas	1.000	2	4	0	0	0

New York Yankees

SEASON IN A SENTENCE: Four fifths of the starting rotation got hurt, high-priced free agents underperformed, Dellin Betances struck out the world and Derek Jeter took his final bows.

HIGH POINT: Derek Jeter's final game at home, when he ended a season filled with pomp, circumstance, naysayers and mediocrity with a game-winning single in the bottom of the ninth in his final game in the Bronx. The Yankees were eliminated from postseason contention for the second straight season, but for a night in New York, September felt like October and 2014 felt like 1998.

LOW POINT: Before Ivan Nova's elbow popped, Masahiro Tanaka's became inflamed and CC Sabathia's knee gave out, the Red Sox caught Michael Pineda putting pine tar on the baseball. Then, two weeks later, they caught him again, reported it to home plate umpire Gerry Davis, and Pineda was ejected. He was suspended for 10 games, but it got worse. While on suspension, the righthander, who had missed two years after labrum surgery, was placed on the disabled list with a balky back. He didn't pitch again until Aug. 13.

NOTABLE ROOKIES: After securing him an extra option and seemingly sealing another season for him in Scranton, Dellin Betances exploded in spring training, earned a spot in the major league bullpen and set the franchise record for most strikeouts by a reliever in a season.

KEY TRANSACTIONS: The Yankees won the bidding for Japanese ace Masahiro Tanaka with a bid of seven years and $155 million. That was only part of a spending spree that included the imports of catcher Brian McCann (five years, $85 million), center fielder Jacoby Ellsbury (seven years, $153 million) and sometime outfielder Carlos Beltran (three years, $45 million). Tanaka finished second on the team in strikeouts with 141 and was among the contenders for the American League's Rookie of the Year honors until his elbow started barking, but McCann, Beltran and Ellsbury combined for just 4.9 wins above replacement.

DOWN ON THE FARM: After a year in 2013 that saw the front office heavily criticized by ownership for failing to produce reliable replacements for its injured players, the farm took significant steps forward. Righthander Luis Severino breezed through three levels and impressed evaluators at every step, and second baseman Rob Refsnyder hit his way into the brains of every New Yorker frustrated with their team's putrid offense.

OPENING DAY PAYROLL: $203,812,506 (2nd)

PLAYERS OF THE YEAR

DAVID SCHOFIELD

MAJOR LEAGUE	MINOR LEAGUE
Dellin Betances	**Rob Refsnyder**
rhp	2b/rf
5-0, 1.40, 0.78 WHIP	(Double-A, Triple-A)
135 SO, 90 IP	.318/.387/.497
13.50 SO/9, 4.6 H/9	14 HR, 63 RBI

ORGANIZATION LEADERS

BATTING		*Minimum 250 AB
MAJORS		
* AVG	Suzuki, Ichiro	.284
* OPS	Gardner, Brett	.749
HR	McCann, Brian	23
RBI	McCann, Brian	75
MINORS		
* AVG	Refsnyder, Robert, Trenton, Scranton/WB	.318
* OBP	Judge, Aaron, Charleston, Tampa	.419
* SLG	O'Brien, Peter, Tampa, Trenton	.593
R	Pirela, Jose, Scranton/WB	87
H	Cave, Jake, Tampa, Trenton	165
TB	Refsnyder, Robert, Trenton, Scranton/WB	256
2B	Refsnyder, Robert, Trenton, Scranton/WB	38
3B	Pirela, Jose, Scranton/WB	11
HR	O'Brien, Peter, Tampa, Trenton	33
RBI	Judge, Aaron, Charleston, Tampa	78
BB	Judge, Aaron, Charleston, Tampa	89
SO	Roller, Kyle, Trenton, Scranton/WB	146
SB	O'Neill, Michael, Charleston	42

PITCHING		#Minimum 75 IP
MAJORS		
W	Tanaka, Masahiro	13
# ERA	Betances, Dellin	1.40
SO	Kuroda, Hiroki	146
SV	Robertson, David	39
MINORS		
W	Long, Jaron, Charleston, Tampa, Trenton	12
L	Camarena, Daniel, Tampa, Trenton	11
# ERA	Long, Jaron, Charleston, Tampa, Trenton	2.18
G	Webb, Tyler, Tampa, Trenton, Scranton/WB	48
GS	Smith, Caleb, Charleston, Tampa	27
SV	Vargas, Cesar, Charleston, Tampa	14
IP	Nuding, Zach, Trenton, Scranton/WB	154
BB	Tracy, Matt, Trenton, Scranton/WB	55
SO	Severino, Luis, Charleston, Tampa, Trenton	127
AVG	Severino, Luis, Charleston, Tampa, Trenton	.220

2014 PERFORMANCE

General Manager: Brian Cashman. **Farm Director:** Mark Newman. **Scouting Director:** Damon Oppenheimer.

Class	Team	League	W	L	PCT	Finish	Manager
Majors	New York Yankees	American	84	78	.519	13th (30)	Joe Girardi
Triple-A	Scranton/W-B RailRiders	International	68	76	.472	10th (14)	Dave Miley
Double-A	Trenton Thunder	Eastern	67	75	.472	8th (12)	Tony Franklin
High A	Tampa Yankees	Florida State	71	68	.511	7th (12)	Al Pedrique
Low A	Charleston RiverDogs	South Atlantic	71	69	.507	6th (14)	Luis Dorante
Short season	Staten Island Yankees	New York-Penn	37	38	.493	t-6th (14)	Mario Garza
Rookie	Yankees1	Gulf Coast	38	22	.633	1st (16)	Travis Chapman
Rookie	Yankees2	Gulf Coast	35	25	.583	5th (16)	Pat Osborn
Overall 2015 Minor League Record			387	373	.509	12th (30)	

ORGANIZATION STATISTICS

NEW YORK YANKEES

AMERICAN LEAGUE

Batting	B-T	HT	WT	DOB	AVG	vLH	vRH	G	AB	R	H	2B	3B	HR	RBI	BB	HBP	SH	SF	SO	SB	CS	SLG	OBP
Almonte, Zoilo	B-R	6-0	205	6-10-89	.139	.200	.129	13	36	2	5	0	0	1	3	0	0	0	0	14	1	0	.222	.139
Anna, Dean	L-R	5-11	180	11-24-86	.136	.000	.200	12	22	3	3	1	0	1	3	2	0	0	1	6	0	0	.318	.200
Beltran, Carlos	B-R	6-1	210	4-24-77	.233	.196	.254	109	403	46	94	23	0	15	49	37	4	0	5	80	3	1	.402	.301
Cervelli, Francisco	R-R	6-1	205	3-6-86	.301	.267	.317	49	146	18	44	11	1	2	13	11	5	0	0	41	1	0	.432	.370
Drew, Stephen	L-R	6-0	190	3-16-83	.150	.161	.147	46	140	7	21	8	0	3	15	13	0	0	2	36	0	0	.271	.219
2-team total (39 Boston)					.162	—	—	85	271	18	44	14	1	7	26	27	0	0	2	75	1	1	.299	.237
Ellsbury, Jacoby	L-L	6-1	195	9-11-83	.271	.300	.258	149	575	71	156	27	5	16	70	49	3	0	7	93	39	5	.419	.328
Gardner, Brett	L-L	5-10	185	8-24-83	.256	.262	.253	148	555	87	142	25	8	17	58	56	6	13	6	134	21	5	.422	.327
Headley, Chase	B-R	6-2	220	5-9-84	.262	.291	.250	58	191	28	50	8	0	6	17	29	4	0	0	49	3	2	.398	.371
Jeter, Derek	R-R	6-3	195	6-26-74	.256	.244	.262	145	581	47	149	19	1	4	50	35	6	8	4	87	10	2	.313	.304
Johnson, Kelly	L-R	6-1	200	2-22-82	.219	.194	.224	77	201	21	44	9	2	6	22	23	2	0	1	50	2	1	.373	.304
3-team total (19 Baltimore, 10 Boston)					.215	—	—	106	265	29	57	14	2	7	27	29	2	0	1	71	2	2	.362	.296
McCann, Brian	L-R	6-3	230	2-20-84	.232	.292	.209	140	495	57	115	15	1	23	75	32	7	0	4	77	0	0	.406	.286
Murphy, J.R.	R-R	5-11	195	5-13-91	.284	.270	.295	32	81	7	23	4	0	1	9	4	0	0	0	22	0	0	.370	.318
Perez, Eury	R-R	6-0	190	5-30-90	.200	1.000	.111	4	10	2	2	0	0	0	0	0	0	0	0	3	1	0	.200	.200
Pirela, Jose	B-R	5-11	210	11-21-89	.333	.833	.167	7	24	6	8	1	2	0	3	1	0	0	0	4	0	0	.542	.360
Prado, Martin	R-R	6-1	190	10-27-83	.316	.421	.274	37	133	18	42	9	0	7	16	3	1	0	0	23	1	0	.541	.336
Richardson, Antoan	B-R	5-8	165	10-8-83	.313	—	.313	13	16	2	5	0	0	0	1	1	0	0	0	5	0	0	.313	.353
Roberts, Brian	S-R	5-9	175	10-9-77	.237	.253	.231	91	317	40	75	16	4	5	21	28	1	1	1	53	7	4	.360	.300
Romine, Austin	R-R	6-0	215	11-22-88	.231	1.000	.167	7	13	2	3	1	0	0	1	0	0	0	0	4	0	0	.308	.231
Ryan, Brendan	R-R	6-2	195	3-26-82	.167	.120	.180	49	114	5	19	4	0	0	8	4	3	1	2	30	0	2	.202	.211
Sizemore, Scott	R-R	6-0	185	1-4-85	.313	.455	.000	6	16	3	5	2	0	0	4	0	0	0	0	8	0	0	.438	.313
Solarte, Yangervis	B-R	5-11	195	7-7-87	.254	.239	.263	75	252	26	64	14	0	6	31	30	3	1	3	34	0	0	.381	.337
Soriano, Alfonso	R-R	6-1	195	1-7-76	.221	.247	.204	67	226	22	50	15	0	6	23	6	2	0	4	71	1	0	.367	.244
Suzuki, Ichiro	L-R	5-11	170	10-22-73	.284	.333	.274	143	359	42	102	13	2	1	22	21	1	2	2	68	15	3	.340	.324
Teixeira, Mark	B-R	6-3	215	4-11-80	.216	.220	.215	123	440	56	95	14	0	22	62	58	6	0	4	109	1	1	.398	.313
Wheeler, Zelous	R-R	5-10	220	1-16-87	.193	.261	.147	29	57	6	11	0	0	2	5	2	1	1	1	12	0	0	.298	.230
Young, Chris	R-R	6-2	200	9-5-83	.282	.250	.286	23	71	9	20	8	0	3	10	7	1	0	0	16	1	0	.521	.354

Pitching	B-T	HT	WT	DOB	W	L	ERA	G	GS	CG	SV	IP	H	R	ER	HR	BB	SO	AVG	vLH	vRH	K/9	BB/9
Aceves, Alfredo	R-R	6-2	205	12-8-82	1	2	6.52	10	0	0	0	19	23	14	14	6	4	16	.288	.379	.235	7.45	1.86
Betances, Dellin	R-R	6-8	260	3-23-88	5	0	1.40	70	0	0	1	90	46	15	14	4	24	135	.149	.163	.135	13.50	2.40
Billings, Bruce	R-R	6-0	210	11-18-85	0	0	9.00	1	0	0	0	4	4	4	4	2	1	7	.250	.250	.250	15.75	2.25
Cabral, Cesar	L-L	6-3	250	2-11-89	0	0	27.00	4	0	0	0	1	4	3	3	0	2	2	.571	.333	.750	18.00	18.00
Capuano, Chris	L-L	6-3	215	8-19-78	2	3	4.25	12	12	0	0	66	67	34	31	7	19	55	.261	.306	.250	7.54	2.60
2-team total (28 Boston)					3	4	4.35	40	12	0	0	97	101	51	47	10	34	84	—	—	—	7.77	3.14
Claiborne, Preston	R-R	6-2	225	1-21-88	3	0	3.00	18	0	0	0	21	24	9	7	1	10	16	.286	.344	.250	6.86	4.29
Daley, Matt	R-R	6-2	180	6-23-82	0	1	5.02	13	0	0	0	14	12	11	8	4	6	10	.222	.294	.189	6.28	3.77
Francis, Jeff	L-L	6-5	220	1-8-81	1	0	5.40	2	0	0	0	2	2	1	1	1	0	1	.286	.400	.000	5.40	0.00
2-team total (9 Oakland)					1	1	6.00	11	0	0	1	15	13	10	10	2	3	11	—	—	—	6.60	1.80
Greene, Shane	R-R	6-4	210	11-17-88	5	4	3.78	15	14	0	0	79	81	38	33	8	29	81	.262	.281	.242	9.27	3.32
Hill, Rich	L-L	6-5	220	3-11-80	0	0	1.69	14	0	0	0	5	6	1	1	0	3	9	.286	.250	.400	15.19	5.06
2-team total (2 Los Angeles)					0	0	3.38	16	0	0	0	5	7	2	2	0	6	9	—	—	—	15.19	10.13
Huff, David	L-L	6-2	215	8-22-84	3	1	1.85	30	0	0	0	39	34	10	8	3	17	28	.231	.250	.215	6.46	3.92
Kelley, Shawn	R-R	6-2	200	4-26-84	3	6	4.53	59	0	0	4	52	45	26	26	5	20	67	.231	.226	.235	11.67	3.48
Kuroda, Hiroki	R-R	6-1	205	2-10-75	11	9	3.71	32	32	0	0	199	191	91	82	20	35	146	.249	.262	.234	6.60	1.58
LeBlanc, Wade	L-L	6-3	215	8-7-84	0	0	18.00	1	0	0	0	1	2	2	2	0	1	0	.500	—	.500	0.00	9.00
2-team total (10 Los Angeles)					1	1	3.94	11	3	0	0	30	27	13	13	2	7	21	—	—	—	6.37	2.12
Leroux, Chris	L-R	6-6	225	4-14-84	0	1	22.50	2	0	0	0	2	7	5	5	0	3	3	.538	.500	.556	13.50	9.00
McCarthy, Brandon	R-R	6-7	200	7-7-83	7	5	2.89	14	14	1	0	90	91	35	29	10	13	82	.257	.255	.259	8.17	1.30
Miller, Jim	R-R	6-1	200	4-28-82	0	0	20.25	2	0	0	0	1	3	4	3	0	2	2	.500	.455	.667	6.75	6.75
Mitchell, Bryan	L-R	6-3	205	4-19-91	0	1	2.45	3	1	0	0	11	10	3	3	0	3	7	.256	.313	.217	5.73	2.45
Nova, Ivan	R-R	6-4	225	1-12-87	2	2	8.27	4	4	0	0	21	32	19	19	6	6	12	.372	.346	.412	5.23	2.61

	B-T	HT	WT	DOB	W	L	ERA	G	GS	CG	SV	IP	H	R	ER	HR	BB	SO	AVG	vLH	vRH	K/9	BB/9
Nuno, Vidal	L-L	5-11	195	7-26-87	2	5	5.42	17	14	0	0	78	86	52	47	15	26	60	.282	.232	.297	6.92	3.00
Outman, Josh	L-L	6-1	205	9-14-84	0	0	0.00	9	0	0	0	4	2	0	0	0	0	2	.182	.111	.500	4.91	0.00
2-team total (31 Cleveland)					4	0	2.86	40	0	0	0	28	24	10	9	4	16	26	—	—	—	8.26	5.08
Phelps, David	R-R	6-2	200	10-9-86	5	5	4.38	32	17	1	1	113	115	62	55	13	46	92	.263	.227	.300	7.33	3.66
Pineda, Michael	R-R	6-7	265	1-18-89	5	5	1.89	13	13	0	0	76	56	18	16	5	7	59	.200	.196	.205	6.96	0.83
Ramirez, Jose	R-R	6-3	190	1-21-90	0	2	5.40	8	0	0	0	10	11	6	6	2	7	10	.275	.063	.417	9.00	6.30
Robertson, David	R-R	5-11	195	4-9-85	4	5	3.08	63	0	0	39	64	45	23	22	7	23	96	.192	.157	.234	13.43	3.22
Roe, Chaz	R-R	6-5	190	10-9-86	0	0	9.00	3	0	0	0	2	3	3	2	0	4	3	.333	.333	.333	18.00	13.50
Rogers, Esmil	R-R	6-3	200	8-14-85	2	0	4.68	18	1	0	0	25	22	13	13	3	10	23	.237	.256	.222	8.28	3.60
2-team total (16 Toronto)					2	0	5.72	34	1	0	0	46	50	30	29	8	17	44	—	—	—	8.67	3.35
Sabathia, C.C.	L-L	6-7	285	7-21-80	3	4	5.28	8	8	0	0	46	58	31	27	10	10	48	.301	.160	.321	9.39	1.96
Tanaka, Masahiro	R-R	6-2	205	11-1-88	13	5	2.77	20	20	3	0	136	123	47	42	15	21	141	.240	.238	.242	9.31	1.39
Thornton, Matt	L-L	6-3	235	9-15-76	0	3	2.55	46	0	0	0	25	23	9	7	0	6	20	.247	.250	.243	7.30	2.19
Warren, Adam	R-R	6-1	200	8-25-87	3	6	2.97	69	0	0	3	79	63	27	26	4	24	76	.219	.178	.252	8.69	2.75
Whitley, Chase	R-R	6-3	215	6-14-89	4	3	5.23	24	12	0	0	76	94	44	44	10	18	60	.308	.315	.301	7.14	2.14

Fielding

Catcher	PCT	G	PO	A	E	DP	PB
Cervelli	.997	42	335	20	1	0	2
McCann	.998	108	859	62	2	4	10
Murphy	.994	30	169	10	1	1	3
Romine	1.000	3	14	2	0	2	0

First Base	PCT	G	PO	A	E	DP
Beltran	1.000	1	3	0	0	0
Cervelli	1.000	5	3	1	0	2
Headley	.981	7	51	2	1	6
Johnson	.981	27	181	25	4	6
McCann	.991	16	100	9	1	7
Romine	1.000	1	2	0	0	0
Ryan	1.000	5	8	1	0	1
Sizemore	1.000	2	8	0	0	1
Teixeira	.994	117	915	66	6	73

Second Base	PCT	G	PO	A	E	DP
Anna	1.000	3	1	5	0	0

	PCT	G	PO	A	E	DP
Drew	.971	34	57	75	4	15
Johnson	1.000	1	0	1	0	0
Pirela	.917	4	4	7	1	2
Prado	.986	17	21	52	1	6
Roberts	.974	91	135	239	10	34
Ryan	.987	19	25	50	1	11
Solarte	.977	17	16	27	1	6

Third Base	PCT	G	PO	A	E	DP
Headley	.986	51	34	110	2	11
Johnson	.934	41	18	53	5	5
Prado	.967	11	7	22	1	
1 Ryan	1.000	2	2	7	0	1
Sizemore	1.000	5	6	6	0	1
Solarte	.947	66	38	105	8	9
Wheeler	.969	18	12	19	1	3

Shortstop	PCT	G	PO	A	E	DP
Anna	.947	9	4	14	1	1

	PCT	G	PO	A	E	DP
Drew	.969	12	13	18	1	5
Jeter	.973	130	144	256	11	48
Ryan	.954	25	18	44	3	7
Solarte	1.000	5	1	5	0	0

Outfield	PCT	G	PO	A	E	DP
Almonte	1.000	10	19	1	0	0
Beltran	.946	32	51	2	3	1
Ellsbury	.997	141	380	3	1	1
Gardner	.993	146	280	5	2	0
Johnson	1.000	4	3	0	0	0
Perez	.727	4	8	0	3	0
Prado	1.000	12	15	0	0	0
Richardson	1.000	6	8	0	0	0
Soriano	.953	35	39	2	2	0
Suzuki	.995	128	189	4	1	0
Wheeler	.900	8	7	2	1	0
Young	.973	19	35	1	1	0

SCRANTON/WILKES-BARRE RAILRIDERS   TRIPLE-A

INTERNATIONAL LEAGUE

Batting	B-T	HT	WT	DOB	AVG	vLH	vRH	G	AB	R	H	2B	3B	HR	RBI	BB	HBP	SH	SF	SO	SB	CS	SLG	OBP
Almonte, Zoilo	B-R	6-0	205	6-10-89	.261	.189	.286	105	421	50	110	18	1	18	69	29	2	0	2	105	6	4	.437	.311
Angelini, Carmen	R-R	6-2	190	9-22-88	.238	.279	.225	84	265	28	63	12	1	4	28	13	0	3	2	54	1	2	.336	.271
Anna, Dean	L-R	5-11	180	11-24-86	.192	.081	.237	36	130	13	25	4	3	1	14	14	4	0	4	20	0	1	.292	.283
2-team total (29 Indianapolis)					.207	—	—	65	198	26	41	8	3	2	21	33	4	1	5	25	1	1	.308	.325
Arcia, Francisco	B-R	5-11	195	9-14-89	.242	.316	.211	38	128	12	31	5	0	0	9	5	3	0	1	26	0	0	.281	.285
Canzler, Russ	R-R	6-2	220	4-11-86	.263	.293	.248	51	175	25	46	12	2	2	24	20	0	0	4	45	1	0	.389	.332
2-team total (61 Lehigh Valley)					.276	—	—	112	388	57	107	32	3	13	58	46	0	0	7	97	3	1	.474	.347
Cervelli, Francisco	R-R	6-1	205	3-6-86	.182	.167	.200	3	11	0	2	0	0	0	0	0	0	0	0	0	0	0	.182	.182
Dugas, Taylor	L-L	5-9	180	12-15-89	.305	.349	.290	57	174	17	53	5	2	0	17	24	3	2	2	30	3	3	.356	.394
Fiorito, Dan	R-R	6-4	215	8-20-90	.250	.600	.000	4	12	0	3	1	0	0	2	1	0	0	0	2	0	0	.333	.308
Flores, Ramon	L-L	5-10	150	3-26-92	.247	.293	.232	63	235	30	58	17	4	7	23	33	1	0	2	45	3	2	.443	.339
Garcia, Adonis	R-R	5-9	190	4-12-85	.319	.248	.349	86	342	58	109	20	3	9	45	17	4	0	5	51	11	3	.474	.353
Gil, Jose	R-R	6-0	205	9-4-86	.273	.250	.286	9	22	2	6	1	0	0	3	4	1	0	0	6	0	0	.318	.407
Joseph, Corban	L-R	6-0	180	10-28-88	.268	.179	.286	70	235	28	63	12	2	4	28	19	0	0	2	31	0	1	.387	.320
Murphy, J.R.	R-R	5-11	195	5-13-91	.246	.264	.238	51	179	17	44	9	0	6	28	13	0	1	3	42	0	0	.397	.292
Mustelier, Ronnier	R-R	5-10	210	8-8-84	.314	.333	.306	13	51	4	16	3	0	0	3	2	0	0	0	9	1	0	.373	.340
Pirela, Jose	B-R	5-11	210	11-21-89	.305	.295	.308	130	535	87	163	21	11	10	60	37	3	2	4	74	15	7	.441	.351
Refsnyder, Rob	R-R	6-1	205	3-26-91	.318	.300	.344	137	287	47	86	19	1	8	33	41	2	1	2	67	4	4	.456	.389
Richardson, Antoan	B-R	5-8	165	10-8-83	.271	.236	.281	93	258	41	70	7	4	3	22	33	14	7	5	56	26	1	.364	.380
Roller, Kyle	L-R	6-1	250	3-27-88	.283	.293	.280	104	378	59	107	24	3	17	51	49	9	0	1	125	0	0	.497	.378
Romine, Austin	R-R	6-2	215	11-22-88	.242	.230	.246	81	285	33	69	17	0	6	33	24	0	3	1	54	1	0	.365	.300
Segedin, Rob	R-R	6-2	220	11-10-88	.143	.130	.148	21	77	7	11	2	0	1	11	4	1	0	3	14	0	0	.208	.188
Sizemore, Scott	R-R	6-0	185	1-4-85	.266	.310	.248	81	289	31	77	17	5	7	41	26	2	0	2	87	0	0	.433	.329
Solarte, Yangervis	B-R	5-11	195	7-7-87	.600	1.000	.579	5	20	3	12	3	1	0	5	1	0	0	0	2	0	0	.850	.619
Toussen, Jose	R-R	6-1	155	11-13-89	.167	.000	.250	3	6	1	0	0	0	0	0	0	0	0	0	1	0	0	.167	.167
Wheeler, Zelous	R-R	5-10	220	1-16-87	.296	.330	.282	82	304	49	90	25	0	9	40	28	6	0	0	61	1	0	.467	.367
Young, Chris	R-R	6-2	200	9-5-83	.200	.000	.214	4	15	1	3	0	0	1	2	1	0	0	0	6	0	0	.400	.250

Pitching	B-T	HT	WT	DOB	W	L	ERA	G	GS	CG	SV	IP	H	R	ER	HR	BB	SO	AVG	vLH	vRH	K/9	BB/9
Aceves, Alfredo	R-R	6-2		8-12-82	0	1	3.49	7	5	0	1	28	30	13	11	1	9	24	.275	.234	.306	7.62	2.86
Banuelos, Manny	L-L	5-10	205	3-13-91	0	3	3.60	4	4	0	0	15	14	6	6	2	10	13	.241	.273	.234	7.80	6.00
Bell, Heath	R-R	6-3	250	9-29-77	0	1	7.50	5	0	0	1	6	7	5	5	1	6	8	.292	.143	.353	12.00	9.00
2-team total (10 Norfolk)					2	1	5.40	15	0	0	2	17	22	11	10	1	12	19	—	—	—	10.26	6.48
Billings, Bruce	R-R	6-0	210	11-18-85	5	5	5.06	15	15	1	0	80	89	49	45	9	27	54	.280	.281	.279	6.08	3.04
Bleich, Jeremy	L-L	6-2	200	6-18-87	0	4	6.68	11	5	0	0	31	37	24	23	2	22	24	.298	.353	.278	6.97	6.39
Burawa, Daniel	R-R	6-2	210	12-30-88	3	1	5.95	31	0	0	3	42	47	28	28	3	26	55	.275	.300	.257	11.69	5.53
Cabral, Cesar	L-L	6-3	250	2-11-89	0	0	9.45	7	0	0	0	7	6	7	7	1	11	7	.240	.273	.214	9.45	14.85

Player	B-T	HT	WT	DOB	W	L	ERA	G	GS	CG	SV	IP	H	R	ER	HR	BB	SO	AVG	vLH	vRH	K/9	BB/9
Claiborne, Preston	R-R	6-2	225	1-21-88	0	1	3.54	15	0	0	2	20	20	10	8	0	11	20	.256	.290	.234	8.85	4.87
Coello, Robert	R-R	6-5	250	11-23-84	2	1	1.69	26	0	0	4	32	21	7	6	1	21	44	.183	.200	.164	12.38	5.91
2-team total (20 Norfolk)					6	2	1.78	46	0	0	6	56	34	17	11	3	36	69	—	—		11.16	5.82
Cotham, Caleb	R-R	6-3	215	11-6-87	0	2	5.40	5	5	0	0	18	25	14	11	1	7	17	.316	.340	.281	8.35	3.44
Daley, Matt	R-R	6-2	180	6-23-82	1	2	4.54	28	0	0	9	36	43	18	18	6	8	48	.301	.313	.291	12.11	2.02
De La Cruz, Joel	B-R	6-1	190	6-9-89	3	5	4.52	17	12	0	0	66	74	43	33	6	18	38	.281	.306	.259	5.21	2.47
Escalona, Edgmer	R-R	6-4	235	10-6-86	1	2	2.08	19	1	0	4	30	26	9	7	1	5	23	.236	.256	.225	6.82	1.48
2-team total (6 Norfolk)					2	4	3.71	25	4	0	4	51	53	23	21	5	10	37	—	—		6.53	1.76
Gerritse, Brett	R-R	6-4	220	3-4-91	0	0	0.00	1	0	0	0	2	0	0	0	0	0	0	.000	.000	.000	0.00	0.00
Gordon, Brian	L-R	6-0	190	8-16-78	4	6	4.75	14	13	0	0	78	89	46	41	7	28	50	.288	.301	.275	5.79	3.24
Greene, Shane	R-R	6-4	210	11-17-88	5	2	4.61	15	13	0	0	66	79	39	34	3	26	57	.295	.317	.275	7.73	3.53
Heredia, Jairo	R-R	6-1	190	10-8-89	1	0	7.53	5	1	0	0	14	22	13	12	0	10	16	.338	.345	.333	10.05	6.28
Herndon, David	R-R	6-5	200	9-4-85	0	2	12.96	5	1	0	0	8	17	12	12	1	3	1	.415	.429	.407	1.08	3.24
Hill, Rich	L-L	6-5	220	3-11-80	0	0	0.00	4	0	0	0	4	2	0	0	0	1	10	.133	.333	.083	22.50	2.25
2-team total (25 Pawtucket)					3	3	2.93	29	0	0	2	43	31	15	14	0	18	55	—	—		11.51	3.77
Kelley, Shawn	R-R	6-2	220	4-26-84	0	0	0.00	1	1	0	0	1	1	0	0	0	0	0	.250	.000	.500	0.00	0.00
Leroux, Chris	L-R	6-6	225	4-14-84	6	4	4.94	12	11	1	0	58	58	35	32	6	21	49	.259	.304	.221	7.56	3.24
Lewis, Freddy	L-L	6-2	210	12-16-86	0	0	7.71	8	0	0	0	9	18	10	8	1	3	8	.429	.533	.370	7.71	2.89
Miller, Jim	R-R	6-1	200	4-28-82	4	4	3.30	36	0	0	2	57	56	24	21	3	20	60	.252	.296	.218	9.42	3.14
Mitchell, Bryan	L-R	6-3	205	4-19-91	4	2	3.67	9	8	0	0	42	45	18	17	5	16	34	.281	.302	.268	7.34	3.46
Montgomery, Mark	R-R	5-11	205	8-30-90	1	1	3.03	22	0	0	2	30	21	12	10	2	18	34	.198	.245	.158	10.31	5.46
Moreno, Diego	R-R	6-1	177	7-21-87	2	3	4.86	30	1	0	2	46	62	25	25	2	15	42	.320	.295	.340	8.16	2.91
Nuding, Zach	R-R	6-4	260	3-29-90	3	5	5.07	14	13	0	0	71	88	44	40	8	22	46	.309	.368	.241	5.83	2.79
Pinder, Branden	R-R	6-3	225	1-26-89	1	0	3.78	13	0	0	1	17	17	7	7	2	5	12	.270	.280	.263	6.48	2.70
Pineda, Michael	R-R	6-7	265	1-18-89	0	1	1.17	2	2	0	0	8	9	1	1	0	1	11	.281	.235	.333	12.91	1.17
Ramirez, Jose	R-R	6-3	190	1-21-90	3	0	1.46	9	0	0	1	12	13	4	2	0	10	16	.265	.190	.321	11.68	7.30
Rondon, Francisco	L-L	6-0	190	4-19-88	3	1	3.32	12	0	0	0	19	18	9	7	2	13	20	.269	.308	.244	9.47	6.16
Rumbelow, Nick	R-R	6-0	190	9-6-91	0	1	4.02	10	0	0	1	16	17	7	7	2	5	19	.274	.200	.344	10.91	2.87
Ruth, Eric	R-R	6-0	195	9-26-90	0	0	1.80	1	1	0	0	5	2	1	1	1	3	3	.118	.222	.000	5.40	5.40
Stoneburner, Graham	R-R	6-0	205	9-29-87	0	0	2.00	3	1	0	0	9	8	3	2	1	2	7	.235	.267	.211	7.00	2.00
Tateyama, Yoshinori	R-R	5-10	165	12-26-75	0	1	6.08	9	0	0	0	13	16	9	9	1	3	17	.286	.357	.214	11.48	2.03
Tracy, Matt	L-L	6-3	215	11-26-88	1	6	4.45	12	11	0	1	63	74	38	31	6	21	39	.298	.288	.303	5.60	3.02
Turley, Nik	L-L	6-4	195	9-11-89	5	3	4.62	13	12	0	0	60	55	36	31	8	43	44	.246	.255	.243	6.56	6.41
Venditte, Pat	R-B	6-1	180	6-30-85	2	5	3.36	26	2	0	0	56	54	21	21	4	17	53	.250	.250	.250	8.47	2.72
Webb, Tyler	R-L	6-6	225	7-20-90	2	0	4.05	17	0	0	1	20	17	10	9	3	7	26	.221	.308	.176	11.70	3.15
Whitley, Chase	R-R	6-3	215	6-14-89	3	2	2.01	10	6	0	0	31	22	7	7	0	8	37	.196	.226	.160	10.63	2.30

Fielding

Catcher	PCT	G	PO	A	E	DP	PB
Arcia	.986	31	200	16	3	2	6
Cervelli	1.000	2	11	1	0	0	0
Gil	.983	9	58	1	1	0	0
Murphy	.995	46	366	22	2	4	7
Romine	.990	62	472	32	5	4	10

First Base	PCT	G	PO	A	E	DP
Arcia	1.000	5	37	1	0	0
Canzler	.977	17	113	14	3	10
Flores	1.000	3	27	2	0	4
Joseph	.995	24	173	21	1	13
Pirela	1.000	12	91	5	0	6
Roller	.993	68	531	22	4	48
Romine	.991	13	101	4	1	
11 Sizemore	1.000	6	43	1	0	1

Second Base	PCT	G	PO	A	E	DP
Anna	1.000	2	3	9	0	1
Fiorito	1.000	1	0	4	0	0

	PCT	G	PO	A	E	DP
Joseph	.960	12	14	34	2	3
Pirela	.979	60	119	161	6	32
Refsnyder	.988	64	98	144	3	34
Sizemore	.882	6	3	12	2	1
Wheeler	1.000	3	3	7	0	1

Third Base	PCT	G	PO	A	E	DP
Arcia	—	1	0	0	0	0
Canzler	.750	5	3	3	2	0
Fiorito	.889	3	1	7	1	1
Garcia	.897	19	7	28	4	1
Joseph	.667	2	0	2	1	0
Segedin	.983	20	12	47	1	6
Sizemore	.939	60	32	91	8	7
Solarte	1.000	4	2	6	0	2
Toussen	.857	2	2	4	1	1
Wheeler	.987	33	28	50	1	8

Shortstop	PCT	G	PO	A	E	DP
Angelini	.970	81	118	206	10	33

	PCT	G	PO	A	E	DP
Anna	.926	34	42	71	9	15
Fiorito	1.000	1	2	1	0	0
Pirela	.947	8	6	12	1	3
Solarte	1.000	1	2	5	0	1
Wheeler	.926	26	28	60	7	7

Outfield	PCT	G	PO	A	E	DP
Almonte	.980	96	191	4	4	0
Arcia	—	1	0	0	0	0
Canzler	.933	8	14	0	1	0
Dugas	.990	54	97	2	1	0
Flores	.967	56	108	8	4	3
Garcia	.984	61	120	7	2	0
Joseph	—	1	0	0	0	0
Mustelier	1.000	5	6	0	0	0
Pirela	.981	50	96	5	2	0
Refsnyder	1.000	9	14	0	0	0
Richardson	.973	88	214	0	6	0
Wheeler	1.000	17	25	3	0	2
Young	1.000	3	6	0	0	0

TRENTON THUNDER   DOUBLE-A

EASTERN LEAGUE

Batting	B-T	HT	WT	DOB	AVG	vLH	vRH	G	AB	R	H	2B	3B	HR	RBI	BB	HBP	SH	SF	SO	SB	CS	SLG	OBP
Angelini, Carmen	R-R	6-2	190	9-22-88	.135	.189	.096	26	89	4	12	5	0	0	6	8	0	1	1	21	1	1	.191	.204
Arcia, Francisco	B-R	5-11	195	9-14-89	.320	.385	.296	26	97	5	31	6	1	1	16	5	0	0	2	16	0	1	.433	.346
Austin, Tyler	R-R	6-1	220	9-6-91	.275	.266	.280	105	396	56	109	26	5	9	47	36	2	0	3	80	3	2	.419	.336
Bichette Jr., Dante	R-R	6-1	215	9-26-92	.224	.200	.234	18	67	7	15	3	0	1	4	6	1	0	0	11	0	0	.313	.297
Bird, Greg	L-R	6-3	215	11-9-92	.253	.324	.207	27	95	16	24	8	0	7	11	18	2	0	1	27	0	0	.558	.379
Blaser, Tyson	R-R	6-2	225	12-8-87	.233	.379	.136	21	73	10	17	4	0	0	4	3	0	0	0	23	0	0	.288	.263
Castillo, Ali	R-R	5-10	165	6-19-89	.254	.311	.225	120	410	46	104	18	3	2	42	36	3	10	1	45	17	5	.327	.318
Cave, Jake	L-L	6-0	180	12-4-92	.273	.239	.295	42	176	24	48	10	5	4	18	18	1	2	0	44	2	3	.455	.344
Cervelli, Francisco	R-R	6-1	225	3-6-86	.133	.125	.143	5	15	2	2	0	0	0	0	4	0	0	0	4	0	0	.133	.350
Dugas, Taylor	L-L	5-9	180	12-15-89	.294	.298	.292	54	177	22	52	10	5	1	23	23	10	4	1	29	4	1	.424	.403
Fiorito, Dan	R-R	6-4	215	8-20-90	.232	.294	.200	102	366	39	85	19	3	4	37	27	2	3	0	71	1	0	.333	.289
Gamel, Ben	L-L	5-11	185	5-17-92	.261	.292	.245	131	544	58	142	31	3	2	51	36	2	1	3	88	13	5	.340	.308
Heathcott, Slade	L-L	6-1	190	9-28-90	.182	.250	.160	9	33	4	6	2	0	0	1	3	0	0	0	13	0	1	.242	.250

	B-T	HT	WT	DOB	AVG	vLH	vRH	G	AB	R	H	2B	3B	HR	RBI	BB	HBP	SH	SF	SO	SB	CS	SLG	OBP
O'Brien, Pete	R-R	6-3	215	7-15-90	.245	.265	.233	72	274	47	67	14	1	23	51	16	4	0	0	77	0	0	.555	.296
Refsnyder, Rob	R-R	6-1	205	3-26-91	.342	.418	.302	60	228	35	78	19	5	6	30	14	2	0	0	38	5	5	.548	.385
Roller, Kyle	L-R	6-1	250	3-27-88	.385	.318	.411	21	78	18	30	6	0	9	23	9	2	0	1	21	1	0	.808	.456
Ryan, Brendan	R-R	6-2	195	3-26-82	.364	.286	.500	3	11	3	4	0	0	0	2	0	0	0	0	1	0	0	.364	.462
Sanchez, Gary	R-R	6-3	235	12-2-92	.270	.297	.255	110	429	48	116	19	0	13	65	43	2	0	3	91	1	1	.406	.338
Sanchez, Yeral	R-R	6-0	210	7-18-85	.167	.233	.119	29	102	13	17	4	0	1	9	7	2	0	0	31	0	0	.235	.234
Segedin, Rob	R-R	6-2	220	11-10-88	.283	.296	.278	92	325	46	92	21	1	8	49	52	13	0	4	60	1	0	.428	.398
Stevenson, Casey	L-R	6-3	200	5-18-88	.204	.179	.211	50	162	20	33	8	0	1	20	16	3	0	6	26	2	0	.272	.278
Toussen, Jose	R-R	6-1	155	11-13-89	.226	.172	.273	19	62	5	14	3	0	0	5	2	0	0	1	12	3	1	.274	.246
Williams, Mason	L-R	6-1	180	8-21-91	.223	.231	.219	128	507	67	113	18	4	5	40	47	1	7	1	68	21	8	.304	.290
Wilson, Zach	R-R	6-1	210	8-6-90	.216	.167	.239	28	97	12	21	4	1	2	12	10	0	0	2	30	0	0	.340	.284

Pitching

	B-T	HT	WT	DOB	W	L	ERA	G	GS	CG	SV	IP	H	R	ER	HR	BB	SO	AVG	vLH	vRH	K/9	BB/9
Banuelos, Manny	L-L	5-10	205	3-13-91	1	3	4.59	17	16	0	0	49	40	28	25	8	19	44	.220	.176	.230	8.08	3.49
Barreda, Manuel	R-R	5-11	195	10-8-88	4	1	3.40	30	0	0	1	50	47	20	19	5	26	58	.250	.185	.299	10.37	4.65
Billings, Bruce	R-R	6-0	210	11-18-85	0	0	0.00	1	1	0	0	1	2	0	0	0	0	0	.500	.333	1.000	0.00	0.00
Bleich, Jeremy	L-L	6-2	200	4-26-87	5	6	3.39	15	15	0	0	80	72	42	30	8	27	68	.233	.163	.260	7.68	3.05
Burawa, Daniel	R-R	6-2	210	12-30-88	0	0	1.59	11	0	0	1	17	13	4	3	0	4	18	.210	.235	.200	9.53	2.12
Cabral, Cesar	L-L	6-3	250	2-11-89	1	3	5.63	25	0	0	0	32	30	25	20	2	23	37	.250	.256	.247	10.41	6.47
Camarena, Daniel	L-L	6-0	200	11-9-92	2	6	5.07	10	10	0	0	55	61	32	31	8	14	43	.284	.200	.306	7.04	2.29
Cotham, Caleb	R-R	6-3	215	11-6-87	0	2	6.04	5	5	0	0	25	25	17	17	3	13	16	.269	.200	.310	5.68	4.62
De La Cruz, Joel	B-R	6-1	190	6-9-89	4	4	4.34	11	10	0	0	56	60	31	27	3	19	39	.278	.330	.227	6.27	3.05
Dott, Aaron	R-L	6-5	210	5-17-88	0	0	3.91	21	0	0	0	25	21	11	11	0	9	17	.228	.179	.250	6.04	3.20
Garrison, Taylor	R-R	5-11	165	5-24-90	4	2	3.46	24	1	0	2	39	32	17	15	2	15	26	.232	.232	.232	6.00	3.46
Goody, Nick	B-R	5-11	195	7-6-91	0	3	6.75	15	0	0	0	16	20	12	12	3	10	19	.313	.227	.357	10.69	5.63
Heredia, Jairo	R-R	6-1	190	10-8-89	4	1	3.53	26	10	0	0	71	71	30	28	2	19	77	.261	.281	.247	9.71	2.40
Kelley, Shawn	R-R	6-2	220	4-26-84	0	0	0.00	1	1	0	0	1	0	0	0	0	1	2	.000	—	.000	27.00	13.50
Kimball, Cole	R-R	6-3	240	8-1-85	0	2	4.73	18	0	0	1	27	19	14	14	2	18	28	.209	.293	.140	9.45	6.08
Lewis, Freddy	L-L	6-2	210	12-16-86	1	3	6.56	19	0	0	2	23	28	18	17	1	28	23	.315	.259	.339	8.87	10.80
Lindgren, Jacob	L-L	5-11	180	3-12-93	1	1	3.86	8	0	0	0	12	6	6	5	0	9	18	.154	.133	.167	13.89	6.94
Long, Jaron	R-R	6-0	185	8-28-91	7	2	2.35	11	10	0	0	69	62	22	18	2	11	50	.237	.206	.258	6.52	1.43
McNamara, Dillon	R-R	6-5	220	10-6-91	0	1	12.00	1	1	0	0	3	2	4	4	0	1	4	.182	.200	.167	12.00	3.00
Mitchell, Bryan	L-R	6-3	205	4-19-91	2	5	4.84	14	13	0	0	61	64	36	33	6	29	60	.268	.230	.302	8.80	4.26
Montgomery, Mark	R-R	5-11	205	8-30-90	1	0	0.83	17	0	0	2	22	13	5	2	1	8	17	.178	.115	.213	7.06	3.32
Moreno, Diego	R-R	6-1	177	7-21-87	1	0	0.79	8	0	0	6	11	5	1	1	0	2	13	.132	.059	.190	10.32	1.59
Nuding, Zach	R-R	6-4	260	3-29-90	7	2	2.71	14	12	1	0	83	70	26	25	7	21	60	.226	.233	.220	7.27	2.28
Pazos, James	R-L	6-3	230	5-5-91	0	1	1.50	28	0	0	6	42	28	7	7	0	19	42	.190	.163	.204	9.00	4.07
Pinder, Branden	R-R	6-3	225	1-26-89	2	0	0.56	12	0	0	4	16	7	1	1	0	2	18	.130	.118	.135	10.13	1.13
Rondon, Francisco	L-L	6-0	190	4-19-88	3	2	3.69	17	1	0	1	32	20	13	13	3	13	22	.183	.083	.212	6.25	3.69
Rumbelow, Nick	R-R	6-0	190	9-6-91	0	0	3.68	7	0	0	1	7	4	4	3	0	1	15	.148	.100	.176	18.41	1.23
Ruth, Eric	R-R	6-0	195	9-26-90	0	0	5.54	3	3	0	0	13	12	9	8	0	6	7	.250	.190	.296	4.85	4.15
Sabathia, C.C.	L-L	6-7	285	7-21-80	0	1	7.36	1	1	0	0	4	5	5	3	0	1	2	.333	.000	.417	4.91	2.45
Severino, Luis	R-R	6-0	195	2-20-94	2	2	2.52	6	6	0	0	25	20	8	7	1	6	29	.213	.250	.190	10.44	2.16
Short, Charlie	R-R	6-0	210	8-13-88	1	2	8.53	7	1	0	0	13	25	12	12	1	2	7	.417	.478	.378	4.97	1.42
Stoneburner, Graham	R-R	6-0	205	9-29-87	2	4	7.04	10	6	0	0	46	61	39	36	4	15	24	.319	.310	.327	4.70	2.93
Tracy, Matt	L-L	6-3	215	11-26-88	8	2	3.26	16	15	0	0	88	97	35	32	3	34	50	.285	.304	.280	5.09	3.46
Venditte, Pat	R-B	6-1	180	6-30-85	0	1	0.82	15	0	0	1	22	11	3	2	2	5	30	.143	.080	.173	12.27	2.05
Webb, Tyler	R-L	6-6	225	7-20-90	1	6	4.04	23	0	0	7	36	35	16	16	2	14	51	.255	.225	.268	12.87	3.53
Wetherall, Phil	R-R	6-5	225	10-9-89	0	4	4.25	27	0	0	1	42	48	27	20	1	21	31	.286	.323	.264	6.59	4.46
Wooten, Eric	L-L	6-3	190	3-18-90	3	3	4.08	7	4	0	0	40	40	21	18	3	11	21	.260	.107	.294	4.76	2.50

Fielding

Catcher	PCT	G	PO	A	E	DP	PB
Arcia	.980	17	135	10	3	1	1
Blaser	.989	12	79	8	1	0	0
Cervelli	1.000	2	14	0	0	0	1
O'Brien	.978	19	123	11	3	1	6
Sanchez	.980	93	737	94	17	8	10

First Base	PCT	G	PO	A	E	DP
Arcia	.961	10	68	6	3	5
Austin	1.000	19	164	9	0	14
Bird	.992	24	234	9	2	15
Blaser	1.000	4	29	0	0	4
Cervelli	1.000	2	16	0	0	0
Fiorito	.988	26	227	13	3	17
O'Brien	.996	27	241	9	1	19
Roller	.989	19	169	12	2	12
Segedin	1.000	5	43	1	0	7
Stevenson	1.000	2	2	0	0	0

	PCT	G	PO	A	E	DP	PB
Wilson	.989	10	84	5	1	8	

Second Base	PCT	G	PO	A	E	DP
Castillo	.972	10	13	22	1	7
Fiorito	.955	27	39	67	5	13
Refsnyder	.968	58	116	158	9	33
Stevenson	.966	42	62	109	6	23
Toussen	.976	10	13	28	1	6

Third Base	PCT	G	PO	A	E	DP
Austin	.862	8	8	17	4	1
Bichette Jr.	.979	15	12	34	1	2
Castillo	1.000	2	2	3	0	0
Fiorito	.953	45	27	94	6	6
Segedin	.955	73	55	176	11	15
Stevenson	1.000	1	0	2	0	0
Toussen	1.000	2	2	2	0	0

Shortstop	PCT	G	PO	A	E	DP
Angelini	.969	23	28	67	3	14
Castillo	.973	109	154	313	13	58
Fiorito	1.000	7	12	18	0	7
Ryan	.917	3	3	8	1	1

Outfield	PCT	G	PO	A	E	DP
Austin	.974	59	109	4	3	2
Cave	.985	35	65	0	1	0
Dugas	.960	47	69	3	3	0
Gamel	.984	112	180	6	3	2
Heathcott	1.000	8	10	1	0	0
O'Brien	.889	5	8	0	1	0
Sanchez	.980	25	48	0	1	0
Stevenson	1.000	6	12	0	0	0
Toussen	.917	6	9	2	1	0
Williams	.990	118	278	7	3	1
Wilson	1.000	10	13	0	0	0

TAMPA YANKEES — HIGH CLASS A

FLORIDA STATE LEAGUE

Batting	B-T	HT	WT	DOB	AVG	vLH	vRH	G	AB	R	H	2B	3B	HR	RBI	BB	HBP	SH	SF	SO	SB	CS	SLG	OBP
Bichette Jr., Dante	R-R	6-1	215	9-26-92	.271	.330	.252	109	402	56	109	27	1	9	64	50	3	0	5	90	1	3	.410	.352

Name	B-T	HT	WT	DOB	AVG	vLH	vRH	G	AB	R	H	2B	3B	HR	RBI	BB	HBP	SH	SF	SO	SB	CS	OBP	SLG
Bird, Greg	L-R	6-3	215	11-9-92	.277	.167	.326	75	274	36	76	22	1	7	32	45	1	0	5	70	1	0	.442	.375
Calderon, Yeicok	L-L	6-2	185	12-23-91	.244	.222	.253	33	123	10	30	11	1	2	16	3	1	1	1	41	2	0	.398	.266
Cave, Jake	L-L	6-0	180	12-4-92	.304	.286	.311	90	385	50	117	18	4	3	24	28	2	1	0	80	10	3	.395	.354
Cervelli, Francisco	R-R	6-1	205	3-6-86	.000	.000	.000	2	6	0	0	0	0	0	0	0	0	0	1	0	0	0	.000	.143
Culver, Cito	R-R	6-0	190	8-26-92	.220	.215	.223	132	508	68	112	21	3	5	48	57	1	7	5	141	12	4	.303	.298
Custodio, Claudio	R-R	5-10	155	10-30-90	.208	.250	.195	53	168	20	35	6	1	0	14	8	2	7	0	58	21	2	.256	.253
Feliz, Anderson	B-R	6-0	175	5-11-92	.190	.250	.175	23	79	7	15	1	1	2	12	4	0	1	2	24	1	1	.304	.224
Ford, Mike	L-R	6-0	225	7-4-92	.354	.357	.353	12	48	7	17	4	0	2	10	4	0	0	0	7	0	0	.563	.404
Garrison, Trent	L-R	6-0	185	5-24-90	.254	.136	.277	82	279	29	71	12	0	1	26	22	1	1	1	44	0	1	.308	.310
Grice, Cody	R-R	6-0	220	1-19-90	.163	.222	.114	25	80	4	13	1	1	0	7	4	0	2	0	29	2	3	.200	.202
Gumbs, Angelo	R-R	6-0	175	10-13-92	.224	.223	.224	90	331	28	74	15	3	5	28	18	2	2	1	97	7	1	.332	.267
Haddad, Radley	L-R	6-1	190	5-11-90	.500	—	.500	1	4	1	2	0	0	0	0	0	0	0	0	1	0	0	.500	.500
Higashioka, Kyle	R-R	6-0	200	4-20-90	.231	.375	.000	9	26	5	6	3	0	1	2	4	0	0	1	4	0	0	.462	.323
Jagielo, Eric	L-R	6-2	195	5-17-92	.259	.239	.267	85	309	43	80	14	0	16	54	38	9	0	3	93	0	0	.460	.354
Judge, Aaron	R-R	6-7	230	4-26-92	.283	.328	.266	66	233	44	66	9	2	8	33	50	1	0	1	72	0	0	.442	.411
Leonora, Ericson	R-R	5-11	175	8-25-92	.203	.111	.250	22	79	9	16	1	1	2	7	3	1	0	0	26	1	0	.316	.241
Nunez, Reymond	R-R	6-4	210	9-25-90	.211	.214	.209	44	152	16	32	9	0	5	22	8	0	1	0	41	0	0	.368	.248
O'Brien, Pete	R-R	6-3	215	7-15-90	.321	.345	.313	30	112	19	36	9	1	10	19	4	2	0	1	29	0	0	.688	.353
Oh, Danny	L-L	6-0	190	12-28-89	.265	.289	.258	49	162	23	43	6	2	0	17	24	2	0	1	30	2	2	.327	.365
Payton, Mark	L-L	5-7	165	12-7-91	.286	.240	.303	26	91	14	26	11	1	2	8	16	2	0	2	17	3	2	.495	.396
Rosario, Jose	R-R	5-11	160	11-29-91	.320	.243	.362	53	197	19	63	7	4	0	21	15	3	1	0	25	1	6	.396	.377
Ryan, Brendan	R-R	6-2	195	3-26-82	.286	.000	.364	4	14	1	4	0	0	0	2	3	0	0	0	3	0	0	.286	.412
Snyder, Matt	L-R	6-5	200	6-17-90	.287	.308	.278	47	178	18	51	15	0	3	25	10	4	0	0	42	0	0	.421	.339
Toussen, Jose	R-R	6-1	155	11-13-89	.234	.276	.215	30	94	11	22	4	0	0	6	10	0	4	0	26	5	2	.277	.308
Wilson, Wes	R-R	6-0	210	8-18-89	.167	.119	.214	26	84	4	14	3	0	0	6	9	6	1	0	25	1	0	.202	.293
Wilson, Zach	R-R	6-1	210	8-6-90	.266	.283	.260	52	192	20	51	7	4	4	23	11	2	1	4	44	0	0	.406	.306

Pitching

Name	B-T	HT	WT	DOB	W	L	ERA	G	GS	CG	SV	IP	H	R	ER	HR	BB	SO	AVG	vLH	vRH	K/9	BB/9
Banuelos, Manny	L-L	5-10	205	3-13-91	0	0	2.84	5	5	0	0	13	10	4	4	0	2	14	.213	.200	.222	9.95	1.42
Benjamin, Ramon	R-L	6-1	195	6-14-87	0	2	3.75	22	0	0	1	36	37	19	15	1	19	34	.278	.261	.287	8.50	4.75
Callahan, Derek	L-L	6-4	205	12-29-92	0	0	2.25	1	1	0	0	4	5	3	1	0	1	2	.278	.000	.333	4.50	2.25
Camarena, Daniel	L-L	6-0	200	11-9-92	5	5	2.35	16	16	0	0	88	77	37	23	6	28	69	.230	.234	.228	7.06	2.86
Clarkin, Ian	L-L	6-2	190	2-14-95	1	0	1.80	1	1	0	0	5	7	1	1	0	1	4	.368	—	.368	7.20	1.80
Cotham, Caleb	R-R	6-3	215	11-6-87	0	0	0.00	4	0	0	0	4	3	0	0	0	0	5	.200	.000	.273	10.38	0.00
De Paula, Rafael	R-R	6-2	215	3-24-91	6	5	4.15	20	17	0	0	89	88	44	41	5	38	104	.257	.245	.266	10.52	3.84
Enns, Dietrich	L-L	6-1	195	5-16-91	3	2	1.42	13	1	0	0	25	16	4	4	1	10	26	.184	.138	.207	9.24	3.55
Garrison, Taylor	R-R	5-11	165	5-24-90	0	0	2.25	10	0	0	0	28	23	7	7	2	8	32	.228	.261	.200	10.29	2.57
Gerritse, Brett	R-R	6-4	220	3-4-91	5	7	4.00	25	12	0	1	92	103	53	41	5	27	53	.281	.298	.265	5.17	2.63
Goody, Nick	B-R	5-11	195	7-6-91	2	0	2.35	12	4	0	0	15	10	4	4	1	5	27	.182	.172	.192	15.85	2.93
Haynes, Kyle	R-R	6-2	190	2-11-91	5	5	3.49	39	0	0	1	70	71	37	27	1	33	55	.262	.276	.252	7.11	4.26
Hebert, Chaz	L-L	6-2	180	9-4-92	0	2	4.05	3	3	0	0	13	15	7	6	0	2	8	.288	.167	.325	5.40	1.35
Hissong, Travis	R-R	6-0	195	7-19-91	0	0	0.00	1	0	0	0	2	0	0	0	0	3	1	.000	.000	.000	5.40	16.20
Kendrick, Conner	L-L	6-1	185	8-18-92	6	8	5.78	19	16	0	0	76	95	52	49	5	34	62	.306	.321	.298	7.31	4.01
Lail, Brady	R-R	6-2	175	8-9-93	3	1	3.38	7	6	0	0	37	30	14	14	2	9	21	.222	.211	.231	5.06	2.17
Lindgren, Jacob	L-L	5-11	180	3-12-93	0	0	0.00	6	0	0	0	7	3	1	0	0	4	17	.111	.000	.136	20.86	4.91
Long, Jaron	R-R	6-0	185	8-28-91	2	2	2.77	6	4	0	0	26	18	8	8	2	3	26	.189	.176	.205	9.00	1.04
Lopez, Stefan	R-R	6-2	190	6-4-91	1	1	8.03	17	0	0	0	25	32	25	22	2	8	25	.317	.309	.326	9.12	2.92
Morban, Jhon	R-R	6-4	190	6-3-92	0	2	11.57	2	2	0	0	7	9	10	9	0	4	4	.321	.273	.353	5.14	5.14
Noteware, Mike	R-R	6-0	190	9-16-90	0	0	9.00	1	0	0	0	1	1	2	1	0	1	1	.200	.000	1.000	9.00	9.00
Pazos, James	R-L	6-3	230	5-5-91	0	2	3.96	18	1	0	4	25	23	13	11	0	6	33	.237	.250	.231	11.88	2.16
Pena, Jose	R-R	6-0	190	3-22-91	0	0	2.00	2	0	0	0	5	0	0	0	0	2	3	.000		.000	5.40	3.60
Rumbelow, Nick	R-R	6-0	190	9-6-91	5	1	2.39	19	0	0	1	26	20	7	7	0	8	29	.215	.200	.226	9.91	2.73
Rutckyj, Evan	R-L	6-5	213	1-31-92	1	0	3.65	12	0	0	0	12	13	9	5	0	15	12	.271	.231	.286	8.76	10.95
Ruth, Eric	R-R	6-0	195	9-26-90	2	1	4.44	7	1	0	0	24	24	13	12	0	5	24	.261	.222	.298	8.88	1.85
Sabathia, C.C.	L-L	6-7	285	7-21-80	0	0	7.71	1	1	0	0	2	3	2	2	0	1	2	.273	.167	.400	7.71	3.86
Severino, Luis	R-R	6-0	195	2-20-94	1	1	1.31	4	4	0	0	21	11	4	3	0	6	28	.151	.065	.214	12.19	2.61
Smith, Alex	R-R	6-0	190	9-29-89	5	5	2.74	46	0	0	7	66	56	23	20	3	21	60	.237	.243	.213	8.22	2.88
Smith, Caleb	R-L	6-2	175	7-28-91	5	2	4.81	9	9	0	0	39	39	22	21	2	11	36	.252	.298	.231	8.24	2.52
Smith, Chris	R-R	6-2	185	8-19-88	0	1	2.70	26	0	0	0	43	36	16	13	3	12	38	.225	.229	.222	7.89	2.49
Sulbaran, Miguel	L-L	5-10	209	3-19-94	4	5	3.52	22	20	0	0	115	106	53	45	6	30	85	.238	.200	.257	6.65	2.35
Vargas, Cesar	R-R	6-1	160	12-30-91	4	0	2.48	27	0	0	11	40	26	14	11	3	7	45	.184	.203	.167	10.13	1.58
Walby, Philip	L-R	6-2	190	7-24-92	0	1	3.07	10	0	0	0	15	10	5	5	0	10	10	.192	.167	.206	6.14	6.14
Webb, Tyler	R-L	6-6	225	7-20-90	0	0	2.77	4	0	0	0	13	7	4	4	0	1	17	.152	.167	.143	11.77	0.69
Wetherell, Phil	R-R	6-5	225	10-9-89	1	3	0.39	18	0	0	3	23	18	7	1	0	9	21	.205	.306	.135	8.10	3.47
Woods, Zach	R-R	6-0	190	11-15-87	1	1	4.05	9	0	0	0	13	11	7	6	0	5	17	.204	.174	.226	11.48	3.38
Wooten, Eric	L-L	6-3	190	3-18-90	2	2	3.25	10	9	0	0	53	61	27	19	2	10	35	.295	.119	.365	5.98	1.71

Fielding

Catcher	PCT	G	PO	A	E	DP	PB
Cervelli	1.000	1	11	0	0	0	0
Garrison	.988	82	594	59	8	3	11
Haddad	1.000	1	8	2	0	1	0
Higashioka	1.000	9	71	7	0	1	0
O'Brien	.986	24	195	10	3	2	7
Wilson	.996	26	215	16	1	1	2

First Base	PCT	G	PO	A	E	DP
Bichette Jr.	1.000	1	0	0	0	0
Bird	.989	61	519	36	6	46
Ford	1.000	8	56	4	0	7
Nunez	.975	40	330	26	9	24
Oh	1.000	3	11	0	0	0
Snyder	.989	19	172	7	2	14
Toussen	1.000	2	11	1	0	1
Wilson	1.000	8	55	6	0	6

Second Base	PCT	G	PO	A	E	DP
Custodio	.971	14	19	48	2	7
Feliz	1.000	1	1	2	0	0
Gumbs	.982	90	158	231	7	48
Rosario	.963	30	49	80	5	15
Toussen	.902	8	17	20	4	2

Third Base	PCT	G	PO	A	E	DP
Bichette Jr.	.927	67	29	111	11	6
Custodio	.750	2	0	3	1	0
Ford	1.000	2	1	0	0	0
Jagielo	.887	62	36	90	16	5
Rosario	.842	8	4	12	3	1
Toussen	.750	3	3	3	2	0

Shortstop	PCT	G	PO	A	E	DP
Culver	.966	130	196	404	21	70

	PCT	G	PO	A	E	DP
Custodio	.964	5	12	15	1	1
Rosario	1.000	1	3	0	0	0
Ryan	1.000	4	9	13	0	4

Outfield	PCT	G	PO	A	E	DP
Calderon	.978	29	44	0	1	0
Cave	.985	89	194	3	3	0
Custodio	.987	33	68	7	1	2
Feliz	.969	20	30	1	1	0
Grice	.907	24	39	0	4	0

	PCT	G	PO	A	E	DP
Judge	.969	61	120	4	4	2
Leonora	.958	20	23	0	1	0
O'Brien	1.000	6	11	2	0	2
Oh	.988	41	79	2	1	0
Payton	.981	24	52	0	1	0
Rosario	1.000	16	20	1	0	0
Toussen	.919	19	30	4	3	
2 Wilson	.913	42	63	0	6	0

CHARLESTON (SC) RIVERDOGS   LOW CLASS A
SOUTH ATLANTIC LEAGUE

Batting	B-T	HT	WT	DOB	AVG	vLH	vRH	G	AB	R	H	2B	3B	HR	RBI	BB	HBP	SH	SF	SO	SB	CS	SLG	OBP
Andujar, Miguel	R-R	6-0	175	3-2-95	.267	.188	.295	127	484	75	129	25	4	10	70	35	3	2	3	83	5	1	.397	.318
Avelino, Abiatal	R-R	5-11	186	2-14-95	.232	.216	.237	53	220	31	51	12	1	2	12	17	3	2	0	44	11	5	.323	.296
Calderon, Yeicok	L-L	6-2	185	12-23-91	.318	.160	.383	24	85	16	27	4	0	3	15	12	0	0	2	19	1	1	.471	.394
Custodio, Claudio	R-R	5-10	155	10-30-90	.321	.250	.364	13	53	8	17	4	0	1	5	2	0	0	0	12	1	0	.453	.345
de Oleo, Eduardo	R-R	5-10	164	1-25-93	.214	.205	.218	78	271	33	58	5	0	12	41	23	1	0	6	71	1	0	.365	.272
Ford, Mike	L-R	6-0	225	7-4-92	.283	.261	.291	93	325	40	92	15	2	11	46	48	5	0	3	39	2	0	.443	.381
Fowler, Dustin	L-L	6-0	185	12-29-94	.257	.268	.253	66	257	33	66	13	6	9	41	13	0	1	1	53	3	2	.459	.292
Jones, Bubba	L-R	6-1	205	8-20-92	.219	.167	.231	9	32	1	7	4	0	0	2	2	0	0	0	10	0	0	.344	.265
Judge, Aaron	R-R	6-7	230	4-26-92	.333	.356	.328	65	234	36	78	15	2	9	45	39	2	0	3	59	1	0	.530	.428
Katoh, Gosuke	L-R	6-2	180	10-8-94	.222	.222	.222	121	383	58	85	19	6	3	37	71	3	4	4	142	20	10	.326	.345
Lopez, Daniel	R-R	6-2	175	1-17-92	.286	.286	—	2	7	0	2	1	0	0	0	0	0	0	0	1	0	0	.429	.286
Murphy, John	L-R	5-11	185	4-2-91	.271	.317	.253	70	229	26	62	8	0	6	30	20	3	3	1	40	17	5	.306	.336
Nunez, Reymond	R-R	6-4	210	9-25-90	.234	.231	.235	33	124	22	29	11	0	5	20	9	4	0	0	36	1	0	.444	.307
O'Neill, Michael	R-R	6-1	195	6-12-92	.256	.233	.264	129	489	80	125	23	5	10	57	42	16	3	3	133	42	9	.384	.333
Oliberto, Mikeson	R-R	5-10	164	8-23-90	.186	.333	.135	22	70	6	13	6	1	1	5	5	2	0	1	24	3	1	.343	.256
Payton, Mark	L-L	5-7	165	12-7-91	.357	.222	.394	22	84	16	30	4	1	2	13	13	0	0	0	15	1	2	.500	.443
Rosario, Jose	R-R	5-11	160	11-29-91	.291	.526	.224	26	86	13	25	6	0	2	8	5	5	1	0	12	3	2	.430	.365
Sumner, Kale	R-R	5-11	205	6-16-91	.233	.303	.208	46	129	19	30	3	1	4	18	39	2	3	1	41	2	0	.364	.415
Thomas, Brandon	B-R	6-3	180	2-7-91	.204	.210	.202	93	299	43	61	11	3	5	39	41	10	1	2	96	22	4	.311	.318
Torrens, Luis	R-R	6-0	175	5-2-96	.154	.000	.235	9	26	4	4	0	0	1	3	6	2	0	0	7	0	0	.269	.353
Valera, Jackson	R-R	6-1	175	4-8-92	.261	.293	.250	63	234	16	61	11	0	0	29	12	2	2	3	30	1	0	.308	.299
Wade, Tyler	L-R	6-1	180	11-23-94	.272	.227	.288	129	507	77	138	24	6	1	51	57	6	2	4	118	22	13	.349	.350

Pitching	B-T	HT	WT	DOB	W	L	ERA	G	GS	CG	SV	IP	H	R	ER	HR	BB	SO	AVG	vLH	vRH	K/9	BB/9
Acevedo, Andury	R-R	6-4	200	8-3-92	1	1	4.38	9	0	0	0	12	13	11	6	0	12	12	.260	.353	.212	8.76	8.76
Bautista, Rony	L-L	6-7	200	9-17-91	0	1	4.76	10	0	0	0	11	12	7	6	1	11	10	.267	.214	.290	7.94	8.74
Benak, Andrew	R-R	6-5	225	1-31-90	0	1	7.15	6	0	0	0	11	14	9	9	2	7	12	.341	.308	.357	9.53	5.56
Beresford, Andy	R-R	6-7	200	2-26-90	1	2	4.35	13	7	0	0	41	42	23	20	1	12	17	.261	.365	.194	3.70	2.61
Clarkin, Ian	L-L	6-2	190	2-14-95	3	3	3.21	16	15	0	0	70	64	28	25	6	22	71	.250	.289	.233	9.13	2.83
Coshow, Cale	R-R	6-5	260	7-16-92	1	1	5.19	6	0	0	0	9	14	6	5	0	1	13	.359	.333	.400	13.50	1.04
Cote, Jordan	R-R	6-5	215	11-13-92	1	1	5.32	12	0	0	1	22	28	14	13	1	9	18	.315	.310	.319	7.36	3.68
Davis, Rookie	R-R	6-3	235	4-29-93	7	8	4.93	27	25	0	0	126	134	73	69	7	42	106	.271	.209	.317	7.53	3.00
Encinas, Gabe	R-R	6-3	195	12-21-91	0	4	5.81	11	11	0	0	31	34	23	20	2	16	29	.270	.404	.176	8.42	4.65
Gallegos, Giovanny	R-R	6-2	210	8-14-91	5	5	4.57	29	6	0	1	89	108	56	45	8	19	91	.298	.319	.286	9.24	1.93
Gerritse, Brett	R-R	6-4	220	3-4-91	1	1	3.86	3	0	0	0	5	5	2	2	2	2	6	.263	.333	.143	11.57	3.86
Hebert, Chaz	L-L	6-2	180	9-4-92	3	3	2.49	15	8	0	1	65	62	26	18	2	26	57	.248	.373	.216	7.89	3.60
Kamplain, Justin	R-L	6-0	175	2-13-93	0	0	2.78	6	6	0	0	23	17	7	7	0	11	21	.210	.200	.211	8.34	4.37
Lail, Brady	R-R	6-2	175	8-9-93	8	4	3.71	18	18	0	0	97	106	46	40	6	17	95	.275	.251	.295	8.81	1.58
Lindgren, Jacob	L-L	5-11	180	3-12-93	1	0	1.80	4	0	0	1	5	1	1	1	0	0	11	.056	.000	.071	19.80	0.00
Long, Jaron	R-R	6-0	185	8-28-91	3	1	1.64	11	4	1	0	49	44	15	9	0	8	46	.228	.239	.221	8.39	1.46
Lopez, Stefan	R-R	6-2	190	6-4-91	1	3	2.42	24	0	0	6	26	17	9	7	3	7	27	.185	.250	.150	9.35	2.42
Luis, Omar	L-L	6-0	210	10-13-92	2	4	5.71	16	3	0	0	41	41	29	26	4	30	25	.265	.320	.238	5.49	6.59
Mullee, Conor	R-R	6-3	185	2-25-88	1	0	0.54	7	0	0	0	17	8	3	1	1	5	9	.143	.111	.158	4.86	2.70
Niebla, Luis	R-R	6-4	185	1-4-91	3	1	2.23	7	5	0	0	36	33	13	9	1	5	16	.234	.245	.227	3.96	1.24
Padilla, Jonathan	R-R	5-10	175	3-30-93	1	0	4.50	1	0	0	0	4	4	2	2	0	1	3	.267	.333	.250	6.75	2.25
Rincon, Angel	R-R	6-1	180	9-26-92	7	3	3.01	26	0	0	3	69	56	25	23	2	18	56	.217	.226	.211	7.34	2.36
Rumbelow, Nick	R-R	6-0	190	9-6-91	0	0	0.00	8	0	0	5	9	4	0	0	0	4	18	.125	.000	.190	18.00	4.00
Rutckyj, Evan	R-L	6-5	213	1-31-92	4	3	3.86	22	0	0	1	37	31	17	16	2	22	46	.228	.216	.232	11.09	5.30
Ruth, Eric	R-R	6-0	195	9-26-90	2	2	2.93	25	0	0	7	46	46	16	15	4	14	56	.260	.307	.225	10.96	2.74
Severino, Luis	R-R	6-0	195	2-20-94	3	2	2.79	14	14	0	0	68	62	24	21	2	15	70	.242	.217	.260	9.31	2.00
Smith, Caleb	R-L	6-2	175	7-28-91	5	7	3.10	18	18	0	0	78	60	33	27	4	35	80	.214	.313	.163	9.19	4.02
Smith, Chris	R-R	6-2	185	8-19-88	1	1	4.50	6	0	0	1	8	9	5	4	2	2	11	.273	.444	.067	12.38	2.25
Taylor, Chad	R-R	6-0	180	3-20-89	4	2	4.50	17	0	0	4	34	36	19	17	1	15	26	.267	.265	.267	6.88	3.97
Vargas, Cesar	R-R	6-1	160	12-30-91	0	2	2.73	17	0	0	3	30	27	12	9	1	7	31	.239	.244	.236	9.40	2.12
Walby, Philip	L-R	6-2	190	7-24-92	2	3	4.66	30	0	0	6	37	27	25	19	0	32	51	.194	.203	.188	12.52	7.85

Fielding

Catcher	PCT	G	PO	A	E	DP	PB
de Oleo	.982	74	599	64	12	4	5
Sumner	.996	27	211	21	1	0	12
Torrens	1.000	9	72	9	0	0	3

	PCT	G	PO	A	E	DP	PB
Valera	.981	33	241	20	5	3	2

First Base	PCT	G	PO	A	E	DP
Ford	.989	74	600	44	7	54
Jones	1.000	9	83	1	0	6

	PCT	G	PO	A	E	DP
Murphy	.987	21	144	11	2	10
Nunez	.993	28	256	13	2	17
Sumner	1.000	2	17	0	0	0
Valera	.977	13	85	1	2	8

Second Base	PCT	G	PO	A	E	DP
Custodio	1.000	2	8	6	0	1
Katoh	.969	108	168	276	14	45
Murphy	.980	13	18	32	1	10
Rosario	.941	4	5	11	1	3
Wade	.986	15	38	34	1	8

Third Base	PCT	G	PO	A	E	DP
Andujar	.919	120	71	223	26	12
Murphy	.912	12	5	26	3	1
Rosario	1.000	2	4	2	0	1

	PCT	G	PO	A	E	DP
Sumner	.938	7	4	11	1	0
Wade	.000	1	0	0	1	0

Shortstop	PCT	G	PO	A	E	DP
Avelino	.960	41	58	110	7	24
Murphy	.870	10	6	14	3	0
Wade	.952	94	132	265	20	51

Outfield	PCT	G	PO	A	E	DP
Calderon	1.000	21	29	1	0	0
Custodio	.963	10	26	0	1	0

	PCT	G	PO	A	E	DP
Fowler	.963	60	103	1	4	0
Judge	.965	55	109	2	4	0
Lopez	1.000	2	2	0	0	0
Murphy	.882	13	14	1	2	0
O'Neill	.990	123	193	9	2	2
Oliberto	.949	22	36	1	2	0
Payton	.974	22	36	1	1	0
Rosario	.926	19	23	2	2	0
Sumner	1.000	2	1	0	0	0
Thomas	.961	84	170	3	7	0

STATEN ISLAND YANKEES

SHORT-SEASON

NEW YORK-PENN LEAGUE

Batting	B-T	HT	WT	DOB	AVG	vLH	vRH	G	AB	R	H	2B	3B	HR	RBI	BB	HBP	SH	SF	SO	SB	CS	SLG	OBP
Anderson, Jake	L-R	6-0	170	12-3-91	.229	.286	.214	14	35	4	8	0	0	2	3	0	0	1	1	11	2	2	.229	.282
Aune, Austin	L-R	6-2	190	9-6-93	.218	.122	.244	59	225	26	49	19	2	4	23	15	4	0	1	97	5	5	.373	.278
Bolasky, Devyn	L-L	5-11	185	1-24-93	.241	.356	.200	44	170	19	41	6	1	0	15	13	0	0	3	30	9	3	.288	.290
Breen, Chris	R-R	6-3	215	3-26-94	.281	.246	.293	63	224	34	63	16	5	8	28	33	3	0	3	71	0	0	.504	.376
Conde, Vince	R-R	6-0	195	10-13-93	.224	.290	.204	38	134	17	30	4	0	0	16	19	1	0	1	31	6	0	.254	.323
Estrada, Thairo	R-R	5-10	155	2-22-96	.271	.412	.214	17	59	11	16	1	0	0	2	6	1	1	0	7	8	1	.288	.348
Fleming, Billy	R-R	6-1	200	9-20-92	.235	.357	.150	9	34	4	8	1	0	0	2	1	1	0	0	10	0	0	.265	.278
Haddad, Radley	L-R	6-1	190	5-11-90	.167	.400	.077	9	18	2	3	1	0	0	2	0	0	0	0	6	0	0	.222	.250
Javier, Jose	R-R	5-10	160	9-16-92	.241	.103	.279	40	133	19	32	4	1	2	16	11	3	2	0	28	8	3	.331	.313
Jones, Bubba	L-R	6-1	205	8-20-92	.132	.111	.136	15	53	1	7	2	0	0	2	4	3	0	0	17	0	0	.264	.179
Lopez, Daniel	R-R	6-2	175	1-17-92	.206	.105	.250	24	63	9	13	4	0	0	4	10	0	0	0	19	1	1	.270	.315
Martini, Renzo	R-R	6-1	190	8-25-92	.199	.182	.204	54	181	19	36	10	1	4	31	17	1	1	1	34	0	2	.331	.270
McFarland, Ty	L-R	6-3	190	10-13-91	.278	.241	.290	62	237	24	66	17	2	5	40	20	4	0	0	37	6	4	.430	.345
Mikolas, Nathan	L-L	6-0	200	12-30-93	.225	.094	.261	48	151	23	34	7	1	2	18	25	6	0	0	54	6	2	.325	.357
Slaybaugh, Collin	L-R	6-2	185	4-3-92	.241	.276	.228	32	108	14	26	5	0	0	12	15	0	0	1	18	5	4	.324	.331
Spencer, Connor	L-R	6-2	215	1-22-93	.364	.288	.390	51	198	22	72	14	1	0	11	6	4	0	3	34	1	5	.444	.389
Steiger, Brady	L-R	6-1	195	12-28-90	.158	.211	.140	24	76	7	12	1	0	1	6	9	3	0	1	25	1	0	.211	.270
Tejeda, Isaias	R-R	6-0	195	10-28-91	.276	.385	.244	51	174	28	48	21	0	5	29	17	3	2	4	27	0	2	.483	.343
Thompson, Bo	R-R	5-10	255	1-27-93	.125	.143	.120	9	32	2	4	0	0	0	6	1	0	0	0	9	0	0	.125	.282
Torrens, Luis	R-R	6-0	175	5-2-96	.270	.217	.288	48	185	27	50	13	3	2	18	14	2	0	1	41	1	2	.405	.327

Pitching	B-T	HT	WT	DOB	W	L	ERA	G	GS	CG	SV	IP	H	R	ER	HR	BB	SO	AVG	vLH	vRH	K/9	BB/9
Acevedo, Andury	R-R	6-4	200	8-23-90	3	3	3.90	23	0	0	1	28	20	16	12	0	24	39	.206	.250	.180	12.69	7.81
Agnew-Wieland, Sam	R-R	6-2	205	5-31-92	3	4	4.19	16	4	0	1	39	42	25	18	0	19	44	.266	.356	.188	10.24	4.42
Bautista, Rony	L-L	6-7	200	9-17-91	1	1	3.28	20	0	0	3	36	24	15	13	2	20	58	.185	.290	.152	14.64	5.05
Beresford, Andy	R-R	6-7	200	2-26-90	1	0	0.46	5	4	0	0	20	15	3	1	0	2	18	.197	.241	.170	8.24	0.92
Borens, Matt	R-R	6-7	195	2-10-93	2	1	3.89	11	6	0	0	37	26	19	16	3	10	29	.197	.214	.184	7.05	2.43
Carley, Sean	R-R	6-4	230	12-28-93	1	4	5.48	10	6	0	0	23	29	21	14	1	4	17	.296	.358	.222	6.65	1.57
Carnes, Ethan	L-L	6-3	205	12-30-91	3	0	1.95	19	0	0	1	32	31	9	7	1	9	35	.254	.281	.244	9.74	2.51
Chin, Andrew	L-L	6-1	180	9-22-92	1	1	6.17	6	1	0	1	12	15	10	8	2	4	9	.294	.250	.314	6.94	3.09
Coshow, Cale	R-R	6-5	260	7-6-92	0	0	0.00	1	1	0	0	3	2	0	0	0	3	3	.182	.000	.222	9.00	0.00
Cote, Jordan	R-R	6-5	215	11-13-92	3	4	6.49	14	9	0	0	51	73	46	37	3	13	37	.329	.308	.348	6.49	2.28
Foley, Jordan	R-R	6-4	215	7-12-93	0	2	4.46	11	5	0	0	34	34	18	17	1	14	37	.262	.283	.247	9.70	3.67
Giel, Tim	R-R	6-2	220	9-29-90	1	1	4.65	18	0	0	3	31	43	24	16	4	5	30	.319	.313	.325	8.71	1.45
Harvey, Joe	R-R	6-2	220	1-9-92	0	2	1.96	13	0	0	1	18	16	6	4	1	3	16	.229	.265	.194	7.85	1.47
Hensley, Ty	R-R	6-4	220	7-30-93	0	0	3.86	4	4	0	0	12	11	6	5	0	2	17	.244	.083	.429	13.11	1.54
Hissong, Travis	R-R	6-0	195	7-19-91	0	0	0.00	2	0	0	0	3	3	1	0	0	0	3	.231	.250	.200	9.00	0.00
Holder, Jonathan	R-R	6-2	235	6-9-93	1	2	3.03	10	7	0	0	33	35	16	11	1	10	30	.285	.328	.246	8.27	2.76
Joseph, Francis	R-R	5-10	165	10-4-93	0	0	4.50	3	0	0	0	4	4	2	2	0	5	6	.267	.333	.250	13.50	11.25
Kamplain, Justin	R-L	6-0	175	2-13-93	1	0	0.43	8	5	0	1	21	9	1	1	0	2	25	.129	.095	.143	10.71	0.86
McNamara, Dillon	R-R	6-5	200	11-2-91	1	2	3.14	12	6	0	0	43	52	18	15	2	10	26	.308	.295	.319	5.44	2.09
Montgomery, Jordan	L-L	6-4	225	12-27-92	1	0	3.38	7	4	0	0	13	11	6	5	0	4	15	.220	.200	.225	10.13	2.70
Mullee, Conor	R-R	6-3	185	2-25-88	2	1	2.01	14	0	0	2	22	15	5	5	0	8	28	.192	.138	.224	11.28	3.22
Niebla, Luis	R-R	6-4	185	1-4-91	2	0	3.18	3	1	0	0	11	14	4	4	0	3	10	.311	.286	.323	7.94	2.38
Palladino, David	R-R	6-8	235	3-15-93	6	5	3.72	14	12	0	0	68	60	35	28	4	30	58	.236	.246	.227	7.71	3.99
Pena, Jose	R-R	6-0	190	3-22-91	1	1	2.89	5	0	0	1	9	8	3	3	0	4	14	.133	.200	.100	13.50	3.86
Perez, Elvin	R-R	6-4	193	8-3-90	0	0	1.93	3	0	0	1	5	1	1	1	0	2	6	.077	.250	.000	11.57	3.86
Reyes, Manolo	R-R	6-1	190	11-14-89	0	1	1.59	5	0	0	0	6	3	1	1	0	5	9	.167	.125	.200	14.29	7.94
Taylor, Chad	R-R	6-0	180	8-29-90	1	0	1.17	4	0	0	1	8	3	1	1	0	5	13	.120	.100	.133	15.26	5.87
Wotherspoon, Matt	R-R	6-1	175	10-6-91	2	3	1.97	17	0	0	2	32	22	11	7	1	9	29	.193	.208	.182	8.16	2.53

Fielding

Catcher	PCT	G	PO	A	E	DP	PB
Haddad	.966	9	50	7	2	1	0
Slaybaugh	1.000	6	56	5	0	0	1
Tejeda	.987	26	208	16	3	3	4
Torrens	.992	39	326	43	3	5	14

First Base	PCT	G	PO	A	E	DP
Breen	.987	17	142	11	2	10
Jones	.976	9	78	5	2	6
Spencer	.987	42	358	22	5	29

	PCT	G	PO	A	E	DP
Steiger	1.000	1	2	0	0	0
Thompson	.985	7	63	4	1	5

Second Base	PCT	G	PO	A	E	DP
Anderson	.961	14	19	30	2	6
Fleming	.946	8	16	19	2	7
Javier	.959	17	34	37	3	7
McFarland	.933	43	76	134	15	23

Third Base	PCT	G	PO	A	E	DP
Fleming	.000	1	0	0	2	0
Martini	.933	53	34	91	9	13
McFarland	.826	16	3	16	4	2
Steiger	.857	10	5	13	3	0

Shortstop	PCT	G	PO	A	E	DP
Conde	.963	38	58	125	7	29
Estrada	.966	17	16	40	2	6
Javier	.906	23	23	64	9	7

BaseballAmerica.com

Outfield	PCT	G	PO	A	E	DP
Aune	.899	59	74	6	9	0
Bolasky	.978	43	88	2	2	1
Breen	.981	36	48	4	1	0
Lopez	.933	22	28	0	2	0
Mikolas	.980	40	49	0	1	0
Slaybaugh	.909	23	38	2	4	2
Spencer	1.000	4	8	0	0	0
Steiger	1.000	7	12	0	0	0

GCL YANKEES1

GULF COAST LEAGUE

ROOKIE

Batting	B-T	HT	WT	DOB	AVG	vLH	vRH	G	AB	R	H	2B	3B	HR	RBI	BB	HBP	SH	SF	SO	SB	CS	SLG	OBP
Avelino, Abiatal	R-R	5-11	186	2-14-95	.355	.333	.364	8	31	7	11	6	0	0	3	2	0	0	0	4	0	0	.548	.394
Bridges, Drew	L-R	6-4	230	2-3-95	.222	.182	.244	52	189	31	42	15	2	5	29	29	3	0	4	65	1	1	.402	.329
Coleman, Kendall	L-L	6-4	190	5-22-95	.130	.222	.071	8	23	4	3	0	0	0	2	8	0	0	0	8	0	0	.130	.355
Cornelius, Kevin	R-R	6-1	180	8-28-92	.333	.667	.000	3	6	0	2	0	0	0	1	1	0	0	0	2	0	0	.333	.429
Cuevas, Bryan	R-R	5-10	179	10-14-93	.356	.348	.359	40	149	25	53	9	8	2	23	13	0	0	1	28	8	5	.564	.405
Diaz, Cesar	B-R	5-10	165	4-12-93	.407	.333	.500	10	27	5	11	2	0	0	6	3	0	0	1	3	2	1	.481	.452
Estrada, Thairo	R-R	5-10	155	2-22-96	.273	.400	.167	6	22	2	6	2	0	0	4	1	0	0	0	4	0	0	.364	.304
Feliz, Anderson	B-R	6-0	175	5-11-92	.571	.333	.750	3	7	3	4	1	0	0	2	2	0	0	0	2	4	0	.714	.667
2-team total (4 Yankees2)					.353	—	—	7	17	6	6	1	0	1	4	5	0	0	0	8	4	0	.588	.500
Fleming, Billy	R-R	6-1	200	9-20-92	.375	.450	.346	22	72	15	27	6	1	0	11	11	3	0	2	8	1	0	.486	.466
Flores, Ramon	L-L	5-10	150	3-26-92	.375	.333	.400	2	8	2	3	2	0	1	2	0	0	0	0	2	0	0	1.000	.375
2-team total (3 Yankees2)					.353	—	—	5	17	4	6	3	0	2	3	1	0	0	0	5	0	0	.882	.389
Gordon, Griff	L-L	6-0	210	2-15-92	.221	.167	.240	24	68	15	15	3	0	0	4	10	1	0	0	13	2	1	.265	.329
2-team total (11 Yankees2)					.230	—	—	35	100	18	23	4	0	0	11	17	1	0	1	21	3	1	.270	.345
Gumbs, Angelo	R-R	6-0	175	10-13-92	.412	.167	.545	4	17	3	7	3	1	0	4	0	0	0	0	2	2	1	.706	.444
Herrera, Roybell	R-R	5-11	177	12-30-90	.172	.250	.125	31	64	9	11	5	0	0	10	4	2	3	0	16	0	0	.250	.243
Higashioka, Kyle	R-R	6-0	200	4-20-90	.217	.167	.235	8	23	3	5	1	0	0	1	3	0	0	1	7	0	0	.261	.296
Jagielo, Eric	L-R	6-2	195	5-17-92	.217	.250	.200	7	23	3	5	0	0	2	4	3	0	0	0	1	0	0	.478	.308
Jose, Dominic	B-R	6-2	180	3-16-93	.300	.298	.301	42	130	17	39	12	3	1	17	10	3	1	0	43	7	4	.462	.364
Leonora, Ericson	R-R	5-11	175	8-25-92	.500	—	.500	1	2	0	1	0	0	0	1	0	0	0	0	0	0	0	.500	.500
2-team total (17 Yankees2)					.353	—	—	18	68	9	24	5	2	4	12	7	0	0	0	16	0	0	.662	.413
Lindemuth, Ryan	R-R	6-0	200	4-15-91	.212	.143	.263	16	33	7	7	1	1	4	2	5	2	0	0	11	0	0	.394	.350
Mateo, Jorge	R-R	6-0	188	6-23-95	.276	.200	.316	15	58	14	16	5	1	0	1	7	0	0	0	17	11	1	.397	.354
Mojica, Miguel	R-R	6-0	180	8-23-92	.215	.270	.190	43	121	26	26	6	2	0	7	18	3	0	0	34	5	1	.298	.331
Molina, Leonardo	R-R	6-2	180	7-31-97	.193	.179	.199	53	192	18	37	10	0	1	21	19	2	0	4	51	6	1	.260	.267
Noriega, Alvaro	R-R	6-0	198	11-9-94	.252	.231	.263	43	147	15	37	6	0	0	9	6	1	0	1	17	0	0	.293	.284
Palma, Alexander	R-R	6-0	201	10-18-95	.305	.397	.262	52	213	22	65	13	3	4	45	3	2	0	2	15	9	0	.451	.318
Palmer, Tyler	R-R	6-0	185	1-13-93	.340	.157	.333	15	47	9	16	3	3	0	3	7	0	1	0	9	9	0	.532	.426
2-team total (36 Yankees2)					.262	—	—	51	149	27	39	6	6	3	24	21	2	4	3	34	17	0	.443	.354
Reyes, Allison	R-R	6-0	165	9-16-92	.273	.400	.167	4	11	1	3	0	0	0	1	0	0	0	0	1	0	0	.273	.333
2-team total (1 Yankees2)					.308	—	—	5	13	1	4	0	0	0	1	0	0	0	0	1	0	0	.308	.357
Reyes, Brian	R-R	6-0	190	6-28-95	.133	.056	.167	33	60	9	8	3	0	0	3	14	0	1	0	17	0	0	.183	.297
Rosario, Jose	R-R	5-11	160	11-29-91	.300	.429	.231	5	20	6	6	0	2	1	4	1	0	0	0	2	1	0	.650	.364
Smith, Dalton	R-R	6-3	205	6-29-94	.245	.292	.218	52	184	21	45	11	0	4	26	19	5	0	3	44	1	1	.370	.327
Toadvine, Derek	R-R	5-10	175	3-20-92	.077	.000	.100	13	26	6	2	0	0	0	2	4	1	2	0	9	2	1	.077	.226
Torrens, Luis	R-R	6-0	175	5-2-96	.250	.571	.000	5	16	1	4	1	0	0	1	0	2	0	0	2	0	0	.313	.333

Pitching	B-T	HT	WT	DOB	W	L	ERA	G	GS	CG	SV	IP	H	R	ER	HR	BB	SO	AVG	vLH	vRH	K/9	BB/9
Batista, Jean	R-R	6-4	175	10-27-91	5	1	3.71	13	7	0	0	51	47	25	21	2	12	37	.242	.297	.215	6.53	2.12
Cabrera, Cristofer	R-R	6-0	180	12-25-92	3	0	1.29	16	0	0	3	28	18	9	4	0	21	31	.184	.161	.194	9.96	6.75
Callahan, Derek	L-L	6-4	205	12-29-92	1	0	2.70	3	3	0	0	13	12	4	4	0	5	7	.240	.200	.250	4.73	3.38
2-team total (7 Yankees2)					1	0	2.94	10	7	0	0	34	41	17	11	1	13	21	—	—	—	5.61	3.48
Carley, Sean	R-R	6-4	230	12-28-90	0	0	3.00	2	0	0	0	3	4	1	1	0	0	3	.286	.000	.364	9.00	0.00
Cedeno, Luis	R-R	5-11	154	7-14-94	1	3	1.13	15	6	0	1	40	23	7	5	0	6	35	.161	.226	.111	7.88	1.35
Chin, Andrew	L-L	6-1	180	9-22-92	0	0	0.00	1	1	0	0	2	1	0	0	0	3	.167	.000	.200	13.50	0.00
Claiborne, Preston	R-R	6-2	225	1-21-88	0	1	15.00	2	2	0	0	3	5	5	5	1	0	1	.385	.200	.500	3.00	0.00
2-team total (2 Yankees2)					0	1	9.53	4	3	0	0	6	8	6	6	1	1	3	—	—		4.76	1.59
Cotham, Caleb	R-R	6-3	215	11-6-87	0	0	0.00	2	0	0	0	4	3	0	0	0	0	2	.214	.000	.300	4.91	0.00
2-team total (2 Yankees2)					0	0	0.00	4	1	0	0	6	4	0	0	0	0	6	—	—		9.00	0.00
Dawe, Dayton	R-R	6-2	175	4-13-94	2	1	6.12	17	0	0	1	25	28	19	17	4	15	21	.275	.256	.286	7.56	5.40
De la Rosa, Simon	R-R	6-3	185	5-11-93	3	3	4.43	12	6	0	0	43	34	21	21	2	25	53	.222	.212	.228	11.18	5.27
DeCarr, Austin	R-R	6-3	218	3-14-95	2	1	4.63	11	8	0	0	23	20	13	12	1	7	24	.222	.185	.238	9.26	2.70
Del Bosque, Andre	R-R	6-0	225	3-14-91	1	0	23.14	4	0	0	0	2	6	6	6	0	3	2	.500	.667	.444	7.71	11.57
Drozd, Jonny	L-L	6-7	200	9-17-91	0	0	0.57	13	0	0	6	16	13	4	1	0	0	23	.224	.200	.226	13.21	0.00
Encinas, Gabe	R-R	6-3	190	12-21-91	0	0	3.24	3	2	0	0	8	10	3	3	0	4	7	.313	.250	.350	7.56	4.32
Harvey, Joe	R-R	6-2	220	1-9-92	0	0	0.00	2	1	0	1	2	2	0	0	0	2	3	.250	.250	.250	11.57	7.71
Hensley, Ty	R-R	6-4	220	7-30-93	0	0	2.37	7	6	0	0	19	16	5	5	2	9	23	.229	.238	.224	10.89	4.26
Hissong, Travis	R-R	6-0	195	7-19-91	1	1	3.24	11	0	0	1	17	17	8	6	1	1	20	.266	.407	.162	10.80	0.54
Jimenez, Juan	R-R	6-2	190	10-6-93	3	1	3.38	6	3	0	0	21	21	10	8	1	8	17	.259	.259	.259	7.17	3.38
Joseph, Francis	R-R	5-10	165	10-4-93	1	3	4.94	14	0	0	3	24	18	13	13	0	11	27	.207	.160	.226	10.27	4.18
Lake, Deshorn	R-R	6-1	210	10-29-93	3	3	6.26	15	0	0	0	23	25	19	16	0	11	16	.278	.257	.291	6.26	4.30
Lindgren, Jacob	L-L	5-11	180	3-12-93	0	0	0.00	1	0	0	0	1	2	0	0	0	0	2	.400	—	.400	18.00	0.00
Marsh, Matt	R-R	6-3	190	7-10-91	0	1	1.84	12	0	0	1	15	15	3	3	0	5	23	.268	.286	.257	14.11	3.07
Mesa Jr., Jose	R-R	6-4	215	8-13-93	2	0	2.79	9	1	0	0	10	10	3	3	1	3	6	.278	.375	.250	5.59	2.79
Niebla, Luis	R-R	6-4	185	1-4-91	0	0	3.86	3	3	0	0	7	5	3	3	0	3	13	.200	.125	.235	16.71	3.86
Polanco, Alex	R-R	6-4	230	5-8-94	1	0	0.00	1	0	0	0	0	0	0	0	0	0	0	.000	—	.000	0.00	0.00
2-team total (13 Yankees2)					2	1	8.04	14	0	0	0	16	15	14	14	0	18	17	—	—	—	9.77	10.34

Name	B-T	HT	WT	DOB	W	L	ERA	G	GS	CG	SV	IP	H	R	ER	HR	BB	SO	AVG	vLH	vRH	K/9	BB/9
Polanco, Reynaldo	R-R	6-2	178	5-20-93	3	1	2.29	17	0	0	0	35	28	13	9	0	13	32	.214	.184	.232	8.15	3.31
Reyes, Manolo	R-R	6-1	190	11-14-89	4	0	3.14	11	3	0	0	29	32	11	10	1	13	26	.286	.326	.258	8.16	4.08
2-team total (1 Yankees2)					4	1	3.48	12	3	0	0	31	34	14	12	1	15	27	—	—	—	7.84	4.35
Sharp, Hayden	R-R	6-6	195	10-30-92	1	0	4.63	4	1	0	0	12	12	7	6	0	7	9	.255	.300	.222	6.94	5.40
Tavares, Orby	L-L	6-4	225	9-16-94	1	1	2.68	13	6	0	0	40	37	15	12	1	21	30	.252	.250	.252	6.69	4.69
Turley, Nik	L-L	6-4	195	9-11-89	0	0	1.93	1	1	0	0	5	4	3	1	0	2	4	.235	.200	.250	7.71	3.86

Fielding

Catcher	PCT	G	PO	A	E	DP	PB
Herrera	.988	18	70	12	1	0	6
Higashioka	.984	7	58	2	1	2	0
Noriega	.987	31	212	24	3	4	5
Reyes	.987	29	134	16	2	2	4
Torrens	1.000	4	29	1	0	0	1

First Base	PCT	G	PO	A	E	DP
Bridges	.966	4	28	0	1	4
Herrera	.987	15	69	5	1	7
Mojica	.959	16	66	5	3	6
Noriega	.986	9	67	3	1	6
Smith	.993	37	251	19	2	13

Second Base	PCT	G	PO	A	E	DP
Cornelius	1.000	1	1	2	0	0
Cuevas	.946	14	25	28	3	3
Feliz	1.000	2	2	2	0	1
Fleming	.946	13	24	29	3	9
Gumbs	1.000	4	12	14	0	3
Lindemuth	.950	12	5	14	1	3

	PCT	G	PO	A	E	DP
Mojica	1.000	1	1	0	0	0
Palmer	1.000	2	0	3	0	1
Reyes	.667	2	3	1	2	1
Rosario	.917	3	6	5	1	3
Smith	.983	14	21	37	1	9
Toadvine	1.000	12	15	18	0	3

Third Base	PCT	G	PO	A	E	DP
Bridges	.920	44	26	77	9	8
Cornelius	1.000	1	0	2	0	0
Fleming	—	2	0	0	0	0
Jagielo	.933	6	5	9	1	0
Lindemuth	.875	4	2	5	1	0
Rosario	.000	1	0	0	1	0
Smith	.882	10	3	12	2	2

Shortstop	PCT	G	PO	A	E	DP
Avelino	.897	7	9	17	3	1
Cornelius	1.000	1	1	1	0	1
Cuevas	.960	25	29	67	4	12
Estrada	1.000	5	5	9	0	0

	PCT	G	PO	A	E	DP
Fleming	.921	8	16	19	3	0
Gordon	—	1	0	0	0	0
Mateo	.983	12	19	39	1	5
Palmer	.925	13	14	23	3	3
Reyes	.875	3	3	4	1	2

Outfield	PCT	G	PO	A	E	DP
Coleman	.941	8	16	0	1	0
Diaz	.941	8	15	1	1	1
Feliz	—	1	0	0	0	0
Flores	1.000	2	1	0	0	0
Gordon	1.000	16	16	0	0	0
Jose	.987	41	74	2	1	0
Leonora	1.000	1	2	0	0	0
Mojica	1.000	31	46	1	0	0
Molina	.973	46	68	3	2	0
Palma	.988	43	77	5	1	3
Palmer	1.000	1	1	0	0	0
Reyes	—	1	0	0	0	0
Rosario	—	1	0	0	0	0
Smith	—	1	0	0	0	0

GCL YANKEES2 — ROOKIE

GULF COAST LEAGUE

Batting	B-T	HT	WT	DOB	AVG	vLH	vRH	G	AB	R	H	2B	3B	HR	RBI	BB	HBP	SH	SF	SO	SB	CS	SLG	OBP
Aguilar, Angel	R-R	6-0	170	6-13-95	.311	.368	.292	39	151	34	47	11	1	7	31	14	1	1	0	28	8	2	.536	.373
Alexander, K.J.	R-R	5-11	210	9-23-91	.304	.278	.316	32	56	7	17	2	0	1	8	15	4	0	1	17	0	0	.393	.474
Anderson, Jake	L-R	6-0	170	12-3-91	.217	.263	.185	15	46	2	10	2	0	1	3	5	0	1	0	12	3	1	.326	.294
Aparicio, Jesus	R-R	5-11	186	8-18-94	.140	.237	.096	47	121	10	17	3	0	0	9	20	3	2	2	38	2	1	.165	.274
Baez, Yancarlos	B-R	6-2	165	9-21-95	.163	.200	.147	14	49	3	8	0	1	0	2	2	0	1	0	18	3	0	.204	.196
Barnes, Jordan	R-R	5-11	180	6-19-94	.180	.231	.157	45	122	15	22	3	1	1	9	15	3	2	0	39	9	1	.246	.286
Coa, Rainiero	R-R	5-10	170	1-2-93	.159	.267	.125	31	63	6	10	1	0	0	1	8	1	0	1	10	1	1	.175	.260
Feliz, Anderson	B-R	6-0	175	5-11-92	.200	.500	.125	4	10	3	2	0	0	1	2	3	0	0	0	6	0	0	.500	.385
2-team total (3 Yankees1)					.353	—	—	7	17	6	6	1	0	1	4	5	0	0	0	8	4	0	.588	.500
Figueroa, Jose	L-R	5-10	170	12-9-92	.290	.175	.341	53	186	34	54	11	2	3	18	16	2	0	0	46	13	5	.419	.353
Flores, Ramon	L-L	5-10	150	3-26-92	.333	.250	.400	3	9	2	3	1	0	1	1	1	0	0	0	3	0	0	.778	.400
2-team total (2 Yankees1)					.353	—	—	5	17	4	6	3	0	2	3	1	0	0	0	5	0	0	.882	.389
Frias, Frank	R-R	6-2	185	3-29-94	.316	.405	.281	41	133	18	42	4	3	0	9	14	1	1	0	22	11	2	.391	.385
Gittens, Chris	R-R	6-4	250	2-9-94	.286	.200	.320	11	35	6	10	4	0	0	5	7	1	0	2	10	0	0	.400	.400
Gordon, Griff	L-L	6-0	210	2-15-92	.250	.222	.261	11	32	3	8	1	0	0	7	7	0	0	1	8	1	0	.281	.375
2-team total (24 Yankees1)					.230	—	—	35	100	18	23	4	0	0	11	17	1	0	1	21	3	1	.270	.345
Hernandez, Jake	R-R	6-1	210	6-5-92	.278	.302	.267	52	194	26	54	12	1	6	25	12	4	0	3	32	0	1	.443	.329
Kirsch, Adam	R-R	6-1	215	11-15-90	.333	.167	.444	5	15	4	5	2	0	2	7	4	0	0	0	2	0	0	.867	.474
Leonora, Ericson	R-R	5-11	175	8-25-92	.348	.333	.354	17	66	9	23	5	2	4	11	7	0	0	0	16	0	0	.667	.411
2-team total (1 Yankees1)					.353	—	—	18	68	9	24	5	2	4	12	7	0	0	0	16	0	0	.662	.413
Palmer, Tyler	B-R	6-0	185	1-13-93	.225	.207	.233	36	102	18	23	3	3	3	21	14	2	3	3	25	8	0	.402	.322
2-team total (15 Yankees1)					.262	—	—	51	149	27	39	6	6	3	24	21	2	4	3	34	17	0	.443	.354
Ramos, Graham	R-R	5-11	170	1-31-91	.244	.235	.250	17	41	5	10	0	0	1	3	11	1	0	1	7	2	1	.317	.407
Reyes, Allison	R-R	6-0	165	9-16-92	.500	1.000	.000	1	2	0	1	0	0	0	1	0	0	1	0	0	0	0	.500	.500
2-team total (4 Yankees1)					.308	—	—	5	13	1	4	0	0	0	1	0	1	0	0	1	0	0	.308	.357
Romero, Wilmer	R-R	6-1	185	12-19-93	.222	.217	.224	32	108	7	24	4	0	2	10	10	0	0	1	30	0	0	.315	.286
Silva, Adam	R-R	6-2	202	3-27-94	.400	—	.400	4	5	2	2	0	0	0	2	0	0	0	0	3	1	0	.400	.571
Thompson, Bo	R-R	5-10	255	7-27-93	.209	.273	.178	22	67	11	14	2	0	1	10	18	5	0	1	20	0	0	.284	.407
Valera, Junior	R-R	6-0	180	9-27-92	.316	.222	.350	38	136	24	43	6	3	2	14	22	0	3	1	25	14	3	.449	.409
Valerio, Allen	R-R	6-1	173	1-11-93	.292	.256	.307	43	144	20	42	14	3	2	24	24	3	0	0	40	4	2	.472	.404

Pitching	B-T	HT	WT	DOB	W	L	ERA	G	GS	CG	SV	IP	H	R	ER	HR	BB	SO	AVG	vLH	vRH	K/9	BB/9
Acevedo, Domingo	R-R	6-7	190	3-6-94	0	1	4.11	5	5	0	0	15	16	8	7	0	6	21	.271	.095	.368	12.33	3.52
Borens, Matt	R-R	6-7	195	2-10-93	0	0	0.00	1	1	0	0	2	1	0	0	0	1		.167	.000	.200	4.50	4.50
Callahan, Derek	L-L	6-4	205	12-29-92	0	0	3.10	7	4	0	0	20	29	13	7	1	8	14	.337	.133	.380	6.20	3.54
2-team total (3 Yankees1)					1	0	2.94	10	7	0	0	34	41	17	11	1	13	21	—	—	—	5.61	3.48
Casas, Lee	R-R	6-7	255	12-17-91	2	0	4.66	15	0	0	0	19	23	18	10	0	19	11	.303	.368	.281	5.12	8.84
Claiborne, Preston	R-R	6-2	225	1-21-88	0	0	3.38	2	1	0	0	3	3	1	1	0	1	2	.273	.250	.286	6.75	3.38
2-team total (2 Yankees1)					0	1	9.53	4	3	0	0	6	8	6	6	1	1	3	—	—	—	4.76	1.59
Cortes, Nestor	R-L	5-11	190	12-10-94	1	2	2.27	11	2	0	0	32	35	13	8	1	5	38	.285	.346		10.80	1.42
Coshow, Cale	R-R	6-5	260	7-16-92	0	1	4.91	3	3	0	0	4	2	2	2	0	1	3	.143	.000	.222	7.36	2.45
Cotham, Caleb	R-R	6-3	215	11-6-87	0	0	0.00	2	1	0	0	2	1	0	0	0	0	4	.125	.500	.000	15.43	0.00

Name	B-T	HT	WT	DOB	W	L	ERA	G	GS	CG	SV	IP	H	R	ER	HR	BB	SO	AVG	vLH	vRH	K/9	BB/9
2-team total (2 Yankees1)					0	0	0.00	4	1	0	0	6	4	0	0	0	0	6	—	—	—	9.00	0.00
Diaz, Carlos	L-L	6-2	170	5-24-95	2	3	4.38	11	6	0	0	37	33	21	18	2	39	40	.254	.222	.262	9.73	9.49
Foley, Jordan	R-R	6-4	215	7-12-93	0	0	0.00	2	1	0	0	3	1	0	0	0	1	0	.100	.000	.125	0.00	3.00
Holder, Jonathan	R-R	6-2	235	6-9-93	1	1	12.27	2	1	0	0	4	7	5	5	0	3	4	.438	.200	.545	9.82	7.36
Leroux, Chris	L-R	6-6	225	4-14-84	0	0	0.00	1	1	0	0	4	1	0	0	0	0	5	.077	.000	.111	11.25	0.00
Maher, Joey	R-R	6-5	200	8-5-92	1	0	0.00	3	0	0	0	3	1	0	0	0	1	2	.091	.000	.167	5.40	2.70
Montgomery, Jordan	L-L	6-4	225	12-27-92	0	1	4.76	3	3	0	0	6	5	4	3	0	2	5	.227	.333	.211	7.94	3.18
Mora, Abel	L-L	6-5	175	12-3-91	2	0	4.13	17	0	0	3	24	23	12	11	0	19	17	.258	.316	.243	6.38	7.13
Morban, Jhon	R-R	6-4	190	6-3-92	5	1	2.79	10	7	0	0	42	29	13	13	2	18	36	.199	.189	.204	7.71	3.86
Morla, Melvin	R-R	6-4	185	5-26-93	2	3	4.15	11	8	0	0	48	41	27	22	3	26	37	.240	.208	.254	6.99	4.91
Noteware, Mike	R-R	6-0	190	9-16-90	3	0	3.03	19	0	0	5	30	30	11	10	1	5	29	.273	.302	.254	8.80	1.52
Padilla, Jonathan	R-R	5-10	175	3-30-93	2	3	3.59	14	3	0	0	43	38	19	17	1	11	44	.238	.217	.250	9.28	2.32
Pena, Jose	R-R	6-0	190	3-22-91	4	0	0.00	13	0	0	2	19	4	1	0	0	3	25	.068	.000	.098	11.64	1.40
Perez, Elvin	R-R	6-4	193	8-3-90	1	4	2.75	12	5	0	0	39	36	16	12	2	7	37	.229	.260	.215	8.47	1.60
Pinder, Branden	R-R	6-3	225	1-26-89	0	0	1.29	4	4	0	0	7	5	1	1	0	2	7	.227	.250	.222	9.00	2.57
Polanco, Alex	R-R	6-4	230	5-8-94	1	1	8.22	13	0	0	0	15	15	14	14	0	18	17	.259	.176	.293	9.98	10.57
2-team total (1 Yankees1)					2	1	8.04	14	0	0	0	16	15	14	14	0	18	17	—	—	—	9.77	10.34
Reyes, Manolo	R-R	6-1	190	11-14-89	0	1	7.71	1	0	0	0	2	2	3	2	0	2	1	.250	.400	.000	3.86	7.71
2-team total (11 Yankees1)					4	1	3.48	12	3	0	0	31	34	14	12	1	15	27	—	—	—	7.84	4.35
Rivera, Eduardo	R-R	6-5	190	9-24-92	0	1	5.02	7	4	0	0	14	10	8	8	2	14	12	.208	.125	.292	7.53	8.79
Rodriguez, David	R-R	5-11	156	1-15-93	4	0	7.54	13	0	0	0	23	28	19	19	1	17	22	.308	.317	.300	8.74	6.75
Santiago, Felix	R-R	6-0	170	12-7-93	2	0	3.12	17	0	0	0	26	22	9	9	0	10	17	.232	.241	.227	5.88	3.46

Fielding

Catcher	PCT	G	PO	A	E	DP	PB
Alexander	.973	20	67	5	2	0	5
Aparicio	.979	43	243	31	6	3	9
Coa	.994	31	152	16	1	2	2
Hernandez	1.000	3	7	3	0	0	0

First Base	PCT	G	PO	A	E	DP
Coa	1.000	1	1	1	0	1
Gittens	.952	3	19	1	1	0
Hernandez	.980	28	217	26	5	20
Johnson	1.000	14	100	4	0	12
Thompson	.993	19	141	6	1	13

Second Base	PCT	G	PO	A	E	DP
Anderson	.984	12	26	36	1	8
Figueroa	—	1	0	0	0	0

	PCT	G	PO	A	E	
Palmer	.957	15	21	23	2	5
Ramos	.893	8	9	16	3	3
Valera	.974	37	66	86	4	19

Third Base	PCT	G	PO	A	E	DP
Anderson	1.000	2	2	0	0	0
Aparicio	.750	4	2	4	2	0
Hernandez	—	2	0	0	0	0
Palmer	.946	12	10	25	2	1
Ramos	.714	5	2	3	2	1
Valerio	.926	42	38	74	9	13

Shortstop	PCT	G	PO	A	E	DP
Aguilar	.949	36	59	90	8	17
Baez	.963	14	19	33	2	7
Palmer	1.000	10	12	25	0	1

	PCT	G	PO	A	E	
Ramos	1.000	5	5	10	0	0
Valerio	1.000	1	1	2	0	0

Outfield	PCT	G	PO	A	E	DP
Aguilar	1.000	1	1	0	0	0
Alexander	.933	9	14	0	1	0
Barnes	.987	44	73	2	1	2
Feliz	—	4	0	0	0	0
Figueroa	1.000	49	82	3	0	0
Flores	1.000	3	5	0	0	0
Frias	.969	38	57	5	2	1
Gordon	1.000	11	9	1	0	0
Kirsch	1.000	2	3	0	0	0
Leonora	.893	15	25	0	3	0
Romero	.977	29	34	9	1	2
Silva	1.000	4	3	0	0	0

DSL YANKEES   ROOKIE

DOMINICAN SUMMER LEAGUE

Batting	B-T	HT	WT	DOB	AVG	vLH	vRH	G	AB	R	H	2B	3B	HR	RBI	BB	HBP	SH	SF	SO	SB	CS	SLG	OBP
Asencio, Hector	R-R	6-0	170	2-22-94	.233	.364	.188	24	43	18	10	0	0	1	5	13	0	1	1	16	9	0	.302	.404
Baez, Yancarlos	B-R	6-2	165	9-21-95	.253	.373	.217	51	217	40	55	8	5	2	33	27	1	0	1	50	16	1	.364	.337
Barrios, Daniel	R-R	5-11	183	4-18-95	.196	.176	.205	21	56	12	11	5	1	0	5	19	1	1	1	14	2	1	.321	.403
Cedeno, Oliver	R-R	5-10	165	5-24-96	.389	—	—	18	36	11	14	1	0	1	6	4	1	0	3	4	0	0	.500	.432
Davis, Eduardo	R-R	6-0	190	11-10-93	.308	.300	.310	49	169	20	52	8	2	2	27	10	4	2	1	24	1	3	.414	.359
De Jesus, Sammy	R-R	6-3	205	1-22-96	.295	.316	.290	28	88	15	26	2	2	0	15	8	2	0	2	25	0	1	.364	.360
Diaz, Andy	L-L	5-11	190	11-21-95	.275	.304	.268	61	236	51	65	7	10	5	49	40	8	1	3	64	4	4	.453	.394
Diaz, Cesar	B-R	5-10	165	4-12-93	.305	.237	.324	44	177	35	54	9	2	2	36	32	4	1	2	16	11	7	.412	.419
Diaz, Fernando	L-R	6-0	185	10-14-94	.211	.167	.224	49	152	26	32	1	4	0	10	38	10	4	2	30	6	3	.270	.396
Encarnacion, Greidy	L-L	5-11	156	4-1-94	.304	.222	.324	38	92	24	28	2	1	1	9	20	1	2	0	21	18	3	.380	.434
Ferreira, Ricardo	B-R	5-11	175	2-3-95	.269	.364	.222	18	67	24	18	2	1	0	10	22	3	1	0	20	15	3	.328	.467
Garabito, Griffin	R-R	5-11	180	8-2-97	.229	.375	.185	10	35	4	8	3	2	0	6	2	1	1	1	9	0	1	.429	.282
Gil, Miguel	R-R	6-2	170	3-9-96	.134	.182	.143	15	39	5	6	2	0	0	3	4	5	0	1	13	1	0	.205	.306
Gonzalez, Kevin	L-R	6-3	230	5-12-97	.329	.200	.357	45	173	21	57	11	1	1	40	19	6	0	3	27	0	1	.422	.408
Guerra, Jesus	L-R	5-11	163	3-15-97	.079	.091	.074	19	38	4	3	0	0	0	2	5	0	0	0	23	1	1	.079	.186
Guzman, Tirson	B-R	6-2	165	6-3-94	.290	.167	.330	41	124	26	36	7	4	1	21	22	2	0	1	35	3	3	.435	.403
Infante, Jose	R-R	5-11	160	9-21-93	.244	—	—	63	221	41	54	6	6	2	33	41	19	3	2	58	17	10	.353	.401
Liranzo, Ozzie	B-R	5-8	182	1-26-93	.344	.667	.310	8	32	5	11	3	2	0	5	3	0	0	0	3	0	0	.563	.400
Mateo, Algeni	R-R	5-9	170	8-1-95	.339	—	—	33	127	25	43	7	3	4	32	9	2	0	2	18	1	3	.535	.386
Mateo, Welfrin	R-R	5-10	170	9-8-96	.290	.244	.301	57	214	34	62	13	1	4	27	32	6	2	4	36	12	7	.416	.391
Mendez, Erick	R-R	6-0	185	4-7-96	.196	.158	.205	27	102	11	20	0	1	1	12	13	3	0	0	50	5	5	.245	.305
Munoz, Miguel	R-R	6-2	170	12-27-95	.206	.158	.219	44	175	19	36	10	2	1	20	12	1	1	0	50	0	0	.303	.261
Navas, Eduardo	B-R	5-10	180	4-5-96	.195	.200	.194	37	128	13	25	7	0	0	13	14	1	1	1	33	1	1	.250	.278
Perez, Bolivar	R-R	5-9	190	3-21-93	.211	.250	.200	7	19	5	4	3	0	0	5	1	4	0	1	0	0	0	.368	.360
Polonia, Jose	R-R	5-11	170	12-11-95	.333	.333	.333	10	36	7	12	0	0	1	3	3	0	0	0	2	2	2	.417	.385
Pujols, Yeangel	R-R	6-0	195	5-27-96	.125	.000	.174	12	32	3	4	2	1	0	5	7	0	0	0	7	0	0	.250	.282
Ramirez, Alan	R-R	6-1	185	2-15-94	.077	.000	.091	3	13	3	1	1	0	0	0	0	0	0	0	4	0	0	.154	.143
Rey, Victor	R-R	6-2	178	6-29-95	.259	.120	.289	47	139	20	36	8	1	1	13	23	4	0	1	50	0	1	.353	.377
Reyes, Allison	R-R	6-0	165	9-16-92	.296	.283	.299	62	230	47	68	13	2	5	32	31	11	3	4	34	8	4	.435	.399
Rodriguez, Ezequiel	R-R	6-0	175	6-22-96	.200	—	.200	11	30	5	6	1	0	0	8	7	4	0	2	16	2	0	.233	.395
Rodriguez, Wascar	R-R	6-2	198	10-6-94	.261	.256	.262	56	203	51	53	20	2	4	28	29	8	1	2	76	2	2	.438	.372

NEW YORK YANKEES

	B-T	HT	WT	DOB	AVG	OBP	SLG	G	AB	R	H	2B	3B	HR	RBI	BB	HBP	SO	SB	CS		vLH	vRH
Rodriguez, Yonauris	R-R	6-1	155	3-10-97	.315	.320	.313	21	89	16	28	1	3	1	17	16	3	1	0	21	2	1	.427	.435
Sanchez, Luis	R-R	5-11	160	5-5-97	.192	.429	.156	22	52	8	10	4	0	0	4	5	1	0	0	14	1	0	.269	.276
Seitz, Jerry	R-R	5-10	180	9-27-94	.333	.333	.333	39	138	22	46	10	5	4	33	10	7	1	0	27	0	2	.565	.406
Silva, Adam	R-R	6-2	202	3-27-94	.000	.000	.000	1	3	0	0	0	0	0	0	0	0	0	0	2	0	0	.000	.000
Suarez, Ronaldo	R-R	5-10	165	8-30-97	.200	.286	.000	7	10	3	2	1	0	0	2	0	0	0	4	0	0	.300	.200
Tamarez, Christopher	R-R	6-2	170	10-25-93	.251	.286	.241	49	183	23	46	2	0	0	18	11	1	0	0	39	2	2	.262	.297
Taveras, Oscar	R-R	5-11	180	9-13-92	.218	.267	.206	64	225	36	49	14	3	2	34	30	13	3	1	62	4	5	.333	.342
Unda, Dario	L-L	5-11	165	5-24-96	.307	.300	.310	55	192	28	59	13	6	2	35	20	4	1	6	36	2	7	.469	.374
Urena, Pedro	R-R	6-3	195	6-1-95	.298	.333	.287	58	225	42	67	13	5	7	40	24	2	0	1	57	1	2	.493	.369
Vergel, David	R-R	6-0	165	1-13-97	.179	.200	.173	23	67	6	12	1	0	0	1	7	4	1	1	18	1	1	.194	.291
Vidal, Carlos	L-L	5-11	160	11-29-95	.361	.385	.356	56	219	65	79	13	7	1	35	42	10	6	1	32	13	12	.498	.482

Pitching

Pitching	B-T	HT	WT	DOB	W	L	ERA	G	GS	CG	SV	IP	H	R	ER	HR	BB	SO	AVG	vLH	vRH	K/9	BB/9
Alcantara, Brayan	R-R	6-1	170	8-6-93	1	4	4.21	18	0	0	5	26	21	17	12	1	9	28	.214	.207	.217	9.82	3.16
Alvarez, Daniel	R-R	6-2	190	6-28-96	4	1	4.55	13	0	0	0	28	18	18	14	3	23	25	.184	.148	.197	8.13	7.48
Arias, Freddery	R-R	6-1	195	10-28-94	3	1	2.67	20	0	0	6	34	27	16	10	0	18	32	.223	.139	.259	8.55	4.81
Baez, Jose	R-R	6-2	210	1-13-92	0	3	3.74	14	9	0	1	43	40	26	18	0	27	33	.248	.267	.241	6.85	5.61
Burgos, Havid	L-L	6-1	188	8-6-94	2	1	3.74	20	0	0	1	22	24	11	9	0	11	23	.267	.267	.267	9.55	4.57
Calvo, Javier	R-R	6-2	180	6-17-93	8	2	2.68	15	1	0	0	37	34	23	11	0	14	34	.234	.275	.213	8.27	3.41
Casanova, Jeris	R-R	6-0	155	5-11-94	1	1	2.45	15	0	0	1	22	23	10	6	0	9	19	.267	.259	.271	7.77	3.68
Castillo, Alexander	R-R	6-6	155	6-22-94	2	1	4.98	17	0	0	0	22	26	13	12	0	10	18	.299	.304	.297	7.48	4.15
Cedeno, Moises	R-R	6-0	188	8-29-95	4	4	3.23	13	13	0	0	53	48	35	19	0	20	59	.239	.228	.243	1.02	3.40
Cortez, Rodrigo	R-R	6-1	174	1-11-97	4	1	3.30	13	0	0	0	30	20	16	11	1	18	12	.190	.154	.212	3.60	5.40
Diaz, Anderson	L-L	6-2	190	12-19-93	0	0	4.50	1	1	0	0	2	1	1	1	0	2	1	.167	.000	.250	4.50	9.00
Duarte, Abel	R-R	6-1	188	5-20-94	0	1	4.14	14	13	0	0	50	59	30	23	1	19	40	.291	.277	.297	7.20	3.42
Escalante, Shailin	R-R	6-3	205	9-18-94	1	0	1.69	6	0	0	0	5	4	1	1	0	9	3	.211	.250	.200	5.06	15.19
Escorcia, Juan	R-R	6-0	170	5-16-96	3	2	3.68	9	1	0	0	22	21	16	9	0	15	14	.247	.212	.269	5.73	6.14
Espinal, Raynel	R-R	6-5	165	10-6-93	2	2	3.54	20	0	0	12	28	22	11	11	1	6	41	.214	.243	.197	13.18	1.93
Garcia, Jairo	R-R	5-11	180	1-25-95	1	2	5.96	14	12	0	0	48	46	47	32	2	23	44	.237	.217	.248	8.19	4.28
Garcia, Leonardo	R-R	6-0	160	12-31-93	2	0	4.25	14	0	0	1	36	28	20	17	1	18	39	.214	.213	.214	9.75	4.50
Garcia, Luis	L-L	6-3	180	9-30-95	0	0	2.87	10	0	0	1	16	13	7	5	1	9	14	.213	.333	.207	8.04	5.17
Giron, Gabriel	R-R	6-0	172	9-20-93	2	2	5.48	10	1	0	0	26	26	23	13	0	15	20	.289	.419	.220	8.44	6.33
Gomez, Anyelo	R-R	6-1	175	3-1-93	4	4	2.72	12	12	0	0	53	41	23	16	1	19	53	.214	.188	.227	9.00	3.23
Guzman, Raudy	R-R	6-1	211	9-27-94	5	3	2.01	14	13	0	0	67	57	22	15	2	10	67	.226	.263	.204	9.00	1.34
Jose, Fernando	R-R	6-2	190	11-27-92	1	0	1.25	10	9	0	0	36	24	10	5	1	10	50	.189	.140	.214	12.50	2.50
Juliana, Hershelon	R-R	6-1	171	2-6-93	1	0	2.70	11	0	0	0	20	15	9	6	1	7	20	.205	.095	.250	9.00	3.15
Magallanes, Kelvin	R-R	6-1	175	7-15-94	1	5	6.04	14	13	0	0	48	47	48	32	0	36	36	.251	.231	.259	6.80	6.80
McCoy, Corby	L-L	6-3	180	10-5-95	2	0	2.87	17	1	0	0	31	22	11	10	0	19	31	.191	.250	.179	8.90	5.46
Ordaz, Rafael	R-R	6-4	201	2-17-95	0	2	5.06	12	0	0	3	16	16	12	9	1	7	18	.242	.111	.292	1.13	3.94
Ovalles, Jordan	R-R	6-1	160	1-17-94	1	1	2.15	14	1	0	0	50	45	23	12	1	10	39	.236	.327	.199	6.97	1.79
Padilla, Isaac	R-R	6-5	210	6-14-96	3	0	9.75	12	0	0	0	24	27	32	26	0	22	28	.281	.308	.271	1.50	8.25
Polanco, Eduardo	L-L	6-0	180	5-31-93	0	0	54.00	2	0	0	0	1	5	4	4	0	1	1	.714	—	.714	13.50	13.50
Pujols, Jose	R-R	6-6	183	11-19-92	2	3	4.25	19	0	0	2	36	30	28	17	0	19	39	.217	.359	.162	9.75	4.75
Ramirez, Jean	R-R	6-4	180	3-1-93	6	1	3.23	14	1	0	0	39	35	19	14	0	19	34	.252	.333	.213	7.85	4.38
Ramirez, Leyfer	R-R	6-0	160	10-19-96	0	1	8.76	10	0	0	0	12	18	13	12	0	11	7	.346	.368	.333	5.11	8.03
Ramos, Daniel	R-R	5-10	170	3-6-95	0	1	.00	1	1	0	0	5	5	4	0	0	1	6	.238	.200	.250	11.57	1.93
Reyes, Aderlis	R-R	6-2	182	10-23-91	1	0	3.97	11	0	0	0	11	12	7	5	0	4	11	.267	.077	.344	8.74	3.18
Rodriguez, Edison	R-R	6-1	180	7-6-92	0	0	14.85	8	0	0	0	7	7	14	11	0	15	12	—	—		16.20	2.25
Rodriguez, Jean	R-R	6-2	175	12-21-96	1	0	36.00	3	0	0	0	1	4	4	4	0	1	1	.571	.500	.600	9.00	36.00
Rosa, Adonis	R-R	6-1	160	11-17-94	1	0	1.62	12	3	0	0	39	32	9	7	0	5	31	.232	.192	.256	7.15	1.15
Rosario, Luis	R-R	6-1	185	12-11-94	1	3	5.13	14	12	0	0	53	50	31	30	2	15	37	.253	.313	.224	6.32	2.56
Rosario, Miguel	R-R	6-1	175	10-5-94	3	1	3.14	12	1	0	0	29	21	12	10	1	17	29	.204	.200	.206	9.10	5.34
Sanchez, Amauris	R-R	6-3	180	3-12-94	1	3	9.30	14	0	0	0	30	46	38	31	2	26	28	.348	.405	.322	8.40	7.80
Severino, Anderson	L-L	5-10	165	9-17-94	0	0	3.97	4	2	0	0	11	13	7	5	0	13	17	.302	.000	.317	13.50	1.32
Vargas, Alexander	R-R	6-4	203	7-24-97	0	0	2.08	5	5	0	0	13	14	5	3	0	6	13	.275	.304	.250	9.00	4.15
Vargas, Daris	R-R	6-3	195	8-12-92	5	4	3.00	15	15	0	0	66	43	28	22	0	32	60	.185	.254	.154	8.18	4.36

Fielding

Catcher	PCT	G	PO	A	E	DP	PB
Cedeno	1.000	5	20	8	0	0	0
Davis	1.000	4	24	2	0	0	2
Mateo	.800	1	4	0	1	0	0
Rey	1.000	1	1	1	0	0	0
Sanchez	.983	19	106	13	2	0	8
Seitz	.982	36	288	39	6	1	5
Vargas	—	1	0	0	0	0	0
Vergel	.995	22	163	38	1	1	7

Catcher	PCT	G	PO	A	E	DP	PB
Cedeno	.969	11	57	6	2	0	3
De Jesus	1.000	2	12	2	0	0	2
Liranzo	.950	3	16	3	1	0	1
Mateo	.971	21	149	20	5	0	10
Navas	.986	34	236	55	4	2	10
Perez	.964	7	45	8	2	1	2
Suarez	1.000	7	18	4	0	0	5

First Base	PCT	G	PO	A	E	DP
Barrios	1.000	4	30	2	0	2
Cedeno	1.000	2	7	0	0	2
Davis	.988	37	314	19	4	20
De Jesus	.957	19	130	5	6	9
Gil	.970	8	63	1	2	2
Gonzalez	.977	39	333	14	8	21
Guzman	1.000	1	7	0	0	1
Liranzo	1.000	2	14	0	0	1
Navas	1.000	3	16	2	0	2
Pujols	1.000	1	11	0	0	1
Rey	.962	9	50	1	2	5
Reyes	1.000	10	57	3	0	6
Sanchez	.971	4	34	0	1	0
Seitz	1.000	1	4	0	0	0
Urena	.990	21	195	7	2	14

Second Base	PCT	G	PO	A	E	DP
Barrios	.932	8	17	24	3	3
Diaz	.930	10	19	21	3	3
Ferreira	.885	11	29	25	7	0
Garabito	1.000	2	5	3	0	0
Guerra	1.000	9	7	11	0	0
Guzman	.924	25	45	64	9	13
Mateo	.951	50	106	145	13	25
Polonia	.955	5	7	14	1	1
Reyes	.922	21	38	57	8	8
Rodriguez	.961	10	21	28	2	5
Tamarez	1.000	1	0	4	0	0

Third Base	PCT	G	PO	A	E	DP
Barrios	1.000	3	3	2	0	0
Gil	.667	3	2	2	2	0
Guerra	.889	5	3	5	1	0
Guzman	—	1	0	0	0	0

	PCT	G	PO	A	E	DP
Rey	.880	34	30	58	12	5
Reyes	.800	8	12	20	8	1
Tamarez	.875	37	21	70	13	7
Taveras	.899	62	58	129	21	10
Shortstop	**PCT**	**G**	**PO**	**A**	**E**	**DP**
Baez	.902	48	79	123	22	19
Barrios	.880	7	6	16	3	2
Ferreira	.828	7	7	17	5	7
Garabito	.938	6	6	9	1	1
Guerra	.000	1	0	0	1	0
Infante	.838	23	33	50	16	8
Mateo	.850	5	5	12	3	1

	PCT	G	PO	A	E	DP
Polonia	.862	5	8	17	4	2
Reyes	.909	24	35	95	13	10
Rodriguez	—	1	0	0	0	0
Rodriguez	.859	19	17	50	11	4
Tamarez	1.000	1	1	2	0	1
Outfield	**PCT**	**G**	**PO**	**A**	**E**	**DP**
Asencio	.923	14	23	1	2	1
Diaz	.945	41	52	0	3	0
Diaz	.924	57	78	7	7	0
Diaz	.983	32	58	1	1	1
Encarnacion	.882	30	28	2	4	0
Guzman	1.000	1	1	0	0	0

	PCT	G	PO	A	E	DP
Infante	1.000	35	57	2	0	0
Mendez	.917	23	33	0	3	0
Munoz	.982	37	51	4	1	1
Padilla	1.000	1	1	0	0	0
Pujols	1.000	7	7	0	0	0
Ramirez	.875	3	7	0	1	0
Rodriguez	.977	49	78	7	2	0
Silva	1.000	1	1	0	0	0
Taveras	—	1	0	0	0	0
Unda	.968	43	59	1	2	0
Urena	.978	27	41	3	1	1
Vidal	.989	46	86	0	1	0

Oakland Athletics

SEASON IN A SENTENCE: A summer filled with hope gave way to another heartbreaking fall, as the Athletics collapsed down the stretch and went out with an extra-inning loss to the Royals in the AL wild-card game.

HIGH POINT: For a time, the A's were the talk of the sport. They put six players on the AL all-star team and looked like the majors' most complete team, ranking second in baseball in both scoring and ERA at the break. When July blockbuster deals brought in Jeff Samardzija and Jon Lester to join Sonny Gray and Scott Kazmir in a fearsome rotation, it looked like things were only getting better. The A's held the majors' best record as late as Aug. 15.

LOW POINT: Everything after mid-August was a nightmare. Losing Yoenis Cespedes crippled the A's offense, although other hitters dropped off as well. Even though the A's pitching largely held up, it wasn't enough to compensate for a lineup that hit .225 as a group from Aug. 1 on. The wild-card loss to the Royals was a microcosm of the season, as the A's blew a 7-3 lead in the eighth inning with Lester on the mound, took the lead again in the top of the 12th, then gave up two in the bottom half to lose 9-8.

NOTABLE ROOKIES: Just three rookies suited up at all for the A's in 2015, and only speedy outfielder Billy Burns received any meaningful playing time.

KEY TRANSACTIONS: The Lester-Cespedes deal will be long debated, given its negative impact on the A's offense. The Samardzija trade cost them their best prospect, shortstop Addison Russell, and 2014 first-round outfielder Billy McKinney. An August waiver deal for Adam Dunn was intended to breathe some life into the offense, but to little effect. General manager Billy Beane also had an active offseason, most notably by scoring big in free agency with the signing of Kazmir but striking out in a trade for Jim Johnson, who flopped as closer.

DOWN ON THE FARM: With Russell and McKinney, among others, leaving the system in trades, most of the A's remaining prospects were concentrated at high Class A Stockton. Led by Daniel Robertson (.310 average) and Matt Olson (37 homers), the Ports posted the California League's best record at 85-55, only to be upset in the first round of the playoffs. Double-A Midland unexpectedly won the Texas League title, doing it with a roster largely devoid of prospects.

OPENING DAY PAYROLL: $77,220,900 (27th)

PLAYERS OF THE YEAR

MAJOR LEAGUE

Josh Donaldson
3b
.255/.342/.456
29 HR, 76 BB, 98 RBI
7th in AL in OPS

MINOR LEAGUE

Matt Olson
1b
(high Class A)
.262/.404/.543
37 HR, 117 BB, 97 RBI

ORGANIZATION LEADERS

BATTING		*Minimum 250 AB
MAJORS		
* AVG	Vogt, Steven	.279
OPS	Donaldson, Josh	.798
HR	Donaldson, Josh	29
RBI	Donaldson, Josh	98
MINORS		
* AVG	Powell, Boog, Beloit, Stockton	.343
* OBP	Powell, Boog, Beloit, Stockton	.451
* SLG	Olson, Matt, Stockton	.543
R	Olson, Matt, Stockton	111
H	Robertson, Daniel, Stockton	170
TB	Olson, Matt, Stockton	278
2B	Peterson, Shane, Sacramento	40
3B	Mercedes, Melvin, Beloit	7
HR	Olson, Matt, Stockton	37
RBI	Olson, Matt, Stockton	97
BB	Olson, Matt, Stockton	117
SO	Coleman, Dusty, Midland	202
SB	Burns, Billy, Midland, Sacramento	54

PITCHING		#Minimum 75 IP
MAJORS		
W	Kazmir, Scott	15
# ERA	Otero, Dan	2.28
SO	Gray, Sonny	183
SV	Doolittle, Sean	22
MINORS		
W	Long, Nate, Midland	13
L	Covey, Dylan, Beloit, Stockton	14
# ERA	Neal, Zach, Stockton, Midland, Sacramento	3.09
G	McBryde, Jeremy, Sacramento	51
GS	Haviland, Shawn, Stockton, Midland	28
SV	House, Austin, Sacramento, Stockton	19
IP	Neal, Zach, Stockton, Midland, Sacramento	166
BB	Granier, Drew ,Sacramento, Midland	76
SO	Buschmann, Matt, Stockton, Sacramento	134
	Lamb, Chris, Beloit, Sacramento, Stockton	134
AVG	Lamb, Chris, Beloit, Sacramento, Stockton	.231

2014 PERFORMANCE

General Manager: Billy Beane. **Farm Director:** Keith Lieppman. **Scouting Director:** Eric Kubota.

Class	Team	League	W	L	PCT	Finish	Manager
Majors	Oakland Athletics	American	88	74	.543	t-8th (30)	Bob Melvin
Triple-A	Sacramento River Cats	Pacific Coast	79	65	.549	4th (16)	Steve Scarsone
Double-A	Midland RockHounds	Texas	77	63	.550	2nd (8)	Aaron Nieckula
High A	Stockton Ports	California	85	55	.607	1st (10)	Ryan Christenson
Low A	Beloit Snappers	Midwest	55	84	.396	16th (16)	Rick Magnante
Short season	Vermont Lake Monsters	New York-Penn	33	43	.434	t-12th (14)	David Newhan
Rookie	Athletics	Arizona	27	28	.491	7th (14)	Ruben Escalera
Overall 2015 Minor League Record			356	338	.513	11th (30)	

ORGANIZATION STATISTICS

OAKLAND ATHLETICS

AMERICAN LEAGUE

Batting	B-T	HT	WT	DOB	AVG	vLH	vRH	G	AB	R	H	2B	3B	HR	RBI	BB	HBP	SH	SF	SO	SB	CS	SLG	OBP
Anderson, Bryan	L-R	6-1	200	12-16-86	.000	—	.000	1	1	0	0	0	0	0	0	0	0	0	0	0	0	0	.000	.000
Barton, Daric	L-R	6-0	205	8-16-85	.158	.200	.143	30	57	7	9	1	0	0	5	5	1	0	1	14	0	0	.175	.234
Blanks, Kyle	R-R	6-6	265	9-11-86	.333	.300	.400	21	45	9	15	1	0	2	7	8	2	0	1	13	0	0	.489	.446
Burns, Billy	B-R	5-9	180	8-30-89	.167	.167	—	13	6	4	1	0	0	0	0	0	0	0	0	0	3	1	.167	.167
Callaspo, Alberto	B-R	5-9	225	4-19-83	.223	.196	.238	127	404	37	90	15	0	4	39	40	1	0	6	50	0	1	.290	.290
Cespedes, Yoenis	R-R	5-10	210	10-18-85	.256	.232	.263	101	399	62	102	26	3	17	67	28	1	0	4	80	3	2	.464	.303
2-team total (51 Boston)					.260	—	—	152	600	89	156	36	6	22	100	35	3	0	7	128	7	2	.450	.301
Crisp, Coco	B-R	5-10	185	11-1-79	.246	.227	.256	126	463	68	114	21	3	9	47	66	0	1	6	66	19	5	.363	.336
Donaldson, Josh	R-R	6-0	220	12-8-85	.255	.275	.248	158	608	93	155	31	2	29	98	76	7	0	4	130	8	0	.456	.342
Dunn, Adam	L-R	6-6	285	11-9-79	.212	.143	.220	25	66	6	14	1	0	2	10	6	4	0	0	27	0	0	.318	.316
2-team total (106 Chicago)					.219	—	—	131	429	49	94	18	0	22	64	71	7	0	4	159	1	1	.415	.337
Freiman, Nate	R-R	6-8	250	12-31-86	.218	.224	.200	36	87	12	19	5	0	5	15	5	1	0	0	23	0	0	.448	.269
Fuld, Sam	L-L	5-10	175	11-20-81	.209	.218	.205	60	187	25	39	6	4	3	19	17	0	3	0	34	9	1	.332	.275
2-team total (53 Minnesota)					.239	—	—	113	351	40	84	16	4	4	36	43	0	6	2	63	21	4	.342	.321
Gentry, Craig	R-R	6-2	190	11-29-83	.254	.266	.241	94	232	38	59	6	1	0	12	17	5	2	0	44	20	2	.289	.319
Gomes, Jonny	R-R	6-1	190	11-22-80	.234	.222	.300	34	64	6	15	1	0	0	5	9	0	0	2	18	0	0	.250	.320
2-team total (78 Boston)					.234	—	—	112	273	28	64	8	0	6	37	35	6	0	7	88	0	0	.330	.327
Jaso, John	L-R	6-2	205	9-19-83	.264	.167	.272	99	307	42	81	18	3	9	40	28	7	0	2	60	2	0	.430	.337
Lowrie, Jed	B-R	6-0	190	4-17-84	.249	.228	.258	136	502	59	125	29	3	6	50	51	5	2	6	79	0	0	.355	.321
Moss, Brandon	L-R	6-0	210	9-16-83	.234	.264	.228	147	500	70	117	23	2	25	81	67	10	0	3	153	1	0	.438	.334
Norris, Derek	R-R	6-0	210	2-14-89	.270	.311	.244	127	385	46	104	19	1	10	55	54	1	1	1	86	2	2	.403	.361
Parrino, Andy	B-R	6-0	190	10-31-85	.152	.150	.154	21	46	4	7	3	0	1	3	3	1	0	1	14	0	0	.283	.216
Punto, Nick	B-R	5-9	195	11-8-77	.207	.238	.175	73	198	21	41	7	2	2	14	25	0	1	0	56	3	1	.293	.296
Reddick, Josh	L-R	6-2	180	2-19-87	.264	.222	.280	109	363	53	96	16	7	12	54	28	1	0	3	63	1	1	.446	.316
Sogard, Eric	L-R	5-10	190	5-22-86	.223	.195	.228	117	291	38	65	10	0	1	22	31	1	4	2	37	11	4	.268	.298
Soto, Geovany	R-R	6-1	235	1-20-83	.262	.318	.200	14	42	3	11	4	0	0	8	6	0	1	0	8	0	0	.357	.354
2-team total (10 Texas)					.250	—	—	24	80	8	20	6	0	1	11	6	0	1	0	19	0	0	.363	.302
Vogt, Stephen	L-R	6-0	215	11-1-84	.279	.205	.291	84	269	26	75	10	2	9	35	16	1	0	1	39	1	0	.431	.321

Pitching	B-T	HT	WT	DOB	W	L	ERA	G	GS	CG	SV	IP	H	R	ER	HR	BB	SO	AVG	vLH	vRH	K/9	BB/9
Abad, Fernando	L-L	6-1	220	12-17-85	2	4	1.57	69	0	0	0	57	34	11	10	4	15	51	.175	.191	.162	8.01	2.35
Chavez, Jesse	R-R	6-2	160	8-21-83	8	8	3.45	32	21	0	0	146	142	64	56	17	49	136	.253	.247	.260	8.38	3.02
Cook, Ryan	R-R	6-2	215	6-30-87	1	3	3.42	54	0	0	1	50	32	19	19	3	22	50	.184	.262	.138	9.00	3.96
Doolittle, Sean	L-L	6-3	210	9-26-86	2	4	2.73	61	0	0	22	63	38	19	19	5	8	89	.169	.118	.195	12.78	1.15
Francis, Jeff	L-L	6-5	220	1-8-81	0	1	6.08	9	0	0	1	13	11	9	9	1	3	10	.224	.286	.200	6.75	2.03
2-team total (2 New York)					1	1	6.00	11	0	0	1	15	13	10	10	2	3	11	—	—	—	6.60	1.80
Gray, Sonny	R-R	5-11	195	11-7-89	14	10	3.08	33	33	2	0	219	187	84	75	15	74	183	.232	.221	.245	7.52	3.04
Gregerson, Luke	L-R	6-3	200	5-14-84	5	5	2.12	72	0	0	3	72	58	20	17	6	15	59	.220	.221	.219	7.34	1.87
Hammel, Jason	R-R	6-6	225	9-2-82	2	6	4.26	13	12	0	0	68	66	34	32	13	21	54	.254	.245	.264	7.18	2.79
Johnson, Jim	R-R	6-6	240	6-27-83	4	2	7.14	38	0	0	2	40	60	33	32	5	23	28	.353	.371	.333	6.25	5.13
2-team total (16 Detroit)					5	2	7.09	54	0	0	2	53	69	46	42	5	35	42	—	—	—	7.09	5.91
Kazmir, Scott	L-L	6-0	185	1-24-84	15	9	3.55	32	32	2	0	190	171	81	75	16	50	164	.238	.273	.227	7.75	2.36
Lester, Jon	L-L	6-4	240	1-7-84	6	4	2.35	11	11	1	0	77	66	24	20	7	16	71	.232	.266	.223	8.33	1.88
2-team total (21 Boston)					16	11	2.46	32	32	1	0	220	194	76	60	16	48	220	—	—	—	9.01	1.97
Lindblom, Josh	R-R	6-4	240	6-15-87	0	0	3.86	1	1	0	0	5	5	2	2	1	2	2	.263	.235	.500	3.86	3.86
Mills, Brad	L-L	6-0	185	3-5-85	1	1	4.41	3	3	0	0	16	19	9	8	2	7	14	.292	.294	.292	7.71	3.86
2-team total (2 Toronto)					1	1	9.15	5	3	0	0	21	29	22	21	5	11	19	—	—	—	8.27	4.79
Milone, Tommy	L-L	6-0	205	2-16-87	6	3	3.55	16	16	0	0	96	91	42	38	12	26	61	.245	.264	.240	5.70	2.43
2-team total (6 Minnesota)					6	4	4.19	22	21	0	0	118	128	63	55	16	37	75	—	—	—	5.72	2.82
O'Flaherty, Eric	L-L	6-2	220	2-5-85	1	0	2.25	21	0	0	1	20	15	5	5	3	4	15	.205	.233	.186	6.75	1.80
Otero, Dan	R-R	6-3	215	2-19-85	8	2	2.28	72	0	0	1	87	80	24	22	4	15	45	.247	.285	.219	4.67	1.56
Pomeranz, Drew	R-L	6-5	240	11-22-88	5	4	2.35	20	10	0	0	69	51	22	18	7	26	64	.204	.232	.196	8.35	3.39
Rodriguez, Fernando	R-R	6-3	235	6-18-84	1	0	1.00	7	0	0	0	9	4	1	1	0	2	4	.129	.091	.150	4.00	2.00
Samardzija, Jeff	R-R	6-5	225	1-23-85	5	6	3.14	16	16	2	0	112	92	42	39	13	12	99	.224	.228	.220	7.98	0.97

	B-T	HT	WT	DOB	W	L	ERA	G	GS	CG	SV	IP	H	R	ER	HR	BB	SO	AVG	vLH	vRH	K/9	BB/9
Savery, Joe	L-L	6-3	235	11-4-85	0	0	0.00	3	0	0	0	4	3	0	0	1	0	.214	.400	.111	0.00	2.25
Scribner, Evan	R-R	6-3	190	7-19-85	1	0	4.63	13	0	0	0	12	11	6	6	4	0	11	.239	.158	.296	8.49	0.00
Straily, Dan	R-R	6-2	215	12-1-88	1	2	4.93	7	7	0	0	38	33	21	21	9	15	34	.232	.231	.234	7.98	3.52

Fielding

Catcher	PCT	G	PO	A	E	DP	PB
Jaso	.997	54	338	10	1	0	1
Norris	.992	114	745	43	6	3	8
Soto	.975	14	103	14	3	3	0
Vogt	1.000	15	71	4	0	0	1

First Base	PCT	G	PO	A	E	DP
Barton	.983	30	166	12	3	16
Blanks	.990	17	93	8	1	11
Callaspo	.986	23	128	17	2	14
Freiman	.986	33	211	7	3	24
Moss	.990	67	487	21	5	48
Vogt	.995	47	341	21	2	28

Second Base	PCT	G	PO	A	E	DP
Callaspo	.978	46	76	104	4	25

	PCT	G	PO	A	E	DP
Parrino	1.000	4	7	11	0	7
Punto	.973	52	89	130	6	41
Sogard	.988	102	154	247	5	49

Third Base	PCT	G	PO	A	E	DP
Callaspo	.953	19	8	33	2	4
Donaldson	.952	150	131	328	23	43
Parrino	1.000	1	1	0	0	0
Punto	1.000	2	0	1	0	0

Shortstop	PCT	G	PO	A	E	DP
Lowrie	.974	130	146	344	13	71
Parrino	.972	14	12	23	1	4
Punto	.982	17	19	36	1	9
Sogard	.896	14	10	33	5	5

Outfield	PCT	G	PO	A	E	DP
Blanks	—	1	0	0	0	0
Burns	.667	1	2	0	1	0
Cespedes	.975	84	144	12	4	0
Crisp	.985	111	194	0	3	0
Fuld	1.000	54	129	4	0	1
Gentry	.994	87	153	8	1	2
Gomes	.962	19	25	0	1	0
Moss	.985	84	123	6	2	1
Parrino	—	2	0	0	0	0
Punto	—	1	0	0	0	0
Reddick	.976	108	195	5	5	2
Vogt	1.000	18	21	0	0	0

SACRAMENTO RIVER CATS   TRIPLE-A

PACIFIC COAST LEAGUE

Batting	B-T	HT	WT	DOB	AVG	vLH	vRH	G	AB	R	H	2B	3B	HR	RBI	BB	HBP	SH	SF	SO	SB	CS	SLG	OBP
Aliotti, Anthony	L-L	6-0	205	7-16-87	.259	.219	.274	72	243	30	63	17	0	2	21	32	2	0	1	76	1	1	.354	.349
Anderson, Bryan	L-R	6-1	200	12-16-86	.381	.000	.421	5	21	4	8	3	1	0	4	1	1	0	1	7	0	0	.619	.417
Barton, Daric	L-R	6-0	205	8-16-85	.261	.261	.261	85	314	46	82	18	1	9	56	51	6	—	4	40	0	1	.411	.371
Blanks, Kyle	R-R	6-6	265	9-11-86	.429	.333	.467	7	21	4	9	0	0	1	3	6	0	0	1	3	0	0	.571	.536
2-team total (27 El Paso)					.298	—	—	34	104	19	31	5	0	10	23	16	4	0	3	27	0	0	.635	.402
Burns, Billy	R-R	5-9	180	8-30-89	.193	.148	.207	28	109	17	21	2	0	0	5	9	0	3	0	19	3	1	.211	.254
Buss, Nick	L-R	6-2	190	12-15-86	.307	.350	.291	110	450	79	138	17	2	4	52	45	4	—	5	75	14	4	.380	.371
2-team total (26 Albuquerque)					.299	—	—	136	542	91	162	20	5	5	68	53	6	1	6	87	14	6	.382	.364
Carrithers, Alden	L-R	5-9	170	11-14-84	.284	.223	.304	101	387	60	110	13	3	2	53	55	7	—	3	45	14	5	.349	.381
DeVoss, Zeke	B-R	5-10	175	7-17-90	.333	—	.333	1	3	0	1	0	0	0	0	1	0	0	0	0	0	0	.333	.500
Elmore, Jake	R-R	5-9	185	6-15-87	.282	.244	.294	47	181	30	51	15	0	0	18	27	1	—	2	26	9	4	.365	.374
Exposito, Luis	R-R	6-3	210	1-20-87	.303	.300	.304	19	66	9	20	6	0	2	11	1	—	0	16	0	0	.394	.410
Freiman, Nate	R-R	6-8	250	12-31-86	.284	.233	.304	80	310	48	88	22	1	15	74	40	7	0	7	73	0	0	.506	.371
Gentry, Craig	R-R	6-2	190	11-29-83	.267	.333	.250	4	15	2	4	0	0	0	5	1	0	0	2	4	0	0	.267	.278
Goebbert, Jake	L-L	6-0	205	9-24-87	.257	.242	.263	31	109	21	28	7	1	6	25	19	2	0	2	20	1	0	.505	.371
2-team total (48 El Paso)					.296	—	—	79	280	58	83	20	3	14	60	52	4	0	3	53	1	0	.539	.410
Kirkland, Wade	R-R	5-10	200	4-4-89	.111	.333	.000	3	9	1	1	1	0	0	0	0	0	0	0	4	1	0	.222	.111
Ladendorf, Tyler	R-R	6-0	210	3-7-88	.297	.395	.255	78	273	44	81	18	3	2	43	35	2	0	4	56	3	1	.407	.376
Lipkin, Ryan	R-R	6-0	205	10-8-87	.269	.250	.286	7	26	1	7	0	0	0	0	0	0	1	0	2	0	0	.269	.269
Lowrie, Jed	B-R	6-0	190	4-17-84	.222	—	.222	2	9	1	2	0	0	0	0	0	0	0	0	1	0	0	.222	.222
Martinez, Jose	R-R	5-11	175	1-24-86	.276	.326	.256	122	446	55	123	19	0	8	61	44	7	—	7	53	2	2	.372	.345
Martinez, Luis	R-R	6-0	210	4-3-85	.150	.111	.161	14	40	1	6	1	0	0	3	5	2	0	0	10	0	0	.175	.277
2-team total (53 Salt Lake)					.242	—	—	67	231	26	56	16	0	4	25	20	6	2	0	43	0	0	.364	.319
Matthes, Kent	R-R	6-2	215	1-8-87	.208	.200	.212	26	101	14	21	5	0	1	12	9	1	0	0	31	2	1	.287	.279
Nakajima, Hiroyuki	R-R	5-11	200	7-31-82	.128	.167	.111	12	39	3	5	2	0	0	4	4	1	0	1	10	1	0	.179	.222
Ortiz, Ryan	R-R	6-3	200	8-7-85	.215	.239	.206	81	247	31	53	9	2	2	22	52	5	2	0	67	0	0	.291	.362
Parrino, Andy	B-R	6-0	190	10-31-85	.286	.290	.285	90	374	57	107	19	2	7	52	44	2	1	1	97	7	0	.404	.363
2-team total (13 Round Rock)					.274	—	—	103	427	61	117	22	2	7	57	47	5	1	1	109	7	0	.384	.352
Peterson, Shane	L-L	6-0	210	2-11-88	.308	.306	.308	137	543	101	167	40	5	11	90	66	2	—	6	139	11	2	.460	.381
Pohl, Phil	R-R	5-11	220	7-22-90	.276	.444	.200	8	29	2	8	4	0	0	6	1	1	0	0	10	0	0	.414	.323
Reddick, Josh	L-R	6-2	180	2-19-87	.438	.429	.444	4	16	1	7	3	0	0	1	0	0	0	1	1	1	1	.625	.471
Taylor, Michael	R-R	6-5	255	12-19-85	.243	.192	.259	59	218	34	53	14	1	5	31	33	6	0	1	50	7	2	.385	.357
Vogt, Stephen	L-R	6-0	215	11-1-84	.364	.240	.413	21	88	18	32	8	2	3	19	8	0	0	1	8	1	0	.602	.412
Walsh, Colin	B-R	6-0	190	9-26-89	.272	.317	.255	47	147	16	40	4	0	2	18	19	3	1	2	38	1	0	.340	.363
Whitaker, Josh	R-R	6-3	225	2-8-89	.238	.389	.197	22	84	9	20	5	0	3	12	6	0	—	2	26	1	0	.405	.283
Wilson, Kenny	B-R	5-11	195	1-30-90	.135	.118	.143	14	52	6	7	1	0	0	5	3	1	—	0	14	2	0	.154	.196

Pitching	B-T	HT	WT	DOB	W	L	ERA	G	GS	CG	SV	IP	H	R	ER	HR	BB	SO	AVG	vLH	vRH	K/9	BB/9
Atherton, Tim	R-R	6-2	209	11-7-89	0	1	54.00	1	1	0	0	1	5	6	6	2	2	0	.625	.500	.750	0.00	18.00
Berger, Eric	L-L	6-2	205	4-22-86	0	0	6.75	3	0	0	0	3	1	1	1	0	3	0	.429	.500	.000	0.00	6.75
Blanton, Joe	R-R	6-3	215	12-11-80	1	0	5.06	2	2	0	0	11	13	7	6	1	3	10	.302	.346	.235	8.44	2.53
Buschmann, Matt	R-R	6-3	215	12-13-84	9	7	4.52	23	22	1	0	133	142	76	67	15	49	123	.275	.229	.308	8.30	3.31
Castro, Angel	R-R	5-11	200	11-14-82	0	3	7.78	4	4	0	0	20	34	20	17	3	6	10	.410	.349	.475	4.58	2.75
2-team total (26 Memphis)					9	9	4.66	30	18	0	1	114	130	71	59	14	32	73	—	—	—	5.76	2.53
Flores, Jose	R-R	6-3	250	6-4-89	2	1	4.60	24	0	0	0	29	33	17	15	2	17	25	.292	.286	.297	7.67	5.22
Frankoff, Seth	R-R	6-5	200	8-18-88	1	1	4.40	22	0	0	1	31	30	16	15	3	10	22	.254	.200	.302	6.46	2.93
Granier, Drew	R-R	6-1	190	11-24-88	0	0	15.75	1	1	0	0	4	12	7	7	0	0	1	.522	.636	.417	2.25	0.00
Healy, Tucker	L-R	6-1	195	6-15-90	1	1	8.14	20	0	0	0	24	31	24	22	4	14	28	.307	.364	.263	10.36	5.18
Hooker, Deryk	R-R	6-4	215	6-21-89	0	4	4.25	22	1	0	0	36	43	22	17	2	16	16	.305	.314	.296	4.00	4.00
House, Austin	R-R	6-4	200	1-24-91	0	0	0.00	4	0	0	0	7	3	0	0	0	4	3	.143	.143	.143	3.86	5.14
Humber, Phil	R-R	6-3	210	12-21-82	6	4	3.65	44	3	0	1	69	67	33	28	8	26	68	.248	.230	.261	8.87	3.39

Pitching	B-T	HT	WT	DOB	W	L	ERA	G	GS	CG	SV	IP	H	R	ER	HR	BB	SO	AVG	vLH	vRH	K/9	BB/9
Lamb, Chris	B-L	6-1	185	6-29-90	0	1	54.00	1	0	0	0	0	2	2	2	0	2	0	1.000	1.000	1.000	0.00	54.00
Leon, Arnold	R-R	6-1	205	9-6-88	10	7	4.97	27	27	0	0	145	170	84	80	12	51	128	.295	.290	.300	7.94	3.17
Lindblom, Josh	R-R	6-4	240	6-15-87	4	3	5.79	17	16	0	0	84	92	60	54	10	26	60	.280	.338	.235	6.43	2.79
Marks, Justin	L-L	6-3	205	1-12-88	0	0	0.00	4	0	0	0	4	0	0	0	0	1	2	.000	.000	.000	4.91	2.45
3-team total (13 Omaha, 5 Round Rock)					3	3	5.03	22	2	0	0	39	44	28	22	4	16	37	—	—	—	8.47	3.66
McBryde, Jeremy	R-R	6-2	225	5-1-87	3	4	2.22	51	1	0	17	65	40	19	16	4	26	66	.181	.220	.154	9.14	3.60
McGuire, Deck	R-R	6-6	220	6-23-89	2	4	8.05	7	6	0	0	35	49	32	31	5	16	16	.340	.381	.309	4.15	4.15
Milone, Tommy	L-L	6-0	205	2-16-87	1	1	6.43	4	4	0	0	21	28	16	15	5	9	17	.318	.417	.281	7.29	3.86
Murphy, Sean	B-R	6-0	215	8-23-88	2	4	7.18	7	7	0	0	36	41	31	29	6	18	20	.283	.207	.333	4.95	4.46
Neal, Zach	R-R	6-3	220	11-9-88	7	7	4.07	20	19	0	0	119	137	70	54	15	16	80	.288	.273	.303	6.03	1.21
Nieve, Fernando	R-R	6-2	220	7-15-82	2	1	7.01	18	0	0	3	26	38	22	20	4	14	24	.342	.346	.339	8.42	4.91
2-team total (15 Salt Lake)					2	3	6.33	33	1	0	3	43	59	32	30	4	26	46	—	—	—	9.70	5.48
O'Flaherty, Eric	L-L	6-2	220	2-5-85	0	1	4.32	7	1	0	0	8	6	4	4	1	3	5	.207	.083	.294	5.40	3.24
Pomeranz, Drew	R-L	6-5	240	11-22-88	3	1	3.69	8	8	0	0	46	45	19	19	6	17	54	.260	.311	.242	10.49	3.30
Rodriguez, Fernando	R-R	6-3	235	6-18-84	3	0	1.97	38	0	0	0	46	40	12	10	2	16	53	.235	.189	.271	10.45	3.15
Savery, Joe	L-L	6-3	235	11-4-85	7	1	2.84	43	0	0	2	44	37	15	14	4	17	45	.228	.216	.239	9.14	3.45
Scribner, Evan	R-R	6-3	190	7-19-85	4	1	3.06	40	0	0	16	47	39	16	16	4	9	72	.223	.230	.218	13.79	1.72
Smyth, Paul	R-R	5-11	210	4-1-87	5	2	3.05	46	0	0	0	59	43	22	20	9	14	56	.202	.186	.213	8.54	2.14
Straily, Dan	R-R	6-2	215	12-1-88	4	3	4.71	10	10	0	0	63	54	33	33	9	26	67	.241	.291	.198	9.57	3.71
2-team total (10 Iowa)					7	8	4.42	20	20	0	0	118	113	67	58	16	46	123	—	—	—	9.38	3.51
Urlaub, Jeff	L-L	6-2	160	4-24-87	0	0	4.05	6	0	0	0	7	7	4	3	1	2	8	.259	.133	.417	10.80	2.70
Walden, Marcus	R-R	6-0	195	9-13-88	2	2	5.73	11	11	0	0	60	69	42	38	6	27	34	.297	.250	.352	5.13	4.07

Fielding

Catcher	PCT	G	PO	A	E	DP	PB
Anderson	1.000	5	37	0	0	0	4
Exposito	.950	19	184	7	10	0	3
Lipkin	1.000	7	42	6	0	1	0
Martinez	1.000	14	102	12	0	5	0
Ortiz	.995	79	590	35	3	1	8
Pohl	.974	7	36	2	1	1	1
Vogt	.988	19	147	14	2	2	2

First Base	PCT	G	PO	A	E	DP
Aliotti	.993	51	401	28	3	47
Barton	.992	42	330	44	3	34
Blanks	1.000	5	23	3	0	4
Freiman	.996	50	420	35	2	50
Ortiz	1.000	1	1	0	0	0
Parrino	1.000	1	2	0	0	0
Peterson	1.000	2	5	0	0	0

Second Base	PCT	G	PO	A	E	DP
Carrithers	.950	4	6	13	1	2
Elmore	.976	29	47	74	3	16
Kirkland	1.000	2	3	4	0	3
Ladendorf	.990	38	87	110	2	28
Martinez	.990	52	87	120	2	34
Nakajima	1.000	1	1	2	0	0
Parrino	1.000	5	9	15	0	3
Walsh	.954	25	36	67	5	13

Third Base	PCT	G	PO	A	E	DP
Carrithers	.970	76	29	100	4	13
Elmore	1.000	4	3	7	0	2
Martinez	.984	56	39	81	2	7
Nakajima	.941	9	7	9	1	1
Ortiz	1.000	1	0	1	0	0
Parrino	.667	1	1	1	0	0
Walsh	.857	3	1	5	1	1

Shortstop	PCT	G	PO	A	E	DP
Elmore	.905	11	13	25	4	8
Kirkland	1.000	1	3	4	0	1
Ladendorf	.964	38	63	124	7	33
Lowrie	.917	2	3	8	1	3
Martinez	.979	11	18	29	1	5
Nakajima	1.000	1	2	3	0	1
Parrino	.966	85	103	236	12	58

Outfield	PCT	G	PO	A	E	DP
Aliotti	.941	9	16	0	1	0
Blanks	1.000	1	1	1	0	0
Burns	.987	28	74	3	1	2
Buss	.985	108	249	8	4	2
Carrithers	1.000	12	19	0	0	0
DeVoss	1.000	1	6	0	0	0
Elmore	1.000	3	3	0	0	0
Gentry	1.000	3	11	0	0	0
Goebbert	1.000	25	49	2	0	1
Ladendorf	1.000	2	3	0	0	0
Matthes	1.000	16	25	2	0	0
Peterson	.974	132	248	10	7	2
Reddick	1.000	3	6	1	0	0
Taylor	.975	58	113	4	3	1
Vogt	1.000	1	1	0	0	0
Walsh	1.000	10	18	2	0	0
Whitaker	.951	19	34	5	2	0
Wilson	1.000	12	14	0	0	0

MIDLAND ROCKHOUNDS   DOUBLE-A
TEXAS LEAGUE

Batting	B-T	HT	WT	DOB	AVG	vLH	vRH	G	AB	R	H	2B	3B	HR	RBI	BB	HBP	SH	SF	SO	SB	CS	SLG	OBP
Aliotti, Anthony	L-L	6-0	205	7-16-87	.277	.114	.321	48	166	26	46	11	1	7	27	28	2	1	0	64	0	0	.482	.388
Barfield, Jeremy	R-L	6-5	220	7-12-88	.261	.258	.261	43	142	16	37	6	2	3	16	29	1	0	1	41	0	1	.394	.387
Burns, Billy	B-R	5-9	180	8-30-89	.250	.270	.242	91	364	57	91	20	3	1	23	44	3	6	4	65	51	5	.330	.333
Chapman, Matt	R-R	6-2	205	4-28-93	.000	.000	.000	1	3	0	0	0	0	0	0	0	0	0	0	0	0	0	.000	.000
Chavez, Jose	R-R	5-11	175	8-5-95	.167	.000	.222	3	12	1	2	1	0	0	1	1	0	0	0	4	0	0	.250	.231
Coleman, Dusty	R-R	6-2	205	4-28-93	.223	.234	.219	135	489	79	109	27	2	18	81	47	9	4	5	202	16	5	.397	.300
Crumbliss, Conner	L-R	5-8	175	4-19-87	.251	.195	.270	118	439	65	110	25	4	10	49	69	7	2	5	66	13	2	.394	.358
Forsythe, Blake	R-R	6-2	220	7-31-89	.224	.247	.213	72	232	26	52	12	1	5	26	27	1	1	1	77	0	1	.349	.307
Head, Miles	R-R	6-0	215	5-2-91	.219	.266	.199	58	210	21	46	7	1	7	28	11	3	0	3	52	1	0	.362	.264
Lamas, Antonio	B-R	5-9	165	12-30-89	.167	.000	.200	2	6	0	1	0	0	0	0	0	0	0	0	2	0	0	.167	.167
Lipkin, Ryan	R-R	6-0	205	10-8-87	.000	.000	.000	1	3	0	0	0	0	0	0	0	0	0	0	1	0	0	.000	.000
Marte, Jefry	R-R	6-1	190	6-21-91	.259	.276	.253	107	405	50	105	17	0	10	53	45	3	1	6	69	9	3	.375	.333
Matthes, Kent	R-R	6-2	215	1-8-87	.241	.325	.211	78	295	43	71	21	1	15	60	20	3	0	1	84	5	0	.471	.295
Maxwell, Bruce	L-R	6-2	235	12-20-90	.141	.296	.069	25	85	8	12	3	0	2	9	8	0	0	0	32	0	1	.176	.223
Muncy, Max	L-R	6-0	205	8-25-90	.264	.248	.272	122	435	59	115	23	3	7	63	87	2	0	6	92	7	2	.379	.385
Myers, D'Arby	R-R	6-3	185	12-9-88	.305	.353	.283	59	213	36	65	14	2	2	21	17	2	4	3	38	9	6	.418	.357
Nakajima, Hiroyuki	R-R	5-11	200	7-31-82	.266	.307	.244	73	256	30	68	8	0	6	31	26	3	1	3	56	3	3	.367	.337
Oberacker, Chad	L-L	5-11	188	1-14-89	.220	.213	.223	86	291	31	64	11	5	2	20	23	0	5	2	52	8	5	.313	.275
Russell, Addison	R-R	6-0	195	1-23-94	.333	.462	.286	13	48	7	16	3	1	1	8	8	1	0	0	8	3	2	.500	.439
Taylor, Beau	L-R	6-0	205	2-13-90	.239	.107	.260	63	209	22	50	15	0	3	26	23	1	2	1	61	1	1	.354	.316
Walsh, Colin	B-R	6-0	190	9-26-89	.287	.231	.307	25	101	13	29	5	0	1	10	11	1	0	3	26	1	1	.366	.353
Whitaker, Josh	R-R	6-3	225	2-8-89	.320	.216	.356	51	197	26	63	11	1	9	42	14	2	0	2	38	3	2	.523	.367
Wilson, Kenny	B-R	5-11	195	1-30-90	.327	.270	.355	27	113	12	37	7	1	0	8	2	1	1	0	24	7	3	.407	.345

Pitching	B-T	HT	WT	DOB	W	L	ERA	G	GS	CG	SV	IP	H	R	ER	HR	BB	SO	AVG	vLH	vRH	K/9	BB/9
Alcantara, Raul	R-R	6-3	225	12-4-92	2	0	2.29	3	3	0	0	20	17	5	5	0	5	10	.250	.273	.239	4.58	2.29

Name	B-T	HT	WT	DOB	W	L	ERA	G	GS	CG	SV	IP	H	R	ER	HR	BB	SO	AVG	vLH	vRH	K/9	BB/9
Castillo, Jesus	R-R	6-0	205	5-31-84	1	0	3.95	8	0	0	1	14	12	6	6	0	6	9	.255	.286	.231	5.93	3.95
Doolittle, Ryan	R-R	6-2	205	3-25-88	5	3	3.23	30	0	0	0	47	47	22	17	4	19	47	.254	.228	.274	8.94	3.61
Dull, Ryan	R-R	5-11	175	10-2-89	5	5	2.88	40	0	0	6	56	52	24	18	6	15	61	.240	.333	.187	9.75	2.40
Duran, Omar	L-L	6-3	220	2-26-90	1	0	3.14	11	0	0	0	14	7	5	5	2	6	18	.146	.120	.174	11.30	3.77
Finnegan, Kyle	R-R	6-2	170	9-4-91	0	1	11.81	1	1	0	0	5	10	7	7	3	1	6	.455	.556	.385	10.13	1.69
Flores, Jose	R-R	6-3	250	6-4-89	1	2	2.96	22	0	0	12	24	16	8	8	1	10	18	.184	.161	.196	6.66	3.70
Frankoff, Seth	R-R	6-5	200	8-27-88	2	2	2.41	27	0	0	15	34	29	10	9	3	11	47	.232	.259	.211	12.56	2.94
Gailey, Frank	L-L	5-9	190	11-18-85	1	0	3.46	40	0	0	0	52	56	20	20	1	21	44	.256	.205	.291	7.62	3.63
Granier, Drew	R-R	6-1	190	11-24-88	7	7	4.56	26	24	0	0	126	131	82	64	15	76	93	.266	.312	.230	6.63	5.41
Hassebrock, Blake	R-R	6-4	212	7-15-89	4	0	7.24	21	0	0	0	32	59	33	26	5	10	20	.391	.418	.369	5.57	2.78
Haviland, Shawn	R-R	6-2	200	11-10-85	7	7	3.87	25	25	0	0	146	137	70	63	14	51	95	.254	.298	.217	5.84	3.14
Healy, Tucker	L-R	6-1	195	6-15-90	0	1	2.33	12	0	0	4	19	17	5	5	1	6	29	.227	.156	.279	13.50	2.79
Hooker, Deryk	R-R	6-4	215	6-21-89	1	0	3.45	12	3	0	0	29	34	11	11	0	11	20	.306	.254	.365	6.28	3.45
Jensen, Chris	R-R	6-4	200	9-30-90	12	8	3.14	26	26	0	0	160	147	65	56	3	62	94	.246	.290	.213	5.28	3.48
Long, Nathan	R-R	6-2	210	2-9-86	13	8	3.18	28	25	0	0	150	147	60	53	17	49	126	.260	.296	.231	7.56	2.94
Murphy, Sean	B-R	6-6	215	8-23-88	4	3	3.95	10	10	0	0	57	66	27	25	3	18	53	.296	.287	.301	8.37	2.84
Neal, Zach	R-R	6-3	220	11-9-88	3	0	0.58	5	5	0	0	31	25	5	2	0	4	25	.212	.213	.211	7.26	1.16
Peters, Tanner	R-R	6-0	155	8-6-90	0	3	3.63	3	3	0	0	17	18	9	7	2	5	7	.273	.206	.344	3.63	2.60
Sexton, Tim	R-R	6-6	185	6-10-87	1	1	5.91	5	0	0	0	11	15	7	7	0	2	11	.333	.200	.440	9.28	1.69
2-team total (1 San Antonio)					2	1	4.02	6	1	0	0	16	19	7	7	0	4	16	—	—	—	9.19	2.30
Smith, Murphy	R-R	6-3	210	8-25-87	2	5	4.73	31	7	0	1	86	84	46	45	4	31	62	.265	.311	.231	6.51	3.26
Urlaub, Jeff	L-L	6-2	160	4-24-87	2	0	1.57	13	0	0	0	23	16	4	4	2	6	19	.198	.250	.175	7.43	2.35
Walden, Marcus	R-R	6-0	195	9-13-88	1	2	3.79	21	0	0	2	36	38	22	15	2	13	26	.273	.356	.213	6.56	3.28
Werner, Andrew	L-L	6-2	215	2-25-87	2	4	6.32	14	8	0	0	47	53	37	33	7	20	36	.285	.295	.282	6.89	3.83

Fielding

Catcher	PCT	G	PO	A	E	DP	PB
Chavez	.969	3	27	4	1	1	0
Forsythe	.984	61	392	39	7	3	3
Lipkin	1.000	1	7	1	0	0	0
Maxwell	1.000	24	181	22	0	1	3
Taylor	.993	57	388	49	3	6	2

First Base	PCT	G	PO	A	E	DP
Aliotti	.988	28	219	24	3	19
Forsythe	1.000	5	36	2	0	4
Head	.992	13	125	7	1	21
Marte	.938	3	27	3	2	2
Muncy	.995	86	737	54	4	78
Nakajima	1.000	4	30	4	0	2
Oberacker	1.000	1	9	0	0	0
Whitaker	.972	5	32	3	1	3

Second Base	PCT	G	PO	A	E	DP
Coleman	1.000	9	20	28	0	10
Crumbliss	.970	83	148	209	11	50
Lamas	1.000	2	3	2	0	2
Nakajima	.979	33	60	80	3	17
Walsh	.980	19	36	61	2	13

Third Base	PCT	G	PO	A	E	DP
Chapman	1.000	1	1	1	0	0
Head	.918	20	16	40	5	4
Marte	.927	91	45	196	19	15
Muncy	.941	22	16	48	4	7
Nakajima	.889	8	3	5	1	0
Walsh	.714	2	2	3	2	0

Shortstop	PCT	G	PO	A	E	DP
Coleman	.964	125	219	365	22	83

	PCT	G	PO	A	E	DP
Nakajima	.762	5	6	10	5	2
Russell	.957	11	15	30	2	11

Outfield	PCT	G	PO	A	E	DP
Aliotti	1.000	12	13	0	0	0
Barfield	1.000	25	40	4	0	0
Burns	.979	87	229	3	5	1
Crumbliss	1.000	34	61	2	0	0
Forsythe	1.000	3	9	0	0	0
Matthes	.983	66	104	11	2	0
Muncy	1.000	1	0	1	0	0
Myers	.963	53	76	1	3	0
Oberacker	.994	76	170	5	1	2
Taylor	1.000	1	3	0	0	0
Walsh	1.000	5	5	1	0	0
Whitaker	.978	42	83	8	2	1
Wilson	1.000	27	51	1	0	0

STOCKTON PORTS

HIGH CLASS A

CALIFORNIA LEAGUE

Batting	B-T	HT	WT	DOB	AVG	vLH	vRH	G	AB	R	H	2B	3B	HR	RBI	BB	HBP	SH	SF	SO	SB	CS	SLG	OBP
Brugman, Jaycob	L-L	6-0	195	1-18-92	.282	.303	.278	50	195	34	55	6	2	13	35	16	0	0	3	50	3	3	.533	.332
Gallaspo, Alberto	B-R	5-9	225	4-19-83	.200	—	.200	1	5	2	1	0	0	0	0	0	0	0	0	0	0	0	.200	.200
Crocker, Bobby	R-R	6-3	220	5-1-90	.271	.244	.280	120	447	59	121	22	6	11	52	37	9	2	4	149	31	6	.421	.336
DeVoss, Zeke	B-R	5-10	175	7-17-90	.167	.167	.167	23	72	9	12	1	0	0	5	18	4	0	1	24	2	2	.181	.358
Gentry, Craig	R-R	6-2	190	11-29-83	.500	.500	—	1	4	0	2	1	0	0	0	0	0	0	0	1	0	1	.750	.500
Gorton, Ryan	R-R	6-2	220	2-27-90	.198	.242	.181	34	116	12	23	2	0	0	7	5	2	1	1	21	1	0	.216	.242
Healy, Ryon	R-R	6-5	205	1-10-92	.285	.221	.308	136	561	73	160	28	2	16	83	28	3	0	8	79	0	0	.428	.318
Kirkland, Wade	R-R	5-10	200	4-4-89	.241	.206	.256	64	228	26	55	17	1	4	27	10	5	0	0	74	6	0	.377	.288
Lipkin, Ryan	R-R	6-0	205	10-8-87	.344	.200	.370	10	32	2	11	2	0	0	4	2	2	0	1	6	0	1	.406	.405
Marincov, Tyler	R-R	6-2	205	10-20-91	.317	.250	.327	16	60	11	19	5	1	2	13	6	1	0	2	22	1	0	.533	.377
Maxwell, Bruce	L-R	6-2	235	12-20-90	.273	.306	.257	79	289	33	79	11	1	6	35	41	2	0	2	58	0	1	.381	.365
McKinney, Billy	L-L	6-1	195	8-23-94	.241	.226	.248	75	290	42	70	12	2	10	33	36	4	0	3	58	5	3	.400	.330
Nunez, Renato	R-R	6-1	185	4-4-94	.279	.320	.266	124	509	75	142	28	3	29	96	34	13	0	6	113	2	0	.517	.336
Oberacker, Chad	L-L	5-11	188	1-14-89	.235	.333	.182	6	17	2	4	2	0	0	0	3	0	0	0	5	1	1	.353	.350
Olson, Matt	L-R	6-4	236	3-29-94	.262	.252	.265	138	512	111	134	31	1	37	97	117	5	0	0	137	2	0	.543	.404
Pinder, Chad	R-R	6-2	195	3-29-92	.288	.307	.283	94	403	61	116	32	5	13	55	22	8	1	2	99	12	9	.489	.336
Powell, Boog	L-L	5-10	185	1-14-93	.377	.400	.370	14	61	11	23	3	1	0	11	8	0	0	0	4	0	2	.459	.449
Reddick, Josh	L-R	6-2	180	2-19-87	.429	.429	.429	5	21	6	9	2	0	3	8	1	0	0	0	6	0	0	.952	.455
Robertson, Daniel	R-R	6-0	190	3-22-94	.310	.326	.304	132	548	110	170	37	3	15	60	72	16	1	5	94	4	4	.471	.402
Robinson, Dusty	R-R	6-0	205	9-9-89	.230	.280	.200	66	239	24	55	14	1	8	28	24	2	0	4	68	9	4	.397	.301
Russell, Addison	R-R	6-0	195	1-23-94	.188	.000	.273	5	16	0	3	0	0	0	1	2	0	0	0	6	1	0	.188	.278
Shipman, Aaron	L-L	6-0	175	1-27-92	.292	.311	.286	52	178	30	52	6	1		16	36	1	0	0	39	13	2	.410	.414
Taylor, Beau	L-R	6-0	205	2-13-90	.333	.474	.305	32	114	21	38	10	0	5	27	22	0	2	3	33	0	0	.553	.435
Walsh, Colin	B-R	6-0	190	9-26-89	.417	.500	.375	6	24	7	10	1	0	1	6	10	1	0	1	0	0	3	.583	.533

Pitching	B-T	HT	WT	DOB	W	L	ERA	G	GS	CG	SV	IP	H	R	ER	HR	BB	SO	AVG	vLH	vRH	K/9	BB/9
Adkins, Hunter	R-R	6-4	190	9-20-90	2	3	5.74	12	11	0	0	58	63	39	37	10	27	37	.283	.354	.241	5.74	4.19
Alderson, Tim	R-R	6-6	220	11-3-88	5	0	4.11	8	7	0	1	46	44	22	21	7	12	42	.249	.207	.284	8.22	2.35

Name	B-T	HT	WT	DOB	W	L	ERA	G	GS	CG	SV	IP	H	R	ER	HR	BB	SO	AVG	vLH	vRH	K/9	BB/9
Atherton, Tim	R-R	6-2	209	11-7-89	6	2	5.04	15	15	0	0	80	88	51	45	10	24	67	.277	.278	.275	7.51	2.69
Avila, Andres	R-R	6-0	185	6-20-90	3	1	3.00	17	0	0	0	36	34	13	12	4	11	41	.250	.232	.263	10.25	2.75
Bowman, Josh	R-R	6-2	195	9-9-88	8	7	5.03	31	20	0	1	131	143	78	73	23	36	89	.280	.291	.273	6.13	2.48
Buschmann, Matt	R-R	6-3	195	2-13-84	1	0	2.70	2	2	0	0	10	5	3	3	2	5	11	.139	.154	.130	9.90	4.50
Castillo, Yeiper	R-R	6-3	185	9-6-88	1	1	9.00	6	5	0	0	23	36	25	23	4	18	8	.387	.417	.377	3.13	7.04
2-team total (2 Inland Empire)					1	2	9.11	8	6	0	0	27	42	30	27	4	22	9	—	—	—	3.04	7.43
Cook, Ryan	R-R	6-2	215	6-30-87	0	0	6.75	3	0	0	0	3	2	2	2	1	2	2	.200	.143	.333	6.75	6.75
Correa, Manuarys	R-R	6-3	170	1-5-89	2	3	5.40	8	8	0	0	37	36	23	22	7	12	29	.263	.279	.250	7.12	2.95
Covey, Dylan	R-R	6-2	195	8-14-91	3	5	7.15	8	8	0	0	39	49	31	31	2	15	22	.312	.246	.354	5.08	3.46
Doolittle, Ryan	R-R	6-2	205	3-25-88	0	1	1.80	6	0	0	0	10	6	2	2		2	13	.167	.143	.200	11.70	1.80
Duran, Omar	L-L	6-3	220	2-26-90	2	2	2.35	26	0	0	1	46	37	13	12	3	22	61	.220	.268	.196	11.93	4.30
Fernandez, Rodolfo	R-R	6-2	220	3-21-90	0	2	4.38	16	0	0	1	25	24	13	12	3	11	26	.261	.258	.262	9.49	4.01
Hall, Kris	R-R	6-3	215	6-8-91	5	0	4.29	40	0	0	3	57	42	28	27	6	38	77	.210	.183	.225	12.23	6.04
Hassebrock, Blake	R-R	6-4	212	7-15-89	0	0	5.23	8	0	0	0	10	15	7	6	1	6	8	.349	.348	.350	6.97	5.23
Haviland, Shawn	R-R	6-2	200	11-10-85	1	2	3.24	3	3	0	0	17	12	8	6	2	4	14	.194	.091	.310	7.56	2.16
Healy, Tucker	L-R	6-1	195	6-15-90	2	1	1.04	13	0	0	3	17	9	2	2	1	4	29	.153	.192	.121	15.06	2.08
Hollstegge, Tyler	L-R	6-1	205	12-17-90	0	0	4.50	2	0	0	0	2	4	1	1	0	1	1	.444	.250	.600	4.50	4.50
House, Austin	R-R	6-4	200	1-24-91	3	4	3.46	46	0	0	19	55	47	22	21	4	19	79	.232	.316	.181	13.01	3.13
Joseph, Jonathan	R-R	6-1	180	5-17-88	7	3	3.58	37	3	0	0	78	68	35	31	5	38	72	.236	.257	.224	8.31	4.38
Lamb, Chris	B-L	6-1	185	6-29-90	4	5	3.21	20	19	0	0	104	92	40	37	5	36	100	.237	.309	.213	8.68	3.13
McCurry, Brendan	R-R	5-10	165	1-7-92	0	0	0.00	1	0	0	0	1	0	0	0	0		1	.000	.000	.000	9.00	0.00
Murphy, Sean	B-R	6-6	215	8-23-88	0	1	2.70	3	3	0	0	13	12	4	4	0	6	19	.250	.250	.250	12.83	4.05
Neal, Zach	R-R	6-3	220	11-9-88	0	0	0.57	2	2	0	0	16	8	2	1	0	0	19	.145	.143	.146	10.91	0.00
O'Flaherty, Eric	L-L	6-2	220	2-5-85	1	0	0.00	1	0	0	0	1	0	0	0	0	0	3	.000	—	.000	27.00	0.00
Sanburn, Nolan	R-R	6-0	175	7-21-91	3	1	3.28	42	0	0	6	71	78	29	26	6	25	73	.279	.252	.297	9.21	3.15
Sanchez, Jake	R-R	6-2	205	8-19-89	8	2	3.42	12	12	0	0	71	71	32	27	7	17	72	.258	.248	.267	9.13	2.15
Streich, Seth	L-R	6-3	210	2-19-91	9	6	3.16	22	22	0	0	114	110	49	40	7	22	116	.253	.247	.257	9.16	1.74
Wahl, Bobby	R-R	6-2	210	3-21-92	0	0	4.22	9	0	0	0	11	8	7	5	2	6	19	.190	.214	.179	16.03	5.06
Ynoa, Michael	R-R	6-7	210	9-24-91	4	2	5.52	31	0	0	0	46	42	28	28	5	21	64	.247	.191	.284	12.61	4.14

Fielding

Catcher	PCT	G	PO	A	E	DP	PB
Gorton	1.000	33	251	15	0	1	4
Lipkin	.979	8	41	6	1	0	0
Maxwell	.990	78	701	56	8	6	16
Taylor	.996	29	265	19	1	0	6

First Base	PCT	G	PO	A	E	DP
Healy	1.000	34	260	21	0	29
Olson	.993	107	845	55	6	80

Second Base	PCT	G	PO	A	E	DP
Callaspo	1.000	1	2	1	0	1
Kirkland	.988	53	95	146	3	29
Pinder	.960	76	146	192	14	42
Robertson	.974	8	20	18	1	6

Walsh	.935	5	13	16	2	3

Third Base	PCT	G	PO	A	E	DP
Callaspo	1.000	1	0	1	0	1
Healy	.937	48	34	84	8	10
Nunez	.931	88	53	150	15	16
Pinder	.889	3	1	7	1	1
Robertson	1.000	3	3	4	0	0

Shortstop	PCT	G	PO	A	E	DP
Kirkland	1.000	2	2	1	0	0
Pinder	.987	14	33	41	1	7
Robertson	.964	123	150	311	17	64
Russell	1.000	4	4	12	0	3

Outfield	PCT	G	PO	A	E	DP
Brugman	.988	50	76	6	1	1
Crocker	.989	115	261	8	3	2
DeVoss	1.000	23	47	1	0	0
Gentry	1.000	1	2	0	0	1
Kirkland	1.000	3	1	0	0	0
Marincov	.941	16	16	0	1	0
McKinney	.981	74	152	1	3	0
Oberacker	1.000	5	14	0	0	0
Olson	.929	9	12	1	1	0
Powell	1.000	14	34	4	0	0
Reddick	1.000	4	4	0	0	0
Robinson	.985	62	120	8	2	0
Shipman	.986	48	71	2	1	0

BELOIT SNAPPERS

LOW CLASS A

MIDWEST LEAGUE

Batting	B-T	HT	WT	DOB	AVG	vLH	vRH	G	AB	R	H	2B	3B	HR	RBI	BB	HBP	SH	SF	SO	SB	CS	SLG	OBP
Akau, Iolana	R-R	5-11	180	8-31-95	.000	—	.000	1	1	0	0	0	0	0	0	0	0	0	0	0	0	0	.000	.000
Baez, Luis	R-R	6-2	200	5-24-91	.237	.293	.221	119	448	41	106	25	1	7	43	12	3	7	3	96	5	3	.344	.260
Boyd, B.J.	L-R	5-11	230	7-16-93	.226	.196	.234	125	464	57	105	15	5	6	38	48	2	5	2	94	15	9	.319	.300
Brugman, Jaycob	L-L	6-0	195	1-18-92	.278	.310	.272	70	248	33	69	19	4	8	37	35	2	1	1	65	5	2	.484	.371
Chapman, Matt	R-R	6-2	205	4-28-93	.237	.275	.227	50	190	22	45	8	3	5	20	7	5	0	0	46	2	1	.389	.282
Chavez, Jose	R-R	5-11	175	8-5-95	.205	.227	.200	46	132	8	27	3	0	0	4	9	4	7	1	23	0	1	.227	.274
Cogswell, Branden	L-R	6-1	180	1-12-93	.203	.161	.216	40	128	14	26	2	1	0	12	17	3	2	1	24	3	1	.234	.309
Freiman, Nate	R-R	6-8	250	12-31-86	.444	—	.444	2	9	2	4	2	0	1	2	0	0	0	0	4	0	0	1.000	.444
Higley, Justin	L-R	6-4	200	12-25-92	.240	.235	.241	48	175	18	42	8	2	2	12	12	1	0	1	59	6	1	.343	.291
Huck, Ryan	R-R	6-5	255	2-24-91	.202	.267	.192	35	119	16	24	2	1	3	13	19	0	0	0	37	1	0	.311	.312
Ludy, Josh	R-R	5-10	210	4-18-90	.218	.214	.220	17	55	7	12	1	0	3	5	11	1	1	0	17	0	0	.400	.358
Marincov, Tyler	R-R	6-2	205	10-20-91	.261	.250	.264	111	399	59	104	29	5	16	64	47	7	0	8	108	17	8	.479	.343
Mathews, Ryan	R-R	6-3	190	8-1-89	.269	.290	.263	90	324	36	87	18	3	12	42	23	1	0	2	85	5	3	.454	.317
Mercedes, Melvin	B-R	5-8	170	1-13-92	.222	.324	.195	98	361	54	80	14	7	2	33	41	4	1	7	70	12	4	.316	.303
Pan, Chih-Fang	B-R	6-1	170	11-12-90	.254	.302	.245	81	284	17	72	13	3	1	24	22	3	4	3	62	4	4	.331	.311
Paz, Andy	R-R	6-0	170	1-5-93	.158	.154	.159	18	57	4	9	2	0	0	7	10	0	3	1	18	1	0	.193	.279
Pohl, Phil	R-R	5-11	220	7-22-90	.238	.224	.241	72	252	26	60	15	0	6	29	10	17	5	0	48	4	1	.369	.312
Powell, Boog	L-L	5-10	185	1-14-93	.335	.383	.324	69	254	43	85	7	4	3	17	53	2	1	1	49	16	13	.429	.452
Roberts, Sam	L-R	6-1	190	2-23-89	.244	—	.244	43	127	7	31	5	0	1	7	10	2	3	1	37	1	1	.307	.307
Soto, Michael	R-R	6-3	215	11-17-91	.274	.351	.252	50	164	26	45	9	2	7	29	15	0	0	3	34	3	0	.482	.330
Vollmuth, B.A.	R-R	6-3	215	12-23-89	.207	.250	.196	99	367	41	76	22	0	9	44	35	3	0	5	91	7	3	.341	.278

Pitching	B-T	HT	WT	DOB	W	L	ERA	G	GS	CG	SV	IP	H	R	ER	HR	BB	SO	AVG	vLH	vRH	K/9	BB/9
Adkins, Hunter	R-R	6-4	190	9-20-90	1	6	5.02	13	9	1	0	57	59	44	32	7	20	37	.259	.257	.260	5.81	3.14
Avila, Andres	R-R	6-0	185	6-20-90	2	3	2.67	24	0	0	8	34	32	14	10	2	6	23	.241	.180	.277	6.15	1.60

OAKLAND ATHLETICS

Name	B-T	HT	WT	DOB	W	L	ERA	G	GS	CG	SV	IP	H	R	ER	HR	BB	SO	AVG	vLH	vRH	K/9	BB/9
Bayless, Trevor	R-R	6-3	210	10-6-91	1	0	5.23	24	0	0	0	41	39	28	24	8	29	22	.248	.211	.284	4.79	6.31
Bragg, Sam	R-R	6-2	190	3-23-93	4	0	3.23	41	1	0	7	75	66	30	27	5	26	68	.237	.261	.219	8.12	3.11
Covey, Dylan	R-R	6-2	195	8-14-91	4	9	4.81	18	17	2	0	101	99	59	54	3	26	70	.258	.237	.272	6.24	2.32
Finnegan, Kyle	R-R	6-2	170	9-4-91	7	9	3.69	23	23	1	0	120	99	53	49	12	52	55	.227	.216	.236	4.14	3.91
Herrera, Ronald	R-R	5-11	185	5-3-95	3	4	3.38	9	9	0	0	51	53	26	19	6	10	35	.272	.290	.262	6.22	1.78
2-team total (17 Fort Wayne)					6	9	3.92	26	25	0	0	133	146	71	58	11	25	82	—	—	—	5.55	1.69
Hollstegge, Tyler	L-R	6-1	205	12-17-90	0	1	11.25	11	0	0	0	12	18	15	15	2	11	9	.340	.333	.344	6.75	8.25
Lamb, Chris	B-L	6-1	185	6-29-90	1	0	2.77	10	3	0	2	26	18	10	8	1	7	34	.191	.194	.190	11.77	2.42
McCurry, Brendan	R-R	5-10	165	1-7-92	2	0	0.34	15	0	0	2	26	12	1	1	1	3	34	.140	.147	.135	11.62	1.03
McMullen, Blake	R-R	6-1	205	2-15-91	1	2	8.04	10	0	0	0	16	21	15	14	3	8	11	.318	.269	.350	6.32	4.60
Mendez, Junior	R-R	6-1	210	9-20-92	2	8	4.77	25	18	0	0	106	107	60	56	16	27	61	.260	.240	.279	5.20	2.30
Michaud, Joe	R-R	6-4	200	4-4-91	3	2	6.32	13	2	0	0	37	51	31	26	5	7	21	.319	.224	.387	5.11	1.70
Powers, Brent	L-L	6-1	185	5-25-89	2	2	6.21	15	4	0	0	38	46	31	26	2	24	31	.297	.262	.310	7.41	5.73
2-team total (12 Lansing)					5	6	5.42	27	15	0	0	86	99	62	52	5	46	66	—	—	—	6.88	4.80
Pudenz, Stuart	R-R	6-5	215	9-15-90	2	3	6.04	18	0	0	0	22	25	19	15	1	17	18	.291	.379	.246	7.25	6.85
Seddon, Joel	R-R	6-1	165	7-13-92	2	2	2.84	19	0	0	1	25	20	9	8	2	8	20	.227	.222	.231	7.11	2.84
Sosa, Lee	R-R	6-2	215	9-3-91	0	0	9.00	14	0	0	1	19	25	22	19	2	14	15	.321	.387	.277	7.11	6.63
Stalcup, Matt	L-L	6-2	195	7-6-90	6	4	3.93	21	14	1	1	89	101	42	39	9	20	70	.277	.238	.289	7.05	2.01
Trivino, Lou	R-R	6-5	225	10-1-91	7	11	5.28	27	26	0	0	140	160	93	82	10	43	95	.290	.289	.291	6.12	2.77
Vail, Tyler	R-R	6-1	208	11-3-91	3	6	4.61	29	0	0	3	41	53	29	21	3	18	24	.314	.307	.319	5.27	3.95
Vattuone, Dominique	R-R	6-4	175	2-12-91	0	0	6.14	5	0	0	0	7	6	5	5	1	8	5	.222	.167	.267	6.14	9.82
Wagman, Joey	L-R	6-0	185	7-25-91	2	2	5.13	6	6	0	0	26	26	15	15	2	7	31	.248	.333	.190	10.59	2.39
Wahl, Bobby	R-R	6-2	210	3-21-92	0	4	5.06	20	7	0	4	43	46	29	24	5	19	43	.267	.305	.233	9.07	4.01

Fielding

Catcher	PCT	G	PO	A	E	DP	PB
Akau	.500	1	1	0	1	0	0
Chavez	.993	46	244	32	2	1	12
Ludy	.990	16	96	7	1	2	1
Paz	.992	18	118	13	1	0	4
Pohl	.991	61	401	41	4	2	1

First Base	PCT	G	PO	A	E	DP
Brugman	1.000	1	1	0	0	0
Freiman	1.000	2	17	3	0	1
Huck	.989	33	254	17	3	23
Mathews	.981	13	97	6	2	12
Soto	.985	43	315	22	5	32
Vollmuth	.985	56	507	22	8	36

Second Base	PCT	G	PO	A	E	DP
Baez	.964	17	31	49	3	14
Mercedes	.965	24	54	57	4	12
Pan	.967	67	102	187	10	39
Roberts	.988	39	77	93	2	15
Vollmuth	1.000	1	1	0	0	0

Third Base	PCT	G	PO	A	E	DP
Baez	.936	58	49	113	11	8
Chapman	.914	38	34	83	11	12
Mercedes	.500	1	0	1	1	0
Soto	.750	2	1	2	1	0
Vollmuth	.939	44	28	80	7	5

Shortstop	PCT	G	PO	A	E	DP
Baez	.915	32	50	80	12	15
Cogswell	.905	37	49	103	16	17
Mercedes	.952	71	113	205	16	41
Roberts	.667	3	1	1	1	0

Outfield	PCT	G	PO	A	E	DP
Baez	1.000	6	10	1	0	1
Boyd	.989	119	252	12	3	4
Brugman	.990	46	102	2	1	0
Higley	.990	47	96	2	1	1
Marincov	.975	101	188	6	5	0
Mathews	.973	36	71	2	2	1
Powell	.976	66	158	6	4	2

VERMONT LAKE MONSTERS — SHORT-SEASON

NEW YORK-PENN LEAGUE

Batting	B-T	HT	WT	DOB	AVG	vLH	vRH	G	AB	R	H	2B	3B	HR	RBI	BB	HBP	SH	SF	SO	SB	CS	SLG	OBP
Alexander, Dayton	R-R	6-1	195	2-4-91	.207	.111	.216	36	111	15	23	7	0	0	7	18	2	1	0	36	11	0	.270	.328
Bennie, Joe	R-R	6-0	200	5-7-91	.288	.333	.279	45	156	15	45	9	1	1	14	21	0	0	2	51	4	1	.378	.369
Brizuela, Jose	L-R	6-0	180	8-31-92	.241	.091	.261	55	187	25	45	9	1	5	22	15	5	0	3	42	2	1	.380	.310
Chavez, Jose	R-R	5-11	175	8-5-95	.093	.000	.143	16	54	3	5	0	0	0	3	3	1	2	0	17	0	0	.093	.155
Gilbert, Trent	L-R	6-1	175	3-17-93	.212	.118	.225	40	137	17	29	6	1	0	10	10	2	0	1	35	1	0	.270	.273
Higley, Justin	L-R	6-4	200	12-25-92	.281	.182	.295	24	89	16	25	6	2	5	25	8	0	0	1	31	10	0	.562	.337
Huck, Ryan	R-R	6-5	255	2-24-91	.188	.200	.187	47	170	11	32	7	1	2	17	13	1	0	1	56	0	1	.276	.249
Kim, Seongmin	R-R	6-2	250	5-12-93	.192	.125	.205	30	99	7	19	5	1	2	19	6	2	0	0	33	0	0	.323	.252
Kuhn, Max	R-R	5-11	185	9-10-92	.277	.259	.280	52	184	26	51	10	2	4	23	17	3	1	0	46	3	2	.418	.348
Masik, Scott	R-R	6-2	180	1-10-91	.218	.258	.209	49	170	20	37	5	1	1	11	13	13	0	0	37	4	2	.276	.321
McQuown, Ben	R-R	5-10	175	2-6-90	.239	.293	.221	52	163	20	39	3	2	2	15	15	3	3	1	33	12	3	.319	.313
Munoz, Yairo	R-R	6-1	165	1-23-95	.298	.298	.298	66	252	29	75	17	3	5	20	7	2	2	2	42	14	6	.448	.319
Nogowski, John	R-L	6-2	210	1-5-93	.259	.286	.252	50	158	18	41	8	0	1	21	20	5	0	2	23	0	0	.329	.357
Paz, Andy	R-R	6-0	170	1-5-93	.120	.200	.111	14	50	7	6	1	0	0	6	3	0	0	1	11	0	0	.180	.167
Santana, Gabriel	R-R	6-0	165	8-23-92	.246	.269	.241	41	134	13	33	4	0	1	9	6	3	1	0	16	2	2	.299	.294
Sportman, J.P.	R-R	5-9	190	1-26-92	.301	.452	.261	38	146	17	44	8	0	3	15	8	0	1	2	22	4	3	.418	.333
Vertigan, Brett	L-L	5-9	175	8-24-90	.265	.400	.255	47	151	23	40	8	2	1	12	9	1	3	1	16	6	2	.364	.309
Wheeler, Kyle	R-R	5-11	195	10-16-90	.181	.111	.189	27	83	4	15	2	0	0	3	4	1	0	0	26	0	1	.205	.227
Wolfe, Chris	B-R	5-11	160	2-2-90	.200	.300	.160	16	35	3	7	1	0	0	4	8	0	1	0	8	0	1	.229	.349

Pitching	B-T	HT	WT	DOB	W	L	ERA	G	GS	CG	SV	IP	H	R	ER	HR	BB	SO	AVG	vLH	vRH	K/9	BB/9
Bayless, Trevor	R-R	6-3	210	10-6-91	0	0	0.00	1	0	0	1	2	3	0	0	0	0	3	.333	.000	.500	13.50	0.00
Burke, A.J.	R-R	6-3	225	7-12-90	6	4	3.89	15	13	0	0	72	76	38	31	5	13	57	.264	.273	.255	7.16	1.63
Cruzado, Fernand	R-R	6-2	210	10-25-88	2	0	1.90	24	0	0	4	24	19	5	5	3	8	20	.221	.289	.167	7.61	3.04
Fagan, Mike	R-L	5-11	160	5-12-92	2	1	4.66	17	0	0	0	19	13	11	10	2	15	25	.191	.120	.233	11.64	6.98
Ferreras, Kevin	L-L	6-0	170	7-5-93	0	0	5.14	6	0	0	0	7	7	4	4	0	5	5	.250	.333	.227	6.43	6.43
Gauna, Koby	R-R	6-3	225	9-10-93	1	0	2.08	15	1	0	12	17	15	4	4	2	2	14	.242	.259	.229	7.27	1.04
Gossett, Daniel	R-R	6-2	185	11-13-92	1	0	2.25	12	1	0	0	24	16	6	6	1	1	25	.188	.206	.176	9.38	0.38
Graves, Brett	R-R	6-1	170	1-30-93	3	2	6.86	8	2	0	0	21	24	18	16	1	6	18	.279	.238	.318	7.71	2.57
Grundy, Jerad	L-L	5-11	200	4-7-90	4	7	4.08	15	15	0	0	90	90	38	34	6	16	51	.303	.288	.307	6.12	1.92
Hollstegge, Tyler	L-R	6-1	205	12-17-90	0	0	5.19	16	0	0	0	17	16	10	10	2	12	18	.250	.258	.242	9.35	6.23
Massad, Jon	R-R	6-1	200	4-19-91	2	2	4.39	21	0	0	0	27	26	13	13	2	8	22	.265	.261	.269	7.43	2.70

Name	B-T	HT	WT	DOB	W	L	ERA	G	GS	CG	SV	IP	H	R	ER	HR	BB	SO	AVG	vLH	vRH	K/9	BB/9
McMullen, Blake	R-R	6-1	205	2-15-91	1	2	4.86	20	0	0	1	33	35	20	18	1	10	25	.267	.250	.284	6.75	2.70
Michaud, Joe	R-R	6-4	200	4-4-91	1	2	3.41	5	5	0	0	29	33	12	11	1	2	23	.289	.327	.254	7.14	0.62
Miller, Corey	R-R	6-3	190	11-13-91	1	3	4.65	12	9	0	0	41	43	21	21	2	16	29	.276	.301	.253	6.42	3.54
Nolasco, Alex	L-L	6-4	190	9-11-90	1	0	0.00	2	0	0	0	2	0	1	0	0	1	0	.000	.000	.000	0.00	5.40
Overton, Dillon	L-L	6-2	172	8-17-91	0	1	2.40	5	5	0	0	15	11	4	4	0	1	22	.200	.208	.194	13.20	0.60
Perez, Cristhian	R-R	6-2	180	9-13-91	2	5	4.90	14	13	0	0	64	76	40	35	5	14	31	.293	.374	.200	4.34	1.96
Rivas, Jesus	R-R	6-0	180	3-22-94	0	0	10.80	2	0	0	0	2	3	2	2	0	3	1	.375	.400	.333	5.40	16.20
Schwartz, Jordan	R-R	6-2	195	2-28-92	1	1	4.82	11	0	0	0	19	21	14	10	0	13	14	.288	.333	.235	6.75	6.27
Sosa, Lee	R-R	6-2	215	9-3-91	3	2	2.39	13	1	0	0	26	21	7	7	1	8	21	.216	.180	.255	7.18	2.73
Torres, Jose	L-L	6-2	175	9-24-93	0	6	4.38	14	9	0	2	62	62	37	30	4	22	47	.267	.222	.288	6.86	3.21
Vattuone, Dominique	R-R	6-4	175	2-12-91	3	1	3.38	19	0	0	1	32	26	14	12	2	12	33	.228	.240	.219	9.28	3.38
Veliz, Victor	L-L	5-11	170	10-6-93	2	0	6.00	4	2	0	0	15	15	12	10	3	6	7	.263	.158	.316	4.20	3.60
Walter, Corey	R-R	6-3	215	8-11-92	2	1	3.10	17	0	0	0	20	16	7	7	0	8	20	.216	.172	.244	8.85	3.54

Fielding

Catcher	PCT	G	PO	A	E	DP	PB
Chavez	.981	16	134	20	3	2	3
Kim	.995	22	167	18	1	3	4
Paz	.970	14	83	15	3	0	1
Wheeler	.976	27	151	15	4	1	2

First Base	PCT	G	PO	A	E	DP
Huck	.996	27	219	23	1	15
Nogowski	.990	48	428	46	5	44
Santana	1.000	2	16	0	0	2
Vertigan	1.000	6	37	2	0	1

Second Base	PCT	G	PO	A	E	DP
Bennie	.957	32	57	97	7	13

	PCT	G	PO	A	E	DP
Gilbert	.967	36	53	93	5	19
Santana	.933	5	5	9	1	1
Wolfe	.971	12	10	24	1	1

Third Base	PCT	G	PO	A	E	DP
Brizuela	.959	53	50	89	6	8
Kuhn	.920	10	6	17	2	0
Munoz	.903	8	7	21	3	1
Santana	.931	6	8	19	2	2
Wolfe	.857	4	4	8	2	0

Shortstop	PCT	G	PO	A	E	DP
Munoz	.941	53	94	178	17	41
Santana	.962	30	40	88	5	8

Outfield	PCT	G	PO	A	E	DP
Alexander	1.000	28	54	1	0	1
Bennie	—	1	0	0	0	0
Higley	1.000	19	23	0	0	0
Huck	.833	8	4	1	1	0
Kuhn	.977	30	39	4	1	0
Masik	.955	40	62	1	3	0
McQuown	1.000	47	81	3	0	0
Sportman	.967	35	52	6	2	1
Vertigan	.986	38	67	3	1	1

AZL ATHLETICS — ROOKIE
ARIZONA LEAGUE

Batting	B-T	HT	WT	DOB	AVG	vLH	vRH	G	AB	R	H	2B	3B	HR	RBI	BB	HBP	SH	SF	SO	SB	CS	SLG	OBP
Akau, Iolana	R-R	5-11	180	8-31-95	.169	.154	.174	18	59	9	10	2	0	0	6	5	1	0	2	19	0	0	.203	.239
Brizuela, Jose	L-R	6-0	180	8-31-92	.429	.600	.333	4	14	2	6	1	1	1	3	1	0	0	0	1	0	0	.857	.467
Brown, Dusty	R-R	6-0	195	6-19-82	.290	.250	.296	10	31	5	9	2	0	2	6	1	1	0	0	9	0	0	.548	.333
Chapman, Matt	R-R	6-2	205	4-28-93	.429	.000	.500	3	14	1	6	1	1	0	0	1	0	0	0	1	0	0	.643	.467
De La Cruz, Vicmal	L-L	6-0	185	11-20-93	.210	.206	.211	46	167	25	35	13	1	0	17	20	4	0	2	43	4	3	.299	.306
Diaz, Edwin	R-R	6-2	195	8-25-95	.241	.212	.250	44	145	21	35	12	1	1	7	17	6	1	1	39	2	0	.359	.343
Duinkerk, Shawn	R-R	6-5	195	8-18-94	.167	.194	.158	35	126	10	21	7	2	0	13	9	0	1	0	39	1	1	.254	.222
Gilbert, Trent	L-R	6-1	175	3-17-93	.327	.429	.286	14	49	7	16	4	1	0	6	4	0	0	0	6	1	0	.449	.377
Kim, Seongmin	R-R	6-2	250	5-12-93	.441	.400	.448	12	34	10	15	2	1	3	6	7	0	0	0	13	1	0	.824	.537
Kubala, A.J.	R-R	6-0	205	6-7-94	.053	.000	.061	13	38	2	2	1	1	0	3	2	1	0	0	21	0	1	.132	.122
Kuhn, Max	R-R	5-11	185	9-10-92	.250	.400	.200	7	20	2	5	2	0	1	6	1	1	0	0	6	0	0	.500	.318
Loehr, Trace	L-R	5-10	175	5-23-95	.244	.262	.237	41	160	22	39	3	2	0	14	15	1	1	0	31	6	2	.288	.313
Lopez, Jesus	B-R	5-11	170	10-5-96	.221	.184	.235	42	136	18	30	5	1	0	13	19	0	2	0	29	4	1	.272	.316
Martinez, Robert	R-R	6-1	180	2-8-94	.219	.289	.195	48	151	24	33	12	1	5	29	26	2	1	1	60	2	2	.411	.339
Mercedes, Miguel	R-R	6-4	200	9-12-95	.221	.263	.213	37	113	9	25	4	0	1	12	11	3	1	1	43	0	0	.283	.305
Montz, Luke	R-R	6-1	230	7-7-83	.333	.000	.400	14	36	11	12	2	0	5	10	10	1	0	0	7	0	0	.806	.489
Myers, D'Arby	R-R	6-3	185	12-9-88	.300	—	.300	3	10	5	3	1	0	0	4	0	0	0	3	1	0	.400	.500
Nogowski, John	R-L	6-2	210	1-5-93	.286	.385	.227	8	35	5	10	3	1	0	11	2	0	0	0	4	0	0	.429	.324
Paz, Andy	R-R	6-0	170	1-5-93	.159	.500	.083	14	44	3	7	2	0	1	4	4	0	0	1	8	0	0	.273	.224
Penalo, Rodolfo	B-R	5-7	130	8-27-92	.276	.167	.304	17	58	16	16	2	0	0	5	8	2	1	1	13	8	4	.310	.377
Raga, Argenis	R-R	6-1	176	7-22-94	.338	.150	.412	26	71	10	24	6	2	0	11	6	2	0	1	11	0	1	.479	.400
Rodriguez, Jean Carlo	R-R	5-10	170	1-12-96	.184	.231	.176	36	98	14	18	2	1	0	8	14	2	0	1	13	3	1	.224	.296
Soto, Michael	R-R	6-3	215	11-17-91	.324	.316	.327	21	74	14	24	8	0	2	17	11	0	0	2	15	2	0	.514	.402
Sportman, J.P.	R-R	5-9	190	1-26-92	.321	.304	.328	22	84	19	27	4	1	0	8	14	0	2	1	9	5	3	.393	.414
Zarraga, Jonesy	R-R	6-1	170	6-3-92	.228	.185	.243	28	101	10	23	4	2	0	7	2	1	3	3	30	5	1	.307	.283

Pitching	B-T	HT	WT	DOB	W	L	ERA	G	GS	CG	SV	IP	H	R	ER	HR	BB	SO	AVG	vLH	vRH	K/9	BB/9
Beasley, Derek	L-L	6-0	185	2-2-92	4	2	6.27	13	0	0	1	19	22	15	13	1	11	21	.286	.200	.316	10.13	5.30
Bracewell, Benjamin	R-R	6-0	195	9-19-90	0	0	0.90	7	0	0	3	10	5	1	1	0	3	9	.143	.063	.211	8.10	2.70
Brown, Dawson	R-R	6-6	200	5-16-93	1	0	2.75	11	0	0	2	20	21	7	6	1	3	16	.280	.235	.317	7.32	1.37
Fagan, Mike	R-L	5-11	160	5-12-92	0	0	2.70	2	0	0	0	3	4	1	1	0	3	4	.286	.000	.333	10.80	8.10
Ferreras, Kevin	L-L	6-0	170	7-5-93	2	3	6.67	12	4	0	0	27	33	22	20	2	12	26	.297	.176	.351	8.67	4.00
Fillmyer, Heath	R-R	6-1	180	5-16-94	1	0	2.79	6	0	0	0	10	5	3	3	0	5	10	.147	.091	.174	9.31	4.66
Gauna, Beau	R-R	6-3	225	9-10-93	0	2	6.14	3	1	0	0	7	4	5	5	0	2	5	.167	.000	.235	6.14	2.45
Graves, Brett	R-R	6-1	195	1-30-93	0	0	0.00	1	0	0	0	1	0	0	0	0	1	1	.000	.000	.000	9.00	9.00
Huber, Rob	R-R	5-11	200	1-8-92	1	0	8.02	15	0	0	1	21	27	19	19	1	13	23	.314	.405	.245	9.70	5.48
Kelliher, Branden	R-R	5-11	175	12-11-95	1	4	4.82	11	7	0	0	28	25	22	15	0	29	37	.229	.255	.204	11.89	9.32
Kurz, Cody	R-R	6-4	225	9-13-92	0	0	13.50	7	0	0	0	7	7	11	10	0	16	11	.259	.333	.200	14.14	21.60
McCurry, Brendan	R-R	5-10	165	1-7-92	0	0	0.00	1	0	0	0	1	2	0	0	0	2	3	.000	.400	13.50	0.00
Miller, Corey	R-R	6-3	190	11-13-91	1	0	5.40	1	0	0	0	3	2	2	2	0	1	3	.167	.000	.182	8.10	2.70
Navas, Carlos	R-R	6-1	170	8-13-92	6	5	3.30	13	11	0	0	71	75	39	26	6	20	61	.272	.276	.269	7.73	2.54
Nolasco, Alex	L-L	6-4	190	9-11-90	0	0	9.75	9	0	0	0	12	17	17	13	1	11	11	.315	.429	.275	8.25	8.25
Ortiz, Phillip	R-R	6-0	190	3-6-95	0	0	7.30	9	0	0	0	12	11	10	10	0	10	16	.268	.263	.273	11.68	7.30

OAKLAND ATHLETICS

OAKLAND ATHLETICS

	B-T	HT	WT	DOB	W	L	ERA	G	GS	CG	SV	IP	H	R	ER	HR	BB	SO	AVG	vLH	vRH	K/9	BB/9
Overton, Dillon	L-L	6-2	172	8-17-91	0	2	1.64	7	7	0	0	22	19	8	4	,0	3	31	.232	.133	.254	12.68	1.23
Painton, Tyler	L-L	6-5	195	2-20-92	0	0	15.75	4	0	0	0	4	3	7	7	0	9	1	.214	.400	.111	2.25	20.25
Peters, Tanner	R-R	6-0	155	8-6-90	0	2	8.44	7	7	0	0	11	18	11	10	0	3	10	.375	.263	.448	8.44	2.53
Pitcher, Travis	R-R	6-4	225	1-30-91	1	2	7.88	12	0	0	0	24	29	26	21	2	19	32	.302	.379	.269	12.00	7.13
Rivas, Jesus	R-R	6-0	180	3-22-94	0	0	2.14	18	0	0	7	21	28	6	5	0	4	10	.318	.333	.309	4.29	1.71
Schwartz, Jordan	R-R	6-2	195	2-28-92	0	0	4.50	1	1	0	0	2	3	1	1	0	0	4	.333	.500	.286	18.00	0.00
Seddon, Joel	R-R	6-1	165	7-13-92	0	0	4.50	1	0	0	0	2	1	1	1	0	2	4	.143	—	.143	18.00	9.00
Stull, Cody	L-L	6-2	160	3-23-92	1	0	1.47	14	1	0	2	18	12	5	3	0	8	27	.182	.250	.160	13.25	3.93
Veliz, Victor	L-L	5-11	170	10-6-93	2	1	2.43	10	4	0	0	33	24	11	9	1	12	17	.203	.087	.232	4.59	3.24
Walter, Corey	R-R	6-3	215	8-11-92	0	0	0.00	4	0	0	0	7	2	2	0	0	3	7	.087	.167	.059	9.45	4.05
Willman, Tyler	R-R	6-6	190	10-8-92	0	2	5.85	12	0	0	0	20	19	13	13	0	11	24	.253	.156	.326	10.80	4.95
Zambrano, Jesus	R-R	5-11	170	8-23-96	6	3	4.33	14	12	0	0	71	66	41	34	3	18	63	.245	.207	.266	8.02	2.29

Fielding

Catcher	PCT	G	PO	A	E	DP	PB
Akau	.957	16	118	15	6	0	2
Brown	.971	5	33	1	1	0	1
Kim	.989	11	83	6	1	0	1
Montz	.980	7	48	2	1	0	1
Paz	.989	11	78	10	1	0	2
Raga	.978	20	112	23	3	0	7

First Base	PCT	G	PO	A	E	DP
Duinkerk	1.000	18	145	10	0	11
Kuhn	1.000	1	1	0	0	1
Mercedes	.967	16	84	3	3	6
Nogowski	1.000	7	53	5	0	2
Raga	1.000	3	20	0	0	3
Soto	.973	20	162	16	5	16

Second Base	PCT	G	PO	A	E	DP
Diaz	.977	14	12	31	1	5
Gilbert	1.000	5	12	19	0	5
Kuhn	.833	2	1	4	1	1
Loehr	.926	5	13	12	2	2
Lopez	.968	30	51	71	4	17
Rodriguez	1.000	5	5	10	0	1

Third Base	PCT	G	PO	A	E	DP
Brizuela	.800	4	1	3	1	0
Chapman	.667	2	0	2	1	0
Diaz	.871	11	6	21	4	3
Gilbert	1.000	8	3	7	0	0
Kubala	.444	4	3	1	5	0
Kuhn	.857	2	1	5	1	1
Mercedes	.848	16	13	26	7	1

Rodriguez	1.000	21	13	31	0	2

Shortstop	PCT	G	PO	A	E	DP
Diaz	.921	16	21	49	6	11
Loehr	.939	32	47	76	8	11
Lopez	.941	11	17	31	3	4

Outfield	PCT	G	PO	A	E	DP
De La Cruz	.942	44	62	3	4	1
Duinkerk	.926	16	19	6	2	0
Martinez	.988	45	79	3	1	0
Myers	1.000	3	4	0	0	0
Penalo	1.000	17	31	2	0	0
Rodriguez	.889	6	6	2	1	0
Sportman	1.000	22	28	2	0	1
Zarraga	.962	25	49	1	2	0

DSL ATHLETICS   ROOKIE
DOMINICAN SUMMER LEAGUE

Batting	B-T	HT	WT	DOB	AVG	vLH	vRH	G	AB	R	H	2B	3B	HR	RBI	BB	HBP	SH	SF	SO	SB	CS	SLG	OBP
Agelvis, Javier	R-R	6-1	170	8-18-97	.149	.214	.119	41	87	17	13	3	0	0	8	20	4	2	1	35	3	2	.184	.330
Barrera, Luis	L-L	6-0	180	11-15-95	.130	.000	.158	16	46	2	6	0	0	0	3	5	0	1	0	12	2	0	.130	.216
Godard, Javier	R-R	6-0	170	12-13-95	.239	.267	.225	38	134	16	32	5	1	1	4	8	2	6	0	18	6	4	.313	.292
Gonzalez, Yhoelnys	R-R	6-0	170	10-30-96	.140	.107	.154	64	179	20	25	7	2	1	12	20	1	2	3	56	15	2	.218	.227
Guzman, Miguel	R-R	6-2	210	3-10-95	.272	.300	.260	53	206	20	56	12	1	1	34	6	3	0	3	30	3	1	.354	.298
Hernandez, Luis	R-R	5-11	203	9-3-94	.220	.258	.196	33	82	6	18	2	0	0	6	22	1	1	1	15	3	0	.244	.387
Hiciano, Carlos	R-R	6-2	175	10-29-96	.143	.185	.126	55	189	20	27	7	0	0	12	13	2	1	1	42	3	5	.180	.205
Marinez, Eric	B-R	6-1	160	9-12-95	.202	.169	.220	66	242	23	49	11	2	1	26	17	0	6	2	70	3	5	.277	.253
Monserratt, Jesus	R-R	6-0	180	1-3-97	.154	.250	.111	26	52	3	8	2	0	0	4	15	0	0	0	14	1	0	.192	.343
Mullen, Robert	R-R	6-0	170	5-23-96	.230	.327	.175	51	152	22	35	10	0	0	9	28	6	4	3	29	6	1	.296	.365
Penalo, Rodolfo	B-R	5-7	130	8-27-92	.274	.225	.301	33	113	37	31	5	3	1	10	38	2	1	0	18	29	6	.398	.464
Pimentel, Sandber	R-R	6-3	216	9-12-94	.311	.321	.306	61	190	25	59	11	4	3	25	31	12	0	3	32	2	2	.458	.432
Rigby, Gean	R-R	6-0	180	1-7-97	.207	.208	.206	52	150	16	31	6	1	0	10	27	5	3	2	48	10	9	.260	.342
Rivas, Raymond	L-R	6-1	180	9-23-95	.162	.182	.152	30	99	6	16	2	1	0	8	4	3	1	1	14	6	1	.202	.215
Rodriguez, Jhonny	L-L	6-3	170	7-20-96	.230	.197	.246	51	183	20	42	13	4	0	18	14	4	2	1	37	2	4	.344	.297
Silva, Andys	R-R	6-0	180	9-12-95	.163	.130	.179	53	160	15	26	3	0	2	10	35	1	1	2	20	6	2	.206	.313

Pitching	B-T	HT	WT	DOB	W	L	ERA	G	GS	CG	SV	IP	H	R	ER	HR	BB	SO	AVG	vLH	vRH	K/9	BB/9
Andueza, Ivan	L-L	5-11	180	2-7-95	2	4	2.94	14	8	0	1	52	43	22	17	0	24	51	.231	.219	.234	8.83	4.15
Aquino, Ruber	R-R	6-2	185	12-29-96	0	1	4.45	18	0	0	1	30	31	19	15	4	11	29	.270	.324	.247	8.60	3.26
Blanco, Argenis	R-R	6-1	165	5-23-96	3	2	2.21	11	11	0	0	53	36	16	13	0	14	53	.189	.143	.213	9.00	2.38
Calderon, Alexander	L-L	6-3	170	2-23-96	0	2	4.30	13	1	0	0	15	16	13	7	0	15	5	.333	.261	.361	3.00	9.20
Duno, Angel	R-R	6-0	180	1-10-94	3	2	1.82	15	15	0	0	84	81	30	17	2	14	63	.248	.260	.242	6.75	1.50
Hoyos, Renaldo	L-L	6-0	170	3-23-94	1	3	3.34	20	0	0	2	35	35	18	13	0	13	33	.263	.063	.291	8.49	3.34
Hurtado, Jhenderson	R-R	6-2	180	3-28-96	1	2	3.45	13	7	0	0	44	49	27	17	1	25	43	.278	.238	.284	8.73	5.08
Magallanes, Wilfredo	R-R	6-2	185	11-15-95	3	2	4.64	14	0	0	1	21	14	12	11	0	23	17	.194	.219	.175	7.17	9.70
Martinez, Jorge	L-L	5-11	170	1-5-96	3	3	3.60	14	5	0	1	50	52	24	20	1	14	45	.281	.238	.287	8.10	2.52
Mendoza, Juan	R-R	6-2	170	4-15-96	1	6	5.85	12	10	0	0	40	49	29	26	1	16	29	.316	.347	.302	6.53	3.60
Nelo, Emerson	R-R	5-11	180	9-13-95	2	3	1.75	14	6	0	0	57	43	18	11	1	27	39	.210	.292	.171	6.19	4.29
Ortiz, Phillip	R-R	6-0	190	3-6-95	0	0	7.50	5	0	0	0	6	7	5	5	0	5	9	.269	.571	.158	13.50	7.50
Rodriguez, Santiago	R-R	6-3	190	3-9-97	1	3	6.23	15	3	0	1	22	18	18	15	0	29	22	.240	.208	.255	9.14	12.05
Ruiz, Jean	R-R	6-1	165	9-6-96	2	4	7.32	14	4	0	0	36	46	38	29	0	29	20	.335	.313	.316	5.05	7.32
Sullivan, Emmanuel	R-R	6-3	195	6-24-96	0	1	7.56	8	0	0	0	8	11	9	7	0	12	5	.314	.300	.320	5.40	12.96
Trejo, Jose	R-R	6-3	175	3-31-96	1	2	14.85	14	0	0	0	13	17	23	22	1	24	9	.354	.286	.382	6.08	16.20
Vargas, Alejandro	R-R	5-11	160	1-29-95	1	3	3.66	22	0	0	6	32	36	21	13	2	15	28	.300	.171	.367	7.88	4.22
Vilchez, Gerardo	R-R	6-4	165	6-6-97	1	2	4.38	19	0	0	0	25	22	17	12	0	23	14	.247	.276	.233	5.11	8.39

Fielding

Catcher	PCT	G	PO	A	E	DP	PB
Guzman	.966	13	67	17	3	0	4
Hernandez	.963	26	132	22	6	1	1
Monserratt	.944	12	39	12	3	0	3

First Base	PCT	G	PO	A	E	DP
Godard	1.000	1	6	0	0	1

Mullen	.969	38	263	47	10	2	5

Guzman	.988	27	227	12	3	24
Hernandez	1.000	1	5	1	0	0
Marinez	.000	1	0	0	1	0
Mullen	1.000	1	13	0	0	0

	PCT	G	PO	A	E	DP
Pimentel	.974	44	395	20	11	28
Silva	1.000	1	3	1	0	0

Second Base	PCT	G	PO	A	E	DP
Agelvis	.964	30	71	61	5	20
Godard	.991	24	46	62	1	10
Hiciano	.895	13	23	28	6	9
Penalo	1.000	2	4	4	0	2
Silva	.935	16	28	30	4	6

Third Base	PCT	G	PO	A	E	DP
Agelvis	.500	3	0	1	1	0

	PCT	G	PO	A	E	DP
Godard	1.000	4	4	6	0	1
Hiciano	.822	15	7	30	8	1
Marinez	.892	32	24	59	10	4
Silva	.904	24	18	48	7	6

Shortstop	PCT	G	PO	A	E	DP
Agelvis	.667	2	0	2	1	0
Godard	.938	2	4	11	1	2
Hiciano	.927	28	41	73	9	12
Marinez	.938	33	48	102	10	16
Silva	.941	10	11	37	3	8

Outfield	PCT	G	PO	A	E	DP
Barrera	1.000	12	12	1	0	0
Godard	1.000	7	9	0	0	0
Gonzalez	.966	63	107	8	4	2
Penalo	1.000	31	49	3	0	0
Pimentel	1.000	3	0	1	0	0
Rigby	.920	51	74	7	7	2
Rivas	1.000	25	45	1	0	0
Rodriguez	.936	47	70	3	5	0
Silva	1.000	2	2	0	0	0

Philadelphia Phillies

SEASON IN A SENTENCE: Armed with a corps of aging veterans, a shaky starting staff behind Cole Hamels and a leaky bullpen, the Phillies performed as expected, losing games in bunches and finishing four games back of the Marlins for last place in the NL East.

HIGH POINT: On Sept. 1, Hamels spun six hitless innings against the Atlanta Braves. Then lefty Jake Diekman pitched a scoreless seventh. Rookie Ken Giles didn't allow a hit in the eighth, and beleaguered closer Jonathan Papelbon finished off the masterpiece with a perfect ninth. It was the first Phillies no-no since Roy Halladay stymied the Reds in the 2010 Division Series.

LOW POINT: Toward the end of the season, with the team's postseason hopes long gone and most fan attention focused on wanting as many front office firings as possible, Papelbon somehow made it worse. On Sept. 14, after allowing four runs in the ninth inning against the Marlins and exiting to a lusty serenade of boos, the closer looked toward the crowd and grabbed his crotch in their general direction, inciting even more boos. He was ejected from the game and suspended for seven games.

NOTABLE ROOKIES: The biggest contributor from the Phillies' system this season was unquestionably righthander Ken Giles, who used an 80-grade fastball, a much-improved slider and better command to breeze through Double-A and Triple-A and reach the majors on June 12. All he did was strike out 64 in 46 innings while allowing just 25 hits and 11 walks.

KEY TRANSACTIONS: The Phillies bolstered their rotation in the offseason by luring A.J. Burnett out of retirement and giving him a one-year deal with an option for a second year, and also adding Roberto Hernandez (the former Fausto Carmona) for one year and $4.5 million. They also added outfielder Marlon Byrd for two years and $16 million with an option for a third year. Hernandez was flipped to the Dodgers at midseason for a pair of prospects, righthander Victor Arano and second baseman Jesmuel Valentin.

DOWN ON THE FARM: No. 1 prospect Maikel Franco also made his debut this past season, gaining an early taste of life in the majors. Shortstop J.P. Crawford tore up two levels of Class A ball, hitting a combined .285/.375/.406 with 23 doubles and 11 homers, and just 74 strikeouts against 65 walks while spending the full season as a 19-year-old.

OPENING DAY PAYROLL: $179,521,056 (3rd)

PLAYERS OF THE YEAR

DAVID SCHOFIELD

MAJOR LEAGUE	MINOR LEAGUE
Cole Hamels lhp	**J.P. Crawford** ss
9-9, 2.46	(Low Class A, High A)
205 IP, 176 H	.285/.375/.406
198 SO, 56 BB	11 HR, 48 RBI

ORGANIZATION LEADERS

BATTING		*Minimum 250 AB
MAJORS		
* AVG	Revere, Ben	.306
* OPS	Byrd, Marlon	.757
HR	Byrd, Marlon	25
RBI	Howard, Ryan	95
MINORS		
* AVG	Astudillo, Willians, Lakewood	.333
* OBP	Crawford, J.P., Lakewood, Clearwater	.375
* SLG	Lavin, Peter, Clearwater, Reading	.441
R	Alonso, Carlos, Reading	76
H	Astudillo, Willians, Lakewood	145
TB	Franco, Maikel, Lehigh Valley	223
2B	Franco, Maikel, Lehigh Valley	33
3B	Tocci, Carlos, Lakewood	8
HR	Fox, Jake, Reading	22
RBI	Franco, Maikel, Lehigh Valley	78
BB	Crawford, J.P., Lakewood, Clearwater	65
SO	Charles, Art, Clearwater	156
SB	Quinn, Roman, Clearwater	32

PITCHING		#Minimum 75 IP
MAJORS		
W	Kendrick, Kyle	10
# ERA	Hamels, Cole	2.46
SO	Hamels, Cole	198
SV	Papelbon, Jonathan	39
MINORS		
W	Milner, Hoby, Reading	10
L	Viza, Tyler, Lakewood	17
# ERA	Loewen, Adam, Clearwater, Reading	3.25
G	Neris, Hector, Reading, Lehigh Valley	48
	Ogando, Nefi, Reading	48
GS	Gonzalez, Severino, Reading	27
	Leiter, Mark, Lakewood, Clearwater	27
SV	Garcia, Luis, Lehigh Valley	22
IP	Gonzalez, Severino, Reading	159
BB	Garner, Perci, Reading, Clearwater	77
SO	Leiter, Mark, Lakewood, Clearwater	141
AVG	Loewen, Adam, Clearwater, Reading	.222

2014 PERFORMANCE

General Manager: Ruben Amaro Jr. **Farm Director:** Joe Jordan. **Scouting Director:** Marti Wolever.

Class	Team	League	W	L	PCT	Finish	Manager
Majors	Philadelphia Phillies	National	73	89	.451	t-22 (30)	Ryne Sandberg
Triple-A	Lehigh Valley IronPigs	International	66	78	.458	11th (14)	Dave Brundage
Double-A	Reading Fightin Phils	Eastern	66	76	.465	t-9th (12)	Dusty Wathan
High A	Clearwater Threshers	Florida State	49	89	.355	12th (12)	Nelson Prada
Low A	Lakewood BlueClaws	South Atlantic	53	84	.387	14th (14)	Greg Legg
Short season	Williamsport Crosscutters	New York-Penn	33	43	.434	t-12th (14)	Shawn Williams
Rookie	Phillies	Gulf Coast	36	23	.610	3rd (16)	Roly de Armas
Overall Minor League Record			303	393	.435	30th (30)	

ORGANIZATION STATISTICS

PHILADELPHIA PHILLIES
NATIONAL LEAGUE

Batting	B-T	HT	WT	DOB	AVG	vLH	vRH	G	AB	R	H	2B	3B	HR	RBI	BB	HBP	SH	SF	SO	SB	CS	SLG	OBP
Altherr, Aaron	R-R	6-5	220	1-14-91	.000	.000	.000	2	5	0	0	0	0	0	0	0	0	0	0	2	0	0	.000	.000
Asche, Cody	L-R	6-1	200	6-30-90	.252	.268	.248	121	397	43	100	25	0	10	46	33	0	3	1	102	0	1	.390	.309
Blanco, Andres	B-R	5-10	190	4-11-84	.277	.308	.238	25	47	4	13	5	0	1	3	2	0	4	0	6	0	0	.447	.306
Brignac, Reid	L-R	6-3	215	1-16-86	.222	.000	.254	37	81	4	18	5	1	1	10	9	0	1	0	33	1	1	.346	.300
Brown, Domonic	L-L	6-5	230	9-3-87	.235	.217	.240	144	473	47	111	22	1	10	63	34	1	0	4	91	7	1	.349	.285
Byrd, Marlon	R-R	6-0	245	8-30-77	.264	.258	.266	154	591	71	156	28	2	25	85	35	8	0	3	185	3	2	.445	.312
Cedeno, Ronny	R-R	6-0	195	2-2-83	.000	.000	.000	7	9	0	0	0	0	0	0	0	0	0	0	2	0	0	.000	.000
Franco, Maikel	R-R	6-1	180	8-26-92	.179	.125	.250	16	56	5	10	2	0	0	5	1	0	0	1	13	0	0	.214	.190
Galvis, Freddy	B-R	5-10	185	11-14-89	.176	.182	.173	43	119	14	21	3	1	4	12	8	0	0	1	30	1	0	.319	.227
Gwynn Jr., Tony	L-R	6-0	190	10-4-82	.152	.000	.190	80	105	14	16	2	1	0	3	15	1	0	0	23	3	0	.190	.264
Hernandez, Cesar	B-R	5-10	166	5-23-90	.237	.290	.217	66	114	13	27	2	0	1	4	9	0	1	1	33	1	1	.281	.290
Hill, Koyie	B-R	6-1	205	3-9-79	.238	.143	.286	10	21	2	5	1	0	0	1	1	0	0	0	5	0	0	.286	.273
Howard, Ryan	L-L	6-4	250	11-19-79	.223	.230	.221	153	569	65	127	18	1	23	95	67	7	0	5	190	0	0	.380	.310
Mayberry Jr., John	R-R	6-6	230	12-21-83	.213	.255	.179	63	122	11	26	7	0	6	21	15	1	0	0	30	0	0	.418	.304
Nieves, Wil	R-R	5-11	190	9-25-77	.254	.200	.272	36	122	9	31	8	0	1	7	1	2	2	1	34	1	0	.344	.270
Nix, Jayson	R-R	5-11	195	8-26-82	.154	.083	.267	18	39	1	6	0	0	1	2	2	1	0	0	18	0	2	.231	.214
2-team total (16 Pittsburgh)					.133	—	—	34	75	2	10	0	0	1	3	3	2	1	0	22	1	2	.173	.188
Revere, Ben	L-R	5-9	165	5-3-88	.306	.341	.291	151	601	71	184	13	7	2	28	13	4	7	1	49	49	8	.361	.325
Rollins, Jimmy	B-R	5-8	180	11-27-78	.243	.237	.246	138	538	78	131	22	4	17	55	64	1	3	3	100	28	6	.394	.323
Ruf, Darin	R-R	6-3	240	7-28-86	.235	.295	.146	52	102	13	24	8	0	3	8	8	4	1	2	32	0	0	.402	.310
Ruiz, Carlos	R-R	5-10	205	1-22-79	.252	.250	.253	110	381	43	96	25	1	6	31	46	12	1	5	60	4	2	.370	.347
Rupp, Cameron	R-R	6-2	250	9-28-88	.183	.000	.208	18	60	4	11	4	0	2	6	4	0	0	0	20	0	0	.250	.234
Sizemore, Grady	L-L	6-2	200	8-2-82	.253	.200	.274	60	162	21	41	9	2	3	12	14	0	0	3	35	1	1	.389	.313
Utley, Chase	L-R	6-1	200	12-17-78	.270	.233	.286	155	589	74	159	36	6	11	78	53	13	0	9	85	10	1	.407	.339

Pitching	B-T	HT	WT	DOB	W	L	ERA	G	GS	CG	SV	IP	H	R	ER	HR	BB	SO	AVG	vLH	vRH	K/9	BB/9
Adams, Mike	R-R	6-5	210	7-29-78	2	1	2.89	22	0	0	0	19	16	8	6	1	8	21	.232	.389	.176	10.13	3.86
Aumont, Phillippe	L-R	6-7	260	1-7-89	0	1	19.06	5	0	0	0	6	14	12	12	3	5	6	.483	.615	.375	9.53	7.94
Bastardo, Antonio	L-L	5-11	200	9-21-85	5	7	3.94	67	0	0	0	64	43	31	28	4	34	81	.188	.175	.195	11.39	4.78
Buchanan, David	R-R	6-3	200	5-11-89	6	8	3.75	20	20	0	0	118	120	55	49	12	32	71	.264	.227	.293	5.43	2.45
Burnett, A.J.	R-R	6-4	225	1-3-77	8	18	4.59	34	34	1	0	214	205	122	109	20	96	190	.256	.250	.261	8.00	4.04
Camp, Shawn	R-R	6-1	205	11-18-75	0	0	5.40	3	0	0	0	3	7	2	2	1	0	1	.467	.143	.750	2.70	0.00
De Fratus, Justin	B-R	6-4	225	10-21-87	3	1	2.39	54	0	0	0	53	45	19	14	4	12	49	.223	.209	.230	8.37	2.05
Diekman, Jake	L-L	6-4	200	1-21-87	5	5	3.80	73	0	0	0	71	66	36	30	4	35	100	.248	.239	.253	12.68	4.44
Garcia, Luis	R-R	6-2	210	1-30-87	1	0	6.43	13	0	0	0	14	14	12	10	2	13	12	.255	.194	.333	7.71	8.36
Giles, Ken	R-R	6-2	205	9-20-90	3	1	1.18	44	0	0	1	46	25	7	6	1	11	64	.164	.152	.174	12.61	2.17
Gonzalez, Miguel Alfredo	R-R	6-3	200	9-23-86	0	1	6.75	6	0	0	0	5	9	4	4	1	3	5	.346	.400	.313	8.44	5.06
Hamels, Cole	L-L	6-3	195	12-27-83	9	9	2.46	30	30	0	0	205	176	60	56	14	59	198	.235	.218	.240	8.71	2.59
Hernandez, Roberto	R-R	6-4	230	8-30-80	6	8	3.87	23	20	0	0	121	108	57	52	11	55	75	.237	.211	.257	5.58	4.09
2-team total (9 Los Angeles)					8	11	4.10	32	29	0	0	165	156	84	75	19	73	105	—	—	—	5.74	3.99
Hollands, Mario	L-L	6-5	200	8-26-88	2	2	4.40	50	0	0	0	47	45	25	23	3	21	35	.253	.241	.263	6.70	4.02
Jimenez, Cesar	L-L	5-11	210	11-12-84	0	0	1.69	16	0	0	0	16	14	3	3	1	7	8	.246	.167	.282	4.50	3.94
Kendrick, Kyle	R-R	6-3	210	8-26-84	10	13	4.61	32	32	0	0	199	214	108	102	25	57	121	.276	.290	.265	5.47	2.58
Lee, Cliff	L-L	6-3	205	8-30-78	4	5	3.65	13	13	1	0	81	100	40	33	7	12	72	.304	.238	.320	7.97	1.33
Lincoln, Brad	L-R	6-0	225	5-25-85	0	0	11.57	2	0	0	0	2	5	3	3	1	0	2	.417	.333	.444	7.71	0.00
Manship, Jeff	R-R	6-2	210	1-16-85	1	2	6.65	20	0	0	0	23	24	17	17	1	14	16	.273	.219	.346	6.26	5.48
Martin, Ethan	R-R	6-2	220	6-6-89	0	0	4.50	2	0	0	0	4	1	2	2	1	3	4	.071	.125	.000	9.00	6.75
Neris, Hector	R-R	6-2	175	6-14-89	1	0	0.00	1	0	0	0	1	0	0	0	0	0	1	.000	.000	.000	9.00	0.00
O'Sullivan, Sean	R-R	6-1	240	9-1-87	0	1	6.39	3	2	0	0	13	15	9	9	3	2	7	.306	.364	.259	4.97	1.42
Papelbon, Jonathan	R-R	6-4	215	11-23-80	2	3	2.04	66	0	0	39	66	45	15	15	2	15	63	.191	.182	.200	8.55	2.04
Pettibone, Jonathan	L-R	6-6	225	7-19-90	0	1	9.00	2	2	0	0	9	17	10	9	2	3	6	.395	.375	.407	6.00	3.00
Rosenberg, B.J.	R-R	6-3	220	9-17-85	1	0	6.75	13	0	0	0	12	20	10	9	5	7	9	.385	.357	.395	6.75	5.25
Williams, Jerome	R-R	6-3	240	12-4-81	4	2	2.83	9	9	0	0	57	48	20	18	5	17	38	.230	.250	.208	5.97	2.67

Fielding

Catcher

Catcher	PCT	G	PO	A	E	DP	PB
Hill	1.000	10	42	3	0	0	0
Nieves	.996	34	246	26	1	4	3
Ruiz	.995	109	852	68	5	9	4
Rupp	.987	18	130	18	2	2	1

First Base

First Base	PCT	G	PO	A	E	DP
Franco	1.000	5	20	2	0	2
Howard	.993	141	1224	80	9	103
Mayberry Jr.	.986	17	66	5	1	2
Nieves	—	1	0	0	0	0
Ruf	1.000	20	106	6	0	9
Utley	1.000	1	2	0	0	0

Second Base

Second Base	PCT	G	PO	A	E	DP
Blanco	1.000	5	1	8	0	1
Brignac	1.000	3	1	3	0	0
Galvis	1.000	7	9	9	0	2
Hernandez	1.000	11	22	14	0	3
Nix	.667	2	0	2	1	0
Utley	.985	147	292	423	11	87

Third Base

Third Base	PCT	G	PO	A	E	DP
Asche	.943	112	59	206	16	18
Blanco	.950	10	1	18	1	0
Brignac	1.000	20	9	22	0	2
Cedeno	1.000	1	2	1	0	0
Franco	.975	12	11	28	1	3
Galvis	1.000	11	1	14	0	1
Hernandez	.889	14	5	19	3	1
Nix	1.000	9	8	16	0	0
Ruf	1.000	1	0	1	0	0

Shortstop

Shortstop	PCT	G	PO	A	E	DP
Blanco	1.000	6	4	10	0	4
Brignac	1.000	3	1	1	0	0
Cedeno	1.000	2	2	4	0	1
Galvis	.991	25	32	79	1	16
Hernandez	1.000	4	6	4	0	1
Nix	.929	4	4	9	1	3
Rollins	.988	131	158	398	7	64

Outfield

Outfield	PCT	G	PO	A	E	DP
Altherr	1.000	1	3	0	0	0
Brown	.989	127	182	4	2	2
Byrd	.982	149	329	6	6	1
Gwynn Jr.	1.000	42	47	2	0	1
Mayberry Jr.	1.000	29	43	1	0	0
Revere	.988	141	323	2	4	2
Ruf	1.000	15	20	0	0	0
Sizemore	.984	42	62	0	1	0

LEHIGH VALLEY IRONPIGS   TRIPLE-A

INTERNATIONAL LEAGUE

Batting	B-T	HT	WT	DOB	AVG	vLH	vRH	G	AB	R	H	2B	3B	HR	RBI	BB	HBP	SH	SF	SO	SB	CS	SLG	OBP
Asche, Cody	L-R	6-1	200	6-30-90	.833	1.000	.800	2	6	3	5	1	0	1	4	1	1	0	0	0	0	0	1.500	.875
Blanco, Andres	B-R	5-10	190	4-11-84	.241	.260	.230	45	137	16	33	6	0	0	11	13	2	2	1	25	3	5	.285	.314
Brignac, Reid	L-R	6-3	215	1-16-86	.266	.211	.289	36	128	23	34	8	1	5	21	16	0	2	3	31	3	0	.461	.340
Canzler, Russ	R-R	6-2	220	4-11-86	.286	.344	.262	61	213	32	61	20	1	11	34	26	0	0	3	52	2	1	.545	.360
2-team total (51 Scranton/W-B)					.276	—		112	388	57	107	32	3	13	58	46	0	0	7	97	3	1	.474	.347
Castro, Leandro	R-R	5-11	195	6-15-89	.259	.209	.280	117	425	59	110	20	4	6	48	27	5	8	5	70	7	7	.367	.307
Cedeno, Ronny	R-R	6-0	195	2-2-83	.286	.286	.286	42	147	10	42	9	0	1	20	9	0	4	0	23	0	4	.367	.327
Davis, Lars	L-R	6-3	205	11-7-85	.235	.167	.250	10	34	1	8	1	0	0	2	0	0	0	0	4	0	0	.265	.235
Duran, Edgar	R-R	5-11	155	2-10-91	.171	.188	.160	14	41	3	7	1	0	0	2	5	0	1	0	11	0	1	.195	.261
Franco, Maikel	R-R	6-1	180	8-26-92	.257	.270	.252	133	521	64	134	33	4	16	78	30	2	0	3	81	3	1	.428	.299
Galvis, Freddy	B-R	5-10	185	11-14-89	.267	.385	.219	35	135	22	36	14	1	3	15	11	0	3	0	25	1	1	.452	.322
Gillies, Tyson	L-R	6-2	205	10-31-88	.214	.146	.237	43	159	13	34	6	0	2	10	6	7	3	2	44	3	2	.289	.270
Gwynn Jr., Tony	L-R	6-0	190	10-4-82	.290	.308	.286	20	69	7	20	2	0	1	7	11	0	0	1	12	2	4	.362	.383
Hanzawa, Troy	R-R	5-9	155	9-12-85	.132	.143	.125	14	38	2	5	1	0	0	3	2	2	1	1	8	0	1	.158	.209
2-team total (10 Toledo)					.119	—	—	24	67	3	8	1	0	0	4	2	2	1		16	0	1	.134	.167
Henson, Tyler	R-R	6-1	205	12-15-87	.272	.285	.267	123	426	63	116	28	3	9	45	38	2	9	5	130	19	6	.415	.331
Hernandez, Cesar	B-R	5-10	166	5-23-90	.256	.373	.200	40	156	23	40	6	3	0	10	15	0	0	0	34	7	4	.333	.322
Hill, Koyie	B-R	6-1	205	3-9-79	.227	.125	.266	53	176	18	40	11	1	3	17	28	0	2	0	45	0	3	.352	.333
Maruszak, Addison	R-R	6-1	190	12-21-86	.174	.100	.231	10	23	1	4	1	0	0	3	2	0	1	1	9	0	1	.217	.231
Mayberry Jr., John	R-R	6-6	230	12-21-83	.182	.182	.182	9	33	4	6	2	0	1	4	2	3	0	0	11	0	0	.333	.289
Murphy, Jim	R-R	6-4	240	9-16-85	.240	.242	.239	116	396	38	95	23	2	11	47	49	6	0	3	107	1	1	.391	.330
Perkins, Cam	R-R	6-5	195	9-27-90	.216	.174	.231	74	255	17	55	9	3	2	17	13	2	2	0	49	3	3	.298	.259
Ruf, Darin	R-R	6-3	240	7-28-86	.265	.235	.273	23	83	6	22	6	0	1	10	6	0	0	2	16	1	0	.373	.308
Rupp, Cameron	R-R	6-2	250	9-28-88	.165	.218	.144	59	194	19	32	8	0	6	19	21	3	0	1	76	0	0	.299	.256
Ryal, Rusty	R-R	6-2	200	3-16-83	.192	.211	.182	20	52	6	10	2	0	1	5	4	1	0	0	14	1	0	.288	.263
Sizemore, Grady	L-L	6-2	200	8-2-82	.283	.211	.333	11	46	5	13	1	0	1	2	5	0	0	0	7	0	0	.370	.353
Spears, Nate	L-R	5-11	180	5-3-85	.299	.138	.339	52	144	18	43	7	3	2	15	13	0	2	2	43	4	2	.431	.352
Susdorf, Steve	L-L	6-1	195	3-28-86	.276	.243	.287	84	272	33	75	17	1	2	29	25	2	1	5	54	7	2	.368	.336
Thomas, Clete	L-R	5-11	200	11-14-83	.247	.214	.258	49	174	22	43	13	0	1	13	23	1	3	0	46	9	2	.339	.338
Tolbert, Matt	B-R	6-0	185	5-4-82	.256	.231	.267	15	43	3	11	1	0	0	1	5	0	2	0	4	1	1	.279	.333
Valle, Sebastian	R-R	6-1	205	7-24-90	.220	.231	.216	38	127	17	28	7	0	4	22	4	0	2	2	33	0	0	.370	.241

Pitching	B-T	HT	WT	DOB	W	L	ERA	G	GS	CG	SV	IP	H	R	ER	HR	BB	SO	AVG	vLH	vRH	K/9	BB/9
Adams, Mike	R-R	6-5	210	7-29-78	0	1	2.25	4	0	0	0	4	3	1	1	0	0	2	.231	.400	.125	4.50	0.00
Aumont, Phillippe	L-R	6-7	260	1-7-89	3	3	3.93	35	0	0	0	55	48	25	24	2	39	65	.240	.226	.252	10.64	6.38
Bootcheck, Chris	R-R	6-5	210	10-24-78	2	5	4.85	8	0	0	0	43	41	24	23	5	20	29	.256	.205	.299	6.12	4.22
Buchanan, David	R-R	6-3	200	5-11-89	6	2	3.95	12	12	0	0	57	67	26	25	3	21	46	.300	.320	.285	7.26	3.32
Camp, Shawn	R-R	6-1	205	11-18-75	0	1	4.20	13	0	0	0	15	20	7	7	1	5	10	.328	.348	.316	6.00	3.00
De Fratus, Justin	B-R	6-4	225	10-21-87	0	0	4.50	15	0	0	3	16	20	8	8	1	4	13	.339	.360	.324	7.31	2.25
Enright, Barry	R-R	6-3	220	3-30-86	4	9	5.58	19	19	1	0	102	129	80	63	17	33	64	.307	.262	.354	5.67	2.92
Friend, Justin	R-R	6-1	210	6-21-86	0	0	0.00	1	0	0	0	1	0	0	0	0	1	1	.250	.000	.500	9.00	9.00
Garcia, Luis	R-R	6-2	210	1-30-87	2	1	0.96	39	0	0	22	47	35	8	5	0	16	52	.205	.205	.204	10.03	3.09
Giles, Ken	R-R	6-3	205	9-20-90	2	0	2.63	11	0	0	5	14	10	4	4	0	8	9	.217	.240	.190	5.93	5.27
Gonzalez, Miguel Alfredo	R-R	6-3	200	9-23-86	0	1	1.62	12	0	0	2	17	10	4	3	0	10	19	.172	.214	.133	10.26	5.40
Hoffman, Matt	L-L	6-2	224	11-8-88	0	0	4.50	3	0	0	0	4	5	2	2	0	2	1	.333	.400	.300	2.25	4.50
2-team total (14 Rochester)					1	0	3.91	17	0	0	2	25	29	12	11	4	11	20	—	—	—	7.11	3.91
Horst, Jeremy	L-L	6-3	235	10-1-85	4	2	3.98	45	3	0	0	63	54	29	28	4	31	57	.234	.236	.232	8.10	4.41
Jimenez, Cesar	L-L	5-11	210	11-12-84	3	2	1.45	38	2	0	3	50	34	9	8	0	15	46	.193	.259	.161	8.34	2.72
Knigge, Tyler	R-R	6-4	215	10-27-88	4	3	4.61	27	0	0	0	41	44	22	21	2	12	25	.270	.243	.290	5.49	2.63
Lincoln, Brad	R-R	6-0	225	5-25-85	6	11	5.11	27	22	1	0	123	123	75	70	13	58	112	.260	.271	.252	8.17	4.23
Manship, Jeff	R-R	6-2	210	1-16-85	0	1	4.62	8	5	1	0	25	29	14	13	1	18	21	.290	.340	.234	7.46	6.39
Marquis, Jason	L-R	6-1	220	8-21-78	3	1	4.63	8	8	0	0	47	46	24	24	5	13	36	.256	.269	.245	6.94	2.51

Name		HT	WT	DOB	W	L	ERA	G	GS	CG	SV	IP	H	R	ER	HR	BB	SO	AVG	vLH	vRH	K/9	BB/9
Martin, Ethan	R-R	6-2	220	6-6-89	2	1	4.15	29	0	0	0	48	46	23	22	2	21	45	.256	.221	.282	8.50	3.97
Neris, Hector	R-R	6-2	175	6-14-89	4	3	4.19	37	1	0	2	58	50	29	27	5	19	58	.228	.264	.203	9.00	2.95
Nesseth, Mike	R-R	6-5	210	4-19-88	0	2	9.39	4	1	0	0	8	13	11	8	2	4	5	.361	.462	.304	5.87	4.70
O'Sullivan, Sean	R-R	6-1	240	9-1-87	6	10	4.30	25	25	1	0	149	154	82	71	17	50	94	.271	.282	.261	5.69	3.03
Pettibone, Jonathan	L-R	6-6	225	7-19-90	2	0	3.42	5	5	0	0	26	22	11	10	0	6	13	.224	.238	.214	4.44	2.05
Reyes, Jo-Jo	L-L	6-2	230	11-20-84	1	3	10.45	5	5	0	0	21	41	28	24	2	8	9	.423	.500	.403	3.92	3.48
Rosenberg, B.J.	R-R	6-3	220	9-17-85	2	1	6.63	18	0	0	1	19	24	14	14	2	12	17	.312	.359	.263	8.05	5.68
Rosin, Seth	R-R	6-6	265	11-2-88	1	3	6.26	17	1	0	2	23	31	17	16	3	9	20	.333	.357	.314	7.83	3.52
Simon, Kyle	R-R	6-6	220	8-18-90	0	2	9.42	10	0	0	0	14	19	16	15	0	10	8	.317	.292	.333	5.02	6.28
Smith, Greg	L-L	6-1	190	12-22-83	9	11	4.40	27	26	1	0	157	176	84	77	17	37	92	.286	.297	.282	5.26	2.12

Fielding

Catcher	PCT	G	PO	A	E	DP	PB
Davis	1.000	9	67	5	0	1	1
Hill	.993	46	277	26	2	1	3
Rupp	.992	56	346	37	3	6	4
Valle	.997	36	271	26	1	2	4

First Base	PCT	G	PO	A	E	DP
Brignac	.857	1	5	1	1	0
Canzler	.992	15	118	9	1	11
Franco	1.000	23	184	11	0	16
Mayberry Jr.	1.000	3	30	1	0	1
Murphy	.995	99	760	58	4	78
Ruf	1.000	8	54	6	0	7

Second Base	PCT	G	PO	A	E	DP
Blanco	1.000	5	6	8	0	1
Brignac	1.000	16	23	33	0	6
Cedeno	.988	17	27	56	1	12
Duran	1.000	1	4	3	0	0
Galvis	1.000	3	8	13	0	2
Hanzawa	.967	8	9	20	1	4
Henson	.977	45	70	101	4	21
Hernandez	.979	21	53	40	2	19
Maruszak	1.000	2	4	2	0	0
Ryal	1.000	7	8	21	0	5
Spears	1.000	29	46	79	0	19
Tolbert	.857	6	9	9	3	3

Third Base	PCT	G	PO	A	E	DP
Asche	1.000	2	0	5	0	0
Brignac	.875	8	6	8	2	0
Canzler	1.000	3	3	3	0	1
Franco	.961	107	69	175	10	13
Galvis	1.000	1	1	3	0	0
Henson	.944	7	4	13	1	2
Hernandez	.750	3	0	6	2	1
Maruszak	.917	5	3	8	1	1
Ryal	.667	2	0	2	1	0
Spears	1.000	9	11	19	0	2
Tolbert	1.000	1	1	1	0	0

Shortstop	PCT	G	PO	A	E	DP
Blanco	.994	39	61	99	1	19
Brignac	1.000	7	10	16	0	5
Cedeno	.971	28	37	62	3	13
Duran	.960	12	17	31	2	6
Galvis	.992	30	39	83	1	27
Hanzawa	.895	6	6	11	2	0
Henson	.889	4	7	9	2	4
Hernandez	.943	16	14	36	3	7
Maruszak	1.000	2	2	6	0	2
Spears	.957	8	8	14	1	2

Outfield	PCT	G	PO	A	E	DP
Canzler	.967	19	29	0	1	0
Castro	.978	109	262	10	6	2
Galvis	1.000	1	1	0	0	0
Gillies	.993	43	137	2	1	1
Gwynn Jr.	1.000	20	41	2	0	2
Henson	.987	67	147	6	2	3
Maruszak	.500	3	1	0	1	0
Mayberry Jr.	.889	6	7	1	1	0
Perkins	1.000	72	145	5	0	1
Ruf	1.000	14	21	1	0	0
Ryal	1.000	5	8	0	0	0
Sizemore	.933	10	14	0	1	0
Susdorf	.970	36	63	2	2	0
Thomas	.972	49	100	3	3	1
Tolbert	1.000	4	9	0	0	0

READING FIGHTIN' PHILS   DOUBLE-A

EASTERN LEAGUE

Batting	B-T	HT	WT	DOB	AVG	vLH	vRH	G	AB	R	H	2B	3B	HR	RBI	BB	HBP	SH	SF	SO	SB	CS	SLG	OBP
Alonso, Carlos	R-R	5-11	205	2-15-88	.272	.256	.281	127	467	76	127	22	3	10	44	60	11	6	1	70	8	4	.396	.367
Altherr, Aaron	R-R	6-5	220	1-14-91	.236	.247	.231	120	449	54	106	27	2	14	57	26	8	4	5	110	12	6	.399	.287
Carman, Chad	R-R	5-10	189	5-9-89	.000	.000	.000	2	7	0	0	0	0	0	0	0	0	0	0	2	0	0	.000	.000
Cartwright, Albert	R-R	5-10	180	10-31-87	.243	.253	.237	119	445	54	108	19	2	3	23	29	4	7	0	111	28	9	.315	.295
Collier, Zach	L-L	6-2	200	9-8-90	.240	.192	.259	86	267	39	64	10	4	9	29	22	9	2	1	82	5	7	.408	.318
Davis, Lars	L-R	6-3	205	11-7-85	.156	.182	.147	16	45	2	7	1	0	1	7	5	1	0	0	10	0	0	.244	.255
Dugan, Kelly	L-R	6-3	215	9-18-90	.284	.281	.306	76	253	35	75	18	1	5	34	28	8	0	1	56	1	0	.435	.383
Duran, Edgar	R-R	5-11	155	2-10-91	.224	.252	.208	105	335	36	75	10	2	4	25	21	4	5	1	57	6	6	.301	.277
Fox, Jake	R-R	6-0	220	7-20-82	.308	.255	.333	78	286	42	88	15	0	22	70	20	11	0	2	49	0	0	.591	.373
Gomez, Raywilly	R-R	5-11	195	1-25-90	.211	.268	.133	26	71	6	15	4	0	1	5	4	0	0	0	5	0	0	.310	.253
Hernandez, Cesar	B-R	5-10	166	5-23-90	.340	.368	.323	26	103	13	35	4	1	3	14	13	0	0	1	13	1	3	.485	.410
Hewitt, Anthony	R-R	6-1	190	4-27-89	.140	.132	.149	34	100	7	14	1	0	1	8	1	0	0	2	39	2	2	.180	.146
James, Jiwan	R-R	6-4	180	4-11-89	.333	.400	.273	9	21	1	7	2	0	0	0	1	0	0	0	7	0	0	.429	.364
Joseph, Tommy	R-R	6-1	225	7-16-91	.282	.250	.304	21	78	8	22	4	1	5	19	5	3	0	1	19	0	0	.551	.345
Lavin, Peter	L-L	5-11	180	12-27-87	.283	.227	.307	74	251	40	71	17	3	5	31	14	2	4	3	31	6	2	.434	.322
Maruszak, Addison	R-R	6-1	190	12-21-86	.200	.125	.227	9	30	2	6	0	1	0	2	2	0	0	0	8	0	1	.267	.250
Mayorga, Jose	R-R	5-10	175	8-20-92	.000	.000	.000	1	3	0	0	0	0	0	0	0	0	0	0	2	0	0	.000	.000
Moore, Logan	L-R	6-2	200	8-22-90	.221	.226	.220	59	190	9	42	12	1	4	17	20	1	2	2	48	0	2	.358	.296
Nieves, Wil	R-R	5-11	190	9-25-77	.083	.000	.200	3	12	0	1	0	0	0	1	0	0	0	0	2	0	0	.083	.083
Perkins, Cam	R-R	6-5	195	9-27-90	.342	.364	.328	52	196	25	67	19	1	3	34	20	2	4	0	30	5	3	.495	.408
Phillips, Anthony	R-R	5-9	160	4-11-90	.237	.167	.279	31	97	9	23	6	1	0	12	12	1	3	1	21	0	0	.320	.324
Ryal, Rusty	R-R	6-2	200	3-16-83	.083	.200	.000	3	12	0	1	0	0	0	0	0	0	0	0	3	0	0	.167	.083
Serna, K.C.	R-R	6-0	185	10-15-89	.273	.368	.222	48	165	20	45	7	1	2	14	4	0	2	0	24	1	2	.364	.290
Serritella, Chris	L-R	6-3	205	2-21-90	.186	.182	.186	35	97	5	18	3	0	2	7	7	0	0	1	34	0	0	.278	.238
Stassi, Brock	L-L	6-2	190	8-7-89	.232	.199	.248	124	440	49	102	12	3	8	44	39	6	2	2	49	3	1	.307	.302
Tolbert, Matt	B-R	6-0	185	5-4-82	.172	.208	.147	21	58	4	10	1	0	0	2	2	1	0		4	0	0	.190	.213
Valle, Sebastian	R-R	6-1	205	7-24-90	.257	.317	.189	37	113	4	29	4	0	1	10	5	0	1	1	19	0	0	.319	.286
Williams, Everett	L-R	5-10	200	10-1-90	.233	.375	.182	9	30	2	7	1	0	0	5	2	0	3		5	0	1	.267	.257

Pitching	B-T	HT	WT	DOB	W	L	ERA	G	GS	CG	SV	IP	H	R	ER	HR	BB	SO	AVG	vLH	vRH	K/9	BB/9
Biddle, Jesse	L-L	6-5	220	10-22-91	3	10	5.03	16	16	0	0	82	78	59	46	11	44	80	.260	.208	.264	8.74	4.81
Bootcheck, Chris	R-R	6-5	210	10-24-78	2	3	5.55	8	8	0	0	36	46	24	22	6	13	24	.322	.319	.324	6.06	3.28
Colvin, Brody	R-R	6-3	195	8-14-90	0	0	0.00	3	0	0	0	3	2	0	0	0	2	3	.200	.250	.167	9.00	6.00
Demmin, Ryan	L-L	6-1	210	4-5-88	1	2	10.00	7	4	0	0	18	24	20	20	4	7	9	.320	.355	.295	4.50	3.50
Friend, Justin	R-R	6-1	210	6-21-86	0	0	0.00	2	0	0	0	2	1	0	0		1	2	.167	.500	.000	9.00	4.50
Garner, Perci	R-R	6-3	225	12-13-88	4	5	4.85	19	16	0	0	82	79	53	44	3	62	62	.260	.236	.277	6.83	6.83

Name	B-T	HT	WT	DOB	W	L	ERA	G	GS	CG	SV	IP	H	R	ER	HR	BB	SO	AVG	vLH	vRH	SO/9	BB/9
Giles, Ken	R-R	6-2	205	9-20-90	0	0	1.20	13	0	0	7	15	8	3	2	0	5	29	.154	.190	.129	17.40	3.00
Gonzalez, Miguel Alfredo	R-R	6-3	200	9-23-86	0	2	3.14	11	0	0	5	14	10	5	5	2	7	24	.192	.192	.192	15.07	4.40
Gonzalez, Severino	R-R	6-1	153	9-28-92	9	13	4.59	27	27	0	0	159	169	89	81	23	34	115	.270	.273	.266	6.52	1.93
Hoffman, Matt	L-L	6-2	224	11-8-88	0	1	3.57	20	0	0	3	23	21	10	9	2	8	30	.247	.146	.341	11.91	3.18
Johnson, Jay	R-L	6-2	210	12-21-89	0	2	13.50	16	0	0	1	13	15	20	19	3	14	11	.288	.208	.357	7.82	9.95
Knigge, Tyler	R-R	6-4	215	10-27-88	3	0	2.06	18	0	0	3	35	27	8	8	0	10	22	.220	.231	.211	5.66	2.57
Loewen, Adam	L-L	6-6	235	4-9-84	4	5	3.31	17	17	1	0	103	84	45	38	7	53	75	.224	.190	.236	6.53	4.62
Milner, Hoby	L-L	6-2	165	1-13-91	10	6	4.21	25	25	1	0	143	146	72	67	25	56	86	.267	.238	.276	5.40	3.52
Murray, Colton	R-R	6-0	195	4-22-90	1	5	2.29	36	2	0	6	59	39	22	15	5	22	60	.188	.163	.205	9.15	3.36
Neris, Hector	R-R	6-2	175	6-14-89	2	0	1.86	11	0	0	0	19	12	4	4	3	10	12	.188	.200	.182	5.59	4.66
Nesseth, Mike	R-R	6-5	210	4-19-88	2	5	5.24	38	8	0	1	81	99	53	47	9	23	59	.305	.338	.281	6.58	2.57
Nola, Aaron	R-R	6-1	195	6-4-93	2	0	2.63	5	5	0	0	24	25	7	7	4	5	15	.272	.234	.311	5.63	1.88
O'Sullivan, Ryan	R-R	6-2	190	9-5-90	7	8	3.91	37	12	1	0	113	112	55	49	10	42	70	.258	.256	.260	5.59	3.36
Ogando, Nefi	R-R	6-2	185	6-3-89	5	1	6.27	48	0	0	7	56	64	41	39	6	28	57	.291	.300	.286	9.16	4.50
Paulino, Luis	R-R	6-1	215	6-16-89	2	0	1.80	2	2	0	0	6	3	2	2	2	6	.162	.188	.143	5.40	1.80
Rosin, Seth	R-R	6-6	265	11-2-88	2	2	2.29	26	0	0	1	35	33	9	9	3	16	24	.252	.250	.253	6.11	2.55
Simon, Kyle	R-R	6-6	220	8-18-90	5	2	2.64	36	0	0	3	61	58	21	18	3	11	33	.259	.292	.237	4.84	1.61
Wright, Austin	L-L	6-4	235	9-26-89	2	4	5.06	32	0	0	0	48	41	31	27	5	44	38	.225	.177	.250	7.13	8.25

Fielding

Catcher	PCT	G	PO	A	E	DP	PB
Carman	1.000	2	8	0	0	0	0
Davis	.955	14	77	7	4	0	1
Fox	1.000	2	10	2	0	0	0
Gomez	.973	21	137	7	4	0	1
Joseph	.995	21	172	12	1	1	0
Mayorga	1.000	1	4	1	0	0	0
Moore	.990	59	379	31	4	2	3
Nieves	1.000	1	3	0	0	0	0
Valle	.985	29	174	20	3	1	4

First Base	PCT	G	PO	A	E	DP
Fox	.993	20	140	9	1	16
Perkins	.986	9	64	4	1	5
Serritella	.984	7	61	2	1	8
Stassi	.993	115	916	74	7	112
Valle	—	1	0	0	0	0

Second Base	PCT	G	PO	A	E	DP
Alonso	.968	61	107	169	9	39
Cartwright	.977	82	166	222	9	65
Duran	.952	4	6	14	1	2
Hernandez	1.000	2	4	6	0	1
Serna	1.000	1	1	4	0	0
Tolbert	1.000	2	2	3	0	0

Third Base	PCT	G	PO	A	E	DP
Alonso	.933	66	30	110	10	11
Duran	1.000	10	2	15	0	2
Fox	.933	18	11	31	3	7
Hernandez	.843	18	9	34	8	3
Maruszak	1.000	1	0	1	0	0
Phillips	.966	23	12	44	2	3
Ryal	.667	1	0	2	1	0
Serna	.727	4	0	8	3	0
Tolbert	.968	12	6	24	1	3

Shortstop	PCT	G	PO	A	E	DP
Alonso	.889	2	3	5	1	0
Duran	.962	89	144	260	16	70
Hernandez	.967	8	13	16	1	3
Maruszak	1.000	2	3	5	0	0
Phillips	.960	6	6	18	1	2
Ryal	.800	1	0	4	1	0
Serna	.963	42	60	124	7	26
Tolbert	1.000	2	3	2	0	0

Outfield	PCT	G	PO	A	E	DP
Altherr	.983	119	283	11	5	4
Cartwright	.976	33	81	1	2	0
Collier	.994	82	152	2	1	0
Dugan	.976	64	123	0	3	0
Hewitt	.880	16	22	0	3	0
James	.750	5	3	0	1	0
Lavin	.983	62	108	7	2	0
Maruszak	1.000	5	6	0	0	0
Perkins	1.000	43	74	5	0	1
Ryal	1.000	1	4	1	0	0
Stassi	.867	8	13	0	2	0
Williams	1.000	8	30	3	0	2

CLEARWATER THRESHERS   HIGH CLASS A

FLORIDA STATE LEAGUE

Batting	B-T	HT	WT	DOB	AVG	vLH	vRH	G	AB	R	H	2B	3B	HR	RBI	BB	HBP	SH	SF	SO	SB	CS	SLG	OBP
Altherr, Aaron	R-R	6-5	220	1-14-91	.250	.750	.167	7	28	6	7	1	2	0	2	5	0	0	0	8	1	0	.429	.364
Bass, Corey	R-R	5-9	200	4-27-91	.202	.087	.239	32	94	7	19	6	0	2	10	8	0	0	0	23	1	0	.330	.265
Brignac, Reid	L-R	6-3	215	1-16-86	.500	.000	.571	3	8	0	4	1	0	0	1	2	0	0	0	1	0	0	.625	.600
Canelo, Malquin	R-R	5-10	156	9-5-94	.208	.333	.167	16	48	2	10	3	0	0	3	3	1	1	0	12	1	1	.271	.269
Carman, Chad	R-R	5-10	189	5-9-89	.071	.000	.083	4	14	1	1	0	0	0	0	0	0	1	0	3	0	0	.071	.071
Carmona, William	B-R	5-11	185	3-9-91	.129	.111	.138	25	85	3	11	1	1	0	4	4	0	0	0	20	0	0	.165	.169
Charles, Art	L-L	6-6	220	11-10-90	.229	.169	.252	127	446	60	102	25	4	19	54	44	5	0	4	156	0	0	.430	.303
Crawford, J.P.	L-R	6-2	180	1-11-95	.275	.279	.274	63	236	32	65	7	0	8	29	28	2	1	4	37	10	7	.407	.352
Ferdinand, Nick	R-R	6-1	210	12-31-89	.142	.139	.143	32	106	10	15	4	1	2	9	5	2	0	0	28	0	0	.255	.195
Fisher, Joel	R-R	6-3	235	1-8-93	.000	—	.000	1	3	0	0	0	0	0	0	0	0	0	0	1	0	0	.000	.000
Galvis, Freddy	B-R	5-10	185	11-14-89	.200	.000	.364	5	20	4	4	0	2	1	3	0	0	0	0	2	0	0	.550	.200
Gillies, Tyson	L-R	6-2	205	10-31-88	.250	.000	.333	2	8	0	2	1	0	0	0	0	0	1	0	1	0	0	.375	.250
Grullon, Deivi	R-R	6-1	180	2-17-96	.200	.500	.125	2	10	0	2	0	0	0	1	0	0	0	0	1	0	0	.200	.200
Hewitt, Anthony	R-R	6-1	190	4-27-89	.129	.222	.091	8	31	2	4	1	0	0	0	0	0	0	0	15	1	1	.161	.129
Knapp, Andrew	B-R	6-1	190	11-9-91	.157	.130	.167	23	83	7	13	1	0	1	7	5	2	0	0	26	1	0	.205	.222
Lavin, Peter	L-L	5-11	180	12-27-87	.292	.289	.293	54	209	27	61	11	2	6	18	16	1	1	1	38	5	5	.450	.344
Lino, Gabriel	R-R	6-3	210	5-17-93	.223	.243	.214	74	238	26	53	7	0	4	28	18	2	1	2	68	0	3	.303	.281
Martinez, Harold	R-R	6-3	210	5-3-90	.251	.260	.248	103	382	36	96	19	1	6	38	10	7	1	1	88	5	1	.353	.283
Moore, Logan	L-R	6-3	190	8-22-90	.238	.250	.232	32	105	5	25	7	0	0	11	7	1	0	2	22	1	0	.305	.287
Mora, Angelo	B-R	5-11	190	2-25-93	.227	.190	.241	107	353	27	80	14	4	3	25	27	2	5	2	81	3	8	.334	.284
Morelos, Jair	L-R	5-10	150	2-2-94	.111	—	.111	3	9	1	1	0	0	0	1	0	0	1	0	0	0	0	.111	.111
Nieves, Wil	R-R	5-11	190	9-25-77	.250	.500	.000	2	4	0	1	0	0	0	0	0	0	0	0	0	0	0	.250	.250
Parr, Justin	L-R	6-2	190	11-29-90	.136	.161	.123	28	88	12	12	2	0	0	3	5	0	2	0	21	0	0	.159	.183
Phillips, Anthony	R-S	5-9	160	4-11-90	.229	.288	.198	72	153	17	35	4	1	2	12	20	1	4	0	36	4	3	.307	.322
Pointer, Brian	L-L	6-0	190	1-28-92	.246	.283	.231	123	415	60	102	19	4	15	53	50	8	4	3	128	16	8	.419	.336
Posso, Jesus	R-R	5-11	201	2-10-95	.250	.000	.333	3	8	1	2	1	0	1	2	0	0	0	0	2	0	0	.750	.250
Quinn, Roman	B-R	5-10	170	5-14-93	.257	.327	.227	88	327	51	84	10	3	7	36	36	9	6	4	80	32	12	.370	.343
Rodriguez, Herlis	L-L	6-0	157	6-10-94	.314	.400	.293	18	51	2	16	3	0	0	3	1	0	3	0	8	0	2	.373	.327
Ruf, Darin	R-R	6-3	240	7-28-86	.250	.000	.300	3	12	0	3	0	0	0	2	1	0	0	0	3	0	0	.250	.308
Ruiz, Carlos	R-R	5-10	205	1-22-79	.176	.000	.200	5	17	4	3	1	0	0	2	1	1	0	0	3	1	0	.235	.263
Serna, K.C.	R-R	6-0	185	10-15-89	.279	.274	.281	76	298	34	83	18	3	3	26	12	3	1	1	37	9	5	.389	.312

	B-T	HT	WT	DOB	AVG	vLH	vRH	G	AB	R	H	2B	3B	HR	RBI	BB	HBP	SH	SF	SO	SB	CS	SLG	OBP
Serritella, Chris	L-R	6-3	205	2-21-90	.216	.156	.234	61	199	20	43	11	1	7	29	24	0	2	3	51	0	1	.387	.296
Short, Brandon	R-R	6-0	190	9-9-88	.215	.243	.203	71	251	23	54	15	3	4	32	18	2	0	3	55	4	4	.347	.270
Swauger, Chris	L-L	6-0	195	8-11-86	.154	.000	.267	8	26	3	4	1	0	0	2	1	0	0	1	6	0	0	.192	.179
Valentin, Jesmuel	B-R	5-9	180	5-12-94	.205	.214	.200	12	44	8	9	2	0	0	3	0	2	0	6	1	1	.250	.255
Williams, Everett	L-R	5-10	200	10-1-90	.280	.182	.296	22	82	10	23	3	2	0	9	6	0	0	0	10	2	1	.366	.330
Zier, Tim	R-R	5-9	195	8-6-91	.000	—	.000	1	2	0	0	0	0	0	0	0	1	0	0	0	0	0	.000	.333

PHILADELPHIA PHILLIES

Pitching

	B-T	HT	WT	DOB	W	L	ERA	G	GS	CG	SV	IP	H	R	ER	HR	BB	SO	AVG	vLH	vRH	K/9	BB/9
Adams, Mike	R-R	6-5	210	7-29-78	0	0	3.38	3	0	0	0	3	3	1	1	0	1	5	.273	.333	.250	16.88	3.38
Baker, Aaron	R-R	6-3	220	12-14-89	1	0	4.32	6	0	0	0	8	10	4	4	1	0	10	.303	.091	.409	10.80	0.00
Biddle, Jesse	L-L	6-5	220	10-22-91	2	0	0.90	2	2	0	0	10	3	1	1	0	6	10	.097	.000	.158	8.10	5.40
Burgess, Chris	R-R	6-2	210	8-24-90	0	1	12.91	8	0	0	1	8	15	11	11	2	4	2	.405	.308	.458	2.35	4.70
Camp, Shawn	R-R	6-1	205	11-18-75	0	0	2.25	3	0	0	0	4	2	1	1	1	0	6	.154	.167	.143	13.50	0.00
Child, Dan	R-R	6-5	230	7-24-92	1	1	5.70	24	0	0	2	36	54	27	23	0	17	24	.351	.408	.295	5.94	4.21
Colvin, Brody	R-R	6-3	195	8-14-90	0	2	7.11	4	4	0	0	13	14	10	10	0	10	2	.298	.269	.333	1.42	7.11
Demmin, Ryan	L-L	6-1	210	4-5-88	2	1	1.29	4	4	0	0	28	20	4	4	0	2	27	.200	.136	.250	8.68	0.64
Forsythe, Cody	L-L	6-0	170	9-17-90	2	3	2.27	22	0	0	3	36	27	14	9	5	11	47	.208	.192	.218	11.86	2.78
Garner, Perci	R-R	6-3	225	12-13-88	0	0	3.00	7	0	0	0	12	9	5	4	0	15	13	.209	.250	.174	9.75	11.25
Gonzalez, Miguel Alfredo	R-R	6-3	200	9-23-86	0	2	4.70	8	3	0	0	15	20	11	8	0	9	11	.317	.419	.219	6.46	5.28
Guth, Jordan	R-R	6-5	215	4-7-91	3	4	3.04	33	8	0	4	77	73	37	26	6	46	47	.252	.270	.235	5.49	5.38
Hamels, Cole	L-L	6-3	195	12-27-83	0	1	2.12	3	3	0	0	17	12	4	4	3	1	12	.211	.227	.200	6.35	0.53
Hanson, Nic	R-R	6-7	210	4-15-92	0	2	12.00	2	2	0	0	6	11	9	8	0	4	2	.407	.571	.350	3.00	6.00
Inch, Steven	R-R	6-4	190	2-11-91	0	0	3.86	3	0	0	0	2	1	1	1	1	1	1	.143	.000	.250	3.86	3.86
Joaquin, Ulises	R-R	5-11	165	6-11-92	2	1	3.57	16	0	0	8	23	25	9	9	2	10	16	.298	.306	.292	6.35	3.97
Kleven, Colin	R-R	6-5	200	4-15-91	6	10	4.83	24	24	1	0	136	155	82	73	13	33	107	.289	.339	.252	7.08	2.18
Lee, Cliff	L-L	6-3	205	8-30-78	0	1	5.06	3	3	0	0	11	13	11	6	1	2	8	.295	.167	.344	6.75	1.69
Leiter Jr., Mark	R-R	6-0	195	3-13-91	4	5	4.31	11	11	1	0	65	69	34	31	5	15	56	.273	.301	.250	7.79	2.09
Loewen, Adam	L-L	6-6	235	4-9-84	1	0	2.61	2	2	0	0	10	7	3	3	0	7	9	.200	.133	.250	7.84	6.10
Martin, Ethan	R-R	6-2	220	6-6-89	0	0	0.00	3	0	0	0	3	3	0	0	0	3	0	.273	.200	.333	0.00	10.13
Martinez, Lino	L-L	6-0	165	9-19-92	0	6	5.32	37	1	0	3	71	64	44	42	6	53	70	.246	.284	.219	8.87	6.72
Meadors, Mark	R-R	6-4	200	2-10-92	0	1	27.00	2	0	0	0	1	1	4	4	0	3	1	.200	.000	.250	6.75	20.25
Murray, Colton	R-R	6-0	195	4-22-90	2	2	2.04	11	0	0	2	18	16	4	4	0	8	17	.242	.316	.213	8.66	4.08
Nola, Aaron	R-R	6-1	195	6-4-93	2	3	3.16	7	6	0	0	31	24	12	11	4	5	30	.214	.245	.190	8.62	1.44
Nunez, Miguel	R-R	6-6	215	10-27-92	6	7	4.49	25	20	0	0	122	125	65	61	8	44	95	.263	.269	.257	6.99	3.24
Oviedo, Ramon	R-R	6-4	175	7-24-90	0	1	5.23	23	0	0	0	31	36	19	18	2	21	20	.298	.333	.274	5.81	6.10
Paulino, Luis	R-R	6-1	215	6-16-89	0	1	5.25	7	2	0	0	24	25	18	14	3	15	17	.266	.359	.200	6.38	5.63
Prosinski, Jon	R-R	6-3	180	2-17-91	0	4	6.56	9	9	0	0	48	69	39	35	7	8	28	.343	.387	.306	5.25	1.50
Ridenhour, Lee	R-R	6-4	230	8-7-89	2	8	4.72	42	0	0	9	55	56	34	29	4	20	37	.267	.240	.289	6.02	3.25
Stefan, Jeb	R-R	6-4	225	4-21-90	6	12	6.44	29	14	0	0	101	112	80	72	11	45	78	.284	.278	.289	6.97	4.02
Stewart, Ethan	L-L	6-7	235	1-19-91	5	7	4.82	28	16	0	0	103	117	66	55	9	58	70	.290	.263	.305	6.14	5.08
Walter, Kevin	R-R	6-5	215	5-1-92	2	3	4.68	34	4	0	0	73	75	47	38	5	39	42	.263	.269	.258	5.18	4.81

Fielding

Catcher	PCT	G	PO	A	E	DP	PB
Bass	.983	32	204	21	4	1	4
Carman	1.000	3	21	4	0	0	0
Fisher	1.000	1	4	0	0	1	0
Grullon	1.000	2	21	2	0	1	0
Lino	.985	70	459	67	8	4	8
Moore	.994	32	153	27	1	1	3
Nieves	1.000	2	7	1	0	0	0
Posso	1.000	3	8	2	0	0	0
Ruiz	1.000	4	25	4	0	0	0

First Base	PCT	G	PO	A	E	DP
Carmona	.977	6	41	1	1	7
Charles	.985	93	752	59	12	85
Lino	1.000	1	9	3	0	1
Martinez	1.000	6	33	2	0	4
Ruf	1.000	2	21	1	0	3
Serna	1.000	1	2	0	0	0
Serritella	.997	35	280	11	1	24

Second Base	PCT	G	PO	A	E	DP
Canelo	1.000	1	5	2	0	1
Galvis	.778	2	2	5	2	0

	PCT	G	PO	A	E	DP
Mora	.971	68	116	188	9	32
Morelos	.909	3	3	7	1	2
Phillips	.992	26	51	75	1	21
Serna	.978	33	70	108	4	37
Valentin	.966	12	27	30	2	11
Zier	1.000	1	2	1	0	0

Third Base	PCT	G	PO	A	E	DP
Brignac	.857	2	1	5	1	1
Carmona	.714	2	1	4	2	1
Galvis	—	1	0	0	0	0
Martinez	.960	96	73	188	11	18
Mora	1.000	1	2	0	0	0
Parr	—	1	0	0	0	0
Phillips	.955	14	6	15	1	2
Serna	.938	30	29	46	5	6

Shortstop	PCT	G	PO	A	E	DP
Brignac	1.000	1	1	2	0	0
Canelo	.914	14	24	29	5	6
Crawford	.940	62	97	169	17	43
Galvis	1.000	2	2	5	0	2
Martinez	1.000	1	2	2	0	1

	PCT	G	PO	A	E	DP
Mora	.967	27	44	74	4	21
Phillips	1.000	9	15	19	0	3
Quinn	.954	17	27	35	3	11
Serna	.981	9	17	34	1	2

Outfield	PCT	G	PO	A	E	DP
Altherr	.923	7	22	2	2	1
Carmona	1.000	6	5	0	0	0
Ferdinand	.969	31	59	3	2	1
Gillies	1.000	2	4	0	0	0
Hewitt	1.000	8	10	1	0	0
Lavin	.981	52	144	14	3	5
Mora	.941	15	15	1	1	0
Parr	.960	24	47	1	2	0
Phillips	1.000	7	8	0	0	0
Pointer	.992	115	224	13	2	2
Quinn	.967	69	171	3	6	2
Rodriguez	.966	17	28	0	1	0
Ruf	—	1	0	0	0	0
Short	.952	51	79	1	4	0
Swauger	1.000	8	19	0	0	0
Williams	1.000	18	41	2	0	2

LAKEWOOD BLUECLAWS   LOW CLASS A
SOUTH ATLANTIC LEAGUE

Batting	B-T	HT	WT	DOB	AVG	vLH	vRH	G	AB	R	H	2B	3B	HR	RBI	BB	HBP	SH	SF	SO	SB	CS	SLG	OBP
Asche, Cody	L-R	6-1	200	6-30-90	.429	.600	.000	3	7	3	3	1	0	2	5	3	0	0	0	2	1	0	1.429	.600
Astudillo, Willians	R-R	5-9	182	10-14-91	.333	.315	.340	117	436	41	145	30	1	4	61	19	6	0	4	20	2	3	.433	.366
Brown, Aaron	L-L	6-2	220	6-20-92	.309	.389	.270	14	55	3	17	6	0	1	5	1	2	0	1	19	0	1	.473	.339
Canelo, Malquin	R-R	5-10	156	9-5-94	.270	.370	.226	45	152	19	41	8	1	1	18	11	1	1	2	31	4	1	.355	.319
Cozens, Dylan	L-L	6-6	235	5-31-94	.248	.255	.245	132	509	69	126	25	6	16	62	40	2	1	4	147	23	7	.415	.303
Crawford, J.P.	L-R	6-2	180	1-11-95	.295	.228	.318	60	227	37	67	16	0	3	19	37	2	1	0	37	14	7	.405	.398

PHILADELPHIA PHILLIES

Batting	B-T	HT	WT	DOB	AVG	vLH	vRH	G	AB	R	H	2B	3B	HR	RBI	BB	HBP	SH	SF	SO	SB	CS	SLG	OBP
Ferdinand, Nick	R-R	6-1	210	12-31-89	.000	.000	.000	3	9	0	0	0	0	0	0	0	0	0	0	0	0	0	.000	.000
Green, Zach	R-R	6-3	210	3-7-94	.268	.263	.271	84	328	41	88	22	2	6	43	24	1	0	5	65	7	1	.402	.316
Greene, Larry	L-R	6-0	235	2-10-93	.183	.132	.201	60	197	23	36	7	3	2	18	22	1	1	3	60	4	2	.279	.265
Grullon, Deivi	R-R	6-1	180	2-17-96	.237	.273	.222	24	76	9	18	5	0	1	7	3	1	1	0	13	0	0	.342	.275
Hernandez, Jan	R-R	6-1	195	1-3-95	.145	.182	.136	17	55	5	8	3	0	1	5	5	0	0	0	23	0	0	.255	.217
Hiciano, Samuel	R-R	6-1	205	1-25-94	.255	.237	.262	93	330	35	84	20	2	9	36	23	3	2	4	86	8	9	.409	.306
Knapp, Andrew	B-R	6-1	190	11-9-91	.290	.250	.309	75	283	39	82	19	4	5	25	27	2	0	2	71	3	3	.438	.354
Lino, Gabriel	R-R	6-3	190	5-17-93	.180	.250	.158	16	50	7	9	5	0	1	6	9	0	0	1	23	0	0	.340	.300
Mayorga, Jose	R-R	5-10	175	8-20-92	.286	.167	.315	38	91	11	26	0	1	0	8	13	3	0	1	11	1	0	.308	.389
Oberto, Wilmer	L-L	5-10	180	11-2-92	.222	.233	.219	43	144	18	32	9	1	3	12	13	0	1	1	45	0	0	.361	.285
Phillips, Anthony	R-R	5-9	160	4-11-90	.167	.000	.333	2	6	1	1	0	0	0	0	0	0	0	0	3	0	0	.167	.167
Pullin, Andrew	L-R	6-0	190	9-25-93	.270	.241	.282	129	492	67	133	18	3	9	61	41	6	2	3	95	6	7	.374	.332
Rodriguez, Herlis	L-L	6-0	157	6-10-94	.111	.000	.125	5	9	1	1	0	1	0	0	2	0	0	0	1	1	0	.333	.273
Serra, Enmanuel	B-R	5-10	166	12-17-92	.224	.292	.186	23	67	6	15	1	0	0	2	8	0	3	0	11	2	2	.239	.307
Stankiewicz, Drew	B-R	5-9	160	6-18-93	.145	.095	.164	23	76	8	11	0	0	0	2	5	0	1	0	21	0	1	.145	.198
Tocci, Carlos	R-R	6-2	160	8-23-95	.242	.267	.232	125	487	59	118	18	8	2	30	25	14	10	2	96	10	11	.324	.297
Torres, Robinson	R-R	5-10	160	2-12-92	.143	.000	.167	11	28	0	4	0	0	0	3	0	0	0	0	8	1	0	.143	.143
Tromp, Jiandido	R-R	5-11	175	9-27-93	.224	.300	.182	27	85	11	19	4	1	1	9	6	2	1	1	30	3	0	.329	.287
Walding, Mitch	L-R	6-3	190	9-10-92	.237	.147	.268	108	371	33	88	25	2	7	55	36	4	3	5	116	1	5	.372	.308

Pitching	B-T	HT	WT	DOB	W	L	ERA	G	GS	CG	SV	IP	H	R	ER	HR	BB	SO	AVG	vLH	vRH	K/9	BB/9
Anderson, Drew	R-R	6-3	185	3-22-94	4	4	3.68	9	9	0	0	44	46	21	18	1	15	46	.266	.278	.255	9.41	3.07
Arteaga, Alejandro	R-R	6-2	176	4-30-94	3	6	9.23	9	9	1	0	39	69	46	40	7	11	25	.392	.413	.375	5.77	2.54
Baker, Aaron	R-R	6-3	220	12-14-89	1	2	4.26	12	0	0	2	25	30	14	12	0	6	27	.286	.388	.196	9.59	2.13
Buckley, Tyler	R-R	6-5	230	11-9-90	1	2	6.64	15	0	0	0	20	27	17	15	1	14	20	.325	.333	.319	8.85	6.20
Casimiro, Ranfi	R-R	6-8	200	7-16-92	5	9	4.92	25	25	1	0	123	128	84	67	12	65	92	.263	.259	.267	6.75	4.77
Child, Dan	R-R	6-5	230	7-24-92	1	1	11.17	9	0	0	2	10	16	15	12	0	7	13	.333	.563	.219	12.10	6.52
Denato, Joey	L-L	5-10	175	3-17-92	2	1	1.38	15	0	0	2	26	24	7	4	1	10	24	.261	.293	.235	8.31	3.46
Dygestile-Therrien, Jesen	R-R	6-2	200	3-18-93	3	0	6.27	27	1	0	2	56	63	42	39	3	25	38	.280	.333	.236	6.11	4.02
Forsythe, Cody	L-L	6-0	170	9-17-90	3	2	2.45	23	0	0	9	29	28	11	8	1	6	25	.239	.333	.187	7.67	1.84
Francisco, Delvy	R-R	6-1	190	8-24-92	1	3	8.29	22	0	0	2	38	43	41	35	0	21	39	.269	.304	.242	9.24	4.97
Harris, Scott	L-L	6-4	230	5-14-93	2	0	4.05	6	0	0	0	13	9	6	6	1	3	10	.184	.333	.097	6.75	2.03
Hockenberry, Matt	R-R	6-3	220	8-30-91	0	0	9.22	10	0	0	1	14	21	16	14	0	9	6	.368	.346	.387	3.95	5.93
Imhof, Matt	L-L	6-5	220	10-26-93	0	2	4.28	7	7	0	0	27	32	14	13	3	6	27	.302	.387	.267	8.89	1.98
Joaquin, Ulises	R-R	5-11	165	6-11-92	0	1	3.97	30	0	0	8	48	42	22	21	4	20	35	.232	.214	.247	6.61	3.78
Leiter Jr., Mark	R-R	6-0	195	3-13-91	5	7	4.38	16	16	0	0	84	91	48	41	5	22	85	.275	.284	.268	9.07	2.35
Martin, Shane	R-R	6-4	210	4-27-91	0	3	10.29	12	3	0	0	28	47	32	32	3	8	15	.385	.421	.354	4.82	2.57
Martinez, Manaure	R-R	6-1	155	12-31-91	0	1	10.29	5	0	0	0	7	9	8	8	0	3	7	.300	.182	.368	9.00	3.86
Mecias, Yoel	L-L	6-2	160	10-11-93	3	3	3.21	7	7	0	0	34	29	12	12	2	9	23	.246	.368	.188	6.15	2.41
Morris, Will	L-R	6-4	180	5-2-93	1	3	3.52	23	0	0	4	46	45	18	18	2	6	51	.250	.209	.287	9.98	1.17
O'Hare, Chris	L-L	6-2	195	9-23-90	0	4	7.94	12	0	0	0	17	19	20	15	0	14	22	.275	.324	.229	11.65	7.41
Prosinski, Jon	R-R	6-3	180	2-17-91	5	5	3.82	17	17	1	0	97	107	52	41	1	24	52	.274	.267	.280	4.84	2.23
Reyes, Julio	R-R	6-3	190	4-19-91	3	4	3.65	33	6	0	0	81	71	39	33	5	24	55	.231	.261	.206	6.09	2.66
Rios, Yacksel	R-R	6-3	185	6-27-93	6	2	3.69	33	13	0	1	102	102	51	42	9	40	73	.256	.234	.274	6.42	3.52
Rivas, Frank	R-R	5-11	180	7-17-92	0	1	4.67	10	0	0	0	17	17	10	9	2	5	19	.254	.222	.275	9.87	2.60
Rodesky, Nick	R-R	6-5	220	3-27-91	0	1	5.68	4	0	0	1	6	7	4	4	1	3	8	.292	.333	.278	11.37	4.26
Rojas, Keivi	R-R	6-0	170	2-26-93	1	0	3.18	11	0	0	0	23	19	11	8	3	13	17	.221	.286	.159	6.75	5.16
Viza, Tyler	R-R	6-3	170	10-21-94	3	17	5.29	24	24	0	0	126	172	88	74	9	24	80	.323	.315	.332	5.71	1.71

Fielding

Catcher	PCT	G	PO	A	E	DP	PB
Astudillo	.984	33	220	25	4	1	8
Grullon	.964	24	142	19	6	2	4
Knapp	.983	42	258	26	5	2	9
Lino	.992	16	109	14	1	0	2
Mayorga	.995	37	189	30	1	0	5
Stankiewicz	.935	8	13	16	2	3	
Torres	1.000	5	7	12	0	2	
Serra	.934	16	16	41	4	11	
Stankiewicz	.966	14	22	35	2	4	
Torres	1.000	3	4	6	0	1	

First Base	PCT	G	PO	A	E	DP
Astudillo	.986	51	457	36	7	20
Green	.993	53	488	43	4	32
Oberto	.990	34	273	25	3	19
Serra	.000	1	0	0	1	0

Second Base	PCT	G	PO	A	E	DP
Pullin	.951	123	172	334	26	42
Serra	1.000	5	5	15	0	2

Third Base	PCT	G	PO	A	E	DP
Asche	.800	3	0	4	1	0
Green	.900	22	17	46	7	1
Hernandez	.917	11	8	14	2	0
Serra	.800	1	1	3	1	1
Torres	1.000	2	4	2	0	0
Walding	.933	101	67	185	18	7

Shortstop	PCT	G	PO	A	E	DP
Canelo	.954	45	58	108	8	18
Crawford	.957	59	84	180	12	27
Hernandez	1.000	1	1	3	0	2
Phillips	1.000	2	2	5	0	0

Outfield	PCT	G	PO	A	E	DP
Astudillo	1.000	4	12	0	0	0
Brown	.963	13	26	0	1	0
Cozens	.962	123	220	8	9	2
Ferdinand	1.000	3	3	0	0	0
Greene	.958	49	89	3	4	1
Hiciano	.980	71	140	4	3	0
Oberto	1.000	1	1	0	0	0
Rodriguez	1.000	5	6	0	0	0
Tocci	.980	124	288	8	6	3
Tromp	1.000	24	54	2	0	2

WILLIAMSPORT CROSSCUTTERS
SHORT-SEASON
NEW YORK-PENN LEAGUE

Batting	B-T	HT	WT	DOB	AVG	vLH	vRH	G	AB	R	H	2B	3B	HR	RBI	BB	HBP	SH	SF	SO	SB	CS	SLG	OBP
Brown, Aaron	L-L	6-2	220	6-20-92	.256	.190	.275	47	180	23	46	7	1	3	16	6	6	0	1	41	8	4	.356	.301
Campbell, Derek	R-R	6-0	175	6-28-91	.250	.245	.252	57	208	25	52	19	2	2	15	3	10	3	0	47	2	4	.389	.294
Canelo, Malquin	R-R	5-10	156	9-5-94	.154	.000	.222	4	13	1	2	0	0	0	1	1	0	0	0	4	0	0	.154	.214
Garcia, Wilson	B-R	5-11	160	1-11-94	.220	.296	.200	37	127	10	28	8	0	0	9	7	2	1	0	7	0	0	.283	.272
Grullon, Deivi	R-R	6-1	180	2-17-96	.225	.184	.235	53	187	14	42	9	1	0	18	9	2	1	0	39	3	0	.283	.268
Harris, Chase	R-R	6-0	195	7-28-91	.200	.100	.236	26	75	3	15	2	0	0	7	5	3	0	0	18	3	4	.227	.277

Name	B-T	HT	WT	DOB	AVG	vLH	vRH	G	AB	R	H	2B	3B	HR	RBI	BB	HBP	SH	SF	SO	SB	CS	SLG	OBP
Hernandez, Jan	R-R	6-1	195	1-3-95	.186	.271	.158	57	194	22	36	9	1	5	15	18	1	2	2	79	4	2	.320	.256
Hoskins, Rhys	R-R	6-4	225	3-17-93	.237	.220	.242	70	245	30	58	15	0	9	40	21	6	0	1	54	3	3	.408	.311
Marrero, Emmanuel	B-R	5-11	169	5-16-93	.214	.146	.235	60	201	12	43	11	1	0	8	11	5	0	0	37	7	5	.279	.272
McHugh, Sean	R-R	5-11	200	4-19-92	.190	.214	.179	16	42	2	8	1	0	0	4	5	1	1	1	9	0	1	.214	.286
Oberto, Wilmer	L-L	5-10	180	11-2-92	.231	.281	.208	32	104	14	24	9	0	1	13	13	1	0	0	24	1	3	.346	.322
Parr, Justin	L-R	6-2	190	11-29-90	.273	.500	.222	3	11	0	3	1	0	0	1	1	0	0	0	1	0	0	.364	.333
Pujols, Jose	R-R	6-3	175	9-29-95	.213	.059	.273	16	61	3	13	5	0	0	5	0	1	0	0	21	0	0	.295	.226
Rodriguez, Herlis	L-L	6-0	157	6-10-94	.176	.000	.200	5	17	5	3	1	0	0	2	2	0	0	0	4	0	1	.235	.263
Sandberg, Cord	L-L	6-3	215	1-2-95	.235	.250	.231	66	264	33	62	5	3	6	24	11	1	6	1	56	8	3	.345	.267
Serra, Enmanuel	B-R	5-10	166	12-17-92	.192	.000	.238	10	26	1	5	1	0	0	0	3	0	2	0	6	1	0	.231	.276
Shortall, Matt	R-R	6-3	215	10-12-90	.264	.267	.263	26	91	11	24	3	2	3	11	2	2	0	1	19	2	1	.440	.292
Stankiewicz, Drew	B-R	5-9	160	6-18-93	.329	.462	.303	23	79	9	26	4	0	1	12	8	1	2	3	7	3	2	.418	.385
Torres, Robinson	R-R	5-10	160	2-12-92	.226	.261	.214	28	93	7	21	3	0	0	5	5	1	2	1	18	3	1	.258	.270
Tromp, Jiandido	R-R	5-11	175	9-27-93	.266	.306	.254	69	259	39	69	14	2	14	33	19	4	5	1	72	16	5	.498	.325

Pitching	B-T	HT	WT	DOB	W	L	ERA	G	GS	CG	SV	IP	H	R	ER	HR	BB	SO	AVG	vLH	vRH	K/9	BB/9
Arteaga, Alejandro	R-R	6-2	176	4-30-94	1	8	4.46	13	13	0	0	73	91	44	36	4	9	44	.311	.306	.315	5.45	1.11
Bielski, Ricky	R-R	6-3	190	10-25-94	1	0	3.63	19	0	0	0	22	15	11	9	2	19	13	.185	.179	.190	5.24	7.66
Denato, Joey	L-L	5-10	175	3-17-92	2	0	3.18	8	0	0	0	11	9	4	4	0	6	15	.225	.176	.261	11.91	4.76
Dygestile-Therrien, Jesen	R-R	6-2	200	3-18-93	1	1	3.00	8	0	0	1	15	9	5	5	1	5	16	.167	.147	.200	9.60	3.00
Francisco, Delvy	R-R	6-1	190	8-24-92	2	0	5.14	8	0	0	0	14	13	8	8	2	11	8	.260	.333	.192	5.14	7.07
Garcia, Elniery	L-L	6-0	155	12-24-94	0	0	5.79	4	0	0	0	5	6	3	3	1	2	5	.273	.400	.235	9.64	3.86
Gueller, Mitch	R-R	6-3	210	11-10-93	5	5	4.69	13	13	1	0	63	65	34	33	2	29	31	.275	.259	.289	4.41	4.12
Harris, Scott	L-L	6-4	230	5-14-93	0	0	3.55	12	0	0	0	13	14	7	5	0	5	13	.292	.286	.294	9.24	3.55
Hockenberry, Matt	R-R	6-3	220	8-30-91	2	0	2.35	9	0	0	1	15	13	5	4	0	3	17	.228	.212	.250	9.98	1.76
Imhof, Matt	L-L	6-5	220	10-26-93	1	0	0.75	3	3	1	0	12	6	1	1	0	4	11	.154	.133	.167	8.25	3.00
Leibrandt, Brandon	L-L	6-4	190	12-13-92	2	3	2.20	7	7	0	0	41	29	10	10	1	8	45	.203	.147	.220	9.88	1.76
Martinez, Manaure	R-R	6-1	155	12-31-91	1	3	3.55	21	0	0	0	25	22	14	10	3	14	27	.232	.234	.229	9.59	4.97
Meadors, Mark	R-R	6-4	200	2-10-92	0	0	3.72	15	0	0	0	19	20	16	8	0	8	16	.253	.250	.257	7.45	3.72
O'Hare, Chris	L-L	6-2	195	9-23-90	0	0	0.00	1	0	0	0	1	0	0	0	0	0	1	.000	.000	.000	9.00	0.00
Oliver, Chris	R-R	6-4	170	7-8-93	0	1	7.71	7	3	0	0	14	19	20	12	2	20	6	.317	.370	.273	3.86	12.86
Packrall, Preston	R-R	6-1	175	10-15-91	1	0	5.92	10	3	0	0	24	29	17	16	1	8	16	.302	.245	.362	5.92	2.96
Pinto, Ricardo	R-R	6-0	165	1-20-94	1	5	2.11	9	9	0	0	47	36	17	11	4	15	48	.203	.205	.202	9.19	2.87
Ramos, Edubray	R-R	6-0	165	12-19-92	1	0	0.79	11	1	0	2	23	12	2	2	0	2	24	.152	.122	.184	9.53	0.79
Rayburn, Calvin	R-R	6-8	195	7-9-92	2	1	1.23	22	0	0	9	29	16	8	4	1	9	16	.152	.211	.083	4.91	2.76
Rivas, Frank	R-R	5-11	180	7-17-92	1	0	1.89	12	0	0	3	19	14	5	4	1	7	19	.206	.250	.167	9.00	3.32
Rojas, Keivi	R-R	6-0	170	2-26-93	1	0	3.55	12	0	0	0	13	8	6	5	3	1	9	.178	.150	.200	6.39	0.71
Sanchez, Feliberto	R-R	6-1	175	9-30-93	3	9	5.43	14	11	0	0	60	75	40	36	6	19	32	.316	.316	.317	4.83	2.87
Sova, Bryan	R-R	5-11	165	8-4-91	1	2	2.70	20	0	0	2	23	39	14	7	1	2	14	.368	.375	.360	5.40	0.77
Thornhill, Nathan	R-R	6-0	180	9-26-91	0	1	18.00	1	0	0	0	2	4	4	4	1	2	0	.400	.500	.250	0.00	9.00
Whitehead, David	R-R	6-4	215	4-21-92	4	4	2.19	13	13	0	0	74	70	27	18	1	8	43	.246	.245	.248	5.23	0.97

Fielding

Catcher	PCT	G	PO	A	E	DP	PB
Garcia	.972	14	94	9	3	1	1
Grullon	.984	53	322	52	6	6	13
McHugh	1.000	12	64	14	0	2	4

First Base	PCT	G	PO	A	E	DP
Garcia	1.000	1	7	1	0	1
Hoskins	.987	68	575	56	8	39
Oberto	.970	9	60	4	2	9

Second Base	PCT	G	PO	A	E	DP
Campbell	.952	27	40	80	6	12
Serra	1.000	3	0	9	0	1

Second Base (cont.)	PCT	G	PO	A	E	DP
Stankiewicz	.949	19	36	39	4	11
Torres	.971	27	49	85	4	12

Third Base	PCT	G	PO	A	E	DP
Campbell	.941	19	20	44	4	5
Hernandez	.885	56	36	102	18	7
Serra	1.000	1	0	3	0	0

Shortstop	PCT	G	PO	A	E	DP
Campbell	.955	4	7	14	1	5
Canelo	1.000	4	5	9	0	2
Marrero	.953	60	101	163	13	27
Serra	1.000	5	11	9	0	1

Shortstop (cont.)	PCT	G	PO	A	E	DP
Stankiewicz	1.000	3	3	6	0	0

Outfield	PCT	G	PO	A	E	DP
Brown	.980	39	95	2	2	2
Harris	.977	20	39	4	1	1
Oberto	1.000	7	12	0	0	0
Parr	1.000	2	4	1	0	0
Pujols	.935	15	27	2	2	1
Rodriguez	1.000	5	13	1	0	0
Sandberg	.986	65	134	5	2	3
Shortall	1.000	13	20	1	0	0
Tromp	.974	64	144	7	4	1

GCL PHILLIES   ROOKIE

GULF COAST LEAGUE

Batting	B-T	HT	WT	DOB	AVG	vLH	vRH	G	AB	R	H	2B	3B	HR	RBI	BB	HBP	SH	SF	SO	SB	CS	SLG	OBP
Biter, Venn	L-R	6-1	185	10-27-94	.210	.205	.212	45	157	19	33	6	5	0	14	10	4	3	0	45	13	1	.312	.275
Cuicas, William	B-R	5-11	160	2-1-95	.310	.464	.261	42	116	22	36	6	0	0	14	23	2	2	0	19	3	4	.431	.433
Cumana, Grenny	B-R	5-5	143	11-10-95	.248	.294	.228	33	113	15	28	8	1	1	10	7	3	1	2	10	6	1	.363	.304
Duran, Carlos	R-R	6-2	170	11-24-94	.299	.286	.304	35	107	20	32	8	1	0	11	16	0	2	0	23	9	3	.393	.390
Encarnacion, Luis	R-R	6-2	185	8-9-97	.229	.185	.239	40	140	18	32	8	1	2	15	9	4	1	0	36	3	1	.343	.294
Fisher, Joel	R-R	6-3	235	1-8-93	.286	.412	.239	29	63	6	18	6	0	1	5	2	1	1	0	13	0	0	.429	.318
Galvis, Freddy	B-R	5-10	185	11-14-89	.250	—	.250	5	16	2	4	1	0	0	3	1	0	0	0	2	1	0	.313	.294
Greene, Larry	L-R	6-0	235	2-10-93	.250	.000	.333	1	4	1	1	0	0	0	2	1	0	0	0	3	0	0	.250	.400
Harris, Chase	R-R	6-0	195	7-28-91	.333	.200	.364	7	27	4	9	1	1	0	1	1	1	0	1	3	4	0	.444	.367
Joseph, Tommy	R-R	6-1	225	7-16-91	.250	.250	.250	6	20	1	5	1	0	0	1	2	0	0	0	5	0	0	.300	.348
Marte, Olvy	R-R	5-9	154	8-8-94	.250	.255	.255	37	128	22	32	7	1	0	16	16	3	1	2	30	7	3	.320	.342
Martinez, Gustavo	R-R	5-11	155	9-22-93	.280	.217	.298	32	107	14	30	5	0	0	8	7	0	1	1	11	2	3	.327	.322
Nieves, Wil	R-R	5-11	190	9-25-77	.263	.250	.267	6	19	3	5	2	0	0	1	1	2	0	0	1	0	0	.368	.364
Numata, Chace	B-R	6-0	175	8-14-92	.231	.273	.200	11	26	5	6	1	0	0	5	0	0	0	0	4	0	0	.269	.259
Posso, Jesus	R-R	5-11	201	2-10-95	.245	.154	.279	39	94	12	23	6	0	1	22	8	2	1	1	15	0	1	.340	.314
Pujols, Jose	R-R	6-3	175	9-29-95	.232	.250	.225	41	151	21	35	8	2	5	28	12	1	1	1	54	1	2	.411	.291

	B-T	HT	WT	DOB	AVG	vLH	vRH	G	AB	R	H	2B	3B	HR	RBI	BB	HBP	SH	SF	SO	SB	CS	SLG	OBP
Rivero, Gregori	R-R	5-11	194	5-27-96	.217	.231	.213	26	60	5	13	2	0	1	11	2	1	0	2	9	0	0	.300	.246
Ruf, Darin	R-R	6-3	240	7-28-86	.130	.000	.176	6	23	3	3	1	0	0	2	3	1	0	0	4	0	0	.174	.259
Sweaney, Jake	R-R	6-3	180	11-17-94	.255	.500	.186	25	55	6	14	3	0	0	6	6	0	0	1	15	4	3	.309	.323
Thomas, Clete	L-R	5-11	200	11-14-83	.250	.000	.278	7	20	3	5	1	0	0	5	5	0	0	0	4	1	0	.300	.400
Tolbert, Matt	B-R	6-0	185	5-4-82	.231	.000	.273	4	13	3	3	0	0	0	2	3	0	0	0	1	2	0	.231	.375
Tomassetti, Scott	R-R	6-1	195	7-3-93	.143	.250	.000	7	7	0	1	1	0	0	3	1	2	0	1	3	0	0	.286	.364
Tomscha, Damek	R-R	6-2	200	8-27-91	.243	.313	.218	54	181	31	44	17	1	2	24	25	13	0	1	32	3	1	.381	.373
Williams, Everett	L-R	5-10	200	10-1-90	.200	.000	.231	4	15	3	3	1	0	0	2	1	0	0	0	3	1	0	.267	.250
Williams, Trey	R-R	6-1	210	3-9-94	.185	.194	.183	37	124	14	23	8	0	2	13	11	5	0	2	32	1	0	.298	.275
Zier, Tim	R-R	5-9	195	8-6-91	.324	.364	.312	41	142	23	46	8	2	0	17	20	2	0	0	14	6	5	.408	.415

Pitching

	B-T	HT	WT	DOB	W	L	ERA	G	GS	CG	SV	IP	H	R	ER	HR	BB	SO	AVG	vLH	vRH	K/9	BB/9
Alejo, Francibel	L-L	6-3	170	1-21-93	2	1	6.00	10	1	0	0	21	20	14	14	0	13	18	.247	.200	.254	7.71	5.57
Alezones, Lewis	R-R	6-3	170	11-29-95	2	1	2.70	9	4	0	0	30	21	12	9	1	5	27	.189	.143	.211	8.10	1.50
Anderson, Drew	R-R	6-3	185	3-22-94	1	1	3.18	2	1	0	0	6	5	2	2	1	3	6	.238	.300	.182	9.53	4.76
Baker, Aaron	R-R	6-3	220	12-14-89	1	0	20.25	1	0	0	0	1	5	3	3	0	0	1	.556	1.000	.500	6.75	0.00
Biddle, Jesse	L-L	6-5	220	10-22-91	0	0	4.50	1	1	0	0	2	1	1	1	1	1	3	.143	1.000	.000	13.50	4.50
Bogese, Kyle	R-R	6-0	195	10-24-90	2	2	5.17	13	0	0	4	16	11	11	9	0	14	17	.190	.059	.244	9.77	8.04
Davis, Austin	L-L	6-4	245	2-3-93	1	1	2.59	14	1	0	3	31	33	14	9	0	7	27	.280	.350	.265	7.76	2.01
de Gruy, Jacques	R-R	6-4	200	10-25-91	0	0	3.06	13	0	0	0	18	20	9	6	1	8	14	.282	.231	.311	7.13	4.08
Dominguez, Seranthony	R-R	6-1	183	11-25-94	2	2	3.12	14	0	0	0	26	26	11	9	1	14	24	.260	.241	.268	8.31	4.85
Fisher, Jared	L-R	6-4	235	9-1-92	2	0	2.86	13	0	0	3	22	18	9	7	0	8	21	.222	.231	.218	8.59	3.27
Garcia, Elniery	L-L	6-0	155	12-24-94	2	2	2.08	7	4	0	0	26	26	9	6	0	4	23	.250	.091	.269	7.96	1.38
Hanson, Nic	R-R	6-7	210	4-15-92	1	1	2.38	3	3	0	0	11	6	3	3	0	6	8	.154	.154	.154	6.35	4.76
Harris, Scott	L-L	6-4	230	5-14-93	0	0	0.00	1	0	0	0	1	1	0	0	0	0	2	.250	.000	.500	18.00	0.00
Hockenberry, Matt	R-R	6-3	220	8-30-91	1	0	0.00	1	0	0	0	3	2	0	0	0	0	5	.200	.000	.286	16.88	0.00
Imhof, Matt	L-L	6-5	220	10-26-93	0	0	0.00	1	1	0	0	3	2	0	0	0	1	2	.222	.250	.200	6.00	3.00
Keys, Denton	L-L	6-3	190	9-30-94	3	2	2.20	11	7	0	0	49	43	16	12	0	12	35	.246	.125	.273	6.43	2.20
Kiest, Tanner	R-R	6-3	200	9-16-94	1	0	8.22	9	0	0	0	8	5	11	7	1	16	6	.172	.231	.125	7.04	18.78
Kilome, Franklyn	R-R	6-6	175	6-25-95	3	1	3.12	11	8	0	0	40	36	17	14	2	11	25	.235	.250	.228	5.58	2.45
Leibrandt, Brandon	L-L	6-4	190	12-13-92	1	2	4.12	5	3	0	1	20	20	10	9	1	2	22	.274	.294	.268	10.07	0.92
Manship, Jeff	R-R	6-2	210	1-16-85	0	0	0.00	2	2	0	0	3	1	0	0	0	1	2	.100	.000	.111	6.00	3.00
Marquis, Jason	L-R	6-1	220	8-21-78	1	0	0.00	1	1	0	0	5	5	0	0	0	0	7	.250	.250	.250	12.60	0.00
McWilliams, Sam	R-R	6-7	190	9-4-95	2	3	5.40	9	5	0	0	25	28	16	15	1	6	10	.298	.267	.313	3.60	2.16
Mecias, Yoel	L-L	6-2	160	10-11-93	0	1	4.76	4	4	0	0	17	19	10	9	0	8	10	.279	.273	.281	5.29	4.24
Morales, Luis	R-R	6-4	212	3-16-93	2	2	3.83	10	9	0	0	42	57	27	18	3	7	30	.326	.338	.317	6.38	1.49
Oliver, Chris	R-R	6-4	170	* 7-8-93	0	1	12.27	2	0	0	0	4	6	7	5	0	3	4	.333	.333	.333	9.82	7.36
Ramos, Edubray	R-R	6-0	165	12-19-92	0	0	0.93	8	0	0	4	10	7	1	1	0	5	13	.200	.250	.174	12.10	4.66
Rivero, Alexis	R-R	6-0	192	10-18-94	2	0	2.61	12	0	0	1	21	21	6	6	1	5	7	.288	.333	.273	3.05	2.18
Rodesky, Nick	R-R	6-5	220	3-27-91	1	0	1.80	3	0	0	2	5	3	1	1	0	0	5	.176	.000	.214	9.00	0.00
Rosenberg, B.J.	R-R	6-3	220	9-17-85	0	0	0.00	2	2	0	0	3	1	0	0	0	0	5	.100	.000	.200	15.00	0.00
Santos, Gregorio	R-R	6-3	190	3-1-93	0	0	4.86	11	0	0	1	17	16	10	9	3	4	6	.239	.240	.238	3.24	2.16
Southard, Matt	R-R	6-9	220	4-18-92	1	1	10.80	6	0	0	0	3	6	4	4	0	5	4	.400	.000	.600	10.80	13.50
Taylor, Josh	L-L	6-5	225	3-2-93	2	0	0.00	3	0	0	0	9	5	0	0	0	4	13	.156	.200	.148	12.54	3.86
Thornhill, Nathan	R-R	6-0	180	9-26-91	0	0	0.00	1	0	0	0	2	3	0	0	0		2	.000		.000	13.50	0.00
Wright, Austin	L-L	6-4	235	9-26-89	1	0	9.00	1	0	0	0	1	2	1	1	0	0	2	.400	—	.400	18.00	0.00
Zgardowski, Jason	R-R	6-5	190	9-27-93	0	1	2.70	3	2	0	0	10	10	4	3	1	2	10	.270	.200	.296	9.00	1.80

Fielding

Catcher	PCT	G	PO	A	E	DP	PB
Fisher	.994	28	141	19	1	2	3
Joseph	1.000	5	29	5	0	0	0
Nieves	1.000	4	20	5	0	1	0
Numata	1.000	10	41	6	0	0	3
Posso	1.000	13	73	19	0	0	3
Rivero	.982	23	88	21	2	2	2
Tomassetti	1.000	7	14	1	0	0	1

First Base	PCT	G	PO	A	E	DP
Encarnacion	.970	24	209	16	7	10
Posso	.991	10	98	10	1	6
Ruf	1.000	1	6	2	0	0
Williams	1.000	26	257	10	0	16

Second Base	PCT	G	PO	A	E	DP
Cuicas	1.000	2	5	3	0	1

	PCT	G	PO	A	E	DP
Galvis	1.000	1	0	2	0	0
Marte	.984	30	55	72	2	8
Tolbert	1.000	1	1	3	0	0
Zier	.966	28	50	65	4	18

Third Base	PCT	G	PO	A	E	DP
Cuicas	.857	8	2	16	3	
0 Galvis	—	1	0	0	0	
Tolbert	1.000	1	0	3	0	0
Tomscha	.924	49	28	105	11	9
Zier	.889	4	3	5	1	1

Shortstop	PCT	G	PO	A	E	DP
Cuicas	.900	33	41	85	14	10
Cumana	.924	32	42	92	11	11
Galvis	1.000	2	2	1	0	0
Tolbert	1.000	1	0	4	0	0

Outfield	PCT	G	PO	A	E	DP
Biter	.974	44	70	5	2	1
Duran	.964	33	51	3	2	1
Encarnacion	.889	4	6	2	1	0
Greene	1.000	1	2	0	0	0
Harris	.958	7	22	1	1	1
Marte	.900	7	8	1	1	0
Martinez	1.000	29	25	4	0	1
Posso	.500	1	1	0	1	0
Pujols	.986	35	66	2	1	0
Ruf	1.000	3	2	1	0	0
Sweaney	1.000	24	34	1	0	0
Thomas	1.000	7	6	0	0	0
Williams	1.000	4	3	0	0	0

DSL PHILLIES   ROOKIE

DOMINICAN SUMMER LEAGUE

Batting	B-T	HT	WT	DOB	AVG	vLH	vRH	G	AB	R	H	2B	3B	HR	RBI	BB	HBP	SH	SF	SO	SB	CS	SLG	OBP
Arrocha, Hugo	R-R	5-11	150	10-2-95	.253	.227	.262	23	83	6	21	4	0	0	9	9	2	1	2	16	3	2	.301	.333
Beaufond, Luis	R-R	5-11	155	10-12-96	.170	.088	.195	51	147	10	25	3	1	0	8	29	2	0	0	38	7	7	.204	.315
Carrasco, Braylin	R-R	6-3	185	6-17-95	.236	.261	.229	31	106	13	25	7	0	0	8	12	1	1	2	23	5	4	.302	.314
Cepeda, Rommel	R-R	5-11	180	11-13-91	.185	.129	.198	52	157	16	29	11	0	1	12	9	5	1	2	19	1	0	.274	.249
Garcia, Enmanuel	R-R	6-0	180	7-23-94	.263	.265	.263	69	243	28	64	7	6	1	29	31	5	2	8	28	19	11	.354	.348
Kamara, Julsan	R-R	6-3	205	12-20-95	.215	.167	.234	21	65	7	14	3	2	0	12	11	7	0	0	24	3	1	.323	.386

Name	B-T	HT	WT	DOB	AVG	vLH	vRH	G	AB	R	H	2B	3B	HR	RBI	BB	HBP	SH	SF	SO	SB	CS	SLG	OBP
Marrero, Ronaldo	R-R	6-0	160	2-7-96	.220	.200	.225	66	227	24	50	7	3	0	17	16	2	4	1	38	7	6	.278	.276
Martelo, Bryan	R-R	6-2	180	10-15-96	.207	.238	.199	56	188	14	39	8	1	0	18	21	6	1	0	53	11	6	.261	.307
Morillo, Leomar	B-R	5-10	165	1-6-94	.000	—	.000	5	9	2	0	0	0	0	0	1	0	0	0	1	0	0	.000	.100
Paulino, Miguel	R-R	5-10	178	11-4-94	.244	.143	.264	32	86	10	21	6	2	0	5	3	3	0	0	28	3	2	.360	.293
Recio, Jonathan	R-R	6-2	185	4-27-96	.100	.000	.113	24	80	5	8	2	0	1	6	3	3	0	1	29	1	0	.163	.161
Reyes, Yunior	R-R	6-3	190	3-11-95	.234	.129	.255	60	192	28	45	8	1	1	20	12	9	0	2	44	6	3	.302	.307
Salas, Emmanuel	R-R	6-2	172	12-18-94	.194	.250	.185	15	31	3	6	2	0	0	3	4	1	1	2	12	0	2	.258	.289
Santana, Henry	B-R	5-3	180	12-19-94	.268	.229	.278	65	224	37	60	11	2	1	18	13	13	1	2	39	7	6	.348	.341
Torres, Wilber	R-R	5-11	206	5-9-94	.244	.189	.260	51	168	24	41	2	2	1	19	30	4	1	1	36	9	8	.298	.369
Valdez, Hector	B-R	5-11	171	3-8-93	.111	.000	.125	4	9	2	1	0	0	0	0	5	2	0	0	2	1	0	.111	.500

Pitching	B-T	HT	WT	DOB	W	L	ERA	G	GS	CG	SV	IP	H	R	ER	HR	BB	SO	AVG	vLH	vRH	K/9	BB/9
Alcantara, Randy	R-R	5-11	150	11-9-96	0	1	2.57	3	1	0	0	7	7	3	2	0	3	3	.250	.231	.267	3.86	3.86
Cabrera, Ismael	R-R	6-1	185	6-19-94	2	2	2.57	11	8	0	0	42	29	15	12	2	20	46	.201	.224	.189	9.86	4.29
Cabrera, Joel	R-R	6-1	175	6-9-94	2	6	2.74	14	13	0	0	85	72	30	26	1	5	50	.224	.229	.221	5.27	0.53
Campusano, Edgar	R-R	6-4	180	11-20-93	1	1	2.65	9	0	0	0	17	13	6	5	0	7	15	.217	.294	.186	7.94	3.71
Carmona, Steiner	R-R	6-3	195	2-14-96	0	2	7.36	12	0	0	0	18	28	22	15	0	5	13	.350	.424	.298	6.38	2.45
De La Cruz, Yan	R-R	6-4	180	4-28-95	4	6	3.13	13	12	0	0	69	65	35	24	2	8	48	.243	.255	.237	6.26	1.04
Emelenciano, Pedro	R-R	6-4	175	7-23-93	0	2	1.84	15	0	0	6	15	14	5	3	1	2	8	.246	.182	.286	4.91	1.23
Familia, Wilkin	R-R	6-1	157	8-29-96	0	0	13.50	5	0	0	0	6	11	10	9	0	4	7	.393	.333	.421	10.50	6.00
Figueroa, Juan	L-L	6-0	185	8-31-92	0	1	3.07	10	0	0	2	15	10	6	5	0	9	15	.192	.182	.195	9.20	5.52
Garcia, Edgar	R-R	6-1	179	10-4-96	2	0	2.10	12	1	0	2	26	20	8	6	0	6	19	.206	.242	.188	6.66	2.10
Gonzalez, Yonathan	R-R	6-3	165	10-31-95	0	3	5.23	12	4	0	1	31	34	25	18	0	18	15	.291	.370	.239	4.35	5.23
Marcelino, Oscar	R-R	6-3	166	6-8-97	0	1	11.25	4	0	0	0	4	6	11	5	0	6	4	.316	.111	.500	9.00	13.50
Medina, Adonis	R-R	6-1	185	12-18-96	2	3	1.37	11	2	0	1	26	22	10	4	0	4	22	.220	.206	.227	7.52	1.37
Nin, Jose	R-R	6-2	170	6-20-95	1	2	2.76	11	4	0	0	29	37	26	9	0	11	27	.289	.275	.299	8.28	3.38
Nunez, Anderson	R-R	5-10	180	5-24-94	1	1	1.46	4	0	0	0	12	7	3	2	0	3	14	.171	.125	.200	10.22	2.19
Paulino, Felix	R-R	6-1	170	3-24-95	1	6	3.61	13	10	0	1	57	68	37	23	1	11	46	.291	.293	.289	7.22	1.73
Taveras, Jose	R-R	6-4	210	11-6-93	8	4	1.05	15	13	1	0	85	61	22	10	1	8	70	.202	.211	.198	7.38	0.84
Torres, Juan	R-R	6-4	197	9-11-92	3	0	2.75	15	1	0	3	39	32	14	12	1	9	46	.213	.196	.223	10.53	2.06
Trinidad, Yonathan	R-R	6-1	175	3-27-95	0	1	1.65	8	1	0	0	16	16	7	3	0	7	10	.246	.226	.265	5.51	3.86
Vasquez, Gerard	R-R	6-2	190	6-3-94	0	0	13.50	1	0	0	0	1	0	1	1	0	4	2	.000	—	.000	27.00	54.00
Vega, Miguel	L-L	6-2	201	4-6-94	0	1	6.23	14	0	0	0	17	16	17	12	0	14	14	.235	.357	.204	7.27	7.27

Fielding

Catcher	PCT	G	PO	A	E	DP	PB
Beaufond	1.000	2	3	0	0	0	0
Cepeda	.991	44	291	31	3	0	4
Paulino	.977	18	78	8	2	0	7
Torres	1.000	21	130	14	0	1	4

First Base	PCT	G	PO	A	E	DP
Beaufond	1.000	2	12	0	0	1
Cepeda	.984	7	56	5	1	5
Garcia	.995	22	173	15	1	9
Paulino	1.000	1	1	0	0	0
Salas	.900	4	25	2	3	1
Santana	.978	11	86	1	2	6
Torres	.982	32	259	18	5	17

Second Base	PCT	G	PO	A	E	DP
Arrocha	.955	4	9	12	1	4
Beaufond	.914	42	51	76	12	14
Garcia	.938	12	17	28	3	4
Marrero	.941	19	28	36	4	5
Morillo	1.000	2	1	1	0	0
Santana	1.000	1	3	1	0	1
Valdez	1.000	2	2	2	0	0

Third Base	PCT	G	PO	A	E	DP
Arrocha	1.000	2	1	2	0	1
Carrasco	.667	2	1	3	2	0
Garcia	.827	28	26	60	18	4
Marrero	.916	20	23	53	7	4
Recio	.826	19	14	43	12	1
Santana	.778	3	1	6	2	0
Valdez	1.000	3	1	3	0	0

Shortstop	PCT	G	PO	A	E	DP
Arrocha	.928	18	27	50	6	2
Carrasco	.893	25	35	57	11	8
Marrero	.930	32	57	90	11	16
Morillo	—	1	0	0	0	0

Outfield	PCT	G	PO	A	E	DP
Beaufond	.500	1	1	0	1	0
Garcia	.920	10	23	0	2	0
Martelo	.962	43	72	3	3	0
Morillo	1.000	1	0	0	0	0
Reyes	.939	53	97	10	7	3
Rodriguez	.953	59	77	4	4	1
Salas	1.000	11	10	0	0	0
Santana	.992	50	118	7	1	2

VSL PHILLIES · ROOKIE

VENEZUELAN SUMMER LEAGUE

Batting	B-T	HT	WT	DOB	AVG	vLH	vRH	G	AB	R	H	2B	3B	HR	RBI	BB	HBP	SH	SF	SO	SB	CS	SLG	OBP
Acosta, Adrian	R-R	5-11	165	3-15-96	.239	.250	.236	53	159	19	38	9	1	0	14	6	2	2	3	37	3	3	.308	.271
Alastre, Jesus	R-R	6-1	155	11-25-96	.314	.265	.329	61	210	35	66	8	2	0	22	13	22	5	2	34	13	12	.371	.409
Antequera, Jose	R-R	5-10	160	8-1-95	.267	.283	.261	61	217	28	58	7	3	0	23	16	1	3	2	12	2	7	.327	.318
Avila, Juanj	L-L	5-9	185	3-17-95	.190	.111	.225	18	58	6	11	2	0	0	4	3	0	1	0	15	1	1	.224	.230
Gamboa, Rafael	R-R	5-11	190	5-14-96	.241	.192	.263	34	83	7	20	4	0	1	11	9	2	1	1	14	0	0	.325	.326
Gonzalez, Damaso	B-R	6-1	152	4-11-96	.174	.211	.160	30	69	7	12	3	1	0	4	7	0	1	0	15	3	0	.246	.250
Isava, Willerker	R-R	5-11	174	1-21-96	.214	.286	.179	19	42	6	9	2	0	0	4	1	0	0	0	6	0	0	.262	.233
Jimenez, Enger	R-R	6-1	165	7-4-95	.270	.357	.250	51	148	20	40	10	3	2	18	14	5	1	1	30	6	3	.419	.351
Mendoza, Luis	L-R	6-1	165	8-7-97	.280	.260	.286	59	218	22	61	10	3	0	29	10	3	5	2	39	8	5	.353	.318
Miranda, Joseph	B-R	6-2	186	4-30-95	.283	.359	.257	64	247	30	70	19	3	5	40	24	1	1	4	47	0	1	.445	.344
Palacios, Cristian	B-R	6-0	155	1-25-94	.258	.179	.286	53	151	29	39	11	2	1	16	11	2	6	2	50	7	5	.377	.313
Perdomo, Alexander	B-R	5-9	155	5-24-93	.216	.256	.203	56	167	28	36	5	4	0	19	39	8	8	2	19	8	8	.293	.384
Pereira, David	R-R	6-3	195	1-10-97	.455	1.000	.333	5	11	1	5	2	0	0	1	1	1	0	0	3	0	0	.636	.538
Rojo, Lucas	R-R	5-6	153	4-5-94	.268	.231	.286	53	164	22	44	10	0	0	20	16	8	3	5	10	4	3	.329	.352
Romero, Daniel	R-R	5-11	155	5-5-97	.252	.162	.281	51	155	27	38	5	0	0	8	13	6	2	0	18	8	5	.285	.335
Subero, Geovanny	R-R	6-2	180	10-25-96	.136	.067	.172	22	44	4	6	0	0	0	4	1	3	0	0	16	1	0	.136	.208
Tabares, Yorbys	R-R	6-0	165	1-24-97	.182	.240	.146	36	66	7	12	1	0	0	3	4	3	1	0	18	3	4	.197	.260
Zorrilla, Freddy	R-R	6-4	195	10-19-94	.222	.179	.245	30	81	10	18	4	0	3	8	7	3	3	1	35	5	1	.383	.304

Pitching	B-T	HT	WT	DOB	W	L	ERA	G	GS	CG	SV	IP	H	R	ER	HR	BB	SO	AVG	vLH	vRH	K/9	BB/9
Armas, Gustavo	R-R	6-1	195	1-15-96	0	0	4.15	5	0	0	0	4	3	2	2	0	2	2	.231	.500	.111	4.15	4.15
Arroyo, Jesus	R-R	6-1	200	9-20-96	0	0	10.13	5	0	0	0	5	12	8	6	1	2	1	.429	.714	.333	1.69	3.38
Bastidas, Miguelangel	R-R	6-1	170	8-3-95	2	1	3.13	14	0	0	0	23	24	11	8	0	11	13	.267	.138	.328	5.09	4.30
Bermudez, Gabriel	R-R	6-3	184	6-24-93	1	3	4.81	11	7	0	0	39	45	25	21	1	11	25	.292	.250	.307	5.72	2.52
Carrasco, Luis	R-R	6-3	170	9-11-94	1	5	3.67	13	13	0	0	49	41	28	20	1	31	32	.228	.314	.194	5.88	5.69
Delgado, Victor	R-R	6-2	182	2-3-95	5	6	3.15	13	13	0	0	66	66	32	23	0	9	49	.262	.333	.237	6.72	1.23
Diaz, Jose	R-R	6-6	200	4-24-96	0	0	8.53	12	0	0	0	13	16	13	12	0	9	3	.327	.222	.350	2.13	6.39
Diaz, Oberdan	R-L	6-1	175	1-27-95	2	0	3.65	14	0	0	1	25	23	12	10	0	11	14	.261	.167	.276	5.11	4.01
Fernandez, Yeisson	L-L	6-4	170	5-17-94	4	2	1.85	11	0	0	0	24	26	9	5	0	10	23	.283	.238	.296	8.51	3.70
Gonzalez, Reiwal	R-R	6-2	196	11-11-94	0	2	2.40	19	0	0	4	30	31	12	8	1	6	26	.261	.313	.241	7.80	1.80
Indriago, Carlos	R-R	6-2	197	6-29-94	5	1	3.19	13	12	0	0	62	59	30	22	1	7	44	.243	.198	.265	6.39	1.02
Lara, Tanis	L-L	6-2	195	6-19-96	1	0	3.95	11	0	0	0	14	13	7	6	0	11	10	.241	.250	.239	6.59	7.24
Melendez, Orestes	L-L	5-11	180	6-8-95	1	0	3.12	13	0	0	0	17	21	7	6	0	4	17	.296	.389	.264	8.83	2.08
Perez, Alfredo	L-L	6-1	176	10-23-94	0	2	7.78	12	0	0	0	20	22	19	17	0	16	8	.282	.222	.290	3.66	7.32
Ramos, Edubray	R-R	6-0	165	12-19-92	1	1	0.75	7	0	0	4	12	11	5	1	0	3	11	.244	.333	.231	8.25	2.25
Salazar, Carlos	R-R	6-2	155	11-19-96	2	1	6.75	14	1	0	0	20	27	24	15	1	16	18	.297	.391	.265	8.10	7.20
Sobil, Victor	R-R	6-2	215	7-17-96	2	0	3.44	12	0	0	0	18	20	8	7	0	6	8	.274	.286	.269	3.93	2.95
Suarez, Ranger	L-L	6-0	177	8-26-95	5	4	1.56	14	14	0	0	81	67	25	14	2	1	78	.218	.182	.226	8.70	0.11
Velis, Sergio	L-L	5-11	182	1-16-95	4	1	2.05	13	8	0	1	53	49	18	12	0	13	43	.241	.162	.259	7.35	2.22

Fielding

Catcher	PCT	G	PO	A	E	DP	PB
Acosta	.987	53	301	68	5	1	8
Gamboa	.936	32	138	24	11	4	9

First Base	PCT	G	PO	A	E	DP
Mendoza	1.000	8	63	4	0	3
Miranda	.989	62	605	29	7	47
Zorrilla	.857	2	6	0	1	1

Second Base	PCT	G	PO	A	E	DP
Antequera	1.000	3	5	6	0	0
Gonzalez	.786	10	9	13	6	2
Isava	.941	6	10	6	1	4

	PCT	G	PO	A	E	DP
Perdomo	.959	29	46	72	5	10
Rojo	1.000	2	2	3	0	0
Romero	.975	36	72	81	4	26

Third Base	PCT	G	PO	A	E	DP
Antequera	1.000	1	0	1	0	0
Gonzalez	1.000	3	3	5	0	0
Isava	.889	11	6	10	2	2
Perdomo	.878	25	18	54	10	4
Rojo	.917	43	33	88	11	6

Shortstop	PCT	G	PO	A	E	DP
Antequera	.938	54	64	162	15	28

	PCT	G	PO	A	E	DP
Gonzalez	.927	15	14	24	3	6
Romero	.814	14	10	25	8	2

Outfield	PCT	G	PO	A	E	DP
Alastre	.971	60	133	3	4	0
Avila	.946	17	34	1	2	0
Jimenez	1.000	38	51	5	0	1
Mendoza	.932	52	67	2	5	1
Palacios	.906	29	45	3	5	1
Subero	1.000	11	7	0	0	0
Tabares	.907	28	35	4	4	1
Zorrilla	1.000	13	22	5	0	1

Pittsburgh Pirates

SEASON IN A SENTENCE: The Pirates followed their playoff-drought-ending 2013 season with another trip to the postseason, albeit another one that ended too quickly for Pittsburghers with a wild-card loss.

HIGH POINT: Following a lackluster first half (49-46), the Pirates were 39-28 after the break, including 17-9 in September to take the first wild card. Pittsburgh won five in a row from Sept. 14-19, then after a loss, won five of six to cement its postseason berth and put a scare into the NL Central champion Cardinals.

LOW POINT: With the wild-card game at a raucous PNC Park, the Giants' Brandon Crawford silenced the crowd with a fourth-inning grand slam off Edinson Volquez, essentially ending the Pirates' season as they were blanked by Madison Bumgarner.

NOTABLE ROOKIES: Gregory Polanco finally got his much-ballyhooed callup in June and was terrific early but went 1-for-30 in one stretch and was sent back to the minors briefly before being recalled in September. Indy ball refugee John Holdzkom was a hidden gem, striking out 14 in nine innings down the stretch and making the postseason roster.

KEY TRANSACTIONS: Looking for first base help for Gaby Sanchez, the Pirates acquired lefthanded-hitting Ike Davis in April from the Mets for righthander Zach Thornton and lefty Blake Taylor. Davis did not provide as much power as Pittsburgh had hoped (.378 slugging), but did post a .343 OBP and played a solid first base. The Pirates also sent righthanded reliever Jason Grilli to the Angels in June for reliever Ernesto Frieri in a deal of two underperforming players. Grilli was excellent for the Angels, but Frieri was designated for assignment in August after compiling a 10.13 ERA.

DOWN ON THE FARM: High Class A Bradenton of the Florida State League, led by righthander Tyler Glasnow, won the FSL South Division but was defeated by eventual champion Fort Myers (Twins) in the playoff semifinals. Glasnow, the FSL's top prospect, was 12-5, 1.74. Among the hitters, Austin Meadows played only 45 games across three levels because of a hamstring injury, but posted an .881 OPS, while JaCoby Jones had an outstanding season in low Class-A West Virginia (.850 OPS, 23 homers).

OPENING DAY PAYROLL: $77,845,999 (26th).

PLAYERS OF THE YEAR

MAJOR LEAGUE	MINOR LEAGUE
Andrew McCutchen of	**Tyler Glasnow** rhp
.314/.410/.542	(high Class A)
25 HR, 83 RBI	12-5, 1.74
38 2B, 18 SB	157 K, 57 BB in 124 IP

ORGANIZATION LEADERS

BATTING		*Minimum 250 AB
MAJORS		
* AVG	Harrison, Josh	.315
* OPS	McCutchen, Andrew	.952
HR	McCutchen, Andrew	25
RBI	McCutchen, Andrew	83
MINORS		
* AVG	Bell, Josh, Bradenton, Altoona	.325
* OBP	Maggi, Drew, Altoona	
SLG	Jones, JaCoby, West Virginia	.503
R	Jones, JaCoby, West Virginia	72
	Weiss, Erich, West Virginia	72
H	Bell, Josh, Bradenton, Altoona	138
TB	Jones, JaCoby, West Virginia	224
2B	McGuiness, Chris, Indianapolis	31
3B	Hanson, Alen, Altoona	12
HR	Jones, JaCoby, West Virginia	23
RBI	Espinal, Edwin, West Virginia	71
BB	Dickson, Cody, West Virginia	58
	Kuchno, John, Bradenton	58
SO	Garcia, Willy, Altoona	145

PITCHING		#Minimum 75 IP
MAJORS		
W	Volquez, Edinson	13
# ERA	Watson, Tony	1.63
SO	Liriano, Francisco	175
SV	Melancon, Mark	33
MINORS		
W	Kuhl, Chad, Bradenton	13
L	Wilk, Adam, Indianapolis	14
ERA	Glasnow, Tyler, Bradenton	1.74
G	Oliver, Andy, Indianapolis	48
GS	Kuhl, Chad, Bradenton	28
	Sampson, Adrian, Altoona, Indianapolis	28
SV	Barrios, Yhonathan, West Virginia, Bradenton	15
IP	Sampson, Adrian, Altoona, Indianapolis	167
BB	Dickson, Cody, West Virginia	58
	Kuchno, John, Bradenton	58
SO	Glasnow, Tyler, Bradenton	157
AVG	Glasnow, Tyler, Bradenton	.174

General Manager: Neal Huntington. **Farm Director:** Larry Broadway. **Scouting Director:** Joe DelliCarri.

Class	Team	League	W	L	PCT	Finish	Manager
Majors	Pittsburgh Pirates	National	88	74	.543	T-8th (30)	Clint Hurdle
Triple-A	Indianapolis Indians	International	73	71	.507	7th (14)	Dean Treanor
Double-A	Altoona Curve	Eastern	61	81	.430	11th (12)	Carlos Garcia
High A	Bradenton Marauders	Florida State	78	61	.561	2nd (12)	Tom Prince
Low A	West Virginia Power	South Atlantic	54	81	.400	T-12th (14)	Michael Ryan
Short season	Jamestown Jammers	New York-Penn	35	40	.467	8th (14)	Brian Esposito
Rookie	Bristol Pirates	Appalachian	22	46	.324	10th (10)	Edgar Varela
Rookie	Pirates	Gulf Coast	20	40	.333	15th (16)	Milver Reyes
Overall Minor League Record			343	420	.450	29th (30)	

ORGANIZATION STATISTICS

PITTSBURGH PIRATES

NATIONAL LEAGUE

Batting	B-T	HT	WT	DOB	AVG	vLH	vRH	G	AB	R	H	2B	3B	HR	RBI	BB	HBP	SH	SF	SO	SB	CS	SLG	OBP
Alvarez, Pedro	L-R	6-3	235	2-6-87	.231	.175	.245	122	398	46	92	13	1	18	56	45	2	0	0	113	8	3	.405	.312
Barmes, Clint	R-R	6-1	200	3-6-79	.245	.238	.247	48	102	15	25	5	0	0	7	9	4	0	1	18	1	1	.294	.328
d'Arnaud, Chase	R-R	6-1	205	1-21-87	—	—	—	8	0	2	0	0	0	0	0	0	0	0	0	0	0	2	—	—
Davis, Ike	L-L	6-4	220	3-22-87	.235	.107	.247	131	336	39	79	18	0	10	46	57	0	0	4	74	0	4	.378	.343
2-team total (12 New York)					.233	—	—	143	360	43	84	19	0	11	51	63	0	0	4	78	0	4	.378	.344
Decker, Jaff	L-L	5-9	190	2-23-90	.000	—	.000	5	5	0	0	0	0	0	0	0	0	0	0	3	0	0	.000	.000
Hague, Matt	R-R	6-3	220	8-20-85	.000	.000	.000	3	2	0	0	0	0	0	0	0	0	0	0	1	0	0	.000	.000
Harrison, Josh	R-R	5-8	200	7-8-87	.315	.345	.307	143	520	77	164	38	7	13	52	22	4	2	2	81	18	7	.490	.347
Ishikawa, Travis	L-L	6-3	220	9-24-83	.206	—	.206	15	34	2	7	1	1	1	3	3	0	0	1	11	0	0	.382	.263
2-team total (47 San Francisco)					.252	—	—	62	107	9	27	4	1	3	18	9	1	0	2	34	0	0	.393	.311
Lambo, Andrew	L-L	6-3	225	8-11-88	.256	—	.256	21	39	3	10	4	0	1	0	0	0	0	0	8	0	0	.359	.256
Marte, Starling	R-R	6-1	185	10-9-88	.291	.303	.288	135	495	73	144	29	6	13	56	33	17	0	11	131	30	11	.453	.356
Martin, Russell	R-R	5-10	215	2-15-83	.290	.257	.298	111	379	45	110	20	0	11	67	59	15	2	5	78	4	4	.430	.402
Martinez, Michael	B-R	5-9	175	9-16-82	.128	.071	.160	26	39	2	5	1	0	0	2	4	0	1	0	13	0	0	.154	.209
McCutchen, Andrew	R-R	5-10	190	10-10-86	.314	.280	.321	146	548	89	172	38	6	25	83	84	10	0	6	115	18	3	.542	.410
Mercer, Jordy	R-R	6-3	205	8-27-86	.255	.314	.236	149	506	56	129	27	2	12	55	35	4	5	5	89	4	1	.387	.305
Morel, Brent	R-R	6-1	225	4-21-87	.179	.130	.250	23	39	1	7	2	0	0	4	2	0	0	0	9	0	0	.231	.220
Nix, Jayson	R-R	5-11	195	8-26-82	.111	.125	.100	16	36	1	4	0	0	0	1	1	1	1	0	4	1	0	.111	.158
2-team total (18 Philadelphia)					.133	—	—	34	75	2	10	0	0	1	3	3	2	1	0	22	1	2	.173	.188
Polanco, Gregory	L-L	6-4	220	9-14-91	.235	.171	.262	89	277	50	65	9	0	7	33	30	0	2	2	59	14	5	.343	.307
Sanchez, Gaby	R-R	6-1	235	9-2-83	.229	.256	.202	123	262	31	60	18	1	7	33	23	2	0	3	58	2	0	.385	.293
Sanchez, Tony	R-R	5-11	225	5-20-88	.267	.077	.306	26	75	3	20	1	0	2	13	3	1	0	1	28	0	0	.360	.300
Snider, Travis	L-L	6-0	235	2-2-88	.264	.381	.246	140	322	37	85	15	1	13	38	34	2	1	0	67	1	1	.438	.338
Stewart, Chris	R-R	6-4	210	2-19-82	.294	.486	.228	49	136	9	40	5	0	0	10	12	3	2	1	27	0	1	.331	.362
Tabata, Jose	R-R	5-11	210	8-12-88	.282	.348	.258	80	174	14	49	5	2	0	17	7	2	1	2	26	1	2	.333	.314
Walker, Neil	B-R	6-3	210	9-10-85	.271	.280	.269	137	512	74	139	25	3	23	76	45	11	1	2	88	2	2	.467	.342

Pitching	B-T	HT	WT	DOB	W	L	ERA	G	GS	CG	SV	IP	H	R	ER	HR	BB	SO	AVG	vLH	vRH	K/9	BB/9
Axford, John	R-R	6-5	220	4-1-83	0	1	4.09	13	0	0	0	11	9	5	5	0	6	12	.231	.000	.300	9.82	4.91
Cole, Gerrit	R-R	6-4	240	9-8-90	11	5	3.65	22	22	0	0	138	127	58	56	11	40	138	.248	.249	.247	9.00	2.61
Cumpton, Brandon	R-R	6-2	220	11-16-88	3	4	4.89	16	10	0	0	70	82	41	38	2	18	46	.295	.304	.289	5.91	2.31
Frieri, Ernesto	R-R	6-2	205	7-19-85	1	1	10.13	14	0	0	0	11	14	12	12	3	5	10	.311	.333	.286	8.44	4.22
Gomez, Jeanmar	R-R	6-3	220	2-10-88	2	2	3.19	44	0	0	1	62	70	24	22	6	23	38	.292	.391	.230	5.52	3.34
Grilli, Jason	R-R	6-4	235	11-11-76	0	2	4.87	22	0	0	11	20	22	11	11	4	11	21	.275	.200	.320	9.30	4.87
Holdzkom, John	R-R	6-7	225	10-19-87	1	0	2.00	9	0	0	1	9	4	2	2	1	2	14	.133	.133	14.00	2.00
Hughes, Jared	R-R	6-7	245	7-4-85	7	5	1.96	63	0	0	0	64	51	21	14	4	19	36	.229	.214	.240	5.04	2.66
LaFromboise, Bobby	L-L	6-4	215	6-25-86	0	0	2.45	6	0	0	0	4	3	1	1	1	0	4	.214	.200	.222	9.82	0.00
Liriano, Francisco	L-L	6-2	215	10-26-83	7	10	3.38	29	29	0	0	162	130	68	61	13	81	175	.218	.270	.206	9.70	4.49
Locke, Jeff	L-L	6-0	185	11-20-87	7	6	3.91	21	21	0	0	131	127	63	57	16	40	89	.257	.190	.274	6.10	2.74
Mazzaro, Vin	R-R	6-2	220	9-27-86	0	0	3.48	5	0	0	0	10	8	4	4	2	5	7	.205	.200	.208	6.10	4.35
Melancon, Mark	R-R	6-2	215	3-28-85	3	5	1.90	72	0	0	33	71	51	15	15	2	11	71	.195	.164	.223	9.00	1.39
Morris, Bryan	L-R	6-3	225	3-28-87	4	0	3.80	21	0	0	0	24	25	11	10	4	12	14	.294	.292	.295	5.32	4.56
2-team total (39 Miami)					8	1	1.82	60	0	0	0	64	58	17	13	6	24	50	—	—	—	6.99	3.36
Morton, Charlie	R-R	6-5	235	11-12-83	6	12	3.72	26	26	0	0	157	143	76	65	9	57	126	.247	.243	.252	7.21	3.26
Pimentel, Stolmy	R-R	6-3	230	2-1-90	2	1	5.23	20	0	0	0	33	34	19	19	5	16	38	.264	.268	.260	10.47	4.41
Rodriguez, Wandy	R-L	5-10	195	1-18-79	0	2	6.75	6	6	0	0	27	37	25	20	10	8	20	.325	.353	.320	6.75	2.70
Sadler, Casey	R-R	6-4	215	7-13-90	0	1	7.84	6	0	0	0	10	12	9	9	0	5	7	.293	.200	.381	6.10	4.35
Volquez, Edinson	R-R	6-0	220	7-3-83	13	7	3.04	32	31	1	0	193	166	75	65	17	71	140	.235	.236	.235	6.54	3.32
Watson, Tony	L-L	6-4	225	5-30-85	10	2	1.63	78	0	0	2	77	64	16	14	5	15	81	.232	.179	.253	9.43	1.75
Wilson, Justin	L-L	6-2	205	8-18-87	3	4	4.20	70	0	0	0	60	49	30	28	4	30	61	.220	.253	.201	9.15	4.50
Worley, Vance	R-R	6-2	230	9-25-87	8	4	2.85	18	17	1	0	111	112	43	35	9	22	79	.265	.255	.274	6.42	1.79

Fielding

Catcher	PCT	G	PO	A	E	DP	PB
Martin	.994	107	785	90	5	7	3
Sanchez	.967	20	135	10	5	0	1
Stewart	.991	46	308	29	3	0	5

First Base	PCT	G	PO	A	E	DP
Alvarez	1.000	5	31	1	0	4
Barmes	1.000	2	5	0	0	0
Davis	.991	117	886	57	9	79
Ishikawa	.990	11	95	6	1	7
Lambo	1.000	1	4	0	0	1
Morel	—	1	0	0	0	0
Sanchez	.995	96	554	38	3	46

Second Base	PCT	G	PO	A	E	DP
Barmes	1.000	14	10	21	0	1

Harrison	.986	17	26	42	1	9
Martinez	.957	6	12	10	1	1
Nix	.946	10	14	21	2	6
Walker	.992	135	251	374	5	87

Third Base	PCT	G	PO	A	E	DP
Alvarez	.924	99	69	233	25	25
Barmes	1.000	2	1	2	0	0
Harrison	.984	72	42	138	3	15
Morel	1.000	13	2	17	0	0
Nix	1.000	6	1	12	0	1

Shortstop	PCT	G	PO	A	E	DP
Barmes	.975	27	22	56	2	10
d'Arnaud	—	1	0	0	0	0
Harrison	.955	8	8	13	1	5

Mercer	.982	144	159	439	11	80
Outfield	PCT	G	PO	A	E	DP
Decker	—	2	0	0	0	0
Harrison	.988	50	75	4	1	1
Lambo	1.000	6	12	0	0	0
Marte	.968	131	178	4	6	0
Martinez	1.000	9	5	0	0	0
McCutchen	.981	146	301	1	6	0
Mercer	—	1	0	0	0	0
Nix	1.000	2	2	0	0	0
Polanco	.987	83	144	5	2	2
Sanchez	—	1	0	0	0	0
Snider	.991	96	108	8	1	2
Tabata	1.000	50	54	3	0	0

INDIANAPOLIS INDIANS

TRIPLE-A

INTERNATIONAL LEAGUE

Batting	B-T	HT	WT	DOB	AVG	vLH	vRH	G	AB	R	H	2B	3B	HR	RBI	BB	HBP	SH	SF	SO	SB	CS	SLG	OBP
Andino, Robert	R-R	6-0	195	4-25-84	.217	.243	.208	109	424	50	92	15	2	7	42	25	1	1	4	85	1	1	.311	.260
Anna, Dean	L-R	5-11	180	11-24-86	.235	.263	.224	29	68	13	16	4	0	1	7	19	0	1	1	5	1	0	.338	.398
2-team total (36 Scranton/W-B)					.207	—	—	65	198	26	41	8	3	2	21	33	4	1	5	25	1	1	.308	.325
Ashley, Nevin	R-R	6-1	215	8-14-84	.246	.299	.221	70	203	21	50	12	1	2	24	22	5	2	2	41	0	0	.345	.332
Barmes, Clint	R-R	6-1	200	3-6-79	.158	.333	.125	5	19	3	3	0	0	1	2	1	0	0	1	1	0	0	.316	.190
Curry, Matt	L-R	6-1	225	7-27-88	.222	.000	.250	7	18	2	4	0	0	0	3	0	0	0	2	8	0	0	.222	.200
d'Arnaud, Chase	R-R	6-1	205	1-21-87	.250	.266	.241	118	376	59	94	16	9	2	23	29	7	1	3	82	30	13	.356	.313
Davis, Blake	L-R	5-11	170	12-22-83	.245	.170	.267	85	233	11	57	10	2	1	23	11	1	3	0	37	3	1	.318	.282
Decker, Jaff	L-L	5-9	190	2-23-90	.257	.207	.272	104	350	41	90	27	1	6	39	51	3	3	2	73	7	6	.391	.355
Diaz, Elias	R-R	6-1	175	11-17-90	.152	.167	.148	10	33	4	5	1	0	0	3	1	0	0	0	6	0	1	.182	.243
Dickerson, Chris	L-L	6-4	230	4-10-82	.309	.274	.322	65	236	44	73	15	2	7	30	33	8	0	3	65	12	5	.479	.407
Field, Tommy	R-R	5-10	185	2-22-87	.297	.500	.174	10	37	6	11	1	0	0	9	6	1	0	1	6	0	0	.324	.400
Hague, Matt	R-R	6-3	220	8-20-85	.267	.277	.262	93	330	52	88	16	1	14	66	46	7	0	3	66	1	2	.448	.365
2-team total (13 Buffalo)					.282	—	—	106	383	60	108	23	1	15	76	49	7	0	3	76	1	3	.465	.371
Henriquez, Ralph	R-R	6-1	205	4-7-87	.000	—	.000	1	3	0	0	0	0	0	0	0	0	0	0	1	0	0	.000	.000
Lambo, Andrew	L-L	6-1	225	8-11-88	.328	.344	.318	61	238	44	78	19	2	11	42	22	2	0	0	47	3	2	.563	.389
Marte, Starling	R-R	6-1	185	10-9-88	.083	.000	.250	3	12	0	1	1	0	0	0	0	0	0	0	5	0	0	.167	.083
Martinez, Michael	B-R	5-9	175	9-16-82	.244	.180	.270	91	315	34	77	6	6	1	32	29	1	8	8	46	7	4	.311	.303
McGuiness, Chris	L-L	6-1	210	4-11-88	.264	.270	.263	126	420	60	111	31	2	9	54	63	1	0	5	72	0	3	.412	.358
Morel, Brent	R-R	6-1	225	4-21-87	.271	.317	.256	92	336	52	91	19	2	4	53	33	2	0	5	67	7	2	.375	.335
Paulino, Carlos	R-R	6-0	175	9-24-89	.207	.167	.235	10	29	4	6	0	0	0	2	1	0	1	1	9	0	0	.207	.226
Polanco, Gregory	L-L	6-4	220	9-14-91	.328	.329	.328	69	274	51	90	17	5	7	51	28	1	0	2	49	16	6	.504	.390
Rojas Jr., Mel	B-R	6-3	215	5-24-90	.277	.329	.254	77	242	35	67	8	4	5	30	32	2	2	2	62	5	3	.405	.363
Sanchez, Tony	R-R	5-11	225	5-20-88	.235	.208	.245	81	268	30	63	17	0	11	45	38	4	1	2	76	0	0	.422	.337
Santos, Adalberto	R-R	5-11	185	9-28-87	.186	.273	.095	23	43	2	8	3	0	0	4	3	0	0	1	15	0	2	.256	.234
Santos, Omir	R-R	6-0	215	4-29-81	.200	.333	.182	11	25	0	5	3	0	0	3	1	1	0	0	8	0	0	.320	.310
Stewart, Chris	R-R	6-4	210	2-19-82	.400	.200	.500	4	15	1	6	1	0	0	1	0	0	1	0	1	0	0	.467	.471
Tabata, Jose	R-R	5-11	210	8-12-88	.281	.321	.258	39	146	18	41	10	0	0	12	10	4	0	3	14	1	2	.349	.337

Pitching	B-T	HT	WT	DOB	W	L	ERA	G	GS	CG	SV	IP	H	R	ER	HR	BB	SO	AVG	vLH	vRH	K/9	BB/9
Brigham, Jake	R-R	6-3	210	2-10-88	3	5	4.29	18	14	0	1	92	92	51	44	12	28	70	.260	.233	.287	6.82	2.73
Cole, Gerrit	R-R	6-4	240	9-8-90	3	1	2.01	4	4	0	0	22	21	5	5	1	5	16	.247	.250	.245	6.45	2.01
Cumpton, Brandon	R-R	6-2	220	11-16-88	5	4	3.03	12	11	1	0	71	69	27	24	7	20	37	.263	.237	.285	4.67	2.52
Eppley, Cody	R-R	6-5	205	10-8-85	2	1	6.43	13	0	0	0	14	20	12	10	1	9	8	.328	.381	.300	5.14	5.79
Frieri, Ernesto	R-R	6-2	205	7-19-85	0	0	3.86	7	0	0	1	7	5	3	3	2	4	4	.200	.154	.250	7.71	5.14
Holdzkom, John	R-R	6-7	225	10-19-87	2	2	2.49	18	0	0	2	22	14	6	6	1	10	27	.179	.182	.179	11.22	4.15
Hughes, Jared	R-R	6-7	245	7-4-85	1	1	1.17	7	0	0	4	8	5	1	1	0	2	7	.200	.400	.067	8.22	2.35
Irwin, Phil	R-R	6-3	210	2-25-87	1	2	8.72	10	2	0	1	22	27	21	21	4	10	18	.314	.250	.360	7.48	4.15
Jackson, Jay	R-R	6-1	195	10-27-87	5	4	4.89	25	12	0	0	85	91	50	46	8	36	87	.270	.245	.291	9.25	3.83
Kasparek, Kenn	R-R	6-10	245	9-23-85	0	0	3.86	5	0	0	0	9	15	4	4	0	3	5	.357	.353	.360	4.82	2.89
Kingham, Nick	R-R	6-5	220	11-8-91	5	4	3.58	14	14	0	0	88	70	40	35	6	27	65	.213	.240	.191	6.65	2.76
Kinney, Josh	R-R	6-0	220	3-31-79	2	3	3.38	47	0	0	4	61	62	26	23	8	29	62	.256	.263	.250	9.10	4.26
LaFromboise, Bobby	L-L	6-4	215	6-25-86	0	0	0.00	5	0	0	0	4	2	0	0	0	4	6	.143	.143	.143	9.00	0.00
Liriano, Francisco	L-L	6-2	215	10-26-83	0	0	0.00	1	1	0	0	6	3	0	0	0	0	8	.150	.000	.200	12.00	0.00
Locke, Jeff	L-L	6-0	185	11-20-87	3	1	4.14	9	9	0	0	50	51	24	23	5	22	37	.263	.188	.288	6.66	3.96
Mazzaro, Vin	R-R	6-2	220	9-27-86	5	3	2.52	33	1	0	4	50	47	17	14	2	20	34	.250	.257	.250	6.12	3.60
Morris, A.J.	R-R	6-2	185	12-1-86	2	4	4.54	7	7	1	0	38	46	20	19	2	11	28	.309	.313	.304	6.69	2.63
Obispo, Wirfin	R-R	6-2	215	9-26-84	0	2	3.77	26	0	0	0	29	25	13	12	2	15	29	.236	.261	.217	9.10	4.71
2-team total (19 Gwinnett)					3	4	4.13	45	0	0	0	48	42	24	22	2	27	50	—	—	—	9.38	5.06
Oliver, Andy	L-L	6-3	215	12-3-87	3	4	2.53	48	0	0	13	64	35	24	18	3	47	85	.157	.129	.170	11.95	6.61
Perez, Rafael	L-L	6-3	195	5-15-82	3	1	1.77	10	8	0	0	56	56	15	11	2	12	34	.259	.188	.280	5.46	1.93
Pimentel, Stolmy	R-R	6-3	230	2-1-90	0	0	0.00	1	0	0	1	2	0	0	0	0	1	0	.000	.000	.000	4.50	0.00
Ramos, Jhonatan	L-L	5-10	190	10-7-89	0	1	3.55	7	1	0	0	13	11	5	5	3	2	7	.229	.100	.263	4.97	1.42
Sadler, Casey	R-R	6-4	215	7-13-90	11	4	3.03	21	21	1	0	125	124	49	42	11	24	77	.263	.266	.260	5.56	1.73

	B-T	HT	WT	DOB	W	L	ERA	G	GS	CG	SV	IP	H	R	ER	HR	BB	SO	AVG	vLH	vRH	K/9	BB/9
Sampson, Adrian	R-R	6-3	200	10-7-91	1	1	6.16	4	4	0	0	19	29	14	13	1	7	10	.358	.300	.415	4.74	3.32
Schlereth, Daniel	L-L	6-0	210	5-9-86	1	2	7.23	21	0	0	0	19	18	19	15	2	18	18	.257	.233	.275	8.68	8.68
2-team total (17 Toledo)					2	3	5.89	38	0	0	0	37	37	32	24	3	29	34	—	—	—	8.35	7.12
Thornton, Zach	R-R	6-3	220	5-19-88	2	0	1.23	4	0	0	0	7	7	2	1	0	1	8	.241	.250	.235	9.82	1.23
Waldron, Tyler	R-R	6-2	185	5-1-89	2	3	3.79	16	4	0	0	40	41	19	17	3	12	33	.265	.288	.244	7.36	2.68
Wall, Josh	R-R	6-6	215	1-21-87	0	3	2.91	28	0	0	3	34	35	15	11	2	14	35	.263	.271	.257	9.26	3.71
Welker, Duke	L-R	6-7	240	2-10-86	1	1	4.91	9	0	0	2	11	9	7	6	0	11	15	.214	.167	.250	12.27	9.00
Wilk, Adam	L-L	6-2	180	12-9-87	7	14	4.73	28	24	1	1	147	166	94	77	18	44	106	.291	.243	.306	6.50	2.70
Worley, Vance	R-R	6-2	230	9-25-87	3	2	4.30	7	7	0	0	46	47	23	22	3	4	43	.264	.247	.278	8.41	0.78

Fielding

Catcher	PCT	G	PO	A	E	DP	PB
Ashley	1.000	52	349	25	0	8	1
Diaz	1.000	9	64	6	0	1	0
Henriquez	1.000	1	2	1	0	0	
Paulino	.985	10	64	3	1	0	1
Sanchez	.983	70	476	37	9	3	7
Santos	.983	10	55	3	1	0	0
Stewart	1.000	4	35	5	0	0	0

First Base	PCT	G	PO	A	E	DP
Davis	1.000	1	5	1	0	0
Hague	1.000	26	169	10	0	13
Lambo	.986	17	126	12	2	13
McGuiness	.994	111	919	64	6	87
Morel	1.000	2	1	0	0	0
Sanchez	.938	2	14	1	1	1

Second Base	PCT	G	PO	A	E	DP
Andino	1.000	3	3	10	0	4

	PCT	G	PO	A	E	DP
Anna	1.000	19	35	50	0	13
d'Arnaud	.976	15	16	25	1	4
Davis	.987	54	94	141	3	24
Field	1.000	7	7	23	0	4
Martinez	.984	55	89	152	4	36
Morel	1.000	6	13	19	0	5
Santos	.882	10	2	13	2	3

Third Base	PCT	G	PO	A	E	DP
d'Arnaud	.854	20	11	24	6	3
Davis	1.000	10	2	8	0	0
Field	1.000	2	3	10	0	3
Hague	.935	40	30	57	6	6
Martinez	.900	5	3	6	1	2
Morel	.958	86	46	157	9	12

Shortstop	PCT	G	PO	A	E	DP
Andino	.963	107	126	292	16	64
Anna	1.000	3	2	10	0	3

	PCT	G	PO	A	E	DP
Barmes	1.000	5	5	6	0	2
Davis	1.000	15	18	36	0	8
Field	1.000	3	3	7	0	0
Martinez	.952	22	25	54	4	5

Outfield	PCT	G	PO	A	E	DP
Curry	1.000	6	11	1	0	0
d'Arnaud	.994	72	157	5	1	1
Decker	.989	96	165	15	2	2
Dickerson	.981	63	149	3	3	1
Hague	1.000	1	2	0	0	0
Lambo	1.000	29	49	1	0	0
Marte	1.000	3	11	0	0	0
Martinez	.931	14	26	1	2	0
Polanco	.955	69	143	5	7	1
Rojas Jr.	.972	67	131	8	4	1
Santos	1.000	1	1	0	0	0
Tabata	.969	33	62	1	2	0

ALTOONA CURVE   DOUBLE-A

EASTERN LEAGUE

Batting	B-T	HT	WT	DOB	AVG	vLH	vRH	G	AB	R	H	2B	3B	HR	RBI	BB	HBP	SH	SF	SO	SB	CS	SLG	OBP
Allie, Stetson	R-R	6-2	238	3-13-91	.246	.270	.232	117	407	60	100	16	0	21	62	71	4	2	2	127	9	6	.440	.362
Barmes, Clint	R-R	6-1	200	3-6-79	.333	.000	.667	2	6	0	2	0	0	0	0	0	0	0	0	0	0	0	.333	.333
Bell, Josh	B-R	6-2	235	8-14-92	.287	.295	.280	24	94	13	27	2	0	0	7	8	0	0	0	12	4	1	.309	.343
Brown, Kelson	R-R	6-3	175	11-7-87	.295	.297	.291	51	129	8	38	3	1	0	8	4	1	3	0	18	3	2	.333	.321
Broxton, Keon	R-R	6-3	195	5-7-90	.275	.233	.300	127	407	67	112	22	9	15	52	59	3	0	2	122	25	6	.484	.369
Cabrera, Ramon	B-R	5-8	195	11-5-89	.239	.143	.320	12	46	5	11	5	0	1	5	3	0	0	0	6	0	1	.413	.286
2-team total (107 Erie)					.273	—	—	119	440	47	120	22	0	6	52	36	0	0	4	43	1	1	.364	.325
Cunningham, Jarek	R-R	6-1	195	12-25-89	.246	.257	.240	101	309	46	76	16	4	8	27	27	8	6	4	69	3	4	.401	.319
Curry, Matt	L-R	6-1	225	7-27-88	.234	.136	.279	58	188	22	44	8	1	4	23	20	0	1	2	50	1	1	.351	.305
Diaz, Elias	R-R	6-1	175	11-17-90	.328	.427	.283	91	326	41	107	20	0	6	54	30	1	2	8	51	3	2	.445	.378
Emsley-Pai, Kawika	B-R	5-11	195	9-3-88	.000	.000	.000	3	8	2	0	0	0	0	0	4	0	0	0	4	0	0	.000	.333
Gamache, Daniel	L-R	5-11	190	11-20-90	.275	.237	.290	39	138	22	38	11	0	6	27	11	3	2	1	32	0	1	.486	.340
Garcia, Willy	R-R	6-3	180	9-4-92	.271	.260	.278	126	439	59	119	27	5	18	63	24	3	4	4	145	8	4	.478	.311
Hanson, Alen	B-R	5-11	170	10-22-92	.280	.292	.274	118	482	64	135	21	12	11	58	31	3	8	3	88	25	11	.442	.326
Henriquez, Ralph	B-R	6-1	205	4-7-87	.129	.156	.113	25	85	7	11	2	0	2	6	1	0	0	0	23	1	0	.224	.140
Howard, Justin	L-L	6-0	205	8-28-87	.233	.152	.265	63	159	18	37	10	0	3	10	15	5	0	1	41	1	0	.352	.317
Maggi, Drew	R-R	6-0	185	5-16-89	.280	.268	.287	110	347	60	97	12	0	3	25	50	9	6	2	58	37	19	.340	.382
Ngoepe, Gift	B-R	5-10	165	1-18-90	.238	.220	.249	131	437	58	104	17	9	9	52	51	2	7	2	135	13	8	.380	.319
Paulino, Carlos	R-R	6-0	175	9-24-89	.296	.367	.244	22	71	5	21	4	0	1	13	3	0	2	2	19	0	1	.394	.316
Rojas Jr., Mel	B-R	6-3	215	5-24-90	.303	.269	.315	53	195	26	59	11	1	5	36	23	1	1	0	34	6	4	.446	.379
Sosa, Junior	L-L	5-10	180	10-3-90	.360	.571	.278	12	25	3	9	2	0	0	1	1	0	2	0	3	1	0	.480	.385
Vasquez, Andy	R-R	5-11	175	10-8-87	.268	.205	.291	96	272	38	73	18	1	11	38	15	0	6	2	61	17	6	.463	.304

Pitching	B-T	HT	WT	DOB	W	L	ERA	G	GS	CG	SV	IP	H	R	ER	HR	BB	SO	AVG	vLH	vRH	K/9	BB/9
Baker, Nate	L-L	6-3	190	12-27-87	3	1	1.71	17	0	0	0	26	24	9	5	1	13	22	.233	.250	.218	7.52	4.44
Balester, Collin	R-R	6-5	200	6-6-86	1	4	6.55	10	0	0	1	11	10	9	8	2	9	10	.227	.238	.217	8.18	7.36
Beckman, Ryan	R-R	6-4	185	1-2-90	3	4	2.62	45	0	0	5	55	44	18	16	2	21	28	.218	.231	.210	4.58	3.44
Benedict, Matt	R-R	6-5	220	2-3-89	0	5	5.77	30	1	0	0	53	62	39	34	2	25	35	.294	.242	.333	5.94	4.25
Castro, Orlando	L-L	5-11	190	3-17-92	0	0	11.25	2	2	0	0	8	13	10	10	1	4	8	.361	.385	.348	9.00	4.50
De Leon, Emmanuel	B-R	6-1	175	12-25-90	1	2	3.56	31	0	0	3	48	57	24	19	2	20	35	.289	.302	.277	6.56	3.75
Dodson, Zack	L-L	6-2	190	7-23-90	4	8	4.62	24	23	0	0	123	139	75	63	11	46	76	.290	.270	.299	5.58	3.38
Harlan, Tom	L-L	6-6	215	3-7-90	3	3	3.71	11	10	0	0	61	60	29	25	6	17	26	.268	.282	.259	3.86	2.52
Holdzkom, John	R-R	6-7	225	10-19-87	1	0	0.00	4	0	0	0	6	1	0	0	0	2	10	.056	.143	.000	15.00	3.00
Inman, Jeff	R-R	6-3	180	11-24-87	5	1	1.09	18	0	0	1	25	18	3	3	0	11	18	.212	.238	.186	6.57	4.01
Kasparek, Kenn	R-R	6-10	245	9-23-85	1	1	2.25	31	0	0	13	40	30	11	10	2	5	37	.201	.242	.172	8.33	1.13
Kingham, Nick	R-R	6-5	220	11-8-91	1	7	3.04	12	12	0	0	71	71	35	24	3	25	54	.259	.274	.245	6.85	3.17
Ludwig, Pat	R-R	6-1	185	10-11-89	3	4	5.63	8	7	0	0	40	53	26	25	4	14	24	.331	.324	.337	5.40	3.15
Mann, Brandon	L-L	6-2	195	5-16-84	1	4	2.91	14	2	0	0	34	33	13	11	1	14	34	.250	.264	.241	9.00	3.71
Miller, Quinton	R-R	6-1	185	11-28-89	1	2	4.04	24	0	0	4	36	37	18	16	3	24	30	.264	.296	.244	7.57	6.06
Montero, Joan	R-R	6-0	186	10-26-88	3	4	6.02	28	7	0	0	61	84	50	41	2	37	31	.326	.316	.333	4.55	5.43
Morris, A.J.	R-R	6-2	185	12-1-86	5	1	1.98	14	9	0	0	59	48	17	13	4	18	40	.224	.234	.214	6.10	2.75
Morton, Charlie	R-R	6-5	235	11-12-83	0	0	4.50	1	1	0	0	4	4	2	2	0	1	6	.250	.250	.250	13.50	2.25

Name	B-T	HT	WT	DOB	W	L	ERA	G	GS	CG	SV	IP	H	R	ER	HR	BB	SO	AVG	vLH	vRH	K/9	BB/9
Nevarez, Matt	R-R	6-4	220	2-26-87	1	1	1.35	6	0	0	1	7	3	1	1	1	5	9	.136	.182	.091	12.15	6.75
Pimentel, Stolmy	R-R	6-3	230	2-1-90	0	0	1.42	5	3	0	0	6	6	3	1	0	5	6	.261	.333	.235	8.53	7.11
Ramos, Jhonatan	L-L	5-10	190	10-7-89	5	6	4.38	31	7	0	2	64	72	41	31	8	22	37	.286	.307	.272	5.23	3.11
Rodriguez, Joely	L-L	6-1	200	11-14-91	6	11	4.84	30	21	2	1	134	151	80	72	10	43	73	.289	.270	.296	4.90	2.89
Rodriguez, Wandy	R-L	5-10	195	1-18-79	0	1	10.38	2	2	0	0	9	11	11	10	3	6	7	.289	.222	.310	7.27	6.23
Sample, Tyler	L-R	6-7	245	6-27-89	3	3	6.49	11	6	0	0	35	35	30	25	2	30	28	.267	.239	.297	7.27	7.79
Sampson, Adrian	R-R	6-3	200	10-7-91	10	5	2.55	24	24	2	0	148	125	45	42	10	30	99	.229	.254	.204	6.02	1.82
Sanchez, Angel	R-R	6-1	190	11-28-89	0	2	4.32	6	5	0	0	33	40	18	16	5	10	21	.303	.355	.257	5.67	2.70
Townsend, Jason	R-R	6-3	190	9-17-88	0	1	7.04	7	0	0	1	8	12	8	6	0	5	11	.316	.444	.200	12.91	5.87
Waldron, Tyler	R-R	6-2	185	5-1-89	0	0	0.00	1	0	0	0	1	0	0	0	0	0	3	.000	.000	.000	27.00	0.00
Yang, Yao-Hsun	L-L	5-11	210	1-22-83	0	1	6.48	11	0	0	0	17	15	12	12	1	18	16	.263	.389	.205	8.64	9.72

Fielding

Catcher	PCT	G	PO	A	E	DP	PB
Cabrera	1.000	11	56	12	0	1	1
Diaz	.992	88	531	75	5	1	8
Emsley-Pai	1.000	3	14	1	0	0	0
Henriquez	.991	22	109	7	1	1	2
Paulino	.993	22	130	12	1	2	4

First Base	PCT	G	PO	A	E	DP
Allie	.991	109	946	72	9	92
Brown	.976	10	73	8	2	6
Curry	.981	17	143	12	3	17
Diaz	1.000	1	1	2	0	0
Gamache	1.000	1	5	1	0	1
Henriquez	1.000	2	14	1	0	1
Howard	.986	9	64	4	1	6
Maggi	1.000	4	15	0	0	2

Second Base	PCT	G	PO	A	E	DP
Brown	1.000	15	30	44	0	7
Gamache	.963	16	29	50	3	11
Hanson	.952	17	24	55	4	10
Maggi	.971	18	22	44	2	7
Ngoepe	.980	86	177	273	9	72
Vasquez	1.000	2	1	2	0	0

Third Base	PCT	G	PO	A	E	DP
Brown	.813	10	4	9	3	0
Cunningham	.899	96	55	168	25	13
Gamache	.765	11	5	21	8	3
Maggi	.962	40	21	79	4	8
Vasquez	.733	7	2	9	4	1

Shortstop	PCT	G	PO	A	E	DP
Barnes	1.000	2	1	3	0	1

	PCT	G	PO	A	E	DP
Hanson	.938	100	134	306	29	66
Maggi	.969	7	10	21	1	7
Ngoepe	.988	44	63	100	2	16

Outfield	PCT	G	PO	A	E	DP
Allie	1.000	1	1	0	0	0
Bell	.956	19	40	3	2	1
Brown	1.000	3	5	0	0	0
Broxton	.990	122	300	6	3	1
Curry	1.000	8	15	1	0	0
Garcia	.950	122	230	19	13	2
Howard	1.000	16	20	1	0	0
Maggi	1.000	37	61	3	0	0
Rojas Jr.	.991	53	103	2	1	1
Sosa	1.000	10	16	1	0	0
Vasquez	.969	80	117	8	4	1

BRADENTON MARAUDERS

HIGH CLASS A

FLORIDA STATE LEAGUE

Batting	B-T	HT	WT	DOB	AVG	vLH	vRH	G	AB	R	H	2B	3B	HR	RBI	BB	HBP	SH	SF	SO	SB	CS	SLG	OBP
Barnes, Barrett	R-R	6-1	195	7-29-91	.238	.250	.235	6	21	3	5	2	0	0	1	3	0	0	0	5	1	0	.333	.333
Bell, Josh	B-R	6-2	235	8-14-92	.335	.320	.342	84	331	45	111	20	4	9	53	25	2	4	1	43	5	4	.502	.384
Crumlich, D.J.	R-R	6-0	190	4-23-90	.190	.273	.158	26	79	7	15	0	0	0	6	9	3	2	4	21	0	0	.190	.284
Fortunato, Raul	R-R	6-0	190	9-5-90	.222	.184	.237	97	311	34	69	9	0	4	29	20	2	6	0	67	13	3	.289	.273
Frazier, Adam	L-R	5-11	170	12-14-91	.252	.233	.260	121	492	62	124	21	2	1	42	37	3	6	2	61	14	8	.309	.307
Gourley, Walker	R-R	6-0	185	6-28-91	.254	.270	.247	101	374	47	95	14	1	1	34	18	5	15	1	88	23	5	.305	.296
Howard, Justin	L-L	6-0	205	8-28-87	.272	.125	.316	32	103	17	28	9	2	2	13	9	2	1	0	27	1	0	.456	.342
Jhang, Jin-De	L-R	5-11	220	11-28-89	.219	.200	.228	77	269	29	59	12	2	2	35	15	2	4	3	36	3	0	.301	.263
Lewis, Taylor	L-L	6-0	200	12-18-89	.246	.308	.232	38	138	15	34	1	3	2	16	6	1	3	0	26	10	6	.341	.283
Maffei, Justin	R-R	6-1	180	8-27-91	.303	.366	.281	49	155	23	47	8	3	1	13	16	2	1	0	35	8	3	.413	.376
Moroff, Max	B-R	6-0	175	5-13-93	.244	.237	.247	130	467	57	114	30	6	1	50	54	3	7	3	129	21	15	.340	.324
Osuna, Jose	R-R	6-2	213	12-12-92	.296	.344	.279	97	365	47	108	23	3	10	57	28	4	4	7	72	4	2	.458	.347
Ponce, Ashley	R-R	5-11	140	1-22-91	.158	.125	.170	39	120	14	19	1	1	0	7	16	1	5	2	17	2	1	.183	.259
Roy, Jeff	L-L	5-9	168	1-24-92	.233	.239	.229	61	215	29	50	3	1	0	14	24	1	8	1	70	18	12	.256	.311
Schwind, Jonathan	R-R	6-0	185	5-30-90	.289	.309	.279	47	166	18	48	8	2	3	16	14	1	0	1	38	4	6	.416	.346
Stallings, Jacob	R-R	6-5	215	12-22-89	.241	.157	.267	68	212	22	51	11	0	4	30	28	2	5	2	52	1	2	.349	.332
Steranka, Jordan	L-R	6-1	205	11-14-89	.278	.274	.279	97	371	39	103	21	1	7	50	15	0	5	4	76	1	4	.396	.303
Stewart, Chris	R-R	6-4	210	2-19-82	.286	.000	.667	3	7	1	2	0	0	0	0	1	0	0	0	1	0	0	.286	.375
Walker, Neil	B-R	6-3	210	9-10-85	.250	—	.250	1	4	1	1	0	0	0	0	1	0	0	0	1	0	0	.250	.400
Wood, Eric	R-R	6-2	195	11-22-92	.271	.259	.276	113	399	51	108	28	6	3	44	41	6	7	3	93	7	3	.393	.345

Pitching	B-T	HT	WT	DOB	W	L	ERA	G	GS	CG	SV	IP	H	R	ER	HR	BB	SO	AVG	vLH	vRH	K/9	BB/9
Barrios, Yhonathan	B-R	5-11	180	12-1-91	0	1	2.25	15	0	0	11	20	12	5	5	1	7	12	.174	.156	.189	5.40	3.15
Benedict, Matt	R-R	6-5	220	3-28-89	0	0	1.69	4	0	0	1	11	10	2	2	1	2	4	.256	.308	.192	3.38	1.69
Carle, Shane	R-R	6-4	185	8-30-91	2	3	3.60	10	10	0	0	55	55	29	22	3	13	36	.255	.270	.241	5.89	2.13
Castro, Orlando	L-L	5-11	190	3-17-92	6	4	3.17	17	16	0	0	94	79	33	33	5	11	68	.230	.269	.209	6.53	1.06
Creasy, Jason	R-R	6-4	197	5-13-92	8	9	3.93	28	27	0	0	149	165	75	65	13	22	100	.284	.265	.300	6.05	1.33
Glasnow, Tyler	L-R	6-7	195	8-23-93	12	5	1.74	23	23	0	0	124	74	29	24	3	57	157	.174	.198	.149	11.36	4.13
Gonzalez, Felipe	R-R	6-1	200	8-15-91	1	0	1.93	3	2	0	0	9	8	2	2	0	6	8	.235	.077	.333	7.71	5.79
Hafner, Ryan	R-R	6-6	205	11-22-91	2	6	4.31	34	0	0	0	77	76	46	37	3	37	54	.259	.233	.279	6.28	4.31
Harlan, Tom	L-L	6-6	215	3-7-90	3	3	2.49	21	0	0	1	51	52	23	14	1	9	41	.255	.165	.312	7.28	1.60
Inman, Jeff	R-R	6-3	180	11-24-87	2	0	4.15	8	0	0	0	9	10	4	4	1	2	5	.278	.333	.238	5.19	2.08
Kuchno, John	R-R	6-5	210	5-21-91	8	9	3.56	26	26	0	0	144	136	64	57	3	58	62	.256	.265	.248	3.88	3.63
Kuhl, Chad	R-R	6-3	215	9-10-92	13	5	3.46	28	28	0	0	153	141	67	59	9	42	100	.251	.258	.245	5.87	2.47
Locke, Jeff	L-L	6-0	185	11-20-87	0	1	3.00	1	1	0	0	6	5	2	2	1	1	10	.217	.167	.235	15.00	1.50
Ludwig, Pat	R-R	6-1	185	10-11-89	3	3	3.84	20	6	0	2	68	70	34	29	7	19	51	.262	.231	.293	6.75	2.51
McKinney, Brett	R-R	6-2	225	11-19-90	0	0	0.00	1	0	0	0	1	0	0	0	0	0	0	.000	—	.000	0.00	0.00
Medina, Jhondaniel	R-R	5-11	158	2-8-93	3	0	0.72	35	0	0	3	50	30	8	4	0	29	47	.174	.139	.204	8.46	5.22
Montero, Joan	R-R	6-0	186	10-26-88	2	0	5.79	9	0	0	1	19	22	12	12	0	11	11	.328	.258	.389	5.30	5.30
Morris, A.J.	R-R	6-2	185	12-1-86	0	0	0.00	1	0	0	0	1	0	0	0	0	0	1	.000	.000	.000	9.00	0.00
Otamendi, Andy	L-L	5-11	170	5-15-92	0	0	7.71	2	0	0	0	4	5	2	2	0	3	2	.333	.125	.750	7.71	11.57
Pimentel, Stolmy	R-R	6-3	230	2-1-90	0	0	0.00	1	0	0	0	2	0	0	0	0	1	2	.000	.000	.000	9.00	4.50

	B-T	HT	WT	DOB	W	L	ERA	G	GS	CG	SV	IP	H	R	ER	HR	BB	SO	AVG	vLH	vRH	K/9	BB/9
Rocha, Oderman	R-R	6-3	165	11-7-92	0	0	0.00	1	0	0	0	2	4	2	0	0	0	2	.333	.286	.400	7.71	0.00
Rowland, Robby	R-R	6-4	215	12-15-91	3	7	6.05	24	0	0	1	39	43	27	26	5	10	21	.281	.243	.316	4.89	2.33
Sample, Tyler	L-R	6-7	245	6-27-89	1	0	6.11	10	0	0	0	18	18	13	12	1	12	20	.273	.222	.308	10.19	6.11
Smith, Josh	L-L	6-3	200	10-11-89	4	2	1.93	35	0	0	8	56	38	13	12	1	25	51	.191	.105	.257	8.20	4.02
Trepagnier, Bryton	R-R	6-4	186	9-18-91	4	1	2.53	38	0	0	9	53	34	16	15	1	33	40	.190	.169	.206	6.75	5.57
Waldron, Tyler	R-R	6-2	185	5-1-89	1	0	0.00	6	0	0	2	10	3	0	0	0	1	10	.100	.077	.118	9.31	0.93

Fielding

Catcher	PCT	G	PO	A	E	DP	PB
Jhang	.985	74	468	57	8	5	9
Stallings	.992	68	431	54	4	8	2
Stewart	1.000	3	18	4	0	0	0

First Base	PCT	G	PO	A	E	DP
Crumlich	.990	10	95	6	1	16
Gourley	.996	25	242	29	1	18
Osuna	.994	62	618	35	4	56
Steranka	.988	43	392	28	5	46

Second Base	PCT	G	PO	A	E	DP
Crumlich	1.000	7	8	18	0	3

Gourley	1.000	2	2	4	0	1
Moroff	.980	123	239	395	13	88
Ponce	.982	11	17	38	1	12
Walker	1.000	1	2	6	0	3

Third Base	PCT	G	PO	A	E	DP
Crumlich	1.000	8	5	19	0	2
Gourley	.886	12	6	25	4	1
Ponce	.917	10	3	19	2	2
Wood	.918	110	65	236	27	25

Shortstop	PCT	G	PO	A	E	DP
Frazier	.938	117	187	361	36	84

Moroff	1.000	5	5	8	0	3
Ponce	.957	18	30	60	4	12

Outfield	PCT	G	PO	A	E	DP
Barnes	1.000	6	11	0	0	0
Bell	.990	62	92	3	1	0
Fortunato	.968	96	177	6	6	3
Gourley	.984	62	116	7	2	0
Howard	.981	32	49	2	1	0
Lewis	1.000	37	73	1	0	0
Maffei	1.000	49	92	5	0	3
Roy	.992	61	120	4	1	1
Schwind	1.000	31	47	3	0	1

WEST VIRGINIA POWER   LOW CLASS A
SOUTH ATLANTIC LEAGUE

Batting	B-T	HT	WT	DOB	AVG	vLH	vRH	G	AB	R	H	2B	3B	HR	RBI	BB	HBP	SH	SF	SO	SB	CS	SLG	OBP
Aponte, Francisco	B-R	5-11	135	2-9-91	.286	.500	.200	2	7	0	2	0	0	0	0	0	0	0	0	2	0	0	.286	.286
Barnes, Barrett	R-R	6-1	195	7-29-91	.154	.200	.125	4	13	1	2	0	0	0	2	2	0	0	0	2	2	0	.154	.267
Collins, Danny	R-R	6-2	205	2-11-91	.259	.238	.268	77	270	29	70	14	1	4	33	25	7	2	6	62	3	0	.363	.331
Diaz, Chris	R-R	6-0	180	11-9-90	.233	.195	.249	82	288	39	67	14	0	0	22	26	7	6	0	44	5	6	.281	.312
Diaz, Francisco	B-R	5-11	185	3-21-90	.209	.256	.190	44	148	15	31	9	1	1	13	13	0	3	2	28	1	0	.304	.270
Emsley-Pai, Kawika	B-R	5-11	195	9-3-88	.205	.220	.198	44	122	13	25	5	0	3	15	28	2	3	2	36	1	1	.320	.357
Escobar, Elvis	L-L	5-10	180	9-6-94	.210	.167	.224	55	200	18	42	11	2	2	29	7	1	2	1	55	3	2	.315	.239
Espinal, Edwin	R-R	6-2	250	1-27-94	.283	.250	.295	122	470	50	133	25	1	7	71	27	6	3	4	71	1	1	.385	.327
Fransoso, Mike	L-R	6-0	180	7-27-90	.242	.302	.225	58	194	30	47	3	4	6	19	33	3	4	2	38	5	3	.392	.358
Jones, JaCoby	R-R	6-3	200	5-10-92	.288	.262	.297	117	445	72	128	21	3	23	70	33	12	3	8	132	17	9	.503	.347
Landecker, Adam	R-R	6-0	200	2-1-91	.244	.229	.250	37	119	19	29	7	0	0	11	8	1	3	2	19	0	3	.303	.292
Maffei, Justin	R-R	6-1	180	8-27-91	.239	.258	.232	63	226	30	54	4	1	1	23	34	7	1	2	53	7	2	.279	.353
Mathisen, Wyatt	R-R	6-1	210	12-30-93	.280	.400	.242	103	375	48	105	17	2	3	42	33	5	3	3	54	6	2	.360	.344
McGuire, Reese	L-R	6-0	181	3-2-95	.262	.225	.275	98	389	46	102	11	4	3	45	24	4		6	44	7	2	.334	.307
Meadows, Austin	L-L	6-3	200	5-3-95	.322	.190	.375	38	146	18	47	13	1	3	15	14	3	0	2	30	2	3	.486	.388
Myles, Candon	L-R	5-10	185	10-24-92	.219	.154	.243	45	146	14	32	6	2	0	10	15	2	0	0	46	10	2	.288	.301
Ponce, Ashley	R-R	5-11	140	1-22-91	.320	.200	.350	7	25	4	8	2	0	0	5	5	2	0	0	3	1	1	.400	.469
Ramirez, Harold	R-R	5-10	210	9-6-94	.309	.352	.293	49	204	30	63	14	1	1	24	11	8	1	2	35	12	3	.402	.364
Rivera, Maximo	R-R	5-11	185	12-22-92	.208	.130	.241	25	77	7	16	3	0	0	9	9	0	1	1	17	1	3	.247	.287
Roy, Jeff	L-L	5-9	168	1-24-92	.234	.167	.259	44	158	22	37	7	2	1	17	12	1	5	1	48	6	4	.323	.291
Weiss, Erich	L-R	6-3	180	9-11-91	.287	.213	.314	130	463	72	133	22	4	4	42	60	10	3	4	117	21	12	.378	.378

Pitching	B-T	HT	WT	DOB	W	L	ERA	G	GS	CG	SV	IP	H	R	ER	HR	BB	SO	AVG	vLH	vRH	K/9	BB/9
Barrios, Yhonathan	B-R	5-11	180	12-1-91	2	6	4.70	26	0	0	4	38	51	26	20	2	16	38	.315	.309	.321	8.92	3.76
Borden, Buddy	R-R	6-3	210	4-29-92	7	9	3.16	27	26	0	0	128	103	52	45	13	48	122	.220	.201	.238	8.58	3.38
Burnette, Jake	R-R	6-4	180	8-10-92	1	0	7.11	2	1	0	0	6	9	6	5	0	5	7	.346	.500	.000	9.95	7.11
Carle, Shane	R-R	6-4	185	8-30-91	2	5	3.72	17	13	0	0	82	96	43	34	9	9	47	.293	.275	.312	5.14	0.98
Dickson, Cody	L-L	6-4	180	4-27-92	7	9	3.90	27	27	0	0	129	138	72	56	11	58	104	.281	.267	.287	7.24	4.04
Gonzalez, Felipe	R-R	6-1	200	8-15-91	2	4	2.81	33	8	0	2	93	79	39	29	10	25	86	.228	.218	.237	8.32	2.42
Heredia, Luis	R-R	6-6	205	8-10-94	2	4	4.15	18	18	0	0	89	87	54	41	9	33	43	.258	.305	.230	4.35	3.34
Hirsch, Henry	R-R	6-3	185	9-29-92	4	6	4.46	38	1	0	1	83	82	45	41	8	41	68	.265	.280	.251	7.40	4.46
Kendall, Will	B-L	6-3	180	9-7-91	0	2	6.06	11	0	0	1	16	20	12	11	1	6	14	.313	.435	.244	7.71	3.31
Lakind, Jared	L-L	6-2	195	3-9-92	0	1	4.44	17	0	0	0	24	34	13	12	2	9	20	.343	.333	.348	7.40	3.33
McKinney, Brett	R-R	6-2	225	11-19-90	4	7	2.20	37	0	0	4	49	36	14	12	6	20	48	.205	.257	.167	8.82	3.67
Mulderig, Jerry	L-R	6-4	205	6-17-92	2	2	4.29	9	1	0	0	21	20	14	10	1	16	19	.247	.184	.302	8.14	6.86
Neverauskas, Dovydas	R-R	6-3	175	1-14-93	6	12	5.60	27	26	1	0	124	151	86	77	12	55	88	.305	.315	.296	6.40	4.00
Otamendi, Andy	L-L	5-11	170	5-15-92	1	0	1.19	14	0	0	0	23	16	3	3	0	7	20	.195	.240	.175	7.94	2.78
Perez, Clario	R-R	6-1	185	8-30-92	4	1	4.08	38	0	0	2	68	71	35	31	5	15	39	.271	.279	.263	5.14	1.98
Rosario, Miguel	R-R	6-0	182	1-30-93	0	1	6.14	6	0	0	0	7	5	5	1		4	6	.233	.357	.125	7.36	4.91
Rowland, Robby	B-R	6-4	215	12-15-91	1	0	7.71	6	0	0	0	12	16	10	10	2	13	10	.333	.391	.280	7.71	10.03
Sanchez, Isaac	R-R	6-0	170	10-14-92	3	4	4.45	42	0	0	6	57	62	31	28	7	20	48	.272	.275	.269	7.62	3.18
Topa, Justin	R-R	6-4	200	3-7-91	4	8	6.09	25	14	0	1	81	109	60	55	8	20	50	.330	.329	.331	5.53	2.21
Von Rosenberg, Zack	R-R	6-5	205	9-24-90	2	2	3.38	16	0	0	0	37	35	16	14	3	5	25	.259	.292	.229	6.03	1.21

Fielding

Catcher	PCT	G	PO	A	E	DP	PB
Diaz	.990	16	90	10	1	0	1
Emsley-Pai	.992	38	216	38	2	1	4
McGuire	.987	84	614	96	9	9	9

First Base	PCT	G	PO	A	E	DP
Collins	.987	18	143	14	2	15
Emsley-Pai	1.000	2	4	0	0	0
Espinal	.992	107	842	82	7	77
Landecker	.992	14	117	7	1	7
Rivera	1.000	4	11	2	0	0

Second Base	PCT	G	PO	A	E	DP
Diaz	.964	12	24	30	2	5
Fransoso	.967	7	16	13	1	4
Landecker	.857	1	1	5	1	0
Ponce	1.000	1	3	5	0	0
Weiss	.962	114	185	323	20	67

Third Base	PCT	G	PO	A	E	DP
Aponte	.750	2	3	0	1	0
Diaz	.968	40	26	95	4	8
Espinal	.500	2	0	1	1	1
Fransoso	1.000	1	0	2	0	0
Landecker	.870	11	6	14	3	2
Mathisen	.910	84	44	148	19	6

Shortstop	PCT	G	PO	A	E	DP
Diaz	.978	32	54	78	3	19

Fransoso	.875	2	2	5	1	1
Jones	.948	99	173	266	24	49
Ponce	.941	6	14	18	2	6

Outfield	PCT	G	PO	A	E	DP
Barnes	1.000	4	7	0	0	0
Collins	.944	33	49	2	3	1
Diaz	1.000	23	36	6	0	0
Escobar	.954	54	122	3	6	1
Fransoso	1.000	44	80	8	0	0

Landecker	—	2	0	0	0	0
Maffei	1.000	62	142	2	0	0
Meadows	.968	38	87	4	3	1
Myles	.960	45	89	6	4	0
Ramirez	.981	47	97	5	2	1
Rivera	1.000	16	23	0	0	0
Roy	.971	44	94	5	3	1

JAMESTOWN JAMMERS

SHORT-SEASON

NEW YORK-PENN LEAGUE

Batting	B-T	HT	WT	DOB	AVG	vLH	vRH	G	AB	R	H	2B	3B	HR	RBI	BB	HBP	SH	SF	SO	SB	CS	SLG	OBP
Anderson, Carl	L-L	6-0	185	9-1-92	.244	.212	.253	60	242	35	59	8	4	0	14	14	5	8	0	33	14	4	.310	.299
Andriese, David	L-R	6-2	210	3-2-91	.224	.241	.219	44	134	15	30	7	0	1	13	16	0	2	1	41	5	1	.299	.305
Aponte, Francisco	B-R	5-11	135	2-9-91	.250	.300	.233	25	80	11	20	4	3	1	15	7	0	2	1	21	0	0	.413	.307
Dennis, Andrew	R-R	6-2	180	3-30-93	.333	—	.333	1	3	0	1	0	0	0	0	0	0	0	0	1	0	0	.333	.333
Escobar, Elvis	L-L	5-10	180	9-6-94	.274	.139	.318	38	146	18	40	6	1	1	9	8	0	3	2	28	6	3	.349	.316
Filliben, Tyler	R-R	6-2	188	8-8-92	.263	.269	.261	33	114	12	30	10	0	1	5	10	8	3	0	24	3	2	.377	.364
Forgione, Erik	B-R	6-0	160	9-9-92	.228	.306	.198	39	127	12	29	1	0	0	9	6	3	3	0	22	5	2	.236	.279
Fransoso, Mike	L-R	6-0	180	7-27-90	.269	.167	.300	16	52	8	14	2	2	0	5	7	0	4	0	11	1	1	.385	.356
Gamache, Daniel	L-R	5-11	190	11-20-90	.235	.167	.273	5	17	1	4	0	0	0	1	2	1	1	0	2	0	0	.235	.350
Garcia, Deybi	R-R	5-11	185	2-11-92	.200	.235	.188	20	65	5	13	3	0	0	3	1	0	1	0	19	0	0	.246	.212
Gushue, Taylor	B-R	6-1	215	12-19-93	.241	.163	.263	54	199	25	48	13	2	5	29	27	2	4	1	37	0	1	.402	.336
Krause, Kevin	R-R	6-2	200	11-23-92	.276	.267	.279	39	134	22	37	9	4	7	32	16	4	3	3	28	6	2	.560	.363
Lambo, Andrew	L-L	6-3	225	8-11-88	.167	.000	.222	4	12	2	2	0	0	0	1	4	0	1	0	2	0	0	.167	.375
Lunde, Erik	L-R	5-9	180	1-14-92	.206	.162	.217	55	175	21	36	3	3	0	23	21	4	6	0	32	3	6	.257	.305
Luplow, Jordan	R-R	6-1	195	9-26-93	.277	.321	.263	62	220	31	61	12	1	6	30	27	3	6	3	44	10	6	.423	.360
Montilla, Ulises	R-R	5-11	170	5-12-92	.286	.250	.333	2	7	1	2	1	0	0	1	0	1	0	0	0	0	0	.429	.375
Ross, Kevin	R-R	6-1	205	9-17-93	.265	.342	.242	44	162	14	43	11	0	1	24	4	0	8	1	13	1	1	.352	.281
Simpson, Chase	B-R	6-1	210	2-17-92	.286	.325	.275	55	189	27	54	14	1	7	31	26	2	2	5	40	0	1	.481	.369
Sopena, Nathan	R-R	5-9	180	5-16-91	.125	.000	.143	3	8	1	1	0	0	0	0	1	0	0	0	5	0	0	.125	.222
Suchy, Michael	R-R	6-3	220	4-15-93	.236	.226	.239	66	237	35	56	8	6	1	17	26	8	3	1	53	7	9	.333	.331
Tam Sing, Trace	R-R	6-0	175	12-7-91	.208	.278	.185	22	72	4	15	5	0	0	4	5	0	1	1	15	2	3	.278	.256
Vallejo, Enyel	R-R	6-1	175	10-15-90	.263	.400	.214	5	19	2	5	0	1	0	3	1	1	1	0	4	2	0	.368	.333

Pitching	B-T	HT	WT	DOB	W	L	ERA	G	GS	CG	SV	IP	H	R	ER	HR	BB	SO	AVG	vLH	vRH	K/9	BB/9
Baker, Nate	L-L	6-3	190	12-27-87	0	0	10.13	2	0	0	0	3	4	3	3	0	2	5	.364	.250	.429	16.88	6.75
Brigham, Jake	R-R	6-3	210	2-10-88	0	0	0.00	2	2	0	0	7	4	1	0	0	3	9	.154	.091	.200	11.57	3.86
Coley, Austin	R-R	6-3	200	7-14-92	0	2	5.23	8	8	0	0	21	28	12	12	3	9	18	.322	.346	.286	7.84	3.92
Dorsch, Eric	R-R	6-8	245	9-23-91	1	1	4.63	19	0	0	3	23	29	16	12	2	9	16	.302	.298	.306	6.17	3.47
Duncan, Frank	R-R	6-4	215	1-30-92	3	3	3.58	14	14	0	0	65	75	30	26	3	11	49	.292	.300	.285	6.75	1.52
DuRapau, Montana	R-R	5-11	175	3-27-92	3	2	2.21	15	11	0	1	61	56	18	15	3	8	57	.243	.289	.193	8.41	1.18
Eppler, Tyler	R-R	6-6	220	1-5-93	3	2	2.49	14	14	0	0	69	54	24	19	6	11	49	.213	.226	.201	6.42	1.44
Eusebio, Julio	R-R	6-2	190	6-2-92	1	1	2.86	19	0	0	3	28	30	12	9	1	8	25	.278	.224	.340	7.94	2.54
Karch, Eric	R-R	6-2	205	10-15-91	2	3	3.22	18	0	0	3	22	22	12	8	1	9	16	.250	.214	.283	6.45	3.63
Lakind, Jared	L-L	6-2	195	3-9-92	0	0	0.82	8	0	0	1	11	5	1	1	0	2	13	.135	.000	.179	10.64	1.64
McRae, Alex	R-R	6-3	185	4-6-93	3	6	6.21	15	15	0	0	67	85	48	46	5	16	44	.306	.377	.243	5.94	2.16
Mendoza, Andres	R-R	6-2	220	6-3-92	1	0	6.32	9	0	0	0	16	24	16	11	5	9	8	.338	.444	.229	5.17	2.87
Minarik, Marek	R-R	6-7	195	6-28-93	1	4	4.86	10	8	0	0	37	34	23	20	2	21	21	.250	.232	.269	5.11	5.11
Minier, Jonathan	R-R	6-1	180	3-8-90	0	0	18.00	2	0	0	0	3	7	6	6	0	4	4	.438	.545	.200	12.00	12.00
Mulderig, Jerry	L-R	6-4	205	6-17-92	1	4	5.45	19	0	0	1	38	36	24	23	2	21	28	.250	.224	.267	6.63	4.97
Neumann, Nick	R-R	6-3	205	4-26-91	3	2	4.50	17	1	0	0	34	38	19	17	4	7	28	.277	.323	.240	7.41	1.85
Otamendi, Andy	L-L	5-11	170	5-15-92	1	0	2.00	5	0	0	0	9	6	2	2	0	0	10	.194	.333	.105	10.00	0.00
Regalado, Jose	R-R	6-3	180	11-22-91	6	3	5.70	15	1	0	0	30	34	23	19	4	13	16	.276	.243	.327	4.80	3.90
Rocha, Oderman	R-R	6-3	165	11-7-92	1	2	2.79	7	0	0	1	10	10	6	3	1	2	5	.250	.211	.286	4.66	1.86
Rosario, Miguel	R-R	6-0	182	1-30-93	2	2	3.27	20	1	0	1	44	33	18	16	0	19	46	.205	.195	.215	9.41	3.89
Street, Sam	R-R	6-3	200	3-18-92	1	1	0.98	16	0	0	5	28	13	5	3	0	4	21	.135	.170	.102	6.83	1.30
Townsend, Jason	R-R	6-3	190	9-17-88	0	0	4.50	2	0	0	0	2	2	1	1	0	0	3	.250	.000	.400	13.50	0.00

Fielding

Catcher	PCT	G	PO	A	E	DP	PB
Dennis	1.000	1	4	1	0	0	0
Garcia	.984	20	116	11	2	2	2
Gushue	.990	36	268	28	3	6	6
Krause	.978	20	118	15	3	1	4

First Base	PCT	G	PO	A	E	DP
Andriese	.988	39	300	26	4	23
Lambo	1.000	2	20	0	0	2
Ross	.986	37	335	21	5	23

Second Base	PCT	G	PO	A	E	DP
Forgione	.957	19	28	60	4	8
Fransoso	1.000	1	2	4	0	0
Gamache	1.000	2	2	7	0	1

Lunde	.972	53	112	166	8	26
Sopena	1.000	3	2	4	0	0

Third Base	PCT	G	PO	A	E	DP
Aponte	.939	16	8	23	2	2
Fransoso	1.000	4	2	4	0	0
Gamache	1.000	3	2	5	0	0
Montilla	.889	2	4	4	1	0
Ross	.867	6	4	9	2	0
Simpson	.908	46	33	66	10	4

Shortstop	PCT	G	PO	A	E	DP
Filliben	.928	33	56	111	13	20
Forgione	.916	21	29	58	8	10
Fransoso	1.000	1	0	6	0	1

Tam Sing	.916	21	29	47	7	10

Outfield	PCT	G	PO	A	E	DP
Anderson	.992	55	124	4	1	1
Andriese	1.000	1	2	0	0	0
Aponte	1.000	9	21	0	0	0
Escobar	.975	37	74	4	2	1
Fransoso	.846	5	10	1	2	0
Krause	1.000	1	6	0	0	0
Lambo	.833	2	5	0	1	0
Luplow	.991	58	94	17	1	3
Suchy	.970	58	96	1	3	0
Vallejo	1.000	3	14	0	0	0

BRISTOL PIRATES

ROOKIE

APPALACHIAN LEAGUE

PITTSBURGH PIRATES

Batting	B-T	HT	WT	DOB	AVG	vLH	vRH	G	AB	R	H	2B	3B	HR	RBI	BB	HBP	SH	SF	SO	SB	CS	SLG	OBP
Arbet, Trae	R-R	6-0	185	7-1-94	.226	.250	.219	57	221	27	50	12	0	1	17	11	9	2	1	69	4	3	.294	.289
Arribas, Danny	R-R	6-0	185	9-30-92	.281	.263	.287	44	160	19	45	7	0	4	23	23	0	0	2	50	3	1	.400	.368
Buckner, Nick	L-L	6-1	205	8-9-95	.276	.250	.285	56	210	24	58	14	2	0	35	25	0	4	2	72	2	0	.362	.350
Dennis, Andrew	R-R	6-2	180	3-30-93	.111	.000	.125	4	9	1	1	0	0	0	0	1	0	1	0	3	0	0	.111	.200
Figueroa, Edgar	L-L	6-1	160	12-2-94	.234	.255	.228	52	209	18	49	9	2	0	17	12	1	5	0	44	3	2	.297	.279
Harvey, Chris	R-R	6-5	220	3-10-93	.292	.231	.308	20	65	7	19	2	0	2	9	10	1	1	0	17	0	0	.415	.395
Meadows, Austin	L-L	6-3	200	5-3-95	.071	.000	.167	5	14	2	1	0	0	0	0	3	0	0	0	3	0	0	.071	.235
Montilla, Ulises	R-R	5-11	170	5-12-92	.308	—	.308	4	13	0	4	1	0	0	1	1	1	0	0	2	0	0	.385	.400
Morales, Tomas	R-R	6-0	190	7-30-91	.267	.292	.260	29	101	12	27	12	1	0	16	2	4	2	0	19	2	1	.406	.308
Munoz, Edgard	B-R	5-9	150	10-30-91	.259	.333	.231	31	108	15	28	3	0	2	9	6	1	5	0	24	1	4	.343	.304
Myles, Candon	R-R	5-10	185	10-24-92	.192	.107	.216	42	125	19	24	3	0	0	9	24	1	3	1	43	8	3	.216	.325
Ozuna, Carlos	B-R	5-11	162	7-19-93	.255	.313	.239	41	149	17	38	8	2	2	13	8	5	0	0	44	0	0	.376	.315
Reyes, Pablo	R-R	5-10	150	9-5-93	.272	.216	.295	46	180	30	49	9	1	2	16	25	3	1	2	31	5	5	.367	.367
Rivera, Maximo	R-R	5-11	185	12-22-92	.310	.375	.291	19	71	8	22	0	2	1	5	5	0	1	0	17	3	2	.408	.355
Salazar, Jose	R-R	6-2	175	7-11-94	.291	.400	.259	30	110	14	32	4	0	0	12	7	2	1	0	14	1	0	.327	.345
Sopena, Nathan	R-R	5-9	180	5-16-91	.100	.200	.080	10	30	3	3	1	0	0	3	3	1	0	0	17	0	1	.133	.206
Suiter, Jerrick	R-R	6-3	210	3-4-93	.279	.271	.282	55	190	35	53	8	2	1	29	41	1	2	4	37	8	3	.358	.403
Tomaszewski, Nathan	L-R	6-4	225	10-10-90	.211	.048	.247	34	114	13	24	5	0	1	12	17	2	0	0	28	0	2	.281	.323
Vallejo, Enyel	R-R	6-1	175	10-15-90	.289	.385	.266	55	197	29	57	12	4	1	26	6	3	5	2	41	5	2	.406	.317

Pitching	B-T	HT	WT	DOB	W	L	ERA	G	GS	CG	SV	IP	H	R	ER	HR	BB	SO	AVG	vLH	vRH	K/9	BB/9
Amedee, Jess	R-R	6-2	205	9-5-93	2	0	6.26	15	0	0	1	27	31	25	19	2	14	38	.279	.188	.349	12.51	4.61
Balester, Collin	R-R	6-5	200	6-6-86	0	0	2.70	6	0	0	0	7	8	5	2	1	2	5	.286	.375	.250	6.75	2.70
Basulto, Omar	L-L	6-3	190	8-24-93	2	4	3.95	14	14	0	0	55	64	30	24	3	13	41	.292	.278	.295	6.75	2.14
Betts, Palmer	R-R	6-1	190	4-13-94	0	1	5.51	11	0	0	0	16	16	10	10	1	7	15	.262	.316	.238	8.27	3.86
Burnette, Jake	R-R	6-4	180	8-10-92	0	2	4.15	3	3	0	0	9	10	4	4	1	3	8	.303	.417	.238	8.31	3.12
Clemens, Michael	R-R	6-4	225	7-27-93	0	0	1.00	13	0	0	3	18	13	7	2	0	5	20	.176	.286	.130	10.00	2.50
De Leon, Christopher	R-R	6-0	158	8-2-92	1	0	4.50	6	0	0	0	8	7	4	4	1	7	6	.226	.250	.211	6.75	7.88
Del Rosario, Mervin	L-L	6-3	190	3-15-92	1	5	6.68	12	3	0	0	32	38	29	24	4	15	22	.292	.200	.314	6.12	4.18
Ferreras, Miguel	R-R	6-5	221	9-19-91	1	1	8.47	11	0	0	0	17	21	22	16	2	16	11	.296	.333	.273	5.82	8.47
Garcia, Hector	L-L	6-0	170	10-4-95	1	5	3.38	13	13	0	0	48	40	22	18	2	19	50	.222	.167	.233	9.38	3.56
Grullon, Adrian	R-R	6-0	180	9-17-92	0	0	1.17	3	3	0	0	8	1	1	1	0	1	8	.043	.100	.000	9.39	1.17
Henriquez, Cristian	L-L	6-0	175	6-20-92	0	2	6.11	14	0	0	0	18	24	14	12	3	11	12	.333	.353	.327	6.11	5.60
Lopez, Junior	R-R	6-2	165	6-27-91	3	4	4.56	13	10	0	0	51	52	31	26	4	9	41	.259	.211	.290	7.19	1.58
Minarik, Marek	R-R	6-7	195	6-28-93	0	2	5.51	5	2	0	0	16	19	14	10	2	7	10	.292	.318	.279	5.51	3.86
Moore, Colter	R-R	6-8	200	10-14-91	1	0	8.44	4	0	0	0	5	5	6	5	0	5	4	.263	.429	.167	6.75	8.44
Paula, Luis	B-R	6-3	205	6-22-93	2	2	1.37	16	0	0	3	26	20	5	4	2	8	22	.213	.200	.220	7.52	2.73
Pimentel, Cesilio	L-L	6-2	185	1-5-93	4	2	1.93	14	0	0	2	37	25	14	8	2	12	31	.184	.143	.198	7.47	2.89
Rhodes, Cory	R-R	6-4	235	8-30-91	0	0	5.40	4	0	0	0	5	9	9	3	2	3	5	.333	.231	.429	9.00	5.40
Rocha, Oderman	R-R	6-3	165	11-7-92	0	0	0.00	2	0	0	0	3	1	0	0	0	1	4	.100	—	.100	12.00	3.00
Roth, Billy	R-R	6-3	184	6-5-95	0	6	6.00	14	11	0	0	45	42	39	30	7	33	36	.251	.232	.265	7.20	6.60
Sanchez, Angel	L-L	6-7	190	3-2-93	1	0	6.17	8	0	0	0	12	6	10	8	0	14	12	.162	.000	.176	9.26	10.80
Sandfort, Jon	B-R	6-6	215	8-27-94	1	4	10.85	15	5	0	0	37	67	46	45	3	14	21	.401	.448	.370	5.06	3.38
Sever, John	L-L	6-5	190	7-26-93	1	3	1.33	16	3	0	1	41	30	10	6	1	17	63	.204	.231	.198	13.94	3.76
Urbina, Dan	R-R	6-3	158	11-27-93	1	3	8.01	13	1	0	1	30	38	31	27	6	17	19	.314	.231	.354	5.64	5.04
Vivas, Julio	R-R	6-2	227	10-1-93	0	0	0.00	2	0	0	1	4	1	0	0	0	1	4	.083	.000	.100	9.82	2.45

Fielding

Catcher	PCT	G	PO	A	E	DP	PB
Arribas	.977	27	194	21	5	3	8
Dennis	1.000	1	4	0	0	0	0
Harvey	.986	18	121	16	2	3	11
Morales	.985	26	171	31	3	2	6

First Base	PCT	G	PO	A	E	DP
Arribas	.987	15	150	6	2	8
Rivera	1.000	3	26	3	0	5
Salazar	.984	7	60	1	1	8
Suiter	.976	16	111	9	3	11
Tomaszewski	.983	28	224	12	4	15

Second Base	PCT	G	PO	A	E	DP
Montilla	1.000	2	0	4	0	0
Munoz	1.000	4	3	11	0	2
Ozuna	.946	25	45	61	6	16
Reyes	.964	33	66	69	5	16
Sopena	.900	8	12	15	3	6

Third Base	PCT	G	PO	A	E	DP
Montilla	.778	1	1	6	2	1
Munoz	.946	27	26	61	5	2
Ozuna	.833	13	10	20	6	4
Rivera	.600	3	2	4	4	0
Salazar	.890	24	22	43	8	4
Sopena	1.000	1	2	1	0	0

Shortstop	PCT	G	PO	A	E	DP
Arbet	.914	56	62	151	20	30
Ozuna	.889	4	5	11	2	2
Reyes	.936	9	12	32	3	2

Outfield	PCT	G	PO	A	E	DP
Buckner	.981	35	49	4	1	0
Figueroa	.984	50	115	7	2	2
Meadows	1.000	5	6	0	0	0
Myles	.956	42	58	7	3	2
Rivera	1.000	9	12	2	0	0
Suiter	.913	19	20	1	2	0
Vallejo	.956	54	101	7	5	2

GCL PIRATES

ROOKIE

GULF COAST LEAGUE

Batting	B-T	HT	WT	DOB	AVG	vLH	vRH	G	AB	R	H	2B	3B	HR	RBI	BB	HBP	SH	SF	SO	SB	CS	SLG	OBP
Barnes, Barrett	R-R	6-1	195	7-29-91	.313	.000	.385	7	16	5	5	2	0	2	5	6	3	0	0	3	1	0	.813	.560
Bastardo, Alexis	R-R	5-11	190	2-26-94	.344	.250	.386	19	64	5	22	4	0	1	7	1	3	2	0	14	6	1	.453	.382
Benitez, Luis	B-R	5-10	165	8-12-93	.252	.225	.265	36	123	13	31	0	2	0	6	5	0	4	1	23	12	4	.285	.279
Cerda, Reggie	R-R	6-0	185	9-10-94	.178	.267	.133	13	45	3	8	0	0	0	3	6	0	0	1	9	0	0	.178	.269
Chourio, Bealyn	B-R	6-0	150	3-31-94	.244	.200	.268	31	86	10	21	4	1	0	6	23	0	4	0	26	5	3	.314	.404

264 · Baseball America 2015 Almanac

BaseballAmerica.com

	B-T	HT	WT	DOB	AVG	vLH	vRH	G	AB	R	H	2B	3B	HR	RBI	BB	HBP	SH	SF	SO	SB	CS	SLG	OBP
De La Cruz, Julio	R-R	6-1	190	10-5-95	.244	.170	.275	41	156	10	38	7	0	2	20	6	3	1	2	32	1	0	.327	.281
de la Cruz, Michael	L-L	6-1	165	7-10-96	.165	.138	.177	32	91	10	15	0	0	1	7	15	1	4	1	25	4	1	.198	.287
Gamache, Daniel	L-R	5-11	190	11-20-90	.286	1.000	.167	2	7	0	2	0	0	0	1	0	0	0	0	0	0	0	.286	.286
Gonzalez, Yoel	R-R	6-1	180	8-1-96	.220	.191	.233	40	150	14	33	7	0	1	12	14	0	4	1	30	1	2	.287	.285
Kennelly, Sam	R-R	6-2	190	1-9-96	.284	.367	.250	30	102	12	29	6	0	0	14	16	2	2	1	17	0	2	.343	.388
Lambo, Andrew	L-L	6-3	225	8-11-88	.154	—	.154	4	13	3	2	0	0	1	1	4	0	0	0	3	0	0	.385	.353
Marquez, Carlos	L-R	6-2	180	4-29-93	.079	.154	.040	13	38	0	3	1	0	0	3	4	0	0	0	19	0	0	.105	.167
Meadows, Austin	L-L	6-3	200	5-3-95	1.000	1.000	1.000	2	4	1	4	2	1	0	1	2	0	0	0	0	0	0	2.000	1.000
Munoz, Carlos	L-L	5-11	225	6-29-94	.284	.318	.267	54	197	20	56	15	0	4	38	30	0	2	1	16	0	2	.421	.377
Munoz, Edgard	B-R	5-9	150	10-30-91	.353	1.000	.313	5	17	2	6	1	0	1	3	0	0	0	0	2	0	0	.588	.353
Paulino, Carlos	R-R	6-0	175	9-24-89	.333	.429	.200	4	12	3	4	1	1	1	3	0	1	0	0	0	0	0	.833	.385
Polo, Tito	R-R	5-11	180	8-23-94	.291	.323	.271	44	158	30	46	8	6	3	25	17	5	4	2	34	8	4	.475	.374
Rosario, Henry	L-L	5-9	180	4-5-93	.301	.300	.301	48	173	25	52	10	6	3	20	20	3	3	0	28	3	5	.480	.383
Salazar, Jose	R-R	6-2	175	7-11-94	.220	.444	.094	17	50	2	11	2	0	0	3	2	1	3	0	11	0	0	.260	.264
Schwind, Jonathan	R-R	6-0	185	5-30-90	.167	.000	.333	2	6	1	1	0	0	0	1	1	0	0	0	1	0	0	.167	.286
Thomas, Eric	B-L	5-10	175	3-30-95	.227	.226	.227	29	97	9	22	1	0	0	11	11	1	2	0	23	5	4	.237	.312
Tucker, Cole	B-R	6-3	185	7-3-96	.267	.227	.289	48	180	39	48	6	2	2	13	26	3	8	0	38	13	5	.356	.368

Pitching	B-T	HT	WT	DOB	W	L	ERA	G	GS	CG	SV	IP	H	R	ER	HR	BB	SO	AVG	vLH	vRH	K/9	BB/9
Agrazal, Dario	R-R	6-3	190	12-28-94	3	4	4.20	12	12	0	0	56	65	30	26	3	5	34	.285	.203	.317	5.50	0.81
Baker, Nate	L-L	6-3	190	12-27-87	0	0	0.00	2	0	0	0	2	1	0	0	0	0	1	.143	.500	.000	4.50	0.00
Balester, Collin	R-R	6-5	200	6-6-86	0	1	54.00	1	0	0	0	1	10	10	8	0	2	1	.667	.800	.600	6.75	13.50
Batista, Jose	L-L	6-2	175	2-1-96	1	1	2.70	15	2	0	0	27	26	9	8	1	7	13	.265	.083	.291	4.39	2.36
Burnette, Jake	R-R	6-4	180	8-10-92	0	2	13.00	5	5	0	0	9	15	15	13	0	8	5	.375	.385	.370	5.00	8.00
De Aza, Remy	R-R	6-3	207	9-8-94	1	2	7.13	15	0	0	0	18	17	14	14	2	11	14	.254	.269	.244	7.13	5.60
De Leon, Christopher	R-R	6-0	158	8-2-92	0	1	2.16	12	0	0	1	17	13	7	4	1	5	13	.213	.385	.167	7.02	2.70
Ferreras, Miguel	R-R	6-5	221	9-19-91	0	0	0.00	6	0	0	0	7	1	0	0	0	1	3	.048	.091	.000	3.86	1.29
Hinsz, Gage	R-R	6-4	210	4-20-96	0	0	3.38	3	2	0	0	8	8	4	3	0	4	7	.267	.333	.222	7.88	4.50
Hutchings, Nick	R-R	6-2	165	2-10-96	2	4	4.53	12	12	0	0	48	52	28	24	2	13	24	.275	.264	.279	4.53	2.45
Keller, Mitch	R-R	6-3	195	4-4-96	0	0	1.98	9	8	0	0	27	19	8	6	0	13	29	.202	.323	.143	9.55	4.28
Kozikowski, Neil	R-R	6-4	180	5-26-95	1	3	7.71	15	3	0	0	33	47	30	28	4	10	16	.329	.333	.327	4.41	2.76
Liao, Jen-Lei	R-R	6-6	255	8-30-93	1	2	5.29	14	0	0	0	17	11	11	10	1	16	12	.183	.250	.154	6.35	8.47
Minier, Jonathan	R-R	6-1	180	3-8-90	0	1	1.53	15	0	0	1	18	13	5	3	0	15	23	.203	.100	.250	11.72	7.64
Montero, Yunior	R-R	6-4	175	2-9-93	1	4	4.68	19	0	0	1	25	24	17	13	1	12	18	.253	.250	.254	6.48	4.32
Morris, A.J.	R-R	6-2	185	12-16-86	0	0	2.57	4	0	0	0	7	4	2	2	1	1	7	.160	.400	.100	9.00	1.29
Mota, Cristian	L-L	5-10	150	9-26-91	0	4	3.10	14	0	0	0	20	15	9	7	0	16	14	.211	.000	.242	7.08	4.87
Navarro, Gerardo	L-R	6-2	194	8-23-93	2	4	4.41	13	10	0	0	51	45	28	25	2	12	21	.232	.271	.215	3.71	2.12
Paredes, Jesus	R-R	6-2	162	1-18-93	0	0	3.43	16	0	0	1	21	15	10	8	1	15	20	.211	.250	.203	8.57	6.43
Ramos, Horelbin	L-L	6-1	180	1-14-94	1	0	0.40	16	0	0	3	22	10	4	1	0	9	12	.135	.000	.154	4.84	3.63
Ruiz, Carlos	R-R	6-2	169	4-13-91	0	2	4.15	14	0	0	1	13	13	9	6	0	2	5	.250	.333	.216	3.46	1.38
Supak, Trey	R-R	6-5	210	5-31-96	1	3	4.88	8	6	0	0	24	27	13	13	4	11	21	.293	.357	.240	7.88	4.13
Vera, Eduardo	R-R	6-2	185	7-3-94	3	1	4.80	17	0	0	0	30	29	17	16	3	5	18	.257	.235	.266	5.40	1.50
Vivas, Jose	R-R	6-2	227	10-1-93	3	1	1.17	15	0	0	2	23	20	4	3	0	1	25	.230	.182	.246	9.78	0.39

Fielding

Catcher	PCT	G	PO	A	E	DP	PB
Cerda	1.000	13	77	8	0	2	3
Gonzalez	.977	38	219	32	6	1	13
Marquez	.930	8	35	5	3	0	1
Paulino	.895	4	15	2	2	0	1
Jorge	.947	36	65	96	9	20	
Kennelly	.960	19	44	52	4	13	
Munoz	1.000	1	1	0	0	0	
Tucker	.939	42	65	134	13	20	

First Base	PCT	G	PO	A	E	DP
Hurst	1.000	3	19	4	0	0
Lambo	1.000	2	14	1	0	1
Munoz	.992	53	472	26	4	43
Salazar	1.000	5	38	3	0	2

Second Base	PCT	G	PO	A	E	DP
Chourio	.950	7	9	10	1	2
Gamache	1.000	1	1	1	0	0

Third Base	PCT	G	PO	A	E	DP
Chourio	.892	12	7	26	4	2
De La Cruz	.919	40	22	102	11	6
Munoz	—					
Salazar	.871	11	8	19	4	4

Shortstop	PCT	G	PO	A	E	DP
Chourio	.938	12	13	17	2	6
Jorge	.867	4	3	10	2	1
Kennelly	.952	6	9	11	1	3
Munoz	1.000	1	0	1	0	0

Outfield	PCT	G	PO	A	E	DP
Barnes	.929	7	13	0	1	0
Bastardo	1.000	16	36	0	0	0
Benitez	.963	31	52	0	2	0
de la Cruz	.973	30	69	3	2	3
Lambo	1.000	2	7	0	0	0
Meadows	1.000	2	1	0	0	0
Munoz	1.000	1	1	0	0	0
Polo	1.000	41	93	4	0	1
Rosario	1.000	37	96	1	0	0
Schwind	1.000	2	4	0	0	0
Thomas	.975	25	38	1	1	0

DSL PIRATES 1 — ROOKIE

DOMINICAN SUMMER LEAGUE

Batting	B-T	HT	WT	DOB	AVG	vLH	vRH	G	AB	R	H	2B	3B	HR	RBI	BB	HBP	SH	SF	SO	SB	CS	SLG	OBP
Adames, Yunerky	L-L	6-1	200	8-26-90	.275	.205	.295	54	171	36	47	2	6	3	38	23	2	2	1	31	9	8	.409	.365
De Jesus, Johan	B-R	6-0	165	8-1-96	.204	.289	.183	66	191	39	39	7	0	1	19	47	2	1	2	68	10	1	.257	.364
Fernandez, Victor	R-R	5-11	175	10-17-94	.289	.324	.278	45	152	35	44	11	3	3	17	23	7	5	0	28	14	5	.461	.407
Fuentes, Huascar	R-R	6-2	195	6-2-92	.250	.500	.214	5	16	3	4	0	0	1	2	2	3	0	0	5	1	0	.438	.429
Granberry, Mikell	R-R	6-1	190	8-19-95	.259	.217	.270	33	112	17	29	5	1	2	13	19	4	2	0	38	3	1	.375	.385
Herrera, Jhoan	L-R	6-1	185	6-14-95	.282	.174	.310	31	110	10	31	8	0	0	14	14	1	1	1	26	0	1	.355	.365
Lantigua, Edison	L-L	6-0	175	1-9-97	.299	.229	.318	47	164	30	49	12	5	0	30	25	2	7	4	36	3	1	.433	.390
Perez, Luis	L-R	5-10	170	1-18-94	.302	.174	.337	36	106	24	32	4	0	0	15	25	6	4	1	13	11	1	.340	.457
Perez, Ramy	R-R	6-0	170	9-29-94	.146	.167	.139	32	96	8	14	0	1	0	11	8	5	1	2	23	2	2	.167	.243
Portorreal, Jeremias	L-L	6-3	195	8-7-97	.167	.140	.174	58	204	22	34	5	2	2	13	35	0	2	0	73	1	2	.240	.289
Ramirez, Eliezer	R-R	6-1	170	11-21-96	.198	.150	.212	36	86	13	17	2	0	0	11	21	1	4	1	26	1	0	.221	.358
Reyes, Patrick	R-R	6-0	190	9-11-92	.243	.125	.276	33	111	19	27	3	2	1	12	11	3	1	2	25	2	1	.333	.323

Name	B-T	HT	WT	DOB	AVG	vLH	vRH	G	AB	R	H	2B	3B	HR	RBI	BB	HBP	SH	SF	SO	SB	CS	SLG	OBP
Ronco, Jesus	R-R	5-11	160	3-31-93	.208	.222	.200	19	24	7	5	1	0	0	2	3	5	1	0	4	0	0	.250	.406
Santos, Sandy	R-R	6-3	185	4-20-94	.262	.268	.260	51	187	34	49	7	3	1	26	21	14	2	0	41	15	6	.348	.378
Siri, Raul	R-R	5-9	175	10-21-94	.324	.283	.333	66	238	52	77	25	5	4	32	41	8	4	3	37	11	4	.521	.434
Valerio, Adrian	B-R	5-11	150	3-13-97	.240	.298	.223	60	250	33	60	14	2	1	29	16	1	10	4	36	6	6	.324	.284
Vinicio, Felix	L-L	5-10	175	10-28-94	.261	.219	.275	46	134	13	35	4	2	1	18	19	2	4	3	16	0	2	.343	.354

Pitching	B-T	HT	WT	DOB	W	L	ERA	G	GS	CG	SV	IP	H	R	ER	HR	BB	SO	AVG	vLH	vRH	K/9	BB/9
Brun, Luis	R-R	6-0	170	12-28-94	1	0	10.47	14	0	0	2	16	28	21	19	1	13	14	.368	.435	.340	7.71	7.16
Bustamante, Carlos	R-R	6-0	170	9-15-95	0	0	4.25	19	0	0	0	36	33	19	17	1	24	19	.248	.355	.216	4.75	6.00
Escobar, Luis	R-R	6-1	155	5-30-96	2	4	4.75	13	13	0	0	55	50	38	29	2	31	34	.242	.231	.246	5.56	5.07
Esqueda, Jherson	L-R	6-1	175	6-9-95	2	0	3.97	13	4	0	0	34	38	16	15	1	5	28	.290	.361	.263	7.41	1.32
Garcia, Ramon	R-R	6-0	195	3-12-92	0	1	5.92	17	0	0	3	24	31	22	16	1	9	18	.307	.464	.247	6.66	3.33
Garcia, Yeudy	R-R	6-3	185	10-6-92	4	3	2.41	13	13	0	0	60	50	23	16	0	20	47	.225	.143	.269	7.09	3.02
Hiciano, Delvin	R-R	6-2	175	12-24-91	0	1	4.40	10	0	0	2	14	14	8	7	1	5	10	.255	.400	.200	6.28	3.14
Leon, Edgardo	R-R	6-3	190	7-4-96	2	4	7.68	23	0	0	0	36	44	37	31	3	37	19	.303	.378	.270	4.71	9.17
Martinez, Alex	R-R	6-3	175	5-8-95	1	1	4.76	13	0	0	0	17	13	12	9	0	12	14	.200	.200	.200	7.41	6.35
Miranda, Luylli	L-L	5-11	180	1-29-92	2	1	1.35	15	0	0	0	27	15	4	4	1	9	18	.161	.250	.143	6.08	3.04
Mitchell, Richard	R-R	6-2	185	7-29-95	7	3	3.05	14	14	0	0	65	56	30	22	0	16	24	.220	.270	.200	3.32	2.22
Mota, Cristian	L-L	5-10	150	9-26-91	0	0	4.50	6	0	0	0	6	2	6	3	0	7	4	.100	.000	.118	6.00	10.50
Oronel, Nestor	L-L	6-1	175	12-13-96	2	7	3.99	14	14	0	0	59	87	45	26	2	14	31	.354	.333	.357	4.76	2.15
Perez, Jesus	R-R	6-2	228	1-1-94	0	0	18.00	1	0	0	0	1	3	2	2	0	2	1	.600	.667	.500	9.00	18.00
Rodriguez, Francis	R-R	6-2	172	11-28-92	1	3	2.91	12	12	0	0	53	43	22	17	0	13	40	.223	.262	.203	6.84	2.22
Rodriguez, Raymond	L-L	6-1	175	3-13-97	1	0	5.19	17	0	0	1	17	16	14	10	0	19	10	.250	.250	.250	5.19	9.87
Santana, Edgar	R-R	6-2	180	10-16-91	1	3	3.66	13	0	0	2	20	27	12	8	0	3	11	.342	.357	.333	5.03	1.37
Santos, Cesar	L-L	6-2	190	4-20-95	0	0	6.43	5	0	0	0	7	6	5	5	0	8	5	.250	—	.250	6.43	10.29
Sepulveda, Eumir	R-R	6-2	170	2-14-96	1	0	7.29	14	0	0	1	21	25	21	17	1	9	12	.294	.429	.228	5.14	3.86
Vasquez, Angel	R-R	6-1	185	4-13-94	1	0	2.31	10	0	0	1	12	6	4	3	0	2	8	.146	.188	.120	6.17	1.54
Villamar, Julian	R-R	6-5	190	4-23-94	4	2	8.31	21	0	0	0	26	32	26	24	3	29	27	.302	.212	.342	9.35	10.04

Fielding

Catcher	PCT	G	PO	A	E	DP	PB
Adames	1.000	1	3	0	0	0	0
Granberry	.963	32	185	24	8	2	12
Perez	.980	17	76	20	2	1	7
Reyes	.977	29	144	23	4	1	5

First Base	PCT	G	PO	A	E	DP
Adames	.982	49	412	20	8	30
Fuentes	1.000	2	16	2	0	3
Herrera	.990	11	98	4	1	9
Perez	.975	12	72	5	2	5
Reyes	.936	5	43	1	3	2

Second Base	PCT	G	PO	A	E	DP
De Jesus	1.000	7	9	17	0	6
Perez	.980	23	47	53	2	12
Siri	.931	47	110	106	16	16

Third Base	PCT	G	PO	A	E	DP
De Jesus	.907	60	64	121	19	9
Fuentes	.600	1	2	1	2	0
Herrera	.946	14	6	29	2	2
Perez	—	2	0	0	0	0
Ronco	.882	11	10	20	4	2

Shortstop	PCT	G	PO	A	E	DP
De Jesus	.929	5	4	9	1	1
Perez	.886	8	16	15	4	2
Ronco	1.000	1	1	3	0	1
Valerio	.943	59	124	188	19	29

Outfield	PCT	G	PO	A	E	DP
Adames	—	1	0	0	0	0
Fernandez	.947	40	69	2	4	1
Fuentes	—	1	0	0	0	0
Lantigua	.966	45	84	0	3	0
Portorreal	.971	55	96	5	3	2
Ramirez	.947	25	34	2	2	1
Santos	.967	47	79	8	3	1
Vinicio	.930	27	36	4	3	1

St. Louis Cardinals

SEASON IN A SENTENCE: St. Louis withstood injuries to Michael Wacha and Yadier Molina to make its fourth straight playoff appearance, only to be the background while Travis Ishikawa did his best Bobby Thomson impression in the NLCS.

HIGH POINT: Entering a doubleheader with the Cubs on Aug. 30, the Cardinals were one game back in the race for the NL Central crown. They dropped the first game, then won the second game. Innocuous as it might have seemed at the time, that win was the first of six straight. By the end of the streak, they were up in the division by four games and would never relinquish that lead on the way to the playoffs.

LOW POINT: It's not often that part of a championship series can be considered a low point, but exceptions can be made when a season ends in such dramatic and deflating fashion. When Ishikawa hit a 2-0 fastball from an obviously rusty Michael Wacha for a three-run, pennant-winning home run, it gave an otherwise-successful Cardinals season an abrupt end.

NOTABLE ROOKIES: Top prospect Oscar Taveras made his major league debut, to middling results. He did hit a key home run in the NLCS, however. Kolten Wong had a nice rebound year, including three postseason homers in 29 at-bats.

KEY TRANSACTIONS: In the offseason, the Cardinals added shortstop Jhonny Peralta for four years and $53 million, giving the team stability at a key position for the foreseeable future. They also brought in outfielders Randal Grichuk and Peter Bourjos from the Angels in exchange for third baseman David Freese. In season, they bolstered their roster at the deadline by adding righthander John Lackey from the Red Sox for righty Joe Kelly and outfielder/first baseman Allen Craig. They also pried Justin Masterson from the Indians for minor league outfielder James Ramsey.

DOWN ON THE FARM: Righthander Sam Tuivailala used his triple-digit heat to whiff a combined 14.6 hitters per nine during his zoom from high Class A Palm Beach all the way to the majors. Though he failed to homer all season, second baseman Breyvic Valera put his name on the map with a .313 average and a .361 on-base percentage between high Class A and Double-A. Lefty Marco Gonzales, a first-rounder from last season, made his major league debut less than a year after being drafted and found himself a part of the team's playoff bullpen.

OPENING DAY PAYROLL: $108,020,360 (13th)

PLAYERS OF THE YEAR

MAJOR LEAGUE	MINOR LEAGUE
Adam Wainwright rhp	**Randal Grichuk** of
20-9, 2.38	(Triple-A)
3rd in NL in ERA	.259/.311/.493
2nd in NL in wins	Led org with 25 HR

ORGANIZATION LEADERS

BATTING		*Minimum 250 AB
MAJORS		
* AVG	Jay, Jon	.303
* OPS	Holliday, Matt	.811
HR	Peralta, Jhonny	21
RBI	Holliday, Matt	90
MINORS		
* AVG	Pham, Tommy, Memphis	.324
* OBP	Pham, Tommy, Memphis	.395
* SLG	Scruggs, Xavier, Memphis	.494
R	Scruggs, Xavier, Memphis	82
H	Valera, Breyvic, Palm Beach, Springfield	163
TB	Scruggs, Xavier, Memphis	233
2B	Piscotty, Stephen, Memphis	32
3B	Bryan, Vaughn, Peoria	9
	Tilson, Charlie, Palm Beach, Springfield	9
HR	Grichuk, Randal, Memphis	25
RBI	Scruggs, Xavier, Memphis	87
BB	Rodriguez, Jonathan, Springfield	56
SO	Wisdom, Patrick, Springfield	149
SB	McElroy, C.J., Peoria	41

PITCHING		#Minimum 75 IP
MAJORS		
W	Wainwright, Adam	20
# ERA	Wainwright, Adam	2.38
SO	Lynn, Lance	181
SV	Rosenthal, Trevor	45
MINORS		
W	Cooney, Tim, Memphis	14
L	Heyer, Kurt, Memphis, Springfield	13
# ERA	Gonzales, Marco, P. Beach, Springfield, Memphis	2.43
G	Kiekhefer, Dean, Springfield, Memphis	55
GS	Heyer, Kurt, Memphis, Springfield	27
SV	Donofrio, Joey, Memphis, Springfield	16
IP	Cooney, Tim, Memphis	158
BB	Reyes, Alex, Peoria	61
SO	Reyes, Alex, Peoria	137
AVG	Gonzales, Marco, P. Beach, Springfield, Memphis	.238

2014 PERFORMANCE

General Manager: John Mozeliak. **Farm Director:** Gary LaRocque. **Scouting Director:** Dan Kantrovitz.

Class	Team	League	W	L	PCT	Finish	Manager
Majors	St. Louis Cardinals	National	90	72	.556	t-5th (30)	Mike Matheny
Triple-A	Memphis Redbirds	Pacific Coast	79	64	.552	3rd (16)	Ron Warner
Double-A	Springfield Cardinals	Texas	68	72	.486	t-5th (8)	Mike Shildt
High A	Palm Beach Cardinals	Florida State	76	63	.547	5th (12)	Dann Bilardello
Low A	Peoria Chiefs	Midwest	72	67	.518	t-5th (16)	Joe Kruzel
Short season	State College Spikes	New York-Penn	48	28	.632	t-1st (14)	Oliver Marmol
Rookie	Johnson City Cardinals	Appalachian	37	31	.544	5th (10)	Johnny Rodriguez
Rookie	Cardinals	Gulf Coast	37	23	.617	2nd (16)	Steve Turco
Overall Minor League Record			417	348	.545	4th (30)	

ORGANIZATION STATISTICS

ST. LOUIS CARDINALS

NATIONAL LEAGUE

Batting	B-T	HT	WT	DOB	AVG	vLH	vRH	G	AB	R	H	2B	3B	HR	RBI	BB	HBP	SH	SF	SO	SB	CS	SLG	OBP
Adams, Matt	L-R	6-3	260	8-31-88	.288	.190	.318	142	527	55	152	34	5	15	68	26	3	0	7	114	3	2	.457	.321
Bourjos, Peter	R-R	6-1	185	3-31-87	.231	.194	.255	119	264	32	61	9	5	4	24	20	4	5	1	78	9	3	.348	.294
Butler, Joey	R-R	6-2	220	3-12-86	.000	.000	.000	6	5	0	0	0	0	0	0	1	0	0	0	3	0	0	.000	.167
Carpenter, Matt	L-R	6-3	215	11-26-85	.272	.262	.277	158	595	99	162	33	2	8	59	95	8	2	9	111	5	3	.375	.375
Craig, Allen	R-R	6-2	215	7-18-84	.237	.256	.231	97	367	34	87	17	1	7	44	26	3	0	2	77	1	1	.346	.291
Cruz, Tony	R-R	5-11	215	8-18-86	.200	.158	.216	50	135	11	27	5	0	1	17	13	0	2	0	28	0	3	.259	.270
Descalso, Daniel	L-R	5-10	190	10-19-86	.242	.364	.211	104	161	20	39	11	0	0	10	20	2	1	0	33	1	3	.311	.333
Ellis, Mark	R-R	5-10	190	6-6-77	.180	.195	.167	73	178	15	32	6	0	0	12	14	4	4	2	38	4	1	.213	.253
Garcia, Greg	L-R	6-0	190	8-8-89	.143	.333	.091	14	14	2	2	1	0	0	1	1	3	0	0	6	0	0	.214	.333
Grichuk, Randal	R-R	6-1	195	8-13-91	.245	.242	.250	47	110	11	27	6	1	3	8	5	0	1	0	31	0	2	.400	.278
Holliday, Matt	R-R	6-4	250	1-15-80	.272	.301	.263	156	574	83	156	37	0	20	90	74	17	0	2	100	4	1	.441	.370
Jay, Jon	L-L	5-11	195	3-15-85	.303	.375	.283	140	413	52	125	16	3	3	46	28	20	3	4	78	6	3	.378	.372
Kottaras, George	L-R	6-0	200	5-10-83	.200	—	.200	4	5	0	1	0	0	0	1	1	0	0	0	2	0	0	.200	.333
Kozma, Pete	R-R	6-0	190	4-11-88	.304	.250	.333	14	23	4	7	3	0	0	3	0	0	0	4	0	0	.435	.385
Molina, Yadier	R-R	5-11	220	7-13-82	.282	.278	.283	110	404	40	114	21	0	7	38	28	6	1	6	55	1	1	.386	.333
Peralta, Jhonny	R-R	6-2	215	5-28-82	.263	.265	.262	157	560	61	147	38	0	21	75	58	6	0	4	112	3	2	.443	.336
Perez, Audry	R-R	5-9	230	12-23-88	—	—	—	1	0	0	0	0	0	0	0	1	0	0	0	0	0	0	—	1.000
Pham, Tommy	R-R	6-1	175	3-8-88	.000	.000	.000	6	2	0	0	0	0	0	0	0	0	0	0	2	0	0	.000	.000
Pierzynski, A.J.	L-R	6-3	235	12-30-76	.244	.286	.240	30	82	6	20	2	0	1	6	5	1	0	0	14	0	1	.305	.295
Robinson, Shane	R-R	5-9	165	10-30-84	.150	.152	.148	47	60	3	9	1	1	0	4	6	0	0	0	10	0	1	.200	.227
Scruggs, Xavier	R-R	6-1	220	9-23-87	.200	.000	.200	9	15	0	3	1	0	0	2	2	1	0	0	7	0	0	.267	.333
Taveras, Oscar	L-L	6-2	200	6-19-92	.239	.238	.240	80	234	18	56	8	0	3	22	12	1	0	1	37	0	1	.312	.278
Wong, Kolten	L-R	5-9	185	10-10-90	.249	.315	.234	113	402	52	100	14	3	12	42	21	4	5	1	71	20	4	.388	.292

Pitching	B-T	HT	WT	DOB	W	L	ERA	G	GS	CG	SV	IP	H	R	ER	HR	BB	SO	AVG	vLH	vRH	K/9	BB/9
Butler, Keith	R-R	6-0	170	1-30-89	0	0	27.00	2	0	0	0	2	6	6	6	0	1	2	.500	.500	.500	9.00	4.50
Choate, Randy	L-L	6-1	210	9-5-75	2	2	4.50	61	0	0	0	36	27	18	18	2	13	32	.213	.093	.385	8.00	3.25
Fornataro, Eric	R-R	6-1	225	1-2-88	0	0	4.66	8	0	0	0	10	11	6	5	0	1	3	.282	.214	.320	2.79	0.93
Freeman, Sam	R-L	5-11	165	6-24-87	2	0	2.61	44	0	0	0	38	34	13	11	2	19	35	.236	.298	.195	8.29	4.50
Garcia, Jaime	L-L	6-2	215	7-8-86	3	1	4.12	7	7	0	0	44	39	20	20	6	7	39	.234	.326	.202	8.04	1.44
Gonzales, Marco	L-L	6-1	195	2-16-92	4	2	4.15	10	5	0	0	35	32	16	16	4	21	31	.241	.143	.267	8.05	5.45
Greenwood, Nick	R-L	6-1	180	9-25-87	2	1	4.75	19	1	0	0	36	36	19	19	5	5	17	.259	.235	.273	4.25	1.25
Kelly, Joe	R-R	6-1	175	6-9-88	2	2	4.37	7	7	0	0	35	41	19	17	3	10	25	.291	.338	.239	6.43	2.57
Lackey, John	R-R	6-6	235	10-23-78	3	3	4.30	10	10	0	0	61	69	34	29	9	15	43	.287	.307	.275	7.12	2.23
Lynn, Lance	R-R	6-5	240	5-12-87	15	10	2.74	33	33	2	0	204	185	72	62	13	72	181	.238	.244	.234	8.00	3.18
Lyons, Tyler	B-L	6-4	200	2-21-88	0	4	4.42	11	4	0	0	37	33	23	18	4	11	36	.236	.091	.280	8.84	2.70
Maness, Seth	R-R	6-0	190	10-14-88	6	4	2.91	73	0	0	3	80	77	29	26	7	11	55	.261	.314	.232	6.16	1.23
Martinez, Carlos	R-R	6-0	185	9-21-91	2	4	4.03	57	7	0	1	89	90	41	40	4	36	84	.266	.297	.244	8.46	3.63
Masterson, Justin	R-R	6-6	250	3-22-85	3	3	7.04	9	6	0	0	31	35	24	24	6	13	23	.294	.281	.306	6.75	3.82
Miller, Shelby	R-R	6-3	215	10-10-90	10	9	3.74	32	31	1	0	183	160	78	76	22	73	127	.236	.238	.235	6.25	3.59
Motte, Jason	R-R	6-0	205	6-22-82	1	0	4.68	29	0	0	0	25	29	14	13	7	9	17	.293	.211	.344	6.12	3.24
Neshek, Pat	B-R	6-3	210	9-4-80	7	2	1.87	71	0	0	6	67	44	14	14	4	9	68	.183	.196	.176	9.09	1.20
Rondon, Jorge	R-R	6-1	215	2-16-88	0	0	0.00	1	0	0	0	1	0	0	0	0	1	0	.000	.000	.000	0.00	9.00
Rosenthal, Trevor	R-R	6-2	220	5-29-90	2	6	3.20	72	0	0	45	70	57	25	25	2	42	87	.223	.181	.257	11.13	5.37
Siegrist, Kevin	L-L	6-5	215	7-20-89	1	4	6.82	37	0	0	0	30	32	23	23	5	16	37	.267	.308	.247	10.98	4.75
Tuivailala, Sam	R-R	6-3	195	10-19-92	0	0	36.00	2	0	0	0	1	5	4	4	2	2	1	.625	.667	.600	9.00	18.00
Wacha, Michael	R-R	6-6	210	7-1-91	5	6	3.20	19	19	0	0	107	95	41	38	6	33	94	.234	.224	.243	7.91	2.78
Wainwright, Adam	R-R	6-7	235	8-30-81	20	9	2.38	32	32	5	0	227	184	64	60	10	50	179	.222	.244	.203	7.10	1.98

Fielding

Catcher	PCT	G	PO	A	E	DP	PB
Cruz	.997	47	275	15	1	1	4
Kottaras	1.000	3	8	0	0	0	0
Molina	.998	107	810	56	2	10	3

	PCT	G	PO	A	E	DP	PB
Pierzynski	.988	23	155	6	2	1	0

First Base	PCT	G	PO	A	E	DP
Adams	.993	133	1115	80	9	111
Craig	1.000	24	194	15	0	13

	PCT	G	PO	A	E	DP
Cruz	1.000	2	4	0	0	0
Descalso	1.000	4	24	2	0	1
Ellis	1.000	3	15	2	0	5
Molina	1.000	1	10	1	0	0

Scruggs	.970	5	29	3	1	4
Second Base	**PCT**	**G**	**PO**	**A**	**E**	**DP**
Descalso	.986	21	21	47	1	14
Ellis	1.000	50	70	123	0	21
Garcia	1.000	4	5	7	0	2
Kozma	1.000	6	10	11	0	2
Wong	.975	107	196	273	12	70
Third Base	**PCT**	**G**	**PO**	**A**	**E**	**DP**
Carpenter	.959	156	90	288	16	23
Cruz	1.000	1	0	1	0	1

Descalso	1.000	14	1	7	0	0
Ellis	.667	3	0	2	1	1
Shortstop	**PCT**	**G**	**PO**	**A**	**E**	**DP**
Descalso	.940	19	18	29	3	6
Garcia	1.000	1	0	1	0	0
Kozma	1.000	8	9	14	0	5
Peralta	.981	152	191	418	12	98
Outfield	**PCT**	**G**	**PO**	**A**	**E**	**DP**
Bourjos	.990	104	194	0	2	0
Butler	1.000	1	1	0	0	0

Carpenter	1.000	2	1	0	0	0
Craig	1.000	74	121	3	0	0
Grichuk	.966	35	54	2	2	0
Holliday	.972	150	240	5	7	1
Jay	.992	125	247	2	2	0
Pham	1.000	2	2	0	0	0
Robinson	1.000	20	20	1	0	0
Taveras	.991	63	107	3	1	1

MEMPHIS REDBIRDS

TRIPLE-A

PACIFIC COAST LEAGUE

Batting	B-T	HT	WT	DOB	AVG	vLH	vRH	G	AB	R	H	2B	3B	HR	RBI	BB	HBP	SH	SF	SO	SB	CS	SLG	OBP
Adams, Matt	L-R	6-3	260	8-31-88	.200	.000	.214	4	15	1	3	1	0	0	2	0	0	0	0	2	0	0	.267	.200
Butler, Joey	R-R	6-2	220	3-12-86	.360	.318	.375	31	86	16	31	4	0	4	20	19	1	0	0	16	0	0	.547	.481
Curtis, Jermaine	R-R	5-11	190	7-10-87	.253	.269	.247	98	225	29	57	8	0	0	26	42	8	2	2	22	5	0	.289	.386
Easley, Ed	R-R	6-0	205	12-21-85	.296	.333	.283	80	277	43	82	17	1	10	43	22	7	3	3	46	0	4	.473	.359
Ellis, Mark	R-R	5-10	190	6-6-77	.333	—	.333	1	3	1	1	0	0	0	0	0	0	0	0	0	0	0	.333	.333
Garcia, Greg	L-R	6-0	190	8-8-89	.272	.219	.290	106	382	60	104	12	3	8	40	41	11	5	2	95	7	5	.382	.358
Grichuk, Randal	R-R	6-1	195	8-13-91	.259	.325	.233	108	436	73	113	23	2	25	71	28	6	0	2	108	8	5	.493	.311
Kozma, Pete	R-R	6-0	190	4-11-88	.248	.233	.254	117	379	59	94	23	0	8	54	41	7	7	3	61	10	7	.372	.330
Mateo, Luis	R-R	6-0	175	5-23-90	.238	.250	.232	73	223	21	53	13	1	3	22	10	3	6	1	36	1	2	.345	.278
Miclat, Greg	B-R	5-8	180	7-23-87	.125	.000	.167	5	8	2	1	0	0	0	0	3	0	0	0	2	1	0	.125	.364
Moore, Scott	L-R	6-2	195	11-17-83	.236	.264	.226	121	416	55	98	22	0	15	58	39	19	1	2	93	1	0	.397	.328
O'Neill, Mike	L-L	5-9	170	2-12-88	.333	.429	.278	26	57	3	19	1	1	0	8	7	0	0	1	4	0	1	.386	.400
Ortega, Rafael	L-R	5-11	160	5-15-91	.238	.429	.143	7	21	5	5	1	0	0	1	2	0	0	0	5	2	0	.286	.304
Perez, Audry	R-R	5-9	230	12-23-88	.292	.313	.285	62	236	27	69	12	0	6	33	4	0	3	5	34	0	1	.419	.298
Pham, Tommy	R-R	6-1	175	3-8-88	.324	.319	.325	104	346	63	112	16	6	10	44	38	4	0	2	81	20	2	.491	.395
Piscotty, Stephen	R-R	6-3	210	1-14-91	.288	.296	.285	136	500	70	144	32	0	9	69	43	10	1	2	61	11	5	.406	.355
Robinson, Shane	R-R	5-9	165	10-30-84	.304	.333	.293	53	191	33	58	12	0	2	16	22	2	0	1	25	4	2	.398	.380
Rosenberg, Dante	R-R	5-11	180	7-5-90	.000	.000	.000	2	3	0	0	0	0	0	0	0	0	0	0	0	0	0	.000	.000
Scruggs, Xavier	R-R	6-1	220	9-23-87	.286	.350	.259	135	472	82	135	29	3	21	87	53	11	0	2	114	3	5	.494	.370
Tartamella, Travis	R-R	6-0	205	12-17-87	.286	.000	.400	2	7	1	2	0	0	0	0	0	0	0	0	4	0	0	.286	.286
Taveras, Oscar	L-L	6-2	200	6-19-92	.318	.329	.314	62	239	36	76	18	1	8	49	19	2	0	2	31	1	1	.502	.370
Wong, Kolten	L-R	5-9	185	10-10-90	.360	.360	.360	18	75	16	27	4	0	3	13	5	0	0	0	9	6	0	.533	.400

Pitching	B-T	HT	WT	DOB	W	L	ERA	G	GS	CG	SV	IP	H	R	ER	HR	BB	SO	AVG	vLH	vRH	K/9	BB/9
Aardsma, David	R-R	6-3	205	12-27-81	4	0	1.29	33	0	0	11	35	20	5	5	1	17	36	.161	.143	.173	9.26	4.37
Almarante, Jose	R-R	6-1	170	10-19-88	2	0	4.01	17	0	0	1	25	25	11	11	4	11	23	.263	.318	.216	8.39	4.01
Blair, Seth	R-R	6-2	185	3-3-89	0	0	6.35	6	0	0	0	6	5	8	4	1	7	4	.217	.333	.091	6.35	11.12
Butler, Keith	R-R	6-0	170	1-30-89	1	0	0.84	9	0	0	0	11	8	1	1	0	2	13	.222	.143	.273	10.97	1.69
Castro, Angel	R-R	5-11	200	11-14-82	9	6	4.01	26	14	0	1	94	96	51	42	11	26	63	.261	.248	.271	6.01	2.48
2-team total (4 Sacramento)					9	9	4.66	30	18	0	1	114	130	71	59	14	32	73	—	—	—	5.76	2.53
Cooney, Tim	L-L	6-3	195	12-19-90	14	6	3.47	26	25	1	0	158	158	66	61	21	47	119	.263	.219	.278	6.78	2.68
Cornelius, Jonathan	L-L	6-1	190	5-31-88	0	2	6.35	2	2	0	0	11	11	8	8	3	5	6	.268	.263	.273	4.76	3.97
Donofrio, Joey	R-R	6-3	185	5-10-89	0	0	5.19	10	0	0	0	9	13	5	5	2	4	6	.371	.429	.333	6.23	4.15
Feliciano, Pedro	L-L	5-10	195	8-25-76	1	4	5.57	22	0	0	1	21	26	15	13	5	8	19	.302	.256	.340	8.14	3.43
Fornataro, Eric	R-R	6-2	225	1-2-88	4	5	2.57	44	0	0	15	56	46	23	16	3	20	35	.225	.231	.222	5.63	3.21
Freeman, Sam	R-L	5-11	165	6-24-87	0	1	3.54	16	0	0	0	20	25	12	8	1	7	26	.291	.313	.278	11.51	3.10
Garcia, Jaime	L-L	6-2	215	7-8-86	0	0	3.60	1	1	0	0	5	3	2	2	1	2	5	.167	.200	.125	9.00	3.60
Gast, John	L-L	6-1	195	2-16-89	3	2	4.85	12	11	0	0	59	55	32	32	8	22	36	.244	.314	.213	5.46	3.34
Gonzales, Marco	L-L	6-1	195	2-16-92	4	1	3.35	8	8	0	0	46	43	18	17	7	9	39	.251	.189	.269	7.69	1.77
Greenwood, Nick	R-L	6-1	180	9-28-87	4	4	3.02	27	5	0	0	51	42	18	17	4	10	37	.230	.196	.244	6.57	1.78
Harris, Mitch	R-R	6-4	215	11-7-85	0	0	0.00	1	0	0	0	1	1	0	0	0	0	2	.333	.333	—	18.00	0.00
Heyer, Kurt	L-R	6-2	185	1-23-91	0	2	7.30	3	2	0	0	12	17	10	10	3	8	6	.362	.500	.290	4.38	5.84
Kelly, Joe	R-R	6-1	175	6-9-88	0	0	2.61	3	1	0	0	10	8	3	3	1	6	4	.222	.238	.200	3.48	5.23
Kiekhefer, Dean	L-L	6-0	175	6-7-89	2	3	2.54	40	0	0	1	57	48	17	16	7	5	52	.226	.125	.288	8.26	0.79
Lyons, Tyler	B-L	6-4	200	2-21-88	8	2	4.43	14	14	2	0	81	94	41	40	9	18	75	.293	.227	.313	8.30	1.99
Martinez, Carlos	R-R	6-0	185	9-21-91	1	0	0.00	2	2	0	0	10	6	0	0	0	1	7	.167	.238	.067	6.10	0.87
Mayers, Mike	R-R	6-4	185	12-6-91	0	0	7.20	1	1	0	0	5	9	5	4	2	1	4	.409	.357	.500	7.20	1.80
McGregor, Scott	R-R	6-2	193	12-19-86	1	6	6.34	13	13	0	0	61	73	45	43	10	33	33	.308	.333	.289	4.87	4.87
Motte, Jason	R-R	6-0	205	6-22-82	0	0	0.00	2	0	0	0	3	2	0	0	0	2	2	.182	.000	.250	6.00	6.00
Petrick, Zach	R-R	6-3	195	7-29-89	7	6	4.62	24	20	1	1	115	119	61	59	16	36	82	.270	.243	.291	6.42	2.82
Rondon, Jorge	R-R	6-1	215	2-16-88	5	4	3.03	51	0	0	10	62	59	23	21	3	20	51	.250	.245	.254	7.36	2.89
Sherriff, Ryan	L-L	6-1	185	5-25-90	0	0	6.75	4	0	0	0	4	9	4	3	1	1	4	.450	.400	.467	9.00	2.25
Siegrist, Kevin	L-L	6-5	215	7-20-89	0	0	1.35	6	0	0	1	7	3	1	1	0	3	11	.130	.222	.071	14.85	4.05
Stoppelman, Lee	L-L	6-2	210	5-24-90	0	1	6.75	10	0	0	0	13	10	10	10	2	11	12	.213	.105	.286	8.10	7.43
Tuivailala, Sam	R-R	6-3	195	10-19-92	0	0	0.00	2	0	0	1	1	0	0	0	0	0	3	.200	.000	.500	20.25	0.00
Whiting, Boone	R-R	6-1	175	8-20-89	4	7	4.19	21	20	1	0	97	96	50	45	9	44	99	.254	.241	.268	9.22	4.10
Wright, Justin	L-L	5-9	175	8-18-89	0	0	6.65	16	1	0	0	22	25	16	16	1	9	17	.294	.259	.310	7.06	3.74
Wyatt, Heath	R-R	6-2	185	8-27-88	1	2	4.34	45	1	0	0	66	64	33	32	5	17	36	.258	.295	.231	4.88	2.31

Fielding

Catcher	PCT	G	PO	A	E	DP	PB
Easley	.995	79	549	38	3	4	6
Perez	.995	62	413	26	2	0	0
Rosenberg	1.000	1	4	1	0	0	0
Tartamella	1.000	2	19	1	0	0	0

First Base	PCT	G	PO	A	E	DP
Adams	1.000	3	25	5	0	4
Moore	1.000	17	116	5	0	13
Scruggs	.992	133	1063	53	9	106

Second Base	PCT	G	PO	A	E	DP
Curtis	.978	10	22	22	1	6
Ellis	1.000	1	1	1	0	1
Garcia	.985	90	209	241	7	68
Kozma	.923	8	14	22	3	3

	PCT	G	PO	A	E	DP
Mateo	1.000	23	37	52	0	11
Miclat	1.000	3	0	4	0	0
Wong	.972	18	46	60	3	15

Third Base	PCT	G	PO	A	E	DP
Curtis	.948	49	31	78	6	9
Garcia	1.000	1	1	2	0	1
Kozma	.938	11	4	26	2	4
Mateo	1.000	3	3	5	0	0
Miclat	1.000	1	1	1	0	0
Moore	.950	95	43	146	10	9

Shortstop	PCT	G	PO	A	E	DP
Garcia	.979	13	14	32	1	8
Kozma	.977	96	134	284	10	58
Mateo	.994	42	50	120	1	24

	PCT	G	PO	A	E	DP
Miclat	1.000	1	0	1	0	0

Outfield	PCT	G	PO	A	E	DP
Butler	1.000	14	17	1	0	0
Easley	—	1	0	0	0	0
Grichuk	.989	96	166	9	2	0
Kozma	—	2	0	0	0	0
Moore	1.000	8	7	1	0	0
O'Neill	1.000	16	25	1	0	0
Ortega	.900	6	9	0	1	0
Pham	.985	87	191	3	3	1
Piscotty	.988	121	241	4	3	0
Robinson	1.000	45	106	5	0	0
Scruggs	1.000	1	1	0	0	0
Taveras	.980	54	96	1	2	0

SPRINGFIELD (MO) CARDINALS — DOUBLE-A

TEXAS LEAGUE

Batting	B-T	HT	WT	DOB	AVG	vLH	vRH	G	AB	R	H	2B	3B	HR	RBI	BB	HBP	SH	SF	SO	SB	CS	SLG	OBP
Cruz, Tony	R-R	5-11	215	8-18-86	.200	.333	.000	2	5	0	1	0	0	0	0	0	0	0	0	2	0	0	.200	.200
Diaz, Aledmys	R-R	6-1	195	8-1-90	.291	.313	.282	34	117	15	34	8	1	3	18	2	2	3	1	24	6	2	.453	.311
Garcia, Greg	L-R	6-0	190	8-8-89	.333	.125	.571	4	15	2	5	2	0	0	1	1	0	0	1	4	1	0	.467	.354
Keener, Jonathan	R-R	6-0	195	12-10-89	.250	.000	.333	4	4	0	1	0	0	0	0	0	0	0	0	1	0	0	.250	.250
Martini, Nick	L-L	5-11	205	6-27-90	.375	.000	.400	6	16	2	6	1	0	0	1	1	0	0	0	1	0	0	.438	.412
Mateo, Luis	R-R	6-0	175	5-23-90	.278	.286	.276	21	79	6	22	3	0	0	7	3	1	3	0	17	2	3	.316	.313
Mejia, Alex	R-R	6-1	200	1-18-91	.270	.286	.266	49	163	13	44	3	1	3	21	13	2	2	3	20	2	2	.356	.326
Miclat, Greg	B-R	5-8	180	7-23-87	.177	.143	.190	50	147	13	26	3	0	0	10	21	1	3	0	35	10	3	.197	.284
Molina, Yadier	R-R	5-11	220	7-13-82	.833	.667	1.000	2	6	2	5	3	0	0	2	0	0	0	0	1	0	0	1.333	.833
O'Neill, Mike	L-L	5-9	170	2-12-88	.269	.255	.274	92	360	57	97	17	4	1	26	41	1	3	3	37	5	7	.347	.343
Ortega, Rafael	L-R	5-11	160	5-15-91	.249	.218	.257	101	358	56	89	8	3	7	31	45	1	6	4	57	16	10	.346	.331
Popkins, David	L-R	6-3	215	11-16-89	.243	.229	.249	90	276	31	67	12	5	1	24	26	7	5	2	70	4	3	.348	.322
Ramsey, James	L-R	6-0	190	12-19-89	.300	.250	.320	67	243	47	73	14	1	13	36	31	5	1	1	66	4	2	.527	.389
Rodriguez, Jonathan	R-R	6-2	205	8-21-89	.266	.282	.261	114	406	45	108	19	2	11	51	56	4	0	3	96	8	2	.404	.358
Rodriguez, Starlin	B-R	5-10	170	12-31-89	.260	.200	.292	33	100	9	26	6	0	2	15	9	2	0	1	21	2	4	.380	.330
Smith, Curt	R-R	5-10	210	9-9-86	.262	.255	.264	114	390	43	102	16	2	11	52	35	3	1	7	66	3	2	.397	.322
Stanley, Cody	L-R	5-10	190	12-21-88	.283	.227	.302	103	385	47	109	16	2	12	43	35	3	1	9	68	13	2	.429	.340
Swauger, Chris	L-L	6-0	195	8-11-86	.200	.462	.045	9	35	1	7	2	0	0	4	1	0	0	0	4	0	0	.257	.222
Tartamella, Travis	R-R	6-0	205	12-17-87	.171	.105	.194	65	217	11	37	6	0	1	20	15	2	0	1	55	0	0	.212	.230
Tilson, Charlie	L-L	5-11	175	12-2-92	.237	.167	.257	31	139	19	33	4	1	2	17	6	0	0	0	28	2	3	.324	.269
Valera, Breyvic	B-R	5-11	160	1-8-92	.286	.296	.283	59	227	31	65	8	2	0	20	15	0	4	1	22	4	5	.339	.329
Vargas, Ildemaro	R-R	6-0	170	7-16-91	.000	.000	.000	8	10	1	0	0	0	0	0	0	0	0	0	1	0	0	.000	.000
Velazco, Gerwuins	R-R	6-1	190	10-7-91	.000	—	.000	1	4	0	0	0	0	0	0	0	0	0	0	0	0	0	.000	.000
Williams, Matt	R-R	6-0	170	8-29-89	.250	.256	.248	100	304	37	76	10	2	1	25	43	2	5	3	62	14	7	.306	.344
Wilson, Jacob	R-R	5-11	180	7-29-90	.305	.386	.264	36	131	15	40	13	0	5	21	11	2	0	1	23	3	1	.519	.366
Wisdom, Patrick	R-R	6-2	210	8-27-91	.215	.242	.205	128	452	49	97	19	4	14	53	39	2	0	5	149	5	1	.367	.277

Pitching	B-T	HT	WT	DOB	W	L	ERA	G	GS	CG	SV	IP	H	R	ER	HR	BB	SO	AVG	vLH	vRH	K/9	BB/9
Baker, Corey	R-R	6-1	170	11-23-89	1	0	5.79	7	1	0	0	14	20	9	9	3	4	7	.351	.429	.276	4.50	2.57
Berg, Jeremy	R-R	6-0	180	7-17-86	2	0	1.27	16	0	0	0	21	13	3	3	1	6	26	.181	.158	.189	10.97	2.53
Billbrough, Logan	R-R	6-5	225	8-4-89	1	1	7.50	25	0	0	0	30	40	29	25	5	16	28	.315	.302	.321	8.40	4.80
Blair, Seth	R-R	6-2	185	3-3-89	5	7	5.99	26	11	0	1	74	78	53	49	9	51	48	.283	.263	.297	5.86	6.23
Cornelius, Jonathan	L-L	6-1	190	5-31-88	11	9	3.99	26	24	1	0	144	143	71	64	19	39	98	.258	.202	.273	6.11	2.43
Donofrio, Joey	R-R	6-3	185	5-10-89	3	3	0.87	43	0	0	16	52	31	9	5	1	17	65	.172	.175	.171	11.32	2.96
Ferrara, Anthony	R-L	6-1	175	9-2-89	2	1	4.80	17	0	0	0	30	30	16	16	8	10	18	.261	.302	.236	5.40	3.00
Garcia, Jaime	L-L	6-2	215	7-8-86	0	0	9.00	1	1	0	0	2	3	2	2	1	1	2	.429	1.000	.333	9.00	4.50
Gaviglio, Sam	R-R	6-2	195	5-22-90	5	12	4.28	25	24	0	0	137	153	79	65	8	46	126	.284	.317	.258	8.30	3.03
Gonzales, Marco	L-L	6-1	195	2-16-92	3	2	2.33	7	7	0	0	39	33	14	10	2	10	46	.220	.300	.200	10.71	2.33
Hald, Kyle	L-L	6-0	190	11-23-87	11	4	3.81	24	23	0	0	137	142	64	58	18	45	105	.266	.191	.282	6.90	2.96
Harris, Mitch	R-R	6-4	215	11-7-85	2	0	3.92	33	0	0	1	44	38	19	19	5	13	34	.230	.258	.212	7.01	2.68
Heyer, Kurt	L-R	6-2	185	1-23-91	5	11	4.63	25	25	0	0	140	144	83	72	18	38	103	.264	.270	.259	6.62	2.44
Kiekhefer, Dean	L-L	6-0	175	6-7-89	0	2	4.30	15	0	0	7	15	18	10	7	2	1	10	.300	.235	.326	6.14	0.61
Llorens, Dixon	R-R	5-10	170	11-18-92	0	0	12.46	5	0	0	0	4	5	6	6	0	8	6	.333	.333	.333	12.46	14.54
Lyons, Tyler	B-L	6-4	200	2-21-88	0	0	4.50	1	1	0	0	2	3	1	1	0	0	3	.333	1.000	.250	13.50	0.00
Mayers, Mike	R-R	6-4	185	12-6-91	6	5	2.83	13	13	0	0	76	81	29	24	2	23	52	.277	.281	.275	6.13	2.71
Miranda, Danny	L-L	6-0	185	8-25-90	0	0	5.25	11	0	0	0	12	9	7	7	1	5	7	.214	.231	.207	5.25	3.75
Motte, Jason	R-R	6-0	205	6-22-82	0	0	0.00	5	0	0	0	5	1	0	0	0	1	5	.067	.000	.083	5.79	1.93
Nazario, Iden	L-L	6-0	190	3-28-89	0	0	2.25	3	0	0	0	4	2	1	1	0	1	5	.167	.500	.000	11.25	2.25
Petree, Nick	R-R	6-1	195	7-16-90	0	0	9.64	1	1	0	0	5	10	7	5	0	1	2	.455	.429	.467	3.86	1.93
Petrick, Zach	R-R	6-3	195	7-29-89	2	0	0.48	3	3	0	0	19	4	1	1	0	5	15	.129	.194	.077	7.23	2.41
Reed, Jimmy	L-L	5-11	185	12-18-90	1	1	4.91	2	2	0	0	11	10	6	6	1	2	6	.244	.000	.286	4.91	1.64
Shaban, Ronnie	L-R	6-1	195	3-8-90	0	2	7.66	24	0	0	2	25	37	22	21	4	8	19	.356	.405	.323	6.93	2.92
Sherriff, Ryan	L-L	6-1	185	5-25-90	2	7	2.64	40	3	0	2	65	63	21	19	3	19	48	.266	.206	.290	6.68	2.64
Siegrist, Kevin	L-L	6-5	215	7-20-89	0	0	0.00	5	0	0	0	5	0	0	0	0	3	5	.222	.200	.231	5.79	5.79

	B-T	HT	WT	DOB	W	L	ERA	G	GS	CG	SV	IP	H	R	ER	HR	BB	SO	AVG	vLH	vRH	K/9	BB/9
Stoppelman, Lee	L-L	6-2	210	5-24-90	1	2	5.00	37	0	0	4	36	36	23	20	3	15	45	.259	.255	.261	11.25	3.75
Thomas, Chris	R-R	6-2	200	3-16-88	1	1	1.63	19	0	0	0	28	18	6	5	1	6	24	.186	.194	.182	7.81	1.95
Tuivailala, Sam	R-R	6-3	195	10-19-92	2	1	2.57	17	0	0	1	21	18	8	6	0	9	30	.234	.276	.208	12.86	3.86
Wacha, Michael	R-R	6-6	210	7-1-91	0	0	0.00	1	1	0	0	2	1	0	0	0	1	1	.143	.000	.333	4.50	4.50
Wright, Justin	L-L	5-9	175	8-18-89	2	1	1.50	31	0	0	9	36	24	6	6	1	11	35	.194	.146	.217	8.75	2.75

Fielding

Catcher	PCT	G	PO	A	E	DP	PB
Cruz	1.000	2	2	1	0	0	0
Molina	1.000	2	9	0	0	0	0
Stanley	.992	76	551	63	5	5	3
Tartamella	.992	65	451	55	4	7	3
Velazco	1.000	1	7	1	0	0	0

First Base	PCT	G	PO	A	E	DP
Rodriguez	.993	94	817	51	6	78
Smith	.991	48	401	18	4	41

Second Base	PCT	G	PO	A	E	DP
Garcia	.500	1	0	1	1	0
Mateo	.966	7	12	16	1	5
Miclat	.980	37	62	88	3	25
Smith	1.000	2	2	6	0	0

	PCT	G	PO	A	E	DP
Valera	.976	58	93	146	6	34
Williams	.983	12	23	34	1	13
Wilson	.976	31	51	72	3	16

Third Base	PCT	G	PO	A	E	DP
Garcia	1.000	1	0	3	0	1
Smith	.667	3	1	3	2	0
Williams	.917	15	5	17	2	1
Wilson	1.000	5	2	8	0	1
Wisdom	.928	125	77	259	26	21

Shortstop	PCT	G	PO	A	E	DP
Diaz	.938	17	29	31	4	11
Garcia	1.000	2	5	6	0	1
Mateo	.987	15	17	57	1	15
Mejia	.941	47	62	115	11	20

	PCT	G	PO	A	E	DP
Miclat	.935	11	16	27	3	7
Williams	.967	56	74	157	8	29

Outfield	PCT	G	PO	A	E	DP
Martini	1.000	6	10	0	0	0
Miclat	—	1	0	0	0	0
O'Neill	.981	85	154	4	3	1
Ortega	.980	98	223	16	5	4
Popkins	.974	81	146	3	4	0
Ramsey	1.000	63	148	5	0	1
Rodriguez	.972	30	66	3	2	1
Smith	1.000	14	15	2	0	1
Swauger	1.000	9	12	1	0	0
Tilson	.972	31	69	1	2	0
Vargas	1.000	6	5	1	0	0
Williams	.903	16	25	3	3	0

PALM BEACH CARDINALS

HIGH CLASS A

FLORIDA STATE LEAGUE

Batting	B-T	HT	WT	DOB	AVG	vLH	vRH	G	AB	R	H	2B	3B	HR	RBI	BB	HBP	SH	SF	SO	SB	CS	SLG	OBP
Acevedo, Johan	R-R	6-1	173	3-28-93	.263	.286	.250	6	19	1	5	1	0	0	2	1	0	0	0	5	0	0	.316	.300
Bosco, Jimmy	L-R	5-10	170	5-21-91	.260	.167	.274	39	131	19	34	9	2	2	18	7	1	0	2	30	3	0	.405	.298
Caldwell, Bruce	L-R	5-11	175	11-27-91	.247	.173	.273	101	369	52	91	19	7	12	51	31	4	7	4	109	3	0	.434	.309
Diaz, Aledmys	R-R	6-1	195	8-1-90	.227	.333	.200	13	44	5	10	2	0	2	6	7	2	0	1	10	1	0	.409	.352
Ehrlich, Adam	L-R	6-1	205	12-13-92	.227	.000	.278	7	22	3	5	0	0	0	1	1	0	0	0	4	0	0	.227	.261
Garcia, Anthony	R-R	6-0	180	1-4-92	.227	.253	.219	100	343	56	78	20	2	10	44	38	9	0	1	64	3	4	.385	.320
Garcia, Ronnierd	R-R	6-2	175	1-1-93	.000	—	.000	2	3	0	0	0	0	0	0	1	0	0	0	1	0	0	.000	.250
Gibson, Derek	L-R	6-2	220	2-25-91	.625	—	.625	2	8	3	5	2	0	1	3	2	1	0	0	0	0	0	1.250	.727
Godoy, Jose	L-R	5-11	180	10-13-94	.000	.000	.000	2	4	0	0	0	0	0	0	0	0	0	0	1	0	0	.000	.000
Herrera, Juan	R-R	5-11	165	6-28-93	.194	.000	.222	10	31	3	6	0	0	0	1	0	0	0	0	5	1	0	.194	.219
Katz, Mason	R-R	5-10	188	8-23-90	.276	.302	.267	49	163	21	45	7	1	6	28	16	1	1	2	36	3	0	.442	.341
Lopez, Joshua	R-R	5-10	188	3-4-96	.000	—	.000	1	3	0	0	0	0	0	0	0	0	0	0	1	0	0	.000	.000
Martini, Nick	L-L	5-11	205	10-29-90	.256	.213	.270	115	438	59	112	25	5	7	59	44	9	2	3	71	5	5	.384	.334
Mejia, Alex	R-R	6-1	200	1-18-91	.284	.303	.276	71	275	30	78	13	1	1	29	9	1	7	2	41	4	2	.349	.307
Miclat, Greg	B-R	5-8	180	7-23-87	.284	.231	.309	22	81	9	23	4	2	1	8	9	1	0	0	12	4	0	.420	.363
Montero, Jesus	R-R	5-10	220	6-21-91	.212	.182	.227	28	99	14	21	1	0	0	6	8	2	1	1	29	1	1	.222	.282
Perez, Luis	R-R	5-10	165	7-24-91	.225	.214	.250	13	40	4	9	2	0	0	3	3	0	3	0	8	0	0	.275	.279
Popkins, David	L-R	6-3	215	11-16-89	.242	.265	.230	25	95	13	23	4	2	2	10	4	2	1	0	20	0	1	.389	.287
Ramos, Steve	R-R	6-0	160	7-4-90	.118	.286	.000	5	17	1	2	0	0	0	1	1	1	0	0	3	0	1	.118	.211
Rasmus, Casey	L-R	5-10	175	3-29-90	.235	.154	.268	38	136	12	32	5	1	0	14	7	2	2	4	26	5	1	.287	.275
Rodriguez, Starlin	B-R	5-10	170	12-31-89	.269	.320	.248	46	175	30	47	11	2	5	24	18	3	0	3	37	2	2	.440	.342
Rosenberg, Dante	R-R	5-11	180	7-7-93	.179	.235	.157	38	117	11	21	3	0	1	6	1	4	4	0	32	0	1	.231	.213
Tilson, Charlie	L-L	5-11	175	12-2-92	.308	.268	.319	89	370	54	114	8	8	5	36	24	4	4	0	76	10	7	.414	.357
Valera, Breyvic	B-R	5-11	160	1-8-92	.333	.300	.346	73	294	35	98	8	4	0	37	25	1	1	2	13	13	10	.388	.385
Valera, Cesar	R-R	6-1	180	3-8-92	.289	.348	.264	24	76	7	22	1	0	0	4	1	1	2	1	9	1	1	.303	.304
Vargas, Ildemaro	R-R	6-0	170	7-16-91	.241	.256	.235	112	431	46	104	17	1	1	40	16	4	20	6	51	1	4	.292	.271
Velazco, Gerwuins	R-R	6-1	190	10-7-91	.281	.318	.270	33	96	13	27	6	1	1	16	15	1	1	0	15	0	0	.396	.384
Voit, Luke	R-R	6-3	225	2-13-91	.276	.281	.275	93	351	57	97	21	5	9	51	32	4	1	2	79	1	1	.442	.342
Washington, David	L-L	6-5	230	11-20-90	.232	.187	.246	89	319	42	74	16	2	15	52	34	3	0	4	106	2	2	.436	.308
Williams, Matt	R-R	6-0	170	8-29-89	.250	.400	.211	7	24	5	6	0	1	1	4	3	2	0	0	7	0	0	.458	.359
Wilson, Jacob	R-R	5-11	180	7-29-90	.298	.214	.323	30	121	18	36	12	0	0	20	12	1	1	3	24	0	0	.397	.358

Pitching	B-T	HT	WT	DOB	W	L	ERA	G	GS	CG	SV	IP	H	R	ER	HR	BB	SO	AVG	vLH	vRH	K/9	BB/9
Alexander, Kevin	R-R	6-1	170	5-4-91	0	1	27.00	1	0	0	0	1	3	4	3	0	2	0	.429	.400	.500	0.00	18.00
Anderson, Will	R-R	6-3	205	8-26-92	0	0	0.00	1	0	0	1	3	4	1	0	0	0	4	.364	.500	.000	12.00	0.00
Baker, Corey	R-R	6-1	170	11-23-89	5	2	2.33	30	4	0	2	77	61	21	20	3	14	57	.214	.153	.277	6.63	1.63
Barraclough, Kyle	R-R	6-3	225	5-23-90	1	1	5.30	16	0	0	1	19	28	13	11	0	11	18	.354	.439	.263	8.68	5.30
Billbrough, Logan	R-R	6-5	225	8-4-89	1	0	2.66	17	0	0	1	24	21	7	7	0	10	31	.239	.324	.176	11.79	3.80
Cuda, Joey	R-R	5-9	195	9-13-89	8	8	5.70	19	19	0	0	101	130	68	64	4	27	75	.313	.329	.302	6.68	2.41
Garcia, Silfredo	R-R	6-2	170	7-19-91	7	4	3.68	17	17	1	0	93	94	41	38	7	27	67	.261	.288	.235	6.48	2.61
Gast, John	L-L	6-1	195	2-16-89	0	0	1.80	1	1	0	0	5	5	1	1	0	2	1	.263	.375	.182	1.80	3.60
Gonzales, Marco	L-L	6-1	195	2-16-92	2	2	1.43	6	6	0	0	38	34	8	6	1	8	32	.239	.262	.230	7.65	1.91
Hald, Kyle	L-L	6-0	190	5-27-89	2	0	2.13	2	2	0	0	13	11	4	3	1	2	9	.224	.214	.229	6.39	1.42
Harris, Mitch	R-R	6-4	215	11-7-85	0	2	4.26	8	0	0	0	13	8	6	6	1	6	9	.178	.176	.179	6.39	4.26
Helisek, Kyle	L-L	6-0	170	4-23-90	5	6	3.80	18	18	0	0	97	90	51	41	11	34	56	.247	.187	.278	5.20	3.15
Herget, Kevin	R-R	5-10	185	4-3-91	2	0	2.00	7	0	0	2	9	8	3	2	0	2	9	.235	.083	.318	9.00	2.00
Jenkins, Tyrell	R-R	6-4	204	7-20-92	6	5	3.28	13	13	0	0	74	74	32	27	6	23	41	.264	.174	.322	4.99	2.80
Jones, Cory	R-R	6-5	225	9-20-91	1	0	7.00	5	5	0	0	18	18	14	14	2	15	13	.261	.222	.303	6.50	7.50

ST. LOUIS CARDINALS

Name	B-T	HT	WT	DOB	W	L	ERA	G	GS	CG	SV	IP	H	R	ER	HR	BB	SO	AVG	vLH	vRH	K/9	BB/9
Lee, Thomas	R-R	6-1	190	10-20-89	8	3	3.34	28	9	0	0	94	112	42	35	7	6	52	.291	.308	.277	4.96	0.57
Littrell, Corey	L-L	6-3	185	3-21-92	0	2	4.55	5	5	0	0	32	45	25	16	4	10	19	.352	.400	.337	5.40	2.84
Llorens, Dixon	R-R	5-10	170	11-18-92	0	1	2.06	33	0	0	9	44	22	12	10	1	27	74	.150	.140	.156	15.25	5.56
Lucas, Aiden	R-R	6-2	225	4-21-88	1	2	3.90	18	0	0	0	32	32	15	14	0	10	19	.269	.229	.296	5.29	2.78
Lucas, Josh	R-R	6-6	185	11-5-90	0	0	1.80	4	0	0	0	5	3	1	1	0	2	5	.167	.125	.200	9.00	3.60
Mayers, Mike	R-R	6-4	185	12-6-91	2	7	3.72	12	12	1	0	73	84	35	30	5	13	61	.294	.319	.270	7.56	1.61
Miranda, Danny	L-L	6-0	225	8-25-90	4	2	4.24	23	0	0	3	34	40	16	16	0	3	25	.294	.224	.333	6.62	0.79
Morales, Andrew	R-R	6-0	185	1-16-93	1	0	1.23	2	0	0	0	7	2	1	1	0	0	6	.083	.111	.067	7.36	0.00
Nazario, Iden	L-L	6-0	190	3-28-89	5	1	2.72	39	0	0	4	56	46	18	17	4	24	56	.227	.244	.215	8.95	3.83
Perdomo, Luis	R-R	6-2	160	5-9-93	0	0	0.00	1	0	0	0	3	2	0	0	0	0	3	.200	.143	.333	9.00	0.00
Perry, Chris	L-R	6-2	215	7-15-90	1	1	1.93	13	0	0	5	14	6	3	3	1	6	18	.122	.190	.071	11.57	3.86
Petree, Nick	R-R	6-1	195	7-16-90	6	5	2.44	17	17	0	0	103	98	32	28	5	22	80	.250	.230	.266	6.97	1.92
Reed, Jimmy	L-L	5-11	185	12-18-90	6	2	3.58	9	9	1	0	55	63	22	22	3	7	35	.288	.295	.284	5.69	1.14
Sabatino, Steve	L-L	6-2	190	3-8-90	0	0	0.00	4	0	0	0	4	3	0	0	0	0	1	.231	.000	.300	2.45	0.00
Shaban, Ronnie	L-R	6-1	195	3-8-90	0	1	5.40	15	0	0	3	15	20	10	9	1	4	18	.323	.409	.275	10.80	2.40
Stock, Robert	L-R	6-1	200	11-21-89	0	0	2.31	11	0	0	1	23	15	8	6	0	25	13	.188	.094	.250	5.01	9.64
Thomas, Chris	R-R	6-2	200	3-16-88	1	1	1.86	9	0	0	3	10	6	2	2	0	2	14	.182	.286	.105	13.03	1.86
Tuivailala, Sam	R-R	6-3	195	10-19-92	0	1	3.58	29	0	0	3	38	29	16	15	1	18	64	.207	.224	.195	15.29	4.30
Weaver, Luke	R-R	6-2	170	8-21-93	0	1	21.60	2	2	0	0	3	11	8	8	1	4	3	.550	.571	.538	8.10	10.80

Fielding

Catcher	PCT	G	PO	A	E	DP	PB
Ehrlich	.981	7	47	4	1	0	2
Godoy	1.000	2	15	3	0	2	0
Lopez	1.000	1	6	1	0	0	1
Montero	.991	28	198	21	2	1	6
Rasmus	.990	37	263	28	3	1	5
Rosenberg	.986	38	249	30	4	3	0
Velazco	.992	33	216	22	2	3	3

First Base	PCT	G	PO	A	E	DP
Katz	1.000	2	15	2	0	1
Valera	1.000	1	6	1	0	0
Vargas	.981	6	46	5	1	3
Voit	.981	82	688	45	14	74
Washington	.984	53	447	39	8	58

Second Base	PCT	G	PO	A	E	DP
Caldwell	.987	30	66	86	2	23
Katz	.976	39	85	116	5	33

Miclat	.917	2	4	7	1	2
Rodriguez	1.000	1	0	1	0	0
Valera	.972	52	110	166	8	53
Vargas	.929	7	13	13	2	4
Wilson	.984	12	17	43	1	8

Third Base	PCT	G	PO	A	E	DP
Caldwell	.908	39	30	79	11	13
Valera	.970	10	11	21	1	4
Valera	1.000	4	2	7	0	2
Vargas	.953	77	51	131	9	17
Voit	—	1	0	0	0	0
Wilson	.929	15	10	29	3	6

Shortstop	PCT	G	PO	A	E	DP
Herrera	.936	9	12	32	3	6
Mejia	.964	67	108	216	12	53
Miclat	.963	19	24	55	3	4
Valera	.800	1	1	3	1	0

Valera	.950	20	19	57	4	15
Vargas	.980	21	29	67	2	10
Williams	.917	6	8	14	2	1

Outfield	PCT	G	PO	A	E	DP
Acevedo	.923	4	12	0	1	0
Bosco	.978	30	42	3	1	1
Garcia	.993	80	137	5	1	0
Gibson	1.000	2	1	1	0	1
Martini	.973	113	276	15	8	5
Perez	1.000	13	14	0	0	0
Popkins	1.000	25	49	1	0	1
Ramos	1.000	5	7	0	0	0
Rasmus	1.000	1	3	0	0	0
Rodriguez	.973	36	66	5	2	3
Tilson	.983	83	174	4	3	2
Valera	1.000	3	6	0	0	0
Vargas	1.000	8	7	1	0	1
Washington	.925	28	46	3	4	0

PEORIA CHIEFS   LOW CLASS A
MIDWEST LEAGUE

Batting	B-T	HT	WT	DOB	AVG	vLH	vRH	G	AB	R	H	2B	3B	HR	RBI	BB	HBP	SH	SF	SO	SB	CS	SLG	OBP
Bean, Steve	L-R	6-2	190	9-15-93	.235	.206	.239	78	260	25	61	12	0	2	30	36	1	2	4	67	0	0	.304	.326
Bosco, Jimmy	L-R	5-10	170	5-21-91	.237	.111	.248	34	114	18	27	6	1	1	6	9	1	1	1	21	4	1	.333	.296
Bryan, Vaugn	R-R	6-0	185	6-5-93	.262	.191	.274	83	317	47	83	17	9	1	15	27	3	3	0	73	11	7	.382	.326
Castillo, Ronard	R-R	6-5	200	6-16-92	.259	.311	.245	92	347	40	90	24	1	6	50	23	2	0	3	75	1	1	.386	.307
Garcia, Ronnierd	R-R	6-2	175	1-1-93	.191	.250	.171	14	47	2	9	3	0	0	1	0	0	0	0	4	0	0	.255	.208
Herrera, Juan	R-R	5-11	165	6-28-93	.274	.247	.282	101	379	50	104	22	3	2	56	24	4	4	5	57	27	13	.364	.320
Katz, Mason	R-R	5-10	188	8-23-90	.212	.304	.191	75	250	36	53	11	1	14	43	29	6	1	1	63	1	1	.432	.308
Kelly, Carson	R-R	6-2	200	7-14-94	.248	.237	.251	98	363	41	90	17	4	6	49	37	7	4	4	54	1	0	.366	.326
McElroy Jr., C.J.	R-R	5-10	180	5-29-93	.267	.323	.254	130	490	74	131	11	2	0	29	40	16	12	0	84	41	18	.298	.342
Medina, Rafael	R-R	6-2	170	10-24-91	.200	.143	.222	34	100	7	20	3	0	2	9	6	3	3	1	13	0	1	.290	.264
Pedroza, Richy	B-R	5-6	150	7-21-91	.239	.269	.232	85	255	28	61	13	6	1	27	28	4	4	5	27	1	3	.349	.318
Peoples-Walls, Kenny	R-R	6-1	180	8-16-93	.234	.280	.224	81	291	27	68	10	0	3	28	5	4	1	3	73	7	6	.299	.254
Perez, Luis	R-R	5-10	165	7-24-91	.286	.333	.267	35	119	11	34	7	2	5	20	5	0	1	1	35	1	1	.504	.312
Reyes, Robelys	B-R	5-9	150	7-25-90	.182	.500	.150	9	22	4	4	0	0	0	2	1	0	0	0	4	2	1	.182	.217
Ringo, Justin	L-R	6-0	195	12-24-90	.294	.180	.325	78	289	46	85	15	0	9	46	27	6	0	1	47	4	1	.439	.365
Schulze, Michael	L-R	6-1	195	5-13-91	.234	.288	.221	105	321	40	75	12	1	0	26	33	1	7	2	46	3	5	.277	.305
Stone, Jake	L-R	6-0	220	10-22-90	.136	.048	.159	34	103	11	14	5	0	0	8	21	2	0	0	24	1	2	.184	.294
Valera, Cesar	R-R	6-1	180	3-8-92	.232	.243	.229	54	190	17	44	7	3	0	16	13	5	1	1	43	4	4	.300	.297
Velazco, Gerwuins	R-R	6-1	190	10-7-91	.409	.400	.412	6	22	2	9	2	0	1	2	1	0	1	0	6	0	0	.636	.435
Wick, Rowan	L-R	6-3	220	11-9-92	.220	.185	.228	39	141	21	31	8	2	6	22	13	3	0	0	60	4	0	.433	.299
Young, Matt	R-R	6-3	230	8-17-90	.169	.182	.163	21	71	8	12	1	1	3	10	12	1	0	0	25	2	3	.338	.298

Pitching	B-T	HT	WT	DOB	W	L	ERA	G	GS	CG	SV	IP	H	R	ER	HR	BB	SO	AVG	vLH	vRH	K/9	BB/9
Barraclough, Kyle	R-R	6-3	225	5-23-90	1	1	1.13	32	0	0	10	40	21	9	5	0	23	60	.152	.203	.114	13.50	5.18
Booden, Jacob	R-R	6-7	235	8-14-90	0	2	2.70	5	0	0	0	7	4	3	2	0	5	6	.167	.167	.167	8.10	6.75
Bray, Tyler	R-R	6-5	200	10-3-91	1	1	4.82	6	0	0	0	9	6	5	5	1	4	10	.188	.182	.190	9.64	3.86
Brookshire, Chase	R-L	6-0	190	3-7-91	4	7	3.96	29	18	0	0	109	123	60	48	7	23	82	.281	.345	.252	6.77	1.90
Garcia, Silfredo	R-R	6-2	170	7-19-91	2	3	4.25	6	6	0	0	30	38	22	14	1	11	21	.297	.385	.237	6.37	3.34
Helisek, Kyle	L-L	6-0	170	4-23-90	2	1	5.84	7	5	0	0	25	31	19	16	3	14	11	.307	.227	.329	4.01	5.11
Herget, Kevin	R-R	5-10	185	4-3-91	6	3	2.81	35	1	0	2	67	59	29	21	6	27	85	.234	.200	.259	11.36	3.61
Holback, Michael	R-R	6-1	195	9-15-92	0	1	4.15	3	3	0	0	13	10	6	6	1	5	13	.222	.400	.133	9.00	3.46

	B-T	HT	WT	DOB	W	L	ERA	G	GS	CG	SV	IP	H	R	ER	HR	BB	SO	AVG	vLH	vRH	K/9	BB/9
Kaminsky, Rob	R-L	5-11	191	9-2-94	8	2	1.88	18	18	0	0	101	71	27	21	2	31	79	.194	.186	.196	7.06	2.77
Lee, Brandon	R-R	6-0	200	11-18-90	1	2	6.33	15	0	0	1	21	28	16	15	2	9	16	.326	.393	.293	6.75	3.80
Loraine, Zach	R-R	6-3	205	8-8-90	2	1	3.09	39	0	0	10	58	61	21	20	6	16	58	.268	.345	.222	8.95	2.47
Lucas, Josh	R-R	6-6	185	11-5-90	1	1	6.23	8	0	0	2	9	14	7	6	0	0	13	.359	.462	.308	13.50	0.00
McKnight, Blake	R-R	6-1	182	2-13-91	5	10	5.17	30	17	0	0	111	129	75	64	6	36	56	.296	.309	.286	4.53	2.91
Perdomo, Luis	R-R	6-2	160	5-9-93	3	6	5.05	11	11	0	0	57	64	44	32	4	21	41	.276	.258	.289	6.47	3.32
Perry, Chris	L-R	6-2	215	7-15-90	4	0	2.20	28	0	0	3	49	29	15	12	4	15	80	.165	.138	.180	14.69	2.76
Petree, Nick	R-R	6-1	195	7-16-90	2	0	1.29	4	4	0	0	21	15	3	3	2	10	24	.200	.263	.179	10.29	4.29
Polanco, Jhonny	R-R	6-3	195	4-28-92	1	2	1.04	37	0	0	0	57	35	15	13	0	30	71	.176	.169	.180	11.15	4.71
Rauh, Jeff	R-R	6-2	200	1-24-90	0	1	23.14	2	0	0	0	2	4	6	6	0	2	2	.333	—	.333	7.71	7.71
Reed, Jimmy	L-L	5-11	185	12-18-90	3	3	3.88	13	13	0	0	72	77	32	31	6	18	62	.268	.280	.263	7.75	2.25
Reyes, Alex	R-R	6-3	185	8-29-94	7	7	3.62	21	21	1	0	109	82	54	44	6	61	137	.207	.186	.224	11.28	5.02
Reyes, Artie	R-R	5-11	185	4-6-92	6	8	3.67	23	22	0	0	123	123	55	50	8	34	104	.258	.268	.252	7.63	2.49
Sabatino, Steve	L-L	6-2	190	3-8-90	5	2	1.94	31	0	0	4	42	29	17	9	1	11	47	.195	.133	.221	10.15	2.38
Scanio, Joe	R-R	6-4	230	1-30-90	2	1	3.86	6	0	0	1	9	8	4	4	0	3	8	.250	.231	.263	7.71	2.89
Stock, Robert	L-R	6-1	200	11-21-89	4	1	5.18	24	0	0	0	40	42	23	23	1	21	30	.278	.311	.256	6.75	4.73
Thomas, Chris	R-R	6-2	200	3-16-88	1	0	1.02	16	0	0	6	18	13	3	2	1	5	26	.197	.143	.222	13.25	2.55

Fielding

Catcher	PCT	G	PO	A	E	DP	PB
Bean	.983	60	524	46	10	6	7
Kelly	.987	79	624	73	9	10	13

First Base	PCT	G	PO	A	E	DP
Garcia	.913	3	21	0	2	1
Katz	.992	27	217	19	2	17
Medina	1.000	5	36	6	0	1
Ringo	.993	71	559	45	4	40
Stone	.993	34	256	9	2	22
Velazco	1.000	3	23	1	0	3

Second Base	PCT	G	PO	A	E	DP
Katz	.959	49	84	128	9	25
Pedroza	.974	51	100	129	6	28

	PCT	G	PO	A	E	DP
Perez	.933	6	8	6	1	0
Reyes	.929	6	5	8	1	0
Schulze	.953	24	37	44	4	7
Valera	.978	12	17	27	1	3

Third Base	PCT	G	PO	A	E	DP
Garcia	.852	10	12	11	4	0
Medina	.914	27	18	46	6	1
Pedroza	1.000	1	1	1	0	0
Schulze	.898	80	44	123	19	13
Valera	.955	25	19	45	3	4

Shortstop	PCT	G	PO	A	E	DP
Herrera	.927	92	107	221	26	37
Pedroza	.944	33	40	79	7	11

	PCT	G	PO	A	E	DP
Reyes	1.000	1	2	1	0	0
Valera	.931	18	30	51	6	13

Outfield	PCT	G	PO	A	E	DP
Bosco	1.000	26	28	2	0	0
Bryan	.965	74	132	4	5	0
Castillo	.906	63	95	1	10	1
McElroy Jr.	.986	122	279	3	4	1
Peoples-Walls	.971	69	93	6	3	0
Perez	.977	21	40	3	1	1
Schulze	—	1	0	0	0	0
Wick	.894	35	51	8	7	2
Young	1.000	12	30	0	0	0

STATE COLLEGE SPIKES — SHORT-SEASON

NEW YORK-PENN LEAGUE

Batting	B-T	HT	WT	DOB	AVG	vLH	vRH	G	AB	R	H	2B	3B	HR	RBI	BB	HBP	SH	SF	SO	SB	CS	SLG	OBP
Acevedo, Johan	R-R	6-1	173	3-28-93	.256	.143	.280	56	199	25	51	7	1	1	21	12	4	0	0	38	11	4	.317	.312
Cruz, Luis	R-R	6-2	180	5-26-93	.290	.333	.279	31	107	13	31	4	0	2	15	4	2	0	0	15	0	0	.383	.327
DeLeon, Alex	R-R	6-1	215	2-9-91	.268	.314	.255	64	239	43	64	17	1	9	29	27	3	0	2	49	2	1	.460	.347
Diekroeger, Danny	L-R	6-2	205	5-25-92	.286	.200	.302	62	262	41	75	13	4	5	35	16	4	0	5	34	2	2	.424	.331
Ehrlich, Adam	L-R	6-1	205	12-13-92	.169	.111	.179	18	65	8	11	5	0	0	4	9	1	0	0	10	0	0	.246	.280
Garcia, Ronnierd	R-R	6-2	175	1-1-93	.230	.154	.262	27	87	8	20	7	0	1	12	10	2	0	3	22	0	3	.345	.314
Medina, Rafael	R-R	6-2	170	10-24-91	.000	—	.000	1	3	0	0	0	0	0	0	0	0	0	0	1	0	0	.000	.000
O'Keefe, Brian	R-R	6-0	210	7-15-93	.239	.323	.218	47	155	23	37	8	0	3	17	16	15	1	0	23	2	0	.348	.366
Peoples-Walls, Kenny	R-R	6-1	180	8-16-93	.224	.273	.213	20	58	9	13	5	0	0	1	2	0	0	1	17	1	0	.310	.262
Pina, Leobaldo	R-R	6-2	160	6-29-94	.170	.286	.150	12	47	9	8	2	0	0	2	4	0	0	0	9	0	0	.213	.235
Radack, Collin	R-R	6-3	205	3-30-92	.287	.394	.252	39	136	11	39	7	1	2	23	4	6	0	0	24	1	1	.397	.336
Raffield, Chase	L-R	6-0	185	8-27-91	.199	.231	.192	47	146	19	29	7	1	4	22	17	0	1	1	31	2	0	.342	.280
Reyes, Robelys	B-R	5-9	150	7-25-93	.284	.302	.279	60	250	36	71	11	3	3	31	14	4	5	3	27	16	9	.388	.328
Rivera, Chris	R-R	5-11	150	3-10-95	.250	—	.250	2	8	1	2	0	0	0	0	0	0	0	0	1	0	0	.250	.250
Seferina, Darren	R-R	5-9	175	1-24-94	.294	.289	.295	51	194	28	57	8	3	0	9	21	0	1	3	48	20	5	.366	.358
Sohn, Andrew	R-R	5-11	185	5-8-93	.324	.400	.313	11	37	7	12	1	1	1	4	1	4	1	0	4	0	2	.486	.405
Sosa, Edmundo	R-R	5-11	170	3-6-96	.200	—	.200	3	5	1	1	0	0	0	0	0	0	0	0	2	0	0	.200	.200
Stone, Jake	L-R	6-0	220	10-22-90	.256	.294	.248	56	199	32	51	8	1	5	40	31	1	0	3	51	0	1	.382	.355
Thompson, Nick	R-R	6-1	210	11-13-92	.282	.333	.271	65	227	47	64	12	1	5	42	39	4	0	0	36	4	1	.410	.396
Vigo-Suarez, Brian	R-R	5-11	150	11-1-93	.667	—	.667	1	3	1	2	0	0	0	1	0	0	0	0	0	0	0	.667	.750
Wick, Rowan	L-R	6-3	220	11-9-92	.378	.462	.355	35	119	30	45	8	1	14	38	20	2	0	0	34	1	1	.815	.475
Wiley, Brett	L-R	5-10	175	11-24-91	.301	.350	.283	19	73	7	22	8	1	0	12	5	0	0	1	18	1	0	.438	.342

Pitching	B-T	HT	WT	DOB	W	L	ERA	G	GS	CG	SV	IP	H	R	ER	HR	BB	SO	AVG	vLH	vRH	K/9	BB/9
Alexander, Kevin	R-R	6-1	170	5-4-91	0	0	0.00	1	0	0	0	1	0	0	0	0	0	3	.000	—	.000	27.00	0.00
Anderson, Will	R-R	6-3	205	8-26-92	6	2	2.43	12	12	0	0	70	72	28	19	1	11	59	.261	.306	.218	7.55	1.41
Baez, Fernando	R-R	6-1	190	2-1-92	2	2	3.94	13	9	0	0	46	32	21	20	2	28	48	.201	.141	.250	9.46	5.52
Barkley, Jeff	R-R	6-5	210	7-7-90	1	0	8.36	7	0	0	1	14	18	13	13	3	7	6	.321	.294	.333	3.86	4.50
Booden, Jacob	R-R	6-7	235	8-14-90	1	2	3.45	21	0	0	1	31	20	17	12	1	17	37	.174	.158	.190	10.63	4.88
Bray, Tyler	R-R	6-5	200	10-3-91	1	2	2.96	17	0	0	0	27	18	10	9	1	14	34	.189	.268	.130	11.20	4.61
Dunnington, Tyler	R-R	6-2	195	2-25-92	1	0	0.00	1	0	0	0	3	2	0	0	0	1	3	.182	.333	.125	9.00	3.00
Farinaro, Steven	R-R	6-0	170	8-18-95	0	0	3.60	1	1	0	0	5	4	2	2	0	0	2	.211	.286	.167	3.60	0.00
Gerdel, Anderson	R-R	6-4	204	3-22-93	2	0	5.00	3	0	0	1	9	12	5	5	1	2	9	.333	.444	.222	9.00	2.00
Gomber, Austin	L-L	6-5	205	11-23-93	2	2	2.30	11	11	0	0	47	55	17	12	3	18	36	.297	.419	.261	6.89	3.45
Grana, Kyle	R-R	6-4	245	4-26-91	3	2	0.89	27	0	0	8	41	25	7	4	0	14	62	.181	.281	.111	13.72	3.10
Hawkins, Dylan	L-L	6-2	215	6-26-93	0	0	0.00	1	0	0	0	1	0	0	0	0	1	1	.000	—	.000	9.00	9.00
Lee, Brandon	R-R	6-0	200	11-18-90	4	1	2.49	12	0	0	0	25	26	7	7	1	2	26	.263	.288	.234	9.24	0.71
Lomascolo, Nick	R-L	6-1	200	11-5-90	1	1	2.77	27	0	0	1	39	27	14	12	1	16	44	.194	.266	.133	10.15	3.69

	B-T	HT	WT	DOB	W	L	ERA	G	GS	CG	SV	IP	H	R	ER	HR	BB	SO	AVG	vLH	vRH	K/9	BB/9
Lucas, Josh	R-R	6-6	185	11-5-90	2	2	0.31	19	0	0	5	29	16	7	1	0	8	32	.167	.216	.136	10.05	2.51
Martinez, Dailyn	R-R	6-2	170	4-19-93	1	0	1.80	1	1	0	0	5	3	2	1	0	2	1	.176	.250	.111	1.80	3.60
McKinney, Ian	L-L	5-11	185	11-18-94	1	1	6.17	2	2	0	0	12	11	8	8	0	2	9	.244	.357	.194	6.94	1.54
Nielsen, Trey	R-R	6-1	190	9-1-91	3	2	2.50	15	8	0	1	50	36	16	14	3	14	49	.201	.235	.170	8.76	2.50
Perdomo, Luis	R-R	6-2	160	5-9-93	1	0	1.50	2	2	0	0	12	11	3	2	1	1	13	.250	.357	.200	9.75	0.75
Perez, Dewin	L-L	6-0	175	9-29-94	6	2	3.68	13	13	0	0	64	62	28	26	0	26	46	.258	.375	.229	6.50	3.68
Poncedeleon, Daniel	R-R	6-4	190	1-16-92	3	3	2.44	12	10	0	0	44	38	13	12	0	14	52	.229	.176	.284	10.56	2.84
Rauh, Jeff	R-R	6-2	200	1-24-90	4	2	4.17	25	1	0	1	45	48	23	21	4	16	28	.281	.316	.253	5.56	3.18
Scanio, Joe	R-R	6-4	230	1-30-90	1	1	3.58	18	0	0	3	28	22	14	11	1	8	24	.214	.208	.220	7.81	2.60
Schumacher, Cody	R-R	6-1	190	12-1-90	1	0	3.58	6	6	0	0	28	22	14	11	4	6	18	.218	.212	.224	5.86	1.95
Villegas, Kender	R-R	6-2	170	6-8-93	0	0	0.00	1	0	0	0	2	3	0	0	0	0	2	.375	.333	.400	7.71	0.00

Fielding

Catcher	PCT	G	PO	A	E	DP	PB
Cruz	.992	30	203	32	2	5	7
Ehrlich	.958	4	22	1	1	0	1
O'Keefe	.985	45	408	38	7	4	14

First Base	PCT	G	PO	A	E	DP
DeLeon	.994	32	295	21	2	26
Garcia	1.000	2	21	0	0	3
Stone	.997	43	361	19	1	39

Second Base	PCT	G	PO	A	E	DP
Diekroeger	1.000	11	16	30	0	8
Reyes	.942	9	22	27	3	8

	PCT	G	PO	A	E	DP
Rivera	1.000	2	3	4	0	1
Seferina	.961	47	71	124	8	36
Wiley	.960	11	15	33	2	11

Third Base	PCT	G	PO	A	E	DP
Diekroeger	.875	49	39	73	16	9
Garcia	.931	25	14	40	4	6
Medina	1.000	1	0	2	0	1
Wiley	.889	5	2	6	1	1

Shortstop	PCT	G	PO	A	E	DP
Pina	.891	12	8	33	5	7
Reyes	.936	50	67	154	15	36

	PCT	G	PO	A	E	DP
Seferina	1.000	1	2	7	0	1
Sohn	.979	11	16	30	1	5
Sosa	.800	2	3	1	1	1
Wiley	1.000	2	4	1	0	2

Outfield	PCT	G	PO	A	E	DP
Acevedo	.966	55	114	1	4	0
Peoples-Walls	1.000	13	16	1	0	0
Radack	1.000	37	63	0	0	0
Raffield	.970	43	65	0	2	0
Thompson	.975	60	76	3	2	0
Vigo-Suarez	1.000	1	2	0	0	0
Wick	.975	33	72	5	2	2

JOHNSON CITY CARDINALS   ROOKIE

APPALACHIAN LEAGUE

Batting	B-T	HT	WT	DOB	AVG	vLH	vRH	G	AB	R	H	2B	3B	HR	RBI	BB	HBP	SH	SF	SO	SB	CS	SLG	OBP
Drake, Blake	R-R	6-1	175	7-11-93	.282	.357	.242	64	241	33	68	15	0	6	35	25	7	4	2	49	7	4	.419	.364
Ehrlich, Adam	L-R	6-1	205	12-13-92	.219	.125	.250	9	32	4	7	0	0	0	2	0	0	0	4	0	0		.219	.265
Franco, Bladimil	R-R	6-0	170	10-29-93	.250	.000	.333	6	20	6	5	0	0	0	1	3	0	0	0	4	1	1	.250	.348
Godoy, Jose	L-R	5-11	180	10-13-94	.331	.382	.310	36	118	15	39	4	0	1	18	18	1	0	0	11	0	0	.390	.423
Gomez, Jose	R-R	5-11	183	1-30-92	.200	.143	.238	12	35	5	7	1	0	0	2	4	0	0	0	4	1	0	.229	.282
Grayson, Casey	L-L	6-1	215	8-24-91	.283	.264	.292	64	226	32	64	17	1	5	46	36	2	0	5	35	3	0	.434	.379
Lacy, Devante	R-R	5-9	180	4-20-94	.186	.182	.188	40	113	19	21	3	0	0	9	12	2	1	0	40	1	1	.212	.276
Lankford, Cole	L-R	6-0	185	9-3-92	.257	.186	.286	57	206	28	53	7	3	5	27	11	5	0	1	56	1	2	.393	.309
Medina, Rafael	R-R	6-2	170	10-24-91	.500	—	.500	1	2	0	1	0	0	0	0	0	0	0	0	0	0	0	.500	.500
Mercado, Oscar	R-R	6-2	175	12-16-94	.224	.240	.218	60	245	41	55	9	1	3	25	20	8	0	1	37	26	7	.306	.303
Muscarello, Christian	R-R	5-10	170	6-16-92	.176	.182	.174	13	34	7	6	2	0	1	4	4	4	0	0	6	0	0	.324	.333
Neil, Charlie	B-R	6-5	195	2-1-90	.138	.130	.140	29	80	4	11	4	0	0	1	14	0	0	0	36	0	0	.188	.266
Ray, Anthony	L-R	6-1	165	3-3-95	.238	.286	.219	44	147	16	35	2	3	0	13	7	2	3	0	25	3	3	.293	.282
Rivera, Chris	R-R	5-11	150	3-10-95	.231	.181	.255	60	225	24	52	13	0	3	24	13	7	0	2	55	3	4	.329	.291
Torres, Carlos	R-R	6-3	160	10-1-92	.218	.186	.230	48	165	22	36	6	1	1	18	8	1	1	2	34	2	3	.285	.256
Turgeon, Casey	R-R	5-10	160	9-28-92	.306	.254	.331	62	222	52	68	13	3	4	26	42	6	1	1	33	7	4	.446	.428
Ustariz, Jesus	R-R	6-1	192	4-26-93	.242	.345	.191	49	165	17	40	8	0	3	18	14	1	0	2	36	0	0	.345	.302

Pitching	B-T	HT	WT	DOB	W	L	ERA	G	GS	CG	SV	IP	H	R	ER	HR	BB	SO	AVG	vLH	vRH	K/9	BB/9
Barkley, Jeff	R-R	6-5	210	7-7-90	0	0	10.47	11	0	0	0	16	37	20	19	1	7	7	.446	.455	.440	3.86	3.86
Beck, Landon	R-R	6-3	215	12-9-92	1	1	3.19	13	8	0	0	42	43	18	15	1	19	51	.259	.197	.295	10.84	4.04
Brito, Ismael	L-L	5-11	170	3-23-93	2	0	4.50	23	0	0	9	30	25	17	15	1	16	37	.225	.313	.211	11.10	4.80
Caballero, Juan	R-R	6-4	175	8-20-92	0	3	3.24	17	0	0	5	25	25	17	9	4	10	21	.248	.242	.250	7.56	3.60
Carlow, Kevin	L-R	6-2	190	8-21-90	3	3	6.00	23	0	0	0	33	39	27	22	4	10	42	.283	.348	.250	11.45	2.73
DeLorenzo, Jordan	L-L	6-1	205	9-8-92	0	3	5.30	6	3	0	0	19	30	17	11	4	5	20	.353	.217	.403	9.64	2.41
Escudero, Jhonatan	R-R	6-1	165	7-7-93	5	1	2.68	20	0	0	2	40	28	12	12	2	16	56	.190	.167	.204	12.50	3.57
Farinaro, Steven	R-R	6-0	170	8-18-95	3	4	4.31	11	11	0	0	48	61	34	23	5	12	30	.305	.338	.287	5.63	2.25
Gerdel, Anderson	R-R	6-4	204	3-22-93	4	0	1.50	19	0	0	5	30	26	8	5	0	5	32	.226	.233	.222	9.60	1.50
Kuebel, Sasha	R-L	6-1	200	7-28-92	1	1	4.22	10	2	0	0	21	26	11	10	1	4	19	.302	.338	.302		1.69
Martinez, Dailyn	R-R	6-2	170	4-19-93	6	3	4.55	11	11	0	0	57	67	37	29	3	20	41	.291	.353	.255	6.44	3.14
Mateo, Julio	R-R	6-3	180	9-29-95	1	1	3.62	6	6	0	0	27	29	17	11	4	5	14	.259	.185	.282	4.61	1.65
McKinney, Ian	L-L	5-11	185	11-18-94	1	0	1.26	6	0	0	0	36	27	5	5	0	7	31	.220	.250	.212	7.82	1.77
Pearce, Matt	R-R	6-3	205	2-24-94	2	4	4.20	10	10	0	0	45	54	25	21	2	9	34	.305	.366	.280	6.80	1.80
Perez, Juan	R-R	6-2	195	7-22-95	5	3	3.24	13	10	0	0	58	48	32	21	5	27	59	.225	.161	.270	9.10	4.17
Silva, Isaac	L-L	6-2	190	9-12-92	0	1	7.71	14	0	0	0	12	9	14	10	1	18	12	.220	.308	.179	9.26	13.89
Villegas, Kender	R-R	6-2	170	6-8-93	1	2	3.00	23	0	0	3	39	34	20	13	4	11	42	.236	.350	.155	9.69	2.54
Wirsu, Josh	R-R	6-0	190	9-4-93	1	1	6.23	5	1	0	0	9	10	9	6	0	8	7	.303	.333	.278	2.08	8.31

Fielding

Catcher	PCT	G	PO	A	E	DP	PB
Ehrlich	.960	9	64	8	3	0	2
Franco	1.000	1	1	0	0	0	0
Godoy	.980	32	259	36	6	1	7
Gomez	.957	10	64	3	3	0	1
Neil	.961	24	164	8	7	3	6

First Base	PCT	G	PO	A	E	DP
Grayson	.989	42	336	23	4	27
Lankford	1.000	2	13	2	0	1
Torres	—	1	0	0	0	0
Ustariz	.985	26	186	16	3	21

Second Base	PCT	G	PO	A	E	DP
Muscarello	.852	9	10	13	4	2
Rivera	.952	7	7	13	1	5
Turgeon	.972	56	87	123	6	29

Third Base	PCT	G	PO	A	E	DP
Lankford	.878	19	13	30	6	4

	PCT	G	PO	A	E	DP
Medina	1.000	1	0	1	0	0
Rivera	.949	51	40	108	8	15
Turgeon	1.000	1	0	1	0	0
Shortstop	**PCT**	**G**	**PO**	**A**	**E**	**DP**
Mercado	.880	60	93	148	33	27

	PCT	G	PO	A	E	DP
Muscarello	1.000	2	4	4	0	2
Rivera	.700	3	0	7	3	0
Turgeon	.882	4	8	7	2	3
Outfield	**PCT**	**G**	**PO**	**A**	**E**	**DP**
Drake	.964	58	127	6	5	2

	PCT	G	PO	A	E	DP
Franco	1.000	4	9	0	0	0
Lacy	.957	36	64	3	3	0
Lankford	1.000	25	25	2	0	0
Neil	—	2	0	0	0	0
Ray	.918	43	43	2	4	1
Torres	.981	47	97	4	2	0

GCL CARDINALS | ROOKIE

GULF COAST LEAGUE

Batting	B-T	HT	WT	DOB	AVG	vLH	vRH	G	AB	R	H	2B	3B	HR	RBI	BB	HBP	SH	SF	SO	SB	CS	SLG	OBP
Alvarez, Eliezer	B-R	5-11	165	10-15-94	.353	.269	.405	21	68	11	24	6	5	1	15	6	1	0	0	7	3	1	.632	.413
Asbury, De'Andre	R-R	6-3	170	8-5-95	.234	.219	.241	43	111	17	26	3	2	0	8	9	1	6	0	35	0	4	.297	.298
Barzilli, Julian	R-R	6-0	185	11-16-90	.211	.143	.232	46	147	19	31	8	1	3	19	21	2	1	2	46	0	2	.340	.314
Bautista, Ricardo	L-R	6-0	185	12-27-95	.278	.214	.299	43	115	13	32	5	1	2	19	22	2	1	0	20	4	1	.391	.403
Castillo, Ronard	R-R	6-5	200	6-16-92	.167	.000	.200	2	6	0	1	1	0	0	0	0	0	0	0	0	0	0	.333	.167
Collymore, Malik	R-R	5-11	190	4-29-95	.333	.267	.356	54	177	34	59	7	8	1	34	18	4	0	2	43	9	5	.480	.403
Gibson, Derek	L-R	6-2	220	2-25-91	.301	.359	.279	42	143	14	43	5	4	2	22	17	3	0	2	18	2	3	.434	.382
Gronsky, Jake	R-R	6-0	210	11-21-91	.288	.273	.293	24	80	9	23	5	1	1	15	8	3	0	1	10	0	0	.413	.370
Lopez, Joshua	R-R	5-10	188	3-4-96	.194	.133	.218	36	108	9	21	6	1	1	12	16	0	0	0	25	0	2	.296	.298
Massi, Michael	R-R	6-0	185	6-19-92	.210	.143	.234	34	105	11	22	5	1	0	8	16	6	0	2	14	2	1	.276	.341
Ortega, Rafael	L-R	5-11	160	5-15-91	.000	—	.000	2	3	0	0	0	0	0	0	1	0	0	0	2	1	0	.000	.250
Pritchard, Michael	L-L	5-11	180	11-10-91	.330	.400	.303	55	182	36	60	7	1	0	22	24	4	1	5	10	10	1	.379	.409
Rodriguez, Elier	B-R	6-2	210	2-15-95	.239	.255	.233	50	176	26	42	13	0	0	18	15	3	0	1	31	1	0	.313	.308
Rodriguez, Frankie	R-R	5-9	175	7-27-95	.266	.077	.303	29	79	18	21	4	0	0	10	16	1	1	0	18	2	0	.316	.396
Sierra, Magneuris	L-L	5-11	160	4-7-96	.386	.400	.380	52	202	42	78	12	3	2	30	16	2	2	1	30	13	3	.505	.434
Sosa, Edmundo	R-R	5-11	170	3-6-96	.275	.213	.294	52	207	37	57	8	5	1	23	18	4	1	3	29	8	5	.377	.341
Washington, David	L-L	6-5	200	11-20-90	.250	.000	.400	3	8	3	2	1	0	1	1	2	0	0	0	3	0	0	.750	.400

Pitching	B-T	HT	WT	DOB	W	L	ERA	G	GS	CG	SV	IP	H	R	ER	HR	BB	SO	AVG	vLH	vRH	K/9	BB/9
Aardsma, David	R-R	6-3	205	12-27-81	0	1	4.50	2	0	0	0	2	3	1	1	0	1	2	.333	.000	.429	9.00	4.50
Alexander, Kevin	R-R	6-1	170	5-4-91	1	2	1.85	20	0	0	3	24	28	9	5	2	2	20	.275	.286	.269	7.40	0.74
Bohannan, Silas	R-R	6-3	245	1-26-93	3	0	4.38	7	0	0	0	12	13	6	6	1	1	10	.277	.077	.353	7.30	0.73
Caballero, Juan	R-R	6-4	175	8-20-92	0	0	1.50	5	0	0	1	6	3	1	1	1	0	6	.143	.286	.071	9.00	0.00
De La Cruz, Steven	R-R	6-1	185	4-26-93	0	0	3.75	15	0	0	0	24	25	12	10	1	5	21	.272	.231	.288	7.88	1.88
Dobzanski, Bryan	R-R	6-4	220	8-31-95	2	1	2.67	8	4	0	0	27	18	11	8	1	7	17	.186	.240	.167	5.67	2.33
Dunnington, Tyler	R-R	6-2	190	2-25-92	3	2	3.41	18	0	0	2	29	30	11	11	0	10	26	.280	.333	.257	8.07	3.10
Flaherty, Jack	R-R	6-4	205	10-15-95	1	1	1.59	8	6	0	0	23	18	9	4	1	4	28	.209	.240	.197	11.12	1.59
Frey, Nick	R-R	6-4	185	8-30-91	1	0	4.85	10	1	0	1	13	12	8	7	0	7	12	.235	.063	.314	8.31	4.85
Hawkins, Dylan	L-L	6-2	215	6-26-93	3	1	3.13	18	4	0	0	32	29	15	11	0	11	25	.250	.355	.212	7.11	3.13
Kuebel, Sasha	R-L	6-1	200	7-28-92	1	0	1.64	7	0	0	2	11	12	2	2	0	1	6	.273	.176	.333	4.91	0.82
Mateo, Julio	R-R	6-3	180	9-29-95	4	2	5.19	6	6	0	0	35	34	20	20	3	7	28	.258	.186	.292	7.27	1.82
Medina, Yeison	R-R	6-2	210	10-2-92	4	1	1.64	19	0	0	3	33	29	7	6	0	8	31	.242	.250	.238	8.45	2.18
Morales, Andrew	R-R	6-0	185	1-16-93	0	1	3.60	3	2	0	0	5	2	3	2	1	3	6	.118	.500	.000	10.80	5.40
Parra, Frederis	R-R	6-3	162	10-22-94	3	2	2.70	10	9	0	0	47	43	18	14	1	15	34	.250	.306	.218	6.56	2.89
Reidt, Drew	R-R	6-6	218	1-8-92	4	1	4.15	16	2	0	0	30	28	18	14	1	3	24	.231	.129	.267	7.12	0.89
Rodriguez, Jorge L.	R-R	6-2	175	3-18-94	4	0	0.98	5	5	2	0	28	13	3	3	0	7	21	.140	.115	.149	6.83	2.28
Santos, Ramon	R-R	6-2	160	9-20-94	1	2	4.50	9	6	0	0	32	29	17	16	2	16	27	.250	.265	.244	7.59	4.50
Scanio, Joe	R-R	6-4	230	1-30-90	0	0	0.00	1	0	0	0	2	2	0	0	0	1	2	.333	.000	.400	10.80	5.40
Then, Jery	R-R	6-2	195	5-6-95	1	1	0.87	12	1	0	2	21	11	2	2	1	5	23	.157	.250	.120	10.02	2.18
Ward, Davis	R-R	6-0	196	2-23-92	1	0	1.69	5	2	0	0	16	19	4	3	0	0	10	.302	.400	.256	5.63	0.00
Weaver, Luke	R-R	6-2	170	8-21-93	0	0	0.00	4	4	0	0	6	4	0	0	0	0	9	.190	.200	.188	13.50	0.00
Williams, Ronnie	R-R	6-0	170	1-6-96	0	5	4.71	10	8	0	1	36	39	22	19	1	9	30	.279	.255	.292	7.43	2.23

Fielding

Catcher	PCT	G	PO	A	E	DP	PB
Lopez	.992	36	227	32	2	1	10
Rodriguez	.974	8	32	5	1	0	1
Rodriguez	.989	25	150	25	2	2	6

First Base	PCT	G	PO	A	E	DP
Massi	1.000	1	6	1	0	0
Pritchard	.994	18	152	1	1	6
Rodriguez	.977	42	327	20	8	21
Washington	1.000	2	17	0	0	2

Second Base	PCT	G	PO	A	E	DP
Alvarez	.979	14	22	24	1	6

	PCT	G	PO	A	E	DP
Collymore	.944	33	54	63	7	9
Gronsky	1.000	5	5	10	0	2
Massi	1.000	12	22	31	0	4

Third Base	PCT	G	PO	A	E	DP
Barzilli	.874	42	25	65	13	4
Gronsky	1.000	9	9	25	0	0
Massi	.964	12	5	22	1	0

Shortstop	PCT	G	PO	A	E	DP
Massi	.875	11	12	23	5	3
Sosa	.954	52	83	145	11	19

Outfield	PCT	G	PO	A	E	DP
Asbury	.943	37	61	5	4	0
Bautista	.980	37	48	2	1	0
Castillo	.750	2	1	1	1	0
Gibson	.979	31	43	3	1	1
Ortega	1.000	2	1	0	0	0
Pritchard	.955	35	39	3	2	0
Sierra	.976	52	115	5	3	3

DSL CARDINALS | ROOKIE

DOMINICAN SUMMER LEAGUE

Batting	B-T	HT	WT	DOB	AVG	vLH	vRH	G	AB	R	H	2B	3B	HR	RBI	BB	HBP	SH	SF	SO	SB	CS	SLG	OBP
Alvarado, Henry	R-R	6-3	195	1-30-96	.168	.278	.146	28	107	4	18	3	0	1	8	1	3	0	0	39	1	1	.224	.198
Bandes, Luis	R-R	6-1	200	5-15-96	.286	.192	.307	37	140	16	40	8	0	6	20	6	3	0	1	20	1	0	.471	.327
Chevalier, Ignacio	R-R	6-1	190	1-10-94	.154	.000	.167	5	13	0	2	1	0	0	0	0	0	0	0	5	0	0	.231	.154
Cordoba, Allen	R-R	6-1	175	12-6-95	.258	.245	.262	62	244	41	63	9	1	2	18	15	2	2	5	46	14	4	.328	.301

	B-T	HT	WT	DOB	AVG	vLH	vRH	G	AB	R	H	2B	3B	HR	RBI	BB	SO	SB	CS	OBP	SLG
Cotes, Oscar	R-R	6-2	165	3-31-97	.127	.111	.131	35	102	12	13	4	0	0	4	9	2	0	0	57	0	3	.167	.212
De La Cruz, Joaquin	R-R	6-2	195	10-13-95	.127	.172	.116	46	158	9	20	1	0	1	8	16	2	2	2	51	0	1	.152	.213
Flores, Luis	B-R	6-0	190	10-22-96	.217	.167	.231	55	217	20	47	6	1	2	12	11	1	6	0	58	9	8	.281	.258
Linares, Hector	R-R	6-0	160	1-13-97	.179	.205	.173	56	212	23	38	8	3	0	9	15	2	0	1	70	6	.5	.245	.239
Luis, Carlos	R-R	6-4	180	8-22-96	.047	.000	.061	15	43	3	2	0	0	0	1	3	2	0	1	25	1	1	.047	.143
Luna, Andres	R-R	5-10	175	7-17-97	.250	.286	.241	19	36	8	9	2	0	1	6	6	3	2	0	10	3	2	.389	.400
Melendez, Dylan	R-R	6-2	180	6-11-95	.435	.500	.421	6	23	1	10	3	0	0	4	1	0	0	1	1	0	0	.565	.440
Ortega, Dennis	R-R	6-2	180	6-11-97	.229	.241	.226	45	153	16	35	2	0	0	13	20	3	3	0	38	1	1	.242	.330
Pena, Dionenrys	R-R	6-1	185	4-20-95	.237	.227	.239	30	93	11	22	2	1	1	4	7	1	0	0	29	3	2	.312	.297
Rivera, Jonathan	R-R	6-1	185	4-27-97	.271	.351	.249	63	258	22	70	12	3	6	40	6	2	0	3	71	3	4	.411	.290
Rodriguez, Carlos	R-R	6-2	215	1-6-97	.181	.143	.192	49	160	15	29	3	0	0	11	30	2	0	1	49	6	5	.200	.316
Talavera, Carlos	B-R	6-1	175	9-20-96	.197	.250	.185	65	233	31	46	8	4	0	13	32	3	2	1	76	16	4	.266	.301
Wilson, Irving	R-R	5-10	168	8-13-96	.211	.500	.176	6	19	2	4	0	0	2	4	2	1	0	0	3	0	0	.526	.318
Ynfante, Wadye	R-R	6-0	160	8-15-97	.200	.138	.215	46	150	15	30	5	3	2	11	21	2	3	0	56	11	2	.313	.306

Pitching	B-T	HT	WT	DOB	W	L	ERA	G	GS	CG	SV	IP	H	R	ER	HR	BB	SO	AVG	vLH	vRH	K/9	BB/9
Alcantara, Sandy	R-R	6-4	170	9-7-95	1	9	3.97	12	11	1	0	57	56	31	25	1	19	55	.253	.358	.193	8.74	3.02
Alvarez, Juan	R-R	6-4	180	12-28-96	1	0	3.27	15	0	0	1	41	40	20	15	2	10	37	.245	.215	.265	8.06	2.18
Bennett, Kerrion	L-L	6-3	160	5-28-96	0	1	1.71	12	0	0	0	21	14	6	4	1	12	15	.173	.176	.172	6.43	5.14
Casadilla, Franyel	R-R	6-3	175	4-5-97	1	3	2.25	19	2	0	0	40	33	18	10	1	11	42	.223	.185	.245	9.45	2.48
Changarotty, Will	R-R	6-0	165	10-19-95	1	4	4.99	13	9	0	0	52	57	32	29	2	22	45	.275	.281	.273	7.74	3.78
De La Cruz, Andy	L-L	6-1	185	8-29-94	2	1	1.93	13	0	0	1	28	26	10	6	0	11	23	.248	.233	.253	7.39	3.54
Diaz, Oneiver	R-R	6-2	160	8-28-96	1	3	2.92	11	5	0	0	37	41	18	12	1	9	21	.279	.200	.314	5.11	2.19
Estevez, Angel	R-R	6-2	175	6-3-97	4	2	2.92	11	4	0	0	37	37	18	12	0	10	17	.270	.255	.279	4.14	2.43
Fernandez, Junior	R-R	6-1	180	3-2-97	0	5	5.79	7	6	0	0	28	29	25	18	1	12	13	.276	.419	.177	4.18	3.86
Gonzalez, Derian	R-R	6-3	190	1-31-95	2	2	3.11	13	11	0	0	55	52	27	19	1	22	62	.246	.317	.202	10.15	3.60
Gonzalez, Junior	R-R	6-3	175	11-7-96	2	3	4.09	13	8	0	0	51	69	31	23	0	16	20	.330	.381	.296	3.55	2.84
Lara, Jose	R-R	6-2	175	3-26-94	0	4	2.49	16	0	0	8	22	27	11	6	0	8	16	.310	.364	.278	6.65	3.32
Narvaez, Jesus	L-L	6-2	180	5-3-97	0	2	6.00	6	2	0	0	15	20	11	10	0	6	6	.317	.333	.316	3.60	3.60
Oca, David	L-L	5-10	165	7-4-95	3	3	2.22	13	12	0	0	65	54	27	16	1	13	67	.223	.317	.204	9.28	1.80
Perez, Enrique	L-L	6-2	180	8-10-97	2	1	3.42	16	0	0	1	24	16	11	9	0	24	21	.213	.333	.190	7.99	9.13
Urena, Rigobert	L-L	6-4	170	2-8-95	1	3	4.67	11	0	0	0	17	18	16	9	2	11	8	.257	.400	.233	4.15	5.71
Vallejo, Esteban	R-R	6-4	190	12-9-93	1	2	5.80	17	0	0	2	36	46	26	23	2	18	26	.319	.321	.318	6.56	4.54

Fielding

Catcher	PCT	G	PO	A	E	DP	PB
Chevalier	.962	5	24	1	1	0	1
Ortega	.978	41	276	40	7	0	9
Pena	.956	26	152	23	8	1	9
Wilson	.978	6	36	8	1	0	0

First Base	PCT	G	PO	A	E	DP
Alvarado	.987	22	208	13	3	17
De La Cruz	.986	16	130	8	2	11
Melendez	1.000	1	6	0	0	0
Rodriguez	.988	34	306	14	4	32

Second Base	PCT	G	PO	A	E	DP
Cordoba	1.000	3	7	6	0	2
Flores	.960	51	116	148	11	26
Ynfante	.954	18	44	39	4	13

Third Base	PCT	G	PO	A	E	DP
Alvarado	1.000	1	0	2	0	0
Cordoba	.904	29	27	58	9	7
Cotes	.863	18	21	48	11	2
De La Cruz	.908	27	21	58	8	11

Shortstop	PCT	G	PO	A	E	DP
Cordoba	.908	34	63	114	18	23

	PCT	G	PO	A	E	DP
Cotes	.938	14	12	33	3	4
Linares	.852	29	41	80	21	10

Outfield	PCT	G	PO	A	E	DP
Bandes	.972	34	62	8	2	3
Luis	.950	11	18	1	1	0
Luna	.958	17	22	1	1	1
Rivera	.938	62	107	14	8	3
Rodriguez	1.000	12	14	1	0	0
Talavera	.966	62	106	8	4	2
Ynfante	.905	25	37	1	4	0

San Diego Padres

SEASON IN A SENTENCE: The pitching was excellent—when healthy—but the Padres were the worst offensive team in baseball and it was not close; San Diego was dead last in average, on-base percent, slugging and runs.

HIGH POINT: As poor as the offense was, the Padres did go 36-31 in the second half, highlighted by a 16-11 August which included a five-game winning streak. The Padres won twice at playoff-bound Pittsburgh before sweeping the Rockies at home.

LOW POINT: The Padres went 10-17 in June, their fewest wins in any full month, and the bottoming out resulted in the firing of general manager Josh Byrnes. He was replaced on an interim basis by Omar Minaya, but A.J. Preller was appointed GM in August.

NOTABLE ROOKIES: Three of San Diego's top 11 prospects entering the season made their major league debuts in 2014. Jace Peterson hit just .113, but the organization and scouts were still impressed with his approach, aggressiveness and lefty swing. Outfielder Rymer Liriano hit just .220/.289/.266 but showed strength when he hit a bomb of a home run in his third game. And Cory Spangenberg was the most impressive Padres rookie with a .764 OPS and two homers in 65 plate appearances.

KEY TRANSACTIONS: Prior to the season, the Padres sent Logan Forsythe, righthanders Brad Boxberger, Matt Andriese and Matt Lollis and shortstop Maxx Tissenbaum to the Rays for lefty reliever Alex Torres and righthander Jesse Hahn. Boxberger performed well in Tampa Bay, but both Hahn and Torres excelled in San Diego. Hahn was 7-4, 3.07 as a starter before he was shut down, while Torres pitched to a 3.33 ERA in 70 appearances out of the bullpen despite control issues.

DOWN ON THE FARM: Catcher Austin Hedges remains the team's top prospect, although the team asked him to put down the glove in the off-season and concentrate on the bat (.589 OPS). No. 1 draft pick Trea Turner blazed through two levels, showing a better bat than expected, flashing his excellent speed and holding his own at shortstop. Speedy Mallex Smith stole 88 bases across two levels. Righthander Matt Wisler was hit hard early in the PCL, but rebounded and was impressive to scouts and opposing managers with his velocity (95-96).

OPENING DAY PAYROLL: $89,881,695 (19th)

ORGANIZATION LEADERS

BATTING   *Minimum 250 AB

MAJORS

*	AVG	Smith, Seth	.266
*	OPS	Smith, Seth	.807
	HR	Grandal, Yasmani	15
	RBI	Gyorko, Jedd	51

MINORS

*	AVG	Smith, Mallex, Fort Wayne, Lake Elsinore	.310
*	OBP	Smith, Mallex, Fort Wayne, Lake Elsinore	.403
*	SLG	Decker, Cody, El Paso	.514
	R	Smith, Mallex, Fort Wayne, Lake Elsinore	99
	H	Asencio, Yeison, San Antonio, El Paso	156
		Goris, Diego, Lake Elsinore, San Antonio	156
	TB	Goris, Diego, Lake Elsinore, San Antonio	243
	2B	Quintana, Gabriel, Lake Elsinore	35
	3B	Spangenberg, Cory, AZL, Eugene, San Antonio	10
	HR	Decker, Cody, El Paso	27
	RBI	Perez, Fernando, Fort Wayne	95
	BB	Smith, Mallex, Fort Wayne, Lake Elsinore	69
	SO	Decker, Cody, El Paso	150
		Quintana, Gabriel, Lake Elsinore	150
	SB	Smith, Mallex, Fort Wayne, Lake Elsinore	88

PITCHING   #Minimum 75 IP

MAJORS

	W	Kennedy, Ian	13
		Ross, Tyson	13
#	ERA	Cashner, Andrew	2.55
	SO	Kennedy, Ian	207
	SV	Street, Huston	24

MINORS

	W	Rea, Colin, Lake Elsinore	11
	L	Geer, Josh, San Antonio	12
#	ERA	Needy, James, San Antonio	2.90
	G	LaFromboise, Bobby, El Paso	58
	GS	two tied with	28
	SV	Barbato, Johnny, San Antonio	16
	SV	Gott, Trevor, Lake Elsinore, San Antonio	16
	IP	Geer, Josh, San Antonio	156
	BB	two tied with 68	68
	SO	Lloyd, Kyle, Fort Wayne	155
	AVG	Needy, James, San Antonio	.246

General Manager: Josh Byrnes. **Farm Director:** Randy Smith. **Scouting Director:** Billy Gasparino.

Class	Team	League	W	L	PCT	Finish	Manager
Majors	San Diego Padres	National	77	85	.475	t-18th (30)	Bud Black
Triple-A	El Paso Chihuahuas	Pacific Coast	72	72	.500	10th (16)	Pat Murphy
Double-A	San Antonio Missions	Texas	68	72	.486	t-5th (8)	Rich Dauer
High A	Lake Elsinore Storm	California	75	65	.536	t-4th (10)	Jamie Quirk
Low A	Fort Wayne TinCaps	Midwest	63	76	.453	12th (16)	Michael Collins
Short season	Eugene Emeralds	Northwest	30	46	.395	7th (8)	Robbie Wine
Rookie	Padres	Arizona	20	36	.357	13th (13)	Anthony Contreras
Overall Minor League Record			328	367	.472	23rd (30)	

ORGANIZATION STATISTICS

SAN DIEGO PADRES

NATIONAL LEAGUE

Batting	B-T	HT	WT	DOB	AVG	vLH	vRH	G	AB	R	H	2B	3B	HR	RBI	BB	HBP	SH	SF	SO	SB	CS	SLG	OBP
Almonte, Abraham	B-R	5-9	205	6-27-89	.265	.250	.276	32	98	9	26	5	0	2	7	6	0	2	1	20	1	2	.378	.305
Alonso, Yonder	L-R	6-1	230	4-8-87	.240	.216	.245	84	267	27	64	19	1	7	27	17	1	0	3	36	6	1	.397	.285
Amarista, Alexi	L-R	5-6	150	4-6-89	.239	.200	.252	148	423	39	101	13	2	5	40	29	1	8	5	69	12	1	.314	.286
Blanks, Kyle	R-R	6-6	265	9-11-86	.200	—	.200	5	10	1	2	0	0	0	0	0	0	0	0	3	0	0	.200	.200
Cabrera, Everth	B-R	5-10	190	11-17-86	.232	.253	.226	90	357	36	83	13	1	3	20	20	1	9	4	86	18	8	.300	.272
Conrad, Brooks	B-R	5-10	190	1-16-80	.100	.000	.158	13	30	2	3	1	0	1	2	3	0	0	1	14	0	0	.233	.176
Denorfia, Chris	R-R	6-0	195	7-15-80	.242	.253	.235	89	248	25	60	10	3	1	16	18	0	2	0	51	8	1	.319	.293
Falu, Irving	B-R	5-10	180	6-6-83	.150	.000	.231	11	20	0	3	0	0	0	3	0	0	0	0	4	1	0	.150	.261
2-team total (11 Milwaukee)					.100	—	—	22	30	0	3	0	0	0	1	4	0	0	1	5	1	0	.100	.200
Francoeur, Jeff	R-R	6-4	220	1-8-84	.083	.143	.000	10	24	2	2	0	0	0	1	3	0	0	1	7	0	0	.083	.179
Goebbert, Jake	L-L	6-0	205	9-24-87	.218	.000	.237	51	101	12	22	1	3	1	10	12	2	0	0	32	2	1	.317	.313
Grandal, Yasmani	B-R	6-2	225	11-8-88	.225	.162	.241	128	377	47	85	19	1	15	49	58	2	0	6	115	3	0	.401	.327
Gyorko, Jedd	R-R	5-10	210	9-23-88	.210	.228	.205	111	400	37	84	17	1	10	51	36	4	0	3	100	3	2	.333	.280
Headley, Chase	B-R	6-2	220	5-9-84	.229	.212	.235	77	279	27	64	12	1	7	32	22	5	0	1	73	4	1	.355	.296
Hundley, Nick	R-R	6-1	200	9-8-83	.271	.273	.271	33	59	1	16	3	0	1	3	0	0	0	0	13	0	0	.373	.271
Liriano, Rymer	R-R	6-0	230	6-20-91	.220	.212	.228	38	109	13	24	2	0	1	6	9	2	0	1	39	4	1	.266	.289
Maybin, Cameron	R-R	6-3	205	4-4-87	.235	.211	.248	95	251	24	59	13	4	1	15	19	1	0	1	56	4	3	.331	.290
Medica, Tommy	R-R	6-3	205	4-9-88	.233	.245	.225	102	240	31	56	11	2	9	27	14	4	0	1	75	6	1	.408	.286
Moore, Adam	R-R	6-3	220	5-8-84	.200	.143	.333	9	10	1	2	1	0	0	1	2	0	0	0	5	0	0	.300	.333
Nady, Xavier	R-R	6-2	215	11-14-78	.135	.200	.091	22	37	4	5	1	0	3	4	5	0	0	0	9	0	0	.405	.238
Nelson, Chris	R-R	5-11	205	9-3-85	.233	.161	.286	27	73	5	17	3	0	0	7	7	0	0	1	14	1	2	.274	.296
Peterson, Jace	L-R	6-0	210	5-9-90	.113	.250	.073	27	53	3	6	0	0	0	0	2	1	2	0	18	2	0	.113	.161
Quentin, Carlos	R-R	6-1	235	8-28-82	.177	.180	.175	50	130	9	23	6	0	4	18	17	4	0	4	33	0	0	.315	.284
Rivera, Rene	R-R	5-10	215	7-31-83	.252	.280	.237	103	294	27	74	18	1	11	44	27	3	3	2	76	0	0	.432	.319
Smith, Seth	L-L	6-3	210	9-30-82	.266	.240	.270	136	443	55	118	31	5	12	48	69	4	0	4	87	1	1	.440	.367
Solarte, Yangervis	B-R	5-11	195	7-7-87	.267	.356	.222	56	217	30	58	5	1	4	17	23	1	2	3	24	0	1	.355	.336
Spangenberg, Cory	L-R	6-0	195	3-16-91	.290	.333	.277	20	62	7	18	2	1	2	9	2	0	1	0	14	4	2	.452	.313
Venable, Will	L-L	6-3	205	10-29-82	.224	.200	.228	146	406	47	91	13	2	8	33	33	4	3	2	107	11	6	.325	.288

Pitching	B-T	HT	WT	DOB	W	L	ERA	G	GS	CG	SV	IP	H	R	ER	HR	BB	SO	AVG	vLH	vRH	K/9	BB/9
Alvarez, R.J.	R-R	6-1	200	6-8-91	0	0	1.13	10	0	0	0	8	3	1	1	0	5	9	.115	.125	.111	10.13	5.63
Ambriz, Hector	L-R	6-2	235	5-24-84	0	0	4.50	1	0	0	0	2	1	2	1	1	0	1	.286	.333	.250	4.50	9.00
Benoit, Joaquin	R-R	6-3	220	7-26-77	4	2	1.49	53	0	0	11	54	28	10	9	3	14	64	.151	.157	.144	10.60	2.32
Boyer, Blaine	R-R	6-3	225	7-11-81	0	1	3.57	32	0	0	0	40	34	16	16	2	8	29	.228	.305	.178	6.47	1.79
Buckner, Billy	R-R	6-2	205	8-27-83	0	1	4.76	1	1	0	0	6	6	3	3	1	4	4	.273	.333	.231	6.35	6.35
Campos, Leonel	R-R	6-3	185	7-7-87	0	0	5.14	6	0	0	0	7	9	5	4	0	4	9	.310	.143	.467	11.57	5.14
Cashner, Andrew	R-R	6-6	220	9-11-86	5	7	2.55	19	19	2	0	123	110	42	35	7	29	93	.235	.240	.230	6.79	2.12
Despaigne, Odrisamer	R-R	6-0	195	4-4-87	4	7	3.36	16	16	0	0	96	85	44	36	6	32	65	.237	.258	.216	6.07	2.99
Erlin, Robbie	L-L	6-0	190	10-8-90	4	5	4.99	13	11	0	0	61	71	34	34	6	15	46	.293	.279	.299	6.75	2.20
Garces, Frank	L-L	5-11	175	1-17-90	0	0	2.00	15	0	0	0	9	8	2	2	1	1	10	.229	.250	.182	10.00	1.00
Hahn, Jesse	R-R	6-5	190	7-30-89	7	4	3.07	14	12	0	0	73	57	26	25	4	32	70	.214	.227	.200	8.59	3.93
Kennedy, Ian	R-R	6-0	190	12-19-84	13	13	3.63	33	33	0	0	201	189	85	81	16	70	207	.250	.240	.259	9.27	3.13
Lane, Jason	R-L	6-2	225	12-22-76	0	1	0.87	3	1	0	0	10	7	1	1	0	6	.179	.000	.250	5.23	0.00
Patton, Troy	B-L	6-1	180	9-3-85	0	0	2.45	8	0	0	0	7	7	2	2	1	1	8	.226	.133	.313	9.82	1.23
Quackenbush, Kevin	R-R	6-4	220	11-28-88	3	3	2.48	56	0	0	6	54	42	15	15	2	18	56	.212	.196	.231	9.28	2.98
Roach, Donn	R-R	6-0	195	12-14-89	1	0	4.75	16	1	0	0	30	36	17	16	2	15	17	.308	.341	.289	5.04	4.45
Ross, Tyson	R-R	6-5	225	4-22-87	13	14	2.81	31	31	2	0	196	165	75	61	13	72	195	.230	.230	.231	8.97	3.31
Stauffer, Tim	R-R	6-1	210	6-2-82	6	2	3.50	44	3	0	0	64	67	25	25	4	23	67	.273	.282	.264	9.37	3.22
Street, Huston	R-R	6-0	195	8-2-83	1	0	1.09	33	0	0	24	33	18	4	4	3	7	34	.158	.189	.131	9.27	1.91
Stults, Eric	L-L	6-2	220	12-9-79	8	17	4.30	32	32	0	0	176	197	93	84	26	45	111	.283	.295	.279	5.68	2.30
Thayer, Dale	R-R	6-0	210	12-17-80	4	5	2.34	70	0	0	0	65	53	19	17	9	16	62	.215	.217	.214	8.54	2.20
Torres, Alex	L-L	5-10	175	12-8-87	2	1	3.33	70	0	0	0	54	46	25	20	2	33	51	.230	.256	.209	8.50	5.50
Vincent, Nick	R-R	5-11	180	7-12-86	1	2	3.60	63	0	0	0	55	44	22	22	5	11	62	.221	.274	.190	10.15	1.80
Wieland, Joe	R-R	6-3	210	1-21-90	1	0	7.15	4	2	0	0	11	16	9	9	3	5	8	.333	.318	.346	6.35	3.97

Fielding

Catcher	PCT	G	PO	A	E	DP	PB
Grandal	.993	76	526	31	4	4	12
Hundley	1.000	14	74	5	0	2	2
Moore	1.000	1	8	0	0	0	0
Rivera	.989	89	680	66	8	7	7

First Base	PCT	G	PO	A	E	DP
Alonso	.997	77	569	43	2	45
Blanks	1.000	3	24	4	0	4
Goebbert	.989	25	166	13	2	6
Grandal	.988	37	235	22	3	18
Medica	.997	46	292	26	1	29
Nady	—	1	0	0	0	0
Nelson	1.000	1	1	1	0	1
Rivera	.917	3	11	0	1	0

Second Base	PCT	G	PO	A	E	DP
Amarista	1.000	21	27	39	0	7
Conrad	1.000	10	17	15	0	5
Falu	1.000	11	14	11	0	4
Gyorko	.977	109	184	281	11	60
Nelson	.923	3	3	9	1	0
Peterson	.964	14	21	32	2	4
Solarte	.972	10	19	16	1	3
Spangenberg	.889	3	3	5	1	0

Third Base	PCT	G	PO	A	E	DP
Alonso	1.000	3	0	1	0	0
Amarista	.960	22	9	39	2	3
Headley	.965	76	43	124	6	14
Nelson	.973	20	10	26	1	2
Peterson	.913	10	2	19	2	0
Solarte	.948	45	23	50	4	10
Spangenberg	.857	9	4	14	3	0

Shortstop	PCT	G	PO	A	E	DP
Amarista	.980	73	103	194	6	33
Cabrera	.967	90	126	254	13	47
Solarte	1.000	3	1	1	0	0

Outfield	PCT	G	PO	A	E	DP
Almonte	.973	25	67	4	2	1
Amarista	.976	26	39	1	1	1
Blanks	—	1	0	0	0	0
Cashner	—	1	0	0	0	0
Denorfia	.993	73	138	2	1	0
Francoeur	.929	7	13	0	1	0
Goebbert	1.000	8	10	0	0	0
Liriano	.937	34	57	2	4	0
Maybin	.988	86	161	1	2	1
Medica	1.000	22	27	0	0	0
Nady	1.000	12	11	0	0	0
Quentin	1.000	32	42	1	0	1
Smith	.996	124	219	5	1	1
Solarte	.857	7	6	0	1	0
Spangenberg	.750	4	3	0	1	0
Venable	1.000	136	254	3	0	0

EL PASO CHIHUAHUAS   TRIPLE-A
PACIFIC COAST LEAGUE

Batting	B-T	HT	WT	DOB	AVG	vLH	vRH	G	AB	R	H	2B	3B	HR	RBI	BB	HBP	SH	SF	SO	SB	CS	SLG	OBP
Alonso, Yonder	L-R	6-1	230	4-8-87	.235	.333	.182	5	17	0	4	0	0	0	1	0	0	0	0	2	0	0	.235	.235
Asencio, Yeison	R-R	6-1	225	11-14-89	.333	.273	.356	21	81	16	27	4	0	5	15	4	1	0	0	9	0	1	.568	.372
Bixler, Brian	R-R	6-1	195	10-22-82	.167	.500	.100	8	12	1	2	0	0	0	1	0	0	0	0	5	0	0	.167	.167
Blanks, Kyle	R-R	6-6	265	9-11-86	.265	.222	.270	27	83	15	22	5	0	9	20	10	4	0	2	24	0	0	.651	.364
2-team total (7 Sacramento)					.298	—	—	34	104	19	31	5	0	10	23	16	4	0	3	27	0	0	.635	.402
Buck, Travis	L-R	6-2	230	11-18-83	.289	.200	.295	54	142	21	41	7	0	3	21	14	4	0	3	30	0	1	.401	.362
Cabrera, Everth	B-R	5-10	190	11-17-86	.350	.167	.429	7	20	4	7	1	0	0	1	4	0	0	1	3	1	0	.400	.458
Castellanos, Alex	R-R	6-0	200	8-4-86	.275	.303	.268	113	360	69	99	25	5	8	42	37	6	3	2	104	8	5	.439	.351
Conrad, Brooks	B-R	5-10	190	1-16-80	.278	.308	.270	78	295	52	82	18	1	18	57	33	2	2	5	79	0	2	.529	.349
Decker, Cody	R-R	5-11	220	1-17-87	.261	.262	.260	134	449	68	117	25	4	27	79	51	4	0	6	150	0	3	.514	.337
Francoeur, Jeff	R-R	6-4	220	1-8-84	.289	.330	.278	115	456	55	132	22	3	15	69	21	3	0	7	95	11	2	.450	.320
Fuentes, Reymond	L-L	6-0	160	2-12-91	.261	.280	.258	46	157	29	41	9	3	1	16	17	1	3	0	27	13	2	.376	.337
Gale, Rocky	R-R	6-1	180	2-22-88	.303	.327	.295	77	228	21	69	12	0	0	35	10	0	2	3	33	1	0	.355	.328
Galvez, Jonathan	R-R	6-2	200	1-18-91	.280	.354	.257	103	343	55	96	24	2	10	52	39	2	2	3	77	3	5	.449	.354
Goebbert, Jake	L-L	6-0	205	9-24-87	.322	.219	.345	48	171	37	55	13	2	8	35	33	2	0	1	33	0	0	.561	.435
2-team total (31 Sacramento)					.296	—	—	79	280	58	83	20	3	14	60	52	4	0	3	53	1	0	.539	.410
Gonzalez, Alberto	R-R	5-10	195	4-18-83	.208	.500	.184	19	53	4	11	3	0	0	2	1	1	1	1	12	0	0	.264	.218
Greene, Tyler	R-R	6-2	200	8-17-83	.307	.322	.303	114	433	70	133	30	3	9	59	29	8	2	5	124	6	4	.453	.358
Gyorko, Jedd	R-R	5-10	210	9-23-88	.292	.375	.250	6	24	7	7	2	0	1	5	4	0	0	0	4	0	0	.500	.393
Jackson, Ryan	R-R	6-3	180	5-10-88	.188	.000	.231	6	16	3	3	1	0	0	0	5	0	1	0	4	0	0	.250	.381
Lemmerman, Jake	R-R	6-1	195	5-4-89	.176	.048	.210	41	102	15	18	7	1	1	10	15	1	1	1	29	0	0	.294	.286
Lindsey, Taylor	L-R	6-0	195	12-2-91	.219	.242	.212	41	146	18	32	6	1	2	17	9	2	0	2	15	0	2	.315	.270
2-team total (75 Salt Lake)					.238	—	—	116	441	68	105	19	5	10	47	40	4	5	2	59	7	4	.372	.306
Liriano, Rymer	R-R	6-0	230	6-20-91	.452	.385	.469	16	62	14	28	11	1	0	13	8	1	0	0	14	3	1	.661	.521
Maybin, Cameron	R-R	6-3	205	4-4-87	.264	.294	.250	15	53	8	14	2	1	1	6	6	0	0	2	10	1	0	.396	.328
Medica, Tommy	R-R	6-3	205	4-9-88	.213	.222	.211	24	89	8	19	6	2	3	18	9	3	0	0	24	0	0	.427	.307
Moore, Adam	R-R	6-3	220	5-8-84	.298	.269	.306	91	312	38	93	20	1	12	34	31	1	0	3	78	1	1	.484	.360
Nelson, Chris	R-R	5-11	205	9-3-85	.293	.247	.317	24	82	13	24	6	1	2	21	18	1	0	1	16	0	0	.463	.422
Noel, Rico	R-R	5-8	170	1-11-89	.258	.306	.245	109	333	49	86	11	1	2	27	41	3	6	2	81	32	6	.315	.343
Peterson, Jace	L-R	6-0	210	5-9-90	.306	.326	.302	68	248	44	76	21	6	2	39	42	1	6	2	50	12	6	.464	.406
Quentin, Carlos	R-R	6-1	235	8-28-82	.250	.000	.286	3	8	1	2	0	0	1	0	0	0	0	0	0	0	0	.625	.250
Robertson, Dan	R-R	5-8	170	9-30-85	.364	.333	.368	5	22	6	8	2	0	2	5	1	0	0	2	3	0	0	.727	.391
2-team total (8 Round Rock)					.300	—	—	13	50	12	15	3	1	3	8	6	0	0	2	7	2	0	.580	.375

Pitching	B-T	HT	WT	DOB	W	L	ERA	G	GS	CG	SV	IP	H	R	ER	HR	BB	SO	AVG	vLH	vRH	K/9	BB/9
Ambriz, Hector	L-R	6-2	235	5-24-84	2	3	3.93	51	0	0	11	55	60	27	24	5	18	43	.278	.281	.275	7.04	2.95
Boyer, Blaine	R-R	6-3	225	7-11-81	1	2	3.10	25	0	0	7	29	26	10	10	2	6	28	.234	.250	.222	8.69	1.86
Branham, Matt	R-R	6-5	220	9-28-87	0	1	6.75	3	1	0	0	4	8	8	3	2	2	2	.400	.364	.444	4.50	4.50
Buckner, Billy	R-R	6-2	205	8-27-83	4	5	5.80	15	14	0	0	64	85	52	41	10	33	44	.324	.312	.336	6.22	4.66
2-team total (4 Nashville)					5	6	5.83	19	16	0	0	76	94	60	49	11	36	59	—	—	—	7.02	4.28
Campos, Leonel	R-R	6-3	185	7-17-87	0	0	11.70	11	0	0	0	10	20	15	13	2	13	13	.408	.435	.385	11.70	11.70
Carter, Anthony	L-R	6-4	215	4-4-86	0	0	6.00	3	0	0	0	3	5	2	2	0	1	0	.385	.333	.429	0.00	3.00
Cashner, Andrew	R-R	6-6	220	9-11-86	0	2	7.04	2	2	0	0	8	7	6	6	3	2	7	.226	.231	.222	8.22	2.35
Despaigne, Odrisamer	R-R	6-0	195	4-4-87	1	3	7.61	5	5	0	0	24	36	20	20	3	13	29	.356	.283	.418	11.03	4.94
Erlin, Robbie	L-L	6-0	190	10-8-90	0	1	9.28	2	2	0	0	11	21	12	11	2	2	8	.438	.273	.486	6.75	1.69
Kloess, Brandon	R-R	6-2	195	12-9-84	3	5	5.90	46	5	0	1	76	78	54	50	11	37	45	.264	.295	.236	5.31	4.36
Kohlscheen, Stephen	R-R	6-3	235	9-20-88	1	0	1.32	13	0	0	1	14	13	5	2	0	2	13	.250	.318	.200	8.56	1.32
2-team total (15 Tacoma)					3	0	2.58	28	0	0	1	38	35	14	11	2	8	35	—	—	—	8.22	1.88
LaFromboise, Bobby	L-L	6-4	215	6-25-86	1	2	4.75	58	0	0	3	53	68	37	28	4	21	45	.309	.290	.325	7.64	3.57
Lane, Jason	R-L	6-2	225	12-22-76	9	9	4.51	24	24	0	0	150	183	88	75	16	26	77	.306	.316	.302	4.63	1.56
Mejia, Ruben	R-R	6-1	175	2-23-92	0	1	189.00	1	1	0	0	0	4	7	7	0	3	1	.800	.667	1.000	27.00	81.00

	B-T	HT	WT	DOB	W	L	ERA	G	GS	CG	SV	IP	H	R	ER	HR	BB	SO	AVG	vLH	vRH	K/9	BB/9
Nix, Michael	R-R	6-5	235	5-21-83	7	3	4.68	27	6	1	1	60	75	36	31	3	23	41	.316	.305	.326	6.18	3.47
O'Grady, Dennis	R-R	5-9	205	5-17-89	7	1	4.42	43	0	0	0	53	61	31	26	6	24	37	.298	.318	.282	6.28	4.08
Oramas, Juan Pablo	L-L	5-10	220	5-11-90	7	7	5.61	23	21	0	0	111	135	76	69	14	45	93	.305	.389	.269	7.56	3.66
Quackenbush, Kevin	R-R	6-4	220	11-28-88	0	0	1.26	13	0	0	6	14	9	2	2	0	4	12	.180	.143	.207	7.53	2.51
Rearick, Chris	L-L	6-3	190	12-5-87	2	0	2.72	33	0	0	0	36	31	13	11	2	9	38	.225	.136	.291	9.41	2.23
Reyes, Jorge	B-R	6-3	195	12-7-87	3	2	3.86	24	0	0	0	30	25	14	13	2	16	26	.227	.229	.226	7.71	4.75
Roach, Donn	R-R	6-0	195	12-14-89	4	6	5.24	19	13	0	0	77	98	56	45	2	40	44	.314	.343	.291	5.12	4.66
Sampson, Keyvius	R-R	6-0	225	1-6-91	2	5	6.68	38	14	0	0	92	91	73	68	19	68	94	.261	.316	.218	9.23	6.68
Sexton, Tim	R-R	6-6	185	6-10-87	1	3	6.45	23	2	0	0	53	67	40	38	7	15	36	.318	.316	.319	6.11	2.55
Sipp, Tony	L-L	6-0	190	7-12-83	1	1	4.30	11	0	0	0	15	14	7	7	1	2	21	.241	.360	.152	12.89	1.23
Smith, Burch	R-R	6-4	215	4-12-90	0	2	18.56	2	2	0	0	5	13	11	11	2	5	3	.481	.615	.357	5.06	8.44
Smith, Chris	R-R	6-0	190	4-9-81	2	1	5.61	14	6	0	0	43	44	29	27	5	19	46	.263	.304	.213	9.55	3.95
Sullivan, Jerry	R-R	6-4	225	1-18-88	2	1	2.65	30	0	0	12	34	24	11	10	2	10	39	.197	.161	.227	10.32	2.65
Wieland, Joe	R-R	6-3	210	1-21-90	2	1	3.42	4	4	0	0	24	22	9	9	1	4	20	.247	.265	.225	7.61	1.52
Wisler, Matt	R-R	6-3	195	9-12-92	9	5	5.01	22	22	0	0	117	131	68	65	19	36	101	.279	.291	.268	7.79	2.78

Fielding

Catcher	PCT	G	PO	A	E	DP	PB
Decker	.982	11	51	4	1	1	0
Gale	.990	71	431	47	5	6	3
Moore	.988	86	524	54	7	4	4

First Base	PCT	G	PO	A	E	DP
Alonso	.970	4	31	1	1	2
Blanks	1.000	20	169	15	0	22
Castellanos	1.000	3	13	1	0	2
Conrad	1.000	2	16	0	0	0
Decker	.993	93	684	71	5	65
Galvez	.990	13	92	7	1	11
Goebbert	.987	9	71	6	1	6
Lane	1.000	3	12	1	0	4
Medica	1.000	15	116	6	0	13
Moore	1.000	2	1	0	0	0
Nelson	1.000	5	34	0	0	5

Second Base	PCT	G	PO	A	E	DP
Bixler	1.000	1	4	6	0	3
Castellanos	1.000	5	8	9	0	2
Conrad	.983	54	100	130	4	34
Gonzalez	—	2	0	0	0	0
Greene	.978	20	34	53	2	13

	PCT	G	PO	A	E	DP
Gyorko	1.000	6	9	15	0	4
Lindsey	.946	33	58	82	8	20
Nelson	.972	6	13	22	1	3
Peterson	.984	25	47	73	2	16
Robertson	.905	5	3	16	2	2

Third Base	PCT	G	PO	A	E	DP
Bixler	1.000	4	1	2	0	0
Castellanos	.917	39	16	72	8	6
Conrad	.936	22	14	30	3	6
Decker	.929	15	9	30	3	8
Galvez	.923	30	23	37	5	4
Gonzalez	1.000	6	3	8	0	1
Greene	.839	13	2	24	5	2
Lemmerman	.944	15	5	12	1	0
Lindsey	.900	6	5	13	2	0
Nelson	.977	14	13	30	1	1
Peterson	.974	15	14	23	1	2

Shortstop	PCT	G	PO	A	E	DP
Cabrera	.909	6	9	11	2	3
Conrad	1.000	4	1	7	0	1
Gonzalez	.930	12	18	22	3	8
Greene	.946	83	100	234	19	50

	PCT	G	PO	A	E	DP
Jackson	1.000	6	5	15	0	2
Lemmerman	.952	20	21	39	3	9
Peterson	.982	28	42	69	2	20

Outfield	PCT	G	PO	A	E	DP
Asencio	.951	21	36	3	2	1
Bixler	—	1	0	0	0	0
Blanks	1.000	5	8	0	0	0
Buck	.970	23	30	2	1	0
Castellanos	1.000	69	126	4	0	1
Francoeur	.972	109	167	9	5	2
Fuentes	.968	41	87	3	3	0
Galvez	.979	38	43	3	1	0
Goebbert	.975	41	76	1	2	0
Lane	1.000	2	1	0	0	0
Liriano	.941	16	31	1	2	0
Maybin	1.000	15	29	0	0	0
Medica	1.000	10	15	1	0	0
Noel	.982	100	266	4	5	1
Quentin	1.000	2	3	0	0	0
Robertson	—	1	0	0	0	0
Sampson	—	1	0	0	0	0
Sipp	—	1	0	0	0	0

SAN ANTONIO MISSIONS

DOUBLE-A

TEXAS LEAGUE

Batting	B-T	HT	WT	DOB	AVG	vLH	vRH	G	AB	R	H	2B	3B	HR	RBI	BB	HBP	SH	SF	SO	SB	CS	SLG	OBP
Asencio, Yeison	R-R	6-1	225	11-14-89	.284	.292	.281	117	455	51	129	21	3	10	44	24	3	3	1	57	8	4	.409	.323
Bixler, Brian	R-R	6-1	195	10-22-82	.207	.202	.209	87	295	30	61	6	1	2	22	28	7	2	0	74	7	6	.254	.291
Buschini, Adam	R-R	6-2	205	5-6-87	.215	.209	.218	100	358	51	77	11	2	9	29	42	0	2	1	74	11	5	.332	.297
Dickerson, Alex	L-L	6-3	230	5-26-90	.321	.314	.324	34	137	20	44	11	2	3	24	9	1	0	0	28	0	1	.496	.367
Fuentes, Reymond	L-L	6-0	160	2-12-91	.324	.273	.336	42	170	25	55	6	2	4	17	16	2	5	1	37	12	1	.453	.386
Gaedele, Kyle	R-R	6-3	220	11-1-89	.159	.179	.148	30	82	5	13	2	0	4	9	9	0	0	1	25	1	0	.329	.239
Goris, Diego	R-R	5-10	215	11-8-90	.247	.233	.252	37	146	18	36	5	0	4	10	2	1	1	1	25	1	2	.363	.260
Guinn, B.J.	B-R	6-1	180	4-4-89	.174	.250	.158	9	23	1	4	0	0	1	3	2	0	1	0	8	0	0	.304	.240
Hagerty, Jason	B-R	6-3	230	9-13-87	.266	.293	.255	97	350	46	93	21	1	10	46	51	6	0	1	72	4	2	.417	.368
Hedges, Austin	R-R	6-1	190	8-18-92	.225	.168	.245	113	427	31	96	19	2	6	44	23	3	2	2	89	1	3	.321	.268
Hunt, Bridger	R-R	5-11	165	7-24-85	.214	.195	.222	41	140	10	30	3	1	1	8	6	2	1	0	19	2	3	.271	.257
Jankowski, Travis	L-R	6-2	190	6-15-91	.240	.174	.260	29	100	14	24	4	1	0	10	8	1	1	2	14	10	2	.300	.297
Kral, Robert	L-R	5-10	195	3-28-89	.181	.194	.179	60	193	20	35	8	0	2	25	35	0	0	2	54	1	1	.301	.304
Lemmerman, Jake	R-R	6-1	195	5-4-89	.181	.161	.188	33	116	13	21	4	0	4	14	14	1	0	0	33	2	1	.319	.275
Liriano, Rymer	R-R	6-0	230	6-20-91	.264	.245	.271	99	371	55	98	20	2	14	53	35	6	0	3	102	17	7	.442	.335
McElroy, Casey	L-R	5-8	180	12-28-89	.248	.246	.248	96	347	56	86	12	1	9	45	47	12	2	3	50	1	3	.366	.355
Orr, Lee	R-R	6-3	215	10-23-88	.171	.177	.168	77	222	21	38	6	0	2	12	21	3	1	3	99	7	1	.315	.221
Overbeck, Cody	R-R	6-1	200	6-5-86	.235	.306	.212	69	251	29	59	7	1	13	32	11	1	0	2	66	0	1	.426	.268
Peterson, Jace	L-R	6-0	210	5-9-90	.311	.294	.316	18	74	10	23	3	0	1	7	9	0	0	0	9	4	3	.392	.386
Renfroe, Hunter	R-R	6-1	200	1-28-92	.232	.242	.228	60	224	17	52	12	0	5	23	25	0	0	2	53	2	1	.353	.307
Spangenberg, Cory	L-R	6-0	195	3-16-91	.331	.347	.325	66	281	38	93	17	8	2	22	15	0	8	0	63	14	9	.470	.365
Tejada, Luis	R-R	6-3	175	10-12-92	.333	.400	.000	2	6	1	2	0	0	0	1	0	1	0	0	1	0	0	.333	.429

Pitching	B-T	HT	WT	DOB	W	L	ERA	G	GS	CG	SV	IP	H	R	ER	HR	BB	SO	AVG	vLH	vRH	K/9	BB/9
Alvarez, R.J.	R-R	6-1	200	6-8-91	0	1	2.76	17	0	0	6	16	16	5	5	0	3	23	.250	.370	.162	12.67	1.65
2-team total (21 Arkansas)					0	1	1.25	38	0	0	7	43	29	7	6	0	13	61	—	—		12.67	2.70
Barbato, Johnny	R-R	6-2	185	7-11-92	2	2	2.87	27	0	0	16	31	26	12	10	3	10	33	.226	.196	.250	9.48	2.87
Branham, Matt	R-R	6-5	220	9-28-87	5	4	4.02	35	6	0	0	87	94	44	39	7	27	74	.277	.289	.266	7.63	2.79
Campos, Leonel	R-R	6-3	185	7-17-87	2	7	5.60	31	14	0	1	72	69	46	45	6	38	95	.249	.238	.259	11.82	4.73
Church, Joe	R-R	6-2	190	9-29-89	0	0	9.00	2	0	0	0	2	4	2	2	1	0	3	.400	.167	.750	13.50	0.00
De La Cruz, Luis	R-R	6-6	225	6-15-89	6	9	2.69	57	0	0	3	67	49	30	20	5	36	63	.204	.204	.205	8.46	4.84

Pitching	B-T	HT	WT	DOB	W	L	ERA	G	GS	CG	SV	IP	H	R	ER	HR	BB	SO	AVG	vLH	vRH	K/9	BB/9
Despaigne, Odrisamer	R-R	6-0	195	4-4-87	0	0	1.17	2	2	0	0	8	4	1	1	0	5	12	.154	.286	.105	14.09	5.87
Dimock, Michael	R-R	6-2	194	10-26-89	1	3	3.64	23	0	0	0	30	29	20	12	5	10	40	.244	.204	.271	12.13	3.03
2-team total (16 Corpus Christi)					2	7	3.47	39	0	0	1	57	55	32	22	6	17	61	—	—	—	9.63	2.68
Enloe, Jeffrey	L-L	6-5	215	8-13-89	0	0	10.80	1	0	0	0	2	3	2	2	0	2	1	.375	—	.375	5.40	10.80
Erlin, Robbie	L-L	6-0	190	10-8-90	0	0	3.48	3	3	0	0	10	12	4	4	1	4	10	.293	.444	.250	8.71	3.48
Garces, Frank	L-L	5-11	175	1-17-90	2	5	1.93	51	0	0	8	65	46	17	14	3	24	74	.196	.124	.240	10.19	3.31
Geer, Josh	R-R	6-3	195	6-2-83	7	12	3.58	30	24	0	0	156	172	74	62	4	30	95	.288	.282	.294	5.49	1.73
Gott, Trevor	R-R	6-0	190	8-26-92	0	0	4.63	10	0	0	0	12	11	8	6	0	9	11	.256	.238	.273	8.49	6.94
2-team total (13 Arkansas)					2	1	2.76	23	0	0	2	29	22	11	9	0	16	29	—	—	—	8.90	4.91
Hahn, Jesse	R-R	6-5	190	7-30-89	2	1	1.91	13	10	0	0	42	34	13	9	1	15	38	.221	.273	.169	8.08	3.19
Hancock, Justin	R-R	6-4	185	10-28-90	3	2	4.12	13	12	0	0	59	69	29	27	5	23	41	.294	.308	.278	6.25	3.51
Hussey, John	R-R	6-3	190	11-22-86	5	5	4.23	37	6	0	0	89	103	51	42	8	24	58	.288	.288	.287	5.84	2.42
Ibarra, Jeff	L-L	6-6	180	8-18-87	2	1	2.59	38	0	0	2	42	41	15	12	5	15	50	.258	.229	.289	10.80	3.24
Jones, Devin	R-R	6-2	170	7-4-90	4	3	7.23	9	7	0	0	37	51	34	30	5	12	20	.329	.345	.309	4.82	2.89
Kelly, Casey	R-R	6-3	210	10-4-89	1	0	0.75	2	2	0	0	12	11	3	1	0	1	8	.250	.200	.292	6.00	0.75
Lemond, Zech	R-R	6-1	170	10-9-92	0	0	0.00	1	0	0	0	4	1	0	0	0	0	2	.071	.000	.100	4.50	0.00
Morrow, Bryce	R-R	6-2	200	1-2-88	4	5	3.13	16	13	0	0	89	84	32	31	6	19	67	.257	.207	.297	6.78	1.92
Needy, James	R-R	6-6	230	3-30-91	10	5	2.90	26	24	0	0	146	133	48	47	6	50	113	.246	.221	.266	6.98	3.09
O'Grady, Dennis	R-R	5-9	205	5-17-89	0	0	3.86	14	0	0	1	16	19	7	7	1	7	21	.292	.235	.355	11.57	3.86
Oramas, Juan Pablo	L-L	5-10	220	5-11-90	3	0	1.05	4	4	0	0	26	24	8	3	0	6	23	.255	.125	.323	8.06	2.10
Patton, Troy	B-L	6-1	180	9-3-85	0	0	0.00	2	1	0	0	2	2	0	0	0	0	4	.250	.200	.333	18.00	0.00
Portillo, Adys	R-R	6-3	235	12-20-91	1	4	3.23	46	0	0	0	56	44	23	20	2	43	68	.220	.221	.219	10.99	6.95
Rearick, Chris	L-L	6-3	190	12-5-87	1	0	3.68	7	0	0	0	7	8	3	3	2	0	9	.267	.286	.250	11.05	0.00
Ross, Joe	R-R	6-4	205	5-21-93	2	0	3.60	4	3	0	0	20	23	8	8	2	1	19	.277	.333	.227	8.55	0.45
Sexton, Tim	R-R	6-6	185	6-10-87	1	0	0.00	1	1	0	0	5	4	0	0	0	2	5	.222	.111	.333	9.00	3.60
2-team total (5 Midland)					2	1	4.02	6	1	0	0	16	19	7	7	0	4	16	—	—	—	9.19	2.30
Sullivan, Jerry	R-R	6-4	225	1-18-88	3	2	1.80	24	0	0	1	25	19	6	5	0	10	27	.211	.209	.213	9.72	3.60
Wieland, Joe	R-R	6-3	210	1-21-90	0	1	2.00	2	2	0	0	9	8	3	2	1	1	6	.242	.125	.353	6.00	1.00
Wisler, Matt	R-R	6-3	195	9-12-92	1	0	2.10	6	6	0	0	30	26	7	7	2	6	35	.234	.233	.235	10.50	1.80
Yardley, Eric	R-R	6-0	165	8-18-90	0	0	3.00	4	0	0	0	6	3	2	2	0	4	7	.150	.100	.200	10.50	6.00

Fielding

Catcher	PCT	G	PO	A	E	DP	PB
Hagerty	.974	7	35	3	1	1	2
Hedges	.985	106	910	80	15	11	6
Kral	.980	32	228	14	5	2	4

First Base	PCT	G	PO	A	E	DP
Buschini	1.000	15	77	6	0	8
Hagerty	.990	56	474	28	5	39
Hunt	1.000	3	26	0	0	3
Kral	.750	1	3	0	1	1
Orr	.993	32	267	13	2	23
Overbeck	.995	44	352	19	2	39
Tejada	1.000	2	7	0	0	0

Second Base	PCT	G	PO	A	E	DP
Buschini	.980	18	37	63	2	13
Goris	1.000	3	7	8	0	2
Guinn	1.000	1	0	4	0	0
Hunt	.923	8	11	25	3	4
Lemmerman	1.000	1	2	4	0	0
McElroy	.991	70	123	190	3	44
Peterson	—	1	0	0	0	0
Spangenberg	.970	48	96	127	7	34

Third Base	PCT	G	PO	A	E	DP
Buschini	.978	42	22	65	2	6
Goris	.935	9	10	19	2	5
Guinn	1.000	3	0	6	0	0
Hunt	.929	29	23	42	5	5
Lemmerman	.918	29	18	49	6	10
McElroy	.985	31	15	50	1	7
Overbeck	1.000	5	4	5	0	1
Peterson	1.000	1	0	2	0	0
Spangenberg	.909	7	6	14	2	3

Shortstop	PCT	G	PO	A	E	DP
Bixler	.946	87	129	236	21	53
Buschini	.871	11	5	22	4	2
Goris	.894	25	36	65	12	12
Guinn	.875	3	4	3	1	0
Lemmerman	1.000	2	1	7	0	1
Peterson	.934	17	25	46	5	7

Outfield	PCT	G	PO	A	E	DP
Asencio	.953	112	195	8	10	4
Buschini	1.000	12	10	0	0	0
Dickerson	.983	28	57	1	1	0
Fuentes	.953	41	97	5	5	0
Gaedele	.976	19	40	1	1	1
Jankowski	.969	28	62	1	2	1
Liriano	.986	92	195	13	3	3
Orr	.978	28	43	1	1	0
Overbeck	.778	6	7	0	2	0
Renfroe	.946	59	100	6	6	1
Spangenberg	.974	14	35	2	1	0

LAKE ELSINORE STORM · HIGH CLASS A

CALIFORNIA LEAGUE

Batting	B-T	HT	WT	DOB	AVG	vLH	vRH	G	AB	R	H	2B	3B	HR	RBI	BB	HBP	SH	SF	SO	SB	CS	SLG	OBP
Adamson, Corey	L-R	6-2	205	2-23-92	.257	.250	.260	89	303	45	78	11	7	6	39	31	8	4	2	66	13	9	.399	.340
Baltz, Jeremy	R-R	6-3	195	9-17-90	.241	.257	.235	97	365	58	88	18	4	12	57	40	17	0	5	101	4	1	.411	.340
Brugeura, Reynaldo	B-R	5-10	170	11-5-91	.169	.167	.171	17	59	6	10	1	0	1	3	2	1	1	0	16	0	1	.237	.210
Carmon, Stephen	L-R	5-7	155	2-19-90	.206	.000	.245	19	63	9	13	2	2	1	5	8	0	3	1	5	1	2	.349	.292
Domoromo, Luis	L-L	6-1	215	2-4-92	.272	.240	.280	106	386	52	105	25	4	10	49	24	1	3	2	90	5	1	.435	.315
Gallego, Niko	R-R	5-11	160	12-29-88	.207	.000	.273	9	29	2	6	1	0	0	2	1	0	1	0	10	0	0	.241	.233
Gonzalez, Benji	R-R	5-11	160	1-16-90	.306	.318	.301	102	376	61	115	28	3	3	41	45	3	11	4	62	13	7	.420	.381
Goris, Diego	R-R	5-10	215	11-8-90	.324	.358	.311	89	370	66	120	27	2	13	61	14	2	0	6	74	5	0	.514	.347
Guinn, B.J.	B-R	6-1	180	4-4-89	.258	.143	.353	11	31	4	8	3	0	0	2	4	0	1	0	10	0	0	.355	.343
Headley, Chase	B-R	6-2	220	5-9-84	.333	.333	.333	4	12	1	4	1	0	0	2	0	0	0	0	4	0	0	.417	.429
Hunt, Bridger	R-R	5-11	165	7-24-85	.167	.000	.500	2	6	1	1	0	0	0	1	0	0	0	1	1	1	0	.167	.143
Jankowski, Travis	L-R	6-2	190	6-15-91	.167	.200	.154	5	18	2	3	1	0	0	1	6	0	1	0	3	1	0	.222	.375
Jensen, Chase	R-R	6-4	195	1-29-91	.455	1.000	.143	3	11	4	5	2	0	0	1	0	0	0	0	3	0	0	.636	.500
Jones, Duanel	R-R	6-3	220	5-11-93	.234	.273	.216	108	389	34	91	20	1	10	56	27	5	2	5	112	4	5	.368	.289
Martinez, Alberth	R-R	6-1	170	1-23-91	.268	.277	.264	132	526	76	141	28	2	12	68	41	6	2	11	97	7	6	.397	.322
McElroy, Casey	L-R	5-8	180	12-28-89	.211	.000	.235	15	57	8	12	2	0	2	6	6	0	1	0	17	0	0	.351	.286
Moreno, Edwin	L-L	6-1	190	10-27-93	.200	—	.200	3	5	0	1	0	0	0	1	0	0	0	0	2	0	0	.200	.200
Nester, John	R-R	6-1	210	5-28-89	.211	.103	.247	36	114	14	24	8	0	1	9	15	0	3	0	33	0	1	.307	.302
Phillips, Dane	L-R	6-1	195	12-18-90	.279	.300	.274	68	251	43	70	16	4	10	48	22	3	1	1	55	3	0	.494	.343
Quentin, Carlos	R-R	6-1	235	8-28-82	.100	.000	.250	4	10	1	1	0	0	0	0	3	0	0	0	2	0	0	.100	.308

SAN DIEGO PADRES

	B-T	HT	WT	DOB	AVG	vLH	vRH	G	AB	R	H	2B	3B	HR	RBI	BB	HBP	SH	SF	SO	SB	CS	SLG	OBP
Quintana, Gabriel	R-R	6-2	190	9-7-92	.263	.282	.256	130	529	77	139	35	0	18	84	21	11	0	5	150	4	1	.431	.302
Renfroe, Hunter	R-R	6-1	200	1-28-92	.295	.363	.268	69	278	46	82	21	3	16	52	28	7	0	3	81	9	3	.565	.370
Rodriguez, Jeremy	B-R	5-8	185	8-30-89	.177	.190	.170	57	175	13	31	5	0	0	16	23	2	8	2	24	0	1	.206	.277
Rondon, Jose	R-R	6-1	160	3-3-94	.301	.314	.297	37	136	18	41	9	0	1	12	13	2	3	0	23	3	1	.390	.371
2-team total (72 Inland Empire)					.319	—	—	109	433	58	138	26	5	1	36	30	2	12	1	73	11	7	.409	.365
Smith, Mallex	L-R	5-9	170	5-6-93	.327	.283	.341	55	223	43	73	16	1	5	16	31	2	5	0	48	40	10	.475	.414
Stevens, River	L-R	6-0	185	1-10-92	.150	.000	.200	7	20	1	3	0	0	0	0	3	0	0	0	4	0	0	.150	.261
Tejada, Luis	R-R	6-3	175	10-12-92	.190	.200	.182	12	42	5	8	2	0	0	2	2	1	0	0	12	0	0	.238	.244
Valdez, Jeudy	R-R	5-10	190	5-5-89	.197	.158	.212	23	71	7	14	4	0	0	7	10	0	0	2	15	3	0	.254	.289

Pitching	B-T	HT	WT	DOB	W	L	ERA	G	GS	CG	SV	IP	H	R	ER	HR	BB	SO	AVG	vLH	vRH	K/9	BB/9
Alger, Brandon	L-L	6-3	190	7-4-91	4	3	2.70	53	0	0	15	63	45	22	19	5	19	73	.191	.206	.178	10.37	2.70
Cashner, Andrew	R-R	6-6	220	9-11-86	0	0	0.00	1	1	0	0	2	1	0	0	0	0	3	.143	—	.143	13.50	0.00
Church, Joe	R-R	6-2	190	9-29-89	0	1	5.40	24	0	0	0	33	34	24	20	2	12	34	.248	.265	.239	9.18	3.24
Cimber, Adam	R-R	6-4	180	8-15-90	5	3	2.90	52	1	0	0	78	80	27	25	5	9	43	.272	.347	.236	4.98	1.04
Cowgill, Coby	R-R	6-1	200	3-23-91	3	2	6.59	13	7	0	0	41	52	36	30	5	26	31	.317	.317	.317	6.80	5.71
De Paula, Rafael	R-R	6-2	215	3-24-91	2	4	6.54	8	8	0	0	47	47	32	31	7	17	41	.281	.314	.258	6.65	3.59
Eflin, Zach	R-R	6-4	200	4-8-94	10	7	3.80	24	24	0	0	128	138	56	54	9	31	93	.281	.283	.279	6.54	2.18
Gott, Trevor	R-R	6-0	190	8-26-92	2	4	3.16	29	0	0	16	31	28	13	11	3	9	31	.239	.218	.258	8.90	2.59
Guerrero, Tayron	R-R	6-7	189	1-9-91	0	0	2.63	14	0	0	3	14	10	4	4	1	8	14	.200	.143	.241	9.22	5.27
Hebner, Cody	R-R	6-0	175	11-21-90	2	3	4.81	31	0	0	2	43	42	30	23	3	24	42	.263	.309	.228	8.79	5.02
Kelly, Casey	R-R	6-3	210	10-4-89	0	0	4.32	2	2	0	0	8	14	4	4	0	0	9	.400	.348	.500	9.72	0.00
Madrid, Roman	R-R	6-0	185	2-26-91	2	1	2.14	12	0	0	0	21	14	6	5	0	8	22	.192	.226	.167	9.43	3.43
Mejia, Ruben	R-R	6-1	175	2-23-92	2	2	5.88	6	5	0	0	26	33	20	17	1	11	15	.311	.293	.323	5.19	3.81
Morris, Elliot	R-R	6-4	210	4-26-92	3	3	3.56	8	8	0	0	48	40	19	19	7	11	33	.226	.175	.254	6.19	2.06
2-team total (9 Inland Empire)					6	6	3.86	17	17	0	0	93	77	42	40	12	39	73	—	—		7.04	3.76
Morrow, Bryce	R-R	6-2	200	1-2-88	1	1	3.75	19	5	0	0	50	56	27	21	7	8	37	.287	.247	.321	6.62	1.43
Mutz, Nick	R-R	6-1	190	6-15-90	0	1	18.56	4	0	0	0	5	10	11	11	2	3	5	.370	.250	.391	8.44	5.06
Nunn, Chris	L-L	6-5	200	10-5-90	4	2	4.30	49	0	0	0	59	52	31	28	7	25	76	.234	.248	.223	11.66	3.84
Oaks, Alan	R-R	6-3	225	4-4-88	0	0	7.59	9	0	0	0	11	11	13	9	3	6	10	.244	.133	.300	8.44	5.06
Paullus, Ben	R-R	6-1	190	8-31-89	1	0	4.65	23	0	0	1	31	45	23	16	4	9	28	.331	.286	.363	8.13	2.61
Rea, Colin	R-R	6-5	220	7-1-90	11	9	3.88	28	28	0	0	139	151	65	60	11	37	118	.274	.253	.289	7.64	2.40
Reyes, Genison	R-R	6-5	190	9-19-91	1	2	5.47	18	0	0	0	25	37	23	15	4	15	21	.343	.324	.351	7.66	5.47
Richardson, Josh	R-R	6-0	175	8-1-91	0	0	9.39	6	0	0	0	8	14	9	8	1	5	5	.412	.333	.440	5.87	5.87
Rizzotti, Tony	R-R	6-4	205	4-21-92	0	0	4.32	8	0	0	0	8	8	5	4	1	4	8	.294	.200	.368	8.64	4.32
Rodriguez, Bryan	R-R	6-5	180	7-6-91	8	9	4.16	27	26	0	0	149	154	81	69	9	46	104	.263	.248	.268	6.27	2.77
Ross, Joe	R-R	6-4	205	5-21-93	8	6	3.98	19	19	0	0	102	101	52	45	6	28	87	.256	.242	.266	7.70	2.48
Shepherd, Matt	R-R	6-3	185	5-2-90	6	1	5.02	43	5	0	1	86	81	50	48	8	37	96	.243	.238	.246	10.05	3.87
Verbitsky, Bryan	R-R	5-11	205	6-11-92	0	1	5.40	1	1	0	0	3	2	2	2	0	6	2	.231	.200	.250	5.40	16.20
Vincent, Nick	R-R	5-11	180	7-12-86	0	0	0.00	2	0	0	0	2	2	0	0	0	0	1	.286	—	.286	4.50	0.00
Wood, Tyler	R-R	6-3	225	10-17-91	0	0	27.00	1	0	0	0	1	5	3	3	1	0	1	.714	—	.714	9.00	0.00

Fielding

Catcher	PCT	G	PO	A	E	DP	PB
Nester	.987	36	280	18	4	2	3
Phillips	.987	54	410	35	6	4	10
Rodriguez	.985	57	419	37	7	5	5

First Base	PCT	G	PO	A	E	DP
Domoromo	.984	50	417	24	7	34
Goris	1.000	3	27	0	0	0
Jones	.992	85	744	49	6	59
Tejada	1.000	5	50	1	0	6
Valdez	1.000	2	14	0	0	2

Second Base	PCT	G	PO	A	E	DP
Brugeura	.981	14	15	37	1	6
Gallego	.950	4	7	12	1	2
Gonzalez	.975	85	144	243	10	46
Goris	.941	10	18	30	3	8
Guinn	.875	4	6	8	2	1
Jones	1.000	1	1	0	0	0

	PCT	G	PO	A	E	DP
McElroy	.984	13	19	44	1	3
Stevens	1.000	6	16	16	0	6
Valdez	.986	13	30	43	1	10

Third Base	PCT	G	PO	A	E	DP
Brugeura	.500	1	0	1	1	0
Gonzalez	.846	6	4	7	2	0
Goris	.600	2	1	2	2	0
Guinn	1.000	2	0	2	0	0
Headley	1.000	2	2	1	0	0
Jones	.889	11	4	12	2	2
Quintana	.920	121	56	219	24	18
Valdez	1.000	1	0	1	0	0

Shortstop	PCT	G	PO	A	E	DP
Brugeura	.769	2	4	6	3	4
Carmon	.938	15	24	52	5	9
Gallego	.950	4	4	15	1	4
Gonzalez	.974	11	8	29	1	3

	PCT	G	PO	A	E	DP
Goris	.962	71	117	209	13	35
Guinn	1.000	2	4	9	0	1
Jensen	.917	2	3	8	1	1
Rondon	.970	36	54	105	5	22
Valdez	.667	1	0	2	1	0

Outfield	PCT	G	PO	A	E	DP
Adamson	.980	61	91	5	2	0
Baltz	.986	78	144	1	2	0
Domoromo	.959	45	66	4	3	0
Gonzalez	1.000	1	2	0	0	0
Jankowski	1.000	4	8	0	0	0
Martinez	.984	124	295	9	5	3
Moreno	—	2	0	0	0	0
Quentin	1.000	3	2	0	0	0
Renfroe	.961	66	114	10	5	1
Smith	.968	45	90	1	3	0
Stevens	.500	1	1	0	1	0
Tejada	1.000	3	7	0	0	0

FORT WAYNE TINCAPS   LOW CLASS A

MIDWEST LEAGUE

Batting	B-T	HT	WT	DOB	AVG	vLH	vRH	G	AB	R	H	2B	3B	HR	RBI	BB	HBP	SH	SF	SO	SB	CS	SLG	OBP
Bauers, Jake	L-L	6-1	195	10-6-95	.296	.300	.294	112	406	59	120	18	3	8	64	51	4	1	5	80	5	6	.414	.376
Brugeura, Reynaldo	B-R	5-10	170	11-5-91	.253	.133	.278	27	87	10	22	3	0	0	6	8	0	0	2	23	0	0	.287	.309
Charles, Henry	L-L	6-1	205	1-3-94	.236	.182	.248	86	309	34	73	9	3	8	39	20	1	2	0	62	4	2	.362	.285
Cordero, Franchy	L-R	6-3	175	9-2-94	.188	.182	.189	22	85	5	16	2	1	0	9	4	2	1	2	36	3	3	.235	.237
Jensen, Chase	R-R	6-4	195	1-29-91	.161	.143	.167	16	56	4	9	2	1	0	5	1	2	0	1	12	0	0	.232	.200
Miller, Ryan	R-R	6-2	200	11-17-92	.243	.239	.244	87	305	38	74	14	0	12	37	19	9	2	2	69	1	1	.407	.304
Moreno, Edwin	L-L	6-0	190	10-27-93	.143	.000	.154	8	28	1	4	1	0	0	1	0	0	0	0	10	0	0	.179	.143
Nester, John	R-R	6-1	210	5-28-89	.300	.091	.359	14	50	11	15	4	0	0	2	5	1	0	0	13	0	0	.380	.375
Perez, Fernando	L-R	6-0	210	9-13-93	.284	.254	.293	116	469	69	133	24	1	18	95	25	5	1	7	106	3	2	.454	.322

Name	B-T	HT	WT	DOB	AVG	vLH	vRH	G	AB	R	H	2B	3B	HR	RBI	BB	HBP	SH	SF	SO	SB	CS	SLG	OBP
Peterson, Dustin	R-R	6-2	180	9-10-94	.233	.252	.228	126	527	64	123	31	3	10	79	25	6	0	5	137	1	3	.361	.274
Phillips, Dane	L-R	6-1	195	12-18-90	.295	.244	.313	40	156	25	46	12	3	2	28	10	0	1	1	30	2	0	.449	.335
Reina, Adolfo	R-R	6-0	210	1-22-90	.243	.261	.238	47	189	24	46	7	0	8	27	8	1	0	1	36	0	1	.407	.276
Reyes, Franmil	R-R	6-5	240	7-7-95	.248	.271	.240	128	508	67	126	24	2	11	59	38	2	1	3	118	1	5	.368	.301
Richardson, Ronnie	B-R	5-6	175	5-5-90	.268	.292	.261	87	306	66	82	16	6	4	27	54	16	4	3	66	12	5	.399	.401
Schulz, Nick	R-R	6-3	220	5-3-91	.341	.333	.344	49	176	30	60	8	2	8	30	11	2	2	0	47	1	1	.545	.386
Smith, Mallex	L-R	5-9	170	5-6-93	.295	.317	.288	65	254	56	75	13	6	0	15	38	4	5	2	55	48	16	.394	.393
Stevens, River	L-R	6-0	185	1-10-92	.248	.346	.213	26	101	14	25	1	2	1	9	4	0	0	1	13	2	0	.327	.274
Tejada, Luis	R-R	6-3	175	10-12-92	.247	.349	.209	46	158	19	39	6	1	3	18	9	6	1	1	36	2	0	.354	.310
Turner, Trea	R-R	6-1	175	6-30-93	.369	.383	.364	46	187	31	69	14	2	4	22	24	3	1	1	48	14	3	.529	.447
Urena, Jose	R-R	6-3	180	1-14-95	.165	.077	.182	19	79	7	13	3	1	2	11	5	2	0	0	27	0	0	.304	.233
VanMeter, Josh	L-R	5-11	165	3-10-95	.254	.304	.238	116	421	49	107	24	0	3	39	34	1	2	0	87	8	4	.333	.311

Pitching	B-T	HT	WT	DOB	W	L	ERA	G	GS	CG	SV	IP	H	R	ER	HR	BB	SO	AVG	vLH	vRH	K/9	BB/9
Baskette, Payton	L-L	6-1	175	10-1-93	4	4	5.29	20	12	0	0	82	113	60	48	5	35	52	.325	.267	.341	5.73	3.86
Blueberg, Colby	R-R	6-0	185	5-11-93	1	0	0.00	2	0	0	0	3	3	0	0	0	2	3	.250	.200	.286	9.00	6.00
Bostjancic, Cory	R-R	6-0	180	7-14-92	1	0	7.04	4	0	0	0	8	11	6	6	0	5	6	.344	.250	.400	7.04	5.87
Brasoban, Yimmi	R-R	6-1	185	6-22-94	2	4	6.54	15	14	0	0	65	79	52	47	4	35	50	.302	.300	.302	6.96	4.87
Butler, Ryan	R-R	6-4	225	2-23-92	1	1	0.83	18	0	0	10	22	17	3	2	0	6	30	.215	.286	.190	12.46	2.49
Cabrera, Erik	R-R	6-1	180	8-15-90	4	7	5.15	36	9	0	0	87	90	60	50	9	37	61	.273	.304	.256	6.29	3.81
Chabot, Matt	R-R	6-2	190	9-11-91	1	0	0.00	1	0	0	0	2	0	0	0	0	1	0	.000	.000	.000	27.00	0.00
Cowgill, Coby	R-R	6-1	200	3-23-91	2	2	7.31	9	7	0	0	32	40	28	26	0	21	24	.315	.261	.346	6.75	5.91
De Horta, Adrian	R-R	6-3	185	3-13-95	0	2	5.32	12	11	0	0	47	49	31	28	2	38	36	.272	.234	.301	6.85	7.23
Enloe, Jeffrey	L-L	6-5	215	8-13-89	6	6	3.84	14	12	0	0	63	65	33	27	3	15	34	.263	.139	.284	4.83	2.13
Fried, Max	L-L	6-4	185	1-18-94	0	1	4.76	2	2	0	0	6	7	3	3	1	2	2	.318	.333	.308	3.18	3.18
Guerrero, Tayron	R-R	6-7	189	1-9-91	6	1	1.00	25	0	0	1	36	22	7	4	2	12	42	.169	.190	.159	10.50	3.00
Guzman, Jorge	R-R	6-1	170	7-15-89	1	1	3.11	25	0	0	0	38	34	17	13	4	14	29	.241	.296	.207	6.93	3.35
Hebner, Cody	R-R	6-0	175	11-21-90	2	5	4.64	11	11	0	0	43	50	32	22	3	14	46	.284	.294	.278	9.70	2.95
Herrera, Ronald	R-R	5-11	185	5-3-95	3	5	4.26	17	16	0	0	82	93	45	39	5	15	47	.288	.316	.273	5.14	1.64
2-team total (9 Beloit)					6	9	3.92	26	25	0	0	133	146	71	58	11	25	82	—	—	—	5.55	1.69
Jester, Jason	R-R	5-10	185	5-4-91	3	1	1.71	19	0	0	0	26	21	9	5	0	8	27	.208	.313	.159	9.23	2.73
Kelich, Pete	R-R	6-2	195	2-16-91	0	3	4.88	5	5	0	0	24	33	21	13	1	3	26	.303	.267	.328	9.75	1.13
Livengood, Justin	R-R	6-3	210	3-2-90	7	1	3.46	35	1	0	1	83	78	35	32	5	30	84	.244	.195	.271	9.07	3.24
Lloyd, Kyle	R-R	6-4	210	10-16-90	6	5	3.61	27	21	0	0	120	114	60	48	8	34	155	.247	.219	.260	11.66	2.56
Lockett, Walker	R-R	6-5	225	5-3-94	0	0	0.00	1	1	0	0	5	3	3	0	0	1	1	.150	.300	.000	1.80	1.80
Mutz, Nick	R-R	6-1	190	6-15-90	2	5	2.29	46	0	0	9	51	48	20	13	2	15	51	.240	.213	.256	9.00	2.65
Reyes, Genison	R-R	6-5	190	9-19-91	2	0	6.69	30	0	0	0	39	47	29	29	2	22	39	.290	.315	.278	9.00	5.08
Richardson, Josh	R-R	6-0	175	8-1-91	1	2	7.11	18	0	0	0	32	48	26	25	2	10	22	.358	.352	.363	6.25	2.84
Rizzotti, Tony	R-R	6-4	205	4-21-92	3	2	5.88	25	0	0	0	49	67	37	32	2	21	41	.318	.289	.336	7.53	3.86
Santos, Wilson	R-R	6-2	200	10-20-91	0	3	7.00	14	0	0	0	18	21	17	14	1	14	16	.288	.318	.275	8.00	7.00
Verbitsky, Bryan	R-R	5-11	205	6-11-92	0	1	13.50	3	2	0	0	8	16	13	12	1	5	8	.410	.313	.478	9.00	5.63
Weickel, Walker	R-R	6-6	195	11-14-93	1	8	6.32	15	15	0	0	73	94	65	51	8	34	39	.308	.306	.310	4.83	4.21
Wieber, Tony	R-R	6-0	200	2-10-91	2	0	5.40	5	0	0	0	12	12	7	7	1	2	5	.273	.154	.323	3.86	1.54
Wood, Tyler	R-R	6-3	225	10-17-91	0	1	7.53	6	0	0	0	14	18	12	12	3	2	10	.300	.292	.306	6.28	1.26
Yardley, Eric	R-R	6-0	165	8-18-90	2	4	2.95	42	0	0	3	58	48	24	19	1	10	52	.218	.209	.222	8.07	1.55

Fielding

Catcher	PCT	G	PO	A	E	DP	PB
Miller	.985	73	524	63	9	4	8
Nester	.992	14	120	9	1	1	1
Phillips	.986	15	121	15	2	1	1
Reina	.991	42	290	48	3	2	3

First Base	PCT	G	PO	A	E	DP
Bauers	.987	103	871	62	12	62
Perez	.985	17	117	12	2	16
Tejada	.983	22	159	12	3	13

Second Base	PCT	G	PO	A	E	DP
Brugeura	.966	21	39	47	3	13
Perez	.972	51	87	119	6	15

	PCT	G	PO	A	E	DP
Stevens	.925	14	40	22	5	2
VanMeter	.965	59	111	111	8	31

Third Base	PCT	G	PO	A	E	DP
Brugeura	1.000	5	1	8	0	0
Perez	.830	35	23	55	16	4
Peterson	.874	101	85	178	38	9
Stevens	1.000	1	1	0	0	0

Shortstop	PCT	G	PO	A	E	DP
Cordero	.793	20	27	42	18	10
Jensen	.967	16	21	38	2	7
Stevens	.864	10	13	38	8	8
Turner	.982	36	66	100	3	25

	PCT	G	PO	A	E	DP
VanMeter	.960	59	78	160	10	20

Outfield	PCT	G	PO	A	E	DP
Brugeura	1.000	1	0	1	0	0
Charles	.970	85	162	0	5	0
Moreno	1.000	7	16	0	0	0
Reyes	.932	107	183	9	14	3
Richardson	.994	82	156	3	1	1
Schulz	1.000	48	69	4	0	3
Smith	.955	63	171	0	8	0
Stevens	1.000	1	1	0	0	0
Tejada	.982	25	53	2	1	1
Urena	.935	14	26	3	2	0

EUGENE EMERALDS   SHORT-SEASON

NORTHWEST LEAGUE

Batting	B-T	HT	WT	DOB	AVG	vLH	vRH	G	AB	R	H	2B	3B	HR	RBI	BB	HBP	SH	SF	SO	SB	CS	SLG	OBP
Blanco, Felipe	R-R	6-1	175	12-9-93	.169	.206	.156	37	130	9	22	8	1	1	5	4	1	2	0	57	3	1	.269	.200
Bousfield, Auston	R-R	5-11	185	7-5-93	.301	.368	.281	45	166	36	50	16	5	3	13	24	4	—	0	37	12	4	.512	.402
Boykin, Rod	R-R	6-1	175	4-17-95	.278	.667	.200	8	18	4	5	0	1	0	0	1	—	0		6	2	0	.389	.316
Bravo, Daniel	R-R	6-0	160	2-16-95	.000	.000	.000	2	7	0	0	0	0	0	0	1	0	0	0	2	0	0	.000	.000
Cordero, Franchy	L-R	6-3	175	9-2-94	.279	.259	.285	61	240	40	67	8	4	9	35	14	4	—	0	75	13	5	.458	.329
Daal, Rodney	R-R	5-11	190	3-23-94	.091	—	.091	3	11	1	1	0	0	0	1	1	0	0	0	3	0	0	.091	.167
Davis, Marcus	L-L	6-3	200	4-26-92	.322	.368	.306	60	214	32	69	23	1	7	31	29	3	—	0	44	4	2	.537	.411
Del Castillo, Miguel	R-R	5-10	170	10-14-91	.203	.158	.217	23	79	12	16	7	1	0	12	4	0	0	1	18	0	0	.316	.238
Dickerson, Alex	R-R	6-3		6-26-90	.300	.000	.333	3	10	3	3	1	0	0	2	0	0	0	0	2	0	0	.400	.462
Epperson, Joey	R-R	6-2	195	2-17-91	.245	.063	.339	31	94	11	23	5	0	1	4	7	5	1	0	19	2	3	.330	.330
Goree, Jalen	R-R	5-10	195	6-15-93	.217	.350	.170	43	152	20	33	9	1	5	21	11	2	—	2	40	8	3	.388	.275

SAN DIEGO PADRES

Name	B-T	HT	WT	DOB	AVG	vLH	vRH	G	AB	R	H	2B	3B	HR	RBI	BB	HBP	SH	SF	SO	SB	CS	SLG	OBP
Jankowski, Travis	L-R	6-2	190	6-15-91	.182	.286	.154	8	33	6	6	0	0	0	1	3	0	0	0	5	4	0	.182	.250
Jensen, Chase	R-R	6-4	195	1-29-91	.278	.412	.242	23	79	5	22	5	0	2	11	1	1—	1	27	0	0	.418	.293
Miller, Michael	R-R	6-2	200	5-27-92	.236	.179	.262	26	89	7	21	3	0	1	9	6	2	0	0	13	2	0	.303	.299
Morales, Mitch	L-R	5-10	165	3-3-93	.214	.143	.238	9	28	1	6	1	0	0	1	1	0	0	0	8	1	0	.250	.241
Moreno, Edwin	L-L	6-1	190	10-27-93	.242	.217	.250	26	95	8	23	7	0	1	5	3	0	0	1	22	3	2	.347	.263
Rosen, Yale	L-L	6-2	210	5-9-93	.247	.160	.262	54	170	16	42	12	0	7	29	26	1—	0	55	1	2	.441	.350
Ruiz, Jose	R-R	6-1	190	10-11-94	.187	.194	.185	43	155	12	29	7	0	0	7	1	2—	1	36	0	0	.232	.201
Santos, Trae	L-L	6-1	235	10-11-92	.204	.237	.194	49	162	15	33	8	1	4	26	20	5	0	1	47	2	0	.340	.309
Schulz, Nick	R-R	6-3	220	5-3-91	.167	.182	.162	12	48	6	8	2	0	1	5	4	0	0	0	13	0	0	.271	.231
Spangenberg, Cory	L-R	6-0	195	3-16-91	.200	.143	.222	6	25	3	5	0	1	0	2	0	0	0	0	6	2	0	.280	.200
Stevens, River	L-R	6-0	185	1-10-92	.267	.118	.304	24	86	12	23	4	0	0	10	7	3	1	1	16	7	2	.314	.340
Torres, Nick	R-R	6-1	220	6-30-93	.254	.293	.242	43	169	20	43	11	0	3	23	7	2—	0	42	2	2	.373	.292
Turner, Trea	R-R	6-1	175	6-30-93	.228	.333	.208	23	92	14	21	2	0	1	2	11	2	0	0	19	9	1	.283	.324
Urena, Jose	R-B	6-3	180	1-14-95	.196	.175	.203	44	158	14	31	8	0	4	13	16	3	0	1	65	0	3	.323	.281
Vilter, Nick	R-R	6-4	220	10-6-93	.216	.176	.228	23	74	11	16	4	1	0	8	15	4	1	0	21	1	1	.297	.376

Pitching

Name	B-T	HT	WT	DOB	W	L	ERA	G	GS	CG	SV	IP	H	R	ER	HR	BB	SO	AVG	vLH	vRH	K/9	BB/9
Baskette, Payton	L-L	6-1	175	10-1-93	0	2	5.52	4	3	0	0	15	14	9	9	0	3	17	.255	.278	.243	10.43	1.84
Beatty, Max	R-R	6-2	225	3-27-91	1	1	4.50	18	1	0	0	28	29	21	14	4	5	25	.257	.294	.241	8.04	1.61
Blueberg, Colby	R-R	6-0	185	5-11-93	2	0	0.55	18	0	0	1	33	24	4	2	0	6	37	.207	.121	.241	10.19	1.65
Bostjancic, Cory	R-R	6-0	180	7-14-92	1	2	14.32	15	0	0	0	22	36	35	35	2	14	17	.379	.516	.313	6.95	5.73
Brasoban, Yimmi	R-R	6-1	185	6-22-94	2	1	6.48	4	4	0	0	17	19	13	12	1	8	15	.275	.375	.222	8.10	4.32
Butler, Ryan	R-R	6-4	225	2-23-92	0	0	8.22	5	0	0	1	8	12	7	7	0	3	6	.375	.444	.348	7.04	3.52
Constanza, Alex	L-L	6-3	190	7-27-94	0	2	14.14	2	2	0	0	7	11	11	11	2	4	6	.344	.333	.350	7.71	5.14
Cox, Taylor	L-L	6-3	210	7-2-93	0	1	27.00	2	0	0	0	2	7	6	5	0	0	1	.538	1.000	.455	5.40	0.00
Cressley, Aaron	L-R	6-1	175	9-2-92	2	1	3.60	21	2	0	0	35	34	17	14	1	15	29	.252	.208	.276	7.46	3.86
De Horta, Adrian	R-R	6-3	185	3-13-95	1	2	5.40	13	7	0	0	30	28	24	18	2	30	26	.246	.282	.227	7.80	9.00
Dorminy, Thomas	L-L	6-0	190	6-1-92	0	1	3.72	11	7	0	0	19	25	13	8	2	9	24	.316	.421	.283	11.17	4.19
Enloe, Jeffrey	L-L	6-5	215	8-13-89	0	0	2.45	1	0	0	0	4	1	1	1	0	1	5	.077	.000	.125	12.27	0.00
Fry, Brandon	L-L	6-3	195	3-28-93	0	1	3.42	12	0	0	0	24	18	12	9	1	13	15	.209	.150	.227	5.70	4.94
Guzman, Jorge	R-R	6-1	170	7-15-89	0	0	0.00	1	0	0	0	2	1	0	0	0	0	3	.143	.000	.250	13.50	0.00
Holland, Sam	R-R	6-4	200	2-20-94	0	1	2.43	27	0	0	0	41	36	20	11	1	8	53	.222	.217	.224	11.73	1.77
Huffman, Chris	R-R	6-1	205	11-25-92	0	1	4.26	15	0	0	0	19	21	11	9	1	6	16	.292	.185	.356	7.58	2.84
Jernigan, Logan	R-R	6-3	185	9-21-92	0	4	5.59	11	10	0	0	37	36	28	23	5	20	39	.257	.320	.222	9.49	4.86
Kelly, Mike	R-R	6-4	185	9-6-92	7	5	4.05	15	14	0	0	73	59	36	33	5	25	71	.224	.268	.199	8.71	3.07
Lemond, Zech	R-R	6-1	170	10-9-92	2	3	3.79	11	8	0	0	38	39	17	16	1	5	34	.262	.327	.230	8.05	1.18
Liriano, Elvin	L-L	6-3	190	10-17-92	0	0	3.86	2	0	0	0	2	1	1	1	0	3	4	.111	.000	.167	15.43	11.57
Lockett, Walker	R-R	6-5	225	5-3-94	0	2	21.94	4	2	0	0	5	13	15	13	0	12	1	.481	.714	.400	1.69	20.25
Lucio, Seth	R-R	5-10	180	4-30-93	3	2	2.96	24	0	0	1	27	16	11	9	1	20	46	.165	.138	.176	15.15	6.59
Radke, Travis	L-L	6-4	200	3-6-93	2	3	3.12	17	2	0	0	35	32	20	12	0	16	44	.241	.242	.240	11.42	4.15
Rizzotti, Tony	R-R	6-4	205	4-21-92	0	0	0.96	5	0	0	1	9	3	1	1	0	2	10	.100	.167	.083	9.64	1.93
Russell, Griffin	L-L	6-0	190	3-5-94	0	3	4.97	11	5	0	0	29	32	18	16	3	18	29	.288	.192	.318	9.00	5.59
Santos, Wilson	R-R	6-2	200	10-20-91	3	2	2.55	24	0	0	0	35	33	14	10	1	12	23	.265	.222	.286	5.86	3.06
Verbitsky, Bryan	R-R	5-11	205	11-12-92	2	2	1.67	23	0	0	5	27			5	0	10	42	.144	.250	.086	14.00	3.33
Weickel, Walker	R-R	6-6	195	11-14-93	0	3	6.09	7	7	0	0	34	47	31	23	3	17	20	.318	.305	.326	5.29	4.50
Wieber, Tony	R-R	6-0	200	2-10-91	1	0	7.90	5	2	0	0	14	21	13	12	1	1	13	.333	.333	.333	8.56	0.66
Wissmann, Danny	L-L	5-10	180	5-6-92	1	0	0.00	1	0	0	0	1	1	0	0	0	0	1	.200	.000	.500	9.00	0.00

Fielding

Catcher	PCT	G	PO	A	E	DP	PB
Del Castillo	.984	14	113	9	2	0	2
Miller	.972	21	158	16	5	1	4
Ruiz	.982	43	383	49	8	1	23

First Base	PCT	G	PO	A	E	DP
Davis	.981	43	335	22	7	30
Del Castillo	1.000	1	3	0	0	0
Santos	.988	36	303	22	4	31

Second Base	PCT	G	PO	A	E	DP
Blanco	.969	13	24	39	2	8
Bravo	1.000	1	0	2	0	0
Del Castillo	1.000	3	2	5	0	1
Epperson	.955	8	25	17	2	4
Goree	.927	39	77	102	14	19
Spangenberg	.958	4	9	14	1	4
Stevens	.965	16	22	33	2	8

	PCT	G	PO	A	E	DP
Vilter	1.000	1	7	1	0	0

Third Base	PCT	G	PO	A	E	DP
Blanco	.863	20	10	34	7	2
Cordero	.750	1	0	3	1	0
Del Castillo	.750	6	1	5	2	0
Epperson	.853	17	7	22	5	0
Jensen	.939	19	11	35	3	2
Miller	1.000	1	0	2	0	1
Vilter	.961	21	7	42	2	5

Shortstop	PCT	G	PO	A	E	DP
Blanco	.885	8	6	17	3	4
Bravo	1.000	1	1	3	0	0
Cordero	.805	36	44	92	33	20
Jensen	.867	3	4	9	2	2
Morales	.923	9	13	23	3	4
Stevens	.920	7	10	13	2	3

	PCT	G	PO	A	E	DP
Turner	.987	14	24	54	1	6
Vilter	.727	2	4	4	3	0

Outfield	PCT	G	PO	A	E	DP
Bousfield	.970	44	93	3	3	0
Boykin	.800	4	4	0	1	0
Davis	.938	13	13	2	1	0
Dickerson	1.000	2	5	1	0	0
Epperson	1.000	4	7	0	0	0
Jankowski	1.000	7	9	0	0	0
Moreno	.960	23	47	1	2	1
Rosen	1.000	50	67	5	0	1
Schulz	1.000	12	13	1	0	0
Spangenberg	1.000	1	1	0	0	0
Torres	.986	39	66	3	1	1
Urena	.981	40	51	2	1	0

AZL PADRES   ROOKIE

ARIZONA LEAGUE

Batting	B-T	HT	WT	DOB	AVG	vLH	vRH	G	AB	R	H	2B	3B	HR	RBI	BB	HBP	SH	SF	SO	SB	CS	SLG	OBP
Alonso, Yonder	L-R	6-1	230	4-8-87	.375	.333	.400	2	8	1	3	0	0	1	4	0	0	0	0	1	0	0	.750	.375
Barahona, Luis	B-R	5-11	170	11-27-93	.296	.182	.317	25	71	8	21	0	1	1	10	11	0	0	0	15	1	2	.366	.390
Belen, Carlos	R-R	6-1	213	2-28-96	.256	.200	.269	37	133	20	34	5	9	5	22	14	6	0	2	61	3	1	.541	.348
Boykin, Rod	R-R	6-1	175	4-17-95	.266	.091	.302	21	64	8	17	6	1	0	12	3	1	0	2	20	5	1	.391	.300
Bravo, Daniel	R-R	6-0	160	2-16-95	.265	.219	.276	42	155	27	41	9	2	2	18	12	2	3	1	44	8	3	.387	.324

Batting	B-T	HT	WT	DOB	AVG	vLH	vRH	G	AB	R	H	2B	3B	HR	RBI	BB	HBP	SH	SF	SO	SB	CS	SLG	OBP
Daal, Rodney	R-R	5-11	190	3-23-94	.258	.600	.192	9	31	5	8	0	0	2	5	4	0	0	1	9	0	0	.452	.333
Dickerson, Alex	L-L	6-3	230	5-26-90	.286	.333	.273	4	14	3	4	1	2	0	0	0	0	0	0	3	0	0	.643	.286
Fitzgerald, Mike	R-R	6-1	210	5-26-91	.167	.091	.184	26	60	9	10	1	0	0	5	19	6	0	1	20	0	1	.183	.407
Gettys, Michael	R-R	6-1	203	10-22-95	.310	.333	.305	52	213	29	66	8	5	3	38	15	1	1	3	66	14	2	.437	.353
Giron, Ruddy	R-R	5-11	175	1-4-97	.168	.111	.181	48	185	23	31	10	0	0	13	8	1	3	1	42	1	2	.222	.205
Guinn, B.J.	B-R	6-1	180	4-4-89	.700	.667	.714	4	10	2	7	3	1	0	1	3	0	0	1	1	1	0	1.200	.714
Jackson, Ryan	R-R	6-3	180	5-10-88	.211	.167	.231	5	19	2	4	0	0	0	0	0	0	0	0	6	1	0	.211	.250
Jankowski, Travis	L-R	6-2	190	6-15-91	.429	.500	.375	4	14	5	6	1	0	0	3	1	1	0	0	1	2	1	.500	.500
Lantigua, Jonas	L-R	6-5	205	12-15-94	.238	.171	.256	43	160	18	38	14	0	4	24	14	1	0	3	48	0	1	.400	.298
Moore, Adam	R-R	6-3	220	5-8-84	.667	—	.667	2	6	3	4	3	0	1	4	1	0	0	0	0	0	0	1.667	.714
Morales, Mitch	L-R	5-10	165	3-3-93	.167	.000	.200	11	24	3	4	1	0	0	2	7	0	1	0	7	0	0	.208	.355
Munoz, Cristian	L-R	5-10	185	7-12-94	.500	—	.500	2	4	1	2	1	0	0	1	1	0	0	0	0	0	0	.750	.600
Nester, John	R-R	6-1	210	5-28-89	.222	.333	.200	6	18	1	4	0	0	0	3	0	0	0	0	4	0	0	.278	.222
Paroubeck, Jordan	R-R	6-2	190	11-2-94	.286	.321	.277	34	140	26	40	8	2	4	24	13	1	1	2	42	4	2	.457	.346
Pena, Jhonatan	R-R	6-2	180	4-18-94	.231	.174	.250	29	91	11	21	2	2	0	9	6	0	1	0	31	4	2	.297	.278
Risedorf, Zach	R-R	5-11	190	3-11-96	.203	.357	.164	23	69	13	14	1	0	1	7	8	1	0	0	18	0	0	.261	.295
Smith, Mason	R-R	6-2	195	3-16-95	.199	.125	.218	44	151	20	30	5	2	1	10	22	9	0	3	53	2	1	.278	.330
Spangenberg, Cory	L-R	6-0	195	3-16-91	.167	—	.167	2	6	3	1	0	1	0	2	2	0	0	0	0	0	0	.500	.375
Torres, Nick	R-R	6-1	220	6-30-93	.000	.000	—	1	1	1	0	0	0	0	0	0	0	0	0	0	0	0	.000	.500
Urias, Luis	R-R	5-9	160	6-3-97	.310	.267	.320	43	155	29	48	5	1	0	14	18	4	1	1	13	10	6	.355	.393
Valenzuela, Ricardo	R-R	6-0	190	8-4-90	.250	.316	.234	34	96	12	24	4	1	1	11	8	3	1	3	17	1	0	.344	.318
Vilter, Nick	R-R	6-4	220	10-6-93	.111	.000	.125	3	9	2	1	0	0	0	1	1	0	0	0	2	0	0	.111	.273

Pitching	B-T	HT	WT	DOB	W	L	ERA	G	GS	CG	SV	IP	H	R	ER	HR	BB	SO	AVG	vLH	vRH	K/9	BB/9
Aikenhead, Taylor	L-L	6-0	175	3-31-92	4	0	1.19	12	2	0	0	23	15	4	3	0	4	30	.185	.176	.188	11.91	1.59
Atwood, Ryan	L-L	6-1	185	8-12-91	0	0	9.00	1	0	0	0	1	2	1	1	0	0	1	.400	.667	.000	9.00	0.00
Constanza, Alex	L-L	6-3	190	7-27-94	2	3	4.75	10	7	0	0	36	37	27	19	7	14	29	.253	.279	.243	7.25	3.50
Cox, Taylor	L-L	6-3	210	7-2-93	1	1	3.71	11	4	0	0	27	35	15	11	0	5	26	.304	.263	.325	8.78	1.69
Diaz, Malcom	R-R	6-2	185	3-2-94	1	1	4.13	21	0	0	2	28	24	21	13	1	17	28	.222	.238	.212	8.89	5.40
Erlin, Robbie	L-L	6-0	190	10-8-90	0	0	0.00	1	1	0	0	2	1	0	0	0	0	5	.111	.000	.167	22.50	0.00
Fried, Max	L-L	6-4	185	1-18-94	0	0	5.40	3	3	0	0	5	8	3	3	0	3	8	.348	.375	.333	14.40	5.40
Fry, Brandon	L-L	6-3	195	3-28-93	0	1	4.50	7	0	0	0	10	13	10	5	1	5	10	.310	.250	.324	9.00	4.50
Gonzalez, Manuel	R-R	6-4	195	10-21-94	1	6	8.04	12	6	0	0	44	66	48	39	3	16	25	.338	.351	.331	5.15	3.30
Hancock, Justin	R-R	6-4	185	10-28-90	0	0	0.00	2	2	0	0	3	4	0	0	0	0	3	.333	.400	.286	0.00	0.00
Jester, Jason	R-R	5-10	185	5-4-91	0	0	0.00	2	0	0	0	3	2	0	0	0	2	7	.200	.000	.250	23.63	0.00
Kimber, Corey	R-R	6-1	175	6-28-94	2	2	5.24	21	0	0	1	34	36	26	20	1	23	37	.288	.385	.244	9.70	6.03
Lebron, Jaimito	R-R	6-2	175	10-20-96	1	3	7.58	12	8	0	0	38	57	38	32	4	17	26	.337	.329	.344	6.16	4.03
Liriano, Elvin	L-L	6-3	190	10-17-92	1	1	1.34	17	0	0	0	34	16	11	5	0	17	18	.139	.259	.102	9.09	4.54
MacNabb, Max	L-L	6-0	195	8-28-92	0	4	5.93	19	0	0	0	27	40	24	18	2	19	21	.351	.314	.367	6.91	6.26
McGrath, Kyle	L-L	6-2	185	7-31-92	1	1	0.79	13	0	0	2	23	8	3	2	0	6	22	.110	.077	.128	8.74	2.38
Patton, Troy	B-L	6-1	180	9-3-85	0	0	0.00	3	2	0	0	3	1	0	0	0	0	4	.100	.000	.125	12.00	0.00
Perez, Mayky	R-R	6-5	235	9-26-96	0	3	7.08	11	4	0	0	34	46	31	27	4	15	30	.315	.328	.304	7.86	3.93
Remillard, Travis	R-R	6-1	190	7-9-93	0	1	3.38	11	0	0	0	11	11	8	4	0	6	10	.275	.316	.238	8.44	5.06
Richardson, Josh	R-R	6-0	175	8-1-91	0	0	0.00	3	0	0	0	4	2	0	0	0	1	7	.143	.167	.125	15.75	2.25
Solano, Leonardo	R-R	6-4	200	1-18-92	1	1	11.70	12	0	0	0	10	9	13	13	3	16	9	.237	.250	.231	8.10	14.40
Stewart, Cam	L-R	6-8	220	9-9-94	0	2	18.00	2	2	0	0	2	3	4	4	0	3	1	.333	.429	.000	4.50	13.50
Watrous, Mitch	R-R	6-0	205	12-31-92	1	0	10.80	2	0	0	0	3	6	4	4	0	1	4	.400	.500	.286	10.80	2.70
Weickel, Walker	R-R	6-6	195	11-14-93	1	0	1.29	2	2	0	0	7	5	1	1	0	2	3	.208	.143	.300	3.86	2.57
Weir, T.J.	R-R	6-0	205	9-15-91	2	0	0.42	12	6	0	0	22	11	2	1	0	6	24	.151	.152	.150	9.97	2.49
Wieland, Joe	R-R	6-3	210	1-21-90	0	1	3.00	3	3	0	0	6	3	2	2	0	1	10	.143	.286	.071	15.00	1.50
Wilson, Tyler	R-R	6-2	215	11-27-91	0	1	1.04	8	0	0	0	9	6	4	1	1	3	17	.194	.133	.250	17.65	3.12
Wood, Tyler	R-R	6-3	225	10-17-91	0	0	1.66	12	0	0	0	22	13	4	4	0	0	22	.167	.200	.151	9.14	0.00
Ynfante, Starling	R-R	6-2	200	2-23-94	0	4	4.42	8	4	0	0	18	9	12	9	4	12	17	.134	.222	.102	8.35	5.89

Fielding

Catcher	PCT	G	PO	A	E	DP	PB
Fitzgerald	1.000	11	54	6	0	0	0
Moore	1.000	1	8	1	0	0	0
Munoz	1.000	1	3	1	0	0	0
Nester	1.000	6	43	4	0	2	1
Risedorf	.964	22	141	18	6	0	2
Valenzuela	.996	30	211	24	1	1	7

First Base	PCT	G	PO	A	E	DP
Alonso	1.000	1	7	0	0	0
Barahona	—	1	0	0	0	0
Fitzgerald	.968	15	114	8	4	8
Lantigua	.982	43	359	21	7	25
Valenzuela	.909	1	7	3	1	3

Second Base	PCT	G	PO	A	E	DP
Bravo	.942	34	64	115	11	18
Guinn	1.000	1	1	2	0	2
Morales	.944	6	8	9	1	1
Spangenberg	1.000	1	1	3	0	2
Urias	.957	22	32	56	4	9

Third Base	PCT	G	PO	A	E	DP
Belen	.846	31	17	60	14	6
Bravo	1.000	3	2	5	0	0
Jackson	.750	1	1	2	1	0
Urias	.959	23	14	57	3	8
Vilter	1.000	2	0	4	0	0

Shortstop	PCT	G	PO	A	E	DP
Bravo	.727	5	1	7	3	0
Giron	.928	48	59	109	13	24
Guinn	1.000	2	2	1	0	0
Jackson	1.000	3	3	6	0	0
Morales	.917	5	4	7	1	0

Outfield	PCT	G	PO	A	E	DP
Barahona	1.000	13	11	1	0	0
Boykin	.971	20	32	1	1	0
Dickerson	1.000	3	4	0	0	0
Gettys	.921	49	111	5	10	3
Jankowski	1.000	4	10	1	0	1
Paroubeck	.875	26	21	0	3	0
Pena	.892	21	32	1	4	0
Smith	.984	39	59	3	1	0

DSL PADRES   ROOKIE

DOMINICAN SUMMER LEAGUE

Batting	B-T	HT	WT	DOB	AVG	vLH	vRH	G	AB	R	H	2B	3B	HR	RBI	BB	HBP	SH	SF	SO	SB	CS	SLG	OBP
Arias, Enmanuel	R-R	6-1	215	12-16-94	.101	.150	.093	42	138	10	14	7	0	0	11	8	2	0	2	66	3	1	.152	.160

					AVG	vLH	vRH	G	AB	R	H	2B	3B	HR	RBI	BB	SO	SB	CS		OBP	SLG
Asuncion, Luis	R-R	6-4	205	2-27-97	.135	.208	.113	26	104	9	14	0	1	2	10	5	3	0	0	33	0	0	.212	.196
Beltre, Moises	R-R	5-11	190	11-15-90	.333	1.000	.000	1	3	0	1	1	0	0	0	0	0	0	0	1	0	0	.667	.333
2-team total (14 Tigers)					.353	—	—	15	17	3	6	2	0	0	2	1	1	0	0	3	0	0	.471	.421
Castillo, Fabian	R-R	6-1	175	9-26-93	.244	.280	.235	37	123	12	30	6	1	2	14	5	3	1	1	10	0	1	.358	.288
Contreras, Ronaldo	R-R	6-3	195	7-15-96	.235	.273	.228	60	213	17	50	10	2	3	26	14	5	0	0	66	0	1	.343	.297
De La Cruz, Wilfri	R-R	5-11	180	12-29-93	.250	.188	.260	34	112	20	28	3	0	2	8	16	3	1	0	18	3	1	.330	.359
Magdaleno, Westhers	R-R	6-1	190	10-30-96	.182	.150	.188	62	231	28	42	5	2	0	17	32	11	1	1	85	6	4	.221	.309
Molina, Leudy	L-R	6-0	160	11-20-94	.301	.176	.326	28	103	17	31	2	3	1	9	10	0	0	0	24	1	0	.408	.363
Olmo, Dayon	B-R	5-11	165	11-15-96	.162	.148	.164	48	167	11	27	1	4	0	14	17	3	1	2	51	6	4	.216	.249
Perez, Aurelio	R-R	6-1	185	4-11-94	.220	.273	.208	45	123	21	27	7	1	1	9	26	3	0	1	34	12	5	.317	.366
Pomare, Derwin	R-R	5-11	160	5-11-95	.211	.207	.212	46	175	16	37	1	3	1	18	9	0	0	2	45	13	2	.269	.247
Savinon, Jose	L-R	6-0	160	2-17-96	.300	.263	.304	50	180	29	54	4	3	0	18	23	1	0	0	15	9	3	.356	.382
Sosa, Carlos	R-R	6-1	190	8-7-95	.241	.357	.212	36	141	17	34	8	1	3	28	12	4	0	1	35	1	1	.376	.316
Sotillo, Jose	R-R		175	5-13-96	.195	.125	.207	56	169	21	33	3	1	0	9	23	11	1	0	68	7	2	.225	.330
Suarez, Felix	R-R	6-0	180	1-9-96	.208	.300	.184	41	144	20	30	8	2	1	10	16	2	2	1	52	9	4	.313	.294
Urias, Luis	R-R	5-9	160	6-3-97	.100	.000	.125	2	10	1	1	0	0	0	0	0	1	0	0	0	1	0	.100	.182
Vizcaino, Manuel	R-R	6-0	165	1-8-96	.265	.350	.246	61	219	29	58	9	5	1	14	24	5	0	1	66	9	7	.365	.349

Pitching	B-T	HT	WT	DOB	W	L	ERA	G	GS	CG	SV	IP	H	R	ER	HR	BB	SO	AVG	vLH	vRH	K/9	BB/9
Caminero, Franly	L-L	5-11	175	12-3-92	0	3	8.20	9	4	0	0	26	49	29	24	0	8	26	.395	.444	.391	8.89	2.73
Carrillo, Jhonathan	L-L	6-1	170	2-2-94	0	3	4.25	8	5	0	0	30	29	21	14	4	9	29	.244	.316	.230	8.80	2.73
Cordova, Eisler	L-L	5-11	180	7-11-95	3	1	2.04	18	3	0	0	35	20	15	8	0	35	38	.157	.176	.155	9.68	8.92
De Los Santos, Erick	R-R	6-4	200	4-23-94	1	2	2.91	16	0	0	0	22	13	11	7	1	18	25	.163	.111	.177	10.38	7.48
Diaz, Adonis	R-R	6-1	185	12-8-94	2	3	5.03	15	0	0	1	20	21	19	11	1	8	20	.263	.208	.286	9.15	3.66
Diaz, Malcom	R-R	6-2	185	3-2-94	0	0	12.79	6	0	0	0	6	12	11	9	1	5	8	.400	.429	.391	11.37	7.11
Garcia, Jean	R-R	6-5	220	12-7-96	0	3	6.00	12	3	0	0	18	21	20	12	0	15	17	.276	.200	.304	8.50	7.50
Garcia, Joel	L-L	6-2	180	8-7-92	1	2	8.59	19	0	0	0	22	16	22	21	0	33	28	.111	.221		11.45	13.50
Gonzalez, Cesar	R-R	6-0	185	12-18-91	0	3	13.24	20	0	0	0	17	18	31	25	1	29	13	.286	.211	.318	6.88	15.35
Lamet, Dinelson	R-R	6-4	187	7-18-92	0	0	0.00	2	0	0	0	4	2	1	0	0	8		.143	.333	.091	18.00	0.00
Lebron, Jaimito	R-R	6-2	175	10-20-96	0	0	1.50	2	2	0	0	6	4	3	1	0	2	7	.190	.167	.200	10.50	3.00
Linares, Joel	R-R	6-1	175	12-8-94	2	7	3.64	15	14	0	0	64	58	37	26	3	15	55	.240	.173	.273	7.69	2.10
Lopez, Diomar	R-R	6-0	165	12-15-96	0	1	2.30	12	0	0	1	16	15	6	4	1	3	8	.246	.357	.213	4.60	1.72
Lora, Carlos	R-R	6-3	190	8-24-91	2	3	2.23	30	0	0	2	36	36	13	9	1	14	27	.252	.341	.212	6.69	3.47
Mejia, Angel	R-R	6-0	160	2-10-95	1	1	2.89	16	0	0	2	19	19	9	6	0	2	22	.253	.172	.304	10.61	0.96
Montas, Ernesto	R-R	6-3	180	7-18-91	2	5	2.35	14	13	0	0	69	63	35	18	1	9	47	.227	.276	.215	6.13	1.17
Pena, Arturo	R-R	6-4	200	5-13-94	0	3	2.77	18	10	0	0	55	39	23	17	4	24	59	.198	.164	.211	9.60	3.90
Perez, Mayky	R-R	6-5	235	9-26-96	0	1	9.00	2	2	0	0	4	7	5	4	0	3	4	.368	.167	.462	9.00	6.75
Purroy, Rosmel	R-R	6-2	170	3-27-95	0	1	11.40	15	0	0	0	15	13	24	19	0	27	13	.236	.333	.209	7.80	16.20
Ramirez, Emmanuel	R-R	6-2	190	7-15-94	3	1	4.56	12	0	0	0	26	25	15	13	0	10	31	.258	.222	.271	10.87	3.51
Ramos, Emmanuel	R-R	6-2	185	7-23-94	0	3	3.71	16	5	0	0	34	38	21	14	1	5	25	.271	.267	.274	6.62	1.32
Reyes, Ramon	L-L	6-3	170	11-23-95	0	8	7.41	11	10	0	0	38	33	35	31	2	39	36	.241	.313	.231	8.60	9.32
Severino, Miguel	R-R	6-3	180	5-30-93	0	0	37.80	4	0	0	0	2	3	8	7	0	9	4	.429	1.000	.333	21.60	48.60
2-team total (5 Astros)					0	0	20.57	9	2	0	0	7	5	17	16	0	20	8	—	—		10.29	25.71
Solano, Eduardo	L-L	6-3	203	5-22-97	0	0	3.38	4	0	0	0	8	10	3	3	0	4	6	.303	.000	.323	6.75	4.50
Vargas, Franklyn	L-L	6-4	205	8-21-94	0	0	11.20	9	0	0	0	14	19	17	17	0	17	16	.322	.333	.321	10.54	11.20

Fielding

Catcher	PCT	G	PO	A	E	DP	PB
Beltre	1.000	1	6	1	0	0	0
Castillo	.987	36	268	39	4	2	5
De La Cruz	.978	32	252	26	6	3	3
Molina	.945	8	58	11	4	0	5

First Base	PCT	G	PO	A	E	DP
Arias	.952	41	302	18	16	19
Molina	1.000	1	8	1	0	0
Pomare	.979	30	258	16	6	16
Savinon	1.000	4	23	2	0	1

Second Base	PCT	G	PO	A	E	DP
Pomare	.889	3	4	4	1	0

	PCT	G	PO	A	E	DP
Savinon	.939	17	31	31	4	6
Suarez	.967	6	14	15	1	1
Urias	1.000	1	2	4	0	1
Vizcaino	.912	47	74	102	17	15

Third Base	PCT	G	PO	A	E	DP
Castillo	1.000	1	0	1	0	0
Molina	.892	10	7	26	4	2
Pomare	.789	11	12	18	8	1
Savinon	.955	6	5	16	1	0
Sosa	.905	34	35	79	12	11
Suarez	.818	4	4	5	2	1
Vizcaino	.867	9	6	20	4	1

Shortstop	PCT	G	PO	A	E	DP
Magdaleno	.881	54	71	121	26	17
Savinon	.897	17	23	38	7	4

Outfield	PCT	G	PO	A	E	DP
Asuncion	.953	26	40	1	2	1
Contreras	.921	52	68	2	6	0
Olmo	.959	47	88	6	4	3
Perez	.942	42	58	7	4	1
Pomare	1.000	4	4	0	0	0
Sotillo	.963	56	96	7	4	1

San Francisco Giants

SEASON IN A SENTENCE: Halfway through the decade we have the Team of the Teens as San Francisco won its third World Series in five years.

HIGH POINT: Picking the finest moment of Madison Bumgarner's outstanding postseason run is difficult. The complete-game shutout in Game 5 of the World Series was excellent but the five shutout innings in relief to finish off Game 7 was even better. Pitching on two days' rest, Bumgarner looked like he could have thrown nine innings.

LOW POINT: When you win the World Series, the low points don't seem all that low. San Francisco chased the Dodgers for most of the second half of the season, but a sweep at the hands of the Royals followed by a loss to the White Sox on Aug. 12 dropped the Giants to 5 1/2 games behind the Dodgers. The Giants never again led the division.

NOTABLE ROOKIES: Second baseman Joe Panik arrived on June 21 and fixed what had been a season-long problem. Panik hit over .300 in the regular season, homered in the LCS and started a difficult but vital double play that proved game-changing in Game 7 of the World Series. Catcher Andrew Susac proved to be an excellent backup to Buster Posey in a late-season callup.

KEY TRANSACTIONS: The Giants' excellent work at building inexpensive depth paid off handsomely as San Francisco survived injuries to righthander Matt Cain, outfielder Angel Pagan, second baseman Marco Scutaro and catcher Hector Sanchez. The Giants covered those holes with former minor league free agent Gregor Blanco, the promotion of Susac and Juan Perez and a waiver pickup of Travis Ishikawa. The Giants picked up free agent outfielder Michael Morse on an inexpensive one-year deal. Righthander Tim Hudson was productive on a two-year deal. Needing rotation help, the Giants dealt lefthander Edwin Escobar and righthander Heath Hembree to the Red Sox for righthander Jake Peavy. Peavy went 6-4, 2.17 in 12 late-season starts after the trade.

DOWN ON THE FARM: Four of the Giants' seven minor league clubs finished with winning records, led by a Richmond club that lost in the Eastern League finals. The club's Dominican Summer League and Arizona League teams lost in their playoff semifinals. Outfielder Adam Duvall led the organization with 27 home runs, but between trades and down seasons by top prospects like Kyle Crick, the farm system has thinned.

OPENING DAY PAYROLL: $148.2 million (6th).

PLAYERS OF THE YEAR

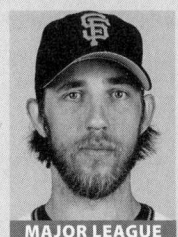

MAJOR LEAGUE	MINOR LEAGUE
Madison Bumgarner lhp	**Adam Duvall** 3b
18-10, 2.98	(Triple-A)
NLCS and World Series MVP	.298/.360/.599 27 HR, 90 RBI

ORGANIZATION LEADERS

BATTING *Minimum 250 AB

MAJORS

*	AVG	Posey, Buster	.311
*	OPS	Posey, Buster	.854
	HR	Posey, Buster	22
	RBI	Posey, Buster	89

MINORS

*	AVG	Duffy, Matt, Richmond	.332
*	OBP	Minicozzi, Mark, San Jose, Fresno	.410
*	SLG	Duvall, Adam, Fresno	.599
	R	Brown, Gary, Fresno	89
	H	Delfino, Mitch, San Jose	154
	TB	Horan, Tyler, Augusta, San Jose	249
	2B	Harris, Devin, Augusta, Richmond	31
	3B	Galindo, Jesus, San Jose	8
	HR	Duvall, Adam, Fresno	27
	RBI	Duvall, Adam, Fresno	90
	BB	Stromsmoe, Skyler, Richmond	58
	SO	Jones, Chuckie, San Jose	150
	SB	Tomlinson, Kelby, Richmond	49

PITCHING #Minimum 75 IP

MAJORS

	W	Bumgarner, Madison	18
#	ERA	Peavy, Jake	2.17
	SO	Bumgarner, Madison	219
	SV	Romo, Sergio	23

MINORS

	W	Fleet, Austin, Richmond, Fresno	12
		Heston, Chris, Fresno	12
		Lujan, Matt, Augusta, San Jose	12
	L	seven tied at	9
#	ERA	Ysla, Luis, Augusta	2.45
	G	Mizenko, Tyler, San Jose	59
	GS	Heston, Chris, Fresno	28
	SV	Okert, Steven, San Jose, Richmond	24
	IP	Heston, Chris, Fresno	173
	BB	Kickham, Mike, Fresno	64
	SO	Lujan, Matt, Augusta, San Jose	135
	AVG	Ysla, Luis, Augusta	.231

General Manager: Brian Sabean. **Farm Director:** Shane Turner. **Scouting Director:** John Barr.

Class	Team	League	W	L	PCT	Finish	Manager
Majors	San Francisco Giants	National	88	74	.543	T-8th (30)	Bruce Bochy
Triple-A	Fresno Grizzlies	Pacific Coast	68	76	.472	13th (16)	Bob Mariano
Double-A	Richmond Flying Squirrels	Eastern	79	63	.556	3rd (12)	Russ Morman
High A	San Jose Giants	California	73	67	.521	6th (10)	Lenn Sakata
Low A	Augusta GreenJackets	South Atlantic	62	76	.449	9th (14)	Mike Goff
Short season	Salem-Keizer Volcanoes	Northwest	38	38	.500	5th (8)	Gary Davenport
Rookie	Giants	Arizona	34	22	.607	2nd (13)	Nestor Rojas
Overall 2015 Minor League Record			354	342	.509	13th (30)	

ORGANIZATION STATISTICS

SAN FRANCISCO GIANTS
NATIONAL LEAGUE

Batting	B-T	HT	WT	DOB	AVG	vLH	vRH	G	AB	R	H	2B	3B	HR	RBI	BB	HBP	SH	SF	SO	SB	CS	SLG	OBP
Abreu, Tony	B-R	5-10	200	11-13-84	.000	.000	.000	3	4	0	0	0	0	0	0	0	0	0	0	0	0	0	.000	.000
Adrianza, Ehire	B-R	6-1	170	8-21-89	.237	.200	.250	53	97	10	23	6	0	0	5	5	1	2	1	22	1	1	.299	.279
Arias, Joaquin	R-R	6-1	165	9-21-84	.254	.305	.193	107	193	18	49	9	0	0	15	8	0	1	2	23	1	0	.301	.281
Belt, Brandon	L-L	6-5	220	4-20-88	.243	.266	.233	61	214	30	52	8	0	12	27	18	2	0	1	64	3	1	.449	.306
Blanco, Gregor	L-L	5-11	175	12-24-83	.260	.296	.243	146	393	51	102	18	6	5	38	41	3	6	1	77	16	5	.374	.333
Brown, Gary	R-R	6-1	190	9-28-88	.429	.200	1.000	7	7	1	3	0	0	0	1	0	0	0	0	0	0	0	.429	.429
Colvin, Tyler	L-L	6-3	210	9-5-85	.223	.300	.210	57	139	16	31	10	3	2	18	8	1	0	1	45	1	0	.381	.268
Crawford, Brandon	L-R	6-2	215	1-21-87	.246	.320	.213	153	491	54	121	20	10	10	69	59	2	2	10	129	5	3	.389	.324
Dominguez, Chris	R-R	6-4	235	11-22-86	.059	.000	.091	8	17	1	1	0	0	1	2	1	0	0	0	4	0	0	.235	.111
Duffy, Matt	R-R	6-2	170	1-15-91	.267	.400	.133	34	60	5	16	2	0	0	8	1	2	1	0	14	0	1	.300	.302
Duvall, Adam	R-R	6-1	205	9-4-88	.192	.184	.200	28	73	8	14	2	0	3	5	3	1	0	0	20	0	0	.342	.234
Hicks, Brandon	R-R	6-2	215	9-14-85	.162	.176	.154	71	204	27	33	6	1	8	22	32	2	3	1	77	0	1	.319	.280
Ishikawa, Travis	L-L	6-3	220	9-24-83	.274	.182	.290	47	73	7	20	3	0	2	15	6	1	0	1	23	0	0	.397	.333
2-team total (15 Pittsburgh)					.252	—	—	62	107	9	27	4	1	3	18	9	1	0	2	34	0	0	.393	.311
Morse, Michael	R-R	6-5	245	3-22-82	.279	.248	.293	131	438	48	122	32	3	16	61	31	9	0	4	121	0	0	.475	.336
Pagan, Angel	B-R	6-2	200	7-2-81	.300	.239	.335	96	383	56	115	21	2	3	27	25	1	1	3	53	16	6	.389	.342
Panik, Joe	L-R	6-1	190	10-30-90	.305	.373	.274	73	269	31	82	10	2	1	18	16	0	1	1	33	0	0	.368	.343
Pence, Hunter	R-R	6-4	220	4-13-83	.277	.284	.274	162	650	106	180	29	10	20	74	52	3	0	3	130	13	6	.445	.332
Perez, Juan	R-R	5-11	185	11-13-86	.170	.163	.176	61	100	13	17	7	0	1	3	5	2	2	0	25	0	1	.270	.224
Posey, Buster	R-R	6-1	215	3-27-87	.311	.304	.314	147	547	72	170	28	2	22	89	47	3	0	8	69	0	1	.490	.364
Quiroz, Guillermo	R-R	6-1	230	11-29-81	.000	—	.000	2	3	0	0	0	0	0	0	0	0	0	0	0	0	0	.000	.000
Sanchez, Hector	B-R	6-0	235	11-17-89	.196	.224	.184	66	163	8	32	8	0	3	28	8	2	0	4	55	0	1	.301	.237
Sandoval, Pablo	B-R	5-11	245	8-11-86	.279	.199	.317	157	588	68	164	26	3	16	73	39	4	0	7	85	0	0	.415	.324
Scutaro, Marco	R-R	5-10	185	10-30-75	.091	.125	.000	5	11	1	1	0	0	0	0	1	0	1	0	3	0	0	.091	.167
Susac, Andrew	R-R	6-1	215	3-22-90	.273	.333	.241	35	88	13	24	8	0	3	19	7	0	0	0	28	0	0	.466	.326
Uggla, Dan	R-R	5-11	210	3-11-80	.000	.000	.000	4	11	1	0	0	0	0	0	1	0	0	0	6	0	0	.000	.083
2-team total (48 Atlanta)					.149	—	—	52	141	14	21	3	0	2	10	11	4	0	1	46	0	0	.213	.229

Pitching	B-T	HT	WT	DOB	W	L	ERA	G	GS	CG	SV	IP	H	R	ER	HR	BB	SO	AVG	vLH	vRH	K/9	BB/9
Affeldt, Jeremy	L-L	6-4	225	6-6-79	4	2	2.28	62	0	0	0	55	47	14	14	1	14	41	.229	.231	.228	6.67	2.28
Bochy, Brett	R-R	6-2	200	8-27-87	0	0	5.40	3	0	0	0	3	1	2	2	1	2	3	.091	.000	.167	8.10	5.40
Bumgarner, Madison	R-L	6-5	235	8-1-89	18	10	2.98	33	33	4	0	217	194	81	72	21	43	219	.240	.224	.244	9.07	1.78
Cain, Matt	R-R	6-3	230	10-1-84	2	7	4.18	15	15	0	0	90	81	47	42	13	32	70	.242	.253	.231	6.97	3.19
Casilla, Santiago	R-R	6-0	210	7-25-80	3	3	1.70	54	0	0	19	58	35	13	11	3	15	45	.177	.200	.161	6.94	2.31
Cordier, Erik	R-R	6-4	250	2-25-86	0	0	1.50	7	0	0	0	6	5	4	1	0	2	9	.217	.091	.333	13.50	3.00
Dunning, Jake	R-R	6-4	190	8-12-88	0	0	0.00	1	0	0	0	1	0	0	0	0	1	0	—	—	0.00	13.50
Gutierrez, Juan	R-R	6-3	245	7-14-83	1	2	3.96	61	0	0	0	64	60	30	28	7	16	44	.247	.226	.258	6.22	2.26
Heston, Chris	R-R	6-3	195	4-10-88	0	0	5.06	3	1	0	0	5	6	3	3	0	3	4	.300	.455	.111	6.75	5.06
Hudson, Tim	R-R	6-1	175	7-14-75	9	13	3.57	31	31	1	0	189	199	86	75	15	34	120	.270	.281	.258	5.70	1.62
Huff, David	L-L	6-2	215	8-24-84	1	0	6.30	16	0	0	0	20	27	15	14	2	6	11	.318	.270	.354	4.95	2.70
Kickham, Mike	L-L	6-4	220	12-12-88	0	0	22.50	2	0	0	0	2	8	5	5	1	1	1	.533	.429	.625	4.50	4.50
Kontos, George	R-R	6-3	215	6-12-85	4	0	2.78	24	0	0	0	32	24	10	10	1	11	27	.211	.143	.250	7.52	3.06
Lincecum, Tim	L-R	5-11	170	6-15-84	12	9	4.74	33	26	1	1	156	154	86	82	19	63	134	.258	.256	.259	7.75	3.64
Lopez, Javier	L-L	6-4	220	7-11-77	1	1	3.11	65	0	0	0	38	31	14	13	2	19	22	.220	.194	.271	5.26	4.54
Machi, Jean	R-R	6-0	255	2-1-82	7	1	2.58	71	0	0	2	66	45	19	19	5	18	51	.201	.226	.186	6.92	2.44
Peavy, Jake	R-R	6-1	195	5-31-81	6	4	2.17	12	12	0	0	79	65	24	19	3	17	58	.231	.210	.247	6.64	1.94
Petit, Yusmeiro	R-R	6-1	250	11-22-84	5	5	3.69	39	12	1	0	117	97	51	48	12	22	133	.223	.257	.193	10.23	1.69
Romo, Sergio	R-R	5-10	185	3-4-83	6	4	3.72	64	0	0	23	58	43	24	24	9	12	59	.203	.256	.172	9.16	1.86
Strickland, Hunter	R-R	6-4	220	9-24-88	1	0	0.00	9	0	0	0	7	5	0	0	0	0	9	.200	.200	.200	11.57	0.00
Vogelsong, Ryan	R-R	6-4	215	7-22-77	8	13	4.00	32	32	1	0	185	178	86	82	18	58	151	.254	.287	.223	7.36	2.83

Fielding

Catcher	PCT	G	PO	A	E	DP	PB					
Posey	.994	111	787	51	5	8	5	Quiroz	1.000	2	6	1 0 0 0
								Sanchez	.990	45	261	28 3 1 4

Susac | 1.000 | 29 | 160 | 20 0 1 2

First Base	PCT	G	PO	A	E	DP
Arias	1.000	16	90	5	0	4
Belt	.993	59	499	55	4	48
Duvall	.994	21	149	8	1	13
Hicks	1.000	1	1	0	0	0
Ishikawa	1.000	31	125	9	0	16
Morse	.991	43	307	24	3	41
Posey	.996	35	246	22	1	20
Sanchez	1.000	1	6	1	0	0

Second Base	PCT	G	PO	A	E	DP
Abreu	1.000	1	2	1	0	0
Adrianza	.975	25	27	52	2	10
Arias	1.000	15	14	23	0	7
Duffy	.962	9	9	16	1	3
Hicks	.983	61	107	180	5	47

	PCT	G	PO	A	E	DP
Panik	.975	70	131	185	8	53
Scutaro	1.000	3	4	5	0	0
Uggla	.920	4	9	14	2	2

Third Base	PCT	G	PO	A	E	DP
Abreu	—	1	0	0	0	0
Adrianza	1.000	3	0	2	0	0
Arias	.979	44	11	36	1	6
Dominguez	—	1	0	0	0	0
Duffy	1.000	2	0	2	0	0
Duvall	—	1	0	0	0	0
Sandoval	.971	151	89	282	11	27

Shortstop	PCT	G	PO	A	E	DP
Adrianza	1.000	7	5	16	0	2
Arias	.950	11	17	21	2	9

	PCT	G	PO	A	E	DP
Crawford	.967	149	185	428	21	85
Duffy	.966	7	15	13	1	5

Outfield	PCT	G	PO	A	E	DP
Belt	—	1	0	0	0	0
Blanco	.996	127	219	6	1	0
Brown	1.000	6	7	0	0	0
Colvin	.982	44	52	2	1	1
Dominguez	1.000	5	12	0	0	0
Hicks	—	1	0	0	0	0
Ishikawa	1.000	8	10	0	0	0
Morse	.982	84	107	2	2	0
Pagan	.995	91	209	3	1	1
Pence	.984	161	308	9	5	0
Perez	.985	59	65	2	1	1

FRESNO GRIZZLIES

PACIFIC COAST LEAGUE

TRIPLE-A

Batting	B-T	HT	WT	DOB	AVG	vLH	vRH	G	AB	R	H	2B	3B	HR	RBI	BB	HBP	SH	SF	SO	SB	CS	SLG	OBP
Abreu, Tony	B-R	5-10	200	11-13-84	.284	.220	.297	80	282	37	80	16	1	7	33	14	8	—	3	33	3	0	.422	.332
Adrianza, Ehire	B-R	6-1	170	8-21-89	.316	.250	.333	6	19	6	6	0	0	1	1	2	0	1	0	4	0	0	.474	.381
Belt, Brandon	L-L	6-5	220	4-20-88	.526	.600	.500	5	19	2	10	3	0	2	5	1	0	0	5	0	1	1.000	.550
Brown, Gary	R-R	6-1	190	9-28-88	.271	.255	.275	136	536	89	145	24	6	10	53	36	13	—	5	119	36	20	.394	.329
Brown, Trevor	R-R	6-2	195	11-15-91	.319	.500	.283	23	72	6	23	3	0	0	13	7	0	1	0	13	0	0	.361	.380
Ciriaco, Juan	R-R	6-0	160	8-15-83	.302	.390	.269	54	149	27	45	8	1	5	19	11	1	2	2	17	13	1	.470	.350
Colvin, Tyler	L-L	6-3	210	9-5-85	.227	.133	.248	50	163	21	37	9	2	2	18	11	1	0	1	43	1	0	.344	.278
Dominguez, Chris	R-R	6-4	235	11-22-86	.274	.234	.285	131	496	66	136	23	3	21	85	22	4	—	6	143	21	10	.460	.307
Duvall, Adam	R-R	6-1	205	9-4-88	.298	.295	.299	91	359	67	107	21	3	27	90	30	5	—	0	82	2	0	.599	.360
Ford, Darren	R-R	5-9	190	10-11-85	.283	.373	.256	107	321	48	91	11	1	3	27	27	2	—	2	77	35	12	.352	.341
Herrera, Javier	R-R	5-11	225	4-9-85	.273	.000	.346	13	33	2	9	2	1	0	4	2	0	0	0	9	1	0	.394	.314
Hicks, Brandon	R-R	6-2	215	9-14-85	.218	.308	.196	41	133	18	29	11	0	6	17	14	4	1	0	49	0	0	.436	.311
Ishikawa, Travis	L-L	6-3	220	9-24-83	.271	.271	.271	71	240	34	65	9	0	11	45	24	6	—	2	62	0	0	.446	.349
Krill, Brett	R-R	6-4	220	1-24-89	.189	.200	.184	29	53	6	10	0	1	0	3	4	0	1	0	15	0	1	.226	.246
LaTorre, Tyler	L-R	6-0	235	4-22-83	.300	.000	.333	10	30	5	9	1	0	0	2	7	0	0	0	4	0	0	.333	.432
Minicozzi, Mark	R-R	6-0	220	2-11-83	.298	.243	.314	89	315	53	94	18	0	12	62	49	5	—	1	83	1	0	.470	.400
Moss, Brad	R-R	5-8	160	10-10-89	.000	—	.000	2	1	1	0	0	0	0	0	1	0	0	0	0	0	0	.000	.500
Noonan, Nick	L-R	6-1	175	5-4-89	.237	.256	.232	104	379	38	90	16	0	3	24	20	4	—	1	98	6	5	.303	.282
Pagan, Angel	B-R	6-2	200	7-2-81	.125	.000	.143	2	8	0	1	0	0	0	1	0	0	0	0	0	0	1	.125	.125
Panik, Joe	L-R	6-1	190	10-30-90	.321	.359	.310	74	293	50	94	14	4	5	45	27	3	1	2	33	3	2	.447	.382
Parker, Jarrett	L-L	6-4	210	1-1-89	.278	.222	.286	24	79	13	22	5	3	0	10	9	1	0	0	23	1	2	.456	.360
Perez, Juan	R-R	5-11	185	11-13-86	.316	.205	.348	48	177	33	56	13	0	7	25	14	3	0	2	32	7	4	.508	.372
Quiroz, Guillermo	R-R	6-1	230	11-29-81	.267	.353	.243	69	240	22	64	13	1	3	23	8	2	1	1	56	0	0	.367	.295
Sanchez, Hector	R-R	6-0	235	11-17-89	.158	.000	.231	7	19	1	3	0	0	1	3	1	0	0	0	5	0	0	.316	.200
Santos, Adalberto	R-R	5-11	185	9-28-87	.250	.429	.222	23	52	8	13	3	0	0	5	7	0	0	0	13	2	0	.308	.339
Scutaro, Marco	R-R	5-10	185	10-30-75	.100	—	.100	3	10	2	1	0	0	0	1	0	0	0	0	6	0	0	.100	.182
Susac, Andrew	R-R	6-1	215	3-22-90	.268	.311	.256	63	213	34	57	9	0	10	32	34	5	—	1	50	0	0	.451	.379
Uggla, Dan	R-R	5-11	210	3-11-80	.286	.000	.333	2	7	1	2	1	0	0	1	2	0	0	0	2	0	0	.429	.444
Villegas, Ydwin	B-R	5-10	178	9-1-90	.147	.154	.145	30	68	6	10	2	2	0	5	5	1	0	0	16	1	0	.235	.216

Pitching	B-T	HT	WT	DOB	W	L	ERA	G	GS	CG	SV	IP	H	R	ER	HR	BB	SO	AVG	vLH	vRH	K/9	BB/9
Affeldt, Jeremy	L-L	6-4	225	6-6-79	0	1	27.00	2	1	0	0	1	3	4	4	0	2	2	.429	.500	.400	13.50	13.50
Berken, Jason	R-R	6-0	210	11-27-83	10	9	4.64	24	21	2	1	132	159	78	68	13	43	89	.304	.315	.294	6.07	2.93
Bochy, Brett	R-R	6-2	200	8-27-87	4	4	3.83	35	2	0	0	54	53	25	23	8	27	47	.264	.253	.273	7.83	4.50
Boggs, Mitchell	R-R	6-4	235	2-15-84	0	1	6.23	10	0	0	0	13	18	9	9	2	7	4	.333	.217	.419	2.77	4.85
Bradley, Ryan	B-L	6-1	180	7-15-88	0	0	3.00	1	1	0	0	3	2	1	1	0	1	3	.182	.200	.167	9.00	3.00
Broadway, Mike	R-R	6-5	215	3-30-87	0	0	9.00	3	0	0	0	4	5	4	4	2	3	5	.333	.333	.333	11.25	6.75
Bucardo, Jorge	R-R	6-1	190	10-18-89	0	1	6.55	8	0	0	0	11	16	8	8	1	11	10	.333	.316	.345	8.18	9.00
Carignan, Andrew	R-R	5-11	235	7-23-86	1	1	5.01	16	1	0	0	23	31	14	13	2	20	23	.333	.404	.261	8.87	7.71
Cordier, Erik	R-R	6-4	250	2-25-86	4	3	3.59	47	0	0	3	53	40	22	21	4	31	68	.211	.275	.164	11.62	5.30
DePaula, Jose	L-L	6-1	170	3-4-88	4	3	4.21	16	10	0	1	51	55	28	24	5	16	41	.266	.286	.258	7.19	2.81
Dolis, Rafael	R-R	6-4	215	1-10-88	0	0	16.62	4	0	0	0	4	8	8	8	0	3	4	.400	.333	.455	8.31	6.23
Dunning, Jake	R-R	6-4	190	8-12-88	0	3	4.57	38	4	0	1	65	65	35	33	5	26	51	.264	.272	.256	7.06	3.60
Escobar, Edwin	L-L	6-1	185	4-22-92	3	8	5.11	20	20	0	0	111	128	69	63	16	37	96	.287	.188	.334	7.78	3.00
Fleet, Austin	R-R	6-2	200	4-17-87	4	-2	3.95	7	7	1	0	43	43	20	19	4	13	33	.262	.257	.266	6.85	2.70
Hembree, Heath	R-R	6-4	210	1-13-89	1	3	3.89	41	0	0	18	39	40	18	17	5	13	46	.263	.349	.202	10.53	2.97
Heston, Chris	R-R	6-3	195	4-10-88	12	9	3.38	28	28	1	0	173	152	76	65	16	51	125	.233	.251	.213	6.50	2.65
Huff, David	L-L	6-2	215	8-22-84	0	0	0.00	1	1	0	0	3	3	0	0	0	1	2	.250	.000	.300	3.00	0.00
Kickham, Mike	L-L	6-4	220	12-12-88	8	8	4.43	27	27	0	0	148	171	92	73	8	64	131	.290	.254	.306	7.95	3.88
Kontos, George	R-R	6-3	215	6-12-85	3	3	2.08	30	0	0	4	48	41	17	11	4	11	58	.228	.226	.229	10.95	2.08
Lively, Mitch	R-R	6-5	255	9-7-85	6	4	5.08	22	15	0	0	90	104	55	51	9	42	80	.295	.315	.275	7.97	4.18
Marte, Kelvin	R-R	5-9	170	11-24-87	1	2	5.45	6	6	0	0	36	42	24	22	6	8	21	.298	.273	.306	5.20	1.98
Reifer, Adam	R-R	6-2	195	6-3-86	5	3	6.11	43	0	0	1	63	62	46	43	11	39	70	.255	.273	.243	9.95	5.54
Rosario, Sandy	R-R	6-1	205	8-22-85	0	1	4.08	17	0	0	1	18	18	9	8	0	9	15	.269	.148	.350	7.64	4.58
Runzler, Dan	L-L	6-4	210	3-30-85	1	1	3.30	39	0	0	1	46	38	23	17	2	36	53	.225	.203	.242	10.29	6.99

	B-T	HT	WT	DOB	W	L	ERA	G	GS	CG	SV	IP	H	R	ER	HR	BB	SO	AVG	vLH	vRH	K/9	BB/9
Tobin, Mason	R-R	6-2	220	7-8-87	1	2	4.24	27	0	0	1	34	36	18	16	3	18	27	.277	.309	.253	7.15	4.76
Willis, Dontrelle	L-L	6-4	225	1-12-82	0	0	0.00	2	0	0	0	1	0	0	0	0	1	0	.000	—	.000	0.00	13.50

Fielding

Catcher	PCT	G	PO	A	E	DP	PB
Brown	1.000	22	143	12	0	1	0
LaTorre	1.000	3	27	0	0	0	0
Quiroz	.992	67	501	23	4	2	10
Sanchez	1.000	5	19	4	0	1	1
Susac	.987	56	424	29	6	1	9

First Base	PCT	G	PO	A	E	DP
Belt	.976	4	36	4	1	3
Ciriaco	1.000	2	15	0	0	0
Dominguez	.988	15	77	8	1	15
Duvall	.988	41	310	26	4	35
Ishikawa	.995	57	406	31	2	44
LaTorre	1.000	7	60	0	0	7
Minicozzi	.997	37	289	21	1	34
Quiroz	1.000	1	5	2	0	1

Second Base	PCT	G	PO	A	E	DP
Abreu	.975	34	52	105	4	22
Adrianza	.905	3	7	12	2	3
Brown	1.000	1	1	0	0	0
Ciriaco	1.000	4	6	10	0	3

	PCT	G	PO	A	E	DP
Hicks	.992	29	52	75	1	15
Noonan	1.000	12	10	25	0	4
Panik	.989	61	110	163	3	51
Santos	.968	8	12	18	1	6
Scutaro	1.000	2	2	6	0	2
Uggla	1.000	2	2	5	0	1

Third Base	PCT	G	PO	A	E	DP
Abreu	.962	31	19	57	3	4
Adrianza	1.000	1	0	4	0	0
Ciriaco	.941	11	4	12	1	2
Dominguez	.939	32	23	54	5	5
Duvall	.915	52	29	89	11	10
Hicks	.889	10	5	19	3	1
Noonan	.929	14	14	25	3	3
Perez	1.000	1	1	0	0	0
Santos	.667	1	2	0	1	1
Villegas	1.000	1	0	1	0	0

Shortstop	PCT	G	PO	A	E	DP
Abreu	.929	6	8	18	2	10
Adrianza	1.000	2	4	8	0	4

	PCT	G	PO	A	E	DP
Ciriaco	.917	3	3	8	1	1
Dominguez	.973	33	46	96	4	23
Hicks	—	1	0	0	0	0
Noonan	.963	77	116	225	13	51
Panik	.952	10	14	26	2	5
Villegas	1.000	20	30	42	0	14

Outfield	PCT	G	PO	A	E	DP
Brown	.984	133	301	13	5	2
Ciriaco	.976	22	38	2	1	0
Colvin	1.000	38	74	4	0	1
Dominguez	.949	60	103	8	6	1
Ford	.979	86	133	6	3	2
Ishikawa	.909	12	20	0	2	0
Krill	.969	21	30	1	1	0
Minicozzi	1.000	29	24	1	0	0
Pagan	1.000	2	6	0	0	0
Parker	.957	22	43	1	2	1
Perez	.975	44	74	4	2	0
Santos	.714	3	5	0	2	0

RICHMOND FLYING SQUIRRELS

DOUBLE-A

EASTERN LEAGUE

Batting	B-T	HT	WT	DOB	AVG	vLH	vRH	G	AB	R	H	2B	3B	HR	RBI	BB	HBP	SH	SF	SO	SB	CS	SLG	OBP
Arnold, Jeff	R-R	6-2	205	1-13-88	.000	.000	.000	1	3	0	0	0	0	0	0	0	0	0	0	3	0	0	.000	.000
Blair, Elliott	R-R	6-1	181	2-3-88	.240	.143	.267	27	96	9	23	4	0	1	11	10	1	1	0	27	4	1	.313	.318
Duffy, Matt	R-R	6-2	170	1-15-91	.332	.349	.324	97	367	53	122	24	4	3	62	42	2	0	6	66	20	4	.444	.398
Graham, Tyler	R-R	6-0	185	12-25-84	.255	.288	.238	106	412	57	105	12	3	1	27	27	8	3	2	72	38	14	.311	.312
Harris, Devin	R-R	6-3	225	4-23-88	.256	.289	.242	108	394	47	101	26	3	13	52	30	2	0	3	121	3	2	.437	.310
Krill, Brett	R-R	6-2	220	1-24-89	.213	.192	.224	21	75	10	16	4	1	0	9	5	3	0	0	13	2	0	.293	.289
LaTorre, Tyler	L-R	6-0	235	4-22-83	.263	.262	.263	48	160	21	42	8	0	1	12	16	0	0	3	43	2	1	.331	.324
Lisson, Mario	R-R	6-2	220	5-31-84	.266	.267	.266	114	379	59	101	22	0	18	76	54	12	0	6	93	11	3	.467	.370
Lollis, Ryan	L-L	6-2	185	12-16-86	.217	.164	.236	70	203	21	44	4	3	1	17	17	1	3	2	28	2	0	.281	.278
Miller, Blake	R-R	6-3	195	4-25-90	.304	.348	.290	26	92	9	28	5	2	0	12	9	1	0	0	21	1	0	.402	.373
Oropesa, Ricky	L-R	6-3	225	12-15-89	.241	.205	.252	116	349	32	84	16	0	5	35	36	3	0	3	89	0	0	.330	.315
Parker, Jarrett	L-L	6-4	210	1-1-89	.275	.231	.293	100	363	52	100	20	6	12	58	45	10	0	1	103	11	4	.463	.370
Schroder, Myles	R-R	5-11	180	8-1-87	.254	.295	.233	110	362	43	92	16	5	5	34	20	8	0	4	76	11	0	.367	.305
Sim, Eric	R-R	6-2	215	1-3-89	.158	.300	.000	7	19	2	3	0	0	0	1	2	1	0	0	4	0	0	.158	.273
Stromsmoe, Skyler	B-R	5-10	175	3-30-84	.233	.218	.239	104	296	49	69	14	2	0	15	58	11	3	4	56	12	8	.294	.374
Tomlinson, Kelby	R-R	6-2	180	6-16-90	.268	.263	.270	126	433	63	116	9	6	1	32	44	5	8	4	82	49	12	.323	.340
Villalona, Angel	R-R	6-3	235	8-13-90	.227	.208	.238	101	365	35	83	18	4	10	54	23	10	0	2	94	1	1	.381	.290
Zambrano, Eliezer	B-R	5-11	195	9-16-86	.268	.302	.252	60	194	15	52	4	0	1	12	10	0	4	0	26	1	1	.304	.304

Pitching	B-T	HT	WT	DOB	W	L	ERA	G	GS	CG	SV	IP	H	R	ER	HR	BB	SO	AVG	vLH	vRH	K/9	BB/9
Alvarado, Carlos	R-R	6-4	175	10-22-89	2	0	5.87	11	0	0	0	15	17	11	10	3	5	11	.279	.353	.250	6.46	2.93
Bandilla, Bryce	L-L	6-4	235	1-17-90	0	2	8.80	15	0	0	0	15	18	16	15	2	15	10	.321	.389	.289	5.87	8.80
Blach, Ty	R-L	6-1	210	10-20-90	8	8	3.13	25	25	1	0	141	142	53	49	8	39	91	.261	.246	.266	5.81	2.49
Blackburn, Clayton	L-R	6-2	260	1-6-93	5	6	3.29	18	18	0	0	93	94	40	34	1	20	85	.268	.281	.259	8.23	1.94
Bradley, Ryan	B-L	6-1	180	7-15-88	0	1	6.75	4	2	0	0	11	15	8	8	1	7	5	.341	.250	.361	4.22	5.91
Carignan, Andrew	R-R	5-11	235	7-23-86	0	1	4.24	14	0	0	0	17	6	8	8	1	19	16	.109	.067	.125	8.47	10.06
Casilla, Jose	R-R	6-1	205	5-21-89	4	1	3.97	41	0	0	0	66	57	30	29	5	22	39	.232	.274	.205	5.35	3.02
Crick, Kyle	L-R	6-2	220	11-30-92	6	7	3.79	23	22	0	0	90	78	42	38	7	61	111	.234	.235	.232	11.06	6.08
Fleet, Austin	R-R	6-2	200	4-17-87	8	1	2.78	26	11	0	0	97	82	31	30	5	36	77	.232	.221	.241	7.14	3.34
Hall, Cody	R-R	6-4	220	1-6-88	1	4	3.14	47	0	0	11	52	42	18	18	3	14	57	.225	.203	.239	9.93	2.44
Law, Derek	R-R	6-2	210	9-14-90	2	0	2.57	27	0	0	13	28	19	8	8	1	14	29	.198	.162	.220	9.32	4.50
Marte, Kelvin	R-R	5-9	170	11-24-87	8	3	3.83	18	15	1	0	87	89	37	37	8	23	55	.265	.282	.259	5.69	2.38
McCormick, Phil	L-L	6-1	185	9-7-88	2	4	3.72	50	0	0	1	65	61	31	27	4	29	62	.239	.212	.253	8.54	3.99
Mejia, Adalberto	L-L	6-3	195	6-20-93	7	9	4.67	22	21	0	0	108	119	62	56	9	31	82	.283	.225	.296	6.83	2.58
Okert, Steven	L-L	6-3	210	7-9-91	0	2	2.73	24	0	0	5	33	24	11	10	3	11	38	.207	.167	.225	10.36	3.00
Osich, Josh	L-L	6-2	230	9-3-88	1	0	3.78	28	0	0	0	33	28	18	14	4	20	27	.233	.222	.237	7.29	5.40
Quirarte, Edwin	R-R	6-2	185	12-20-86	11	7	3.23	51	1	0	1	84	75	37	30	4	28	51	.238	.281	.214	5.49	3.01
Slania, Dan	R-R	6-5	275	5-24-92	0	0	0.79	10	0	0	0	11	10	2	1	0	3	3	.244	.167	.276	2.38	2.38
Snodgrass, Jack	L-L	6-6	210	12-16-87	11	6	3.56	24	22	1	0	131	130	58	52	1	41	86	.265	.248	.272	5.89	2.81
Stratton, Chris	R-R	6-3	186	8-22-90	1	1	3.52	5	5	0	0	23	29	10	9	2	12	61	.318	.342	.296	7.04	4.70
Strickland, Hunter	R-R	6-4	220	9-24-88	1	1	2.02	38	0	0	11	36	25	10	8	3	4	48	.195	.217	.183	12.11	1.01

Fielding

Catcher	PCT	G	PO	A	E	DP	PB
Arnold	1.000	1	6	1	0	0	0
LaTorre	.990	47	376	20	4	0	5
Schroder	.986	42	242	35	4	3	3
Sim	1.000	7	44	8	0	1	1
Zambrano	.987	52	337	35	5	3	5

First Base	PCT	G	PO	A	E	DP
Lisson	1.000	11	61	5	0	9
Lollis	1.000	1	1	0	0	0

SAN FRANSISCO GIANTS

	PCT	G	PO	A	E	DP
Oropesa	.987	55	442	18	6	43
Schroder	1.000	3	6	0	0	0
Villalona	.994	85	761	44	5	87

Second Base	PCT	G	PO	A	E	DP
Duffy	1.000	3	5	7	0	0
Miller	.989	23	34	55	1	18
Schroder	.958	9	8	15	1	5
Stromsmoe	.973	52	93	122	6	29
Tomlinson	.986	73	146	196	5	62

Third Base	PCT	G	PO	A	E	DP
Duffy	1.000	3	3	5	0	0
Lisson	.964	80	42	174	8	18
Oropesa	.864	17	10	28	6	4
Schroder	.967	44	25	93	4	9
Stromsmoe	1.000	17	8	17	0	1

Shortstop	PCT	G	PO	A	E	DP
Duffy	.962	89	102	277	15	60
Miller	.800	3	1	3	1	0
Stromsmoe	1.000	5	5	15	0	4
Tomlinson	.941	50	67	140	13	37

Outfield	PCT	G	PO	A	E	DP
Blair	1.000	27	62	0	0	0
Graham	.983	100	227	4	4	0
Harris	.981	93	156	2	3	0
Krill	.970	20	31	1	1	0
Lisson	1.000	5	5	1	0	0
Lollis	1.000	60	93	4	0	0
Parker	.989	96	184	3	2	1
Quirarte	—	1	0	0	0	0
Schroder	.833	15	24	1	5	0
Stromsmoe	.980	31	44	6	1	1

SAN JOSE GIANTS
CALIFORNIA LEAGUE
HIGH CLASS A

Batting	B-T	HT	WT	DOB	AVG	vLH	vRH	G	AB	R	H	2B	3B	HR	RBI	BB	HBP	SH	SF	SO	SB	CS	SLG	OBP
Bednar, Brandon	R-R	6-4	185	3-21-92	.241	.283	.228	48	195	23	47	7	0	5	16	12	4	0	1	27	3	3	.354	.297
Belt, Brandon	L-L	6-5	220	4-20-88	.500	.500	.500	2	6	2	3	0	0	1	1	0	2	0	0	1	0	0	1.000	.625
Blair, Elliott	R-R	6-1	181	2-3-88	.316	.300	.322	94	345	50	109	22	5	5	35	33	5	1	3	87	8	6	.452	.381
Brown, Trevor	R-R	6-2	195	11-15-91	.215	.196	.221	54	195	19	42	5	1	2	22	12	1	0	4	33	0	0	.282	.259
Carbonell, Daniel	R-R	6-3	196	3-29-91	.344	.375	.333	21	93	17	32	3	3	3	12	6	1	0	0	19	7	2	.538	.390
Deacon, Jared	L-R	6-0	190	8-25-91	.217	.333	.143	8	23	3	5	2	0	0	2	2	0	1	0	5	0	0	.304	.280
Delfino, Mitch	R-R	6-2	210	1-13-91	.289	.352	.269	131	533	78	154	28	4	12	77	34	2	0	2	77	5	2	.424	.333
Galindo, Jesus	B-R	5-11	175	8-23-90	.268	.276	.265	101	396	61	106	22	8	2	30	31	9	8	1	87	31	13	.379	.334
Horan, Tyler	L-R	6-2	230	12-2-90	.321	.318	.321	28	106	17	34	5	1	10	27	9	1	0	1	31	6	4	.670	.376
Jones, Chuckie	R-R	6-3	235	7-28-92	.256	.228	.265	131	485	79	124	19	4	15	66	48	5	4	5	150	17	9	.404	.326
Krill, Brett	R-R	6-4	220	1-24-89	.160	.333	.122	14	50	7	8	3	0	0	3	5	0	0	1	18	1	1	.220	.232
Lofton, Chris	L-R	6-1	175	5-20-90	.189	.200	.188	20	74	13	14	2	3	0	4	9	0	0	0	27	4	2	.297	.277
Lollis, Ryan	L-L	6-2	185	12-16-86	.275	.360	.250	26	109	15	30	3	0	3	11	7	0	2	0	8	4	0	.385	.319
Mende, Sam	R-R	6-3	195	1-9-90	.191	.143	.204	18	68	5	13	2	1	0	1	4	0	0	0	26	0	1	.250	.236
2-team total (17 Modesto)					.175	—	—	35	126	11	22	5	2	0	1	8	5	1	0	38	2	2	.246	.252
Miller, Blake	R-R	6-3	195	4-25-90	.299	.295	.301	96	364	47	109	24	4	8	73	26	9	2	8	80	5	1	.453	.354
Minicozzi, Mark	R-R	6-0	220	2-11-83	.393	.455	.353	8	28	6	11	2	0	2	7	6	1	0	0	5	0	0	.679	.514
Moreno, Rando	R-R	5-11	165	6-6-92	.218	.143	.242	27	87	6	19	0	0	0	3	7	0	5	1	17	10	4	.218	.274
Navarro, Jesus	R-R	6-0	180	1-3-88	.182	.000	.222	7	22	0	4	1	0	0	1	2	1	1	0	9	0	0	.227	.280
Noonan, Nick	L-R	6-1	175	5-4-89	.158	.100	.222	4	19	1	3	1	0	1	2	1	0	0	0	4	0	0	.368	.200
Pare, Matt	L-R	6-0	205	11-17-90	.238	.000	.263	13	42	3	10	4	0	0	9	4	5	1	2	12	0	0	.333	.358
Payne, Shawn	R-R	6-1	190	7-13-89	.256	.311	.237	81	281	39	72	19	4	5	32	36	7	1	1	76	14	7	.406	.354
Price, Scott	L-R	6-3	205	1-9-92	.125	—	.125	3	8	1	1	1	0	0	0	1	0	0	0	4	0	0	.250	.222
Ragira, Brian	R-R	6-2	220	1-22-92	.260	.196	.279	120	457	58	119	24	0	20	82	37	6	0	6	127	2	2	.444	.320
Robles, Alberto	R-R	6-1	155	9-14-90	.224	.217	.226	60	214	23	48	8	1	2	23	12	2	4	2	30	9	5	.299	.270
Turner, Ben	R-R	6-5	220	4-27-90	.298	.301	.297	106	383	47	114	20	1	2	40	34	2	5	6	37	0	0	.371	.353
Villegas, Ydwin	B-R	5-10	178	9-1-90	.205	.111	.232	50	161	18	33	5	2	2	12	12	7	6	1	48	5	6	.298	.287
Williamson, Mac	R-R	6-5	240	7-15-90	.318	.259	.345	23	85	16	27	7	0	3	11	13	2	0	0	14	6	1	.506	.420

Pitching	B-T	HT	WT	DOB	W	L	ERA	G	GS	CG	SV	IP	H	R	ER	HR	BB	SO	AVG	vLH	vRH	K/9	BB/9
Affeldt, Jeremy	L-L	6-4	225	6-6-79	0	0	0.00	2	0	0	0	3	2	0	0	0	0	3	.200	.200	.200	9.00	0.00
Agosta, Martin	R-R	6-1	180	4-7-91	3	3	9.23	11	11	0	0	39	51	42	40	5	34	25	.325	.292	.348	5.77	7.85
Bandilla, Bryce	L-L	6-4	235	1-17-90	0	1	3.15	36	0	0	8	34	27	12	12	3	16	47	.216	.265	.184	12.32	4.19
Biagini, Joe	R-R	6-5	265	5-29-90	10	9	4.01	23	23	0	0	128	133	58	57	5	46	103	.275	.242	.304	7.24	3.23
Black, Ray	R-R	6-5	225	6-26-90	1	0	2.25	4	0	0	0	4	1	1	1	0	2	7	.083	.000	.100	15.75	4.50
Bradley, Ryan	B-L	6-1	180	7-15-88	0	4	8.76	21	4	0	0	49	72	50	48	6	20	37	.341	.309	.362	6.75	3.65
Bucardo, Jorge	R-R	6-1	190	10-18-89	1	2	3.81	33	0	0	0	54	59	27	23	6	19	41	.280	.269	.288	6.79	3.15
Casilla, Santiago	R-R	6-0	210	7-25-80	0	0	0.00	2	2	0	0	3	0	0	0		1	3	.000	.000	.000	9.00	3.00
Flores, Kendry	R-R	6-2	175	11-24-91	4	6	4.09	20	20	0	0	106	101	57	48	14	32	112	.249	.249	.249	9.54	2.73
Gardeck, Ian	R-R	6-2	215	11-21-90	1	2	9.38	17	0	0	0	24	23	27	25	2	28	19	.256	.341	.184	7.13	10.50
Gregorio, Joan	R-R	6-7	180	1-12-92	2	2	6.75	6	5	0	0	23	27	18	17	2	13	27	.303	.158	.412	10.72	5.16
Johnson, Stephen	R-R	6-5	215	2-21-91	7	4	3.65	49	0	0	1	69	62	31	28	5	36	77	.238	.235	.241	10.04	4.70
Kurrasch, Joe	L-L	6-0	205	6-19-91	8	4	3.05	18	15	0	0	91	80	34	31	3	33	49	.242	.229	.248	4.83	3.25
Lujan, Matt	L-L	6-1	210	8-23-88	6	2	3.42	12	12	0	0	71	66	29	27	8	23	69	.248	.205	.268	8.75	2.92
McVay, Mason	L-L	6-7	230	8-15-90	0	5	4.38	47	0	0	1	72	62	45	35	6	26	83	.232	.214	.245	10.38	3.25
Mizenko, Tyler	R-R	6-1	200	4-9-90	4	3	3.48	59	0	0	14	62	65	26	24	5	17	48	.272	.286	.261	6.97	2.47
Okert, Steven	L-L	6-3	210	7-9-91	1	2	1.53	33	0	0	19	35	33	6	6	2	11	54	.241	.164	.293	13.75	2.80
Rogers, Tyler	R-R	6-5	187	12-17-90	4	0	2.00	47	0	0	2	72	61	17	16	1	22	72	.234	.269	.209	9.00	2.75
Smith, Jake	R-R	6-4	190	6-2-90	0	1	10.80	3	1	0	0	7	8	8		2	4	8	.296	.000	.333	10.80	5.40
Soptic, Jeff	R-R	6-6	220	4-8-91	2	1	4.60	36	0	0	0	63	55	36	32	4	62	64	.238	.280	.206	9.19	8.90
Stratton, Chris	R-R	6-3	186	8-22-90	7	8	5.07	19	18	0	0	99	103	61	56	13	36	102	.270	.268	.271	9.24	3.26
Strickland, Hunter	R-R	6-4	220	9-24-88	0	0	3.00	3	0	0	0	3	2	1	1	0	0	7	.182	.167	.200	21.00	0.00
Vander Tuig, Nick	R-R	6-3	190	12-9-91	3	2	5.06	6	6	0	0	32	45	21	18	5	5	19	.331	.344	.320	5.34	1.41
Young, Pat	R-R	6-5	200	3-24-92	9	6	6.13	24	23	0	0	112	137	82	76	13	47	93	.305	.297	.313	7.50	3.79

Fielding

Catcher	PCT	G	PO	A	E	DP	PB
Brown	.995	41	378	29	2	3	9
Deacon	1.000	8	52	5	0	1	1
Navarro	.984	7	54	9	1	0	0
Turner	.995	87	688	52	4	7	7

First Base	PCT	G	PO	A	E	DP
Bednar	1.000	6	54	6	0	12
Brown	1.000	5	43	4	0	6

Lollis	1.000	2	15	2	0	1
Minicozzi	1.000	3	21	5	0	3
Price	1.000	3	31	1	0	4
Ragira	.983	104	867	61	16	101
Turner	.993	20	130	7	1	12

Second Base	PCT	G	PO	A	E	DP
Bednar	.977	10	14	29	1	6
Brown	1.000	8	18	26	0	7
Mende	.988	18	35	45	1	15
Miller	.993	48	108	157	2	54
Moreno	.975	20	46	73	3	15
Noonan	1.000	4	9	14	0	5

Robles	.966	32	50	92	5	22
Villegas	1.000	3	9	2	0	0

Third Base	PCT	G	PO	A	E	DP
Bednar	.900	6	0	9	1	2
Delfino	.950	126	101	239	18	31
Miller	.929	8	5	8	1	1

Shortstop	PCT	G	PO	A	E	DP
Bednar	.955	24	26	80	5	18
Miller	.955	36	50	100	7	26
Moreno	.957	6	8	14	1	4
Robles	.953	28	43	78	6	20

Villegas	.971	47	68	135	6	40

Outfield	PCT	G	PO	A	E	DP
Blair	.973	90	138	6	4	0
Carbonell	.963	19	51	1	2	0
Galindo	.982	101	212	7	4	1
Horan	.931	22	26	1	2	1
Jones	.979	125	225	12	5	4
Krill	.957	14	21	1	1	0
Lofton	1.000	20	34	1	0	0
Lollis	1.000	20	32	0	0	0
Mende	—	1	0	0	0	0
Payne	.941	24	29	3	2	0

AUGUSTA GREENJACKETS
SOUTH ATLANTIC LEAGUE

LOW CLASS A

Batting	B-T	HT	WT	DOB	AVG	vLH	vRH	G	AB	R	H	2B	3B	HR	RBI	BB	HBP	SH	SF	SO	SB	CS	SLG	OBP
Arroyo, Christian	R-R	6-1	180	5-30-95	.203	.188	.206	31	118	10	24	3	1	1	14	4	0	1	2	22	1	2	.271	.226
Bednar, Brandon	R-R	6-4	185	3-21-92	.275	.288	.271	74	291	38	80	9	2	1	24	14	4	1	3	51	8	6	.330	.314
Callaway, Will	R-R	6-0	190	12-14-89	.262	.241	.270	31	103	6	27	6	1	0	8	8	2	1	0	22	2	3	.340	.327
Chavez, Matt	R-R	6-2	195	3-6-89	.194	.000	.212	10	36	4	7	3	0	0	3	1	0	0	0	14	0	0	.278	.216
Cornier, Gabriel	B-R	6-0	190	6-10-92	.200	.206	.197	36	110	14	22	5	0	2	21	20	1	1	2	35	2	0	.300	.323
Escalante, Geno	R-R	5-11	210	6-25-91	.176	.091	.200	16	51	7	9	3	0	0	3	5	0	0	0	10	0	0	.235	.250
Harris, Devin	R-R	6-3	225	4-23-88	.236	.333	.224	16	55	7	13	5	0	2	7	8	0	0	0	12	1	0	.436	.333
Horan, Tyler	L-R	6-2	230	12-2-90	.273	.183	.303	102	370	59	101	22	5	15	54	39	6	0	2	97	9	4	.481	.350
Jones, Ryan	R-R	5-10	175	9-8-90	.242	.214	.252	46	153	20	37	9	0	1	11	29	0	3	1	35	5	4	.320	.361
Jones, Ryder	L-R	6-2	200	6-7-94	.220	.181	.239	91	369	43	81	21	1	7	49	18	9	2	1	93	6	1	.339	.272
Lofton, Chris	L-R	6-1	175	5-20-90	.250	.203	.266	76	276	36	69	16	3	2	29	28	1	2	1	69	17	6	.351	.320
Massoni, Craig	R-R	6-2	215	10-29-91	.255	.189	.276	44	153	18	39	11	0	1	10	15	1	0	0	45	2	0	.346	.325
Mende, Sam	R-R	6-3	195	1-9-90	.308	.200	.375	4	13	2	4	1	0	0	2	2	0	1	0	1	0	0	.385	.400
Moreno, Rando	R-R	5-11	165	6-6-92	.197	.152	.214	93	330	36	65	7	0	1	30	22	7	14	3	44	16	5	.227	.260
Ortiz, Randy	R-R	5-11	185	6-15-93	.259	.216	.272	51	162	15	42	3	1	0	13	13	3	2	0	43	8	6	.290	.326
Paulino, Cristian	R-R	5-10	170	9-4-91	.240	.274	.227	92	271	36	65	8	4	3	31	15	5	4	1	56	20	5	.332	.291
Payne, Shawn	R-R	6-1	190	7-13-89	.246	.308	.231	18	65	10	16	3	0	0	1	11	0	0	0	14	4	2	.292	.355
Polonius, John	R-R	6-1	160	1-13-91	.257	.455	.196	44	140	24	36	3	1	2	20	13	6	3	2	22	5	2	.336	.342
Price, Scott	L-R	6-3	205	1-9-92	.250	.500	.194	13	44	6	11	2	1	0	2	3	4	0	0	13	1	0	.341	.353
Rodriguez, Rafael	R-R	6-5	198	7-13-92	.269	.300	.256	77	283	36	76	10	0	5	41	11	6	0	1	33	2	2	.357	.309
Rojas, Leo	R-R	5-11	200	6-11-90	.264	.417	.233	20	72	9	19	4	0	1	7	1	0	0	0	19	0	1	.361	.274
Ross, Ty	R-R	6-1	203	1-17-92	.246	.281	.233	117	415	45	102	24	0	6	48	38	6	6	7	87	1	6	.347	.313
Sim, Eric	R-R	6-2	215	1-3-89	.195	.277	.159	43	154	17	30	6	0	3	23	15	5	3	2	49	2	0	.292	.284
Sy, Jeremy	R-R	5-8	180	10-14-89	.216	.188	.227	92	338	52	73	13	4	13	36	50	5	2	2	93	16	8	.393	.324
Tuntland, Ryan	R-R	6-1	190	4-30-91	.195	.190	.197	65	205	24	40	14	1	1	17	28	2	0	0	76	0	2	.288	.298

Pitching	B-T	HT	WT	DOB	W	L	ERA	G	GS	CG	SV	IP	H	R	ER	HR	BB	SO	AVG	vLH	vRH	K/9	BB/9
Alvarado, Carlos	R-R	6-4	175	10-22-89	6	1	2.03	32	0	0	0	62	47	22	14	3	13	55	.205	.204	.206	7.98	1.89
Black, Ray	R-R	6-5	225	6-26-90	1	3	3.73	33	0	0	1	31	16	15	13	1	14	64	.147	.109	.175	18.38	4.02
Castillo, Luis	R-R	6-2	170	12-12-92	2	2	3.07	48	0	0	10	59	56	23	20	6	25	66	.247	.232	.258	10.13	3.84
Connolly, Mike	R-R	6-1	180	10-31-91	0	0	1.93	4	0	0	0	5	5	1	1	0	3	6	.263	.143	.333	11.57	5.79
Diaz, Carlos	L-L	6-2	176	11-18-93	6	6	4.16	29	14	0	0	102	105	53	47	5	37	76	.269	.263	.271	6.73	3.28
Farley, Brandon	R-R	6-2	215	8-1-90	0	0	7.71	9	0	0	0	16	27	17	14	2	7	14	.391	.310	.450	7.71	3.86
Gregorio, Joan	R-R	6-7	180	1-12-92	2	7	3.57	13	12	0	1	68	50	33	27	2	27	65	.204	.210	.198	8.60	3.57
Johnson, Chase	R-R	6-3	185	1-9-92	4	7	4.57	23	22	0	0	110	111	69	56	5	40	94	.260	.247	.274	7.67	3.26
Johnson, Chris	R-R	6-4	205	8-24-91	0	1	9.00	1	1	0	0	2	3	2	2	0	2	0	.375	.750	.000	0.00	9.00
Jones, Christian	L-L	6-3	210	1-27-91	5	9	3.33	22	22	0	0	111	96	54	41	6	26	100	.232	.204	.246	8.13	2.11
Jones, Nick	L-L	6-6	215	9-15-91	1	0	0.00	4	0	0	1	5	3	0	0	0	3	5	.176	.000	.231	9.64	5.79
Kaden, Connor	R-R	6-4	200	10-27-92	0	1	3.60	7	0	0	0	10	14	5	4	0	3	7	.341	.429	.296	6.30	2.70
Lujan, Matt	L-L	6-2	210	8-23-88	6	2	2.19	12	10	0	0	70	67	20	17	0	21	66	.255	.200	.277	8.49	2.70
Mella, Keury	R-R	6-2	200	8-2-93	3	3	3.93	12	12	1	0	66	69	36	29	1	13	63	.265	.299	.238	8.55	1.76
Messner, Steven	L-L	6-1	185	12-10-89	7	5	4.17	31	12	0	0	110	139	67	51	3	39	82	.308	.287	.318	6.71	3.19
Montero, Raymundo	R-R	6-2	195	6-26-89	1	6	5.26	30	0	0	5	38	34	29	22	3	23	36	.233	.206	.256	8.60	5.50
Ramer, Robert	R-R	6-5	195	7-4-90	3	5	4.73	9	8	0	0	46	47	28	24	4	13	40	.263	.277	.250	7.88	2.56
Rogers, Tyler	R-R	6-5	187	12-17-90	0	0	1.02	9	0	0	0	18	10	2	2	0	5	11	.164	.120	.194	5.60	2.55
Slania, Dan	R-R	6-5	275	5-24-92	2	5	3.99	43	0	0	12	59	56	31	26	5	21	46	.253	.287	.228	7.06	3.22
Smith, Jake	R-R	6-4	190	6-2-90	3	5	2.79	48	0	0	5	58	47	24	18	1	30	77	.221	.250	.203	11.95	4.66
Snelten, D.J.	L-L	6-6	215	5-29-92	4	1	1.23	20	0	0	0	29	24	4	4	0	16	32	.226	.194	.240	9.82	4.91
Vander Tuig, Nick	R-R	6-3	190	12-9-91	0	0	11.17	6	2	0	0	10	17	13	12	1	5	6	.395	.278	.480	5.59	4.66
Ysla, Luis	L-L	6-1	185	4-27-92	6	7	2.45	24	23	0	0	121	104	42	33	8	45	115	.231	.201	.244	8.53	3.34

Fielding

Catcher	PCT	G	PO	A	E	DP	PB
Cornier	1.000	7	63	6	0	0	2
Rojas	.960	9	68	4	3	0	3
Ross	.990	96	742	74	8	2	4
Sim	.989	29	251	26	3	3	5

First Base	PCT	G	PO	A	E	DP
Bednar	.988	25	232	13	3	25
Cornier	.991	22	199	10	2	19
Jones	—	1	0	0	0	0
Massoni	1.000	24	193	13	0	16
Price	1.000	7	59	5	0	6

Rojas	.986	6	63	7	1	4
Ross	1.000	3	23	0	0	2
Tuntland	.991	60	490	43	5	40

Second Base	PCT	G	PO	A	E	DP
Arroyo	.984	26	26	96	2	17
Bednar	.979	9	17	29	1	4

	PCT	G	PO	A	E	DP
Callaway	.926	4	4	21	2	3
Jones	.963	28	53	76	5	21
Jones	—	1	0	0	0	0
Moreno	1.000	1	1	2	0	1
Paulino	.833	2	0	5	1	1
Polonius	.983	23	40	74	2	14
Sy	.959	48	69	139	9	24

Third Base	PCT	G	PO	A	E	DP
Arroyo	—	1	0	0	0	0
Bednar	.978	33	21	68	2	2
Callaway	.893	24	20	30	6	2
Jones	.974	11	12	25	1	3

	PCT	G	PO	A	E	DP
Jones	.891	50	21	101	15	9
Mende	1.000	4	2	5	0	1
Polonius	.902	15	7	30	4	2
Rojas	.833	1	0	5	1	1
Tuntland	1.000	1	0	3	0	0

Shortstop	PCT	G	PO	A	E	DP
Arroyo	.913	5	7	14	2	2
Jones	1.000	3	6	4	0	0
Jones	.912	34	55	79	13	28
Moreno	.947	93	140	289	24	54
Polonius	.950	6	3	16	1	2

Outfield	PCT	G	PO	A	E	DP
Callaway	1.000	2	1	0	0	0
Escalante	.833	16	14	1	3	0
Harris	.895	13	16	1	2	0
Horan	.977	97	166	7	4	1
Lofton	.986	75	134	3	2	2
Massoni	1.000	16	15	3	0	0
Ortiz	.967	48	81	6	3	2
Paulino	.958	87	134	4	6	2
Payne	1.000	11	15	0	0	0
Price	.889	4	8	0	1	0
Rodriguez	.957	76	87	2	4	0

SALEM-KEIZER VOLCANOES · SHORT-SEASON

NORTHWEST LEAGUE

Batting	B-T	HT	WT	DOB	AVG	vLH	vRH	G	AB	R	H	2B	3B	HR	RBI	BB	HBP	SH	SF	SO	SB	CS	SLG	OBP
Arroyo, Christian	R-R	6-1	180	5-30-95	.333	.319	.337	58	243	39	81	14	2	5	48	18	2	0	4	31	6	1	.469	.378
Callaway, Will	R-R	6-0	190	12-14-89	.294	.298	.293	43	163	20	48	11	0	3	23	9	3	0	0	36	4	2	.417	.343
Cole, Hunter	R-R	6-1	179	10-3-92	.239	.294	.227	27	92	17	22	5	0	4	10	8	2	1	1	20	1	0	.424	.311
Davis, Dylan	R-R	6-0	205	7-20-93	.200	.222	.194	23	85	11	17	0	0	4	7	7	1	0	0	23	1	0	.341	.269
Deacon, Jared	L-R	6-0	190	8-25-91	.219	.077	.255	21	64	8	14	1	0	0	5	8	1	3	1	9	0	0	.234	.311
Escalante, Geno	R-R	5-11	210	6-25-91	.172	.143	.189	18	58	3	10	3	0	0	4	2	6	0	0	10	1	0	.224	.273
Ewing, Skyler	R-R	6-1	225	8-22-92	.291	.282	.294	51	182	35	53	9	0	8	31	36	6	0	0	28	0	1	.473	.417
Fargas, Johneshwy	R-R	6-1	165	12-15-94	.240	.326	.210	49	167	33	40	6	0	3	13	24	12	4	1	27	15	6	.329	.373
Fuentes, Leonardo	R-R	6-4	215	11-29-92	.150	.000	.176	7	20	3	3	0	0	0	1	0	2	0	1	6	0	0	.150	.217
Garcia, Aramis	R-R	6-2	195	1-12-93	.229	.375	.210	20	70	5	16	3	0	2	12	5	1	0	0	19	0	0	.357	.289
Harrison, Seth	R-R	6-0	200	7-22-92	.266	.314	.252	37	158	24	42	10	2	0	20	8	1	2	4	42	11	4	.354	.298
Hollick, Tyler	L-R	6-1	205	9-16-92	.241	.143	.258	43	141	24	34	5	3	0	12	22	0	0	1	37	6	4	.319	.341
Jones, Jonathan	R-R	6-5	230	2-15-92	.196	.133	.222	32	102	14	20	7	0	1	12	21	1	0	2	26	0	0	.294	.333
Jones, Ryan	R-R	5-10	175	9-8-90	.310	.353	.293	14	58	8	18	3	0	0	4	6	1	1	0	18	4	0	.362	.385
Jones, Ryder	L-R	6-2	200	6-7-94	.243	.261	.238	27	107	17	26	5	1	3	18	7	1	1	1	21	1	0	.393	.293
Kay, Brett	R-R	5-11	165	4-11-91	.222	.226	.221	40	117	22	26	7	0	0	8	17	0	3	0	35	3	2	.282	.321
Lichtenthaler, Christian	B-R	5-10	165	10-8-91	.286	—	.286	3	7	0	2	0	0	0	0	1	0	1	0	0	1	0	.286	.375
Massoni, Craig	R-R	6-2	215	10-29-91	.244	.172	.286	21	78	7	19	4	0	2	12	16	2	0	1	22	0	0	.372	.381
McCall, Shilo	R-R	6-1	210	6-2-94	.200	.189	.205	46	165	20	33	13	0	3	21	19	2	0	2	53	2	1	.333	.287
Melendez, Rene	R-R	6-1	190	1-20-95	.182	.000	.222	5	11	0	2	0	0	0	3	3	0	0	0	2	0	0	.182	.357
Mende, Sam	R-R	6-3	195	1-9-90	.227	.182	.242	12	44	8	10	1	0	2	7	8	0	0	0	11	1	0	.386	.346
Ortiz, Randy	R-R	5-11	185	6-15-93	.000	—	.000	1	5	0	0	0	0	0	0	0	0	0	0	1	1	0	.000	.000
Pujadas, Fernando	R-R	6-1	210	1-2-92	.254	.250	.256	36	114	9	29	7	1	2	18	4	1	1	1	17	0	0	.386	.283
Relaford, Travious	R-R	5-11	180	5-13-92	.283	.328	.267	70	258	45	73	10	2	3	28	37	5	3	3	39	9	0	.372	.380
Rojas, Leo	R-R	5-11	200	6-11-90	.206	.364	.130	12	34	4	7	2	0	0	3	4	0	0	1	7	0	0	.265	.282
Slater, Austin	R-R	6-2	194	12-13-92	.347	.526	.313	29	118	21	41	6	0	2	23	10	4	0	0	17	7	1	.449	.417

Pitching	B-T	HT	WT	DOB	W	L	ERA	G	GS	CG	SV	IP	H	R	ER	HR	BB	SO	AVG	vLH	vRH	K/9	BB/9
Beede, Tyler	R-R	6-4	200	5-23-93	0	0	2.70	2	2	0	0	7	8	2	2	0	3	7	.308	.385	.231	9.45	4.05
Encinosa, E.J.	R-R	6-5	230	8-5-91	4	1	2.39	27	0	0	1	26	20	8	7	2	10	22	.211	.214	.208	7.52	3.42
Forjet, Jason	R-R	6-2	185	1-4-90	7	1	3.10	15	14	0	0	87	84	33	30	6	16	87	.257	.288	.236	9.00	1.66
Gardeck, Ian	R-R	6-2	185	11-21-90	2	1	2.70	12	0	0	1	13	7	5	4	0	11	24	.156	.250	.121	16.20	7.43
Gonzalez, Nick	L-L	6-4	220	6-26-92	2	5	4.06	15	14	0	0	71	69	45	32	2	28	47	.251	.308	.233	5.96	3.55
Knight, Dusten	R-R	6-0	185	9-7-90	1	3	3.65	24	0	0	1	37	26	18	15	4	20	44	.202	.256	.174	10.70	4.86
Leenhouts, Drew	L-L	6-3	225	3-28-90	3	4	4.73	18	11	0	0	72	87	46	38	8	11	71	.290	.281	.294	8.83	1.37
McCasland, Jake	R-R	6-2	215	9-13-91	2	3	7.76	22	0	0	0	27	26	23	23	1	23	32	.260	.273	.254	10.80	7.76
McVey, Cameron	R-R	6-5	205	10-18-88	1	2	5.86	22	0	0	1	28	24	18	18	2	15	32	.233	.132	.292	10.41	4.88
Mella, Keury	R-R	6-2	200	8-2-93	1	1	1.83	6	6	0	0	20	16	5	4	0	6	20	.222	.229	.216	9.15	2.75
Miller, Ethan	R-R	6-2	220	11-19-90	5	3	4.60	14	14	0	0	78	89	44	40	2	15	57	.285	.289	.283	6.55	1.72
Montero, Raymundo	R-R	6-2	185	6-26-89	0	0	0.00	6	0	0	1	7	3	0	0	0	3		.120	.100	.133	11.05	3.68
Neff, Steven	L-L	6-2	205	2-24-89	1	3	3.90	26	0	0	0	30	36	14	13	3	10	34	.290	.250	.313	10.20	3.00
Paniagua, Armando	R-R	5-11	155	11-10-90	0	2	6.48	18	0	0	0	25	21	20	18	1	17	26	.221	.313	.175	9.36	6.12
Reyes, Jose	R-R	6-1	184	1-3-91	6	4	3.89	15	15	0	0	83	78	42	36	6	16	64	.245	.267	.228	6.91	1.73
Sanchez, Eury	R-R	5-10	170	11-8-92	3	3	3.48	28	0	0	14	34	25	17	13	5	15	50	.203	.190	.210	13.37	4.01
Singer, Kirk	R-R	6-2	170	12-1-89	0	2	6.82	23	0	0	0	32	37	30	24	5	20	39	.282	.311	.267	11.08	5.68
Snelten, D.J.	L-L	6-6	215	5-29-92	0	0	6.75	9	0	0	0	9	12	7	7	1	4	12	.300	.278	.318	11.57	3.86

Fielding

Catcher	PCT	G	PO	A	E	DP	PB
Deacon	.994	21	156	12	1	1	4
Escalante	1.000	5	39	4	0	0	1
Garcia	.981	18	138	20	3	1	1
Melendez	1.000	5	25	5	0	0	0
Pujadas	.993	34	258	30	2	0	6
Rojas	.952	6	36	4	2	1	1

First Base	PCT	G	PO	A	E	DP
Callaway	—	1	0	0	0	0
Cole	1.000	3	25	0	0	2
Ewing	.998	45	379	29	1	32
Jones	.985	22	188	13	3	9
Massoni	.980	11	95	5	2	3

Second Base	PCT	G	PO	A	E	DP
Callaway	1.000	2	1	2	0	0
Jones	.973	10	17	19	1	4
Kay	.978	37	59	75	3	18
Lichtenthaler	.889	2	0	8	1	2
Relaford	.971	34	63	71	4	15

Third Base	PCT	G	PO	A	E	DP
Callaway	.976	30	24	58	2	2
Cole	.800	3	0	4	1	0
Jones	1.000	2	1	4	0	0
Jones	.943	27	19	47	4	2
Mende	.941	9	7	9	1	1
Relaford	.955	12	8	13	1	1

Shortstop	PCT	G	PO	A	E	DP
Arroyo	.965	58	88	185	10	33
Lichtenthaler	1.000	1	1	1	0	0

	PCT	G	PO	A	E	DP
Relaford	.976	21	23	59	2	6
Outfield	**PCT**	**G**	**PO**	**A**	**E**	**DP**
Callaway	.917	7	10	1	1	0
Cole	1.000	9	11	0	0	0

	PCT	G	PO	A	E	DP
Davis	1.000	15	15	1	0	1
Escalante	1.000	4	4	0	0	0
Fargas	.959	47	66	4	3	0
Fuentes	1.000	4	6	0	0	0
Harrison	.959	36	70	1	3	0

	PCT	G	PO	A	E	DP
Hollick	.985	38	60	4	1	0
Massoni	1.000	9	14	0	0	0
McCall	.971	41	65	3	2	1
Ortiz	1.000	1	1	0	0	0
Slater	.943	27	49	1	3	0

AZL GIANTS   ROOKIE

ARIZONA LEAGUE

Batting	B-T	HT	WT	DOB	AVG	vLH	vRH	G	AB	R	H	2B	3B	HR	RBI	BB	HBP	SH	SF	SO	SB	CS	SLG	OBP
Abreu, Tony	B-R	5-10	200	11-13-84	.000	.000	—	1	2	0	0	0	0	0	1	0	0	0	1	0	0	1	.000	.000
Amion, Richard	R-R	5-10	190	2-24-93	.267	.324	.245	38	135	25	36	4	3	2	17	22	3	2	1	36	8	5	.385	.379
Arenado, Jonah	R-R	6-4	195	2-3-95	.250	.235	.256	50	184	20	46	10	0	0	21	21	4	0	0	43	0	0	.304	.340
Carbonell, Daniel	R-R	6-3	196	3-29-91	.314	.400	.280	10	35	10	11	3	0	1	4	2	1	0	0	4	4	0	.486	.368
Cartagena, Carlos	R-R	6-2	190	12-22-93	.182	.105	.222	22	55	9	10	2	1	1	7	10	1	0	0	14	0	0	.309	.318
Cole, Hunter	R-R	6-1	179	10-3-92	.444	.750	.200	2	9	2	4	1	0	0	1	0	0	0	0	1	1	0	.556	.444
Compton, Chase	L-R	6-2	210	9-26-91	.282	.250	.294	33	117	21	33	5	1	0	21	13	8	1	0	33	1	0	.342	.391
Davis, Dylan	R-R	6-0	205	7-20-93	.297	.167	.360	9	37	6	11	7	0	0	8	3	0	0	1	12	0	0	.486	.341
Ewing, Skyler	R-R	6-1	225	8-22-92	.237	.182	.259	11	38	4	9	4	0	1	8	4	1	0	1	9	0	0	.421	.318
Garcia, Aramis	R-R	6-2	195	1-12-93	.219	.250	.200	8	32	6	7	3	0	0	3	5	0	1	0	6	0	0	.313	.324
Harrison, Seth	R-R	6-0	200	7-22-92	.067	.000	.083	4	15	5	1	0	1	0	3	3	0	0	0	6	1	0	.200	.222
Javier, Nathanael	R-R	6-3	185	10-10-95	.172	.125	.190	9	29	3	5	0	0	0	2	0	0	0	0	11	1	0	.172	.172
Lacen, Luis	R-R	6-3	195	10-13-96	.250	.000	.308	19	48	8	12	1	0	0	5	5	0	0	0	20	3	0	.271	.321
Leslie, Ben	L-L	6-1	185	6-28-94	.200	.182	.207	16	40	8	8	3	0	0	7	14	2	0	0	11	0	0	.275	.429
Lichtenthaler, Christian	B-R	5-10	165	10-8-91	.235	.172	.269	25	81	9	19	2	1	0	9	13	2	0	3	20	3	1	.284	.343
Melendez, Rene	R-R	6-1	190	1-20-95	.123	.143	.115	24	73	5	9	3	0	0	4	4	1	0	0	20	0	0	.164	.179
Mercedes, Hector	R-R	6-3	185	10-25-91	.296	.267	.309	31	98	15	29	6	4	1	12	5	1	1	2	26	0	1	.469	.330
Metzger, Brennan	R-R	5-11	180	12-15-89	.354	.296	.382	33	82	24	29	6	3	0	10	16	1	1	1	8	4	0	.500	.460
Murray, Byron	R-R	5-10	195	7-26-95	.279	.238	.298	19	68	10	19	5	2	0	12	6	1	0	0	15	1	0	.412	.347
Ortiz, Randy	R-R	5-11	185	6-15-93	.390	.483	.333	20	77	20	30	2	3	1	9	8	1	1	1	12	16	1	.532	.448
Pagan, Angel	B-R	6-2	200	7-2-81	.600	—	.600	2	5	2	3	2	0	0	1	0	0	0	0	0	0	0	1.000	.667
Pare, Matt	L-R	6-0	205	11-17-90	.286	.000	.400	4	7	2	2	0	0	0	1	0	1	0	0	1	0	0	.286	.375
Parra, Nicoll	L-L	5-9	160	7-28-94	.254	.111	.306	25	67	13	17	2	0	0	8	6	3	1	1	9	3	0	.284	.338
Pena, Julio	R-R	6-0	185	12-13-92	.205	.233	.195	33	117	16	24	6	3	2	15	9	0	0	1	45	3	2	.359	.260
Potter, Evan	R-R	6-1	170	6-9-92	.130	.120	.134	37	92	9	12	1	1	0	7	14	1	2	2	27	2	0	.163	.204
Price, Scott	L-R	6-3	205	1-9-92	.275	.400	.224	21	69	12	19	5	1	0	4	6	0	1	0	13	0	0	.377	.363
Riley, John	R-R	6-0	210	2-14-94	.188	.148	.200	34	112	20	21	6	1	2	19	15	2	0	2	43	1	0	.313	.290
Rivas, Kleiber	L-R	5-11	200	6-22-95	.077	.000	.083	11	13	3	1	0	0	0	1	5	0	0	0	4	0	0	.077	.333
Rivera, Kevin	R-R	5-11	170	6-12-96	.228	.111	.274	48	162	23	37	5	3	0	18	12	1	2	3	38	1	0	.296	.281
Scutaro, Marco	R-R	5-10	185	10-30-75	.231	.250	.222	7	13	2	3	1	0	0	1	2	0	0	0	0	0	0	.308	.333
Slater, Austin	R-R	6-1	194	12-13-92	.333	.200	.500	2	9	2	3	0	1	0	2	0	0	0	0	2	0	0	.556	.333
Villalona, Angel	R-R	6-3	255	8-13-90	.273	.429	.200	6	22	4	6	3	0	0	3	0	0	0	0	3	0	0	.409	.273

Pitching	B-T	HT	WT	DOB	W	L	ERA	G	GS	CG	SV	IP	H	R	ER	HR	BB	SO	AVG	vLH	vRH	K/9	BB/9
Agosta, Martin	R-R	6-1	180	4-7-91	1	0	4.50	4	4	0	0	14	16	8	7	0	2	19	.286	.235	.308	12.21	1.29
Beede, Tyler	R-R	6-4	200	5-23-93	0	1	3.12	4	4	0	0	9	8	4	3	0	4	11	.242	.364	.182	11.42	4.15
Blackburn, Clayton	L-R	6-2	260	1-6-93	0	1	3.60	2	2	0	0	5	4	2	2	0	0	9	.222	.429	.091	16.20	0.00
Bochy, Brett	R-R	6-2	200	8-27-87	1	0	0.00	2	0	0	0	2	0	0	0	0	1	1	.000	.000	.000	4.50	0.00
Boggs, Mitchell	R-R	6-4	235	2-15-84	1	0	0.00	2	0	0	0	2	2	0	0	0	1	1	.286	.333	.250	4.50	9.00
Broadway, Mike	R-R	6-5	215	3-30-87	0	0	1.50	5	0	0	0	6	8	1	1	1	1	6	.333	.286	.353	9.00	1.50
Brody, Greg	R-R	6-2	185	10-22-91	1	1	0.63	14	0	0	2	14	12	6	1	0	3	27	.211	.333	.154	16.95	1.88
Brooks, Dylan	R-R	6-7	230	8-20-95	2	1	3.18	18	1	0	0	34	33	14	12	1	15	45	.258	.235	.273	11.91	3.97
Connolly, Mike	R-R	6-1	180	10-31-91	2	1	2.70	11	0	0	0	17	8	5	5	2	5	14	.148	.043	.226	7.56	2.70
Coonrod, Sam	R-R	6-2	190	9-22-92	1	0	3.90	15	5	0	0	28	32	14	12	0	6	25	.291	.366	.246	8.13	1.95
Farley, Brandon	R-R	6-2	215	8-1-90	1	1	0.64	13	0	0	4	14	11	2	1	0	3	17	.224	.300	.172	10.93	1.93
Gage, Matt	L-R	6-4	240	2-11-93	2	0	1.89	13	6	0	0	33	27	8	7	1	8	32	.225	.189	.241	8.64	2.16
Hernandez, Rayan	R-R	6-4	230	9-24-95	0	3	1.53	21	0	0	0	29	21	6	5	0	9	25	.202	.256	.169	7.67	2.76
Hughes, Garrett	L-L	6-9	230	8-27-91	1	0	2.84	11	0	0	0	13	14	6	4	0	10	11	.298	.500	.243	7.82	7.11
Johnson, Jordan	R-R	6-3	195	9-15-93	0	0	0.00	3	0	0	0	3	0	0	0	0	2	3	.000	.000	.000	10.13	6.75
Jones, Nick	L-L	6-6	215	9-15-91	2	0	6.61	19	0	0	1	16	26	16	12	0	12	11	.356	.375	.351	6.06	6.61
Kaden, Connor	R-R	6-4	200	10-27-92	1	0	2.79	9	0	0	0	10	11	4	3	0	4	16	.282	.286	.280	14.90	3.72
Loux, Shane	R-R	6-2	225	8-31-79	0	0	2.45	7	0	0	0	7	7	2	2	0	0	7	.226	.091	.300	11.05	0.00
Martinez, Rodolfo	R-R	6-2	180	4-4-94	1	5	8.78	15	7	0	0	28	45	32	27	1	16	35	.375	.356	.387	11.39	5.20
Melo, Kendry	R-R	6-3	210	1-7-94	1	2	9.50	3	3	0	0	18	21	24	19	2	21	19	.296	.310	.286	9.50	10.50
Moronta, Reyes	R-R	6-0	175	1-6-93	0	1	4.66	20	0	0	5	19	10	11	10	1	11	30	.222	.353	.182	13.97	5.12
Pino, Luis	R-R	6-1	185	10-8-92	2	0	6.07	16	1	0	0	30	38	21	20	3	11	24	.317	.383	.274	7.28	3.34
Reyes, Mark	R-L	6-1	185	10-8-92	1	1	3.00	5	3	0	0	12	13	8	4	0	3	14	.277	.364	.250	10.50	2.25
Riggs, Nolan	R-R	6-8	235	5-22-93	0	0	5.40	1	0	0	0	10	8	7	6	0	6	14	.211	.300	.179	12.60	5.40
Rosario, Sandy	R-R	6-1	205	8-22-85	0	0	4.26	3	0	0	0	6	7	3	3	1	0	8	.280	.273	.286	11.37	0.00
Sabo, Nick	R-L	6-5	220	6-14-93	1	0	6.75	3	0	0	0	3	3	2	2	0	2	1	.300	.000	.500	3.38	6.75
Santos, Michael	R-R	6-4	170	5-29-95	4	3	2.56	12	12	0	0	60	59	26	17	3	13	50	.259	.261	.256	7.54	1.96
Smith, Caleb	R-L	6-2	205	10-4-92	1	1	4.35	13	0	0	0	10	6	5	5	0	13	18	.139	.111	.148	10.45	11.32
Vander Tuig, Nick	R-R	6-3	190	12-9-91	0	0	0.95	5	0	0	0	19	15	3	2	0	4	18	.217	.185	.238	8.53	1.89
Webb, Logan	R-R	6-2	195	11-18-96	0	0	2.25	3	1	0	0	4	3	2	1	0	3	5	.200	.000	.333	11.25	6.75
Woods, Stetson	R-R	6-8	200	1-15-95	5	1	2.25	10	0	0	0	16	11	4	4	0	4	20	.190	.238	.162	11.25	2.25
Yanez, Cesar	R-R	6-5	175	9-30-94	0	0	15.53	16	0	0	0	13	27	27	23	2	23	14	.409	.364	.432	9.45	15.53

Fielding

Catcher	PCT	G	PO	A	E	DP	PB
Garcia	.973	7	66	7	2	0	6
Melendez	.975	24	171	21	5	1	7
Pare	1.000	4	14	3	0	2	0
Riley	.990	28	249	34	3	3	7
Rivas	.970	11	29	3	1	1	1

First Base	PCT	G	PO	A	E	DP
Arenado	1.000	4	25	3	0	1
Compton	.993	30	250	16	2	21
Ewing	.985	8	64	3	1	9
Price	1.000	17	128	6	0	14
Villalona	.974	5	38	0	1	2

Second Base	PCT	G	PO	A	E	DP
Abreu	1.000	1	1	2	0	0
Lichtenthaler	1.000	10	13	25	0	2

Metzger	1.000	1	1	0	0	0
Potter	.889	5	6	10	2	1
Rivera	.958	47	78	125	9	27
Scutaro	.950	7	6	13	1	4

Third Base	PCT	G	PO	A	E	DP
Arenado	.902	47	26	75	11	6
Cole	.833	2	0	5	1	0
Compton	.000	2	0	0	1	0
Javier	.917	7	3	8	1	0
Potter	1.000	6	1	9	0	0

Shortstop	PCT	G	PO	A	E	DP
Lichtenthaler	1.000	17	14	48	0	9
Mercedes	.901	25	29	53	9	11
Potter	.989	31	27	67	1	17

Outfield	PCT	G	PO	A	E	DP
Amion	1.000	36	46	2	0	1
Carbonell	1.000	9	10	1	0	0
Cartagena	.950	17	18	1	1	1
Davis	1.000	8	12	3	0	0
Harrison	1.000	3	7	0	0	0
Lacen	.769	10	9	1	3	0
Leslie	.882	12	14	1	2	0
Metzger	.970	22	26	6	1	0
Murray	1.000	11	8	1	0	1
Ortiz	.935	19	27	2	2	0
Pagan	1.000	2	1	0	0	0
Parra	.923	20	22	2	2	0
Pena	.913	25	39	3	4	0
Slater	1.000	1	5	0	0	0

DSL GIANTS   ROOKIE

DOMINICAN SUMMER LEAGUE

Batting	B-T	HT	WT	DOB	AVG	vLH	vRH	G	AB	R	H	2B	3B	HR	RBI	BB	HBP	SH	SF	SO	SB	CS	SLG	OBP
Angomas, Jean	L-R	6-0	170	6-5-95	.298	.319	.292	57	218	37	65	7	7	0	33	25	2	0	1	24	8	5	.394	.374
Antunez, Robert	R-R	5-10	160	3-22-96	.188	.135	.208	57	138	35	26	1	2	0	18	29	12	4	2	35	15	1	.225	.370
Beltre, Kelvin	R-R	5-11	170	9-25-96	.235	.357	.204	22	68	21	16	5	0	3	10	22	2	0	1	11	7	4	.441	.430
Coronado, Mecky	R-R	6-0	180	12-13-96	.289	.256	.305	41	121	12	35	6	3	1	18	15	7	0	2	21	0	0	.413	.393
Edie, Mikey	R-R	5-11	175	7-3-97	.298	.256	.311	48	188	54	56	8	1	2	24	22	19	3	0	30	14	8	.383	.424
Geraldo, Manuel	R-R	6-1	170	9-23-96	.251	.196	.265	62	231	35	58	8	6	0	29	14	11	2	1	54	16	5	.338	.323
Gomez, Anthony	R-R	6-3	200	11-23-94	.238	.152	.263	47	151	17	36	8	0	2	21	29	8	0	5	28	2	2	.331	.378
Gomez, Miguel	B-R	5-10	185	12-17-92	.318	.339	.308	65	258	35	82	18	1	5	60	17	5	0	3	37	3	0	.453	.367
Gonzalez, Yendrys	R-R	6-3	185	12-28-96	.040	.000	.045	14	25	5	1	0	0	0	0	2	0	0	0	12	0	0	.040	.111
Guzman, Marco	R-R	6-0	170	8-7-94	.265	.313	.242	14	49	6	13	2	0	2	5	4	1	0	0	4	1	1	.429	.333
Medina, Hengerber	R-R	5-11	158	10-12-94	.220	.194	.229	49	132	28	29	2	1	0	9	22	4	1	2	17	6	2	.250	.344
Medrano, Robinson	R-R	6-3	180	4-20-96	.268	.255	.272	55	209	38	56	6	5	2	31	27	6	0	0	50	3	3	.373	.368
Mora, Jose	R-R	5-11	175	1-16-93	.133	.333	.103	16	45	2	6	0	0	1	10	6	1	2	0	8	0	1	.200	.250
Morles, Jose	L-R	5-10	180	8-18-94	.287	.313	.282	33	87	18	25	3	0	0	9	19	2	3	1	14	1	1	.322	.422
Rodriguez, Alilzon	R-R	6-3	200	9-22-96	.208	.200	.211	17	24	3	5	1	0	0	2	4	0	0	0	7	0	0	.250	.321
Rodriguez, Juan	R-R	6-0	175	8-29-94	.295	.368	.280	26	95	12	28	8	0	1	16	7	1	0	0	17	3	2	.411	.350
Rodriguez, Richard	R-R	6-1	170	10-3-92	.352	.349	.353	64	247	55	87	8	0	0	37	40	0	1	3	25	14	11	.385	.438
Valdez, Carlos	R-R	5-11	180	6-22-94	.240	.261	.235	31	121	18	29	7	1	3	24	16	2	1	2	17	2	0	.388	.333

Pitching	B-T	HT	WT	DOB	W	L	ERA	G	GS	CG	SV	IP	H	R	ER	HR	BB	SO	AVG	vLH	vRH	K/9	BB/9
Benitez, Julio	R-R	6-3	185	11-1-94	2	1	0.84	16	0	0	2	43	26	8	4	0	16	42	.173	.170	.175	8.79	3.35
Bolivar, Deiyerbert	L-L	5-11	155	4-3-96	7	1	1.27	15	10	0	3	64	41	13	9	2	20	67	.192	.286	.169	9.42	2.81
Concepcion, Victor	R-R	6-0	170	11-23-96	6	1	3.18	14	14	0	0	65	65	29	23	4	15	75	.255	.282	.245	10.38	2.08
De La Cruz, Jose	L-L	6-2	175	6-19-93	2	2	5.90	13	1	0	1	29	32	21	19	0	19	20	.288	.222	.310	6.21	5.90
Diaz, Alvaro	R-R	6-3	190	6-13-93	2	3	3.25	24	0	0	8	28	22	14	10	1	15	37	.220	.250	.211	12.04	4.88
Flores, Alejandro	R-R	6-0	180	9-25-93	4	1	2.86	12	11	0	0	63	52	26	20	1	12	56	.220	.239	.209	8.00	1.71
Gomez, Shawn	R-R	6-4	180	8-24-94	1	1	1.38	12	0	0	2	26	23	12	4	0	11	15	.240	.207	.254	5.19	5.88
Guzman, Eber	R-R	6-3	195	4-8-93	4	3	3.38	14	14	0	0	77	83	37	29	3	23	46	.282	.296	.274	5.35	2.68
Morel, Jose	R-R	6-2	190	9-6-93	7	1	1.73	20	0	0	5	52	46	15	10	0	15	55	.240	.313	.200	9.52	2.60
Parra, Olbis	R-R	6-2	180	10-1-94	4	0	1.24	6	4	0	0	29	19	5	4	2	4	23	.186	.171	.194	7.14	1.24
Revolledo, Dainer	L-L	6-3	200	12-1-93	0	0	7.27	7	1	0	0	9	9	8	7	2	7	2	.290	.286	.292	2.08	7.27
Reyes, Prebito	L-L	6-3	175	10-21-95	3	3	3.11	14	14	0	0	67	77	36	23	2	16	48	.295	.362	.276	6.48	2.16
Rodriguez, Reymi	R-R	6-2	195	8-30-94	2	2	3.20	13	0	0	1	25	22	13	9	0	10	28	.229	.300	.179	9.95	3.55
Villa, Eduin	R-R	6-2	170	3-12-96	1	2	9.90	11	1	0	0	20	26	24	22	5	14	22	.313	.368	.297	9.90	6.30
Vizcaino, Raffi	R-R	6-1	195	12-2-95	0	0	0.00	2	0	0	1	2	3	1	0	0	1	2	.429	.667	.250	9.00	4.50
Yan, Weilly	R-R	6-0	175	1-30-96	1	2	3.81	13	0	0	0	26	24	14	11	0	8	18	.245	.375	.182	6.23	2.77

Fielding

Catcher	PCT	G	PO	A	E	DP	PB
Coronado	1.000	2	2	1	0	0	0
Gomez	.982	33	229	48	5	2	4
Mora	.981	15	87	15	2	0	1
Morles	.974	31	199	23	6	0	3
Rodriguez	.944	5	15	2	1	0	0

First Base	PCT	G	PO	A	E	DP
Gomez	.988	35	320	18	4	24
Gomez	.987	29	220	11	3	26
Medina	1.000	1	2	0	0	1
Mora	1.000	1	2	0	0	0
Rodriguez	1.000	1	1	0	0	1
Rodriguez	1.000	15	93	7	0	10

Second Base	PCT	G	PO	A	E	DP
Antunez	.981	45	92	110	4	27
Geraldo	.985	14	29	36	1	9
Guzman	1.000	3	3	3	0	0
Medina	1.000	3	5	8	0	1
Rodriguez	.954	20	39	44	4	12

Third Base	PCT	G	PO	A	E	DP
Antunez	.848	10	11	17	5	3
Beltre	.857	2	3	9	2	3
Gomez	.944	7	5	12	1	1
Guzman	.889	5	4	12	2	3
Medina	.920	39	22	59	7	5
Rodriguez	.867	22	21	31	8	1

Shortstop	PCT	G	PO	A	E	DP
Beltre	.944	14	25	42	4	7
Geraldo	.896	49	94	148	28	28
Medina	1.000	9	10	21	0	4

Outfield	PCT	G	PO	A	E	DP
Angomas	.976	51	77	3	2	1
Edie	.952	47	77	3	4	1
Gomez	—	1	0	0	0	0
Gonzalez	—	10	0	0	0	0
Guzman	1.000	8	8	0	0	0
Medrano	.934	55	79	6	6	2
Rodriguez	1.000	25	34	2	0	0
Rodriguez	1.000	15	20	2	0	0
Valdez	1.000	17	24	1	0	0

SAN FRANSISCO GIANTS

Seattle Mariners

SEASON IN A SENTENCE: Seattle's streak of seasons without a playoff appearance extended to 13, but the 2015 season did have a much-needed turnaround when the Mariners stayed in the play-off race until the final day of the season.

HIGH POINT: After hovering around .500 for most of the first half, Seattle won nine of 10 in early August, culminating with a 7-2 win over the Tigers on Aug. 15 thanks to a Robinson Cano home run and an excellent start by rookie James Paxton. The win pushed the Mariners ahead of the Tigers and into second place in the wild card race.

LOW POINT: Seattle stayed in the thick of the wild card race for the rest of August and September. A half-game back on Sept. 19, the Mariners' pitching fell apart. They allowed eight or more runs in four straight games as part of a five-game losing streak that proved costly when the M's ended up finishing one game out in the wild-card race.

NOTABLE ROOKIES: Righthander Roenis Elias (10-12, 3.85) was a fixture in the rotation. Lefthander James Paxton (6-4, 3.04) was even better in a second-half stint as a starter. Center fielder James Jones (.250/.278/.311, 27-for-28 on SBs) showed off his speed, but struggled at the plate. Shortstop Chris Taylor (.287/.347/.346) more than adequately replaced Nick Franklin, traded away in the deal that brought Austin Jackson.

KEY TRANSACTIONS: The biggest move of the offseason for the Mariners was the biggest move in baseball, as they signed second baseman Robinson Cano to a 10-year, $240 million deal. That move paid off, at least for year one. The midseason acquisition of Jackson in a three-team deal that was more noteworthy for shipping David Price from Tampa Bay to Detroit didn't turn out as well, as Jackson struggled offensively in Seattle. A deadline deal to acquire DH Kendrys Morales for righthander Stephen Pryor also fell flat as Morales failed to hit.

DOWN ON THE FARM: The Mariners finished 22nd in overall minor league record. D.J. Peterson had an excellent first full season as a middle-of-the-lineup bat. He led the organization with 31 home runs and 111 RBIs. High Desert first baseman Jordy Lara took advantage of his home park's hitter-friendly conditions to lead the organization in batting average (.337) while finishing second to Peterson with 26 home runs. Taijuan Walker battled injuries, but touched 97 mph.

OPENING DAY PAYROLL: $89.5 million (21st).

PLAYERS OF THE YEAR

MAJOR LEAGUE	MINOR LEAGUE
Felix Hernandez rhp	**D.J. Peterson** 1b/3b
15-6, 2.14	(High-A, Double-A)
236 IP, 248 SO, 46 BB	.297/.360/.552
Led AL in ERA	31 HR, 111 RBI

ORGANIZATION LEADERS

BATTING		*Minimum 250 AB
MAJORS		
* AVG	Cano, Robinson	.314
* OPS	Cano, Robinson	.836
HR	Seager, Kyle	25
RBI	Seager, Kyle	96
MINORS		
* AVG	Lara, Jordy, High Desert, Jackson	.337
* OBP	Henry, Jabari, High Desert	.398
* SLG	Henry, Jabari, High Desert	.584
R	Guerrero, Gabby, High Desert	97
H	Lara, Jordy, High Desert, Jackson	177
TB	Lara, Jordy, High Desert, Jackson	305
2B	Lara, Jordy, High Desert, Jackson	40
3B	Kivlehan, Patrick, High Desert, Jackson	9
3B	Landry, Leon, Jackson	9
HR	Peterson, D.J., High Desert, Jackson	31
RBI	Peterson, D.J., High Desert, Jackson	111
BB	Pike, Tyler, High Desert, Jackson	80
SO	Simpson, Corey, Clinton, Tacoma, Everett	151
AVG	Lara, Jordy, High Desert, Jackson	0.337

PITCHING		#Minimum 75 IP
MAJORS		
W	Hernandez, Felix	15
# ERA	Hernandez, Felix	2.14
SO	Hernandez, Felix	248
SV	Rodney, Fernando	48
MINORS		
W	Olson, Tyler, High Desert, Jackson	12
L	Misell, Carlos, Clinton	12
# ERA	Diaz, Edwin, Clinton	3.33
G	Kensing, Logan, Tacoma	49
GS	Campbell, Eddie, Clinton	27
	Olson, Tyler, High Desert, Jackson	27
	Pike, Tyler, High Desert, Jackson	27
SV	Pagan, Emilio, Clinton	16
IP	Pries, Jordan, Jackson, Tacoma	154
BB	Pike, Tyler, High Desert, Jackson	80
SO	Olson, Tyler, High Desert, Jackson	127
AVG	Diaz, Edwin, Clinton	.226

2014 PERFORMANCE

General Manager: Jack Zduriencik. **Farm Director:** Chris Gwynn. **Scouting Director:** Tom McNamara.

Class	Team	League	W	L	PCT	Finish	Manager
Majors	Seattle Mariners	American	87	75	.537	11th (30)	Lloyd McClendon
Triple-A	Tacoma Rainiers	Pacific Coast	74	70	.514	T-7th (16)	Roy Howell
Double-A	Jackson Generals	Southern	63	76	.453	7th (10)	Jim Horner
High A	High Desert Mavericks	California	66	74	.471	7th (10)	Eddie Menchaca
Low A	Clinton LumberKings	Midwest	61	77	.442	T-14th (16)	Scott Steinmann
Short season	Everett AquaSox	Northwest	28	48	.368	8th (8)	Dave Valle
Rookie	Pulaski Mariners	Appalachian	36	30	.545	4th (10)	Rob Mummau
Rookie	Mariners	Arizona	31	22	.585	3rd (13)	Darrin Garner
Overall 2015 Minor League Record			359	397	.475	22nd (30)	

ORGANIZATION STATISTICS

SEATTLE MARINERS

AMERICAN LEAGUE

Batting	B-T	HT	WT	DOB	AVG	vLH	vRH	G	AB	R	H	2B	3B	HR	RBI	BB	HBP	SH	SF	SO	SB	CS	SLG	OBP
Ackley, Dustin	L-R	6-1	195	2-26-88	.245	.212	.259	143	502	64	123	27	4	14	65	32	3	3	2	90	8	4	.398	.293
Almonte, Abraham	B-R	5-9	205	6-27-89	.198	.257	.169	27	106	10	21	5	1	1	8	6	1	0	0	40	3	1	.292	.248
Bloomquist, Willie	R-R	5-11	190	11-27-77	.278	.282	.274	47	133	15	37	6	0	1	14	4	0	1	1	32	1	1	.346	.297
Buck, John	R-R	6-3	245	7-7-80	.226	.243	.213	27	84	9	19	2	0	1	6	8	0	0	0	24	0	0	.286	.293
2-team total (5 Los Angeles)					.225	—	—	32	89	9	20	2	0	1	6	8	0	0	0	26	0	0	.281	.289
Cano, Robinson	L-R	6-0	210	10-22-82	.314	.294	.327	157	595	77	187	37	2	14	82	61	6	0	3	68	10	3	.454	.382
Chavez, Endy	L-L	5-11	170	2-7-78	.276	.069	.305	80	232	22	64	12	2	2	23	15	0	9	2	30	5	2	.371	.317
Denorfia, Chris	R-R	6-0	195	7-15-80	.195	.164	.259	32	82	11	16	2	1	2	5	7	0	0	1	19	1	2	.317	.256
Franklin, Nick	B-R	6-1	195	3-2-91	.128	.000	.154	17	47	3	6	0	1	0	2	3	1	0	1	21	1	0	.170	.192
2-team total (11 Tampa Bay)					.160	—	—	28	81	7	13	2	1	1	6	6	1	0	2	32	2	0	.247	.222
Gillespie, Cole	R-R	6-1	215	6-20-84	.254	.280	.190	34	71	9	18	2	0	1	5	6	0	1	0	13	2	2	.324	.312
2-team total (1 Toronto)					.243	—	—	35	74	9	18	2	0	1	5	6	0	1	0	13	2	2	.311	.300
Hart, Corey	R-R	6-6	230	3-24-82	.203	.196	.207	68	232	17	47	9	0	6	21	16	6	0	1	59	2	0	.319	.271
Jackson, Austin	R-R	6-1	185	2-1-87	.229	.257	.215	54	223	19	51	5	1	0	14	12	0	0	1	59	11	2	.260	.267
2-team total (100 Detroit)					.256	—	—	154	597	71	153	30	6	4	47	47	2	1	9	144	20	6	.347	.308
Jones, James	L-L	6-4	200	9-24-88	.250	.247	.251	108	312	46	78	9	5	0	9	12	0	4	0	67	27	1	.311	.278
Miller, Brad	L-R	6-2	200	10-18-89	.221	.170	.238	123	367	47	81	15	4	10	36	34	2	3	3	95	4	2	.365	.288
Montero, Jesus	R-R	6-3	235	11-28-89	.235	.273	.167	6	17	1	4	0	0	1	2	0	0	0	0	3	0	0	.412	.235
Morales, Kendrys	B-R	6-1	225	6-20-83	.207	.232	.191	59	213	16	44	9	0	7	24	21	3	0	2	41	0	0	.347	.285
2-team total (39 Minnesota)					.218	—	—	98	367	28	80	20	0	8	42	27	3	0	4	68	0	0	.338	.274
Morrison, Logan	L-L	6-3	245	8-25-87	.262	.333	.236	99	336	41	88	20	0	11	38	24	3	0	2	59	5	2	.420	.315
Quintero, Humberto	R-R	5-9	215	8-2-79	.000	—	.000	3	2	0	0	0	0	0	1	0	0	0	1	0	0	0	.000	.000
Romero, Stefen	R-R	6-2	220	10-17-88	.192	.207	.164	72	177	19	34	6	2	3	11	4	6	2	1	48	0	4	.299	.234
Saunders, Michael	L-R	6-4	225	11-19-86	.273	.262	.276	78	231	38	63	11	3	8	34	26	0	2	4	59	4	5	.450	.341
Seager, Kyle	L-R	6-0	210	11-3-87	.268	.242	.283	159	590	71	158	27	4	25	96	52	8	1	3	118	7	5	.454	.334
Smoak, Justin	B-L	6-4	230	12-5-86	.202	.222	.186	80	248	28	50	13	0	7	30	24	2	0	2	66	0	1	.339	.275
Sucre, Jesus	R-R	6-0	225	4-30-88	.213	.182	.231	21	61	4	13	2	0	0	5	0	0	3	0	17	0	0	.246	.213
Taylor, Chris	R-R	6-1	190	8-29-90	.287	.276	.295	47	136	16	39	8	0	0	9	11	2	1	1	39	5	2	.346	.347
Zunino, Mike	R-R	6-2	220	3-25-91	.199	.252	.176	131	438	51	87	20	2	22	60	17	17	0	4	158	0	3	.404	.254

Pitching	B-T	HT	WT	DOB	W	L	ERA	G	GS	CG	SV	IP	H	R	ER	HR	BB	SO	AVG	vLH	vRH	K/9	BB/9
Beavan, Blake	R-R	6-7	245	1-17-89	0	1	4.50	1	1	0	0	4	6	2	2	2	0	1	.375	.429	.333	2.25	0.00
Beimel, Joe	L-L	6-3	205	4-19-77	3	1	2.20	56	0	0	0	45	39	12	11	4	14	25	.236	.188	.282	5.00	2.80
Elias, Roenis	L-L	6-1	190	8-1-88	10	12	3.85	29	29	1	0	164	151	77	70	16	64	143	.248	.212	.257	7.86	3.52
Farquhar, Danny	R-R	5-9	185	2-17-87	3	1	2.66	66	0	0	1	71	58	23	21	5	22	81	.221	.240	.206	10.27	2.79
Furbush, Charlie	L-L	6-5	215	4-11-86	1	5	3.61	67	0	0	1	42	40	17	17	4	9	51	.247	.241	.253	10.84	1.91
Hernandez, Felix	R-R	6-3	225	4-8-86	15	6	2.14	34	34	0	0	236	170	68	56	16	46	248	.200	.201	.197	9.46	1.75
Iwakuma, Hisashi	R-R	6-3	210	4-12-81	15	9	3.52	28	28	0	0	179	167	70	70	20	21	154	.244	.273	.210	7.74	1.06
Leone, Dominic	R-R	5-11	210	10-26-91	8	2	2.17	57	0	0	0	66	52	18	16	4	25	70	.217	.295	.166	9.50	3.39
Luetge, Lucas	L-L	6-4	205	3-24-87	0	0	5.00	12	0	0	0	9	6	5	5	3	5	7	.182	.133	.222	7.00	5.00
Maurer, Brandon	R-R	6-5	220	7-3-90	1	4	4.65	38	7	0	0	70	74	39	36	6	19	55	.267	.237	.289	7.11	2.45
Medina, Yoervis	R-R	6-3	245	7-27-88	5	3	2.68	66	0	0	0	57	48	18	17	3	28	60	.229	.195	.250	9.47	4.42
Noesi, Hector	R-R	6-3	205	1-26-87	0	1	27.00	2	0	0	0	1	2	3	3	1	0	2	.400	.333	.500	18.00	0.00
3-team total (28 Chicago, 3 Texas)					8	12	4.75	33	27	1	0	172	180	98	91	28	56	123	—	—	—	6.42	2.92
Paxton, James	L-L	6-4	220	11-6-88	6	4	3.04	13	13	0	0	74	60	29	25	3	29	59	.223	.205	.227	7.18	3.53
Pryor, Stephen	R-R	6-4	245	7-23-89	0	0	0.00	3	0	0	0	2	1	1	0	0	2	1	.200	.000	.333	5.40	10.80
Ramirez, Erasmo	R-R	5-11	200	5-2-90	1	6	5.26	17	14	0	0	75	82	44	44	13	34	60	.277	.282	.270	7.17	4.06
Rodney, Fernando	R-R	5-11	220	3-18-77	1	6	2.85	69	0	0	48	66	61	24	21	3	28	76	.244	.289	.178	10.31	3.80
Smith, Carson	R-R	6-6	215	10-19-89	1	0	0.00	9	0	0	0	8	2	0	0	0	3	10	.077	.000	.133	10.80	3.24
Walker, Taijuan	R-R	6-4	230	8-13-92	2	3	2.61	8	5	1	0	38	31	12	11	2	18	34	.223	.253	.179	8.05	4.26
Wilhelmsen, Tom	R-R	6-6	220	12-16-83	3	2	2.27	57	2	0	1	79	47	22	20	6	36	72	.171	.165	.176	8.17	4.08
Young, Chris	R-R	6-10	255	5-25-79	12	9	3.65	30	29	0	0	165	140	70	67	26	60	108	.234	.260	.199	5.89	3.27

Fielding

Catcher	PCT	G	PO	A	E	DP	PB
Buck	.993	19	132	9	1	2	1
Quintero	1.000	3	4	0	0	0	0
Sucre	.994	21	151	10	1	0	2
Zunino	.995	130	1010	84	5	5	8

First Base	PCT	G	PO	A	E	DP
Bloomquist	1.000	7	51	5	0	6
Buck	1.000	1	3	2	0	0
Hart	1.000	2	15	0	0	1
Montero	1.000	1	8	0	0	0
Morales	.992	14	117	4	1	15
Morrison	.996	79	639	46	3	48
Smoak	.997	79	588	31	2	60

Second Base	PCT	G	PO	A	E	DP
Bloomquist	1.000	10	6	13	0	2
Cano	.987	150	261	427	9	103
Franklin	1.000	5	11	18	0	4
Miller	.952	13	5	15	1	3

Third Base	PCT	G	PO	A	E	DP
Bloomquist	1.000	5	1	12	0	1
Franklin	—	1	0	0	0	0
Miller	—	2	0	0	0	0
Seager	.981	157	87	327	8	36

Shortstop	PCT	G	PO	A	E	DP
Bloomquist	1.000	16	13	21	0	4
Franklin	1.000	7	1	15	0	3
Miller	.958	107	145	267	18	48

Taylor	.962	47	50	127	7	23

Outfield	PCT	G	PO	A	E	DP
Ackley	.992	133	245	4	2	2
Almonte	.923	26	58	2	5	0
Bloomquist	1.000	3	6	0	0	0
Chavez	1.000	60	79	1	0	0
Denorfia	.977	28	41	1	1	0
Franklin	1.000	2	2	0	0	0
Gillespie	.957	25	45	0	2	0
Hart	.929	8	13	0	1	0
Jackson	.985	54	131	2	2	1
Jones	.988	98	158	1	2	0
Morrison	1.000	10	18	1	0	0
Romero	.986	49	67	1	1	0
Saunders	1.000	71	127	1	0	0

TACOMA RAINIERS   TRIPLE-A

PACIFIC COAST LEAGUE

Batting	B-T	HT	WT	DOB	AVG	vLH	vRH	G	AB	R	H	2B	3B	HR	RBI	BB	HBP	SH	SF	SO	SB	CS	SLG	OBP
Almonte, Abraham	B-R	5-9	205	6-27-89	.267	.275	.264	72	277	42	74	10	3	6	31	28	0	6	1	66	7	4	.390	.333
Avery, Xavier	L-L	6-0	190	1-1-90	.275	.222	.287	120	400	70	110	21	2	10	38	42	1	2	2	91	31	8	.413	.344
Blash, Jabari	R-R	6-5	225	7-4-89	.210	.214	.209	45	162	23	34	8	0	12	37	17	8	0	2	57	2	2	.481	.312
Bonilla, Leury	R-R	6-2	195	2-8-85	.234	.229	.236	90	278	29	65	16	1	2	27	22	1	12	1	64	5	4	.320	.291
Brady, Patrick	R-R	5-10	176	2-5-88	.100	.333	.059	7	20	2	2	0	0	0	1	4	0	0	1	8	1	0	.100	.240
Chavez, Endy	L-L	5-11	170	2-7-78	.272	.462	.248	37	114	16	31	2	0	0	6	13	1	4	2	17	0	4	.289	.346
Choi, Ji-Man	L-R	6-1	225	5-19-91	.283	.260	.289	70	237	41	67	7	2	5	30	36	3	3	2	42	2	2	.392	.381
Franklin, Nick	B-R	6-1	195	3-2-91	.294	.254	.306	52	279	45	82	16	1	9	47	47	1	1	5	60	9	5	.455	.392
Gillespie, Cole	R-R	6-1	215	6-20-84	.362	.000	.438	16	58	14	21	5	1	5	14	9	1	0	0	9	2	0	.741	.456
Hart, Corey	R-R	6-6	230	3-24-82	.286	.154	.316	19	70	8	20	4	2	4	9	7	0	0	0	13	0	0	.571	.351
Hebert, Brock	R-R	5-10	180	5-11-91	.200	.000	.222	3	10	0	2	0	0	0	0	1	0	0	0	2	0	0	.200	.273
Hicks, John	R-R	6-2	210	8-31-89	.277	.333	.263	28	101	13	28	2	1	2	20	7	2	0	2	24	1	0	.376	.330
Jones, James	L-L	6-4	200	9-24-88	.282	.400	.254	37	156	24	44	6	3	2	15	13	1	3	0	31	7	3	.397	.341
Kelly, Ty	L-R	6-0	185	7-20-88	.263	.271	.261	134	456	81	120	19	2	15	80	85	3	3	2	96	11	3	.412	.381
Mack, Chantz	L-L	5-10	205	5-4-91	.400	.250	1.000	2	5	1	2	0	0	0	1	0	0	0	0	3	0	0	.400	.500
Marte, Ketel	B-R	6-1	180	10-12-93	.313	.571	.220	19	80	16	25	5	0	2	9	8	0	0	2	13	6	0	.450	.367
Montero, Jesus	R-R	6-3	235	11-28-89	.286	.319	.277	97	364	55	104	24	1	16	74	37	2	0	6	79	1	0	.489	.350
Morban, Julio	L-L	6-1	210	2-13-92	.242	.357	.197	29	99	10	24	4	1	0	7	10	0	0	0	32	0	0	.303	.312
Morrison, Logan	L-L	6-3	245	8-25-87	.308	.263	.326	18	65	13	20	2	0	3	8	11	1	0	0	8	2	0	.477	.416
Nady, Xavier	R-R	6-2	215	11-14-78	.236	.174	.258	22	89	8	21	3	0	2	9	4	4	0	1	17	0	0	.337	.296
Noriega, Gabriel	R-R	6-2	180	9-13-90	.281	.232	.292	101	367	36	103	21	0	3	36	10	3	3	3	86	3	2	.362	.303
Pina, Manny	R-R	6-0	215	6-5-87	.214	.333	.182	4	14	1	3	1	0	0	3	0	0	0	0	2	0	0	.286	.214
Quintero, Humberto	R-R	5-9	215	8-2-79	.290	.291	.289	73	259	29	75	17	3	4	27	7	2	6	2	49	2	3	.425	.311
Romero, Stefen	R-R	6-2	220	10-17-88	.358	.419	.333	36	151	26	54	7	2	12	36	8	1	0	3	28	1	3	.669	.387
Saunders, Michael	L-R	6-4	225	11-19-86	.327	.348	.313	15	55	11	18	3	1	1	9	16	0	0	0	15	0	0	.473	.479
Simpson, Corey	R-R	6-2	210	12-8-93	.167	.000	.200	2	6	0	1	0	0	0	0	0	0	0	0	4	0	0	.167	.167
Smoak, Justin	B-L	6-4	230	12-5-86	.337	.367	.324	56	205	29	69	13	0	7	40	33	3	0	8	41	0	2	.502	.422
Sucre, Jesus	R-R	6-0	225	4-30-88	.274	.379	.253	48	175	13	48	7	1	2	16	4	1	0	1	29	0	1	.360	.293
Taylor, Chris	R-R	6-1	190	8-29-90	.328	.302	.335	75	302	63	99	22	7	5	37	35	3	1	5	74	14	6	.497	.397
Taylor, Wayne	L-R	6-1	205	11-4-92	.000	—	.000	1	1	0	0	0	0	0	0	0	0	0	0	1	0	0	.000	.000
Tenbrink, Nate	L-R	6-2	200	12-21-86	.237	.273	.231	23	76	8	18	4	0	2	12	8	0	0	0	30	0	0	.368	.310

Pitching	B-T	HT	WT	DOB	W	L	ERA	G	GS	CG	SV	IP	H	R	ER	HR	BB	SO	AVG	vLH	vRH	K/9	BB/9
Arias, Jonathan	R-R	6-3	210	2-8-88	1	1	9.82	8	0	0	0	15	20	16	16	2	7	10	.308	.323	.294	6.14	4.30
Bawcom, Logan	R-R	6-2	220	11-2-88	4	4	4.93	40	0	0	6	46	48	26	25	6	25	32	.287	.312	.267	6.31	4.93
Beavan, Blake	R-R	6-7	245	1-17-89	4	1	3.69	19	2	1	0	39	38	18	16	7	14	31	.255	.233	.270	7.15	3.23
Carraway, Andrew	R-R	6-2	205	9-4-86	8	5	5.10	30	22	0	0	125	151	76	71	13	32	83	.298	.301	.296	5.96	2.30
Coffey, Todd	R-R	6-4	240	9-9-80	4	1	1.93	36	0	0	11	37	31	10	8	3	16	34	.220	.237	.207	8.20	3.86
Elias, Roenis	L-L	6-1	190	8-1-88	1	0	0.00	1	1	0	0	5	0	0	0	0	1	6	.000	.000	.000	10.80	1.80
Fernandez, Anthony	L-L	6-4	215	6-8-90	1	1	3.86	5	5	0	0	26	24	16	11	3	14	27	.250	.353	.194	9.47	4.91
Gillheeney, Jimmy	L-L	6-1	205	11-9-85	3	11	5.62	24	23	0	0	106	117	73	66	16	44	110	.280	.282	.279	9.37	3.75
Hill, Nick	L-L	6-0	195	1-30-85	0	2	9.90	11	1	0	0	10	14	12	11	1	12	8	.341	.294	.375	7.20	10.80
Iwakuma, Hisashi	R-R	6-3	210	4-12-81	0	0	4.50	1	1	0	0	4	5	2	2	0	0	2	.353	.333	.375	4.50	0.00
Kensing, Logan	L-R	6-1	190	7-3-82	6	3	3.58	49	1	0	2	88	85	40	35	5	33	79	.254	.273	.239	8.08	3.38
Kohlscheen, Stephen	R-R	6-6	235	9-20-88	2	0	3.28	15	0	0	0	25	22	9	9	2	6	22	.237	.387	.161	8.03	2.19
2-team total (13 El Paso)					3	0	2.58	28	0	0	1	38	35	14	11	2	8	35	—	—	—	8.22	1.88
Luetge, Lucas	L-L	6-4	205	3-24-87	3	2	3.32	42	0	0	3	62	58	24	23	6	27	70	.249	.261	.241	10.11	3.90
MacDougal, Mike	B-R	6-4	180	3-5-77	0	0	8.25	12	0	0	0	12	16	11	11	1	7	13	.308	.259	.360	9.75	5.25
Maurer, Brandon	R-R	6-5	220	7-3-90	1	0	2.79	12	1	0	3	19	18	8	6	2	8	24	.247	.160	.292	11.17	3.72
Miller, Trevor	R-R	6-3	190	6-13-91	0	0	24.30	2	0	0	0	3	10	9	9	1	2	4	.526	.500	.545	10.80	5.40
Miner, Zach	R-R	6-4	205	3-12-82	0	2	8.60	21	1	0	0	38	57	43	36	9	15	25	.341	.376	.305	5.97	3.58
Palmer, Matt	R-R	6-2	235	3-21-79	2	8	5.42	18	13	0	2	73	82	54	44	9	36	51	.281	.275	.287	6.29	4.44
Paxton, James	L-L	6-4	220	11-6-88	0	1	4.35	3	3	0	0	10	13	7	5	2	6	14	.295	.455	.242	12.19	5.23

	B-T	HT	WT	DOB	W	L	ERA	G	GS	CG	SV	IP	H	R	ER	HR	BB	SO	AVG	vLH	vRH	K/9	BB/9
Pries, Jordan	B-R	6-1	195	1-27-90	9	8	4.06	25	24	0	0	142	135	66	64	14	53	111	.254	.206	.294	7.04	3.36
Pryor, Stephen	R-R	6-4	245	7-23-89	2	1	4.65	24	0	0	1	31	26	16	16	4	18	27	.226	.236	.217	7.84	5.23
Ramirez, Erasmo	R-R	5-11	200	5-2-90	6	5	3.65	15	14	0	0	86	92	43	35	8	13	67	.270	.312	.240	6.98	1.36
Ramirez, Ramon	R-R	5-11	200	8-31-81	0	0	10.38	4	0	0	0	4	6	5	5	0	3	5	.300	.571	.154	10.38	6.23
Rapada, Clay	R-L	6-5	195	3-9-81	4	1	4.12	14	0	0	0	20	17	13	9	5	7	16	.246	.147	.343	7.32	3.20
Rogers, Mark	R-R	6-3	240	1-30-86	1	0	3.86	2	1	0	0	7	5	3	3	1	7	5	.185	.250	.091	6.43	9.00
Ruffin, Chance	R-R	6-0	210	9-8-88	3	3	5.31	22	7	0	2	61	65	38	36	9	25	50	.266	.256	.276	7.38	3.69
Smith, Carson	R-R	6-6	215	10-19-89	1	3	2.93	39	0	0	10	43	44	19	14	1	13	45	.265	.244	.286	9.42	2.72
Snow, Forrest	R-R	6-6	220	12-30-88	2	3	4.05	16	10	0	0	60	57	29	27	8	21	61	.247	.229	.262	9.15	3.15
Walker, Taijuan	R-R	6-4	230	8-13-92	6	4	4.81	14	14	1	0	73	68	40	39	13	25	74	.243	.224	.256	9.12	3.08

Fielding

Catcher	PCT	G	PO	A	E	DP	PB
Hicks	.996	28	210	17	1	1	0
Pina	1.000	4	24	2	0	1	0
Quintero	.990	71	526	46	6	4	5
Sucre	.995	48	362	35	2	5	2
Taylor	—	1	0	0	0	0	0

First Base	PCT	G	PO	A	E	DP
Bonilla	1.000	15	74	6	0	6
Choi	.997	40	291	18	1	26
Montero	.971	44	317	23	10	27
Morrison	1.000	6	31	5	0	5
Nady	1.000	8	73	6	0	6
Quintero	1.000	2	6	1	0	0
Smoak	.997	43	351	16	1	23

Second Base	PCT	G	PO	A	E	DP
Bonilla	1.000	1	1	0	0	0
Brady	1.000	3	5	5	0	0
Franklin	.959	35	60	81	6	13
Kelly	.984	64	119	133	4	29

	PCT	G	PO	A	E	DP
Noriega	1.000	24	50	75	0	12
Romero	1.000	1	3	5	0	1
Taylor	.979	21	33	62	2	13

Third Base	PCT	G	PO	A	E	DP
Bonilla	.926	50	32	80	9	7
Brady	.714	4	2	3	2	1
Hebert	1.000	3	2	1	0	0
Kelly	.905	36	24	62	9	5
Noriega	.955	48	43	104	7	11
Tenbrink	.829	15	11	18	6	0

Shortstop	PCT	G	PO	A	E	DP
Bonilla	.957	10	13	32	2	3
Franklin	.973	34	51	93	4	18
Hebert	1.000	1	1	2	0	1
Marte	.961	19	21	53	3	8
Noriega	.946	29	35	53	5	10
Taylor	.959	54	65	143	9	26

Outfield	PCT	G	PO	A	E	DP
Almonte	.973	69	177	5	5	0

	PCT	G	PO	A	E	DP
Avery	.970	112	218	6	7	0
Blash	.953	41	80	1	4	1
Bonilla	1.000	18	34	2	0	0
Brady	1.000	1	1	0	0	0
Chavez	1.000	23	55	1	0	0
Choi	1.000	26	40	0	0	0
Franklin	1.000	2	1	0	0	0
Gillespie	1.000	15	19	1	0	0
Hart	1.000	1	2	0	0	0
Jones	.988	37	82	3	1	0
Kelly	1.000	20	40	2	0	0
Mack	1.000	2	2	0	0	0
Morban	.925	21	35	2	3	1
Nady	.958	12	21	2	1	0
Romero	1.000	32	59	2	0	0
Saunders	.944	10	17	0	1	0
Simpson	1.000	2	7	0	0	0
Tenbrink	1.000	7	14	0	0	0

JACKSON GENERALS — DOUBLE-A
SOUTHERN LEAGUE

Batting	B-T	HT	WT	DOB	AVG	vLH	vRH	G	AB	R	H	2B	3B	HR	RBI	BB	HBP	SH	SF	SO	SB	CS	SLG	OBP
Austin, Jamal	R-R	5-9	170	8-26-90	.262	.326	.247	63	244	30	64	12	2	1	16	7	8	10	0	38	19	3	.340	.305
Baron, Steve	R-R	6-0	205	12-7-90	.275	.000	.288	21	69	5	19	4	1	0	6	7	0	0	0	12	1	1	.362	.342
Blash, Jabari	R-R	6-5	225	7-24-89	.236	.136	.257	37	127	27	30	7	1	6	22	28	5	0	3	35	4	1	.449	.387
Brady, Patrick	R-R	5-10	176	2-5-88	.248	.143	.267	42	141	17	35	4	1	6	17	2	1	1	0	34	2	1	.418	.264
Choi, Ji-Man	L-R	6-1	225	5-19-91	.273	.000	.333	4	11	3	3	1	0	1	5	4	0	0	0	2	0	0	.636	.467
Dowd, Mike	R-R	5-9	205	4-10-90	.209	.192	.212	55	182	12	38	5	1	1	13	12	3	1	0	36	1	0	.264	.269
Hebert, Brock	R-R	5-10	185	5-11-91	.177	.250	.157	39	113	12	20	2	0	0	10	10	3	3	0	37	3	0	.195	.262
Hicks, John	R-R	6-2	210	8-31-89	.296	.378	.271	53	189	29	56	10	2	3	27	20	0	1	1	42	6	3	.418	.362
Kivlehan, Patrick	R-R	6-2	210	12-22-89	.300	.323	.295	104	377	60	113	23	7	11	68	44	4	0	5	78	9	4	.485	.374
Landry, Leon	L-R	5-11	185	9-20-89	.280	.209	.294	108	421	60	118	21	9	2	30	19	3	6	1	48	25	10	.387	.315
Lara, Jordy	R-R	6-3	180	5-21-91	.286	.333	.282	33	126	14	36	14	0	4	24	8	1	0	3	19	0	0	.492	.326
Marder, Jack	R-R	5-11	185	2-21-90	.277	.311	.269	74	238	36	66	11	2	5	24	27	12	4	3	40	2	0	.403	.375
Marlette, Tyler	R-R	5-11	195	1-23-93	.250	.500	.192	9	32	3	8	2	0	2	2	4	0	0	0	10	0	1	.500	.333
Marte, Ketel	R-B	6-1	180	10-12-93	.302	.290	.305	109	443	63	134	27	6	2	46	19	1	4	5	65	23	10	.404	.329
Melendres, Nate	R-R	5-10	190	4-4-90	.243	.184	.264	43	148	14	36	7	2	1	12	8	0	0	2	28	6	4	.338	.278
Morban, Julio	L-L	6-1	210	2-13-92	.252	.267	.250	30	115	14	29	5	1	1	11	9	1	1	2	35	0	0	.339	.307
Noriega, Gabriel	R-R	6-2	180	9-13-90	.182	.200	.176	7	22	4	4	1	0	2	2	0	1	1	0	6	0	0	.318	.240
Paolini, Dan	R-R	6-0	190	10-11-89	.268	.296	.263	116	410	58	110	34	1	13	65	56	5	1	4	75	3	2	.451	.360
Peterson, D.J.	R-R	6-1	190	12-31-91	.261	.273	.259	58	222	32	58	8	0	13	38	22	3	0	1	51	1	1	.473	.335
Pina, Manny	R-R	6-0	215	6-5-87	.279	.400	.239	17	61	11	17	4	0	2	10	8	0	0	0	8	0	0	.443	.362
Pizzano, Dario	L-R	5-11	200	4-25-91	.228	.122	.247	81	272	32	62	14	5	8	55	45	5	0	6	38	1	1	.404	.341
Rivers, Kevin	L-R	6-2	204	8-24-88	.231	.180	.241	97	320	33	74	23	4	3	34	38	1	0	5	71	2	1	.356	.310
Smith, Tyler	R-R	6-0	195	7-1-91	.271	.000	.306	20	70	12	19	3	1	1	4	16	1	0	0	13	1	1	.386	.414
Tanabe, Carlton	R-R	6-0	190	10-28-91	.222	.250	.217	9	27	1	6	1	0	0	4	1	1	0	0	7	0	0	.259	.276
Wiswall, Mickey	L-R	6-1	213	11-25-88	.217	.167	.223	45	166	15	36	5	0	5	16	7	3	0	2	47	0	0	.337	.258

Pitching	B-T	HT	WT	DOB	W	L	ERA	G	GS	CG	SV	IP	H	R	ER	HR	BB	SO	AVG	vLH	vRH	K/9	BB/9
Anderson, Matt	R-R	6-1	210	11-18-91	3	5	5.16	13	13	0	0	66	80	44	38	5	14	45	.297	.314	.287	6.11	1.90
Arias, Jonathan	R-R	6-3	210	2-8-88	0	0	0.00	1	0	0	0	1	0	0	0	0	0	1	.000	.000	.000	9.00	0.00
Brazis, Matt	R-R	6-3	205	9-6-89	1	1	1.64	17	0	0	2	33	20	6	6	1	10	34	.179	.186	.174	9.27	2.73
Colvin, David	R-R	6-3	215	1-7-89	0	1	3.10	19	0	0	3	29	23	11	10	2	6	26	.217	.237	.206	8.07	1.86
Gillheeney, Jimmy	L-L	6-1	205	11-8-87	1	0	1.29	3	3	0	0	14	12	3	2	0	3	7	.231	.294	.200	4.50	1.93
Guaipe, Mayckol	R-R	6-3	175	8-11-90	1	3	2.89	40	0	0	12	56	45	20	18	4	9	56	.215	.254	.197	9.00	1.45
Hernandez, Moises	R-R	6-1	168	3-18-84	1	8	5.93	31	2	0	0	61	76	43	40	6	23	36	.313	.316	.311	5.34	3.41
Hill, Nick	L-L	6-0	195	1-30-85	1	1	6.97	18	0	0	0	21	28	18	16	1	11	24	.329	.303	.346	10.45	4.79
Hobson, Cameron	L-L	6-0	190	4-10-89	8	11	4.60	29	18	0	0	129	153	78	66	10	47	70	.301	.220	.325	4.88	3.28
Hunter, Kyle	L-L	6-2	207	6-18-89	5	3	3.25	38	3	0	1	75	79	28	27	8	21	46	.273	.277	.272	5.54	2.53
Kittredge, Andrew	R-R	6-1	200	3-17-90	0	0	6.75	3	0	0	0	4	6	3	3	0	6	3	.316	.333	.308	6.75	13.50
Kohlscheen, Stephen	R-R	6-6	235	9-20-88	1	1	2.25	23	0	0	6	32	31	10	8	4	8	33	.250	.265	.240	9.28	1.13

Name	B-T	HT	WT	DOB	W	L	ERA	G	GS	CG	SV	IP	H	R	ER	HR	BB	SO	AVG	vLH	vRH	K/9	BB/9
Landazuri, Steve	R-R	6-0	175	1-6-92	6	5	4.33	19	19	0	0	96	78	51	46	13	39	79	.223	.229	.220	7.43	3.67
Miller, Trevor	R-R	6-3	190	6-13-91	5	8	3.81	31	13	0	4	111	100	59	47	5	43	87	.243	.289	.211	7.05	3.49
Ogando, Jochi	R-R	6-5	210	5-27-93	0	3	5.54	4	4	0	0	13	18	14	8	0	13	14	.333	.480	.207	9.69	9.00
Olson, Tyler	R-L	6-3	190	10-2-89	10	7	3.52	22	22	1	0	125	126	55	49	8	25	100	.260	.207	.275	7.18	1.80
Pike, Tyler	L-L	6-3	180	1-26-94	3	4	7.35	13	13	0	0	49	57	42	40	5	34	33	.300	.305	.298	6.06	6.24
Pries, Jordan	B-R	6-1	195	1-27-90	1	0	1.50	2	2	0	0	12	3	2	2	2	0	9	.079	.063	.091	6.75	0.00
Pryor, Stephen	R-R	6-4	245	7-23-89	0	1	14.73	4	0	0	0	4	5	6	6	2	3	3	.333	.500	.222	7.36	7.36
Sanchez, Victor	R-R	6-0	255	1-30-95	7	6	4.19	23	23	1	0	125	128	66	58	17	34	97	.268	.292	.253	7.00	2.45
Shackleford, Stephen	R-R	6-2	205	5-5-89	6	2	3.11	44	0	0	0	64	57	24	22	3	30	70	.245	.324	.208	9.90	4.24
Shipers, Jordan	R-L	5-10	168	6-27-91	0	3	6.55	12	1	0	0	22	25	20	16	2	18	11	.281	.333	.265	4.50	7.36
Snow, Forrest	R-R	6-6	220	12-30-88	1	1	3.86	4	2	0	0	16	14	8	7	2	4	14	.233	.250	.227	7.71	2.20
Vargas, Richard	R-R	6-3	185	4-19-91	1	2	4.71	36	0	0	5	50	39	28	26	2	34	48	.213	.217	.211	8.70	6.16
Walker, Taijuan	R-R	6-4	230	8-13-92	1	0	0.00	1	1	0	0	5	3	0	0	0	1	10	.167	.000	.273	18.00	1.80

Fielding

Catcher	PCT	G	PO	A	E	DP	PB
Baron	.993	20	139	10	1	1	0
Dowd	.990	53	359	33	4	5	4
Hicks	.997	43	286	31	1	6	2
Marlette	.986	9	65	6	1	1	0
Pina	.963	10	70	9	3	0	1
Tanabe	1.000	9	46	7	0	1	0
Hebert	.945	25	45	59	6	14	
Marder	.979	59	116	163	6	42	
Marte	.969	7	6	25	1	5	
Melendres	.990	21	53	48	1	12	
Noriega	1.000	2	4	6	0	2	
Paolini	1.000	1	1	0	0	0	
Smith	1.000	1	3	2	0	2	
Marder	1.000	2	0	5	0	0	
Marte	.937	102	139	280	28	55	
Melendres	1.000	2	2	7	0	2	
Noriega	1.000	3	7	10	0	1	
Smith	.970	19	33	63	3	16	

First Base	PCT	G	PO	A	E	DP
Choi	1.000	3	23	0	0	1
Kivlehan	.990	26	194	12	2	25
Lara	.985	7	61	4	1	4
Morla	1.000	3	6	0	0	0
Paolini	.992	61	451	24	4	46
Peterson	1.000	9	78	7	0	11
Wiswall	.994	37	300	18	2	31

Second Base	PCT	G	PO	A	E	DP
Austin	1.000	2	3	2	0	0
Brady	1.000	31	54	79	0	23

Third Base	PCT	G	PO	A	E	DP
Hebert	1.000	2	2	0	0	0
Kivlehan	.888	58	39	88	16	9
Marder	.951	12	15	24	2	3
Melendres	.917	4	4	7	1	0
Morla	.930	23	5	48	4	4
Noriega	1.000	3	1	3	0	1
Peterson	.962	45	27	75	4	13

Shortstop	PCT	G	PO	A	E	DP
Brady	.962	6	12	13	1	4
Hebert	.925	11	21	28	4	9

Outfield	PCT	G	PO	A	E	DP
Austin	.986	58	143	0	2	0
Blash	.949	23	54	2	3	0
Brady	1.000	6	14	0	0	0
Kivlehan	1.000	22	45	2	0	0
Landry	.974	106	262	4	7	0
Lara	.974	15	37	1	1	0
Marder	1.000	4	3	0	0	0
Melendres	1.000	18	45	5	0	1
Morban	.983	26	54	3	1	2
Paolini	.953	27	41	0	2	0
Pizzano	.968	50	89	3	3	0
Rivers	.967	78	139	9	5	1

HIGH DESERT MAVERICKS

HIGH CLASS A

CALIFORNIA LEAGUE

Batting	B-T	HT	WT	DOB	AVG	vLH	vRH	G	AB	R	H	2B	3B	HR	RBI	BB	HBP	SH	SF	SO	SB	CS	SLG	OBP
Austin, Jamal	R-R	5-9	170	8-26-90	.346	.111	.471	6	26	5	9	0	0	2	2	1	1	0	0	3	1	0	.577	.393
Barbosa, Aaron	L-R	5-10	160	4-14-92	.256	.250	.257	34	125	26	32	1	1	0	12	28	2	0	0	27	10	5	.280	.400
Baron, Steve	R-R	6-0	205	12-7-90	.254	.095	.281	39	142	18	36	10	1	1	23	10	3	0	4	27	3	1	.359	.308
Blanco, Dominic	L-R	6-2	215	11-10-95	.000	.000	—	1	2	0	0	0	0	0	0	1	0	0	0	2	0	0	.000	.333
Brady, Patrick	R-R	5-10	176	2-5-88	.222	.200	.227	22	81	15	18	3	2	3	19	9	1	0	0	26	0	2	.420	.308
Brito, Bryan	R-R	6-2	170	2-16-92	.244	.263	.239	27	86	12	21	1	0	2	12	4	1	—	0	21	4	5	.326	.286
Caballero, Luis	R-R	6-0	185	7-8-92	.194	.167	.200	9	31	5	6	1	1	0	1	3	0	0	0	12	2	1	.290	.265
DeMello, Toby	R-R	6-2	220		.107	.200	.087	10	28	2	3	1	0	0	0	4	0	0	0	8	0	0	.143	.219
Guerrero, Gabby	R-R	6-3	190	12-11-93	.307	.356	.291	131	538	97	165	28	2	18	96	34	2	1	5	131	18	6	.467	.347
Hebert, Brock	R-R	5-10	180	5-11-91	.267	.173	.301	50	195	35	52	12	4	3	30	13	3	1	2	55	9	2	.415	.319
Henry, Jabari	R-R	6-1	200	11-11-90	.291	.293	.290	114	430	79	125	26	5	30	95	69	9	—	2	109	6	9	.584	.398
Kauppila, Lonnie	R-R	6-1	179	1-17-92	.308	.238	.333	24	78	7	24	1	0	0	6	6	0	1	1	12	2	1	.321	.353
Kivlehan, Patrick	R-R	6-2	210	12-22-89	.282	.308	.272	34	142	24	40	9	2	9	35	12	0	0	3	32	2	0	.563	.331
Lara, Jordy	R-R	6-3	180	5-21-91	.353	.348	.355	102	399	77	141	26	5	22	80	38	5	—	4	82	1	3	.609	.413
Littlewood, Marcus	B-R	6-3	208	3-18-92	.212	.300	.174	9	33	4	7	3	0	1	5	3	0	0	0	11	0	0	.394	.278
Lopes, Timmy	R-R	5-11	180	6-24-94	.238	.212	.245	114	421	54	100	16	7	4	44	37	6	—	1	81	18	7	.337	.308
Mack, Chantz	L-L	5-10	205	5-4-91	.222	.214	.224	17	63	5	14	3	0	2	4	4	0	0	0	13	2	1	.365	.269
Marlette, Tyler	R-R	5-11	195	1-23-93	.301	.402	.265	81	312	51	94	23	0	15	49	24	1	—	2	61	9	2	.519	.351
Nieto, Arturo	R-R	6-2	190		.000	.000	.000	6	13	0	0	0	0	0	0	1	0	0	0	6	0	0	.000	.133
Peterson, D.J.	R-R	6-1	190	12-31-91	.326	.313	.330	65	273	51	89	23	1	18	73	23	2	0	1	65	6	0	.615	.381
Pimentel, Guillermo	L-L	6-1	206	10-5-92	.333	.200	.400	6	15	4	5	1	0	2	6	4	0	0	0	5	0	0	.800	.474
Pizzano, Dario	L-R	5-11	200	4-25-91	.275	.270	.277	35	138	33	38	16	2	3	21	23	0	0	1	16	0	0	.486	.377
Reinheimer, Jack	R-R	6-1	186	7-19-92	.341	.263	.364	20	85	15	29	5	1	1	12	4	0	1	1	12	5	2	.459	.367
Reynolds, Burt	R-R	6-1	212	9-13-88	.257	.246	.260	78	284	37	73	17	3	12	46	18	10	—	2	97	12	7	.465	.322
Shank, Zach	R-R	6-1	180	1-6-91	.260	.237	.268	55	227	35	59	9	5	4	26	20	4	—	2	43	3	2	.396	.300
Smith, Mario	R-R	6-0	195	7-1-91	.286	.293	.284	108	423	81	121	19	7	9	44	57	7	—	2	81	11	7	.428	.378
Witherspoon, Travis	R-R	6-2	190	4-16-89	.252	.258	.250	99	357	69	90	23	1	15	44	43	4	—	1	89	25	7	.448	.338

Pitching	B-T	HT	WT	DOB	W	L	ERA	G	GS	CG	SV	IP	H	R	ER	HR	BB	SO	AVG	vLH	vRH	K/9	BB/9
Anderson, Matt	R-R	6-1	210	11-18-91	3	3	4.59	14	7	0	1	51	47	26	26	4	19	46	.245	.188	.308	8.12	3.35
Beavan, Blake	R-R	6-7	245	1-17-89	0	0	9.00	1	0	0	0	2	3	2	2	1	0	0	.375	.500	.250	0.00	4.50
Bordonaro, Mark	R-R	6-0	167	8-17-90	1	1	7.20	8	0	0	0	15	16	14	12	3	13	11	.271	.235	.320	6.60	7.80
Brazis, Matt	R-R	6-3	205	9-6-89	3	0	2.97	23	0	0	4	39	34	15	13	4	8	50	.230	.197	.256	11.44	1.83
Chen, Min-Sih	R-R	6-3	205	12-6-89	2	6	8.03	36	8	0	1	77	104	81	69	14	39	62	.321	.308	.333	7.22	4.54
DeCecco, Scott	R-L	6-0	175	5-8-91	7	11	5.46	28	25	0	0	140	164	101	85	27	88	90	.296	.298	.298	6.24	3.73
Garcia, Oliver	R-R	6-2	180	12-7-90	2	1	3.50	28	0	0	3	54	45	24	21	8	20	63	.225	.236	.211	10.50	3.33
Hauser, Blake	R-R	6-2	180	4-14-91	2	3	5.66	28	0	0	2	41	38	31	26	7	29	43	.239	.296	.193	9.36	6.31

Name	B-T	HT	WT	DOB	W	L	ERA	G	GS	CG	SV	IP	H	R	ER	HR	BB	SO	AVG	vLH	vRH	K/9	BB/9
Herb, Tyler	R-R	6-2	175	4-28-92	0	2	6.43	4	0	0	0	7	12	7	5	1	2	9	.364	.286	.421	11.57	2.57
Hermann, Spencer	L-L	6-4	235	8-6-93	0	1	11.88	2	2	0	0	8	11	11	11	2	4	6	.324	.389	.250	6.48	4.32
Holman, David	R-R	6-6	220	5-31-90	3	1	4.07	16	5	0	0	55	59	29	25	8	12	25	.273	.241	.306	4.07	1.95
Huijer, Lars	R-R	6-4	203	9-22-93	2	4	6.54	12	12	0	0	52	69	43	38	8	27	32	.324	.357	.287	5.50	4.64
Kim, Seon Gi	R-R	6-2	185	9-1-91	0	1	16.05	7	0	0	0	12	23	22	22	1	11	8	.390	.433	.345	5.84	8.03
Kittredge, Andrew	R-R	6-1	200	3-17-90	6	1	4.35	42	0	0	8	83	91	47	40	11	25	112	.269	.288	.254	12.19	2.72
Mathis, Will	L-L	6-3	180	8-18-90	5	8	4.86	46	3	0	7	76	91	54	41	9	35	60	.285	.319	.261	7.11	4.14
Ogando, Jochi	R-R	6-5	210	5-27-93	4	2	7.10	22	11	0	0	58	72	51	46	6	36	52	.309	.298	.318	8.02	5.55
Olson, Tyler	R-L	6-3	190	10-2-89	2	1	3.13	5	5	0	0	23	21	8	8	0	10	27	.236	.200	.250	10.57	3.91
Pike, Tyler	L-L	6-0	180	1-26-94	2	4	5.72	14	14	0	0	61	56	44	39	10	46	57	.243	.302	.201	8.36	6.75
Pineda, Rafael	L-R	6-5	217	2-3-91	1	0	3.38	5	2	0	0	13	16	6	5	1	3	10	.291	.188	.435	6.75	2.03
Ramirez, Erasmo	R-R	5-11	200	5-2-90	0	1	7.50	1	1	0	0	6	8	6	5	2	2	7	.308	.273	.333	10.50	3.00
Shankin, Brett	R-R	6-0	200	10-30-89	5	5	4.97	28	11	0	0	80	102	68	44	6	35	59	.311	.299	.322	6.67	3.95
Shipers, Jordan	R-L	5-10	168	6-27-91	2	1	2.84	15	0	0	0	32	39	10	10	1	10	35	.305	.292	.313	9.95	2.84
Unsworth, Dylan	R-R	6-1	175	9-23-92	6	9	5.88	26	26	0	0	119	153	87	78	17	19	119	.309	.306	.312	8.97	1.43
Valenza, Nick	R-L	5-10	180	3-31-93	0	1	4.85	8	0	0	0	13	20	15	7	3	12	14	.328	.276	.375	9.69	8.31
Walker, Taijuan	R-R	6-4	230	8-13-92	0	0	2.08	1	1	0	0	4	4	2	1	0	1	7	.235	.375	.111	14.54	2.08
Wood, Grady	R-R	6-2	195	5-18-90	6	4	3.29	40	0	0	6	82	80	39	30	5	22	82	.254	.272	.238	9.00	2.41
Zokan, Jake	R-L	6-1	198	4-27-91	2	2	7.85	7	7	0	0	29	39	26	25	8	8	26	.328	.380	.290	8.16	2.51

Fielding

Catcher	PCT	G	PO	A	E	DP	PB
Baron	.977	39	304	33	8	4	6
Blanco	.909	1	8	2	1	0	0
Brito	1.000	1	5	0	0	0	2
DeMello	.986	10	65	6	1	0	2
Littlewood	1.000	9	64	6	0	0	0
Marlette	.983	81	633	71	12	3	22
Nieto	.962	6	24	1	1	0	0

First Base	PCT	G	PO	A	E	DP
Brito	1.000	3	4	0	0	1
Kivlehan	.982	13	102	6	2	7
Lara	.980	77	678	46	15	69
Peterson	.988	10	75	4	1	3
Reynolds	.990	25	187	15	2	20
Shank	.961	17	139	10	6	16

Second Base	PCT	G	PO	A	E	DP
Brady	1.000	4	6	19	0	4
Brito	.955	5	11	10	1	2

	PCT	G	PO	A	E	DP
Caballero	1.000	4	8	8	0	4
Hebert	.978	10	17	27	1	8
Kauppila	1.000	4	13	9	0	5
Lopes	.978	106	166	322	11	62
Smith	1.000	9	14	22	0	6

Third Base	PCT	G	PO	A	E	DP
Brady	.879	10	8	21	4	2
Brito	.810	8	5	12	4	3
Caballero	1.000	4	2	5	0	0
Hebert	.951	17	11	28	2	5
Kauppila	.885	13	8	15	3	3
Kivlehan	.822	14	13	24	8	3
Peterson	.885	45	25	75	13	8
Shank	.930	36	33	60	7	3

Shortstop	PCT	G	PO	A	E	DP
Brito	.850	9	9	25	6	3
Caballero	1.000	1	2	2	0	1
Hebert	.952	17	25	54	4	15

	PCT	G	PO	A	E	DP
Lopes	.750	1	1	2	1	0
Reinheimer	.978	19	35	52	2	13
Shank	1.000	3	3	13	0	2
Smith	.948	91	162	240	22	60

Outfield	PCT	G	PO	A	E	DP
Austin	1.000	4	10	0	0	0
Barbosa	1.000	34	70	2	0	0
Brady	1.000	8	14	5	0	0
Guerrero	.956	118	207	10	10	2
Hebert	1.000	6	12	1	0	0
Henry	.994	83	148	7	1	3
Lara	1.000	7	8	2	0	0
Mack	1.000	13	32	0	0	0
Pimentel	.800	4	4	0	1	0
Pizzano	1.000	26	38	0	0	0
Reynolds	.913	35	38	4	4	0
Witherspoon	.996	94	226	5	1	0

CLINTON LUMBERKINGS   LOW CLASS A

MIDWEST LEAGUE

Batting	B-T	HT	WT	DOB	AVG	vLH	vRH	G	AB	R	H	2B	3B	HR	RBI	BB	HBP	SH	SF	SO	SB	CS	SLG	OBP
Barbosa, Aaron	L-R	5-10	160	4-14-92	.293	.291	.293	81	314	53	92	8	2	0	15	43	1	3	1	47	42	7	.331	.379
Caballero, Luis	R-R	6-0	185	7-8-92	.205	.100	.222	48	146	15	30	5	0	1	11	8	1	1	6	42	5	1	.260	.242
Carmichael, Christian	R-R	5-11	187	4-25-92	.234	.267	.228	57	201	20	47	9	3	2	22	15	4	5	1	41	3	1	.338	.299
DeCarlo, Joe	R-R	5-10	210	9-13-93	.246	.192	.259	80	268	29	66	19	1	5	42	36	9	1	3	84	0	1	.381	.351
Fields, Arby	B-R	5-9	192	6-25-91	.071	.200	.043	9	28	4	2	0	0	0	0	5	0	0	0	9	1	1	.071	.212
Guarnaccia, Luke	R-R	5-11	210	7-11-92	.250	.250	.250	5	16	1	4	0	0	0	2	0	0	0	0	5	0	0	.250	.250
Kauppila, Lonnie	R-R	6-1	179	1-17-92	.281	.286	.280	50	160	18	45	9	0	0	13	12	1	4	0	20	2	2	.338	.335
Littlewood, Marcus	B-R	6-3	208	3-18-92	.250	.320	.236	77	292	42	73	14	2	8	43	40	2	0	3	58	4	1	.394	.341
Mack, Chantz	L-L	5-10	205	5-4-91	.282	.302	.278	73	273	32	77	11	4	8	50	29	2	2	4	40	7	3	.440	.351
Martinez, Wilton	R-R	6-0	195	12-11-93	.150	.111	.161	13	40	2	6	4	0	1	5	3	1	0	0	12	0	1	.325	.227
Miller, Ian	L-R	6-0	171	2-21-92	.271	.303	.263	45	166	33	45	5	4	0	13	16	0	1	2	35	16	2	.349	.332
O'Neill, Tyler	R-R	5-11	210	6-22-95	.247	.240	.249	57	219	31	54	9	0	13	38	20	5	0	1	79	5	0	.466	.322
Peguero, Martin	R-R	6-1	206	11-3-93	.263	.263	.263	80	270	26	71	15	0	2	24	8	2	6	2	42	4	5	.341	.287
Peterson, Andy	R-R	5-10	178	4-19-92	.241	.200	.250	8	29	2	7	0	0	0	2	2	0	0	0	6	1	0	.241	.290
Reinheimer, Jack	R-R	6-1	186	7-19-92	.264	.315	.250	110	436	69	115	17	4	2	46	39	7	4	2	76	34	9	.335	.333
Reynolds, Burt	R-R	6-1	212	9-13-88	.326	.400	.306	14	46	12	15	3	2	4	10	6	2	0	0	15	4	1	.739	.426
Seager, Justin	R-R	6-1	211	5-15-92	.240	.299	.228	110	383	41	92	11	2	3	37	35	11	3	4	101	2	3	.303	.319
Shank, Zach	R-R	6-1	180	1-6-91	.302	.250	.314	69	235	49	71	17	1	6	30	21	9	4	2	39	7	3	.460	.378
Simpson, Corey	R-R	6-2	210	12-8-93	.199	.300	.174	53	201	16	40	6	1	3	18	9	1	1	1	91	1	0	.284	.236
Thomas, Brett	L-R	6-1	190	2-21-92	.250	.083	.267	39	132	16	33	5	0	0	11	20	0	1	1	35	2	1	.288	.346
Ward, Nelson	L-R	5-11	175	8-6-92	.232	.222	.234	18	56	8	13	3	2	0	3	4	0	2	1	10	3	3	.357	.279
Wilson, Austin	R-R	6-4	249	2-7-92	.291	.173	.321	72	261	38	76	17	3	12	54	26	10	1	1	65	1	1	.517	.376
Yates, Isaiah	R-L	5-9	185	8-31-94	.182	.238	.169	30	110	14	20	5	0	2	15	8	0	0	0	41	0	1	.282	.237
Zimmerman, Jeff	R-L	6-3	223	7-5-92	.212	.311	.190	94	340	30	72	22	3	6	31	34	3	0	3	66	0	4	.347	.289

Pitching	B-T	HT	WT	DOB	W	L	ERA	G	GS	CG	SV	IP	H	R	ER	HR	BB	SO	AVG	vLH	vRH	K/9	BB/9
Bordonaro, Mark	R-R	6-0	167	8-17-90	1	0	2.63	7	0	0	1	14	13	4	4	0	7	12	.271	.250	.286	7.90	4.61
Brooks, Aaron	R-R	6-6	210	5-15-92	5	4	3.22	40	0	0	4	73	81	32	26	5	13	51	.282	.319	.256	6.32	1.61
Burns, Tommy	R-R	6-1	200	9-27-93	0	4	10.59	15	3	0	0	26	33	33	31	4	18	24	.303	.292	.311	8.20	6.15
Campbell, Ed	L-L	6-0	200	1-17-92	9	9	5.15	27	27	0	0	135	142	84	77	9	74	105	.276	.260	.280	7.02	4.95
Cleto, Ramire	R-R	6-0	220	4-4-93	0	1	9.00	6	0	0	0	14	21	15	14	2	8	7	.339	.190	.415	4.50	5.14

	B-T	HT	WT	DOB	W	L	ERA	G	GS	CG	SV	IP	H	R	ER	HR	BB	SO	AVG	vLH	vRH	K/9	BB/9
De Meyer, Dylan	R-R	6-4	165	9-16-92	0	0	6.75	1	0	0	0	1	2	3	1	0	1	2	.286	.250	.333	13.50	6.75
Diaz, Edwin	R-R	6-2	178	3-22-94	6	8	3.33	24	24	1	0	116	96	50	43	5	42	111	.226	.232	.222	8.59	3.25
Flores, Jose	R-R	6-2	190	12-31-92	3	5	4.29	21	20	0	0	101	107	57	48	9	36	50	.276	.288	.265	4.47	3.22
Fry, Paul	L-L	6-0	190	7-26-92	4	4	2.71	38	0	0	2	66	52	23	20	1	33	77	.221	.260	.203	10.45	4.48
Garcia, Rigoberto	R-R	6-5	202	9-23-93	0	1	81.00	1	1	0	0	1	4	6	6	0	1	0	.667	1.000	.500	0.00	13.50
Herb, Tyler	R-R	6-2	175	4-28-92	2	1	3.57	11	0	0	1	23	27	10	9	1	6	24	.287	.333	.250	9.53	2.38
Holovach, Blake	L-L	6-5	205	3-27-91	7	6	4.10	26	10	0	0	86	92	45	39	6	38	62	.277	.313	.263	6.51	3.99
Huijer, Lars	R-R	6-4	203	9-22-93	4	5	4.02	16	12	1	0	72	59	36	32	2	34	44	.230	.301	.183	5.53	4.27
Kim, Seon Gi	R-R	6-2	185	9-1-91	2	3	3.04	23	10	0	0	80	79	34	27	5	21	70	.256	.259	.253	7.88	2.36
McCoy, Kevin	L-R	6-4	220	7-12-91	0	2	4.34	17	0	0	1	29	21	16	14	0	16	30	.208	.325	.131	9.31	4.97
Misell, Carlos	R-R	6-1	191	4-25-92	8	12	4.90	26	26	0	0	127	149	82	69	15	48	96	.292	.336	.248	6.82	3.41
Munoz, Leoncio	L-L	6-4	221	8-18-90	0	0	9.00	8	0	0	0	15	19	17	15	0	7	10	.302	.267	.313	6.00	4.20
Pagan, Emilio	L-R	6-3	207	5-7-91	2	3	2.89	42	0	0	16	56	43	19	18	4	14	62	.214	.218	.211	9.96	2.25
Pereira, Cruz	L-L	5-10	175	12-18-90	1	0	7.71	5	0	0	0	12	15	11	10	1	4	5	.306	.250	.333	3.86	3.09
Pereira, Ricardo	B-R	6-3	150	4-18-91	1	0	1.17	6	1	0	1	15	9	2	2	0	4	8	.173	.150	.188	4.70	2.35
Pineda, Rafael	L-R	6-5	217	2-3-91	4	4	2.42	40	0	0	3	78	82	27	21	5	18	52	.274	.289	.262	6.00	2.08
Valenza, Nick	R-L	5-10	180	3-31-93	0	2	2.75	14	0	0	1	20	22	11	6	0	8	15	.286	.263	.293	6.86	3.66
Vieira, Thyago	R-R	6-2	210	1-7-93	1	1	5.23	13	0	0	1	21	16	12	12	1	14	23	.232	.238	.229	10.02	6.10
Zokan, Jake	R-L	6-1	198	4-27-91	1	1	2.21	4	4	0	0	20	24	6	5	1	4	17	.293	.333	.281	7.52	1.77

Fielding

Catcher	PCT	G	PO	A	E	DP	PB
Carmichael	.991	57	403	46	4	3	5
Guarnaccia	.972	5	32	3	1	0	0
Littlewood	.987	76	559	51	8	0	7

First Base	PCT	G	PO	A	E	DP
Caballero	1.000	1	3	0	0	0
DeCarlo	.976	9	74	7	2	6
Seager	.975	63	506	42	14	47
Shank	1.000	6	9	1	0	1
Zimmerman	.983	69	520	43	10	52

Second Base	PCT	G	PO	A	E	DP
Caballero	.950	14	20	37	3	8
Kauppila	.994	29	64	98	1	24
Peguero	.990	26	50	50	1	9
Peterson	.968	7	16	14	1	3
Reinheimer	.965	21	50	61	4	16
Shank	.977	37	75	96	4	23
Ward	.983	11	30	28	1	5

Third Base	PCT	G	PO	A	E	DP
Caballero	.800	7	3	9	3	0
DeCarlo	.907	68	42	134	18	10
Kauppila	1.000	5	5	6	0	2
Peguero	.948	36	33	59	5	7
Peterson	1.000	1	2	1	0	0
Reinheimer	1.000	2	3	4	0	0
Seager	.880	17	9	35	6	4
Shank	1.000	9	7	17	0	0

Shortstop	PCT	G	PO	A	E	DP
Caballero	.956	24	41	67	5	10
Kauppila	.929	8	13	26	3	7
Peguero	.935	7	7	22	2	5
Reinheimer	.965	86	143	246	14	51
Shank	.973	11	15	21	1	7
Ward	.955	6	9	12	1	1

Outfield	PCT	G	PO	A	E	DP
Barbosa	.989	76	181	5	2	0
Fields	1.000	9	22	0	0	0
Mack	.946	57	99	6	6	1
Martinez	.938	11	14	1	1	0
Miller	.988	42	79	3	1	2
O'Neill	.961	47	68	5	3	1
Reynolds	.964	11	26	1	1	0
Seager	1.000	2	1	0	0	0
Shank	.941	9	16	0	1	0
Simpson	.949	45	73	2	4	0
Thomas	.969	29	63	0	2	0
Wilson	.983	60	110	7	2	1
Yates	.981	28	47	6	1	1

EVERETT AQUASOX
SHORT-SEASON

NORTHWEST LEAGUE

Batting	B-T	HT	WT	DOB	AVG	vLH	vRH	G	AB	R	H	2B	3B	HR	RBI	BB	HBP	SH	SF	SO	SB	CS	SLG	OBP
Alfonso, James	R-R	5-10	195	9-3-91	.254	.188	.279	19	59	6	15	2	0	2	6	7	1	0	0	15	0	0	.390	.343
Brady, Patrick	R-R	5-10	176	2-5-88	.571	.500	.600	2	7	3	4	3	0	1	1	2	0	0	0	1	1	0	1.429	.667
Brito, Bryan	R-R	6-2	170	2-16-92	.214	.000	.231	5	14	1	3	0	0	0	1	0	0	1	0	5	1	0	.214	.214
Brito, Kristian	R-R	6-5	240	12-20-94	.213	.156	.229	40	141	15	30	9	0	6	21	12	0	0	1	57	0	0	.404	.273
Caballero, Luis	R-R	6-0	185	7-8-92	.180	.125	.206	14	50	4	9	2	1	0	6	3	1	0	0	23	4	0	.260	.241
Castillo, Phillips	R-R	6-2	200	2-2-94	.227	.075	.270	54	181	24	41	11	0	7	30	16	9	0	3	58	1	1	.403	.316
Cousino, Austin	L-L	5-10	178	4-17-93	.266	.281	.261	66	271	40	72	17	1	6	28	28	4	4	2	54	23	4	.402	.341
Cowan, Jordan	L-R	6-0	160	4-13-95	.231	.150	.250	63	216	24	50	6	1	1	11	19	1	8	1	36	2	6	.282	.295
DeCarlo, Joe	R-R	5-10	210	9-13-93	.222	.333	.167	3	9	2	2	1	0	0	1	1	1	0	0	5	0	0	.333	.364
DeMello, Toby	R-R	6-2	220	1-3-90	.190	.000	.222	7	21	1	4	1	0	0	0	1	0	0	0	3	1	1	.444	.222
Fields, Arby	B-R	5-9	192	6-25-91	.222	.000	.333	3	9	0	2	0	0	0	0	0	0	1	0	1	1	0	.222	.222
Guarnaccia, Luke	B-R	5-11	210	7-11-92	.266	.286	.260	21	64	8	17	1	0	1	4	5	1	0	0	28	2	1	.328	.329
Mariscal, Chris	R-R	5-10	170	4-26-93	.262	.273	.259	51	187	25	49	9	1	2	16	24	3	3	0	52	2	3	.353	.355
Martin, Adam	R-R	6-2	230	12-7-91	.260	.239	.266	58	200	27	52	12	0	5	24	31	5	1	1	50	2	0	.395	.371
Martinez, Wilton	R-R	6-4	195	12-7-91	.165	.235	.141	37	133	11	22	6	1	2	16	14	0	0	0	33	0	0	.271	.245
O'Neill, Tyler	R-R	5-11	210	6-22-95	.400	.333	.429	3	10	2	4	2	0	0	2	1	0	0	0	5	0	0	.600	.455
Peterson, Andy	R-R	5-10	178	4-19-92	.192	.150	.208	22	73	10	14	2	0	0	3	5	1	5	0	23	5	0	.219	.253
Petty, Kyle	R-R	6-5	215	3-1-91	.251	.246	.253	63	231	29	58	19	1	2	23	18	6	1	2	67	8	1	.368	.319
Planas-Arteaga, Sheehan	L-R	6-2	195	3-2-93	.181	.061	.211	52	166	24	30	5	0	0	12	38	1	1	1	50	0	1	.211	.335
Simpson, Corey	R-R	6-2	210	12-8-93	.222	.240	.217	53	207	28	46	7	0	9	35	19	4	0	1	56	2	1	.386	.299
Smart, Taylor	R-R	5-10	175	2-24-92	.220	.282	.196	44	141	11	31	4	0	0	12	16	5	3	1	43	4	2	.248	.319
Tenbrink, Nate	L-R	6-2	200	12-21-86	.500	—	.500	1	2	1	1	0	0	0	0	4	1	0	0	0	0	0	2.000	.750
Thomas, Brett	L-R	6-1	190	12-21-91	.178	.000	.205	14	45	5	8	1	0	1	4	8	0	0	0	12	1	3	.267	.302
Ward, Nelson	L-L	5-11	175	8-6-92	.223	.235	.221	31	94	12	21	2	1	2	11	16	1	0	1	17	3	3	.330	.339
Yates, Isaiah	R-L	5-9	185	8-31-94	.188	.077	.263	9	32	4	6	3	0	3	6	4	0	0	0	2	1	1	.281	.308

Pitching	B-T	HT	WT	DOB	W	L	ERA	G	GS	CG	SV	IP	H	R	ER	HR	BB	SO	AVG	vLH	vRH	K/9	BB/9
Altavilla, Dan	R-R	5-11	200	9-8-92	5	3	4.36	14	14	0	0	66	74	36	32	7	32	66	.288	.292	.285	9.00	4.36
Ash, Brett	R-R	6-2	195	5-27-91	2	1	3.58	8	0	0	0	28	22	11	11	0	12	23	.227	.364	.156	7.48	3.90
Bawcom, Logan	R-R	6-2	220	11-2-88	0	0	0.00	2	0	0	1	2	0	0	0	0	2	0	.000	.000	.000	13.50	9.00
Buchanan, Hawtin	R-R	6-8	230	4-29-93	2	0	2.97	19	0	0	0	30	26	10	10	3	25	45	.232	.209	.246	13.35	7.42
Cleto, Ramire	R-R	6-0	200	4-4-93	3	2	4.97	14	7	0	0	63	78	41	35	1	22	38	.311	.327	.299	5.40	3.13
Cochran-Gill, Trey	R-R	5-10	190	12-10-92	2	0	0.00	7	0	0	4	11	8	0	0	0	4	11	.216	.188	.238	9.28	3.38

	B-T	HT	WT	DOB	W	L	ERA	G	GS	CG	SV	IP	H	R	ER	HR	BB	SO	AVG	vLH	vRH	K/9	BB/9
De La Cruz, Noel	R-R	6-3	180	12-17-91	1	2	3.67	6	4	0	0	27	22	13	11	3	14	22	.218	.222	.215	7.33	4.67
De Meyer, Dylan	R-R	6-4	165	9-16-92	1	0	0.93	4	0	0	0	10	5	1	1	0	4	9	.147	.273	.087	8.38	3.72
Garcia, Oliver	R-R	6-2	205	12-7-90	0	0	0.00	2	0	0	0	2	2	1	0	0	0	4	.250	.200	.333	18.00	0.00
Garcia, Rigoberto	R-R	6-5	202	9-23-93	0	2	8.25	4	2	0	0	12	11	14	11	0	15	16	.250	.308	.226	12.00	11.25
Gohara, Luiz	L-L	6-3	210	7-31-96	0	6	8.20	11	11	0	0	37	46	43	34	6	24	37	.293	.277	.300	8.92	5.79
Holovach, Blake	L-L	6-5	205	3-27-91	0	1	2.59	4	4	0	0	24	24	9	7	0	0	17	.264	.267	.263	6.29	0.00
Kerski, Kody	R-R	5-10	185	4-18-92	4	3	2.95	25	0	0	3	40	39	18	13	0	17	46	.244	.321	.206	10.44	3.86
Kiel, Nick	R-L	5-11	205	11-30-92	0	1	5.28	6	0	0	0	15	24	9	9	0	6	6	.375	.368	.378	3.52	3.52
Kittredge, Andrew	R-R	6-1	200	3-17-90	1	0	0.00	1	0	0	0	3	1	0	0	0	0	2	.111	.000	.167	6.00	0.00
Lindquist, Sam	R-R	6-7	250	3-30-92	0	3	7.29	19	0	0	0	21	27	19	17	1	22	9	.321	.257	.367	3.86	9.43
Medina, Jefferson	R-R	6-2	184	5-31-94	2	8	4.19	13	13	0	0	69	77	41	32	2	22	43	.283	.284	.282	5.64	2.88
Munoz, Leoncio	L-L	6-4	221	8-18-90	2	3	4.38	22	1	0	3	51	49	28	25	6	20	51	.257	.134	.323	8.94	3.51
Nittoli, Vinny	R-R	6-1	210	11-11-90	1	1	4.03	12	0	0	0	22	20	11	10	2	9	18	.253	.385	.189	7.25	3.63
Paxton, James	R-L	6-4	220	11-6-88	0	1	6.75	1	1	0	0	3	2	2	2	1	1	2	.222	.500	.143	6.75	3.38
Pereira, Cruz	L-L	5-10	175	12-18-90	0	3	3.43	21	0	0	2	45	38	19	17	2	14	42	.224	.146	.254	8.46	2.82
Pereira, Ricardo	B-R	6-3	150	4-18-91	1	2	4.15	4	0	0	0	13	16	8	6	1	3	3	.302	.077	.375	2.08	2.08
Schiraldi, Lukas	R-R	6-6	210	7-25-93	1	2	5.18	8	8	0	0	24	25	15	14	3	10	29	.263	.273	.258	10.73	3.70
Scott, Troy	R-R	6-3	200	11-17-93	0	0	9.00	1	0	0	0	3	4	3	3	1	1	4	.308	.400	.250	12.00	9.00
Seifrit, Logan	B-R	5-11	165	8-25-94	0	1	9.90	7	0	0	2	10	15	12	11	0	6	9	.333	.235	.393	8.10	5.40
Yarbrough, Ryan	R-L	6-5	205	12-31-91	0	1	1.40	12	10	0	0	39	25	7	6	1	4	53	.180	.222	.165	12.34	0.93
Zokan, Jake	R-L	6-1	198	4-27-91	0	0	0.00	1	1	0	0	2	1	0	0	0	1	2	.167	.500	.000	9.00	4.50

Fielding

Catcher	PCT	G	PO	A	E	DP	PB
Alfonso	1.000	9	49	5	0	0	0
DeMello	1.000	7	42	7	0	3	1
Guarnaccia	.978	13	78	13	2	0	3
Martin	.989	47	392	41	5	1	6
Petty	.980	8	44	6	1	2	3

First Base	PCT	G	PO	A	E	DP
Brito	.982	37	311	20	6	27
Castillo	1.000	1	3	0	0	2
Guarnaccia	1.000	1	1	0	0	0
Martin	.889	1	8	0	1	2
Petty	.975	34	291	15	8	31
Planas-Arteaga	.973	10	66	7	2	8

Second Base	PCT	G	PO	A	E	DP
Alfonso	—	1	0	0	0	0
Caballero	1.000	1	4	1	0	0
Cowan	.991	47	85	146	2	30

	PCT	G	PO	A	E	DP
Mariscal	.950	5	7	12	1	1
Peterson	.988	14	30	52	1	13
Smart	.971	8	11	22	1	5
Ward	.966	6	15	13	1	2

Third Base	PCT	G	PO	A	E	DP
Brady	1.000	1	1	3	0	1
Brito	.727	5	3	5	3	1
Caballero	.800	2	3	1	1	0
Cowan	1.000	4	2	6	0	0
DeCarlo	1.000	2	1	2	0	0
Mariscal	.844	26	17	48	12	5
Peterson	.923	6	4	8	1	1
Petty	.930	18	9	31	3	3
Smart	.982	18	17	39	1	3

Shortstop	PCT	G	PO	A	E	DP
Caballero	.886	10	16	23	5	5
Cowan	.957	13	28	38	3	11

	PCT	G	PO	A	E	DP
Mariscal	.916	17	24	52	7	5
Peterson	.889	2	3	5	1	1
Smart	.944	14	26	41	4	12
Ward	.992	23	39	78	1	18

Outfield	PCT	G	PO	A	E	DP
Brady	1.000	1	2	0	0	0
Castillo	.982	41	51	4	1	0
Cousino	.992	62	117	3	1	1
Fields	.667	3	2	0	1	0
Martinez	.971	34	60	6	2	2
O'Neill	1.000	2	2	0	0	0
Planas-Arteaga	.979	33	43	3	1	1
Simpson	.923	42	65	7	6	0
Tenbrink	1.000	1	3	0	0	0
Thomas	1.000	8	22	0	0	0
Ward	1.000	3	1	0	0	0
Yates	.929	7	13	0	1	0

PULASKI MARINERS
APPALACHIAN LEAGUE
ROOKIE

Batting	B-T	HT	WT	DOB	AVG	vLH	vRH	G	AB	R	H	2B	3B	HR	RBI	BB	HBP	SH	SF	SO	SB	CS	SLG	OBP
Baum, Jay	R	6-0	185	10-25-92	.273	.299	.261	57	205	24	56	7	1	0	33	21	1	2	3	28	12	7	.317	.339
Calderon, Yordyn	R-R	6-2	185	2-15-94	.184	.164	.192	55	185	25	34	6	3	1	20	22	9	4	2	62	11	1	.265	.298
Fernandez, Rafael	B-R	5-10	180	4-21-94	.303	.400	.266	31	109	27	33	4	0	0	12	16	3	10	1	14	7	2	.339	.403
Fields, Arby	B-R	5-9	192	6-25-91	.331	.271	.354	54	175	32	58	10	4	4	13	27	3	12	0	56	19	10	.503	.429
Leal, Jose	R-R	6-3	215	2-16-95	.243	.167	.280	23	74	4	18	3	1	1	10	8	0	1	1	37	1	2	.351	.313
Morales, Estarlyn	R-R	6-3	180	10-28-92	.303	.293	.307	57	208	43	63	16	3	6	34	25	4	2	6	46	17	3	.495	.379
Nyman, Chase	L-R	5-11	170	10-2-93	.171	.032	.217	42	123	13	21	2	1	0	12	12	0	2	2	51	0	2	.203	.241
Palma, Alexy	R-R	6-3	195	12-24-92	.050	.000	.080	14	40	2	2	0	0	0	5	1	0	0	1	17	1	2	.050	.174
Perez, Georvic	B-R	6-0	198	4-15-95	.207	.136	.233	26	82	8	17	3	0	1	10	9	1	2	0	17	0	0	.280	.293
Tanabe, Carlton	R-R	6-0	190	10-28-91	.326	.341	.320	39	141	20	46	13	1	1	21	10	5	2	2	15	5	1	.454	.386
Taylor, Wayne	L-R	6-1	205	11-4-92	.275	.203	.308	55	207	36	57	17	1	6	38	24	3	0	3	72	3	1	.454	.354
Thomas, Brett	L-R	6-1	190	2-21-92	.125	.250	.000	2	8	0	1	0	0	0	0	0	0	0	0	4	0	0	.125	.125
Torres, Dan	R-R	6-0	175	5-29-92	.243	.225	.250	41	136	18	33	4	1	0	15	19	1	2	4	26	1	2	.287	.331
Verdi, Tom	R-R	6-2	185	4-2-92	.238	.333	.193	25	84	16	20	1	0	0	4	6	3	3	0	11	5	2	.250	.312
Ward, Nelson	L-R	5-11	175	8-6-94	.350	.500	.269	11	40	6	14	3	1	1	8	4	0	1	0	7	5	1	.550	.409
Wawoe, Gianfranco	B-R	5-11	170	7-25-94	.275	.226	.293	56	200	30	55	9	1	2	19	11	1	5	1	30	7	4	.360	.315
Zeutenhorst, Taylor	L-R	6-4	200	10-25-91	.191	.114	.222	46	152	18	29	7	1	1	11	15	0	0	1	58	1	0	.270	.262

Pitching	B-T	HT	WT	DOB	W	L	ERA	G	GS	CG	SV	IP	H	R	ER	HR	BB	SO	AVG	vLH	vRH	K/9	BB/9
Brown, Jarrett	R-L	6-3	169	12-15-92	3	2	4.32	19	0	0	1	25	23	17	12	3	18	17	.253	.056	.301	6.12	6.48
Byrd, Taylor	L-L	6-2	195	8-15-92	0	2	5.02	12	10	0	0	38	44	26	21	2	15	25	.288	.344	.273	5.97	3.58
Cochran-Gill, Trey	R-R	5-10	190	12-10-92	3	0	0.35	18	0	0	8	26	14	2	1	0	3	33	.154	.171	.143	11.57	1.05
Garcia, Rigoberto	R-R	6-5	202	9-23-93	0	2	13.75	10	4	0	0	18	25	31	27	2	21	20	.333	.370	.313	10.19	10.70
Hermann, Spencer	L-L	6-4	235	8-6-93	1	0	1.69	5	1	0	0	21	16	4	4	1	5	22	.205	.091	.224	9.28	2.11
Littell, Zack	B-R	6-3	190	10-5-95	5	5	4.52	13	13	0	0	70	75	38	35	3	12	64	.275	.313	.248	8.27	1.55
Medina, Jefferson	R-R	6-2	184	5-31-94	0	0	0.00	1	1	0	0	5	4	2	0	0	1	5	.200	.125	.250	9.00	1.80
Miller, Ryan	R-R	6-1	195	4-27-92	2	1	1.35	22	0	0	9	33	26	9	5	1	8	39	.213	.239	.197	10.53	2.16
Missaki, Daniel	R-R	6-0	170	4-9-96	6	3	2.76	11	11	1	0	59	46	20	18	3	16	62	.212	.247	.183	9.51	2.45
Pereira, Ricardo	B-R	6-3	150	4-18-91	3	2	1.73	9	2	0	0	36	24	10	7	2	14	33	.194	.250	.167	8.17	3.47
Peterson, Pat	R-L	6-3	190	3-8-93	2	2	3.26	11	11	0	0	50	43	21	18	2	18	54	.235	.189	.247	9.79	3.26

Name	B-T	HT	WT	DOB	W	L	ERA	G	GS	CG	SV	IP	H	R	ER	HR	BB	SO	AVG	vLH	vRH	K/9	BB/9
Pierce, Rohn	R-R	6-3	210	1-21-93	5	1	3.40	18	0	0	0	42	33	17	16	4	13	56	.217	.172	.245	11.91	2.76
Pina, Luis	L-L	6-2	178	12-6-93	1	3	4.98	17	2	0	2	47	60	32	26	3	13	34	.305	.190	.335	6.51	2.49
Ratliff, Lane	L-L	6-3	185	3-22-95	0	0	15.00	2	1	0	0	3	7	6	5	0	1	4	.438	.000	.467	12.00	3.00
Scott, Troy	R-R	6-3	200	11-17-93	2	3	4.57	10	10	0	0	41	59	33	21	6	11	35	.322	.343	.310	7.62	2.40
Thieben, Daniel	R-R	6-4	195	9-18-93	2	1	2.73	18	0	0	0	26	23	12	8	0	24	15	.242	.308	.217	5.13	8.20
Urbina, Ugueth	R-R	6-1	185	10-28-94	1	2	5.55	20	0	0	1	36	51	32	22	1	20	34	.323	.365	.302	8.58	5.05
Yarbrough, Ryan	R-L	6-5	205	12-31-91	0	0	0.00	2	0	0	1	4	1	0	0	0	1	5	.071	.000	.077	11.25	2.25

Fielding

Catcher	PCT	G	PO	A	E	DP	PB
Perez	.936	13	81	7	6	1	5
Tanabe	.990	13	78	26	1	0	3
Taylor	.972	15	126	11	4	1	4
Torres	.989	30	240	41	3	2	12

First Base	PCT	G	PO	A	E	DP
Calderon	.983	37	338	11	6	21
Nyman	.984	14	115	5	2	10
Tanabe	.965	19	156	11	6	21

Second Base	PCT	G	PO	A	E	DP
Baum	.966	5	9	19	1	5
Fernandez	.957	22	36	52	4	15
Nyman	1.000	12	16	32	0	9

	PCT	G	PO	A	E	DP
Verdi	1.000	3	7	5	0	0
Ward	1.000	7	18	19	0	6
Wawoe	.962	20	45	56	4	15

Third Base	PCT	G	PO	A	E	DP
Baum	.923	40	19	77	8	4
Calderon	.783	14	8	28	10	3
Nyman	.909	12	6	14	2	0
Tanabe	—	1	0	0	0	0
Wawoe	1.000	4	2	4	0	1

Shortstop	PCT	G	PO	A	E	DP
Baum	.982	11	21	33	1	7
Fernandez	.909	6	11	9	2	3
Nyman	—	1	0	0	0	0

	PCT	G	PO	A	E	DP
Verdi	.976	22	41	83	3	18
Ward	1.000	2	2	11	0	1
Wawoe	.936	28	44	87	9	13

Outfield	PCT	G	PO	A	E	DP
Baum	—	1	0	0	0	0
Fields	.967	50	84	3	3	0
Leal	.833	15	20	0	4	0
Morales	.955	55	83	2	4	1
Palma	.875	7	7	0	1	0
Taylor	.983	39	55	4	1	1
Thomas	1.000	2	1	0	0	0
Zeutenhorst	1.000	39	57	5	0	0

AZL MARINERS   ROOKIE

ARIZONA LEAGUE

Batting	B-T	HT	WT	DOB	AVG	vLH	vRH	G	AB	R	H	2B	3B	HR	RBI	BB	HBP	SH	SF	SO	SB	CS	SLG	OBP
Alcantara, Ismael	R-R	6-0	185	12-15-93	.222	.152	.258	34	99	16	22	7	0	1	9	12	2	1	1	23	1	1	.323	.316
Alfonso, James	R-R	5-10	195	9-3-91	.216	.357	.130	12	37	4	8	4	0	1	5	2	0	0	0	9	0	0	.405	.256
Ascanio, Rayder	R-R	5-11	155	3-17-96	.248	.298	.224	51	145	28	36	9	0	0	15	25	2	1	3	46	5	3	.310	.360
Blanco, Dominic	L-R	6-2	215	11-10-95	.296	.111	.389	17	27	2	8	1	0	2	5	2	0	0		15	0	0	.407	.441
Capriata, Alexander	R-R	5-11	190	8-3-92	.268	.333	.250	18	41	2	11	1	0	2	3	0	1	0	4	2	0	.293	.318
DeCarlo, Joe	R-R	5-10	210	9-13-93	.500	.000	1.000	1	2	1	1	0	0	0	0	0	0	0	0	0	0	0	.500	.500
Fernandez, Rafael	R-R	5-10	180	4-21-94	.211	.000	.267	7	19	4	4	0	0	0	1	7	0	1	0	4	0	1	.211	.423
Fontaine, Lachlan	L-R	6-2	210	8-27-95	.179	.138	.202	51	179	17	32	8	1	2	20	5	0	1	1	62	1	4	.268	.200
Jackson, Alex	R-R	6-2	215	12-25-95	.280	.348	.254	23	82	11	23	6	2	2	16	9	0	1	2	24	0	1	.476	.344
Keyes, Kavin	R-R	5-11	190	4-25-92	.236	.152	.286	25	89	14	21	4	0	1	9	6	1	0	0	14	2	1	.315	.292
Leal, Jose	R-R	6-3	215	2-16-95	.250	.000	.333	9	32	8	8	4	0	1	5	6	0	0	0	17	1	0	.469	.368
Liberato, Luis	L-L	6-1	175	12-18-95	.211	.217	.209	49	175	28	37	6	3	2	14	29	1	4	1	47	14	2	.314	.325
Martinez, Hersin	R-R	6-5	220	2-27-95	.248	.250	.247	45	145	22	36	4	0	4	14	11	9	0	0	68	5	1	.359	.339
Mejia, Erick	R-R	5-11	155	11-9-94	.283	.341	.256	38	127	23	36	3	6	1	13	16	0	3	1	25	13	2	.425	.361
Morgan, Gareth	R-R	6-4	220	4-12-96	.148	.188	.131	45	155	15	23	8	1	2	12	16	4	2	1	73	4	1	.252	.244
Nieto, Arturo	R-R	6-2	195	12-9-92	.179	.167	.188	12	28	4	5	0	0	0	4	6	1	0	0	7	0	1	.179	.343
O'Neill, Tyler	R-R	5-11	210	6-22-95	.000	.000	.000	1	2	0	0	0	0	0	0	0	0	0	0	1	0	0	.000	.000
Palma, Alexy	R-R	6-3	195	12-24-92	.244	.150	.320	18	45	2	11	4	0	0	5	2	1	2	1	17	0	0	.333	.286
Peterson, Andy	R-R	5-10	178	4-19-92	.000	.000	.000	3	6	0	0	0	0	0	0	0	0	0	0	3	0	0	.000	.000
Pimentel, Guillermo	L-L	6-1	206	10-5-92	.333	.667	.000	3	6	1	2	0	0	2	0	0	0	0	3	0	0	.333	.333
Quevedo, Johan	R-R	6-1	212	11-6-93	.281	.278	.282	33	114	12	32	7	3	0	18	6	0	0	1	19	1	0	.395	.314
Schuetzle, Austin	R-R	6-3	175	3-9-95	.316	.200	.333	16	38	6	12	2	0	0	2	2	0	1	0	14	1	1	.368	.350
Tenbrink, Nate	L-R	6-2	200	12-21-86	.500	1.000	.455	5	12	2	6	3	0	0	3	4	0	0	0	4	0	0	.750	.625
Vargas, Leurys	L-R	6-3	225	8-30-96	.190	.280	.132	20	63	5	12	1	0	0	6	4	0	0	1	29	3	0	.206	.235
Verdi, Tom	R-R	6-2	185	4-2-92	.111	.176	.053	14	36	5	4	0	1	0	3	6	2	0	0	8	1	0	.167	.273
Wilson, Austin	R-R	6-4	249	2-7-92	.625	1.000	.250	3	8	3	5	1	1	1	1	0	0	0	1	0	0	0	.875	.667
Yates, Isaiah	R-L	5-9	185	8-31-94	.421	.333	.462	4	19	4	8	3	0	2	7	2	0	0		2	1	0	.895	.476

Pitching	B-T	HT	WT	DOB	W	L	ERA	G	GS	CG	SV	IP	H	R	ER	HR	BB	SO	AVG	vLH	vRH	K/9	BB/9
Arias, Jefferson	R-R	6-4	185	4-8-93	2	2	6.02	10	9	0	0	46	55	38	31	2	22	42	.301	.365	.257	8.16	4.27
Ash, Brett	R-R	6-2	195	5-27-91	1	0	0.00	4	0	0	2	6	4	2	0	0	2	8	.182	.125	.214	12.00	3.00
Cano, Joselito	L-L	6-5	190	9-16-92	0	0	0.00	6	0	0	2	9	3	2	0	0	1	7	.094	.400	.037	6.75	0.96
Dominguez, Ronald	R-R	6-2	180	1-13-94	5	1	0.43	17	0	0	2	42	21	3	2	0	11	36	.153	.204	.125	7.65	2.34
Gadea, Kevin	R-R	6-5	188	12-6-94	0	0	7.71	3	1	0	0	9	13	10	8	0	9	11	.342	.091	.444	10.61	8.68
Gohara, Luiz	L-L	6-3	210	7-31-96	1	1	2.13	2	2	0	0	13	11	4	3	0	2	16	.234	.300	.216	11.37	1.42
Gorgas, Marvin	R-R	5-9	185	1-19-96	0	0	0.00	2	1	0	0	3	1	0	0	0	3	3	.125	.000		10.13	10.13
Herb, Tyler	R-R	6-2	175	4-28-92	1	1	6.14	5	0	0	1	7	12	6	5	0	1	12	.333	.214	.409	14.73	1.23
Hermann, Spencer	L-L	6-4	235	8-6-93	3	0	0.00	4	0	0	0	11	7	1	0	0	2	11	.189	.182	.192	9.28	1.69
Hill, Nick	L-L	6-0	195	1-30-85	0	0	0.00	2	0	0	0	2	1	0	0	0	2	2	.125	.000	.200	9.00	9.00
Horstman, Ryan	L-L	6-1	185	7-20-92	0	0	0.00	4	0	0	0	4	1	0	0	0		7	.250	.667	.111	9.45	2.70
Kiel, Nick	R-L	5-11	205	11-30-92	4	0	1.31	12	0	0	3	21	12	5	3	1	2	25	.160	.211	.143	10.89	0.87
McCoy, Kevin	L-R	6-4	220	7-12-91	0	0	0.00	1	0	0	0	1	0	0	0	0	1		.000	.000		9.00	9.00
Millord, Yohailys	R-R	6-2	180	12-4-93	0	0	6.29	18	0	0	0	24	27	22	17	1	27	19	.273	.300	.263	7.03	9.99
Morales, Osmel	R-R	6-3	196	3-30-92	5	2	2.20	11	8	0	0	49	40	12	12	1	15	65	.227	.293	.195	11.94	2.76
Morla, Ramon	R-R	6-1	205	11-20-89	0	0	2.84	5	0	0	1	6	2	2	2	0	4	8	.105	.000	.200	11.37	5.68
Muhammad, Jay	R-R	6-2	195	11-14-94	1	1	7.82	12	0	0	0	36	26	33	31	2	35	21	.213	.250	.198	5.30	8.83
Peralta, Freddy	R-R	5-11	175	6-4-96	1	6	5.29	12	12	0	0	51	55	38	30	3	24	42	.275	.338	.238	7.41	4.24
Perez, Ulises	R-R	6-3	160	7-14-97	0	1	2.16	7	0	0	1	8	5	2	2	0	6	10	.179	.100	.222	10.80	4.32

Name	B-T	HT	WT	DOB	W	L	ERA	G	GS	CG	SV	IP	H	R	ER	HR	BB	SO	AVG	vLH	vRH	K/9	BB/9
Ratliff, Lane	L-L	6-3	185	3-22-95	0	1	0.00	4	0	0	1	5	2	1	0	0	3	6	.111	.333	.067	10.13	5.06
Roy, Alex	L-L	6-2	165	7-28-95	0	0	3.38	3	0	0	0	3	3	1	1	0	1	3	.273	.000	.333	10.13	3.38
Santiago, Jose	R-R	6-1	190	3-1-94	5	1	2.80	9	8	0	0	45	31	18	14	1	20	45	.190	.237	.163	9.00	4.00
Seifrit, Logan	B-R	5-11	165	8-25-94	1	3	9.92	12	0	0	0	16	24	22	18	0	12	11	.329	.440	.271	6.06	6.61
Torres, Jose	R-R	6-4	165	9-1-93	0	0	6.65	17	0	0	1	22	16	18	16	0	24	18	.211	.226	.200	7.48	9.97
Zokan, Jake	R-L	6-1	198	4-27-91	0	1	3.00	3	2	0	0	6	8	2	2	0	0	7	.320	.667	.211	10.50	0.00

Fielding

Catcher	PCT	G	PO	A	E	DP	PB
Alfonso	1.000	3	19	0	0	1	
Blanco	1.000	12	40	8	0	0	5
Capriata	.975	17	93	23	3	2	1
Nieto	.981	10	46	6	1	1	1
Quevedo	.985	31	231	35	4	1	3

First Base	PCT	G	PO	A	E	DP
Alcantara	.987	24	149	7	2	7
Alfonso	1.000	6	37	5	0	10
Fontaine	1.000	1	1	0	0	0
Keyes	.993	16	136	8	1	8
Nieto	1.000	1	8	2	0	3
Vargas	.970	17	125	4	4	7

Second Base	PCT	G	PO	A	E	DP
Alcantara	1.000	4	8	9	0	4

	PCT	G	PO	A	E	DP	PB
Ascanio	.958	25	36	56	4	9	
Fernandez	1.000	4	5	6	0	2	
Keyes	.969	7	14	17	1	5	
Mejia	.976	14	19	22	1	2	
Peterson	1.000	3	3	5	0	0	
Quevedo	1.000	1	1	1	0	1	
Verdi	1.000	9	12	20	0	2	

Third Base	PCT	G	PO	A	E	DP
Alcantara	.722	6	3	10	5	0
DeCarlo	—	1	0	0	0	0
Fontaine	.910	47	32	90	12	10
Keyes	.800	2	1	3	1	0

Shortstop	PCT	G	PO	A	E	DP
Ascanio	.926	29	47	66	9	9
Fernandez	1.000	3	4	7	0	1

	PCT	G	PO	A	E	DP
Mejia	.945	23	34	52	5	14
Verdi	.950	5	8	11	1	2

Outfield	PCT	G	PO	A	E	DP
Alcantara	1.000	3	1	0	0	0
Jackson	.960	19	23	1	1	0
Leal	1.000	5	4	1	0	0
Liberato	.942	49	76	5	5	1
Martinez	.891	28	41	0	5	0
Morgan	.956	41	64	1	3	0
O'Neill	1.000	1	1	0	0	0
Palma	1.000	12	19	1	0	1
Pimentel	1.000	1	2	0	0	0
Schuetzle	1.000	11	16	2	0	2
Tenbrink	1.000	3	2	0	0	0
Wilson	1.000	2	3	0	0	0
Yates	1.000	3	4	3	0	0

DSL MARINERS

DOMINICAN SUMMER LEAGUE

ROOKIE

Batting	B-T	HT	WT	DOB	AVG	vLH	vRH	G	AB	R	H	2B	3B	HR	RBI	BB	HBP	SH	SF	SO	SB	CS	SLG	OBP
Almonte, Adalfi	R-R	6-1	170	4-19-96	.263	.289	.256	56	194	35	51	14	0	4	20	27	11	2	2	45	13	6	.397	.380
Almonte, Miguel	R-R	6-0	180	1-5-94	.226	.231	.225	21	53	7	12	1	1	1	8	5	2	0	1	15	3	2	.340	.311
Andrade, Greifer	R-R	6-0	170	1-27-97	.125	.000	.143	5	16	2	2	0	0	0	0	0	0	1	0	4	0	0	.250	.125
Baez, Cesar	L-R	6-0	160	7-6-95	.240	.129	.264	57	175	36	42	4	4	0	16	28	5	5	1	45	12	8	.309	.359
Cano, Jose	R-R	5-11	190	12-18-96	.125	.083	.143	14	40	2	5	2	0	0	2	2	1	0	0	24	0	0	.175	.186
De la Cruz, Adonis	R-R	6-2	170	12-20-94	.229	.261	.223	43	144	17	33	5	0	4	23	12	3	1	1	22	4	5	.347	.300
Dominguez, Anthony	R-R	6-0	170	6-6-96	.200	.182	.203	59	175	25	35	1	3	0	14	24	6	4	0	32	3	6	.240	.317
Franco, Joshua	R-R	5-11	193	9-10-93	.244	.136	.261	47	164	10	40	9	0	2	18	15	3	1	1	47	3	5	.335	.317
Gonzalez, Ivan	R-R	6-0	175	10-28-95	.310	.250	.327	50	187	35	58	14	1	2	23	14	6	1	3	26	7	5	.428	.371
Jimenez, Angel	R-R	6-1	180	9-8-94	.280	.296	.277	53	189	29	52	10	2	3	34	27	10	0	0	36	14	6	.403	.399
Joseph, Luis	B-R	5-9	160	9-20-96	.226	.188	.234	54	186	22	42	11	1	0	13	12	1	3	1	36	3	10	.296	.275
Morales, Jhonbaker	R-R	6-0	170	7-17-94	.297	.333	.291	36	138	23	41	10	1	3	22	13	4	3	2	27	7	3	.449	.369
Pena, Onil	R-R	6-0	180	11-6-96	.302	.263	.308	38	149	20	45	9	2	2	22	8	6	3	1	26	8	3	.430	.360
Perez, Yeison	R-R	6-0	185	4-9-96	.184	.250	.176	13	38	7	7	2	0	0	3	9	1	2	0	14	0	0	.237	.354
Ramirez, Gregory	R-R	6-4	190	7-24-95	.160	.059	.176	45	125	15	20	2	0	0	9	13	3	3	0	40	2	4	.176	.255
Rojas, Brayan	R-R	6-2	180	1-5-96	.279	.276	.279	52	201	38	56	9	2	2	23	27	5	3	2	54	15	4	.373	.374
Rosa, Jose	R-R	6-0	175	3-7-94	.214	.292	.193	38	112	17	24	4	0	2	12	12	10	1	1	26	4	2	.304	.341
Rosario, Ronald	L-L	6-2	165	2-8-97	.198	.227	.189	29	96	12	19	1	0	0	9	12	0	1	1	39	4	1	.229	.284

Pitching	B-T	HT	WT	DOB	W	L	ERA	G	GS	CG	SV	IP	H	R	ER	HR	BB	SO	AVG	vLH	vRH	K/9	BB/9
Asencio, Oliver	L-L	6-2	199	1-18-93	3	4	3.90	13	8	0	0	55	67	38	24	2	17	51	.306	.298	.308	8.30	2.77
Brito, Frankely	R-R	6-0	170	11-1-92	0	1	10.24	10	2	0	0	19	22	26	22	0	29	18	.282	.345	.245	8.38	13.50
Encarnacion, Frank	R-R	6-3	195	2-13-95	1	1	5.71	14	5	0	0	35	23	28	22	0	36	30	.184	.229	.156	7.79	9.35
Feliz, Jose	R-R	6-0	170	12-23-94	2	1	2.81	10	1	0	1	32	37	10	10	2	8	22	.289	.255	.312	6.19	2.25
Guzman, Carlos	R-L	6-1	170	1-28-97	0	1	14.90	8	3	0	1	10	12	17	16	0	20	7	.324	.500	.240	6.52	18.62
Jimenez, Luis	R-R	6-0	180	5-28-93	1	4	2.91	22	0	0	4	46	46	21	15	2	18	40	.266	.246	.279	7.77	3.50
Manzueta, Romulo	L-L	6-2	160	10-9-95	2	4	4.21	14	13	0	0	51	44	29	24	1	35	51	.230	.220	.233	8.94	6.14
Martinez, Edwin	R-R	6-6	240	7-31-95	1	1	2.22	17	8	0	2	57	44	20	14	0	18	42	.217	.217	.216	6.67	2.86
Paulino, Roberto	R-R	6-2	187	11-16-93	0	0	4.02	21	0	0	2	31	25	22	14	2	30	23	.217	.176	.235	6.61	8.62
Pedie, Raul	R-R	6-0	175	8-14-92	6	4	4.10	23	0	0	1	48	49	29	22	5	21	62	.262	.259	.264	11.54	3.91
Reyes, Ricardo	R-R	6-7	198	10-17-93	3	2	10.29	14	1	0	0	28	39	42	32	1	27	21	.333	.314	.348	6.75	8.68
Santiago, Jose	R-R	6-1	190	3-1-94	2	2	3.51	6	6	0	0	25	19	10	10	0	13	31	.202	.154	.236	10.87	4.56
Severino, Robert	L-R	6-2	185	2-14-94	2	4	4.04	22	0	0	1	42	34	25	19	0	28	56	.231	.273	.214	11.91	5.95
Tamarez, Albert	R-R	6-1	185	11-30-93	1	3	8.19	15	5	0	0	30	38	38	27	3	29	16	.302	.286	.312	4.85	8.80
Urquides, Melchor	B-L	6-0	180	7-26-95	0	3	9.31	14	0	0	0	29	46	45	30	2	29	31	.357	.367	.354	9.62	9.00
Zabala, Aneurys	R-R	6-2	175	12-21-96	4	4	4.33	14	12	1	0	54	56	40	26	0	38	32	.276	.260	.285	5.33	6.33

Fielding

Catcher	PCT	G	PO	A	E	DP	PB
Almonte	.979	12	82	12	2	0	3
Pena	.968	33	263	44	10	1	11
Perez	.949	12	74	19	5	3	2
Rosa	.978	19	119	14	3	1	3

First Base	PCT	G	PO	A	E	DP
Almonte	1.000	1	8	0	0	0
Cano	.989	11	90	3	1	3
Dominguez	.857	2	5	1	1	0

	PCT	G	PO	A	E	DP
Franco	.977	27	209	5	5	21
Gonzalez	.983	9	53	4	1	7
Jimenez	.992	16	114	3	1	15
Morales	1.000	2	19	0	0	2
Rosa	.968	16	118	3	4	11
Rosario	1.000	1	4	0	0	0

Second Base	PCT	G	PO	A	E	DP
Andrade	1.000	1	1	1	0	0
Baez	.934	16	31	26	4	9

	PCT	G	PO	A	E	DP
Dominguez	.921	12	28	42	6	6
Gonzalez	.989	21	41	52	1	16
Joseph	.984	30	54	66	2	10

Third Base	PCT	G	PO	A	E	DP
Cano	1.000	2	1	0	0	1
Dominguez	.920	19	19	27	4	5
Gonzalez	.854	18	12	29	7	5
Jimenez	.813	34	24	41	15	3
Morales	.920	11	5	18	2	5

SEATTLE MARINERS

Ramirez	1.000	1	1	1	0	0
Rosa	.000	1	0	0	1	0

Shortstop	PCT	G	PO	A	E	DP
Andrade	.818	3	3	6	2	0
Baez	.750	5	3	9	4	1
Dominguez	.878	26	38	41	11	7

Jimenez	1.000	1	2	6	0	0
Joseph	.864	22	29	60	14	10
Morales	.907	19	44	54	10	8

Outfield	PCT	G	PO	A	E	DP
Almonte	.942	55	89	8	6	0
Baez	.896	31	57	3	7	0

De la Cruz	.953	29	40	1	2	1
Dominguez	1.000	2	1	0	0	0
Ramirez	.925	38	43	6	4	1
Rojas	.971	50	95	6	3	0
Rosa	1.000	1	1	0	0	0
Rosario	.967	24	27	2	1	0

VSL MARINERS

ROOKIE

VENEZUELAN SUMMER LEAGUE

Batting	B-T	HT	WT	DOB	AVG	vLH	vRH	G	AB	R	H	2B	3B	HR	RBI	BB	HBP	SH	SF	SO	SB	CS	SLG	OBP
Andrade, Greifer	R-R	6-0	170	1-27-97	.308	.267	.316	26	91	17	28	8	0	0	13	5	3	2	1	14	8	1	.396	.360
Arocha, Hector	R-R	5-11	180	1-15-97	.147	.167	.143	16	34	2	5	0	0	0	2	4	2	1	0	9	0	1	.147	.275
Ascanio, Rayder	B-R	5-11	155	3-17-96	.133	.000	.182	5	15	1	2	0	0	0	0	1	0	0	0	3	0	0	.133	.188
Guedez, Jose	R-R	6-2	175	9-6-94	.178	.143	.190	49	107	12	19	4	1	1	9	7	2	0	0	29	2	5	.262	.241
Helder, Eugene	R-R	5-11	165	2-26-96	.267	.236	.276	61	225	40	60	11	4	1	27	22	3	2	3	19	6	2	.364	.336
Herrera, Albert	R-R	5-11	160	3-7-96	.170	.160	.173	41	100	16	17	2	1	0	6	10	2	0	1	30	4	2	.210	.257
Jimenez, Anthony	R-R	5-11	165	10-21-95	.294	.333	.282	64	218	45	64	19	4	0	28	32	5	2	5	38	23	5	.417	.388
Laya, Alexdray	R-R	6-1	185	10-6-95	.237	.200	.248	43	139	17	33	3	1	0	7	13	3	1	1	19	3	4	.273	.314
Leal, Bryan	L-R	6-0	164	8-20-96	.208	.190	.212	39	106	14	22	4	2	0	9	10	5	0	1	18	3	3	.283	.303
Montilla, Geoandry	R-R	6-0	165	5-14-96	.223	.276	.207	44	121	10	27	6	0	0	11	11	1	1	1	34	3	1	.273	.291
Munoz, Oberto	R-R	6-0	170	2-18-97	.113	.316	.000	20	53	2	6	1	0	0	1	7	0	0	0	13	1	0	.132	.217
Rengifo, Luis	B-R	5-10	165	2-26-97	.198	.119	.226	64	227	39	45	11	2	1	20	39	5	6	1	45	11	5	.278	.327
Sandoval, Jose	R-R	6-2	195	10-23-96	.235	.162	.256	51	166	20	39	4	1	1	21	6	0	1	2	44	3	3	.289	.259
Sojo, Danilo	R-R	6-4	211	4-29-95	.223	.241	.218	39	130	17	29	6	0	3	12	12	7	0	0	32	4	1	.338	.322
Talos, Felipe	L-R	5-11	170	2-3-95	.147	.143	.147	45	116	17	17	4	1	0	12	16	1	0	2	20	3	2	.198	.252
Tenias, Raymon	R-R	5-8	185	4-15-94	.261	.303	.248	47	134	19	35	8	1	2	10	15	0	1	4	19	4	2	.381	.327
Velasquez, Alberto	L-L	6-5	240	3-7-94	.319	.200	.360	64	238	27	76	18	1	6	56	18	5	0	4	16	3	1	.479	.374

Pitching	B-T	HT	WT	DOB	W	L	ERA	G	GS	CG	SV	IP	H	R	ER	HR	BB	SO	AVG	vLH	vRH	K/9	BB/9
Berroteran, Jose	L-L	5-10	178	8-3-94	1	3	8.42	12	0	0	1	26	36	24	24	0	17	29	.327	.500	.302	10.17	5.96
Breto, Liarvis	L-L	5-11	175	4-10-93	2	2	3.50	14	0	0	1	36	36	20	14	1	15	35	.255	.227	.261	8.75	3.75
Carrillo, Rohimard	R-L	5-11	175	8-19-94	0	0	1.96	15	1	0	3	41	31	11	9	0	9	29	.215	.286	.203	6.31	1.96
Fernandez, Alvaro	R-R	6-0	170	9-1-96	0	1	2.45	7	6	0	0	18	10	5	5	1	9	7	.164	.100	.195	3.44	4.42
Hernandez, Anjul	R-R	6-2	192	1-2-96	3	1	4.18	13	11	0	0	60	69	36	28	2	10	41	.288	.341	.255	6.12	1.49
Hernandez, Carlos	R-R	6-3	195	2-26-96	2	2	1.93	9	3	0	1	28	32	8	6	0	6	19	.291	.294	.289	6.11	1.93
Hidalgo, Hector	R-R	6-1	182	9-21-92	2	3	2.87	14	0	0	2	31	36	19	10	0	4	25	.293	.333	.278	7.18	1.15
Lopez, Robinson	R-R	6-1	175	6-2-96	0	1	6.75	3	2	0	0	5	9	4	4	1	3	5	.429	.500	.412	8.44	5.06
Marruffo, Wladimir	R-R	6-0	173	5-29-93	5	2	5.79	21	0	0	6	33	39	25	21	1	15	17	.307	.179	.364	4.68	4.13
Miliani, Eduardo	R-R	5-11	178	7-8-93	1	2	2.79	11	2	0	2	29	29	13	9	0	6	19	.257	.258	.256	5.90	1.86
Osorio, Neritzon	R-R	6-1	180	12-29-93	6	1	2.55	9	4	0	0	42	35	14	12	1	14	37	.223	.250	.211	7.87	2.98
Padovani, Paolo	R-R	6-2	175	8-22-94	1	2	5.66	11	1	0	0	21	19	15	13	1	10	12	.232	.207	.245	5.23	4.35
Pena, Michael	R-R	6-3	190	1-16-95	1	1	4.23	10	10	0	0	28	25	17	13	0	16	29	.243	.083	.291	9.43	5.20
Perez, Ulises	R-R	6-3	160	7-14-97	0	5	5.09	12	12	0	0	46	63	37	26	1	16	28	.332	.358	.317	5.48	3.13
Rodriguez, Carlos	R-R	6-0	190	5-23-95	1	3	3.86	12	0	0	1	33	28	18	14	0	11	19	.233	.143	.282	5.23	3.03
Salinas, Edward	R-R	6-2	175	1-3-96	0	3	5.84	8	0	0	0	12	11	10	8	0	9	16	.234	.182	.250	7.30	6.57
Suarez, Michael	L-L	6-2	180	3-21-95	6	0	1.72	13	9	0	0	58	41	18	11	1	16	60	.195	.139	.207	9.36	2.50
Torres, Andres	R-R	6-3	185	10-31-95	3	1	1.39	10	6	0	0	45	30	11	7	0	8	42	.183	.151	.198	8.34	1.59

Fielding

Catcher	PCT	G	PO	A	E	DP	PB
Arocha	.987	11	72	6	1	1	2
Montilla	.985	23	106	23	2	0	5
Munoz	.991	17	94	19	1	1	0
Tenias	.987	34	203	28	3	3	7

First Base	PCT	G	PO	A	E	DP
Laya	1.000	1	1	0	0	0
Montilla	.950	3	18	1	1	2
Sandoval	1.000	1	7	0	0	0
Sojo	1.000	12	67	3	0	4
Velasquez	.985	57	446	26	7	30

Second Base	PCT	G	PO	A	E	DP
Herrera	.926	22	45	43	7	7

Laya	1.000	3	2	1	0	0
Montilla	.833	3	3	2	1	0
Rengifo	.965	53	116	106	8	21

Third Base	PCT	G	PO	A	E	DP
Andrade	.893	7	8	17	3	1
Ascanio	1.000	2	1	0	0	0
Helder	.940	24	18	45	4	1
Herrera	.850	8	7	10	3	2
Laya	.864	35	36	66	16	4
Sandoval	.750	5	1	5	2	0

Shortstop	PCT	G	PO	A	E	DP
Andrade	.892	19	30	61	11	6
Ascanio	1.000	2	0	7	0	0

Guedez	.600	1	1	2	2	2
Helder	.922	37	58	95	13	11
Herrera	—	1	0	0	0	0
Laya	.938	4	7	8	1	2
Rengifo	.927	15	16	35	4	3

Outfield	PCT	G	PO	A	E	DP
Guedez	.943	44	61	5	4	1
Helder	—	1	0	0	0	0
Herrera	1.000	5	12	0	0	0
Jimenez	.955	63	139	8	7	3
Leal	.909	35	45	5	5	2
Sandoval	.929	41	58	7	5	0
Sojo	1.000	18	27	3	0	1
Talos	.968	30	56	5	2	0

SEATTLE MARINERS

Tampa Bay Rays

SEASON IN A SENTENCE: Expected to contend for a playoff spot after four straight seasons with 90-plus victories, the Rays had their worst season since they were the Devil Rays in 2007.

HIGH POINT: After a dreadful first half, the Rays were essentially a .500 team in the second half of the season, led by a 17-6 record in July, their only month with a winning record. Alex Cobb and Chris Archer were effective young starters, while Jake McGee and Brad Boxberger became one of the game's best bullpen duos, with the two combining for 194 strikeouts in 136 innings.

LOW POINT: A June 10 loss to the Cardinals marked the 14th loss in 15 games for the Rays, who dropped 15 games back in the American League East and carried the worst record in baseball at 24-42. Right fielder Wil Myers had a disappointing sophomore campaign, while third baseman Evan Longoria was solid but had his quietest offensive year yet in seven major league seasons.

NOTABLE ROOKIES: Kevin Kiermaier was a revelation at the plate, hitting .263/.315/.450 in 108 games while playing Gold Glove-caliber defense in the outfield. Righthander Jake Odorizzi had a promising debut, striking out 174 batters in 168 innings while maintaining a 4.13 ERA. Outfielder Brandon Guyer was also productive and a pleasant surprise, hitting .266/.344/.367 in 294 plate appearances as a 28-year-old rookie.

KEY TRANSACTIONS: While the Rays have become accustomed to trading off star talent in the offseason that they can't afford to re-sign, they found themselves in the unfamiliar position of making such a deal in-season due to their poor record. That meant ace David Price went to the Tigers in a three-team deal that netted the Rays big league lefty Drew Smyly and low Class A shortstop Willy Adames from Detroit, along with shortstop Nick Franklin from the Mariners. Smyly performed well in Price's stead (3-1, 1.70) and Adames could jump to the top of the Rays' prospect list.

DOWN ON THE FARM: The farm system is no longer the powerful pipeline it used to be, as several thin drafts have taken a toll on the team's prospects. Adames immediately becomes one of the system's best prospects. Outfielder Mikie Mahtook and catcher Justin O'Conner had productive years, while the organization must hope righthander Taylor Guerrieri returns to form in 2015 in his return from Tommy John surgery.

PAYROLL: $82,035,490 (25th)

PLAYERS OF THE YEAR

MAJOR LEAGUE

Ben Zobrist
of/if
.272/.354/.395
10 HR, 10 SB, 34 2B
Versatile and durable

MINOR LEAGUE

Justin O'Conner
c
(High A/Double-A)
.282/.321/.486
33 CS in 60 SBA

ORGANIZATION LEADERS

BATTING		*Minimum 250 AB
MAJORS		
* AVG	Loney, James	.290
* OPS	Kiermaier, Kevin	.765
HR	Longoria, Evan	22
RBI	Longoria, Evan	91
MINORS		
* AVG	Wong, Kean, Bowling Green	.306
* OBP	Field, Johnny, Bowling Green, Charlotte	.376
* SLG	Field, Johnny, Bowling Green, Charlotte	.488
R	Field, Johnny, Bowling Green, Charlotte	95
H	Mahtook, Mikie, Durham	143
TB	Field, Johnny, Bowling Green, Charlotte	228
2B	Christian, Justin, Durham	37
3B	four tied at	8
HR	Shaffer, Richie, Montgomery	19
RBI	Mahtook, Mikie, Durham	68
BB	Belnome, Vince, Durham	72
SO	Betemit, Wilson, Durham	144
SB	Coyle, Thomas, Charlotte	30

PITCHING		#Minimum 75 IP
MAJORS		
W	Price, David	11
	Odorizzi, Jake	11
# ERA	Cobb, Alex	2.87
SO	Price, David	189
SV	McGee, Jake	19
MINORS		
W	Mateo, Victor, Montgomery	12
L	Floro, Dylan, Montgomery	13
# ERA	Kelly, Merrill, Durham	2.76
G	Liberatore, Adam, Durham	54
GS	Floro, Dylan, Montgomery	28
	Mateo, Victor, Montgomery	28
SV	Yates, Kirby, Durham	16
IP	Floro, Dylan, Montgomery	179
BB	Karns, Nate, Durham	62
SO	Karns, Nate, Durham	153
AVG	Snell, Blake, Bowling Green, Charlotte	.225

General Manager: Andrew Friedman. **Farm Director:** Mitch Lukevics. **Scouting Director:** R.J. Harrison

Class	Team	League	W	L	PCT	Finish	Manager
Majors	Tampa Bay Rays	American	77	85	.475	t-18th (30)	Joe Maddon
Triple-A	Durham Bulls	International	75	69	.521	6th (14)	Charlie Montoyo
Double-A	Montgomery Biscuits	Southern	66	74	.471	6th (10)	Brady Williams
High A	Charlotte Stone Crabs	Florida State	63	70	.474	9th (12)	Jared Sandberg
Low A	Bowling Green Hot Rods	Midwest	61	77	.442	t-14th (16)	Michael Johns
Short season	Hudson Valley Renegades	New York-Penn	46	30	.605	3rd (14)	Tim Parenton
Rookie	Princeton Rays	Appalachian	40	28	.588	1st (10)	Danny Sheaffer
Rookie	Rays	Gulf Coast	32	28	.533	8th (16)	Jim Morrison
Overall Minor League Record			383	376	.505	16 (30)	

ORGANIZATION STATISTICS

TAMPA BAY RAYS

AMERICAN LEAGUE

Batting	B-T	HT	WT	DOB	AVG	vLH	vRH	G	AB	R	H	2B	3B	HR	RBI	BB	HBP	SH	SF	SO	SB	CS	SLG	OBP
Belnome, Vince	L-R	5-11	205	3-11-88	.100	—	.100	4	10	1	1	1	0	0	1	3	0	0	1	3	0	0	.200	.286
Casali, Curt	R-R	6-2	225	11-9-88	.167	.125	.179	30	72	10	12	3	0	0	3	8	2	2	0	23	0	0	.208	.268
DeJesus, David	L-L	5-11	190	12-20-79	.248	.143	.251	83	238	24	59	15	2	6	19	30	5	0	0	43	0	3	.403	.344
Escobar, Yunel	R-R	6-2	215	11-2-82	.258	.270	.255	137	476	33	123	18	0	7	39	43	4	4	2	60	1	1	.340	.324
Figueroa, Cole	L-R	5-10	175	6-30-87	.233	.000	.238	23	43	6	10	2	1	0	6	4	0	0	2	4	0	0	.326	.286
Forsythe, Logan	R-R	6-1	195	1-14-87	.223	.241	.206	110	301	32	67	12	1	6	26	25	4	2	4	71	2	1	.329	.287
Franklin, Nick	B-R	6-1	195	3-2-91	.206	.286	.185	11	34	4	7	2	0	1	4	3	0	0	1	11	1	0	.353	.263
2-team total (17 Seattle)					.160	—	—	28	81	7	13	2	1	1	6	6	1	0	2	32	2	0	.247	.222
Guyer, Brandon	R-R	6-2	195	1-28-86	.266	.297	.243	97	259	37	69	15	1	3	26	16	11	7	1	52	6	1	.367	.334
Hanigan, Ryan	R-R	6-0	210	8-16-80	.218	.143	.239	84	225	18	49	9	0	5	34	31	3	2	2	39	1	0	.324	.318
Jennings, Desmond	R-R	6-2	200	10-30-86	.244	.265	.238	123	479	64	117	30	2	10	36	47	6	9	1	108	15	6	.378	.319
Joyce, Matt	L-R	6-2	200	8-3-84	.254	.147	.263	140	418	51	106	23	2	9	52	62	4	0	9	111	2	5	.383	.349
Kiermaier, Kevin	L-R	6-1	195	4-22-90	.263	.203	.280	108	331	35	87	16	8	10	35	23	3	5	2	71	5	4	.450	.315
Loney, James	L-L	6-3	235	5-7-84	.290	.256	.304	155	600	59	174	27	0	9	69	41	4	0	6	80	4	0	.380	.336
Longoria, Evan	R-R	6-2	210	10-7-85	.253	.273	.247	162	624	83	158	26	1	22	91	57	9	1	9	133	5	0	.404	.320
Molina, Jose	R-R	6-0	250	6-3-75	.178	.255	.155	80	225	4	40	2	0	0	10	14	2	4	2	55	3	0	.187	.230
Myers, Wil	R-R	6-3	205	12-10-90	.222	.192	.235	87	325	37	72	14	0	6	35	34	0	0	2	90	6	1	.320	.294
Rodriguez, Sean	R-R	6-0	200	4-26-85	.211	.221	.200	96	237	30	50	13	3	12	41	10	6	3	3	66	2	1	.443	.258
Sands, Jerry	R-R	6-4	220	9-28-87	.190	.091	.300	12	21	1	4	0	0	1	4	0	1	0	0	6	0	0	.333	.227
Solis, Ali	R-R	6-0	175	9-29-87	.000	.000	.000	8	6	0	0	0	0	0	0	1	0	0	1	4	0	0	.000	.000
Zobrist, Ben	B-R	6-3	210	5-26-81	.272	.340	.246	146	570	83	155	34	3	10	52	75	1	2	6	84	10	5	.395	.354

Pitching	B-T	HT	WT	DOB	W	L	ERA	G	GS	CG	SV	IP	H	R	ER	HR	BB	SO	AVG	vLH	vRH	K/9	BB/9
Archer, Chris	R-R	6-3	190	9-26-88	10	9	3.33	32	32	0	0	195	177	85	72	12	72	173	.243	.228	.262	8.00	3.33
Balfour, Grant	R-R	6-2	200	12-30-77	2	6	4.91	65	0	0	12	62	49	34	34	3	41	57	.217	.200	.234	8.23	5.92
Bedard, Erik	L-L	6-1	200	3-5-79	4	6	4.76	17	15	0	0	76	84	46	40	10	29	64	.275	.273	.275	7.61	3.45
Beliveau, Jeff	L-L	6-1	195	1-17-87	0	0	2.63	30	0	0	1	24	19	7	7	1	7	28	.213	.146	.271	10.50	2.63
Bell, Heath	R-R	6-3	250	9-29-77	1	1	7.27	13	0	0	0	17	24	16	14	1	8	12	.324	.279	.387	6.23	4.15
Boxberger, Brad	R-R	6-2	220	5-27-88	5	2	2.37	63	0	0	2	65	34	17	17	9	20	104	.155	.107	.198	14.47	2.78
Cobb, Alex	R-R	6-3	200	10-7-87	10	9	2.87	27	27	0	0	166	142	56	53	11	47	149	.231	.207	.252	8.06	2.54
Colome, Alex	R-R	6-2	210	12-31-88	2	0	2.66	5	3	0	0	24	19	7	7	1	10	13	.221	.217	.225	4.94	3.80
Geltz, Steve	R-R	5-10	170	11-1-87	0	1	3.24	11	0	0	0	8	6	3	3	3	5	14	.200	.100	.250	15.12	5.40
Gomes, Brandon	R-R	5-11	195	7-15-84	2	2	3.71	29	0	0	0	34	28	14	14	5	11	24	.222	.245	.208	6.35	2.91
Hellickson, Jeremy	R-R	6-1	190	4-8-87	1	5	4.52	13	13	0	0	64	71	35	32	8	21	54	.276	.213	.353	7.63	2.97
Karns, Nathan	R-R	6-3	230	11-25-87	1	1	4.50	2	2	0	0	12	7	6	6	3	6	13	.163	.111	.200	9.75	3.00
Lueke, Josh	R-R	6-5	245	12-4-84	1	2	5.64	25	0	0	0	30	38	20	19	7	5	19	.299	.261	.345	5.64	1.48
McGee, Jake	L-L	6-3	235	8-6-86	5	2	1.89	73	0	0	19	71	48	15	15	2	16	90	.189	.236	.170	11.36	2.02
Moore, Matt	L-L	6-3	200	6-18-89	0	2	2.70	2	2	0	0	10	10	3	3	1	5	6	.256	.333	.233	5.40	4.50
Odorizzi, Jake	R-R	6-2	185	3-27-90	11	13	4.13	31	31	0	0	168	156	79	77	20	59	174	.242	.230	.257	9.32	3.16
Oviedo, Juan Carlos	R-R	6-2	195	3-15-82	3	3	3.69	32	0	0	1	32	27	14	13	3	16	26	.225	.242	.207	7.39	4.55
Peralta, Joel	R-R	5-11	210	3-23-76	3	4	4.41	69	0	0	1	63	60	31	31	9	15	74	.244	.247	.240	10.52	2.13
Price, David	L-L	6-6	210	8-26-85	11	8	3.11	23	23	2	0	171	156	68	59	20	23	189	.238	.255	.233	9.97	1.21
2-team total (11 Detroit)					15	12	3.26	34	34	3	0	248	230	100	90	25	38	271				9.82	1.38
Ramos, Cesar	L-L	6-2	200	6-22-84	2	6	3.70	43	7	0	0	83	73	39	34	8	39	66	.233	.244	.227	7.19	4.25
Riefenhauser, C.J.	L-L	6-0	180	1-30-90	0	0	8.44	7	0	0	0	5	6	5	5	0	3	2	.286	.111	.417	3.38	5.06
Smyly, Drew	L-L	6-3	190	6-13-89	3	1	1.70	7	7	1	0	48	25	9	9	4	11	44	.155	.154	.156	8.31	2.08
2-team total (21 Detroit)					9	10	3.24	28	25	1	0	153	136	57	55	18	42	133				7.82	2.47
Yates, Kirby	R-R	5-10	195	3-25-87	0	2	3.75	37	0	0	1	36	33	16	15	4	15	42	.241	.250	.238	10.50	3.75

Fielding

Catcher	PCT	G	PO	A	E	DP	PB
Casali	.996	29	212	11	1	0	3
Hanigan	.998	79	540	32	1	5	1
Molina	.997	80	659	30	2	2	4
Solis	1.000	8	27	0	0	0	1

First Base	PCT	G	PO	A	E	DP
Forsythe	1.000	1	1	0	0	0
Loney	.992	152	1111	58	9	78

	PCT	G	PO	A	E	DP			PCT	G	PO	A	E	DP			PCT	G	PO	A	E	DP
Myers	1.000	2	1	0	0	0		Longoria	.967	155	121	262	13	27		Escobar	—		1	0	0	0	0
Rodriguez	1.000	18	101	8	0	9		Rodriguez	.944	9	6	11	1	1		Forsythe	1.000	3	2	0	0	0
Second Base	**PCT**	**G**	**PO**	**A**	**E**	**DP**		**Shortstop**	**PCT**	**G**	**PO**	**A**	**E**	**DP**		Guyer	1.000	72	122	0	0	0
Figueroa	.977	16	19	24	1	4		Escobar	.965	136	168	267	16	50		Jennings	1.000	118	307	2	0	0
Forsythe	.991	74	82	149	2	22		Forsythe	1.000	2	0	3	0	0		Joyce	.982	94	156	5	3	1
Franklin	.905	7	8	11	2	4		Franklin	.917	3	3	8	1	2		Kiermaier	.976	108	237	5	6	2
Rodriguez	.971	23	32	35	2	5		Rodriguez	1.000	1	0	1	0	0		Myers	.976	78	161	5	4	1
Zobrist	.980	79	105	185	6	32		Zobrist	.973	31	16	57	2	12		Rodriguez	1.000	18	16	0	0	0
Third Base	**PCT**	**G**	**PO**	**A**	**E**	**DP**		**Outfield**	**PCT**	**G**	**PO**	**A**	**E**	**DP**		Zobrist	1.000	54	101	2	0	0
Forsythe	1.000	6	4	6	0	0		DeJesus	1.000	15	25	0	0	0								

DURHAM BULLS — TRIPLE-A

INTERNATIONAL LEAGUE

Batting	B-T	HT	WT	DOB	AVG	vLH	vRH	G	AB	R	H	2B	3B	HR	RBI	BB	HBP	SH	SF	SO	SB	CS	SLG	OBP
Acosta, Mayobanex	R-R	6-1	205	11-20-87	.133	.217	.100	30	83	4	11	5	0	0	6	9	0	1	1	38	0	0	.193	.215
Beckham, Tim	R-R	6-0	195	1-27-90	.258	.462	.204	15	62	8	16	2	0	0	4	2	0	1	0	14	0	2	.290	.281
Belnome, Vince	L-R	5-11	205	3-11-88	.245	.198	.259	118	413	59	101	25	1	10	49	72	3	0	4	128	2	0	.383	.358
Betemit, Wilson	B-R	6-2	220	11-2-81	.217	.184	.228	111	396	53	86	17	0	18	50	49	0	0	8	144	1	0	.396	.298
Casali, Curt	R-R	6-2	225	11-9-88	.237	.200	.255	46	156	11	37	10	0	3	15	22	2	1	2	50	0	0	.359	.335
Christian, Justin	R-R	6-1	195	4-3-80	.271	.241	.281	127	461	68	125	37	4	10	37	43	10	3	3	71	16	4	.434	.344
Figueroa, Cole	L-R	5-10	175	6-30-87	.282	.278	.284	71	262	33	74	13	3	3	33	39	1	5	5	29	4	1	.389	.371
Fontenot, Mike	L-R	5-9	165	6-6-80	.276	.243	.288	113	398	35	110	24	1	3	48	43	4	5	4	85	5	2	.364	.350
Franklin, Nick	B-R	6-1	195	3-2-91	.210	.154	.230	27	100	8	21	2	0	2	9	10	1	2	0	34	2	0	.290	.288
Guyer, Brandon	R-R	6-2	195	1-28-86	.400	.000	.533	5	20	8	8	2	2	0	1	6	0	0	0	4	0	0	.700	.538
Kiermaier, Kevin	L-R	6-1	195	4-22-90	.305	.250	.323	34	128	28	39	7	2	3	13	12	0	2	1	23	11	1	.461	.362
Lee, Hak-Ju	L-R	6-2	170	11-4-90	.203	.222	.198	93	315	36	64	9	1	4	23	37	0	5	0	86	12	5	.276	.287
Mahtook, Mikie	R-R	6-1	200	11-30-89	.292	.387	.260	132	489	56	143	33	6	12	68	46	10	0	5	137	18	5	.458	.362
Moore, Jeremy	L-R	6-1	190	6-29-87	.262	.322	.235	55	195	24	51	7	1	12	34	22	0	0	1	62	0	1	.492	.335
Myers, Wil	R-R	6-3	205	12-10-90	.250	.400	.211	7	24	3	6	1	0	2	6	7	0	0	0	7	3	0	.542	.419
Nix, Jayson	R-R	5-11	195	8-26-82	.272	.296	.263	55	191	25	52	15	1	3	16	20	1	1	3	36	2	2	.408	.340
Olmedo, Ray	B-R	5-11	165	5-31-81	.224	.208	.231	104	362	32	81	11	3	0	25	28	1	12	1	79	9	3	.271	.281
Price, Robby	L-R	5-10	188	4-20-88	.216	.234	.208	68	213	25	46	6	1	3	18	27	2	6	1	26	1	0	.296	.309
Rodriguez, Eddy	R-R	6-0	220	12-1-85	.152	.235	.103	13	46	5	7	1	0	1	4	1	2	0	0	17	0	0	.239	.204
Sands, Jerry	R-R	6-4	220	9-28-87	.268	.279	.265	54	190	32	51	12	0	9	36	26	0	0	3	53	1	0	.474	.352
Solis, Ali	R-R	6-0	175	9-29-87	.203	.217	.199	73	251	20	51	7	2	3	25	6	4	2	3	75	0	1	.283	.231

Pitching	B-T	HT	WT	DOB	W	L	ERA	G	GS	CG	SV	IP	H	R	ER	HR	BB	SO	AVG	vLH	vRH	K/9	BB/9
Andriese, Matt	R-R	6-3	210	8-28-89	11	8	3.77	28	25	0	0	162	153	73	68	18	48	129	.254	.272	.236	7.15	2.66
Bedard, Erik	L-L	6-1	200	3-5-79	0	0	2.25	1	1	0	0	4	2	1	1	0	1	5	.167	.000	.222	11.25	2.25
Beliveau, Jeff	L-L	6-1	195	1-17-87	0	0	1.50	30	0	0	11	36	19	7	6	0	14	51	.151	.081	.180	12.75	3.50
Boxberger, Brad	R-R	6-2	220	5-27-88	1	0	1.93	6	0	0	2	9	4	2	2	1	4	18	.125	.118	.133	17.36	3.86
Burns, Cory	R-R	6-0	205	10-9-87	2	2	2.77	7	0	0	1	13	17	5	4	0	3	8	.309	.273	.333	5.54	2.08
Colome, Alex	R-R	6-2	210	12-31-88	7	6	3.77	15	15	0	0	86	84	40	36	2	30	73	.261	.281	.243	7.64	3.14
Geltz, Steve	R-R	5-10	170	11-1-87	3	3	2.38	29	0	0	1	42	27	11	11	3	17	60	.184	.154	.207	12.96	3.67
Gomes, Brandon	R-R	5-11	195	7-15-84	0	2	3.62	27	0	0	0	37	36	18	15	4	12	42	.250	.283	.226	10.13	2.89
Hellickson, Jeremy	R-R	6-1	190	4-8-87	1	4	7.23	5	5	0	0	19	38	20	15	1	5	16	.413	.413	.413	7.71	2.41
Karns, Nathan	R-R	6-3	230	11-25-87	9	9	5.08	27	27	0	0	145	142	89	82	16	62	153	.257	.239	.276	9.47	3.84
Kelly, Merrill	R-R	6-2	190	10-14-88	9	4	2.76	28	15	0	0	114	107	39	35	10	37	108	.244	.236	.251	8.53	2.92
Lara, Braulio	L-L	6-1	180	12-20-88	0	3	9.00	9	0	0	0	11	7	11	11	2	12	11	.194	.182	.200	9.00	9.82
Liberatore, Adam	L-L	6-3	225	5-12-87	6	1	1.66	54	0	0	4	65	43	14	12	1	15	86	.187	.176	.192	11.91	2.08
Lueke, Josh	R-R	6-5	245	12-5-84	0	1	3.38	32	0	0	12	37	32	17	14	3	9	40	.227	.226	.228	9.64	2.17
Mathis, Doug	R-R	6-3	230	6-7-83	2	3	3.63	26	3	0	0	67	73	30	27	5	37	54	.280	.300	.262	7.25	4.97
Montgomery, Mike	L-L	6-4	200	7-1-89	10	5	4.29	25	25	0	0	126	117	68	60	9	48	98	.245	.248	.244	7.00	3.43
Oviedo, Juan Carlos	R-R	6-2	195	3-15-82	0	0	3.86	7	0	0	0	7	5	3	3	1	1	10	.200	.167	.231	12.86	1.29
Patterson, Jimmy	R-L	6-0	190	2-9-89	1	1	2.70	5	1	0	0	10	10	3	3	1	3	5	.263	.077	.360	4.50	2.70
Riefenhauser, C.J.	L-L	6-0	180	1-30-90	3	3	1.40	39	0	0	1	58	41	13	9	3	11	53	.195	.119	.231	8.27	3.90
Romero, Enny	L-L	6-3	210	1-24-91	5	11	4.50	25	25	0	0	126	128	69	63	13	52	117	.261	.342	.235	8.36	3.71
Sandoval, Juan	R-R	6-2	170	1-12-81	0	1	3.12	14	1	0	1	26	21	12	9	2	14	15	.228	.310	.160	5.19	4.85
Stowell, Bryce	R-R	6-2	205	9-23-86	0	0	0.00	1	0	0	0	2	2	0	0	1	1	1	.286	.500	.200	4.50	4.50
Thompson, Jake	R-R	6-2	225	8-8-89	4	1	3.15	24	1	0	0	34	42	12	12	1	11	30	.304	.234	.365	7.86	2.88
Yates, Kirby	R-R	5-10	195	3-25-87	1	0	0.36	21	0	0	16	25	10	1	1	0	9	35	.118	.050	.178	12.60	3.24

Fielding

Catcher	PCT	G	PO	A	E	DP	PB		Second Base	PCT	G	PO	A	E	DP			PCT	G	PO	A	E	DP
Acosta	.991	26	205	19	2	2	2		Beckham	.889	1	3	11	3	3		Fontenot	.950	7	4	15	1	2
Casali	.994	41	326	27	4	3			Figueroa	1.000	4	4	10	0	2		Franklin	1.000	2	1	1	0	0
Rodriguez	1.000	12	122	8	0	0	0		Fontenot	.974	82	125	215	9	55		Nix	1.000	12	4	16	0	3
Solis	.995	69	550	62	3	3	7		Franklin	.959	16	33	37	3	9		Olmedo	.932	54	31	78	6	6
First Base	**PCT**	**G**	**PO**	**A**	**E**	**DP**			Nix	.990	21	34	63	1	11		Price	.957	19	6	38	2	3
Belnome	.992	76	613	33	5	54			Olmedo	1.000	8	13	25	0	8		**Shortstop**	**PCT**	**G**	**PO**	**A**	**E**	**DP**
Betemit	1.000	47	351	19	0	37			Price	.968	10	11	19	1	4		Beckham	.938	5	12	18	2	6
Nix	.991	12	102	7	1	8			**Third Base**	**PCT**	**G**	**PO**	**A**	**E**	**DP**		Figueroa	.976	21	24	57	2	10
Olmedo	1.000	1	8	1	0	0			Belnome	.889	4	2	6	1	0		Franklin	.963	7	6	20	1	4
Price	1.000	1	1	0	0	0			Betemit	.909	7	3	17	2	2		Lee	.952	92	113	221	17	48
Sands	.964	12	76	4	3	7			Figueroa	.933	43	28	83	8	8		Nix	1.000	1	0	3	0	0
																	Olmedo	.953	23	27	54	4	15

Outfield	PCT	G	PO	A	E	DP
Belnome	1.000	11	23	0	0	0
Christian	.996	127	257	4	1	1
Figueroa	—	1	0	0	0	0
Guyer	1.000	2	5	0	0	0

	PCT	G	PO	A	E	DP
Kiermaier	.989	33	91	2	1	0
Mahtook	.983	131	288	5	5	1
Moore	.980	50	90	6	2	0
Myers	.889	4	7	1	1	0
Nix	1.000	3	5	0	0	0

	PCT	G	PO	A	E	DP
Olmedo	.943	20	32	1	2	1
Price	.982	35	52	3	1	1
Sands	.985	38	60	7	1	1

MONTGOMERY BISCUITS   DOUBLE-A

SOUTHERN LEAGUE

Batting	B-T	HT	WT	DOB	AVG	vLH	vRH	G	AB	R	H	2B	3B	HR	RBI	BB	HBP	SH	SF	SO	SB	CS	SLG	OBP
Argo, Willie	R-R	6-1	220	10-15-89	.203	.170	.213	120	384	48	78	11	2	4	42	62	10	3	5	109	24	7	.273	.325
Bailey, Luke	R-R	6-0	198	3-11-91	.220	.154	.243	17	50	3	11	2	0	0	5	6	1	0	1	16	0	0	.260	.310
Brett, Ryan	R-R	5-9	180	10-9-91	.303	.329	.297	107	422	64	128	25	6	8	38	24	5	5	3	74	27	7	.448	.346
Carter, Kes	L-L	6-2	205	3-3-90	.241	.200	.253	56	199	27	48	14	2	3	19	23	7	0	1	46	8	6	.377	.339
Casali, Curt	R-R	6-2	225	11-9-88	.314	.250	.323	22	70	7	22	5	0	1	13	23	3	0	0	16	0	0	.429	.500
DePew, Jake	R-R	6-0	225	3-1-92	.179	.111	.191	17	56	5	10	2	0	1	5	8	0	1	0	13	0	0	.268	.281
Guevara, Hector	R-R	6-0	192	10-7-91	.216	.174	.228	33	102	7	22	9	0	1	11	8	1	2	3	10	0	0	.333	.272
Hager, Jake	R-R	6-1	170	3-4-93	.271	.287	.267	114	447	42	121	27	4	4	47	30	2	6	5	91	4	4	.376	.316
Maile, Luke	R-R	6-3	220	2-6-91	.268	.310	.257	97	351	43	94	19	4	5	37	35	5	0	2	76	1	1	.387	.341
Malm, Jeff	L-L	6-3	225	10-31-90	.258	.257	.258	96	326	37	84	18	0	5	38	22	8	0	1	72	3	2	.359	.319
Moore, Jeremy	L-R	6-1	190	6-29-87	.183	.185	.183	38	120	13	22	4	0	6	16	9	1	1	0	29	1	1	.367	.246
Motter, Taylor	R-R	6-1	190	9-18-89	.274	.310	.266	119	452	60	124	19	3	16	61	34	5	6	9	71	15	7	.436	.326
O'Conner, Justin	R-R	6-0	190	3-31-92	.263	.133	.292	21	80	9	21	4	0	2	3	1	3	0	0	20	0	0	.388	.298
Reginatto, Leonardo	R-R	6-2	179	4-10-90	.130	.154	.122	17	54	2	7	0	0	0	6	6	3	0	0	9	0	0	.130	.254
Rickard, Joey	R-L	6-1	185	5-21-91	.243	.239	.244	68	206	33	50	8	0	1	17	28	4	4	5	39	9	4	.296	.337
Segovia, Alejandro	R-R	6-0	185	4-27-90	.224	.237	.219	88	295	31	66	14	1	10	33	40	6	0	2	69	2	1	.380	.327
Seitzer, Cameron	L-R	6-5	220	1-11-90	.242	.157	.267	123	450	60	109	27	0	14	65	53	8	0	8	89	3	2	.396	.328
Shaffer, Richie	R-R	6-3	218	3-15-91	.222	.233	.220	119	427	58	95	28	4	19	64	56	5	1	2	119	4	0	.440	.318
Torrez, Riccio	R-R	6-0	205	10-14-89	.179	.286	.141	34	106	17	19	3	2	1	8	3	1	0	0	29	1	0	.274	.209

Pitching	B-T	HT	WT	DOB	W	L	ERA	G	GS	CG	SV	IP	H	R	ER	HR	BB	SO	AVG	vLH	vRH	K/9	BB/9
Bellatti, Andrew	R-R	6-1	190	8-5-91	2	6	3.68	46	0	0	6	71	69	32	29	6	22	80	.253	.230	.263	10.14	2.79
Brandt, Kevin	R-L	6-1	195	11-24-89	0	0	7.20	6	0	0	0	10	15	8	8	0	8	8	.375	.556	.323	7.20	7.20
Burns, Cory	R-R	6-0	205	10-9-87	1	1	2.00	16	0	0	4	18	9	4	4	2	3	21	.150	.136	.158	10.50	1.50
Colla, Mike	R-R	6-2	220	12-23-86	7	12	4.38	28	26	0	0	144	174	91	70	11	40	108	.303	.229	.343	7.38	2.50
Floro, Dylan	L-R	6-2	175	12-27-90	11	13	3.48	28	28	3	0	179	209	80	69	4	24	112	.294	.357	.260	5.64	1.21
Garrido, Santiago	R-R	6-1	195	10-4-89	1	3	3.41	47	0	0	7	58	58	27	22	4	29	48	.257	.250	.260	7.45	4.50
Garvin, Grayson	L-L	6-6	225	10-27-89	1	8	3.77	20	20	0	0	74	76	32	31	5	15	60	.271	.246	.280	7.30	1.82
Gomez, Roberto	R-R	6-5	178	8-3-89	2	4	5.97	8	8	0	0	38	51	28	25	2	6	21	.331	.271	.358	5.02	1.43
Hellickson, Jeremy	R-R	6-1	190	4-8-87	0	0	1.50	1	1	0	0	6	5	1	1	0	0	11	.227	.400	.176	16.50	0.00
Lara, Braulio	L-L	6-1	180	12-20-88	2	1	5.01	36	0	0	3	47	49	27	26	2	19	46	.266	.236	.279	8.87	3.66
Lollis, Matt	R-R	6-9	250	9-11-90	6	2	4.03	49	0	0	3	74	76	41	33	8	32	70	.271	.313	.255	8.55	3.91
Markel, Parker	R-R	6-4	220	9-15-90	0	1	3.78	16	0	0	0	17	17	10	7	0	9	14	.258	.167	.310	7.56	4.86
Mateo, Victor	R-R	6-5	175	7-27-89	12	11	3.90	28	28	2	0	166	172	84	72	12	55	99	.267	.260	.270	5.37	2.98
Mortensen, Jared	L-R	5-11	205	6-1-88	5	1	5.73	12	9	0	0	55	58	40	35	5	31	42	.270	.284	.264	6.87	5.07
Neil, Matt	R-R	6-6	225	9-5-86	1	2	7.40	7	3	0	0	21	34	17	17	3	4	19	.366	.407	.348	8.27	1.74
Patterson, Jimmy	R-L	6-0	190	2-9-89	4	0	4.08	35	4	0	2	64	67	29	29	6	12	52	.269	.254	.275	7.31	1.69
Ramsey, Matt	R-R	5-11	205	9-24-89	3	0	1.07	24	0	0	6	34	16	4	4	0	23	46	.148	.231	.101	12.30	6.15
2-team total (20 Jacksonville)					3	2	1.47	44	0	0	14	61	35	16	10	2	30	80	—	—	11.74	4.40
Runion, Sam	R-R	6-4	220	11-9-88	0	0	5.27	9	0	0	0	14	14	11	8	2	6	12	.264	.000	.400	7.90	3.95
Sanchez, Angel	R-R	6-1	190	11-28-89	0	1	8.00	2	2	0	0	9	11	8	8	2	2	6	.289	.364	.188	6.00	2.00
3-team total (3 Birmingham, 12 Jacksonville)					1	11	6.96	17	17	0	0	76	102	66	59	6	25	45	—	—	5.31	2.95
Stowell, Bryce	R-R	6-2	205	9-23-86	4	2	1.99	38	0	0	3	50	39	16	11	1	20	54	.218	.308	.181	9.73	3.62
Suarez, Albert	R-R	6-3	235	10-8-89	3	6	4.34	11	11	0	0	56	67	34	27	4	19	32	.303	.341	.277	5.14	3.05
Thompson, Jake	R-R	6-2	225	8-8-89	1	0	2.08	10	0	0	1	17	18	6	4	1	4	14	.261	.276	.250	7.27	2.08

Fielding

Catcher	PCT	G	PO	A	E	DP	PB
Bailey	.963	15	93	10	4	1	6
Casali	1.000	15	120	6	0	2	0
DePew	.975	17	107	12	3	0	1
Maile	.995	80	588	62	3	7	11
O'Conner	.964	14	90	18	4	1	0

First Base	PCT	G	PO	A	E	DP
Malm	.978	21	127	9	3	17
Segovia	.996	25	212	11	1	18
Seitzer	.998	100	848	37	2	95

Second Base	PCT	G	PO	A	E	DP
Brett	.956	100	189	272	21	78
Guevara	.947	16	20	34	3	8

		G	PO	A	E	DP
Motter	.972	16	25	44	2	7
Reginatto	.980	11	15	33	1	8
Torrez	.857	5	5	7	2	2

Third Base	PCT	G	PO	A	E	DP
Guevara	.929	10	6	20	2	2
Motter	.857	2	2	4	1	1
Seitzer	1.000	2	1	2	0	0
Shaffer	.914	109	73	205	26	15
Torrez	.896	19	14	29	5	2

Shortstop	PCT	G	PO	A	E	DP
Guevara	.941	7	10	22	2	7
Hager	.957	112	147	316	21	74
Motter	.932	11	13	28	3	7

		G	PO	A	E	DP
Reginatto	1.000	6	8	20	0	3
Seitzer	1.000	2	2	6	0	0
Torrez	.947	5	9	9	1	3

Outfield	PCT	G	PO	A	E	DP
Argo	.983	116	227	5	4	1
Carter	.966	56	137	4	5	1
Malm	.971	64	125	7	4	1
Moore	.982	33	55	0	1	0
Motter	.981	93	183	24	4	6
Rickard	.981	68	151	7	3	4
Segovia	1.000	3	9	0	0	0
Torrez	—	2	0	0	0	0

CHARLOTTE STONE CRABS   HIGH CLASS A

FLORIDA STATE LEAGUE

Batting	B-T	HT	WT	DOB	AVG	vLH	vRH	G	AB	R	H	2B	3B	HR	RBI	BB	HBP	SH	SF	SO	SB	CS	SLG	OBP
Bailey, Luke	R-R	6-0	198	3-11-91	.173	.217	.138	15	52	6	9	2	0	2	7	4	0	0	0	18	0	0	.327	.232

Player	B-T	HT	WT	DOB	AVG	vLH	vRH	G	AB	R	H	2B	3B	HR	RBI	BB	HBP	SH	SF	SO	SB	CS	OBP	SLG
Beckham, Tim	R-R	6-0	195	1-27-90	.167	.250	.125	3	12	2	2	0	0	0	0	1	0	0	0	4	0	0	.167	.231
Carter, Kes	L-L	6-2	205	3-3-90	.230	.222	.233	61	222	24	51	10	3	2	25	25	0	3	1	55	5	1	.329	.306
Casali, Curt	R-R	6-2	225	11-9-88	.000	—	.000	2	7	0	0	0	0	0	0	0	0	0	0	3	0	0	.000	.000
Coyle, Tommy	R-R	5-7	170	10-24-90	.249	.264	.244	117	461	72	115	13	8	5	37	52	6	2	4	97	30	4	.345	.331
DeJesus, David	L-L	5-11	190	12-20-79	.227	.500	.200	7	22	1	5	0	0	0	2	4	1	0	1	4	1	1	.227	.357
DePew, Jake	R-R	6-1	220	3-1-92	.245	.370	.194	30	94	10	23	2	0	0	5	15	1	1	1	19	0	0	.266	.351
Escobar, Yunel	R-R	6-2	215	11-2-82	.143	1.000	.000	2	7	2	1	0	0	0	1	0	0	0	0	1	0	0	.143	.143
Field, Johnny	R-R	5-10	190	2-20-92	.320	.405	.287	40	150	33	48	13	3	5	17	13	6	0	0	28	5	4	.547	.396
Gantt, Marty	R-L	5-11	179	2-11-90	.262	.277	.256	86	282	42	74	14	6	4	31	38	7	2	3	62	9	5	.397	.361
Goeddel, Tyler	R-R	6-4	186	10-20-92	.269	.207	.294	113	424	41	114	25	8	6	61	46	7	0	2	98	20	9	.408	.349
Goetzman, Granden	R-R	6-4	200	11-14-92	.213	.167	.230	50	174	14	37	6	2	1	13	6	5	0	0	53	3	3	.287	.259
Guevara, Hector	R-R	6-0	192	10-7-91	.207	.235	.190	24	92	9	19	5	0	0	4	6	0	2	2	11	1	0	.261	.250
Hanigan, Ryan	R-R	6-0	210	8-16-80	.250	.500	.143	6	20	4	5	0	0	1	2	2	2	0	0	3	0	0	.400	.375
Leonard, Patrick	R-R	6-4	225	10-20-92	.284	.256	.293	122	455	79	129	26	5	13	58	49	7	0	4	107	14	0	.448	.359
O'Conner, Justin	R-R	6-0	190	3-31-92	.282	.287	.280	80	319	40	90	31	2	10	44	15	4	0	2	78	0	0	.486	.321
Querecuto, Juniel	B-R	5-9	155	9-19-92	.194	.167	.203	27	93	9	18	0	2	0	8	2	0	0	0	19	0	1	.237	.211
Quinonez, Jonathan	R-R	6-1	187	11-27-90	.221	.211	.224	54	172	18	38	6	1	2	24	10	7	2	2	38	3	0	.302	.288
Reginatto, Leonardo	R-R	6-2	179	4-10-90	.316	.346	.304	94	364	45	115	16	2	0	35	38	5	2	4	46	14	2	.371	.384
Ridings, Julian	L-R	6-2	175	3-1-92	.272	.304	.263	29	103	7	28	5	4	2	8	3	1	2	0	22	2	2	.456	.299
Sale, Josh	L-R	6-0	215	7-5-91	.238	.179	.259	90	323	34	77	14	4	4	46	35	1	0	2	109	0	4	.344	.313
Soriano, Ariel	R-R	5-11	160	11-24-91	.276	.303	.264	31	105	11	29	9	2	1	19	7	2	0	1	18	4	1	.429	.330
Tissenbaum, Maxx	B-R	5-10	185	7-25-91	.288	.307	.282	86	333	41	96	15	2	6	51	19	3	0	6	35	0	0	.399	.327
Toles, Andrew	L-R	5-10	185	5-24-92	.261	.278	.255	46	199	28	52	10	1	1	13	12	1	3	3	34	18	10	.337	.302
Zobrist, Ben	B-R	6-3	210	5-26-81	.250	.000	.333	1	4	0	1	0	0	0	0	1	0	0	0	0	0	0	.250	.400

Pitching	B-T	HT	WT	DOB	W	L	ERA	G	GS	CG	SV	IP	H	R	ER	HR	BB	SO	AVG	vLH	vRH	K/9	BB/9
Ames, Jeff	R-R	6-4	225	1-31-91	1	6	6.29	8	7	0	0	34	44	27	24	7	16	21	.319	.267	.359	5.50	4.19
Brandt, Kevin	R-L	6-1	195	11-24-89	3	2	1.17	30	0	0	4	54	39	10	7	2	20	45	.204	.261	.172	7.50	3.33
Cabrera, Luis	R-R	6-2	185	8-14-90	0	0	10.80	2	0	0	1	3	7	6	4	1	3	3	.368	.000	.538	8.10	8.10
Cobb, Alex	R-R	6-3	200	10-7-87	1	0	0.00	1	1	0	0	5	3	0	0	0	0	9	.176	.091	.333	16.20	0.00
Colome, Alex	R-R	6-2	210	12-31-88	0	1	1.64	3	3	0	0	11	7	2	2	0	5	10	.179	.235	.136	8.18	4.09
Cooper, Zach	R-R	5-10	185	1-6-90	0	3	5.92	22	0	0	7	24	24	17	16	3	12	22	.261	.250	.269	8.14	4.44
Echarry, Eli	R-R	6-1	150	7-1-92	0	0	4.00	5	0	0	0	9	10	9	4	1	5	8	.270	.200	.353	8.00	5.00
Gabay, Willie	R-R	6-0	180	7-3-91	0	0	1.35	3	0	0	0	7	6	1	1	0	4	4	.240	.111	.313	5.40	5.40
Garton, Ryan	R-R	5-11	170	12-5-89	6	2	3.07	40	0	0	4	67	61	29	23	3	28	44	.244	.184	.286	5.88	3.74
Gomez, Roberto	R-R	6-5	178	8-3-89	1	2	4.50	7	7	0	0	40	47	21	20	2	15	19	.301	.279	.329	4.28	3.38
Griset, Ben	L-L	6-1	175	3-12-92	1	1	0.71	5	0	0	0	13	11	4	1	0	3	9	.239	.300	.192	6.39	2.13
Harrison, Jordan	R-L	6-1	180	4-9-91	3	3	3.45	14	4	0	1	44	35	19	17	2	15	41	.215	.228	.208	8.32	3.05
Hellickson, Jeremy	R-R	6-1	190	4-8-87	0	1	2.25	2	2	0	0	8	9	4	2	0	2	6	.281	.292	.250	6.75	2.25
Lopez, Reinaldo	R-R	6-3	221	4-27-91	7	5	3.49	26	25	0	0	142	135	70	55	6	58	79	.249	.250	.248	5.01	3.68
Markel, Parker	R-R	6-4	220	9-15-90	2	3	5.18	29	0	0	2	49	54	31	28	2	17	37	.281	.333	.246	6.84	3.14
Molina, Jose	L-L	5-11	160	6-26-91	5	5	3.78	39	0	0	1	64	66	30	27	0	33	45	.262	.288	.250	6.30	4.62
Mortensen, Jared	L-R	5-11	205	6-1-88	2	1	2.93	7	7	0	0	31	25	12	10	3	9	30	.219	.241	.200	8.80	2.64
Peralta, Joel	R-R	5-11	210	3-23-76	0	0	0.00	1	1	0	0	1	1	0	0	0	0	1	.250	.333	.000	9.00	0.00
Proctor, Marcus	R-R	6-3	170	8-21-91	5	7	3.93	35	2	0	5	87	96	46	38	5	20	55	.284	.270	.296	5.69	2.07
Pruitt, Austin	R-R	5-11	165	8-31-89	9	7	3.73	26	25	0	0	147	144	70	61	12	31	106	.255	.261	.250	6.49	1.90
Reavis, Colton	R-R	6-0	195	12-16-89	1	2	1.02	15	0	0	7	18	10	4	2	1	5	13	.164	.065	.267	6.62	2.55
Rodriguez, Jorge	R-R	5-11	187	12-15-91	0	0	2.70	1	0	0	0	3	4	1	1	0	1	3	.308	.125	.600	8.10	2.70
Santiago, Leonel	R-R	6-0	180	12-23-89	2	6	6.03	17	14	0	0	75	87	57	50	1	24	49	.284	.303	.265	5.91	2.89
Sawyer, Nick	R-R	5-11	175	9-23-91	1	0	6.35	20	0	0	0	23	19	21	16	1	36	18	.238	.188	.271	7.15	14.29
Schultz, Jaime	R-R	5-10	200	6-20-91	2	0	3.13	5	5	0	0	23	19	9	8	0	15	21	.226	.263	.196	8.22	5.87
Slaton, D.J.	R-R	6-2	195	10-10-92	0	1	13.50	2	0	0	0	3	7	6	5	1	5	0	.389	.455	.286	0.00	13.50
Snell, Blake	L-L	6-4	180	12-4-92	5	5	3.94	16	16	1	0	75	69	40	33	1	37	77	.245	.205	.263	9.20	4.42
Stanek, Ryne	R-R	6-4	180	7-26-91	1	1	5.54	3	3	0	0	13	13	8	8	0	5	4	.277	.304	.250	2.77	3.46
Suarez, Albert	R-R	6-3	235	10-8-89	1	0	0.64	3	3	0	0	14	14	1	1	0	1	10	.255	.323	.167	6.43	0.64
Suero, Bruedlin	L-L	6-4	170	2-28-90	3	3	4.82	16	8	0	1	62	71	37	33	6	12	36	.285	.219	.313	5.25	1.75
Weathers, Casey	R-R	6-1	205	6-10-85	0	2	13.06	8	0	0	0	10	14	15	15	1	12	8	.359	.412	.318	6.97	10.45

Fielding

Catcher	PCT	G	PO	A	E	DP	PB
Bailey	.962	8	49	2	2	0	1
Casali	1.000	1	4	1	0	1	0
DePew	.992	21	106	14	1	1	4
Hanigan	1.000	3	17	0	0	0	0
O'Conner	.975	68	439	66	13	6	13
Tissenbaum	.992	36	218	22	2	0	17

First Base	PCT	G	PO	A	E	DP
Leonard	.990	104	957	58	10	84
Quinonez	.983	32	269	22	5	23

Second Base	PCT	G	PO	A	E	DP
Beckham	.923	3	5	7	1	1
Coyle	.974	114	205	357	15	67

	PCT	G	PO	A	E	DP
Guevara	.923	9	14	34	4	8
Soriano	1.000	6	15	21	0	2
Zobrist	1.000	1	3	3	0	1

Third Base	PCT	G	PO	A	E	DP
Goeddel	.920	106	65	221	25	20
Guevara	.952	6	3	17	1	0
Leonard	.923	6	2	10	1	1
Quinonez	.932	17	12	29	3	2

Shortstop	PCT	G	PO	A	E	DP
Escobar	1.000	2	4	4	0	0
Guevara	.947	7	13	23	2	3
Querecuto	.981	27	38	67	2	17
Quinonez	—	1	0	0	0	0

	PCT	G	PO	A	E	DP
Reginatto	.943	94	142	269	25	54
Soriano	.947	5	7	11	1	3

Outfield	PCT	G	PO	A	E	DP
Carter	.979	61	132	5	3	2
DeJesus	1.000	3	3	0	0	0
Field	1.000	40	93	2	0	1
Gantt	.980	85	191	5	4	1
Goetzman	.971	41	65	2	2	1
Quinonez	.750	2	2	1	1	0
Ridings	.986	29	65	4	1	0
Sale	.965	79	134	2	5	0
Soriano	1.000	20	38	4	0	1
Toles	.983	46	107	7	2	2

BOWLING GREEN HOT RODS

MIDWEST LEAGUE

Batting	B-T	HT	WT	DOB	AVG	vLH	vRH	G	AB	R	H	2B	3B	HR	RBI	BB	HBP	SH	SF	SO	SB	CS	SLG	OBP
Adames, Willy	R-R	6-1	180	9-2-95	.278	.125	.309	27	97	15	27	5	2	2	11	15	1	0	1	30	3	0	.433	.377
2-team total (98 West Michigan)					.271	—	—	125	450	55	122	19	14	8	61	54	4	4	2	126	6	6	.429	.353
Araiza, Armando	R-R	5-11	185	6-19-93	.214	.194	.219	93	345	36	74	11	0	8	43	35	3	1	1	101	0	2	.316	.292
Araujo, Yoel	R-R	6-0	190	12-3-93	.226	.222	.227	61	217	31	49	5	2	10	27	11	4	2	2	90	6	6	.406	.274
Blair, Pat	R-R	5-10	180	10-1-91	.252	.333	.236	96	337	53	85	16	3	3	32	44	2	7	1	60	12	4	.344	.341
Duran, Douglas	B-R	5-10	150	11-17-92	.158	.000	.176	13	38	2	6	1	0	0	5	4	0	1	0	10	0	1	.184	.238
Edwards, Spencer	R-R	6-0	170	4-7-93	.202	.132	.219	54	193	21	39	4	2	0	13	16	2	4	0	64	12	3	.244	.270
Field, Johnny	R-R	5-10	190	2-20-92	.290	.315	.285	82	317	62	92	23	5	7	41	33	7	2	3	74	18	4	.461	.367
George, Darryl	R-R	6-1	213	3-14-93	.255	.278	.249	70	251	31	64	11	3	4	29	17	3	6	3	51	9	2	.371	.307
Goetzman, Granden	R-R	6-4	200	11-14-92	.315	.405	.295	60	235	40	74	20	3	7	31	10	3	0	1	53	7	7	.515	.349
Harris, James	R-R	6-1	180	8-7-93	.230	.321	.202	70	244	22	56	8	0	7	25	23	1	0	0	69	11	3	.348	.299
Hernandez, Oscar	R-R	6-0	196	7-9-93	.249	.242	.250	94	362	43	90	18	5	9	63	25	4	1	5	78	3	6	.401	.301
Querecuto, Juniel	B-R	5-9	155	9-19-92	.291	.304	.288	88	354	45	103	13	1	2	37	25	1	6	1	44	5	5	.350	.339
Ridings, Julian	L-R	6-2	175	3-1-92	.252	.263	.250	37	139	17	35	3	2	2	9	7	0	0	1	37	4	2	.345	.286
Simon, Alexander	B-R	6-2	182	9-28-92	.281	.305	.276	122	430	49	121	22	3	4	49	25	3	5	3	110	10	6	.374	.323
Smedley, Sean	R-R	6-1	195	9-28-90	.136	.231	.097	15	44	1	6	0	0	0	2	8	0	0	0	16	0	1	.136	.269
Soriano, Ariel	R-R	5-11	160	11-24-91	.250	.273	.245	33	128	16	32	13	0	2	16	6	0	0	0	20	2	1	.398	.284
Torres, Elias	R-R	6-1	176	2-22-92	.261	.185	.278	42	142	13	37	10	0	2	17	9	1	1	1	45	2	0	.373	.307
Wong, Kean	L-R	5-11	190	4-17-95	.306	.256	.317	106	422	56	129	15	3	2	24	27	1	2	2	73	13	7	.370	.347
Young, Ty	L-R	5-10	173	7-17-92	.252	.246	.254	97	333	52	84	17	8	9	50	42	12	1	2	95	9	6	.432	.355

Pitching	B-T	HT	WT	DOB	W	L	ERA	G	GS	CG	SV	IP	H	R	ER	HR	BB	SO	AVG	vLH	vRH	K/9	BB/9
Cabrera, Luis	R-R	6-2	185	8-14-90	1	1	4.50	17	0	0	1	30	25	16	15	4	18	24	.229	.220	.235	7.20	5.40
Faria, Jacob	R-R	6-3	175	7-30-93	7	9	3.46	23	23	1	0	120	113	60	46	9	32	107	.248	.263	.239	8.05	2.41
Gabay, Willie	R-R	6-0	180	7-3-91	2	1	2.13	21	0	0	1	42	35	10	10	4	7	39	.230	.245	.223	8.29	1.49
Gil, Isaac	R-R	6-5	230	10-8-91	1	2	5.88	7	5	0	0	26	33	20	17	2	5	27	.306	.362	.262	9.35	1.73
Griffin, Aaron	R-R	6-4	200	6-17-91	3	4	5.82	17	0	0	1	39	48	29	25	6	14	29	.300	.233	.340	6.75	3.26
Griset, Ben	L-L	6-1	175	3-12-92	2	8	3.86	15	12	0	0	72	95	40	31	8	13	56	.315	.220	.333	6.97	1.62
Hanse, Andrew	R-R	6-7	210	5-13-91	1	3	4.96	32	0	0	0	65	80	48	36	5	15	45	.301	.302	.300	6.20	2.07
Harrison, Jordan	R-L	6-1	180	4-9-91	1	1	3.30	6	6	0	0	30	30	17	11	2	9	11	.254	.304	.242	3.30	2.70
Kendall, Ian	R-R	6-0	205	11-11-91	3	1	2.48	17	0	0	1	29	16	13	8	0	23	27	.162	.094	.194	8.38	7.14
Kimborowicz, Josh	R-R	6-3	215	3-17-92	0	0	2.91	17	0	0	2	34	24	11	11	4	7	29	.197	.116	.241	7.68	1.85
Kirsch, Chris	L-L	6-2	185	11-15-91	9	8	2.83	24	24	0	0	134	121	55	42	9	41	82	.239	.178	.255	5.52	2.76
Marquez, German	R-R	6-1	184	2-22-95	5	7	3.21	22	18	0	0	98	83	43	35	5	29	95	.228	.200	.245	8.72	2.66
Miller, Brian	R-R	6-4	200	7-15-92	0	1	6.75	7	0	0	3	8	15	6	6	0	1	8	.395	.545	.333	9.00	1.13
Reavis, Colton	R-R	6-0	195	12-16-89	2	1	2.60	27	0	0	7	45	29	17	13	1	21	55	.187	.200	.179	11.00	4.20
Rodriguez, Jorge	R-R	5-11	187	12-15-91	2	6	6.35	16	2	0	1	40	51	33	28	6	15	30	.313	.273	.333	6.81	3.40
Schreiber, Brad	R-R	6-3	225	2-13-91	2	7	3.57	35	0	0	1	68	55	33	27	2	24	82	.214	.227	.207	10.85	3.18
Schultz, Jaime	R-R	5-10	200	6-20-91	2	1	1.95	9	9	0	0	37	27	9	8	2	14	58	.203	.220	.189	14.11	3.41
Slaton, D.J.	R-R	6-2	195	10-10-92	0	3	9.51	9	5	0	0	24	37	28	25	6	13	20	.359	.262	.426	7.61	4.94
Snell, Blake	L-L	6-4	180	12-4-92	3	2	1.79	8	8	0	0	40	26	10	8	1	19	42	.184	.173	.188	9.37	4.24
Speer, Stone	L-L	5-11	180	6-10-91	6	3	3.55	36	0	0	4	79	64	42	31	5	51	77	.226	.176	.242	8.81	5.83
Stanek, Ryne	R-R	6-4	180	7-26-91	3	4	3.63	9	9	0	0	45	47	23	18	2	13	46	.275	.266	.280	9.27	2.62
Suero, Bruedlin	L-L	6-4	170	2-28-90	5	4	4.23	11	11	0	0	66	79	39	31	12	11	59	.296	.235	.310	8.05	1.50
Wood, Hunter	R-R	6-1	175	8-12-93	1	0	4.07	6	6	0	0	24	22	13	11	4	12	21	.244	.241	.246	7.77	4.44

Fielding

Catcher	PCT	G	PO	A	E	DP	PB
Araiza	.979	68	488	81	12	9	5
Hernandez	.982	69	523	80	11	4	12
Smedley	1.000	1	2	1	0	0	0

First Base	PCT	G	PO	A	E	DP
Blair	1.000	2	17	0	0	1
George	.992	28	233	15	2	20
Simon	.988	111	917	80	12	87

Second Base	PCT	G	PO	A	E	DP
Blair	.963	32	61	70	5	14
Duran	1.000	3	5	4	0	1
George	.952	10	20	20	2	6

	PCT	G	PO	A	E	DP
Wong	.985	97	191	255	7	58

Third Base	PCT	G	PO	A	E	DP
Blair	.951	35	12	66	4	3
Duran	.900	10	2	16	2	2
George	.974	15	14	23	1	2
Smedley	1.000	1	0	1	0	0
Young	.890	85	52	134	23	14

Shortstop	PCT	G	PO	A	E	DP
Adames	.955	25	42	65	5	9
Blair	.904	27	38	84	13	19
George	1.000	1	2	4	0	2
Querecuto	.950	86	126	233	19	44

Outfield	PCT	G	PO	A	E	DP
Araujo	.953	55	95	6	5	3
Blair	—	1	0	0	0	0
Edwards	.955	50	102	3	5	0
Field	.989	78	179	5	2	1
George	.889	13	14	2	2	0
Goetzman	.966	52	82	4	3	0
Harris	.964	66	101	6	4	2
Kimborowicz	—	1	1	0	0	0
Ridings	.975	34	75	4	2	0
Smedley	—	1	0	0	0	0
Soriano	1.000	29	50	4	0	2
Torres	.972	41	60	9	2	1

HUDSON VALLEY RENEGADES

NEW YORK-PENN LEAGUE

Batting	B-T	HT	WT	DOB	AVG	vLH	vRH	G	AB	R	H	2B	3B	HR	RBI	BB	HBP	SH	SF	SO	SB	CS	SLG	OBP
Alexander, John	L-L	6-5	200	4-25-93	.500	—	.500	1	2	0	1	0	0	0	1	0	0	0	0	0	0	0	.500	.667
Blanchard, Coty	R-R	6-0	180	12-16-91	.298	.268	.307	66	248	35	74	15	5	2	30	24	2	1	1	47	22	12	.423	.364
Conrad, Jace	L-R	5-11	195	12-15-92	.265	.352	.241	65	257	35	68	9	5	2	24	10	3	2	3	40	19	5	.362	.297
Correa, Leopoldo	L-R	6-0	186	12-3-91	.256	.235	.260	26	90	6	23	3	0	0	5	2	0	0	1	18	0	1	.289	.269
Dominguez, Wilmer	R-R	5-10	180	6-19-91	.248	.242	.250	47	165	13	41	4	1	0	24	9	1	1	2	54	0	2	.285	.288
Duran, Douglas	B-R	5-10	150	11-17-92	.176	.111	.200	13	34	0	6	2	0	0	0	0	0	1	0	12	0	0	.235	.176
Garcia, David	R-R	5-9	190	3-30-91	.231	.000	.300	5	13	1	3	0	0	0	0	0	0	0	0	7	0	1	.231	.231

Batting	B-T	HT	WT	DOB	AVG	vLH	vRH	G	AB	R	H	2B	3B	HR	RBI	BB	HBP	SH	SF	SO	SB	CS	SLG	OBP
Gillaspie, Casey	B-L	6-4	240	1-25-93	.262	.305	.250	71	263	27	69	16	1	7	42	42	1	0	2	65	2	3	.411	.364
Henning, Clayton	L-L	6-3	180	11-9-93	.211	.143	.222	29	95	11	20	6	0	0	18	6	1	0	1	43	4	0	.274	.262
Jackson, Bralin	R-L	6-2	183	12-2-93	.279	.310	.273	62	229	37	64	13	4	1	23	25	0	3	1	64	17	4	.384	.349
James, Mac	R-R	6-1	195	6-2-93	.263	.231	.273	16	57	7	15	3	0	0	1	6	3	0	0	6	1	1	.316	.364
Kay, Grant	R-R	6-0	185	5-29-93	.314	.429	.290	42	159	27	50	14	4	2	20	12	5	0	2	30	2	4	.409	.376
Lee, Braxton	L-R	5-10	185	8-23-93	.287	.273	.291	51	202	36	58	7	1	0	13	19	1	4	1	33	12	9	.332	.350
Lockwood, Hunter	R-R	5-10	180	9-16-92	.266	.232	.274	70	271	47	72	13	5	13	46	15	5	0	3	98	2	2	.494	.313
Marberry, Zach	R-R	6-4	200	2-1-91	.244	.364	.206	14	45	2	11	1	0	0	3	5	1	1	1	20	1	0	.267	.327
Miles, Daniel	R-R	6-2	190	8-9-91	.219	.217	.219	28	96	11	21	7	1	0	6	8	4	0	0	21	3	1	.313	.306
Montes, Hector	R-R	6-0	235	2-21-92	.000	.000	.000	2	8	0	0	0	0	0	0	1	0	0	0	3	0	0	.000	.111
Sole, Alec	L-R	6-2	200	6-1-93	.199	.220	.194	63	206	19	41	5	2	0	16	21	5	4	3	34	13	2	.243	.285
Talley, Chris	R-R	6-0	220	3-14-90	.196	.364	.143	14	46	3	9	2	0	0	2	1	1	1	0	16	0	0	.239	.229
Torres, Elias	R-R	6-1	176	2-22-92	.270	.333	.255	17	63	6	17	1	1	0	1	5	0	1	0	11	8	2	.317	.324

Pitching	B-T	HT	WT	DOB	W	L	ERA	G	GS	CG	SV	IP	H	R	ER	HR	BB	SO	AVG	vLH	vRH	K/9	BB/9
Alonzo, Jose	R-R	6-4	191	2-24-93	1	2	4.94	7	7	0	0	31	35	20	17	3	10	23	.289	.217	.361	6.68	2.90
Armenta, Oscar	R-L	5-11	170	10-15-93	4	3	3.66	13	13	1	0	64	66	30	26	4	17	50	.268	.347	.236	7.03	2.39
Dunlap, Trevor	R-R	6-7	230	6-15-92	0	3	3.12	9	0	0	0	17	20	7	6	1	2	12	.294	.222	.341	6.23	1.04
Echarry, Eli	R-R	6-1	150	7-1-92	2	1	2.84	17	1	0	3	38	33	18	12	1	9	30	.234	.211	.257	7.11	2.13
Fernandez, Mario	R-R	6-0	206	9-7-93	0	0	0.00	1	0	0	0	3	2	0	0	0	2	2	.182	.000	.250	6.00	6.00
Fierro, Edwin	R-R	6-1	200	8-30-93	0	2	4.38	7	0	0	2	12	14	6	6	0	1	6	.280	.304	.259	4.38	0.73
Fischer, Darren	L-L	6-2	185	8-8-92	1	1	7.27	14	0	0	0	26	38	22	21	2	19	18	.352	.364	.347	6.23	6.58
Franco, Enderson	R-R	6-2	170	12-29-92	7	3	3.28	13	13	1	0	69	74	34	25	4	8	50	.277	.279	.276	6.55	1.05
Franco, Mike	R-R	5-11	200	11-20-91	0	1	4.11	10	1	0	2	15	24	9	7	1	2	18	.353	.417	.281	10.57	1.17
Gannon, Nolan	R-R	6-5	195	11-3-93	6	2	2.84	11	11	0	0	57	50	19	18	1	9	47	.234	.231	.236	7.42	1.42
Gauthier, Tyler	L-R	6-5	245	6-3-92	0	0	0.00	1	0	0	0	2	1	0	0	1	1	.143	.250	.000	4.50	4.50
Gil, Isaac	R-R	6-5	230	10-8-91	5	0	0.00	7	0	0	2	19	9	0	0	0	7	23	.145	.040	.216	11.09	3.38
Gomez, Edgar	R-R	5-11	190	1-5-93	4	4	2.44	16	2	0	1	48	31	14	13	4	13	41	.182	.227	.154	7.69	2.44
Kimborowicz, Josh	R-R	6-3	215	3-17-92	0	1	1.08	4	0	0	0	8	5	1	1	0	2	6	.200	.286	.167	6.48	2.16
McCalvin, Justin	R-R	6-0	180	1-14-92	1	1	2.66	13	0	0	2	24	21	7	7	2	7	18	.239	.308	.184	6.85	2.66
McKenzie, Kyle	R-R	6-1	205	9-13-90	1	0	1.06	11	0	0	3	17	11	6	2	0	7	16	.175	.125	.205	8.47	3.71
Miller, Brian	R-R	6-4	200	7-15-92	0	0	0.00	7	0	0	3	13	2	1	0	0	1	16	.045	.000	.074	11.08	0.69
Pennell, Ryan	R-L	6-4	210	7-14-92	1	0	4.22	16	0	0	0	21	22	13	10	1	9	22	.262	.167	.300	9.28	3.80
Pike, Chris	R-R	6-0	175	10-11-92	4	1	2.72	12	10	0	0	53	41	16	16	2	15	44	.219	.268	.167	7.47	2.55
Reyes, Gerardo	R-R	5-11	190	5-13-93	2	1	4.09	20	0	0	3	33	32	16	15	2	9	39	.258	.279	.238	10.64	2.45
Slaton, D.J.	R-R	6-2	195	10-10-92	1	1	0.64	6	5	0	0	28	19	5	2	1	7	23	.184	.182	.188	7.39	2.25
Tzamtzis, Anthony	R-R	6-0	185	11-4-90	0	0	18.00	1	0	0	0	1	1	2	2	0	1	0	.333	.000	.500	0.00	9.00
Wallace, Bradley	R-R	6-2	175	9-12-92	1	0	0.00	3	0	0	1	6	5	0	0	0	1	6	.238	.250	.231	9.00	1.50
Wood, Hunter	R-R	6-1	175	8-12-93	3	4	3.08	13	13	0	0	64	53	24	22	3	16	57	.219	.219	.219	7.97	2.24

Fielding

Catcher	PCT	G	PO	A	E	DP	PB
Dominguez	.994	44	324	35	2	1	3
James	.967	11	78	11	3	0	5
Marberry	.989	12	70	20	1	2	1
Talley	.990	12	89	7	1	2	11

First Base	PCT	G	PO	A	E	DP
Correa	.975	11	72	5	2	5
Dominguez	.909	1	10	0	1	1
Gillaspie	.997	65	557	43	2	41

Second Base	PCT	G	PO	A	E	DP
Blanchard	1.000	11	20	31	0	6

	PCT	G	PO	A	E	DP
Conrad	.988	61	76	165	3	30
Duran	1.000	4	2	6	0	0
Kay	1.000	3	3	8	0	2

Third Base	PCT	G	PO	A	E	DP
Blanchard	.944	33	22	63	5	7
Correa	1.000	7	4	7	0	0
Duran	.875	3	0	7	1	0
Garcia	1.000	4	2	7	0	2
Kay	.862	12	5	20	4	2
Miles	.809	19	12	26	9	2
Montes	.833	2	1	4	1	0

Shortstop	PCT	G	PO	A	E	DP
Blanchard	.976	12	15	26	1	4
Duran	.889	5	7	9	2	3
Sole	.967	63	91	170	9	23

Outfield	PCT	G	PO	A	E	DP
Blanchard	1.000	8	23	0	0	0
Henning	.980	26	48	0	1	0
Jackson	.988	61	159	7	2	1
Kay	1.000	15	30	1	0	0
Lee	.993	51	131	7	1	1
Lockwood	.948	51	87	4	5	2
Torres	1.000	17	28	2	0	1

PRINCETON RAYS
ROOKIE
APPALACHIAN LEAGUE

Batting	B-T	HT	WT	DOB	AVG	vLH	vRH	G	AB	R	H	2B	3B	HR	RBI	BB	HBP	SH	SF	SO	SB	CS	SLG	OBP
Burgess, Carter	R-R	6-1	200	4-6-93	.307	.431	.262	53	192	21	59	14	0	2	17	16	3	1	0	35	8	0	.411	.370
Ciuffo, Nick	L-R	6-1	205	3-7-95	.224	.143	.252	52	192	25	43	7	1	4	20	17	1	0	1	45	2	1	.333	.289
Garcia, David	R-R	5-9	190	3-30-91	.280	.333	.263	17	50	4	14	0	0	0	2	4	2	2	0	13	3	2	.280	.357
Grady, Patrick	R-L	6-0	230	12-23-91	.231	.226	.234	36	108	17	25	4	2	3	16	20	7	0	0	29	2	2	.389	.385
Grant-Parks, Blake	R-R	6-1	190	7-15-93	.242	.294	.224	21	66	5	16	3	0	0	8	8	3	0	1	16	0	0	.288	.346
Hawkins, Taylor	R-R	5-11	188	9-17-93	.211	.154	.240	21	76	6	16	4	0	1	4	4	0	0	0	26	1	0	.303	.250
Milone, Thomas	L-L	5-11	190	1-26-95	.266	.241	.274	61	233	30	62	12	4	2	23	28	2	2	1	61	12	5	.378	.348
Montes, Hector	R-R	6-0	235	2-21-92	.325	.386	.304	46	169	23	55	14	0	4	23	12	2	1	1	43	1	1	.479	.375
Moreno, Angel	R-R	6-2	180	7-31-96	.235	.229	.236	48	196	15	46	8	3	4	22	3	5	0	2	52	10	1	.367	.262
Paez, Jose	B-R	6-0	165	8-11-93	.264	.206	.292	34	106	15	28	2	2	1	10	12	1	2	0	32	5	4	.349	.345
Paulino, Enmanuel	R-R	6-1	175	11-28-93	.182	.310	.119	26	88	6	16	5	0	1	8	5	4	1	0	27	3	1	.273	.258
Pujols, Bill	R-R	5-11	160	7-19-94	—	—	—	1	0	0	0	0	0	0	0	0	0	0	0	0	0	0	—	—
Sanay, Oscar	R-R	5-7	185	2-23-92	.000	.000	.000	1	6	1	0	0	0	0	0	0	0	0	0	0	0	0	.000	.000
Sanchez, Manny	R-R	6-0	220	10-6-95	.240	.200	.255	55	208	21	50	12	2	3	17	15	2	0	1	72	2	0	.361	.296
Toribio, Cristian	R-R	5-11	170	9-3-94	.250	.359	.250	46	164	14	35	5	2	2	25	13	3	0	0	35	4	4	.485	.339
Unroe, Riley	B-R	5-10	180	8-3-95	.226	.250	.219	61	243	32	55	11	2	3	19	29	3	0	1	47	7	5	.335	.315
Wilson, Nic	R-R	6-6	240	7-21-92	.207	.210	.206	54	217	22	45	10	0	10	29	14	4	0	1	88	0	0	.392	.267

Pitching	B-T	HT	WT	DOB	W	L	ERA	G	GS	CG	SV	IP	H	R	ER	HR	BB	SO	AVG	vLH	vRH	K/9	BB/9
Alonzo, Jose	R-R	6-4	191	2-24-93	2	1	2.67	6	6	0	0	30	37	11	9	1	5	29	.314	.239	.361	8.60	1.48
Alvarez, Freddy	R-R	5-10	203	9-10-93	3	4	3.47	13	11	0	0	57	56	23	22	3	19	37	.276	.321	.246	5.84	3.00
Ascher, Steve	L-L	6-0	185	10-18-93	2	1	2.35	15	0	0	3	23	21	6	6	1	5	24	.241	.125	.268	9.39	1.96
Bird, Kyle	L-L	6-2	175	4-12-93	1	0	4.19	12	0	0	1	19	15	11	9	3	6	15	.214	.273	.203	6.98	2.79
Carroll, Damion	R-R	6-3	198	1-31-94	1	0	1.59	16	0	0	0	28	17	8	5	0	21	38	.179	.194	.169	12.07	6.67
Centeno, Henry	R-R	6-2	174	8-24-94	1	0	3.60	1	1	0	0	5	6	2	2	0	0	4	.353	.250	.385	7.20	0.00
Chirinos, Yonny	R-R	6-2	170	12-26-93	3	0	2.09	14	2	0	0	43	39	14	10	2	11	33	.244	.204	.264	6.91	2.30
Cordova, Rafael	R-R	6-2	175	11-16-94	2	4	4.75	16	0	0	2	30	33	17	16	3	7	31	.284	.171	.333	9.20	2.08
Dahlson, Bret	R-R	6-1	200	8-19-91	2	1	1.62	9	0	0	0	17	14	5	3	0	4	11	.250	.238	.257	5.94	2.16
Fernandez, Mario	R-R	6-0	206	9-7-93	3	1	3.50	15	1	0	2	36	46	14	14	2	15	35	.324	.275	.352	8.75	3.75
Formo, Hyrum	R-R	6-1	185	4-13-92	3	1	3.93	11	11	1	0	50	45	26	22	5	8	46	.236	.282	.204	8.23	1.43
Honeywell, Brent	R-R	6-2	180	3-31-95	2	1	1.07	9	8	0	0	34	19	7	4	1	6	40	.161	.204	.130	10.69	1.60
Lubking, Trevor	L-L	6-0	205	9-4-92	2	4	3.51	12	10	0	0	49	44	24	19	7	10	43	.234	.244	.231	7.95	1.85
Maisto, Greg	L-L	6-1	180	11-17-94	3	3	4.50	11	7	0	0	44	45	26	22	2	11	33	.262	.222	.276	6.75	2.25
McCalvin, Justin	R-R	6-0	180	1-14-92	1	0	0.00	4	0	0	2	5	3	0	0	0	1	5	.176	.000	.333	9.64	1.93
McKenzie, Kyle	R-R	6-1	205	9-13-90	0	1	2.08	6	0	0	1	9	12	4	2	0	1	11	.316	.250	.346	11.42	1.04
Michelson, Tomas	L-R	6-4	185	4-7-92	0	1	2.13	18	0	0	3	25	25	11	6	1	6	23	.245	.278	.227	8.17	2.13
Paredes, Ruben	R-R	6-1	180	9-21-93	2	2	2.03	18	0	0	7	31	25	10	7	3	11	39	.219	.208	.227	11.32	3.19
Ramirez, Roel	R-R	6-1	205	5-26-95	6	2	1.86	12	6	0	2	53	41	19	11	2	6	29	.206	.247	.180	4.89	1.01
Varga, Cameron	R-R	6-2	189	8-19-94	1	1	4.74	5	5	0	0	19	26	12	10	1	7	11	.338	.293	.389	5.21	3.32
Velasquez, Mike	L-L	6-1	215	2-28-93	0	0	5.40	2	0	0	0	3	3	2	2	1	0	1	.250	.000	.333	2.70	0.00

Fielding

Catcher	PCT	G	PO	A	E	DP	PB
Ciuffo	.987	42	322	55	5	6	9
Grant-Parks	1.000	8	50	4	0	0	2
Hawkins	.963	21	151	30	7	2	6

	PCT	G	PO	A	E	DP
Garcia	.986	14	30	39	1	11
Paulino	.923	3	5	7	1	0
Sanay	1.000	1	2	3	0	0
Unroe	.982	37	60	104	3	13

Shortstop	PCT	G	PO	A	E	DP
Paulino	.986	13	28	42	1	6
Toribio	.913	35	49	88	13	17
Unroe	.926	21	31	57	7	15

First Base	PCT	G	PO	A	E	DP
Grant-Parks	1.000	7	51	2	0	3
Montes	.988	28	246	5	3	21
Wilson	.994	35	312	15	2	26

Third Base	PCT	G	PO	A	E	DP
Burgess	.879	38	31	63	13	2
Garcia	1.000	3	3	4	0	2
Montes	.867	10	5	8	2	3
Paulino	.893	10	3	22	3	5
Toribio	.964	9	6	21	1	0

Outfield	PCT	G	PO	A	E	DP
Grady	1.000	25	43	2	0	0
Milone	.977	57	122	3	3	1
Moreno	.970	46	90	6	3	2
Paez	1.000	32	57	0	0	0
Sanchez	.969	50	88	6	3	1

Second Base	PCT	G	PO	A	E	DP
Burgess	.987	16	25	49	1	9

GCL RAYS   ROOKIE

GULF COAST LEAGUE

Batting	B-T	HT	WT	DOB	AVG	vLH	vRH	G	AB	R	H	2B	3B	HR	RBI	BB	HBP	SH	SF	SO	SB	CS	SLG	OBP
Alcantar, Isias	R-R	6-0	215	9-24-91	.171	.276	.132	32	105	8	18	3	0	1	17	2	6	0	3	15	4	0	.229	.224
Ayende, Jaime	B-R	6-1	170	5-28-96	.105	.148	.082	30	76	9	8	2	0	1	15	0	2	0	0	39	0	2	.132	.253
Beckham, Tim	R-R	6-0	195	1-27-90	.476	.556	.417	6	21	5	10	2	1	1	4	3	0	0	1	4	1	0	.810	.520
Clark, Mark	R-R	6-5	205	6-26-96	.000	.000	.000	7	17	1	0	0	0	0	0	1	1	0	0	5	0	0	.000	.105
DeJesus, David	L-L	5-11	190	12-20-79	.000	.000	—	1	1	1	0	0	0	0	0	1	0	0	0	0	0	0	.000	.500
DeMorais, Chris	L-R	6-0	195	6-18-92	.253	.148	.297	30	91	7	23	3	0	0	8	8	1	0	0	24	0	0	.286	.320
Ford, Matt	L-R	5-11	195	2-15-91	.218	.216	.218	48	170	15	37	11	1	0	15	12	3	0	1	36	1	3	.294	.280
Freemyer, Jonathan	R-R	6-6	280	11-24-94	.255	.368	.188	14	51	7	13	2	0	0	5	3	2	0	0	12	3	0	.294	.321
Gotta, Cade	R-R	6-4	205	8-1-91	.245	.246	.245	49	159	34	39	11	3	2	21	30	3	1	2	39	16	3	.390	.371
Grady, Patrick	R-L	6-0	230	12-23-91	.250	.167	.333	4	12	3	3	1	0	0	1	2	0	0	0	1	1	0	.333	.438
Hadley, Jeremy	R-R	6-0	205	11-21-94	.175	.208	.152	18	57	10	10	1	1	1	5	7	1	0	0	20	0	1	.281	.277
Harris, James	R-R	6-1	180	8-7-93	.267	.250	.286	4	15	2	4	1	0	0	0	1	1	0	0	2	1	0	.333	.353
Knott, Chris	R-R	6-0	215	7-20-92	.248	.290	.234	39	125	20	31	9	4	0	15	18	5	0	1	31	4	3	.384	.362
Law, Zac	R-R	5-8	180	7-8-96	.255	.244	.262	29	102	20	26	5	2	0	10	8	3	0	3	18	5	0	.343	.319
Marberry, Zach	R-R	6-4	200	2-1-91	.167	.091	.231	11	24	4	4	0	0	1	3	2	1	0	0	10	0	0	.292	.259
Mitchell, Jamie	R-R	6-0	205	2-7-90	.250	.222	.257	18	44	5	11	3	0	0	3	2	1	1	0	3	0	1	.318	.298
Pujols, Bill	R-R	5-11	160	7-19-94	.239	.220	.248	57	184	19	44	12	2	1	25	18	4	1	1	38	1	3	.342	.319
Rapacz, Josh	R-R	6-1	205	7-30-94	.139	.053	.170	30	72	4	10	1	1	0	4	3	3	0	0	9	0	0	.181	.205
Reida, Matt	L-R	5-10	160	11-24-91	.295	.176	.352	42	156	29	46	8	3	3	20	16	5	1	0	26	9	2	.442	.379
Rodriguez, David	R-R	5-11	200	2-25-96	.273	.360	.218	38	128	15	35	10	2	0	23	9	6	0	3	31	3	0	.383	.342
Rojas, Jose	R-R	6-0	175	3-11-93	.258	.209	.282	39	128	14	33	11	0	1	16	6	2	0	2	21	2	4	.367	.297
Sanay, Oscar	R-S	5-7	185	2-23-92	.329	.364	.314	43	146	15	48	8	0	0	11	15	1	0	3	17	3	2	.384	.388
Toles, Andrew	L-R	5-10	185	5-24-92	.292	.273	.308	6	24	4	7	0	1	0	2	0	1	0	0	6	6	0	.375	.320

Pitching	B-T	HT	WT	DOB	W	L	ERA	G	GS	CG	SV	IP	H	R	ER	HR	BB	SO	AVG	vLH	vRH	K/9	BB/9
Adames, Mario	R-R	6-6	210	5-29-92	1	0	1.38	6	0	0	0	13	10	2	2	0	3	8	.227	.100	.333	5.54	2.08
Alvarado, Jose	L-L	6-0	180	5-21-95	1	5	3.79	12	11	0	0	40	28	28	17	1	29	46	.190	.158	.195	10.26	6.47
Bivens, Blake	R-R	6-2	205	8-11-95	0	1	4.05	8	4	0	0	20	23	10	9	0	10	16	.311	.161	.419	7.20	4.50
Burke, Brock	L-L	6-2	170	8-4-96	0	3	10.80	8	5	0	0	13	16	20	16	1	12	12	.286	.333	.273	8.10	8.10
Cano, Joselito	L-L	6-5	190	9-16-92	0	0	2.57	5	0	0	0	14	14	6	4	1	7	15	.255	.167	.279	9.64	4.50
Casanas, Alberto	R-R	6-2	158	11-27-93	2	1	3.57	11	0	0	0	35	38	17	14	2	11	16	.273		.382	4.08	2.80
Castillo, Jose	L-L	6-4	200	1-10-96	0	0	3.86	3	0	0	0	5	3	2	2	0	2	4	.188	.000	.200	7.71	3.86
Centeno, Henry	R-R	6-2	174	8-24-94	4	2	1.50	11	11	0	0	54	38	18	9	0	11	51	.203	.211	.198	8.50	1.83
Cooper, Zach	R-R	5-10	185	1-6-90	1	0	0.00	1	0	0	0	3	2	0	0	0	3	3	.200	.250	.167	9.00	0.00
Crisostomo, Christopher	L-L	6-2	180	3-8-94	1	2	3.24	7	0	0	0	17	13	7	6	0	5	11	.220	.111	.240	5.94	2.70
Dahlson, Bret	R-R	6-1	200	8-19-91	1	0	4.00	5	0	0	0	9	7	4	4	0	2	6	.206	.000	.292	6.00	2.00

Name	B-T	HT	WT	DOB	W	L	ERA	G	GS	CG	SV	IP	H	R	ER	HR	BB	SO	AVG	vLH	vRH	K/9	BB/9
Dunlap, Trevor	R-R	6-7	230	6-15-92	1	0	0.00	4	0	0	1	5	4	2	0	0	4	4	.211	.214	.200	6.75	6.75
Feliz, Junior	R-R	6-0	160	1-17-94	4	1	2.11	12	4	0	0	43	36	14	10	2	18	30	.228	.264	.198	6.33	3.80
Fierro, Edwin	R-R	6-1	200	8-30-93	0	1	0.00	4	0	0	3	6	8	2	0	0	1	2	.333	.222	.400	2.84	1.42
Franco, Mike	R-R	5-11	200	11-20-91	1	0	0.00	1	0	0	0	2	1	0	0	0	0	2	.143	.000	.250	9.00	0.00
Gomez, Roberto	R-R	6-5	178	8-3-89	0	2	7.04	3	3	0	0	8	10	8	6	1	6	9	.313	.200	.412	10.57	7.04
Guerrieri, Taylor	R-R	6-3	195	12-1-92	0	0	0.00	5	5	0	0	9	7	3	0	0	2	10	.194	.200	.188	9.64	1.93
Harrison, Jordan	R-L	6-1	180	4-9-91	0	0	0.00	2	0	0	1	7	7	0	0	0	0	9	.250	.000	.292	11.57	0.00
Lawrence, Tommy	R-R	5-11	195	11-25-90	1	0	2.52	12	0	0	0	25	27	12	7	1	8	18	.278	.273	.281	6.48	2.88
Mendez, Deivy	R-R	6-2	160	10-27-95	2	5	6.63	11	2	0	0	37	41	32	27	6	20	29	.287	.390	.214	7.12	4.91
Moran, Spencer	R-R	6-6	180	4-2-96	4	0	4.24	7	0	0	0	17	22	9	8	0	4	10	.344	.370	.324	5.29	2.12
Mujica, Jose	R-R	6-2	200	6-29-96	0	0	0.00	2	2	0	0	3	4	1	0	0	0	2	.333	.250	.375	6.00	0.00
Nunez, Luis	R-R	5-10	185	10-29-91	1	1	8.44	7	0	0	2	11	10	10	10	1	8	9	.244	.238	.250	7.59	6.75
Quinonez, Eduar	R-R	6-3	190	8-9-89	0	0	3.00	2	2	0	0	3	2	1	1	0	0	4	.182	.333	.000	12.00	0.00
Rodriguez, Abrahan	R-R	6-2	182	4-20-95	0	1	4.50	3	0	0	0	6	9	3	3	0	0	1	.360	.385	.333	1.50	0.00
Romero, Orlando	R-R	6-0	185	9-26-96	0	0	9.64	3	0	0	0	5	5	5	5	0	2	6	.263	.200	.333	11.57	3.86
Sawyer, Nick	R-R	5-11	175	9-23-91	2	0	1.84	10	0	0	0	15	6	4	3	0	9	24	.120	.038	.208	14.73	5.52
Stanek, Ryne	R-R	6-4	180	7-26-91	0	0	0.00	1	1	0	0	1	0	0	0	0	0	0	.000	.000	.000	0.00	0.00
Varga, Cameron	R-R	6-2	189	8-19-94	2	0	2.51	5	1	0	0	14	12	4	4	0	1	14	.226	.250	.207	8.79	0.63
Velasquez, Mike	L-L	6-1	215	2-28-93	1	0	3.97	8	0	0	1	11	17	7	5	1	1	13	.340	.231	.378	10.32	0.79
Yepez, Angel	R-R	6-1	215	4-27-95	2	3	1.74	12	9	0	0	52	48	16	10	1	7	38	.245	.227	.256	6.62	1.22

Fielding

Catcher	PCT	G	PO	A	E	DP	PB
Clark	.778	2	6	1	2	0	0
Marberry	1.000	3	14	1	0	1	0
Mitchell	1.000	7	43	2	0	1	1
Rapacz	.984	13	52	9	1	2	1
Rodriguez	.982	28	193	25	4	1	7
Rojas	.985	20	116	19	2	2	12

First Base	PCT	G	PO	A	E	DP
Alcantar	.990	24	184	19	2	24
Freemyer	.989	10	84	7	1	6
Marberry	1.000	7	54	2	0	4
Rapacz	1.000	13	71	8	0	9
Rojas	.992	18	111	10	1	8

Second Base	PCT	G	PO	A	E	DP
Beckham	1.000	1	2	0	0	0
Pujols	.983	29	54	63	2	18
Reida	.941	4	6	10	1	1
Sanay	.984	32	53	67	2	19

Third Base	PCT	G	PO	A	E	DP
Alcantar	.958	6	5	18	1	3
Ford	.667	1	3	1	2	0
Pujols	.966	19	12	45	2	2
Reida	.886	35	21	80	13	11

Shortstop	PCT	G	PO	A	E	DP
Beckham	1.000	2	3	10	0	0
Ford	.934	47	73	126	14	31
Pujols	.936	12	16	28	3	6
Reida	1.000	3	3	6	0	1

Outfield	PCT	G	PO	A	E	DP
Ayende	.977	28	42	1	1	0
DeMorais	1.000	21	29	1	0	0
Gotta	.988	48	76	7	1	2
Grady	1.000	3	8	0	0	0
Hadley	.968	18	29	1	1	1
Harris	1.000	2	2	0	0	0
Knott	.983	38	46	11	1	2
Law	.956	29	40	3	2	0
Toles	1.000	5	9	0	0	0

DSL RAYS   ROOKIE

DOMINICAN SUMMER LEAGUE

Batting	B-T	HT	WT	DOB	AVG	vLH	vRH	G	AB	R	H	2B	3B	HR	RBI	BB	HBP	SH	SF	SO	SB	CS	SLG	OBP
Arias, Juan Carlos	R-R	6-3	199	9-16-95	.236	.175	.248	67	258	43	61	13	3	7	42	29	9	0	5	68	1	0	.391	.329
Astacio, Joseph	L-R	6-0	155	6-5-94	.392	.286	.410	39	143	33	56	3	2	0	15	13	1	1	1	14	18	6	.441	.443
Guzman, Carlos	R-R	6-1	145	6-22-97	.228	.261	.221	40	136	18	31	8	0	1	13	11	3	2	1	27	6	3	.309	.298
Hernandez, Miguel	R-R	6-2	175	12-28-95	.223	.333	.207	65	265	36	59	15	1	5	22	28	6	0	1	73	21	7	.343	.310
Lorenzo, Rafelin	R-R	6-2	200	1-15-97	.274	.259	.277	41	157	18	43	8	2	5	33	12	2	0	2	31	0	3	.446	.329
Maria, Eric	R-R	6-0	180	6-30-94	.198	.286	.190	26	86	7	17	3	0	0	14	9	2	1	0	13	0	0	.233	.289
Marrero, Gilbert	L-L	6-2	195	8-9-96	.284	.321	.277	53	183	27	52	10	2	5	22	32	1	0	2	42	0	1	.443	.390
Perez, Angel	R-R	6-2	185	1-10-95	.290	.324	.284	66	262	41	76	12	4	1	37	29	7	4	2	48	18	7	.378	.373
Perez, Carlos	L-L	6-1	150	6-1-97	.105	.154	.098	29	95	6	10	1	1	0	8	11	1	1	3	22	1	0	.137	.200
Rodriguez, Darinel	R-R	5-10	175	6-28-95	.206	.136	.221	43	126	18	26	9	1	1	13	25	1	2	2	30	3	4	.317	.338
Rodriguez, Juan	R-R	6-0	175	2-13-97	.227	.185	.234	54	194	31	44	7	1	6	23	32	5	0	5	39	2	3	.366	.343
Rosario, Jilber	B-R	5-11	175	9-20-94	.276	.273	.277	36	134	33	37	0	2	0	10	25	4	2	3	22	20	3	.306	.398
Santana, Jefry	R-R	6-2	170	11-26-94	.219	.167	.229	32	114	14	25	5	0	0	6	9	3	1	1	17	6	1	.263	.291
Trinidad, Jesus	R-R	5-11	166	1-11-95	.123	.167	.113	21	65	5	8	1	0	0	3	6	3	1	1	20	0	0	.138	.227
Vasquez, Jose	R-R	6-1	205	4-4-96	.244	.250	.243	44	160	25	39	4	2	2	25	11	8	3	2	47	6	6	.331	.320

Pitching	B-T	HT	WT	DOB	W	L	ERA	G	GS	CG	SV	IP	H	R	ER	HR	BB	SO	AVG	vLH	vRH	K/9	BB/9
Brito, Sandy	R-R	6-1	170	7-19-96	1	4	4.35	12	0	0	0	21	12	18	10	0	20	28	.158	.167	.154	12.19	8.71
Cabrera, Genesis	L-L	6-0	155	10-10-96	2	1	2.45	14	1	0	0	29	20	9	8	0	3	26	.187	.200	.186	7.98	0.92
Castillo, Diego	R-R	6-3	195	1-18-94	3	3	3.96	18	0	0	2	25	26	11	11	0	11	26	.274	.263	.281	9.36	3.96
Castillo, Erodis	R-R	6-1	173	11-29-93	0	1	4.68	12	4	0	0	25	24	25	13	2	13	16	.247	.167	.295	5.76	4.68
Cedeno, Estarly	R-R	6-3	180	11-7-96	1	2	6.75	15	0	0	0	28	33	27	21	2	7	14	.308	.262	.338	4.50	2.25
Collado, Oscar	R-R	6-1	180	8-30-93	0	0	2.84	4	0	0	0	6	3	4	2	0	8	6	.143	.250	.118	8.53	11.37
De La Cruz, Miguel	R-R	5-10	150	3-28-96	1	1	1.89	12	1	0	0	19	22	13	4	1	12	7	.289	.360	.255	3.32	5.68
Disla, Jose	R-R	6-2	165	3-11-96	0	3	4.05	14	14	0	0	47	43	25	21	1	29	41	.239	.179	.266	7.91	5.59
Done, Jeffry	R-R	6-5	195	6-5-95	0	2	2.78	13	9	0	0	32	17	14	10	0	19	23	.156	.176	.147	6.40	5.29
Germoso, Herminio	R-R	6-2	178	10-21-94	0	3	6.83	17	0	0	0	24	34	32	22	0	34	25	.216	.306	.173	7.76	10.55
Gracia, Ariel	L-L	5-11	173	9-17-94	2	0	3.11	14	14	0	0	64	64	26	22	0	17	50	.271	.167	.290	7.07	2.40
Guilamo, Robert	R-R	6-4	200	10-2-92	0	0	7.99	17	0	0	1	24	22	30	21	0	24	24	.247	.357	.197	9.13	11.41
Henriquez, Jean Carlos	R-R	6-3	231	7-23-93	1	1	4.91	17	0	0	0	29	26	19	16	3	19	26	.250	.333	.211	7.98	5.83
Inoa, Odelis	R-R	6-1	180	9-2-94	0	5	3.53	14	14	0	0	51	41	29	20	0	23	42	.218	.280	.177	7.41	4.06
Mena, Francisco	R-R	6-4	195	11-4-93	3	3	2.66	15	0	0	2	24	15	7	7	1	8	16	.174	.227	.156	6.08	3.04
Nunez, Luis	R-R	5-10	185	10-29-91	3	0	1.64	12	0	0	2	22	16	6	4	0	9	20	.195	.144	.222	8.18	3.68
Ortiz, Willy	R-R	6-1	174	7-20-95	5	4	4.21	13	13	0	0	51	52	34	24	2	10	34	.261	.250	.266	5.96	1.75
Pena, Francisco	R-R	5-11	190	2-28-93	2	2	4.67	17	0	0	0	27	25	23	14	1	25	18	.243	.278	.224	6.00	8.33
Salvador, Kendri	R-R	6-2	200	8-14-94	2	2	5.27	19	0	0	3	27	32	25	16	2	27	17	.311	.281	.324	5.60	8.89

Sanchez, Cristopher	L-L	6-5	165	12-12-96	1	3	7.77	13	0	0	0	22	36	26	19	0	16	13	.379	.333	.390	5.32	6.55
Thomas, Luigence	R-R	6-3	160	10-12-94	3	0	4.24	11	0	0	0	17	18	10	8	0	10	14	.273	.346	.225	7.41	5.29

Fielding

Catcher	PCT	G	PO	A	E	DP	PB
Lorenzo	.958	39	236	58	13	1	19
Maria	.945	25	172	35	12	1	4
Trinidad	.952	11	63	16	4	1	4

First Base	PCT	G	PO	A	E	DP
Maria	1.000	1	5	0	0	0
Marrero	.973	53	444	17	13	29
Rodriguez	1.000	9	83	7	0	5
Trinidad	.988	10	76	3	1	6

Second Base	PCT	G	PO	A	E	DP
Astacio	.963	14	22	30	2	6

Rodriguez	.934	19	23	34	4	7
Rosario	.955	34	63	86	7	14
Santana	.912	7	17	14	3	3

Third Base	PCT	G	PO	A	E	DP
Arias	.897	41	36	77	13	6
Astacio	1.000	2	4	1	0	0
Rodriguez	.714	6	1	9	4	1
Astacio	.865	24	31	46	12	5

Shortstop	PCT	G	PO	A	E	DP
Astacio	.947	16	17	37	3	3
Guzman	.859	38	56	84	23	18

Rodriguez	1.000	1	2	4	0	1
Santana	.892	23	40	59	12	4

Outfield	PCT	G	PO	A	E	DP
Astacio	1.000	11	13	0	0	
Hernandez	.940	64	136	6	9	2
Perez	.957	66	166	10	8	3
Perez	.936	29	39	5	3	0
Rodriguez	.929	7	12	1	1	0
Vasquez	.952	37	78	1	4	0

VSL RAYS — ROOKIE

VENEZUELAN SUMMER LEAGUE

Batting	B-T	HT	WT	DOB	AVG	vLH	vRH	G	AB	R	H	2B	3B	HR	RBI	BB	HBP	SH	SF	SO	SB	CS	SLG	OBP
Alvarez, Alexander	R-R	5-11	200	9-14-96	.231	.219	.235	40	134	14	31	10	0	1	12	8	2	0	1	31	2	1	.328	.283
Apaez, Cesar	R-R	6-1	182	5-19-95	.201	.103	.236	45	149	17	30	4	1	0	11	9	2	0	0	39	6	2	.242	.256
Auciello, Kreiber	R-R	5-10	176	2-23-95	.288	.282	.289	44	153	10	44	7	2	2	19	7	2	0	0	32	1	1	.399	.327
Balcazar, Randhi	R-R	6-0	160	12-19-96	.236	.167	.263	53	191	16	45	4	2	0	10	5	4	2	1	55	10	10	.277	.269
Barrios, Kevin	R-R	6-1	190	8-28-95	.277	.276	.278	54	202	18	56	11	1	4	34	6	2	0	1	27	5	2	.401	.303
Cabrera, Eleardo	L-R	5-10	185	11-8-95	.234	.114	.292	31	107	14	25	6	3	0	6	11	7	0	1	29	0	2	.346	.341
Cantillo, Anthony	R-R	5-10	145	8-6-95	.319	.277	.336	50	160	25	51	5	2	0	17	15	7	2	4	13	6	8	.375	.392
Fiorello, Pascual	R-R	6-0	155	1-16-97	.202	.208	.200	52	183	19	37	11	0	0	11	8	2	0	1	46	3	1	.262	.242
Lugo, Henry	R-R	5-11	160	11-30-95	.208	.152	.230	46	168	15	35	4	1	1	14	5	4	1	2	29	1	3	.262	.246
Perez, Ricardo	R-R	5-10	155	5-20-95	.265	.309	.243	52	204	30	54	13	6	0	17	22	3	0	1	24	9	4	.387	.343
Pinto, Rene	R-R	5-10	180	11-2-96	.264	.225	.279	40	144	15	38	9	0	1	11	10	2	0	1	25	4	0	.347	.318
Rincon, Santiago	L-L	6-0	195	12-20-96	.181	.238	.163	51	177	19	32	12	1	1	9	14	4	0	0	74	2	0	.277	.256
Rojas, Oscar	R-R	5-11	165	7-5-96	.282	.234	.301	55	220	30	62	18	1	2	21	10	2	1	1	30	18	3	.400	.338
Silva, Darwin	R-R	6-0	187	4-29-97	.167	.111	.185	27	72	7	12	2	0	1	5	5	1	1	0	19	0	0	.236	.231

Pitching	B-T	HT	WT	DOB	W	L	ERA	G	GS	CG	SV	IP	H	R	ER	HR	BB	SO	AVG	vLH	vRH	K/9	BB/9
Bastardo, Armando	R-R	6-0	172	7-11-94	0	2	2.45	18	0	0	10	29	28	13	8	1	5	28	.252	.308	.222	8.59	1.53
Cazorla, Kevin	R-R	6-2	190	10-14-93	1	0	1.37	12	10	0	0	46	36	14	7	0	10	29	.216	.175	.240	5.67	1.96
Da Silva, Miguel	R-R	6-1	195	4-11-96	0	2	5.79	12	0	0	0	19	25	16	12	0	14	12	.333	.360	.320	5.79	6.75
Duarte, Jorman	R-R	6-2	190	11-16-94	2	4	1.99	13	13	0	0	54	45	26	12	1	10	19	.227	.188	.246	3.15	1.66
Guarecuco, Roimar	R-R	6-1	170	1-25-95	0	7	7.71	13	7	0	0	33	47	36	28	2	14	16	.343	.468	.278	4.41	3.86
Hernandez, E, Edgardo	R-R	6-3	201	11-9-94	3	1	3.09	13	0	0	1	23	19	10	8	0	5	15	.216	.303	.164	5.79	1.93
Lopez, Hector	R-R	6-4	190	6-10-95	0	0	3.24	4	1	0	0	8	6	3	0	6	3	.313	.556	.217	6.48	6.48
Marval, Johan	R-R	6-1	195	11-24-93	3	0	1.98	15	0	0	3	36	30	13	8	2	4	22	.222	.196	.236	5.45	0.99
Mujica, Arturo	L-L	6-3	181	6-4-96	1	1	1.20	9	0	0	0	15	9	3	2	1	10	13	.180	.250	.174	7.80	6.00
Pilar, Daniel	R-R	6-4	185	6-6-95	1	2	2.72	16	6	0	0	40	31	16	12	1	14	21	.218	.240	.207	4.76	3.18
Prado, Enderson	R-R	6-1	165	1-3-95	1	0	2.91	15	0	0	2	34	30	18	11	0	16	28	.240	.367	.200	7.41	4.24
Rivas, Frehumar	L-L	6-1	175	9-25-95	0	1	6.75	4	0	0	0	5	2	8	4	0	9	2	.100	.000	.111	3.38	15.19
Rodriguez, Abrahan	R-R	6-2	182	4-20-95	1	5	3.08	12	12	0	0	38	36	18	13	2	8	26	.259	.286	.244	6.16	1.89
Rodriguez, Jesus	L-L	6-2	145	8-19-95	2	3	7.15	14	0	0	0	23	25	20	18	0	14	14	.294	.067	.343	5.56	5.56
Romero, Orlando	R-R	6-0	185	9-26-96	2	4	3.86	12	9	0	0	33	34	16	14	0	15	28	.283	.205	.321	7.71	4.13
Sanchez, Jesus	R-R	6-2	190	3-1-95	2	4	3.38	16	1	0	0	32	25	23	12	0	22	19	.216	.189	.228	5.34	6.19
Sanz, Chander	R-R	6-4	185	6-4-96	0	1	54.00	2	0	0	0	1	5	7	6	1	4	1	.714	.667	.750	9.00	36.00
Serrano, Luis	R-R	6-1	180	3-22-97	3	1	3.46	14	0	0	0	26	19	12	10	1	11	13	.204	.289	.145	4.50	3.81
Torres, Jesus	R-R	6-1	190	5-1-96	1	2	7.71	12	0	0	0	16	19	15	14	1	14	16	.292	.190	.341	8.82	7.71
Veliz, Oliver	R-R	6-0	175	2-22-96	2	0	6.75	14	0	0	0	28	32	26	21	1	17	22	.288	.333	.272	7.07	5.46
Yepez, Angel	R-R	6-1	215	4-27-95	0	0	1.71	7	6	0	0	21	16	9	4	1	6	15	.211	.304	.170	6.43	2.57
Zerpa, Jose	R-R	6-4	185	3-29-97	1	1	3.65	14	2	0	0	25	23	18	10	2	16	12	.253	.167	.274	4.38	5.84

Fielding

Catcher	PCT	G	PO	A	E	DP	PB
Alvarez	.975	29	156	40	5	1	13
Pinto	.979	27	146	45	4	3	12
Silva	.970	21	67	30	3	1	3

First Base	PCT	G	PO	A	E	DP
Auciello	.974	12	107	7	3	3
Barrios	.983	50	405	48	8	30
Rincon	.920	9	44	2	4	2

Second Base	PCT	G	PO	A	E	DP
Cabrera	1.000	1	1	3	0	1

Cantillo	.963	21	51	52	4	14
Fiorello	.975	10	23	16	1	1
Lugo	.913	6	12	9	2	3
Perez	.939	34	99	85	12	18

Third Base	PCT	G	PO	A	E	DP
Auciello	.885	19	19	35	7	3
Cantillo	.882	15	13	32	6	3
Fiorello	.842	41	31	65	18	3

Shortstop	PCT	G	PO	A	E	DP
Cantillo	.951	11	19	39	3	4

Lugo	.897	40	61	104	19	15
Perez	.923	16	19	53	6	6

Outfield	PCT	G	PO	A	E	DP
Apaez	.917	39	73	4	7	1
Auciello	1.000	1	2	1	0	1
Balcazar	.964	53	155	4	6	1
Barrios	—	1	0	0	0	0
Cabrera	.971	22	33	1	1	1
Cantillo	.833	5	5	0	1	0
Rincon	.930	37	51	2	4	0
Rojas	.966	55	105	9	4	5

Texas Rangers

SEASON IN A SENTENCE: Everything that could possibly go wrong went wrong, as injuries mounted up at a stunning rate to turn the Rangers from one of the best teams in baseball into a complete disaster.

HIGH POINT: The Rangers finished the season on a 13-3 run, with closer Neftali Feliz showing promising signs that he could be dangerous when healthy next season.

LOW POINT: Where to start? Derek Holland, Yu Darvish, Prince Fielder, Matt Harrison, Jurickson Profar, Martin Perez and Alexi Ogando were among the Rangers who missed all or a significant portion of the 2015 season. After getting pounded 15-6 by the Angels on July 10, the Rangers had the worst record in baseball and were in the middle of a stretch in which they lost 14 of 15 games. After the Angels swept them on Sept. 11, the Rangers dropped to 54-92, still the worst record in MLB. Manager Ron Washington resigned with less than a month left in the season for undisclosed reasons.

NOTABLE ROOKIES: With Ian Kinsler traded to Detroit for Fielder and Profar out due to injury, the Rangers rushed Rougned Odor to the big leagues. He flashed a promising swing but looked like a player who belonged in the minors as he hit .259/.297/.402 in 114 games. Righthander Nick Martinez also looked rushed into the big league rotation, while outfielder Michael Choice, a .182/.250/.320 hitter in 86 games, simply looked overmatched.

KEY TRANSACTIONS: In the rare position to be in the seller's market for major league talent, the Rangers sold high on Joakim Soria in late July and capitalized on Detroit's desperation to upgrade its bullpen, pulling a potential mid-rotation starter in righthander Jake Thompson and a reliever with high-octane stuff in righthander Corey Knebel. Thompson immediately became one of the Rangers' top pitching prospects.

DOWN ON THE FARM: Joey Gallo's 42 home runs were one behind minor league leader Kris Bryant. The 20-year-old third baseman, who split the season between high Class A Myrtle Beach and Double-A Frisco, also tied for fifth in the minors with 87 walks and tied for third in strikeouts with 179, producing a .271/.394/.615. Outfielder Nomar Mazara had a breakout year, hitting .271/.362/.478 with 22 homers mostly with low Class A Hickory before an August promotion to Double-A.

OPENING DAY PAYROLL: $132,491,596 (8th)

PLAYERS OF THE YEAR

MAJOR LEAGUE	MINOR LEAGUE
Adrian Beltre	**Joey Gallo**
3b	**3b**
.324/.388/.492	(High A/Double-A)
19 HR, 77 RBI, 33 2B	.271/.394/.615
4th in AL in WAR (8.0)	Led org with 42 HR

ORGANIZATION LEADERS

BATTING *Minimum 250 AB

MAJORS

*	AVG	Beltre, Adrian	.324
*	OPS	Beltre, Adrian	.88
	HR	Beltre, Adrian	19
	RBI	Beltre, Adrian	77

MINORS

*	AVG	Cordell, Ryan, Hickory, Myrtle Beach	.318
*	OBP	Gallo, Joey, Myrtle Beach, Frisco	.394
*	SLG	Gallo, Joey, Myrtle Beach, Frisco	.615
	R	Gallo, Joey, Myrtle Beach, Frisco	97
	H	Herrera, Odubel, Myrtle Beach, Frisco	151
	TB	Gallo, Joey, Myrtle Beach, Frisco	270
	2B	Adams, Trever, Frisco	36
	3B	Garia, Chris, Myrtle Beach	11
	HR	Gallo, Joey, Myrtle Beach, Frisco	42
	RBI	Gallo, Joey, Myrtle Beach, Frisco	106
	BB	Gallo, Joey, Myrtle Beach, Frisco	87
	SO	Gallo, Joey, Myrtle Beach, Frisco	179
	SB	Garia, Chris, Myrtle Beach	45

PITCHING #Minimum 75 IP

MAJORS

	W	Lewis, Colby	10
		Darvish, Yu	10
#	ERA	Darvish, Yu	3.06
	SO	Darvish, Yu	182
	SV	Soria, Joakim	17

MINORS

	W	Faulkner, Andrew, Myrtle Beach, Frisco	12
		Gonzalez, Alex Myrtle Beach, Frisco	12
	L	Germano, Justin, Round Rock	13
#	ERA	Gonzalez, Alex, Myrtle Beach, Frisco	2.66
	G	Mendoza, Francisco, Frisco	45
	GS	Asher, Alec, Frisco	28
	SV	Leclerc, Jose, Myrtle Beach	14
	IP	Eickhoff, Jerad, Frisco	154
	BB	Payano, Victor, Myrtle Beach	90
	SO	Eickhoff, Jerad, Frisco	144
#	AVG	Eickhoff, Jerad, Frisco	.226

2014 PERFORMANCE

General Manager: Jon Daniels. **Farm Director:** Mike Daly. **Scouting Director:** Kip Fagg.

Class	Team	League	W	L	PCT	Finish	Manager
Majors	Texas Rangers	American	67	95	.414	28th (30)	Ron Washington/Tim Bogar
Triple-A	Round Rock Express	Pacific Coast	70	74	.486	t-11th (16)	Steve Buechele
Double-A	Frisco RoughRiders	Texas	80	59	.576	1st (8)	Jason Wood
High A	Myrtle Beach Pelicans	Carolina	82	56	.594	1st (8)	Joe Mikulik
Low A	Hickory Crawdads	South Atlantic	80	59	.576	5th (14)	Corey Ragsdale
Short season	Spokane Indians	Northwest	40	36	.526	4th (8)	Tim Hulett
Rookie	Rangers	Arizona	26	30	.464	8th (14)	Kenny Holmberg
Overall Minor League Record			378	314	.546	3rd (30)	

ORGANIZATION STATISTICS

TEXAS RANGERS

AMERICAN LEAGUE

Batting	B-T	HT	WT	DOB	AVG	vLH	vRH	G	AB	R	H	2B	3B	HR	RBI	BB	HBP	SH	SF	SO	SB	CS	SLG	OBP
Adduci, Jim	L-L	6-2	210	5-15-85	.168	.000	.183	44	101	13	17	3	0	1	8	10	0	1	2	27	3	1	.228	.239
Andrus, Elvis	R-R	6-0	200	8-26-88	.263	.310	.247	157	619	72	163	35	1	2	41	46	3	9	7	96	27	15	.333	.314
Arencibia, J.P.	R-R	6-0	205	1-5-86	.177	.239	.147	62	203	20	36	9	0	10	35	10	7	0	2	62	0	0	.369	.239
Beltre, Adrian	R-R	5-11	220	4-7-79	.324	.351	.316	148	549	79	178	33	1	19	77	57	3	0	5	74	1	1	.492	.388
Carp, Mike	L-R	6-2	210	6-30-86	.125	.000	.132	17	40	2	5	0	0	0	4	5	0	0	1	14	0	0	.125	.217
2-team total (42 Boston).175—			—	59	126	11	22	5	1	0	13	16	5	0	2	31	0	1	.230.289					
Chirinos, Robinson	R-R	6-1	205	6-5-84	.239	.237	.239	93	306	36	73	15	0	13	40	17	7	4	4	71	0	1	.415	.290
Choice, Michael	R-R	6-0	215	11-10-89	.182	.203	.172	86	253	20	46	6	1	9	36	21	3	0	3	69	1	0	.320	.250
Choo, Shin-Soo	L-L	5-11	205	7-13-82	.242	.236	.244	123	455	58	110	19	1	13	40	58	12	0	4	131	3	4	.374	.340
Fielder, Prince	L-R	5-11	275	5-9-84	.247	.237	.253	42	150	19	37	8	0	3	16	25	2	0	1	24	0	0	.360	.360
Gimenez, Chris	R-R	6-2	220	12-27-82	.262	.241	.269	33	107	13	28	10	0	1	11	11	0	0	0	26	0	1	.355	.331
2-team total (8 Cleveland).241—			—	41	116	13	28	10	0	0	11	12	0	0	0	29	0	1	.328.313					
Kouzmanoff, Kevin	R-R	6-1	210	7-25-81	.362	.462	.324	13	47	8	17	6	0	2	10	2	2	0	0	7	0	0	.617	.412
Martin, Leonys	L-R	6-2	190	3-6-88	.274	.250	.282	155	533	68	146	13	7	7	40	39	2	7	2	114	31	12	.364	.325
Moreland, Mitch	L-L	6-2	230	9-6-85	.246	.120	.268	52	167	18	41	9	1	2	23	12	1	2	2	43	0	0	.347	.297
Murphy, Donnie	R-R	5-10	190	3-10-83	.196	.233	.183	45	112	11	22	3	0	4	14	11	1	1	3	38	0	1	.330	.268
Odor, Rougned	L-R	5-11	190	2-3-94	.259	.248	.264	114	386	39	100	14	7	9	48	17	5	6	3	71	4	7	.402	.297
Pena, Carlos	L-L	6-2	225	5-17-78	.136	.077	.152	18	59	4	8	3	0	1	2	4	0	0	0	11	1	0	.237	.190
Rios, Alex	R-R	6-5	210	2-18-81	.280	.325	.266	131	492	54	138	30	8	4	54	23	1	0	5	93	17	9	.398	.311
Robertson, Dan	R-R	5-8	190	9-5-85	.271	.330	.200	70	177	23	48	9	1	0	21	17	0	2	1	28	6	4	.333	.333
Rodriguez, Guilder	B-R	6-1	190	7-24-83	.167	.000	.250	7	12	2	2	0	0	0	1	1	0	1	0	5	0	0	.167	.231
Rosales, Adam	R-R	6-1	195	5-20-83	.262	.281	.250	56	164	20	43	7	0	4	19	13	3	0	0	42	4	2	.378	.328
Rua, Ryan	R-R	6-2	205	3-11-90	.295	.387	.257	28	105	11	31	7	0	2	14	2	2	0	0	18	1	0	.419	.321
Sardinas, Luis	B-R	6-1	150	5-16-93	.261	.333	.239	43	115	12	30	6	0	0	8	5	2	3	0	21	5	1	.313	.303
Smolinski, Jake	R-R	5-11	215	2-9-89	.349	.476	.308	24	86	12	30	5	0	3	12	3	3	0	0	24	0	0	.512	.391
Snyder, Brad	L-L	6-3	220	5-25-82	.167	—	.167	10	30	3	5	1	0	2	3	4	0	0	0	10	0	0	.400	.265
Soto, Geovany	R-R	6-1	235	1-20-83	.237	.167	.269	10	38	5	9	2	0	1	3	0	0	0	0	11	0	0	.368	.237
2-team total (14 Oakland).250—			—	24	80	8	20	6	0	1	11	6	0	1	0	19	0	0	.363.302					
Telis, Tomas	B-R	5-8	200	6-18-91	.250	.200	.259	18	68	7	17	2	0	0	8	1	1	1	0	10	0	0	.279	.271
Wilson, Josh	R-R	6-0	175	3-26-81	.239	.393	.128	24	67	7	16	4	0	0	8	2	1	2	0	14	1	0	.299	.271

Pitching	B-T	HT	WT	DOB	W	L	ERA	G	GS	CG	SV	IP	H	R	ER	HR	BB	SO	AVG	vLH	vRH	K/9	BB/9
Adcock, Nate	R-R	6-4	235	2-25-88	0	0	4.50	7	0	0	0	10	11	5	5	2	5	9	.289	.316	.263	8.10	4.50
Baker, Scott	R-R	6-4	215	9-19-81	3	4	5.47	25	8	0	0	81	82	49	49	15	14	55	.262	.259	.265	6.14	1.56
Bonilla, Lisalverto	R-R	6-0	175	6-18-90	3	0	3.05	5	3	0	0	21	13	8	7	2	12	17	.186	.179	.194	7.40	5.23
Claudio, Alex	L-L	6-3	160	1-31-92	0	0	2.92	15	0	0	0	12	14	4	4	0	4	14	.280	.190	.345	10.22	2.92
Cotts, Neal	L-L	6-1	200	3-25-80	2	9	4.32	73	0	0	2	67	66	33	32	6	23	63	.257	.270	.250	8.51	3.11
Darvish, Yu	R-R	6-5	215	8-16-86	10	7	3.06	22	22	2	0	144	133	54	49	13	49	182	.241	.246	.233	11.35	3.06
Edwards, Jon	R-R	6-5	230	1-8-88	0	0	4.32	9	0	0	0	8	13	5	4	0	5	9	.351	.438	.286	9.72	5.40
Feierabend, Ryan	L-L	6-3	225	8-22-85	0	0	6.14	6	0	0	0	7	12	5	5	0	2	4	.375	.235	.533	4.91	2.45
Feliz, Neftali	R-R	6-3	225	5-2-88	2	1	1.99	30	0	0	13	32	20	7	7	5	11	21	.183	.127	.241	5.97	3.13
Figueroa, Pedro	L-L	6-0	215	11-23-85	2	1	4.00	10	0	0	0	9	10	7	4	1	3	3	.278	.111	.444	3.00	3.00
Frasor, Jason	R-R	5-9	180	8-9-77	1	1	3.34	38	0	0	0	30	27	14	11	2	14	30	.243	.233	.250	9.10	4.25
2-team total (23 Kansas City)4		1		2.66	61	0	0	0	47	40	17	14	3	18	46	—	—	8.75	3.42				
Germano, Justin	R-R	6-2	210	8-6-82	0	0	11.81	2	0	0	0	5	8	7	7	1	3	3	.348	.286	.375	5.06	5.06
Harrison, Matt	L-L	6-4	240	9-16-85	1	1	4.15	4	4	0	0	17	20	8	8	1	12	10	.286	.231	.298	5.19	6.23
Holland, Derek	B-L	6-2	210	10-9-86	2	0	1.46	6	5	0	0	37	34	8	6	0	5	25	.248	.265	.243	6.08	1.22
Irwin, Phil	R-R	6-3	210	2-25-87	0	1	6.75	1	1	0	0	4	6	3	3	1	2	2	.353	.250	.444	4.50	4.50
Kirkman, Michael	L-L	6-4	220	9-18-86	0	1	1.59	12	0	0	0	6	5	1	1	0	1	3	.263	.357	.000	4.76	1.59
Klein, Phil	R-R	6-6	240	4-30-89	1	2	2.84	17	0	0	0	19	11	6	6	3	10	23	.164	.308	.073	10.89	4.74
Lewis, Colby	R-R	6-4	240	8-2-79	10	14	5.18	29	29	2	0	170	211	107	98	25	48	133	.304	.320	.288	7.03	2.54
Martinez, Nick	L-R	6-1	175	8-5-90	5	12	4.55	29	24	0	0	140	150	79	71	18	55	77	.275	.279	.271	4.94	3.53
McCutchen, Daniel	R-R	6-2	215	9-26-82	0	0	7.71	1	0	0	0	2	4	3	2	1	2	0	.333	—	.333	0.00	7.71
Mendez, Roman	R-R	6-3	190	7-25-90	0	1	2.18	30	0	0	0	33	20	8	8	2	17	22	.174	.175	.172	6.00	4.64

Name	B-T	HT	WT	DOB	W	L	ERA	G	GS	CG	SV	IP	H	R	ER	HR	BB	SO	AVG	vLH	vRH		
Mikolas, Miles	R-R	6-5	220	8-23-88	2	5	6.44	10	10	0	0	57	64	43	41	8	18	38	.278	.266	.294	5.97	2.83
Noesi, Hector	R-R	6-3	205	1-26-87	0	0	11.81	3	0	0	0	5	11	7	7	0	2	4	.423	.294	.667	6.75	3.38
3-team total (28 Chicago, 2 Seattle)					8	12	4.75	33		27	1	0	172	180	98	91	28	56	123	—	—	6.42	2.92
Ogando, Alexi	R-R	6-4	200	10-5-83	2	3	6.84	27	0	0	1	25	33	19	19	1	15	22	.314	.300	.327	7.92	5.40
Patton, Spencer	R-R	6-1	185	2-20-88	1	0	0.96	9	0	0	0	9	6	1	1	0	2	8	.182	.273	.136	7.71	1.93
Perez, Martin	L-L	6-0	190	4-4-91	4	3	4.38	8	8	2	0	51	50	25	25	3	19	35	.269	.256	.273	6.14	3.33
Poreda, Aaron	L-L	6-6	240	10-1-86	2	1	5.91	26	0	0	0	21	30	14	14	2	7	21	.337	.333	.339	8.86	2.95
Rosin, Seth	R-R	6-6	265	11-2-88	1	0	6.75	3	0	0	0	4	6	3	3	0	1	3	.333	.500	.125	6.75	2.25
Ross, Robbie	L-L	5-11	215	6-24-89	3	6	6.20	27	12	0	0	78	103	65	54	9	30	51	.319	.283	.336	5.86	3.45
Rowen, Ben	R-R	6-4	190	11-15-88	0	0	4.15	8	0	0	0	9	10	4	4	0	4	7	.313	.556	.217	7.27	4.15
Saunders, Joe	L-L	6-3	215	6-16-81	0	5	6.13	8	8	0	0	40	62	32	27	8	20	22	.356	.326	.367	4.99	4.54
2-team total (6 Baltimore)					0	5	6.70	14	8	0	0	43	65	37	32	9	24	23	—	—	4.81	5.02	
Scheppers, Tanner	R-R	6-4	200	1-17-87	0	1	9.00	8	4	0	0	23	31	24	23	6	10	17	.320	.318	.323	6.65	3.91
Soria, Joakim	R-R	6-3	200	5-18-84	1	3	2.70	35	0	0	17	33	25	12	10	0	4	42	.198	.259	.089	11.34	1.08
2-team total (13 Detroit)					2	4	3.25	48	0	0	18	44	38	19	16	2	6	48	—	—	9.74	1.22	
Tepesch, Nick	R-R	6-4	225	10-12-88	5	11	4.36	23	22	0	0	126	128	66	61	15	44	56	.267	.234	.311	4.00	3.14
Tolleson, Shawn	R-R	6-2	210	1-19-88	3	1	2.76	64	0	0	0	72	56	23	22	10	28	69	.214	.216	.212	8.67	3.52
West, Matt	R-R	6-1	200	11-20-88	0	0	6.75	3	0	0	0	4	6	3	3	0	1	3	.353	.545	.000	6.75	2.25
Williams, Jerome	R-R	6-3	240	12-4-81	1	1	9.90	2	2	0	0	10	18	11	11	0	3	6	.400	.452	.286	5.40	2.70
2-team total (26 Houston)					2	5	6.71	28	2	0	0	58	77	44	43	7	19	44	—	—	6.87	2.97	

Fielding

Catcher	PCT	G	PO	A	E	DP	PB
Arencibia	.988	22	160	7	2	1	3
Chirinos	.994	91	585	45	4	7	5
Gimenez	.991	26	203	11	2	1	1
Soto	1.000	10	91	2	0	0	0
Telis	.991	17	105	6	1	0	0

First Base	PCT	G	PO	A	E	DP
Adduci	1.000	3	13	1	0	0
Arencibia	.987	22	144	13	2	17
Carp	.973	12	67	4	2	7
Fielder	.989	39	333	14	4	36
Gimenez	1.000	5	22	0	0	1
Moreland	.989	22	158	14	2	15
Murphy	1.000	6	28	4	0	4
Pena	.991	16	105	9	1	12
Rosales	.996	32	215	22	1	32
Rua	1.000	9	54	7	0	7
Snyder	.985	10	63	4	1	9

Second Base	PCT	G	PO	A	E	DP
Murphy	1.000	21	36	49	0	17
Odor	.981	110	194	275	9	70
Robertson	1.000	1	2	1	0	0
Rodriguez	1.000	2	6	6	0	1
Rosales	.944	5	7	10	1	3
Sardinas	1.000	19	26	33	0	10
Wilson	1.000	19	24	55	0	11

Third Base	PCT	G	PO	A	E	DP
Beltre	.967	136	144	206	12	25
Kouzmanoff	.909	13	2	18	2	1
Murphy	1.000	5	3	2	0	0
Rodriguez	.833	3	3	2	1	0
Rosales	1.000	7	6	8	0	0
Rua	—	1	0	0	0	0
Sardinas	.917	7	4	7	1	1
Wilson	.917	4	0	11	1	4

Shortstop	PCT	G	PO	A	E	DP
Andrus	.971	153	237	371	18	94
Rodriguez	—	1	0	0	0	0
Rosales	1.000	3	2	6	0	1
Sardinas	.935	13	14	29	3	6
Wilson	1.000	3	4	3	0	1

Outfield	PCT	G	PO	A	E	DP
Adduci	1.000	28	60	1	0	0
Carp	1.000	2	1	0	0	0
Choice	.969	65	119	5	4	0
Choo	.971	75	129	4	4	0
Martin	.982	152	415	11	8	3
Moreland	.800	2	4	0	1	0
Rios	.977	114	250	6	6	2
Robertson	.981	63	98	7	2	0
Rua	1.000	17	33	0	0	0
Smolinski	1.000	21	41	0	0	0

ROUND ROCK EXPRESS

TRIPLE-A
PACIFIC COAST LEAGUE

Batting	B-T	HT	WT	DOB	AVG	vLH	vRH	G	AB	R	H	2B	3B	HR	RBI	BB	HBP	SH	SF	SO	SB	CS	SLG	OBP
Adduci, Jim	L-L	6-2	210	5-15-85	.296	.267	.333	7	27	3	8	1	0	0	3	2	0	0	0	8	2	1	.333	.345
Arencibia, J.P.	R-R	6-0	205	1-5-86	.279	.358	.248	48	190	31	53	8	0	14	41	10	2	0	1	53	1	0	.542	.320
Arroyo, Carlos	L-R	5-11	150	6-28-93	.214	.250	.200	3	14	2	3	1	0	0	1	0	0	0	0	2	0	0	.286	.214
Beltre, Engel	L-L	6-2	180	11-1-89	.106	.125	.097	11	47	2	5	1	0	0	2	1	1	1	0	7	0	0	.128	.143
Brown, Jordan	L-L	6-0	220	12-18-83	.242	.214	.263	9	33	4	8	2	0	0	1	2	0	0	0	7	0	0	.303	.306
Buchholz, Alex	R-R	6-0	185	9-30-87	.283	.368	.235	13	53	9	15	4	0	0	10	3	1	0	1	7	0	0	.358	.328
Choice, Michael	R-R	6-0	215	11-10-89	.267	.257	.270	43	150	25	40	8	0	7	31	23	6	0	3	47	2	1	.460	.379
Donald, Jason	R-R	6-1	195	9-4-84	.236	.269	.229	44	144	22	34	6	2	3	8	15	0	3	1	44	3	1	.368	.306
2-team total (25 Omaha)					.234	—	—	69	222	29	52	9	2	4	13	18	2	3	3	65	4	2	.347	.294
Felix, Jose	R-R	5-10	200	6-28-88	.000	—	.000	1	3	0	0	0	0	0	0	0	0	0	0	0	0	0	.000	.000
Garay, Carlos	R-R	6-0	210	10-5-94	.176	.000	.188	5	17	0	3	0	0	0	2	1	0	0	0	4	0	0	.176	.222
Gimenez, Chris	R-R	6-2	220	12-27-82	.284	.302	.275	39	134	18	38	4	2	6	22	19	0	0	3	30	0	1	.478	.365
Hoying, Jared	L-R	6-3	190	5-18-89	.271	.270	.271	135	509	86	138	33	7	26	78	40	2	1	3	140	20	7	.517	.325
Kouzmanoff, Kevin	R-R	6-2	210	7-25-81	.313	.000	.357	4	16	1	5	1	0	0	1	0	0	0	1	3	0	0	.375	.294
Lillibridge, Brent	R-R	5-11	185	9-18-83	.234	.295	.203	89	312	48	73	14	3	10	41	28	4	2	3	95	15	5	.394	.303
Murphy, Donnie	R-R	5-10	190	3-10-83	.053	.125	.000	6	19	1	1	0	0	0	1	3	1	0	1	7	0	0	.053	.208
Nicholas, Brett	L-R	6-2	215	7-18-88	.274	.296	.265	127	452	40	124	20	1	10	58	27	7	1	4	112	4	1	.389	.322
Parrino, Andy	B-R	6-0	190	10-31-85	.189	.133	.211	13	53	4	10	3	0	0	5	3	0	0	1	12	0	0	.245	.271
2-team total (90 Sacramento)					.274	—	—	103	427	61	117	22	2	7	57	47	5	1	1	109	7	0	.384	.352
Patton, Cory	L-L	5-9	220	6-18-82	.333	—	.333	2	6	2	2	0	0	1	2	0	0	0	0	2	0	0	.833	.333
Pena, Carlos	L-L	6-2	225	5-17-78	.297	.300	.296	20	74	12	22	3	0	4	8	5	1	0	0	15	0	0	.500	.350
Petersen, Bryan	L-R	6-0	200	4-9-86	.252	.286	.240	120	452	72	114	30	3	13	65	45	2	0	2	152	6	3	.418	.321
Profar, Juremi	R-R	6-1	185	1-30-96	.333	1.000	.000	2	6	1	2	0	0	0	0	0	0	0	0	0	0	0	.333	.333
Robertson, Dan	R-R	5-8	190	9-30-85	.250	.231	.260	8	28	6	7	1	1	1	3	5	0	0	0	4	2	0	.464	.364
2-team total (5 El Paso)					.300	—	—	13	50	12	15	3	1	3	8	6	0	0	0	7	2	0	.580	.375
Robinson, Drew	L-R	6-1	200	4-20-92	.304	.000	.318	8	23	3	7	2	0	1	5	6	1	0	0	7	3	0	.522	.467
Rodriguez, Guilder	B-R	6-1	190	7-24-83	.167	.222	.143	9	30	4	5	1	0	0	1	4	0	1	0	5	0	0	.200	.265
Rosales, Adam	R-R	6-1	195	5-20-83	.276	.291	.269	72	272	42	75	16	3	7	43	28	4	0	3	61	3	0	.434	.349
Rua, Ryan	R-R	6-2	205	3-11-90	.313	.327	.309	58	214	31	67	13	2	8	35	21	0	0	2	42	1	0	.505	.382

TEXAS RANGERS

Player	B-T	HT	WT	DOB	AVG	vLH	vRH	G	AB	R	H	2B	3B	HR	RBI	BB	HBP	SH	SF	SO	SB	CS	SLG	OBP
Sardinas, Luis	B-R	6-1	150	5-16-93	.290	.286	.291	60	262	39	76	15	2	1	28	8	0	2	1	39	9	4	.374	.310
Smolinski, Jake	R-R	5-11	215	2-9-89	.267	.222	.286	8	30	7	8	6	0	0	6	4	0	0	0	5	0	0	.467	.353
Snyder, Brad	L-L	6-3	220	5-25-82	.284	.289	.282	61	232	46	66	11	1	18	51	25	0	0	3	82	3	0	.573	.350
Snyder, Chris	R-R	6-4	235	2-12-81	.238	.375	.154	7	21	3	5	1	0	0	2	4	0	0	0	8	0	0	.286	.360
Soto, Geovany	R-R	6-1	235	1-20-83	.188	.278	.071	10	32	2	6	2	0	1	2	1	0	0	0	10	0	0	.344	.212
Strausborger, Ryan	R-R	6-0	180	3-4-88	.258	.337	.230	88	325	50	84	17	4	5	22	29	2	2	2	55	21	0	.382	.321
Tanaka, Kensuke	L-R	5-9	170	5-20-81	.258	.200	.284	62	213	29	55	8	2	4	27	27	1	1	3	28	12	2	.371	.340
Telis, Tomas	B-R	5-8	200	6-18-91	.345	.343	.346	36	139	18	48	7	2	3	17	6	1	1	0	12	1	1	.489	.377
Teschner, Brett	R-R	6-3	225	8-23-91	.000	—	.000	1	1	0	0	0	0	0	0	1	0	0	0	0	0	0	.000	.500
Towles, J.R.	R-R	6-2	200	2-11-84	.176	.000	.188	6	17	1	3	3	0	0	4	5	0	0	0	5	0	0	.353	.364
Wilson, Josh	R-R	6-0	175	3-26-81	.246	.244	.247	92	305	37	75	11	1	5	33	16	7	0	4	87	1	2	.338	.295
Wise, J.T.	R-R	6-0	210	6-2-86	.000	—	.000	1	1	0	0	0	0	0	0	0	0	0	0	0	0	0	.000	.000

Pitching	B-T	HT	WT	DOB	W	L	ERA	G	GS	CG	SV	IP	H	R	ER	HR	BB	SO	AVG	vLH	vRH	K/9	BB/9
Adcock, Nate	R-R	6-4	235	2-25-88	1	0	2.95	18	0	0	2	21	14	7	7	1	11	22	.189	.178	.207	9.28	4.64
Baker, Scott	R-R	6-4	215	9-19-81	4	1	3.32	6	6	0	0	38	35	16	14	5	11	30	.252	.351	.183	7.11	2.61
Bell, Chad	R-L	6-3	200	2-28-89	0	0	135.00	1	0	0	0	0	6	5	5	0	1	0	.857	1.000	.833	0.00	27.00
Bonilla, Lisalverto	R-R	6-0	175	6-18-90	4	2	4.10	39	6	0	1	75	73	36	34	9	25	92	.253	.222	.276	11.09	3.01
Burns, Cory	R-R	6-0	205	10-9-87	2	2	7.44	20	1	0	0	33	55	29	27	6	10	29	.374	.393	.363	7.99	2.76
Cabrera, Edwar	L-L	6-0	195	10-20-87	2	3	4.50	8	7	0	0	38	51	19	19	4	11	31	.333	.279	.355	7.34	2.61
Claudio, Alex	L-L	6-3	160	1-31-92	0	1	3.38	2	1	0	0	5	6	2	2	0	2	6	.300	.143	.385	10.13	3.38
Edwards, Jon	R-R	6-5	230	1-8-88	1	1	2.87	12	0	0	0	16	15	6	5	0	9	26	.250	.276	.226	14.94	5.17
Feierabend, Ryan	L-L	6-3	225	8-22-85	8	6	5.11	25	20	0	0	125	148	82	71	18	29	81	.297	.270	.307	5.83	2.09
Feliz, Neftali	R-R	6-3	225	5-2-88	1	1	3.14	24	0	0	7	29	19	10	10	6	8	31	.188	.216	.172	9.73	2.51
Garcia, Martire	L-L	6-0	170	3-1-90	0	0	7.11	4	0	0	0	6	8	5	5	0	4	7	.320	.300	.333	9.95	5.68
Germano, Justin	R-R	6-2	210	8-6-82	4	13	4.51	21	21	3	0	132	145	72	66	22	22	82	.279	.293	.268	5.61	1.50
2-team total (3 Albuquerque)					5			24	23	3	0	145.2	165	87	81	26	24	96	—	—		5.94	1.49
Henry, Randy	R-R	6-3	190	5-10-90	1	0	6.75	14	0	0	0	19	27	15	14	2	7	12	.355	.278	.379	5.79	3.38
Holland, Derek	B-L	6-2	210	10-9-86	2	1	5.87	4	4	0	0	15	20	15	10	5	8	19	.308	.217	.357	11.15	4.70
Irwin, Phil	R-R	6-3	210	2-25-87	5	2	3.51	11	10	0	0	51	51	21	20	0	25	56	.268	.256	.280	9.82	4.38
Jackson, Luke	R-R	6-2	205	8-24-91	1	3	10.35	11	10	0	0	40	56	49	46	9	28	43	.333	.309	.365	9.68	6.30
Kirkman, Michael	L-L	6-4	220	9-18-86	5	5	4.47	36	4	0	1	54	50	34	27	6	29	62	.240	.198	.268	10.27	4.80
Klein, Phil	R-R	6-7	260	4-30-89	0	0	0.00	9	0	0	0	18	7	0	0	0	6	28	.119	.172	.067	13.75	2.95
Knebel, Corey	R-R	6-3	195	11-26-91	1	0	3.75	9	0	0	0	12	9	5	5	2	5	20	.205	.136	.273	15.00	3.75
Lewis, Colby	R-R	6-4	240	8-2-79	0	1	3.60	1	1	0	0	5	4	4	2	0	3	2	.211	.000	.235	3.60	5.40
Marks, Justin	L-L	6-3	205	1-12-88	0	1	5.06	5	0	0	0	5	6	3	3	0	4	8	.273	.222	.308	13.50	6.75
3-team total (13 Omaha, 4 Sacramento)					3	3	5.03	22	2		0	39	44	28	22	4	16	37	—	—		8.47	3.66
Mathis, Doug	R-R	6-3	230	6-7-83	0	0	4.50	2	0	0	0	4	2	2	2	1	3	2	.143	.250	.100	4.50	6.75
Mavare, Jose	R-R	6-0	175	2-19-90	0	0	20.25	1	0	0	0	1	5	3	3	1	1	5	.556	.500	.571	6.75	6.75
McCutchen, Daniel	R-R	6-2	215	9-26-82	2	5	7.05	15	8	1	0	60	79	47	47	22	13	54	.311	.364	.272	8.10	1.95
Mendez, Roman	R-R	6-3	190	7-25-90	0	1	4.02	25	0	0	3	31	39	16	14	4	12	30	.302	.353	.269	8.62	3.45
Mikolas, Miles	R-R	6-5	220	8-23-88	5	1	3.22	16	6	0	2	45	53	20	16	3	3	38	.283	.310	.260	7.66	0.60
Monegro, Jose	R-R	6-3	200	9-19-89	0	0	3.38	2	1	0	0	5	4	2	2	0	2	3	.200	.000	.250	5.06	3.38
Patton, Spencer	R-R	6-1	185	2-20-88	1	1	3.38	15	0	0	4	16	16	6	6	1	3	25	.258	.270	.240	14.06	1.69
2-team total (34 Omaha)					5	4	3.90	49	0		18	62	42	27	27	10	25	85	—	—	—	12.27	3.61
Perez, Rafael	L-L	6-3	195	5-15-82	0	1	7.36	4	0	0	0	4	8	3	3	1	0	4	.267	.400	.200	9.82	0.00
Poreda, Aaron	L-L	6-6	240	10-1-86	0	1	6.06	16	0	0	3	16	21	11	11	0	7	28	.300	.231	.341	15.43	3.86
Reyes, Jimmy	L-L	5-10	200	3-7-89	1	2	8.31	13	2	0	0	26	36	25	24	7	5	19	.327	.243	.370	6.58	1.73
Richmond, Scott	R-R	6-5	220	8-30-79	1	6	7.65	21	9	0	0	58	81	55	49	7	21	42	.328	.355	.307	6.55	3.28
Ross, Robbie	L-L	5-11	215	6-24-89	5	4	4.33	12	9	2	0	60	66	29	29	7	16	43	.286	.284	.287	6.41	2.39
Rowen, Ben	R-R	6-4	190	11-15-88	3	0	3.45	34	0	0	5	47	47	22	18	2	9	31	.253	.246	.256	5.94	1.72
Saunders, Joe	L-L	6-3	215	6-16-81	0	1	2.25	2	2	0	0	12	15	3	3	1	5	8	.319	.000	.341	6.00	3.75
2-team total (4 Omaha)					1	3	4.99	6	6	0		31	42	20	17	5	10	14	—	—	—	4.11	2.93
Scheppers, Tanner	R-R	6-4	200	1-17-87	0	0	12.27	3	1	0	0	4	7	5	5	3	1	3	.389	.625	.200	7.36	2.45
Schwinden, Chris	R-R	6-3	215	9-22-86	1	2	11.25	3	3	0	0	12	20	17	15	4	3	11	.351	.133	.429	8.25	2.25
Segovia, Zack	R-R	6-2	245	4-11-83	0	1	8.31	2	2	0	0	13	9	8	1	5	8		.342	.286	.412	8.31	5.19
Tepesch, Nick	R-R	6-4	225	10-12-88	6	1	1.58	7	7	1	0	46	36	8	8	1	9	41	.218	.250	.204	8.08	1.77
West, Matt	R-R	6-1	200	11-21-88	3	3	4.15	33	1	0	1	43	52	25	20	4	16	54	.294	.338	.264	11.22	3.32
Williams, Jerome	R-R	6-3	240	12-4-81	0	1	6.10	2	2	0	0	10	16	8	7	3	1	3	.348	.259	.474	2.61	0.87

Fielding

Catcher	PCT	G	PO	A	E	DP	PB
Arencibia	.995	23	187	10	1	0	1
Felix	1.000	1	5	1	0	0	0
Garay	1.000	5	40	1	0	0	0
Gimenez	.986	18	125	12	2	2	2
Nicholas	.992	74	586	42	5	5	9
Snyder	1.000	6	48	4	0	2	1
Soto	1.000	7	29	4	0	1	0
Telis	.993	19	126	11	1	1	0

First Base	PCT	G	PO	A	E	DP
Adduci	.982	6	50	4	1	3
Arencibia	.986	20	130	13	2	9
Brown	.987	7	63	11	1	5
Donald	.905	4	19	0	2	4
Gimenez	1.000	14	99	11	0	12
Kouzmanoff	1.000	1	7	2	0	0
Nicholas	.997	44	339	32	1	41
Pena	.991	14	103	10	1	10
Robinson	1.000	3	19	0	0	1
Rodriguez	1.000	1	7	1	0	1
Rosales	1.000	15	124	9	0	17
Rua	1.000	4	40	4	0	5
Snyder	1.000	2	14	1	0	2
Snyder	.750	1	3	0	1	0
Strausborger	1.000	2	19	1	0	1
Telis	1.000	9	72	5	0	12
Towles	1.000	5	40	2	0	2
Wilson	1.000	4	9	1	0	0
Wise	.667	1	2	0	1	0

Second Base	PCT	G	PO	A	E	DP
Donald	.983	33	36	77	2	20
Lillibridge	.961	44	91	108	8	25
Murphy	1.000	1	1	1	0	0
Robertson	1.000	1	3	0	0	0
Rodriguez	.941	4	8	8	1	4
Rosales	1.000	2	3	3	0	1
Rua	1.000	3	6	3	0	1
Strausborger	.933	2	5	9	1	3
Tanaka	.971	49	70	130	6	34
Wilson	.973	10	14	22	1	7

Third Base	PCT	G	PO	A	E	DP
Buchholz	.976	12	9	32	1	2
Donald	.778	3	1	6	2	0

Gimenez	1.000	3	2	11	0	1		Lillibridge	.936	18	27	46	5	12		Donald	—	2	0	0	0	0
Kouzmanoff	1.000	2	2	8	0	1		Parrino	.962	13	15	35	2	8		Hoying	.997	129	284	7	1	0
Lillibridge	.818	10	8	10	4	0		Rodriguez	.909	2	5	5	1	2		Lillibridge	1.000	10	21	0	0	0
Murphy	1.000	5	1	20	0	6		Rosales	1.000	6	10	14	0	5		Patton	—	1	0	0	0	0
Profar	.900	2	1	8	1	1		Sardinas	.966	60	87	170	9	45		Petersen	.963	79	122	7	5	2
Rodriguez	1.000	1	0	3	0	1		Wilson	.977	45	56	112	4	24		Robertson	.941	7	13	3	1	0
Rosales	.978	50	34	99	3	8		**Outfield**	**PCT**	**G**	**PO**	**A**	**E**	**DP**		Robinson	1.000	4	7	0	0	0
Rua	.932	27	19	49	5	5		Adduci	1.000	1	2	0	0	0		Rodriguez	1.000	1	4	0	0	0
Wilson	.944	33	12	55	4	2		Arroyo	.833	3	5	0	1	0		Rua	1.000	24	29	2	0	0
Shortstop	**PCT**	**G**	**PO**	**A**	**E**	**DP**		Beltre	.947	11	17	1	1	0		Smolinski	.944	8	17	0	1	0
Donald	.909	2	3	7	1	1		Choice	1.000	36	61	2	0	0		Snyder	.989	43	87	1	1	0
																Strausborger	.982	79	155	5	3	0

FRISCO ROUGHRIDERS

DOUBLE-A

TEXAS LEAGUE

Batting	B-T	HT	WT	DOB	AVG	vLH	vRH	G	AB	R	H	2B	3B	HR	RBI	BB	HBP	SH	SF	SO	SB	CS	SLG	OBP
Adams, Trever	R-R	6-0	210	9-30-88	.278	.284	.276	125	482	71	134	36	2	14	61	38	4	4	3	100	7	4	.448	.334
Adduci, Jim	L-L	6-2	210	5-15-85	.318	.333	.313	6	22	3	7	1	1	1	6	0	0	0	1	5	1	0	.591	.304
Alberto, Hanser	R-R	5-11	175	10-17-92	.275	.161	.299	50	178	23	49	6	1	2	15	6	4	2	0	17	6	4	.354	.314
Alfaro, Jorge	R-R	6-2	185	6-11-93	.261	.357	.243	21	88	12	23	4	0	4	14	6	5	0	0	23	0	0	.443	.343
Beltre, Engel	L-L	6-2	180	11-1-89	.500	.333	1.000	1	4	1	2	0	0	0	1	0	0	0	0	0	0	0	.500	.500
Brown, Jordan	L-L	6-0	220	12-18-83	.200	.136	.224	23	80	12	16	3	0	4	10	9	0	0	1	13	0	0	.388	.278
Cantwell, Pat	R-R	6-2	210	4-10-90	.268	.324	.249	76	276	43	74	15	1	1	33	20	22	3	4	58	1	2	.341	.360
De Leon, Michael	R-R	6-1	160	1-14-97	.333	—	.333	1	3	1	1	0	0	0	0	0	0	0	0	1	0	0	.667	.333
Gallo, Joey	L-R	6-5	205	11-19-93	.232	.183	.247	68	250	44	58	10	0	21	56	36	3	1	1	115	2	0	.524	.334
Garay, Carlos	R-R	6-0	210	10-5-94	.000	.000	.000	2	5	0	0	0	0	0	0	0	0	0	0	0	0	0	.000	.000
Garcia, Edwin	B-R	6-1	185	3-1-91	.206	.161	.225	30	102	14	21	4	0	0	6	8	0	0	2	21	1	0	.245	.259
Grayson, Chris	R-R	6-0	215	9-15-89	.241	.125	.270	44	158	20	38	8	0	2	20	19	1	1	2	44	3	7	.329	.322
Herrera, Odubel	L-R	5-11	200	12-29-91	.321	.207	.353	96	368	47	118	16	4	2	48	29	3	6	2	70	12	7	.402	.373
Martinez, Teodoro	R-R	6-0	180	3-16-92	.273	.292	.268	87	311	33	85	16	0	3	44	17	5	0	4	56	3	8	.354	.318
Mazara, Nomar	L-L	6-4	195	4-26-95	.306	.111	.358	24	85	10	26	7	1	3	16	9	2	0	1	22	0	0	.518	.381
Odor, Rougned	L-R	5-11	170	2-3-94	.279	.250	.289	32	129	21	36	2	1	6	17	7	0	1	1	22	6	3	.450	.314
Robinson, Drew	L-R	6-1	200	4-20-92	.190	.138	.209	96	331	41	63	15	5	11	40	37	2	4	3	125	6	5	.366	.273
Rodriguez, Guilder	B-R	6-1	190	7-24-83	.269	.239	.278	81	305	36	82	7	1	0	20	37	0	6	1	45	10	7	.298	.347
Rua, Ryan	R-R	6-2	205	3-11-90	.300	.262	.313	71	257	34	77	13	1	10	38	30	1	0	0	55	5	3	.475	.375
Sardinas, Luis	B-R	6-1	150	5-16-93	.253	.167	.286	21	87	12	22	5	1	0	9	3	0	0	0	12	1	1	.333	.278
Skole, Jake	L-R	6-1	195	1-17-92	.216	.211	.218	103	342	46	74	16	2	6	33	40	0	2	2	103	6	2	.327	.297
Smolinski, Jake	R-R	5-11	215	2-9-89	.267	.229	.281	72	266	43	71	15	3	10	35	32	4	0	5	54	6	2	.459	.349
Soto, Geovany	R-R	6-1	235	1-20-83	.368	.000	.438	6	19	4	7	2	0	0	1	3	0	0	0	6	0	0	.474	.455
Strausborger, Ryan	R-R	6-0	180	3-4-88	.417	.444	.407	8	36	9	15	1	2	1	4	0	0	0	0	6	1	0	.639	.417
Telis, Tomas	B-R	5-8	200	6-18-91	.303	.235	.327	70	267	31	81	16	2	2	33	17	1	3	7	29	7	1	.401	.339
Williams, Nick	L-L	6-3	195	9-8-93	.256	.111	.245	15	62	4	14	2	1	0	4	2	0	0	0	21	1	1	.290	.250
Wise, J.T.	R-R	6-0	210	6-2-86	.319	.286	.325	38	141	27	45	13	0	11	34	13	3	0	0	40	0	0	.645	.389
Zaneski, Zach	R-R	6-2	215	6-27-86	.000	.000	.000	3	10	0	0	0	0	0	0	0	1	0	0	2	0	0	.000	.167
2-team total (19 Arkansas)	.239	—	—	22	71	9	17	3	0	3	7	6	1	0	0	14	0	0.408	.308					

Pitching	B-T	HT	WT	DOB	W	L	ERA	G	GS	CG	SV	IP	H	R	ER	HR	BB	SO	AVG	vLH	vRH	K/9	BB/9
Asher, Alec	R-R	6-4	225	10-4-91	11	11	3.80	28	28	0	0	154	139	74	65	18	32	122	.238	.271	.213	7.13	1.87
Bores, Ryan	R-R	6-3	205	10-10-90	2	3	2.79	16	2	0	0	29	37	17	9	1	7	14	.314	.362	.267	4.34	2.17
Cabrera, Edwar	L-L	6-0	195	10-20-87	4	6	2.99	22	17	0	1	108	104	42	36	6	32	84	.254	.266	.252	6.98	2.66
Claudio, Alex	L-L	6-3	160	1-31-92	2	2	2.17	8	6	0	0	37	31	17	9	1	2	22	.223	.182	.236	5.30	0.48
Downs, Brodie	R-R	6-4	235	7-19-91	1	0	7.56	7	0	0	0	8	11	7	7	0	6	4	.314	.353	.278	4.32	6.48
Edwards, Jon	R-R	6-5	230	1-8-88	1	2	5.13	22	0	0	0	33	27	26	19	4	23	36	.225	.308	.162	9.72	6.21
Eickhoff, Jerad	R-R	6-4	240	7-2-90	10	9	4.08	27	26	0	0	154	129	76	70	17	52	144	.226	.241	.213	8.40	3.03
Faulkner, Andrew	R-L	6-3	180	9-12-92	2	4	4.99	7	6	0	0	31	28	22	17	3	14	33	.237	.214	.244	9.68	4.11
Font, Wilmer	R-R	6-4	265	5-24-90	2	1	3.48	29	0	0	3	31	25	13	12	2	17	31	.214	.229	.203	9.00	4.94
Garcia, Martire	L-L	6-0	170	3-1-90	1	1	1.37	13	1	0	0	20	12	3	3	1	9	22	.169	.105	.192	10.07	4.12
Gonzalez, Alex	R-R	6-2	195	1-15-92	7	4	2.70	15	14	0	0	73	67	30	22	3	25	64	.245	.220	.267	7.85	3.07
Hamren, Erik	R-R	6-1	195	8-21-86	0	1	1.13	15	0	0	1	16	7	2	2	1	8	21	.135	.188	.111	11.81	4.50
Harrison, Matt	L-L	6-4	240	9-16-85	1	0	1.69	3	3	0	0	16	12	4	3	0	4	10	.207	.056	.275	5.63	2.25
Henry, Randy	R-R	6-3	190	5-10-90	1	1	3.38	9	0	0	1	13	15	5	5	0	3	6	.283	.154	.407	4.05	2.03
Holland, Derek	B-L	6-2	210	10-9-86	0	0	0.00	2	2	0	0	5	3	0	0	0	2	8	.176	.000	.250	14.40	3.60
Jackson, Luke	R-R	6-2	205	8-24-91	8	2	3.02	15	14	0	1	83	58	28	28	5	24	83	.191	.198	.186	8.96	2.59
Kela, Keone	R-R	6-1	225	4-16-93	2	1	1.86	36	0	0	5	39	22	14	8	1	27	55	.162	.204	.138	12.80	6.28
Klein, Phil	R-R	6-7	260	4-30-89	3	0	0.81	24	0	0	10	33	15	3	3	0	14	42	.139	.171	.119	11.34	3.78
Lamb, Will	L-L	6-6	180	9-9-90	4	2	1.09	26	0	0	3	33	18	5	4	1	26	42	.168	.171	.167	9.27	7.09
Lotzkar, Kyle	L-R	6-5	210	10-24-89	3	2	4.93	30	8	0	1	66	65	39	36	6	40	65	.254	.261	.248	8.91	5.48
Martinez, Nick	L-R	6-1	175	8-5-90	0	0	1.86	2	2	0	0	10	8	2	2	0	7	9	.222	.143	.241	8.38	6.52
McElwee, Josh	R-R	6-4	227	6-12-89	0	0	1.00	6	0	0	0	9	4	1	1	0	2	8	.129	.273	.050	8.00	2.00
Mendoza, Francisco	R-R	6-0	200	12-7-87	4	1	2.63	45	0	0	8	65	50	24	19	6	30	66	.215	.209	.218	9.14	4.15
Monegro, Jose	R-R	6-3	200	9-19-89	0	1	15.75	2	1	0	0	4	6	7	7	1	2	4	.333	.444	.222	9.00	4.50
Ortiz, Joe	L-L	5-7	175	8-13-90	0	2	4.50	13	0	0	1	16	24	9	8	2	2	8	.348	.429	.293	4.50	1.13
Reyes, Jimmy	L-L	5-10	200	3-7-89	3	2	5.34	27	0	0	0	30	33	20	18	1	13	30	.280	.262	.289	8.90	3.86
Rodebaugh, Ryan	L-R	6-0	190	3-30-89	3	0	5.73	33	0	0	0	38	48	25	24	2	18	50	.304	.371	.250	11.95	4.30

Name	B-T	HT	WT	DOB	W	L	ERA	G	GS	CG	SV	IP	H	R	ER	HR	BB	SO	AVG	vLH	vRH	K/9	BB/9
Saunders, Joe	L-L	6-3	215	6-16-81	0	1	5.79	2	2	0	0	9	11	7	6	3	2	6	.314	.250	.348	5.79	1.93
Scheppers, Tanner	R-R	6-4	200	1-17-87	0	0	0.00	2	1	0	0	2	2	1	0	0	1	1	.250	.000	.400	4.50	4.50
Thompson, Jake	R-R	6-4	235	1-31-94	3	1	3.28	7	6	0	0	36	28	13	13	3	18	44	.219	.222	.216	11.10	4.54
West, Matt	R-R	6-1	200	11-21-88	2	0	0.68	8	0	0	3	13	7	1	1	1	2	10	.156	.176	.143	6.75	1.35

Fielding

Catcher	PCT	G	PO	A	E	DP	PB
Alfaro	1.000	15	139	14	0	0	5
Cantwell	.991	62	476	61	5	4	5
Garay	1.000	1	8	0	0	0	0
Soto	1.000	4	26	1	0	0	0
Telis	.990	46	364	48	4	2	3
Wise	.980	12	96	4	2	0	2
Zaneski	1.000	2	10	0	0	0	0
Telis	1.000	1	6	1	0	0	
Wise	1.000	8	70	3	0	4	

First Base	PCT	G	PO	A	E	DP
Adams	.998	76	594	35	1	45
Adduci	.964	4	25	2	1	2
Alfaro	.941	1	16	0	1	1
Brown	1.000	17	119	6	0	11
Gallo	.971	7	65	1	2	5
Garcia	1.000	1	7	0	0	0
Robinson	.969	10	59	4	2	6
Rodriguez	.986	9	65	3	1	5
Rua	1.000	6	51	3	0	4
Smolinski	1.000	4	25	1	0	1

Second Base	PCT	G	PO	A	E	DP
Garcia	1.000	4	8	12	0	4
Herrera	.975	91	155	195	9	43
Odor	.969	31	75	83	5	22
Robinson	1.000	3	0	8	0	0
Rodriguez	.967	7	9	20	1	3
Rua	1.000	4	5	9	0	2
Sardinas	1.000	1	3	2	0	1

Third Base	PCT	G	PO	A	E	DP
Gallo	.943	53	37	96	8	4
Robinson	.855	16	13	34	8	5
Rodriguez	.980	19	14	35	1	3
Rua	.908	50	38	71	11	8
Telis	.600	1	0	3	2	0

Shortstop	PCT	G	PO	A	E	DP
Alberto	.988	50	87	152	3	20

	PCT	G	PO	A	E	DP
De Leon	1.000	1	3	5	0	1
Garcia	.932	25	31	51	6	11
Rodriguez	.960	45	69	121	8	21
Sardinas	.956	20	23	42	3	10

Outfield	PCT	G	PO	A	E	DP
Adams	.952	25	40	0	2	0
Adduci	1.000	2	2	0	0	0
Beltre	1.000	1	3	0	0	0
Grayson	1.000	40	83	0	0	0
Herrera	1.000	3	5	0	0	0
Martinez	.972	83	137	2	4	1
Mazara	.897	23	35	0	4	0
Robinson	.961	64	118	5	5	1
Rodriguez	—	1	0	0	0	0
Rua	1.000	2	4	1	0	0
Skole	.980	103	238	5	5	0
Smolinski	.990	55	92	4	1	1
Strausborger	1.000	8	25	1	0	0
Williams	.917	15	22	0	2	0

MYRTLE BEACH PELICANS   HIGH CLASS A

CAROLINA LEAGUE

Batting	B-T	HT	WT	DOB	AVG	vLH	vRH	G	AB	R	H	2B	3B	HR	RBI	BB	HBP	SH	SF	SO	SB	CS	SLG	OBP
Alberto, Hanser	R-R	5-11	175	10-17-92	.271	.264	.273	70	262	37	71	15	3	5	43	10	3	6	4	25	10	4	.408	.301
Alfaro, Jorge	R-R	6-2	185	6-11-93	.261	.275	.258	100	398	63	104	22	5	13	73	23	12	0	4	100	6	5	.440	.318
Beck, Preston	L-R	6-2	190	10-26-90	.255	.220	.264	121	436	66	111	33	1	11	77	80	7—		3	93	8	2	.411	.376
Bolinger, Royce	R-R	6-2	200	8-12-90	.280	.234	.294	93	346	41	97	23	2	7	44	29	7—		4	82	3	2	.419	.345
Bostick, Chris	R-R	5-11	185	3-24-93	.251	.276	.244	130	495	81	124	31	8	11	62	47	7—		4	116	24	11	.412	.322
Brinson, Lewis	R-R	6-3	170	5-8-94	.246	.256	.243	46	183	17	45	8	1	3	22	15	1—		0	50	5	5	.350	.307
Castillo, Elio	R-R	6-1	160	3-1-94	.000	—	.000	1	3	0	0	0	0	0	0	0	0	1	0	0	0	0	.000	.250
Cone, Zach	R-R	6-2	205	12-14-89	.181	.267	.160	43	149	14	27	5	0	1	15	15	2	0	1	59	3	2	.235	.263
Cordell, Ryan	R-R	6-4	205	3-31-92	.306	.286	.313	16	62	12	19	2	2	5	19	7	0	0	1	13	3	1	.645	.371
De Leon, Michael	R-R	6-1	160	1-14-97	.292	.667	.238	7	24	5	7	3	0	1	6	3	0	1	0	4	0	0	.542	.370
Deglan, Kellin	L-R	6-2	195	5-3-92	.217	.000	.286	12	46	3	10	3	0	1	8	1	0	0	2	16	0	0	.348	.224
Gallo, Joey	L-R	6-5	205	11-19-93	.323	.359	.313	58	189	53	61	9	3	21	50	51	2	0	4	64	5	3	.735	.463
Garcia, Edwin	B-R	6-1	185	1-31-93	.263	.321	.241	53	198	21	52	9	0	0	11	14	0—		0	31	3	4	.308	.311
Garia, Chris	R-R	6-0	165	12-16-92	.284	.207	.305	101	398	75	113	7	11	4	24	29	7—		0	81	45	12	.387	.343
Gonzalez, Jose	B-R	6-1	175	3-16-94	.182	.250	.167	7	22	2	4	0	0	0	0	0	0	0	0	1	0	0	.182	.182
Grayson, Chris	L-L	6-0	215	9-15-89	.289	.179	.315	45	152	27	44	12	2	3	16	21	5	1	3	41	9	5	.454	.387
Herrera, Odubel	L-R	5-11	200	12-29-91	.297	.393	.265	29	111	26	33	3	1	0	11	23	0	1	2	21	9	3	.342	.412
Jarmon, Jamie	R-R	6-1	190	6-21-94	.091	.000	.100	5	11	1	1	0	0	0	0	1	0	0	0	9	0	0	.091	.167
Lyon, David	B-R	5-11	190	1-19-90	.227	.157	.251	80	277	26	63	18	3	8	35	30	5	0	2	90	2	1	.401	.312
Mendez, Luis	B-R	5-9	155	1-1-93	.228	.279	.215	72	224	24	51	9	0	0	15	24	12—		0	48	12	4	.268	.335
Perez, Brallan	R-R	5-10	165	1-27-96	.000	—	.000	1	1	0	0	0	0	0	0	0	0	0	0	0	0	0	.000	.000
Torres, Kevin	L-R	6-3	195	2-24-90	.217	.125	.235	40	143	12	31	3	2	0	16	8	0—		4	33	0	0	.266	.252
Triunfel, Alberto	R-R	5-11	160	2-1-94	.235	—	.235	5	17	3	4	0	0	2	2	0	0	0	0	3	1	0	.588	.235
Vickerson, Nick	R-R	5-11	205	7-8-89	.149	.037	.181	43	121	13	18	3	0	0	10	28	3	1	1	37	1	0	.223	.320
Williams, Nick	L-L	6-3	195	9-8-93	.292	.286	.294	94	377	61	110	28	4	13	68	19	11—		1	117	5	7	.491	.343

Pitching	B-T	HT	WT	DOB	W	L	ERA	G	GS	CG	SV	IP	H	R	ER	HR	BB	SO	AVG	vLH	vRH	K/9	BB/9
Bell, Chad	R-L	6-3	200	2-28-89	6	3	3.52	13	13	0	0	61	65	25	24	4	20	36	.274	.250	.280	5.28	2.93
Bores, Ryan	R-R	6-3	205	10-10-90	1	4	3.60	15	6	0	2	55	70	36	22	5	15	21	.311	.306	.314	3.44	2.45
Buckel, Cody	R-R	6-1	185	6-18-92	5	6	5.73	34	4	0	0	60	53	45	38	0	56	73	.249	.205	.280	11.01	8.45
Claudio, Alex	L-L	6-3	160	1-31-92	4	0	1.09	17	2	0	4	49	38	9	6	2	9	56	.216	.213	.217	10.22	1.64
De Los Santos, Abel	R-R	6-2	180	11-21-92	5	2	1.97	33	0	0	8	46	29	12	10	1	17	53	.177	.161	.186	10.45	3.35
Ege, Cody	L-L	6-1	185	5-8-91	4	1	3.88	37	0	0	2	63	62	28	27	4	17	76	.261	.167	.292	10.91	2.44
Faulkner, Andrew	R-L	6-3	180	9-12-92	10	1	2.07	21	18	0	1	104	86	26	24	1	31	100	.228	.280	.215	8.63	2.67
Garcia, Martire	L-L	6-0	170	3-1-90	1	2	2.25	6	1	0	0	16	10	4	4	2	10	11	.192	.250	.167	6.19	5.63
Gonzalez, Alex	R-R	6-2	195	1-15-92	5	2	2.62	11	11	0	0	65	56	22	19	3	16	49	.222	.233	.217	6.75	2.20
Harvey, Ryan	R-R	6-2	200	2-25-91	0	0	2.25	5	0	0	0	8	5	4	2	0	5	11	.289	.429	.208	12.38	10.13
James, Chad	L-L	6-3	180	1-23-91	4	3	2.74	8	8	0	0	43	36	16	13	3	22	35	.231	.176	.246	7.38	4.64
Kela, Keone	R-R	6-1	225	4-16-93	0	1	2.61	8	0	0	5	10	9	3	3	0	4	13	.225	.333	.160	11.32	3.48
Kendall, Cody	R-R	6-2	210	12-12-89	1	1	1.46	9	0	0	0	12	9	4	2	0	1	9	.200	.167	.222	6.57	0.73
Knapp, Jason	R-R	6-5	235	8-31-90	1	2	2.78	17	3	0	0	32	26	14	10	4	20	36	.224	.250	.211	10.02	5.57
Lamb, Will	L-L	6-6	180	9-9-90	1	1	2.41	14	0	0	2	19	17	5	5	0	9	25	.236	.182	.260	12.05	4.34
Leclerc, Jose	R-R	6-0	165	12-19-93	4	1	3.30	42	0	0	14	57	39	23	21	8	37	79	.193	.220	.175	12.40	5.81
McElwee, Josh	R-R	6-4	227	6-12-89	2	0	0.42	11	0	0	0	22	11	1	1	0	9	27	.151	.152	.150	11.22	3.74
Monegro, Jose	R-R	6-3	200	9-19-89	2	2	2.86	9	0	0	0	22	17	7	7	3	1	12	.202	.250	.173	4.91	0.41

	B-T	HT	WT	DOB	W	L	ERA	G	GS	CG	SV	IP	H	R	ER	HR	BB	SO	AVG	vLH	vRH	K/9	BB/9
Parra, Luis	L-L	6-2	160	11-21-91	10	7	4.71	27	24	1	1	138	132	81	72	14	62	82	.253	.225	.261	5.36	4.05
Payano, Victor	L-L	6-5	185	10-17-92	5	8	4.58	29	25	0	0	126	123	69	64	11	90	86	.258	.254	.259	6.16	6.45
Pucetas, Kevin	R-R	6-4	225	11-27-84	0	0	7.62	5	0	0	0	13	11	12	11	0	15	6	.224	.200	.241	4.15	10.38
Sprenger, Justin	R-R	6-4	179	6-11-91	0	3	3.60	22	0	0	0	45	49	29	18	3	18	30	.280	.371	.219	6.00	3.60
Stafford, Sam	L-L	6-4	200	4-27-90	2	1	4.34	23	0	0	1	37	30	23	18	3	41	37	.217	.172	.229	8.92	9.88
Wolff, Sam	R-R	6-1	190	4-14-91	9	5	3.37	24	23	0	0	120	106	47	45	9	35	81	.238	.232	.243	6.06	2.62

Fielding

Catcher	PCT	G	PO	A	E	DP	PB
Alfaro	.979	75	527	65	13	5	18
Deglan	1.000	12	98	18	0	2	3
Lyon	.988	47	379	40	5	2	7
Torres	.972	4	31	4	1	1	0

First Base	PCT	G	PO	A	E	DP
Alfaro	.986	17	131	6	2	15
Beck	.984	76	677	40	12	70
Garcia	.920	3	23	0	2	4
Lyon	.971	8	65	3	2	10
Torres	.986	36	346	16	5	31

Second Base	PCT	G	PO	A	E	DP
Bostick	.968	122	243	323	19	94
Garcia	.917	2	5	6	1	1
Herrera	.958	6	10	13	1	4

	PCT	G	PO	A	E	DP
Mendez	.921	9	12	23	3	3
Perez	1.000	1	2	0	0	0
Triunfel	1.000	1	2	6	0	1

Third Base	PCT	G	PO	A	E	DP
Alberto	.923	5	2	10	1	2
Castillo	—	1	0	0	0	0
Gallo	.939	54	45	125	11	16
Garcia	1.000	2	1	3	0	1
Lyon	1.000	1	0	1	0	0
Mendez	.935	40	28	87	8	10
Triunfel	1.000	4	1	10	0	1
Vickerson	.926	40	24	76	8	7

Shortstop	PCT	G	PO	A	E	DP
Alberto	.974	64	103	194	8	48
De Leon	1.000	7	7	22	0	4

	PCT	G	PO	A	E	DP
Garcia	.973	46	63	116	5	21
Mendez	.953	26	34	87	6	20

Outfield	PCT	G	PO	A	E	DP
Beck	.983	32	55	2	1	0
Bolinger	.983	80	169	6	3	4
Brinson	.950	38	92	4	5	0
Cone	.982	35	51	5	1	0
Cordell	1.000	15	25	2	0	0
Garia	.984	91	176	3	3	1
Gonzalez	1.000	6	7	0	0	0
Grayson	.978	33	42	2	1	0
Herrera	1.000	10	10	0	0	0
Jarmon	1.000	3	2	0	0	0
Lyon	1.000	1	2	0	0	0
Vickerson	—	1	0	0	0	0
Williams	.969	79	123	4	4	0

HICKORY CRAWDADS

LOW CLASS A

SOUTH ATLANTIC LEAGUE

Batting	B-T	HT	WT	DOB	AVG	vLH	vRH	G	AB	R	H	2B	3B	HR	RBI	BB	HBP	SH	SF	SO	SB	CS	SLG	OBP
Beras, Jairo	R-R	6-5	178	12-25-94	.242	.191	.258	110	389	38	94	18	0	7	33	33	3	1	1	133	5	4	.342	.305
Brinson, Lewis	R-R	6-3	170	5-8-94	.335	.387	.323	43	164	36	55	8	1	10	28	18	2	1	1	46	7	4	.579	.405
Castro, JanLuis	B-R	5-9	165	1-4-94	.225	.207	.230	40	129	14	29	8	0	1	10	16	1	2	2	30	1	1	.310	.311
Cone, Zach	R-R	6-2	205	12-14-89	.215	.188	.227	31	107	17	23	5	0	3	13	10	7	0	1	29	1	2	.346	.320
Cordell, Ryan	R-R	6-4	205	3-31-92	.321	.219	.358	73	274	53	88	18	4	8	40	27	4	3	2	53	18	3	.504	.388
De Leon, Michael	R-R	6-1	160	1-14-97	.244	.264	.237	85	336	42	82	10	2	1	26	28	1	5	3	40	3	3	.295	.302
Deglan, Kellin	L-R	6-2	195	5-3-92	.251	.259	.248	89	327	46	82	21	2	15	60	34	4	3	3	87	2	0	.465	.326
Demeritte, Travis	R-R	6-0	178	9-30-94	.211	.216	.209	118	398	77	84	16	2	25	66	50	9	5	4	171	6	2	.450	.310
Greene, Marcus	R-R	5-11	195	8-19-94	.179	.200	.172	13	39	5	7	1	1	0	1	9	1	0	0	15	0	0	.256	.347
Guzman, Ronald	L-L	6-5	205	10-20-94	.218	.212	.220	118	445	46	97	32	0	6	63	37	5	0	5	107	6	3	.330	.283
Jackson, Joe	L-R	6-1	180	5-5-92	.293	.266	.302	86	341	46	100	18	4	6	53	36	4	4	0	59	2	2	.422	.364
Kiner-Falefa, Isiah	R-R	5-10	165	3-23-95	.194	.200	.190	19	62	8	12	0	0	0	6	1	4	0	0	12	1	0	.194	.275
Lantigua, Smerling	R-R	6-2	180	2-3-94	.083	.000	.100	3	12	1	1	0	0	0	0	0	0	0	0	7	0	0	.083	.083
Marte, Luis	R-R	6-1	180	12-15-93	.270	.385	.232	72	259	33	70	9	0	1	20	10	0	6	0	51	14	2	.317	.297
Mazara, Nomar	L-L	6-4	195	4-26-95	.264	.214	.283	106	398	68	105	21	2	19	73	57	3	0	3	99	4	3	.470	.358
Pinto, Eduard	L-L	5-11	150	10-23-94	.158	.143	.164	23	76	6	12	3	0	0	6	4	0	3	0	12	0	1	.197	.200
Profar, Juremi	R-R	6-1	185	1-30-96	.269	1.000	.240	7	26	3	7	0	0	1	4	2	0	0	0	3	1	0	.385	.321
Torres, Kevin	L-R	6-3	195	2-24-90	.226	.194	.240	30	106	15	24	4	0	4	12	7	2	1	1	25	0	0	.377	.284
Urbanus, Nick	R-R	6-1	175	3-29-92	.212	.226	.209	48	165	18	35	7	3	0	11	8	1	8	1	44	5	3	.291	.251
Van Hoosier, Evan	R-R	5-11	185	12-24-93	.268	.230	.283	111	437	79	117	27	8	11	58	44	5	3	4	85	14	2	.442	.339
Vickerson, Nick	R-R	5-11	205	7-8-89	.299	.171	.341	51	167	34	50	13	0	4	25	38	7	2	0	37	11	2	.449	.448

Pitching	B-T	HT	WT	DOB	W	L	ERA	G	GS	CG	SV	IP	H	R	ER	HR	BB	SO	AVG	vLH	vRH	K/9	BB/9
Bard, Daniel	R-R	6-4	215	6-25-85	0	0	175.50	4	0	0	0	1	0	13	13	0	9	1	.000	.000	.000	13.50	121.50
Bell, Chad	R-L	6-3	200	2-28-89	2	0	4.10	6	6	1	0	26	32	13	12	5	7	14	.308	.417	.250	4.78	2.39
Bostick, Akeem	R-R	6-4	180	5-4-95	5	6	5.17	21	20	0	0	92	98	59	53	10	28	64	.271	.283	.260	6.24	2.73
Carvallo, Felix	L-L	6-0	175	10-5-93	4	4	3.41	34	0	0	0	66	69	30	25	6	26	58	.268	.320	.236	7.91	3.55
De Los Santos, Abel	R-R	6-2	180	11-21-92	0	1	1.69	8	0	0	0	11	7	3	2	1	1	12	.179	.211	.150	10.13	0.84
Harvey, Ryan	L-R	6-2	220	1-31-91	0	0	10.29	6	0	0	0	7	7	10	8	0	9	8	.280	.250	.308	10.29	11.57
Kaminska, Pat	R-R	6-3	215	2-5-91	5	1	2.70	11	0	0	0	27	22	8	8	3	2	19	.224	.227	.222	6.41	0.68
Kendall, Cody	R-R	6-2	210	12-12-89	7	2	1.02	29	0	0	7	44	35	7	5	1	15	42	.213	.222	.205	8.53	3.05
Leclerc, Angelo	R-R	6-0	170	10-9-91	3	4	2.33	24	7	0	4	66	63	19	17	4	24	71	.251	.226	.276	9.73	3.29
Ledbetter, David	L-R	5-11	188	2-13-92	6	7	5.38	17	16	0	0	75	96	55	45	15	19	52	.315	.354	.280	6.21	2.27
Ledbetter, Ryan	R-R	6-1	190	2-13-92	1	0	4.76	3	0	0	0	5	7	3	3	0	5	7	.292	.182	.385	11.12	7.94
Lopez, Frank	L-L	6-1	175	2-18-94	4	3	2.82	16	15	1	0	73	69	25	23	4	23	80	.247	.247	.247	9.82	2.82
McElwee, Josh	R-R	6-4	227	6-12-89	2	0	4.25	25	0	0	6	36	35	19	17	4	14	57	.246	.263	.235	14.25	3.50
Mendez, Yohander	L-L	6-4	178	1-17-95	3	0	2.32	7	6	0	0	31	26	9	8	4	2	28	.232	.295	.191	8.13	0.58
Monegro, Jose	R-R	6-3	200	9-19-89	0	1	3.98	12	0	0	1	32	31	16	14	0	4	33	.248	.241	.254	9.38	1.14
Ortiz, Luis	R-R	6-3	230	9-22-95	0	0	1.29	3	1	0	1	7	4	1	1	1	3	4	.154	.182	.133	5.14	3.86
Pollorena, Luis	L-L	5-8	170	1-14-91	0	0	4.91	2	0	0	0	4	6	3	2	1	1	2	.375	.286	.444	4.91	2.45
Pucetas, Kevin	R-R	6-4	225	11-27-84	1	1	3.32	13	1	1	1	41	38	15	15	3	18	26	.250	.316	.184	5.75	3.98
Rodriguez, Ricardo	R-R	6-2	220	8-31-92	5	5	3.07	29	12	0	1	103	101	45	35	7	28	72	.263	.245	.283	6.31	2.45
Schwendel, Paul	R-R	6-5	220	8-9-89	0	1	14.40	2	0	0	0	5	8	9	8	3	5	6	.364	.429	.250	10.80	9.00
Slack, Ryne	L-L	6-2	221	7-22-92	9	2	3.28	39	1	0	5	82	65	31	30	5	42	94	.217	.204	.223	10.28	4.59
Smith, Tyler	R-R	6-3	195	2-3-92	7	6	3.67	29	19	0	0	125	131	65	51	9	38	125	.260	.304	.219	9.00	2.74
Valdespina, Jose	R-R	6-6	220	3-22-92	2	2	2.18	26	0	0	9	33	26	10	8	0	9	34	.217	.268	.172	9.27	2.45

Name	B-T	HT	WT	DOB	W	L	ERA	G	GS	CG	SV	IP	H	R	ER	HR	BB	SO	AVG	vLH	vRH	K/9	BB/9
Vasquez, Kelvin	R-R	6-4	195	4-6-93	3	1	4.35	12	8	0	1	52	44	26	25	2	18	58	.228	.198	.261	10.10	3.14
Wiles, Collin	R-R	6-4	212	5-30-94	2	3	4.06	17	8	0	0	58	66	30	26	4	13	42	.287	.303	.275	6.55	2.03
Williams, Scott	R-R	6-2	195	11-17-93	2	1	9.00	13	0	0	0	17	21	18	17	1	16	14	.300	.378	.212	7.41	8.47
Wiper, Cole	R-R	6-4	185	6-3-92	7	8	3.83	24	19	0	0	101	92	48	43	13	45	96	.241	.205	.274	8.55	4.01

Fielding

Catcher	PCT	G	PO	A	E	DP	PB
Deglan	.991	82	666	94	7	4	6
Greene	.987	8	69	9	1	1	1
Jackson	.988	31	228	14	3	0	4
Torres	.986	19	126	18	2	0	0

First Base	PCT	G	PO	A	E	DP
Cordell	.985	8	56	8	1	3
Guzman	.988	115	994	48	13	71
Jackson	.941	2	15	1	1	5
Torres	.987	9	70	8	1	7
Urbanus	1.000	1	2	0	0	0
Vickerson	1.000	7	61	5	0	7

Second Base	PCT	G	PO	A	E	DP
Castro	.955	10	17	25	2	5
De Leon	.930	9	13	27	3	4

	PCT	G	PO	A	E	DP
Demeritte	.967	92	135	248	13	46
Urbanus	1.000	19	24	48	0	10
Van Hoosier	.969	15	18	45	2	7

Third Base	PCT	G	PO	A	E	DP
Castro	.965	27	14	41	2	4
Demeritte	.857	12	7	23	5	0
Lantigua	1.000	1	2	1	0	0
Marte	.938	38	36	69	7	3
Profar	.765	7	5	8	4	1
Urbanus	.909	17	9	31	4	2
Vickerson	.865	40	32	64	15	5

Shortstop	PCT	G	PO	A	E	DP
Castro	1.000	3	1	5	0	3
De Leon	.967	76	101	218	11	37
Demeritte	1.000	1	0	4	0	0

	PCT	G	PO	A	E	DP
Kiner-Falefa	.962	19	26	50	3	11
Marte	.962	33	40	86	5	14
Urbanus	.973	10	14	22	1	6

Outfield	PCT	G	PO	A	E	DP
Beras	.959	96	181	6	8	2
Brinson	.991	43	105	2	1	1
Cone	1.000	29	62	3	0	1
Cordell	.985	53	131	3	2	0
Greene	1.000	3	1	0	0	0
Guzman	1.000	2	7	0	0	0
Jackson	1.000	25	37	4	0	0
Mazara	.973	91	132	12	4	2
Pinto	1.000	15	18	4	0	1
Urbanus	—	1	0	0	0	0
Van Hoosier	.973	70	141	5	4	1

SPOKANE INDIANS — SHORT-SEASON

NORTHWEST LEAGUE

Batting	B-T	HT	WT	DOB	AVG	vLH	vRH	G	AB	R	H	2B	3B	HR	RBI	BB	HBP	SH	SF	SO	SB	CS	SLG	OBP
Cedeno, Diego	L-L	5-11	160	5-19-92	.312	.280	.320	36	125	18	39	4	0	0	8	14	3	1	0	21	3	0	.344	.394
Cone, Zach	R-R	6-2	205	12-14-89	.230	.313	.202	36	126	29	29	9	1	8	26	21	6	0	2	35	3	0	.508	.361
Gonzalez, Jose	B-R	6-1	175	3-16-94	.333	.522	.250	20	75	8	25	5	1	0	10	6	0	0	1	9	3	1	.427	.378
Greene, Marcus	R-R	5-11	195	8-19-94	.318	.297	.324	42	148	30	47	9	2	3	24	26	9	0	1	30	7	0	.466	.446
Jarmon, Jamie	R-R	6-1	190	6-21-94	.189	.200	.188	10	37	2	7	2	0	0	1	2	0	0	0	13	0	0	.243	.231
Johnson, Saquan	R-R	6-2	175	2-26-93	.206	.265	.192	52	180	16	37	4	1	3	17	11	0	1	1	79	8	0	.289	.250
Kiner-Falefa, Isiah	R-R	5-10	165	3-23-95	.260	.260	.260	58	223	27	58	8	2	0	16	19	4	2	0	34	2	4	.314	.329
Moorman, Chuck	R-R	5-11	200	1-9-94	.181	.200	.174	31	94	4	17	4	0	1	14	7	2	0	1	28	1	0	.255	.250
Morgan, Josh	R-R	5-11	185	11-16-95	.303	.381	.279	23	89	11	27	1	0	0	9	10	3	0	0	10	1	1	.315	.392
Pinto, Eduard	L-L	5-11	150	10-23-94	.335	.313	.342	59	251	43	84	11	0	1	27	20	1	5	3	16	5	3	.382	.390
Profar, Juremi	R-R	6-1	185	1-30-96	.247	.267	.241	67	251	26	62	10	0	1	36	22	2	3	5	47	1	1	.299	.307
Spivey, Seth	L-R	5-11	180	7-6-92	.332	.219	.369	67	259	51	86	12	4	3	27	39	4	1	2	45	3	2	.444	.424
Tendler, Luke	L-R	5-11	190	8-25-91	.316	.295	.323	67	256	48	81	18	2	11	57	29	3	0	2	46	9	4	.531	.390
Trevino, Jose	R-R	5-11	195	11-28-92	.257	.194	.276	72	288	58	74	22	3	9	49	23	3	5	5	50	2	0	.448	.313
Triunfel, Alberto	R-R	5-11	160	2-1-94	.255	.200	.270	13	47	7	12	3	0	1	3	2	0	0	2	6	1	1	.383	.275
Vivili, Fernando	R-R	6-3	210	1-9-94	.215	.224	.212	51	186	21	40	13	0	4	23	10	6	0	2	55	4	2	.349	.275
Votoloto, Doug	B-R	6-2	190	6-29-91	.000	.000	.000	2	7	0	0	0	0	0	0	0	0	0	0	6	0	0	.000	.000

Pitching	B-T	HT	WT	DOB	W	L	ERA	G	GS	CG	SV	IP	H	R	ER	HR	BB	SO	AVG	vLH	vRH	K/9	BB/9
Barnett, Andrew	R-R	6-0	185	5-1-92	5	3	5.72	16	13	0	1	68	76	47	43	10	23	51	.286	.346	.247	6.78	3.06
Dignacco, Nick	L-L	6-3	185	4-1-92	2	2	4.01	13	1	0	0	25	21	12	11	4	7	25	.228	.087	.275	9.12	2.55
Dula, Chris	R-R	6-2	200	8-6-92	0	0	5.40	13	0	0	0	17	9	11	10	0	10	22	.155	.211	.128	11.88	5.40
Fasola, John	R-R	6-2	195	12-12-91	0	1	2.05	19	0	0	5	26	21	6	6	1	5	40	.223	.219	.226	13.67	1.71
Gardewine, Nick	R-R	6-1	160	8-15-93	6	3	4.54	15	15	0	0	71	62	38	36	6	23	60	.234	.283	.201	7.57	2.90
Garrett, Reed	R-R	6-2	170	1-2-93	6	1	4.06	16	9	0	0	58	54	29	26	3	21	46	.244	.200	.275	7.18	3.28
Hoppe, Jason	R-R	6-1	170	6-13-92	1	4	5.50	15	4	0	1	34	40	23	21	3	10	33	.292	.163	.364	8.65	2.62
Hunter, Darrell	R-R	6-3	200	7-20-90	0	0	3.86	14	0	0	0	19	16	8	8	1	6	23	.219	.280	.188	11.09	2.89
Ledbetter, Ryan	R-R	6-1	190	2-13-92	1	3	7.34	15	1	0	0	31	40	30	25	2	18	16	.323	.400	.292	4.70	5.28
Matthews, Kevin	R-L	5-11	180	11-29-92	1	0	6.57	8	0	0	0	12	8	9	9	0	10	15	.174	.200	.167	10.95	7.30
McCain, Shane	L-L	6-4	185		2	0	0.31	15	0	0	3	29	17	2	1	0	1	39	.170	.194	.159	12.24	0.31
Parks, Adam	R-R	6-3	220	10-10-92	2	2	2.13	18	0	0	0	25	19	6	6	1	5	31	.207	.353	.121	11.01	1.78
Pena, Richelson	R-R	6-1	170	9-29-93	5	5	3.36	14	14	0	0	72	68	31	27	3	15	67	.250	.189	.289	8.34	1.87
Perez, David	R-R	6-5	200	12-20-92	1	0	3.90	14	2	0	0	28	19	13	12	2	21	24	.192	.200	.189	7.81	6.83
Pettibone, Austin	R-R	6-3	180	9-10-92	2	2	5.45	15	4	0	0	40	48	25	24	5	8	32	.298	.311	.290	7.26	1.82
Pollorena, Luis	L-L	5-8	170	1-14-91	1	2	2.79	17	0	0	3	29	26	9	9	1	13	14	.245	.138	.286	4.34	4.03
Swanson, Erik	R-R	6-3	220	9-4-93	1	2	4.63	15	0	0	0	23	19	12	12	0	7	24	.229	.310	.185	9.26	2.70
Thompson, Derek	L-L	6-4	180	8-8-92	4	6	3.21	14	13	0	0	70	66	27	25	5	15	73	.251	.283	.241	9.39	1.93
Williams, Greg	L-L	6-4	205	12-30-89	0	0	9.00	1	0	0	0	1	2	2	1	0	1	3	.400	1.000	.250	27.00	9.00

Fielding

Catcher	PCT	G	PO	A	E	DP	PB
Greene	.988	30	242	10	3	1	2
Moorman	1.000	16	91	8	0	3	2
Spivey	.875	1	7	0	1	0	0
Trevino	.980	31	268	33	6	4	7
Vivili	1.000	3	25	7	0	0	0

First Base	PCT	G	PO	A	E	DP
Cedeno	.991	14	99	8	1	5
Moorman	1.000	13	80	5	0	4
Profar	1.000	8	66	3	0	6

	PCT	G	PO	A	E	DP
Vivili	.987	45	366	27	5	34

Second Base	PCT	G	PO	A	E	DP
Kiner-Falefa	.978	2	28	16	1	4
Morgan	.981	13	22	30	1	5
Profar	.960	5	10	14	1	4
Spivey	.955	41	73	95	8	23
Trevino	.972	7	11	24	1	2

Third Base	PCT	G	PO	A	E	DP
Profar	.941	41	11	69	5	5

	PCT	G	PO	A	E	DP
Spivey	.974	16	8	30	1	1
Trevino	.964	23	22	58	3	5
Vivili	—	1	0	0	0	0

Shortstop	PCT	G	PO	A	E	DP
Kiner-Falefa	.974	48	73	116	5	24
Morgan	.973	10	12	24	1	3
Profar	.818	3	1	8	2	1
Spivey	1.000	2	2	4	0	1
Trevino	1.000	1	3	1	0	1
Triunfel	.932	13	19	36	4	7

TEXAS RANGERS

Outfield	PCT	G	PO	A	E	DP
Cedeno	1.000	20	28	1	0	1
Cone	.987	32	76	1	1	0
Gonzalez	1.000	20	51	2	0	1

	PCT	G	PO	A	E	DP
Greene	1.000	1	2	0	0	0
Jarmon	.923	9	12	0	1	0
Johnson	.983	48	55	3	1	0
Pinto	.950	48	110	5	6	1

	PCT	G	PO	A	E	DP
Pollorena	—	1	0	0	0	0
Tendler	.992	56	113	6	1	3
Votoloto	.800	2	4	0	1	0

AZL RANGERS   ROOKIE

ARIZONA LEAGUE

Batting	B-T	HT	WT	DOB	AVG	vLH	vRH	G	AB	R	H	2B	3B	HR	RBI	BB	HBP	SH	SF	SO	SB	CS	SLG	OBP
Almonte, Jose	R-R	6-3	205	9-9-96	.164	.184	.158	50	171	16	28	2	1	2	18	10	5	0	0	51	5	3	.222	.231
Arroyo, Carlos	L-R	5-11	150	6-28-93	.286	.239	.302	49	185	34	53	6	2	0	17	18	1	2	0	23	14	4	.341	.353
Beltre, Engel	L-L	6-2	180	11-1-89	.000	—	.000	1	2	0	0	0	0	0	0	0	0	0	0	0	0	0	.000	.000
Bolinger, Royce	R-R	6-2	200	8-12-90	.400	.000	.500	4	10	3	4	1	0	0	3	2	0	0	0	3	0	0	.500	.500
Caraballo, Oliver	R-R	6-1	180	8-25-94	.277	.293	.270	41	130	17	36	7	4	1	22	9	5	0	3	26	3	1	.415	.340
Castillo, Elio	R-R	6-1	160	3-1-94	.248	.190	.262	36	105	16	26	1	0	0	15	18	2	0	1	19	4	1	.257	.365
Castro, Rubell	R-R	6-3	180	8-13-96	.071	.000	.083	7	14	2	1	0	0	0	0	4	0	0	0	5	0	0	.071	.278
Cedeno, Diego	L-L	5-11	160	5-19-92	.235	.200	.250	7	17	3	4	0	0	0	3	2	0	0	0	0	2	0	.235	.316
Day, Darius	L-L	5-11	175	8-25-94	.245	.269	.238	36	110	16	27	2	1	1	7	16	3	1	0	43	4	2	.309	.357
Forbes, Ti'quan	R-R	6-3	180	8-26-96	.241	.304	.219	48	174	27	42	3	2	0	16	23	4	0	3	47	10	1	.282	.338
Garay, Carlos	R-R	6-0	210	10-5-94	.071	.333	.000	6	14	3	1	0	0	0	1	1	0	1	0	3	0	0	.071	.133
Gonzalez, Jose	R-R	6-1	175	3-16-94	.316	.400	.295	20	76	9	24	4	2	0	11	4	0	0	0	14	8	0	.421	.350
Kiner-Falefa, Isiah	R-R	5-10	165	3-23-95	.250	.500	.167	2	8	1	2	0	0	0	0	0	0	0	0	0	1	0	.250	.250
Lacrus, Sherman	R-R	5-11	180	12-23-93	.263	.250	.267	45	152	22	40	9	2	3	25	24	3	0	4	22	2	3	.408	.366
Lantigua, Smerling	R-R	6-2	180	2-3-94	.229	.100	.263	31	96	13	22	5	2	1	9	5	1	1	2	23	2	2	.354	.269
McDonald, Todd	R-R	6-3	180	10-23-95	.245	.333	.216	17	49	5	12	2	0	1	4	3	0	0	0	14	1	0	.347	.288
Morgan, Josh	R-R	5-11	185	11-16-95	.336	.172	.393	33	113	26	38	2	1	0	10	19	9	0	0	13	2	2	.372	.468
Quiroz, Isaias	R-R	5-10	195	10-22-96	.205	.200	.206	25	78	9	16	4	1	0	7	12	6	0	2	32	1	0	.282	.347
Stephens, Zach	R-R	6-0	225	12-13-91	.309	.361	.290	41	136	19	42	9	0	3	22	11	1	1	1	27	2	1	.441	.362
Urbanus, Nick	B-R	6-1	175	3-29-92	.333	.000	.357	5	15	2	5	0	0	0	2	2	0	0	0	3	0	0	.333	.412
Williams, Nick	L-L	6-3	195	9-8-93	.308	.500	.222	3	13	3	4	0	1	0	2	1	0	0	0	4	0	0	.462	.357
Yrizarri, Yeyson	R-R	6-0	175	2-2-97	.237	.222	.241	50	190	23	45	13	1	1	19	9	2	2	3	36	5	3	.332	.275

Pitching	B-T	HT	WT	DOB	W	L	ERA	G	GS	CG	SV	IP	H	R	ER	HR	BB	SO	AVG	vLH	vRH	K/9	BB/9
Abreu, Gio	R-R	6-1	170	9-7-94	0	0	8.56	12	0	0	0	14	16	15	13	1	9	9	.291	.118	.368	5.93	5.93
Beltre, Dario	R-R	6-3	170	11-19-92	0	1	0.00	6	0	0	0	5	3	1	0	0	6	.176	.200	.167	11.57	1.93
Clark, Michael	L-L	6-1	175	6-11-91	0	0	6.00	7	0	0	0	6	7	5	4	0	5	6	.280	.125	.353	9.00	7.50
Dian, Adam	R-R	6-4	205	6-4-93	0	0	5.40	6	0	0	0	5	5	3	3	0	6	8	.278	.250	.300	14.40	10.80
Filomeno, Jean	R-L	5-11	235	12-31-92	2	0	3.00	10	0	0	1	9	7	3	3	0	7	13	.241	.333	.217	13.00	7.00
Green, Nick	R-R	6-1	165	3-25-95	4	3	3.83	14	5	0	0	42	29	19	18	1	19	32	.193	.247	.137	6.80	4.04
Jurado, Ariel	R-R	6-1	180	1-30-96	2	1	1.63	14	3	0	0	39	35	15	7	1	8	35	.233	.203	.256	8.15	1.86
Kaminska, Pat	R-R	6-3	215	2-5-91	0	0	0.00	6	0	0	4	10	3	0	0	0	0	12	.091	.071	.105	10.45	0.00
Lanphere, Luke	R-R	6-2	175	9-30-95	2	2	3.42	14	8	0	1	47	51	20	18	3	14	54	.274	.244	.298	10.27	2.66
Ledbetter, David	L-R	5-11	188	2-13-92	1	0	0.00	4	0	0	2	13	6	0	0	0	2	9	.140	.000	.222	6.39	1.42
Lin, Che-Hsuan	R-R	6-0	180	9-21-88	1	1	5.84	14	0	0	2	12	12	8	8	2	3	14	.261	.267	.258	10.22	2.19
Lopez, Frank	L-L	6-1	175	2-18-94	0	0	1.50	4	0	0	0	6	2	1	1	1	7	.091	.000	.118	10.50	1.50
Lopez, Omarlin	R-R	6-3	175	10-8-93	3	2	4.95	14	0	0	0	44	53	36	24	2	15	42	.303	.338	.282	8.66	3.09
Martin, Brett	L-L	6-4	190	4-28-95	1	4	5.40	15	6	0	1	35	36	26	21	3	12	39	.261	.256	.263	10.03	3.09
Martinez, Emerson	R-R	6-0	190	1-11-95	0	1	4.18	12	4	0	0	32	35	17	15	0	10	37	.280	.250	.299	10.30	2.78
Matthews, Kevin	R-L	5-11	180	11-29-92	1	0	9.00	5	2	0	0	9	16	11	9	0	7	5	.410	1.000	.361	5.00	7.00
Mavare, Jose	R-R	6-0	175	2-19-90	0	1	12.27	4	0	0	0	4	5	6	5	0	1	6	.294	.417	.000	14.73	2.45
Mendez, Yohander	L-L	6-4	178	1-17-95	0	1	4.76	3	3	0	0	6	8	4	3	0	2	7	.320	.250	.353	11.12	3.18
Napiontek, Easton	R-R	6-8	250	4-18-93	1	1	5.59	11	0	0	0	10	9	6	6	1	3	6	.243	.235	.250	5.59	2.79
Ortiz, Joe	L-L	5-7	175	8-13-90	0	0	0.00	2	0	0	0	2	2	0	0	0	1	.250	.000	.333	4.50	0.00
Ortiz, Luis	R-R	6-3	230	9-22-95	1	1	2.03	6	5	0	0	13	12	3	3	0	3	15	.240	.143	.310	10.13	2.03
Palmquist, Cody	R-R	6-5	190	4-8-94	0	1	2.70	15	0	0	3	20	13	8	6	1	6	25	.178	.152	.200	11.25	2.70
Palumbo, Joe	L-L	6-1	150	10-26-94	1	4	2.32	14	7	0	0	43	29	14	11	0	15	49	.190	.178	.194	10.34	3.16
Raffaele, Jacob	L-L	6-3	210	2-23-91	1	3	1.72	13	0	0	0	16	11	3	3	1	7	11	.208	.125	.222	6.32	4.02
Rynard, Storm	R-R	6-0	165	9-25-95	0	0	14.63	10	0	0	0	8	13	15	13	1	9	7	.382	.462	.333	7.88	10.13
Watson, Joe	R-R	6-3	225	9-24-92	0	0	13.50	2	0	0	0	1	2	2	2	0	3	1	.333	.333	.333	6.75	20.25
Wiles, Collin	R-R	6-4	212	5-30-94	1	0	6.35	3	1	0	0	6	6	4	4	0	2	6	.273	.333	.231	9.53	3.18
Williams, Greg	L-L	6-4	205	12-30-89	0	0	12.00	3	0	0	0	3	3	4	4	1	3	5	.273	.500	.222	15.00	9.00
Wynn, Sterling	B-L	6-2	175	11-23-93	1	2	6.20	13	2	0	0	20	25	20	14	1	12	23	.301	.207	.352	10.18	5.31

Fielding

Catcher	PCT	G	PO	A	E	DP	PB
Caraballo	.867	3	24	2	4	0	4
Garay	1.000	4	34	0	0	0	1
Lacrus	.985	31	230	30	4	0	12
Quiroz	1.000	22	192	23	0	3	10

First Base	PCT	G	PO	A	E	DP
Caraballo	1.000	10	83	8	0	9
Castillo	.950	2	18	1	1	3
Cedeno	1.000	2	11	0	0	2
Lantigua	.991	14	112	3	1	9
Stephens	.997	33	266	21	1	19

Second Base	PCT	G	PO	A	E	DP
Arroyo	.911	8	12	29	4	6
Castillo	1.000	14	19	29	0	5
Kiner-Falefa	1.000	1	1	6	0	0
Morgan	.964	17	27	53	3	10
Urbanus	1.000	1	1	2	0	0
Yrizarri	.989	20	41	53	1	8

Third Base	PCT	G	PO	A	E	DP
Arroyo	1.000	5	0	2	0	0
Castillo	.931	15	4	23	2	2
Forbes	.864	33	16	54	11	3
Lantigua	.867	9	2	11	2	0
Urbanus	1.000	2	4	2	0	0
Yrizarri	.600	1	2	1	2	0

Shortstop	PCT	G	PO	A	E	DP
Arroyo	.750	1	1	2	1	0
Castillo	.909	4	7	3	1	2
Forbes	.880	11	11	33	6	7
Kiner-Falefa	1.000	1	2	5	0	2
Morgan	.943	13	11	39	3	7
Yrizarri	.940	28	39	87	8	17

TEXAS RANGERS

Outfield	PCT	G	PO	A	E	DP
Almonte	1.000	43	52	5	0	0
Arroyo	.965	37	50	5	2	1
Beltre	.000	1	0	0	1	0
Bolinger	1.000	3	2	0	0	0
Caraballo	1.000	28	43	1	0	1
Castillo	—	2	0	0	0	
Castro	1.000	5	2	0	0	0
Cedeno	1.000	4	2	0	0	0
Day	.915	34	40	3	4	0
Gonzalez	1.000	20	37	4	0	3
Lacrus	1.000	4	8	0	0	0
Lantigua	1.000	3	6	0	0	0
McDonald	—	2	0	0	0	0
Urbanus	.500	1	1	0	1	0
Williams	1.000	3	9	1	0	0

DSL RANGERS

ROOKIE

DOMINICAN SUMMER LEAGUE

Batting	B-T	HT	WT	DOB	AVG	vLH	vRH	G	AB	R	H	2B	3B	HR	RBI	BB	HBP	SH	SF	SO	SB	CS	SLG	OBP
Adames, Crisford	B-R	6-1	160	1/26/95	.278	.200	.292	65	237	47	66	14	6	0	26	39	5	5	1	43	5	3	.388	.390
Almonte, Jose	R-R	6-3	205	9/9/96	.317	.308	.321	10	41	3	13	2	0	0	5	3	1	0	1	8	0	0	.366	.370
Alonzo, Yimmelvyn	R-R	6-1	185	3/10/97	.286	.211	.300	60	238	43	68	10	6	3	40	13	6	0	2	61	2	1	.416	.336
Barrios, Ciro	R-R	6-0	178	9/27/96	.240	.429	.167	10	25	5	6	1	0	0	1	2	0	0	0	4	0	0	.280	.296
Brujan, Luis	R-R	6-0	170	7/20/96	.176	.091	.217	16	34	3	6	0	0	0	3	1	2	0	0	11	0	0	.176	.243
Carvajal, Ronny	R-R	6-3	180	10/9/95	.216	.238	.211	60	208	29	45	5	4	1	30	22	8	1	2	74	7	1	.293	.313
Castro, Rubell	R-R	6-3	180	8/13/96	.210	.250	.201	58	200	26	42	14	3	5	31	24	12	0	1	92	1	1	.385	.329
Contreras, Jose	R-R	6-3	180	2/13/96	.179	.300	.141	36	84	15	15	1	1	1	13	18	2	2	1	34	2	1	.250	.333
Cordero, Andretty	R-R	6-1	170	5/3/97	.266	.423	.234	43	154	16	41	9	0	0	18	10	5	1	2	16	0	2	.325	.327
Diaz, Willy	R-R	6-3	200	4/19/94	.197	.180	.201	67	229	44	45	8	2	2	27	45	10	2	3	63	4	3	.275	.348
Encarnacion, Cristian	R-R	6-3	185	9/9/96	.286	.400	.222	11	42	10	12	3	2	0	8	2	0	0	2	10	1	0	.452	.304
Fajardo, Kelvin	R-R	5-11	160	3/8/96	.332	.167	.367	65	205	37	68	10	3	0	34	25	5	1	5	32	1	4	.410	.408
Gonzalez, Jesus	R-R	6-1	180	9/12/94	.257	.196	.272	62	241	30	62	17	2	1	36	27	2	4	3	38	1	4	.357	.333
Lugo, Jose	R-R	6-0	180	10/29/96	.231	—	—	42	78	13	18	3	0	0	6	9	2	1		23	4	3	.269	.371
Martinez, Jesus	L-L	5-10	165	5/7/95	.300	.297	.300	67	270	65	81	8	1	0	34	43	1	2	3	33	22	9	.337	.394
Martinez, Porfirio	L-R	6-1	190	3/23/96	.177	.143	.188	24	62	6	11	3	1	0	4	3	2	1	1	23	1	0	.258	.235
Mejias, Luis	R-R	5-10	165	3/11/96	.210	.195	.214	70	233	35	49	7	1	0	17	42	3	5	3	54	13	2	.249	.335
Mendez, Luis	R-R	5-10	165	3/30/95	.324	—	—	38	105	16	34	5	3	1	23	9	4	1	2	21	1	2	.457	.392
Mendoza, Kevin	B-R	5-10	155	8/16/95	.323	.333	.321	28	99	15	32	4	1	1	18	10	1	0	1	8	0	0	.414	.387
Novoa, Melvin	R-R	5-11	200	6/17/96	.238	—	—	49	168	24	40	10	2	3	28	13	11	3	2	26	0	0	.375	.330
Ogando, Pedro	L-R	6-0	170	6/10/94	.273	.000	.286	14	22	3	6	1	0	0	7	1	0	0	1	8	1	0	.409	.292
Parra, Eduardo	R-R	5-10	155	2/16/97	.278	—	—	11	18	2	5	0	1	0	4	1	0	2	0	6	0	0	.389	.316
Perez, Brallan	R-R	5-10	165	1/27/96	.280	.333	.272	64	214	49	60	12	1	0	27	43	10	12	3	19	16	4	.346	.419
Pozo, Yohel	R-R	6-0	175	6/14/97	.273	.267	.274	50	198	22	54	12	0	0	29	11	7	2	3	18	1	0	.333	.329
Rivera, Eudys	R-R	6-1	152	6/3/97	.195	.269	.172	37	113	12	22	1	0	0	4	12	6	3	0	36	1	3	.204	.305
Rojas, Alejandro	R-R	5-10	175	8/6/94	.341	.429	.324	28	82	18	28	4	0	0	12	9	6	2	0	11	3	0	.390	.443
Rollin, Franklin	R-R	5-11	165	8/26/95	.269	.137	.297	70	290	68	78	15	5	1	28	15	30	3	4	46	23	7	.366	.363
Rosa, Abel	L-L	5-11	165	7/20/94	.257	.191	.277	53	206	36	53	6	4	1	33	29	2	2	2	28	7	4	.340	.351
Santana, Angelo	L-L	6-2	195	7/24/95	.230	.250	.224	25	61	8	14	2	0	0	5	18	1	0	0	23	1	3	.262	.413
Silva, Luis	R-R	5-11	170	6/30/95	.278	.462	.250	63	198	39	55	7	5	0	26	19	9	5	4	32	2	5	.364	.361
Suarez, Jose	R-R	5-11	180	4/21/95	.282	—	—	41	124	26	35	12	0	0	23	23	5	1	2	15	1	2	.379	.409
Terrero, Luis	R-R	6-0	185	11/11/95	.358	—	—	68	260	51	93	15	5	0	50	26	9	4	8	28	30	11	.454	.422
Valencia, Ricardo	R-R	6-0	185	1/13/93	.238	.000	.250	7	21	6	5	0	1	1	5	5	1	0	0	5	0	0	.476	.407
Yrizarri, Yeyson	R-R	6-0	175	2/2/97	.302	.154	.367	10	43	7	13	3	1	0	6	3	1	0	1	4	1	1	.419	.354

Pitching	B-T	HT	WT	DOB	W	L	ERA	G	GS	CG	SV	IP	H	R	ER	HR	BB	SO	AVG	vLH	vRH	K/9	BB/9
Brito, Pedro	L-L	5-11	155	4/4/95	0	0	4.02	9	0	0	0	16	13	9	7	0	8	18	.228	.333	.200	1.34	4.60
Cedeno, Rafael	R-R	6-5	210	10/5/94	2	1	1.50	17	0	0	2	36	29	9	6	0	9	28	.228	.190	.247	7.00	2.25
Civil, Henrry	R-R	6-5	194	12/14/94	0	0	0.00	1	0	0	0	1	0	0	0	0	1	0	.250	.000	.500	0.00	9.00
Cruz, Israel	R-R	6-1	170	6/1/97	2	0	4.15	11	5	0	0	30	29	14	14	0	12	18	—	—	—	5.34	3.56
Decena, Albert	R-R	6-3	185	5/12/91	1	1	3.33	24	0	0	10	27	21	12	10	0	11	25	.219	.182	.238	8.33	3.67
Diplan, Marcos	R-R	6-0	160	9/18/96	7	2	1.54	13	13	0	0	64	32	18	11	2	36	57	.155	.152	.156	7.97	5.04
Fracchiolla, Gionny	L-L	5-7	156	9/10/91	3	4	3.88	20	6	0	0	63	58	34	27	2	27	63	.246	.309	.227	9.05	3.88
Garcia, Christopher	R-R	6-4	220	8/26/95	2	3	2.82	21	0	0	2	45	46	25	14	0	12	38	.266	.196	.291	7.66	2.42
Hernandez, Jonathan	R-R	6-2	150	7/6/96	5	2	2.85	14	14	0	0	76	72	32	24	6	17	57	.246	.223	.256	6.78	2.02
Jimenez, Luis	R-R	6-2	195	3/28/97	2	0	2.63	6	2	0	0	14	9	4	4	0	3	18	.188	.278	.133	11.85	1.98
Juan, Johan	R-R	6-1	180	4/14/94	5	2	3.49	16	3	0	2	49	46	20	19	2	12	29	.258	.279	.248	5.33	2.20
Leal, Werner	R-R	6-1	160	7/8/95	1	1	6.55	8	0	0	0	11	18	9	8	0	5	6	.391	.333	.419	4.91	4.09
Linares, Jesus	R-R	6-4	216	1/10/97	0	1	4.91	8	0	0	0	11	8	6	6	0	7	11	.231	.133	.136	9.00	5.73
Liriano, Roberto	L-L	5-11	165	8/4/93	5	0	0.80	20	0	0	4	45	25	8	4	0	24	59	.170	.133	.174	11.80	4.80
Lopez, Ismel	R-R	6-1	190	8/24/94	0	1	3.75	14	0	0	0	24	30	17	10	1	13	31	—	—	—	11.63	4.88
Lopez, Luis	R-R	6-4	185	7/25/96	1	7	4.73	14	14	0	0	53	65	41	28	1	27	35	.294	.364	.248	5.91	4.56
Mancebo, Jorge	R-R	5-11	155	4/25/95	2	1	6.86	14	0	0	1	20	29	15	15	1	8	8	.358	.355	.360	3.66	3.66
Martinez, Greidy	R-R	6-0	155	4/2/94	3	1	2.22	21	0	0	0	28	22	8	7	2	13	29	.214	.262	.180	9.21	4.13
Martinez, Yancarlos	R-R	6-5	227	11/18/95	1	0	4.82	6	0	0	0	9	6	8	5	0	9	9	.162	.091	.192	8.68	9.64
Mavo, Daniel	L-L	5-10	170	7/20/95	6	5	4.02	22	0	0	2	40	38	26	18	2	15	28	.255	.387	.220	6.25	3.35
Morrobel, Eddy	R-R	5-11	185	3/26/93	0	0	11.25	9	0	0	1	12	19	16	15	0	9	11	—	—	—	8.25	6.75
Munoz, Yelfri	R-R	6-3	210	11/24/93	3	0	4.60	12	3	0	0	29	28	21	15	0	16	25	—	—	—	7.67	4.91
Nunez, Nerfy	L-R	6-3	210	8/12/92	2	0	2.67	11	1	0	1	27	28	11	8	1	11	24	.283	.467	.250	8.00	3.67
Payano, Pedro	R-R	6-2	170	9/27/94	7	2	2.95	14	14	1	0	76	68	31	25	3	17	65	.241	.301	.207	7.66	2.00
Pichardo, Yonelvy	L-L	6-2	165	7/12/96	1	1	2.44	14	11	0	0	55	36	17	15	2	29	42	.194	.306	.167	6.83	4.72
Rodriguez, Argenis	R-R	6-3	190	3/7/96	2	3	4.35	14	9	0	0	50	56	27	24	1	18	39	—	—	—	7.07	3.26
Rojas, Yhonson	L-L	6-0	160	10/1/96	0	0	9.00	1	0	0	0	1	1	1	1	0	0	3	.250	0.00	.333	27.00	0.00
Rosario, Luis	R-R	5-11	165	2/8/97	2	3	5.37	17	11	0	1	59	79	43	35	4	20	45	.320	.305	.329	6.90	3.07

					W	L	ERA	G	GS	CG	SV	IP	H	R	ER	HR	BB	SO	AVG	vLH	vRH	BB/9	SO/9
Sosa, Kevin	R-R	6-1	192	1/6/95	1	0	1.13	6	0	0	1	8	5	2	1	1	0	10	.167	.167	.167	11.25	0.00
Suarez, Sergio	L-L	6-0	180	5/24/95	6	2	3.38	18	1	0	0	40	41	18	15	1	17	33	.275	.240	.282	7.43	3.83
Taveras, Francisco	R-R	5-11	195	6/21/94	1	3	4.13	15	8	0	0	52	59	33	24	2	14	26	—	—	—	4.47	2.41
Taveras, Juan	R-R	6-1	170	1/28/95	0	0	4.5	6	0	0	0	6	4	5	3	0	10	4	.200	.143	.231	6.00	15.00
Vivas, Samir	R-R	5-11	170	2/1/95	8	0	1.61	22	0	0	6	45	35	12	8	1	14	33	.224	.306	.187	6.65	2.82
Volquez, Rafael	R-R	6-5	200	4/25/95	5	2	2.65	14	14	0	0	71	70	26	21	1	23	53	.264	.348	.220	6.69	2.90
Zazueta, Samuel	L-L	5-11	170	11/21/96	5	0	1.63	14	11	0	2	66	49	19	12	0	12	91	.203	.244	.195	12.35	1.63

Fielding

Catcher	PCT	G	PO	A	E	DP	PB
Barrios	—	1	0	0	0	0	0
Contreras	1.000	1	3	0	0	0	0
Gonzalez	.989	34	234	48	3	0	8
Mendez	.975	6	33	6	1	0	4
Mendoza	.979	12	83	10	2	1	1
Novoa	.969	29	159	29	6	1	9
Pozo	.982	36	274	45	6	1	5
Rojas	1.000	9	45	4	0	1	5
Rollin	1.000	1	1	0	0	0	1
Suarez	.980	22	122	24	3	0	3
Suarez	.982	5	45	9	1	0	4
Valencia	1.000	5	40	4	0	0	1

First Base	PCT	G	PO	A	E	DP
Adames	.993	62	513	38	4	52
Castro	.917	10	75	2	7	7
Contreras	.969	10	60	3	2	7
Cordero	1.000	1	6	0	0	0
Gonzalez	.996	30	245	15	1	21
Martinez	.986	9	71	2	1	5
Mendez	1.000	6	50	0	0	6
Mendoza	1.000	1	1	0	0	0
Novoa	1.000	1	8	0	0	0
Pozo	1.000	7	58	2	0	8
Rojas	.990	14	97	4	1	9

	PCT	G	PO	A	E	DP
Santana	—	1	0	0	0	0
Suarez	1.000	2	2	0	0	1
Valencia	1.000	1	8	0	0	1

Second Base	PCT	G	PO	A	E	DP
Barrios	.960	8	10	14	1	2
Fajardo	.959	12	23	24	2	8
Mejias	1.000	4	12	12	0	5
Ogando	—	1	0	0	0	0
Parra	1.000	2	2	2	0	0
Perez	.962	38	83	96	7	30
Rollin	.969	62	166	174	11	36
Silva	.983	21	25	34	1	7
Terrero	.951	10	21	18	2	4

Third Base	PCT	G	PO	A	E	DP
Contreras	1.000	2	1	5	0	0
Cordero	.956	12	10	33	2	2
Diaz	.916	65	79	149	21	17
Fajardo	.931	56	47	87	10	8
Martinez	.870	9	9	11	3	0
Mendoza	.905	6	6	13	2	2
Ogando	1.000	4	2	6	0	0
Silva	1.000	1	2	0	0	0
Suarez	.875	4	4	3	1	0

Shortstop	PCT	G	PO	A	E	DP
Mejias	.944	67	95	175	16	36
Parra	.786	6	4	18	6	3
Perez	.959	28	53	64	5	15
Silva	.941	40	70	106	11	26
Yrizarri	.898	8	18	26	5	7

Outfield	PCT	G	PO	A	E	DP
Almonte	1.000	9	10	1	0	1
Alonzo	.920	57	98	5	9	3
Brujan	.905	14	17	2	2	1
Carvajal	.951	56	93	5	5	0
Castro	.906	22	28	1	3	1
Contreras	.941	16	15	1	1	0
Encarnacion	.909	9	9	1	1	0
Fajardo	—	1	0	0	0	0
Lugo	.957	40	43	2	2	0
Martinez	.971	67	126	9	4	4
Mendez	.963	22	21	5	1	0
Ogando	1.000	4	3	0	0	0
Rivera	.957	37	85	4	4	2
Rollin	.900	11	18	0	2	0
Rosa	.948	52	84	8	5	1
Santana	.800	5	4	0	1	0
Suarez	1.000	7	9	1	0	0
Terrero	.933	53	75	8	6	0

Toronto Blue Jays

SEASON IN A SENTENCE: After a season of high expectations in 2013 cratered, the Jays entered 2014 with low expectations from fans and pundits and initially exceeded them, racing into first place, only to devolve into a third-place finish.

HIGH POINT: The Blue Jays hit their high point on June 6 when they reached 14 games over .500 at 38-24. They were six games ahead of the Yankees in first place in the AL East at that point, but it didn't last.

LOW POINT: The Jays, who were still in first place as late as July 3, went 9-17 in August to fall to .500 with a loss to lowly Boston on Aug. 26. Toronto did rebound to finish the season at 83-79, thanks to a 14-12 September, but it was not enough to avoid a third-place finish.

NOTABLE ROOKIES: Marcus Stroman had a shaky start out of the bullpen before stabilizing as a solid rotation option, going 11-6, 3.65 overall, but posting a 3.29 ERA as a starter. He'll certainly be in the rotation to begin 2015. Hard-throwing righthander Aaron Sanchez, the No. 1 prospect to begin the season, was dominant out of the bullpen. Ryan Goins was given a shot to be the everyday second baseman but didn't hit (.188/.209/.271). Outfielder and hometown guy Dalton Pompey flashed exciting tools in limited playing time, and lefthander Daniel Norris rocketed from the Florida State League to Toronto in one season, although he had arthroscopic surgery on his left elbow in October.

KEY TRANSACTIONS: The Jays did not make many impactful transactions during the season, although they did swap Dominican infielder Gustavo Pierre to Philadelphia in August for outfielder John Mayberry Jr. Following an explosive 2013 offseason, 2014's was quiet, although they did bring in backup catcher Erik Kratz and lefthander Rob Rasmussen from Philadelphia for righthanded reliever Brad Lincoln.

DOWN ON THE FARM: With the callups of Pompey, Sanchez, Stroman and Norris, most of Toronto's high-end talent saw the majors last season. But the Jays still have players such as shortstop Franklin Barreto, the top prospect in the Northwest League at just 18; Third baseman Mitch Nay, the club's No. 4 prospect entering 2015 who has yet to show much power, and lefthander Jairo Labourt and righthander Miguel Castro, who ranked Nos. 3-4, respectively, on the Northwest Top 20 Prospects list.

OPENING DAY PAYROLL: $129,427,700 (9th)

PLAYERS OF THE YEAR

MAJOR LEAGUE	MINOR LEAGUE
Jose Bautista rf	**Daniel Norris** lhp
.286/.403/.524	(High Class A/
35 HR, 103 RBI	Double-A/Triple-A)
Led team in HR, RBI	12-2, 2.53

ORGANIZATION LEADERS

BATTING		*Minimum 250 AB
MAJORS		
* AVG	Cabrera, Melky	.321
* OPS	Bautista, Jose	.927
HR	Bautista, Jose	35
RBI	Bautista, Jose	103
MINORS		
* AVG	Pillar, Kevin, Buffalo	.323
* OBP	Pompey, Dalton, Dunedin, New Hamp., Buff.	.392
SLG	Pillar, Kevin, Buffalo	.509
R	Pompey, Dalton, Dunedin, New Hamp., Buff.	84
H	Berti, Jon, New Hampshire	146
TB	Smith Jr., Dwight, Dunedin	214
2B	Pillar, Kevin, Buffalo	39
3B	Loveless, Derrick, Lansing	9
	Pompey, Dalton, Dunedin, New Hamp., Buff.	9
HR	Schimpf, Ryan, New Hampshire, Buffalo	24
RBI	Hobson, K.C., Dunedin, New Hampshire	78
BB	Tirado, Alberto, Lansing, Vancouver	67
SO	Davis, D.J., Lansing	167
SB	Fields, Roemon, Vancouver	48

PITCHING		#Minimum 75 IP
MAJORS		
W	Dickey, R.A.	14
ERA	Redmond, Todd	3.24
SO	Hutchison, Drew	184
SV	Janssen, Casey	25
MINORS		
W	Graveman, Kendall, Lansing, Dun., New Hamp., Buff.	14
L	Cole, Taylor, New Hampshire, Dunedin	11
L	Hernandez, Jesse, Dunedin	11
ERA	Graveman, Kendall, Lansing, Dun., New Hamp., Buff.	1.83
G	Sikula, Arik, New Hampshire, Dunedin	56
GS	Gabryszwski, Jeremy, Dunedin, Lansing	28
SV	Sikula, Arik, New Hampshire, Dunedin	31
IP	Graveman, Kendall, Lansing, Dun., New Hamp., Buff.	167
BB	Tirado, Alberto, Lansing, Vancouver	67
SO	Cole, Taylor, New Hampshire, Dunedin	181
AVG	Norris, Daniel, Dunedin, New Hamp., Buff.	.212

General Manager: Alex Anthopoulos. **Farm Director:** Charlie Wilson. **Scouting Director:** Brian Parker.

Class	Team	League	W	L	PCT	Finish	Manager
Majors	Toronto Blue Jays	American	83	79	.512	14th (30)	John Gibbons
Triple-A	Buffalo Bisons	International	77	66	.538	4th (14)	Gary Allenson
Double-A	New Hampshire Fisher Cats	Eastern	66	76	.465	t-9th (12)	Bobby Meacham
High A	Dunedin Blue Jays	Florida State	77	61	.558	3rd (8)	Omar Malave
Low A	Lansing Lugnuts	Midwest	62	77	.446	13th (16)	John Tamargo
Short season	Vancouver Canadians	Northwest	46	30	.605	2nd (8)	John Schneider
Rookie	Bluefield Blue Jays	Appalachian	33	35	.485	7th (10)	Dennis Holmberg
Rookie	Blue Jays	Gulf Coast	18	41	.305	16th (16)	Kenny Graham
Overall 2015 Minor League Record			379	386	.495	18th (30)	

ORGANIZATION STATISTICS

TORONTO BLUE JAYS

AMERICAN LEAGUE

Batting	B-T	HT	WT	DOB	AVG	vLH	vRH	G	AB	R	H	2B	3B	HR	RBI	BB	HBP	SH	SF	SO	SB	CS	SLG	OBP
Bautista, Jose	R-R	6-0	205	10-19-80	.286	.345	.270	155	553	101	158	27	0	35	103	104	9	1	6	96	6	2	.524	.403
Cabrera, Melky	B-L	5-10	210	8-11-84	.301	.276	.310	139	568	81	171	35	3	16	73	43	3	2	5	67	6	2	.458	.351
Diaz, Jonathan	R-R	5-9	155	4-10-85	.158	.118	.190	23	38	3	6	1	0	0	4	3	2	2	0	14	1	0	.184	.256
Encarnacion, Edwin	R-R	6-1	230	1-7-83	.268	.263	.270	128	477	75	128	27	2	34	98	62	2	0	1	82	2	0	.547	.354
Francisco, Juan	L-R	6-2	245	6-24-87	.220	.116	.238	106	287	40	63	16	2	16	43	27	3	0	3	116	0	2	.456	.291
Getz, Chris	L-R	6-0	185	8-30-83	.160	.000	.211	10	25	1	4	1	0	0	0	1	1	1	0	4	2	0	.200	.222
Gillespie, Cole	R-R	6-1	215	6-20-84	.000	.000	.000	1	3	0	0	0	0	0	0	0	0	0	0	0	0	0	.000	.000
2-team total (34 Seattle)					.243	—		35	74	9	18	2	0	1	5	6	0	1	0	13	2	2	.311	.300
Glenn, Brad	R-R	6-2	220	4-2-87	.067	.067	—	6	15	0	1	0	0	0	0	1	0	0	0	5	0	0	.067	.125
Goins, Ryan	L-R	5-10	185	2-13-88	.188	.158	.196	67	181	14	34	6	3	1	15	5	0	6	1	42	0	1	.271	.209
Gose, Anthony	L-L	6-1	190	8-10-90	.226	.180	.238	94	239	31	54	8	1	2	13	25	5	4	1	74	15	5	.293	.311
Izturis, Maicer	B-R	5-8	155	9-12-80	.286	.357	.238	11	35	3	10	1	0	0	1	2	0	1	0	4	1	0	.314	.324
Johnson, Dan	L-R	6-2	210	8-10-79	.211	.200	.214	15	38	8	8	2	0	1	7	7	1	0	2	10	0	0	.342	.333
Kawasaki, Munenori	L-R	5-11	175	6-3-81	.258	.283	.253	82	240	31	62	7	1	0	17	22	3	8	1	49	1	0	.296	.327
Kottaras, George	L-R	6-0	200	5-10-83	.000	.000	.000	4	4	0	0	0	0	0	0	1	0	0	0	3	0	0	.000	.200
2-team total (10 Cleveland)					.240	—		14	25	4	6	0	0	3	4	5	0	1	1	14	0	0	.600	.355
Kratz, Erik	R-R	6-4	240	6-15-80	.198	.195	.200	34	81	8	16	3	0	3	10	3	0	0	0	12	0	0	.346	.226
2-team total (13 Kansas City)					.218	—		47	110	12	24	4	0	5	13	4	0	0	1	22	0	0	.391	.243
Lawrie, Brett	R-R	6-0	210	1-18-90	.247	.197	.263	70	259	27	64	9	0	12	38	16	5	0	2	49	0	0	.421	.301
Lind, Adam	L-L	6-2	195	7-17-83	.321	.061	.354	96	290	38	93	24	2	6	40	28	0	0	0	48	0	0	.479	.381
Mastroianni, Darin	R-R	5-11	190	8-26-85	.156	.120	.286	14	32	4	5	0	0	1	2	0	0	0	0	5	0	0	.250	.156
2-team total (7 Minnesota)					.116	—		21	43	7	5	0	0	1	2	1	0	0	0	10	1	0	.186	.136
Mayberry Jr., John	R-R	6-6	230	12-21-83	.208	.200	.222	15	24	4	5	3	0	1	2	5	0	0	1	5	0	0	.458	.333
Navarro, Dioner	B-R	5-9	205	2-9-84	.274	.280	.272	139	481	40	132	22	0	12	69	32	1	0	6	76	3	0	.395	.317
Pillar, Kevin	R-R	6-0	205	1-4-89	.267	.304	.243	53	116	19	31	9	0	2	7	4	1	0	1	28	1	2	.397	.295
Pompey, Dalton	B-R	6-2	195	12-11-92	.231	.071	.320	17	39	5	9	1	2	1	4	4	0	0	0	12	1	0	.436	.302
Rasmus, Colby	L-L	6-2	195	8-11-86	.225	.195	.236	104	346	45	78	21	1	18	40	29	1	0	0	124	4	0	.448	.287
Reimold, Nolan	R-R	6-4	205	10-12-83	.212	.231	.192	22	52	3	11	4	0	2	9	6	0	0	2	22	1	0	.404	.283
Reyes, Jose	B-R	6-0	195	6-11-83	.287	.281	.289	143	610	94	175	33	4	9	51	38	1	2	4	73	30	2	.398	.328
Sierra, Moises	R-R	6-1	220	9-24-88	.059	.000	.087	13	34	2	2	0	0	0	2	1	0	0	0	9	0	0	.059	.086
2-team total (83 Chicago)					.230	—		96	161	22	37	8	2	2	9	8	0	0	1	43	3	1	.342	.265
Thole, Josh	L-R	6-1	205	10-28-86	.248	.294	.232	57	133	11	33	4	0	0	7	14	0	3	0	25	0	3	.278	.320
Tolleson, Steve	R-R	5-11	185	11-1-83	.253	.319	.123	108	170	21	43	7	2	3	16	12	2	4	1	49	3	1	.371	.308
Valencia, Danny	R-R	6-2	220	9-19-84	.240	.277	.224	50	154	12	37	11	1	2	19	7	1	0	3	35	1	1	.364	.273
2-team total (36 Kansas City)					.258	—		86	264	20	68	16	1	4	30	14	2	0	4	62	1	1	.371	.296

Pitching	B-T	HT	WT	DOB	W	L	ERA	G	GS	CG	SV	IP	H	R	ER	HR	BB	SO	AVG	vLH	vRH	K/9	BB/9
Buehrle, Mark	L-L	6-2	240	3-23-79	13	10	3.39	32	32	0	0	202	228	83	76	15	46	119	.287	.269	.293	5.30	2.05
Cecil, Brett	R-L	6-3	220	7-2-86	2	3	2.70	66	0	0	5	53	46	16	16	2	27	76	.227	.247	.213	12.83	4.56
Delabar, Steve	R-R	6-5	220	7-17-83	3	0	4.91	30	0	0	0	26	19	14	14	3	19	21	.211	.135	.264	7.36	6.66
Dickey, R.A.	R-R	6-3	215	10-29-74	14	13	3.71	34	34	1	0	216	191	101	89	26	74	173	.233	.221	.242	7.22	3.09
Drabek, Kyle	R-R	6-2	205	12-8-87	0	0	0.00	2	0	0	0	3	2	0	0	0	2	5	.182	.333	.125	15.00	6.00
Graveman, Kendall	R-R	6-2	195	12-21-90	0	0	3.86	5	0	0	0	5	4	2	2	0	0	4	.222	.250	.200	7.71	0.00
Happ, J.A.	L-L	6-5	205	10-19-82	11	11	4.22	30	26	0	0	158	160	79	74	22	51	133	.261	.268	.259	7.58	2.91
Hendriks, Liam	R-L	6-1	205	2-10-89	1	0	6.08	3	3	0	0	13	12	9	9	3	4	8	.235	.292	.185	5.40	2.70
2-team total (6 Kansas City)					1	2	5.23	9	6	0	0	33	38	21	19	3	7	23	—	—	—	6.34	1.93
Hutchison, Drew	L-R	6-3	195	8-22-90	11	13	4.48	32	32	1	0	185	173	92	92	23	60	184	.245	.263	.224	8.97	2.92
Janssen, Casey	R-R	6-4	205	9-17-81	3	3	3.94	50	0	0	25	46	47	22	20	6	7	28	.261	.260	.262	5.52	1.38
Jeffress, Jeremy	R-R	6-1	205	9-21-87	0	0	10.80	3	0	0	0	3	8	4	4	0	3	4	.533	.500	.571	10.80	8.10
Jenkins, Chad	R-R	6-4	235	12-22-87	1	1	2.56	21	0	0	0	32	34	10	9	2	6	18	.264	.315	.227	5.12	1.71
Korecky, Bobby	R-R	5-11	185	9-16-79	0	0	8.10	2	0	0	0	3	3	3	3	0	1	2	.308	.500	.143	5.40	2.70
Loup, Aaron	L-L	5-11	205	12-19-87	4	4	3.15	71	0	0	4	69	50	25	24	4	30	56	.207	.159	.235	7.34	3.93

TORONTO BLUE JAYS

Name	B-T	HT	WT	DOB	W	L	ERA	G	GS	CG	SV	IP	H	R	ER	HR	BB	SO	AVG	vLH	vRH		
McGowan, Dustin	R-R	6-3	240	3-24-82	5	3	4.17	53	8	0	1	82	80	41	38	13	33	61	.253	.257	.250	6.70	3.62
Mills, Brad	L-L	6-0	185	3-5-85	0	0	27.00	2	0	0	0	4	10	13	13	3	4	5	.455	.800	.167	10.38	8.31
2-team total (3 Oakland)					1	1	9.15	5	3	0	0	21	29	22	21	5	11	19	—	—	—	8.27	4.79
Morrow, Brandon	R-R	6-3	210	7-26-84	1	3	5.67	13	6	0	0	33	37	21	21	2	18	30	.287	.303	.270	8.10	4.86
Nolin, Sean	L-L	6-4	230	12-26-89	0	0	9.00	1	0	0	0	1	1	1	1	0	0	0	.250	.000	.333	0.00	0.00
Norris, Daniel	L-L	6-2	180	4-25-93	0	0	5.40	5	1	0	0	7	5	4	4	1	5	4	.208	.091	.308	5.40	6.75
Rasmussen, Rob	R-L	5-10	170	4-2-89	0	0	3.18	10	0	0	0	11	8	4	4	1	7	13	.195	.133	.231	10.32	5.56
Redmond, Todd	R-R	6-3	200	5-17-85	1	4	3.24	42	0	0	1	75	73	33	27	5	27	60	.263	.287	.245	7.20	3.24
Rogers, Esmil	R-R	6-3	200	8-14-85	0	0	6.97	16	0	0	0	21	28	17	16	5	7	21	.318	.386	.250	9.15	3.05
2-team total (18 New York)					2	0	5.72	34	1	0	0	46	50	30	29	8	17	44	—	—	—	8.67	3.35
Sanchez, Aaron	R-R	6-4	200	7-1-92	2	2	1.09	24	0	0	3	33	14	5	4	1	9	27	.128	.150	.116	7.36	2.45
Santos, Sergio	R-R	6-3	215	7-4-83	0	3	8.57	26	0	0	5	21	28	22	20	5	18	29	.326	.244	.415	12.43	7.71
Stroman, Marcus	R-R	5-9	185	5-1-91	11	6	3.65	26	20	1	1	131	125	56	53	7	28	111	.250	.232	.269	7.65	1.93
Wagner, Neil	R-R	6-0	215	1-1-84	0	0	8.10	10	0	0	0	10	12	9	9	1	4	6	.279	.333	.211	5.40	3.60

Fielding

Catcher	PCT	G	PO	A	E	DP	PB
Kottaras	1.000	3	10	0	0	0	1
Kratz	1.000	25	141	9	0	1	1
Navarro	.996	112	782	35	3	3	7
Thole	.997	53	295	11	1	3	9

First Base	PCT	G	PO	A	E	DP
Bautista	1.000	12	75	6	0	6
Encarnacion	.988	80	625	33	8	51
Francisco	.985	20	129	6	2	12
Johnson	.980	8	44	4	1	2
Lind	.992	47	357	23	3	41
Mayberry Jr.	1.000	6	40	2	0	3
Valencia	.987	20	71	5	1	3

Second Base	PCT	G	PO	A	E	DP
Diaz	1.000	5	3	5	0	2
Getz	1.000	10	8	22	0	1

	PCT	G	PO	A	E	DP
Goins	.995	57	79	124	1	24
Izturis	1.000	10	10	22	0	8
Kawasaki	.977	64	78	139	5	28
Lawrie	.984	32	53	69	2	19
Tolleson	.963	55	56	75	5	14

Third Base	PCT	G	PO	A	E	DP
Francisco	.933	74	37	88	9	11
Kawasaki	.956	19	6	37	2	1
Lawrie	.984	63	42	82	2	10
Tolleson	1.000	43	11	28	0	1
Valencia	.978	40	24	67	2	5

Shortstop	PCT	G	PO	A	E	DP
Diaz	1.000	14	12	23	0	6
Goins	1.000	15	12	25	0	5
Kawasaki	1.000	4	2	2	0	0
Reyes	.965	142	160	371	19	75

	PCT	G	PO	A	E	DP
Tolleson	1.000	2	1	1	0	0

Outfield	PCT	G	PO	A	E	DP
Bautista	.987	133	282	12	4	2
Cabrera	.992	136	240	13	2	3
Diaz	1.000	3	2	0	0	0
Encarnacion	1.000	2	2	0	0	0
Gillespie	1.000	1	2	0	0	0
Glenn	1.000	4	8	0	0	0
Gose	.995	88	187	2	1	0
Mastroianni	1.000	12	17	1	0	0
Mayberry Jr.	1.000	5	2	0	0	0
Pillar	1.000	47	71	2	0	0
Pompey	1.000	11	17	0	0	0
Rasmus	.996	87	234	3	1	0
Reimold	.947	10	17	1	1	0
Sierra	1.000	7	13	0	0	0
Tolleson	.900	7	9	0	1	0

BUFFALO BISONS — TRIPLE-A

INTERNATIONAL LEAGUE

Batting	B-T	HT	WT	DOB	AVG	vLH	vRH	G	AB	R	H	2B	3B	HR	RBI	BB	HBP	SH	SF	SO	SB	CS	SLG	OBP
Aldridge, Cory	L-R	6-1	225	6-13-79	.226	.158	.265	16	53	5	12	1	0	2	8	7	0	0	2	17	0	1	.358	.306
Carroll, Brett	R-R	5-11	210	10-3-82	.179	.227	.147	19	56	5	10	1	0	0	3	2	1	1		19	0	1	.196	.242
Chambers, Adron	L-L	5-10	200	10-8-86	.286	.190	.314	25	91	11	26	2	0	3	14	9	0	3	1	18	0	3	.407	.347
Diaz, Jonathan	R-R	5-9	155	4-10-85	.205	.225	.190	92	244	37	50	13	3	1	23	37	5	15	2	43	4	4	.295	.319
Encarnacion, Edwin	R-R	6-1	180	1-7-83	.250	—	.250	2	8	1	2	0	0	1	2	0	0	0	0	0	0	0	.625	.250
Francisco, Juan	L-R	6-2	245	6-24-87	.341	.273	.364	12	44	9	15	2	1	2	11	6	0	0	0	9	0	0	.568	.420
Getz, Chris	L-R	6-0	185	8-30-83	.309	.417	.286	18	68	8	21	2	0	0	9	8	0	0	0	11	6	1	.338	.382
Gillespie, Cole	R-R	6-1	215	6-20-84	.354	.500	.300	26	82	15	29	4	1	2	16	14	1	0	7	14	3	0	.500	.423
Gimenez, Hector	B-R	5-10	230	9-28-82	.286	.286	—	3	7	1	2	0	0	1	2	0	0	1	0	0	0	0	.286	.400
2-team total (16 Charlotte)					.129	—	—	19	62	6	8	1	0	1	5	11	0	0	1	14	0	0	.194	.257
Glenn, Brad	R-R	6-2	220	4-2-87	.303	.353	.281	61	221	26	67	13	1	6	37	19	1	1	5	54	2	1	.452	.360
Goedert, Jared	R-R	6-1	210	5-25-85	.250	.274	.239	98	344	49	86	14	1	10	40	45	2	0	0	78	3	0	.384	.340
Goins, Ryan	L-R	5-10	185	2-13-88	.284	.279	.286	97	363	36	103	21	2	0	30	28	2	7	2	64	4	4	.353	.337
Gose, Anthony	L-L	6-1	190	8-10-90	.244	.286	.219	51	205	29	50	5	2	4	25	17	1	1	0	65	21	8	.346	.305
Hague, Matt	R-R	6-3	220	8-20-85	.377	.500	.276	13	53	8	20	7	0	1	10	3	0	0	0	10	0	1	.566	.411
2-team total (93 Indianapolis)					.282	—	—	106	383	60	108	23	1	15	76	49	7	0	3	76	1	3	.465	.371
Jimenez, A.J.	R-R	6-0	225	5-1-90	.260	.280	.250	58	219	21	57	13	1	2	24	13	0	0	5	33	1	1	.356	.295
Johnson, Dan	L-R	6-2	210	8-10-79	.232	.195	.253	107	362	62	84	19	0	18	56	86	5	0	6	81	0	0	.434	.381
Kawasaki, Munenori	L-R	5-11	175	6-3-81	.276	.355	.247	44	116	12	32	11	1	0	9	8	0	4	1	17	1	1	.388	.320
Kottaras, George	L-R	6-0	200	5-10-83	.262	.278	.250	13	42	6	11	1	0	3	8	7	0	0	0	14	0	0	.500	.367
2-team total (14 Columbus)					.190	—	—	27	84	10	16	1	0	4	13	11	0	1	0	32	0	0	.345	.284
Kratz, Erik	R-R	6-4	240	6-15-80	.299	.259	.317	27	87	13	26	10	0	3	17	9	0	1	3	18	0	1	.517	.354
LaRoche, Andy	R-R	6-0	205	9-13-83	.248	.241	.252	60	202	25	50	15	0	5	29	16	3	1	2	33	0	0	.396	.309
Mastroianni, Darin	R-R	5-11	190	8-26-85	.267	.336	.232	88	344	52	92	18	1	5	21	40	4	3	2	67	20	5	.369	.349
2-team total (4 Rochester)					.277	—	—	92	364	56	101	20	1	5	23	40	4	3	2	71	20	6	.379	.354
McDade, Mike	B-B	6-1	250	5-8-89	.136	.000	.176	7	22	0	3	0	0	0	1	0	0	0	1	5	0	0	.136	.174
Mesa, Melky	R-R	6-1	190	1-31-87	.250	.200	.286	3	12	1	3	1	0	0	0	0	0	0	0	7	0	0	.333	.250
Murphy, Jack	B-R	6-4	235	4-6-88	.206	.167	.214	11	34	3	7	3	0	0	2	5	0	0	0	7	0	0	.294	.308
Nanita, Ricardo	L-L	6-1	195	6-12-81	.118	.000	.125	6	17	2	2	1	0	0	0	0	0	0	0	5	0	0	.176	.118
Nickeas, Mike	R-R	6-0	210	2-13-83	.207	.208	.206	49	150	13	31	2	0	3	17	18	0	5	4	30	1	0	.280	.285
Nolan, Kevin	R-R	6-2	205	12-13-87	.239	.214	.246	21	71	8	17	1	1	0	3	5	1	0	0	10	0	0	.282	.299
Ochinko, Sean	R-R	5-11	205	10-21-87	.231	.000	.250	8	26	2	6	1	0	1	5	2	0	0	0	3	0	0	.385	.286
Pillar, Kevin	R-R	6-1	205	1-4-89	.323	.355	.310	100	405	57	131	39	3	10	59	21	4	0	4	48	27	6	.509	.359
Pompey, Dalton	B-R	6-2	195	12-11-92	.358	.393	.320	12	53	15	19	5	0	0	5	3	0	0	0	10	6	0	.453	.393
Rasmus, Colby	L-L	6-2	195	8-11-86	.130	.250	.000	6	23	0	3	0	0	0	2	1	0	0	0	9	0	0	.130	.167
Schimpf, Ryan	L-R	5-9	190	4-11-88	.189	.104	.213	67	212	29	40	7	1	9	21	24	7	1	2	59	0	1	.358	.290
Tolleson, Steve	R-R	5-11	185	11-1-83	.236	.250	.232	19	72	12	17	2	1	1	9	12	0	0	0	13	6	1	.333	.345

Batting	B-T	HT	WT	DOB	AVG	vLH	vRH	G	AB	R	H	2B	3B	HR	RBI	BB	HBP	SH	SF	SO	SB	CS	SLG	OBP
Tuiasosopo, Matt	R-R	6-2	225	5-10-86	.206	.209	.204	59	214	17	44	8	0	2	18	25	1	0	2	64	1	1	.271	.289
2-team total (63 Charlotte)					.240	—	—	122	409	59	98	18	0	13	50	71	5	0	2	120	1	1	.379	.357
Wallace, Brett	L-R	6-2	235	8-26-86	.323	.300	.330	38	133	12	43	5	0	7	23	15	3	0	0	33	0	0	.519	.404
2-team total (90 Norfolk)					.282	—	—	128	472	62	133	17	0	17	58	44	7	0	2	131	0	1	.426	.350
Wilson, Kenny	B-R	5-11	195	1-30-90	.239	.182	.265	21	71	7	17	3	2	0	5	9	1	1	0	15	5	4	.338	.333

Pitching	B-T	HT	WT	DOB	W	L	ERA	G	GS	CG	SV	IP	H	R	ER	HR	BB	SO	AVG	vLH	vRH	K/9	BB/9
Ayala, Luis	R-R	6-2	205	1-12-78	1	2	5.40	11	0	0	0	12	19	8	7	1	4	9	.365	.588	.257	6.94	3.09
Bibens-Dirkx, Austin	R-R	6-1	210	4-29-85	2	2	3.89	17	4	0	0	39	40	18	17	4	11	35	.261	.250	.270	8.01	2.52
Bleier, Richard	L-L	6-3	215	4-16-87	0	0	4.50	1	0	0	0	2	3	1	1	1	0	2	.333	.500	.286	9.00	0.00
Boone, Randy	R-R	6-0	200	8-6-84	0	0	0.00	2	0	0	0	2	1	0	0	0	1	0	.167	.000	.200	0.00	4.50
Cecil, Brett	R-L	6-3	220	7-2-86	1	0	4.50	2	0	0	0	2	2	1	1	1	0	1	.286	—	.286	4.50	0.00
Copeland, Scott	R-R	6-3	210	12-15-87	3	1	1.80	4	4	0	0	25	19	7	5	0	7	16	.209	.267	.152	5.76	2.52
Delabar, Steve	R-R	6-5	220	7-17-83	2	2	2.89	24	0	0	1	28	21	9	9	3	18	38	.208	.093	.293	12.21	5.79
Drabek, Kyle	R-R	6-2	205	12-8-87	7	7	4.18	32	13	0	0	99	116	57	46	12	30	68	.293	.283	.301	6.18	2.73
Graveman, Kendall	R-R	6-2	195	12-21-90	3	2	1.88	6	6	0	0	38	34	8	8	1	5	22	.245	.293	.188	5.17	1.17
Happ, J.A.	L-L	6-5	205	10-19-82	0	0	1.93	1	1	0	0	5	5	1	1	2	6	.278	.400	.231	11.57	3.86
Hendriks, Liam	R-R	6-1	205	2-10-89	8	1	2.33	18	16	1	0	108	92	32	28	6	7	91	.231	.227	.235	7.56	0.58
Hill, Shawn	R-R	6-2	225	4-28-81	2	1	4.85	6	4	0	0	30	31	17	16	5	14	21	.277	.305	.245	6.37	4.25
3-team total (10 Charlotte, 4 Toledo)					7	6	4.49	20	17	0	0	112	133	61	56	13	27	56	—	—	—	4.49	2.16
Hynes, Colt	L-L	5-11	200	6-28-85	0	1	1.04	7	0	0	0	9	4	1	1	1	7	.133	.000	.190	7.27	1.04
Infante, Greg	R-R	6-2	215	7-10-87	2	1	2.35	5	0	0	0	8	2	2	2	0	2	10	.080	.071	.091	11.74	2.35
Jenkins, Chad	R-R	6-4	235	12-22-87	1	3	4.70	21	4	0	2	44	45	26	23	5	9	27	.263	.281	.252	5.52	1.84
Korecky, Bobby	R-R	5-11	185	9-16-79	5	3	1.97	55	0	0	22	64	47	14	14	3	18	60	.199	.216	.187	8.44	2.53
Liz, Radhames	R-R	6-2	185	10-6-83	1	0	5.21	4	4	0	0	19	21	11	11	3	13	11	.300	.286	.310	5.21	6.16
McGuire, Deck	R-R	6-6	220	6-23-89	3	5	5.56	10	10	0	0	55	57	37	34	12	23	38	.265	.263	.267	6.22	3.76
Mills, Brad	L-L	6-0	185	3-5-85	2	1	3.06	6	6	0	0	32	26	11	11	2	5	26	.228	.259	.218	7.24	1.39
Morrow, Brandon	R-R	6-3	210	7-26-84	0	0	3.86	2	0	0	0	2	2	1	1	0	0	1	.222	.500	.143	3.86	0.00
Nolin, Sean	L-L	6-4	230	12-26-89	4	6	3.50	17	17	0	0	87	74	36	34	6	35	74	.225	.192	.235	7.63	3.61
Norris, Daniel	L-L	6-2	180	4-25-93	3	1	3.18	5	4	0	0	23	14	8	8	2	8	38	.182	.211	.172	15.09	3.18
Rasmussen, Rob	R-L	5-10	170	4-2-89	1	1	2.72	35	0	0	1	43	32	15	13	0	17	44	.203	.226	.190	9.21	3.56
Rogers, Esmil	R-R	6-3	200	8-14-85	2	2	3.14	12	7	0	0	49	42	17	17	2	18	41	.237	.211	.255	7.58	3.33
Romero, Ricky	R-L	6-1	210	11-6-84	0	3	5.50	9	9	0	0	38	37	24	23	4	42	28	.268	.240	.274	6.69	10.04
Rowland-Smith, Ryan	L-L	6-3	250	1-26-83	1	0	5.14	12	0	0	0	14	10	8	8	4	3	11	.204	.250	.189	7.07	1.93
2-team total (12 Louisville)					1	0	4.66	24	1	0	0	29	29	17	15	4	7	20	—	—	—	6.21	2.17
Sanchez, Aaron	R-R	6-4	200	7-1-92	0	3	4.19	8	6	0	0	34	36	20	16	4	17	27	.281	.327	.247	7.08	4.46
Santos, Sergio	R-R	6-3	215	7-4-83	1	0	0.00	11	0	0	2	11	3	1	0	0	6	16	.083	.067	.095	13.50	5.06
Stilson, John	R-R	6-3	205	7-28-90	2	0	3.18	25	0	0	1	34	37	14	12	2	18	32	.272	.268	.275	8.47	4.76
Storey, Mickey	R-R	6-1	185	3-16-86	0	1	10.80	4	0	0	0	3	7	4	4	0	5	2	.467	.667	.417	5.40	13.50
Stroman, Marcus	R-R	5-9	185	5-1-91	2	4	3.03	7	7	1	0	36	34	14	12	1	9	45	.239	.268	.218	11.36	2.27
Tepera, Ryan	R-R	6-1	190	11-5-87	7	3	3.66	51	0	0	2	64	66	29	26	4	24	67	.264	.291	.243	9.34	3.38
Valdes, Raul	L-L	5-11	190	11-27-77	5	5	4.00	23	12	0	0	81	84	40	36	9	24	78	.263	.238	.271	8.67	2.67
Wagner, Neil	R-R	6-0	215	1-1-84	0	1	4.00	9	0	0	4	9	6	4	4	0	3	11	.182	.333	.095	11.00	3.00
Walden, Marcus	R-R	6-0	195	9-13-88	0	1	13.50	3	0	0	0	4	5	6	6	1	3	1	.313	.000	.556	2.25	6.75
Walters, P.J.	R-R	6-4	215	3-12-85	4	2	4.56	9	9	0	0	49	54	27	25	5	17	41	.277	.308	.250	7.48	3.10
Zagurski, Mike	L-L	6-0	240	1-27-83	2	1	1.83	30	0	0	9	44	31	11	9	0	19	61	.197	.277	.164	12.38	3.86
2-team total (16 Columbus)					4	1	2.08	46	0	0	0	61	42	16	14	1	29	83	—	—	—	12.31	4.30

Fielding

Catcher	PCT	G	PO	A	E	DP	PB
Gimenez	1.000	3	18	1	0	0	1
Jimenez	1.000	48	340	25	0	5	2
Kottaras	.988	11	78	1	1	0	2
Kratz	.989	20	165	8	2	1	0
Murphy	.990	11	93	5	1	1	1
Nickeas	.995	47	368	16	2	0	0
Ochinko	1.000	8	64	2	0	0	0

First Base	PCT	G	PO	A	E	DP
Encarnacion	1.000	1	6	0	0	0
Goedert	1.000	17	119	11	0	15
Johnson	.999	81	690	40	1	67
LaRoche	1.000	1	1	0	0	0
McDade	1.000	6	51	2	0	8
Nolan	.500	1	0	1	1	0
Tuiasosopo	1.000	14	101	9	0	13
Wallace	.992	29	230	19	2	28

Second Base	PCT	G	PO	A	E	DP
Diaz	.992	28	53	68	1	21
Getz	.956	14	24	41	3	6

	PCT	G	PO	A	E	DP
Goins	.983	49	90	140	4	34
Kawasaki	.984	13	22	38	1	10
LaRoche	1.000	1	0	1	0	0
Nolan	1.000	4	9	9	0	4
Schimpf	.983	38	68	103	3	28
Tolleson	.973	7	16	20	1	6

Third Base	PCT	G	PO	A	E	DP
Diaz	1.000	10	3	2	0	0
Francisco	.944	7	7	10	1	1
Goedert	.919	71	35	123	14	9
Hague	.884	13	8	30	5	1
Johnson	1.000	1	0	1	0	0
Kawasaki	.800	1	2	2	1	0
LaRoche	.936	34	16	57	5	7
Nolan	.870	7	3	17	3	2
Schimpf	.958	8	3	20	1	5
Tolleson	1.000	4	1	6	0	0

Shortstop	PCT	G	PO	A	E	DP
Diaz	.987	56	61	162	3	40
Goins	.995	51	63	138	1	30

	PCT	G	PO	A	E	DP
Kawasaki	.990	28	32	68	1	16
Nolan	1.000	10	10	28	0	3
Tolleson	.900	9	10	17	3	3

Outfield	PCT	G	PO	A	E	DP
Aldridge	.917	8	11	0	1	0
Carroll	.960	12	23	1	1	1
Chambers	.971	21	33	1	1	0
Diaz	1.000	1	3	0	0	0
Gillespie	.974	20	36	1	1	0
Glenn	.990	51	91	4	1	2
Gose	.991	49	110	5	1	2
Mastroianni	1.000	85	163	6	0	2
Mesa	.909	3	10	0	1	0
Nanita	1.000	4	6	0	0	0
Pillar	.989	95	173	6	2	1
Pompey	.931	11	27	0	2	0
Rasmus	1.000	4	11	0	0	0
Schimpf	1.000	14	23	1	0	0
Tuiasosopo	.983	39	54	3	1	1
Wilson	.972	21	31	4	1	1

NEW HAMPSHIRE FISHER CATS

DOUBLE-A

EASTERN LEAGUE

Batting	B-T	HT	WT	DOB	AVG	vLH	vRH	G	AB	R	H	2B	3B	HR	RBI	BB	HBP	SH	SF	SO	SB	CS	SLG	OBP
Aldridge, Cory	L-R	6-1	225	6-13-79	.271	.188	.290	22	85	11	23	1	0	5	18	4	0	0	0	20	0	1	.459	.303

Name	B-T	HT	WT	DOB	AVG	vLH	vRH	G	AB	R	H	2B	3B	HR	RBI	BB	HBP	SH	SF	SO	SB	CS	OBP	SLG
Berti, Jon	R-R	5-10	175	1-22-90	.270	.277	.266	136	541	69	146	21	7	7	50	35	9	5	4	82	40	15	.373	.323
Burns, Andy	R-R	6-2	205	8-7-90	.255	.301	.232	133	495	71	126	32	5	15	63	41	6	3	8	99	18	8	.430	.315
Carter, Yusuf	R-R	6-2	205	2-6-85	.183	.200	.174	23	71	6	13	3	0	0	5	3	1	0	1	19	1	0	.225	.224
Chung, Derrick	R-R	5-9	185	2-23-88	.240	.229	.244	47	171	13	41	6	0	0	12	6	3	1	2	14	0	3	.275	.275
Crouse, Michael	R-R	6-4	215	11-22-90	.243	.292	.213	109	346	45	84	17	6	9	34	37	4	1	2	104	15	6	.405	.321
Fermin, Andy	L-R	6-0	180	7-27-89	.262	.150	.283	42	126	17	33	6	0	5	16	8	1	0	2	10	0	0	.429	.307
Flores, Jorge	R-R	5-5	160	11-25-91	.293	.306	.286	64	205	19	60	8	1	0	16	11	3	3	0	27	5	5	.341	.338
Gimenez, Hector	B-R	5-10	230	9-28-82	.235	.125	.286	13	51	6	12	3	0	2	5	2	0	0	0	14	0	0	.412	.264
Glenn, Brad	R-R	6-2	220	4-2-87	.231	.284	.200	48	182	31	42	10	1	9	23	20	2	0	2	53	0	0	.445	.311
Hobson, K.C.	L-L	6-2	205	8-22-90	.215	.222	.213	53	177	18	38	8	0	5	21	15	0	0	0	41	1	1	.345	.276
Jacobo, Gabe	R-R	6-3	200	4-14-87	.146	.188	.124	35	137	5	20	5	0	4	15	6	1	0	2	37	1	0	.270	.185
Jimenez, A.J.	R-R	6-0	225	5-1-90	.223	.289	.179	25	94	11	21	8	0	1	13	6	1	0	1	19	1	0	.340	.275
Jones, Jonathan	R-R	5-11	185	8-2-89	.233	.182	.264	56	172	21	40	7	2	1	15	16	1	7	0	26	7	3	.314	.302
McDade, Mike	B-R	6-1	250	5-8-89	.250	.214	.270	78	276	25	69	11	0	7	36	20	4	0	3	57	0	0	.366	.307
Mesa, Melky	R-R	6-1	190	1-31-87	.256	.220	.273	35	129	17	33	9	1	4	10	5	4	0	0	33	1	2	.434	.304
Mooney, Peter	L-R	5-6	155	8-19-90	.161	.000	.179	9	31	2	5	1	0	0	4	1	0	0	0	7	0	0	.194	.188
Munoz, Aaron	R-R	5-9	190	12-24-88	.043	.143	.000	8	23	2	1	0	0	0	2	1	0	0	1	7	0	0	.043	.080
Murphy, Jack	B-R	6-4	235	4-6-88	.225	.189	.250	42	129	19	29	4	0	6	15	15	1	1	0	30	0	0	.395	.310
Newman, Matt	L-L	5-10	170	9-20-88	.242	.279	.230	80	298	25	72	22	4	6	39	16	1	3	5	81	1	3	.403	.278
Nolan, Kevin	R-R	6-2	205	12-13-87	.257	.231	.273	102	354	42	91	22	1	5	38	26	3	0	3	47	9	4	.367	.311
Ochinko, Sean	R-R	5-11	205	10-21-87	.204	.240	.172	16	54	5	11	2	0	2	8	1	1	0	0	5	0	0	.352	.232
Pierre, Gustavo	R-R	6-2	202	12-28-91	.214	.200	.222	9	28	2	6	1	0	1	3	1	0	0	1	11	0	0	.357	.233
Pompey, Dalton	B-R	6-2	195	12-11-92	.295	.226	.321	31	112	20	33	5	3	3	12	14	1	0	0	18	8	5	.473	.378
Rankin, Pierce	R-R	6-1	190	4-26-89	.209	.294	.154	12	43	5	9	1	0	0	0	1	1	0	15	0	0	.233	.227
Schimpf, Ryan	L-R	5-9	190	4-11-88	.270	.217	.296	50	185	35	50	17	1	15	37	28	3	0	3	56	3	0	.616	.370
Van Kirk, Brian	R-R	6-1	200	8-10-85	.217	.235	.207	12	46	5	10	2	0	0	4	3	0	1	0	16	0	1	.261	.265
Wilson, Kenny	B-R	5-11	195	1-30-90	.241	.236	.243	44	170	24	41	4	4	2	15	11	4	5	2	58	17	6	.347	.299
2-team total (11 New Britain)					.232	—	—	55	211	30	49	7	4	2	16	17	6	6	2	58	17	6	.332	.305

Pitching

Name	B-T	HT	WT	DOB	W	L	ERA	G	GS	CG	SV	IP	H	R	ER	HR	BB	SO	AVG	vLH	vRH	K/9	BB/9
Anderson, John	L-L	6-2	200	11-9-88	3	3	4.59	27	6	0	1	69	57	39	35	7	32	72	.229	.230	.229	9.44	4.19
Antolin, Dustin	R-R	6-2	195	8-9-89	4	6	3.38	37	0	0	0	43	42	17	16	0	15	52	.259	.258	.260	10.97	3.16
Bibens-Dirkx, Austin	R-R	6-1	210	4-29-85	6	4	3.16	17	12	0	1	74	67	30	26	11	12	57	.240	.254	.228	6.93	1.46
Bleier, Richard	L-L	6-3	215	4-16-87	6	5	3.93	34	5	0	1	85	100	47	37	13	11	43	.292	.217	.319	4.57	1.17
Boone, Randy	R-R	6-0	200	8-6-84	1	4	2.89	43	0	0	10	56	48	21	18	3	17	55	.234	.217	.246	8.84	2.73
Boyd, Matt	L-L	6-3	215	2-2-91	1	4	6.96	10	10	0	0	43	55	33	33	5	13	44	.307	.257	.319	9.28	2.74
Browning, Wil	R-R	6-3	190	9-8-88	1	0	7.11	6	0	0	0	6	6	6	5	1	5	7	.261	.400	.222	9.95	7.11
Cole, Taylor	R-R	6-1	190	8-20-89	0	2	7.30	2	2	0	0	12	12	11	10	1	7	10	.250	.304	.200	7.30	5.11
Copeland, Scott	R-R	6-3	210	12-15-87	8	8	3.74	27	22	1	0	140	140	72	58	11	48	89	.260	.305	.228	5.74	3.09
Davis, Tony	B-L	5-9	180	1-16-88	1	1	5.70	17	0	0	1	24	23	16	15	1	22	17	.277	.294	.273	6.46	8.37
Gracey, Scott	R-R	6-2	190	10-15-86	3	4	5.50	35	0	0	3	52	55	33	32	7	19	53	.263	.297	.244	9.11	3.27
Graveman, Kendall	R-R	6-2	195	12-21-90	1	0	1.50	1	1	0	0	6	8	1	1	0	2	4	.364	.429	.333	6.00	3.00
Hill, Shawn	R-R	6-2	225	4-28-81	0	2	5.09	3	3	1	0	18	15	11	10	2	3	7	.221	.243	.194	3.57	1.53
Infante, Greg	R-R	6-2	215	7-10-87	0	1	1.86	36	0	0	22	39	28	8	8	0	16	34	.207	.204	.210	7.91	3.72
Jackson, Justin	R-R	6-2	190	12-11-88	0	1	6.23	6	0	0	0	9	15	7	6	0	3	5	.357	.286	.429	5.19	3.12
Janssen, Casey	R-R	6-4	205	9-17-81	0	0	0.00	3	2	0	0	3	3	0	0	0	0	2	.250	.000	.429	6.00	0.00
Lawrence, Casey	R-R	6-2	170	10-28-87	9	9	3.69	26	22	1	0	151	161	72	62	9	29	93	.276	.296	.262	5.53	1.72
Lee, Mike	R-R	6-7	235	11-18-86	2	1	2.25	5	5	0	0	32	24	8	8	4	7	30	.200	.115	.265	8.44	1.97
Liz, Radhames	R-R	6-2	185	10-6-83	2	2	1.93	8	8	1	0	42	32	9	9	0	11	33	.212	.176	.247	7.07	2.36
McFarland, Blake	R-R	6-5	230	2-2-88	0	2	2.04	19	1	0	2	35	25	9	8	1	15	37	.197	.154	.216	9.42	3.82
McGuire, Deck	R-R	6-3	210	6-23-89	3	4	2.98	10	10	0	0	60	58	28	20	3	17	47	.249	.264	.236	7.01	2.54
Norris, Daniel	L-L	6-2	180	4-25-93	3	1	4.54	8	8	0	0	36	32	18	18	5	17	49	.235	.212	.243	12.36	4.29
Sanchez, Aaron	R-R	6-4	200	7-1-92	3	4	3.82	14	14	0	0	66	52	34	28	2	40	57	.222	.225	.220	7.77	5.45
Santos, Sergio	R-R	6-3	215	7-4-83	0	0	18.00	2	1	0	0	2	4	4	4	1	1	3	.400	.500	.333	13.50	4.50
Sikula, Arik	R-R	6-0	200	12-21-88	1	0	3.00	12	0	0	15	15	19	5	5	1	4	20	.322	.350	.308	12.00	2.40
Storey, Mickey	R-R	6-1	185	3-16-86	1	0	2.45	8	0	0	2	15	12	4	4	2	3	18	.222	.154	.286	11.05	1.84
Walters, P.J.	R-R	6-4	215	3-12-85	2	3	2.60	8	8	0	0	52	47	20	15	5	10	50	.237	.212	.257	8.65	1.73
White, Ben	R-R	6-2	185	5-10-89	1	1	5.73	2	2	0	0	11	10	7	7	2	4	14	.233	.273	.190	11.45	3.27
Ybarra, Tyler	L-L	6-2	210	12-11-89	4	4	4.42	38	0	0	0	53	42	28	26	8	30	43	.227	.220	.230	7.30	5.09

Fielding

Catcher	PCT	G	PO	A	E	DP	PB
Carter	.977	6	38	4	1	1	3
Chung	.990	46	333	53	4	3	4
Gimenez	.988	9	73	11	1	1	2
Jimenez	.994	24	143	17	1	2	6
Munoz	.980	8	44	4	1	0	0
Murphy	.997	38	281	22	1	0	4
Ochinko	1.000	9	72	2	0	0	2
Rankin	.982	9	49	7	1	1	0

First Base	PCT	G	PO	A	E	DP
Burns	.981	7	49	2	1	3
Carter	1.000	5	46	2	0	1
Glenn	1.000	4	44	1	0	5
Hobson	.975	39	318	26	9	21

	PCT	G	PO	A	E	DP
Jacobo	.997	28	268	17	1	19
McDade	.995	61	570	38	3	65
Nolan	1.000	4	25	1	0	4

Second Base	PCT	G	PO	A	E	DP
Berti	.968	84	150	272	14	61
Burns	1.000	7	8	18	0	2
Fermin	.986	15	25	43	1	6
Flores	.977	20	36	49	2	14
Mooney	1.000	3	4	12	0	1
Nolan	1.000	3	6	6	0	2
Schimpf	.967	13	18	40	2	7

Third Base	PCT	G	PO	A	E	DP
Berti	1.000	6	6	12	0	0
Burns	.935	94	46	200	17	18

	PCT	G	PO	A	E	DP
Fermin	.930	18	9	31	3	3
Nolan	1.000	9	5	10	0	1
Pierre	.955	9	5	16	1	1
Schimpf	.917	8	4	18	2	1

Shortstop	PCT	G	PO	A	E	DP
Berti	1.000	1	3	1	0	0
Burns	.947	14	18	36	3	5
Flores	.950	43	48	124	9	29
Mooney	.913	6	5	16	2	1
Nolan	.949	83	110	259	20	58

Outfield	PCT	G	PO	A	E	DP
Aldridge	.939	18	29	2	2	0
Berti	1.000	31	42	2	0	0
Burns	1.000	5	9	1	0	0

Crouse	.975	102	180	14	5	3	Mesa	1.000	31	57	4 0 1
Glenn	1.000	32	58	1	0	0	Newman	.987	76	150	6 2 1
Hobson	—	1	0	0	0	0	Pompey	1.000	30	56	4 0 2
Jones	.983	51	110	5	2	0	Schimpf	1.000	14	19	0 0 0

Van Kirk	1.000 7 11 0 0 0
Wilson	.982 41 105 3 2 0

DUNEDIN BLUE JAYS   HIGH CLASS A
FLORIDA STATE LEAGUE

Batting	B-T	HT	WT	DOB	AVG	vLH	vRH	G	AB	R	H	2B	3B	HR	RBI	BB	HBP	SH	SF	SO	SB	CS	SLG	OBP
Baligod, Nick	L-R	5-11	190	9-28-87	.249	.208	.259	95	354	45	88	10	2	6	35	33	3	1	1	36	5	2	.339	.317
Chung, Derrick	R-R	5-9	185	2-23-88	.320	.340	.313	49	178	18	57	15	0	2	16	19	3	1	0	20	1	2	.438	.395
Dantzler, L.B.	L-R	5-11	200	5-22-91	.241	.261	.234	48	174	17	42	11	0	3	29	16	1	0	2	37	0	0	.356	.306
Encarnacion, Edwin	R-R	6-1	230	1-7-83	.250	.500	.000	2	4	0	1	0	0	0	0	0	0	0	0	1	0	0	.250	.250
Fermin, Andy	L-R	6-0	180	7-27-89	.276	.400	.250	14	58	7	16	3	2	1	6	4	0	0	0	9	0	0	.448	.323
Flores, Jorge	R-R	5-5	160	11-25-91	.308	.160	.354	32	104	20	32	6	0	0	14	8	3	3	0	10	4	2	.365	.374
Gillespie, Cole	R-R	6-1	215	6-20-84	.375	—	.375	2	8	1	3	1	0	0	3	1	0	0	0	2	0	0	.500	.444
Guerrero, Emilio	R-R	6-4	189	8-21-92	.258	.226	.268	105	392	50	101	21	1	9	46	21	6	2	3	107	4	2	.385	.303
Hobson, K.C.	L-L	6-2	205	8-22-90	.238	.203	.250	61	227	21	54	13	0	7	57	28	1	0	6	30	2	0	.388	.317
Knecht, Marcus	R-R	6-1	200	6-21-90	.250	.223	.258	107	400	48	100	24	5	7	52	41	7	0	3	87	7	3	.388	.328
Lawrie, Brett	R-R	6-0	210	1-18-90	.400	—	.400	3	10	3	4	1	0	0	2	0	0	0	0	2	0	0	.500	.500
Lind, Adam	L-L	6-2	195	7-17-83	.286	.167	.375	4	14	5	4	2	0	1	2	0	0	0	0	3	0	0	.429	.375
Lopes, Christian	R-R	6-0	185	10-1-92	.243	.261	.236	106	346	52	84	26	1	3	33	42	3	2	1	67	3	4	.350	.329
Mooney, Peter	L-R	5-6	155	8-19-90	.234	.170	.255	54	184	20	43	8	0	0	15	27	4	4	5	32	1	1	.277	.336
Munoz, Aaron	R-R	5-9	190	12-24-88	.000	.000	.000	4	14	0	0	0	0	0	0	0	0	0	0	5	0	0	.000	.000
Nay, Mitch	R-R	6-3	195	9-20-93	.189	.100	.222	11	37	2	7	1	0	0	1	3	0	0	0	9	0	0	.216	.250
Nessy, Santiago	R-R	6-2	230	12-8-92	.211	.143	.224	25	90	9	19	8	0	0	12	7	2	0	1	22	0	0	.300	.280
Newman, Matt	L-L	5-10	170	9-20-88	.292	.385	.254	25	89	10	26	8	0	1	14	14	0	0	2	20	1	1	.416	.381
Opitz, Shane	L-R	6-1	180	1-10-92	.305	.250	.318	29	105	14	32	1	1	0	8	6	0	0	0	18	4	1	.333	.342
Parmley, Ian	L-L	5-11	175	12-19-89	.261	.000	.273	15	46	2	12	3	0	0	1	7	0	1	0	7	3	0	.326	.358
Patterson, Kevin	L-R	6-4	220	9-28-88	.196	.218	.191	81	285	35	56	14	1	11	35	37	3	0	3	94	3	0	.368	.293
Pierre, Gustavo	R-R	6-2	202	12-28-91	.263	.326	.245	107	392	45	103	23	3	7	40	12	0	3	0	101	8	6	.390	.285
Pompey, Dalton	S-R	6-2	195	12-11-92	.319	.315	.320	70	276	49	88	12	6	6	34	35	2	2	2	56	29	2	.471	.397
Rankin, Pierce	R-R	6-1	190	4-26-89	.222	.182	.231	18	63	4	14	5	0	1	8	6	0	0	1	25	1	0	.349	.286
Reeves, Mike	L-R	6-2	195	9-16-90	.196	.083	.227	17	56	5	11	2	0	0	4	4	1	0	0	10	0	0	.232	.262
Reyes, Jose	S-R	6-0	195	6-11-83	.000	—	.000	2	6	3	0	0	0	0	1	2	0	0	0	0	0	0	.000	.250
Saez, Jorge	S-R	6-0	195	10-26-90	.248	.281	.236	38	121	16	30	5	2	2	15	19	0	0	1	33	0	0	.372	.348
Smith Jr., Dwight	L-R	5-11	180	10-26-92	.284	.300	.278	121	472	83	134	28	8	12	60	58	1	1	5	69	15	4	.453	.363
Sweeney, Kellen	L-R	6-0	180	9-14-91	.222	.250	.214	10	36	3	8	4	0	1	2	1	0	0	0	10	0	0	.333	.282

Pitching	B-T	HT	WT	DOB	W	L	ERA	G	GS	CG	SV	IP	H	R	ER	HR	BB	SO	AVG	vLH	vRH	K/9	BB/9
Barnes, Dan	L-R	6-1	195	10-21-89	0	5	4.19	36	0	0	7	39	36	20	18	4	12	49	.245	.260	.237	11.41	2.79
Boyd, Matt	L-L	6-3	215	2-2-91	5	3	1.39	16	16	1	0	91	65	20	14	4	20	103	.196	.208	.190	10.22	1.99
Browning, Wil	R-R	6-3	190	9-8-88	5	1	1.65	43	0	0	0	44	31	9	8	1	17	57	.194	.250	.175	11.75	3.50
Carnevale, Hunter	R-R	5-11	200	8-27-88	0	0	4.15	5	0	0	0	4	5	6	2	0	4	2	.263	.333	.250	4.15	8.31
2-team total (7 St. Lucie)					1	0	4.30	12	0	0	0	15	10	11	7	1	10	10	—	—	—	6.14	6.14
Castro, Miguel	R-R	6-5	190	12-24-94	1	0	3.12	2	1	0	0	9	4	3	3	2	3	5	.143	.000	.250	5.19	3.12
Champlin, Kramer	R-R	6-6	200	3-8-90	4	2	2.70	17	1	0	0	30	23	12	9	1	11	18	.217	.176	.236	5.40	3.30
Cole, Taylor	R-R	6-1	190	8-20-89	8	9	3.07	24	23	0	0	132	114	55	45	4	39	171	.232	.202	.258	11.66	2.66
Davis, Tony	L-L	5-9	180	11-6-90	2	2	3.53	34	0	0	0	43	41	19	17	3	16	53	.253	.228	.267	11.01	3.32
Gabryszwski, Jeremy	R-R	6-4	195	3-16-93	1	1	5.40	2	2	0	0	10	13	6	6	2	3	9	.302	.250	.348	8.10	2.70
Girodo, Chad	L-L	6-1	195	2-6-91	7	3	2.47	47	1	0	3	77	70	25	21	2	20	81	.241	.224	.253	9.51	2.35
Graveman, Kendall	R-R	6-2	195	12-21-90	8	4	2.23	16	16	0	0	97	89	29	24	1	18	64	.243	.278	.210	5.96	1.68
Happ, J.A.	L-L	6-5	205	10-19-82	1	0	3.60	1	1	0	0	5	3	2	2	0	1	5	.176	.375	.000	9.00	1.80
Hernandez, Jesse	R-R	6-1	200	8-23-88	6	11	4.67	27	23	0	0	129	165	82	67	20	27	59	.317	.338	.302	4.12	1.88
Jackson, Justin	R-R	6-2	190	12-11-88	4	2	4.38	40	0	0	1	49	54	28	24	5	22	40	.284	.310	.269	7.30	4.01
Janssen, Casey	R-R	6-4	205	9-17-81	0	0	0.00	1	1	0	0	1	1	0	0	0	1	1	.250	.333	.000	9.00	9.00
McFarland, Blake	R-R	6-5	230	2-2-88	2	0	4.00	16	0	0	2	27	21	12	12	3	8	36	.226	.209	.240	12.00	2.67
Meyer, Ajay	L-R	6-6	185	7-19-87	1	0	2.45	4	0	0	0	7	6	2	2	0	2	5	.231	.300	.188	6.14	2.45
Morrow, Brandon	R-R	6-3	210	7-26-84	0	0	0.00	1	0	0	0	1	0	0	0	0	0	1	.000	.000	.000	9.00	0.00
Murphy, Griffin	R-L	6-3	230	1-16-91	2	1	6.00	15	0	0	0	21	23	15	14	3	15	15	.267	.281	.259	6.43	6.43
Nieves, Efrain	L-L	6-0	169	11-15-89	3	5	2.29	44	4	0	1	86	80	25	22	2	21	57	.245	.221	.263	5.94	2.19
Nolin, Sean	L-L	6-4	230	12-26-89	1	0	3.68	2	2	0	0	7	4	3	3	0	4	9	.143	.125	.150	11.05	4.91
Norris, Daniel	L-L	6-2	180	4-25-93	6	0	1.22	13	13	0	0	66	50	11	9	0	18	76	.209	.297	.177	10.31	2.44
Osuna, Roberto	R-R	6-2	230	2-7-95	0	2	6.55	7	7	0	0	22	28	16	16	3	9	30	.318	.366	.277	12.27	3.68
Sikula, Arik	R-R	6-0	200	12-21-88	2	1	1.66	44	0	0	31	43	31	9	8	2	8	60	.200	.157	.235	12.46	1.66
Usui, Kamakami	R-R	6-1	180	2-27-90	1	0	0.00	2	0	0	0	4	0	0	0	0	2	2	.000	.000	.000	4.50	0.00
Viola III, Frank	R-R	6-4	190	6-19-84	1	2	12.06	4	4	0	0	16	26	22	21	1	15	4	.406	.405	.407	2.30	8.62
Wandling, Jon	R-R	6-3	205	3-28-92	1	0	0.00	4	0	0	0	6	10	4	0	0	2	4	.357	.364	.353	6.35	3.18
White, Ben	R-R	6-2	185	5-10-89	6	6	5.03	26	23	0	0	125	160	73	70	12	32	79	.313	.318	.309	5.67	2.30

Fielding

Catcher	PCT	G	PO	A	E	DP	PB
Chung	.996	49	411	45	2	5	2
Munoz	.967	4	28	1	1	0	0
Nessy	.986	25	181	25	3	1	3
Rankin	1.000	6	60	6	0	0	0

	PCT	G	PO	A	E	DP	PB
Reeves	.985	17	117	15	2	1	1
Saez	.987	37	276	29	4	3	1
First Base	**PCT**	**G**	**PO**	**A**	**E**	**DP**	
Dantzler	.995	45	372	16	2	36	
Hobson	.992	52	445	26	4	37	

	PCT	G	PO	A	E	DP
Lind	1.000	2	10	3	0	2
Opitz	1.000	4	33	3	0	5
Patterson	.983	30	273	14	5	27
Rankin	.980	6	46	3	1	4

TORONTO BLUE JAYS

Second Base	PCT	G	PO	A	E	DP
Fermin	1.000	2	5	7	0	3
Flores	.979	19	36	56	2	12
Lawrie	1.000	1	2	4	0	1
Lopes	.966	103	153	271	15	61
Mooney	.967	16	37	52	3	13

Third Base	PCT	G	PO	A	E	DP
Fermin	.933	5	2	12	1	3
Guerrero	.833	9	6	19	5	2
Lawrie	.833	2	4	1	1	0
Mooney	1.000	2	1	1	0	0

	PCT	G	PO	A	E	DP
Nay	.905	11	7	12	2	1
Pierre	.909	104	52	189	24	15
Sweeney	1.000	7	3	11	0	0

Shortstop	PCT	G	PO	A	E	DP
Flores	.952	14	21	38	3	6
Guerrero	.939	76	85	209	19	55
Mooney	.965	33	52	85	5	16
Opitz	.983	14	11	46	1	8
Pierre	.889	2	1	7	1	3
Reyes	1.000	2	1	5	0	1

Outfield	PCT	G	PO	A	E	DP
Baligod	.988	86	157	9	2	3
Gillespie	—	1	0	0	0	0
Guerrero	.976	20	39	1	1	0
Knecht	1.000	89	158	8	0	3
Newman	1.000	17	43	3	0	2
Parmley	1.000	14	33	1	0	0
Patterson	1.000	1	2	0	0	0
Pompey	.981	70	157	2	3	2
Rankin	1.000	2	1	0	0	0
Smith Jr.	.963	117	192	16	8	4

LANSING LUGNUTS
LOW CLASS A
MIDWEST LEAGUE

Batting	B-T	HT	WT	DOB	AVG	vLH	vRH	G	AB	R	H	2B	3B	HR	RBI	BB	HBP	SH	SF	SO	SB	CS	SLG	OBP
Alford, Anthony	R-R	6-1	193	7-20-94	.320	.250	.333	5	25	3	8	1	0	1	3	0	0	0	0	8	4	0	.480	.320
Atkinson, Justin	R-R	6-1	205	7-24-93	.291	.407	.257	77	265	34	77	8	3	1	29	17	3	0	4	54	0	2	.355	.336
Conner, Seth	R-R	6-2	205	1-29-92	.200	.333	.176	6	20	1	4	0	0	0	3	1	0	0	0	5	0	0	.200	.238
Dantzler, L.B.	L-R	5-11	200	5-22-91	.248	.231	.252	43	161	22	40	8	1	3	35	25	2	0	3	21	0	0	.366	.351
Davis, D.J.	L-R	6-1	180	7-25-94	.213	.161	.224	121	494	56	105	13	7	8	52	36	3	4	5	167	19	20	.316	.268
Dean, Matt	R-R	6-3	215	12-22-92	.281	.307	.275	113	448	58	126	29	5	9	51	27	8	0	2	117	2	1	.429	.332
Frank, Chaz	L-L	5-10	170	10-18-90	.245	.179	.257	72	261	36	64	4	3	0	23	39	2	5	0	40	17	7	.284	.348
Harris, David	R-R	6-1	190	8-10-91	.254	.137	.289	59	224	36	57	10	3	6	27	7	8	2	0	62	8	5	.406	.301
Klein, Dan	R-R	5-10	185	8-29-90	.252	.280	.244	36	107	9	27	6	1	2	10	5	3	1	2	33	0	0	.383	.299
Leblebijian, Jason	R-R	6-1	205	5-19-91	.248	.175	.263	99	323	56	80	23	2	5	48	28	9	1	3	71	8	6	.378	.322
Loveless, Derrick	L-R	6-1	200	3-7-93	.264	.169	.285	119	428	58	113	18	9	6	55	66	3	6	5	120	17	7	.390	.363
Lugo, Dawel	R-R	6-0	190	12-31-94	.259	.352	.238	117	474	40	123	17	2	4	53	18	1	1	4	72	3	3	.329	.286
Nay, Mitch	R-R	6-3	195	9-20-93	.285	.218	.301	120	473	57	135	34	3	3	59	39	3	0	3	79	6	2	.389	.342
Nessy, Santiago	R-R	6-2	230	12-8-92	.243	.208	.250	44	148	20	36	9	2	1	16	18	2	0	0	35	0	0	.351	.333
Parmley, Ian	L-L	5-11	175	12-19-89	.209	.077	.227	41	110	16	23	2	0	0	9	20	0	6	1	17	11	1	.227	.328
Ramirez, Carlos	R-R	6-5	205	4-24-91	.176	.143	.190	28	91	15	16	4	1	0	3	8	1	1	0	29	6	1	.242	.250
Reeves, Mike	L-R	6-2	195	9-16-90	.223	.222	.224	29	94	12	21	3	0	0	7	13	0	1	0	19	1	0	.255	.318
Saez, Jorge	R-R	5-10	195	8-28-90	.291	.200	.312	42	134	18	39	10	1	2	21	26	1	1	4	28	1	1	.425	.400
Schaeffer, Chris	R-R	5-10	195	11-19-87	.325	.250	.344	13	40	6	13	4	0	1	4	2	2	0	1	10	0	0	.500	.386
Tellez, Rowdy	L-L	6-4	220	3-16-95	.357	.222	.394	12	42	6	15	0	0	2	7	7	0	0	0	10	0	0	.500	.449
Thon, Dickie Joe	R-R	6-2	185	11-16-91	.265	.207	.281	103	393	57	104	20	4	3	40	42	1	7	8	71	7	8	.359	.314

Pitching	B-T	HT	WT	DOB	W	L	ERA	G	GS	CG	SV	IP	H	R	ER	HR	BB	SO	AVG	vLH	vRH	K/9	BB/9
Allen, Brad	L-R	6-4	220	3-26-89	4	5	3.11	15	15	0	0	75	71	30	26	7	23	82	.252	.226	.267	9.80	2.75
2-team total (4 South Bend)					7	5	3.44	19	19	0	0	97	89	41	37	10	33	107	—			9.96	3.07
Cardona, Adonys	R-R	6-2	198	1-16-94	0	3	8.44	5	3	0	0	11	13	13	10	0	8	11	.289	.400	.257	9.28	6.75
Castro, Miguel	R-R	6-5	190	12-24-94	1	1	3.74	4	4	0	0	22	10	9	9	2	7	20	.133	.100	.156	8.31	2.91
Cordero, Jimmy	R-R	6-3	215	10-19-91	3	2	3.06	25	0	0	0	32	36	17	11	2	20	34	.286	.348	.250	9.46	5.57
Dawson, Shane	R-L	6-1	180	9-9-93	3	5	3.38	14	10	0	0	56	55	22	21	4	24	46	.257	.190	.273	7.39	3.86
DeJong, Chase	L-R	6-4	200	12-29-93	1	6	4.82	23	21	0	0	97	113	59	52	12	22	73	.290	.301	.283	6.77	2.04
Del Rosario, Yeyfry	R-R	6-2	182	4-27-94	1	1	3.86	9	0	0	0	19	17	13	8	3	5	20	.236	.278	.222	9.64	2.41
Dermody, Matt	R-L	6-5	190	7-4-90	4	6	4.67	27	12	0	0	96	113	62	50	5	36	65	.294	.239	.312	6.07	3.36
Dragmire, Brady	R-R	6-1	180	2-5-93	3	6	2.91	43	0	0	5	77	70	33	25	2	9	45	.241	.309	.209	5.24	1.05
Espinosa, Roberto	R-R	6-2	180		2	2	4.37	40	0	0	1	70	73	40	34	2	36	72	.265	.314	.235	9.26	4.63
Gabryszwski, Jeremy	R-R	6-4	195	3-16-93	6	7	4.27	26	26	1	0	141	176	80	67	10	21	91	.304	.309	.302	5.79	1.34
Gonzalez, Alonzo	L-L	6-5	212	1-15-92	2	1	5.11	34	2	0	1	79	87	49	45	9	30	90	.274	.237	.286	10.21	3.40
Gracesqui, Francisco	L-L	6-0			1	2	2.11	10	0	0	0	21	5	5	5	1	9	28	.266	.190	.293	11.81	3.80
Graveman, Kendall	R-R	6-2	195	12-21-90	2	0	0.34	4	0	0	0	26	11	2	1	0	6	26	.126	.059	.143	8.54	2.05
Kelly, Adaric	R-R	5-10	180	12-1-92	1	3	6.19	19	0	0	0	32	39	25	22	2	17	19	.310	.289	.321	5.34	4.78
Kish, Phil	R-R	5-10	180	8-30-89	5	5	2.77	35	0	0	3	62	61	24	19	3	11	48	.263	.343	.228	7.01	1.61
Labourt, Jairo	L-L	6-4	204	3-7-94	0	0	6.43	6	3	0	0	14	15	13	10	1	20	11	.300	.200	.325	7.07	12.86
Lovecchio, Joey	R-R	6-2	190	9-6-90	0	0	2.35	4	0	0	0	8	7	2	2	0	3	5	.250	.154	.333	5.87	3.52
Murphy, Griffin	R-L	6-3	230	1-16-91	2	2	2.00	28	0	0	16	36	31	12	8	1	8	47	.231	.160	.248	11.75	2.00
Powers, Brent	L-L	6-1	185	5-25-89	3	4	4.81	12	11	0	0	49	53	31	26	3	22	36	.277	.308	.270	6.47	4.07
2-team total (15 Beloit)					5	6	5.42	27	15	0	0	86	99	62	52	5	46	66	—			6.88	4.80
Robson, Tom	R-R	6-4	210	6-27-93	2	4	6.25	8	8	0	0	32	37	26	22	1	18	22	.303	.351	.262	6.25	5.12
Silverstein, Scott	L-L	6-6	260	5-27-90	11	4	4.08	47	0	0	4	64	70	33	29	2	17	67	.276	.212	.298	9.42	3.80
Suriel, Starlyn	R-R	5-11	180	11-17-93	2	4	3.21	9	8	0	0	42	38	17	15	6	10	32	.241	.317	.189	6.86	2.14
Tirado, Alberto	R-R	6-0	180	12-10-94	1	2	6.30	13	7	0	1	40	45	30	28	3	39	40	.283	.250	.301	9.00	8.78
Viola III, Frank	R-R	6-4	190	6-19-84	2	2	3.86	5	5	0	0	23	24	10	10	1	15	13	.279	.241	.298	5.01	5.79
Wellbrock, Chase	L-R	5-10	200	1-6-92	0	0	5.14	2	0	0	0	7	7	4	4	2	1	5	.250	.182	.294	6.43	1.29

Fielding

Catcher	PCT	G	PO	A	E	DP	PB
Conner	1.000	1	2	0	0	0	0
Klein	.988	34	225	19	3	4	4
Nessy	.994	40	271	46	2	2	13
Reeves	.984	29	217	28	4	2	1
Saez	.991	31	212	21	2	3	7
Schaeffer	.983	13	111	8	2	2	0

First Base	PCT	G	PO	A	E	DP
Atkinson	.994	34	307	13	2	28
Conner	1.000	1	3	0	0	2
Dantzler	.997	34	282	13	1	32
Dean	.982	64	575	16	11	40
Leblebijian	1.000	4	30	1	0	3
Saez	—	1	0	0	0	0

	PCT	G	PO	A	E	DP
Tellez	.982	8	53	1	1	3

Second Base	PCT	G	PO	A	E	DP
Atkinson	.985	14	24	41	1	10
Harris	.927	11	12	26	3	6
Leblebijian	.974	53	97	130	6	23
Thon	.974	68	123	179	8	51

Third Base	PCT	G	PO	A	E	DP
Atkinson	.938	16	6	24	2	3
Dean	.932	16	12	29	3	3
Harris	.857	3	1	11	2	3
Leblebijian	.917	9	3	8	1	2
Nay	.940	104	64	234	19	23

Shortstop	PCT	G	PO	A	E	DP
Leblebijian	.992	30	45	86	1	21
Lugo	.943	110	148	286	26	53

Outfield	PCT	G	PO	A	E	DP
Alford	1.000	4	8	0	0	0
Davis	.939	116	269	7	18	3

Frank	.959	67	114	2	5	1
Harris	.985	39	66	1	1	0
Loveless	.957	106	213	7	10	1
Parmley	.984	36	61	2	1	1
Ramirez	1.000	25	44	2	0	1
Thon	.984	33	55	7	1	0

VANCOUVER CANADIANS   SHORT-SEASON
NORTHWEST LEAGUE

Batting	B-T	HT	WT	DOB	AVG	vLH	vRH	G	AB	R	H	2B	3B	HR	RBI	BB	HBP	SH	SF	SO	SB	CS	SLG	OBP
Barreto, Franklin	R-R	5-9	174	2-27-96	.311	.300	.315	73	289	65	90	23	4	6	61	26	10	0	3	64	29	5	.481	.384
Carlson, Chris	L-L	5-7	180	4-29-91	.312	.349	.302	59	215	30	67	13	1	0	35	36	2	0	4	25	4	1	.381	.409
Collins, Boomer	R-R	6-0	200	6-13-89	.222	.212	.225	62	212	22	47	11	0	2	28	25	4	0	3	50	8	1	.302	.311
Conner, Seth	R-R	6-2	205	1-29-92	.221	.267	.208	27	68	9	15	3	0	0	6	9	0	1	0	15	0	0	.265	.312
Davis, Jonathan	R-R	5-8	188	5-12-92	.216	.333	.164	27	88	14	19	4	4	1	10	6	1	6	1	26	7	1	.386	.271
De La Cruz, Michael	R-R	5-10	175	5-15-93	.232	.176	.250	47	142	15	33	6	1	1	21	19	1	0	2	23	1	2	.310	.323
Fields, Roemon	L-L	5-11	180	11-28-90	.269	.269	.269	72	294	64	79	13	4	1	26	27	5	0	2	61	48	9	.350	.338
Garcia, Kevin	R-R	5-10	190	9-17-92	.269	.600	.190	10	26	4	7	1	0	0	2	3	1	0	2	5	0	0	.308	.344
Harris, David	R-R	6-1	190	8-10-91	.292	.286	.294	5	24	3	7	1	1	0	6	1	0	0	0	8	2	1	.417	.320
Heidt, Gunnar	R-R	5-11	195	9-12-92	.262	.278	.258	23	84	10	22	9	1	1	11	7	2	0	0	17	2	0	.429	.333
Hurley, Sean	R-R	6-4	235	5-5-92	.120	.167	.094	18	50	6	6	1	0	1	9	9	1	0	1	14	1	0	.200	.262
Kalfus, Brenden	B-R	6-0	190	8-22-91	.140	.077	.159	25	57	4	8	0	1	0	2	5	1	0	0	13	0	0	.175	.222
Klein, Dan	R-R	5-10	185	8-29-90	.000	.000	.000	1	5	0	0	0	0	0	0	0	0	0	0	2	0	0	.000	.000
Locastro, Tim	R-R	6-1	175	7-14-92	.313	.295	.318	67	256	49	80	11	0	1	27	12	32	5	5	23	32	4	.367	.407
Maldonado, Alex	R-R	5-9	175	6-12-91	.303	.289	.307	46	152	24	46	7	1	1	14	14	1	0	1	31	5	2	.382	.365
McBroom, Ryan	R-L	6-3	220	4-9-92	.297	.277	.303	70	273	37	81	23	0	11	59	13	7	0	5	52	1	0	.502	.339
Metzler, Ryan	R-R	6-3	190	3-20-93	.239	.233	.241	35	113	14	27	3	0	0	9	18	2	0	1	27	2	2	.265	.351
Miller, Trent	R-R	6-1	215	8-5-91	.250	.000	.353	8	24	2	6	1	0	0	0	0	0	0	0	5	0	0	.292	.250
Pentecost, Max	R-R	6-2	191	3-10-93	.313	.389	.292	19	83	15	26	2	3	0	9	2	0	0	2	18	2	1	.410	.322
Reeves, Mike	L-R	6-2	195	9-16-90	.212	.067	.270	17	52	4	11	1	0	1	5	10	1	0	0	9	0	0	.288	.349
Urena, Richard	L-R	6-1	170	2-26-96	.242	.000	.286	9	33	3	8	2	1	0	3	5	1	0	0	5	1	0	.364	.297
Vazquez, Christian	B-R	5-10	170	9-11-89	.160	.059	.188	29	81	8	13	2	0	0	6	2	1	0	0	12	0	0	.185	.236

Pitching	B-T	HT	WT	DOB	W	L	ERA	G	GS	CG	SV	IP	H	R	ER	HR	BB	SO	AVG	vLH	vRH	K/9	BB/9
Barber, Brett	R-R	6-1	180	11-1-90	0	1	6.91	16	0	0	6	14	16	12	11	0	5	11	.281	.444	.205	6.91	3.14
Biggs, Mark	R-R	6-3	205	5-10-93	2	0	6.91	18	0	0	0	29	33	23	22	0	19	26	.280	.244	.299	8.16	5.97
Borucki, Ryan	L-L	6-4	175	3-31-94	1	1	1.90	5	4	0	1	24	13	8	5	1	3	22	.159	.139	.174	8.37	1.14
Case, Andrew	R-R	6-2	190	1-6-93	0	1	2.45	24	1	0	2	44	38	13	12	3	10	37	.233	.280	.212	7.57	2.66
Castro, Miguel	R-R	6-5	190	12-24-94	6	2	2.15	10	10	0	0	50	36	13	12	2	20	53	.202	.211	.196	9.48	3.58
Del Rosario, Yeyfry	R-R	6-2	182	4-27-94	3	1	4.07	18	0	0	1	24	18	14	11	2	19	35	.205	.267	.172	12.95	7.03
Fernandez, Jose	L-L	6-3	170	2-13-93	1	1	4.01	21	0	0	2	25	29	13	11	0	11	24	.284	.212	.319	8.76	4.01
Gracesqui, Francisco	L-L	6-0	175	11-26-91	2	0	0.00	11	0	0	1	14	6	1	0	0	7	16	.133	.267	.067	10.05	4.40
Kelly, Adaric	R-R	5-10	180	12-1-92	3	1	1.64	10	0	0	1	11	10	3	2	0	5	10	.238	.231	.241	8.18	4.09
Kish, Phil	R-R	5-10	180	8-30-89	0	0	0.00	11	0	0	9	14	6	1	0	0	4	12	.133	.059	.179	7.71	2.57
Kraft, Michael	L-L	5-11	175	9-3-91	1	0	0.86	16	0	0	1	21	7	2	2	0	13	25	.103	.030	.171	10.71	5.57
Labourt, Jairo	L-L	6-4	204	3-7-94	5	3	1.77	15	15	0	0	71	47	17	14	0	37	82	.188	.246	.171	10.35	4.67
Lietz, Daniel	L-L	6-2	200	6-1-94	1	1	5.73	9	7	0	0	33	37	24	21	2	22	27	.294	.242	.312	7.36	6.00
Lovecchio, Joey	R-R	6-2	190	9-6-91	1	1	4.37	17	0	0	2	23	27	14	11	3	7	23	.290	.346	.269	6.75	3.18
Mallard, Chase	R-R	6-2	185	11-22-91	4	3	2.75	12	9	0	0	52	47	21	16	2	11	48	.232	.281	.193	8.25	1.89
Mayza, Tim	L-L	6-3	205	1-15-92	2	3	6.75	12	0	0	0	20	31	20	15	2	12	17	.356	.343	.365	7.65	5.40
Pickens, Garrett	R-R	6-1	185	4-17-90	0	0	0.00	4	0	0	0	5	2	2	0	0	4	7	.125	.000	.167	13.50	7.71
Shafer, Justin	R-R	6-2	195	9-18-92	1	3	5.16	11	2	0	1	23	26	15	13	1	7	23	.286	.344	.254	9.13	2.78
Smoral, Matt	L-L	6-8	220	3-18-94	2	0	2.70	5	3	0	0	20	14	6	6	0	15	19	.219	.259	.189	8.55	6.75
Suriel, Starlyn	R-R	5-11	180	11-17-93	4	1	3.41	8	7	0	0	37	34	15	14	5	14	26	.245	.306	.211	6.32	3.16
Tirado, Alberto	R-R	6-0	180	12-10-94	1	0	3.53	17	3	0	0	36	25	17	14	1	28	36	.191	.205	.184	9.08	7.07
Usui, Kamakami	R-R	6-1	180	2-27-90	0	1	7.88	14	0	0	4	16	22	16	14	2	6	12	.324	.381	.298	6.75	3.38
Wandling, Jon	R-R	6-3	205	5-28-92	2	0	4.63	4	1	0	0	12	12	6	6	1	5	6	.279	.333	.240	4.63	3.86
Wasilewski, Zak	L-L	6-1	190	6-16-93	4	6	7.32	15	14	0	0	63	79	56	51	7	35	39	.311	.191	.355	5.60	5.03

Fielding

Catcher	PCT	G	PO	A	E	DP	PB
Conner	.986	12	67	5	1	0	6
De La Cruz	.989	43	339	32	4	1	6
Garcia	1.000	9	58	6	0	0	1
Klein	1.000	1	5	1	0	0	0
Pentecost	.972	6	34	1	1	0	0
Reeves	.993	17	119	14	1	0	1

First Base	PCT	G	PO	A	E	DP
Collins	1.000	2	10	0	0	0
Conner	1.000	12	73	2	0	6
McBroom	.994	69	574	38	4	55

Second Base	PCT	G	PO	A	E	DP
Heidt	.972	20	42	64	3	13

	PCT	G	PO	A	E	DP
Locastro	.975	33	77	80	4	13
Metzler	.974	13	33	42	2	11
Urena	.969	5	16	15	1	4
Vazquez	.960	5	13	11	1	3

Third Base	PCT	G	PO	A	E	DP
Harris	.818	3	3	6	2	0
Maldonado	.927	42	28	73	8	6
Metzler	.897	20	16	36	6	6
Urena	1.000	3	0	4	0	0
Vazquez	.974	10	10	28	1	2

Shortstop	PCT	G	PO	A	E	DP
Barreto	.913	68	91	181	26	38
Urena	1.000	1	1	5	0	0

	PCT	G	PO	A	E	DP
Vazquez	1.000	14	18	24	0	7

Outfield	PCT	G	PO	A	E	DP
Carlson	.978	55	85	3	2	0
Collins	.986	54	69	4	1	1
Davis	.977	23	41	2	1	0
Fields	.987	69	149	5	2	4
Harris	1.000	1	2	0	0	0
Hurley	1.000	11	10	0	0	0
Kalfus	1.000	21	22	1	0	0
Locastro	1.000	6	5	1	0	0
Miller	1.000	7	6	0	0	0

TORONTO BLUE JAYS

BLUEFIELD BLUE JAYS — ROOKIE
APPALACHIAN LEAGUE

TORONTO BLUE JAYS

Batting	B-T	HT	WT	DOB	AVG	vLH	vRH	G	AB	R	H	2B	3B	HR	RBI	BB	HBP	SH	SF	SO	SB	CS	SLG	OBP
Alford, Anthony	R-R	6-1	193	7-20-94	.207	.200	.208	9	29	5	6	0	0	1	2	5	1	0	0	13	1	0	.310	.343
Almonte, Josh	R-R	6-3	193	1-28-94	.307	.400	.281	62	251	35	77	6	4	3	24	8	6	1	0	69	15	5	.398	.343
Anderson, Jake	R-R	6-4	190	11-22-92	.100	.000	.143	3	10	0	1	0	0	0	0	0	1	0	0	2	0	0	.100	.182
Attaway, Aaron	R-R	5-7	170	3-6-92	.206	.250	.188	36	97	11	20	6	2	0	7	19	4	0	1	32	3	1	.309	.355
Cenas, Gabriel	R-R	6-1	155	10-16-93	.221	.204	.226	53	195	22	43	6	0	2	24	19	2	1	2	43	2	0	.282	.294
Davis, Austin	L-R	5-10	170	4-26-93	.216	.091	.237	46	153	12	33	0	0	0	10	9	2	8	0	37	0	0	.216	.268
Garcia, Kevin	R-R	5-10	190	9-17-92	.250	.294	.236	23	72	11	18	2	0	1	7	5	2	1	0	9	1	1	.319	.316
Gonzalez, Jesus	R-R	6-0	180	1-11-95	.188	.229	.178	49	170	11	32	3	2	2	15	9	0	1	2	68	3	2	.265	.227
Hurley, Sean	R-R	6-4	235	5-5-92	.185	.214	.176	23	65	6	12	1	1	2	8	7	1	1	1	21	1	1	.323	.270
Jansen, Danny	R-R	6-2	215	4-15-95	.282	.250	.292	38	124	22	35	10	0	5	17	16	6	0	0	17	2	1	.484	.390
Lynch, James	L-R	6-2	195	4-5-92	.132	.182	.126	36	106	7	14	3	0	1	6	5	1	1	1	37	0	1	.189	.177
Miller, Trent	R-R	6-1	215	8-5-91	.257	.237	.265	38	140	20	36	11	0	3	14	9	1	0	0	27	2	2	.400	.307
Moseby, Lydell	R-R	6-6	230	3-15-91	.211	.212	.210	30	95	14	20	3	0	5	16	12	2	0	1	24	0	0	.400	.309
Rojas, Angel	R-R	5-11	160	4-7-93	.206	.429	.203	34	100	15	25	4	1	0	13	7	3	1	2	22	1	0	.310	.315
Segovia, Rolando	B-R	5-11	165	10-26-94	.244	.194	.256	49	164	30	40	12	0	3	16	20	4	4	3	42	7	6	.372	.335
Sotillo, Andres	R-R	5-11	180	12-28-93	.200	.286	.174	13	30	2	6	0	1	0	1	1	2	0	0	9	1	0	.267	.273
Tellez, Rowdy	L-L	6-4	220	3-16-95	.293	.303	.291	53	191	26	56	11	1	4	36	19	3	0	5	27	3	2	.424	.358
Thomas, Lane	R-R	6-1	210	8-23-95	.323	.383	.264	18	65	10	21	4	0	1	8	6	1	0	1	16	2	0	.431	.384
Urena, Richard	L-R	6-1	170	2-26-96	.318	.283	.327	53	217	35	69	15	2	2	20	16	0	2	1	51	5	4	.433	.363

Pitching	B-T	HT	WT	DOB	W	L	ERA	G	GS	CG	SV	IP	H	R	ER	HR	BB	SO	AVG	vLH	vRH	K/9	BB/9
Aquino, Joey	R-R	6-0	195	8-13-90	2	3	2.48	13	11	0	0	54	47	19	15	4	10	32	.229	.205	.246	5.30	1.66
Autrey, J.T.	R-R	6-5	215	5-12-92	0	1	12.91	8	0	0	0	8	12	11	11	1	9	6	.364	.385	.350	7.04	10.57
Borucki, Ryan	L-L	6-4	175	3-31-94	2	1	2.70	8	6	0	0	33	26	11	10	2	6	30	.211	.242	.200	8.10	1.62
Burgos, Miguel	L-L	5-9	155	6-16-95	1	0	1.69	4	3	0	0	16	13	6	3	2	3	14	.217	.091	.245	7.88	1.69
Cabrera, Oscar	L-L	6-2	215	5-22-94	3	1	1.98	14	1	0	1	36	27	11	8	1	21	36	.208	.273	.202	8.92	5.20
Fisk, Conor	R-R	6-2	210	4-4-92	5	1	2.67	15	0	0	0	34	27	12	10	2	12	36	.213	.184	.231	9.62	3.21
Greene, Conner	R-R	6-3	165	4-4-95	1	4	4.23	6	5	0	0	28	26	16	13	1	12	21	.250	.273	.239	6.83	3.90
Guzman, Alberto	R-R	6-1	180	12-7-92	1	4	7.84	14	3	0	0	31	44	31	27	3	20	32	.341	.292	.370	9.29	5.81
Huffman, Grayson	L-L	6-2	195	5-6-95	0	1	0.82	3	3	0	0	11	11	3	1	0	7	11	.268	.000	.306	9.00	5.73
Isaacs, Dusty	R-R	6-1	190	8-7-91	0	1	3.41	21	0	0	8	29	33	14	11	1	5	36	.292	.349	.257	11.17	1.55
Kraft, Michael	L-L	5-11	175	9-3-91	2	0	0.00	6	0	0	1	10	4	0	0	2	9	.129	.000	.167	8.38	1.86
Lietz, Daniel	L-L	6-2	200	6-1-94	1	2	2.03	4	2	0	0	13	13	3	3	0	2	15	.265	.231	.278	10.13	1.35
Mallard, Chase	R-R	6-2	185	11-22-91	0	0	2.61	3	1	0	1	10	7	8	3	1	4	7	.179	.105	.250	6.10	0.00
Mayza, Tim	L-L	6-3	205	1-15-92	1	0	6.75	4	0	0	1	7	7	5	5	0	4	3	.304	.000	.318	4.05	5.40
Rios, Francisco	R-R	6-1	180	5-6-95	3	2	5.91	13	9	0	0	53	79	42	35	5	18	38	.351	.367	.342	6.41	3.04
Romano, Jordan	R-R	6-4	200	4-21-93	1	1	2.16	11	0	0	0	25	19	7	6	0	9	33	.209	.176	.188	11.88	3.24
Smith, Evan	R-L	6-5	190	8-17-95	3	2	4.05	9	7	0	1	40	42	20	18	3	12	34	.259	.391	.237	7.65	2.70
Smoral, Matt	L-L	6-8	220	3-18-94	2	3	3.48	9	5	0	0	34	31	15	13	0	18	51	.230	.231	.229	13.63	4.81
Tinoco, Jesus	R-R	6-4	190	4-30-95	1	9	4.95	13	12	0	1	56	62	44	31	4	20	47	.270	.326	.234	7.51	3.20
Usui, Kamakami	R-R	6-1	180	2-27-90	2	0	3.60	4	0	0	0	5	3	2	2	1	1	6	.176	.167	.182	10.80	1.80
Wellbrock, Chase	L-R	5-10	200	1-6-92	2	2	0.37	20	0	0	2	24	13	3	1	0	1	34	.153	.121	.173	12.58	0.37

Fielding

Catcher	PCT	G	PO	A	E	DP	PB
Cenas	.941	2	15	1	1	0	3
Garcia	.979	23	164	25	4	1	7
Jansen	.991	38	293	29	3	1	9
Sotillo	.988	12	72	11	1	1	8

First Base	PCT	G	PO	A	E	DP
Cenas	1.000	6	45	3	0	6
Moseby	.985	14	127	6	2	12
Rojas	.833	3	5	0	1	0
Tellez	.987	49	429	18	6	37

Second Base	PCT	G	PO	A	E	DP
Attaway	1.000	1	1	4	0	0

	PCT	G	PO	A	E	DP
Rojas	.960	22	35	61	4	15
Segovia	.941	47	84	123	13	29

Third Base	PCT	G	PO	A	E	DP
Attaway	.833	10	4	11	3	1
Cenas	.891	37	25	81	13	5
Davis	.765	9	6	7	4	1
Rojas	1.000	7	3	8	0	1
Thomas	.793	10	6	17	6	3

Shortstop	PCT	G	PO	A	E	DP
Attaway	.919	16	15	42	5	8
Rojas	.917	3	5	6	1	1
Segovia	—	1	0	0	0	0

	PCT	G	PO	A	E	DP
Urena	.917	50	64	146	19	31

Outfield	PCT	G	PO	A	E	DP
Alford	1.000	7	7	0	0	0
Almonte	.943	61	126	7	8	4
Anderson	.667	2	2	0	1	0
Davis	.973	26	30	6	1	1
Gonzalez	1.000	49	73	8	0	1
Hurley	.909	12	19	1	2	0
Lynch	.967	20	28	1	1	0
Miller	.966	28	54	2	2	0
Thomas	1.000	6	13	0	0	0

GCL BLUE JAYS — ROOKIE
GULF COAST LEAGUE

Batting	B-T	HT	WT	DOB	AVG	vLH	vRH	G	AB	R	H	2B	3B	HR	RBI	BB	HBP	SH	SF	SO	SB	CS	SLG	OBP
Barreto, Deiferson	R-R	5-10	165	5-19-95	.288	.333	.275	51	170	21	49	15	0	2	16	5	1	1	2	14	2	3	.412	.309
Bell, Dean	R-R		175	10-14-92	.191	.133	.208	21	68	7	13	1	0	0	5	3	0	0	0	21	0	0	.206	.225
Brantley, Cliff	L-R	5-9	170	9-15-92	.232	.190	.246	25	82	11	19	1	2	0	4	4	2	1	0	14	3	1	.293	.284
Davis, Jonathan	R-R	5-8	188	5-12-92	.000	.000	—	1	3	0	0	0	0	0	0	0	0	0	0	0	0	0	.000	.000
De Aza, Andres	R-R	6-4	190	11-17-94	.193	.353	.152	27	83	5	16	3	1	0	11	5	1	0	1	24	0	0	.253	.244
DeSouza, Nathan	R-R	6-0	185	7-13-94	.263	.222	.271	17	57	7	15	6	0	0	5	6	1	0	0	8	0	0	.368	.344
Florides, Andrew	R-R	6-1	170	1-22-95	.083	.000	.143	5	12	0	1	0	0	0	2	1	0	0	0	4	0	0	.083	.267
Fuentes, Edwin	R-R	6-0	170	8-14-94	.203	.333	.155	48	158	10	32	6	2	1	21	8	4	0	5	24	2	0	.285	.251
Gillespie, Cole	R-R	6-1	215	6-20-84	.333	.500	.250	2	6	0	2	0	0	0	1	0	0	0	0	1	0	1	.333	.429
Gomez, Angel	B-R	6-2	180	1-12-92	.320	.444	.271	30	97	12	31	5	2	0	7	13	2	1	0	16	7	4	.412	.411

Batting	B-T	HT	WT	DOB	AVG	vLH	vRH	G	AB	R	H	2B	3B	HR	RBI	BB	HBP	SH	SF	SO	SB	CS	SLG	OBP
Gudino, Yeltsin	R-R	6-0	150	1-17-97	.145	.116	.158	40	138	17	20	3	0	0	12	13	1	0	3	28	0	1	.167	.219
Heidt, Gunnar	R-R	5-11	195	9-12-92	.273	.167	.313	6	22	5	6	1	1	0	4	3	0	0	0	6	0	0	.409	.360
Hernandez, Javier	R-R	6-1	180	7-21-96	.385	.000	.417	6	13	2	5	0	0	0	1	0	0	0	0	4	0	0	.385	.429
Kelly, Juan	L-R	5-10	155	7-16-94	.287	.255	.298	54	188	22	54	10	4	0	21	21	2	0	1	36	1	0	.383	.363
Lind, Adam	L-L	6-2	195	7-17-83	1.000	—	1.000	1	2	1	2	2	0	0	0	0	0	0	0	0	0	0	2.000	1.000
Morgan, Matt	R-R	6-1	190	1-27-96	.092	.107	.088	39	119	8	11	2	0	1	7	14	0	0	0	56	0	2	.134	.188
Opitz, Shane	L-R	6-1	180	1-10-92	.111	.000	.200	3	9	1	1	0	0	0	1	0	0	0	0	0	0	0	.222	.111
Pascazi, Trey	B-R	6-1	175	8-7-93	.141	.077	.173	30	78	4	11	0	0	1	3	10	0	0	0	34	1	0	.179	.239
Pentecost, Max	R-R	6-2	191	3-10-93	.364	.500	.313	6	22	2	8	2	0	0	3	0	0	0	0	3	0	1	.455	.364
Pepe, Dave	L-R	5-9	170	10-15-91	.304	.294	.308	27	69	11	21	4	0	0	11	14	2	0	1	6	2	2	.362	.430
Rodriguez, Freddy	L-R	6-1	180	11-15-96	.239	.222	.244	34	113	12	27	4	2	1	6	10	1	5	0	30	1	1	.336	.306
Silviano, John	L-R	5-11	190	7-11-94	.154	.167	.150	7	26	2	4	0	0	0	1	2	0	0	0	10	0	0	.154	.214
Sotillo, Andres	R-R	5-11	180	12-28-93	.107	.083	.125	9	28	4	3	1	0	0	1	1	3	0	0	7	0	0	.143	.219
Tejada, Juan	R-R	6-3	180	2-13-94	.241	.267	.233	47	174	18	42	8	4	5	21	10	3	0	1	60	9	0	.420	.293
Thomas, Lane	R-R	6-1	210	8-23-95	.260	.244	.267	34	131	21	34	8	4	0	11	21	0	0	0	33	7	3	.382	.362
Wellman, Brett	L-R	6-0	200	11-22-91	.077	.000	.100	17	26	3	2	0	0	0	1	6	2	1	0	11	0	0	.077	.294

Pitching	B-T	HT	WT	DOB	W	L	ERA	G	GS	CG	SV	IP	H	R	ER	HR	BB	SO	AVG	vLH	vRH	K/9	BB/9
Autrey, J.T.	R-R	6-5	215	5-12-92	0	2	6.43	4	0	0	0	7	11	6	5	0	7	5	.379	.333	.429	6.43	9.00
Brentz, Jake	L-L	6-2	175	9-14-94	1	3	4.08	12	6	0	2	40	30	21	18	1	26	34	.208	.097	.239	7.71	5.90
Champlin, Kramer	R-R	6-6	200	3-8-90	0	0	0.00	3	3	0	0	5	3	0	0	0	0	7	.176	.286	.100	12.60	0.00
Claver, Joe	L-L	6-2	170	10-9-91	1	1	11.95	13	0	0	0	20	33	31	27	3	15	11	.375	.412	.366	4.87	6.64
Diaz, Francisco	R-R	6-5	200	2-27-93	1	1	2.57	15	0	0	1	28	16	15	8	0	32	18	.168	.189	.155	5.79	10.29
Eduardo, Francis	R-R	6-2	190	5-24-94	0	3	4.85	16	0	0	4	26	26	15	14	3	12	27	.252	.194	.278	9.35	4.15
Greene, Conner	R-R	6-3	165	4-4-95	2	2	1.99	7	4	0	0	32	25	11	7	2	6	30	.216	.100	.276	8.53	1.71
Hinkle, Brandon	L-R	5-11	180	11-15-90	1	2	4.58	16	0	0	0	20	17	12	10	2	9	18	.258	.250	.260	8.24	4.12
Huffman, Grayson	L-L	6-2	195	5-6-95	1	0	1.00	8	7	0	0	27	7	3	3	0	13	23	.086	.100	.082	7.67	4.33
Lee, Turner	R-L	6-3	215	8-30-91	1	3	7.89	15	1	0	1	30	43	27	26	1	11	23	.341	.278	.352	6.98	3.34
Murphy, Patrick	R-R	6-4	195	6-10-95	0	1	11.25	3	2	0	0	4	8	6	5	0	2	4	.400	.375	.417	9.00	4.50
Nolin, Sean	L-L	6-4	230	12-26-89	0	0	0.00	1	1	0	0	2	1	0	0	0	0	5	.125	.000	.143	19.29	0.00
Osuna, Roberto	R-R	6-2	230	2-7-95	0	0	0.00	1	1	0	0	1	0	0	0	0	0	2	.000	.000	.000	18.00	0.00
Perdomo, Angel	L-L	6-6	200	5-7-94	3	2	2.54	13	3	0	1	46	36	13	13	1	21	57	.209	.208	.220	11.15	4.11
Ratcliffe, Sean	L-R	6-4	200	4-11-95	1	2	8.16	11	0	0	0	14	20	16	13	1	17	7	.333	.192	.441	4.40	10.67
Reid-Foley, Sean	R-R	6-3	220	8-30-95	1	2	4.76	9	6	0	0	23	21	12	12	0	10	25	.244	.292	.226	9.93	3.97
Rodriguez, Dalton	R-R	6-1	180	8-20-96	1	5	7.02	12	5	0	0	41	65	37	32	3	12	28	.378	.433	.343	6.15	2.63
Rodriguez, Hansel	R-R	6-2	170	2-27-97	0	3	7.11	9	6	0	0	19	18	18	15	0	12	13	.257	.300	.240	6.16	5.68
Romano, Jordan	R-R	6-4	200	4-21-93	0	0	0.00	2	0	0	0	3	2	0	0	0	4	1	.182	.000	.400	3.00	12.00
Smith, Evan	R-L	6-5	190	8-17-95	1	0	1.50	3	2	0	0	12	11	3	2	0	3	13	.244	.154	.281	9.75	2.25
Storey, Mickey	R-R	6-1	185	3-16-86	0	0	1.13	5	2	0	1	8	8	1	1	0	1	8	.286	.500	.250	9.00	1.13
Torres, Jonathan	L-L	6-4	190	12-31-94	0	0	5.06	7	0	0	0	5	5	10	3	0	15	6	.217	.000	.238	10.13	25.31
Wagner, Neil	R-R	6-0	215	1-1-84	0	1	—	1	0	0	0	1	1	1	1	0	0	1	0	1.000	—	1.000	—
Wandling, Jon	R-R	6-3	205	5-28-92	1	1	3.65	4	1	0	0	12	9	5	5	1	3	9	.214	.286	.200	6.57	2.19
Wells, Nick	L-L	6-5	175	2-21-96	1	3	5.71	11	4	0	0	35	44	27	22	1	11	18	.303	.375	.289	4.67	2.86
Wheatley, Bobby	L-L	6-5	220	2-4-92	1	5	9.37	12	5	0	1	33	54	36	34	4	19	24	.383	.423	.374	6.61	5.23

Fielding

Catcher	PCT	G	PO	A	E	DP	PB
Hernandez	.938	6	27	3	2	0	2
Kelly	.990	15	92	8	1	0	4
Morgan	.983	34	213	25	4	3	15
Pentecost	1.000	4	26	0	0	0	0
Sotillo	1.000	8	47	8	0	0	0
Wellman	1.000	9	11	2	0	0	1

First Base	PCT	G	PO	A	E	DP
Fuentes	.992	18	122	10	1	17
Kelly	.987	37	278	18	4	25
Silviano	.984	7	56	6	1	6

Second Base	PCT	G	PO	A	E	DP
Barreto	.990	44	96	108	2	30
Bell	.959	13	16	31	2	5

	PCT	G	PO	A	E	DP
Fuentes	.889	2	4	4	1	0
Heidt	1.000	5	10	3	0	0
Opitz	1.000	1	1	0	0	0
Pascazi	1.000	1	0	1	0	0
Pepe	—	1	0	0	0	0

Third Base	PCT	G	PO	A	E	DP
Barreto	.750	1	2	1	1	0
Bell	.875	4	3	4	1	0
Fuentes	.894	16	10	32	5	4
Kelly	1.000	1	0	2	0	0
Pascazi	.897	28	10	42	6	5
Thomas	.872	15	13	28	6	5

Shortstop	PCT	G	PO	A	E	DP
Barreto	.960	5	8	16	1	3

	PCT	G	PO	A	E	DP
Florides	.867	5	4	9	2	1
Fuentes	.903	12	15	41	6	9
Gudino	.935	40	47	98	10	17
Opitz	1.000	2	3	4	0	1

Outfield	PCT	G	PO	A	E	DP
Brantley	1.000	23	36	1	0	0
Davis	1.000	1	3	0	0	0
De Aza	.971	15	30	4	1	1
DeSouza	1.000	15	30	3	0	0
Gillespie	—	1	0	0	0	0
Gomez	.957	24	44	1	2	0
Pepe	1.000	19	19	2	0	0
Rodriguez	.966	30	53	3	2	1
Tejada	.969	41	93	2	3	0
Thomas	.973	16	35	1	1	0

DSL BLUE JAYS

DOMINICAN SUMMER LEAGUE

ROOKIE

Batting	B-T	HT	WT	DOB	AVG	vLH	vRH	G	AB	R	H	2B	3B	HR	RBI	BB	HBP	SH	SF	SO	SB	CS	SLG	OBP
Alcantara, Eddy	R-R	6-3	185	7-22-94	.244	.154	.267	51	131	13	32	5	1	0	15	19	0	1	0	37	10	4	.298	.340
Almanzar, Jean	R-R	6-0	150	2-12-95	.118	.143	.100	13	17	1	2	0	0	0	1	3	0	3	0	4	1	2	.118	.250
Almonte, Miguel	R-R	5-11	165	11-26-96	.242	.417	.186	48	149	29	36	8	0	0	18	21	7	1	2	41	11	3	.295	.358
Demorizi, Ronniel	B-R	6-0	170	7-19-95	.238	.368	.201	52	172	22	41	11	0	2	18	20	2	1	0	38	8	4	.337	.325
Dominguez, Luis	R-R	6-2	190	4-16-96	.160	.182	.157	26	81	9	13	4	0	0	7	9	1	2	0	21	1	1	.210	.253
Fuentes, Antony	R-R	5-11	160	9-26-95	.323	.500	.280	10	31	6	10	3	0	0	5	6	1	0	0	3	2	1	.419	.447
Garcia, Leudy	R-R	6-4	195	4-18-95	.182	.208	.172	34	88	11	16	3	0	0	8	12	0	3	0	34	4	1	.216	.280
Herazo, Manuel	B-R	5-10	175	3-17-95	.250	.300	.236	28	92	15	23	3	0	0	17	6	7	0	4	30	4	1	.283	.330
Hernandez, Javier	R-R	6-1	180	7-21-96	.241	.167	.261	51	195	34	47	18	2	0	21	13	2	2	4	29	2	5	.354	.290

Lizardo, Bryan	B-R	6-0	205	7-26-97	.263	.176	.286	67	240	46	63	17	5	0	29	41	6	2	3	75	7	4	.375 .379
Moreta, Enmanuel	R-R	6-3	215	2-8-95	.287	.345	.270	65	254	42	73	21	7	1	37	21	11	0	0	58	1	6	.437 .367
Olivares, Edward	R-R	6-2	186	3-6-96	.314	.032	.394	40	140	31	44	5	3	1	22	20	11	1	1	23	12	3	.414 .436
Orozco, Rodrigo	B-R	5-11	155	4-2-95	.274	.306	.265	61	234	49	64	9	2	2	33	40	3	3	1	32	20	8	.355 .385
Rodriguez, Francisco	R-R	6-1	220	9-22-94	.259	.267	.257	65	212	49	55	16	4	1	28	40	10	1	2	61	10	9	.387 .398
Severino, Jesus	L-R	6-1	175	6-11-97	.211	.250	.200	63	242	34	51	4	4	0	35	36	2	3	1	63	10	4	.260 .317
Vasquez, Junior	B-R	5-8	165	6-3-95	.200	.222	.196	45	110	14	22	4	1	0	11	10	3	1	0	19	4	0	.255 .285

Pitching	B-T	HT	WT	DOB	W	L	ERA	G	GS	CG	SV	IP	H	R	ER	HR	BB	SO	AVG	vLH	vRH	K/9	BB/9
Aleton, Wilfri	L-L	6-3	165	11-18-95	2	2	3.97	15	0	0	1	34	29	20	15	1	17	27	.220	.200	.223	7.15	4.50
Cordova, Manuel	R-R	6-3	190	1-17-95	0	4	15.19	11	3	0	0	16	29	29	27	1	12	15	.397	.370	.413	8.44	6.75
De La Cruz, Guillermo	L-L	6-1	170	5-13-97	0	1	4.57	15	1	0	1	22	19	12	11	1	13	17	.244	.333	.222	7.06	5.40
Diaz, Denis	R-R	6-1	180	11-20-94	4	4	3.91	14	9	0	0	53	45	28	23	4	16	49	.231	.175	.254	8.32	2.72
Diaz, Jose	R-R	6-1	180	8-17-92	2	1	6.75	13	0	0	1	21	26	20	16	0	16	18	.306	.250	.323	7.59	6.75
Diaz, Pedro	R-R	6-1	187	12-10-94	2	1	2.70	23	1	0	5	30	22	11	9	2	13	31	.202	.278	.164	9.30	3.90
Gomez, Luis	R-R	6-3	160	10-9-92	4	1	1.77	14	1	0	1	41	38	15	8	1	10	36	.233	.209	.242	7.97	2.21
Gutierrez, Osman	R-R	6-4	185	12-15-94	0	1	1.91	12	10	0	0	47	44	26	10	0	25	42	.256	.222	.271	8.04	4.79
Herdenez, Yonardo	R-R	6-1	170	9-20-95	4	0	4.14	15	3	0	0	50	60	31	23	6	10	34	.288	.224	.313	6.12	1.80
Higuera, Juliandry	L-L	6-1	180	9-6-94	3	3	3.50	11	10	0	0	46	42	22	18	1	19	45	.250	.138	.273	8.74	3.69
Hurtado, Erick	L-L	6-4	190	11-21-94	3	3	2.87	15	0	0	2	38	37	19	12	0	20	37	.259	.176	.270	8.84	4.78
Jose, Kelyn	L-L	6-4	195	5-19-95	0	0	8.00	11	5	0	0	18	22	23	16	0	19	25	.293	.071	.344	12.50	9.50
Lara, Wilmin	R-R	6-2	175	6-5-94	1	1	4.56	15	2	0	3	26	25	20	13	0	24	16	.260	.158	.286	5.61	8.42
Martinez, Jeffry	R-R	6-1	180	7-11-93	0	1	5.40	7	0	0	0	8	7	8	5	1	4	9	.233	.143	.313	9.72	4.32
Nova, Jose	L-L	6-1	170	4-6-95	1	3	3.97	13	12	0	0	48	53	29	21	0	16	42	.282	.226	.293	7.93	3.02
Nunez, Juan	R-R	6-2	185	1-23-96	0	2	9.64	6	5	0	0	14	22	19	15	1	15	17	.338	.429	.328	10.93	9.64
Rosario, Jairo	R-R	6-4	190	10-21-93	1	3	3.93	22	0	0	1	34	32	25	15	1	19	29	.252	.256	.250	7.60	4.98
Sanchez, Luis	R-R	6-3	200	2-20-94	5	3	3.38	14	8	0	1	56	57	33	21	0	17	48	.256	.164	.286	7.71	2.73
Torres, Jonathan	L-L	6-4	190	12-31-94	1	0	1.80	4	1	0	0	10	6	3	2	0	4	11	.188	.000	.214	9.90	3.60
Vinicio, Thony	R-R	6-5	175	3-25-94	0	0	11.57	6	0	0	0	5	6	6	6	0	4	5	.316	.333	.313	9.64	7.71
Zambrano, William	R-R	6-1	190	2-19-94	0	3	10.13	13	0	0	0	11	17	15	12	0	13	13	.333	.467	.278	10.97	10.97

Fielding

Catcher	PCT	G	PO	A	E	DP	PB
Dominguez	.969	11	79	14	3	0	5
Herazo	.961	22	173	22	8	2	16
Hernandez	.975	43	336	47	10	3	25

First Base	PCT	G	PO	A	E	DP
Alcantara	1.000	1	3	0	0	1
Demorizi	1.000	2	12	0	0	2
Dominguez	1.000	8	51	1	0	5
Moreta	.985	65	496	34	8	33

Second Base	PCT	G	PO	A	E	DP
Almanzar	.941	5	5	11	1	1
Almonte	.926	47	71	91	13	20
Demorizi	1.000	1	0	1	0	0
Orozco	.000	1	0	0	1	0
Vasquez	.942	38	62	67	8	13

Third Base	PCT	G	PO	A	E	DP
Almanzar	—	1	0	0	0	0
Almonte	1.000	1	0	1	0	0
Demorizi	1.000	8	5	14	0	1
Lizardo	.905	67	54	136	20	5
Orozco	1.000	1	2	0	0	0

Shortstop	PCT	G	PO	A	E	DP
Almanzar	.833	3	1	4	1	0
Almonte	—	1	0	0	0	0
Demorizi	.902	8	24	13	4	2
Severino	.881	62	109	151	35	32
Vasquez	—	1	0	0	0	0

Outfield	PCT	G	PO	A	E	DP
Alcantara	.984	49	61	2	1	2
Demorizi	.667	2	2	0	1	0
Fuentes	.857	6	6	0	1	0
Garcia	.947	33	51	3	3	1
Olivares	.955	40	77	8	4	1
Orozco	.992	59	117	10	1	3
Rodriguez	.929	49	61	4	5	0

Washington Nationals

SEASON IN A SENTENCE: Washington won the National League East by 17 games and posted the best record in the NL, but its season ended with a bitterly disappointing loss to the Giants in the Division Series.

HIGH POINT: The Nationals carried incredible momentum into the postseason, as Jordan Zimmermann threw the first no-hitter in Nats history against the Marlins on the final day of the regular season. Steven Souza recorded the final out with an incredible diving catch on the warning track in left-center field. "Just an epic day for an epic season," said center fielder Denard Span, who set a Nationals record with his 184th hit of the season.

LOW POINT: The Nats lost both of their home playoff games against the Giants, including an 18-inning heartbreaker in Game Two, en route to a series loss in four games. Washington's No. 3 and No. 4 hitters, Jayson Werth and Adam LaRoche, went a combined 2-for-35 in the series.

NOTABLE ROOKIES: Washington was a veteran club, but a pair of rookies emerged as quality complementary pieces on the mound. Aaron Barrett posted a 2.66 ERA in 50 relief appearances before struggling with the season on the line in the playoffs. Fellow righty Blake Treinen posted a 2.49 in 51 innings split between the bullpen and rotation.

KEY TRANSACTIONS: The Nationals led the majors with a 3.03 ERA, and their stellar pitching staff was boosted last winter by the acquisition of righthander Doug Fister in a trade for Steve Lombardozzi, Robbie Ray and Ian Krol. Fister posted the third-best WAR and ERA of any pitcher on the staff.

DOWN ON THE FARM: Three Nationals affiliates—Triple-A Syracuse, high Class A Potomac and low Class A Hagerstown—reached the playoffs in their respective leagues. Potomac won the Carolina League crown, while Hagerstown fell in the decisive fifth game of the South Atlantic League finals. Several Nationals prospects took big steps forward, led by Michael Taylor, who harnessed his five-tool ability and established himself as one of baseball's best outfield prospects. Souza and Tony Renda also had strong seasons offensively, while Lucas Giolito cemented his status as one of the game's top pitching prospects, and fellow righties Austin Voth and A.J. Cole also posted standout seasons.

OPENING DAY PAYROLL: $134 million (seventh)

PLAYERS OF THE YEAR

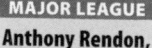

MAJOR LEAGUE

Anthony Rendon, 3b
.287/.351/.473
21 HR, 39 2B, 83 RBI
Led team in WAR (6.5)

MINOR LEAGUE

Michael Taylor, of
(Double-A/Triple-A)
.296/.376/.512,
24 HR, 37 SB

ORGANIZATION LEADERS

BATTING		*Minimum 250 AB
MAJORS		
* AVG	Span, Denard	.302
* OPS	Werth, Jayson	.849
HR	LaRoche, Adam	26
RBI	LaRoche, Adam	92
MINORS		
* AVG	Souza Jr., Steven, Hagerstown, Potomac, Syr.	.345
* OBP	Souza Jr., Steven, Hagerstown, Potomac, Syr.	.427
* SLG	Souza Jr., Steven, Hagerstown, Potomac, Syr.	.577
R	Bautista, Rafael, Hagerstown	97
H	Difo, Wilmer, Hagerstown	176
TB	Difo, Wilmer, Hagerstown	263
2B	Laird, Brandon, Syracuse	32
3B	Ballou, Isaac, Hagerstown, Potomac	12
HR	Keyes, Kevin, Potomac, Harrisburg	24
RBI	Difo, Wilmer, Hagerstown	90
BB	Mooneyham, Brett, Potomac, Aub., Hgrstwn	62
SO	Taylor, Michael, Harrisburg, Syracuse	144
SB	Bautista, Rafael, Hagerstown	69

PITCHING		#Minimum 75 IP
MAJORS		
W	Fister, Doug	16
# ERA	Fister, Doug	2.41
SO	Strasburg, Stephen	242
SV	Soriano, Rafael	32
MINORS		
W	Cole, A.J.M Harrisburg, Syracuse	13
	Pivetta, Nick, Hagerstown	13
L	Simms, John, Hgrstwn, Potomac, Harrisburg	10
ERA	Voth, Austin, Hgrstwn, Potomac, Harrisburg	2.77
G	Grace, Matt, Harrisburg, Syracuse	50
	Herron, Tyler, Syracuse, Harrisburg	50
GS	Cole, A.J., Harrisburg, Syracuse	25
GS	Pivetta, Nick, Hagerstown	25
SV	Benincasa, Robert, Potomac, Harrisburg	18
IP	Laffey, Aaron, Syracuse	147
BB	Mooneyham, Brett, Potomac, Aub., Hgrstwn	62
SO	Voth, Austin, Hgrstwn, Potomac, Harrisburg	133
# AVG	Voth, Austin, Hgrstwn, Potomac, Harrisburg	.197

General Manager: Mike Rizzo. **Farm Director:** Mark Scialabba. **Scouting Director:** Kris Kline.

Class	Team	League	W	L	PCT	Finish	Manager
Majors	Washington Nationals	National	96	66	.593	t-2nd (30)	Matt Williams
Triple-A	Syracuse Chiefs	International	81	62	.566	1st (14)	Billy Gardner
Double-A	Harrisburg Senators	Eastern	53	89	.373	12th (12)	Brian Daubach
High A	Potomac Nationals	Carolina	78	58	.574	2nd (8)	Tripp Keister
Low A	Hagerstown Suns	South Atlantic	87	53	.621	t-3rd (14)	Patrick Anderson
Short season	Auburn Doubledays	New York-Penn	34	41	.453	9th (14)	Gary Cathcart
Rookie	Nationals	Gulf Coast	25	35	.417	t-12th (16)	Michael Barrett
Overall Minor League Record			358	338	.514	10th (30)	

ORGANIZATION STATISTICS

WASHINGTON NATIONALS

NATIONAL LEAGUE

Batting	B-T	HT	WT	DOB	AVG	vLH	vRH	G	AB	R	H	2B	3B	HR	RBI	BB	HBP	SH	SF	SO	SB	CS	SLG	OBP
Cabrera, Asdrubal	B-R	6-0	205	11-13-85	.229	.255	.219	49	175	20	40	9	2	5	21	22	0	1	2	29	3	0	.389	.312
Desmond, Ian	R-R	6-3	215	9-20-85	.255	.273	.248	154	593	73	151	26	3	24	91	46	6	0	3	183	24	5	.430	.313
Dobbs, Greg	L-R	6-1	205	7-2-78	.214	.500	.192	21	28	0	6	1	0	0	2	1	0	0	1	4	0	0	.250	.233
2-team total (15 Miami)					.171	—	—	36	41	0	7	1	0	0	2	1	0	0	1	8	0	0	.195	.186
Espinosa, Danny	B-R	6-0	205	4-25-87	.219	.301	.183	114	333	31	73	14	3	8	27	18	12	0	1	122	8	1	.351	.283
Frandsen, Kevin	R-R	6-0	190	5-24-82	.259	.303	.236	105	220	17	57	8	0	1	17	6	7	2	1	26	0	0	.309	.299
Hairston, Scott	R-R	6-0	200	5-25-80	.208	.250	.120	61	77	6	16	4	0	1	8	4	2	0	4	26	0	0	.299	.253
Harper, Bryce	L-R	6-3	225	10-16-92	.273	.263	.276	100	352	41	96	10	2	13	32	38	1	3	1	104	2	2	.423	.344
Kobernus, Jeff	R-R	6-2	195	6-30-88	.000	.000	.000	4	6	2	0	0	0	0	0	1	0	0	0	0	0	0	.000	.250
LaRoche, Adam	L-L	6-3	205	11-6-79	.259	.204	.280	140	494	73	128	19	0	26	92	82	2	0	8	108	3	0	.455	.362
Leon, Sandy	B-R	5-10	220	3-13-89	.156	.217	.122	20	64	7	10	1	0	1	3	6	0	0	0	20	0	0	.219	.229
Lobaton, Jose	B-R	6-0	215	10-21-84	.234	.230	.235	66	214	18	50	9	0	2	12	15	1	0	0	61	0	0	.304	.287
McLouth, Nate	L-R	5-10	180	10-28-81	.173	.190	.169	79	139	10	24	6	0	1	7	16	5	1	1	35	4	1	.237	.280
Moore, Tyler	R-R	6-2	220	1-30-87	.231	.207	.242	42	91	8	21	2	0	4	14	7	2	0	0	29	0	0	.385	.300
Ramos, Wilson	R-R	6-0	235	8-10-87	.267	.325	.249	88	341	32	91	12	0	11	47	17	0	0	3	57	0	0	.399	.299
Rendon, Anthony	R-R	6-1	200	6-6-90	.287	.313	.278	153	613	111	176	39	6	21	83	58	5	2	5	104	17	3	.473	.351
Schierholtz, Nate	L-R	6-2	215	2-15-84	.225	.250	.222	23	40	3	9	1	1	1	4	2	0	0	0	8	0	1	.375	.262
2-team total (99 Chicago)					.195	—	—	122	353	32	69	11	4	7	37	20	4	0	6	84	4	5	.309	.243
Souza, Steven	R-R	6-4	225	4-24-89	.130	.500	.000	21	23	2	3	0	0	2	2	3	0	0	0	7	0	0	.391	.231
Span, Denard	L-L	6-0	210	2-27-84	.302	.269	.314	147	610	94	184	39	8	5	37	50	2	3	3	65	31	7	.416	.355
Taylor, Michael	R-R	6-3	210	3-26-91	.205	.333	.182	17	39	5	8	3	0	1	5	3	1	0	0	17	0	2	.359	.279
Walters, Zach	B-R	6-2	210	9-5-89	.205	.444	.133	32	39	7	8	1	0	3	5	4	0	0	0	16	0	0	.462	.279
Werth, Jayson	R-R	6-5	240	5-20-79	.292	.331	.280	147	534	85	156	37	1	16	82	83	9	0	3	113	9	1	.455	.394
Zimmerman, Ryan	R-R	6-3	220	9-28-84	.280	.288	.278	61	214	26	60	19	1	5	38	22	0	0	4	37	0	0	.449	.342

Pitching	B-T	HT	WT	DOB	W	L	ERA	G	GS	CG	SV	IP	H	R	ER	HR	BB	SO	AVG	vLH	vRH	K/9	BB/9
Barrett, Aaron	R-R	6-3	225	1-2-88	3	0	2.66	50	0	0	0	41	33	17	12	1	20	49	.220	.275	.192	10.84	4.43
Blevins, Jerry	L-L	6-6	185	9-6-83	2	3	4.87	64	0	0	0	57	48	31	31	3	23	66	.229	.160	.298	10.36	3.61
Cedeno, Xavier	L-L	6-0	205	8-26-86	0	0	3.86	9	0	0	0	7	10	4	3	1	0	5	.333	.400	.267	6.43	0.00
Clippard, Tyler	R-R	6-3	200	2-14-85	7	4	2.18	75	0	0	1	70	47	22	17	5	23	82	.188	.237	.130	10.49	2.94
Detwiler, Ross	R-L	6-5	210	3-6-86	2	3	4.00	47	0	0	1	63	68	34	28	5	21	39	.282	.226	.312	5.57	3.00
Fister, Doug	L-R	6-8	210	2-4-84	16	6	2.41	25	25	1	0	164	153	52	44	18	24	98	.246	.263	.228	5.38	1.32
Gonzalez, Gio	L-L	6-0	205	9-19-85	10	10	3.57	27	27	0	0	159	134	66	63	10	56	162	.230	.221	.233	9.19	3.18
Hill, Taylor	R-R	6-3	235	3-12-89	0	1	9.00	3	1	0	0	9	16	9	9	0	3	5	.410	.389	.429	5.00	3.00
Jordan, Taylor	R-R	6-5	200	1-17-89	0	3	5.61	5	5	0	0	26	34	20	16	3	8	17	.309	.386	.388	5.96	2.81
Mattheus, Ryan	R-R	6-3	220	11-10-83	0	0	1.04	7	0	0	0	9	7	1	1	0	4	4	.233	.250	.222	4.15	4.15
Roark, Tanner	R-R	6-2	230	10-5-86	15	10	2.85	31	31	1	0	199	178	64	63	16	39	138	.239	.235	.242	6.25	1.77
Soriano, Rafael	R-R	6-4	230	12-19-79	4	1	3.19	64	0	0	32	62	51	23	22	4	19	59	.223	.218	.227	8.56	2.76
Stammen, Craig	R-R	6-4	225	3-9-84	4	5	3.84	49	0	0	0	73	78	34	31	5	14	56	.276	.286	.268	6.94	1.73
Storen, Drew	B-R	6-1	195	8-11-87	2	1	1.12	65	0	0	11	56	44	8	7	2	11	46	.215	.253	.184	7.35	1.76
Strasburg, Stephen	R-R	6-4	230	7-20-88	14	11	3.14	34	34	0	0	215	198	86	75	23	43	242	.245	.234	.254	10.13	1.80
Thornton, Matt	L-L	6-6	235	9-15-76	1	0	0.00	18	0	0	0	11	10	0	0	2	8	8	.238	.250	.222	6.35	1.59
Treinen, Blake	R-R	6-5	215	6-30-88	2	3	2.49	15	7	0	0	51	57	17	14	1	13	30	.286	.337	.238	5.33	2.31
Zimmermann, Jordan	R-R	6-2	220	5-23-86	14	5	2.66	32	32	3	0	200	185	67	59	13	29	182	.244	.258	.231	8.20	1.31

Fielding

Catcher	PCT	G	PO	A	E	DP	PB
Leon	.994	20	154	9	1	1	1
Lobaton	.996	64	497	46	2	3	1
Ramos	.993	87	626	54	5	2	4

First Base	PCT	G	PO	A	E	DP
Dobbs	1.000	3	31	3	0	3
Frandsen	1.000	9	51	1	0	5
LaRoche	.994	136	1100	93	7	101

	PCT	G	PO	A	E	DP
Moore	.984	24	172	16	3	16
Zimmerman	.958	5	23	0	1	2

Second Base	PCT	G	PO	A	E	DP
Cabrera	.995	48	73	132	1	29
Espinosa	.990	89	157	231	4	58
Frandsen	1.000	13	21	31	0	6
Kobernus	1.000	3	1	9	0	4
Rendon	1.000	28	51	52	0	8

	PCT	G	PO	A	E	DP
Walters	1.000	1	2	1	0	0

Third Base	PCT	G	PO	A	E	DP
Frandsen	.947	16	14	22	2	0
Rendon	.958	134	106	235	15	30
Walters	1.000	3	0	2	0	0
Zimmerman	.948	23	18	37	3	4

Shortstop	PCT	G	PO	A	E	DP
Cabrera	1.000	1	0	1	0	0
Desmond	.963	154	203	416	24	82
Espinosa	.978	12	16	28	1	7
Walters	1.000	3	1	3	0	0

Outfield	PCT	G	PO	A	E	DP
Frandsen	.967	21	27	2	1	0
Hairston	.926	16	25	0	2	0
Harper	.978	98	166	9	4	0
McLouth	.970	50	64	0	2	0
Moore	1.000	4	8	0	0	0
Schierholtz	1.000	10	8	0	0	0

	PCT	G	PO	A	E	DP
Souza	.909	13	10	0	1	0
Span	.990	147	377	7	4	3
Taylor	1.000	14	31	0	0	0
Walters	1.000	1	2	0	0	0
Werth	.981	139	247	8	5	1
Zimmerman	1.000	30	48	2	0	0

SYRACUSE CHIEFS

INTERNATIONAL LEAGUE

TRIPLE-A

Batting	B-T	HT	WT	DOB	AVG	vLH	vRH	G	AB	R	H	2B	3B	HR	RBI	BB	HBP	SH	SF	SO	SB	CS	SLG	OBP
Burriss, Emmanuel	B-R	6-0	190	1-17-85	.300	.275	.310	116	444	80	133	18	7	6	46	48	8	9	1	41	22	10	.412	.377
Dobbs, Greg	L-R	6-1	205	7-2-78	.247	.231	.254	35	97	12	24	4	0	2	11	5	0	0	0	23	0	0	.351	.284
Goodwin, Brian	L-L	6-0	200	11-2-90	.219	.193	.231	81	274	31	60	10	4	4	32	50	1	4	0	95	6	4	.328	.342
Hairston, Scott	R-R	6-0	200	5-25-80	.100	.143	.000	3	10	0	1	1	0	0	1	2	0	0	0	4	0	0	.200	.250
Hood, Destin	R-R	6-1	225	4-3-90	.294	.312	.289	84	309	43	91	24	2	10	36	22	2	0	1	65	4	3	.482	.344
Howell, Jeff	R-R	5-11	200	4-1-83	.208	.200	.213	24	77	6	16	5	0	0	7	7	0	3	0	20	0	0	.273	.274
Johnson, Josh R.	B-R	5-10	190	1-11-86	.236	.226	.242	90	258	30	61	7	2	0	30	45	0	9	6	42	6	5	.279	.343
Kobernus, Jeff	R-R	6-2	195	6-30-88	.257	.254	.259	59	206	28	53	13	1	2	23	23	3	1	2	44	15	3	.359	.338
Komatsu, Erik	L-L	5-10	175	10-1-87	.188	.000	.273	18	48	7	9	1	0	1	4	13	1	0	1	11	1	2	.271	.365
Laird, Brandon	R-R	6-1	215	9-11-87	.300	.350	.278	130	463	67	139	32	1	18	85	34	4	1	4	96	0	0	.490	.350
Leon, Sandy	B-R	5-10	220	3-13-89	.229	.195	.240	51	170	26	39	9	0	5	25	23	0	0	0	36	1	0	.371	.321
Lozada, Jose	B-R	6-0	180	12-29-85	.237	.250	.230	44	114	14	27	2	0	1	9	12	1	2	1	30	3	3	.281	.313
Moore, Tyler	R-R	6-2	220	1-30-87	.265	.278	.261	84	302	45	80	21	0	10	44	47	3	0	2	77	0	2	.434	.367
Nicol, Sean	R-R	5-10	175	9-25-86	.250	.000	.313	6	20	2	5	2	0	0	2	0	1	0	0	2	0	0	.350	.318
Perez, Eury	R-R	6-0	190	5-30-90	.311	.338	.299	57	212	30	66	13	2	1	11	13	8	4	1	35	20	3	.406	.372
Peterson, Brock	R-R	6-3	230	11-20-83	.250	.238	.256	72	264	37	66	11	1	6	31	29	5	0	3	76	0	0	.367	.332
Rhymes, Will	L-R	5-8	170	4-1-83	.255	.230	.264	114	392	55	100	22	5	5	42	33	3	3	6	54	5	2	.375	.313
Schierholtz, Nate	L-R	6-2	215	2-15-84	.158	.200	.143	4	19	1	3	0	0	1	4	0	0	0	0	6	0	0	.316	.158
Solano, Jhonatan	R-R	5-9	210	8-12-85	.251	.292	.232	93	343	45	86	15	1	10	53	23	5	0	3	49	1	0	.388	.305
Souza, Steven	R-R	6-4	225	4-24-89	.350	.322	.359	96	346	62	121	25	2	18	75	52	3	0	6	75	26	7	.590	.432
Taylor, Michael	R-R	6-3	210	3-26-91	.227	.182	.242	12	44	7	10	3	1	1	3	7	0	1	0	14	3	1	.409	.333
Walters, Zach	R-R	6-2	210	9-5-89	.300	.339	.287	60	237	38	71	18	5	15	48	20	2	1	1	62	0	2	.608	.358
2-team total (7 Columbus)					.310	—	—	67	268	42	83	22	5	17	56	20	2	1	1	67	0	2	.619	.361

Pitching	B-T	HT	WT	DOB	W	L	ERA	G	GS	CG	SV	IP	H	R	ER	HR	BB	SO	AVG	vLH	vRH	K/9	BB/9
Barrett, Aaron	R-R	6-3	225	1-2-88	1	0	0.00	10	0	0	2	10	5	0	0	0	1	8	.139	.267	.048	6.97	0.87
Cedeno, Xavier	L-L	6-0	205	8-26-86	5	1	2.29	35	0	0	4	39	22	10	10	3	12	57	.163	.133	.178	13.04	2.75
Cole, A.J.	R-R	6-5	200	1-5-92	7	0	3.43	11	11	0	0	63	69	30	24	9	17	50	.283	.293	.276	7.14	2.43
Delcarmen, Manny	R-R	6-2	225	2-16-82	4	4	3.13	46	1	0	4	60	58	22	21	2	23	55	.252	.208	.287	8.20	3.43
Dupra, Brian	R-R	6-3	200	12-15-88	0	0	6.23	1	1	0	0	4	5	3	3	1	1	4	.294	.500	.182	2.08	2.08
Espino, Paolo	R-R	5-10	190	1-10-87	0	0	1.35	1	1	0	0	7	2	1	1	0	1	4	.091	.143	.000	5.40	1.35
Garcia, Christian	R-R	6-5	230	8-24-85	1	1	2.45	10	0	0	0	15	9	5	4	1	4	17	.180	.200	.171	10.43	2.45
Gonzalez, Mike	R-L	6-2	200	5-23-78	1	1	2.78	21	0	0	6	23	20	8	7	1	10	18	.238	.273	.215	7.15	3.97
Grace, Matt	L-L	6-3	190	12-14-88	2	0	1.30	28	0	0	0	42	28	6	6	1	13	30	.194	.113	.242	6.48	2.81
Herron, Tyler	R-R	6-3	190	8-5-86	1	0	16.20	2	0	0	0	2	2	4	3	0	3	2	.250	.400	.000	16.20	16.20
Hill, Taylor	R-R	6-3	235	3-12-89	11	7	2.81	25	24	4	1	144	136	48	45	15	25	86	.249	.243	.253	5.38	1.56
Holland, Neil	R-R	6-0	190	8-14-88	1	1	4.66	6	1	0	0	12	9	5	5	2	4	3	.293	.267	.308	2.79	2.79
Jackson, Zach	L-L	6-5	225	5-13-83	2	3	6.06	26	0	0	0	36	43	28	24	1	13	26	.301	.250	.330	6.56	3.28
Jordan, Taylor	R-R	6-5	200	1-17-89	0	2	4.06	6	6	0	0	31	31	15	14	3	8	28	.256	.306	.222	8.13	2.32
Kroenke, Zach	R-L	6-2	215	4-21-84	1	0	4.22	2	2	0	0	11	12	5	5	0	4	9	.293	.200	.323	2.53	3.38
Laffey, Aaron	L-L	6-0	200	4-15-85	12	6	3.67	25	21	2	0	147	159	64	60	8	37	91	.275	.258	.282	5.57	2.27
Lively, Mitch	R-R	6-5	255	9-7-85	5	2	3.86	9	7	0	0	37	42	18	16	2	14	36	.286	.258	.309	8.68	3.38
Madrigal, Warner	R-R	6-1	235	3-21-84	0	4	3.94	30	0	0	7	32	38	14	14	2	9	35	.288	.339	.247	9.84	2.53
Martin, Rafael	R-R	6-3	215	5-16-84	1	1	0.80	25	0	0	10	34	20	4	3	0	7	42	.168	.244	.122	11.23	1.87
Mattheus, Ryan	R-R	6-3	220	11-10-83	1	3	5.80	34	0	0	2	40	47	31	26	5	12	32	.283	.319	.258	7.14	2.68
McGregor, Scott	R-R	6-2	193	12-19-86	1	2	3.91	4	4	0	0	23	31	10	10	2	6	13	.330	.341	.321	5.09	2.35
Ohlendorf, Ross	R-R	6-4	240	8-8-82	1	0	0.00	2	2	0	0	8	2	0	0	1	6	.080	.000	.133	6.75	1.13
Poveda, Omar	R-R	6-3	235	9-28-87	1	4	6.38	9	8	0	0	42	48	31	30	4	17	36	.289	.266	.310	7.65	3.61
Robertson, Tyler	L-L	6-5	285	12-23-87	0	0	4.08	12	0	0	1	18	23	9	8	3	4	14	.329	.545	.229	7.13	2.04
Roenicke, Josh	R-R	6-3	205	8-4-82	4	6	5.45	23	15	0	0	79	105	58	48	9	31	37	.319	.318	.320	4.20	3.52
Rosenbaum, Danny	R-L	6-2	210	10-10-87	1	1	4.50	4	4	0	0	20	22	10	10	1	5	9	.272	.227	.288	4.05	2.25
Runion, Sam	R-R	6-4	220	11-9-88	0	1	4.76	5	1	0	0	11	14	6	6	0	2	13	.298	.333	.276	10.32	1.59
Simmons, James	R-R	6-3	220	9-29-86	2	2	5.68	4	4	0	0	25	24	16	16	5	6	17	.253	.296	.195	6.04	2.13
Stange, Daniel	R-R	6-3	235	12-22-85	2	3	3.64	44	0	0	0	59	61	26	24	2	34	43	.274	.284	.263	6.52	5.16
Tatusko, Ryan	R-R	6-5	200	3-27-85	5	5	2.85	14	14	0	0	79	61	29	25	5	30	51	.216	.239	.193	5.81	3.42
Treinen, Blake	R-R	6-5	215	6-30-88	8	2	3.35	16	16	0	0	81	78	34	30	4	20	64	.253	.289	.228	7.14	2.23

Fielding

Catcher	PCT	G	PO	A	E	DP	PB
Howell	1.000	21	123	7	0	0	2
Leon	1.000	42	290	28	0	2	3
Solano	.989	81	527	37	6	3	8

First Base	PCT	G	PO	A	E	DP
Dobbs	.986	16	130	7	2	13
Laird	1.000	4	37	1	0	7
Lozada	.980	5	45	3	1	4
Moore	.995	64	519	44	3	60
Peterson	.998	58	507	28	1	48

Second Base	PCT	G	PO	A	E	DP
Burriss	.917	11	20	24	4	6
Johnson	.976	27	58	64	3	15
Kobernus	.947	11	16	20	2	4
Lozada	1.000	3	10	16	0	7
Nicol	1.000	3	4	8	0	1

Rhymes	1.000	70	114	189	0	53
Walters	.971	27	51	84	4	20

Third Base	PCT	G	PO	A	E	DP
Johnson	1.000	11	3	11	0	1
Laird	.965	116	65	264	12	28
Lozada	1.000	2	0	5	0	0
Nicol	—	1	0	0	0	0
Rhymes	.912	12	4	27	3	1
Walters	.931	11	6	21	2	1

Shortstop	PCT	G	PO	A	E	DP
Burriss	.962	103	146	309	18	71
Johnson	.971	21	21	79	3	11
Lozada	.947	8	5	13	1	5
Nicol	.800	2	1	7	2	1
Walters	.934	14	18	39	4	6

Outfield	PCT	G	PO	A	E	DP
Goodwin	.984	80	179	3	3	1
Hairston	1.000	3	3	0	0	0
Hood	.980	75	142	3	3	0

Johnson	.958	28	46	0	2	0
Kobernus	.978	44	90	0	2	0
Komatsu	1.000	12	30	1	0	0
Lozada	1.000	20	30	0	0	0
Moore	1.000	15	23	0	0	0
Perez	.971	57	98	3	3	0
Schierholtz	1.000	2	3	0	0	0
Souza	.982	88	214	4	4	0
Taylor	.976	12	38	2	1	0
Walters	1.000	7	10	1	0	0

HARRISBURG SENATORS

DOUBLE-A

EASTERN LEAGUE

Batting	B-T	HT	WT	DOB	AVG	vLH	vRH	G	AB	R	H	2B	3B	HR	RBI	BB	HBP	SH	SF	SO	SB	CS	SLG	OBP
Bantz, Brandon	R-R	6-1	205	1-7-87	.271	.389	.231	22	70	7	19	5	0	0	6	4	1	0	0	14	0	0	.343	.320
Bloxom, Justin	R-B	6-1	205	4-29-88	.252	.229	.263	35	111	11	28	8	0	1	10	12	0	0	1	31	1	0	.351	.323
Canham, Mitch	L-R	6-2	205	9-25-84	.204	.200	.205	34	103	12	21	1	1	1	11	9	0	3	2	18	3	0	.262	.263
Dykstra, Cutter	R-R	5-11	180	6-29-89	.274	.286	.267	96	358	46	98	18	3	6	49	41	4	1	7	82	10	6	.391	.349
Hague, Rick	R-R	6-2	190	9-18-88	.231	.260	.212	101	321	31	74	20	0	4	27	27	2	1	2	74	9	4	.330	.293
Harper, Bryce	L-R	6-3	225	10-16-92	.600	—	.600	3	10	4	6	1	0	3	7	3	0	0	0	1	2	1	1.600	.692
Hood, Destin	R-R	6-1	225	4-3-90	.329	.333	.326	19	73	9	24	1	0	1	5	2	1	0	0	8	6	0	.384	.355
Jeroloman, Brian	L-R	6-0	205	5-10-85	.188	.218	.173	72	234	22	44	6	0	6	21	30	0	3	2	59	0	2	.291	.278
Keyes, Kevin	R-R	6-3	225	3-15-89	.236	.273	.216	114	402	52	95	15	1	20	64	43	3	1	4	104	1	4	.428	.312
Kobernus, Jeff	R-R	6-2	195	6-30-88	.292	.500	.250	6	24	2	7	1	0	0	3	2	0	0	0	4	2	0	.333	.346
LaRoche, Adam	L-R	6-3	—	11-6-79	.333	.333	—	1	3	0	1	0	0	0	0	1	0	0	0	1	0	0	.333	.500
Latimore, Quincy	R-R	5-11	175	2-3-89	.277	.263	.286	108	303	48	84	10	2	11	41	36	2	5	4	75	14	6	.432	.354
Leonida, Cole	R-R	6-2	220	12-25-88	.236	.280	.196	33	106	12	25	10	0	0	5	14	0	0	0	29	0	1	.330	.325
Lozada, Jose	R-B	6-0	180	12-29-85	.373	.318	.414	16	51	5	19	2	0	0	5	1	0	1	1	5	2	1	.412	.377
Martinson, Jason	R-R	6-1	190	10-15-88	.236	.249	.229	132	466	56	110	17	5	10	42	45	3	4	4	127	23	2	.358	.305
Nicol, Sean	R-R	5-10	175	9-25-86	.247	.273	.234	36	97	17	24	6	0	0	3	8	0	0	0	19	5	0	.309	.305
Oduber, Randolph	R-L	6-3	190	3-18-89	.000	.000	—	1	2	0	0	0	0	0	0	0	0	0	0	0	0	0	.000	.000
Ramos, Wilson	R-R	6-0	235	8-10-87	.182	.000	.286	3	11	1	2	0	1	0	4	0	0	0	0	1	0	0	.455	.182
Ramsey, Caleb	L-R	6-2	215	10-7-88	.245	.290	.226	127	473	44	116	16	2	1	43	42	2	2	3	75	20	5	.294	.308
Sanchez, Adrian	B-R	6-0	160	8-16-90	.223	.253	.208	89	269	34	60	6	0	3	29	23	3	1	2	42	7	3	.279	.290
Skole, Matt	L-R	6-4	225	7-30-89	.241	.221	.252	132	461	58	111	29	1	14	68	78	2	1	2	127	3	1	.399	.352
Taylor, Michael	R-R	6-3	210	3-26-91	.313	.324	.305	98	384	74	120	17	2	22	61	50	4	2	1	130	34	8	.539	.396
Tejeda, Oscar	R-R	6-1	170	12-26-89	.204	.118	.243	18	54	6	11	0	1	1	4	1	1	0	1	13	0	1	.296	.228
Vettleson, Drew	L-R	6-1	185	7-19-91	.246	.282	.227	75	248	24	61	14	3	8	28	11	1	2	5	75	3	3	.423	.275

Pitching	B-T	HT	WT	DOB	W	L	ERA	G	GS	CG	SV	IP	H	R	ER	HR	BB	SO	AVG	vLH	vRH	K/9	BB/9
Alfaro, Gabriel	R-R	6-5	225	6-14-83	0	0	11.48	10	0	0	0	13	23	17	17	1	10	9	.383	.250	.472	6.08	6.75
Bates, Colin	R-R	6-1	175	3-10-88	1	3	3.81	39	1	0	3	87	103	41	37	4	15	50	.294	.300	.289	5.15	1.55
Benincasa, Robert	R-R	6-2	180	9-5-90	1	3	3.10	25	0	0	7	29	26	14	10	4	10	30	.241	.260	.224	9.31	3.10
Brach, Brett	R-R	6-2	190	3-29-88	1	4	4.88	6	5	0	0	31	49	18	17	2	6	17	.383	.391	.378	4.88	1.72
Cole, A.J.	R-R	6-5	200	1-5-92	6	3	2.92	14	14	1	0	71	79	30	23	1	15	61	.273	.269	.278	7.73	1.90
Demny, Paul	R-R	6-2	200	8-3-89	2	1	2.88	22	1	0	0	41	39	13	13	3	21	36	.255	.258	.253	7.97	4.65
Dupra, Brian	R-R	6-3	200	12-15-88	2	6	5.60	24	12	0	0	90	102	61	56	7	42	57	.291	.281	.300	5.70	4.20
Espino, Paolo	R-R	5-10	190	1-10-87	6	5	3.98	24	16	0	0	113	98	52	50	12	23	112	.229	.213	.240	8.92	1.83
Fister, Doug	L-R	6-8	210	2-4-84	0	0	4.91	1	1	0	0	4	2	2	2	0	3	5	.154	.000	.400	12.27	7.36
Gilliam, Rob	R-R	6-1	195	11-29-87	0	0	5.09	5	4	0	0	18	15	10	10	3	9	13	.231	.240	.225	6.62	4.58
Grace, Matt	L-L	6-3	190	12-14-88	3	1	1.02	22	0	0	3	35	32	10	4	0	12	32	.229	.176	.258	8.15	3.06
Harper, Bryan	L-L	6-5	205	12-29-89	1	0	4.70	12	0	0	1	15	20	10	8	1	8	11	.323	.364	.300	6.46	4.70
Herron, Tyler	R-R	6-3	190	8-5-86	3	2	2.73	48	0	0	6	63	58	24	19	4	26	50	.256	.211	.297	7.18	3.73
Holland, Neil	R-R	6-0	190	8-14-88	6	3	3.22	40	0	0	1	67	57	28	24	4	20	60	.230	.161	.292	8.06	2.69
Jackson, Zach	L-L	6-5	200	5-13-83	0	0	0.00	5	0	0	0	8	4	0	0	0	2	7	.160	.000	.235	8.22	0.00
Kroenke, Zach	R-L	6-2	215	4-21-84	3	9	6.72	18	16	0	0	83	119	74	62	13	32	44	.339	.326	.343	4.77	3.47
Madrigal, Warner	R-R	6-1	235	3-21-84	0	0	1.50	6	0	0	1	6	5	1	1	1	2	6	.217	.500	.067	9.00	3.00
Manno, Chris	L-L	6-3	170	11-4-88	1	0	3.38	4	0	0	0	5	3	3	2	0	4	5	.150	.286	.077	10.13	6.75
Martin, Rafael	R-R	6-3	195	5-16-84	2	1	2.70	11	0	0	4	20	15	7	6	1	5	20	.205	.250	.162	9.00	2.25
McGregor, Scott	R-R	6-2	193	12-19-86	2	1	5.22	8	6	0	0	29	28	18	17	2	8	22	.252	.314	.200	6.75	2.45
Meyers, Brad	R-R	6-6	205	9-13-85	1	4	7.13	6	6	0	0	24	39	22	19	4	13	11	.371	.382	.360	4.13	4.88
Mirowski, Richie	R-R	6-2	190	4-30-89	0	1	6.23	10	0	0	1	13	17	10	9	1	2	12	.309	.370	.250	8.31	1.38
Perry, Ryan	R-R	6-5	215	2-13-87	0	0	5.63	5	0	0	0	8	9	5	5	0	3	6	.290	.188	.400	6.75	3.38
Poveda, Omar	R-R	6-3	235	9-28-87	1	3	5.34	6	6	0	0	32	36	21	19	6	7	39	.281	.262	.299	10.97	1.97
Purke, Matt	L-L	6-4	215	7-17-90	1	6	8.04	8	8	0	0	31	42	32	28	5	18	22	.330	.200	.363	6.32	5.17
Rivero, Felipe	L-L	6-2	195	7-5-91	2	7	4.12	10	10	0	0	44	45	30	20	4	18	38	.260	.154	.299	7.83	3.71
Runion, Sam	R-R	6-4	220	11-9-88	0	1	4.26	9	0	0	0	13	11	6	6	1	1	11	.239	.238	.240	7.82	0.71
Schwartz, Blake	R-R	6-3	200	10-9-89	0	7	7.04	8	8	0	0	38	54	39	30	6	16	23	.333	.412	.247	5.40	3.76
Self, Derek	R-R	6-3	205	1-14-90	2	4	3.38	25	0	0	1	40	44	21	15	7	13	29	.281	.386	.212	6.98	2.93
Simmons, James	R-R	6-3	220	9-29-86	3	3	5.47	21	11	0	0	81	88	52	49	10	27	60	.272	.288	.259	6.69	3.01
Simms, John	R-R	6-3	205	1-17-92	2	6	5.03	11	11	1	0	59	73	34	33	6	15	42	.308	.336	.282	6.41	2.29
Solis, Sammy	R-L	6-5	250	8-10-88	0	1	21.60	1	1	0	0	3	9	9	8	0	1	1	.500	.000	.563	2.70	2.70
Voth, Austin	R-R	6-1	190	6-26-92	1	3	6.52	5	5	0	0	19	22	14	14	4	9	19	.286	.250	.306	8.84	4.19

Fielding

Catcher
Catcher	PCT	G	PO	A	E	DP	PB
Bantz	.980	20	137	8	3	4	0
Canham	1.000	23	144	7	0	0	1
Jeroloman	.994	72	489	33	3	7	3
Leonida	.996	30	214	19	1	2	0
Ramos	1.000	3	20	1	0	0	0

First Base
First Base	PCT	G	PO	A	E	DP
Bloxom	1.000	16	124	9	0	9
Canham	1.000	5	49	2	0	5
Keyes	.982	30	211	9	4	21
LaRoche	1.000	1	7	0	0	2
Leonida	1.000	1	2	1	0	0
Ramsey	1.000	4	12	0	0	2
Skole	.989	97	680	56	8	59
Tejeda	1.000	2	6	0	0	1

Second Base
Second Base	PCT	G	PO	A	E	DP
Dykstra	.969	87	152	226	12	46
Hague	.975	19	33	44	2	11
Lozada	1.000	2	1	0	0	0
Nicol	.900	5	7	11	2	4
Sanchez	.969	34	69	85	5	20
Tejeda	1.000	1	0	3	0	0

Third Base
Third Base	PCT	G	PO	A	E	DP
Bloxom	.909	8	3	7	1	0
Canham	.750	2	2	1	1	0
Hague	.888	45	22	57	10	2
Lozada	1.000	7	4	12	0	2
Nicol	.865	14	6	26	5	2
Sanchez	.949	44	20	74	5	14
Skole	.828	29	18	30	10	4
Tejeda	.931	13	8	19	2	1

Shortstop
Shortstop	PCT	G	PO	A	E	DP
Hague	.944	16	27	40	4	12
Lozada	1.000	2	1	2	0	0
Martinson	.969	119	160	316	15	59
Nicol	1.000	6	7	18	0	3
Sanchez	.800	4	0	4	1	0

Outfield
Outfield	PCT	G	PO	A	E	DP
Bloxom	.833	5	10	0	2	0
Hague	1.000	9	13	2	0	2
Harper	1.000	2	4	0	0	0
Hood	1.000	17	29	1	0	0
Keyes	.988	50	82	1	1	0
Kobernus	1.000	6	22	0	0	0
Latimore	.981	85	197	5	4	2
Lozada	1.000	4	10	0	0	0
Nicol	1.000	5	6	0	0	0
Oduber	—	1	0	0	0	0
Ramsey	.987	116	217	9	3	3
Sanchez	1.000	4	4	0	0	0
Taylor	.997	88	276	10	1	4
Vettleson	.980	72	144	4	3	0

POTOMAC NATIONALS

HIGH CLASS A

CAROLINA LEAGUE

Batting	B-T	HT	WT	DOB	AVG	vLH	vRH	G	AB	R	H	2B	3B	HR	RBI	BB	HBP	SH	SF	SO	SB	CS	SLG	OBP
Ballou, Isaac	L-R	6-2	205	3-17-90	.260	.238	.264	33	127	17	33	6	3	4	20	11	1	2	2	31	3	2	.449	.319
Dent, Cody	L-R	5-11	190	8-1-91	.122	.267	.038	13	41	2	5	0	0	0	4	4	0	2	0	12	1	0	.122	.200
Harper, Bryce	L-R	6-3	225	10-16-92	.750	—	.750	2	4	3	3	0	0	1	4	2	0	0	0	0	0	0	1.500	.833
Keyes, Kevin	R-R	6-3	225	3-15-89	.284	.214	.300	19	74	12	21	2	1	4	17	6	1	0	0	17	1	0	.500	.346
Kobernus, Jeff	R-R	6-2	195	6-30-88	.333	1.000	.286	4	15	5	5	0	0	0	3	3	0	0	0	2	5	0	.333	.444
LaRoche, Adam	L-L	6-3	225	11-6-79	.000	—	.000	1	2	0	0	0	0	0	0	0	0	0	0	0	0	0	.000	.000
Leonida, Cole	R-R	6-2	220	12-25-88	.260	.188	.279	28	77	16	20	9	0	4	11	19	2	0	0	17	2	0	.532	.418
Manuel, Craig	L-R	6-1	205	5-22-90	.203	.056	.255	24	69	4	14	2	0	0	5	11	0	0	0	13	0	0	.232	.313
Martinez, Estarlin	R-R	6-1	185	3-8-92	.269	.270	.269	73	223	28	60	9	3	0	19	13	0	0	2	38	6	5	.336	.307
McQuillan, Mike	L-R	5-11	175	11-28-82	.207	.171	.215	80	246	26	51	11	3	6	37	49	7	1	1	75	4	8	.350	.353
Mesa, Narciso	R-R	5-11	175	11-16-91	.156	.250	.143	20	64	3	10	2	0	0	1	4	1	1	0	14	0	0	.188	.217
Miller, Brandon	R-R	6-2	215	10-8-89	.178	.282	.153	60	202	28	36	7	0	13	31	28	1	0	0	71	2	1	.406	.281
Miller, Justin	R-R	6-0	180	11-28-88	.218	.229	.214	62	193	27	42	14	0	3	21	20	0	3	2	53	3	1	.337	.288
Norfork, Khayyan	R-R	5-10	190	1-19-89	.264	.239	.273	102	348	52	92	20	5	2	38	31	7	5	4	74	13	4	.368	.333
Oduber, Randolph	R-L	6-3	190	3-18-89	.266	.240	.276	125	462	66	123	26	5	6	51	16	9	6	2	115	16	8	.383	.303
Perez, Eury	R-R	6-0	190	5-30-90	.321	.333	.316	9	28	6	9	1	0	1	4	3	0	2	0	4	6	1	.464	.387
Perez, Stephen	B-R	5-11	185	12-16-90	.258	.250	.260	124	431	70	111	25	2	2	50	72	3	7	5	90	27	6	.339	.364
Piwnica-Worms, Will	R-R	6-3	215	4-1-90	.241	.200	.257	61	195	29	47	10	0	4	29	23	3	0	4	48	3	2	.354	.324
Pleffner, Shawn	L-R	6-5	225	8-17-89	.298	.333	.286	95	356	45	106	26	1	2	44	35	2	0	3	62	9	1	.393	.361
Ramos, Wilson	R-R	6-0	235	8-10-87	.556	—	.556	2	9	1	5	1	0	1	5	0	0	0	0	0	0	0	1.000	.556
Renda, Tony	R-R	5-8	180	1-24-91	.307	.276	.317	107	414	75	127	21	4	0	47	43	10	5	5	59	19	5	.377	.381
Sanchez, Adrian	B-R	6-0	160	8-16-90	.271	.261	.274	29	96	6	26	3	1	0	9	5	2	0	3	14	4	1	.323	.311
Severino, Pedro	R-R	6-1	180	7-20-93	.247	.211	.256	94	291	41	72	15	1	9	36	21	5	6	3	57	2	0	.399	.306
Souza, Steven	R-R	6-4	225	4-24-89	.111	—	.111	3	9	0	1	0	0	0	1	0	0	1	0	4	1	0	.111	.200
Tejeda, Oscar	R-R	6-1	170	12-26-89	.270	.326	.253	94	359	57	97	18	1	16	65	27	0	0	4	74	9	1	.460	.318
Wooten, John	R-R	6-3	190	1-19-91	.269	.348	.243	26	93	16	25	5	1	4	17	6	1	1	0	20	1	0	.473	.320
Zimmerman, Ryan	R-R	6-3	220	9-28-84	.357	.500	.333	4	14	0	5	1	0	0	3	0	0	0	1	1	0	1	.429	.333

Pitching	B-T	HT	WT	DOB	W	L	ERA	G	GS	CG	SV	IP	H	R	ER	HR	BB	SO	AVG	vLH	vRH	K/9	BB/9
Bacus, Dakota	R-R	6-2	200	4-2-91	7	6	4.41	27	20	0	1	129	143	70	63	9	40	89	.285	.303	.273	6.23	2.80
Benincasa, Robert	R-R	6-2	180	9-5-90	4	2	5.47	21	0	0	11	26	27	16	16	5	12	21	.265	.318	.224	7.18	4.10
Brach, Brett	R-R	6-2	190	3-29-88	1	0	2.81	3	3	0	0	16	13	7	5	0	2	12	.213	.235	.205	6.75	1.13
Davis, Cody	R-R	5-9	170	7-21-90	2	0	2.70	11	0	0	0	17	14	5	5	0	8	13	.222	.111	.306	7.02	4.32
Demny, Paul	R-R	6-2	200	8-3-89	0	0	4.50	1	0	0	0	2	2	1	1	0	2	2	.286	.333	.250	9.00	9.00
Dickson, Ian	R-R	6-5	215	9-16-90	5	9	4.37	30	15	0	0	124	116	65	60	9	47	100	.253	.269	.244	7.28	3.42
Dupra, Brian	R-R	6-3	200	12-15-88	3	0	1.25	6	0	0	0	22	15	3	3	0	2	26	.190	.138	.220	10.80	0.83
Encarnacion, Pedro	R-R	6-4	175	6-26-91	3	4	5.28	13	7	0	0	44	61	27	26	3	19	34	.343	.309	.371	6.90	3.86
Fister, Doug	L-R	6-8	210	2-4-84	0	0	0.00	1	1	0	0	4	6	3	0	0	0	3	.353	.500	.273	6.75	0.00
Gonzalez, Gio	R-L	6-0	205	9-19-85	0	0	10.57	2	2	0	0	8	9	9	9	1	8	9	.281	.400	.259	10.57	9.39
Harper, Bryan	L-L	6-5	205	12-29-89	2	0	2.66	27	0	0	3	44	33	18	13	2	17	40	.199	.146	.220	8.18	3.48
Henke, Travis	R-R	6-6	241	7-9-88	5	2	5.79	36	0	0	0	65	81	47	42	7	22	45	.310	.330	.296	6.20	3.03
Lee, Nick	L-L	5-11	185	1-13-91	0	2	10.05	5	4	0	0	14	17	18	16	0	8	23	.283	.333	.267	14.44	5.02
Manno, Chris	L-L	6-3	170	11-4-88	2	0	3.46	8	0	0	0	13	11	5	5	1	8	18	.220	.250	.200	12.46	5.54
Martin, Rafael	R-R	6-3	215	5-16-84	0	0	0.00	2	0	0	0	5	0	0	0	0	0	7	.000	.000	.000	7.71	0.00
Mendez, Gilberto	R-R	6-2	165	11-17-92	7	4	3.14	41	0	0	15	52	37	18	18	4	9	49	.196	.247	.161	8.54	1.57
Mirowski, Richie	R-R	6-2	190	4-30-89	1	0	2.31	12	0	0	0	23	22	10	6	1	8	27	.247	.268	.229	10.41	3.09
Mooneyham, Brett	L-L	6-5	235	1-24-90	2	4	7.36	10	7	0	0	33	35	33	27	2	35	18	.294	.395	.247	4.91	9.55
Ohlendorf, Ross	R-R	6-4	240	8-8-82	0	1	11.81	2	2	0	0	5	13	7	7	1	1	4	.464	.385	.533	6.75	1.69
Pena, Ronald	R-R	6-4	195	9-19-91	3	2	5.96	13	11	0	0	51	63	37	34	7	20	19	.303	.314	.295	3.33	3.51
Rauh, Brian	R-R	6-2	200	7-23-91	2	4	4.39	17	12	0	0	66	66	43	32	5	23	51	.257	.207	.298	6.99	3.15
Runion, Sam	R-R	6-4	220	11-9-88	1	0	2.00	5	0	0	0	9	8	2	2	1	2	10	.229	.154	.273	10.00	2.00

Name	B-T	HT	WT	DOB	W	L	ERA	G	GS	CG	SV	IP	H	R	ER	HR	BB	SO	AVG	vLH	vRH	K/9	BB/9
Schwartz, Blake	R-R	6-3	200	10-9-89	2	1	4.40	8	6	0	0	29	27	15	14	3	10	12	.250	.256	.246	3.77	3.14
Self, Derek	R-R	6-3	205	1-14-90	3	0	1.69	17	0	0	3	27	19	5	5	1	5	30	.196	.152	.235	10.13	1.69
Silvestre, Hector	L-L	6-3	180	12-14-92	1	2	4.45	6	6	0	0	28	32	14	14	6	3	21	.283	.389	.263	6.67	0.95
Simms, John	R-R	6-3	205	1-17-92	2	4	4.36	10	10	0	0	54	50	27	26	2	16	49	.253	.298	.219	8.22	2.68
Solis, Sammy	R-L	6-5	250	8-10-88	1	0	1.69	1	1	0	0	5	7	1	1	0	1	4	.292	.167	.333	6.75	1.69
Spann, Matt	L-L	6-6	185	2-17-91	9	5	3.81	23	18	0	1	106	109	50	45	4	38	63	.266	.228	.278	5.33	3.22
Suero, Wander	R-R	6-3	175	9-15-91	2	1	7.57	12	0	0	0	27	33	23	23	4	10	21	.303	.372	.258	6.91	3.29
Swynenberg, Matt	R-R	6-5	215	2-16-89	0	0	5.40	2	1	0	0	5	4	3	3	0	3	2	.238	.100	.364	3.60	5.40
Turnbull, Kylin	R-L	6-5	205	9-12-89	3	3	4.41	19	4	0	0	49	68	28	24	1	9	37	.329	.345	.322	6.80	1.65
Ullmann, Ryan	R-R	6-6	230	8-12-91	0	0	6.00	1	0	0	0	3	4	2	2	0	0	3	.308	.500	.143	9.00	0.00
Voth, Austin	R-R	6-1	190	6-26-92	2	1	1.43	6	6	0	0	38	16	6	6	2	7	40	.126	.167	.082	9.56	1.67
Walsh, Jake	L-L	6-3	195	1-1-91	3	0	1.71	14	0	0	2	21	12	4	4	1	4	27	.160	.111	.175	11.57	1.71

Fielding

Catcher	PCT	G	PO	A	E	DP	PB
Leonida	.980	27	171	23	4	2	1
Manuel	1.000	24	137	22	0	2	1
Ramos	1.000	2	17	0	0	0	0
Severino	.986	93	590	90	10	5	9

First Base	PCT	G	PO	A	E	DP
Keyes	1.000	13	118	4	0	3
LaRoche	1.000	1	6	0	0	0
Martinez	1.000	19	127	7	0	9
Miller	1.000	16	136	3	0	8
Pfeffner	.994	86	724	60	5	67
Wooten	1.000	9	73	5	0	2

Second Base	PCT	G	PO	A	E	DP
Norfork	.994	39	66	93	1	18
Renda	.980	91	160	237	8	44

	PCT	G	PO	A	E	DP
Sanchez	.977	9	19	24	1	5
Third Base	PCT	G	PO	A	E	DP
Dent	.909	6	0	10	1	0
McQuillan	—	1	0	0	0	0
Miller	.929	6	3	10	1	1
Norfork	.955	53	45	82	6	9
Sanchez	.909	16	14	26	4	2
Tejeda	.918	47	31	92	11	9
Wooten	.833	15	9	26	7	2
Shortstop	PCT	G	PO	A	E	DP
Dent	1.000	1	3	5	0	1
Perez	.954	119	163	355	25	60
Renda	.923	8	11	13	2	4
Sanchez	.900	3	5	4	1	0
Tejeda	.929	6	4	9	1	2

Outfield	PCT	G	PO	A	E	DP
Ballou	.973	33	71	1	2	0
Dent	1.000	6	12	0	0	0
Harper	1.000	2	1	0	0	0
Kobernus	1.000	2	2	0	0	0
Martinez	.990	48	87	8	1	1
McQuillan	.978	36	45	0	1	0
Mesa	.974	18	38	0	1	0
Miller	.965	57	102	9	4	1
Miller	.976	39	79	2	2	0
Oduber	.979	119	219	11	5	4
Perez	.955	9	20	1	1	1
Piwnica-Worms	1.000	61	118	2	0	0
Souza	1.000	3	5	0	0	0
Tejeda	1.000	3	4	2	0	0
Zimmerman	1.000	3	2	0	0	0

HAGERSTOWN SUNS

LOW CLASS A

SOUTH ATLANTIC LEAGUE

Batting	B-T	HT	WT	DOB	AVG	vLH	vRH	G	AB	R	H	2B	3B	HR	RBI	BB	HBP	SH	SF	SO	SB	CS	SLG	OBP
Ballou, Isaac	L-R	6-2	205	3-17-90	.271	.253	.276	100	377	74	102	20	9	6	53	47	14	1	2	65	23	8	.419	.370
Bautista, Rafael	R-R	6-2	165	3-8-93	.290	.318	.279	134	487	97	141	20	5	5	54	33	8	10	5	72	69	15	.382	.341
Chubb, Austin	R-R	6-1	200	4-17-89	.221	.278	.200	21	68	8	15	4	0	1	5	6	2	0	1	22	0	0	.324	.299
Davidson, Austin	L-R	6-0	180	1-3-93	.188	.500	.143	4	16	3	3	0	0	1	4	2	0	0	0	3	1	1	.375	.278
Dent, Cody	L-R	5-11	190	8-1-91	.204	.200	.205	36	103	18	21	1	2	1	6	14	1	1	0	23	4	2	.282	.305
Difo, Wilmer	R-B	6-0	175	4-2-92	.315	.324	.311	136	559	91	176	31	7	14	90	37	6	2	6	65	49	9	.470	.360
Kieboom, Spencer	R-R	6-0	220	3-16-91	.309	.321	.306	87	330	50	102	28	4	9	61	21	4	0	6	67	2	2	.500	.352
Kobernus, Jeff	R-R	6-2	195	6-30-88	.231	.250	.222	4	13	6	3	0	0	1	2	3	0	0	0	3	2	1	.462	.375
Langlois, Bryan	R-R	6-1	200	10-30-91	.182	.200	.167	3	11	2	2	0	0	0	1	1	0	0	1	0	0		.182	.308
Lopez, Carlos	R-R	6-2	220	1-18-90	.260	.229	.274	78	262	39	68	21	0	6	34	33	0	0	5	54	3	2	.408	.337
Manuel, Craig	L-R	6-1	205	5-22-90	.270	.313	.255	37	126	16	34	6	0	4	15	17	2	0	1	14	0	2	.413	.363
Martinez, Estarlin	R-R	6-1	185	3-8-92	.304	.217	.326	35	115	15	35	5	1	1	16	17	3	0	2	17	6	3	.391	.401
Masters, David	R-R	6-1	185	4-23-93	.182	.133	.198	51	176	25	32	8	1	0	10	20	5	2	0	49	4	2	.239	.284
Medina, Willie	R-R	5-10	160	1-25-91	.207	.185	.214	44	111	13	23	0	1	0	5	12	4	4	3	17	13	5	.225	.300
Mesa, Narciso	R-R	5-11	175	11-16-91	.273	.253	.280	74	286	31	78	15	3	4	31	10	3	5	1	52	24	6	.388	.303
Middleton, Brennan	R-R	6-0	190	11-20-90	.253	.238	.259	69	225	31	57	7	0	0	17	17	4	6	1	33	5	3	.284	.316
Norfork, Khayyan	R-R	5-10	190	1-19-89	.190	.000	.308	6	21	5	4	2	0	0	2	3	0	0	0	5	1	0	.286	.292
Ramos, Wilson	R-R	6-1	235	8-10-87	.667	.667	—	1	3	1	2	0	0	1	3	1	0	0	0	0	0	0	1.667	.750
Rodriguez, Wilman	R-R	6-1	175	6-7-91	.257	.191	.278	57	191	23	49	15	1	3	22	9	4	3	1	33	16	6	.393	.302
Souza, Steven	R-R	6-4	225	4-24-89	.500	.500	—	1	2	0	1	0	0	0	2	3	0	0	0	1	1	0	.500	.500
Span, Denard	L-L	6-0	210	2-27-84	.500	—	.500	2	4	3	2	0	0	0	2	3	0	0	0	0	1	0	.500	.714
Ward, Drew	L-R	6-4	210	11-25-94	.269	.268	.270	115	431	45	116	26	3	10	73	42	5	0	0	121	2	2	.413	.341
Wooten, John	R-R	6-3	190	1-19-91	.309	.328	.303	72	275	40	85	21	2	8	54	15	4	0	7	41	4	4	.487	.346
Yezzo, Jimmy	L-R	6-0	200	2-22-91	.271	.268	.271	123	466	56	126	22	1	13	56	20	5	0	2	77	3	4	.406	.306
Zebrack, Greg	R-R	6-1	200	8-28-90	.171	.100	.200	12	35	7	6	1	1	0	5	6	1	1	0	8	2	0	.257	.310

Pitching	B-T	HT	WT	DOB	W	L	ERA	G	GS	CG	SV	IP	H	R	ER	HR	BB	SO	AVG	vLH	vRH	K/9	BB/9
Anderson, Dixon	R-R	6-5	225	7-2-89	4	0	6.38	7	3	0	0	24	27	19	17	2	10	13	.284	.286	.283	4.88	3.75
Cooper, Andrew	R-R	6-1	200	6-27-92	7	4	5.91	28	5	0	2	70	103	48	46	8	15	37	.342	.368	.324	4.76	1.93
Davis, Cody	R-R	5-9	170	7-21-90	0	1	3.63	12	0	0	2	17	18	8	7	1	4	16	.273	.375	.176	8.31	2.08
Dickey, Robbie	R-R	6-3	205	4-6-94	1	0	3.00	2	2	0	0	9	10	4	3	0	5	5	.270	.286	.250	5.00	5.00
Estevez, Wirkin	R-R	6-1	170	3-15-92	0	2	9.18	5	5	0	0	17	25	17	17	1	8	10	.352	.516	.225	5.40	4.32
Giolito, Lucas	R-R	6-6	255	7-14-94	10	2	2.20	20	20	0	0	98	70	28	24	7	28	110	.197	.220	.175	10.10	2.57
Hollins, L.J.	R-R	6-3	185	7-31-91	2	0	5.91	9	0	0	0	11	14	7	7	0	8	10	.318	.467	.241	8.44	6.75
Johansen, Jake	R-R	6-6	235	1-23-91	5	6	5.19	29	18	0	0	101	120	70	58	3	55	89	.302	.253	.344	7.96	4.92
Johns, Sam	R-R	6-2	205	7-12-91	3	2	4.05	13	0	0	3	20	18	9	9	2	4	11	.247	.194	.297	4.95	1.80
Lee, Nick	L-L	5-11	185	1-13-91	1	0	7.56	5	0	0	0	8	11	7	7	1	6	8	.314	.368	.250	6.48	9.72
Lopez, Reynaldo	R-R	6-0	185	1-4-94	4	1	1.33	9	9	0	0	47	27	7	7	1	11	39	.167	.200	.138	7.42	2.09
Mooneyham, Brett	L-L	6-5	235	1-24-90	2	0	3.94	7	5	0	0	30	27	13	13	1	23	26	.250	.220	.269	7.89	6.98
Napoli, David	R-L	5-10	180	10-3-90	2	0	2.53	18	0	0	7	32	19	9	9	0	15	31	.171	.186	.162	8.72	4.22
Orlan, R.C.	R-L	6-0	185	9-28-90	0	2	6.28	6	0	0	0	14	17	10	10		7	21	.288	.316	.275	13.19	4.40

	B-T	HT	WT	DOB	W	L	ERA	G	GS	CG	SV	IP	H	R	ER	HR	BB	SO	AVG	vLH	vRH	K/9	BB/9
Ott, Travis	L-L	6-4	170	6-29-95	0	2	7.59	3	3	0	0	11	15	11	9	1	4	8	.349	.313	.370	6.75	3.38
Pena, Ronald	R-R	6-4	195	9-19-91	1	0	3.00	1	0	0	0	3	4	1	1	0	0	0	.364	.500	.333	0.00	0.00
Pivetta, Nick	R-R	6-5	220	2-14-93	13	8	4.22	26	25	0	0	132	142	66	62	15	39	98	.277	.280	.275	6.66	2.65
Ramos, David	R-R	6-0	175	9-13-91	1	0	6.46	8	0	0	1	15	27	14	11	3	1	16	.380	.481	.318	9.39	0.59
Rivero, Felipe	L-L	6-2	195	7-5-91	0	0	0.00	1	1	0	0	4	3	1	0	0	0	6	.200	.000	.375	13.50	0.00
Rodriguez, Jefry	R-R	6-5	185	7-26-93	0	2	6.88	4	4	0	0	17	27	15	13	0	5	11	.380	.359	.406	5.82	2.65
Silvestre, Hector	L-L	6-3	180	12-14-92	6	7	4.14	18	18	0	0	91	91	45	42	10	21	49	.259	.240	.267	4.83	2.07
Simms, John	R-R	6-3	205	1-17-92	0	0	0.98	5	0	0	3	18	13	2	2	0	2	20	.194	.226	.167	9.82	0.98
Solis, Sammy	R-L	6-5	250	8-10-88	1	0	0.00	1	1	0	0	6	4	0	0	0	0	7	.190	.200	.182	10.50	0.00
Spann, Matt	L-L	6-6	185	2-17-91	2	0	1.20	4	0	0	2	15	13	2	2	0	4	15	.228	.207	.250	9.00	2.40
Suero, Wander	R-R	6-3	175	9-15-91	4	1	2.13	17	6	0	3	72	59	22	17	3	11	62	.227	.212	.242	7.75	1.38
Swynenberg, Matt	R-R	6-5	215	2-16-89	0	0	0.00	1	1	0	0	4	1	0	0	0	1	3	.077	.167	.000	6.75	2.25
Sylvestri, Mike	R-R	5-10	180	6-14-90	0	0	6.30	6	0	0	0	10	11	7	7	1	2	12	.268	.143	.333	10.80	1.80
Thomas, Justin	L-L	6-2	195	10-21-90	3	5	2.78	34	0	0	4	71	66	27	22	3	11	64	.249	.150	.309	8.07	1.39
Turnbull, Kylin	R-L	6-5	205	9-12-89	0	0	3.60	1	1	0	0	5	6	3	2	1	1	3	.316	.250	.364	5.40	1.80
Ullmann, Ryan	R-R	6-6	230	8-12-91	4	1	4.44	30	0	0	3	73	82	45	36	5	22	49	.278	.246	.307	6.04	2.71
Valdez, Phillip	R-R	6-2	160	11-16-91	2	0	3.68	18	0	0	1	29	19	16	12	1	18	28	.178	.127	.231	8.59	5.52
Voth, Austin	R-R	6-1	190	6-26-92	4	3	2.45	13	13	0	0	70	51	25	19	1	22	74	.206	.223	.189	9.56	2.84
Walsh, Jake	L-L	6-3	195	1-1-91	1	2	1.45	23	0	0	10	31	17	7	5	1	10	27	.157	.161	.156	7.84	2.90
Webb, Joey	L-L	6-5	230	9-27-90	4	1	2.45	19	0	0	1	29	21	9	8	1	19	24	.206	.231	.190	7.36	5.83

Fielding

Catcher	PCT	G	PO	A	E	DP	PB
Chubb	.985	21	122	11	2	0	2
Kieboom	.997	86	638	68	2	5	7
Manuel	.996	37	229	36	1	2	3

First Base	PCT	G	PO	A	E	DP
Dent	1.000	3	17	1	0	0
Lopez	1.000	22	220	11	0	19
Martinez	1.000	2	9	1	0	2
Wooten	.996	27	234	27	1	19
Yezzo	.991	90	814	46	8	60

Second Base	PCT	G	PO	A	E	DP
Davidson	.917	1	3	8	1	2
Dent	1.000	5	8	9	0	2
Difo	.976	66	92	194	7	36
Medina	.983	26	46	73	2	13

	PCT	G	PO	A	E	DP
Middleton	.972	45	73	133	6	22
Norfork	1.000	1	2	4	0	1

Third Base	PCT	G	PO	A	E	DP
Davidson	1.000	2	1	4	0	0
Dent	.951	13	8	31	2	2
Lopez	.750	7	3	9	4	0
Middleton	1.000	5	1	10	0	0
Norfork	1.000	5	4	10	0	0
Ward	.920	92	48	158	18	7
Wooten	.985	20	19	45	1	4

Shortstop	PCT	G	PO	A	E	DP
Difo	.965	70	103	200	11	38
Masters	.974	51	89	172	7	28
Medina	.949	12	10	27	2	4
Middleton	.982	9	21	34	1	10

Outfield	PCT	G	PO	A	E	DP
Ballou	.976	99	157	9	4	1
Bautista	.974	134	296	9	8	3
Dent	.947	14	17	1	1	0
Kobernus	1.000	3	2	1	0	0
Langlois	1.000	2	8	0	0	0
Lopez	.900	4	9	0	1	0
Martinez	.962	29	48	3	2	0
Mesa	.969	74	118	7	4	1
Rodriguez	.988	47	77	3	1	0
Souza	1.000	1	2	0	0	0
Span	1.000	2	2	0	0	0
Wooten	1.000	10	15	0	0	0
Zebrack	1.000	12	21	0	0	0

AUBURN DOUBLEDAYS

SHORT-SEASON

NEW YORK-PENN LEAGUE

Batting	B-T	HT	WT	DOB	AVG	vLH	vRH	G	AB	R	H	2B	3B	HR	RBI	BB	HBP	SH	SF	SO	SB	CS	SLG	OBP
Abreu, Osvaldo	R-R	6-0	170	6-13-94	.229	.205	.235	58	210	31	48	7	3	1	15	9	6	5	1	41	10	6	.305	.279
Allen, Brenton	L-L	6-1	200	11-2-91	.154	.500	.091	4	13	1	2	0	0	0	2	0	0	0	3	0	0		.154	.267
Bacak, Kyle	R-R	5-9	175	11-15-91	.143	.000	.167	10	28	0	4	0	0	0	2	2	0	2	0	0	0		.143	.200
Carey, Dale	R-R	6-3	185	11-14-91	.248	.268	.241	47	157	21	39	8	0	3	18	19	7	0	1	26	6	2	.357	.353
Chubb, Austin	R-R	6-1	200	4-17-89	.286	.500	.200	3	7	3	2	0	0	0	2	4	1	0	0	1	0	0	.286	.583
Davidson, Austin	L-R	6-0	180	1-3-93	.248	.438	.226	43	153	17	38	13	1	2	22	11	1	0	3	26	1	0	.386	.298
Dykstra, Cutter	R-R	5-11	180	6-29-89	.389	.500	.375	5	18	5	7	3	0	0	1	3	1	0	0	3	1	1	.556	.500
Eusebio, Diomedes	R-R	6-0	185	9-8-92	.246	.206	.263	34	114	11	28	8	0	4	15	3	0	0	2	24	0	1	.421	.261
Gardner, Jeff	L-R	6-2	210	1-21-92	.206	.174	.211	49	165	20	34	6	1	4	11	16	2	0	0	54	2	5	.327	.284
Gordon, Garrett	R-R	6-0	210	2-26-93	.230	.308	.189	38	113	15	26	4	0	2	11	8	1	0	0	55	4	3	.319	.287
Gunter, Cody	L-R	6-3	195	4-18-94	.233	.171	.248	54	172	19	40	9	2	4	28	23	1	2	3	51	0	1	.378	.322
Hood, Destin	R-R	6-1	225	4-3-90	.143	—	.143	3	7	0	1	1	0	0	1	3	0	0	0	5	0	0	.286	.400
Keller, Alec	L-R	6-2	200	5-13-92	.100	—	.100	2	10	0	1	0	0	0	0	2	0	0	0	5	0	0	.100	.100
Langlois, Bryan	R-R	6-1	200	10-30-91	.241	.379	.205	41	141	25	34	8	0	0	9	17	3	1	1	35	4	1	.298	.333
Marmolejos-Diaz, Jose	L-L	6-1	185	1-2-93	.265	.333	.253	65	234	30	62	19	3	1	31	28	1	0	4	50	0	1	.385	.341
Marquez, Alex	R-R	5-11	190	12-10-92	.154	.000	.190	13	26	2	4	0	0	0	1	2	0	0	0	3	0	0	.154	.214
Masters, David	R-R	6-1	185	4-23-93	.292	.500	.250	8	24	4	7	2	0	2	3	2	1	0	0	4	0	0	.625	.370
Medina, Willie	R-R	5-10	160	1-25-91	.247	.105	.296	27	73	10	18	1	1	0	2	7	1	3	0	12	6	2	.288	.321
Mejia, Bryan	B-R	6-1	170	3-2-94	.259	.206	.277	45	135	19	35	5	5	2	14	5	0	1	2	22	8	2	.415	.282
Miller, Brandon	R-R	6-2	215	10-8-89	.357	.250	.400	3	14	1	5	1	0	0	1	1	0	0	0	3	0	0	.429	.400
Page, Matt	L-L	6-3	210	10-22-91	.248	.368	.224	38	117	10	29	5	2	1	13	14	1	0	1	30	1	0	.350	.331
Read, Raudy	R-R	6-0	170	10-29-93	.281	.370	.256	57	210	27	59	20	0	6	35	14	3	0	2	37	0	3	.462	.332
Riopedre, Chris	R-R	5-9	175	4-16-93	.216	.235	.211	23	74	5	16	3	0	0	7	1	0	2	0	15	3	0	.257	.227
Rodriguez, Wilman	R-R	6-1	175	6-7-91	.304	.667	.250	6	23	4	7	2	0	0	1	2	0	0	0	6	1	0	.391	.360
Ruiz, Adderling	R-R	6-1	175	5-3-91	.240	.333	.211	11	25	3	6	0	0	0	2	5	2	0	1	9	1	1	.240	.394
Valdez, Jean Carlos	R-R	6-2	190	3-14-93	.235	.000	.333	5	17	2	4	2	0	0	3	1	0	0	0	4	0	0	.353	.278
Vettleson, Drew	L-R	6-1	185	7-19-91	.318	.500	.300	8	22	3	7	1	1	0	2	3	1	0	0	5	1	0	.455	.423
Williamson, Clay	L-R	6-1	205	6-1-93	.236	.083	.255	37	106	10	25	5	0	0	6	11	7	0	0	34	4	4	.283	.347
Wooten, John	R-R	6-3	190	1-19-91	.167	.333	.133	5	18	0	3	2	0	0	1	2	0	0	0	6	0	1	.278	.250
Zebrack, Greg	R-R	6-1	190	8-28-90	.143	.000	.182	5	14	1	2	0	0	0	2	0	0	0	0	4	0	0	.143	.250

Pitching	B-T	HT	WT	DOB	W	L	ERA	G	GS	CG	SV	IP	H	R	ER	HR	BB	SO	AVG	vLH	vRH	K/9	BB/9
Bach, Connor	L-L	6-4	195	6-24-92	0	0	3.52	14	1	0	0	31	23	13	12	0	28	26	.215	.179	.228	7.63	8.22

	B-T	HT	WT	DOB	W	L	ERA	G	GS	CG	SV	IP	H	R	ER	HR	BB	SO	AVG	vLH	vRH	K/9	BB/9
Bafidis, Cory	L-L	6-0	190	8-22-90	0	1	4.50	4	0	0	1	6	11	5	3	0	3	4	.367	.333	.375	6.00	4.50
Bourque, James	R-R	6-4	190	7-9-93	3	5	4.19	11	10	0	0	43	52	33	20	1	16	31	.294	.321	.273	6.49	3.35
Derosier, Matt	R-R	6-2	200	7-13-94	1	2	6.33	6	2	0	0	21	28	15	15	3	5	18	.326	.333	.319	7.59	2.11
Dickey, Robbie	R-R	6-3	205	4-6-94	0	2	2.25	5	5	0	0	20	18	8	5	0	3	13	.231	.205	.265	5.85	1.35
Feliz, John	R-R	6-2	180	10-28-93	0	1	6.00	5	0	0	0	9	9	6	6	1	6	7	.273	.231	.300	7.00	6.00
Fischer, David	R-R	6-5	175	4-10-90	0	1	21.60	2	0	0	0	2	2	4	4	0	3	1	.333	.000	.500	5.40	16.20
Johns, Sam	R-R	6-2	205	7-12-91	0	0	4.50	3	0	0	1	4	4	2	2	1	0	1	.250	.125	.375	2.25	0.00
Joyce, Jake	R-R	6-0	185	8-19-91	0	0	0.00	4	0	0	1	3	0	0	0	0	1	4	.000	.000	.000	10.80	2.70
Lopez, Reynaldo	R-R	6-0	185	1-4-94	3	2	0.75	7	7	0	0	36	15	5	3	0	15	31	.125	.131	.119	7.75	3.75
Mancini, Domenick	R-R	6-3	190	9-28-93	1	0	0.00	3	0	0	0	3	0	1	0	0	1	1	.000	.000	.000	2.70	2.70
Mapes, Tyler	R-R	6-2	205	7-18-91	1	1	1.25	15	0	0	5	22	20	4	3	1	6	14	.256	.268	.243	5.82	2.49
Martinez, Anderson	R-R	6-3	180	2-22-93	2	3	3.76	8	0	0	0	41	41	18	17	5	7	18	.261	.273	.250	3.98	1.55
McDowell, Chase	L-R	6-2	195	12-14-90	1	3	4.50	14	1	0	2	28	40	20	14	1	3	15	.333	.393	.281	4.82	0.96
Mooneyham, Brett	L-L	6-5	235	1-24-90	0	0	6.75	2	0	0	0	4	4	3	3	1	4	3	.286	.000	.308	6.75	9.00
Napoli, Chris	R-L	5-10	180	10-3-90	0	0	0.00	1	0	0	1	1	0	0	0	0	1	2	.000	—	.000	18.00	9.00
Orlan, R.C.	R-L	6-0	185	9-28-90	1	0	4.19	17	0	0	1	34	35	17	16	4	11	37	.254	.149	.308	9.70	2.88
Ott, Travis	L-L	6-4	170	6-29-95	1	2	3.05	10	10	0	0	44	33	16	15	2	22	37	.210	.167	.223	7.51	4.47
Ramos, David	R-R	6-0	175	9-13-91	1	2	7.97	15	0	0	1	20	28	20	18	5	9	16	.326	.294	.346	7.08	3.98
Reyes, Luis	R-R	6-2	175	9-26-94	0	1	2.63	5	5	0	0	24	19	7	7	1	6	19	.218	.257	.192	7.13	2.25
Rodriguez, Jefry	R-R	6-5	185	7-26-93	1	0	2.76	3	3	0	0	16	16	5	5	0	4	9	.267	.280	.200	4.96	2.20
Sanchez, Mario	R-R	6-1	166	10-31-94	6	1	4.11	18	0	0	3	35	30	20	16	1	11	25	.236	.286	.188	6.43	2.83
Swynenberg, Matt	R-R	6-5	215	2-16-89	0	0	3.00	3	0	0	0	6	8	2	2	0	1	5	.296	.214	.385	7.50	1.50
Torres, Luis	R-R	6-3	190	6-4-94	1	2	2.27	12	5	0	0	36	30	15	9	3	9	25	.221	.258	.186	6.31	2.27
Valdez, Phillip	R-R	6-2	160	11-16-91	2	0	0.68	8	0	0	0	13	5	1	1	0	3	11	.111	.087	.136	7.43	2.03
Van Orden, Drew	R-R	6-4	200	1-19-92	2	3	4.39	10	8	0	0	41	47	22	20	4	11	35	.296	.264	.322	7.68	2.41
Webb, Joey	L-L	6-5	230	9-27-90	1	0	5.40	3	0	0	0	7	7	4	4	0	1	5	.241	.100	.316	6.75	1.35
Williams, Austen	R-R	6-3	220	12-19-92	4	3	4.66	9	9	0	0	39	42	24	20	2	8	26	.276	.292	.263	6.05	1.86
Williams, Deion	R-R	6-3	190	11-11-92	1	3	5.90	14	0	0	0	29	32	25	19	3	14	28	.281	.333	.246	8.69	4.34
Yrizarri, Deibi	R-R	6-1	170	10-3-94	1	1	0.00	4	0	0	0	6	7	1	2	0	5	5	.269	.250	.286	7.94	7.94

Fielding

Catcher	PCT	G	PO	A	E	DP	PB
Bacak	.986	10	61	12	1	0	0
Chubb	1.000	2	19	0	0	0	1
Marquez	1.000	12	46	10	0	1	1
Read	.980	50	294	54	7	4	10
Ruiz	.942	9	43	6	3	1	1

First Base	PCT	G	PO	A	E	DP
Eusebio	.977	19	155	15	4	14
Gunter	.500	1	1	0	1	0
Marmolejos-Diaz	.996	56	489	27	2	38
Valdez	1.000	3	25	2	0	0
Wooten	1.000	3	21	3	0	3

Second Base	PCT	G	PO	A	E	DP
Davidson	1.000	18	30	52	0	8
Dykstra	1.000	4	3	10	0	0

	PCT	G	PO	A	E	DP
Medina	.962	17	32	43	3	12
Mejia	.951	37	60	94	8	16
Riopedre	.976	8	22	18	1	7

Third Base	PCT	G	PO	A	E	DP
Davidson	.903	22	14	42	6	4
Eusebio	.824	6	5	9	3	1
Gunter	.924	49	31	102	11	5

Shortstop	PCT	G	PO	A	E	DP
Abreu	.917	57	79	142	20	28
Masters	1.000	7	9	17	0	0
Medina	.875	6	10	18	4	4
Mejia	—	1	0	0	0	0
Riopedre	.980	14	13	37	1	4

Outfield	PCT	G	PO	A	E	DP
Allen	1.000	2	1	0	0	0
Carey	.983	46	111	5	2	1
Gardner	.939	38	61	1	4	1
Gordon	.950	34	56	1	3	0
Hood	1.000	2	2	0	0	0
Keller	1.000	1	1	0	0	0
Langlois	.951	36	56	2	3	0
Marmolejos-Diaz	1.000	4	5	0	0	0
Mejia	1.000	1	1	0	0	0
Miller	1.000	3	2	1	0	0
Page	.941	22	29	3	2	0
Rodriguez	1.000	4	5	0	0	0
Vettleson	1.000	7	11	1	0	0
Williamson	.986	34	68	0	1	0
Wooten	1.000	1	1	0	0	0
Zebrack	1.000	5	10	1	0	0

GCL NATIONALS   ROOKIE

GULF COAST LEAGUE

Batting	B-T	HT	WT	DOB	AVG	vLH	vRH	G	AB	R	H	2B	3B	HR	RBI	BB	HBP	SH	SF	SO	SB	CS	SLG	OBP
Aguero, Younaifred	R-R	6-2	170	4-10-93	.274	.269	.275	38	95	11	26	9	0	1	5	6	2	1	0	10	1	1	.400	.330
Alvarez, Thomas	R-R	6-1	165	2-15-95	.226	.320	.205	48	137	27	31	8	5	1	6	26	2	7	0	35	4	3	.380	.358
Bacak, Kyle	R-S	5-9	175	11-15-91	.000	.000	.000	1	2	0	0	0	0	0	0	0	0	0	0	1	0	1	.000	.333
Corredor, Aldrem	L-L	6-0	202	10-27-95	.235	.227	.238	32	85	15	20	3	0	0	19	25	1	1	1	18	2	2	.271	.411
Encarnacion, Randy	R-R	6-3	180	7-31-94	.216	.222	.214	23	74	5	16	4	0	1	14	6	0	0	1	25	1	3	.311	.272
Florentino, Darryl	L-R	6-2	175	1-1-96	.195	.269	.176	44	128	14	25	5	1	1	12	3	2	2	2	26	8	3	.273	.222
Gutierrez, Kelvin	R-R	6-3	185	8-28-94	.286	.359	.268	53	192	27	55	6	3	0	25	23	1	0	2	29	4	6	.349	.362
Guzman, Luis	L-L	5-11	183	9-10-95	.255	.220	.266	50	165	27	42	8	2	1	17	14	4	2	1	23	3	4	.345	.326
Keniry, Conor	L-R	6-1	195	12-2-91	.236	.091	.274	40	106	14	25	4	0	0	11	14	1	2	1	24	5	2	.274	.328
Lora, Edwin	R-R	6-1	150	9-14-95	.293	.319	.284	52	181	27	53	8	0	0	15	11	0	6	0	37	13	6	.337	.333
Miller, Brandon	R-R	6-2	215	10-8-89	.133	.000	.167	6	15	1	2	0	0	0	1	1	1	0	0	4	0	0	.133	.235
Ortiz, Oliver	L-L	6-0	170	5-6-96	.219	.278	.200	51	146	16	32	7	3	2	24	17	2	0	2	46	1	1	.349	.305
Perez, Eury	R-R	6-0	190	5-30-90	.000	—	.000	1	2	0	0	0	0	0	0	0	0	0	0	1	0	0	.000	.000
Ramirez, Gilberto	R-R	6-4	180	11-14-92	.264	.300	.254	32	91	13	24	1	1	0	16	10	1	3	0	22	7	5	.297	.343
Reetz, Jakson	R-R	6-1	195	1-3-96	.274	.231	.286	43	117	20	32	6	1	1	15	26	8	1	3	30	6	3	.368	.429
Ripken, Ryan	L-L	6-6	205	7-26-93	.157	.273	.125	16	51	5	8	1	0	1	6	4	0	0	0	10	0	0	.235	.218
Rosario, Dionicio	R-R	6-3	180	2-14-94	.222	.200	.230	50	162	29	36	12	1	2	25	14	7	0	0	30	3	2	.346	.311
Serrata, Brayan	R-R	6-3	175	6-17-94	.238	.167	.267	22	42	3	10	1	0	1	4	1	0	0	1	15	0	0	.333	.250
Tillero, Jorge	R-R	5-11	160	12-21-93	.300	.524	.232	33	90	5	27	4	0	0	10	6	1	0	0	8	2	1	.344	.351

Pitching	B-T	HT	WT	DOB	W	L	ERA	G	GS	CG	SV	IP	H	R	ER	HR	BB	SO	AVG	vLH	vRH	K/9	BB/9
Bach, Connor	L-L	6-4	195	6-24-92	1	0	0.00	1	0	0	0	2	0	0	0	0	1	1	.000	.000	.000	4.50	4.50
Baez, Joan	R-R	6-3	190	12-26-94	1	3	3.78	4	3	0	0	17	18	13	7	2	3	12	.254	.444	.189	6.48	1.62
Bourque, James	R-R	6-4	190	7-9-93	0	0	0.00	1	1	0	0	2	1	0	0	0	1	2	.143	.333	.000	9.00	4.50

Player	B-T	HT	WT	DOB	W	L	ERA	G	GS	CG	SV	IP	H	R	ER	HR	BB	SO	AVG	vLH	vRH	K/9	BB/9
Costa, John	R-R	6-2	180	5-1-93	0	2	11.57	2	2	0	0	2	2	4	3	0	0	1	.200	.500	.125	3.86	0.00
Davis, Weston	R-R	6-3	185	7-6-96	0	2	9.92	9	3	0	0	16	20	20	18	1	9	11	.308	.167	.362	6.06	4.96
De La Cruz, Kida	R-R	6-5	240	8-10-94	0	0	4.50	13	0	0	0	18	19	11	9	0	11	12	.288	.292	.286	6.00	5.50
Dickey, Robbie	R-R	6-3	205	4-6-94	0	2	12.71	3	2	0	0	6	11	9	8	0	3	5	.407	.429	.400	7.94	4.76
Encarnacion, Pedro	R-R	6-4	175	6-26-91	0	0	6.00	4	4	0	0	9	10	7	6	0	2	13	.263	.286	.250	13.00	2.00
Estevez, Wirkin	R-R	6-1	170	3-15-92	0	0	2.25	3	3	0	0	8	4	2	2	1	0	6	.143	.091	.176	6.75	0.00
Feliz, John	R-R	6-2	180	10-28-93	3	1	1.08	10	0	0	1	17	9	4	2	0	3	13	.164	.188	.154	7.02	1.62
Fischer, David	R-R	6-5	175	4-10-90	0	0	4.50	2	0	0	0	4	2	2	2	0	2	5	.143	.200	.111	11.25	4.50
Jauss, D.J.	R-R	6-2	200	9-5-90	1	0	6.35	14	0	0	0	17	20	14	12	0	12	11	.299	.429	.239	5.82	6.35
Johns, Sam	R-R	6-2	205	7-12-91	0	0	0.00	1	0	0	0	2	0	0	0	0	0	0	.000	.000	.000	0.00	0.00
Lee, Nick	L-L	5-11	185	1-13-91	1	0	6.75	5	0	0	0	8	9	6	6	4	4	6	.290	.333	.280	6.75	4.50
Mancini, Domenick	R-R	6-3	190	9-28-93	0	2	3.18	9	0	0	0	11	13	7	4	0	6	8	.302	.455	.250	6.35	4.76
Mapes, Tyler	R-R	6-2	205	7-18-91	0	0	0.00	2	0	0	0	2	1	0	0	0	0	2	.167	.000	.200	9.00	0.00
Martinez, Anderson	R-R	6-3	180	2-22-93	2	0	1.04	5	1	0	0	17	15	2	2	1	1	14	.246	.278	.233	7.27	0.52
Mattheus, Ryan	R-R	6-3	220	11-10-83	0	0	7.71	2	1	0	0	2	3	2	2	0	0	4	.273	.000	.429	15.43	0.00
McDowell, Chase	L-R	6-2	195	12-14-90	1	0	8.31	2	0	0	0	4	5	4	4	1	1	4	.294	.444	.125	8.31	2.08
Mills, McKenzie	L-L	6-4	205	11-19-95	1	2	5.87	10	5	0	1	23	31	18	15	2	18	13	.333	.409	.310	5.09	7.04
Morales, Jose	R-R	6-3	180	2-12-95	0	5	4.68	13	3	0	1	33	44	22	17	2	11	18	.324	.390	.295	4.96	3.03
Ohlendorf, Ross	R-R	6-4	240	8-8-82	0	0	5.40	1	1	0	0	2	2	1	1	0	1	3	.286	.500	.200	16.20	5.40
Pena, Ronald	R-R	6-4	195	9-19-91	0	0	0.00	1	0	0	0	2	0	0	0	0	0	3	.000	.000	.000	13.50	0.00
Perry, Ryan	R-R	6-5	215	2-13-87	0	0	0.00	1	0	0	1	1	0	0	0	0	1	6	.250	1.000	.000	9.00	0.00
Plouck, Cole	L-L	6-2	175	4-25-94	1	1	3.55	8	0	0	2	13	13	5	5	0	4	9	.277	.250	.290	6.39	2.84
Poveda, Omar	R-R	6-3	235	9-28-87	0	1	5.40	4	1	0	0	8	11	8	5	0	7	8	.314	.125	.370	8.64	7.56
Ramirez, Jean	R-R	6-4	180	10-24-94	3	1	3.41	14	0	0	1	32	33	16	12	0	13	18	.262	.217	.288	5.12	3.69
Reyes, Luis	R-R	6-2	175	9-26-94	1	4	4.42	9	5	0	0	37	40	19	18	1	12	24	.282	.286	.280	5.89	2.95
Reynoso, Yorlin	L-L	6-2	200	11-20-95	1	0	3.38	13	0	0	0	24	29	11	9	0	13	14	.293	.346	.274	5.25	4.88
Rivero, Felipe	L-L	6-2	195	7-5-91	0	0	0.00	3	3	0	0	6	4	0	0	0	1	6	.190	.286	.143	9.00	1.50
Salazar, Melvi	R-R	6-1	175	12-17-94	0	1	6.46	13	0	0	0	15	17	13	11	0	8	12	.283	.353	.256	7.04	4.70
Simmons, Kyle	R-R	6-6	205	9-25-91	1	1	5.03	9	3	0	0	20	19	14	11	0	16	14	.253	.417	.176	6.41	7.32
Sisk, Brandon	L-L	6-2	220	7-13-85	0	0	0.00	3	0	0	0	4	1	0	0	0	2	5	.083	.333	.000	12.27	4.91
Solis, Sammy	R-L	6-5	250	8-10-88	0	0	0.00	2	2	0	0	4	1	0	0	0	1	5	.083	.000	.125	12.27	2.45
Torres, Luis	R-R	6-3	190	6-4-94	1	0	0.79	3	2	0	0	11	7	1	1	0	0	7	.179	.125	.194	5.56	0.00
Turnbull, Kylin	R-L	6-5	205	9-12-89	0	0	0.00	1	0	0	0	2	2	0	0	0	0	0	.286	.000	.333	0.00	0.00
Valerio, Maximo	R-R	6-2	175	7-22-95	3	0	5.23	16	0	0	2	31	29	18	18	2	16	25	.248	.298	.214	7.26	4.65
Van Orden, Drew	R-R	6-4	200	1-19-92	0	1	3.60	2	1	0	0	5	6	2	2	0	0	7	.286	.286	.286	12.60	0.00
Vasquez, Daury	R-R	6-4	170	11-21-92	1	2	6.94	11	5	0	0	23	27	19	18	0	17	11	.287	.276	.292	4.24	6.56
Williams, Austen	R-R	6-3	220	12-19-92	0	0	1.93	2	2	0	0	5	5	1	1	0	2	1	.263	.333	.231	1.93	3.86
Yrizarri, Deibi	R-R	6-1	170	10-3-94	2	4	9.08	11	6	0	0	37	50	44	37	2	17	14	.336	.390	.300	3.44	4.17

Fielding

Catcher	PCT	G	PO	A	E	DP	PB
Bacak	1.000	1	2	1	0	0	0
Reetz	.972	33	185	20	6	2	7
Serrata	.986	20	60	10	1	0	2
Tillero	.993	26	113	23	1	1	4

First Base	PCT	G	PO	A	E	DP
Aguero	.976	14	76	5	2	7
Ripken	.990	12	98	4	1	10
Rosario	.975	44	295	20	8	45

Second Base	PCT	G	PO	A	E	DP
Aguero	.931	6	13	14	2	6

	PCT	G	PO	A	E	DP
Alvarez	.976	43	91	109	5	38
Keniry	.986	18	29	43	1	7
Lora	1.000	1	4	1	0	0

Third Base	PCT	G	PO	A	E	DP
Aguero	.882	14	12	18	4	2
Gutierrez	.934	47	42	114	11	10
Keniry	.833	3	1	4	1	1

Shortstop	PCT	G	PO	A	E	DP
Gutierrez	1.000	4	3	8	0	1
Keniry	.925	16	16	33	4	7
Lora	.939	50	78	138	14	38

Outfield	PCT	G	PO	A	E	DP
Aguero	—	1	0	0	0	0
Alvarez	1.000	3	5	0	0	0
Corredor	1.000	22	42	2	0	1
Encarnacion	.966	18	28	0	1	0
Florentino	.986	43	67	2	1	0
Guzman	1.000	45	66	3	0	0
Miller	1.000	5	7	1	0	0
Ortiz	1.000	43	84	6	0	1
Perez	1.000	1	1	0	0	0
Ramirez	.967	28	57	1	2	0
Rosario	1.000	3	4	0	0	0

DSL NATIONALS

ROOKIE

DOMINICAN SUMMER LEAGUE

Batting	B-T	HT	WT	DOB	AVG	vLH	vRH	G	AB	R	H	2B	3B	HR	RBI	BB	HBP	SH	SF	SO	SB	CS	SLG	OBP
Agustin, Telmito	L-L	5-10	160	10-9-96	.300	.308	.298	60	220	56	66	14	10	3	41	40	6	4	5	47	25	7	.495	.413
Baez, Jeyner	R-R	6-1	175	7-25-95	.273	.250	.280	44	139	26	38	5	2	0	17	20	5	1	2	19	1	7	.338	.380
Franco, Anderson	R-R	6-3	190	8-15-97	.272	.238	.280	57	206	26	56	8	1	4	35	26	0	0	5	46	4	2	.379	.346
Guerrero, Sandy	B-R	6-1	175	7-25-95	.193	.269	.158	38	83	16	16	1	1	2	8	16	0	1	1	36	6	3	.301	.320
Martinez, Andres	R-R	6-1	170	7-7-95	.302	.320	.296	58	202	33	61	6	3	1	26	31	7	2	0	33	8	4	.376	.413
Mota, Israel	R-R	6-2	165	1-3-96	.310	.351	.299	67	268	48	83	19	2	8	47	17	3	0	2	60	14	4	.485	.355
Peguero, Francys	R-R	6-2	170	10-4-95	.248	.212	.263	35	109	14	27	2	0	1	14	6	1	0	2	21	1	0	.294	.288
Perdomo, Luis	L-L	5-11	170	5-21-97	.212	.188	.220	23	66	5	14	2	0	0	6	5	1	1	0	10	3	1	.242	.278
Pilier, Neivy	R-R	6-1	185	8-1-96	.171	.121	.190	37	117	16	20	2	1	0	8	12	3	0	1	21	0	2	.205	.265
Pimentel, Davinson	R-R	5-9	170	2-12-97	.350	.304	.364	55	200	44	70	18	2	6	38	23	11	0	1	35	4	4	.550	.443
Ramirez, Gilberto	R-R	6-4	180	11-14-92	.350	.318	.358	29	103	20	36	1	2	1	16	7	1	3	1	19	18	6	.427	.393
Ramirez, Joshual	R-R	6-2	185	5-20-96	.302	.319	.296	52	182	28	55	6	2	2	24	15	4	1	4	31	8	7	.390	.361
Rengel, Luis	R-R	6-0	165	7-20-95	.208	.132	.231	45	159	26	33	4	0	2	24	17	7	3	4	23	2	8	.270	.305
Robles, Victor	R-R	6-0	185	5-19-97	.313	.333	.308	47	182	46	57	14	4	3	25	16	13	2	0	26	22	9	.484	.408
Rojas, Dany	L-L	5-9	160	1-8-97	.182	.000	.207	20	33	2	6	0	1	0	8	0	0	0	1	13	1	1	.242	.341
Trejos, Edward	R-R	5-11	170	3-12-97	.091	.250	.000	14	22	3	2	0	0	1	4	5	1	0	0	8	0	0	.227	.286
Vilorio, Luis	R-R	6-1	180	8-28-93	.345	.344	.345	41	145	24	50	9	1	1	16	7	5	1	2	9	6	1	.441	.390

Pitching	B-T	HT	WT	DOB	W	L	ERA	G	GS	CG	SV	IP	H	R	ER	HR	BB	SO	AVG	vLH	vRH	K/9	BB/9
Acevedo, Carlos	R-R	6-3	200	9-27-94	3	3	3.56	14	10	0	0	56	74	40	22	2	16	44	.323	.356	.303	7.11	2.59
Archibald, Michael	L-L	6-2	165	3-15-95	1	0	7.36	12	0	0	0	15	20	22	12	1	13	11	.299	.563	.216	6.75	7.98
Avila, Aroon	R-R	6-3	175	5-26-97	0	0	2.08	3	0	0	0	4	2	1	1	1	1	4	.143	.000	.222	8.31	2.08
Baez, Joan	R-R	6-3	190	12-26-94	4	1	1.15	11	11	0	0	55	33	16	7	1	17	49	.168	.169	.168	8.07	2.80
Bermudez, Juan	R-R	6-2	180	9-29-94	5	5	2.08	15	14	0	0	61	44	27	14	4	20	61	.194	.181	.200	9.05	2.97
Cespedes, Angher	R-R	6-1	190	7-25-94	4	0	3.94	22	0	0	9	32	24	16	14	0	13	39	.211	.270	.182	10.97	3.66
Charlis, Fiyeral	R-R	6-2	180	9-17-94	3	2	6.15	17	0	0	1	26	26	24	18	2	8	31	.243	.239	.246	10.59	2.73
Fuentes, Steven	R-R	6-2	175	5-4-97	2	3	2.30	15	9	0	0	55	50	24	14	2	17	62	.236	.171	.272	10.21	2.80
Garcia, Yordani	R-R	6-5	180	2-19-96	0	1	0.00	1	0	0	0	2	2	2	0	0	2	3	.250	1.000	.143	13.50	9.00
Guance, Hector	R-R	6-6	200	7-12-95	0	1	4.60	7	0	0	0	16	18	9	8	0	3	7	.286	.238	.310	4.02	1.72
Guillen, Angel	R-R	6-2	150	1-24-97	0	0	7.94	5	0	0	0	6	7	8	5	0	4	2	.304	.333	.273	3.18	6.35
Jimenez, Jose	L-L	6-1	190	12-7-96	0	0	0.00	1	0	0	0	1	1	0	0	0	0	1	.250	—	.250	9.00	0.00
Lopez, Franklyn	R-R	6-3	190	9-9-94	1	0	0.00	2	1	0	0	7	1	0	0	0	2	5	.048	.143	.000	6.43	2.57
Morel, Melvin	L-L	6-2	185	12-14-93	3	1	5.71	17	0	0	0	35	37	31	22	1	19	39	.272	.289	.265	10.13	4.93
Nunez, Jose	R-R	6-4	175	5-19-96	0	0	8.25	12	4	0	0	24	36	31	22	2	24	16	.350	.318	.373	6.00	9.00
Pena, Malvin	R-R	6-2	180	6-24-97	1	1	5.46	13	3	0	0	30	37	23	18	2	11	20	.306	.310	.304	6.37	3.34
Pena, Wilber	R-R	6-2	185	9-14-95	4	4	2.70	14	14	0	0	63	46	22	19	2	32	59	.201	.259	.169	8.38	4.55
Pinto, Francisco	R-R	6-2	165	4-26-97	1	0	3.38	5	0	0	0	8	10	4	3	0	4	5	.294	.273	.304	5.63	4.50
Ramirez, Nector	R-R	6-0	170	9-4-96	5	3	4.40	12	2	0	0	29	28	17	14	2	17	35	.264	.267	.262	10.99	5.34
Ramirez, Yonathan	L-L	5-11	165	4-13-97	3	0	2.63	11	0	0	2	27	19	10	8	1	6	29	.204	.118	.224	9.55	1.98
Rosario, Ramses	R-R	6-3	180	10-18-95	1	2	2.25	18	1	0	2	36	38	19	9	1	11	26	.266	.306	.245	6.50	2.75
Silfa, Isaias	L-L	6-0	180	2-9-94	0	0	0.00	1	1	0	0	1	0	0	0	0	1	1	.000	—	.000	9.00	9.00
Vargas, Miguel	R-R	6-4	190	3-5-95	1	1	5.26	24	0	0	4	38	46	29	22	1	15	33	.297	.211	.347	7.88	3.58

Fielding

Catcher	PCT	G	PO	A	E	DP	PB
Baez	.991	24	192	34	2	0	15
Pimentel	.963	14	92	11	4	2	6
Trejos	1.000	2	5	0	0	0	
Vilorio	.967	36	280	47	11	1	6

First Base	PCT	G	PO	A	E	DP
Baez	.986	16	133	7	2	6
Guerrero	1.000	2	1	0	0	0
Martinez	1.000	7	33	1	0	2
Peguero	.930	12	78	2	6	1
Perdomo	.976	14	74	6	2	5
Pilier	.966	18	105	9	4	1
Pimentel	.983	22	173	5	3	14

Second Base	PCT	G	PO	A	E	DP
Pilier	.933	5	7	7	1	0
Ramirez	.942	49	91	105	12	19
Rengel	.971	25	36	64	3	7

Third Base	PCT	G	PO	A	E	DP
Franco	.884	35	29	70	13	2
Martinez	.891	22	21	36	7	4
Peguero	.706	11	6	18	10	2
Pilier	.743	12	8	18	9	0

Shortstop	PCT	G	PO	A	E	DP
Franco	.929	20	23	55	6	7
Martinez	.908	33	56	62	12	11
Ramirez	1.000	3	1	2	0	0

Rengel	.904	24	32	43	8	4

Outfield	PCT	G	PO	A	E	DP
Agustin	.961	49	94	5	4	2
Baez	1.000	5	4	0	0	0
Guerrero	.909	21	30	0	3	0
Mota	.939	65	87	5	6	3
Peguero	1.000	1	1	0	0	0
Perdomo	1.000	7	8	0	0	0
Ramirez	.973	18	33	3	1	1
Robles	.949	45	91	3	5	0
Rojas	.870	17	19	1	3	0
Trejos	—	1	0	0	0	0
Vilorio	.800	4	5	3	2	1

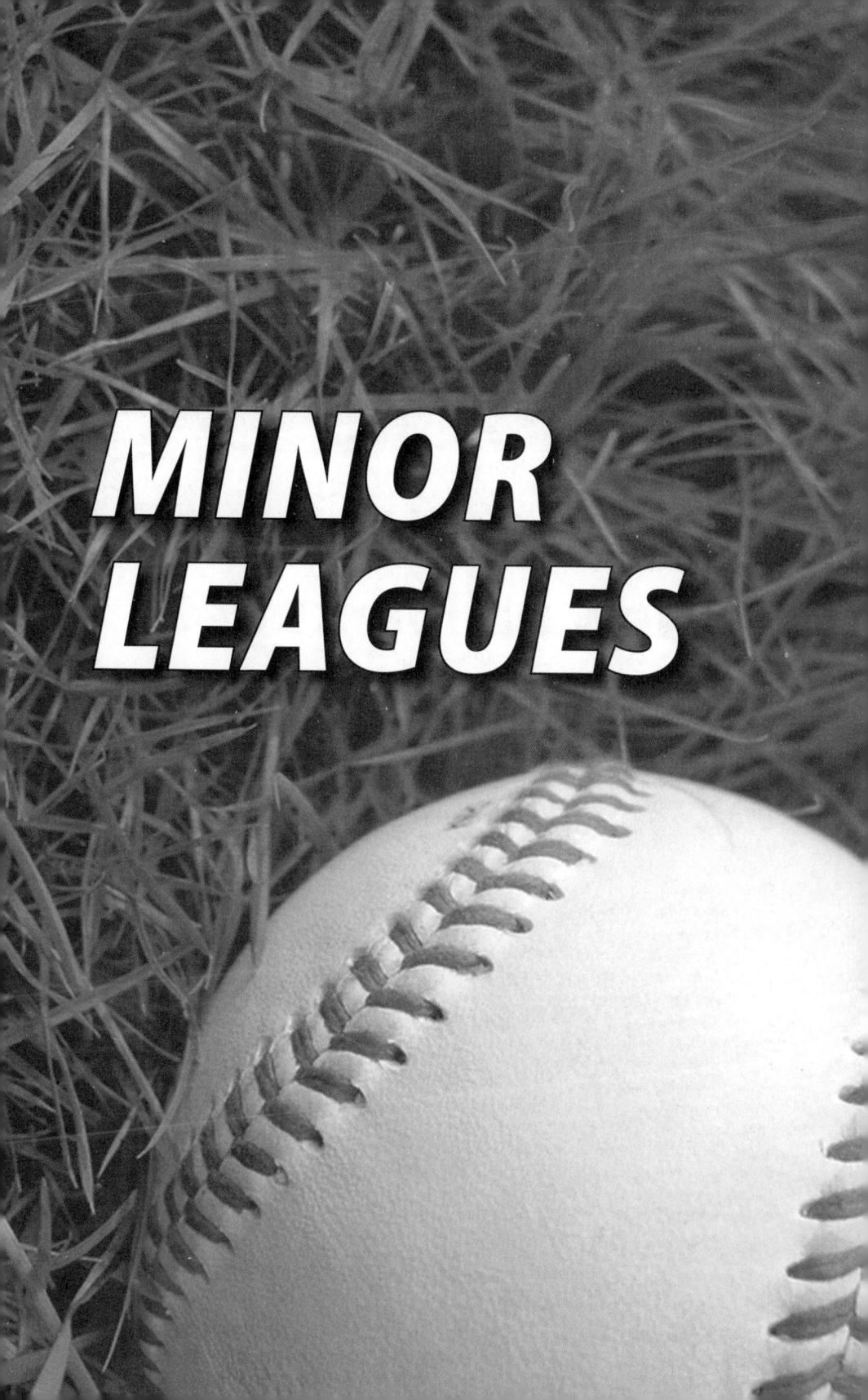

MINOR LEAGUES

The Charlotte Knights topped the minors in attendance during their first year at BB&T Ballpark

New ballparks get minors back on track

COMPILED BY JOSH LEVENTHAL

At first glance, the 2014 season played out in similar fashion to those of recent years. That is, it helped turn minor league baseball into a major attraction.

Promotions grabbed headlines (the Brooklyn Cyclones' Seinfeld Night was a sensation), prospects offered promise (Kris Bryant and Joey Gallo led a home run race into the final days of the season) and familiar faces finished in first (the Omaha Storm Chasers repeated as Triple-A champions).

However, the addition of two new ballparks, and the subsequent rebirth of two struggling franchises, set 2014 apart and snapped the industry out of a six-season slump at the gate.

The Charlotte Knights, long the cellar-dwellers of International League attendance, topped all of minor league baseball with 687,715 fans during its first season at a new downtown ballpark. Likewise, the El Paso Chihuahuas made their Pacific Coast League debut after three disappointing seasons in Tucson and attracted 560,997 spectators to a unique new ballpark just over the border from Juarez, Mexico.

And as a result, minor league baseball totaled 42,411,194 fans—the most since 2008.

"I think so much of what we gained this year we can attribute back to Charlotte and El Paso," Minor League Baseball president Pat O'Conner said.

That's for sure. Charlotte and Tucson combined for 1,248,712 fans—a 793,801 increase over the 454,911 the two franchises attracted in 2013—and accounted for the bulk of MiLB's 857,413 increase over the previous year's total of 41,553,781. Without the new ballparks, the minors would have continued its three-year trend of holding steady at the gate. And although average attendance grew 2.1 percent to 4,099 a game in 2014, the number of teams that saw an increase at the gate dropped from 86 in 2013 to 76.

The difference was Charlotte and El Paso's new ballparks—and how their fan bases responded.

After 23 years of playing in Fort Mill, S.C., at a ballpark to which few Charlotte residents felt was worth making the 12-mile drive down Interstate-85, the Knights sold out 31 of 71 home dates at their new $54 million home despite finishing an IL-worst 63-81.

"You always have a special type of situation when you bring a team to a city that hasn't had baseball," IL president Randy Mobley said on

Opening Day. "This has a lot of those elements. It was almost like (Charlotte) hadn't had baseball even though it was only 10 or 12 miles away."

El Paso hadn't had an affiliated minor league club since the Double-A Diablos left town in 2005. That changed with the opening of Southwest University Ballpark, a downtown gem whose $72 million price tag is among the most expensive in minor league history and included the leveling of city hall to make room for it.

"I expected it to be nice, but I didn't expect it to be this nice," El Paso manager Pat Murphy said. "You mix the stadium and the fans together, and it's been the best professional experience I've been a part of."

Minor league baseball had plenty of success stories beyond Charlotte and El Paso in 2014, and rebounded well after a second straight year with disastrous April weather. Teams totaled 140 lost openings the first month, 10 more than the previous year, and regularly opened ballparks in freezing temperatures and with few fans in the seats.

But as the weather turned in May, fans returned to ballparks and attendance steadily increased over the final four months. By the end of the season, six teams had set single-season attendance records.

The Indianapolis Indians (International), who topped the minors in overall attendance last season, drew 15,520 fans to their season finale to help top their previous season-high set in 1998. The Durham Bulls' (International) first season at the newly renovated Durham Bulls Athletic Park included a packed house for the Triple-A all-star game and a record-high 525,199 fans—topping the mark set in 2007. The Tennessee Smokies (Southern) increased their average attendance 9.5 percent and totaled a franchise-record 283,038. The Clearwater Threshers (Florida State), South Bend SilverHawks (Midwest) and Spokane Indians (Northwest) set new highs for overall attendance.

Everybody's Shuffling

Minor league fans may want to bring a map before heading to the ballpark next season, because 20 minor league teams will welcome new parent organizations following the busiest offseason affiliation shuffle since 2006.

The biggest turnover comes in the Pacific Coast League, where six of the league's 16 teams changed affiliates. Rumors turned into reality when the Sacramento River Cats cut ties with the Athletics—the only affiliate Sacramento has known since debuting in 2000—in exchange for the Giants.

And that was just the beginning. Rather than move into the Giants' former home of 16 years in

Fresno, Oakland opted to relocate to Nashville. The Sounds had spent 10 seasons as a Brewers affiliate, but felt the A's would give them a better chance to win at their new ballpark. Milwaukee had not fielded a playoff team in Nashville since 2007. Oakland, however, made 11 PCL playoff appearances during its 15 years in Sacramento and won four league championships.

"We consider winning at this level as a major part of the relationship, a major part of development," A's general manager Billy Beane said at a press conference in Nashville. "It's one thing to say it, but it's another thing to do it."

Meanwhile, Rockies ownership had long been saying that they wanted a new ballpark in Colorado Springs. When it became clear that wasn't going to happen, they ended their 21-year relationship with the Sky Sox and moved on to Albuquerque. The Isotopes had been a Dodgers affiliate since 2009, but were available after Los Angeles followed minority owner Peter Guber to Oklahoma City when he purchased the club from Mandalay Baseball a few weeks earlier. The Astros, which had previously been in Oklahoma City, ended up in

Fresno and the Brewers landed in Colorado Springs.

No big league team had a busier affiliation shuffle than the Cubs, who wielded the power of their brand to find ballpark upgrades for three of its affiliates. The Cubs ditched high Class A Daytona (Florida State) for better weather and a more modern ballpark in Myrtle Beach (Carolina) and ended their affiliation with low Class A Kane County after just two seasons to sign a four-year pact with South Bend (Midwest).

Chicago had seemed likely to renew its affiliation with Kane County, which is just an hour away from Wrigley Field, after Cougars ownership announced in early September plans for several upgrades to Fifth Third Bank Ballpark, including batting cages to be built to the Cubs' specifications. But Chicago got a better offer in South Bend, which put $8 million into Coveleski Regional Stadium in 2010, and this offseason is adding a new grass playing surface and an 11,000-square-foot indoor hitting and pitching facility.

The Cubs also landed the most modern ballpark in the Northwest League by leaving Boise for Eugene, which plays at 6-year-old PK Park on the University of Oregon campus.

The Braves and Rangers were the last two teams standing at the high Class A level. Each team was hoping to team up with the Carolina Mudcats, the Carolina League's last available team, or else be sent to the unfriendly confines of the High Desert Mavericks (California). Atlanta won the spot by playing up its connection to the area as a former Durham Bulls affiliate.

"This is where we wanted to be," Braves president John Schuerholz said during a press conference at the Mudcats' Five County Stadium, to which as a show of appreciation, the Braves also sent general manager John Hart, Hall of Fame manager Bobby Cox and manager Fredi Gonzalez. "We decided that Zebulon is open, so let's do everything we can to be in the heart of Braves country."

The Rangers, who had spent four years in Myrtle Beach, put a good face on landing in High Desert, where high winds make Mavericks Stadium a tough place for pitchers.

"It is what it is," Rangers farm director Mike Daley said. "When you play in the big leagues, you don't get to choose where you pitch or hit."

Cyclones Steal Promo Show

Each offseason, team officials gather for the Promotional Seminar to share success stories and pass out Golden Bobbleheads for the best promotions of the season. The Brooklyn Cyclones took home the Best Theme Night honors and the coveted Best Overall Promotion award for its Seinfeld

ORGANIZATION STANDINGS

Cumulative domestic farm club records for major league organizations, with winning percentages going back five years. Most organizations have six affiliates.

	2014						
	W	L	PCT	2013	2012	2011	2010
1. Mets	434	330	.568	.546	.509	.498	.511
2. D-backs	431	337	.561	.510	.499	.488	.489
3. Rangers	378	314	.546	.528	.517	.565	.522
4. Cardinals	417	348	.545	.494	.505	.518	.569
5. Red Sox	368	328	.529	.504	.504	.490	.491
6. Twins	366	327	.528	.546	.525	.490	.434
7. Cubs	361	330	.522	.504	.470	.507	.542
8. Astros	397	368	.519	.570	.546	.408	.436
9. Tigers	360	337	.516	.484	.482	.467	.485
10. Nationals	358	338	.514	.550	.506	.511	.501
11. Athletics	356	338	.513	.497	.496	.514	.527
12. Giants	354	342	.509	.564	.506	.539	.524
Yankees	387	373	.509	.495	.529	.494	.538
14. Brewers	350	339	.508	.449	.459	.466	.493
15. Indians	349	340	.507	.445	.506	.515	.504
16. Rays	383	376	.505	.524	.515	.497	.534
17. Marlins	347	350	.498	.497	.524	.495	.490
18. Blue Jays	379	386	.495	.493	.524	.515	.506
19. Braves	339	348	.493	.485	.461	.471	.457
20. Reds	339	354	.489	.426	.449	.503	.466
21. Angels	337	356	.486	.501	.449	.507	.507
22. Mariners	359	397	.475	.497	.528	.483	.530
23. Padres	328	367	.472	.496	.455	.515	.485
24. Rockies	332	381	.466	.482	.540	.495	.480
25. Orioles	324	373	.465	.481	.456	.487	.463
26. Dodgers	316	374	.458	.486	.528	.543	.508
27. White Sox	315	376	.456	.488	.504	.500	.489
28. Pirates	343	420	.450	.515	.505	.512	.511
Royals	317	387	.450	.463	.492	.494	.492
30. Phillies	303	393	.435	.468	.498	.522	.508

POSTSEASON RESULTS

LEAGUE	CHAMPION	RUNNER-UP
International	Pawtucket	Durham
Pacific Coast	Omaha	Reno
Eastern	Binghamton	Richmond
Southern	Jacksonville	Chattanooga
Texas	Midland	Tulsa
California	Lancaster	Visalia
Carolina	Potomac	Myrtle Beach
Florida State	Fort Myers	Daytona
Midwest	Kane County	Lake County
South Atlantic	Asheville	Hagerstown
New York-Penn	State College	Tri-City
Northwest	Hillsboro	Vancouver
Appalachian	Johnson City	Danville
Pioneer	Billings	Orem
Arizona	Indians	Giants
Gulf Coast	Red Sox	Yankees

Night event in August.

The Cyclones pulled out all the stops in celebration of the 25th anniversary of the iconic show's pilot episode. MCU Park was renamed Vandelay Industries Park, a guy named George Costanza drove down from Rhode Island to throw out the first pitch, the first 3,000 fans received a Keith Hernandez "Magic Loogie" bobblehead, and a

Brooklyn fans compete for the best impression of Elaine's awful dance moves at Seinfeld Night

group of Elaine lookalikes held a dance-off.

Cyclones pitching coach Tom Signore, who donned one of the puffy shirts the team wore during batting practice, says he quotes the show when giving advice on the mound. He once told a pitcher on the verge of giving up a lead that "we don't want to be 'Even Steven,'" and he had no idea what I was talking about."

There was no shortage promotional brilliance at ballparks around the sport. The Myrtle Beach Pelicans (Carolina) took an unusual approach to their prostate cancer awareness event, with general manager Andy Milovich taking a prostate exam while leaning out the press box window and signing "Take Me Out to the Ballgame" over a microphone during the seventh-inning stretch.

The event went viral, and several teams followed suit by hosting their own version of the promotion later dubbed the "two-knuckle challenge."

"I bent over to the pressure," said Lake Elsinore GM Dave Oster, who was challenged by local sports-talk radio hosts to take a press-box exam.

Other promotional hits this season included a "Ghostsbusters" anniversary celebration by the Toledo Mud Hens that included special jerseys, the Akron Aeros' series of Rock 'n Bobble giveaways of local rock stars (Devo, Joe Walsh, Chrissie Hynde), and the emergence of the Cowboy Monkey Rodeo that features monkeys riding dogs herding sheep.

The Great Home Run Race

A quartet of minor leaguers paid little attention to the hand-wringing over the lack of power in baseball these days. While home run totals were down again in the majors—only one player reached the 40-homer mark on the senior circuit—four sluggers put on a nightly show and offered promise of what may soon be coming to a big league ballpark near you.

As the calendar flipped to August, Rangers third baseman Joey Gallo, Cubs third baseman Kris Bryant, Athletics first baseman Matt Olson

BRYANT'S PLACE IN HISTORY

Minor league hitters brought the power this season. Here's a look at how home run champion Kris Bryant's performance measures up against previous champs over the last 60 years.

Year	Champion	Homer Total	Year	Champion	Homer Total
1974	Bill McNulty	55	2008	Dallas McPherson	42
1982	Ron Kittle	50	1996	Phil Hiatt	42
1968	Tony Solaita	49	1981	Tim Laudner	42
2004	Ryan Howard	46	1977	Danny Walton	42
1998	Chris Hatcher	46	1976	Roger Freed	42
1966	Dave Duncan	46	1999	J.R. Phillips	41
2001	Phil Hiatt	44	1979	Rick Lancellotti	41
2014	Kris Bryant	43	1963	Arlo Engel	41
1985	Danny Tartabull	43	2013	Joey Gallo	40
1971	Adrian Garrett	43	1995	Todd Greene	40

and Diamondbacks catcher Peter O'Brien (who began the season in the Yankees system) had each swatted 30 or more homers. In the end, Bryant, the Minor League Player of the Year, came away with the title by slugging 43 bombs—one more than Gallo. Bryant hit his stride, and most anything thrown his way, in the final month of the season at Triple-A Iowa. He hit eight homers in August—perhaps a fitting farewell for the minors' most well-rounded hitter.

"I've seen him hit everything," said righthander Corey Black, a teammate of Bryant's for the first half of the year at Double-A Tennessee. "It's hard to really have a game plan against a guy like that, that you've seen hit so many home runs on so many different types of pitches and different types of locations. It's hard to throw to guys like that."

Yet, it may be Gallo who left the biggest mark this season—on seatbacks, bare hands and even pick-up trucks—with his majestic moon shots.

Gallo's batting practices became the stuff of legend, particularly his showing at the Futures Game, when ball after ball left the yard, including one that cracked the windshield of a pick-up truck on

CONTINUED ON PAGE 355

Bryant blasts away challenges

BY J.J. COOPER

Time after time, Cubs front-office officials believed they finally cracked the code on challenging Kris Bryant, only to see him step in the box, hit a few home runs and respond, "Is that all you've got?"

Chicago's front office thought high Class A Daytona would be a steep test for a hitter just weeks into his pro career. Bryant, the 2013 College Player of the Year, hit .333 with five home runs and a .719 slugging percentage in 16 games, then went 7-for-20 in the Florida State League playoffs to help lead the team to a championship.

So the Cubs decided to raise the bar by aggressively sending him to the Arizona Fall League. Bryant hit .364/.457/.727 with an AFL-leading six homers and was the league MVP.

Kris Bryant

Not tough enough? The Cubs had debated sending Bryant back to Daytona to start the season this year, but ended up pushing him to Double-A Tennessee when spring training wrapped up.

It didn't stretch Bryant. He led the Southern League in most offensive categories in June, forcing a midseason promotion to Triple-A Iowa. Bryant has yet to find the level that challenges him. He's been the best around wherever he's played the last three years.

"He's exceeded our expectations at every level," Cubs general manager Jed Hoyer said. "At three different junctures we felt we were pushing him into struggles."

In his first full pro season, Bryant hit .325/.438/.661 between Tennessee and Iowa. He led the minors in home runs (43), extra-base hits (78), slugging and OPS (1.098). He wasn't just a swing-for-the fences slugger, for Bryant posted his gaudy home run numbers while compiling the minor's second-best on-base percentage. He joins Alex Gordon as the second player to win the College and the Minor League Player of the Year Awards.

Bryant's 43 home runs are the second most ever for a Minor League POY, topped only by Ron Kittle's 50 in 1983. Last year, Bryant hit 31 home runs with the NCAA's BBCOR bats,

which was a total that not only led Division I by double digits but was more than most teams hit.

But even with power evaporating from the game, it's Bryant's hitting approach that is more notable. It's hard to find a power hitter who can hit 25-30 home runs consistently. But a slugger who can hit for power and hit for average? That's limited to the best players in the game.

At the Futures Game in Minneapolis this July, Javier Baez reached the upper deck in left field during batting practice. Joey Gallo hit a ball that shattered a windshield and another that almost bounced out of the ballpark. Kennys Vargas, Hunter Renfroe, Jorge Alfaro and Michael Taylor all impressed with second-deck shots.

"When you see those guys Gallo and Baez hitting cars, I'm sure there is a temptation to let it out," Hoyer said.

Bryant hit some nice line drives to the right-field power alley. His batting practice was studious, it was professional and it was completely unmemorable.

Bryant doesn't care.

"It's kind of tempting to launch some balls to the upper deck, but you can create some bad habits," Bryant said. "I'm big on having a routine and sticking to it. Just because it's an all-star game doesn't mean I should go away from my routine. My routine has gotten me to that type of game."

PREVIOUS WINNERS

2004: Jeff Francis, lhp, Tulsa/Colorado Springs (Rockies)
2005: Delmon Young, of, Montgomery/Durham (Devil Rays)
2006: Alex Gordon, 3b, Wichita (Royals)
2007: Jay Bruce, of, Sarasota/Chattanooga/Louisville (Reds)
2008: Matt Wieters, c, Frederick/Bowie (Orioles)
2009: Jason Heyward, Myrtle Beach/Mississippi (Braves)
2010: Jeremy Hellickson, Montgomery/Durham (Rays)
2011: Mike Trout, Arkansas (Angels)
2012: Wil Myers, Northwest Arkansas/Omaha (Royals)
2013: Byron Buxton, Cedar Rapids/Fort Myers (Twins)

Full list: BaseballAmerica.com/awards

A man of many titles

To describe Sam Bernabe simply as a front-office executive would be selling him short.

Yes, Bernabe is president and general manager of the Iowa Cubs—the Pacific Coast League franchise he joined as an intern in 1983 before working his way up to general manager in 1986 and part-owner in 1999. But Bernabe's influence on minor league baseball extends well beyond the Des Moines border. He has helped oversee Minor League Baseball grow into a booming industry as chairman of MiLB's board of trustees. He serves on the PCL executive committe, is MiLB's representative on the Major League Baseball rules committee, and (quite uniquely) oversees the Iowa Cubs Sports Turf Management company.

"He's a leader in the community and a leader in the league," MiLB president Pat O'Conner said of Bernabe.

Amid his other responsibilities, Bernabe keeps the I-Cubs running steadily as one of the smallest markets in Triple-A. Iowa ranked fifth in the 16-team league in attendance and

EXECUTIVE OF THE YEAR

PREVIOUS WINNERS

2003: Chuck Domino, Reading Phillies (Eastern)
2004: Chris Kemple, Wilmington Blue Rocks (Carolina)
2005: Jay Miller, Round Rock Express (Pacific Coast)
2006: Alan Ledford, Sacramento River Cats (Pacific Coast)
2007: Mike Moore, Minor League Baseball
2008: Naomi Silver, Rochester Red Wings (International)
2009: Ken Young, Norfolk Tides (International)
2010: Monty Hoppel, Midland Rockhounds (Texas)
2011: Todd Parnell, Richmond Flying Squirrels (Eastern)
2012: Bob Richmond, Northwest League
2013: Martie Cordaro, Omaha Storm Chasers (Pacific)

Full list: BaseballAmerica.com/awards

enjoyed a slight tick up in average attendance to 7,029. All the while Bernabe stays on top of industry trends and has a keen understanding of what interests local fans.

"They have always stayed faithful to their fans," PCL president Branch Rickey said.

CONTINUED FROM PAGE 353

the concourse in right field of Target Field. Twins pitching prospect Alex Meyer got a good look while shagging flies in the outfield, and said Gallo's performance lived up to the billing.

"He was hitting balls out of the stadium like it was nothing," Meyer said. "And that's not to take a shot at (Miguel) Sano or anybody at that game. I didn't think it was close. That's plus-plus power that I don't think you can really find at the big league level. To watch it, it was incredible."

Olson spent the season at high Class A Stockton and found the California League to his liking. After hitting 23 homers in his first full pro season at low Class A Beloit in 2013, the lefty-hitting Olson topped the Cal League with 37.

O'Brien, who was traded by the Yankees to the Diamondbacks at the July 31 deadline for Martin Prado, had his season come to an end just four days later with a left shin injury—and one day after his first (and final) home run at Double-A Mobile. He finished the year with 34.

History Makers

Of course, Bryant and company have a ways to go to catch Mike Hessman, the veteran minor league third baseman who hit his 259th career home run in International League play in June, establishing an all-time record for a league that traces its roots back to 1884.

Hessman broke the longstanding record held by Ollie Carnegie, who clubbed 258 homers for Buffalo between 1931-41 and '45. Hessman returned to Triple-A Toledo (Tigers) this season, where he previously played from 2005-09, and the 36-year-old hit 28 homers to bring his overall career minor league total to 417.

"It obviously feels good to get it out of the way," Hessman told reporters after the historic shot. "I'd been sitting on it for a while, with injuries and stuff, just trying to get back on the field . . . It's one of those things where I'm finally glad it's over with."

Meanwhile, Dodgers outfielder Joc Pederson earned Pacific Coast League MVP and rooke of the year honors at Triple-A Albuquerque. The 22-year-old hit .303/.435/.582 with 33 homers, 78 RBIs and 106 runs. He drew 100 walks and had an OPS of 1.017. And with 30 steals, Pederson became the first 30-30 player in the modern history of the PCL, and the first since Frank Demaree accomplished the feat in 1934. He's just the fourth in PCL history, joining baseball greats Tony Lazzeri and Lefty O'Doul.

MINOR LEAGUES

Johnson overcomes turnovers

BY GORDON WITTENMYER

Few managers in professional baseball this year dealt with the kind of roster turnover that Mark Johnson did at low Class A Kane County.

And nobody else did it as successfully.

With 51 different players—not counting a pair of injury-rehab assignments from the parent Cubs—clicking through his turnstile this year, Johnson took his Cougars to 98 wins, including a 7-0 run through the Midwest League playoffs.

Only the Angels had as many wins in professional baseball, and it took them 18 more games.

"It wasn't as weird as you would think," said Johnson, the former big league catcher.

"As many moves as we had, the one thing that really stayed put was our starting pitching," he said. "And up the middle we stayed pretty much the same."

But the Cougars also had big turnover in the bullpen, lost their leadoff hitter (Jacob Hannemann) to a promotion in July, and 2014

MANAGER OF THE YEAR

PREVIOUS 10 WINNERS

2004: Marty Brown, Buffalo (Indians)
2005: Ken Oberkfell, Norfolk (Mets)
2006: Todd Claus, Portland (Red Sox)
2007: Matt Wallbeck, Erie (Tigers)
2008: Rocket Wheeler, Myrtle Beach (Braves)
2009: Charlie Montoyo, Durham (Rays)
2010: Mike Sarbaugh, Columbus (Indians)
2011: Ryne Sandberg, Lehigh Valley (Phillies)
2012: Dave Miley, Scranton/Wilkes-Barre (Yankees)
2013: Gary DiSarcina, Pawtucket (Red Sox)

Full list: BaseballAmerica.com/awards

No. 4 overall draft pick Kyle Schwarber (1.050 OPS in 23 games) was long gone by the time Johnson's crew reeled off 13 consecutive victories in a 25-4 finish to the season.

Just four members of the Opening Day lineup were in Kane County lineup for the final game.

Storm Chasers Repeat

The Omaha Storm Chasers lived up to both their name and their title on a sopping wet evening in September.

They entered Triple-A National Championship, held at the Charlotte Knights' BB&T Ballpark, as the defending kings of the classification and the Pacific Coast League. After sitting through a thunderstorm that lasted about two hours, they topped the International League-champion Pawtucket Red Sox 4-2 to keep their crown.

Afterward, when the dogpile on the mound and the infield was gone, Omaha manager Brian Poldberg said that the win spoke to his team's resilience not just that day, but throughout the season.

"It's been unbelievable," Poldberg said. "The heart that they showed every day, the camaraderie, the chemistry. They show up and they have fun and they enjoy being around each other."

Pawtucket reached the Triple-A final for the second time in three years and continued its run as the top team in the IL, where it has made three straight championship apperances.

News Of The Weird

In a strange twist, former baseball oddball (and all-time great hitter) turned into a mentor as a player/coach for the Cubs' Triple-A Iowa affiliate in the PCL. Ramirez, 42, hit just .222 with three home runs but made more of an impact as a role model for young Cubs prospects.

"He was great. I learned a lot of stuff from him," shortstop prospect Javier Baez said of Ramirez, who in June joined Iowa in an unorthodox signing by Cubs team president Theo Epstein.

"He helped my approach to right-center (field)," Baez said. "(I followed) his routine every day, going to the cage, the way he works. He's always got a bat in his hand, doing something, either swinging or just hitting in the cage. He talked to a lot of the guys. A lot of people learned from him."

Meanwhile, a Mariners scout lost his job after reportedly heckling one of his own players. Seattle crosschecker Butch Baccala reportedly yelled at first baseman Jesus Montero—rehabbing an oblique injury at short-season Everett—for not leaving the field as quickly enough at the end of an inning after coaching first base.

Baccala then had an ice cream sundae in a mini batting helmet delivered to Montero in the dugout—a dig at Montero's weight. Montero left the dugout, approached the scout in the stands, and threw the dessert at him before being pulled away.

TRIPLE-A

Pos	Player, Team (Org)	League	AVG	OBP	SLG	G	AB	R	H	2B	3B	HR	RBI	BB	SO	SB
C	James McCann, Toledo (Tigers)	IL	.295	.343	.427	109	417	49	123	34	0	7	54	25	90	9
1B	Jesus Aguilar, Columbus (Indians)	IL	.304	.395	.511	118	427	69	130	31	0	19	77	64	96	0
2B	Rob Refsnyder, Scranton/W-B (Yankees)	IL	.300	.389	.456	77	287	47	86	19	1	8	33	41	67	4
3B	Adam Duvall, Fresno (Giants)	PCL	.298	.360	.599	91	359	67	107	21	3	27	90	30	82	2
SS	Chris Taylor, Tacoma (Mariners)	PCL	.328	.397	.497	75	302	63	99	22	7	5	37	35	74	14
CF	Joc Pederson, Albuquerque (Dodgers)	PCL	.303	.435	.582	121	445	106	135	17	4	33	78	100	149	30
OF	Gregory Polanco, Indianapolis (Pirates)	IL	.328	.390	.504	69	274	51	90	17	5	7	51	28	49	16
OF	Steven Souza, Syracuse (Nationals)	IL	.350	.432	.590	96	346	62	121	25	2	18	75	52	75	26
DH	Andy Wilkins, Charlotte (White Sox)	IL	.293	.338	.558	127	491	79	144	38	1	30	85	34	91	0

Pos	Pitcher, Team (Org)	League	W	L	ERA	G	GS	SV	IP	H	HR	BB	SO	AVG	SO/9	WHIP
SP	Kyle Hendricks, Iowa (Cubs)	PCL	10	5	3.59	17	17	0	103	98	5	23	97	.251	8.5	1.18
SP	Liam Hendriks, Buffalo/Omaha (Jays/Royals)	IL/PCL	12	2	2.45	23	21	0	143	125	7	13	126	.233	7.9	0.96
SP	Jimmy Nelson, Nashville (Brewers)	PCL	10	2	1.46	17	16	0	111	70	3	32	114	.177	9.2	0.92
SP	Anthony Ranaudo, Pawtucket (Red Sox)	IL	14	4	2.61	24	24	0	138	112	9	54	111	.220	7.2	1.20
SP	Nick Tropeano, Oklahoma City (Astros)	PCL	9	5	3.03	23	20	0	125	90	11	33	120	.200	8.7	0.99
RP	Adam Liberatore, Durham (Rays)	IL	6	1	1.66	54	0	4	65	43	1	15	86	.186	11.9	0.89

Player of the Year: Joc Pederson, of, Albuquerque (Dodgers). **Pitcher of the Year:** Jimmy Nelson, rhp, Nashville (Brewers).

DOUBLE-A

Pos	Player, Team (Org)	League	AVG	OBP	SLG	G	AB	R	H	2B	3B	HR	RBI	BB	SO	SB
C	J.T. Realmuto, Jacksonville (Marlins)	SL	.299	.369	.461	97	375	66	112	25	6	8	62	41	59	18
1B	Christian Walker, Bowie (Orioles)	EL	.301	.367	.516	96	366	58	110	15	2	20	77	38	83	2
2B	Darnell Sweeney, Chattanooga (Dodgers)	SL	.288	.387	.463	132	490	88	141	34	5	14	57	77	117	15
3B	Kris Bryant, Tennessee (Cubs)	SL	.355	.458	.702	68	248	61	88	20	0	22	58	43	77	8
SS	Deven Marrero, Portland (Red Sox)	EL	.291	.371	.433	68	268	42	78	19	2	5	39	34	57	12
CF	Michael Taylor, Harrisburg (Nationals)	EL	.313	.396	.539	98	384	74	120	17	2	22	61	50	130	34
OF	Steven Moya, Erie (Tigers)	EL	.276	.306	.555	133	515	81	142	33	3	35	105	23	161	16
OF	Scott Schebler, Chattanooga (Dodgers)	SL	.280	.365	.556	135	489	82	137	23	14	28	73	45	110	10
DH	Jake Lamb, Mobile (Diamondbacks)	SL	.318	.399	.551	103	374	60	119	35	5	14	79	50	99	0

Pos	Pitcher, Team (Org)	League	W	L	ERA	G	GS	SV	IP	H	HR	BB	SO	AVG	SO/9	WHIP
SP	Tyler Anderson, Tulsa (Rockies)	TL	7	4	1.98	23	23	0	118	91	3	40	106	.212	8.1	1.11
SP	Brian Johnson, Portland (Red Sox)	EL	10	2	1.75	20	20	0	118	78	6	32	99	.186	7.6	0.93
SP	Steve Matz, Binghamton (Mets)	EL	6	5	2.27	12	12	0	71	66	3	14	69	.244	8.7	1.12
SP	Justin Nicolino, Jacksonville (Marlins)	SL	14	4	2.85	28	28	0	170	162	10	20	81	.245	4.3	1.07
SP	Henry Owens, Portland (Red Sox)	EL	14	4	2.60	20	20	0	121	89	6	47	126	.201	9.4	1.12
RP	Chasen Shreve, Mississippi (Braves)	SL	3	2	2.48	36	0	7	54	42	2	9	76	.213	12.6	0.94

Player of the Year: Michael Taylor, of, Harrisburg (Nationals). **Pitcher of the Year:** Henry Owens, lhp, Portland (Red Sox).

HIGH CLASS A

Pos	Player, Team (Org)	League	AVG	OBP	SLG	G	AB	R	H	2B	3B	HR	RBI	BB	SO	SB
C	Justin O'Conner, Charlotte (Rays)	FSL	.282	.321	.486	80	319	40	90	31	2	10	44	15	78	0
1B	Matt Olson, Stockton (Athletics)	CAL	.262	.404	.543	138	512	111	134	31	1	37	97	117	137	2
2B	Jose Peraza, Lynchburg (Braves)	CL	.342	.365	.454	66	284	44	97	13	8	1	27	10	32	35
3B	Brandon Drury, Visalia (Diamondbacks)	CAL	.300	.366	.519	107	430	73	129	35	1	19	81	41	76	3
SS	Corey Seager, Rancho Cucamonga (Dodgers)	CAL	.352	.411	.633	80	327	61	115	34	2	18	70	30	76	5
CF	Teoscar Hernandez, Lancaster (Astros)	CAL	.294	.376	.550	96	391	72	115	33	8	17	75	49	117	31
OF	Josh Bell, Bradenton (Pirates)	FSL	.335	.384	.502	84	331	45	111	20	4	9	53	25	43	5
OF	Dwight Smith Jr., Dunedin (Blue Jays)	FSL	.284	.363	.453	121	472	83	134	28	8	12	60	58	69	15
DH	Joey Gallo, Myrtle Beach (Rangers)	CL	.323		.735	58	189	53	61	9	3	21	50	51	64	5

Pos	Pitcher, Team (Org)	League	W	L	ERA	G	GS	SV	IP	H	HR	BB	SO	AVG	SO/9	WHIP
SP	Jose Berrios, Fort Myers (Twins)	FSL	9	3	1.96	16	16	0	96	78	4	23	109	.216	10.2	1.05
SP	Tyler Glasnow, Bradenton (Pirates)	FSL	12	5	1.74	23	23	0	124	74	3	57	157	.171	11.4	1.05
SP	Kendall Graveman, Dunedin (Blue Jays)	FSL	8	4	2.23	16	16	0	97	89	1	18	64	.239	6.0	1.11
SP	Ben Lively, Bakersfield (Reds)	CAL	10	1	2.28	13	13	0	79	57	6	16	95	.200	10.8	0.92
SP	Glenn Sparkman, Wilmington (Royals)	CL	8	3	1.56	29	18	1	121	94	2	25	117	.211	8.7	0.98
RP	Sam Tuivailala, Palm Beach (Cardinals)	FSL	0	1	3.58	29	0	3	38	29	1	18	64	.204	15.3	1.25

Player of the Year: Corey Seager, ss, Rancho Cucamonga (Dodgers). **Pitcher of the Year:** Tyler Glasnow, rhp, Bradenton (Pirates).

MINOR LEAGUES

LOW CLASS A

Pos	Player, Team (Org)	League	AVG	OBP	SLG	G	AB	R	H	2B	3B	HR	RBI	BB	SO	SB
C	Clint Coulter, Wisconsin (Brewers)	MWL	.287	.410	.520	126	429	84	123	28	3	22	89	73	103	6
1B	Nellie Rodriguez, Lake County (Indians)	MWL	.268	.349	.482	130	485	67	130	32	3	22	88	60	142	0
2B	Wilmer Difo, Hagerstown (Nationals)	SAL	.315	.360	.470	136	559	91	176	31	7	14	90	37	65	49
3B	Ryan McMahon, Asheville (Rockies)	SAL	.282	.358	.502	126	482	93	136	46	3	18	102	54	143	8
SS	Andrew Velazquez, South Bend (D-backs)	MWL	.290	.367	.428	134	544	94	158	18	15	9	56	62	136	50
CF	Brett Phillips, Quad Cities (Astros)	MWL	.302	.362	.521	103	384	68	116	21	12	13	58	36	76	18
OF	David Dahl, Asheville (Rockies)	SAL	.309	.347	.500	90	392	69	121	33	6	10	41	23	65	18
OF	Nomar Mazara, Hickory (Rangers)	SAL	.264	.358	.470	106	398	68	105	21	2	19	73	57	99	4
DH	Chance Sisco, Delmarva (Orioles)	SAL	.340	.406	.448	114	426	56	145	27	2	5	63	42	79	1

Pos	Pitcher, Team (Org)	League	W	L	ERA	G	GS	SV	IP	H	HR	BB	SO	AVG	SO/9	WHIP
SP	Steven Brault, Delmarva (Orioles)	SAL	9	8	3.05	22	21	0	130	107	4	28	115	.223	8.0	1.04
SP	Lucas Giolito, Hagerstown (Nationals)	SAL	10	2	2.20	20	20	0	98	70	7	28	110	.196	10.1	1.00
SP	Rob Kaminsky, Peoria (Cardinals)	MWL	8	2	1.88	18	18	0	101	71	2	31	79	.192	7.1	1.01
SP	Trevor Williams, Wisconsin (Brewers)	MWL	8	1	2.36	22	12	4	107	78	4	23	112	.197	9.4	0.94
SP	Kevin Ziomek, West Michigan (Tigers)	MWL	10	6	2.27	23	23	0	123	89	5	53	152	.197	11.1	1.15
RP	Akeel Morris, Savannah (Mets)	SAL	4	1	0.63	41	0	16	57	19	1	22	89	.101	14.1	0.72

Player of the Year: Brett Phillips, of, Quad Cities (Astros). **Pitcher of the Year:** Lucas Giolito, rhp, Hagerstown (Nationals).

SHORT-SEASON

Pos	Player, Team (Org)	League	AVG	OBP	SLG	G	AB	R	H	2B	3B	HR	RBI	BB	SO	SB
C	Mark Zagunis, Boise (Cubs)	NWL	.299	.429	.422	41	154	32	46	9	2	2	27	31	31	11
1B	A.J. Reed, Tri-City (Astros)	NYP	.306	.420	.516	34	124	22	38	11	0	5	30	22	22	2
2B	Seth Spivey, Spokane (Rangers)	NWL	.332	.424	.444	67	259	51	86	12	4	3	27	39	45	2
3B	Jhoan Urena, Brooklyn (Mets)	NYP	.300	.356	.431	75	283	30	85	20	1	5	47	27	58	7
SS	Franklin Barreto, Vancouver (Blue Jays)	NWL	.311	.384	.481	73	289	65	90	23	4	6	61	26	64	29
CF	Bradley Zimmer, Mahoning Valley (Indians)	NYP	.304	.401	.464	45	168	32	51	11	2	4	30	19	30	11
OF	Auston Bousfield, Eugene (Padres)	NWL	.301	.402	.512	45	166	36	50	16	5	3	13	24	37	12
OF	Michael Conforto, Brooklyn (Mets)	NYP	.331	.403	.448	42	163	30	54	10	0	3	19	16	29	3
DH	Rowan Wick, State College (Cardinals)	NYP	.378	.475	.815	35	119	30	45	8	1	14	38	20	34	1

Pos	Pitcher, Team (Org)	League	W	L	ERA	G	GS	SV	IP	H	HR	BB	SO	AVG	SO/9	WHIP
SP	Nolan Gannon, Hudson Valley (Rays)	NYP	6	2	2.84	11	11	0	57	50	1	9	47	.234	7.4	1.04
SP	Jairo Labourt, Vancouver (Blue Jays)	NWL	5	3	1.77	15	15	0	71	47	0	37	82	.186	10.4	1.18
SP	Marcos Molina, Brooklyn (Mets)	NYP	7	3	1.77	12	12	0	76	46	2	18	91	.169	10.7	0.84
SP	Joe Musgrove, Tri-City (Astros)	NYP	7	1	2.81	15	13	0	77	64	4	10	67	.222	7.8	0.96
SP	Corey Oswalt, Brooklyn (Mets)	NYP	6	2	2.26	12	11	0	67	55	1	15	59	.214	7.9	1.03
RP	Zac Curtis, Hillsboro (Diamondbacks)	NWL	2	1	1.00	24	0	14	27	18	0	12	42	.186	14.0	1.11

Player of the Year: Franklin Barreto, ss, Vancouver (Blue Jays). **Pitcher of the Year:** Marcos Molina, rhp, Brooklyn (Mets).

ROOKIE

Pos	Player, Team (Org)	League	AVG	OBP	SLG	G	AB	R	H	2B	3B	HR	RBI	BB	SO	SB
C	Jakson Reetz, GCL Nationals	GCL	.274	.429	.368	43	117	20	32	6	1	1	15	26	30	6
1B	Bobby Bradley, AZL Indians	AZL	.361	.426	.652	39	155	39	56	13	4	8	50	16	36	3
2B	Forrest Wall, Grand Junction (Rockies)	PIO	.318	.416	.490	41	157	48	50	6	6	3	24	27	32	18
3B	Kevin Padlo, Grand Junction (Rockies)	PIO	.300	.421	.594	48	160	32	48	15	4	8	44	31	38	6
SS	Yu-Cheng Chang, AZL Indians	AZL	.346	.420	.566	42	159	39	55	9	4	6	25	18	28	6
CF	Alex Verdugo, AZL Dodgers	AZL	.353	.421	.511	54	190	31	67	15	3	3	41	20	18	11
OF	Aristides Aquino, Billings (Reds)	PIO	.292	.342	.577	71	284	48	83	23	5	16	64	15	66	21
OF	Amaurys Minier, GCL Twins	GCL	.292	.405	.520	53	171	25	50	11	2	8	33	29	52	2
DH	Max Murphy, Elizabethton (Twins)	APP	.378	.483	.723	35	119	34	45	7	2	10	26	22	34	4

Pos	Pitcher, Team (Org)	League	W	L	ERA	G	GS	SV	IP	H	HR	BB	SO	AVG	SO/9	WHIP
SP	Agapito Barrios, Greeneville (Astros)	APP	5	0	2.09	13	6	0	56	39	0	11	46	.190	7.4	0.89
SP	Henry Centeno, GCL Rays/Princeton (Rays)	APP	5	2	1.68	12	0	0	59	44	0	11	55	.214	8.4	0.93
SP	Felix Jorge, Elizabethton (Twins)	APP	4	2	2.59	12	12	0	66	58	2	14	61	.234	8.3	1.09
SP	Tyler Mahle, Billings (Reds)	PIO	5	4	3.87	15	15	0	77	80	5	15	71	.260	8.3	1.24
SP	Daniel Missaki, Pulaski (Mariners)	APP	6	3	2.76	11	11	0	58	46	3	16	62	.212	9.5	1.06
RP	John Sever, Bristol (Pirates)	APP	1	3	1.33	16	3	1	41	30	1	17	63	.204	13.9	1.16

Player of the Year: Bobby Bradley, 1b, AZL Indians. **Pitcher of the Year:** Henry Centeno, rhp, GCL Rays. .

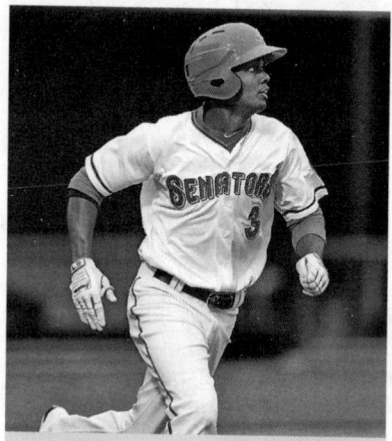

A breakout season has Michael Taylor closing in on the Nationals' outfield

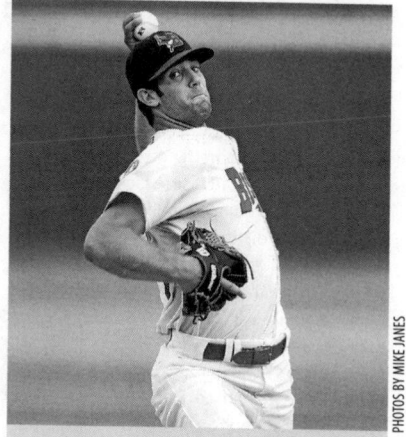

Toronto's Daniel Norris jumped from the Florida State League to the majors

PHOTOS BY MIKE JANES

MINOR LEAGUES

FIRST TEAM

Pos.	Player, Level (Organization)	Age	AVG	OBP	SLG	G	AB	R	H	2B	3B	HR	RBI	BB	SO	SB
C	Blake Swihart, AA/AAA (Red Sox)	22	.293	.341	.469	110	416	53	122	26	4	13	64	31	80	8
1B	Matt Olson, Hi A (Athletics)	20	.262	.404	.543	138	512	111	134	31	1	37	97	117	137	2
2B	Mookie Betts, AA/AAA (Red Sox)	21	.346	.431	.529	99	399	87	138	30	5	11	65	61	50	33
3B	Kris Bryant, AAA/AA (Cubs)	22	.325	.438	.661	138	492	118	160	34	1	43	110	86	162	15
SS	Seager, Corey, Hi A/AA (Dodgers)	20	.349	.402	.602	118	475	89	166	50	5	20	97	40	115	6
OF	Joc Pederson, AAA (Dodgers)	22	.303	.435	.582	121	445	106	135	17	4	33	78	100	149	30
OF	Steven Souza, AAA (Nationals)	25	.345	.427	.577	100	357	62	123	25	2	18	77	52	80	28
OF	Michael Taylor, AA/AAA (Nationals)	23	.304	.390	.526	110	428	81	130	20	3	23	64	57	144	37
DH	Joey Gallo, AA/Hi A (Rangers)	20	.271	.394	.615	126	439	97	119	19	3	42	106	87	179	7

Pos.	Pitcher, Level (Organization)	Age	W	L	ERA	G	GS	SV	IP	H	HR	BB	SO	AVG	SO/9	WHIP
SP	Tyler Glasnow, Hi A (Pirates)	20	12	5	1.74	23	23	0	124	74	3	57	157	.174	11.4	1.05
SP	Kendall Graveman, Hi A/AAA/Lo A/AA (Blue Jays)	23	14	6	1.83	27	27	0	167	142	2	31	115	.231	6.2	1.03
SP	Jimmy Nelson, AAA (Brewers)	25	10	2	1.46	17	16	0	111	70	3	32	114	.179	9.2	0.92
SP	Daniel Norris, Hi A/AA/AAA (Blue Jays)	21	12	2	2.53	26	25	0	125	96	7	43	163	.212	11.8	1.11
SP	Henry Owens, AA/AAA (Red Sox)	21	17	5	2.94	26	26	0	159	121	10	59	170	.208	9.6	1.13
RP	Cam Bedrosian, AA/AAA (Angels)	22	2	1	2.00	43	0	18	45	16	1	18	82	.109	16.4	0.76

SECOND TEAM

Pos.	Player, Level (Organization)	Age	AVG	OBP	SLG	G	AB	R	H	2B	3B	HR	RBI	BB	SO	SB
C	J.T. Realmuto, AA (Marlins)	23	.299	.369	.461	97	375	66	112	25	6	8	62	41	59	18
1B	Christian Walker, AA/AAA (Orioles)	23	.288	.357	.489	139	532	73	153	25	2	26	96	56	132	2
2B	Dilson Herrera, AA /Hi A (Mets)	20	.323	.379	.479	128	524	98	169	33	5	13	71	47	96	23
3B	Jake Lamb, AA/AAA (Diamondbacks)	23	.327	.407	.566	108	392	63	128	39	5	15	84	53	103	2
SS	J.P. Crawford, Hi A/ Lo A (Phillies)	19	.285	.375	.406	123	463	69	132	23	0	11	48	65	74	24
CF	Dalton Pompey, Hi A/AA /AAA (Blue Jays)	21	.317	.392	.469	113	441	84	140	22	9	9	51	52	84	43
OF	Scott Schebler, AA (Dodgers)	23	.280	.365	.556	135	489	82	137	23	14	28	73	45	110	10
OF	Brett Phillips, Lo A/Hi A (Astros)	20	.310	.375	.529	134	493	87	153	29	14	17	68	50	96	23
DH	Aaron Judge, Hi A/Lo A (Yankees)	22	.308	.419	.486	131	467	80	144	24	4	17	78	89	131	1

Pos.	Pitcher, Level (Organization)	Age	W	L	ERA	G	GS	SV	IP	H	HR	BB	SO	AVG	SO/9	WHIP
SP	Jose Berrios, Hi A/AA/AAA (Twins)	20	12	8	2.76	25	25	0	140	118	6	38	140	.227	9.0	1.11
SP	Josh Hader, Hi A/AA (Astros)	20	10	3	3.28	27	19	2	123	92	11	54	136	.208	9.9	1.18
SP	Brian Johnson, AA/Hi A (Red Sox)	23	13	3	2.13	25	25	0	144	101	6	39	132	.197	8.3	0.97
SP	Steve Matz, AA/Hi A (Mets)	23	10	9	2.24	24	24	0	141	132	3	35	131	.251	8.4	1.19
SP	Luis Severino, Lo A/AA/Hi A (Yankees)	20	6	5	2.46	24	24	0	113	93	3	27	127	.220	10.1	1.06
RP	Enrique Burgos, Hi A (Diamondbacks)	23	3	3	2.47	55	0	29	55	37	5	26	83	.188	13.7	1.15

Portland packs a punch

BY ALEX SPEIER

When Mookie Betts stepped to the plate on April 3 to open the season for Double-A Portland, he had something to prove. He had delivered a singularly spectacular breakout season in 2013, going from a performer without particular distinction in 2012 with short-season Lowell to someone who had landed very much on the prospect map with standout performances in low Class A Greenville and high Class A Salem in 2013.

Still, it remained to be seen whether Betts' eruption in 2013—a 15-homer season after he hadn't gone deep once in 2012—was a harbinger or an outlier.

"You never know how guys are going to adapt to a new level. Double-A is filled with rosters of prospects," Portland manager Billy McMillon said. "With better players, with the travel of the Eastern League, you just never know how some guys are going to respond."

Betts responded by taking five pitches and then turning on the sixth from Reading lefthander Jesse Biddle—who entered the season as the Phillies' top pitching prospect—hammering the pitch over the left-center field fence to set in motion a 4-for-4 day.

Shortstop Deven Marrero, who showed little extra-base pop in his first full pro season in 2013, slammed a pair of doubles. Catcher Blake Swihart went 2-for-3 with a triple. And on the mound, lefthander Henry Owens tossed six no-hit innings while punching out nine.

"In hindsight, we can say that kind of set the pattern," McMillon said of his team. "But we didn't know what exactly the guys were going to do, how they were going to respond. It was really nice as you look back on it, but I don't think anyone could have projected we would win 88 games."

Portland went on to post a .620 winning percentage, the best mark in the 21-year history of the Double-A franchise. That regular season excellence (which preceded a five-game, first-round EL playoff exit against eventual-champion Binghamton) was driven by a number of superb prospect performances.

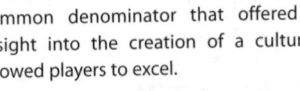

Deven Marrero

TEAM OF THE YEAR

A trio of 2011 high school draftees excelled, including Betts (.355/.443/.551 with six homers and 22 steals in 54 games before his promotion to Triple-A and then the majors), Swihart (.300/.353/.487 with 12 homers before his move up to Triple-A) and Owens (14-4, 2.60, 9.4 strikeouts per nine). Likewise, a pair of 2012 college first-rounders flourished: Marrero (.291/.371/.433 in 68 games) and lefthander Brian Johnson (10-2, 1.75, the lowest ERA by a qualifying starter in the EL since 1985). First baseman Travis Shaw (.305/.406/.548 with 11 homers in 47 games) mashed his way to Triple-A.

The list went on. Prospects whose stock had slipped in prior years, such as second baseman Sean Coyle (.295/.371/.512 with 16 homers in 97 games) and shortstop Derrik Gibson (.302/.390/.395 in 85 games), reestablished their prospect credentials. Late-season additions, most notably lefthander Eduardo Rodriguez (3-1, 0.96, 9.4 SO/9 following his July 31 trade from the Orioles) and Justin Haley (3-2, 1.19 in six starts) hit the ground running upon joining the Sea Dogs.

In short, the prospect-laden team saw virtually every player flourish. While the performances took on a variety, there was a visual common denominator that offered some insight into the creation of a culture that allowed players to excel.

PREVIOUS 10 WINNERS

2004: Lancaster/California (Diamondbacks)
2005: Jacksonville/Southern (Dodgers)
2006: Tucson/Pacific Coast (Diamondbacks)
2007: San Antonio/Texas (Padres)
2008: Frisco/Texas (Rangers)
2009: Akron/Eastern (Indians)
2010: Northwest Arkansas/Texas (Royals)
2011: Mobile BayBears/Southern (Diamondbacks)
2012: Springfield Cardinals/Texas (Cardinals)
2013: Daytona Cubs/Florida State (Cubs)

Full list: BaseballAmerica.com/awards

BY JOHN MANUEL

For scouts, front-office executives and fans who have lamented that the power has gone out of the game in the major leagues, just hold tight: Javier Baez and Joey Gallo are coming.

At the Futures Game at Target Field, two of the minors' best prospects played a game of 'Can you top this?'. Baez struck first both times, first with a rousing, exciting round of batting practice, then with an opposite-field home run in the top of the sixth for the World team.

But Gallo outshined Baez on both counts. He wowed media and fans alike with a windshield-breaking BP performance, denting the upper deck at Target Field repeatedly. Then, after striking out in each of his first two at-bats, Gallo got a 2-0 pitch from the Astros' Michael Feliz, a 95 mph fastball, and sent it 419 feet over the right-field fence for a two-run homer.

The blast powered Gallo to the MVP award and allowed the U.S. to retake the lead, one it held for a 3-2 victory. It's the fifth straight victory for U.S. prospects against the World, running the all-time ledger to 10-6 Americans since the first game in 1999.

"After the first two at-bats I just wanted to make contact and not embarrass myself too much by striking out," Gallo said. "I got a 2-0 pitch and was just like, 'I'm going to try to hit this one out.'"

The U.S. took an early 1-0 lead during a shaky inning by lefty Edwin Escobar (Giants). Jesse Winker (Reds) doubled to left to lead off the inning, moved to third on Padres farmhand Hunter Renfroe's single to center and scored on a fielder's choice. Escobar wobbled more, loading the bases with two outs, but retired Kris Bryant (Cubs) on a harmless fly to right.

Baez's homer and Gallo's were the game's only other scoring. U.S. relievers Robert Stephenson (Reds) and Noah Syndergaard (Mets) wrapped up the game, with Syndergaard earning the save while Jake Thompson (Tigers) got credit for the victory, getting two outs by strikeout.

"It was a good game," World manager Bert Blyleven said. "We had a lot of impressive young arms, a lot of young guys in low (Class) A even, who really showed well. I got everybody into the game and nobody got hurt. I thought it was a great game and TK (U.S. manager Tom Kelly) will tell you the same thing."

The World team's standouts, other than Baez, were mostly pitchers. Center fielder Dalton Pompey (Blue Jays) had two hits in four trips and scored ahead of Baez's homer. Rockies infielder Rosell Herrera singled in both of his at-bats as a DH.

Four World pitchers made their mark, starting with Jose Berrios (Twins) tossing a scoreless inning, followed by Domingo German (Marlins), who struck out Bryant and Gallo to start his second scoreless inning. German got Bryant by throwing six straight fastballs, all between 94-96 mph, and fanned Bryant on an 83-mph slider.

FUTURES GAME BOX SCORE

JULY 13 IN MINNEAPOLIS
UNITED STATES 3, WORLD 2

WORLD	AB	R	H	BI	U.S.	AB	R	H	BI
Pompey, CF	4	1	2	0	Taylor, CF	4	0	1	0
Lindor, SS	2	0	0	0	Coyle, 2B	2	0	0	0
Baez, J SS	2	1	1	2	Johnson, M 2B	2	0	0	0
Peraza, 2B	2	0	1	0	Seager, SS	1	0	0	0
Rondon, 2B	2	0	0	0	Crawford, SS	2	1	1	0
Vargas, 1B	4	0	1	0	Bryant, 3B	3	0	0	0
Moya, LF	3	0	0	0	Gallo, DH	4	1	1	2
Alvarez, RF	2	0	0	0	Peterson, 1B	2	0	1	0
Santana, D, RF	2	0	0	0	O'Brien, 1B	2	0	0	0
Guerrero, G, DH	2	0	0	0	Winker, LF	2	1	1	0
a-Herrera, R, PH-DH	2	0	2	0	Ramsey, J LF	1	0	0	0
Nunez, R, 3B	2	0	1	0	Renfroe, RF	2	0	1	0
Franco, 3B	2	0	0	0	Bell, RF	1	0	0	0
Alfaro, C	2	0	0	0	Plawecki, C	2	0	0	1
Jimenez, C	1	0	0	0	O'Conner, C	1	0	1	0
TOTALS	**34**	**2**	**8**	**2**	**Totals**	**31**	**3**	**7**	**3**

a-Singled for Guerrero, G in the 7th

WORLD		000	002	000	2	8 0
UNITED STATES		001	002	00X	3	7 0

LOB: World 6, U.S. 6. **2B:** Vargas (1 Harvey); Winker (1, Escobar, Ed); Peterson (1, Severino, L.). **HR:** Baez, J (1, 6th inning off Giolito, 1 on, 0 out); Gallo (1, 6th off Feliz, M, 1 on, 1 out). Runners left in scoring position, 2 out: Alvarez; Vargas; Bryant 2; Renfroe; Johnson, M. **GIDP:** Alfaro. **SB:** Crawford (1, 2nd base off Feliz, M/Jimenez, A.).

WORLD	IP	H	R	ER	BB	SO	U.S.	IP	H	R	ER	BB	SO
Berrios	1	0	0	0	0	1	Owens	1	1	0	0	0	1
German, D	1	0	0	0	0	2	Norris	1	0	0	0	0	1
Escobar, Ed	1	3	1	1	0	0	Binford	1	0	0	0	0	1
Severino, L	1	1	0	0	0	1	Harvey	1	1	0	0	1	2
Urias, J	1	0	0	0	0	1	Meyer, A	1	1	0	0	0	0
Feliz, M (L)	1	2	2	2	0	2	Giolito	.2	2	2	2	1	1
Romero	1	1	0	0	0	0	Thompson (W)	.2	0	0	0	0	2
Lopez, J	0.1	0	0	0	0	0	Shipley	.2	1	0	0	0	0
Alcantara	0.1	0	0	0	0	0	Stephenson	1	1	0	0	0	1
Guerrero, T	0.1	0	0	0	0	1	Syndergaard (S)	1	1	0	0	0	1

Umpires—HP: Travis Eggert. **1B:** Jansen Visconti. **2B:** Nate White. **3B:** Matt McCoy.
T: 2:33. **A:** 39,553.

MINOR LEAGUES

TRIPLE-A: Before the Durham faithful could find their seats, the International League jumped out to a hefty lead over the Pacific Coast League. The PCL never overcame the early deficit and lost 7-3.

With two outs and two runners on in the bottom of the first inning, Durham DH Wilson Betemit singled to right field off the glove of Reno first baseman Mike Jacobs (Diamondbacks) for a 2-0 lead. After Buffalo righthander Liam Hendriks (Blue Jays) worked his second efficient inning for the IL—he needed just 25 pitches to strike out four and record six outs—his offense went back to work. Gwinnett third baseman Phil Gosselin (Braves) hit a chopper to left, and Syracuse catcher Jhonatan Solano (Nationals) hammered a fastball over the left-field wall for a 4-0 lead.

Steven Moya

EASTERN: Erie right fielder Steven Moya (Tigers) hit a grand slam in the fifth inning to lead the Western Division to a 5-2 victory. Moya's homer came against New Hampshire righthander Dustin Antolin (Blue Jays). Altoona righthander Ryan Beckman (Pirates) got the win with one scoreless inning, giving up two hits and striking out two. Moya, who topped the EL in home runs with 35 at season's end, was named MVP.

SOUTHERN: The Southern Division cranked out six runs on 14 hits, in the process limiting Tennessee third baseman Kris Bryant (Cubs) to a single in five trips to the plate. Montgomery right fielder Taylor Motter (Rays) connected for a solo homer in the sixth for the South's fifth and deciding run. The Northern Division made things interesting in the bottom of the ninth, scoring twice thanks to a two-run bomb by Chattanooga first baseman O'Koyea Dickson (Dodgers).

TEXAS: The Northern Division got a two-run homer from Springfield catcher Cody Stanley (Cardinals) in the fourth inning against Corpus Christi righthander Kyle Smith (Astros) en route to a 3-1 victory. Springfield lefty Kyle Hald pitched two innings for the victory, while Smith took the loss. The Southern Division had taken a

1-0 lead in the top of the fourth on an RBI single by Midland right fielder Josh Whitaker (Athletics) that drove in San Antonio center fielder Rymer Liriano (Padres), who singled.

CALIFORNIA-CAROLINA: Bakersfield left fielder Kyle Waldrop (Reds) did most of the damage in this one. He drove home all three Cal League runs, including a two-run homer to center off Wilmington righty Christian Binford (Royals) to lift the Cal League to a 3-2 win. Carolina made it interesting in the ninth after Carolina third baseman Erik Gonzalez (Indians) and Wilmington catcher Cam Gallagher scored consecutive singles off Inland Empire righthander Austin Adams (Angels). San Jose lefty Steven Okert (Giants) then entered and retired the side.

FLORIDA STATE: The Northern Division mounted a ninth-inning comeback, erasing a two-run deficit to win 6-4. Tampa teammates Dante Bichette Jr. and Jake Cave (Yankees) set the table in the top of the ninth, reaching on a single and a walk, before RBI singles by Lakeland catcher Austin Green (Tigers) and Daytona shortstop Marco Hernandez (Cubs) tied the score. Daytona second baseman Gioskar Amaya then hit a game-winning two-run double.

MIDWEST: The Western Division relied on lucky No. 7, tallying seven runs and no-hitting the Eastern Division through seven innings in a 7-0 win. The West punctuated its victory with a four-run sixth inning in which Beloit's Boog Powell (Athletics) hit a two-run double and Burlington's Chad Hinshaw (Angels) later hit a two-run homer to left.

SOUTH ATLANTIC: After a rain-shortened, seven-inning game last year, the SAL all-stars played to a 4-4 tie in 2014, the result of both teams running out of pitchers after the 10th inning. The Northern Division tied the score at two in the bottom of the eighth to force extras, but neither side was done scoring. Lexington center fielder Dominique Taylor (Royals) drove in two runs in the top of the 10th to give the Southern Division all-stars the edge, but the North rallied again for two runs in the bottom of the inning.

DEPARTMENT LEADERS

*Full-season teams only

TEAM

WINS

Kane County (Midwest)	91
Asheville (South Atlantic)	89
Portland (Eastern)	88
Greensboro (South Atlantic)	87
Hagerstown (South Atlantic)	87

LONGEST WINNING STREAK*

Kane County (Midwest)	13
Asheville (South Atlantic)	12
Hickory (South Atlantic)	12
Visalia (California)	12
Chattanooga (Southern)	11
New Britain (Eastern)	11
Pawtucket (International)	11
Savannah (South Atlantic)	11

LOSSES

Modesto (California)	97
Colorado Springs (Pacific Coast)	91
Clearwater (Florida State)	89
Harrisburg (Eastern)	89
Jupiter (Florida State)	87
Northwest Arkansas (Texas)	87

LONGEST LOSING STREAK*

Greenville (South Atlantic)	17
West Virginia (South Atlantic)	14
Bowling Green (Midwest)	13
Fort Wayne (Midwest)	13
Reading (Eastern)	12
Visalia (California)	12

BATTING AVERAGE*

Salt Lake (Pacific Coast)	.293
Reno (Pacific Coast)	.293
Asheville (South Atlantic)	.292
Bakersfield (California)	.286
Greensboro (South Atlantic)	.285

RUNS

Las Vegas (Pacific Coast)	880
High Desert (California)	841
Lancaster (California)	837
Bakersfield (California)	816
Reno (Pacific Coast)	790

HOME RUNS

Charlotte (International)	176
High Desert (California)	176
Stockton (California)	174
Las Vegas (Pacific Coast)	172
Albuquerque (Pacific Coast)	169

STOLEN BASES

Hagerstown (South Atlantic)	235
Asheville (South Atlantic)	209
Great Lakes (Midwest)	183
DSL Cubs (Dominican)	175
DSL Indians (Dominican)	171

EARNED RUN AVERAGE*

Kane County (Midwest)	2.85
Savannah (South Atlantic)	3.03
West Michigan (Midwest)	3.05
Wilmington (Carolina)	3.09
Brevard County (Florida State)	3.25

STRIKEOUTS

Great Lakes (Midwest)	1,256
Stockton (California)	1,254
Nashville (Pacific Coast)	1,236
Durham (International)	1,220
Visalia (California)	1,209

INDIVIDUAL BATTING

BATTING AVERAGE

Corey Seager (R.Cucamonga, Chattanooga)	.349
T.J. Rivera (St. Lucie, Binghamton)	.349
Mookie Betts (Portland, Pawtucket)	.346
Steven Souza (Hagerstown, Potomac, Syr)	.345
Phil Gosselin (Gwinnett)	.344

RUNS

Tony Kemp (Lancaster, Corpus Christi)	121
Kris Bryant (Tennessee, Iowa)	118
Matt Olson (Stockton)	111
Daniel Robertson (Stockton)	110
Sherman Johnson (Inland Empire)	107

HITS

Jordy Lara (High Desert, Jackson)	177
Wilmer Difo (Hagerstown)	176
Daniel Robertson (Stockton)	170
Dilson Herrera (St. Lucie, Binghamton)	169
Tony Kemp (Lancaster, Corpus Christi)	167
Shane Peterson (Sacramento)	167

TOP HITTING STREAKS

Rangel Ravelo (Birmingham)	26
Harold Ramirez (West Virginia)	23
Nick Buss (Sacramento)	22
Wilmer Flores (Las Vegas)	22
Pat Valaika (Asheville)	22
Andrew Velazquez (South Bend)	22

MOST HITS (ONE GAME)

Carlos Garcia (Lexington)	6
Carlos Lopez (Greensboro)	6

TOTAL BASES

Kris Bryant (Tennessee, Iowa)	325
Jordy Lara (High Desert, Jackson)	305
Steven Moya (Erie)	286
Corey Seager (R. Cucamonga, Chattanooga)	286
Matt Olson (Stockton)	278

EXTRA-BASE HITS

Kris Bryant (Tennessee, Iowa)	78
Corey Seager (R. Cucamonga, Chattanooga)	75
Jordy Lara (High Desert, Jackson)	71
Steven Moya (Erie)	71
Correlle Prime (Asheville)	71

DOUBLES

Corey Seager (R. Cucamonga, Chattanooga)	50
Correlle Prime (Asheville)	47
Ryan McMahon (Asheville)	46
Jantzen Witte (Greenville, Salem)	44
Brandon Drury (Visalia, Mobile)	42

TRIPLES

Mike Yastrzemski (Delmarva, Frederick, Bowie)	16
Roberto Caro (DSL Cubs)	15
Andrew Velazquez (South Bend)	15
Willy Adames (West Michigan, Bowling Green)	14
Brett Phillips (Quad Cities, Lancaster)	14
Scott Schebler (Chattanooga)	14

HOME RUNS

Kris Bryant (Tennessee, Iowa)	43
Joey Gallo (Myrtle Beach, Frisco)	42
Matt Olson (Stockton)	37
Steven Moya (Erie)	35
Pete O'Brien (Tampa, Trenton, Mobile)	34

RUNS BATTED IN

Marquez Smith (Pensacola, Bakersfield)	131
D.J. Peterson (High Desert, Jackson)	111
Kris Bryant (Tennessee, Iowa)	110
Joey Gallo (Myrtle Beach, Frisco)	106
Steven Moya (Erie)	105

MOST RBIS (ONE GAME)

Brett Eibner (Omaha)	9
Kent Matthes (Midland)	9
Jimmy Paredes (Omaha)	8
21 players tied	7

WALKS

Matt Olson (Stockton)	117
Joc Pederson (Albuquerque)	100
Aaron Judge (Charleston, Tampa)	89
Sherman Johnson (Inland Empire)	88
Taylor Brennan (Wisconsin)	87
Joey Gallo (Myrtle Beach, Frisco)	87
Max Muncy (Midland)	87

INTENTIONAL WALKS

Justin Bour (New Orleans)	11
Kris Bryant (Tennessee, Iowa)	8
Kyle Kubitza (Mississippi)	8
Preston Tucker (Corpus Christi, Okla. City)	8
Joey Gallo (Myrtle Beach, Frisco)	7
Nick Ramirez (Huntsville)	7

STRIKEOUTS

Dusty Coleman (Midland)	202
Rudy Flores (Visalia)	189
Joey Gallo (Myrtle Beach, Frisco)	179
Jacob Morris (Kannapolis)	179
Grant Fink (Lake County)	174

STOLEN BASES

Mallex Smith (Fort Wayne, Lake Elsinore)	88
Gabriel Mejia (DSL Indians)	72
Rafael Bautista (Hagerstown)	69
Jose Peraza (Lynchburg, Mississippi)	60
Billy Burns (Midland, Sacramento)	54
Delino DeShields (Corpus Christi)	54

CAUGHT STEALING

Mallex Smith (Fort Wayne, Lake Elsinore)	26
Johnny Davis (Wisconsin)	21
Omar Garcia (Wisconsin)	21
Gary Brown (Fresno)	20
D.J. Davis (Lansing)	20
Gabriel Mejia (DSL Indians)	20

ON-BASE PERCENTAGE*

Boog Powell (Beloit, Stockton)	.451
Kris Bryant (Tennessee, Iowa)	.438
Joc Pederson (Albuquerque)	.435
Mookie Betts (Portland, Pawtucket)	.431
Chad Wallach (Jupiter, Greensboro)	.431

SLUGGING PERCENTAGE*

Kris Bryant (Tennessee, Iowa)	.661
Brennan Boesch (Salt Lake)	.636
Joey Gallo (Myrtle Beach, Frisco)	.615
Corey Seager (R. Cucamonga, Chattanooga)	.602
Marquez Smith (Pensacola, Bakersfield)	.601

ON-BASE PLUS SLUGGING (OPS)*

Kris Bryant (Tennessee, Iowa)	1.098
Marquez Smith (Pensacola, Bakersfield)	1.025
Brennan Boesch (Salt Lake)	1.017
Joc Pederson (Albuquerque)	1.017
Joey Gallo (Myrtle Beach, Frisco)	1.009

HIT BY PITCH

Tim Locastro (Vancouver)	32
Franklin Rollin (DSL Rangers2)	30
Chad Hinshaw (Burlington, Inland Empire)	29
Jesus Alastre (VSL Phillies)	22
Pat Cantwell (Frisco)	22
Daniel Carroll (Rome, Mississippi, Lynchburg)	22
Nathan Orf (Brevard County)	22
Scott Schebler (Chattanooga)	22

SACRIFICE BUNTS

Ruben Sosa (Lancaster, Corpus Christi, Ok. City)	22
Ramon Torres (Lexington, Wilmington)	21
Ronald Torreyes (Okla. City)	21
Ildemaro Vargas (Palm Beach, Springfield)	20
Rando Moreno (San Jose, Augusta)	19

SACRIFICE FLIES

Jantzen Witte (Greenville, Salem)	13
Eric Aguilera (Inland Empire, Burlington)	12
Jordan Edgerton (Danville)	11
Mike Jacobs (Reno)	11
Alberth Martinez (Lake Elsinore)	11
Alex Yarbrough (Arkansas)	11

GROUNDED INTO DOUBLE PLAY

Matt Duffy (Corpus Christi, Okla. City)	22
Trey Mancini (Delmarva, Frederick)	22
Albert Almora (Daytona, Tennessee)	21
Mason Williams (Trenton)	21
5 players tied	20

BATTING AVERAGE*

CATCHERS

Chance Sisco (Delmarva)	.340
Chad Wallach (Jupiter, Greensboro)	.322
Tomas Telis (Frisco, Round Rock)	.318

Elias Diaz (Altoona, Indianapolis) .312
Kevin Plawecki (Binghamton, Las Vegas) .309

FIRST BASEMEN

Jordy Lara (High Desert, Jackson) .337
Willians Astudillo (Lakewood) .333
Clint Robinson (Albuquerque) .312
Jantzen Witte (Greenville, Salem) .312
Marquez Smith (Pensacola, Bakersfield) .311

SECOND BASEMEN

Jose Peraza (Lynchburg, Mississippi) .339
Dilson Herrera (St. Lucie, Binghamton) .323
Avery Romero (Jupiter, Greensboro) .320
Enrique Hernandez (Corp Christi, OKC, New Orleans) .319
Robert Refsnyder (Trenton, Scranton/WB) .318

THIRD BASEMEN

Phil Gosselin (Gwinnett) .344
Andy Marte (Reno) .329
Jake Lamb (Mobile, Reno) .327
Kris Bryant (Tennessee, Iowa) .325
Niuman Romero (Bowie) .320

SHORTSTOPS

Corey Seager (R. Cucamonga, Chattanooga) .349
T.J. Rivera (St. Lucie, Binghamton) .349
Matt Reynolds (Las Vegas, Binghamton) .343
Matt Duffy (Richmond) .332
Jose Rondon (Inland Empire, Lake Elsinore) .319

OUTFIELDERS

Mookie Betts (Portland, Pawtucket) .346
Steven Souza Jr. (Hagerstown, Potomac, Syr.) .345
Boog Powell (Beloit, Stockton) .343
Kyle Waldrop (Bakersfield, Pensacola) .338
Matt den Dekker (Las Vegas) .334

INDIVIDUAL PITCHING

EARNED RUN AVERAGE*

Glenn Sparkman (Wilmington) 1.56
Tyler Glasnow (Bradenton) 1.74
Kendall Graveman (Lansing, Dunedin, NH, Buff) 1.83
Tyler Wagner (Brevard County) 1.86
Tyler Anderson (Tulsa) 1.98

WORST ERA*

Drew Cisco (Bakersfield) 6.78
Scott Diamond (Rochester, Louisville) 6.57
Jake Pettit (Norfolk, Bowie) 6.27
Barry Enright (Lehigh Valley, Albuquerque) 6.20
Bo Schultz (Reno) 6.18

WINS

Henry Owens (Portland, Pawtucket) 17
Antonio Senzatela (Asheville) 15
11 players tied 14

LOSSES

Zach Bird (Great Lakes) 17
Tyler Viza (Lakewood) 17
9 players tied 14

GAMES

Bobby LaFromboise (El Paso, Indianapolis) 63
Brent Leach (Huntsville, Nashville) 63
Tyler Mizenko (San Jose) 59
Ryan Dennick (Pensacola, Louisville) 58
Daniel Gibson (South Bend, Visalia) 58

GAMES STARTED

Charles Brewer (Mobile, Reno) 29
27 players tied 28

COMPLETE GAMES

Robert Gsellman (Savannah) 4
Taylor Hill (Syracuse) 4
Virgil Vasquez (New Britain, Rochester) 4
Tyler Cloyd (Columbus) 3
Dylan Floro (Montgomery) 3
Justin Germano (Round Rock, Albuquerque) 3
Henry Owens (Portland, Pawtucket) 3
Brandon Sinnery (Visalia) 3

SHUTOUTS

13 players tied 2

GAMES FINISHED

Enrique Burgos (Visalia) 47
Oliver Drake (Bowie) 47
David Goforth (Huntsville) 44

Arik Sikula (New Hampshire, Dunedin) 44
Austin House (Sacramento, Stockton) 43

HOLDS

Ryan Dennick (Pensacola, Louisville) 19
Daniel Gibson (South Bend, Visalia) 19
Brent Leach (Huntsville, Nashville) 17
Kevin Munson (Reno) 16
Miguel Socolovich (Las Vegas) 16

SAVES

Oliver Drake (Bowie) 31
Arik Sikula (New Hampshire, Dunedin) 31
Enrique Burgos (Visalia) 29
Jake Barrett (Mobile, Reno) 28
David Goforth (Huntsville) 27

INNINGS PITCHED

Dylan Floro (Montgomery) 178
Chris Heston (Fresno) 173
Chien-Ming Wang (Louisville, Charlotte) 173
Justin Nicolino (Jacksonville) 170
Brandon Sinnery (Visalia) 170

WALKS

Fabio Martinez (R. Cucamonga, Albuquerque) 93
Victor Payano (Myrtle Beach) 90
Cody Kukuk (Greenville, Salem) 83
Tyler Pike (High Desert, Jackson) 80
Mark Sappington (Arkansas, Inland Empire) 79

STRIKEOUTS

Taylor Cole (New Hampshire, Dunedin) 181
Aaron Blair (South Bend, Visalia, Mobile) 171
Ben Lively (Bakersfield, Pensacola) 171
Henry Owens (Portland, Pawtucket) 170
Daniel Norris (Dunedin, NH, Buffalo) 163

HITS ALLOWED

Drew Cisco (Bakersfield) 210
Dylan Floro (Montgomery) 209
Chien-Ming Wang (Louisville, Charlotte) 200
Pat Dean (New Britain) 192
Jeremy Gabryszwski (Dunedin, Lansing) 189
Derek Hankins (Toledo) 189

HOME RUNS ALLOWED

Daniel McCutchen (Round Rock, Charlotte) 29
Scott DeCecco (High Desert) 27
Tyler Cloyd (Columbus) 26
Justin Germano (Round Rock, Albuquerque) 26
Jarrett Grube (Salt Lake) 26

STRIKEOUTS PER NINE INNINGS (STARTERS)*

Daniel Norris (Dunedin, NH, Buffalo) 11.74
Tyler Glasnow (Bradenton) 11.36
Taylor Cole (Dunedin, New Hampshire) 11.32
Kevin Ziomek (West Michigan) 11.12
Sean Manaea (Wilmington) 10.80

STRIKEOUTS PER NINE INNINGS (RELIEVERS)*

Sam Tuivailala (P. Beach, Springfield, Memphis) 14.55
Akeel Morris (Savannah) 14.05
Chris Perry (Peoria, Palm Beach) 14.00
Armando Rivero (Tennessee, Iowa) 13.85
Michael Johnson (Great Lakes) 12.80

OPPONENT BATTING AVERAGE (STARTERS)*

Tyler Glasnow (Bradenton) .174
Austin Voth (Harrisburg, Hagrstwn, Potomac) .197
Brian Johnson (Salem, Portland) .197
Tyler DeLoach (Inland Empire, Arkansas) .198
Kevin Ziomek (West Michigan) .201

OPPONENT BATTING AVERAGE (RELIEVERS)*

Akeel Morris (Savannah) .103
Austin Adams (Inland Empire) .141
Cody Wheeler (Visalia, Mobile) .150
Chris Perry (Peoria, Palm Beach) .156
Andy Oliver (Indianapolis) .157

MOST STRIKEOUTS, ONE GAME

Chris Lamb (Stockton) 17
Blayne Weller (Visalia) 16
Jose De Leon (Great Lakes) 14
John Simms (Potomac) 14

WILD PITCHES

Henry Rodriguez (New Orleans, AZL, Charlotte) 32
Mitch Brown (Lake County) 24
Andrew Mitchell (Kannapolis) 23
Johendi Jiminian (Asheville) 22
Manuel Cordova (DSL Blue Jays) 21
Jhenderson Hurtado (DSL Athletics) 21

BALKS

Matt Carasiti (Asheville) 8
Luis Carrasco (VSL Phillies) 7
Miguel Almonte (Wilmington) 6
Jefferson Arias (AZL Mariners) 6
Leandro Linares (AZL Indians) 6

HIT BATTERS

Lars Huijer (Clinton, High Desert) 26
Tyler DeLoach (Inland Empire, Arkansas) 22
Matt Milroy (Greensboro, Jupiter) 21
Lucas Sims (Lynchburg) 17
Daniel Corcino (Pensacola, Louisville) 16

GROUND BALL DOUBLE PLAYS

John Kuchno (Bradenton) 31
Dylan Floro (Montgomery) 30
Chien-Ming Wang (Louisville, Charlotte) 28
Jason Hursh (Mississippi) 25
Reinaldo Lopez (Charlotte) 24

INDIVIDUAL FIELDING

ERRORS

Franchy Cordero (Fort Wayne, Eugene) 52
Carlton Daal (Dayton) 39
Wilson Amador (DSL Astros Orange) 39
Jorge Polanco (Fort Myers, New Britain) 38
Dustin Peterson (Fort Wayne) 38

Tyler Glasnow

DAVID SCHOFIELD

MINOR LEAGUES

	INTERNATIONAL LEAGUE	PACIFIC COAST LEAGUE	EASTERN LEAGUE	SOUTHERN LEAGUE	TEXAS LEAGUE	CALIFORNIA LEAGUE	CAROLINA LEAGUE	FLORIDA STATE LEAGUE	MIDWEST LEAGUE	SOUTH ATLANTIC LEAGUE
Best Batting Prospect	Gregory Polanco, Indianapolis	Joc Pederson, Albuquerque	Michael Taylor, Harrisburg	Kris Bryant, Tennessee	Ryan Rua, Frisco	Corey Seager, Rancho Cucamonga	Joey Gallo, Myrtle Beach	Josh Bell, Bradenton	Kean Wong, Bowling Green	David Dahl, Asheville
Best Power Prospect	Steven Souza, Syracuse	Javier Baez, Iowa	Steven Moya, Erie	Kris Bryant, Tennessee	Joey Gallo, Frisco	Matt Olson, Stockton	Joey Gallo, Myrtle Beach	Adam Brett Walker, Fort Myers	Daniel Palka, South Bend	Aaron Judge, Charleston
Best Strike-Zone Judgment	Mikie Mahtook, Durham	Joc Pederson, Albuquerque	Niuman Romero, Bowie	Darnell Sweeney, Chattanooga	Max Muncy, Midland	Tony Kemp, Lancaster	Reed Gragnani, Salem	Brandon Nimmo, St. Lucie	Boog Powell, Beloit	Chance Sisco, Delmarva
Best Baserunner	Steven Souza, Syracuse	Austin Wates, Oklahoma City	Kelby Tomlinson, Richmond	Josh Prince, Huntsville	Billy Burns, Midland	Juan Silva, Bakersfield	Jose Peraza, Lynchburg	Dalton Pompey, Dunedin	Chan Moon, Quad Cities	Rafael Bautista, Hagerstown
Fastest Baserunner	Ezequiel Carrera, Toledo	Paulo Orlando, Omaha	Michael Taylor, Harrisburg	Jose Peraza, Mississippi	Billy Burns, Midland	Juan Silva, Bakersfield	Terrance Gore, Wilmington	Dalton Pompey, Dunedin	Mallex Smith, Fort Wayne	Rafael Bautista, Hagerstown
Best Pitching Prospect	Marcus Stroman, Buffalo	Jimmy Nelson, Nashville	Henry Owens, Portland	Robert Stephenson, Pensacola	Jon Gray, Tulsa	Josh Hader, Lancaster	Andrew Faulkner, Myrtle Beach	Jose Berrios, Fort Myers	Kohl Stewart, Cedar Rapids	Hunter Harvey, Delmarva
Best Fastball	Alex Meyer, Rochester	Aaron Poreda, Round Rock	Kyle Crick, Richmond	Robert Stephenson, Pensacola	Sam Tuivailala, Springfield	Enrique Burgos, Visalia	Francellis Montas, Winston-Salem	Sam Tuivailala, Palm Beach	Nick Burdi, Cedar Rapids	Ray Black, Augusta
Best Breaking Pitch	Alex Meyer, Rochester	Jimmy Nelson, Nashville	Henry Owens, Portland	Chris Reed, Chattanooga	R.J. Alvarez, Arkansas	Austin Adams, Inland Empire	Madison Younginer, Salem	Jose Berrios, Fort Myers	Buck Farmer, West Michigan	Lucas Giolito, Hagerstown
Best Changeup	Allen Webster, Pawtucket	Rafael Montero, Las Vegas	Henry Owens, Portland	Justin Nicolino, Jacksonville	J.C. Sulbaran, Northwest Arkansas	Chris Devenski, Lancaster	Ryan Merritt, Carolina	Jose Berrios, Fort Myers	Joe Mantiply, West Michigan	Luis Ysla, Augusta
Best Control	Liam Hendriks, Buffalo	Kyle Hendricks, Iowa	Casey Lawrence, New Hampshire	Dylan Floro, Montgomery	Alec Asher, Frisco	Seth Streich, Stockton	Christian Binford, Wilmington	Tim Shibuya, Fort Myers	Buck Farmer, West Michigan	James Dykstra, Kannapolis
Best Reliever	Juan Jaime, Gwinnett	Blake Parker, Iowa	Oliver Drake, Bowie	Shae Simmons, Mississippi	Cam Bedrosian, Arkansas	Enrique Burgos, Visalia	Mark Peterson, Wilmington	Arik Sikula, Dunedin	Silvino Bracho, South Bend	Akeel Morris, Savannah
Best Defensive Catcher	Christian Vazquez, Pawtucket	Juan Centeno, Las Vegas	Elias Diaz, Altoona	J.T. Realmuto, Jacksonville	Austin Hedges, San Antonio	Roberto Pena, Lancaster	Cam Gallagher, Wilmington	Justin O'Conner, Charlotte	Armando Araiza, Bowling Green	Reese McGuire, West Virginia
Best Defensive First Baseman	Jordan Lennerton, Toledo	Efren Navarro, Salt Lake	Christian Walker, Bowie	Nick Ramirez, Huntsville	Anthony Aliotti, Midland	Matt Olson, Stockton	Shawn Pleffner, Potomac	Patrick Leonard, Charlotte	Dominic Ficciello, West Michigan	Dominic Smith, Savannah
Best Defensive Second Baseman	Carlos Sanchez, Charlotte	Arismendy Alcantara, Iowa	Mookie Betts, Portland	Ryan Brett, Montgomery	Odubel Herrera, Frisco	Sherman Johnson, Inland Empire	Jose Peraza, Lynchburg	Breyvic Valera, Palm Beach	Kean Wong, Bowling Green	Wilmer Difo, Hagerstown
Best Defensive Third Baseman	Maikel Franco, Lehigh Valley	Kris Bryant, Iowa	Niuman Romero, Bowie	Jake Lamb, Mobile	Jayson Langfels, Tulsa	Brandon Drury, Visalia	Yandy Diaz, Carolina	Gustavo Pierre, Dunedin	Mitch Nay, Lansing	Cleuis Rondon, Kannapolis
Best Defensive Shortstop	Hernan Perez, Toledo	Nick Ahmed, Reno	Francisco Lindor, Akron	Sean Jamieson, Mobile	Alex Mejia, Springfield	Carlos Correa, Lancaster	Daniel Castro, Lynchburg	Jorge Polanco, Fort Myers	Andrew Velasquez, South Bend	Ryan McMahon, Asheville
Best Infield Arm	Maikel Franco, Lehigh Valley	Javier Baez, Iowa	Francisco Lindor, Akron	Kris Bryant, Tennessee	Jayson Langfels, Tulsa	Carlos Correa, Lancaster	Joey Gallo, Myrtle Beach	Niko Goodrum, Fort Myers	Willy Adames, West Michigan	Johan Camargo, Rome
Best Defensive Outfielder	Kevin Kiermaier, Durham	Matt Szczur, Iowa	Michael Taylor, Harrisburg	D'Vontrey Richardson, Huntsville	Lane Adams, Northwest Arkansas	Evan Marzilli, Visalia	Bubba Starling, Wilmington	Albert Almora, Daytona	Breland Almadova, South Bend	David Dahl, Asheville
Best Outfield Arm	Steven Souza, Syracuse	Jake Marisnick, New Orleans	Michael Taylor, Harrisburg	Jorge Soler, Tennessee	Drew Robinson, Frisco	Hunter Renfroe, Lake Elsinore	Bubba Starling, Wilmington	Aaron Judge, Tampa	Stryker Trahan, South Bend	Nomar Mazara, Hickory
Most Exciting Player	Gregory Polanco, Indianapolis	Joc Pederson, Albuquerque	Michael Taylor, Harrisburg	Kris Bryant, Tennessee	Lane Adams, Northwest Arkansas	Carlos Correa, Lancaster	Joey Gallo, Myrtle Beach	Dalton Pompey, Dunedin	Andrew Velasquez, South Bend	David Dahl, Asheville
Best Manager Prospect	Ron Johnson, Norfolk	Phil Nevin, Reno	Pedro Lopez, Binghamton	Andy Green, Mobile	Vance Wilson, Northwest Arkansas	Rodney Linares, Lancaster	Joe Mikulik, Myrtle Beach	Doug Mientkiewicz, Fort Myers	Mark Johnson, Kane County	Luis Rojas, Greensboro

BY VINCENT LARA-CINISOMO

Pawtucket and Durham have been frequent visitors to the International League playoffs in the past decade, but it was a late addition that decided the championship.

The Bulls were one strike from winning their fifth Governor's Cup since 1998—and beating Pawtucket for the second year in a row—when Cuban defector Rusney Castillo stepped to the plate. Castillo, who signed with the Red Sox in August and played with the PawSox in the playoffs, singled off Bulls closer Adam Liberatore to tie Game Four before Ivan DeJesus provided the game-winning homer in the 13th.

In Game Five, Castillo, 27, went 2-for-4 with a run and Pawtucket took its second Governor's Cup in three seasons with a 4-1 win. Pawtucket lost the Triple-A Championship to Omaha.

Keith Couch, a 24-year-old righthander making his Triple-A debut, blanked the Bulls on one hit over 6 ⅔ innings in the Governor's Cup finale.

"They always have good starters and a good bullpen," Durham manager Charlie Montoyo said.

And Couch isn't even among the top prospects the PawSox possessed for part of the season.

Catcher Blake Swihart, shortstop Deven Marrero and lefthanders Brian Johnson, Henry Owens and Eduardo Rodriguez all starred for the IL champs in the playoffs.

"We were fortunate to have guys here who not only contributed to our success, but also, I believe, can have an impact with Boston," Pawtucket first-year manager Kevin Boles said.

The Bulls didn't boast a similar stable of prospects. Center fielder Mikie Mahtook took a step forward by hitting .292/.362/.458 with an .820 OPS and 18 steals. Righthander Nate Karns, acquired from the Nationals for catcher Jose

Lobaton, was strong in the playoffs, when he struck out 12 against Columbus to help the Bulls advance to the IL finals.

The league's MVP was a story of redemption. A drug suspension in 2010 and a lousy 2011 caused Steven Souza's star to fall in the Nationals system. He entered 2013 as the Nats' No. 25 prospect, but he rebounded with a 1.022 OPS, which included winning the batting title at .350, and he was rewarded with a promotion to the major leagues.

Pawtucket righthander Anthony Ranaudo, who also made his major league debut in 2014, led the IL with 14 wins, flashing a plus fastball and solid-average curveball.

Charlotte, which played host to the Triple-A National Championship in its first season in new BB&T Ballpark in downtown Charlotte, drew 687,715—more than doubling the Knights' attendance from 2013, their last season in Fort Mill, S.C.

TOP 20 PROSPECTS

1. Gregory Polanco, of, Indianapolis (Pirates)
2. Mookie Betts, 2b/of, Pawtucket (Red Sox)
3. Francisco Lindor, ss, Columbus (Indians)
4. Maikel Franco, 3b/1b, Lehigh Valley (Phillies)
5. Steven Souza, of, Syracuse (Nationals)
6. Anthony Ranaudo, rhp, Pawtucket (Red Sox)
7. A.J .Cole, rhp, Syracuse (Nationals)
8. Alex Meyer, rhp, Rochester (Twins)
9. Robbie Ray, lhp, Toledo (Tigers)
10. Christian Bethancourt, c, Gwinnett (Braves)
11. Casey Sadler, rhp, Indianapolis (Pirates)
12. Giovanny Urshela, 3b, Columbus (Indians)
13. Rob Refsnyder, 2b/of, Scranton/WB (Yankees)
14. Micah Johnson, 2b, Charlotte (White Sox)
15. Alex Colome, rhp, Durham (Rays)
16. Christian Vazquez, c, Pawtucket (Red Sox)
17. Trevor May, rhp, Rochester (Twins)
18. Hernan Perez, ss/2b, Toledo (Tigers)
19. Allen Webster, rhp, Pawtucket (Red Sox)
20. Nick Kingham, rhp, Indianapolis (Pirates)

OVERALL STANDINGS

North Division	W	L	PCT	GB	Manager(s)	Attendance	Average	Last Pennant
Syracuse Chiefs (Nationals)	81	62	.556	—	Billy Gardner	247,046	3,743	1976
Pawtucket Red Sox (Red Sox)	79	65	.549	2 ½	Kevin Boles	515,665	7,367	2014
Buffalo Bisons (Blue Jays)	77	66	.538	4	Gary Allenson	535,275	8,110	2004
Rochester Red Wings (Twins)	77	67	.535	4 ½	Gene Glynn	422,454	6,401	1997
Scranton/Wilkes-Barre RailRiders (Yankees)	68	76	.472	13 ½	Dave Miley	401,618	5,906	2008
Lehigh Valley IronPigs (Phillies)	66	78	.458	15 ½	Dave Brundage	614,888	9,042	1995

South Division	W	L	PCT	GB	Manager(s)	Attendance	Average	Last Pennant
Durham Bulls (Rays)	75	69	.521	—	Charlie Montoyo	533,033	7,615	2013
Gwinnett Braves (Braves)	65	77	.458	9	Brian Snitker	303,959	4,281	2007
Norfolk Tides (Orioles)	65	79	.451	10	Ron Johnson	358,147	5,267	1985
Charlotte Knights (White Sox)	63	81	.438	12	Joel Skinner	687,715	9,686	1999

West Division	W	L	PCT	GB	Manager(s)	Attendance	Average	Last Pennant
Columbus Clippers (Indians)	79	65	.549	—	Chris Tremie	628,980	8,985	2010
Indianapolis Indians (Pirates)	73	71	.507	6	Dean Treanor	660,289	9,433	2000
Toledo Mud Hens (Tigers)	69	74	.483	9 ½	Larry Parrish	545,265	7,680	2006
Louisville Bats (Reds)	68	75	.476	10 ½	Jim Riggleman	567,256	7,990	2001

Semifinals: Pawtucket defeated Syracuse 3-0 and Durham defeated Columbus 3-1 in best-of-five series. **Finals:** Pawtucket defeated Durham 3-2 in a best-of-five series.

CLUB BATTING

	AVG	G	AB	R	H	2B	3B	HR	RBI	BB	SO	SB	OBP	SLG
Scranton/W-B	.273	144	4834	642	1318	254	43	113	591	438	1013	73	.337	.413
Gwinnett	.271	142	4788	607	1298	243	26	88	561	425	921	102	.334	.388
Norfolk	.269	144	4918	636	1322	227	30	79	587	469	1008	102	.333	.375
Syracuse	.268	143	4719	668	1265	256	34	116	624	515	991	113	.344	.410
Rochester	.266	144	4800	618	1278	299	26	89	581	414	1007	73	.327	.395
Charlotte	.261	144	4828	699	1261	259	29	176	657	511	1163	70	.336	.436
Columbus	.261	144	4783	672	1247	284	25	121	635	533	1041	82	.337	.406
Buffalo	.260	143	4726	609	1228	250	22	101	566	518	981	111	.335	.386
Indianapolis	.259	144	4784	645	1241	253	39	91	599	513	987	94	.335	.386
Louisville	.257	143	4836	586	1245	263	20	76	545	451	975	50	.323	.367
Pawtucket	.256	144	4835	639	1240	269	24	110	590	496	1154	66	.329	.390
Toledo	.253	143	4789	618	1211	259	29	131	567	464	1138	145	.323	.401
Lehigh Valley	.249	144	4726	556	1179	267	27	91	522	418	1084	77	.313	.375
Durham	.248	144	4755	573	1180	246	28	101	520	527	1198	87	.326	.375

CLUB PITCHING

	ERA	G	CG	SHO	SV	IP	H	R	ER	HR	BB	SO	AVG
Buffalo	3.52	143	2	6	35	1246	1157	540	488	105	438	1106	.246
Rochester	3.53	144	8	12	39	1244	1123	556	488	99	501	1141	.240
Durham	3.59	144	0	15	49	1267	1169	565	505	97	473	1220	.245
Pawtucket	3.60	144	4	11	40	1263	1135	557	505	92	518	1095	.241
Syracuse	3.63	143	6	15	37	1233	1230	554	498	91	373	928	.260
Columbus	3.71	144	7	11	39	1258	1187	578	519	135	410	1072	.250
Indianapolis	3.76	144	4	11	37	1262	1243	606	527	109	448	1020	.258
Toledo	3.90	143	2	14	31	1254	1284	593	543	91	443	910	.267
Scranton/W-B	4.27	144	2	10	35	1234	1324	666	585	104	508	1087	.274
Gwinnett	4.34	142	1	7	35	1232	1264	652	594	107	550	1064	.267
Lehigh Valley	4.42	144	5	9	40	1245	1295	677	611	104	482	969	.270
Norfolk	4.42	144	1	5	34	1272	1318	716	625	127	459	1088	.267
Louisville	4.68	143	3	6	42	1268	1408	741	659	92	538	927	.283
Charlotte	4.99	144	1	4	27	1247	1376	767	692	130	551	1034	.283

CLUB FIELDING

	PCT	PO	A	E	DP		PCT	PO	A	E	DP
Buffalo	.984	3738	1433	85	141	Rochester	.980	3734	1270	101	122
Lehigh Valley	.983	3736	1355	89	124	Charlotte	.979	3742	1507	110	151
Pawtucket	.983	3791	1373	88	124	Gwinnett	.979	3698	1319	110	148
Toledo	.983	3764	1480	92	141	Indianapolis	.978	3786	1463	117	125
Syracuse	.982	3700	1490	97	138	Scranton/W-B	.978	3702	1294	110	103
Columbus	.981	3774	1327	101	143	Louisville	.977	3805	1454	123	153
Durham	.980	3802	1349	106	118	Norfolk	.976	3817	1328	125	112

INDIVIDUAL BATTING LEADERS

Batter, Club	AVG	G	AB	R	H	HR	RBI
Souza Jr., Steven, Syracuse	.350	96	346	62	121	18	75
Gosselin, Phil, Gwinnett	.344	96	378	58	130	5	31
Pillar, Kevin, Buffalo	.323	100	405	57	131	10	59
Carrera, Ezequiel, Toledo	.307	97	374	68	115	6	41
Pirela, Jose, Scranton-WB	.305	130	535	87	163	10	60
Aguilar, Jesus, Columbus	.304	118	427	69	130	19	77
Laird, Brandon, Syracuse	.300	130	463	67	139	18	85
Burriss, Emmanuel, Syracuse	.300	116	444	80	133	6	46
McCann, James, Toledo	.295	109	417	49	123	7	54
Wilkins, Andy, Charlotte	.293	127	491	79	144	30	85

INDIVIDUAL PITCHING LEADERS

Pitcher, Club	W	L	ERA	IP	H	BB	SO
Ranaudo, Anthony, Pawtucket	14	4	2.61	138	112	54	111
Hill, Taylor, Syracuse	11	7	2.81	144	136	25	86
Sadler, Casey, Indianapolis	11	4	3.03	125	124	24	77
Webster, Allen, Pawtucket	4	4	3.10	122	107	44	100
Johnson, Kris, Rochester	10	7	3.48	132	115	55	102
Martin, Cody, Gwinnett	7	8	3.52	156	151	56	142
Meyer, Alex, Rochester	7	7	3.52	130	116	64	153
Darnell, Logan, Rochester	7	6	3.60	115	108	49	90
Jones, Chris, Norfolk	8	8	3.61	119.2	124	36	85
Laffey, Aaron, Syracuse	12	6	3.67	147	159	37	91

ALL-STAR TEAM

C: Josh Phegley, Charlotte. **1B:** Andy Wilkins, Charlotte. **2B:** Jose Pirela, Scranton/WB. **3B:** Brandon Laird, Syracuse. **SS:** Emmanuel Burriss, Louisville. **DH:** Mike Hessman, Toledo. **OF:** Ezequiel Carrera, Toledo. **OF:** Kevin Pillar, Buffalo; Steven Souza Jr., Syracuse. **IF:** Phil Gosselin, Gwinnett. **SP:** Anthony Ranaudo, Pawtucket. **RP:** Bobby Korecky, Buffalo. **Most Valuable Player:** Steven Souza Jr., Syracuse. **Most Valuable Pitcher:** Anthony Ranaudo, Pawtucket. **Rookie of the Year:** Steven Souza Jr., Syracuse. **Manager of the Year:** Charlie Montoyo, Durham.

DEPARTMENT LEADERS

BATTING

OBP	Souza Jr., Steven, Syracuse	.432
SLG	Souza Jr., Steven, Syracuse	.590
OPS	Souza Jr., Steven, Syracuse	1.022
R	Pirela, Jose, Scranton/Wilkes-Barre	87
H	Pirela, Jose, Scranton/Wilkes-Barre	163
TB	Wilkins, Andy, Charlotte	274
XBH	Wilkins, Andy, Charlotte	69
2B	Pillar, Kevin, Buffalo	39
3B	Pirela, Jose, Scranton/Wilkes-Barre	11
HR	Wilkins, Andy, Charlotte	30
RBI	Laird, Brandon, Syracuse	85
	Wilkins, Andy, Charlotte	85
SAC	Diaz, Jonathan, Buffalo	15
BB	Johnson, Dan, Buffalo	
HBP	Guez, Ben, Toledo	17
SO	Davidson, Matt, Charlottte	164
SB	Carrera, Ezequiel, Toledo	43
CS	Carrera, Ezequiel, Toledo	13
	d'Arnaud, Chase, Indianapolis	13
AB/SO	Burriss, Emmanuel, Syracuse	10.83

PITCHING

G	Dennick, Ryan, Louisville	57
GS	Wang, Chien-Ming, L-ville/Charlotte	28
GF	Korecky, Bobby, Buffalo	41
SV	Garcia, Luis, Lehigh Valley	22
	Korecky, Bobby, Buffalo	22
W	Ranaudo, Anthony, Pawtucket	14
L	Hankins, Derek, Toledo	14
	Wilk, Adam, Indianapolis	14
IP	Wang, Chien-Ming, L-ville/Char.	17
H	Wang, Chien-Ming, L-ville/Char.	200
R	Diamond, Scott, Rochester/L-ville	96
ER	Diamond, Scott, Rochester/L-ville	90
HB	Lincoln, Brad, Lehigh Valley	11
BB	Smith, Josh, Louisville	66
SO	Karns, Nate, Durham	153
	Meyer, Alex, Rochester	153
SO/9	Meyer, Alex, Rochester	10.57
SO/9(RP)	Zagurski, Mike, Columbus	12.31
BB/9	Hill, Taylor, Syracuse	1.56
WP	Montgomery, Mike, Durham	11
BK	Darnell, Logan, Rochester	4
HR	Cloyd, Tyler, Columbus	26
AVG	Ranaudo, Anthony, Pawtucket	.223

FIELDING

C	PCT	McCann, James, Toledo	0.993
	PO	Phegley, Josh, Charlotte	799
	A	Phegley, Josh, Charlotte	86
	DP	Ashley, Nevin, Indianapolis	8
	E	Ward, Brian, Norfolk	11
	PB	Ward, Brian, Norfolk	4
1B	PCT	Lennerton, Jordan, Toledo	1.000
	PO	Lennerton, Jordan, Toledo	1,058
	A	Lennerton, Jordan, Toledo	69
	DP	Lennerton, Jordan, Toledo	107
	E	Terdoslavich, Joey, Gwinnett	8
2B	PCT	Beresford, James, Rochester	.982
	PO	Beresford, James, Rochester	272
	A	Beresford, James, Rochester	325
	DP	Beresford, James, Rochester	85
	E	Beresford, James, Rochester	11
3B	PCT	Urshela, Giovanny, Columbus	.977
	PO	Franco, Maikel, Lehigh Valley	69
	A	Laird, Brandon, Syracuse	264
	DP	Laird, Brandon, Syracuse	28
	E	Romero, Deibinson, Rochester	21
SS	PCT	Perez, Hernan, Toledo	.970
	PO	Perez, Hernan, Toledo	175
	A	Perez, Hernan, Toledo	334
	DP	Burriss, Emmanuel, Syracuse	71
		Perez, Hernan, Toledo	71
	E	Burriss, Emmanuel, Syracuse	18
OF	PCT	Farris, Eric, Norfolk	1.000
	PO	Cunningham, Todd, Gwinnett	319
	A	Moncrief, Carlos, Columbus	22
	DP	Moncrief, Carlos, Columbus	6
	E	Collins, Tyler, Toledo	9

BY VINCENT LARA-CINISOMO

The Storm Chasers of Omaha will spend next season chasing history.

The Royals affiliate won its third Pacific Coast League title in four seasons by defeating the Reno Aces (Diamondbacks) 4-3 in the deciding Game Five.

Omaha became just the second team to win three titles in four years since 1963, when the PCL adopted a formal final round. Albuquerque won three in a row from 1980-82.

Omaha then went on to win the Triple-A National Championship, defeating Pawtucket 4-2 at the Charlotte Knights' BB&T Ballpark to repeat as the champ of that classification.

"It's been unbelievable," Omaha manager Brian Poldberg said. "The heart that they showed every day, the camaraderie, the chemistry. They show up and they have fun and they enjoy being around each other."

And the Storm Chasers did it without much help from top prospects. Omaha did not place a player among the league's Top 20 Prospects

In the PCL playoffs, Omaha did have the services of righthander Christian Binford, who started the Triple-A National Championship game, and Kyle Zimmer, who struck out four over two innings.

But the Storm Chasers during the season relied on the likes of Aaron Brooks, who pitched a two-hit shutout in Game Five over Reno, and leadoff man Whit Merrifield, who walked just 17 times but posted a .373 OPS thanks to .340 batting average.

Although the champs were not chockfull of prospects, the league was. Minor League Player

of the Year Kris Bryant spent half a season in Iowa (Cubs), but Joc Pederson (Dodgers) won the league's MVP after compiling the first 30-30 season in the modern history of the PCL and the first in the league since Frank Demaree pulled the feat in 1934.

Other hitting stars included Iowa's Javier Baez and Jorge Soler and Memphis' Oscar Taveras, each of whom went on to play in the majors.

Don't sell the pitchers short, either. Andrew Heaney, Noah Syndergaard and Jimmy Nelson were among the hurlers who had dominant stretches despite the often hitter-friendly climates and ballparks.

Lefthander Tim Cooney (Cardinals) led the PCL with 14 victories. The third-round pick from Wake Forest in 2012 lacks elite velocity but has pitchability and a No. 4-5 starter profile.

TOP 20 PROSPECTS

1. Kris Bryant, 3b, Iowa (Cubs)
2. Joc Pederson, of, Albuquerque (Dodgers)
3. Javier Baez, 2b, Iowa (Cubs)
4. Noah Syndergaard, rhp, Las Vegas (Mets)
5. Andrew Heaney, lhp, New Orleans (Marlins)
6. Oscar Taveras, of, Memphis (Cardinals)
7. Jon Singleton, 1b, Oklahoma City (Astros)
8. Jimmy Nelson, rhp, Nashville (Brewers)
9. Taijuan Walker, rhp, Tacoma (Mariners)
10. Arismendy Alcantara, ss/2b/of, Iowa (Cubs)
11. Rafael Montero, rhp, Las Vegas (Mets)
12. Andrew Susac, c, Fresno (Giants)
13. Tim Cooney, lhp, Memphis (Cardinals)
14. Stephen Piscotty, of, Memphis (Cardinals)
15. Kyle Hendricks, rhp, Iowa (Cubs)
16. Kevin Plawecki, c, Las Vegas (Mets)
17. Matt Wisler, rhp, El Paso (Padres)
18. Nick Ahmed, ss, Reno (Diamondbacks)
19. Mike Foltynewicz, rhp, Oklahoma City (Astros)
20. Luis Sardinas, ss, Round Rock (Rangers)

OVERALL STANDINGS

American Northern	W	L	PCT	GB	Manager(s)	Attendance	Average	Last Pennant
Omaha Storm Chasers (Royals)	76	67	.531	—	Brian Poldberg	393,946	5,628	2014
Iowa Cubs (Cubs)	74	70	.514	2 ½	Marty Pevey	492,060	7,029	Never
Oklahoma City RedHawks (Astros)	74	70	.514	2 ½	Ton Lawless; Tony DeFrancesco	429,190	6,045	1965
Colorado Springs Sky Sox (Rockies)	53	91	.368	23 ½	Glenallen Hill	350,374	5,078	1995

American Southern	W	L	PCT	GB	Manager(s)	Attendance	Average	Last pennant
Memphis Redbirds (Cardinals)	79	64	.552	—	Ron Warner	381,429	5,693	2009
Nashville Sounds (Brewers)	77	67	.535	2 ½	Rick Sweet	323,961	4,909	2005
New Orleans Zephyrs (Marlins)	70	74	.486	9 ½	Andy Haines	348,796	4,913	2001
Round Rock Express (Rangers)	70	74	.486	9 ½	Steve Buechele	595,700	8,390	Never

Pacific Northern	W	L	PCT	GB	Manager(s)	Attendance	Average	Last pennant
Reno Aces (Diamondbacks)	81	63	.563	—	Phil Nevin	379,439	5,270	2012
Sacramento River Cats (Athletics)	79	65	.549	2	Steve Scrasone	607,839	8,561	2008
Tacoma Rainiers (Mariners)	74	70	.514	7	Roy Howell	305,446	4,699	2010
Fresno Grizzlies (Giants)	68	76	.472	13	Bob Mariano	467,862	6,781	Never

Pacific Southern	W	L	PCT	GB	Manager(s)	Attendance	Average	Last pennant
Las Vegas 51s (Mets)	81	63	.563	—	Wally Backman	329,429	4,640	1998
El Paso Chihuahuas (Padres)	72	72	.500	9	Pat Murphy	560,997	7,901	Never
Albuquerque Isotopes (Dodgers)	62	80	.437	18	Damon Berryhill	564,625	8,066	1994
Salt Lake Bees (Angels)	60	84	.417	21	Keith Johnson	470,565	6,722	1979

Semifinals: Reno defeated Las Vegas 3-1 and Omaha defeated Memphis 3-1 in best-of-five series; **Finals:** Omaha defeated Reno 3-2 in a best-of-five series.

CLUB BATTING

	AVG	G	AB	R	H	2B	3B	HR	RBI	BB	SO	SB	OBP	SLG
Reno	.293	144	5059	790	1480	296	51	127	736	510	996	71	.359	.447
Salt Lake	.293	144	5037	788	1477	295	57	128	725	453	933	102	.355	.451
Omaha	.285	143	4927	711	1404	274	31	156	659	391	1097	147	.340	.448
Albuquerque	.283	142	4833	730	1369	270	46	169	688	490	1171	95	.353	.463
Las Vegas	.283	144	4985	880	1413	290	36	172	816	650	1115	76	.372	.460
Oklahoma City	.283	144	4901	722	1388	250	31	114	669	527	1037	127	.356	.417
Tacoma	.281	144	4931	727	1384	249	34	131	678	523	1091	107	.351	.425
El Paso	.279	144	4988	761	1392	300	38	145	717	510	1204	92	.349	.442
Sacramento	.274	144	4973	745	1363	273	24	83	696	628	1024	82	.359	.389
Memphis	.273	143	4757	712	1301	250	18	133	665	451	910	80	.346	.417
Fresno	.270	144	4939	708	1332	240	27	139	661	396	1165	132	.331	.414
Nashville	.266	144	4715	634	1252	257	35	130	595	384	1060	77	.325	.418
Colorado Springs	.265	144	4880	639	1294	281	35	110	594	422	1054	89	.325	.405
Round Rock	.265	144	4856	700	1285	253	36	148	659	416	1197	109	.327	.423
New Orleans	.260	144	4926	668	1282	245	24	151	633	435	1166	82	.325	.412
Iowa	.254	144	4762	644	1209	245	26	140	612	469	1280	135	.326	.404

CLUB PITCHING

	ERA	G	CG	SHO	SV	IP	H	R	ER	HR	BB	SO	AVG
Salt Lake Bees	5.78	144	3	4	33	1259	1523	885	809	154	533	1055	.302
Albuquerque Isotopes	5.50	142	3	6	35	1224	1466	828	749	145	468	976	.299
Colorado Springs Sky Sox	5.43	144	3	12	24	1252	1501	839	756	150	466	1055	.299
El Paso Chihuahuas	5.15	144	1	2	42	1273	1465	824	728	146	503	1013	.290
Round Rock Express	4.91	144	7	6	29	1247	1417	751	681	168	393	1135	.285
Las Vegas 51s	4.64	144	1	7	38	1274	1453	750	657	129	475	1172	.287
Tacoma Rainiers	4.63	144	2	7	40	1272	1325	728	654	151	495	1106	.268
Sacramento River Cats	4.60	144	1	5	40	1286	1361	735	658	144	465	1114	.274
New Orleans Zephyrs	4.51	144	2	9	36	1270	1324	724	637	127	542	1150	.269
Fresno Grizzlies	4.38	144	4	8	32	1269	1333	703	618	126	532	1103	.271
Reno Aces	4.36	144	2	8	40	1276	1342	687	618	121	537	1071	.272
Omaha Storm Chasers	4.27	143	1	7	38	1251	1247	665	594	149	475	1105	.260
Oklahoma City RedHawks	4.19	144	1	7	35	1270	1275	658	592	106	454	1089	.263
Memphis Redbirds	3.97	143	5	13	43	1234	1220	593	545	141	410	967	.259
Iowa Cubs	3.88	144	3	15	40	1255	1237	602	541	118	423	1153	.260
Nashville Sounds	3.85	144	1	11	39	1230	1136	587	526	101	484	1236	.245

CLUB FIELDING

	PCT	PO	A	E	DP		PCT	PO	A	E	DP
Memphis	.984	3704	1396	82	129	New Orleans	.980	3811	1371	107	118
Nashville	.980	3690	1405	102	99	Oklahoma City	.980	3811	1461	108	156
Iowa	.979	3767	1441	114	142	Omaha	.978	3755	1320	115	130
Albuquerque	.978	3674	1518	119	149	Reno	.980	3830	1667	111	151
Colorado Springs	.977	3756	1530	123	153	Round Rock	.982	3742	1433	97	135
Fresno	.977	3808	1442	125	148	Sacramento	.980	3859	1417	108	149
El Paso	.975	3819	1496	137	143	Salt Lake	.980	3778	1403	104	153
Las Vegas	.975	3823	1453	136	151	Tacoma	.977	3817	1335	122	104

INDIVIDUAL BATTING LEADERS

Batter, Club	AVG	G	AB	R	H	HR	RBI
Boesch, Brennan, Salt Lake	.332	95	374	68	124	25	85
Marte, Andy, Reno	.329	126	471	81	155	19	80
Pham, Tommy, Memphis	.324	104	346	63	112	10	44
Shuck, J.B., Salt Lake	.320	102	406	64	130	5	57
Robinson, Clint, Albuquerque	.312	119	429	77	134	18	80
Ahmed, Nick, Reno	.312	104	407	57	127	4	47
Velez, Eugenio, Nashville	.309	116	404	57	125	7	51
Giavotella, Johnny, Omaha	.308	114	441	66	136	7	61
Peterson, Shane, Sacramento	.308	137	543	101	167	11	90

INDIVIDUAL PITCHING LEADERS

Pitcher, Club	W	L	ERA	IP	H	BB	SO
Tropeano, Nick Oklahoma City	9	5	3.03	124.2	90	33	120
Heston, Chris, Fresno	12	9	3.38	173	152	51	125
Beeler, Dallas, Iowa	9	6	3.40	124.1	112	32	83
Cooney, Tim, Memphis	14	6	3.47	158	158	47	119
Jokisch, Eric, Iowa	9	10	3.58	158.1	155	31	143
Bennett, Jeff, Albuquerque	8	6	3.83	120	137	44	82
Brooks, Aaron, Omaha	12	3	3.88	139	151	25	97
Lamb, John, Omaha	8	10	3.97	138.1	137	68	131
Pries, Jordan, Tacoma	9	8	4.06	142	143	53	111
Flynn, Brian, New Orleans	8	10	4.06	139.2	169	50	104

ALL-STAR TEAM

C: Francisco Pena, Omaha. **1B:** Adam Duvall, Fresno. **2B:** Arismendy Alcantara, Iowa. **3B:** Andy Marte, Reno. **SS:** Nick Ahmed, Reno. **CF:** Matt den Dekker, Las Vegas. **DH:** Brennan Boesch, Salt Lake. **OF:** Shane Peterson, Sacramento. **P:** Jimmy Nelson, Nashville. **P:** Tsuyoshi Wada, Iowa. **RP:** Blake Parker, Iowa.

Most Valuable Player: Joc Pederson, Albuquerque. **Pitcher of the Year:** Jimmy Nelson, Nashville. **Rookie of the Year:** Joc Pederson, Albuquerque. **Manager of the Year:** Wally Backman, Las Vegas.

DEPARTMENT LEADERS

BATTING

OBP	Pederson, Joc, Albuquerque	.435
SLG	Boesch, Brennan, Salt Lake	.636
OPS	Boesch, Brennan, Salt Lake	1.017
R	Pederson, Joc, Albuquerque	106
H	Peterson, Shane, Sacramento	167
TB	Hoying, Jared, Round Rock	263
XBH	Hoying, Jared, Round Rock	66
2B	Peterson, Shane, Sacramento	40
3B	Alcantara, Arismendy, Iowa	11
HR	Pederson, Joc, Albuquerque	33
RBI	Jacobs, Mike, Reno	97
SAC	Torreyes, Ronald, Oklahoma City	21
BB	Pederson, Joc, Albuquerque	100
HBP	Puello, Cesar, Las Vegas	21
SO	Fields, Matt, Omaha	156
SB	Wates, Austin, OKC/New Orleans	37
CS	Brown, Gary, Fresno	20
AB/SO	Torreyes, Ronald, Oklahoma City	17.69

PITCHING

G	Leach, Brent, Nashville	59
GS	Heston, Chris, Fresno	28
GF	Patton, Spencer, Omaha/R. Rock	40
SV	Parker, Blake, Iowa	25
W	Cooney, Tim, Memphis	14
L	Germano, Justin, Round Rock	14
IP	Heston, Chris, Fresno	173
H	Verrett, Logan, Las Vegas	188
R	Schultz, Bo, Reno	109
ER	Schultz, Bo, Reno	93
HB	Jungmann, Taylor, Nashville	12
	McGregor, Scott, Memphis	12
BB	Harrell, Lucas, Reno	77
SO	Syndergaard, Noah, Las Vegas	145
SO/9	Pena, Ariel, Nashville	9.82
SO/9(RP)	Scribner, Evan, Sacramento	13.79
BB/9	Neal, Zach, Sacramento	1.21
WP	Evans, Bryan, New Orleans	15
BK	Foltynewicz, Michael, Okla. City	4
HR	Germano, Justin, Round Rock	26
	Grube, Jarrett, Salt Lake	26
AVG	Tropeano, Nick, Oklahoma City	.202

FIELDING

C	PCT	Marte, Andy, Reno	.956
	PO	Marte, Andy, Reno	67
	A	Pena, Francisco, Omaha	60
	DP	Wilson, Bobby, Reno	9
	E	Perez, Carlos, Oklahoma City	12
	PB	Perez, Carlos, Oklahoma City	8
1B	PCT	Jacobs, Mike, Reno	.995
	PO	Scruggs, Xavier, Memphis	1.063
	A	Decker, Cody, El Paso	71
	DP	Scruggs, Xavier, Memphis	106
	E	Fields, Matt, Omaha	12
2B	PCT	Lindsey, Taylor, Salt Lake/El Paso	.967
	PO	Garcia, Greg, Memphis	209
	A	Nina, Angelys, Colorado Springs	261
	DP	Nina, Angelys, Colorado Springs	71
	E	Lindsey, Taylor, Salt Lake/El Paso	15
3B	PCT	Marte, Andy, Reno	.956
	PO	Marte, Andy, Reno	67
	A	Marte, Andy, Reno	236
	DP	Jimenez, Luis, Salt Lake	25
	E	Marte, Andy, Reno	14
SS	PCT	Kozma, Pete, Memphis	.977
	PO	Diaz, Juan, New Orleans	156
	A	Diaz, Juan, New Orleans	325
	DP	Diaz, Juan, New Orleans	70
	E	Diaz, Juan, New Orleans	20
OF	PCT	Hoying, Jared, Round Rock	.997
	PO	Orlando, Paulo, Omaha	329
	A	Brown, Gary, Fresno	13
	DP	Orlando, Paulo, Omaha	4
	E	Peguero, Carlos, Omaha	8
		Puello, Cesar, Las Vegas	8

MINOR LEAGUES

BY JOSH NORRIS

In the regular season, the Eastern League belonged to the Portland Sea Dogs. After the season, the Eastern League belonged to the Binghamton Mets.

Prospect-packed Portland opened the year in a fashion that served as a near-perfect epitome for their first half: Lefthander Henry Owens spun a rain-shortened no-hitter against the Reading Fightin Phils, and second baseman Mookie Betts led off the game with a home run.

Owens finished his stint in Portland with marks of 14-4, 2.60 and took home the league's pitcher of the year honors. Betts blitzed through the EL, then did the same in the International League with Triple-A Pawtucket, and finished the year in center field in Fenway Park as part of a complicating but tantalizing group of young outfielders in Boston.

Owens and Betts were just the beginning of Portland's riches. Owens was beaten out for the league's ERA title by another lefthander, Brian Johnson, who finished his turn with the Sea Dogs with a 1.75 mark. The staff added a third talented southpaw, Eduardo Rodriguez, who has arguably the best stuff of the trio, in a deadline deal that sent lefty Andrew Miller to the Orioles.

Betts was surrounded in the lineup by even more talented prospects, including athletic switch-hitting catcher Blake Swihart, superlative defensive shortstop Deven Marrero and sneaky powerful infielder Sean Coyle.

Of course, when prospects perform, as everybody in the Sea Dogs' enviable group did, they get promoted. So by the time the playoffs rolled around, they were noticeably depleted. It also didn't help that they ran into the Binghamton Mets, who had recently gained talented outfielder Brandon Nimmo and electric lefthander Steven Matz, in the first round of the playoffs.

Behind a walk-off bomb from T.J. Rivera in the opener and a .364 average throughout the series from Nimmo, Binghamton rallied from a 2-1 deficit and take the series in five games.

They met the Richmond Flying Squirrels—who had knocked off Akron in the opening round—in the championship series, and quickly built on the momentum they'd established in the previous round. After establishing a quick 2-0 edge in the series, they finished the sweep with a little bit of drama. Tied 1-1 in the ninth, pinch-hitter Jayce Boyd doubled off of reliever Steven Okert to send home pinch-runner Gavin Cecchini with the run that won the game and delivered Binghamton its first championship since 1994.

Erie outfielder Steven Moya, who led the EL with 35 homers, doubled 33 times and stole 16 bases in 20 tries, was named the league's MVP. Harrisburg outfielder Michael Taylor, who took four categories in our annual Best Tools survey, was the league's rookie of the year.

TOP 20 PROSPECTS

1. Michael Taylor, of, Harrisburg (Nationals)
2. Mookie Betts, 2b/of, Portland (Red Sox)
3. Francisco Lindor, ss, Akron (Indians)
4. Steve Matz, lhp, Binghamton (Mets)
5. Aaron Sanchez, rhp, New Hampshire (Blue Jays)
6. Henry Owens, lhp, Portland (Red Sox)
7. Eduardo Rodriguez, lhp, Bowie/Portland, (Orioles/Red Sox)
8. Blake Swihart, c, Portland (Red Sox)
9. Brian Johnson, lhp, Portland (Red Sox)
10. Elias Diaz, c, Altoona (Pirates)
11. Gary Sanchez, c, Trenton (Yankees)
12. Dilson Herrera, 2b/ss, Binghamton (Mets)
13. Rob Refsnyder, 2b, Trenton (Yankees)
14. Kevin Plawecki, c, Binghamton (Mets)
15. A.J. Cole, rhp, Harrisburg (Nationals)
16. Kennys Vargas, 1b, New Britain (Twins)
17. Willy Garcia, of, Altoona (Pirates)
18. Steven Moya, of, Erie (Tigers)
19. Deven Marrero, ss, Portland (Red Sox)
20. Nick Kingham, rhp, Altoona (Pirates)

OVERALL STANDINGS

Eastern Division	W	L	PCT	GB	Manager(s)	Attendance	Average	Last Pennant
Portland Sea Dogs (Red Sox)	88	54	.620	—	Billy McMillon	359,427	5,530	2006
Binghamton Mets (Mets)	83	59	.585	5	Pedro Lopez	171,279	2,676	1994
New Britain Rock Cats (Twins)	73	69	.514	15	Jeff Smith	302,865	4,454	2001
Trenton Thunder (Yankees)	67	75	.472	21	Tony Franklin	361,369	5,090	2013
New Hampshire Fisher Cats (Blue Jays)	66	76	.465	22	Bobby Meacham	340,299	5,156	2011
Reading Fightin Phils (Phillies)	66	76	.465	22	Dusty Wathan	394,458	5,801	2001

Western Division	W	L	PCT	GB	Manager(s)	Attendance	Average	Last Pennant
Richmond Flying Squirrels (Giants)	79	63	.556	—	Russ Morman	418,147	6,336	2014
Akron RubberDucks (Indians)	73	69	.514	6	Dave Wallace	350,704	5,157	2012
Bowie Baysox (Orioles)	72	70	.507	7	Gary Kendall	248,630	3,603	Never
Erie SeaWolves (Tigers)	71	71	.500	8	Lance Parrish	209,299	3,124	Never
Altoona Curve (Pirates)	61	81	.430	18	Carlos Garcia	275,823	4,117	2010
Harrisburg Senators (Nationals)	53	89	.373	26	Brian Daubach	273,645	4,146	1999

Semifinals: Richmond defeated Akron 3-1 and Binghamton defeated Portland 3-2 in best-of-five series; **Finals:** Binghamton defeated Richmond 3-0 in a best-of-five series.

CLUB BATTING

	AVG	G	AB	R	H	2B	3B	HR	RBI	BB	SO	SB	OBP	SLG
Binghamton	.278	142	4699	718	1304	273	23	122	668	492	1005	77	.353	.423
Bowie	.275	142	4841	652	1330	268	21	109	600	411	839	46	.333	.406
Erie	.273	142	4771	655	1301	278	27	113	604	408	907	117	.332	.413
Portland	.268	142	4611	658	1234	256	30	105	613	461	1010	108	.341	.404
Altoona	.265	142	4672	632	1236	231	43	124	575	457	1155	159	.333	.412
Akron	.261	142	4744	604	1239	234	39	74	557	436	1020	114	.325	.374
Richmond	.256	142	4691	586	1200	207	37	74	525	453	1068	168	.329	.363
Trenton	.256	142	4813	607	1232	252	37	99	564	441	927	75	.323	.385
New Britain	.254	142	4658	599	1182	283	24	100	564	402	1032	98	.319	.389
Reading	.250	142	4705	558	1178	222	27	103	518	367	944	80	.313	.375
Harrisburg	.248	142	4729	580	1171	203	21	113	538	491	1165	145	.320	.371
New Hampshire	.245	142	4731	571	1159	236	36	114	529	352	996	125	.302	.382

CLUB PITCHING

	ERA	G	CG	SHO	SV	IP	H	R	ER	HR	BB	SO	AVG
Portland	3.41	142	9	14	38	1216	1176	512	461	80	362	992	.254
Richmond	3.60	142	3	11	42	1238	1161	546	496	76	458	1003	.250
New Hampshire	3.73	142	4	10	43	1249	1193	599	518	106	414	1046	.252
Trenton	3.84	142	1	9	36	1255	1176	601	535	83	476	1093	.248
Binghamton	3.86	142	7	12	34	1214	1202	585	520	95	359	1106	.257
New Britain	3.89	142	7	9	38	1216	1240	603	526	96	351	1071	.263
Akron	3.98	142	1	9	44	1237	1217	605	547	122	405	945	.259
Altoona	4.00	142	4	6	32	1225	1263	641	545	88	482	836	.267
Bowie	4.09	142	1	7	43	1241	1244	638	564	107	468	1092	.262
Reading	4.21	142	3	8	37	1235	1201	654	578	136	513	946	.256
Harrisburg	4.63	142	2	9	25	1237	1375	735	637	120	415	963	.281
Erie	4.71	142	4	7	36	1224	1318	701	641	141	468	975	.276

CLUB Fielding

	PCT	PO	A	E	DP		PCT	PO	A	E	DP
Akron	.982	3712	1479	95	140	New Britain	.977	3650	1238	114	115
Portland	.982	3649	1416	94	114	New Hampshire	.977	3748	1574	124	130
Binghamton	.980	3642	1243	100	97	Harrisburg	.976	3713	1287	125	117
Bowie	.979	3724	1467	112	125	Trenton	.976	3765	1506	132	119
Richmond	.979	3716	1494	112	150	Reading	.974	3706	1455	140	148
Erie	.978	3674	1322	113	111	Altoona	.971	3676	1597	158	133

INDIVIDUAL BATTING LEADERS

Batter, Club	AVG	G	AB	R	H	HR	RBI
Duffy, Matt, Richmond	.332	97	367	53	122	3	62
Romero, Niuman, Bowie	.320	130	482	86	154	5	48
Taylor, Michael, Harrisburg	.313	98	384	74	120	22	61
Green, Dean, Erie	.311	113	409	51	127	10	65
Jones, Corey, Erie	.304	113	415	42	126	5	42
Walker, Christian, Bowie	.301	95	366	58	110	20	77
Travis, Devon, Erie	.298	100	396	68	118	10	52
Coyle, Sean, Portland	.295	96	336	60	99	16	61
Krizan, Jason, Erie	.293	124	464	68	136	7	56
Boyd, Jayce, Binghamton	.293	119	413	60	121	8	59

INDIVIDUAL PITCHING LEADERS

Pitcher, Club	W	L	ERA	IP	H	BB	SO
Johnson, Brian, Portland	10	2	1.75	118	78	32	99
Sampson, Adrian, Altoona	10	5	2.55	148	125	30	99
Owens, Henry, Portland	14	4	2.60	121	89	47	126
Peavey, Greg, Binghamton	11	3	2.90	115	93	26	99
Blach, Ty, Richmond	8	8	3.13	141	142	39	91
Rogers, Taylor, New Britain	11	6	3.29	145	150	37	113
Colon, Joseph, Akron	8	7	3.39	138	132	55	96
Berry, Tim, Bowie	6	7	3.51	133	122	45	108
Snodgrass, Jack, Richmond	11	6	3.56	131	130	41	86
Rodriguez, Eduardo, Portland/Bowie	6	8	3.60	120	120	37	108

ALL-STAR TEAM

C: Elias Diaz, Altoona. **1B:** Christian Walker, Bowie. **2B:** Devon Travis, Erie. **3B:** Niuman Romero, Bowie. **SS:** Matt Duffy, Richmond. **CF:** Michael Taylor, Harrisburg. **DH:** Reynaldo Rodriguez, New Britain. **OF:** Dariel Alvarez, Bowie. **OF:** Steven Moya, Erie. **IF:** Brian Burgamy, Binghamton. **P:** Henry Owens, Portland. **SP:** Adrian Sampson, Altoona. **RP:** Oliver Drake, Bowie. **Most Valuable Player:** Steven Moya, Erie. **Manager of the Year:** Billy McMillon, Portland. **Rookie of the Year:** Michael Taylor, Harrisburg. **Pitcher of the Year:** Henry Owens, Portland.

DEPARTMENT LEADERS

BATTING

OBP	Romero, Niuman, Bowie	.417
SLG	Moya, Steven, Erie	.555
OPS	Taylor, Michael, Harrisburg	.935
R	Romero, Niuman, Bowie	86
H	Romero, Niuman, Bowie	154
TB	Moya, Steven, Erie	286
XBH	Moya, Steven, Erie	71
2B	Rodriguez, Reynaldo, New Britain	36
3B	Hanson, Alen, Altoona	12
HR	Moya, Steven, Erie	35
RBI	Moya, Steven, Erie	105
SAC	Albernaz, Craig, Erie	13
BB	Romero, Niuman, Bowie	84
HBP	Segedin, Rob, Trenton	13
SO	Moya, Steven, Erie	161
SB	Tomlinson, Kelby, Richmond	49
CS	Maggi, Drew, Altoona	19
AB/SO	Cabrera, Ramon, Erie/Altoona	10.23

PITCHING

G	Quirarte, Edwin, Richmond	51
GS	Gonzalez, Severino, Reading	27
	Roberts, Will, Akron	27
	Saupold, Warwick, Erie	27
GF	Drake, Oliver, Bowie	47
SV	Drake, Oliver, Bowie	31
W	Owens, Henry, Portland	14
L	Gonzalez, Severino, Reading	13
IP	Roberts, Will, Akron	161
H	Dean, Pat, New Britain	192
R	Saupold, Warwick, Erie	92
ER	Ferrell, Jeff, Erie	85
HB	Espino, Paolo, Harrisburg	11
BB	Saupold, Warwick, Erie	65
SO	Owens, Henry, Portland	126
SO/9	Owens, Henry, Portland	9.37
SO/9(RP)	Leathersich, Jack, Binghamton	15.46
BB/9	Augliera, Mike, Portland	1.22
WP	Saupold, Warwick, Erie	16
BK	Rodriguez, Eduardo, Bowie/Portland	5
HR	Milner, Hoby, Reading	25
AVG	Johnson, Brian, Portland	.189

FIELDING

C	PCT	Knudson, Kyle, New Britain	.995
	PO	Sanchez, Gary, Trenton	737
	A	Sanchez, Gary, Trenton	94
	DP	Sanchez, Gary, Trenton	8
	E	Sanchez, Gary, Trenton	17
	PB	Ohlman, Mike, Bowie	10
		Sanchez, Gary, Trenton	10
1B	PCT	Stassi, Brock, Reading	.993
	PO	Allie, Stetson, Altoona	946
	A	Westlake, Aaron, Erie	76
	DP	Stassi, Brock, Reading	112
	E	Allie, Stetson, Altoona	9
		Hobson, K.C., New Hampshire	9
		Walker, Christian, Bowie	9
		Westlake, Aaron, Erie	9
2B	PCT	Travis, Devon, Erie	.974
	PO	Travis, Devon, Erie	183
	A	Wendle, Joe, Akron	280
	DP	Wendle, Joe, Akron	73
	E	Berti, Jon, New Hampshire	14
3B	PCT	Cunningham, Jarek, Altoona	.899
	PO	Waring, Brandon, New Britain	56
	A	Burns, Andy, New Hampshire	200
	DP	Romero, Niuman, Bowie	22
	E	Cunningham, Jarek, Altoona	25
SS	PCT	Castillo, Ali, Trenton	.973
	PO	Machado, Dixon, Erie	164
	A	Martinson, Jason, Harrisburg	316
	DP	Duran, Edgar, Reading	70
	E	Hanson, Alen, Altoona	29
OF	PCT	Wilkerson, Shannon, Portland	.996
	PO	Broxton, Keon, Altoona	300
	A	Garcia, Willy, Altoona	19
	DP	Altherr, Aaron, Reading	4
		Alvarez, Dariel, Bowie	4
		Taylor, Michael, Harrisburg	4
	E	Garcia, Willy, Altoona	13

MINOR LEAGUES

BY MATT EDDY

Though Tennessee finished under .500 in both halves of the season and did not qualify for the playoffs, the Cubs affiliate had the best collection of prospects in the league, bar none.

Third baseman Kris Bryant led the SL in average (.355), home runs (22), RBIs (58) and nearly every other category prior to his promotion to Triple-A in June. Acquired by the Cubs in early July, Addison Russell hit with more authority (.872 OPS) than any other shortstop in the league.

Center fielder Albert Almora, like Russell a 2012 first-rounder out of high school, joined the Smokies in August, playing plus defense but not hitting much. Plagued by hamstring trouble, right fielder Jorge Soler still managed 16 extra-base hits in 22 games at Tennessee but didn't play enough to qualify for either the Southern or Pacific Coast league prospect lists as he rocketed to Chicago.

Tennessee's rotation featured righthanders C.J. Edwards, Pierce Johnson and Corey Black. Edwards had one of the best arms in the league (a strikeout per inning) but missed three months with a shoulder injury, Johnson recovered from an injury-plagued first half to log a 1.80 ERA in the final two months, while Black handed out too many free passes but demonstrated power stuff.

League champion Jacksonville won six of seven playoff games, sweeping Chattanooga in the finals, with a roster packed with Marlins prospects, especially on the pitching staff and at the up-the-middle positions. Lefthander Justin Nicolino and righty Jose Urena went a combined 3-0 in four playoff starts. Catcher J.T. Realmuto had a breakthrough season, hitting .299/.369/.461 in 97 games. Shortstop Austin Nola and second baseman Austin Barnes also have big league potential.

The quality of SL pitching prospects did not compare favorably with 2013. Top righties such as Pensacola's Robert Stephenson, Edwards and Mobile's Archie Bradley pitched ineffectively for long stretches or spent significant time on the disabled list (or both). Picking up the slack was a quintet of college righthanders from the 2013 draft

who zoomed to Double-A. Mobile's Aaron Blair and Pensacola's Michael Lorenzen and Ben Lively made the Top 20, while Mississippi's Jason Hursh just missed the cut. First-rounder Braden Shipley (Mobile) might have had the best arm in the league but pitched just 20 innings.

MVP Jake Lamb powered the Mobile offense through July, when he turned over third base to fellow hard-hitting prospect Brandon Drury. Shortstop Sean Jamieson and center fielder Evan Marzilli contributed on both sides of the ball.

TOP 20 PROSPECTS

1. Kris Bryant, 3b, Tennessee (Cubs)
2. Addison Russell, ss, Tennessee (Cubs)
3. Corey Seager, ss, Chattanooga (Dodgers)
4. Robert Stephenson, rhp, Pensacola (Reds)
5. C.J. Edwards, rhp, Tennessee (Cubs)
6. Jose Peraza, 2b, Mississippi (Braves)
7. J.T. Realmuto, c, Jacksonville (Marlins)
8. D.J. Peterson, 1b/3b, Jackson (Mariners)
9. Jake Lamb, 3b, Mobile (Diamondbacks)
10. Archie Bradley, rhp, Mobile (Diamondbacks)
11. Aaron Blair, rhp, Mobile (Diamondbacks)
12. Michael Lorenzen, rhp, Pensacola (Reds)
13. Andrew Heaney, lhp, Jacksonville (Marlins)
14. Chris Reed, lhp, Chattanooga (Dodgers)
15. Ketel Marte, ss/2b, Jackson (Mariners)
16. Micah Johnson, 2b, Birmingham (White Sox)
17. Scott Schebler, of, Chattanooga (Dodgers)s
18. Albert Almora, of, Tennessee (Cubs)
19. Justin Nicolino, lhp, Jacksonville (Marlins)
20. Ben Lively, rhp, Pensacola (Reds)

STANDINGS: SPLIT SEASON

FIRST HALF

NORTH	W	L	PCT	GB
Huntsville	46	24	.657	—
Tennessee	33	36	.478	12 ½
Jackson	31	38	.449	14 ½
Birmingham	29	41	.414	17
Chattanooga	26	44	.371	20

SOUTH	W	L	PCT	GB
Mobile	42	27	.609	—
Mississippi	39	30	.565	3
Jacksonville	36	34	.514	6 ½
Montgomery	35	35	.500	7 ½
Pensacola	31	39	.443	11 ½

SECOND HALF

NORTH	W	L	PCT	GB
Chattanooga	35	33	.515	—
Tennessee	33	37	.471	3
Jackson	32	38	.457	4
Birmingham	31	39	.443	5
Huntsville	31	39	.443	5

SOUTH	W	L	PCT	GB
Jacksonville	45	25	.643	—
Mississippi	44	26	.629	1
Mobile	37	31	.544	5
Montgomery	31	39	.443	14
Pensacola	29	41	.414	16

Playoffs—Semifinals: Jacksonville defeated Mobile 3-1 and Chattanooga defeated Huntsville 3-2 in best-of-five series.
Finals: Jacksonville defeated Chattanooga 3-0 in a best-of-five series.

OVERALL STANDINGS

Team (Organization)	W	L	PCT	GB	Manager(s)	Attendance	Average	Last pennant
Mississippi Braves (Braves)	83	56	.597	—	Aaron Holbert	211,200	3,152	2008
Jacksonville Suns (Marlins)	81	59	.579	2 ½	Andy Barkett	300,538	4,624	2014
Mobile BayBears Diamondbacks	79	58	.577	3	Andy Green	106,297	1,687	2012
Huntsville Stars (Brewers)	77	63	.550	6 ½	Carlos Subero	94,929	1,460	2001
Tennessee Smokies (Cubs)	66	73	.475	17	Buddy Bailey	283,038	4,102	2004
Montgomery Biscuits (Rays)	66	74	.471	17 ½	Brady Williams	244,534	3,821	2007
Jackson Generals (Mariners)	63	76	.453	20	Jim Horner	244,534	3,821	2000
Chattanooga Lookouts (Dodgers)	61	77	.442	21 ½	Razor Shines	242,627	3,516	1998
Birmingham Barons (White Sox)	60	80	.429	23 ½	Julio Vinas	437,612	6,252	2013
Pensacola Blue Wahoos (Reds)	60	80	.429	23 ½	Delino DeShields	311,687	4,453	Never

CLUB BATTING

	AVG	G	AB	R	H	2B	3B	HR	RBI	BB	SO	SB	OBP	SLG
Mississippi	.266	139	4620	609	1228	238	40	63	551	428	920	141	.336	.376
Jackson	.261	139	4641	603	1210	251	48	92	564	430	894	109	.329	.395
Birmingham	.259	140	4702	604	1216	260	42	96	560	441	966	106	.327	.393
Mobile	.258	137	4550	610	1175	242	37	97	572	456	1064	56	.331	.392
Chattanooga	.257	138	4647	608	1192	256	60	108	575	431	1013	78	.326	.407
Tennessee	.254	139	4669	605	1185	249	25	100	566	463	958	83	.327	.382
Pensacola	.251	140	4628	569	1163	228	30	101	529	437	1032	55	.319	.379
Huntsville	.248	140	4511	609	1118	214	32	83	555	562	952	116	.335	.365
Jacksonville	.246	140	4623	618	1135	221	35	76	572	546	1026	98	.331	.358
Montgomery	.246	140	4597	566	1131	239	28	101	528	471	997	102	.324	.376

CLUB PITCHING

	ERA	G	CG	SHO	SV	IP	H	R	ER	HR	BB	SO	AVG
Mobile	3.30	137	2	8	40	1209	1084	502	443	72	497	1020	.243
Mississippi	3.37	139	3	16	42	1223	1117	513	458	70	381	1043	.244
Huntsville	3.57	140	1	11	36	1224	1138	556	485	110	427	969	.248
Jacksonville	3.58	140	3	16	40	1233	1228	576	491	97	307	872	.260
Tennessee	3.93	139	0	11	31	1219	1058	610	532	99	597	1026	.237
Montgomery	3.99	140	5	10	35	1219	1304	630	540	80	383	985	.275
Pensacola	3.99	140	3	6	34	1219	1139	619	540	106	548	1087	.249
Chattanooga	4.06	138	3	11	27	1226	1200	667	553	88	580	987	.256
Jackson	4.15	139	2	9	33	1215	1210	640	561	102	434	959	.261
Birmingham	4.52	140	4	7	26	1229	1275	688	617	93	511	874	.269

CLUB FIELDING

	PCT	PO	A	E	DP		PCT	PO	A	E	DP
Mobile	.982	3628	1469	91	139	Jackson	.975	3646	1342	128	136
Mississippi	.981	3670	1378	98	114	Jacksonville	.975	3699	1454	133	131
Tennessee	.978	3659	1483	117	126	Pensacola	.975	3657	1328	130	126
Birmingham	.977	3688	1384	121	134	Montgomery	.972	3658	1394	143	145
Huntsville	.976	3672	1524	130	143	Chattanooga	.965	3678	1428	186	120

INDIVIDUAL BATTING LEADERS

Batter, Club	AVG	G	AB	R	H	HR	RBI
Lamb, Jake, Mobile	.318	103	374	60	119	14	79
Ravelo, Rangel, Birmingham	.309	133	476	72	147	11	66
Belza, Tom, Mobile	.305	123	413	56	126	1	31
Brett, Ryan, Montgomery	.303	107	422	64	128	8	38
Marte, Ketel, Jackson	.302	109	443	63	134	2	46
Mayora, Daniel, Chattanooga	.302	131	493	69	149	9	75
Kivlehan, Patrick, Jackson	.300	104	377	60	113	11	68
Realmuto, J.T., Jacksonville	.299	97	375	66	112	8	62
Kubitza, Kyle, Mississippi	.295	132	440	76	130	8	55
Hunter, Cedric, Mississippi	.295	120	400	60	118	14	72

INDIVIDUAL PITCHING LEADERS

Pitcher, Club	W	L	ERA	IP	H	BB	SO
Nicolino, Justin, Jacksonville	14	4	2.85	170	162	20	81
Perez, Williams, Mississippi	7	6	2.91	133	119	39	94
Lorenzen, Michael, Pensacola	4	6	3.13	121	112	44	84
Moscot, Jon, Pensacola	7	10	3.13	149	145	43	111
Reed, Chris, Chattanooga	4	8	3.22	137	114	55	116
Urena, Jose, Jacksonville	13	8	3.33	162	155	29	121
Beck, Chris, Birmingham	5	8	3.39	117	116	31	57
Schugel, A.J., Mobile	6	4	3.47	148	142	50	117
Black, Corey, Tennessee	6	7	3.47	124	100	71	119
Floro, Dylan, Montgomery	11	13	3.48	179	209	24	112

ALL-STAR TEAM

C: J.T. Realmuto, Jacksonville. **1B:** Rangel Ravelo, Birmingham. **2B:** Ryan Brett, Montgomery. **3B:** Jake Lamb, Mobile. **SS:** Ketel Marte, Jackson. **LF:** Josh Prince, Huntsville. **DH:** Nick Ramirez, Huntsville. **OF:** Cedric Hunter, Mississippi; Scott Schebler, Chattanooga; Taylor Motter, Montgomery; Tom Belza, Mobile. **IF:** Patrick Kivlehan, Jackson. **P:** Justin Nicolino, Jacksonville. **P:** Williams Perez, Mississippi. **RP:** David Goforth, Huntsville.
Most Valuable Player: Jake Lamb, Mobile. **Most Outstanding Pitcher:** Justin Nicolino, Jacksonville. **Manager of the Year:** Andy Green, Mobile.

DEPARTMENT LEADERS

BATTING

OBP	Kubitza, Kyle, Mississippi	.405
SLG	Schebler, Scott, Chattanooga	.556
OPS	Lamb, Jake, Mobile	.949
R	Sweeney, Darnell, Chattanooga	88
H	Mayora, Daniel, Chattanooga	149
TB	Schebler, Scott, Chattanooga	272
XBH	Schebler, Scott, Chattanooga	65
2B	Ravelo, Rangel, Birmingham	37
3B	Schebler, Scott, Chattanooga	14
HR	Schebler, Scott, Chattanooga	28
RBI	Ramirez, Nick, Huntsville	82
SAC	Cuevas, Noel, Chattanooga	12
BB	Kubitza, Kyle, Mississippi	77
	Nola, Austin, Jacksonville	77
	Sweeney, Darnell, Chattanooga	77
HBP	Schebler, Scott, Chattanooga	22
SO	Ramirez, Nick, Huntsville	152
SB	Prince, Josh, Huntsville	37
CS	Sweeney, Darnell, Chattanooga	16
AB/SO	Landry, Leon, Jackson	8.77

PITCHING

G	Fleck, Kaleb, Mobile	56
GS	Floro, Dylan, Montgomery	28
	Gagnon, Drew, Huntsville	28
	Mateo, Victor, Montgomery	28
	Nicolino, Justin, Jacksonville	28
GF	Goforth, David, Huntsville	44
SV	Goforth, David, Huntsville	27
W	Nicolino, Justin, Jacksonville	14
L	Floro, Dylan, Montgomery	13
IP	Floro, Dylan, Montgomery	179
H	Floro, Dylan, Montgomery	209
R	Colla, Mike, Montgomery	91
ER	Jaye, Myles, Birmingham	78
HB	Corcino, Daniel, Pensacola	16
BB	Stephenson, Robert, Pensacola	74
SO	Stephenson, Robert, Pensacola	140
SO/9	Stephenson, Robert, Pensacola	9.22
SO/9(RP)	Shreve, Chasen, Mississippi	12.59
BB/9	Nicolino, Justin, Jacksonville	1.06
WP	Black, Corey, Tennessee	15
BK	Rogers, Jay, Jacksonville	3
HR	Gagnon, Drew, Huntsville	18
	Stephenson, Robert, Pensacola	18
AVG	Stephenson, Robert, Pensacola	.224

FIELDING

C	PCT	Maile, Luke, Montgomery	.995
	PO	O'Brien, Chris, Chattanooga	652
	A	O'Brien, Chris, Chattanooga	74
	DP	Thomas, Mark, Mobile	11
	E	Smith, Kevan, Birmingham	10
	PB	Smith, Kevan, Birmingham	10
1B	PCT	Seitzer, Cameron, Montgomery	.998
	PO	Ramirez, Nick, Huntsville	1,084
	A	Dickson, O'Koyea, Chattanooga	76
	DP	Ramirez, Nick, Huntsville	114
	E	Dickson, O'Koyea, Chattanooga	18
2B	PCT	Bruno, Stephen, Tennessee	.973
	PO	Brett, Ryan, Montgomery	189
	A	Brett, Ryan, Montgomery	272
	DP	Brett, Ryan, Montgomery	78
	E	Brett, Ryan, Montgomery	21
3B	PCT	Lamb, Jake, Mobile	.959
	PO	Kubitza, Kyle, Mississippi	80
	A	Mayora, Daniel, Chattanooga	256
	DP	Mayora, Daniel, Chattanooga	26
	E	Shaffer, Richie, Montgomery	26
SS	PCT	Nola, Austin, Jacksonville	.962
	PO	Nola, Austin, Jacksonville	180
	A	Nola, Austin, Jacksonville	381
	DP	Hager, Jake, Montgomery	74
	E	Marte, Ketel, Jackson	28
OF	PCT	Galloway, Isaac, Jacksonville	.991
	PO	Thompson, Trayce, Birmingham	329
	A	Motter, Taylor, Montgomery	24
	DP	Motter, Taylor, Montgomery	6
	E	Duran, Juan, Pensacola	14

BY JOSH LEVENTHAL

Midland won its second Texas League crown in six years with a team short on prospects but full of minor league veterans. The Athletics affiliate didn't place a player in the top 20 but knocked off prospect-rich Tulsa in five games behind home runs from Dusty Coleman and Conner Crumbliss. The Drillers may have given Midland a better run if top Rockies pitching prospect Jon Gray was available or ace Dan Winkler wasn't lost to injury.

This year's prospect ranking was not completely representatve of the talent that passed through Texas League ballparks in 2014 and would have been significantly deeper if several top performers had not fallen short of qualifying. Righthanders Mark Appel (Astros) and Gray, two of the top three picks in the 2013 draft, pitched in the Texas League but only Gray made it in top 20. Appel, the top pick of the Astros out of Stanford, saw his season take a turn for better after escaping the hitter-friendly California League in late July and posted a 3.69 ERA over 39 innings in the TL—down from his unsightly 9.74 mark high Class A Lancaster. He tossed eight shutout innings and struck out 10 in his second-to-last start against Frisco, but inconsistent performances drew mixed reviews from league observers.

"The first time we saw him he was throwing hard and had good stuff. You could see why he was the No. 1 pick," one league manager said. "The second time it was just down to being normal again, nothing that stood out."

Meanwhile, Frisco second baseman Rougned Odor would have ranked near the top if he had gotten only one more plate appearance before he was summoned to the Rangers. Likewise, his double-play partner Luis Sardinas would have ranked among the top prospects but he got called up to the majors one day after Odor on May 6. Springfield ace Marco Gonzales quickly handled TL hitters before moving on to Triple-A and then the majors.

Other non-qualifiers included San Antonio righthanders Jesse Hahn and Matt Wisler (Padres), Corpus Christi third baseman Colin Moran (Astros), and Frisco catcher Jorge Alfaro (Rangers).

Frisco third baseman Joey Gallo (Rangers) made his Double-A debut in in mid-June after blasting 21 home runs in just 58 Carolina League games, and he homered in four of his first five games with Frisco. He was neck and neck with Cubs phenom Kris Bryant in the minor league home run race before hitting just .179 with five home runs over his final 106 at-bats, when he proved vulnerable to breaking pitches on the outer half.

TOP 20 PROSPECTS

1. Joey Gallo, 3b, Frisco (Rangers)
2. Jon Gray, rhp, Tulsa (Rockies)
3. Eddie Butler, rhp, Tulsa (Rockies)
4. Austin Hedges, c, San Antonio (Padres)
5. Alex Gonzalez, rhp, Frisco (Rangers)
6. Hunter Dozier, 3b, Northwest Arkansas (Royals)
7. Luke Jackson, rhp, Frisco (Rangers)
8. Rymer Liriano, of, San Antonio (Padres)
9. Ryan Rua, 3b, Frisco (Rangers)
10. Jorge Bonifacio, of, Northwest Arkansas (Royals)
11. Tyler Anderson, lhp, Tulsa (Rockies)
12. Alec Asher, rhp, Frisco (Rangers)
13. James Ramsey, of, Springfield (Cardinals)
14. Alex Yarbrough, 2b, Arkansas (Angels)
15. Tony Kemp, 2b, Corpus Christi (Astros)
16. Dan Winkler, rhp, Tulsa (Rockies)
17. Cam Bedrosian, rhp, Arkansas (Angels)
18. Jason Adam, rhp, Northwest Arkansas (Royals)
19. R.J. Alvarez, rhp, Arkansas/San Antonio (Angels/Padres)
20. Delino DeShields, of, Corpus Christi (Astros)

STANDINGS: SPLIT SEASON

FIRST HALF

NORTH	W	L	PCT	GB
Tulsa	38	31	.551	—
Arkansas	34	36	.486	4 ½
Springfield	34	36	.486	4 ½
NW Arkansas	25	45	.357	13 ½

SOUTH	W	L	PCT	GB
Frisco	40	29	.580	—
Midland	38	32	.543	2 ½
San Antonio	36	34	.514	4 ½
Corpus Christi	34	36	.486	6 ½

SECOND HALF

NORTH	W	L	PCT	GB
Arkansas	41	29	.586	—
Springfield	34	36	.486	7
Tulsa	33	37	.471	8
NW Arkansas	28	42	.400	13

SOUTH	W	L	PCT	GB
Frisco	40	30	.571	—
Midland	39	31	.557	1
Corpus Christi	33	37	.471	7
San Antonio	32	38	.457	8

Semifinals: Midland defeated Frisco 3-1 and Tulsa defeated Arkansas 3-1 in best-of-five series. **Finals:** Midland defeated Tulsa 3-2 in a best-of-five series.

OVERALL STANDINGS

Team (Organization)	W	L	PCT	GB	Manager(s)	Attendance	Average	Last Pennant
Frisco RoughRiders (Rangers)	80	59	.576	—	Jason Wood	449,773	6,614	2004
Midland RockHounds (Athletics)	77	63	.550	3 ½	Aaron Nieckula	299,586	4,471	2014
Arkansas Travelers (Angels)	75	65	.536	5 ½	Phillip Wellman	326,179	5,097	2008
Tulsa Drillers (Rockies)	71	68	.511	9	Kevin Riggs	403,732	6,211	1998
San Antonio Missions (Padres)	68	72	.486	12 ½	Rich Dauer	294,539	4,269	2013
Springfield Cardinals (Cardinals)	68	72	.486	12 ½	Mike Shildt	354,227	5,134	2012
Corpus Christi Hooks (Astros)	67	73	.479	13 ½	Keith Bodie	393,769	5,625	2006
Northwest Arkansas Naturals (Royals)	53	87	.379	27 ½	Vance Wilson	319,109	4,625	2010

CLUB BATTING

	AVG	G	AB	R	H	2B	3B	HR	RBI	BB	SO	SB	OBP	SLG
Frisco	.266	139	4664	642	1239	234	29	114	598	419	1069	85	.332	.402
Corpus Christi	.252	140	4656	645	1174	202	30	112	599	539	984	170	.337	.381
Midland	.252	140	4714	628	1189	247	28	107	595	541	1154	137	.332	.385
Springfield	.252	140	4667	553	1178	195	26	91	502	453	968	105	.321	.364
Tulsa	.252	139	4598	570	1160	200	37	97	515	413	1137	130	.319	.375
Arkansas	.251	140	4559	569	1145	212	26	79	523	421	994	134	.318	.361
San Antonio	.243	140	4826	562	1172	200	27	115	516	424	1079	105	.309	.367
Northwest Arkansas	.241	140	4644	505	1118	206	17	84	462	436	1067	110	.309	.347

CLUB PITCHING

	ERA	G	CG	SHO	SV	IP	H	R	ER	HR	BB	SO	AVG
San Antonio	3.36	140	0	11	38	1281	1242	557	478	81	437	1156	.256
Arkansas	3.37	140	2	8	44	1219	1084	508	456	75	520	1073	.242
Frisco	3.39	139	0	12	38	1216	1048	538	458	89	465	1136	.231
Tulsa	3.61	139	1	11	38	1223	1125	576	491	89	441	903	.246
Midland	3.71	140	0	10	41	1240	1231	592	511	98	460	981	.261
Springfield	3.90	140	1	9	43	1233	1219	611	534	117	415	1021	.259
Corpus Christi	3.92	140	1	8	36	1248	1178	614	544	132	412	1118	.249
Northwest Arkansas	4.26	140	2	7	34	1234	1248	678	584	118	496	1064	.264

CLUB FIELDING

	PCT	PO	A	E	DP		PCT	PO	A	E	DP
Arkansas	.981	3657	1422	97	112	Springfield	.977	3699	1421	123	132
Corpus Christi	.978	3746	1363	116	108	Tulsa	.972	3671	1504	147	130
Frisco	.978	3650	1268	113	94	San Antonio	.971	3845	1427	155	137
Midland	.977	3720	1495	125	138	NW Arkansas	.968	3704	1371	166	112

INDIVIDUAL BATTING LEADERS

Batter, Club	AVG	G	AB	R	H	HR	RBI
Herrera, Odubel, Frisco	.321	96	368	47	118	2	48
Hernandez, Brian, Arkansas	.308	119	458	53	141	7	60
Yarbrough, Alex, Arkansas	.285	136	544	66	155	5	77
Asencio, Yeison, San Antonio	.284	117	455	51	129	10	44
Stanley, Cody, Springfield	.283	103	385	47	109	12	43
Casteel, Ryan, Tulsa	.280	113	436	63	122	16	56
Adams, Trever, Frisco	.278	125	482	71	134	14	61
Humphries, Brian, Tulsa	.276	112	402	35	111	4	45
Cuthbert, Cheslor, NW Arkansas	.276	96	355	35	98	10	48
Gonzalez, Maikol, Arkansas	.270	89	319	57	86	1	21

INDIVIDUAL PITCHING LEADERS

Pitcher, Club	W	L	ERA	IP	H	BB	SO
Anderson, Tyler, Tulsa	7	4	1.98	118	91	40	106
Roth, Michael, Arkansas	11	7	2.62	140	121	53	79
Hernandez, Carlos, Tulsa	5	7	2.68	124	130	21	94
Needy, James, San Antonio	10	5	2.90	145	133	50	113
Ferguson, Andy, Northwest Arkansas	11	10	2.93	147	130	41	118
Jensen, Chris, Midland	12	8	3.14	160	147	62	94
Rucinski, Drew, Arkansas	10	6	3.15	148	142	41	140
Long, Nate, Midland	13	8	3.18	150	147	49	126
Sulbaran, J.C., Northwest Arkansas	8	10	3.25	127	128	54	116
Geer, Josh, San Antonio	7	12	3.58	155	172	30	95

ALL-STAR TEAM

C: Cody Stanley, Springfield. **1B:** Trever Adams, Frisco. **2B:** Alex Yarbrough, Arkansas. **3B:** Joey Gallo, Frisco. **SS:** Cristhian Adames, Tulsa. **DH:** Brian Hernandez, Arkansas. **OF:** James Ramsey, Springfield; Lane Adams, Northwest Arkansas; Preston Tucker, Corpus Christi; Yeison Asencio, San Antonio. **IF:** Odubel Herrera, Frisco; Taylor Featherston, Tulsa. **P:** Andy Ferguson, Northwest Arkansas; Cam Bedrosian, Arkansas; Chris Jensen, Midland; James Needy, San Antonio; Michael Roth, Arkansas; Tommy Shirley, Corpus Christi; Tyler Anderson, Tulsa.

DEPARTMENT LEADERS

BATTING

OBP	Muncy, Max, Midland	.385
SLG	Adams, Trever, Frisco	.448
OPS	Casteel, Ryan, Tulsa	.786
R	Coleman, Dusty, Midland	79
H	Yarbrough, Alex, Arkansas	155
TB	Featherston, Taylor, Tulsa	218
XBH	Featherston, Taylor, Tulsa	53
2B	Yarbrough, Alex, Arkansas	38
3B	Spangenberg, Cory, San Antonio	8
HR	Nash, Telvin, Corpus Christi	22
RBI	Coleman, Dusty, Midland	81
SAC	DeShields, Delino, Corpus Christi	18
BB	Muncy, Max, Midland	87
HBP	Cantwell, Pat, Frisco	22
SO	Coleman, Dusty, Midland	202
SB	DeShields, Delino, Corpus Christi	54
CS	DeShields, Delino, Corpus Christi	14
AB/SO	O'Neill, Mike, Springfield	9.73

PITCHING

G	De La Cruz, Luis, San Antonio	57
GS	Asher, Alec, Frisco	28
GF	White, Cole, Tulsa	38
SV	Triggs, Andrew, NW Arkansas	19
W	Long, Nate, Midland	13
L	Castillo, Richard, Tulsa	12
	Gaviglio, Sam, Springfield	12
	Geer, Josh, San Antonio	12
	Rodgers, Brady, Corpus Christi	12
IP	Jensen, Chris, Midland	160
H	Geer, Josh, San Antonio	172
R	Castillo, Richard, Tulsa	97
ER	Castillo, Richard, Tulsa	82
HB	Jensen, Chris, Midland	13
BB	Granier, Drew, Midland	76
SO	Eickhoff, Jerad, Frisco	144
SO/9	Rucinski, Drew, Arkansas	8.48
SO/9(RP)	Donofrio, Joey, Springfield	11.32
BB/9	Rodgers, Brady, Corpus Christi	1.42
WP	Eickhoff, Jerad, Frisco	12
	Gaviglio, Sam, Springfield	12
BK	Anderson, Tyler, Tulsa	3
	Castillo, Richard, Tulsa	3
HR	Cornelius, Jonathan, Springfield	19
AVG	Anderson, Tyler, Tulsa	.216

FIELDING

C	PCT	Bandy, Jett, Arkansas	.996
	PO	Hedges, Austin, San Antonio	910
	A	Bandy, Jett, Arkansas	84
	DP	Hedges, Austin, San Antonio	11
	E	Hedges, Austin, San Antonio	15
	PB	Hedges, Austin, San Antonio	6
1B	PCT	Rodriguez, Jonathan, Springfield	.993
	PO	Rodriguez, Jonathan, Springfield	817
	A	Muncy, Max, Midland	54
	DP	Muncy, Max, Midland	78
		Rodriguez, Jonathan, Springfield	78
	E	Casteel, Ryan, Tulsa	8
		Hernandez, Brian, Arkansas	8
		Threlkeld, Mark, NW Arkansas	8
2B	PCT	Yarbrough, Alex, Arkansas	.982
	PO	Yarbrough, Alex, Arkansas	250
	A	Yarbrough, Alex, Arkansas	297
	DP	Yarbrough, Alex, Arkansas	76
	E	Trapp, Justin, NW Arkansas	15
3B	PCT	Cowart, Kaleb, Arkansas	.929
	PO	Cowart, Kaleb, Arkansas	81
	A	Wisdom, Patrick, Springfield	259
	DP	Wisdom, Patrick, Springfield	21
	E	Wisdom, Patrick, Springfield	26
SS	PCT	Stamets, Eric, Arkansas	.976
	PO	Coleman, Dusty, Midland	219
	A	Coleman, Dusty, Midland	365
	DP	Coleman, Dusty, Midland	83
	E	Calixte, Orlando, NW Arkansas	25
OF	PCT	Chapman, Ethan, NW Arkansas	1.000
	PO	Adams, Lane, NW Arkansas	262
	A	Massey, Tyler, Tulsa	17
	DP	Massey, Tyler, Tulsa	5
	E	Massey, Tyler, Tulsa	12

MINOR LEAGUES

BY JIM SHONERD

With two No. 1 overall picks and several other blue-chip prospects on their roster for much of the season, the Lancaster JetHawks were the Cal League's most star-studded team. They also proved to be its best.

The JetHawks' lineup was dotted with prospects, like 2012 No. 1 pick Carlos Correa at shortstop, along with third baseman Rio Ruiz and outfielder Teoscar Hernandez. Correa was the league's top prospect despite having his season end in late June with a broken leg. The JetHawks' other No. 1 pick, righthander Mark Appel, didn't fare as well. The Stanford product endured a tumultuous stint that included being sent back to extended spring, though he was eventually given a (somewhat controversial) promotion to Double-A.

While Appel fell victim to pitching in hitter-friendly Lancaster, lefthander Josh Hader went 9-2, 2.70 and the first Lancaster pitcher to win Cal League pitcher of the year honors. Righthanders Vince Velasquez and Lance McCullers Jr., gave the JetHawks a couple more marquee arms.

Appel, Correa, Hader and several of Lancaster's other big names were gone by the playoffs, but the JetHawks found new faces to contribute while sweeping Inland Empire in the semifinals before taking a five-game series from Visalia.

The one team that could've challenged Lancaster for the title of most talented roster didn't get to do it on the field. Stockton boasted a prospect-laden infield led by first baseman Matt Olson, shortstop Daniel Robertson and third baseman Renato Nunez. Olson won the Cal League home run title with 37, the most homers by a Cal League player since 2008, while Robertson emerged as the best prospect remaining the Athletics system. The Ports posted the Cal League's best overall record in the regular season at 85-55, seven games better than their closest competitor. They were even able to keep Olson, Robertson and the rest of the core of their lineup together in the postseason, but they were upset by Visalia in the first round.

Beyond just Lancaster and Stockton, it was a deep year for prospects in the Cal League. The league's Top 20 prospects featured 13 first- or supplemental first-round picks—not including Appel, who didn't pitch enough to qualify. Rancho Cucamonga shortstop Corey Seager was right with Correa for the top spot, winning the minor league batting title and Cal League MVP honors, while teammate Julio Urias posted a 2.36 ERA while pitching most of the season at age 17.

TOP 20 PROSPECTS

1. Carlos Correa, ss, Lancaster (Astros)
2. Corey Seager, ss, Rancho Cucamonga (Dodgers)
3. Julio Urias, lhp, Rancho Cucamonga (Dodgers)
4. Braden Shipley, rhp, Visalia (Diamondbacks)
5. Aaron Blair, rhp, Visalia (Diamondbacks)
6. Joe Ross, rhp, Lake Elsinore (Padres)
7. Daniel Robertson, ss/2b, Stockton (Athletics)
8. Vince Velasquez, rhp, Lancaster (Astros)
9. Hunter Renfroe, of, Lake Elsinore (Padres)
10. D.J. Peterson, 1b/3b, High Desert (Mariners)
11. Chris Anderson, rhp, Rancho Cucamonga (Dodgers)
12. Jesse Winker, of, Bakersfield (Reds)
13. Matt Olson, 1b, Stockton (Athletics)
14. Gabby Guerrero, of, High Desert (Mariners)
15. Renato Nunez, 3b, Stockton (Athletics)
16. Ben Lively, rhp, Bakersfield (Reds)
17. Billy McKinney, of, Stockton (Athletics)
18. Brandon Drury, 3b, Visalia (Diamondbacks)
19. Teoscar Hernandez, of, Lancaster (Astros)
20. Lance McCullers Jr., rhp, Lancaster (Astros)

STANDINGS: SPLIT SEASON

FIRST HALF

NORTH	W	L	PCT	GB
Bakersfield	45	25	.643	—
Stockton	37	33	.529	8
Visalia	36	34	.514	9
San Jose	34	36	.486	11
Modesto	23	47	.329	22

SOUTH	W	L	PCT	GB
Lancaster	44	26	.629	—
Lake Elsinore	40	30	.571	4
High Desert	34	36	.486	10
R. Cucamonga	32	38	.457	12
Inland Empire	25	45	.357	19

SECOND HALF

NORTH	W	L	PCT	GB
Stockton	48	22	.686	—
San Jose	39	31	.557	9
Visalia	39	31	.557	9
Bakersfield	33	37	.471	15
Modesto	20	50	.286	28

SOUTH	W	L	PCT	GB
Inland Empire	37	33	.529	—
Lake Elsinore	35	35	.500	2
Lancaster	34	36	.486	3
R. Cucamonga	33	37	.471	4
High Desert	32	38	.457	5

Playoffs—Mini Series: Inland Empire defeated Lake Elsinore 2-0 and Visalia defeated Stockton 2-0 in best-of-three series. **Semifinals:** Lancaster defeated Inland Empire 3-0 and Visalia defeated Bakersfield 3-1 in best-of-five series. **Finals:** Lancaster defeated Visalia 3-2 in a best-of-five series.

OVERALL STANDINGS

Team (Organization)	W	L	PCT	GB	Manager(s)	Attendance	Average	Last Pennant
Stockton Ports (Athletics)	85	55	.607	—	Ryan Christenson	195,500	2,793	2008
Bakersfield Blaze (Reds)	78	62	.557	7	Pat Kelly	57,057	827	1989
Lancaster JetHawks (Astros)	78	62	.557	7	Rodney Linares	170,532	2,436	2014
Lake Elsinore Storm (Padres)	75	65	.536	10	Jamie Quirk	220,069	3,144	2011
Visalia Rawhide (Diamondbacks)	75	65	.536	10	Robby Hammock	120,003	1,714	1978
San Jose Giants (Giants)	73	67	.521	12	Lenn Sakata	200,124	2,859	2010
High Desert Mavericks (Mariners)	66	74	.471	19	Eddie Menchaca	147,231	2,103	1997
Rancho Cucamonga Quakes (Dodgers)	65	75	.464	20	P.J. Forbes	166,993	2,386	1994
Inland Empire 66ers (Angels)	62	78	.443	23	Denny Hocking	195,841	2,838	2013
Modesto Nuts (Rockies)	43	97	.307	42	Don Sneddon	172,902	2,470	2004

CLUB BATTING

	AVG	G	AB	R	H	2B	3B	HR	RBI	BB	SO	SB	OBP	SLG
Bakersfield	.286	140	4858	816	1390	298	21	146	748	531	1001	147	.359	.446
Lancaster	.285	140	4833	837	1375	300	59	130	741	590	980	141	.366	.452
High Desert	.281	140	4947	841	1391	277	50	176	786	483	1121	149	.350	.464
Visalia	.278	140	4916	736	1367	269	39	142	676	402	1165	146	.337	.435
Stockton	.276	140	4941	761	1364	273	35	174	697	546	1152	94	.354	.451
San Jose	.267	140	4829	655	1291	239	42	103	602	403	1059	137	.330	.398
Lake Elsinore	.265	140	4855	697	1287	286	33	121	641	423	1120	116	.330	.412
Inland Empire	.262	140	4772	682	1250	237	53	109	620	444	1180	147	.333	.402
Rancho Cucamonga	.257	140	4844	699	1245	283	43	142	639	464	1283	118	.328	.421
Modesto	.246	140	4699	588	1157	233	55	93	547	409	1226	146	.312	.379

CLUB PITCHING

	ERA	G	CG	SHO	SV	IP	H	R	ER	HR	BB	SO	AVG
Stockton	4.08	140	0	8	35	1264	1216	630	573	134	470	1254	.254
Lake Elsinore	4.30	140	0	6	38	1261	1313	690	603	115	414	1084	.268
Rancho Cucamonga	4.43	140	1	7	30	1258	1262	739	620	125	537	1171	.261
Inland Empire	4.48	140	1	9	32	1240	1239	708	617	118	504	1118	.262
San Jose	4.51	140	0	5	45	1255	1275	689	629	110	533	1169	.266
Visalia	4.52	140	3	8	45	1250	1325	715	628	142	457	1209	.270
Bakersfield	4.73	140	0	7	36	1233	1358	746	648	157	390	1018	.280
Lancaster	4.75	140	0	4	43	1248	1332	739	658	149	391	1134	.274
Modesto	4.96	140	2	3	20	1221	1376	786	673	119	490	1008	.284
High Desert	5.26	140	0	5	32	1239	1421	870	725	167	509	1122	.286

CLUB FIELDING

	PCT	PO	A	E	DP		PCT	PO	A	E	DP
Stockton	.981	3792	1290	97	117	Lake Elsinore	.973	3784	1499	148	116
San Jose	.979	3766	1437	113	159	Visalia	.973	3750	1323	140	96
Inland Empire	.976	3722	1464	130	134	R. Cucamonga	.972	3776	1502	151	126
Lancaster	.975	3744	1461	133	119	Modesto	.968	3665	1414	169	144
Bakersfield	.974	3700	1510	137	125	High Desert	.965	3719	1416	185	131

INDIVIDUAL BATTING LEADERS

Batter, Club	AVG	G	AB	R	H	HR	RBI
Lara, Jordy, High Desert	.353	102	399	77	141	22	80
Goris, Diego, Lake Elsinore	.324	89	370	66	120	13	61
Smith, Marquez, Bakersfield	.323	120	424	89	137	29	126
Rondon, Jose, Inland Empire, Lake Elsinore	.319	109	433	58	138	1	36
Blair, Elliott, San Jose	.316	94	345	50	109	5	35
Robertson, Daniel, Stockton	.310	132	548	110	170	15	60
Guerrero, Gabby, High Desert	.307	131	538	97	165	18	96
Gonzalez, Benji, Lake Elsinore	.306	102	376	61	115	3	41
Navarro, Raul, Visalia	.304	114	437	72	133	7	53
Flores, Rudy, Visalia	.301	132	525	76	158	28	100

INDIVIDUAL PITCHING LEADERS

Pitcher, Club	W	L	ERA	IP	H	BB	SO
Streich, Seth, Stockton	9	6	3.16	114	110	22	116
DeLoach, Tyler, Inland Empire	10	4	3.21	112	87	49	122
Eflin, Zach, Lake Elsinore	10	7	3.80	128	138	31	93
Rea, Colin, Lake Elsinore	11	9	3.88	139	151	37	118
Biagini, Joe, San Jose	10	9	4.01	128	133	46	103
Sinnery, Brandon, Visalia	14	7	4.02	170	175	44	109
Cotton, Jharel, Rancho Cucamonga	6	10	4.05	126	113	34	138
Rodriguez, Bryan, Lake Elsinore	8	9	4.16	149	154	46	104
Westwood, Kyle, Lancaster	8	7	4.23	132	146	26	88
Windle, Tom, Rancho Cucamonga	12	8	4.26	139	147	44	111

ALL-STAR TEAM

C: Roberto Pena, Lancaster. **1B:** Matt Olson, Stockton. **2B:** Tony Kemp, Lancaster. **3B:** Renato Nunez, Stockton. **SS:** Corey Seager, Rancho Cucamonga. **UT:** Marquez Smith, Bakersfield. **DH:** Jordy Lara, High Desert. **OF:** Alex Glenn, Visalia; Teoscar Hernandez, Lancaster; Jabari Henry, High Desert. **LHP:** Josh Hader, Lancaster, Tyler DeLoach, Inland Empire. **RHP:** Enrique Burgos, Visalia; Seth Streich, Stockton. **Most Valuable Player:** Corey Seager, Rancho Cucamonga. **Pitcher of the Year:** Josh Hader, Lancaster. **Rookie of the Year:** Jose Rondon, Lake Elsinore. **Manager of the Year:** Ryan Christenson, Stockton.

DEPARTMENT LEADERS

BATTING

OBP	Smith, Marquez, Bakersfield		.438
SLG	Smith, Marquez, Bakersfield		.623
OPS	Smith, Marquez, Bakersfield		1.061
R	Olson, Matt, Stockton		111
H	Robertson, Daniel, Stockton		170
TB	Olson, Matt, Stockton		278
XBH	Olson, Matt, Stockton		69
2B	Robertson, Daniel, Stockton		37
	Ruiz, Rio, Lancaster		37
3B	Johnson, Sherman, Inland Empire		13
HR	Olson, Matt, Stockton		37
RBI	Smith, Marquez, Bakersfield		126
SAC	Garvey, Robbie, R. Cucamonga		13
BB	Olson, Matt, Stockton		117
HBP	Baltz, Jeremy, Lake Elsinore		17
	Jacobs, Chris, Rancho Cucamonga		17
SO	Flores, Rudy, Visalia		189
SB	Smith, Mallex, Lake Elsinore		40
CS	Towey, Cal, Inland Empire		15
AB/SO	Turner, Ben, San Jose		10.35

PITCHING

G	Mizenko, Tyler, San Jose	59
GS	Alsup, Ben, Modesto	28
	Peralta, Wandy, Bakersfield	28
	Rea, Colin, Lake Elsinore	28
	Sinnery, Brandon, Visalia	28
GF	Burgos, Enrique, Visalia	47
SV	Burgos, Enrique, Visalia	29
W	Sinnery, Brandon, Visalia	14
L	Alsup, Ben, Modesto	14
IP	Sinnery, Brandon, Visalia	170
H	Cisco, Drew, Bakersfield	210
R	Cisco, Drew, Bakersfield	119
ER	Cisco, Drew, Bakersfield	108
HB	DeLoach, Tyler, Inland Empire	16
BB	Martinez, Fabio, R. Cucamonga	91
SO	Anderson, Chris, R. Cucamonga	146
SO/9	Cotton, Jharel, R. Cucamonga	9.81
SO/9(RP)	Burgos, Enrique, Visalia	13.66
BB/9	Unsworth, Dylan, High Desert	1.43
WP	Martinez, Fabio, R. Cucamonga	17
BK	Atherton, Tim, Stockton	3
	Carpenter, Ryan, Modesto	3
	Martinez, Fabio, Rancho Cucamonga	3
	Rodriguez, Bryan, Lake Elsinore	3
	Santos, Eduard, Inland Empire	3
	Sinnery, Brandon, Visalia	3
HR	DeCecco, Scott, High Desert	27
AVG	DeLoach, Tyler, Inland Empire	.213

FIELDING

C	PCT	Pena, Roberto, Lancaster	.996
	PO	Pena, Roberto, Lancaster	755
	A	Wright, Zach, Inland Empire	97
	DP	Pena, Roberto, Lancaster	9
	E	Marlette, Tyler, High Desert	12
	PB	Marlette, Tyler, High Desert	22
1B	PCT	Olson, Matt, Stockton	.993
	PO	Jacobs, Chris, R. Cucamonga	995
	A	Jacobs, Chris, R. Cucamonga	84
	DP	Ragira, Brian, San Jose	101
	E	Ragira, Brian, San Jose	16
2B	PCT	Johnson, Sherman, In. Empire	.991
	PO	Johnson, Sherman, In. Empire	205
	A	Lopes, Tim, High Desert	322
	DP	Johnson, Sherman, Inland Empire	72
	E	Dixon, Brandon, R. Cucamonga	20
3B	PCT	Delfino, Mitch, San Jose	.950
	PO	Delfino, Mitch, San Jose	101
	A	Delfino, Mitch, San Jose	239
	DP	Delfino, Mitch, San Jose	31
	E	Proscia, Steven, R. Cucamonga	27
SS	PCT	Rondon, Jose, Inland Empire	.965
	PO	Smith, Tyler, High Desert	162
	A	Rondon, Jose, Inland Empire	326
	DP	Vincej, Zach, Bakersfield	76
	E	Smith, Tyler, High Desert	22
		Vincej, Zach, Bakersfield	22
OF	PCT	Witherspoon, Travis, Hi Desert	.996
	PO	Martinez, Alberth, Lake Elsinore	295
	A	Jones, Chuckie, San Jose	12
		Kandilas, David, Modesto	12
	DP	Kandilas, David, Modesto	5
	E	Glenn, Alex, Visalia	13

MINOR LEAGUES

BY LACY LUSK

At every opportunity, the Potomac Nationals and the Myrtle Beach Pelicans separated themselves from the pack in the Carolina League in 2014, so it was no surprise that those two teams met for the Mills Cup.

Potomac won the best-of-five series in four games, defeating the only other club in the eight-team league that had a winning overall record. The Nationals went 78-58 in the regular season, taking the first- and second-half titles in the Northern Division. Meanwhile, Myrtle Beach won both halves in the South and went 82-56 in its final year as a Rangers affiliate.

In Potomac's clinching game, the lineup featured four key players who spent the whole year with the P-Nats in catcher Pedro Severino, second baseman Tony Renda, shortstop Stephen Perez and first baseman Shawn Pleffner.

"We had a lot of guys with high baseball IQs," said Potomac's Tripp Keister, the Carolina League's manager of the year.

Pleffner, Perez, Renda and Potomac DH Oscar Tejeda all made the postseason all-star team.

First baseman-DH John Wooten was playoff MVP for helping the P-Nats win their third league crown in seven years and first since 2010. He went 8-for-14 with three home runs in the final series against a Pelicans team still loaded with talent despite the midseason promotion of third baseman Joey Gallo, the league's No. 1 prospect. Gallo hit 21 homers for Myrtle Beach and another 21 for Double-A Frisco.

Gallo, who turned 21 after the season, was the league's MVP despite his early June departure for the Texas League. With the Pelicans, the 2012 supplemental first-round pick hit .323/.463/.735 with 50 RBIs in 189 at-bats. His average fell off at Frisco, where he hit .232/.334/.524 with 56 RBIs in 250 at-bats, but he dominated in the Carolina League, which is usually a challenge for hitters on their way through farm systems.

Gallo, catcher Jorge Alfaro and outfielders Nick Williams and Chris Garia represented Myrtle Beach on the postseason all-star list.

Righthander Glenn Sparkman, a 22-year-old who was the Royals' 20th-round selection in 2013, was pitcher of the year after going 8-3, 1.56 with 117 strikeouts in 121 innings.

After the season, three Carolina League teams changed affiliations. The Cubs took over at Myrtle Beach, the Indians switched their club from Carolina to Lynchburg and the Braves went from Lynchburg to Carolina after a full-on sales pitch that featured team president John Schuerholz, interim general manager John Hart, Hall of Fame manager Bobby Cox, senior vice president Chip Moore and manager Fredi Gonzalez.

STANDINGS: SPLIT SEASON

FIRST HALF					SECOND HALF				
NORTH	**W**	**L**	**PCT**	**GB**	**NORTH**	**W**	**L**	**PCT**	**GB**
Potomac	38	31	.551	—	Potomac	40	27	.597	—
Lynchburg	34	36	.486	4 ½	Lynchburg	34	35	.493	7
Wilmington	33	35	.485	4 ½	Frederick	33	37	.471	8 ½
Frederick	32	35	.478	5	Wilmington	32	37	.464	9
SOUTH	**W**	**L**	**PCT**	**GB**	**SOUTH**	**W**	**L**	**PCT**	**GB**
Myr Beach	44	24	.647	—	Myr Beach	38	32	.543	—
Salem	33	35	.485	11	Salem	35	33	.515	2
W-S	30	39	.435	14 ½	Carolina	33	36	.478	4 ½
Carolina	29	38	.433	14 ½	W-S	31	39	.443	7

Playoffs—Semifinals: Potomac defeated Lynchburg 2-0 and Myrtle Beach defeated Salem 2-1 in best-of-three series. **Finals:** Potomac defeated Myrtle Beach 3-1 in a best-of-five series.

OVERALL STANDINGS

Team (Organization)	W	L	PCT	GB	Manager(s)	Attendance	Average	Last Pennant
Myrtle Beach Pelicans (Rangers)	82	56	.594	—	Joe Mikulik	294,539	4,269	2000
Potomac (Nationals)	78	58	.574	3	Tripp Keister	449,773	6,614	2014
Salem Salem (Red Sox)	68	68	.500	13	Carlos Febles	354,227	5,134	2013
Lynchburg Hillcats (Braves)	68	71	.489	14 ½	Luis Salazar	299,586	4,471	2012
Frederick Keys (Orioles)	65	72	.474	16 ½	Luis Pujols	326,179	5,097	2011
Wilmington Blue Rocks (Royals)	65	72	.474	16 ½	Darryl Kennedy	403,732	6,211	1999
Carolina Mudcats (Indians)	62	74	.456	19	Scotter Tucker	393,769	5,625	2006
Winston-Salem Dash (White Sox)	61	78	.439	21 ½	Tommy Thompson	319,109	4,625	2003

CLUB BATTING

	AVG	G	AB	R	H	2B	3B	HR	RBI	BB	SO	SB	OBP	SLG
Carolina	.263	136	4567	612	1200	230	35	68	542	552	996	106	.348	.373
Lynchburg	.261	139	4619	613	1207	261	39	57	541	431	943	146	.329	.372
Salem	.261	136	4538	648	1186	265	47	72	582	478	1012	122	.338	.388
Winston-Salem	.260	139	4619	588	1203	267	46	76	525	391	995	130	.321	.388
Myrtle Beach	.258	138	4645	683	1200	246	48	111	627	479	1134	154	.336	.404
Potomac	.258	136	4442	635	1146	234	31	82	572	452	965	137	.331	.380
Frederick	.256	137	4547	591	1165	277	29	87	543	372	996	95	.315	.387
Wilmington	.224	137	4362	475	977	202	38	68	427	369	1042	131	.292	.334

CLUB PITCHING

	ERA	G	CG	SHO	SV	IP	H	R	ER	HR	BB	SO	AVG
Wilmington	3.09	137	1	17	37	1164	1056	469	400	48	330	1083	.243
Myrtle Beach	3.43	138	1	9	40	1223	1095	550	466	80	564	1044	.240
Carolina	3.89	136	2	3	33	1185	1118	606	513	79	390	978	.248
Winston-Salem	3.91	139	5	6	28	1204	1263	671	523	74	433	1087	.267
Salem	4.09	136	3	11	32	1177	1176	618	535	79	434	1013	.262
Frederick	4.26	137	4	9	34	1183	1187	635	560	86	503	887	.261
Potomac	4.32	136	0	6	37	1167	1177	627	561	83	402	928	.262
Lynchburg	4.36	139	0	5	34	1208	1212	669	585	92	468	1063	.260

CLUB FIELDING

	PCT	PO	A	E	DP		PCT	PO	A	E	DP
Frederick	.978	3551	1496	113	115	Carolina	.972	3557	1323	139	105
Wilmington	.977	3492	1295	114	96	Myrtle Beach	.972	3671	1484	149	144
Lynchburg	.976	3624	1349	122	93	Salem	.971	3531	1362	146	120
Potomac	.976	3503	1396	121	103	Winston-Salem	.963	3614	1452	194	114

INDIVIDUAL BATTING LEADERS

Batter, Club	AVG	G	AB	R	H	HR	RBI
Renda, Tony, Potomac	.307	107	414	75	127	0	47
Gragnani, Reed, Salem	.300	99	360	64	108	5	43
Pleffner, Shawn, Potomac	.298	95	356	45	106	2	44
Davis, Glynn, Frederick	.295	89	352	65	104	1	31
Williams, Nick, Myrtle Beach	.292	94	377	61	110	13	68
Coats, Jason, Winston-Salem	.291	115	429	64	125	15	72
Medina, Yhoxian, Potomac	.288	99	385	60	111	1	36
Garia, Chris, Myrtle Beach	.284	101	398	75	113	4	24
Bolinger, Royce, Myrtle Beach	.280	93	346	41	97	7	44
Johnson, Matty, Salem	.276	132	510	104	141	4	55

INDIVIDUAL PITCHING LEADERS

Pitcher, Club	W	L	ERA	IP	H	BB	SO
Sparkman, Glenn, Wilmington	8	3	1.56	121	94	25	117
Dziedzic, Jonathan, Wilmington	6	7	2.52	125	122	37	113
Merritt, Ryan, Carolina	13	3	2.58	160	128	25	127
Manaea, Sean, Wilmington	7	8	3.11	121	102	54	146
Blackmar, Mark, Frederick	10	1	3.18	130	109	32	83
Wolff, Sam, Myrtle Beach	9	5	3.37	120	106	35	81
Kline, Branden, Frederick	8	6	3.84	126	143	32	95
Bucciferro, Tony, Winston-Salem	7	10	3.90	129	139	16	94
Miller, Jarrett, Lynchburg	8	9	4.04	151	164	50	127
Sims, Lucas, Lynchburg	8	11	4.19	156	146	57	107

ALL-STAR TEAM

C: Jorge Alfaro, Myrtle Beach. **1B:** Shawn Pleffner, Potomac. **2B:** Tony Renda, Potomac. **3B:** Joey Gallo, Myrtle Beach. **SS:** Stephen Perez, Potomac. **DH:** Oscar Tejeda, Potomac. **OF:** Chris Garia, Myrtle Beach; Courtney Hawkins, Winston-Salem; OF: Jason Coats, Winston-Salem; Michael Burgess, Frederick; Nick Williams, Myrtle Beach. **IF:** Reed Gragnani, Salem. **SP:** Ryan Merritt, Carolina. **RP:** Mark Peterson, Wilmington.

Most Valuable Player: Joey Gallo, Myrtle Beach. **Pitcher of the Year:** Glenn Sparkman, Wilmington. **Manager of the Year:** Tripp Keister.

DEPARTMENT LEADERS

BATTING

OBP	Gragnani, Reed, Salem	.409
SLG	Burgess, Michael, Frederick	.579
OPS	Coats, Jason, Winston-Salem	.837
R	Johnson, Matty, Salem	104
H	Johnson, Matty, Salem	141
TB	Coats, Jason, Winston-Salem	209
XBH	Coats, Jason, Winston-Salem	52
2B	Ahrens, Kevin, Lynchburg	41
3B	Mondesi, Raul, Wilmington	12
HR	Gallo, Joey, Myrtle Beach	21
RBI	Hawkins, Courtney, Winston-Salem	84
SAC	Garia, Chris, Myrtle Beach	12
	May, Jacob, Winston-Salem	12
BB	Beck, Preston, Myrtle Beach	80
HBP	Heller, Kevin, Salem	17
SO	Barnum, Keon, Winston-Salem	163
SB	Garia, Chris, Myrtle Beach	45
CS	Johnson, Matty, Salem	17
AB/SO	Gragnani, Reed, Salem	7.06

PITCHING

G	Sides, Grant, Carolina	43
GS	Miller, Jarrett, Lynchburg	28
	Sims, Lucas, Lynchburg	28
GF	Leclerc, Jose, Myrtle Beach	37
SV	Peterson, Mark, Wilmington	22
W	Merritt, Ryan, Carolina	13
L	Sulser, Cole, Carolina	13
IP	Merritt, Ryan, Carolina	160.1
H	Wendelken, J.B., Winston-Salem	181
R	Wendelken, J.B., Winston-Salem	105
ER	Wendelken, J.B., Winston-Salem	85
HB	Sims, Lucas, Lynchburg	17
BB	Payano, Victor, Myrtle Beach	90
SO	Manaea, Sean, Wilmington	146
SO/9	Manaea, Sean, Wilmington	10.8
SO/9(RP)	Leclerc, Jose, Myrtle Beach	12.4
BB/9	Bucciferro, Tony, Winston-Salem	1.11
WP	Peoples, Michael, Carolina	17
BK	Almonte, Miguel, Wilmington	6
HR	Wendelken, J.B., Winston-Salem	15
AVG	Sparkman, Glenn, Wilmington	.213

FIELDING

C	PCT	Gallagher, Cam, Wilmington	.991
	PO	Gallagher, Cam, Wilmington	691
	A	Gallagher, Cam, Wilmington	101
	DP	Marjama, Mike, Winston-Salem	6
	E	Alfaro, Jorge, Myrtle Beach	13
	PB	Alfaro, Jorge, Myrtle Beach	18
1B	PCT	Barnum, Keon, Winston-Salem	.985
	PO	Barnum, Keon, Winston-Salem	1,146
	A	Barnum, Keon, Winston-Salem	67
	DP	Barnum, Keon, Winston-Salem	99
	E	Barnum, Keon, Winston-Salem	19
2B	PCT	DeMichele, Joey, Winston-Salem	.972
	PO	Bostick, Christopher, Myrtle Beach	243
	A	Bostick, Christopher, Myrtle Beach	323
	DP	Bostick, Christopher, Myrtle Beach	94
	E	Bostick, Christopher, Myrtle Beach	19
3B	PCT	Esposito, Jason, Frederick	.960
	PO	Esposito, Jason, Frederick	83
	A	Esposito, Jason, Frederick	257
	DP	Ahrens, Kevin, Lynchburg	19
		Esposito, Jason, Frederick	19
	E	Basto, Nick, Winston-Salem	31
SS	PCT	Marin, Adrian, Frederick	.972
	PO	Marin, Adrian, Frederick	179
	A	Perez, Stephen, Potomac	355
	DP	Marin, Adrian, Frederick	67
	E	Anderson, Tim, Winston-Salem	31
OF	PCT	Starling, Bubba, Wilmington	.993
	PO	Johnson, Matty, Salem	275
	A	Starling, Bubba, Wilmington	14
	DP	Starling, Bubba, Wilmington	5
	E	Hawkins, Courtney, Winston-Salem	14

MINOR LEAGUES

BY JOHN MANUEL

The Fort Myers Miracle didn't need a miracle, or even top prospect Byron Buxton, to win the first Florida State League championship in the franchise's 22-year history.

But it didn't hurt to get an infusion of talent from the Twins' last two drafts. Righthander Nick Burdi, the club's 2014 second-round pick, flashed 100 mph heat and struck out eight of 19 batters he faced in the playoffs. Meanwhile 2013 third-rounder Stuart Turner hit .304 and handled the staff well all season. Manager Doug Mientkiewicz led the Miracle to a 5-1 postseason mark, beating defending champ Daytona in the final.

Fort Myers was a worthy champion, posting the league's best regular season record thanks to a deep lineup that led the league with 712 runs, despite Buxton's prolonged absence. The game's No. 1 prospect entering 2014, Buxton missed most of the first half with a sprained wrist, then was promoted in August to Double-A (where he was injured in his first game).

But his teammates, many of whom teamed with Buxton to win a Rookie-level Appalachian League title in 2012 with Elizabethton, picked him up. Elizabethton alumni Adam Brett Walker (who led the FSL in homers) and D.J. Hicks combined for 170 RBIs in the middle of the lineup. Shortstop Niko Goodrum stole a team-best 35 bases, while '12 Elizabethton ace Jose Berrios led the team in strikeouts despite being promoted in early July.

"They got hits when they needed them," Daytona manager Dave Keller said. "They had the whole package—good defense, speed, and they filled their different roles as a lineup. And against us, their pitching was off the charts."

Both finalists had talent, including the Cubs' Kyle Schwarber, the No. 4 overall pick in the 2014 draft, but Bradenton produced the league's official hitter and pitcher of the year in outfielder Josh Bell and righthander Tyler Glasnow. Dunedin had the

best record in the North Division and also produced three players who finished the season in the major leagues in righthander Kendall Graveman, lefthander Daniel Norris and outfielder Dalton Pompey. The Jays also had righthander Taylor Cole, who led the minors with 171 strikeouts.

TOP 20 PROSPECTS

1. Tyler Glasnow, rhp, Bradenton (Pirates)
2. J. P. Crawford, ss, Clearwater (Phillies)
3. Daniel Norris, lhp, Dunedin (Blue Jays)
4. Kyle Schwarber, c/of, Daytona (Cubs)
5. Dalton Pompey, of, Dunedin (Blue Jays)
6. Jose Berrios, rhp, Fort Myers (Twins)
7. Steve Matz, lhp, St. Lucie (Mets)
8. Josh Bell, of, Bradenton (Pirates)
9. Orlando Arcia, ss/2b, Brevard County (Brewers)
10. Justin O'Conner, c, Charlotte (Rays)
11. Albert Almora, of, Daytona (Cubs)
12. Dilson Herrera, 2b/ss, St. Lucie (Mets)
13. Jake Thompson, rhp, Lakeland (Tigers)
14. Jorge Polanco, 2b/ss, Fort Myers (Twins)
15. Aaron Judge, of, Tampa (Yankees)
16. Tyrone Taylor, of, Brevard County (Brewers)
17. Brandon Nimmo, of, St. Lucie (Mets)
18. Billy McKinney, of, Daytona (Cubs)
19. Dwight Smith Jr., of, Dunedin (Blue Jays)
20. Colin Moran, 3b, Jupiter (Marlins)

STANDINGS: SPLIT SEASON

FIRST HALF

NORTH	W	L	PCT	GB
Dunedin	46	23	.667	—
Lakeland	42	25	.627	3
Brevard Co.	36	30	.545	8 ½
Tampa	33	37	.471	13 ½
Daytona	26	42	.382	19 ½
Clearwater	17	51	.250	28 ½

SOUTH	W	L	PCT	GB
Fort Myers	41	28	.594	—
St. Lucie	40	29	.580	1
Palm Beach	36	33	.522	5
Bradenton	35	34	.507	6
Charlotte	31	36	.463	9
Jupiter	27	42	.391	14

SECOND HALF

NORTH	W	L	PCT	GB
Daytona	41	27	.603	—
Tampa	38	31	.551	3 ½
Brevard Co.	37	32	.536	4 ½
Clearwater	32	38	.457	10
Dunedin	31	38	.449	10 ½
Lakeland	20	50	.286	22

SOUTH	W	L	PCT	GB
Bradenton	43	27	.614	—
Fort Myers	41	29	.586	2
Palm Beach	40	30	.571	3
St. Lucie	36	33	.522	6 ½
Charlotte	32	34	.485	9
Jupiter	23	45	.338	19

Playoffs—Semifinals: Fort Myers defeated Bradenton 2-0 and Daytona defeated Dunedin 2-0 in best-of-three series. **Finals:** Fort Myers defeated Daytona 3-1 in best-of-five series.

OVERALL STANDINGS

Team (Organization)	W	L	PCT	GB	Manager(s)	Attendance	Average	Last Pennant
Fort Myers Miracle (Twins)	82	57	.590	—	Doug Mientkiewicz	119,102	1,861	2014
Bradenton Marauders (Pirates)	78	61	.561	4	Tom Prince	104,584	1,609	1963
Dunedin Blue Jays (Blue Jays)	77	61	.558	4 ½	Omar Malave	60,044	896	Never
St. Lucie Mets (Mets)	76	62	.551	5 ½	Ryan Ellis	94,650	1,479	2006
Palm Beach Cardinals (Cardinals)	76	63	.547	6	Dann Bilardello	74,887	1,101	2005
Brevard County Manatees (Brewers)	73	62	.541	7	Joe Ayrault	78,465	1,286	2001
Tampa Yankees (Yankees)	71	68	.511	11	Al Pedrique	111,521	1,640	2010
Daytona Cubs (Cubs)	67	69	.493	13 ½	Dave Keller	143,273	2,470	2011
Charlotte Stone Crabs (Rays)	63	70	.474	18	Jared Sandberg	118,430	1,850	1990
Lakeland Flying Tigers (Tigers)	62	75	.453	19	Dave Huppert/Bill Dancy	64,396	1,006	2012
Jupiter Hammerheads (Marlins)	50	87	.365	29	Brian Schneider	71,713	1,138	1991
Clearwater Threshers (Phillies)	49	89	.355	32 ½	Nelson Prada	195,063	2,787	2007

CLUB BATTING

	AVG	G	AB	R	H	2B	3B	HR	RBI	BB	SO	SB	OBP	SLG
St. Lucie	.272	138	4582	643	1246	240	31	70	575	456	856	70	.342	.384
Brevard County	.262	135	4343	522	1136	234	27	55	462	414	814	153	.333	.366
Charlotte	.262	133	4489	572	1176	222	55	65	511	403	959	129	.329	.379
Fort Myers	.261	139	4612	712	1203	248	32	84	661	523	985	131	.339	.383
Palm Beach	.261	139	4695	623	1225	217	47	82	573	371	925	63	.321	.380
Bradenton	.259	139	4599	561	1191	221	37	50	510	380	958	136	.319	.356
Jupiter	.259	137	4602	511	1190	205	32	49	465	360	852	84	.316	.349
Dunedin	.257	138	4541	587	1169	255	32	78	541	456	922	91	.329	.379
Tampa	.256	139	4610	562	1181	236	31	87	526	449	1154	70	.326	.377
Daytona	.255	136	4433	618	1131	231	37	85	570	483	999	103	.333	.381
Lakeland	.249	137	4570	526	1137	210	33	77	472	358	1080	77	.310	.360
Clearwater	.233	138	4493	497	1049	199	34	91	454	360	1077	98	.296	.354

CLUB PITCHING

	ERA	G	CG	SHO	SV	IP	H	R	ER	HR	BB	SO	AVG
Brevard County	3.25	135	8	16	44	1151	1019	482	416	98	361	977	.240
Bradenton	3.27	139	0	18	39	1223	1095	518	444	60	413	916	.241
Dunedin	3.30	138	1	13	45	1191	1153	508	437	75	347	1095	.254
Fort Myers	3.34	139	10	16	37	1208	1214	544	449	60	377	936	.261
Palm Beach	3.47	139	3	7	38	1235	1233	542	477	69	369	992	.261
Tampa	3.48	139	0	8	33	1206	1123	562	466	52	399	1089	.244
Lakeland	3.70	137	4	12	37	1201	1150	572	494	80	472	940	.255
Charlotte	3.92	133	1	8	33	1163	1158	607	507	61	449	834	.260
St. Lucie	4.12	138	1	8	45	1185	1201	611	542	71	442	989	.261
Daytona	4.22	136	1	6	30	1161	1187	631	545	90	477	973	.264
Jupiter	4.22	137	2	9	28	1174	1233	646	550	58	391	921	.270
Clearwater	4.62	138	2	8	32	1201	1268	711	617	99	516	919	.273

CLUB FIELDING

	PCT	PO	A	E	DP		PCT	PO	A	E	DP
Brevard County	.978	3453	1377	109	133	Clearwater	.975	3604	1410	127	143
Lakeland	.978	3604	1408	112	122	Dunedin	.973	3574	1395	140	126
Daytona	.977	3485	1455	115	113	Jupiter	.973	3523	1445	138	124
Fort Myers	.977	3625	1509	120	147	Charlotte	.972	3489	1434	144	119
Palm Beach	.976	3707	1516	128	154	Tampa	.972	3624	1379	143	107
Bradenton	.975	3671	1595	137	152	St. Lucie	.969	3557	1351	155	113

INDIVIDUAL BATTING LEADERS

Batter, Club	AVG	G	AB	R	H	HR	RBI
Bell, Josh, Bradenton	.335	84	331	45	111	9	53
Reginatto, Leonardo, Charlotte	.316	94	364	45	115	0	35
Tilson, Charlie, Palm Beach	.308	89	370	54	114	5	36
Cave, Jake, Tampa	.304	90	385	50	117	3	24
Osuna, Jose, Bradenton	.296	97	365	47	108	10	57
Moran, Colin, Jupiter	.294	89	361	34	106	5	33
Rosa, Viosergy, Jupiter	.291	116	446	52	130	13	78
Polanco, Jorge, Fort Myers	.291	94	378	61	110	6	45
Arcia, Orlando, Brevard County	.289	127	498	65	144	4	50
Orf, Nathan, Brevard County	.288	123	451	66	130	2	43

INDIVIDUAL PITCHING LEADERS

Pitcher, Club	W	L	ERA	IP	H	BB	SO
Glasnow, Tyler, Bradenton	12	5	1.74	124	74	57	157
Wagner, Tyler, Brevard County	13	6	1.86	150	118	48	118
Williams, Trevor, Jupiter	8	6	2.79	129	138	29	90
Johnson, Hobbs, Brevard County	12	8	2.93	147	118	43	105
Cole, Taylor, Dunedin	8	9	3.07	132	114	39	171
De La Rosa, Edgar, Lakeland	7	9	3.30	139	116	53	91
Kuhl, Chad, Bradenton	13	5	3.46	153	141	42	100
Lopez, Reinaldo, Charlotte	7	5	3.49	142	135	58	79
Tomshaw, Matt, Fort Myers	11	6	3.50	136	152	28	82
Sulbaran, Miguel, Tampa	4	5	3.52	115	106	30	85

ALL-STAR TEAM

P: Jose Berrios, Fort Myers; Taylor Cole, Dunedin; Tyler Glasnow, Bradenton; Tyler Wagner, Brevard County **C:** Cam Maron, St. Lucie. **C:** Justin O'Conner, Charlotte. **1B:** Viosergy Rosa, Jupiter. **2B:** Gioskar Amaya, Daytona. **3B:** Colin Moran, Jupiter. **SS:** Leonardo Reginatto, Charlotte. **LF:** Jake Cave, Tampa. **CF:** Charlie Tilson, Palm Beach. **RF:** Josh Bell, Bradenton. **DH:** Adam Brett Walker II, Fort Myers. **OF:** Dwight Smith Jr., Dunedin. **IF:** Nathan Orf, Brevard County. **RP:** Angel Nesbitt, Lakeland; Arik Sikula, Dunedin.
Most Valuable Player: Josh Bell, Bradenton. **Most Valuable Pitcher:** Tyler Glasnow, Bradenton.

DEPARTMENT LEADERS

BATTING

OBP	Reed, Michael, Brevard County	.396
SLG	Bell, Josh, Bradenton	.502
OPS	Smith Jr., Dwight, Dunedin	.816
R	Smith Jr., Dwight, Dunedin	83
H	Arcia, Orlando, Brevard County	144
TB	Walker II, Adam Brett, Fort Myers	220
XBH	Charles, Art, Clearwater	48
	Smith Jr., Dwight, Dunedin	48
2B	Taylor, Tyrone, Brevard County	36
3B	Four tied at	8
HR	Walker II, Adam Brett, Fort Myers	25
RBI	Walker II, Adam Brett, Fort Myers	94
SAC	Vargas, Ildemaro, Palm Beach	20
BB	Reed, Michael, Brevard County	78
HBP	Orf, Nathan, Brevard County	22
SO	Charles, Art, Clearwater	156
	Walker II, Adam Brett, Fort Myers	156
SB	Goodrum, Niko, Fort Myers	35
CS	Moroff, Max, Bradenton	15
AB/SO	Baligod, Nick, Dunedin	9.83

PITCHING

G	Girodo, Chad, Dunedin	47
GS	Kuhl, Chad, Bradenton	28
GF	Sikula, Arik, Dunedin	42
SV	Sikula, Arik, Dunedin	31
W	Kuhl, Chad, Bradenton	13
	Wagner, Tyler, Brevard County	13
L	Lopez, Yorfrank, Lakeland	12
	Stefan, Jeb, Clearwater	12
IP	Kuhl, Chad, Bradenton	153
H	Creasy, Jason, Bradenton	165
	Hernandez, Jesse, Dunedin	165
R	Lopez, Yorfrank, Lakeland	90
ER	Lopez, Yorfrank, Lakeland	75
HB	Kuhl, Chad, Bradenton	15
BB	Kuchno, John, Bradenton	58
	Lopez, Reinaldo, Charlotte	58
	Stewart, Ethan, Clearwater	58
SO	Cole, Taylor, Dunedin	171
SO/9	Cole, Taylor, Dunedin	11.66
SO/9(RP)	Drummond, Calvin, Lakeland	12.90
BB/9	Creasy, Jason, Bradenton	1.33
WP	Brice, Austin, Jupiter	17
	Cole, Taylor, Dunedin	17
BK	De La Rosa, Edgar, Lakeland	4
HR	Hernandez, Jesse, Dunedin	20
AVG	Glasnow, Tyler, Bradenton	.174

FIELDING

C	PCT	Contreras, Willson, Daytona	.998
	PO	Maron, Cam, St. Lucie	713
	A	Contreras, Willson, Daytona	72
	DP	Stallings, Jacob, Bradenton	8
	E	O'Conner, Justin, Charlotte	13
	PB	O'Conner, Justin, Charlotte	13
1B	PCT	Vogelbach, Dan, Daytona	.995
	PO	Robbins, James, Lakeland	1,077
	A	Robbins, James, Lakeland	70
	DP	Hicks, Dalton, Fort Myers	112
	E	Voit, Luke, Palm Beach	14
2B	PCT	Moroff, Max, Bradenton	.980
	PO	Moroff, Max, Bradenton	239
	A	Moroff, Max, Bradenton	395
	DP	Moroff, Max, Bradenton	88
	E	Coyle, Thomas, Charlotte	15
		Lopes, Christian, Dunedin	15
3B	PCT	Martinez, Harold, Clearwater	.960
	PO	Martinez, Harold, Clearwater	73
	A	Wood, Eric, Bradenton	236
	DP	Wood, Eric, Bradenton	25
	E	Wood, Eric, Bradenton	27
SS	PCT	Culver, Cito, Tampa	.966
	PO	Culver, Cito, Tampa	196
	A	Culver, Cito, Tampa	404
	DP	Frazier, Adam, Bradenton	84
	E	Frazier, Adam, Bradenton	36
OF	PCT	Harrell, Connor, Lakeland	.997
	PO	Harrell, Connor, Lakeland	296
	A	Smith Jr., Dwight, Dunedin	16
	DP	Lavin, Peter, Clearwater	5
		Martini, Nick, Palm Beach	5
	E	Pina, Eudy, St. Lucie	11
		Rademacher, Bijan, Daytona	11

MINOR LEAGUES

MINOR LEAGUES

BY J.J. COOPER

In 2013, the Kane County Cougars were one of the better assemblies of prospects in the minors. But prospects don't always make for winners, and the Cougars proved that, finishing with the second-worst record in the Midwest League.

The 2014 Cougars had a number of interesting prospects, but nothing like the firepower of the previous year. What they do have is a title.

Kane County dominated the Midwest League in 2014. The Cougars had the best record in the league in the first half of the season. They had the best record in the second half. Their 91-49 record was 7 ½ games better than anyone in the league and 18 games more than their closest division foe.

Kane County went a perfect 7-0 in the playoffs to easily win the league title. It was a drama-free playoffs. Kane County knocked off Lake County in the championship series, winning the final two games 6-0 and 7-2—with neither game ever really in doubt. Mark Zagunis hit .429 with two home runs in the playoffs. Shawon Dunston Jr. stole seven bases and scored nine runs and Jen-Ho Tseng went 2-0 in two postseason starts.

The Cougars' dominance overshadowed a nearly as impressive season by the West Michigan Whitecaps. Dubbed an "All-SEC" rotation by some Midwest League managers, the Whitecaps had five prominent draft picks from prominent college programs in their rotation. They lived up to expectations as Kevin Ziomek led the league in ERA, Austin Kubitza was second, Jonathan Crawford was sixth and Chad Green was ninth.

There were plenty of notable moments during the season. None more notable than the steady day-after-day consistency of South Bend shortstop Andrew Velazquez, whose 74-game on-base streak is the longest in recorded minor league history.

TOP 20 PROSPECTS

1. Alex Reyes, rhp, Peoria (Cardinals)
2. Trea Turner, ss, Fort Wayne (Padres)
3. Braden Shipley, rhp, South Bend (Diamondbacks)
4. Michael Feliz, rhp, Quad Cities (Astros)
5. Willy Adames, ss, West Michigan/Bowling Green (Tigers/Rays)
6. Kohl Stewart, rhp, Cedar Rapids (Twins)
7. Clint Coulter, c, Wisconsin (Brewers)
8. Brett Phillips, of, Quad Cities (Astros)
9. Clint Frazier, of, Lake County (Indians)
10. Buck Farmer, rhp, West Michigan (Tigers)
11. Amir Garrett, lhp, Dayton (Reds)
12. Jesmuel Valentin, 2b, Great Lakes (Dodgers)
13. Carson Kelly, c, Peoria (Cardinals)
14. Austin Kubitza, rhp, West Michigan (Tigers)
15. Zach Bird, rhp, Great Lakes (Dodgers)
16. Andrew Velazquez, ss/2b, South Bend (Diamondbacks)
17. Kyle Farmer, c, Great Lakes (Dodgers)
18. Duane Underwood, rhp, Kane County (Cubs)
19. Mitch Brown, rhp, Lake County (Indians)
20. Jake Bauers, 1b, Fort Wayne (Padres)

STANDINGS: SPLIT SEASON

FIRST HALF

EAST	W	L	PCT	GB
W. Michigan	41	29	.586	—
South Bend	40	29	.580	½
Dayton	36	32	.529	4
Great Lakes	34	36	.486	7
B. Green	32	37	.464	8 ½
Lansing	32	37	.464	8 ½
Fort Wayne	30	39	.435	10 ½
Lake County	27	43	.386	14

WEST	W	L	PCT	GB
Kane County	45	25	.643	—
Burlington	38	31	.551	6 ½
Peoria	37	32	.536	7 ½
Wisconsin	36	33	.522	8 ½
Quad Cities	35	34	.507	9 ½
Cedar Rapids	31	39	.443	14
Clinton	30	38	.441	14
Beloit	30	40	.429	15

SECOND HALF

EAST	W	L	PCT	GB
South Bend	43	27	.614	—
W. Michigan	41	29	.586	2
Lake County	38	31	.551	4 ½
Fort Wayne	33	37	.471	10
Great Lakes	32	37	.464	10 ½
Dayton	32	38	.457	11
Lansing	30	40	.429	13
B. Green	29	40	.420	13 ½

WEST	W	L	PCT	GB
Kane County	46	24	.657	—
Cedar Rapids	42	28	.600	4
Wisconsin	36	34	.514	10
Peoria	35	35	.500	11
Quad Cities	35	35	.500	11
Clinton	31	39	.443	15
Burlington	30	40	.429	16
Beloit	25	44	.362	20 ½

Quarterfinals: Lake County defeated South Bend 2-0, Kane County defeated Wisconsin 2-0, Cedar Rapids defeated Burlington 2-1 and Fort Wayne defeated West Michigan 2-1 in best-of-three series. **Semifinals:** Lake County defeated Fort Wayne 2-0 and Kane County defeated Cedar Rapids 2-0 in best-of-three series. **Finals:** Kane County defeated Lake County 3-0 in a best-of-five series.

OVERALL STANDINGS

Team (Organization)	W	L	PCT	GB	Manager(s)	Attendance	Average	Last pennant
Kane County Cougars (Cubs)	91	49	.650	—	Mark Johnson	63,505	977	2014
South Bend Silver Hawks (Diamondbacks)	83	56	.597	7 ½	Mark Haley	258,836	3,751	2005
West Michigan Whitecaps (Tigers)	82	58	.586	9	Andrew Graham	391,653	5,595	2007
Cedar Rapids Kernels (Twins)	73	67	.521	18	Jake Mauer	171,011	2,552	1994
Peoria Chiefs (Cardinals)	72	67	.518	18 ½	Joe Kruzel	217,632	3,297	2002
Wisconsin Timber Rattlers (Brewers)	72	67	.518	18 ½	Matt Erickson	250,131	3,970	2012
Quad Cities River Bandits (Astros)	70	69	.504	20 ½	Omar Lopez	237,005	3,885	2013
Dayton Dragons (Reds)	68	70	.493	22	Jose Nieves	573,709	8,437	Never
Burlington Bees (Angels)	68	71	.489	22 ½	Bill Richardson	70,649	1,054	2008
Great Lakes Loons (Dodgers)	66	73	.475	24 ½	Bill Haselman	230,019	3,334	2000
Lake County Captains (Indians)	65	74	.468	25 ½	Mark Budzinski	226,454	3,484	2010
Fort Wayne TinCaps (Padres)	63	76	.453	27 ½	Michael Collins	406,715	5,810	2009
Lansing Lugnuts (Blue Jays)	62	77	.446	28 ½	John Tamargo	338,249	4,832	2003
Bowling Green Hot Rods (Rays)	61	77	.442	29	Michael Johns	180,350	2,818	Never
Clinton LumberKings (Mariners)	61	77	.442	29	Scott Steinmann	111,329	1,713	1991
Beloit Snappers (Athletics)	55	84	.396	35 ½	Rick Magnante	63,505	977	1995

CLUB BATTING

	AVG	G	AB	R	H	2B	3B	HR	RBI	BB	SO	SB	OBP	SLG
Fort Wayne	.263	139	4857	683	1277	236	37	102	622	393	1111	107	.324	.390
Kane County	.261	140	4640	647	1211	254	36	74	578	404	958	139	.324	.379
Quad Cities	.261	139	4501	656	1175	261	45	104	589	510	1044	142	.340	.408
Bowling Green	.260	138	4628	605	1203	215	42	80	524	382	1120	126	.321	.376
Cedar Rapids	.259	140	4649	633	1202	213	45	77	567	433	1120	113	.330	.373
Lansing	.258	139	4755	616	1226	223	47	57	555	425	1115	110	.324	.360
West Michigan	.257	140	4817	574	1237	210	36	57	500	403	970	116	.319	.351
South Bend	.254	139	4699	694	1194	226	58	104	610	481	1208	131	.328	.393
Clinton	.252	138	4622	601	1166	214	34	78	535	439	1074	145	.324	.364
Wisconsin	.248	139	4512	644	1121	200	33	88	570	491	1103	150	.330	.366
Lake County	.246	139	4648	604	1144	228	42	119	541	447	1370	58	.317	.390
Peoria	.246	139	4492	555	1105	206	36	62	500	391	901	115	.314	.349
Dayton	.244	138	4534	582	1106	211	48	64	503	434	1097	149	.316	.354
Beloit	.243	139	4558	531	1109	219	41	92	482	436	1067	107	.315	.370
Great Lakes	.242	139	4682	551	1135	233	35	62	469	433	1101	183	.313	.347
Burlington	.241	139	4680	541	1128	217	37	80	485	407	1119	147	.308	.354

CLUB PITCHING

	ERA	G	CG	SHO	SV	IP	H	R	ER	HR	BB	SO	AVG
Kane County	2.85	140	3	12	39	1226	1017	449	388	71	417	1060	.227
West Michigan	3.05	140	0	10	49	1278	1143	513	434	59	389	1207	.240
Burlington	3.46	139	1	4	44	1251	1127	581	481	81	462	1140	.241
Great Lakes	3.49	139	1	8	38	1248	1183	555	484	96	401	1256	.250
South Bend	3.49	139	7	10	43	1226	1145	570	475	81	397	1128	.246
Peoria	3.53	139	1	12	39	1201	1116	570	471	68	436	1146	.244
Dayton	3.63	138	3	12	40	1214	1116	595	490	84	442	1177	.245
Bowling Green	3.69	138	1	9	22	1195	1156	615	490	99	407	1069	.253
Cedar Rapids	3.73	140	2	9	33	1210	1102	587	501	77	418	1145	.243
Quad Cities	3.79	139	2	7	33	1186	1186	601	500	71	394	1064	.261
Wisconsin	4.05	139	1	6	28	1206	1204	636	543	78	458	1051	.260
Lansing	4.07	139	1	4	31	1233	1295	663	557	84	447	1047	.270
Clinton	4.11	138	2	13	32	1202	1209	635	549	76	469	958	.264
Lake County	4.28	139	1	7	33	1211	1173	687	581	90	472	1129	.253
Beloit	4.54	139	5	7	29	1196	1221	702	603	110	431	856	.263
Fort Wayne	4.56	139	0	9	24	1232	1346	758	625	75	469	1045	.275

CLUB FIELDING

	PCT	PO	A	E	DP		PCT	PO	A	E	DP
Great	.977	3746	1366	119	104	Clinton	.970	3606	1414	155	123
Kane County	.977	3680	1450	119	101	South Bend	.970	3679	1450	158	102
West Michigan	.977	3536	1536	128	130	Dayton Dragons	.969	3643	1481	164	139
Quad Cities	.973	3558	1399	137	121	Bowling Green	.968	3585	1437	168	121
Lansing	.971	3699	1418	151	124	Wisconsin	.967	3618	1369	172	101
Beloit	.970	3589	1395	152	110	Lake County	.966	3665	1418	177	114
Burlington	.970	3754	1452	163	123	Peoria	.966	3606	1305	172	97
Cedar Rapids	.970	3631	1358	153	125	Fort Wayne	.960	3697	1350	208	103

INDIVIDUAL BATTING LEADERS

Batter, Club	AVG	G	AB	R	H	HR	RBI
Bernard, Wynton, West Michigan	.323	131	507	91	164	6	47
Wong, Kean, Bowling Green	.306	106	422	56	129	2	24
Phillips, Brett, Quad Cities	.302	103	384	68	116	13	58
Garver, Mitch, Cedar Rapids	.298	120	430	65	128	16	79
Bauers, Jake, Fort Wayne	.296	112	406	59	120	8	64
Aguilera, Eric, Burlington	.292	124	469	59	137	14	71
Querecuto, Juniel, Bowling Green	.291	88	354	45	103	2	37
Velazquez, Andrew, South Bend	.290	134	544	94	158	9	56
Hendrix, Paul, Lake County	.287	115	415	63	119	12	46
Coulter, Clint, Wisconsin	.287	126	429	84	123	22	89

INDIVIDUAL PITCHING LEADERS

Pitcher, Club	W	L	ERA	IP	H	BB	SO
Ziomek, Kevin, West Michigan	10	6	2.27	123	89	53	152
Kubitza, Austin, West Michigan	10	2	2.34	131	98	43	140
Cooney, Harrison, Burlington	9	8	2.65	129	108	51	91
Torrez, Daury, Kane County	11	7	2.74	131	110	21	81
Kirsch, Chris, Bowling Green	9	8	2.83	133	121	41	82
Crawford, Jonathon, West Michigan	8	3	2.85	123	93	50	85
Travieso, Nick, Dayton	14	5	3.03	142	123	44	114
Banda, Anthony, South Bend, Wisconsin	9	6	3.03	118	116	45	117
Green, Chad, West Michigan	6	4	3.11	130	121	28	125
Blackburn, Paul, Kane County	9	4	3.23	117	108	31	75

ALL-STAR TEAM

C: Mitch Garver, Cedar Rapids. **1B:** Jake Bauers, Fort Wayne. **2B:** Kean Wong, Bowling Green. **3B:** Mitch Nay, Lansing. **SS:** Andrew Velazquez, South Bend. **DH:** Clint Coulter, Wisconsin. **OF:** Brett Phillips, Quad Cities; Joey Curletta, Great Lakes; Wynton Bernard, West Michigan. **P:** Buck Farmer, West Michigan; Kevin Ziomek, West Michigan. **RP:** Silvino Bracho, South Bend; Will Locante, South Bend. **Most Valuable Player:** Wynton Bernard, West Michigan. **Manager of the Year:** Mark Johnson, Kane County. **Prospect of the Year:** Andrew Velazquez, South Bend.

DEPARTMENT LEADERS

BATTING

OBP	Coulter, Clint, Wisconsin	.410
SLG	Phillips, Brett, Quad Cities	.521
OPS	Coulter, Clint, Wisconsin	.930
R	Velazquez, Andrew, South Bend	94
H	Bernard, Wynton, West Michigan	164
TB	Rodriguez, Nellie, Lake County	234
XBH	Rodriguez, Nellie, Lake County	57
2B	Eaves, Kody, Burlington	37
	Hoenecke, Paul, Great Lakes	37
3B	Velazquez, Andrew, South Bend	15
HR	Coulter, Clint, Wisconsin	22
	Palka, Daniel, South Bend	22
	Rodriguez, Nellie, Lake County	22
RBI	Perez, Fernando, Fort Wayne	95
SAC	Betancourt, Javier, West Michigan	15
BB	Brennan, Taylor, Wisconsin	87
HBP	Coulter, Clint, Wisconsin	21
SO	Fink, Grant, Lake County	174
SB	Velazquez, Andrew, South Bend	50
CS	Davis, Johnny, Wisconsin	21
	Garcia, Omar, Wisconsin	21
AB/SO	Carhart, Ben, Kane County	9.65

PITCHING

G	Carlson, Ben, Burlington	52
GS	Kime, Dace, Lake County	28
	Romano, Sal, Dayton	28
GF	Frank, Trevor, Lake County	40
SV	Bracho, Silvino, South Bend	26
W	Travieso, Nick, Dayton	14
L	Bird, Zachary, Great Lakes	17
IP	Romano, Sal, Dayton	149
H	Gabryszwski, Jeremy, Lansing	176
R	Trivino, Lou, Beloit	93
ER	Trivino, Lou, Beloit	82
HB	Huijer, Lars, Clinton	18
BB	Campbell, Eddie, Clinton	74
SO	Lloyd, Kyle, Fort Wayne	155
SO/9	Lloyd, Kyle, Fort Wayne	11.66
SO/9(RP)	Perry, Chris, Peoria	14.69
BB/9	Gabryszwski, Jeremy, Lansing	1.34
WP	Brown, Mitch, Lake County	24
BK	six tied at 3	3
HR	Lugo, Luis, Lake County	16
	Mendez, Junior, Beloit	16

FIELDING

C	PCT	Perez, Michael, South Bend	.993
	PO	Perez, Michael, South Bend	756
	A	Hudson, Joe, Dayton	84
	DP	Kelly, Carson. Peoria	10
		McGee, Stephen, Burlington	10
	E	Haase, Eric, Lake County	16
	PB	Haase, Eric, Lake County	19
1B	PCT	Rogers, Jacob, Kane County	.993
	PO	Rodriguez, Nellie, Lake County	1,047
	A	Rogers, Jacob, Kane County	121
	DP	Ficociello, Dominic, West Michigan	94
	E	Seager, Justin, Clinton	14
2B	PCT	Wong, Kean, Bowling Green	.985
	PO	Bautista, Claudio, Lake County	233
	A	Eaves, Kody, Burlington	359
	DP	Betancourt, Javier, West Michigan	75
	E	Eaves, Kody, Burlington	30
3B	PCT	Rahier, Tanner, Dayton	.948
	PO	Peterson, Dustin, Fort Wayne	85
	A	Nay, Mitch, Lansing	234
		Rahier, Tanner, Dayton	234
	DP	Rahier, Tanner, Dayton	31
	E	Peterson, Dustin, Fort Wayne	38
SS	PCT	Salcedo, Erick, Burlington	.971
	PO	Penalver, Carlos, Kane County	208
	A	Penalver, Carlos, Kane County	376
	DP	Adames, Willy, West Michigan	72
	E	Daal, Carlton, Dayton	39
OF	PCT	Martin, Trey, Kane County	.996
	PO	McElroy, C.J., Peoria	279
	A	Phillips, Brett, Quad Cities	14
	DP	Boyd, B.J., Beloit	4
		Curletta, Joey, Great Lakes	4
		Kanzler, Jason, Cedar Rapids	4
	E	Davis, D.J., Lansing	18

MINOR LEAGUES

BY J.J. COOPER

aseball playoffs are often described as a roll of the dice. In a short series anything can happen, and the better team over a long season may not be the team that gets the season-ending dogpile.

But in the South Atlantic League, no one could complain about the worthy being honored when Asheville's players rushed the field to celebrate their Game Five win over Hagerstown to clinch the best-of-five championship series.

Asheville, owner of the best record in the Southern Division, had one of the best lineups in recent South Atlantic League history. As a team, the Tourists hit .292 and led the league in most offensive categories. From David Dahl and Ryan McMahon to Correlle Prime and Ramiel Tapia, the Tourists were the lineup no pitcher wanted to face.

What made the championship series so special is that the Tourists lineup was facing the pitching staff no one wanted to face. The Nationals shut down ace Lucas Giolito because he hit his innings limit late in the season. But they had a suitable substitute in Reynaldo Lopez. Lopez was the best pitcher in the league over the second half of the season. Coming into the championship round, he had allowed one earned run in his last 46 innings.

With the series tied 1-1, Asheville knocked around Lopez in a Game Three 4-1 win. It was the first time Lopez had struggled since he joined the Suns in late July. Hagerstown rallied to win Game Four, but Tapia homered and Zach Osborne doubled in two more as Asheville rolled to another 4-1 win in the deciding game.

While he didn't win the title, the playoffs were a suitable send-off to the Sally League for Hagerstown shortstop/second baseman Wilmer

Difo. The league MVP, Difo hit .433 with two home runs in the playoffs.

TOP 20 PROSPECTS

1. Lucas Giolito, rhp, Hagerstown (Nationals)
2. J.P. Crawford, ss, Lakewood (Phillies)
3. Reynaldo Lopez, rhp, Hagerstown (Nationals)
4. Luis Severino, rhp, Charleston (Yankees)
5. Reese McGuire, c, West Virginia (Pirates)
6. Austin Meadows, of, West Virginia (Pirates)
7. David Dahl, of, Asheville (Rockies)
8. Aaron Judge, of, Charleston (Yankees)
9. Manuel Margot, of, Greenville (Red Sox)
10. Hunter Harvey, rhp, Delmarva (Orioles)
11. Ryan McMahon, 3b, Asheville (Rockies)
12. Raimel Tapia, of, Asheville (Rockies)
13. Nomar Mazara, of, Asheville (Rangers)
14. Wilmer Difo, 2b/ss/ Hagerstown (Nationals)
15. Ian Clarkin, lhp, Charleston (Yankees)
16. Domingo German, rhp, Greensboro (Marlins)
17. Wendell Rijo, 2b, Greenville (Red Sox)
18. Chance Sisco, c, Delmarva (Orioles)
19. Mike Yastrzemski, of, Delmarva (Orioles)
20. Lewis Brinson, of, Asheville (Rangers)

STANDINGS: SPLIT SEASON

FIRST HALF

NORTH	W	L	PCT	GB
Greensboro	44	26	.629	—
Hagerstown	44	26	.629	—
Hickory	41	28	.594	2 ½
Delmarva	38	31	.551	5 ½
Kannapolis	29	38	.433	13 ½
Lakewood	27	42	.391	16 ½
West Virginia	20	48	.294	23

SOUTH	W	L	PCT	GB
Savannah	44	22	.667	—
Asheville	41	28	.594	4 ½
Augusta	34	34	.500	11
Greenville	34	35	.493	11 ½
Charleston	33	37	.471	13
Lexington	29	41	.414	17
Rome	24	46	.343	22

SECOND HALF

NORTH	W	L	PCT	GB
Hagerstown	43	27	.614	—
Greensboro	43	27	.614	—
Hickory	39	31	.557	4
West Virginia	34	33	.507	7 ½
Kannapolis	33	37	.471	10
Delmarva	28	42	.400	15
Lakewood	26	42	.382	16

SOUTH	W	L	PCT	GB
Asheville	48	21	.696	—
Savannah	41	29	.586	7 ½
Charleston	38	32	.543	10 ½
Rome	32	38	.457	16 ½
Augusta	28	42	.400	20 ½
Lexington	28	42	.400	20 ½
Greenville	26	44	.371	22 ½

Playoffs—Semifinals: Hagerstown defeated Greensboro 2-0 and Asheville defeated Savannah 2-0 in best-of-three series. **Finals:** Asheville defeated Hagerstown 3-2 in best-of-five series.

OVERALL STANDINGS

Team (Organization)	W	L	PCT	GB	Manager(s)	Attendance	Average	Last Pennant
Asheville Tourists (Rockies)	89	49	.645	—	Fred Ocasio	174,893	2,572	2014
Savannah Sand Gnats (Mets)	85	51	.625	3	Luis Rojas	124,013	2,067	2013
Greensboro Grasshoppers (Marlins)	87	53	.621	3	Dave Berg	369,170	5,429	2011
Hagerstown Suns (Nationals)	87	53	.621	3	Patrick Anderson	346,187	5,017	Never
Hickory Crawdads (Rangers)	80	59	.576	9 ½	Corey Ragsdale	61,683	979	2004
Charleston RiverDogs (Yankees)	71	69	.507	19	Luis Dorante	148,414	2,151	Never
Delmarva Shorebirds (Orioles)	66	73	.475	23 ½	Ryan Minor	210,130	3,233	2001
Kannapolis Intimidators (White Sox)	62	75	.453	26 ½	Pete Rose Jr.	119,377	1,925	2005
Augusta GreenJackets (Giants)	62	76	.449	27	Mike Goff	169,194	2,525	2008
Greenville Drive (Red Sox)	60	79	.432	29 ½	Darren Fenster	346,187	5,017	1998
Lexington Legends (Royals)	57	83	.407	33	Brian Buchanan	282,158	4,211	2001
West Virginia Power (Pirates)	54	81	.400	33 ½	Michael Ryan	140,484	2,266	1990
Rome Braves (Braves)	56	84	.400	34	Jonathan Schuerholz	177,531	2,573	2003
Lakewood BlueClaws (Phillies)	53	84	.387	35 ½	Greg Legg	380,573	5,597	2010

CLUB BATTING

	AVG	G	AB	R	H	2B	3B	HR	RBI	BB	SO	SB	OBP	SLG
Asheville	.292	138	4763	772	1389	334	33	122	704	361	1087	209	.349	.452
Greensboro	.285	140	4884	746	1394	245	33	94	677	459	817	74	.351	.407
Hagerstown	.273	140	4693	699	1283	253	41	88	621	389	843	235	.336	.401
Delmarva	.267	139	4753	592	1267	230	39	53	538	369	1129	110	.327	.365
West Virginia	.262	135	4485	577	1173	208	29	62	517	419	936	111	.332	.362
Greenville	.261	139	4640	660	1213	268	37	80	582	531	1049	132	.341	.387
Charleston	.257	140	4628	653	1190	224	38	91	573	511	1085	159	.337	.381
Lakewood	.256	137	4570	546	1172	242	36	74	492	373	1034	93	.317	.374
Lexington	.255	140	4701	591	1197	236	36	94	524	308	1076	129	.309	.380
Savannah	.255	136	4418	619	1126	206	50	63	533	528	993	154	.337	.367
Hickory	.252	139	4657	685	1174	239	29	122	602	474	1145	101	.327	.394
Rome	.249	140	4702	586	1170	210	44	65	529	433	1002	106	.319	.354
Kannapolis	.246	137	4526	568	1114	234	37	72	515	466	1248	118	.323	.362
Augusta	.238	138	4577	574	1088	211	25	67	504	411	1052	130	.309	.339

CLUB PITCHING

	ERA	G	CG	SHO	SV	IP	H	R	ER	HR	BB	SO	AVG
Savannah	3.03	136	11	17	40	1165	1076	486	392	55	392	1089	.243
Greensboro	3.49	140	2	12	43	1238	1211	578	480	87	351	1146	.256
Augusta	3.56	138	1	6	35	1207	1147	590	477	56	432	1129	.250
Charleston	3.66	140	1	11	36	1207	1159	579	491	65	427	1140	.250
Hagerstown	3.74	140	0	11	44	1214	1182	575	505	76	399	1006	.256
Asheville	3.75	138	0	7	46	1240	1243	641	516	98	380	974	.262
Hickory	3.76	139	3	8	36	1222	1201	592	511	106	424	1124	.256
Delmarva	3.80	139	2	10	37	1210	1173	606	511	70	394	1105	.253
Kannapolis	3.92	137	5	7	28	1194	1204	615	520	75	442	975	.263
West Virginia	4.15	135	1	6	22	1170	1223	637	539	111	425	902	.272
Greenville	4.63	139	1	6	31	1206	1227	719	621	93	527	999	.263
Rome	4.67	140	1	4	21	1219	1333	760	633	83	536	914	.277
Lexington	4.72	140	1	8	32	1205	1258	737	632	95	490	999	.270
Lakewood	4.88	137	3	8	30	1181	1313	753	641	77	413	934	.279

CLUB FIELDING

	PCT	PO	A	E	DP		PCT	PO	A	E	DP
Hagerstown	.977	3642	1484	118	108	Greenville	.970	3620	1322	152	114
Greensboro	.974	3714	1497	137	116	Lexington	.970	3616	1487	160	134
Delmarva	.972	3631	1487	146	104	Augusta	.969	3622	1512	162	121
Hickory	.972	3666	1397	148	103	Kannapolis	.969	3584	1499	160	133
Charleston	.971	3623	1370	147	101	Lakewood	.969	3543	1399	156	81
Savannah	.971	3495	1340	143	100	Asheville	.967	3720	1548	182	135
West Virginia	.971	3510	1452	146	110	Rome	.967	3658	1454	175	105

INDIVIDUAL BATTING LEADERS

Batter, Club	AVG	G	AB	R	H	HR	RBI
Sisco, Chance, Delmarva	.340	114	426	56	145	5	63
Astudillo, Williams, Lakewood	.333	117	436	41	145	4	61
Tapia, Raimel, Asheville	.326	122	481	93	157	9	72
Lopez, Carlos, Greensboro	.323	130	507	85	164	7	74
Romero, Avery, Greensboro	.320	92	366	51	117	5	46
Difo, Wilmer, Hagerstown	.315	136	559	91	176	14	90
Dosch, Drew, Delmarva	.314	128	500	76	157	5	50
Dahl, David, Asheville	.309	90	392	69	121	10	41
Dean, Austin, Greensboro	.308	99	403	67	124	9	58
Asuaje, Carlos, Greenville	.305	90	325	59	99	11	73

INDIVIDUAL PITCHING LEADERS

Pitcher, Club	W	L	ERA	IP	H	BB	SO
Ysla, Luis, Augusta	6	7	2.45	121	104	45	115
German, Domingo, Greensboro	9	3	2.48	123	116	25	113
Gsellman, Robert, Savannah	10	6	2.55	116	122	34	92
Gant, John, Savannah	11	5	2.56	123	107	40	114
Brault, Steven, Delmarva	9	8	3.05	130	107	28	115
Senzatela, Antonio, Asheville	15	2	3.11	144	134	36	89
Borden, Buddy, West Virginia	7	9	3.16	128	103	48	122
Gil, Yean Carlos, Rome	7	6	3.35	126	117	26	93
Wade, Konner, Asheville	8	8	3.61	142	154	35	94
Smith, Tyler, Hickory	7	6	3.67	125	131	38	125

ALL-STAR TEAM

C: Chance Sisco, Delmarva. **1B:** Felix Munoz, Greensboro. **2B:** Wilmer Difo, Hagerstown. **3B:** Ryan McMahon, Asheville. **SS:** JaCoby Jones, West Virginia. **DH:** Willians Astudillo, Lakewood. **OF:** Carlos Lopez, Greensboro; David Dahl, Asheville; Rafael Bautista, Hagerstown; Raimel Tapia, Asheville. **IF:** Carlos Asuaje, Greenville. **P:** John Gant, Savannah; Luis Ysla, Augusta. **RP:** Akeel Morris, Savannah. **Most Valuable Player:** Wilmer Difo, Hagerstown. **Most Outstanding Pitcher:** Lucas Giolito, Hagerstown.

DEPARTMENT LEADERS

BATTING

OBP	Sisco, Chance, Delmarva	.406
SLG	Asuaje, Carlos, Greenville	.542
OPS	Asuaje, Carlos, Greenville	.933
R	Bautista, Rafael, Hagerstown	97
H	Difo, Wilmer, Hagerstown	176
TB	Prime, Correlle, Asheville	264
XBH	Prime, Correlle, Asheville	71
2B	Prime, Correlle, Asheville	47
3B	Asuaje, Carlos, Greenville	10
	Yastrzemski, Mike, Delmarva	10
HR	Demeritte, Travis, Hickory	25
RBI	McMahon, Ryan, Asheville	102
	Prime, Correlle, Asheville	102
SAC	Camargo, Johan, Rome	15
	Torres, Ramon, Lexington	15
BB	Hayes, Danny, Kannapolis	73
HBP	Patterson, Jordan, Asheville	17
SO	Morris, Jacob, Kannapolis	179
SB	Bautista, Rafael, Hagerstown	69
CS	Tapia, Raimel, Asheville	16
AB/SO	Astudillo, Willians, Lakewood	21.80

PITCHING

G	Daniel, Trent, Asheville	53
GS	Dickson, Cody, West Virginia	27
	Jemiola, Zach, Asheville	27
	Jiminian, Johendi, Asheville	27
GF	Castillo, Luis, Augusta	31
	Perez, Pete, Rome	31
SV	Morris, Akeel, Savannah	16
W	Senzatela, Antonio, Asheville	15
L	Viza, Tyler, Lakewood	17
IP	Jiminian, Johendi, Asheville	151
H	Viza, Tyler, Lakewood	172
R	Jemiola, Zach, Asheville	96
ER	Callahan, Jamie, Greenville	84
HB	Dickson, Cody, West Virginia	13
BB	Mitchell, Andrew, Kannapolis	67
SO	Horacek, Mitch, Delmarva	151
SO/9	Horacek, Mitch, Delmarva	9.90
SO/9(RP)	Morris, Akeel, Savannah	14.05
BB/9	Garcia, Jarlin, Greensboro	1.41
WP	Mitchell, Andrew, Kannapolis	23
BK	Carasiti, Matt, Asheville	8
HR	Jemiola, Zach, Asheville	18
AVG	Borden, Buddy, West Virginia	.220

FIELDING

C	PCT	Kieboom, Spencer, Hagerstown	.997
	PO	Ross, Ty, Augusta	742
	A	Plaia, Colton, Savannah	100
	DP	McGuire, Reese, West Virginia	9
	E	Briceno, Jose, Asheville	14
	PB	Briceno, Jose, Asheville	11
1B	PCT	Munoz, Felix, Greensboro	.994
	PO	Prime, Correlle, Asheville	1,185
	A	Espinal, Edwin, West Virginia	82
	DP	Prime, Correlle, Asheville	107
	E	Prime, Correlle, Asheville	18
2B	PCT	Katoh, Gosuke, Charleston	.969
	PO	Rijo, Wendell, Greenville	205
	A	Pullin, Andrew, Lakewood	334
	DP	Weiss, Erich, West Virginia	67
	E	Pullin, Andrew, Lakewood	26
3B	PCT	Walding, Mitch, Lakewood	.933
	PO	McMahon, Ryan, Asheville	99
	A	McMahon, Ryan, Asheville	248
	DP	McMahon, Ryan, Asheville	28
	E	McMahon, Ryan, Asheville	32
SS	PCT	Arteaga, Humberto, Lexington	.970
	PO	Arteaga, Humberto, Lexington	191
	A	Camargo, Johan, Rome	330
	DP	Arteaga, Humberto, Lexington	76
	E	Camargo, Johan, Rome	33
OF	PCT	Perez, Yefri, Greensboro	.995
	PO	Bautista, Rafael, Hagerstown	296
	A	Lopez, Carlos, Greensboro	16
		Lorenzo, Gregory, Delmarva	16
	DP	Bautista, Rafael, Hagerstown	3
		Lorenzo, Gregory, Delmarva	3
		Morris, Jacob, Kannapolis	3
		Oliver, Connor, Rome	3
		Taylor, Dominique, Lexington	3
		Tocci, Carlos, Lakewood	3
	E	Tapia, Raimel, Asheville	15

MINOR LEAGUES

BY AARON FITT

For the second straight year, the State College Spikes and Tri-City ValleyCats met in the best-of-three New York-Penn League championship series. After the teams split the first two games, the Spikes avenged last year's finals loss by scoring six runs in the first inning of the decisive third game and cruising to an 11-2 win, securing their first NYPL crown in their nine-year history.

"That was a great game and a great series," State College manager Oliver Marmol said afterward. "They did a nice job all year and we competed against them in the same situation last year. It was a good battle tonight. Getting on the board early was what we stressed before the game, and we came out hot."

State College sent 10 batters to the plate in the first inning, which was sparked by Nick Thompson's two-run homer. The six-run outburst proved more than enough support for righthander Daniel Poncedeleon, who allowed just three hits and a walk while striking out five over six scoreless innings to earn the win.

The Spikes went 48-28 in the regular season to win the Pinckney Division and match Tri-City for the best record in the league. State College led the NYPL in batting (.269), home runs (55, led by Rowan Wick's 14 longballs in just 35 games) and runs (398). The Spikes also ranked second in the league with a 2.97 ERA and 644 strikeouts.

The ValleyCats, who reached the finals for the fourth time in the last five years, had some of the best college talent in the league, as usual, while State College was also an older club once again.

But the most talented team in the league was Brooklyn, which landed four players among the league's top 10 prospects, including three exciting young talents from Latin America. Brooklyn led the NYPL with a 2.74 staff ERA and 666 strikeouts, led by righthander Marcos Molina, the league's top prospect. Molina won the NYPL's pitching triple crown, tying for the league lead with seven wins while leading outright in ERA (1.77) and strikeouts (91).

"It was a real good group, they played real well together as a team," Brooklyn manager Tom Gamboa said. "We had a phenomenal pitching staff. In all my years, I've never seen a pitching staff with a collective ERA under 3. We were in virtually every game."

Talent in the 75-year-old NYPL was as strong as it has been in years, with a strong contingent of young international players blended with an excellent crop of premium 2014 draft picks. Last year, just one 2013 first-round pick (and five college players) cracked the Top 20. This year's list features three 2014 first-rounders plus a supplemental first-rounder, part of a strong group of nine college draftees.

TOP 20 PROSPECTS

1. Marcos Molina, rhp, Brooklyn (Mets)
2. Reynaldo Lopez, rhp, Auburn (Nationals)
3. Amed Rosario, ss, Brooklyn (Mets)
4. Luis Torrens, c, Staten Island (Yankees)
5. Bradley Zimmer, of, Mahoning Valley (Indians)
6. Yairo Munez, ss, Vermont (Athletics)
7. Michael Conforto, of, Brooklyn (Mets)
8. Derek Fisher, of, Tri-City (Astros)
9. Francisco Mejia, c, Mahoning Valley (Indians)
10. Jhoan Urena, 3b, Brooklyn (Mets)
11. A.J. Reed, 1b, Tri-City (Astros)
12. Casey Gillaspie, 1b, Hudson Valley (Rays)
13. Raudy Read, c, Auburn (Nationals)
14. Enderson Franco, rhp, Hudson Valley (Rays)
15. Sam Travis, 1b, Lowell (Red Sox)
16. Joe Musgrove, rhp, Tri-City (Astros)
17. Rowan Wick, of, State College (Cardinals)
18. Aaron Brown, of, Williamsport (Phillies)
19. Joe Jimenez, rhp, Connecticut (Tigers)
20. Kevin McAvoy, rhp, Lowell (Red Sox)

OVERALL STANDINGS

McNamara Division	W	L	PCT	GB	Manager(s)	Attendance	Average	Last Pennant
Hudson Valley Renegades (Rays)	46	30	.605	—	Tim Parenton	159,084	4,300	2012
Brooklyn Cyclones (Mets)	42	34	.553	4	Tom Gamboa	231,628	6,260	2001
Staten Island Yankees (Yankees)	37	38	.493	8 ½	Mario Garza	122,442	3,401	2011
Aberdeen IronBirds (Orioles)	27	48	.360	18 ½	Matt Merullo	150,300	4,175	1983

Pinckney Division	W	L	PCT	GB	Manager(s)	Attendance	Average	Last Pennant
State College Spikes (Cardinals)	48	28	.632	—	Oliver Marmol	134,927	3,647	2014
Jamestown Jammers (Pirates)	35	40	.467	12 ½	Brian Esposito	24,246	758	1991
Auburn Doubledays (Nationals)	34	41	.453	13 ½	Gary Cathcart	44,640	1,240	2007
Batavia Muckdogs (Marlins)	34	42	.447	14	Angel Espada	33,376	954	2008
Mahoning Valley Scrappers (Indians)	33	42	.440	14 ½	Ted Kubiak	109,545	3,130	2004
Williamsport Crosscutters (Phillies)	33	43	.434	15	Shawn Williams	61,249	1,750	2003

Stedler Division	W	L	PCT	GB	Manager(s)	Attendance	Average	Last Pennant
Tri-City ValleyCats (Astros)	48	28	.632	—	Ed Romero	161,171	4,241	2013
Connecticut Tigers (Tigers)	42	34	.553	6	Mike Rabelo	78,118	2,111	1998
Lowell Spinners (Red Sox)	37	38	.493	10 ½	Joe Oliver	165,129	4,346	Never
Vermont Lake Monsters (Athletics)	33	43	.434	15	David Newhan	84,091	2,273	1996

MINOR LEAGUES

CLUB BATTING

	AVG	G	AB	R	H	2B	3B	HR	RBI	BB	SO	SB	OBP	SLG
State College	.269	76	2619	398	705	138	19	55	357	252	494	63	.343	.399
Lowell	.267	75	2556	337	682	115	32	32	290	177	603	88	.319	.374
Tri-City	.262	76	2551	355	669	141	18	48	318	265	543	65	.341	.388
Connecticut	.260	76	2577	345	671	138	24	24	297	222	505	54	.324	.360
Hudson Valley	.260	76	2549	323	663	121	30	27	276	212	622	106	.323	.363
Brooklyn	.254	76	2531	307	642	114	19	22	260	214	653	62	.316	.340
Batavia	.251	76	2524	294	634	114	21	20	254	170	548	43	.308	.337
Jamestown	.249	75	2414	302	600	117	28	31	269	232	474	65	.323	.359
Staten Island	.248	75	2490	314	618	149	17	35	277	245	602	59	.322	.364
Auburn	.243	75	2440	299	593	135	19	32	260	220	545	53	.313	.353
Vermont	.242	76	2529	289	611	116	18	33	256	204	581	73	.307	.341
Mahoning Valley	.240	75	2514	319	604	122	19	27	281	241	499	67	.317	.336
Williamsport	.234	76	2477	264	580	127	13	44	239	150	563	64	.289	.349
Aberdeen	.230	75	2435	247	561	107	16	30	212	207	654	55	.297	.324

CLUB PITCHING

	ERA	G	CG	SHO	SV	IP	H	R	ER	HR	BB	SO	AVG
Brooklyn	2.74	76	0	10	20	671	566	268	204	22	234	666	.226
State College	2.97	76	0	8	22	679	587	271	224	27	229	644	.234
Hudson Valley	3.06	76	2	8	22	670	609	270	228	32	175	568	.242
Connecticut	3.13	76	0	7	18	664	624	293	231	24	181	565	.246
Tri-City	3.42	76	2	8	23	667	613	295	254	34	205	628	.241
Staten Island	3.46	75	0	6	19	653	617	327	251	26	226	661	.247
Williamsport	3.47	76	2	4	18	658	634	322	254	37	216	489	.253
Auburn	3.71	75	0	4	16	638	621	332	263	39	219	483	.254
Mahoning Valley	3.73	75	0	7	13	658	645	319	273	34	240	497	.258
Aberdeen	3.79	75	0	3	13	648	660	322	273	26	209	572	.266
Batavia	3.87	76	0	5	21	660	669	347	284	40	243	556	.265
Jamestown	3.95	75	0	3	21	651	658	336	286	40	188	503	.260
Vermont	4.06	76	0	3	21	664	667	338	300	43	202	531	.262
Lowell	4.20	75	0	5	19	660	663	353	308	36	244	523	.260

CLUB FIELDING

	PCT	PO	A	E	DP		PCT	PO	A	E	DP
Hudson Valley	.976	2010	750	69	54	Williamsport	.967	1974	809	95	61
Mahoning Valley	.972	1975	783	80	54	Batavia	.966	1981	841	100	74
Vermont Lake	.971	1994	895	86	67	Jamestown	.966	1953	778	97	60
State College	.970	2038	758	87	81	Auburn	.965	1916	806	100	63
Tri-City	.970	2003	837	88	59	Connecticut	.963	1994	785	108	54
Lowell	.969	1982	764	89	69	Brooklyn	.961	2013	764	113	55
Aberdeen	.968	1946	878	93	69	Staten Island	.961	1959	775	110	65

INDIVIDUAL BATTING LEADERS

Batter, Club	AVG	G	AB	R	H	HR	RBI
Spencer, Connor, Staten Island	.364	51	198	22	72	0	11
Dubon, Mauricio, Lowell	.320	66	256	40	82	3	34
Davis, Mason, Batavia	.319	56	216	39	69	3	29
Tanielu, Nick, Tri-City	.300	62	233	29	70	3	40
Urena, Jhoan, Brooklyn	.300	75	283	30	85	5	47
Blanchard, Coty, Hudson Valley	.298	66	248	35	74	2	30
Munoz, Yairo, Vermont	.298	66	252	29	75	5	20
Fuentes, Steven, Connecticut	.295	55	200	30	59	3	19
Seferina, Darren, State College	.294	51	194	28	57	0	9
Pankake, Joey, Connecticut	.292	64	240	37	70	2	36

INDIVIDUAL PITCHING LEADERS

Pitcher, Club	W	L	ERA	IP	H	BB	SO
Molina, Marcos, Brooklyn	7	3	1.77	76	46	18	91
Whitehead, David, Williamsport	4	4	2.19	74	70	8	43
DuRapau, Montana, Jamestown	3	2	2.21	61	56	8	57
Oswalt, Corey, Brooklyn	6	2	2.26	67	55	15	59
Anderson, Will, State College	6	2	2.43	70	72	11	50
Eppler, Tyler, Jamestown	3	2	2.49	68	54	11	49
Brady, Sean, Mahoning Valley	2	4	2.79	71	68	27	44
Musgrove, Joe, Tri-City	7	1	2.81	77	64	10	67
Edwards, Chase, Connecticut	6	3	2.99	87	99	13	52
Wood, Hunter, Hudson Valley	3	4	3.08	64	53	16	57

DEPARTMENT LEADERS

BATTING

OBP	Ritchie, Jamie, Tri-City	.455
SLG	Wick, Rowan, State College	.815
OPS	Breen, Chris, Staten Island	.881
R	Lockwood, Hunter, Hudson Valley	47
	Thompson, Nick, State College	47
H	Urena, Jhoan, Brooklyn	85
TB	Lockwood, Hunter, Hudson Valley	134
XBH	Lockwood, Hunter, Hudson Valley	31
2B	Tejeda, Isaias, Staten Island	21
3B	Meyers, Mike, Lowell	9
HR	Tromp, Jiandido, Williamsport	14
	Wick, Rowan, State College	14
RBI	Castillo, Leo, Mahoning Valley	49
SAC	Hyde, Mott, Tri-City	15
BB	Gillaspie, Casey, Hudson Valley	42
HBP	Two tied at	15
SO	Lockwood, Hunter, Hudson Valley	98
SB	Allen, Greg, Mahoning Valley	30
CS	Blanchard, Coty, Hudson Valley	12
AB/SO	Dubon, Mauricio, Lowell	9.85

PITCHING

G	Grana, Kyle, State College	27
	Lomascolo, Nick, State College	27
GS	Edwards, Chase, Connecticut	15
	Grundy, Jerad, Vermont	15
	McRae, Alex, Jamestown	15
GF	Pinales, Carlos, Lowell	24
SV	Bay, Shane, Brooklyn	15
	Pinales, Carlos, Lowell	15
W	Five tied at	7
L	Sanchez, Feliberto, Williamsport	9
	Santana, Juan, Mahoning Valley	9
IP	Edwards, Chase, Connecticut	87
H	Edwards, Chase, Connecticut	99
R	McRae, Alex, Jamestown	48
	Santana, Juan, Mahoning Valley	48
ER	McRae, Alex, Jamestown	46
HB	Rosario, Miguel, Jamestown	9
	Tarpley, Stephen, Aberdeen	9
BB	Castellanos, Gabriel, Batavia	41
SO	Molina, Marcos, Brooklyn	91
SO/9	Molina, Marcos, Brooklyn	10.73
SO/9(RP)	Bautista, Rony, Staten Island	14.64
BB/9	Whitehead, David, Williamsport	.97
WP	Hemmer, Gabe, Connecticut	15
BK	Arteaga, Alejandro, Williamsport	4
	Zapata, Jose, Mahoning Valley	4
HR	Cavanerio, Jorgan, Batavia	9
AVG	Molina, Marcos, Brooklyn	.170

FIELDING

C	PCT	Dominguez, Wilmer, Hudson Valley	.994
	PO	O'Keefe, Brian, State College	408
	A	Read, Raudy, Auburn	54
	DP	Grullon, Deivi, Williamsport	6
		Gushue, Taylor, Jamestown	6
	E	Mejia, Francisco, Mahoning Valley	11
	PB	Mejia, Francisco, Mahoning Valley	9
1B	PCT	Gillaspie, Casey, Hudson Valley	.997
	PO	Hoskins, Rhys, Williamsport	575
	A	Hoskins, Rhys, Williamsport	56
	DP	Nogowski, John, Vermont	44
	E	Fisher, Eric, Batavia	9
2B	PCT	Conrad, Jace, Hudson Valley	.988
	PO	Lunde, Erik, Jamestown	112
	A	Lunde, Erik, Jamestown	166
	DP	Seferina, Darren, State College	36
	E	McFarland, Ty, Staten Island	15
3B	PCT	Brizuela, Jose, Vermont	.959
	PO	Brizuela, Jose, Vermont	50
	A	Urena, Jhoan, Brooklyn	125
	DP	Martini, Renzo, Staten Island	13
	E	Hernandez, Jan, Williamsport	18
SS	PCT	Sole, Alec, Hudson Valley	.967
	PO	Dubon, Mauricio, Lowell	130
	A	Hyde, Mott, Tri-City	204
	DP	Munoz, Yairo, Vermont	41
	E	Mattlage, Garrett, Connecticut	24
OF	PCT	Gonzalez, Jay, Aberdeen	1.000
		Tharp, Tucker, Brooklyn	1.000
	PO	Jackson, Bralin, Hudson Valley	159
	A	Luplow, Jordan, Jamestown	17
	DP	Meyers, Mike, Lowell	4
	E	Aune, Austin, Staten Island	9

MINOR LEAGUES

BY JOHN MANUEL

Age is just a number, but it's a number that mattered greatly in the Northwest League playoffs.

In just its second year in the league, Hillsboro won the title, sweeping Vancouver in the best-of-three league finals after sweeping Boise in the first round of the playoffs. The Diamondbacks affiliate moved from Yakima, which had not won the NWL title since 2000.

As usual, the Diamondbacks stocked their NWL affiliate with somewhat older players—it had the oldest roster in the league—including six independent league signees. That group included 26-year-old Stewart Ijames, the league's playoff MVP after playing the vast majority of the regular season at Rookie-level Missoula; 23-year-old shortstop Steve Nyisztor, a former Rutgers star who had a five-hit game July 10 against Boise; and 23-year-old German righty Markus Solbach.

Meanwhile, Vancouver started 19-year-old righty Alberto Tirado and 20-year-old lefty Matt Smoral in the finals. The Canadians also featured the league's MVP in 18-year-old Franklin Barreto, a shortstop who led the league in hits (90), RBIs (61), runs (65), doubles (23) and total bases (139) while ranking third in stolen bases with 29.

"Taking into account he's playing against 22-, 23-, 24-year-olds, that's really, really hard," Tri-City manager Drew Saylor said. "This kid would be a freshman, maybe a sophomore in college. Imagine the hype if he were in the States. He'd be a first-rounder."

The Hops, who had the league's best regular season record at 48-28, had prospects too, chiefly relievers Mason McCullough, who hit 100 mph in a limited look late in the year, and closer Zac Curtis, who racked up 18 saves counting his four in the playoffs. The last save came in the title clincher, as he preserved a 4-3 victory.

But Ijames, who hit two homers in four playoff games, and third baseman Nate Robertson also were playoff heroes. Robertson went 5-for-12 with three extra-base hits (one double, two triples) in

four playoff games, after hitting just five doubles in 57 regular season games.

Vancouver posted the league's second-best regular season mark and also had four of the top eight prospects in the league, led by Barreto and including 2014 first-round pick Max Pentecost. Other first-rounders who played in the league included No. 4 pick Kyle Schwarber with Boise (Cubs) and shortstop Trea Turner (Padres) with Eugene. Neither stuck around long, with Schwarber going 12-for-20 with four homers in five games. He went on to hit 18 homers overall in his pro debut.

TOP 20 PROSPECTS

1. Franklin Barreto, ss, Vancouver (Blue Jays)
2. Christian Arroyo, ss, Salem-Keizer (Giants)
3. Jairo Labourt, lhp, Vancouver (Blue Jays)
4. Miguel Castro, rhp, Vancouver (Blue Jays)
5. Trea Turner, ss, Eugene (Padres)
6. Jeffrey Baez, of, Boise (Cubs)
7. Franchy Cordero, ss, Eugene (Padres)
8. Max Pentecost, c, Vancouver (Blue Jays)
9. Mark Zagunis, c/of, Boise (Cubs)
10. Josh Morgan, 2b/ss/ Spokane (Rangers)
11. Ryan Castellani, rhp, Tri-City (Rockies)
12. Ryan Yarbrough, lhp, Everett (Mariners)
13. Richelson Pena, rhp, Spokane (Rangers)
14. Erick Leal, rhp, Boise (Cubs)
15. Jose Trevino, c/3b/ss/ Spokane (Rangers)
16. Austin Cousino, of, Everett (Mariners)
17. Helmis Rodriguez, lhp, Tri-City (Rockies)
18. Rashad Crawford, of, Boise (Cubs)
19. Zac Curtis, lhp, Hillsboro (Diamondbacks)
20. Roemon Fields, of, Vancouver (Blue Jays)

STANDINGS: SPLIT SEASON

FIRST HALF					SECOND HALF				
NORTH	**W**	**L**	**PCT**	**GB**	**NORTH**	**W**	**L**	**PCT**	**GB**
Spokane	25	13	.658	—	Vancouver	21	17	.553	—
Vancouver	25	13	.658	—	Tri-City	19	19	.500	2
Tri-City	14	24	.368	11	Everett	17	21	.447	4
Everett	11	27	.289	14	Spokane	15	23	.395	6
SOUTH	**W**	**L**	**PCT**	**GB**	**SOUTH**	**W**	**L**	**PCT**	**GB**
Hillsboro	22	16	.579	—	Hillsboro	26	12	.684	—
Boise	22	16	.579	—	Salem-Keizer	20	18	.526	6
Salem-Keizer	18	20	.474	4	Boise	19	19	.500	7
Eugene	15	23	.395	7	Eugene	15	23	.395	11

Playoffs—Semifinals: Hillsboro defeated Boise 2-0 and Vancouver defeated Spokane 2-0 in best-of-three series. **Finals:** Hillsboro defeated Vancouver 2-0 in best-of-three series.

OVERALL STANDINGS

Team (Organization)	W	L	PCT	GB	Manager(s)	Attendance	Average	Last Pennant
Hillsboro Hops (Diamondbacks)	48	28	.632	—	J.R. House	138,732	3,651	2014
Vancouver Canadians (Blue Jays)	46	30	.605	2	John Schneider	180,187	4,870	2013
Boise Hawks (Cubs)	41	35	.539	7	Gary Van Tol	87,519	2,303	2004
Spokane Indians (Rangers)	40	36	.526	8	Tim Hulett	193,865	5,240	2008
Salem-Keizer Volcanoes (Giants)	38	38	.500	10	Gary Davenport	95,083	2,502	2009
Tri-City Dust Devils (Rockies)	33	43	.434	15	Drew Saylor	85,679	2,255	Never
Eugene Emeralds (Padres)	30	46	.395	18	Robbie Wine	108,067	2,844	1980
Everett AquaSox (Mariners)	28	48	.368	20	Dave Valle	92,642	2,504	2010

MINOR LEAGUES

CLUB BATTING

	AVG	G	AB	R	H	2B	3B	HR	RBI	BB	SO	SB	OBP	SLG
Boise	.274	76	2643	438	725	141	27	44	392	299	641	69	.353	.398
Spokane	.274	76	2642	399	725	135	16	45	354	261	524	53	.347	.389
Vancouver	.266	76	2621	402	698	137	22	27	345	251	505	145	.343	.366
Salem-Keizer	.258	76	2661	397	686	132	11	47	343	300	557	73	.342	.369
Hillsboro	.253	76	2584	376	655	122	17	47	328	267	639	105	.330	.368
Tri-City Dust	.251	76	2568	328	644	138	24	29	279	260	656	142	.327	.357
Eugene	.239	76	2584	318	618	151	17	50	277	218	698	78	.308	.369
Everett	.231	76	2563	317	591	127	7	48	276	291	710	65	.318	.342

CLUB PITCHING

	ERA	G	CG	SHO	SV	IP	H	R	ER	HR	BB	SO	AVG
Hillsboro	3.64	76	0	6	25	686	655	330	278	32	250	591	.251
Vancouver	3.75	76	0	6	31	680	615	332	283	32	322	630	.241
Spokane	4.15	76	0	4	17	677	631	340	312	47	219	638	.247
Everett	4.24	76	0	2	15	679	686	374	320	40	293	614	.263
Salem-Keizer	4.24	76	0	1	19	686	668	377	323	48	243	677	.253
Boise	4.43	76	1	2	11	675	691	388	332	57	252	615	.263
Eugene	4.53	76	0	4	14	675	664	417	340	39	288	672	.255
Tri-City	4.68	76	0	3	20	679	732	417	353	42	280	493	.275

CLUB FIELDING

	PCT	PO	A	E	DP		PCT	PO	A	E	DP
Boise	.963	2025	847	109	72	Salem-Keizer	.976	2059	786	71	50
Eugene	.954	2025	808	136	64	Spokane	.975	2032	716	70	58
Everett	.968	2038	841	96	79	Tri-City	.961	2037	886	120	84
Hillsboro	.970	2060	835	91	64	Vancouver	.972	2040	787	80	70

INDIVIDUAL BATTING LEADERS

Batter, Club	AVG	G	AB	R	H	HR	RBI
Pinto, Eduard, Spokane	.335	59	251	43	84	1	27
Arroyo, Christian, Salem-Keizer	.333	58	243	39	81	5	48
Spivey, Seth, Spokane	.332	67	259	51	86	3	27
Hoelscher, Shane, Tri-City	.332	53	193	31	64	2	27
Davis, Marcus, Eugene	.322	60	214	32	69	7	31
Tendler, Luke, Spokane	.316	67	256	48	81	11	57
Heyman, Grant, Hillsboro	.315	57	222	31	70	5	37
Locastro, Tim, Vancouver	.313	67	256	49	80	1	27
Carlson, Chris, Vancouver	.312	59	215	30	67	0	35
Barreto, Franklin, Vancouver	.311	73	289	65	90	6	61

INDIVIDUAL PITCHING LEADERS

Pitcher, Club	W	L	ERA	IP	H	BB	SO
Labourt, Jairo, Vancouver	5	3	1.77	71	47	37	82
Rodriguez, Helmis, Tri-City	4	7	1.97	91	82	18	41
Doran, Ryan, Hillsboro	4	3	2.56	63	69	10	48
Forjet, Jason, Salem-Keizer	7	1	3.10	87	84	16	87
Thompson, Derek, Boise	4	6	3.21	70	66	15	73
Pena, Richelson, Spokane	5	5	3.36	72	68	15	67
Clifton, Trevor, Boise	4	2	3.69	61	59	30	54
Leal, Erick, Boise	6	2	3.73	62	68	18	31
Reyes, Jose, Salem-Keizer	6	4	3.89	83	78	16	64
Kelly, Michael, Eugene	7	5	4.05	73	59	25	71

DEPARTMENT LEADERS

BATTING

OBP	Hoelscher, Shane, Tri-City	.427
SLG	Davis, Marcus, Eugene	.537
OPS	Davis, Marcus, Eugene	.948
R	Barreto, Franklin, Vancouver	65
H	Barreto, Franklin, Vancouver	90
TB	Barreto, Franklin, Vancouver	139
XBH	McBroom, Ryan, Vancouver	34
	Trevino, Jose, Spokane	34
2B	Barreto, Franklin, Vancouver	23
	Davis, Marcus, Eugene	23
	McBroom, Ryan, Vancouver	23
3B	Crawford, Rashad, Boise	7
HR	McBroom, Ryan, Vancouver	11
	Tendler, Luke, Spokane	11
RBI	Barreto, Franklin, Vancouver	61
SAC	Cowan, Jordan, Everett	8
BB	Spivey, Seth, Spokane	39
HBP	Locastro, Tim, Vancouver	32
SO	Hodges, Jesse, Boise	84
SB	Fields, Roemon, Vancouver	48
CS	Fields, Roemon, Vancouver	9
	Galvez, Cesar, Tri-City	9
AB/SO	Pinto, Eduard, Spokane	15.69

PITCHING

G	Sanchez, Eury, Salem-Keizer	28
GS	Four tied at	15
GF	Michalec, Josh, Tri-City	23
SV	Curtis, Zac, Hillsboro	14
	Sanchez, Eury, Salem-Keizer	14
W	Forjet, Jason, Salem-Keizer	7
	Kelly, Michael, Eugene	7
L	Medina, Jefferson, Everett	8
IP	Rodriguez, Helmis, Tri-City	91
H	Miller, Ethan, Salem-Keizer	89
R	Wasilewski, Zak, Vancouver	56
ER	Wasilewski, Zak, Vancouver	51
HB	Shouse, Blake, Tri-City	12
BB	Warner, Ryan, Tri-City	38
SO	Forjet, Jason, Salem-Keizer	87
SO/9	Labourt, Jairo, Vancouver	10.35
SO/9(RP)	Lucio, Seth, Eugene	15.15
BB/9	Leenhouts, Andrew, Salem-Keizer	1.37
WP	Lang, Trey, Boise	16
BK	Three tied at	3
HR	Barnett, Andrew, Spokane	10
AVG	Labourt, Jairo, Vancouver	.188

FIELDING

C	PCT	De La Cruz, Michael, Vancouver	.989
	PO	Martin, Adam, Everett	392
	A	Ruiz, Jose, Eugene	49
	DP	Trevino, Jose, Spokane	4
	E	Ruiz, Jose, Eugene	8
	PB	Ruiz, Jose, Eugene	23
1B	PCT	McBroom, Ryan, Vancouver	.994
	PO	McBroom, Ryan, Vancouver	574
	A	McBroom, Ryan, Vancouver	38
	DP	McBroom, Ryan, Vancouver	55
	E	Canela, Danny, Boise	8
		Petty, Kyle, Everett	8
2B	PCT	No qualifiers	
	PO	Bumpers, Sam, Tri-City	91
	A	Cowan, Jordan, Everett	146
	DP	Cowan, Jordan, Everett	30
	E	Goree, Jalen, Eugene	14
3B	PCT	Hodges, Jesse, Boise	.930
	PO	Hodges, Jesse, Boise	46
	A	Hodges, Jesse, Boise	141
	DP	Hodges, Jesse, Boise	13
	E	Hodges, Jesse, Boise	14
SS	PCT	Arroyo, Christian, Salem-Keizer	.965
	PO	Barreto, Franklin, Vancouver	91
	A	Arroyo, Christian, Salem-Keizer	185
	DP	Barreto, Franklin, Vancouver	38
		Rabago, Chris, Tri-City	38
	E	Cordero, Franchy, Eugene	33
OF	PCT	Cousino, Austin, Everett	.992
	PO	Crawford, Rashad, Boise	162
	A	Simpson, Corey, Everett	7
	DP	Fields, Roemon, Vancouver	4
	E	Pinto, Eduard, Spokane	6
		Simpson, Corey, Everett	6

MINOR LEAGUES

BY CLINT LONGENECKER

The Elizabethton Twins were the top Appalachian League team in the early part of the 21st century, winning five league titles in a 10-year stretch. The Johnson City Cardinals have staked an early claim to the top franchise of the next decade after winning their third league title in five years.

Johnson City has had a winning record for seven consecutive years. Elizabethton topped the Cardinals by one game to win the Western Division crown in the regular season before the Cardinals beat the Twins in the first round of the playoffs. The Twins won 7-6 in the series opener that went 13 innings, but then the Cardinals won back-to-back one-run games to win the series.

The Cardinals defeated the Danville Braves by a score of 4-2 in the decisive third game of the championship bout. Second baseman Casey Turgeon drew a bases-loaded walk in the second inning to get the Cardinals on the scoreboard before his double-play partner, shortstop Oscar Mercado, plated two on a single to give the Cardinals a 3-0 lead. Turgeon provided a seventh-inning home run to give the Cardinals a 4-1 lead before Danville scored once in the ninth, which summoned lefthander Ismael Brito to seal the victory. Brito, 21, led the league in saves with nine during the regular season.

The lefthanded-hitting Turgeon, a 24th-round pick out of Florida in 2014, was a driving offensive force for the Cardinals, finishing in the top-10 in all three triple-slash categories (.306/.428/.446) and second in the league in on-base percentage while pacing the league in runs scored (52). Johnson City had one player, No. 17 Oscar Mercado, make the Top 20 Prospects list. The young, athletic shortstop led the league in stolen bases with 26 while stealing at a 79 percent clip.

The earlier signing deadline continued to bolster the talent in the League, which had an above-average year for talent and featured the No. 5 overall pick in the 2014 draft (Elizabethton shortstop Nick Gordon) and 10 selections from the top two rounds of the past two drafts. Eight of those players made the Top 20, while in contrast, no first-rounders qualified for last year's ranking.

A trio of exciting shortstops—Danville's Ozhaino Albies, Gordon and Bluefield's Richard Urena—headlined the prospect list. The 17-year-old Albies separated himself as the youngest player in the league while drawing rave reviews for his defense at shortstop, instincts for the game and hitting ability from both sides of the plate.

Though the Appy League champion came out of the Western Division (Johnson City), the East boasted a bountiful batch of prospects that included 16 of the 20 to make the list. Burlington placed more prospects on the list than any other team with five, including a trio of 2014 draftees who signed for more than a million dollars (lefthander Foster Griffin, catcher Chase Vallot and righthander Scott Blewett) and a million-dollar international signee in Italian shortstop Marten Gasparini.

TOP 20 PROSPECTS

1. Ozhaino Albies, ss, Danville (Braves)
2. Nick Gordon, ss, Elizabethton (Twins)
3. Richard Urena, ss, Bluefield (Blue Jays)
4. Foster Griffin, lhp, Burlington (Royals)
5. Brent Honeywell, rhp, Princeton (Rays)
6. Scott Blewett, rhp, Burlington (Royals)
7. Matt Smoral, rhp, Bluefield (Blue Jays)
8. Alec Grosser, rhp, Danville (Braves)
9. Nick Ciuffo, ss, Princeton (Rays)
10. Angel Moreno, of, Princeton (Rays)
11. Chase Vallot, c, Burlington (Royals)
12. Ryan Borucki, lhp, Bluefield (Blue Jays)
13. Riley Unroe, 2b/ss, Princeton (Rays)
14. Marten Gasparini, ss, Burlington (Royals)
15. Tanner Murphy, c, Danville (Braves)
16. Dan Jansen, c, Bluefield (Blue Jays)
17. Oscar Mercado, ss, Johnson City (Cardinals)
18. Wuilmer Becerra, of, Kingsport (Mets)
19. Michael Cederoth, rhp, Elizabethton (Twins)
20. Niklas Stephenson, rhp, Burlington (Royals)

OVERALL STANDINGS

East Division	W	L	PCT	GB	Manager(s)	Attendance	Average	Last Pennant
Princeton (Rays)	40	28	.588	—	Danny Sheaffer	24,848	753	1994
Danville (Braves)	38	30	.559	2	Randy Ingle	30,385	950	2009
Pulaski (Mariners)	36	30	.545	3	Rob Mummau	26,160	818	2013
Bluefield (Blue Jays)	33	35	.485	7	Dennis Holmberg	26,446	826	2001
Burlington (Royals)	28	40	.412	12	Tommy Shields	40,497	1,191	1993

West Division	W	L	PCT	GB	Manager(s)	Attendance	Average	Last Pennant
Elizabethton (Twins)	38	30	.559	—	Ray Smith	26,590	806	2012
Johnson City (Cardinals)	37	31	.544	1	Johnny Rodriguez	40,351	1,261	2014
Kingsport (Mets)	34	34	.500	4	Jose Leger	30,464	952	1995
Greeneville (Astros)	32	34	.485	5	Josh Bonifay	48,619	1,430	2004
Bristol (Pirates)	22	46	.324	16	Edgar Varela	25,743	858	2002

Semifinals: Danville defeated Princeton 2-0 and Johnson City defeated Elizabethton 2-1 in best-of-three series. **Finals:** Johnson City defeated Danville 2-1 in a best-of-three series.

CLUB BATTING

	AVG	G	AB	R	H	2B	3B	HR	RBI	BB	SO	SB	OBP	SLG
Danville	.266	68	2250	320	598	108	14	26	281	259	558	72	.345	.361
Elizabethton	.262	68	2263	345	592	112	19	34	289	203	548	64	.335	.373
Kingsport	.258	68	2316	335	598	113	10	47	290	218	571	50	.329	.377
Bristol	.257	68	2276	293	584	110	16	17	252	230	575	45	.332	.341
Pulaski	.257	66	2169	322	557	105	19	24	260	234	551	95	.335	.356
Johnson City	.250	68	2276	325	568	104	12	32	267	233	465	55	.329	.348
Princeton	.249	68	2317	271	576	120	19	43	243	200	621	60	.319	.372
Bluefield	.248	68	2274	294	564	97	14	35	244	192	566	48	.316	.349
Greeneville	.239	66	2155	303	516	106	15	29	243	260	522	51	.324	.343
Burlington	.232	68	2196	265	510	88	23	31	232	187	538	88	.304	.336

CLUB PITCHING

	ERA	G	CG	SHO	SV	IP	H	R	ER	HR	BB	SO	AVG
Princeton	2.92	68	1	2	23	611	572	252	198	38	160	538	.250
Elizabethton	3.00	68	2	14	13	584	536	252	195	16	175	634	.242
Danville	3.39	68	0	4	13	589	513	260	222	24	201	575	.233
Bluefield	3.59	68	0	4	16	592	578	303	236	33	211	555	.253
Greeneville	3.60	66	0	4	13	580	550	295	232	19	240	595	.247
Pulaski	3.81	66	1	5	22	580	577	316	246	35	215	572	.257
Johnson City	3.93	68	0	4	24	588	618	340	257	42	209	550	.268
Burlington	3.96	68	0	3	15	586	569	319	258	40	258	510	.254
Kingsport	4.05	68	1	5	19	591	562	348	266	22	293	493	.251
Bristol	4.74	68	0	2	12	575	588	388	303	49	254	508	.263

CLUB FIELDING

	PCT	PO	A	E	DP		PCT	PO	A	E	DP
Danville	.972	1767	669	70	58	Burlington	.961	1758	712	101	50
Princeton	.968	1833	720	84	59	Bluefield	.957	1776	709	111	61
Elizabethton	.965	1753	672	88	53	Bristol	.956	1727	691	111	55
Greeneville	.963	1741	643	91	56	Johnson City	.954	1764	647	116	55
Pulaski	.962	1742	726	97	60	Kingsport	.952	1773	742	126	58

INDIVIDUAL BATTING LEADERS

Batter, Club

	AVG	G	AB	R	H	HR	RBI
Moon, Logan, Burlington	.332	59	226	23	75	2	24
Fields, Arby, Pulaski	.331	54	175	32	58	4	13
Montes, Hector, Princeton	.325	46	169	23	55	4	23
Vavra, Trey, Elizabethton	.319	50	185	32	59	1	34
Urena, Richard, Bluefield	.318	53	217	35	69	2	20
Rodriguez, Jean, Kingsport	.312	49	173	30	54	3	17
Burgess, Carter, Princeton	.307	53	192	21	59	2	17
Almonte, Josh, Bluefield	.307	62	251	35	77	3	24
Turgeon, Casey, Johnson City	.306	62	222	52	68	4	26
Morales, Estarlyn, Pulaski	.303	57	208	43	63	6	34

INDIVIDUAL PITCHING LEADERS

Pitcher, Club

	W	L	ERA	IP	H	BB	SO
Barrios, Agapito, Greeneville	5	0	2.09	56	39	11	46
Stephenson, Niklas, Burlington	3	3	2.14	59	45	9	47
Aquino, Joey, Bluefield	2	3	2.48	54	47	10	32
Jorge, Felix, Elizabethton	4	2	2.59	66	58	14	61
Missaki, Daniel, Pulaski	6	3	2.76	58	46	16	62
Perez, Juan, Johnson City	5	3	3.24	58	48	27	59
Alvarez, Freddy, Princeton	3	4	3.47	57	56	19	37
Ubiera, Andry, Danville	4	3	3.68	63	57	26	56
Grosser, Alec, Danville	4	3	3.68	63	60	22	63
Cordero, Daniel, Danville	4	3	3.81	59	58	17	50

ALL-STAR TEAM

C: Daniel Arribas, Bristol. **1B:** Carlton Tanabe, Pulaski. **2B:** Casey Turgeon, Johnson City. **3B:** Jordan Edgerton, Danville. **SS:** Nick Gordon, Elizabethton; Richard Urena, Bluefield. **DH:** Casey Grayson, Johnson City. **OF:** Arby Fields, Pulaski; Estarlyn Morales, Pulaski; Max Murphy, Elizabethton; Wuilmer Becerra, Kingsport. **P:** Felix Jorge, Elizabethton; Matthew Smoral, Bluefield. **RP:** Trey Cochran-Gill, Pulaski.

Player of the Year: Max Murph, Elizabethton. **Manager of the Year:** Ray Smith, Elizabethton. **Pitcher of the Year:** Felix Jorge, Elizabethton.

DEPARTMENT LEADERS

BATTING

OBP	Fields, Arby, Pulaski	.429
SLG	Murphy, Max, Elizabethton	.723
OPS	Fields, Arby, Pulaski	.932
R	Turgeon, Casey, Johnson City	52
H	Almonte, Josh, Bluefield	77
TB	Morales, Estarlyn, Pulaski	103
XBH	Morales, Estarlyn, Pulaski	25
2B	Vavra, Trey, Elizabethton	20
3B	Fukofuka, Amalani, Burlington	7
HR	Wilson, Ivan, Kingsport	11
RBI	Grayson, Casey, Johnson City	46
SAC	Fields, Arby, Pulaski	12
BB	Turgeon, Casey, Johnson City	42
HBP	Diemer, Austin, Elizabethton	12
SO	Wilson, Ivan, Kingsport	99
SB	Mercado, Oscar, Johnson City	26
CS	Fields, Arby, Pulaski	10
AB/SO	Caraballo, Oswald, Kingsport	9.58

PITCHING

G	Three tied at	23
GS	Basulto, Omar, Bristol	14
	Waszak, Andrew, Danville	14
GF	Cochran-Gill, Trey, Pulaski	17
	Isaacs, Dusty, Bluefield	17
SV	Brito, Ismael, Johnson City	9
	Miller, Peter, Pulaski	9
W	Martinez, Dailyn, Johnson City	6
	Missaki, Daniel, Pulaski	6
	Ramirez, Roel, Princeton	6
L	Tinoco, Jesus, Danville	9
IP	Waszak, Andrew, Danville	73
H	Rios, Francisco, Bluefield	79
R	Sandfort, Jonathan, Bristol	46
ER	Sandfort, Jonathan, Bristol	45
HB	Nuez, Yoryi, Kingsport	11
BB	Nuez, Yoryi, Kingsport	38
SO	Littell, Zack, Pulaski	64
SO/9	Missaki, Daniel, Pulaski	9.51
SO/9(RP)	Sever, John, Bristol	14.67
BB/9	Stephenson, Niklas, Burlington	1.37
WP	Urbina, Ugueth, Pulaski	15
BK	Three tied at	3
HR	Lubking, Trevor, Princeton	7
	Roth, Billy, Bristol	7
AVG	Barrios, Agapito, Greeneville	.193

FIELDING

C	PCT	Jansen, Dan, Bluefield	.991
	PO	Nottingham, Jacob, Greeneville	371
	A	Ciuffo, Nick, Princeton	55
	DP	Ciuffo, Nick, Princeton	6
	E	Garcia, Jose, Kingsport	8
	PB	Garcia, Jose, Kingsport	13
1B	PCT	Banuelos, Joshua, Burlington	.996
	PO	Tellez, Rowdy, Bluefield	429
	A	Banuelos, Joshua, Burlington	39
	DP	Tellez, Rowdy, Bluefield	37
	E	Calderon, Yordi, Pulaski	6
		Tanabe, Carlton, Pulaski	6
		Tellez, Rowdy, Bluefield	6
2B	PCT	Obregon, Omar, Danville	.992
	PO	Obregon, Omar, Danville	102
	A	Obregon, Omar, Danville	136
	DP	Segovia, Rolando, Bluefield	29
		Turgeon, Casey, Johnson City	29
	E	Segovia, Rolando, Bluefield	13
3B	PCT	Rivera, Chris, Johnson City	.949
	PO	Rivera, Chris, Johnson City	40
	A	Edgerton, Jordan, Danville	110
	DP	Rivera, Chris, Johnson City	15
	E	Dale, Ryan, Burlington	14
SS	PCT	Gordon, Nick, Elizabethton	.964
	PO	Mercado, Oscar, Johnson City	93
	A	Guillorme, Luis, Kingsport	187
	DP	Guillorme, Luis, Kingsport	33
	E	Mercado, Oscar, Johnson City	33
OF	PCT	Gonzalez, Jesus, Bluefield	1.000
	PO	Wilson, Ivan, Kingsport	139
	A	Moon, Logan, Burlington	10
	DP	Almonte, Josh, Bluefield	4
		Wilson, Ivan, Kingsport	4
	E	Almonte, Josh, Bluefield	8

MINOR LEAGUES

MINOR LEAGUES

BY BILL MITCHELL

The Billings Mustangs overcame a lackluster first half of the season to win the North Division second-half title, and then went undefeated through both playoff rounds to capture the league championship. The Reds affiliate, managed by first-time skipper Dick Schofield, were paced by top prospect Aristides Aquino, who led the league in doubles and RBIs and finished second in home runs and stolen bases.

Other key contributors in the Mustangs' regular lineup were first baseman Argenis Aldazoro, who led the team in batting (.325) and trailed only Aquino in home runs (11), and shortstop Alex Blandino, a 2014 first-round pick who batted .309/.412/.527 before a midseason promotion to low Class A Dayton. Lefthanded closer Brennan Bernardino finished with nine saves and a sparkling 1.01 ERA before securing the championship with the tying run on third base with no outs.

The Orem Owlz (Angels) reached the championship round by sweeping Ogden in the semifinals. The strength of their offense in the early part of the season came from third baseman Zach Houchins (.388 batting average) and outfielder Bo Way (.354), both of whom were promoted to low Class A Burlington at midseason, although Way returned for the championship series to replenish an outfield thinned by injuries. Righthander Arjenis Fernandez led all Pioneer League pitchers with nine wins.

The Grand Junction Rockies posted the league's best overall record (43-33), but missed the postseason after fading down the stretch to finish second in both halves of the season. The league's youngest team contributed five players to the league Top 20 Prospects list, with second baseman Forrest Wall placing second after batting .318/.416/.490.

A pair of unlikely candidates earned MVP and Pitcher of the Year honors. Idaho Falls first baseman Ryan O'Hearn, the Royals eighth round pick from Sam Houston State, burst into the Pioneer League with a 5-for-5 night in his first game and finished as MVP with a .361/.444/.590 average. Ogden righthander Jose De Leon was a 24th-

round pick from Southern in 2013 who didn't garner any prospect acclaim in his first pro season, but made adjustments and increased velocity in 2014 to become the Pioneer League's top hurler. He went undefeated in five decisions and finished with a 2.65 ERA and 77-19 K-BB rate.

In a lean year for blue-chip prospects, Blandino was the only first-round pick who played enough to qualify for the prospect list before his July promotion to the Midwest League. The only other first rounders to make appearances were Kyle Freeland (Grand Junction), Touki Toussaint (Missoula) and Grant Holmes (Odgen).

TOP 20 PROSPECTS

1. Aristides Aquino, of, Billings (Reds)
2. Forrest Wall, 2b, Grand Junction (Rockies)
3. Jose De Leon, rhp, Ogden (Dodgers)
4. Alex Blandino, ss, Billings (Reds)
5. Ryan O'Hearn, 1b, Idaho Falls (Royals)
6. Julian Leon, c, Ogden (Dodgers)
7. Justin Williams, of, Missoula (Diamondbacks)
8. Wyatt Strahan, rhp, Billings (Reds)
9. Sergio Alcantara, ss, Diamondbacks
10. Cody Bellinger, 1b, Ogden (Dodgers)
11. Kevin Padlo, 3b, Grand Junction (Rockies)
12. Taylor Sparks, 3b, Billings (Reds)
13. Jeff Brigham, rhp, Ogden (Dodgers)
14. Dom Nunez, c, Grand Junction (Rockies)
15. Tyler Mahle, rhp, Billings (Reds)
16. Devin Williams, rhp, Helena (Brewers)
17. Samir Duenez, 1b, Idaho Falls (Royals)
18. Wes Rogers, of, Grand Junction (Rockies)
19. Natanael Delgado, of, Orem (Angels)
20. Luis Jean, ss/2b, Grand Junction (Rockies)

STANDINGS: SPLIT SEASON

FIRST HALF

NORTH	W	L	PCT	GB
Great Falls	23	15	.605	—
Billings	17	21	.447	6
Missoula	17	21	.447	6
Helena	13	25	.342	10

SOUTH	W	L	PCT	GB
Billings	24	14	.632	—
Missoula	19	19	.500	5
Great Falls	16	22	.421	8
Helena	14	24	.368	10

SECOND HALF

NORTH	W	L	PCT	GB
Orem	24	14	.632	—
G. Junction	23	15	.605	1
Idaho Falls	20	18	.526	4
Ogden	15	23	.395	9

SOUTH	W	L	PCT	GB
Ogden	22	15	.595	—
G. Junction	20	18	.526	2½
Orem	18	19	.486	4
Idaho Falls	18	20	.474	4½

Playoffs—Semifinals: Orem defeated Ogden 2-0 and Billings defeated Great Falls 2-0 in best-of-three series. **Finals:** Billings defeated Orem 2-0 in best-of-three series.

OVERALL STANDINGS

Team (Organization)	W	L	PCT	GB	Manager(s)	Attendance	Average	Last Pennant
Grand Junction Rockies (Rockies)	43	33	.566	—	Anthony Sanders	81,382	2,200	Never
Orem Owlz (Angels)	42	33	.560	½	Dave Stapleton	83,179	2,248	2009
Billings Mustangs (Reds)	41	35	.539	2	Dick Schofield	105,358	2,927	2014
Great Falls Voyagers (White Sox)	39	37	.513	4	Charles Poe	49,520	1,338	2011
Idaho Falls Chukars (Royals)	38	38	.500	5	Omar Ramirez	79,895	2,283	2013
Ogden Raptors (Dodgers)	37	38	.493	5½	Jack McDowell	108,504	3,014	Never
Missoula Osprey (Diamondbacks)	36	40	.474	7	Audo Vicente	84,429	2,345	2012
Helena Brewers (Brewers)	27	49	.355	16	Tony Diggs	30,764	855	2010

CLUB BATTING

	AVG	G	AB	R	H	2B	3B	HR	RBI	BB	SO	SB	OBP	SLG
Grand Junction	.303	76	2574	499	780	142	31	58	429	283	551	167	.379	.450
Orem	.291	75	2608	489	758	158	35	74	428	242	577	86	.358	.463
Idaho Falls	.290	76	2640	446	766	155	37	44	392	252	546	82	.356	.427
Missoula	.280	76	2573	384	720	120	17	62	337	236	601	45	.347	.412
Ogden	.278	75	2594	428	720	136	31	61	378	246	555	95	.347	.424
Great Falls	.274	76	2642	392	723	134	28	70	347	255	632	39	.343	.425
Helena	.265	76	2556	358	678	125	17	36	282	245	629	122	.337	.370
Billings	.255	76	2581	421	659	145	31	78	375	212	617	117	.320	.426

CLUB PITCHING

	ERA	G	CG	SHO	SV	IP	H	R	ER	HR	BB	SO	AVG
Great Falls	3.74	76	0	5	18	664	686	345	276	48	225	606	.266
Billings	4.31	76	2	2	15	668	748	440	320	44	244	604	.279
Orem	4.68	75	0	3	17	648	705	422	337	54	235	525	.275
Grand Junction	4.69	76	0	1	21	658	785	451	343	77	199	575	.295
Idaho Falls	4.78	76	1	2	16	649	670	404	345	53	280	621	.269
Ogden	5.12	75	0	2	19	658	743	477	374	60	312	648	.283
Missoula	5.15	76	0	4	20	648	711	441	371	79	254	612	.280
Helena	5.32	76	0	2	15	652	756	470	386	68	222	517	.288

CLUB FIELDING

	PCT	PO	A	E	DP		PCT	PO	A	E	DP
Great Falls	.968	1993	848	95	66	Grand Junction	.957	1975	841	127	76
Missoula	.966	1946	812	98	70	Orem	.957	1945	898	129	71
Idaho Falls	.962	1949	844	109	68	Billings	.956	2004	827	130	60
Helena	.959	1958	818	118	62	Ogden	.953	1974	807	138	57

INDIVIDUAL BATTING LEADERS

Batter, Club	AVG	G	AB	R	H	HR	RBI
Williams, Justin, Missoula	.386	46	189	31	73	2	23
Daza, Yonathan, Grand Junction	.370	47	192	38	71	4	35
O'Hearn, Ryan, Idaho Falls	.361	64	249	61	90	13	54
Ahart, Devan, Ogden	.358	48	190	40	68	2	20
Daniel, Andrew, Orem	.340	63	259	49	88	6	39
Toups, Corey, Idaho Falls	.335	57	203	49	68	3	32
Pehl, Robert, Idaho Falls	.332	63	241	38	80	3	41
Leon, Julian, Ogden	.332	63	223	39	74	12	57
Mitsui, Trevor, Missoula	.330	68	264	46	87	12	52
Bellinger, Cody, Ogden	.328	46	195	49	64	3	34

INDIVIDUAL PITCHING LEADERS

Pitcher, Club	W	L	ERA	IP	H	BB	SO
Deshazier, Torey, Idaho Falls	5	3	3.17	65	59	22	66
Mahle, Tyler, Billings	5	4	3.87	76	80	15	71
Stone, Dane, Great Falls	6	3	3.99	79	95	20	76
Hernandez, Carlos, Missoula	5	4	4.22	70	76	36	61
Ortega, Jorge, Helena	4	5	4.23	83	90	8	46
Fernandez, Arjenis, Orem	9	5	4.23	78	103	19	46
Williams, Devin, Helena	4	7	4.48	66	74	20	66
Newberry, Jake, Idaho Falls	6	4	4.50	68	74	22	65
Bolaski, Michael, Orem	5	3	4.52	67	62	32	51
Moran, Luke, Billings	5	5	4.60	74	77	12	60

ALL-STAR TEAM

C: Julian Leon, Ogden. **1B:** Ryan O'Hearn, Idaho Falls. **2B:** Jake Peter, Great Falls. **3B:** Mike Hill, Idaho Falls. **SS:** Corey Toups, Idaho Falls. **OF:** Aristides Aquino, Billings; Justin Williams, Missoula; Robert Pehl, Idaho Falls. **DH:** Trevor Mitsui, Missoula. **P:** Jose DeLeon, Ogden; Dan Stone, Great Falls; Tyler Mahle, Billings; Torey Deshazier, Idaho Falls; Michael Bolaski, Orem.
Most Valuable Player: Ryan O'Hearn, Idaho Falls. **Pitcher of the Year:** Jose DeLeon, Ogden.
Manager of the Year: Anthony Sanders, Grand Junction.

DEPARTMENT LEADERS

BATTING

OBP	Toups, Corey, Idaho Falls	.453
SLG	O'Hearn, Ryan, Idaho Falls	.590
OPS	O'Hearn, Ryan, Idaho Falls	1.034
R	O'Hearn, Ryan, Idaho Falls	61
H	O'Hearn, Ryan, Idaho Falls	90
TB	Aquino, Aristides, Billings	164
XBH	Aquino, Aristides, Billings	44
2B	Aquino, Aristides, Billings	23
3B	Hill, Mike, Idaho Falls	8
HR	Chigbogu, Justin, Ogden	20
RBI	Aquino, Aristides, Billings	64
SAC	Soto, Wendell, Orem	7
BB	Alcantara, Sergio, Missoula	48
HBP	Wass, Wade, Orem	10
SO	Chigbogu, Justin, Ogden	101
SB	Diaz, Brandon, Helena	22
CS	Ahart, Devan, Ogden	10
	Carrizales, Omar, Grand Junction	10
AB/SO	Ahart, Devan, Ogden	10.56

PITCHING

G	Solis, Jency, Missoula	27
GS	Six tied at	15
GF	Crawford, Alec, Grand Junction	22
SV	Greer, Brody, Missoula	10
W	Fernandez, Arjenis, Orem	9
L	Ortega, Luis, Helena	9
IP	Ortega, Jorge, Helena	83
H	Fernandez, Arjenis, Orem	103
	Palacios, Javier, Grand Junction	103
R	Palacios, Javier, Grand Junction	69
ER	Palacios, Javier, Grand Junction	57
HB	Bolton, Tyler, Missoula	10
BB	Hernandez, Carlos, Missoula	36
SO	De Leon, Jose, Ogden	77
SO/9	Moya, Gabriel, Missoula	9.71
SO/9(RP)	Bello, Yoely, Grand Junction	12.91
BB/9	Ortega, Jorge, Helena	.87
WP	Bolaski, Michael, Orem	13
	Hernandez, Carlos, Missoula	13
	Keller, Brad, Missoula	13
BK	Four tied at	3
HR	Palacios, Javier, Grand Junction	15
AVG	Deshazier, Torey, Idaho Falls	.243

FIELDING

C	PCT	Leon, Julian, Ogden	.991
	PO	Leon, Julian, Ogden	404
	A	Leon, Julian, Ogden	53
	DP	Gutierrez, Yosbel, Missoula	3
		Leon, Julian, Ogden	3
		Long, Shedric, Billings	3
	E	Mejia, Natanael, Helena	8
	PB	Mejia, Natanael, Helena	4
1B	PCT	No qualifiers	
	PO	Sharkey, Alan, Helena	411
	A	Sharkey, Alan, Helena	44
	DP	Mitsui, Trevor, Missoula	34
		Sharkey, Alan, Helena	34
	E	Franklin, Kevin, Billings	9
2B	PCT	Daniel, Andrew, Orem	.976
	PO	Daniel, Andrew, Orem	103
	A	Daniel, Andrew, Orem	178
	DP	Daniel, Andrew, Orem	43
	E	Three tied at	10
3B	PCT	Ahmed, Michael, Ogden	.921
	PO	Neuhaus, Tucker, Helena	36
	A	Hill, Mike, Idaho Falls	115
	DP	Houchins, Zachary, Orem	10
		Palmeiro, Patrick, Great Falls	10
	E	Neuhaus, Tucker, Helena	16
SS	PCT	Alcantara, Sergio, Missoula	.950
	PO	Alcantara, Sergio, Missoula	114
	A	Alcantara, Sergio, Missoula	225
	DP	Alcantara, Sergio, Missoula	42
	E	Aviles, Luis, Helena	21
		George, Max, Grand Junction	21
OF	PCT	Diaz, Brandon, Helena	.994
	PO	Diaz, Brandon, Helena	153
	A	Aquino, Aristides, Billings	13
		McFarland, Dane, Missoula	13
	DP	Diaz, Brandon, Helena	7
	E	Gomez, Brawlun, Idaho Falls	7
		McFarland, Dane, Missoula	7

BY BILL MITCHELL

The Indians proved to be quite the juggernaut while dominating the 13-team Arizona League from start to finish. They compiled the league's top record (37-16), finished first in the Central Division in both halves of the season, and ended the year with a 14-0 trouncing of the defending champion Giants in the playoff finals.

Indians first baseman Bobby Bradley took home the most awards, with Cleveland's 2014 third-round pick earning MVP honors and leading the league in six different categories: batting average, home runs, RBIs, OPS, slugging percentage and runs scored. He became the first triple crown winner since 1989. Indians skipper Anthony Medrano was named manager of the year.

The Indians used more than just Bradley while rolling through the AZL season. Yu-Cheng Chang put together a strong first professional season while manning both spots on the left side of the infield. The native of Taiwan, who signed for a $500,000 bonus in 2013, hit .346/.420/.556 while playing solid infield defense. Fellow countryman Li-Jen Chu batted .348/.431/.596 as the Indians' primary catcher. The pitching staff was paced by a pair of 2013 draft choices, with righthander Casey Shane and lefty Thomas Pannone returning for their second AZL seasons. Lefthander Justus Sheffield, one of two Cleveland first round picks in 2014, also contributed with a 3-1 record. Yoiber Marquina, who earlier in the year converted from behind the plate to the mound, relied on an upper-90s fastball to save seven games and record a 2.57 ERA.

The Giants continued their Arizona League success, defeating the Mariners in a semifinal. Each of the parent club's top 11 draft picks in 2014 made appearances in the Arizona League, but their most impressive player was Dominican 19-year-old righthander Michael Santoswho finished with a 4-3, 2.56 record in his first season in the states.

Mariners outfielder Alex Jackson, the sixth overall pick in 2014, ranked as the league's top prospect. The rest of the prospect landscape was dominated by pitchers, with nine of the Top 20 being hurlers, including 2014 first rounders Sheffield and Grant Holmes (Dodgers).

TOP 20 PROSPECTS

1. Alex Jackson, of, Mariners
2. Grant Holmes, rhp, Dodgers
3. Bobby Bradley, 1b, Indians
4. Justus Sheffield, lhp, Indians
5. Spencer Adams, rhp, White Sox
6. Alex Verdugo, of, Dodgers
7. Monte Harrison, of, Brewers
8. Michael Gettys, of, Padres
9. Carson Sands, lhp, Cubs
10. Michael Santos, rhp, Giants
11. Cody Reed, lhp, Diamondbacks
12. Yu-Cheng Chang, ss/3b, Indians
13. Eloy Jimenez, of, Cubs
14. Gleyber Torres, ss, Cubs
15. Jose Herrera, c, Diamondbacks
16. Ricardo Sanchez, lhp, Angels
17. Dillon Overton, lhp, Athletics
18. Miguel Diaz, rhp, Brewers
19. Josh Morgan, ss/2b, Rangers
20. Yeyson Yrizarri, ss, Rangers

STANDINGS: SPLIT SEASON

FIRST HALF

EAST	W	L	PCT	GB
Angels	18	10	.643	—
D-backs	16	12	.571	2
Giants	14	14	.500	4
Cubs	13	15	.464	5
Athletics	12	16	.429	6

CENTRAL	W	L	PCT	GB
Indians	17	11	.607	—
Brewers	14	14	.500	3
Dodgers	12	16	.429	5
Reds	11	17	.393	6

WEST	W	L	PCT	GB
Rangers	18	10	.643	—
White Sox	15	13	.536	3
Mariners	14	14	.500	4
Padres	8	20	.286	10

SECOND HALF

EAST	W	L	PCT	GB
Giants	20	8	.714	—
Athletics	15	12	.556	4 ½
D-backs	13	15	.464	7
Angels	12	15	.444	7 ½
Cubs	9	19	.321	11

CENTRAL	W	L	PCT	GB
Indians	20	5	.800	—
Dodgers	13	15	.464	8 ½
Reds	13	15	.464	8 ½
Brewers	10	17	.370	11

WEST	W	L	PCT	GB
Mariners	17	8	.680	—
White Sox	15	12	.556	3
Padres	12	16	.429	6 ½
Rangers	8	20	.286	10 ½

OVERALL STANDINGS

Team (Organization)	W	L	PCT	GB	Manager(s)	Last Pennant
Indians	37	16	.698	—	Anthony Medrano	2014
Giants	34	22	.607	4 ½	Nestor Rojas	2013
Mariners	31	22	.585	6	Darrin Garner	2009
Angels	30	25	.545	8	Elio Sarmiento	Never
White Sox	30	25	.545	8	Mike Gellinger	Never
Diamondbacks	29	27	.518	9 ½	Luis Urueta	Never
Athletics	27	28	.491	11	Ruben Escalera	2001
Rangers	26	30	.464	12 ½	Kenny Holmberg	2012
Dodgers	25	31	.446	13 ½	John Shoemaker	2011
Brewers	24	31	.436	14	Nestor Corredor	2010
Reds	24	32	.429	14 ½	Eli Marrero	Never
Cubs	22	34	.393	16 ½	Jimmy Gonzalez	2002
Padres	20	36	.357	18 ½	Anthony Contreras	2006

Playoffs—Quarterfinals: Rangers defeated Angels and Mariners defeated Dodgers in one-game playoffs. **Semifinals:** Giants defeated Mariners and Indians defeated Rangers in one-game playoffs. **Finals:** Indians defeated Giants in a one-game playoff.

CLUB BATTING

	AVG	G	AB	R	H	2B	3B	HR	RBI	BB	SO	SB	OBP	SLG
Indians	.269	53	1837	332	495	87	24	35	280	193	437	74	.345	.400
Cubs	.261	56	1842	261	480	90	21	20	219	156	415	82	.326	.365
Angels	.256	56	1867	295	478	91	26	10	231	210	476	67	.340	.349
Diamondbacks	.254	56	1909	283	485	67	37	13	243	218	506	62	.335	.348
Rangers	.254	56	1858	269	472	70	20	13	213	193	406	65	.335	.334
Padres	.253	56	1907	285	483	89	30	26	243	192	524	57	.330	.372
Dodgers	.248	56	1888	282	469	95	13	32	232	212	581	62	.338	.363
Giants	.245	56	1943	316	476	98	29	11	247	216	492	53	.330	.342
Athletics	.241	56	1868	274	451	105	20	22	222	219	473	44	.328	.354
White Sox	.241	55	1848	278	446	77	25	29	232	219	515	39	.331	.357
Reds	.237	56	1884	251	447	86	26	24	215	154	498	55	.302	.349
Mariners	.233	53	1731	239	403	86	19	20	188	185	540	56	.314	.339
Brewers	.227	55	1834	259	417	69	11	16	206	203	537	106	.315	.303

CLUB PITCHING

	ERA	G	CG	SHO	SV	IP	H	R	ER	HR	BB	SO	AVG
Dodgers	3.20	56	1	4	10	487	425	244	173	20	157	476	.228
Indians	3.51	53	0	2	19	468	386	258	183	17	196	509	.222
White Sox	3.68	55	0	3	12	486	435	257	199	21	201	563	.237
Cubs	3.82	56	0	6	9	466	437	283	198	20	189	467	.245
Angels	3.84	56	0	0	12	502	486	270	214	16	190	482	.251
D-backs	3.86	56	0	2	13	498	493	268	214	17	156	466	.256
Giants	3.93	56	0	3	13	503	511	275	220	18	216	546	.264
Mariners	3.93	53	0	4	15	460	394	248	201	12	237	449	.232
Reds	3.93	56	0	2	10	492	497	295	215	25	185	510	.258
Rangers	4.12	56	0	1	14	482	458	275	221	21	188	496	.249
Padres	4.45	56	0	2	5	489	490	317	242	32	212	469	.256
Athletics	4.65	56	0	1	16	487	484	306	252	18	232	486	.257
Brewers	4.73	55	0	2	14	488	506	328	257	34	211	481	.261

CLUB FIELDING

	PCT	PO	A	E	DP		PCT	PO	A	E	DP
Giants	.966	1511	616	76	53	Padres	.954	1469	605	99	46
Rangers	.965	1448	605	75	47	Indians	.952	1406	529	98	43
Athletics	.964	1463	567	76	40	Dodgers	.951	1461	596	105	40
Angels	.961	1506	659	88	52	Brewers	.949	1466	582	109	44
Mariners	.961	1384	554	78	39	Cubs	.948	1398	626	110	53
White Sox	.959	1461	594	88	42	Reds	.946	1477	592	119	41
Diamondbacks	.957	1496	582	94	53						

INDIVIDUAL BATTING LEADERS

Batter, Club	AVG	G	AB	R	H	HR	RBI
Bradley, Bobby, Indians	.361	39	155	39	56	8	50
Verdugo, Alex, Dodgers	.347	49	170	28	59	3	33
Chang, Yu-Cheng, Indians	.346	42	159	39	55	6	25
Gettys, Michael, Padres	.310	52	213	29	66	3	38
Urias, Luis, Padres	.310	43	155	29	48	0	14
Mateo, Steven, Angels	.306	45	157	20	48	1	26
Vargas, Hector, Reds	.297	41	155	28	46	1	9
Mitchell, Kevonte, Cubs	.294	39	143	30	42	0	12
Hernandez, Gerard, Diamondbacks	.293	47	184	29	54	1	24
Barraza, Jose, White Sox	.287	37	136	28	39	5	19

INDIVIDUAL PITCHING LEADERS

Pitcher, Club	W	L	ERA	IP	H	BB	SO
Torres, Joshua, Brewers	4	0	1.92	51	47	10	37
Morales, Osmel, Mariners	5	2	2.20	49	40	15	65
Pacheco, Jairo, Dodgers	4	3	2.27	47	39	16	54
Santos, Michael, Giants	4	3	2.56	59	59	13	50
Shane, Casey, Indians	5	0	2.72	46	38	15	40
Santiago, Jose, Mariners	5	1	2.80	45	31	20	45
Pannone, Thomas, Indians	5	0	3.20	45	32	24	62
Navas, Carlos, Athletics	6	5	3.30	71	75	20	61
Guzman, Kevin, Dodgers	3	4	3.33	54	50	12	48
Boyles, Ty, Reds	4	2	3.35	45	30	16	52

ALL-STAR TEAM

C: Sherman Lacrus, Rangers. **1B:** Bobby Bradley, Indians. **2B:** Henry Castillo, Diamondbacks. **2B:** Josh Morgan, Rangers. **3B:** Gavin LaValley, Reds. **SS:** Yu-Cheng Chang, Indians. **DH:** Fran Whitten, Angels. **OF:** Alex Verdugo, Dodgers; Matt McPhearson, Diamondbacks; Michael Gettys, Padres. **P:** Thomas Pannone, Indians; Yefrey Ramirez, Diamondbacks. **RP:** Joe Palumbo, Rangers; Ronald Dominguez, Mariners.

Most Valuable Player: Bobby Bradley, Indians. **Manager of the Year:** Anthony Medrano, Indians.

DEPARTMENT LEADERS

BATTING

OBP	Morgan, Josh, Rangers	.468
SLG	Bradley, Bobby, Indians	.652
OPS	Bradley, Bobby, Indians	1.078
R	Bradley, Bobby, Indians	39
	Chang, Yu-Cheng, Indians	39
H	Gettys, Michael Padres	66
TB	Bradley, Bobby, Indians	101
XBH	Bradley, Bobby, Indians	25
2B	Lantigua, Jonas, Padres	14
	Verdugo, Alex, Dodgers	14
3B	Belen, Carlos, Padres	9
	Castillo, Henry, Diamondbacks	9
HR	Bradley, Bobby, Indians	8
RBI	Bradley, Bobby, Indians	50
SAC	Perez, Ayendy, Angels	6
BB	Harrison, Monte, Brewers	31
HBP	Harrison, Monte, Brewers	12
SO	Adolfo, Micker, White Sox	85
SB	Harrison, Monte, Brewers	32
CS	Belonis, Carlos, Brewers	8
	Gatewood, Jake, Brewers	8
AB/SO	Verdugo, Alex, Dodgers	12.14

PITCHING

G	Three tied at	21
GS	Armstrong, Mark, Reds	13
GF	Rivas, Jesus, Athletics	14
SV	Marquina, Yoiber, Indians	7
	Rivas, Jesus, Athletics	7
W	Navas, Carlos, Athletics	6
	Ventura, Angel, Brewers	6
	Zambrano, Jesus, Athletics	6
L	Four tied at	6
IP	Navas, Carlos, Athletics	71
H	Mendoza, Jose, Angels	81
R	Gonzalez, Manuel, Padres	48
	Mendoza, Jose, Angels	48
ER	Gonzalez, Manuel, Padres	39
HB	Arias, Jefferson, Mariners	10
	Muhammad, Jeremiah, Mariners	10
BB	Muhammad, Jeremiah, Mariners	35
SO	Morales, Osmel, Mariners	65
SO/9	Pannone, Thomas, Indians	12.4
SO/9(RP)	Mendonca, Tanner, White Sox	17.3
BB/9	Chiang, Shao-Ching, Indians	.59
WP	Lopez, Eduar, Angels	17
BK	Two tied at	6
HR	Constanza, Alex, Padres	7
AVG	Boyles, Ty, Reds	.175

FIELDING

C	PCT	Valenzuela, Ricardo, Padres	.996
	PO	Herrera, Jose, Diamondbacks	331
	A	Herrera, Jose, Diamondbacks	42
	DP	Castillo, Erick, Cubs	4
		Scott, Ryan, Dodgers	4
	E	Herrera, Jose, Diamondbacks	7
	PB	Herrera, Jose, Diamondbacks	7
1B	PCT	Lantigua, Jonas, Padres	.982
	PO	Lantigua, Jonas, Padres	359
	A	Four tied at	21
	DP	Alcala, Roney, Cubs	26
	E	Kronenfeld, Paul, Reds	9
2B	PCT	Rivera, Kevin, Giants	.958
	PO	Rivera, Kevin, Giants	78
	A	Rivera, Kevin, Giants	125
	DP	Rivera, Kevin, Giants	27
	E	Mardirosian, Shane, Reds	12
3B	PCT	Herrera, Jose, Diamondbacks	.936
	PO	Fontaine, Lachlan, Mariners	32
	A	Herrera, Jose, Diamondbacks	96
	DP	Fontaine, Lachlan, Mariners	10
	E	Walker, Jared, Dodgers	19
SS	PCT	Gatewood, Jake, Brewers	.955
	PO	Gatewood, Jake, Brewers	74
	A	Torres, Gleyber, Cubs	125
	DP	Torres, Gleyber, Cubs	25
	E	Tirado, Lucas, Dodgers	23
OF	PCT	Three tied at	1.000
	PO	Gettys, Michael, Padres	111
	A	Crook, Narciso, Reds	8
	DP	Medina, Michael, Dodgers	4
	E	Gettys, Michael, Padres	10

MINOR LEAGUES

BY BEN BADLER

Boston's international scouting has provided plenty of talent to the lower levels of the farm system in recent years. Those efforts paid off in the Gulf Coast League, where the Red Sox won 8-1 over the Yankees1 in the decisive Game 3 of the championship series.

The Red Sox led the league in runs and allowed the second-fewest runs in the GCL as well. Rafael Devers was a big part of the lineup once he arrived in early July following a midseason promotion from the Dominican Summer League. Devers, a 17-year-old third baseman who signed for $1.5 million in July 2013, hit .312/.374/.484 in 42 games, demolishing pitchers beyond his years to rank as the GCL's top prospect. Devers formed a dynamic left side of the infield with Panamanian shortstop Javier Guerra, who impressed scouts with his smooth glove work, while first-rounder Michael Choice also split time between shortstop and third base.

For the second straight season, the Yankees fielded two teams in the GCL. Both won their divisions thanks in largely to their young Latin American players, but the Yankees1 club went the furthest, reaching the finals.

Shortstop Jorge Mateo received limited playing time due to injury, but he made a loud impression with his blazing speed and quick-twitch athleticism. Middle infielder Bryan Cuevas showed polish while batting .356/.405/.564 in 40 games, and outfielder Alexander Palma flashed offensive potential with a .305/.318/.451 average. Among Yankees2 players, shortstop Angel Aguilar emerged from obscurity to rank second in the league in slugging and tied for second in homers.

The Cardinals won the GCL East division thanks behind center fielder Magneuris Sierra, who led the GCL in batting average and OBP while placing fourth in slugging. Sierra impressed both with his bat and his glove in center field. He and shortstop Edmundo Sosa, who hit .275/.341/.377, were vital to the Cardinals' success, as was right-hander Jack Flaherty, a first-round pick who held down a 1.56 ERA and a 28-4 K-BB mark in 23 innings with a strong fastball/changeup combination and excellent control. All three players ranked among the league's top 20 prospects.

Amaurys Minier didn't crack the GCL Top 20, but he made progress in his return to the league as an 18-year-old. Moved from third base to left field and first base, Minier led the league with eight home runs. The switch-hitter batted .292/.405/.520 in 53 games overall.

TOP 20 PROSPECTS

1. Rafael Devers, 3b, Red Sox
2. Tyler Kolek, rhp, Marlins
3. Ozhaino Albies, ss, Braves
4. Jorge Mateo, ss, Yankees
5. Jack Flaherty, rhp, Cardinals
6. Derek Hill, of, Tigers
7. Javier Guerra, ss, Red Sox
8. Sean Reid-Foley, rhp, Blue Jays
9. Michael Chavis, ss/3b, Red Sox
10. Edmundo Sosa, ss, Cardinals
11. Cole Tucker, ss, Pirates
12. Braxton Davidson, of, Braves
13. Mitch Keller, rhp, Pirates
14. Jakson Reetz, c, Nationals
15. Angel Aguilar, ss, Yankees
16. Magneuris Sierra, of, Cardinals
17. Jose Alvarado, lhp, Rays
18. Jomar Reyes, 3b, Orioles
19. Francis Martes, rhp, Marlins/Astros
20. Isael Soto, of, Marlins

OVERALL STANDINGS

East Division	W	L	PCT	GB	Manager(s)	Last Pennant
Cardinals	37	23	.617	—	Steve Turco	Never
Mets	33	27	.550	4	Jose Carreno	Never
Marlins	25	35	.417	12	Julio Garcia	Never
Nationals	25	35	.417	12	Michael Barrett	2009

Northeast Division	W	L	PCT	GB	Manager(s)	Last Pennant
Yankees2	35	25	.583	—	Pat Osborn	Never
Tigers	34	25	.576	½	Basilio Cabrera	Never
Braves	29	30	.492	5 ½	Rocket Wheeler	2003
Astros	28	32	.467	7	Marty Malloy	Never

Northwest Division	W	L	PCT	GB	Manager(s)	Last Pennant
Yankees1	38	22	.633	—	Travis Chapman	2011
Phillies	36	23	.610	1 ½	Roly de Armas	2010
Pirates	20	40	.333	18	Milver Reyes	2012
Blue Jays	18	41	.305	19 ½	Kenny Graham	Never

South Division	W	L	PCT	GB	Manager(s)	Last Pennant
Red Sox	36	24	.600	—	Tom Kotchman	2014
Rays	32	28	.533	4	Jim Morrison	Never
Orioles	29	31	.483	7	Orlando Gomez	Never
Twins	23	37	.383	13	Ramon Borrego	Never

Playoffs—Semifinals: Yankees 1 defeated Yankees 2 and Red Sox defeated Cardinals in one-game playoffs. **Finals:** Red Sox defeated Yankees 1 2-1 in a best-of-three series.

CLUB BATTING

	AVG	G	AB	R	H	2B	3B	HR	RBI	BB	SO	SB	OBP	SLG
Cardinals	.283	60	1917	299	542	96	33	15	256	225	341	55	.365	.391
Tigers	.262	59	1882	292	494	92	19	25	251	235	372	65	.347	.371
Yankees1	.260	60	1990	294	518	126	27	22	251	203	437	71	.336	.384
Yankees2	.258	60	1964	279	507	94	20	40	245	266	482	79	.353	.387
Astros	.254	60	1943	257	494	98	19	19	219	218	490	91	.337	.354
Braves	.251	59	1939	287	487	95	15	14	234	210	411	56	.340	.337
Phillies	.251	59	1928	276	484	116	19	15	241	193	394	65	.332	.354
Red Sox	.250	60	1919	306	479	109	14	16	263	223	437	61	.338	.346
Pirates	.249	60	1978	236	493	80	22	22	213	231	441	66	.336	.345
Mets	.247	60	1841	270	454	88	20	11	230	184	402	89	.327	.334
Nationals	.247	60	1881	259	464	87	17	12	215	208	394	60	.330	.333
Marlins	.241	60	1885	234	454	65	13	24	199	163	437	46	.315	.327
Rays	.241	60	1908	251	460	104	21	11	209	182	407	60	.321	.335
Orioles	.234	60	1878	210	439	89	19	16	174	166	423	52	.304	.327
Blue Jays	.227	59	1894	206	429	83	22	11	172	173	460	35	.298	.311
Twins	.226	60	1880	218	424	74	13	11	183	199	434	108	.307	.296

CLUB PITCHING

	ERA	G	CG	SHO	SV	IP	H	R	ER	HR	BB	SO	AVG
Red Sox	2.83	60	0	5	17	505	444	204	159	8	150	394	.235
Cardinals	3.01	60	2	8	15	493	444	199	165	17	123	418	.241
Rays	3.26	60	0	3	14	502	468	247	182	18	183	422	.248
Mets	3.27	60	1	4	20	503	449	250	183	18	225	434	.240
Yankees1	3.36	60	0	5	17	521	469	230	195	17	208	500	.239
Phillies	3.37	59	0	5	19	510	488	239	191	18	175	417	.252
Orioles	3.38	60	0	5	17	503	403	248	189	10	232	452	.218
Tigers	3.41	59	1	3	10	501	451	240	190	21	205	434	.241
Yankees2	3.57	60	0	5	11	516	466	247	205	16	256	467	.245
Twins	3.65	60	0	3	17	508	487	286	206	18	205	433	.249
Astros	3.90	60	1	3	17	528	526	292	229	23	227	497	.259
Braves	4.02	59	0	5	15	510	492	269	228	23	208	398	.254
Pirates	4.13	60	0	1	10	523	500	284	240	26	189	358	.251
Marlins	4.39	60	2	5	10	488	487	294	238	8	214	372	.262
Nationals	4.81	60	0	6	8	501	534	319	268	19	218	350	.273
Blue Jays	5.05	59	0	3	11	492	514	326	276	24	261	416	.272

CLUB FIELDING

	PCT	PO	A	E	DP		PCT	PO	A	E	DP
Rays	.969	1508	650	68	61	Red Sox	.965	1516	637	77	53
Tigers	.968	1505	630	70	54	Cardinals	.964	1479	577	77	36
Yankees1	.968	1565	613	71	47	Nationals	.963	1505	631	81	67
Yankees2	.968	1549	603	70	53	Marlins	.962	1464	646	83	51
Pirates	.967	1568	630	76	50	Mets	.962	1509	655	85	54
Blue Jays	.966	1477	577	72	53	Astros	.961	1585	660	91	52
Braves	.966	1530	630	77	55	Orioles	.961	1509	603	85	43
Phillies	.966	1530	678	78	41	Twins	.960	1524	638	91	53

INDIVIDUAL BATTING LEADERS

Batter, Club	AVG	G	AB	R	H	HR	RBI
Sierra, Magneuris, Cardinals	.386	52	202	42	78	2	30
Cuevas, Bryan, Yankees1	.356	40	149	25	53	2	23
Collymore, Malik, Cardinals	.333	54	177	34	59	1	34
Pritchard, Michael, Cardinals	.330	55	182	36	60	0	22
Sanay, Oscar, Rays	.329	43	146	15	48	0	11
Gonzalez, David, Tigers	.326	49	181	26	59	2	23
Zier, Tim, Phillies	.324	41	142	23	46	0	17
Valera, Junior, Yankees2	.316	38	136	24	43	2	14
Devers, Rafael, Red Sox	.312	42	157	21	49	4	36
Aguilar, Angel, Yankees2	.311	39	151	34	47	7	31

INDIVIDUAL PITCHING LEADERS

Pitcher, Club	W	L	ERA	IP	H	BB	SO
Centeno, Henry, Rays	4	2	1.50	54	38	11	51
Yepez, Angel, Rays	2	3	1.74	51	48	7	38
Keys, Denton, Phillies	3	2	2.20	49	43	12	35
Easton, Brandon, Twins	2	2	2.70	50	48	20	46
Caicedo, Oriel L, Braves	4	2	2.81	48	46	3	32
Baez, Sandy, Tigers	1	2	3.06	61	62	16	48
Jimenez, Dedgar, Red Sox	5	2	3.28	49	54	8	37
Batista, Gean, Yankees1	5	1	3.71	51	47	12	37
Gonzalez, Francisco, Braves	3	3	4.06	57	64	17	41
Castro, Anthony, Tigers	6	3	4.10	59	53	30	50

ALL-STAR TEAM

C: Arvicent Perez, Tigers. **1B:** Carlos Munoz, Pirates. **2B:** Malik Collymore, Cardinals. **3B:** Rafael Devers, Red Sox. **SS:** Angel Aguilar, Yankees 2. **UT:** Bryan Cuevas, Yankees 1. **DH:** Amaurys Minier, Twins. **OF:** Alexander Palma, Yankees 2; Michael Pritchard, Cardinals; Magneuris Sierra, Cardinals. **RHP:** Henry Centeno, Rays. **LHP:** Denton Keys, Phillies. **RP:** Trevor Hildenberger, Twins. **Most Valuable Player:** Magneuris Sierra, Cardinals. **Manager of the Year:** Tom Kotchman, Red Sox.

DEPARTMENT LEADERS

BATTING

OBP	Sierra, Magneuris, Cardinals	.434
SLG	Cuevas, Bryan, Yankees1	.564
OPS	Cuevas, Bryan, Yankees1	.969
R	Sierra, Magneuris, Cardinals	42
H	Sierra, Magneuris, Cardinals	78
TB	Sierra, Magneuris, Cardinals	102
XBH	Bridges, Drew	22
2B	Tomscha, Damek, Phillies	17
3B	Collymore, Malik, Cardinals	8
	Cuevas, Bryan, Yankees1	8
HR	Minier, Amaurys, Twins	8
RBI	Palma, Alexander, Yankees1	45
SAC	Tucker, Cole, Pirates	8
BB	Gotta, Cade, Rays	30
	Munoz, Carlos, Pirates	30
HBP	Tomscha, Damek, Phillies	13
SO	Bridges, Drew, Yankees1	65
SB	Guzman, Manuel. Twins	18
	Medina, Edwin, Astros	18
	Ramirez, Raphael, Mets	18
CS	Zabala, Enmanuel, Mets	12
AB/SO	Pritchard, Michael, Cardinals	18.20

PITCHING

G	Hildenberger, Trevor, Twins	23
GS	Four tied at	12
GF	Hildenberger, Trevor, Twins	22
SV	Hildenberger, Trevor, Twins	10
	Palsha, Alex, Mets	10
W	Rodriguez, Javier, Red Sox	8
L	Fulenchek, Garrett, Braves	7
IP	Baez, Sandy, Tigers	62
H	Agrazal, Dario, Pirates	65
	Rodriguez, Daniel, Blue Jays	65
R	Yrizarri, Deibi, Nationals	44
ER	Yrizarri, Deibi, Nationals	37
HB	Yrizarri, Deibi, Nationals	10
BB	Diaz, Carlos, Yankees2	39
SO	Perdomo, Angel, Blue Jays	57
SO/9	Centeno, Henry, Rays	8.5
SO/9(RP)	Pena, Jose, Yankees2	11.64
BB/9	Caicedo, Oriel L, Braves	.56
WP	Diaz, Francisco, Blue Jays	16
BK	Two tied at	4
HR	Mendez, Deivy, Marlins	6
AVG	Centeno, Henry, Rays	.203

FIELDING

C	PCT	Coa, Rainiero, Yankees2	.994
	PO	Aparicio, Jesus, Yankees2	243
	A	Heim, Jonah, Orioles	34
	DP	Heim, Jonah, Orioles	5
	E	Aparicio, Jesus, Yankees2	6
		Gonzalez, Yoel, Pirates	6
		Reetz, Jakson, Nationals	6
	PB	Aparicio, Jesus, Yankees2	9
1B	PCT	Munoz, Carlos, Pirates	.992
	PO	Munoz, Carlos, Pirates	472
	A	Hernandez, Jake, Yankees2	26
		Munoz, Carlos, Pirates	26
	DP	Rosario, Dionicio, Nationals	45
	E	Lee, Alexander, Orioles	8
		Rodriguez, Elier, Cardinals	8
		Rosario, Dionicio, Nationals	8
2B	PCT	Barreto, Deiferson, Blue Jays	.990
	PO	Barreto, Deiferson, Blue Jays	96
	A	Alvarez, Thomas, Nationals	109
	DP	Alvarez, Thomas, Nationals	38
	E	Juvier, Alejandro, Orioles	10
3B	PCT	Gutierrez, Kelvin	.934
	PO	Gutierrez, Kelvin	42
	A	Gutierrez, Kelvin, Nationals	114
	DP	Valerio, Allen, Yankees2	13
	E	Four tied at	13
SS	PCT	Sosa, Edmundo, Cardinals	.954
	PO	Sosa, Edmundo, Cardinals	83
	A	Sosa, Edmundo, Cardinals	145
	DP	Lora, Edwin, Nationals	38
	E	Three tied at	14
OF	PCT	Four tied at	1.000
	PO	Sierra, Magneuris, Cardinals	115
	A	Knott, Christian, Rays	11
	DP	Mercedes, Alex, Orioles	6
	E	Garrett, Stone, Marlins	5

MINOR LEAGUES

DOMINICAN SUMMER LEAGUE

The two teams with the best regular season records met in the Dominican Summer League finals, with the Rangers1 taking the title by beating the Red Sox three games to one.

In leading the league in winning percentage, the Rangers1 allowed the second-fewest runs in the league and ranks third in runs scored. Marcos Diplan, a 17-year-old Dominican righthander who signed for $1.3 million on July 2, 2013, was a key part of their team, ranking sixth in the league with a 1.54 ERA.

Run prevention was the strength of the Red Sox, who allowed the third-fewest runs in the DSL. Their most notable player, however, was third baseman Rafael Devers, another July 2 signing from 2013 who signed for $1.5 million. Devers hit .337/.445/.538 in 28 games and established himself as the league's best prospect before the Red Sox promoted him to the Gulf Coast League in early July.

STANDINGS

BOCA CHICA NORTH

TEAM	W	L	PCT	GB
Rangers1	54	16	.771	—
Cubs	42	28	.600	12
Rangers2	38	32	.543	16
Yankees2	38	32	.543	16
Pirates	34	36	.486	20
Angels	31	39	.443	23
Astros 1	31	39	.443	23
DSL Mets2	28	42	.400	26
DSL Marlins	27	43	.386	27
DSL Phillies	27	43	.386	27

BOCA CHICA SOUTH

TEAM	W	L	PCT	GB
Red Sox	50	19	.725	—
Giants	46	23	.667	4
Nationals	42	28	.600	8 ½
Yankees1	41	28	.594	9
Mets1	35	34	.507	15
Rockies	35	35	.500	15 ½
Orioles2	30	40	.429	20 ½
Mariners	27	43	.386	23 ½
Cardinals	22	48	.314	28 ½
Rojos	20	50	.286	30 ½

BOCA CHICA NORTHWEST

TEAM	W	L	PCT	GB
Royals	42	28	.600	—
Indians	41	28	.594	½
Dodgers	36	34	.514	6
Astros Blue	35	34	.507	6 ½
Rays	30	40	.429	12
Athletics	25	45	.357	17

BOCA CHICA BASEBALL CITY

TEAM	W	L	PCT	GB
Orioles1	47	23	.671	—
Twins	43	27	.614	4
D-backs	42	28	.600	5
Reds	32	39	.451	15 ½
White Sox	30	40	.429	17
Padres	17	54	.239	30 ½

SAN PEDRO DE MACORIS

TEAM	W	L	PCT	GB		TEAM	W	L	PCT	GB
Tigers	51	20	.718	—		Braves	30	40	.429	20 ½
Blue Jays	33	38	.465	18		Brewers	27	43	.386	23 ½

PLAYOFFS—First Round: Royals defeated Orioles1 2-1 and Giants defeated Tigers 2-1 in best-of-three series. **Semifinals:** Rangers1 defeated Giants 2-0 and Red Sox defeated Royals 2-1 in best-of-three series; **Finals:** Rangers1 defeated Red Sox 1 3-1 in a best-of-three series.

INDIVIDUAL BATTING LEADERS

PLAYER, TEAM	AVG	G	AB	R	H	2B	3B	HR	RBI	BB	SO	SB
Segovia, Joantgel, Brewers	.384	58	224	40	86	6	4	0	21	24	19	6
Joseph, Manuel, Tigers	.379	60	211	55	80	10	7	7	45	27	23	16
Vidal, Carlos, Yankees	.361	56	219	65	79	13	7	1	35	42	32	13
Terrero, Luis, Rangers	.358	68	260	51	93	15	5	0	50	26	28	30
Santana, Felix G., Tigers	.358	53	193	40	69	14	2	2	29	21	36	14
Rodriguez, Richard, Giants	.352	64	247	55	87	8	0	0	37	40	25	14
Pimentel, Davinson, Nats	.350	55	200	44	70	18	2	6	38	23	35	4
Gonzalez, Cesar, Tigers	.342	59	225	57	77	15	6	1	29	29	52	31
Mejia, Gabriel, Indians	.335	70	263	67	88	6	5	0	20	51	50	72
Fajardo, Kelvin, Rangers	.332	65	205	37	68	10	3	0	34	25	32	1

INDIVIDUAL PITCHING LEADERS

PLAYER, TEAM	W	L	ERA	G	GS	CG	SV	IP	H	R	ER	BB	SO
Bautista, Gerson	2	1	1.03	13	12	0	0	61	37	15	7	21	32
Taveras, Jose	8	4	1.05	15	13	1	0	85	61	22	10	8	70
Pena, Juan	4	2	1.16	13	10	0	0	70	50	18	9	10	54
Bolivar, Deiyerbert	7	1	1.27	15	10	0	3	64	41	13	9	20	67
Gomez, Daniel	7	3	1.39	14	10	0	0	64	45	16	10	10	55
Diplan, Marcos	7	2	1.54	13	13	0	0	64	32	18	11	36	57
Urena, Miguel	5	5	1.60	13	13	0	0	62	50	18	11	18	36
Bautista, Miguel	9	1	1.61	15	5	0	1	61	42	15	11	16	63
Diaz, Jhonathan	6	2	1.63	14	14	0	0	66	46	15	12	16	54
Zazueta, Samuel	5	0	1.63	14	11	0	2	66	49	19	12	12	91

VENEZUELAN SUMMER LEAGUE

With the series tied 1-1, the Tigers edged the Phillies 3-2 in the decisive Game Three to win the VSL championship.

The Tigers ran away with the regular season crown, leading the league in runs while also allowing the fewest. Tigers outfielder Jose Azocar won the batting title by hitting .340, while Tigers lefty Eudis Idrogo won the ERA crown at 0.91.

The Phillies and Tigers were the only teams in the five-team circuit to finish over .500, with the Phillies getting strong work from lefthander Ranger Suarez, who led the league in strikeouts and walks per nine innings with an incredible 78-1 K-BB mark in 80⅔ innings and a 1.56 ERA.

Cubs 17-year-old third baseman Wladimir Galindo made his mark on the league in his pro debut by hitting .278/.356/.462 and leading the VSL with seven home runs.

PLAYOFFS—Finals: Tigers defeated Phillies 2-1 in a best-of-three series.

STANDINGS

TEAM	W	L	PCT	GB		TEAM	W	L	PCT	GB
Tigers	45	23	.662	—		Cubs	28	40	.412	17
Phillies	36	32	.529	9		Rays	27	41	.397	18
Mariners	34	34	.500	11						

INDIVIDUAL BATTING LEADERS

PLAYER, TEAM	AVG	G	AB	R	H	2B	3B	HR	RBI	BB	SO	SB
Azocar, Jose, Tigers	.340	65	250	39	85	7	6	1	36	11	48	13
Ledezma, Junnell, Tigers	.326	46	172	31	56	5	8	1	29	14	20	11
Velasquez, Alberto, Mariners	.319	64	238	27	76	18	1	6	56	18	163	1
Cantillo, Anthony, Mariners	.319	50	160	25	51	5	2	0	17	15	13	6
Alastre, Jesus, Phillies	.314	61	210	35	66	8	2	2	13	34	13	13
Jimenez, Anthony, Mariners	.294	64	218	45	64	19	4	0	28	32	38	23
Miranda, Joseph, Phillies	.283	64	247	30	70	19	3	5	40	24	47	0
Rojas, Oscar, Rays	.282	55	220	30	62	18	1	2	21	10	30	18
Mendoza, Luis, Phillies	.280	59	218	22	61	10	1	0	3	29	10	39	8
Galindo, Wladimir, Cubs	.278	62	223	29	62	18	1	7	30	20	55	3

INDIVIDUAL PITCHING LEADERS

PLAYER, TEAM	W	L	ERA	G	GS	CG	SV	IP	H	R	ER	BB	SO
Idrogo, Eudis, Tigers	4	1	0.91	13	12	1	0	59	44	15	6	12	42
Rodriguez, Carlos A., Cubs	0	3	1.23	12	10	0	0	58	53	19	8	5	56
Gomez, Yapson, Cubs	6	2	1.51	13	12	1	0	71	50	19	12	8	37
Suarez, Ranger, Phillies	5	4	1.56	14	14	0	0	80	67	25	14	1	78
Vasquez, Angel, Tigers	8	2	1.71	13	13	1	0	68	48	17	13	10	32
Suarez, Michael, Mariners	6	0	1.72	13	9	0	0	57	41	18	11	16	60
Duarte, Jorman, Rays	2	4	1.99	13	13	0	0	54	45	26	12	10	19
Delgado, Victor, Phillies	5	6	3.15	13	13	0	0	65	66	32	23	9	49
Indriago, Carlos, Phillies	5	1	3.19	13	12	0	0	62	59	30	22	7	44
De Los Rio, Enrique, Cubs	2	5	3.76	14	14	0	0	67	74	33	28	9	42

Awards honor sustained success

TRIPLE-A
CHARLOTTE KNIGHTS (INTERNATIONAL)

The image of a new downtown ballpark is what kept Dan Rajkowski, Don Beaver and the rest of the Charlotte Knights staff going during the lean years at their old home in Fort Mill, S.C. Even as they attracted meager crowds to a stadium few Charlotte residents felt was worth the 12-mile drive down I-85 year after year, the team's leadership kept pushing for a new ballpark in downtown Charlotte that would certainly become the place to be on summer nights.

"We kept a vision of what could be something special and it did turn out to be special," said Rajkowski, the Knights' president who joined the team in 2005 and pushed for a new ballpark.

More special than even they imagined. That downtown ballpark became a reality on April 11, 2014, when the Knights hosted their first of 31 sellouts at BB&T Ballpark—the newdowntown venue with one of the best skyline views in minor league baseball. It lifted the Knights from the bottom of the International League in attendance to top the draw in all of the minors.

DOUBLE-A
MONTGOMERY BISCUITS (SOUTHERN)

Montgomery was without baseball since 1980 after the Rebels final season at Paterson Field. Sherrie Myers and Tom Dickson—a wife and husband team with marketing backgrounds—were part of a nationwide search for operators of a new franchise and in 2002 were chosen as the owners by the city of Montgomery, which agreed to build a $26 million ballpark.

Riverwalk Stadium opened on April 16, 2004, and in its first three seasons of operation, the Biscuits averaged better than 320,000 fans a season. It was the second-best figure in the Southern League despite being one of the league's smallest

markets. The ballpark has since spurred the development of downtown Montgomery.

"We approached it like it was no different than it was launching a package of soap or a magazine," Myers said. "It had to be a brand that had appeal that was contemporary and exciting."

CLASS A
WEST MICHIGAN WHITECAPS (MIDWEST)

Just three days into the year, the West Michigan Whitecaps organization experienced heartbreak at Fifth Third Ballpark, seeing half of what had been there for more than two decades burn to the ground in front of them. Rather than mourn the loss of a second home, team officials were determined to rebuild and had ballpark ready for Opening Day and back to normal in time to host the Midwest League all-star game in June.

"In a very real sense, watching that place burn was like watching your own house burn down," owner Lew Chamberlin said. "It was pretty devastating for our staff and the community, but that only underscored our urgency to get it rebuilt and rebuilt the right way."

SHORT-SEASON
BROOKLYN CYCLONES (NEW YORK-PENN)

Brooklyn's MCU Park suffered over $5 million in damages as a result of Hurricane Sandy in 2012. The water that flowed in from the Atlantic Ocean reached the third row of seats and a swell of five feet of water covered the field. The next several months were spent not only cleaning up the ballpark, but helping their neighbors as well.

Miraculously the 2013 season started on time with a new playing surface and the Cyclones haven't missed a beat since, remaining active in the community and entertaining at the ballpark with one of the best schedule of promotions in the minors. This season that included Seinfeld Night, a tribute to the popular sitcom.

PREVIOUS WINNERS

TRIPLE-A	DOUBLE-A	CLASS A	SHORT-SEASON
2004: Sacramento (Pacific Coast)	2004: Round Rock (Texas)	2004: Dayton (Midwest)	2004: Burlington (Appalachian)
2005: Toledo (International)	2005: Tulsa (Texas)	2005: Lakewood (South Atlantic)	2005: Brooklyn (New York-Penn)
2006: Durham (International)	2006: Altoona (Eastern)	2006: Daytona (Florida State)	2006: Aberdeen (New York-Penn)
2007: Albuquerque (Pacific Coast)	2007: Frisco (Texas)	2007: Lake Elsinore (California)	2007: Missoula (Pioneer)
2008: Columbus (International)	2008: Birmingham (Southern)	2008: Greensboro (South Atlantic)	2008: Greeneville (Appalachian)
2009: Iowa (Pacific Coast)	2009: New Hamshire (Eastern)	2009: San Jose (California)	2009: Tri-City (New York-Penn)
2010: Louisville (International)	2010: Corpus Christi (Texas)	2010: Lynchburg (Carolina)	2010: Idaho Falls (Pioneer)
2011: Colo. Springs (Pacific Coast)	2011: Harrisburg (Eastern)	2011: Fort Wayne (Midwest)	2011: Vancouver (Northwest)
2012: Lehigh Valley (International)	2012: N-West Arkansas (Texas)	2012: Greenville (South Atlantic)	2012: Billings (Pioneer)
2013: Indianapolis (International)	2013: Tulsa (Texas)	2013: Clearwater (Florida State)	2013: State College (NY-Penn)

MINOR LEAGUES

BY JOHN MANUEL

The Arizona Fall League was created for players such as Eddie Rosario, players who for one reason or another need to make up for lost development time and need extra playing time.

The Twins farmhand missed the first 50 games of the 2014 season for a second violation of MLB's drug of abuse policy, and he never found his rhythm in 86 games this season, batting just .242/.286/.387 overall in the regular season.

But the AFL gave Rosario another chance to write a different ending to his season, and it would be hard to top his finish in the finale. He hit a first-inning solo homer, the start of a loud 4-for-5, two-RBI day that helped key a 14-7 win for Salt River in the AFL championship game. The Rafters won their first title, with a seven-run seventh inning sealing their win against the Peoria Javelinas.

"Anytime you can say you're a champion, it's pretty special," Salt River manager Andy Haines (Marlins) said. "It was just our day. Our guys did what champions do . . . It's a good feeling at the end of the day to be a champion.

"Major league teams aren't developing players to just get their work in. They're developing guys to be championship baseball players."

Salt River—with prospects from the Astros, Diamondbacks, Marlins, Rockies and Twins organizations—had been the AFL's best team throughout the regular season. The Rafters went 17-11, their 3.10 ERA led the league by nearly a full run, and they ranked first in the league in batting (.272) while ranking second in runs.

They showed many ways to win in the championship. Rosario and first baseman Ryan Casteel (Rockies) homered, with Casteel's two-run shot in the bottom of the sixth knotting the game at 7-7.

"I just tried to lock in because it was a big game, and every at-bat was important," said Casteel, who had three RBIs. "Thankfully I got a slider up (for the home run), and I hit it (well). I thought it was gone off the bat . . . Thankfully it cleared that fence."

The Rafters played cleaner than Peoria, issuing just three walks as a pitching staff, committing one error and getting some sterling plays with the glove by third baseman Brandon Drury (Diamondbacks) and center fielder Evan Marzilli (Diamondbacks).

But their seven-run explosion in the seventh was the deciding factor. Two walks issued by righthander Nathan Hyatt (Braves), sandwiched around a double by Rosario, loaded the bases.

Peoria reliever Sam Selman (Royals) got ahead of Max Kepler (Twins) 0-and-2 but missed with his next four pitches, walking in a run to put the Rafters up to stay.

The inning was far from over. Justin Bohn (Marlins) jumped on a 2-0 pitch for a two-run single, and Casteel brought another run home with a single to left off reliever Brandon Cunniff (Braves). Drury walked to load the bases again, and Taylor Featherston capped the inning with a hit to right that Edward Salcedo (Braves) muffed, clearing the bases.

Eight pitchers appeared for Salt River, and Peoria had some success at the plate. The Javelinas hit just 11 home runs during the regular season but hit five in the title game. Trailing 3-0 entering the fourth inning against Salt River starter Anthony DeSclafani (Marlins), Hunter Dozier (Royals) and Justin O'Conner (Rays) went back-to-back to start the inning, both with home runs to left. Two outs later, Kes Carter (Rays) chased DeSclafani with a solo shot that tied the game.

O'Conner also hit a two-run homer in the top of the fifth as the Javelinas took a short-lived 6-5 lead. Bubba Starling (Royals) hit the fifth and final homer, a solo shot in the sixth. But Rafters relievers retired 12 of the last 13 Javelinas batters, with Taylor Rogers (Twins), Reid Redman (Marlins), Mitchell Lambson (Astros) and Enrique Burgos (Diamondbacks) tossing the last four innings.

Joe Sclafani (Astros) reached base four times, scoring twice for Salt River. O'Conner's two homers made him the only multi-hit batter for the Javelinas, who got four innings out of starter Miguel Almonte (Royals). He gave up three runs but also struck out seven while hitting 97 mph with his fastball in the first inning.

Scottsdale first baseman Greg Bird (Yankees) won the Joe Black award as the AFL's MVP. Surprise corner infielder Patrick Kivlehan (Mariners) took home the Dernell Stenson sportsmanship award.

TOP 10 PROSPECTS

1. Byron Buxton, of, Salt River (Twins)
2. Corey Seager, ss, Glendale (Dodgers)
3. Francisco Lindor, ss, Peoria (Indians)
4. Addison Russell, ss, Mesa (Cubs)
5. Tyler Glasnow, rhp, Scottsdale (Pirates)
6. Mark Appel, rhp, Salt River (Astros)
7. Hunter Renfroe, of, Surprise (Padres)
8. Archie Bradley, rhp, Salt River (D-backs)
9. Jesse Winker, of, Surprise (Reds)
10. Rusney Castillo, of, Surprise (Red Sox)

STANDINGS

EAST	W	L	PCT	GB	WEST	W	L	PCT	GB
Salt River Rafters	17	11	.607	—	Peoria Javelinas	15	14	.517	—
Mesa Solar Sox	15	14	.517	2½	Surprise Saguaros	16	15	.516	—
Scottsdale Scorpions	12	20	.375	7	Glendale Desert Dogs	14	15	.483	1

(Minimum 2 Plate Appearances/League Games)

Player, Team	AVG	G	AB	R	H	HR	RBI
Winker, Jesse, Surprise	.338	19	68	14	23	3	18
Rosario, Eddie, Salt River	.330	24	100	10	33	0	18
Bohn, Justin, Salt River	.328	17	58	11	19	1	5
Marrero, Deven, Surprise	.328	17	58	13	19	0	2
Sweeney, Darnell, Glendale	.316	19	79	14	25	2	12
Bird, Greg, Scottsdale	.313	26	99	21	31	6	21
Schebler, Scott, Glendale	.310	23	84	17	26	5	13
Rosa, Garabez, Glendale	.308	21	78	13	24	3	11
Kepler, Max, Salt River	.307	18	75	13	23	0	7
Smith, Mallex, Surprise	.305	15	59	12	18	0	5

INDIVIDUAL PITCHING LEADERS
(Minimum .4 Innings Pitched/League Games)

Player, Team	W	L	ERA	IP	H	BB	SO
McFarland, Blake, Mesa	1	0	0.00	13	9	8	15
Roberts, Ken, Salt River	0	0	0.00	14	8	4	9
Perez, Tyson, Salt River	0	2	0.63	14	11	1	11
Bassitt, Chris, Glendale	1	1	0.69	13	9	3	22
Reed, Jake, Salt River	1	0	0.71	13	10	3	10
Self, Derek, Mesa	1	0	1.20	15	12	5	6
Lambson, Mitch, Salt River	0	0	1.26	14	6	7	17
Tuivailala, Sam, Peoria	1	0	1.29	14	10	8	13
Doolittle, Ryan, Mesa	0	1	1.38	13	10	0	11
Scott, Robby, Surprise	0	0	1.38	13	11	5	14

GLENDALE DESERT DOGS

BATTERS	AVG	AB	R	H	2B	3B	HR	RBI	BB	SO	SB
Anderson, Tim	.301	93	14	28	6	0	2	9	4	28	6
Basto, Nick	.209	43	5	9	1	0	0	3	8	9	0
Coulter, Clint	.174	23	4	4	0	0	1	3	2	5	0
Esposito, Jason	.253	91	6	23	2	2	1	12	2	24	0
Fields, Daniel	.255	47	7	12	0	0	1	3	6	15	3
Gomez, Hector	.255	47	7	12	4	0	1	5	3	10	1
Leyba, Domingo	.171	41	2	7	0	0	0	1	4	9	0
Moya, Steven	.289	90	17	26	6	1	5	19	6	29	5
Ohlman, Mike	.244	41	3	10	2	0	1	2	4	15	0
Ramirez, Nick	.214	70	7	15	2	0	3	8	7	20	0
Rosa, Garabez	.308	78	13	24	3	0	3	11	4	16	1
Schebler, Scott	.310	84	17	26	3	0	5	13	5	20	0
Seager, Corey	.281	89	6	25	10	2	1	14	9	23	0
Smith, Kevan	.244	45	4	11	4	1	0	5	3	9	0
Sweeney, Darnell	.316	79	14	25	6	0	2	12	8	19	3
Taylor, Tyrone	.271	85	12	23	1	1	0	7	5	7	3
Zarraga, Shawn	.355	31	3	11	0	0	0	5	5	5	0

PITCHERS	W	L	ERA	G	GS	SV	IP	H	BB	SO	AVG
Bassitt, Chris	1	1	0.69	6	0	0	13	9	3	22	.184
Bridwell, Parker	0	1	7.94	8	0	0	11	9	8	9	.209
Coulombe, Daniel	0	0	0.00	4	0	0	3	1	3	6	.125
Davies, Zach	3	0	1.75	7	7	0	25	18	10	23	.205
Givens, Mychal	0	2	3.09	10	0	0	11	12	8	8	.273
Hall, Brooks	1	0	3.38	8	2	0	18	11	3	13	.175
Magill, Matt	2	3	3.96	7	6	0	25	21	14	21	.228
Mantiply, Joe	0	1	2.57	11	0	1	14	12	2	15	.226
Montas, Francellis	1	0	3.52	6	6	0	23	22	10	19	.253
Olacio, Jefferson	0	1	9.72	9	0	0	8	14	9	4	.368
Ray, Robbie	1	1	2.45	4	4	0	11	9	6	13	.225
Reininger, Zac	0	1	8.25	11	0	0	12	15	8	14	.294
Shelton, Matt	0	0	5.40	6	0	0	8	9	5	6	.273
Smith, Blake	0	2	9.00	11	0	2	11	17	11	13	.347
Smith, Chad	0	1	9.00	4	0	0	4	6	4	3	.316
Snodgress, Scott	1	0	8.53	11	0	0	12	16	13	9	.333
Strong, Michael	1	0	1.98	11	0	2	13	8	3	14	.167
Thomas, Mike	1	0	4.85	11	0	1	13	12	6	13	.240
Tolliver, Ashur	0	0	2.70	4	0	0	3	3	0	2	.250
Wagner, Tyler	0	1	7.43	9	0	1	13	13	7	7	.245
Wang, Wei-Chung	2	0	2.74	6	6	0	23	22	2	12	.253

MESA SOLAR SOX

BATTERS	AVG	AB	R	H	2B	3B	HR	RBI	BB	SO	SB
Berti, Jon	.292	65	10	19	0	0	3	8	12	16	6
Cowart, Kaleb	.185	81	11	15	0	3	0	6	4	15	3

	AVG	AB	R	H	2B	3B	HR	RBI	BB	SO	SB
Hannemann, Jacob	.279	61	5	17	4	2	0	7	5	12	0
Hinshaw, Chad	.284	67	12	19	4	0	0	6	12	16	7
Kieboom, Spencer	.324	34	3	11	2	0	1	7	5	4	0
Lockhart, Danny	.250	20	3	5	0	0	0	3	2	0	1
Ochinko, Sean	.310	42	4	13	5	0	1	11	3	4	0
Olson, Matt	.257	35	11	9	1	1	4	8	10	9	2
Pompey, Dalton	.257	70	7	18	4	2	0	2	11	14	9
Powell, Boog	.300	70	8	21	3	0	2	10	12	11	3
Rademacher, Bijan	.350	40	11	14	2	1	1	9	5	3	4
Renda, Tony	.200	85	12	17	3	1	0	7	3	19	1
Robertson, Daniel	.301	73	13	22	1	0	1	12	11	20	0
Russell, Addison	.196	46	8	9	1	0	2	10	3	13	1
Severino, Pedro	.250	44	1	11	2	1	0	5	2	7	0
Smith Jr., Dwight	.262	42	7	11	1	1	0	5	4	5	3
Stamets, Eric	.279	61	10	17	1	1	1	6	1	7	1
Towey, Cal	.279	68	11	19	4	0	2	13	9	20	3
Vogelbach, Dan	.261	69	8	18	4	0	0	8	17	11	1

PITCHERS	W	L	ERA	G	GS	SV	IP	H	BB	SO	AVG
Cates, Zach	0	0	9.28	9	0	0	10	17	6	8	.347
Concepcion, Gerardo	1	1	5.87	9	0	0	15	16	9	7	.291
Doolittle, Ryan	0	1	1.38	8	0	0	13	10	0	11	.217
Edwards, C.J.	1	0	1.80	6	6	0	15	8	8	13	.154
Gott, Trevor	0	0	6.14	8	0	1	7	11	2	4	.344
Grace, Matt	0	0	3.18	10	0	0	11	10	5	8	.227
Granier, Drew	0	0	6.91	9	0	0	14	18	9	9	.321
Holland, Neil	1	2	10.80	8	0	0	11	20	8	8	.392
House, Austin	0	0	4.76	9	0	1	11	11	7	8	.244
McFarland, Blake	1	0	0.00	9	0	0	12	9	8	15	.196
Nolin, Sean	2	1	4.03	7	7	0	22	20	6	24	.230
O'Grady, Chris	3	0	1.42	8	0	1	12	5	6	8	.125
Osuna, Roberto	0	3	9.49	6	0	0	12	22	4	15	.393
Peters, Tanner	0	1	3.77	8	1	0	14	15	6	15	.273
Pineyro, Ivan	1	0	1.98	7	4	0	13	11	4	16	.208
Rivero, Felipe	2	4	6.08	7	7	0	23	26	11	15	.283
Sappington, Mark	0	0	5.25	10	0	1	12	10	7	8	.238
Self, Derek	1	0	1.20	9	0	0	15	12	5	6	.235
Sikula, Arik	1	0	2.61	9	0	2	10	11	2	7	.268
Smith, Nate	1	3	3.27	6	6	0	22	23	8	21	.267

PEORIA JAVELINAS

BATTERS	AVG	AB	R	H	2B	3B	HR	RBI	BB	SO	SB
Carter, Kes	.191	68	8	13	3	2	2	13	7	26	2
Castro, Daniel	.190	58	5	11	3	0	0	3	5	8	1
Dozier, Hunter	.256	86	13	22	6	0	1	11	18	29	0
Leonard, Patrick	.182	66	8	12	3	0	2	5	10	19	1
Lindor, Francisco	.265	98	15	26	5	1	3	9	8	13	2
McElroy, C.J.	.200	40	4	8	1	0	0	2	6	12	7
Mondesi, Raul	.233	73	8	17	6	1	0	2	0	14	5
O'Conner, Justin	.303	66	7	20	6	0	1	10	4	6	1
Salcedo, Edward	.260	96	11	25	9	0	1	10	8	25	2
Smith, James	.304	69	9	21	6	0	1	10	4	16	1
Stanley, Cody	.292	72	9	21	4	1	0	12	7	9	2
Starling, Bubba	.177	79	7	14	5	0	0	5	3	30	0
Valera, Breyvic	.333	39	5	13	1	0	0	5	5	3	3
Wilson, Jacob	.289	90	12	26	7	1	0	13	7	15	2
Wolters, Tony	.255	55	5	14	3	0	0	8	7	7	0
Wren, Kyle	.238	42	2	10	2	0	0	1	4	4	4

PITCHERS	W	L	ERA	G	GS	SV	IP	H	BB	SO	AVG
Almonte, Miguel	1	1	2.84	7	4	0	19	16	9	16	.239
Baker, Dylan	0	1	4.24	6	6	0	17	17	5	10	.274
Cooper, Zach	0	0	10.45	9	0	1	10	13	9	3	.361
Cunniff, Brandon	2	0	3.21	11	0	3	14	16	5	10	.291
Harper, Ryne	2	0	3.97	9	0	0	11	9	4	13	.214
Harris, Mitch	0	2	4.26	11	0	0	12	13	3	12	.271
Head, Louis	0	0	2.45	10	0	0	11	13	3	12	.289
Hyatt, Nate	0	0	4.35	11	0	0	10	6	7	12	.167
Jenkins, Tyrell	2	2	2.22	6	6	0	24	23	10	18	.256
Lollis, Matt	0	1	15.12	9	0	0	8	16	5	5	.410
Maronde, Nick	1	1	8.36	10	0	0	14	20	5	11	.345
Northcraft, Aaron	2	3	2.42	6	6	0	22	17	9	14	.205
Perry, Chris	0	0	8.22	9	0	0	7	9	10	3	.300
Reavis, Colton	0	0	4.09	9	0	0	11	10	4	10	.256
Schultz, Jaime	2	3	4.61	7	7	0	20	20	23	28	.198
Selman, Sam	0	0	2.08	11	0	0	13	12	3	12	.245
Sides, Grant	1	0	1.59	10	0	0	11	7	5	13	.167
Stumpf, Daniel	1	0	3.72	7	0	0	9	6	4	11	.188
Tuivailala, Sam	1	0	1.29	12	0	5	14	10	8	13	.196
Williams, Ali	0	0	1.42	10	0	0	12	6	4	17	.136
Zimmer, Kyle	0	0	2.79	3	3	0	9	5	4	15	.156

MINOR LEAGUES

SALT RIVER RAFTERS

BATTERS	AVG	AB	R	H	2B	3B	HR	RBI	BB	SO	SB
Aplin, Andrew	.269	67	13	18	1	1	1	9	12	18	4
Bohn, Justin	.328	58	11	19	1	1	1	5	8	11	1
Buxton, Byron	.263	57	8	15	2	0	0	6	4	12	5
Casteel, Ryan	.258	93	11	24	9	0	0	15	10	23	0
Drury, Brandon	.219	96	12	21	4	1	3	11	13	21	1
Featherston, Taylor	.294	68	15	20	2	3	1	10	7	23	4
Heineman, Tyler	.400	5	1	2	0	0	0	2	1	0
Kepler, Max	.307	75	13	23	4	3	0	7	6	14	3
Marzilli, Evan	.303	76	15	23	1	1	1	9	6	18	7
Nola, Austin	.298	47	9	14	4	1	0	6	10	2	2
O'Brien, Peter	.256	86	15	22	7	0	5	12	17	24	0
O'Dowd, Chris	.231	26	3	6	2	0	1	6	2	13	0
Rosario, Eddie	.330	100	10	33	4	2	0	18	5	19	10
Ruiz, Rio	.187	75	9	14	3	0	0	7	12	17	0
Sclafani, Joe	.370	46	7	17	5	0	1	10	5	11	1
Story, Trevor	.256	86	8	22	9	1	1	14	11	26	3
Wallach, Chad	.192	52	4	10	2	0	0	5	3	7	0
PITCHERS	W	L	ERA	G	GS	SV	IP	H	BB	SO	AVG
Adam, Jason	1	1	5.40	10	0	0	13	23	6	7	.371
Appel, Mark	1	0	2.61	7	7	0	31	18	8	24	.167
Aquino, Jayson	2	0	3.38	4	4	0	16	16	4	13	.258
Bergman, Christian	2	0	4.34	7	3	0	18	19	2	17	.260
Bradley, Archie	0	2	7.13	6	6	0	17	28	11	12	.364
Burgos, Enrique	1	1	3.65	10	0	4	12	10	4	11	.227
DeSclafani, Anthony	1	0	2.67	6	6	0	27	24	4	24	.242
Ellington, Brian	0	0	2.77	10	0	0	13	9	4	12	.196
Fleck, Kaleb	0	1	3.12	8	0	2	8	8	4	12	.250
Gonzalez, Nelson	2	0	3.14	10	0	0	14	16	3	11	.281
Jones, Zack	0	0	0.00	11	0	0	11	7	12	11	.171
Lambson, Mitch	0	0	1.26	10	0	0	14	6	7	17	.128
Olmos, Edgar	1	1	7.36	9	0	0	11	11	6	7	.244
Perez, Tyson	0	2	0.63	10	0	1	14	11	1	11	.200
Redman, Reid	2	1	3.14	11	0	0	14	9	2	11	.180
Reed, Jake	1	0	0.71	10	0	1	12	10	3	10	.213
Roberts, Ken	0	0	0.00	11	0	1	14	8	4	9	.163
Rogers, Taylor	0	0	1.59	3	2	0	5	4	2	4	.211
Sherfy, Jimmie	1	0	0.93	9	0	0	9	5	3	10	.156
Velasquez, Vincent	2	2	6.59	5	4	0	13	14	3	13	.264

SCOTTSDALE SCORPIONS

BATTERS	AVG	AB	R	H	2B	3B	HR	RBI	BB	SO	SB
Austin, Tyler	.304	69	12	21	2	1	2	13	10	12	4
Bell, Josh	.214	84	9	18	8	0	0	7	12	13	2
Bichette Jr., Dante	.260	73	3	19	1	0	0	11	7	18	1
Bird, Greg	.313	99	21	31	6	0	6	21	13	23	1
Carbonell, Daniel	.190	58	6	11	0	1	1	6	2	16	0
Diaz, Elias	.260	50	7	13	2	2	0	6	10	7	1
Gamache, Dan	.186	59	7	11	4	0	1	6	11	13	0
Higashioka, Kyle	.409	22	4	9	3	0	1	2	3	2	1
Judge, Aaron	.278	90	15	25	5	0	4	15	13	22	0
Mazzilli, L.J.	.306	49	9	15	3	1	1	7	9	12	1
Miller, Blake	.193	57	8	11	1	0	0	5	7	11	1
Moore, Logan	.146	41	4	6	1	0	0	3	5	11	0
Nimmo, Brandon	.202	84	11	17	3	0	0	8	12	28	2
Quinn, Roman	.250	92	19	23	0	2	2	9	16	16	14
Reynolds, Matt	.234	77	11	18	5	1	3	15	11	17	3
Tomlinson, Kelby	.111	63	5	7	1	1	0	3	7	10	8
PITCHERS	W	L	ERA	G	GS	SV	IP	H	BB	SO	AVG
Alvarez, Dario	1	0	6.75	6	0	0	9	11	6	11	.289
Blackburn, Clayton	1	2	5.40	6	0	0	11	14	0	9	.280
Cotham, Caleb	0	0	6.08	10	0	0	13	18	2	14	.321
Glasnow, Tyler	1	2	3.72	7	7	0	19	20	12	20	.278

SURPRISE SAGUAROS

BATTERS	AVG	AB	R	H	2B	3B	HR	RBI	BB	SO	SB
Cantwell, Pat	.162	37	2	6	1	0	0	1	4	9	0
Castillo, Rusney	.278	36	10	10	3	0	0	1	3	6	1
Coyle, Sean	.209	67	8	14	4	1	1	7	7	22	5
De Leon, Michael	.240	50	7	12	2	0	0	8	4	8	0
Hicks, John	.304	46	9	14	4	0	2	11	6	7	2
Kivlehan, Patrick	.280	93	18	26	4	1	4	22	14	17	0
Maile, Luke	.214	28	3	6	1	0	1	4	3	10	1
Marrero, Deven	.328	58	13	19	5	0	0	2	11	19	2
Mejias-Brean, Seth	.194	72	9	14	2	0	1	5	8	16	1
Miller, Mike	.000	11	2	0	0	0	0	1	2	3	0
Perez, Juan	.286	28	4	8	1	0	1	3	2	9	1
Peterson, D.J.	.169	59	5	10	4	0	1	6	10	15	1
Peterson, Jace	.262	84	14	22	4	1	0	9	14	13	8
Renfroe, Hunter	.284	102	15	29	9	1	6	20	8	23	0
Smith, Mallex	.305	59	12	18	2	0	0	5	11	12	4
Turner, Trea	.400	35	10	14	0	0	0	5	1	8	7
Waldrop, Kyle	.300	80	14	24	3	2	1	14	3	14	2
Williams, Nick	.277	112	9	31	6	2	2	19	1	32	0
Winker, Jesse	.338	68	14	23	4	1	3	18	14	17	1
PITCHERS	W	L	ERA	G	GS	SV	IP	H	BB	SO	AVG
Alger, Brandon	0	1	5.40	11	0	2	11	17	3	12	.340
Anderson, Matt	0	1	10.80	9	0	1	13	23	5	13	.377
Bonilla, Lisalverto	0	1	5.68	4	3	0	12	11	7	13	.224
Brazis, Matt	1	0	5.11	10	0	0	12	14	5	11	.298
Couch, Keith	3	2	5.59	7	7	0	29	39	6	14	.339
DeCecco, Scott	0	0	0.00	4	0	0	4	1	4	2	.077
Dennick, Ryan	1	0	1.08	7	0	1	8	4	1	6	.148
Gonzalez, Carlos	1	0	4.61	11	0	1	13	16	8	9	.302
Guerrero, Tayron	0	2	22.50	4	0	0	4	9	5	5	.474
Hancock, Justin	1	0	6.19	6	6	0	16	20	12	8	.333
Howard, Nick	2	1	4.43	6	6	0	20	19	9	15	.260
Iglesias, Raisel	0	0	0.00	7	0	0	7	1	3	7	.045
Kendall, Cody	1	0	3.18	10	0	0	11	12	2	6	.273
Klimesh, Ben	0	2	2.77	11	0	2	13	9	8	13	.200
Kurcz, Aaron	1	0	3.86	10	0	1	14	12	9	15	.231
Landazuri, Stephen	1	5	6.95	8	5	0	22	32	9	19	.356
McElwee, Josh	0	0	1.93	12	0	1	14	12	4	20	.245
Scott, Robby	0	0	1.38	10	0	0	13	11	5	14	.229
Smith, Burch	3	0	5.52	9	0	0	14	18	5	9	.321
Vasquez, Kelvin	0	0	0.00	2	0	0	1	3	3	.143
Walker, Taijuan	0	0	2.00	2	2	0	9	7	2	11	.206
Wolff, Sam	0	0	5.27	9	3	0	13	15	6	8	.273
Younginer, Madison	1	0	7.36	7	0	0	7	10	6	3	.313

The following SURPRISE SAGUAROS pitching lines appear at the top right of the page:

PITCHERS	W	L	ERA	G	GS	SV	IP	H	BB	SO	AVG
Harlan, Tom	0	4	9.64	6	6	0	14	21	8	11	.339
Haynes, Kyle	0	0	2.31	10	0	2	11	11	8	9	.244
Hilario, Julian	1	1	5.06	10	0	0	16	16	6	15	.254
Kuebler, Jake	0	0	0.00	4	0	0	5	6	1	2	.286
Mizenko, Tyler	0	0	13.50	1	0	0	0	2	2	0	.500
Morgan, Adam	1	2	6.61	6	5	0	16	26	3	11	.356
Murray, Colton	0	2	4.91	11	0	0	14	15	2	13	.259
O'Sullivan, Ryan	1	2	9.39	10	1	0	15	24	5	7	.364
Ogando, Nefi	0	0	3.07	12	0	3	14	13	4	15	.236
Okert, Steven	0	0	0.75	10	0	1	12	5	1	17	.119
Rodriguez, Joely	3	0	2.38	7	7	0	22	27	6	22	.310
Rogers, Tyler	0	0	2.13	10	0	0	12	15	2	7	.306
Sampson, Adrian	0	0	2.25	10	0	1	12	10	4	6	.238
Sanchez, Angel	1	0	2.25	8	0	0	12	11	5	11	.234
Sewald, Paul	0	2	7.59	9	0	0	10	17	4	17	.347
Smith, Alex	1	1	10.45	10	0	0	10	25	8	7	.446
Stewart, Ethan	0	0	7.56	7	0	0	8	5	10	12	.156
Whalen, Rob	0	2	6.87	6	6	0	18	18	10	15	.254

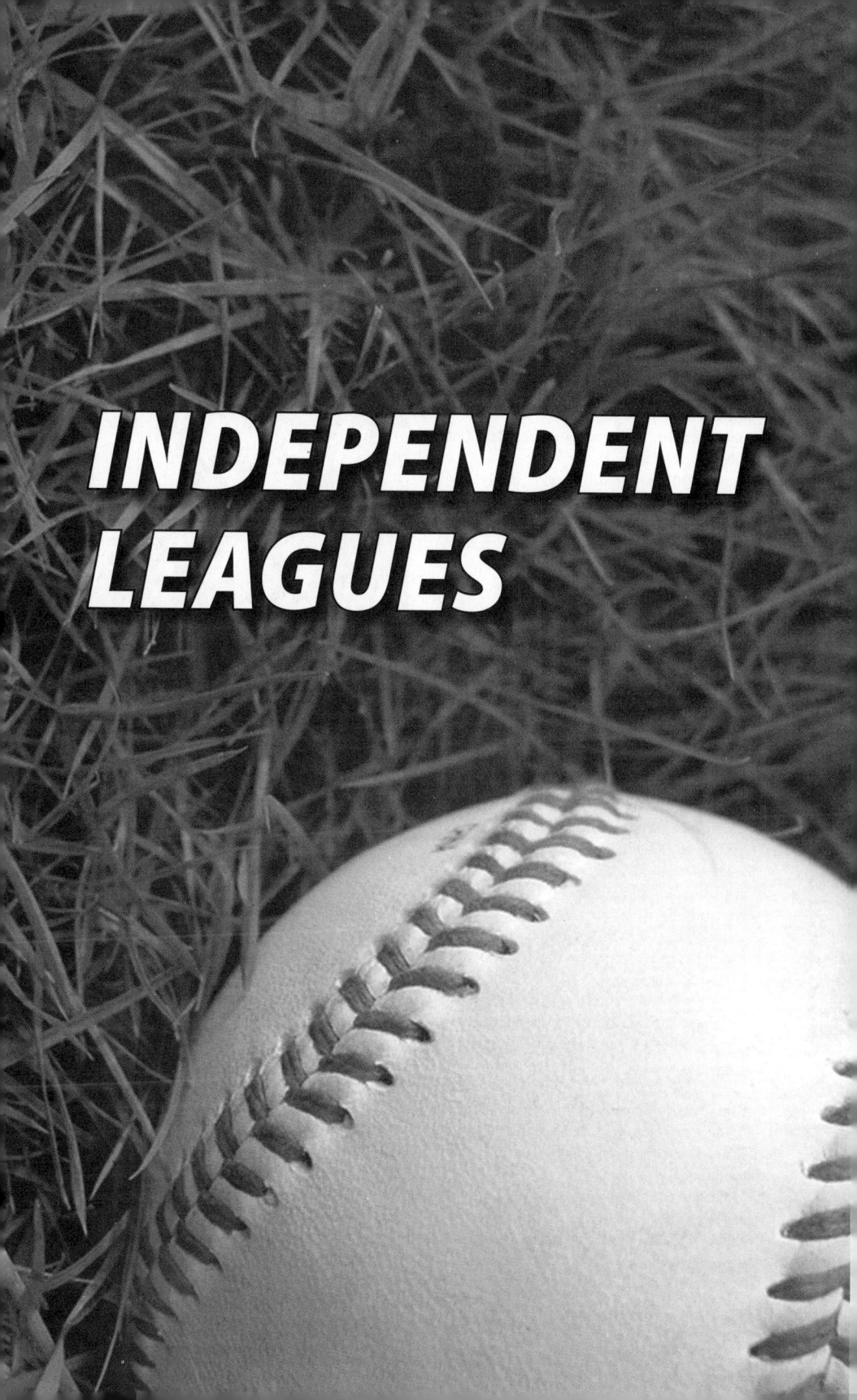

INDEPENDENT LEAGUES

Indy ball gets boost from better pitching

BY J.J. COOPER

Plenty of success stories have sprung from the independent leagues over the past two decades. From position players Kevin Millar to Daniel Nava and from pitchers Brian Tollberg to Steve Delabar, numerous players can credit the independent leagues for keeping their dream of a big league career alive.

But in 2014, indy ball became nearly mainstream. John Holdzkom went from hard-throwing, control-troubled righthander scuffling for an independent league job to one of the best stories in baseball. Just two months after Pirates independent leagues consultant Mal Fichman signed him, he was pitching in the big leagues. A month later, he was part of the Pirates' playoff roster.

Holdzkom's success story served as a reminder for players all around the independent leagues that the gap between big league success and indy league struggles isn't always all that far.

In Arizona, outfielder David Peralta was making a case to be part of the Rookie of the Year discussion with a .286/.320/.450 half-season with the Diamondbacks.

Success stories like that keep Fichman and Chris Carminucci, the independent leagues coordinator for the D-backs, flying around the country finding players. Carminucci and the Diamondbacks were especially active this year, signing 21 players by the middle of October. Six of those signees ended up helping short-season Hillsboro win a Northwest League title in the franchise's second year of existence.

With the D-backs signing 21 players, the Braves adding another 13, and 25 teams signing at least one player, a total of 92 independent league players had signed with affiliated clubs in 2014 by the end of the Atlantic League season, including a record 40 from the Frontier League. The independent leagues have never been as well-scouted by affiliated ball as they are today.

Major League Baseball's decision to reduce the draft from 50 rounds to 40 has benefitted indy ball teams, as a number of productive college players now go undrafted with the shorter draft. Also the increased velocity seen throughout the game

John Holdzkom's quick rise was one of the best stories of the 2014 season

GEORGE GOJKOVICH

has filtered down to independent ball. The overall competition level has improved.

While indy games are a better brand of baseball than ever before, better games haven't paid off in more fans.

With more leagues and teams, indy ball drew more than 8 million fans in 2010. This year, they drew a little less than 6.1 million fans, down more than 500,000 fans from 2013. Every indy league drew fewer fans in 2014 than 2013. The American Association saw the biggest drop with more than 250,000 fewer fans than in 2013. New teams opening in Joplin, Mo. (American Association) and Ottawa (Can-Am) may provide a boost for 2015.

The Atlantic League made plenty of news with an initiative to try to shorten the length of games. The league allowed only three in-inning timeouts (or mound meetings) per game per team. Batters were required to stay in the batter's box during their at-bats and pitchers were on a 12-second clock when no batters were on base. Warm-up pitches were cut from eight to six and batters were waved to first base on intentional walks.

Slugger thankful for opportunity

On a pretty regular basis, Balbino Fuenmayor would come up to Quebec manager Patrick Scalabrini this year and just say, 'Thanks.'

When you've been released from affiliated ball, you quickly realize what you're missing. Fuenmayor had spent most of his first year out of affiliated ball on a travel team, so he was quite happy to have a regular home with the Can-Am League's Quebec club.

He was thankful for a job playing baseball. He was thankful for another chance. Talk to Fuenmayor, 24, for more than five minutes and the thank-yous pour out. He's thankful to Jon Hunton, an indy ball pitcher/player-development official who helped him land a job with the travel-team Frontier Greys. He's thankful to Greys manager Brent Matheny for helping him develop last year. And he's thankful to Scalabrini and the Capitales club for helping him take a big step forward.

But in reality, Scalabrini says it's the club who should be thanking Fuenmayor. After all, he hit .347/.383/.610 this year with 23 home runs in 95 games with Quebec. He finished second in the league in batting, second in home runs and first in RBIs (99). With that kind of production, he was more than earning his keep.

He also earned the Baseball America Independent Leagues Player of the Year award, becoming the first Can-Am Leaguer to win the award since future Twins big leaguer Chris Colabello won it in 2011.

When Scalabrini picked up Fuenmayor in time for the Can-Am playoffs in 2013, it was with an eye on putting him in the Capitales lineup for 2014 as well. Scalabrini thought that Fuenmayor, a former Blue Jays prospect who had quickly gone from intriguing youngster to a stuck-in-Lansing, former prospect, could help

PLAYER OF THE YEAR

the club by providing power. But the expectations were pretty limited.

Fuenmayor had always struck out a lot. He'd never hit for average. And because of that, his power numbers had never matched his lofty power potential.

When the season began, Fuenmayor batted eighth. But a 2-for-4 Opening Day chock full of impressive at-bats quickly convinced Scalabrini to move him up to the sixth spot in the lineup.

A week later, he was hitting cleanup. Scalabrini and the rest of the Can-Am League were learning that the old scouting reports on Fuenmayor were no longer applicable.

Pitches on the outer half were no longer being rolled over on mistaken attempts to pull the ball. Fuenmayor's two-strike approach went from grip and rip to a shorter, controlled swing.

Signed as a 16-year-old, Fuenmayor was released by the Blue Jays when he was 23. At an age when some college players are making their pro minor league debuts, Fuenmayor was told that his career may be over.

The raw power that Fuenmayor was expected to turn into towering home runs never showed up for the Blue Jays. The hitting ability he was projected to have as a youngster had been buried under too many overly aggressive swings on pitches outside the zone.

At 24, he's young enough that it's quite plausible that an improved approach and confidence at the plate that comes from experiencing success could make him a significantly better hitter. He's going to play with Caribes in the Venezuelan League this winter to try to catch scouts' eyes again.

Now that he's signed with the Royals, his new club will be sure to hear plenty of thank yous from Fuenmayor.

PREVIOUS WINNERS

1996: Darryl Motley, of, Fargo-Moorhead (Northern)
1997: Mike Meggers, of, Winnipeg/Duluth (Northern)
1998: Morgan Burkhart, 1b, Richmond (Frontier)
1999: Carmine Cappucio, of, New Jersey (Northeast)
2000: Anthony Lewis, 1b, Duluth-Superior (Northern)
2001: Mike Warner, of, Somerset (Atlantic)
2002: Bobby Madritsch, lhp, Winnipeg (Northern)
2003: Jason Shelley, rhp, Rockford (Frontier)
2004: Victor Rodriguez, ss, Somerset (Atlantic)

2005: Eddie Lantigua, 3b, Quebec (Can-Am)
2006: Ian Church, of, Kalamazoo (Frontier)
2007: Darryl Brinkley, of, Calgary (Northern)
2008: Patrick Breen, of, Orange County (Golden)
2009: Greg Porter, of, Wichita (American Association)
2010: Beau Torbert, of, Sioux Falls (American Association)
2011: Chris Collabello, 1b, Worcester (Can-Am League)
2012: Blake Gailen, of, Lancaster (Atlantic)
2013: C.J. Ziegler, 1b, Wichita (American Association)

INDEPENDENT STATISTICS

AMERICAN ASSOCIATION

The Wichita Wingnuts have been one of the best teams in the American Association for several years. They won their division in 2011, 2012 and 2013, including a league-best 68-32 record in 2013. For an expansion team that only joined the league in 2008, it's been an impressive run. But all of that regular season success had never paid off in a title.

That's no longer the case. Wichita put together its best season, posting a 73-27 mark that was 10 games better than anyone else. But more importantly, the Wingnuts followed it up by winning six of their seven games in the playoffs, sweeping the Lincoln Saltdogs in the championship series for the club's first American Association title.

League MVP Brent Clevlen led the way for the Wingnuts with a league leading .372 average to go with 20 home runs.

NORTH DIVISION	W	L	PCT	GB
Winnipeg Goldeyes	63	37	.630	-
St. Paul Saints	48	52	.480	15
Fargo-Moorhead RedHawks	43	56	.434	19.5
Sioux Falls Canaries	33	67	.330	30

CENTRAL DIVISION	W	L	PCT	GB
Lincoln Saltdogs	54	46	.540	-
Gary SouthShore RailCats	53	47	.530	1
Kansas City T-Bones	48	52	.480	6
Sioux City Explorers	47	53	.470	7

SOUTH DIVISION	W	L	PCT	GB
Wichita Wingnuts	73	27	.730	-
Laredo Lemurs	58	42	.580	15
Grand Prairie AirHogs	40	60	.400	33
Amarillo Sox	37	62	.374	35.5

PLAYOFFS: Semifinals—Wichita defeated Laredo 3-1 and Lincoln defeated Winnipeg 3-2 in best-of-5 series. **Finals**—Wichita defeated Lincoln 3-0 in best-of-5 series.

ATTENDANCE: Winnipeg Goldeyes 258,429; Kansas City T-Bones 248,989; St Paul Saints 248,106; Fargo-Moorhead RedHawks 186,306; Gary SouthShore RailCats 164,286; Lincoln Saltdogs 166,503; Wichita Wingnuts 147,706; Sioux Falls Canaries 139,784; Laredo Lemurs 132,562; Amarillo Sox 81,834; Grand Prairie AirHogs 60,747; Sioux City Explorers 50,746.

MANAGERS: Amarillo Sox—Bobby Brown. **Fargo-Moorhead Redhawks**—Doug Simunic. **Gary SouthShore RailCats**—Greg Tagert. **Grand Prairie AirHogs**—Ricky VanAsselberg and Eric Champion. **Kansas City T-Bones**—John Massarelli. **Laredo Lemurs**—Pete Incaviglia. **Lincoln Saltdogs**—Ken Oberkfell. **Sioux City Explorers**—Steve Montgomery. **Sioux Falls Canaries**—Steve Shirley. **St. Paul Saints**—George Tsamis. **Wichita Wingnuts**—Kevin Hooper. **Winnipeg Goldeyes**—Rick Forney.

ALL-STAR TEAM: C—Chris McMurray (Wichita). **1B**—Casey Haerther (Winnipeg). **2B**—Travis Denker (Laredo). **3B**—Abel Nieves (Grand Prairie/Wichita). **SS**—Tyler Kuhn (Winnipeg). **OF**—Drew Martinez (Gary SouthShore); Brent Clevlen (Wichita); Nick Van Stratten (Laredo). **DH**—Ian Gac (Lincoln).
SP—Nick Hermandez (Winnipeg). **RP**—Marshall Schuler (Lincoln). **Defensive Player**—Ryan Khoury (Wichita).
PLAYER OF THE YEAR: Brent Clevlen, Wichita. **MANAGER OF THE YEAR:** Kevin Hooper, Wichita.

BATTING LEADERS

BATTER	TEAM	AVG	AB	R	H	HR	RBI
Clevlen, Brent	WI	.372	360	76	134	20	80
Haerther, Casey	WP	.360	389	49	140	13	72
*Kuhn, Tyler	WP	.360	411	70	148	5	56
*Martinez, Drew	GR	.358	427	64	153	2	62
Nieves, Abel	WI	.354	362	52	128	2	45
*Nunez, Alex	GP	.354	274	40	97	1	27
Gac, Ian	LN	.349	321	63	112	27	77
Van Stratten, Nick	LL	.349	416	81	145	6	49
*Thaut, Devin	SP	.342	272	50	93	3	33
Alonso, John	LL	.340	335	59	114	17	67

PITCHING LEADERS

PITCHER	TEAM	W	L	ERA	IP	H	BB	SO
Carrillo, Cesar	LL	8	5	2.80	116	109	49	78
*Hernandez, Nick	WP	12	2	3.06	121	117	22	93
Brown, Tim	WI	10	4	3.12	130	150	19	76
Crenshaw, Dustin	GR	9	8	3.16	148	146	22	76
Link, Jon	WI	11	2	3.26	127	123	33	100
Broussard, Geoff	SC	8	1	3.26	88	75	31	83
*Salamida, Chris	WP	7	4	3.29	126	120	26	91
Wilkerson, Aaron	GP	3	1	3.35	81	74	33	84
Van Skike, Jason	WI	12	5	3.36	110	121	31	55
Fleming, Marquis	LN	10	3	3.38	120	104	52	100

AMARILLO SOX

PLAYER	AVG	AB	R	H	HR	RBI	BB	SO	SB
Luna, Omar	.333	54	2	18	0	3	2	5	1
Valentin, Geraldo	.333	150	21	50	0	24	14	17	2
*Perren, Derek	.322	298	39	96	1	32	33	39	2
Pinckney, Brandon	.313	80	12	25	4	16	4	13	1
Rodriguez, Andres	.312	125	9	39	0	21	8	24	1
Weik, Joe	.304	253	40	77	4	32	26	26	2
LaLonde, Ransom	.295	61	9	18	0	4	9	9	1
*Mahoney, Kevin	.286	217	28	62	2	21	12	52	4
Bladel, Johnny	.286	70	7	20	0	7	3	13	4
Weaver, Travis	.285	137	23	39	0	11	15	30	4
Martin, Jason	.276	351	52	97	7	39	24	56	5
*Patton, Cory	.275	258	31	71	7	36	27	35	3
Bellows, Kyle	.271	221	31	60	4	25	11	46	5
Nichols, Kyle	.268	287	34	77	11	53	17	58	0
Morales, Cory	.265	34	4	9	0	0	2	7	1
Miller, Josh	.256	82	14	21	1	8	10	19	0
Farnham, Jeff	.250	308	43	77	3	30	34	61	17
*Figueroa, Christian	.250	12	4	3	0	3	2	5	1
Williams, Jeremy	.241	58	5	14	0	5	2	8	1
Estill, Lyndon	.233	30	2	7	0	4	4	10	0
*Brachold, Keith	.214	154	14	33	1	20	12	26	2
Henk, Thomas	.176	17	2	3	0	1	0	3	1
O'Gorman, Connar	.111	27	1	3	0	0	1	9	0
*Mirabel, Charlie	.105	38	5	4	0	1	3	14	1
Broad, Michael	.098	51	6	5	1	2	3	9	1

PLAYER	W	L	ERA	G	SV	IP	H	BB	SO
*Rogers, Kevin	0	0	0.00	5	0	2	2	3	2
Holdzkom, John	0	0	1.17	9	0	8	6	2	7
Gooding, Jeremy	0	0	1.50	2	0	12	8	3	19
Draxton, Erik	0	1	2.18	22	6	21	19	12	25
Hamrick, Randy	2	1	2.37	19	7	19	5	14	30
Figliolia, Anthony	2	1	3.33	5	0	27	25	5	17
Moen, Kellen	3	6	3.62	41	1	60	65	33	54
Larkins, Matt	7	7	3.98	28	0	124	131	33	98
*Quist, Dayne	1	3	3.98	8	0	43	54	17	23
Howard, Cephas	1	1	4.00	11	0	9	8	2	7
Maxon, Adam	1	0	4.15	8	0	9	11	5	6
*Tanner, Clayton	3	3	4.23	12	0	72	83	25	43
Bellows, Kyle	0	0	4.50	8	0	8	9	1	4
*Linares, Kristhiam	3	2	4.77	16	0	23	25	7	23
Blacksher, Derek	4	10	4.98	29	1	99	119	28	73
Polanco, Celson	0	1	5.00	9	1	9	11	9	11
Feckley, Jake	0	2	5.33	21	0	25	28	9	18
Nannini, Michael	3	2	5.68	5	0	25	34	7	14
Zeller, Joe	2	3	5.74	8	0	42	54	20	29
Oliver, Brian	0	0	6.00	2	0	3	6	0	2
Hale, Tyler	1	1	6.05	21	0	22	22	10	18
Brooks, Andrew	0	2	6.20	12	0	20	29	11	9

*Williamson, Logan	1	2	6.62	3	0	18	27	8	10
Casillas, David	1	2	6.65	5	0	22	23	11	21
Lintz, Seth	0	0	6.75	3	0	1	1	2	1
Vaughn, Derek	0	0	6.75	1	0	1	2	0	2
Stephens, Coleman	1	3	6.91	9	0	43	65	19	37
*Rogers, Joseph	0	1	7.56	2	0	8	10	3	5
Bladel, Johnny	0	0	8.10	5	0	10	17	4	4
Weinshank, Scott	0	0	8.10	2	0	3	5	1	0
Kadish, Ian	0	0	8.31	4	0	4	6	8	2
Kadish, Ian	0	0	8.31	4	0	4	6	8	2
*Rogers, Ryan	1	1	9.00	4	0	3	6	1	2
*Patton, Cory	0	0	11.46	9	0	11	23	5	7
*Smith, Brian	0	1	11.57	5	0	9	17	4	7
Beck, Casey	0	2	13.50	16	0	15	19	21	15
*Spence, Josh	0	0	18.69	3	0	4	10	5	3
Egan, Jordan	0	1	20.25	2	0	4	8	3	4
Cuneo, Cameron	0	1	23.63	1	0	3	7	3	4
Barnard, Chandler	0	1	24.92	3	0	4	14	2	2
Schlact, Michael	0	1	81.00	2	0	1	4	2	0

FARGO-MOORHEAD REDHAWKS

PLAYER	AVG	AB	R	H	HR	RBI	BB	SO	SB
Salerno, Frank	.327	52	10	17	1	10	4	6	3
*Castro, Erik	.319	119	12	38	1	14	10	14	0
Retherford, C.J.	.312	385	53	120	12	72	32	35	3
Penprase, Zach	.276	362	55	100	4	32	41	82	19
Higgs, Travis	.271	192	24	52	6	25	12	56	3
Thompson, Michael	.268	41	5	11	0	5	0	6	0
*Tripp, Brandon	.263	160	25	42	5	25	23	52	1
White, Andy	.261	23	7	6	0	2	4	7	0
*Carroll, Sawyer	.258	345	58	89	7	51	64	64	3
*Newton, Brandon	.258	151	22	39	1	9	16	28	4
*Jackson, Nic	.257	374	43	96	8	45	37	61	8
Paramore, Petey	.254	280	37	71	6	36	45	33	0
*Bourquin, Ronnie	.240	350	62	84	13	52	68	95	4
Robinson, Dusty	.228	57	8	13	0	3	7	15	1
Alberts, Tim	.225	160	13	36	2	15	16	44	2
Kaskadden, Anthony	.213	211	20	45	3	22	17	44	6

PLAYER	W	L	ERA	G	SV	IP	H	BB	SO
Roemer, Wes	1	0	0.00	2	0	3	2	2	1
*Harris, Joe	4	3	2.31	36	0	47	43	18	42
Camilli, Curtis	2	2	2.91	5	0	22	24	12	15
McCully, Nick	1	1	3.32	3	0	19	21	3	16
*Laber, Jake	8	11	3.53	21	0	133	142	34	89
Montoya, Jhonny	0	0	4.00	7	0	9	9	5	8
Draxton, Erik	0	0	4.35	25	0	29	34	17	28
Bowlin, Drew	2	4	4.45	17	0	55	57	31	44
Garcia, Nate	0	4	4.46	36	18	40	40	18	43
Ernst, Brian	9	6	4.72	20	0	116	118	68	80
Fuqua, Kevin	5	3	4.86	40	0	46	52	20	36
Stanton, Taylor	6	11	4.90	20	0	118	142	33	77
Schuld, Matthew	1	0	4.97	2	0	13	13	5	9
Woods, Coty	0	0	5.00	26	1	27	34	7	21
Erasmus, Justin	2	2	5.07	25	2	55	53	24	38
*O'Neill, Shawn	0	3	5.29	4	0	17	24	10	9
Gutierrez, Danny	2	3	5.36	11	0	44	45	23	30
*Opsahl, Ethan	0	0	5.40	2	0	8	11	3	7
*Kline, Eric	0	1	6.05	16	0	19	25	16	13
Orosey, Brad	0	0	6.75	3	0	9	13	3	5
Sanz, Luis	0	1	9.00	3	0	11	19	7	9
*Miller, Adam	0	0	9.00	2	0	1	1	2	2
Carroll, Sawyer	0	0	36.00	1	0	1	3	2	1
Mooney, Josh	0	1	45.00	1	0	1	4	4	1

GARY SOUTHSHORE RAILCATS

PLAYER	AVG	AB	R	H	HR	RBI	BB	SO	SB
Luna, Omar	.333	54	2	18	0	3	2	5	1
Valentin, Geraldo	.333	150	21	50	0	24	14	17	2
*Perren, Derek	.322	298	39	96	1	32	33	39	2
Pinckney, Brandon	.313	80	12	25	4	16	4	13	1
Rodriguez, Andres	.312	125	9	39	0	21	8	24	1
Weik, Joe	.304	253	40	77	4	32	26	26	2
LaLonde, Ransom	.295	61	9	18	0	4	9	7	3
*Mahoney, Kevin	.286	217	28	62	2	21	12	52	4
Bladel, Johnny	.286	70	7	20	0	7	3	13	4
Weaver, Travis	.285	137	23	39	0	11	15	30	4
Martin, Jason	.276	351	52	97	7	39	24	56	5

*Patton, Cory	.275	258	31	71	7	36	27	35	3
Bellows, Kyle	.271	221	31	60	4	25	11	46	5
Nichols, Kyle	.268	287	34	77	11	53	17	58	0
Morales, Cory	.265	34	4	9	0	0	2	7	1
Miller, Josh	.256	82	14	21	1	8	10	19	0
Farnham, Jeff	.250	308	43	77	3	30	34	61	17
*Figueroa, Christian	.250	12	4	3	0	3	2	5	1
Williams, Jeremy	.241	58	5	14	0	5	2	8	1
Estill, Lyndon	.233	30	2	7	0	4	4	10	0
*Brachold, Keith	.214	154	14	33	1	20	12	26	2
Henk, Thomas	.176	17	2	3	0	1	0	3	1
OGorman, Connar	.111	27	1	3	0	0	1	9	0
*Mirabel, Charlie	.105	38	5	4	0	1	3	14	1
Broad, Michael	.098	51	6	5	1	2	3	9	1

PLAYER	W	L	ERA	G	SV	IP	H	BB	SO
Kadish, Ian	2	1	2.03	22	1	27	21	5	28
Kadish, Ian	2	1	2.03	22	1	27	21	5	28
Crenshaw, Dustin	9	8	3.16	22	0	148	146	22	76
Quintero, A.J.	0	0	3.18	5	0	6	4	2	2
Gibbons, Ethan	2	2	3.77	37	2	45	43	20	28
Hopkins, Kagen	4	3	4.04	30	0	65	70	15	47
Parr, James	2	2	4.13	21	8	24	21	3	25
*Brahney, Kevin	5	3	4.41	32	3	33	35	11	22
*Fontana, Chuck	1	1	4.46	28	4	38	41	21	27
Hiscock, Stephen	10	6	4.53	23	0	147	178	33	105
Bougher, Stephen	8	7	4.80	23	0	122	138	34	58
Fowler, Barry	0	0	4.91	8	2	11	13	0	2
Wagoner, Jack	1	0	4.91	3	0	4	4	6	3
Stephens, Coleman	1	1	5.22	15	0	29	34	18	24
McGee, Travis	1	1	5.23	4	0	10	12	4	8
Coombs, Morgan	7	9	5.40	23	0	142	154	48	72
*Loomis, Andy	0	0	6.00	9	2	9	9	2	11
*Giulietti, James	0	0	6.00	3	1	3	5	2	0
McCully, Nick	0	2	7.00	3	0	9	15	7	9
Testa, Joe	0	1	7.94	5	1	6	11	3	8
Weatherly, Mike	0	0	13.50	2	0	1	2	1	0
O'Neill, Shawn	1	0	18.90	5	0	3	8	4	1

GRAND PRAIRIE AIRHOGS

PLAYER	AVG	AB	R	H	HR	RBI	BB	SO	SB
*Nunez, Alex	.354	274	40	97	1	27	22	45	10
Nieves, Abel	.326	319	41	104	2	35	35	37	1
#Botts, Jason	.320	378	50	121	12	68	54	55	0
Karr, Palmer	.295	129	18	38	4	19	13	23	0
Mojica, Jimmy	.284	317	58	90	2	25	24	60	9
Pinckney, Brandon	.255	106	15	27	3	16	12	17	0
*Hall, Frazier	.253	237	37	60	7	31	33	68	2
*Myrow, Brian	.251	195	21	49	3	21	33	55	0
Hur, Michael	.250	96	10	24	1	10	8	14	2
Carter, Madison	.248	117	12	29	0	9	7	24	4
DiFazio, Vince	.238	193	27	46	2	20	25	39	2
Peterson, Brian	.235	136	13	32	3	14	3	33	0
Abeita, Mitch	.230	74	6	17	0	3	10	17	0
Baker, Eric	.224	304	31	68	0	22	21	59	7
Rodriguez, Andres	.213	188	23	40	3	31	9	45	0
*Gasporra, Ryan	.200	45	1	9	1	4	4	15	0
Rodriguez, Ryde	.171	82	4	14	0	6	0	10	0
Castano, Miguel	.164	61	3	10	0	3	0	17	0

PLAYER	W	L	ERA	G	SV	IP	H	BB	SO
*Hinshaw, Alex	0	1	1.59	6	1	6	3	2	13
*Gaynor, Jared	0	2	1.74	2	0	10	12	1	4
*Whitmore, Bennett	3	2	2.42	25	0	41	50	9	22
Wallach, Brett	4	0	3.24	31	0	33	36	11	29
Wilkerson, Aaron	3	1	3.35	13	0	81	74	33	84
Gutierrez, Danny	1	4	3.70	11	0	66	67	20	57
Searle, Ryan	5	9	4.39	20	0	131	149	39	89
Harden, Trevor	6	5	4.40	20	0	108	123	25	77
Bozeman, T.J.	1	3	4.53	15	0	46	41	35	49
Harris, TyRelle	4	4	4.55	26	0	30	28	14	30
Watts, Dakota	0	4	4.56	44	21	49	70	17	46
Brazoban, Yhency	1	1	4.77	5	0	6	6	4	6
Jarvis, Jason	6	5	5.38	15	0	92	124	27	40
*Bargas, Brandon	2	6	5.84	12	0	57	73	19	43
Cameron, Dustin	2	2	6.28	14	0	14	17	3	7
Lopez, Caesar	0	1	6.52	8	0	10	11	4	8
*Spainhoward, Shawn	0	5	7.01	7	0	35	54	9	22

INDEPENDENT LEAGUES

PLAYER	W	L	ERA	G	SV	IP	H	BB	SO
Wilkerson, Brandon	0	1	8.68	7	1	9	15	4	9
Tietze, Jeremy	0	0	9.00	5	0	5	9	3	3
Mateychick, Tobin	1	1	10.47	18	0	16	21	16	8
Shirley, Hayden	0	1	10.80	6	0	7	8	9	7
Hunter, Brett	1	1	10.80	5	0	7	10	5	5
*Keeling, Thomas	0	0	12.34	10	0	12	23	15	16
*Nunez, Luis	0	0	74.25	3	0	1	10	1	4

KANSAS CITY T-BONES

PLAYER	AVG	AB	R	H	HR	RBI	BB	SO	SB
Lusardi, Jeff	.333	15	2	5	0	1	0	3	0
*Padgett, Matt	.328	125	24	41	6	27	25	23	0
Sabatella, Bryan	.307	371	59	114	3	45	36	62	40
Espinosa, David	.290	238	39	69	1	29	48	46	9
Kuzdale, Robby	.275	327	44	90	7	39	34	59	16
#Frias, Vladamir	.273	330	43	90	2	33	24	34	23
*Richar, Danny	.272	331	46	90	7	61	31	46	6
*Wiley, Byron	.269	130	22	35	3	23	25	47	3
*Mittelstaedt, TJ	.268	351	74	94	16	52	92	107	12
*Schwaner, Nick	.265	298	41	79	5	40	26	54	8
Sadler, Ray	.249	197	30	49	8	24	6	47	2
Erie, Brian	.236	296	29	70	1	41	28	58	3
Giarraputo, Nick	.224	107	11	24	2	12	12	30	2
#Hudson, Darrell	.214	112	13	24	0	10	12	27	7
Masiello, Danny	.174	23	2	4	0	0	1	6	0
Kaplan, Jonny	.170	47	8	8	0	8	3	6	2
Bianchi, Christopher	.143	21	1	3	0	2	3	6	0

PLAYER	W	L	ERA	G	SV	IP	H	BB	SO
*Regas, Kris	7	3	2.70	47	22	67	47	32	60
*Loera, Derek	0	2	3.05	24	1	41	49	13	25
Barone, Daniel	5	3	3.09	10	0	64	66	9	50
*Fowler, Zach	0	1	3.57	9	0	18	16	13	10
DeVore, Kyle	5	6	3.90	17	0	92	104	16	74
Noga, Andy	2	6	4.68	23	0	94	117	26	47
Messer, Jared	5	3	4.87	33	2	68	80	15	55
Doyle, Pat	7	4	5.11	36	1	79	98	34	56
Mincey, Patrick	2	0	6.00	19	1	24	29	7	22
Barnes, Casey	3	6	6.02	12	0	67	95	14	47
VanMeter, Joe	2	1	6.03	7	0	31	35	13	29
Nannini, Michael	0	2	6.35	3	0	17	26	4	8
Gordon, Derek	1	1	6.49	14	0	26	28	23	12
*Zagone, Rick	6	5	6.93	14	0	74	100	33	39
Squires, Chris	2	3	7.89	25	1	30	39	17	23
*Linares, Kristhiam	0	1	7.94	8	0	11	11	10	14
Shore, Bobby	0	1	8.44	3	0	5	8	1	8
Smith, Matt	1	3	8.71	10	0	31	46	14	13
*Bennett, Hamilton	0	0	10.07	15	0	20	31	11	13
D'Alessandro, Justin	0	1	17.47	3	0	6	8	7	4
Sweeney, Kevin	0	0	36.00	1	0	1	4	2	0

LAREDO LEMURS

PLAYER	AVG	AB	R	H	HR	RBI	BB	SO	SB
Van Stratten, Nick	.349	416	81	145	6	49	36	28	19
Monteagudo, Victor	.346	26	4	9	0	2	1	8	0
Alonso, John	.344	331	59	114	17	66	37	44	0
Phipps, Denis	.335	251	51	84	15	47	33	57	9
*Avila, Gerardo	.329	146	15	48	3	22	12	23	0
Denker, Travis	.305	371	78	113	25	85	62	60	5
*Ramirez, JP	.304	391	57	119	11	60	22	79	5
Goodwin, Devin	.288	385	77	111	17	68	32	60	26
*Wiley, Byron	.287	150	27	43	6	23	31	51	3
Flores, Angel	.276	134	22	37	4	19	17	22	0
Scheffert, Josh	.268	149	21	40	2	14	15	23	1
Kain, Harrison	.256	289	47	74	2	26	26	50	18
#Brandenburg, Kyle	.242	62	7	15	0	2	1	16	2
Ramirez, Carlos	.221	262	30	58	6	41	33	39	0
Flynn, Ryan	.200	10	3	2	0	1	0	2	0
Taveras, Danny	.182	22	3	4	0	1	0	4	1

PLAYER	W	L	ERA	G	SV	IP	H	BB	SO
Capellan, Victor	0	0	0.00	1	0	1	0	2	0
Cruz, Joe	0	0	0.00	3	0	2	3	0	3
Minnich, Byron	0	0	1.80	5	1	5	4	2	4
Weismann, Scott	1	0	1.80	18	1	20	12	4	18
Wagoner, Jack	0	0	2.08	5	0	4	3	2	3
Strawn, Jeremy	9	0	2.46	14	0	73	70	17	51
Carrillo, Cesar	8	5	2.80	19	0	116	109	49	78

PLAYER	W	L	ERA	G	SV	IP	H	BB	SO
Haynes, Mark	0	1	3.00	8	0	9	9	6	6
Suk, Michael	5	2	3.44	31	0	68	66	26	45
Piazza, Mike	2	1	3.45	6	0	31	27	14	17
Graham, Caleb	2	1	3.51	42	2	41	44	14	53
Strawn, Josh	6	9	4.00	24	0	124	157	39	61
*Harman, Casey	6	2	4.18	17	0	84	101	12	50
Pearson, Tyler	7	8	4.28	29	1	101	81	72	97
Povich, Chad	2	5	4.32	44	15	42	43	19	50
Shreves, Michael	5	3	5.60	24	0	64	83	27	34
Tracey, Sean	3	3	6.43	7	0	28	25	23	18
Lintz, Seth	0	0	7.03	20	0	24	24	24	19
Uriegas, Estevan	1	2	9.11	36	0	28	42	22	38
*Linares, Kristhiam	0	0	10.13	4	0	3	4	1	3
Goodwin, Devin	0	0	81.00	1	0	1	0	1	2

LINCOLN SALTDOGS

PLAYER	AVG	AB	R	H	HR	RBI	BB	SO	SB
Gonzalez, Maikol	.417	36	5	15	1	7	1	6	4
Gac, Ian	.349	321	63	112	27	77	35	75	0
Nunez, Luis	.320	259	46	83	8	30	10	26	10
*Howard, Kevin	.310	187	16	58	3	39	13	12	10
Joynt, Brian	.307	371	59	114	10	58	40	79	1
Gaston, Jon	.287	178	36	51	12	42	20	39	2
Mozingo, Chad	.283	286	42	81	6	34	36	53	21
*Gilmartin, Mike	.262	317	38	83	7	37	25	78	4
Viger, Tony	.261	23	4	6	0	1	5	5	2
Forgatch, Matt	.253	384	64	97	9	42	36	74	35
Pinckney, Brandon	.248	101	10	25	0	14	6	21	0
*Hamilton, Jeremy	.245	261	36	64	1	33	37	37	4
Smith, Tyler	.231	156	21	36	1	16	19	30	0
Luna, Omar	.226	137	17	31	2	10	11	12	3
Vargas, Leonardo	.214	14	1	3	0	0	0	7	2
Anderson, Chris	.211	209	33	44	3	24	29	75	0
Young, Eddie	.193	171	15	33	0	13	17	35	7
Martin, Trevor	.170	88	8	15	1	8	7	27	0

PLAYER	W	L	ERA	G	SV	IP	H	BB	SO
Brooks, Eric	3	1	3.00	2	0	12	9	3	8
*Spink, Conor	4	1	3.05	29	0	44	35	13	40
Fleming, Marquis	10	3	3.38	19	0	120	104	52	100
Bisenius, Joe	6	2	3.46	13	0	81	70	29	100
Varce, Zach	5	9	4.20	19	0	118	130	47	77
*McGovern, Kevin	3	3	4.22	10	0	64	69	17	60
Schuler, Marshall	4	6	4.26	50	34	51	46	23	51
Montoya, Jhonny	4	2	4.59	26	0	35	35	24	27
Kadish, Ian	0	0	4.61	11	0	14	17	6	18
Bozeman, T.J.	1	2	4.74	8	0	19	17	13	20
*Barham, Trey	3	1	4.78	37	0	43	44	20	34
Kuks, Justin	5	6	5.35	18	1	101	128	41	54
Meiers, Jake	3	3	5.72	23	1	39	40	20	21
Green, Nick	4	5	5.82	18	0	108	133	43	71
Click, Michael	2	2	6.43	10	0	14	16	6	12
King, Mackenzie	0	0	7.71	2	0	2	2	2	4

SIOUX FALLS CANARIES

PLAYER	AVG	AB	R	H	HR	RBI	BB	SO	SB
*Ford, Shelby	.336	110	17	37	6	19	7	9	2
*Valencia, Chris	.312	375	44	117	6	44	24	51	10
Tinoco, Steven	.282	373	53	105	7	41	30	56	6
Kirby-Jones, A.J.	.280	321	54	90	23	69	50	92	1
Mendez, Carlos	.276	384	45	106	5	39	24	55	3
*Jones, Brandon	.270	378	43	102	6	47	32	54	0
Branca, Stephen	.260	327	32	85	2	29	7	60	3
Hitt, Matt	.250	68	8	17	2	12	6	26	1
*Duffy, Chris	.242	364	50	88	15	52	46	118	4
*Lind, Sam	.242	182	26	44	5	20	27	41	4
Forney, Tv	.237	114	13	27	0	11	3	20	3
Dultz, Kevin	.234	252	38	59	2	25	28	52	4
*Muren, Drew	.192	73	9	14	1	2	6	13	1
Burch, Chase	.146	48	4	7	1	4	1	9	0

PLAYER	W	L	ERA	G	SV	IP	H	BB	SO
Meyer, Mike	0	0	1.59	4	0	6	6	0	7
Brebbia, John	3	2	3.31	34	1	65	63	22	76
*Testa, Joe	0	2	3.32	31	0	41	42	18	35
DeRatt, Alan	3	7	3.72	40	14	39	45	9	29
*Bircher, Joe	4	8	4.37	18	0	107	121	37	60
Moore, Ben	6	6	4.97	18	0	112	143	17	93

PLAYER	W	L	ERA	G	SV	IP	H	BB	SO
Downing, Kaohi	0	1	5.79	4	0	5	4	3	2
Ruwe, Kyle	6	8	5.79	20	0	143	194	30	58
Vazquez, Kyle	5	9	6.02	18	0	99	121	35	66
*Wickswat, Matt	3	9	6.21	22	0	104	139	60	69
Gonzalez, Erick	0	3	6.75	13	0	19	20	14	12
Winter, Kye	2	3	6.90	20	0	44	69	15	19
Giles, Josh	1	5	7.02	31	1	33	42	28	31
Boruff, Chase	0	2	8.68	20	0	28	35	21	23
Clark, Kirk	0	1	10.45	10	0	10	18	6	9
Kingsley, Kyle	0	1	12.86	6	0	7	17	3	3

SIOUX CITY EXPLORERS

PLAYER	AVG	AB	R	H	HR	RBI	BB	SO	SB
Kjeldgaard, Brock	.358	53	15	19	3	15	9	18	2
Samson, Nate	.335	164	26	55	2	23	17	5	9
#Mesa, Oscar	.327	294	45	96	0	35	46	56	18
*Colwell, Tim	.307	228	46	70	1	34	14	39	19
Lang, Michael	.295	295	53	87	0	18	34	69	15
Perez, Andres	.285	340	54	97	3	43	36	42	12
Barrows, Peter	.283	364	62	103	17	76	43	97	7
*Tosoni, Rene	.277	394	66	109	7	57	50	61	12
Ramon, Amos	.272	235	25	64	5	35	23	38	5
Jennings, Todd	.262	210	19	55	1	29	19	24	1
*Mendonca, Tommy	.250	360	41	90	3	55	22	86	4
Murton, Luke	.244	90	8	22	2	8	3	21	0
*Usiak, Dillon	.209	230	27	48	2	33	26	58	5
Sobolewski, Mark	.204	103	10	21	2	7	6	20	2
#Escobar, Chris	.173	98	13	17	1	4	17	32	2

PLAYER	W	L	ERA	G	SV	IP	H	BB	SO
Mendonca, Tommy	0	0	0.00	1	0	1	0	0	0
Usiak, Dillon	0	0	0.00	1	0	1	1	0	0
Wort, Rob	2	1	0.97	24	1	37	24	14	58
Burnett, Alex	6	1	2.17	28	3	54	52	13	50
Bodishbaugh, Chris	1	4	2.63	36	14	41	35	11	40
Kennedy, Jimmer	3	5	2.90	48	1	71	53	30	52
Broussard, Geoff	8	1	3.26	41	2	88	75	31	83
Tsukada, Kohei	1	2	3.35	8	0	38	38	18	23
*Long, Kenny	2	0	3.76	40	0	41	35	21	24
Straka, John	9	5	4.14	21	0	130	162	38	90
Morrison, Wade	0	4	4.54	10	0	42	48	24	36
Johnson, Patrick	9	7	4.59	23	0	112	106	65	106
Pagano, Alex	0	1	5.21	11	0	19	19	15	13
Holt, Greg	3	8	5.35	12	0	69	74	31	50
Allen, Kyle	0	1	6.30	6	0	10	14	6	6
*Liguori, Lars	2	4	6.36	9	0	47	61	19	26
Mitchell, Ryan	0	4	7.17	4	0	21	27	7	12
Caldera, Alex	1	3	7.58	8	0	38	42	44	27
*English, Jesse	0	2	11.74	7	0	23	39	22	13
Engle, Elliott	0	0	67.50	1	0	1	3	2	0

ST. PAUL SAINTS

PLAYER	AVG	AB	R	H	HR	RBI	BB	SO	SB
*Thaut, Devin	.342	272	50	93	3	33	34	62	1
Maus, Sam	.323	133	18	43	0	9	28	27	1
Cabrera, Willie	.317	325	48	103	12	39	26	30	0
Bonfe, Joe	.300	293	44	88	4	39	31	42	1
Elliott, Mitch	.300	40	6	12	0	9	2	11	1
Wrigley, Henry	.297	306	36	91	14	68	17	42	1
Bigley, Evan	.292	360	52	105	5	52	29	68	17
Becker, Joey	.284	317	40	90	1	21	42	54	2
Taylor, Jake	.283	223	39	63	9	34	16	48	6
*Tripp, Brandon	.277	173	18	48	3	14	14	42	1
*Brachold, Keith	.270	137	15	37	3	21	16	18	1
*Songco, Angelo	.269	375	58	101	16	66	26	83	1
*McDonald, Jared	.258	97	18	25	2	19	10	27	3
DiFazio, Vince	.256	43	6	11	0	3	6	4	0
*Wikoff, Brandon	.230	61	8	14	0	2	12	7	1
Peterson, Tyler	.229	48	8	11	0	4	2	9	0
Escobar, Carlos	.207	82	12	17	1	8	9	20	0
Childs, Dwight	.201	169	16	34	0	14	7	36	2

PLAYER	W	L	ERA	G	SV	IP	H	BB	SO
Sattler, Dan	3	4	1.80	35	19	40	23	30	56
King, Mackenzie	1	0	1.96	13	0	23	16	12	22
Mehlich, Mikey	6	2	3.11	44	2	64	49	28	60
Gay, Drew	5	2	3.54	22	0	86	97	35	42
Claggett, Anthony	6	7	3.55	19	0	127	119	42	85

PLAYER	W	L	ERA	G	SV	IP	H	BB	SO
*Meyer, Matt	0	1	3.60	19	1	20	20	13	14
Barnese, Nick	6	9	3.85	21	0	122	142	46	98
Shields, Jeff	6	8	4.31	19	0	104	117	30	61
Danczyk, Tommy	0	1	4.50	4	0	4	2	1	1
Johnson, Andy	1	0	4.85	10	0	13	13	10	6
*Nelson, Cole	2	5	5.67	8	0	40	43	31	21
Hughes, Ben	4	3	5.90	21	0	58	62	33	46
Coe, Robert	5	7	6.60	16	0	90	109	44	64
Thomas, Dylan	2	1	8.31	17	0	35	53	18	25
Klipp, Justin	0	0	8.78	3	0	13	22	7	10
*Bollinger, Ryan	1	0	9.00	7	0	6	14	3	3
Plefka, Jon	0	0	9.31	8	0	10	14	6	3
Seidel, RJ	0	0	12.15	4	0	7	7	7	4
Hentges, Chase	0	0	13.50	6	0	8	13	8	5
Ghelfi, Drew	0	2	34.71	2	0	2	8	4	1

WICHITA WINGNUTS

PLAYER	AVG	AB	R	H	HR	RBI	BB	SO	SB
Nieves, Abel	.558	43	11	24	0	10	8	4	2
Clevlen, Brent	.372	360	76	134	20	80	51	55	14
*Luce, Jake	.341	123	25	42	2	15	9	33	10
*Testa, Carlo	.338	397	79	134	10	58	36	76	24
Espinosa, David	.338	136	36	46	6	22	28	26	5
Kahaulelio, Jake	.327	309	52	101	7	59	22	42	16
Dean, Brent	.317	63	11	20	3	11	3	9	2
Khoury, Ryan	.315	387	87	122	12	61	76	62	31
Wise, J.T.	.297	185	33	55	12	42	14	36	1
*McClendon, Chris	.296	314	47	93	2	49	21	39	21
Oldham, Taylor	.285	144	15	41	3	25	19	32	6
McDonald, Jared	.279	43	10	12	0	5	6	13	3
Loehrs, Colt	.276	87	15	24	2	7	7	7	2
McMurray, Chris	.261	310	44	81	7	60	30	43	1
Amberson, David	.258	298	49	77	1	15	20	80	24
Diaz, Victor	.240	50	2	12	0	12	2	15	0
Hernandez, Michael	.229	48	5	11	1	9	2	11	0
*Whyte, Trevor	.211	90	13	19	4	11	7	20	1
Hazlett, Dillon	.184	38	2	7	0	1	3	11	2
Chen, Chun-Hsiu	.182	22	3	4	0	5	3	9	1

PLAYER	W	L	ERA	G	SV	IP	H	BB	SO
Oldham, Taylor	0	0	0.00	1	1	1	0	0	0
Johnson, Chase	1	0	1.13	8	1	8	7	4	7
Nevarez, Matt	4	0	1.59	35	23	34	26	12	42
*Hinshaw, Alex	2	1	2.08	34	4	30	16	19	43
Sattler, Dan	0	0	2.25	5	3	4	2	5	4
Polanco, Celson	1	0	2.92	2	0	12	16	3	12
*Capra, Anthony	7	2	3.03	14	0	74	57	46	72
Zouzalik, Michael	4	0	3.06	47	0	47	46	16	31
Brown, Tim	10	4	3.12	22	0	130	150	19	76
Bennett, Daniel	6	1	3.17	46	1	48	51	12	27
Link, Jon	11	2	3.26	20	0	127	123	33	100
Van Skike, Jason	12	5	3.36	26	0	110	121	31	55
Mincey, Patrick	2	3	3.42	27	0	26	23	9	20
Robertson, Luke	1	0	3.60	1	0	5	6	1	2
Klipp, Justin	7	3	3.92	18	0	103	107	39	50
*Del Valle, Frank	1	1	5.70	9	0	36	43	26	24
Robertson, Matthew	2	0	6.03	28	0	34	44	11	19
Peacock, Chris	2	0	7.50	6	0	6	9	3	4
*Gaynor, Jared	0	0	8.16	10	0	14	19	4	7
*Williams, Alan	2	3	9.60	14	0	30	39	29	16

WINNIPEG GOLDEYES

PLAYER	AVG	AB	R	H	HR	RBI	BB	SO	SB
*Kuhn, Tyler	.360	411	70	148	5	56	43	42	11
Haerther, Casey	.360	389	49	140	13	72	21	48	0
Bond, Brock	.326	227	53	74	0	20	50	21	6
Blackwood, Jake	.321	330	50	106	10	49	22	45	1
#Webb, Donnie	.292	359	60	105	10	50	43	79	32
Alen, Luis	.289	325	29	94	6	50	24	16	3
Abercrombie, Reggie	.284	398	73	113	19	74	15	98	23
Guida, Jordan	.281	121	22	34	2	10	9	35	0
Pineda, Ryan	.274	252	45	69	5	31	32	59	5
Mazzola, Josh	.265	373	61	99	16	68	26	64	17
Sadler, Ray	.234	201	33	47	10	31	13	47	8
*Kimmel, Sam	.139	36	1	5	0	2	3	4	1

PLAYER	W	L	ERA	G	SV	IP	H	BB	SO
*Anderson, Kyle	3	2	1.64	8	0	49	41	9	29

INDEPENDENT LEAGUES

*Lafferty, Brendan	0	3	2.66	55	6	51	41	23	52
Fowler, Barry	1	0	2.70	3	0	7	5	2	1
Sewitt, Taylor	1	1	2.95	42	0	43	42	12	27
*Hernandez, Nick	12	2	3.06	20	0	121	117	22	93
*Bratton, Taylor	0	0	3.07	12	0	15	15	7	4
Kissock, Chris	0	5	3.18	47	17	45	49	11	45
*Salamida, Chris	7	4	3.29	19	0	126	120	26	91
*Aguilar, Gabe	7	2	3.38	41	0	48	41	15	39
Hollingsworth, Ethan	8	1	3.39	15	0	93	86	20	50
Stoner, Jeffrey	0	0	3.60	5	0	5	4	1	3
Jackson, Matthew	11	7	4.18	21	0	121	140	34	82
Barnard, Chandler	4	2	4.28	8	0	40	41	21	20
Downing, Kaohi	1	1	4.97	34	0	29	30	16	27
*Bollinger, Ryan	3	0	6.00	4	0	21	29	5	11
Johnson, Chase	0	0	6.00	3	0	3	4	3	2
Bellamy, Kyle	3	2	7.64	21	5	18	22	14	16
Howard, Cephas	1	0	9.00	5	0	3	4	2	3
DeLaCruz, Alex	0	0	9.82	3	0	4	8	3	2
Jarvis, Jason	1	3	9.95	4	0	19	38	6	10
Sintes, Jonathan	0	2	14.73	2	0	7	18	2	5

	TEAM	AVG	AB	R	H	HR	RBI	BB	SO
Simmons, James	BPT	.295	545	103	161	20	67	37	151
Valdez, Wilson	YRK	.292	442	69	129	2	38	42	42

PITCHING LEADERS

PITCHER	TEAM	G	W	L	ERA	IP	H	BB	SO
Schwinden, Chris	LAN	25	14	5	2.57	165	163	32	105
Pauley, David	SL	24	13	7	2.67	142	135	38	102
Blevins, Bobby	LI	27	9	5	2.95	189	175	32	119
Martinez, Jorge	YRK	27	11	8	3.21	135	125	39	93
Lansford, Jared	LI	25	8	5	3.22	159	155	41	123
*Zielinski, Matt	SOM	27	10	8	3.21	151	147	32	85
*Hammond, Steve	SL	27	10	8	3.3	150	149	67	121
Watanabe, Shunsuke	LAN	39	8	2	3.37	120	97	33	91
*Maloney, Matt	SOM	22	10	8	3.4	138	134	34	90
Wright, Matt	SL	26	12	9	3.48	155	136	50	137

BRIDGEPORT BLUEFISH

PLAYER	AVG	AB	R	H	HR	RBI	BB	SO	SB
*Burroughs, Sean	.344	270	34	93	1	25	22	28	1
#Almonte, Denny	.203	256	21	52	9	33	25	99	9
*Gallagher, Austin	.164	165	13	27	4	12	12	35	1
*Lewis, Fred	.285	186	27	53	3	24	22	40	9
Castro, Ramon	.271	480	63	130	7	59	46	90	5
Gonzalez, Billy	.163	49	2	8	0	1	2	17	0
Lopez, Luis	.222	451	37	100	7	48	42	46	0
Martinez, Juan	.230	447	53	103	8	37	26	96	5
Mather, Joe	.242	120	14	29	2	14	20	26	1
Redman, Prentice	.270	508	57	137	16	65	49	65	0
Richard, Mike	.281	256	42	72	0	18	28	36	17
Rodriguez, Luis	.232	327	20	76	2	39	17	63	1
Simmons, James	.295	545	103	161	20	67	37	151	15
Wells, Casper	.267	176	18	47	2	19	17	41	3
Overbeck, Cody	.276	123	17	34	7	23	7	32	0
Towles, JR	.292	216	35	63	11	37	30	43	0
*Gilmartin, Michael	.000	13	1	0	0	1	1	7	0
#Boggs, Brandon	.324	68	9	22	1	7	7	11	2

PLAYER	W	L	ERA	G	SV	IP	H	BB	SO
Bonser, Boof	2		2.16	12	0	17	14	4	15
Gustafson, Tim	2	5	2.39	57	6	64	50	19	71
Parr, James	1	0	2.79	5	0	10	12	0	11
Texeira, Kanekoa	3	2	3.31	9	0	52	60	16	31
Accardo, Jeremy	0	0	3.57	23	0	23	23	9	11
Bateman, Joe	2	4	3.80	54	1	83	82	16	50
Chapman, Jay	2	3	3.86	50	0	54	55	24	58
Rodriguez, Julio	2	2	4.31	9	0	40	28	32	35
*Iannazzo, Matt	4	11	4.38	32	0	125	145	38	60
Mitchell, DJ	9	11	4.63	27	0	156	169	82	110
Abreu, Winston	3	7	4.85	54	17	52	43	36	54
*Maine, Scott	2	3	4.95	19	0	20	19	4	23
*Jones, Hunter	5	10	5.04	21	0	125	148	28	58
Ohka, Tomo	7	12	5.15	26	0	157	190	74	49
Sommo, Matt	2	0	6.04	18	0	28	46	9	20
*Willis, Dontrelle	0	2	6.40	2	0	13	14	5	9
Harris, TyRelle	0	6	6.94	8	0	36	38	27	27
McMillen, Kyle	0	7	7.78	31	0	59	72	50	38
*English, Jesse	0	1	8.03	17	0	25	22	28	20
Fruto, Emiliano	0	0	8.10	6	0	7	9	4	4
Hiscock, Stephen	0	1	8.10	2	0	10	15	7	4
Rodriguez, Luis	0	0	8.22	3	0	8	13	1	1
Harvey, Ryan	0	1	9.31	10	1	10	7	14	12
*Gibson, Glenn	1	0	9.45	6	0	7	12	6	5
*Braddock, Zach	0	1	10.39	3	0	9	14	5	7
Omogrosso, Brian	0	3	13.50	7	0	6	12	5	7

CAMDEN RIVERSHARKS

PLAYER	AVG	AB	R	H	HR	RBI	BB	SO	SB
*Gomez, Yasser	.308	289	41	89	1	28	31	22	12
*Julio-Ruiz, Jose	.308	377	61	116	15	66	25	59	2
Strieby, Ryan	.293	256	42	75	4	33	35	62	0
Hudak, Alex	.287	286	40	82	7	39	29	80	5
#Batista, Wilson	.284	81	7	23	1	5	4	11	3
Pounds, Bryan	.283	480	72	136	16	70	53	106	0
Zazueta, Amadeo	.274	62	4	17	0	1	2	3	1
#Morales, Jose	.269	260	15	70	1	22	12	41	0
Van Kirk, Brian	.268	407	44	109	11	58	40	72	0
#Susini, Norberto	.250	16	1	4	0	3	2	9	0

ATLANTIC LEAGUE

Gabe Jacobo had the moment that every young baseball player dreams of while swinging a bat in their backyard.

With one out in the bottom of the 13th inning, Jacobo hit a walk-off home run to lift the Lancaster Barnstormers to an 8-7 win over Sugar Land. The home run finished off Lancaster's three-game sweep of the Skeeters.

FREEDOM DIVISION	W	L	PCT	GB
&Lancaster Barnstormers	81	59	.579	–
*Sugar Land Skeeters	80	60	.571	1
^York Revolution	78	62	.557	3
Southern Maryland Blue Crabs	68	72	.486	13

LIBERTY DIVISION	W	L	PCT	
&^Somerset Patriots	85	55	.607	—
Long Island Ducks	73	67	.521	12
Camden Riversharks	48	92	.343	37
Bridgeport Bluefish	47	93	.336	38

^ First-half champion & second-half champion. *Wild Card.

PLAYOFFS: Semifinals—Sugar Land defeated York 3-2 and Lancaster defeated 3-2 in best-of-5 series. **Finals**—Lancaster defeated Sugar Land 3-0 in best-of-5 series.

MANAGERS: Bridgeport Bluefish: Willie Upshaw; Camden Riversharks: Ron Karkovice; Lancaster Barnstormers: Butch Hobson; Long Island Ducks: Kevin Baez; Somerset Patriots: Brett Jodie; Southern Maryland Blue Crabs: Lance Burkhart; Sugar Land Skeeters: Gary Gaetti; York Revolution: Mark Mason.

ATTENDANCE: Sugar Land 383,465; Somerset 348,512; Long Island 344,543; Lancaster 301,935; York 267,695; Southern Maryland 221,694; Camden 214,891; Bridgeport 150,284.

ALL-STAR TEAM: C—Adam Donachie, Somerset; 1B—Chad Tracy, York; 2B—Eric Patterson, York; 3B—Corey Smith, Somerset; SS—Wilson Valdez, York; Utl.—Bryan Pounds, Camden; OFs—Lew Ford, Long Island; Cole Garner, Lancaster; Adam Bailey, Long Island; Justin Greene, York. DH—Delwyn Young, Sugar Land.

LHP—Matt Zielinski, Somerset; RHP—Chris Schwinden, Lancaster RP.—Jason Lowey, Somerset. Closer—Jon Hunton, Somerset.

PLAYER OF THE YEAR: Lew Ford, Long Island. **PITCHER OF THE YEAR:** Chris Schwinden, Lancaster.

BATTING LEADERS

BATTER	TEAM	AVG	AB	R	H	HR	RBI	BB	SO
Greene, Justin	YRK	.358	444	81	159	7	45	47	79
Ford, Lew	LI	.347	544	100	189	15	95	53	65
Garner, Cole	LAN	.313	530	84	166	26	92	28	114
Smith, Corey	SOM	.305	488	75	149	13	79	65	62
*Julio-Ruiz, Jose	CMD	.302	470	73	142	18	76	33	74
*Patterson, Eric	YRK	.301	498	94	150	15	86	66	103
*Bailey, Adam	LI	.301	489	65	147	20	89	41	88
Puckett, Cody	LI	.298	568	64	169	10	77	36	73

Albaladejo, Michael	.249	297	34	74	1	37	21	37	4
Perez, Eric	.244	82	7	20	0	5	7	22	0
#Nelson, Bryant	.238	172	15	41	0	18	12	10	1
Matera, Paddy	.236	398	51	94	3	39	37	49	6
Phillips, PJ	.236	110	9	26	2	9	6	27	1
Sams, Kalian	.232	56	4	13	2	6	8	19	1
Chaves, Brandon	.231	225	24	52	2	17	22	53	3
*Cortes, Jorge	.224	85	12	19	0	9	15	10	2
Brown, Tyler	.214	14	0	3	0	0	1	4	0
*Dunigan, Joe	.212	33	3	7	1	2	2	10	0
Stevens, Bobby	.209	86	10	18	0	7	13	21	2
MacPhee, Zack	.200	451	58	90	2	35	47	71	20
Galarraga, Joel	.200	50	4	10	0	6	3	6	1
*Valencia, Chris	.200	10	1	2	0	0	2	3	0
#Hughes, Carlos	.200	15	1	3	1	1	0	3	0
Patterson, Chase	.083	12	2	1	1	2	2	5	0

PLAYER	W	L	ERA	G	SV	IP	H	BB	SO
*Murphy, Bill	1	0	0.00	2	0	10	4	3	3
Gorgen, Matt	2	2	1.82	38	21	40	34	8	40
Kimball, Cole	2	2	1.91	29	2	33	22	27	34
Hose, T.J.	4	8	2.04	50	0	53	43	28	47
MacDougal, Mike	0	0	2.25	4	0	4	3	0	7
*Morgado, Bryan	1	2	2.29	25	0	20	20	15	15
Simmons, James	0	0	2.70	2	0	10	12	2	8
Clark, Zachary	2	3	3.00	7	0	36	34	8	21
Click, Michael	4	0	3.53	29	0	36	23	15	37
Hale, Jake	5	3	3.86	12	0	82	69	16	37
*Kline, Eric	0	1	3.94	7	0	16	17	9	4
Blewett, Dan	5	3	4.04	39	0	71	63	28	61
Lujan, John	1	1	4.36	34	0	43	44	18	21
Torrez, Wes	5	5	4.39	22	0	117	123	51	54
*Testa, Joe	0	1	4.50	6	0	8	7	5	8
*Ni, Fu-Te	2	5	4.72	11	0	61	74	15	58
Miller, Greg	0	8	5.27	26	0	68	77	33	39
Liriano, Pedro	3	11	5.35	29	0	109	137	33	61
*Teufel, Shawn	0	1	5.40	46	0	28	29	18	25
*Voss, Jay	1	3	5.44	11	0	46	58	28	20
Toler, Sean	3	1	5.57	23	0	32	34	13	22
Montefusco, Anthony	0	1	5.73	2	0	11	14	2	8
*Kulik, Ryan	2	8	5.80	13	0	71	97	25	39
Sanchez, Cesar	0	4	6.57	5	0	25	31	14	16
Gorgen, Scott	3	6	7.12	11	0	49	70	24	29
Semerano, Rob	1	4	7.32	18	0	20	23	11	14
Johnston, Andrew	0	0	7.66	19	0	25	40	8	13
Lucas, Jonathan	0	1	7.71	4	0	5	7	0	3
DeBarr, Nick	1	4	8.18	20	0	47	54	38	34
Pelzer, Wynn	0	1	9.45	6	0	7	10	4	6
Tullo, Aaron	0	3	16.20	4	0	10	19	15	7

LONG ISLAND DUCKS

PLAYER	AVG	AB	R	H	HR	RBI	BB	SO	SB
Crawford, Evan	.378	45	8	17	0	3	4	9	7
Ford, Lew	.347	544	100	189	15	95	53	65	8
Retherford, C.J.	.314	70	10	22	2	8	5	11	0
*Bailey, Adam	.301	489	65	147	20	89	41	88	2
Puckett, Cody	.298	568	64	169	10	77	36	73	4
Ruiz, Randy	.298	178	29	53	9	40	10	37	1
Lentini, Fehlandt	.290	593	96	172	6	63	31	61	46
Harris, Brendan	.286	409	68	117	8	53	71	41	1
Bantz, Brandon	.257	183	17	47	5	29	15	33	1
Lyons, Dan	.256	386	56	99	4	37	43	67	14
#Brodin, Joash	.254	503	56	128	9	60	42	81	28
Peacock, Brian	.244	45	6	11	0	1	4	14	0
Myers, Jon	.243	177	26	43	4	16	15	31	1
Hall, Bill	.239	138	22	33	4	19	27	42	1
*Vazquez, Jan	.232	168	26	39	2	20	20	35	2
#Castillo, Keith	.216	116	14	25	3	17	14	22	0
2 Strieby, Ryan	.206	68	6	14	1	8	7	16	0
*Miranda, Sergio	.203	123	12	25	0	7	10	21	1
*McClendon, Chris	.125	72	9	9	0	0	8	15	0

PLAYER	W	L	ERA	G	SV	IP	H	BB	SO
Rosales, Leo	0	0	1.35	13	9	13	7	6	12
*Organ, Tommy	0	1	2.29	20	0	20	15	5	18
Perez, Sergio	1	1	2.37	20	1	19	17	9	13
Lorin, Brett	3	4	2.77	53	2	52	54	18	35
Hernandez, Fernando	2	3	2.78	10	0	36	35	15	24
Lansford, Josh	5	3	2.91	43	1	43	48	10	32

Blevins, Bobby	9	5	2.95	27	0	189	175	32	119
*Niesen, Eric	4	3	3.06	59	0	53	46	40	65
Lansford, Jared	8	5	3.22	25	0	159	155	41	123
*Arguello, Doug	1	2	3.38	8	0	21	24	9	17
Kopp, David	1	3	3.55	30	7	33	27	11	33
Zimmermann, Bob	3	3	3.60	18	0	45	43	23	18
Brownell, John	13	9	3.61	29	0	202	208	54	130
Whitenack, Rob	1	3	3.72	10	0	29	21	21	14
*Regas, Kris	1	0	3.86	8	0	7	7	1	5
Talbot, Mitch	3	2	4.14	9	0	37	36	13	26
Meloan, Jon	0	4	4.50	25	9	24	29	11	18
Accardo, Jeremy	4	7	4.89	37	0	39	51	10	29
Holt, Brad	0	0	4.91	4	0	4	3	4	6
Garceau, Shaun	13	4	4.99	28	0	166	181	54	117
Barnes, Casey	0	2	5.24	13	0	33	42	11	25
*Way, Matt	1	1	7.20	3	0	15	16	5	12
*Garrison, Steve	0	2	7.50	14	0	12	23	4	4

LANCASTER BARNSTORMERS

PLAYER	AVG	AB	R	H	HR	RBI	BB	SO	SB
Rosario, Olmo	.364	99	12	36	3	15	2	6	3
*Gailen, Blake	.350	246	54	86	18	52	51	33	13
4#Castillo, Keith	.347	75	11	26	1	8	8	12	0
#Pedroza, Jaime	.327	55	7	18	1	2	8	11	2
#Batista, Wilson	.319	204	33	65	7	39	13	18	6
Garner, Cole	.313	530	84	166	26	92	28	114	18
Golson, Greg	.312	199	47	62	2	20	14	40	13
Delmonico, Tony	.304	46	8	14	1	6	7	7	1
*Clark, Andrew	.284	303	42	86	14	51	46	52	2
*Kajimoto, Yusuke	.283	371	66	105	4	36	48	65	12
Jacobo, Gabe	.281	295	37	83	9	48	14	60	1
Apodaca, Juan	.277	260	31	72	5	32	30	56	0
Carroll, Brett	.265	268	45	71	13	49	16	74	3
*Walton, Jamar	.263	19	2	5	1	5	0	6	0
Tsuboi, Tomo	.263	19	2	5	0	2	0	6	0
#Kielty, Bobby	.257	35	4	9	1	9	2	10	0
Francisco, Ben	.242	223	20	54	6	27	19	30	4
*Zawadzki, Lance	.238	484	54	115	11	53	32	101	15
*Gallagher, Austin	.232	82	10	19	3	11	8	15	0
Kjeldgaard, Brock	.223	238	32	53	13	30	22	90	4
*Lewis, Fred	.222	135	16	30	3	15	18	34	4
*Skelton, James	.203	123	21	25	8	15	21	32	4
#Corona, Reegie	.192	73	11	14	0	3	8	9	3
Frawley, Casey	.188	245	30	46	3	33	14	64	2
Ramon, Amos	.176	85	12	15	1	7	10	18	2
Buller, Dayton	.167	42	2	7	0	4	1	11	0
Zawadski, Grant	.109	46	5	5	0	2	6	18	0
*Owens, Jerry	.038	26	3	1	0	1	1	3	0

PLAYER	W	L	ERA	G	SV	IP	H	BB	SO
Kadish, Ian	0	1	1.50	7	0	6	4	6	7
Eppley, Cody	4	0	1.59	26	0	34	24	12	15
Englebrook, Evan	1	1	1.86	8	0	10	12	4	7
*Packer, Matt	2	0	1.93	4	0	23	22	5	15
*Braddock, Zach	0	0	2.00	9	1	9	7	3	10
Urquidez, Jason	3	2	2.37	48	28	49	40	21	65
Gardner, Joe	3	2	2.51	8	0	43	43	19	38
Schwinden, Chris	14	5	2.57	25	0	165	163	32	105
McCully, Nick	1	0	3.00	2	0	12	10	3	13
*Peeples, Ross	5	2	3.09	60	0	47	47	16	13
Watanabe, Shunsuke	8	2	3.37	39	1	120	97	33	91
Parise, Peter	4	2	3.57	18	1	23	26	8	12
Andrelczyk, Pete	5	8	3.66	70	5	93	81	48	83
*Loop, Derrick	0	0	3.68	6	0	7	6	3	6
Patterson, Scott	0	1	3.77	17	1	14	18	4	18
*Osterbrock, Dan	11	4	3.79	31	0	145	150	28	89
Downs, Brodie	2	3	3.82	29	3	35	34	13	24
*Mann, Brandon	2	2	4.09	20	0	51	47	17	48
Rogers, Mark	5	6	4.17	18	0	86	90	59	44
Beck, Chad	1	1	4.70	3	0	15	17	4	8
Scarpetta, Cody	0	2	5.13	8	0	40	39	24	37
Richardson, Jason	1	2	5.29	38	1	34	34	14	36
Wade, Cory	4	6	5.45	19	0	73	97	11	43
*Ni, Fu-Te	0	1	6.14	24	0	22	32	5	25
Blair, Kyle	1	0	6.23	8	0	9	9	6	4
*Tanner, Clayton	2	3	6.94	8	0	36	56	11	28
Grening, Brian	3	8	8.23	8	0	27	34	18	17

INDEPENDENT LEAGUES

SOUTHERN MARYLAND BLUE CRABS

PLAYER	AVG	AB	R	H	HR	RBI	BB	SO	SB
Arrojo, Junior	.600	10	1	6	0	2	0	2	2
Sappelt, Dave	.295	122	18	36	2	11	10	13	5
Moss, Steve	.294	163	27	48	5	24	24	41	5
*McDonald, Jared	.293	92	7	27	0	9	8	27	2
Sanchez, Angel	.288	52	12	15	1	4	10	6	0
#Zazueta, Amadeo	.284	394	33	112	4	43	6	27	3
Hankerd, Cyle	.283	237	31	67	6	30	39	43	3
*Opitz, Jake	.282	482	83	136	18	78	43	86	8
*Julio-Ruiz, Jose	.280	93	12	26	3	10	8	18	0
*Mitchell, Jermaine	.279	455	82	127	5	46	75	117	27
Ziegler, C.J.	.276	478	64	132	17	79	60	89	2
Stevens, Bobby	.274	288	43	79	7	40	22	43	15
Chavez, Angel	.269	260	24	70	4	38	18	30	4
*Schwartz, Mike	.269	67	11	18	1	9	6	10	0
Skelton, James	.268	179	32	48	0	25	32	45	11
#Castillo, Keith	.250	20	3	5	1	2	5	6	1
Bowden, John	.243	37	6	9	2	2	5	12	0
*Walton, Jamar	.233	193	23	45	1	18	10	44	3
Delmonico, Tony	.231	117	11	27	2	13	5	28	0
Murton, Luke	.231	290	29	67	10	37	13	77	0
de San Miguel, Allan	.203	187	20	38	5	21	20	51	0
Kaplan, Jonny	.200	60	6	12	0	6	5	8	2
*Schwaner, Nick	.200	45	1	9	0	3	0	4	0
Chavez, Johermyn	.194	62	4	12	1	3	2	13	0
Maruszak, Addison	.153	85	8	13	2	7	5	27	0
Barton, Brian	.131	107	12	14	2	7	8	21	1
Medina, Juan	.122	41	1	5	0	3	3	7	0
*Dziomba, Jon	.122	41	3	5	0	2	2	13	0

PLAYER	W	L	ERA	G	SV	IP	H	BB	SO
Slama, Anthony	0	0	1.04	17	7	17	9	8	19
Marban, Jorge	0	0	1.13	10	2	8	5	6	15
*Burres, Brian	3	2	1.64	9	0	49	46	20	31
Warden, Jim Ed	3	0	1.90	42	17	43	28	9	30
Parise, Peter	1	1	1.93	13	0	19	15	3	14
Jannis, Mickey	4	1	2.37	10	0	57	51	21	36
Santos, Orlando	2	0	2.41	21	0	19	11	7	20
Hamren, Erik	1	3	2.41	36	0	37	34	11	42
*Korpi, Wade	6	3	2.79	56	2	74	59	32	63
Toler, Sean	1	0	2.84	6	0	6	6	0	5
Berg, Justin	2	2	3.20	26	6	25	29	11	21
Baker, Brian	1	4	3.25	10	0	53	65	13	28
Keeler, Sean	0	1	3.38	7	0	5	8	2	6
Gannon, Joe	0	0	3.60	4	0	10	9	4	5
Hale, Jake	2	0	3.93	13	1	34	24	9	16
Marshall, Ian	10	10	4.09	27	0	156	181	44	78
*Brown, Jake	6	4	4.11	40	0	88	78	43	60
Morlan, Eduardo	3	3	4.29	36	1	36	33	17	23
*Manning, Charlie	1	8	4.50	52	1	46	49	25	40
Hernandez, Gabriel	8	9	4.73	28	0	158	158	53	128
Thompson, Daryl	7	6	4.76	22	0	123	131	40	99
*Hinson, Ryan	0	4	5.29	9	0	32	27	44	21
Meyers, Brad	2	2	5.64	7	0	30	35	5	14
Grening, Brian	2	5	6.16	24	0	57	70	18	35
Massingham, Eric	2	4	6.16	42	1	38	31	12	28
*Septimo, Leyson	0	0	14.85	8	0	7	10	10	4
Nelo, Hector	0	0	18.00	2	0	1	3	2	1

SOMERSET PATRIOTS

PLAYER	AVG	AB	R	H	HR	RBI	BB	SO	SB
Fox, Jake	.375	16	2	6	0	2	2	2	0
Smith, Corey	.305	488	75	149	13	79	65	62	1
Martinez-Esteve, Edd	.290	138	19	40	1	16	19	20	2
Montanez, Luis	.289	491	69	142	17	74	38	50	5
Wilson, Mike	.284	81	20	23	3	12	16	22	3
Donachie, Adam	.277	242	34	67	9	45	44	61	1
#Dominguez, Jeff	.273	220	37	60	3	25	23	38	13
Wright, Ty	.265	419	55	111	13	64	34	57	6
Tucker, Jonny	.262	416	68	109	2	34	47	70	18
Espino, Damaso	.252	242	17	61	1	18	8	30	2
*Eggleston, Aharon	.251	259	46	65	1	25	35	32	8
*Spears, Nate	.248	145	21	36	4	21	12	28	2
Ward, Daryle	.239	197	25	47	8	34	25	27	0
Barden, Brian	.238	290	30	69	7	30	23	63	5
Maysonet, Edwin	.226	336	37	76	4	26	18	75	12
*Harrilchak, Cory	.225	244	30	55	5	27	30	59	7
*Kotch, Kevin	.222	36	3	8	1	6	2	15	1
*Widlansky, Robbie	.214	126	10	27	0	16	10	14	4
Sulcoski, Steve	.200	15	2	3	0	1	0	2	0
Kelly, Scott	.193	243	32	47	0	10	11	31	20

PLAYER	W	L	ERA	G	SV	IP	H	BB	SO
Brach, Brett	1	0	0.00	1	0	5	2	1	3
Newby, Kyler	0	0	0.00	11	1	11	7	2	10
Fisher, Carlos	1	1	1.33	20	0	20	7	4	28
Lowey, Jason	5	1	1.91	59	1	57	35	15	59
Hunton, Jon	0	1	2.08	59	49	56	49	12	33
*Kroenke, Zach	2	1	2.19	4	0	25	20	7	13
Lowey, Josh	3	0	2.57	5	0	28	25	12	23
Rincon, Juan	2	0	2.59	26	0	24	23	10	14
*Merritt, Roy	1	1	2.63	3	0	14	10	5	11
*Purcey, David	3	0	2.72	9	0	40	30	18	36
*Zielinski, Matt	10	8	3.27	27	0	151	147	32	85
*Maloney, Matt	10	8	3.40	22	0	138	134	34	90
Langwell, Matt	5	6	3.42	14	0	79	73	27	61
*Herrera, Daniel	4	0	3.43	36	0	45	40	7	35
McCall, Derell	6	6	3.43	33	1	100	113	25	50
Sommo, Matt	2	1	3.67	24	0	27	22	19	22
Moran, Gary	11	5	4.07	25	0	146	157	37	108
Arnesen, Erik	7	6	4.18	18	0	112	114	8	64
Hyde, Lee	2	0	4.26	15	0	13	11	6	12
DeMark, Mike	7	2	4.39	43	2	39	40	20	35
Solbach, Mike	0	1	4.45	35	0	32	37	15	28
Harden, David	3	6	4.97	13	0	38	48	10	22
*Reichenbach, J.D.	1	0	5.17	18	0	16	14	7	17
*Harrilchak, Cory	0	0	6.97	11	0	10	18	3	6
Sanchez, Salvador	0	1	7.20	5	0	5	6	2	2
Lucas, Jonathan	0	1	13.50	6	0	6	11	3	6

SUGAR LAND SKEETERS

PLAYER	AVG	AB	R	H	HR	RBI	BB	SO	SB
Moss, Steve	.389	18	1	7	0	3	1	3	1
Barton, Brian	.294	252	32	74	3	37	21	36	7
Jennings, Todd	.293	75	9	22	0	10	5	11	0
Hunt, Bridger	.291	110	16	32	0	12	14	13	1
#Young, Delwyn	.289	530	63	153	20	88	40	61	2
*Langerhans, Ryan	.279	434	84	121	13	56	91	86	6
Harbin, Taylor	.276	152	23	42	2	17	11	19	4
Ramos, Dominic	.271	458	55	124	1	43	39	72	7
Lehmann, Danny	.266	124	15	33	0	9	16	27	3
*Martin, Dustin	.261	46	5	12	0	3	3	7	2
Ryal, Rusty	.255	106	14	27	5	16	15	20	2
Stavinoha, Nick	.252	337	33	85	14	54	20	55	0
Godwin, Adam	.247	332	37	82	1	20	19	38	13
*Medchill, Neil	.231	147	29	34	4	13	19	39	2
*Scott, Travis	.228	408	59	93	12	51	62	57	1
Rockett, Michael	.228	351	34	80	8	38	4	67	6
#Lambin, Chase	.202	382	47	77	5	31	38	94	0
Clemens, Koby	.190	105	10	20	1	6	10	36	0
#Almonte, Denny	.189	74	11	14	3	9	8	25	2
*Tosoni, Rene	.170	53	3	9	1	8	4	5	0
Denker, Travis	.158	19	0	3	0	1	5	4	0
*Nunez, Alex	.103	39	2	4	0	2	0	7	10
Wood, Brandon	.098	82	4	8	1	5	6	29	0

PLAYER	W	L	ERA	G	SV	IP	H	BB	SO
Nix, Michael	2	1	2.00	5	0	27	21	13	23
*VanAllen, Cory	2	0	2.11	44	0	47	45	13	29
Smith, Chris	6	0	2.15	12	0	50	40	10	55
Corcoran, Roy	4	0	2.30	60	1	63	58	21	60
Broderick, Brian	0	2	2.31	60	11	62	51	9	65
Johnston, Andrew	1	0	2.51	23	0	29	28	4	17
Pauley, David	13	7	2.67	24	0	142	135	38	102
Delgado, Ramon	5	2	2.88	46	0	69	66	18	50
Majewski, Gary	8	3	3.06	57	24	65	71	7	35
*Kozlowski, Ben	3	4	3.29	54	1	63	74	16	41
*Hammond, Steve	8	8	3.30	27	0	150	149	67	121
Wright, Matt	12	9	3.48	26	0	155	136	50	137
*Meadows, Dan	3	5	3.77	21	0	57	57	20	47
Wells, Jared	3	2	3.83	55	1	56	48	33	54
Gallagher, Sean	3	4	4.98	13	0	69	73	31	33
Everts, Clint	5	11	5.82	25	0	119	127	63	71
McGrady, Tracy	0	2	6.75	4	0	7	4	10	0

Hensley, Clay	0	0	13.50	3	0	3	5	3	1

YORK REVOLUTION

PLAYER	AVG	AB	R	H	HR	RBI	BB	SO	SB
*Limonta, Johan	.302	321	34	97	7	58	32	54	3
*Patterson, Eric	.301	498	94	150	15	86	66	103	26
#Espinosa, Alberto	.210	162	12	34	1	11	7	49	3
#Chaves, Brandon	.127	63	7	8	0	5	7	13	3
#Nelson, Bryant	.253	225	19	57	2	17	15	26	3
Battle, Tim	.185	146	14	27	1	13	5	42	4
Flores, Angel	.264	91	7	24	1	2	6	15	0
Garcia, Travis	.256	442	45	113	14	61	20	92	4
Greene, Justin	.358	444	81	159	7	45	47	79	31
Luna, Omar	.265	68	3	18	0	5	2	8	1
Paniagua, Salvador	.249	289	23	72	6	36	7	64	0
Smith, Sean	.243	453	72	110	8	32	52	133	41
Tracy, Chad	.272	493	76	134	23	97	63	83	1
Valdez, Wilson	.292	442	69	129	2	38	42	42	55
Castro, Ofilio	.247	356	30	88	2	38	25	59	1
Repko, Jason	.196	97	13	19	2	8	9	22	1
Sulcoski, Steve	.176	17	0	3	0	0	0	3	0
*Bumbry, Steve	.231	26	5	6	0	2	3	10	0
#Torres, Tim	.220	59	12	13	0	5	16	21	10
#Yan, Ruddy	.087	23	0	2	0	1	1	3	1

PLAYER	W	L	ERA	G	SV	IP	H	BB	SO
DeMark, Mike	0	0	0.00	6	0	6	3	1	7
Gomez, Ricardo	0	0	0.00	4	0	4	3	3	4
Neil, Matt	2	0	1.47	3	0	18	15	3	13
*Hendrickson, Mark	2	0	1.54	55	9	53	40	11	34
*Lewis, Rommie	3	1	2.15	45	28	46	37	14	35
Lerew, Anthony	1	1	2.25	5	0	24	21	9	24
Penney, Stephen	3	2	2.32	45	1	43	40	8	40
Vaughan, Beau	8	3	2.33	51	2	77	49	15	56
DePaula, Julio	3	2	2.48	28	1	29	24	8	30
*Paredes, Edward	3	3	2.70	43	0	57	45	19	57
*Williamson, Logan	6	7	2.72	20	0	109	116	56	62
*Harris, Joe	0	0	2.84	7	0	6	5	3	4
Durham, Ian	5	2	3.02	54	0	63	52	20	65
*Morgado, Bryan	0	0	3.16	24	0	31	31	15	28
Martinez, Jorge	11	8	3.21	27	0	135	125	39	93
*Cody, Chris	5	4	3.93	12	0	69	69	19	50
Thurman, Corey	9	7	3.97	25	0	138	135	34	73
McClendon, Mike	2	2	4.22	7	0	32	35	7	20
*Quijano, Alain	10	10	4.59	28	0	169	201	40	89
Wuertz, Michael	2	2	4.70	18	1	15	9	22	17
Gorgen, Scott	3	5	5.59	18	0	76	88	26	36
Miller, Greg	1	1	5.73	7	0	11	17	3	5
DeSalvo, Matt	0	1	6.00	1	0	6	4	3	3
Cortes, Dan	0	1	13.50	8	0	7	11	11	2

CAN-AM LEAGUE

Quebec's hold on the Can-Am League title has finally been broken.

The Capitales had won five straight Can-Am League titles. The streak finally ended as Rockland, a club that didn't even exist when Quebec's streak began, rallied to edge New Jersey for the title.

Rockland used plenty of late-inning heroics to win its first championship. Matt Nandin hit a walk-off single to win Game 3 of the series. In the next game, Rockland scored on a walk-off wild pitch. The final two games took less drama. Rockland scored seven runs in the first on their way to a 14-4 win in Game 5, and Bo Budkevics and two relievers combined on a 4-0 shutout in the clinching Game 6.

CAN-AM LEAGUE	W	L	PCT	GB
Rockland Boulders	56	40	.583	-
New Jersey Jackals	55	41	.573	1
Quebec Capitales	46	50	.479	10
Trois-Rivieres Aigles	37	59	.385	19

PLAYOFFS: Rockland defeated New Jersey 4-2 in best-of-7 series.

ATTENDANCE: Rockland 146,383; Quebec 121,305; New Jersey 76,423; Trois-Rivieres 72,543.

MANAGERS: New Jersey: Joe Calfapietra; Quebec: Pat Scalabrini; Rockland: Jamie Keefe; Trois-Rivieres: Pete LaForest.

ALL-STARS: C—Kyle Lafrenz, Trois-Rivieres. **1B**—Jerod Edmondson, Rockland. **2B**—Jose Cuevas, New Jersey/Trois-Rivieres. **3B**—Balbino Fuenmayor, Quebec. **SS**—Jonathan Malo, Quebec. **OF**—Sebastien Boucher, Quebec; Ryan Stovall, Rockland; Antone DeJesus, Rockland. **DH**—Joe Dunigan, New Jersey.

SP—Michael Antonini, New Jersey. **RP**—Salvador Sanchez, New Jersey.

MOST VALUABLE PLAYER: Balbino Fuenmayor, 3B, Quebec. **ROOKIE OF THE YEAR:** Matt Helms, OF, Quebec. **MANAGER OF THE YEAR:** Jamie Keefe, Rockland.

BATTING LEADERS

PLAYER	TEAM	AVG	AB	R	H	HR	RBI	BB	SO
Boucher, Sebastien	QC	.366	314	67	115	8	48	53	44
Fuenmayor, Balbino	QC	.347	377	67	131	23	99	22	64
Helms, Matt	QC	.315	324	56	102	3	32	24	39
Stovall, Ryan	ROC	.312	375	63	117	17	72	25	86
DeJesus, Antone	ROC	.308	386	70	119	7	43	39	28
Shah, Asif	QC	.303	347	53	105	2	43	38	29
Cardullo, Stephen	ROC	.298	352	43	105	6	51	16	46
Nandin, Matt	ROC	.296	388	69	115	2	40	31	33
Harris, Alonzo	NJ	.290	355	54	103	7	52	35	75
Malo, Jonathan	QC	.285	365	61	104	5	36	36	52

PITCHING LEADERS

PLAYER	W	L	ERA	G	IP	H	BB	SO
Bierman, Sean	8	6	2.44	17	114	108	17	63
Rusch, Matthew	9	7	2.72	20	126	128	34	110
Antonini, Michael	9	3	2.84	19	117	106	20	115
Harrold, Stephen	7	4	2.87	23	122	103	41	83
Gelinas, Karl	8	6	3.48	21	137	141	16	123
Salazar, Richard	10	5	3.72	21	109	116	24	84
Pavlik, Issac	9	5	3.75	19	115	119	32	75
Perez, Leondy	6	7	3.95	18	107	107	35	93
Bilodeau, Keith	6	7	4.00	19	115	109	49	53
Terhune, Greg	3	6	4.45	19	83	92	29	42

NEW JERSEY JACKALS

PLAYER	AVG	AB	R	H	HR	RBI	BB	SO	SB
Adams, Ryan	.300	40	5	12	0	4	3	8	0
Harris, Alonzo	.290	355	54	103	7	52	35	75	34
*Cortes, Jorge	.278	209	29	58	4	34	34	28	4
#Sanchez, Felix	.272	360	62	98	0	20	23	95	36
Childs, Dwight	.261	23	2	6	0	2	5	4	0
Barnes, Jeremy	.260	315	49	82	11	39	41	52	0
Caldwell, Tony	.257	261	31	67	4	32	25	77	1
Arias, Richard	.251	299	27	75	1	23	17	43	5
*Dunigan, Joe	.249	358	58	89	27	71	22	141	10
Nikorak, Steve	.248	254	29	63	4	25	24	76	6
*Talley, Jon	.245	335	45	82	13	50	21	76	1
Zinsmeister, Rob	.238	21	3	5	0	0	1	6	5
Shepherd, JaRon	.223	103	11	23	0	11	19	31	2
Cabezas, Yaniel	.216	74	7	16	0	7	3	8	0
Cuevas, Jose	.206	107	17	22	3	13	9	18	2
Mesa, Carlos	.204	54	5	11	1	3	0	15	0

PLAYER	W	L	ERA	G	SV	IP	H	BB	SO
Shields, Jeff	1	0	1.50	1	0	6	5	2	3
Fennell, Ryan	1	0	1.63	34	0	50	30	39	50
Ellis, Shaun	3	1	2.27	43	3	52	40	15	56
Smith, Eric	1	0	2.35	3	0	15	14	7	12
Sanchez, Salvador	4	2	2.40	42	25	41	33	12	46
*Antonini, Michael	9	3	2.84	19	0	117	106	20	115
Lucas, Jon	0	0	2.84	4	0	6	9	1	2
Kelley, Ty	2	3	3.33	39	0	54	51	10	48
Staniewicz, Zach	1	1	3.31	4	0	17	13	10	8
*Pavlik, Isaac	9	5	3.75	19	0	115	119	32	75
Bilodeau, Keith	6	7	4.00	19	0	115	109	49	53
Perez, Gabriel	8	5	4.01	13	0	74	55	38	54
*Ferrara, Anthony	5	5	4.85	15	0	69	77	34	36
Beaulac, Eric	0	2	5.79	14	0	19	19	12	18
Soren, Matt	0	2	6.43	7	0	7	7	5	7
*Vessella, Tom	5	5	6.60	20	0	61	92	30	48

INDEPENDENT LEAGUES

PLAYER	W	L	ERA	G	SV	IP	H	BB	SO	
Wynn, David	0	0	7.27	6	0	9	10	5	8	
Adamek, Brady	0	0	10.13	8	0	8	11	10	6	

QUEBEC CAPITALES

PLAYER	AVG	AB	R	H	HR	RBI	BB	SO	SB
*Boucher, Sebastien	.356	309	65	110	8	44	53	44	8
Fuenmayor, Balbino	.347	375	66	130	23	95	21	63	2
Gurriel, Yuniesky	.321	78	10	25	1	11	6	11	3
*Helms, Matt	.313	319	53	100	3	32	24	38	9
*Shah, Asif	.297	343	51	102	2	43	37	28	2
Peley, Josue	.286	227	28	65	6	28	7	22	1
Malo, Jonathan	.285	361	61	103	5	36	36	50	15
Provencher, Mike	.273	311	51	85	9	46	24	56	12
Blaquiere, Jean-Luc	.261	222	25	58	7	30	19	47	0
Leveret, Rene	.257	334	37	86	8	42	19	46	4
Smith, Tim	.238	122	12	29	0	15	15	12	2
Balkwill, Larry	.200	35	3	7	0	4	4	14	0
Domingue, Samuel	.146	48	8	7	0	4	6	15	
3 Brill, Aaron	.139	72	10	10	0	6	6	19	1
Haney, Bobby	.080	50	1	4	0	1	2	11	5

PLAYER	W	L	ERA	G	SV	IP	H	BB	SO
Leach, Ryan	0	0	0.00	6	0	7	3	4	6
*McDonald, Sheldon	3	1	2.02	38	1	36	29	11	48
Dubois, Derek	0	1	2.84	5	0	6	3	2	9
Moskovits, Danny	2	2	3.03	8	0	30	29	12	24
Gelinas, Karl	8	6	3.48	21	0	137	141	16	123
Perez, Leondy	6	7	3.95	18	0	107	107	35	93
*Regnault, Kyle	4	6	4.47	22	3	87	83	24	90
Sanford, Shawn	9	4	4.97	18	0	109	138	18	64
Staniewicz, Zach	6	7	5.26	20	0	91	89	63	65
Schreiber, Brett	0	1	5.40	8	0	12	17	3	6
Housey, Joey	0	3	5.86	20	0	28	29	10	22
Johnson, Jay	2	4	6.08	25	8	27	27	9	34
Marino, Harry	0	2	6.30	7	0	10	8	1	6
Clark, Kirk	0	0	6.35	28	0	23	28	13	14
*Ronick, Ari	2	1	6.67	7	0	30	41	14	26
Pierce, Joel	0	1	7.04	13	1	15	22	4	14
Cox, Chris	2	2	7.36	30	4	33	39	17	36
Riley, Joe	1	0	7.50	3	0	6	6	2	5
Bayne, Cameron	0	1	11.57	5	0	7	11	3	6

ROCKLAND BOULDERS

PLAYER	AVG	AB	R	H	HR	RBI	BB	SO	SB
*DeJesus, Antone	.308	386	70	119	7	43	39	28	20
Nandin, Matt	.296	388	69	115	2	40	31	33	6
*Edmondson, Jerod	.277	365	65	101	11	68	51	89	9
Stovall, Ryan	.312	375	63	117	17	72	25	86	14
Maloney, Sean	.271	295	56	80	17	66	31	85	10
Cardullo, Stephen	.298	352	43	105	6	51	16	46	8
Nidiffer, Marcus	.251	243	35	61	14	49	18	65	0
Nyisztor, Steve	.341	164	30	56	2	24	5	22	8
Arrojo, Junior	.261	184	27	48	2	18	16	31	3
#O'Hare, Sean	.210	157	23	33	0	10	17	24	6
*Walsh, Will	.205	151	19	31	7	17	11	31	3
Papaccio, Giuseppe	.239	92	11	22	1	9	5	24	0
Dalles, Justin	.147	34	3	5	0	3	1	6	0
Guzman, Carlos	.282	39	2	11	0	4	2	3	0
Fischer, Michael	.050	20	0	1	0	0	1	13	0

PLAYER	W	L	ERA	G	SV	IP	H	BB	SO
Robinson, Chad	2	1	1.04	31	14	35	18	13	45
Mangum, Taylor	4	0	2.08	19	0	22	22	6	16
Sanz, Luis	2	1	2.16	19	2	25	19	11	31
Bierman, Sean	8	6	2.44	17	0	114	108	17	63
Budkevics, Bo	3	2	2.64	5	0	31	29	10	25
Harrold, Stephen	7	4	2.87	23	0	122	103	41	83
*Gilblair, Shawn	1	2	3.47	43	0	47	37	15	54
Martinez, Fray	3	1	3.68	38	0	44	37	16	36
*Salazar, Richard	10	5	3.72	21	0	109	116	24	84
Roe, Nathaniel	5	1	3.81	29	1	59	52	21	56
Kreis, Alex	1	2	4.19	18	7	19	17	15	24
Donino, Joe	5	4	4.31	10	0	56	52	25	53
*Terhune, Greg	3	6	4.45	19	0	83	92	29	42
Law, Charlie	1	5	5.85	11	0	52	64	24	28
Hur, Min	1	0	7.20	2	0	10	14	7	1

TROIS-RIVIERES AIGLES

PLAYER	AVG	AB	R	H	HR	RBI	BB	SO	SB
Walsh, Will	.346	26	4	9	1	2	4	6	3
Cuevas, Jose	.295	217	40	64	10	35	22	35	15
Side, Joey	.274	146	31	40	3	18	21	23	2
Hernandez, Michael	.271	273	35	74	9	36	32	79	0
#Mateo, Daniel	.270	37	6	10	4	12	2	4	0
Lafrenz, Kyle	.267	307	44	82	5	29	36	73	0
Grabe, Eric	.264	326	49	86	5	33	54	60	4
Guzman, Carlos	.254	307	41	78	6	41	33	47	2
Brown, Steve	.252	309	54	78	11	44	37	101	15
Millan Jr., Elvin	.250	140	15	35	3	19	4	46	0
Brown, Felix	.238	126	15	30	1	14	21	36	9
Newton, Brandon	.231	108	11	25	0	3	8	26	4
*LaGarde, Sasha	.230	113	13	26	0	7	5	33	3
*Miller, Drew	.224	313	47	70	7	51	29	71	1
Hampton, Josh	.224	76	5	17	0	4	2	15	0
Dostaler, Pier-Olivi	.220	109	11	24	1	16	6	26	1
Weaver, Travis	.169	83	3	14	0	6	2	18	3
Nichols, Kyle	.163	49	3	8	0	3	5	12	0
Zorrilla, Janelfry	.143	21	0	3	0	3	2	4	0

PLAYER	W	L	ERA	G	SV	IP	H	BB	SO
Kreis, Alex	1	1	2.57	18	1	21	17	12	21
Rusch, Matthew	9	7	2.72	20	0	126	128	34	110
Bradstreet, Mike	4	1	3.42	8	0	55	62	7	22
Sarianides, Nick	1	2	3.52	16	6	15	14	6	14
Schmeltzer, Jadd	0	1	3.72	22	0	29	21	15	18
Keeler, Sean	0	3	3.89	36	11	42	35	27	36
*Szymanski, Alex	1	3	4.54	7	0	38	38	11	20
Leblanc, David	4	1	4.59	36	0	53	56	26	29
Purdy, Nick	4	6	4.67	39	0	44	43	21	44
Alvarez, Edilson	4	8	4.68	17	0	102	120	34	60
Britton-Foster, Dan	0	1	4.73	8	0	27	28	5	13
Bollinger, Ryan	4	7	4.73	13	0	65	78	10	49
LaFreniere, Francois	3	11	5.35	19	0	98	128	34	46
Scheiner, Jordan	0	0	5.40	1	0	5	3	6	2
Wilson, Tyler	1	4	7.22	11	0	62	89	23	30
Cooper, Rob	0	0	9.24	18	0	13	15	11	7
Burkard, Alexander	0	2	10.03	3	0	12	19	15	5
Ferreira, Andrew	0	0	10.80	7	0	7	10	6	6

FRONTIER LEAGUE

When Seth Webster was on the mound, Schaumburg didn't have to worry.

In a one-game, loser-goes-home first round of the playoffs, Webster was sensational. He shut out Lake Erie, striking out 13 in a 1-0 win where any mistake might have been a season-ender. He then pitched Schaumburg to the finals, allowing one run in seven innings in a 2-1 win over Southern Illinois.

And with Schaumburg trying to finish off a sweep of River City in the championship series, Webster was excellent once again, allowing one run in seven innings in a 6-2 victory. Three starts, three wins, three dog-piles.

By winning back-to-back Frontier League titles, Schaumburg is the first team to repeat as Frontier League champ since Windy City won back-to-back titles in 2006-2007. Richmond (2001-2002) is the only other repeat champion.

EAST DIVISION	W	L	PCT	GB
Southern Illinois Miners	60	36	.625	-
Evansville Otters *	57	37	.606	2
Washington Wild Things *	57	39	.594	3
Lake Erie Crushers *	52	43	.547	7.5
Florence Freedom	41	55	.427	19
Traverse City Beach Bums	38	58	.396	22
Frontier Greys	29	66	.305	30.5

WEST DIVISION	W	L	PCT	GB
River City Rascals	61	35	.635	-
Schaumburg Boomers *	61	35	.635	-

Gateway Grizzlies	50	46	.521	11
Normal CornBelters	48	47	.505	12.5
Rockford Aviators	40	56	.417	21
Joliet Slammers	40	56	.417	21
Windy City ThunderBolts	35	60	.368	25.5

* Wild Card.

PLAYOFFS: Wild Card—Washington defeated Evansville and Schaumburg defeated Lake Erie in one-game series. **Semifinals**—River City defeated Washington 2-0 and Schaumburg defeated Southern Illinois 2-1 in best-of-3 series. **Finals**—Schaumburg defeated River City 3-1 in best-of-5 series.

ATTENDANCE: Schaumburg 157,393; Gateway 156,840; Southern Illinois 147,287; Traverse City 143,585; Evansville 111,709; Normal 109,952; Lake Erie 106,009; Florence 105,539; Joliet 92,992; Washington 84,533; River City 81,662; Windy City 74,481 Rockford 72,340.

MANAGERS: Evansville—Andy McCauley; Florence—Fran Riordan; Frontier—Kyle Haines; Gateway—Phil Warren; Joliet—Jeff Isom; Lake Erie—Chris Mongiardo; Normal—Brooks Carey; River City—Steve Brook; Rockford—James Frisbie; Schaumburg—Jamie Bennett; Southern Illinois—Mike Pinto; Traverse City—Dan Rohn; Washington—Bart Zeller; Windy City—Ron Biga.

ALL-STARS: C—Tyler Shover, Normal. **1B**—Sam Eberle, Florence. **2B**—Vincent Mejia, Lake Erie. **3B**—Shayne Houck, Evansville. **SS**—Michael Wing, Gateway. **OF**—Mike Schwartz, Normal; Kyle Robinson, Windy City; Sam Judah, Normal. **DH**—C.J. Beatty, Washington. **SP**—Matt Bywater, Southern Illinois. **RP**—Jonathan Kountis, Washington.

MOST VALUABLE PLAYER: Shayne Houck, Evansville. **PITCHER OF THE YEAR:** Matt Bywater, Southern Illinois Miners. **ROOKIE OF THE YEAR:** Tanner Witt, Rockford. **MANAGER OF THE YEAR:** Andy McCauley, Evansville.

BATTING LEADERS

BATTER	TEAM	AVG	AB	R	H	HR	RBI
Robinson, Kyle	WIN	.366	309	52	113	13	70
DeBruin, Grant	JOL	.355	380	63	135	12	67
Eberle, Sam	FLO	.346	318	53	110	8	45
*Schwartz, Mike	NOR	.336	348	79	117	16	68
*Nelson, Mark	SCH	.323	310	53	100	4	5
#Martinez, Frank	SOU	.317	312	57	99	9	64
*Dudley, Aaron	NOR	.316	332	69	105	14	64
Mejia, Vincent	LER	.314	299	45	94	15	53
*Redal, Curran	RIV	.312	247	29	77	0	24
*Vasquez, Justin	SCH	.312	340	62	106	7	49

PITCHING LEADERS

PITCHER	TEAM	W	L	ERA	IP	H	BB	SO
*Kibby, Todd	LER	6	2	2.12	81	70	31	75
*Fuesser, Zac	WSH	9	2	2.26	96	88	32	74
*Bywater, Matt	SOU	8	4	2.37	129	86	60	114
Snodgrass, Jessie	WIN	3	1	2.61	76	57	34	62
Weaver, Chuck	FLO	7	6	2.65	109	93	28	77
Henn, Casey	FLO	9	6	2.72	123	91	52	111
Olson, Preston	EVA	9	3	2.72	109	82	41	106
Cody, Eddie	SCH	8	1	2.86	79	81	23	65
Treece, Zac	LER	7	3	2.97	97	73	30	88
Zimmerman, Ryan	RCK	9	6	3.21	112	89	47	87

EVANSVILLE OTTERS

PLAYER	AVG	AB	R	H	HR	RBI	BB	SO	SB
#Del Valle, Jaime	.320	25	4	8	0	2	3	4	0
Houck, Shayne	.307	349	66	107	23	66	29	79	2
Sweeney, Chris	.297	279	52	83	21	54	27	91	6
Allen, Josh	.290	221	42	64	5	30	33	78	11
*Balog, Nik	.283	325	44	92	9	31	20	69	1
*Schwaner, Nick	.283	46	6	13	2	8	4	1	4
*Elder, Chris	.277	296	35	82	4	36	23	42	14
*Schultz, John	.276	294	48	81	8	35	45	57	5
Urquhart, Cory	.268	209	27	56	1	20	25	48	4
#Nowak, Jeremy	.265	257	38	68	7	45	29	87	6
Wilson, Phillip	.265	200	24	53	3	31	4	44	1

Conner, Kolin	.245	196	21	48	4	23	13	48	1
Higley, J.R.	.227	229	47	52	2	26	37	62	4
Cruz, David	.176	85	12	15	1	7	6	31	0
Rodgers, Stephen	.171	35	7	6	0	1	8	11	2

PLAYER	W	L	ERA	G	SV	IP	H	BB	SO
Massingham, Eric	0	0	0.75	10	8	12	9	2	13
Lopez, Edgar	2	0	1.33	7	0	20	11	13	19
Ramer, Robert	7	0	1.90	8	0	47	33	11	36
Oliver, Will	3	1	1.95	5	0	32	29	10	29
*Fowler, Zach	2	1	2.04	3	0	18	19	10	14
Marin, Terance	4	1	2.06	6	0	39	25	6	39
*Velez, Jose	2	5	2.53	30	1	57	44	33	82
Mott, Evan	3	2	2.70	27	0	40	28	13	39
Olson, Preston	9	3	2.72	17	0	109	82	41	106
Little, Connor	2	1	2.92	4	0	25	24	12	25
*Collazo, Anthony	5	2	2.93	35	0	43	32	15	50
Shimo, Brandon	1	1	3.07	37	3	41	42	13	34
Santos, Orlando	4	3	3.21	24	9	28	23	16	22
Walch, Trevor	5	3	3.73	18	0	89	81	37	87
*Monar, Blake	1	4	5.02	13	0	38	30	36	50
*James, Chad	4	2	5.05	9	0	46	32	37	67
Robinson, Chad	0	0	5.14	5	0	7	8	7	8
Dennis, Taylor	2	1	5.45	12	0	38	38	31	30
Petersime, Zach	1	4	5.64	7	0	38	48	15	26
*Kerins, Conor	0	1	5.91	2	0	11	11	11	4

FLORENCE FREEDOM

PLAYER	AVG	AB	R	H	HR	RBI	BB	SO	SB
Eberle, Sam	.346	318	53	110	8	45	64	53	3
*Taylor, Adam	.282	170	24	48	4	20	12	28	9
*Miles, Cole	.272	313	44	85	6	33	31	59	29
*Blair, Zach	.271	177	28	48	0	18	20	31	2
#Staley, Joe	.261	176	29	46	7	34	37	38	8
Solberg, Ryan	.247	81	10	20	1	6	10	38	2
Juarbe, Gaby	.244	90	11	22	0	9	5	24	0
Kline, Ben	.238	151	12	36	1	15	9	25	0
*Sosnoskie, Buddy	.236	203	31	48	5	24	11	38	10
*Kelly, Rob	.230	209	18	48	8	35	13	32	1
*Gomez, Rolando	.227	75	10	17	4	13	11	21	6
Stein, Nick	.225	102	10	23	4	14	10	36	10
#Tannehill, Bobby Joe	.220	109	13	24	4	8	13	33	2
Miller, James	.217	83	11	18	1	4	20	26	2
Overbey, Preston	.214	28	2	6	0	0	0	8	0
Ross, Chance	.202	129	9	26	1	16	5	30	0
Soloman, Bryan	.200	40	6	8	1	2	2	12	0
Tanis, Jacob	.197	127	10	25	6	17	7	36	0
Sears, Orrin	.178	45	5	8	1	9	3	13	1
Joyce, Doug	.177	62	5	11	0	2	4	17	2
*Wilson, Michael	.176	85	10	15	3	8	7	27	1
Bryson, Caleb	.157	51	8	8	1	3	7	20	0
Bluestein, Kyle	.132	68	3	9	1	5	8	23	4
Gallego, Niko	.109	55	3	6	0	1	2	10	1

PLAYER	W	L	ERA	G	SV	IP	H	BB	SO
DeSimone, Daniel	4	3	2.53	44	3	53	48	29	43
Weaver, Chuck	7	6	2.65	17	0	109	93	28	77
Henn, Casey	9	6	2.72	19	0	123	91	52	111
Kohout, Ed	2	3	3.88	39	8	49	42	17	72
*Gehle, Peter	5	7	4.15	19	0	117	126	29	48
Marban, Jorge	4	6	4.27	34	11	46	32	45	65
Levitt, Pete	1	3	4.53	44	2	52	46	26	39
*Cummins, Chris	1	1	4.61	23	0	27	31	4	20
*Middendorf, Dave	5	8	4.78	20	0	107	135	22	64
Squires, Chris	0	1	5.87	12	0	15	14	13	14
Valle, Edgar	0	1	6.00	13	0	15	13	10	14
*O'Neal, Michael	2	7	7.13	11	0	42	47	23	17
McDaniel, Gregory	1	1	7.15	3	0	11	8	12	3
Krebs, Adam	0	0	7.54	12	0	14	14	11	17
*Choban, Brent	0	2	8.04	3	0	16	18	5	8
Allen, Brad	0	0	9.00	1	0	5	6	3	7

GATEWAY GRIZZLIES

PLAYER	AVG	AB	R	H	HR	RBI	BB	SO	SB
*Beaird, Madison	.289	342	54	99	4	48	52	67	21
Vasquez, Niko	.287	181	37	52	7	34	37	39	5
Wing, Michael	.284	317	49	90	14	59	25	72	6

INDEPENDENT LEAGUES

PLAYER	AVG	AB	R	H	HR	RBI	BB	SO	SB
Hernandez, Landon	.273	245	37	67	12	42	40	63	1
*Bennett, TJ	.269	208	25	56	2	37	23	48	4
*Johnson, Jonathan	.269	119	26	32	1	6	23	17	15
#Kiser, Kale	.258	120	18	31	2	8	10	20	0
*Seigel, Richard	.258	287	52	74	10	36	55	96	10
*Waldrip, Ben	.252	333	42	84	12	51	18	89	1
Richards, Tommy	.248	270	40	67	3	24	17	74	6
Bieser, Cole	.244	45	6	11	0	3	8	9	2
*Johnson, Michael	.241	241	24	58	3	26	22	62	5
Vail, Garrett	.236	110	15	26	2	13	12	28	0
Shepherd, Blake	.212	52	4	11	1	9	4	18	3
Adams, Josh	.211	90	8	19	2	11	9	17	0
Macklin, Xavier	.201	179	29	36	7	24	30	74	11
Backlund, Nick	.133	30	0	4	0	3	2	14	0
*Faulkner, Michael	.091	22	2	2	0	1	8	0	
Obermark, Jimmy	.074	27	0	2	0	1	2	12	0

PLAYER	W	L	ERA	G	SV	IP	H	BB	SO
West, JaVaun	7	3	3.62	16	0	102	89	31	116
Aizenstadt, Andrew	3	4	6.65	26	1	65	81	30	43
DeBoo, Chris	5	1	4.67	37	1	64	74	35	42
Arneson, Zach	1	0	3.78	13	0	17	11	8	18
Thompson, Tyler	3	4	3.82	16	0	78	77	24	77
Cropper, Daniel	0	2	9.88	4	0	14	19	7	7
Barrett, Richard	2	2	2.89	37	19	37	28	14	38
*Westphal, Luke	3	5	2.91	35	1	53	43	39	68
Newcomb, Aaron	9	6	6.95	16	0	79	91	46	48
Stephens, Jake	0	1	4.97	7	0	13	15	8	12
*Waldrip, Ben	0	0	0.00	1	0	1	0	3	1
Hernandez, Landon	0	0	0.00	1	0	1	1	1	0
Baker, Aaron	1	0	0.51	13	1	18	11	7	16
Zawacki, Brett	1	0	1.54	11	0	12	6	1	12
Higginbotham, Brett	0	0	1.59	4	0	6	4	2	5
Jensen, Tucker	9	4	4.39	19	0	123	128	40	81
Houston, John	0	1	5.19	8	0	9	9	6	8
Oliver, Dejai	3	4	5.29	22	0	68	61	57	44
*Kelley, Kerry	3	8	5.50	13	0	70	79	31	47
Buckley, Tyler	0	0	10.29	6	0	7	11	3	5
Van Zant, Oliver	0	0	11.25	3	0	4	7	7	3
Reamy, Phillip	0	0	11.25	4	0	4	5	3	4
Mabry, Brett	0	1	11.32	6	0	10	23	8	9

FRONTIER GREYS

PLAYER	AVG	AB	R	H	HR	RBI	BB	SO	SB
Monger, Cameron	.307	300	46	92	2	19	22	55	8
*Dziomba, Jon	.279	197	26	55	5	28	11	39	5
*Ellison, Chris	.267	341	52	91	14	51	48	67	10
Minucci, Jon	.265	298	34	79	8	33	23	76	15
Rapp, Joe	.256	371	58	95	19	55	44	109	0
Tanner, Zach	.250	284	25	71	6	29	30	78	1
Bachman, Greg	.234	184	18	43	4	19	14	41	0
*Florio, Frank	.233	240	29	56	8	32	12	63	0
Tucker, Chase	.228	290	27	66	0	23	25	58	8
*Pierce, Logan	.225	120	11	27	1	10	11	15	0
Vaughn, Michael	.222	212	32	47	5	22	20	52	0
Chavez, Matt	.218	55	6	12	4	6	2	19	0
#Ortega, Ramon	.208	106	14	22	1	7	23	30	2
*Rogers, Steve	.208	77	10	16	3	8	9	17	2
Blunt, Donald	.196	92	8	18	1	9	7	24	6
Scruggs, Matthew	.152	66	1	10	0	2	6	32	2

PLAYER	W	L	ERA	G	SV	IP	H	BB	SO
Mittura, Paul	2	4	2.10	22	1	34	29	10	22
*Leverett, Jarret	0	6	2.72	33	5	46	41	22	44
DeJiulio, Frank	0	0	3.00	4	0	6	6	2	8
*Pearson, Devon	1	3	3.72	21	2	46	48	24	43
Lamb, Cameron	3	3	3.96	33	9	36	38	17	21
Hartman, Ryan	0	1	4.00	2	0	9	6	3	9
Wright, Clint	8	6	4.50	20	0	120	141	50	71
Blair, Kyle	1	2	4.59	7	0	35	40	27	21
*Rohde, Brandon	7	7	5.07	20	0	103	120	30	78
Hyatt, B.J.	0	1	6.00	1	0	15	15	10	11
Belcastro, Matt	2	2	6.00	8	0	36	43	30	14
Picht, Keith	2	9	6.93	22	0	88	122	49	64
Kovalik, John	0	0	7.71	0	0	23	42	17	20
Rey, Lamarre	3	8	7.71	20	0	82	113	40	42
*Liedka, Jacob	0	1	8.12	26	0	41	59	23	33
Hildebrand, Josh	0	2	8.85	13	0	19	27	11	9

PLAYER	W	L	ERA	G	SV	IP	H	BB	SO
Van Zant, Oliver	0	2	9.00	9	0	15	20	18	9
Jackson, Justin	1	3	11.05	4	0	15	26	6	7
Lowery, Patrick	0	2	12.96	3	0	8	4	13	3
*Perrault, Eric	0	1	17.10	12	0	10	10	19	9

JOLIET JACKHAMMERS

PLAYER	AVG	AB	R	H	HR	RBI	BB	SO	SB
Gronsky, Jake	.385	26	6	10	0	4	2	3	1
DeBruin, Grant	.355	380	63	135	12	67	21	59	5
English, Adrian	.313	144	15	45	2	9	10	7	2
Stang, Chadwin	.304	23	2	7	0	2	3	5	0
*Riley, Marquis	.302	169	24	51	4	24	18	16	7
*Moldenhauer, Russell	.298	332	42	99	9	62	57	56	3
*Giacalone, Adam	.265	351	38	93	10	56	43	63	1
Casper, Max	.257	343	54	88	1	31	34	65	5
Weaver, Matt	.255	102	10	26	3	15	10	26	4
Dorgan, JD	.247	85	12	21	2	13	2	18	1
*Epps, Christopher	.237	241	48	57	3	29	49	61	13
Scheffert, Josh	.229	96	8	22	0	7	3	17	1
*Granger, Seth	.227	211	29	48	4	20	5	50	7
Epperson, CJ	.216	37	5	8	0	2	4	9	1
*Lewis, Adam	.209	163	20	34	0	12	20	27	2
Garcia, Jose	.206	180	24	37	2	13	13	23	7
#Sandford, Darian	.196	56	9	11	0	3	10	14	3
Hernandez, Danny	.191	115	9	22	0	16	6	26	2
Grogg, Tyler	.160	25	4	4	0	2	3	2	1
*Miller, Bill	.154	26	2	4	0	3	3	8	0
Roberts, Tyler	.145	83	9	12	1	7	12	24	0
Johnson, Tre-von	.129	31	4	4	0	2	4	5	1

PLAYER	W	L	ERA	G	SV	IP	H	BB	SO
Giacalone, Adam	0	0	0.00	2	0	3	2	0	4
Kubiak, David	3	1	1.52	20	7	30	19	8	35
Bradshaw, Travis	2	1	2.66	5	0	20	22	7	17
*Walters, Blair	2	4	2.74	11	0	76	59	28	54
*Costello, Matt	3	1	2.92	8	0	37	42	10	26
Zawacki, Brett	3	4	3.08	22	1	38	37	20	28
Wellander, Jordan	4	1	3.31	40	5	54	48	22	53
Strenge, Andrew	0	2	3.32	6	0	19	15	5	17
Moore, Sam	2	5	3.99	39	1	50	47	28	45
Maloney, John	0	1	4.05	8	0	13	11	6	18
McNorton, Kevin	2	1	4.18	25	0	28	34	6	21
McFarland, Kody	4	5	4.55	20	0	91	89	32	81
Manzanillo, Santo	2	3	4.58	14	1	20	18	9	14
Hillier, Bobby	0	0	4.70	4	0	8	8	5	10
Busby, Ryan	3	6	4.82	19	0	103	123	29	73
Carter, Ethan	2	2	5.19	7	0	26	35	7	11
*Hermsen, Jake	1	1	5.19	9	0	35	51	18	25
Gotzon, Caleb	1	1	5.75	4	0	20	25	12	9
Hernandez, Daniel	0	1	5.91	2	0	11	15	2	7
Connolly, Ryan	1	2	6.05	14	1	19	22	11	12
Reboulet, Travis	0	0	6.08	8	0	13	17	11	5
*Crim, Matt	2	4	6.63	10	0	37	53	14	36
Dillon, Matt	0	4	7.14	6	0	29	35	18	21
*Marino, Harry	0	0	7.31	16	0	16	21	9	10
Doremus, Chase	2	1	7.78	15	0	20	26	13	15
*Thicke, Tyler	0	0	9.72	12	0	17	22	10	8
Kaminsky, Alex	0	2	18.78	2	0	8	18	6	4

LAKE ERIE CRUSHERS

PLAYER	AVG	AB	R	H	HR	RBI	BB	SO	SB
Mejia, Vincent	.314	299	45	94	15	53	43	69	8
*Hertler, Craig	.302	311	59	94	2	40	50	39	15
#Stevens, Trevor	.297	195	33	58	2	26	29	37	9
Hutchison, Ryan	.297	306	39	91	11	40	21	62	3
Hidalgo, Anderson	.295	329	47	97	7	64	51	44	6
Burney, Joey	.266	139	24	37	6	28	24	21	4
#Davis, Andrew	.265	272	36	72	3	38	30	60	0
Sanchez, Juan	.263	338	51	89	2	27	32	52	7
Quiles, Emmanuel	.242	260	23	63	2	36	5	56	1
*Granger, Seth	.228	92	14	21	1	12	11	33	4
*Haggett, Brian	.217	69	10	15	1	5	8	15	1
Ford, Adam	.215	228	37	49	2	27	32	51	21
*Bricknell, Zachary	.215	65	7	14	1	3	1	19	4
Dickason, Matt	.154	39	4	6	0	3	3	4	0
Franchetti, Kevin	.144	146	15	21	1	7	17	60	2
Torres, P.J.	.132	38	4	5	0	5	3	13	0

Berard, Kevin .114 35 1 4 0 2 1 9 2

PLAYER	W	L	ERA	G	SV	IP	H	BB	SO
Masters, Brant	1	0	0.00	12	0	10	5	2	5
Maxon, Adam	0	0	1.13	7	0	8	7	6	5
Litzinger, Matt	1	0	1.50	7	0	6	3	3	4
*Rosario, Jose	1	1	1.66	8	0	22	18	17	11
*Kibby, Todd	6	2	2.12	15	0	81	70	31	75
Longfellow, Trevor	5	3	2.14	40	8	59	43	19	60
Connolly, Ryan	2	1	2.19	18	1	25	20	9	12
Duffy, Brad	2	1	2.20	48	1	41	33	15	58
McCoy, Jordan	1	1	2.83	46	1	41	25	22	37
Zambron, Brad	3	0	2.96	46	2	49	43	15	44
Treece, Zac	7	3	2.97	31	0	97	73	30	88
Smith, Brandon	2	2	3.89	40	0	39	41	13	32
Wilson, Jason	8	6	4.02	37	5	69	62	18	57
Jannis, Mickey	3	4	4.45	12	0	65	68	29	57
*Whalen, Connor	3	3	4.73	9	0	46	49	14	36
Gordon, Zach	3	5	4.85	14	0	59	68	19	23
*Roberts, Andy	2	2	4.97	7	0	25	26	9	9
*Rein, Matt	1	5	5.29	14	0	65	89	26	47
*Padilla, Roberto	1	4	6.84	5	0	26	27	16	15

NORMAL CORNBELTERS

PLAYER	AVG	AB	R	H	HR	RBI	BB	SO	SB
*Schwartz, Mike	.336	348	79	117	16	68	55	44	11
*Dudley, Aaron	.316	332	69	105	14	64	44	48	1
Judah, Sam	.307	361	62	111	13	82	35	64	1
*Micowski, Mark	.301	113	23	34	1	11	13	22	4
Chirino, Santiago	.300	380	61	114	2	31	27	29	9
*Shover, Tyler	.296	270	38	80	2	34	22	36	2
Veras, Jhiomar	.293	266	40	78	6	25	21	77	7
Lucas, Richard	.285	340	57	97	13	54	35	74	12
Chavarria, Jorge	.267	30	2	8	0	5	3	5	1
McKenna, Patrick	.257	253	44	65	10	32	44	86	0
*Guillen, Ozney	.255	255	36	65	5	45	21	32	8
Hernandez, Roman	.244	127	21	31	1	15	21	25	4
*Kelly, Dylan	.239	71	6	17	0	10	2	22	0
Bistagne, Brian	.214	42	4	9	0	5	6	8	0

PLAYER	W	L	ERA	G	SV	IP	H	BB	SO
Brocker, Cole	1	1	1.50	19	1	30	17	9	36
Postill, Jason	7	3	2.61	36	0	59	46	30	50
Anderson, Eric	1	1	2.65	23	7	34	29	9	40
*Packer, Matt	4	2	2.67	11	0	67	71	15	65
Carmain, Chris	4	0	2.75	19	0	52	48	15	41
Oaks, Alan	0	3	3.18	25	10	28	21	12	30
Short, Charley	7	4	4.37	29	0	47	43	19	57
*Frey, Stephen	1	2	4.42	19	0	18	13	10	21
Elias, Ethan	1	2	4.47	19	1	58	49	29	66
Babin, Cullen	6	7	4.73	22	0	103	111	31	61
MacDonald, Corey	3	2	4.99	11	0	52	69	24	38
*Erickson, Eric	1	0	5.00	5	0	9	8	3	3
*Mascheri, Rich	0	1	5.06	3	0	5	5	3	7
Shore, Bobby	4	7	5.40	16	0	82	89	34	76
*Wynn, David	0	0	6.14	5	0	7	9	5	6
Schweiss, Michael	4	2	6.17	11	0	42	46	17	33
Provence, Drew	2	4	6.57	7	0	37	48	14	20
Rosan, Joe	0	0	6.75	5	0	4	4	7	2
Devine, Mike	2	2	6.99	10	0	48	66	17	40
Schluter, Kurt	0	2	8.24	5	0	20	22	8	16
Ghysels, Chuck	0	2	10.13	5	0	5	8	7	7
Mitchell, Ryan	0	0	11.25	2	0	8	13	4	4

RIVER CITY RASCALS

PLAYER	AVG	AB	R	H	HR	RBI	BB	SO	SB
Ludy, Josh	.362	185	36	67	16	50	24	26	0
Ard, Taylor	.338	204	40	69	9	33	17	32	9
Kometani, Zach	.313	208	28	65	8	38	15	44	11
*Redal, Curran	.312	247	29	77	0	24	16	16	12
Crespo, Hector	.310	332	62	103	6	47	42	52	38
Morales, Johnny	.302	308	62	93	2	39	34	43	5
*Butler, Saxon	.297	370	55	110	7	84	35	51	4
Carrillo, Steve	.291	148	24	43	3	26	15	41	6
*McConkey, Brian	.290	162	30	47	11	34	18	48	4
#Staley, Joe	.279	129	28	36	5	24	24	31	8
Myers, Jon	.269	104	19	28	4	20	9	17	0
Hansen, Brian	.248	141	26	35	6	18	14	45	7

Crawford, Evan .238 202 28 48 4 17 23 52 11
Fernandez, Blaise .231 78 12 18 3 12 9 21 2
*Williams, Eric .224 321 72 72 2 26 90 64 12
Aanderud, Bryan .220 59 12 13 1 9 15 13 1

PLAYER	W	L	ERA	G	SV	IP	H	BB	SO
Stone, Dane	3	1	0.93	5	0	29	23	3	17
*Hvozdovic, Paul	0	0	1.23	18	0	15	14	5	10
*Crider, Patrick	7	0	1.43	65	0	50	28	24	62
Samayoa, Jose	2	0	1.64	3	0	11	8	4	6
Kennedy, Nick	4	3	2.47	58	1	62	56	14	53
Shaw, Gabriel	4	0	3.34	53	28	59	49	10	57
Mendoza, Tommy	9	3	3.40	17	0	87	91	25	63
Hanson, Ray	4	1	3.53	8	0	36	36	10	37
*Brockett, Ryan	0	1	3.86	7	0	14	16	5	7
Lambert, Trey	3	1	4.10	27	0	37	45	18	25
Jagodzinski, Chandle	5	1	4.95	44	1	60	69	17	45
*Organ, Tommy	3	1	4.97	9	0	29	26	10	26
Brady, Kyle	2	3	4.98	25	0	60	53	33	72
Koons, Tim	5	4	5.14	13	0	68	64	32	63
Carter, Ethan	2	4	6.20	13	1	41	50	4	24
Goodman, Craig	1	2	6.31	5	0	26	34	9	14
Urban, Andy	0	1	6.38	15	0	18	31	9	13
*Caruso, Cory	1	4	6.87	7	0	37	50	17	23
Shafer, Bryce	2	2	7.07	17	0	28	36	18	35
Bracewell, Ben	1	0	7.56	4	0	17	18	10	13
Cuda, Joe	2	2	7.83	5	0	23	29	8	26
Cendejas, Eric	0	0	8.31	6	0	9	18	4	11
Doremus, Chase	1	1	8.36	5	0	14	27	6	11
Bader, Ethan	0	0	10.80	5	0	5	7	4	2

ROCKFORD RIVERHAWKS

PLAYER	AVG	AB	R	H	HR	RBI	BB	SO	SB
Hur, Michael	.346	130	18	45	2	20	13	22	4
Martinez, Jose	.337	104	17	35	3	14	10	12	6
*Kremer, Jeff	.309	220	28	68	0	17	25	28	2
Witt, Tanner	.305	367	58	112	4	39	39	63	5
#Corcino, Edgar	.302	371	63	112	11	51	26	57	10
#Breen, Ryan	.283	180	23	51	4	21	22	48	3
*Bryant, Kenny	.279	341	43	95	5	51	30	65	6
Bistagne, Brian	.272	276	32	75	3	27	26	46	5
Robinson, Dusty	.250	156	22	39	9	27	14	33	4
Kahoohalahala, Kalai	.227	181	20	41	1	19	6	40	9
Ramos, Wander	.212	33	0	7	0	3	2	9	1
Gonzalez, Danny	.210	124	9	26	0	9	8	24	1
Dhanani, Kyle	.206	233	25	48	2	16	16	63	13
Morioka, Mason	.204	152	15	31	1	11	11	40	3
Trail, Elijah	.197	66	6	13	1	3	3	20	0
*Pederson, Tyger	.187	134	10	25	0	15	20	48	2
Martinez, Adrian	.136	22	1	3	0	0	9	6	0
Gerig, Brad	.120	25	0	3	0	1	1	7	0

PLAYER	W	L	ERA	G	SV	IP	H	BB	SO
Sanchez, Gerardo	0	3	1.54	39	18	41	37	12	55
Wagman, Joey	6	2	3.05	12	0	77	56	18	85
Hassna, Kyle	2	4	3.09	18	0	67	61	27	65
Zimmerman, Ryan	9	6	3.21	21	0	112	89	47	87
Frahm, Matt	1	1	3.28	31	0	36	41	10	34
Brueggemann, Kyle	7	8	3.84	20	0	122	128	34	88
*Smoker, Josh	1	0	4.03	28	0	29	29	23	57
Cendejas, Eric	0	2	4.21	20	0	26	34	7	20
*Meyer, Dan	1	1	4.22	4	0	11	15	5	9
Masters, Brant	0	1	4.50	6	0	10	18	3	6
Odom, Logan	4	0	4.57	24	0	22	17	23	24
Schaub, Michael	1	6	4.63	40	0	47	46	20	58
*Cicio, Nick	0	2	4.96	3	0	16	18	3	10
Slaats, Josh	3	5	5.61	12	0	61	68	44	41
Green, Cole	2	5	5.89	11	0	47	42	35	47
*Bonnot, Ryan	0	2	6.75	2	0	11	9	6	9
*Butler, Tony	1	2	7.36	7	0	22	22	28	22
Grim, Nick	0	3	7.61	8	0	24	16	24	23
*Russo, David Wayne	2	1	9.43	17	0	21	32	13	20
Ormseth, Michael	0	1	13.50	2	0	4	11	2	0
Shull, Trevor	0	1	27.00	3	0	2	7	5	2

SOUTHERN ILLINOIS MINERS

PLAYER	AVG	AB	R	H	HR	RBI	BB	SO	SB
Vasquez, Niko	.336	152	39	51	6	33	29	26	1

INDEPENDENT LEAGUES

PLAYER	AVG	AB	R	H	HR	RBI	BB	SO	SB
#Martinez, Frank	.317	312	57	99	9	64	42	37	5
#Cavan, Ryan	.309	333	67	103	5	44	60	59	14
#Eisen, Jon	.305	187	35	57	0	13	35	21	10
Jones, Matt	.301	93	10	28	2	15	7	15	1
*Austin, Jay	.292	233	35	68	0	19	22	44	28
*Gates, Aaron	.284	320	51	91	10	59	43	52	6
*Riley, Marquis	.263	156	24	41	1	20	19	15	6
Howard, Matt	.261	157	29	41	0	11	13	36	9
*Booth, Tyler	.251	211	25	53	1	24	16	60	6
Marino, Steve	.245	327	34	80	6	51	33	57	1
Burke, Chris	.244	340	58	83	17	77	56	73	6
Butler, Phil	.228	197	24	45	3	24	30	37	1
Gonzalez, Jose	.225	40	6	9	0	2	15	10	0
Windster, Sundrendy	.206	34	2	7	0	1	1	7	0
*McDonald, Jared	.194	93	16	18	1	9	16	19	5

PLAYER	W	L	ERA	G	SV	IP	H	BB	SO
*Levin, Jon	1	0	0.00	4	0	7	7	4	2
Montefusco, Anthony	2	0	0.38	4	0	24	21	6	14
Brase, Stew	1	2	1.43	46	2	44	32	22	41
Kubiak, David	4	1	1.47	13	0	18	11	5	21
*Woods, James	1	0	1.54	24	0	23	18	11	26
Miramontes, Derrick	4	1	1.57	42	20	52	29	14	62
*Ackerman, Hunter	2	0	1.69	8	0	11	8	3	12
*Bywater, Matt	8	4	2.37	21	0	129	86	60	114
Bierlein, James	2	2	2.97	32	1	33	23	13	32
Robertshaw, Britt	3	2	3.08	37	1	50	41	27	53
*Carden, Michael	6	4	3.57	20	0	108	113	36	55
*Teasley, Rick	11	5	3.57	20	0	116	106	33	81
Hyatt, B.J.	0	0	3.60	5	0	5	5	2	6
Parmenter, Race	0	0	3.86	13	0	12	13	7	6
*Crim, Matt	0	0	4.42	6	0	18	22	4	16
Ramirez, Miguel	10	4	4.49	19	0	108	108	33	72
Hagen, Steve	1	0	4.91	3	1	11	15	6	4
Lavigne, Tyler	4	5	5.82	12	0	65	67	29	49
Miller, Matt	0	3	8.00	16	0	18	21	7	7
Weismann, Scott	0	0	9.53	4	0	6	8	3	1
*McGeary, Jack	0	2	12.15	2	0	7	7	10	6

SCHAUMBURG BOOMERS

PLAYER	AVG	AB	R	H	2B	3B	HR	RBI	BB
Delmonico, Tony	.356	146	47	52	10	0	12	41	28
Sciacca, Tyler	.337	187	23	63	7	0	1	26	11
*Nelson, Mark	.323	310	53	100	19	3	4	55	50
*Vasquez, Justin	.312	340	62	106	16	6	7	49	47
Nelson, Ty	.305	213	39	65	12	0	2	39	16
#Hall, Gerard	.302	235	47	71	12	4	8	43	33
*Mahley, Sean	.300	70	12	21	3	1	0	7	9
De Pinto, Joe	.291	189	47	55	11	1	6	30	36
*Colon, Alexi	.269	324	62	87	17	5	11	45	58
Dean, Jordan	.261	356	54	93	13	2	3	43	29
Valadez, Michael	.255	255	25	65	9	1	3	49	14
*McConkey, Brian	.250	156	24	39	14	0	4	21	20
Solberg, Ryan	.226	31	2	7	3	0	0	4	0
*McChesney, Ryan	.224	98	13	22	7	0	1	14	7
Martin, Bobby	.219	196	34	43	8	0	4	20	22
Chavez, Denver	.208	24	5	5	1	0	0	4	3
Kline, Ben	.192	26	6	5	1	1	0	2	6
*Sherrer, Cameron	.152	46	3	7	1	0	0	4	6

PLAYER	W	L	ERA	G	SV	IP	H	BB	SO
*Mahley, Sean	0	0	1.08	10	1	8	5	6	8
Labitan, Clark	3	3	2.20	41	3	41	29	16	43
Cody, Eddie	8	1	2.86	15	0	79	81	23	65
Hatfield, Heith	2	2	3.24	35	0	42	33	23	38
Smith, Anthony	6	2	3.28	24	2	58	57	11	37
Webster, Seth	7	5	3.36	19	0	118	119	24	87
*Brahney, Kevin	1	0	3.52	10	1	8	6	8	3
Price, Dexter	4	5	3.80	45	21	47	48	16	37
*Rodriguez, Rey	2	2	3.86	8	0	40	38	20	18
Erasmus, Justin	3	0	4.21	8	1	26	28	6	24
*Jimenez, Danny	7	3	4.23	15	0	83	104	24	64
*Gomez, Anthony	0	0	4.64	11	0	21	29	10	14
Spurgeon, Ross	1	1	4.67	19	0	27	30	13	26
Carroll, Kevin	0	0	4.70	6	0	8	7	6	6
Rosario, Charle	2	0	4.77	7	0	40	46	12	34
Bierlein, James	2	1	5.09	12	0	18	16	7	24
*Ackerman, Hunter	3	3	5.24	24	1	69	89	15	65
Bowling, Cal	9	7	5.27	19	0	96	104	53	48

PLAYER	W	L	ERA	G	SV	IP	H	BB	SO
Duval, Max	0	0	6.75	3	0	5	8	3	3
*Singh, Kris	1	0	9.95	3	0	6	9	4	5

TRAVERSE CITY

PLAYER	AVG	AB	R	H	HR	RBI	BB	SO	SB
Rosa, Jovan	.279	323	44	90	9	49	46	67	0
*DeBlieux, Jeff	.274	307	47	84	7	37	37	67	23
*Rhodes, Jake	.271	192	16	52	3	30	24	46	0
*Taylor, Kevin	.271	203	32	55	3	18	20	27	0
Harisis, Greg	.267	172	26	46	3	13	16	50	18
Cooper, Shaun	.266	64	9	17	1	6	6	14	0
Vargas, Jose	.266	188	27	50	6	37	12	37	2
*Gusrang, Sean	.260	219	24	57	2	15	18	50	1
Benedict, Rob	.255	239	47	61	3	23	14	49	21
*Arbelo, Yazy	.249	345	38	86	17	61	36	93	0
Rossi, Drew	.245	53	3	13	0	5	6	10	0
*Wrenn, Taylor	.238	63	8	15	2	4	3	13	1
Cowell, Chris	.235	132	13	31	3	17	15	41	0
Miller, Josh	.226	221	21	50	1	18	13	52	1
*Woodward, Scott	.213	225	36	48	3	27	28	67	17
Barber, George	.196	112	13	22	2	8	13	33	5
Roche, Casey	.180	50	5	9	0	2	2	8	1

PLAYER	W	L	ERA	G	SV	IP	H	BB	SO
Rankin, Will	5	2	1.08	47	8	58	33	21	57
Johnson, D.J.	0	3	1.30	24	14	28	18	10	35
Ruch, Clayton	0	0	1.93	7	0	5	4	5	3
Eck, Eric	0	0	2.61	10	0	10	12	12	5
Ghysels, Chuck	2	3	2.94	36	1	49	34	33	72
*MacDougall, Ian	6	4	3.25	22	0	108	107	29	60
Delgado, Casey	7	6	3.25	19	0	116	115	31	118
Gillingham, Alex	2	2	3.57	4	0	18	19	19	13
Devine, Mike	1	3	3.72	5	0	29	28	12	19
*Alexander, Corey	0	0	3.86	8	0	16	19	6	18
Tripp, Tanner	4	8	4.28	18	0	101	124	26	41
*Phillips, Alex	4	9	4.85	15	0	78	87	31	45
Bossendery, Chris	0	1	4.91	4	0	4	4	4	1
Vachon, Scott	2	4	5.00	15	0	45	59	16	18
*Shellhorn, Rusty	4	5	5.75	19	0	83	95	45	70
*O'Bryan, Nate	1	2	5.76	22	0	25	31	10	14
Giannini, Cameron	0	1	7.43	18	0	27	37	20	22
*Camacho, Vladimir	0	0	11.57	4	0	5	8	7	5
*Brasser, Ryan	0	3	13.00	7	0	9	20	4	1
*Merkling, Patrick	0	2	13.50	3	0	5	6	7	7

WASHINGTON WILD THINGS

PLAYER	AVG	AB	R	H	HR	RBI	BB	SO	SB
*Ijames, Stewart	.319	188	38	60	15	45	16	37	3
Poma, Daniel	.308	312	52	96	2	31	22	53	30
*Kalamar, Scott	.300	283	45	85	9	48	25	51	17
Bell, Carter	.289	308	38	89	4	37	35	64	30
#Beatty, C.J.	.275	265	45	73	18	57	44	66	15
Dore, Jose	.273	88	15	24	2	11	11	34	2
Heck, Andrew	.261	46	9	12	2	7	7	20	3
Rau, Garrett	.258	326	43	84	1	28	37	57	23
Kregeloh, Pat	.250	20	3	5	0	1	1	6	0
Tejeda, Yeury	.244	41	3	10	0	1	0	9	1
Vahalik, Jim	.237	253	37	60	5	25	22	61	5
*Beckwith, William	.223	206	30	46	7	36	28	50	14
*Lewis, Connor	.222	72	4	16	1	8	3	18	1
Garrett, Maxx	.217	157	22	34	8	18	15	58	3
*Kresky, Ryan	.215	209	35	45	4	24	27	66	7
Montgomery, Sam	.211	76	9	16	0	7	8	17	4
Fernandez, Blaise	.188	32	2	6	0	1	1	9	1
*Wobrock, Austin	.171	41	4	7	0	6	4	9	0
*Ratajczak, Nick	.087	46	2	4	0	2	6	4	2

PLAYER	W	L	ERA	G	SV	IP	H	BB	SO
Sergey, Matt	3	1	1.79	18	0	50	30	22	60
Rau, Garrett	0	0	2.25	4	0	4	4	1	2
*Fuesser, Zac	9	2	2.26	21	1	96	88	32	74
Marks, Troy	5	1	2.46	8	0	48	36	8	55
Kountis, Jonathan	1	4	2.51	41	32	43	35	10	50
*Yevoli, Alfonso	4	5	2.92	48	1	49	48	16	46
Purnell, Matt	5	2	3.23	42	1	47	36	12	38
Dunn, Scott	8	5	3.28	19	0	107	110	27	59
*Flight, Tim	2	0	3.42	5	0	24	17	10	21
Blackwell, Shawn	10	4	3.70	21	0	100	101	39	75

INDEPENDENT LEAGUES

PLAYER	W	L	ERA	G	SV	IP	H	BB	SO
*LeBarron, Zach	1	3	4.02	15	0	40	42	12	30
Butler, Pat	2	3	4.15	42	1	39	39	10	37
Phelan, Chris	5	2	4.36	8	0	43	48	6	19
Kaminsky, Alex	2	5	4.97	10	0	54	62	10	37
*O'Hare, Christopher	0	0	5.63	9	0	8	10	5	9
Elrod, Tyler	0	0	5.65	21	0	37	48	13	20
Malone, Devin	0	0	6.92	9	0	13	9	4	8
Newcomb, Aaron	0	0	7.20	2	0	5	7	1	2
Holland, A.J.	0	2	13.50	2	0	6	10	1	4

WINDY CITY THUNDERBOLTS

PLAYER	AVG	AB	R	H	HR	RBI	BB	SO	SB
Robinson, Kyle	.366	309	52	113	13	70	39	57	12
*McIntyre, Ryan	.300	120	23	36	6	21	6	24	5
Soares, Ryan	.277	372	50	103	3	45	15	52	3
*Torres, Mike	.274	332	65	91	1	23	58	43	18
Castro, Spencer	.273	22	3	6	0	1	1	7	0
Mestas, Jon	.268	127	17	34	2	14	16	27	2
*Button, Evan	.265	211	24	56	2	25	18	39	17
*Peguero, Davidson	.247	154	6	38	1	18	6	41	0
Brauer, Andrew	.242	265	36	64	1	24	26	66	19
*Aldrich, Daniel	.239	92	4	22	0	4	1	32	0
White, Max	.239	285	27	68	3	49	24	64	7
Scioscia, Matt	.238	63	4	15	0	6	2	10	0
Carey, Garrett	.227	194	22	44	2	12	6	32	1
Tufts, Ryan	.217	69	6	15	0	7	1	19	0
*Stetson, Ty	.217	92	13	20	0	6	11	13	2
Joyce, Doug	.202	114	13	23	1	8	10	34	4
McGuckin, Mike	.194	129	11	25	0	7	6	37	1
Allen, Michael	.155	58	4	9	3	6	6	24	0
Viger, Tony	.097	31	3	3	0	1	2	15	0
Dalles, Justin	.077	26	0	2	0	0	0	6	0

PLAYER	W	L	ERA	G	SV	IP	H	BB	SO
Solbach, Markus	1	1	0.86	3	0	21	9	5	16
Snodgrass, Jessie	3	1	2.61	48	3	76	57	34	62
Anderson, Eli	2	8	6.62	14	0	67	101	26	47
Tingle, Travis	8	6	4.69	19	0	104	125	22	93
Larez, Victor	3	3	4.77	30	0	45	48	11	57
Oliver, Brian	0	2	10.80	2	0	10	23	0	8
Kafka, Jason	2	1	7.86	20	0	34	55	28	26
*Ferguson, James	1	0	2.89	13	0	28	30	15	21
Mejia, Jordan	0	1	1.93	4	0	5	7	6	3
McGraw, Reese	1	2	2.23	37	5	40	24	14	48
Carela, Daniel	1	2	2.28	26	7	28	15	17	39
*Whittingslow, Pete	1	1	4.35	9	0	20	30	22	25
Cropper, Daniel	6	7	4.39	16	0	96	117	22	65
*Spence, Josh	1	10	5.23	14	0	76	94	30	58
*Fisher, Jake	5	10	5.31	21	0	117	146	27	104
Barton, Tad	0	2	11.12	2	0	6	12	2	6
*Robb, Hein	0	2	13.14	4	0	12	18	16	6
Shirley, Hayden	0	0	13.50	7	0	6	4	11	9
McGee, Travis	0	1	14.29	2	0	6	10	6	6

PACIFIC ASSOCIATION

San Rafael won its second consecutive Pacific Association title, helped by the change of rules in 2014 that handed the title to the regular season champion.

TEAM	W	L	PCT	GB
San Rafael Pacifics	48	30	.615	-
Vallejo Admirals	44	34	.564	4
Sonoma Stompers	42	36	.538	6
Pittsburg Mettle	22	56	.282	26

CHAMPIONSHIP: San Rafael declared champion after regular season.

BATTING LEADERS

PLAYER	TEAM	AVG	AB	R	H	HR	RBI
Ray, Jayce	SON	.355	234	62	83	8	44
Hinshaw, Jordan	VAL	.339	239	59	81	12	43
Boggan, Nicholas	VAL	.333	303	52	101	14	58
Pace, Zack	SRF	.321	271	63	87	2	37
Jova, Maikel	SRF	.319	301	46	96	7	57
Orefice, Mike	SRF	.318	280	59	89	4	31
Boyd, Evan	SRF	.315	254	47	80	4	41
Claudio, Ricky	PIT	.305	190	30	58	3	30
Pugh, Tillman	VAL	.303	274	77	83	11	44
Phillips, P.J.	VAL	.300	217	31	65	1	32

PITCHING LEADERS

PLAYER	TEAM	W	L	ERA	IP	H	BB	SO
Neal, Dennis	VAL	5	4	2.76	75	75	22	62
DeJesus, Ryan	SRF	7	2	2.92	71	83	13	45
Flory, Nick	VAL	8	2	3.41	71	70	23	52
Garcia, Gabriel	SON	4	2	3.69	76	73	15	50
Smith, Jesse	SRF	6	7	3.75	98	103	36	73
Schwieger, Eric	SON	5	5	3.77	74	74	22	51
Conroy, Patrick	SRF	9	2	3.93	92	95	32	76
Scott, Will	SON	8	6	4.53	101	116	38	71
Ramirez, Devin	VAL	4	4	4.56	81	81	37	74
Gonsalves, Erik	SON	7	5	4.67	106	119	33	51

UNITED LEAGUE

Rio Grande Valley had the United League's best player (Roger Bernal), its best pitcher (Celson Polanco) and its best reliever (Byron Minnich). So it can't be much of a surprise that it also had the league's best team.

After rolling through the regular season, the Whitewings swept Fort Worth in three games to win the United League title. It was Rio Grande Valley's first championship since winning the then-Texas Louisiana League title in 2000.

TEAM	W	L	PCT	GB
Rio Grande Valley WhiteWings	51	27	.654	--
Fort Worth Cats	42	35	.545	8.5
San Angelo Colts	33	39	.458	15
Brownsville Charros	24	49	.329	24.5

PLAYOFFS: Rio Grande Valley defeated Fort Worth 3-0 in best-of-5 series.
ATTENDANCE: Fort Worth 60,314; Rio Grande Valley 27,374; San Angelo 18,008.
MOST VALUABLE PLAYER: Roger Bernal, Rio Grande Valley. **BEST HITTER:** Chris Grossman, San Angelo and Ryan Lashey, Fort Worth. **BEST RELIEVER:** Byron Minnich, Rio Grande Valley. **BEST PITCHER:** Celson Polanco, Rio Grande Valley. **MANAGER OF THE YEAR:** Chris Paterson, Rio Grande Valley.

BATTING LEADERS

PLAYER	TEAM	AVG	AB	R	H	HR	RBI
Lashley, Ryan	FW	.369	214	46	79	6	45
Grossman, Chris	SA	.339	280	43	95	5	48
Kam, Adam	FW	.325	191	29	62	0	31
Fabry, Jacob	RGV	.322	267	34	86	0	28
Muse, J.J.	SA	.317	268	42	85	3	36
Rodriguez, Ryde	BC	.317	183	31	58	2	21
Kruse, Chad	FW	.304	240	35	73	0	23
Bernal, Roger	RGV	.301	312	60	94	1	35
McAllister, K.J.	SA	.296	189	31	56	0	20
Luce, Jake	BC	.294	177	24	52	5	26

PITCHING LEADERS

PLAYER	TEAM	W	L	ERA	IP	H	BB	SO
Orosey , Brad	RGV	6	4	2.06	70	52	21	67
Polanco, Celson	RGV	6	2	2.12	85	74	21	81
Evins, Trent	BC	5	3	2.85	66	65	20	54
Medina, Eddie	FW	5	3	3.36	80	81	40	69
Budkevics, Bo	SA	2	3	3.70	58	65	13	42
Banks, Demetrius	SA	4	4	4.36	85	103	22	60
Cowan, Brandon	FW	4	5	4.36	87	91	45	60
Bonnot, Ryan	RGV	5	3	4.48	86	94	43	77
Weatherly, Mike	SA	3	1	4.70	59	63	32	34
Montgomery, Trent	FW	6	5	4.82	95	116	22	53

INDEPENDENT LEAGUES

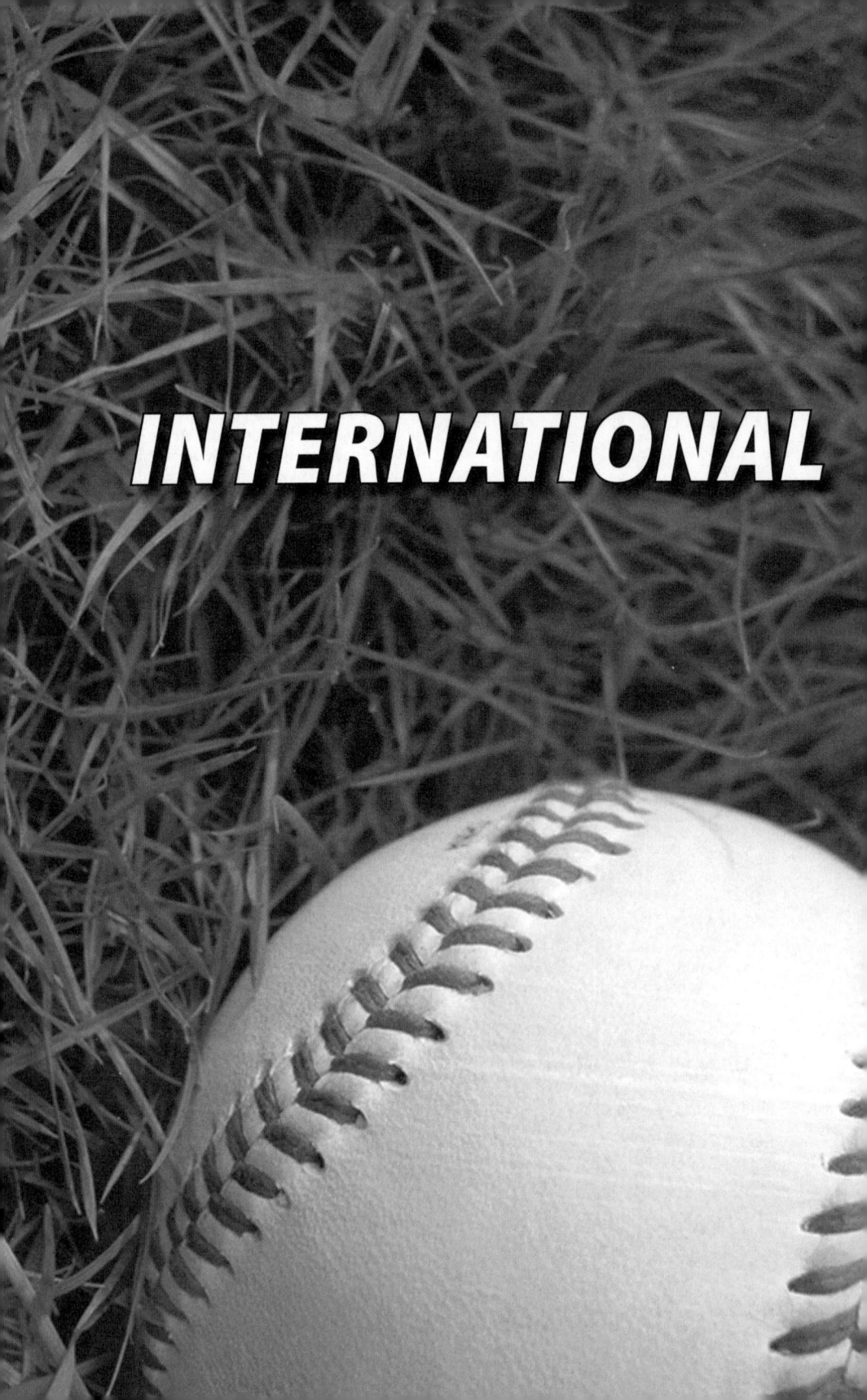

INTERNATIONAL

Amateurs highlight limited 2014 schedule

COMPILED BY JOHN MANUEL

The 2013 international baseball calendar was so jam-packed, it bled into 2014.

The schedule included the Caribbean Series in its usual Febuary spot, though with a new participant and tweaked format. There also was a counterpoint to the Caribbean Series on the other side of the globe in November 2013, when the Asia Series expanded for the first time to include the champion of the European Cup alongside usual suspects such as Japan, Korea, host Taiwan and Australia.

International baseball's schedule gets heavier in 2015 with the November debut of the Premier 12, which is expected to feature professional teams from the top 12-ranked countries in the IBAF rankings.

The next step could be getting baseball and softball—in a one-sport, two-disciplines approach—back on the Olympic program. While that effort once appeared dead, International Olympic Committee reforms and a new IOC president appear destined to give local organizing committees greater flexibility to choose sports for their particular Olympiad. With Tokyo scheduled to host the 2020 Games, baseball and softball are likely to be included, giving the international game and national governing bodies around the world a financial shot in the arm.

But for now, there was no great professional international tournament in 2014. Amateurs dominated the rest of the international schedule, with the U.S. College National Team winning Haarlem Honkbal Week, while the American 18U team dominated the 18U championship for the Americas, held in Mexico.

And while Cuba's national team didn't make much noise internationally in 2014, its players did, as the stream of players leaving the island continued both with and without the Cuban government's permission.

Out Of Mexico

USA Baseball's 18-and-under National Team went undefeated at the COPABE 18U Pan American Championships in Mexico with a run differential of 110-5, and qualified for the 2015 18U World Cup. Despite such dominance on the field, Team USA faced numerous obstacles during

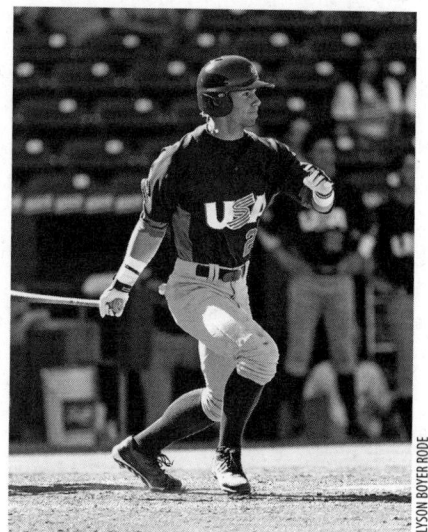

Freshman Nick Banks (Texas A&M) was one of Team USA's top performers

the tournament and in coming back home.

A 5-4 victory over Cuba to move to 7-0 was the only time the U.S. did not run-rule its opponent or allowed more than a single run. The teams met two days later in the championship game, which was scheduled for 7:30 p.m. local time despite Hurricane Odile's looming presence.

Team USA had a 1-0 lead and starting pitcher Kolby Allard struck out seven of the first 11 hitters he faced through three innings, when play was halted because of the weather. The International Baseball Federation declared the U.S. the gold-medal winner, but COPABE (the Baseball Confederation of the Americas) ruled the U.S. and Cuba dual gold medalists.

"We were up 1-0 and they were going to call the game due to weather," 18U director Shaun Cole said. "Cuba did not take the field and there was confusion. The committee tried to say that a co-champion was going to be declared. I argued for about 40 minutes because we were undefeated, we had already beaten Cuba and we were beating them in the championship game.

"Cuba had two losses, which didn't make sense how there could be co-champs. So they tried to

INTERNATIONAL

tell me it was a rule in the rulebook and I said that I wanted to see the rulebook. They didn't give us a rulebook when we were at the official meeting before the tournament started and they never sent us one after it started. So I asked them to see the rule in the rulebook they kept referring to. They said they would get it. But it took them about 15 to 20 minutes and they couldn't produce the rulebook."

Multiple reports from Spanish-speaking media outlets said that the U.S. and Cuba were declared co-champions, but the ceremony to honor a single champion was made before both teams left the stadium.

"Then they came back about five minutes later and said that we won the gold medal," Cole said. "We were not going to be satisfied with being co-champions because of the way we played and dominated at the tournament."

COPABE, the continental organization running the tournament, did not respond to multiple calls and emails.

The end result was that Team USA claimed its fourth straight gold medal in international play dating back to the summer of 2011 when it won the 2011 COPABE Pan American Championship. Team USA will vie for a third straight World Cup title next summer, which would be the first World Cup three-peat in U.S. 18U history and the first three-peat for any country since Cuba from 1984-87.

The hurricane hit after the gold-medal game was canceled, and the U.S. and Canadian teams and staffs had to stay in Mexico for four extra days before finally getting military transport planes to get them back home.

"We are glad to have everyone back home safely," USA Baseball executive director and CEO Paul Seiler said. "Team USA and Team Canada were aided by the Mexican military to get everyone home, and we owe a huge thank you to each individual that was involved with the process."

The team excelled in all facets. The pitching staff produced an 0.71 ERA, which was the lowest in 18U history and broke the previous mark set by the Clayton Kershaw-led 2005 team (0.86 ERA). Team USA averaged 13.75 runs per game, which was also the best in 18U history, topping the 2002 team (13.0), which featured two of the top five picks in the draft the following year.

Right fielder Trenton Clark led the team in all three triple-slash categories and had the second-highest batting average of any player at the event (.565/.694/1.043).

Allard, one of the top prep pitchers in the class, struck out 59 percent of the hitters he faced in

Mexico after striking out 10 of 18 against Canada, when he walked two and allowed one earned run. Although the team had two rising juniors who are in the 2016 class, the 17-year-old Allard was the youngest player on the team by nearly two months. He has an easy delivery and curveball that shows at least plus potential.

CNT Wins Honkbal

Just four teams participated in Haarlem Honkbal Week in the Netherlands this year, down from the usual four, with defending champion Cuba pulling out of the event. The U.S. defeated Japan 6-3 in the championship game behind two RBIs apiece from rising sophomores Nick Banks (Texas A&M) and Chris Okey (Clemson). The Americans lost their opener 1-0 to Japan but won seven straight games to finish the event, giving up just five runs in the seven-game win streak.

However, the CNT was swept in a five-game series in Cuba, dropping the team to a final 18-8-1 record.

"We didn't finish quite like we had hoped down here in Cuba, but our players really kept a great

INTERNATIONAL

attitude," head coach Dave Van Horn (Arkansas) said. "We just couldn't get over the hump. It was hot and the travel was definitely a grind but the bottom line was that we played a great team, full of grown men. We lost three one-run games and just didn't field and hit like we were capable of."

Christin Stewart (Tennessee) finished as the lone Team USA player to hit above .300; he hit a blistering .383/.474/.605 on the summer with two homers, 16 RBIs and 12 doubles. Stewart was the breakout star of a fairly balanced offense.

The pitching staff had more than its share of stars, and its bullpen was nearly untouchable. Relievers Tyler Jay (Illinois), A.J. Minter (Texas A&M) and Ryan Burr (Arizona State) posted a combined 0.00 ERA in 40 innings over 36 appearances. Righthanders Carson Fulmer (Vanderbilt), James Kaprielian (UCLA), Kyle Funkhouser (Louisville) and Justin Garza (Cal State Fullerton) made at least four starts apiece and all posted ERAs below 2.00. By and large, the staff pounded the strike zone and missed plenty of bats.

Australia Wins Asia Series

The Asia Series, played in Nov. 2013, was the last significant international event with professional players before the scheduled Nov. 2014 21U World Cup, which was not completed by Almanac press time.

For the first time in the tournament's nine-year history, the winner of the European Cup was invited into the field. This year that was the Italian Baseball League's Fortitudo Baseball Bologna, which featured former major leaguer Chris Aguila. The Marlins' third-round selection in 1997, Aguila spent parts of four seasons with the Marlins and the Mets and made a 14-game cameo with the Japanese League's Softbank Hawks in 2009.

Bologna lost both games it played, but its presence alone was a big step forward for the advancement of international baseball.

Canberra punctuated its championship, the first by a non-Asian team in the tournament's history, with seven RBIs—including a two-run single and a grand slam from catcher Jack Murphy, to rout the Uni-President Lions of the Chinese Baseball League. Murphy was named the Asia Series MVP, with past winners including Benny Agbayani (2005) and Yu Darvish (2006).

Japan and Australia sent teams with professionals to the 21U World Cup, but the United States and Cuba were noticeable by the absence, meaning the 21U event lacked the two top-ranked countries in the IBAF rankings.

Cuba's No. 2 ranking appeared to be threatened as a steady stream of defections continued to

Cuban Rusney Castillo left the island and signed with the Red Sox for $72 million

siphon talent away from the island nation. Players such as outfielders Rusney Castillo (who signed for $72 million with the Red Sox), Yoan Moncada and Yosmany Tomas, second baseman Jose Fernandez, shortstop Erisbel Arrubarrena and righthander Raicel Iglesias had been key players either in Serie Nacional or the Cuban national team (or both) but all had left Cuba to chase major league dreams.

Other Cuban players who did not want to defect were allowed to play overseas. Veterans Frederich Cepeda and Youliesky Gourriel played in Japan in Nippon Professional Baseball, though a passport scheme wound up blocking outfielder Alfredo Despaigne from continuing to play for pay in the Mexican League.

The Cuban baseball diaspora and Cuba's inclusion presented some unusual situations at the 2014 Caribbean Series. Yunesky Maya, a former Cuban star who defected in 2009 and signed with the Nationals in July 2010, refused to pitch against his former country in the first game of the Caribbean Series, which pitted Licey, his Dominican team, against the Cubans.

"The first thing I would do is (greet) them . . . but not play against them." Maya told a Dominican television station toward the beginning of January.

Mexico's Yunesky Sanchez, also born in Cuba, did not make the same decision. He not only played against his home country, but went 3-for-5 with a double, a run and an RBI in their only matchup, which opened the series.

INTERNATIONAL

Red Devils roll opponents on way to title

Major League Baseball had a wild-card World Series, with two teams that ranked seventh and ninth in the majors in winning percentage meeting in the World Series.

Not so in the Mexican League, though, as the top team in the Triple-A circuit's regular season also dominated the postseason. The Mexico Red Devils won their 16th Mexican Baseball League title, following a 70-win regular season in which the Red Devils nearly won the North Division by 10 games.

Shortstop Juan Carlos "Haper" Gamboa hit a game-winning homer in the fourth and deciding game of the championship series to defeat Puebla. Gamboa, 23, was named MVP of the playoffs, hitting five homers in three series, and batting .370 with 20 RBIs overall in 14 games. It was his first full season in Mexico after playing parts of three season in the Mets farm system, including two straight years at short-season Brooklyn.

The Red Devils' lineup skewed younger with key players such as Gamboa, rookie of the year Carlos Figueroa, 22, in center field and 25-year-old Jesus Avila, the third baseman who led the team in runs scored (88). But the team's veteran core played a key role as well, such as first baseman John Lindsey, 37, who led the league with 33 home runs and 99 RBIs. Lefthander Arturo Lopez, who reached the major leagues for four games with the Padres in 2009, won four of his five playoff starts after leading the team in wins and innings in the regular season. Righties Manny Acosta and Juan Sandoval, both 33-year-old Dominicans, held down the bullpen's biggest roles, with Sandoval posting a 9-1, 2.00 mark in the regular season before becoming the playoff closer. Acosta, who spent six seasons in the majors and 2013 in Japan, vultured four victories in the playoffs after ranking fifth in the league with 20 regular season saves.

Runner-up Puebla had finished second in the South Division in the regular season and survived and advanced through two grueling playoff series, rallying from a 2-1 deficit to beat Campeche in seven games in the first round before holding off South regular season winner Quintana Roo in six games in the semifinals. Puebla was the league's top-hitting club at .322 (third in runs at 634) while the Red Devils ranked second at .315 and first in runs with 721.

Puebla DH Sandy Madera, who spent most of 2000-09 in the U.S. affiliated minors, won the MVP after winning the batting title while ranking tied for third in home runs (26) and RBIs (98) during a .403/.477/.696 campaign. Quintana Roo's Amauri Sanit, part of a strong Cuban presence in the LMB, was the league's pitcher of the year and ERA champion, going 11-1, 2.00.

STANDINGS & LEADERS

NORTH	W	L	PCT	GB
Diablos Rojos del Mexico	70	42	.625	—
Acereros del Norte	60	51	.541	9 ½
Sultanes de Monterrey	61	52	.540	9 ½
Vaqueros de la Laguna	58	54	.518	12
Saraperos de Saltillo	56	54	.509	13
Toros de Tijuana	55	58	.487	15 ½
Rieleros de Aguascalientes	51	61	.455	19
Broncos de Reynosa	42	70	.375	28

SOUTH	W	L	PCT	GB
Tigres de Quintana Roo	65	48	.575	—
Pericos de Puebla	61	48	.560	2
Piratas de Campeche	56	53	.514	7
Delfines de Ciudad del Carmen	57	54	.514	7
Guerreros de Oaxaca	55	57	.491	9 ½
Rojos del Aguila de Veracruz	52	60	.464	12 ½
Leones de Yucatan	46	64	.418	17 ½
Olmecas de Tabasco	46	65	.414	18

INDIVIDUAL BATTING LEADERS

PLAYER, TEAM	AVG	AB	R	H	2B	3B	HR	RBI	BB	SO	SB
Madera, Sandy, PUE	.403	362	64	146	26	1	26	98	47	45	3
Roberson, Chris, MTY	.384	401	98	154	29	4	15	71	39	53	26
Rodriguez, Arturo, TIJ	.379	330	46	125	28	3	15	71	22	52	0
Del Campo, Jon, PUE	.367	311	62	114	27	1	12	62	16	68	24
Borges, Luis, SAL	.363	476	88	173	31	3	3	50	18	27	5
Gutierrez, Gabriel, MEX	.356	323	71	115	33	3	6	58	41	40	4
Mustelier, Ronnier, LAG	.351	302	65	106	17	1	10	60	30	35	13
Tapia, Cesar, PUE	.350	357	48	125	25	0	4	52	20	28	3
Agramon, Ruben, REY	.349	335	50	117	21	3	5	34	29	50	2
Linares, Donell, TAB	.347	317	39	110	23	0	5	38	21	14	0
Rodriguez, Jose M., SAL	.344	439	77	151	28	0	28	96	23	50	10
Murillo, Agustin, MTY	.340	424	98	144	29	1	24	95	52	45	32
Rios, Ramon, MTY	.339	454	73	154	20	2	6	50	14	43	13
Sanchez, Yunesky, OAX	.337	392	62	132	22	1	12	68	28	49	8
Castillo, Jesse, AGS	.335	409	67	137	25	1	17	91	59	57	14

INDIVIDUAL PITCHING LEADERS

PITCHER, TEAM	W	L	ERA	G	GS	CG	SV	IP	H	HR	BB	SO
Sanit, Amauri, TIG	11	1	2	21	21	0	0	126	103	6	32	103
Castro, Fabio, TIG	13	3	2.16	21	21	0	0	117	86	4	48	107
Gonzalez, Mario, CDC	10	7	2.8	23	23	4	0	141	122	13	30	120
Pina, Jose, VER	10	7	2.84	24	24	2	0	152	135	3	51	109
Zambrano, Baudel, CDC	10	3	2.98	21	21	1	0	124	123	6	38	50
Castellanos, Jonathan, YUC	10	9	3.06	22	21	0	0	129	129	6	30	74
Garcia, Ramon, MTY	9	3	3.13	46	10	0	1	92	82	5	21	80
Valdez, Rolando, CAM	10	7	3.25	21	21	0	0	125	133	11	21	100
Meza, Andres Ivan, PUE	11	4	3.4	22	22	0	0	127	130	9	28	88
Contreras, Jose, TIJ	10	3	3.49	23	23	1	0	134	114	15	40	140
Tovar, James, VER	9	2	3.58	21	21	1	0	118	103	11	44	88
Solis, Tomas, VER	4	8	3.58	18	18	0	0	93	98	14	30	48
Rodriguez, Jesus, YUC	5	5	3.74	21	21	0	0	108	125	4	40	56
Castillo, Jorge, MTY	6	8	3.87	22	22	0	0	114	124	18	41	84
Barcelo, Lorenzo, AGS	12	7	3.9	23	23	2	0	152	180	22	15	101

Cubans leave mark in NPB

BY WAYNE GRACZYK

The Fukuoka SoftBank Hawks, led by outgoing manager Koji Akiyama, defeated the Hanshin Tigers four games to one in the 2014 Japan Series and claimed a second Japanese baseball championship in the last four seasons. The Hawks also won the Japan Series in 2011.

Fukuoka won the Pacific League pennant by the slimmest of margins, finishing just two percentage points ahead of the second-place Orix Buffaloes of Osaka. SoftBank then qualified for the Japan Series by beating Orix four games to three in the best-of-seven Climax Series of playoffs.

Hanshin, under manager Yutaka Wada, finished second in the Central League regular-season standings, seven games behind the first-place Yomiuri Giants, but secured a berth against SoftBank in the Japan Series by knocking off the Giants four games to one in the Central's Climax Series.

A total of 72 foreigners played

Brad Eldred

in the Japan pro leagues in 2014, including a host of Cuban players signed by Japanese teams to take advantage of the recent decision by the Havana government to allow Cuban stars to play in foreign leagues without having to defect to other countries.

Besides Cuba, players from the U.S., Canada, Mexico, Puerto Rico, Venezuela, the Dominican Republic, Curacao, Australia, Italy, the Netherlands, South Korea and Taiwan also saw action in the Central and Pacific Leagues.

Home run crowns were won by foreign sluggers Brad Eldred of the Hiroshima Carp (37) in the Central League and Ernesto Mejia in the Pacific (34). Mejia tied with teammate Takeya Nakamura.

All four foreign players on the Hanshin club claimed leadership in some C.L. category. Tigers outfielder Matt Murton was the batting champion (.338), first baseman Mauro Gomez won the RBI title (109), Randy Messenger was the league's winningest pitcher (tied at 13 victories with Daisuke Yamai of the Chunichi Dragons), and Korean closer Oh Seung-Hwan had the most saves (39).

Other foreign standouts in the Central League included Chunichi third baseman Hector Luna who batted .317, Yakult Swallows slugger Wladimir Balentien who hit .301 with 31 homers

and Yomiuri closer Scott Mathieson, who notched 30 saves.

In the Pacific division, Wily Mo Pena of Orix slammed 32 home runs, SoftBank pitcher Jason Standridge won 11 games, and Hawks closer Dennis Sarfate saved 37.

The "Cuban invasion" began in April when Yomiuri announced the signing of slugger Frederich Cepeda. The Yokohama DeNA Baystars followed by acquiring infielder Yulieski Gourriel, and the Chiba Lotte Marines picked up outfielder Alfredo Despaigne. All are veterans of Cuban national teams, Olympic Games and World Baseball Classics.

Japanese players rumored as possible candidates for Major League service through posting or free agency in coming years enjoyed successful seasons. These include Orix pitcher Chihiro Kaneko, Buffaloes outfielder Yoshio Itoi and Hiroshima hurler Kenta Maeda. Kaneko led both leagues with 16 victories and a 1.98 ERA, while Itoi was the P.L. batting champion, hitting .331. Maeda went 11-9, 2.60.

The two leagues split their two-game 2014 mid-summer all-star series, and the Pacific League leads the all-time series, 80-75 with 10 ties.

Five of the 12 Japanese teams will start the 2015 season with new managers. SoftBank's Akiyama, despite winning the Japan Series, has decided to step down after six seasons as the Hawks pilot. He is being replaced by former Hawks pitcher Kimiyasu Kudo.

Veteran skipper Senichi Hoshino, who led the Tohoku Rakuten Golden Eagles to the 2013 Japan Series title, also resigned for health reasons, and the new Rakuten manager is ex-Seibu Lions and Yomiuri Giants catcher Hiromoto "Dave" Okubo. Norio Tanabe, a batting coach with Seibu, took over as interim manager at midseason in 2014 and was given the Lions field-boss job full time.

Kenjiro Nomura managed the Hiroshima Carp to third-place finishes and Climax Series appearances in 2013 and 2014 but resigned after five years at the helm. His successor is ex-Hiroshima outfielder and batting coach Koichi Ogata. The Yakult Swallows, after consecutive last-place showings, also promoted a hitting coach, Mitsuru Manaka, to replace manager Junji Ogawa.

CENTRAL LEAGUE

	W	L	T	PCT	GB
Yomiuri Giants	82	61	1	.573	—
Hanshin Tigers	75	68	1	.524	7
Hiroshima Carp	74	68	2	.521	7 ½
Chunichi Dragons	67	73	4	.479	13 ½
Yokohama DeNA Baystars	67	75	2	.472	14 ½
Tokyo Yakult Swallows	60	81	3	.426	21

CLIMAX SERIES PLAYOFFS—First Stage: Hokkaido Nippon Ham defeated Orix 2-1 in best-of-three series. **Final Stage:** Fukuoka SoftBank defeated Hokkaido Nippon Ham 4-3 in best-of-seven series

INDIVIDUAL BATTING LEADERS
(Minimum 446 Plate Appearances)

PLAYER, TEAM	AVG	AB	R	H	2B	3B	HR	RBI	SB
Murton, Matt, Tigers	.338	532	58	180	32	0	14	84	2
Kikuchi, Ryosuke, Carp	.325	579	88	188	39	2	11	58	23
Yamada, Tetsuto, Carp	.324	596	106	193	39	1	29	89	15
Oshima, Yohei, Dragons	.318	585	92	186	18	2	2	28	28
Luna, Hector, Dragons	.317	467	80	148	25	5	17	73	8
Takai, Yuhei, Swallows	.316	547	97	173	28	3	23	90	10
Toritani, Takashi, Tigers	.313	550	96	172	28	2	8	73	10
Hatakeyama, Kazuhiro, Swallows	.310	422	52	131	19	1	17	79	2
Maru, Yoshihiro, Carp	.310	536	106	166	30	5	19	67	26
Kawabata, Shingo, Swallows	.305	580	86	177	33	2	10	69	2
Balentien, Wladimir, Swallows	.301	366	61	110	12	0	31	69	2
Tsutsugo, Yoshitomo, Baystars	.300	410	58	123	24	2	22	77	2
Chono, Hisayoshi, Giants	.297	472	67	140	29	1	13	62	8
Morino, Masahiko, Dragons	.288	507	64	146	34	0	13	86	3
Gomez, Mauro, Tigers	.283	537	81	152	30	2	26	109	1

REMAINING NORTH AMERICAN AND LATIN PLAYERS

PLAYER, TEAM	AVG	AB	R	H	2B	3B	HR	RBI	SB
Rosario, Rainel, Carp	.336	238	32	80	13	2	14	49	1
Anderson, Leslie, Giants	.319	295	32	94	11	1	15	50	1
Gourriel, Yulieski, Baystars	.305	239	46	73	22	0	11	30	3
Blanco, Tony, Baystars	.283	311	32	88	14	0	17	60	0
Hernandez, Anderson, Dragons	.262	279	34	73	14	1	5	32	2
Ka'aihue, Kila, Carp	.257	288	25	74	13	0	11	40	0
Lopez, Jose, Giants	.243	375	43	91	17	0	22	57	1
Milledge, Lastings, Swallows	.231	39	3	9	2	0	1	6	0
Cepeda, Frederich, Giants	.194	108	11	21	3	0	6	18	0
Gomez, Alexis, Dragons	.077	13	0	1	0	0	0	0	0

INDIVIDUAL PITCHING LEADERS
(Minimum 144 innings)

PITCHER, TEAM	W	L	ERA	G	SV	IP	H	BB	SO
Sugano, Tomoyuki, Giants	12	5	2.33	23	0	159	138	36	122
Iwata, Minoru, Tigers	9	8	2.54	22	0	149	123	43	116
Maeda, Kenta, Carp	11	9	2.60	27	0	187	164	41	161
Ono, Yudai, Dragons	10	8	2.89	25	0	165	156	47	119
Sugiuchi, Toshiya, Giants	10	6	3.16	26	0	159	144	41	145
Utsumi, Tetsuya, Giants	7	9	3.17	22	0	145	139	36	105
Messenger, Randy, Tigers	13	10	3.20	31	0	208	188	69	226
Yamai, Daisuke, Dragons	13	5	3.21	27	0	174	156	66	103
Kubo, Yasutomo, Baystars	12	6	3.33	28	0	178	181	54	119
Moscoso, Guillermo, Baystars	9	9	3.39	24	0	146	133	45	96
Fujinami, Shintaro, Tigers	11	8	3.53	25	0	163	150	64	172
Nomi, Atsushi, Tigers	9	13	3.99	26	0	169	170	48	151
Ino, Shoichi, Baystars	11	9	4.01	25	0	159	163	49	104
Osera, Daichi, Carp	10	8	4.05	26	0	151	165	40	116
Ishikawa, Masanori, Swallows	10	10	4.75	27	0	165	181	49	101

REMAINING NORTH AMERICAN AND LATIN PLAYERS

PITCHER, TEAM	W	L	ERA	G	SV	IP	H	BB	SO
Roman, Orlando, Swallows	1	0	0.56	16	5	16	11	7	9
Soto, Enyelbert, Baystars	1	1	1.57	26	1	23	17	6	10
Heath, Deunte, Carp	3	0	2.38	7	0	42	29	20	35
Mickolio, Kam, Carp	1	1	2.45	51	25	48	39	18	29
Payano, Nelson, Dragons	0	2	2.59	23	0	24	14	16	26
Phillips, Zach, Carp	1	0	3.27	9	0	11	8	3	7
Barnette, Tony, Swallows	1	2	3.34	33	14	32	27	11	42
Mathieson, Scott, Giants	6	6	3.58	64	30	65	59	23	75
Cabrera, Daniel, Dragons	5	7	4.09	14	0	77	77	39	59
Narveson, Chris, Swallows	4	11	4.53	24	0	137	136	53	96
Bullington, Bryan, Carp	9	8	4.58	23	0	131	145	32	85
Seddon, Chris, Giants	4	5	4.67	10	0	52	58	20	37
Carpenter, Chris, Swallows	1	2	4.73	32	0	32	30	24	27
Sosa, Jorge, Baystars	0	3	4.94	27	3	24	35	14	14

PACIFIC LEAGUE

	W	L	T	PCT	GB
Fukuoka SoftBank Hawks	78	60	6	.565	—
Orix Buffaloes	80	62	2	.563	0
Hokkaido Nippon Ham Fighters	73	68	3	.518	6 ½
Chiba Lotte Marines	66	76	2	.465	14
Saitama Seibu Lions	63	77	4	.450	16
Tohoku Rakuten Golden Eagles	64	80	0	.444	17

INDIVIDUAL BATTING LEADERS
(Minimum 446 Plate Appearances)

PLAYER, TEAM	AVG	AB	R	H	2B	3B	HR	RBI	SB
Itoi, Yoshio, Buffaloes	.331	502	73	166	36	2	19	81	31
Akaminai, Ginji, Eagles	.327	459	59	150	26	0	4	70	1
Yanagida, Yuuki, Hawks	.317	524	91	166	18	4	15	70	33
Nakamura, Akira, Eagles	.308	571	75	176	22	4	4	61	10
Uchikawa, Seiichi, Hawks	.307	488	50	150	26	1	18	74	0
Lee, Dae Ho, Hawks	.300	566	60	170	30	0	19	68	0
Hasegawa, Yuya, Hawks	.300	473	58	142	30	3	6	55	7
Yo, Daikan, Fighters	.293	471	77	138	18	1	25	85	20
Matsui, Kazuo, Eagles	.291	444	57	129	32	3	8	46	9
Mejia, Ernesto, Lions	.290	396	56	115	11	1	34	73	2
Kuriyama, Takumi, Lions	.288	532	64	153	34	4	3	61	3
Suzuki, Daichi, Marines	.287	533	60	153	29	7	3	43	7
Okajima, Takero, Eagles	.283	545	77	154	27	3	7	53	9
Kakunaka, Katsuya, Marines	.277	451	62	125	22	5	8	57	9
Asamura, Hideto, Lions	.273	440	52	120	19	1	14	55	3

REMAINING NORTH AMERICAN AND LATIN PLAYERS

PLAYER, TEAM	AVG	AB	R	H	2B	3B	HR	RBI	SB
Lutz, Zach, Eagles	.314	51	11	16	3	0	5	18	1
Despaigne, Alfredo, Marines	.311	161	26	50	13	1	12	33	0
Canizares, Barbaro, Hawks	.308	13	1	4	3	0	0	2	0
Brazell, Craig, Marines	.276	76	8	21	5	0	3	14	0
Huffman, Chad, Marines	.270	185	23	50	20	0	4	28	0
Abreu, Abner, Lions	.250	16	4	4	0	1	0	4	1
Bowker, John, Eagles	.248	214	18	53	12	1	7	22	3
Butler, Joey, Buffaloes	.231	52	5	12	2	0	2	6	0
Miranda, Juan, Fighters	.227	375	43	85	19	0	14	57	0
Youkilis, Kevin, Eagles	.215	65	6	14	4	0	1	11	0
Ransom, Cody, Lions	.212	118	8	25	8	0	2	12	0
Abreu, Michel, Fighters	.211	19	2	4	0	0	1	1	0
Betancourt, Yuniesky, Buffaloes	.141	71	1	10	1	0	0	4	0
Evans, Nick, Lions	.111	18	0	2	0	0	0	1	0

INDIVIDUAL PITCHING LEADERS

PITCHER, TEAM	W	L	ERA	G	SV	IP	H	BB	SO
Kaneko, Chihiro, Buffaloes	16	5	1.98	26	0	191	157	42	199
Kishi, Takayuki, Lions	13	4	2.51	23	0	161	126	36	126
Otani, Shohei, Fighters	11	4	2.61	24	0	155	125	57	179
Norimoto, Takahiro, Eagles	14	10	3.02	30	0	203	187	39	204
Nishi, Yuuki, Buffaloes	12	10	3.29	24	0	156	146	35	119
Standridge, Jason, Hawks	11	8	3.30	26	0	172	156	57	129
Dickson, Brandon, Buffaloes	9	10	3.33	26	0	154	156	55	118
Ishikawa, Ayumu, Marines	10	8	3.43	25	0	160	165	37	111
Makita, Kazuhisa, Lions	8	9	3.74	26	0	171	170	50	98
Karashima, Wataru, Eagles	8	13	3.79	25	0	154	160	46	99
Mendoza, Luis, Fighters	7	13	3.89	26	0	162	170	45	119
Wakui, Hideaki, Marines	8	12	4.21	26	0	165	158	63	116
Nakata, Kenichi, Hawks	11	7	4.34	25	0	145	139	65	116

REMAINING NORTH AMERICAN AND LATIN PLAYERS

PITCHER, TEAM	W	L	ERA	G	SV	IP	H	BB	SO
Sarfate, Dennis, Hawks	7	1	1.05	64	37	68	50	22	96
Maestri, Alessandro, Buffaloes	3	1	1.97	36	0	50	31	30	48
Crotta, Mike, Fighters	4	5	2.62	61	6	58	49	16	36
Falkenborg, Brian, Eagles	3	5	2.87	39	20	38	31	8	45
Williams, Randy, Lions	6	4	2.96	60	0	52	54	25	59
Rosa, Carlos, Marines	1	4	3.02	45	0	42	35	17	27
Wolfe, Brian, Hawks	4	2	3.04	8	0	47	44	14	32
Barrios, Edison, Hawks	0	0	3.38	2	0	3	3	0	3
Carter, Anthony, Fighters	0	5	3.97	48	0	45	42	24	33
Cruz, Rhiner, Eagles	2	2	3.99	29	0	29	34	17	24
Van Mil, Loek, Eagles	0	1	4.15	9	0	9	7	7	7
Bowden, Michael, Lions	2	1	4.50	36	0	40	38	24	30
Reynolds, Greg, Lions	3	7	5.46	12	0	61	77	23	29
Blackley, Travis, Eagles	1	2	5.54	3	0	13	21	5	7
Oseguera, Paul, Hawks	0	2	9.75	3	0	12	19	5	7

Lions do it again

The dynasty continues.

Samsung won its fourth straight KBO title, trouncing Nexen 11-1 in the deciding Game Six of their best-of-7 championship series.

The Lions have been the class of the league for the entirety of this decade. This was their fifth consecutive Korean Series appearance and they finished with the league's best record.

The rest of the league hoped that this would be the year that Samsung's experienced veterans would finally falter due to age. They'll be wondering the same thing next year.

Samsung's lineup and rotation are filled with veterans who are well accustomed to postseason play. Outfielders Park Han Yi, 35 and Choi Hyoung Woo, 31, first baseman Lee Seung Yeop, 38, and infielder Chae Tae In, 32, are all long-time Korean league stars. Samsung even got some contributions from 40-year-old catcher Jin Kab Yong.

The pitching staff isn't much younger.

Maybe the Lions will wear down next year, but so far, the dynasty just keeps rolling along.

STANDINGS & LEADERS

North	W	L	T	PCT	GB
Samsung Lions	78	47	3	.624	—
Nexen Heroes	78	48	2	.619	½
NC Dinos	70	57	1	.551	9
LG Twins	62	64	2	.492	16½
SK Wyverns	61	65	2	.484	17½
Doosan Bears	59	68	1	.465	20
Lotte Giants	58	69	1	.457	21
Kia Tigers	54	74	0	.422	25½
Hanwha Eagles	49	77	2	.389	29½

INDIVIDUAL BATTING LEADERS

PLAYER, TEAM	AVG	AB	R	H	2B	3B	HR	RBI	SB
Seo, Geon Chang, Nexen	.370	543	135	201	41	17	7	67	48
Kim, Tae Kyun, Hanwha	.365	422	66	154	30	0	18	84	0
Son, A Seop, Lotte	.362	483	105	175	25	3	18	80	10
Kang, Jung Ho, Nexen	.356	418	103	149	36	2	40	117	3
Choi, Hyoung Woo, Samsung	.356	430	92	153	33	0	31	100	4
Kim, Joo Chan, Kia	.346	399	72	138	32	4	9	46	22
Min, Byung Hun, Doosan	.345	470	85	162	31	3	12	79	16
Thames, Eric, NC	.343	443	95	152	30	6	37	121	11
Park, Yong Taik, LG	.343	464	71	159	24	2	9	73	11
An, Chi Hong, Kia	.339	434	65	147	31	2	18	88	19

INDIVIDUAL PITCHING LEADERS

PITCHER, TEAM	W	L	ERA	G	SV	IP	H	BB	SO
Vandenhurk, Rick, Samsung	13	4	3.18	25	0	153	125	45	180
Kim, Kwang Hyun, SK	13	9	3.42	28	0	173	178	81	145
Van Hekken, Andy, Nexen	20	6	3.51	31	0	187	193	53	178
Shirek, Charlie, NC	12	8	3.81	28	0	165	184	55	92
Nippert, Dustin, Doosan	14	7	3.81	30	0	179	186	48	158
Riordan, Cory, LG	9	10	3.96	28	0	168	177	37	77
Hacker, Eric, NC	8	8	4.01	30	0	173	169	62	112
Woo, Kyu Min, LG	11	5	4.04	29	0	153	170	34	103
Jang, Won Sam, Samsung	11	5	4.11	24	0	129	149	37	63
Oxspring, Chris, Lotte	10	8	4.20	32	0	184	184	63	130

Lamigo claims CPBL crown

The Lamigo Monkeys won their second Chinese Professional Baseball League championship in three years, winning the best-of-seven finals in five games against Chinatrust Brother Elephants with an 8-3 victory in the clincher. The Monkeys had finished third in the four-team league in the second half but nevertheless cruised to the top regular season record of 66-51-3.

The Monkeys' mix of players included Puerto Rican reliever Miguel Mejia, who set a league record by converting 34 consecutive save chances and went 5-1, 1.24 with 35 saves overall. Mejia, a former Tigers and Marlins farmhand who played collegiately at Florida International, also had three saves in the championship series. The pitching staff also included Taiwan league vet Ken Ray (9-5, 2.17), former Southern University ace Roy Merritt (6-4, 2.82) and an offense led by native players such as catcher Lin Hung-Yu (.313/.372/.488, 16 HR).

Another native, Yu Teh-Lung, earned championship series MVP after moving from outfield to shortstop and hitting .389 in the series after batting .270/.292/.321 in the regular season.

Brother Elephants finished with the league's worst overall record, but the team won the second half of the 120-game season, which is split into two 60-game segments. Lefty Chris Cody, a former Tigers farmhand, tossed a complete-game shutout with 14 strikeouts to clinch the second half.

STANDINGS & LEADERS

TEAM	W	L	T	PCT
Lamigo Monkeys	66	51	3	.564
Uni-7-11 Lions	58	55	7	.513
EDA Rhinos	58	60	2	.492
Brother Elephants	50	66	4	.431

INDIVIDUAL BATTING LEADERS

PLAYER, TEAM	AVG	AB	R	H	2B	3B	HR	RBI	OPS	SLG	SB
Hu Chin Lung, EDA	.350	463	81	162	27	4	5	55	.391	.458	12
Lin Yi Quan, EDA	.346	465	81	161	32	1	14	88	.398	.510	1
Chang Cheng Wei, BE	.320	481	68	154	25	3	3	34	.375	.403	19
Chen Yung Chi, Uni	.314	353	55	111	21	3	6	54	.367	.442	14
Lin Hung Yu, Lamigo	.313	387	55	121	16	2	16	60	.372	.488	0

INDIVIDUAL PITCHING LEADERS

PITCHER, TEAM	W	L	ERA	G	GS	IP	H	HR	BB	SO
Zhen Kai Wen, BE	11	3	2.48	22	22	153	150	6	27	108
Shairon Martis, Uni	8	7	3.15	28	23	152	142	5	44	67
Freddy Garcia, EDA	11	9	3.19	25	25	161	172	9	20	108
Nelson Figueroa, Uni	8	7	3.39	22	21	138	172	9	27	94
Lin Yu Ching, BE	9	10	3.41	23	23	148	157	5	39	100

EUROPE

Ex-MLBers lead Bologna to crown in Italy

Bologna defeated Rimini four games to three tow in the Italy Series. The teams split the first two games of the series in Bologna. Rimini then won two of three at home to take a three games to two lead. But after returning to Gianni Falchi Stadium, Bologna reeled off convincing 8-1 and 4-0 victories to claim their first national championship since 2009.

Guillermo Rodriguez was voted Italy Series MVP. Formerly a big league catcher with the Giants and Orioles, Rodriguez hit .379 in the series with five extra-base hits and 10 RBIs. Bologna's Claudio Liverziani batted .357 and scored eight runs in the series. Liverziani, 39, hit his 100th career Italian Baseball League homer in mid July. He played his first top flight game in 1991 and has been with Bologna since 2002.

Guillermo Rodriguez

Rodriguez was not the only MLB alumnus in Bologna's Italy Series lineup. Former Diamondbacks and Dodgers outfielder Trent Oeltjen joined Bologna in midseason and became the club's center fielder.

Bologna starter Joey Williamson won the pivotal sixth game of the series and could have easily won two more. The ex-Rockies farm hand left Games One and Three with 4-1 and 2-1 leads, respectively, but Rimini battled back and won both in the late innings. Williamson finished the series with a 1.21 ERA and a 0.85 WHIP. The Bologna pitching staff held Rimini to a cumulative .209 batting average.

The Italian Baseball League regular season schedule format was overhauled in 2014. The eight-team loop was broken up into two groups. An opening, unbalanced round saw each team play 20 games. The top two teams in each group advanced to an 18-game, balanced semifinal round. The best two semi-finalists qualified for the Italy Series.

The IBL included a pair of clubs from Nettuno. Simply referred to as "Nettuno" and "Nettuno 2", neither team made it past the first round.

Nettuno 2 had solid pitching but struggled at the plate and were often overmatched. They batted .157 as a team and were on the wrong end of two no-hitters: a 13-0 pasting by Rimini on April 18 and a 10-0 loss to Parma on May 23. Multiple pitchers shared both no-hitters.

San Marino beat Rimini to win its third European Cup. It was the fourth straight season in which the continental club championship final was an all-Italian affair. San Marino won the best-of-three series in three games.

STANDINGS & LEADERS

GROUP A	W	L	T	GB
Bologna	17	3	.850	-
San Marino	13	7	.650	4
Padua	7	13	.350	10
Godo	7	13	.350	10

GROUP B	W	L	T	GB
Parma	12	8	.650	-
Rimini	12	8	.650	-
Nettuno	8	12	.400	4
Nettuno	4	16	.200	8

INDIVIDUAL BATTING LEADERS

PLAYER, TEAM	AVG	AB	R	H	2B	3B	HR	RBI	BB
Nosti, Nick, PDO	.380	50	9	19	5	2	1	7	5
Ramos, G. Jairo r., RSM	.371	70	6	26	4	0	1	15	7
Duran, Carlos, RSM	.346	78	21	27	7	2	0	9	10
Vasquez, C. Wuillians, RSM	.342	73	21	25	7	0	2	17	14
Molina, G. Rolexis, GOD	.342	76	10	26	7	0	0	10	7
Retrosi, Ennio, NET	.333	72	9	24	2	1	0	6	7
Romero, G. Alexander, RIM	.333	66	11	22	4	0	1	15	23
Albanese, Simone, RSM	.327	52	9	17	3	0	0	7	3
Marval, G. Osman J., PAR	.324	74	12	24	8	0	1	16	12
Chapelli, Laidel, PDO	.319	72	10	23	2	1	1	10	11
Sambucci, Alex, PAR	.313	67	10	21	5	1	0	9	6
Ambrosino, Paolino, BOL	.309	55	8	17	4	1	0	6	5
Desimoni, Stefano, PAR	.307	75	15	23	1	0	0	13	13
Sanchez, L. Danilo, GOD	.306	62	5	19	4	0	2	12	16
Paoletti, Alessandro, NET	.300	50	3	15	2	1	0	5	3

INDIVIDUAL PITCHING LEADERS

PITCHER, TEAM	W	L	ERA	SV	IP	H	R	ER	BB	SO
Marquez, Enorbel, RIM	2	0	0.00	0	22	10	0	0	12	26
Rivero, Raul, BOL	2	0	0.68	6	27	14	2	2	6	28
Williamson, Joey, BOL	7	1	0.74	0	61	32	7	5	15	76
Eckstrom, Michael, RIM	5	1	1.16	0	54	25	9	7	17	76
Guerra, Junior, RSM	8	1	1.29	0	63	30	12	9	32	99
Florian, Frailyn, NET	3	1	1.30	0	48	35	11	7	19	40
Rodriguez, Rodney, NET	4	0	1.40	1	45	29	12	7	15	76
Yepez, Jesus, PAR	1	2	1.46	5	25	10	4	4	16	31
Giovanelli, Nicolas, POR	3	1	1.83	0	34	27	7	7	14	19
Sanchez, Jose, PAR	7	0	1.91	0	61	37	14	13	18	71
de Santis, Riccardo, BOL	1	0	2.08	3	26	15	8	6	15	27
Uviedo, Ronald, PDO	4	4	2.20	0	61	59	24	15	21	52
Gonzalez, Norberto, NE2	1	7	2.29	0	59	51	22	15	29	47
Calero, Angel Gust, GOD	5	1	2.40	0	56	39	16	15	21	60
Richetti, Carlos, NE2	1	3	2.88	1	34	34	16	11	11	36

KEVIN PATAKY

INTERNATIONAL

Neptunus wins 15th Dutch title

In winning its 15th Dutch Major League title, Neptunus of Rotterdam became comeback kids, rallying from 2-0 and 3-1 deficits to defeat the Amsterdam Pirates four games to three in the Holland Series.

The Pirates won the first two games of the series in Rotterdam, then split the next two at home. Neptunus righthander Berry van Driel earned Holland Series MVP after allowing one run in 15 2/3 innings while earning victories in Game Five and Game Seven. The 6-foot-6, 29-year old went 1-1, 1.82 with six saves this season. He first joined Neptunus in 2008 and has never started a regular season game for them.

His hero turn came against longtime Dutch League ace Rob Cordemans of Amsterdam. In Game Seven, the Pirates' Cordemans (8-0, 1.53) lost 1-0 but went the distance for a series record fifth time .

MORRIS FOSTOFF

Robbie Cordemans

Without van Driel in the bullpen, Kevin Kelly emerged as Neptunus' closer in the Series. Kelly, a Curacao native who pitched for Southwestern Oklahoma State JC in 2012-13, saved Games Five, Six and Seven. It was the first time that a pitcher had three saves in the Holland Series.

Neptunus won the Series without manager Evert-Jan t'Hoen. The former minor leaguer was suspended after being ejected in Games Two and Four. Bench coach Jan Collins took his place and steered Neptunus to victory. Game Two was a wild run fest that featured a bench clearance and multiple ejections. The Pirates won the game 17-7. The last time that Neptunus gave up that many runs was in a 1997 regular season game.

Hoofddorp Pioniers outfielder Dirk van't Klooster set two DML all-time records in late July. The 38-year-old Amsterdam native eclipsed Marcel Joost when he notched hit number 1,167. Shortly thereafter, he played his 860th DML game. Joost, a long-time national team player who retired after the 2002 season, was the previous holder of that record as well.

Bryan Engelhardt of Kinheim won his seventh DML home run crown. The 32-year-old Curacao native hit nine round trippers, just one shy of his personal best in 2011.

Former Phillies farmhand Mike Bolsenbroek pitched a seven-inning perfect game for the Netherlands against Greece in the European Championships. Six days later, Bolsenbroek held Italy to three hits in a 5-0 win. Going into the game, Italy had reeled off twenty consecutive victories in the competition. The Netherlands went on to win their twenty-first continental title, their first since 2007.

Long-time minor leaguer Curt Smith hit two home runs in the final and was voted the tournament's MVP.

STANDINGS & LEADERS

REGULAR SEASON	W	L	T	GB
Neptunus	34	7	1	—
Amsterdam Pirates	32	10	0	2 ½
Kinheim	29	13	0	5 ½
Hoofddorp Pioniers	27	14	1	7
UVV	14	25	3	19
HCAW	12	28	2	21 ½
ADO	9	32	1	25
Dordrecht Hawks	6	34	2	27 ½

INDIVIDUAL BATTING LEADERS

PLAYER, TEAM	AVG	AB	R	H	2B	3B	HR	RBI	BB
Jong, de Bas, AMS	.373	134	28	50	16	2	3	42	19
Rooi, Vince, PIO	.360	136	35	49	14	0	4	42	34
Flanegin, De, PIO	.355	107	18	38	7	0	0	23	23
Lampe, Gilmer, UVV	.355	141	29	50	8	0	1	15	22
Meer, vd Stijn, NEP	.354	113	32	40	2	0	1	11	14
Diaz, Christian, ADO	.338	148	21	50	10	2	6	25	14
Quint, de Dennis, UVV	.333	129	15	43	8	1	1	21	14
Duursma, Michael, AMS	.326	132	37	43	7	1	0	28	31
Rombley, Danny, PIO	.325	154	36	50	7	3	1	36	21
Legito, Raily, NEP	.319	141	34	45	6	0	4	26	28
Moorman, Mark Jan, PIO	.318	107	16	34	13	0	1	29	11
Boekhoudt, Gianison, NEP	.316	136	37	43	9	2	7	42	34
Klooster, vt Dirk, PIO	.314	169	39	53	3	1	1	26	20
Berkenbosch, Kenny, AMS	.313	147	33	46	10	0	7	39	29
Cuba, de Quintin, KIN	.309	139	22	43	9	1	2	24	23

INDIVIDUAL PITCHING LEADERS

PITCHER, TEAM	W	L	ERA	SV	IP	H	R	ER	BB	SO
Yntema, Orlando, NEP	8	1	1.15	0	86	50	13	11	26	73
Heijstek, Kevin, AMS	10	3	1.33	0	101	63	19	15	17	77
Cordemans, Rob, AMS	8	0	1.53	0	65	44	12	11	9	60
Harcksen, Misja, NEP	5	0	1.59	0	34	23	7	6	11	22
Asjes, Aschwin, KIN	5	0	1.72	9	37	29	10	7	15	28
Markwell, Diegomar, NEP	8	1	1.97	0	82	67	19	18	29	65
Koeiman, Elton, PIO	6	3	1.98	0	59	55	24	13	12	33
Bergman, David, KIN	5	4	2.16	0	79	68	24	19	16	67
Koks, Jurrian, AMS	1	2	2.34	5	35	28	12	9	9	19
Karel, Sedley, PIO	1	2	2.38	2	34	26	12	9	12	33
Martijn, Jerrold, KIN	4	0	2.45	0	59	63	26	16	28	39
Jong, de Jos, AMS	4	3	2.66	0	51	43	19	15	8	29
Branden vd, Kenny, UVV	2	3	2.70	2	70	57	29	21	21	56
Mowday, Chris, AMS	4	0	2.80	1	45	48	20	14	5	30
Hernandez, Ricardo, PIO	9	4	3.06	0	82	71	34	28	28	83

Island exodus continues

The talent exodus from Cuba continues to grow, with star players, young prospects and a wave of marginal players leaving the island and giving teams headaches trying to keep track of them all.

Outfielder Yasmany Tomas and second baseman Hector Olivera were among the former national team stars who left Cuba after the 2013-14 season, while young up-and-coming infielders Yoan Moncada and Andy Ibanez also left, much to the excitement of international scouts.

While the caliber of play in Cuba has decreased due to defections, there is still talent to watch in Serie Nacional. Pinar Del Rio won the 2013-14 championship, defeating a Matanzas team led by Cuban national team manager Victor Mesa. Matanzas had more star power, with two national teamers in second baseman Jose Fernandez and center fielder Guillermo Heredia, along with corner outfielder

ALYSON BOYER RODE

Jose Fernandez

Yadiel Hernandez (who finished third in MVP voting) and 17-year-old Victor Mesa, who's the son of the manager and a rising star, a spectacular defender who won a Gold Glove in center field.

The Pinar Del Rio club did it more with veteran savvy than talent that would attract major league scouts. Righthander Yosvani Torres, a 33-year-old with a mid-to-high 80s fastball, led the rotation and won the league MVP award, edging Industriales star third baseman Yulieski Gourriel for the honor. Righthander Vladimir Gutierrez chipped in key innings during the postseason and won the rookie of the year award, showing a fastball up to 93 mph and a plus curveball.

Gourriel remains the best player in Cuba, a dynamic player with lightning bat speed, plus power to all fields and strong defense with a plus arm. Right behind him is Granma outfielder Alfredo Despaigne, who has 80 power on the 20-80 scale, tremendous bat speed and an unconventional swing that works for him. Among pitch-

ers, 20-year-old righthander Norge Ruiz continued his ascent as the country's top pitching prospect by major league standards and one of the best pitchers in Serie Nacional right now.

Cuba also loosened its restrictions by allowing some top players to participate in foreign professional leagues. The Cuban government brokered the contracts with foreign professional teams (and took a commission of the salaries), allowing the players to join the team for the summer during the Cuban offseason, with the players returning to Cuba when their foreign season finished.

Gourriel starred for the Yokohama DeNA BayStars, while Despaigne mashed for the Chiba Lotte Marines in Japan. The Yomiuri Giants also brought over Frederich Cepeda, though he struggled and was sent to the minors, and young righthander Hector Mendoza, who never pitched in a game as he had trouble building back up his arm strength.

STANDINGS & LEADERS

TEAM	SECOND HALF	FIRST HALF
Matanzas	62-36	28-17
Pinar Del Rio	61-39	28-17
Villa Clara	52-40	27-18
Industriales	53-41	27-18
Holguin	48-39	26-19
Artemisa	42-44	25-20
Isla De La Juventud	40-46	24-21
Santiago De Cuba	36-51	24-21
Ciego De Avila	N/A	24-21
Las Tunas	N/A	22-23
Mayabeque	N/A	21-24
Granma	N/A	20-25
Cienfuegos	N/A	18-27
Camaguey	N/A	17-28
Guantanamo	N/A	15-30
Sancti Spiritus	N/A	14-31

INDIVIDUAL BATTING LEADERS

PLAYER, TEAM	AVG	AB	R	H	2B	3B	HR	RBI	BB	SO	SB
Michel Enriquez, IJV	.367	248	32	91	17	0	7	44	37	16	0
Maikel Caceres, HOL	.363	344	58	125	28	2	3	31	37	31	12
Giorvis Duverge, GTM	.343	230	42	79	22	0	9	41	21	19	3
Ariel Sanchez, MTZ	.341	320	59	109	13	5	11	51	35	28	2
Yordanis Linares, VCL	.333	207	43	69	10	2	8	46	33	40	11
Andres Reyna, SCU	.333	219	27	73	5	1	5	29	36	17	0
Alejandro Ortiz, IJV	.327	257	41	84	9	8	0	23	21	43	7
Jose Fernandez, MTZ	.326	239	44	78	16	0	5	42	65	10	2
Lisban Correa, IND	.324	250	36	81	24	0	7	41	36	63	0
Luis Yander La O, SCU	.324	278	39	90	11	2	2	21	18	17	24

INDIVIDUAL PITCHING LEADERS

PITCHER, TEAM	W	L	ERA	G	GS	CG	SV	IP	H	HR	BB	SO
Yasmany Hernandez, VCL	7	5	1.66	19	19	0	0	114	110	5	34	67
Julio A. Martinez, PRI	7	3	1.71	19	18	1	0	110	79	3	52	72
Yusmel Velazquez, HOL	9	2	1.74	17	16	0	0	98	77	1	45	45
Yosvani Torres, PRI	15	3	1.78	20	20	5	0	152	130	6	28	88
Vladimir Garcia, CAV	5	4	2.19	18	18	2	0	111	91	4	31	91
Yoanni Yera, MTZ	10	3	2.45	21	20	0	1	121	94	8	36	89
Norge Luis Ruiz, CMG	8	7	2.48	21	21	2	0	145	117	5	46	94
Ismel Jimenez, VCL	9	8	2.64	20	20	1	0	130	127	2	44	76
Yulieski Gonzalez, ART	6	9	2.64	20	20	0	0	129	123	2	57	73
Lazaro Blanco, GRA	9	6	2.77	29	10	2	0	94	83	7	46	52

Phillies farmhand Sebastian Valle hit a key grand slam to help Mexico win the Caribbean Series

MIKE JANES

Mexico wins Caribbean for 3rd time in 4 years

In its second consecutive Caribbean Series victory and third in the last four years, Mexico hit .285/.350/.455 over six games, all of which were tops for the tournament. Their seven homers, including a game-breaking grand slam from catcher Sebastian Valle in the championship, also paced the field.

Chris Roberson, a 34-year-old outfielder who spent time in the Phillies and Orioles systems, led the offense for Mexico with 10 hits, including a double, triple and two homers, in 27 at-bats. The output helped him earn the tournament's MVP honors. Juan Delgadillo, who started and won the clincher, pitched 14 shutout innings while allowing just eight hits and no walks, striking out nine.

To claim victory, Mexico beat Puerto Rico 7-0 in the finale. Along the way, Mexico also dispatched Venezuela, the Dominican Republic and, for the first time in 54 years, Cuba, which went 1-3 in its return to Caribbean Series play.

AUSTRALIAN LEAGUE

	W	L	PCT	GB
Perth Heat	32	14	.696	—
Sydney Blue Sox	23	23	.500	9
Canberra Cavalry	22	24	.478	10
Melbourne Aces	22	24	.478	10
Adelaide Bite	21	25	.457	11

| Brisbane Bandits | | | 18 | 28 | .391 | 14 |

Championship: Perth def. Canberra 2-0

INDIVIDUAL BATTING LEADERS

PLAYER, TEAM	AVG	AB	R	H	2B	3B	HR	RBI	BB	SO	SB
Casteel, Ryan, MEL	.343	166	23	57	10	1	11	36	17	20	1
Tripp Brandon, PER	.333	174	32	58	15	1	10	41	13	36	4
Barnes, Jeremy, CAN	.326	175	19	57	16	1	1	33	15	20	0
Schlehuber, Jared, MEL	.310	168	26	52	9	0	7	31	19	30	0
Berti, Jon, CAN	.309	178	46	55	11	3	1	18	30	13	31
Murphy, Jack, CAN	.306	160	13	49	9	0	2	27	14	21	0
Frawley, Casey, CAN	.306	170	37	52	17	5	5	30	27	33	3
Barron, Jesse, PER	.306	108	18	33	6	0	0	13	25	19	2
Kennelly, Tim, PER	.303	132	18	40	5	1	4	16	9	13	4
Kennelly, Matt, PER	.298	151	17	45	3	0	5	25	12	14	2

INDIVIDUAL PITCHING LEADERS

PITCHER, TEAM	W	L	ERA	G	SV	IP	H	BB	SO	AVG
Elkstrom, Mike, PER	5	1	0.72	7	0	50	31	10	57	.176
Olson, Richard, ADE	3	1	0.74	22	2	37	32	12	26	.242
Frawley, Jack, PER	7	2	2.07	12	0	74	64	18	54	.233
Thorpe, Lewis, MEL	3	2	2.45	7	0	37	34	10	30	.241
Burns, Joe, MEL	5	3	2.47	12	0	73	58	9	62	.215
Harris, Vaughan, SYD	1	2	2.58	10	0	15	34	16	25	.204
Searle, Ryan, BRI	3	4	2.78	8	0	55	46	7	50	.220
Williams, Matthew, ADE	3	5	2.89	21	8	44	40	9	36	.252
Claggett, Anthony, PER	4	3	2.96	12	0	70	57	30	44	.223
Jannis, Mickey, BRI	2	4	3.05	15	1	44	40	15	36	.245

DOMINICAN LEAGUE

	W	L	PCT	GB
Leones del Escogido	31	19	.620	—
Aguilas Cibaenas	31	19	.620	—
Tigres del Licey	29	21	.580	2
Gigantes del Cibao	22	28	.440	9

INTERNATIONAL

	W	L	PCT	GB
Estrellas de Oriente	19	31	.380	12
Toros del Este	18	32	.360	13

Championship: Licey def. Escogido 5-3

	W	L	PCT	GB
Indios de Mayaguez	21	19	.525	—
Gigantes de Carolina	19	21	.475	2
Cangrejeros de Santurce	18	22	.450	3

INDIVIDUAL BATTING LEADERS

PLAYER, TEAM	AVG	AB	R	H	2B	3B	HR	RBI	BB	SO	SB
Ynoa, Rafael, AGU	.333	141	26	47	9	2	4	10	11	23	5
Polanco, Gregory, ESC	.331	166	28	55	10	1	5	28	28	34	7
Sierra, Moises, GIG	.331	154	23	51	4	0	4	21	16	33	6
Gonzalez, Erik, ESC	.325	163	23	53	6	6	1	20	3	47	6
Almonte, Zoilo, AGU	.316	174	22	55	10	1	4	20	7	36	6
Polanco, Jorge, ESC	.294	180	23	53	9	2	1	17	21	29	4
Perez, Juan, AGU	.285	158	26	45	10	0	0	17	13	32	13
Navarro, Yamacio, LIC	.277	159	25	44	9	1	8	38	30	27	2
Ozuna, Marcell, GIG	.278	141	13	39	8	0	2	12	3	29	1
Black, Dan, AGU	.270	122	15	33	11	0	5	25	21	31	2

INDIVIDUAL BATTING LEADERS

PLAYER, TEAM	AVG	AB	R	H	2B	3B	HR	RBI	BB	SO	SB
Taylor, Michael, MAY	.365	137	20	50	7	2	3	10	13	38	3
Padilla, Jorge, CAG	.342	117	19	40	7	0	1	13	14	22	4
Lennerton, Jordan, PON	.340	141	17	48	13	0	5	21	19	32	0
Bates, Aaron, CAG	.333	114	14	38	6	0	0	11	16	30	0
Gotay, Ruben, CAR	.312	141	21	44	11	0	4	14	22	34	2
Gonzales, Andy, CAG	.309	123	17	38	8	0	3	20	20	22	3
Feliciano, Jesus, CAR	.308	146	28	45	4	1	0	12	16	9	3
Garcia, Anthony, CAR	.305	131	20	40	11	0	5	26	12	28	0
Ruiz, Randy, MAY	.305	118	17	36	4	1	6	22	7	32	0
Soto, Neftali, SAN	.292	137	12	40	8	0	4	22	6	21	1

INDIVIDUAL PITCHING LEADERS

PITCHER, TEAM	W	L	ERA	G	SV	IP	H	BB	SO	AVG
Castro, Angel, AGU	4	3	1.29	8	0	49	41	13	37	.228
MacLane, Evan , EST	2	2	1.93	12	0	56	58	7	35	.274
Noesi, Hector, EST	3	1	2.3	9	0	43	35	8	33	.220
Valdez, Edward, ESC	4	2	2.45	10	0	51	47	11	43	.240
Owens, Rudy, GIG	3	2	2.68	10	0	54	37	16	49	.191
Villanueva, Elih, TOR	3	2	3.73	11	0	53	50	7	42	.241
Maya, Yunesky, LIC	2	4	2.96	10	0	55	50	10	43	.237
Valdes, Raul, TOR	2	2	3.09	8	0	44	44	5	34	.259
Cody, Chris, AGU	3	3	3.18	9	0	45	40	13	24	.242
Barcelo, Lorenzo, AGU	4	2	3.42	9	0	50	49	6	31	.258

INDIVIDUAL PITCHING LEADERS

PITCHER, TEAM	W	L	ERA	G	SV	IP	H	BB	SO	AVG
Burgos, Hiram, MAY	2	2	1.4	11	0	39	25	12	35	.191
Colon, Joseph, SAN	1	0	1.93	7	0	33	22	8	22	.204
Martinez, Jorge, SAN	3	3	2.49	11	0	47	44	11	36	.262
Brownell, John, CAG	3	3	2.68	9	0	47	38	11	37	.220
Mateo, Victor, SAN	4	3	3.05	11	0	44	50	11	46	.284
Collazo, Willie, CAR	2	1	3.09	11	0	35	40	16	18	.299
Iida, Yuya, CAR	2	1	3.13	8	0	46	35	8	35	.215
Higashihama, Nao, CAR	1	4	3.15	8	0	40	34	10	42	.225
Albaladejo, Jonathan, MAY	2	5	3.51	10	0	49	54	7	36	.280
Alvarado, Giancarlo, PON	3	2	3.56	9	0	43	39	21	34	.248

MEXICAN PACIFIC LEAGUE

	W	L	PCT	GB
Naranjeros de Hermosillo	42	25	.627	—
Aguilas de Mexicali	38	30	.559	5
Caneros de los Mochis	36	31	.537	6
Mayos de Navojoa	36	31	.537	6
Tomateros de Culiacan	34	33	.507	8
Algodoneros de Guasave	30	38	.441	13
Yaquis de Obregon	27	41	.397	16
Venados de Mazatlan	26	40	.394	16

INDIVIDUAL BATTING LEADERS

PLAYER, TEAM	AVG	AB	R	H	2B	3B	HR	RBI	BB	SO	SB
Owens, Jerry, HER	.361	249	37	90	10	4	1	29	23	35	8
Fonseca, Luis, NAV	.335	242	34	81	14	0	8	35	24	51	7
Acosta, Rolando, NAV	.321	218	31	70	10	0	6	25	23	39	3
Avla, Emmanuel, MOC	.311	225	33	70	9	3	6	27	13	44	1
Aguilar, Jose, HER	.307	192	30	59	14	1	3	23	20	31	3
Robertson, Dan, OBR	.293	263	36	77	13	2	3	20	29	26	20
Burgamy, Brian, MOC	.290	231	50	67	13	0	15	47	50	56	2
Robertson, Chris, MXC	.288	267	46	77	11	3	11	33	28	43	17
Canizares, Barbaro, OBR	.286	203	24	58	5	0	11	31	31	18	2
Arredondo, Eduardo, GSV	.285	267	36	76	7	0	1	18	16	23	9

INDIVIDUAL PITCHING LEADERS

PITCHER, TEAM	W	L	ERA	G	SV	IP	H	BB	SO	AVG
Sanit, Amauri, CUL	7	0	2.13	12	0	72	53	21	43	.209
Velazquez, Hector, NAV	8	1	2.17	13	0	75	50	26	60	.191
Solano, Javier, MXC	5	2	2.28	21	0	71	60	22	56	.236
Meza, Andrews Ivan, CUL	3	3	2.36	12	0	69	75	15	48	.276
Martinez, Alejandro, MAZ	4	4	2.488	14	0	73	54	29	60	.209
Osuna, Edgar, MXC	7	2	2.54	13	0	71	57	18	54	.219
Solis, Tomas, MOC	7	4	2.58	13	0	77	66	25	44	.233
Doyle, Terry, MXC	5	5	2.99	13	0	75	65	33	58	.236
Oyervidez, Jose, NAV	6	5	3.03	13	0	74	59	22	56	.217
Melgarejo, Thomas, MOC	5	3	3.04	13	0	68	67	23	43	.253

PUERTO RICAN LEAGUE

	W	L	PCT	GB
Criollos de Caguas	21	19	.525	—
Leones de Ponce	21	19	.525	—

VENEZUELAN LEAGUE

NORTH	W	L	PCT	GB
Caribes de Anzoategui	39	24	.619	—
Aguilas del Zulia	34	29	.540	5
Leones de Caracas	34	29	.540	5
Navagentes del Magallanes	33	30	.524	6
Tiburones de La Guaira	32	31	.508	7
Cardenales de Lara	28	35	.444	11
Tigres de Aragua	29	34	.460	10
Bravos de Margarita	23	40	.365	16

INDIVIDUAL BATTING LEADERS

PLAYER, TEAM	AVG	AB	R	H	2B	3B	HR	RBI	BB	SO	SB
Cabrera, Alex, LAG	.391	215	41	84	13	0	21	59	32	36	0
Aldridge, Cory, ORI	.378	209	46	79	14	1	14	46	36	55	0
Sanchez, Carlos, LAG	.348	221	48	77	10	4	1	31	30	35	5
Castillo, Jose, ORI	.340	250	44	85	12	1	9	46	14	31	3
Pirela, Jose, ZUL	.332	247	58	82	13	7	6	44	33	28	5
Retherford, C.J., LAG	.328	235	48	77	11	0	11	45	24	30	1
Aguilar, Jesus, CAR	.327	226	49	74	7	0	18	50	27	43	0
Anderson, Leslie, ORI	.325	166	29	54	12	0	4	27	25	18	2
Garcia, Adonis, MAG	.325	231	38	75	15	1	8	39	7	30	3
Abreu, Bobby, CAR	.322	180	25	58	10	3	3	28	30	35	0

INDIVIDUAL PITCHING LEADERS

PITCHER, TEAM	W	L	ERA	G	SV	IP	H	BB	SO	AVG
Lively, Mitch, MAG	6	1	1.70	10	0	58	44	29	41	.215
Berger, Eric, MAR	4	4	3.04	12	0	56	45	27	30	.226
Merritt, Roy, ZUL	2	2	3.16	14	0	68	68	24	59	.263
Escalona, Edgmer, LAG	2	3	3.34	10	0	57	57	19	34	.258
Rivero, Raul, LAR	3	3	3.62	14	0	60	70	14	41	.299
Jakubauskas, Chris, LAR	2	2	3.63	14	0	62	67	21	32	.286
Monasterios, Carlos, MAR	3	4	4.02	13	0	54	52	20	42	.255
Negrin, Yoanner, CAR	4	3	4.06	13	0	62	58	22	38	.254
Pino, Yohan, ARA	4	6	4.33	14	0	69	78	24	42	.281
Ramirez, Ramon A., ORI	0	5	6.62	12	0	53	69	28	40	.318

COLLEGE

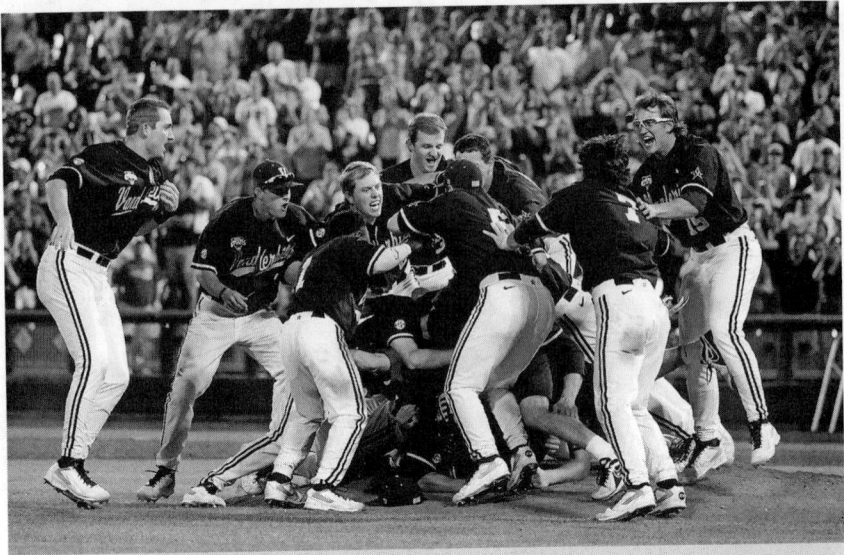

Vanderbilt bested Virginia in a compelling CWS Finals to win its first national championship

Norwood's homer lifts Vanderbilt to CWS title

BY AARON FITT

OMAHA

Sometimes, immortality comes to those who wait. Warren Morris waited through a wrist injury that sidelined him for much of the 1996 season. He ended it with a College World Series-winning home run.

John Norwood waited two seasons for a chance to play every day at Vanderbilt. He earned that chance in 2014, and on the last day of the season, he ensured that his name will be remembered forever, alongside those of Morris and Whit Merrifield and the other select few who have provided some of the most indelible moments in CWS lore.

Norwood blasted a tie-breaking home run in the eighth inning of the decisive third game of the CWS Finals, propelling Vanderbilt to a 3-2 win against Virginia and its first national championship.

But if Norwood had his way, the names of Carson Fulmer and Dansby Swanson, Vince Conde, Hayden Stone, Rhett Wiseman and so many others would go down in history right there with his. All of them will be remembered as part of the team that brought Vanderbilt its second national championship in any sport (the other came in women's bowling in 2007).

"I didn't bring it to them," Norwood insisted on the field after the game. "It was the people way before us, and they caused us to be here. Coach (Tim) Corbin did a great job getting a bunch of great guys year-in and year-out, and he finally got one. So it's an amazing feeling to do that for the university."

As the Commodores celebrated on the field, their alumni celebrated from afar. One Vanderbilt big leaguer after another rejoiced on Twitter, sending out heartfelt expressions of gratitude and joy for Corbin, a man they love like another father.

Corbin and his fine coaching staff have built a model program in part through their incredible ability to recruiting marquee players with winning makeup. The current groups of sophomores and juniors both rated as the No. 1 recruiting classes in college baseball when they showed up on campus in the falls of 2011 and 2012. Vanderbilt has gotten plenty of meaningful contributions from

COACHING CAROUSEL

SCHOOL	IN (PREVIOUS JOB)	OUT (REASON/NEW JOB)
Arizona State	Tracy Smith (Indiana head coach)	Tim Esmay (resigned)
Arkansas-Little Rock	Chris Curry (Northwestern State assistant)	Scott Norwood (resigned)
Brown	Grant Achilles (Brown assistant)	Marek Drabinski (resigned)
UC Riverside	Troy Percival (Moreno Valley, Calif., HS head coach)	Doug Smith (retired)
Campbell	Justin Haire (Campbell assistant)	Greg Goff (Louisiana Tech head coach)
East Carolina	Cliff Godwin (Mississippi assistant)	Billy Godwin (fired)
Eastern Michigan	Mark Van Ameyde (Michigan State assistant)	Jay Alexander (fired)
Illinois State	Bo Durkac (ISU associate head coach)	Mark Kingston (South Florida head coach)
Indiana	Chris Lemonis (Louisville assistant)	Tracy Smith (Arizona State head coach)
Long Island-Brooklyn	Alex Trezza (Sacred Heart assistant)	Don Maines (resigned)
Longwood	Ryan Mau (Navy assistant)	Brian McCullough (served as interim coach)
Louisiana Tech	Greg Goff (Campbell head coach)	Wade Simoneaux (fired)
Louisiana-Monroe	Bruce Peddie (ULM assistant)	Jeff Schexnaider (fired)
Murray State	Kevin Moulder (Saint Louis assoc head coach)	Rob McDonald (fired)
New Mexico State	Brian Green (Kentucky assistant)	Rocky Ward (fired)
UNC Asheville	Scott Friedholm (Boston College assistant)	Tom Smith (retired)
Quinnipiac	John Delaney (Quinnipiac assoc head coach)	Dan Gooley (retired)
Rhode Island	Raphael Cerrato (URI assistant)	Jim Foster (Boston College associate head coach)
Sam Houston State	Matt Deggs (Louisiana-Lafayette assistant)	David Pierce (Tulane head coach)
San Diego State	Mark Martinez (SDSU associate head coach)	Tony Gwynn (died)
South Florida	Mark Kingston (Illinois State head coach)	Lelo Prado (USF administrative role)
Tennessee-Martin	Rick Robinson (Young Harris, Ga., head coach)	Bubba Cates (UTM teaching role)
Tulane	David Pierce (Sam Houston State head coach)	Rick Jones (retired)

talented freshmen in recent years, but Norwood and righthander Adam Ravenelle were raw talents when they arrived in Nashville in 2011, and both played sparingly for loaded Vandy teams over their first two seasons.

But they kept working hard, they stayed patient and waited for their opportunities. The coaching staff stayed patient too, and helped them develop into key cogs on a championship team. With a national title hanging in the balance, it was Norwood who gave Vanderbilt the lead, and Ravenelle who preserved it, working two scoreless innings of relief for his second save of the Finals, and third of the CWS. He had no saves in his career before Omaha.

"You know who I think has to be just as patient as them is their parents, because I think a lot of times in today's world, parents have a lot of influence on their kids," Corbin said. "And for parents to sit back and say, 'It will happen, just stay with it, just stick with it,' the Ravenelles are that way, Johnny Norwood's mother is that way, and they have been patient. Because I told them they would have to wait their turn in order to get out there. But through that, and their stick-to-it-iveness, and training, and the coaches, (Travis) Jewett and (Scott) Brown, those guys have really taken off."

Virginia had erased a 2-0 deficit with two runs in the sixth inning to chase Carson Fulmer, but unlike in the sixth inning a day earlier, the

Cavaliers could not surge ahead. They stranded the bases loaded that inning against Hayden Stone, leaving the game tied heading into the eighth.

Norwood, who finished 3-for-3 with two of Vandy's three runs, came to the plate with one out in the top of the eighth and tomahawked a 97 mph fastball from UVa. closer Nick Howard into the left-field bullpen. It was just the third home run of the CWS, and the first for Vanderbilt since May 16. It was the first home run allowed all season by Howard, a first-round pick who had been dominant in his two previous CWS appearances, allowing just two hits over five shutout innings.

"I was just hoping that it didn't have enough topspin that it would hit the fence," Corbin said. "But Johnny's strength and bat speed, with the velocity of Howard—that doesn't happen to that kid. A 97 mile an hour fastball and someone to turn it around like that takes a great amount of ability. I'm just happy for Johnny . . . The kid has grown so much as a person and as a player, even in the last four weeks. You can talk to the players about his approach at the plate, his calmness, and just his overall offensive productivity. So just a big moment."

But once again, Virginia fought back in the bottom of the frame. The Cavaliers put runners on first and second with no outs in the bottom of the eighth, prompting Vanderbilt to summon Ravenelle to take over for Stone. After a sacrifice

bunt put the tying run at third and the go-ahead run at second, Ravenelle hit Kenny Towns to load the bases with one out. Then he got John La Prise to hit a chopper back to the mound and threw home for the force out. The dangerous Brandon Downes followed with a ground ball toward the hole on the left side of the infield, and Conde fielded it cleanly and made a quick transfer to get the force at second base, extinguishing the threat.

Ravenelle then worked a 1-2-3 ninth inning, striking out Branden Cogswell and Daniel Pinero to end the game and trigger a dogpile around Ravenelle on the mound.

"Coming into the College World Series, I couldn't tell you that I was going to be closing games out here," Ravenelle said. "But it's just an opportunity, and I was just trying to take it pitch by pitch, and let my defense work, and I've trusted these guys all year. These guys are the best defense in the country, so that's all I was trying to do."

With the game on the line, the sure-handed Conde made the crucial play in the eighth inning, atoning for his uncharacteristic error in the sixth,

which allowed Virginia to score the tying run. Swanson also made a standout defensive play in the sixth, diving to his left to snare a Branden Cogswell hot shot and help prevent Virginia from putting together a bigger inning. Swanson was the best all-around player in Omaha, repeatedly impacting the game with his stellar defense as well as his timely hitting. He had two more hits in the final game, including a single that led to Vanderbilt's first run in the first inning.

And Fulmer, pitching on three days' rest, held Virginia's explosive offense scoreless on one hit for the first five innings. After issuing six walks in his last start against Texas, Fulmer was much sharper in the winner-take-all showdown against UVa., walking two and allowing just three hits over 5 1/3 strong innings. It was the best outing of the CWS for a Vanderbilt starter, and it allowed the Commodores to head into the second half of the game from a position of strength. He said he did not make any adjustments from one start to the next; he was simply resolved to rise to the huge occasion—which so many Commodores have

COLLEGE WORLD SERIES CHAMPIONS

YEAR	CHAMPION	COACH	RECORD	RUNNER-UP	MOST OUTSTANDING PLAYER
1948	Southern California	Sam Barry	40-12	Yale	None selected
1949	Texas*	Bibb Falk	23-7	Wake Forest	Charles Teague, 2b, Wake Forest
1950	Texas	Bibb Falk	27-6	Washington State	Ray VanCleef, of, Rutgers
1951	Oklahoma*	Jack Baer	19-9	Tennessee	Sid Hatfield, 1b-p, Tennessee
1952	Holy Cross	Jack Barry	21-3	Missouri	Jim O'Neill, p, Holy Cross
1953	Michigan	Ray Fisher	21-9	Texas	J.L. Smith, p, Texas
1954	Missouri	Hi Simmons	22-4	Rollins	Tom Yewcic, c, Michigan State
1955	Wake Forest	Taylor Sanford	29-7	Western Michigan	Tom Borland, p, Oklahoma State
1956	Minnesota	Dick Siebert	33-9	Arizona	Jerry Thomas, p, Minnesota
1957	California*	George Wolfman	35-10	Penn State	Cal Emery, 1b-p, Penn State
1958	Southern California	Rod Dedeaux	35-7	Missouri	Bill Thom, p, Southern California
1959	Oklahoma State	Toby Greene	27-5	Arizona	Jim Dobson, 3b, Oklahoma State
1960	Minnesota	Dick Siebert	34-7	Southern California	John Erickson, 2b, Minnesota
1961	Southern California*	Rod Dedeaux	43-9	Oklahoma State	Littleton Fowler, p, Oklahoma State
1962	Michigan	Don Lund	31-13	Santa Clara	Bob Garibaldi, p, Santa Clara
1963	Southern California	Rod Dedeaux	37-16	Arizona	Bud Hollowell, c, Southern Californ
1964	Minnesota	Dick Siebert	31-12	Missouri	Joe Ferris, p, Maine
1965	Arizona State	Bobby Winkles	54-8	Ohio State	Sal Bando, 3b, Arizona State
1966	Ohio State	Marty Karow	27-6	Oklahoma State	Steve Arlin, p, Ohio State
1967	Arizona State	Bobby Winkles	53-12	Houston	Ron Davini, c, Arizona State
1968	Southern California*	Rod Dedeaux	45-14	Southern Illinois	Bill Seinsoth, 1b, Southern Californ
1969	Arizona State	Bobby Winkles	56-11	Tulsa	John Dolinsek, of, Arizona State
1970	Southern California	Rod Dedeaux	51-13	Florida State	Gene Ammann, p, Florida State
1971	Southern California	Rod Dedeaux	53-13	Southern Illinois	Jerry Tabb, 1b, Tulsa
1972	Southern California	Rod Dedeaux	50-13	Arizona State	Russ McQueen, p, Southern Califor
1973	Southern California*	Rod Dedeaux	51-11	Arizona State	Dave Winfield, of-p, Minnesota
1974	Southern California	Rod Dedeaux	50-20	Miami	George Milke, p, Southern Californ
1975	Texas	Cliff Gustafson	56-6	South Carolina	Mickey Reichenbach, 1b, Texas
1976	Arizona	Jerry Kindall	56-17	Eastern Michigan	Steve Powers, dh-p, Arizona
1977	Arizona State	Jim Brock	57-12	South Carolina	Bob Horner, 3b, Arizona State
1978	Southern California*	Rod Dedeaux	54-9	Arizona State	Rod Boxberger, p, Southern Californ
1979	Cal State Fullerton	Augie Garrido	60-14	Arkansas	Tony Hudson, p, Cal State Fullerton
1980	Arizona	Jerry Kindall	45-21	Hawaii	Terry Francona, of, Arizona
1981	Arizona State	Jim Brock	55-13	Oklahoma State	Stan Holmes, of, Arizona State

dreamed about for so long.

"You think back to the moment where you lay in bed, you toss the baseball up and you're like, 'OK.' Last year I was laying there and I said, 'Man, I just really want a national championship,'" Fulmer said while hugging the national championship trophy to his chest in a hallway underneath TD Ameritrade Park. "Going out there you throw everything away, throw the mechanics away, and you go, 'OK, I'm here to compete. I'm here to give my team a chance to win.' I couldn't tell you the first couple innings because it just goes by so quick. It's something special holding this trophy, that's for sure."

A Progression To Greatness

As talented as the Commodores were, they were the clear underdogs heading into the Finals. Virginia was the older club, with six upperclassmen in its starting lineup compared to just two for Vanderbilt. Tyler Beede was the lone upperclassman in Vandy's rotation, while Brian Miller and Ravenelle were juniors in the bullpen.

But by this point in the season, freshmen aren't freshmen anymore; both teams were battle-tested, tough and confident. Virginia, the preseason No. 1, had been a bit more consistent from start to finish this year. The Cavaliers had played like a veteran team on a mission, and their focus had never really wavered. Vanderbilt had more growing pains with its younger team. After all, the Commodores had to replace six everyday stalwarts and the ace from their 2013 team that won a record 26 games in Southeastern Conference play, earned the No. 2 national seed and lost in a super regional to Louisville.

The Commodores still brought back enough talent to rank 10th in BA's preseason Top 25, and they got off to a 16-2 start against a solid nonconference slate.

But from mid-March to mid-April, Vandy lost four series in five weeks. The Commodores rebounded with series wins against Georgia, Missouri and Florida down the stretch, then lost a home series to South Carolina to close the regular season and earn the No. 6 seed in the SEC tourna-

*Undefeated

YEAR	CHAMPION	COACH	RECORD	RUNNER-UP	MOST OUTSTANDING PLAYER
1982	Miami	Ron Fraser	57-18	Wichita State	Dan Smith, p, Miami
1983	Texas	Cliff Gustafson	66-14	Alabama	Calvin Schiraldi, p, Texas
1984	Cal State Fullerton	Augie Garrido	66-20	Texas	John Fishel, of, Cal State Fullerton
1985	Miami*	Ron Fraser	64-16	Texas	Greg Ellena, dh, Miami
1986	Arizona	Jerry Kindall	49-19	Florida State	Mike Senne, of, Arizona
1987	Stanford	Mark Marquess	53-17	Oklahoma State	Paul Carey, of, Stanford
1988	Stanford	Mark Marquess	46-23	Arizona State	Lee Plemel, p, Stanford
1989	Wichita State	Gene Stephenson	68-16	Texas	Greg Brummett, p, Wichita State
1990	Georgia	Steve Webber	52-19	Oklahoma State	Mike Rebhan, p, Georgia
1991	Louisiana State*	Skip Bertman	55-18	Wichita State	Gary Hymel, c, Louisiana State
1992	Pepperdine*	Andy Lopez	48-11	Cal State Fullerton	Phil Nevin, 3b, Cal State Fullerton
1993	Louisiana State	Skip Bertman	53-17	Wichita State	Todd Walker, 2b, Louisiana State
1994	Oklahoma*	Larry Cochell	50-17	Georgia Tech	Chip Glass, of, Oklahoma
1995	Cal State Fullerton*	Augie Garrido	57-9	Southern California	Mark Kotsay, of-p, Cal State Fullerton
1996	Louisiana State*	Skip Bertman	52-15	Miami	Pat Burrell, 3b, Miami
1997	Louisiana State*	Skip Bertman	57-13	Alabama	Brandon Larson, ss, Louisiana State
1998	Southern California	Mike Gillespie	49-17	Arizona State	Wes Rachels, 2b, Southern California
1999	Miami*	Jim Morris	50-13	Florida State	Marshall McDougall, 2b, Florida State
2000	Louisiana State*	Skip Bertman	52-17	Stanford	Trey Hodges, rhp, Louisiana State
2001	Miami*	Jim Morris	53-12	Stanford	Charlton Jimerson, of, Miami
2002	Texas*	Augie Garrido	57-15	South Carolina	Huston Street, rhp, Texas
2003	Rice	Wayne Graham	58-12	Stanford	John Hudgins, rhp, Stanford
2004	Cal State Fullerton	George Horton	47-22	Texas	Jason Windsor, rhp, Cal State Fullerton
2005	Texas*	Augie Garrido	56-16	Florida	David Maroul, 3b, Texas
2006	Oregon State	Pat Casey	50-16	North Carolina	Jonah Nickerson, rhp, Oregon State
2007	Oregon State*	Pat Casey	49-18	North Carolina	Jorge Reyes, rhp, Oregon State
2008	Fresno State	Mike Batesole	47-31	Georgia	Tommy Mendonca, 3b, Fresno State
2009	Louisiana State	Paul Mainieri	56-17	Texas	Jared Mitchell, of, Louisiana State
2010	South Carolina	Ray Tanner	54-16	UCLA	Jackie Bradley Jr., of, South Carolina
2011	South Carolina*	Ray Tanner	55-14	Florida	Scott Wingo, 2b, South Carolina
2012	Arizona*	Andy Lopez	48-17	South Carolina	Robert Refsnyder, of, Arizona
2013	UCLA*	John Savage	49-17	Mississippi State	Adam Plutko, rhp, UCLA
2014	Vanderbilt	Tim Corbin	51-21	Virginia	Dansby Swanson, 2b, Vanderbilt

ment. After a 1-2 showing in Hoover, Corbin was despondent. His pitching staff's inability to consistently throw strikes had become a major concern.

Beede, Fulmer and Walker Buehler responded the next week, giving Vandy three straight quality starts in its 3-0 run through the Nashville Regional. The Commodores beat Oregon twice in a row to win that regional, then faced another Pac-12 foe in a home super regional, after Stanford stunned national seed Indiana to win the Bloomington Regional.

Vandy's starting pitching faltered in the series against the Cardinal, but its bats and its bullpen picked up the slack. The 'Dores scored 23 runs in their two wins that weekend, sandwiched around a 5-4 loss. In a harbinger of things to come, Stone came out of the bullpen to work six brilliant innings after Buehler struggled in the decisive third game.

In Omaha, the Commodores never got a quality start in seven games, and still they won the College World Series. Stone and Ravenelle repeatedly came up huge in relief, and Buehler came out of the bullpen to fire 5 1/3 innings of no-hit relief in a win against UC Irvine. Miller followed with crucial long relief in a losing cause against Texas, working 7 1/3 innings to spare the Vandy bullpen after starter Tyler Ferguson failed to get out of the first inning.

The Commodores beat Texas the next day behind Stone, who threw 5 2/3 innings of sparkling relief after Fulmer struggled with his control in the fifth. Stone entered the game with the bases loaded and one out in the fifth, and he escaped the jam with a double play ball.

And when Stone tried to sneak a fastball past C.J Hinojosa in the 10th inning of that game, Rhett Wiseman had his back, making an improbable diving catch on the warning track. That catch, which set the stage for Tyler Campbell's walk-off infield single in the bottom of the inning, will go down as one of the great plays in Vanderbilt history.

Wiseman's catch will be remembered, and so will Campbell's hustle down the line to beat out the game-winning hit, and Stone's unhittable slider. Norwood's CWS-winning home run will be remembered most of all.

Like all champions, the Commodores caught their share of breaks along the way. But great teams create their own greatness, and this group of Commodores fought for every inch.

Cavaliers Come Close

The two most talented teams in college baseball were the last two standing in Omaha. That does

RPI RANKINGS

The Ratings Percentage Index is an important tool used by the NCAA in selecting at-large teams for the 64-team Division I regional tournament. The NCAA now releases its RPI rankings during the season. These were the top 100 finishers for 2014. A team's rank in the final Baseball America Top 25 is indicated in parentheses, and College World Series teams are in bold.

1. **Virginia** (2)	53-16	51. UC Santa Barbara 34-17
2. **Vanderbilt** (1)	51-21	52. Kennesaw State (16) 40-24
3. **Texas** (4)	46-21	53. Tennessee 31-23
4. **Mississippi** (3)	48-21	54. Western Carolina 37-18
5. Houston (11)	48-18	55. Clemson 36-25
6. La.-Lafayette (7)	58-10	56. Illinois 32-21
7. **Texas Christian** (5)	48-18	57. California 26-27
8. Florida (18)	40-23	58. Georgia 26-29
9. Indiana (21)	44-15	59. N.C. State 32-23
10. Florida State (19)	43-17	60. Ball State 39-18
11. Louisiana State (22)	46-16	61. Southern California 29-24
12. **Texas Tech** (9)	45-21	62. High Point 33-22
13. Oregon State (13)	45-14	63. Campbell 41-21
14. Rice	42-20	64. Southern Miss. 35-25
15. South Carolina (25)	44-18	65. San Diego 34-20
16. Cal Poly (20)	47-12	66. Creighton 32-17
17. Miami (23)	44-19	67. Southeastern La. 38-25
18. **Louisville** (6)	50-17	68. Canisius 40-16
19. Oklahoma State (10)	48-18	69. New Mexico 37-20
20. Kentucky	37-25	70. William & Mary 34-22
21. Maryland (14)	40-23	71. Samford 35-25
22. Pepperdine (12)	43-18	72. Southeast Mo. State 37-20
23. **UC Irvine** (8)	41-25	73. Auburn 28-28
24. Alabama	37-24	74. East Carolina 33-26
25. Washington (24)	41-17	75. Baylor 26-31
26. Oregon	44-20	76. Arkansas State 32-27
27. Stanford (15)	35-26	77. Florida Gulf Coast 39-22
28. Mississippi State	39-24	78. Alabama-Birmingham 35-21
29. Arkansas	40-25	79. Wichita State 31-28
30. Long Beach State	34-26	80. Evansville 34-21
31. Texas A&M	36-26	81. Wake Forest 30-26
32. Indiana State	35-18	82. Oklahoma 29-29
33. Nebraska	41-21	83. UC Riverside 26-28
34. Sam Houston State	43-19	84. Duke 33-25
35. UNLV	36-25	85. Va. Commonwealth 37-20
36. Georgia Tech	37-27	86. Ga. Southern 40-23
37. Dallas Baptist	40-21	87. Illinois State 33-22
38. West Virginia	28-26	88. Florida International 36-20
39. Liberty	41-18	89. Rutgers 30-25
40. San Diego State	42-21	90. Middle Tenn. State 31-27
41. Col. of Charleston (17)	44-19	91. Xavier 30-29
42. Columbia	29-20	92. Jacksonville State 36-27
43. Old Dominion	36-26	93. Texas State 30-28
44. Kansas	35-26	94. Saint Joseph's 35-16
45. North Carolina	35-27	95. Oral Roberts 30-26
46. Arizona State	33-24	96. UNC Wilmington 30-27
47. Mercer	38-17	97. Texas-Arlington 33-26
48. Cal State Fullerton	34-24	98. Radford 33-23
49. Bryant	42-16	99. Fla. Atlantic 28-25
50. Central Florida	36-23	100. Michigan State 31-26

not usually happen.

Vanderbilt and Virginia gave us a compelling series worthy of their greatness. It wasn't always clean baseball—walks and errors factored prominently in the outcome of the first and third games—but it was intense theater.

The Cavaliers outplayed the 'Dores for much of the best-of-three Finals, but Vanderbilt found

COLLEGE ALL-AMERICA TEAM

FIRST TEAM

POS.	NAME	YEAR	AVG	OBP	SLG	AB	R	H	HR	RBI	BB	SO	SB
C	Max Pentecost, Kennesaw State	Jr.	.422	.482	.627	268	59	113	9	61	30	26	17
1B	Casey Gillaspie, Wichita State	Jr.	.389	.520	.682	211	50	82	15	50	58	28	8
2B	Jace Conrad, Louisiana-Lafayette	Jr.	.364	.438	.564	264	63	96	9	65	18	27	22
3B	Dustin DeMuth, Indiana	Sr.	.374	.449	.531	211	40	79	5	40	20	40	4
SS	Trea Turner, N.C. State	Jr.	.321	.418	.516	215	65	69	8	36	37	25	26
OF	Caleb Adams, Louisiana-Lafayette	Jr.	.381	.502	.673	223	67	85	11	42	46	60	7
OF	Michael Conforto, Oregon State	Jr.	.345	.504	.547	203	52	70	7	56	55	38	4
OF	Bradley Zimmer, San Francisco	Jr.	.368	.461	.573	220	42	81	7	31	31	34	21
DH	Kyle Schwarber, Indiana	Jr.	.358	.464	.659	232	66	83	14	48	44	30	10
UT	A.J. Reed, Kentucky	Jr.	.336	.476	.735	223	60	75	23	73	49	48	0

		YEAR	W	L	ERA	G	CG	SV	IP	H	BB	SO	AVG
SP	Kyle Freeland, Evansville	Jr.	10	2	1.90	14	2	0	100	79	13	128	.214
SP	Nathan Kirby, Virginia	So.	9	3	2.06	18	1	0	113	68	33	112	.175
SP	Aaron Nola, Louisiana State	Jr.	11	1	1.47	16	2	0	116	69	27	134	.172
SP	Ben Wetzler, Oregon State	Sr.	12	1	0.78	14	4	0	104	49	31	83	.143
RP	Jacob Lindgren, Mississippi State	Jr.	6	1	0.88	25	0	3	51	20	21	93	.116
UT	A.J. Reed, Kentucky	Jr.	12	2	2.09	16	1	0	112	98	29	71	.236

SECOND TEAM

POS.	NAME	YEAR	AVG	OBP	SLG	AB	R	H	HR	RBI	BB	SO	SB
C	Grayson Greiner, South Carolina	Jr.	.311	.389	.486	212	35	82	5	38	22	28	2
1B	Sam Travis, Indiana	Jr.	.347	.415	.576	245	55	85	12	58	25	26	8
2B	Mark Mathias, Cal Poly	So.	.376	.448	.483	205	48	77	2	39	23	18	12
3B	Alex Blandino, Stanford	Jr.	.310	.397	.531	226	49	70	12	44	30	33	2
SS	Blake Trahan, Louisiana-Lafayette	So.	.355	.455	.465	256	58	91	4	49	44	37	15
OF	Jordan Luplow, Fresno State	Jr.	.377	.475	.609	215	40	81	9	48	36	22	10
OF	D.J. Stewart, Florida State	So.	.351	.472	.557	194	45	68	7	50	40	30	4
OF	Drew Weeks, North Florida	Jr.	.430	.478	.606	221	52	95	6	38	18	20	10
DH	Michael Katz, William & Mary	Jr.	.363	.445	.646	240	64	87	14	75	32	43	0
UT	Aaron Brown, Pepperdine	Jr.	.314	.354	.554	242	44	76	13	49	9	52	5

		YEAR	W	L	ERA	G	CG	SV	IP	H	BB	SO	AVG
SP	Thomas Eshelman, Cal State Fullerton	So.	8	3	1.89	16	5	0	124	100	8	99	.222
SP	Jace Fry, Oregon State	Jr.	11	2	1.80	16	4	0	120	83	30	98	.196
SP	Andrew Morales, UC Irvine	Sr.	11	2	1.53	19	3	0	136	89	33	141	.185
SP	Preston Morrison, Texas Christian	Jr.	9	4	1.32	18	5	0	130	90	21	95	.197
RP	Brendan McCurry, Oklahoma State	Sr.	5	0	0.38	35	0	19	47	29	8	54	.178
UT	Aaron Brown, Pepperdine	Jr.	13	1	1.95	17	1	0	116	84	40	104	.212

THIRD TEAM

POS.	NAME	YEAR	AVG	OBP	SLG	AB	R	H	HR	RBI	BB	SO	SB
C	Brett Austin, N.C. State	Jr.	.344	.414	.516	215	42	74	5	31	27	29	8
1B	Connor Joe, San Diego	Jr.	.367	.462	.606	218	59	80	9	51	32	24	3
2B	Dansby Swanson, Vanderbilt	So.	.333	.411	.475	282	63	94	3	34	37	49	22
3B	Matt Chapman, Cal State Fullerton	Jr.	.312	.412	.498	205	37	64	6	48	27	26	6
SS	Michael Russell, North Carolina	Jr.	.339	.424	.496	230	43	78	4	32	29	27	13
OF	Auston Bousfield, Mississippi	Jr.	.336	.393	.476	286	61	96	6	50	20	27	19
OF	Zach Fish, Oklahoma State	Jr.	.308	.390	.517	240	41	74	11	48	32	56	4
OF	Mark Payton, Texas	Sr.	.315	.456	.444	241	33	76	2	39	57	27	19
DH	Ty France, San Diego State	So.	.356	.450	.498	233	55	83	5	45	28	25	3
UT	Louie Lechich, San Diego	Sr.	.342	.396	.542	225	45	77	7	46	16	30	3

		YEAR	W	L	ERA	G	CG	SV	IP	H	BB	SO	AVG
SP	Brandon Finnegan, Texas Christian	Jr.	9	3	2.04	17	1	0	106	79	29	134	.210
SP	Kyle Funkhouser, Louisville	So.	13	3	1.94	18	0	0	120	85	65	122	.201
SP	Sean Newcomb, Hartford	Jr.	8	2	1.25	14	1	0	93	51	38	106	.162
SP	Josh Prevost, Seton Hall	Sr.	12	1	1.62	15	6	0	116	64	20	111	.158
RP	Ryan Thompson, Campbell	Sr.	7	2	1.33	39	0	17	88	71	29	87	.219
UT	Louie Lechich, San Diego	Sr.	8	3	1.51	13	1	0	82	82	21	50	.265

a way to win the national championship anyway. In Game One, UVa. first-team All-America ace Nathan Kirby shockingly and abruptly lost the ability to throw strikes in the third inning, leading to a nine-run frame for Vanderbilt.

Virginia still almost found a way to win that game, cutting the deficit to 9-8 in the eighth inning and putting the tying run on third base, but the Cavaliers could not get the big hit to push the runner home. The story was the same in the

decisive third game; Virginia came from behind for the second straight day to tie the score in the sixth inning, but it stranded the bases loaded in that frame. Vandy took the lead on Norwood's eighth-inning home run, and again UVa. fought back to load the bases with one out in the bottom of the inning. And again, the Cavaliers failed to push across the tying run.

"Throughout the course of the game, we did a good job getting guys on base," Virginia outfielder Joe McCarthy said. "But it comes down to we never got that big hit to bust it open. Guys were hitting the ball hard, but just couldn't get that big one."

CWS NOTES

■ The SEC has been college baseball's best conference over the last decade. Vanderbilt is the sixth different SEC school to reach the finals over the past seven years, joining Georgia, LSU, Florida, South Carolina (three straight years) and Mississippi State. That is a loud testament to the SEC's famous depth. The conference also has won four national titles in the past six years, and 10 championships in the past 25 years—quite a stretch of prolonged excellence. In that same 25-year period, the Pacific-12/Pac-10 has won five titles, the second-most of any league. And nine of the SEC's 14 current members have been to the College World Series at least once in the last seven years. Mississippi is the newest member of that club after it finally returned to Omaha in 2014 for the first time since 1972.

■ The overall College World Series attendance of 347,740 was a new record, but its per-game attendance declined dramatically from a year ago, dropping from 24,392 to 21,733. The CWS averaged 22,977 fans per game in the first year at TD Ameritrade park in 2011, and 21,782 per game in 2012. So the 2014 attendance is actually in line with the norm. But the attendance for the final game was still disappointing. Only 18,344 fans showed up to watch a winner-takes-the-title showdown, down from 27,127 in the second (and last) game of last year's Finals.

But CWS officials aren't concerned about the drop. CWS Inc. president Jack Diesing Jr. told the Associated Press that the 2013 attendance was an "anomaly" because LSU and Mississippi State brought strong fan followings to Omaha.

"Actually, we think it's quite an accomplishment to average 22,000 people watching college baseball where there is no home run," Diesing told the AP.

■ There were just three home runs in the CWS for the second straight year, but one of them—Norwood's shot in the eighth inning of the last game—proved to be the title-winner. It's not just power that's down—the eight CWS teams hit an aggregate .219, down from .237 a year ago, .234 in 2012 and .239 in 2011. The CWS also tied the metal-bat record for most sacrifice bunts in a Series (37), set in 2011.

■ If Virginia had won the final game against Vanderbilt, senior righty Artie Lewicki would likely have won the CWS Most Outstanding Player award. Lewicki, an eighth-round pick of the

COLLEGE WORLD SERIES

STANDINGSB

BRACKET ONE	W	L
Vanderbilt	3	1
Texas	2	2
UC Irvine	1	2
Louisville	0	2

BRACKET TWO	W	L
Virginia	3	0
Mississippi	2	2
Texas Christian	1	2
Texas Tech	0	2

CWS FINALS (BEST OF THREE)
June 23: Vanderbilt 9, Virginia 8
June 24: Virginia 7, Vanderbilt 2
June 24: Vanderbilt 3, Virginia 2

ALL-TOURNAMENT TEAM
C: Nate Irving, Virginia. **1B:** Kevin Cron, TCU. **2B:** Branden Cogswell, Virginia. **3B:** Tyler Campbell, Vanderbilt. **SS:** C.J Hinojosa, Texas. **OF:** Brandon Downes, Virginia; John Norwood, Vanderbilt; Rhett Wiseman, Vanderbilt. **DH:** *Dansby Swanson, Vanderbilt. **P:** Artie Lewicki, Virginia; Brandon Waddell, Virginia. *Named Most Outstanding Player.

BATTING
(Minimum 8 PA)

PLAYER AVG	AB	R	H	2B	3B	HR	RBI	SB
Adam Kirsch, TTU	.500	0	4	0	1	0	0	0
Stephen Smith, TTU	.429	0	3	0	0	0	0	0
Kyle Gibson, UofL	.429	0	3	0	0	0	1	0
John Norwood, Vandy	.400	5	10	1	0	1	6	4
Robbie Coman, UVa	.400	1	4	1	0	0	2	0
Branden Cogswell, UVa	.391	4	9	2	0	0	2	0
Alex Chittenden, UofL	.375	0	3	0	0	0	0	0
Adam Alcantara, UCI	.375	2	3	0	0	1	0	0
Collin Shaw, Texas	.333	2	6	1	0	0	0	0
Zane Gurwitz, Texas	.333	2	6	1	1	0	2	0

PITCHING
(Minimum 6 IP)

PITCHER	W-L	ERA	G	SV	IP	H	BB	SO
Artie Lewicki, UVa	2-0	0.00	0	13	5	3	10	
Chad Hollingsworth, Texas	1-0	0.00	1	8	4	0	5	
Christian Trent, Ole Miss	0-0	0.00	1	0	8	6	1	6
Ryan Moseley, TTU	0-0	0.00	1	0	7	4	3	6
Brandon Waddell, UVa	1-0	1.12	2	0	16	11	3	10
Brandon Finnegan, TCU	0-0	1.12	1	0	8	9	2	5
Nathan Thornhill, Texas	1-1	1.17	2	0	15	12	2	9
Evan Brock, UC Irvine	1-0	1.17	3	0	8	4	1	8
Preston Morrison, TCU	0-0	1.23	1	0	7	5	2	10
Chris Sadberry, TTU	0-0	1.29	1	0	7	3	2	5

Detroit Tigers, was brilliant in four relief appearances in Omaha, allowing just one unearned run over 13 innings of work while striking out 10. He yielded just five hits and three walks, and he gave Virginia a chance in the final game by working six sterling innings of relief on three days' rest.

"You go to somebody that started his whole career, and you go to him the day before the first game in Omaha, and you have an honest, man-to-man conversation with somebody that this is what we need to do to win in Omaha: We need to put you in the bullpen," O'Connor said. "And the response being, 'Coach, whatever I need to do to help the team win.'"

REGIONALS

MAY 30-JUNE 2

64 teams, 16 four-team, double-elimination tournaments. Winners advance to super regionals.

CORVALLIS, ORE.

Host: Oregon State (No. 1 national seed).
Participants: No. 1 Oregon State (42-14), No. 2 UNLV (35-23), No. 3 UC Irvine (35-22), No. 4 North Dakota State (25-24).
Champion: UC Irvine (3-1).
Runner-up: Oregon State (3-2).
Outstanding player: Connor Spencer, 1b, UC Irvine.

STILLWATER, OKLA.

Host: Oklahoma State.
Participants: No. 1 Oklahoma State (45-16), No. 2 Nebraska (40-19), No. 3 Cal State Fullerton (32-22), No. 4 Binghamton (25-25).
Champion: Oklahoma State (3-0).
Runner-up: Cal State Fullerton (2-2).
Outstanding player: Donnie Walton, ss, Oklahoma State.

HOUSTON

Host: Rice.
Participants: No. 1 Rice (41-18), No. 2 Texas (38-18), No. 3 Texas A&M (33-24), No. 4 George Mason (34-20).
Champion: Texas (3-1).
Runner-up: Texas A&M (3-2).
Outstanding player: Chad Hollingsworth, rhp, Texas; Mark Payton, of, Texas.

BATON ROUGE, LA.

Host: Louisiana State (No. 8 national seed).
Participants: No. 1 Louisiana State (44-14-1), No. 2 Houston (44-15), No. 3 Bryant (42-14), No. 4 Southeastern Louisiana (37-23).
Champion: Houston (4-1).
Runner-up: Louisiana State (2-2).
Outstanding player: Kyle Survance, of, Houston.

TALLAHASSEE, FLA.

Host: Florida State (No. 5 national seed).
Participants: No. 1 Florida State (43-15), No. 2 Alabama (34-22), No. 3 Kennesaw State (37-21), No. 4 Georgia Southern (39-21).
Champion: Kennesaw State (3-1).
Runner-up: Alabama (3-2).
Outstanding player: Travis Bergen, lhp, Kennesaw State.

LOUISVILLE

Host: Louisville.
Participants: No. 1 Louisville (45-15), No. 2 Kentucky (35-23), No. 3 Kansas (34-24), No. 4 Kent State (36-21).
Champion: Louisville (3-0).
Runner-up: Kentucky (2-2).
Outstanding player: Cole Sturgeon, of/lhp, Louisville.

NASHVILLE

Host: Vanderbilt.
Participants: No. 1 Vanderbilt (41-18), No. 2 Oregon (42-18), No. 3 Clemson (36-23), No. 4 Xavier (29-17).
Champion: Vanderbilt (3-0).
Runner-up: Oregon (2-2).
Outstanding player: Tyler Beede, rhp, Vanderbilt.

BLOOMINGTON, IND.

Host: Indiana (No. 4 national seed).
Participants: No. 1 Indiana (42-13), No. 2 Indiana State (35-16), No. 3 Stanford (30-23), No. 4 Youngstown State (16-36).
Champion: Stanford (4-1).
Runner-up: Indiana (2-2).
Outstanding player: Tommy Edman, ss, Stanford.

GAINESVILLE

Host: Florida (No. 2 national seed).
Participants: No. 1 Florida (40-21), No. 2 Long Beach State (32-24), No. 3 North Carolina (34-25), No. 4 College of Charleston (41-17).
Champion: College of Charleston (3-0).
Runner-up: Long Beach State (2-2).
Outstanding player: Tyler Thornton, rhp, College of Charleston.

CORAL GABLES, FLA.

Host: Miami.
Participants: No. 1 Miami (41-17), No. 2 Texas Tech (40-18), No. 3 Columbia (29-18), No. 4 Bethune-Cookman (26-31).
Champion: Texas Tech (3-1).
Runner-up: Miami (3-2).
Outstanding player: Dylan Dusek, lhp, Texas Tech.

SAN LUIS OBISPO, CALIF.

Host: Cal Poly.
Participants: No. 1 Cal Poly (45-10), No. 2 Arizona State (33-22), No. 3 Pepperdine (39-16), No. 4 Sacramento State (39-22).
Champion: Pepperdine (3-0).
Runner-up: Cal Poly (2-2).
Outstanding player: Bryan Langlois, of, Pepperdine.

FORT WORTH, TEXAS

Host: Texas Christian (No. 7 national seed).
Participants: No. 1 Texas Christian (42-15), No. 2 Dallas Baptist (40-19), No. 3 Sam Houston State (41-17), No. 4 Siena (26-31).
Champion: Texas Christian (3-0).
Runner-up: Sam Houston State (2-2).
Outstanding player: Boomer White, of, Texas Christian.

LAFAYETTE, LA.

Host: Louisiana-Lafayette (No. 6 national seed).
Participants: No. 1 Louisiana-Lafayette (53-7), No. 2 Mississippi State (37-22), No. 3 San Diego State (42-19), No. 4 Jackson State (31-23).
Champion: Louisiana-Lafayette (4-1).
Runner-up: Mississippi State (2-2).
Outstanding player: Jace Conrad, 2b, Louisiana-Lafayette.

OXFORD, MISS.

Host: Mississippi.
Participants: No. 1 Mississippi (41-18), No. 2 Washington (39-15-1), No. 3 Georgia Tech (36-25), No. 4 Jacksonville State (36-25).
Champion: Mississippi (3-0).
Runner-up: Washington (2-2).
Outstanding player: Sikes Orvis, 1b, Mississippi.

COLUMBIA, S.C.

Host: South Carolina.
Participants: No. 1 South Carolina (42-16), No. 2 Maryland (36-21), No. 3 Old Dominion (36-24), No. 4 Campbell (40-19).
Champion: Maryland (3-0).
Runner-up: South Carolina (2-2).
Outstanding player: Charlie White, of, Maryland.

CHARLOTTESVILLE, VA.

Host: Virginia (No. 3 national seed).
Participants: No. 1 Virginia (44-13), No. 2 Arkansas (38-23), No. 3 Liberty (41-16), No. 4 Bucknell (30-19-1).
Champion: Virginia (3-0).
Runner-up: Arkansas (2-2).
Outstanding player: Nathan Kirby, lhp, Virginia.

SUPER REGIONALS

JUNE 6-9

16 teams, best-of-three series. Winners advance to College World Series.

UC IRVINE AT OKLAHOMA STATE

Site: Stillwater, Okla.
UC Irvine wins 2-0, advances to CWS.

HOUSTON AT TEXAS

Site: Austin, Texas.
Houston wins 2-0, advances to CWS.

KENNESAW STATE AT LOUISVILLE

Site: Louisville.
Louisville wins 2-0, advances to CWS.

STANFORD AT VANDERBILT

Site: Nashville.
Vanderbilt wins 2-1, advances to CWS.

COLLEGE OF CHARLESTON AT TEXAS TECH

Site: Lubbock, Texas.
Texas Tech wins 2-0, advances to CWS.

PEPPERDINE AT TEXAS CHRISTIAN

Site: Fort Worth, Texas.
Texas Christian wins 2-1, advances to CWS.

MISSISSIPPI AT LOUISIANA-LAFAYETTE

Site: Lafayette, La.
Mississippi wins 2-1, advances to CWS.

MARYLAND AT VIRGINIA

Site: Charlottesville, Va.
Virginia wins 2-1, advances to CWS.

Reed makes mark as two-way star

PLAYER OF THE YEAR

Not since John Olerud has a college baseball player had the kind of two-way impact A.J. Reed did for Kentucky in 2014.

Olerud, the 1988 Baseball America College Player of the Year for Washington State, has been the gold standard for two-way brilliance since hitting .464 with 23 homers and going 15-0, 2.49 on the mound 26 years ago. But in a number of ways, Reed raised the bar this spring, earning him the 2014 BA Player of the Year Award.

Using deadened BBCOR bats, Reed smacked 23 home runs as well, matching Olerud's total with supercharged bats. Reed led the nation in homers, slugging percentage (.735) and OPS (1.211), while ranking third in total bases (164) and RBIs (73). He hit .336 with a .476 on-base percentage, walking (49) more than he struck out (48).

That offensive season alone would make him worthy of the Player of the Year award, but Reed also went 12-2, 2.09 in 112 innings as Kentucky's Friday night ace in the rugged Southeastern Conference. He led the SEC in wins, falling one win shy of the national lead..

We asked Reed's coach, and those who coached against him, to weigh in on his historic season.

Coaches' Take

"He's grown up through the three years he's been with us, which is awesome to see. He and I had some real heart-to-hearts in August. You illustrate the path that they need to travel in order to get better, and he bought in.

"I'm saying, 'You've got to lose 25 pounds and you've got to start looking at yourself as a real guy. You've got to take the steps necessary to do that.' What's that mean, what's that entail? That's not a five-minute conversation; it's not a one-time conversation either . . . The guy made a commitment to become great, he really did. And I'm just really proud of him."

—Gary Henderson, Kentucky

"He is a threat every time he comes to the plate. He handles himself very well. He does everything that you want your National Player of the Year to do. He reminds me of (College Baseball Hall of Famer) Brad Wilkerson that was at Florida; he reminds me of (1993 BA Player of the Year) Brooks Kieschnick that was at Texas—great two-way players in this game."

—Scott Stricklin, Georgia

"The numbers he's put up in this conference, it's unbelievable to be honest with you. And not only what he's done at the plate, but what he's done on the mound . . . You don't put up those type of numbers in what I feel like is the best conference in America, especially in today's era where the bats have changed."

—Dave Serrano, Tennessee

"To watch him take BP and to watch him in the games, a lot of different teams played the shift on him and tried a lot of different things and obviously pitched around him every chance they got—I know we did—and it didn't matter. He still made a difference in each and every game. Just special."

—Rob Childress, Texas A&M

ROBERT GURGANUS

A.J. Reed

PREVIOUS WINNERS

1982: Jeff Ledbetter, of/lhp, Florida State
1983: Dave Magadan, 1b, Alabama
1984: Oddibe McDowell, of, Arizona State
1985: Pete Incaviglia, of, Oklahoma State
1986: Casey Close, of, Michigan
1987: Robin Ventura, 3b, Oklahoma State
1988: John Olerud, 1b/lhp, Washington St.
1989: Ben McDonald, rhp, Louisiana State
1990: Mike Kelly, of, Arizona State
1991: David McCarthy, 1b, Stanford
1992: Phil Nevin, 3b, Cal State Fullerton

1993: Brooks Kieschnick, dh/rhp, Texas
1994: Jason Varitek, c, Georgia Tech
1995: Todd Helton, 1b/lhp, Tennessee
1996: Kris Benson, rhp, Clemson
1997: J.D. Drew, of, Florida State
1998: Jeff Austin, rhp, Stanford
1999: Jason Jennings, rhp, Baylor
2000: Mark Teixeira, 3b, Georgia Tech
2001: Mark Prior, rhp, Southern California
2002: Khalil Greene, ss, Clemson
2003: Rickie Weeks, 2b, Southern

2004: Jered Weaver, rhp, Long Beach State
2005: Alex Gordon, 3b, Nebraska
2006: Andrew Miller, lhp, North Carolina
2007: David Price, lhp, Vanderbilt
2008: Buster Posey, c/rhp, Florida State
2009: Stephen Strasburg, rhp, San Diego St.
2010: Anthony Rendon, 3b, Rice
2011: Trevor Bauer, rhp, UCLA
2012: Mike Zunino, c, Florida
2013: Kris Bryant, 3b, San Diego

Corbin raises bar at Vandy again

BY AARON FITT

OMAHA

Finally, Tim Corbin was in the middle of the party.

As Vanderbilt players celebrated the program's first national championship on the makeshift dais on the field at TD Ameritrade Park, they hefted Corbin onto their shoulders. He looked around at the scene, his face a picture of fatherly pride while he fought back tears. It was an unfamiliar spot for Corbin, who usually watches on-field celebrations from the dugout when his Commodores win regionals, super regionals or other big games.

"It's the best feeling in the world. It's the parent just watching your kids open the Christmas gift," Corbin said after watching his team celebrate a trip to the CWS Finals a few days earlier. "You don't hustle under the tree and start opening yours with them. I don't want to be in that mess; I just want to watch it. I think that's the part that coaches get. That's the gratification of watching your kids celebrate moments like that and just being able to take it in, and I just enjoy it."

Corbin can't help but view his team as a father would view his children. He often speaks of the family atmosphere surrounding the Vanderbilt program, and his players have bought in to that vision. It's a major reason Vanderbilt has become a model program, and a big reason Corbin is Baseball America's 2014 College Coach of the Year.

COACH OF THE YEAR

"The Vanderbilt way. First off, it's a brotherhood," Vandy second baseman Dansby Swanson said before the CWS Finals. "It's a family. It's faith in one another. It's loving the guy to your left, right, no matter what. And on the field it's trying to be the best at everything . . . It's the whole package. And we pride ourselves on loving each other and always being there and just creating that type of family atmosphere."

After Swanson was announced as Most Outstanding Player of the College World Series, Corbin wrapped him in a huge bear hug before he climbed the dais to accept his award. Both were overcome with emotion.

Tim Corbin

"You know, he's like my second dad," Swanson said moments later. "He's the greatest guy, and to win something like this for him, as a team, you can't even control your emotions with it, really. I mean, I've already cried twice hugging him. I love him to death, and I know every other player does, and we respect him. I think he's the best coach in college baseball. He's a leader, he's a mentor, and he lives out his life the way he preaches. And that means a lot."

When Vanderbilt hired Corbin to take over its baseball program after the 2002 season, the Commodores had been to just three regionals ever, and none since 1980. They had never sniffed Omaha. Vandy has made 10 regionals since 2004, winning five of them. The 'Dores broke through to Omaha for the first time in 2011. Now, Corbin has led them to the very pinnacle of college baseball.

PREVIOUS WINNERS

1982: Gene Stephenson, Wichita State	**1993:** Gene Stephenson, Wichita State	**2004:** David Perno, Georgia
1983: Barry Shollenberger, Alabama	**1994:** Jim Morris, Miami	**2005:** Rick Jones, Tulane
1984: Augie Garrido, Cal State Fullerton	**1995:** Pat Murphy, Arizona State	**2006:** Pat Casey, Oregon State
1985: Ron Polk, Mississippi State	**1996:** Skip Bertman, Louisiana State	**2007:** Dave Serrano, UC Irvine
1986: Skip Bertman, LSU/Dave Snow, LMU	**1997:** Jim Wells, Alabama	**2008:** Mike Fox, North Carolina
1987: Mark Marquess, Stanford	**1998:** Pat Murphy, Arizona State	**2009:** Paul Mainieri, Louisiana State
1988: Jim Brock, Arizona State	**1999:** Wayne Graham, Rice	**2010:** Ray Tanner, South Carolina
1989: Dave Snow, Long Beach State	**2000:** Ray Tanner, South Carolina	**2011:** Kevin O'Sullivan, Florida
1990: Steve Webber, Georgia	**2001:** Dave Van Horn, Nebraska	**2012:** Mike Martin, Florida State
1991: Jim Hendry, Creighton	**2002:** Augie Garrido, Texas	**2013:** John Savage, UCLA
1992: Andy Lopez, Pepperdine	**2003:** George Horton, Cal State Fullerton	

Collins adds to Miami's legacy

FRESHMAN OF THE YEAR

BY AARON FITT

Zack Collins is the sixth Miami Hurricane to win Baseball America's Freshman of the Year Award, following in the footsteps of Chris Hernandez, Ryan Braun, Kevin Howard, Pat Burrell and Alex Fernandez. Adding his name to that prestigious list means something to Collins, a lifelong Miami fan with a deep appreciation for the program's heritage.

"I grew up as a Hurricanes fan, I knew a lot of guys who played there, and a lot of alumni I grew up watching, they helped me out," Collins said.

When Collins showed up on campus as a college freshman last fall, he was the team's best hitter. So coach Jim Morris didn't panic when he started his collegiate career in an 0-for-17 slump. And

Zack Collins

Collins rewarded his coach's faith by putting together the loudest offensive season by any freshman in college baseball in 2014, hitting .298/.427/.556 with 11 home runs and 54 RBIs.

Midway through the season, Collins also took over as Miami's everyday catcher, after spending time in the first half at first base.

Morris said Miami's veteran weekend rotation isn't easy to catch, as Chris Diaz has late, hard movement on his sinker, and Bryan Radziewski relies heavily on his breaking ball, frequently burying it in the dirt.

"I think he's got some work to do, but to me, he's a prototype pro catcher . . . If he hits, they'll find a place for him to play," Morris said. "But I think he has a chance to catch at the next level, and when I say that, I mean in the bigs. He's going to hit. He's got a natural swing, he's got lift, and the ball screams off his bat."

PREVIOUS WINNERS

1982: Cory Snyder, 3b, Brigham Young
1983: Rafael Palmeiro, of, Mississippi State
1984: Greg Swindell, lhp, Texas
1985: Jack McDowell, rhp, Stanford
1986: Robin Ventura, 3b, Oklahoma State
1987: Paul Carey, of, Stanford
1988: Kirk Dressendorfer, rhp, Texas
1989: Alex Fernandez, rhp, Miami
1990: Jeffrey Hammonds, of, Stanford
1991: Brooks Kieschnick, rhp-dh, Texas
1992: Todd Walker, 2b, Louisiana State
1993: Brett Laxton, rhp, Louisiana State
1994: R.A. Dickey, rhp, Tennessee
1995: Kyle Peterson, rhp, Stanford
1996: Pat Burrell, 3b, Miami
1997: Brian Roberts, ss, North Carolina
1998: Xavier Nady, 2b, California
1999: James Jurries, 2b, Tulane
2000: Kevin Howard, 3b, Miami
2001: Michael Aubrey, of/lhp, Texas
2002: Stephen Drew, ss, Florida State
2003: Ryan Braun, ss, Miami
2004: Wade LeBlanc, lhp, Alabama
2005: Joe Savery, lhp, Rice
2006: Pedro Alvarez, 3b, Vanderbilt
2007: Dustin Ackley, 1b, North Carolina
2008: Chris Hernandez, lhp, Miami
2009: Anthony Rendon, 3b, Rice
2010: Matt Purke, lhp, Texas Christian
2011: Colin Moran, 3b, North Carolina
2012: Carlos Rodon, lhp, N.C. State
2013: Alex Bregman, ss, Louisiana State

FRESHMAN ALL-AMERICA TEAMS

FIRST TEAM

POS.	AVG	OBP	SLG	AB	R	H	HR	RBI	SB
C Aaron Barnett, Pepperdine	.359	.384	.390	223	23	80	0	27	1
1B Nick Pappas, Col. of Charleston	.269	.321	.406	197	33	53	5	26	3
2B Brandon Lowe, Maryland	.348	.464	.464	181	35	63	1	42	8
3B Sheldon Neuse, Oklahoma	.304	.369	.521	240	43	73	7	47	7
SS Garrett Hampson, Long Beach	.300	.419	.389	203	34	61	1	47	21
OF Austin Miller, Loyola Marymount	.374	.474	.451	206	46	77	0	18	25
OF Bryan Reynolds, Vanderbilt	.341	.397	.494	261	51	89	4	53	13
OF Heath Quinn, Samford	.319	.398	.533	229	49	73	9	48	2
DH Zack Collins, Miami	.298	.427	.556	205	32	61	11	54	0
UT Alex Robles, Austin Peay	.349	.444	.444	169	35	73	1	39	2

	W	L	ERA	G	SV	IP	H	BB	SO	BAA
SP Bailey Ober, Col. of Charleston	10	3	1.52	17	0	107	73	19	85	.192
SP Cal Quantrill, Stanford	7	5	2.68	18	0	111	90	34	98	.221
SP Logan Shore, Florida	7	4	2.16	16	0	96	86	20	68	.241
SP Keegan Thompson, Auburn	5	3	2.01	14	1	90	61	23	73	.192
RP Bryan Garcia, Miami	7	4	1.75	31	15	51	40	19	56	.220
UT Alex Robles, Austin Peay State	6	2	3.63	16	0	84	97	20	56	.284

SECOND TEAM

C—Tres Barrera, Texas (.265-5-35). **1B**—Bobby Dalbec, Arizona (.266-2-30). **2B**—Jake Noll, Florida Gulf Coast (.367-0-29). **3B**—Andrew Knizner, North Carolina State (.330-4-47). **SS**—David Fletcher, Loyola Marymount (.329-0-28). **OF**—Nick Banks, Texas A&M (.327-2-26); Ryan Boldt, Nebraska (.311-2-31); J.B. Woodman (.298-2-20). **DH**—Nick Solak, Louisville (.351-2-25). **UT**—Trenton Brooks, Nevada (.330-3-35; 3-1, 3.86, 28 IP/20 SO). **SP**—Tyler Alexander, Texas Christian (10-3, 2.16, 96 IP/58 SO); Wil Crowe, South Carolina (8-3, 2.75, 92 IP/59 SO); Jared Piche', Louisiana State (9-3, 2.45, 92 IP/52 SO); Mike Shawaryn, Maryland (11-4, 3.12, 92 IP/72 SO). **RP**—Hayden Stone, Vanderbilt (2-0, 1.78, 3 SV, 51 IP/68 SO)

COLLEGE

HITTING
Minimum 3.0 plate appearances per team game. Players must appear in 75 percent of team games.

BATTING AVERAGE

RANK NAME, TEAM	CL	G	AB	H	AVG
1. Drew Weeks, North Florida	Jr.	53	221	95	.430
2. Max Pentecost, Kennesaw State	Jr.	64	268	113	.422
3. Caleb Howell, Eastern Ill.	Jr.	55	224	94	.420
4. Casey Jones, Elon	Jr.	53	196	82	.418
5. Scott Schaub, Jacksonville	Sr.	47	172	70	.407
6. DJ Miller, Delaware State	Sr.	43	151	61	.404
7. Derek Gibson, Southeast Mo. State	Sr.	57	226	91	.403
8. Robbie Knightes, St. John's	Fr.	46	138	55	.399
9. Andrew Utterback, Alabama A&M	Jr.	53	171	68	.398
10. Bobby Ison, Charleston So.	Jr.	56	230	91	.396
11. Tim Swatek, Fordham	Sr.	54	186	73	.392
12. Spencer Angelis, High Point	Jr.	55	212	83	.392
13. Brandon Rawe, Morehead State	Jr.	57	251	98	.390
14. Bennie Robinson, Florida A&M	Sr.	52	213	83	.390
15. Jameson Fisher, Southeastern La.	So.	63	239	93	.389
16. Tj Olesczuk, Winthrop	Sr.	49	180	70	.389
17. Casey Gillaspie, Wichita State	Jr.	59	211	82	.389
18. Matt Tellor, Southeast Mo. State	Sr.	57	233	90	.386
19. Scotty Peavey, Alcorn	Jr.	47	171	66	.386
20. Brian Rowry, Southern	Sr.	35	127	49	.386
21. Mark Mathias, Cal Poly	So.	58	210	81	.386
22. Mike Alexander, Delaware State	Sr.	43	153	59	.386
23. Caleb Adams, La.-Lafayette	Jr.	67	223	85	.381
24. Griff Gordon, Jacksonville State	Sr.	63	263	100	.380
25. Daniel Miles, Tennessee Tech	Sr.	58	237	90	.380
26. Doug Votolato, Central Ark.	Sr.	52	219	83	.379
27. Hunter King, UNC Greensboro	Jr.	48	198	75	.379
Lee Longo, Eastern Mich.	Sr.	52	198	75	.379
29. Tim Colwell, North Dakota State	Sr.	51	201	76	.378
30. Jordan Luplow, Fresno State	Jr.	57	215	81	.377
31. Chase Harris, New Mexico	Sr.	58	247	93	.377
32. Joey Epperson, UC Santa Barbara	Sr.	52	197	74	.376
33. Dustin DeMuth, Indiana	Sr.	57	211	79	.374
34. Austin Miller, Loyola Marymount	Fr.	56	206	77	.374
35. Robby Enslen, Oakland	Jr.	45	180	67	.372
36. Justin Korenblatt, La Salle	Jr.	49	191	71	.372
37. Byron Campbell, Md.-Eastern Shore	Sr.	46	167	62	.371
38. Connor Marabell, Jacksonville	So.	48	178	66	.371
39. David Kimbrough, Delaware State	Jr.	36	108	40	.370
40. Andrew Daniel, San Diego	Jr.	52	222	82	.369
41. Bobby Webb, LIU Brooklyn	Jr.	48	176	65	.369
42. Andrew Clow, Mt. St. Mary's	Jr.	41	141	52	.369
43. Robby Sunderman, Dayton	Sr.	54	217	80	.369
44. Lee Miller, Davidson	So.	46	152	56	.368
45. Bradley Zimmer, San Francisco	Jr.	54	220	81	.368
46. Aramis Garcia, Fla. International	Jr.	45	163	60	.368
47. Nick Thompson, William & Mary	Jr.	56	231	85	.368
48. Ryan Bottger, Texas-Arlington	Jr.	55	204	75	.368
49. Ryan Solberg, Milwaukee	Sr.	49	185	68	.368
50. Anthony Azar, Sam Houston State	Sr.	60	234	86	.368
Dylan Bosheers, Tennessee Tech	Jr.	59	234	86	.368
52. Jordan McDonald, UNC Greensboro	Jr.	45	166	61	.367
53. Jake Noll, Fla. Gulf Coast	Fr.	61	275	101	.367
54. Connor Joe, San Diego	Jr.	53	218	80	.367
55. Bill Bereszniewicz, Binghamton	Sr.	52	210	77	.367
56. David MacKinnon, Hartford	Fr.	41	131	48	.366
57. Payden Cawley Lamb, Gonzaga	Sr.	48	172	63	.366
58. John Ziznewski, LIU Brooklyn	Sr.	51	197	72	.365
59. Jake Yacinich, Iowa	Jr.	53	208	76	.365
60. Anthony Massicci, Canisius	So.	52	173	63	.364
61. Connor Spencer, UC Irvine	Jr.	66	250	91	.364
62. Forrest Brandt, Davidson	Sr.	48	187	68	.364
Jace Conrad, La.-Lafayette	Jr.	68	264	96	.364
64. Jimmy Luppens, Canisius	Sr.	55	190	69	.363
65. Michael Katz, William & Mary	Jr.	56	240	87	.363
Brett Pirtle, Mississippi State	Jr.	63	240	87	.363
67. Reagan Fowler, Creighton	So.	50	185	67	.362
68. Aaron Nardone, Delaware State	Sr.	47	152	55	.362
69. Jarred Mederos, St. John's	Jr.	42	141	51	.362
Connor Panas, Canisius	Jr.	53	188	68	.362
71. Alex Miklos, Kent State	Jr.	46	177	64	.362
72. Sean Guite, UNC Greensboro	Sr.	49	202	73	.361
73. Scott Heath, Maine	Jr.	48	155	56	.361
74. Curtis Jones, Houston Baptist	Jr.	51	227	82	.361
Alex Tomasovich, Charleston So.	Sr.	56	227	82	.361
76. Sam Bumpers, Lamar	Sr.	55	230	83	.361
77. D.J. Ruhlman, Seton Hall	Jr.	48	181	65	.359
78. Robert Currie, Navy	So.	51	195	70	.359
79. Bobby Melley, UConn	So.	58	209	75	.359
80. Aaron Barnett, Pepperdine	Fr.	60	223	80	.359
81. Kristian Gayday, IPFW	Sr.	54	173	62	.358
Corbin Olmstead, North Florida	So.	45	173	62	.358
83. Charles Sikes, Savannah State	Jr.	53	201	72	.358
84. Kyle Schwarber, Indiana	Jr.	59	232	83	.358
85. Brett Sullivan, Pacific	So.	53	207	74	.357
86. Alexander Lee, Radford	Sr.	53	199	71	.357
87. Bobby Burns, Morehead State	Sr.	50	185	66	.357
88. Tyler France, San Diego State	So.	63	233	83	.356
89. Chase Raffield, Georgia State	Sr.	56	205	73	.356
90. Austin Hulsey, Alabama A&M	So.	50	191	68	.356
91. Cameron Cecil, Delaware State	Sr.	44	177	63	.356
92. Bobby Boyd, West Virginia	Jr.	53	222	79	.356
93. Wes Satzinger, North Dakota State	Sr.	48	163	58	.356
94. Blake Trahan, La.-Lafayette	So.	68	256	91	.355
95. Collin Forgey, Saint Joseph's		51	203	72	.355
96. Jacob McNamara, Ill.-Chicago	Sr.	43	158	56	.354
97. Alex Call, Ball State	Fr.	53	206	73	.354
Patrick Mazeika, Stetson	So.	59	206	73	.354
99. Joel Rosencrance, St. Bonaventure	Sr.	42	144	51	.354
100. Kyle Teaf, South Florida	Jr.	58	209	74	.354

ONBASE PERCENTAGE

RANK NAME, TEAM	PCT
1. Aaron Nardone, Delaware State	.521
2. Casey Gillaspie, Wichita State	.520
3. Andrew Utterback, Alabama A&M	.509
4. Michael Conforto, Oregon State	.504
5. Casey Jones, Elon	.502
6. Caleb Adams, La.Lafayette	.502
7. Caleb Howell, Eastern Ill.	.492
8. Tim Swatek, Fordham	.491
9. Scott Schaub, Jacksonville	.490
10. Mike Alexander, Delaware State	.490
11. Jimmy Luppens, Canisius	.490
12. Anthony Massicci, Canisius	.489
13. Evan Harasta, Albany	.484
14. Joey Epperson, UC Santa Barbara	.483
15. Max Pentecost, Kennesaw State	.482
16. Jameson Fisher, Southeastern La.	.481
17. Daniel Miles, Tennessee Tech	.481
18. Kyle Teaf, South Florida	.479
19. Patrick Mazeika, Stetson	.479
20. Nick Thompson, William & Mary	.479
21. Drew Weeks, North Florida	.478
22. Spencer Angelis, High Point	.477
23. Bennie Robinson, Florida A&M	.476
24. AJ Reed, Kentucky	.476
25. Jordan Luplow, Fresno State	.475
Bobby Melley, UConn	.475
27. Austin Miller, Loyola Marymount	.474
28. Ryan Plourde, Fairfield	.473
29. Alex Harris, Dayton	.472
30. DJ Stewart, Florida State	.472
31. Kristian Gayday, IPFW	.472
32. Ryan Bottger, TexasArlington	.472
33. Michael Medina, New Mexico State	.471
34. Jacob McNamara, Ill.Chicago	.469
35. Bo Thompson, Citadel	.468
36. Luke Tendler, N.C. A&T	.467
37. Einar Muniz, Alabama State	.465
38. Alexander Lee, Radford	.465
39. Byron Campbell, Md.Eastern Shore	.465
40. Kyle Schwarber, Indiana	.464
41. Chris Cook, George Mason	.464
42. Reagan Fowler, Creighton	.464
Tyler Leffler, Bradley	.464
44. Christ Conley, Canisius	.464
45. Brandon Lowe, Maryland	.464
46. Connor Joe, San Diego	.462
47. Bradley Zimmer, San Francisco	.461
48. Robbie Knightes, St. John's	.458
49. Scott Kingery, Arizona	.456
50. Wes Satzinger, North Dakota State	.456

SLUGGING PERCENTAGE

RANK NAME, TEAM	SLG PCT
1. AJ Reed, Kentucky	.735
2. Brandon Thomasson, Tenn. Tech	.721
3. Nic Wilson, Georgia State	.683
4. Casey Gillaspie, Wichita State	.682
5. Caleb Adams, La.-Lafayette	.673
6. Casey Jones, Elon	.668
7. Kyle Schwarber, Indiana	.659
8. Matt Tellor, Southeast Mo. State	.657
9. Chase Raffield, Georgia State	.654
10. Kristian Gayday, IPFW	.653
11. Michael Katz, William & Mary	.646
12. Shaun Chase, Oregon	.634
13. Max Pentecost, Kennesaw State	.627
14. Aramis Garcia, Fla. International	.626
15. Forrest Brandt, Davidson	.626
16. Austin Byler, Nevada	.624
17. Clinton Freeman, East Tenn. State	.620
18. Lee Miller, Davidson	.618
19. Bryan Soloman, Eastern Ky.	.612
20. Aaron Nardone, Delaware State	.612
21. Jordan Luplow, Fresno State	.609
22. Drew Weeks, North Florida	.606
23. Connor Joe, San Diego	.606
24. Corbin Olmstead, North Florida	.601
25. Daniel Miles, Tennessee Tech	.599
26. Max Murphy, Bradley	.598
27. Paul DeJong, Illinois State	.596
28. Brandon Rawe, Morehead State	.594
29. Alex Miklos, Kent State	.593
30. Ryan Seiz, Liberty	.593
31. Charles Sikes, Savannah State	.592
32. John Ziznewski, LIU Brooklyn	.589
33. Drew Ferguson, Belmont	.589
34. Ryan Bottger, Texas-Arlington	.588
35. Matt Shortall, Texas-Arlington	.586
36. Matt Weckerle, NJIT	.583
37. Nathan Becker, Davidson	.583
38. Andrew Utterback, Alabama A&M	.579
39. Stephen Wallace, Southern	.577
40. Dylan Bosheers, Tennessee Tech	.577
41. DJ Miller, Delaware State	.576
42. Sam Travis, Indiana	.576
43. Mike Alexander, Delaware State	.575
44. Connor Panas, Canisius	.574
45. Adam Martin, Western Caro.	.574
46. Brad Haynal, San Diego State	.573
47. Ryan Solberg, Milwaukee	.573
48. Rhys Hoskins, Sacramento State	.573
49. Bradley Zimmer, San Francisco	.573
50. Nick Thompson, William & Mary	.571

HOME RUNS

RANK NAME, TEAM	HR
1. AJ Reed, Kentucky	23
2. Brandon Thomasson, Tenn. Tech	22
3. Zach Stephens, Tennessee Tech	19
4. Nic Wilson, Georgia State	18
5. Casey Gillaspie, Wichita State	15
Matt Tellor, Southeast Mo. State	15
7. Austin Byler, Nevada	14
Shaun Chase, Oregon	14
Jacob Hoyle, Western Caro.	14
Michael Katz, William & Mary	14
Adam Martin, Western Caro.	14
Sikes Orvis, Ole Miss	14
Chase Raffield, Georgia State	14
Kyle Schwarber, Indiana	14
Bryan Soloman, Eastern Ky.	14
16. Aaron Brown, Pepperdine	13
Clinton Freeman, East Tenn. State	13
Aaron Mizell, Ga. Southern	13
19. Alex Blandino, Stanford	12
Forrest Brandt, Davidson	12
Matt Dacey, Richmond	12
Kristian Gayday, IPFW	12
Eric Gutierrez, Texas Tech	12
Brad Haynal, San Diego State	12
Rhys Hoskins, Sacramento State	12
Max Murphy, Bradley	12
Ryan Seiz, Liberty	12
Sam Travis, Indiana	12
Tommy Williams, UCF	12
30. Caleb Adams, La.-Lafayette	11
Nathan Becker, Davidson	11
Dylan Bosheers, Tennessee Tech	11
Zack Collins, Miami	11
Dillon Dobson, Appalachian State	11
Zach Fish, Oklahoma State	11
Mike Gerber, Creighton	11
Tripp Martin, Samford	11
Greg McCall, Texas-Arlington	11
Daniel Miles, Tennessee Tech	11
Mike Papi, Virginia	11
Matt Rose, Georgia State	11
Nick Thompson, William & Mary	11
Kurt Wertz, Towson	11

RUNS BATTED IN

RANK NAME, TEAM	RBI
1. Brandon Thomasson, Tenn. Tech	76
2. Michael Katz, William & Mary	75
3. AJ Reed, Kentucky	73
4. Matt Tellor, Southeast Mo. State	71
5. Derek Gibson, Southeast Mo. State	70
6. Jeff Gardner, Louisville	68
7. Jace Conrad, La.-Lafayette	65
Seth Harrison, La.-Lafayette	65
Adam Martin, Western Caro.	65
10. Will Allen, Ole Miss	64
Dylan Davis, Oregon State	64
12. Chase Harris, New Mexico	63
13. Max Pentecost, Kennesaw State	61
14. Waldyvan Estrada, Alabama State	60
15. Chase Raffield, Georgia State	59
16. Caleb Bryson, Samford	58
Matt Burgess, Arkansas State	58
Andrew Godbold, Southeastern La.	58
Eric Gutierrez, Texas Tech	58
Max Kuhn, Kentucky	58
Emmanuel Marrero, Alabama State	58
Sam Travis, Indiana	58
23. Sean Godfrey, Ball State	57
Matt Shortall, Texas-Arlington	57
Zach Stephens, Tennessee Tech	57
26. Dylan Bosheers, Tennessee Tech	56
Michael Conforto, Oregon State	56
Cody Koch, Kent State	56
Cody Leichman, Central Mich.	56
Mike Papi, Virginia	56
James Vasquez, UCF	56
32. Bill Cullen, VCU	55
Pat Kelly, Nebraska	55
Bryan Soloman, Eastern Ky.	55
John Ziznewski, LIU Brooklyn	55
36. Zack Collins, Miami	54
Daniel Miles, Tennessee Tech	54
Paschal Petrongolo, Jacksonville State	54
Bryan Reynolds, Vanderbilt	54
Carl Wise, Col. of Charleston	54
41. Clinton Freeman, East Tenn. State	53
Rhys Hoskins, Sacramento State	53
Jacob Hoyle, Western Caro.	53
Casey Jones, Elon	53
Aaron Mizell, Ga. Southern	53
Sikes Orvis, Ole Miss	53
Bradley Strong, Western Caro.	53
Demetre Taylor, Eastern Ill.	53

DOUBLES

RANK NAME, TEAM	2B
1. Kewby Meyer, Nevada	27
Dansby Swanson, Vanderbilt	27
3. Matt Shortall, Texas-Arlington	26
4. Trent Miller, Middle Tenn.	25
Alex Real, New Mexico	25
Nick Rivera, Fla. Gulf Coast	25
7. Will Allen, Ole Miss	24
Michael Katz, William & Mary	24
Hutton Moyer, Pepperdine	24
Max Pentecost, Kennesaw State	24
Bryan Reynolds, Vanderbilt	24
12. Derek Peterson, Temple	23
13. Juan Bueno, Grambling	22
Sean Godfrey, Ball State	22
Blaise Salter, Michigan State	22
16. Craig Brinkerhoff, Utah Valley	21
Bryant Burleson, Texas Tech	21
Paul DeJong, Illinois State	21
Blaise Fernandez, George Mason	21
Matt Gonzalez, Georgia Tech	21
Shane Hoelscher, Rice	21
Connor Joe, San Diego	21
Adam Kirsch, Texas Tech	21
Jordan Luplow, Fresno State	21
Michael Pritchard, Nebraska	21
Brandon Rawe, Morehead State	21
Garrett Russini, Stetson	21
Alex Tomasovich, Charleston So.	21
29. Jordan Betts, Duke	20
Jace Conrad, La.-Lafayette	20
Andrew Daniel, San Diego	20
Jeff Gardner, Louisville	20
Casey Jones, Elon	20
Doug Kraeger, Richmond	20
Lee Longo, Eastern Mich.	20
Heath Quinn, Samford	20
Michael Russell, North Carolina	20
Bradley Strong, Western Caro.	20
Brandon Thomasson, Tenn. Tech	20
Nic Wilson, Georgia State	20
41. Jackson Glines, Michigan	19
Brendan Hendriks, San Francisco	19
Tim Hoehn, William & Mary	19
Tyler Jones, Air Force	19
Kevin Kaczmarski, Evansville	19
Stuart Levy, Arkansas State	19
Grant Massey, Lipscomb	19
Paschal Petrongolo, Jacksonville State	19
Chase Raffield, Georgia State	19
Christin Stewart, Tennessee	19
DJ Stewart, Florida State	19
Wade Wass, Alabama	19

TRIPLES

RANK NAME, TEAM	3B
1. Taylor Sparks, UC Irvine	9
2. Trent Gilbert, Arizona	8
Anthony Gonsolin, St. Mary's	8
Michael Hill, Long Beach State	8
Emmanuel Marrero, Alabama State	8
Daniel Spingola, Georgia State	8
7. Caleb Adams, La.-Lafayette	7
Tyler Baumgartner, Oregon	7
Jaylin Davis, Appalachian State	7
Seth Harrison, La.-Lafayette	7
Connor Jones, Villanova	7
Jared Kujawa, Western Mich.	7
Alex Miklos, Kent State	7
Sheldon Neuse, Oklahoma	7
Paschal Petrongolo, Jacksonville State	7
Daniel Salters, Dallas Baptist	7
J.P. Sportman, Central Conn. State	7
Cole Sturgeon, Louisville	7

Name, Team	
Bradley Zimmer, San Francisco	7
20. Greg Allen, San Diego State	6
Ryan Boldt, Nebraska	6
Bill Cullen, VCU	6
Edwin Drexler, Grambling	6
Hunter Haley, Oklahoma	6
Justin Korenblatt, La Salle	6
Andre Moore, Norfolk State	6
Taylor Murphy, Pacific	6
Tyler Neslony, Texas Tech	6
Rob Pescitelli, Quinnipiac	6
Casey Rodrigue, Indiana	6
Kyle Schwarber, Indiana	6
Austin Slater, Stanford	6
Andrew Sohn, Western Mich.	6
Christin Stewart, Tennessee	6
Bradley Strong, Western Caro.	6
Preston Troutman, Appalachian State	6
Bret Underwood, Northwestern State	6
Tyler Ware, A&M-Corpus Chris	6
39. Jonathan Allison, Lipscomb	5
Patrick Armstrong, UNLV	5
Brett Austin, North Carolina State	5
Bill Bereszniewicz, Binghamton	5
C.T. Bradford, Mississippi State	5
Hunter Burton, Furman	5
Austin Byler, Nevada	5
Keenan Cook, Rice	5
Chris Cook, East Tenn. State	5
Robert Currie, Navy	5
Charles Dailey, Delaware State	5
J.D. Davis, Cal State Fullerton	5

STOLEN BASES

RANK NAME, TEAM	SB	CS
1. Hunter Burton, Furman	41	10
Nick Richter, Rider	41	5
3. Derek Jenkins, Seton Hall	38	11
4. Sutton Whiting, Louisville	37	6
5. Nick Regnier, Central Mich.	35	3
6. Ben Crumpton, UALR	33	3
7. Gavin Golsan, Jacksonville State	32	4
8. Carl Anderson, Bryant	31	3
Joe Daru, NYIT	31	3
Nick Sinay, Buffalo	31	4
Kyle Survance, Houston	31	6
12. Braxton Lee, Ole Miss	30	5
13. Brandon Angus, VMI	29	5
Moses Charles, Alcorn	29	8
Anthony Cheky, Michigan State	29	6
Cody Jones, TCU	29	5
Alex Witkus, Fairfield	29	2
18. Joe Torres, Iona	28	5
19. Devan Ahart, Akron	27	6
Sean Beesley, Illinois State	27	9
Mason Davis, Citadel	27	6
Jack Sundberg, UConn	27	7
23. Jose Carrera, Manhattan	26	3
Robert Currie, Navy	26	5
Harold Earls, Army	26	4
Tyler Grogg, Toledo	26	7
Clay Holcomb, Troy	26	6
Trea Turner, North Carolina State	26	4
Doug Votolato, Central Ark.	26	5
30. Greg Allen, San Diego State	25	5
Steven Duggar, Clemson	25	3
Austin Miller, Loyola Marymount	25	4
Jake Noll, Fla. Gulf Coast	25	5
Jordan Serena, Columbia	25	5
Charlie White, Maryland	25	5
Jake Yacinich, Iowa	25	4
37. Chase Fields, Seattle	24	6
Jerry Ford, Texas Southern	24	11
Dalton Herrington, La.-Monroe	24	4
Josh Hyman, Wofford	24	3

Name, Team		
Colton Konvicka, Longwood	24	3
Will Maddox, Tennessee	24	6
Evan Ocello, Holy Cross	24	4
Ryan Solberg, Milwaukee	24	1
Matt Weckerle, NJIT	24	0
46. Bill Bereszniewicz, Binghamton	23	3
Jason Blum, Southeast Mo. State	23	2
Brandon Howard, Bowling Green	23	1
Chris Kalousdian, Manhattan	23	4
Grant Kay, Louisville	23	3
John Rubino, Eastern Mich.	23	7
Joseph Runco, Fordham	23	6

RUNS

RANK NAME, TEAM	R
1. Nick Thompson, William & Mary	69
2. Max Kuhn, Kentucky	68
3. Caleb Adams, La.-Lafayette	67
Daniel Miles, Tennessee Tech	67
5. Richard Amion, Alabama State	66
Dylan Bosheers, Tennessee Tech	66
Kyle Schwarber, Indiana	66
8. Trea Turner, North Carolina State	65
9. Michael Katz, William & Mary	64
10. Jace Conrad, La.-Lafayette	63
Ryan Leonards, La.-Lafayette	63
Dansby Swanson, Vanderbilt	63
13. Auston Bousfield, Ole Miss	61
14. Jason Blum, Southeast Mo. State	60
AJ Reed, Kentucky	60
Matt Tellor, Southeast Mo. State	60
Brandon Thomasson, Tenn. Tech	60
18. Connor Joe, San Diego	59
Max Pentecost, Kennesaw State	59
20. Austin Cousino, Kentucky	58
Brian O'Keefe, Saint Joseph's	58
Bradley Strong, Western Caro.	58
Cole Sturgeon, Louisville	58
Blake Trahan, La.-Lafayette	58
25. Austin Anderson, Ole Miss	57
Jacob Bruce, Kennesaw State	57
Skyler Ewing, Rice	57
Andrew Guillotte, McNeese State	57
Sam Haggerty, New Mexico	57
Chris Hueth, Saint Joseph's	57
31. Michael Bishop, Jacksonville State	56
Jackson Gooch, McNeese State	56
Dalton Herrington, La.-Monroe	56
Braxton Lee, Ole Miss	56
Jake Noll, Fla. Gulf Coast	56
Zach Stephens, Tennessee Tech	56
John Welborn, UTSA	56
Zach Zarzour, Tennessee Tech	56
39. Tyler France, San Diego State	55
Griff Gordon, Jacksonville State	55
Austin Listi, Dallas Baptist	55
Joe McCarthy, Virginia	55
Mike Papi, Virginia	55
Ryan Seiz, Liberty	55
Sam Travis, Indiana	55
46. Cody Koch, Kent State	54
Nathan Lukes, Sacramento State	54
Michael Suchy, Fla. Gulf Coast	54
Jude Vidrine, Lamar	54

HITS

RANK NAME, TEAM	H
1. Max Pentecost, Kennesaw State	113
2. Jake Noll, Fla. Gulf Coast	101
3. Griff Gordon, Jacksonville State	100
4. Brandon Rawe, Morehead State	98
5. Auston Bousfield, Ole Miss	96
Jace Conrad, La.-Lafayette	96
7. Bryan Reynolds, Vanderbilt	95
Drew Weeks, North Florida	95

Name, Team	
9. Will Allen, Ole Miss	94
Caleb Howell, Eastern Ill.	94
Dansby Swanson, Vanderbilt	94
12. Jameson Fisher, Southeastern La.	93
Chase Harris, New Mexico	93
14. Derek Gibson, Southeast Mo. State	91
Bobby Ison, Charleston So.	91
Connor Spencer, UC Irvine	91
Blake Trahan, La.-Lafayette	91
18. Nathan Lukes, Sacramento State	90
Daniel Miles, Tennessee Tech	90
Matt Tellor, Southeast Mo. State	90
21. Matt Shortall, Texas-Arlington	88
22. Austin Anderson, Ole Miss	87
Michael Katz, William & Mary	87
Brett Pirtle, Mississippi State	87
Cole Sturgeon, Louisville	87
26. Anthony Azar, Sam Houston State	86
Dylan Bosheers, Tennessee Tech	86
Ryan Leonards, La.-Lafayette	86
29. Caleb Adams, La.-Lafayette	85
Nick Thompson, William & Mary	85
Sam Travis, Indiana	85
Bo Way, Kennesaw State	85
33. Zach Houchins, East Carolina	84
Max Kuhn, Kentucky	84
Boomer White, TCU	84
36. Spencer Angelis, High Point	83
Colt Atwood, Sam Houston State	83
Sam Bumpers, Lamar	83
Tyler France, San Diego State	83
Sam Haggerty, New Mexico	83
Bennie Robinson, Florida A&M	83
Kyle Schwarber, Indiana	83
Doug Votolato, Central Ark.	83
44. Andrew Daniel, San Diego	82
Casey Gillaspie, Wichita State	82
Andrew Godbold, Southeastern La.	82
Seth Harrison, La.-Lafayette	82
Casey Jones, Elon	82
Curtis Jones, Houston Baptist	82
Kyle Martin, South Carolina	82
Daniel Spingola, Georgia Tech	82
Brandon Thomasson, Tenn. Tech	82
Alex Tomasovich, Charleston So.	82
Zach Zarzour, Tennessee Tech	82

TOTAL BASES

RANK NAME, TEAM	TB
1. Brandon Thomasson, Tenn. Tech	176
2. Max Pentecost, Kennesaw State	168
3. AJ Reed, Kentucky	164
4. Michael Katz, William & Mary	155
5. Kyle Schwarber, Indiana	153
Matt Tellor, Southeast Mo. State	153
7. Caleb Adams, La.-Lafayette	150
Matt Shortall, Texas-Arlington	150
9. Jace Conrad, La.-Lafayette	149
Brandon Rawe, Morehead State	149
11. Casey Gillaspie, Wichita State	144
12. Daniel Miles, Tennessee Tech	142
13. Sam Travis, Indiana	141
14. Seth Harrison, La.-Lafayette	140
Nic Wilson, Georgia State	140
16. Will Allen, Ole Miss	139
17. Austin Byler, Nevada	138
Chase Harris, New Mexico	138
19. Clinton Freeman, East Tenn. State	137
Griff Gordon, Jacksonville State	137
Ryan Seiz, Liberty	137
22. Auston Bousfield, Ole Miss	136
23. Dylan Bosheers, Tennessee Tech	135
Bryan Reynolds, Vanderbilt	135
Zach Stephens, Tennessee Tech	135
26. Aaron Brown, Pepperdine	134

Name, Team	
Chase Raffield, Georgia State	134
Dansby Swanson, Vanderbilt	134
Drew Weeks, North Florida	134
30. Eric Gutierrez, Texas Tech	132
Connor Joe, San Diego	132
Aaron Mizell, Ga. Southern	132
Nick Thompson, William & Mary	132
34. Casey Jones, Elon	131
Jordan Luplow, Fresno State	131
Bradley Strong, Western Caro.	131
37. Paul DeJong, Illinois State	130
38. Derek Gibson, Southeast Mo. State	129
Brad Haynal, San Diego State	129
40. Sean Godfrey, Ball State	128
Max Kuhn, Kentucky	128
Bryan Soloman, Eastern Ky.	128
Taylor Sparks, UC Irvine	128
44. Anthony Azar, Sam Houston State	127
Jacob Hoyle, Western Caro.	127
Sikes Orvis, Ole Miss	127
47. Sam Bumpers, Lamar	126
Jeff Gardner, Louisville	126
Adam Kirsch, Texas Tech	126
Bradley Zimmer, San Francisco	126

WALKS

RANK NAME, TEAM	BB
1. Mike Papi, Virginia	61
2. Casey Gillaspie, Wichita State	58
3. Mark Payton, Texas	57
4. Michael Conforto, Oregon State	55
5. Casey Grayson, Houston	52
Mark Lumpa, Duke	52
7. Michael Medina, New Mexico State	50
8. AJ Reed, Kentucky	49
9. Justin Gonzalez, Florida State	48
Aaron Nardone, Delaware State	48
11. Tim Arakawa, Oklahoma State	47
Brooks Marlow, Texas	47
13. Caleb Adams, La.-Lafayette	46
Cody Jones, TCU	46
Pat MacKenzie, Central Mich.	46
Jude Vidrine, Lamar	46
17. Daniel Salters, Dallas Baptist	45
18. Justin Protacio, Kansas	44
Kyle Schwarber, Indiana	44
Blake Trahan, La.-Lafayette	44
21. Mitchell Gunsolus, Gonzaga	43
Max Kuhn, Kentucky	43
John Nogowski, Florida State	43
Evan Stephens, Wake Forest	43
Boomer Synek, Evansville	43
Sutton Whiting, Louisville	43
27. Branden Cogswell, Virginia	42
Zack Collins, Miami	42
Anthony Massicci, Canisius	42
Reed Seeley, Samford	42
Tyler Slaton, Clemson	42
Kane Sweeney, Morehead State	42
Kyle Teaf, South Florida	42
Nick Thompson, William & Mary	42
Jake Welch, Southern Ill.	42
36. Vince Conde, Vanderbilt	41
Jacob Cronenworth, Michigan	41
T.J. Dixon, Samford	41
Mike Fitzgerald, Indiana State	41
Dalton Herrington, La.-Monroe	41
Melvin Rodriguez, Jackson State	41
Bo Thompson, Citadel	41

Name, Team	
Keaton Wright, SIUE	41
44. Austin Baker, Arkansas State	40
Eric Cheray, Missouri State	40
Garrett Copeland, Austin Peay	40
Dominic Fratantuono, Towson	40
Rolando Gautier, Austin Peay	40
Logan Ice, Oregon State	40
Saige Jenco, Virginia Tech	40
Spencer Mahoney, Valparaiso	40
Grant Massey, Lipscomb	40
DJ Stewart, Florida State	40
Luke Tendler, N.C. A&T	40
Peter Van Gansen, Cal Poly	40

TOUGHEST TO STRIKE OUT

RANK NAME, TEAM	AB/SO
1. Bobby Ison, Charleston So.	38.3
2. Carter Yagi, Kansas State	29
3. Payden Cawley Lamb, Gonzaga	28.7
4. Cameron Berra, Eastern Ill.	22.9
5. Kewby Meyer, Nevada	22.5
6. Dan Walsh, Miami (OH)	22.4
7. DJ Miller, Delaware State	21.6
Matt Weckerle, NJIT	21.6
9. Brett Sullivan, Pacific	20.7
10. Chris Ayers, VCU	20.7
11. T.J. Sutton, Kent State	19.9
Deion Tansel, Toledo	19.9
13. Mike Alexander, Delaware State	19.1
14. Ryan Plourde, Fairfield	18.8
15. Aaron Barnett, Pepperdine	18.6
16. Zachary Brigham, Savannah State	18.4
17. Mike Brosseau, Oakland	18
18. Edwin Gomez, Northwestern State	17.6
19. Nick Murphy, CSUN	17.4
20. Blair Beck, Kansas	17.1
21. Pat Wilson, Milwaukee	17.1
22. Ty Warrington, Delaware	17
23. Mac James, Oklahoma	16.8
24. Joey Cujas, VCU	16.6
25. James Cantu, McNeese State	16.1

HIT BY PITCH

RANK NAME, TEAM	HBP
1. Chris Cook, George Mason	31
Aaron Payne, Oregon	31
3. Tyler Bigler, Morehead State	30
4. Chase Compton, La.-Lafayette	25
Jimmy Luppens, Canisius	25
Jarod Perry, Evansville	25
Nick Sinay, Buffalo	25
8. Joel Atkinson, Northwestern State	23
Drew Ferguson, Belmont	23
10. Braden Bishop, Washington	22
Alex Jensen, Army	22
Tyler Leffler, Bradley	22
Steven Leonard, Campbell	22
Ryan Lindemuth, William & Mary	22
Kevin Nutter, William & Mary	22
Bo Thompson, Citadel	22
Elijah Trail, Campbell	22
18. Blake Davey, UConn	21
Zack Lee, N.C. Central	21
Austin Miller, Loyola Marymount	21
Brady Sheetz, Hartford	21
Bryce Taylor, Jackson State	21
Woody Woodward, UC Santa Barbara	21
24. Mike Allen, Siena	20
James Bunn, VCU	20
Andrew Godbold, Southeastern La.	20

Name, Team	
Adam Goss, Villanova	20
Alex Harris, Dayton	20
James Sheltrown, Akron	20
Blake Sipe, Radford	20
Mitchell Tolman, Oregon	20
Matt Weckerle, NJIT	20
Charlie White, Maryland	20

SACRIFICE BUNTS

RANK NAME, TEAM	SH
1. Andrew Ely, Washington	26
2. Brett Michael Doran, Stanford	23
Chris Rabago, UC Irvine	23
4. Brandon Healy, Oral Roberts	22
Donnie Walton, Oklahoma State	22
6. Daniel Pinero, Virginia	20
Jomarcos Woods, UCF	20
8. Joey Hawkins, Missouri State	19
Aaron Siple, New Mexico	19
10. Kyle Bacak, TCU	18
Keegan Dale, Cal State Fullerton	18
Thomas Simoneaux, Louisiana Tech	18
Leo Vargas, Nicholls State	18
14. Mark Karaviotis, Oregon	17
John Reilly, Campbell	17
Lamonte Wade, Maryland	17
17. Branden Cogswell, Virginia	16
Ryan Fitzgerald, Creighton	16
CJ Hinojosa, Texas	16
Tyler Palmer, Miami	16
Andy Peterson, Oregon State	16
22. Hughston Armstrong, Citadel	15
Joel Atkinson, Northwestern State	15
Colby Brenner, Long Beach State	15
Madison Carter, Texas	15
David Fletcher, Loyola Marymount	15
Steven Leonard, Campbell	15
Dane McDermott, High Point	15
Grant Miller, Western Mich.	15
Cody Sharrow, South Dakota State	15
A.J. Simcox, Tennessee	15
Justin Treece, Central Ark.	15

SACRIFICE FLIES

RANK NAME, TEAM	SF
1. Derek Gibson, Southeast Mo. State	12
2. Tommy Cheek, Loyola Marymount	11
Taylor Gushue, Florida	11
Seth Harrison, La.-Lafayette	11
Brian Mundell, Cal Poly	11
6. Carl Wise, Col. of Charleston	10
7. Michael Suchy, Fla. Gulf Coast	9
Matt Tellor, Southeast Mo. State	9
Blake Trahan, La.-Lafayette	9
10. Brian Anderson, Arkansas	8
Cavan Biggio, Notre Dame	8
Alex Blandino, Stanford	8
Garrett Boulware, Clemson	8
Mason Davis, Citadel	8
David Del Grande, Sacramento State	8
Nick Favatella, Rutgers	8
Aramis Garcia, Fla. International	8
Matt Gonzalez, Georgia Tech	8
Kyle Grimm, Seton Hall	8
Kevin Kaczmarski, Evansville	8
Cole Lankford, Texas A&M	8
Vimael Machin, VCU	8
Jerry McClanahan, UC Irvine	8
Patrick Porter, Ohio State	8
Luke Willis, George Mason	8

PITCHING Minimum 1 IP per team game

EARNED RUN AVERAGE

RANK NAME, TEAM	YEAR	G	IP	R	ER	ERA
1. Ben Wetzler, Oregon State	Sr.	14	104	12	9	0.78
2. Mike Franco, Fla. International	Sr.	15	99	18	12	1.09
3. Kyle Davis, Southern California	So.	26	56	11	7	1.12
4. James Cooksey, Sacred Heart	Jr.	24	62	16	8	1.16

5. Tyler Ford, Houston	Sr.	27	69	10	9	1.17
6. Jason Richman, Ga. Southern	So.	47	90	26	12	1.20
7. Sean Newcomb, Hartford	Jr.	14	93	16	13	1.25
8. Jimmy Herget, South Florida	So.	15	107	15	19	1.26
9. Preston Morrison, TCU	Jr.	18	130	25	19	1.32
10. Ryan Thompson, Campbell	Sr.	39	88	21	13	1.33
11. Zach Rodgers, UCF	Jr.	26	79	19	12	1.36
12. Dylan Stuart, UC Riverside	Sr.	26	69	21	11	1.44
13. Blake Fox, Rice	So.	15	105	17	17	1.46
14. Aaron Nola, LSU	Jr.	16	116	19	19	1.47
15. Nathan Thornhill, Texas	Sr.	21	113	20	19	1.51
16. Vince Wheeland, Oklahoma State	Sr.	31	83	16	14	1.52
17. Bailey Ober, Col. of Charleston	Fr.	17	107	24	18	1.52
18. Marc Skinner, Troy		31	65	17	11	1.52
19. Anthony Parenti, Navy	Jr.	12	83	16	14	1.52
20. Cas Silber, High Point	Fr.	22	59	10	10	1.53
21. Andrew Morales, UC Irvine	Sr.	19	136	27	23	1.53
22. A.J. Ladwig, Wichita State	Jr.	15	105	28	18	1.54
23. Chase Mallard, UAB	Sr.	15	110	20	19	1.55
24. Casey Bloomquist, Cal Poly	So.	16	98	21	17	1.56
25. Matt Cooper, Hawaii	Sr.	15	107	29	19	1.60
Tyler Davis, Washington	Jr.	17	107	22	19	1.60
27. Montana Durapau, Bethune-Cookman	Sr.	19	117	25	21	1.61
28. Scott Schultz, Oregon State	Sr.	24	67	17	12	1.61
29. Josh Prevost, Seton Hall	Sr.	15	116	26	21	1.62
30. Matt Eckelman, Saint Louis	So.	22	61	16	11	1.63
31. Koby Gauna, Cal State Fullerton	Jr.	27	60	13	11	1.64
32. Grahamm Wiest, Cal State Fullerton	Jr.	15	113	37	21	1.68
33. Alex Luna, UAB	Jr.	15	87	21	17	1.76
34. Erick Fedde, UNLV	Jr.	11	77	22	15	1.76
Trent Swart, Duke	Jr.	11	61	13	12	1.76
Aaron Myers, Longwood	Jr.	16	107	28	21	1.76
37. Connor Cuff, Penn	Jr.	10	66	19	13	1.77
38. Jace Fry, Oregon State	Jr.	16	120	29	24	1.80
39. Kevin Duchene, Illinois	So.	9	55	16	11	1.80
40. Ryan Williams, East Carolina	Sr.	32	100	27	20	1.81
41. Craig Schlitter, Bryant	Sr.	15	95	29	19	1.81
42. Sam Street, Tex.-Pan American	Sr.	15	129	33	26	1.81
43. Joey DeNato, Indiana	Sr.	17	109	26	22	1.82
44. Harry Thomas, Delaware State	Fr.	14	49	15	10	1.82
45. Matt Ditman, Rice	So.	26	69	16	14	1.83
46. Michael Murray, Fla. Gulf Coast	So.	15	107	30	22	1.85
47. Michael Byrne, Cornell	So.	9	53	16	11	1.86
48. David Speer, Columbia	Sr.	12	87	19	18	1.86
49. Scott Kerrigan, Notre Dame	Jr.	14	58	26	12	1.87
50. Thomas Eshelman, Cal State Fullerton	So.	16	124	32	26	1.89
51. Zac Curtis, Middle Tenn.	Sr.	15	114	31	24	1.89
52. Kyle Freeland, Evansville	Jr.	14	100	29	21	1.90
53. Corey Miller, Pepperdine	Sr.	16	118	34	25	1.90
54. Taylor Byrd, Nicholls State	Sr.	14	89	22	19	1.92
55. Daniel Gossett, Clemson	Jr.	15	107	25	23	1.93
56. Dylan Dusek, Texas Tech	Fr.	14	74	17	16	1.94
57. Josh Frye, Long Beach State	Sr.	17	83	19	18	1.94
Dalton Lundeen, Valparaiso	So.	13	83	26	18	1.94
59. Kyle Funkhouser, Louisville	So.	18	120	33	26	1.94
60. Aaron Brown, Pepperdine	Jr.	17	116	29	25	1.95
61. Andro Cutura, Southeastern La.	Jr.	16	106	30	23	1.95
62. Christopher Mourelle, FIU	Fr.	15	78	21	17	1.95
63. Carson Fulmer, Vanderbilt	So.	26	91	22	20	1.98
64. Jalen Beeks, Arkansas	Jr.	13	82	24	18	1.98
65. Carlos Rodon, North Carolina State	Jr.	14	99	39	22	2.01
66. Keegan Thompson, Auburn	Fr.	14	90	23	20	2.01
67. Alex Robinett, Army	Jr.	13	89	25	20	2.02
68. Matt Warren, Creighton	So.	14	84	21	19	2.03
69. Jared Gaynor, George Mason	Sr.	16	115	35	26	2.03
70. Christian Morris, Indiana	So.	16	84	31	19	2.04
71. Brandon Finnegan, TCU	Jr.	17	106	26	24	2.04
72. Christian Trent, Ole Miss	So.	17	110	28	25	2.05
73. Andrew Rohrbach, Long Beach State	So.	16	110	34	25	2.05
74. Nathan Kirby, Virginia	So.	18	113	34	26	2.06
Santos Saldivar, Southern	Jr.	9	57	20	13	2.06
76. Jonny Drozd, Texas Tech	Sr.	28	73	20	17	2.09
77. Bryan Sova, Creighton	Sr.	29	60	14	14	2.09
78. AJ Reed, Kentucky	Jr.	16	112	39	26	2.09
79. Dan Savas, Illinois State	Jr.	16	103	31	24	2.10
80. Zach Plesac, Ball State	Fr.	25	85	25	20	2.11
81. Kyle Bouman, LSU	Jr.	17	64	15	15	2.12
82. Dillon Peters, Texas	Jr.	13	80	24	19	2.13
83. Phil Bickford, Cal State Fullerton	Fr.	20	76	25	18	2.13
84. Dylan Craig, Illinois State	So.	15	93	32	22	2.14
85. Kaleb Jon Fontenot, McNeese State	So.	16	80	25	19	2.14
86. Thomas Thorpe, Oregon	Jr.	16	105	30	25	2.14
87. Chance Sinclair, Nebraska	Jr.	16	101	37	24	2.15
88. Brennan Leitao, Sacramento State	Jr.	19	117	31	28	2.15
89. Logan Shore, Florida	Fr.	16	96	27	23	2.16
90. Rohn Pierce, Canisius	Jr.	15	112	32	27	2.18
91. Brandon Jackson, Nicholls State	Sr.	13	70	23	17	2.19
92. Anthony Montefusco, George Mason	Sr.	16	107	32	26	2.19
93. Gunnar Carroll, Army	Sr.	13	82	33	20	2.20
94. Tyler Mapes, Tulane		13	82	22	20	2.20
95. Tanner Tully, Ohio State	Fr.	16	93	35	23	2.22
Spencer Turnbull, Alabama	Jr.	15	93	28	23	2.22
97. Cale Elam, Wichita State	Sr.	14	89	26	22	2.22
98. Trey Lambert, Liberty	Sr.	16	109	34	27	2.23
Cody Crouse, Fla. International	Fr.	14	73	23	18	2.23
100. Reed Garrett, VMI	Jr.	13	89	32	22	2.23

WINS

RANK NAME, TEAM	W	L
1. Aaron Brown, Pepperdine	13	1
Joey DeNato, Indiana	13	1
Michael Murray, Fla. Gulf Coast	13	1
Kyle Funkhouser, Louisville	13	3
5. Blake Fox, Rice	12	0
Ben Wetzler, Oregon State	12	1
Casey Bloomquist, Cal Poly	12	1
Walker Buehler, Vanderbilt	12	2
Zach Plesac, Ball State	12	2
Josh Prevost, Seton Hall	12	2
AJ Reed, Kentucky	12	2
Sam Street, Tex.-Pan American	12	2
13. Montana Durapau, Beth.-Cookman	11	1
Aaron Nola, LSU	11	1
Carson Baranik, La.-Lafayette	11	2
Tyler Davis, Washington	11	2
Jace Fry, Oregon State	11	2
Alex Ledford, Samford	11	2
Andrew Morales, UC Irvine	11	2
Trey Lambert, Liberty	11	3
Rohn Pierce, Canisius	11	3
Ryan Williams, East Carolina	11	3
John Richy, UNLV	11	4
Mike Shawaryn, Maryland	11	4
Thomas Thorpe, Oregon	11	4
26. Joseph Camacho, Alabama State	10	1
Jason Inghram, William & Mary	10	1
Craig Schlitter, Bryant	10	1
Matt Warren, Creighton	10	1
Vince Wheeland, Oklahoma State	10	1
Luke Cahill, Seton Hall	10	2
Andro Cutura, Southeastern La.	10	2
Kyle Freeland, Evansville	10	2
Sam Odom, Sam Houston State	10	2
Daniel Thorpe, Saint Joseph's	10	2
Colin Welmon, Loyola Marymount	10	2
Tyler Alexander, TCU	10	3
Chris Ellis, Ole Miss	10	3
Alex Godzak, Canisius	10	3
Jeff Gold, Oregon	10	3
John Hochstatter, Stanford	10	3
Bailey Ober, Col. of Charleston	10	3
Brandon Waddell, Virginia	10	3
Heath Bowers, Campbell	10	4
Jordan Carter, Saint Joseph's	10	4
Taylor Clarke, Col. of Charleston	10	4
Matt Imhof, Cal Poly	10	4
Drew Morovick, Kansas	10	4

SAVES

RANK NAME, TEAM	SV
1. Sam Moore, UC Irvine	23
2. Josh Michalec, Baylor	21
3. Nick Howard, Virginia	20
Michael Cederoth, San Diego State	20
5. Brendan McCurry, Oklahoma State	19
6. Nick Burdi, Louisville	18
7. Ryan Thompson, Campbell	17
8. Eric Karch, Pepperdine	16
Michael Hanzlik, Col. of Charleston	16
Justin McClavin, Kennesaw State	16
11. Joel Seddon, South Carolina	15
Travis Stout, Jacksonville State	15
Ian Hamilton, Washington State	15
Skylar Hunter, Citadel	15
Riley Ferrell, TCU	15
Bryan Garcia, Miami	15
17. Ian Tompkins, Western Ky.	14
Andres Gracia, Samford	14
19. Kevin Mooney, Maryland	13
Andrew Elliott, Wright State	13
Joe Kuzia, St. John's	13
Jeff Kinley, Michigan State	13
Jake Reed, Oregon	13
24. Jacob Cronenworth, Michigan	12

Bradley Roney, Southern Miss.	12
Ryan Pennell, Elon	12
Ashton Perritt, Liberty	12
Tyler Powell, Western Caro.	12
Josh Roeder, Nebraska	12
Chase Wellbrock, Houston	12
Eric Eck, Wofford	12
Reed Reilly, Cal Poly	12
Dillon Tate, UC Santa Barbara	12
Jordan Romano, Oral Roberts	12
Ryan Burr, Arizona State	12
Brad Gero, Old Dominion	12
37. Karch Kowalczyk, Valparaiso	11
Thomas Burrows, Alabama	11
Sam Johns, Evansville	11
Ryan Keaffaber, Indiana State	11
Clinton Freeman, East Tenn. State	11
Houston Hibberd, San Francisco	11
Hunter Lemke, Texas State	11
Austin Weekley, Charleston So.	11
David Berg, UCLA	11
Reece Karalus, Santa Clara	11
47. Brandon Gonnella, Towson	10
Victor Sanchez, New Mexico	10
Tyler Jay, Illinois	10
Carson Fulmer, Vanderbilt	10
Seth Lucio, Tennessee Tech	10
Eric Dorsch, Kent State	10
Aaron Fossas, Wake Forest	10
Trevor Hildenberger, California	10
Robert Huber, Duke	10
Tyler Warmoth, Stetson	10
Bret Dahlson, Loyola Marymount	10

STRIKEOUTS

RANK NAME, TEAM	SO
1. Andrew Morales, UC Irvine	141
2. Zac Curtis, Middle Tenn.	136
3. Brandon Finnegan, TCU	134
Aaron Nola, LSU	134
5. Jake Stinnett, Maryland	132
6. Kyle Freeland, Evansville	128
7. Matt Imhof, Cal Poly	124
8. Seth Varner, Miami (OH)	123
9. Kyle Funkhouser, Louisville	122
10. Carlos Rodon, North Carolina State	117
T.J. Weir, Ball State	117
12. Tyler Beede, Vanderbilt	116
13. John Richy, UNLV	113
14. Mike Franco, Fla. International	112
Nathan Kirby, Virginia	112
16. Walker Buehler, Vanderbilt	111
Josh Prevost, Seton Hall	111
Bryan Radziewski, Miami	111
19. Jordan Schwartz, Niagara	109
20. Matt Fraudin, Gardner-Webb	108
James Kaprielian, UCLA	108
22. Daniel Gossett, Clemson	107
23. Matt Cooper, Hawaii	106
Sean Newcomb, Hartford	106
25. Mat Batts, UNCW	105
26. Aaron Brown, Pepperdine	104
David Hess, Tennessee Tech	104
28. Montana Durapau, Beth.-Cookman	103
29. Heath Bowers, Campbell	101
Shane McCain, Troy	101

31. Matt Borens, Eastern Ill.	100
Bubba Derby, San Diego State	100
James Farris, Arizona	100
Jacob Lindgren, Mississippi State	100
35. Andro Cutura, Southeastern La.	99
Thomas Eshelman, Cal State Fullerton	99
37. Dylan Craig, Illinois State	98
Jace Fry, Oregon State	98
Cal Quantrill, Stanford	98
40. Tommy Lawrence, Maine	97
41. Austen Williams, Texas State	96
42. Adam Bray, South Dakota State	95
Carson Fulmer, Vanderbilt	95
Daniel Mengden, Texas A&M	95
Jordan Montgomery, South Carolina	95
Preston Morrison, TCU	95
47. Andrew Barnett, Gardner-Webb	94
Sam Howard, Ga. Southern	94
Chase Mallard, UAB	94
Kevin McAvoy, Bryant	94
Eric Skoglund, UCF	94
Cameron White, Air Force	94

STRIKEOUTS PER NINE INNINGS

RANK NAME, TEAM	SO/9
1. Michael Fagan, Princeton	11.95
2. Kyle Freeland, Evansville	11.56
3. Brandon Finnegan, TCU	11.41
4. Reilly Hovis, North Carolina	11.39
5. T.J. Fussell, Western Caro.	11.33
6. DJ Roche, NJIT	11.25
7. Matt Imhof, Cal Poly	11.23
8. Jeremy Rhoades, Illinois State	10.80
9. Zac Curtis, Middle Tenn.	10.74
10. Carlos Rodon, North Carolina State	10.67
11. Michael Matuella, Duke	10.65
12. Seth Varner, Miami (OH)	10.61
13. T.J. Weir, Ball State	10.57
14. Aaron Nola, LSU	10.37
15. Jordan Schwartz, Niagara	10.29
16. Sean Newcomb, Hartford	10.22
17. Mike Franco, Fla. International	10.18
18. Kevin Hill, South Ala.	10.17
19. Eric Peterson, North Carolina State	10.13
20. Matt Ditman, Rice	10.09
21. Jake Stinnett, Maryland	10.07
22. David Bednar, Lafayette	9.97
23. Bryan Radziewski, Miami	9.92
24. Alex Daniele, NJIT	9.90
25. Cory Taylor, Dallas Baptist	9.84
26. Connor Bach, VMI	9.78
27. Walker Buehler, Vanderbilt	9.76
28. Marc Skinner, Troy	9.69
29. Colin Gotzon, Lehigh	9.68
30. Erick Fedde, UNLV	9.63
31. Jeff Hoffman, East Carolina	9.62
32. David Hess, Tennessee Tech	9.62
33. Parker Bean, Liberty	9.57
34. Dylan Craig, Illinois State	9.48
35. Mitchell Schulewitz, Ill.-Chicago	9.48
36. Adam Choplick, Oklahoma	9.46
37. Dan Gautieri, Penn	9.41
38. Carson Fulmer, Vanderbilt	9.40
39. Drew Van Orden, Duke	9.38
40. Andrew Morales, UC Irvine	9.35
41. Cas Silber, High Point	9.31

42. Anthony Misiewicz, Michigan State	9.27
43. Tyler Bray, La.-Monroe	9.27
44. Austin Coley, Belmont	9.25
45. Clay Murphy, Missouri State	9.23
46. Tyler Beede, Vanderbilt	9.21
47. Luke Leftwich, Wofford	9.20
48. Max Povse, UNC Greensboro	9.19
49. James Kaprielian, UCLA	9.17
50. Tim Koons, Oakland	9.13

FEWEST HITS PER NINE INNINGS

RANK NAME, TEAM	H/9
1. Ben Wetzler, Oregon State	4.24
2. Sean Newcomb, Hartford	4.92
3. Josh Prevost, Seton Hall	4.95
4. Aaron Nola, LSU	5.34
5. Nathan Kirby, Virginia	5.40
6. Andy Cox, Tennessee	5.47
7. Andrew Zapata, UConn	5.57
8. Cas Silber, High Point	5.80
9. David Koll, Bradley	5.80
10. Spencer Turnbull, Alabama	5.88
11. Matt Imhof, Cal Poly	5.89
12. Andrew Morales, UC Irvine	5.90
13. Montana Durapau, Beth.-Cookman	5.91
14. Josh Frye, Long Beach State	5.94
15. Carson Fulmer, Vanderbilt	6.03
16. Chase Mallard, UAB	6.05
17. Kevin Roy, Columbia	6.12
18. Keegan Thompson, Auburn	6.12
19. Tyler Ford, Houston	6.13
20. Bailey Ober, Col. of Charleston	6.16
21. Michael Matuella, Duke	6.17
22. Mike Franco, Fla. International	6.18
23. Reilly Hovis, North Carolina	6.19
24. Harry Thomas, Delaware State	6.20
25. Jace Fry, Oregon State	6.21

FEWEST WALKS PER NINE INNINGS

RANK NAME, TEAM	BB/9
1. Thomas Eshelman, CS Fullerton	0.58
2. Tyler Ford, Houston	0.65
3. Tanner Tully, Ohio State	0.68
4. Mikey Ramirez, Ark.-Pine Bluff	0.72
5. David Speer, Columbia	0.72
6. Jeff Gold, Oregon	0.72
7. Matt McClain, Delaware State	0.82
8. Gage Smith, Florida State	0.84
9. Aaron Garza, Houston	0.92
10. Cameron White, Air Force	0.95
11. Grahamm Wiest, Cal State Fullerton	0.96
12. Ryan Williams, East Carolina	0.99
13. Tyler Alexander, TCU	1.00
14. Jack Wynkoop, South Carolina	1.02
15. Logan Rice, East Tenn. State	1.04
16. Frank Duncan, Kansas	1.06
17. Jacob Evans, Oklahoma	1.07
18. Kyle Freeland, Evansville	1.08
19. Josh Walker, New Mexico	1.09
20. Kalei Contrades, San Jose State	1.13
21. Michael Murray, Fla. Gulf Coast	1.18
22. Anthony Montefusco, George Mason	1.18
23. Koby Gauna, Cal State Fullerton	1.19
24. Connor Cuff, Penn	1.23
Tanner Perkins, Eastern Ky.	1.23

TEAM LEADERS

SCORING

RANK TEAM	G	R	R/G
1. Tennessee Tech	59	488	8.3
2. Delaware State	47	386	8.2
3. William & Mary	56	452	8.1
4. La.-Lafayette	68	530	7.8
5. Kentucky	62	472	7.6
6. Canisius	56	410	7.3
7. Alabama State	57	412	7.2
8. Southeast Mo. State	57	408	7.2
9. Western Caro.	55	388	7.1
10. San Diego	54	380	7.0
11. Saint Joseph's	51	350	6.9
12. Seton Hall	53	356	6.7
13. Davidson	48	322	6.7
14. Samford	60	401	6.7
15. Bryant	58	386	6.7
16. Ill.-Chicago	51	338	6.6

17.	Morehead State	57	374	6.6	29.	VCU	57	357	6.3	41.	Cal Poly	59	350	5.9
18.	Ga. Southern	63	413	6.6	30.	LSU	63	394	6.3	42.	Central Mich.	58	342	5.9
19.	Florida State	60	393	6.6	31.	Austin Peay	56	349	6.2	43.	Ole Miss	69	406	5.9
20.	St. John's	55	352	6.4		Radford	56	349	6.2	44.	Eastern Ky.	55	323	5.9
21.	New Mexico	58	370	6.4	33.	Louisville	67	417	6.2	45.	Arkansas State	59	346	5.9
22.	UNC Greensboro	49	312	6.4	34.	Texas-Arlington	59	365	6.2	46.	Texas Tech	66	387	5.9
23.	Iowa	53	337	6.4	35.	Ball State	57	352	6.2	47.	Nebraska	62	363	5.9
24.	Georgia State	56	356	6.4	36.	Oklahoma State	66	400	6.1	48.	Furman	59	345	5.8
25.	Kent State	59	375	6.4	37.	Jacksonville State	63	379	6.0	49.	Fla. Gulf Coast	61	356	5.8
26.	Dallas Baptist	61	387	6.3	38.	Kennesaw State	64	384	6.0	50.	Arizona State	57	331	5.8
27.	New Mexico State	54	340	6.3		Evansville	55	330	6.0					
28.	Indiana	59	370	6.3	40.	Jackson State	57	341	6.0					

BATTING AVERAGE

RANK TEAM	BA
1. Delaware State	.331
2. La.-Lafayette	.317
3. San Diego	.315
4. Canisius	.314
5. New Mexico	.312
6. UNC Greensboro	.310
7. William & Mary	.310
8. Tennessee Tech	.309
9. Southeast Mo. State	.306
10. Morehead State	.306

HOME RUNS

RANK TEAM	HR
1. Tennessee Tech	83
2. La.-Lafayette	68
3. Ga. Southern	61
4. Kentucky	60
Georgia State	60
6. Samford	57
7. William & Mary	55
8. Oklahoma State	53
9. Eastern Ky.	50
Davidson	50

DOUBLES

RANK TEAM	2B
1. William & Mary	149
2. Vanderbilt	145
3. La.-Lafayette	141
4. Fla. Gulf Coast	128
5. Jacksonville State	126
6. Texas Tech	125
Texas-Arlington	125
8. Georgia State	124
9. Tennessee Tech	121
Ole Miss	121
Kentucky	121
San Diego	121

TRIPLES

RANK TEAM	3B
1. La.-Lafayette	31
2. Oregon	27
3. Texas Tech	26
4. Arizona	25
Miami (OH)	25
East Tenn. State	25
Canisius	25
8. Bakersfield	24
Rutgers	24
Pacific	24

SLUGGING PERCENTAGE

RANK TEAM	SLG PCT
1. Tennessee Tech	.495
2. La.-Lafayette	.493
3. William & Mary	.471
4. Delaware State	.469
5. Georgia State	.460
6. Davidson	.459
7. San Diego	.453
8. Kentucky	.446
9. Bryant	.436
10. Indiana	.434

STOLEN BASES

RANK TEAM	SB	CS
1. Wofford	153	38
2. Louisville	133	34
3. Vanderbilt	120	45
4. Seton Hall	111	30
5. La.-Lafayette	109	43
6. Fordham	101	41
7. Bryant	99	21
Rider	99	24
9. Army	98	22
10. Southeast Mo. State	97	24

WALKS

RANK TEAM	BB
1. Florida State	330
2. Oklahoma State	324
3. Tennessee Tech	312
4. Virginia	294
5. Oregon State	293
6. Houston	292
7. Dallas Baptist	291
8. Texas	288
9. La.-Lafayette	278
Canisius	278

PITCHING

EARNED RUN AVERAGE

RANK TEAM	ERA
1. TCU	2.22
2. Virginia	2.23
3. Cal State Fullerton	2.24
4. Texas	2.25
5. Fla. International	2.29
6. Oregon State	2.29
7. Indiana	2.33
8. Houston	2.35
9. South Carolina	2.43
10. Pepperdine	2.55
11. Nicholls State	2.60
12. LSU	2.60
13. Rice	2.61
14. Liberty	2.62
15. Arkansas	2.63
16. Ole Miss	2.72
17. Sam Houston State	2.73
18. Col. of Charleston	2.73
19. UC Irvine	2.76
20. Louisville	2.80
21. Bryant	2.84
22. UTSA	2.84
23. Army	2.86
24. UAB	2.87
25. Vanderbilt	2.90
26. Seton Hall	2.90
27. Southeastern La.	2.92
28. Miami	2.94
29. Long Beach State	2.97
30. East Carolina	2.99
31. Cal Poly	3.03
32. Notre Dame	3.05
33. Mississippi State	3.06
34. Oregon	3.06
35. Northeastern	3.08
36. Florida State	3.08
37. Michigan State	3.09
38. Hartford	3.09
39. Texas Tech	3.11
40. Washington	3.11
41. Duke	3.14
42. Ga. Southern	3.15
43. Alabama	3.19
44. UNLV	3.19
45. UConn	3.19
46. North Carolina	3.21
47. Michigan	3.21
48. High Point	3.24
49. Illinois	3.25
50. North Carolina State	3.27

STRIKEOUTS PER NINE INNINGS

RANK TEAM	K/9
1. Illinois State	9.4
2. North Carolina State	9.3
3. Vanderbilt	8.9
4. Duke	8.6
5. Louisville	8.4
6. TCU	8.4
7. Wofford	8.4
8. Cal Poly	8.4
9. Dallas Baptist	8.3
10. Miami	8.2

FEWEST WALKS PER NINE INNINGS

RANK TEAM	PG
1. Cal State Fullerton	1.52
2. Houston	1.82
3. Mercer	2.08
4. UC Irvine	2.15
5. TCU	2.22
6. Central Conn. State	2.28
7. East Tenn. State	2.35
8. Illinois	2.37
9. Missouri	2.39
10. Long Beach State	2.41

FIELDING

FIELDING PERCENTAGE

RANK TEAM	PCT
1. Creighton	.984
2. Stony Brook	.983
3. Washington	.982
4. Virginia	.981
5. Mississippi State	.981
6. Texas Tech	.981
7. Tennessee Tech	.979
8. La.-Lafayette	.979
9. Dartmouth	.979
10. Oregon State	.979
11. TCU	.977
12. Cal Poly	.977
13. Long Beach State	.977
14. Rice	.977
15. Oregon	.976
16. West Virginia	.976
17. Bakersfield	.976
18. LSU	.976
19. Stanford	.976
20. Old Dominion	.976
21. Nebraska	.976
22. Central Conn. State	.975
23. UAB	.975
24. Florida	.975
25. Maryland	.975

DOUBLE PLAYS

RANK TEAM	DP
1. Georgia Tech	77
2. Texas	71
3. Old Dominion	68
Nicholls State	68
5. Siena	67
6. Lipscomb	65
Texas Tech	65
8. Washington	64
9. Tulane	63
Southeast Mo. State	63

COLLEGE *TOP 25*

Batters: 10 or more at-bats. **Pitchers:** 5 or more innings.

1. VANDERBILT

Coach: Tim Corbin. **Record:** 51-21.

PLAYER, POS., YEAR	AVG	AB	R	H	2B	3B	HR	RBI	SB
Bryan Reynolds, of, Fr.	.338	281	53	95	24	2	4	54	14
Dansby Swanson, 2b, So.	.333	282	63	94	27	2	3	34	22
John Norwood, of, Jr.	.298	218	32	65	12	1	3	32	17
Chris Harvey, c, Jr.	.294	68	8	20	3	0	0	8	0
Xavier Turner, 3b, So.	.284	250	35	71	15	0	2	38	18
Vince Conde, ss, Jr.	.284	243	45	69	9	1	4	50	15
Rhett Wiseman, of, So.	.277	238	37	66	18	4	0	30	12
Zander Wiel, 1b, So.	.260	235	43	61	14	3	5	44	13
Jason Delay, c, Fr.	.246	114	26	28	9	0	0	13	1
Ro Coleman, of, Fr.	.217	115	16	25	2	0	1	13	4
Tyler Campbell, 3b, So.	.212	33	6	7	3	0	0	6	0
Nolan Rogers, dh, Fr.	.203	148	20	30	6	0	0	14	3
Karl Ellison, c, Fr.	.192	73	8	14	0	1	0	9	0
Will Cooper, cf, Jr.	.182	22	4	4	1	0	0	1	1
Kyle Smith, dh, So.	.154	39	7	6	2	0	0	5	0

PLAYER, POS., YEAR	W	L	ERA	G	SV	IP	H	BB	SO
Adam Ravenelle, rhp, Jr.	3	2	1.35	24	3	40	19	14	37
John Kilichowski, lhp, Fr.	0	0	1.57	13	0	23	13	8	22
Hayden Stone, rhp, Fr.	4	0	1.71	23	3	58	41	14	80
Brian Miller, rhp, Jr.	1	1	1.93	30	5	42	24	8	37
Carson Fulmer, rhp, So.	7	1	1.98	26	10	91	61	41	95
Walker Buehler, rhp, So.	12	2	2.64	19	0	102	85	31	111
Tyler Ferguson, rhp, So.	8	4	2.69	17	0	77	55	30	65
Ben Bowden, lhp, Fr.	0	0	3.48	12	0	10	8	6	10
Tyler Beede, rhp, Jr.	8	8	4.05	19	0	113	92	53	116
Jared Miller, lhp, Jr.	7	2	4.35	17	0	62	58	27	46
T.J. Pecoraro, rhp, Sr.	1	1	8.20	13	0	19	29	12	16

2. VIRGINIA

Coach: Brian O'Connor. **Record:** 53-16.

Player, Pos., Year	AVG	AB	R	H	2B	3B	HR	RBI	SB
John La Prise, dh, So.	.348	178	24	62	10	0	1	17	5
Mike Papi, 1b, Jr.	.307	244	55	75	11	0	11	56	8
Branden Cogswell, 2b, Jr.	.301	259	47	78	11	1	0	23	8
Joe McCarthy, of, So.	.301	256	55	77	16	2	6	49	11
Robbie Coman, c, So.	.283	106	18	30	4	1	1	15	1
Kenny Towns, 3b, Jr.	.278	187	25	52	14	1	2	36	6
Matt Thaiss, c, Fr.	.265	68	11	18	5	0	0	7	0
Nick Howard, dh, Jr.	.261	153	20	40	6	1	1	20	1
Daniel Pinero, ss, Fr.	.261	241	39	63	6	0	0	22	10
Derek Fisher, of, Jr.	.260	177	24	46	7	1	3	29	5
Nate Irving, c, Jr.	.242	153	19	37	5	0	1	18	1
Brandon Downes, of, Jr.	.241	237	31	57	10	2	7	40	9
Tony Butler, if, Fr.	.182	11	1	2	0	0	0	1	0
Robert Bennie, of/if, So.	.150	20	4	3	0	1	0	3	0

PLAYER, POS., YEAR	W	L	ERA	G	SV	IP	H	BB	SO
Alec Bettinger, rhp, Fr.	6	0	1.23	11	0	37	24	12	32
Artie Lewicki, rhp, Sr.	8	1	1.31	16	1	69	37	13	57
Whit Mayberry, rhp, Sr.	6	1	1.60	30	2	56	38	12	59
Austin Young, rhp, Sr.	1	0	1.75	19	0	26	18	4	27
Nick Howard, rhp, Jr.	2	2	1.91	31	20	38	23	14	60
Nathan Kirby, lhp, So.	9	3	2.06	18	0	113	68	33	112
Brandon Waddell, lhp, Fr.	10	3	2.45	18	0	114	98	19	73
David Rosenberger, lhp, So.	1	1	2.82	16	0	22	20	8	16
Josh Sborz, rhp, So.	6	4	2.92	17	0	77	57	44	72
Kevin Doherty, lhp, So.	0	0	3.09	10	0	12	7	7	6
Connor Jones, rhp, Fr.	4	1	3.13	25	1	55	42	23	40

3. MISSISSIPPI

Coach: Mike Bianco. **Record:** 48-21.

PLAYER, POS., YEAR	AVG	AB	R	H	2B	3B	HR	RBI	SB
Will Allen, c, Sr.	.339	277	44	94	24	0	7	64	0

PLAYER, POS., YEAR	AVG	AB	R	H	2B	3B	HR	RBI	SB
Auston Bousfield, of, Jr.	.336	286	61	96	18	2	6	50	19
Holt Perdzock, c, So.	.324	37	4	12	1	0	0	6	0
Austin Anderson, 3b, Sr.	.323	269	57	87	18	1	5	41	10
Brantley Bell, if, Fr.	.304	102	16	31	6	0	0	11	2
Austin Knight, c, Jr.	.303	33	5	10	0	0	0	0	0
J.B. Woodman, of, Fr.	.298	168	31	50	10	3	2	20	10
Errol Robinson, ss, Fr.	.294	214	23	63	7	0	0	19	5
Sikes Orvis, 1b, Jr.	.294	235	40	69	14	1	14	53	1
Braxton Lee, of, So.	.281	270	56	76	9	1	0	25	30
Preston Overbey, 2b, Sr.	.271	225	28	61	10	2	4	34	2
Dalton Dulin, 2b, Fr.	.264	53	6	14	0	0	0	7	6
Colby Bortles, dh, Fr.	.250	68	10	17	2	1	2	14	0
Will Jamison, of, Jr.	.248	129	14	32	1	4	2	13	6
John Gatlin, if, Sr.	.133	30	1	4	0	0	0	6	1
Henri Lartique, c, Fr.	.100	10	0	1	1	0	0	2	0
Cameron Dishon, of, So.	.071	14	8	1	0	0	0	1	0

PLAYER, POS., YEAR	W	L	ERA	G	SV	IP	H	BB	SO
Josh Laxer, rhp, Jr.	3	2	1.47	23	6	37	30	11	43
Preston Tarkington, rhp, So.	0	1	1.69	19	0	16	13	6	17
Aaron Greenwood, rhp, Sr.	3	2	2.03	22	5	44	29	12	35
Christian Trent, lhp, So.	9	0	2.05	17	0	110	95	20	86
Evan Anderson, rhp, So.	2	0	2.11	10	0	21	9	10	20
Scott Weathersby, rhp, Jr.	4	1	2.13	20	2	38	28	10	51
Chris Ellis, rhp, Jr.	10	3	2.55	19	0	116	11	42	67
Wyatt Short, lhp, Fr.	3	3	2.59	23	3	31	19	13	34
Jeremy Massie, lhp, Sr.	4	3	2.69	21	1	64	61	17	46
Sam Smith, rhp, Jr.	5	4	3.61	18	0	95	108	21	54
Jacob Waguespack, rhp, So.	1	0	3.77	9	0	14	15	9	11
Matt Denny, lhp, So.	1	1	4.20	15	0	15	16	5	11
Cheyne Bickel, rhp, Fr.	3	1	4.26	12	0	13	19	1	8
Hawtin Buchanan, rhp, Jr.	0	0	8.18	12	0	11	11	9	16
Austin Blunt, rhp, Sr.	0	0	9.64	7	0	5	7	3	2

4. TEXAS

Coach: Augie Garrido. **Record:** 46-21.

PLAYER, POS., YEAR	AVG	AB	R	H	2B	3B	HR	RBI	SB
Carter, Madison, dh, Sr.	.322	188	27	38	6	0	1	12	3
Payton, Mark, of, Sr.	.315	241	33	76	15	5	2	39	19
Hinojosa, C.J., ss, So.	.298	242	31	72	13	0	2	35	5
Gurwitz, Zane, 3b, Fr.	.284	208	26	59	10	1	2	28	9
Marlow, Brooks, 2b,	.268	261	41	70	11	4	3	21	4
Shaw, Collin, of, Jr.	.264	193	22	51	5	1	0	23	13
Johnson, Ben, of, So.	.263	247	46	65	11	3	6	33	21
Barrera, Tres, c, Fr.	.261	241	32	63	13	3	5	35	0
Clemens, Kacy, 1b, Fr.	.212	208	20	44	4	0	1	21	0
Felts, Jacob, dh, Sr.	.214	56	4	12	1	1	0	6	0
Montalbano, Jeremy, c, So.	.171	82	5	14	6	0	0	4	0
McGuire, Andy, inf, Fr.	.113	71	6	8	1	0	0	7	1

PLAYER, POS., YEAR	W	L	ERA	G	SV	IP	H	BB	SO
Duke, Travis, lhp, So.	2	1	0.29	29	2	31	22	7	27
Hollingsworth, Chad, rhp, So.	4	0	1.15	25	2	55	34	13	28
Thornhill, Nathan, rhp, Sr.	3	1.51	21		21	13	82	37	68
Culbreth, Ty, lhp, So.	2	0	1.98	20	0	27	16	18	20
Peters, Dillon, lhp, Jr.	7	3	2.17	13	0	80	72	21	53
Curtiss, John, rhp, Jr.	2	3	2.28	28	9	43	34	15	33
French, Parker, rhp, Jr.	7	5	2.41	20	1	105	88	44	62
Cooper, Morgan, rhp, Fr.	4	2	2.89	29	3	56	53	9	41
Goins, Blake, rhp, Fr.	1	0	3.38	7	0	11	10	8	7
Schiraldi, Lukas, rhp, Jr.	7	3	4.08	13	0	64	58	39	35
Sawyer, Josh, lhp, Fr.	1	0	5.59	7	0	10	14	6	8

5. TEXAS CHRISTIAN

Coach: Jim Schlossnagle. **Record:** 48-18.

PLAYER, POS., YEAR	AVG	AB	R	H	2B	3B	HR	RBI	SB
Pennington, Walker, of, Fr.	.400	10	0	4	2	0	0	3	0
Crain, Garrett, 2b, Jr.	.324	179	31	58	9	2	1	19	8
White, Boomer, of, So.	.315	267	49	84	14	0	2	49	12

PLAYER, POS., YEAR	AVG	AB	R	H	2B	3B	HR	RBI	SB
Fitzgerald, Dylan, of, Sr.	.307	244	34	75	16	3	2	34	6
Cron, Kevin, 1b, Jr.	.279	247	37	69	18	2	6	41	2
Suiter, Jerrick, dh, Jr.	.273	172	24	47	12	0	0	29	5
Bacak, Kyle, c, Sr.	.269	171	23	46	4	0	0	18	7
Jones, Keaton, ss, Jr.	.266	241	28	64	4	1	0	21	9
Odell, Derek, 3b, Jr.	.265	253	34	67	8	2	1	35	8
Jones, Cody, of, Jr.	.265	257	51	68	9	2	0	18	29
Delso, Dylan, So.	.257	35	2	9	1	0	0	6	0
Castellano, Connor, inf, Jr.	.219	96	14	21	3	0	0	6	6
Fagnan, Jeremie, of, Jr.	.203	74	4	15	1	0	2	11	1

PLAYER, POS., YEAR	W	L	ERA	G	SV	IP	H	BB	SO
Burnett, Ryan, lhp, Fr.	0	0	0.00	4	0	8	6	3	10
Ferrell, Riley, rhp, So.	3	1	0.79	31	15	45	20	14	70
Morrison, Preston, rhp, Jr.	9	4	1.32	18	0	130	90	21	95
Finnegan, Brandon, lhp, Jr.	9	3	2.04	17	0	106	79	29	134
Teakell, Trey, rhp, Jr.	6	1	2.34	26	2	62	47	13	41
Alexander, Tyler, lhp, Fr.	10	3	2.36	20	0	99	88	11	59
Young, Alex, lhp, So.	1	3	2.51	22	1	43	35	16	40
Howard, Brian, rhp, Fr.	0	0	2.77	9	0	13	9	10	14
Kipper, Jordan, rhp, Jr.	8	3	3.23	17	0	75	67	17	74
Evans, Travis, lhp, Jr.	0	0	3.60	18	0	15	14	9	18
Trieglaff, Brian, rs-Fr.	2	0	4.76	16	0	17	22	8	19

6. LOUISVILLE

Coach: Dan McDonnell. Record: 50-17.

PLAYER, POS., YEAR	AVG	AB	R	H	2B	3B	HR	RBI	SB
Solak, Nick, dh, Fr.	.351	97	29	34	5	0	2	25	9
Gibson, Kyle, c, Sr.	.325	126	20	41	4	0	1	21	4
Ray, Corey, of, Fr.	.325	77	11	25	5	2	1	17	4
Sturgeon, Cole, of, Sr.	.323	269	58	87	16	7	2	35	19
Gardner, Jeff, of, Sr.	.313	240	37	75	20	2	9	68	2
Crain, Shane, c, Sr.	.296	81	11	24	9	0	2	24	3
Chittenden, Alex, 3b, Sr.	.294	211	39	62	10	1	1	30	2
Kay, Grant, 1b, Jr.	.285	207	49	59	9	0	5	35	23
Lucas, Zach, 2b, Jr.	.270	237	38	64	13	2	5	44	7
Rosenbaum, Danny, 1b/3b, So.	.295	129	20	38	9	0	2	24	3
Lyman, Colin, of, Fr.	.263	114	21	30	4	2	0	16	10
Taylor, Logan, of, Fr.	.238	80	10	19	1	0	0	7	3
White, Mike, of, Jr.	.235	51	12	12	2	0	0	3	7
Smith, Will, inf, Fr.	.221	77	10	17	4	0	0	12	3
Whiting, Sutton, ss, Jr.	.216	218	51	47	4	3	2	18	37

PLAYER, POS., YEAR	W	L	ERA	G	SV	IP	H	BB	SO
Burdi, Nick, rhp, Jr.	3	1	0.49	32	18	37	18	10	65
McGrath, Kyle, lhp, Jr.	2	1	1.34	23	0	40	25	14	40
Strader, Robert, lhp, Fr.	0	0	1.93	14	0	1	9	10	9
Funkhouser, Kyle, rhp, So.	13	3	1.94	18	0	120	85	65	122
Sturgeon, Cole, lhp, Sr.	3	0	1.98	25	1	36	19	14	37
Ruxer, Jared, rhp, Jr.	7	1	2.27	13	0	75	62	16	68
Alphin, Brandon, rhp, Jr.	1	1	2.77	12	0	13	13	4	4
Sparger, Jake, rhp, Fr.	2	1	3.20	17	0	45	48	16	26
Kidston, Anthony, rhp, So.	9	1	3.40	14	0	77	56	36	69
Philley, Jonah, rhp, So.	1	0	3.48	17	0	10	9	8	6
Rogers, Josh, lhp, Fr.	3	3	3.63	14	0	52	44	12	47
Burdi, Zack, rhp, Fr.	1	0	4.35	13	0	10	8	7	6
Harrington, Drew, lhp, Fr.	3	2	4.95	21	1	36	62	7	34

7. LOUISIANA LAFAYETTE

Coach: Tony Robichaux. Record: 58-10.

PLAYER, POS., YEAR	AVG	AB	R	H	2B	3B	HR	RBI	SB
Adams, Caleb, of, Jr.	.381	223	67	85	18	7	11	42	7
Conrad, Jace, 2b, Jr.	.364	264	63	96	20	7	9	65	22
Trahan, Blake, ss, So.	.355	256	58	91	12	2	4	49	15
Leonards, Ryan, utl, Sr.	.328	262	63	86	16	4	4	35	18
Girouard, Tyler, 3b, Jr.	.324	179	33	58	11	2	3	32	4
Harrison, Seth, of, Jr.	.323	254	53	82	17	7	9	65	15
Davis, Greg, 3b, Jr.	.314	86	20	27	5	1	3	23	6
Butler, Dylan, of, Jr.	.298	171	40	51	11	2	6	31	4
Compton, Chase, 1b, Sr.	.290	176	37	51	8	0	3	44	5
Powell, Evan, utl, Jr.	.250	60	15	15	2	1	4	14	2
Wilson, Ryan, of, Sr.	.246	65	12	16	4	0	2	13	5
Strentz, Michael, c, Jr.	.231	225	47	52	1	1	10	43	6
Thurman, Nick, c, So.	.222	54	10	12	3	1	0	13	0

PLAYER, POS., YEAR	W	L	ERA	G	SV	IP	H	BB	SO
Hicks, Matt, lhp, Sr.	8	1	1.41	25	1	45	33	12	41
Wilson, Ryan, lhp, Sr.	6	0	2.08	23	7	61	51	20	44
Bazar, Reagan, rhp, Fr.	4	0	2.27	25	6	32	26	17	20
Robichaux, Austin, rhp, Jr.	8	3	3.11	14	0	90	69	24	80
Baranik, Carson, rhp, Jr.	11	2	3.31	17	0	106	93	27	74
Boutte, Cody, lhp, Sr.	9	1	3.36	16	0	86	81	27	56
Cooper, Riley, lhp, Fr.	0	0	3.48	15	0	10	12	4	9
Plitt, Matt, rhp, Sr.	2	0	3.68	28	5	59	43	30	44
Griffit, Chris, lhp, Jr.	0	0	4.09	12	1	11	5	4	14
Carter, Ben, rhp, Sr.	1	0	4.34	16	1	29	27	8	33
Charpentier, Chris, rhp, Fr.	1	0	4.67	8	0	17	15	7	9
Milhorn, Greg, rhp, Jr.	5	2	7.12	16	2	37	47	14	23

8. UC IRVINE

Coach: Mike Gillespie. Record: 41-25.

PLAYER, POS., YEAR	AVG	AB	R	H	2B	3B	HR	RBI	SB
Spencer, Connor, 1b, Jr.	.364	250	36	91	15	5	1	44	8
Alcantara, Adam, of, Fr.	.323	62	8	20	0	0	0	9	1
Sparks, Taylor, 3b, Jr.	.308	253	45	78	17	9	5	37	8
McClanahan, Jerry, c, Jr.	.304	207	17	63	5	0	1	36	3
Munoz, Jonathan, dh, So.	.281	167	21	47	10	0	0	18	1
Palmer, Grant, 2b, So.	.268	228	29	61	8	0	0	13	3
Rabago, Chris, ss, Jr.	.246	240	36	59	9	2	0	20	2
Duarte, Mikey, inf, So.	.241	79	7	19	2	0	0	8	1
Cassolato, Evan, of, rs-Fr.	.238	105	11	25	2	1	0	8	2
Castro, Justin, of, Jr.	.231	130	15	30	4	0	0	8	2
Paulino, Kris, of/inf, Jr.	.216	204	34	44	8	2	5	25	3
Cooper, Ryan, of, Jr.	.200	80	11	16	2	2	0	11	3
Brontsema, John, inf, Fr.	.197	66	10	13	1	2	0	4	0
Martinez, Renae, c, rs-Fr.	.152	33	2	5	1	0	0	5	0
Herkins, Jonathan, of, So.	.100	10	4	1	0	0	0	1	0

PLAYER, POS., YEAR	W	L	ERA	G	SV	IP	H	BB	SO
Davis, Kyle, rhp, So.	2	0	1.37	11	0	20	10	6	15
Morales, Andrew, rhp, Sr.	11	2	1.53	19	0	136	89	33	141
Moore, Sam, rhp, Jr.	0	3	1.85	32	23	44	35	11	39
Surrey, Elliot, lhp, So.	8	5	2.32	19	1	113	97	29	76
Manarino, Evan, lhp, Jr.	4	4	2.66	23	1	65	77	9	56
Brock, Evan, rhp, Jr.	9	6	3.02	19	0	107	109	23	70
Litchfield, Jimmy, lhp, Sr.	3	2	3.55	27	2	38	35	12	22
Fielding, Matt, lhp, Jr.	2	0	4.00	23	0	27	27	2	12
Merten, Mitch, rhp, Sr.	2	2	6.58	24	0	26	32	12	21
Sparling, Sean, rhp, Fr.	0	0	9.95	7	0	6	12	1	7

9. TEXAS TECH

Coach: Tim Tadlock. Record: 45-21.

PLAYER, POS., YEAR	AVG	AB	R	H	2B	3B	HR	RBI	SB
Nelsony, Tyler, of, So.	.375	160	29	60	12	6	4	34	2
Davis, Zach, of, So.	.367	30	20	11	1	0	0	9	9
Randolph, Mason, c, Sr.	.350	20	6	7	3	1	1	7	0
Humphreys, Alec, inf, So.	.322	87	18	23	3	2	0	15	3
Proudfoot, Tim, ss, Jr.	.309	149	26	46	5	1	0	19	1
Kirsch, Adam, dh, Sr.	.307	225	37	69	21	3	10	51	0
Gutierrez, Eric, inf, So.	.302	245	46	74	18	2	12	85	0
Smith, Stephen, inf, Sr.	.287	195	41	56	12	3	1	20	2
Lyons, Anthony, of, Fr.	.286	70	10	22	2	0	0	8	1
Barrios, Jake, inf, Sr.	.272	184	36	50	8	1	0	23	2
Burleson, Bryant, 2b,	.272	254	38	69	21	3	2	37	2
Conley, Devon, of, Sr.	.269	104	18	28	1	1	0	8	5
Redman, Hunter, c, Jr.	.246	142	11	35	3	0	0	17	1
Floyd, Tyler, c, So.	.241	58	12	14	2	2	0	8	0
Broadbent, Matt, inf, Fr.	.228	79	7	18	6	0	0	11	1
Long, Ryan, 3b, Fr.	.212	156	18	33	7	1	0	22	1

PLAYER, POS., YEAR	W	L	ERA	G	SV	IP	H	BB	SO
Dusek, Dylan, lhp, Fr.	8	0	1.94	14	0	74	63	14	38
Drozd, Jonny, lhp, Sr.	7	1	2.09	28	5	73	64	15	48
Taylor, Corey, rhp, Jr.	5	3	2.61	21	2	48	49	8	32
Tripp, Jonathan, rhp, So.	0	1	2.73	12	1	26	24	5	16
Smith, Cameron, lhp, Jr.	8	3	2.79	25	1	68	49	29	44
Moseley, Ryan, rhp, Fr.	1	2	2.84	22	3	51	36	25	41
Sadberry, Chris, lhp, Jr.	5	3	3.03	18	0	95	88	25	65
Moreno, Dominic, rhp, Jr.	4	5	3.14	22	2	66	68	24	56

	W	L	ERA	G	SV	IP	H	BB	SO
Brown, Dalton, rhp, So.	2	0	4.05	15	1	20	16	11	17
Winthrow, Matt, rhp, So.	3	3	5.65	12	0	37	36	21	42

10. OKLAHOMA STATE

Coach: Josh Holliday. **Record:** 48-18.

PLAYER, POS., YEAR	AVG	AB	R	H	2B	3B	HR	RBI	SB
Green, Gage, of, Jr.	.310	239	45	74	14	2	3	30	20
Walton, Donnie, ss, So.	.310	252	45	78	15	0	3	36	7
Fish, Zach, dh, Jr.	.308	240	41	74	17	0	11	48	4
McConaughy, Criag, 3b, Sr.	.300	160	22	48	6	0	1	23	5
Sluder, Ryan, of, Fr.	.284	67	11	19	10	0	0	7	1
Krietmeier, Tanner, 1b, Sr.	.275	262	48	72	13	2	10	52	5
Saxon, Saulyer, of, Sr.	.273	161	34	44	5	0	1	24	5
Arakawa, Tim, 2b, Jr.	.265	230	43	61	6	1	4	44	15
Case, Bryan, c, Jr.	.262	84	21	22	5	1	4	14	2
Rosa, Andrew, inf, Fr.	.243	37	9	9	1	0	1	6	2
Costello, Conor, of, So.	.240	192	28	46	10	0	9	27	4
Rojas, Robie, c, Fr.	.235	34	6	8	0	1	0	4	0
Hagler, Hunter, inf, Jr.	.227	22	4	5	0	0	1	3	0
Cornell, Aaron, of, Sr.	.227	75	16	17	1	0	1	8	2
Williams, Garrett, 1b, Fr.	.22	18	3	4	0	0	1	7	0
Williams, Dustin, 1b, Fr.	.216	102	20	22	1	4	3	21	2

PLAYER, POS., YEAR	W	L	ERA	G	SV	IP	H	BB	SO
McCurry, Brendan, rhp, Sr.	5	0	.0.38	35	19	47	29	8	54
Wheeland, Vince, rhp, Sr.	10	1	1.52	31	0	83	65	16	45
Battenfield, Blak, rhp, Fr.	4	0	1.69	27	0	53	42	20	38
Perrin, Jon, rhp, Jr.	8	5	2.38	21	0	102	94	29	81
Buffett, Tyler, rhp, Jr.	2	1	2.95	14	0	55	52	24	36
Hackerrott, Alex, lhp, So.	4	1	3.00	28	0	27	19	9	26
Cobb, Trey, rhp, Fr.	0	0	3.12	18	0	35	37	18	28
Robinette, Mark, rhp, Sr.	3	2	3.58	12	0	28	32	13	25
Hatch, Thomas, rhp, Fr.	2	2	5.28	13	0	46	50	19	36
Freeman, Michael, lhp, Jr.	2	1	6.28	10	0	14	16	9	17
Nurdin, Tyler, lhp, Jr.	4	3	6.54	17	0	52	70	39	31

11. HOUSTON

Coach: Todd Whitting. **Record:** 48-18.

PLAYER, POS., YEAR	AVG	AB	R	H	2B	3B	HR	RBI	SB
Grayson, Casey, 1b, Sr.	.321	243	37	78	16	1	6	48	1
Hollis, Connor, 3b, Fr.	.321	106	15	34	4	0	0	8	1
Survance, Kyle, of, So.	.308	253	53	78	11	2	2	32	31
Montenayor, Justin, dh, So.	.298	248	36	74	15	0	1	31	0
Pyeatt, Michael, of, Jr.	.297	172	20	51	4	2	1	21	5
Vidales, Josh, 2b, So.	.285	235	45	67	5	0	0	30	11
Ratcliff, Frankie, ss, Sr.	.278	223	40	62	9	1	2	28	17
Fulmer, Ashford, of, So.	.267	187	26	50	9	0	4	322	12
Barker, Caleb, c, Sr.	.225	204	26	46	8	2	1	28	2
Stading, Jordan, inf, Fr.	.225	102	13	23	1	0	0	13	0
Smith, Daniel, rhp, Sr.	.250	12	0	3	1	0	0	1	0
Luenenerg, Jacob, inf, Sr.	.247	73	10	18	8	0	0	11	0
Appling, Landon, of, Sr.	.222	90	16	20	1	1	0	11	5

PLAYER, POS., YEAR	W	L	ERA	G	SV	IP	H	BB	SO
Ford, Tyler, lhp, Sr.	9	0	1.17	27	4	69	47	5	49
Wellbrock, Chase, rhp, Sr.	5	0	1.17	23	12	46	38	5	37
Robinson, Jared, rhp, Jr.	5	1	1.35	23	0	47	31	16	41
Locus, Matt, lhp, Jr.	1	0	1.42	8	0	13	10	5	8
Cobb, Taylor, rhp, Jr.	0	0	1.80	4	0	5	2	2	2
Lantrip, Andrew, rhp, Fr.	6	0	1.87	14	0	43	33	7	33
Lemoine, Jake, rhp, Fr.	6	8	2.87	17	0	107	98	29	87
Longville, David, rhp, Jr.	1	0	2.88	14	0	59	68	8	36
West, Jared, lhp, So.	2	2	2.90	14	0	50	38	18	39
Garza, Aaron, rhp, Jr.	9	5	2.92	17	0	108	102	11	57
Peek, Kirby, rhp, Fr.	0	0	3.00	3	0	9	7	2	6
Maxwell, Bubba, rhp, So.	3	0	3.24	15	1	25	23	5	20
Stewart, Aaron, lhp, Sr.	1	2	4.32	17	0	8	7	6	11

12. PEPPERDINE

Coach: Steve Rodriguez. **Record:** 43-18.

PLAYER, POS., YEAR	AVG	AB	R	H	2B	3B	HR	RBI	SB
Fornaci, Chris, dh, So.	.405	42	8	17	3	0	2	12	0
Barnett, Aaron, c, Fr.	.359	223	23	80	5	1	0	27	1

PLAYER, POS., YEAR	AVG	AB	R	H	2B	3B	HR	RBI	SB
Brown, Aaron, of, Jr.	.314	242	44	76	13	3	13	49	5
Moyer, Hutton, 2b, So.	.306	232	52	71	24	4	0	22	15
Rodriguez, Ben, inf, Fr.	.300	10	0	3	0	0	0	2	0
Caruso, Brandon, of, Fr.	.283	184	35	52	8	1	4	28	3
Anderson, Brad, 1b, So.	.282	220	31	62	13	0	5	33	1
Langlois, Bryan, of, Jr.	.281	231	40	65	9	1	3	34	6
Davidson, Austin, 3b, Jr.	.266	241	36	64	15	2	4	33	0
Carter, Devin, of, So.	.263	57	9	15	2	0	1	7	1
Jefferson, Manny, ss, Fr.	.227	176	17	40	10	0	1	28	1
Perri, Michael, inf, Fr.	.219	32	4	7	0	1	0	2	0
Yamaguchi, Kolten, inf, Jr.	.173	75	8	13	0	0	2	9	0
Ross, Jack, of, Fr.	.162	99	13	16	1	1	1	11	2

PLAYER, POS., YEAR	W	L	ERA	G	SV	IP	H	BB	SO
Dilda, Ivan, lhp, So.	0	0	16	0	9	4	0	6
Blanchard, Chandler, rhp, Fr.	1	1	1.12	26	0	32	24	9	23
Miller, Corey, rhp, Sr.	9	5	1.90	16	0	118	102	33	82
Brown, Aaron, lhp, Jr.	13	1	1.95	17	0	116	84	40	104
Karch, Eric, rhp, Sr.	4	2	2.12	30	16	34	22	11	23
Maurer, Matt, lhp, Sr.	4	3	3.04	19	0	71	70	40	44
McClelland, Jackson, rhp, So.	8	3	3.48	16	0	83	83	23	49
Puckett, A.J., rhp, Fr.	2	2	3.58	23	0	50	44	24	43
Dunn, Evan, rhp, Jr.	0	1	3.72	16	0	19	18	6	16

13. OREGON STATE.

Coach: Pat Casey. **Record:** 45-14.

PLAYER, POS., YEAR	AVG	AB	R	H	2B	3B	HR	RBI	SB
Hendrix, Jeff, of, So.	.351	171	42	60	11	5	2	32	4
Conforto, Michael, of, Jr.	.345	203	52	70	16	2	7	56	4
Keyes, Kavin, 1b, Sr.	.329	152	22	50	7	2	1	23	3
Rulli, Nick, of, Sr.	.298	47	8	14	3	2	0	7	4
Davis, Dylan, of, Jr.	.283	237	33	67	14	0	7	64	4
Clark, Gabe, dh, So.	.280	157	24	44	10	1	1	34	0
Howard, Michael, of, Jr.	.260	123	15	32	6	0	0	12	1
Ice, Logan, c, Fr.	.250	172	23	43	5	0	0	19	5
Peterson, Andy, 2b, Sr.	.237	207	42	49	8	2	0	14	9
Hamilton, Caleb, 3b, Fr.	.231	182	21	42	6	1	1	18	7
Morrison, Trever, ss, Fr.	.225	204	40	46	3	5	0	17	8
Casper, Jerad, 3b, Sr.	.157	51	6	8	2	0	2	8	3
King, Billy, if, Fr.	.091	11	1	1	0	0	1	0	1

PLAYER, POS., YEAR	W	L	ERA	G	SV	IP	H	BB	SO
Wetzler, Ben, lhp, Jr.	12	1	0.78	14	0	104	49	9	31
Davis, Dylan, rhp, Jr.	0	0	1.12	5	0	16	7	14	14
Schultz, Scott, rhp, Sr.	7	2	1.61	24	6	67	47	15	40
Reser, Zack, lhp, Jr.	5	0	1.71	19	1	26	24	7	14
Fry, Jace, lhp, Jr.	11	2	1.80	16	0	120	83	30	98
Moore, Andrew, rhp, So.	6	5	2.77	16	0	94	97	26	68
Engelbrekt, Max, lhp, So.	0	1	2.84	17	1	13	13	4	7
Flemer, Kevin, rhp, Fr.	0	0	3.68	9	0	7	3	6	3
Fox, Mak, lhp, Fr.	1	0	3.86	6	0	7	8	0	3
Jackson, Brandon, rhp, So.	0	1	3.97	16	0	11	9	3	7
Thompson, Jake, rhp, Fr.	3	2	4.25	14	0	36	25	21	23
Shelton, Trent, lhp, Fr.	0	0	4.25	16	2	13	15	6	9
Eden, Chandler, rhp, Fr.	0	0	6.75	11	1	8	7	4	6
Belding, Philip, rhp, Jr.	0	0	15.00	7	0	6	9	4	4

14. MARYLAND

Coach: John Szefc. **Record:** 40-23.

PLAYER, POS., YEAR	AVG	AB	R	H	2B	3B	HR	RBI	SB
Lowe, Brandon, 2b, Rs-Fr.	.348	181	35	63	12	3	1	42	8
Schmit, Blake, ss, Sr.	.309	207	42	64	18	1	1	31	16
White, Charlie, of, So.	.290	245	49	71	14	0	2	29	15
Cuas, Jose, 3b, So.	.279	204	23	57	13	0	5	42	3
Papio, Anthony, of, Sr.	.271	177	23	48	9	0	2	29	7
Lewis, Tim, of, Jr.	.270	111	22	30	2	0	0	15	2
Maritr, Kevin, c, So.	.269	171	29	46	8	0	4	26	3
Cieri, Nick, Fr.	.248	133	17	33	8	0	0	18	2
Wade, LaMonte, 1b, So.	.247	227	39	56	12	1	2	25	4
Convissar, Kyle, dh, Sr.	.242	124	15	30	5	0	1	16	4
Rescigno, Mike, inf, Fr.	.241	83	12	20	4	0	0	11	4
Montville, Michael, of, Jr.	.230	61	14	14	4	0	1	3	1
Amaro, Andrew, inf, Jr.	.193	57	13	11	1	0	0	7	3
Leal, Krysthian, inf, Fr.	.188	48	5	9	2	0	0	6	3

PLAYER, POS., YEAR	W	L	ERA	G	SV	IP	H	BB	SO
Stinnett, Jake, rhp, Sr.	8	6	2.67	17	1	118	85	30	132
Drossner, Jake, lhp, So.	4	1	2.45	13	0	62	55	23	59
Morris, Zach, lhp, S.	2	1	2.77	10	0	39	37	23	19
Robinson, Alex, lhp, So.	1	0	2.87	18	0	16	13	15	19
Brewster, Ben, lhp, Sr.	0	0	3.00	23	2	24	11	11	29
Shawaryn, Mike, rhp, Fr.	11	4	3.12	16	0	92	89	24	72
Ruse, Bobby, rhp, Jr.	7	3	3.52	31	1	64	51	15	36
Stiles, Tayler, lhp, Fr.	5	2	4.05	22	1	47	51	14	34
Mooney, Kevin, rhp, So.	1	2	4.33	26	13	35	36	18	45
Pashuck, Jamie, lhp, Sr.	0	0	6.00	7	0	6	9	6	6
Price, Jared, rhp, So.	1	2	6.83	19	0	29	32	21	31
Casas, Brandon, rhp, So.	0	1	7.27	13	0	17	19	9	12
Galligan, Robert, lhp, So.	0	1	9.95	6	0	6	9	2	6

15. STANFORD

Coach: Mark Marquess. **Record:** 35-26.

PLAYER, POS., YEAR	AVG	AB	R	H	2B	3B	HR	RBI	SB
Slater, Austin, of,	.341	229	39	78	17	6	2	40	6
Hoffpauir, Zach, of, So.	.324	219	36	71	9	5	7	35	3
Diekroeger, Danny, 1b, Sr.	.313	230	43	72	13	0	2	22	8
Blandino, Alex, 3b, Jr.	.310	226	49	70	14	0	12	44	2
Whiting, Brant, c,	.281	160	13	45	7	0	1	24	0
Edman, Tommy, ss, Fr.	.256	195	21	50	8	0	3	18	3
Klein, Jack, of, Fr.	.256	43	13	11	2	0	1	6	2
Taylor, Wayne, of, Jr.	.247	158	20	39	7	5	5	25	2
Dunlap, Alex, of, Fr.	.237	118	5	28	3	0	0	14	0
Doran, Brett Michael, 2b, Jr.	.228	193	22	44	6	2	1	22	3
Jose, Dominic, of, So.	.204	108	11	22	3	0	1	14	3
Barr, Austin, cf, So.	.146	41	4	6	2	0	1	3	0
Jackson, Drew, of, So.	.167	108	14	18	3	1	0	4	1
Locher, Jonny, of, So.	.059	17	2	1	0	0	0	1	0

PLAYER, POS., YEAR	W	L	ERA	G	SV	IP	H	BB	SO
Vanegas, AJ, rhp, Sr.	4	3	2.63	20	7	41	34	19	29
Quantrill, Cal, rhp, Fr.	7	5	2.68	18	0	111	90	34	98
Lindquist, Sam, rhp, Jr.	2	0	2.81	15	0	16	10	12	8
Hanewich, Brett, rhp, Fr.	4	4	3.17	16	0	77	79	31	49
Hochstatter, John, lhp, Jr.	10	3	3.36	16	0	80	60	35	38
Brakeman, Marcus, rhp, So.	1	3	3.80	19	1	45	36	33	41
Castellanos, Chris, lhp, Fr.	0	1	4.12	22	3	24	26	11	15
Weir, Griffin, rhp, Fr.	0	0	4.15	10	0	8.2	11	6	4
Stairwalt, Daniel, rhp, So.	0	0	4.50	9	0	10	8	6	9
Viall, Chris, rhp, Fr.	2	3	4.74	17	0	44	45	31	18
Thorne, Tyler, rhp, Fr.	2	0	4.76	19	2	28	27	16	17
James, Logan, lhp, So.	3	4	5.31	24	0	61	53	32	42

16. KENNESAW STATE

Coach: Mike Sansing. **Record:** 40-24.

PLAYER, POS., YEAR	AVG	AB	R	H	2B	3B	HR	RBI	SB
Pentecost, Max, c, Jr.	.422	268	59	113	24	2	9	61	17
Liquori, Alex, of, So.	.354	178	37	63	13	5	1	42	7
Way, Bo, of, Sr.	.353	241	40	85	17	2	2	31	11
Bennett, Colin, 1b, Sr.	.333	57	9	19	0	0	2	8	1
Erwin, Chris, lhp, Fr.	.318	22	2	7	1	1	0	4	0
Bruce, Jacob, of, Jr.	.281	263	57	74	12	4	1	28	12
Morgan, Brennan, dh, So.	.281	210	40	59	6	2	4	41	2
Wynn, Clint, inf, So.	.281	32	8	9	2	0	0	3	0
Simmons, Kal, ss, So.	.272	268	46	73	6	1	1	26	3
McGowan, Chris, 1b, Jr.	.272	224	29	61	8	2	4	46	2
Bahnick, Matt, 3b, Jr.	.259	162	12	42	6	0	2	15	1
Motley, Justin, of, Jr.	.257	70	13	18	5	1	1	9	1
Nixon, Cornell, 2b, Fr.	.228	127	17	29	3	0	0	15	4
Ivey, Dylan, inf, Jr.	.167	84	8	14	0	0	0	4	1
Howell, Jeremy, inf, Fr.	.162	68	5	11	0	0	0	8	0

PLAYER, POS., YEAR	W	L	ERA	G	SV	IP	H	BB	SO
McCalvin, Justin, rhp, Jr.	5	3	2.21	39	16	61	42	19	60
Connell, James, rhp, Sr.	7	4	2.49	37	2	47	45	16	66
Hawkins, Kendall, rhp, So.	1	1	2.70	6	0	13	17	8	8
Bergen, Travis, lhp, So.	9	5	2.89	17	0	100	105	15	78
Erwin, Chris, lhp, Fr.	3	1	3.16	15	0	43	44	24	33
Friese, Gabe, rhp, Fr.	2	2	3.19	17	0	73	76	15	41
Hillyer, Jordan, lhp, So.	7	3	3.48	18	0	101	100	41	75

PLAYER, POS., YEAR	W	L	ERA	G	SV	IP	H	BB	SO
Solomon, Will, lhp, Jr.	1	0	4.31	19	0	31	31	10	25
Ward, Mason, lhp, Fr.	1	0	4.36	10	0	10	7	9	8
Lowman, Will, lhp, So.	0	0	4.50	11	0	10	7	11	9
Harsh, Nathan, rhp, Jr.	3	3	4.92	16	0	53	56	25	42
McArthur, Cole, rhp, So.	1	1	5.02	14	0	29	38	15	15
Austin, Andrew, rhp, Sr.	0	1	7.25	13	0	14	18	10	6

17. COLLEGE OF CHARLESTON

Coach: Monte Lee. **Record:** 46-16.

PLAYER, POS., YEAR	AVG	AB	R	H	2B	3B	HR	RBI	SB
Heidt, Gunnar, inf, Jr.	.327	168	39	55	10	1	4	30	15
Wise, Carl, 3b, So.	.295	227	24	67	11	4	3	54	2
Butler, Blake, 2b, So.	.282	255	48	72	11	2	3	24	7
Pappas, Nick, 1b, Fr.	.269	197	33	53	12	0	5	26	3
Murray, Brandon, of, Sr.	.266	139	25	73	9	1	6	23	1
Phillips, Morgan, of, So.	.247	182	23	45	14	2	2	25	4
Welke, Ryan, c, Sr.	.238	151	21	36	7	0	4	17	2
Reed, Devon, inf, Jr.	.235	17	1	4	0	0	0	1	1
Boykin, Ben, dh, So.	.233	120	14	28	5	2	3	17	1
Rowland, Champ, ss, Jr.	.228	136	24	31	5	0	0	9	6
Pastorius, Alex, of, So.	.221	104	15	23	3	1	0	10	1
Glazer, Brandon, of, Jr.	.221	222	23	49	4	2	5	30	7
Jones, Bradley, inf, Fr.	.210	100	6	21	3	0	1	8	2
Bello, Austin, of, So.	.190	42	5	8	1	0	0	4	0
Roper, Erven, c, Fr.	.167	30	2	5	1	0	0	1	0

PLAYER, POS., YEAR	W	L	ERA	G	SV	IP	H	BB	SO
Ober, Bailey, rhp, Fr.	10	3	1.52	17	0	107	73	19	85
McCutcheon, Hayde, rhp, Fr.	1	0	2.08	7	2	13	9	2	10
Bauer, Eric, lhp, So.	6	2	2.09	13	0	52	45	8	27
Henry, Chase, rhp, Jr.	2	0	2.27	28	2	48	38	13	51
Clarke, Taylor, rhp, So.	10	4	2.51	18	0	104	81	31	92
Ross, Blake, rhp, Sr.	0	0	3.00	8	0	6	3	11	5
Thorton, Tyler, rhp, Fr.	7	5	3.03	22	0	98	81	17	71
Hanzlik, Michael, rhp, Sr.	2	1	3.35	31	16	38	23	13	37
Helvey, Nathan, rhp, So.	3	4	3.78	21	0	69	79	19	54
Rice, Hunter, rhp, Jr.	1	0	4.15	14	0	17	18	14	17
Smith, Derrick, rhp, Sr.	1	0	4.38	8	0	12	6	11	12
Morris, Marlin, lhp, Jr.	0	0	9.00	8	0	6	10	2	6

18. FLORIDA

Coach: Kevin O'Sullivan. **Record:** 40-23.

PLAYER, POS., YEAR	AVG	AB	R	H	2B	3B	HR	RBI	SB
Bader, Harrison, of, So.	.337	169	27	57	6	2	2	24	13
Gushue, Taylor, c, Jr.	.316	225	30	71	16	0	6	49	1
Tobias, Josh, 3b, Jr.	.305	105	15	32	4	1	3	8	2
Larson, Ryan, of, Fr.	.274	84	9	23	0	0	0	7	2
Mattson, Braden, of, Jr.	.270	200	28	54	5	1	1	28	5
Martin, Richie, ss, Jr.	.265	249	49	66	11	2	1	27	18
Alonso, Peter, inf, Fr.	.264	197	18	52	6	2	4	32	1
Turgeon, Casey, 2b, Jr.	.259	247	36	64	11	0	4	33	4
Reed, Buddy, of, Fr.	.244	172	26	42	7	0	0	6	5
Sternagel, John, inf, Fr.	.238	101	16	24	0	0	1	12	1
Powers, Zack, 1b, Fr.	.231	121	14	28	3	1	3	13	1
Puk, A.J, dh, Fr.	.222	63	4	14	3	0	0	6	0
Shafer, Justin, rhp, Jr.	.211	95	10	20	1	0	1	10	3
Fahrman, Mike, c, Jr.	.167	24	1	4	3	0	0	5	0
Lombardozzi, Jason, inf, So.	.120	25	6	3	0	0	0	0	1

PLAYER, POS., YEAR	W	L	ERA	G	SV	IP	H	BB	SO
Shore, Logan, rhp, Fr.	7	4	2.16	16	0	96	86	20	68
Young, Danny, lhp, So.	5	0	2.23	25	1	48	55	18	36
Rubio, Frank, rhp, Fr.	0	0	2.25	0	0	8	9	2	5
Snead, Kirby, lhp, Fr.	3	0	2.40	32	2	41	43	5	22
Rhoades, Aaron, rhp, So.	5	2	2.48	20	3	54	43	15	19
Harris, Ryan, rhp, Jr.	3	2	3.00	27	5	36	29	12	19
Puk, A.J., lhp, Fr.	5	2	3.19	20	1	42	33	18	46
Poyner, Bobby, lhp, Jr.	4	5	3.47	28	4	57	58	10	46
Whitson, Karsten, rhp, Jr.	1	1	3.86	14	37	34	18	23	21
Shafer, Justin, rhp, Jr.	1	0	4.17	18	0	37	44	7	27
Hanhold, Eric, rhp, So.	4	3	4.20	25	3	49	45	18	36
Dunning, Dane, rhp, Fr.	1	1	4.50	17	0	24	17	11	31
Anderson, Shaun, rhp, Fr.	0	2	5.60	14	1	18	27	3	8
Morales, Brett, rhp, Fr.	0	2	6.56	11	0	23	25	10	16

19. FLORIDA STATE

Coach: Mike Martin. **Record:** 43-17.

PLAYER, POS., YEAR	AVG	AB	R	H	2B	3B	HR	RBI	SB
Stewart, DJ, of, So.	.351	194	45	68	19	0	7	50	4
Brizuela, Jose, 3b, Jr.	.321	218	46	70	14	2	3	38	14
Montgomery, Ladson, c, Sr.	.320	25	3	8	0	0	0	4	0
Nogowski, John, 1b, Jr.	.307	212	47	65	12	1	5	49	3
Smit, Casey, dh, Sr.	.297	145	25	43	2	0	1	25	3
Truluck, Hank, inf, Fr.	.286	21	3	6	1	0	0	3	2
DeLuzio, Ben, of, Fr.	.281	171	35	48	7	5	1	27	16
Delph, Josh, of, Jr.	.268	194	34	52	14	1	0	20	2
Knief, Brett, of, Jr.	.264	159	26	42	5	0	2	22	4
Gonzalez, Justin, ss, Sr.	.245	196	43	48	16	2	3	39	3
Graganella, Nick, of, So.	.231	13	7	3	0	0	0	3	0
Danny De La Calle, c, Jr.	.224	174	27	39	3	0	0	29	1
Sansone, John, 2b, So.	.221	199	38	44	13	0	2	39	6
West, Gage, rhp, Sr.	.161	31	6	5	1	1	2	8	0
Winston, Jameis, of, Fr.	.128	39	6	5	2	0	0	4	0

PLAYER, POS., YEAR	W	L	ERA	G	SV	IP	H	BB	SO
Winston, Jameis, rhp, Fr.	1	0	1.08	24	7	33	18	31	3
Leibrandt, Brandon, lhp, Jr.	4	1	1.83	6	0	39	31	9	30
Silva, Dylan, lhp, So.	4	0	1.90	17	1	24	16	14	28
Smith, Gage, rhp, Sr.	5	2	2.39	40	1	64	57	6	31
Weaver, Luke, rhp, Jr.	8	4	2.62	16	0	106	88	23	85
Strode, Billy, lhp, Jr.	2	1	2.62	24	0	48	38	23	49
Compton, Mike, rhp, So.	7	3	3.23	15	0	84	93	19	50
Johnson, Brandon, lhp, Jr.	0	0	3.31	12	1	16	19	4	11
Holtmann, Bryant, lhp, Jr.	5	1	3.68	14	0	37	31	12	30
Voyles, Jim, rhp, Fr.	1	0	4.05	5	0	7	7	2	3
Byrd, Alec, lhp, Fr.	1	1	4.20	10	0	15	16	8	13
Miller, Peter, rhp, Sr.	3	4	5.14	17	1	42	38	31	53
Blatch, Taylor, rhp, Fr.	1	0	6.23	14	0	17	13	19	11
Burkhead, Kenny, rhp, So.	1	0	8.44	10	0	11	13	5	8

20. CAL POLY

Coach: Larry Lee. **Record:** 47-12.

PLAYER, POS., YEAR	AVG	AB	R	H	2B	3B	HR	RBI	SB
Morgan, Kevin, of, Fr.	.538	13	2	7	2	0	0	3	0
Mathias, Mark, 2b, So.	.386	210	48	81	14	1	2	39	12
Torres, Nick, of, Jr.	.322	242	39	78	17	2	6	52	4
Zehner, Zack, of, Jr.	.316	174	32	55	7	3	3	16	5
Hoo, Chris, c, Sr.	.301	186	33	56	13	2	1	37	1
Allen, Jimmy, 3b, Sr.	.298	235	33	70	13	3	6	39	4
Wise, Tim, of, Sr.	.289	149	30	43	5	2	0	20	2
Van Gansen, Peter, ss, So.	.286	175	29	50	2	2	0	26	2
Schuknecht, John, 1b, Sr.	.286	84	17	24	7	3	1	11	2
Barbier, Brett, c, rs-Fr.	.280	25	3	7	2	0	0	6	0
Mundell, Brian, dh, So.	.279	215	40	60	12	2	4	41	1
Lesinsky, Jake, c, Fr.	.250	8	1	2	0	0	0	0	0
Ellis, Jordan, of, Jr.	.245	208	26	51	8	0	0	23	10
Drobny, Ryan, inf, Jr.	.217	60	11	13	1	1	0	6	0
Michaels, Alex, of, So.	.182	11	1	2	0	0	0	0	0
Pluschkell, Tommy, inf, Jr.	.167	12	2	2	0	0	0	0	0
Hoo, Michael, inf, Jr.	.091	11	2	1	0	0	0	0	2

PLAYER, POS., YEAR	W	L	ERA	G	SV	IP	H	BB	SO
Bloomquist, Casey, rhp, So.	12	2	1.56	16	1	98	87	20	74
Chris, Taylor, lhp, Jr.	4	1	1.61	24	5	56	38	23	53
Reilly, Reed, rhp, Jr.	3	1	1.71	28	12	47	24	17	53
Imhof, Matt, lhp, Jr.	10	4	2.45	15	0	99	65	27	43
Granger, Bryan, rhp, Jr.	2	0	2.73	21	0	26	24	17	22
Zandona, Danny, rhp, Jr.	4	0	3.49	20	0	49	54	16	43
Calomeni, Justin, rhp, Fr.	8	2	3.68	15	0	73	74	18	66
Dingilian, Michael, rhp, jr	1	0	5.59	8	0	10	14	5	6
Lee, Slater, rhp, Fr.	3	2	6.20	14	0	49	48	22	34
Suniga, Nick, rhp, Fr.	0	0	10.22	12	0	12	19	9	7

21. INDIANA.

Coach: Chris Lemonis. **Record:** 44-15.

PLAYER, POS., YEAR	AVG	AB	R	H	2B	3B	HR	RBI	SB
DeMuth, Dustin, 3b, Sr.	.374	211	40	79	16	1	5	40	4
Schwarber, Kyle, c, Jr.	.358	232	66	83	16	6	14	48	10

PLAYER, POS., YEAR	AVG	AB	R	H	2B	3B	HR	RBI	SB
Travis, Sam, 1b, Jr.	.347	245	55	85	16	2	12	58	8
Donley, Scott, dh, Jr.	.324	219	33	71	16	2	5	47	5
Hartong, Brad, of, Jr.	.313	160	27	50	11	1	3	36	7
Nolden, Will, of, Jr.	.302	172	33	52	9	1	0	24	5
Rodrigue, Casey, 2b, Jr.	.264	246	48	65	12	6	0	22	12
Ramos, Nick, ss, So.	.260	169	22	44	8	2	2	21	4
Cangelosi, Austin, inf, Fr.	.257	35	5	9	0	0	1	3	0
Dedelow, Craig, of, Fr.	.232	69	6	16	2	1	0	8	1
Alfonso, Ricky, of, Jr.	.222	27	4	6	0	0	1	7	0
Wilhite, Brian, inf, So.	.222	27	4	6	0	0	0	2	1
Clark, Chad, inf, Jr.	.194	31	2	3	0	0	0	2	0
O'Connor, Tim, of, Jr.	.188	138	16	26	3	0	0	19	9
Smith, Casey, of, Sr.	.179	56	5	10	1	0	0	2	1
Sujka, Chris, of, Jr.	.125	16	0	2	0	0	0	0	1
Cureton, Luke, of, Fr.	.059	17	4	1	0	0	0	0	0

PLAYER, POS., YEAR	W	L	ERA	G	SV	IP	H	BB	SO
DeNato, Joey, lhp, Sr.	13	1	1.82	17	0	109	91	39	81
Belcher, Thomas, rhp, rs-Fr.	1	0	1.91	15	4	33	33	4	23
Effross, Scott, rhp, So.	5	3	1.98	32	5	55	56	11	40
Morris, Christian, rhp, So.	6	3	2.04	16	0	84	76	21	47
Harrison, Luke, rhp, Jr.	6	0	2.21	27	3	53	47	10	57
Hart, Kyle, lhp, Jr.	3	1	2.29	9	1	35	19	14	25
Korte, Brian, lhp, Sr.	3	0	2.45	16	0	40	36	13	30
Stadler, Sullivan, lhp, So.	2	1	2.70	13	0	27	19	12	18
Kelzer, Jake, rhp, rs-Fr.	1	3	3.13	25	3	32	27	9	44
Bell, Evan, rhp, So.	2	1	3.32	12	0	22	23	7	16
Coursen, Carr, Will, lhp, So.	2	2	3.49	16	0	39	35	25	24

22. LOUISIANA STATE

Coach: Paul Mainieri. **Record:** 46-14.

PLAYER, POS., YEAR	AVG	AB	R	H	2B	3B	HR	RBI	SB
Fraley, Jake, of, Fr.	.372	121	31	45	7	1	3	29	8
Stevenson, Andrew, of, So.	.335	203	41	68	7	5	0	32	9
Bregman, Alex, ss, So.	.316	244	35	77	16	0	6	47	12
Hale, Connor, 2b, Jr.	.306	209	38	64	11	1	4	29	0
Scivicque, Kade, c, Jr.	.304	184	32	56	9	0	7	31	0
Moore, Tyler, 1b, Jr.	.301	153	30	46	10	0	6	37	1
Laird, Mark, of, So.	.291	223	38	65	10	2	0	27	10
McMullen, Sean, dh, Sr.	.288	205	44	59	18	3	7	40	5
Zardon, Danny, inf, Fr.	.268	56	8	15	2	0	1	10	0
Sciambra, Chris, of, Jr.	.265	49	9	13	3	0	1	13	0
Chinea, Chris, c, So.	.250	76	9	19	5	0	2	13	0
Stone, Cade, of, Fr.	.250	16	11	4	1	1	0	1	0
Ibarra, Christian, 3b, Sr.	.238	172	35	41	7	0	3	22	0
Robertson, Kramer, inf, Fr.	.200	100	19	20	6	0	1	20	3
DeHart, Jarret, of, Fr.	15	4	3	1	1	0	2	0	
Foster, Jared, of, Jr.	.115	61	8	7	4	0	0	8	1
Dean, Dakota inf, Fr.	.000	11	2	0	0	0	0	0	0

PLAYER, POS., YEAR	W	L	ERA	G	SV	IP	H	BB	SO
Broussard, Joe, rhp, Jr.	3	2	1.05	32	8	34	19	17	37
Nola, Aaron, rhp, Jr.	11	1	1.47	16	0	116	69	27	134
Bouman, Kyle, lhp, Jr.	5	2	2.12	17	0	64	49	16	32
Fury, Natem rhp, Sr.	3	1	2.15	26	0	29	22	11	22
Cartwright, Alden, rhp, Fr.	1	1	2.41	21	0	34	28	13	25
Poche, Jared, lhp, Fr.	9	3	2.45	16	0	92	72	26	52
Person, Zac, lhp, Jr.	3	1	2.57	31	0	28	25	12	29
Bugg, Parker, rhp, Fr.	2	2	2.75	26	2	36	27	5	29
Devall, Hunter, lhp, So.	1	0	3.10	18	0	20	16	8	
16 McCune, Kurt, rhp, Sr.	2	2	3.86	30	5	35	30	11	24
Faucheux, Henri, lhp, Jr.	3	0	4.22	16	0	21	16	11	14
Glenn, Cody, (?)	1	1	5.51	13	0	33	42	9	18
Domangue, Brady, rhp, Jr	2	0	5.59	19	1	19	21	12	11

23. MIAMI

Coach: Jim Morris. **Record:** 41-17.

PLAYER, POS., YEAR	AVG	AB	R	H	2B	3B	HR	RBI	SB
Thompson, David, 3b, So.	.322	87	14	28	5	1	0	11	0
Carey, Dale, of, Sr.	.313	230	51	72	15	1	7	28	16
Collins, Zack, c, Fr.	.300	190	30	57	13	3	9	49	0
Palmer, Tyler, of, Sr.	.294	218	42	64	14	4	2	33	18
Abreu, Willie, of, Fr.	.291	206	28	60	8	1	1	28	4
Eusebio, Ricky, of, So.	.268	56	16	15	2	0	0	7	6

PLAYER, POS., YEAR	AVG	AB	R	H	2B	3B	HR	RBI	SB
Rivera, Laz, inf, Fr.	.263	19	6	5	1	0	0	3	1
Hernandez, Alex, 2b, Sr.	.254	197	25	50	1	1	0	25	3
Lopez, Brandon, ss, So.	.235	170	23	40	6	1	0	29	6
Ruiz, Johnny, 3b, Fr.	.234	111	21	26	7	0	0	11	2
Kennedy, Garrett, c, Jr.	.220	109	13	24	3	0	2	15	1
Fieger, Brad, inf, Sr.	.211	180	19	38	9	0	1	29	0
Heyward, Jacob, of, Fr.	.205	39	8	8	2	0	0	4	0
Michelangeli, Edgar, inf, So.	.196	46	4	9	3	0	0	9	0
Diaz, Sebastian, inf, Fr.	.179	28	8	5	2	0	1	3	0
Zunica, Brad, 1b, Fr.	.175	40	4	7	2	0	0	6	0

PLAYER, POS., YEAR	W	L	ERA	G	SV	IP	H	BB	SO
Beauprez, Derik, rhp, Fr.	1	0	1.02	5	0	18	12	6	15
Garcia, Bryan, rhp, Fr.	6	4	1.86	30	15	48	40	18	53
Diaz, Chris, lhp, Jr.	9	0	2.31	15	0	94	83	38	80
Woodrey, Thomas, lhp, So.	4	0	2.45	28	0	44	32	9	31
Hammond, Cooper, rhp, Fr.	5	1	2.51	32	2	32	27	11	33
Salas, Javi, rhp, Sr.	4	3	3.04	13	1	47	44	12	38
Radziewski, Bryan, lhp, Jr.	7	2	3.14	15	0	92	78	47	102
Suarez, Andrew, lhp, Jr.	5	3	3.22	15	0	101	101	15	77
Sargent, Adam, rhp, Sr.	0	0	5.68	9	0	6	11	5	7
Garcia, Danny, lhp, Fr.	0	1	6.30	11	0	20	22	10	18
Salcines, AJ, lhp, Sr.	0	1	6.75	13	1	11	15	10	11
Sosa, Enrique, rhp, So.	0	1	7.04	11	0	15	12	11	14

24. WASHINGTON

Coach: Lindsay Meggs. Record: 41-17.

PLAYER, POS., YEAR	AVG	AB	R	H	2B	3B	HR	RBI	SB
Wolfe, Brian, of, Sr.	.352	176	32	62	10	0	5	36	2
Mitsui, Trevor, dh,	.328	198	35	65	9	0	5	32	1
Jackson, Matt, inf, So.	.318	22	8	7	0	0	0	2	2
Rei, Austin, c, So.	.314	153	24	48	11	2	2	28	1
Bishop, Braden, of, So.	.304	217	43	66	8	2	0	27	21
Ely, Andrew, 2b, Jr.	.300	207	38	62	8	3	3	34	2
Berry, Braden, 1b, So.	.262	164	26	43	9	0	1	18	2
Pehl, Robert, of, Jr.	.259	220	27	57	13	1	5	36	2
Baker, Chris, 3b, Fr.	.256	39	10	10	3	0	0	7	1
Sparks, Will, of, Jr.	.250	24	2	6	1	0	0	7	0
Guinn, Parker, c, Jr.	.235	17	2	4	0	0	0	3	1
Schmidt, Alex, inf, Jr.	.233	172	16	40	7	0	5	26	0
Forgione, Erik, ss, Jr.	.228	171	28	39	8	1	0	22	5
London, Kyle, of, Fr.	.222	18	12	4	0	0	0	3	1
Wiggins, Ryan, c, Sr.	.205	39	6	8	2	1	0	6	0
Meggs, Jack, of, Fr.	.188	69	13	13	3	0	0	8	0
Cushing, Josh, inf, rs-Fr.	.100	10	1	1	0	0	0	1	1

PLAYER, POS., YEAR	W	L	ERA	G	SV	IP	H	BB	SO
Kim, Dae Yang, rhp, Sr.	1	0	1.00	6	0	9	5	4	6
Davis, Tyler, rhp, Jr.	11	2	1.60	17	1	107	88	15	62
Rallings, Troy, rhp, So.	5	1	2.30	31	9	43	39	9	34
Ballowe, Will, lhp, So.	4	1	2.30	30	1	55	49	9	25
Choate, Brandon, rhp, Jr.	4	1	2.54	21	0	28	23	14	24
Brigham, Jeff, rhp, Jr.	7	4	2.90	16	0	90	79	23	45
Dunlap, Trevor, rhp, Sr.	2	2	3.36	31	6	59	49	23	50
Fisher, Jared, rhp, Jr.	6	4	4.07	16	0	95	91	47	60
Nesbitt, Alex, rhp, So.	0	1	4.63	10	0	12	13	7	9
Baker, Henry, lhp, Fr.	1	0	7.31	6	0	16	17	6	16
Wright, Zach, rhp, Sr.	0	1	10.66	7	0	13	18	13	7

25. SOUTH CAROLINA

Coach: Chad Holbrook. Record: 44-18.

PLAYER, POS., YEAR	AVG	AB	R	H	2B	3B	HR	RBI	SB
Martin, Kyle, 1b, Jr.	.336	244	35	82	11	0	5	38	2
Pike, Weber, inf, rs-Fr.	.333	18	1	6	0	0	0	3	0
Greiner, Grayson, c, Jr.	.311	212	39	66	13	0	8	50	0
Bright, Connor, of, Jr.	.311	161	25	50	11	0	0	24	4
Pankake, Joey, 3b, Jr.	.303	221	52	67	11	0	5	31	4
Schrock, Max, dh,	.299	127	26	38	5	1	5	20	4
Koch, Logan, c, Fr.	.286	28	2	8	1	0	0	0	0
English, Tanner, of, Jr.	.284	215	30	61	9	1	1	25	21
Mooney, Marcus, ss, So.	.274	215	32	59	10	1	0	22	2
Arendas, DC, 2b, So.	.271	177	32	48	6	0	4	29	1
Caldwell, Elliot, of, Jr.	.254	122	10	31	5	0	0	14	4
Gore, Jordan, ss, Fr.	.226	62	8	14	0	0	2	6	0
Cone, Gene, of, Fr.	.221	104	22	23	3	2	0	18	4
Widener, Taylor, 1b, Fr.	.191	47	6	9	0	0	0	2	0
Celek, Brison, 1b, Sr.	.188	85	4	16	4	0	1	7	0
Harrington, Patrick, of, Jr.	.172	58	5	10	1	0	0	9	1

PLAYER, POS., YEAR	W	L	ERA	G	SV	IP	H	BB	SO
Privette, Hunter, rhp, Sr.	1	0	0.00	10	0	10	3	3	5
Reagan, Josh, lhp, Fr.	3	0	0.36	14	0	25	25	4	21
Mincey, Cody, rhp, Jr.	5	0	1.04	29	1	35	20	17	44
Fiori, Vince, lhp, So.	1	0	1.37	17	0	20	14	10	18
Seddon, Joel, rhp, Jr.	3	2	1.66	27	14	49	37	12	59
Widener, Taylor, rhp, Fr.	3	0	1.79	21	0	40	24	15	38
Scott, Reed, rhp, Fr.	2	0	1.94	14	0	42	34	8	31
Britt, Curt, rhp, So.	3	0	2.35	8	0	23	22	11	19
Crowe, Wil, rhp, Fr.	8	3	2.75	15	0	92	76	19	59
Wynkoop, Jack, lhp, So.	7	6	2.86	17	0	88	94	10	58
Montgomery, Jordan, lhp, Jr.	8	5	3.42	16	0	100	93	29	95
Beal, Evan, rhp, Jr.	0	1	3.29	5	0	14	12	4	8
Vogel, Matthew, rhp, Fr.	0	1	6.91	8	0	14	12	11	15

CONFERENCE STANDINGS & LEADERS

NCAA regional teams in bold. Conference category leaders in bold.
*Team won conference's automatic regional bid. #Category leader who did not qualify for batting or pitching title.

AMERICA EAST CONFERENCE

Team	Conference		Overall	
	W	L	W	L
Stony Brook	18	5	34	16
Hartford	16	7	31	21
Massachusetts-Lowell	10	10	20	22
*Binghamton	11	12	21	25
Maine	10	11	24	28
Maryland-Baltimore County	7	17	17	29
Albany	7	17	12	33

ALL-CONFERENCE TEAM: C—Kevin Krause, Jr., Stony Brook. **1B**—Kevin Courtney, Sr., Stony Brook. **2B**—Brian Bullard, Sr., Albany. **SS**—Cole Peragine, Jr., Stony Brook. **3B**—Matt Sanchez, Jr., UMass-Lowell. **OF**—Bill Bereszniewicz, Sr., Binghamton; Ian Strom, Fr., UMass-Lowell; Jake Thomas, Jr., Binghamton. **DH**—Scott Heath, Jr., Maine. **SP**—Tommy Lawrence, Sr., Maine; Brandon McNitt, Sr., Stony Brook; Sean Newcomb, Jr., Hartford; Frankie Vanderka, Sr., Stony Brook. **RP**—Cameron Stone, Fr., Stony Brook. **Player of the Year:** Kevin Krause, Stony Brook. **Pitcher of the Year:** Sean Newcomb, Hartford. **Coach of the Year:** Matt Senk, Stony Brook. **Rookie of the Year:** Cameron Stone, Stony Brook.

INDIVIDUAL BATTING LEADERS
(Minimum 2.5 at-bats per team game)

	AVG	AB	R	H	2B	3B	HR	RBI	SB
Bill Bereszniewicz, Binghamton	.367	210	43	**77**	12	5	0	25	**23**
Scott Heath, Maine	.362	152	23	55	13	2	4	29	0
Matthew Sanchez, UMass-Lowell	.357	157	27	56	8	1	0	23	14
Kevin Krause, Stony Brook	.354	198	**46**	70	15	0	**8**	**51**	8
Kevin Courtney, Stony Brook	.341	208	44	71	14	2	2	41	5
Brian Bullard, Albany	.329	155	30	51	11	0	2	20	14
Colin Gay, Maine	.328	201	29	66	**16**	0	0	24	10
Troy Black, Maine	.326	**218**	29	71	12	2	2	27	15
Danny Mendick, UMass-Lowell	.314	159	27	50	9	1	5	34	11
Brian Doran, Maine	.314	191	27	60	15	3	0	20	4
Evan Harasta, Albany	.314	137	19	43	7	0	2	28	1
Matt Mottola, UMass-Lowell	.311	106	15	33	4	0	3	13	2
Eddie Posavec, Binghamton	.309	152	20	47	10	0	0	18	11
Hunter Dolshun, UMBC	.304	135	18	41	7	0	3	22	2
Mark Esposito, UMBC	.303	142	18	43	7	0	1	18	6
James Alfonso, Hartford	.302	192	29	58	14	2	5	31	0
Daniel Nevares, Binghamton	.298	188	33	56	13	3	5	35	4
Ryan Lukach, Hartford	.296	196	35	58	9	3	5	33	4
Robert Chavarria, Stony Brook	.292	185	40	54	3	0	0	17	8
Ian Strom, UMass-Lowell	.290	138	21	40	9	0	0	23	8
Brady Sheetz, Hartford	.288	184	27	53	10	3	0	27	1
Sam Balzano, Maine	.288	160	28	46	1	0	0	14	12
Cole Peragine, Stony Brook	.287	188	34	54	6	4	1	36	13
Luke Reynolds, UMass-Lowell	.287	129	23	37	5	2	1	11	7
Alex Calbick, Maine	.284	194	26	55	11	0	4	25	2
Reed Gamache, Binghamton	.283	173	25	49	8	0	1	26	5
D.J. Hoagboon, Albany	.278	151	26	42	5	2	2	9	5
Jack Parenty, Stony Brook	.277	184	37	51	6	3	1	22	10
Zach Blanden, Binghamton	.276	210	33	58	7	3	1	22	7
Craig Lepre, Albany	.273	154	10	42	7	0	1	28	0

INDIVIDUAL PITCHING LEADERS
(Minimum 1 IP per team game)

	W	L	ERA	G	SV	IP	H	BB	SO
Sean Newcomb, Hartford	8	2	**1.25**	14	0	93	51	38	**106**
Kevin Archbold, Albany	3	3	2.49	10	0	61	55	27	62
#Charlie Butler, Maine	1	5	2.54	**21**	5	39	35	15	26
#Alex Gouin, Hartford	1	2	2.74	17	**9**	23	21	8	15
Greg Ostner, Binghamton	3	2	2.81	21	4	58	59	10	23
Brandon McNitt, Stony Brook	8	1	2.89	13	0	72	66	22	71
Tyler Honahan, Stony Brook	7	2	2.89	15	0	72	50	33	55
Tommy Lawrence, Maine	**8**	5	3.18	14	0	**105**	100	29	97
Brendan Ryan, Albany	3	2	3.28	12	0	47	47	23	20
Frankie Vanderka, Stony Brook	4	5	3.33	12	0	81	65	22	49

Joe Vanderplas, UMBC	1	3	3.34	11	0	62	60	9	28
Mike Calzetta, UMass-Lowell	4	2	3.36	12	1	64	62	15	36
Cole, UMass Lowell	3	1	3.59	14	0	43	38	10	15
Jack Rogalla, Binghamton	5	8	3.77	14	0	86	81	27	63
Shaun Coughlin, Maine	4	5	3.84	16	1	61	66	11	41
Jake Cryts, Binghamton	5	6	3.89	17	0	88	80	35	37
Brian Hunter, Hartford	4	8	4.13	15	1	81	76	35	64
Christian Lavoie, UMass-Lowell	1	4	4.13	12	0	61	72	11	28
Shane Beauchemin, UMass-Lowell	4	5	5.03	11	0	68	82	21	38
Riley Stephenson, UMBC	2	7	6.44	11	0	57	78	13	19
Mac Gill, UMBC	1	7	6.64	11	0	61	102	9	16

AMERICAN ATHLETIC CONFERENCE

Team	Conference		Overall	
	W	L	W	L
Louisville	19	5	50	17
Central Florida	17	7	36	23
*Houston	14	9	48	18
Rutgers	14	9	30	25
South Florida	10	14	27	31
Connecticut	9	14	27	31
Temple	9	14	15	32
Memphis	8	16	30	29
Cincinnati	6	18	22	31

ALL-CONFERENCE TEAM: C—Caleb Barker, Sr., Houston; Max McDowell, So., UConn. **1B**—Bobby Melley, So., UConn. **2B**—Nick Favatella, Sr., Rutgers. **3B**—Alex Chittenden, Sr., Louisville. **SS**—Tommy Williams, Jr., UCF. **OF**—Blake Davey, Jr., UConn; Jeff Gardner, Sr., Louisville; Ian Happ, So., Cincinnati. **DH**—Justin Montemayor, So. Houston. **SP**—Kyle Funkhouser, So., Louisville; Jimmy Herget, So., USF; Eric Skoglund, Jr., UCF; Caleb Wallingford, Jr., Memphis. **RP**—Nick Burdi, Jr., Louisville. **Player of the Year:** Jeff Gardner, Louisville. **Pitcher of the Year:** Erik Skoglund, UCF. **Rookies of the Year:** Andrew Lantrip, Houston; Gaby Rosa, Rutgers.

INDIVIDUAL BATTING LEADERS
(Minimum 2.5 at-bats per team game)

	AVG	AB	R	H	2B	3B	HR	RBI	SB
Bobby Melley, UConn	.359	209	32	75	16	1	4	47	2
Kyle Teaf, USF	.354	209	41	74	7	3	0	22	7
James Vazquez, UCF	.340	206	41	70	11	1	8	56	1
Pat Sweeney, Rutgers	.331	166	35	55	11	4	1	26	4
Matt Williams, Cincinnati	.330	182	30	60	11	4	0	25	14
Brian O'Grady, Rutgers	.328	204	40	67	12	5	5	30	13
Vinny Zarrillo, Rutgers	.328	198	31	65	12	0	1	43	14
Cole Sturgeon, Louisville	.323	**269**	**58**	**87**	16	**7**	2	35	19
Robert Amaro, Temple	.322	180	25	58	10	2	3	39	7
Ian Happ, Cincinnati	.322	171	32	55	13	1	5	27	19
Casey Grayson, Houston	.321	243	37	78	16	1	6	48	1
Kane Barrow, Memphis	.319	191	34	61	10	0	3	28	3
Mike Carter, Rutgers	.318	211	35	67	10	3	0	34	9
Blake Davey, UConn	.313	201	48	63	10	0	10	32	8
Jeff Gardner, Louisville	.313	240	37	75	20	2	9	**68**	2
Dylan Moore, UCF	.310	232	47	72	17	0	2	35	10
Jimmy Kerrigan, Temple	.310	174	15	54	8	1	1	16	8
Derrick Salberg, UCF	.310	216	42	67	6	0	1	26	12
Kyle Survance, Houston	.308	253	53	78	11	2	2	32	31
Jake Little, Memphis	.308	237	39	73	10	0	5	37	15
Erik Barber, UCF	.302	162	41	49	9	2	6	30	5
Justin Montemayor, Houston	.298	248	36	74	15	0	1	31	0
Nick Favatella, Rutgers	.298	205	43	61	16	3	4	33	5
Michael Pyeatt, Houston	.297	172	20	51	4	2	1	21	5
Alex Chittenden, Louisville	.294	211	39	62	10	1	1	30	2
Carter White, Memphis	.288	170	30	49	7	0	2	35	6
Justin Glass, Cincinnati	.288	184	36	53	8	1	5	31	10
Josh Vidales, Houston	.285	235	45	67	5	0	0	31	11
Grant Kay, Louisville	.285	207	49	59	9	0	5	35	23
Derek Peterson, Temple	.283	180	32	51	**23**	1	2	22	8

	AVG	AB	R	H	2B	3B	HR	RBI	SB
#Tommy Williams, UCF	.263	224	37	59	8	1	12	45	16
#Sutton Whiting, Louisville	.216	218	51	47	4	3	2	18	37

INDIVIDUAL PITCHING LEADERS
(Minimum 1 IP per team game)

	W	L	ERA	G	SV	IP	H	BB	SO
#Nick Burdi, Louisville	3	1	0.49	32	18	37	18	10	65
Tyler Ford, Houston	9	0	1.17	27	4	69	47	5	49
Jimmy Herget, USF	8	6	1.26	15	0	107	91	27	90
Zach Rodgers, UCF	7	1	1.36	26	5	79	66	14	52
Kyle Funkhouser, Louisville	13	3	1.94	18	0	120	85	65	122
Ruxer, Louisville	7	1	2.27	13	0	75	62	16	68
Howie Brey, Rutgers	6	3	2.36	13	1	76	55	27	40
Caleb Wallingford, Memphis	6	5	2.44	16	0	89	78	24	70
Eric Skoglund, UCF	9	3	2.54	15	0	110	86	27	94
Andrew Zapata, UConn	3	2	2.57	15	0	63	39	36	35
Jake Lemoine, Houston	6	8	2.87	17	0	107	98	29	87
Gaby Rosa, Rutgers	6	3	2.91	15	0	74	66	19	30
Aaron Garza, Houston	9	5	2.92	17	0	108	102	11	57
Anthony Marzi, UConn	5	7	3.11	16	0	93	75	40	69
Jon Reed, Memphis	8	3	3.23	15	0	100	90	31	63
Brian Ward, UConn	4	3	3.30	13	0	63	64	28	39
Anthony Kidston, Louisville	9	1	3.40	14	0	77	56	36	69
Jordan Tabakman, UConn	4	4	3.40	14	0	77	89	26	42
Matt Hockenberry, Temple	5	6	3.47	15	0	93	105	23	71
Anthony Kay, UConn	5	4	3.49	18	2	67	62	40	56
Ryan Kuehn, Temple	4	2	3.54	15	0	53	50	19	24

ATLANTIC COAST CONFERENCE

Team	Conference		Overall	
Atlantic	**W**	**L**	**W**	**L**
Florida State	21	9	43	15
Maryland	15	14	36	21
Clemson	15	14	36	23
Wake Forest	15	15	30	26
N.C. State	13	17	32	23
Boston College	10	20	22	33
Notre Dame	9	21	22	31
Coastal				
Miami	24	6	41	17
Virginia	22	8	44	13
Duke	16	14	33	25
North Carolina	15	15	34	25
*Georgia Tech	14	16	36	25
Pittsburgh	11	19	22	20
Virginia Tech	9	21	21	31

ALL-CONFERENCE TEAM: C—Brett Austin, Jr. N.C. State. **1B**—Mike Papi, Jr., Virginia; John Nogowski, Jr. Florida State. **2B**—Branden Cogswell, Jr., Virginia. **3B**—Jose Brizuela, Jr., Florida State. **SS**—Trea Turner, Jr., N.C. State. **OF**—Joe McCarthy, So., Virginia; Chris Shaw, So., Boston College; D.J. Stewart, So., Florida State. **DH/UT**—Nick Howard, Jr., Virginia. **SP**—Chris Diaz, Jr., Miami; Daniel Gossett, Jr., Clemson; Nathan Kirby, So., Virginia; Carlos Rodon, Jr., N.C. State; Luke Weaver, Jr., Florida State. **RP**—Reilly Hovis, So., North Carolina.

INDIVIDUAL BATTING LEADERS
(Minimum 2.5 at-bats per team game)

	AVG	AB	R	H	2B	3B	HR	RBI	SB
D.J. Stewart, Florida State	.351	194	45	68	19	0	7	50	4
John La Prise, Virginia	.348	178	24	62	10	0	1	17	5
Brandon Lowe, Maryland	.348	181	35	63	12	3	1	42	8
Brett Austin, N.C. State	.344	215	42	74	12	5	5	31	8
Michael Russell, North Carolina	.339	230	43	78	20	2	4	32	13
Tyler Krieger, Clemson	.338	219	49	74	18	0	2	32	19
Grant Shabley, Wake Forest	.331	151	30	50	4	1	0	20	5
Andrew Knizner, N.C. State	.330	209	34	69	11	1	4	47	0
Mark Zagunis, Virginia Tech	.330	209	44	69	10	2	2	39	16
Chris Shaw, Boston College	.329	207	25	68	18	0	6	45	1
Saige Jenco, Virginia Tech	.323	192	38	62	5	0	1	16	20
Jose Brizuela, Florida State	.321	218	46	70	14	2	3	38	14
Trea Turner, N.C. State	.321	215	65	69	12	3	8	36	26
Daniel Spingola, Georgia Tech	.319	257	45	82	9	8	3	36	15
Matt Berezo, Duke	.318	151	23	48	4	1	1	16	4

	AVG	AB	R	H	2B	3B	HR	RBI	SB
Steve Wilkerson, Clemson	.317	205	33	65	18	1	6	42	8
Jordan Betts, Duke	.316	196	31	62	20	2	5	32	2
Matt Gonzalez, Georgia Tech	.314	255	34	80	21	1	1	37	9
Blake Schmit, Maryland	.309	207	42	64	18	1	1	31	16
Ryan Deitrich, Duke	.309	175	25	54	11	2	9	34	3
Mike Papi, Virginia	.307	244	55	75	11	0	11	56	8
John Nogowski, Florida State	.307	212	47	65	12	1	5	49	3
Landon Lassiter, North Carolina	.305	223	41	68	7	1	1	21	3
Dale Carey, Miami	.305	246	53	75	16	1	7	29	16
Garrett Boulware, Clemson	.302	225	38	68	16	0	4	35	1
Brendon Hayden, Virginia Tech	.302	199	35	60	16	1	7	43	2
Thomas Smith, Georgia Tech	.301	229	35	69	10	1	2	36	5
Branden Cogswell, Virginia	.301	259	47	78	11	1	0	22	8
Joe McCarthy, Virginia	.301	256	55	77	16	2	6	49	11
Evan Stephens, Wake Forest	.300	210	42	63	10	1	1	15	10
#Zack Collins, Miami	.298	205	32	61	14	3	11	54	0

INDIVIDUAL PITCHING LEADERS
(Minimum 50 IP)

	W	L	ERA	G	SV	IP	H	BB	SO
Sam Clay, Georgia Tech	4	1	1.26	31	8	57	38	29	64
Artie Lewicki, Virginia	8	1	1.31	16	1	69	37	13	57
Whit Mayberry, Virginia	6	1	1.60	30	2	56	38	12	59
Bryan Garcia, Miami	7	4	1.75	31	15	51	40	19	56
Trent Swart, Duke	5	2	1.76	11	0	61	48	21	54
Scott Kerrigan, Notre Dame	3	1	1.87	14	0	58	46	16	31
#Nick Howard, Virginia	2	2	1.91	31	20	38	23	14	60
Dusty Isaacs, Georgia Tech	8	5	1.92	29	7	61	48	21	53
Daniel Gossett, Clemson	7	2	1.93	15	0	107	78	30	107
Carlos Rodon, N.C. State	6	7	2.01	14	0	99	84	31	117
Nathan Kirby, Virginia	9	3	2.06	18	0	113	68	33	112
Devin Stanton, Georgia Tech	5	3	2.24	18	0	76	68	22	57
Reilly Hovis, North Carolina	9	1	2.25	34	6	64	44	24	81
Sean Fitzgerald, Notre Dame	3	3	3.29	10	0	71	52	19	48
John McLeod, Wake Forest	5	2	2.33	10	0	58	50	28	48
Gage Smith, Florida State	5	2	2.39	40	1	64	57	6	31
Chris Diaz, Miami	9	1	2.41	16	0	101	88	41	86
Brandon Waddell, Virginia	10	3	2.45	18	0	114	98	19	73
Jake Drossner, Maryland	4	1	2.45	13	0	62	55	23	59
Michael Hearne, Notre Dame	5	6	2.51	19	0	86	82	13	48
Thomas Woodrey, Miami	4	0	2.54	31	0	50	38	11	36
#Jake Stinnett, Maryland	8	6	2.67	17	1	118	85	30	132
#Mike Shawaryn, Maryland	11	4	3.12	16	0	92	89	24	72

ATLANTIC SUN CONFERENCE

Team	Conference		Overall	
	W	**L**	**W**	**L**
Florida Gulf Coast	19	8	39	22
Mercer	18	9	38	17
*Kennesaw State	17	9	37	21
Lipscomb	17	10	33	28
Jacksonville	13	13	21	33
East Tennessee State	13	13	27	30
Stetson	13	14	26	34
North Florida	11	16	22	31
Northern Kentucky	6	21	14	37
South Carolina-Upstate	6	20	17	38

ALL-CONFERENCE TEAM: C—Max Pentecost, Jr., Kennesaw State. **1B**—Clinton Freeman, Sr., ETSU. **2B**—Jake Noll, Fr., FGCU. **3B**—Scott Schaub,Sr., Jacksonville. **SS**—Michael Massi, Sr., Mercer. **OF**—Sasha Lagarde, Sr., Mercer; Michael Suchy, Jr., FGCU; Drew Weeks, Jr., North Florida. **DH**—Corbin Olmstead, So., North Florida. **SP**—Michael Murray, So., FGCU; Eric Nyquist, Jr., Mercer; David Trexler, Sr., North Florida. **RP**—Justin McCalvin, Jr., Kennesaw State. **Player of the Year:** Max Pentecost, Kennesaw State. **Pitcher of the Year:** Michael Murray, FGCU. **Defensive Player of the Year:** Michael Massi, FGCU. **Freshman of the Year:** Jake Noll, FGCU. **Coach of the Year:** Dave Tollett, FGCU.

INDIVIDUAL BATTING LEADERS
(Minimum 2 at-bats per team game)

	AVG	AB	R	H	2B	3B	HR	RBI	SB
Drew Weeks, North Florida	.430	221	52	95	13	4	6	38	10
Max Pentecost, Kennesaw St.	.422	268	59	113	24	2	9	61	17

Scott Schaub, Jacksonville	.407	172	23	70	7	3	1	47	9
Connor Marabell, Jacksonville	.371	178	32	66	13	1	5	31	9
Jake Noll, FGCU	.367	275	56	101	18	1	0	29	**25**
Corbin Olmstead, North Florida	.358	173	39	62	10	1	10	33	0
Patrick Mazeika, Stetson	.354	206	42	73	18	0	2	27	1
Alex Liquori, Kennesaw State	.354	178	37	63	13	**5**	1	42	7
Bo Way, Kennesaw State	.353	241	40	85	17	2	2	31	11
Logan Spurlin, N. Kentucky	.350	183	26	64	16	0	4	32	0
Clinton Freeman, ETSU	.348	221	40	77	17	2	**13**	53	0
Chesny Young, Mercer	.348	204	32	71	10	0	4	38	3
Michael Massi, Mercer	.346	214	51	74	13	2	5	35	8
Cole Bauml, Northern Kentucky	.337	178	29	60	18	1	7	39	7
Trent Higginbothem, N. Florida	.335	206	28	69	13	1	6	50	0
Nick Rivera, FGCU	.330	221	45	73	**25**	0	6	48	0
Patrick Ervin, North Florida	.329	170	18	56	5	0	0	17	3
Colton Bottomley, FGCU	.328	174	38	57	11	0	6	25	1
Grant Massey, Lipscomb	.322	239	47	77	18	3	3	24	14
Michael Suchy, FGCU	.318	239	54	76	16	4	8	49	10
Sasha Lagarde, Mercer	.314	210	51	66	8	1	9	45	9
Zack Tillery, FGCU	.314	185	29	58	10	1	6	39	0
Tyler Lesch, USC Upstate	.313	230	35	72	11	2	1	25	10
Zac Asman, Northern Kentucky	.308	198	34	61	15	2	1	24	9
Kyle Zech, Stetson	.303	165	28	50	7	0	0	20	15
Garrett Russini, Stetson	.297	222	32	66	21	4	4	37	3
Erik Samples, USC Upstate	.294	201	27	59	17	2	2	22	2
Kyle Brooks, North Florida	.293	215	41	63	8	1	0	14	3
Josh Lee, Lipscomb	.288	184	32	53	14	0	2	22	5
Derrick Workman, Mercer	.287	181	21	52	8	0	5	27	2
Tyler Roach, ETSU	.287	181	26	52	6	2	4	25	4
#Jonathan Allison, Lipscomb	.274	241	44	66	15	**5**	4	33	3
#Chris Cook, ETSU	.269	186	39	50	9	**5**	1	14	6
#Trey York, ETSU	.231	186	28	43	9	**5**	1	17	11

INDIVIDUAL PITCHING LEADERS

(Minimum 1 IP per team game)

	W	L	ERA	G	SV	IP	H	BB	SO
Michael Murray, FGCU	**13**	1	**1.85**	15	0	107	92	14	**79**
#Justin McCalvin, KSU	5	3	2.21	**39**	**16**	61	42	19	60
Brady Anderson, FGCU	5	3	2.45	24	7	70	72	14	50
Travis Bergen, Kennesaw State	9	5	2.89	17	0	100	105	15	78
Jack English, FGCU	4	4	3.00	18	0	75	67	32	55
Eric Nyquist, Mercer	8	1	3.12	14	0	87	70	17	49
Gabe Friese, Kennesaw State	2	2	3.19	17	0	73	76	15	41
Logan Rice, ETSU	3	2	3.26	24	0	61	69	7	46
Nick Andros, Lipscomb	5	3	3.28	19	2	69	52	18	57
Denton Norman, Lipscomb	7	6	3.43	15	0	87	75	33	57
Jordan Hillyer, Kennesaw State	7	3	3.48	18	0	101	99	41	75
Ryan Askew, Mercer	3	3	3.54	22	0	69	81	11	49
David Trexler, North Florida	6	4	3.62	14	0	87	92	39	59
Nick Deckert, FGCU	7	5	3.72	18	0	82	103	19	76
Ian Martinez-McGraw, Lipscomb	9	3	3.77	19	0	**112**	**128**	42	64
Brandon Barker, Mercer	4	4	3.84	15	0	68	87	16	63
Jimmy Nesselt, ETSU	7	5	4.06	20	1	102	121	25	62
Grant Papelian, Mercer	5	4	4.13	20	0	81	89	18	44
Taylor Cockrell, Stetson	5	4	4.35	19	0	97	103	29	72
Justin Russel, Jacksonville	6	3	4.56	14	0	75	83	27	39
Hunter Brothers, Lipscomb	3	2	4.57	15	0	65	48	53	55

ATLANTIC 10 CONFERENCE

Team	Conference		Overall	
	W	L	W	L
Saint Louis	18	7	34	21
St. Joseph's	18	8	56	16
***George Mason**	16	9	34	20
Virginia Commonwealth	15	10	37	20
Richmond	13	12	24	28
Dayton	14	13	24	30
Fordham	13	14	24	30
George Washington	12	15	20	30
Massachusetts	12	15	15	31
La Salle	9	15	14	34
Rhode Island	7	18	13	40
St. Bonaventure	6	17	12	30

ALL-CONFERENCE TEAM: C—Brian O'Keefe, Saint Joseph's. **1B**—Mike Vigliarolo, Saint Louis. **2B**—Chris Cook, George Mason. **SS**—Alec Solé, Jr., Saint Louis. **3B**—Stefan Kancylarz, Saint Joseph's. **OF**—Collin Forgey, Saint Joseph's; Justin Korenblatt, La Salle; Tim Swatek, Fordham. **DH**—Tommy Cunningham, Saint Joseph's. **SP**—Jordan Carter, Saint Joseph's; James Norwood, Saint Louis. **RP**—Matt Eckelman, Saint Louis. **Player of the Year:** Collin Forgey, Saint Joseph's. **Pitcher of the Year:** Jordan Carter, Saint Joseph's. **Rookie of the Year:** Mike Geannelis, UMass. **Coach of the Year:** Fritz Hamburg, Saint Joseph's.

INDIVIDUAL BATTING LEADERS

(Minimum 2.5 at-bats per team game)

	AVG	AB	R	H	2B	3B	HR	RBI	SB
Tim Swatek, Fordham	**.392**	186	30	73	12	4	3	36	22
Justin Korenblatt, La Salle	.372	191	38	71	11	**6**	3	34	9
Robby Sunderman, Dayton	.369	217	52	**80**	17	1	1	22	21
Joel Rosencrance, St. Bonaventure	.366	145	24	53	13	1	5	26	0
Collin Forgey, St. Joseph's	.355	203	51	72	12	4	6	47	13
Alec Sole, Saint Louis	.352	179	31	63	8	2	1	29	10
Brian O'Keefe, St. Joseph's	.350	214	**58**	75	11	2	7	43	3
Stefan Kancylarz, St. Joseph's	.349	172	26	60	13	3	4	29	2
A.J. Ryan, Dayton	.338	160	15	54	15	0	4	38	2
Ryan Xepoleas, GW	.337	190	27	64	11	3	2	27	12
Owen Beightol, GW	.337	193	31	65	14	0	2	21	4
Alex Harris, Dayton	.333	180	44	60	15	0	2	32	15
Mike Vigliarolo, Saint Louis	.332	232	36	77	18	0	7	37	13
Mike Muha, St. Joseph's	.331	169	33	56	11	0	3	37	2
Chris Ayers, VCU	.323	186	21	60	7	2	1	28	1
Tommy Cunningham, St. Joseph's	.322	208	32	67	15	0	6	44	0
James Bunn, VCU	.315	200	44	63	9	3	0	15	12
Doug Kraeger, Richmond	.308	214	39	66	20	0	5	34	3
Cameron Johnson, La Salle	.308	169	20	52	11	1	5	26	2
Chris Hueth, St. Joseph's	.307	215	57	66	13	4	4	30	10
Brandon Gum, GMU	.307	202	36	62	7	0	0	27	5
Vimael Machin, VCU	.307	199	40	61	11	1	3	52	2
Logan Farrar, VCU	.305	174	32	53	4	2	1	26	10
Bill Cullen, VCU	.302	215	49	65	18	**6**	4	**55**	11
Thad Johnson, St. Bonaventure	.302	169	31	51	8	3	1	20	3
Luke Willis, Mason	.302	232	37	70	12	3	2	34	21
Joseph Runco, Fordham	.301	206	35	62	9	2	0	25	**23**
Chris Cook, Mason	.301	173	37	52	13	0	4	27	2
Joey Bartosic, GW	.298	151	21	45	1	0	0	12	20
Kevin Baron, La Salle	.297	192	36	57	11	1	1	17	2
#Cody Acker, VCU	.291	**237**	39	69	7	0	0	27	11
#Blaise Fernandez, GMU	.294	228	38	67	**21**	3	4	41	3
#Matt Dacey, Richmond	.269	197	38	53	8	1	**12**	47	2

INDIVIDUAL PITCHING LEADERS

(Minimum 1 inning pitched per team game)

	W	L	ERA	G	SV	IP	H	BB	SO
Matt Eckelman, Saint Louis	7	2	**1.63**	22	**9**	61	51	12	35
Jared Gaynor, George Mason	8	5	2.03	16	0	**115**	101	27	73
Anthony Montefusco, GMU	9	4	2.19	16	0	107	112	14	**82**
Steve Moyers, Richmond	2	5	2.30	13	0	82	66	19	60
Jordan Carter, St. Joseph's	**10**	4	2.45	14	0	96	78	14	81
James Norwood, Saint Louis	8	2	2.68	15	0	94	84	28	64
John Williams, Mason	5	2	2.82	10	0	61	58	19	30
Daniel Thorpe, St. Joseph's	**10**	2	3.10	16	0	96	83	26	73
JoJo Howie, VCU	7	3	3.15	15	0	100	98	26	78
Zak Sterling, Richmond	5	5	3.35	18	0	91	104	16	67
Brett Kennedy, Fordham	6	7	3.36	14	0	88	106	24	75
Bobby LeWarne, GW	2	5	3.38	14	0	77	88	27	57
Daniel Concepcion, VCU	6	3	3.39	19	1	85	83	32	48
Tyler Pallante, St. Joseph's	1	2	3.57	10	1	58	50	17	50
Heath Dwyer, VCU	7	2	3.58	13	0	83	80	27	53
Josh Moore, Saint Louis	3	2	3.63	13	0	62	49	32	47
Charlie Dant, Dayton	6	5	3.69	16	0	100	100	30	68
Lou Distasio, Richmond	3	4	3.71	14	0	78	70	31	63
Jacob Williams, GW	4	5	3.72	13	0	82	74	33	25
Aaron Plunkett, UMass	1	6	3.74	12	0	65	63	30	37
#J.C. Porter, Fordham	5	5	4.63	**26**	2	56	69	18	32
#Noah Buettgen, Dayton	6	7	4.37	17	1	**115**	132	24	65

BIG EAST CONFERENCE

Team	Conference		Overall	
	W	L	W	L
Creighton	14	4	32	17
St. John's	13	5	35	20
Seton Hall	11	7	39	15
*Xavier	8	10	31	28
Butler	7	11	20	30
Georgetown	5	13	19	29
Villanova	5	13	16	34

ALL-CONFERENCE TEAM: C—Daniel Rizzie, So. Xavier. **1B**—Reagan Fowler, So., Creighton. **2B**—Jake Peter, Jr., Creighton. **SS**—D.J. Ruhlman, Jr., Seton Hall. **3B**—Kyle Grimm, Jr., Seton Hall. **OF**—Michael Donadio, Fr., St. John's; Mike Gerber, Sr., Creighton; Derek Jenkins, So., Seton Hall. **DH**—Nick Collins, So., Georgetown. **SP**—James Lomangino, Sr., St. John's; Vinny Nittoli, Sr., Xavier; Josh Prevost, Sr., Seton Hall; Matt Warren, So., Creighton. **RP**—Joe Kuzia, Jr., St. John's. **Player of the Year:** Reagan Fowler, Creighton; D.J. Ruhlman, Seton Hall. **Pitcher of the Year:** Josh Prevost, Seton Hall. **Rookie of the Year:** Michael Donadio, St. John's. **Coach of the Year:** Ed Servais, Creighton.

INDIVIDUAL BATTING LEADERS
(Minimum 2.5 at-bats per team game)

	AVG	AB	R	H	2B	3B	HR	RBI	SB
Robbie Knightes, St. John's	.399	138	20	55	6	1	0	26	2
Reagan Fowler, Creighton	.362	185	38	67	16	3	0	27	9
Jarred Mederos, St. John's	.362	141	24	51	8	1	2	34	2
D.J. Ruhlman, Seton Hall	.351	185	43	65	11	2	3	28	15
Nick Collins, Georgetown	.351	188	31	66	8	0	2	38	2
Bret Dennis, St. John's	.346	127	30	44	5	0	2	23	2
Steve Anderson, Georgetown	.344	183	28	63	13	1	5	47	2
Sal Annunziata, Seton Hall	.330	197	35	65	17	1	5	49	1
Michael Donadio, St. John's	.328	189	50	62	7	4	5	45	7
Alex Caruso, St. John's	.326	181	36	59	5	2	0	14	7
Derek Jenkins, Seton Hall	.324	176	43	57	2	1	0	27	38
Ryan Busch, Georgetown	.317	167	39	53	13	1	1	14	13
Derek Hasenbeck, Xavier	.309	236	36	73	10	0	6	28	0
Chris Maranto, Butler	.309	162	21	50	7	2	1	22	8
Daniel Rizzie, Xavier	.307	218	41	67	16	1	5	38	9
Todd Czinege, Villanova	.306	196	26	60	7	3	4	38	5
Max Beermann, Villanova	.304	181	36	55	16	3	4	30	1
Marcos Calderon, Butler	.303	188	34	57	10	1	3	26	9
Jake Peter, Creighton	.299	197	43	59	8	3	4	36	4
Emmanuel Morris, Villanova	.299	117	25	35	2	0	0	14	3
Zach Lauricela, St. John's	.296	196	41	58	14	3	4	39	7
Zack Weigel, Seton Hall	.292	195	48	57	5	4	0	27	12
Chris Selden, Seton Hall	.291	175	32	51	8	0	1	25	6
Dillon Hamlin, Seton Hall	.290	131	18	38	7	1	2	26	6
Matt Harris, St. John's	.290	207	43	60	9	2	6	47	5
Kyle Grimm, Seton Hall	.286	189	39	54	10	2	2	38	4
Brian Bruening, Xavier	.283	219	30	62	8	3	1	28	12
Joe Forney, Xavier	.282	248	33	70	17	0	0	33	7
Stephen Schoettmer, Xavier	.281	203	36	57	5	1	5	24	3
Brad McKewon, Creighton	.279	208	33	58	11	1	1	25	8
Robert Wayman, St. John's	.276	210	46	58	7	1	0	27	10
#Connor Jones, Villanova	.272	195	35	53	7	4	4	29	5
#Mike Gerber, Creighton	.274	208	34	57	10	2	11	49	2

INDIVIDUAL PITCHING LEADERS
(Minimum 1 IP per team game)

	W	L	ERA	G	SV	IP	H	BB	SO
#Joe Kuzia, St. John's	0	2	0.97	28	13	37	24	9	29
Josh Prevost, Seton Hall	12	2	1.62	15	0	116	64	20	111
Matt Warren, Creighton	10	1	2.03	14	0	84	62	25	45
Bryan Sova, Creighton	6	1	2.09	29	9	60	47	9	36
Vinny Nittoli, Xavier	6	4	2.38	14	0	87	73	23	66
#Nick Highberger, Creighton	4	0	2.58	31	0	38	45	13	13
Luke Cahill, Seton Hall	10	2	2.65	15	0	78	74	15	58
Anthony Elia, Seton Hall	4	3	2.77	16	0	75	66	21	48
Anthony Pacillo, Seton Hall	4	2	2.98	13	0	63	59	13	36
Matt Hollenbeck, Georgetown	3	2	3.18	18	0	51	48	31	50
Matt Smith, Georgetown	5	5	3.21	13	0	84	75	38	55
David Ellingson, Georgetown	2	4	3.38	13	0	59	49	37	40
Billy Laing, Butler	2	2	3.51	21	7	59	45	36	53
James Lomangino, St. John's	6	5	3.65	15	0	91	78	33	85
Gunner Johnson, Butler	3	5	3.88	12	1	58	57	19	47
Chris Kalica, St. John's	6	3	3.94	19	0	59	74	17	37
Scott Klever, Xavier	7	6	3.96	16	0	105	95	32	44
Ryan McCormick, St. John's	7	2	4.28	14	0	69	76	25	59
Trent Astle, Xavier	5	4	4.46	17	1	77	72	23	28
Hunter Schryver, Villanova	2	7	4.55	14	0	57	55	25	43
Kyle Allen, Butler	3	4	5.33	20	0	51	61	17	30
Max Almonte, Villanova	1	6	5.55	12	0	58	78	24	25

BIG SOUTH CONFERENCE

Team	Conference		Overall	
North	W	L	W	L
Liberty	23	3	41	18
*Campbell	18	8	41	21
High Point	18	9	33	22
Radford	17	10	33	23
Virginia Military Institute	11	16	25	23
Longwood	9	18	22	33
South				
Winthrop	14	13	27	33
Coastal Carolina	13	13	24	33
Charleston Southern	12	14	30	26
Gardner-Webb	11	15	24	31
Presbyterian	9	18	19	34
UNC Asheville	4	22	13	40

ALL-CONFERENCE TEAM: C—Danny Grauer, Sr., Liberty. **Infield**—Spencer Angelis, Jr., High Point; Alex Close, Jr., Liberty; Ryan Seiz, Jr., Liberty; Alex Tomasovich, Sr., Charleston Southern. **OF**—Bobby Ison, Jr., Charleston Southern; Patrick Marshall, Jr., Radford; T.J. Olesczuk, Jr., Winthrop. **DH**—Andrew Widell, Jr., Charleston Southern **Utility**—Connor Owings, So. Coastal Carolina. **SP**—Parker Bean, Fr. Liberty; Trey Lambert, Sr., Liberty; Aaron Myers, Jr., Longwood. **RP**—Ryan Thompson, Sr., Campbell. **Player of the Year:** Ryan Seiz, Liberty. **Pitcher of the Year:** Trey Lambert, Liberty. **Freshman of the Year:** Parker Bean, Liberty. **Coach of the Year:** Jim Toman, Liberty.

INDIVIDUAL BATTING LEADERS
(Minimum 2.5 at-bats per team game)

	AVG	AB	R	H	2B	3B	HR	RBI	SB
Bobby Ison, Charleston So.	.396	230	47	91	17	0	3	34	16
Spencer Angelis, High Point	.390	213	37	83	15	1	3	37	0
T.J. Olesczuk, Winthrop	.389	180	17	70	18	3	2	30	7
Alex Tomasovich, Charleston So.	.361	227	50	82	21	2	5	44	6
Alexander Lee, Radford	.357	199	37	71	14	1	3	37	5
Ryan Seiz, Liberty	.351	231	55	81	16	2	12	43	0
Chase Shelton, Charleston So.	.348	221	32	77	17	0	4	44	3
Patrick Marshall, Radford	.338	198	26	67	13	0	3	45	2
Nick Berry, Charleston So.	.338	160	22	54	9	0	5	26	4
Brandon Angus, VMI	.333	186	23	62	9	3	0	21	29
#Matt Nadolski, Campbell	.303	244	45	74	17	2	5	47	11
#Josh Greene, High Point	.276	276	32	54	10	4	2	30	9
#John Menken, Winthrop	.248	210	28	52	8	4	2	21	9

INDIVIDUAL PITCHING LEADERS
(Minimum 1 IP per team game)

	W	L	ERA	G	SV	IP	H	BB	SO
Ryan Thompson, Campbell	7	2	1.33	39	17	88	71	29	87
Cas Silber, High Point	5	0	1.53	22	0	59	38	38	61
Aaron Myers, Longwood	7	4	1.76	16	1	107	82	28	89
Trey Lambert, Liberty	11	3	2.23	16	0	109	85	28	71
Reed Garrett, VMI	6	6	2.23	13	0	89	64	36	71
Hector Cedano, Campbell	8	0	2.31	17	0	93	79	36	48
John McGillicuddy, High Point	6	2	2.37	15	0	102	74	37	52
Matt Fraudin, Gardner Webb	4	7	2.41	16	0	108	88	28	108
Andrew Woods, VMI	5	2	2.70	13	0	77	76	25	71
Ryan Meisinger, Radford	5	1	2.80	19	5	61	52	27	61
#Heath Bowers, Campbell	10	4	3.04	19	0	115	111	33	101

BIG TEN CONFERENCE

Team	Conference		Overall	
	W	L	W	L
*Indiana	21	3	44	14
Nebraska	18	6	41	21
Illinois	17	7	32	21
Minnesota	13	11	27	24
Michigan	13	11	30	29
Michigan State	11	13	31	26
Iowa	10	14	30	23
Ohio State	10	14	30	28
Northwestern	7	16	19	33
Purdue	6	18	13	37
Penn State	5	18	18	32

ALL-CONFERENCE TEAM: C—Kyle Schwarber, Jr., Indiana. **1B**—Sam Travis, Jr., Indiana. **2B**—Pat Kelly, Jr., Nebraska. **SS**—Jake Yacinich, Sr., Iowa. **3B**—Dustin DeMuth, Sr., Indiana. **OF**—Brad Hartong, Jr., Indiana; Jimmy Pickens, Jr., Michigan State; Michael Pritchard, Sr., Nebraska. **DH**—Scott Donley, Jr., Indiana. **SP**—Joey DeNato, Sr., Indiana; Christian Morris, So., Indiana; Chance Sinclair, Jr., Nebraska. **RP**—Luke Harrison, Jr., Indiana. **Player of the Year:** Sam Travis, Indiana. **Pitcher of the Year:** Joey DeNato, Indiana. **Freshman of the Year:** Tanner Tully, Ohio State. **Coach of the Year:** Tracy Smith, Indiana.

INDIVIDUAL BATTING LEADERS
(Minimum 115 at bats)

	AVG	AB	R	H	2B	3B	HR	RBI	SB
Dustin DeMuth, Indiana	.374	211	40	79	16	1	5	40	4
Jake Yacinich, Iowa	.365	208	45	76	6	4	1	32	25
Kyle Schwarber, Indiana	.358	232	66	83	16	6	14	48	10
Sam Travis, Indiana	.347	245	55	85	16	2	12	58	8
Ronnie Dawson, Ohio State	.337	205	28	69	10	1	4	25	10
Matt Hopfner, Northwestern	.335	197	30	66	6	1	0	25	1
Jackson Glines, Michigan	.332	214	38	71	19	3	1	43	14
Tyler Peyton, Iowa	.331	142	23	47	9	0	2	28	2
Dan Potempa, Iowa	.330	176	15	58	13	0	3	40	0
Adam Walton, Illinois	.329	149	22	49	5	3	1	19	13
Scott Donley, Indiana	.324	219	33	71	16	2	5	47	5
Blake Headley, Nebraska	.323	201	22	65	8	2	2	27	2
Steve Snyder, Penn State	.321	193	28	62	7	1	0	15	9
Jimmy Pickens, Michigan State	.318	201	38	64	10	3	5	35	22
Nick Sergakis, Ohio State	.318	151	29	48	6	2	1	13	3
Scott Heelan, Northwestern	.317	189	26	60	13	1	1	33	1
Blaise Salter, Michigan State	.317	221	34	70	22	0	5	50	0
Ben Miller, Nebraska	.316	117	19	37	3	0	2	13	0
Jason Goldstein, Illinois	.316	193	26	61	11	0	4	28	2
Cam Gibson, Michigan State	.315	222	35	70	8	4	2	18	16
Jake Mangler, Iowa	.315	216	38	68	11	1	1	45	5
Zach Jones, Northwestern	.315	162	15	51	7	1	0	17	0
Michael Pritchard, Nebraska	.314	239	45	75	21	4	3	49	5
Brad Hartong, Indiana	.313	160	27	50	11	1	3	36	7
#Ryan Boldt, Nebraska	.311	238	47	74	12	6	2	31	7
#Casey Rodriguez, Indiana	.264	246	48	65	12	6	0	22	12
#Anthony Cheky, Michigan State	.273	227	38	62	5	2	1	14	29

INDIVIDUAL PITCHING LEADERS
(Minimum 50 IP)

	W	L	ERA	G	SV	IP	H	BB	SO
Zach Hirsch, Nebraska	5	2	1.72	31	4	52	36	14	50
Kevin Duchene, Illinois	4	1	1.80	9	0	55	43	11	35
Joey DeNato, Indiana	13	1	1.82	17	0	109	91	39	81
Scott Effross, Indiana	5	3	1.98	32	5	55	56	11	40
Christian Morris, Indiana	6	3	2.04	16	0	84	76	21	47
Chance Sinclair, Nebraska	9	1	2.15	16	0	101	87	26	52
Luke Harrison, Indiana	6	0	2.21	27	3	53	47	10	57
Tanner Tully, Ohio State	6	3	2.22	16	0	93	91	7	53
Ben Meyer, Minnesota	4	5	2.39	15	0	98	83	28	67
Travis Lakins, Ohio State	3	3	2.45	25	2	55	49	21	55
#Jeff Kinley, Michigan State	2	2	2.45	30	13	37	32	13	22
Christian DeLeon, Nebraska	5	2	2.46	11	0	80	71	16	39
Calvin Matthews, Iowa	3	3	2.72	13	1	73	55	20	60
Justin Alleman, Michigan State	6	2	2.75	14	0	95	70	32	57
Mick VanVossen, Minnesota	8	3	2.82	16	0	99	82	29	77
Brett Adcock, Michigan	7	4	2.87	26	1	53	45	20	61
Drasen Johnson, Illinois	5	7	2.91	15	0	96	106	20	79
Tim Dunn, Penn State	2	4	2.98	13	0	57	53	19	21
John Kravetz, Illinois	6	1	3.00	13	0	78	82	15	42
Cam Vieaux, Michigan State	6	5	3.18	18	0	71	66	18	57
Evan Hill, Michigan	5	6	3.24	16	1	89	80	28	63

BIG 12 CONFERENCE

Team	Conference		Overall	
	W	L	W	L
Oklahoma State	18	6	48	16
*Texas Christian	17	7	45	15
Kansas	15	9	35	26
Texas Tech	14	10	43	19
Texas	13	11	41	19
West Virginia	9	14	28	26
Baylor	8	15	26	31
Oklahoma	8	16	29	29
Kansas State	5	19	25	30

ALL-CONFERENCE TEAM: C—Gage Green, Jr., Oklahoma State. **IF**—Billy Fleming, Jr., West Virginia; Eric Gutierrez, So., Texas Tech; Sheldon Neuse, Fr., Oklahoma; Tim Proudfoot, Jr., Texas Tech; Donnie Walton, So., Oklahoma State. **OF**—Bobby Boyd, Jr., West Virginia; Zach Fish, Jr., Oklahoma State; Mark Payton, Sr., Texas; Boomer White, So., TCU. **DH**—Adam Kirsch, Sr., Texas Tech; Mac James, Jr., Oklahoma. **P**—Frank Duncan, Sr., Kansas; Riley Ferrell, So., TCU; Brandon Finnegan, Jr., TCU; Brendan McCurry, Sr., Oklahoma State; Josh Michalec, Sr., Baylor; Preston Morrison, Jr., TCU; Jon Perrin, Jr., Oklahoma State; Vince Wheeland, Sr., Oklahoma State. Player of the Year: Zach Fish, Oklahoma State. **Pitcher of the Year:** Preston Morrison, TCU. **Freshman of the Year:** Sheldon Neuse, Oklahoma. **Newcomer of the Year:** Adam Kirsch, Texas Tech. **Coach of the Year:** Josh Holliday, Oklahoma State.

INDIVIDUAL BATTING LEADERS
(Minimum 2.5 at-bats per team game)

	AVG	AB	R	H	2B	3B	HR	RBI	SB
Bobby Boyd, West Virginia	.356	222	46	79	8	2	1	24	18
Billy Fleming, West Virginia	.351	222	35	78	8	2	1	30	6
Ryan McBroom, West Virginia	.341	211	32	72	12	0	8	49	1
Dakota Smith, Kansas	.337	187	33	63	11	3	2	43	3
R.J. Santigate, Kansas State	.335	197	34	66	6	1	0	27	15
Ross Kivett, Kansas State	.333	210	49	70	13	1	4	33	21
Mac James, Oklahoma	.330	218	32	72	15	1	5	41	4
Craig Aikin, Oklahoma State	.326	239	47	78	7	4	0	25	5
Garrett Crain, TCU	.324	179	31	58	9	2	1	19	8
Michael Suiter, Kansas	.322	239	47	77	11	1	3	42	3
Mark Payton, Texas	.315	241	33	76	15	5	2	39	19
Boomer White, TCU	.315	267	49	84	14	0	2	49	12
Colby Wright, Kansas	.314	156	35	49	11	1	1	21	1
Gage Green, Oklahoma State	.310	239	45	74	14	2	3	30	20
Donnie Walton, Oklahoma State	.310	252	45	78	15	0	3	36	70
Tucker Tharp, Kansas	.310	210	34	65	15	0	6	39	11
Zach Fish, Oklahoma State	.308	240	41	74	17	0	11	48	4
Dylan Fitzgerald, TCU	.307	244	34	75	16	3	2	34	62
Adam Kirsch, Texas Tech	.307	225	37	69	21	3	10	51	0
Sheldon Neuse, Oklahoma	.304	240	43	73	17	7	7	47	7
Eric Gutierrez, Texas Tech	.302	245	46	74	18	2	12	58	0
Austin Fisher, Kansas State	.300	207	36	62	7	1	2	34	6
C.J. Hinojosa, Texas	.298	242	31	72	13	0	2	35	5
Adam Toth, Baylor	.296	216	33	64	9	4	3	26	13
Shane Conlon, Kansas State	.296	189	38	56	8	2	1	29	8
Jacob Rice, West Virginia	.296	206	25	61	9	1	1	31	22
Hunter Kelley, Oklahoma	.294	218	43	64	9	6	6	34	12
Anthony Hermelyn, Oklahoma	.289	211	24	61	7	1	2	28	1
Stephen Smith, Texas Tech	.287	195	41	56	12	3	1	20	2
Zane Gurwitz, Texas	.284	208	26	59	10	1	2	28	9
#Justin Protacio, Kansas	.280	236	53	66	6	2	0	16	4
#Bryant Burleson, Texas Tech	.272	254	38	69	21	3	2	37	2
#Cody Jones, TCU	.265	257	51	68	9	2	0	18	29

INDIVIDUAL PITCHING LEADERS
(Minimum 1 IP per team game)

	W	L	ERA	G	SV	IP	H	BB	SO
#Brendan McCurry, Okla. State	5	0	0.38	35	11	47	29	8	54
Preston Morrison, TCU	9	4	1.32	18	0	130	90	21	95

	W	L	ERA	G	SV	IP	H	BB	SO
Nathan Thornhill, Texas	9	3	1.51	21	2	113	82	37	68
Vince Wheeland, Okla. State	10	1	1.52	31	0	83	65	16	45
Dylan Dusek, Texas Tech	8	0	1.94	14	0	74	63	14	38
Brandon Finnegan, TCU	9	3	2.04	17	0	106	79	29	**134**
Jonny Drozd, Texas Tech	7	1	2.09	28	5	73	64	15	48
Dillon Peters, Texas	7	3	2.13	13	0	80	72	21	53
Tyler Alexander, TCU	10	3	2.36	20	0	99	88	11	59
Jon Perrin, Oklahoma State	8	5	2.38	21	0	102	94	29	81
Parker French, Texas	7	5	2.41	20	1	105	88	44	62
Frank Duncan, Kansas	6	4	2.58	16	0	119	110	14	82
Harrison Musgrave, WVU	5	3	2.62	15	0	106	90	22	87
Cameron Smith, Texas Tech	8	3	2.79	25	1	68	49	29	44
Sean Carley, West Virginia	5	3	2.95	18	4	73	74	26	47
Chris Sadberry, Texas Tech	5	3	3.03	18	0	95	88	25	65
John Means, West Virginia	5	2	3.13	12	0	69	73	18	46
Dominic Moreno, Texas Tech	4	5	3.14	22	2	66	68	24	56
Jordan Kipper, TCU	9	3	3.23	17	0	75	67	17	74
Brad Kuntz, Baylor	4	2	3.23	11	0	62	51	34	51
Daniel Castano, Baylor	4	2	3.34	20	0	70	72	22	39
#Drew Morovick, Kansas	10	4	5.00	25	0	77	86	26	44

BIG WEST CONFERENCE

Team	Conference		Overall	
	W	L	W	L
*Cal Poly	19	5	47	12
Long Beach State	17	7	34	26
UC Irvine	15	9	38	23
Cal State Fullerton	14	10	34	24
UC Santa Barbara	12	12	34	17
UC Riverside	12	12	26	28
UC Davis	7	17	23	31
Hawaii	6	18	22	31
Cal State Northridge	6	18	18	38

ALL-CONFERENCE TEAM: C—Chris Hoo, Sr., Cal Poly. 1B—Connor Spencer, Jr., UC Irvine. 2B—Mark Mathias, So., Cal Poly. SS—Garrett Hampson, Fr., Long Beach State. 3B—Matt Chapman, Jr., Cal State Fullerton. OF—Richard Prigatano, Jr., Long Beach State; Nick Torres, Jr., Cal Poly; Thomas Walker, Jr., UC Riverside. DH—Jonathan Munoz, So., UC Irvine. UT—J.D. Davis, Jr., Cal State Fullerton. SP—Josh Frye, Sr., Long Beach State; Matt Imhof, Jr., Cal Poly; Andrew Morales, Sr., UC Irvine. RP—Taylor Chris, Jr., Cal Poly; Dylan Stuart. Sr., UC Riverside. CP—Sam Moore, Jr., UC Irvine; Reed Reilly, Jr., Cal Poly. Player of the Year—Mark Mathias, Cal Poly. Pitcher of the Year: Andrew Morales, UC Irvine. Defensive Player of the Year: Chris Hoo, Cal Poly. Freshman Pitcher of the Year: Phil Bickford, Cal State Fullerton. Freshman Player of the Year: Garrett Hampson, Long Beach State. Coach of the Year: Larry Lee, Cal Poly.

INDIVIDUAL BATTING LEADERS
(Minimum 2.5 at-bats per team game)

	AVG	AB	R	H	2B	3B	HR	RBI	SB
Mark Mathias, Cal Poly	.386	210	48	81	14	1	2	39	12
Joey Epperson, UCSB	.376	197	45	74	12	1	4	31	15
Connor Spencer, UC Irvine	.364	250	36	91	15	5	1	44	8
J.D. Davis, CS Fullerton	.338	237	34	80	16	5	6	43	7
Adam Young, UC Davis	.337	175	26	59	7	0	0	22	2
Devyn Bolasky, UC Riverside	.336	226	30	76	6	1	2	26	14
Kevin Barker, UC Davis	.335	188	17	63	10	1	1	21	7
Thomas Walker, UC Riverside	.328	174	24	57	15	1	1	27	1
Steven Patterson, UC Davis	.326	144	19	47	7	4	1	24	1
Robby Nesovic, UCSB	.325	194	17	63	15	0	1	33	5
Nick Torres, Cal Poly	.322	242	39	78	17	2	6	43	4
Francisco Tellez, UC Riverside	.319	210	33	67	13	1	3	45	4
Zack Zehner, Cal Poly	.316	174	32	55	7	3	3	16	5
Matt Chapman, CS Fullerton	.312	205	37	64	16	2	6	48	6
Andrew Calica, UCSB	.310	145	25	45	6	0	0	20	10
Ino Patron, Long Beach	.310	226	32	70	13	3	3	36	7
Garrett Hampson, Long Beach	.308	240	44	74	13	2	1	19	9
Taylor Sparks, UC Irvine	.308	253	45	78	17	9	5	37	8
Nick Lynch, UC Davis	.308	185	20	57	11	0	4	34	2
Kaeo Alviado, Hawaii	.307	212	36	65	9	2	0	27	3
Adam Hurley, Hawaii	.306	144	18	44	7	0	1	15	3
Jerry McClanahan, UC Irvine	.304	207	17	63	5	0	1	36	3

	AVG	AB	R	H	2B	3B	HR	RBI	SB
Marc Flores, Hawaii	.303	185	25	56	12	1	5	44	1
Nick Blaser, CSUN	.302	182	16	55	9	0	0	23	2
Chris Hoo, Cal Poly	.301	186	33	56	13	2	1	37	1
Johnny Bekakis, Long Beach	.301	193	26	58	5	0	2	22	8
Richard Prigatano, Long Beach	.300	203	34	61	7	4	1	47	21
Jimmy Allen, Cal Poly	.298	235	33	70	13	3	6	39	4
Tanner Pinkston, CS Fullerton	.298	188	16	56	6	0	1	19	4
Nick Vilter, UC Riverside	.294	160	37	47	9	1	**10**	33	5
#Joe Chavez, UC Riverside	.281	217	45	61	10	3	2	24	**22**

INDIVIDUAL PITCHING LEADERS
(Minimum 40 IP)

	W	L	ERA	G	SV	IP	H	BB	SO
Dylan Stuart, UC Riverside	3	0	**1.44**	26	4	69	68	12	38
Dillon Tate, UCSB	2	1	1.45	28	12	43	32	17	46
Andrew Morales, UC Irvine	11	2	1.53	19	0	**136**	89	33	**141**
Casey Bloomquist, Cal Poly	**12**	2	1.56	16	1	98	87	20	74
Matt Cooper, Hawaii	6	5	1.60	15	0	107	83	28	106
Taylor Chris, Cal Poly	4	1	1.61	24	5	56	38	23	53
Koby Gauna, CS Fullerton	5	3	1.64	27	5	60	53	8	54
Grahamm Wiest, CS Fullerton	5	4	1.68	15	0	113	89	12	86
Reed Reilly, Cal Poly	3	1	1.71	28	12	47	24	17	53
#Sam Moore, UC Irvine	0	3	1.85	**32**	**23**	44	35	11	39
Thomas Eshelman, CS Fullerton	8	3	1.89	16	0	124	100	8	99
Josh Frye, Long Beach	8	1	1.94	17	0	83	55	19	52
Andrew Rohrbach, Long Beach	7	2	2.05	16	0	110	91	20	69
Ryan Millison, Long Beach	4	1	2.06	19	1	52	46	13	30
Phil Bickford, CS Fullerton	6	3	2.13	20	0	76	66	13	74
Elliot Surrey, UC Irvine	8	5	2.32	19	1	113	97	29	76
Matt Imhof, Cal Poly	10	4	2.45	15	0	99	65	43	124
Justin Jacome, UCSB	8	2	2.61	12	0	79	75	19	47
Evan Manarino, UC Irvine	4	4	2.66	23	1	64	77	9	56
Greg Mahle, UCSB	6	5	2.70	**32**	1	70	66	22	42
Jarrett Arakawa, Hawaii	2	1	2.76	11	0	49	50	11	20

COLONIAL ATHLETIC ASSOCIATION

Team	Conference		Overall	
	W	L	W	L
William & Mary	15	5	34	22
*College of Charleston	15	6	44	19
UNC Wilmington	10	9	30	27
Delaware	10	10	26	27
Northeastern	9	12	26	29
James Madison	8	12	17	36
Hofstra	7	11	20	24
Towson	4	13	22	25

ALL-CONFERENCE TEAM: C—Ryan Hissey, So., William & Mary. 1B—Matt Tenaglia, Sr., James Madison. 2B—Zach Lopes, Jr., Delaware. SS—Jason Vosler, Jr., Northeastern. 3B—Ty McFarland, Sr., James Madison. OF—Tyler Gregory, Sr., James Madison; Michael Katz, Jr., William & Mary; Nick Thompson, Jr., William & Mary. DH—Charley Gould, So., William & Mary. UT—Gunnar Heidt, Jr., College of Charleston. SP—Matt Batts, Sr., UNC Wilmington; Bailey Ober, Fr., College of Charleston. RP—Joseph Gaouette, Jr., William & Mary. Player of the Year: Michael Katz, William & Mary. Pitcher of the Year: Mat Batts, UNC Wilmington. Defensive Player of the Year: Matt Ford, Hofstra. Rookie of the Year: Bailey Ober, College of Charleston. Coach of the Year: Brian Murphy, William & Mary.

INDIVIDUAL BATTING LEADERS
(Minimum 125 at-bats)

	AVG	AB	R	H	2B	3B	HR	RBI	SB
Nick Thompson, William & Mary	.368	231	69	85	14	0	11	37	2
Michael Katz, William & Mary	.363	240	64	87	24	1	14	75	0
Connor Lyons, Northeastern	.335	227	49	76	10	5	0	23	11
Charley Gould, William & Mary	.333	150	25	50	14	0	7	42	0
Robbie Cafiero, Hofstra	.331	142	23	47	15	1	2	21	10
Gunnar Heidt, CofC	.327	168	39	55	10	1	4	30	15
E.J. Stoltzfus, Delaware	.323	198	34	64	12	0	2	29	2
Jason Vosler, Northeastern	.322	211	24	68	13	2	1	29	1
Zach Lopes, Delaware	.320	200	31	64	8	2	1	29	5
Brian MacDonald, Hofstra	.318	151	20	48	12	0	4	29	4
Ty McFarland, James Madison	.317	227	47	72	12	2	9	37	3
Norm Donkin, Delaware	.316	209	35	66	16	1	3	30	10

Corey Dick, UNC Wilmington	.315	184	21	58	3	0	6	38	1
Joe Giacchino, Delaware	.314	207	39	65	14	5	2	23	4
Matt Tenaglia, James Madison	.314	185	32	58	12	2	6	41	0
Ryan Hissey, William & Mary	.313	147	35	46	8	2	8	39	2
Kevin Husum, James Madison	.309	207	45	64	9	3	0	20	6
Luke Dunlap, UNC Wilmington	.305	177	22	54	15	0	1	22	1
Peter Bowles, Towson	.304	181	25	55	10	1	3	35	3
Kyle Weston, James Madison	.300	200	30	60	14	2	2	26	5
Michael Foster, Northeastern	.299	221	38	66	10	1	3	36	18
Ryan Lindemuth, William & Mary	.297	145	50	43	11	2	6	34	3
Carl Wise, CofC	.295	227	24	67	11	4	3	54	2
Josh Smith, William & Mary	.294	136	20	40	7	1	2	17	4
T.J. Ehrsam, Hofstra	.294	126	14	37	3	0	0	14	21
Matt Ford, Hofstra	.293	164	23	48	9	1	2	16	10
Kevin Casey, William & Mary	.291	220	44	64	15	2	2	32	1
Conner Brown, James Madison	.290	193	32	56	15	3	4	34	4
Kevin Nutter, William & Mary	.290	231	36	67	14	0	0	29	3
Kenny Jackson, Hofstra	.289	173	26	50	10	2	4	29	12
#Blake Butler, CofC	.282	255	48	72	11	2	3	24	7

INDIVIDUAL PITCHING LEADERS
(Minimum 50 IP)

	W	L	ERA	G	SV	IP	H	BB	SO
Bailey Ober, CofC	10	3	1.52	17	0	107	73	19	85
Joseph Gaouette, William & Mary	3	1	1.84	26	4	54	39	21	54
Eric Bauer, CofC	6	2	2.09	13	0	52	45	8	27
Chris Carmain, Northeastern	7	2	2.27	14	0	91	82	21	57
Dustin Hunt, Northeastern	6	1	2.50	14	0	83	67	30	73
Taylor Clarke, CofC	10	4	2.51	18	0	104	81	31	92
Mat Batts, UNC Wilmington	6	3	2.69	15	0	104	91	18	105
Jason Inghram, William & Mary	10	2	2.71	15	0	110	93	21	91
Tyler Thornton, CofC	7	5	3.03	22	0	98	81	17	71
#Michael Hanzlik, CofC	2	1	3.35	31	16	38	23	13	37
Ryan Foster, UNC Wilmington	2	3	3.47	16	1	62	63	24	36
Dan Gatto, Delaware	5	6	3.71	16	0	107	120	30	68
Nathan Helvey, CofC	3	4	3.78	21	0	69	79	19	54
Nick Berger, Northeastern	3	6	3.83	15	0	92	92	31	85
John Sheehan, William & Mary	5	6	4.00	13	0	81	81	31	46
Nick Monroe, UNC Wilmington	1	4	4.23	16	0	55	49	19	30
Nick Brown, William & Mary	5	1	4.27	23	1	59	73	20	46
Nick Kozlowski, Hofstra	6	5	4.45	12	0	63	57	38	44
Lee Lawler, Towson	2	3	4.53	14	0	52	56	32	32
Brandon Hinkle, Delaware	5	1	4.61	10	0	55	51	27	55
Bruce Zimmermann, Towson	5	5	5.00	14	0	67	74	21	53

CONFERENCE USA

Team	Conference		Overall	
	W	L	W	L
*Rice	23	7	42	20
Alabama-Birmingham	20	10	35	21
Southern Mississippi	19	11	35	25
Middle Tennessee	17	13	31	27
Old Dominion	17	13	36	26
Florida International	16	14	35	20
East Carolina	16	14	33	26
Texas-San Antonio	16	14	35	26
Florida Atlantic	14	16	28	25
Tulane	10	18	23	29
Marshall	10	19	20	31
Charlotte	10	19	19	31
Louisiana Tech	5	25	15	35

ALL-CONFERENCE TEAM: C—Aramis Garcia, Jr., FIU. IF—Skyler Ewing, Jr., Rice; Shane Hoelscher, Sr., Rice; Zach Houchins, Sr., East Carolina; Trent Miller, Sr., Middle Tennessee. OF—Jared Allen, Jr., Middle Tennessee; Michael Aquino, Sr., Rice; Nick Walker, Fr., Old Dominion. DH/UT—Drew Reynolds, Sr., East Carolina. P—Zac Curtis, Sr., Middle Tennessee; Mike Franco, Sr., FIU; Blake Fox, So., Rice; Chase Mallard, Sr., UAB. RP—Ryan Williams, Sr., East Carolina. Player of the Year: Aramis Garcia, FIU. Pitcher of the Year: Chase Mallard, UAB. Freshman of the Year: Chris Mourelle, FIU. Newcomer of the Year: John Clay Reeves, Rice. Coach of the Year: Brian Shoop, UAB.

INDIVIDUAL BATTING LEADERS
(Minimum 150 at-bats)

	AVG	AB	R	H	2B	3B	HR	RBI	SB
Aramis Garcia, FIU	.368	163	34	60	14	2	8	37	4
Zach Houchins, East Carolina	.347	242	27	84	16	0	3	26	6
Trent Miller, Middle Tennessee	.339	230	25	78	25	1	5	45	0
Skyler Ewing, Rice	.335	242	57	81	16	0	9	48	0
Brendon Sanger, Florida Atlantic	.332	193	36	64	11	2	2	29	6
Shane Hoelscher, Rice	.330	227	43	75	21	0	0	27	0
Stephen Kerr, Florida Atlantic	.324	207	38	67	10	0	0	15	10
Taylor Love, Louisiana Tech	.318	176	24	56	12	0	2	17	11
Mike Warren, UTSA	.317	230	32	73	11	2	4	48	6
John Clay Reeves, Rice	.317	221	32	70	7	1	6	41	1
Drew Reynolds, East Carolina	.316	231	33	73	8	1	2	21	2
Michael Aquino, Rice	.316	244	38	77	17	2	7	46	4
R.J. Perucki, UTSA	.314	229	40	72	11	1	3	40	3
Tyler Rocklein, Florida Atlantic	.310	200	25	62	13	4	3	36	6
Nick Walker, Old Dominion	.309	194	43	60	11	1	4	26	16
P.J. Higgins, Old Dominion	.308	250	44	77	15	0	0	36	7
Taylor Ostrich, Old Dominion	.306	229	34	70	12	4	1	22	3
Dustin Delgado, MTSU	.306	216	34	66	12	1	0	30	3
Ryan Jones, Louisiana Tech	.301	153	21	46	4	1	1	12	6
Josh Anderson, FIU	.300	220	37	66	13	0	5	43	3
C.J. Chatham, Florida Atlantic	.300	200	27	60	11	0	4	26	1
Griffin Gum, UAB	.296	216	28	64	5	0	2	22	11
Edwin Rios, FIU	.296	230	30	68	14	2	2	38	3
Josh Eldridge, Old Dominion	.295	220	30	65	9	3	1	31	8
John Welborn, UTSA	.295	237	56	70	15	3	3	26	5
Corey Bird, Marshall	.292	168	19	49	3	1	0	12	15
John Bormann, UTSA	.288	208	23	60	12	0	4	24	4
Julius Gaines, FIU	.288	226	43	65	8	0	1	27	8
Luke Lowery, East Carolina	.288	160	14	46	6	0	4	19	3
Michael Adkins, MTSU	.286	196	27	56	6	1	1	22	1
#Horacio Correa, UTSA	.270	252	30	68	11	2	1	25	3
#Keenan Cook, Rice	.278	245	46	68	11	5	0	30	12
#Jared Allen, MTSU	.257	218	37	56	11	3	10	33	8
#Tyler Hibbert, FIU	.258	194	39	50	4	2	1	22	16

INDIVIDUAL PITCHING LEADERS
(Minimum 1 IP per team game)

	W	L	ERA	G	SV	IP	H	BB	SO
Mike Franco, FIU	9	3	1.09	15	0	99	68	27	112
#Bradley Roney, Southern Miss	2	0	1.24	18	12	36	18	16	38
Blake Fox, Rice	12	0	1.46	15	0	105	88	27	69
Chase Mallard, UAB	9	3	1.55	15	0	110	74	22	94
Alex Luna, UAB	7	1	1.76	15	0	87	75	17	58
Ryan Williams, East Carolina	11	3	1.81	32	7	100	88	11	76
Matt Ditman, Rice	5	6	1.83	26	9	69	50	12	77
Zac Curtis, MTSU	9	3	1.89	15	0	114	84	29	136
Chris Mourelle, FIU	9	3	1.95	15	0	78	75	11	37
Tyler Mapes, Tulane	5	5	2.20	13	0	82	83	15	59
Cody Crouse, FIU	4	3	2.23	14	0	73	72	18	38
Richie Navari, Louisiana Tech	5	6	2.23	14	0	97	89	29	51
Brett Mabry, East Carolina	4	3	2.24	19	0	76	61	19	41
Brock Hartson, UTSA	7	3	2.24	16	0	104	101	30	88
Logan Onda, UTSA	3	2	2.34	30	8	62	57	11	54
Tyler Bolton, East Carolina	2	5	2.42	14	0	71	64	27	35
Nolan Bertrain, UTSA	9	3	2.43	15	0	81	79	19	41
Randy LeBlanc, Tulane	4	5	2.46	14	0	91	89	20	66
Conor Fisk, Southern Miss	7	2	2.62	13	0	89	71	24	84
Christian Talley, Southern Miss	4	4	2.67	13	0	78	80	14	74
Johnny Lieske, UAB	5	2	2.69	14	0	74	61	41	56
#Brad Gero, Old Dominion	3	4	2.87	39	12	53	52	8	44

HORIZON LEAGUE

Team	Conference		Overall	
	W	L	W	L
Wright State	25	4	35	22
Illinois-Chicago	17	13	24	27
Valparaiso	12	12	25	28
Wisconsin-Milwaukee	10	14	21	29
Oakland	7	17	12	33
*Youngstown State	6	17	17	38

ALL-CONFERENCE TEAM: C—Alex Jurich, Sr., UIC. **1B**—Jeff Boehm, Jr., UIC. **2B**—Michael Timm, Jr., Wright State. **SS**—Mike Brosseau, So., Oakland. **3B**—Michael Morman, Sr., Valparaiso. **OF**—Tyler Detmer, Jr., UIC; Robby Enslen, Jr., Oakland; Jeff Limbaugh, Sr., Wright State; Ryan Solberg, Sr., Milwaukee. **DH**—Jacob McNamara, Sr., UIC. **UT**—John Coen, Sr., UIC. **P**—Joey Hoelzel, Sr., Wright State; Dalton Lundeen, Valparaiso. **Player of the Year:** Ryan Solberg, Milwaukee. **Pitchers of the Year:** Joey Hoelzel, Wright State; Dalton Lundeen, Valparaiso. **Relief Pitcher of the Year:** Andrew Elliott, Wright State. **Freshman of the Year:** Sean Murphy, Wright State. **Coach of the Year:** Greg Lovelady, Wright State.

INDIVIDUAL BATTING LEADERS
(Minimum 125 at-bats)

	AVG	AB	R	H	2B	3B	HR	RBI	SB
Robby Enslen, Oakland	.378	180	35	68	12	1	4	38	3
Ryan Solberg, UWM	.369	185	33	68	15	1	7	43	24
Jacob McNamara, UIC	.354	158	39	56	6	0	0	21	3
Alex Jurich, UIC	.339	186	40	63	8	2	5	46	2
Tyler Detmer, UIC	.330	185	38	61	9	1	5	39	2
John Coen, UIC	.327	168	32	55	5	1	2	22	7
Michael Timm, Wright State	.325	212	41	69	17	2	3	38	7
Phil Lipari, YSU	.323	186	40	60	9	3	5	26	8
Mike Brosseau, Oakland	.321	162	26	52	12	0	2	27	0
Josh White, YSU	.314	140	12	44	8	2	1	21	0
Jeff Limbaugh, Wright State	.311	180	32	56	10	1	1	26	8
Alex Lee, UIC	.309	178	39	55	6	1	1	23	1
Jeff Beohm, UIC	.302	162	32	49	16	1	7	30	1
Pat Wilson, UWM	.302	162	32	49	16	1	7	30	1
Sean Murphy, Wright State	.301	205	25	62	9	2	4	31	10
Mickey McDonald, UIC	.297	145	22	43	6	1	2	24	3
Michael Morman, Valparaiso	.296	206	26	61	10	0	1	26	20
Chris Manning, Valparaiso	.296	206	35	61	6	2	3	31	13
Jason DeFevers, Wright State	.296	142	19	42	7	0	1	24	3
Trent Pell, Oakland	.292	106	18	31	1	3	0	9	2
Ryan McShane, UWM	.290	145	18	42	3	0	2	16	11
Brad Macciocchi, Wright State	.288	184	33	53	8	3	0	23	2
Conor Philbin, UIC	.281	153	20	43	8	1	1	30	4
Jake Nath, UIC	.280	132	23	37	4	2	1	15	14
Tyler Hermann, UWM	.280	161	21	45	5	0	3	17	5
Zach Sterry, Oakland	.279	136	20	38	4	1	3	18	0
Nick Unes, UWM	.276	170	19	47	10	0	1	18	3
Andrew McCafferty, Wright St.	.274	219	36	60	17	1	3	33	5
Alex Larivee, YSU	.274	190	21	52	7	2	0	18	7
Mike Porcaro, UWM	.271	177	34	48	10	1	1	24	6
#Joe Ford, Wright State	.267	221	37	59	15	2	2	31	10
#Jared Theisen, Oakland	.244	164	18	40	2	4	1	27	9

INDIVIDUAL PITCHING LEADERS
(Mimimum 50 IP)

	W	L	ERA	G	SV	IP	H	BB	SO
#Andrew Elliot, Wright State	2	0	0.65	27	13	42	22	16	61
Dalton Lundeen, Valparaiso	5	6	1.94	13	0	83	73	12	65
Robby Sexton, WSU	8	4	2.95	14	0	82	69	34	61
Mitchell Schulewitz, UIC	4	7	3.54	31	3	56	64	12	59
Joey Hoelzel, Wright State	7	6	3.57	15	0	93	93	31	59
Jake Paulson, Oakland	4	8	3.68	12	0	66	77	27	45
Tim Koons, Oakland	3	2	3.86	12	0	70	59	37	71
Ian Lewandowski, Oakland	4	6	4.02	14	0	94	126	26	28
Mario Losi, Valparaiso	2	7	4.05	14	1	60	66	20	21
Jason Hager, Oakland	3	4	4.12	12	0	79	83	26	51
Cole Webb, Valparaiso	7	4	4.17	14	0	86	87	34	57
Brian Keller, UWM	2	7	4.26	14	0	82	85	24	54
Tomas Michelson, UIC	6	5	4.82	14	0	93	102	20	61
Ellis Foreman, Valparaiso	4	6	4.88	14	0	72	91	15	41
Tyler Thicke, UWM	6	5	5.13	20	0	60	58	34	43
Cody Peterson, UWM	4	3	5.23	14	1	53	60	23	34
Jake Anderson, UIC	3	4	6.17	13	0	57	73	19	18

IVY LEAGUE

Team	Conference		Overall	
Gehrig	**W**	**L**	**W**	**L**
*Columbia	15	5	29	20
Pennsylvania	15	5	24	17
Cornell	9	11	18	21

Princeton	8	12	14	26
RolfeYale	11	9	19	22
Dartmouth	11	9	18	21
Brown	6	14	13	24
Harvard	5	15	11	28

ALL-CONFERENCE TEAM: C—Austin Bossart, Jr., Penn. **1B**—Dustin Selzer, Sr., Dartmouth. **2B**—Will Savage, Fr., Columbia. **SS**—Cale Hanson, Sr., Yale; Ryan Mincher, So., Penn. **3B**—David Vandercook, Jr., Columbia. **OF**—Rick Brebner, Sr., Penn; Gus Craig, Jr., Columbia; Mike Martin, Jr., Harvard. **DH**—Ryan Karl, Jr., Cornell. **UT**—Alec Keller, Sr., Princeton. **P**—Connor Cuff, Jr., Penn; Mike Fagan, Sr., Princeton; David Speer, Sr., Columbia. **RP**—Duncan Robinson, So., Dartmouth. **Player of the year:** Alec Keller, Princeton. **Pitcher of the Year:** David Speer, Columbia. **Rookie of the Year:** Will Savage, Columbia.

INDIVIDUAL BATTING LEADERS
(Minimum 2.5 at-bats per team game)

	AVG	AB	R	H	2B	3B	HR	RBI	SB
Alec Keller, Princeton	.327	147	20	48	8	4	2	19	7
Will Savage, Columbia	.320	153	27	49	8	1	1	15	14
Carlton Bailey, Harvard	.319	113	15	36	7	0	0	13	3
Jeff McGarry, Penn	.316	152	28	48	12	0	4	30	2
Jeff Keller, Dartmouth	.308	146	29	45	15	1	2	17	11
Danny Baer, Princeton	.306	108	17	33	5	1	0	10	2
Jordan Serena, Columbia	.305	187	41	57	9	3	0	14	25
Mike Martin, Harvard	.304	148	22	45	6	2	1	12	17
Michael Vilardo, Penn	.304	148	21	45	14	2	1	23	4
Robert Baldwin, Yale	.304	125	21	38	10	0	3	22	4
Thomas Roulis, Dartmouth	.300	150	20	45	5	4	1	25	2
Austin Bossart, Penn	.297	158	29	47	9	0	4	19	1
J.J. Franco, Brown	.296	135	29	40	5	3	1	17	2
Robb Paller, Columbia	.296	186	25	55	12	1	3	35	3
Daniel Massey, Brown	.296	115	20	34	9	0	6	21	4
Dustin Selzer, Dartmouth	.294	119	12	35	7	0	2	22	0
Danny Hoy, Princeton	.285	151	25	43	9	1	3	15	7
Kyle Larrow, Harvard	.285	151	22	43	3	1	0	16	7
Rick Brebner, Penn	.285	151	33	43	10	1	8	31	5
Green Campbell, Yale	.283	127	23	36	3	0	1	20	9
Zack Belski, Princeton	.280	125	8	35	3	0	1	19	0
Ryan Karl, Cornell	.280	143	23	40	10	1	9	32	3
Dan Kerr, Brown	.280	118	16	33	4	0	2	14	1
Gus Craig, Columbia	.277	159	27	44	9	3	6	26	3
Nick Lombardi, Dartmouth	.277	141	18	39	9	3	5	26	0
Paul Tupper, Princeton	.275	142	18	39	3	1	2	20	0
Matt Parisi, Dartmouth	.273	139	18	38	2	0	3	12	2
Ryan Mincher, Penn	.271	133	19	36	10	0	4	24	2
Eric Hsieh, Yale	.267	116	16	31	5	0	0	11	4
Jack Colton, Harvard	.266	143	13	38	6	0	0	14	4
#David Vandercook, Columbia	.252	159	22	40	15	0	5	34	2

INDIVIDUAL PITCHING LEADERS
(Minimum 1 IP per team game)

	W	L	ERA	G	SV	IP	H	BB	SO
Connor Cuff, Penn	5	3	1.77	10	0	66	63	9	49
Michael Byrne, Cornell	3	4	1.86	9	0	53	40	20	49
David Speer, Columbia	7	2	1.86	12	0	87	69	7	75
Michael Fagan, Princeton	4	2	2.33	9	0	58	46	18	77
Brent Jones, Cornell	2	3	2.50	9	0	50	45	13	47
Sean Poppen, Harvard	2	4	2.51	10	1	57	51	19	51
Christian Taugner, Brown	2	4	2.56	8	0	53	52	9	49
George Thanopoulos, Columbia	5	2	2.60	15	2	52	43	18	40
Duncan Robinson, Dartmouth	7	3	2.96	16	2	55	42	18	40
Kevin Roy, Columbia	6	5	3.06	12	0	68	46	23	49
Glenn Ronnie, Penn	5	2	3.46	10	0	55	57	16	48
Louis Cohen, Dartmouth	1	2	3.60	9	1	45	47	17	14
Chris Lanham, Yale	7	2	3.77	12	0	62	59	16	46
Michael Concato, Dartmouth	2	3	3.81	10	0	54	65	13	28
#Chris Bodurian, Princeton	0	3	4.03	18	0	29	20	14	20
Nick Gruener, Harvard	1	4	4.24	9	0	51	47	13	38
Anthony Galan, Brown	2	3	4.38	6	0	37	54	8	24
#Jonathan York, Princeton	0	1	4.85	17	7	26	31	17	20
Chad Powers, Princeton	3	4	4.91	9	0	40	39	19	14
Dan Gautieri, Penn	2	6	4.97	9	0	50	56	16	53
Michael Danielak, Dartmouth	1	5	5.26	8	1	39	46	8	26
Chasen Ford, Yale	3	4	5.37	11	0	54	60	20	32

METRO ATLANTIC ATHLETIC CONFERENCE

Team	Conference		Overall	
	W	L	W	L
Canisius	20	4	10	16
*Siena	17	7	27	33
Fairfield	15	8	32	24
Monmouth	12	10	24	25
Quinnipiac	12	10	18	31
Manhattan	11	13	17	32
Iona	9	15	13	31
Niagara	8	14	20	31
Rider	7	15	16	33
Saint Peter's	6	17	11	41

ALL-CONFERENCE TEAM: C—Ryan Plourde, Fairfield. **1B**—Justin Thomas, Rider. **2B**—Jake Gronsky, Monmouth. **SS**—Anthony Massicci, Canisius. **3B**—Connor Panas, Canisius. **OF**—Brett Siddall, Canisius; Craig Sweeney, Monmouth; Joe Torres, Iona. **DH**—Jake Salpietro, Fairfield; Christian Santisteban, Manhattan. **UT**—Ronnie Bernick, Canisius. **P**—E.J. Ashworth, Fairfield; Alex Godzak, Canisius; Rohn Pierce, Canisius. **Player of the Year:** Connor Panas, Canisius. **Pitcher of the Year:** Rohn Pierce, Canisius. **Relief Pitcher of the Year:** Neil Fryer, Siena; Ryan Thomas, Marist. **Rookie of the Year:** Dan Swain, Siena. **Coach of the Year:** Mike McRae, Canisius.

INDIVIDUAL BATTING LEADERS
(Minimum 125 at-bats)

	AVG	AB	R	H	2B	3B	HR	RBI	SB
Anthony Massicci, Canisius	.364	173	48	63	8	4	1	31	11
Jimmy Luppens, Canisius	.363	190	37	39	15	1	3	42	3
Connor Panas Canisius	.362	188	38	68	16	3	6	51	16
Ryan Plourde, Fairfield	.346	191	45	66	10	3	2	30	15
Justin Thomas, Rider	.341	179	24	61	11	2	4	45	2
Vincent Guglietti, Quinnipiac	.341	185	29	63	13	1	5	38	2
Christ Conley, Canisius	.336	119	17	40	5	1	1	23	1
Jimmy Guiliano, Iona	.336	122	15	41	7	1	0	15	5
Vincent Citro, Siena	.335	239	51	80	10	0	0	23	18
Brett Siddall, Canisius	.333	168	27	56	11	3	3	43	2
Jake Gronsky, Monmouth	.330	182	31	60	12	1	0	28	8
Jose Torralba, Canisius	.324	145	41	47	11	0	0	33	12
Brendan Slattery, Manhattan	.324	136	13	44	4	0	1	25	1
Nick Richter, Rider	.321	190	41	61	11	0	0	18	41
Craig Sweeney, Monmouth	.315	165	24	52	10	0	3	29	1
Christian Santisteban, Manhattan	.314	175	21	55	17	0	2	22	1
Taylor Hackett, Niagara	.310	113	15	35	4	1	1	22	6
Greg Rodgers, Niagara	.308	172	27	53	9	1	0	33	3
Joe Bamford, Monmouth	.308	182	27	56	5	3	0	14	7
Rob Moore, Saint Peter's	.307	163	24	50	11	1	5	30	1
Jake Salpietro, Fairfield	.307	199	36	61	16	2	5	44	11
Jon Kristofferse, Saint Peter's	.305	220	37	67	11	3	1	17	6
Danny Avella, Monmouth	.302	172	21	52	14	0	4	36	2
Ronnie Bernick, Canisius	.301	136	33	41	3	1	1	17	1
Mike Allen, Siena	.301	196	32	59	13	1	1	20	8
Steve Laurino, Marist	.299	167	29	50	10	0	0	27	8
Nick Henriquez, Saint Peter's	.297	182	25	54	4	1	2	21	0
Jesse Puscheck, Siena	.295	193	39	57	14	2	3	40	3
Dan Swain, Siena	.293	208	21	61	10	0	2	27	12
Michael Fuhrman, Niagara	.292	161	35	47	8	3	3	27	4
#Rob Pescitelli, Quinnipiac	.242	120	20	29	3	6	3	18	8

INDIVIDUAL PITCHING LEADERS
(Minimum 55 IP)

	W	L	ERA	G	SV	IP	H	BB	SO
Rohn Pierce, Canisius	11	3	2.18	15	0	112	86	16	63
Alex Godzak, Canisius	10	3	2.63	15	1	89	76	42	51
E.J. Ashworth, Fairfield	6	2	2.85	13	0	82	84	18	47
Chris McKenna, Monmouth	4	4	2.93	14	0	74	62	11	51
Jordan sainSchwartz, Niagara	5	6	3.12	15	0	95	76	35	109
Joey Rocchietti, Manhattan	2	6	3.26	16	1	97	78	30	41
Mike Wallace, Fairfield	5	5	3.32	14	0	87	100	15	54
William Fabra, Manhattan	3	4	3.46	13	0	55	46	21	26
Andrew McGee, Monmouth	4	6	3.89	13	0	76	82	16	45
#Neil Fryer, Siena	4	4	3.95	26	8	41	48	14	26
Thomas Jankins, Quinnipiac	5	7	4.02	14	0	87	88	33	48

	W	L	ERA	G	SV	IP	H	BB	SO
Evan Davis, Marist	2	5	4.03	17	0	58	56	31	44
Max Bruckner, Iona	2	2	4.08	17	0	46	49	9	27
Bill Maier, Iona	3	7	4.15	12	0	69	78	24	28
Jordan Eich, Marist	3	6	4.20	13	0	75	75	33	46
Justin Thomas, Quinnipiac	2	5	4.20	13	0	71	54	30	42
#Matt Quintana, Siena	4	3	4.26	28	2	51	63	15	31
Joe Jacques, Manhattan	2	5	4.29	19	1	65	66	34	39
Devon Stewart, Canisius	6	5	4.38	15	0	90	88	23	43
Kenny Dietrich, Iona	2	5	4.42	15	0	59	69	22	31
Matt Gage, Siena	4	7	4.50	16	0	110	117	39	90

MID-AMERICAN CONFERENCE

Team	Conference		Overall	
East	W	L	W	L
*Kent State	20	11	36	23
Miami	19	11	30	27
Bowling Green	15	13	25	26
Akron	15	16	28	29
Buffalo	14	15	25	26
Ohio	7	20	11	40
West				
Ball State	23	6	39	18
Central Michigan	19	10	35	23
Western Michigan	13	18	24	31
Toledo	11	16	24	31
Northern Illinois	11	16	22	32
Eastern Michigan	6	21	19	34

ALL-CONFERENCE TEAM: C—T.J. Losby, Bowling Green. **1B**—Tyler Mautner, Buffalo. **2B**—Ryan Spaulding, Ball State. **SS**—Brian Bien, Bowling Green. **3B**—Dan Walsh, Miami. **OF**—Sean Godfrey, Ball State; Alex Miklos, Kent State; Matt Pollock, Buffalo. **SP**—Pat Kaminska, Central Michigan; Zach Plesac, Ball State; Seth Verner, Miami; T.J. Weir, Ball State. **RP**—Tim Black, Central Michigan. **DH**—Zarley Zalewski, Ball State. **UT**—Jarrett Rindfleisch, Ball State. **Player of the Year:** Sean Godfrey, Ball State. **Pitcher of the Year:** Seth Varner, Miami. **Freshman of the Year:** Zach Plesac, Ball State. **Coach of the Year:** Rich Maloney, Ball State.

INDIVIDUAL BATTING LEADERS
(Minimum 125 at-bats)

	AVG	AB	R	H	2B	3B	HR	RBI	SB
Lee Longo, Eastern Michigan	.379	198	38	75	20	2	3	49	1
Alex Miklos, Kent State	.362	177	44	64	18	7	3	36	17
Alex Call, Ball State	.354	206	40	73	15	0	1	24	2
Zarley Zalewski, Kent State	.350	214	38	75	16	2	2	40	0
Brian Bien, Bowling Green	.350	203	37	71	8	1	0	22	17
Tyler Mautner, Buffalo	.337	193	34	65	17	2	4	52	3
Sean Godfrey, Ball State	.333	237	48	79	22	0	9	57	20
Jon Wilson, Kent State	.333	210	34	70	7	5	0	32	9
Cody Koch, Kent State	.330	218	54	72	12	2	7	56	9
Tyler Huntey, Central Michigan	.329	237	41	78	10	3	5	51	13
John Rubino, Eastern Michigan	.329	213	36	70	10	1	1	34	23
Patrick Lancaster, Bowling Green	.326	193	30	63	6	2	0	19	14
Matt Pollock, Buffalo	.324	188	43	61	15	3	3	36	14
Andrew Sohn, W. Michigan	.323	192	34	62	7	6	0	28	17
Jake Madsen, Ohio	.322	208	29	67	9	0	0	17	1
Kris Simonton, Akron	.320	194	39	62	5	0	1	23	12
T.J. Losby, Bowling Green	.317	186	26	59	9	2	1	36	4
Sean Kennedy, Ball State	.315	197	29	62	5	1	0	17	3
Cody Leichman, C. Michigan	.315	213	38	67	15	1	7	56	4
Max Andresen, Miami	.314	175	25	55	10	4	2	28	0
Dan Walsh, Miami	.313	224	33	70	8	3	2	33	4
Jeremy Shay, Bowling Green	.312	173	32	54	13	2	2	38	6
Devan Ahart, Akron	.311	225	35	70	8	2	3	32	27
Sam Ott, Eastern Michigan	.311	209	45	65	13	2	0	33	7
Logan Regnier, C. Michigan	.311	222	48	69	6	2	0	22	22
Steve Sada, Miami	.309	178	29	55	15	3	0	21	9
Brian Sisler, Northern Illinois	.307	166	19	51	9	1	0	16	5
T.J. Sutton, Kent State	.307	212	29	65	14	2	2	35	2
Matt Honchel, Miami	.305	174	19	53	3	1	0	24	7
Deion Tansel, Toledo	.304	214	27	65	7	1	0	19	10
#Gary Russo, Miami	.284	218	38	62	16	2	10	40	4
#Nick Regnier, C. Michigan	.290	231	50	67	2	1	1	28	35

INDIVIDUAL PITCHING LEADERS
(Minimum 50 IP)

	W	L	ERA	G	SV	IP	H	BB	SO
Zach Plesac, Ball State	12	2	2.11	25	6	85	75	33	67
Alex Klowowski, N. Illinois	4	5	2.39	13	0	90	69	26	57
Pat Kaminska, C. Michigan	8	3	2.47	15	0	95	85	14	70
Chad Mayle, Western Michigan	6	5	2.59	15	0	94	86	44	50
Ryan Wilkinson, Toledo	6	5	2.66	14	0	102	94	21	66
John Valek, Akron	6	4	2.77	15	0	91	103	21	28
Seth Varner, Miami	7	3	2.85	15	0	104	95	25	123
Kevin Hughes, Buffalo	5	6	2.96	17	2	85	81	23	55
Steve Laudicina, W. Michigan	5	7	3.16	16	0	111	111	32	66
Andrew Lacinak, Bowling Green	5	3	3.24	15	0	78	70	26	34
Eric Lauer, Kent State	8	4	3.26	15	0	80	58	36	64
Mike Burke, Buffalo	6	5	3.34	15	0	97	91	21	78
Akin Keegan, W. Michigan	6	4	3.46	16	0	88	85	49	62
Eli Anderson, Northern Illinois	4	6	3.50	13	0	93	93	25	74
#Eric Dorsch	2	4	3.60	26	10	30	24	10	27
T.J. Weir, Ball State	8	2	3.61	19	1	100	100	39	117
Jordan Foley, Central Michigan	6	5	3.69	15	0	98	104	28	81
Adam Aldred, Central Michigan	5	5	3.75	18	2	82	88	30	54
Brian Clark, Kent State	6	6	3.78	15	0	83	71	32	65
Anthony Andres, N. Illinois	3	7	3.92	18	0	67	69	38	27
J.T. Brubaker, Akron	3	5	4.02	14	0	72	74	37	45
Pat Dyer, Akron	4	5	4.04	12	0	65	77	22	48
Scott Baker, Ball State	7	5	4.04	17	0	89	93	18	61
Nick Deeg, Central Michigan	5	4	4.08	14	0	82	90	26	64
Sam Shutes, Toledo	3	4	4.17	14	0	69	71	26	46
#Tyler Wells, Ohio	1	3	6.23	28	5	26	30	17	11

MID-EASTERN ATHLETIC CONFERENCE

Team	Conference		Overall	
NORTH	W	L	W	L
Delaware State	17	7	30	17
Norfolk State	14	10	20	25
Coppin State	9	15	12	33
Maryland-Eastern Shore	8	16	13	35
SOUTH				
Florida A&M	14	10	25	25
*Bethune-Cookman	14	10	24	31
North Carolina Central	12	12	19	32
Savannah State	11	13	21	30
North Carolina A&T	9	15	17	32

ALL-CONFERENCE TEAM: C—Mike Alexander, Sr., Delaware State. 1B—Bennie Robinson, Sr., Florida A&M. 2B—Todd Hagen, Sr., Savannah State. SS—D.J. Miller, Sr., Delaware State. 3B—Tyson Simpson, Sr., North Carolina Central. OF—Stephen Bull, Sr., Maryland Eastern Shore; Byron Campbell, Sr., Maryland Eastern Shore; Aarron Nardone, Sr., Delaware State. DH—Charles Sikes, Jr., Savannah State. P—Montana Durapau, Sr. Bethune-Cookman; Matt McClain, Sr., Delaware State. RP—Kevin Herlihy, Sr., Savannah State. Player of the Year: Bennie Robinson, Florida A&M. Pitcher of the Year: Montana Durapau, Bethune-Cookman. Rookie of the Year: Carlos Ortiz, North Carolina Central. Coach of the Year: Jamey Shouppe, Florida A&M.

INDIVIDUAL BATTING LEADERS
(Minimum 2 at-bats per team game)

	AVG	AB	R	H	2B	3B	HR	RBI	SB
D.J. Miller, Delaware State	.404	151	40	61	14	3	2	29	4
Ben Robinson, Florida A&M	.390	213	45	83	15	0	6	42	11
Mike Alexander, Delaware State	.386	153	41	59	8	0	7	33	16
Byron Campbell, UMES	.371	167	30	62	10	2	4	37	10
Aaron Nardone Delaware State	.362	152	47	55	10	2	8	43	19
Charles Sikes, Savannah State	.358	201	41	72	15	1	10	51	1
Cameron Cecil, Delaware State	.356	177	39	63	15	1	4	30	12
Luke Tendler, N.C. A&T	.350	163	34	57	11	0	7	32	13
Charles Dailey, Delaware State	.349	149	37	52	10	5	0	34	6
Stephen Bull, UMES	.349	195	41	68	12	1	0	16	12
Carter Williamson, N.C. Central	.344	183	28	63	12	0	4	42	1
Tyson Simpson, N.C. Central	.341	182	33	62	10	0	2	36	1
Marlon Gibbs, Florida A&M	.333	198	27	66	11	1	1	21	13
Ross Cardwell, Norfolk State	.331	139	19	46	12	1	2	27	1
Ron Farley, Delaware State	.331	133	29	44	10	0	2	33	3

	AVG	AB	R	H	2B	3B	HR	RBI	SB
Carlos Ortiz, N.C. Central	.321	159	33	51	5	1	6	25	5
Cameron Day, Norfolk State	.321	131	20	42	5	1	0	17	2
Parker Nix, Savannah State	.315	181	24	57	3	1	0	23	10
Eric Sams, B-CU	.310	226	43	70	15	1	1	17	6
Andre Moore, Norfolk State	.306	157	34	48	5	6	0	15	18
Zack Lee, N. Carolina Central	.305	203	49	62	9	3	0	18	
18John Kraft, Coppin State	.305	128	17	39	5	4	0	25	4
Ryan Kennedy, Florida A&M	.303	198	28	60	5	0	8	40	1
Todd Hagen, Savannah State	.297	175	44	52	7	1	0	19	5
Lester Salcedo, N.C. A&T	.292	144	18	42	6	1	1	25	3
Mike Escanilla, UMES	.289	187	32	54	7	1	0	16	11
Zach Markel, Norfolk State	.286	154	32	44	12	1	1	24	0
Eros Modena, B-CU	.283	184	21	52	10	3	0	25	8
Matt Noble, B-CU	.281	196	30	55	13	0	2	24	0
Jerem Barlow, Florida A&M	.280	164	11	46	6	0	3	22	1
#Josh Johnson, B-CU	.254	228	40	58	3	2	2	15	16
#Ryan Hill, N.C. A&T	.279	129	24	36	2	1	0	5	20
#Justin Lee, Norfolk State	.228	167	34	38	9	2	0	20	20

INDIVIDUAL PITCHING LEADERS
(Minimum 1 IP per team game)

	W	L	ERA	G	SV	IP	H	BB	SO
Montana Durapau, B-CU	11	1	1.61	19	3	117	77	23	103
Harry Thomas, Delaware State	5	2	1.82	14	0	49	34	21	38
Matt McClain, Delaware State	7	0	2.34	14	0	88	102	8	58
Devin Hemmerich, Norfolk St.	5	3	2.49	21	5	61	58	13	38
Keith Zuniga, B-CU	8	4	2.70	15	0	100	89	19	57
Matt Outman, Norfolk State	8	2	2.96	15	0	76	78	32	55
George Michael, Delaware St.	5	3	3.00	15	0	66	74	12	37
Charles Cantrell, N.C. A&T	4	4	3.21	12	0	67	68	17	50
Chas Jarrell, Florida A&M	5	2	3.42	16	0	79	80	16	47
Tyler Boone, N.C. A&T	2	7	4.14	14	1	72	71	30	50
Jesse Stinnett, UMES	4	5	4.26	12	0	80	89	25	49
John Sever, B-CU	3	5	4.27	21	4	59	52	36	49
Bran Fleming, Florida A&M	5	4	4.36	31	3	54	48	18	40
Austin Denney, Savannah St.	5	5	4.42	16	0	77	86	27	46
Gabriel Hernandez, B-CU	1	4	4.43	15	0	65	79	27	45
Carrasco, Florida A&M	3	6	4.57	22	2	61	68	25	28
David Duncan, Florida A&M	5	5	4.60	16	1	72	79	24	57
Terry McNabb, N.C. Central	2	9	4.66	13	0	75	89	16	69
Austin Robinson, Savannah St.	1	4	4.74	16	0	44	47	22	20
Stephen Butt, Norfolk State	3	3	4.82	16	0	62	66	31	59
#Andrew Vernon, N.C. Central	2	2	5.31	24	7	42	40	20	39

MISSOURI VALLEY CONFERENCE

Team	Conference		Overall	
	W	L	W	L
Evansville	15	6	34	21
Indiana State	14	7	35	18
*Dallas Baptist	14	7	38	21
Wichita State	13	8	31	28
Illinois State	10	11	33	21
Missouri State	9	12	26	30
Bradley	5	16	24	27
Southern Illinois	4	17	26	31

ALL-CONFERENCE TEAM: C—Kyle Pollock, Jr., Evansville. 1B—Casey Gillaspie, Jr., Wichita State. 2B—Paul DeJong, So., Illinois State. SS—Tyler Wampler, Sr., Indiana State. 3B—Jake Mahon, Sr., Evansville. OF—Kevin Kaczmarski, Jr., Evansville; Austin Listi, So., Dallas Baptist; Tate Matheny, So., Missouri State. DH—Greg Parypa, Sr., Bradley. UT—Dayne Parker, Sr., Wichita State. SP—Kyle Freeland, Jr., Evansville; A.J. Ladwig, Jr., Wichita State; Paul Voelker, So., Dallas Baptist. RP—Ryan Keaffaber, Fr., Indiana State; Brandon Koch, So., Dallas Baptist. Player of the Year: Casey Gillaspie, Wichita State. Pitcher of the Year: Kyle Freeland, Evansville. Newcomer of the Year: Brad Lombard, Indiana State. Freshman of the Year: Ryan Keaffaber, Indiana State. Defensive Player of the Year: Tyler Wampler, Indiana State. Coach of the Year: Wes Carroll, Evansville.

INDIVIDUAL BATTING LEADERS
(Minimum 2.5 at-bats per team game)

	AVG	AB	R	H	2B	3B	HR	RBI	SB
Casey Gillaspie, Wichita State	.389	211	50	82	15	1	15	50	8
Tyler Leffler, Bradley	.354	181	34	64	13	1	2	29	

	AVG	AB	R	H	2B	3B	HR	RBI	SB
2 Paul Dejong, Illinois State	.349	218	44	76	**21**	3	9	48	2
Mike Hollenbeck, Illinois State	.338	201	34	68	18	0	2	41	1
Cody Daily, Southern Illinois	.333	210	36	70	17	2	6	28	0
Tate Matheny, Missouri State	.330	218	42	72	9	2	10	37	7
Camden Duzenack, Dallas Baptist	.321	165	28	53	14	2	0	27	6
Daniel Dwyer, Illinois State	.318	211	39	67	7	1	0	32	8
Kevin Kaczmarski, Evansville	.315	219	40	69	19	5	4	**50**	7
Max Murphy, Bradley	.314	194	47	61	15	2	12	42	10
Greg Partyka, Bradley	.313	179	27	56	8	2	6	38	0
Daniel Kihle, Wichita State	.313	160	21	50	12	1	3	22	10
Kyle Pollock, Evansville	.310	229	36	71	15	3	5	**50**	4
Mike Wesolowski, Dallas Baptist	.305	**246**	50	75	13	0	6	34	1
Dayne Parker, Wichita State	.302	179	25	54	9	1	5	30	2
Derek Hannahs, Indiana State	.301	183	22	55	6	0	0	34	3
Isaac Smith, Bradley	.299	154	27	46	4	2	2	26	17
Josh Jyawook, Evansville	.298	215	41	64	8	0	0	31	4
Jake Mahon, Evansville	.295	217	44	64	12	0	1	35	1
Spencer Gaa, Bradley	.294	187	32	55	14	2	0	22	15
Shain Showers, Evansville	.294	160	28	47	13	0	4	33	7
Mike Fitzgerald, Indiana State	.293	174	25	51	10	0	3	26	7
Eric Cheray, Missouri State	.290	210	37	61	10	2	3	32	6
Landon Curry, Indiana State	.285	228	43	65	4	1	0	20	18
Eric McKibban, Evansville	.285	172	30	49	8	2	0	17	3
Cody Zimmerman, Indiana State	.284	204	30	58	11	1	1	24	3
Joe Kelch, Illinois State	.283	138	16	39	3	1	1	16	0
Patrick Drake, Missouri State	.282	117	9	33	13	0	0	21	2
Brett Synek, Evansville	.281	185	35	52	9	2	2	41	3
Austin Listi, Dallas Baptist	.278	230	**54**	64	13	1	10	45	4
Connor McClain, Indiana State	.276	152	23	42	6	2	1	1	9
Tyler Wampler, Indiana State	.275	193	29	53	5	1	0	16	12
#Daniel Salters, Dallas Baptist	.251	223	49	56	14	**7**	6	40	3
#Sean Beesley, Illinois State	.258	209	43	54	4	2	0	25	**27**

INDIVIDUAL PITCHING LEADERS
(Minimum 1 IP per team game)

	W	L	ERA	G	SV	IP	H	BB	SO
A.J. Ladwig, Wichita State	3	6	1.54	15	0	**105**	95	17	73
Kyle Freeland, Evansville	**10**	2	1.90	14	0	100	79	12	**128**
Dan Savas, Illinois State	8	5	2.10	16	0	103	77	39	93
Dylan Craig, Illinois State	6	2	2.14	15	0	93	73	29	98
Cale Elam, Wichita State	7	2	2.22	14	1	89	66	17	71
Jeremy Rhoades, Illinois State	6	4	2.35	19	4	77	64	25	92
Cody Schumacher, Mo. State	6	2	2.45	13	0	77	56	26	66
Elliot Ashbeck, Bradley	6	3	2.57	12	0	74	69	15	46
Clay Murphy, Missouri State	4	4	2.69	14	0	77	67	25	79
#Aaron LaBrie, Wichita State	5	2	2.77	**33**	1	49	49	12	43
Sam Coonrod, Southern Illinois	2	6	2.87	15	0	85	70	47	77
Eric Scheuermann, Bradley	2	2	3.00	18	0	54	48	18	47
Jon Harris, Missouri State	3	5	3.16	15	2	80	66	28	66
David Stagg, Indiana State	7	5	3.22	15	0	95	74	45	89
Ryan Keaffaber, Indiana State	3	2	3.26	24	**11**	61	46	19	38
Sam Tewes, Wichita State	8	3	3.27	15	0	83	76	30	50
Paul Voelker, Dallas Baptist	8	4	3.41	16	1	87	84	39	74
Cy Sneed, Dallas Baptist	3	3	3.46	16	0	104	98	36	82
Brad Lombard, Indiana State	6	3	3.48	14	0	85	84	30	55
Cory Taylor, Dallas Baptist	4	4	3.50	16	0	82	73	51	90
Aaron Hauge, Southern Illinois	3	4	3.60	12	0	60	53	30	42

MOUNTAIN WEST CONFERENCE

Team	Conference		Overall	
	W	L	W	L
New Mexico	20	10	37	20
UNLV	20	10	36	25
*San Diego State	17	13	42	21
Nevada	15	15	31	27
Fresno State	13	17	28	29
Air Force	10	20	20	34
San Jose State	10	20	19	38

ALL-CONFERENCE TEAM: C—Alex Real, Jr., New Mexico. **1B**—Austin Byler, Jr., Nevada. **2B**—Tim Zier, Sr., San Diego State. **SS**—Sam Haggerty, So., New Mexico. **3B**—Tyler France, So., San Diego State. **OF**—Brad Gerig, Sr., Nevada; Chase Harris, Sr., New Mexico; Jordan Luplow, Jr., Fresno State. **DH/UT**—Patrick Armstrong, Sr., UNLV. **P**—Bubba Derby, So., San Diego State; Erick Fedde, Jr., UNLV; John Richy, Jr., UNLV. **RP**—Michael Cederoth, Jr., San Diego State. **Player of the Year:** Jordan Luplow, Fresno State. **Pitcher of the Year:** Erick Fedde, UNLV. **Freshman of the Year:** Danny Collier, New Mexico. **Coach of the Year:** Tim Chambers, UNLV.

INDIVIDUAL BATTING LEADERS
(Minimum 125 at-bats)

	AVG	AB	R	H	2B	3B	HR	RBI	SB
Jordan Luplow, Fresno State	**.377**	215	40	81	21	1	9	48	10
Chase Harris, New Mexico	**.377**	247	46	**93**	11	5	8	**63**	13
Ty France, San Diego State	.356	233	55	83	18	0	5	45	3
Sam Haggerty, New Mexico	.340	244	**57**	83	9	2	2	38	14
Tyler Jones, Air Force	.338	195	30	66	19	2	4	31	7
Morgan Stotts, UNLV	.337	196	23	66	12	1	3	36	2
Trenton Brooks, Nevada	.330	188	23	62	8	0	3	35	4
Kewby Meyer, Nevada	.328	247	48	81	**27**	2	3	29	6
Austin Byler, Nevada	.326	221	51	72	14	5	**14**	47	7
John Pustay, New Mexico	.324	204	34	66	11	3	2	37	5
Alex Real, New Mexico	.320	228	34	73	25	1	2	47	3
Taylor Ward, Fresno State	.320	219	29	70	8	0	6	41	3
Tim Zier, San Diego State	.319	251	44	80	15	0	1	33	13
T.J. White, UNLV	.318	236	46	75	15	2	2	38	18
Brett Bautista, San Jose State	.313	195	24	61	12	0	0	17	0
Brad Haynal, San Diego State	.313	224	37	70	15	4	12	50	2
Andre Vigil, New Mexico	.311	180	26	56	8	2	0	30	3
Kyle Gallegos, San Jose State	.308	224	27	69	15	0	0	24	9
Patrick Armstrong, UNLV	.303	228	40	69	13	5	8	49	5
Joey Armstrong, UNLV	.302	205	36	62	8	3	4	27	7
Greg Allen, San Diego State	.302	**255**	52	77	8	**6**	0	26	**25**
Brad Gerig, Nevada	.300	180	23	54	11	0	4	23	3
Noah Pierce, Air Force	.296	196	30	58	13	2	3	25	2
Edgar Montes, UNLV	.296	186	33	55	14	1	3	27	1
Scott Kaplan, Nevada	.295	166	28	49	5	0	0	17	2
Seby Zavala, San Diego State	.293	232	38	68	13	2	2	36	2
Chris Mariscal, Fresno State	.293	222	29	65	10	0	4	27	6
Tyler Adkinson, San Diego St.	.292	178	28	52	12	2	1	26	7
Joey Swanner, UNLV	.292	161	28	47	6	1	0	15	4
Erik Vanmeetren, UNLV	.291	213	36	62	14	1	2	29	7

INDIVIDUAL PITCHING LEADERS
(Minimum 50 IP)

	W	L	ERA	G	SV	IP	H	BB	SO
#Colby Blueberg, Nevada	4	2	1.22	**35**	2	52	36	17	46
Erick Fedde, UNLV	8	2	**1.76**	11	0	77	58	21	82
#Michael Cederoth, San Diego St.	6	2	2.29	32	**20**	51	35	28	55
Kalei Contrades, San Jose State	5	2	2.50	17	2	79	70	10	52
Jason Deitrich, Nevada	3	2	2.80	18	2	84	84	23	41
Jordan Brink, Fresno State	5	3	2.87	15	1	85	66	44	62
Bryan Bonnell, UNLV	7	5	2.90	16	0	115	107	22	48
Tim Borst, Fresno State	4	5	3.02	18	0	92	95	30	65
Bubba Derby, San Diego State	8	4	3.08	17	1	105	96	39	100
Kenny Oakley, UNLV	4	8	3.15	18	2	97	80	34	79
John Richy, UNLV	**11**	4	3.20	16	0	**121**	113	24	**113**
Colton Thomson, New Mexico	6	6	3.68	15	0	88	94	26	65
Josh Walker, New Mexico	7	5	3.87	15	0	107	129	13	36
Mark Seyler, San Diego State	8	6	3.90	17	0	99	101	36	78
Michael Fain, Nevada	4	5	3.90	14	0	85	80	33	55
Cameron White, Air Force	4	8	4.30	18	1	105	132	11	94
Barry Timko, Nevada	6	3	4.40	20	0	72	69	27	29
Mike Robards, San Diego State	5	4	4.41	17	0	86	102	32	62
Bo Wilson, Air Force	5	3	4.92	27	0	57	68	13	43
Jonathan Hernandez, San Jose St.	0	7	5.32	14	0	68	105	15	24
Steven Trojan, Air Force	3	6	5.33	16	0	78	80	35	60
Griffin Jax, Air Force	3	8	5.86	15	0	91	122	19	43

NORTHEAST CONFERENCE

Team	Conference		Overall	
	W	L	W	L
*Bryant	19	5	42	16
Central Connecticut State	14	10	27	22
Sacred Heart	13	11	29	28
Long Island-Brooklyn	11	13	25	25
Wagner	11	13	19	35

Mount St. Mary's	10 14		17 24	
Fairleigh Dickinson	6 18		15 32	

ALL-CONFERENCE TEAM: C—Andrew Clow, Jr., Mount St. Mary's. **1B**—Robby Rinn, So., Bryant. **2B**—Josh Ingham, Sr., Central Connecticut. **SS**—John Ziznewski, Sr., LIU-Brooklyn. **3B**—John Mullen, Jr., Bryant. **OF**—Carl Anderson, Jr., Bryant; Pete Leonello, Sr., LIU-Brooklyn; J.P. Sportman, Sr., Central Connecticut. **DH**—Buck McCarthy, So., Bryant. **UT**—Dan St. George, Jr., Bryant. **SP**—Kevin McAvoy, Jr., Bryant; Craig Schlitter, Sr., Bryant. **RP**—James Cooksey, So., Sacred Heart. **Player of the Year:** John Ziznewski, LIU-Brooklyn. **Pitcher of the Year:** Craig Schlitter, Bryant. **Rookie of the Year:** Matt Albanese, Bryant. **Coach of the Year:** Steve Owens, Bryant.

INDIVIDUAL BATTING LEADERS
(Minimum 125 at-bats)

	AVG	AB	R	H	2B	3B	HR	RBI	SB
Bobby Webb, LIU-Brooklyn	.369	176	32	65	12	1	1	38	1
Andrew Clow, Mount St. Mary's	.369	141	21	52	6	1	2	26	5
John Ziznewski, LIU-Brooklyn	.365	197	50	72	13	2	9	55	18
Buck McCarthy, Bryant	.340	141	30	48	14	0	4	29	2
J.P. Sportman, Central Conn.	.337	187	36	63	7	7	3	23	15
Kory Britton, Mount St. Mary's	.329	143	14	47	9	0	3	27	2
Josh Ingham, Central Conn.	.327	168	20	55	5	2	0	23	2
Carl Anderson, Bryant	.324	225	49	73	11	3	7	41	31
Zack Short, Sacred Heart	.324	204	43	66	10	2	1	26	11
Matt Albanese, Bryant	.322	214	53	69	16	4	2	36	11
Tom Gavitt, Bryant	.320	128	31	41	8	4	6	29	0
Jon McAllister, LIU-Brooklyn	.315	203	43	64	3	1	0	25	12
John Mullen, Bryant	.308	201	31	62	11	0	4	37	15
Pete Leonello, LIU-Brooklyn	.307	199	46	61	10	4	1	26	12
Jayson Sullivan, Sacred Heart	.304	204	35	62	11	2	5	39	9
Chris Smith, Wagner	.302	169	29	51	14	1	5	21	10
Robby Rinn, Bryant	.302	189	37	57	13	1	2	36	0
Mark Hernandez, LIU-Brooklyn	.302	189	32	57	7	0	1	40	9
Zach Tondi, Fairleigh Dickinson	.301	136	20	41	6	0	0	20	0
Keith Klebart, Sacred Heart	.298	171	21	51	10	2	0	19	6
John Giakas, Fairleigh Dickinson	.294	160	16	47	8	0	0	19	1
Joel Roman, Fairleigh Dickinson	.293	150	15	44	15	0	0	19	0
Nick Mascelli, Wagner	.293	205	26	60	3	1	0	13	5
Jason Gordon, Wagner	.293	147	9	43	6	1	0	18	3
Dominic Severino, Central Conn.	.292	168	21	49	6	0	2	23	2
Ryan Brennan, Fairleigh Dickinson	.285	144	25	41	8	1	0	15	2
Matt McCann, Fairleigh Dickinson	.281	146	13	41	3	0	0	18	12
Riley Moonan, Fairleigh Dickinson	.280	168	25	47	7	2	3	26	8
Anthony Turgeon, Central Conn.	.277	173	23	48	2	0	1	19	4
Shaun Flynn, Wagner	.273	194	23	53	10	1	2	26	4

INDIVIDUAL PITCHING LEADERS
(Minimum 50 IP)

	W	L	ERA	G	SV	IP	H	BB	SO
James Cooksey, Sacred Heart	6	2	1.16	24	2	62	43	11	25
Craig Schlitter, Bryant	10	1	1.81	15	0	95	77	18	70
Nick Neumann, Central Conn.	6	3	2.38	12	1	72	71	15	50
Vaughn Hayward, Bryant	9	2	2.41	15	1	71	63	23	47
Kody Kerski, Sacred Heart	7	3	2.42	13	0	86	69	15	74
Kevin McAvoy, Bryant	9	1	2.62	15	0	100	77	28	94
Tom Coughlin, Central Conn.	5	5	2.94	11	0	70	52	29	46
Kyle Wilcox, Bryant	3	3	3.02	13	0	60	43	36	46
Matt McCormick, LIU-Brooklyn	5	3	3.03	13	0	68	66	19	36
Matt Blandino, Central Conn.	4	4	3.09	15	2	76	71	12	38
Jason Foley, Sacred Heart	3	3	3.30	16	2	63	54	30	53
Jeff Stoddard, Sacred Heart	5	2	3.45	13	0	63	59	25	39
Ryan Casey, Wagner	4	6	3.84	13	0	80	96	17	32
Matt Morris, Wagner	3	7	3.89	13	0	79	83	22	34
#Nick Riley, Mount St. Mary's	2	1	3.89	25	9	42	44	9	24
Vincent Molesky, Mount St. Mary's	5	4	3.92	11	0	57	66	14	42
John Chalupa, Fairleigh Dickinson	2	3	4.09	14	0	51	41	39	29
Nick Leiningen, Sacred Heart	2	3	4.25	20	1	55	69	9	26
Nick Morrissey, Sacred Heart	4	6	4.50	15	2	60	64	21	29
Danny Marsh, Wagner	4	3	4.67	13	0	54	63	11	30
Bobby Maxwell, LIU-Brooklyn	4	5	5.35	13	0	66	69	27	27
#Yonah Perline, Fairleigh Dickinson	0	1	7.40	30	0	24	31	5	10

OHIO VALLEY CONFERENCE

Team	Conference		Overall	
	W	L	W	L
Southeast Missouri State	23	7	37	20
Tennessee Tech	18	12	40	19
*Jacksonville State	18	12	36	27
Morehead State	16	14	29	28
Southern Illinois-Edwardsville	16	14	21	33
Eastern Illinois	15	14	22	33
Murray State	14	16	23	29
Austin Peay State	14	16	23	33
Belmont	13	16	24	31
Eastern Kentucky	12	18	24	31
Tennessee-Martin	5	25	9	42

ALL-CONFERENCE TEAM: C—Sean Hagen, Eastern Kentucky. **1B**—Matt Tellor, Southeast Missouri. **2B**—Eddie Mora-Loera, Jacksonville State. **SS**—Dylan Bosheers, Tennessee Tech. **3B**—Daniel Miles, Tennessee Tech. **OF**—Derek Gibson, Southeast Missouri; Brandon Thomasson, Tennessee Tech; Brandon Rawe, Morehead State. **DH**—Bryan Soloman, Eastern Kentucky. **UT**—Ridge Smith, Austin Peay. **SP**—Brock Downey, Murray State; Ryan Daniels, SIU-Edwardsville; Travis Hayes, Southeast Missouri. **RP**—Travis Scout, Jacksonville State. **Player of the Year:** Matt Tellor, Southeast Missouri. **Pitcher of the Year:** Brock Downey, Murray State; Travis Hayes, Southeast Missouri. **Rookie of the Year:** Alex Robles, Austin Peay. **Coach of the Year:** Steve Bieser, Southeast Missouri.

INDIVIDUAL BATTING LEADERS
(Minimum 2.5 at-bats per team game)

	AVG	AB	R	H	2B	3B	HR	RBI	SB
Caleb Howell, EIU	.420	224	51	94	11	0	0	32	9
Derek Gibson, Southeast Mo.	.403	226	42	91	12	4	6	70	9
Brandon Rawe, Morehead St.	.390	251	50	98	21	0	10	48	5
Matt Tellor, Southeast Mo.	.386	233	60	90	18	0	15	71	2
Griff Gordon, JSU	.380	263	55	100	6	5	7	50	10
Daniel Miles, Tenn. Tech	.380	237	67	90	17	1	11	54	5
Dylan Bosheers, Tenn. Tech	.368	234	66	86	14	1	11	56	8
Bobby Burns, Morehead State	.357	185	26	66	11	2	2	28	2
Alex Robles, Austin Peay	.349	209	35	73	14	2	1	39	3
Bryan Soloman, EKU	.344	209	39	72	12	1	14	55	1
Drew Ferguson, Belmont	.344	192	44	66	15	1	10	35	12
Taylor Douglas, UTM	.341	179	33	61	15	0	7	29	16
Brandon Thomasson, Tenn. Tech	.336	244	60	82	20	4	22	76	2
Zach Zarzor, Tenn. Tech	.336	244	56	82	18	2	0	37	6
Chris Robinson, Morehead St.	.332	226	37	75	6	4	1	40	
8Cayce Bredlau, Austin Peay	.331	169	40	56	11	1	2	21	14
Jeff Birkofer, Morehead State	.330	179	34	59	10	1	0	22	1
Jake Rowland, Tenn. Tech	.328	238	43	78	11	0	6	46	8
Paschal Petrongolo, JSU	.328	232	38	76	19	7	5	54	0
Anthony Bayus, Murray State	.327	199	37	65	15	3	3	31	8
Andrew Bishop, JSU	.324	238	40	77	17	2	4	40	6
Robby Spencer, Morehead St.	.323	223	39	72	15	5	3	36	1
Nick Lombardo, SIU-E	.321	215	45	69	12	1	2	21	13
Eddie Mora-Loera, JSU	.317	230	45	73	17	2	3	36	1
Tyler Schweigert, EIU	.314	169	29	53	7	1	3	26	6
Sean Hagen, EKU	.313	182	37	57	8	1	9	36	17
Tyler Lawrence, Murray State	.313	208	34	65	11	1	1	36	1
Andy Lennington, Southeast Mo.	.312	231	34	72	18	5	0	45	9
Ridge Smith, Austin Peay	.312	208	34	65	11	1	1	36	11
Demetre Taylor, EIU	.309	207	39	64	16	5	7	53	6
#Gavin Golsan, JSU	.256	176	27	45	7	0	0	15	32

INDIVIDUAL PITCHING LEADERS
(Minimum 50 IP)

	W	L	ERA	G	SV	IP	H	BB	SO
#Tracis Stout, JSU	3	1	1.82	27	15	40	26	18	29
Austin Coley, Belmont	5	1	2.72	15	0	83	68	42	85
Brock Downey, Murray State	9	3	2.76	15	0	108	72	25	74
James Buckelew, Belmont	5	5	3.21	15	0	84	72	44	67
Travis Hayes, Southeast Mo.	8	2	3.23	17	0	86	73	33	61
David Hess, Tenn. Tech	9	3	3.24	16	0	97	81	34	104
Matt Borens, EIU	6	4	3.39	16	0	109	101	36	100
Alex Winkelman, Southeast Mo.	6	2	3.48	15	1	75	60	28	62
Ryan Daniels, SIU-E	7	0	3.53	14	0	97	83	14	69

Player	W	L	ERA	G	SV	IP	H	BB	SO
Alex Robles, Austin Peay	6	2	3.63	16	0	84	97	20	56
Zachary Fowler, JSU	7	8	4.06	17	0	89	83	33	60
Chase Cunningham, Belmont	5	7	4.31	27	0	65	73	18	44
Caleb Johnson, EKU	5	0	4.34	13	0	56	69	20	26
Taylor Shields, JSU	4	4	4.40	18	0	90	106	34	52
Carter Smith, UTM	2	3	4.61	17	0	55	60	22	45
Tyler Iago, Southeast Mo.	4	3	4.80	16	0	75	97	22	48
Tanner Perkins, EKU	3	9	4.91	14	0	88	116	12	48
Brent Cobb, EKU	4	6	4.91	14	0	81	102	44	29
Cameron Finch, Murray State	4	7	5.19	16	0	85	111	28	66
Adam Polk, JSU	5	4	5.35	20	0	66	75	28	46
Joe Greenfield, EIU	6	6	5.40	23	1	73	99	36	49
#Jake Corum, Austin Peay	2	2	6.61	31	0	33	37	16	25

PACIFIC-12 CONFERENCE

Team	Conference W	L	Overall W	L
*Oregon State	23	7	45	14
Washington	21	9	41	17
Arizona State	21	9	41	17
Oregon	18	12	44	20
Stanford	16	14	34	24
Southern California	16	14	29	24
Washington State	14	16	24	29
California	13	17	26	27
UCLA	12	18	25	30
Arizona	9	21	22	33
Utah	4	26	16	36

ALL-CONFERENCE TEAM: C—Shaun Chase, Jr., Oregon; Austin Rei, So., Washington; Shane Zeile, Jr., UCLA. 1B—Nate Causey, Jr., Arizona State; Danny Diekroeger, Sr., Stanford. 2B—Andrew Ely, Jr., Oregon State. 3B—Alex Blandino, Jr., Stanford; Nick Tanielu, So., Washington State; Mitchell Tolman, So., Oregon. SS—Drew Stankiewicz, Jr., Arizona State. OF—Michael Conforto, Jr., Oregon State; Dylan Davis, Jr. Oregon State; Jeff Hendrix, So., Oregon State; Scott Kingery, So., Arizona; Austin Slater, Jr., Stanford. P—David Berg, Jr., UCLA; Kyle Davis, So., USC; Tyler Davis, Jr., Washington; Jace Fry, Jr., Oregon State; Ian Hamilton, Fr., Washington State; John Hochstatter, Jr., Stanford; James Kaprielian, So., UCLA; Ryan Kellogg, So., Arizona State; Brett Lilek, Jr., Arizona State; Cal Quantrill, Fr., Stanford; Jake Reed, Jr., Oregon; Wyatt Strahan, Jr., USC; Tommy Thorpe, Jr., Oregon; Ben Wetzler, Sr., Oregon State. Player of the Year: Michael Conforto, Oregon State. Pitcher of the Year: Jace Fry, Oregon State. Defensive Player of the Year: Erik Forgione, Washington. Freshman of the Year: Cal Quantrill, Stanford. Coach of the Year: Lindsay Meggs, Washington.

INDIVIDUAL BATTING LEADERS
(Minimum 2.5 at-bats per team game)

Player	AVG	AB	R	H	2B	3B	HR	RBI	SB
Scott Kingery, Arizona	.354	195	41	69	11	4	1	26	19
Brian Wolfe, Washington	.352	176	32	62	10	0	5	36	2
Jeff Hendrix, Oregon State	.351	171	42	60	11	5	2	32	4
Michael Conforto, Oregon State	.345	203	52	70	16	2	7	56	4
Austin Slater, Stanford	.341	229	39	78	17	6	2	40	6
Nick Tanielu, WSU	.340	206	29	70	16	1	1	33	5
Zach Gibbons, Arizona	.338	216	29	73	7	0	0	25	7
Drew Stankiewicz, Ariz. State	.331	178	34	59	11	2	3	26	10
Trevor Mitsui, Washington	.328	198	35	65	9	0	5	32	1
Jake Hernandez, USC	.327	171	17	56	8	0	0	20	0
Trent Gilbert, Arizona	.324	225	38	73	16	8	2	39	2
Zach Hoffpauir, Stanford	.324	219	36	71	9	5	7	35	3
Shane Zeile, UCLA	.324	216	25	70	9	3	2	28	5
Nathaniel Causey, Ariz. State	.323	201	33	65	14	0	4	31	0
Mitchell Tolman, Oregon	.315	219	45	69	18	5	2	48	5
Austin Rei, Washington	.314	153	24	48	11	2	2	28	1
Danny Diekroeger, Stanford	.313	230	43	72	13	0	2	22	8
Alex Blandino, Stanford	.310	226	49	70	14	0	12	44	2
Johnny Sewald, Arizona State	.305	203	44	62	7	1	0	19	16
Kevin Newman, Arizona	.304	230	39	70	10	4	0	34	13
Braden Bishop, Washington	.303	218	43	66	8	2	0	27	21
Andrew Ely, Washington	.300	207	38	62	8	3	3	34	2
Collin Slaybaugh, WSU	.299	214	19	64	8	3	0	17	7
Kevin Swick, USC	.299	204	27	61	10	0	0	24	4
Jeremy Martinez, USC	.297	185	23	55	10	0	1	29	2

Player	AVG	AB	R	H	2B	3B	HR	RBI	SB
Yale Rosen, WSU	.294	197	24	58	13	2	5	28	4
Dalton Dinatale, Arizona State	.294	197	29	58	12	1	3	36	7
Ty Moore, UCLA	.294	211	28	62	14	3	2	24	2
Vince Bruno, California	.294	143	16	42	3	1	2	20	1
Trent Chatterton, UCLA	.291	189	21	55	9	0	0	17	0
#Tyler Baumgartner, Oregon	.286	255	50	73	16	7	3	42	7
#Dylan Davis, Oregon State	.283	237	33	67	14	0	7	64	4

INDIVIDUAL PITCHING LEADERS
(Minimum 1 IP per team game)

Player	W	L	ERA	G	SV	IP	H	BB	SO
Ben Wetzler, Oregon State	12	1	0.78	14	0	104	49	31	83
Kyle Davis, USC	3	4	1.12	26	9	56	39	18	57
#Max Schuh, UCLA	0	1	1.55	37	0	29	22	10	34
Tyler Davis, Washington	11	2	1.60	17	1	107	88	15	62
Scott Schultz, Oregon State	7	2	1.61	24	6	67	47	15	40
Jace Fry, Oregon State	11	2	1.80	16	0	120	83	30	98
Tommy Thorpe, Oregon	11	4	2.14	16	0	105	80	33	90
James Kaprielian, UCLA	7	6	2.29	15	0	106	76	35	108
Brett Lilek, Arizona State	4	5	2.68	16	1	84	59	39	79
Cal Quantrill, Stanford	7	5	2.68	18	0	111	90	34	98
#Ian Hamilton, Washington	2	2	2.70	28	15	30	34	12	24
Andrew Moore, Oregon State	6	5	2.77	16	0	94	97	26	68
Jeff Brigham, Washington	7	4	2.90	16	0	90	79	23	45
Kyle Porter, California	6	5	3.01	15	0	93	85	22	72
Ryan Mason, California	7	1	3.04	16	0	68	60	21	32
Kyle Twomey, USC	2	2	3.11	19	0	55	50	20	50
Brett Hanewich, Stanford	4	4	3.17	16	0	77	79	31	49
Jeff Gold, Oregon	10	3	3.17	16	0	99	95	8	61
Wyatt Strahan, USC	6	5	3.28	16	1	104	91	49	89
Joe Pistorese, WSU	4	3	3.31	16	0	98	87	27	48
Trevor Dunlap, Washington	1	2	3.36	31	6	59	49	23	50
John Hochstatter, Stanford	10	3	3.36	16	0	80	60	35	38

PATRIOT LEAGUE

Team	Conference W	L	Overall W	L
*Bucknell	15	5	31	21
Army	15	5	33	18
Lehigh	10	10	25	24
Navy	9	11	23	28
Lafayette	5	13	15	26
Holy Cross	4	14	13	31

ALL-CONFERENCE TEAM: C—Jon Mayer, So., Bucknell. 1B—Kash Manzelli, Sr., Navy. 2B—Mike Garzillo, So., Lehigh. SS—Travis Blue, Fr., Navy. 3B—Drew Hayes, So., Navy. OF—Anthony Gingerelli, Jr., Bucknell; Evan Ocello, Jr., Holy Cross; Justin Pacchioli, Jr., Lehigh. DH—Corey Furman, Sr., Bucknell. SP—Gunnar Carroll, Sr., Army; Nick Dignacco, Sr., Army; Anthony Parenti, Jr., Navy; Dan Weigel, Sr., Bucknell. RP—Cory Spera, Jr., Lafayette. Player of the Year: Kash Manzelli, Navy. Pitcher of the Year: Anthony Parenti, Navy. Rookie of the Year: Brett Smith, Bucknell. Coach of the Year: Scott Heather, Bucknell.

INDIVIDUAL BATTING LEADERS
(Minimum 2.5 at-bats per team game)

Player	AVG	AB	R	H	2B	3B	HR	RBI	SB
#Corey Furman, Bucknell	.388	116	18	45	4	5	2	24	2
Justin Pacchioli, Lehigh	.362	127	19	46	3	0	0	7	16
Robert Currie, Navy	.359	195	39	70	7	5	1	24	26
Evan Ocello, Holy Cross	.329	173	34	57	10	3	2	13	24
Daniel Cortes, Army	.311	135	19	42	7	1	0	18	2
Joe Ogren, Bucknell	.309	181	32	56	9	3	0	28	6
Anthony Gingerelli, Bucknell	.309	152	29	47	7	4	5	27	3
Mike Garzillo, Lehigh	.308	182	26	56	12	3	0	33	10
Kash Manzelli, Navy	.307	192	19	59	12	1	3	39	0
Joe Abeln, Lehigh	.301	176	32	53	12	0	0	19	9
Brandon Cipolla, Holy Cross	.301	163	29	49	13	1	4	28	7
Anthony Critelli, Holy Cross	.299	147	16	44	11	0	2	19	0
Andrew Santomauro, Lafayette	.299	154	33	46	11	1	3	21	12
Jacob Page, Army	.297	182	23	54	11	2	1	27	11
Connor Perry, Holy Cross	.296	115	15	34	5	0	3	20	0
Jon Crucitti, Army	.289	166	34	48	5	3	0	20	5
Brett Smith, Bucknell	.288	184	46	53	1	2	0	15	9
Travis Blue, Navy	.284	176	27	50	5	1	0	26	6

	AVG	AB	R	H	2B	3B	HR	RBI	SB
Jack St. Clair, Holy Cross	.280	150	25	42	12	0	1	25	3
Drew Hayes, Navy	.274	168	17	46	3	1	0	20	3
Kris Lindner, Army	.270	126	25	34	3	0	1	15	13
Nick Lovullo, Holy Cross	.266	169	20	45	5	1	0	15	9
Andrew Barry, Holy Cross	.260	150	14	39	8	0	1	12	3
John Elson, Lehigh	.259	162	29	42	9	0	2	25	11
Tyler Hudson, Lafayette	.259	112	9	29	2	1	2	19	2
Tyler Brong, Lehigh	.253	158	17	40	9	0	3	24	1
Parker Hills, Lafayette	.243	107	8	26	3	0	0	7	1
Connor Faust, Lehigh	.240	150	17	36	7	0	0	19	7
Leland Saile, Navy	.229	144	18	33	8	2	0	21	0
Mark McCants, Army	.226	177	28	40	6	1	1	17	11
Alex Jensen, Army	.224	161	29	36	11	0	3	22	8
#Harold Earls, Army	.215	177	27	38	3	1	0	25	26

INDIVIDUAL PITCHING LEADERS
(Minimum 1 IP per team game)

	W	L	ERA	G	SV	IP	H	BB	SO
Anthony Parenti, Navy	8	3	1.52	12	0	83	60	17	74
Alex Robinett, Army	6	3	2.02	13	1	89	70	26	85
Gunnar Carroll, Army	8	3	2.20	13	0	82	89	12	52
Nick Dignacco, Army	6	3	2.34	13	0	81	65	17	79
Stephen Moore, Navy	3	5	2.49	13	0	80	68	12	60
Brian Hapeman, Army	0	2	2.85	17	3	41	43	17	25
Dan Weigel, Bucknell	8	4	2.86	15	0	98	100	22	52
#Nick Cassell, Lehigh	5	3	3.07	19	7	41	40	16	42
Colin Gotzon, Lehigh	5	1	3.12	11	0	58	52	16	62
Ben White, Holy Cross	0	5	3.18	11	0	51	43	20	42
Kevin Long, Lehigh	4	5	3.21	15	2	56	52	14	44
Connor Ortolf, Lafayette	2	7	3.27	11	0	63	62	25	30
Luke Gillingham, Navy	2	6	3.33	12	0	68	69	21	59
Xavier Hammond, Bucknell	3	5	3.67	18	4	74	72	13	45
Mitch Leeds, Lafayette	2	4	3.90	10	0	55	62	21	47
Mike Burke, Lehigh	3	4	3.97	11	0	59	58	24	43
Andrew Andreychik, Bucknell	5	5	4.00	12	0	63	68	10	49
David Bednar, Lafayette	1	4	4.15	9	0	43	33	13	48
Bryson Hough, Bucknell	8	5	4.22	14	0	85	89	21	44
Phil Reese, Holy Cross	2	4	4.43	10	0	45	50	21	22
#George Capen, Holy Cross	2	0	4.66	25	0	37	44	5	27
Donny Murray, Holy Cross	2	6	6.55	9	0	44	59	10	33

SOUTHEASTERN CONFERENCE

Team	Conference		Overall	
	W	L	W	L
Eastern				
Florida	21	9	40	21
South Carolina	18	12	42	16
Vanderbilt	17	13	41	18
Kentucky	14	16	35	23
Tennessee	12	18	31	23
Georgia	11	18	26	29
Missouri	6	24	20	33
Western				
Mississippi	19	11	41	18
*Louisiana State	17	11	44	14
Mississippi State	18	12	37	22
Arkansas	16	14	38	23
Alabama	15	14	34	22
Texas A&M	14	16	33	24
Auburn	10	20	28	28

ALL-CONFERENCE TEAM: C—Taylor Gushue, Jr., Florida. **1B**—Sikes Orvis, Jr., Ole Miss. **2B**—Dansby Swanson, So., Vanderbilt. **SS**—Vince Conde, Jr., Vanderbilt. **3B**—Austin Anderson, Sr., Ole Miss. **OF**—Auston Bousfield, Jr., Ole Miss; Christin Stewart, So., Tennessee; Ka'ai Tom, So., Kentucky. **DH/UTIL**—A.J. Reed, Jr., Kentucky. **SP**—Aaron Nola, Jr., LSU; Logan Shore, Fr., Florida. **RP**—Jacon Lindgren, Jr., Mississippi State. **Player of the Year:** A.J. Reed, Kentucky. **Pitcher of the Year:** Aaron Nola, LSU. **Freshman of the Year:** Logan Shore, Florida. **Coach of the Year:** Kevin O'Sullivan, Florida.

INDIVIDUAL BATTING LEADERS
(Minimum 2.5 at bats per team game)

	AVG	AB	R	H	2B	3B	HR	RBI	SB
Brett Pirtle, Miss. State	.363	240	35	87	10	1	2	31	4
Jordan Ebert, Auburn	.353	204	28	72	5	1	0	29	9
Will Allen, Ole Miss	.339	277	44	94	24	0	7	64	0
Bryan Reynolds, Vanderbilt	.338	281	53	95	24	2	4	54	14
A.J. Reed, Kentucky	.336	223	60	75	18	1	23	73	0
Kyle Martin, South Carolina	.336	244	35	82	11	0	5	38	2
Auston Bousfield, Ole Miss	.336	286	61	96	18	2	6	50	19
Andrew Stevenson, LSU	.335	203	41	68	7	5	0	32	9
Dansby Swanson, Vanderbilt	.333	282	63	94	27	2	3	34	22
Christin Stewart, Tennessee	.330	218	45	72	19	6	5	39	7
Dylan Kelly, Missouri	.330	179	20	59	13	0	3	27	2
Ka'ai Tom, Kentucky	.328	204	40	67	13	0	3	41	14
Brian Anderson, Arkansas	.328	241	39	79	14	3	7	51	9
Nick Banks, Texas A&M	.327	199	29	65	10	2	2	26	7
Max Kuhn, Kentucky	.324	259	68	84	18	1	8	58	3
Austin Anderson, Ole Miss	.323	269	57	87	18	1	5	41	10
Hunter Cole, Georgia	.319	207	26	66	14	0	3	31	3
Cole Lankford, Texas A&M	.319	251	30	80	11	0	5	47	3
Alex Bregman, LSU	.316	244	35	77	16	0	6	47	12
Taylor Gushue, Florida	.316	225	30	71	16	0	6	49	1
Austen Smith, Alabama	.316	187	29	59	14	0	6	39	5
Michael Thomas, Kentucky	.315	219	47	69	11	1	8	45	2
Nick Senzel, Tennessee	.315	181	37	57	12	2	1	38	14
Damek Tomscha, Auburn	.313	176	37	55	8	0	5	29	4
Grayson Greiner, South Carolina	.311	212	39	66	13	0	8	50	0
C.T. Bradford, Mississippi State	.310	197	23	61	7	5	1	31	2
Austin Cousino, Kentucky	.308	263	58	81	15	4	4	38	19
Conner Hale, LSU	.306	209	38	64	11	1	4	29	0
Nelson Ward, Georgia	.306	209	29	64	13	3	2	34	10
Ryan Tella, Auburn	.306	183	30	56	6	1	3	18	13
#Braxton Lee, Ole Miss	.281	270	56	76	9	1	0	25	35

INDIVIDUAL PITCHING LEADERS
(Minimum 1 IP per team game)

	W	L	ERA	G	SV	IP	H	BB	SO
Aaron Nola, LSU	11	1	1.47	16	0	116	69	27	134
#Joel Seddon, South Carolina	3	2	1.66	27	14	49	37	12	59
Carson Fulmer, Vanderbilt	7	1	1.98	26	10	91	61	41	95
Jalen Beeks, Arkansas	6	4	1.98	13	0	82	67	20	68
Keegan Thompson, Auburn	5	3	2.01	14	1	90	61	23	73
Christian Trent, Ole Miss	9	0	2.05	17	0	110	95	20	86
A.J. Reed, Kentucky	12	2	2.09	16	0	112	98	29	71
Kyle Bouman, LSU	5	2	2.12	17	0	64	49	16	32
Logan Shore, Florida	7	4	2.16	16	0	96	86	20	68
Spencer Turnbull, Alabama	5	7	2.22	15	0	93	61	47	61
Trey Killian, Arkansas	4	9	2.30	14	0	94	74	18	62
Andy Cox, Tennessee	5	1	2.44	27	2	77	47	33	70
Jared Poche', LSU	9	3	2.45	16	0	92	72	26	52
Chris Oliver, Arkansas	9	4	2.51	16	0	93	68	36	59
Ross Mitchell, Mississippi State	8	5	2.53	19	0	110	93	30	49
Chris Ellis, Ole Miss	10	3	2.55	19	0	116	111	42	67
Trevor Fitts, Mississippi State	5	3	2.58	16	0	70	70	15	58
Walker Buehler, Vanderbilt	12	2	2.64	19	0	102	85	31	111
Robert Tyler, Georgia	6	4	2.68	15	0	81	60	22	64
Tyler Ferguson, Vanderbilt	8	4	2.69	17	0	77	55	30	65
Dillon Ortman, Auburn	9	5	2.70	15	0	100	95	16	62
#Andrew Vinson, Texas A&M	3	2	2.95	32	2	37	26	11	34

SOUTHERN CONFERENCE

Team	Conference		Overall	
	W	L	W	L
Western Carolina	20	6	37	18
Davidson	17	8	29	19
*Georgia Southern	15	12	40	23
Samford	15	12	35	25
Wofford	12	14	32	28
Appalachian State	12	14	21	34
Elon	12	15	27	26
Furman	11	15	26	33
UNC Greensboro	8	16	21	28
The Citadel	8	18	24	23

ALL-CONFERENCE TEAM: C—Adam Martin, Western Carolina. **1B**—Jacob Hoyle, Western Carolina. **2B**—Hunter King, UNCG. **SS**—Dillon Dobson, Appalachian State. **3B**—Sean Guite, UNCG. **OF**—Forrest Brandt, Davidson; Lee Miller, Davidson; Casey Jones, Elon. **DH**—Ryan Lowe,

Davidson. **SP**—Josh Wirsu, Georgia Southern; Jordan Smith, Western Carolina. **RP**—Andres Garcia, Samford. **Co-Players of the Year:** Forrest Brandt, Davidson; Casey Jones, Elon. **Pitcher of the Year:** Josh Wirsu, Georgia Southern. **Freshman of the Year:** Heath Quinn, Samford. **Coach of the Year:** Dick Cooke, Davidson.

INDIVIDUAL BATTING LEADERS
(Minimum 2.5 at-bats per team game)

	AVG	AB	R	H	2B	3B	HR	RBI	SB
Casey Jones, Elon	.418	196	42	82	20	4	7	53	11
Hunter King, UNCG	.382	199	39	76	18	2	3	46	6
Lee Miller, Davidson	.368	152	39	56	11	0	9	36	3
Sean Guite, UNCG	.366	202	52	74	15	3	3	21	1
Forrest Brandt, Davidson	.364	187	50	68	9	2	12	51	14
Jordan McDonald, UNCG	.364	165	29	60	14	2	5	40	1
Michael Pierson, App. State	.343	201	41	69	16	1	7	33	0
Garrett Chapman, GSU	.341	226	43	77	7	0	8	32	6
Bradley Strong, WCU	.339	239	58	81	20	6	6	53	20
Drew DeKerlegand, Citadel	.338	207	36	70	10	3	3	25	6
Ryan Lowe, Davidson	.337	184	35	62	12	1	3	27	3
Hunter Burton, Furman	.333	234	49	78	8	5	0	28	41
Greg Harrison, Furman	.333	231	40	77	14	2	5	41	6
Drew McWhorter, Samford	.332	235	45	78	14	1	9	50	0
Jacob Hoyle, WCU	.332	223	43	74	11	0	14	53	6
David Daniels, Davidson	.332	205	46	68	15	2	4	30	6
Zac MacAneney, UNCG	.325	206	42	67	4	2	2	21	2
Stryker Brown, GSU	.323	220	49	71	9	1	10	44	11
Heath Quinn, Samford	.319	229	49	73	20	1	9	48	2
Chris Ohmstede, Furman	.318	223	40	74	11	2	10	47	6
Eric Kalbfleisch, UNCG	.317	126	28	40	9	0	5	26	1
Bo Thompson, Citadel	.315	200	39	63	3	0	9	42	2
Nathan Becker, Davidson	.314	159	39	50	9	0	11	38	5
Mason Davis, Citadel	.310	242	45	75	13	0	1	25	27
Aaron Mizell, GSU	.309	246	44	76	13	2	13	53	8
Jake Jones, Furman	.309	149	31	46	3	1	2	23	5
Cody Jones, WCU	.308	237	43	73	16	1	1	40	7
Adam Martin, WCU	.307	202	48	62	10	1	14	65	9
Caleb Bryson, Samford	.306	216	38	66	13	1	10	58	1
Kody Adams, GSU	.301	229	46	69	12	2	5	28	
12#Jordan Simpson, Furman	.295	251	38	74	10	2	5	35	7
#Jaylin Davis, App. State	.280	211	28	59	2	7	4	38	5

INDIVIDUAL PITCHING LEADERS
(Miminum 1 IP per team game)

	W	L	ERA	G	SV	IP	H	BB	SO
Jason Richman, GSU	5	1	1.20	47	3	90	87	16	78
#Skylar Hunter, Citadel	2	4	1.67	29	15	43	22	23	44
Sam Howard, GSU	7	5	2.35	16	0	96	81	22	94
Josh Wirsu, GSU	9	3	2.53	16	0	96	75	37	92
Danny Mooney, Davidson	6	3	2.75	12	0	72	56	20	68
Jeremy Null, WCU	6	4	2.94	15	0	101	87	29	93
Jordan Smith, WCU	8	5	3.26	16	0	105	109	32	82
Nick Neitzel, Davidson	7	2	3.38	13	0	61	55	29	57
Ryan Clark, UNCG	3	6	3.68	14	0	93	87	22	68
Lucas Bakker, Elon	7	3	3.81	15	0	87	86	23	64
Matt Solter, Furman	3	5	3.90	15	0	90	85	33	67
Matt McCall, GSU	4	2	3.92	40	9	66.2	63	20	59
Matthew Milburn, Wofford	4	6	3.95	16	0	93	97	27	77
Jake Stalzer, ELON	5	4	3.97	14	0	77	72	26	33
Connell Anderson, Wofford	1	2	4.20	14	0	70	81	43	13
Tyler Moore, App. State	9	5	4.28	15	0	103	107	32	64
Bryan Sammons, WCU	7	2	4.50	21	2	60	62	36	57
Logan Cribb, Citadel	4	4	4.44	15	0	85	90	29	61
Alex Ledford, Samford	11	2	4.70	17	0	103	107	32	64
Jesse Morris, Wofford	9	6	4.71	20	0	84	91	21	84
Tyler Wood, Furman	5	2	4.73	18	0	63	75	19	55

SOUTHLAND CONFERENCE

Team	Conference		Overall	
	W	L	W	L
Sam Houston State	22	8	43	19
Nicholls State	21	9	32	26
Northwestern State	19	11	33	26
Texas A&M-Corpus Christi	19	11	31	27
*Southeastern Louisiana	18	12	38	25
Central Arkansas	17	13	32	22
McNeese State	17	13	30	28
Lamar	16	14	31	25
Oral Roberts	15	15	30	26
Houston Baptist	12	18	23	28
Incarnate Word	9	15	18	32
Stephen F. Austin State	11	19	20	35
Abilene Christian	6	18	18	36
New Orleans	2	28	11	38

ALL-CONFERENCE TEAM: C—Anthony Azar, Sr., Sam Houston State. **1B**—Chayse Marion, Sr., McNeese State. **2B**—Andrew Guillotte, Jr., McNeese State. **SS**—Sam Bumpers, Sr., Lamar. **3B**—Brandon Tierney, Sr., A&M Corpus Christi. **OF**—Tyler Boss, Sr., Oral Roberts; Jackson Gooch, Sr., McNeese State; Doug Votolato, Sr., Central Arkansas. **DH**—Mackenzie Handel, Sr., Stephen F. Austin. **P**—Taylor Byrd, Sr., Nicholls; Andro Cutura, Jr., Southeastern La.; Pepe Gomez, Sr., Oral Roberts. **Player of the Year:** Anthony Azar, Sam Houston State. **Hitter of the Year:** Sam Bumpers, Lamar. **Pitcher of the Year:** Taylor Byrd, Nicholls. **Relief Pitcher of the Year:** Andrew Godbold, Southeastern Louisiana. **Freshman of the Year:** Adam Oller, Northwestern State. **Newcomer of the Year:** Andrew Godbold, Southeastern Louisiana. **Coach of the Year:** Seth Thibodeaux, Nicholls.

INDIVIDUAL BATTING LEADERS
(Minimum 125 At-bats)

	AVG	AB	R	H	2B	3B	HR	RBI	SB
Jameson Fisher, SLU	.389	239	53	93	17	1	0	39	9
Doug Votolato, Central Ark.	.379	219	50	83	10	2	1	24	26
Anthony Azar, SHSU	.368	234	40	86	10	2	9	49	1
Sam Bumpers, Lamar	.361	230	45	83	17	4	6	37	8
Curtis Jones, Houston Baptist	.357	227	33	81	5	0	0	21	6
Andrew Godbold, SLU	.349	235	42	82	10	1	9	58	8
Tyler Boss, Oral Roberts	.347	202	34	70	15	1	3	34	6
Samuel Capielano, New Orleans	.341	205	28	70	9	1	0	19	3
Brandon Tierney, TAMU-CC	.341	214	36	73	13	2	3	32	4
Jordan McCoy, Houston Baptist	.335	206	30	69	7	2	3	31	2
Josh Martinez, Houston Baptist	.333	189	25	63	6	2	0	22	2
Seth Spivey, Abilene Christian	.332	205	44	68	14	3	5	32	10
Chase Daughdrill, NW State	.324	222	38	72	9	1	2	38	5
Chayse Marion, McNeese State	.322	227	41	73	12	1	4	40	11
Brandon Grudzielanek, Abilene	.320	200	18	64	2	0	0	34	7
Jude Vidrine, Lamar	.320	219	54	70	14	2	1	36	14
Jackson Gooch, McNeese State	.319	229	56	73	12	1	3	41	12
Russell Vaughan, TAMU-CC	.318	151	37	48	9	3	1	25	6
Andrew Guillotte, McNeese	.316	247	57	78	14	1	0	17	20
Brett Hoffman, SLU	.312	234	31	73	17	0	1	41	0
Corey Toups, SHSU	.310	187	43	58	17	0	7	29	11
Jesse Hoover, Incarnate Word	.309	191	25	59	16	1	2	36	2
Aaron Draper, Abilene Christian	.309	191	28	59	8	1	0	21	2
Nate Ferrell, Central Ark.	.309	178	32	55	11	0	0	31	0
Jordan Lee, TAMU-CC	.309	230	43	71	8	4	2	29	18
Brett Thornell, SFA	.306	196	30	60	10	0	1	29	4
Colt Atwood, SHSU	.306	271	40	83	10	2	0	40	6
Jose Trevino, Oral Roberts	.304	230	37	70	11	1	10	43	4
Brandon Provost, Lamar	.301	186	25	56	9	0	1	31	3
Kevin Santana, Lamar	.300	160	19	48	12	0	1	19	0
#Zach Marberry, SFA	.272	191	27	52	18	1	3	29	0
#Bret Underwood, NW State	.289	204	28	59	10	6	0	17	18
#Tyler Ware, TAMU-CC	.287	204	34	60	6	6	3	33	
7#Mackenzie Handel, SFA	.299	201	31	60	10	0	10	43	4

INDIVIDUAL PITCHING LEADERS
(Minimum 50 IP)

	W	L	ERA	G	SV	IP	H	BB	SO
Taylor Byrd, Nicholls State	8	3	1.92	14	0	89	79	27	80
Andro Cutura, SLU	10	2	1.95	16	0	106	87	21	99
Kaleb Fontenot, McNeese State	6	2	2.14	16	1	80	75	20	49
Brandon Jackson, Nicholls State	3	2	2.19	14	0	70	66	22	49
Adam Oller, NW State	6	2	2.44	16	1	92	86	20	58
Sam Odom, SHSU	10	2	2.61	16	1	79	61	33	38
Geno Encina, Incarnate Word	7	7	2.64	15	0	95	89	15	62
Jason Simms, SHSU	5	3	2.67	23	4	81	68	16	46
Dillon Mangham, SFA	6	5	2.83	15	0	86	92	22	70
Brant Borne, Nicholls State	8	3	2.97	15	0	100	90	35	81

	W	L	ERA	G	SV	IP	H	BB	SO
Connor Gilmore, Central Ark.	7	3	2.98	16	0	103	90	40	53
Tate Scioneaux, SLU	7	6	3.02	17	1	**110**	101	20	77
Bryce Biggerstaff, Central Ark.	7	6	3.03	16	1	104	102	19	58
Pepe Gomez, Oral Roberts	8	3	3.08	16	0	76	68	29	49
Guillermo Trujilllo, Oral Roberts	3	4	3.11	14	0	81	77	25	63
Ryan Lower, Houston Baptist	6	4	3.12	13	0	81	92	16	53
Tyler Eppler, SHSU	9	6	3.20	16	0	**110**	106	30	67
Gavin Glanz, Oral Roberts	3	5	3.27	14	0	83	76	31	50
Steven O'Bryant, McNeese State	3	5	3.55	**30**	**7**	58	49	25	48
Darron McKigney, New Orleans	1	7	3.57	19	1	63	59	45	49

SOUTHWESTERN ATHLETIC CONFERENCE

Team	Conference		Overall	
East	**W**	**L**	**W**	**L**
Alabama State	21	3	37	20
Alabama A&M	12	9	21	32
Alcorn State	10	12	21	32
*Jackson State	9	15	32	25
Mississippi Valley State	4	18	4	38
West				
Arkansas-Pine Bluff	16	7	22	28
Texas Southern	13	9	23	29
Prairie View A&M	11	12	21	30
Grambling State	11	13	16	32
Southern	6	16	10	26

ALL-CONFERENCE TEAM: C—Richard Gonzalez, Alabama State. **1B**—Austin Hulsey, Alabama A&M. **2B**—Einar Muniz, Alabama State. **SS**—Emmanuel Marrero, Alabama State. **3B**—Melvin Rodriguez, Jackson State. **OF**—Richard Amion, Alabama State; Andrew Utterback, Alabama A&M; D.J. Wallace, Southern. **DH**—Waldyvan Estrada, Alabama State. **SP**—Joseph Camacho, Alabama State; Desmond Russell, Jackson State. **RP**—Kevin Walsh, Arkansas-Pine Bluff. **Player of the Year:** Emmanuel Marrero, Alabama State. **Pitcher of the Year:** Joseph Camacho, Alabama State. **Hitter of the Year:** Andrew Utterback, Alabama A&M. **Newcomer of the Year:** Tilur Smith, Jackson State. **Freshman of the Year:** Cody Den Beste, Prairie View A&M. **Coach of the Year:** Mervyl Melendez, Alabama State.

INDIVIDUAL BATTING LEADERS
(Minimum 100 at-bats)

	AVG	AB	R	H	2B	3B	HR	RBI	SB
Andrew Utterback, Ala. A&M	**.398**	171	28	68	12	2	5	42	6
Brian Rowry, Southern	.386	127	18	49	12	1	2	24	1
Scotty Peavey, Alcorn State	.382	170	25	65	12	1	3	20	11
Austin Hulsey, Alabama A&M	.356	191	32	68	15	1	5	37	4
Waldyvan Estrada, Ala. State	.347	202	51	70	12	2	6	**60**	7
Yariel Medina, Grambling	.339	186	28	63	10	1	4	38	5
Robert Cossey, Prairie View	.338	195	39	66	15	3	5	35	7
Richard Amion, Alabama State	.336	211	**66**	71	14	4	4	27	17
Einar Muniz, Alabama State	.335	173	41	58	9	1	1	21	5
Julio Nunez, Alabama A&M	.332	199	52	66	16	1	8	45	14
Tilur Smith, Jackson State	.331	169	38	56	17	3	3	27	5
Jose DeLaTorre, Southern	.330	115	22	38	5	2	5	22	0
Emmanuel Marrero, Ala. State	.329	**222**	44	**73**	16	**8**	4	58	7
Isias Alcantar, UAPB	.328	180	23	59	9	0	6	43	3
Dominic Harris, Prairie View	.328	177	34	58	16	0	7	51	5
Korey Hall, Grambling	.323	161	21	52	7	2	3	25	5
Christian Hickman, Alcorn State	.322	146	19	47	8	0	4	19	4
Brandyn Crutcher, Ala. A&M	.321	134	27	43	4	2	0	18	18
Moses Charles, Alcorn State	.320	200	34	64	7	0	0	16	**27**
Juan Bueno, Grambling	.315	200	36	63	**22**	2	2	42	8
Jerry Ford, Texas Southern	.311	180	28	56	5	1	0	15	21
Cody Den Beste, Prairie View	.309	178	41	55	10	3	3	30	8
D.J. Wallace, Southern	.309	149	20	46	11	1	**9**	37	1
Kirby Campbell, UAPB	.307	137	16	42	5	0	0	12	4
Melvin Rodriguez, Jackson State	.307	199	33	61	11	2	3	46	5
Zach Welz, Texas Southern	.304	168	25	51	8	0	2	34	10
Greg Salcido, Prairie View	.303	188	28	57	16	1	3	38	1
Kris Minter, Grambling	.299	201	32	60	5	3	1	27	12
Dexter Price, Alabama State	.299	201	40	60	9	0	7	40	6
Jordan Friend, Alabama A&M	.295	122	16	36	9	1	3	20	0

INDIVIDUAL PITCHING LEADERS
(Minimum 50 IP)

	W	L	ERA	G	SV	IP	H	BB	SO
Santos Saldivar, Southern	3	0	**2.06**	9	0	57	46	23	49
Joseph Camacho, Ala. State	**10**	1	2.44	14	0	96	87	25	63
Darius McClelland, Texas So.	2	4	2.63	14	0	51	41	25	42
Michael Starkey, Texas So.	4	6	3.18	16	0	74	65	38	43
Rios Ryan, Texas Southern	4	5	3.23	19	1	61	51	21	34
Mikey Ramirez, UAPB	6	5	3.29	13	0	88	101	7	40
Tyler Howe, Alabama State	5	1	3.29	16	1	63	60	26	47
Jim Ploeger, UAPB	4	3	3.34	14	0	70	64	20	68
Desmond Russell, Jackson State	9	5	3.46	17	2	**109**	102	32	**90**
Ryan Fuentes, Alcorn State	5	4	3.69	16	1	100	110	29	54
Felix Gomez, Texas Southern	1	4	3.79	21	3	59	53	22	47
Alexander Juday, Jackson State	3	7	3.97	21	4	95	102	26	68
T.J. Renda, Alabama State	5	5	4.10	14	0	86	103	17	72
Normando Valentin, Ala. State	4	0	4.14	14	0	50	57	10	23
Devin Kanorik, Texas Southern	4	2	4.15	14	0	65	51	24	47
Jonathan Mata, Prairie View	4	6	4.54	13	0	73	74	29	50
Devin Smith, Alabama A&M	4	7	4.91	16	1	84	90	30	52
Kyle Schwartz, UAPB	3	6	4.98	15	0	81	91	23	45
T.J. Murphy, Grambling	4	7	5.01	18	0	79	93	31	35
Zach Moreau, Grambling	3	3	5.02	15	2	75	79	26	52
#Kevin Walsh, UAPB	2	1	2.57	**24**	**5**	21	17	16	18
#Hunter Mcintosh, Ala. State	3	3	4.15	**24**	2	35	36	19	28

SUMMIT LEAGUE

Team	Conference		Overall	
	W	**L**	**W**	**L**
Nebraska-Omaha	15	9	31	20
South Dakota State	11	11	28	29
Western Illinois	11	13	21	32
IPFW	11	13	19	36
*North Dakota State	10	12	25	26

ALL-CONFERENCE TEAM: C—Michael Leach, Sr., North Dakota State. **1B**—Aaron Machbitz, Sr., South Dakota State. **2B**—Clayton Taylor, So., Omaha. **SS**—Caleb Palensky, Sr., Omaha. **3B**—Tanner Glore, Sr., Western Illinois. **OF**—Tim Colwell, Sr., North Dakota State; Neil DeCook, Sr., Western Illinois; Scott Splett, Sr., South Dakota State. **DH**—Carter DeBoe, Sr., Fort Wayne. **UTIL**—Steve Lowden, Sr., Fort Wayne. **SP**—Adam Bray, Jr., South Dakota State; Tyler Fox, So., Omaha; Tyler Willman, Jr., Western Illinois. **RP**—J.D. Moore, Jr., South Dakota State. **Player of the Year:** Tim Colwell, North Dakota State. **Pitcher of the Year:** Tyler Fox, Omaha. **Newcomer of the Year:** Matt Johnson, South Dakota State. **Coach of the Year:** Bob Herold, Omaha.

INDIVIDUAL BATTING LEADERS
(Minimum 2.5 plate appearances per team game)

	AVG	AB	R	H	2B	3B	HR	RBI	SB
Tim Colwell, NDSU	**.378**	201	44	**76**	9	4	1	22	19
Kristian Gayday, IPFW	.358	173	44	62	13	1	**12**	37	0
Wes Satzinger, NDSU	.356	163	38	58	**18**	1	2	31	3
Clayton Taylor, UNO	.342	187	40	64	17	2	9	**48**	4
Tanner Gore, Western Illinois	.335	170	25	57	10	0	0	34	13
Daniel Jewett, UNO	.333	138	21	46	5	2	1	29	4
Steve Lowden, IPFW	.333	144	26	48	10	0	2	28	0
Brandon Soat, IPFW	.328	131	23	43	8	0	0	13	4
Carter Deboe, IPFW	.321	193	38	62	10	3	4	35	9
Neil DeCook, Western Illinois	.321	193	25	62	7	2	0	28	18
Cole Gruber, UNO	.319	188	**47**	60	7	2	1	18	**34**
Aaron Machbitz, SDSU	.318	217	39	69	13	0	7	34	3
Malcolm White, IPFW	.311	135	25	42	3	1	2	24	1
Kyle Kleinendorst, NDSU	.310	174	42	54	10	**5**	4	42	10
Jameson Henning, W. Illinois	.310	197	29	61	8	2	1	23	12
Caleb Palensky, UNO	.306	186	29	57	15	2	4	40	5
Scott Splett, SDSU	.305	**223**	40	68	12	1	3	27	8
Tyler Splichal, UNO	.302	162	22	49	3	0	0	18	0
Alex Schultz, UNO	.302	182	43	55	7	1	1	23	10
Brett Bass, UNO	.299	164	25	49	9	1	1	32	6
Travis Stafford, Western Illinois	.297	138	18	41	4	1	1	11	2
Kevin Wirth, IPFW	.295	190	28	56	13	0	2	34	0
Greg Kaiser, IPFW	.289	166	28	48	9	4	8	38	4
Zach Coppola, SDSU	.288	163	23	47	7	0	0	17	14

Nick Altavilla, NDSU	.282	142	15	40	10	0	0	25	3
Adam McGinnis, W. Illinois	.281	135	26	38	3	0	2	19	4
Paul Jacobson, SDSU	.278	133	21	37	6	1	0	17	4
Jon Hechtner, NDSU	.278	151	27	42	3	1	0	17	6
Zack Burling, Western Illinois	.274	201	32	55	5	2	0	18	20
Shane Trevino, IPFW	.273	183	25	50	11	0	2	37	2

INDIVIDUAL PITCHING LEADERS
(Minimum 1 IP per team game)

	W	L	ERA	G	SV	IP	H	BB	SO
Steven Schoonover, UNO	3	2	**1.58**	9	0	51	47	5	20
Tyler Fox, UNO	**9**	1	2.29	13	0	79	65	17	57
Chris Anderson, SDSU	1	4	2.48	14	0	83	84	21	55
Parker Trewin, NDSU	7	3	2.57	14	0	77	62	28	68
Adam Bray, SDSU	5	7	2.80	15	0	**103**	106	17	**95**
Reed Pfannenstein, NDSU	4	1	2.86	13	0	44	39	17	28
Chad Hodges, SDSU	8	5	3.00	14	0	81	73	24	46
#J.D. Moore, SDSU	4	3	3.07	24	8	29	21	23	27
Zach Williamsen, UNO	3	3	3.47	12	0	57	56	16	39
David Ernst, NDSU	5	5	3.60	15	0	95	108	30	43
Tyler Willman, Western Illinois	3	3	3.66	16	0	84	81	50	63
Aaron Michel, Western Illinois	3	6	4.02	12	0	65	56	30	49
Ryan Wells, IPFW	3	3	4.81	16	1	73	82	33	71
Tom Constand, Western Illinois	2	8	5.15	19	0	73	86	24	56
Trent Keefer, NDSU	4	5	5.34	14	0	57	80	24	54
Marcus Ethen, UNO	4	3	5.44	11	0	45	58	18	34
Connor Lawhead, IPFW	3	5	5.60	**25**	6	45	36	38	57
Dane Davis, IPFW	1	6	6.27	15	0	70	92	44	28
Nate White, IPFW	1	7	6.32	14	0	47	55	44	33
Steve Danielak, IPFW	2	4	8.74	14	0	59	87	38	28

SUN BELT CONFERENCE

Team	Conference		Overall	
	W	L	W	L
*Louisiana-Lafayette	26	4	58	10
Texas-Arlington	19	11	32	36
Arkansas State	18	12	32	26
Texas State	16	14	30	28
Western Kentucky	15	15	29	28
Troy	11	18	25	32
South Alabama	11	18	22	33
Arkansas-Little Rock	11	19	25	39
Georgia State	11	19	25	31
Louisiana-Monroe	11	19	23	36

ALL-CONFERENCE TEAM: C—Joey Roach, Georgia State. **1B**—Nic Wilson, Georgia State. **2B**—Jace Conrad, Louisiana-Lafayette. **SS**—Blake Trahan, Louisiana-Lafayette. **3B**—Ben Crumpton, UALR. **OF**—Chase Raffield, Georgia State; Caleb Adams, Louisiana-Lafayette; Ryan Bottger, UT Arlington. **DH**—Matt Shortall, UT Arlington. **UTIL**—Cory Geisler, Texas State. **SP**—Carson Baranik, Louisiana-Lafayette; Cody Boutte, Louisiana-Lafayette; Justin Hageman, Western Kentucky. **RP**—Ian Tompkins, Western Kentucky. **Player of the Year:** Jace Conrad, Louisiana-Lafayette. **Pitcher of the Year:** Carson Baranik, Louisiana-Lafayette. **Freshman of the Year:** Marc Skinner, Troy. **Coach of the Year:** Tony Robichaux, Louisiana-Lafayette.

INDIVIDUAL BATTING LEADERS
(Minimum 2.5 at-bats per team game)

	AVG	AB	R	H	2B	3B	HR	RBI	SB
Caleb Adams, ULL	**.384**	219	67	84	18	**7**	11	42	6
Jace Conrad, ULL	.369	**260**	63	**96**	20	3	9	**65**	22
Ryan Bottger, UTA	.368	204	49	75	18	3	7	42	5
Blake Trahan, ULL	.359	251	58	90	12	2	4	49	13
Chase Raffield, Georgia State	.356	205	44	73	19	0	14	59	7
David Hall, Troy	.344	209	33	72	17	0	9	48	3
Matt Shortall, UTA	.344	256	42	88	**26**	3	10	57	2
Anderson Miller, WKU	.335	200	40	67	11	4	3	33	3
Cole Gleason, South Alabama	.333	204	27	68	12	0	3	33	0
Tyler Girouard, ULL	.331	175	32	58	11	2	3	31	4
Ben Crumpton, UALR	.324	207	40	67	8	1	3	23	**33**
Nic Wilson, Georgia State	.322	205	50	66	20	0	**18**	52	0
Ryan Leonards, UL-L	.322	258	62	83	14	4	4	34	18
Tanner Rockwell, UALR	.321	209	35	67	16	3	7	43	4
Garrett Pitts, Troy	.320	225	36	72	15	2	3	35	4

Seth Harrison, ULL	.316	250	53	79	16	**7**	9	64	15
Matt Burgess, Arkansas State	.313	230	34	72	13	0	4	58	2
Regan Flaherty, WKU	.313	230	29	72	18	1	3	35	0
Zach Maggio, Arkansas State	.312	205	51	64	11	0	0	22	9
Matt Rose, Georgia State	.312	202	33	63	12	0	11	34	4
Garrett Mattlage, Texas State	.308	214	37	66	11	1	5	44	11
Ryan Church, WKU	.306	229	34	70	11	0	7	38	7
Derek Miller, UTA	.304	247	46	75	15	0	0	30	6
Levi Scott, UTA	.303	185	18	56	7	2	3	19	0
Joey Roach, Georgia State	.301	146	18	44	8	1	3	23	1
Darin McLemore, UTA	.301	166	33	50	8	0	4	31	2
Scott Wilcox, WKU	.297	222	39	66	15	0	3	32	1
Keelin Rasch, ULM	.289	242	33	70	16	3	4	30	0
Chase Compton, ULL	.289	173	36	50	8	0	3	44	5
Cody Wofford, WKU	.288	156	28	45	6	3	5	26	2

INDIVIDUAL PITCHING LEADERS
(Minimum 1 IP per team game)

	W	L	ERA	G	SV	IP	H	BB	SO
Marc Skinner, Troy	6	1	**1.52**	31	5	65	58	16	70
#Ian Tompkins, WKU	0	1	2.42	26	**14**	26	23	22	46
Justin Hageman, WKU	6	2	2.63	15	1	96	86	38	68
Daniel Milliman, UTA	6	0	2.69	14	0	60	56	23	35
Taylor Black, Texas State	6	4	2.85	15	0	101	98	25	88
Cody Boutte, ULL	9	0	3.09	15	0	82	76	26	54
Austin Robichaux, ULL	8	3	3.11	14	0	90	69	24	80
Locke St. John, S. Alabama	6	3	3.24	15	0	97	96	29	52
Carson Baranik, ULL	**11**	2	3.31	17	0	**106**	93	27	74
Tyler Bray, ULM	8	5	3.36	**33**	5	67	58	20	69
Shane McCain, Troy	4	4	3.38	15	0	101	82	40	**101**
Austen Williams, Texas State	8	3	3.65	15	0	99	88	29	96
Lucas Humpal, Texas State	4	6	3.76	15	0	89	87	27	82
Travis McDonald, UALR	4	6	4.04	14	0	69	67	29	54
Cameron Allen, UALR	5	6	4.07	13	0	80	74	11	49
David Owen, Arkansas State	5	6	4.19	15	0	77	76	30	76
Jake Thompson, WKU	4	4	4.29	15	0	78	73	31	61
Bradley Wallace, Ark. State	4	5	4.37	15	0	78	86	25	69
Josh Bartley, WKU	5	4	4.61	16	1	66	72	29	38
Zach Thompson, UTA	5	4	4.64	16	0	87	97	32	62
Kevin Hill, South Alabama	4	5	4.70	13	0	82	85	34	93

WEST COAST CONFERENCE

Team	Conference		Overall	
	W	L	W	L
*Pepperdine	18	9	43	18
Loyola Marymount	17	10	32	24
Gonzaga	17	10	26	29
Santa Clara	16	11	26	30
San Diego	16	11	34	20
Pacific	15	12	26	26
Brigham Young	12	15	22	31
San Francisco	11	16	25	28
Saint Mary's	8	19	16	38
Portland	5	22	11	41

ALL-CONFERENCE TEAM: C—Jesse Jenner, Jr., San Diego. **INF**—Andrew Daniel, Jr., San Diego; Austin Davidson, Jr., Pepperdine; David Fletcher, Fr., Loyola Marymount; Connor Joe, Jr., San Diego; Hutton Moyer, So., Pepperdine; Dillon Robinson, Jr., BYU; Brett Sullivan, So., Pacific; Jose Vizcaino, So., Santa Clara; Caleb Wood, So., Gonzaga;. **OF**—Derek Atikinson, Jr., San Francisco; Payden Cawley-Lamb, Sr., Gonzaga; DonAndre Clark, Jr., Saint Mary's; Brennon Lund, Fr., BYU; Austin Miller, Fr., Loyola Marymount; Bradley Zimmer, Jr., San Francisco. **UT**—Louie Lechich, Sr., San Diego. **P**—Brandon Bailey, Fr., Gonzaga; Aaron Brown, Jr., Pepperdine; Bret Dahison, Sr., Loyola Marymount; Jake Jenkins, So., Pacific; Reece Karalus, So., Santa Clara; Eric Karch, Sr., Pepperdine; Corey Miller, Sr., Pepperdine; Colin Welmon, Jr., Loyola Marymount. **Player of the Year:** Connor Joe, San Diego. **Pitcher of the Year:** Aaron Brown, Pepperdine. **Freshman of the Year:** Austin Miller, Loyola Marymount. **Coach of the Year:** Steve Rodriguez, Pepperdine.

INDIVIDUAL BATTING LEADERS
(Minimum 3 plate appearances per team game)

	AVG	AB	R	H	2B	3B	HR	RBI	SB
Austin Miller, LMU	**.374**	206	46	77	10	3	0	18	**25**

Player	AVG	AB	R	H	2B	3B	HR	RBI	SB
Dillon Robinson, BYU	.372	148	24	55	6	1	2	27	0
Payden Lamb, Gonzaga	.369	203	31	75	12	1	1	29	8
Andrew Daniel, San Diego	.369	222	51	82	20	3	5	43	13
Bradley Zimmer, USF	.368	220	42	81	10	7	7	31	21
Connor Joe, San Diego	.367	218	59	80	21	2	9	51	3
Aaron Barnett, Pepperdine	.364	220	23	80	5	1	0	28	1
Brett Sullivan, Pacific	.357	207	36	74	15	5	4	40	9
Brock Whitney, BYU	.348	204	43	71	13	1	3	32	2
Jesse Jenner, San Diego	.348	161	31	56	7	0	3	35	4
Louie Lechich, San Diego	.342	225	45	77	18	3	7	46	3
Jarrett Jarvis, BYU	.339	168	15	57	15	0	0	16	0
Derek Atikinson, USF	.330	215	32	71	15	1	1	44	8
David Fletcher, LMU	.329	222	37	73	6	2	0	28	17
Austin Bailey, San Diego	.328	204	44	67	11	2	0	32	3
Bret Lopez, BYU	.325	151	23	49	9	2	2	26	1
Jose Vizcaino, Santa Clara	.323	201	33	65	8	3	2	28	11
Stevie Berman, Santa Clara	.322	183	35	59	13	0	4	23	4
Tanner Donnels, LMU	.321	218	27	70	14	3	1	36	8
Kelton Caldwell, BYU	.319	213	32	68	12	2	6	37	2
Eric Urry, BYU	.318	151	26	48	4	1	1	21	6
Taylor Murphey, Pacific	.315	200	35	63	9	6	5	34	8
Tyler Sullivan, Pacific	.315	216	43	68	7	4	2	16	11
Jos Goossen-Brown, San Diego	.314	175	19	55	10	2	4	27	2
Anthony Gonsolin, St. Mary's	.308	208	37	64	9	8	2	24	
8 Hutton Moyer, Pepperdine	.307	228	52	70	24	4	0	22	15
Aaron Brown, Pepperdine	.307	238	43	73	12	3	12	47	5
Cole Trezek, LMU	.303	155	17	47	6	2	0	14	2
Brennon Lund, BYU	.303	228	39	69	5	1	0	19	11
Caleb Wood, Gonzaga	.300	227	32	68	12	0	2	24	9

INDIVIDUAL PITCHING LEADERS
(Minimum 1 IP per team game)

Player	W	L	ERA	G	SV	IP	H	BB	SO
Corey Miller, Pepperdine	9	5	1.90	16	0	118	102	33	82
Aaron Brown, Pepperdine	13	1	1.95	17	0	116	84	40	104
#Eric Karch, Pepperdine	1	1	2.12	30	16	34	22	11	23
#Reece Karalus, Santa Clara	6	2	2.25	34	11	48	34	13	46
Colin Welmon, LMU	10	2	2.37	14	0	106	89	19	58
Lucas Long, San Diego	4	3	2.41	20	2	71	58	20	62
Louie Lechich, San Diego	8	3	2.51	13	0	82	82	21	50
Jake Jenkins, Pacific	6	3	2.55	15	0	92	79	26	74
Hayden Rogers, BYU	2	3	2.93	25	1	55	50	15	33
Matt Maurer, Pepperdine	4	3	3.09	18	0	70	70	40	44
Jackson McClelland, Pepperdine	8	3	3.53	15	0	79	78	19	47
Ryan Brockett, St. Mary's	5	7	3.56	15	0	94	88	36	67
Brandon Bailey, Gonzaga	6	7	3.69	15	0	102	118	25	62
Andrew Sopko, Gonzaga	5	4	3.74	15	0	96	108	23	61
Jeff Barker, BYU	6	5	3.80	15	0	88	85	38	55
Sheldon Lee, USF	5	3	3.83	17	0	54	48	21	32
Jacob Steffens, Santa Clara	2	5	3.90	16	0	65	73	13	43
Kolton Mahoney, BYU	6	6	3.97	16	1	88	75	29	69
Patrick McGrath, LMU	3	4	4.07	15	0	73	81	18	49
Desmond Poulson, BYU	5	5	4.13	17	0	94	99	40	58
Christian Cecilio, USF	5	8	4.15	15	0	91	93	25	76
Mike Hager, Pacific	4	5	4.19	13	0	73	75	19	44

WESTERN ATHLETIC CONFERENCE

Team	Conference		Overall	
	W	L	W	L
*Sacramento State	21	6	40	24
Grand Canyon	19	8	30	23
Texas-Pan American	17	10	27	30
Utah Valley	16	11	28	30
Cal State Bakersfield	15	12	26	33
Seattle	13	11	26	27
New Mexico State	11	13	23	31
North Dakota	8	16	10	29
Chicago State	5	19	17	37
Northern Colorado	4	23	10	43

ALL-CONFERENCE TEAM: C—Brian Olson, Jr., Seattle. **IF**—Chad De La Guerra, Jr., Grand Canyon; Rhys Hoskins, Jr., Sacramento State. **1B/OF**—Michael Pomeroy, Sr., Grand Canyon. **OF**—Landon Cray, So., Seattle; Alex Howe, Sr., Texas-Pan American; Nathan Lukes, So., Sacramento State; Michael Medina, Sr., New Mexico State; David Walker, Jr., Grand Canyon. **DH**—Mark Krueger, So., Utah Valley. **P**—Taylor Aikenhead, Sr., Bakersfield; Brennan Leitao, Jr., Sacramento State; Andrew Naderer, So., Grand Canyon; Sam Street, Sr., Texas-Pan American. **Player of the Year:** Rhys Hoskins, Sacramento State. **Pitcher of the Year:** Sam Street, Texas-Pan American. **Freshman of the Year:** Sam Long, Sacramento State. **Coach of the Year:** Reggie Christiansen.

INDIVIDUAL BATTING LEADERS
(Minimum 2.5 at-bats per team game)

Player	AVG	AB	R	H	2B	3B	HR	RBI	SB
Chad De La Guerra, Grand Canyon	.373	209	45	78	12	4	6	49	16
David Walker, Grand Canyon	.360	200	49	72	10	3	0	16	22
Landon Cray, Seattle	.350	177	26	62	8	2	2	22	6
Nathan Lukes, Sacramento St.	.347	259	54	90	10	3	0	26	10
Alex Howe, UTPA	.345	206	34	71	18	4	5	42	12
Tyler Follis, North Dakota	.331	130	17	43	4	0	0	11	4
Kyle Moses, Sacramento State	.330	182	39	60	10	0	1	18	13
Derek Umphres, NMSU	.328	201	35	66	12	2	3	40	0
Julian Russell, Chicago State	.328	189	38	62	14	0	0	22	15
Brian Olson, Seattle	.320	203	29	65	15	2	3	47	2
Chase Fields, Seattle	.319	213	40	68	13	2	1	24	24
Rhys Hoskins, Sacramento St.	.319	213	45	68	18	0	12	53	6
Michael Paulson, NMSU	.317	202	41	64	10	1	1	40	2
Ryan Reese, North Dakota	.314	105	10	33	4	0	0	17	2
Mattingly Romanin, Chicago St.	.312	202	39	63	9	3	1	32	13
David Metgar, Bakersfield	.312	154	19	48	5	2	0	11	4
Sanford Hunt, Chicago State	.310	171	20	53	9	3	0	17	4
Chance Gusbeth, Bakersfield	.309	220	28	68	7	5	3	37	2
Michael Pomeroy, Grand Canyon	.309	217	21	67	9	1	1	31	0
Jordan Stroschein, Chicago St.	.308	214	30	66	7	4	2	33	13
Kristoffer Koerper, NMSU	.308	198	40	61	12	1	5	45	1
Mark Krueger, Utah Valley	.306	219	36	67	12	1	7	42	4
Taylor Peterson, North Dakota	.305	151	27	46	15	0	5	26	0
Jensen Park, Northern Colo.	.304	148	20	45	9	5	4	22	1
Scotty Burcham, Sacramento St.	.300	237	38	71	14	1	0	23	8
Mylz Jones, Bakersfield	.300	207	25	62	9	4	2	24	5
Humberto Aranda, Grand Canyon	.299	117	16	35	8	1	2	22	1
Oscar Sanay, Bakersfield	.299	201	40	60	9	5	0	25	13
Griffin Andreychuk, Seattle	.297	111	23	33	3	0	0	36	3
Craig Brinkerhoff, Utah Valley	.295	190	34	56	21	4	6	40	3

INDIVIDUAL PITCHING LEADERS
(Minimum 1 IP per team game)

Player	W	L	ERA	G	SV	IP	H	BB	SO
Sam Street, UTPA	12	2	1.81	15	0	129	104	25	91
Sutter McLoughlin, Sacramento St.	4	2	1.81	29	9	45	33	10	36
Alex Palsha, Sacramento State	6	1	1.82	37	4	59	35	28	57
Brennan Leitao, Sacramento St.	9	4	2.15	19	0	117	103	23	79
Coley Bruns, Grand Canyon	6	0	2.24	15	0	88	74	22	69
Grant Gunning, Seattle	3	1	2.36	17	0	42	35	20	31
Blake English, UTPA	5	4	2.61	17	0	93	86	21	42
Alex Henson, UTPA	3	2	2.88	14	0	75	70	29	52
Riley Barr, NMSU	5	3	2.94	27	0	64	71	22	46
Garrett Anderson, Seattle	3	2	3.00	23	3	48	50	19	38
Sam Long, Sacramento State	8	2	3.03	17	0	95	83	26	50
Taylor Aikenhead, Bakersfield	8	7	3.05	15	0	106	105	35	76
Will Dennis, Seattle	6	5	3.25	21	2	69	69	17	51
Andrew Naderer, Grand Canyon	9	3	3.26	14	0	99	83	28	61
Andrew Padron, UTPA	2	3	3.29	20	2	41	39	14	22
Ethan Evanko, Grand Canyon	6	1	3.42	15	0	74	75	19	41
Jorge Perez, Grand Canyon	1	6	3.43	14	3	63	59	12	38
Zach Muckenhirn, N. Dakota	2	4	3.44	11	0	65	59	30	44
Eric Hall, Chicago State	3	6	3.45	14	1	86	93	23	23
Jared Paderez, Sacramento St.	1	3	3.59	14	0	43	42	17	14

SMALL COLLEGES

NCAA DIVISION II

BY JACOB EMMERT

Southern Indiana bookended its stay at USA Baseball's National Training Complex in Cary, N.C. with a pair of one-run victories. The first was a 4-3 win over Tampa, the nation's top team, to open the NCAA Division II tournament. The last was a 3-2, 12-inning battle with Colorado Mesa resulting in USI's second national title in school history (2010).

Southern Indiana entered the championship round with a 4-0 record, needing to topple the once-beaten Mavericks just once to capture the title. With the game tied at two in the top of the 12th, Matt Bowles, 1-for-5 on the day, drew a bases loaded, one-out walk to put the Screaming Eagles ahead for good.

Junior Matt Chavarria, who was named the tournament's Most Outstanding Player and shares his time between the pitching rubber and shortstop, threw his fourth scoreless inning of the night in the bottom of the 12th, stranding Garrett Woodward, Colorado Mesa's final hope, at third base. Chavarria went 1-0 with two saves in the finals without giving up an earned run and struck out four while working the final four innings.

After USI jumped out to an early lead in the top of the first on a Chavarria RBI double, the Mavericks scored two of their own, both unearned, in the bottom of the third, taking advantage of a pair of Screaming Eagles errors. The game remained 2-1 in favor of Colorado Mesa until the top of the eighth, when a throwing error by Mavericks reliever Ryan Reno allowed right fielder Kyle Kempf to score and tie the game at two.

"What a great game," USI head coach Tracy Archuleta told NCAA.com. "I think everyone enjoyed it. I'm so proud of each and every one of our guys."

Archuleta's squad defeated the top four teams in the country en route to the national title. Outfielder Kyle Kempf batted .379 in the postseason, hitting one home run, three doubles and scoring six runs. Kempf, Wright and Chavarria were joined by Brent Wenzapfel, the USI DH who batted .375 in the postseason, as Screaming Eagles on the all-tournament team.

DIVISION II WORLD SERIES

Site: Cary, N.C.
Participants: Chico State, Calif. (43-12); Colorado Mesa (43-11); Lander, S.C. (50-7); Minnesota State-Mankato (45-8); St. Thomas Aquinas, N.Y. (39-15); Seton Hill, Pa. (39-15); Southern Indiana (44-12); Tampa (51-1).
Champion: Southern Indiana.
Runner-up: Colorado Mesa.
Outstanding player: Matt Chavarria, ss/rhp, Southern Indiana.

PRELIMINARIES

Southern Indiana 4, Tampa 3
Lander 6, Chico State 4
Seton Hill 4, Minnesota State-Mankato 2
Colorado Mesa 5, St. Thomas Aquinas 4
Tampa 14, Chico State 6 (Chico State eliminated)
Southern Indiana 6, Lander 5
Minnesota State-Mankato 6, St. Thomas Aquinas 1 (St. Thomas Aquinas eliminated)
Colorado Mesa 6, Seton Hill 2
Tampa 7, Lander 3 (Lander eliminated)
Minnesota State-Mankato 3, Seton Hill 1 (Seton Hill eliminated)

SEMIFINALS

Minnesota State-Mankato 5, Southern Indiana 1
Southern Indiana 4, Minnesota State-Mankato 3 (Mankato eliminated)
Tampa 3, Colorado Mesa 1
Colorado Mesa 3, Tampa 2 (Tampa eliminated)

FINALS

Southern Indiana 3, Colorado Mesa 2 (Colorado Mesa eliminated)

NCAA DIVISION III

Wisconsin-Whitewater cruised to its second NCAA Division III title by winning all four of its games by at least three runs (and three of them by at least six) while going undefeated in the postseason. The clincher came in a 7-0 rout of Emory in Appleton, Wis.

The victory gave Whitewater a sweep of D-III titles, as it also won football and men's basketball championships this year.

Emory, which lost its opening round game 5-4 to Baldwin-Wallace but fought off elimination by winning four in a row to reach the finals, was no match for the Warhawks, winners of their last 11 games of the season.

Backing up a seven-hit shutout by junior righthander Scott Plaza—who was named the tournament's Most Outstanding Player—Whitewater put up runs in the second, third, fourth, and seventh innings.

"There is no way they were taking me out of that game," Plaza, who posted a 3-0, 1.23 postseason record, told NCAA.com. "(I) tried to

make them hit my stuff. I knew I had (defense) behind me and if I did my job, they're going to do their job."

Plaza started two of the Warhawks' four games at the finals, posting a perfect ERA through 16 innings of work. He struck out 14. Plaza struck out 106 batters while walking only 19 this season.

"He was about 60 percent," Whitewater head coach John Vodenlich, who also led the team to a title in 2005, said to NCAA.com. "We talk a lot about giving 100 percent of whatever you have. If his 100 percent was 75, percent that's good enough for me."

Emory came into the game hitting .355 on the year and scoring more than nine runs per game, but that was all put to an end by Plaza's dominant performance.

DIVISION III WORLD SERIES

Site: Appleton, Wis.
Participants: Baldwin Wallace, Ohio (28-18); Emory, Ga. (34-10); Linfield, Ore. (37-6); St. Thomas, Minn. (36-7); Salisbury (37-6); Southern Maine (35-12); SUNY Cortland (34-8); Wisconsin-Whitewater (39-7).
Champion: Wisconsin-Whitewater.
Runner-up: Emory.
Outstanding player: Scott Plaza, rhp, Wisconsin-Whitewater.

RESULTS
St. Thomas 10, Linfield 0
Baldwin Wallace 5, Emory 4
SUNY Cortland 4, Salisbury 3
Wisconsin-Whitewater 8, Southern Maine 1
Emory 8, Linfield 5 (Linfield eliminated)
Southern Maine 6, Salisbury 3 (Salisbury eliminated)
St. Thomas 5, Baldwin Wallace 4
Wisconsin-Whitewater 9, SUNY Cortland 6
Emory 9, SUNY Cortland 7 (SUNY Cortland eliminated)
Southern Maine 11, Baldwin Wallace 5 (Baldwin Wallace eliminated)
Wisconsin-Whitewater 10, St. Thomas 4
Emory 15, Southern Maine 3 (Southern Maine eliminated)
Emory 10, St. Thomas 7 (St. Thomas eliminated)
FINALS
Wisconsin-Whitewater 7, Emory 0 (Emory eliminated)

NAIA

Cumberland (Tenn.) became the first No. 10 seed to win the 10-team Avista-NAIA World Series since its current format was adopted in 2003. Cumberland (Tenn.) won five of six games in Lewiston, Idaho, including a 3-0 win in the championship over host Lewis-Clark State to avenge a 2006 loss to the Warriors in the title game. With

its third national title, Cumberland moved into a tie for third place on the NAIA's all-time champions chart.

Senior lefthander Anthony Gomez threw his second complete game against Lewis-Clark State at the World Series in the championship game, scattering six hits while striking out four. His performance sealed the first shutout victory in the World Series finale since 1996.

"I knew it was going to be really tough," Cumberland coach Woody Hunt said. "Gomez pitched another terrific game for us. This team has a special makeup. We've grinded it out every tournament, with nothing coming easy to us."

Senior second baseman Sam Lind went 13-for-24 (.542) with three doubles, two home runs, 12 RBIs and six runs scored in the World Series to earn Most Valuable Player honors.

Site: Lewiston, Idaho.
Participants: Cumberland, Tenn. (44-19); Faulkner, Ala. (49-14); Georgetown, Ky. (46-9); Georgia Gwinnett (52-11); Lewis-Clark State, Idaho (43-7); Oklahoma Baptist (53-7); Oklahoma Wesleyan (55-6); San Diego Christian (42-18); Southern Poly, Ga. (45-17); Tabor, Kan. (49-11).
Champion: Cumberland.
Runner-up: Lewis-Clark State.
Outstanding player: Sam Lind, 2b, Cumberland.

NJCAA DIVISION I

For the third time in the past five years, Iowa Western CC is the top team in NJCAA Division I. The Reivers led Miami Dade by a run before scoring five in the seventh and six in the ninth en route to a 17-5 win in the championship game at Grand Junction.

Iowa Western outfielder Alex Krupa was named tournament MVP after going 4-for-5. He helped the Reivers get on the scoreboard first with a two-run single in the second inning. Western Iowa led 6-0 heading into the bottom of the fourth, when Miami Dade made things interesting with a five-run outburst. But Drake Robison came out of the bullpen to pick up the win with 5 1/3 innings of two-hit, shutout ball, allowing just one walk and striking out five. Western Iowa's Ryan Merrill capped the scoring with a three-run homer to right field in the ninth.

Erik Swanson, who struck out nine in a seven-inning complete-game shutout against Midland (Texas), was named the tournament's most outstanding pitcher.
Site: Grand Junction, Colo.
Participants: Blinn, Texas (34-26); Chattahoochee, Ala. (47-9); Cochise, Ariz. (37-27); Columbia State, Tenn. (44-11);

Delgado, La. (43-11); Iowa Western (51-11); Johnson County, Kan. (50-12); Midland, Texas (40-23).

Champion: Iowa Western.

Runner-up: Miami Dade.

Outstanding player: Alex Krupa, of, Iowa Western.

NJCAA DIVISION II

Jordan Zimmerman's 14 RBIs during the NJCAA D-II World Series set a new tournament record, but it was what he did with the bases empty that propelled Mesa (Ariz.) CC to a 9-7 win over Hinds (Miss.) CC. Leading off the top of the 11th in a ballgame tied at six, Zimmerman tripled, beginning a three-run rally. It was one of three hits in the game for the tournament MVP. Hinds got a run back in the bottom of the 11th and loaded the bases with two outs, but reliever Joseph Carvalho worked his way out of the jam to seal Mesa's first national title in 42 years. The Thunderbirds won the NJCAA World Series three years in a row in 1970-72, when the organization sponsored just one division of the sport.

Mesa entered the tournament as the nation's No. 1 team but lost its opening game to Vincennes (Ind.), then had to win four straight games in the loser's bracket to reach the winner-takes-all title game.

Site: Enid, Okla.

Participants: Hinds, Miss. (35-19); Lincoln Land, Ill. (44-15); Madison, Wis. (42-15); Mercer County, N.J. (39-6); Mesa, Ariz. (47-12); Northern Oklahoma-Enid (38-21); Pasco-Hernando State, Fla. (25-16); Southeastern, Iowa (44-20); Vincennes, Ind. (42-16); Westchester, N.Y. (33-15).

Champion: Mesa.

Runner-up: Hinds.

Outstanding player: Jordan Zimmerman, 3b, Mesa.

NJCAA DIVISION III

In its final year as host of the NJCAA D-III national championship, Tyler (Texas) made sure to keep the hardware at home, beating Cumberland County (N.J.) 6-3 to win its second national title (and its first since 2007). Anthony Soriano, who had two hits and one RBI in the final, went 7-for-15 over the week and was named tournament MVP. Cody Broussard went 2-for-5 with a triple and two RBIs in the championship game, while shortstop Tim Hunter went 2-for-3 with a double, two runs and two RBIs.

The tournament will be held in Kinston, N.C., for three years starting in 2015.

Site: Tyler, Texas.

Participants: Cumberland County, N.J. (46-8); Herkimer County, N.Y. (37-9); Northern Essex, Mass. (20-12); Prince George's, Md. (12-21); St. Cloud Tech, Minn. (27-7); Suffolk County, N.Y. (22-10); Tyler, Texas (38-17); Waubonsee, Ill.

(37-23).

Champion: Tyler.

Runner-up: Cumberland County.

Outstanding player: Anthony Soriano, of, Tyler.

CALIFORNIA CC ATHLETIC ASSOCIATION

Orange Coast won its fifth state championship in school history (and its first since 2009), beating San Joaquin Delta 5-3 in the title game of the California Community College Athletic Association state tournament. The Pirates finished the season on a 15-game winning streak, as coach John Altobelli earned the second title of his 22-year career at Orange Coast.

Orange Coast lefthander Jacob Hill threw eight strong innings in the championship semifinals, and twin brother David Hill followed with seven innings in the finals. The righthander battled battled with a tender ankle, scattering 11 hits but striking out seven and earning the win. The Pirates took the lead for good on Chris Iriart's two-run single in the fifth. Lefthander Art Vidro, who threw seven innings in Orange Coast's opening game, was named tournament MVP.

Site: Fresno, Calif.

Participants: College of the Sequoias (33-11); Orange Coast (33-9); Oxnard (33-9); San Joaquin Delta (33-9).

Champion: Orange Coast.

Runner-up: San Joaquin Delta.

Outstanding player: Art Vidro, lhp, Orange Coast.

NORTHWEST ATHLETIC CONFERENCE

Edmonds (Wash.) beat Bellevue (Wash.) 7-6 in the championship game to secure its seventh NWAC title, and its first since 2008. Tyler Baker's RBI single in the bottom of the eighth plated the game-winning run for the Tritons, who had to win two games on the last day of the tournament. They beat Lane 9-2 earlier in the day to reach the title game for the 11th time in school history. Edmonds third baseman Chris Osborne went 4-for-4 in the final game and hit .500 with five RBIs in the tournament to win MVP honors.

Site: Longview Wash.

Participants: Bellevue, Wash. (28-23); Clark, Wash. (31-15); Columbia Basin, Wash. (28-17); Edmonds, Wash. (39-8); Lane, Ore. (30-18); Pierce, Wash. (28-13); Tacoma, Wash. (39-8); Treasure Valley, Ore. (35-12).

Champion: Edmonds.

Runner-up: Bellevue.

Outstanding player: Chris Osborne, of, Edmonds.

The USA Baseball Collegiate National Team's summer ended with a whimper, as Cuba completed a five-game sweep of Team USA in Cuba. Team USA finished the summer with an 18-8-2 record. Though it ended on a sour note, the American campaign featured a pair of notable successes in a Honkbal Week tournament championship in the Netherlands and a series win against Japan on American soil.

"I am really proud of this team and all that we accomplished this summer," Team USA head coach Dave Van Horn (Arkansas) said. "Starting with our tour of the Coastal Plain League when we were in something like 10 different hotels in 12 nights, these players have always had great attitudes, have never complained and really bonded as a squad.

"We started out really strong, winning a five-game series against Chinese Taipei and a hard-fought three-game series over Japan. Then, we took the first overseas trip for pretty much every player on the team and I felt like they responded really well. They showed up to play every day and played hard. We didn't panic after losing the first game at Honkbal Week and ran off seven straight wins to accomplish one of our biggest goals of the summer, which was to win that tournament."

Team USA beat Japan 6-3 in the championship game, giving Team USA its fourth Honkbal title

since 2000. The Americans are now 29-5 all-time in the tournament, having previously won the title in 2000, 2002 and 2008.

Alex Bregman (Louisiana State) won the Honkbal Week Most Valuable Player award after hitting .367 with six stolen bases and playing strong infield defense in the tournament. Christin Stewart (Tennessee) led Team USA with a .455/.538/.591 slash line in Haarlem to win the event's "Best Hitter" award. Clemson's Chris Okey was named "Carl Angelo Most Popular Player."

Team USA's pitching was dominant in the tournament, posting a 0.62 staff ERA, as the Americans outscored their opponents 34-6 in seven games. Carson Fulmer (Vanderbilt) and James Kaprielian (UCLA) started two games apiece, working 11 innings apiece without allowing an earned run. Kyle Funkhouser (Louisville) also started two games, including the championship game against Japan, when he allowed two runs over 4 1/3 innings. Tyler Jay (Illinois) followed with 1 1/3 innings of scoreless relief to earn the win in the title game. Okey went 2-for-3 with two RBIs to lead USA's 10-hit attack in the finale. Nick Banks (Texas A&M) hit a two-run single to highlight Team USA's three-run fourth inning, giving the Americans a commanding 4-0 lead they would never relinquish.

Japan beat Team USA 1-0 to start the week, but

COLLEGIATE NATIONAL TEAM STATS

Year indicates 2014-15 class standing

PLAYER, POS.	YEAR	SCHOOL	AVG	OBP	SLG	G	AB	R	H	2B	3B	HR	RBI	BB	SO	SB
Christin Stewart, of	Jr.	Tennessee	.383	.474	.605	25	81	15	31	12	0	2	16	12	18	4
Dansby Swanson, 2b	Jr.	Vanderbilt	.288	.342	.364	18	66	14	19	5	0	0	3	5	13	3
Tate Matheny, of	Jr.	Missouri State	.288	.329	.350	26	80	4	23	2	0	1	11	3	17	6
Chris Okey, c	So.	Clemson	.286	.407	.429	22	49	8	14	4	0	1	6	8	12	3
Zack Collins, c/1b	So.	Miami	.273	.403	.491	21	55	8	15	3	0	3	7	12	16	0
Blake Trahan, ss	Jr.	Louisiana-Lafayette	.267	.313	.300	25	90	12	24	3	0	0	9	6	11	7
Mark Mathias, 3b/2b	Jr.	Cal Poly	.263	.390	.368	28	95	15	25	7	0	1	10	19	15	5
Alex Bregman, ss	Jr.	Louisiana State	.257	.317	.330	28	109	20	28	5	0	1	17	9	7	10
Bryan Reynolds, of	So.	Vanderbilt	.246	.358	.351	18	57	7	14	3	0	1	14	9	19	2
Nick Banks, of	So.	Texas A&M	.241	.290	.333	26	87	11	21	2	0	2	13	4	22	1
D.J. Stewart, of	Jr.	Florida State	.232	.362	.316	28	95	14	22	6	1	0	12	17	14	4
Taylor Ward, c	Jr.	Fresno State	.176	.348	.235	12	17	5	3	1	0	0	1	3	6	1

PITCHER, POS.	YEAR	SCHOOL	W	L	ERA	G	SV	IP	H	R	ER	BB	SO	AVG
Tyler Jay, lhp	Jr.	Illinois	2	0	0.00	15	1	17	7	2	0	6	21	.130
A.J. Minter, lhp	Jr.	Texas A&M	0	0	0.00	9	0	12	4	2	0	7	10	.100
Ryan Burr, rhp	Jr.	Arizona State	0	0	0.00	12	3	11	1	1	0	7	18	.029
Walker Buehler, rhp	Jr.	Vanderbilt	0	0	0.00	1	0	6	4	1	0	3	3	.167
Carson Fulmer, rhp	Jr.	Vanderbilt	3	1	0.73	5	4	25	11	4	2	12	19	.141
Dillon Tate, rhp	Jr.	UC Santa Barbara	0	0	0.79	11	3	11	7	2	1	3	7	.171
James Kaprielian, rhp	Jr.	UCLA	3	1	1.07	5	0	25	13	4	3	7	29	.149
Kyle Funkhouser, rhp	Jr.	Louisville	1	1	1.27	6	0	28	15	7	4	8	36	.152
Justin Garza, rhp	Jr.	Cal State Fullerton	2	1	1.35	8	0	27	16	4	4	7	27	.178
Andrew Moore, rhp	Jr.	Oregon State	2	0	2.12	7	1	17	16	4	4	5	19	.254
Thomas Eshelman, rhp	Jr.	Cal State Fullerton	2	0	2.14	8	1	21	16	6	5	2	20	.213
Jake Lemoine, rhp	Jr.	Houston	2	2	2.45	5	0	18	13	7	5	9	15	.194
Trey Killian, rhp	Jr.	Arkansas	1	1	4.76	3	0	6	5	4	3	2	8	.208

the Americans bounced back to beat the Japanese 6-0 later in the event, then won the third meeting between the teams in the gold-medal game.

But Team USA's bats went cold in Cuba, where the Americans managed just seven runs total in five games and were shut out twice, including a 1-0 loss in the finale.

Stewart finished as the lone Team USA player to hit above .300; he hit a blistering .383/.474/.605 on the summer with two homers, 16 RBIs and 12 doubles. Stewart was the breakout star of a fairly balanced offense.

The pitching staff had more than its share of stars, and its bullpen was nearly untouchable. Relievers Tyler Jay (Illinois), A.J. Minter (Texas A&M) and Ryan Burr (Arizona State) posted a combined 0.00 ERA in 40 innings over 36 appearances. Righthanders Carson Fulmer (Vanderbilt), James Kaprielian (UCLA), Kyle Funkhouser (Louisville) and Justin Garza (Cal State Fullerton) made at least four starts apiece and all posted ERAs below 2.00. By and large, the staff pounded the strike zone and missed plenty of bats.

It will go down as a solid summer, despite its disappointing conclusion.

Y-D Wins Cape Title

After starting the season 5-11, the Yarmouth-Dennis Red Sox caught fire in the final month of the Cape Cod League season and stayed hot through the playoffs to win the league championship for the first time in seven years. Y-D completed a two-game sweep of Falmouth in the championship series with a come-from-behind 10-4 win in Game Two. The Red Sox erased a 4-2 deficit with six runs in the sixth inning, highlighted by Jordan Tarsovich's three-run double.

"They grouped together," Yarmouth-Dennis coach Scott Pickler told the Cape Cod Times. "They started believing in each other."

Coaches and scouts generally agreed that there was less top-end talent than usual in the Cape in 2014, though the depth was still solid.

"I have to agree with the scouts who are saying the talent was down; it was definitely down this year," longtime Chatham coach John Schiffner said. "It's a combination of the teams signing more high school players, and the college coaches shutting down more of their position players and their pitchers."

SUMMER LEAGUE ROUNDUP

■ The Lakeshore Chinooks won the Northwoods League championship in just the franchise's third year of existence. The Chinooks compiled the best regular-season record, 50-21 for a .704 winning percentage, before going undefeated in the playoffs. Lakeshore became just the third team in the history of the league to win at least 50 regular-season games. Run prevention was the strength of the team, as the Chinooks had the best ERA in the league (2.92) by more than half a run over the team with the second-lowest ERA (3.58). Lakeshore defeated the Mankato MoonDogs by a score of 3-0 to clinch the best-of-three championship. Joe Pavlovich (Wisconsin-Oshkosh) threw six shutout innings while striking out seven before being relieved by Jake Tuttle (UW-Milwaukee). The MoonDogs lost in the championship series for the third time in four years.

After expanding to 18 teams, the NWL continued to outdraw every other summer league, becoming the first summer college league to draw more than 1 million fans in a year.

■ The Newport Gulls went 15-3 in their final 18 games—regular season and playoffs—to storm from fourth place in its division at the start of that stretch all the way to the NECBL title. After defeating Ocean State and Plymouth, each in three games, on its way to the finals, Newport swept Sanford in two games to finish its run. Vanderbilt's John Kilichowski threw seven scoreless innings in Game One of the finals, while an eight-run sixth inning powered the Gulls to an 8-5 win in Game Two, lifting the Gulls to their second championship in three years.

■ The Peninsula Pilots repeated as Coastal Plain League champions by beating the Florence RedWolves in the best-of-three championship series. After the teams split the first two games, Peninsula erased a 4-3 deficit in the decisive third game by exploding for eight runs in the seventh inning to win 11-4. Kyle Kempf (Southern Indiana) hit the go-ahead double to put Peninsula ahead for good, after an error extended the inning. A packed house of 3,698 fans watched the final game.

■ For the second consecutive year, the Alaska Goldpanners produced the best record in Alaska League games (21-8) and won the league championship. The Goldpanners defeated the Mat-Su Miners in the best-of-three championship series by sweeping the first two games to finish with a 33-9 record and .786 winning percentage. Alaska pushed across two runs in the fifth inning to defeat Mat-Su 2-1 in the clinching game. League batting champion Scott Hurst (Cal State Fullerton), drove in the game-winning run.

■ The Los Angeles Brewers went 26-7 to win the California Collegiate League's South Division by 12 games, then rallied through the losers' bracket in the playoffs to win the championship. The Brewers lost their postseason opener 6-3 to Neptune Beach, then reeled off four straight wins, capped by back-to-back victories against Neptune Beach. Austin Boyle threw five shutout innings to lead the Brewers to a 3-1 win in the finale.

■ The Santa Barbara Foresters finished 31-8 in CCL play but did not participate in the league playoffs, instead traveling to Wichita for the National Baseball Congress World Series. The Foresters repeated as champions in Wichita, winning the world series for the fifth time since 2006. Jaylin Davis (Appalachian State) doubled twice, scored two runs and made a game-saving defensive play in center field to lead the Foresters to a 3-2 win in 12 innings against the Seattle Studs in the finals.

CAPE COD LEAGUE

East Division	W	L	T	PTS
Harwich Mariners	26	16	2	54
Orleans Firebirds	24	18	2	50
Yarmouth-Dennis Red Sox	24	19	1	49
Brewster Whitecaps	17	25	2	36
Chatham Anglers	17	26	1	35

West Division	W	L	T	PTS
Bourne Braves	28	15	1	57
Falmouth Commodores	26	17	1	53
Hyannis Harbor Hawks	19	24	1	39
Cotuit Kettleers	18	25	1	37
Wareham Gatemen	14	28	2	30

CHAMPIONSHIP: Yarmouth-Dennis defeated Falmouth Commodores 2-0 in best-of-three championship series.

TOP 30 PROSPECTS: 1. Walker Buehler, rhp, Yarmouth-Dennis (Jr., Vanderbilt). **2.** Kyle Cody, rhp, Wareham (Jr., Kentucky). **3.** Cody Ponce, rhp, Brewster (Jr., Cal Poly Pomona). **4.** Gio Brusa, of, Brewster (Jr., Pacific). **5.** Ian Happ, of, Harwich (Jr., Cincinnati). **6.** Phil Bickford, rhp, Yarmouth-Dennis (So., CC of Southern Nevada). **7.** Marc Brakeman, rhp, Hyannis (Jr., Stanford). **8.** Richie Martin, ss, Bourne (Jr., Florida). **9.** Kevin Newman, ss, Falmouth (Jr., Arizona). **10.** C.J Hinojosa, ss, Harwich (Jr., Texas). **11.** Alex Young, lhp, Falmouth (Jr., Texas Christian). **12.** Steven Duggar, of, Falmouth (Jr., Clemson). **13.** Chris Shaw, of/1b, Chatham (Jr., Boston College). **14.** Kyle Twomey, lhp, Orleans (Jr., Southern California). **15.** Eric Hanhold, rhp, Orleans (Jr., Florida). **16.** Mikey White, ss, Brewster (Jr., Alabama). **17.** Garrett Cleavinger, lhp, Falmouth (Jr., Oregon). **18.** Joe McCarthy, of, Harwich (Jr., Virginia). **19.** Kevin Duchene, lhp, Yarmouth-Dennis (Jr., Illinois). **20.** Zack Erwin, lhp, Harwich (Jr., Clemson). **21.** Josh Sborz, rhp, Orleans (Jr., Virginia). **22.** Kal Simmons, ss, Chatham (Jr., Kennesaw State). **23.** Kyri Washington, of, Wareham (Jr., Longwood). **24.** Garrett Williams, lhp, Chatham (So., Oklahoma State). **25.** Justin Jacome, lhp, Yarmouth-Dennis (Jr., UC Santa Barbara). **26.** Kolton Mahoney, rhp, Orleans (Jr., Brigham Young). **27.** Ryan Perez, lhp/rhp, Hyannis (Jr., Judson, Ill.). **28.** Rhett Wiseman, of, Cotuit (Jr., Vanderbilt). **29.** David Thompson, 1b/3b, Orleans (Jr., Miami). **30.** Andrew Stevenson, of, Yarmouth-Dennis (Jr., Louisiana State).

INDIVIDUAL BATTING LEADERS

	AVG	AB	R	H	2B	3B	HR	RBI	SB
Kevin Newman, Falmouth	.380	121	20	46	7	0	1	20	10
Richard Martin, Bourne	.364	162	36	59	6	1	3	20	17
Mark Laird, Bourne	.358	137	23	49	4	2	1	22	17
Billy Fleming, Bourne	.357	112	18	40	7	0	0	18	1
Jake Madsen, Falmouth	.346	107	23	37	9	0	2	17	1
Donnie Dewees, Hyannis	.340	150	31	51	9	1	3	20	19
David Thompson, Orleans	.331	163	27	54	10	0	4	29	2
Steven Duggar, Falmouth	.329	161	32	53	6	0	0	11	15
Ian Happ, Harwich	.329	149	25	49	12	1	4	26	8
Conner Hale, Falmouth	.327	171	17	56	12	1	4	38	0
Andrew Stevenson, Y-D	.327	168	30	55	9	1	1	16	21

INDIVIDUAL PITCHING LEADERS

	W	L	ERA	SV	IP	H	BB	SO
Adam Whitt, Cotuit	5	0	1.00	4	36	19	12	34
Justin Jacome, Y-D	5	1	1.66	0	38	40	8	28
Zack Erwin, Harwich	2	2	1.80	0	40	34	8	32
Michael Boyle, Harwich	3	1	1.85	0	39	29	10	24
Kolton Mahoney, Orleans	3	2	1.93	1	37	27	12	47
Matt Hall, Falmouth	3	1	2.11	0	43	41	10	47
Kyle Twomey, Orleans	2	0	2.23	0	40	36	10	39
Andrew Naderer, Brewster	3	1	2.27	2	36	34	8	27
Kevin McCanna, Falmouth	6	2	2.47	0	47	41	13	28

BOURNE

BATTING	AVG	AB	R	H	2B	3B	HR	RBI	SB
Richard Martin	.364	162	36	59	6	1	3	20	17
Mark Laird	.358	137	23	49	4	2	1	22	17

Billy Fleming	.357	112	18	40	7	0	0	18	1
Logan Ratledge	.308	13	0	4	1	0	0	1	1
Brett Sullivan	.281	146	22	41	8	3	1	17	1
Blake Davey	.270	148	30	40	10	2	5	21	1
Blake Allemand	.268	123	19	33	9	1	0	15	6
Zander Wiel	.265	83	10	22	4	0	5	20	1
Harrison Bader	.234	141	20	33	4	0	3	16	8
Jason Delay	.226	31	2	7	1	0	0	4	0
Gavin Collins	.223	112	10	25	10	0	1	11	0
Stephen Wrenn	.198	96	12	19	2	0	0	6	5
Brian Serven	.172	58	5	10	2	0	1	9	0
Sutton Whiting	.123	57	10	7	1	0	0	7	4
Ryan Howard	.100	20	0	2	1	0	0	1	0

PITCHING	W	L	ERA	G	SV	IP	H	BB	SO
Joey Strain	1	0	0.53	15	6	17	16	1	18
John Gorman	0	1	2.04	13	4	18	12	7	21
Travis Bergen	3	2	2.25	6	0	32	32	4	36
Dylan Hecht	0	0	2.35	6	0	8	7	2	11
Ryan Kellogg	4	2	2.63	7	0	41	41	3	37
Lucas Laster	0	0	2.91	13	1	22	23	6	20
Joseph Kuzia	0	0	3.00	2	0	3	3	0	0
Dylan Nelson	1	2	3.81	13	0	26	29	10	24
Josh Rogers	2	1	3.96	5	0	25	31	11	11
Thomas Hatch	0	1	4.00	4	0	9	11	4	4
Andrew Sopko	3	1	4.26	8	0	32	42	6	36
Eric Nyquist	2	2	4.45	10	0	28	30	9	18
Jimmy Herget	2	2	4.64	7	0	33	33	10	37
Jacob Sparger	1	0	4.77	11	0	17	21	4	8
Samuel Kmiec	3	1	4.79	6	0	26	38	1	25
Brett Morales	2	0	5.56	10	0	23	35	9	16
Brad Raley	1	0	7.11	5	0	6	6	1	5

BREWSTER

BATTING	AVG	AB	R	H	2B	3B	HR	RBI	SB
Jackson Glines	.421	19	1	8	1	0	0	2	0
Andrew Lee	.333	63	10	21	4	0	1	13	0
Travis Maezes	.329	73	14	24	3	0	1	6	2
Gio Brusa	.322	121	16	39	3	3	6	20	3
Kyle Overstreet	.322	87	11	28	4	0	0	8	0
Scott Kingery	.312	125	14	39	5	1	2	12	5
Mikey White	.310	87	14	27	6	0	3	11	1
Justin Hazard	.308	13	2	4	2	0	0	1	0
Bradon Bishop	.270	89	15	24	1	0	1	7	2
Wade Wass	.268	41	6	11	2	0	3	18	2
Josh Vidales	.261	69	8	18	2	0	0	3	3
Zach Gibbons	.259	81	15	21	2	0	3	18	1
Levi MaVorhis	.250	4	0	1	0	0	0	0	0
Dalton DiNatale	.235	17	4	4	0	0	0	3	1
Luke Lowery	.231	78	9	18	2	0	5	14	1
Kevin Martir	.225	71	6	16	1	0	1	2	2
John Sansone	.223	103	18	23	4	2	2	11	4
Danny De La Calle	.221	68	5	15	1	0	0	4	0
Justin Montemayor	.217	83	6	18	2	0	0	3	1
Georgie Salem	.209	86	11	18	0	1	0	8	5
LaMonte Wade	.145	55	10	8	0	0	1	6	4

PITCHING	W	L	ERA	G	SV	IP	H	BB	SO
Ryan Mason	0	0	0.00	6	0	13	13	0	12
Ryan McCormick	2	0	0.93	3	0	10	6	3	4
Danny De La Calle	0	0	1.54	8	0	12	10	6	6
Pat Ruotolo	1	1	2.25	16	3	24	16	11	26
Andrew Naderer	3	1	2.27	10	2	36	34	8	27
Cody Ponce	4	1	2.83	8	1	35	33	11	32
Doug Willey	0	0	2.92	7	0	12	17	4	8
Tyger Talley	1	1	3.21	4	1	14	14	3	7
Evan Hill	0	3	3.46	11	4	26	31	7	16
Joey McCarthy	1	3	4.13	10	0	28	25	14	21
Garrett Mundell	1	2	4.21	10	0	41	42	12	27
Andrew Lee	2	3	4.22	7	0	32	26	18	19
Levi MaVorhis	0	2	4.77	12	0	34	40	7	28

	W	L	ERA	G	SV	IP	H	BB	SO
Zach Morris	0	2	5.32	12	0	24	31	14	18
Kenneth Oakley	2	4	7.00	8	0	27	38	16	26
Dylan Silva	0	2	25.07	3	0	5	13	5	4

CHATHAM

BATTING	AVG	AB	R	H	2B	3B	HR	RBI	SB
Matthew Peters	.500	10	3	5	0	0	0	0	0
Blake Butera	.326	43	5	14	3	0	0	5	1
Ty Moore	.323	158	25	51	7	1	2	20	8
AJ Murray	.317	161	32	51	6	0	6	32	5
Nick Collins	.310	87	12	27	1	0	1	13	0
Nicholas Sciortino	.300	10	0	3	0	0	0	2	0
Chris Shaw	.275	167	24	46	10	0	8	34	1
Kal Simmons	.275	102	15	28	2	0	1	7	5
Garrett Hampson	.268	56	10	15	0	0	0	4	1
Jake Fraley	.265	98	11	26	2	1	0	7	11
Mitch Gunsolus	.244	90	10	22	3	0	1	5	3
Robert Baldwin	.228	57	4	13	2	0	0	5	0
Landon Lassiter	.226	53	10	12	1	0	0	4	0
Landon Cray	.214	117	17	25	6	0	0	13	8
Patrick Mazeika	.207	82	17	17	3	0	2	10	1
Bryant Burleson	.177	62	4	11	0	0	0	4	0
Kevin Fagan	.150	60	6	9	2	0	0	6	1
Justin Jones	.108	37	2	4	0	1	1	6	0
Joseph Cronin	.100	10	0	1	0	0	1	0	0

PITCHING	W	L	ERA	G	SV	IP	H	BB	SO
Jordan Hillyer	5	0	1.60	7	1	34	26	12	32
Jerry Keel	1	0	2.31	5	0	12	7	3	4
Paul Covelle	0	0	3.09	9	0	12	10	10	10
Andrew Chin	2	1	3.49	6	0	28	27	14	20
Zack Burdi	1	1	3.50	12	1	18	18	8	18
Lou Distasio	1	1	4.00	12	0	18	18	3	12
Zac Gallen	0	5	4.35	7	0	29	29	11	16
Bryan Goossens	0	1	4.36	11	0	21	35	6	19
Max Tishman	2	4	4.67	10	0	35	51	8	19
Garrett Williams	1	3	4.74	10	0	25	31	14	23
Kyle Davis	2	1	5.16	17	5	30	30	14	33
Jeff Gelinas	0	2	5.24	13	0	22	29	11	19
Charlie Dant	2	2	5.48	7	0	23	25	9	22
P.J. Conlon	0	3	6.03	12	0	34	47	7	35
Jeff Burke	0	0	6.97	9	0	21	18	18	16
Michael Wallace	0	1	9.72	6	1	8	20	2	2

COTUIT

BATTING	AVG	AB	R	H	2B	3B	HR	RBI	SB
Grant Kay	.538	26	9	14	4	0	2	3	1
DC Arendas	.500	14	3	7	0	0	0	2	2
John Norwood	.324	71	15	23	3	0	3	12	3
Jackson Glines	.320	103	17	33	4	0	1	18	5
Richard Carthon	.304	23	1	7	0	0	0	0	3
Jameson Fisher	.300	130	14	39	6	0	0	9	3
Brendan Hendriks	.298	94	11	28	5	0	1	15	1
Logan Taylor	.296	162	17	48	3	1	5	20	7
Austin Byler	.286	42	8	12	1	0	4	7	2
Jake Fincher	.277	119	14	33	4	2	0	12	4
Kyle Holder	.274	73	6	20	2	0	0	3	0
Ian Rice	.270	63	12	17	5	0	2	11	1
Rhett Wiseman	.261	69	11	18	2	1	1	12	5
Jordan Ebert	.260	50	5	13	4	0	1	7	0
Jeremy Taylor	.239	67	8	16	2	0	0	6	4
Tres Barrera	.205	73	9	15	3	0	4	12	0
Drew Jackson	.196	107	16	21	1	0	1	7	6
Ashton Perritt	.176	17	3	3	1	0	0	1	0
Caleb Whalen	.170	47	9	8	0	1	0	2	8
Casey Schroeder	.107	28	4	3	0	0	1	2	1
Collin Shaw	.083	12	2	1	0	0	0	1	0

PITCHING	W	L	ERA	G	SV	IP	H	BB	SO
Adam Whitt	5	0	1.00	19	4	36	19	12	34
Jeff Kinley	2	0	1.41	16	3	32	25	10	19
Ashton Perritt	1	1	2.30	7	0	16	10	4	16
A.J. Minter	0	0	2.35	4	1	8	5	2	11

Bailey Clark	0	0	2.70	5	0	7	5	4	4
Mason Klotz	0	1	3.14	8	0	14	14	8	8
Nick Eicholtz	0	1	3.75	8	0	24	21	21	17
Gabe Berman	0	1	4.50	7	1	10	13	3	6
Vincent Fiori	4	2	4.55	8	0	30	33	11	24
Jackson McClelland	1	2	4.79	9	0	21	27	8	14
Luke Leftwich	1	2	4.88	13	0	28	26	16	17
Trey Wingenter	2	2	5.13	11	0	33	38	21	26
Sean Beckman	0	1	5.79	3	0	5	6	2	3
Blake Stevens	0	1	6.00	2	0	6	8	2	8
Travis Duke	0	2	6.08	10	0	13	15	7	8
Grayson Jones	0	1	7.07	7	0	14	12	12	14
Sam Tewes	1	2	7.45	3	0	10	14	1	5
Reagan Bazar	0	0	7.79	13	0	17	22	18	15
Logan James	1	3	7.86	10	0	26	31	22	27
Daniel Lewis	0	1	8.00	4	0	9	8	9	7

FALMOUTH

BATTING	AVG	AB	R	H	2B	3B	HR	RBI	SB
Kevin Newman	.380	121	20	46	7	0	1	20	10
Jake Madsen	.346	107	23	37	9	0	2	17	1
Steven Duggar	.329	161	32	53	6	0	0	11	15
Conner Hale	.327	171	17	56	12	1	4	38	0
Matthew Eureste	.292	120	19	35	6	0	3	13	4
Austin Afenir	.289	90	13	26	6	0	0	16	0
Boomer White	.289	97	14	28	4	1	0	9	2
Leon Byrd Jr.	.250	32	2	8	1	0	0	3	3
Shaun Chase	.250	76	10	19	4	0	5	16	0
Cameron O'Brien	.248	105	18	26	4	1	1	14	2
Evan Ocello	.240	25	5	6	2	0	0	0	1
Sam Gillikin	.235	115	13	27	2	0	1	11	2
Conor Costello	.233	86	10	20	3	1	3	12	0
Tate Matheny	.222	27	3	6	1	0	1	3	1
Trever Morrison	.189	90	15	17	1	1	0	10	2
Nicholas Ramos	.176	74	6	13	2	0	0	11	1
Connor Marabell	.105	19	1	2	1	0	0	2	0

PITCHING	W	L	ERA	G	SV	IP	H	BB	SO
Conor Costello	0	0	0.00	5	1	5	2	3	5
Matthew Eckelman	1	0	0.47	15	5	19	11	1	17
Matt Hollenbeck	1	0	1.35	9	0	13	6	6	14
Taylor Durand	0	0	1.50	5	0	6	2	4	4
Alex Young	3	0	1.50	5	0	30	29	3	28
Matt Hall	3	1	2.11	8	0	43	41	10	47
Kevin McCanna	6	2	2.47	8	0	47	41	13	28
Travis Stout	0	1	2.70	16	2	20	19	7	16
Charles Mulholland	1	5	3.63	9	0	40	42	17	25
Jared Price	0	1	4.12	7	0	20	16	10	19
Garrett Cleavinger	1	0	4.15	12	2	13	11	4	29
Nicholas Cooney	1	0	4.26	12	0	19	14	11	18
Kevin Mooney	2	1	4.86	15	3	17	15	6	19
Kyle Zimmerman	2	1	6.52	13	0	19	31	11	13
Chandler Eden	1	0	6.88	12	0	17	23	13	14
Ryan Moseley	3	1	6.94	8	0	23	19	12	27
Donny Murray	1	2	7.24	10	0	14	20	6	15
Brad Labozzetta	0	2	7.80	6	0	15	18	11	12

HARWICH

BATTING	AVG	AB	R	H	2B	3B	HR	RBI	SB
Ian Happ	.329	149	25	49	12	1	4	26	8
Anthony Hermelyn	.323	99	20	32	3	0	1	10	0
Robert Youngdahl	.321	28	6	9	3	0	0	5	1
Kyle Barrett	.317	120	22	38	3	1	0	6	10
Joe McCarthy	.314	51	10	16	4	0	0	6	4
Danny Zardon	.305	95	17	29	5	0	0	12	2
Craig Aikin	.279	68	11	19	0	0	1	13	3
Angelo Amendolare	.278	108	13	30	3	0	0	13	15
Matt Gonzalez	.278	126	18	35	4	0	4	22	4
C.J. Hinojosa	.264	87	13	23	2	1	3	20	5
Brendon Sanger	.260	100	10	26	8	0	1	14	1
Sal Annunziata	.258	120	22	31	6	0	5	21	0
Kenny Towns	.250	52	7	13	2	0	0	4	2

	AVG	AB	R	H	2B	3B	HR	RBI	SB
Alex Perez	.211	19	4	4	1	0	0	2	2
Skye Bolt	.205	112	16	23	4	0	0	11	11
Cavan Biggio	.203	64	12	13	1	0	1	5	0
Matt Winn	.181	72	8	13	2	0	0	4	0

PITCHING	W	L	ERA	G	SV	IP	H	BB	SO
Jacob Evans	2	0	0.32	11	1	28	16	5	27
Ronnie Glenn	0	1	1.24	13	1	29	17	16	25
Robby Kalaf	3	0	1.40	9	1	26	18	6	25
Johnathan Frebis	2	0	1.44	11	3	31	24	8	24
Zack Erwin	2	2	1.80	7	0	40	34	8	32
Michael Boyle	3	1	1.85	8	0	39	29	10	24
Jared Poche	2	1	2.70	4	0	20	20	5	19
Jason Inghram	1	1	3.10	4	0	20	24	2	18
Seth McGarry	0	1	3.72	13	2	19	14	7	21
James Mulry	3	0	3.89	8	0	42	46	15	35
Jon Harris	4	2	4.36	8	0	33	41	15	29
Gavin Pittore	1	1	6.10	8	0	21	18	10	12
Jake Drossner	1	2	6.62	6	0	18	29	8	10
Ray Castillo	0	4	7.71	9	1	12	17	4	9

HYANNIS

BATTING	AVG	AB	R	H	2B	3B	HR	RBI	SB
John La Prise	.407	81	9	33	1	0	0	11	5
Donnie Dewees Jr.	.340	150	31	51	9	1	3	20	19
Matthew Britton	.303	33	3	10	1	0	0	4	2
Sam Haggerty	.261	138	21	36	6	0	1	11	12
Daniel Kihle	.261	142	32	37	8	0	5	28	12
Carl Wise	.260	127	20	33	4	1	6	22	5
Dylan Bosheers	.254	142	14	36	8	0	1	14	6
Austin Slater	.247	77	7	19	4	2	0	13	8
Bobby Melley	.231	104	8	24	7	0	0	20	3
Cam Gibson	.210	62	9	13	2	0	0	3	5
Kyle Survance	.209	110	21	23	1	0	1	5	14
Joe Purritano	.200	10	1	2	1	0	0	1	1
David Houser	.169	65	7	11	4	0	0	10	2
Ben DeLuzio	.163	98	10	16	4	1	1	6	9
Arden Pabst	.138	65	7	9	0	0	0	2	1
Jarret DeHart	.133	30	2	4	1	0	0	3	1

PITCHING	W	L	ERA	G	SV	IP	H	BB	SO
Ryan Perez	0	1	1.98	13	1	27	30	13	39
Matt Denny	0	0	2.00	7	2	18	15	3	19
Marc Brakeman	3	1	2.18	9	1	33	29	7	47
Sarkis Ohanian	1	0	2.35	3	0	8	8	4	8
Nick Bates	0	0	2.70	7	0	17	17	4	22
Tate Scioneaux	4	2	2.78	8	0	45	42	12	29
Jordan Minch	2	1	2.79	5	0	19	18	9	20
Shaefer Shepard	1	0	3.38	2	0	8	9	4	3
Lance Thonvold	1	1	3.86	11	5	26	22	11	23
Nick Deeg	1	3	3.89	8	0	37	45	6	18
Blake Hickman	3	3	4.29	8	0	36	38	16	31
Matthew Margaritonda	0	1	5.19	4	1	9	15	3	8
Chris Mourelle	0	0	5.68	4	0	6	10	1	6
Ian Gibaut	1	2	5.79	14	2	14	11	6	19
Peter Fairbanks	0	4	6.42	9	0	34	52	10	11
Chris Lanham	1	0	6.52	5	0	10	13	3	4
Alec Byrd	0	1	6.75	9	0	15	17	9	11
Joseph Shaw	1	2	12.41	6	0	12	24	9	6

ORLEANS

BATTING	AVG	AB	R	H	2B	3B	HR	RBI	SB
David Thompson	.331	163	27	54	10	0	4	29	2
Timmy Robinson	.308	39	5	12	3	1	2	7	1
Edwin Rios	.303	89	17	27	5	1	4	20	1
David Fletcher	.299	154	24	46	4	0	0	17	7
Geoff DeGroot	.291	110	19	32	1	0	0	8	4
Korey Dunbar	.280	25	3	7	1	0	0	1	0
Christin Stewart	.276	29	4	8	1	0	2	5	0
Mitchell Tolman	.272	114	24	31	7	0	1	9	4
Johnny Sewald	.265	136	19	36	2	0	2	11	13
Dathan Prewett	.250	16	1	4	0	0	0	1	1
RJ Ybarra	.246	138	15	34	3	0	3	19	0

	AVG	AB	R	H	2B	3B	HR	RBI	SB
Bobby Dalbec	.228	92	14	21	3	0	5	18	0
Taylor Ward	.222	18	2	4	1	0	1	2	0
Cole Peragine	.221	122	11	27	6	0	0	6	0
Brett Lang	.212	52	8	11	1	0	0	7	0
Brett Stephens	.192	78	8	15	1	0	0	7	3
Jerry McClanahan	.184	38	5	7	0	0	0	1	1
Jacob Cronenworth	.132	38	1	5	0	0	0	0	1

PITCHING	W	L	ERA	G	SV	IP	H	BB	SO
Hayden Stone	1	1	0.82	8	0	11	8	4	13
Bobby Dalbec	1	0	1.32	11	1	14	13	4	16
Reilly Hovis	1	1	1.54	15	2	23	16	8	33
Kyle Wilcox	0	1	1.59	5	0	6	1	7	7
Kolton Mahoney	3	2	1.93	7	1	37	27	12	47
Tyler Honahan	0	1	2.19	4	0	12	8	8	8
Kyle Twomey	2	0	2.23	14	0	40	36	10	39
Cody Moffett	0	0	2.25	13	0	24	21	2	16
Nathan Bannister	4	1	2.37	7	0	30	21	5	21
Trent Thornton	3	2	2.79	6	0	29	23	5	25
Jacob Cronenworth	1	2	3.04	15	5	24	17	8	27
Brett Lilek	0	0	3.12	3	0	9	3	6	9
Bobby Poyner	3	0	3.16	10	0	26	24	2	19
Eric Hanhold	1	2	3.42	6	0	24	33	6	24
Sam Moore	2	1	3.68	11	1	15	14	8	5
Josh Sborz	1	1	4.50	5	0	16	18	4	13
Trevor Megill	0	1	4.77	4	0	6	10	4	6
Tommy Bergjans	0	1	5.51	9	0	16	16	11	14
Gianni Zayas	0	1	5.79	2	0	5	6	2	4
Ryne Combs	1	0	9.22	12	1	14	21	14	9

WAREHAM

BATTING	AVG	AB	R	H	2B	3B	HR	RBI	SB
Chris Chinea	.310	87	7	27	4	0	0	18	0
Keaton Aldridge	.293	92	8	27	1	0	1	10	1
Andrew Knizner	.281	57	4	16	3	0	0	10	1
Jake Little	.277	112	19	31	3	1	4	10	3
Kramer Robertson	.277	112	18	31	2	0	1	4	3
John Bormann	.255	51	9	13	3	0	0	5	0
Anderson Miller	.253	79	5	20	1	0	0	3	4
Charlie Warren	.252	111	11	28	1	0	0	1	7
Corey Ray	.250	92	6	23	4	0	1	8	2
Willie Calhoun	.245	139	22	34	12	0	0	12	2
Nick Halamandaris	.233	116	9	27	6	1	1	12	0
Errol Robinson	.231	13	2	3	0	0	0	1	3
Danny Rosenbaum	.224	67	6	15	5	1	0	5	1
Blake Lacey	.214	103	6	22	8	0	0	9	1
Kyri Washington	.204	93	10	19	1	1	1	10	6
Jose Cuas	.198	81	6	16	2	0	0	6	2
Justin Brock	.167	12	1	2	0	0	0	2	0
Blair Beck	.111	18	2	2	1	0	1	1	0
Preston Palmeiro	.091	11	1	1	0	0	0	0	0

PITCHING	W	L	ERA	G	SV	IP	H	BB	SO
Drew Harrington	1	2	1.71	7	0	21	17	6	19
Sean Adler	1	1	1.80	4	1	20	13	5	18
Anthony Kay	2	2	2.75	15	1	39	39	17	24
Kyle Cody	2	3	2.80	8	0	35	33	11	33
Scott Effross	0	3	3.30	14	3	30	24	13	27
Ryan Olson	1	3	3.66	12	1	39	44	15	37
Brock Hartson	2	2	4.05	5	0	27	21	10	33
Willie Kuhl	0	0	4.15	10	0	17	14	9	15
Jason Richman	2	2	4.50	11	1	12	15	6	10
Jake Kalish	0	3	4.83	6	0	32	41	10	29
Keaton Aldridge	0	1	5.06	6	1	5	2	3	5
Liam OSullivan	1	0	5.55	12	0	37	38	9	24
Nick Fuller	1	1	5.84	4	0	12	13	5	8
Andrew Zapata	1	2	5.84	13	0	12	20	13	13
Brock Downey	0	2	6.62	6	0	18	24	5	7
Ryan Williamson	0	1	9.31	6	0	10	14	2	9

YARMOUTH-DENNIS

BATTING	AVG	AB	R	H	2B	3B	HR	RBI	SB
Hunter Cole	.353	85	11	30	6	0	4	25	3
Andrew Stevenson	.327	168	30	55	9	1	1	16	21
Jordan Tarsovich	.322	152	26	49	4	0	3	21	11
Robert Fonseca	.315	127	19	40	8	0	4	20	1
Marcus Mastrobuoni	.313	16	2	5	1	0	0	1	0
Timothy Wharton	.310	29	1	9	1	0	1	8	0
Jesse Jenner	.304	69	13	21	3	0	2	11	1
Derek Atkinson	.282	39	6	11	1	0	0	1	0
Nico Giarratano	.279	86	9	24	3	0	0	8	0
Josh Lester	.279	111	16	31	4	0	0	14	4
A.J. Simcox	.246	118	8	29	2	0	0	11	3
Vincent Jackson	.244	78	9	19	1	0	1	8	2
Michael Foster	.205	44	5	9	3	1	0	4	0
Brennon Lund	.195	77	12	15	2	0	0	6	1
Michael Donadio	.182	11	0	2	1	0	0	0	0
Ramsey Romano	.182	33	2	6	0	0	0	2	0
Donnie Walton	.179	56	8	10	1	0	0	3	1
Jason Goldstein	.163	49	7	8	4	0	0	8	0
Joey Armstrong	.157	51	6	8	1	0	0	1	0
Ryan Hissey	.111	27	3	3	0	0	1	1	0

PITCHING	W	L	ERA	G	SV	IP	H	BB	SO
Walker Buehler	2	0	1.35	3	0	13	16	3	11
Justin Jacome	5	1	1.66	8	0	38	40	8	28
William Strode	1	0	1.86	13	1	19	10	7	23
Tyler Jay	0	0	1.93	3	1	5	4	1	4
Phil Bickford	1	1	2.25	14	8	20	17	5	33
Cody Poteet	4	0	3.10	7	0	41	36	11	43
Kevin Duchene	3	3	3.38	8	0	43	39	12	37
Nicholas Kozlowski	1	0	3.38	8	0	8	5	4	6
Gregory Ostner	0	0	3.38	1	0	5	3	0	4
Michael Murray	1	6	3.53	8	0	36	35	11	24
Dimitri Kourtis	1	1	3.80	15	5	21	22	6	23
Josh Staumont	2	2	3.86	8	0	21	19	19	19
Josh Pierce	1	1	3.93	14	0	18	22	6	12
Doug Willey	0	0	4.26	7	0	13	12	5	13
Zac Favre	0	0	5.16	13	0	23	23	12	19
Drake Owenby	0	2	5.52	15	0	15	17	11	12
Parker Bugg	1	0	8.66	12	0	18	31	4	15
Bryan Bonnell	1	2	9.42	4	0	14	17	7	12

ALASKA LEAGUE

	League			Overall		
American League	W	L	PCT	W	L	PCT
Alaska Goldpanners	21	8	.724	33	9	.786
Anchorage Bucs	18	14	.563	26	18	.591
Peninsula Oilers	11	22	.333	20	25	.447
National League	W	L	PCT	W	L	PCT
Mat-Su Miners	21	12	.636	26	14	.646
Anchorage Glacier Pilots	17	18	.486	20	22	.476
Chugiak Chinooks	9	23	.281	13	25	.342

CHAMPIONSHIP: Alaska Goldpanners defeated the Mat-Su Miners 2-0 in best-of-three series.
TOP 10 PROSPECTS: 1. Tyler Stubblefield, lhp, Mat-Su (So., Texas A&M). **2.** Kyle Serrano, rhp, Mat-Su (So., Tennessee). **3.** Scott Hurst, of, Alaska Goldpanners (Fr., Cal State Fullerton). **4.** Riley Adams, c, Anchorage Glacier Pilots (Fr., San Diego). **5.** Ryan Hendrix, rhp, Mat-Su (So., Texas A&M). **6.** Mylz Jones, ss/3b, Peninsula (Jr., Cal State Bakersfield). **7.** Cameron Frost, of, Mat-Su (So., Washington State). **8.** Josh Meyer, c, Mat-Su (So., Grand Canyon). **9.** Cody Nulph, ss, Alaska Goldpanners (Jr., Auburn). **10.** Devon Stewart, rhp, Anchorage Bucs (Sr., Canisius).

INDIVIDUAL BATTING LEADERS

	AVG	AB	R	H	2B	3B	HR	RBI	SB
Scott Hurst, Alaska	.429	91	30	39	4	1	1	15	5
Jacob Hayes, Alaska	.378	135	48	51	8	4	9	42	8
Cameron Newell, Mat-Su	.353	116	22	41	8	0	7	38	9
Andy Crowley, Bucs	.345	139	27	48	16	3	2	21	4
Mark Krueger, Bucs	.338	139	23	47	10	4	5	31	2

Dylan Butler, Bucs	.338	133	26	45	6	0	4	19	8
Cameron Frost, Matsu	.327	150	39	49	12	7	5	25	6
Cade Reiten, Bucs	.325	126	21	41	11	0	3	20	2
Cody Nulph, Alaska	.322	143	34	46	10	1	9	38	2
Vahn Bozoian, Alaska	.308	130	27	40	10	0	9	38	2
Mylz Jones, Peninsula	.307	140	13	43	11	1	2	21	13
Tanner Pinkston, Alaska	.307	153	35	47	7	1	4	31	3

INDIVIDUAL PITCHING LEADERS

	W	L	ERA	G	SV	IP	H	BB	SO
Tyler Stubblefield, Matsu	5	0	1.06	7	0	43	30	9	45
Henri Faucheux, Pilots	3	2	1.73	8	0	36	28	12	28
Dallas DeVrieze, Peninsula	1	1	1.76	8	0	46	38	14	34
Trevor Lacosse, Bucs	3	0	1.82	10	0	40	29	14	49
Bret Marks, Bucs	2	2	1.90	12	0	43	32	15	49
Ryan Hendrix, Matsu	3	1	3.07	10	0	44	30	20	43
Kyle McDorman, Chugiak	3	3	3.29	9	0	52	43	14	26
Mike Benson, Alaska	4	0	3.32	9	0	43	34	13	42
Jimmy Nesselt, Peninsula	3	3	3.53	10	0	43	42	6	36
Jace Puckett, Alaska	6	0	3.74	10	0	43	39	15	37
Daniel Przeniczny, Chugiak	2	5	3.78	11	0	48	50	29	35

ATLANTIC COLLEGIATE LEAGUE

	W	L	PCT	GB
Allentown Railers	28	12	.700	—
Trenton Generals	25	14	.638	2 ½
South Jersey Giants	24	16	.600	4
Staten Island Tide	21	17	.551	6
Quakertown Blazers	19	21	.475	9
North Jersey Eagles	15	24	.385	12 ½
Lehigh Valley Catz	13	25	.342	14
Jersey Pilots	11	27	.289	16

CHAMPIONSHIP: Trenton Generals defeated Staten Island Tide in championship game.
TOP 10 PROSPECTS: 1. C.J. Moore, of, Staten Island (Fr., Lamar). **2.** Matt Swarmer, rhp, Allentown (Jr., Kutztown, Pa.). **3.** Anthony Pacillo, lhp, North Jersey (So., Seton Hall). **4.** David Moyer, 1b/rhp, Lehigh Valley (Fr., St. John's). **5.** Andrew Schorr, lhp, South Jersey (Jr., Coastal Carolina). **6.** Brandon Kulp, rhp, Quakertown (Jr., Lehigh). **7.** Mike Garzillo, 2b, Lehigh Valley (Jr., Lehigh). **8.** Xavier Hammond, lhp, Allentown (Sr., Bucknell). **9.** Matt Festa, rhp, Staten Island (Jr., East Stroudsburg, Pa.). **10.** Shaine Hughes, 3b, South Jersey (So., Monmouth).

INDIVIDUAL BATTING LEADERS

	AVG	AB	R	H	2B	3B	HR	RBI	SB
Mike Garzillo, Lehigh Valley	.417	120	20	50	7	1	5	16	12
Jacen Nalesnik, Allentown	.398	108	25	43	12	0	1	23	7
Patrick Donnelly, Quakertown	.385	122	16	47	9	3	1	30	5
Shane Hughes, South Jersey	.361	133	21	48	13	2	2	24	1
Ian Glassman, Jersey	.359	131	20	47	7	1	2	22	4
Anthony Renz, Allentown	.356	135	29	48	12	2	4	41	0
Chris Melillo, Quakertown	.342	117	15	40	11	0	2	26	2
Kyle Cullen, North Jersey	.336	119	16	40	3	1	5	21	13
Tyle Kirkpatrick, Quakertown	.333	102	21	34	2	0	2	18	8
Kyle Grimm, North Jersey	.325	126	16	41	14	0	0	17	4

INDIVIDUAL PITCHING LEADERS

	W	L	ERA	G	SV	IP	H	BB	SO
Paul Balestrieri, Trenton	5	0	0.96	9	0	38	23	14	22
John Geffre, Quakertown	4	2	1.53	6	0	35	34	4	11
Delio Coutinho Jr., SI	3	1	1.57	8	0	46	31	24	60
Sean Keenan, Trenton	4	2	2.30	10	0	43	40	8	37
Matthew Kostalos, SI	1	2	2.50	7	1	36	38	12	32
Anthony Pacillo, North Jersey	3	3	2.51	9	0	47	46	12	36
Matthew Festa, Staten Island	5	0	2.63	7	0	51	34	16	44
Matthew Swarmer, Allentown	6	3	2.64	9	0	58	43	13	68
Michael Macchia, SI	5	3	2.72	10	0	46	48	7	24
Adam Schreck, Trenton	1	1	2.73	10	0	36	32	13	23

CAL RIPKEN COLLEGIATE LEAGUE

	W	L	PCT	GB
Bethesda Big Train	31	9	.775	—
Baltimore Redbirds	25	15	.625	6
Rockville Express	24	16	.600	7
Gaithersburg Giants	23	17	.575	8
Alexandria Aces	23	17	.575	8
Youse's Orioles	18	22	.450	13
Vienna River Dogs	18	22	.450	13
Herndon Braves	17	23	.425	14
D.C. Grays	15	25	.375	16
Baltimore Dodgers	13	27	.325	18
Silver Spring Takoma T Bolts	13	27	.325	18

CHAMPIONSHIP: Baltimore Redbirds defeated Bethesda Big Train in championship game.

TOP 10 PROSPECTS: 1. Brady Bramlett, rhp, Baltimore Redbirds, (R-So., Mississippi). **2.** J.B. Woodman, of, Baltimore Redbirds (So., Mississippi). **3.** Justin Morris, c, Bethesda (Fr., Maryland). **4.** Brandon Lowe, 2b, Bethesda (So., Maryland). **5.** Willie Rios, lhp, Baltimore Redbirds (Fr., Maryland). **6.** Nolan Riggs, rhp, Baltimore Redbirds (SIGNED: Giants). **7.** Nick Cieri, c, Baltimore Redbirds (So., Maryland). **8.** Garrett Pearson, rhp, Silver Spring-Takoma (Fr., Virginia Commonwealth). **9.** Justin Dunn, rhp, Baltimore Redbirds (So., Boston College). **10.** Tanner Anderson, rhp, Youse's Orioles (Sr., Harvard).

INDIVIDUAL BATTING LEADERS

	AVG	AB	R	H	2B	3B	HR	RBI	SB
Webb Bobo, D.C.	.365	115	27	42	9	3	3	20	6
Josh Swirchak, Alexandria	.352	128	24	45	6	7	0	29	5
Justin Morales, Dodgers	.342	120	18	41	6	2	3	23	7
Mac Caples, Redbirds	.336	128	33	43	8	0	3	26	6
Brandon Lowe, Bethesda	.329	82	24	27	4	1	4	29	1
Nick Cieri, Redbirds	.325	114	16	37	7	1	2	18	0
Stephen Alemais, Bethesda	.320	150	28	48	6	0	1	21	26
Brad Elwood, Alexandria	.313	96	22	30	7	0	0	15	2
J.D. Long, Alexandria	.311	106	21	33	5	0	0	5	5
Garrett Hudson, Redbirds	.308	146	26	45	10	1	0	22	10

INDIVIDUAL PITCHING LEADERS

	W	L	ERA	G	SV	IP	H	BB	SO
Andrew Witczak, Alexandria	3	1	0.84	7	1	32	28	9	20
Octavio Rodriguez, Youse's	4	2	1.29	7	0	42	25	14	40
Jake Enterlin, Dodgers	3	1	1.37	8	0	53	31	16	42
Tyler Tobin, Alexandria	3	2	1.40	7	0	39	26	11	26
Mike Bittel, Rockville	2	2	1.62	6	0	33	20	8	38
Aaron McGarity, Redbirds	4	1	1.76	7	0	46	24	8	52
Kit Scheetz, Bethesda	5	1	1.90	7	0	38	29	6	31
Anton Constantino, Rockville	5	2	2.05	8	0	53	36	15	31
Brandon Holsworth, SS-T	3	2	2.16	10	1	42	38	13	20
Brandon Casas, Youse's	2	1	2.19	6	1	37	32	12	22
Tim Davis, Vienna	1	2	2.27	8	0	40	29	12	29

CALIFORNIA COLLEGIATE LEAGUE

North	W	L	PCT	GB
Walnut Creek Crawdads	16	16	.500	—
Neptune Beach Pearl	16	16	.500	—
Pacific Union Capitalists	12	20	.375	4
Menlo Park Legends	12	20	.375	4

Central	W	L	PCT	GB
Santa Barbara Foresters	31	8	.795	—
San Luis Obispo Blues	29	11	.725	2 ½
Conejo Oaks	14	23	.378	16

South	W	L	PCT	GB
Los Angeles Brewers	26	7	.788	—
SoCal Catch	14	19	.424	12
Academy Barons	10	23	.303	16
Santa Paula Halos	9	24	.273	17

CHAMPIONSHIP: Los Angeles Brewers defeated Neptune Beach Pearl in championship.

TOP 10 PROSPECTS: 1. Jon Duplantier, rhp, Santa Barbara (So., Rice).

2. Alec Hansen, rhp, San Luis Obispo (So., Oklahoma). **3.** Jaylin Davis, of, Santa Barbara (Jr., Appalachian State). **4.** Sheldon Neuse, 3b/ss/rhp, San Luis Obispo (So., Oklahoma). **5.** Andrew Lantrip, rhp, Santa Barbara (So., Houston). **6.** Bret Boswell, 3b/ss, Santa Barbara (R-Fr., Texas). **7.** Matt Esparza, rhp, Los Angeles (Jr., UC Irvine). **8.** Dillon Dobson, ss/2b, Santa Barbara (Jr., Appalachian State). **9.** Matt Withrow, rhp, Santa Barbara (Jr., Texas Tech). **10.** Dylan Moore, ss/2b, Los Angeles (Sr., Central Florida).

INDIVIDUAL BATTING LEADERS

	AVG	AB	R	H	2B	3B	HR	RBI	SB
Jon Torres, Los Angeles	.429	63	10	27	3	0	0	5	0
Billy Frederick, Santa Paula	.396	101	16	40	9	1	1	15	3
Ford Stainback, SB	.396	96	20	38	9	2	0	16	10
Cal Stevenson, PUF	.392	74	17	29	2	1	2	13	12
Dylan Moore, Los Angeles	.386	114	30	44	12	0	5	26	7
Granger Studdard, SB	.362	130	29	47	12	5	5	35	6
Philip Caulfield, WC	.357	84	14	30	6	0	0	9	3
Collin Ferguson, SLO	.353	68	9	24	8	1	2	22	1
Louis Payetta, Los Angeles	.352	71	13	25	3	0	0	16	1
Matt MacLaughlin, PUF	.349	86	11	30	2	0	0	6	2

INDIVIDUAL PITCHING LEADERS

	W	L	ERA	G	SV	IP	H	BB	SO
Matt Esparza, Los Angeles	4	0	0.31	6	0	29	15	12	33
Sam Odom, Santa Barbara	2	0	0.75	5	0	24	16	7	15
Zach Fox, Neptune Beach	5	0	1.06	7	0	34	29	4	15
Andrew Vinson, SLO	2	0	1.13	17	4	24	15	5	26
Zach Merciez, SLO	4	0	1.36	12	0	33	25	8	19
Doug Druckenmiller, Academy	1	1	1.38	11	2	33	19	12	31
Jon Duplantier, SB	3	2	1.50	6	0	36	23	13	52
Jon Woodcock, SB	4	0	1.57	5	0	29	15	15	47
Matthew Blais, Menlo Park	0	0	1.78	6	0	30	22	9	37
Cameron Avila-Leeper, PUF	0	0	1.88	7	0	29	17	13	40

COASTAL PLAIN LEAGUE

East	W	L	PCT
Peninsula Pilots	41	15	.732
Edenton Steamers	36	16	.692
Wilson Tobs	27	27	.500
Fayetteville SwampDogs	25	29	.462
Wilmington Sharks	24	30	.444
Morehead City Marlins	19	31	.380
Petersburg Generals	15	40	.273

West	W	L	PCT
Florence RedWolves	36	20	.643
Gastonia Grizzlies	32	22	.593
Forest City Owls	30	25	.545
High Point-Thomasville HiToms	26	28	.481
Asheboro Copperheads	26	29	.473
Columbia Blowfish	26	30	.464
Martinsville Mustangs	18	38	.321

CHAMPIONSHIP: Peninsula Pilots defeated Florence RedWolves 2-1 in best-of-three championship series..

TOP 10 PROSPECTS: 1. Cal Quantrill, rhp, Morehead City (So., Stanford). **2.** Josh Roeder, rhp, Edenton (Sr., Nebraska). **3.** Alex Close, c, Peninsula (So., Liberty). **4.** Taylor Ostrich, of/1b, Peninsula (Sr., Old Dominion). **5.** Jared Cheek, rhp, Gastonia (Sr., Georgia). **6.** Mike Morrison, rhp, Florence (Jr., Coastal Carolina). **7.** J.D. Crowe, c/3b, Columbia (Jr., Francis Marion, S.C.). **8.** Hunter Bryant, 3b, Forest City (Sr., UNC Asheville). **9.** Jon Olczak, rhp, Wilmington (Jr., North Carolina State). **10.** Brandon Vick, lhp, Peninsula (Jr., Longwood).

INDIVIDUAL BATTING LEADERS

	AVG	AB	R	H	2B	3B	HR	RBI	SB
Gene Cone, Florence	.385	161	40	62	18	2	0	25	4
Weston Lawing, Gastonia	.375	176	44	66	15	0	3	28	17
Anthony Marks, Asheboro	.374	155	41	58	11	3	0	19	24
Ryan Raslowsky, Edenton	.369	149	26	55	5	2	0	21	24
J.D. Crowe, Columbia	.368	174	34	64	11	3	2	25	9
P.J. Huggins, Peninsula	.356	160	26	57	7	4	0	28	5
Michael Bozarth, Fayetteville	.356	118	25	42	9	0	1	12	22

Chris Robinson, Gastonia	.354	164	30	58	7	3	0	23	13
Gavin Stupienski, Martinsville	.342	193	32	66	14	2	3	42	3
Jeremy Wolf, Petersburg	.331	175	32	58	21	2	1	33	3

INDIVIDUAL PITCHING LEADERS

	W	L	ERA	G	SV	IP	H	BB	SO
Gunnar Kines, Edenton	6	2	1.26	9	0	50	34	9	56
Travis Burnette, Florence	6	1	1.29	13	0	49	43	18	31
Josh Reagan, Columbia	5	1	1.59	7	0	45	31	12	39
Ryan Otero, Gastonia	6	0	2.17	10	1	46	27	13	33
Nick Nietzel, Forest City	4	3	2.23	12	0	61	42	22	61
Jonathan Olczak, Wilmington	4	2	2.29	10	0	59	41	27	64
Jordy Farthing, Fayetteville	2	5	2.31	10	0	47	51	26	66
Christian Slazinik, Wilson	3	2	2.34	10	0	50	49	17	39
Max Beerman, Martinsville	3	3	2.40	10	1	45	35	17	41
Bennett Schiltz, Fayetteville	4	4	2.56	10	0	46	49	5	30

FLORIDA COLLEGIATE SUMMER LEAGUE

	W	L	PCT	GB
Sanford River Rats	23	13	.639	—
Winter Park Diamond Dawgs	25	17	.595	1
Winter Garden Squeeze	22	18	.550	3
Leesburg Lightning	18	17	.514	4 ½
DeLand Suns	16	23	.410	8 ½
College Park Freedom	9	25	.265	13

CHAMPIONSHIP: Winter Park Diamond Dawgs defeated Sanford River Rats in championship game.

TOP 10 PROSPECTS: 1. Austin Hays, of, DeLand (So., Jacksonville). **2.** Rock Rucker, 1hp/of, Sanford (R-So., Seminole State JC, Fla.). **3.** Chase Williams, rhp, Sanford (R-So., Wichita State). **4.** Casey Schroeder, c, Winter Park (Jr., Coastal Carolina). **5.** Alex Kline, 1hp, Winter Park (So., Nova Southeastern, Fla.). **6.** Josh Greene, of, Winter Park (So., High Point). **7.** Spencer Trayner, rhp, Winter Garden (So., North Carolina). **8.** Alex Deise, 1hp, Winter Park (Jr., Florida State). **9.** Hunter Melton, 1b, Sanford (Jr., Texas A&M). **10.** Damon Haecker, 2b/ss, Winter Garden (So., Auburn).

INDIVIDUAL BATTING LEADERS

	AVG	AB	R	H	2B	3B	HR	RBI	SB
Rock Rucker, Sanford	.424	92	22	39	7	1	3	23	4
Keith Skinner, Sanford	.384	112	19	43	6	0	1	23	0
Austin Hays, DeLand	.349	152	27	53	9	2	4	18	4
Demetrius Sims, Sanford	.344	93	22	32	3	0	0	8	10
Brett Jones, Leesburg	.333	99	21	33	14	0	1	21	13
Hunter Melton, Sanford	.330	115	22	38	10	2	3	33	1
Damon Haecker, WG	.326	138	30	45	8	1	3	18	11
Daniel Portales, WG	.319	138	17	44	5	0	0	24	8
Alex Young, College Park	.318	88	18	28	1	0	0	5	15
Shea Pierce, Leesburg	.314	102	19	32	10	0	2	14	4
Edwin Bonilla, College Park	.308	78	9	24	5	1	2	12	2

INDIVIDUAL PITCHING LEADERS

	W	L	ERA	G	SV	IP	H	BB	SO
Arturo Martoral, Sanford	5	0	1.46	9	1	37	25	8	47
Alexander Kline, Winter Park	4	1	1.69	9	0	43	25	9	51
Chris Fee, WG	3	3	2.34	6	0	35	36	7	21
Austin Glorius, WG	3	1	2.51	10	0	43	43	17	23
Jonny Ortiz, Winter Park	5	1	2.54	9	0	46	35	19	26
Corey Tufts, WG	1	4	2.83	7	0	35	20	11	39
Brett Porter, DeLand	2	3	2.93	10	1	40	40	13	32
Alexander Smith, Sanford	6	0	2.98	9	0	39	23	16	38
Devin Raftery, Winter Park	6	0	3.00	9	0	48	35	11	61
Brandon Caples, Leesburg	5	4	3.00	11	0	42	59	14	14
Brett Jones, Leesburg	3	1	3.00	8	0	36	41	14	32

FUTURES COLLEGIATE LEAGUE

East	W	L	PCT	GB
Martha's Vineyard Sharks	30	23	.566	—
Brockton Rox	30	25	.545	1
North Shore Navigators	26	29	.473	5

Seacoast Mavericks	24	29	.453	6
Old Orchard Beach Raging Tide	19	34	.358	11

West	W	L	PCT	GB
Worcester Bravehearts	32	22	.593	—
Torrington Titans	28	25	.528	3 ½
Nashua Silver Knights	28	26	.519	4
Pittsfield Suns	26	27	.491	5 ½
Wachusett Dirt Dawgs	26	29	.473	6 ½

CHAMPIONSHIP: Worcester Bravehearts defeated Martha's Vineyard Sharks in championship game.

TOP 10 PROSPECTS: 1. Will Toffey, 3b, Martha's Vineyard (Fr., Vanderbilt). **2.** Luke Bonfield, of, Martha's Vineyard (Fr., Arkansas). **3.** Mike Gibbons, rhp, Torrington (SIGNED: Mets). **4.** Joe Freiday, c, Brockton (Fr., Virginia Tech). **5.** Nick Fuller, 1hp, Martha's Vineyard (SIGNED: Marlins). **6.** Mike Odenwaelder, of, Torrington (Jr., Amherst, Mass.). **7.** James Vernon, rhp, Seacoast (Jr., North Carolina Central). **8.** Iam Strom, 1hp/of, Worcester (So., Massachusetts-Lowell). **9.** Carson Helms, of, Nashua (R-Jr., Southern New Hampshire). **10.** John Mayer, c, Martha's Vineyard (Jr., Bucknell).

INDIVIDUAL BATTING LEADERS

	AVG	AB	R	H	2B	3B	HR	RBI	SB
Mike Odenwaelder, Torrington	.370	181	30	67	16	1	7	49	20
Jack St. Clair, Torrington	.362	188	45	68	10	1	2	24	17
Brian Campbell, MV	.352	162	33	57	11	0	4	33	12
Michael Mastroberti, Seacoast	.348	132	24	46	5	2	2	15	12
Ryan Kelly, MV	.336	149	43	50	9	1	6	16	17
Joe Breen, Wachusett	.324	179	34	58	15	2	9	31	2
Will Toffey, MV	.322	149	47	48	11	0	7	30	11
Martin Tavares, Seacoast	.322	146	21	47	12	0	3	21	8
Langston Calhoun, Torrington	.320	147	24	47	9	0	2	30	5
Nick Johnson, Brockton	.319	160	20	51	5	0	2	16	4

INDIVIDUAL PITCHING LEADERS

	W	L	ERA	G	SV	IP	H	BB	SO
Matt Quintana, MV	6	1	1.29	9	0	56	37	6	
65 Jamin McCann, Pittsfield	7	0	1.54	9	0	58	40	20	32
Simon Mathews, Brockton	7	0	1.66	11	0	60	48	8	37
Soren Hanson, MV	3	1	2.08	13	0	52	38	13	59
Mike Lundin, Wachusett	5	1	2.67	10	0	57	42	10	63
Sam Nepiarsky, Nashua	5	1	2.81	10	0	58	56	8	50
Jon Pusateri, Brockton	3	6	3.07	13	0	59	43	22	57
Connor Landers, Torrington	5	1	3.25	8	0	44	41	13	37
Phil Reese, Pittsfield	3	1	3.33	10	0	51	51	14	22
Perry Kulaga, Pittsfield	4	5	3.42	15	0	55	51	17	42

GOLDEN STATE LEAGUE

	League			Overall		
	W	L	PCT	GB	W	L	PCT	GB
---	---	---	---	---	---	---	---	---
Top Speed Baseball	28	7	.800	—	46	10	.821	—
South Bay Storm	22	12	.647	5 ½	25	23	.521	17
Healdsburg Prune Packers	22	13	.629	6	36	19	.655	9 ½
Alameda Merchants	20	14	.588	7 ½	28	23	.549	15 ½
California Warriors	15	17	.469	11 ½	28	23	.549	15 ½
San Francisco Seagulls	14	18	.438	12 ½	25	24	.510	17 ½
Atwater Aviators	12	20	.375	14 ½	19	31	.380	24
Sacramento Heat	12	20	.375	14 ½	19	31	.380	24
Nevada Big Horns	4	28	.125	22 ½	11	37	.229	31

CHAMPIONSHIP: Alameda Merchants defeated Top Speed Baseball in championship game.

TOP 5 PROSPECTS: 1. Brandon Poulson, rhp, Healdsburg (SIGNED, Twins). **2.** Francis Christy, c, Healdsburg (So., Palomar JC, Calif.). **3.** Denis Karas, 3b, California (Fr., California). **4.** Ransom Lalonde, ss, Top Speed Baseball (SIGNED, Amarillo Sox). **5.** Nick Sanchez, rhp, Top Speed Baseball (So., Menlo College, Calif.).

INDIVIDUAL BATTING LEADERS

	AVG	AB	R	H	2B	3B	HR	RBI	SB
Nick McGrew, San Francisco	.415	130	34	54	11	2	0	27	11
Troy Dixon, San Francisco	.404	156	35	63	17	2	5	45	5
Anthony Roberts, Nevada	.394	109	27	43	7	1	4	21	1
Ricky Rodriguez, Top Speed	.379	182	56	69	20	0	7	33	3

	AVG	AB	R	H	2B	3B	HR	RBI	SB
Wes Koenig, Top Speed	.367	180	35	66	15	3	6	50	0
Michael Echavia, Alameda	.365	126	30	46	9	3	5	38	4
Zachary Muenster, Nevada	.352	122	25	43	6	3	3	20	2
Lance VanNoy, Atwater	.350	160	27	56	8	0	3	27	6
Michael Eaton, Healdsburg	.347	176	36	61	16	0	3	26	6
Brian Hamm, Alameda	.346	127	33	44	12	2	1	18	6
Rob Smith Jr., Top Speed	.346	156	32	54	4	0	5	31	6

INDIVIDUAL PITCHING LEADERS

	W	L	ERA	G	SV	IP	H	BB	SO
Nick Hudson, Alameda	4	2	1.60	6	0	45	37	7	39
Ross Slaney, South Bay	7	1	2.34	11	0	62	49	26	70
Kurtis Sargent, Healdsburg	4	4	2.94	12	0	46	38	29	45
Jerad Hawkins, Healdsburg	8	0	2.94	10	0	67	84	6	24
Blake Oliver, Healdsburg	4	2	2.95	12	0	58	72	11	39
Tim Gretter, South Bay	2	1	2.98	20	1	42	46	9	25
John Tierney, San Francisco	5	1	2.98	10	1	45	37	21	27
Julian Barron, Sacramento	4	3	3.07	12	1	59	62	17	45
Alex Fernandez, California	3	2	3.07	10	2	44	36	13	34
Kyle Treadway, Atwater	3	2	3.19	8	0	59	68	6	33
Justin Eclavea, San Francisco	2	3	3.19	12	2	48	50	13	13

GREAT LAKES LEAGUE

	W	L	PCT	GB
Lima Locos	27	13	.675	—
Southern Ohio Copperheads	23	16	.590	3 ½
Xenia Scouts	21	19	.525	6
Cincinnati Steam	21	19	.525	6
Licking County Settlers	19	18	.514	6 ½
Hamilton Joes	19	21	.475	8
Lake Erie Monarchs	18	21	.462	8 ½
Grand Lake Mariners	16	23	.410	10 ½
Lexington Hustlers	11	25	.306	14

CHAMPIONSHIP: Licking County Settlers defeated Southern Ohio Copperheads 2-0 in best-of-three championship series.
TOP 10 PROSPECTS: 1. Cory Wilder, rhp, Lima (So., North Carolina State). **2.** Austin Sexton, rhp, Lima (So., Mississippi State). **3.** Kyle Lewis, of, Lima (So., Mercer). **4.** Luke Crumley, rhp, Lima (Sr., Georgia). **5.** Kyle Fiala, ss, Lake Erie (So., Notre Dame). **6.** Brandyn Sittinger, rhp, Lima (Jr., Santa Clara). **7.** Brandyn Sittinger, rhp, Southern Ohio (Jr., Marshall). **8.** Jacob Bodner, rhp, Cincinnati (R-Jr., Xavier). **9.** Nick Paxton, of, Licking County (R-Sr., Liberty). **10.** Tanner Rainey, rhp/1b, Licking County (Sr., West Alabama).

INDIVIDUAL BATTING LEADERS

	AVG	AB	R	H	2B	3B	HR	RBI	SB
Nick Paxton, LC	.438	96	26	42	7	1	0	10	12
Kolin McMillen, LC	.404	94	21	38	6	1	0	16	7
TJ Braff, So. Ohio	.388	103	26	40	7	0	3	22	8
Kyle Fiala, Lake Erie	.388	129	19	50	8	3	2	18	4
Kyle Lewis, Lima	.342	152	41	52	9	1	6	36	4
Brett Carlson, Lima	.333	123	16	41	6	1	1	13	7
Jake Farr, So. Ohio	.333	114	26	38	4	0	3	18	5
Braden Boggetto, So. Ohio	.333	111	22	37	3	0	2	21	7
TJ Nichting, Hamilton	.329	161	19	53	7	4	1	30	7
Daniel Garner, Lima	.327	153	25	50	13	1	8	32	2
Andrew Carrillo, Xenia	.326	92	15	30	6	0	0	10	13

INDIVIDUAL PITCHING LEADERS

	W	L	ERA	G	SV	IP	H	BB	SO
Rob Gustitus, Lake Erie	2	0	0.95	10	1	38	25	14	33
Daniel Sexton, Lima	3	0	1.63	5	0	39	30	9	21
Jake Miller, So. Ohio	3	2	1.76	10	3	41	37	7	40
Brandyn Sittinger, So. Ohio	4	0	1.86	9	0	44	32	16	51
Lucas Hamelink, Xenia	3	3	2.29	9	0	55	59	16	39
Curtis Wilson, Grand Lake	5	1	2.36	7	0	42	41	8	27
Duncan Robinson, LC	3	1	2.38	7	0	34	32	5	30
Cory Wilder, Lima	3	1	2.64	8	0	44	29	16	60
Alec Tuohy, Grand Lake	1	1	2.65	9	0	34	28	9	22
Jacob Banks, Hamilton	2	2	2.76	6	0	33	26	12	32
Matt Dennis, LC	4	1	2.78	10	0	36	32	11	26

HAMPTONS COLLEGIATE LEAGUE

	W	L	T	GB
Southampton	22	18	0	—
Sag Harbor	22	18	0	—
Shelter Island	21	19	0	1
North Fork	21	19	0	1
Riverhead	20	20	0	2
Westhampton	19	20	1	2 ½
Montauk	14	25	1	7 ½

CHAMPIONSHIP: Southampton Breakers swept Shelter Island in championship series.
TOP 10 PROSPECTS: 1. Mike Donadio, of, Riverhead (So., St. John's). **2.** Ricky Surum, ss, Southampton (So., Virginia Tech). **3.** Dan Rizzie, c, Sag Harbor (Jr., Xavier). **4.** Corbin Burnes, rhp, Riverhead (So., St. Mary's). **5.** Stephen Woods, rhp, North Fork (So., Albany). **6.** Max Watt, rhp, Shelter Island (Jr., Lynn, Fla.). **7.** Casey Baker, if, North Fork (So., Stony Brook). **8.** Matt LaRocca, rhp/1b, Westhampton (Sr., Akron). **9.** Chris Hall, rhp/c, Sag Harbor (So., Elon). **10.** Andrew Burnick, rhp, North Fork (So., Pennsylvania).

INDIVIDUAL BATTING LEADERS

	AVG	AB	R	H	2B	3B	HR	RBI	SB
Mike Donadio, Riverhead	.378	127	27	48	9	2	0	25	9
Rob Moore, Southampton	.351	111	23	39	7	0	3	18	5
Dan Rizzie, Sag Harbor	.337	92	17	31	6	1	0	18	4
Trevor Freeman, SI	.330	106	20	35	9	0	2	10	19
Casey Baker, North Fork	.325	151	21	49	5	0	1	17	16
Troy Scocca, SI	.325	120	25	39	10	2	2	20	11
Marquise Gill, Southampton	.312	138	29	43	4	0	1	18	39
Connor Hawthorne, West.	.311	122	15	38	12	0	1	21	0
Donovan May, Southampton	.308	104	19	32	3	1	0	23	8
Mike Palladino, Montauk	.308	91	16	28	3	1	2	19	8
Mitchell McGeein, South.	.308	133	26	41	7	0	5	29	6

INDIVIDUAL PITCHING LEADERS

	W	L	ERA	G	SV	IP	H	BB	SO
Alex Person, Sag Harbor	2	4	1.13	9	1	48	36	10	30
Issac OBear, SI	3	1	1.38	9	0	33	20	5	15
Cody McPartland, West.	3	2	1.65	9	0	55	39	15	40
Mark Wilson, Southampton	2	1	1.84	7	0	49	48	8	28
Dylan Mouzakes, Montauk	3	2	1.91	6	0	38	35	9	30
Jake Cousins, North Fork	3	1	1.93	8	0	47	33	13	42
Justin Thomas, Sag Harbor	2	1	2.27	8	0	44	48	15	27
Brenton Arriaga, SI	0	1	2.47	8	0	44	43	12	33
Ian Searles, Sag Harbor	3	0	2.55	9	0	49	42	15	25
Greg Weissert, Westhampton	2	2	2.64	12	1	48	40	13	56
Max Watt, SI	5	2	2.76	10	0	49	52	19	30

JAYHAWK LEAGUE

	W	L	PCT	GB
Wellington Heat	28	6	.824	—
Hays Larks	21	13	.618	7
Derby Twins	16	18	.471	12
El Dorado Broncos	14	20	.412	14
Liberal BeeJays	13	21	.382	15
Dodge City A's	10	24	.294	18

CHAMPIONSHIP: None.
TOP 10 PROSPECTS: 1. Blake Rogers, rhp, Liberal (Jr., Oklahoma). **2.** Max Hogan, 2b, El Dorado (Jr., Arkansas). **3.** Dylan Dillard, of, Derby (Jr., Jacksonville). **4.** Stuart Patke, rhp, Derby (Jr., Abilene Christian). **5.** Luke Doyle, 3b, Wellington (So., Yavapai JC, Ariz.). **6.** Tyler Detmer, c/of, Hays (Sr., Illinois-Chicago). **7.** Chase Rader, 3b, Derby (Jr., Wichita State). **8.** Jeremy McGowan, rhp, El Dorado (Sr., Troy). **9.** Tyler Leffler, ss, Hays (Jr., Bradley). **10.** Jagger Harjo, rhp, Dodge City (Jr., Emporia State, Kan.).

INDIVIDUAL BATTING LEADERS

	AVG	AB	R	H	2B	3B	HR	RBI	SB
Michael Burns, Hays	.381	118	19	45	8	0	2	14	8
Dylan Dillard, Derby	.373	118	34	44	7	1	10	30	9
Tyler Eager, Derby	.364	88	18	32	5	1	5	30	2
Ben Craft, Dodge City	.343	99	11	34	9	0	3	16	1

	AVG	AB	R	H	2B	3B	HR	RBI	SB
Tyler Lefler, Hays	.336	119	21	40	8	1	3	12	1
Luke Doyle, Wellington	.333	105	18	35	8	0	4	16	1
Ty Detmer, Hays	.330	115	24	38	5	0	7	32	1
Juan Rivera, Derby	.322	118	17	38	3	2	0	13	3
Rowdy Andrews, Wellington	.318	88	18	28	4	1	1	12	8
Derek Birginske, Hays	.312	93	19	29	5	0	7	22	0
Mikel Mucha, El Dorado	.310	113	13	35	9	2	2	17	6

INDIVIDUAL PITCHING LEADERS

	W	L	ERA	G	SV	IP	H	BB	SO
Derek Fischer, Wellington	5	1	1.80	7	0	50	46	4	48
Ray Ashford, Liberal	3	0	1.95	9	0	37	24	17	31
Jeremy McGowan, El Dorado	3	0	2.13	8	0	42	31	18	52
Brady Bowen, Wellington	2	1	2.20	5	0	29	22	14	21
Jagger Harjo, Dodge City	4	2	2.25	11	0	52	48	16	56
Stuart Patke, Derby	2	2	2.54	8	1	46	34	12	40
J.B. Olson, Liberal	2	3	2.75	7	0	36	45	9	26
Matt Gunderson, Dodge City	1	1	3.54	12	1	28	33	5	17
Trever Ezell, El Dorado	0	3	3.58	7	0	28	27	7	18
Robert Dugger, Liberal	2	2	3.62	5	0	27	28	9	26

MIDWEST COLLEGIATE LEAGUE

	Conference				Overall			
	W	L	PCT	GB	W	L	PCT	GB
Southland Vikings	27	12	.692	—	29	12	.707	—
DuPage County Hounds	26	14	.650	1 ½	26	14	.650	2 ½
Northwest Indiana Oilmen	24	16	.600	3 ½	26	17	.605	4
Lexington Snipes	23	18	.561	5	23	18	.561	6
Joliet Admirals	11	30	.268	17	11	30	.268	18
Chicago Zephyrs	8	29	.216	18	8	29	.216	19

CHAMPIONSHIP: Southland Vikings swept DuPage County Hounds in championship series.

INDIVIDUAL BATTING LEADERS

	AVG	AB	R	H	2B	3B	HR	RBI	SB
Bobby Shepard, Southland	.427	124	32	53	12	1	6	28	5
Garrett Walter, Michigan City	.400	15	2	6	3	0	0	1	0
Chase Fieldhouse, Southland	.384	99	23	38	5	1	3	18	0
Jeff Boehm, Southland	.375	144	27	54	11	1	5	27	3
Brandon Mallder, Southland	.351	134	32	47	7	0	2	16	8
Erik Phillis, Lexington	.339	121	13	41	9	0	4	25	8
KJ Zelenika, Michigan City	.333	18	1	6	1	0	0	3	0
Jerry Hodges, Michigan City	.333	18	3	6	1	1	0	2	0
Chris Maranto, Lexington	.329	140	31	46	13	2	2	30	5
Stefano Belmonte, Southland	.328	128	25	42	9	0	4	30	0
Adam Casson, Lexington	.325	126	25	41	10	0	7	23	3

INDIVIDUAL PITCHING LEADERS

	W	L	ERA	G	SV	IP	H	BB	SO
Joe Ucho, Michigan City	0	0	0.00	1	0	4	1	2	7
Patrick Bellinger, DuPage	3	0	0.74	8	1	37	20	17	44
John Munyon, Lexington	3	2	1.57	7	0	46	26	9	43
Casey Young, Michigan City	0	1	1.93	1	0	5	6	1	5
Cameron Linck, NW Indiana	5	2	1.94	10	0	51	43	18	45
Matt Frawley, DuPage County	2	3	2.06	8	0	39	35	10	36
Keith Mahler, NW Indiana	5	4	2.06	9	0	48	45	7	43
Danny Pobereyko, NW Indiana	6	2	2.53	12	0	46	35	4	52
Tyler House, Southland	2	2	2.65	7	0	34	33	7	27
Brandon White, Southland	4	1	2.82	6	0	38	36	9	28
Quinn Ahern, Joliet	2	5	2.89	8	0	56	71	13	48
Kyle Weller, Lexington	2	2	3.09	5	0	35	23	13	43

MINK LEAGUE

	League				Overall			
North Division	W	L	PCT	GB	W	L	PCT	GB
St. Joseph Mustangs	29	14	.674	—	42	16	.724	—
Chillicothe Mudcats	26	18	.591	3 ½	29	18	.617	7 ½
Clarinda A's	19	23	.452	9 ½	26	25	.510	12 ½
Omaha Diamond Spirit	18	24	.429	10 ½	20	24	.455	15
South Division	**W**	**L**	**PCT**	**GB**	**W**	**L**	**PCT**	**GB**
Sedalia Bombers	27	16	.628	—	28	18	.609	—
Joplin Outlaws	25	19	.568	2 ½	26	19	.578	1 ½
Nevada Griffons	21	22	.488	6	24	22	.522	4
Ozark Generals	14	26	.350	11 ½	15	28	.349	11 ½
Branson Nationals	14	31	.311	14	14	31	.311	13 ½

CHAMPIONSHIP: St. Joseph's Mustangs defeated Sedalia Bombers 2-1 in best-of-three championship series.

TOP 10 PROSPECTS: 1. Brett Ash, rhp, St. Joseph's (SIGNED: Mariners). 2. Trent Hill, lhp/if, St. Joseph's (So., Arkansas). 3. Cody Farrell, of, Nevada (Jr., Texas-Arlington). 4. Todd Czinege, 2b/3b, Chillicothe (So., Villanova). 5. Matt Jones, 1b/of, Sedalia (SIGNED: Dodgers). 6. Taylor Love, ss, Nevada (Sr., Louisiana Tech). 7. Tanner Lubach, c, St. Joseph's (Sr., Nebraska). 8. Trey Hair, 2b, Sedalia (So., Fort Scott CC, Kan.). 9. Austin Aspegren, rhp, St. Joseph's (Jr., Arkansas State). 10. Danny Chambliss, rhp, Sedalia (Graduated Sr., Harris Stowe, Mo.).

INDIVIDUAL BATTING LEADERS

	AVG	AB	R	H	2B	3B	HR	RBI	SB
Kurt Becker, Nevada	.350	157	21	55	9	1	1	23	8
Joe Koerper, St. Joseph	.333	195	34	65	9	2	1	30	12
Daniel Midyett, Nevada	.333	147	21	49	6	5	2	20	3
Zac Stewart, Joplin	.329	161	22	53	15	2	0	20	5
Jacob Alexander, Nevada	.327	156	23	51	9	0	1	26	3
Kolby Follis, Branson	.325	126	23	41	0	1	0	6	23
Gavin Golsan, Clarinda	.324	145	31	47	4	2	0	5	17
Corban Williams, Chillicothe	.317	161	31	51	3	3	0	13	19
Trey Hair, Sedalia	.313	147	27	46	6	1	2	20	22
Trevor Bowling, Ozark	.312	109	14	34	7	1	0	12	5

INDIVIDUAL PITCHING LEADERS

	W	L	ERA	G	SV	IP	H	BB	SO
Grant Hamilton, Joplin	2	1	1.23	11	1	37	20	16	28
Danny Chambliss, Sedalia	1	1	1.47	20	1	43	33	15	32
Ryker Fox, St. Joseph	8	2	1.52	10	0	65	46	25	46
Winston Lavender, Sedalia	3	2	1.66	8	0	49	45	10	35
Robert Beltran, Chillicothe	3	1	1.80	10	0	45	44	8	34
Garret Stockton, Joplin	4	1	2.08	8	0	48	31	19	53
Connor Eller, Joplin	4	2	2.11	7	0	43	43	7	31
Jacob Howel, Clarinda	4	1	2.23	10	0	61	44	14	51
Addison Russ, Nevada	5	2	2.35	10	0	54	48	13	43
Tyler Omlid, Joplin	3	2	2.68	6	0	37	34	9	24

NEW ENGLAND COLLEGIATE LEAGUE

Northern Division	W	L	PCT	GB
Vermont Mountaineers	27	15	.643	—
Sanford Mainers	24	18	.571	3
Keene Swamp Bats	21	21	.500	6
Laconia Muskrats	20	22	.476	7
North Adams SteepleCats	19	23	.452	8
Valley Blue Sox	14	28	.333	13

Southern Division	W	L	PCT	GB
Plymouth Pilgrims	31	11	.738	—
Newport Gulls	25	17	.595	6
Ocean State Waves	24	18	.571	7
Mystic Schooners	23	19	.548	8
Danbury Westerners	13	29	.310	18
New Bedford Bay Sox	11	31	.262	20

CHAMPIONSHIP: Newport Gulls defeated Sanford Mainers 2-0 in best-of-three championship series.

TOP 10 PROSPECTS: 1. Alex Robinson, lhp, Keene (Jr., Maryland). 2. Jordan Sheffield, rhp, Laconia (R-Fr., Vanderbilt). 3. Blake Tiberi, 3b, Vermont (So., Louisville). 4. Nolan Long, rhp, Mystic (So., Wagner). 5. Tommy Edman, ss, Newport (So., Stanford). 6. Blaise Salter, c, Newport (Sr., Michigan State). 7. Vincent Gulietti, 1b, Plymouth (Sr., Quinnipiac). 8. Jack English, rhp, Laconia (Sr., Florida Gulf Coast). 9. Cam Hatch, lhp, Sanford (Jr., St. Edward's, Texas). 10. Jared Gesell, rhp, Vermont (Jr., UNC Wilmington).

INDIVIDUAL BATTING LEADERS

	AVG	AB	R	H	2B	3B	HR	RBI	SB
Stephen Laurino, Mystic	.381	139	27	53	10	0	0	21	3
Blake Tiberi, Vermont	.372	113	22	42	7	1	2	13	2
Toby Handley, Mystic	.351	134	28	47	11	0	1	16	15

David Mackinnon, NB	.349	109	10	38	3	0	0	10	3
Blaise Salter, Newport	.340	144	25	49	11	0	9	42	1
Vinny Zarrillo, Laconia	.333	171	25	57	10	0	2	20	16
Dan Hoy, Mystic	.331	136	21	45	12	1	2	29	9
James Bunn, Plymouth	.328	116	26	38	2	0	1	9	14
Colton Bottomley, Laconia	.328	131	13	43	7	0	2	20	1
Trey Amburgey, Vermont	.327	107	18	35	2	1	1	22	12

INDIVIDUAL PITCHING LEADERS

	W	L	ERA	G	SV	IP	H	BB	SO
Thomas Jankins, Plymouth	5	0	0.41	11	1	44	22	8	41
Nicholas Berger, Plymouth	4	0	0.75	8	0	48	35	23	47
Christian Lavoie, Sanford	3	2	1.20	8	0	45	36	2	19
Danny Garcia, Plymouth	4	0	1.45	8	0	43	32	16	36
Brad Applin, Ocean State	1	0	1.51	16	0	36	33	8	29
Jack English, Laconia	4	1	1.52	9	0	41	26	24	40
Michael Concato, Mystic	2	0	1.62	7	0	39	38	8	36
Dominic Severino, Keene	1	1	1.79	7	0	40	28	6	22
Shea Spitzbarth, Laconia	4	2	1.93	10	1	47	32	15	50
Andrew Schwaab, Danbury	0	2	2.10	10	1	34	31	10	25

NEW YORK COLLEGIATE LEAGUE

Eastern Division	W	L	PCT	GB
Geneva Red Wings	30	16	.652	—
Oneonta Outlaws	27	19	.587	3
Sherrill Silversmiths	23	23	.500	7
Syracuse Salt Cats	23	23	.500	7
Syracuse JR Chiefs	16	30	.348	14
Cortland Crush	15	31	.326	15

Western Division	W	L	PCT	GB
Hornell Dodgers	38	8	0.826	—
Geneva Twins	28	18	.609	10
Rochester Ridgemen	27	19	.587	11
Niagara Power	22	24	.478	16
Genesee Rapids	21	25	.457	17
Olean Oilers	16	30	.348	22
Wellsville Nitros	13	33	.283	25

CHAMPIONSHIP: Hornell Dodgers defeated Oneonta Outlaws 2-0 in best-of-three championship series.

INDIVIDUAL BATTING LEADERS

	AVG	AB	R	H	2B	3B	HR	RBI	SB
Kevin Brice, Sherrill	.400	155	29	62	10	0	4	32	15
Fernando Garcia, Twins	.364	118	22	43	5	4	3	23	10
Ted Dilts, Olean Oilers	.363	146	23	53	16	1	0	27	0
Nick Wolyniec, Rochester	.362	130	16	47	10	1	2	26	6
Anthony Massicci, Salt Cats	.354	144	27	51	3	8	0	21	12
Hank Morrison, Hornell	.354	178	33	63	12	3	3	47	2
Reid Neal, Sherrill	.353	167	36	59	10	3	3	27	14
Jimmy Latona, Hornell	.348	112	43	39	10	2	2	18	7
Thad Johnson, Hornell	.342	184	42	63	9	2	0	36	8
Mike Annone, Twins	.333	147	29	49	10	4	4	35	5

INDIVIDUAL PITCHING LEADERS

	W	L	ERA	G	SV	IP	H	BB	SO
Drew Doring, Red Wings	5	0	0.89	7	0	41	19	21	42
David Anderson, Twins	8	0	0.98	15	0	46	41	11	23
Billy Whaley, Red Wings	4	2	1.36	7	0	46	34	19	44
Seth Cornell, Hornell	6	1	1.49	13	2	48	33	12	43
Blaise Whitman, Salt Cats	2	1	1.58	6	0	40	31	8	38
Jordon Accetta, Hornell	9	0	1.79	9	0	55	42	19	45
Alex Lopez, Olean	1	4	1.92	9	0	56	44	16	40
Austin Bizzle, Olean	4	2	1.97	10	0	64	47	19	59
Connor Hamilton, Rochester	5	2	2.00	9	0	72	59	6	24
Zachary Krivda, Olean	4	1	2.02	9	1	49	35	19	52
Iannick Remillard, JR Chiefs	2	2	2.10	6	0	39	34	7	27

NORTHWOODS LEAGUE

North Division	W	L	PCT	GB
Willmar Stingers	46	26	.639	—
Waterloo Bucks	45	27	.625	1

Mankato MoonDogs	42	30	.583	4
St. Cloud Rox	37	35	.514	9
Rochester Honkers	37	35	.514	9
Eau Claire Express	36	36	.500	10
Duluth Huskies	30	42	.417	16
Thunder Bay Border Cats	23	49	.319	23
Alexandria Blue Anchors	22	50	.306	24

South Division	W	L	PCT	GB
Lakeshore Chinooks	50	21	.704	—
Wisconsin Woodchucks	42	30	.583	8 ½
Kenosha Kingfish	41	30	.577	9
Madison Mallards	39	33	.542	11 ½
Green Bay Bullfrogs	36	36	.500	14 ½
La Crosse Loggers	33	39	.458	17 ½
Battle Creek Bombers	32	40	.444	18 ½
Kalamazoo Growlers	29	43	.403	21 ½
Wisconsin Rapids Rafters	27	45	.375	23 ½

CHAMPIONSHIP: Lakeshore Chinooks defeated Mankato MoonDogs 2-0 in best-of-three championship series.

TOP 10 PROSPECTS: 1. Ryan Boldt, of, Rochester (So., Nebraska). **2.** Zach Jackson, rhp, Wisconsin Rapids (So., Arkansas). **3.** Connor Jones, lhp, Lakeshore (So., Georgia). **4.** Peter Alonso, 1b, Madison (So., Florida). **5.** Dalton Sawyer, lhp, St. Cloud (Jr., Minnesota). **6.** Buddy Reed, of, Kenosha (So., Florida). **7.** Andy Ravel, rhp, Wisconsin (So., Kent State). **8.** Chad Hockin, rhp, St. Cloud (So., Cal State Fullerton). **9.** Mitchell Traver, rhp, Mankato (R-So., Texas Christian). **10.** Daniel Salters, c, Eau Claire (R-Jr., Dallas Baptist).

INDIVIDUAL BATTING LEADERS

	AVG	AB	R	H	2B	3B	HR	RBI	SB
Zack Domingues, Wisconsin	.376	213	49	80	5	1	0	30	15
Pat MacKenzie, Waterloo	.374	214	57	80	15	1	0	29	26
Pete Alonso, Madison	.354	226	43	80	5	1	18	53	2
Tyler Sullivan, Mankato	.352	261	65	92	10	2	1	23	36
Chris Godinez, Kenosha	.342	202	49	69	5	0	6	21	11
Ryne Birk, La Crosse	.340	209	27	71	11	0	2	34	11
Keelin Rasch, Wisconsin	.340	247	38	84	19	1	8	57	5
Peter Maris, Mankato	.337	199	26	67	7	3	2	45	12
Daniel Salters, Eau Claire	.327	196	33	64	11	1	7	40	0
Jordan Lee, Alexandria	.325	197	35	64	11	1	9	33	12
Pat Porter, Kenosha	.324	256	53	83	16	5	10	63	2

INDIVIDUAL PITCHING LEADERS

	W	L	ERA	G	SV	IP	H	BB	SO
Reese Gregory, St. Cloud	7	2	1.70	12	0	69	50	16	71
Jacob Waguespack, BC	1	3	1.80	11	0	60	51	23	50
Rico Garcia, Kenosha	5	1	1.90	11	0	66	49	12	51
Ryan Smoyer, Kalamazoo	8	1	2.01	13	2	81	65	21	43
Matt Kent, Rochester	3	3	2.09	12	0	78	63	10	69
Roberto Baroniel, Green Bay	4	3	2.75	13	0	75	62	21	57
Austin Caspersen, St. Cloud	5	4	3.09	12	0	58	61	15	19
Spencer Greer, Rochester	5	1	3.24	13	0	58	57	16	39
Cody Sedlock, Waterloo	5	3	3.27	13	0	63	69	29	53
Trevor Haas, Kenosha	4	4	3.52	14	0	61	70	16	19

PROSPECT LEAGUE

East Division	W	L	PCT	GB
Chillicothe Paints	40	20	.667	—
Butler Blue Sox	40	20	.667	—
West Virginia Miners	38	22	.633	2
Richmond RiverRats	24	35	.407	15 ½
Champion City Kings	21	39	.350	19
Lorain County Ironmen	20	40	.333	20

West Division	W	L	PCT	GB
Quincy Gems	39	20	.661	—
Terre Haute Rex	37	23	.617	2 ½
Danville Dans	31	29	.517	8 ½
Hannibal Cavemen	25	35	.417	14 ½
Springfield Sliders	14	46	.233	25 ½

CHAMPIONSHIP: Quincy Gems defeated Chillicothe Paints 2-0 in best-of-three championship series.

TOP 10 PROSPECTS: 1. Ronnie Dawson, of, Chillicothe (So., Ohio State). **2.** C.J. Burdick, rhp, Danville (So., San Diego). **3.** Ronnie Jebavy, of, Danville (Jr., Middle Tennessee State). **4.** Travis Lakins, rhp, Chillicothe (So., Ohio State). **5.** Chase Boster, rhp, West Virginia (Jr., Marshall). **6.** Adam McGinnis, c, Quincy (So., Western Illinois). **7.** Kurt Hoekstra, 2b/of, Chillicothe (Jr., Western Michigan). **8.** Adam Bleday, lhp, Butler (So., Gulf Coast State JC, Fla.). **9.** Kolin Stanley, rhp, West Virginia (Redshirt Sr., Marshall). **10.** Michael Paez, ss, Richmond (So., Coastal Carolina).

INDIVIDUAL BATTING LEADERS

	AVG	AB	R	H	2B	3B	HR	RBI	SB
Kurt Hoekstra, Chillicothe	.342	155	24	53	5	3	0	19	2
Jake Bennett, Champion City	.342	193	24	66	12	4	0	22	2
Manuel De Jesus, Terre Haute	.336	232	43	78	15	0	0	37	25
Adam McGinnis, Quincy	.335	200	43	67	16	1	6	50	5
Austin Bryant, Danville	.318	195	26	62	9	3	1	31	8
TJ Diffenderfer, Chillicothe	.309	175	32	54	18	1	6	33	3
Mike Brosseau, West Virginia	.309	217	32	67	8	1	0	24	18
Ryan Uhl, Butler	.308	143	22	44	8	0	3	25	2
Grant Massey, West Virginia	.307	199	48	61	11	1	0	21	27
Joe Hoscheit, Chillicothe	.307	153	21	47	6	5	2	28	2
Justin Paulsen, Richmond	.306	183	31	56	8	0	1	33	8

INDIVIDUAL PITCHING LEADERS

	W	L	ERA	G	SV	IP	H	BB	SO
Chase Boster, West Virginia	5	2	0.75	9	0	60	28	10	60
Adam Bleday, Butler	5	3	1.66	9	0	54	30	23	58
Jason Byers, Chillicothe	5	2	1.67	9	0	59	46	10	50
Brandon Allen, Terre Haute	4	3	2.04	9	0	53	45	17	28
Lance Elder, Chillicothe	4	1	2.15	10	0	54	37	9	38
Luke Mamer, Champion City	6	3	3.26	13	0	68	57	3	34
Ben Hartz, Butler	5	1	2.28	9	0	51	49	19	30
JT Brubaker, Lorain County	4	3	2.57	10	0	70	49	20	56
Preston Church, Quincy	2	2	2.59	14	1	56	44	24	40
Tyler Feece, Springfield	4	2	2.71	13	1	66	51	30	30
Denis Lyman, Butler	3	3	2.90	10	0	50	37	18	48

SUNBELT COLLEGIATE LEAGUE

West	W	L	PCT	GB
Phenix City Crawdads	19	14	.576	—
Douglasville Bulls	15	14	.517	2
Home Plate Chukars	10	17	.370	6
East Cobb Patriots	10	18	.357	6 ½

East	W	L	PCT	GB
Atlanta Crackers	22	10	.688	—
Brookhaven Bucks	19	10	.655	1 ½
Gwinnett Tides	12	16	.429	8
Windward Braves	10	18	.357	10

CHAMPIONSHIP: Atlanta Crackers defeated Phenix City Crawdads 3-0 in best-of-five championship series.

TOP 10 PROSPECTS: 1. Gabe Friese, rhp, East Cobb, (So., Kennesaw State). **2.** Morgan Bunting, 1b, Brookhaven (Jr., Georgia). **3.** Nathaniel Lowe, 1b, East Cobb (So., Mercer). **4.** Bryan Headley, rhp, Phenix City (Sr., Columbus State, Ga.). **5.** Ryan Peurifoy, of, Home Plate (So., Georgia Tech). **6.** Devin Vanier, lhp, Brookhaven (So., Georgia Perimeter JC). **7.** Christian Turnipseed, rhp, Douglasville (Sr., Georgia-Gwinnett). **8.** Jake Wright, of/lhp, Atlanta (Jr., TBA). **9.** Cole Miller, 1b, Gwinnett (So., Georgia Tech). **10.** J.J. Shaffer, of, Brookhaven (So., Auburn).

INDIVIDUAL PITCHING LEADERS

	AVG	AB	R	H	2B	3B	HR	RBI	SB
Will Price, Atlanta	.371	105	30	39	5	2	3	19	5
Nathaniel Lowe, East Cobb	.370	73	13	27	6	0	3	20	1
Corey Greeson, Douglasville	.370	73	18	27	4	1	3	19	11
Deric Boone, Brookhaven	.355	93	22	33	0	0	0	14	24
Phillip Bates, Atlanta	.350	100	28	35	3	0	2	8	6
Carson Bowers, Phenix City	.348	112	25	39	7	0	2	19	8
Cletis Avery, Home Plate	.346	81	21	28	6	3	0	18	15
Andrew Gordon, Douglasville	.342	73	13	25	5	1	1	12	5
Tyler Martin, Brookhaven	.329	82	10	27	6	1	0	17	4
Alex McGill, East Cobb	.322	87	18	28	4	0	0	15	4
Morgan Bunting, Brookhaven	.317	82	19	26	4	3	1	14	6

INDIVIDUAL PITCHING LEADERS

	W	L	ERA	G	SV	IP	H	BB	SO
Ben Burns, Brookhaven	6	2	0.89	9	0	50	35	4	35
Clay Garner, Atlanta	2	1	1.38	17	5	33	24	13	40
Ty Alvey, Home Plate	3	2	1.83	8	1	44	27	21	63
Gabe Friese, East Cobb	2	2	1.88	6	0	38	33	5	45
Avery Fagan, Atlanta	1	0	2.03	14	3	27	20	11	29
Doug Heath, East Cobb	1	3	2.10	7	0	34	36	9	19
Ryan Turner, Douglasville	3	0	2.13	8	0	25	13	8	19
Ethan Hunter, Douglasville	1	1	2.19	11	0	25	19	8	23
Alex Roberts, Atlanta	5	1	2.30	9	0	59	49	19	53
Garrett Kriston, East Cobb	0	4	2.46	4	0	33	33	8	30

TEXAS COLLEGIATE LEAGUE

Texas Collegiate League	W	L	PCT	GB
Brazos Valley Bombers	42	14	.750	—
Victoria Generals	38	23	.623	6 ½
Acadiana Cane Cutters	31	24	.564	10 ½
East Texas Pump Jacks	24	33	.421	18 ½
Texas Marshals	19	37	.339	23
Woodlands Strykers	18	41	.305	25 ½

CHAMPIONSHIP: Brazos Valley Bombers defeated Victoria Generals 2-1 in best-of-three championship series.

TOP 10 PROSPECTS: 1. Connor Barron, of, Acadiana (Sr., Southern Mississippi). **2.** Hunter Haley, of, Brazos Valley (Jr., Oklahoma). **3.** Gandy Stubblefield, rhp, Woodlands (Sr., Texas A&M). **4.** Cannon Chadwick, rhp, Brazos Valley (So., Arkansas). **5.** Justin Pacchioli, of, Victoria (Sr., Lehigh). **6.** Marshall Kasowski, rhp, East Texas (So., Houston). **7.** Logan Nottebrok, 3b/of, Brazos Valley (Sr., Texas A&M). **8.** Carson Shaddy, c, Texas (R-Fr., Arkansas). **9.** Andrew Godail, lhp, Woodlands (Sr., Sam Houston State). **10.** Alvaro Rondon, ss, Victoria (SIGNED: Diamondbacks).

INDIVIDUAL BATTING LEADERS

	AVG	AB	R	H	2B	3B	HR	RBI	SB
Justin Pacchioli, Victoria	.369	157	40	58	7	2	3	22	22
Connor Barron, Acadiana	.344	183	45	63	10	5	4	20	34
G.R. Hinsley, BV	.320	178	35	57	8	0	2	30	18
Brian Portelli, Victoria	.311	206	25	64	13	5	3	35	0
Spence Rahm, Woodlands	.306	183	26	56	12	0	5	24	0
Joe Moroney, East Texas	.296	159	27	47	6	0	0	18	22
Carlos Contreras, Texas	.295	166	18	49	13	1	1	29	1
Dustin Williams, East Texas	.293	147	19	43	9	0	3	30	0
Chase Daughdrill, Texas	.291	172	31	50	9	2	3	31	10
Horacio Correa III, BV	.286	147	25	42	4	0	2	22	6

INDIVIDUAL PITCHING LEADERS

	W	L	ERA	G	SV	IP	H	BB	SO
Kris Looper, Victoria	5	2	0.99	11	1	55	36	5	47
Ryan Benitez, Victoria	5	0	1.29	9	0	56	53	23	51
Ty Schlottmann, Victoria	3	1	2.16	9	0	50	34	15	42
Garrett Harris, BV	5	0	2.17	14	0	46	34	25	45
John Jaeger, East Texas	3	1	2.20	16	0	61	51	22	49
Jeremy Hallonquist, E. Texas	3	3	2.36	11	0	61	62	13	55
Cody Brannon, BV	6	1	2.49	9	0	47	39	23	46
Nick Johnson, BV	5	2	2.50	23	2	50	58	11	17
Mike Walker, BV	3	2	2.96	9	0	49	49	23	30
Austin Hilton, Texas	1	4	3.38	9	0	48	47	9	35

VALLEY LEAGUE

	W	L	PCT	GB
Harrisonburg Turks	29	13	.690	—
Waynesboro Generals	27	16	.628	2 ½
Front Royal Cardinals	26	17	.605	3 ½
Staunton Braves	25	18	.581	4 ½
Charles Town Cannons	23	19	.548	6
Strasburg Express	21	22	.488	8 ½
Aldie Senators	19	25	.432	11
Covington Lumberjacks	18	24	.429	11
Winchester Royals	17	27	.386	13
Woodstock River Bandits	15	26	.366	13 ½
New Market Rebels	15	28	.349	14 ½

CHAMPIONSHIP: Waynesboro Generals defeated Charles Town Cannons 2-1 in best-of-three championship series.
TOP 10 PROSPECTS: 1. J.C. Escarra, c, Staunton (So., Florida International). **2.** Matt Rose, 3b/rhp, Harrisonburg (Jr., Georgia State). **3.** Stephen Kerr, 2b, Charles Town (So., Florida Atlantic). **4.** Reece Karalus, rhp, Aldie (Jr., Santa Clara). **5.** Mike Vinson, rhp, Strasburg (R-So., Florida). **6.** Gunnar McNeill, 1b, Staunton (So., Florida International). **7.** Garrett Kelly, rhp, New Market (Jr., Wake Forest). **8.** Keegan Long, rhp, Front Royal (Jr., St. Joseph's College, Ind.). **9.** Mike Carpenter, rhp, Winchester (Jr., Virginia Commonwealth). **10.** Logan Longwith, rhp, Front Royal (R-So., Tennessee Wesleyan).

INDIVIDUAL BATTING LEADERS

	AVG	AB	R	H	2B	3B	HR	RBI	SB
Gunnar McNeill, Staunton	.402	169	28	68	16	0	6	50	6
Cole Gruber, Waynesboro	.385	122	31	47	5	1	0	16	23
Jerry Downs, Winchester	.355	155	30	55	7	0	5	25	15
Joey Rodriguez, Staunton	.355	152	42	54	12	1	2	22	20
Hunter Thomas, Staunton	.348	115	23	40	1	1	1	13	10
Mike Marcinko, Waynesboro	.344	131	39	45	7	2	0	18	13
Matt Rose, Harrisonburg	.342	149	25	51	7	1	6	29	1
Nick Sinay, Front Royal	.341	126	43	43	3	0	0	10	28
Anthony Payne, Strasburg	.336	122	22	41	13	0	3	21	3
Blake Edwards, Covington	.335	167	34	56	5	1	0	19	21
Alex Mata, Winchester	.335	161	22	54	8	1	3	22	4

INDIVIDUAL PITCHING LEADERS

	W	L	ERA	G	SV	IP	H	BB	SO
Keegan Long, Front Royal	4	2	1.61	11	0	45	35	13	41
Austin Stephens, Charles Town	3	0	1.77	6	0	41	32	14	21
Lucas Mould, Winchester	1	2	2.04	15	4	35	32	8	34
Jeff Schank, Waynesboro	4	0	2.09	10	0	43	38	9	35
Mike Vinson, Strasburg	3	1	2.15	10	2	38	37	5	34
Humberto Delatorre, Aldie	3	3	2.17	8	0	50	34	21	50
Jake Harper, Front Royal	5	0	2.22	8	0	53	42	11	47
Brock Hunter, Strasburg	3	3	2.36	12	0	42	37	15	47
Michael O'Reilly, Woodstock	2	5	2.55	10	0	60	52	18	50
Garrett Ford, Harrisonburg	4	2	2.95	6	0	40	47	11	13

WEST COAST LEAGUE

East Division

	W	L	PCT	GB
Yakima Valley Pippins	35	19	.648	—
Wenatchee AppleSox	30	24	.556	5
Walla Walla Sweets	28	26	.519	7
Kelowna Falcons	14	39	.264	20 ½

South Division

	W	L	PCT	GB
Corvallis Knights	35	19	.648	—
Bend Elks	31	23	.574	4
Medford Rogues	26	28	.481	9
Klamath Falls Gems	15	39	.278	20

West Division

	W	L	PCT	GB
Bellingham Bells	37	17	.685	—
Victoria HarbourCats	25	29	.463	12
Cowlitz Black Bears	24	30	.444	13
Kitsap BlueJackets	23	30	.434	13 ½

CHAMPIONSHIP: Bellingham Bells defeated Corvallis Knights 2-1 in best-of-three championship series.
TOP 10 PROSPECTS: 1. David Peterson, lhp, Medford Rogues (Fr., Oregon). **2.** Sean Bouchard, 3b, Walla Walla (Fr., UCLA). **3.** Vince Fernandez, of, Yakima Valley (So., UC Riverside). **4.** Elliott Cary, of, Cowlitz (Fr., Oregon State). **5.** Dalton Kelly, of/1b, Corvallis (Jr., UC Santa Barbara). **6.** John Pomeroy, rhp, Wenatchee (So., Oregon State). **7.** Justin Calomeni, rhp, Corvallis (So., Cal Poly). **8.** Drew Rasmussen, rhp, Wenatchee (Fr., Oregon State). **9.** Nick Kern, rhp, Yakima Valley (R-So., UCLA). **10.** Seth Martinez, rhp, Bellingham (So., Arizona State).

INDIVIDUAL BATTING LEADERS

	AVG	AB	R	H	2B	3B	HR	RBI	SB
Steven Packard, Kelowna	.394	155	26	61	14	1	0	24	11
Hunter Mercado-Hood, Victoria	.385	200	32	77	10	0	2	46	6
Tyler Frost, Wenatchee	.373	134	40	50	5	3	3	22	5
Caleb Wood, Wenatchee	.360	136	20	49	6	0	2	17	4
Vince Fernandez, YV	.359	170	38	61	13	3	10	51	11
Michael Duarte, WW	.353	136	27	48	11	3	6	31	3
Andrew Mendenhall, WW	.349	209	38	73	17	2	8	39	4
Justin Jacobs, Yakima Valley	.348	141	28	49	6	0	1	17	5
Daniel Woodrow, Kitsap	.346	133	29	46	4	4	0	19	17
Nick Lopez, Bend	.345	139	30	48	5	0	0	17	6
Nathan Lukes, Victoria	.343	172	35	59	9	1	2	24	7
Nathan Etheridge, Medford	.343	181	27	62	11	3	4	32	0

INDIVIDUAL PITCHING LEADERS

	W	L	ERA	G	SV	IP	H	BB	SO
Seth Martinez, Bellingham	6	0	2.07	9	0	57	28	16	50
Aaron Sandefur, Bellingham	5	3	2.16	9	0	58	31	25	55
Brandon Williams, YV	5	2	2.33	10	0	50	45	13	34
Andrew Woods, YV	5	3	2.38	12	0	72	57	22	58
Angel Landazuri, Corvallis	4	0	2.44	10	0	48	36	6	35
Billy Sahlinger, Cowlitz	4	0	2.68	9	0	57	39	30	32
Jackson Lockwood, Corvallis	8	2	2.83	13	0	54	53	13	43
Jackson Bertsch, Medford	6	2	2.91	10	1	53	45	25	40
Mikey Wright, Victoria	4	5	2.96	10	0	55	43	18	39
Eli Morgan, YV	8	0	3.05	11	1	62	57	22	56

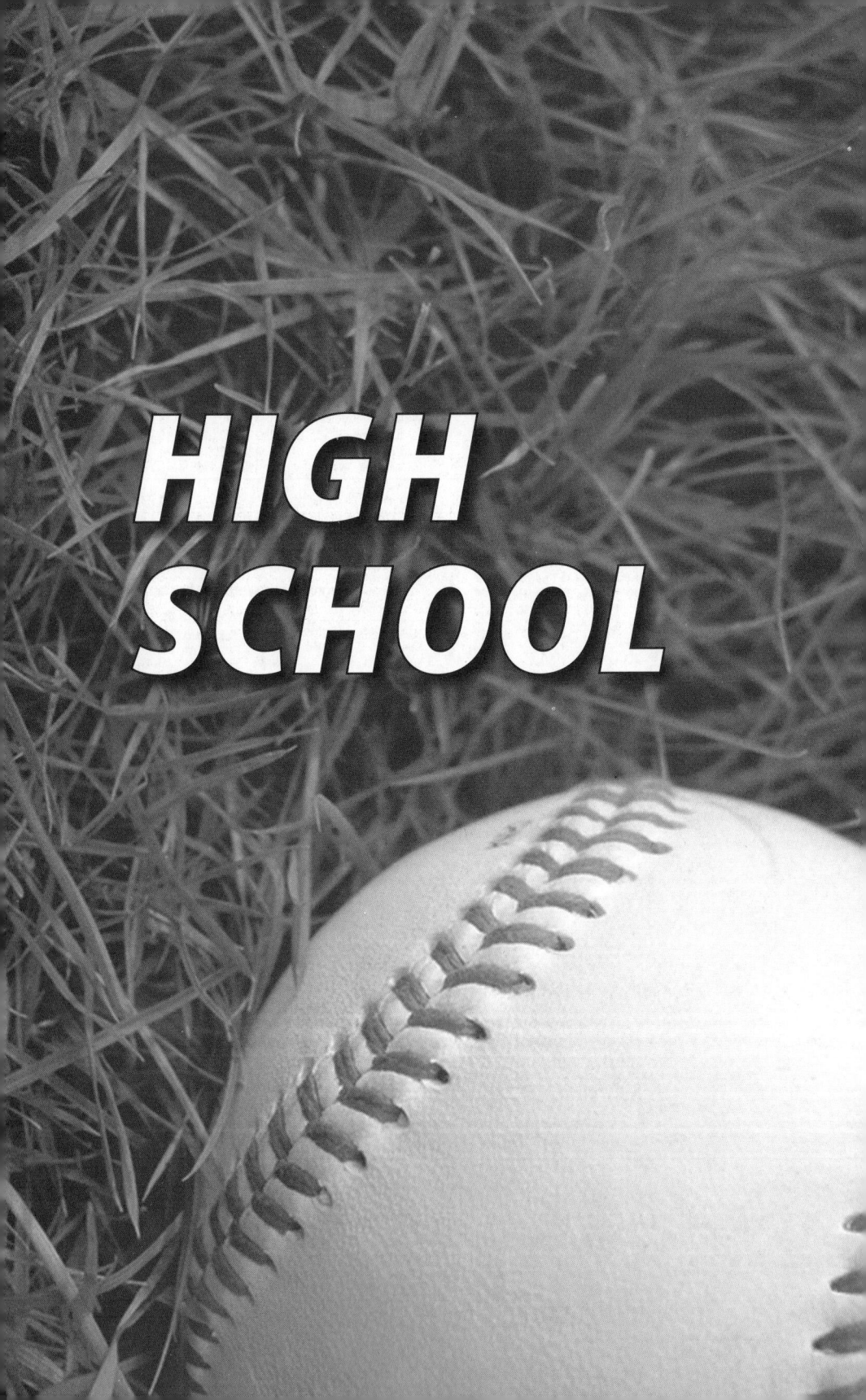

HIGH SCHOOL

KIRK MECHE

Barbe High had reason to cheer after winning a seventh state title and first national crown

Barbe High hits goal, wins national title

Well before Opening Day rolled around at Barbe High in Lake Charles, La., head coach Glenn Cecchini had already drawn up his goals for the 2014 season.

When he discussed them with his players in a preseason meeting, the team decided those goals were theirs as well.

So the Buccaneers, ranked sixth in the national preseason, made the goals visible. In the locker room, in the dugout, in the Barbe Baseball Book each player was assigned, there was a paper with season's goals in plain sight for all to see:

2014 State Champion.

2014 National Champion.

"People can say, 'Gosh dang, that's over the top. That's really arrogant,' " Cecchini said. "But we really believe in goal-setting. You got to make your goals visible where you can see them every day."

The Buccaneers had won a state title six times before, most recently in 2012. But if Barbe was going to win its first national title it realized the commitment and dedication it would take.

It was then that the four steps it would take to achieve them were laid out.

First, they would have to work harder than ever. In the past, biweekly workouts were canceled

when weeks were filled with games. This year, that wouldn't be the case. No matter the circumstances, the team participated in two workouts a week.

The newfound resolve came on the practice field. Two drills in every practice, one bunting and one fielding, would never be less than perfect.

Twenty-one outs, a simulated defensive game, had to be completed flawlessly. One mistake and the counter reset to zero.

In a practice before the state tournament, the team reached 20 outs four times before finally finishing the drill.

"I mean, I love being at the baseball field, and I love practicing, but once you get to 45 minutes and you're still doing the same drill it gets kind of frustrating," outfielder Beau Jordan said. "Even if you're frustrated though, you can't get down. You have to tell your teammate, 'Come on, man, come on,' and pick them up."

Barbe finished with a .974 fielding percentage.

The second step was to remain process-driven.

Hitting the ball hard, fielding a ground ball, making a pitch became valued over getting a hit, never making an error or striking out hitters. It was the reason individual stats were never posted.

"You can't do it alone," Jordan said. "One

HIGH SCHOOL TOP 50

Rank	School	Record	Season conclusion
1	Barbe HS, Lake Charles, La.	39-2	5A State Champ
2	Lambert HS, Suwanee, Ga.	36-2	6A State Champ
3	Hamilton HS, Chandler, Ariz.	30-3	Division I State Champ
4	Clovis (Calif.) HS	33-5	CIF Central Section D-I Champion
5	South Dade HS, Homestead, Fla.	23-6	8A State Champ
6	Stillwater (Okla.) HS	32-3	6A State Champ
7	American Senior HS, Hialeah, Fla.	26-5	7A State Champ
8	Greenway HS, Phoenix	29-4	Division II State Champ
9	West Lauderdale HS, Collinsville, Miss.	33-2	4A State Champ
10	Puyallup (Wa.) HS	28-0	4A State Champ
11	Sumter (S.C.) HS	26-2	4A State Champ
12	Spanish Fork (Ala.) HS	42-6	5A State Champ
13	Houston County HS, Perry, Ga.	31-7	5A State Champ
14	Liberty HS, Las Vegas	30-5	Division I State
15	North Florida Christian HS, Tallahasse, Fla.	26-4	3A State Champ
16	Leland HS, San Jose	23-9	CIF Central Coast Section Champion
17	Omaha (Neb.) Westside HS	35-3	Class A State Champ
18	Flower Mound (Texas) HS	34-12	5A State Champ
19	Aledo (Texas) HS	34-6	4A State Champ
20	New Hope HS, Columbus, Miss.	32-4	5A State Champ
21	Bryant (Ark.) HS	30-2	7A State Champ
22	Oak Grove HS, Hattiesburg, Miss.	27-7	6A State Champ
23	Western Branch HS, Chesapeake,Va.	27-2	6A State Champ
24	La Cueva HS, Albuquerque, N.M.	24-3	5A State Champ
25	Bloom Carroll (Ohio) HS	29-2	Division II State Champ
26	Mater Academy Charter, Hialeah, Fla.	30-8	6A State Champ
27	Santa Margarita HS, Rancho Santa Margaritita, Calif.	20-10	CIF Southern Section D-I Champion
28	De La Salle HS, Concord, Calif.	22-7	CIF North Coast Section D-I Champion
29	St. Thomas More HS, Layayette, La.	31-5	4A State Champ
30	St. Xavier HS, Louisville, Ky.	30-10	KHSAA State Champ
31	Rocky Mountain HS, Fort Collins, Colo.	21-5	5A State Champ
32	Buchanan HS, Clovis, Calif.	25-8	CIF Central Section D-I Champion Runner Up
33	Carl Albert HS, Midwest City, Okla.	38-4	5A State Champ
34	Jackson HS, Massillon, Ohio	26-5	Division I State Champ
35	Granite Hills HS, El Cajon, Calif.	26-7	CIF San Diego Section Champion
36	Milton (Ga.) HS	28-9	6A State Champ Runner Up
37	Winter Haven (Fla.) HS	25-6	6A State Champ Runner Up
38	Jordan HS, Sandy, Utah	25-6	5A State Champ
39	Temecula Valley HS, Calif.	24-8	CIF Southern Section D-II Champion
40	Cardozo HS, New York	20-2	PSAL Division A Champion
41	Farragut (Tenn.) HS	34-13	3A State Champ
42	Leominster (Mass.) HS	24-1	Division I State Champ
43	Live Oak HS, Denham Springs, La.	30-10	5A State Runner Up
44	West Forsyth HS, Clemmons, N.C.	27-8	5A State Runner Up
45	St. Thomas Aquinas, Overland Park, Kan.	21-4	5A State Champ
46	Blue Valley HS, Stilwell, Kan.	18-7	6A State Champ
47	St. John Vianney Regional HS, Holmdel, N.J.	23-7	Non-Public Group A State Champ
48	Bellarmine HS, San Jose	26-8	CIF Central Coast Section Runner Up
49	Newton (Mass.) North HS	20-1	Division 1A State Champ
50	Reservoir HS, Fulton, Md.	22-2	3A State Runner Up

pitcher or one player isn't going to get you to 39-2. That's what we bought in to."

Then came learning how to deal with failure. When something negative happened the team adopted a "so what, move on" attitude.

Taking deep breaths after letting up an extra-base hit, removing the helmet to let out all the negative thoughts after a bad swing or shaking out a glove after an error, players were determined not to let the last pitch's outcome affect the next one's.

"At first it was a little uncomfortable," shortstop Kennon Fontenot said. "But everybody bought into it. It worked. Once it started to work we all kept doing it, and it elevated our game even more."

The final step was spiritual. Player-led Bible studies, pregame devotions, joint postgame prayers with opposing teams, all in an effort to remind the players how fortunate they were to be ballplayers.

It was a combination of these four steps, team unity and tremendous talent that led to the ultimate goal being realized: finishing atop the Baseball America national rankings.

Still, it wasn't a cakewalk to the championship. After losing two of its first 13 games, Barbe's chances of finishing first were falling fast.

"We wanted to be the first Barbe team to (win the national title). Early we dropped a couple games and we knew it probably wasn't going to be

possible for us to win it all," said Fontenot. "We just went out there, played our game.

"All of a sudden we hear that everyone else is losing. Then, when that national title was back in our grasps, we took off. We knew we were not going to lose again. That was our goal, and we achieved it."

Beginning with a 9-5 win on March 15, which improved the team's record to 12-2, Barbe rattled off one win after another. By the season's concluding contest the win streak sat at 28.

It wasn't all smooth sailing, despite outscoring opponents 371-94, hitting .384/.488/.592 as a team and averaging more than nine runs a game. Already in "can't lose again" territory, Barbe found itself trailing by a sizable margin against Comeaux High on March 27.

"We had our backs against the wall there. It was 6-1 going into the fourth or fifth inning," said Fontenot. "We were just doing what we do. We didn't have a big meeting or a group talk. Somebody just got a hit, than the next guy did, and we kept rolling."

Staying true to the four steps they had all bought into, Barbe scored 15 unanswered runs and won via the 10-run mercy rule, 16-6.

"That might be the best and deepest lineup I have ever seen from a high school team," a scout said during the season. "I would put it up against any lineup in the country. Their lineup is led by a tremendous group of seniors and they are just a factory that produces ballplayers."

Senior lefthander Gunner Leger and freshman lefty Adam Goree combined to go 23-0 and toss 14 complete games, marching Barbe through the rest of the year and into the state tournament.

The Bucaneers outscored their playoff opponents 47-12 on their way to the title game.

While the championship stage was a large one, it paled in comparison to one five Barbe players had been on six years earlier. As members of the South Lake Charles Little League team, Jordan, his twin brother Bryce—who was the first catcher Cecchini ever allowed to call his own game— Leger, Fontenot, and Nicholas Abshire made it to the 2008 Little League U.S. title game of the Little League World Series in Williamsport, Pa.

"I guess being a kid we didn't realize how big of a stage we were on," Beau Jordan said. "But just the crowds and not being overwhelmed, that carried over to the state tournament. Knowing you have more than a normal group of people watching you. I guess that's the biggest part of it."

Barbe fell behind Live Oak 1-0 in the first inning of the state title game with Leger pitching. By the time players flooded from the dugout and charged from their respective positions at game's end to meet in the celebratory dog pile, Barbe rattled off seven straight runs to win 7-1.

One last time, the best team in the country— the one that decided before the season's first game they'd come together to do something remarkable—won in convincing fashion.

First Academy Wins NHSI

Clovis High came close to keeping the third National High School Invitational trophy in the hands of a California school, just like the first two.

But Orlando's The First Academy wouldn't let it happen.

Second baseman Chadwick Word hit a bases-loaded double in the sixth, clearing the bases and turning a 3-2 deficit into a 5-3 The First Academy victory. Reliever Peyton Hopkins got out of a bases-loaded, one-out jam in the fourth and finished with 3 2/3 innings of scoreless relief for the Royals, who won all four of their NHSI contests.

Hopkins also closed out TFA's semifinal win against Regis Jesuit. Hopkins entered the game versus Clovis holding a 3-2 lead, having scored its three runs on six hits in the fourth inning, and had the bases juiced. He didn't realize when he got to the mound that preseason All-American Jacob Gatewood was the first hitter he would face.

"They told me it was Gatewood hitting, and I was like, 'Oh.' But I knew I had to keep it low," said Hopkins, who fell behind in the count 3-0. Clovis coach James Patrick said he usually gives Gatewood the green light on 3-0 counts, but because Hopkins had just come in and not thrown a strike, he had Gatewood take on 3-0.

Hopkins got a strike, then located his fastball down and away, and Gatewood rolled over for a 5-2 forceout. With sophomore catcher Cody Oerther calling the pitches, Hopkins then retired Alan Crowley on another fielder's choice grounder to third baseman Trenton Fiscus, who had a strong day defensively, as TFA escaped the jam.

"Their pitcher did a great job by executing pitches," Patrick said. "I was really proud of the way our kids fought back and put up those runs after they had scored and taken the lead. We got right back into it and got the lead."

Clovis held the lead until The First Academy's two-out rally in the bottom of the sixth. Reliever Masyn Ashworth gave up a leadoff single but a popped-up bunt double play brought Nick Gavin to the plate, and the shortstop prolonged the inning with a single. Clovis went to knuckleballing righthander Gavin Brar, who gave up a single and then walked Adam Haseley to load the bases.

That's when Word drilled a knuckler down the left-field line for a game-winning double. All three

runs scored. Coach Scott Grove, in his first year at TFA, said his team had been able to scout Brar the night before and was able to tell his players the knuckler lacked velocity, but Word said he had never hit against a knuckleballer.

"I just wanted to get a good swing, and he left it up," said Word, who had doubled home a run and scored in TFA's two-run third inning.

"The whole week was amazing, and I'm just so happy for the kids because it was a total team effort," coach Grove said of the Royals, whose 16-player roster was by far the smallest in the event. "The kids stayed resilient and came up big when they needed to. It was just a lot of fun."

The First Academy was led by strong pitching, headlined by one of the top duos of lefthanders in the country with Haseley and Foster Griffin, both All-NHSI first teamers. Haseley, the leadoff hitter, hit .417/.533/.583 and threw a complete game shutout with nine strikeouts. Griffin, the Royals' first-rounder, threw a complete game shutout while striking out eight.

U.S. Claims 18U Title

With Hurricane Odile about to hit Mexico on the evening of the championship game, USA Baseball's 18-and-under National Team was declared the winner of the COPABE 18U Pan American Championships.

It marks the fourth straight summer Team USA's 18U program has emerged victorious in international play after winning the 2011 COPABE Pan American Championship in Colombia and consecutive World Cups in 2012 and 2013.

Cuba and the U.S. squared off in the championship game, with the game scheduled for a 7:30 p.m. local start, following the bronze medal game.

For the second straight year, a Southern California lefthander committed to UCLA who is very young for the draft class pitched the team to a gold medal game victory, as Kolby Allard (San Clemente High, South Coast, Calif.) followed in the footsteps of Brady Aiken.

The U.S. took a 1-0 lead in the bottom of the first inning when speedy leadoff hitter Nick Madrigal of Elk Grove (Calif.) High reached on an error and advanced to second before scoring on a single to center field by right fielder Trenton Clark (Richland High, North Richland Hills, Texas).

Allard, who struck out 10 of the 18 hitters he faced in five innings in his first start against Canada, was off to a strong start against Cuba, striking out seven of the 11 hitters he faced in his first three scoreless innings while allowing a walk.

In the bottom of the third inning, the Cubans refused to take the field for Team USA's turn at the plate. As soon as the Cubans took the field, the umpires pulled them off because of a concern about lightning strikes from the looming hurricane. The game was then called off.

There was initially talk of naming co-champions, but officials declared Team USA the champs.

The U.S. squad dominated the field in their eight games, producing a 110-5 run differential. Four of the five runs Team USA allowed were against the Cubans in a 5-4 victory.

"This is one of the most dominating teams that I have ever been a part of," 18U National Team manager Andy Stankiewicz said. "We used the word relentless a lot and they totally bought in. They were relentless in every facet. They didn't give up at-bats and every pitcher came in and topped the guy before him.

"It was an unbelievably competitive group. When you have talented young men like this and they play together, you are going to have success. We had lots of fun playing."

This year's U.S. squad produced a statistical dominance over its international opponents that is unparalleled in 18U history.

The pitching staff produced a 0.71 ERA, breaking the mark of 0.86 from the 2005 team that had first-round picks Clayton Kershaw and Jeremy Bleich, as well as major leaguers Brett Anderson, Dellin Betances, Shawn Tolleson and Tyson Ross. The team allowed 0.63 runs per game, the lowest ever, also behind the 2005 squad.

Team USA's pitching staff recorded strikeouts at a prodigious pace, striking out 11.8 per nine and 36 percent of all hitters against 3.4 walks per nine and a 10.2 walk percent.

The defense was surehanded and committed only three errors in eight games in 51 defensive innings, producing a fielding percentage of .985, which led all teams at the event. Strong-armed backstop Lucas Herbert (San Clemente High, South Coast, Calif.) threw out the lone baserunner who tried to attempt a steal.

The offensive attack averaged 13.75 runs per game, the most in Team USA history dating back to 1987, the first year 18U statistics were recorded. This tops the previous high of 13.0 by the 2002 team that had No. 1 overall pick Delmon Young and No. 5 overall pick Chris Lubanski, as well as major leaguers Allen Craig, Lastings Milledge, Jarrod Saltalamacchia and Ian Stewart.

The team hit .432/.539/.657 with 12 home runs, drawing almost two walks for every strikeout. The lineup swiped 22 bases at a 95.7 percent clip. Last year's gold medal–winning team hit three home runs with an isolated slugging of .098, compared to 12 home runs this year with an .225 ISO.

USA BASEBALL

Event	Site	Champion	Runner-up
Tournament of Stars (18U)	Cary, N.C.	Pride	Brave
USA Baseball 17U—East	Palm Beach Co., Fla.	Marlins Scout Team	Easton Rockets 17u
USA Baseball 17U—West	Goodyear, Ariz.	GBG Marucci	Nor Cal Valley
USA Baseball 15U—East	Fort Myers, Fla.	Team Phenom	Palm Beach County PAL
USA Baseball 15U—West	Goodyear, Ariz.	BPA Gold	NorCal DeMarini
USA Baseball 14U—East	Cary, N.C.	Miami Suns	Central Florida Gators
USA Baseball 14U—West	Goodyear, Ariz.	West Covina Dukes National	San Diego Show

ALL-AMERICAN AMATEUR BASEBALL ASSOCIATION (AAABA) · Headquarters: Zanesville, Ohio

Event	Site	Champion	Runner-up
World Series (21-and-Under)	Johnstown, Pa.	Des Plaines Patriots	Philadelphia Bandits

AMATEUR ATHLETIC UNION (AAU) · Headquarters: Lake Buena Vista, Fla.

Event	Site	Champion	Runner-up
10-and-Under Diamond (60-foot)	Orlando	First Strike	Virginia Young Guns
10-and-Under Gold (60-foot)	Orlando	FS Elite (FL)	QBA Bad Boyz
11-and-Under Diamond (70-foot)	Orlando	CBC Riverhawks Black	Team Florida
11-and-Under Gold (70-foot)	Orlando	East Cobb Braves	Oviedo Knights
12-and-Under Diamond (70-foot)	Orlando	Hamden Yard Dogs	Jax Rockets
12-and-Under Gold (70-foot)	Orlando	GPA Hooks	Ocala Venom
13-and-Under Diamond (90-foot)	Orlando	Mountain Expos Black	Team Elite
13-and-Under Gold (90-foot)	Orlando	Connecticut Capitals	Reg Rage
14-and-Under Super Showcase	Orlando	Puerto Rico Hawks	Mizuno Taylormade
Upperclassmen Super Showcase	Orlando	Brazos Valley Renegades	LB Warriors

AMERICAN AMATEUR BASEBALL CONGRESS (AABC) · Headquarters: Farmington, N.M.

Event	Site	Champion	Runner-up
Gil Hodges	Brooklyn, N.Y.	Bonnie Seals	Youth SVC
Pee Wee Reese (12 & U)	Toa Baja, P.R.	Dallas Bombers	Cachorros Levittown
Sandy Koufax (14 & U)	Bartlesville, Okla.	Seymour Mudcats	Aquilas de Carolina
Ken Griffey, Jr. (15 & U)	Surprise, Ariz.	Frozen Ropes	South Troy
Mickey Mantle (16 & U)	McKinney, Texas	DBAT – Bonesio	Midland Tomahawks
Don Mattingly (17 & U)	Surprise, Ariz.	Colton Nighthawks	McKinney Marshals
Connie Mack (18 & U)	Farmington, N.M.	DBAT-Gallegos	Midland Redskins
Stan Musial (open)	Farmingdale, N.Y.	Braintree White Sox	New York Bluehawks

AMERICAN LEGION BASEBALL · Headquarters: Indianapolis

Event	Site	Champion	Runner-up
World Series (19 & U)	Shelby, N.C.	Brooklawn, N.J.	Midland, Mich.

BABE RUTH BASEBALL · Headquarters: Trenton, N.J.

Event	Site	Champion	Runner-up
Cal Ripken (10 & U)	Winchester, Va.	Marlton, N.J.	Lexington, Ky.
Cal Ripken 12-year-old (60 feet)	Alachua, Fla.	Bismarck, N.D.	Bronx, N.Y.
Cal Ripken 13-year-old (70 feet)	Aberdeen, Md.	West Raleigh, N.C.	Japan
13-year-old	Greg Allen, Va.	Broomall-Newtown, Pa.	Phoenix, Ariz.
14-year-old	Longview, Wash.	Tri-Counties, Texas	Oahu, Hawaii
13-15-year-olds	Longview, Wash.	Broomall-Newtown, Pa.	Lumber River, N.C.
16-18-year-old	Ephrata, Wash.	Alabama Rawdogs	Klamath Falls, Ore.

CONTINENTAL AMATEUR BASEBALL ASSOCIATION (CABA) · Headquarters: Westerville, Ohio

Event	Site	Champion	Runner-up
9-and-Under	Mason, Ohio	Midland Blackhawks	Triple Crown Defenders
12-and-Under	Mason, Ohio	Apaches Baseball	Cincy Flames
13-and-Under	Westfield, Ind.	East Cobb Astros	NA
14-and-Under (60x90)	Lebanon, Tenn.	Tennessee Knights	Middle Tennessee Bruins
15-and-Under (Aluminum)	Jacksonville, Ill.	Rijo Athletics	Team Missouri

Clark had the second-highest batting average of any hitter at the event while producing a .565/.694/1.043 line. Clark drew a team-high 10 walks while striking out once. After getting on base in more than two-thirds of his plate appearances, he stole five bases. He led the team in extra-base hits with three home runs and two doubles.

"It was a lot of fun, it always is when you are playing for something bigger than yourself, for a bigger purpose," Clark said. "I got to be a part of that earlier this summer playing for a national championship for Connie Mack. Coming here I knew it was going to be even better playing for and representing my country."

Third baseman Ke'Bryan Hayes (Concordia Lutheran High, Tomball, Texas) also hit better than .500 with his .542/.656/.625 line, walking seven times against a lone strikeout.

15-and-Under (Wood)	Charleston, S.C.	Blue Chip Bulls	Palmetto Gators
16-and-Under	Marietta, Ga.	East Cobb Astros	Team Elite Roadrunner
17-and-Under/HS (Aluminum)	Euclid, Ohio	Florida Legends	Lake Erie Bulldogs
17-and-Under/HS (Wood)	Charleston, S.C.	Knoxville Stars	Palmetto Gators
18-and-Under (Wood)	Charleston, S.C.	Diamond Devils	East Cobb Yankees

LITTLE LEAGUE BASEBALL · Headquarters: Williamsport, Pa.

Event	Site	Champion	Runner-up
Little League (11-12)	Williamsport, Pa.	South Korea	Chicago, Illinois
Junior League (13-14)	Taylor, Mich.	Chinese Taipei	Corpus Christi, Texas
Senior League (15-16)	Bangor, Maine	Houston, Texas	Curacao
Big League (17-18)	Easley, S.C	Florida District 12	Puerto Rico

NATIONAL AMATEUR BASEBALL FEDERATION (NABF) · Headquarters: Bowie, Md.

Event	Site	Champion	Runner-up
Sophomore (14 & U)	Knoxville, Tenn.	Creekside Fitness	Diamond Elite 96ers
Junior (16 & U)	Toledo, Ohio	Sayo Grays	Youngstown Astro Falcons
High School (17 & U)	Knoxville, Tenn.	Toronto Mets	HCYP 17s
Senior (18 & U)	Struthers, Ohio	Ohio Glaciers	Creekside Fitness

PERFECT GAME/BCS FINALS · Headquarters: Cedar Rapids, Iowa

Event	Site	Champion	Runner-up
13-and-Under	Fort Myers, Fla.	Banditos Black	Florida Stealth
14-and-Under	Fort Myers, Fla.	Connecticut Wolfpack	East Cobb Astros
15-and-Under	Fort Myers, Fla.	Georgia Jackets	Scorpions Panhandle
16-and-Under	Fort Myers, Fla.	Elite Squad Prime	Team Elite Prime
17-and-Under	Fort Myers, Fla.	Texas Sun Devils	East Cobb Astros
18-and-Under	Fort Myers, Fla.	Midwest Elite	Next Level Upperclass

PERFECT GAME/WORLD WOOD BAT ASSOCIATION SUMMER CHAMPIONSHIPS · Headquarters: Cedar Rapids, Iowa

Event	Site	Champion	Runner-up
14-and-Under	Fort Myers, Fla.	Upstate Mavericks	6-4-3 DP Tigers
15-and-Under	Marietta, Ga.	Georgia Jackets	Tri-State Arsenal
16-and-Under	Marietta, Ga.	BPA DeMarini Elite	Team Elite Roadrunners
17-and-Under	Marietta, Ga.	EvoShield Canes	Elite Squad Prime
18-and-Under	Marietta, Ga.	Knights Baseball National	Georgia Roadrunners

PONY BASEBALL · Headquarters: Washington, Pa.

Event	Site	Champion	Runner-up
Mustang (9-10)	Burleson, Texas	Mission Viejo, Calif.	San Cristobal, D.R.
Bronco (11-12)	Chesterfield, Va.	Chesterfield (CBC), Va.	Los Alamitos, Calif.
Pony (13)	Fullerton, Calif.	Sinaloa, Mexico	Evansville, Ind.
Pony (13-14)	Washington, Pa.	Hilo, Hawaii	Chinese Taipei
Colt (15-16)	Lafayette, Ind.	Los Gatos, Calif.	Caguas, P.R.
Palomino (17-18)	Compton, Calif.	Urban Youth Academy, Calif.	NA

REVIVING BASEBALL IN INNER CITIES (RBI) · Headquarters: New York

Event	Site	Champion	Runner-up
Junior (13-15)	Arlington, Texas	Venice, Fla.	Detroit, Mich.
Senior (16-18)	Arlington, Texas	Jersey City, N.J.	Los Angeles, Calif.

U.S. SPECIALTY SPORTS ASSOCIATION (USSSA) · Headquarters: Petersburg, Va.

Event	Site	Champion	Runner-up
10-and-Under/Majors Elite	Orlando	South Texas Longhorn Academy	Central Florida Wolverines
11-and-Under/Majors Elite	Orlando	Diamond Club	Team Halo
12-and-Under/Majors Elite	Orlando	Team Panama	Team Select
13-and-Under/Majors Elite	Orlando	Weston Black Hawks	EM Majors
14-and-Under/Majors Elite	Orlando	Team Rawlings Moulton	NorCal Naturals

Madrigal was a table-setter who hit .481/.559/.556 with a team-high seven steals and 17 runs scored. Madrigal has exceptional bat control and was the only hitter on the team who did not strike out, accruing 36 plate appearances.

The pitching staff combined to throw consecutive no-hitters against Guatemala and Ecuador. Only one no-hitter had ever been thrown in Team USA's 18U history before 2014.

Righthander Kyle Molnar (Aliso Niguel High, Aliso Viejo, Calif.) threw two one-hitters in victories over Panama and Mexico. He led the team in strikeouts.

The victory clinches the United States' spot in the 2015 IBAF 18U World Cup in Japan, as the squad will try for its first World Cup three-peat. Cuba, Canada and Mexico also qualified.

– BY JACOB EMERT

Jackson Has Superlative Prep Career

Alex Jackson has been a baseball player for his entire life.

From when he was 2 years old, inspecting his first tee-ball set, to the nights in high school when he would take extra cuts in the batting cage. For Jackson, baseball is life.

His father Dorian recalls when Alex first started getting serious about the game.

"At 4, he became more consistent with wanting to play and it kind of blossomed from there," he said. "Right away he just absolutely loved the sport. That's where he got started."

That drive to play the game has become instilled in Jackson. The reason he hit .379/.513/.844 with 47 home runs throughout his high school career. The reason he became the first two-time Under Armour All-American. The reason he was drafted No. 6 overall.

Jackson looks back to the many Friday nights when he passed on football games and went to the batting cage. Baseball became serious—more than just a game he loved to play—when he made the varsity roster at famed Rancho Bernardo High in San Diego.

"I always wanted to play baseball my whole life," Jackson said. "And so when I had the opportunity to be able to start on the varsity team and coach Blalock told me I had a chance, that's when it kind of kicked in."

Jackson was a freshman, young, but talented and determined to make varsity.

"I was like, 'You know what? I've got to work my butt off, I've got to go get the starting position,'" he said.

Jackson quickly began turning heads.

"People that we've known over the years that are in baseball," Dorian Jackson said. "They were the ones who were telling us, 'This kid, he's been good for a long time, but he's pretty special and he's got pretty special talents.'

"I think one of the first things that his head coach (Blalock) said to me is, 'You know, you'll be watching your kid play for a long time.'"

His performance during showcases bolstered his track record with Rancho Bernardo.

Steve Bernhardt is the executive vice president of Baseball Factory, and one of his responsibilities is to evaluate players for the Under Armour All-American Game. He still remembers the first time he saw Jackson.

"It was the summer after his sophomore

PLAYER OF THE YEAR

PREVIOUS WINNERS

1992: Preston Wilson, of/rhp, Bamberg-Ehrhardt (S.C.) HS
1993: Trot Nixon, of/lhp, New Hanover HS, Wilmington, N.C.
1994: Doug Million, lhp, Sarasota (Fla.) HS
1995: Ben Davis, c, Malvern (Pa.) Prep
1996: Matt White, rhp, Waynesboro Area (Pa.) HS
1997: Darnell McDonald, of, Cherry Creek HS, Englewood, Colo.
1998: Drew Henson, 3b/rhp, Brighton (Mich.) HS
1999: Josh Hamilton, of/lhp, Athens Drive HS, Raleigh, N.C.
2000: Matt Harrington, rhp, Palmdale (Calif.) HS
2001: Joe Mauer, c, Cretin-Derham Hall HS, St. Paul, Minn.
2002: Scott Kazmir, lhp, Cypress Falls HS, Houston
2003: Jeff Allison, rhp, Veterans Memorial HS, Peabody, Mass.
2004: Homer Bailey, rhp, LaGrange (Texas) HS
2005: Justin Upton, ss, Great Bridge HS, Chesapeake, Va.
2006: Adrian Cardenas, ss/2b, Mons. Pace HS, Opa Locka, Fla.
2007: Mike Moustakas, ss, Chatsworth (Calif.) HS
2008: Ethan Martin, rhp/3b, Stephens County HS, Toccoa, Ga.
2009: Bryce Harper, c, Las Vegas HS
2010: Kaleb Cowart, rhp/3b, Cook HS, Adel, Ga.
2011: Dylan Bundy, rhp, Owasso (Okla.) HS
2012: Byron Buxton, of, Appling County HS, Baxley, Ga.
2013: Clint Frazier, of, Loganville (Ga.) HS

year," Bernhardt said. "The thing that stood out was the ability to hit, plus the power. The ability to fit in with older players who are also talented for their class (stood out). You just kind of sensed that he was a pretty special player."

He showed an advanced hitting approach.

"Especially at that young age it's not often that you see somebody with a polished approach," Bernhardt said. "He could handle velocity, he recognized offspeed stuff and handled that very well. And you know they say a lot of times with certain guys that it sounds different off the bat, and when he was hitting with a wood bat it was certainly the case."

Jackson signed with the Mariners for a $4.2 million bonus, and was moved to the outfield, which he did not mind.

"That's one of those things that just doesn't really matter," Jackson said. "Honestly, I just want to go out and play baseball."

He's still the same kid who used to take extra cuts in the cage on Friday nights. Still the young boy who was always seen carrying around his first tee-ball bat.

He's just a bit bigger now. And a little bit closer to fulfilling his dream of playing major league baseball.

ALL-AMERICA TEAM

Alex Jackson

BILL MITCHELL

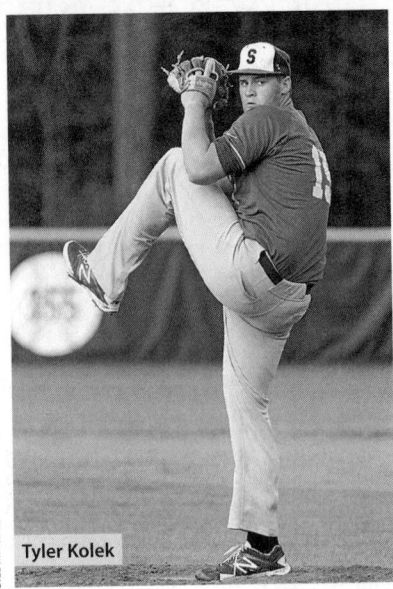

Tyler Kolek

MARK ANDERSON

FIRST TEAM

Pos.	Name	School	Yr.	AVG	AB	R	H	2B	3B	HR	RBI	SB	DRAFTED
C	Alex Jackson	Rancho Bernardo HS, Escondido, Calif.	Sr.	.400	100	45	40	7	4	11	31	8	Mariners (1)
IF	Gavin LaValley	Carl Albert HS, Oklahoma City	Sr.	.554	115	62	63	11	1	18	73	5	Reds (4)
IF	Nick Gordon	Olympia HS, Orlando	Sr.	.512	86	31	44	11	2	6	28	14	Twins (1)
IF	Michael Chavis	Sprayberry HS, Marietta, Ga.	Sr.	.580	81	30	47	9	1	13	37	21	Red Sox (1)
IF	JJ Matijevic	Norwin HS, North Huntingdon, Pa.	Sr.	.607	NA	29	34	9	1	10	37	8	Red Sox (22)
OF	Braxton Davidson	Roberson HS, Asheville, N.C.	Sr.	.449	78	33	35	7	1	4	21	NA	Braves (1)
OF	Derek Hill	Elk Grove (Calif.) HS	Sr.	.500	94	26	47	11	7	0	30	21	Tigers (1)
OF	Lane Thomas	Bearden HS, Knoxville, Tenn.	Sr.	.410	100	57	41	8	4	17	40	NA	Blue Jays (5)
DH	Chase Vallot	St. Thomas More HS, Lafayette, La.	Sr.	.545	99	45	54	15	1	13	62	3	Royals (1)
UT	Jack Flaherty	Harvard-Westlake HS, Studio City, Calif.	Jr.	.280	82	22	23	3	3	2	18	21	Cardinals (1)

Pos.	Name	School	Yr.	W	L	ERA	G	SV	IP	H	BB	K	DRAFTED
RHP	Cameron Varga	Cincinnati Hills Academy, Loveland, Ohio	Sr.	8	0	0	8	0	58	8	6	141	Rays (2)
LHP	Cody Reed	Ardmore (Ala.) HS	Sr.	10	2	0.46	12	0	92	28	17	226	D'backs (2)
RHP	JB Bukauskas	Stone Bridge HS, Ashburn, Va.	Sr.	7	0	0	9	0	47	14	7	105	D'backs (20)
LHP	Justus Sheffield	Tullahoma (Tenn.) HS	Sr.	10	0	0.34	12	0	62	17	22	137	Indians (1S)
RHP	Tyler Kolek	Shepherd (Texas) HS	Sr.	5	2	0.35	10	0	60	23	8	126	Marlins (1))
UT	Jack Flaherty	Harvard-Westlake HS, Studio City, Calif.	Sr.	10	0	0.63	12	0	78	32	12	125	Cardinals (1)

SECOND TEAM

Pos.	Name	School	Yr.	AVG	AB	R	H	2B	3B	HR	RBI	SB	DRAFTED
C	Jakson Reetz	Norris HS, Firth, Neb.	Sr.	.486	74	37	36	13	1	8	37	13	Nationals (3)
IF	Justin Twine	Falls City (Texas) HS	Sr.	.538	52	28	28	7	5	6	22	19	Marlins (2)
IF	Isan Diaz	Springfield (Mass.) Central HS	Sr.	.529	NA	27	27	9	2	4	15	NA	D'backs (2)
IF	Forrest Wall	Orangewood Christian HS, Winter Park, Fla.	Sr.	.500	56	31	28	9	4	1	16	29	Rockies (1)
IF	Aaron Pilkington	Ardrey Kell HS, Charlotte	So.	.400	80	35	32	4	1	19	43	4	Not eligible
OF	Kyle Tucker	Plant HS, Tampa	Jr.	.415	82	34	34	7	3	9	35	6	Not eligible
OF	Clay Casey	Desoto Central HS, Southaven, Miss.	Sr.	.464	110	43	51	8	5	14	47	9	Nationals (33)
OF	Alec Allred	Faith Christian Academy, Goldsboro, N.C.	Sr.	.585	NA	47	38	11	0	3	35	65	Undrafted
DH	Hunter Taylor	Nandua HS, Olney, Va.	Sr.	.554	56	31	31	5	3	12	39	9	Undrafted
UT	Adam Haseley	The First Academy, Orlando	Sr.	.425	80	35	34	5	2	5	18	6	Undrafted

Pos.	Name	School	Yr.	W	L	ERA	G	SV	IP	H	BB	K	DRAFTED
LHP	Brendan McKay	BlackHawk HS, Beaver Falls, Pa.	Sr.	10	0	0.63	11	0	56	NA	8	119	Padres (34)
LHP	Justin Steele	George County HS, Lucedale, Miss.	Sr.	5	1	0.98	8	0	43	16	12	92	Cubs (5)
LHP	Nick Wells	Battlefield HS, Haymarket, Va.	Sr.	7	1	1.06	9	0	53	21	18	102	Blue Jays (3)
RHP	Michael Kopech	Mount Pleasant (Texas) HS	Sr.	3	0	0.44	11	0	64	25	18	129	Red Sox (1)
LHP	Kodi Medeiros	Waiakea HS, Hilo, Hawaii	Sr.	5	1	1.12	8	0	44	18	15	81	Brewers (1)
UT	Adam Haseley	The First Academy, Orlando	Sr.	6	2	0.34	11	0	41	18	16	69	Undrafted

DRAFT

Aiken, Astros dispute leaves draft unsettled

BY JOHN MANUEL AND CLINT LONGENECKER

The Houston Astros drafted Brady Aiken first overall in the 2014 draft. And yet Brady Aiken is not a member of the Astros organization.

It's just the third time in draft history that the No. 1 pick failed to sign, with Aiken joining Danny Goodwin (1971, White Sox) and Tim Belcher (1983, Twins) in dubious draft history. Goodwin, a catcher, went to Southern and was drafted No. 1 overall again four years later and had a modest big league career. Belcher went on to be a first-rounder again in January 1984 and had a 14-season, 146-win big league career.

How Aiken's career unfolds is anyone's guess, because as the Almanac went to press, Aiken's future plans remained a mystery. He had a UCLA commitment in the spring but was not attending the school, and Bruins coaches do not expect him to attend. He had yet to attend a junior college yet or announce plans of any kind. Attempts to reach him or his adviser, Casey Close of Excel Sports Management, have been met with polite silence.

Excel represented both Aiken and righthander Jacob Nix, whom the Astros drafted in the fifth

Brady Aiken became the first high school lefthander to go No. 1 overall since 1991

FIRST-ROUND BONUS PROGRESSION

Current draft rules have been effective in slowing overall draft spending, but teams continue to pay for premium talent, spending an average of $2,612,109 on first-round picks in 2014, the third-highest ever. This marks a slight decrease (1.1 percent) from last year, which can be largely attributed for the first overall pick (which held a pick value of nearly eight million dollars) not signing. Had Brady Aiken signed for what had publically been reported ($6.5 million), the slight decrease would have been a 3.2 percent increase.

The highest ever was the $2,653,375 average from 2011, the last year of the old draft rules.

After the first draft in 1965, first-round bonuses rose by an average of just 0.6 percent annually for the rest of the 1960s and 5.2 percent per year in the 1970s. Bonus inflation picked up in the 1980s, averaging 10.2 percent annually, and soared to 26.9 percent per year in the 1990s.

Below are the annual averages for first-round bonuses since the draft started in 1965. The 1996 total does not include four players who became free agents through a draft loophole.

YEAR	AVERAGE	CHANGE	YEAR	AVERAGE	CHANGE	YEAR	AVERAGE	CHANGE
1965	$42,516	—	1982	$82,615	+5.1%	1999	$1,809,767	+10.5%
1966	$44,430	+4.5%	1983	$87,236	+5.6%	2000	$1,872,586	+3.5%
1967	$42,898	-3.4%	1984	$105,391	+20.8%	2001	$2,154,280	+15.0%
1968	$43,850	+2.2%	1985	$118,115	+12.1%	2002	$2,106,793	-2.2%
1969	$43,504	-0.8%	1986	$116,300	-1.6%	2003	$1,765,667	-16.2%
1970	$45,230	+3.9%	1987	$128,480	+10.5%	2004	$1,958,448	+10.9%
1971	$45,197	-0.1%	1988	$142,540	+10.9%	2005	$2,018,000	+3.0%
1972	$44,952	-0.5%	1989	$176,008	+23.5%	2006	$1,933,333	-4.2%
1973	$48,832	+8.6%	1990	$252,577	+43.5%	2007	$2,098,083	+8.5%
1974	$53,333	+9.2%	1991	$365,396	+44.7%	2008	$2,458,714	+17.2%
1975	$49.333	-7.5%	1992	$481,893	+31.9%	2009	$2,434,800	-1.0%
1976	$49,631	+0.6%	1993	$613,037	+27.2%	2010	$2,220,966	-8.8%
1977	$48,813	-1.6%	1994	$790,357	+28.9%	2011	$2,653,375	+19.5%
1978	$67,892	+39.1%	1995	$918,019	+16.1%	2012	$2,475,167	-6.7%
1979	$68,094	+0.2%	1996*	$944,404	+2.9%	2013	$2,641,538	+6.7%
1980	$74,025	+8.7%	1997	$1,325,536	+40.4%	2014	$2,612,109	-1.1%
1981	$78,573	+6.1%	1998	$1,637,667	+23.1%			

round. The Astros and Nix were reported to have agreed to terms on a $1.5 million bonus, one that required Houston to sign Aiken to a bonus below the $7.9 million slot allocated for the No. 1 overall pick. Aiken and the Astros also were reported widely to have agreed to terms on a $6.5 million deal, and Aiken came to Houston in early July to take his physical and sign the contract.

That's where things went off course. What's certain is the Astros didn't like what they found in the physical and pulled their offer, leaving both Aiken and Nix in limbo. Close made few public comments, but in an interview with FoxSports.com's Ken Rosenthal, he lashed out at Houston and general manager Jeff Luhnow.

"We are extremely disappointed that Major League Baseball is allowing the Astros to conduct business in this manner with a complete disregard for the rules governing the draft and the 29 other clubs who have followed those same rules," Close told Rosenthal.

Rosenthal reported that Aiken's physical revealed a "significant abnormality" in the area of his elbow ligament; the point of contention was whether the abnormality was a legitimate cause for concern. Aiken touched 97 mph in his final start before the draft, and Close called the elbow issue "asymptomatic."

"Brady has been seen by some of the most experienced and respected orthopedic arm specialists in the country, and all of those doctors have acknowledged that he's not injured and that he's ready to start his professional career," Close said.

Luhnow and an MLB spokesman both told Rosenthal that the club was adhering to major league rules, but a grievance was filed in August with MLB on Close's behalf by the MLB Player's Association.

"Today, two young men should be one step closer to realizing their dreams of becoming major league ballplayers. Because of the actions of the Houston Astros, they are not," the union's first-year executive director, ex-big league first baseman Tony Clark, said in a July 18 statement. "The MLBPA, the players and their advisers are exploring all legal options."

Commissioner Bud Selig clouded the issue with a clumsy interview in San Diego in August, saying there was still a chance Aiken could sign with the Astros. But Excel, the union and the Astros had been very quiet on the subject, and it was believed only Nix had filed a grievance.

His future is key to the Astros. If they are not forced to sign Nix, then they stayed under their bonus pool for 2014 and will get the No. 2 pick in

BONUS SPENDING BY TEAM

Teams combined to spend $222.8 million on draft bonuses in 2014, the second-highest total ever, topping the $219.3 total in 2013 that held the distinction as the second-highest in history. The record was set in 2011, the final year of the previous Collective Bargaining Agreement, when clubs spent $228 million on bonuses and another $8.1 million on guaranteed salaries that were part of major league contracts.

The current labor agreement took effect in 2012 and drastically changed the draft rules. Rather than having the freedom to spend whatever they wanted on the draft, clubs now are assigned a bonus pool for the first 10 rounds and lose draft picks if they exceed it by more than 5 percent. Also, major league contracts are no longer permitted. In the first year under the new rules, teams spent $207.9 million on bonuses.

Teams at the top of the draft get more money in their pools, so it's no surprise that the clubs selecting second (Marlins, $13,112,900) and third (White Sox, $10,460,600) led the industry in spending. The Marlins expenditure was the most of any team in the last three drafts under the current CBA. The Orioles ($3,410,600) did not pick on the first day of the draft due to forfeiting draft picks because of free agent compensation. Baltimore's first selection was 90th overall.

TEAM	2014	2013	2012
Marlins	$13,112,900	$7,951,000	$5,755,700
White Sox	$10,460,600	$5,810,800	$6,452,100
Blue Jays	$9,308,700	$3,747,280	$10,486,000
Cubs	$9,783,000	$11,724,900	$9,164,700
Royals	$9,888,700	$9,581,900	$7,573,000
Indians	$9,317,800	$6,713,600	$5,330,000
Rockies	$8,853,800	$10,368,200	$6,978,700
Brewers	$8,102,300	$4,637,300	$7,200,100
Pirates	$8,186,400	$9,887,400	$3,830,700
Twins	$8,067,600	$8,776,400	$12,602,400
Diamondbacks	$8,357,900	$8,049,100	$4,594,800
Mariners	$8,237,500	$7,376,700	$9,325,200
Reds	$7,929,900	$6,757,800	$7,450,400
Cardinals	$7,613,800	$8,526,400	$9,909,490
Phillies	$7,187,800	$6,186,900	$4,787,800
Red Sox	$7,814,800	$7,210,900	$7,908,000
Giants	$7,275,900	$6,063,800	$4,630,500
Rays	$7,141,319	$7,147,000	$4,427,300
Padres	$6,637,600	$7,895,000	$10,993,000
Angels	$6,387,500	$3,168,200	$2,289,800
Mets	$6,488,800	$7,854,400	$7,007,400
Dodgers	$5,901,100	$6,366,100	$6,277,300
Astros	$6,154,500	$11,441,000	$12,074,200
Rangers	$6,089,200	$7,696,500	$7,394,400
Tigers	$5,405,300	$6,839,100	$3,172,300
Athletics	$5,386,000	$6,506,100	$8,301,600
Braves	$5,069,800	$5,410,500	$4,758,000
Nationals	$5,188,600	$3,176,200	$4,880,500
Yankees	$4,050,200	$9,197,400	$4,898,400
Orioles	$3,410,600	$7,235,000	$7,433,200
Total	**$222,809,919**	**$219,302,880**	**$207,886,990**
Average	**$7,426,997**	**$7,310,096**	**$6,929,566**

2015 (as compensation for not signing Aiken), in addition to already earning the fourth spot in the draft order (which will be the No. 5 overall pick). The Astros would be in position to have by far the largest bonus pool in the draft (and the largest since the current rules came into play in 2012) and could influence the draft even more than they have the last three years, when they held the No. 1 overall pick each year.

However, if Nix wins his grievance and the Astros are ordered to honor their deal with him, they go over their pool and have to give up two draft picks—the two from the top five in the 2015 draft.

In the end, at the July 18 deadline, Aiken did not sign, with Luhnow conducting negotiations from Mexico and the Astros failing to land the No. 1 player on the BA 500. The Marlins wound up spending more money than any other team at $12,741,700, more than $3 million more than the White Sox, who picked third.

But Chicago shelled out the largest bonus for any single player in North Carolina State lefthander Carlos Rodon, who signed for $6,582,000, the fifth-largest bonus in draft history and the second-largest under the current CBA. Rodon finished the year in Triple-A. The second-largest bonus, $6 million, went to Marlins pick Tyler Kolek, the Texas prep righthander and No. 2 overall pick. Kolek tied a record, most recently tied by Jameson Taillon (2010), as the highest-drafted high-school righty.

On draft day itself, the Cubs pulled one of the

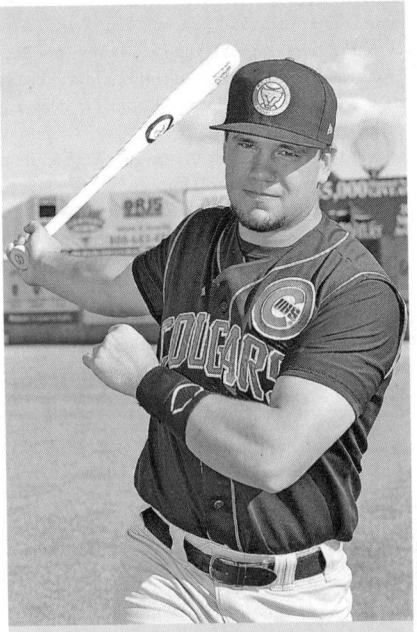

PAUL GIERHART

Kyle Schwarber went fourth overall and had an outstanding minor league debut

bigger surprises when they picked Indiana catcher Kyle Schwarber with the No. 4 pick. Schwarber signed for a below-slot $3.125 million bonus, freeing the Cubs to aggressively pursue and sign above-slot prep pitchers in rounds 4-6 in lefthanders Carson Sands ($1.1 million bonus) and Justin Steele ($1 million) and righthander Dylan Cease ($1.5 million), who required Tommy John surgery.

Schwarber made the pick look tremendous in the early returns on his own, hitting 18 homers in the regular season as he mashed his way to high Class A.

The Mariners and Brewers also had intriguing drafts, with Seattle investing more than 90 percent of its bonus pool in two high school outfielders—High School Player of the Year Alex Jackson ($4.2 million) and Canadian slugger Gareth Morgan ($2 million in the supplemental second round).

Bonuses for the 2014 draft totaled $222,809,919, the largest yet under the current Collective Bargaining Agreement and the second-largest in draft history.

The 2014 draft could have had the highest draft expenditure in history, surpassing the $228,009,050 spent in the last draft under the previous CBA in 2011. Had Aiken signed for the original $6.5 million deal he and the Astros agreed to in early June, or if Aiken had signed for the

HIGHEST BONUSES EVER

The 2014 draft saw just two players, Carlos Rodon and Tyler Kolek, join the list of top bonuses. Three of the top five bonuses in draft history, including the record, came in the 2011 draft. Only five bonuses from the last three years under the current CBA have made the list that runs 27 players deep.

PLAYER, POS.	TEAM, YEAR (PICK)	BONUS
Gerrit Cole, rhp	Pirates, 2011 (No. 1)	$8,000,000
Stephen Strasburg, rhp	Nationals, 2009 (No. 1)	*$7,500,000
Bubba Starling, of	Royals, 2011 (No. 5)	+$7,500,000
Kris Bryant, 3b	Cubs, 2013 (No. 2)	$6,708,400
Carlos Rodon, lhp	White Sox, 2014 (No. 3)	$6,582,000
Jameson Taillon, rhp	Pirates, 2010 (No. 2)	$6,500,000
Danny Hultzen, lhp	Mariners, 2011 (No. 2)	*$6,350,000
Mark Appel, rhp	Astros, 2013 (No. 1)	$6,350,000
Donavan Tate, of	Padres, 2009 (No. 3)	+$6,250,000
Bryce Harper, of	Nationals, 2010 (No. 1)	*$6,250,000
Buster Posey, c	Giants, 2008 (No. 5)	$6,200,000
Tim Beckham, ss	Rays, 2008 (No. 1)	+$6,150,000
Justin Upton, ss	Diamondbacks, 2005 (No. 1)	+$6,100,000
Matt Wieters, c	Orioles, 2007 (No. 5)	$6,000,000
Pedro Alvarez, 3b	Pirates, 2008 (No. 2)	*$6,000,000
Eric Hosmer, 1b	Royals, 2008 (No. 3)	$6,000,000
Dustin Ackley, of	Mariners, 2009 (No. 2)	*$6,000,000
Anthony Rendon, 3b	Nationals, 2011 (No. 6)	*$6,000,000
Byron Buxton, of	Twins, 2012 (No. 2)	$6,000,000
Tyler Kolek, rhp	Marlins, 2014 (No. 2)	$6,000,000
David Price, lhp	Rays, 2007 (No. 1)	*$5,600,000
Joe Borcahrd, of	White Sox, 2000 (No. 12)	+$5,300,000
Manny Machado, ss	Orioles, 2010 (No. 3)	$5,250,000
Zach Lee, rhp	Dodgers, 2010 (No. 28)	+$5,250,000
Joe Mauer, c	Twins, 2001 (No. 1)	+$5,150,000
Archie Bradley, rhp	Diamondbacks, 2011 (No. 7)	+$5,000,000
Josh Bell, of	Pirates, 2011 (2nd Rd, No. 61)	$5,000,000

*Part of major league contract.
+Bonus spread over multiple years under MLB provisions for two-sport athletes.

reported $5 million offered on deadline day and fifth-rounder Jacob Nix signed for his reported $1.5 million deal, the 2014 receipt would have surpassed 2011 by more than $1 million.

Teams are taxed 75 percent on every dollar spent over their bonus pool allotment, but showed a greater willingness to spend more than their bonus pool. In 2012, the first year under the current CBA, nine teams paid a tax and 10 paid in 2013. But this year 15 teams paid the tax, totaling $3,569,219 over their bonus pools.

If teams exceed their bonus pool by more than 5 percent, they forfeit two future picks. No team in the current CBA has forfeited a pick. As teams gain greater experience and comfort working within the constructs of the current CBA, more teams have shown a willingness to creatively approach this 5 percent threshold. In 2012, only three teams spent at least 4 percent over their bonus pool. That total doubled to six in 2013. This year, nine teams went at least 4.69 percent over their bonus allotment. The Nationals, who signed No. 18 pick Erick Fedde for $2,511,100 and lost their second-round bonus slot when Andrew Suarez did not sign, went right up to the threshold of 5 percent.

Including teams that spent less than their bonus pool allotment, teams collectively spent $2.11 million more than the cumulative bonus pools. That total was $7.88 million below in 2013 and $5.62 below in 2012.

The White Sox, who finished second in total spending ($10.46 million) and bonus pool spending ($9.98 million), paid the most tax money at $356,175. Chicago's draft expenditure this season is the largest in franchise history. Under the previous CBA from 2007-2011, the White Sox averaged $3.665 million per draft, the least of any team and just 57 percent of the average of all teams ($6.355 million). Chicago has totaled $21,178,500 bonus pool spending under the current CBA, the 11th most of any team.

Just 13 teams did not pay any tax and the teams that receive revenue sharing money are incentivized to not exceed their bonus pool. The 75 percent tax on the $3.569 million spent over the bonus pool allotment equates to $2,676,914. Teams that receive revenue sharing money and do not exceed their bonus pools receive an equal amount of the tax money. Nine teams qualified to receive $297,435 each. All but one of the teams (Miami, who was $448,300 under their pool allotment), was under their allotment by less than they will receive through the tax distributions. Six of the teams (Royals: 41,200, Brewers: 1,500, Diamondbacks:

NO. 1 OVERALL PICKS

YEAR	TEAM: PLAYER, POS., SCHOOL	BONUS
1965	Athletics: Rick Monday, of, Arizona State	$100,000
1966	Mets: Steve Chilcott, c, Antelope Valley HS, Lancaster, Calif.	$75,000
1967	Yankees: Ron Blomberg, 1b, Druid Hills HS, Atlanta	$65,000
1968	Mets: Tim Foli, ss, Notre Dame HS, Sherman Oaks, Calif.	$74,000
1969	Senators: Jeff Burroughs, of, Centennial HS, Long Beach	$88,000
1970	Padres: Mike Ivie, c, Walker HS, Atlanta	$75,000
1971	White Sox: Danny Goodwin, c, Peoria (Ill.) HS	Did Not Sign
1972	Padres: Dave Roberts, 3b, Oregon	$70,000
1973	Rangers: David Clyde, lhp, Westchester HS, Texas	*$65,000
1974	Padres: Bill Almon, ss, Brown	*$90,000
1975	Angels: Danny Goodwin, c, Southern	*$125,000
1976	Astros: Floyd Bannister, lhp, Arizona State	$100,000
1977	White Sox: Harold Baines, of, St. Michaels (Md.) HS	$32,000
1978	Braves: Bob Horner, 3b, Arizona State	*$162,000
1979	Mariners: Al Chambers, 1b, Harris HS, Harrisburg, Pa.	$60,000
1980	Mets: Darryl Strawberry, of, Crenshaw HS, Los Angeles	$152,500
1981	Mariners: Mike Moore, rhp, Oral Roberts	$100,000
1982	Cubs: Shawon Dunston, ss, Jefferson HS, New York	$135,000
1983	Twins: Tim Belcher, rhp, Mount Vernon Nazarene (Ohio)	Did Not Sign
1984	Mets: Shawn Abner, of, Mechanicsburg (Pa.) HS	$150,500
1985	Brewers: B.J. Surhoff, c, North Carolina	$150,000
1986	Pirates: Jeff King, 3b, Arkansas	$180,000
1987	Mariners: Ken Griffey Jr., of, Moeller HS, Cincinnati	$160,000
1988	Padres: Andy Benes, rhp, Evansville	$235,000
1989	Orioles: Ben McDonald, rhp, Louisiana State	*$350,000
1990	Braves: Chipper Jones, ss, The Bolles School, Jacksonville	$275,000
1991	Yankees: Brien Taylor, lhp, East Carteret HS, Beaufort, N.C.	$1,550,000
1992	Astros: Phil Nevin, 3b, Cal State Fullerton	$700,000
1993	Mariners: Alex Rodriguez, ss, Westminster Christian HS, Miami	*$1,000,000
1994	Mets: Paul Wilson, rhp, Florida State	$1,550,000
1995	Angels: Darin Erstad, of, Nebraska	$1,575,000
1996	Pirates: Kris Benson, rhp, Clemson	$2,000,000
1997	Tigers: Matt Anderson, rhp, Tigers	$2,505,000
1998	Phillies: Pat Burrell, 3b, Miami	*$3,150,000
1999	Devil Rays: Josh Hamilton, of, Athens Drive HS, Raleigh	$3,960,000
2000	Marlins: Adrian Gonzalez, 1b, Eastlake HS, Chula Vista, Calif.	$3,000,000
2001	Twins: Joe Mauer, c, Cretin-Derham Hall, St. Paul	$5,150,000
2002	Pirates: Bryan Bullington, rhp, Ball State	$4,000,000
2003	Devil Rays: Delmon Young, of, Camarillo (Calif.) HS	*$3,700,000
2004	Padres: Matt Bush, ss, Mission Bay HS, San Diego	$3,150,000
2005	Diamondbacks: Justin Upton, ss, Great Bridge HS, Chesapeake, Va.	$6,100,000
2006	Royals: Luke Hochevar, rhp, Fort Worth (American Association)	*$3,500,000
2007	Devil Rays: David Price, lhp, Vanderbilt	*$5,600,000
2008	Rays: Tim Beckham, ss, Griffin (Ga.) HS	$6,150,000
2009	Nationals: Stephen Strasburg, rhp, San Diego State	*$7,500,000
2010	Nationals: Bryce Harper, of, JC of Southern Nevada	*$6,250,000
2011	Pirates: Gerrit Cole, rhp, UCLA	$8,000,000
2012	Astros: Carlos Correa, ss, Puerto Rico Baseball Academy, Gurabo, P.R.	$4,800,000
2013	Astros: Mark Appel, rhp, Stanford	$6,350,000
2014	Astros: Brady Aiken, lhp, Cathedral Catholic, San Diego	Did Not Sign

*Part of major league contract.

22,400, Reds: 15,000, Padres: 0, Athletics: 3,300) were less than $50,000 below their bonus pools and will receive $297,435 reach.

The Marlins spent the most of any team in the draft by both total spending ($13.11 million) and bonus pool spending ($12.74). This marked the largest draft expenditure during the current CBA and made the Marlins the only team to spend more than $12 million in the last three drafts. The previous high water mark belonged to the 2012 Minnesota Twins ($11,938,900), who signed No. 2 pick Byron Buxton to the highest bonus in the draft class ($6,000,000).

Draft Trends And Tidbits

■ The current Collective Bargaining Agreement and its bonus pools have created incentives for teams to select high school players early in the draft before spending less in the back half of the top 10 rounds, and 2014 saw the most aggressive use of that strategy in the three years under the current CBA. Nearly half of the high school players drafted in the top 10 rounds (47.1 percent) went in the top two rounds. More prep players went in the first 89 picks (43) than in the next 225 picks (42). The percentage of high school players taken in each round fell in every round in the top 10 (with the exception of ties). Only one high school player was selected in the senior-heavy 10th round.

Teams that haven't had first-round picks have been severely hampered in their ability to draft high school players because they lack the financial ammunition at the top of the draft. Nearly 40 percent (39.2) of the high school players picked in the top 10 rounds over the last three drafts have been gone by the end of the second round.

■ The American League champion Royals were the only team to sign more lefthanded pitchers (12) than righthanders (7). For a baseline of comparison, 28.1 percent of the pitchers who signed were lefthanders. The Royals signed as many lefthanders as the six least lefthanded-heavy teams combined: the Dodgers (1), Pirates (1), Braves (2), Red Sox (2), Indians (3) and Tigers (3). This was not a one-year anomaly: the Royals have signed more lefthanders (26) than righthanders (24) over the last three drafts. This is true at the top of the draft and in the later rounds. The Royals have drafted 10 pitchers in the top three rounds during the last three drafts and seven were lefthanders: Brandon Finnegan, Foster Griffin, Eric Skoglund (all 2014), Sean Manaea, Cody Reed (2013), Sam Selman and Colin Rodgers (2012).

■ The Marlins, tied for the most selections in the top 10 rounds (12), signed more high school

THE BONUS RECORD

Rick Monday, the No. 1 overall pick in baseball's first draft in 1965, signed with the Athletics for $100,000—a figure that no draftee bettered for a decade. The record has been broken many times since, with Gerrit Cole setting a new standard in 2011 when he signed for $8 million with the Pirates as the No. 1 overall pick and no draftee under the CBA has eclipsed him in the three years under the new rules. In fact, no signee during that timeframe has topped $7 million.

The list below represents only cash bonuses and doesn't include guaranteed money from major league deals, college scholarship plans or incentives. It also considers only players who signed with the clubs that drafted them and doesn't include draft picks who signed after being granted free agency, such as Bill Bordley ($200,000 from the Giants after the Reds selected him in the January 1979 draft) and Matt White ($10.2 million from the Devil Rays after the Giants chose him in the 1996 draft).

YEAR	PLAYER, POS., CLUB (ROUND)	BONUS
1965	Rick Monday, of, Athletics (1)	$100,000
1975	Danny Goodwin, c, Angels (1)	$125,000
1978	Kirk Gibson, of, Tigers (1)	$150,000
	*Bob Horner, 3b, Braves (1)	$162,000
1979	Todd Demeter, 1b, Yankees (2)	$208,000
1988	Andy Benes, rhp, Padres (1)	$235,000
1989	Tyler Houston, c, Braves (1)	$241,500
	*Ben McDonald, rhp, Orioles (1)	$350,000
	*John Olerud, 1b, Blue Jays (3)	$575,000
1991	Mike Kelly, of, Braves (1)	$575,000
	Brien Taylor, lhp, Yankees (1)	$1,550,000
1994	Paul Wilson, rhp, Mets (1)	$1,550,000
	Josh Booty, 3b, Marlins (1)	$1,600,000
1996	Kris Benson, rhp, Pirates (1)	$2,000,000
1997	Rick Ankiel, lhp, Cardinals (2)	$2,500,000
	Matt Anderson, rhp, Tigers (1)	$2,505,000
1998	*J.D. Drew, of, Cardinals (1)	$3,000,000
	*Pat Burrell, 3b, Phillies (1)	$3,150,000
	Mark Mulder, lhp, Athletics (1)	$3,200,000
	Corey Patterson, of, Cubs (1)	$3,700,000
1999	Josh Hamilton, of, Devil Rays (1)	$3,960,000
2000	Joe Borchard, of, White Sox (1)	$5,300,000
2005	Justin Upton, ss, Diamondbacks (1)	$6,100,000
2008	Tim Beckham, ss, Rays (1)	$6,150,000
	Buster Posey, c, Giants (1)	$6,200,000
2009	Donavan Tate, cf, Padres (1)	$6,250,000
	*Stephen Strasburg, rhp, Nationals (1)	$7,500,000
2011	Gerrit Cole, rhp, Pirates (1)	$8,000,000

*Part of major league contract.

players than any other team, with most of the prep draftees (7) coming in the top 10 rounds. Three of the four prep players the Marlins drafted after the 10th round signed for over-slot bonuses of at least $200,000. This Marlins' draft is the most athletic that has entered the system in years and includes speedsters Justin Twine and Anfernee Seymour and athletic outfielders with great bodies such as Stone Garrett and Zach Sullivan.

■ The Indians, known in the recent past as a college-centric drafting team, signed the lowest percentage of college players (53.3 percent) of any team in the draft. No American League team signed more high school players than the Indians with nine prep players, led by first-round lefthander Justus Sheffield, second-round right-

hander Grant Hockin and third-round first baseman Bobby Bradley. That was the most prep signees the Indians have had since the 2001 draft, when they took prep right-handers with their first four picks. Cleveland also signed the third-most junior college players (6) of any team after signing six junior college players last year.

■ No team had high school players comprise a higher percent-age of their draft signings than the Mets (35.7 percent), who signed the second-most high school play-ers of any team (10). While more than half of the (57.7 percent) of all high school players that signed were drafted in the top 10 rounds, the Mets drafted all but two of their prep players after the 10th round (third-round shortstop Milton Ramos and eighth-round first base-man Dash Winningham), signing many of them to bonuses exceeding $100,000 such as righthanders Erik Manoah and Gabe Llanes, outfield-er Raphael Ramirez and shortstop Dale Burdick. There were 60 prep players who signed after the 10th round, and the Mets drafted eight of them (13.3 percent).

In the last two drafts there have been five teams (2013: Brewers, Angels and Nationals, 2012: Yankees and Orioles) that did not have first-round picks. Four of those teams have drafted only one high school player in the top 10 rounds, while the Brewers drafted three. They have had to grab their high school players early with their limited picks, as all five of the clubs drafted their prep players within the first two picks. These teams got prep players with 15.6 percent of their picks in the top 10 rounds compared to the more-than-double rate of 32.1 percent for all other drafts.

■ The current CBA has caused teams in many cases to move their signing bonuses around in the top 10 rounds to find the best finan-cial fit for each draft pick and their corresponding bonuses. More teams than ever signed players below the draft pick bonus value in the back half

BONUSES VS. PICK VALUES

Just as they did in 2012 and 2013 in the first two drafts under the revamped rules, the signing bonuses and the assigned pick values for 2014 tracked each other nicely. To give the worst teams extra spending power, the values for the selections at the top of the draft have been set higher than the perceived market value. As a result, just two of the top 10 signees received more than their full pick value, and three received less.

But all told, the top 50 bonuses added up to $111.3 million, while the first 50 pick values totaled $116.5 million, a 4.4 percent shortfall. By comparison, when MLB unilaterally determined slot recommendations in the last year of the previous Collective Bargaining Agreement (2011) but had no enforcement mechanism, the total of the first 50 bonuses ($120.5 million) dwarfed that of the top 50 slots ($70 million).

PLAYER, POS., TEAM (ROUND/OVERALL PICK)	BONUS	PICK VALUE
1. Carlos Rodon, lhp, White Sox (1st round/No. 3)	$6,582,000	$7,922,100
2. Tyler Kolek, rhp, Marlins (1st round/No. 2)	$6,000,000	$6,821,800
3. Alex Jackson, of, Mariners (1st round/No. 6)	$4,200,000	$5,721,500
4. Nick Gordon, ss, Twins (1st round/No. 5)	$3,851,000	$4,621,200
5. Aaron Nola, rhp, Phillies (1st round/No. 7)	$3,300,900	$3,851,000
6. Kyle Schwarber, c/of, Cubs (1st round/No. 4)	$3,125,000	$3,575,900
7. Jeff Hoffman, rhp, Blue Jays (1st round/No. 9)	$3,080,800	$3,300,900
8. Michael Conforto, of, Mets (1st round/No. 10)	$2,970,800	$3,190,800
9. Trea Turner, ss, Padres (1st round/No. 13)	$2,900,000	$3,080,800
10. Max Pentecost, c, Blue Jays (1st round/No. 11)	$2,888,300	$2,970,800
11. Touki Toussaint, rhp, Diamondbacks (1st round/No. 16)	$2,700,000	$2,888,300
12. Tyler Beede, rhp, Giants (1st round/No. 14)	$2,613,200	$2,805,700
13. Sean Newcomb, lhp, Angels (1st round/No. 15)	$2,518,400	$2,723,300
14. Erick Fedde, rhp, Nationals (1st round/No. 18)	$2,511,100	$2,613,200
15. Kodi Medeiros, lhp, Brewers (1st round/No. 12)	$2,500,000	$2,475,600
Grant Holmes, rhp, Dodgers (1st round/No. 22)	$2,500,000	$2,338,200
17. Kyle Freeland, lhp, Rockies (1st round/No. 8)	$2,300,000	$2,200,600
18. Brandon Finnegan, lhp, Royals (1st round/No. 17)	$2,200,600	$2,145,600
19. Casey Gillaspie, 1b, Rays (1st round/No. 20)	$2,035,500	$2,090,500
20. Derek Hill, of, Tigers (1st round/No. 23)	$2,000,000	$2,035,500
Jack Flaherty, rhp, Cardinals (1st round/No. 34)	$2,000,000	$2,008,100
Forrest Wall, 2b, Rockies (supp. 1st/No. 35)	$2,000,000	$1,980,500
Gareth Morgan, of, Mariners (supp. 2nd round/No. 74)	$2,000,000	$1,953,100
24. Nick Howard, rhp, Reds (1st round/No. 19)	$1,990,500	$1,925,500
25. Foster Griffin, lhp, Royals (1st round/No. 28)	$1,925,000	$1,898,000
26. Bradley Zimmer, of, Indians (1st round/No. 21)	$1,900,000	$1,870,500
27. Michael Chavis, ss/3b, Red Sox (1st round/No. 26)	$1,870,500	$1,843,000
28. Luke Weaver, rhp, Cardinals (1st round/No. 27)	$1,843,000	$1,815,500
29. Jacob Gatewood, ss, Brewers (supp. 1st/No. 41)	$1,830,000	$1,788,000
30. Cole Tucker, ss, Pirates (1st round/No. 24)	$1,800,000	$1,760,500
Monte Harrison, of, Brewers (2nd round/No. 50)	$1,800,000	$1,733,000
Scott Blewett, rhp, Royals (2nd round/No. 56)	$1,800,000	$1,705,400
33. Alex Blandino, ss, Reds (1st round/No. 29)	$1,788,000	$1,678,000
34. Matt Chapman, 3b, Athletics (1st round/No. 25)	$1,750,000	$1,650,400
Luis Ortiz, rhp, Rangers (1st round/No. 30)	$1,750,000	$1,614,500
36. Braxton Davidson, 1b, Braves (1st round/No. 32)	$1,705,000	$1,573,900
37. Justus Sheffield, lhp, Indians (1st round/No. 31)	$1,600,000	$1,534,100
38. Derek Fisher, of, Astros (supp. 1st/No. 37)	$1,534,100	$1,495,400
39. Michael Kopech, rhp, Red Sox (1st round/No. 33)	$1,500,000	$1,457,600
Dylan Cease, rhp, Cubs (6th round/No. 169)	$1,500,000	$1,420,800
41. Chase Vallot, c, Royals (supp. 1st/No. 40)	$1,350,000	$1,384,900
A.J. Reed, 1b, Astros (2nd round/No. 42)	$1,350,000	$1,350,000
43. Justin Twine, ss, Marlins (2nd round/No. 43)	$1,316,000	$1,316,000
44. Michael Gettys, of, Padres (2nd round/No. 51)	$1,300,000	$1,282,700
45. Spencer Adams, rhp, White Sox (2nd round/No. 44)	$1,282,700	$1,250,400
46. Mike Papi, of, Indians (supp. 1st/No. 38)	$1,250,000	$1,218,800
Connor Joe, of, Pirates (supp. 1st/No. 39)	$1,250,000	$1,187,900
48. Nick Burdi, rhp, Twins (2nd round/No. 46)	$1,218,800	$1,158,000
49. Joe Gatto, rhp, Angels (2nd round/No. 53)	$1,200,000	$1,128,800
Ti'quan Forbes, ss, Rangers (2nd round/No. 59)	$1,200,000	$1,100,300
Total	**$111,381,200**	**$116,456,900**

of the top 10 rounds, evidenced by 20 seniors drafted in the 10th round. The draft bonus values in these rounds totaled $1,286,000 compared to $4,160,400 for the bonus slots, which was only 30.9 percent of the bonus slot values.

BRIAN WESTERHOLT

Carlos Rodon made a strong first impression on the White Sox after they took him third overall

TEAM, PLAYER, POS., SCHOOL	BONUS
1. Astros. Brady Aiken, lhp, HS—San Diego	Did not sign
2. Marlins. Tyler Kolek, rhp, HS—Shepherd, Texas	$6,000,000
3. White Sox. Carlos Rodon, lhp, North Carolina State	$6,582,000
4. Cubs. Kyle Schwarber, c, Indiana	$3,125,000
5. Twins. Nick Gordon, ss, HS—Orlando, Fla.	$3,851,000
6. Mariners. Alex Jackson, of, HS—San Diego	$4,200,000
7. Phillies. Aaron Nola, rhp, Louisiana State	$3,300,900
8. Rockies. Kyle Freeland, lhp, Evansville	$2,300,000
9. Blue Jays. Jeff Hoffman, rhp, East Carolina	$3,080,800
10. Mets. Michael Conforto, of, Oregon State	$2,970,800
11. Blue Jays. Max Pentecost, c, Kennesaw State	$2,888,300
12. Brewers. Kodi Medeiros, lhp, HS—Hilo, Hawaii	$2,500,000
13. Padres. Trea Turner, ss, North Carolina State	$2,900,000
14. Giants. Tyler Beede, rhp, Vanderbilt	$2,613,200
15. Angels. Sean Newcomb, lhp, Hartford	$2,518,400
16. D-backs. Touki Toussaint, rhp, HS—Coral Springs, Fla.	$2,700,000
17. Royals. Brandon Finnegan, lhp, Texas Christian	$2,200,600
18. Nationals. Erick Fedde, rhp, Nevada-Las Vegas	$2,511,100
19. Reds. Nick Howard, rhp, Virginia	$1,990,500
20. Rays. Casey Gillaspie, 1b, Wichita State	$2,035,500
21. Indians. Bradley Zimmer, of, San Francisco	$1,900,000
22. Dodgers. Grant Holmes, rhp, HS—Conway, S.C.	$2,500,000
23. Tigers. Derek Hill, of, HS—Elk Grove, Calif.	$2,000,000
24. Pirates. Cole Tucker, ss, HS—Phoenix	$1,800,000
25. Athletics. Matt Chapman, 3b, Cal State Fullerton	$1,750,000
26. Red Sox. Michael Chavis, ss, HS—Marietta, Ga.	$1,870,500
27. Cardinals. Luke Weaver, rhp, Florida State	$1,843,000
28. Royals. Foster Griffin, lhp, HS—Orlando, Fla.	$1,925,000
29. Reds. Alex Blandino, 3b, Stanford	$1,788,000
30. Rangers. Luis Ortiz, rhp, HS—Sanger, Calif.	$1,750,000
31. Indians. Justus Sheffield, lhp, HS—Tullahoma, Tenn.	$1,600,000
32. Braves. Braxton Davidson, of, HS—Asheville, N.C.	$1,705,000
33. Red Sox. Michael Kopech, rhp, HS—Mount Pleasant, Texas	$1,500,000
34. Cardinals. Jack Flaherty, rhp, HS—Studio City, Calif.	$2,000,000
35. Rockies. Forrest Wall, 2b, HS—Maitland, Fla.	$2,000,000
36. Marlins. Blake Anderson, c, HS—Collinsville, Miss.	$1,170,000
37. Astros. Derek Fisher, of, Virginia	$1,534,100
38. Indians. Mike Papi, of, Virginia	$1,250,000
39. Pirates. Connor Joe, of, San Diego	$1,250,000
40. Royals. Chase Vallot, c, HS—Lafayette, La.	$1,350,000
41. Brewers. Jacob Gatewood, ss, HS—Clovis, Calif.	$1,830,000
42. Astros. A.J. Reed, 1b, Kentucky	$1,350,000
43. Marlins. Justin Twine, ss, HS—Falls City, Texas	$1,316,000
44. White Sox. Spencer Adams, rhp, HS—Cleveland, Ga.	$1,282,700
45. Cubs. Jake Stinnett, rhp, Maryland	$1,000,000
46. Twins. Nick Burdi, rhp, Louisville	$1,218,800
47. Phillies. Aaron Imhof, lhp, Cal Poly	$1,187,900
48. Rockies. Ryan Castellani, rhp, HS—Phoenix	$1,100,000
49. Blue Jays. Sean Reid-Foley, rhp, HS—Jacksonville	$1,128,800
50. Brewers. Monte Harrison, of, HS—Lee's Summit West, Mo.	$1,800,000

TEAM, PLAYER, POS., SCHOOL	BONUS
51. Padres. Michael Gettys, of, HS—Gainesville, Ga.	$1,300,000
52. Giants. Aramis Garcia, c, Florida International	$1,100,000
53. Angels. Joe Gatto, rhp, HS—Richland, N.J.	$1,200,000
54. Diamondbacks. Cody Reed, lhp, HS—Ardmore, Ala.	$1,034,500
55. Yankees. Jacob Lindgren, lhp, Mississippi State	$1,018,700
56. Royals. Scott Blewett, rhp, HS—Baldwinsville, N.Y.	$1,800,000
57. Nationals. Andrew Suarez, lhp, Miami	Did not sign
58. Reds. Taylor Sparks, 3b, UC Irvine	$972,800
59. Rangers. Ti'quan Forbes, ss, HS—Columbia, Miss.	$1,200,000
60. Rays. Cameron Varga, rhp, HS—Cincinnati	$1,097,500
61. Indians. Grant Hockin, rhp, HS—Damien, Calif.	$1,100,000
62. Dodgers. Alex Verdugo, of, HS—Tucson, Ariz.	$914,600
63. Tigers. Spencer Turnbull, rhp, Alabama	$900,000
64. Pirates. Mitch Keller, rhp, HS—Cedar Rapids, Iowa	$1,000,000
65. Athletics. Daniel Gossett, rhp, Clemson	$750,000
66. Braves. Garrett Fulenchek, rhp, HS—Howe, Texas	$1,000,000
67. Red Sox. Sam Travis, 1b, Indiana	$846,800
68. Cardinals. Ronnie Williams, rhp, HS—Hialeah, Fla.	$833,900
69. D-backs. Marcus Wilson, of, HS—Gardena, Calif.	$1,000,000
70. Diamondbacks. Isan Diaz, ss, HS—Springfield, Mass.	$750,000
71. Cardinals. Andrew Morales, rhp, UC Irvine	$546,100
72. Rays. Brent Honeywell, rhp, Walters State (Tenn.) CC	$800,000
73. Pirates. Trey Supak, rhp, HS—La Grange, Texas	$1,000,000
74. Mariners. Gareth Morgan, of, HS—Toronto, Ont.	$2,000,000
75. Astros. J.D. Davis, 3b, Cal State Fullerton	$748,600
76. Marlins. Brian Anderson, 2b, Arkansas	$600,000
77. White Sox. Jace Fry, lhp, Oregon State	$760,000
78. Cubs. Mark Zagunis, c, Virginia Tech	$615,000
79. Twins. Michael Cederoth, rhp, San Diego State	$703,900
80. Mariners. Austin Cousino, of, Kentucky	$400,000
81. Phillies. Aaron Brown, of, Pepperdine	$750,000
82. Rockies. Sam Howard, lhp, Georgia Southern	$672,100
83. Blue Jays. Nick Wells, lhp, HS—Haymarket, Va.	$661,800
84. Mets. Milton Ramos, ss, HS—Plantation, Fla.	$750,000
85. Brewers. Cy Sneed, rhp, Dallas Baptist	$400,000
86. Padres. Zech Lemond, rhp, Rice	$600,000
87. Giants. Dylan Davis, of, Oregon State	$650,000
88. Angels. Chris Ellis, rhp, Mississippi	$575,000
89. Diamondbacks. Matt Railey, of, HS—Tallahassee, Fla.	$600,000
90. Orioles. Brian Gonzalez, lhp, HS—Southwest Ranches, Fla.	$700,000
91. Yankees. Austin DeCarr, rhp, HS—Salisbury, Conn.	$1,000,000
92. Royals. Eric Skoglund, lhp, Central Florida	$576,100
93. Nationals. Jakson Reetz, c, HS—Firth, Neb.	$800,000
94. Reds. Wyatt Strahan, rhp, Southern California	$558,700
95. Rangers. Josh Morgan, ss, HS—Orange, Calif.	$800,000
96. Rays. Brock Burke, lhp, HS—Evergreen, Colo.	$897,500
97. Indians. Bobby Bradley, 1b, HS—Gulfport, Miss.	$912,500
98. Dodgers. John Richy, rhp, Nevada-Las Vegas	$534,400
99. Tigers. Grayson Greiner, c, South Carolina	$529,400
100. Pirates. Jordan Luplow, of, Fresno State	$500,000

2014 CLUB-BY-CLUB SELECTIONS

ORDER OF SELECTION IN PARENTHESES PLAYERS SIGNED IN BOLD

ARIZONA DIAMONDBACKS

1. **Touki Toussaint, rhp, Coral Springs (Fla.) Christian Academy**
2. **Cody Reed, lhp, Ardmore (Ala.) HS**
2s. **Marcus Wilson, of, Serra HS, Gardena, Calif. (Competitive balance pick, obtained in trade from Padres)**
2s. **Isan Diaz, ss, Springfield (Mass.) HS (Competitive balance pick)**
3. **Matt Railey, of, North Florida Christian HS, Tallahassee, Fla.**
4. **Brent Jones, rhp, Cornell**
5. **Mason McCullough, rhp, Lander (S.C.)**
6. **Zac Curtis, lhp, Middle Tennessee State**
7. **Tyler Humphreys, 3b, St. Johns River State (Fla.) JC**
8. **Grant Heyman, of, JC of Southern Nevada**
9. **Justin Gonzalez, ss, Florida State**
10. **Scott Schultz, rhp, Oregon State**
11. **Jared Miller, lhp, Vanderbilt**
12. **Holden Helmink, rhp, San Jacinto (Texas) JC**
13. C.J. Moore, of, Suffield (Conn.) Academy
14. **Kevin Cron, 1b, Texas Christian**
15. **Tyler Baker, c, Wichita State**
16. **Kevin Simmons, rhp, Wallace State (Ala.) CC**
17. **Mike Abreu, 2b, Hillsborough (Fla.) CC**
18. Garrett Mundell, rhp, Fresno State
19. **Dan Savas, rhp, Illinois State**
20. Jacob Bukauskas, rhp, Stone Bridge HS, Ashburn, Va.
21. **Gerard Hernandez, of, Pinnacle HS, Phoenix**
22. **Michael Branigan, c, Forsyth Central HS, Cumming, Ga.**
23. John Fidanza, c, Georgia-Gwinnett
24. **Mike Cetta, rhp, Central Florida**
25. **Brando Tessar, rhp, Oregon**
26. Willie Rios, lhp, St. Bernard HS, Montville, Conn.
27. **Nate Robertson, ss, Colorado Mesa**
28. **Bennie Robinson, 1b, Florida A&M**
29. **Nick Baker, rhp, Chico State (Calif.)**
30. **Trevor Mitsui, 1b, Washington**
31. **Roberto Cancio, lhp, Broward (Fla.) CC**
32. Cameron Bishop, lhp, Brea Olinda HS, Brea, Calif.
33. **Tyler Bolton, rhp, East Carolina**
34. **Nate Irving, c, Virginia**
35. Justin Morris, c, Dematha HS, Hyattsville, Md.
36. **Will Landsheft, rhp, Drury (Mo.)**
37. Keith Holcombe, of, Hillcrest HS, Tuscaloosa, Ala.
38. **Lawrence Pardo, lhp, South Florida**
39. Drew Rasmussen, rhp, Mt. Spokane HS, Mead, Wash.
40. Zach Gahagan, ss, North Henderson HS, Hendersonville, N.C.

ATLANTA BRAVES

1. (Pick lost for signing free agent Ervin Santana)
1. **Braxton Davidson, of, Roberson HS, Asheville, N.C. (Compensation pick for loss of free agent Brian McCann)**
2. **Garrett Fulenchek, rhp, Howe (Texas) HS**
3. **Max Povse, rhp, UNC Greensboro**
4. **Chad Sobotka, rhp, South Carolina-Upstate**
5. **Chris Diaz, lhp, Miami**
6. **Keith Curcio, of, Florida Southern**
7. **Luke Dykstra, 2b, Westlake HS, Westlake Village, Calif.**
8. **Bradley Roney, rhp, Southern Mississippi**
9. **Jordan Edgerton, 3b, UNC Pembroke**
10. **Matt Tellor, 1b, Southeast Missouri State**
11. **Luis Gamez, rhp, Cienega HS, Tucson**
12. **Patrick Dorrian, 2b, Kingston (N.Y.) HS**
13. **Caleb Beech, rhp, Shelton State (Ala.) CC**
14. **Joseph Daris, of, Azusa Pacific (Calif.)**
15. **Caleb Dirks, rhp, California Baptist**
16. **Brandon Barker, rhp, Mercer**
17. Ashton Perritt, rhp, Liberty
18. **Jacob Webb, rhp, Tabor (Kan.)**
19. **Codey McElroy, ss, Cameron (Okla.)**
20. **Wigberto Nevarez, c, Lubbock Christian (Texas)**
21. Jake Godfrey, rhp, Providence Catholic HS, New Lenox, Ill.
22. **Sean Godfrey, of, Ball State**
23. **Tanner Krietemeier, 1b, Oklahoma State**
24. **Kevin Reiher, c, Prairie State (Ill.) JC**
25. **Kyle Kinman, lhp, Bellevue (Neb.)**
26. **Trevor Sprowl, 2b, Auburn-Montgomery**
27. Carl Stajduhar, 1b, Rocky Mountain HS, Fort Collins, Colo.
28. **Matt Sims, rhp, Texas-San Antonio**
29. Dazon Cole, rhp, West Bloomfield (Mich.) HS
30. Jared James, of, McClatchy HS, Sacramento
31. **Sal Giardina, c, Lynn (Fla.)**
32. Tucker Baca, lhp, North Gwinnett HS, Suwanee, Ga.
33. Doug Still, lhp, Sikeston (Mo.) HS
34. Nick Leonard, rhp, Mountain Vista HS, Highlands Ranch, Colo.
35. Ryan Kokora, rhp, Fairview HS, Boulder, Colo.
36. Larry Crisler, of, Bishop Noll Institute, Hammond, Ind.
37. Gavin Sheets, 1b, Gilman School, Baltimore
38. **J.J. Franco, 2b, Brown**
39. Grayson Byrd, ss, King's Ridge Christian HS, Alpharetta, Ga.
40. Randy Santiesteban, 2b, Peru State (Neb.)

BALTIMORE ORIOLES

1. (Pick lost for signing free agent Ubaldo Jimenez)
2. (Pick lost for signing free agent Nelson Cruz)
3. **Brian Gonzalez, lhp, Archbishop McCarthy HS, Southwest Ranches, Fla.**
4. **Pat Connaughton, rhp, Notre Dame**
5. **David Hess, rhp, Tennessee Tech**
6. **Tanner Scott, lhp, Howard (Texas) JC**
7. **Max Schuh, lhp, UCLA**
8. **Steve Wilkerson, 2b, Clemson**
9. **Austin Anderson, 3b, Mississippi**
10. **Jay Gonzalez, of, Mount Olive (N.C.)**
11. **John Means, lhp, West Virginia**
12. **Nigel Nootbaar, rhp, Southern California**
13. **Matt Trowbridge, lhp, Central Michigan**
14. **Gerrion Grim, of, Jefferson (Mo.) JC**
15. **Alejandro Juvier, 2b, Doral (Fla.) Academy**
16. **Tanner Chleborad, rhp, Washington State**
17. **Jean Cosme, rhp, Colegio Sagrada Familia HS, San Juan, P.R.**
18. **Matt Grimes, rhp, Georgia Tech**
19. Connor Seabold, rhp, Newport Harbor HS, Newport Beach, Calif.
20. **Zach Albin, rhp, Connecticut-Avery Point JC**
21. **John McLeod, lhp, Wake Forest**
22. **Josh Walker, rhp, New Mexico**
23. **Zeke McGranahan, rhp, Georgia-Gwinnett**
24. **Lucas Long, rhp, San Diego**
25. Brandon Bonilla, lhp, Grand Canyon
26. Gage Burland, rhp, East Valley HS, Spokane, Wash
27. **Austin Pfeiffer, ss, Arkansas-Little Rock**
28. James Carter, rhp, Chabot (Calif.) JC
29. **Patrick Baker, rhp, Anne Arundel (Md.) CC**
30. **Mike Burke, rhp, Buffalo**
31. **Riley Palmer, 3b, Southern New Hampshire**
32. **Jamill Moquete, of, Massachusetts-Boston**
33. **Brandon Koch, rhp, Temecula Valley HS, Temecula, Calif.**
34. Garrett Pearson, rhp, St. John's College HS, Washington, D.C.
35. **Tad Gold, of, Endicott (Mass.)**
36. **Alexander Lee, 1b, Radford**
37. Hunter Hart, rhp, St. Joseph (Ill.) Ogden HS
38. **Keegan Ghidotti, rhp, Ouachita Baptist (Ark.)**
39. Tucker Simpson, rhp, Chipola (Fla.) JC
40. **T.J. Olesczuk, of, Winthrop**

BOSTON RED SOX

1. **Michael Chavis, ss, Sprayberry HS, Marietta, Ga.**
1. **Michael Kopech, rhp, Mount Pleasant (Texas) HS (Compensation pick for loss of free agent Jacoby Ellsbury)**

2. Sam Travis, 1b, Indiana
3. Jake Cosart, rhp, Seminole State (Fla.) JC
4. Kevin McAvoy, rhp, Bryant
5. Josh Ockimey, 1b, Neumann-Goretti HS, Philadelphia
6. Danny Mars, of, Chipola (Fla.) JC
7. Reed Reilly, rhp, Cal Poly
8. Ben Moore, c, Alabama
9. Kevin Steen, rhp, Oak Ridge (Tenn.) HS
10. Cole Sturgeon, of, Louisville
11. Karsten Whitson, rhp, Florida
12. Jalen Beeks, lhp, Arkansas
13. Chandler Shepherd, rhp, Kentucky
14. Jordan Procyshen, c, Northern Kentucky
15. Trenton Kemp, of, Buchanan HS, Clovis, Calif.
16. Michael Gunn, lhp, Arkansas
17. Jeremy Rivera, ss, El Paso CC
18. Jordan Betts, 3b, Duke
19. Tyler Hill, of, Delaware Military Academy, Wilmington, Del.
20. Devon Fisher, c, Western Branch HS, Chesapeake, Va.
21. Ian Rice, c, Chipola (Fla.) JC
22. J.J. Matijevic, ss, Norwin HS, North Huntingdon, Pa.
23. Derek Miller, of, Texas-Arlington
24. Cisco Tellez, 1b, UC Riverside
25. Gabriel Klobosits, rhp, Galveston (Texas) CC
26. Ryan Harris, rhp, Florida
27. Taylor Nunez, rhp, Southern Mississippi
28. David Peterson, lhp, Regis Jesuit HS, Aurora, Colo.
29. Josh Pennington, rhp, Lower Cape May Regional HS, Cape May, N.J.
30. Jeren Kendall, of, Holmen (Wis.) HS
31. Alex McKeon, c, Texas A&M-International
32. Case Rolen, rhp, Sherman (Texas) HS
33. Luis Alvarado, of, Puerto Rico Baseball Academy, Gurabo, P.R.
34. Kuehl McEachern, rhp, Flagler (Fla.)
35. Ross Puskarich, 3b, Liberty HS, Bakersfield, Calif.
36. Bradley Wilpon, rhp, Brunswick School, Greenwich, Conn.
37. Hector Lorenzana, ss, Oklahoma
38. Brandon Show, rhp, San Diego
39. Mike Gretler, ss, Bonney Lake (Wash.) HS
40. Joe Winterburn, c, La Verne (Calif.)

CHICAGO CUBS

1. Kyle Schwarber, c, Indiana
2. Jake Stinnett, rhp, Maryland
3. Mark Zagunis, c, Virginia Tech
4. Carson Sands, lhp, North Florida Christian HS, Tallahassee, Fla.
5. Justin Steele, lhp, George County HS, Lucedale, Miss.
6. Dylan Cease, rhp, Milton (Ga.) HS
7. James Norwood, rhp, Saint Louis
8. Tommy Thorpe, lhp, Oregon
9. James Farris, rhp, Arizona
10. Ryan Williams, rhp, East Carolina
11. Jordan Brink, rhp, Fresno State
12. Tanner Griggs, rhp, Angelina (Texas) JC
13. Kevonte Mitchell, 3b, Kennett (Mo.) HS
14. Chesny Young, 2b, Mercer
15. Jeremy Null, rhp, Western Carolina
16. Jason Vosler, ss, Northeastern
17. John Michael Knighton, rhp, Central Alabama CC
18. Austyn Willis, rhp, Barstow (Calif.) HS
19. Brad Markey, rhp, Virginia Tech
20. Alex Tomasovich, ss, Charleston Southern
21. Charlie White, of, Maryland
22. Joe Martarano, 3b, Boise State
23. Isiah Gilliam, of, Parkview HS, Lilburn, Ga.
24. Daniel Spingola, of, Georgia Tech
25. Tyler Pearson, c, Texas State
26. Zach Hedges, rhp, Azusa Pacific (Calif.)
27. Calvin Graves, of, Franklin Pierce (N.H.)
28. Jake Niggemeyer, rhp, Olentangy Liberty HS, Powell, Ohio
29. Gianni Zayas, rhp, Seminole State (Fla.) JC

30. Michael Cantu, c, Moody HS, Corpus Christi, Texas
31. Brad Depperman, rhp, East Lake HS, Tarpon Springs, Fla.
32. Andrew Ely, 2b, Washington
33. Brad Bass, rhp, Lincoln-Way Central HS, New Lenox, Ill.
34. Stephen Kane, rhp, Cypress (Calif.) JC
35. Jordan Minch, lhp, Purdue
36. D.J. Peters, of, Glendora (Calif.) HS
37. Riley Adams, c, Canyon Crest Academy, San Diego
38. Daniel Wasinger, c, Eastlake HS, El Paso
39. David Petrino, c, Central Arizona JC
40. Diamond Johnson, of, Hillsborough HS, Tampa

CHICAGO WHITE SOX

1. Carlos Rodon, lhp, North Carolina State
2. Spencer Adams, rhp, White County HS, Cleveland, Ga.
3. Jace Fry, lhp, Oregon State
4. Brett Austin, c, North Carolina State
5. Zach Thompson, rhp, Texas-Arlington
6. Louie Lechich, of, San Diego
7. Jake Peter, ss, Creighton
8. John Ziznewski, ss, Long Island
9. Brian Clark, lhp, Kent State
10. Jake Jarvis, 2b, Klein Collins HS, Spring, Texas
11. Zach Fish, of, Oklahoma State
12. Connor Walsh, rhp, Cincinnati
13. Mike Gomez, lhp, Florida International
14. Bryce Montes de Oca, rhp, Lawrence (Kan.) HS
15. Ben Brewster, lhp, Maryland
16. Matt Cooper, rhp, Hawaii
17. David Trexler, rhp, North Florida
18. Tanner Banks, lhp, Utah
19. Aaron Bummer, lhp, Nebraska
20. Brannon Easterling, rhp, St. Edward's (Texas)
21. Ryan Leonards, 3b, Louisiana-Lafayette
22. Kevin Swick, 3b, Southern California
23. Michael Hollenbeck, c, Illinois State
24. Michael Suiter, of, Kansas
25. Mason Robbins, of, Southern Mississippi
26. Ethan Gross, ss, Memphis
27. Ryan Jones, 1b, Arizona Christian
28. Blair Moore, 3b, California Baptist
29. Evin Einhardt, rhp, Brewton-Parker (Ga.)
30. Marc Flores, 1b, Hawaii
31. Josh Goossen-Brown, rhp/inf, San Diego
32. Adam Choplick, lhp, Oklahoma
33. Louis Silverio, of, Florida International
34. Michael Danner, of, Tampa
35. Jared Koenig, lhp, Central Arizona JC
36. Dayne Wagoner, c, Great Oak HS, Temecula, Calif.
37. Jed Sprague, 1b, St. Mary's HS, Stockton, Calif.
38. Anthony Justiniano, ss, Clemente HS, Chicago
39. James Davison, of, Morgan Park HS, Chicago
40. Julian Service, of, Howard (Texas) JC

CINCINNATI REDS

1. Nick Howard, rhp, Virginia
1. Alex Blandino, ss, Stanford (Compensation pick for loss of free agent Shin-Soo Choo)
2. Taylor Sparks, 3b, UC Irvine
3. Wyatt Strahan, rhp, Southern California
4. Gavin LaValley, 3b, Albert HS, Midwest City, Okla.
5. Tejay Antone, rhp, Weatherford (Texas) JC
6. Jose Lopez, rhp, Seton Hall
7. Shane Mardirosian, 2b, King HS, Riverside, Calif.
8. Brian O'Grady, 1b, Rutgers
9. Brian Hunter, rhp, Hartford
10. Seth Varner, lhp, Miami (Ohio)
11. Mitch Trees, c, Sacred Heart-Griffin HS, Springfield, Ill.
12. Montrell Marshall, 3b, South Gwinnett HS, Snellville, Ga.
13. Zac Correll, rhp, Case HS, Swansea, Mass.
14. Jake Ehret, rhp, UCLA
15. Jimmy Pickens, of, Michigan State

16. **Garrett Boulware, c, Clemson**
17. **Jacob Moody, lhp, Memphis**
18. Roderick Bynum, of, Monroe Catholic HS, Fairbanks, Alaska
19. Isaac Anderson, rhp, JC of Southern Idaho
20. **Conor Krauss, rhp, Seton Hall**
21. **Tyler Parmenter, rhp, Arizona**
22. Robert Byckowski, 3b, Blyth Academy, Toronto
23. **Ty Sterner, lhp, Rhode Island**
24. **Shane Crouse, rhp, Lake Sumter (Fla.) CC**
25. **Paul Kronenfeld, 1b, Catawaba (N.C.)**
26. **Brennan Bernardino, lhp, Cal State Dominguez Hills**
27. **Jake Paulson, rhp, Oakland**
28. Dustin Cook, rhp, San Jacinto (Texas) JC
29. **Michael Sullivan, lhp, Gloucester County (N.J.) CC**
30. **Josciel Veras, ss, Cumberland (Tenn.)**
31. Josh Palacios, of, San Jacinto (Texas) JC
32. Dalton Viner, rhp, San Jacinto (Texas) JC
33. **Jose Lopez, c, King HS, Tampa**
34. **Keenan Kish, rhp, Florida**
35. Brandon Vicens, of, American Heritage HS, Plantation, Fla.
36. Logan Browning, lhp, Lakeland (Fla.) Christian HS
37. Walker Whitworth, 2b, Ada (Okla.) HS
38. Bo Tucker, lhp, Rome (Ga.) HS
39. Seth Roadcap, c, Capital HS, Charleston, W.Va.
40. Michael Mediavilla, lhp, Mater Academy, Hialeah Gardens, Fla.

CLEVELAND INDIANS

1. **Bradley Zimmer, of, San Francisco**
1. **Justus Sheffield, lhp, Tullahoma (Tenn.) HS (Compensation pick for loss of free agent Ubaldo Jimenez)**
1s. **Mike Papi, of, Virginia (Competitive balance pick)**
2. **Grant Hockin, rhp, Damien HS, La Verne, Calif.**
3. **Bobby Bradley, 1b, Harrison Central HS, Gulfport, Miss.**
4. **Sam Hentges, lhp, Mounds View HS, Arden Hills, Minn.**
5. **Julian Merryweather, rhp, Oklahoma Baptist**
6. **Greg Allen, of, San Diego State**
7. **Simeon Lucas, c, Grant Community HS, Fox Lake, Ill.**
8. **Micah Miniard, rhp, Boyle County HS, Danville, Ky.**
9. **Alexis Pantoja, ss, Puerto Rico Baseball Academy, Gurabo, P.R.**
10. **Steven Patterson, 2b, UC Davis**
11. **Jared Robinson, rhp, Cerritos (Calif.) JC**
12. **Jordan Dunatov, rhp, Nevada**
13. **Austin Fisher, ss, Kansas State**
14. Grayson Jones, rhp, Shelton State (Ala.) CC
15. **Luke Eubank, rhp, Oxnard (Calif.) JC**
16. **J.P. Feyereisen, rhp, Wisconsin-Stevens Point**
17. **Cameron Hill, rhp, Redlands (Calif.) CC**
18. **Taylor Murphy, of, Pacific**
19. **Argenis Angulo, rhp, Ranger (Texas) JC**
20. **Gianpaul Gonzalez, c, Puerto Rico Baseball Academy, Gurabo, P.R.**
21. **Bobby Ison, of, Charleston Southern**
22. **Jordan Carter, rhp, St. Joseph's**
23. **David Armendariz, of, Cal Poly Pomona**
24. **Jodd Carter, of, Hilo (Hawaii) HS**
25. K.J. Harrison, c, Punahou HS, Honolulu
26. Reese Cooley, of, Fleming Island HS, Orange Park, Fla.
27. **David Speer, lhp, Columbia**
28. **Nate Winfrey, 3b, Maple Woods (Mo.) CC**
29. **Drake Roberts, 2b, St. Mary's (Texas)**
30. Nick Hynes, rhp, Riverside (Calif.) CC
31. **Dominic DeMasi, rhp, Valdosta State (Ga.)**
32. Jared West, lhp, Houston
33. Peter Dolan, 3b, Gilmour Academy, Gates Mills, Ohio
34. Cody Calloway, 3b, Midview HS, Grafton, Ohio
35. Joe Dunand, 3b, Gulliver Prep, Miami
36. Max Bartlett, ss, Gulf Coast (Fla.) CC
37. **Juan Gomes, c, Odessa (Texas) JC**
38. Cody Jones, of, Texas Christian
39. Jake Morton, rhp, Oakland

40. Ryder Ryan, rhp, North Mecklenburg HS, Huntersville, N.C.

COLORADO ROCKIES

1. **Kyle Freeland, lhp, Evansville**
1s. **Forrest Wall, 2b, Orangewood Christian HS, Maitland, Fla. (Competitive balance pick)**
2. **Ryan Castellani, rhp, Brophy Prep, Phoenix**
3. **Sam Howard, lhp, Georgia Southern**
4. **Wes Rogers, of, Spartanburg Methodist (S.C.) JC**
5. **Kevin Padlo, 3b, Murrieta Valley HS, Murrieta, Calif.**
6. **Max George, ss, Regis Jesuit HS, Aurora, Colo.**
7. **Drew Weeks, of, North Florida**
8. **Harrison Musgrave, lhp, West Virginia**
9. **Andrew Rohrbach, rhp, Long Beach State**
10. **Troy Stein, c, Texas A&M**
11. **Richard Prigatano, of, Long Beach State**
12. **Dylan Craig, lhp, Illinois State**
13. **Chris Rabago, ss, UC Irvine**
14. **Grahamm Wiest, rhp, Cal State Fullerton**
15. **Alec Kenilvort, rhp, Marin (Calif.) CC**
16. **Roberto Ramos, 1b, JC of the Canyons (Calif.)**
17. **Shane Hoelscher, 3b, Rice**
18. **James Lomangino, rhp, St. John's**
19. **Nate Causey, 1b, Arizona State**
20. **Jordan Parris, c, Tennessee Tech**
21. **Josh Michalec, rhp, Baylor**
22. **Sam Bumpers, ss, Lamar**
23. **Gavin Glanz, rhp, Oral Roberts**
24. **Jerry Vasto, lhp, Felician (N.J.)**
25. **Alec Crawford, rhp, Minnesota**
26. **Taylor Black, rhp, Texas State**
27. **Craig Schlitter, rhp, Bryant**
28. Landon Lassiter, 3b, North Carolina
29. **Logan Sawyer, rhp, Lincoln Memorial (Tenn.)**
30. **Hunter Brothers, rhp, Lipscomb**
31. **Dylan Thompson, rhp, UNC Greensboro**
32. Pavin Smith, 1b, Palm Beach Gardens (Fla.) HS
33. Jake Kolterman, rhp, Decatur HS, Federal Way, Wash.
34. Cory Voss, c, Pueblo (Colo.) South HS
35. Brody Westmoreland, ss, Thunderridge HS, Highlands Ranch, Colo.
36. Lucas Gilbreath, lhp, Legacy HS, Broomfield, Colo.
37. Tolly Filotei, of, Daphne (Ala.) HS
38. Griffin Canning, rhp, Santa Margarita HS, Rancho Santa Margarita, Calif.
39. Nathan Rodriguez, c, El Dorado HS, Placentia, Calif.
40. Taylor Lewis, rhp, Chipola (Fla.) JC

DETROIT TIGERS

1. **Derek Hill, of, Elk Grove (Calif.) HS**
2. **Spencer Turnbull, rhp, Alabama**
3. **Grayson Greiner, c, South Carolina**
4. **Adam Ravenelle, rhp, Vanderbilt**
5. **Shane Zeile, c, UCLA**
6. **Ross Kivett, of, Kansas State**
7. **Joey Pankake, 3b, South Carolina**
8. **Artie Lewicki, rhp, Virginia**
9. **Josh Laxer, rhp, Mississippi**
10. **Paul Voelker, rhp, Dallas Baptist**
11. **A.J. Ladwig, rhp, Wichita State**
12. **Garrett Mattlage, ss, Texas State**
13. **Will Allen, c, Mississippi**
14. **Josh Heddinger, rhp, Georgia Tech**
15. **Mike Gerber, of, Creighton**
16. Chase Rader, 3b, Coffeyville (Kan.) CC
17. **Corey Baptist, 1b, St. Petersburg (Fla.) JC**
18. **Will Maddox, 3b, Tennessee**
19. Parker French, rhp, Texas
20. **Trent Szkutnik, lhp, Michigan**
21. **Whit Mayberry, rhp, Virginia**
22. **Michael Thomas, c, Kentucky**
23. **Brett Pirtle, 2b, Mississippi State**
24. **Gabe Hemmer, rhp, San Diego Christian**

25. Gage Smith, rhp, Florida State
26. Jack Fischer, rhp, Wake Forest
27. Tyler Ford, lhp, Houston
28. Will Kengor, ss, Slippery Rock (Pa.)
29. Jacob Butler, rhp, St. Francis (Ill.)
30. Spenser Watkins, rhp, Western Oregon
31. Grant Reuss, lhp, Cranbrook HS, Bloomfield, Mich.
32. Locke St. John, lhp, South Alabama
33. Jonathan Perrin, rhp, Oklahoma State
34. Sammy Stevens, c, Brother Rice HS, Bloomfield Hills, Mich.
35. Dave Hollins, 3b, Orchard Park (N.Y.) HS
36. Nate Fury, rhp, Louisiana State
37. Pat Mahomes Jr., rhp, Whitehouse (Texas) HS
38. Magglio Ordonez Jr., 1b, American Heritage HS, Plantation, Fla.
39. Taylor Sanagorski, c, Bishop Carroll Catholic HS, Wichita
40. Alex Faedo, rhp, Alonso HS, Tampa

HOUSTON ASTROS

1. Brady Aiken, lhp, Cathedral Catholic HS, San Diego
1s. Derek Fisher, of, Virginia (Competitive balance pick, obtained from Orioles in trade)
2. A.J. Reed, 1b, Kentucky
3. J.D. Davis, 3b, Cal State Fullerton
4. Daniel Mengden, rhp, Texas A&M
5. Jacob Nix, rhp, Los Alamitos (Calif.) HS
6. Brock Dykxhoorn, rhp, Central Arizona JC
7. Derick Velazquez, rhp, Fresno State
8. Bobby Boyd, of, West Virginia
9. Bryan Radziewski, lhp, Miami
10. Jay Gause, rhp, Faulkner (Ala.)
11. Dean Deetz, rhp, Northeastern Oklahoma A&M JC
12. Ryan Bottger, of, Texas-Arlington
13. Jamie Ritchie, c, Belmont
14. Nick Tanielu, 2b, Washington State
15. Connor Goedert, 3b, Neosho County (Kan.) CC
16. Ramon Laureano, of, Northeastern Oklahoma A&M JC
17. Ben Smith, lhp, Coastal Carolina
18. Antonio Nunez, ss, Western Oklahoma State JC
19. Ruben Castro, c, Puerto Rico Baseball Academy, Gurabo, P.R.
20. Trent Woodward, c, Fresno State
21. Mac Marshall, lhp, Parkview HS, Lilburn, Ga.
22. Bryan Muniz, 1b, Southeastern (Fla.)
23. Ryan Thompson, rhp, Campbell
24. Vince Wheeland, rhp, Oklahoma State
25. Zach Davis, lhp, Central Missouri
26. Mott Hyde, 2b, Georgia Tech
27. Brandon McNitt, rhp, Stony Brook
28. Aaron Greenwood, rhp, Mississippi
29. Richard Gonzalez, c, Alabama State
30. Sean McMullen, of, Louisiana State
31. Dex McCall, 1b, Hillsborough (Fla.) CC
32. Robert Kahana, rhp, Kansas
33. Edwin Medina, of, St. Thomas (Fla.)
34. Josh James, rhp, Western Oklahoma State JC
35. Keegan Yuhl, rhp, Concordia (Cal.)
36. Justin Ferrell, rhp, Connors State (Okla.) JC
37. Eric Peterson, rhp, North Carolina State
38. Michael Foster, 2b, Northeastern
39. Brad Antchak, ss, Northeastern Oklahoma A&M JC
40. Alex Hernandez, 2b, Miami

KANSAS CITY ROYALS

1. Brandon Finnegan, lhp, Texas Christian
1. Foster Griffin, lhp, First Academy, Orlando (Compensation pick for loss of free agent Ervin Santana)
1s. Chase Vallot, c, St. Thomas More HS, Lafayette, La. (Competitive balance pick)
2. Scott Blewett, rhp, Baker HS, Baldwinsville, N.Y.
3. Eric Skoglund, lhp, Central Florida
4. D.J. Burt, ss, Fuquay-Varina (N.C.) HS
5. Corey Ray, rhp, Texas A&M

6. Logan Moon, of, Missouri Southern State
7. Brandon Downes, of, Virginia
8. Ryan O'Hearn, 1b, Sam Houston State
9. Brandon Thomasson, of, Tennessee Tech
10. Nick Green, lhp, Utah
11. Robert Pehl, 1b, Washington
12. Emilio Ogando, lhp, St. Thomas (Fla.)
13. Eric Stout, lhp, Butler
14. Ian Tompkins, lhp, Western Kentucky
15. Corey Toups, ss, Sam Houston State
16. Manny Olloque, 3b, Torrance (Calif.) HS
17. Brennan Henry, lhp, Bellevue (Neb.)
18. Alberto Rodriguez, rhp, Northwest Florida State JC
19. Scott Heineman, of, Oregon
20. Kyle Pollock, c, Evansville
21. Evan Beal, rhp, South Carolina
22. Mike Hill, ss, Long Beach State
23. Eric Sandness, rhp, San Joaquin Delta (Calif.) JC
24. Brandon Thomas, lhp, San Diego State
25. Rudy Martin, of, Lewisburg HS, Olive Branch, Miss.
26. Michael Arroyo, c, Puerto Rico Baseball Academy, Gurabo, P.R.
27. Alex Close, c, Liberty
28. Josh Banuelos, 1b, Fresno Pacific
29. Vance Vizcaino, 3b, Glendale (Ariz.) CC
30. Ryan Lillard, 3b, Urbandale (Iowa) HS
31. Rocky McCord, rhp, Auburn
32. Tim Hill, lhp, Bacone (Okla.)
33. DonAndre Clark, of, St. Mary's
34. Todd Eaton, rhp, Southern Illinois
35. Andrew Sykes, lhp, Valparaiso (Ind.) HS
36. Brandon Gonzalez, of, Villa Park (Calif.) HS
37. David Noworyta, c, Holy Cross HS, Delran, N.J.
38. Cole Way, lhp, Tulsa
39. Jeff Hendrix, of, Oregon State
40. Diego Francisco, 2b, Palm Beach Central HS, Wellington, Fla.

LOS ANGELES ANGELS

1. Sean Newcomb, lhp, Hartford
2. Joe Gatto, rhp, St. Augustine Prep, Richland, N.J.
3. Chris Ellis, rhp, Mississippi
4. Jeremy Rhoades, rhp, Illinois State
5. Jake Jewell, rhp, Northeastern Oklahoma A&M JC
6. Alex Abbott, of, Tift County HS, Tifton, Ga.
7. Bo Way, of, Kennesaw State
8. Jake Yacinich, ss, Iowa
9. Jordan Kipper, rhp, Texas Christian
10. Caleb Adams, of, Louisiana-Lafayette
11. Andrew Daniel, 3b, San Diego
12. Jared Ruxer, rhp, Louisville
13. Zach Houchins, 3b, East Carolina
14. Justin Anderson, rhp, Texas-San Antonio
15. Greg Mahle, lhp, UC Santa Barbara
16. Blaine Prescott, 2b, Midland (Texas) JC
17. Ryan Seiz, 1b, Liberty
18. Austin Robichaux, rhp, Louisiana-Lafayette
19. Justin Bormann, c, Texas-San Antonio
20. Kyle Martin, 1b, South Carolina
21. Tyler Palmer, of, Miami
22. Adam McCreery, lhp, Azusa Pacific (Calif.)
23. Zach Varela, rhp, UC Riverside
24. Eason Spivey, c, North Georgia College and State
25. Tyler Carpenter, rhp, Georgia-Gwinnett
26. James Connell, rhp, Kennesaw State
27. Cody Lavalli, of, Lewis-Clark State (Idaho)
28. Jordan Piche, rhp, Kansas
29. Alex Klonowski, rhp, Northern Illinois
30. Ronnie Muck, rhp, Illinois
31. Nick Wagner, rhp, Cal State Dominguez Hills
32. Kholton Sanchez, c, New Mexico JC
33. Jake Petersen, lhp, California Lutheran
34. Jose Rodriguez, ss, Colegio Hector Urdaneta, Rio Grande, P.R.

35. Caleb Wallingford, lhp, Memphis
36. **Brandon Gildea, c, Westmont (Calif.)**
37. **Fran Whitten, 1b, St Leo (Fla.)**
38. **Tyler Watson, lhp, McLennan (Texas) CC**
39. **Patrick Armstrong, of, Nevada-Las Vegas**
40. **Eric Alonzo, rhp, Georgia Southern**

LOS ANGELES DODGERS

1. **Grant Holmes, rhp, Conway (S.C.) HS**
2. **Alex Verdugo, of, Sahuaro HS, Tucson**
3. **John Richy, rhp, Nevada-Las Vegas**
4. **Jeff Brigham, rhp, Washington**
5. **Jared Walker, 3b, McEachern HS, Powder Springs, Ga.**
6. **Brock Stewart, rhp, Illinois State**
7. **Trevor Oaks, rhp, California Baptist**
8. **Hunter Redman, c, Texas Tech**
9. **Matt Campbell, rhp, Clemson**
10. **Colin Hering, of, Coastal Carolina**
11. **A.J. Vanegas, rhp, Stanford**
12. **Kam Uter, rhp, Pace Academy, Atlanta**
13. **Ryan Taylor, rhp, Arkansas Tech**
14. **Kelvin Ramos, ss, San Jacinto (Texas) JC**
15. **Joe Broussard, rhp, Louisiana State**
16. **Devan Ahart, of, Akron**
17. **Tyler Wampler, ss, Indiana State**
18. **Clint Freeman, 1b, East Tennessee State**
19. Gary Cornish, rhp, Palomar (Calif.) JC
20. **Brian Wolfe, of, Washington**
21. **Osvaldo Vela, ss, Oklahoma Baptist**
22. **Bubby Rossman, rhp, Cal State Dominguez Hills**
23. **Andrew Godbold, of, Southeastern Louisiana**
24. **Jimmy Allen, 2b, Cal Poly**
25. **Matt Jones, of, Hutchinson (Kan.) CC**
26. **Deion Ulmer, 2b, Holmes (Miss.) JC**
27. **Harlan Richter, rhp, Bossier Parrish (La.) CC**
28. **Billy Bereszniewicz, of, Binghamton**
29. Christian Trent, lhp, Mississippi
30. **Brant Whiting, c, Stanford**
31. **Derrick Sylvester, rhp, Southern New Hampshire**
32. **Scott De Jong, 1b, Felician (N.J.)**
33. **Carson Baranik, rhp, Louisiana-Lafayette**
34. Hunter Bross, of, Notre Dame Prep, Scottsdale, Ariz.
35. Tanner Chauncey, ss, Brigham Young
36. Kyle Kocher, rhp, Mountain View HS, Mesa, Ariz.
37. **Karch Kowalczyk, rhp, Valparaiso**
38. **Caleb Ferguson, lhp, West Jefferson (Ohio) HS**
39. Jeff Bain, rhp, San Marino (Calif.) HS
40. **Sam Moore, rhp, UC Irvine**

MIAMI MARLINS

1. **Tyler Kolek, rhp, Shepherd (Texas) HS**
1s. **Blake Anderson, c, West Lauderdale HS, Collinsville, Miss. (Compensation pick for failure to sign 2013 supplemental first-round pick Matt Krook)**
2. **Justin Twine, ss, Falls City (Texas) HS**
3. **Brian Anderson, 2b, Arkansas**
3s. **Michael Mader, lhp, Chipola (Fla.) JC (Compensation pick for failure to sign 2013 third-round pick Ben DeLuzio)**
4. **Brian Schales, ss, Edison HS, Huntington Beach, Calif.**
5. **Casey Soltis, of, Granada HS, Livermore, Calif.**
6. **Chris Sadberry, lhp, Texas Tech**
7. **Anfernee Seymour, ss, American Heritage HS, Delray Beach, Fla.**
8. **Stone Garrett, of, George Ranch HS, Richmond, Texas**
9. **Ben Holmes, lhp, Oregon State**
10. **Dillon Peters, lhp, Texas**
11. **Nick White, rhp, Berryhill HS, Tulsa**
12. **Roy Morales, c, Colegio Angel David HS, San Juan, P.R.**
13. **Jacob Smigelski, rhp, UC Riverside**
14. **Zach Sullivan, ss, Corning-Painted Post East HS, Corning, N.Y.**
15. **Connor Overton, rhp, Old Dominion**
16. **Scott Squier, lhp, Hawaii**

17. **Eric Fisher, 1b, Arkansas**
18. **Brad Haynal, c, San Diego State**
19. **Mason Davis, 2b, The Citadel**
20. **Jordan Holloway, rhp, Ralston Valley HS, Arvada, Colo.**
21. D.J. King, ss, Fort Meade (Fla.) HS
22. Mitchell Robinson, 3b, Clayton Heights SS, Surrey, B.C.
23. **Steven Farnworth, rhp, Cal Poly Pomona**
24. **Ryan Cranmer, 2b, Newberry (S.C.)**
25. **Christian MacDonald, lhp, UNC Wilmington**
26. **Nick Williams, rhp, Tennessee**
27. **Chris Hoo, c, Cal Poly**
28. Christian Williams, 1b, Gulf Coast (Fla.) CC
29. **Greg Greve, rhp, Ohio State**
30. **Kyle Fischer, rhp, St. Cloud State (Minn.)**
31. **Kyle Porter, rhp, California**
32. **Nestor Bautista, lhp, Ball State**
33. **Austen Smith, 1b, Alabama**
34. Taylor Lehman, lhp, Keystone Oaks HS, Pittsburgh
35. Keith Zuniga, rhp, Bethune-Cookman
36. **Justin Hepner, rhp, San Diego State**
37. Chase Williams, rhp, Eastern Oklahoma State JC
38. Parker Ray, rhp, Texas A&M
39. Matt Pope, rhp, Walters State (Tenn.) CC
40. Hunter Aguirre, of, Westmoore HS, Oklahoma City

MILWAUKEE BREWERS

1. **Kodi Medeiros, lhp, Waiakea HS, Hilo, Hawaii**
1s. **Jacob Gatewood, ss, Clovis (Calif.) HS (Competitive balance pick)**
2. **Monte Harrison, of, Lee's Summit (Mo.) West HS**
3. **Cy Sneed, rhp, Dallas Baptist**
4. **Troy Stokes, of, Calvert Hall College HS, Baltimore**
5. **Dustin DeMuth, 3b, Indiana**
6. **David Burkhalter, rhp, Ruston (La.) HS**
7. **Mitch Meyer, of, Kansas State**
8. **J.B. Kole, rhp, Villanova**
9. **Greg McCall, c, Texas-Arlington**
10. **Javi Salas, rhp, Miami**
11. **Brandon Woodruff, rhp, Mississippi State**
12. **Jordan Yamamoto, rhp, St. Louis HS, Honolulu**
13. **Kaleb Earls, rhp, Limestone (S.C.)**
14. **Jonathan Oquendo, ss, Maria Teresa Pineiro HS, Toa Baja, P.R.**
15. **Caleb Smith, rhp, Rice**
16. Ben Onyshko, lhp, Vauxhall Academy, Winnipeg
17. J.J. Schwarz, c, Palm Beach Gardens (Fla.) HS
18. **Luke Curtis, rhp, Pittsburgh**
19. **Zach Hirsch, lhp, Nebraska**
20. Tate Blackman, ss, Lake Brantley HS, Altamonte Springs, Fla.
21. **Donnie Hissa, rhp, Notre Dame**
22. Patrick Weigel, rhp, Oxnard (Calif.) JC
23. Kolton Mahoney, rhp, Brigham Young
24. **Bubba Blau, rhp, Dixie State (Utah)**
25. C.D. Pelham, lhp, Spartanburg Methodist (S.C.) JC
26. Cre Finfrock, rhp, Martin County HS, Stuart, Fla.
27. **Matt Martin, c, Wake Forest**
28. Turner Larkins, rhp, Martin HS, Arlington, Texas
29. Aaron Garza, rhp, Houston
30. **Taylor Stark, rhp, Delta State (Miss.)**
31. **Brock Hudgens, rhp, Charlotte**
32. Eric White, rhp, Parkers Chapel HS, El Dorado, Ark.
33. **Chad Reeves, lhp, Louisiana State-Eunice JC**
34. **Carlos Leal, rhp, Delta State (Miss.)**
35. **David Carver, lhp, Lamar**
36. Hunter Tackett, of, Anderson County HS, Clinton, Tenn.
37. Eric Ramirez, 1b, Rio Mesa HS, Oxnard, Calif.
38. Carl Chester, of, Lake Brantley HS, Altamonte Springs, Fla.
39. John Gavin, lhp, St. Francis HS, Mountain View, Calif.
40. Taylor Lane, ss, IMG Academy, Bradenton, Fla.

MINNESOTA TWINS

1. **Nick Gordon, ss, Olympia HS, Orlando**

2. **Nick Burdi, rhp, Louisville**
3. **Michael Cederoth, rhp, San Diego State**
4. **Sam Clay, lhp, Georgia Tech**
5. **Jake Reed, rhp, Oregon**
6. **John Curtiss, rhp, Texas**
7. **Andro Cutura, rhp, Southeastern Louisiana**
8. **Keaton Steele, rhp, Missouri**
9. **Max Murphy, of, Bradley**
10. **Randy LeBlanc, rhp, Tulane**
11. **Tanner English, of, South Carolina**
12. **Pat Kelly, 2b, Nebraska**
13. **Zach Tillery, rhp, Florida Gulf Coast**
14. **Tyler Mautner, 3b, Buffalo**
15. **Roberto Gonzalez, of, University HS, Orlando**
16. **Tyler Kuresa, 1b, UC Santa Barbara**
17. **Mat Batts, lhp, UNC Wilmington**
18. **T.J. White, 3b, Nevada-Las Vegas**
19. **Jarrard Poteete, c, Connors State (Okla.) JC**
20. McCarthy Tatum, 3b, Clovis (Calif.) HS
21. **Onas Farfan, lhp, Ridgewater (Minn.) JC**
22. **Trevor Hildenberger, rhp, California**
23. **Miles Nordgren, rhp, Birmingham-Southern**
24. **Alex Real, c, New Mexico**
25. Taylor Hearn, lhp, San Jacinto (Texas) JC
26. **Blake Schmit, ss, Maryland**
27. **Gabriel Ojeda, c, Colegio Hector Urdaneta HS, Rio Grande, P.R.**
28. **Austin Diemer, of, Cal State Fullerton**
29. Cameron Avila-Leeper, lhp, Grant HS, Sacramento
30. **Michael Theofanopoulos, lhp, California**
31. Sam Hilliard, lhp, Crowder (Mo.) JC
32. Orynn Veillon, rhp, St. Thomas More HS, Lafayette, La.
33. **Trey Vavra, 1b, Florida Southern**
34. Mike Baumann, rhp, Mahtomedi (Minn.) HS
35. Brad Mathiowetz, c, Mayo HS, Rochester, Minn.
36. Kirvin Moesquit, ss, Highlands Christian Academy, Pompano Beach, Fla.
37. **Tyree Davis, of, Centennial HS, Compton, Calif.**
38. **Brett Doe, c, Baylor**
39. John Jones, c, Orangewood Christian HS, Maitland, Fla.
40. Dalton Guthrie, ss, Venice (Fla.) HS

NEW YORK METS

1. **Michael Conforto, of, Oregon State**
2. (Pick lost for signing free agent Curtis Granderson)
3. **Milton Ramos, ss, American Heritage HS, Plantation, Fla.**
4. **Eudor Garcia, 3b, El Paso (Texas) CC**
5. **Josh Prevost, rhp, Seton Hall**
6. **Tyler Moore, c, Louisiana State**
7. **Brad Wieck, lhp, Oklahoma City**
8. **Dash Winningham, 1b, Trinity Catholic HS, Ocala, Fla.**
9. **Michael Katz, of, William & Mary**
10. **Kelly Secrest, lhp, UNC Wilmington**
11. **Connor Buchmann, rhp, Oklahoma**
12. **Alex Durham, rhp, Southern Alamance HS, Graham, N.C.**
13. **Erik Manoah, rhp, South Dade HS, Homestead, Fla.**
14. **Darryl Knight, c, Embry-Riddle (Fla.)**
15. **Gabe Llanes, rhp, Downey (Calif.) HS**
16. **Joel Huertas, lhp, Colegio Carmen Sol, Bayamon, P.R.**
17. **David Roseboom, lhp, South Carolina-Upstate**
18. **Raphael Ramirez, of, Pace Academy, Atlanta**
19. **Bryce Beeler, rhp, Memphis**
20. **Jimmy Duff, rhp, Stonehill (Mass.)**
21. Luke Bonfield, of, IMG Academy, Bradenton, Fla.
22. **William Fulmer, 2b, Montevallo (Ala.)**
23. Richard Moesker, rhp, Trinity Christian Academy, Lake Worth, Fla.
24. **Tyler Badamo, rhp, Dowling (N.Y.)**
25. **Nicco Blank, rhp, Central Arizona JC**
26. Tommy Pincin, c, Upland (Calif.) HS
27. **Alex Palsha, rhp, Sacramento State**
28. Keaton McKinney, rhp, Ankeny (Iowa) HS
29. **Matt Blackham, rhp, Middle Tennessee State**

---

30. **Tucker Tharp, of, Kansas**
31. **Kurtis Horne, lhp, Milne Community School, Sooke, B.C.**
32. Chris Glover, rhp, Rockwall (Texas) HS
33. Brady Puckett, rhp, Riverdale HS, Murfreesboro, Tenn.
34. Jordan Hand, c, Shadow Ridge HS, Las Vegas
35. Jonathan Teaney, rhp, Quartz Hill (Calif.) HS
36. Garett King, rhp, Orange (Calif.) Lutheran HS
37. Tristan Gray, ss, Elkins HS, Missouri City, Texas
38. Kyle Dunster, rhp, Greenwich (Conn.) HS
39. **Arnaldo Berrios, of, Beltran Baseball Academy, Florida, P.R.**
40. **Dale Burdick, ss, Summit HS, Spring Hill, Tenn.**

NEW YORK YANKEES

1. (Pick lost for signing free agent Brian McCann)
1. (Compensation pick for loss of free agent Robinson Cano; pick lost for signing free agent Carlos Beltran)
1. (Compensation pick for loss of free agent Curtis Granderson; pick lost for signing free agent Jacoby Ellsbury)
2. **Jacob Lindgren, lhp, Mississippi State**
3. **Austin DeCarr, rhp, Salisbury (Conn.) School**
4. **Jordan Montgomery, lhp, South Carolina**
5. **Jordan Foley, rhp, Central Michigan**
6. **Jonathan Holder, rhp, Mississippi State**
7. **Mark Payton, of, Texas**
8. **Connor Spencer, 1b, UC Irvine**
9. **Vince Conde, ss, Vanderbilt**
10. **Ty McFarland, 2b, James Madison**
11. **Matt Borens, rhp, Eastern Illinois**
12. **Chris Gittens, 1b, Grayson County (Texas) CC**
13. **Bo Thompson, 1b, The Citadel**
14. **Sean Carley, rhp, West Virginia**
15. **Andrew Chin, lhp, Boston College**
16. **Derek Callahan, lhp, Gonzaga**
17. Garrett Cave, rhp, South Sumter HS, Bushnell, Fla.
18. **Justin Kamplain, lhp, Alabama**
19. **Joe Harvey, rhp, Pittsburgh**
20. **Corey Holmes, rhp, Concordia (Texas)**
21. Porter Clayton, lhp, Oregon
22. Jake Kelzer, rhp, Indiana
23. Will Toffey, 3b, Salisbury (Conn.) School
24. **Dominic Jose, of, Stanford**
25. Dylan Barrow, rhp, Tampa
26. **Collin Slaybaugh, c, Washington State**
27. **Griff Gordon, of, Jacksonville State**
28. **Lee Casas, rhp, Southern California**
29. Mariano Rivera Jr., rhp, Iona
30. Jorge Perez, rhp, Grand Canyon (Ariz.)
31. **Devyn Bolasky, of, UC Riverside**
32. Jordan Ramsey, rhp, UNC Wilmington
33. David Graybill, rhp, Arizona State
34. **Matt Wotherspoon, rhp, Pittsburgh**
35. Christopher Hudgins, c, Valhalla HS, El Cajon, Calif.
36. William Gaddis, rhp, Brentwood (Tenn.) HS
37. **Ryan Lindemuth, 2b, William & Mary**
38. **Andre Del Bosque, rhp, Houston-Victoria**
39. Cameron Warren, 1b, Albert HS, Midwest City, Okla.
40. Madison Stokes, ss, Flora HS, Columbia, S.C.

OAKLAND ATHLETICS

1. **Matt Chapman, 3b, Cal State Fullerton**
2. **Daniel Gossett, rhp, Clemson**
3. **Brett Graves, rhp, Missouri**
4. **Jordan Schwartz, rhp, Niagara**
5. **Heath Fillmyer, rhp, Mercer County (N.J.) JC**
6. **Trace Loehr, ss, Putnam HS, Milwaukie, Ore.**
7. **Branden Cogswell, ss, Virginia**
8. **Branden Kelliher, rhp, Lake Stevens (Wash.) HS**
9. **Mike Fagan, lhp, Princeton**
10. **Corey Miller, rhp, Pepperdine**
11. **Joel Seddon, rhp, South Carolina**
12. **Tyler Willman, rhp, Western Illinois**

13. Max Kuhn, 2b, Kentucky
14. Casey Schroeder, c, Polk State (Fla.) JC
15. Trent Gilbert, 2b, Arizona
16. Jose Brizuela, 3b, Florida State
17. Eric Cheray, c, Missouri State
18. Michael Nolan, lhp, Oklahoma City
19. Tom Gavitt, c, Bryant
20. Koby Gauna, rhp, Cal State Fullerton
21. Tim Proudfoot, ss, Texas Tech
22. Brendan McCurry, rhp, Oklahoma State
23. Collin Ferguson, 1b, St. Mary's
24. Dawson Brown, rhp, West Florida
25. Joseph Estrada, of, Colegio Hector Urdaneta HS, Ceiba, P.R.
26. Rob Huber, rhp, Duke
27. J.P. Sportman, of, Central Connecticut State
28. Corey Walter, rhp, West Virginia
29. Cody Stull, lhp, Belmont Abbey (N.C.)
30. Derek Beasley, lhp, South Carolina-Aiken
31. Tyler Schimpf, rhp, Capital Christian HS, Sacramento
32. Denz'l Chapman, of, Serra HS, Gardena, Calif.
33. Michael Rivera, c, Venice (Fla.) HS
34. John Nogowski, 1b, Florida State
35. Austen Swift, of, Bishop Allen Academy, Toronto
36. Tyler Spoon, of, Arkansas
37. Brock Lundquist, of, Fountain Valley (Calif.) HS
38. Colt Atwood, of, Sam Houston State
39. Payton Squier, 2b, Greenway HS, Phoenix
40. Bryson Brigman, ss, Valley Christian HS, San Jose

PHILADELPHIA PHILLIES

1. Aaron Nola, rhp, Louisiana State
2. Matt Imhof, lhp, Cal Poly
3. Aaron Brown, of, Pepperdine
4. Chris Oliver, rhp, Arkansas
5. Rhys Hoskins, 1b, Sacramento State
6. Brandon Leibrandt, lhp, Florida State
7. Emmanuel Marrero, ss, Alabama State
8. Sam McWilliams, rhp, Beech HS, Hendersonville, Tenn.
9. Matt Hockenberry, rhp, Temple
10. Matt Shortall, of, Texas-Arlington
11. Drew Stankiewicz, ss, Arizona State
12. Austin Davis, lhp, Cal State Bakersfield
13. Nathan Thornhill, rhp, Texas
14. Chase Harris, of, New Mexico
15. Jared Fisher, rhp, Washington
16. Calvin Rayburn, rhp, Barry (Fla.)
17. Damek Tomscha, 3b, Auburn
18. Sean McHugh, c, Purdue
19. Joey Denato, lhp, Indiana
20. Derek Campbell, 2b, California
21. Tim Zier, 2b, San Diego State
22. Ryan Powers, rhp, Miami (Ohio)
23. Joel Fisher, c, Michigan State
24. Preston Packrall, rhp, Tampa
25. Bryan Sova, rhp, Creighton
26. Jacques de Gruy, rhp, Furman
27. Scott Harris, lhp, Buena Vista (Iowa)
28. Tanner Kiest, rhp, Chaffee (Calif.) CC
29. Al Molina, ss, Red Bank (N.J.) Catholic HS
30. Brandon Murray, rhp, Hobart (Ind.) HS
31. Shane Gonzales, rhp, Fullerton (Calif.) JC
32. Tom Flacco, of, Eastern HS, Voorhees Township, N.J.
33. James Harrington, rhp, Mesquite HS, Gilbert, Ariz.
34. Scott Tomassetti, c, JC of Southern Nevada
35. Thomas Gamble, of, Moorestown (N.J.) HS
36. Blake Wiggins, c, Pulaski Academy, Little Rock, Ark.
37. Keith Rogalla, rhp, Oak Park & River Forest HS, Oak Park, Ill.
38. Kollin Schrenk, rhp, Kell HS, Charlotte
39. Keenan Eaton, of, Chaparral HS, Parker, Colo.
40. Jesse Berardi, ss, Commack (N.Y.) HS

PITTSBURGH PIRATES

1. Cole Tucker, ss, Mountain Pointe HS, Phoenix
1s. Connor Joe, of, San Diego (Competitive balance pick obtained from Marlins in trade)
2. Mitch Keller, rhp, Xavier HS, Cedar Rapids, Iowa
2s. Trey Supak, rhp, La Grange (Texas) HS (Competitive balance pick)
3. Jordan Luplow, of, Fresno State
4. Taylor Gushue, c, Florida
5. Michael Suchy, of, Florida Gulf Coast
6. Tyler Eppler, rhp, Sam Houston State
7. Nelson Jorge, ss, International Baseball Academy, Ceiba, P.R.
8. Austin Coley, rhp, Belmont
9. Kevin Krause, c, Stony Brook
10. Alex McRae, rhp, Jacksonville
11. Gage Hinsz, rhp, Billings (Mont.) West HS
12. Tyler Filliben, ss, Samford
13. Frank Duncan, rhp, Kansas
14. Chase Simpson, 3b, Wichita State
15. Eric Dorsch, rhp, Kent State
16. Sam Street, rhp, Texas-Pan American
17. Michael Clemens, rhp, McNeese State
18. Erik Lunde, 2b, Lander (S.C.)
19. Carl Anderson, of, Bryant
20. John Sever, lhp, Bethune-Cookman
21. Eric Thomas, of, Langham Creek HS, Houston
22. Eric Karch, rhp, Pepperdine
23. Zach Warren, lhp, St. Augustine Prep, Richland, N.J.
24. Denis Karas, 3b, Campolindo HS, Moraga, Calif.
25. Erik Forgione, ss, Washington
26. Jerrick Suiter, of, Texas Christian
27. Jess Amedee, rhp, Texas-Arlington
28. Nick Neumann, rhp, Central Connecticut State
29. Zach Lucas, 2b, Louisville
30. David Andriese, of, UC Riverside
31. Luis Paula, rhp, North Carolina
32. Montana DuRapau, rhp, Bethune-Cookman
33. Zach Lewis, rhp, Wabash Valley (Ill.) CC
34. Colin Welmon, rhp, Loyola Marymount
35. Chris Eades, rhp, Delgado (La.) JC
36. Palmer Betts, rhp, Chipola (Fla.) JC
37. Bryant Holtmann, lhp, Florida State
38. Paul DeJong, c, Illinois State
39. Daniel Keating, 3b, Gulfport (Miss.) HS
40. Tyler Brown, 2b, JC of Southern Nevada

ST. LOUIS CARDINALS

1. Luke Weaver, rhp, Florida State
1. Jack Flaherty, rhp, Harvard-Westlake HS, Studio City, Calif. (Compensation pick for loss of free agent Carlos Beltran)
2. Ronnie Williams, rhp, American Senior HS, Hialeah, Fla.
2s. Andrew Morales, rhp, UC Irvine (Competitive balance pick)
3. Trevor Megill, rhp, Loyola Marymount
4. Austin Gomber, lhp, Florida Atlantic
5. Darren Seferina, 2b, Miami Dade JC
6. Andrew Sohn, ss, Western Michigan
7. Brian O'Keefe, c, St. Joseph's
8. Nick Thompson, of, William & Mary
9. Daniel Poncedeleon, rhp, Embry-Riddle (Fla.)
10. Danny Diekroeger, 3b, Stanford
11. Justin Bellinger, 1b, St. Sebastian's HS, Needham, Mass.
12. Jordan DeLorenzo, lhp, West Florida
13. Matt Pearce, rhp, Polk State (Fla.) JC
14. Chris Shaw, c, Midland (Texas) JC
15. Matt Ditman, rhp, Rice
16. Tristan Hildebrandt, ss, Esperanza HS, Anaheim
17. Dustin Beggs, rhp, Georgia Perimeter JC
18. Blake Drake, of, Concordia (Ore.)
19. Dominic Thompson-Williams, cf, Iowa Western CC
20. Collin Radack, of, Hendrix (Ark.)

DRAFT

21. Casey Grayson, 1b, Houston
22. Derek Casey, rhp, Hanover HS, Mechanicsville, Va.
23. Joe Gillette, 3b, Scotts Valley (Calif.) HS
24. Casey Turgeon, 2b, Florida
25. Landon Beck, rhp, Anderson (S.C.)
26. Tyler Bray, rhp, Louisiana-Monroe
27. Cole Lankford, c, Texas A&M
28. Tyler Dunnington, rhp, Colorado Mesa
29. Bryan Dobzanski, rhp, Delsea Regional HS, Franklinville, N.J.
30. Josh Wirsu, rhp, Georgia Southern
31. Julian Barzilli, 3b, Whittier (Calif.)
32. Anthony Herron, rhp, Affton HS, St. Louis
33. Dominic Moreno, rhp, Texas Tech
34. George Iskenderian, ss, Indian River State (Fla.) JC
35. Michael Bono, rhp, Buchanan HS, Clovis, Calif.
36. Cody Schumacher, rhp, Missouri State
37. Chase Raffield, of, Georgia State
38. Sasha Kuebel, lhp, Iowa
39. Kyle Ruchim, 2b, Northwestern
40. Davis Ward, rhp, Ouachita Baptist (Ark.)

SAN DIEGO PADRES

1. Trea Turner, ss, North Carolina State
2. Michael Gettys, of, Gainesville (Ga.) HS
3. Zech Lemond, rhp, Rice
4. Nick Torres, of, Cal Poly
5. Auston Bousfield, of, Mississippi
6. Zach Risedorf, c, Northwestern Regional HS, Winchester, Conn.
7. Ryan Butler, rhp, Charlotte
8. Mitch Watrous, rhp, Utah
9. Nick Vilter, ss, UC Riverside
10. Thomas Dorminy, lhp, Faulkner (Ala.)
11. Yale Rosen, of, Washington State
12. Seth Lucio, rhp, Tennessee Tech
13. Joey Epperson, 3b, UC Santa Barbara
14. Chris Huffman, rhp, James Madison
15. Logan Jernigan, rhp, North Carolina State
16. Taylor Cox, lhp, Tennessee-Martin
17. T.J. Weir, rhp, Ball State
18. Max MacNabb, lhp, San Diego
19. Justin Lewis, rhp, Greater Atlanta Christian HS, Norcross, Ga.
20. Tyler Wilson, rhp, Tennessee Wesleyan
21. Peter Solomon, rhp, Mount St. Joseph HS, Baltimore
22. Danny Wissmann, lhp, South Carolina-Aiken
23. Jason Jester, rhp, Texas A&M
24. Colby Blueberg, rhp, Nevada
25. Travis Radke, lhp, Portland
26. Aaron Cressley, rhp, Pittsburgh-Bradford
27. Mike Fitzgerald, c, Indiana State
28. Johnny Manziel, ss, Texas A&M
29. Mitch Morales, ss, Florida Atlantic
30. Ryan Atwood, lhp, Florida Gulf Coast
31. Logan Sowers, of, McCutcheon HS, Lafayette, Ind.
32. Taylor Aikenhead, lhp, Cal State Bakersfield
33. Devin Smeltzer, lhp, Bishop Eustace Prep, Pennsauken, N.J.
34. Brendan McKay, lhp, Blackhawk HS, Beaver Falls, Pa.
35. Cobi Johnson, rhp, Mitchell HS, Trinity, Fla.
36. Kyle McGrath, lhp, Louisville
37. Tyler Wood, rhp, Furman
38. Louis-Phillipe Pelletier, 2b, Maisonneuve (Quebec) JC
39. Richard Negron, 3b, Tallahassee (Fla.) CC
40. Bryce Carter, c, Cascia Hall Prep, Tulsa

SAN FRANCISCO GIANTS

1. Tyler Beede, rhp, Vanderbilt
2. Aramis Garcia, c, Florida International
3. Dylan Davis, of, Oregon State
4. Logan Webb, rhp, Rocklin (Calif.) HS
5. Sam Coonrod, rhp, Southern Illinois
6. Skyler Ewing, 1b, Rice

7. Seth Harrison, of, Louisiana-Lafayette
8. Austin Slater, of, Stanford
9. Stetson Woods, rhp, Liberty HS, Madera, Calif.
10. Matt Gage, lhp, Siena
11. Greg Brody, rhp, Belmont
12. Jameson Henning, ss, Western Illinois
13. Luis Lacen, of, Beltran Baseball Academy, Florida, P.R.
14. Kevin Rivera, 2b, Beltran Baseball Academy, Florida, P.R.
15. Benton Moss, rhp, North Carolina
16. Kevin Ginkel, rhp, Southwestern (Calif.) JC
17. Caleb Smith, lhp, South Carolina-Aiken
18. Edrick Agosto, rhp, International Baseball Academy, Cieba, P.R.
19. Richard Amion, of, Alabama State
20. Bret Underwood, of, Northwestern State
21. Matthew Crownover, lhp, Clemson
22. Mark Reyes, lhp, Crowder (Mo.) JC
23. Jordan Johnson, rhp, Cal State Northridge
24. Michael Petersen, rhp, Riverside (Calif.) CC
25. Byron Murray, of, Trinity Christian Academy, Deltona, Fla.
26. Hunter Cole, 3b, Georgia
27. Connor Kaden, rhp, Wake Forest
28. Nick Sabo, lhp, Long Beach State
29. Ryan Cruz, rhp, JC of the Canyons (Calif.)
30. Cliff Covington, 1b, West Florida
31. Nick Nelson, rhp, Rutherford HS, Panama City, Fla.
32. Hunter Williams, lhp, Cosby HS, Midlothian, Va.
33. Jared Deacon, c, Cal State Fullerton
34. Tim Susnara, c, St. Francis HS, Mountain View, Calif.
35. Mitch Hart, rhp, Granite Bay HS, Sacramento
36. Zach Taylor, c, Horizon HS, Scottsdale, Ariz.
37. Garrett Christman, ss, Noblesville (Ind.) HS
38. Benito Santiago Jr., c, Coral Springs (Fla.) Christian Academy
39. Joe Ryan, rhp, Sir Francis Drake HS, San Anselmo, Calif.
40. Riles Mahan, ss, Moeller HS, Cincinnati

SEATTLE MARINERS

1. Alex Jackson, of, Rancho Bernardo HS, San Diego
1. (Pick lost for signing free agent Robinson Cano)
2s. Gareth Morgan, of, North Toronto Collegiate HS (Competitive balance pick)
3. Austin Cousino, of, Kentucky
4. Ryan Yarbrough, lhp, Old Dominion
5. Dan Altavilla, rhp, Mercyhurst (Pa.)
6. Lane Ratliff, lhp, Jones County (Miss.) JC
7. Taylor Byrd, lhp, Nicholls State
8. Kody Kerski, rhp, Sacred Heart
9. Peter Miller, rhp, Florida State
10. Adam Martin, c, Western Carolina
11. Jay Muhammad, rhp, Coral Springs (Fla.) Christian Academy
12. Nelson Ward, ss, Georgia
13. Marvin Gorgas, rhp, East Hampton (Conn.) HS
14. Chris Mariscal, ss, Fresno State
15. Lukas Schiraldi, rhp, Texas
16. Wayne Taylor, c, Stanford
17. Trey Cochran-Gill, rhp, Auburn
18. Nick Kiel, lhp, Bellevue (Wash.) CC
19. Rohn Pierce, rhp, Canisius
20. Hawtin Buchanan, rhp, Mississippi
21. Jay Baum, ss, Clemson
22. Jarrett Brown, lhp, Georgia
23. Pat Peterson, lhp, North Carolina State
24. Sheehan Planas-Arteaga, 1b, Barry (Fla.)
25. Vinny Nittoli, rhp, Xavier
26. Taylor Smart, ss, Tennessee
27. Andy Peterson, 2b, Oregon State
28. Dominic Blanco, c, Gulf Coast HS, Naples, Fla.
29. Tyler Herb, rhp, Coastal Carolina
30. James Alfonso, c, Hartford
31. DeAires Moses, of, East Nashville (Tenn.) Magnet School
32. Chase Nyman, 2b, East Mississippi JC
33. Tom Verdi, ss, Connecticut
34. Andrew Summerville, lhp, Lakeside HS, Seattle

35. Chris McGrath, lhp, Marist School, Atlanta
36. **Spencer Hermann, lhp, Fisher (Mass.)**
37. **Sam Lindquist, rhp, Stanford**
38. **Taylor Zeutenhorst, of, Iowa**
39. **Kavin Keyes, 3b, Oregon State**
40. Scott Manea, c, St John's HS, Shrewsbury, Mass.

TAMPA BAY RAYS

1. **Casey Gillaspie, 1b, Wichita State**
2. **Cameron Varga, rhp, Cincinnati Hills Christian Academy, Cincinnati**
2s. **Brent Honeywell, rhp, Walters State (Tenn.) CC (Competitive balance pick)**
3. **Brock Burke, lhp, Evergreen (Colo.) HS**
4. **Blake Bivens, rhp, Washington HS, Danville, Va.**
5. **Michael Russell, ss, North Carolina**
6. **Mac James, c, Oklahoma**
7. **Mike Franco, rhp, Florida International**
8. **Daniel Miles, 3b, Tennessee Tech**
9. **Chris Pike, rhp, Oklahoma City**
10. **Bradley Wallace, rhp, Arkansas State**
11. **Spencer Moran, rhp, Mountain View HS, Mesa, Ariz.**
12. **Braxton Lee, of, Mississippi**
13. **Jace Conrad, 2b, Louisiana-Lafayette**
14. **Trevor Lubking, lhp, Pacific Lutheran (Wash.)**
15. **Brian Miller, rhp, Vanderbilt**
16. **Greg Maisto, lhp, McLennan (Texas) CC**
17. **Steve Ascher, lhp, Oneonta State (N.Y.)**
18. **Alec Sole, ss, Saint Louis**
19. **Justin McCalvin, rhp, Kennesaw State**
20. **Kyle McKenzie, rhp, Tulane**
21. **Jaime Ayende, of, Beltran Baseball Academy, Florida, P.R.**
22. **Ryan Pennell, lhp, Elon**
23. **Zac Law, of, Robinson HS, Waco, Texas**
24. **Nic Wilson, 1b, Georgia State**
25. Tyler Wells, lhp, Nevada
26. **Cade Gotta, of, San Diego Christian**
27. **Grant Kay, 2b, Louisville**
28. **Carter Burgess, 3b, Sam Houston State**
29. **Tomas Michelson, rhp, Illinois-Chicago**
30. **Trevor Dunlap, rhp, Washington**
31. **Andrew Woeck, rhp, North Carolina State**
32. Josh Davis, of, Union HS, Tulsa
33. **Patrick Grady, of, Lander (S.C.)**
34. **Chris Knott, of, East Stroudsburg (Pa.)**
35. **Kyle Bird, lhp, Flagler (Fla.)**
36. **Isias Alcantar, c, Arkansas-Pine Bluff**
37. Matt Plitt, rhp, Louisiana-Lafayette
38. **Chris DeMorais, of, New Haven (Conn.)**
39. **Blake Grant-Parks, 1b, Cal State Monterey Bay**
40. Conor Harber, rhp, Western Nevada JC

TEXAS RANGERS

1. (Pick lost for signing free agent Shin-Soo Choo)
1. **Luis Ortiz, rhp, Sanger (Calif.) HS (Compensation pick for loss of free agent Nelson Cruz)**
2. **Ti'quan Forbes, ss, Columbia (Miss.) HS**
3. **Josh Morgan, ss, Orange (Calif.) Lutheran HS**
4. **Brett Martin, lhp, Walters State (Tenn.) CC**
5. **Wes Benjamin, lhp, Kansas**
6. **Jose Trevino, 3b, Oral Roberts**
7. **Nick Green, rhp, Indian Hills (Iowa) CC**
8. **Erik Swanson, rhp, Iowa Western CC**
9. **Doug Votolato, of, Central Arkansas**
10. **Seth Spivey, c, Abilene Christian (Texas)**
11. **Scott Williams, rhp, State JC of Florida**
12. **Joe Watson, rhp, Catawba (N.C.)**
13. Gabe Gonzalez, rhp, Arbor View HS, Las Vegas
14. **Gio Abreu, rhp, St. Raymond HS, Bronx, N.Y.**
15. **Joe Filomeno, lhp, Louisville**
16. **Reed Garrett, rhp, Virginia Military Institute**
17. David Berg, rhp, UCLA

18. J.T. Phillips, rhp, Georgia Perimeter JC
19. Tramayne Holmes, 2b, Rickards HS, Tallahassee, Fla.
20. **Isaias Quiroz, c, St. Joseph HS, Montvale, N.J.**
21. **Sterling Wynn, lhp, McLennan (Texas) CC**
22. **Tripp Martin, 3b, Samford**
23. **Darius Day, of, Simeon HS, Chicago**
24. **Austin Pettibone, rhp, UC Santa Barbara**
25. Daniel Sweet, of, Polk State (Fla.) JC
26. Jayce Vancena, rhp, Lake HS, Millbury, Ohio
27. **Jason Hoppe, rhp, Minnesota State-Mankato**
28. Chris Mathewson, rhp, Kaiser HS, Fontana, Calif.
29. **Luke Tendler, of, North Carolina A&T State**
30. **Cody Palmquist, rhp, Palm Beach State (Fla.) JC**
31. **John Fasola, rhp, Kent State**
32. Andre Jackson, rhp, Cienega HS, Tucson
33. **Adam Parks, rhp, Liberty**
34. **Storm Rynard, rhp, Cowley County (Kan.) CC**
35. Will Carter, rhp, Walters State (Tenn.) CC
36. **Cody Chartrand, rhp, Lewis-Clark State (Idaho)**
37. Andrew Bechtold, ss, Garnet Valley HS, Glen Mills, Pa.
38. Tyree Johnson, lhp, New Hannover HS, Wilmington, N.C.
39. Travis Jones, of, Atascocita HS, Humble, Texas
40. **Nick Dignacco, lhp, Army**

TORONTO BLUE JAYS

1. **Jeff Hoffman, rhp, East Carolina**
1. **Max Pentecost, c, Kennesaw State (Compensation pick for failure to sign 2012 first-round pick Phil Bickford)**
2. **Sean Reid-Foley, rhp, Sandalwood HS, Jacksonville**
3. **Nick Wells, lhp, Battlefield HS, Haymarket, Va.**
4. **Matt Morgan, c, Thorsby (Ala.) HS**
5. **Lane Thomas, of, Bearden HS, Knoxville**
6. **Grayson Huffman, lhp, Grayson County (Texas) CC**
7. Zach Zehner, of, Cal Poly
8. **Justin Shafer, rhp, Florida**
9. **Ryan Metzler, 2b, South Carolina-Aiken**
10. **Jordan Romano, rhp, Oral Roberts**
11. Jake Latz, lhp, Lemont (Ill.) HS
12. Tanner Houck, rhp, Collinsville (Ill.) HS
13. **Gunnar Heidt, 2b, College of Charleston**
14. **Chase Mallard, rhp, Alabama-Birmingham**
15. **Ryan McBroom, 1b, West Virginia**
16. Mike Papierski, c, Lemont (Ill.) HS
17. Quinn Carpenter, rhp, Iowa Western CC
18. **Dusty Isaacs, rhp, Georgia Tech**
19. **Cliff Brantley, of, Adelphi (N.Y.)**
20. **Aaron Attaway, ss, Western Carolina**
21. Drew Lugbauer, c, Arlington HS, Lagrangeville, N.Y.
22. Todd Isaacs, of, American Heritage HS, Plantation, Fla.
23. Zach Pop, rhp, Notre Dame SS, Brampton, Ontario
24. **Conor Fisk, rhp, Southern Mississippi**
25. Rob Winemiller, rhp, Case Western Reserve (Ohio)
26. **Bobby Wheatley, lhp, Southern California**
27. Owen Taylor, 1b, Grand Junction (Colo.) HS
28. **Chris Carlson, of, Cal Poly Pomona**
29. Chris Murphy, rhp, Billerica (Mass.) Memorial HS
30. **Kevin Garcia, c, Loyola Marymount**
31. **Dave Pepe, 2b, Pace (N.Y.)**
32. **J.T. Autrey, rhp, Lamar**
33. **Chase Wellbrock, rhp, Houston**
34. **Brandon Hinkle, lhp, Delaware**
35. **Joey Aquino, rhp, San Diego Christian**
36. Yan Rivera, ss, Colegio Catolico Notre Dame HS, Caguas, P.R.
37. **Michael Kraft, lhp, Texas-San Antonio**
38. Keith Weisenberg, rhp, Osceola HS, Seminole, Fla.
39. **James Lynch, of, Pima (Ariz.) CC**
40. **Trent Miller, of, Middle Tennessee State**

WASHINGTON NATIONALS

1. **Erick Fedde, rhp, Nevada-Las Vegas**
2. Andrew Suarez, lhp, Miami

3. Jakson Reetz, c, Norris HS, Firth, Neb.
4. Robbie Dickey, rhp, Blinn (Texas) JC
5. Drew Van Orden, rhp, Duke
6. Austen Williams, rhp, Texas State
7. Dale Carey, of, Miami
8. Jeff Gardner, of, Louisville
9. Austin Byler, 1b, Nevada
10. Matt Page, of, Oklahoma Baptist
11. Weston Davis, rhp, Manatee HS, Bradenton, Fla.
12. Domenick Mancini, rhp, Miami Dade JC
13. Austin Davidson, 3b, Pepperdine
14. James Bourque, rhp, Michigan
15. Ryan Ripken, 1b, Indian River State (Fla.) JC
16. Cole Plouck, lhp, Pima (Ariz.) CC
17. Alec Keller, of, Princeton
18. McKenzie Mills, lhp, Sprayberry HS, Marietta, Ga.
19. Clay Williamson, of, Cal State Fullerton
20. Bryan Langlois, of, Pepperdine
21. Connor Bach, lhp, Virginia Military Institute

22. Daniel Salters, c, Dallas Baptist
23. Chris Riopedre, ss, East Tennessee State
24. Kyle Simmons, rhp, Texas Lutheran
25. Kyle Bacak, c, Texas Christian
26. Chase McDowell, rhp, Rice
27. Conor Keniry, ss, Wake Forest
28. Kida De La Cruz, rhp, Volunteer State (Tenn.) CC
29. D.J. Jauss, rhp, Massachusetts
30. Tyler Mapes, rhp, Tulane
31. Sam Johns, rhp, Evansville
32. Elliott Cary, of, Clackamas (Ore.) HS
33. Clay Casey, of, Desoto Central HS, Southaven, Miss.
34. Evan Skoug, c, Libertyville (Ill.) HS
35. Tommy Doyle, rhp, Flint Hill HS, Oakton, Va.
36. John Henry Styles, lhp, Episcopal HS, Bellaire, Texas
37. Quinn Brodey, lhp, Loyola HS, Los Angeles
38. Stuart Fairchild, of, Seattle Prep
39. Jon Littell, of, Stillwater (Okla.) HS
40. Jacob Hill, lhp, Orange Coast (Calif.) JC

DRAFT

APPENDIX

■ **Mark Ballinger,** a righthander who pitched in one big league season, died June 13 in Okeechobee, Fla. He was 65.

A second-round pick by the Indians in the 1967 draft out of a California high school, Ballinger played 12 seasons in pro ball but only made the majors once. He appeared in 18 games, all in relief, for the Indians in 1971, going 1-2, 4.67 in 35 innings.

■ **Bruce Barmes,** an outfielder who played in one big league season with the Washington Senators, died Jan. 25 in Garner, N.C. He was 84.

Barmes won two minor league batting titles while he was coming up through the Senators system in the early 1950s, but he only got one chance to play in the majors. Called up in September 1953, he played in five games for Washington and had one hit. Barmes continued playing in the minors through 1960 before leaving the game, other than a one-game return in 1966. He was an uncle of Pirates shortstop Clint Barmes.

■ **John "Zeke" Bella,** an outfielder who played in two big league seasons, died Nov. 17, 2013, in Greenwich, Conn. He was 83.

Bella was 27 when he got his first callup in September 1957, appearing in five games for the Yankees and going 1-for-10 at the plate. His only other time in the majors came two years later, when he logged 47 appearances with the Kansas City Athletics and hit .207 in 82 at-bats. Bella played one more season in the minors before retiring in 1960.

■ **Vern Benson,** an outfielder who played in parts of five big league seasons in the 1940s and '50s, died Jan. 20 in Salisbury, N.C. He was 89.

Benson received brief callups with the Philadelphia Athletics in 1943 (two games) and 1946 (seven). He also missed two seasons in between to serve in the military. After 1946, Benson didn't get another call to the major leagues until 1951 with the Cardinals, when he got into 13 games and hit .261 with one homer in 46 at-bats. He played in 33 more games for St. Louis over the next two seasons but hit just .176 (9-for-51).

The 1953 season was Benson's last in the majors and he began serving as a player-manager in the minors in 1956. He went on to a long coaching career in the minors and majors. He got back to the big leagues as a coach with the Cardinals in 1961 and was a member of their staff when they won the 1964 World Series. Benson coached through 1980 with the Yankees, Reds, Braves and Giants.

■ **Buddy Bicknell,** a righthander who pitched two seasons for the Phillies in the late 1940s, died Nov. 24, 2013, in Livingston, Mont. He was 85.

Bicknell debuted with the Phillies as a 19-year-old in 1948, working 26 innings over 17 appearances, including one start, and going 0-1, 5.96. He logged another 13 relief appearances and 28 innings in 1949 with a 7.62 ERA. Bicknell spent the rest of his career in the minor leagues, pitching through 1957 despite missing the 1951 season to serve in the military.

■ **Werner "Babe" Birrer,** a righthander who pitched in three big league seasons, died Nov. 19, 2013, in Clarence, N.Y. He was 84.

Birrer pitched six years in the minors from 1947-52 before going into the military. He returned to baseball in 1955 and got his first big league callup that year, going 4-3, 4.15 in 80 innings, mostly in relief, for the Tigers. The Orioles claimed Birrer on waivers shortly before the 1956 season, but he made just four appearances in the majors that season. His only other big league time came with the Dodgers in 1958, when he logged 34 innings over 16 relief appearances, posting a 4.50 ERA without figuring in any decisions.

■ **Paul Blair,** an outfielder who was a two-time all-star and played 17 years in the majors, died Dec. 26, 2013, in Baltimore. He was 69.

Blair was best known as the everyday center fielder for the powerhouse Orioles squads of the 1960s and '70s. He excelled on defense, winning eight Gold Gloves in his career, including seven in a row from 1969-75, but he developed into a capable hitter as well. Blair took over the everyday job in 1965 and had a breakout year with the bat in 1967, leading the American League in triples with 12 and hitting .293 with 11 homers as well. He made his first All-Star Game in 1969, when he belted a career-best 26 homers and hit .285. He reached double figures in homers four more times and made a second all-star appearance in 1973, when he hit .280 with 10 longballs.

With Blair patrolling center field, the Orioles won four pennants and two World Series, in 1966 and '70. He won two more rings late in his career with the Yankees in 1977 and '78. Blair had his best showing in the Fall Classic in 1970, when he hit .474 (9-for-19) as the Orioles defeated the Reds in five games. In all, he played in 52 postseason games in his career and hit .260 in 146 at-bats.

Blair finished his career with the Yankees in 1980, ending with 1,513 hits. After his playing days, he went on to coach in the minor leagues and at the college level with Fordham and Coppin State.

■ **Lou Brissie,** a lefthander who pitched in the majors from 1947-53, died Nov. 15, 2013, in Augusta, Ga. He was 89.

Brissie was best known for his time with the Philadelphia Athletics, making his debut there in 1947 after serving as a paratrooper in World War II. He won 14 games with a 4.13 ERA over 194 innings in his first full season for the A's in 1948, then followed that with an all-star campaign in 1949, going 16-11, 4.28 in 229 innings. He finished in the top 10 in the American League in strikeouts each year from 1948-50, his best showing in '48 when he finished fourth with 127.

After he went just 7-19, 4.02 in 1950, the A's traded him to the Indians the following April. Cleveland moved him to the bullpen and he flourished in 1951, going 4-3, 3.20. He pitched two more seasons, enjoying another solid year in 1952 but then logging just 16 appearances in 1953 before calling it a career.

■ **Jim Brosnan,** a righthander who pitched nine seasons in the majors, died June 28 in Park Ridge, Ill. He was 84.

Brosnan split time between starting and relieving early in his career after debuting with the Cubs in 1954. After being traded twice, he found his stride with the Reds, converting to the bullpen full-time in 1960. He posted his best season that year, going 7-2, 2.36 with 12 saves in 57 appearances. A year later, he went 10-4, 3.04 with 16 saves for the Reds' pennant-winning 1961 club. Brosnan finished his career in 1963 with a 3.54 lifetime ERA and 67 saves. Along the way, he also gained notoriety for authoring two books about his experiences, "The Long Season" and "Pennant Race," which are still held in high regard for their honest portrayal of life in baseball.

■ **Jophery Brown,** a righthander who pitched in one big league game in 1968, died Jan. 11 in Inglewood, Calif. He was 68.

Brown pitched in the minors from 1966-69, making his lone appearance in the majors on Sept. 21, 1968, with the Cubs. He came out of the bullpen in the fifth and threw two innings against the Pirates, allowing a run on two hits. After his baseball career, Brown worked for many years as a Hollywood stunt man.

■ **Jim Burton,** a lefthander who pitched in two seasons for the Red Sox, died Dec. 12, 2013, in Charlotte. He was 64.

Burton had a fine rookie season for the Red Sox in 1975, going 1-2, 2.89 in 53 innings, mostly out of the Boston bullpen. However, his greatest claim to fame was being the losing pitcher in Game Seven of the '75 World Series against Reds, allowing a run in the top of the ninth after entering with the score tied 3-3. Burton made only one more big league appearance after that game, on Sept. 17, 1977. He retired a year later.

■ **Frank Cashen,** who helped build the Orioles dynasty of the late 1960s and early '70s and rebuilt the laughingstock Mets into a World Series winner in 1986, died June 30 in Easton, Md. He was 88.

Cashen spent 26 continuous years in the front office of a major league team, starting in 1966 as executive vice president with the Orioles, who that year won the first of their six American League pennants. Promoted to general manager in October 1971, he presided over two division titles in Baltimore before stepping down following the 1975 season. He remained as assistant GM in Baltimore until 1980.

Through a series of trades, Cashen turned the Mets from a doormat into a perennial contender after taking the club's GM job in 1980. His most famous deals netted first baseman Keith Hernandez from the Cardinals in June 1983 and catcher Gary Carter from the Expos in December 1984.

The Mets' poor records in the late 1970s and early '80s helped the franchise accumulate high draft choices. New York drafted first overall in Cashen's first year on the job in 1980 and took Darryl Strawberry. They also snagged Dwight Gooden fifth overall in 1982. Those players, along with complementary pieces picked up in trades, such as starters Ron Darling and Sid Fernandez and third baseman Howard Johnson, culminated in a World Series title in 1986.

■ **Bobby Castillo,** a righthander who pitched nine seasons for the Dodgers and Twins, died June 30 in Los Angeles. He was 59.

Castillo saw limited action with the Dodgers from 1977-79 but became a regular out of their bullpen in 1980, going 8-6, 2.75 in 61 appearances. He was also part of the Dodgers' World Series-winning 1981 team. Los Angeles traded him to the Twins after the '81 season and he moved into a starting role, winning 13 games in 1982, though he would go back to relieving in 1984. He returned to the Dodgers for his final season in 1985.

■ **Mel Clark,** an outfielder who played in the big leagues from 1951-55 and in 1957, died May 1 in West Columbia, W.Va. He was 89.

Clark spent most of his big league career with the Phillies, appearing in 210 games from 1951-55 and hitting .277. A knee injury in 1955 set

APPENDIX

his career back, and he only made it back to the majors briefly in 1957, getting into five games with the Tigers.

■ **Jerry Coleman,** a second baseman who played nine years in the majors and became a Hall of Fame broadcaster, died Jan. 5 in La Jolla, Calif. He was 89.

Coleman spent his entire big league playing career with the Yankees from 1949-57. He took over as their everyday second baseman at age 24 in 1949 and hit .275 as a rookie. He earned his only All-Star Game appearance in 1950 when he hit .287 with six homers and 69 RBIs, setting career-bests in all three categories. Coleman's playing career was twice interrupted by military service, first from 1943-45 during World War II while he was in the minors and then again in 1952 and '53, when he missed all but a few games of those seasons to serve in Korea. He returned to the Yankees full-time in 1954 but was used mostly as a utility player for the rest of his career. Coleman played in six World Series, winning four, before retiring as a player in 1957.

A few years after his playing days ended, Coleman got into broadcasting big league games for NBC in 1960. He worked Yankees games throughout 1960s but was best known for his long tenure calling San Diego Padres games. Coleman joined the Padres' booth in 1972 and was a fixture there all the way through 2013, with the only exception being 1980 when he stepped in to manage the team. Coleman received the Ford Frick Award, the Hall of Fame's honor for broadcasters, in 2005, and he'd previously been inducted into the Padres hall of fame in 2001.

■ **Drew Denson,** a first baseman and 1984 first-round pick who played in 16 big league games, died Feb. 13 in Cincinnati. He was 48.

Taken by the Braves 19th overall in the 1984 draft out of a Cincinnati-area high school, Denson reached the big leagues in September 1989, playing in 12 games for the Braves and hitting .250. He returned to the big leagues only one other time, getting into four games for the White Sox at the tail end of the 1993 season. Denson last played pro ball in 1997 in the Mexican League.

■ **Jack Dittmer,** a second baseman who played six years in the majors from 1952-57, died May 31 in Strawberry Point, Iowa. He was 86.

Dittmer came up with the Boston Braves in 1952 and, following the team's move to Milwaukee, was the Braves' regular second baseman in 1953. He hit .266 with nine homers over 504 at-bats that year, however he would play a reduced role over the next three seasons, never getting into more than 70 games. The Braves traded him to the Tigers before the 1957 season but he made just 16 appearances in a Detroit uniform before being sent down, and he played out the final two seasons of his pro career in Triple-A.

■ **Jim Fregosi,** a six-time all-star shortstop in the big leagues who had a long managerial career, died Feb. 14 in Miami. He was 71.

Fregosi first came to prominence as a player with the Angels. He was just 19 when he made his big league debut in 1961, and he took over as everyday shortstop as a 21-year-old in 1963. He had his best all-around offensive season in 1964, hitting .277/.369/.463 with 18 homers and 72 RBIs to earn his first All-Star Game appearance. He went on to make five straight All-Star Games from 1966-70, including during his career-best 22-homer season in 1970.

After the 1971 season, however, Fregosi was part of one of the most infamous trades in baseball history, going from the Angels to the Mets for a package of four players that included Nolan Ryan. Fregosi was plagued by injuries and played less than two full seasons in New York before being sold to the Rangers, and he went on to play part-time roles with Texas (1973-77) and the Pirates (1977-78). He recorded 1,726 hits for his career and 151 homers.

Fregosi retired from the Pirates in the midst of the 1978 season because the Angels wanted to hire him as their manager. He skippered the Angels through the middle of 1981, going 237-248. After a three-year stint leading the White Sox from 1986-88 (he succeeded Tony La Russa), Fregosi enjoyed the highlight of his managerial career with the Phillies. He took over in 1991 and led the Phillies to 97 wins and the National League pennant in 1993, though they famously lost to the Blue Jays on Joe Carter's walk-off homer in the World Series. Fregosi managed in Philadelphia through 1996 and worked his final managerial job with the Blue Jays in 1999 and 2000. In total, he won 1,028 games over parts of 15 seasons. He went on to work for the Braves as a special assistant to the general manager through 2013.

■ **Bill Gabler,** a first baseman who played briefly for the White Sox in 1958, died Jan. 4 in St. Louis. He was 83.

Gabler was an accomplished minor league slugger, producing six 20-homer seasons and one 30-homer season in 1961. His pro career spanned 1950-61, but he only got to the major leagues once, for three games with the White Sox in

September 1958. He made three pinch-hitting appearances and went 0-for-3.

■ **Mike Gordon,** a catcher who played in two big league seasons, died May 26 in Boston. He was 60.

Gordon received brief callups with the Cubs in 1977 and '78, appearing in a total of 12 major league games and going 2-for-28 at the plate. A third-round pick by the Cubs out of high school in the 1972 draft, he played eight seasons in the pros from 1972-79.

Johnny Gray, a righthander who pitched four years in the majors in the 1950s, died May 21 in Boca Raton, Fla. He was 87.

Gray had a long, well traveled pro career, pitching from 1950-60 and appearing with three different big league teams between 1954 and 1958. Gray got his longest exposure to the big leagues with the Philadelphia Athletics in 1954, when he worked 105 innings and spent much of the second half in their rotation. However, pitching for a last-place team, he went just 3-12, 6.51. He saw limited time with the A's, Indians and Phillies through 1958, posting a 5.63 ERA between '55 and '58.

■ **Tony Gwynn,** who had a Hall of Fame career as a player and a successful one as San Diego State's head baseball coach, died June 16 in Poway, Calif. He was 54.

Gwynn, born in Long Beach, had become synonymous with San Diego since attending San Diego State to play basketball and baseball in the late 1970s. A third-round pick in 1981, he chose baseball over basketball, where he had played point guard and was drafted in the 10th round by the then-San Diego Clippers. Gwynn reached the majors a year later, and led the Padres to both of their National League pennants, in 1984 and 1998.

He finished with 3,141 hits in 20 seasons and was the 22nd player to get 3,000 hits. He batted .338 in his career, the 18th-best average in major league history. He also had 319 stolen bases and a .388 on-base percentage. Gwynn was inducted into the Hall of Fame in 2007, having received 97.6 percent of the vote.

■ **Mike Hegan,** an outfielder and first baseman who played 12 major league seasons with the Yankees, Athletics, Seattle Pilots and Brewers, died Dec. 25, 2013, in Hilton Head, S.C. He was 71.

The son of former major leaguer Jim Hegan, Mike hit .242 with 53 homers and 229 RBIs in 965 career games. He reached the World Series with the Yankees in 1964 and helped Oakland win the Series in '72. He was also a radio and TV

broadcaster with the Brewers for 12 seasons and the Indians for 23 years until he retired after the 2011 season.

■ **Bill Henry,** a lefthander who pitched 16 seasons in the majors, died April 11 in Round Rock, Texas. He was 86.

Henry pitched for six different big league teams between 1952 and 1969. After working as a starter for the Red Sox from 1952-55, he was sent back to the minors for the entire 1956 and '57 seasons, then converted to relief in 1958. He got back to the majors with the Cubs and spent the rest of his career as a reliever. He led the NL in appearances with 65 in 1959 while going 9-8, 2.68 with 12 saves. He made his only All-Star Game in 1960 with the Reds, going 1-5, 3.19 with 17 saves, though he continued pitching through age 41 in 1969. He finished his career with 90 saves and a 3.26 ERA over 527 appearances.

■ **Ed Herrmann,** a catcher who played in 11 big league seasons and was an all-star in 1974, died Dec. 22, 2013, in San Diego. He was 67.

Herrmann spent the bulk of his career with the White Sox, debuting in 1967 and becoming their primary catcher in 1969. He had his best offensive season in 1970 at age 23, hitting 19 homers in 96 games to go with a .283/.356/.505 batting line. He never came very close to equaling that .283 average over a full season again, but he did continue to put up solid power numbers, hitting double-digit home runs in each of the next four seasons. Along the way, Herrmann led American League catchers in throwing out base stealers in 1972, catching exactly 50 percent in 112 games behind the dish. He made his only All-Star Game appearance in 1974, during a season in which he hit .259 with 10 homers.

The White Sox traded Herrmann, then 28, to the Yankees shortly before the start of the 1975 season, and he spent the last four years of his career as more of a journeyman. After brief stints with the Yankees and Angels, Herrmann landed with the Astros in June 1976. He played parts of three seasons in Houston, though mostly in a reserve role. He finished his career as a backup with the Montreal Expos in 1978. In all, Herrmann played in 922 big league games, hitting .240 with 80 career home runs.

■ **John Hoover,** a righthander who pitched briefly in the majors in 1990, died July 8 in Fresno. He was 51.

Hoover made his name at Fresno State, still holding Division I records for complete games in a season (19) and career (42). Hoover was the

Bulldogs' ace from 1981-84 and was Baseball America's Pitcher of the Year in 1984, when he had a season for the ages. Hoover went 18-3, 2.09 and struck out 205 with just 39 walks in 177 innings. He completed 19 of his 21 starts that season and earned a spot on the first U.S. Olympic team. The Orioles picked him 25th overall that year in the draft, and Hoover reached the major leagues for two outings in May 1990 with the Rangers.

■ **Tim Hosley,** a catcher who played in parts of nine big league seasons between 1970 and 1981, died Jan. 21 in Moore, S.C. He was 66.

Hosley came up through the Tigers organization, reaching the big leagues in 1970. He never secured a full-time job in the majors, serving as a reserve for the Tigers, Athletics and Cubs. The only season in which he surpassed 100 plate appearances in the majors came in 1975, when he hit .255 with six homers for the Cubs. He had multiple stints with the A's, playing there from 1973-74 and then returning in 1976. He remained in the Oakland organization, playing in the majors and minors, through the end of his career in 1981.

■ **Art Kenney,** a lefthander who pitched briefly in the majors in 1938, died March 12 in Littleton, N.H. He was 97.

The Boston Bees signed Kenney out of Holy Cross in June 1938 and brought him to the majors just a few weeks later. The 22-year-old Kenny appeared in two games for the Bees, both in relief, and allowed four runs in 2 1/3 innings, spending the rest of the year in the minors. He only pitched professionally for one more season. Kenney was the third-oldest former big leaguer at the time of his passing.

■ **Ralph Kiner,** a Hall of Fame player in a career spent mostly with the Pirates who went on to have an equally prominent career as a broadcaster for the Mets, died Feb. 6 in Rancho Mirage, Calif. He was 91.

Kiner played for the Pirates, Cubs and Indians in a 10-year career and hit more than 40 homers five years in a row, averaging nearly 47 home runs a season in that stretch, and he ended up with 369 home runs. He started his major league career at age 23 in 1946, after serving three years as a Navy pilot during World War II. Kiner finished in the top 10 in MVP voting five consecutive seasons and hit .297/.398/.548 for his career. Despite his success with the Pirates, he was traded to the Cubs on June 4, 1953, after continual salary disputes with Pittsburgh general manager Branch Rickey.

Chronic back problems forced Kiner to retire after the 1955 season at age 32. He was elected to the Hall of Fame in 1975, getting 273 votes from the Baseball Writers Association of America, one more than required, in his final year on the ballot. As successful as he was on the field—Kiner was one of the most feared righthanded hitters in his era—he became equally beloved for his work on Mets broadcasts and on his TV postgame show, "Kiner's Korner."

■ **Chuck Kress,** a first baseman who played in four big league seasons, died March 4 in Colville, Wash. He was 92.

Kress lost three years to military service while he was coming up through the minors and didn't make his big league debut until he was 25 in 1947, when he played in 11 games for the Reds. His only season as a big league regular came two years later, when he played in 124 games combined between stints with the Reds and White Sox, batting .272 with one homer in 382 at-bats. He played briefly for the White Sox in 1950, and his only other big league time came in 1954 when he got into 37 games with the Tigers and Brooklyn Dodgers. He continued on in the minors through 1959.

■ **Les Layton,** an outfielder who played one season with the New York Giants, died March 1 in Scottsdale, Ariz. He was 92.

Layton had four 20-homer seasons in the minors but only got one crack at the majors, appearing in 63 games for the Giants in 1948 at age 26. He hit .231 with two homers and 12 RBIs while playing most of his time in left field. Layton played pro ball in the minors through 1954.

■ **Jerry Lumpe,** a second baseman who played 12 years in the majors from 1956-67, died Aug. 15 in Springfield, Mo. He was 81.

Lumpe broke into the majors with the Yankees in 1956 and won a World Series with them in 1958, but he didn't get a chance at regular playing time until a trade to the Kansas City Athletics in May 1959. He served as the everyday second baseman for the A's (1959-63) and Tigers (1964-65) over the next six years, earning an all-star appearance as a Tiger in 1964, although his best season was 1962 with Kansas City, when he hit .301 with 10 homers and 83 RBIs. He finished his career in 1967 with a .268 lifetime average, 47 homers and 454 RBIs.

■ **Connie Marrero,** a righthander who pitched five seasons for the Washington Senators, died April 23 in Havana, Cuba. He was 102.

A Cuban who didn't make his big league debut until he was nearly 39 in 1950, Marrero was a regular member of the Senators' rotation from 1950-54. He made the All-Star Game at age 40

in his second season, going 11-9, 3.90. He posted a 2.88 ERA in 22 starts in 1952 and nearly had another sub-3.00 ERA in 1953, finishing 8-7, 3.03. Marrero was the oldest living former major leaguer at the time of his passing.

■ **Rod Miller,** an outfielder and third baseman who played in one big league game, died Nov. 8, 2013, in Cascade, Idaho. He was 73.

Miller's lone big league callup came at the tail end of the 1957 season when the Brooklyn Dodgers summoned him to the majors. He pinch-hit in the ninth inning on Sept. 28 against the Phillies and struck out in his only big league at-bat. He went on to play three more seasons in the minors through 1960.

■ **Billy McCool,** a lefthander who pitched seven years in the majors from 1964-70, died June 8 in Summerfield, Fla. He was 69.

McCool debuted as a 19-year-old with the Reds in 1964, having pitched only one season in the minors. He made a splash as a rookie, going 6-5, 2.42 in 89 innings, mostly in relief. The Sporting News named him its rookie of the year for '64. He made his only all-star appearance in 1966 during a season in which he logged 105 innings out of the Reds' bullpen and went 8-8, 2.48 with 18 saves. However, his numbers fell off subsequently. He posted a cumulative 3.95 ERA from 1967-68, then the Padres snapped him up in the 1968 expansion draft. He lasted only one season in San Diego before being traded to the Cardinals, where he last pitched in the majors in 1970.

■ **Pete Naton,** a catcher who played briefly in the majors in 1953, died Dec. 10, 2013, in Springfield, Mass. He was 82.

A member of Holy Cross' 1952 College World Series championship team, Naton signed with the Pirates in June 1953 and debuted in the majors four days later. He played in six games for Pittsburgh over the remainder of the season, going 2-for-12 at the plate. He went on to play professionally through 1958 but never got back to the big leagues.

■ **Eddie O'Brien,** a shortstop and righthanded pitcher who played in five big league seasons, died Feb. 21 in Seattle. He was 83.

O'Brien broke into the majors with the Pirates in 1953 and got to be the double play partner for his twin brother Johnny in 1953, '55 and '56. Both brothers missed the 1954 season to serve in the military. Eddie had his best offensive season in 1956, batting .264 in 63 appearances for Pittsburgh, but he began working more as a pitcher in the latter half of his career. He pitched

in three big league games for the Pirates in 1957 and served mainly as a pitcher, also seeing some time as an outfielder, for Triple-A Salt Lake City in 1958. He also made one pitching appearance for the Pirates in '58, which would be his last stop in the majors.

■ **Charlie Osgood,** a righthander who pitched in one big league game as part of a five-year pro career, died Jan. 23 in Tewksbury, Mass. He was 87.

Osgood was just 17 years old when he signed with the Brooklyn Dodgers and made his lone big league appearance on June 18, 1944. He pitched three innings of relief against the Phillies and allowed one run. He spent the rest of the '44 season in the minors, then went into the military in 1945. He returned to the diamond in 1946 but never got back to the majors, playing in the minors through 1949.

■ **Mike Palagyi,** a righthander who pitched in one big league game, died Nov. 21, 2013, in Conneaut, Ohio. He was 96.

Palagyi pitched three seasons in the minors before getting his lone big league call with the Washington Senators on Aug. 18, 1939. He entered in the ninth inning of the club's game against the Red Sox, faced four hitters and walked three of them. Following his glimpse of the majors, Palagyi pitched one more season in the minors before entering the military, and he only returned to baseball briefly in 1946.

■ **Clarence "Ace" Parker,** a shortstop who played two seasons in the majors in the 1930s, died Nov. 6, 2013, in Portsmouth, Va. He was 101.

Parker played in 94 major league games for the Philadelphia Athletics from 1937-38 but had a much more accomplished career as a football player. He played seven seasons as a running back in the NFL and ran for 4,698 career yards in 68 games from 1937-41 and 45-46, also missing three years to serve in the military. He was inducted into both the college and pro football halls of fame in 1955 and 1972, respectively. Interestingly, Parker continued playing minor league baseball during football offseasons, even winning a batting title with Portsmouth (Eastern) in 1946. He also stayed in baseball as a minor league player-manager after his football career ended. Parker was the second-oldest living former big leaguer at the time of his passing.

■ **Joe Pittman,** a second baseman who played three seasons in the majors, died June 13 in Lake Jackson, Texas. He was 60.

A Houston native, Pittman played parts of two

seasons for the Astros from 1981-82, hitting .276 in 145 at-bats. The Astros traded him to the Padres in June 1982, and he finished out the year hitting .254 in 55 games for San Diego. Pittman was kept in the minors in 1983 and, following a trade to the Giants, reached the majors one more time in 1984, getting into 17 games and hitting .227. He returned to the Astros organization after his playing career, working as a scout and minor league instructor from 1988-2003.

■ **Bob Powell,** a righthander who played briefly for the White Sox in 1955 and 1957, died April 26 in Muscle Shoals, Ala. He was 80.

Powell signed with the White Sox out of Michigan State and went straight to the majors under the bonus baby rules in place at the time. He was originally a position player and appeared in two big league games, both as a pinch-runner, once in 1955 and once in '57. He was released in May 1957 and spent two years pitching in the minors before giving up baseball.

■ **Bruce Seid,** the Brewers' scouting director since 2008, died Sept. 2 in Las Vegas. He was 53.

Seid had worked for the Brewers since 1998 when he was hired as an area scout. He rose through the ranks to become scouting director when Jack Zduriencik left for the Mariners' GM job. He had played two seasons in the minor leagues in the early 1980s and began his scouting career with the Padres in 1992.

■ **Hal Smith,** a catcher who played 7 seasons in the major leagues, died April 12 in Fort Smith, Ark. He was 82.

Smith was a two-time all-star for the Cardinals, with whom he played from 1956-61. His best season came in 1959, when he hit .270 with 13 homers and 50 RBIs while logging a career-high 142 games. A heart condition ended his playing career at age 30 in 1961, other than a brief comeback with the Pirates in 1965, and he went on to serve as a scout and coach for several teams.

■ **George Spencer,** a righthander who pitched eight seasons in the majors, died Sept. 10 in Columbus, Ohio. He was 88.

Spencer was a bullpen mainstay with the 1951 Giants in his first full season in the majors, going 10-4, 3.75 for the team that ultimately won the pennant on Bobby Thompson's "Shot Heard 'Round the World." He made 35 appearances for New York in 1952 but largely stayed in the minors for the remainder of his career, seeing limited time with the Giants (through 1955) and Tigers (1958, 1960).

■ **Russ Sullivan,** an outfielder who played in

parts of three seasons for the Tigers, died Nov. 2, 2013, in Fredericksburg, Va. He was 90.

Sullivan hit 191 home runs in the minors, his career spanning from 1948-57. Despite a solid track record of hitting in the minors, he played in just 45 games with the Tigers over the 1951-53 seasons, hitting a combined .267 with five homers in 150 at-bats.

■ **Oscar Taveras,** an outfielder who was the Cardinals' top prospect and made his big league debut in 2014, died Oct. 26 in the Dominican Republic. He was 22.

Taveras signed with the Cardinals as a 16-year-old in 2008 and took off when he hit .386 in low Class A in 2011. He was ranked as the Cardinals' top prospect for both the 2013 and 2014 seasons and reached the majors for the first time in 2014. Although he hit .239 for St. Louis in the regular season, he delivered a memorable game-tying, pinch-hit home run in Game 2 of the National League Championship against the Giants. He had returned to his native Dominican Republic following the Cardinals' loss in the NLCS when he and his girlfriend, Edilia Arvelo, lost their lives in an automobile accident.

■ **Frank Torre,** a first baseman who played in seven big league seasons, died Sept. 13 in Palm Beach Gardens, Fla. He was 82.

The older brother of Joe Torre, Frank reached the majors at age 24 with the Milwaukee Braves in 1956. Sharing time at first base with Joe Adcock, Torre was a productive hitter for his first three seasons in the majors, hitting .285 cumulatively from 1956-58 while earning a reputation as a sound defensive first baseman. Torre helped the Braves to two World Series, in 1957 and '58. He hit two homers in the '57 Series, which the Braves won in seven games against the Yankees.

Torre's hitting fell off in 1959, and he spent most of the 1960 and '61 seasons in Triple-A. He got back to the majors in 1962 with the Phillies and played well, hitting .310 in 168 at-bats. However, the '63 season was his last in the majors, during which he hit .250 in 130 at-bats for the Phillies.

■ **Bill Tremel,** a righthander who pitched in three seasons with the Cubs, died Dec. 22, 2013, in Hollidaysburg, Pa. He was 84.

Tremel pitched five years in the minors before joining the Cubs in 1954. He made 33 relief appearances for them, the second most on the team that year, and he went 1-2, 4.21 in 51 innings. Tremel posted a 3-0, 3.72 mark over 23 appearances, again all in relief, in 1955, but he

got into only one game for the Cubs in 1956 and spent the rest of his career in the minors, pitching through 1959.

■ **Roberto Vargas,** a lefthander who pitched one season in the majors, died May 27 in Puerto Rico. He was 84.

Vargas was one of the first Puerto Ricans to play in the big leagues, making 25 relief appearances with the Milwaukee Braves in 1955. He recorded an 8.76 ERA in 25 innings. He had a long pro career, having spent a year in the Negro Leagues in 1948 when he was 19 and continuing to pitch through 1961.

■ **Tom Veryzer,** a shortstop who played 12 seasons in the majors from 1973-84, died July 8 in Islip, N.Y. He was 61.

Veryzer came up with the Tigers in 1973 and played five seasons in Detroit, but he saw his most extensive playing time following a trade to the Indians after the 1977 season. He served as Cleveland's regular shortstop from 1978-81, hitting a combined .251 with 108 RBIs. He finished out his career with the Mets (1982) and Cubs (1983-84).

■ **Bob Welch,** a righthander who pitched 17 seasons in the majors and won the 1990 American League Cy Young Award, died June 9 in Seal Beach, Calif. He was 57.

The Dodgers made Welch the 20th overall pick in 1977 out of Eastern Michigan and he debuted with Los Angeles a year later in June. At the tender age of 21, he pitched effectively for the pennant-winning Dodgers, going 7-4, 2.02 in 111 innings as a swingman. Welch joined the rotation full time in 1980 and made the first of two All-Star Games. He went 9-5, 3.44 for the World Series-champion Dodgers in 1981.

Traded to the Athletics in December 1987, Welch went on to pitch his final seven seasons in Oakland. He settled in as the No. 2 starter behind Dave Stewart for the A's teams that dominated the AL, winning three straight pennants from 1988-90 and the '89 World Series. Welch won at least 17 games in each of those seasons, peaking when he went 27-6, 2.95 in 1990 to win the Cy Young at age 33. He is the only pitcher since 1973 to win more than 25 games in a season, and he compiled a 211-146, 3.47 record in total.

■ **George Werley,** a righthander who pitched in one big league game in 1956, died Nov. 21, 2013, in St. Louis. He was 75.

Werley signed with the Orioles as an 18-year-old at the tail end of the 1956 season and made his lone big league appearance that Sept. 29. He pitched one inning of a 7-1 loss against the Washington Senators, allowing one run. Werley subsequently pitched three seasons in the minors before ending his baseball career in 1959.

■ **Don Zimmer,** who spent 66 years in baseball as a player, coach and manager and was best known as skipper for the Red Sox and bench coach for the Yankees under Joe Torre, died June 4 in Dunedin, Fla. He was 83.

Zimmer began his career with the Brooklyn Dodgers and was a member of the 1955 "Dem Bums" team that won the franchise's lone World Series in Brooklyn. After a largely undistinguished 12-year playing career, he began coaching in 1966 as a player-manager in the Reds system.

His major league managerial career began with the Padres in 1972. He then moved to the Red Sox as third-base coach, taking over as manager in mid-1976. Though Boston did not finish first during his tenure, Zimmer had arguably his best run as a manager with the franchise—though the 1978 team infamously blew a 14-game lead in July to the hard-charging Yankees.

Fired by the Red Sox after the 1980 season, Zimmer managed the Rangers in 1981-82, though he didn't land another managerial job after that until 1988 with the Cubs. He led Chicago to an improbable National League East title in 1989 but was fired when the team got off to a slow start in 1991.

In his time with the Yankees as Torre's bench coach, the once-fiery Zimmer came to be viewed as a beloved figure, especially by Derek Jeter and other players. He coached with New York from 1996-2003, collecting four World Series rings along the way. He closed out his life in baseball as a senior adviser for the Rays from 2004-14.

■ **George Zuverink,** a righthander who pitched eight seasons in the big leagues, died Sept. 8 in Tempe, Ariz. He was 90.

Zuverink pitched for the Indians, Reds and Tigers between 1951 and 1955 before emerging as a reliever with the Orioles in the mid- to late 1950s. He led the American League in both appearances (62) and saves (16) with the Orioles in 1956, and he led in appearances again in '57 (56) while posting a 2.48 ERA. Shoulder problems ended his career in 1959.

APPENDIX

APPENDIX

MAJOR LEAGUES

AMERICAN LEAGUE
Baltimore	66
Boston	77
Chicago	98
Cleveland	117
Detroit	135
Houston	145
Kansas City	156
Los Angeles	165
Minnesota	203
New York	223
Oakland	236
Seattle	296
Tampa Bay	307
Texas	317
Toronto	328

NATIONAL LEAGUE
Arizona	45
Atlanta	56
Chicago	87
Cincinnati	107
Colorado	126
Los Angeles	175
Miami	185
Milwaukee	195
New York	212
Philadelphia	246
Pittsburgh	257
St. Louis	267
San Diego	277
San Francisco	287
Washington	339

TRIPLE-A

INTERNATIONAL LEAGUE
Bufalo	330
Charlotte	100
Columbus	119
Durham	309
Gwinnett	58
Indianapolis	259
Lehigh Valley	248
Louisville	109
Norfolk	68
Pawtucket	79
Rochester	205
Scranton/WB	225
Syracuse	341
Toledo	137

PACIFIC COAST LEAGUE
Albuquerque	177
Colorado Springs	128
El Paso	279
Fresno	289
Iowa	89
Las Vegas	214
Memphis	269
Nashville	197
New Orleans	187
Oklahoma City	147
Omha	158

Reno	47
Round Rock	319
Sacramento	238
Salt Lake	167
Tacoma	298

DOUBLE-A

EASTERN LEAGUE
Akron	120
Altoona	260
Binghamton	215
Bowie	69
Erie	138
Harrisburg	342
New Britain	206
New Hampshire	331
Portland	80
Reding	249
Richmond	290
Trenton	226

SOUTHERN LEAGUE
Birmingham	101
Chattanooga	178
Huntsville	198
Jackson	299
Jacksonville	188
Mississippi	59
Mobile	48
Montgomery	310
Pensacola	110
Tennessee	90

TEXAS LEAGUE
Arkansas	168
Corpus Christi	148
Frisco	321
Midland	239
Northwest Arkansas	159
San Antonio	280
Springfield	270
Tulsa	129

HIGH CLASS A

CAROLINA LEAGUE
Carolina	121
Frederick	70
Lynchburg	60
Myrtle Beach	322
Potomac	343
Salem	81
Wilmington	160
Winston-Salem	102

CALIFORNIA LEAGUE
Bakersfield	111
High Desert	300
Inland Empire	169
Lake Elsinore	281
Lancaster	149
Modesto	130
Rancho Cucamonga	179
San Jose	291
Stockton	240
Visalia	49

FLORIDA STATE LEAGUE
Bradenton	261
Brevard County	199
Charlotte	310
Clearwater	250
Daytona	91
Dunedin	333
Fort Myers	207
Jupiter	189
Lakeland	139
Palm Beach	271
St. Lucie	216
Tampa	227

LOW CLASS A

MIDWEST LEAGUE
Beloit	241
Bowling Green	312
Burlington	171
Cedar Rapids	208
Clinton	301
Dayton	112
Fort Wayne	282
Great Lakes	180
Kane County	92
Lake County	122
Lansing	334
Peoria	272
Quad Cities	150
South Bend	50
West Michigan	140

SOUTH ATLANTIC LEAGUE
Asheville	131
Augusta	292
Charleston	227
Dellmrva	71
Greensboro	190
Greenville	82
Hagerstown	344
Hickory	323
Kannapolis	103
Lakewood	251
Lexington	161
Rome	61
Savannah	217
West Virginia	262

SHORT-SEASON

NEW YORK-PENN LEAGUE
Aberdeen	72
Auburn	345
Batavia	191
Brooklyn	218
Connecticut	140
Hudson Valley	312
Jamestown	263
Lowell	83
Mahoning Valley	123
State College	273
Staten Island	230
Tri-City	151
Vermont	242
Williamsport	252

NORTHWEST LEAGUE
Hillsboro	51
Boise	93
Tri-City	132
Eugene	283
Salem-Keizer	293
Everett	302
Spokane	324
Vancouver	335

ROOKIE

APPALACHIAN LEAGUE
Bluefield	336
Bristol	264
Burlington	162
Danville	62
Elizabethton	209
Greeneville	152
Johnson City	274
Kingsport	218
Princeton	313
Pulaski	303

PIONEER LEAGUE
Billings	114
Grand Junction	133
Great Falls	105
Helena	201
Idaho Falls	163
Missoula	53
Ogden	182
Orem	172
Angels	171
Athletics	243
Brewers	200
Cubs	94
Diamondbacks	52
Dodgers	181
Giants	294
Indians	124
Mariners	304
Padres	284
Rangers	325
Reds	113
Tigers	141
White Sox	104

GULF COAST LEAGUE
Astros	153
Blue Jays	337
Braves	63
Cardinals	275
Marlins	192
Mets	219
Nationals	346
Orioles	73
Phillies	253
Pirates	264
Rays	314
Red Sox	84
Twins	210
Yankees	231